Notable Black American Women

To my mother, Vesona Bigelow Carney Graves
—my most notable black American woman—
and to all black American foremothers and mothers and sisters,
who together have made our history.

Notable Black American Women

Jessie Carney Smith,
Editor

Jessie Carney Smith, *Editor*

Gale Research Inc. Staff

Mary Beth Trimper, *Production Manager*
Evi Seoud, *Assistant Production Manager*
Mary Winterhalter, *Production Assistant*

Arthur Chartow, *Art Director*
Jeanne M. Moore, *Graphic Designer*

Library of Congress Cataloging-in-Publication Data

Notable Black American women / edited by Jessie Carney Smith.
p. cm.
Includes bibliographical references and index.
ISBN 0-8103-4749-0
1. Afro-American women—Biography. I. Smith, Jessie Carney.
E185.96.N68 1991
920.72'08996073—dc20
[B] 91-35074

A CIP catalogue record for this book is available from the British Library.

∞™ This book is printed on acid-free paper that meets the minimum requirements of American National Standard for Information Sciences—Permanence Paper for Printed Library Materials, ANSI Z39.48-1984.

This book is printed on recycled paper that meets Environmental Protection Agency standards.

ISBN 0-8103-4749-0
Printed in the United States of America
Published simultaneously in the United Kingdom
by Gale Research International Limited
(An affiliated company of Gale Research Inc.)

10 9 8 7 6 5 4

Contents

Contents by Area of Endeavor

Coach

Collector

College dean of women

College president

Comedienne

Commentator

Community activist

Community leader

Community organizer

Community worker

Composer

Consultant

Critic

Culinary anthropologist

Dance company director

Dancer

Introduction

"I was not born with a silver spoon in mouth; but instead with a clothes basket almost upon my head," said Maggie Lena Walker, a versatile black woman whose achievements in the early part of this century as entrepreneur, feminist, civil rights advocate, newspaper founder, and lecturer won for her the respect, honor, and recognition that she deserved. Her wide range of interests and accomplishments reflect only some of the areas in which black American women have achieved. Whatever the circumstances of their lives, black American women have a rich and varied history that has been only partially told. Now that their story is being discovered, African-American and general histories will need to be rewritten. This first edition of *Notable Black American Women* is a pioneering attempt to fill a long-existing gap in reference sources as it chronicles the lives of five hundred African-American women, living and dead. Of the women represented, the earliest birth is approximately 1730, when poet and orator Lucy Terry Prince was born, while the most recent is 1956, the year in which astronaut Mae C. Jemison was born. This book is a tribute to these and other black women not chronicled here and to their accomplishments in the face of racial and gender discrimination and abuse.

To illustrate the range of experiences and achievements of this group of women from colonial times to the present, *Notable Black American Women* presents five hundred biographies. In the original design of the book one hundred seventy-five women were to be the subject of longer biographies of about thirty-five hundred words while the rest were to be about twelve hundred. These limits were generously interpreted as the work progressed and a clear distinction between longer and shorter biographies is much effaced; they now form a continuum in which length is determined in part by the desire to present material which previously has been difficult to find. In some instances, as seen, for example, with Geraldine Pindell Trotter, a woman was quite productive yet her life and achievements became publicly subordinate to her husband's, and she was generally overlooked in known published sources. To help future research the biographies include reference notes and, as far as possible, the identification of local or archival material. A further goal was to allow the women to comment upon their lives and concerns in their own words through apt use of quotations. When possible, those written about were asked to review their essays and correct inaccuracies. In addition, this volume includes the likenesses of one hundred seventy-nine of the women.

Selection Process Aims at Diversity

The women selected as subjects of biographies do not constitute a list of the five hundred most important African-American women—that would be a foolish and presumptuous goal. The selection includes a consensus of the editor and an advisory board on a number of women whose listing was essential and a further selection which is as widely representative as possible geographically, historically, and professionally. The board advised the editor in identifying the women who should be included and in screening the list that was subsequently drawn up. The initial list of some thousand women was drawn from an exhaustive search of works ranging from the obscure to well-known sources, both published and unpublished. Examples of works drawn upon are Constance R. Marteena, "Checklist of Afro-American Women Who Began Their Careers Prior to the Twentieth Century and Have Made Significant Achievements in the United States" (manuscript, Marteena Collection, Bennett College Archives); Hallie Q. Brown, *Homespun*

Heroines and Other Women of Distinction; M. A. Majors, *Noted Negro Women*; Rayford W. Logan and Michael R. Winston, *Dictionary of American Negro Biography*; *Notable American Women*; other specialized and general biographical directories; *Golden Jubilee of the General Association of Colored Baptists in Kentucky*; journals such as *Crisis* and *Opportunity*; and local sources, such as *Herstory Silhouettes, Profiles of Black Womanhood.* Women in this initial selection satisfied one or more of these criteria:

a pioneer in a particular area, such as first black woman elected to public office in a state or first black woman editor of a newspaper, or

an important entrepreneur, such as a manufacturer of cosmetics for black women or developer of hair care products, or

a leading businesswoman, such as president of an advertising firm or vice-president of a major bank, or

a literary or creative figure of stature, such as outstanding poet, well-known writer, author of works on a unique theme, important artist, outstanding sculptor, or

a leader for social or human justice, such as abolitionist, freedom fighter, suffragist, outstanding participant in the civil rights movement, or

a major governmental or organizational official, such as director of the Women's Bureau, president of the National Medical Association, president of the National Education Association, first black president of the American Library Association, or

a creative figure in the performing arts, such as the first black to perform at the Metropolitan Opera, outstanding popular singer or performer, prima ballerina, actress, or composer, or

a noted orator, elocutionist, or public speaker (particularly for nineteenth and early twentieth century women), or

a distinguished educator, such as first woman principal of an early high school, president of a college, founder of a college, first black woman to receive a doctoral degree, or

a noted scholar, such as a scientist, a mathematician, an historian, or a sociologist, or

a leader, pioneer, or contributor in other fields or areas who meets the basic criteria suggested above for selection as an outstanding black American woman.

Other scholars, including those who contributed essays to this volume, also nominated women for inclusion in the book. The editor made the final choice. New candidates for inclusion became evident as the work progressed; some have been selected and others regretfully omitted due to the pressures of space, time, and the inability to locate readily sufficient biographical information to prepare an entry of appropriate length. The final list includes some women who stand alone in the magnitude of their accomplishments, such as abolitionist, lecturer, and preacher Sojourner Truth; Underground Railroad conductor Harriet Tubman; and poet Phillis Wheatley. It is my hope that a second edition will in time allow the inclusion of further biographies and the correction of errors in this one.

All efforts were made to make *Notable Black American Women* as accurate as possible, but perfection is an unobtainable goal, especially in a work that breaks new ground as this does. Many, if not most, of these five hundred women have not previously been the objects of known scholarly investigation into their biographies. It has not always been possible to locate and use the local sources which might resolve contradictory statements in the available sources. The aid of family members, friends, and local historians would be most welcome in supplying additional material, filling omissions, and correcting errors which, unfortunately, often have been transmitted from one published work to another. This material will be placed on file in view of a revision of the present volume.

Arrangement of Entries

The entries in this book are arranged alphabetically by the surname, in this case also the name by which the women are known. Women with compound surnames are arranged under the first of these names whether or not the names are hyphenated. The index, which gives important names, places, and events, further guides the reader to the subjects.

Contributions to *Notable Black American Women* Acknowledged

Notable Black American Women represents the generous contributions of the scholars who took the time from their busy professional lives to serve on the advisory board and provide much-needed direction. As well, the help of those scholars who interrupted their schedules to prepare the individual biographies is gratefully acknowledged. Whenever possible, the choice fell upon persons who had already shown a special interest in the subjects of the biographies. The editor expresses her gratitude to all those who contributed their time and expertise in writing the entries, from those who contributed a single essay to those who prepared multiple entries.

It is impossible to thank individually all the libraries and repositories whose generous help to the contributors and the editor made the work possible, but I cannot omit three: Schomburg Center for Research in Black Culture, New York City; Moorland-Spingarn Research Center, Howard University, Washington, D.C.; and Special Collections, Fisk University, Nashville, Tennessee. Through the assistance of Deborah Willis and James Huffman at Schomburg and Karen Jefferson at Moorland-Spingarn, these repositories also provided many of the photographs that illustrate this volume.

I am grateful to the following members of the Fisk University family for their encouragement and support: Gregory Engleberg, Dorothy G. Lake, Beth Madison Howse, Marion T. Roberts, Vando Rogers, Sharon Williams, and many interested students and faculty. I am grateful also to my colleague at Tennessee State University library, Vallie P. Pursley.

Standing alone in a special category is my Fisk faculty colleague Robert L. Johns, who edited each of the five hundred essays, wrote twenty-three of them, and shared the agony and ecstasy of producing this pioneer work on America's notable black women. I am eternally grateful to him.

The editors at Gale Research who provided expertise during the research and writing stage and to whom I owe special gratitude are James Lesniak, Diane Dupuis, Christine Nasso, Christine Hammes, and, finally, Lawrence Baker, who carefully guided the work through the last few months.

Finally, I must acknowledge the patience, understanding, and moral support of my family as well as many friends, acquaintances, and colleagues through the nation who maintained high interest in the project and lent support by asking "How's the book?"

Jessie Carney Smith

Advisory Board

Darlene Clark-Hine, John A. Hannah Professor of History, Michigan State University

Arlene Clift-Pellow, director, Division of Humanities and Fine Arts, Fisk University

Johnnetta B. Cole (Robinson), president, Spelman College

Bettye Collier-Thomas, director, Center for Black Culture and History, Temple University

Beverly Guy-Sheftall, director, Women's Research and Resource Center, Spelman College

Jean Blackwell Hutson, retired director, Schomburg Center for Research in Black Culture

Dorothy Porter (Wesley), director emerita, Moorland-Spingarn Research Center, Howard University

Gloria Randle Scott, president, Bennett College

Dr. Elinor DesVerney Sinnett, acting director, Moorland-Spingarn Research Center, Howard University

Susan L. Taylor, editor-in-chief, *Essence* Magazine

Photo Credits

Photographs appearing in *Notable Black American Women* were received from the following sources:

Rae Alexander-Minter 584; ***American Libraries:*** 594, 606; **Atlanta History Center, The Atlanta Historical Society** 445; **Patricia Bell-Scott** 245; **Bennett College Library** 855, 993; **Ida Berman** 190; **Bethune Museum-Archives National Historic Site** 86; **Charles L. Blockson Afro-American Collection, Temple University** 336, 374, 412, 942; **Cynthia S. Brown** 190; **Mary Elizabeth Carnegie** 156; **Janet Charles** 783; **Jewell Plummer Cobb** 195; **Johnnetta Betsch Cole** 198; **Cardiss Collins** 204; **Marva Collins** 212; **Miriam DeCosta-Willis** 828, 837; **Frank Driggs** 913; **Tyrone Drummond** 568; **Ramona Hoage Edelin** 307; **Helen G. Edmunds** 313; **Episcopal Diocese of Massachusetts** 462; **Essex Institute** 929; **Elton Fax** 172; **Fisk University Library** 48, 57, 98, 137, 217, 239, 250, 264, 276, 388, 404, 458, 477, 537, 616, 646, 701, 736, 775, 793, 950, 962, 998, 1006, 1038, 1077, 1079, 1096, 1107, 1145, 1147, 1165, 1176, 1189, 1205, 1251, 1260; **Edward Fontenette** 64; **Mary Hatwood Futrell** 376; **Georgia Department of Archives and History** 650; **Gores-Fields Agency** 932; **Hackley Collection, Detroit Public Library** 430; **Marcelite J. Harris** 467; **Michael A. Hooks** 512; **Huston-Tillotson College** 102; **Library of Congress** 285; **Lyndon B. Johnson Space Center** 572; **Thura Mack** 887; **Martin Luther King, Jr., Center for Social Change** 632; **Mississippi Valley Collection, John Willard Brister Library, Memphis State University** 512; **Jack Mitchell** 568; **Moorland-Spingarn Research Center, Howard University** 78, 80, 121, 219, 417, 468, 695, 770, 830, 970, 1115, 1121; **Constance Baker Motley** 779; **Robert Nemiroff Estate, Jewell Handy, Executor** 452; **North Carolina Division of Archives and History** 109, 502; **Northwestern State University of Louisiana, Eugene P. Watson Library, Cammie G. Henry Research Center, The Mildred Bailey Collection** 530; **Oberlin College Archives** 826; **Episcopal Church Center, Office of Black Ministries, New York City** 783; **Carl Owens** 430; **Linda Perkins** 224; **Ernesta G. Procope** 885; **Bernice J. Reagon** 926; **Rick Reinhard** 310; **Rosetta Reitz** 1041; **Seaver Center for Western History Research, Natural History Museum of Los Angeles County** 733; **Schomburg Center for Research in Black Culture** 14, 23, 29, 32, 35, 40, 43, 105, 126, 141, 142, 231, 281, 293, 296, 346, 359, 365, 398, 441, 483, 518, 524, 557, 579, 601, 638, 653, 663, 703, 724, 752, 859, 874, 890, 954, 958, 979, 983, 1062, 1074, 1108, 1151, 1160, 1167, 1174, 1202, 1225, 1233, 1244; **South Caroliniana Library, University of South Carolina** 1011; **Southern Education Foundation** 918; **Niara Sudarkasa** 1089; **Rosalyn Terborg-Penn** 899; **Tuskegee Archives, Tuskegee University** 1217, 1221; **United Methodist Communications** 622; **University of Massachusetts, Amherst; University of North Florida, Thomas G. Carpenter Library, Eartha White Collection** 1250; **Carl Van Vechten Estate, Joseph Solomon, Executor** 543; **Voorhees College** 1280; **Margaret Walker Alexander National Archives** 1193; **Walker Collection of A'Lelia Perry Bundles** 1184; **Ben Wallace** 6, 51, 394, 486, 764, 821, 1172, 1238; **Jean Weisinger** 1178; **Western Reserve Historical Society** 533; **Wilberforce University, Rembert E. Stokes Learning Resources Center, Archives and Special Collections** 116; ***Women in Congress,*** **Raymond W. Smock, Historian** 130, 185, 610; **Irene Young** 1142

Contributors

Adele Logan Alexander, *Howard University*
Gloria Long Anderson, *Morris Brown College*
Phyllis W. Anderson, *Payne College*
A.B. Assensoh, *Martin Luther King, Jr., Center for Social Change*
Joan Adams Bahner, *Fisk University*
Ben E. Bailey, *Tougaloo College*
Gerri Bates, *Howard University*
Roseanne P. Bell, *Memphis, Tennessee*
Patricia Bell-Scott, *University of Georgia*
Esme E. Bhan, *Howard University*
Rosia Bobia, *Kennesaw State College*
Tonya Bolden, *Bronx, New York*
A. Lynn Bolles, *University of Maryland*
Lena Boyd-Brown, *Hampton University*
Margaret Bernice Smith Bristow, *Hampton University*
Annette K. Brock, *Savannah State College*
Barnsley Brown, *University of North Carolina, Chapel Hill*
Cynthia Stokes Brown, *Dominican College of San Rafael*
T.J. Bryan, *Coppin State College*
Violet Harrington Bryan, *Dillard University*
Cozetta W. Buckley, *Jackson State University*
Penelope L. Bullock, *Clark-Atlanta University*
Margaret Burroughs, *Chicago, Illinois*
Marva Griffin Carter, *Morehouse College*
Floris Barnett Cash, *State University of New York, Stony Brook*
Jean Elder Cazort, *Nashville, Tennessee*
Ralph J. Cazort, *Meharry Medical College*
Keith Clark, *University of North Carolina, Chapel Hill*
Darlene Clark-Hine, *Michigan State University*
Arlene Clift-Pellow, *Fisk University*
Bettye Collier-Thomas, *Temple University*
Grace E. Collins, *Coppin State College*
Helen C. Cooks, *University of Toledo*
Guy C. Craft, *Clark-Atlanta University*
Sarah Elizabeth Crest, *Towson State University*
Adelaide M. Cromwell, *Boston University*
Carolyn Cunningham, *Oberlin College*
Richelle Curl, *South Orange, New Jersey*
Vonita White Dandridge, *Virginia Union University*
Nancy A. Davidson, *Illinois State University*

Althea T. Davis, *Brooklyn, New York*
Pamala S. Deane, *Lanham, Maryland*
Alice A. Deck, *University of Illinois*
Miriam DeCosta-Willis, *University of Maryland, Baltimore County*
Vanessa D. Dickerson, *Rhodes College*
Rita D. Disroe, *University of Illinois*
Carolyn A. Dorsey, *University of Missouri*
Alan Duckworth, *Claremont College*
James Duckworth, *University of Richmond*
Margaret Duckworth, *Virginia Union University*
Lois L. Dunn, *Nashville, Tennessee*
De Witt S. Dykes, Jr., *Oakland University*
Maalik Edwards, *Oberlin College*
Nina T. Eliott, *University of Tennessee*
Joan Curl Elliott, *Tennessee State University*
Sharynn Owens Etheridge, *University of Tennessee*
V. P. Franklin, *Drexel University*
Karla Y. E. Frye, *University of Missouri, Saint Louis*
Marie Garrett, *University of Tennessee*
Frances K. Gateward, *University of Maryland*
Sandra E. Gibbs, *National Council of Teachers of English*
Paula Giddings, *Rutgers University*
Glenda E. Gill, *Michigan Technological University*
Carmen Renee Gillespie, *Fairfax, Virginia*
Iva Gloudon, *Spelman College*
Sandra Y. Govan, *University of North Carolina, Charlotte*
Jenifer Lyn Grady, *Oberlin College*
Maryemma Grahamn, *Northeastern University*
Jacquelyn Grant, *Interdenominational Theological Center*
Mildred Green, *LeMoyne-Owen College*
Betty K. Gubert, *Schomburg Center for Research in Black Culture*
Beverly Guy-Sheftall, *Spelman College*
Debra Newman Ham, *Library of Congress*
James E. Haney, *Tennessee State University*
Violette J. Harris, *University of Illinois*
Daphne Duval Harrison, *University of Maryland, Baltimore County*
Lynda Roscoe Hartigan, *National Museum of American Art*
Valerie S. Hartman, *Teaneck, New Jersey*
Lisa Beth Hill, *Emory University*
Roy L. Hill, *Lane College*
Ruth Edmonds Hill, *Radcliffe College*
Carolyn R. Hodges, *University of Tennessee*
Felicia Harris (Felder) Hoehne, *University of Tennessee*
Mary R. Holley, *Montclair State College*
Ellistine P. Holly, *Jackson State University*
Alton Hornsby, Jr., *Morehouse College*
Juanita R. Howard, *Baruch College*
Delores Hudson, *Los Angeles Harbor College*
Jean McMahon Humez, *University of Massachusetts, Boston*
Helen R. Huston, *Tennessee State University*

Jean Blackwell Hutson, *New York City, New York*
Brenda J. Ingram, *Albright College*
Elwana D. Ingram, *Winston-Salem State University*
Dona L. Irvin, *Oakland, California*
Adrienne M. Israel, *Guilford College*
Jacquelyn L. Jackson, *Middle Tennessee State University*
Laura C. Jarmon, *Middle Tennessee State University*
La Vinia Delois Jennings, *University of Tennessee*
Margaret Jerrido, *Temple University*
Robert L. Johns, *Fisk University*
Adrienne Lash Jones, *Oberlin College*
Casper LeRoy Jordan, *Atlanta, Georgia*
Shirley M. Jordan, *Hampton University*
E. J. Josey, *University of Pittsburgh*
Donald Franklin Joyce, *Austin Peay State University*
Ibrahim Kargbo, *Coppin State College*
Juanita Karpf, *University of Georgia*
Arthur R. LaBrew, *Michigan Music Research Center*
Evonne Lack, *Oberlin College*
Jo Ann Lahmon, *University of Tennessee*
Helena Carney Lambeth, *Montgomery County (Md.) Schools*
Candis LaPrade, *University of North Carolina, Chapel Hill*
Sandra M. Lawson, *Library of Congress*
Theresa A. Leininger, *Yale University*
Mamie E. Locke, *Hampton University*
Dorothy E. Lyles, *Carter G. Woodson Library*
Maureen A. McCarthy, *Oberlin College*
Lois C. McDougald, *Tennessee State University*
Jo Dawn McEwan, *University of North Carolina, Chapel Hill*
Thura R. Mack, *University of Tennessee*
Nellie Y. McKay, *University of Wisconsin*
Genna Rae McNeil, *University of North Carolina, Chapel Hill*
Julianne Malveaux, **Essence** *Magazine*
Diana Marre, *University of Puget Sound*
Dianne Marshall, *New York City, New York*
Larry L. Martin, *Coppin State College*
Denis Mercier, *Glassboro State College*
Ronald E. Mickens, *Clark-Atlanta University*
Reavis L. Mitchell, Jr., *Fisk University*
Maria K. Mootry, *Grinnell College*
Cynthia Neverdon-Morton, *Coppin State College*
Richard Newman, *New York Public Library*
Virginia J. Newsome, *University of the District of Columbia*
Dolores Nicholson, *Fisk University*
Kelley Norman, *Northeastern University*
Lucius Outlaw, *Haverford College*
Margaret D. Pagan, *Baltimore, Maryland*
Nell Irvin Painter, *Princeton University*
Susanna Bartmann Pathak, *Johns Hopkins University*
Elizabeth Patrick, *Fisk University*

David H. K. Pellow, *Fisk University*
Huel D. Perkins, *Louisiana State University*
Kathy A. Perkins, *University of Illinois*
Linda M. Perkins, *University of Illinois*
Margaret Perry, *Valparaiso University*
Patsy B. Perry, *North Carolina Central University*
Harriette A. Peterson, *Tennessee State University*
William D. Piersen, *Fisk University*
Diane M. Pinderhughes, *University of Illinois*
Margaret Ann Reid, *Morgan State University*
Rosetta Reitz, *Rosetta Records, New York City, New York*
Marilyn Richardson, *Africa Meeting House, Boston, Massachusetts*
Florence Crim Robinson, *Clark-Atlanta University*
Jacqueline A. Rouse, *The American University*
Sue Rowland, *Slidell, Louisiana*
Marva Rudolph, *University of Tennessee*
Deborah Tulani Salahu-Din, *Blacks in Wax Museum, Baltimore, Maryland*
Sandra G. Shannon, *Howard University*
Spencer G. Shaw, *University of Washington*
John C. Shields, *Illinois State University*
Bonnie Shipp, *Middle Tennessee State University*
Simmona E. Simmons, *University of Maryland, Baltimore County*
Oscar L. Sims, *University of California, Los Angeles*
Janet Sims-Wood, *Howard University*
Robert E. Skinner, *Xavier University*
Dorothea W. Slocum, *Washington, D.C.*
Elaine M. Smith, *Alabama State University*
J. Clay Smith, Jr., *Howard University*
Jessie Carney Smith, *Fisk University*
Linda Anderson Smith, *North Carolina State University*
Theresa Snyder, *University of Pennsylvania*
Raymond R. Sommerville, *Fisk University*
E. Delores B. Stephens, *Morehouse College*
Robert W. Stephens, *Montclair State University*
Deborah Stewart, *Oberlin College*
Lisa Studier, *Oberlin College*
Lester Sullivan, *Xavier University*
Katheryn Talalay, *Symbolic Systems, Summit, New Jersey*
Rosalyn Terborg-Penn, *Morgan State University*
Darius L. Thieme, *Fisk University*
Donald Thieme, *DuVall and Associates*
Anne Trapasso, *University of North Carolina, Chapel Hill*
Toni-Michelle C. Travis, *George Mason University*
Patricia Turner, *University of Minnesota*
Marsha C. Vick, *University of North Carolina, Chapel Hill*
Gloria Wade-Gales, *Spelman College*
Susan Brown Wallace, *Wake Forest University*
Virginia Wilson Wallace, *Dallas Public Library*
Nagueyalti Warren, *Emory University*
Carole McAlpine Watson, *National Endowment for the Humanities*

Monda Raquel Webb, *Silver Spring, Maryland*
Carolyn Wedin, *University of Wisconsin, Whitewater*
Maurice B. Wheeler, *Detroit Public Library*
Lillian Williams, *State University of New York, Albany*
Pearl Williams-Jones, *Bible Way Church, Washington, D.C.*
Leslie Wilson, *Montclair State College*
Ollie Wilson, *University of California, Berkeley*
Emery Wimbish, Jr., *Lincoln University (Pa.)*
Julie Winch, *Harvard University*
Keith A. Winsell, *Amistad Research Center*
Kari Winter, *Fisk University*
Elaine P. Witty, *Norfolk State University*
Phyllis Wood, *Wake County (N.C.) Public Schools and Wake Technical Community College*
Helena Woodard, *University of North Carolina, Chapel Hill*
Barbara A. Woods, *University of South Carolina*
Linda T. Wynn, *Tennessee Historical Commission*
Barbara Lynne Ivey Yarn, *Atlanta, Georgia*
Kris Anne Yohe, *University of North Carolina, Chapel Hill*
Dyhana Ziegler, *University of Tennessee*
Amanda Beth Zola, *Oberlin College*

Notable Black American Women

Clara Leach Adams-Ender

(1939-)

Nursing administrator

Brigadier General Clara Adams-Ender, chief of the Army Nurse Corps, is the highest-ranking nurse in the U.S. Army. In July 1967 she became the first woman in the army to be awarded the Expert Field Medical Badge, and in 1976 she became the first black, female, and nurse to graduate with a master's degree from the U.S. Army Command Staff and General College. Also the first black Army Nurse Corps officer to graduate, in 1982, from the U.S. Army War College, two years later Adams-Ender became the first black nurse appointed chief of the department of nursing at Walter Reed Army Medical Center in Washington, D.C.

Clara Mae Leach Adams-Ender was born on July 11, 1939, in Willow Springs, Wake County, near Raleigh, North Carolina. She was the fourth child in a family of ten children born to Otha Leach and Caretha Bell (Sapp) Leach. Adams Ender's parents came from large families, and both left school at an early age to help support their families. Although her parents did not complete their education, they placed a high value on the education of their children. Her parents were hard-working farmers who at one time were sharecroppers. Adams-Ender lived on a farm owned by a landlord until 1955, prior to her senior year in high school. Then her parents moved to another farm and subsequently purchased their own in North Carolina. This farm is currently owned by Adams-Ender, who chose to keep the land in the family.

Adams-Ender attended Fuquay Springs Consolidated High School, which comprised primary grades through high school. From the age of five until she entered college, she worked on the farm while going to school. She always enjoyed reading and often read between sixty and one hundred books during summer recess. In 1956 she graduated from high school at the age of sixteen and entered North Carolina Agricultural and Technical State University School of Nursing at Greensboro. During her college years, Adams-Ender joined an army program that financed her junior and senior years in college. As an army reservist in college, her rank was private and thereafter private first class. She was commissioned a second lieutenant in March 1961, three months prior to graduation. She graduated from the basic nursing program at North Carolina in 1961 and entered the active U.S. Army Nurse Corps. Adams-Ender stated that "the Army is known for their ability to educate people and the Army gave a lot of folks their start."

Adams-Ender began her active army career as a second lieutenant and a general duty nurse from 1961 to 1963 at Walson Army Hospital in Fort Dix, New Jersey. For thirteen months in 1963 and 1964, she was stationed overseas in Ascom, Korea, with the 121st Evacuation Hospital, working with a close-knit group of lieutenant staff nurses. During this assignment, she learned a great deal about nursing administration, leading nursing assistants, and "how to manage nursing practice and to do this well." She also discovered that she had an affinity for teaching.

To develop her teaching skills, Adams-Ender was assigned to be a nursing instructor at the U.S. Army Medical Training Center at Fort Sam Houston in Texas from 1965 until 1967. That year she began graduate studies at the University of Minnesota, majoring in medical surgical nursing. After graduating in 1969 with a master of science degree in nursing, she was assigned as a nursing instructor and then as an assistant professor at WRAIN Center of the University of Maryland in Washington, D.C.

For a year, beginning in 1974, Adams-Ender served as assistant chief of the department of nursing at Kimborough Army Hospital in Fort Meade, Maryland. She then entered the U.S. Army Command and General Staff College at Fort Leavenworth, Kansas, and completed a master's degree in military art and science. She was subsequently assigned for two years to the Health Services Command at Fort Sam Houston as the inspector general of all services in army hospitals.

Adams-Ender began her second overseas assignment at the Army Regional Medical Center in Frankfurt, West Germany, in 1978. She began as the assistant chief of the department of nursing, then, after a year, became chief. At the age of thirty-nine, while in Germany, she was promoted to full colonel, a promotion she was quite proud to receive at that age. She described her experience in Germany as a tremendously exciting time, a learning experience, and an exchange of learning. The American nurses had a collaborative working relationship with German nurses at a nearby trauma hospital, and she learned the German language, local customs, and culture. While assigned in Germany, she was a member of two organizations—one of which taught conversational English to German citizens and another that promoted German-American relations among healthcare professionals. While in Germany, she also met her husband, a German doctor, Heinz Ender. They married in 1981, three months after she returned to the United States.

Adams-Ender Becomes Brigadier General

In 1981 Adams-Ender was assigned to the U.S. Army Recruiting Command in Fort Sheridan, Illinois, as chief of the Army Nurse Corps division. In 1984 she was appointed chief of the department of nursing at Walter Reed Army Medical Center. "Military nursing offers a great deal of diversity," Adams-Ender stated, and, by 1987, she had engaged in clinical practice, teaching, nursing administration, and nursing research and had taken numerous military courses. Her experiences and education provided a broad base of for her next assignment. In 1987 she was appointed to the Office of the Surgeon General as chief of the U.S. Army Nurse Corps. Her military career had been an impressive climb from private in the reserves to second lieutenant in the active army to brigadier general.

In addition to holding the chief nurse position of the U.S. Army Nurse Corps, Adams-Ender has taken various military and civilian consultant positions and adjunct assistant professor-ships. She enjoys consulting and sharing with people the wealth of experience she has gained. She is currently an adjunct faculty member of Georgetown University School of Nursing in Washington, D.C., and of Oakland University School of Nursing in Rochester, Michigan. In 1989 she gave eighty-eight presentations at national and international conferences on various topics. She enjoys research for presentations, writes her own speeches, and has authored numerous articles.

Adams-Ender believes that nurses should be educated with an eclectic approach, and that two major professional issues of the day are the nursing shortage and the image of nursing. The increasing levels of high technology, a maturing society, and emerging diseases such as AIDS have had an impact on the nursing shortage. She has stated that the image of nursing must be improved in order to attract a pool of qualified people into the profession. Adams-Ender is presently involved in media projects aimed at improving the image of nursing.

Adams-Ender belongs to numerous professional societies, including the American Nurses Association, Council of Nursing Administration, Nurses Association, American Red Cross Nurses, Chi Eta Phi Nursing Sorority, National Association for Female Executives, Drug and Alcohol Nurses Association, National League of Nursing, and Sigma Theta Tau. She is chair of the Impaired Nurses Committee of the D.C. Nurses Association.

Adams-Ender is active in numerous community organizations as well. She is president of the Officers Bowling Club and a board member of the Northeast Illinois Council of the Boy Scouts of America and of the Arlington Symphony. She is a life member of the NAACP, and a member of the National Council of Negro Women.

Of the many mentors in her life, two army officers stand out significantly—Brigadier General Lillian Dunlap and Colonel Katherine Frances Galloway. In particular, Galloway helped Adams-Ender grow and develop as a nursing administrator and taught her to reward herself and celebrate her success. Adams-Ender also admires Leah Curtin, the editor of *Nursing Management*.

Adams-Ender has dark brown skin and is approximately five feet six inches with a medium build. She has a dynamic personality and a good sense of humor. Her philosophy is that "new experiences are a way of living." Her hobbies are reading, fashion design and construction, volksmarching, bowling, and traveling. She actively maintains a rigid physical fitness program that includes running, walking, biking, and swimming.

Important to Adams-Ender are such national issues as teenage pregnancy, the drug problem, the increase in teenage suicide, and the high school dropout rate. She questions the disenfranchisement of minorities through the way they have been educated and believes that teenagers need role models and someone with whom they can communicate.

Adams-Ender stated that most of her success emanates from her humble beginnings and her parents' influence. Her parents always emphasized two concepts: "We are somebody" and "You can do anything you want if you put your mind to it." Adams-Ender says, "Having goals is important, and persistance is the greatest quality that anybody can ever have."

References

Adams-Ender, Clara Mae, Curriculum Vitae, 1990.

Adams-Ender, Clara Mae. Interview with Althea T. Davis, 6 March 1990.

Carnegie, Elizabeth. *The Path We Tread.* New York: Lippincott, 1986.

Althea T. Davis

Cecelia Adkins

(1923-)

Business executive

The first woman and the first lay person to be named executive director of the Sunday School Publishing Board of the National Baptist Convention, U.S.A., Cecelia Antoinette Nabrit Adkins is a talented administrator and a role model for black women in the business world. Adkins was born on September 3, 1923, in Atlanta, Georgia, the youngest of eight children of Gertrude (West) Nabrit and James Madison Nabrit, a Baptist minister and church administrator. Adkins attended grade school in the Atlanta public system for three years before transferring to Oglethorpe School (now the Atlanta University Demonstration School). She was later briefly enrolled at Atlanta University Laboratory High School. In 1937 James Nabrit was appointed president of American Baptist Theological Seminary, and the Nabrit family moved to Nashville, Tennessee. Nabrit's life and that of her siblings reflect their parents' strong will to succeed. James M., Jr., a noted civil rights attorney as early as the 1930s, was president of Howard University. Samuel Milton became president of Texas Southern University while Henry Clarke became a minister and lawyer. The Nabrit sisters were notable in their professions of social work and library science, and were active in civic and social affairs as well.

Adkins entered Pearl High School in Nashville and graduated as valedictorian of her class of 1939. She enrolled in Fisk University on a Gabriel Scholarship, in September of that year. She decided early at Fisk that although she was a liberal arts student, she would pursue studies that would prepare her for the business field. She completed a major in English and a minor in speech and drama and took her baccalaureate degree summa cum laude in 1943. Elected to membership in Sigma Upsilon Pi honorary scholastic fraternity, the forerunner of the Phi Beta Kappa chapter at Fisk, Adkins was also listed in *Who's Who in American Universities and Colleges.*

Of her years as a student at Fisk, Adkins recalls, "Under Professor Theodore Currier I learned an invaluable skill—how to think. I believe that if you can develop the ability to think clearly, you can be successful in almost any enterprise. Professor Ross, who was head of the speech and drama department, helped me to develop the artistic side of myself. And, of course, Professor [Isaiah] Creswell presented business in such an interesting fashion that my inclination in that direction became my life's profession." As a student in Creswell's accounting class, Adkins researched the history of the Morris Memorial Building, which housed the offices and printing facilities of the Sunday School Publishing Board, located at the corner of Third and Charlotte avenues in Nashville. Little did she know that one day she would become executive director of the Sunday School Publishing Board of the National Baptist Convention, U. S. A., and as such, would be the first woman and the first layperson to be appointed to this prominent position.

"Our parents always told us to do our best, no matter what we were doing," Adkins explained her parents' great influence on her life. "When I came to the publishing board in 1943 as an accountant, my father told me to perform even the most mundane task with excellence. He encouraged me to learn as much about the operation as possible. That's how I got to be head of the department. My mother instilled in me a strong sense of organization, and she always told me there's more to managing money than making it."

This distinguished administrator remains convinced that an educational background in the liberal arts tradition constitutes the best possible preparation for subsequent scholastic and professional endeavor on the part of any individual. "There is," Adkins maintains, "no substitute for the cultural background that you are exposed to in working for a liberal arts degree. An education in the liberal arts tradition has helped me enjoy a better life and has enhanced my appreciation of what life has to offer."

Adkins Pioneers in Business

During the course of her career, Adkins has broken new ground in a variety of fields. In addition to becoming the first woman to serve as chief accountant of the Sunday School Publishing Board, in 1965 she became the first woman to serve as chief fiscal agent of the board. A decade later, she assumed leadership of the publishing house, becoming the first woman to head a denominational publishing establishment, an operation serving more than thirty-five thousand Baptist churches making up a constituency of over 7.5 million persons. Adkins is the first female member of the Protestant Church-owned Publisher's Association, and the first black person on the executive committee of this organization. In February of 1989 she was elected vice president of the association.

Adkins, a certified public accountant, was the first woman to serve on the Board of Directors of the Nashville Branch of the Federal Reserve Bank of Atlanta, and she served two terms as its chair. Adkins was the first black woman to be appointed to the Board of Education of Nashville/Davidson County, and served that body for six years.

Among the citations and awards Adkins has received are designation as "Woman of the Year" by the Nashville Business and Professional Woman's Club and by the Nashville Press and Radio Club; an award for "Outstanding Leadership and Community Service" given by the Alpha Kappa Alpha Sorority, Southeastern Regional Conference, 1984; and recognition as "Link of the Year" by the Nashville Chapter of Links, Inc. She is a member of various civic, social, and religious boards and committees, including the YMCA, YWCA, Travelers Aid Society, United Way, Senior Citizens, Inc., Davidson County Department of Human Service, Nashville Chamber of Commerce, and the Nashville Convention Center.

Nabrit married John Willis Adkins on May 26, 1943. They had no children. In 1948 they established the J. W. Adkins Funeral Home in south Nashville, and after John Adkins died in 1984, Cecelia Adkins continues to operate the business. She is a licensed funeral director and serves as an attendant at numerous funerals entrusted to her company.

Adkins is in great demand as a public speaker. As a part of her professional duties, she travels frequently throughout the United States and abroad. In Nashville she is an active member of Progressive Baptist Church, where she serves as church organist. Additionally, Adkins manifests a profound and continuing commitment to the operation of Fisk University. She has served on its board of trustees since 1970 and is currently board chair. She declares, "When I'm asked how I find the time to be on the Board of Trustees when I have so many other obligations, I say that there are two things that continue to impress me about Fisk. First, our product. Fisk continues to turn out top-flight individuals. As long as we continue to fulfill our educational mission, I'm willing to sacrifice for it. And second, Fisk maintains its interest in quality education. We may lack fine facilities, but the one thing we do not lack is interest in maintaining high scholarship."

References

Adkins, Cecelia Nabrit, Resume.

"Fisk Profile: Cecelia Nabrit Adkins, '43," *Fisk News* (Spring 1979): 12-13.

Sheeler, J. Reuben. "The Nabrit Family." *Negro History Bulletin* 20 (October 1956): 3-9.

Who's Who Among Black Americans, 1990/91. Detroit: Gale Research, 1990.

Collections

Photographs and materials on Cecelia Nabrit Adkins are in the Sunday School Publishing Board, Morris Memorial Building, Nashville, and in the Special Collections at Fisk University.

Lois L. Dunn

Octavia Albert

(1853-c. 1899)

Writer

Octavia Albert's *The House of Bondage*, though inspired and informed by faith, is an objective, journalistic approach to the recording of life in bondage. Her interviews with former slaves are a valuable source of history and one of few attempts to document a dark time in American life.

Octavia Victoria Rogers Albert was born a slave on December 24, 1853, in Oglethorpe, Georgia, and died about 1899 in Louisiana. After general emancipation as a young woman, she studied at Atlanta University to be a teacher. She then taught school in Montezuma, Georgia. She married the Reverend A. E. P. Albert on October 21, 1874. Reverend Albert also taught at the school, where they had met in 1873. They had one daughter, Laura T. F. Albert.

Prior to her marriage, Octavia Albert had been a member of the African Methodist Episcopal (AME) church. She joined the Methodist Episcopal church, her husband's denomination, in 1878. Reverend Albert himself baptized her in Houma, Louisiana.

Octavia V. R. Albert is the author of *The House of Bondage, or Charlotte Brooks and Other Slaves* (1890), a series of conversations with former slaves. The sketches were published originally in serial form "some months after her death" in the *Southwestern Christian Advocate*, a journal published by the Methodist Episcopal church. The response from readers was positive and extensive. As a result, her family arranged for the publication of the sketches as a separate volume (Preface, *Bondage)*.

In *Bondage*, Albert articulates the rationale for such a book:

> I believe we should not only treasure [our history], but should transmit [it] to our children's children. That's what the Lord commanded Israel to do in reference to their deliverance from Egyptian bondage, and I verily believe that the same is his will concerning us and our bondage and deliverance in this country. After thirty-three centuries the Jews are more faithful in the observance of the facts connected with their bondage and deliverance than we are in those touching ours, although our deliverance took place scarcely a quarter of a century ago (130).

Religion is a major unifying theme in the book. Albert notes: "It is, indeed, a mystery to those who have witnessed the cruelty of the whites in the South toward the poor, ignorant, innocent, degraded, and helpless people whom God, in his own good time, has liberated. Here, with an open Bible, a Christian land of prosperity for the Caucasian; but, alas! what for the negro?" (58). The question is followed by a call for religious leaders of all denominations to send missionaries to the South rather than abroad.

Catholic slave owners are depicted negatively; they are accused of not honoring the Sabbath nor allowing their slaves to do so. Some former slaves also say that Catholicism lacks the emotional depth of the "'Merican" or Protestant denominations.

The opening chapters focus on Albert's talks with former slave Charlotte Brooks, who suffered much but remained strong, especially helped by her faith. Aunt Charlotte, as Brooks is termed, speaks often of another especially pious slave, Jane Lee. In the book's closing chapter, Albert witnesses and assists the reunion of Jane Lee with her long-lost son, Dr. Coleman Lee. Dr. Lee, a minister, gives a moving speech at the 1884 Cotton Centennial Exposition in New Orleans.

The book's concluding chapters generally stress the progress blacks have been able to make since slavery. Along with Dr. Lee, there is the example of Albert's interview with Colonel Douglass Wilson, a former slave who fought during the Civil War. Wilson cites battles demonstrating incidents of bravery by colored soldiers during the Civil War (132), and he notes positive colored leaders during the Reconstruction (142).

Other historical matters discussed in *The House of Bondage* include the treatment of Union soldiers at Andersonville prison (82-85) and the terrorist activities of the Ku Klux Klan (135-40). Another example of the special perspective of those enslaved in Louisiana is information on the activities of some 'Cadiens (Cajuns) during slavery (106).

The book is clearly written and straightforward. Albert allows the center stage to belong to those she is interviewing. Even as the religious orientation unifies the book, a variety of situations and views are presented. Completed very close to the end of slavery, *The House of Bondage* remains a very valuable resource.

References

Albert, Octavia V. Rogers. *The House of Bondage, or Charlotte Brooks and Other Slaves.* New York: Hunt and Eaton, 1890. Reprinted. New York: Oxford University Press, 1988. (The Schomburg Library of Nineteenth-Century Black Women Writers) Introduction by Frances Smith Foster.

Fleming, John E. "Octavia Victoria Rogers Albert." *Dictionary of American Negro Biography.* Eds. Rayford W. Logan and Michael R. Winston. New York: Norton, 1982. 7-8.

Hagood, L. M. *The Colored Man in the Methodist Episcopal Church.* 1890. Reprinted. New York: Negro Universities Press, 1970. 192, 229.

Majors, M. A. *Noted Negro Women.* Chicago: Donohue and Henneberry, 1893. 219-227.

Slave Testimony: Two Centuries of Letters, Speeches, Interviews, and Autobiographies. Ed. John W. Blassingame. Baton Rouge: Louisiana State University Press, 1977.

Arlene Clift-Pellow

Sadie Alexander

(1898-1989)

Lawyer, civil rights activist

The life of Sadie Tanner Mossell Alexander spanned just over nine decades, from her birth in Philadelphia on January 2, 1898, to her death on November 1, 1989. Sadie Alexander's ancestry was the strong roots from which she grew to become a pioneer for black American women and a role model for anyone striving to end predjudice and discrimination. She played a leadership role in legal, political, and civic arenas, accomplished a list of "firsts," and can count becoming a comic-book hero as one of her finest achievements.

Sadie Alexander was proud of her forebears, and with good reason. Her maternal grandmother, Sadie Elizabeth Miller, was born into slavery in 1840. Her family escaped to Pennsylvania, and in 1858 Sadie Miller and Benjamin Tucker Tanner were married. Tanner became the editor of the *Christian Recorder* 1868-1884, founding editor of the *African Methodist Episcopal Church Review* 1884-1888, and bishop in the African Methodist Episcopal (AME) church. Sadie and Benjamin Tanner had seven children, one of whom was the acclaimed expatriate painter, Henry Ossawa Tanner. Another child, Mary Louise Tanner, married Aaron Albert Mossell.

Aaron Albert Mossell was born in Hamilton, Ontario, Canada, in 1863. Following the Civil War his family settled in Lockport, New York. His father, having donated all the brick for the building of the Lockport Public School, argued successfully against segregated education. As a result, Aaron Mossell and his siblings were the first black Americans to attend an integrated school in Lockport. He attended Lincoln University in Pennsylvania and then the University of Pennsylvania Law School, and in 1888, he was the first black American to graduate from the law school. After graduation, he established a legal practice in Philadelphia with two partners. On September 23, 1890, he was married to Mary Louise Tanner by Bishop Tanner. Aaron and Mary Louise Tanner had three children, Elizabeth, Aaron Albert, and Sadie Tanner. In 1899, despairing of success, Aaron Mossell left the city and his family and settled in Cardiff, Wales, where he championed civil rights for people of color as the chairman of the United Committee of Colored and Colonial Peoples' Organization ("Dr. Mossell's Kin Fights Housing Bias in Wales," Alexander Papers).

Aaron Albert, Jr., was educated in pharmacy at Howard University; he returned to Philadelphia and continued in this line of work. Elizabeth Mossell Anderson attended the

Sadie Alexander

University of Pennsylvania and Columbia University. She held the position of dean at Virginia State College and later at Wilberforce University.

Sadie Mossell Alexander's impressive academic career began in Washington, D.C. She and her family had moved between Washington, where her maternal aunt (her namesake) and uncle, Sarah "Sadie" Elizabeth Tanner Moore and Dr. Lewis Baxter Moore, lived, and Philadelphia, the home of Bishop Benjamin Tucker Tanner and Sadie Alexander's birthplace. When she reached high school, Alexander moved back to Washington to live with Lewis Moore, the dean at Howard University. While attending the M Street High School in Washington, D.C., she was profoundly influenced by Carter G. Woodson.

After completing high school, Alexander was eager to attend Howard University, where she had come to love the campus and the school during her high school years and where she had won a scholarship. Her mother, however, had already investigated the possibility of Alexander attending the University of Pennsylvania and insisted that she return to Philadelphia to attend the university (Interview with Sadie Tanner Mossell Alexander, 12 October 1977, Alexander Papers). As a black American woman, her time at the university was difficult. In 1972 Sadie Alexander wrote:

> I recall praying every night beginning that fall [1916]: "God, give me the strength to do my assignment the very best I have the ability" and "Dear Lord, teach me to walk alone and not be lonely, knowing Thou art at my side." The latter prayer stemmed from the fact that not one woman in my class spoke to me in class or when I passed one or more than one woman on the walks to College Hall or the Library. Can you imagine looking for classrooms and asking persons the way, only to find the same unresponsive person you asked for directions seated in the classroom, in which you entered late because you could not find your way? Let us imagine you came from Outer Space and entered the University of Pennsylvania School of Education. You spoke perfect English, but no one spoke to you. Such circumstances made a student either dropout or a survivor so strong that she could not be overcome, regardless of the indignities (Alexander, 30).

Alexander was given a small broom at graduation as an award for making a clean sweep of her grades, receiving all "Distinguished" grades that year. Enduring prejudice, but remaining focused on academic achievement, she spent very little time on social activities. She did, nevertheless, develop a deep and lasting friendship during her undergraduate years with Virginia Alexander, who later continued her professional studies at the Women's Medical College in Philadelphia. It was through this friendship that Sadie Mossell met Raymond Pace Alexander, Virginia's brother. Virginia and Sadie both became active in the Gamma Chapter of the Delta Sigma Theta Sorority, the first black American sorority at the University of Pennsylvania. Sadie Alexander was to be elected the first president of the Grand Chapter, the national organization, in 1921.

By 1918 she completed her undergraduate program, receiving a bachelor's of science in education with senior honors. She was awarded a master of arts degree in economics, 1919, and won the Francis Sergeant Pepper Fellowship in economics, 1920-1921, one of five grants awarded to women in the graduate school. Her dissertation, entitled "The Standard of Living Among One Hundred Negro Migrant Families in Philadelphia, 1921," qualified her for the honor of the first black American to receive a Ph.D. in economics and one of the first three ever to receive the degree, all in that year. She often recounted in later life, with justifiable pride, how she was followed along the commencement procession route by photographers and reporters from across the country (Sadie T. Mossell to Raymond P. Alexander, 21 May 1921, Alexander Papers; interviews, 1974, 1976, 1979, Alexander Papers).

As a black woman, Sadie Alexander had a great deal of difficulty securing a suitable position. She was finally employed, from 1921 to 1923, as assistant actuary of the North Carolina Mutual Life Insurance Company, Durham, North Carolina, a black-owned company. Her years in North Carolina were lonely and filled with occasions of prejudice from blacks as well because she came from the north and attended a northern university (Interview, 12 October 1977). In 1923 she returned to Philadelphia. On Thanksgiving Day, November 29, 1923, Reverend J. Albert Johnson married Sadie Tanner Mossell and Raymond Pace Alexander at the Tanner homestead on Diamond Street in North Philadelphia.

Sadie Mossell Alexander remained at home during the first year of their marriage while Raymond Pace Alexander, who had just completed his law degree at Harvard University and passed the Pennsylvania bar examination, established his private practice. After her early achievements, the role of housewife left Sadie Alexander feeling unfulfilled. In 1924 she entered the School of Law at the University of Pennsylvania, where she was the first black American woman to be enrolled, to serve as associate editor of the *Law Review,* and in 1927, to graduate. Later that year she passed the Pennsylvania bar examination and, continuing a succession of "firsts," became the first black woman to practice law in Pennsylvania.

Immediately after graduation, Sadie T. M. Alexander joined Raymond Pace Alexander's law office, gradually becoming the firm's specialist in estate and family law. While his civil and criminal cases brought high visibility to the firm, Sadie Alexander was known for the thoroughness of her presentations, her knowledge of the finer points of law, and the extraordinary quality and quantity of her work. By 1931 the Alexander firm had expanded to four more lawyers and a support staff of five. The firm's practice flourished; in 1934 it moved into newly constructed offices at 1900 Chestnut Street, in Philadelphia's commercial center, where real estate had previously been closed to blacks. Ten years later the law offices moved into nearby space on Nineteenth Street, adding three more lawyers.

In addition to her caseload with the Alexander law offices, Sadie Alexander also served as assistant city solicitor of Philadelphia from 1927 to 1931, and from 1936 to 1940, again as the first black American woman to hold the post. In November 1943, Sadie Alexander was elected secretary of the National Bar Association; she remained in office until 1947. Few women held memberships in the National Bar Association; Sadie Alexander was the first to hold national office. As secretary, she was responsible for the publication of three national directories of black American attorneys and was often consulted on the publication of future directories and other association business well after her service. Raymond and Sadie Alexander continued their private practice together until 1959, when Raymond was appointed judge in the Philadelphia Court of Common Pleas.

Law Office Opened

In 1959 Sadie Alexander opened her own law office. The majority of her work remained domestic relations, divorce, adoption, and juvenile care, with the smaller portion of her work, approximately one quarter, dedicated to civil and probate work. Her clients were for the most part schoolteachers, government clerks, professional and business men and women or their spouses, and industrial workers. She did not limit herself to cases in which she was assured a high level of compensation. Sadie Alexander felt, as she once wrote: "If a domestic worker or laborer comes to me with a deserving case in the field in which I practice, which case cries out for competent counsel, I accept the case for a nominal fee. I consider this as much my duty as I consider it the duty of a physician to serve a dying patient" (Personal data questionnaire of the Judicial Nominating Commission, Alexander Papers). She was active in the Philadelphia Bar Association, the Pennsylvania Bar Association, the American Bar Association, the Lawyers' Club of Philadelphia, and the American Judicare Society. She practiced independently until 1976, when she joined the firm of Atkinson, Myers, and Archie as Counsel.

Together the Alexanders fought against discrimination and segregation in Philadelphia hotels, restaurants, and theaters, and it is in the area of civil rights and human relations for which Sadie Alexander is most known. In 1947 she was appointed by President Harry S. Truman to the President's Committee on Civil Rights. The committee was created to prepare a report to address the need for "more adequate and effective means and procedures for the protection of the civil rights of the people of the United States," and its report, entitled *To Secure These Rights,* served as a foundation of the civil rights movement and the basis for future civil rights policy decisions and legislation for decades to follow (VIII).

From 1946 to 1965, Sadie Alexander also served as a prominent member of the Philadelphia Fellowship Commission. When in 1949 the City of Philadelphia was ordered by the General Assembly of Pennsylvania to draft a new city charter, the Fellowship Commission formed a special committee, for which Sadie Alexander served as chairperson, to ensure that the new charter would contain provisions that would guarantee equal treatment and equal opportunity in the city's administration. In her role as chairperson of this committee, Sadie Alexander authored a section of the Home Rule Charter of 1952, the city's new charter, which called for the formation of the Philadelphia Commission on Human Relations. She served as a member of the board for more than fifteen years until 1968, when for political reasons, she resigned from office (Interview, 12 October 1977).

Her national status in the area of civil rights and human relations was recognized in 1978 with her appointment by President Jimmy Carter as chairperson, at the age of eighty-one, of the White House Conference on Aging. The conference was charged to address a broad range of social and economic needs of the nation's elderly. She worked from 1978 until 1981, giving speeches and holding meetings in preparation for the conference. In 1981 President Ronald Reagan removed her from the position as chair before the conference took place.

As early as 1945 Sadie Alexander was nationally recognized as an inspiration for black American achievement. She was featured in a series entitled "Interesting People" and as the 1948 "Woman of the Year" in *Negro Heroes,* a comic book published by the National Urban League in conjunction with the Delta Sigma Theta Sorority. This series was typical of many publications aimed at black youth. It described and emphasized the value of education, training, and perseverance as seen through role models such as Sadie Alexander, Jackie Robinson, and Booker T. Washington.

Not only did Sadie Alexander make valuable contributions to the legal and political field, but she actively participated in and played leadership roles in more than thirty local and national civic organizations. Some of these include: the American Civil Liberties Union, the Americans for Democratic Action, the National Urban League, National Association for the Advancement of Colored People, the Philadelphia Housing Authority, The Benezet Committee, National Welfare Assembly, Lawyer's Committee on Civil Rights, United States Committee of the International Conference on Social Work, Committee on Religion and Public Education, National Conference on Christians and Jews, National Defense Conference on Negro Affairs, National Midcentury Committee for Children and Youth, Philadelphia Council for Community Advancement, Philadelphia Household Institute, Philadelphia USO Council, Philadelphia Service Organization, National Committee on Segregation in the Nation's Capitol, Texas Centennial Commission, Wharton Settlement, and Women's International League for Peace and Freedom.

She and Raymond Pace Alexander had two children, Mary Elizabeth Alexander (who later married Melvin F. Brown), and Rae Pace Alexander (who married Archie C. Epps, III and, later, Thomas Kendall Minter). Balancing her professional and civic life with family was just one more example of Sadie Alexander's abilities. In 1974 she received a fifth, richly deserved degree from the University of Pennsylvania—an honorary degree of Doctor of Laws. Her citation read:

> Through her singular legacy of womanhood, family, and race, Sadie Tanner Mossell Alexander has given us all a special heritage of accomplishment to be admired and emulated. . . . As an active worker for civil rights, she has been a steady and forceful advocate on the national, state, and municipal scene, reminding people everywhere that freedoms are won not only by idealism but by persistence and will over a long time.

Drexel University, Lincoln University, Medical College of Philadelphia, Spelman College, Swarthmore College, and Wilson College also awarded her honorary degrees.

In 1982 Alzheimer's disease forced Sadie's Alexander's retirement from practice and public life. She lived the last years of her life at Cathedral Village, a retirement community in the Roxborough section of Philadelphia.

References

Alexander, Sadie. "'A Clean Sweep:' Reflections on the Rocky Road to Winning a 'Broom Award' in 1918." *Pennsylvania Gazette* (March 1972): 30.

Alexander, Sadie Tanner Mossell. Interview, Sadie Tanner Mossell Alexander Papers, 1974, 1976, 1977, 1979. Sadie Tanner Mossell Alexander Papers, Box 1, folders 19-21.

"Autobiography of Nathan Francis Mossell." Alexander Papers, Sadie Tanner Mossell Alexander Papers, Box 78, folder 2.

"Dr. Mossell's Kin Fights Housing Bias in Wales." Alexander Papers, Box 78, folder 11.

Mossell, Sadie T. to Raymond P. Alexander, 21 May 1921. Alexander Papers, Box 3, folder 1.

Personal Data Questionnaire of the Judicial Nominating Commission, 1964. Sadie Tanner Mossell Alexander Papers, Box 1, folder 12.

To Secure These Rights: The Report of the President's Committee on Civil Rights. Washington, D.C.: U.S. Government Printing Office, 1947.

"The Tanner Family." *Negro History Bulletin* 10 (April 1947): 148.

Collections

The Alexander Papers, located at the University of Pennsylvania Archives, consist of five series: the Raymond Pace Alexander papers; the Sadie Tanner Mossell papers; the joint papers of Raymond and Sadie Alexander; the Elizabeth Mossell Anderson papers; and the Virginia M. Alexander papers. There are slides, tapes, film footage, and hundreds of photographs throughout the collection documenting the visual history of this prominent black American family.

Theresa Snyder

Elreta Alexander Ralston

(1919-)

Lawyer, judge

Elreta Narcissus Melton Alexander Ralston is distinguished as the first black woman popularly elected to the judiciary in the United States and the second black person to hold this honor. Already widely known and respected as an able, skillful criminal lawyer before her judgeship, she was responsible for many judicial reforms in her North Carolina district. Often the target of attacks by some to remove her from the bench, she effectively withstood the tactics and remained a highly respected judge until she chose an early retirement from the bench in 1981.

Alexander Ralston was born March 21, 1919, in Smithfield, North Carolina, the youngest of three children of Joseph C. Melton, a Baptist minister and teacher, and Alian A. (Reynolds) Melton. Alexander Melton received her elementary school education in Danville, Virginia, and in 1934, at the age of fifteen, she received her diploma from James B.

Dudley High School in Greensboro, North Carolina. In 1937 she graduated from North Carolina Agricultural and Technical College (now University) in Greensboro, receiving her bachelor's degree at age eighteen. When Columbia University School of Law awarded her the L.L.B. degree in 1945, Alexander Ralston became the school's first black woman graduate. On June 7, 1938, she married Girardeau Alexander, a surgeon, and had one son, Alexander III. After her husband's death in 1979, she married John D. Ralston, who had retired from the IRS Appellate Division.

Prior to pursuing a law degree, Alexander Ralston taught history and mathematics and directed music in South Carolina and North Carolina for four years. Afterwards she became a law clerk in the firm of Dyer & Stevens in New York City, a position which she held from 1945 to 1947. That year, until December 1968, she practiced law in Greensboro, becoming the first black woman to practice law in North Carolina and the first to try a case in the state supreme court. In 1965 she became a senior partner in the first integrated firm in the state.

Alexander Ralston had a colorful career as an attorney. She represented a group that brought suit against the Greensboro City Council for its attempt to block the rezoning of a tract to permit a private housing project for blacks. The suit resulted in the granting of the first federal housing project to blacks and the election of the first black to the Greensboro City Council. She was a leader in establishing the first city-owned golf course for blacks in Greensboro and the attorney for its incorporation. In 1950 she personally integrated Montaldos, an exclusive women's store in downtown Greensboro. Later, upon her insistence, the owner promoted a black woman elevator operator to salesperson.

For twenty-one years Alexander Ralston represented both blacks and whites in state and federal courts, and for many years, was the only female attorney practising. She has been described in local press editorials as ''flamboyant,''which she disclaims, although she does admit to being stylishly dressed. And Alexander Ralston has also been labelled ''formidable''. Indeed, she represented a number of Ku Klux Klan men, who, after their trials, left the Klan because of her fair and effective representation of them.

Alexander Ralston Elected District Judge

The new Constitutional Court System of 1968 subjected all regular judges in the state of North Carolina to election, except interim appointments and special superior court judges. Alexander Ralston's district, Guilford County, was phased in with the election of six district court judges from the nominees of the Republican and Democratic parties. She changed parties, ran as one of five nominees of the Republican party, and polled the third highest vote—without actually campaigning, Alexander Ralston was elected the only Republican woman in her district and the only black in the state. This was the first time a black woman had been elected to the judiciary in the United States by popular election, and she was only the second black elected in the country.

Alexander Ralston ran as a Republican in the belief that her election would help create an effective two-party system in North Carolina and pressure the reigning Democratic party to appoint qualified minorities to governmental positions, particularly in the courts. The Democrats responded by appointing a black judge who is now a state appellate judge. This practise gained momentum, and soon the party had appointed women of both races and black men to all of the courts of the state and to prime positions in state government. Alexander Ralston's views on the treatment of ethnic groups in the courts were expressed in an article in *Ebony* magazine in 1971:

> ''I don't practice ethnic law. . . . I don't consider myself a black judge. I think of We, the People. I don't want Black Power or White Power. . . . The duty of the judge is to interpret the law fairly, impersonally and accurately . . . to the end that the judge does not make law, but causes other people to abide by the law'' (''Black Judges in the South,'' 33).

Alexander Ralston is also a ''law and order'' person, observing that ''the law of the universe is built on order. Order leads to liberty and chaos to destruction'' (33).

When President Richard M. Nixon was reelected in 1974, a Republican governor was elected in North Carolina for the first time since Reconstruction. Also in 1974, the position of chief justice of the state supreme court became subject to statewide election, and it was assumed that no Republican would run for that position since all members of the bench were Democrats. Furthermore, the Republicans were thought to have a tacit understanding that no Republican would run for that position to assure that the senior jurist, who was female, would be elected. Alexander Ralston filed for the nomination but learned later that another Republican, who was not a lawyer, had also filed. He won as the Republican nominee with 52 percent of the votes in the primary. The results so enraged the public that only a few of the Republican candidates won in the general election. After that, Alexander Ralston became targeted for some campaigns to ''get her at all costs.'' She was reelected for two more consecutive terms to the district court bench, leading the ticket. She retired in April 1981, after having been elected four consecutive terms, to practise law in the integrated firm of Alexander Ralston, Pell & Speckhard.

Alexander Ralston's persuasiveness brought about many reforms in the judiciary. She stopped the practice of the public demeaning of minority lawyers by judges, officials, and the majority public who addressed them by first name. She started assigning probation officers to offenders regardless of either's color or gender. In 1969 she began a rehabilitation program for youthful and other offenders, a deferred sentencing program with alternatives to incarceration and a criminal record. The program was called ''Judgment Day,'' which was a special day set aside for those in the program to report and testify on their progress, each offender providing support for the others in a system similar to that practiced in

Alcoholics Anonymous. When a new state code was enacted in 1973, effective in 1975, by which the district attorney had the authority to dismiss criminal cases, Alexander Ralston's assignment was restricted. The concerted attack on ''Judgment Day'' and attempts from high state officers to censure her were never supported. Much of her program has now become statutory and the original ''Judgment Day'' concept enables its participants to enhance their lives or the life of a loved one or friend.

When the local press conducted a judicial rating poll among the local bar, Alexander Ralston was at the top, leading every judge in a significant category. The bar and the public continued to rate her highly and support her efforts. She encouraged student participation in court proceedings and often allowed classes to attend her court to learn the court system.

Alexander Ralston, an attractive, fair-skinned, silver-haired, ''stylishly''dressed woman of five feet two and one half inches, is poised, assertive, articulate, commanding, and self-assured. As a member of the bench, and as a practicing attorney, she has a reputation of being just and exacting. Yet, she has time for matters other than law: she is active in civic organizations and is a frequent speaker for civic, religious, educational, governmental, fraternal, youth, and senior citizens organizations. She has served on the Board of Disadvantaged Students at the University of North Carolina at Greensboro, the board of visitors of the Appalachian State University, the board of advisors of the North Carolina Symphony, and, continuing her interest in drug action programs, the board of the Drug Action Council.

Alexander Ralston has also written a book of poetry, *When Is a Man Free*, and a commencement speech that she delivered was published in *Vital Speeches of Today*. The high esteem in which she is held extends to community groups. In 1969 Alexander Ralston received the Dolly Madison Award from the Greensboro Chamber of Commerce for her contribution to womanpower in the community; Guys and Dolls, Inc., a national family organization, named her the most admired black citizen of Greensboro in 1969 and 1970 and inducted her as an honorary member; she received the Citizenship Award from the Cherokee Council of the Boy Scouts of America in 1970; in 1976 she was awarded the ''Brotherhood Citation'' from the Greensboro Chapter of the National Conference of Christians and Jews; the North Carolina Federation of Womens Clubs in 1977 selected her one of the twenty-five most distinguished women in the state; and in 1980 she attended a reception given by Mrs. Roslyn Carter at the White House in honor of Distinguished Negro Women. She has received numerous other recognitions and citations for outstanding leadership and distinction in the judicial system and in the community.

References

Alexander Ralston, Elreta. Resume.

''Black Judges in the South.'' *Ebony* (March 1971): 31-34, 36, 38, 40.

Horton, Luci. ''The Distaff Side of Politics.'' *Ebony* (December 1973): 48-50, 52-54.

Jackson, Donald Dale. *Judges*. n.p., 1974.

Paths Toward Freedom. Raleigh: Center for Urban Affairs, North Carolina State University, 1976.

Wake Forest Jurist. Wake Forest Law School, Spring 1975.

Who's Who Among Black Americans, 1990/91. Detroit: Gale Research, 1990.

Jessie Carney Smith

Debbie Allen

(1950-)

Actress, television producer, writer and director, singer, dancer

Deborah ''Debbie'' Allen has arrived as one of American show business's brightest stars. She has spent a lifetime preparing for her current breaks. Her philosophy is that ''luck is when opportunity meets preparation'' (*Current Biography Yearbook*, 3). Actress, singer, dancer, director, producer Allen was born in Houston, Texas, on January 16, 1950, to a Pulitzer Prize-nominee for poetry, Vivian (Ayers) Allen, and a dentist, Andrew Allen. She is the third of four children (one sister and two brothers) in a rather artistic family that includes Phylicia Rashad—Clare on the ''Cosby Show''—and Andrew ''Tex'' Allen—a jazz musician.

At the age of three, Allen began her dance training. By age eight she had settled on a future in musical theater, inspired by a performance of *Revelations* by Alvin Ailey's ballet troupe. Her mother, whom she considers her mentor, was an active participant in her training, so much so that when she attempted to enroll Allen in the Houston Foundation for Ballet and was denied due to what was perceived to be existing segregation practices, Vivian Allen contracted a former dancer with the Ballet Russe to give her daughter private lessons. Later she took her three older children and moved to Mexico City where Allen trained with the Ballet Nacional de Mexico. There Allen became fluent in Spanish and attended performances of the Ballet Folklorico de Mexico. Back in Houston, at age fourteen, she was finally admitted to the Houston Foundation for Ballet on full scholarship. Allen was the only black in the company.

The Houston Foundation for Ballet was not the final racial obstacle to Allen's training. As her senior year of high school approached she sought but was denied admission to the North Carolina School of the Arts in Winston-Salem. Though the director cited inappropriate body type as the reason for refusal, Allen credited this rejection to a racial quota system, since she had been asked to demonstrate technique to others auditioning at that time. This rejection proved to be difficult for the young dancer to accept, causing her to stop training for a year; instead, she studied Greek classics, speech, and theater arts at Howard University, Washington, D.C.

At Howard, choreographer Mike Malone reintroduced Allen to dance. After recruiting her for his dance troupe, he gave her a part in the Burn Brae Dinner Theater's production of *The Music Man*. Allen began to perform with student groups at the university while also studying at the National Ballet School. Additionally, the busy dancer became the head of the dance department at the Duke Ellington School of the Performing Arts. She received her bachelor of fine arts degree cum laude from Howard in 1971.

Although she loved teaching, she also yearned for the stage and decided to go to New York after her graduation. Her first Broadway performance there was in the chorus of the musical adaptation of Ossie Davis's play *Purlie Victorious*, titled *Purlie*. After just six weeks in that show, Allen left to become a principal dancer in George Faison's modern dance troupe, the Universal Dance Experience.

In 1973 she returned to the Broadway stage in *Raisin*, a musical rendering of the Lorraine Hansberry classic *A Raisin in the Sun*. She "added a kick and a turn to her dance assignment whenever possible" and was quickly elevated to the featured role of Beneatha (*Current Biography Yearbook*, 4). The theater critic for the *New York Post*, Richard Watts, noted "I liked the attractively humorous and zestful Debbie Allen as the ambitious [young woman]." *Women's Wear Daily*'s Martin Gottfried found her "enchanting . . . and [with] chance enough to show a special talent for dance and a delightful quality altogether" (*New York Theatre Critic's Reviews*, No. 26).

After a nearly two-year run in *Raisin*, Allen began working in television in both commercials and series. Her first commercial, selling disposable diapers, gave her a chance to work with her sister. Though her next effort, a comedy-variety series titled *3 Girls 3* was a critical success, it did poorly in the ratings and was quickly canceled. Subsequently, she took on television specials, working with Ben Vereen on his special *Stompin' at the Savoy* and with Jimmie Walker in the made-for-television movie *The Greatest Thing That Almost Happened.*

Back on stage in 1977, Allen starred with Leslie Uggams and Richard Roundtree as Miss Adelaide in the National Company's revival of *Guys and Dolls*. In 1978 she was selected for the lead in a disco version of *Alice in Wonderland*. The production was a disappointing failure and closed after only a short run. Allen described the *Alice* flop as devastating.

Displaying Texas-sized enthusiasm and energy, she returned to television in 1979 as Alex Haley's wife in the top-rated autobiographical miniseries *Roots: The Next Generation*. On stage, she joined the cast of *Ain't Misbehavin'*. That year also marked Allen's film debut in *The Fish That Saved Pittsburgh*. The hard-working actress and dancer worked in both capacities on the film, behind the camera as choreographer, and in front of it as a cheerleader.

In 1980 it was back to Broadway in a revival of *West Side Story*. The Jerome Robbins' choreography provided the perfect vehicle to display Allen's talent. This role would finally be the one she had hoped for, one that would place her in that charmed circle of stars who could name their own projects. Indeed, she so overwhelmed the critics that Clive Barnes of the *New York Post* was led to believe that this role would catapult her to stardom. Walter Kerr of the *New York Times* concurred, commenting that "Debbie Allen is worth checking out on the double. . . . She whips across the stage floor dizzyingly" (*New York Theatre Critics Review,* Number 3). Her peers agreed with the public and critical assessment of her performance and nominated her for the Antoinette Perry ("Tony") Award and gave her the Drama Desk Award.

That year Allen also took a bit part in the hit movie *Fame*, playing the dance instructor Lydia Grant in the fictionalized look at New York City's High School for the Performing Arts. She only had two lines but was able to execute them in such a way as to make them her ticket to an enduring on-screen presence. The movie became a television spin-off with Allen reprising the part of the strong yet empathetic dance instructor. She also contracted to choreograph the show. "Fame" achieved critical acclaim but declined in the ratings due to its mid-season arrival and being scheduled against an established hit, "Magnum P.I." *Current Biography Yearbook* commented that it may also have been impeded by "a national viewing public possibly nonplussed by the most ethnically diverse cast on television" (5). Despite its ratings the show ran from 1982 to 1983 on NBC, winning five Emmy Awards (two to Allen for choreography) and a Golden Globe Award for best actress in a series. The show was quickly picked up as an independent project and was distributed to 116 nonaffiliated stations. Seen in thirty states in syndication markets, the show gained a new level of popularity. It also became a number one show in syndication in Great Britain, continental Europe, and Australia. For the show's fourth season (1985-1986), Allen was contracted to produce and direct the show in addition to the choreography.

In 1981 Allen returned to film, taking a part in the movie *Ragtime*. In a cast of seasoned big-screen stars, including James Cagney, Moses Gunn, and Howard Rollins, Jr., she was able to create a "believable portrait of a distraught woman trying to cope with disastrous circumstances" (*Current Biography Yearbook,* 5). Other film parts were scarce due to the lack of roles for blacks.

During her 1983 work on *Fame*, Allen took time off to make a television movie titled *Women of San Quentin*, in which she played a hard prison guard. In 1985 she again made time for a television production, choreographing, cowriting, and performing in the special "Dancin' in the Wings."

Back on the big screen in 1986, Allen starred with Richard Pryor in his "semi-autobiography," *Jo Jo Dancer, Your Life is Calling*. Bob Fosse's choreography in the revival of *Sweet Charity* beckoned her back to the Broadway stage that same year. The show won Allen her second Tony nomination. She also filled out her busy year by directing episodes of "Family Ties" and "Bronx Zoo."

The 1987-1988 season was a rocky one for "the Cosby Show" spin-off, "A Different World." The show consistently attained top ratings on the coattails of "the Cosby Show" but received critical jeers. Executive producer Bill Cosby challenged Allen to take over behind the camera. Accepting the challenge, she was able to revive the show through creative directing and meatier, more realistic plots.

Allen's natural talent and effervescence was most visible in choreographical achievements in "Polly" and "Polly—Coming Home," a black adaptation of the Polly Anna stories, which aired on ABC in 1989 and 1990. For the 1990 "Motown 30 Special," a chronology of the thirty years of the black-founded record company, Allen created a dance retrospective that traced the roots of break dancing. The 1990-1991 television season saw her named producer, director, occasional writer, and guest star on "A Different World."

This versatile performer recorded her first album, *Special Look*, in 1989. Her plans are to rival Paula Abdul and Janet Jackson with her own triple threat of singing, dancing, and exciting stage and visual presence.

Allen's whirlwind career has not precluded a personal life. She has been married twice. Her first marriage in 1975 to CBS Records executive Winfred Wilford was a bicoastal affair. She worked on her career in New York, and he on his in Los Angeles. The marriage did not survive and the couple divorced in 1983. In 1984 she married Norman Nixon, a former basketball star with the Los Angeles Lakers and the Los Angeles Clippers. The two had been friends since 1978, though Nixon did not see her perform until 1982, and she did not see him play until later that year. Two children have been born to the marriage, Vivian Nichole and Norman Nixon, Jr. Debbie Allen credits Nixon with supporting her in a way that allows her to aggressively pursue her career. "Being rooted in a really good family life situation allows me creative freedom. . . . I've found myself even more creative since I've had my children," she remarks of her family ("Debbie Allen," 57).

References

Cohen-Strayner, Barbara Naomi. *Biographical Dictionary of Dance*. New York: Schirmer Books, 1982.

Contemporary Theatre, Film, and Television. Vol. 6. Detroit: Gale Research, 1989.

Current Biography Yearbook. New York: H. W. Wilson, 1987.

"Debbie Allen—Doing It All, Her Way!!" *Ebony* 45 (November 1989): 54-58.

Mapp, Edward. *Directory of Blacks in the Performing Arts*. Metuchen, N.J.: Scarecrow Press, 1978.

"Mothers and Daughters: The Special Connection." *Ebony* 43 (February 1988): 158-62.

New York Theatre Critics' Reviews. 34, No. 26 (1973): 218-21; 51, No. 3 (1980): 366-71.

Ploski, Harry A., and James Williams, eds. *Negro Almanac*. Detroit: Gale Research, 1989.

Who's Who among Black Americans. 5th ed. Lake Forest, Ill.: Educational Communications, 1988.

Sarah Crest

Caroline Still Anderson

(1848-1919)

Physician, educator

Prominent nineteenth-century physicians Caroline Virginia Still Wiley Anderson, was born in Philadelphia, Pennsylvania, on November 1, 1848. Her career as a physician and educator included an active participation as a decision-maker in her community.

Her father, William Still, the son of fugitive slaves, became a successful businessman, abolitionist, and prominent figure in the Philadelphia station of the Underground Railroad. In fact, Still conducted "passengers," or escaped slaves, to the New York homes of prominent black abolitionists David Ruggles, Jermain Loguen, and Frederick Douglass. In 1883 Still published his seminal work, *The Underground Railroad*, which recorded many of the authentic events of escaped slaves in the railroad's history.

In 1860 William Still had invested in the coal-mining business. By 1867 his Lehigh and Schuylkill Coal Business was flourishing and provided him a respectable income. Having achieved prominence and financial security for his family, William Still was able to send his daughter to Mrs. Henry Gordon's Private School and the Friends Raspberry Allen School for her early education. In 1861 Caroline Still entered the Institute for Colored Youth, now Cheyney State

College, in Pennsylvania and went on to complete her high school education.

Anderson was almost sixteen years old when she entered Oberlin College in 1865. While a student at Oberlin, some of her expenses were paid by her father while her remaining fees were paid from other support. She graduated from the Oberlin College Literary Course in August 1868, the youngest and only "colored" in a class of forty-five. During the commencement exercises, was elected to preside over the annual meeting of the Ladies' Literary Society of Oberlin—an honor never before bestowed upon one of her race.

After graduation, Anderson returned to Philadelphia and taught school. On December 28, 1869, she married Edward A. Wiley in her parents' home. The wedding was covered by the press and an account from the *Loraine County News* stated that "sixty or seventy persons were present at the wedding, including Lucretia Mott, Wm. Whipper, James Grant, and many others who have been earnest and active in the anti-slavery movement."

Wiley was born a slave in Alabama. Anderson apparently met him at Oberlin College while they were students. Wiley supported himself at Oberlin by doing "hard, physical labor outside of college hours"(*Loraine County News* 20 January 1870). He worked and attended college for three years. Unable to keep up with his studies and hold to a rigorous work schedule, he left Oberlin. Due to poor health he died in 1873, never having the opportunity to enjoy the growth of their two children, William and Letitia.

Interest in Medical Career Develops

After teaching for another year in Philadelphia, Anderson went to Howard University in Washington, D.C., and taught drawing and speech. In 1875 she decided to enroll in Howard's medical school. The following year she transferred to the Woman's Medical College of Pennsylvania. When she graduated on March 14, 1878, Anderson was one of two black women in a class of seventeen to receive her medical degree; the other was Georgiana E. Patterson Young of New York.

Anderson did her internship in 1878 and 1879 at the New England Hospital for Women and Children in Boston. Initially she was refused a position on account of her race, but after a meeting of the hospital's board of management she was unanimously accepted. After completing her internship, she returned to Pennsylvania, where she was to spend the majority of her life.

On August 17, 1880, Caroline Still married Matthew Anderson. He was born in Green Castle, Pennsylvania, on January 25, 1848, the son of Timothy and Mary (Croog) Anderson. Matthew Anderson had graduated from Oberlin College in 1874 with a Bachelor of Arts degree, and went on to attend and receive a Doctor of Divinity from Lincoln University near Philadelphia, Pennsylvania. Soon after graduation Anderson helped found the Berean Presbyterian Church in Philadelphia.

In 1899 the Berean Manual Training and Industrial School was established. According to the school's 1907 catalogue, the institution was formed "for the purpose of educating and training minors and adults in cooking, carpentering, upholstering, sewing, millinery, or any and all kinds of manual and industrial employment, and also instruction in the branches of a practical liberal education" (15).

Anderson was instrumental in helping to establish the school, and served as its instructor in elocution, physiology, and hygiene as well as its assistant principal. Her personal life was equally demanding. The Andersons had five children, three of whom survived—Helen, Maude, and Margaret.

Involvement in community activities and events was very much a part of Anderson's life before she suffered a stroke that left her paralyzed for five or six years before her death on June 1, 1919. She had served as treasurer of the Woman's Medical College of Pennsylvania Alumnae Association in 1888. She was a member of the Board of the Home for Aged and Infirm Colored People of Philadelphia, president of the Bureau Women's Christian Temperance Union, and one of the main organizers of the YWCA for black people in Philadelphia.

References

Berean Manual Training and Industrial School. Catalogue, 1907/08.

Blockson, Charles. *Pennsylvania's Black History*. Edited by Louise D. Stone. Philadelphia: Portfolio Associates, 1975.

———. *The Underground Railroad in Pennsylvania*. Jacksonville, N.C.: Flame International, 1981.

Caroline Still Papers. Charles L. Blockson Afro-American Collection, Temple University, Philadelphia, Pa.

News, (Loraine County) 20 January 1870.

Still, William. *The Underground Railroad*. Philadelphia: Porter, 1883.

Collections

Papers of Caroline Virginia Still Wiley Anderson are in the Archives and Special Collections on Women in Medicine, the Medical College of Pennsylvania; Berean Institute; Charles L. Blockson Afro-American Historical Collection, Temple University; Historical Society of Pennsylvania (includes photographs), and Oberlin College Archives (also includes photographs).

Margaret Jerrido

Marian Anderson

(c. 1900-)

Singer

Marian Anderson rose from inauspicious beginnings to become one of the twentieth century's most celebrated singers. The contralto who first sang in her church choir, astonished audiences around the world, and in doing so became a symbol of overcoming discrimination in the arts. Furthermore, she never compromised her position: she included beloved black spirituals among the traditional pieces of her repertoire.

Anderson, the first of three daughters of John Berkeley Anderson and Anna D. Anderson, was born in Philadelphia, Pennsylvania, on February 27, circa 1900. (Anderson's birth year is most frequently reported as 1902, although some biographies show her birth year as 1908.) John Anderson worked at the Reading Terminal Market and sold ice and coal in Philadelphia communities. Anna Anderson, originally from Virginia, had taught school in Lynchburg, Virginia. Unable to find a teaching position in Philadelphia, however, she contributed to the family income by doing laundry for others in her home.

The family lived in south Philadelphia, first in small quarters on Webster Street, then at 713 Colorado Street, near the home of the paternal grandparents. Anderson's memories of her early childhood suggest a warm, loving environment with church and school central. John Anderson was a member and officer of the large Union Baptist Church; Anna Anderson was a member of the Methodist church. Marian Anderson was taken to the Union Baptist Church at an early age by her father, and it was at the church that her musical ability was nurtured. She became a member of the church's junior choir, which was directed by Alexander Robinson. She recalls learning the hymn "Dear to the Heart of the Shepherd," which Robinson had asked her to memorize. She made her first public appearance singing this hymn, with her friend Viola Johnson singing soprano, at the main service at Union Baptist Church.

Marian Anderson

Anderson's musical experiences expanded and developed in Union Baptist Church, where she remained a member of the junior choir and joined the senior choir by age thirteen. She usually sang alto but often substituted for absent choir members by singing soprano and tenor or singing the bass line up one octave. Her voice had a range of three octaves from low D to high C. Her singing ability was known throughout the community. At a young age she was singing beyond her own church, and she was identified as the "baby contralto."

Music was the center of what one biographer has termed a life of "artistic compulsion." In recalling her early years in her autobiography and in interviews, Anderson speaks of this urge to make music. She ran errands for neighbors and scrubbed their steps to earn $3.45 to buy a violin from a neighborhood pawn shop. When the violin was no longer playable, she persuaded her father to buy a piano from his brother. Although the piano was purchased, there were no funds for lessons. So, using a keyboard note guide, Anderson and her sisters taught themselves to play.

When Anderson was about ten years old, her father was injured at work and never recovered. Anna Anderson and her daughters moved into the home of John Anderson's parents, and she worked in other people's homes as a cleaning woman and laundress. When her daughters were older, she took a job as a cleaning woman at Wanamaker's Department Store.

Anderson went to William Penn High School, where she was enrolled in the commercial course, taking classes in shorthand and typing so that she could obtain a job to assist her family. She sang at churches and for various community activities, often earning small fees that she shared with her mother and sisters. Through a family friend, John Thomas Butler, she was introduced to soprano Mary Saunders Patterson, who gave her vocal lessons gratis. Penn High School had limited musical courses, but Anderson participated in all available music activities.

After Anderson sang for some school visitors, one of them, a Dr. Rohrer, spoke with the school principal urging that Anderson be transferred to a high school with college preparatory courses. She was transferred to South Philadelphia High School for Girls, from which she graduated on June 20, 1921. Anderson also joined and sang with the Philadelphia Choral Society. Throughout her high school years she embarked on a schedule of singing at nearby churches and schools that often meant missing and having to make up her high school classes. G. Grant Williams, editor of the *Philadelphia Tribune*, became her first manager. She continued voice study with Patterson, who encouraged her to get additional training. Anderson studied with Agnes Reifsnyder, a contralto, who concentrated her teaching on the development of Anderson's medium and low tones.

In the summer of 1919, Anderson was in Chicago at the inaugural meeting of the National Association of Negro Musicians. She was the recipient of a first scholarship from this organization, which was to be used for study at a conservatory of music. Although Anderson was accepted by Yale University, the full funds pledged by members of this organization were not forthcoming, so those received were used for her continued study with the Philadelphia teacher, Giuseppe Boghetti.

Anderson was taken to Boghetti's studio for an audition through the intervention of her high school principal, Lucy Wilson, and Wilson's friend Lisa Roma, who was Boghetti's student. This well-known and very busy teacher, on hearing her, agreed to accept her as a student. There was initially no money for the cost of this instruction, but the members of the Union Baptist Church sponsored a concert with Roland Hayes as the soloist, and the money was raised for her instruction. Boghetti remained her voice teacher for many years and continued as her musical advisor until his death.

Anderson's concertizing continued, but while formerly she was her own accompanist, she now was accompanied by William (Billy) King, who became her manager and encouraged her to add "E" as her middle initial and to expand her touring itinerary. They traveled by train to southern schools and churches. A regularly scheduled concert was given at Hampton Institute, where R. Nathaniel Dett encouraged her and advised her never to compromise in her study of music. Her earnings, contributed to her family, made it possible for them to purchase their own home.

By 1924 Anderson felt competent enough to make a New York concert debut. She sang to a very small audience at Town Hall in what she considered a major career fiasco. She sang lieder, and the critic's comment about her German so depressed her that she stopped studying music and put aside any hope for a musical career. Although this was not the first time her lack of extensive language study was mentioned, it was the most devastating. Anderson had studied French in high school, was tutored in French in Boghetti's studio, and was also coached in French songs by Leon Rothier in New York City. She learned Italian from Boghetti as well, and was urged by many to go to Europe to study and develop language proficiency.

Eventually Anderson returned to music—to her concerts and classes with Boghetti. In the summer of 1925 he entered her in the auditions sponsored by the National Music League, with the award being an appearance with the New York Philharmonic Orchestra. Anderson won over approximately three hundred contestants. The centerpiece of music she prepared for the contest was the aria "O mio Fernando" from Donizetti's *La Favorita*. On August 26, 1925, she appeared at Lewisohn Stadium with the Philharmonic Orchestra conducted by Willem Van Hoogstraten and accompanied by King.

After this concert Anderson was managed by the Arthur Judson Company of New York. Judson's management produced no discernable change in her itinerary or audiences during this period. For Anderson there remained a sense of the need for additional study. Her attempt to enroll in a school of music in Philadelphia was met with the comment, "We don't take colored." Judson encouraged her to study with Frank LaForge, and she was able to do so with a scholarship but incurred the animosity of her longtime teacher, Boghetti. She concentrated on lieder in her studies with LaForge and later returned to her study with Boghetti.

By 1928 Anderson saved enough money to go to England, intent on studying with Raimund von Zur Mühlen, with whom Lawrence Brown suggested she study German lieder. She was also given the address of Roger Quilter, the English composer who had befriended Roland Hayes and other black musicians. Quilter was ill and she was unable to see him. She was welcomed by the composer and baritone, John Payne however, and stayed at his Regent Park Road quarters, as did many musicians, including singers Nell Pierce Hunter, the Paul Robesons, and Alberta Hunter. She had only two lessons with the aged and ill von Zur Mühlen. When Quilter was finally able to see her, he told Anderson to consider studying with Mark Raphael, a student of von Zur Mühlen. She did study with Raphael and also with Amanda Ira Aldridge, the daughter of actor Ira Aldridge.

Anderson sang for guests of Quilter and made her English debut at Wigmore Hall on September 16, 1930, followed by an appearance at a Promenade Concert with conductor Sir Henry Wood. After about a year in England, Anderson returned to the United States, still with the unfulfilled desire to become an accomplished and expert singer of lieder. She resumed concertizing under Judson's management with King as her accompanist.

Anderson, an honorary member of the Alpha Kappa Alpha sorority, sang at a Chicago concert that they sponsored. After the concert Ray Field and George Arthur, representatives of the Julius Rosenwald Fund, spoke with her. They invited her to apply for a Rosenwald Fellowship for additional study in Europe. Anderson was granted a six-month fellowship, with exception made to the usual one year required. She returned to Europe, this time to Berlin, to live with a German family, the von Edburgs, in order to absorb and master the German language. She studied music for a short period with Sverre Joran and had more extensive coaching with Michael Raucheisen.

Berlin Concert Brings Critical Acclaim

Anderson's concert in the Bach Saal in Berlin in October of 1930 brought her critical acclaim. She embarked on an extensive European career, making occasional returns to the United States, and she received a second Rosenwald Grant in 1933. She credits Kosti Vehanen, her new accompanist, for her extended repertoire and her career advancement. She sang more than 108 concerts in a twelve-month period in the Scandinavian countries, learning songs in Swedish, Norwegian, and Finnish. She visited the home of Sibelius and sang for him. He dedicated his composition "Solitude" to her.

Anderson continued to study in Europe—French repertoire with Germaine de Castro and Mahler songs with Madame Charles Cahier [Sara Jane Layton-Walker], who had studied with Mahler. Her programs now showed works by the composers Handel, Scarlatti, Pergolesi, Strauss, Brahms, Schubert, Schuman, Dvorak, Rimsky-Korsakov, and Rachmaninoff. Audiences all over the world, including those in the Soviet Union, called for her to sing or repeat Schubert's "Ave Maria." Always a part of a Anderson concert were spirituals. She usually sang those as arranged by her friend Harry Burleigh, but she also sang and recorded the spirituals of Lawrence Brown, Hall Johnson, Roland Hayes, R. Nathaniel Dett, and Florence Price.

At Salzburg in 1935, Arturo Toscanini made his often repeated remark regarding Anderson. Vehanen records it: "Arturo Toscanini told Mme. Cahier, 'What I heard today one is privileged to hear only in a hundred years.' He did not say the voice he heard, but *what* he heard—not the voice alone but the whole art" (Vehanen, 130). Another highlight of Anderson's European career was her performance of Brahm's "Alto Rhapsody" in Vienna with the orchestra conducted by Bruno Walter.

At a concert at the Salle Gaveau in Paris, Anderson was heard by the impresario Sol Hurok, who introduced himself and told her that he wished to become her manager. Since she had not signed the extension of her contract with Judson, she signed with Hurok. On December 31, 1935, Anderson's career under Hurok Management began with a critically acclaimed concert at Town Hall in New York City, followed by a January 1936 concert at Carnegie Hall. Under Hurok, Anderson began a most intensive and extensive concert career. Vehanen retired as her accompanist in 1941; Franz Rupp became her accompanist from 1941 through her final farewell concert in 1965.

Daughters of the American Revolution (DAR) Actions Stir Controversy

Events of February 1939 catapulted this serene and dedicated artist from the music review pages of newspapers to front page stories. The refusal of the Daughters of the American Revolution (DAR) to schedule Anderson in concert in their Constitution Hall captured the most headlines. Howard University, the original sponsor of the Anderson concert, was caught in the furor of the DAR refusal, the resignation of Eleanor Roosevelt from the DAR, and the subsequent Lincoln Memorial concert on April 9, 1939. This was a free concert given through the auspices of Harold Ickes, the Secretary of the Interior. The audience, estimated to be seventy-five thousand, included congressmen, Supreme Court justices, and ordinary citizens.

In July 1939 Eleanor Roosevelt was selected to present the NAACP's Spingarn Medal to Anderson. Additional recognition came to Anderson when she received the ten-thousand-dollar Bok Award for the year 1940, presented in March of 1941. This award, created by Philadelphian Edward Bok in 1921, was designated for an individual making a contribution to Philadelphia and the surrounding community. Anderson used the funds to establish a scholarship award for young singers. She divorced herself from the award process and selected her sister Ethel, William Lawrence, Boghetti, and others to make the award decisions. A few of the many recipients are Judith Raskin, McHenry Boatwright, William Brown, and Camilla Williams. Anderson replenished this fund for many years.

On July 24, 1943, at Bethel Methodist Church in Bethel, Connecticut, Anderson was married to Orpheus Hodge Fisher, a New York architect. Rumors of their impending marriage had surfaced over the years. "King," as she called him, was the boyfriend of her youth. She met him in Wilmington, Delaware, when they were both in high school; Anderson sang at a benefit concert and attended a reception at the Fisher home afterwards. The newltweds purchased a farm in Danbury, Connecticut, and King designed and assisted in the building of their home. There she had her music studio and engaged in her hobbies of photography, playing jazz piano, collecting jazz recordings, sewing, and upholstery.

Anderson's extraordinarily busy concert schedule continued in the 1940s with additional concerts given for servicemen and for bond drives. One such concert was given at Constitution Hall in December 1942. She requested that on this occasion the audience not be separated in the usual racial seating; the DAR would not agree to this stipulation. In the end, Anderson chose to sing in the interest of the benefit for the Army Emergency Relief Fund. After World War II she resumed her international concertizing.

Anderson Debuts at Metropolitan Opera

In September 1954 an extraordinary event occurred which, as with other events in Anderson's life, had implications in the broader musical world for other black singers. Langston Hughes wrote of this as "a precedent-shattering moment in American musical history" ("Marian Anderson," 127). She was asked by Rudolph Bing, general manager of the Metropolitan Opera, to join the Metropolitan Opera in the role of Ulrica in Verdi's *Un Ballo in Maschera*. After studying the role, she agreed to sing it and made her debut on January 7, 1955. Her colleagues in that performance were Zinka Milanov, Roberta Peters, Richard Tucker, Leonard Warren, Nicola Moscona, and Norman Scott, with Dimitri Mitropoulos as the conductor. Anderson's debut at the Metropolitan Opera was of such significance in the history of American race relations that it was given a front page story the next morning in the *New York Times* with a picture of Anderson and her mother taken after the performance. Critics have often written about Anderson's age and voice at this debut; few have commented on Bing's astute casting of her in the role of Ulrica, the sorceress/fortune teller who need not have a fresh, youthful voice.

Anderson sang with the Metropolitan Opera for seven performances, including a performance of the opera on tour in her home city at the Philadelphia Academy of Music. An RCA recording was made of excerpts of the opera featuring Anderson and other cast members. This was her only operatic run.

After *Un Ballo in Maschera* Anderson resumed touring. In September 1957 she embarked on a ten-week tour of south Asia and the Far East sponsored by the U.S. Department of State. This tour was filmed by the television crew of the CBS television program "See It Now" as the "Lady from Philadelphia." A soundtrack record of some of the program was issued by RCA Victor.

In 1958 Anderson was named by U.S. President Dwight D. Eisenhower as an alternate delegate to the United Nations. As one of the ten-member U.S. delegation to the United Nations, she was a member of the Human Rights Committee. She had never been identified as a militant, but in this capacity she did disagree with the official U.S. position in the 1958 debate over the colonial status of the Cameroons.

In 1964 Hurok and Anderson announced her farewell tour to take place during the 1964-65 season. The tour began at Constitution Hall, in Washington, D.C., on October 24, 1964, and ended with a concert at Carnegie Hall, on Easter Sunday in 1965. After this extensive tour, in which she revisited cities of her many recitals over the years, Anderson generally lived in retirement on Marianna Farm in Danbury.

After Anderson's retirement she sang in Paris at the Sainte Chappelle and on behalf of the First World Festival of Negro Arts, which was held at Dakar, Senegal, in 1966. She also appeared as narrator on several occasions with various orchestras in Aaron Copland's *Lincoln Portrait*. In 1977 a seventy-fifth birthday gala concert was sponsored by Young Artists Presents with performers including Clamma Dale, Mignon Dunn, Shirley Verrett, James Levine, and others. In 1982 an eightieth birthday concert in Anderson's honor was given at Carnegie Hall with Verrett and Grace Bumbry.

Anderson was recently honored by the Danbury community and many others in a gala concert that served to establish a Marian Anderson Award, reestablishing the award she started in 1941 with the ten-thousand-dollar Bok Award. Musicians performing at this gala included Jessye Norman and Isaac Stern, with Julius Rudel conducting the Ives Symphony Orchestra.

Anderson Records For Four Decades

Recordings by Anderson span four decades—from the acoustic recordings—spirituals with orchestra led by Joseph Pasternak—of the mid-1920s to the long-playing album of Brahms and Schubert lieder that was recorded at Webster Hall in New York City in 1966 and released by RCA in 1978. Several recent recordings are compact disk reissues of earlier works.

Anderson recorded extensively in Europe on the HMV/Gramophone labels with Vehanen as accompanist. Several 78 RPM recordings were made for Artiphone, a German label. These have been dubbed and reissued on the 78 RPM labels Belvox, Davis, Concertone, Masterpiece, and Royale. Long-playing issues of these were issued on Halo, Allegro, Royale, Varsity, and, more recently, on the Pearl label. After 1935 her recordings appeared on Victor Red Seal and RCA Victor. Most of the European recordings from HMV were issued on Victor Red Seal. Lebow (1949) and Turner (1990) provide listings of her 78 RPM recordings. See Turner (1977) for listings of original long-playing recordings. Long-playing issues of 78 RPM recordings are noted in Turner (1990), but must be supplemented with examination of current catalogs and review journals such as *American Record Guide*, *Fanfare*, and *Grammophone*.

Steane (1974) provides an overview that is valuable for mentions of Anderson's recordings of specific works:

> On records, where we can turn backwards and forwards from one kind of song to another at will, the variety of her singing, and the conscious direction of the voice are still more impressive. One feature of the change is the appearance and disappearance of vibrato. The art-songs have a distinctively European fast vibrato, and a more sharply edged tone to go with it: it is there, for instance in "Langsamt som kvällskyn," one of the Sibelius songs which became a cherished part of her repertoire . . . in Brahms's "Die Mainacht." Her performance of this on 78 is extremely fine: the breath-control is admirable, and the song makes great demands upon it. She grades and shades her tone with much skill, and captures too the kind of yearning happiness-in-melancholy which often proves elusive. . . . This, together with the range of the voice, makes us realise afresh what an operatic artist she might have been. The Schubert song takes her down to a fine unforced low D, and in other recordings she sounds sufficiently comfortable above the stave to suggest that the great Verdi mezzo-soprano roles would have been within her powers. . . . It is the recordings of that period [1940s], or earlier still, that we return to hear the gorgeous voice and the inimitable artist in finest form" (278-79).

Henry Fogel, recently reviewing a recording that gives an overview of Anderson's career, writes:

> Separating out the fact that one wants Marian Anderson to have been a fine singer isn't easy, but any objective analysis of what is heard here does indeed show her be a superb artist even if one knew nothing of her role in the struggle for racial equality. As with any singer she was not equally at home in all music, and the value of this record is that it does present a complete picture. One is impressed by the schooling of the technique, the security of production, the depth of emotional commitment in most of what she sang, and most of all by the variety of color in the voice, from a deep, rich port to a gossamer lightness and delicacy. This is what is meant by singing with a "face" (*Fanfare*, 277).

Michel Moe provides these physical descriptions of Anderson from his first in 1925 and a second interview in 1937:

> 1925—Into the room strode a tall tobacco-colored girl with large, melting eyes, who wore her crisp gingham frock as though it were a Paris model. She was cool, poised, dignified.
>
> 1937—The reporter was received by Miss Anderson's secretary.
>
> Presently there strode into the room a tall, tobacco-colored girl with large, melting eyes. She was not a particle different. The only difference was that instead of wearing a gingham frock as though it were a Paris creation, she did wear a Paris model—a silver lame afternoon dress by Chanel.
>
> She was poised and dignified, but not more so than in her mother's little parlor back in 1925. For a moment she looked intently into her visitor's face. Then she smiled a warm broad smile. She recognized him (*Philadelphia Record*, 8 May 1937).

Often descriptions incorporate the physical with her vocalism or descriptions of Anderson in performance. Lucien H. White wrote:

> To me, this night's program was one of considerable interest, as it gave me a chance to hear for the first time, the voice of that muchly praised and widely heralded Philadelphia girl Marian Anderson, contralto. Her singing was a surprise—not entirely from the artistry of her work, for there remains something yet to be done before she has attained full stature in an artistic way—but from the sheer, natural glory of her voice. I have heard some wonderful contraltos, but not yet has there come within my ken such an organ as this girl possesses (*New York Age*, 7 August 1920).

The terms dignified, queenly, calm, sincere, and majestic are used constantly in descriptions of Anderson. Although at the 1989 gala concert in her honor at the Charles Ives Center for the Arts she was described as "frail, white-haired," it was also noticed that "She sat regally, a slight smile on her classically beautiful face, accepting the showers of admiration and love, listening once again to shouts of 'Brava! Brava!'" ("A Tribute to Marian Anderson," 182).

Anderson received many honorary degrees and awards, including the previously mentioned Bok Award and Spingarn Medal, a Congressional Gold Medal (1977), Litteris et Artibus, awarded by the Swedish Government (1952), and the Presidential Medal of Freedom (1963).

In a recent article in *National Review*, Sweeley summed up Anderson's artistry and that symbolic place in America forced upon her:

> For just such reasons, Marian Anderson has become an American symbol—so much so that one may forget how accomplished a singer she really was. The extraordinary range, power and richness of her voice were wedded to a remarkable musicality. The quick, bright vibrato in the middle range, the seemingly boundless top, and the wonderful depth of the lower notes were all combined into one marvelous vocal instrument (65).

Similarly, Donald Bogle writes:

> If there is a tragic aspect to Marian Anderson's career, it is simply that later generations, black and white, would view her as something of a tattered social symbol rather than as the greatest contralto of the twentieth century. Her position, with its layers of meaning and the relentless flow of myth, legend, symbol, image, and dream that swirled about it, was a complex one. Yet she handled her situation with unending reserves of intelligence and poise (110).

References

Abdul, Raoul. *Blacks in Classical Music: A Personal History*. New York: Dodd, Mead and Co., 1977.

———. "Marian Anderson: Symbolic Challenge of Culture in America." *New York Amsterdam News*, 6 February 1982.

Allen, Cleveland G. "Marian Anderson Given Tremendous Ovation as 7,500 Pack New York Stadium." *Pittsburgh Courier*, 5 September 1925.

Anderson, Marian. *My Lord, What a Morning: An Autobiography*. New York: Viking Press, 1956.

———. "Hall Johnson, 1888-1970." *The New York Times*, 24 May 1970.

"At Home with Marian Anderson." *Ebony* 9 (February 1954): 52-59.

Bogle, Donald. *Brown Sugar: Eighty Years of America's Black Female Superstars*. New York: Harmony Books, 1980.

Collins, Leslie M. *A Song, A Dance, and A Play: An Interpretative Study of Three American Artists*. Ph.D. Dissertation. Cleveland: Case Western Reserve University, 1945.

Current Biography Yearbook. New York: H. W. Wilson, *1940:* 17-19, *1950:* 8-10.

De Coverley, Roy. "Marian Anderson in Denmark: An Appreciation." *Opportunity* 12 (September 1934): 270-271.

De Schauenesee, Max. "Marian Anderson." *The New Grove Dictionary of Music and Musicians*. Vol. 1. Edited by Stanley Sadie. Washington, D.C.: Grove's Dictionaries of Music, 1981.

Embree, Edwin R. *13 Against the Odds*. New York: Viking Press, 1944.

Ewen, David. "Marian Anderson." *The Negro in Music and Art*. Edited by Linday Patterson. New York: Publishers Company, 1967.

———. *Musicians Since 1900: Performers in Concert and Opera*. New York: H. W . Wilson, 1978.

"An 80th Birthday Tribute to Marian Anderson." *Ebony* 37 (May 1982): 48-50.

Fisher, Isaac. "Marian Anderson: Ambassador of Beauty from Her Race." *Southern Workman* 65 (March 1936): 72-80.

Fogel, Henry. Review of "The Art of Marian Anderson." *Fanfare* 10 (September/October 1986): 276-277.

Fraser, C. Gerald. "Marian Anderson: A National Treasure is Saluted at 75." *The New York Times*, 25 February 1977.

Gibbs, Margaret. *The DAR*. New York: Holt, Rinehart and Winston, 1969.

Hare, Maud Cuney. *Negro Musicians and Their Music*. Washington, D.C.: Associated Publishers, 1936.

Heylbut, Rose. "Some Reflections on Singing." *Etude* 57 (October 1939): 631-632.

Hughes, Langston. *Black Magic: A Pictorial History of the Negro in American Entertainment*. Englewood Cliffs, N.J.: Prentice-Hall, 1967.

———. *Famous Negro Music Makers*. New York: Dodd, Mead, 1955.

Hurok, Sol. *Impresario, a Memoir*. New York: Random House, 1946.

Klaw, Barbara. "'A Voice One Hears Once in a Hundred Years': An Interview with Marian Anderson." *American Heritage* 28 (February 1977): 50-57.

Kuyper, George. "Marian Anderson." *Southern Workman* 61 (March 1932): 125-27.

"Lady from Philadelphia: Marian Anderson's Far East Trip is Television's Finest Hour." *Ebony* 13 (March 1958): 31-32.

Lebow, Bernard, and Stephen Fassett, eds. and comps. *The American Record Index*. New York: Elaine Music Shop, 1950.

Lovinggood, Penman. *Famous Modern Negro Musicians*. Brooklyn, N.Y.: Press Forum Co., 1921.

"Marian Anderson, American Product." *The Bulletin* (1 April 1929): 1.

Moe, Michael. "12 Years After: Marian Anderson Comes Back Home—A Laundress' Daughter Whose Voice Thrilled All Europe." *Philadelphia Record*, 8 May 1937.

"NAACP Salutes a Living Legend." *Crisis* 89 (April 1982): 25.

Neal, Steve. "Marian Anderson Cherishes Her Privacy." *Philadelphia Inquirer*, 23 February 1975.

Noble, Jeanne L. *Beautiful, Also, Are the Souls of My Black Sisters: A History of the Black Woman in America*. Englewood Cliffs, N.J.: Prentice-Hall, 1982.

Novak, Benjamin J. "Opening Doors in Music." *Negro History Bulletin* 34 (January 1971): 1-14.

"'Of Men and Music': Story of Marian Anderson is Told in Series of Music Films." *Ebony* 6 (May 1951): 49-50.

Reif, Rita. "Marian Anderson at 70: 'We Never Felt Poor.'" *New York Times*, 28 February 1972.

Robinson, Wilhelmena S. *Historical Negro Biographies*. 2d ed., rev. New York: Publishers Co., 1969.

Rogers, Joel Augustus. *World's Great Men of Color*. Edited by John Henrik Clarke. Vol. 2. New York: Macmillan, 1972.

Sims, Janet L. *Marian Anderson: An Annotated Bibliography and Discography*. Westport, Conn.: Greenwood Press, 1981.

Steane, John B. *The Grand Tradition: Seventy Years of Singing on Record*. New York: Scribner, 1974.

Stecklow, Steve. "Marian Anderson Returns with Memories, Thanks." Philadelphia *Evening Bulletin*, 13 May 1977.

"Story of Marian Anderson." *Literary Digest* 123 (May 22, 1937): 30.

Story, Rosalyn M. *And So I Sing: African-American Divas of Opera and Concert.* New York: Warner Books, 1990.

Sweeley, Michael. "The First Lady." *National Review* 41 (September 29, 1989): 65-66.

Thompson, Bill. "To Penn, Fondly, From Marian Anderson." *Philadelphia Inquirer*, 14 April 1977.

"A Tribute to Marian Anderson." *Ebony* 45 (November 1989): 182.

"Triumphs in Berlin." *Norfolk Journal and Guide*, 8 November 1930.

Turner, Patricia. *Afro-American Singers: An Index and Preliminary Discography of Long-Playing Recordings of Opera, Choral Music and Song.* Minneapolis: Challenge Productions, 1977.

———. *Dictionary of Afro-American Performers, 78 RPM and Cylinder Recordings @1900 to 1949.* New York: Garland, 1990. 3-25.

Vehanen, Kosti. *Marian Anderson: A Portrait.* New York: Whittlesey House, 1941.

Westlake, Neda M., and Otto E. Albrecht. *Marian Anderson: A Catalog of the Collection at the University of Pennsylvania Library.* Philadelphia: University of Pennsylvania Press, 1981.

White, Al. "Triumph of Marian Anderson." *Our World* 10 (April 1955): 60-67.

White, Lucien H. Review of New York concert. *New York Age*, 7 August 1920.

Collections

The Marian Anderson Collection is in Special Collections, Van Pelt Library, University of Pennsylvania. Her gift, which established the collection, includes correspondence, photographs, programs, music, diaries, financial records, awards, and honorary degrees. Westlake's publication (1981) is a catalog of that collection. Programs and clippings about Anderson are to be found in many library collections. A scrapbook of programs and clippings was compiled in the Music Department of the Boston Public Library. Other libraries holding similar files are the Woodruff Library of the Atlanta Center; the Free Library of Philadelphia; the James Weldon Johnson Collection of the Beinecke Rare Book Library, Yale University; and the Schomburg Center for Research in Black Culture, New York Public Library. The Schomburg Center also has a tabulation of more than 12,000 clippings about the Marian Anderson-DAR incident. The compilation was made by the Press Section of the study supported by the Carnegie Foundation by Gunnar Myrdal of *The Negro in America.*

Patricia Turner

Regina M. Anderson

(1901-)

Librarian, playwright, arts patron

Regina M. Anderson, librarian, playwright, and proponent of the arts, was an integral figure in the Harlem Renaissance of the 1920s and early 1930s. She was born on May 21, 1901, at 4609 Vincennes Avenue in Chicago, the daughter of William Grant Anderson, an attorney, and Margaret (Simons) Anderson. She attended Normal Training School and Hyde Park High School in Chicago. She studied at Wilberforce University in Ohio and at the University of Chicago. From there she studied at City College of New York, and later received her library science degree from Columbia University Library School.

Regina Anderson found the bourgeois social circle of her lawyer father constricting and dull. Instead, she was drawn to the liberating atmosphere of New York City, where her skills as a librarian, honed in the Chicago public libraries, secured her a job. She became the assistant to Ernestine Rose in the 135th Street (Harlem) Branch of the New York Public Library System (later renamed the Schomburg Center for Research in Black Culture). Her position put her in close contact with the young artists of Harlem. As Nathan Irvin Huggins writes, "Harlem was filled with young Negro men and women who were writing and singing and dancing and painting and acting, and she was in the midst of it all" (25). Regina Anderson's job enabled her to meet the artists and intellectuals of the time and as a result, she became a crucial member of the movement for black arts. During her library career she worked at various branches of the New York Public Library, including the Woodstock and Rivington Street branches. From 1936 to 1945 she acted in the position and was later named supervising librarian at the 115th Street branch. From 1947 to 1967, when she retired, she was the supervising librarian at the Washington Heights branch. Here she instituted "Family Night," a popular lecture series.

Before her marriage in 1926 to lawyer and New York assemblyman William T. Andrews and the birth of their daughter, Regina A., Regina Anderson shared an apartment with Ethel Ray Nance and Louella Tucker on Sugar Hill, the most posh residential area of Harlem. The apartment at 580 Nicholas Avenue on Sugar Hill became a sort of Harlem Renaissance USO, "offering a couch, a meal, sympathy, and proper introduction to wicked Harlem for newcomers on the Urban League approved list'' (Lewis, 127). In effect, Regina Anderson's apartment functioned as a modern day literary salon and ''a combination probation office and intelligence outpost for the Urban League'' (Lewis, 128). Duties at ''580,'' as the apartment was commonly called, were carefully parceled out. Ethel Ray Nance was responsible for alerting Charles S. Johnson, executive director of research and publicity for the National Urban League and her employer, of any problems with a newcomer. Regina Anderson, on the other hand, would convince her employer and the director of the library, Ernestine Rose, that a new artist had joined the community and deserved a chance to present his or her works at the 135th Street Branch. Gatherings or time spent at 580 could thus launch an artist's or writer's career. Indeed, the apartment became such an important meeting place for Harlem intellectuals that Carl Van Vechten immortalized it in his controversial fifth novel, *Nigger Heaven* (1926).

Not only did Ethel Ray Nance and Regina Anderson make their apartment famous by their support of the arts, but they also helped instigate the famous Civic Club dinner. The dinner was originally intended as a party celebrating the pending publication of Jessie Fauset's novel, *There is Confusion.* But as Charles Johnson organized the dinner, spurred on by Regina Anderson, Ethel Ray Nance, and Gwendolyn Bennett, the evening grew into what Bruce Kellner terms, ''a dress rehearsal for the Harlem Renaissance'' (74). Johnson invited Jean Toomer, Countee Cullen, and Langston Hughes as well as about ten other young and fairly unknown writers. They were all to dine on March 21, 1924, at the headquarters of the Civic Club on Twelfth Street off Fifth Avenue. The evening was well-advertised and 110 guests attended. Alain Locke presided as master of ceremonies and speeches were delivered by members of the older black generation, such as W. E. B. Du Bois and James Weldon Johnson. The younger generation of writers gave readings to an audience that included a number of powerful white publishers and editors—Frederick Allen of *Harper's,* Freda Kimberly of *Nation,* Carl Van Doren of the *Century,* Walter Bartlett of *Scribner's,* and Paul Kellog of *Survey Graphic,* to name a few. Not only did the literary symposium and dinner result in the establishment of a patron/advisor relationship for several writers, but Paul Kellog was also so impressed by the talent demonstrated that he offered an entire issue of *Survey Graphic* for the publication of black writing (Kellner, 74). This special issue was published in March 1925 under the guest editorship of Alain Locke. Later in 1925, it was combined with drawings by Winold Reiss to form the definitive volume of the Harlem Renaissance, *The New Negro* (Bontemps, 228).

In the same year as the Civic Club dinner, W. E. B. Du Bois began promoting black theater by founding the Crigwa Theatre. He derived the acronym from *Crisis* Guild of Writers and Artists, a reference to *Crisis Magazine,* the official publication of the NAACP. Annually, *Crisis Magazine* sponsored prizes, known as the Amy Spingarn Awards, for new manuscripts. Du Bois also wanted to encourage black writers, especially playwrights, so he established the Crigwa Players, soon to become known as the Krigwa Players. His philosophy for a Negro art theater was that it should be a theater about blacks, by blacks, for blacks, and near blacks (Mitchell, 70). Consequently, the Krigwa Players settled right in the midst of Harlem at the 135th Street Public Library. The library's basement theater became the headquarters for the group as well as the performance space for prize-winning Krigwa productions such as *The Fool's Errand* by Eulalie Spence. Unfortunately, after several years and substantial financial difficulties, ''the Krigwa suffered the fate of numerous black theatre groups'' and had to disband (Mitchell, 72). However, Du Bois had succeeded in fulfilling his philosophy of a Negro art theater, if only for a short period.

Indeed, the Krigwa Players served as the ''parent dramatic group in New York City'' of the Negro Experimental Theatre (also known as the Harlem Experimental Theatre), founded in 1929 (Mitchell, 69). In her position as librarian assistant, Regina Anderson had been directly involved in the organization of the Krigwa Players. Like Du Bois, she advocated serious black drama as opposed to the musical comedy, the ''Cinderella-type theatre'' (Mitchell, 712), pervading both white and black theater. Regina Anderson explains:

> Somewhere along the line a few of us [probably Dorothy Peterson, Harold Jackman, and one or two others] sat in the basement of the 135th Street library one night, and we began to talk about wanting to write and produce our own dramas. Plays and revues of black people were on downtown stages, but few were presented in Harlem where the black playwright's audience lived. We had few plays to work with and almost none of recent date (Mitchell, 69).

According to Anderson, the group members decided not to limit themselves to Negro plays until they could produce their own. Therefore, their first production was Mary Cass Canfield's *The Duchess Saw Her Prayers* and Paul Green's *The No 'Count Boy.* Regina Anderson notes that North Carolina playwright Paul Green was well known in the South before he became known in New York. The production of his *The No 'Count Boy* at the Negro Experimental Theatre was an encouragement because ''the play was a great success according to the drama critics of the day'' (Mitchell, 75).

In 1931, after several years at the 135th Street Library, the Negro Experimental Theatre moved to Saint Philip's Parish House and produced a number of plays, including Ridgely Torrence's *Rider of Dreams.* The group also produced a number of plays written by some of its original participants: *Coastwise* by Isadore Bennett, *The Prodigal Son* by Harry Camp, *Get Thee Behind Me, Satan* by Robert Dorsey, and *The Little Stone House* by George Cogman. The company was joined by Rose McClendon, a Broadway star, who gave professional direction and expertise and encouraged the production of original scripts.

Playwright's Works Produced

The Negro Experimental Theatre also produced several plays by Regina Anderson, including one of her first, *Climbing Jacob's Ladder* (1931), a serious folk drama about a lynching. Anderson maintains that she wrote her plays under the pseudonym of Ursala Trelling because of her professional connection with the 135th Street Library. But as Loften Mitchell writes:

> I had read the rave reviews about her work, and I think it is an indication of her character that she wrote under an assumed name and remained in the background, modestly. And many, many people told me of the way she blushed when a newspaper reporter broke the story and told all of Harlem that Regina M. Andrews was the real name of the highly acclaimed playwright (63).

Climbing Jacob's Ladder was evidently a great success, described by the forthright and critical Du Bois as "thrilling," and led to roles on Broadway for many members of the cast. The production was an example of the cooperative nature of the little theater group: "The Harlem Experimental Theatre actually served as a creative production center for the playwright, the actor, the costume and stage designer and the director" (Mitchell, 76). In addition, the Negro Experimental Theatre was recognized as one of the early groups that helped bring the Federal Theatre (WPA) to New York and to Harlem. Many of the group's actors were, in fact, sought by the Federal Theatre.

As a part of the so-called little theater movement in New York and elsewhere, the Negro Experimental Theatre was not only a re-creation of the Krigwa Players but also an inspiration to theater groups all over the country. The pioneering Negro Experimental Theatre provided a forum for the specifically black theater Du Bois had envisioned. By encouraging serious black drama during the Harlem Renaissance, Regina Anderson and Du Bois paved the way for black playwrights such as Langston Hughes, Lorraine Hansberry, James Baldwin, Imamu Amiri Baraka (LeRoi Jones), Ossie Davis, Douglas Turner Ward, Ron Milner, Ed Bullins, and August Wilson. Yet to Regina Anderson the efforts to establish a thriving black drama must continue. She says, "It gives me a great deal of personal satisfaction to have lived to see much of what we and other pioneers worked to achieve becoming a reality. However, we need more and more opportunities for our actors, writers, and directors" (Mitchell, 81). Regina Anderson's actions as a librarian, playwright, and promoter of the arts speak for themselves and give resonance to her voice, one of the voices of the Harlem Renaissance as well as of the black theater itself.

Before her retirement in 1967, Regina Anderson had become second vice-president of the National Council of Women as well as National Urban League representative to the United States Commission for UNESCO. She also worked with the State Commission for Human Rights. In recognition of her work, she received the Musical Art Group Award and the Community Heroine Award. An Asian Foundation Award later enabled her to visit India, Hong Kong, Japan, Iran, Thailand, and Afghanistan, to see some of the visiting scholars who had been guest speakers in the programs that she directed. When the 1939 World's Fair was held in New York City and recognized the contributions of ten black women, Anderson, Jessie Fauset, and Gwendolyn Bennett were among them.

Regina Anderson Andrews and Ethel Ray Nance have maintained contact over the years and in 1971 they coedited *Chronology of African-Americans in New York, 1621-1966*. Anderson Andrews lives in upstate New York.

References

Anderson, Jervis. *This Was Harlem: A Cultural Portrait, 1900-1950*. New York: Farrar Straus Giroux, 1981.

Bontemps, Arna, ed. *The Harlem Renaissance Remembered: Essays Edited with a Memoir*. New York: Dodd, Mead, 1972.

Huggins, Nathan Irvin. *Harlem Renaissance*. New York: Oxford University Press, 1971.

Kellner, Bruce, ed. *The Harlem Renaissance: A Historical Dictionary for the Era*. Westport, Conn.: Greenwood Press, 1984.

Lewis, David Levering. *When Harlem Was in Vogue*. New York: Vintage, 1982. 89, 127-29. Includes photograph.

Mitchell, Loften. *Black Drama: The Story of the American Negro in the Theater*. New York: Hawthorn Books, 1967.

———. *Voices of the Black Theatre*. Clifton, N.J.: James T. White, 1975. 58-81. Includes photograph.

Roses, Lorraine E., and Ruth E. Randolph. "Regina M. Anderson" [Ursula Trelling]. *Harlem Renaissance and Beyond: 100 Black Women Writers 1900-1945*. Boston: G. K. Hall, 1990.

Collections

Books from her private library as well as papers, a scrapbook, and an oral history videotape of Regina Anderson Andrews are in the Schomburg Center for Research on Black Culture.

Barnsley Brown

Maya Angelou

(1928-)

Writer, poet

Any biography of Maya Angelou must necessarily rely on Angelou's own account of her colorful life. To date Angelou has written five volumes of a serial autobiography: *I Know Why the Caged Bird Sings* (1970); *Gather Together In My Name* (1974); *Singin' and Swingin' and Gettin' Merry Like Christmas* (1976); *The Heart of a Woman* (1981); and *All God's Children Need Traveling Shoes* (1986). These works chronicle more than thirty-five years of the author's life, from her childhood in Stamps, Arkansas, to her return to the United States in the 1960s from Africa, where she had spent several years. In addition to her autobiography, Angelou has written several volumes of poetry. At various times in her life she has been a dancer, actress, scriptwriter, director and producer, songwriter, and editor. She currently holds an endowed chair as Reynolds Professor of American Studies at Wake Forest University in Winston-Salem, North Carolina. The themes of Angelou's autobiographies, writes Dolly McPherson, "are courage, perseverance, the persistence or renewal of innocence against overwhelming obstacles, and the often difficult process of attaining selfhood. Related to these is the theme of survival" (12). Angelou's life story is the story of a young, poor, black girl pursuing the American dream during several major transitional periods in United States history. Always elusive, the dream required adjustments, but never exacted compromise.

Maya Angelou

Maya Angelou was born Marguerite Johnson on April 4, 1928, in Saint Louis, Missouri. When she was three years old, she and her four-year-old brother, Bailey, Jr., were sent on a train by their divorced parents, Bailey, a doorman and later a naval dietician, and Vivian (Baxter) Johnson, a registered nurse, to live in Stamps, Arkansas, with their paternal grandmother, Annie Henderson. Angelou remembers the journey that she and her brother, Bailey, made alone "wearing tags on our wrists which instructed—'To Whom It May Concern'—that we were Marguerite and Bailey Johnson, Jr., from Long Beach, California, en route to Stamps, Arkansas, c/o Mrs. Annie Henderson" (Angelou, *Caged Bird,* 4). Angelou remembers that the trip south was uneventful except that the other "Negro passengers who always traveled with loaded lunch boxes felt sorry for 'the poor little motherless darlings' and plied us with cold fried chicken and potato salad." No doubt the passengers were used to the scores of "frightened Black children traveling alone to their newly affluent parents in Northern cities, or back to grandmothers in Southern towns when the Urban North reneged on its economic promises" (4).

Despite the hardships of the depression, and of a segregated environment, their grandmother, "Momma" Henderson, supported her family on meager proceeds from her general store, without having to resort to government welfare. Momma Henderson became one of Angelou's role models, and "from her, Angelou learned common sense, practicality and the ability to control one's own destiny that comes from constant hard work and courage, 'grace under pressure'" (Bloom, 2-3). Although living during the depression years in the South was a struggle for blacks, Maya Angelou, nevertheless, found love and the sense of the black tradition in Stamps, Arkansas, primarily from her grandmother and from the local Episcopal church. Angelou especially remembers her graduation from eighth grade, a time that filled the young girl with dreams but also with the realization of the burden of being black in America. Her classmate, Henry Reed, delivered the valedictory address on the theme from "Invictus": "I am master of my fate, I am captain of my soul," despite the denigrating, conciliatory words of the white speaker, Edward Donleavy, who offered no hope to the black 1940 graduating class of Lafayette Training School. Angelou says in *I Know Why the Caged Bird Sings:*

> The man's dead words fell like bricks around the auditorium and too many settled in my belly. Constrained by hard-learned manners I couldn't look behind me, but to my left and right the proud graduating class of 1940 had dropped their heads. Every girl had found something to do with her handkerchief. Some folded the tiny squares into love knots, some into triangles, but most were wadding them, then pressing them flat on their yellow laps (152).

Angelou says later in the book that she thought at the time: "It was awful to be a Negro and have no control over my life" (153).

When Angelou was seven and a half, she spent eight months with her mother in Saint Louis. There Maya Angelou's trust in the adult world crumbled: her mother's boyfriend, Mr. Freeman, raped her. After an initial close encounter with Freeman, she says that she thought "he held me so softly that I wished he wouldn't ever let me go. I felt at home. From the way he was holding me I knew he'd never let me go or let anything bad ever happen to me. This was probably my real father and we had found each other at last. But then he rolled leaving me in a wet place, and stood up" (McPherson, 41).

On a subsequent encounter, when he did rape her, Angelou was confused and felt increasingly guilty, especially at Freeman's trial. When Freeman was kicked to death, Angelou, feeling responsible for his murder, entered a self-imposed world of silence that lasted five years. Annoyed by her daughter's stony silence, Vivian Baxter sent Maya back to Stamps. However, just as an adult had forced Maya to retreat into a world of silence, so an adult, Bertha Flowers, another role model, helped to draw Maya out again. According to critic Dolly McPherson, "Mrs. Flowers throws Maya her 'first life line' by accepting her as an individual not in relation to another person. Moreover, Mrs. Flowers ministers to Maya's growing hunger and quest for individuality by giving her books of poetry, talking to her philosophically about books, and encouraging her to recite poems" (McPherson, 43). Angelou also began writing poetry.

Angelou remembers her grandmother's support. "In another society I'm sure I would have been ruled out. But my grandma told me all the time: 'Sister, Mama don't care what these people be saying about you being a moron, being a idiot. Mama don't care, Mama know, Sister, when you and the good Lord get ready, you're gonna be a preacher'" ("Maya Angelou," B 10-11). Shortly after Angelou's graduation from eighth grade, at the top of her class, she and Bailey left the security of their grandmother's home to live with their mother in San Francisco. Vivian Baxter, now a professional gambler, introduced Angelou to a world vastly different from Stamps, Arkansas. While attending George Washington High School and taking drama and dance lessons on scholarship at the California Labor School, Angelou met a variety of people at her mother's rooming house. From her mother, stepfather, and boarders, Angelou learned everything from etiquette to card playing. During one summer, Angelou stayed with her father; however, she and her father's girlfriend often quarreled, so much so that Angelou, after one stormy scene, ran away and for a month lived among homeless children in an abandoned van in a car lot. Ironically, it was these children who taught her the meaning of tolerance. She says in *Caged Bird* that the children's "own natural brotherhood set a tone of tolerance for my life" (quoted in Bloom, 5). Dolly McPherson credits this experience with initiating young Angelou into adulthood.

The experience of living among the homeless children was only one way that Angelou tested the waters of emerging adolescence. Another achievement that helped to give her a sense of control over her life was her obtaining, while in high school, a position as the first female streetcar collector in San Francisco. A more serious and permanent testing of her emerging adulthood was her unplanned pregnancy and motherhood at age sixteen. *Current Biography* quotes part of an interview in 1974, when Angelou was asked her reason for ending *Caged Bird* with the birth of her son, Guy. Angelou replied to the query: "And I tell them I wanted to end it on a happy note. It was the best thing that ever happened to me" (13).

Motherhood as well as the growing need for independence from her mother prompted Angelou to move from her mother's home. The events of the next two years are narrated in *Gather Together in My Name.* Angelou first tried to get a job as a telephone operator, but was unsuccessful. McPherson states that when Angelou tried to enlist in the WACS, she was rejected because at time the California Labor School in which she was enrolled "was prescribed as communist"(68-69). She finally accepted a position as a cook in a Creole restaurant even though she knew nothing about Creole cooking. A subsequent job as a nightclub waitress in San Diego inadvertently plunged Angelou briefly into the world of prostitution; for a short while, she "managed" two lesbian lovers. Angelou states:

> "At eighteen I had managed in a few tense years to become a snob at all levels, racial, cultural and intellectual. I was a madam and thought myself morally superior to the whores. I was a waitress and believed myself cleverer than the customers I served. I was a lonely unmarried mother and held myself to be freer than the married women I met" (Bloom, 6).

McPherson sees this period in Angelou's life as paralleling the general climate of post World War II disillusionment of black Americans. Black soldiers, maintains McPherson, were returning from war, only to be confronted with America's pervasive racism, unemployment, and an assault on their self-esteem. The uncertain times for blacks was also an uncertain time for the young Angelou, who, moving frequently from place to place, sought her independence from constricting society as well as from her mother. Displaced, Angelou returned briefly to Stamps, Arkansas, to the childhood security of her grandmother's home. However, after returning an insult to a white store owner, her grandmother forced her to leave, since the South still did not sanction black "insubordination." The next few years found Angelou trying different jobs and experimenting with drugs. However, her brother Bailey's downfall from drug addiction coupled with her concerned lover's showing her the horrors of administering a "fix" to himself pulled Angelou from the disaster into which she was headed.

In an effort to give order to her chaotic existence, at age twenty-two, Angelou married a white man, a former sailor, Tosh Angelos. The two-and-a-half-year marriage failed because of Angelou's insistent need for freedom from a constricting life. Leaving again a security that had its price—her freedom—Angelou began her career as a dancer in a bar. Soon performers from the well-known Purple Onion, impressed by her dancing, offered Angelou a job dancing at the establishment. This move proved a turning point in Angelou's halting career. It also modified her view of the white world: "There whites were treating me as an equal, as if I could do whatever they could do. They did not consider that race, height, gender or lack of education might have crippled me and that I should be regarded as someone invalided" (Bloom, 7).

Angelou got more opportunities to develop as an entertainer. She appeared not only at the Purple Onion but also at Chicago's Mr. Kelly's and at both the Blue Angel and Village Vanguard in New York. In 1954-55 she toured Europe and Africa in *Porgy and Bess*. Around this time, Angelou adopted her present name, derived from her brother's nickname of her (Maya) and a variation of her first husband's surname, Angelos. McPherson describes this time in Angelou's life as one of liberation:

> Even so, Angelou's travels and experiences with *Porgy and Bess,* particularly her visit to Africa, do much to enhance her maturity and her feeling of self-worth. The triumph of the opera company is not only the dramatic success of a talented company of Black artists, but it is also the triumphal blooming of a talented, determined young Black woman into the adult self and into a fully liberated woman (88).

Angelou Becomes Social Activist

Returning to the United States after the tour, Angelou resumed her career as a nightclub performer. During this time, she also became a social activist and with comedian Godfrey Cambridge co-wrote a revue, "Cabaret for Freedom," a benefit for Martin Luther King's Southern Christian Leadership Conference (SCLC). Recognizing her commitment to the civil rights cause, King asked her to serve as northern coordinator for SCLC in 1960-61. In May 1961 she played the Queen in Jean Genet's controversial *The Blacks*, off-Broadway at the Saint Mark's Playhouse in New York. Angelou left the successful production before it closed in 1964 because of a dispute with the director-producer over his refusal to pay Angelou and actress Ethel Ayler for music they wrote.

According to Bloom, "By the time she was thirty, Angelou had made a commitment to become a writer" (8). She was introduced to the Harlem Writer's Guild by social activist author John Killens and began to attend the guild's weekly meetings. Angelou states, "If I wanted to write, I had to be willing to develop a kind of concentration found mostly in people awaiting execution. I had to learn technique and surrender my ignorance" (Bloom, 8). Undoubtedly her close association with such noted authors as James Baldwin, Paule Marshall, and John Henrik Clarke inspired Angelou. In fact, it was James Baldwin who introduced Angelou to Jules and Judy Feiffer. Judy Feiffer, intrigued by Angelou's life story, prompted a friend of hers at Random House to encourage Angelou, interested only in writing poetry, to write her autobiography (McPherson, 22).

In late 1961, Angelou left the United States with her son and Vusumzi Make, a South African freedom fighter, who persuaded her to accompany him to Cairo, Egypt, saying that their union would be "the joining of Africa and Africa-America" (Bloom, 9). Angelou never married Make; however, they lived together for several years. Because of Make's poor management of their mounting financial obligations, Angelou did the unheard of—she sought employment as an editor of the *Arab Observer,* a move that infuriated Make. Their disagreement over her new independence as well as his adultery confirmed Angelou's decision to leave Make and move to Ghana. Although she had not planned to stay long in Ghana, her son Guy's automobile accident in Ghana changed her mind. McPherson quotes a passage from *All God's Children Need Traveling Shoes* to illustrate Angelou's connecting Ghana with her past in Arkansas and California:

> Their skins were the colors of my childhood cravings: peanut butter, licorice, chocolate, caramel. There was the laughter of home, quick and without artifice. The erect and graceful walk of the women reminded me of my Arkansas Grandmother, Sunday-hatted, on her way to church. I listened to men talk, and whether or not I understood their meaning, there was a melody as familiar as sweet potato pie, reminding me of my Uncle Tommy Baxter in Santa Monica, California (108).

However, Ghanians viewed Angelou as an American, with "American faults." In fact, she was never completely accepted by native Africans, who regarded her, despite her African heritage, as an outsider. While in Ghana, Angelou held several positions. In addition to serving as a feature editor of *The African Review* in Accra, she wrote articles for the *Ghanian Times* as well as for Accra's Ghanaian Broadcasting Corporation. She also taught at the University of Ghana.

Since her return from Ghana, Angelou has demonstrated her versatile talent in several areas. In 1966 she had a part in Jean Anouilh's *Medea* produced in Hollywood. She also was busy writing songs as well as a television series on "Africanisms in American Life." In 1972 Angelou achieved the distinction of being the first black woman to have a screenplay, *Georgia, Georgia*, produced. One critic applauded the play, saying "Georgia is admirable for the honesty with which it tries to get a psychic fix on the contemporary black woman" (quoted in *Current Biography,* 14). In 1979 her first autobiography, *I Know Why the Caged Bird Sings,* was made into a television movie, for which Angelou wrote the script and music. In 1977 Angelou's performance in the television production of Alex Haley's *Roots* earned her an Emmy nomination.

During this time Angelou also acted in plays such as the short-lived drama *Look Away*, produced on Broadway in 1973. In 1974 her adaptation of Sophocles's *Ajax* played at the Mark Taper Forum in Los Angeles. Her first full-length effort was her film *Sister, Sisters*. In the national arena, the versatile Angelou was appointed by President Gerald Ford to the Bicentennial Commission and by President Jimmy Carter to the Commission of International Woman's Year. Her marriage in 1973 to Paul de Feu ended in 1981.

Since 1981, Angelou has held the lifetime appointment position as Reynolds Professor of American Studies at Wake Forest University in Winston-Salem, North Carolina. She combines teaching one course each semester with lecturing engagements across the country. She is currently writing another volume of her autobiography. She says, "It's a hard one to do, and it's coming very thin on the ground" (Grossmann, C 3).

Autobiographical Works Contribute to Scholarship

Angelou has also published several volumes of poetry about issues in the black experience and in society as a whole: *Just Give Me a Cool Drink of Water 'fore I Diiie* (1971); *Oh Pray My Wings Are Gonna Fit Me Well* (1975); *Shaker Why Don't You Sing*, and *And Still I Rise* (1978); and *I Shall Not be Moved* (1990). Most critics agree that Angelou's most outstanding works are *I Know Why the Caged Bird Sings* (nominated for the National Book Award in 1974) and *The Heart of a Woman*. Critics find that Angelou, in her autobiographies, "mixes fact with fantasy." However, in an interview in Florida in 1989, Angelou stated that in telling her life, she tells the "truth" as distinguished from "facts": "There's a world of difference between truth and facts. Facts can obscure the truth. You can tell so many facts that you fill the stage but haven't got one iota of truth" ("Maya Angelou," B 10-11).

Most critics assess Maya Angelou's autobiographies as a significant contribution to American literature of the self and to black American literature in particular. Placing the autobiographies firmly within the tradition of such black autobiographies as those of Frederick Douglass, Anne Moody, Richard Wright, and Malcom X, critics appreciate Angelou's growing awareness of the environment and of the self within that environment. However, Dolly McPherson credits Angelou's autobiographies with going beyond the usual theme of the impact of the external environment on the narrator: according to McPherson, Angelou uses the external environment only to show the emergence of the internal—Angelou's "growing awareness of her environment—her response to that environment and to the people who made up that environment; their manners, talk, gestures of bravado, their thoughts and dreams" (12). Perhaps what McPherson is noting is what critic Selwyn Cudjue describes as the essential element of black autobiography, the narrating of the "collective experience," the collective history of black American people that takes the black autobiographer away from concentration on the individual 'I' and places the autobiographer within the collective 'we' (9-10).

For her valuable contributions to the arts, Angelou has received many honorary degrees, including Smith College, Mills College, and Sarah Lawrence University. Critic Eugenia Collier notes another achievement of the autobiographies:

> The pervasive theme, naturally developed in all the autobiographies, is the strength of the Black woman, her ability to prevail despite the awful hurting put upon her by the world, even by her own Black man, who often assuages his own hurt by further oppressing her. Yet there is no blatant preaching, no anti-male rhetoric (24).

Critics view Angelou's life as a journey to selfhood, the gradual appreciation of herself as a unique individual. In the same vein, Angelou's distinction between the "facts" and "truth" of her life story emphasizes the special self-examination and insight into self that every black American woman needs to achieve in a male-dominated society. Angelou selects those events in her life that helped her to grow emotionally, psychologically, spiritually—the "stuff of life" that truly counts in building self-acceptance. Knowing oneself—one's strengths as well as one's limitations—as Angelou does, is a difficult achievement. However, reading Angelou's autobiographies convinces the world that she has defied the external limitations that were placed upon her as a young child—a testament to her inner strength.

References

Angelou, Maya. *The Heart of a Woman*. New York: Bantam Books, 1982.

———. *I Know Why the Caged Bird Sings*. New York: Bantam Books, 1970.

Bloom, Lynn Z. "Maya Angelou." *Afro-American Writers after 1955: Dramatisits and Prose Writers*. Edited by Thadious M. Davis and Trudier Harris. Detroit: Gale Research, 1985.

Collier, Eugenia. "Maya Angelou: From *Caged Bird to All God's Childen* [sic]." New York: *New Directions* 13 (October 1986): 22-27.

Cudjoe, Selwyn R. "Maya Angelou and the Autobiographical Statement." In *Black Women Writers (1950-1980): A Critical Evaluation*. Edited by by Mari Evans. New York: Doubleday, 1984. 6-24.

Current Biography. New York: H. W. Wilson, 1974. 12-15. Photograph, p. 13.

Grossman, Mary Ann. "Maya Angelou's Life is a Touch of Elegance." *St. Paul Pioneer Press Dispatch* 18 June 1989. In *Newsbank*, Literature, August 1989. 75: C 3.

"Maya Angelou." *Tampa Tribune* 17 March 1989. In *Newsbank,* Literature, April 1989. 34: B 10-11.

McPherson, Dolly A. "Order Out of Chaos: The Autobiographical Works of Maya Angelou." *Studies in African and African American Culture.* Vol. 1. Edited by James L. Hill. New York: Peter Lang, 1990.

Collections

Maya Angelou's papers are housed in the Z. Smith Reynolds Library at Wake Forest University.

Grace E. Collins

Lillian "Lil" Hardin Armstrong

(1898-1971)

Musician, composer

Lillian "Lil" Hardin Armstrong ranks alongside Jelly Roll Morton and James P. Johnson as one of the great early jazz pianists. "I was just born to swing, that's all," she once said. "Call it what you want, blues, swing, jazz, it caught hold of me way back in Memphis and it looks like it won't ever let go" (Placksin, 58). Armstrong's statement, ironically, was portentous. After a distinguished fifty-year musical career, she died on stage, at a memorial concert for Louis Armstrong.

Armstrong was born on February 3, 1898, in Memphis, Tennessee. She received piano and organ lessons as a child in Memphis and served as a pianist and organist in church and in her school. Her mother and grandmother hated popular music and considered the blues vulgar. In fact, she was beaten for having a copy of W. C. Handy's "St. Louis Blues." Later, she recalled playing "Onward Christian Soldiers" in church one day "with a definite beat" (Placksin, 58), somewhat to the consternation of her minister.

Armstrong received her formal music training at Fisk University, the Chicago College of Music (earning a teacher's certificate in 1924), and the New York College of Music (earning a diploma in 1929). She left Fisk in 1917 when her family moved to Chicago, and her professional career began there with a job as a "song-plugger" at Jones's Music Store on South State Street.

At Jones's Music Store, Armstrong learned and demonstrated all the music available at the store and was billed as "The Jazz Wonder Child." It was here that she met Jelly Roll Morton, probably the greatest jazz pianist of the era. Their encounter has become legendary among jazz historians. Armstrong and Morton traded renditions of standards of the day, and he demonstrated his heavy, foot-stomping style. She took this as an important lesson. From that day forward, she played with a heavy-handed, aggressive rhythmic style that became her trademark throughout her career.

Armstrong was well known and respected by her peers. Compliments by musicians were typically like those of George "Pops" Foster, the great bass player, who referred to her as "a great piano player and a great musician" (Foster, 162). In her day the piano was the centerpiece of the rhythm section, charged with maintaining the beat and fundamental chord structure to free the clarinet, trumpet, or cornet soloists for their flights of fancy. The piano was not necessarily a focus for solo playing, as Armstrong herself attests: "It wasn't the style during the King Oliver days for the pianist to play many solos. Sometimes I'd get the urge to run up and down the piano and make a few runs and things, and Joe ("King" Oliver) would turn around and look at me and say, 'We have a clarinet in the band'" (Placksin, 60-61).

Her four-beat, solid style guaranteed Armstrong's acceptance among her peers and a good following among devotees. As a pianist, her early jobs included accompanying singers, among them the blues great Alberta Hunter. Armstrong was also a good organizer and led her own band for many years. Her other talents included arranging, composing, and singing.

Armstrong's career in jazz extended more than fifty years and centered in Chicago and New York. She got her first playing jobs through contacts made at Jones's Music Store. Her first major band experience was with the Original New Orleans Creole Jazz Band, playing at the De Luxe Cafe. The band included Lawrence Duhé on clarinet, Sugar Johnson and Freddie Keppard on cornets, Roy Palmer on trombone, Sidney Bechet on clarinet and soprano saxophone, Tubby Hall on drums, Jimmy Palao on violin, Bob Frank on piccolo, Wellman Braud on bass. It is about this band that Armstrong told one of her most famous tales: When she asked in what key they were playing their first number, they told her, "'Key, we don't know what key. Just when you hear two knocks, start playing.' So I just hit everything on the piano, so whatever key they was in, I would be in it too. Oh, after a second I could feel what key they were playing, because at that time I don't think they used over five chords. In fact, I'm sure they didn't" (Placksin, 59).

The Original New Orleans Creole Jazz Band played in a pure, swinging New Orleans style and was quite successful. The audience frequently contained some of the leading musicians and stars of the day, including Bill "Bojangles" Robinson, the vaudeville team of Walker and Williams, Eddie Cantor, Al Jolson, and Sophie Tucker. King Oliver and Johnny Dodds came over one evening to hear the band and invited Armstrong to join their band, King Oliver's Creole Jazz Band, playing at the Lincoln Gardens (later the Royal Gardens). In 1922, Louis Armstrong joined him, and the full complement of Oliver's band then included Oliver and Louis Armstrong on cornets, Honoré Dutrey on trombone, Johnny Dodds on clarinet, Baby Dodds on drums, Bill Johnson on banjo, and Armstrong on piano. This band, of course, has become one of the most famous in all of jazz history and formed the nucleus for Louis Armstrong's Hot Five and Hot Seven recording sessions.

Armstrong Called Major Figure in Jazz Field

It must have been quite a heady experience for a young woman in her first few engagements to be playing with the jazz greats of her day who brought the pioneering New Orleans style of traditional jazz to Chicago. It is certainly a testament to Armstrong's talent and ability. Moreover, she was apparently the first woman to enter the jazz field as a major figure and retain that stature and acceptance throughout her career.

Becoming friends almost from the day he joined the band, she and Louis Armstrong were married in 1924. Lil Armstrong eventually "encouraged Louis to leave Oliver and join Fletcher Henderson in New York. It was she who helped Louis Armstrong to become a better music reader and it was she, with her formal training and broad knowledge of musical form, who realized his enormous talent" (Nanry, 121-22). In New York with Henderson, when Louis Armstrong played at the Roseland Ballroom, Lil Armstrong was not satisfied seeing that her husband was not given featured billing. She organized a band in Chicago and brought him back to the Dreamland, where he was featured as "The World's Greatest Trumpet Player." His other ventures included the recording sessions with his Hot Five and Hot Seven from 1925 through 1928. From this point Louis Armstrong's career took off like a rocket. The Armstrong marriage followed the course of their careers: fused at first, but then divergent, and they were divorced in 1938.

Lil Armstrong's subsequent experiences were diverse. She played with many bands, including those of Oliver, Freddie Keppard, Elliot Washington, Hugh Swift, and Louis Armstrong. She led and played in an all-woman swing group called the Harlem Harlicans from about 1932 to 1936. The group included such notables as Alma Scott (Hazel Scott's mother) on reeds, Leora Mieux (Fletcher Henderson's wife) on trombone, and Dolly Hutchinson on trumpet. She also led her own group out of Buffalo, remnants of Stuff Smith's band, including Jonah Jones and George Clarke, from 1933 to 1935. She fronted this band "wearing slinky white gowns, top hat, and wielding a baton" (Placksin, 62). This was, of course, during the depth of the Great Depression, and it is a testament to Armstrong's talent and skill that she was able to get jobs and keep the band together.

Armstrong worked as a session pianist for Decca Records in the late 1930s and appeared in the Broadway shows *Hot Chocolate* (1929) and *Shuffle Along* (1933). While at Decca, she recorded under the name Lil Hardin with soloists and a pick-up band that included numerous stars of the day, among them Red Allen, Chu Berry, Buster Bailey, and Jonah Jones. She returned to Chicago in the 1940s and continued her career with several long engagements at local clubs, including The Three Deuces. She made several tours, including one to Europe in 1952. She was coaxed out of semi-retirement to play at a memorial concert for Louis Armstrong in 1971 and died on stage on August 27.

Among Armstrong's many compositions, most of which she recorded, are "My Heart," "You're Next," "The King of the Zulus," "Skid Dat De Dat," "Jazz Lips," "Lonesome Blues," "Brown Gal," "Perdido Street Blues," "Ol' Man Mose," "Struttin' with Some Barbecue," and "Just For a Thrill." Through her many recordings-with Oliver's Creole Jazz Band, Louis Armstrong's Hot Five and Hot Seven, her own bands, including her Harlem Harlicans and the New Orleans Wanderers (of 1926), and with sundry other artists—this great lady of "hot" jazz has left a permanent legacy for lovers of jazz.

References

Berendt, Joachim E. *The Jazz Book*. Westport, Conn.: Lawrence Hill, 1981.

Cerulli, Dom, Burt Korall, and Mort L. Nasatir. *The Jazz Word*. New York: Da Capo Press, 1987.

Chilton, John. *Who's Who of Jazz; Storyville to Swing Street*. Philadelphia: Chilton Book Co., 1972.

Collier, James L. *Louis Armstrong; An American Genius*. New York: Oxford University Press, 1983.

Dahl, Linda. *Stormy Weather: The Music and Lives of a Century of Jazzmen*. New York: Pantheon Books, 1984.

Foster, George M. *Pops Foster*. Berkeley: University of California Press, 1971.

Harrison, Max, Charles Fox, and Eric Thacker. *The Essential Jazz Records*. Vol. 1. *Ragtime to Swing*. Westport, Conn.: Greenwood Press, 1984.

Hazeldine, Mike. "Lill(ian) Armstrong." *Grove's Dictionary of Jazz*. Vol. 1. New York: Macmillan, 1988.

Hodier, Andre. *Jazz: Its' Evolution and Essence*. New York: Grove Press, 1956.

Jones, Max, and John Chilton. *Louis: The Louis Armstrong Story*. New York: Da Capo Press, 1988.

Mezzrow, Milton "Mezz." *Really the Blues*. New York: Random House, 1946.

Nanry, Charles. *The Jazz Text*. New York: Van Nostrand, 1979.

Placksin, Sally. *American Women in Jazz, 1900 to the Present*. New York: Seaview Books, 1982.

Darius L. Thieme

Gertrude Elise Ayer

(1884-1971)

Activist, educator, writer

Gertrude McDougald Ayer is known as an activist, educator, and writer. Her writings, especially articles related to racial and gender inequality, address a crucial social concern in the early twentieth century and have numerous implications for conditions of inequality prevailing today.

Ayer was born on October 13, 1884, in New York City. Her father, Peter Augustus Johnson, was the third black American admitted to practice medicine in New York City, the founder of McDonough Memorial Hospital, an organizer of the partners at Pennsylvania Railroad Station, and a member of the founding committee of the National Urban League. Her mother, Mary Elizabeth (Whittle) Johnson, was English and was born in the Isle of Wight, north of England. She was an expert needlewoman.

Ayer attended elementary school in New York. Later she was president of her high school class, and after graduating she attended New York Training School for Teachers from 1903 to 1905. During this period, she also completed studies at Hunter College, Columbia University, College of the City of New York, and New York University. In 1905 Ayer was appointed as a class teacher at Public School 11 in Manhattan. She was only twenty-one when she began teaching, and her monthly salary was fifty dollars. She remained at the school until 1911.

Gertrude Elise Ayer

Ayer married Cornelius W. McDougald in 1911, and they had two children: Cornelius McDougald, Jr., and Elizabeth Johnson McDougald. Her husband was the initial counsel for Marcus Garvey when his trial for mail fraud began on May 28, 1923. Later he was appointed United States Assistant District Attorney.

Black Women in New York Surveyed

During Ayer's temporary leave from teaching, she became active with the New York Urban League. She held the position of Assistant Industrial Secretary, beginning in 1915, and obtained the interest of the Women's Trade Union League and the financial support of the YWCA to conduct a survey on black women in New York titled "New Day for the Colored Woman Worker."

After a period of employment as head of the Woman's Department in the United States Labor Department Employment Bureau in Harlem, Ayer became a counselor at the Henry Street Settlement. She felt that young women needed vocational counseling early in their lives. She felt that it was futile to provide training if it resulted in indefinite employment opportunities. Learning and earning had to be complementary goals, she believed. The Board of Education in 1918 asked her to initiate the counseling program in the New York public schools.

In an address, "The Schools and the Vocational Life of Negroes," delivered before the Section on the School at the National Conference of Social Work in Washington, D.C., May 16, 1923, Ayer specifically notes the problem of education and vocation for Negroes:

> A discussion of the school and its relation to the vocational life of the Negro brings us to the consideration of two of the most vital activities of human life-learning and earning. These are vital to all: and, to the Negro, who is like all other folk, the effort to secure, a chance to learn and earn, has brought about an heroic change. Within a year, 84,000 Negroes left the states of South Carolina, Alabama, Arkansas, Georgia and Tennessee. It is significant that all of these states rank in the lowest third of states in educational progress in the nation. After years of patient endurance, the Negro by migrating has made the problem of education and vocation, a national, rather than a sectional one.
>
> Now that the problem is nation-wide, its relation to the problem of the human race in general is becoming more apparent. It is, after all, simply a phase of the big struggle of the modern era—the struggle of the Common Man for the fullest development. The Negro is regarded as the com-

> monest of common men in America, and any consideration of his welfare, in any field of endeavor, is highly in accord with the tendency of the present era—"appreciation of the genius of the common man" (Johnson, "The Schools and the Vocational Life of Negroes," 8).

The speech goes on to describe the dismal vocational opportunities for Negroes in the North and South, yet ends on an optimistic note:

> Education is on the increase—the Negro must get his just share. Industry is becoming more humanized—the Negro must also be regarded in the new light. The two agencies for human good—the school and industry, must work together more effectively. . . . Limited opportunity, a lack of knowledge of the opportunities which exist and a lack of help in making the necessary adjustments are the potent factors in the trouble. It appears that one of the greatest needs of the Negro youth is, not only training in all branches of learning according to ability and interest, but adequate coordination and guidance both in education and work, toward the fullest use of that training (Johnson, "The Schools," 10).

Ayer's speech certainly reflected her acute awareness of the necessity for blacks to have knowledge as well as skills in an increasingly industrial society.

Ayer passed a competitive examination and was appointed as assistant principal of Public School 89 in Manhattan in 1924, where she remained until 1927. While in that position she wrote the article, "The Task of Negro Womanhood," which examines the stratification of black women in employment and the discrimination encountered.

According to Ayer, in terms of stratification the leisure group is among the upper class. This is a small group comprised of wives and daughters of men employed in business, the professions, and a few well-paid personal service occupations. Women in this group have certain luxuries: fine homes, modest motors, tennis, golf and country club memberships, and travel opportunities. The major problem confronting this group is to become acquainted with similar members of the race who have compatible achievements ("The Task of Negro Womanhood," 371).

The second group consists of women in business and the professions. Ayer contends that "a spirit of stress characterizes the second two groups" (371). For example, many have dual tasks. They are wives and mothers whose husbands are inadequately paid; numerous women are widows. They are gainfully employed primarily in businesses owned by Negro men. Many are qualified for civil service positions but have encountered discriminatory practices in this area. In other areas—legal, dental, and medical professions—black women are dependent on their own group for steady income. Nursing, teaching, and library professions have provided employment opportunities for women in this group (371-73).

Women in trades and industry comprise the third group. The major problem for them is the competition encountered in an open field and denial of credit to obtain capital for a partnership in one's own business (377).

The last group, the domestic and casual workers, provide a significant contribution to America. Ayer says:

> The Negro woman is sought after for this unpopular work largely because her honesty, loyalty and cleanliness have stood the test of time. Through her drudgery, the women of other groups find leisure time for progress. This is one of her contributions to America (379).

With respect to gender equality, Ayer viewed this as secondary to racial equality for black women:

> In this matter of sex equality, Negro women have contributed few outstanding militants, a notable instance being the historic Sojourner Truth. On the whole the Negro woman's feminist efforts are directed chiefly toward the realization of the equality of the races, the sex struggle assuming the subordinate place (381).

Finally, she believed in the enduring courage and strength of the black woman:

> We find the Negro woman figuratively struck in the face by contempt from the world about her. Within her soul, she knows little of peace and happiness. But through it all, she is courageously standing erect, developing within herself the moral strength to rise above and conquer false attitudes. She is maintaining her natural beauty and charm and improving her mind and opportunity. She is measuring up to the needs of her family, community and race, and radiating a hope throughout the land.
>
> The wind of the race's destiny stirs more briskly because of her striving (382).

New York City Appoints First Black Woman School Principal

Ayer became the first black woman to have a full-time principalship in a New York City public school in 1936. Subsequently, in 1945 she assumed the principalship of Public School 119 and remained there until she retired in 1954 ("Human Principal," 70). She never obtained a college degree. She said, "Too many people with B.A.'s only know their subject matter and don't know how to teach" (70). Her teaching philosophy was that there should be a combination of academic and practical learning. Quoted in *Newsweek*, she said "neighborhood carpenters, butchers and grocers (whom pupils call 'experts') speak to classes." This, Ayer feels, helps break down the "blackboard curtain" between teacher and pupil and shows youngsters that there are sources of learning outside books. "The informality helps teachers, too" she says. "Sometimes they develop a lot of resistance to being a human being ("Human Principal," 70).

Newsweek described Ayer as a "sprightly 69" in 1954 (70). According to *Who's Who in Harlem*, 1949-1956, she was a member of numerous organizations: Workers' Defense League, New York Chapter; National Council of Women in Administration; Advisory Committee of the Hope Day Nursery and Neighborhood Children's Center; honorary member, Alpha Kappa Alpha Sorority; Ladies Auxiliary of Lincoln University; and secretary, Workshop for Cultural Democracy. In 1928 she had married a second time, to Dr. A. V. Ayer, district health officer in Harlem. He died about April 22, 1976, at his home in New York City at age 83.

Ayer had a strong commitment to the education and training of black Americans. Both of her spouses also were committed to this endeavor. Her generous participation in numerous organizations and principalships—as the first black, in many instances—are indicative of her social philosophy. She died on July 10, 1971, in her home, at age 86.

German-American artist Weinold Reiss captured the beauty of Ayer in his portrait sketch published in the March 1925 special edition of *Survey Graphic,* "Harlem: Mecca of the New Negro," and subsequently reprinted in a variety of sources.

References

"Human Principal." *Newsweek* (5 July 1954): 70. Includes photograph.

Jet, 5 August 1971.

McDougald, Elise Johnson. "The Schools and the Vocational Life of Negroes." *Opportunity* 1 (June 1923): 8-11.

——. "The Task of Negro Womanhood." In *The New Negro*. Edited by Alain Locke. New York: Boni, 1925. Reprinted. New York: Arno Press, 1968.

New York Amsterdam News 17 July 1971.

New York Post, 12 July 1971.

Ottley, Roi, and William J. Weatherby, eds. *The Negro in New York: An Informal Social History*. New York: Ocena Publications, 1967.

"Social Progress." *Opportunity* 3 (January 1925): 28.

Who's Who in Colored America. 7th ed. New York: James G. Fleming Christian E. Burchel, 1950.

Who's Who in Harlem, 1949-1956. Edited by B. S. B. Trottman. New York: Magazine and Periodical Printing and Pub. Co., 1956. Includes photograph.

Mary R. Holley

B

Pearl Bailey

(1918-1990)

Singer, actress, comedienne, author

She was appointed "Ambassador of Love" by President Nixon in 1970, a designation that indisputably belonged to Pearl Bailey, who loved and was loved by people around the world. Bailey was an entertainer and actress who was respected and revered throughout her lengthy career not only for her style and her singing but because of her humanity, generosity, wit, and involvement in social, civic and charitable activities.

Pearl Bailey was born in Newport News, Virginia, on March 29, 1918. She was known as Pearlie Mae to her audiences and close friends, and her family called her Dick, a name that her father gave her during her childhood.

Pearl Bailey

Pearl Bailey was the youngest of four children. Her father was Joseph James Bailey, and her mother was Ella Mae Bailey. Pearl Bailey had two sisters, Virgie Murray and Eura Robinson, and one brother, Willie "Bill" Bailey, a well-known tap dancer, later a minister. Bailey's father was a revivalist minister with the House of Prayer. Her parents were divorced when she was a child, and her mother later married Walter Robinson. Bailey's father died in 1966, and her mother died in 1969. Pearl Bailey was a descendent of Creek Indians on both sides of her family.

Pearl Bailey was married to a musician in the 1930s and the marriage lasted eighteen months. She married John Randolph Pinkett, Jr., on August 31, 1948, and they were divorced on March 20, 1952. She married jazz drummer and musician Louis Bellson, Jr., on November 19, 1952. This was an interracial marriage and continued until her death thirty-seven years later. With Bellson, she adopted two children, a son, Tony, and a daughter, Dee Dee.

At the age of four, Bailey moved with her family to Washington, D.C. Later, she moved with her mother and stepfather to Philadelphia, where she attended public school and began her early career as an entertainer. In Philadelphia, she attended Joseph Singerly School and William Penn High School. Her early ambition was to be a schoolteacher, but at the age of fifteen, she dropped out of school and joined the vaudeville entertainment circuit. Later in life, in 1978, Pearl Bailey reentered school as a full-time student, attending Georgetown University in Washington, D.C., and graduating with a bachelor's degree in theology at the age of sixty-seven. She also received from Georgetown an honorary doctorate degree in 1978. Bailey received no formal training in music, and developed much of her technique from her father's Holy Roller style in the church, where she sang and danced as early as the age of three.

Bailey's career in entertainment began in 1933, when at the age of fifteen she won an amateur contest at the Pearl Theater in Philadelphia, where her brother, Bill Bailey, was appearing. For the contest, she danced and sang "Poor Butterfly" and "Talk of the Town." She won the first prize of five dollars and a two-week engagement at the theater with a promise of thirty to thirty-five dollars a week for performing; although she performed, she was never paid for her engagement because the theater closed. She also won twelve dollars as a prize for her buck-and-wing dance performance at the Jungle Inn in Washington, D.C., where she was visiting with her sister during a summer.

These early contests were Bailey's introduction to show business, and in the depression era she persevered in her decision to become an entertainer. While still in her teens, she toured with vaudeville troupes, singing and dancing throughout the coal-mining towns of Pennsylvania, earning about fifteen dollars a week in the cafes of Pottsville and Wilkes-Barre, among many others. During this time of her life, she also performed at small nightclubs in Washington, D.C., working on U Street N.W., then known as the city's elite black entertainment site. She also won an amateur contest at the Apollo Theatre in Harlem, after which she performed for a brief period as a specialty dancer with Noble Sissle's band.

During the forties, Bailey's career began to take on the forms that brought her worldwide fame. From 1941 through the last year of her life, she performed on United Service Organization (USO) tours. In 1943-1944 she toured with such groups as those of Charles "Cootie" Williams, William "Count" Basie, and Noble Sissle. In August 1988 Bailey and her husband, along with their band, performed aboard a naval flagship, the *Coronado*, on behalf of American troops involved in the Gulf crisis.

In the early forties, Bailey began working more closely with Big-Band groups and performers and began to develop as a solo performer. She sang in nightclubs in New York City, Baltimore, and Washington, D.C. She was a featured vocalist with Edgar Hayes's orchestra and with the Sunset Royal Band. Her debut as a soloist came when she performed at the Village Vanguard in 1944, in the company of Huddie Ledbetter and Richard Dyer-Bennet. During this same year, she began working an eight-month engagement at Manhattan's exclusive Blue Angel, and while working there, appeared in Cab Calloway's act at the Strand Theatre, replacing Sister Rosetta Tharpe, who was ill at the time. She worked with Calloway for three weeks and later worked with him again for sixteen weeks in the late show at Broadway's Zanzibar Nightclub.

Actress Makes Debut

In 1946 Bailey made her debut as an actress when she starred on Broadway in *St. Louis Woman*, in the role of Butterfly. She was hailed as the best newcomer to Broadway for her performance in this all-black drama with Nat King Cole, produced by Johnny Mercer and Harold Arlen. The play opened at the Marten Beck Theatre on March 30, 1946, and it ran for 113 performances. Following this introduction to the stage, she became well-known for her performances on Broadway as well as in movies and television. In the forties she played a runaway slave girl in *Arms and the Girl*, a Theatre Guild operetta. As well, she performed roles in two Paramount pictures, *Variety Girl* (1947), in which she introduced her popular song "Tired," and *Isn't It Romantic?* (1948).

During the fifties Bailey worked both on stage and in motion pictures. In 1954 she had her first Broadway role as a solo star, appearing in *House of Flowers*, a musical produced by Truman Capote and Harold Arlen. The production opened in December and ran for 165 engagements with Bailey as Madame Fleur, a madam at a West Indian bordello. The production cost $269,000 and included such well-known performers as Juanita Hall as Madame Tango, Diahann Carroll as Otillie, and Geoffrey Holder as the voodoo practitioner. Enid Moser and Ada Moore also appeared in the show.

Bailey also played in the screen version of *Carmen Jones* (1954). She was the exuberant and earthy Frankie, one of Carmen's friends, in the film starring Dorothy Dandridge and Harry Belafonte. The movie was a Twentieth Century Fox production of Georges Bizet's opera, arranged for Broadway by Oscar Hammerstein and produced on screen by Otto Preminger. In addition, Bailey performed in other movies of the decade. She was cast as Gussie, the narrator and crafty matchmaker, in Paramount's *That Certain Feeling* (1956), starring Bob Hope and Eva Marie Saint. She appeared in the biographical *St. Louis Blues* (1958), playing the role of Aunt Hagar, kinswoman of the famous W. C. Handy, father of the blues. In 1959 she played Maria, the cookshop woman, in MGM's *Porgy and Bess*, which featured Sammy Davis, Jr., as Sportin' Life. For this film version of George Gershwin's folk opera, according to *Current Biography*, "it was largely at [Bailey's] insistence that director Otto Preminger and producer Sam Goldwyn decided to avoid what she considered to be the exaggerated Negro dialect called for by the script" (1969, 24).

In what is regularly called the high point of Bailey's career, she appeared in the Broadway musical comedy, *Hello, Dolly!* (1967), where she held the starring role in David Merrick's all-black production. The earlier version of the show had been a hit since 1964, with Carol Channing in the starring role of Dolly Gallagher Levi. Bailey played opposite Cab Calloway, and was, according to *Current Biography*, responsible for Calloway's having been cast in the role (1969, 24). As well, when the show previewed in Washington's National Theater, Bailey invited then President Lyndon Baines Johnson and the First Lady on stage for the curtain calls. Bailey's performance was highly acclaimed for her exquisite timing and her remarkable singing.

Bailey's career also included television and records. From the fifties onward, she appeared on many television shows, including "The Perry Como Show," "The Ed Sullivan Show," "What's My Line?," and "The Mike Douglas Show." She appeared on "Toast of the Town" and on the "Colgate Summer Comedy Hour." For the recording industry, she released albums with Coral, Mercury, Columbia, and Decca, accompanied by famous bands. She considered herself most of all a singer, and songs for which she is well-known include "Bill Bailey, Won't You Please Come Home?" "Saint Louis Blues," "Row, Row, Row," "That's Good Enough For Me," "Toot, Toot, Tootsie, Goodbye," "Tired," and "Takes Two to Tango." In 1968 RCA-Victor released the sound track for *Hello, Dolly!*, with Bailey as head of the cast.

Performance Style Appeals to Audience

Bailey's performance style was original and appealed to a broad audience. Repeatedly, she is characterized by her "sexy, throaty drawl and droll sense of humor" ("Pearl Bailey, 'Ambassador of Love,'" 6; "America's Pearlie Mae Dies at 72"). She was also described as a "singer with insouciant charm, expressive hands, and a lazy way with a song" (*Current Biography*, 34). A further observation is that as a performer, she was "raffish and brassy, sometimes delivering her lyrics in a style she called preaching, or sometimes talking them in a deep throated rumble akin to a growl" ("Entertainer, Legend Pearl Bailey Dies," A-2). Most of her audience is familiar with her endearing penchant for embellishing a song by ad-libbing and employing chit-chat and asides. The technique is frequently referred to as Pearlie Mae's throwaway style of delivery. Her delivery was further enhanced by her stylish feather boa, or her rhinestones, or her chinchilla, all contributing their part in the unique presence that this consummate entertainer represented for her audience.

During her fifty-seven years as a performer, Bailey traveled widely. She considered herself clairvoyant and practiced yoga. She both read books and wrote books, completing two autobiographies as well as humorous and inspirational books. Her two autobiographies are *The Raw Pearl* (1968) and *Talking to Myself* (1971). In 1973 she wrote *Pearl's Kitchen*. Her *Between You and Me* was scheduled to be published by Doubleday in the fall of 1990, the year of her death.

Bailey's observations of her fellow man resulted in her often-quoted declaration that "we are humans." In the midst of the various crises faced by the world during her last years, she was a woman of great feeling and sympathy. She observed, for example, "The biggest mistake most people make is to want to become something before they are something. You first have to be something and be it wholeheartedly, and then you can become what you want." She was not afraid to demonstrate social consciousness: "A couple of things hurt me: seeing the homeless curled up in fetal positions as if they're trying to crawl back into their mother's womb. And that if you get a gray hair, you have to quit working. I bleed for the world. If we get a few more bleeders out here, we'll get something done" ("It's the Best of Times," 11).

Bailey's career began with awards for outstanding performance, and it continued with such acknowledgements. She was honored for her role as an entertainer as well as for her role in national, international, and other civic affairs. Her performance in *St. Louis Woman* won her the Donaldson Award as the best newcomer on Broadway (1946). In 1967 she was voted Entertainer of the Year by the editors of *Cue*. In 1968 she received a special award for her performance in *Hello, Dolly!*, accepted during the presentations of the twenty-second Tony Awards of the American Theatre Wing for Distinguished Achievement in the New York Theatre.

In humane affairs, Bailey was honored for her interest and participation. She began suffering heart problems during the sixties, but she continued to perform. She received the March of Dimes annual award (1968), the USO "Woman of the Year" Award (1969), and the "Heart of the Year" award presented her by the American Heart Association (1972).

Known at home and abroad, Bailey was applauded for her role in civic affairs. She made frequent appearances at the White House. In 1957 she was one of the featured entertainers at the festivities following President Dwight D. Eisenhower's second inauguration. She received citations from New York City's mayor, John Lindsay, and from Egypt's president, Anwar Sadat. In 1970 President Richard Nixon appointed her "Ambassador of Love." In 1975 she was appointed special representative in the United States delegation to the United Nations, an appointment that was continued under the administrations of subsequent presidents Gerald Ford, Ronald Reagan, and George Bush. At her death, she was a United Nations senior public delegate. In 1988 President Ronald Reagan presented her the Medal of Freedom.

Bailey performed for most of her seventy-two years. She worked with the greats of the industry from her early associates in the Big Band era to her later activities; for much of the period, she was accompanied by her husband, Louis Bellson. For twenty-five years her manager was Sam Irwin, and for much of this time her road manager was E. B. Smith.

Pearl Bailey died of heart disease on August 17, 1990 at Thomas Jefferson University Hospital in Philadelphia, Pennsylvania, and was buried at Rolling Green Memorial Park. She was seventy-two. Her funeral was attended by more than two thousand people. Cab Calloway, who had starred opposite her in *Hello, Dolly!*, was one of the pallbearers and remembered her, addressing her in words from the musical: "You'll always be here in our hearts where you belong" ("2,000 Bid Bailey Farewell").

References

"America's Pearlie Mae Dies at 72." *Tennessean* 18 August 1990.

Bailey, Pearl, *The Raw Pearl*. New York: Harcourt, Brace, 1968.

"Bailey Serenading Soldiers in Gulf." *Tennessean* 16 August 1988.

Chilton, John. *Who's Who in Jazz*. New York: Da Capo Press, 1985.

Current Biography Yearbook. New York: H. W. Wilson, 1955.

"Entertainer, Legend Pearl Bailey Dies: Heart Suspected." (Nashville) *Banner* 18 August 1990.

Feather, Leonard. *The Encyclopedia of Jazz*. New York: Da Capo Press, 1960.

"It's the Best of Times." *USA Weekend* 17-19 February 1989.

"Pearl Bailey, 'Ambassador of Love,' Dies at Age 72; Was Stage, Film, TV Star." *Jet* 78 (9 March 1990): 4-10. Photographs, pp. 4-5, 8-10.

"Pearl Bailey Returns to Broadway." *Ebony* 10 (April 1955): 60-64.

Shaw, Arnold. "Pearl Bailey." *The New Grove Dictionary of American Music.* Eds. H. Wiley Hitchcock and Stanley Sadie. New York: Macmillan, 1986.

Southern, Eileen. *Biographical Dictionary of Afro-American and African Musicians.* Westport, Conn.: Greenwood Press, 1982.

"That Certain Feeling." *Ebony* 11 (June 1956): 75-79.

"2,000 Bid Bailey Farewell." (Nashville) *Banner* 24 August 1990.

Who's Who in America. Vol. 35. Chicago: Marquis, 1969.

Laura C. Jarmon

Augusta Baker

(1911-)

Storyteller, librarian

Augusta Braxton Baker provided guidance for generations of children through her work as a librarian, author, educator, storyteller, and promoter of honest portrayals of ethnic, cultural, and religious groups in children's literature. She was born April 1, 1911, in Baltimore, Maryland. The daughter and only child of teachers, Winfort J. and Mabel (Gough) Braxton, she was reared and influenced by parents who provided guidance with their beliefs in the value of education and exemplified these precepts through their own actions.

Baker's childhood was further enriched through her close relationship with her grandmother, Augusta Fax Gough, a member of this closely-knit household. Raised on a Maryland plantation and the daughter of a house servant, Gough was educated and tutored at the plantation school. Imbued with a strong intellectual drive, she came to Baltimore as an adult and shared her knowledge with other former slaves, including her future husband, Walter Gough. She knew that "in order for the black person to succeed he must be

Augusta Baker

educated, and this belief she fostered in all she came in contact with down through the years" (Merriman, 61).

Sitting beside her grandmother, young Augusta Braxton absorbed the stories she told, that had been handed down from generation to generation. In Baker's recollections she recounted the impact that these shared moments had upon her as a child:

> There were the positive values of these stories. They gave pure, unrestrained joy to a sometimes lonely child who needed it. I was an only child and I had a lively imagination. These stories strengthened it and guided it into constructive and aesthetic channels. I learned new words—long, difficult, beautiful words—for my grandmother did not know about vocabulary control and short sentences. I think that was the time when I developed a sense of humor. . . . Over the years I have been grateful for whatever small sense I have. . . . . As I look back on my childhood I recognize the influence which storytelling and folktales had on my personal development. I am grateful that I heard these stories when I was "knee-high to a grasshopper" (Baker, "Once Upon a Time," 10-11).

Completing her public school education with her graduation from the high school in which her father taught, Baker matriculated at the University of Pittsburgh in 1927 at the age of sixteen. This movement from an all-black environment into a predominantly white world was a challenging obstacle to overcome, but with perseverance, determination, and a desire to learn, Baker succeeded. During this period she experienced several noteworthy events. At the age of seventeen she was introduced to society in Baltimore at a cotillion ball during the Christmas season. She also pledged the Delta Sigma Theta Sorority. Completing her sophomore year, Augusta Braxton married a fellow student, James Baker, who was a graduate student in the field of social work.

The young couple moved to Albany, New York, where her husband was employed in the Albany Interracial Council, a branch of the National Urban League. Eager to pursue her education, Baker applied for admission to Albany State Teachers College, an institution that was reluctant to admit her. Confronted with obvious racial discrimination, she was supported in her efforts by the University of Pittsburgh, her husband's council, and also Eleanor Roosevelt, who was then the governor's wife.

Graduating June 19, 1933, with her bachelor of arts degree in English, Baker realized eventually that teaching was not a priority for her. After conferring with Martha Caroline Pritchard, director of the library school at Albany, and Madeline Gilmore, she enrolled as a student. She received her bachelor of science degree in library science in 1934.

With a subsequent move to New York City, James Baker was employed with the Home Relief Bureau; however, these years of the Great Depression forestalled any opportunity for Augusta Baker to secure a library position. Disappointments were tempered with the birth of their son, James Baker III, in 1936. Known affectionately as ''Buddy,'' he was their only child.

Baker Enters Library Service for Children

A cherished dream became a reality for Baker in 1937 when she entered the field of library service to children with an appointment as an assistant to Priscilla Edie Morgan, the children's librarian at the New York Public Library's 135th Street Branch Library in Harlem. From this time until her retirement thirty-seven years later, Baker's perceptive, progressive qualities of leadership permeated every sphere of her work. With enthusiasm and sensitive understanding, she gave evidence of an ability to communicate with all age groups. Respecting the potential of her young patrons, she combined her engaging personality with her professional skills to provide needed inspiration and motivation. For many she was a mentor, a confidante, and one with whom dreams and concerns could be shared. With such positive attributes, Baker made a lasting impact upon children, upon library services for youth, and upon those adults and agencies concerned with this age group. In her own words she acknowledges:

> Working with the children was one of the most exciting parts of my professional life. I was with them for seventeen years and I was where I belonged and where I was happiest. . . . I brought all that I could to the boys and girls who came to that children's room in Harlem, and I have been repaid many times by the success which has come to many of these children. James Baldwin pays tribute to the Library and speaks warmly of the influence that the library and librarians had on him. . . . Yes, these were the happiest seventeen years of my professional life (Baker, ''My Years,'' 119-20).

Renamed the Countee Cullen Branch in 1951, this cultural, social, and educational center became a mecca for the citizens of Harlem. With Ernestine Rose as the branch librarian, the institution was one of the primary locations for the emergence of the Harlem Renaissance. It housed the renowned Arthur Schomburg Collection, which was sold to the New York Public Library in 1926. The American Negro Theater Group performed in the basement while the children and adults benefited from the talents of promising figures in the fields of humanities and the arts, including such luminaries as the poets Countee Cullen, Langston Hughes, and James Weldon Johnson, the artist Aaron Douglas, and the actor Frederick O'Neal.

Seeking to supplement these programs with appropriate books that would foster racial pride and a sense of racial identity, Baker surveyed the children's collection and recognized a lack of materials that focused upon black history and culture:

> I came to work at the 135th Street Branch . . . of the New York Public Library in 1937 and found that the children in Harlem had little knowledge of their cultural heritage and background. . . . There was little interest in the subject on the part of the schools, teachers and parents . . . and libraries. . . .
>
> Those people who were interested in sharing their knowledge with the children soon discovered that there were practically no books on the subject written specifically for children. . . . Most of the books which included black characters represented them as shiftless, happy, grinning, dialect-speaking menials. This was what was being written for children and what they read. I was distressed and frustrated but I found I was not alone. Others were recognizing the need for a special kind of children's literature—books about black history and culture (Baker, ''My Years,'' 117-18).

Supported in her concerns by Schomburg and Charlemae Rollins through her pamphlet *We Build Together*, Baker considered ways to remedy the situation. The needed catalyst was sparked by the poignant, bittersweet reactions of a child to the negative portrayals of the black characters in the 1939 book *The Mule Twins* by Inez Hogan after Baker had read it aloud. This incident prompted her to initiate a move that in 1939 led to the formation of a black collection devoted to an honest portrayal of blacks. Later designated the James Weldon Johnson Memorial Collection, it received financial support from black women who were members of the Library Group named after Johnson. Working diligently, Baker carefully evaluated and selected books to fulfill a basic purpose:

> It is the purpose of this collection to bring together books for children that give an unbiased, accurate, well rounded picture of Negro life in all parts of the world. . . . In order to give children more democratic attitudes toward all the racial groups that make America the great nation, we must use literature that will strengthen the growth of democracy. Those of us who knew James Weldon Johnson realize that his life was devoted to this cause. The books placed in this collection are chosen to further this purpose (Baker, "Reading for Democracy," 144).

Fulfilling her responsibilities as a children's librarian, Baker provided meaningful services and programs. Young people derived immeasurable benefits from concerts, reading clubs, guest appearances of black artists, writers, dramatists, diplomats, and other role models. The children came in class visits from all areas of Manhattan; they toured the library and the Schomburg Collection. Highlighting all of her activities was Baker's entry into and her growing love for the art of storytelling. She explained:

> I began to tell stories because it was part of the job of being a children's librarian. Then as time passed I grew to love it. I liked the way the children reacted. I also enjoyed reading the literature that folktales came from and wanted to share this enjoyment with children who came to the library (Maxine Modell Merriman, Interview with Augusta Baker, 27 April 1983. In Modell, 182-83).

Realizing the importance of working with adults, Baker immersed herself in community activities, sharing her knowledge and professional interest with parents, teachers, and allied agencies. Never relinquishing her efforts to enhance the field of children's literature with books relating to the black experience, she gained the unstinting support of Frederick Melcher, the respected publisher of the R. R. Bowker Company. When Baker spoke before a gathering of publishers and editors of children's books concerning the problems of stereotypical representations of blacks in juvenile literature and a lack of substantive material, the reception accorded her was mixed; yet, in the intervening years some of the more liberal-minded publishing houses such as Viking, Doubleday, and Harper began to respond to this obvious need. Support for this worthy cause was received from the Child Study Association, the Bureau of Intercultural Education, and the National Council for Christians and Jews.

During her tenure at the 135th Street Branch Library, a change occurred in the private life of Baker. A separation from her husband was followed by a divorce. During World War II she met Gordon Alexander, and they were married on November 23, 1944. An outgoing, generous individual, he had a wonderful sense of humor that was a perfect match for his wife's. In 1948 the couple relocated in Saint Albans, Queens, New York, where they had their home for thirty-two years until their relocation in 1980 to Columbia, South Carolina.

Baker Becomes Storyteller Specialist and Administrator

In 1953 Baker made a significant professional advancement. Following the appointment of Frances Lander Spain as coordinator of work with children in the New York Public Library, Baker was urged by John Cory, chief of the circulation department, to apply for the newly created position of assistant coordinator and storytelling specialist. Speaking of Baker's subsequent promotion and her talent, Cory said:

> In 1951 when I became Chief of the Circulation Department of the New York Public Library, one of the first and most impressive children's librarians whom I met was Mrs. Augusta Baker, who had pioneered in children's services at the Countee Cullen Branch in Harlem. She was so impressive, so gifted and so humane in her approach to the library needs of children that it was a pleasure to participate in her promotion in 1953 as Assistant Coordinator of Children's Services and in 1961 as Coordinator of Children's Services. Any administrator is, by definition, suspect as to his interests in the support of children's library services. Augusta Baker made my life easy by her very presence which insured the best possible treatment for children's library activities in the New York Public Library. She is a close personal friend, a fellow gardener, a dedicated librarian, and a memorable human being (Cory, [Augusta Baker . . . as Administrator]. In Izard, 353-54).

Relocated with expanded responsibilities, Baker and Spain, had exciting times together as they guided children's services throughout the entire borough of Manhattan, the Bronx, and Staten Island. The first of several international trips occurred for Baker when she was invited in 1955 by Carleton Comma, director of the Trinidad Public Library, to consult with the children's librarians in the system. She conducted workshops, established new programs, and gave expert guidance on programs that would serve as prototypes for future replication. During the same year she entered into a new sphere of endeavor when she became a visiting lecturer in the school of library service at Columbia University. Baker taught oral narration, and Frances Henne taught objectives in services of library work with children and young adults.

Never forsaking her love for storytelling, Baker directed the program throughout the library system for eight years. Through workshops, lectures, training, and teaching the techniques of this art form to others, she followed in the footsteps of her predecessors Mary Gould Davis, Frances Clarke Sayers, and Eulalie Steinmetz Ross. As storytelling specialist, she edited one of the established reference tools for all storytellers, *Stories: A List of Stories to Tell and to Read Aloud*. In 1955, from her gathering of folk literature culled from various cultures, Baker completed another notable collection, *The Talking Tree*, and in 1960 *Golden Lynx*.

Maintaining her deep concern for honest portrayals of minorities, especially blacks, in literature for young people, Baker lectured on this subject at conferences and workshops. A standard example of her beliefs is revealed in an extract from her work, *The Black Experience in Children's Books*:

> Books can perform a unique function in the plan for intercultural education. They provide a means for gaining knowledge, improving social skills, and influencing attitudes and ways of thinking so that they reinforce each other. . . . They help develop awareness and can carry readers into experiences and feelings of people different from themselves. Books cannot take the place of first hand contacts with other people. However, they can prepare children to meet people, to discount unimportant differences, and to appreciate cultural traditions and values unlike their own. The black child is given pride in his heritage at the same time that the white child gains knowledge of another culture and history (Baker, i).

As the recipient of the American Library Association Dutton-Macrae Award in 1953, Baker continued her research "to define the role of books in intercultural education" (Baker, "My Years," 121). Subsequently, she published a bibliography, *Books about Negro Life for Children*, which included forty titles. In 1971 it was retitled *The Black Experience in Children's Books*, with revisions made every five years since 1974. The importance of this work was recognized by Barbara Rollock, a colleague:

> Mrs. Baker's bibliography . . . was to be a benchmark for selection of materials for all minority representations in literature, since in formulating specific criteria she insisted on respecting the dignity of the child and stressed positive representations of a culture (Rollock, 336-37).

The ultimate administrative achievement occurred when Spain retired from her position on July 31, 1931. On the next day, history was made when Baker became coordinator of work with children in the nation's largest public library system. Her elevation as a member of an ethnic minority group to a high-level policy-making position was based upon merit, coupled with a clear recognition of her innovative, visionary leadership abilities and professional competence.

Accepting the broad scope and functions of her role as a major department head, Baker assumed her duties with an intellectual approach that revealed her abilities to be both an idealist and a pragmatist. She continued the well-established coordinated supervision of library service to children in the system's eighty-two branch libraries and its six bookmobiles. Administratively, Baker became an advocate in the interpretation of sociological, educational, and technological trends as they affected the policies and practices in service to youth, both within and beyond the library system. Throughout her thoughtful analyses, new dimensions were propounded that were consonant with the larger goals and objectives of the New York Public Library. She maintained an important liaison with other units in the system, thus assuring that service to children was an integral part of total library service. Participating in personnel decisions, Baker helped to maintain the high standards of professionalism for which the library had an enviable reputation. Her skill in budgetary matters resulted in fiscal decisions that supported meaningful services and programs.

Based upon her previous experience in the area of collection development, Baker directed the department's evaluation and selection processes. She recognized the growing interest in media in addition to books; thus with properly developed criteria, the department included phonograph records and cassettes. With a well-established relationship with publishers, authors, and illustrators of children's literature, she was frequently consulted in matters relating to the field of literature for children. The central children's room in the Forty-second Street Library became a rich reference and research center for scholars, authors, illustrators, and students enrolled in children's literature courses. Baker's steadfast endeavors to have the collection reflect diversity, with honest portrayals of all ethnic, cultural, and religious groups, were recognized in a tribute to her by the librarians of Fisk University:

> To the children of all races, colors, and creeds her legacy to them was her ability to mirror universality in the imaginative world of books ("Augusta Baker Retires," 1).

The department of work with children was renowned for its excellent offerings of services and programs. Through her personal example, Baker furthered the and innovative approaches in serving children and adults who were concerned with this age group. She represented the library before professional library and educational associations in lectures, workshops, and seminars. With the use of media she extended the influence of the library when she initiated the series of weekly radio broadcasts "The World of Children's Literature" in 1971. Called upon as a consultant, she participated in the preparation of bibliographies for the popular television program "Sesame Street," contributing to the Parents and Teachers Guide. The television audience recognized her as the moderator on the television program "It's Fun to Read."

Baker's prestige and authority have been realized nationally and internationally by a wide array of institutions. In the educational sphere she lectured or taught at many universities, including Rutgers, Syracuse, Southern Florida, Atlanta, North Carolina Central, and Long Island universities, the universities of Nevada at Las Vegas and of Washington, Banks Street College of Education, and New School for Social Research. She has been a visiting faculty member at Texas Women's University since 1975, and has been storyteller-in-residence, at the University of South Carolina since 1980.

According to Baker, it was Spain, a former president of the American Library Association (ALA), who indicated to her the importance of becoming involved in professional organizations. The advice prompted her to assume important roles in the American Library Association, including member of the executive board, (1968-72), and of the ALA Council (1965-72). In the ALA's Children's Services Division she was a member of the board of directors (1958-61), vice-president (1966), and president (1967), and chair of the Newbery/Caldecott Awards Committee (1966). Additional assignments include ALA Children's Book Council Joint Committee; representative to UNICEF for the ALA international board on books for young people; chair, the ALA advisory committee to the Westinghouse Broadcasting Company; member of the Notable Books Committee, Children's Services Division; of the Children's Services Division advisory committee, Library USA, New York World's Fair, 1964-65; and various committees of the Public Library Association.

Baker's professional affiliation with other associations and agencies has been extensive. Serving as a member, committee, or board appointee, she has been active in the New York Library Association, the Women's National Book Association, the New York Folklore Society, the South Carolina Library Association, the Association for Early Childhood Education International, and the Good Neighbor Civic Association. Additionally, she is a member of the advisory board of the Center for the Study of Children's Literature at Simmons College, Boston; is co-chair of the Friends of the New York Public Library Children's Services, was a delegate to the White House Conference on Children in 1950 and 1972, and is a consultant to the Council on Library Resources, the Teen-Age Book Club of the Scholastic Book Services, and the *Children's Digest Magazine*.

Her numerous awards include doctor of humane letters, St. John's University, 1978, and University of South Carolina, 1986; Grolier Foundation Award, ALA, 1968; Constance Lindsay Skinner Award, Women's National Book Association, 1971; Clarence Day Award, American Publishers Institute, 1974; honorary membership for life (storyteller par excellence), ALA, 1975; Regina Medal, Catholic Library Association, 1981; and first recipient, Zora Neale Hurston Award presented by the Association of Black Storytellers, 1989.

Completing thirty-seven years of dedicated, influential library and professional service to children, agencies, and adults concerned with the important young public, Baker retired in March, 1974. The legacy that she leaves for us is also a challenge:

> Library work with children has had a great past and has a still greater future. Young black men and women have an opportunity to be part of this exciting future and for the sake of their children they should be. Today they can contribute to the awakening interest in the black man. They have a chance to work with authors, illustrators, and editors in the creation of still much needed materials. Black authors and illustrators are coming into their own and black librarians have a chance to advise them, to help them, and support them. The black child needs the image of a black librarian—and white children need this image also. . . . The community needs the black children's librarian who will relate to it and understand the unique problems. . . . I predict a great and exciting future for black children—and for black librarians (Baker, "My Years," 122-23).

References

Baker, Augusta. "Children's Books in a Changing Culture." In *Diversity in Our Society: Challenge to the School Conference, 1960*. New York: Bank Street College of Education, 1960.

———. "My Years as a Children's Librarian." *The Black Librarian in America*. Edited by E. J. Josey. Metuchen, N.J.: Scarecrow Press, 1970.

———. "Once Upon a Time." *Come Higher!* Edited by Lawrence Clark Powell. Los Angeles: The Yeasayers Press, 1966.

———. "Reading for Democracy." *Wilson Library Bulletin* 18 (October 1943): 140-144.

Baker, Augusta, selector. *The Black Experience in Children's Books*. New York: The New York Public Library, 1971.

"Augusta Baker: Storyteller Retires." *Black Caucus Newsletter* 2 (May 1974): 1.

Izard, Anne. "Augusta Baker, Coordinator of Children's Services of the New York Public Library, Retired on March 1, 1974." *Top of the News* 30 (June 1964): 353-54. Includes photograph.

Merriman, Maxine Modell. *Augusta Baker: Exponent of the Oral Art of Storytelling: Utilizing Video as a Medium*. Ph. D. Dissertation. Graduate School of Library Science, Texas Women's University, 1983. Includes oral interviews with Augusta Baker.

Rollock, Barbara. "Augusta Baker: Storyteller and Librarian." *Catholic Library World* 52 (March 1981): 336-37.

Shaw, Spencer G. "Augusta Baker, (1911-)." *ALA World Encyclopedia of Library and Information Service*. Edited by Robert Wedgeworth. Chicago: American Library Association, 1980.

Something about the Author. Vol. 3. Detroit: Gale Research, 1970. Includes photograph.

Who's Who in Library and Information Services. Edited

by Joel M. Lee. Chicago: American Library Association, 1982.

Collections

Augusta Baker's personal library of children's books has been given to the Queensborough Public Library and has been named the Augusta Baker Collection. A taped interview with Baker is in the Black Oral History Collection, Special Collections, Fisk University Library. Baker's personal papers are in her possession.

Spencer G. Shaw

Ella Baker

(1903-1986)

Community organizer, civil rights and domestic activist, education consultant

Although Ella Jo Baker was not highly visible during the civil rights movement, the supportive role she played greatly influenced its direction. An officer of the National Association for the Advancement of Colored People, a founder of the Southern Christian Leadership Conference, a supporter of the Student Nonviolent Coordinating Committee, and an organizer of many small community groups, Baker attracted grass-roots support for the fight for civil and human rights.

Ella Baker

Born in Norfolk, Virginia, in 1903, Baker grew up in a small town in North Carolina. Her grandfather was a rebellious black slave minister, while her grandmother, equally rebellious, refused to marry a light-skinned slave whom her master had selected for her. As a result she was banished from working in the "big house" to toiling as a field hand. In spite of this, she married the grandfather. With this kind of background, Baker had no choice but to grow up militant.

Baker attended Shaw University in Raleigh, North Carolina, and graduated as valedictorian of her class. As a young woman, she yearned to be a missionary, but instead studied sociology. She came in contact with radical politics for the first time when she arrived in New York in 1927—at the beginning of the Great Depression. Harlem provided new social and political ideas for her; Washington Square Park became the scene for debates over such ideas as communism, socialism, and capitalism, and she was drawn into organizations that strove for social change and political action.

In 1932 Baker allied with George Schuyler, a black writer with the *Pittsburgh Courier*. Together they organized the Young Negro Cooperative League, whose goal was to promote consumer cooperatives. In her role as a group organizer, Baker learned to understand group dynamics. Throughout the thirties, she identified with workers' education, consumer protection, and community organization movements. By now, she identified with the problems of the unemployed and became aware of the suffering and poverty that the Depression produced.

In the early 1940s Baker began her affiliation with the National Association for the Advancement of Colored People (NAACP) as an assistant field secretary. Eventually she became national field secretary for the NAACP, and traveled throughout the South to organize NAACP branches and develop membership drives. In two years, she attended 362 meetings and traveled 16,244 miles. Eventually, she was promoted to the national director of branches of the NAACP. Under Baker's leadership, the New York branch became the best organized and the most active, and as president of that branch, she assisted in the implementation of community action against de facto segregation in the New York public schools.

Baker became disillusioned with the NAACP, however, because it was directed from the top rather than by the branches. She wanted the branches to be more active and in complete control. In spite of the fact that she resigned her national position, Baker remained active with the New York branch. In fact, when the U.S. Supreme Court handed down its decision in the *Brown* v. *Board of Education of Topeka, Kansas* court case of 1954, Baker was serving as chair of the Educational Committee of the New York branch. The committee analyzed the evidence which revealed that de facto segregation caused the achievement levels of black children to go down rather than up after the children entered elementary schools. She served on the mayor's committee on school integration, including the subcommittee on zoning. In 1957, Baker organized a group called Parents in Action for Quality Education:

> I went to the upper West Side, and the people very eagerly said they wanted school integration. But when you raised the question of whether they would permit or would welcome blacks to live in the same house with them, which was the only practical way at that stage to achieve integration, they squirmed. Integration certainly had to be pushed concurrently with changing the quality of education that the black children were getting, and changing the attitudes of the educational establishment toward the black community (Lerner, 348).

From her NAACP experiences, Baker had a firsthand knowledge of the South, southern blacks, southern communities, and southern organizations and leadership and had cultivated personal contacts with persons across the South.

By 1955, when the bus boycott had erupted in Montgomery, Alabama, she and Stanley Levison offered financial assistance to the boycott movement through a group called In Friendship. On June 4, 1956, the federal court ruled in favor of the Montgomery Improvement Association to end segregation in public accommodations, which included segregation of the buses. On November 13, the U.S. Supreme Court confirmed the lower court's ruling and by December 20, 1956, the court order reached Montgomery, Alabama. After the success of the bus boycott, according to Baker, the integration movement literally came to a halt, for no plans existed for a continuance of activities.

Activist Coordinates SCLC Activities

Baker consequently exhorted the leadership of the Montgomery Improvement Association to continue its fight against widespread racial injustice, not for just the desegregation of buses. Through Baker's efforts, in 1957 the Southern Christian Leadership Conference (SCLC) was formed to fight all types of racial injustice. She was an associate director of the movement, and her organizational expertise and unique leadership style were crucial to the SCLC's success. She felt that the leadership of the civil rights movement should be in the South, counterbalancing the NAACP, whose leadership was mainly in the North. Baker also felt that the leadership in Montgomery had not realized how important it was to keep the momentum going. Martin Luther King, Jr., became the leader of the SCLC, but it was Baker who ran and developed its office and coordinated the program. The SCLC, headquartered in Atlanta, grew into an organization comprising sixty-five affiliates in various southern cities, all directed by local black leadership. Baker, then fifty-two years old, intended to work for six weeks. However, due to the SCLC's inability to replace her skills and expertise, she remained as its coordinator for two-and-a-half years. Her responsibilities were varied. Eventually friction developed between Baker and the SCLC leadership; she preferred a people-centered movement, while the SCLC centered its activities around a charismatic leader.

Baker was a key in the network of sit-ins in the summer of 1960. Since the demonstrations were led for the most part by students in historically black colleges, she saw the need for the schools to form one cohesive umbrella organization. She persuaded the SCLC to organize a conference in Raleigh. Anticipating about one hundred young student leaders, she found two hundred dynamic students in attendance.

On April 15, 1960, at Shaw University in Raleigh, North Carolina, Baker helped organize student leaders into the Student Nonviolent Coordinating Committee (SNCC) as the sit-in demonstrations began to sweep the South. Baker, executive secretary of the SCLC, asked that the SCLC give support in the amount of $800 for the sit-in campaign. As a result, SNCC was formed at this meeting but decided to remain independent of the SCLC. SNCC sponsored sit-ins, wade-ins, kneel-ins, and boycotts of retail establishments. As a founder and supporter of SNCC, Baker continued her work with the young students:

> I had no difficulty relating to the young people. I spoke their language in terms of the meaning of what they had to say. I didn't change my speech pattern and they didn't have to change their speech pattern. But we were able to communicate (Lerner, 350).

Baker also assisted the students in the organization of voter registration drives. SNCC became the most significant student-activist movement in U.S. history. Baker's touch was felt as the students pricked the conscience of the nation over the Vietnam War, the free speech movement, and the women's movement. She supported the right of students to make SNCC an independent organization, and as a result of her stand, she broke with the SCLC.

Baker Recognized for Organizational Skills

Baker was known for her fearlessness when organizing community groups to protest and to vote, Barbara Omolade recalls. Baker went to the people, went to the streets, knocked on doors—she went where the people were. And she went whether the group was large or small or whether the problem was big or little:

> Ms. Baker was a subversive who mobilized people to organize for decent wages for Black teachers, for paved streets in the Black community, against police brutality and for the right to vote (Omolade, 54).

Baker helped people understand that there was strength in unity when she served as a NAACP field worker. In spite of danger, she organized in the rural South during the 1940s when lynching and shotgun justice were the norm and membership in the NAACP could mean death. In addition, she believed very firmly in the right of people to be the ones to decide what actions they were going to take to get out from under their oppression.

In 1964 Baker helped establish the Mississippi Freedom Democratic Party (MFDP), gave the keynote address at its founding convention, and helped prepare its challenge to the National Democratic Party in Atlantic City. She moved to Washington, D.C., until the convention was over, closed up the office, and moved back to New York from Atlanta.

Civil rights activist James Foreman credited Baker among all black leaders with understanding the significance of the student sit-in movement and helping to organize these campus groups into SNCC. The established civil rights groups, such as the SCLC, NAACP, and CORE wanted SNCC to ally with them as the youth wing of the parent group. Since Baker at the time identified with the SCLC, the latter group thought it automatically had an inroad to SNCC. However, Baker supported an independent student-oriented group rather than a leader-centered group. In a December 1970 interview Baker stated:

> I have always felt it was a handicap for oppressed peoples to depend so largely upon a leader, because unfortunately in our culture, the charismatic leader usually becomes a leader because he has found a spot in the public limelight. It usually means he has been touted through the public media, which means that the media made him, and the media may undo him (Lerner, 351).

In one instance the feminist issue in the civil rights movement was no different than in any other patriarchal society. Black women were placed in the back to do daily administrative tasks, to perform the legwork, organize the fund-raising, and provide shelter for freedom fighters, while the men made the speeches and took the credit for progress. Baker wanted no credit for her work, although she provided ideas, energy, money, and hard work, but she was instrumental in awakening the nation to women's struggle for equality and justice and fought against the tendency to relegate women to subordinate positions in the movement. She maintained:

> The movement of the '50's and '60's was carried largely by women, since it came out of church groups. It was sort of second nature to women to play a supportive role. How many made a conscious decision on the basis of the larger goals, how many on the basis of habit pattern, I don't know. But it's true that the number of women who carried the movement is much larger than that of men. Black women have had to carry this role, and I think the younger women are insisting on an equal footing (Lerner, 251).

Baker, who is not as well known as some of the other black civil rights leaders, knew that among a group of ministers she would not play a major role in the circle of leaders. However, the movement and its result were more important to her than her visibility on a television screen. She acknowledged that women have always played a supportive role in church groups, and the civil rights movement was no different. Baker continuously served black people without fame, publicity, or recognition. Many people have heard of the SNCC, but without Baker the SNCC may not have existed.

As a community organizer, civil rights advocate, and voice of many activists, Baker both made history and observed it during a career of leadership that started in 1929 and continued over five decades. Like Martin Luther King, Jr., Baker was an effective leader and bold strategist, pioneering the direct-action tactics that were so successful in the 1960s. She is considered one of the foremost organizers of the freedom movement. Known as a woman of determination and conviction, she quietly planned strategies to overcome prejudice and discrimination in the United States.

In 1983, Public Television Broadcast System presented a documentary on her life called "Fundi: The Story of Ella Baker." *Fundi*, a Swahili word, means "one who hands down a craft from one generation to another." Baker died on her eighty-third birthday in December 1986.

References

"About Ella Baker." *Jet* (19 January 1987): 71:18.

Bergman, Peter M. *The Chronological History of the Negro in America.* New York: Harper, 1969.

Blumberg, Rhoda L. *Social Movements Past and Present.* Boston: Twayne Publishers, 1984.

Branch, Taylor. *Parting the Waters: America in the King Years 1954-63.* New York: Simon and Schuster, 1988.

Canterow, Ellen, O'Malley Gushee, and Sharon Hartman Strom. *Moving the Mountain.* Old Westburg, N.Y.: Feminist Press, 1979.

Forman, James. *Making of Black Revolutionaries.* New York: Macmillan, 1972.

Giddings, Paula. *When and Where I Enter: The Impact of Black Women on Race and Sex in America.* New York: Bantam Books, 1984.

Hentoff, Nat. "A New Year's Toast to Those Who Reject Fate." *Village Voice* 1 January 1979: 30.

Lerner, Gerda. *Black Women in White America: A Documentary History.* New York: Vintage Books, 1973.

Morris, Aldon D. *The Origins of the Civil Rights Movement.* New York: Free Press, 1984.

Mueller, Carol. "Ella Baker and the Origins of 'Participatory Democracy.'" In *Women in the Civil Rights Movement: Trailblazers and Torchbearers, 1941-1965.* Edited by Vicki L. Crawford, Jacqueline Anne Rouse, and Barbara Woods. Brooklyn: Carlson Publishing, 1990.

Omolade, Barbara. "Black Womanhood Images of Dignity: Ella Baker and Miriam Makeba.'' *Black Collegian* (April/May 1981): 52-60.

Payne, Charles. ''Ella Baker and Models of Social Change.'' *Signs* 14 (Summer 1989): 885.

Seitz, Michael H. Review of ''Fundi: The Story of Ella Baker.'' *The Progressive*, January 1983.

Wiley, Jean. ''On the Front Lines; Four Women Activists Whose Worked Touched Millions of Lives.'' *Essence* 20 (February 1990): 45.

Collections

An oral history interview with Ella Baker is in the Civil Rights Documentation Project, Moorland-Spingar Research Center, Howard University.

Joan Curl Elliott

Josephine Baker

(1906-1975)

Dancer, entertainer

Flamboyant and colorful on and off the stage, controversial, erratic, difficult, eccentric, and domineering, Josephine Baker was a singer, entertainer, dancer, French spy, and a woman who tried to create a utopian community in a world that doesn't truly allow such impracticalities. Baker, along with all the adjectives that could apply to her complex personality, was a consummate and working showperson until the day of her death, a vigorous spokesperson for causes she believed in, and a brave woman who tried, but didn't always succeed, to make her dreams come true.

Josephine Baker

Josephine Baker was born in Saint Louis, Missouri, on June 3, 1906. Her mother, who worked as a domestic, was Carrie McDonald, and she was not married to Baker's father, Eddie Carson, a local musician who played the drums. According to Lynn Haney in *Naked at the Feast,* after the birth of her brother, Richard, Carson abandoned the family, and then Carrie McDonald married Arthur Martin when Josephine Baker was five and gave birth to two more children, Margaret and Willie Mae (9-10). Martin informally adopted Josephine. (In *Jazz Cleopatra,* Phyllis Rose says that Carson left immediately after Josephine's birth and that Richard is the son of Martin (1). There are significant differences between the two biographies in the treatment of the family background, apparently due to the greater credence Rose is prepared to give to Baker's own rather unreliable biographies. Haney's biography is not documented, but she interviewed among her other informants Margaret Wallace, Baker's sister, and Richard Martin, Jr., Baker's nephew. The account of the Saint Louis background given here relies for the most part on Haney.)

Josephine Baker was jealous of Richard and Carrie but very fond of Willie Mae, especially after Willie Mae lost an eye due to an incident with the family dog. Abandoned by her real father and living with a stepfather who was liable to become quickly violent and abusive—a tendency that was aggravated by his inability to provide adequately for the family, Josephine Baker developed a mistrust of men and a feeling that she must rely on herself. Her mother's temperament added little to the stability of the family. The family lived in extreme poverty, moving often and struggling for survival. Street-wise, Josephine Baker was a rebel in school. The law at that time permitted a child eight years old to be sent out to do domestic work, providing the child was sent to school, so Baker was sent out to work at that age. Baker had the misfortune of encountering an abusive employer in her first job. This job ended when the woman reached the final point in her continuing mistreatment of Baker by plunging the child's arm into a pot of boiling water. Her second employer treated her much better. The precariousness of black existence in the United States was further impressed on the young Josephine Baker when in 1917 she watched some 1,500 blacks crossing the bridge to Saint Louis with what possessions they could carry as they fled the East Saint Louis riot in which thirty-nine black Americans were killed and thousands left homeless.

Before she was fourteen, Baker had run away from home, found a job supporting herself by waiting on tables, and married and discarded a husband, Willie Wells. Her pregnancy by Wells ended either by early miscarriage or by abortion. Strongly attracted by show business, she then joined a street band, the Jones Family. Shortly thereafter the group was incorporated into the Dixie Fliers, a traveling show that featured Clara Smith. Josephine Baker worked as a dresser for Smith and developed her skills as a dancer. Her strong point was comedy; she could perform the most amazing series of moves with her whole body while keeping her eyes crossed. Thus she had the unenviable experience of touring on the Theatre Owners Booking Association (TOBA) circuit, where performers faced very harsh living and working conditions. When the troupe reached Philadelphia, she met and married William Howard Baker in 1921, much to his family's dismay.

Josephine Baker was turned down for the original production of Sissle and Blake's *Shuffle Along* (1921) because she was not yet sixteen, the minimum age to work in New York theaters. She managed to get a job in the road company, and eventually she found a place in Sissle and Blake's new production, *Chocolate Dandies* (1924). When the show closed in May 1925, Baker found work at the Plantation Club. Caroline Dudley, a wealthy white Chicago woman with a passion for black shows, conceived the idea of taking authentic black performers to Paris. Dudley offered a position to her, and after hesitating, Baker accepted. Originally, Baker was not the most important member of the troupe, but when she reached Paris the balance began to turn quickly. Paul Colin, who soon became her lover, selected Baker for the central figure of his poster for the *Revue Nègre* rather than the nominal star, Maude de Forest. Colin was her first guide in Paris, and a little later Ada "Bricktop" Smith, also served as a mentor as the long, tense relationship between the two women began in friendship.

As rehearsals progressed, the producers became worried about the success of the show, and they persuaded Josephine Baker to dance nude. The *Revue Nègre* opened on October 2 at the Thèâtre des Champs-Elysées. As she first appeared dancing the Charleston to "Yes, Sir, That's My Baby!" there were some hostile reactions from a small part of the audience scandalized by the "vulgarity" of the dancer, but Baker's nude dance with Joe Alex overwhelmed the spectators. Her first French lesson came as she looked for her name in French newspaper reviews. They ranged from raves to attacks, but they all added up to the fact that she and the show were definitely noticed.

Josephine Baker became the rage of Paris. She attracted the attention of writers and artists who knew little or nothing of black life in Saint Louis and saw in her their vision of the African woman. Picasso is reputed to have said, "She is the Nefertiti of now" (Haney, 67). Couturiers saw a new ideal in her body, and she eagerly adopted Parisian fashions. Some designers sent in their bills; others did not. Foreshadowing her lifelong attraction for pets, the modest hotel suite into which she moved was soon sheltering a parakeet, a parrot, two baby rabbits, a snake, and a baby pig. Following the Paris engagement, the *Revue Nègre* was scheduled to go on to Berlin and Russia, but Baker had already agreed to go to the Folies Bergère. This commitment would preclude her completing the tour. When matters came to a head in Berlin and Baker decided to return to Paris, the *Revue* closed. Baker's appearance at the Folies Bergère in *La Folie Du Jour,* was a legendary success—this was the occasion that she appeared in the famous costume of rhinestoned bananas around her hips—and little else.

During this early period in Europe, Josephine Baker was notoriously promiscuous and greedy. As Rose puts it, "For Josephine Baker, sex was a pleasurable form of exercise, like dancing, and she wasn't notably fussy about her partners" (107). Few of the men who flocked around her gave her any reason to trust them. An automobile manufacturer, whom she names only as Marcel, was willing to support her, but he made it plain that he had no intention of marrying her. The young man who was to become famous as Georges Simenon, the author and the creator of Inspector Maigret, was her secretary (and lover) for a few months. He was a cold and compulsive womanizer and conspicuously failed in all of his relationships with women, including his wife—whom he had married before meeting Baker—and his daughter. Josephine Baker took up with a former stonemason from Sicily, Guiseppe Abatino, who was passing himself off as the Count Pepito de Abatino, a claim that did not deceive Baker, who already knew his cousin Zito as a non-aristocratic habitué of Montmartre dives. The relationship would provide stability in her life over the next nine years as Abatino became lover and business manager. Baker was by no means faithful to him, but she was no longer widely promiscuous.

Together, they opened a nightclub, Chez Joséphine, on December 14, 1926, while Baker was still performing at the Folies Bergère. To regularize the situation, she avoided the tedious process of getting her former marriages straightened out by simply declaring to the press in the summer of 1927 that she and Abatino had slipped away and gotten married. The publication in that year of her first autobiography, *Les Mémoires de Joséphine Baker,* led to an even closer entanglement of their affairs. Threatened by a suit by the French Association of Mutilated War Veterans for her remarks about her horror of maimed men, she put her assets in Abatino's name. In this same year she also acted in a quite bad and only partially preserved French feature film *La Sirène des Tropiques.*

Baker Makes World Tour

Fearing that her vogue in Paris was waning, Baker embarked on a world tour in 1928. While traveling through Europe and South America, Baker also worked on her voice and her dancing. Some critics alleged that she was a jumped-up chorus girl, her abilities as a dancer nowhere near the level of that of genuine stars like Florence Mills. This assessment of her dancing may reflect her proficiency in the African-American heritage of dancing styles and a relative unfamiliarity with European-derived styles. There was a genuine problem with the voice. The range and expressiveness were fine, but she lacked the power of projection needed to fill large theatrical spaces in the days before microphones. Baker did not like to record, feeling a need to be in contact with her audience, but there are some recordings she made in 1927 that enable one to hear her early singing. The same sort of criticism of her dancing and singing continued when she returned to appear in Paris in 1930, but there was a genuine difference in her performances. The comic elements had disappeared; she struck many people as a much-changed performer, and not all people liked the change, seeing the toning down of her "vulgarity" as a loss of vigor. A further by-product of the tour was a rather bad novel that Baker wrote with Abatino, *Mon Sang Dans Tes Veines.* (*My Blood in Your Veins*).

In preparation for the new period in Paris, in 1929 Baker bought a house in Le Vésinet, a village about forty-five minutes from Paris and much favored by artists and people in show business. There she was a gracious hostess in a beautifully-appointed house and very popular in the village because of her generosity and directness. To those who worked for her, however, she was known for completely unpredictable mood swings, passing from affability to rage on some unknown schedule. The immediate cause was often quite disproportionate to her intense reaction. This tendency only increased with age. By now Abatino was in the category of employee, but he was able to stand up to her because of his mastery of her financial affairs. He also continued to insist on her continuing to work on her performing skills and polishing her social skills. Her singing had improved to the point that she issued a dozen more records from 1931 to 1935.

Her performance for the revue *Paris Qui Remue* in 1930 represented a step upward in show business, since the Casino de Paris was considered to be a cut above the Folies Bergère. This advancement brought Baker into conflict with the aging but still-reigning queen of Paris music halls, Mistinguett; there was one public confrontation where the two women spat at each other. The song that became Baker's theme, performed at every subsequent appearance, was written for this show—"J'ai Deux Amours," "I have two loves, my country and Paris." As publicity for the show, she led a baby leopard about Paris on a leash. The leopard's collar was a diamond choker that was sold for twenty-two thousand dollars later when she was desperate for money.

Josephine Baker continued to work at the Casino de Paris the following year. Abatino had forced her to take ballet instruction from George Balanchine, and she was able to perform a ballet number in this 1931 revue, *La Joie de Paris.* She also took on as a lover and protégé the aspiring young singer Jacques de Pills, who had a long and successful career in Paris and is perhaps as famous as a partner in one of Edith Piaff's spectacular failures at marriage. The affair ran on into 1935, when as a now-established performer, de Pills felt he had to break away from Baker's attempts to completely dominate his life. At the end of an engagement at the Casino de Paris in 1933, Baker undertook another European tour, beginning with poorly-received but break-even appearances in London. On her return to Paris, Baker appeared successfully in an adaptation of Jacques Offenbach's operetta *La Créole* on December 15, 1934. Baker's best motion picture, *Zouzou,* costarring Jean Gabin, was made in 1934, and another, *Princesse Tam-Tam,* in 1935.

The time had come to try to return to the United States. After considerable hesitation, Josephine Baker accepted an offer to appear in the 1936 *Ziegfeld Follies.* She knew she was in her homeland when the Saint Moritz hotel in New York City gave her and Abatino a suite but asked her to use the back entrance to avoid offending the sensibilities of visiting Southerners. She took advantage of the trip to arrange for a divorce from William Baker and to visit Saint Louis. There her sister Willie Mae had died, apparently the victim of a self-induced abortion. Her step-father had also died in the mental institution where he had been confined because of the increase in the frequency and violence of his rages. In New York the opening night of the *Ziegfeld Follies* was a triumph for the other stars but a fiasco for Baker. Both sides were glad to cancel the contract. In the wake of the recriminations which followed this event and which were compounded by her moderate success in a nightclub engagement, Abatino returned alone to France, where he very soon died of cancer of the kidneys, leaving in his will all the money and property held in his name to Baker. She returned to France to appear in the 1936 production of the Folies Bergère.

Josephine Baker now fell deeply in love with Jean Lion. The son of moderately prosperous Jewish parents, he had entered the stock exchange at the age of eighteen and found that he had a flair for making money. Blond, very handsome, and athletic, he was now a millionaire several times over. He taught Baker to fly and proposed one day while they were in the air. They were married in the spring of 1937, and after the shock of the wedding the family accepted her. By this marriage Baker became a French citizen. She became pregnant but had an early miscarriage, and the incompatibility of each partner's goals in the marriage soon became evident. They separated but the divorce did not take place until 1942. Baker hoped for some time for the possibility of a reconciliation which never took place.

Her grief over the breakdown of her marriage did not exclude Baker's taking new lovers, and it was while she was traveling with Claude Meunier, whose family fortune came from chocolate, that she saw and rented a château, Les Milandes, which at this point did not have electricity or heat.

Baker Recruited for French Resistance

Josephine Baker's opening in the Casino de Paris's revue *Paris-Londres* in September 1939 coincided with the opening of World War II. In the late spring of 1940 she was recruited as a spy by Jacques Abtey. Her potential lay in the fact that she was a persona grata at the Italian Embassy because of the favorable remarks she had made about Mussolini during her appearances in Italy in 1935. When the German invasion of France came, she and Abtey joined the flight from Paris. They went first to Les Milandes, and then they made their way to Lisbon. They returned to Marseille in late 1940 and set up operations there. Barred from performing in

German-occupied France, Baker arranged a revival of *La Créole*. She cut short the run of the operetta to go to Casablanca in January 1940. As a performer she had freedom to travel from there to Portugal through Spain. During this period she continued to function as a spy; thus, she was a member of the French Resistance from the very beginning. Her conduct earned her the Medal of the Resistance with rosette at the end of the war, and later she was awarded the Legion of Honor.

In December 1941, Josephine Baker delivered a stillborn child in a Casablanca clinic—the father is unknown. There were complications, and to the doctor in charge an emergency hysterectomy seemed the only way to save her life. Until June 1942, Baker's life was in serious danger from the resulting complications; at one point United Press International carried the news that she had died. Even in the hospital, she continued to serve the Resistance, since visiting her offered a convenient pretext for Resistance workers to meet and exchange messages. When the American Army landed in Morocco on November 8, 1942, Baker had recovered. She spent the time after the landing entertaining the Allied troops in North Africa, striving in the face of the official segregation policy of the United States Army to see that black soldiers had a fair share in the seating.

Soon after the liberation of Paris on August 25, 1944, Josephine Baker returned to her beloved city. She was beginning to focus her energies on the development of her ideal community at Les Milandes. On June 23, 1947, she married Jo Bouillon, an orchestra leader. It was not a marriage for deep love on either side; she saw in him qualities she wanted in a father for the children she intended to adopt. Bouillon initially agreed to accept four. In 1948 he led the orchestra as Baker toured the United States. She persuaded her mother, Carrie, and her sister, Margaret, along with Margaret's husband, to come to France to live at Les Milandes; Carrie's husband refused to follow her. Four years later Baker's brother, Richard, followed the others. Carrie was isolated by her inability to speak French, but Margaret and Richard would be involved in quarrels and reconciliations with Baker as they either accepted her domination or tried to build lives for themselves. Bouillon, who gave up his music to manage Les Milandes, would be treated in the same way. Eventually, he moved out in 1957, though they never divorced. He later established himself as a restaurateur in Argentina. Carrie died in 1959.

Josephine Baker made a very successful return trip to the United States in 1951. She attracted wide attention with her statements against segregation and her refusal to perform at segregated venues. Baker was the first black American performer to appear before integrated audiences in a Miami Beach hotel and the first to house her entire troupe in a Las Vegas hotel; she canceled engagements in such places as Atlanta and Saint Louis when her conditions were not met. On May 29 Harlem turned out to honor her on Josephine Baker Day. The NAACP honored her as the Most Outstanding Woman of the Year. Concluding her tour in the fall, Baker began a well-received run of performances at the Roxy. On October 16 she was a guest at the Stork Club; the others at the table were served, but her order was "forgotten." Furious at this insult, she made her grievance known to the press. Unfortunately, the Stork Club was Walter Winchell's favorite nightclub. He wielded immense power through his newspaper column and radio broadcast. He counterattacked, labeling Baker a Communist, a Nazi sympathizer, and an anti-Semite. Baker had her defenders, but she had become "controversial," and in those days a "controversial" performer's career was blocked when people were afraid to employ such a person. In addition, on December 26, the *Chicago Daily News* gave space to black attorney Edith Sampson's attack on Baker for her pro-French remarks in light of French behavior in the colonies. Her difficulties in the United States were soon compounded when she briefly fell under the spell of Juan Peron during a stay in Argentina in 1952. Her remarks caused Adam Clayton Powell, Jr., to denounce her and the State Department to hint that her visa might be canceled.

Baker Adopts Rainbow Tribe

Josephine Baker continued working outside the United States and began to transform Les Milandes into a tourist center, the showpiece of the ideal community she wished to show the world. Between 1954 and 1965 she adopted twelve children of differing ethnic backgrounds and nationalities—ten boys and two girls, her Rainbow Tribe. After the success of the initial years, the efforts at Les Milandes began to unravel, due in large part to Baker's long absences performing and her management by caprice. Relations with the neighbors became very strained. By being unable to pay employees or by refusing to pay them, she made them feel entitled to steal what they could get their hands on. Lynn Taney states that between 1953 and 1963 Baker spent more than $1.5 million and was $400,000 in debt (280).

In August 1963 Josephine Baker returned to the United States to appear at the March on Washington. After a manager was found, she gave a benefit in New York on October 12 for the Student Nonviolent Coordinating Committee(SNCC), the Congress of Racial Equality (CORE), and the National Association for the Advancement of Colored People (NAACP). By this time it was not easy for her to find managers, since she had become notorious for refusing to pay them the money they had earned. Baker returned to Europe, where she had her first heart attack while performing in Denmark in 1964.

Her financial affairs were becoming increasingly disordered, and she no longer automatically commanded the highest fees. Finally in the spring of 1969 Les Milandes was seized. Baker had to be carried out bodily. For seven hours she sat barefoot, cap on head, crying on the back door steps until an ambulance removed her to a local clinic, where she was treated for exhaustion. The subsequent sale of the château and what remained of its furnishings brought in very little money.

Grace Kelly, now Princess Grace of Monaco, came to

Josephine Baker's rescue by providing the down payment on a villa at Roquebrune, near the principality. The four bedrooms provided scant room for twelve children. Baker worked when she could; when she could not, she would from time to time wander the streets begging for her children. Without her fine clothes, make-up, and wig, she now appeared to be an old woman, but she retained the ability to appear glamorous and beautiful the moment she stepped onto the stage, in a transformation that could surprise observers. Because of the use of lye over the years to straighten her hair, she was now practically bald. In the stress of her later years she joined the Catholic church in search of consolation. Despite her cares, she took under her wing another young man, whom she called her thirteenth son. He was a Belgian, Jean-Claude Baker, born Rouzard. By the time he became master of ceremonies on her 1973 tour of the United States and asked for a salary, the break became inevitable. He went on to become a successful producer for French television.

In the first part of 1973, Josephine Baker returned to the United States for a very successful appearance at Carnegie Hall. Encouraged by her reception, she planned a seventeen-city tour beginning in the fall. In July she had a second heart attack and a stroke that left her face partly paralyzed while performing in Denmark. In spite of her memory lapses, the United States tour went well until her Christmas season performances at the Palace flopped. Since she had dropped Jean-Claude by this point, in desperation she called in her nephew, Richard, from Saint Louis for support.

The Société des Bains de Mer, the company that runs the Monte Carlo casino, provided the last turn in Josephine Baker's career as a performer by sponsoring a show starring Baker and simply called *Joséphine* in August 1974. This revue was so successful that the company decided to take it to Paris. No large theater would entertain the idea because of the questions about Baker's health. A small music hall was located and rehearsals begun. In rehearsal, Baker was still able to summon up immense energy and pay close attention to detail. She was to be on stage almost continuously, sing many songs, and dance the Charleston. *Joséphine* officially opened on April 8, 1975, after several trial performances. Performances sold out many days in advance. That evening a gala was held at the Hotel Bristol to celebrate Baker's fifty years as a performer in Paris. Two nights later she was the last to leave a party, where she had tried in vain to persuade someone to take her to see a young black man who was doing impressions of her in a nightclub.

The following afternoon she did not wake up from her regular nap; she had suffered a massive cerebral hemorrhage and was in a coma. She died early in the morning of April 14, 1975. Her televised state funeral the following day at the Madeleine church drew twenty thousand people, and she is the only American woman to receive an official twenty-one gun salute from the French government. A quiet, private funeral service for her children was held in Monaco, and Josephine Baker of Saint Louis finally found a resting-place in the cemetery of Monaco.

References

Ehrlich, Karla (producer). *Chasing a Rainbow: The Life of Josephine Baker* (video). Csaky Production, 1986.

Haney, Lynn. *Naked at the Feast.* New York: Dodd, Mead, 1981.

Papich, Steven. *Remembering Josephine.* Indianapolis: Bobbs-Merrill, 1976.

Rose, Phyllis. *Jazz Cleopatra: Josephine Baker in Her Time.* New York: Doubleday, 1989.

Spradling, Mary Mace. *In Black and White.* 3rd ed. Vol. 1. Detroit: Gale Research, 1980. This work and the supplement provide extensive references to newspapers and magazines.

———. *In Black and White.* 3rd ed. Supplement. Detroit: Gale Research, 1985.

Robert L. Johns

Maria "Mollie" Louise Baldwin

(1856-1922)

Educator, community worker

For forty years Maria Louise Baldwin was principal of the Agassiz school in Cambridge, Massachusetts. Hers was one of the most distinguished positions in the teaching field in this country at the turn of the twentieth century, particularly since Agassiz's students represented the city's professional and well-established families. In time, black principals in Northern schools with predominantly white enrollments became more common, but Baldwin headed such a school when the practice was a rarity.

Baldwin was born September 13, 1856, in Cambridge, Massachusetts, the oldest of two daughters and a son of Peter L. and Mary E. Baldwin. An emigrant from Haiti, Baldwin's father was for many years a letter carrier in Boston, and her mother was from Baltimore. Baldwin received all of her education in Cambridge's schools. When she was five years old she entered the Sargent Primary School, later attended the Allston Grammar School, and in June 1874 graduated from the Cambridge High School. A year later she graduated from the Cambridge training school for teachers.

Baldwin's first teaching assignment was in Chestertown, Maryland, where she stayed for two years. In 1881 she was appointed as primary grade teacher in Agassiz Grammar

Maria "Mollie" Louise Baldwin

School, near Harvard University's campus. The school was named for the great scientist Louis Agassiz, who in public debate in 1863, said of her race: "I have no hesitation in saying that they should be equal . . . before the law" (*AME Church Review*, 217). In 1889, after teaching all grades from the first to the seventh, Baldwin became principal of the school. A modest person, she had misgivings about accepting the position and her ability to follow her predecessor effectively; however, once persuaded to do so, she and the Board of Education agreed that any dissatisfaction with her service on the part of either would cause her to return to her former position as teacher.

In April 1916 the school building was demolished and a new one, which Baldwin helped to plan, was erected. Since higher grades were added, the board decided that a master was needed rather than a principal. In her position as master, Baldwin supervised twelve teachers and five hundred students. She too remained a student, enrolling in courses at Harvard and other colleges. Baldwin was also an instructor in the summer normal courses for teachers at Hampton Institute in Virginia and at the Institute for Colored Youth in Cheyney, Pennsylvania. Aside from her professional activities, she was an intensive and extensive reader and developed a large private library.

Baldwin Empowered with Special Talents

Baldwin served the Agassiz school for forty years—from 1881 until 1922—and whether in the classroom or in her position as master, she gave herself fully to teaching the young. She was known for her great wisdom and gentleness in dealing with students; it was said she maintained order without discipline through the special love and respect that she had for them. Agassiz school reflected her personality and the extraordinary power that she had over students. And just as others were aware of her principles, "she was conscious of her ideals. She was conscious, too, of her powers and the difficulties that were around her and around the people of her own race. Yet it never led to any self-consciousness and bitterness. She would take no praise for herself, no recognition in this or in any community which could not be given to every one of her own race" (Brown, 185).

Baldwin was acquainted with and treasured her autographed letters from such notables as Elizabeth A. Agassiz, Alice Freeman Palmer, Thomas Wentworth Higginson, Alice M. Longfellow, Charles W. Eliot, Edward Everett Hale, and Julia Ward Howe. While she moved freely through Boston's society and "racial feelings were not overtly hostile," Baldwin was mindful of some Bostonians' attitudes toward race. For example, when the film *Birth of a Nation* was presented in Boston, she felt that it insulted her race. When asked to read from Paul Laurence Dunbar's poems during a session held after the film's showing, which was to be followed by the singing of "My country, 'tis of thee," Baldwin commented: "Please do not sing that then for it would break my heart when I know of the feeling of so many in Boston and throughout the country, who do not recognize truly the fact that this is our country. I might sing it another time, but not now" (Brown, 187).

A small group of prominent black Bostonians were also Baldwin's close friends. She came to know them through her work with the Women's Era Club, the Banneker Club, and the Omar Circle, of which William Monroe Trotter was a member. Baldwin was active in many community organizations including the Twentieth Century Club, the Cantabrigia Club, the Boston Ethical Society, the League of Women for Community Service, and the Teachers' Association. A lover of books and reading, she held weekly reading classes in her home on Prospect Street for black students at Harvard.

Baldwin lectured extensively and spoke throughout the country on such luminaries as Paul Laurence Dunbar, George Washington, Abraham Lincoln, Thomas Jefferson, and James Madison and on such themes as woman's suffrage, poetry, and history. In 1897 she gave the Washington Birthday Memorial Address before the Brooklyn Institute of Arts and Sciences and selected as her subject "The Life and Services of the late Harriet Beecher Stowe." The first black woman invited to deliver the annual address, Baldwin was known for her pure English and was a respected elocutionist. Of medium height and somewhat keen features, Baldwin was dark complexioned and had a stocky build. "She possessed a voice of remarkable sweetness and compass" and had "an unusual charm and manner" ("Maria L. Baldwin," 107).

While she was addressing the council of the Robert Gould Shaw House Association at the Copley Plaza Hotel in Boston on January 9, 1922, Baldwin collapsed and died suddenly of heart disease, having lived her last years in declining health. She was mourned nationally, but especially in Boston, where her body lay in state for two days so that friends and students might honor her. Noted clergy from different denominations participated in the funeral services held in Boston's Arlington Street Church. Prominent men of Boston were pallbearers. Baldwin's ashes were buried in the local Forest Hill Cemetery.

Maria Baldwin's biography in the *AME Church Review,* written to celebrate her life, said that she was:

> above everything, harmonious in every detail of her personality and her work; in the frictionless running of her perfect school machine; in her relations with her teachers and pupils; in her charming manners and conversation; in her quiet dress and her extremely handsome presence, of which we were all so proudly conscious; in her melodious voice, the invariably courteous tones of which had unfailing power to smooth all roughness of manner, temper, voice and nerves in her fortunate hearers—hearers who were vaguely conscious, even at the time, that they were fortunate (219).

In addition to the numerous other tributes that were written by her colleagues, students, and friends, about a year after her death the Agassiz school unveiled a tablet to her memory—a gift from the class of 1922, the last class that she taught. Other memorials were given in the form of a scholarship established in Baldwin's honor, naming the Agassiz school auditorium Baldwin Hall, the dedication on December 24, 1923, of the Maria L. Baldwin Memorial Library at the League of Women for Community Service, and naming a women's dormitory at Howard University in Washington, D.C., Maria Baldwin Hall.

An article in the Cambridge *Chronicle* paid a tribute to Baldwin that helps to summarize her notable contribution:

> Children and adults have learned from contact with Miss Baldwin a new respect and appreciation for the Negro race, whose noble possibilities her whole life exemplified. She has left to all whose lives touched hers the memory of a rare and radiant nature, the keynote of whose character was service (*Southern Workman*, 108).

References

AME Church Review 38 (April 1922): 216-20.

Brawley, Benjamin G. *Negro Builders and Heroes*. Chapel Hill: University of North Carolina Press, 1937.

Brown, Hallie Q. "Maria Louise Baldwin." In *Homespun Heroines and Other Women of Distinction*. Xenia, Ohio: Aldine Publishing Co., 1926. Includes photograph.

"Maria L. Baldwin." *Southern Workman* 51 (March 1922): 107-108.

Lerner, Gerda, ed. *Black Women in White America*. New York: Pantheon Books, 1972.

Porter, Dorothy B. "Maria Louise Baldwin." *Dictionary of American Negro Biography*. Edited by Rayford W. Logan and Michael R. Winston. New York: Norton, 1982.

———. "Maria Louise Baldwin." *Notable American Women, 1607-1950*. Vol. I. Cambridge: Harvard University Press, 1971. Includes bibliography.

———. "Maria Louise Baldwin, 1856-1922." *Journal of Negro Education* 21 (Winter 1952): 94-96.

Helena Carney Lambeth

Carnella Barnes

(1911-)

Religious leader, community worker

Carnella Jamison Barnes devoted her life to developing community organizations and to the fights and concerns of senior citizens. Ordained a minister in 1939—a rare occurance at that time—she became president of the United Christian Missionary Society and was affiliated with the Los Angeles Department of Senior Citizens Affairs for fifteen years. Barnes was born on January 11, 1911, in Edwards, Mississippi, the youngest of eight children of Samuel and Anna (Harris) Jamison. The Jamisons provided a good and healthy environment for their family in spite of the poor living conditions for blacks in Mississippi. Though poorly educated, they were people ahead of their time. Independent landowners and cash-renters, the Jamisons were able to produce on their farm nearly everything that they ate.

After her mother's death, five-year-old Carnella was raised by her father, who later married Roberta Perry, also a homemaker. The entire family was active at Friendship Baptist Church—with Samuel even serving as a church officer—but Barnes later joined the Disciples of Christ, a denomination that took the name Christian Churches in 1957. "Early, I learned to read the Bible and to pray. My first very own library book was a Bible story book," Barnes says. (The Herstory Committee, 48).

Barnes was introduced to the world of work early in life. In fact, from the eighth grade through junior college, she financed her own education from her wages. At age fourteen, Barnes was accepted to Southern Christian Institute as a boarding student. Only one other sister had gone to boarding school; her other siblings attended day school. Because the family could afford to pay, the president refused to accept

Barnes as a work student. Her father insisted that she work, explaining, that she was the last of his children and that, as he grew older, he wanted her to be able to take care of herself. The president persisted in his refusal. When two girls unexpectedly canceled out, he went to the farm to see if Barnes could come that same afternoon. Because her father was not home at the time, she could not go that day. However, her stepmother washed her two dresses and prepared her other clothing, and the next day her father took her to school. There she studied part-time while working in the milk room, where she was responsible for making such products as cream and butter. The school raised much of the produce consumed by the students, and students worked in the various areas of production. After twelve months, Barnes was able to go to school full-time and worked part-time for the school.

One of Barnes's early involvements in the struggle for equality took place at this school. There were two dining areas, one for faculty and their families and one for students. The one black family was forced to eat in a corner of the student dining room. Upon the protest of the students, the black family was able to join the white families in the regular faculty dining room.

After completing the associate of arts degree in education at the Southern Christian Institute, Barnes taught in a community elementary school where she made twenty dollars a month—the salary of a cotton-field worker. Her second year of teaching she earned only $19.95 a month. After moving to another school system nearby, Barnes's monthly salary increased to thirty dollars. Feeling the need for further qualifications, Barnes became a scholarship student at Talladega College in Talladega, Alabama, where she received a bachelor of arts degree in elementary education. Her salary for the next two years of teaching in Tuscumbia, Alabama, was fifty and fifty-five dollars a month, respectively.

It was during these early teaching days that Barnes's noteworthy work in the church began. A particular point of distinction is that she became the president of the first national youth movement in the Disciples of Christ Church. That position brought more national recognition as Barnes moved to serve with the United Christian Missionary Society, located at the headquarters of the Disciples of Christ in Indianapolis, Indiana.

Barnes tells many vivid stories of her experiences while holding this national position in a predominantly white denomination. One story reflects the racism present both in society and within the church. Because she was a church executive, Barnes was able to send a worker to the train station to pick up a ticket for her trip from Indianapolis to Miami. Since the ticket seller assumed the executive to be white, Barnes was put in a "white" car on the train. At a certain point in the trip, within the South, the conductor told her to move to one of the cars reserved for "coloreds." Barnes refused. This scene was repeated several times, and though Barnes expected to be arrested upon her arrival for disobeying the conductor, she was not. She had learned this strategy of nonviolent direct action from the Fellowship of Reconciliation while in junior college.

Upon her return to Indianapolis, Barnes proceeded to protest the illtreatment, reasoning, "I have four nephews overseas fighting for democracy. The least I can do is speak up for it." Having typed Barnes's dictated letter of protest to the railroad company, the secretary, rather than return it to Barnes for signature, took it to the vice-president. The vice-president interrogated Barnes, asking, "Why did you write this?" She responded, "Am I going to have to fight this railroad alone, or will the missionary society stand behind me?" The vice-president then said, "Mail your letter" (Interview with Carnella Barnes, July 1990).

While working for the missionary society, Barnes began her path towards the ministry. In 1939, when it was still unusual for women, particularly black women, to pursue seminary education, Barnes obtained a master's degree in religious education from Chicago Theological Seminary. She was ordained in the Christian ministry in 1939.

Her quest for knowledge did not end with the completion of the master's degree. Later Barnes studied adult education at the University of California, in Los Angeles. Still perceiving a gap in her education, she pursued further courses in gerontology at the Ethel Percy Andrus Gerontology Center at the University of Southern California and later took courses in social work at that instituion's school of social work.

In Los Angeles, Barnes worked as the executive secretary of the Avolon Community Center from 1945 to 1958. This was the first black community center in the Los Angeles area. During this time she met and married Anderson B. Barnes. A set of triplets—two girls and one boy—resulted from this marriage.

In 1952 Barnes tried her hand at politics by running for citywide representative on the Los Angeles City Board of Education. Barnes's candidacy was met with the red-baiting often used to challenge any black activist fighting for the rights of black Americans and other minorities. In response, Barnes boldly claimed that her political, communal and religious interests were not attributable to communism, but "originated from a much higher source" (Interview with Carnella Barnes, July 1990.) The more than one hundred thousand votes she obtained represented a major milestone: for a black woman to have amassed that kind of political support in the 1950s was nothing short of phenomenal.

Needs of Senior Citizens Addressed

In 1962 Barnes joined the newly created Department of Senior Citizens Affairs in Los Angeles, where she worked as coordinator, supervising coordinator, assistant director, and deputy director. This was the beginning of Barnes's work with issues of aging and the aged. Upon her retirement in 1976, Barnes became a program consultant with the Los Angeles County Area Agency on Aging.

Many significant senior citizens' programs in the Los

Angeles area can be attributed directly to Barnes's work. She was one of the founders and organizers of Senior Adult Camp, Older American Recognition Day, Affiliated Committees on Aging, and the Southern California Interfaith Coalition on Aging. Barnes was responsible for the organization of the first chapter of the American Association of Retired Persons in Los Angeles County, and the South Central, Crenshaw, and South West Committees on Aging. She also initiated the first Senior Citizens Observation of Negro History Week and, in conjunction with the Los Angeles City Department of Recreation and Parks, coordinated observance of El Dia de Personas Mayores.

Barnes was adamant about providing quality care for senior citizens. This concern led her to staff and conduct the first county-wide staff and volunteer training seminar for improving and developing effective services to senior citizens. This involvement attests to Barnes's commitment to total care and welfare for the elderly. Not only was she aware of the health, recreational, political, and religious needs of the elderly, but she was concerned about the living conditions as reflected in her work in the Los Angeles County Model Neighborhood Program and the Willowbrook Senior Citizen Center. In addition, seeing the need for bringing meaning into the lives of older people while addressing the needs of the younger generations, Barnes was instrumental in the continued work of the Foster Grandparents Program.

One would have thought that Barnes's well-earned retirement in 1979 would have ushered in a life of rest and relaxation. However, nine years into her retirement, she accepted a position with the Watts Health Foundation of the United Senior Services Center as program director of Respite Care/Transportation for senior citizens.

Barnes served as the president of the Los Angeles unit of Church Women United. But her work extends much beyond California and the United States, for she also served as president of the International Christian Women's Fellowship of the Disciples of Christ church.

Barnes has been widely recognized for her accomplishments. Among her awards are the Los Angeles County Board of Supervisors' Humanitarian Award; the Doctor of Humane Letters from Jarvis Christian College in Hawkins, Texas; the Doctor of Letters from Chicago Theological Seminary; the Zeta Phi Beta Woman of the Year in Religion award; and the Disciple of the Year award from the Christian Churches, of the Disciples of Christ. Barnes claims as her most distinguished award the Rosa Parks Award from the Southern Christian Leadership Conference and the Martin Luther King Legacy Association, commemorating the first national observance of the birthday of Martin Luther King, Jr.

Barnes continues her involvement in the community through the church and organizational memberships. At United Christian Church, she is chair of the Division of Mission Strategy and Outreach, which, among other things, sponsors a supplemental feeding and clothing project for the homeless and hungry as well as a job referral program. Her memberships include Church Women United, Los Angeles Council of Churches, National Council of Negro Women, NAACP, Foster Grandparents, Zeta Phi Beta Sorority, and the Affiliated Agency on Aging.

Of her own life, Carnella Barnes says in a 1990 interview, "Service to and with others has been my way of life."

References

The Herstory Committee. *Christian Women Share Their Faith*. Indianapolis: Department of Church Women, Division of Homeland Ministries, Christian Church, Disciples of Christ, n.d.

Barnes, Carnella. Interview with Jacquelyn Grant, July 1990.

Jacquelyn Grant

Etta Moten Barnett

(1902-)

Singer, actress, lecturer, community worker, arts patron

Her long and successful career as a singer and actress

Etta Moten Barnett

assures Etta Moten Barnett's place in show business history and included special honors—a personal invitation to sing at the White House for Franklin and Eleanor Roosevelt, and a personal request from George Gershwin to play the part of Bess in *Porgy and Bess*. But Barnett also built a successful career as a lecturer, civic and community worker and organizer, arts patron, and African affairs specialist.

Etta Moten Barnett was born in Weimar, Texas, the only child of Ida (Norman) Moten and Freeman Moten. The Normans were ranchers in Glidden and Columbus, Texas, where Barnett's mother was born. Her father was born in Winchester, Texas, where the Moten family had a large farm.

In 1895, as a young minister just out of the theological school of Paul Quinn College, Freeman Moten went to Glidden, Texas, to pastor an African Methodist Episcopal (AME) church. There he met and married Ida Norman, who later became a schoolteacher. With Reverend Moten's transfers to other pastorates, Barnett attended elementary and junior high school in Texas and California, and senior high school in Kansas City, Kansas. Ministers in the AME church were usually transferred in the fall, every five years for established ministers, but often annually for young ministers. Realizing that this would constantly interfere with his daughter's education, Freeman Moten decided to send her to Paul Quinn College (actually a secondary school at the time) in Waco, Texas.

At the age of ten in the fourth grade, she received a scholarship—free schooling at Paul Quinn—because of the quality of her singing voice, and she became a member of the choral club. During summer vacations she was a Sunday school teacher in her father's church, though only ten and eleven years old. Childhood summers were spent at the Moten farm, where Etta Barnett learned about nature from her grandmother and her cousins. The family spent Christmas holidays with the Normans. Because of happy childhood memories, when she herself became a grandmother, she had a big house so that her grandchildren might visit.

Around 1914 her father was transferred to a church in Los Angeles. Barnett attended school there for two years. The family then moved to Kansas, and she went to high school at Western University (a high school and junior college combined) in Quindaro. Again she was a member of the choir.

Her first professional experience as a singer was with the Jackson Jubilee Singers, traveling to rural towns on the Chautauqua circuit. The group consisted of R. G. Jackson as pianist, four male singers, and two women: Mrs. Jackson as soprano and Etta Moten as alto. This was a summer activity that earned money for her to attend Western University, and later the University of Kansas.

At the age of seventeen, Etta Moten married Curtis Brooks, one of the teachers at Western University, and moved with him to Oklahoma. After six years of marriage and the birth of three daughters, they were divorced. With her children, Sue, Gladys, and Etta Vee, she went back home to her parents in Kansas City.

Mrs. R. G. Jackson was enrolled at the University of Kansas at Lawrence, about forty miles away, and encouraged Barnett to do the same. Her parents offered to look after the children so that she could attend school. She returned to school, going home on weekends to see her children and to conduct a church choir, earning a little money. Again summers were spent touring with the Jackson Jubilee Singers. With the money earned from these tours she was able to pay her way through the university. She majored in voice and speech, with a minor in public school music teaching. She had her own program on the university radio station, singing Negro spirituals and the popular songs of the day. She formed and taught a quartet similar to the Jackson Jubilee Singers, which also sang on the university station. After seeing her in a play at the university during her junior year, the dean of the School of Fine Arts advised her to combine singing and acting. Others also encouraged her to go to New York to work.

In 1931 she received the bachelor of fine arts degree from the University of Kansas, having given a senior concert recital that led to an invitation to join the world-renowned Eva Jessye Choir. She decided to accept and to go to New York City for the summer to try her luck. Being uncertain about the outcome, she first got a teaching contract at Lincoln University in Jefferson City, Missouri. With success in New York, she never did go into teaching.

Several people told her that some day she should meet Claude Barnett. A graduate of Tuskegee Institute, he headed the Associated Negro Press, which he had founded in 1919, based on the format of the Associated Press. He had correspondents throughout the country and in Africa who sent him news items that he compiled and syndicated. On the way to New York in 1931 Etta Brooks stopped in Chicago to visit a college classmate with the idea that she might also call Barnett. She met the classmate's father, who immediately introduced her by phone to Barnett, who arranged to interview her. Another person invited her to a dance and asked Barnett to pick her up. It seemed that they were destined to meet. When she left Chicago, he gave her letters to people who might be helpful in New York. She kept in touch with Barnett, writing him letters about her experiences, some of which he published through his news service.

Career in Acting and Singing Begins

Eva Jessye was often asked for an appraisal of vocal talent. It was with Eva Jessye's recommendation, after only two weeks in New York, that Etta Barnett was rehearsing for the Broadway show *Fast and Furious*. Many musicians and comedians who were stars of the black world were involved, but it was to be their first Broadway appearance. Zora Neale Hurston was one of the writers. The show closed after only two nights, but Barnett was invited to appear in another Broadway musical, *Zombie*. It played for about two months in New York, then toured to Chicago and California. In

Chicago she again saw Claude Barnett, and began to think about remarrying someday.

Zombie closed in California in 1932. Later Broadway shows included *Sugar Hill* and *Lysistrata*. She was expecting a role in a film, but they wanted only her voice for *Ladies of the Big House*. Her singing voice was used in several films, but finally, in *The Gold Diggers of 1933,* she actually was seen on the screen, singing "My Forgotten Man." A Chicago critic wrote that her voice "cut through like a trumpet" (*Black Women Oral History Project Interview,* 21). Reviews were syndicated through the Associated Negro Press, and blacks in the South and in the big northern cities crowded in to see the picture. In an interview for the *Chicago Tribune,* she said "When you stop to look for me, you have to look real fast, but it meant so much to the Negro people to break the stereotype of Blacks playing menial roles" *(Chicago Tribune* 7 February 1986). She received no screen credit; later the credit was added because so many people asked for it. Out of this film appearance came invitations for lecture concerts, and RKO wanted her to sing "Carioca" in the film *Flying Down to Rio,* which starred Ginger Rogers and Fred Astaire. The movie came out in 1934, and she received screen credit for the first time. In fact, often when the film was shown in a black neighborhood, she received top billing, and the name of the film and that of the two stars appeared in much smaller letters.

In 1934 she married Claude Barnett in Capahosic, Virginia, at the home of Robert Russa Moton, president of Tuskegee Institute. When her daughters were teenagers they went to Chicago to live with Etta and Claude Barnett. They all chose to change their surname and were adopted by Barnett.

The Barnetts had decided that after marriage, Etta would pretty much continue her work. She made personal appearances for *Flying Down to Rio* in 1935 and in 1936 went to Rio de Janeiro with the picture. *Gold Diggers* was still being shown around, and with *Flying Down to Rio* came additional invitations for lecturing at black colleges and universities. Also, Barnett's contacts through the Associated Negro Press and other organizations led to prominent black citizens sponsoring her concert tours and lectures. She said in her interview for the Black Women Oral History Project at Radcliffe College, "the Negro people made me their star" (26).

On one of the occasions that *Flying Down to Rio* was being shown in Washington, D.C., Etta Barnett attended a presidential birthday ball. There she met Lizzie McDuffie, who worked as a maid in the White House. McDuffie told her how much President Franklin Roosevelt enjoyed hearing her sing "My Forgotten Man," and invited her to the White House to meet him. The next day she received a hand-delivered note from Eleanor Roosevelt inviting her to come and meet the Roosevelts and their guests. Ordinarily all such invitations were handled through Steinway Hall in New York and took a long time to work out. But that evening she visited the White House and gave a short concert, including some Negro spirituals and "My Forgotten Man."

After *Flying Down to Rio,* Lou Brock, the producer of the picture, told her that if she had been white, RKO would have signed her up as one of their stars. Since he knew that they would not do so, he wanted to sign her to a contract and become her personal manager. She would be paid whether or not she worked—fifty dollars a week.

He first got her a radio job in San Francisco with her own program called "Etta Moten Sings." The National Broadcasting Company also signed her as a soloist on Meredith Wilson's radio show, "Carefree Karnival." She later was the mistress of ceremonies for the West Coast salute in 1932 to the newly opened Radio City Music Hall in New York City. With attention coming then from the East Coast, Lou Brock sent her to Robins and Shewing, an agency that booked her into theaters and women's clubs, especially in New England, and finally into the Palace Theater in New York, "which was the crowning thing for vaudeville in those days" (*Black Women Oral History Interview,* 30).

As she and Barnett had agreed that she would go on with her career, she made short three and four-week tours so as to have some time at home. She eventually drifted away from Lou Brock and the other agents, and Barnett began to do the booking. She continued the short tours until the early 1940s, with Barnett as her manager.

Although she was receiving praise all around, she decided to make a concert debut in Town Hall in order to get the comments of the New York critics. To prepare for this, she rented rehearsal space in Steinway Hall. Upstairs they were casting for *Carmen Jones,* a black version of Bizet's *Carmen.* After hearing her rehearsing arias from Carmen, someone arranged for her to audition for *Carmen Jones.* She sang before Arthur Judson, head of Columbia Concerts; Oscar Hammerstein, who had written *Carmen Jones;* Alexander Smallens, a conductor; and Herman Merkin, a concert producer. They wanted to book her for *Carmen Jones,* but Smallens said that he needed someone for the role of Bess in *Porgy and Bess.* Anne Brown, who had originated the role in 1935, was getting ready to leave the 1942 revival of the show. Etta Moten said, "Gershwin was very particular about this work and before it was produced on Broadway, he talked with me and said that I was the kind of Bess he had in mind" (*Chicago Defender,* 4 May 1977). He wanted her to take the role, but she said that the voice was not right for her. By 1942 she felt that her voice was more adequate for the role. Some of the songs had to be lowered for her, but she went into the show singing opposite Todd Duncan as Porgy. The show played for a year on Broadway, then toured throughout the country from 1942 to 1945. When it played the University of Kansas in 1943, her alma mater presented her with a citation of merit, which is bestowed in lieu of an honorary degree. Because of this significant change in her life, the recital in Town Hall never took place.

Before *Porgy and Bess* ended, she found that she was having trouble with hoarseness in her voice. As a mezzo-soprano singing a soprano role almost every day for three years, she had pushed her voice too much. In 1947 she had a cyst removed from her throat and was ordered to rest her voice. Claude Barnett was a trustee of the Phelps Stokes Fund. Since each trustee was given an opportunity to travel in Africa, they decided to go at this time, giving her further opportunity to rest her voice. They visited Liberia, Gambia, Sierra Leone, Gold Coast, Nigeria, Dahomey, Togoland, and other countries. Although Barnett had long been interested in Africa and already knew many African leaders, this was his first trip. They met President Tubman of Liberia; young about-to-be leaders, such as Nkrumah, Azikiwe, and Ojukwu, whom he had known as students in America; and Olympio, who later became president of Togo.

They traveled many times to Africa, often as official representatives of the United States government. In 1957 they were members of the United States delegation to the independence celebration in Ghana, and in 1960 for the inauguration of the first president. They also represented the United States at the independence ceremonies of Nigeria, Zambia, and Lusaka. In 1958 they were guests at the All African People's Conference, and in 1960 Etta Moten Barnett attended the All African Women's Conference. Because of their travels, the Associated Negro Press began to carry many more stories about African affairs. In 1964, with his health failing, Claude Barnett closed his news service. He died in 1967.

It was during these last years that Etta Moten Barnett's career as a singer tapered off, because she felt that she had to be close to home. She had sung with the Chicago Symphony at Ravenia Park summer concerts, performed in festivals in Grant Park in Chicago, hosted "Etta Moten—with Music and Conversation" on NBC's Chicago outlet, and had been community relations director for station WNUS in Chicago. From 1947 to 1952 she toured throughout the United States, and in Canada, Argentina, Brazil, England, and many African countries. With her husband's illness and death, she gave more time to civic affairs, such as the Chicago Lyric Opera, the DuSable Museum, the Field Museum, the South Side Community Arts Center, and the National Conference of Christians and Jews. She became active again in her sorority, Alpha Kappa Alpha, later being appointed to the board of directors.

Barnett Becomes Active in Women's Affairs

In 1970 the Links, a service organization for black women, made her an honorary member and, because of her knowledge of Africa, a consultant for international trends. They later invited her to become a full member, and appointed her head of the international program. In 1971 as part of this work, she presented the idea of becoming involved in the International Woman's Year. She herself headed the United States nongovernmental delegation to the International Women's Year Conference (The Tribune) in Mexico City in 1975. She continued her work for the Links on international affairs, keeping them informed in all areas of women's issues from economics to the arts, including what was happening at the United Nations and plans for the 1985 United Nations Decade for Women World Conference. In preparation for the 1985 meeting, Etta Moten Barnett and others, appointed by the president of the United States as members of the National Women's Conference Committee, met annually until 1984 to develop a plan of action. She attended The Forum (formerly The Tribune) at the mid-decade meeting in Copenhagen in 1980, and headed the Links delegation to the 1985 meeting in Nairobi.

Since 1960 she has been a member of the board of the African-American Institute, particularly involved in the women's department. In 1985 she represented the institute as part of the women's task force in Africa. The task force included many organizations such as the American Association of University Women, National Council of Negro Women, Alpha Kappa Alpha, the Girl Scouts, and Planned Parenthood. In 1988 she received a citation from the institute recognizing her many years of service to Africa.

Etta Moten Barnett has found time to take advanced graduate study in speech and psychology at Northwestern University (1949-1950). She has also been artist-in-residence at Florida Agricultural and Mechanical University and Dillard University. Other activities have included membership on the advisory committee of Delta International of the Diaspora, a Delta Sigma Theta program to study the lives of people of African descent throughout the world; the National Council for Community Service to International Visitors; the Women's Board of the University of Chicago; and the Women's Board of the Chicago Urban League. She is a life member of Alpha Kappa Alpha, the NAACP, and the National Council of Negro Women.

In addition to her citation of merit from the University of Kansas, awards have included a citation for service from the National Association of Business and Professional Women (1958); a citation in recognition of her contributions to Afro-American Music from the Africana Center at Atlanta University (1973); and from radio station WAIT, in recognition of her outstanding contributions to the city of Chicago (1974). In 1988 the Northshore Links established a scholarship in her name for young minority students at the Chicago Academy for the Performing Arts. She has received honorary degrees from Atlanta University (1976), Spelman College (1983), University of Illinois (1987), Lincoln University in Pennsylvania (1989), and North Carolina Central University (1989).

She continues to travel and to lecture for the Links, Alpha Kappa Alpha, the African American Institute, and many other organizations, going to Brazil in 1988 and to China in 1990. During her many years of lecturing, Etta Moten Barnett has spoken on heritage, including folklore and music; African history and politics, economics, and art; women of the Third World; and of her own life as a performer. She also has given poetry readings of Afro-American literature, and taught master classes for choral groups, for concert singers, and those interested in the stage.

Etta Moten Barnett summed up her philosophy of life in her interview for the Black Women Oral History Project. She said, "Be the very best person that you can, and be as happy a person as you possibly can, and create as much happiness in others as you possibly can, and make them glad to have known you" (*Black Women Oral History Project Interview*, 88).

References

Black Women Oral History Project Interview with Etta Moten Barnett. Cambridge: Schlesinger Library, Radcliffe College, 1988.

Chicago Defender (4 May 1977). 22.

Chicago Tribune (7 February 1986).

Evans, Linda J. "Claude Barnett and the Associated Negro Press." In *Chicago History* 12 (Spring 1983): 44-56.

Mimeographed information in files at Schlesinger Library, Radcliffe College.

Women of Courage. Based on the Black Women Oral History Project. Ed. Ruth Edmonds Hill. Cambridge: Schlesinger Library, Radcliffe College, 1984. 46-47. Photograph, 47.

Ruth Edmonds Hill

Marguerite Ross Barnett

(1942-)

Educator

When Marguerite Ross Barnett was appointed president of the University of Houston in 1990, she became the first black and the first woman chief administrator of the flagship of the four-campus Houston system. She had already made her mark at the University of Missouri, Saint Louis, where she was chancellor and tenured professor in political science. The distinguished political scientist has boosted the prestige of both institutions—at Saint Louis as one of its most successful fundraisers and at Houston a major player in the upcoming $350-million fundraising campaign.

Born May 22, 1942, in Charlottesville, Virginia, Barnett is the daughter of Dewey Ross and Mary (Douglass) Barnett. She completed elementary school and in 1959 graduated from Bennett High School, both in Buffalo, New York. In 1964 she graduated from Antioch College with an A.B. degree in political science. She continued her studies in political science at the University of Chicago, where in 1966 she received an M.A. degree and in 1972 a Ph.D. degree. As a child her plans were to become a scientist but while studying a course on Indian politics, she changed her career interests. As a part of her doctoral studies, she conducted research in south India for two years. For her subsequent book on ethnic and cultural pluralism, *The Politics of Cultural Nationalism in South India* (Princeton, N.J.: Princeton University Press, 1976), the American Political Science Association awarded her its top book prize in 1981.

Marguerite Ross Barnett's career as teacher of political science began with her appointment as lecturer at the University of Chicago, a position that she held from September 1969 to September 1970. She was then assistant professor of political science, 1970-1976, and James Madison Bicentennial Preceptor, 1974-1976, at Princeton University. She became professor of political science at Howard University in 1976, and she chaired the department of political science there from July 1977 to June 1980. In 1980, while still at Howard, Barnett was codirector of the Ethnic Heritage Project: Study of an Historic Black Community, Gum Springs, Virginia, funded by the Ethnic Heritage Program, United States Department of Education. Barnett moved to Columbia University and from August 1980 to August 1983 she was professor of politics and education, professor of political science, and director of the Institute for Urban and Minority Education. In 1982-83 she was co-principal investigator on the Constitution and American Culture and the Training Program for Special Project Directors, sponsored by the National Endowment for the Humanities. From February to August 1983, Barnett was also consultant for the Presbyterian Church of the United States of America. She was appointed professor of political science and vice-chancellor for academic affairs at the City University of New York, for the twenty-one college system which serves 180,000 students. She remained there from September 1983 to May 1986. She was then named chancellor and professor of political science, University of Missouri-Saint Louis. She held the post from June 1986 to September 1990. During the spring of 1990 she was appointed president of the University of Houston.

University of Houston Appoints Its First Woman President

While Barnett, the first black and the first woman to head the University of Houston, has been in her position only a brief time, having taken office in the fall of 1990, she continues to gain widespread press coverage. An article on her in the March 6, 1991, issue of the *Chronicle of Higher Education* again put her in the national spotlight as head of an institution that she says is "literally on the cusp of greatness" (Mangan, A-3). Barnett is one of three women to lead universities with more than thirty thousand students. The fact that she is the only black leading a major research institution is less significant to her than her agenda at the University of Houson and the role that public urban universities should play in addressing a wide range of issues, from homelessness to space exploration. The role of urban research universities into the twenty-first century is to help society "solve its key conundrums," she says, and they must do so "in the same way land-grant institutions helped solve the problems of the 19th century'' (Mangan, A-3).

Barnett has been described as ''an animated women'' who outpaces her highly energetic colleagues, an effective school booster, and a woman with strong views as well as a willingness to hear the views of others before making a decision (Mangan, A-3). Self-confident though not conceited, Barnett is as comfortable in the corporate boardroom as she is in her staff meetings and has been praised equally by business people and academics.

During her career Barnett has been involved with numerous community activities and has served on a number of boards. Currently her board memberships are with the Monsanto Company, the Educational Testing Services, the Student Loan Marketing Association (SALLIE MAE), the American Council on Education, and the Committee on Economic Development. Her cultural affiliations include member of the board of directors of the Houston Grand Opera and the board of advisors of the Houston Symphony. Her professional memberships are with associations in political science and South Asian studies. She is also a member of the Overseas Development Council, the Council on Foreign Relations, and the Cleveland Council.

The author of fifty articles, Barnett is also author or editor of five books. In addition to her award-winning book on South India she coedited *Public Policy for the Black Community: Strategies and Perspectives* (Los Angeles: Alfred Press, 1976); *Readings on Equal Education,* vol. 7 (New York: AMS Press, 1984); *Comparing Race, Sex, and National Origin Desegregation: Public Attitudes of Desegregation,* Readings on Equal Education, vol. 8 (AMS Press, 1985); and *Educational Policy in an Era of Conservative Reform,* Readings on Equal Education, Vol. 9 (AMS Press, 1986).

Her awards include Bethune-Tubman-Truth Women of the Year Award, 1983; Association of Black Women in Higher Education Award for Educational Excellence, 1986; American Political Science COBPS Award for Excellence in Scholarship and Service to the Profession, 1986; Golden GAZELLE Award from the Project on Equal Education of the NOW Legal Defense Fund (1987); and Award of Achievement, Jefferson City NAACP, 1988. Barnett was named Woman of the Year by the Saint Louis Variety Club in 1989. In 1990 the Women's International Leadership Forum presented her with the Woman Who Has Made a Difference Award. While at the University of Missouri-Saint Louis, she designed and implemented the Partnerships for Progress Program and in 1991 the American Council on Education recognized the program and awarded the program the Anderson Medal. She is developing a similar program at the University of Houston called the Texas Center for University-School Partnerships.

Marguerite Ross Barnett is the mother of one daughter, Amy (Douglass) Barnett, who was born on December 18, 1962, during a previous marriage to Stephen A. Barnett; she is now a senior at Brown University. On June 30, 1980, Barnett married Walter Eugene King, who is a former member of Parliament in Bermuda and a former professional golfer. He is currently in real estate.

References

Curriculum vitae, n.d.

Mangan, Katherine S. ''New President Sees U. of Houston on 'the Cusp of Greatness.''' *Chronicle of Higher Education* 37 (6 March 1991): A-3. Includes photograph.

''Marguerite Ross Barnett. Biographical Sketch.'' n.d.

Who's Who Among Black Americans, 1990/91. 6th ed. Detroit: Gale Research, 1990. 1100.

Who's Who in America. 46th ed. Wilmette, Ill.: Marquis, 1990. 177.

Who's Who of American Women. 16th ed. Wilmette, Ill.: Marquis, 1988.

Jessie Carney Smith

Janie Porter Barrett

(1865-1948)

Social welfare leader, rehabilitation reform activist, clubwoman

Distinguished social activist Janie Porter Barrett was born in Athens, Georgia on August 9, 1865. In an era when most Southern black families were characterized by extreme poverty, the Porters were considered as being well-off. Oddly enough, Porter's early years of comparative ease were to become the foundation for a life's work in social reform. She established and devoted twenty-five years of her life to the Virginia Industrial School for Colored Girls, one of the first rehabilitation centers for black female delinquents. Additionally, she helped found and presided over the Virginia State Federation of Colored Women's clubs.

Janie's mother, Julia, worked as a housekeeper and seamstress for a transplanted New Yorker who was married to a Georgia aristocrat and, as a live-in servant, she was able to raise her daughter in an environment which drastically contrasted with that of most Southern blacks. Janie not only played with the three Skinner children, she received the same education and enjoyed the same privileges. Being fair-skinned and with an abundance of glossy, curly hair, Janie was a beautiful young girl, and could have easily passed for white.

Life changed, however, when Julia married a relatively

Janie Porter Barrett

well-off railway worker. This necessitated her constant going back and forth between her new home and that of the Skinner's, for whom she still worked. The decision was made that Janie would continue to live in the "big house" with her "other" family. As she matured, though, it became apparent that this cozy arrangement could not last forever. Mrs. Skinner, who truly loved her young charge, and only desired the very best for her, thought that the best course of action would be to send Janie to a northern school where she could live as a white person. To solidify her position, Skinner decided that she should be appointed as Janie's legal guardian in order to be able to carry out her plan. But Julia eventually asserted herself as Janie's rightful and only mother. She decided that her daughter, as a young black woman, should live as a black person in a black environment and that Hampton Institute in Virginia would be that environment. Skinner suffered great remorse at this turn of events, for she believed that the refined and cultured life of southern gentility she had given Janie would ill suit her for the harsh demands of the Hampton life. Now, Janie was being forced to choose between her two mothers, but, blood being thicker than water, she followed Julia's demands.

Some biographical accounts portray Porter as being very noble about suddenly being cut off forever from her lifelong friends and home. In response to Skinner's concerns about her having to scrub floors, Porter said: "I don't believe you've ruined my life. I don't see why I can't do something for my people yet that will be worth all you've done for me—and worth the floor scrubbing, too" (Daniel, 55). Actually, Porter had never even lived among blacks, nor among unlettered, rural poor people of any race. Neither had had she been required to do any manual labor. She had to truly adjust to the Hampton philosophy of the late 1800s, one stressing "a respect for the dignity and necessity of labor."

Hampton offered prototypical vocational education, focusing on training that stressed morality and housekeeping as requirements for wives or domestics. Thus Porter faced a difficult adjustment as a young teenager of privilege suddenly uprooted from familiar and comfortable surroundings. One account characterized her as feeling alienated from her new schoolmates and somewhat estranged. Another quoted her as having "no special sympathy for the poor and ignorant of her race" (Ovington, 182).

Porter rose above her situation and overcame her homesickness, gradually adapting to the Hampton regimen. This adaptation was intensified after she read a novel in which the heroine, a cultured and refined girl whose circumstances closely paralleled her own, devoted her life to social service. During Porter's metamorphosis, she had once remarked how tired she was of hearing about duty to one's race. Neverdon-Morton wrote of her saying, upon awakening one Sunday: "Today I don't have to do a single thing for my race!" (Neverdon-Morton, 105).

Locust Street Settlement Center Instituted

Porter survived the Hampton experience and became one of its outstanding graduates. While still enrolled, she began community involvements that would thereafter characterize her life of service to others. Her first jobs after graduation were in Georgia, where she taught school in the town of Dawson and at Haines Normal and Industrial Institute in Augusta. In 1886 she returned to Hampton to teach night school classes and, three years later, married Harris Barrett, the Hampton Institute cashier and bookkeeper.

At this juncture of her life, the young matron seemed to come into her own. She could easily have lived a life of ease. Ovington referred to Barrett's home as the "Palace of Delight," but instead of hosting soirees and teas for her socialite peers, Barrett opened her home to neighborhood girls in need of a sewing class. This group expanded into a fully organized club whose membership included virtually all of the neighborhood constituents. Activities were an outgrowth of the club's objective to improve home and community life. The Barretts even diverted monies earmarked for house renovations and constructed a practice house on the lot for the girls' home-management activities.

Within three years, the club had outgrown the Barrett home and a new community center, the Locust Street Social Settlement, was instituted. This venture was really a testament to Barrett's organizational, leadership, and managerial skills and talents. An auxiliary committee was charged with overall support, and eventually it turned over all supervisory activities to the Hampton Institute Extension Work Committee. By 1909 there were clubs for girls, boys, women, and older citizens. A forerunner of the contemporary Mother's Day-Out was a feature in the form of mothers' outings on Chesapeake Bay; more than two thousand mothers participated in a 1915 outing. With settlement activities being wholly supervised by committees, Barrett began turning her energies to sponsorship of large-scale annual events, each geared to a specific age group. Hampton students also directed many of the childrens' clubs and activities; therefore, the populations being served were really quite diverse.

By 1908 Barrett's expertise in the field of community service was recognized throughout the state of Virginia. She helped organize the Virginia State Federation of Colored Women's Clubs, whose major objective was philanthropic endeavors, particularly social-service activities. Most state federations were affiliates of one of two national organizations, either the National Federation of Afro-American Women or the National League of Colored Women. These groups merged in 1896 to become the National Association of Colored Women's Clubs (NACW). The membership rolls read like a *Who's Who* of local, state, and national black female leaders. Many were the wives of prominent professionals or were, in their own right, churchwomen, educators, nursing professionals, or social workers. The impetus for the first national convention was to officially refute a widely-circulated letter that slandered the character and morals of black women. Known as the "Jacks Letter," it was written by a Missouri newsman and had been sent to the group by an Englishwoman who was an anti-lynching official.

The NACWC and its predecessors served as a training ground and important outlet for the talents and skills of black women who, in the nineteenth century, were primarily known through the accomplishments of their husbands. Unmarried black women did not even have that advantage. This, however, had little to do with race; it was the result of sexism. Virtually any black woman whose name became known through her social, civic, or political endeavors was a national member or member of an affiliate. Stellar examples of black leaders who worked in the NACWC were Ida Wells Barnett of Memphis and Chicago, Margaret Murray Washington of Tuskegee, Josephine St. Pierre Ruffin of Boston, Julia Hooks of Memphis, and, from the nation's capitol, Mary Church Terrell and Josephine Beall Bruce.

Rehabilitation Center Established Through Women's Club Movement

With Hampton Institute serving as the seed of social service, the NACWC was the professional training ground for the work to which Barrett would devote the remainder of her life. The Virginia State Federation focused its efforts on the plight of black female juvenile delinquents, some of whom were being committed to asylums and jails. Barrett provided the impetus for founding a rehabilitation center; the federation raised funds to open the Industrial Home for Wayward Colored Girls. This school was located in Hanover County, a rural area north of Richmond. The Virginia Assembly, recognizing the need for such a facility, appropriated the sum of three thousand dollars in 1915 and 1916 for maintenance and improvements. With the hiring of a matron to guide the fifteen girls and a farmer to oversee the property—reports as to the amount of acreage purchased range from 147 to 400 acres—Barrett became secretary of the board of trustees. The name was changed a number of times, from the Industrial Home School for Wayward Colored Girls to the Virginia Industrial School for Colored Girls.

During this period of intense activity, Barrett, now the mother of four children, became a widow, her husband having suffered many years as an invalid. She turned down an offer to become dean of women at Tuskegee Institute and moved to the training school to become the resident superintendent. With her move, Barrett hoped to offset the antagonism of area residents who disliked having such a facility in their midst. This was also affecting state funding, without which the school could not operate. Barrett was forced to draw upon her specialized skills and unique resources to keep the school functional but also to make it the prototype of progressive reform in institutional care.

All such successful institutions functioned under the guidance and supervision of a trustee board composed largely of white women with power derived from their social standing or their husbands' professional standing. They were comfortable with black women of culture because their values, moral beliefs, educational backgrounds, and societal goals were much alike. Of great importance was the fact that they all appreciated and had full natural command of the social graces. It definitely cannot be overlooked that Barrett was "comfortable" with white women and they with her. "She understands the differences within the white race. What she might have achieved as a white woman we can never know, but there is little likelihood that she would have been given the impulse to service that came from Hampton Institute. She has achieved much, and I love to think of her as she sits among her girls, never nervous or fidgeting, a serene, happy presence, filled with a beautiful and practical love of humanity" (Ovington, 193). This overly sentimental picture provides a key to Barrett's success in getting things done.

The board of the training school stood solidly behind Barrett's demands to future white employers of her paroled charges that these girls should be treated in a humane fashion, even in service positions. Barrett was also instrumental in getting local benefactors and northern philanthropists to donate funds to build residence cottages. It was no small feat to get regular state appropriations and this certainly involved close working relationships with white women who could influence state legislators. One major source of expertise and funding was the Russell Sage Foundation, a leading proponent of social welfare reform. Raised as an aristocrat, Barrett had no trouble in relating to the Southern upper middle class, but, as Ovington obliquely stated, she still knew her place.

Barrett handpicked Jeannette Layton Forrester of Nashville, Tennessee, a young Howard University English major, as her successor. Forrester remembers the special programs when the boys' band from the Virgina Manual Labor School for black male delinquents was invited to participate, and of honor students from both schools having dress-up affairs. Forrester, however, declined to follow in Barrett's footsteps after an unfortunate incident at the girls' training school.

During the summer of either her junior or senior year at Howard, Forrester was helping out, and it was one of the few times that girls escaped. Forrester was shaken by the resulting chaos and disorder. (Interview with Jeannette Layton Forrester, April 8, 1990).

Despite that incident, the school was highly regarded as one focusing on building character and fostering moral development. In the 1920s it was ranked as one of the five best such schools in the country. Barrett picked the minds of the leading experts in the slowly evolving field of progressive reform; therefore, the school was run on the honor system—with no corporal punishment allowed—and it functioned as a community of individuals living in homes. It was known as a place where school windows had no bars. Because Barrett was able to get the full support of the Virginia Legislature, the federation turned the property over to the state, which began to finance its operations totally. Not until the late 1920s did any other state institution attend to the needs of black female delinquents. Barrett's greatest happiness and satisfaction was derived from her charges' release, employment, marriages, and setting up of happy homes, for these actions were the sure indications of successful rehabilitation.

Barrett Recognized as Social Servant to the Underprivileged

Barrett was recognized as an authority in the area of social service to the underprivileged. In 1929 she was awarded the William E. Harmon Award for Distinguished Achievement among Negroes, and the next year was invited to be participant at the White House Conference on Child Health and Protection. Barrett served as president of the Virginia State Federation of Colored Women's Clubs for twenty-five years and as chair of the executive board of the National Association of Colored Women for four years. She also held membership in the Richmond Urban League and Southern Commission on Interracial Cooperation.

In 1940, Barrett retired, and Phyllis S. O'Kelly succeeded her as superintendent of the school. Barrett lived in Hampton until her death in 1948 from the effects of diabetes mellitus and arteriosclerosis. As a final tribute to one whose life had been devoted to the welfare and uplifting of others, the girls' training school was renamed the Janie Porter Barrett School for Girls in 1950. One last dream of Barrett's has been realized in that the school now houses 120 boys and it is racially integrated. In the 1920's, Barrett said, "You know, we cannot do the best social welfare work unless, as in this school, the two races undertake it together" (Ovington, 190).

The gift of privilege was bestowed upon Barrett as a child, stripped from her as an adolescent, and honed as an adult. An upbringing that could have transformed a beautiful girl with a sweet disposition into a selfish social butterfly was, instead, used to its full advantage. Just as Barrett was raised to be a success, so did she encourage those in her care to strive to be the best if they so desired. With both Julia Porter Jackson and Mrs. Skinner serving as mothers, each bestowed her special gift on the young, impressionable Barrett—that of true, unselfish love which seeks no reward for itself.

Reference

Daniel, Sadie. *Women Builders*. Washington, D.C.: Associated Publishers, 1931. Includes photographs.

Forrester, Jeannette Layton. Interview with Dolores Nicholson, 8 April 1990.

History of the Club Movement among the Colored Women of the United States of America as Contained in the Minutes of the Conventions, Held in Boston, July 29, 30, 31, 1895, and of the National Federation of Afro-American Women, Held in Washington, D.C., July 20, 21, 22, 1896. Washington, D.C.: National Association of Colored Women Clubs, Inc., 1902. Reprinted, 1978.

Ihle, Elizabeth L. *History of Black Women's Education in the South, 1895-Present*. Module II. Harrisonburg, Virginia: James Madison University, Women's Educational Equity Act Program, U. S. Department of Education, 1986.

Layton, William Wendell. Letter to Jeanette Layton Forrester, 6 April 1990.

McDowell, Deborah E. "The Neglected Dimension of Jessie Redmon Fauset." In *Conjuring: Black Women, Fiction, and Literary Tradition*. Edited by Marjorie Pryse and Hortense J. Spillers. Bloomington: Indiana University Press, 1985.

Neverton-Morton, Cynthia. *Afro-American Women of the South and the Advancement of the Race, 1895-1925*. Knoxville: University of Tennessee Press. 1989. Includes photographs.

Ovington, Mary White. *Portraits in Color*. New York: Viking Press, 1927.

The Negro in Virginia. Compiled by workers of the Writers' Program of the Work Projects Administration in the State of Virginia. Sponsored by the Hampton Institute. Roscoe Lewis, supervisor. New York: Hastings House, 1940.

St. Clair, Sadie Daniel. "Janie Porter Barrett." *Notable American Women 1607-1950: A Biographical Dictionary*. Vol. 1. Cambridge: Harvard University Press, 1971.

The Virginia State Federation of Colored Women's Clubs. Undated Fact Sheet.

The Virginia State Federation of Colored Women's Clubs. Fiftieth Anniversary Booklet: 1908-1958.

Dolores Nicholson

Willie B. Barrow "Little Warrior"

(1924-)

Religious leader, organization executive

"Humanity will be saved and served only when justice is done for all people." This quotation from the Operation PUSH platform could easily be considered the personal motto for the Reverend Willie B. Taplin Barrow, until recently the National Executive Director for Operation PUSH. When the Reverend Jesse Jackson founded PUSH in 1971, he described its intentions: "To push for a greater share of economic and political power for all poor people in America in the spirit of Dr. Martin Luther King, Jr." (Baskin and Runes, 348). While these ideals of community action and fighting for justice clearly occupy Barrow in her present position, they also defined her life's work long before PUSH was founded.

Born on December 7, 1924, in Burton, Texas, Willie B. Taplin Barrow was one of six children. She grew up on a farm in a rural community where her father, Nelson Taplin, was a pastor. This early religious influence led Willie B. Taplin herself to become active in the ministry by age seventeen.

After attending high school in Texas, Barrow went on to the Warner Pacific School of Theology in Portland, Oregon, where she was an active student, serving as president of the Student Council. While in Portland, she organized the first black Church of God, which went on to become a thriving congregation. Barrow continued her education in Chicago at the Moody Bible Institute, as well as briefly attending the Central Conservatory of Music. She completed her studies at the University of Monrovia in Monrovia, Liberia, where she received the doctorate of divinity.

As a devoted preacher, Willie B. Taplin Barrow has served in numerous offices in the Church of God, both on the local and international levels. She is currently the associate minister and a member of the Board of Trustees of Vernon Park Church of God in Chicago. But Barrow's dedication to the ministry is not limited to traditional church work. She explains her perspective:

> Some people think ministers are concerned only with the soul of man. Not so. For the soul must travel encased in a body . . . and the body is on earth. Here not only to survive, but to have justice. Ministers need to tend to that, too (Smith).

In another level of her preaching duties and in conjunction with her responsibilities at Operation PUSH, Barrow participated in Jesse Jackson's Saturday church services in Chicago. In the context of these weekly gatherings, Barbara A. Reynolds describes Jackson as "the Country Preacher," fellow pastor Henry Hardy as "the Dean of Alliteration," and Barrow as "the Princess of Protest" (Reynolds, 6). This appellation is clearly appropriate for Barrow, since she has tenaciously fought for equality while maintaining her refined, gentle composure. Over the years, Willie Barrow has organized many activist causes, such as boycotting the A&P grocery chain for not hiring enough blacks and the national Spring Offensive of April 4, 1973, a cooperative movement among more than seventy-five organizations to protest President Nixon's budget cuts.

Involved in Chicago social movements with Jesse Jackson as long ago as the late 1960s, Barrow has proven her loyalty to his cause by serving as national deputy campaign and road manager on his presidential campaigns in the 1980s. This Barrow-Jackson alliance began in 1969 when they worked together in the fight to prove that hunger was alive and making the poor unwell in Chicago. In this context, Barrow was described as one of Jackson's "lieutenants" who assisted him in his city-wide efforts to convince Mayor Richard Daley that this problem needed attention (Reynolds, 198). On behalf of this cause, Barrow served as state coordinator for the Illinois Coalition Against Hunger as well as leading a Special Hunger Task Force. Also an element in the fight against hunger was Barrow's stint as Special Projects Director for the Southern Christian Leadership Conference's (SCLC) Operation Breadbasket.

Barrow's career has run the gamut from preaching and social programs to politics. Most recently, she served as a member of the insiders' power base for Jesse Jackson's 1988 presidential campaign. In her book on the 1988 campaign, former Jackson press secretary Elizabeth O. Colton describes Barrow as a key member of Jackson's "core staff" (58). Barrow was a natural and loyal part of his "rainbow staff," having worked with him on behalf of civil rights in Chicago for years. But Barrow's primary profession and most of her contact with Jackson have resulted from her involvement with Operation PUSH.

Operation PUSH (originally People United to Save Humanity, and then revised to People United to Serve Humanity) was founded December 25, 1971, by Jesse Jackson to "unite people, provide action, urgency, and pushing" (Baskin and Runes, 348). PUSH is a nationally-renowned organization that promotes civil rights among blacks and all poor people. PUSH members like Barrow have worked for humane conditions in general, as well as specific economic equality. Since its inception, PUSH has negotiated with national businesses to encourage them to invest in the black community, both through jobs and through other methods, such as banking and advertising with black-owned businesses.

Leadership Position with Operation PUSH Held

Barrow's connection with Operation PUSH began when she became the first female national vice-president in the mid-1970s. Later, in order to run for the presidency, Jesse Jackson went on leave from heading Operation PUSH in 1984. Thereafter, the position was occupied by several people, including Barrow and others, such as the Reverend Hycel B. Taylor. In 1986, Barrow assumed the helm full-time. When she announced her retirement in 1989, *Jet* magazine said that Barrow, "better known as the 'Little Warrior' . . . won't be on the war path against discrimination like she used to be." At her retirement banquet, she said "I am not moving down, I am moving over" ("Director of Chicago's Operation PUSH to Retire," 24) Also affectionately known as "A Little Ball of Fire" and "The Little Lady with the Big Voice," she continues her work with Operation PUSH as vice-chairperson and chief consultant.

Willie Taplin Barrow is described in a piece in *Essence* magazine as charging American women "that the power and responsibility of the nation rest with them" (70). Willie Barrow herself meets this charge every day, constantly striving for personal excellence while helping her fellow citizens better themselves. By various accounts, Barrow is described as being energetic, talkative, humorous, tenacious, enthusiastic, charismatic, gentle, and loyal. Not only does this great lady do battle with the universal powers of discrimination, but she also pushes for uniquely individual improvement.

When she recognizes problems in her community, Barrow instantly seeks to rectify them: "My life's breath is dealing with problems before those problems become crises. America oftentimes reacts to crises before reacting to the problems which may have precipitated the crises. And then it's too late" (Quoted in Smith, 45). The majority of Barrow's energy is devoted to preventing these social problems. This dedication was recognized early in Barrow's career when she was named Chicago's "Woman of the Year" in 1969.

While maintaining numerous civic responsibilities in the arena of Chicago's civil rights and social programs, Barrow has still repeatedly been described as a loving mother and a devoted wife. She is married to Clyde Barrow, a native of Honduras and a former labor leader there. They had one son, Keith Errol Barrow, who was born in the mid-1950s, but he is now deceased. Keith Barrow earned his master's degree in psychology from New York University and had a successful career as a recording artist before his death. Clyde and Willie Barrow currently live in Chicago, where their concern for human dignity, equality, and justice continue on into the nineties.

References

Baskin, Wade, and Richard N. Runes. *Dictionary of Black Culture*. New York: Philosophical Library, 1973.

"Biographical Sketch." Special Collections, Fisk University Library.

Calloway, Earl. "Keith Barrow, Soul Stylist." *Pittsburgh Courier* (2 December 1978): 9.

Colton, Elizabeth O. *The Jackson Phenomenon: The Man, The Power, the Message*. New York: Doubleday, 1989.

"Director of Chicago's Operation PUSH to Retire." *Jet* 77 (4 December 1989): 24. Includes photograph.

Ginsburg, Jane. "Willie Barrow." *Ms*. 2 (January 1974): 75. Includes photograph.

House, Ernest R. *Jesse Jackson & the Politics of Charisma: The Rise and Fall of the PUSH/Excel Program*. Boulder, Colo.: Westview Press, 1988.

Ploski, Harry A., and James Williams, eds. *The Negro Almanac: A Reference Work of the African American*. 5th ed. Detroit: Gale Research, 1989.

Reynolds, Barbara A. *Jesse Jackson: America's David*. Washington, D.C.: JFJ Associates, 1985.

Smith, Fran. "The Little Warrior." Undated document. Special Collections, Fisk University Library. Includes photograph.

Who's Who Among Black Americans, 1990-1991. 6th ed. Detroit: Gale Research, 1990.

"Windy City Warmers." *Essence* 7 (October 1976): 70. Includes photograph.

Kristine Anne Yohe

Charlotta Spears Bass

(1880-1969)

Political theorist, activist, editor

Win or lose, we win by raising the issues.

Charlotta Spears Bass

Any serious study of the role of black women in the American political arena must include Charlotta Spears Bass. Her distinction as a pioneer newspaper editor and political activist lay in her ability to work tirelessly to combat inequality, racism, and sexism wherever it surfaced.

Bass, born in Sumter, South Carolina, in October of 1880, was the sixth of eleven children and the third of four daughters born to Hiram and Kate Spears. When she was twenty she moved to Providence, Rhode Island, to live with her oldest brother, Ellis, and to work for the *Providence*

Watchman, a local newspaper. After ten years at the paper, on the verge of exhaustion and following the advice of a physician, Bass moved to Los Angeles, California. Although the two-year period was intended to be for "health-recuperation in the sunshine" (*Memoirs*, 27), it became a prelude to the development of a political and social consciousness that spanned a lifetime.

After a few months, financial difficulties forced Bass to forego her physician's advice and earn a partial living collecting and soliciting subscriptions for the *Eagle*, the oldest black newspaper on the West Coast, then edited by John Neimore. Neimore's ill health and the poor management of the paper brought Bass more into contact with the day-to-day administration of the paper. In 1912 she took over the *Eagle*, thus making strides toward her goals of aiding black people and addressing the issues of the day. Once the paper was under her firm control, Bass renamed the publication the *California Eagle* and began a new thrust by discussing the sociopolitical issues of the day in an effort to attract the "patriotically inclined." Bass, as managing editor, could successfully effect meaningful change in the lives of her people.

In 1912 the fledgling managing editor also met her future husband, John Bass, the founder of the *Topeka Plaindealer* and the recently named editor of *California Eagle*. Their combined efforts and firm resolve to combat racial discrimination in all of its forms placed the Basses in the vanguard of the struggle for equality. They sought to bring forth a new nation conceived in the hearts of the people.

During World War I and the 1920s, the Basses escalated their fearless campaign against clusters of injustice around the country. For instance, the paper was opposed to D. W. Griffith's film *The Birth of a Nation*, a contrived tale of the antebellum and Civil War South. In the film the white-robed Ku Klux Klan emerged as glorified victors, heralding the restoration of peace and order in the South, while blacks are depicted as innately inferior. Griffith's stereotypical portrayal of southern blacks on the silver screen was detrimental to blacks around the world.

The Basses were equally concerned about social injustice in the military during the war years. A major example of the problem is an incident in Houston, Texas, in September of 1917, involving the men of the Twenty-Fourth Infantry. They had attempted unsuccessfully to board a street car reserved for whites. Faced with a white mob, these black soldiers had seized their arms in self-defense and in the confusion some whites were killed. A mere semblance of a trial—based largely on circumstantial evidence— resulted in a number of the soldiers being sentenced to hang for murder and mutiny. Some received life sentences, while others were only detained pending further investigation. The severity of punishments given to the men of the Twenty-Fourth Infantry, perhaps, did more to anger blacks—particularly the Basses—than any other event during the war, and caused many to question their faith in America.

Scottsboro Case Supported

After World War I, the Basses' fight for racial equality did not stop with criticism of the motion picture industry and the war department. Charlotta Bass attended the 1919 Pan-African Conference convened by W. E. B. Du Bois in Paris and later became the co-president of the Los Angeles branch of Marcus Garvey's United Negro Improvement Association of the 1920s. Additionally, she and Leon Washington of the *Los Angeles Sentinel* were joint promoters of the "Don't Buy Where You Can't Work" campaign of the mid-1930s. Meanwhile, the Basses defied the Ku Klux Klan once when some Klansmen invaded their newspaper office and verbally threatened them. Charlotta Bass drew a gun on the "hooded guests" and ordered them to clear the premises. After this incident was revealed, the Klan brought the *California Eagle* to court on libel charges. Fortunately, the paper won the case, and it did not deter the Basses from their path. With their resolve strengthened and a renewed sense of mission, the two forged ahead with the campaign for equality.

Over the ensuing years the Basses had a number of opportunities to work conscientiously on behalf of their people. In 1931, when nine black teenagers of Scottsboro, Alabama, were charged with the alleged rape of two white women aboard a freight train, they supported the "Scotsboro Boys" and were outraged by the speedy trial and the harsh sentencing of the youth—to the electric chair. At the beginning of World War II, the Basses joined A. Philip Randolph, president of the Brotherhood of Sleeping Car Porters, in his quest to secure an executive order from the Roosevelt administration, reaffirming the U.S. Government's policy of nondiscrimination in employment. With others in California, Charlotta Bass organized the Industrial Business Council to support black businessmen and to work for fair employment practices. She fought to eradicate restrictive covenants in housing so that blacks could live peacefully in all white neighborhoods, as proposed by the Home Protective Association. She waged successful campaigns to end job discrimination at the Los Angeles General Hospital, the Los Angeles Rapid Transit Company, the Southern California Telephone Company, and the Boulder Dam Project.

In 1934, following the death of her husband, Bass had to manage the *California Eagle* singlehandedly for the first time in twenty-two years. She remained undaunted in her quest to help black people, however, and became even more involved in civic and political affairs. Indeed, visibility in the community characterized nearly all of Bass's actions through the 1940s. As a longtime Republican, she was selected as the western regional director for the Wendell Wilkie Presidential Campaign. Later Bass became the first black grand jury member for the Los Angeles County Court. Within two years, she ran unsuccessfully as the people's candidate for the seventh district city council seat, opposing incumbent Carl Rassmussen. The people's candidate committee, composed of city representatives, chose Bass because of her many years of "unselfish service to the community, championing the rights of people of all races and support of labor" (*Memoirs*, 132).

The Bass platform was as follows: to fight for postwar job security; build homes for all who need them regardless of race, color, or creed; institute health and recreational facilities; support adequate wages and the right of labor to organize and bargain collectively; reduce water, power, and light rates to the consumer; clean the streets; and establish a rehabilitation program for veterans. Bass pledged to "work faithfully for the adoption of every plank" (Los Angeles *Sentinel*, 26 April 1945). Black representation on the City Council was a must, and every black organization in the seventh district worked hard for the Bass campaign. Some support came in the form of newspaper advertisements endorsing Bass. Of these, one of the most important was signed by Thomas Griffith, Jr., then president of the NAACP. He urged Bass to "work for the uplift of the people" (*California Eagle*, 1 May 1945). Although the primary election did not give the incumbent a clear majority, Bass lost in the general election. But her first venture into politics was a milestone not just for Los Angeles blacks but for all minorities in their quest for full equality.

The loss of the city council general election to Rassmussen did not discourage Bass from the political arena. It catapulted her, on the contrary, from the local to the congressional level. She made an unsuccessful bid for the fourteenth district congressional seat—this time running on the Progressive Party ticket. Bass defected to the Progressive party because the two traditional political parties had not developed strong civil rights legislation. In the *Black Dispatch* she stated her reasons for leaving the Republican Party:

> Thirty years of broken promises and vain hopes finally convinced me. . . that even though we celebrate 1776 as Independence year for the colonies of Great Britain, that independence has not yet come to fifteen million Black Americans, mostly of the Republican Party. And as these millions of Americans continue on the downward road to second class citizenship, other American minorities . . . are caught in the maelstrom with them (*Memoirs*, 174).

Bass saw the Progressive party as "the only party in which there is any hope for civil rights."

In 1952 the Progressive party chose the sixty-two-year-old Bass as its vice-presidential candidate. As the first black woman to run for the nation's second highest office, she was on the ticket with Vincent Hallinan, a white male of Irish decent and a California civil liberties lawyer. One analyst states that the two candidates were a deliberate choice by the party to attract ethnic and black Americans, civil libertarians, and women. The party hoped the unpopularity of the Korean conflict (1950), coupled with Democratic wrongdoing and economic woes, would capture the disenchanted voter's interest. Generally, the platform called for an immediate end to the Korean War, peaceful relations with the Soviet Union, recognition of the Peoples's Republic of China, and a neutral Germany. Also proposed was a stronger emphasis on civil rights, civil liberties, and women's rights. Unlike the two previous campaigns, Bass was more vocal and her criticisms were more terse and hard hitting, especially when it came to the junior senator from California, Richard M. Nixon, who was the Republican vice-presidential candidate. She saw him as the personification of all that was evil in the cold war struggle.

Although many Progressive supporters expected a large vote on November 4, the campaign was a dismal failure. Hallinan and Bass received 0.2 percent of the sixty-one million votes cast. This was Bass's third unsuccessful political campaign. However, it must be deemed successful because both candidates called the voters' attention to the issues, domestic, foreign, and racial. In addition, the campaign signalled to the two traditional parties that black people refused to be taken for granted any longer.

History will remember Bass as an outstanding black female who devoted forty years of her life to building a better world for all people of color. Her aggressive approach to the issue of race relations as early as World War I meant that she was out of step with many of her contemporaries, even some blacks, until the rise of the civil rights movement and Martin Luther King, Jr.

As a journalist, Bass used the *California Eagle* as a platform in several ways: to denounce society's ills, to fight injustice, and to promote civil rights. *Forty Years: Memoirs from the Pages of a Newspaper*, published in 1960 after she retired, is a combined autobiographical and historical work. Bass's narrative is inextricably bound up with the part blacks played in the development of Los Angeles. She helped develop a black presence in the field of journalism by encouraging, hiring, and training young blacks. Her memoirs' recurring themes of equality, peace, unity, and liberation provide substantive proof of her commitment to basic human rights. Bass's ability to write well and argue effectively equipped her with the necessary tools for the struggle. She became a political theorist as well as an activist who lived out her creed by running for three political offices. She died on April 29, 1969; that month Tom Bradley won the primary election in his quest to become the first black mayor of Los Angeles.

References

Abajain, James de T. *Blacks in Selected Newspapers, Censuses and Other Sources*. Boston: G. K. Hall, 1977.

Afro American Encyclopedia. Vol. 1. Edited by Rywell, Martin. North Miami: Educational Books, 1974.

Baskin, Wade, and Richard N. Runes. *Dictionary of Black Culture*. New York: Philosophical Library, 1973.

Bass, Charlotta A. *Forty Years: Memoirs from the Pages of a Newspaper*. Los Angeles: Charlotta A. Bass, 1960.

Beasley, Delilah L. *The Negro Trailblazers of California 1919*. Foreword by Charlotta A. Bass. New York: Negro Universities Press, 1969.

Buni, Anthony, and Carol Hurd Green. "Charlotta Spears Bass." *Notable American Women: The Modern Period*. Cambridge: Harvard University Press, 1980.

California Eagle, 1 May 1945.

Contributions of Black Women to America. Edited by Marianna W. Davis. Vol. 1. New York: Kenday Press, 1982.

Harley, Sharon, and Rosalyn Terborg-Penn, eds. *The Afro-American Women: Struggles and Images*. Port Washington: Kennikat Press, 1978.

"Leaders Pledge Support to Council Candidate at Meet." *California Eagle*, 1 March 1945.

Lerner, Gerda, ed. *Black Women in White America: A Documentary History*. New York: Pantheon Books, 1972.

Morris, Dan, and Inez Morris. *Who Was Who in American Politics*. New York: Hawthorn Books, 1974.

"Mrs. Bass Makes Final Appeal for Election." Los Angeles *Sentinel*, 26 April 1945.

"Mrs. Charlotta A. Bass Celebrates 40 Years as Local Newspaper Editor." *Herald-Dispatch*, 28 April 1960.

Ploski, Harry A., and James Williams. *The Negro Almanac: A Reference Work on the Afro American*. New York: John Wiley, 1983.

"Progressive Party's Candidate for Vice President Tells Why Her Ticket Should Win November 4." *The Black Dispatch*, 25 October 1952.

Sentinel (Los Angeles), 26 April 1945.

Who's Who in Colored America. Vol. 1. Brooklyn: Thomas Yenser, 1927.

Collections

Buni and Green's essay on Charlotte Spears Bass locates Bass's papers at the California Library for Social Studies in Los Angeles. Letters from her are in the Calvin Benham Baldwin Papers at the University of Iowa. The Schomburg Center for Research on Black Culture, New York City, and the Moorland-Spingarn Research Center, Howard University, have clipping files on Bass.

Sharynn Owens Etheridge

Daisy Bates

(1920-)

Journalist, civil rights activist

Daisy Lee Gatson Bates—one of the twentieth century's most prominent civil rights activists—was born in 1920 in Huttig, a small town in the lumbering region of southeast Arkansas. She was raised by adoptive parents, Orlee and Susie Smith, and she never knew her real parents. In the autobiographical sections of her 1962 work *The Long Shadow of Little Rock*, Bates remarked that the circumstances of her biological mother's death and her father's subsequent flight were surrounded in secrecy. When she was eight years old, some neighborhood children taunted her for being "so uppity. If you knew what happened to your mother, you wouldn't act so stuck up" (10). She inquired of a cousin what the children meant and was told that her mother was ravished and murdered, allegedly by three white men, and her body was found submerged in a local pond. Her father fled Huttig for fear of reprisals from whites should he attempt to prosecute the suspects.

The relationship with the Smiths was warm and close, and Bates was raised as a somewhat spoiled and willful only child. She was indulged by her loving mother and hardworking though extremely sensitive father. In her autobiography

Daisy Bates

Bates spent a great deal of time examining the nature of their father/daughter interactions and presented a revealing account of their final moments together. "You're filled with hatred. Hate can destroy you," he warned. Orlee Smith understood the hostile feelings Bates's mother's death had generated. He continued:

> Don't hate white people just because they're white. If you hate, make it count for something. Hate the humiliations we are living under in the south. Hate the discrimination that eats away at the soul of every black man and women. Hate the insults hurled at us by white scum—then try to do something about it, or your hate won't spell a thing (29).

Bates attended the segregated public schools in Huttig, where the students used "the worn-out textbooks handed down to us from the white school." The school's physical condition also left much to be desired, and Bates recalled that "with the first frosts the teacher wrestled with the potbellied stove" (15). When she was fifteen years old and still in school, Bates met Lucius Christopher Bates, an insurance agent and close friend of her father. L. C. Bates had been born in Mississippi, attended the segregated county public schools, went on to Wilberforce College, the African Methodist Episopal (AME) church-supported school in Ohio, and majored in journalism. Upon graduation, he worked on the *Kansas City Call* in Missouri but soon lost this position due to the hard times created by the Great Depression. Bates turned to selling insurance and was quite successful, but he wanted to return to journalism.

Shortly after the death of Orlee Smith, L. C. Bates proposed to Daisy, and she accepted. They were married in 1941 and finally settled in Little Rock. L. C. soon convinced his new wife to join him in a newspaper venture, and the Bateses used their savings to lease the *Arkansas State Press*. Initially, the paper was fairly successful, and within the first few months reached a circulation of ten thousand. Daisy enrolled in business administration and public relations courses at Shorter College, an AME school in Little Rock, and the paper was able to attract a large number of advertisers from the local business community.

With the outbreak of World War II, nearby Camp Robinson was reopened at the request of local businessmen and politicians, and soon large numbers of black soldiers filled the streets of Little Rock on weekends. Incidents of police brutality involving blacks were regularly reported in the *State Press*, but on March 2, 1942, a much more horrible incident occurred. According to eyewitness accounts, military police had taken Private Albert Glover into custody, and when Sargeant Thomas Foster inquired about the arrest, local policeman A. J. Hay intervened, struck Foster with his nightstick, threw him to the ground, and fired five shots into his prostrate form. Daisy was on the scene soon after and reported the details of the incident in the *State Press*. Subsequently, indignation meetings were held in the black community, and protests were filed with U.S. Army officials, but nothing was done to prosecute Hay, since this was the way that the local police traditionally handled blacks. The Bateses' coverage of the incident, however, enraged local white businessmen, who feared that this bad publicity could lead to the closing of Camp Robinson. The white businessmen withdrew all their advertisements from the *State Press*. This was a potentially crippling blow to the fledgling newspaper. "Let's face it," Daisy recalled telling L. C., "we can't operate without advertisers. Let's quit now while we still have train fare." L. C. was not ready to throw in the towel, however, and convinced Daisy that they could keep the venture going by "taking the paper to the people" (Bates, 37). The two doubled their efforts, working twelve to sixteen hours a day, and gradually circulation began to increase. Within a year the newspaper reached twenty thousand readers.

The *State Press* gained the reputation of an independent voice of the people and worked for the improvement of social and economic circumstances for blacks throughout the state. In Little Rock, the *State Press* continued to expose police brutality and eventually changes were made. Black policemen were hired to patrol the black neighborhoods, and the state of race relations improved noticeably. As Daisy noted, by the end of the war Little Rock had gained "a reputation as a liberal southern city"(Bates, 38).

When the U.S. Supreme Court declared segregation in public schools unconstitutional in May 1954, the Arkansas school officials felt obliged to respond publicly to the decision. Later in the month Little Rock school superintendent Virgil Blossom called several prominent blacks into his office to preview the school board's statement. L. C., as editor of the *State Press* and an outspoken supporter of the integration of Little Rock public schools, attended the meeting, but was generally disappointed that the board intended to pursue the integration of the public schools gradually. Daisy had been president of the state conference of NAACP branches since 1952; the expectation on the part of some NAACP officials in liberal Little Rock was that the city's public schools would be integrated by September 1954. The meeting with Blossom made it clear that any significant movement toward integration in local public schools would only come through activities launched by members of the black community.

Bates Involved in Little Rock Crisis

The Little Rock School Board was going to continue to act along the regular segregatory patterns established previously, "until the Supreme Court of the United States makes its decision on 12 May 1954 more specific." There were "questions of time and methods for the accomplishment of integration" still unanswered by the courts, and in the interim, the school board would draw up a plan for the gradual implementation of integration (Blossom, 11). Eventually, the state and local NAACP's decision to challenge the school board's policy of gradualism placed Daisy and a group of children at the center of national and international attention for several months.

The NAACP strategy that Bates as state conference president and J. C. Crenshaw as president of the Little Rock branch were to implement called for two things: the compilation of cases of denial of admission to a Little Rock public school solely on the basis of race, and litigation to speed up the plans for integrating the schools. Ultimately, it fell upon Daisy and her "children" to go to the white public school with photographers from the *State Press* and other newspapers present to record the event and attempt to enroll black children. The litigious approach was delivered an important setback on May 31, 1955, when the Supreme Court announced its opinion that the segregationist states must draw up plans in a move toward implementation of public school integration "with all deliberate speed." In June 1955 the NAACP national headquarters issued a statement to all its branches outlining the procedures for undertaking litigation at the local level to bring about the speedy desegregation of the local public educational system. In Little Rock this meant a continuation of the policy of sending Daisy Bates and her children into the white public schools and having them recorded and photographed being denied admission.

Throughout the 1955-56 and 1956-57 school years, the NAACP leadership kept the pressure on the Little Rock School Board to move on its announced integration program while countervailing pressures and influences were building among the more radical and extreme elements in the Little Rock white community. White supremacists took every opportunity to denounce the growing possibility of race mixing in the public schools. Outraged white citizens held meetings, conferences, and rallies where they issued manifestos, resolutions, petitions, and legislative initiatives in vain attempts to slow or halt the coming integration of the Little Rock public schools. Battle lines were drawn in Hoxie, Arkansas, in the summer of 1955, when black parents demanded enrollment of their children in the white schools, and the Hoxie School Board, without sufficient funds to finance the dual system, was forced to integrate its public schools. White racists mobilized a broad-based opposition, but the Hoxie School Board, citing the Supreme Court decision, held its ground. In many ways the confrontations in Hoxie set the tenor and tone for white opposition to public school integration in Little Rock.

The "Blossom Plan" called for integration to start in the highest grades at Central High School, rather than at the elementary level where black students were more numerous, beginning in September 1957. In February 1956, NAACP attorneys Wiley Branton and U. Simpson Tate filed suit in federal court to gain the admittance of several of Daisy's children to white public schools at mid-semester. Federal Judge John Miller decided to go along with the Little Rock School Board's timetable for integration, but it confirmed the federal court's interest in overseeing the scheduled launch date of September 4, 1957.

During the 1956-57 school year, black students were polled and it was estimated by school officials that "only about eighty out of several hundred eligible Negro children" applied for admission to Central High School. Public school officials then did some winnowing of their own, and when additional factors were taken into account, such as "necessary scholastic achievement and emotional stability," the number was reduced to seventeen (Blossom, 20). But at minimum, eighty black teenagers were willing to become one of Daisy's children, seventeen were chosen, and ultimately, nine entered the pages of twentieth-century black history under the protective custody of the courageous and capable Daisy Bates.

Little Rock Nine Begin School Integration Efforts

Threats of violence and economic retaliation during the last two weeks of August 1957 helped to reduce the list to nine. Bates opened her personal account of the Little Rock affair with the hurling of a rock through the front window of her home on August 22, 1957. "Instinctively I threw myself to the floor. I was covered with shattered glass. L. C. rushed into the room. He bent over me as I lay on the floor. 'Are you hurt? Are you hurt?' he cried. 'I don't think so'" (Bates, 4). The failure of angry white supremacist leaders in Arkansas to gain a "legal" halt in the plans to integrate Central High School encouraged the more radical elements to threaten and try to intimidate blacks pushing for first-class citizenship rights. The rock that came through the Bateses' front window had a note attached: "STONE THIS TIME. DYNAMITE NEXT." This was merely a harbinger of the frightening terrorist tactics to be used by the "good white citizens" of Little Rock (Bates, 4).

The nine teenage students who volunteered to attend Central High School and were finally approved by school officials were Carlotta Walls, Jefferson Thomas, Elizabeth Eckford, Thelma Mothershed, Melba Patillo, Ernest Green, Terrence Roberts, Gloria Ray, and Minnijean Brown. All of the children's parents, and some of the students themselves, had *some* misgivings about putting themselves or their children in such a potentially dangerous situation. But both the parents and the children had faith in Daisy, who agreed to take responsibility for the operation. Daisy had put herself on the line for this cause many times already—she had successfully challenged white school authorities, and she had the legal backing of the NAACP. The parents' faith in her would be sorely tested over the next few months.

Arkansas Governor Orval Faubus had not taken an official position on public school integration, noting only that this was something that should be settled by local school officials. But the first important indication of a more proactive stance on the part of the governor came in August 1957 when he testified for the plaintiffs in the Mother League of Central High School's attempt to get a temporary injunction from the Chancery Court to halt the integration on the grounds of "a rumor that the white and Negro youths were forming gangs and some of them were armed with guns and knives." Faubus testified that he had information that weapons were confiscated from Negro teenagers by police. On August 29 Judge Murray O. Reed issued an injunction halting the integration of Central High School. That evening in the streets of Little Rock exuberant white racists chanted: "Daisy, Daisy, Did you hear the news? The coons won't be going to Central'' (Bates, 57).

NAACP lawyers Branton and Thurgood Marshall immediately appealed the decision to federal courts and, four days later, newly appointed federal judge Ronald N. Davis overturned the ruling of the Chancery Court. The first day of school was set, but on September 2, 1957, Labor Day, Faubus sent units of the Arkansas National Guard to Central High School to prevent the possibility of ''disorder and violence.'' The Guard units were ''to maintain or restore the peace and good order of this community.'' Brigidier General Sherman T. Clinger's orders were, according to Little Rock school officials, ''No Negroes will be permitted to enter.'' The school board issued a statement asking the black students not to attempt to enroll at any white public schools. The next day Branton and Marshall went back to Davis, who took the governor at his word and ordered the school board to put its plan into action.

Blossom's insistence at a meeting with Daisy and the black students' parents that no parents or adults accompany the students to Central High School seemed more and more unreasonable as eyewitness reports came in describing mobs of whites forming around the high school and in other areas of the city. Bates decided to contact the members of the Interracial Ministerial Alliance and ask that a group of ministers accompany the students to the school. With the assistance of Reverend Dunbar Ogdon, Jr., she found some ministers willing to go, and they agreed to assemble at 8:30 a.m. at Twelfth Street and Park Avenue. Bates called the parents of all the children except Elizabeth Eckford to inform them of the change in plans. Too tired to drive to the Eckfords (who had no telephone), Bates went to bed. The next morning Eckford went alone to Central High School and was taunted and berated, jeered at and accosted by hundreds of white students and citizens in front of cameras, reporters, and photographers from around the world. The photographs of Eckford's grace under pressure captured her agony and youthful determination, and she became a symbol of the oppression of black children in the United States that included the Scottsboro Boys, Angelo Herndon, and Emmett Till. In the ensuing months and years there would be many other black teenagers and young adults who, when placed in similar circumstances, would demonstrate strength and commitment well beyond their years.

The attack on Eckford set off a round of mob violence in Little Rock that lasted for the next seventeen days. On September 22, 1957, following the issuance of a court injunction against the Arkansas National Guard's further interference with public school integration, Faubus went on television and asked that the black students make no attempt to enroll at Central High School. Chief of Police Marvin Potts was now in charge of the operation, and Daisy received his personal assurances that the police would protect the children. The next morning at 9:23 a.m., the children gathered at the Bateses' home and in two cars drove to a side entrance at Central High School while the white mob was attacking several black reporters. The nine students were quickly escorted into the building.

This touched off mob action in the downtown Central High School area and throughout Little Rock. Indiscriminate acts of violence were committed against northern reporters and photographers, television personnel, and any blacks the mob encountered. By two o'clock in the afternoon, Potts recognized that he could not guarantee the safety of the students inside the high school, and they were taken out secretly through a delivery entrance. Later that day, Potts declared that the city was experiencing a ''reign of terror.''

The students remained home the next day as crowds of whites surrounded the high school. Mayor Woodrow Wilson Mann and Potts requested help from the U.S. Department of Justice. Later that afternoon news filtered in that U.S. President Dwight D. Eisenhower had federalized all units of the Arkansas National Guard and ordered Secretary of Defense Charles Wilson to enforce the integration order issued by the U.S. District Court. Wilson ordered one thousand paratroopers from the 101st Airborne ''Screaming Eagle'' Division of the 327th Infantry Regiment to Little Rock. Later that evening Eisenhower went on national television and made it clear that the ''disorderly mobs have deliberately prevented the carrying out of proper orders from the federal court. . . I have today issued an executive order directing the use of troops under federal authority to aid in the execution of federal law in Little Rock'' (Record and Record, 65).

The next morning, September 25, 1957, the nine children met at the Bateses' home and under the protection of the soldiers were taken to Central High School, where they entered at 9:22 a.m. with hundreds of reporters, photographers, and news cameras present. Inside the school Major General Edwin A. Walker, commander of the federal troops, informed the white students that they had nothing to fear from the soldiers as they went about their regular school routine. More than eighty students decided to leave after the general's talk, but most remained. At the end of the day, the Little Rock Nine were escorted by paratroopers back to the Bateses' home.

The paratroopers remained at Central High School until September 30, when they were withdrawn to Camp Robinson, about twelve miles from Little Rock. The federalized Arkansas National Guard remained on patrol at the school as efforts were made by southern politicians to get Faubus to agree to protect the students in return for an end of federal occupation. Unfortunately, the governor had fallen under the spell of the state's staunch segregationists and would make no public concessions or guarantees of protection for the Little Rock Nine.

On October 31, 1957, the Little Rock City Council ordered the chief of police to arrest ''Daisy Bates, Reverend J. C. Crenshaw, and all other NAACP officials he could find'' (Bates, 107). The next day they surrendered themselves to the police along with Birdie Williams and W. A. Fair, officers for the North Little Rock NAACP branch. The charge was violation of a recently enacted statute requiring an organization to supply to the city clerk's office information regarding its membership, contributors, and expenditures. The arrest of Daisy and other NAACP officers was reported and generally denounced in editorials and statements from all over the country and abroad. At the trial before Judge Harry C. Robinson on December 3, 1957, charges were dropped against Crenshaw when it could not be demonstrated that he had received any previous notice of the ordinance. The NAACP lawyers also sought dismissal of the charges against Daisy, since she was not president of the Little Rock branch and had no records in her possession. "I am going to take judicial notice of the fact that she is not head of the NAACP," declared Judge Robinson, "but she heads some branch or something of the NAACP. I am going to hold that the ordinance is valid." He fined her one hundred dollars, plus court costs; the NAACP immediately moved for appeal to the circuit court. Although they again lost at the appeals level, the conviction was ultimately reversed by the U.S. Supreme Court.

Meanwhile, Daisy's nine children were on their own inside Central High School, but they were not alone in their struggle for acceptance and equal treatment. Some of the students remembered that positive overtures were made by some white students, but die-hard segregationists continually harassed them with name-calling, pushing, shoving, and overt threats of violence. Bates kept in close contact with them and their parents and always accompanied them to meetings with school officials when incidents occurred. Elizabeth Huckaby, vice-principal of Central High School, recalled that at one such meeting Bates complained about the lack of discipline and control by school officials and also about the black students being kicked and shoved with little being done to prevent it. "Mrs. Bates then further chided us for not doing anything to educate our pupils to accept integration." Although she attempted to defend herself and other Central High School officials, Huckaby concluded, "I can see why Mrs. Bates was successful as president of the state NAACP. She was a good infighter, persistent, intelligent, unintimidated—a woman who made a choice of this career fully aware of its dangers to her person and also its rewards in the prestige and service of her people" (Huckaby, 94).

Daisy's vigilance in the protection and support of her children earned for her the resentment and enmity of some white citizens in Little Rock and a secure place for herself in twentieth-century history. Throughout December 1957, newspaper headlines and petitions from outraged white parents claimed that Bates had been given "the right of cross-examination of our children at Central High School when fights or trouble break out between the white and Negro children." White children "have been told that anytime a child crosses one of Daisy Bates' children that the white child will have to give an account to Daisy Bates personally" (Blossom, 163-64). Although the facts were incorrect, the underlying reality was not. Despite the continual opposition of many elements within the white community, Daisy was there until all of her children received the training and education they sought.

In the early 1960s, Daisy traveled throughout the United States on behalf of the Democratic National Committee supporting the cause of voter education. Although the involvement of the Bateses in the Little Rock desegregation efforts kept them from finding meaningful employment in Arkansas, they became intimately involved in the voter registration campaigns throughout the state for the next two decades. One of the Daisy's more recent involvements has been with the Community Revitalization Profect in Mitchelville, Arkansas. There she has worked with federal, state, and local officials and volunteers to bring running water, sanitation, improved health care, and educational programs to the residents of this predominantly black town.

When their newspaper, the *Arkansas State Press*, was forced to close in 1959, the Bateses hoped that some day the paper would reemerge and carry on the activities begun in the 1940s. In 1985 the *Arkansas State Press* was reestablished and continues to serve the social, political, and economic interests of blacks throughout the state. Despite some recent illnesses, Daisy remains active on numerous boards in community organizations and is sought out by the press, politicians, and the people to address the pressing contemporary problems facing the black community.

The crisis at Little Rock's Central High School in 1957 demonstrated to the nation and the entire world the strength and commitment of black youth to the attainment of full citizenship rights in the land of their birth. Little Rock was merely the first round of an extended struggle to desegregate the public elementary, secondary, and higher educational institutions throughout the United States. Black parents and children knew that their cause was just, and they were encouraged by the strength and persistence of Daisy Lee Gatson Bates and the example set by her children.

References

Bates, Daisy. *The Long Shadow of Little Rock*. New York: McKay, 1962.

Blossom, Virgil T. *It Has Happened Here*. New York: Harper, 1959.

Freyer, Tony. *The Little Rock Crisis: A Constitutional Interpretation*. Westport, Conn.: Greenwood Press, 1984.

Huckaby, Elizabeth. *Crisis at Central High School: Little Rock, 1957-1958*. Baton Rouge: Louisiana State University Press, 1980.

Jacoway, Elizabeth. "Taken By Surprise: Little Rock Business Leaders and Desegregation." In *Southern Businessmen and Desegregation*. Edited by Elizabeth Jacoway and David Colburn. Baton Rouge: Louisiana State University Press, 1982.

New York Times, 23-30 September 1957.

Record, Wilson and Jane C. Record, eds. *Little Rock, U. S. A.: Material for Analysis*. San Francisco: Chandler Pub. Co., 1960.

Williams, C. Fred., et. al. *A Documentary History of Arkansas*. Fayetteville: University of Arkansas Press, 1984.

Williams, Juan. *Eyes on the Prize: America's Civil Rights Years, 1954-1965*. New York: Penguin Books, 1987.

Collections

The Daisy Bates Papers, which includes an interview with Mrs. Bates, are located at the State Historical Society of Wisconsin, Archives Division, Madison, Wisconsin.

V. P. Franklin

Flora Batson "Queen of Song"

(1864-1906)

Singer

Flora Batson, one of the three greatest black female concert singers of the nineteenth century, was known as the "Double-Voiced Queen of Song" because her voice ranged from baritone to high soprano. Like other female traveling singers of her time, Batson included in her repertory ballads and arias, mostly from operas by Bellini, Donizetti, and Rossini.

Batson was born on April 16, 1864, in Washington, D.C. Her father died from Civil War wounds when she was very small. After his death, the three-year-old went with her mother, Mary A. Batson, to Providence, Rhode Island, where she attended school and studied music until the age of thirteen. She began her career while still quite young by singing in local church choirs.

By the early 1880s, Batson was appearing in local concerts in Providence and Boston, where she became a favorite with audiences. She spent two years singing for Storer's College at Harper's Ferry, West Virginia, and two years with the People's Church of Boston. Also for two years, beginning in 1883, Batson performed temperance work under the management of Thomas Doutney. During one temperance revival in New York City, Batson sang "Six Feet of Earth Make Us All One Size" for ninety successive nights in the great hall of the city's Masonic Temple. Thousands were reportedly moved to tears by the pathos and sweetness of her voice. The manager of the Bergen Star Concert Company, James G. Bergen, heard her sing as well and later invited her to become a member of his company.

Within two years, by the end of 1887, Batson had achieved national fame and was a great boon to the Bergen Star Concert Company. Bergen made his reputation as a white promoter of black performers, and Batson was his greatest discovery. Shortly after joining the company, Batson made her first major appearance in Steinway Hall in New York City on December 8, 1885, singing with Adelaide Smith, Sam Lucas, and the Walker Male Quartet. She had another successful debut that same year in Philadelphia. Her lucky break came soon after that, when Nellie Brown Mitchell, the company's popular leading soprano, was unable to appear in Providence due to a tour in the South. Batson was called in as a last-minute replacement. Bergen was so impressed by Batson's performance that she quickly become the company's prima donna, and she soon rivaled Madame Marie Selika in her appeal to American and foreign audiences. Batson then toured widely in the United States and abroad, performing before large audiences and receiving rave reviews.

When Batson married Bergen in 1887, in New York on December 13, 1887, an article in the *New York World* sensationalized the union. Indeed, hundreds of newspapers in the United States and in Europe covered the marriage of this famous black concert singer to her successful white manager. Until his death, Bergen managed his wife's concert career and featured her as the star of his productions. Though one source reports that Batson severed their relationship in 1896, it is more likely that it ended with his death at about that same time. Their marriage was mutually beneficial, nonetheless. As Bergen promoted his wife, her success helped his career as a concert manager and allowed him to become less dependent on collaborations with black churches for financial support.

Batson Called "Queen of Song"

Just one week after her marriage, Batson was declared "Queen of Song" in Philadelphia and was presented with a crown of jewels to mark the occasion. In January 1888 an audience at New York City's Steinway Hall gave her a diamond crown and necklace. Similarly, audiences in Pittsburgh and Providence affectionately gave Batson jewels. A poster announcing a concert at Steinway Hall on April 5, 1888, bills Flora Batson as:

> "probably the greatest ballad singer in the world" and notes that "the gifts of three cities will be worn by the great songstress in the coming concert . . . the magnificent crown with which the citizens of Philadelphia crowned Miss Batson 'Queen of Song' in December last, the solid gold diamond cut bead necklace presented to her by the Committee at Steinway Hall in New York January 31st, and the superb diamond ear rings presented by the citizens of Providence [on]

February 22nd'' (Southern, *Black Prima Donnas*, 99).

Photographs and concert posters from the 1890s typically show Batson and other singers regally dressed and bejewelled. Yet Batson was, according to Scruggs, ''a lady of medium size, beautiful form, modest, [and] free from affectation'' (27). *The Californian* reported that she was ''unaffected, almost child-like in her bearing'' and that her pleasing presence ''combined with her wonderful singing, captivated the heart of the listener, regardless of the color line'' (Majors, 93). Scruggs claimed she cut, fit, and made all her magnificent costumes herself, not out of necessity but because she could do it so well.

Batson's voice was remarkable. Her astounding range, her ability to elicit the most enthusiastic responses from audiences, and the sweetness of her voice accounted for her great popularity with audiences and the press. ''Her voice showed a compass of three octaves,'' reported the Pittsburgh *Commercial Gazette*, ''from the purest, clear-cut soprano, sweet and full, to the rich, round notes of the baritone register'' (Scruggs, 29). Similarly, the Charleston *News and Courier* described her as a ''highly cultivated mezzo-soprano, of great sweetness, power and compass, and of dramatic quality'' (Scruggs, 28). Audiences most frequently requested Batson to sing ballads such as ''The Last Rose of Summer,'' ''The Cows Are in the Corn,'' and ''The Ship of Fire,'' and standing ovations and numerous encores were commonplace at her concerts.

Batson made several worldwide tours in her career and appeared before England's Queen Victoria, Pope Leo XIII, and royalty in New Zealand and Hawaii. While touring the British Isles, she received a vase from Queen Victoria in recognition of her great artistry. When in Honolulu on a second world tour, Batson sang for Queen Liliuokalani at the queen's private theater during an eleven-week engagement. She gave concerts in Fiji, India, China, and Japan. In 1899 Batson toured Africa and Australia with basso Gerard Millar, appearing in Australia with the South Before the War Company and the Orpheus McAdoo Minstrels and Vaudeville Company. Millar became Batson's manager and they eventually married. His biography of her was published after her death.

The public apparently tired of black prima donnas by the mid-1890s, and Batson's repertoire changed to meet the demand for popular rather than strictly classical entertainment. Concert singers like Batson and Sisserietta Jones (1869-1933) joined touring companies and sang in vaudeville. Company managers were likely to stage a large production number featuring a former prima donna singing arias from grand operas with the assistance of the company's other soloists and a chorus. In her later career, Batson preferred to do church concerts and performances for charities because of her intense religious feelings. Batson gave her last concert at Philadelphia's Bethel AME Church to a standing-room-only audience. She died suddenly in Philadelphia, on December 1, 1906.

References

Cuney Hare, Maud. *Negro Musicians and Their Music*. 1936. Reprinted. Washington, D.C.: Associated Publishers, 1974.

De Lerma, Dominique-René. ''Flora Batson.'' *New Grove Dictionary of American Music*. Vol. 1. Edited by H. Wiley Hitchcock and Stanley Sudie. New York: Macmillan, 1986.

Gray, John. ''Flora Batson.'' *Blacks in Classical Music: A Bibliographical Guide to Composers, Performers and Ensembles*. Westport, Conn.: Greenwood Press, 1988.

Indianapolis Freeman, 26 December 1896; 24 December 1898; 12 May 1900; 15 February 1901.

Majors, Monroe A. *Noted Negro Women*. Chicago: Donohue & Henneberry Printers, 1893.

McGinty, Doris. ''Flora Batson.'' *Dictionary of American Negro Biography*. Edited by Rayford W. Logan and Michael R. Winston. New York: Norton, 1982.

Millar, Gerard. *Life, Travels, and Works of Miss Flora Batson, Deceased Queen of Song*. T.M.R.M. Company, 190?. Held by the Library of Congress, the Music Collection of the Boston Public Library, and Brown University.

New York Age, 3 December 1887; 6 December 1906.

New York Freeman, 25 April 1885; 24 October 1885.

Scruggs, Lawson A. ''Madam Flora Batson.'' In *Women of Distinction*. Raleigh, N.C.: Privately printed 1893.

Southern, Eileen. *Biographical Dictionary of Afro-American and African Musicians*. Westport, Conn.: Greenwood Press, 1982.

———. *Music of Black Americans: A History*. 2nd ed. New York: Norton, 1983.

Southern, Eileen, ed. ''In Retrospect: Black Prima Donnas of the Nineteenth Century.'' *The Black Perspective in Music* 7 (Spring 1979): 95-106.

Susanna Bartmann Pathak

Bessye Bearden

(1888-1943)

Political and civic worker

Bessye Jeanne Banks Bearden was a prominent figure in

civic and political activities from the 1920s to the early 1940s. Although most of her accomplishments were centered in New York, she was known nationwide, particularly for her work with the Democratic party. The daughter of George T. Banks of Virginia and Clara (Carrie Ocott) Banks of North Carolina, Bessye Banks was born in Goldsboro, North Carolina, in October 1888. She was raised in Atlantic City, New Jersey, and is often fondly referred to as a native of that city. She attended Hartshorn Memorial College in Richmond, Virginia, and graduated from Virginia Normal Industrial Institute in Petersburg, Virginia. She pursued postgraduate work at the University of Western Pennsylvania in Pittsburgh, Pennsylvania, and at Columbia University in New York City, where she studied journalism.

Banks married Richard Howard Bearden of Charlotte, North Carolina. They lived for a while in New York City but moved to Charlotte, just before Bessye Bearden gave birth to their only son, Romare, on September 2, 1914. The Beardens soon returned to New York City, then lived in Canada for a brief period during World War I, and finally moved back to New York City.

After settling in Harlem, R. Howard Bearden found employment as an inspector for the Department of Health. Bessye Bearden was able to maintain steady employment in a variety of interesting positions. She worked as a cashier at the Lafayette Theater box office, where she met many performing artists as well as patrons of the arts. For a number of years she managed the New York office of the E. C. Brown Real Estate Company of Philadelphia. In 1922 she was appointed to the New York City Board of Education, and served as secretary of the fifteenth District. Later, when the district was changed from the fifteenth to the twelfth, she was elected chair, becoming the first black woman member of the board and the first to sign diplomas in the United States public school system. In 1927 she was offered the position of editor of the society column of the weekly African-American newspaper the *Chicago Defender*. In July 1935, she was named deputy collector in internal revenue for the Third New York Collection District—the first black person appointed to that position. She began her municipal government service in the processing tax division and later moved to the income tax division as an auditor.

Despite Bearden's wishes for her son Romare to become a doctor, he decided to pursue a career as an artist. He was influenced more by the many creative talents of the Harlem Renaissance and other socially prominent figures whom his mother knew and entertained in their home including, Arna Bontemps, Langston Hughes, Aaron Douglas, Countee Cullen, Paul Robeson, and Marcus Garvey. Romare became one of the most popular black artists of the twentieth century.

Democratic League for Black Women Founded

During the 1930s, when blacks were beginning to shift their political alliances from the Republican party to the Democratic party, Bessye Bearden became very active in Democratic party politics. She was the founder and first president of the Colored Women's Democratic League in New York. Other branches of the league were formed in Chicago, Saint Louis, Philadelphia, and New Jersey. In 1937 Bearden was elected delegate to the First Judicial District Convention from the Thirteenth Assembly District, of the county of New York. She was involved in congressional campaigns and addressed rallies around the nation during the campaign to reelect President Franklin Roosevelt. In a letter dated September 10, 1940, to the chair of the Speakers' Bureau of the Women's Division, Bearden wrote:

> Having been active in the Democratic Party since I first entered the political field in 1921, my name is now known in association with it throughout the country. This year, however, I am more than ever before anxious to voluntarily serve in whatever way I can to aid in the reelection of President Roosevelt, since he has not only already made a vital and noble contribution to our country, but also because I sincerely believe he is the only persons able to carry us safely through these dark days of world disorder and chaos (Bessye J. Bearden to Mrs. Charles Poletti, 10 September 1940, Bessye J. Bearden Papers).

The National Council of Negro Women was another organization with which Bearden was closely aligned. Mary McLeod Bethune, the national president, conferred with Bearden on many issues—social, economic, and political. Bearden served as national treasurer and vice-president of the New York Metropolitan Council, and in 1942 she was asked by Bethune to serve as deputy organizer for the New York area for the National Council. Later, probably after her death, the Bessye Bearden Achievement Club, affiliated with the metropolitan New York chapter of the National Council, was established.

In 1935 Bearden was appointed to the advisory committee to the special assistant on racial problems in the Emergency Relief Bureau. The committee was charged with the responsibility "to give advice and suggestions on questions pertaining to the Emergency Relief Bureau in its relations to Negroes" (Oswald W. Knauth to Precinct Administrators, 15 July 1935, Bessye J. Bearden Papers). Samuel A. Allen, representative on racial problems, wrote to Bearden, "You have done much to bring about a larger economic justice for the Negroes in New York City" (Samuel A. Allen to Bessye Bearden, 18 June 1935, Bessye J. Bearden Papers).

Untiring, Beardon also served as chair of the New York State Committee to Abolish the Poll Tax. She was elected to the executive board of the New York Urban League, served on the planning committee of the Negro March on Washington Committee, and was secretary of Lodge 657 of the American Federation of Government Employees.

Bearden's service to her community was immeasurable. She served on the executive boards of the Citizens Welfare Council, the Harlem Community Council—heading the

Widow Pension Bureau—and the Harlem Tuberculosis and Health Committee of the New York Tuberculosis and Health Association. In addition, she was a member of the NAACP, the Harlem Hospital Board, and the Utopia Neighborhood Club. She rendered service and spoke on several occasions to the members of the YWCA of the City of New York.

The Citizens' Welfare Council awarded Bearden a gold medal in 1929 for public service and leadership in civic movements and on May 16, 1939, she was awarded the prestigious American Citizenship Medal by the Gerrit Smith Miller Post of the Veterans of Foreign Wars, and was made an honorary life member of the post. She was also an honorary member of Phi Delta Kappa Sorority and Lambda Kappa Nu.

Bearden played a major role in the political, civic, and social activities both in her community and nationwide. She died on September 16, 1943, in Harlem Hospital after a long illness.

References

Campbell, Mary Schmidt. "Romare Bearden: A Creative Mythology." Ph.D. dissertation. Syracuse University, 1982.

Current Biography. New York: H. W. Wilson, *1943:* 33, *1972:* 28.

Fax, Elton C. *Seventeen Black Artists*. New York: Dodd, Mead, 1971.

Schomburg Center for Research in Black Culture, clipping file, 1925-1974. Alexandria, Va.: Chadwyck, 1985.

Schwartzmann, Myron. *Romare Bearden: His Life and Art*. New York: Abrams, 1990.

Who's Who in Colored America. New York: Who's Who in Colored America, 1929.

Collections

Papers of Bessye J. Bearden, including photographs, may be found in the Manuscript Division of the Schomburg Center for Research in Black Culture, New York City. Photos of her have been published in numerous sources including *Who's Who in Colored America*, 1929, and the *New York Amsterdam News*, 29 June, 1940. A portrait of Bearden, reproduced from an oil painting by Robert M. Jackson, was featured on the cover of *Opportunity: Journal of Negro Life*, Vol. 18, September 1940.

Sandra M. Lawson and Ibrahim Kargbo

Delilah Leontium Beasley

(1867-1934)

Historian, journalist

Delilah Leontium Beasley is significant as a pioneer historian of the black American presence in the history of California. She aimed to show the commingling of black history and white history; from the beginning of the exploration of the area that was to become the states, blacks were present and actively involved in all the major events. They were also a presence apt to be overlooked. Beasley aimed to fill the gaps and also build black pride founded on recognition of the accomplishments of black Americans. After the publication of her major work in 1919, she became a regular columnist for the *Oakland Tribune* and continued her efforts to destroy negative stereotypes of blacks and to support black achievements.

The current knowledge of Beasley's early years is not terribly complete; Lorraine J. Crouchett's book, *Delilah Leontium Beasley: Oakland's Crusading Journalist*, tells us what is known at present. Beasley appears to have been born in Cincinnati, Ohio, about 1867, the first of five children of Daniel Beasley, born in Ohio about 1823, and Margaret (Heines) Beasley, born in Tennessee about 1838. The father appears to be at least a semi-skilled worker and, to judge by the daughter's early writing skills, the family background was favorable to education. A piece of her writing apparently appeared in the *Cleveland Gazette* when she was twelve, and she was involved in a column called "Mosaics" appearing in the Sunday *Cincinnati Enquirer*. She also received an offer to learn newspaper work in the plant of the *Colored Catholic Tribune*. Misfortune intervened.

Sometime during her mid-teens, Beasley lost both of her parents within nine months. Forced to support herself, she took a job as a maid to the Hagen family and accompanied them to their summer home in Elmhurst, Illinois. Dissatisfied, she left the job and went to Chicago, where she earned a living by giving massages. Returning to Springfield, Ohio, she continued this line of work and took further courses. At some point she studied hydrotherapy and massage at a school established by graduates of the Battle Creek Sanitarium and then went to Buffalo Sanatorium in New York, where she studied diagnosis, Swedish movement, and medical gymnastics while specializing in massage during pregnancy. Beasley had a successful career as a masseuse and for a time ran a school of massage, scalp treatment, and manicuring for blacks. A former patient asked her to come to California and she accepted.

There is no clear explanation for what must have been a near obsession with writing the history of black Americans in California, but the seed probably germinated during this trip. Beasley's interest in black history existed before this time; while she was living in Springfield, Ohio, she had been given permission to pursue her interests in three private libraries. It was in that city that she began her reading on the history of blacks in California. Finally, she went to California in 1910 to devote the next eight years of her life to her history.

Beasley lived in both northern and southern California—Berkeley, Oakland, and Los Angeles. It is unclear how she supported herself while doing the immense volume of work. For example, she examined all of the California newspapers at the Bancroft Library at the University of California, Berkeley, from 1848 to the 1890s and all of the black ones from the first in 1855 to 1919, when her book came out. She sought the advice of authorities. She traveled through much of the state, inspecting records and collecting oral testimony. She collected the words of people like Annie Peters, then the oldest living black pioneer in California, who had arrived in 1851. Beasley did receive encouragement along the way, especially from the people whose memories she was striving to preserve. As the war in Europe came to an end, she delayed the publication of her book for a year so that she could compile an accurate record of the blacks who had served during the war. During this time she was gravely ill and supported by the monetary contributions of friends, whose generous aid she acknowledges in her preface.

The Negro Trail Blazers of California appeared in 1919. It is not the work of a professional historian, and professionals tended to receive it poorly. Crouchett quotes Carter G. Woodson's review in the 1920 volume of the *Journal of Negro History*: "It is much hodge podge that one is inclined to weep like the minister who felt that his congregation consisted of too many to be lost but not enough to be saved" (39-40). Nonetheless, it remains an invaluable source for information on the subject of the presence of black Americans in the history of California. Not only is it a work reminding us of the constant presence of blacks, it remains a precious repository of knowledge about individual lives. An excellent popular local history, it continues as a source of information to the present day: various essays in the present volume of biographies draw upon the work of Delilah Beasley.

Derogatory Terminology for Blacks Condemned

Beasley's connection with the *Oakland Tribune* can be traced as far back as 1915, when she became a news contributor. On September 12, 1923, she became a regular columnist for the newspaper; she would write "Activities Among Negroes" until her death in 1934. In addition to reporting on the activities of local blacks she also used her column to advocate reform. For example, she waged a vigorous and successful local campaign to abolish derogatory racial designations and to capitalize the word Negro. She extended her efforts nationwide as a result of the discriminatory treatment Hallie Q. Brown and black singers received at the Quinquennial Convention of the International Council of Women in Washington, D.C., in 1925, which she was covering for the *Oakland Tribune*. She protested the use of words like "darkie" and "nigger" in newspaper reports of the incident to a conference of the press representatives to the convention and followed up her campaign with personal visits to editors in California.

Beasley was involved in several organizations, such as the League of Nations Association of Northern California and the World Forum and later the League of Women Voters. She was continually active in organizing and supporting interracial activities wherever possible, always pushing for the inclusion of blacks. In 1925 she applauded the invitation of twenty black clubwomen to a luncheon with 250 white clubwomen at a fashionable restaurant. Beasley was an early and enthusiastic supporter of the NAACP. She claimed major credit for bringing the 1925 national convention of the National Association of Colored Women to Oakland. In 1929 she organized a display of books and portraits to celebrate Negro History Week, as it was known then, at the request of the Oakland Free Library; this exhibit inaugurated the yearly celebration of the week by the library. In 1931 she was a member of the standing committee that organized a fund drive for the Community Chest in the black community—this was an effort to increase black inclusion and influence in the affairs of the community. She worked with the NAACP to buy a picture from the traveling Harmon Foundation exhibition for the Oakland Museum of Art; Eugene Burk's *The Slave Mother* was presented to the museum in 1931.

Lorraine J. Crouchett's interviews with people who knew Beasley reveal a woman who was "short, well proportioned, and speaking quickly in a shrill, light voice. She wore long dresses and was viewed as eccentric and ahead of her time" (59).

This very active woman died of arteriosclerotic heart disease with hypertension at Fairmont Hospital in San Leandro, California, on August 18, 1934. Her residence was given as 705 Thirty-fourth Street in Oakland. Her funeral was held at Saint Francis de Sales Church, where "members of the Delilah Beasley Club served as ushers and placed in the hands of every person present a mimeographed card bearing the following words":

My Pledge
In Memoria
Miss Delilah L. Beasley

> Every life casts its shadow, my life plus others make a power to move the world. I, therefore, pledge my life to the living world of brotherhood and mutual understanding between the races (Crouchett, 54).

References

Beasley, Delilah L. *The Negro Trail Blazers of California.* Los Angeles: Privately printed, 1919. Photograph as frontispiece.

Crouchett, Lorraine J. *Delilah Leontium Beasley: Oakland's Crusading Journalist.* El Cerrito, Calif.: Downey Place Publishing House, 1990.

Dannett, Sylvia G. L. *Profiles of Negro Womanhood.* Vol. 1. Yonkers, N.Y.: Educational Heritage, 1964.

Dillon, Richard. "Delilah L. Beasley." *Humbugs and Heroes: A Gallery of California Pioneers.* Garden City, N.Y.: Doubleday, 1970.

Robert L. Johns

Phoebe Beasley

(1943-)

Radio station executive, artist

Through hard work and perseverance, Phoebe Arlene Audrey Beasley has established herself in two disparate careers. She is a senior media executive and a fine artist whose work has been exhibited at various galleries around the world.

Beasley was born on June 3, 1943, in Cleveland, Ohio. Her mother died when Beasley was seven years old and her father, George Beasley, remarried Mildred Gaines, an individual whom Beasley herself names as her role model and a major influence on her life. After receiving her B.F.A. at Ohio University in 1965, Beasley pursued graduate study at Kent State University. She then spent the next few years as an employee of the Cleveland Board of Education, working as an art teacher at Glenville High School. In 1969 she opted for a career change. Beasley moved to Los Angeles, California, and obtained a position as an advertising account executive for KFI/KOST Radio. Now, almost twenty years later, she is senior account executive at the station, deftly handling large volumes of business with important local and national enterprises. Her contributions to broadcasting have not gone unnoticed by her peers.

In 1977 Beasley became the first black woman to be appointed president of American Women in Radio and Television, the same organization that had presented her with a merit award just two years earlier. In 1974 she received an award from the National Association of Media Women. She is listed in the 1990-91 edition of *Who's Who among Black Americans*, which also makes mention of her achievement of holding the first one-woman art exhibition at the Polly Friedlander Gallery in 1976.

Beasley stated in the October 1989 edition of *Ebony* magazine, that she "can't remember a time when she didn't want to be an artist" (Nipson, 129). As for her life in the business world, she confessed to the Atlanta *Constitution*, "I could never operate in one world. I need people and conversation (1 November 1989).

It is apparent that for Beasley the rigors of maintaining a dual career have their advantages. Logging almost one hundred miles of driving time each day turns out not to be a bane, but a source of inspiration, since for Beasley everything is "fodder for art" (*Atlanta Constitution*, 1 November 1983). Also, as she explained in a story appearing in her hometown paper:

> [Painting is] such a solitary pursuit . . . I need both jobs: I like the interaction in business. I enjoy it and it's not just a job to pay for my painting (Cleveland *Plain Dealer*, 19 May 1985, F10).

These are the words of a woman who, in a relatively short period of time, has managed an almost endless list of impressive achievements.

Beasley studied art at the Art Center of Design at Los Angeles and later at Otis Art Institute, where she studied the art of lithography for some eight years. Beasley's list of solo exhibitions is extensive and includes shows at Flavia Gallery in Huntington Beach, California (1976); the Statsinger Gallery in Venice, California (1981); the Crystal Britton Gallery in Atlanta, Georgia (1983); the Karamu Gallery in Cleveland, Ohio (1985); the Isobel Neal Gallery in Chicago, Illinois (1988); and a show at the Alex Gallery in Washington, D.C. (1989). More recently her works appeared at Arizona State University, where she also delivered an informal lecture.

Beasley works not only in oils-on-canvas, but does prints and collage, a medium she discovered during her years as an art teacher. Her collages and lithographs are included in the corporate collections of the American National Can Company, Johnson Publishing Company, Hanes Hosiery, Atlanta Life Insurance Company, Savannah College of Arts & Design, Katersky Financial, and the Denver Broncos Football Team.

Beasley was commissioned by television and film personality Oprah Winfrey to do a series of paintings and lithographs based on Winfrey's award-winning mini-series "The Women of Brewster Place." In this collection Beasley depicts all of the major characters of the series in her unusual, inimitable style: brilliant in color, meticulous in composition, and often cubist in style.

Official Poster for Presidential Inauguration Designed

Beasley was asked to do the artwork and the official poster for the 1989 presidential inauguration. Of this work, which appeared at the Alex Gallery, a critic for the *Washington Times* commented: "This piece is one of the best in a show featuring collages dating back to the early 80's" (15 June 1989).

The beauty of Beasley's work, it seems, lies in its truth. Her paintings tell stories about the lives of real people: the frailty of old age, the plight of the underclass, moments of intimacy, love, humor. Her work has been described as "a visual facet of humanism" (*Chicago Defender*, 29 October 1988). "You have to subordinate emotion to good composition," Beasley described her approach. "You try to put history in it but you need the composition, too" (*Atlanta Constitution*, 1 November 1983).

Beasley's work is known worldwide and was showcased at the Holler Museum in Bonn, West Germany, in 1989. Her work also appeared at the Eva Dorong Gallery in West Hollywood, California (1983); the Phoenix Arts Gallery in Atlanta, Georgia (1983); Howard University (1984); Museum of African-American Art (1985); Artis Lane Gallery (1986); American Telephone and Telegraph Exhibit (1987); and the Gallery/Tanner (1987, 1988). In addition, she has an impressive list of private collectors, including Maya Angelou, Bill Russell, Winfrey, Ron and Charlayne (Hunter) Gault, Gordon Parks, and Marla Gibbs.

Judging from of her successes as an artist, one might assume that Beasley's vivid treatments of African-American culture have always been received in a spirit of open-minded objectivity. Unfortunately, this has not always been the case. While making the rounds at various galleries, she was surprised to find that so-called established galleries did not, as a rule, showcase what they categorize as "black art." Beasley speaks candidly about this in the *Ebony* article, stating that she was even more surprised at the comments of her contemporaries who asked "Why do you always paint Black subjects?" "It was strange," she confessed, "especially when they were painting nothing but White subjects."(Nipson, 132). Biased opinions aside, Beasley has managed to garner a loyal following and increased recognition and competitive prices for her work.

In addition to the sometimes all-consuming task of carving out a living, Beasley manages also to devote a portion of her efforts to those organizations whose main focus is not necessarily the bottom line. She has always been involved with the work of cultural, education, and non-profit organizations, including the design of the 1986-87 Sickle Cell Anemia National Campaign Poster and the Neighborhood of Watts Organization Twentieth Century Anniversary Poster. She has served as a grants panelist on the California Arts Council and as a member of the executive board of the state/local Arts Task Force.

Beasley's other achievements include being chosen as one of six artists honored by the Museum of African Art for her contributions to contemporary art; she was named official artist for the 1987 Los Angeles Marathon; she was selected to design the International Tennis Trophy and Medal for the 1984 Summer Olympics; and she won the Museum of Science and Industry's 1984 Black Creativity Juried Art Show for her work, "Waiting Room."

Juggling two careers seems to suit Beasley. In a very short time, she has managed the kind of achievements that many people never see in a lifetime.

References

Calloway, Earl. "Phoebe Beasley's Art Show is a Visual Facet of Humanism." *Chicago Defender*, 20 October 1988.

"Collages are Full of Life." Cleveland *Plain Dealer*, 15 May 1985.

Cullinan, Helen. "Beasley Brings 'Homeward Bound' to Karamu." Cleveland *Plain Dealer* 5 May 1985.

Fox, Catherine. "Beasley Goes to Art from Business." *Atlanta Constitution*, 1 November 1983.

Jet 66 (25 June 1984): 31.

Nipson, Herbert. "Newest 'In' Artist is Tops in Two Fields." *Ebony* 44 (October 1989): 128-32.

"People." *Essence* 19 (February 1989): 34.

"The Talented Twelve." *Chicago Defender*, 6 February 1984.

Thorson, Alice. "Arts & Entertainment: Galleries." *Washington Times*, 15 June 1989.

Who's Who Among Black Americans, 1990/91. 6th ed. Detroit: Gale Research, 1990.

Pamala S. Deane

Louise Beavers

(1902-1962)

Actress

One of the most popular character actresses in Hollywood during the 1930s and 1940s, Louise Beavers was born in Cincinnati, Ohio, on March 8, 1902, and moved to California with her parents when she was eleven years old. She graduated from Pasadena High School in June 1920, and according to a *Philadelphia Tribune* reporter, she was "discovered" when she and a group of sixteen young women, calling themselves "The Lady Minstrels," began presenting amateur plays and vaudeville acts at Lowes State Theatre. Beavers was spotted by an agent for Universal pictures and offered a part in the first movie version of *Uncle Tom's*

Cabin. Thus her film career began with this 1927 silent movie starring James B. Lowe.

Another version of how Beavers entered the world of Hollywood movies is given in an article written by Beavers for *Negro Digest*. In "My Biggest Break" she writes:

> It was back in 1927 and I was a concert singer then, believe it or not. I was looking for my first break in the music business. . . . walked past the Philharmonic Auditorium in Los Angeles, my home, and saw a small sign telling about an amateur contest. . . . Acting on impulse, I went to the box office and asked for an application. As I was filling it out, I stopped and laughed at myself. What was a concert singer doing in an amateur show? Shows like that are for comedians and singers and dancers—but not for concert people interested in classical music. But I had been getting nowhere, and in desperation, I finished the form and signed my name with a flourish, "Louise Beavers, concert singer."

She appeared on the show and sang "Pal of My Cradle Days." While she did not win the contest, she recalls that three days after appearing in the contest she was telephoned by Charles Butler, an agent from Central Casting in Hollywood and offered a part in Universal Studio's *Uncle Tom's Cabin*.

Beavers Plays Stereotypical Roles

During her thirty-year career in film, Beavers worked steadily, appearing in more than 125 films. She was forced to play stereotypical parts because of her race and gender, however, such as a maid or "Aunt Jemima" figure. In spite of the roles' limitations, Beavers brought a subtle finesse to her acting that revealed genuine talent.

Donald Bogle, describing Beavers as "big-boned, heavy-set, brown-skinned," called her the personification of "the ever-enduring, resourceful mammy goddess" (*Blacks in American Films and Television, 358*). Beavers often was used for comic relief; one blatant example is her role in a film ironically titled *What Price Hollywood*. In this 1932 motion picture directed by George Cukor, Beavers is dumped into a swimming pool.

The 1934 film *Imitation of Life* brought Beavers both praise and criticism. Finally she was given the opportunity to exhibit her talent and demonstrate her loving kindness in the role of a black mother. Bogle admits that the film was a breakthrough for Beavers, but he is critical her stereotypical portrayal in the "perfect Depression-era fantasy: the perpetually sturdy, all-nurturing, hard-working, God-fearing mammy, ready for self-sacrifice and self-denial" (359).

If the role remained stereotypical, the talent that Beavers brought to it did not go unnoticed. Jimmie Fidler, reviewing *Imitation of Life*, wrote:

> I also lament the fact that the motion picture industry has not set aside racial prejudice in naming actresses. I don't see how it is possible to overlook the magnificent portrayal of Negro actress Louise Beavers who played the mother in 'Imitation of Life.' If the industry chooses to ignore Miss Beavers' performance, please let this reporter . . . tender a special award of praise to Louise Beavers for the finest performance of 1935 (*Dictionary of American Negro Biography*, 35).

Ironically, *Imitation of Life* ultimately did little more than promote Beavers as the eternal "Aunt Jemima" figure posing with the pancakes and grinning from under the chef's hat. Only infrequently did Beavers have the opportunity to play parts that exhibited her talent and confirmed her humanity. *The Jackie Robinson Story* allowed her an escape from the usual role. She plays a loving and concerned mother in this story.

In the early 1950s, Beavers replaced Hattie McDaniel on the CBS radio and television series "Beulah". According to Bogle, "Beavers' Beulah is so jolly, wide-eyed and giggly girlish that at times you just want to tell her to quit the simp act. Yet what saves her is, as always, a fundamental sweetness of temper that, like it or not, is frequently endearing" (259).

Beavers and Mae West Share Friendship

Beavers was especially close friends with Mae West, since the first time they worked together in the early 1930s in the film *Bombshell*. In 1954 the two veteran actresses took Las Vegas by storm, where they earned loud applause and plenty of money at the Congo Room. Beavers, who was still playing the part of the maid, was very popular, and several reviewers thought her time on stage should be longer.

Beavers was married to LeRoy Moore. At the age of sixty, suffering from diabetes and the fatigue of the Las Vegas tour, she was hospitalized. On October 26, 1962, she died of a heart attack in Cedars of Lebanon Hospital in Los Angeles. She was survived by her husband.

Louise Beavers was a member of the board of the Screen Actors Guild. She frequently made appearances in the black community and gave talks in local high schools. On these occasions she was fond of telling young people the story of her discovery, and explained to others her life code: "Always do your best when you are performing because you never know who is watching you. You never know what will come out of what you do when it's your turn to do a job" (*Negro Digest*, 22).

Beavers Credited with Many Films

Louise Beavers's film credits are extensive, and include the following: 1927 *Uncle Tom's Cabin*; 1929 *Wall Street*, *Golddiggers of Broadway*, *Glad Rag Doll*, *Barnum Was Right*, *Coquette*, *Nix on Dames*; 1930 *Our Blushing Brides*, *Back Pay*, *She Couldn't Say No*, *Wide Open*, *Safety in*

Numbers, Up for Murder, Party Husband, Reckless Living, Sundown Trail, Annabelle's Affairs, Six-Cylinder Love, Good Sport, Girls about Town; 1932 *Freaks, Ladies of the Big House, Old Man Minick, Unashamed, It's Rough to Be Famous, Night World, What Price Hollywood?, Street of Women, We Humans, The Expert, Wild Girl, Jubilo, Young America, Divorce in the Family, Too Busy to Work*; 1933 *Girl Missing, What Price Innocence?, Her Bodyguard, Bombshell, Her Splendid Folly, Notorious but Nice, She Done Him Wrong, Pick Up, A Shriek in the Night, I'm No Angel*; 1934 *Imitation of Life, I've Got Your Number, Beside, The Merry Frinks, Cheaters, Glamour, I Believe in You, I Give My Love, Merry Wives of Reno, A Modern Hero, Registered Nurse, Hat, Coat and Glove, Dr. Monica, West of the Pecos*; 1935 *Annapolis Farewell*; 1936 *Bullets or Ballots, General Spanky, Wives Never Know, Rainbow on the River*; 1937 *The Last Gangster, Make Way for Tomorrow, Wings over Honolulu, Love in a Bungalow*; 1938 *Scandal Street, The Headleys at Home, Life Goes On, Brother Rad, Reckless Living*; 1939 *Peck's Bad Boy with the Circus, Made for Each Other, The Lady from Kentucky, Reform School*; 1940 *Parole Fixer, Women without Names, I Want a Divorce, No Time for Comedy*; 1941 *Virginia, Sign of the Wolf, Belle Starr, Shadow of the Thin Man*; 1942 *The Vanishing Virginian, Reap the Wild Wind, Holiday Inn, The Big Street, Seventeen Sweethearts, Tennessee Johnson*; 1943 *There's Something about a Soldier, Good Morning Judge, DuBary Was a Lady, All by Myself, Top Man*; 1944 *Jack London, Dixie Jamboree, South of Dixie, Follow the Boys, Barbary Coast Gents*; 1945 *Delightfully Dangerous*; 1946 *Young Widow*; 1947 *Banjo*; 1948 *Mr. Blandings Builds His Dream House, For the Love of Mary, Good Sam*; 1949 *Tell It to the Judge, My Blue Heaven*; 1950 *Girls School, The Jackie Robinson Story*; 1952 *Colorado Sundown, I Dream of Jeannie*; 1953 *Never Wave at a Wac*; 1956 *Goodbye My Lady, You Can't Run Away from It, Teenage Rebel*; 1957 *Tammy and the Bachelor*; 1958 *The Goddess*; 1960 *All the Fine Young Cannibals*; and 1961 *The Facts of Life*.

Beavers appeared in the following television shows: "Beulah" (series 1951-1953), "Cleopatra Collins" (1956), "The Hostess With the Mostest" (*Playhouse 90*) 1957, "The Swamp Fox" (*World of Disney*) 1959, Groucho Marx's "You Bet Your Life," 1959.

In 1957 Louise Beavers was inducted into the Black Filmmakers Hall of Fame.

References

Aylesworth, Thomas, and John Bowman, eds. *The World Almanac Who's Who of Film*. New York: Pharos Books, Scripps Howard, 1987.

Beavers, Louise. "My Biggest Break." *Negro Digest* (December 1949): 20-22.

Bogle, Donald. *Blacks in American Films and Television*. New York: Garland, 1988.

"Louise Beavers and Mae West: Las Vegas." *Ebony* (November 1954): 103-106.

Mapp, Edward. *Directory of Blacks in the Performing Arts*. Metuchen, N. J.: Scarecrow Press, 1978.

Steward, William, et. al. *International Film Necrology*. London: Garland, 1981.

Traylor, Eleanor. "Louise Beavers." *Dictionary of American Negro Biography*. Edited by Rayford W. Logan and Michael R. Winston. New York: Norton, 1982.

Variety Obituaries, 1957-1963. New York: Garland, 1988.

Collection

Photographs are available from the Schomburg Center for Research in Black Culture, New York City.

Nagueyalti Warren

Gwendolyn Bennett

(1902-1981)

Poet, author, graphic artist, educator, journalist, editor

Gwendolyn Bennett lived an exciting and full life as a poet, short fiction writer, graphic artist, art and English teacher, columnist for the National Urban League's *Opportunity* magazine, contributing editor of *Fire!!*—the avant-garde magazine produced by young writers of the Harlem Renaissance— and head of the Harlem Community Arts Center. For more than twenty years she was actively involved in black culture and the New York arts community.

Although Bennett knew she was born on July 8, 1902, in Giddings, Texas, no record of her birth exists because the state of Texas did not issue birth certificates to blacks at that time. She was the only child of Joshua Robin Bennett, the youngest son of R.B. Bennett, a prosperous barber in Giddings, and Mayme F. (Abernathy) Bennett of San Antonio, Texas. Both parents came from middle-class backgrounds, were well-educated, and had been teachers. In a 1979 interview, Bennett said that some of her earliest childhood memories were recollections of being taken as a toddler to attend meetings on the Indian reservation where her parents taught (Interview with Gwendolyn Bennett, 23 March 1979).

In the early 1900s, when Bennett was four or five, her family moved to Washington, D.C., where her father began to study law and her mother worked as a manicurist and

Gwendolyn Bennett

hairdresser at a fashionable girl's school. Shortly after their move, the Bennetts began to experience marital problems and separated. During subsequent divorce proceedings, Mayme Bennett was awarded custody of her daughter. This verdict, however, did not please Bennett's father, who kidnapped her when she was nearly eight years old, on the pretext of taking her to see the Mt. Vernon home of George Washington. Bennett recalled spending the next several years living with him in hiding, traveling up and down the eastern seaboard states and living in several small Pennsylvania towns before her father finally settled in Brooklyn, New York. Bennett neither saw nor heard from her biological mother again until 1924, when she completed her studies in art at Pratt Institute and accepted a faculty position teaching design, watercolor, and crafts in the newly established fine arts department at Howard University.

The vagabond life the Bennetts led before settling in Brooklyn gave young Gwen a varied education. At Central High in Harrisburg, Pennsylvania, Bennett had performed well, making the honor roll her freshman and sophomore years. When she transferred to Brooklyn's Girls High, she struggled at first to maintain her grades, the move to the new school being a traumatic experience for her. Eventually, however, she adjusted and became very active in the school's literary and drama societies. She was, in fact, the first black student ever elected to either club. A clipping Bennett saved from the school newspaper acknowledges her achievements:

> Miss Gwendolyn B. Bennett was unanimously elected a member of the Dramatic Society of the Girls School on Monday, September 29. On Monday, October 6, she was duly initiated into the society and is now a full fledged member. Miss Bennett is the first and only colored member of this society. Membership to this society is gained only through one's dramatic ability.

In addition to these activities, Bennett wrote poetry, the lyrics to her class graduation song, and the class graduation speech and actively participated in art projects; in fact, one of her poster designs won first prize in the school art contest. Though Bennett had "always wanted to be a writer but nobody knew," she was, at the same time, "doing a little art work, too." Both talents were cultivated while she was still in high school, with her third-year English teacher, Cordelia Went, having a great influence. Bennett's classmates even constructed a yearbook rhyme about the unusually close student-teacher relationship between the white teacher and her "colored" charge: "And Gwennie followed where Cordelia Went." Her art teacher, whom Bennett also respected, never made the same impression. "Although I loved [her] very much—a very fascinating-looking woman—I never loved her in the same way I loved Miss Went. And she didn't have that kind of influence on me."

In 1921, following her graduation from Girls High, Bennett did not retreat into the comfortable shelter of her parents' home—Joshua Bennett had remarried in 1914—nor did she study law or go immediately into education, the two professions her parents deemed safe for a young Negro woman. Instead, she chose to live out some of the lyrics to the class song she had written earlier, and "dauntless, strong and unfraid," she took the highly unusual step of enrolling for classes in the fine arts department of Columbia University, and later, at Pratt Institute. Although the risks facing a black woman at this time were great and the support minimal, Bennett had chosen to become a graphic or visual artist and a writer, in an era when the New Negro movement was just beginning. The early 1920s saw her develop in both of these fields. She began submitting the poetry she had written in private to major journals open to black artists. In 1923, *Opportunity* published her poem "Heritage" and the NAACP's *Crisis* carried a cover that she illustrated.

Bennett Joins the Harlem Renaissance Movement

The five years from 1923 to 1928 were very significant for Bennett. Older and more established writers, like the NAACP's W. E. B. Du Bois and Charles S. Johnson of the Urban League, encouraged the growing cadre of younger writers and artists that Bennett moved among. This group, as Bennett recalled, was "in and out of the *Crisis* office just like it belonged to us. We also were in and out of the Urban League office because that's where Charles S. Johnson was." Members of the group comprised the informal but apparently close-knit Harlem Writers Guild. In addition to Bennett, guild members or associates were Langston Hughes, Countee Cullen, Eric Walrond, Helene Johnson, Wallace Thurman, Bruce Nugent, and Aaron and Alta Douglass. Bennett enjoyed this era, when, as Hughes wrote in his autobiography, "the Negro was in vogue," more than any other period in her life. "It was fun to be alive and to part of this . . . like nothing else I've ever been a part of. [There was] nothing like this particular life in which you saw the same group of people over and over again. You were always glad to see them. You always had an exciting time when you were with them."

In 1924 Bennett left the excitement of New York to go to Howard University in Washington. She was at Howard for one year when she was awarded a one-thousand-dollar Delta Sigma Theta sorority scholarship, which allowed her to study art in Paris during the 1925-26 academic year. She took classes at the Académie Julian, the Académi Coloraossi, and the École du Panthéon. Bennett found Paris both exhilarating and lonely—the two short stories she published, "Tokens" and "Wedding Day," reflect the somber, isolated mood she frequently felt, though neither story is autobiographical. Both works feature black expatriates—a jazz musician down with the blues and a black ex-prize fighter—men who had remained in France following World War I.

When she returned to New York in 1926, Bennett faced several difficulties squarely. Her beloved father died; she could not find a job; most of the paintings, batiks, and other art pieces she had brought home from Paris were destroyed in a fire in her stepmother's home; and she was not keen to return to Howard. Although she had attended Washington parties and occasional dances, she found its Negro social set too staid. A vivacious, attractive young woman of exuberant spirits, her heart remained in New York.

Bennett was also resilient, involved, and hard working. Perhaps these traits were the reason that Johnson pressed her into service as a writer and eventually as a regular columnist for *Opportunity*. Bennett had contributed several poems to both *Crisis* and *Opportunity*; she had also written book reviews and done some journalistic rewriting for the latter. In August of 1926, with Johnson's blessing, Bennett inaugurated "The Ebony Flute"—a "literary and social chit-chat" column for *Opportunity*. From the column, readers learned what new books were coming or were already on the market, what paying contests for artists were available, which of the new musical revues were good, what new role Paul Robeson had. Readers following the activities of Hughes, Aaron Douglass, or Zora Neale Hurston merely turned to "The Ebony Flute" to find out what these young artists and other people involved in various artistic endeavors across the country were doing.

"The Ebony Flute" came to an abrupt end in 1928. Bennett, who, in 1927 had married Alfred Joseph Jackson, a Morehouse College graduate and doctor, removed herself from the New York and Washington intellectual circuits. Jackson wanted to establish his practice in his native Florida, and Bennett joined him in Eustis, where he decided to settle, in 1928. But Bennett was never happy in Florida. Barring a summer school teaching experience at Nashville's Tennessee Agricultural and Industrial State College in 1927, she had never lived in the South and had not experienced active segregation. She found being denied access to such amenities as the public library an unnecessary offense, and there was so little for her to do in the small Negro community that she gained sixty pounds in the four years she lived there.

When Bennett was finally able to persuade her husband that they needed to return to New York, it was 1932 and the Great Depression had begun. The Negro was out of "vogue," and making a living had become very difficult. It was indeed a grim period, for shortly after they settled into their Hemstead, Long Island, community, Alfred Jackson died. Following his death, Bennett moved back to the city and alternated between living with her stepmother and living in the home and studio of the noted sculptor, Augusta Savage. She found work with one of the largest of President Franklin D. Roosevelt's New Deal programs, the Works Progress Administration (WPA)'s Federal Writers Project. Savage, however, convinced her that she should join her in working in the WPA's Federal Arts Project (FPA) instead. Under the auspices of the WPA/FAP, Savage had initiated and become the first director of the Harlem Community Art Center in 1937. When Savage was commissioned to design and create a sculpture for the upcoming 1939 New York World's Fair, however, Bennett replaced her as director of the center. But Bennett's tenure was short-lived; in 1944 she was suspended and then removed from this position allegedly because of her "political convictions" (Porter, 130). The *Amsterdam News* carried the screaming headline, "Suspend HAC Head in Red Probe! Miss Gwen Bennett Suspended on Word from Washington." Ever resilient, by 1943 Bennett had become director of the George Washington Carver School, a labor school geared toward political education. But, by 1947, Bennett wearied of the battle to keep herself above the fray while working in the public arena. Consequently, she withdrew from active public involvement in the arts.

Bennett, having remarried, spent the last years of her life as a housewife and antique dealer in the small Berks County community of Kutztown, Pennsylvania. On May 30, 1981, she died in a hospital in Reading. The cause of death is listed as congestive heart failure, but a contributing cause was unquestionably the unexpected death of Richard Crosscup, her second husband, on January 9, 1980, and an abiding loneliness.

Though no collected volume of her published work exists, Bennett is best known for her striking poetry, largely composed during the 1920s. Several of her poems recall the major themes of the Harlem Renaissance or New Negro movement: Africa, pride in one's heritage, militancy, and the folk. Other poems are of the more personal, poignant variety, lyrical pieces reflecting the poet's absorption in contemplative moods or strong feelings. One such poem, "Quatrains," illustrates the artistic tension Bennett still felt as both graphic artist and writer:

> Brushes and paints are all I have
> To speak the music in my soul
> While silently there laughs at me
> A copper jar beside a pale green bowl
> (*Caroling Dusk*, 155).

For Bennett, by her own testimony in later years and as indicated by the lack of scholarly attention a life as full as hers merits, the New Negro movement of the 1920s was the special shining moment in her life. She recognized that she was not a Wallace Thurman—not, as she called him, "a spearhead," who "was full of enthusiasm" and "[who] thought things up while the rest of us went along." And while Bennett is considered by some merely a minor writer of the time, certainly her many and varied accomplishments both during and following the Harlem renaissance should in no way be summarily dismissed. By her own measure, Bennett was an active and enthusiastic member of the group that "went along," doing her part to further the arts, to give the movement vitality and validity. For Bennett, "It was a very special thing to be an artist and a writer in those days, and to know the arts and have fun participating in them and forwarding them."

References

Bennett, Gwendolyn. Interview with author, 23 March 1979.

———. "Quatrains." In *Caroling Dusk*. Edited by Countee Cullen. New York: Harper and Row, 1927.

Daniel, Walter C., and Sandra Y. Govan. "Gwendolyn Bennett." *Dictionary of Literary Biography*. Edited by Trudier Harris and Thadious Davis. Detroit: Gale Research, 1987.

Govan, Sandra Y. "After the Renaissance: Gwendolyn Bennett and the WPA Years." *Mid Atlantic Writers Association* 3 (December 1988): 27-31.

———. *Rubbing Shoulders: The Life of Gwendolyn Bennett*. In progress.

Hughes, Langston. *The Big Sea: An Autobiography*. 1940. Reprinted. New York: Hill and Wang, 1968.

Porter, James A. *Modern Negro Art*. New York: Dryden Press, 1943.

Collections

Gwendolyn Bennett's personal papers and literary effects are in the Schomburg Center for Research in Black Culture, New York Public Library. Letters from Bennett are included in the Countee Cullen Papers in the Amistad Research Center at Tulane University, the Woodruff Library, at Atlanta University Center, and the Alain Locke Papers in the Moorland-Spingarn Research Center at Howard University. Photographs of Bennett are in the Schomburg Center.

Sandra Y. Govan

Mary Frances Berry

(1938-)

Historian, educator, lawyer, government official, civil and human rights activist

Mary Frances Berry is internationally recognized as an historian, educator, lawyer, public servant, and civil and human rights activist. A member of the United States Commission on Civil Rights under both the Carter and Reagan administrations and an expert on U.S. Constitutional history, she has written such books as *Black Resistance/White Law* to call attention to government sanctioned racism in the United States.

The second of three children, including George, Jr., and Troy Merritt, Mary Frances Berry was born on February 17, 1938, to Frances Southall Berry (now Wiggins) and George Ford Berry in Nashville, Tennessee. Economic and personal hardships beset the family in Mary Berry's earliest years; insurmountable difficulties compelled Frances Berry to place George and Mary in an orphanage for a time. While yet a child, the ravages of poverty and the capacity of human beings for cruelty, selfishness, and racial prejudice created for Mary Frances Berry a period in her life akin to a "horror story" (Lanker, 84).

Mary Frances Berry

Neither poverty, hunger, nor inhumane treatment at the orphanage, however, prevented Berry from demonstrating at an early age exceptional determination, resilience, and intellectual ability. She obtained her first years of formal education in the segregated schools of Nashville and its environs. It was while Berry was in Pearl High School, however, with "no idea of what [she] was going to do with [her] life," that a black teacher, Minerva Hawkins, saw in the teenager a "diamond in the rough" and changed Berry's life irrevocably (Harris, 80; see also Poinsette, 58-60, 65-66). Berry recalls that as a tenth-grade high school student she "felt unchallenged" and "had the usual number of adolescent problems" (Harris, 82):

> I would hang out of school, leave school early, leave for lunch. It wasn't that I couldn't do the work. I always finished ahead of the other students. I was just bored with school. When I got to Ms. Hawkins' class, she noticed that. She started giving me extra books and extra assignments. Then she would talk to me about it. She would even invite me over to her house after school. She then started talking to me about my life and got me interested in intellectual pursuits (Harris, 82).

Hawkins mentored the young Berry, encouraging her to explore new ideas and to stretch in order to reach her full potential. As teacher and mentor, Hawkins also appreciated Berry's capacity to cope with life's vicissitudes and society's harsh realities. They discussed segregation and racism, as well as academic subjects and Berry's plans for the future. The prelude to one of many critical conversations was recently recalled by Berry:

> I was walking down the street with my teacher in Nashville the day *Brown* v. *Board of Education* was decided. I saw the headline in the newspaper and I remembered saying, "Look at this! This is going to be great! Starting next year the kids will all be going to school together!" And she looked at me and said, "I'm not sure it's going to happen quite next year" (Lanker, 84).

The training and expectations of Berry's mentor motivated the high school student. The encouragement, love, faith, and hard work of her mother (who, although she had remarried, still struggled against the odds to provide better opportunities for her children) affected both the consciousness and the conduct of Berry. As a consequence, she excelled and was graduated from Pearl High School with honors in 1956.

Upon graduation from high school, Berry sought and found work, but she began her college education at Hawkin's alma mater, Fisk University. She planned to major in chemistry but read with intensity in many fields. Berry was determined to become a professional. A thirst for knowledge generally and in particular, intellectual curiosity about philosophy, history, and chemistry caused Berry to be dissatisfied with obtaining higher education in any location except Washington, D.C.

Berry applied to and was accepted as a transfer student by Howard University. The absence of financial aid did not deter her; she was accustomed to combining hard work with her studies. Emboldened and excited by such inspiring teachers and role models as Elsie M. Lewis and Lorraine A. Williams, Berry earned her bachelor of arts degree in 1961 and continued at Howard University as a graduate student in the department of history. Under the tutelage of such excellent and dedicated scholar-teachers as Rayford W. Logan and Merze Tate, Berry learned historical methodology and historiography, became acquainted with the bibliographies of several fields of history, and honed skills in research as well as argumentation so that she might develop fully as a scholar. She plunged into specific primary research on the black experience and U.S. history. Subsequently Berry produced a thesis of eighty-one pages for her master of arts degree, titled "The History of the Seventy-third and Seventy-fifth United States Colored Infantry Regiments."

Possessed of an indomitable spirit and clarity about the importance of understanding the nation and its history, Berry decided to pursue a Ph.D. After working as a teaching assistant at Howard University from 1962 to 1963, Berry was admitted to the doctoral program in history at the University of Michigan in Ann Arbor. There Berry focused upon U.S. history with a special concentration in Constitutional history. Although the luxury of having only the task of studying was never Berry's—she worked the evening or night shift in hospital laboratories throughout her undergraduate and graduate years—her outstanding academic record won her the Civil War Roundtable Dissertation Fellowship in 1965. The next year the doctor of philosophy degree was awarded following the completion and successful defense of her dissertation "The Negro Soldier Movement and the Adoption of National Conscription," which was written under the direction of Professor William R. Leslie.

Having been told by her mother years ago that being qualified would never be enough for a black, Berry decided to take her mother's advice literally: "Always have more qualifications than anybody else you're sitting in the room with. If there are people there who have one degree, you get two. If they got two, you get three" (Lanker, 84). Berry was appointed in 1966 an assistant professor of history at Central Michigan University in Mount Pleasant, but applied for further study at the University of Michigan Law School. While studying for the juris doctor degree, Berry continued her teaching career as an assistant and later associate professor of history at Eastern Michigan University in Ypsilanti and associate professor of history at the University of Maryland at College Park. Prior to graduating from the law school of the University of Michigan, she began writing and publishing in scholarly journals. By 1970 she had not only earned her J. D. degree but had also been named the University of Maryland's acting director of Afro-American Studies and been appointed to the faculty of the University of Michigan as an adjunct associate professor of history.

Berry Writes on Constitutional Interpretation

Berry's first major scholarly labor of love was the completion of her manuscript for a book on the history, concept, and practice of Constitutional racism. While yet in law school, she became determined to argue, based upon her historical research and analysis, that "whether its policy was action or inaction, the national government has used the Constitution in such a way as to make law the instrument for maintaining a racist status quo" (Berry, *Black Resistance/White Law*, x). Berry solicited and responded to the critique of junior and senior scholars such as John Wesley Blassingame, professor of Southern and African American history at Yale and Arthur Link of Princeton in the process of completing her manuscript. Berry's first book, *Black Resistance/White Law: A History of Constitutional Racism in America*, was published by Appleton-Century-Crofts in 1971. It "deals in depth, with the way in which racism has been perpetuated through pro-racist interpretations of the Constitution," and as a result, editors of scholarly periodicals sought reviewers (John Hope Franklin to Genna Rae McNeil, 6 May 1988). The controversial monograph was reviewed in journals widely read by professors of history and other educators, such as *The Journal of American History*, the *Journal of Negro History*, *The American Historical Review*, and *Freedomways*. A second printing by Prentice-Hall in 1974 signaled recognition of the young scholar's work by a wider audience. *Black Resistance/White Law* has remained required reading for any who would understand the particular impact of constitutional interpretations on black Americans.

Berry Takes the Helm in Academe

Berry has enthusiastically and energetically developed a career in academe, which began with and continues to include teaching. One important objective has been to teach effectively whether in the classroom or another academic setting. Wide dissemination of her publications has enabled Berry to teach students in far greater numbers than her class enrollments. Berry's teaching activities as a professor of U.S. history and U.S. legal history have included the incorporation of racially plural materials into traditional courses, the introduction of new courses, and instruction of young scholars pursuing graduate degrees in history. Berry's career as a scholar-educator has been marked by a series of noteworthy achievements beyond teaching. In 1972 she was named the first director of the Afro-American Studies Program at the University of Maryland and the interim chairperson of Maryland's Division of Behavioral and Social Sciences for the College Park campus. She was appointed provost for the same division in 1974, becoming the highest ranking black woman at College Park.

In 1976 Berry accepted the invitation of the board of regents of the University of Colorado to become chancellor at that institution, thereby becoming the first black woman and one of only two women to join the ranks of presidents and chancellors of major research universities. (The only other woman at the time of Berry's appointment was Lorene Rogers, president of the University of Texas.) Unquestionably, the most prominent and significant academic administrative post in which Berry has served has been the chancellorship of this 21,000-student campus (then 3 percent black, 14 percent Hispanic), with a faculty of 2,300 members and an annual budget of 113.3 million dollars. Her concerns and her goals during the period of her chancellorship were best described by Berry on the occasion of the university's 163rd commencement: "My task . . . will be to foster and continue the effort to attain excellence in our academic programs, despite the increasing difficulty of explaining the value and power of knowledge and its creation, to . . . many constituencies" (Poinsette, 65). She has accepted two subsequent academic appointments. In 1980 Berry joined the faculty of her undergraduate alma mater, Howard University, as a professor of history and law and became a senior fellow at Howard's Institute for the Study of Educational Policy. After nearly a decade, Berry resigned from the faculty of Howard University to accept a professorship at the University of Pennsylvania, where she now serves as the Geraldine R. Segal Professor of Social Thought and Professor of History.

Unrelenting Researcher Explores Race, Gender, and Law in Publications

Berry has achieved particular distinction among scholars for her research, critical analyses, lucid writing style, coverage of timely issues from a historical perspective, and specific expertise in legal and African-American history. Berry's work is frequently cited in the work of others, given ever-increasing scholarly and general public attention and adopted by colleagues as either required or recommended reading for both graduate and undergraduate students. Berry was elected to the presidency of the Organization of American Historians in March 1990. She has written and published in excess of a dozen articles in scholarly journals or chapters in scholarly books, a score of general articles, and numerous book-review essays and book reviews in a variety of publications.

In addition to *Black Resistance/White Law*, Berry has written five major books: *Military Necessity and Civil Rights Policy: Black Citizenship and the Constitution, 1861-1868* (Kennikat Press, 1977), *Stability, Security, and Continuity: Mr. Justice Burton and Decision-Making in the Supreme Court, 1945-1958* (Greenwood Press, 1978), *Long Memory: The Black Experience in America* (coauthor, John W. Blassingame; Oxford University Press, 1982), *Why ERA Failed* (Indiana University Press, 1986), and *The Politics of Motherhood* (Viking Press, forthcoming). Blassingame has perceptively argued that Berry's "works tend to close debate. Rarely does one put down a book she has written with the feeling that the subject should be explored again. Instead her books . . . [have become] standards in the field" (John W. Blassingame to G. R. McNeil, 15 May 1988).

Beyond *Black Resistance/White Law*, two of Berry's works have made significant contributions to the field of black American history. In *Military Necessity and Civil Rights Policy*, Berry offers the thesis that blacks have gained greatest benefits with respect to civil rights during times of national crises. Focusing on the Civil War period, she noted the federal government's concurrent need for black soldiers and violation of their constitutional rights. She also provided evidence of the instrumental role of black soldiers in effecting the abolition of slavery. While scholars have disagreed as to how critical a force black soldiers were "in extracting civil rights concessions from the white majority," Berry has amply documented—with reference to primary and secondary sources—a direct relationship between military policy and Constitutional/social change from 1861 to 1865. As Benjamin Quarles observed in his review for the *Journal of American History*, "This thoughtful study makes it necessary to weigh . . . these points [and thereafter] take due note that the civil rights laws of the 1860s would . . . be flouted . . . largely unenforced" (478).

In contrast to this monograph stands *Long Memory*, which is the fruit of Berry's collaboration with Blassingame. *Long Memory* has been acclaimed as "a major interpretative survey of the black experience by two distinguished historians" (*Choice*, 1477). Topical organization renders the work particularly suitable for the many survey courses on the African American experience shorter than the needed two terms. It was not intended to supplant the encyclopedic *From Slavery to Freedom* by John Hope Franklin; reviewers who implied this were straining comparisons. For the experience of blacks through 1980, it "offers a wide historical sweep and masterful weaving of cultural, literary and social patterns," as one reviewer noted (*Library Journal*, 2390). Additionally, *Long Memory* makes excellent use of primary sources—such as autobiographies, poetry, and newspapers—in the documentation of self-determination, nationalism, and the responses of black Americans to oppression and racism. Of lasting significance is Berry's unrelenting search not only for the antecedents of and the reasons for racial reform, quests for justice, and the black American liberation struggle, but also the relation of racial reform to the self-interest of the white majority in the United States.

Berry has sometimes worked in relatively unexplored areas of constitutional and legal history. At other times she has examined current legal issues from a historical perspective. Her *Stability, Security and Continuity* (1978) examines decision making and other elements of the normal activity of the U.S. Supreme Court through an essentially "average" justice, Harold H. Burton, in the belief that a competent judge's career—explored through the primary sources of his conference notes, opinions, and correspondence—"informs us more rather than less about the Court as an institution within the American system" (Berry, *Stability*, 234). This work stripped away, as one historian has observed, "much of the mystery about the way that the Supreme Court operates" (John W. Blassingame to G. R. McNeil, 15 May 1988). Although early reviewers raised questions regarding the adequacy of the attention given to the general subject of decision making in small groups, Berry's study has come to be viewed as an effective examination of the court, that contains "useful insights and splendid examples of the problems faced by the justices in grappling with the complexities of their docket" (*Journal of American Studies*, 167).

Why ERA Failed, a widely reviewed and successful book, has examined the legal process, gender, race, and cultural conflict as well as external and internal factors impacting on social movements designed to amend the Constitution. Berry clearly and incisively identified the essential elements required to create the sense of need for alteration of the Constitution and, within a broad historical analysis, addressed specifically the problems of the movement to obtain an Equal Rights Amendment (ERA). As John Hope Franklin has commented, *Why ERA Failed* is "an excellent analysis of the historical as well as current forces that doomed this effort to extend equal rights to women by Constitutional amendment" (John Hope Franklin to G. R. McNeil, 15 May 1988). Berry makes a persuasive, straight-forward argument that the ERA advocates ignored the lessons of history, by demonstrating that the movement "did too little, too late of what [was] required for ratification of a substantive proposal" (Berry, *Why ERA Failed*, 3). Berry's forthcoming study, *The Politics of Motherhood* will present a historical view of culture, gender, race, politics, and economics in an effort to facilitate understanding of the status of women as mothers, the policy and political questions germane to childcare, and concepts of the good and just within society.

In her role as a researcher, Berry has a penchant for detail; as a research scholar-educator, she is consistently concerned with the sufficient use of a variety of primary sources, not only to "creat[e] new knowledge," but also "to give students a more realistic picture of the times" (Poinsette, 65; Berry, "A Love-Hate Relationship with the National Archives," 36). Because of her training in both history and law, Berry's method of research emphasizes the study of court records, including transcripts of oral arguments, briefs, published reports of opinions, memoranda, or conference notes of jurists, and state as well as U.S. statutes. This emphasis has grown out of her conviction "that law is one of the most influential forces in the existence of human beings, a prism through which one can examine the human experience" (Berry, "A Love-Hate Relationship with the National Archives," 36). However intense Berry has been about her scholarly and prodigious research, she also has enjoyed it: "I cannot understand how anybody couldn't think that [research] was exciting—useful, we hope, for man and womankind" (Poinsette, 65).

Nation's First Black Chief Educational Officer Appointed

From 1977 to 1979, Berry was the first black woman to serve as chief educational officer of the United States. Under Secretary of Health, Education, and Welfare Joseph Califano and later Secretary Patricia Roberts Harris, Berry ably administered a thirteen-billion-dollar annual budget and had responsibility for the Fund for the Improvement of Postsecondary Education, the Institute of Museum Services, the National Center for Education Statistics, the National Institute of Education, and the Office of Education. Among her multiple duties, was "constituent-oriented liaison" with the black higher education community, "political leader of a broad spectrum of education interests," academician "with a highly developed interest in black history," and "administrative leader" within the Department of Health, Education and Welfare (HEW) (Pinderhughes, 301-307).

Bennett's duties involved but were not limited to selection of major educational issues for HEW's special attention, determination of recommendations regarding appropriate federal responses to educational issues or problems, establishment of funding levels within the perimeters of congressional allocations for education, and development or identification of suitable guidelines for implementation of court decisions on desegregation and affirmative action.

Some of Berry's goals with respect to equal opportunities, equity, and justice were met in her creation of a Graduate and Professional Opportunities Program that augmented graduate opportunities for racial minorities and women, the establishment of a sizable budget increase for the education of the disabled, and the institutionalization of federal guidelines for the Carter administration with respect to the enhancement of historically black colleges and universities. Consistent with knowledge gained from research and study, Berry was attentive to constituency development in the broadest sense as well as enforcement of legal protections and policies. In an interview she emphasized the critical importance of law in support of equal opportunities and justice, asserting that she had "always maintained as a scholar, before [she] became an administrator, that the major problem is enforcing laws, not passing laws" (Berry interview, *Guidepost*, quoted in *Journal of American History*, 479).

Berry Appointed by President to Civil Rights Commission

Berry has been best known in her public service as a commissioner of the United States Commission on Civil Rights. Berry's association with the commission preceded her appointment. She had prepared for it in 1975 an extensively researched and well-documented special study, *Constitutional Aspects of the Right to Limit Childbearing*. Subsequent to her service as assistant secretary for education, President Jimmy Carter appointed Berry to the United States Civil Rights Commission, which had been established in 1957 to function as an independent, bipartisan agency within the executive branch. Responsible for the investigation of discrimination, the commission had engaged in monitoring and fact-finding, but it had also been the recommending body for the Civil Rights Act of 1964 and Voting Rights Act of 1965. However distinguished Berry's service as commissioner and vice-chairperson from 1980 to 1982, President Ronald Reagan sought to dismiss her before the 1984 election. This effort to remove Berry and two other appointees holding viewpoints opposed to Reagan's was characterized by Berry as the reduction of the commission from the "watchdog of civil rights" to "a lapdog for the administration" (*Washington Post*, 18 January 1984). Berry's prestige and notoriety increased when she successfully challenged in federal court Reagan's attempt to remove her from the commission.

Berry has continued to be a national public figure outspoken in her opposition to the emasculated Civil Rights Commission:

> Our job is to investigate and make recommendations to Congress and the President on what should be done to move us toward real economic opportunity. . . . The Commission is the conscience of the nation on civil rights. [President Reagan and his administration, however,] have . . . destroyed it. They have taken it over so that they could use the wreckage for their own ends—to do studies that will prove that Blacks are to blame for our social and economic problems, that government has no role to play and that racial discrimination is insignificant. The[ir] point is to get Blacks to accept the idea of not asking the government to do anything to overcome the legacy of discrimination and, indeed, to forget about this legacy altogether" (Reynolds, 12).

Berry's continued service on the commission "reflects . . . a commitment to easing . . . barriers for others less able" and a stubborn determination to remind the commission of the duties it was originally created to discharge (Derrick Bell to G. R. McNeil, 13 May 1988).

Scholar-Activist Takes Uncompromising Stand on Justice

Berry has taken a principled and uncompromising stand on justice since her days of student activism. An outspoken critic of oppression, exploitation, and denials of human as well as civil rights, whether the victims be a race of people, a small nation, women, the poor, the marginalized or disabled, Berry has a record of and reputation for articulate, historically grounded advocacy of justice. At various periods the issues addressed by Berry have been the Vietnam War (about which she was protesting in light of her historical analyses as well as her time spent in 1967 as a civilian journalist with a Marine battalion in combat areas), women's rights, federal remedies for past institutionalized racism in the United States, black American civil rights and liberation, African liberation, or the specific recognition of black self-determination required by the principle of justice in South Africa. Her ideological clarity and her activism have been a matter of the public record. For example, Berry has testified before Congress on numerous occasions, participated in the preparation of *amicus curiae* briefs supporting affirmative action, and appeared as an expert on national television broadcasts such as "Nightline."

Berry's leadership in the Free South Africa Movement—of which she is a founder—and her Thanksgiving 1984 arrest at the South African embassy while protesting apartheid and U.S. policy toward South Africa have catapulted Berry to greater national and international prominence. Viewed variously as either abrasive and radical or persuasive and factual, her responses to the government and the media on matters of justice for persons of African descent in United States and for black Africans in South Africa caused her to be a recognizable public figure throughout the United States. She is a spokesperson for justice, moving with ease from the terse, blunt statement to eloquent, research-rooted testimony. She consistently participates in protests, whether they be authorized public demonstrations or actions of civil disobedience. Her praxis has established Berry as one of the outstanding scholar-activists of the second half of the twentieth century. "When it comes to the cause of justice," she has explained, "I take no prisoners and I don't believe in compromising" (Lanker, 84).

Berry has sought to be an especially sensitive and committed activist in the United States. She has valued, however, that which places the activism in a broader context. Therefore a 1990 trip with Jesse Jackson to visit Winnie and Nelson Mandela in South Africa on the occasion of the latter's release from prison and Berry's continuing such public service activities as membership on the Council of the United Nations University and the board of directors of People for the American Way have been viewed by Berry as appropriate and significant uses of her time. Her critics have labeled her an extremist for precisely the same reason that she has become a respected and appreciated leader among many black Americans, namely, her "radical vision of civil rights, of America, and of the world" (*Washington Post*, 16 September 1983).

Career and Public Service Prompt Honors and Awards

In addition to these activities and responsibilities, Berry has been a consultant to and board or council member for a variety of organizations, foundations, governmental agencies, and universities. These have included the American Association of University Professors (1972-73; 1983-1986); Committee on Women Historians of the American Historical Association (1972-74); Metropolitan Washington Planning and Housing Association (1974); "Project 87" (On Women and the Constitution) (1978-); Tuskegee University (1980 -); Delta Sigma Theta (1979 -); District of Columbia Chapter of the American Red Cross (1980); Center for Athletes' Rights and Education (1983-); Minority Legislative Education Program (1981-); Joint Center for Political and Economic Studies (1981-); Marcus Garvey Papers (1981-); National Coalition of 100 Black Women (1984-); Gannett Newspapers (1984); "We the People 200." (in celebration of the Constitution; 1985-1988); and the National Wildlife Federation (1988-).

That Berry is considered a thought-provoking speaker, much in demand, has been affirmed by the numerous institutions of higher education for which she has given addresses and from which she has received honorary degrees. She has been awarded honorary degrees from more than eighteen colleges and universities, among them Howard University (1977), the University of Maryland (1979), Oberlin College (1983), Langston University (1983), City College of the City University of New York (1986), DePaul University (1987), and Smith College (1990). For her contributions to the struggle for justice, the community, the nation, and historical scholarship she has received not only honorary degrees, but such awards as the Athena (Distinguished Alumni) Award (University of Michigan, 1977), the Roy Wilkins Civil Rights Award (National Association for the Advancement of Colored People), the NAACP Image Award (1983), Commission on Human Relations' Farmer Human Rights Award (City of Philadelphia, 1984), Rosa Parks Award (Southern Christian Leadership Conference, 1985), President's Award (Congressional Black Caucus Foundation, 1985), Hubert H. Humphrey Civil Rights Award (Leadership Conference on Civil Rights, 1986), "Woman of the Year" Award (*Ms. Magazine*, 1986), Frito Lay and the National Council of Negro Women's "Salute [to] Black Women Who Make It Happen" Achievement Award (1987), and "Gallery of Greats" (Black Educators) Award (Miller Brewing Company, 1988).

Although this diminutive black woman (approximately 5 feet 3 inches) is a highly visible, formidable opponent in the struggle for justice and a virtually indefatigable scholar-activist, her friends—among whom may be counted Derrick A. Bell, Blassingame, John Hope Franklin, Minerva Hawkins, Jesse Jackson, Elaine Jones, and Roger Wilkins—have found Mary Frances Berry equally genial, generous, witty, loyal, and intellectually stimulating when there have been opportunities to relax as well as work together. Berry's schedule of speech-making, traveling, writing, researching, and reading is punctuated weekly by a game or two of tennis except when Saturday engagements have interfered with her regimen (Interview with Mary Frances Berry).

Berry has both written and made history. Her contributions to the cause of justice and to scholarship have been significant and constructive. While she has not sought to be a public figure, she has also never failed to act on her commitment to the struggle for racial and economic justice.

References

Bell, Derrick. Letter to G. R. McNeil, 13 May 1988.

Berry, Mary Frances. *Black Resistance/White Law*. Englewood Cliffs, N.J.: Prentice-Hall, 1971.

———. Curriculun Vita, 1979.

———. Interview with G. R. McNeil, 15 May 1990; 21 May 1990.

———. "A Love-Hate Relationship with the National Archives." In *Afro-American History: Sources for Research*. Edited by Robert Clarke, Wahington,D.C.: Howard University, 1981.

———. *Stability, Security, and Continuity*. Westport, Conn: Greenwood Press, 1978.

———. *Why ERA Failed*. Bloomington: Indiana University Press, 1986.

Blassingame, John W. Letter to G. R. McNeil, 15 May 1988.

Carroll, Susan J. Review Essay. *American Political Science Review* 81 (December 1987): 1339-41.

Choice 19 (June 1982): 1477.

Franklin, John Hope. Letter to G. R. McNeil, 15 May 1988.

Guidepost, 22 December 1977.

Harris, Ron. "The Turning Point, That Changed Their Lives." *Ebony* 34 (January 1979): 80, 82.

Lanker, Brian. *I Dream A World:* New York: Stewart, Tabori and Chang, 1989.

Library Journal 106 (December 1981): 2390.

Pinderhughes, Dianne M. "Black Women and National Educational Policy." *Journal of Negro Education* 51 (Summer 1982): 301-307.

Poinsette, Alex. "Colorado University's Chancellor." *Ebony* 30 (January 1977): 58-60, 65-66.

Quarles, Benjamin. Review of *Military Necessity and Civil Rights Policy. Journal of American History* 45 (September 1978): 478.

Reynolds, Barbara. "The Woman the President Couldn't Fire." *Essence* 15 (October 1984): 12, 158.

"Rights Panel Backs Reagan in Opposing Quota." *Washington Post,* 18 January 1984.

Smith, Carol Hobson. "Black Female Achievers in Academe." *Journal of Negro History* 51 (Summer 1982): 323-27.

Wattenberg, Ben. Editorial. *Washington Post,* 16 September 1983.

Who's Who Among Black Americans, 1990/91. 6th ed. Detroit: Gale Research, 1991.

Williams, Richard. Review of *Stability, Security, and Continuity. Journal of American Studies* 14 (April 1980): 167.

Winston, Michael R. *The Howard University Department of History: 1913-1973*. Washington, D.C.: 1973.

Collections

Papers of Mary Frances Berry, including correspondence and photographs, are held by the Moorland-Spingarn Research Center, Howard University, Washington, D.C.

Genna Rae McNeil

Mary McLeod Bethune

(1875-1955)

Educator, civil and women's rights activist, government official

A champion of humanitarian and democratic values throughout the United States for more than thirty years, Mary McLeod Bethune made essential contributions to the development of black America. Through her prominent position in the administration of President Franklin D. Roosevelt—she was responsible for facilitating the infusion of much-needed dollars into black education and vocational training—she assumed the role of race reader at large. As such she became the most illustrious black New Dealer and most influential black woman in the annals of the country. Bethune provided the leadership to raise black women from the social and political invisibility they suffered to a sustained presence in national affairs. Vital to her effectiveness was the exercise of well-honed skills in establishing alliances with influential whites while ensuring positive cooperation among influential blacks.

Born in 1875 in Sumter County near Mayesville, South

Mary McLeod Bethune

Carolina, Mary McLeod Bethune was the fifteenth of seventeen children of Sam McLeod and Patsy (McIntosh) McLeod. Her father was of African and Indian descent while her mother was African. Her parents and most of her brothers and sisters were slaves emancipated through the Union victory in the Civil War. One major consequence of freedom for the McLeod family was the acquisition, in the early 1870s, of a farm of about thirty-five acres.

During the post-Reconstruction era in white-controlled Sumter County, the overwhelming black majority had access to little public schooling. Therefore, Bethune was fortunate to attend the rural Trinity Presbyterian Mission School four or five miles from her home when it opened in 1885. There she came under the benevolent and dynamic influence of her first teacher, Emma Jane Wilson. Three years later she attended Scotia Seminary (later Barber-Scotia College) in Concord, North Carolina. Bethune spent six years at this outreach of northern white Presbyterians. Beyond academics she was submerged in a regime emphasizing religious concerns, "culture and refinement," and "industrial education"—sewing, cooking, laundering, and cleaning.

Upon graduation Bethune, preparing to be an African missionary, entered the Bible Institute for Home and Foreign Missions (later Moody Bible Institute), an interdenominational school in Chicago. Upon applying to the Presbyterian Mission Board for an assignment after a year's study, however, Bethune was greatly disappointed, learning that it did not place African-Americans in such positions. Though time and again life would jolt Bethune, she later certified that this blow was the greatest disappointment of her life.

Haines Institute Enriches Career

Believing that foreign missions were closed to her, Bethune entered virtually the only field open to a black woman of her inclination and training—teaching black students. For the next five years she taught in Georgia and South Carolina. The greatest career experience of the period was at the Presbyterian-sponsored Haines Institute in Augusta, Georgia, because it allowed her to observe up close the school's founder-principal, Lucy Craft Laney. The arresting thing about Laney was that in a field dominated by males—both black and white—and by white females, she was perhaps the only black woman educator who ran a school that compared favorably in size, appearance, curriculum, and student achievement with the best of southern secondary institutions for blacks.

While teaching at the Presbyterian Kendall Institute in Sumter, South Carolina, she met Albertus Bethune, a handsome and tall, man five years her senior, who was from the nearby community of Wedgefield. In May 1898 the couple married and they soon made Savannah their home. Here he found work as a porter, and their only child, Albert Bethune, was born. Though the couple remained together for at least eight years and were legally married until Albertus's death in 1918, theirs was not a happy union. Because marriage and family experiences were unsatisfying for her, Bethune ultimately failed to accord these institutions priority status in advancing black Americans.

Bethune saw education as the primary route to racial uplift, and this field consumed her youthful energies. In 1900 she established a Presbyterian parochial school in Palatka, Florida. Two years later, she opened an independent school that she maintained in conjunction with rendering volunteer social services and selling life insurance. After two more years she left the declining Palatka for greener pastures on the state's east coast.

Bethune Founds Educational Institution

In Daytona, Florida, on October 3, 1904, in a rented house sparsely furnished with dry-goods boxes for benches and other improvised essentials, Bethune founded the Daytona Educational and Industrial Institute, with her assets of "five little girls, a dollar and a half, and faith in God" (Bethune-Cookman College, 1). In addition, she had her own five-year-old son. She also possessed well-formed ideas of the school she wanted, a re-creation of "dear old Scotia." But she would modify the model by having her students work a large farm to put food on the institute's table and to provide cash income from the sale of produce. Bethune hoped in time to offer nurse training and advanced subjects and attain national respectability.

Fortunately, Bethune had chosen well the city in which to realize her ambition. Daytona's black leaders eagerly assisted her, particularly A. L. James, pastor of Mount Bethel Baptist Church, one of the two black houses of worship in this town of two thousand. In 1905, besides Bethune, he became the only other black member of the school's trustee board, which meant that the whites gave the institute critical assistance. Socially prominent white women frequently exerted hands-on influence in the school's regular activities and even more in special events. Beginning in 1905 the most energetic of them were organized into a Ladies' Advisory Board to the institute consisting of both local residents and winter tourists. Though on occasion Bethune used her female supporters as a means of interesting their husbands in the Daytona Institute, her largest individual contributors were white males with whom she dealt directly, including James N. Gamble of Proctor and Gamble Manufacturing Company.

By 1922, with black and white support, Bethune had developed a thriving institution that enrolled three hundred girls, and had a dedicated faculty and staff of about twenty-five. Among them was Frances Reynolds Keyser, a previous director of the White Rose Mission in New York City, who stood shoulder-to-shoulder with the founder.

Bethune conducted her institute in the head-heart-hand tradition, yet she factored into it a sweep of experiences that, taken together, appeared to have been broader than those found in the run-of-the-mill black school. Initially, intellectual fare translated into instruction to the eighth grade, but after World War I it included a high school incorporating teacher-training. From 1911 to 1927, through the institute's hospital, a respectable nurse training course was offered.

Heart education at the school meant worship, Bible study, and temperance training. But it also meant outreach programs: farmer conferences on campus, a mission school in a turpentine camp, a summer school and playground for local children, and community holiday projects. Hand education centered on producing and handling food and then sewing. The institute sent students out to do housework as well as to bake cookies and serve tea at the afternoon tea parties of the wealthy.

Beyond study, religion, and work, the girls at the Daytona Institute benefited from contact with an incomparable professional role model, Bethune. With her extremely dark skin, flat nose, and full lips, which clashed sharply with America's ideal of physical attractiveness and which both blacks and whites deemed liabilities to leadership in middle class black America, Bethune transcended the restricted sphere that society usually assigned to one of her color and, for that matter, one of her gender. Her sense of an unfettered self was so great that she defied Jim Crow customs and ordinances, most notably in her insistence on desegregated seating at the Daytona Institute. And despite Ku Klux Klan threats, she and her entire faculty and staff voted in 1920 and afterwards. With a vision of better opportunities for blacks and black women in particular, role model Bethune extended her influence throughout black America.

Merged Institutions Form Bethune-Cookman College

Though seeing herself as uniquely fitted to nurture the potential and aspirations of girls, Bethune took on the direct education of boys as opposed to providing them, as previously, with adjunct classes and services. This came about in 1923 through a merger of her school, then the Daytona Normal and Industrial Institute, with the coeducational Cookman Institute in Jacksonville, Florida. Though declining at the time, the latter claimed a distinguished fifty-one-year-old heritage and sponsorship of the Methodist Episcopal church. The church had arranged for the institutional marriage between Daytona and Cookman on the basis of developing the union, under Bethune's leadership, into a junior college. This relieved Bethune of raising her school's total annual budget, which at the time was close to $58,000, and it provided her with an array of technical services and professional contacts. It also promoted her aspirations for a college. To reflect the collegiate direction, the institution officially changed its name to Bethune-Cookman College in 1929. Six years later, when the Southern Association of Colleges and Secondary Schools evaluated black colleges, Bethune-Cookman earned accreditation with a "B" rating. By 1935, having weathered the worst of the Great Depression, its development won for Mary Bethune the NAACP's coveted Spingarn Medal. But it was under Bethune's handpicked successor, the competent James A. Colson, that ten years later the standing of the junior college was upgraded to an "A" and that in 1943 a senior college was sufficiently advanced to award its first bachelor of science degrees in elementary education.

Bethune's relationship to her beloved school had taken a momentous turn in 1936 when she accepted a full-time government position in Washington, D.C. Consequently, the college suffered from her divided attention until 1942. At that time, after a life-threatening illness, Bethune resigned the presidency. Yet when a great measure of her political effectiveness in Washington ended, she worked her way back into the school's presidential office. In 1947, however, she seemed to have accepted the fact that the escalating rigors of the job required a younger person and consequently vacated the position. At this time Bethune basked in a phenomenal educational record. No other woman of her generation created an institution for disadvantaged youth and developed it into a senior college.

Bethune's success hinged in part upon her interaction with whites in the Daytona resort area. In the early years, having trained her female students to render black folk music movingly, she led them into fashionable hotels to entertain the guests. After singing, she exhibited her magnetic speaking abilities in relating her life's story and aspirations for her school. Then she accepted contributions. By 1912 the white tourists flocked to her, thus boosting the school into "a crossroads of culture and human relations." Essential to this development was Bethune's positive stance before Caucasian friends. She touted constantly the identity of interest between blacks and whites.

Leadership in Black Women's Club Movement Begins

Establishing a school, the achievement for which traditionally Bethune has been best known, assumes augmented significance when it is understood that it was the foundation of her exalted stature in the women's club movement. By hosting state and regional conclaves and channeling personnel and other resources into club work, Bethune progressively made her school a hub of clubwomen's activity. This occurred in tandem with her presidency of state, regional, and national federations beginning with the Florida Association of Colored Women in June 1917. In keeping with self-help trends in other Southern states, on September 10, 1920, Bethune led Florida's women in opening a home in Ocala for wayward and delinquent girls. Her remaining four years in office constituted a relentless, self-sacrificing struggle to keep it open for up to fourteen girls. Her successor faced this situation also until relief came in 1929 in the form of the appropriation from the Florida legislature that Bethune and others had long sought. And like the best of patriotic leaders during World War I, Bethune directed her constituents into well-publicized war-support endeavors. Bethune's presidency of the Southeastern Association of Colored Women, which she established in 1920 and presided over for five years, encompassed especially a turning outward to the broader society. The striking development occurred in 1922 when the Southeastern's Interracial Committee became the black contingent of the Women's General Committee of the Atlanta-based Commission on Interracial Cooperation. In this way was formed the most representative female leadership corps in the South.

But from 1924 to 1928, in the presidency of the ten-thousand-member National Association of Colored Women (NACW), the premier black women's secular organization, Bethune found her greatest platform for leadership in the established voluntary organization. Bethune's stature within the NACW derived in part from her brilliant vision of an activist public affairs role for black women in both national and international arenas. Like some other association leaders, particularly Margaret Murray Washington, Bethune determined to reach out to "the scattered people of African descent." She declared to her members, "we must make this national body of colored women a significant link between the peoples of color throughout the world." But her vision was even broader. In juxtaposition to global agitation, she maintained "This organization must assume an attitude toward all big questions involving the welfare of the nation, public right and especially the present and future of our race" (Bethune, NACW Presidential Address, August 2, 1926).

One available means of promoting the NACW's broad perspective was the National Council of Women in the United States, consisting in 1925 of thirty-eight organizations. In this, Bethune refused to settle for the peripheral position that usually accompanied the status of the only Negro group among many others. Instead, she pushed NACW participation to new limits, and through the National Council affiliation, the NACW projected itself onto the international stage of organized womanhood as a participant in the essentially white International Council of Women, which met in May 1925 in Washington, D.C. Despite a segregated seating ruckus, Bethune obtained significant benefits from this meeting. One of them was stimulation to promote an NACW Friendship Tour of Europe. Though Bethune's tour dwindled into virtually a presidential parade, she profited greatly from the trip, as did the European leaders who greeted her in the summer of 1927 as the emissary of black women.

To achieve her primary goal, effective representation of black women in public affairs, Bethune sought to transform the amorphous NACW into a cohesive body with a common program in all constituent regional, state, city, and individual club entities. For her this necessitated, above all, a permanent, fixed, national headquarters employing an executive secretary. Bethune crossed the country raising money for the project. On July 31, 1928, in Washington, D.C., the association proudly dedicated its newly acquired headquarters. The NACW was the first all-black group geared to operate in the nation's capital as scores of other national organizations already did.

Bethune Establishes National Council of Negro Women

Under the brutality of the Great Depression, Bethune's focus upon black women's energetic presence in national affairs and the mechanisms that she had vitalized to achieve this goal languished within the NACW. Increasingly reasserting its historic decentralized character, the organization retreated from her emphasis upon a cohesive body. Given these developments, coupled with Bethune's domineering personality and her belief in the necessity of linkages between the distaff leadership of black Americans and New Deal administrators, on December 5, 1935, in New York City, she established the National Council of Negro Women (NCNW). Essentially Bethune transferred to the council the brilliant vision that she had once vested in the NACW. As council president for fourteen years, she poured into the new entity all of her fine-tuned organizational skills. By 1949, when Bethune left office, the NCNW included twenty-two national professional and occupational groups and sororities, with eighty-two metropolitan councils.

While developing its internal operations, Bethune pushed the NCNW into extensive lobbying in official Washington. One dramatic device for doing so was a Conference on Governmental Cooperation in the Approach to the Problems of Negro Women and Children held April 4, 1938. At this time, sixty-five black women went to the White House in an effort to gain a toehold in planning and administering federal programs. Another prominent means for council involvement in federal activities was through membership on the advisory committee of the Women's Interest Section (WIS), lodged in the War Department's Bureau of Public Relations. Created in October 1941, it was then one of very few federally sponsored niches for female leadership in the defense effort, but black women had been totally excluded from the WIS Committee. Although the WIS Committee was restricted to organizations of at least one hundred thousand members, with the application of behind-the-scenes pressure the eight-hundred-thousand member NCNW joined the advisory committee.

This victory vindicated Bethune's council concept. "The scattered work and independent programs of national organizations of Negro women," Bethune proclaimed, "needed the strength that unity could bring" (Bethune, NCNW Annual Report, October 1941). With the NCNW's admission to the National Council of Women in late 1941, private organizations acknowledged the NCNW's role as the authoritative voice of black women in public affairs. The council interacted with a multiplicity of interracial, interfaith, and intercultural programs.

Internationalism was just one concern of the NCNW. Considering the economically disadvantaged status of its constituents, the council focused upon the expansion of public housing, Social Security, and other social welfare programs. In light of rampant racism, it also concentrated upon such issues as disenfranchisement, lynching, and discrimination in employment. In grappling with these problems, the council brought a much-needed emphasis upon the advancement of black women, because its members experienced a gender handicap as well as one of class and race. Through various programs the NCNW endeavored to counteract prejudice, as in the "We Serve America" celebrations and in sponsoring the S.S. *Harriet Tubman* (1944), the first liberty ship to honor a black woman. During World War II the council sponsored "Hold Your Job!" clinics and monitored conditions affecting black soldiers on the homefront. But the NCNW's shining hour under Bethune was in relationship to women in the armed forces. When the Women's

Army Auxiliary Corps (WAAC) was just an idea, army leaders favored excluding black Americans; in a series of consultations, Bethune successfully helped dissuade them.

Bethune's pivotal advocacy of minorities in the military revolved around the women's army officer cadre. She prevailed upon Director Oveta Culp Hobby and other officials to allot almost 10 percent of the spaces in the WAAC's first officer candidate class to black Americans. Mirroring this development was her appointment as a special assistant to the Secretary of War to select prospective female officers. Later when the Women's Army solicited recommendations from the NCNW, Bethune's foundational strategy for race advancement was promoted, in that the NCNW responded with proposals emphasizing equality of opportunity for black leadership.

Bethune Heads NYA's Division of Negro Affairs

Bethune's NCNW success derived in part from her contacts and insider status in the Franklin Roosevelt administration. Her base was the National Youth Administration (NYA), an agency that race liberals in Washington shaped and administered. Established in 1935 to assist young people aged sixteen to twenty-four in the Great Depression and continuing to exist during World War II primarily to provide youth with vocational training and then placement in vital defense industries, the NYA served several million constituents for more than eight years at a cost of more than $685,000,000. This agency established the concept of direct federal assistance to deserving youth both in and out of school, which was to have a permanent impact on the country long after its termination in 1944. Bethune had first become affiliated with this youth program in August 1935 as one of thirty-five members of its national advisory committee. After zealously and effectively promoting its work, in June 1936 the NYA provided her greater latitude through a staff position similar to those that dozens of other black race relations specialists held in the New Deal.

Consequently, with administrative sanction, Bethune established herself as the director of the Division of Negro Affairs, an arrangement that the Civil Service Commission made official in January 1939. In this way she occupied a slot in government higher than that of any other black woman in the history of the country up to that time. Although it was only a low-echelon berth within the broad framework of the federal bureaucracy, it was one of twenty or so of the highest appointed positions held by women in the New Deal. Regardless of Bethune's place on an organizational chart, she consistently operated on a level requiring consummate political skill in navigating through disputes in which her white colleagues and her black constituents were at odds and both expected her loyalty. She brought tremendously impressive assets to her job: a charismatic personality, an unexcelled platform style, keen insight into race relations, superb abilities to influence people, and a well-known reputation. Along with the job came not only the support of the NYA hierarchy, headed by administrator Aubrey Williams, but that of the White House as well.

Though institutionalized racism made it impossible for any government program to achieve parity between white and black benefits, from her small stronghold Bethune worked towards this end. She monitored breaking NYA developments to assure that black Americans got in on the ground floor, as in the Civilian Pilot Training Program, which paved the way for black pilots in the military. Bethune viewed her specialized role as one of interpreting the NYA to black Americans and interpreting the needs of black Americans to white Americans.

Throughout her NYA work, Bethune adhered to a grand strategy that she labeled Negro leadership. She believed that opportunities for such leadership were essential for American democracy. In keeping with this idea Bethune lobbied for black college students to receive both extra and regular NYA support on the basis of their greatest needs. With this in mind, she told her NYA chief, "Give it to me on my desk; let me say where it will go. Let me be the boss of that" (NYA Regional Conference Minutes, September 6, 1940). The positive response promoted greater equity in NYA disbursements at the collegiate level and also made Bethune the only black American in New Deal Washington controlling the use of money. In seven years Bethune spent more than six hundred thousand dollars on slightly more than forty-one hundred students.

The Special Negro Fund was secondary to Bethune's advancing the employment and support of qualified blacks on the staffs of state and local organizations—a policy particularly relevant because for seven years the NYA was a decentralized agency in which state directors enjoyed considerable autonomy. By 1941 Bethune's diligent work had led to the employment of black assistants to state directors in twenty-seven states, including all of the South except Mississippi, as well as in New York City and the District of Columbia. Though the administrators' authority varied greatly from one state to another, the fact that they were in place increased both the quantity and quality of the services rendered to black youth. In 1942, when the NYA instituted a regional-based system, it hired black assistants in nine of its eleven office. The new setup greatly augmented opportunities for young black Americans to receive vocational training, and, in addition, virtually guaranteed them employment in defense plants. This meant, in part, that the NYA was a significant channel through which black women became "Rosie the Riveter," a development that director Bethune encouraged.

While employed in the NYA, the politically astute Bethune not only maintained her revered status among both the grass roots and leadership of black America, but she greatly enhanced it. Though continuing to address predominantly white audiences, more frequently she mesmerized black Americans. She also wrote a column in the *Pittsburgh Courier*, the era's premier black weekly. In the fall of 1936 she accepted the presidency of Carter G. Woodson's Association for the Study of Negro Life and History. She swelled the troops of the rising protest movement most literally when she joined the New Negro Alliance's picket line around a drugstore chain that refused to hire black clerks. Of greater importance was her endorsement of A. Philip Randolph's March on Washington Movement in 1941, which led to the celebrated executive order banning racial discrimination in employment in both government and defense industries and the creation of the Fair Employment Practices Commission to monitor compliance.

Aware of her impeccable race leadership credentials, the Roosevelt Administration drafted Bethune to help sell its policies to black America. In both depression and war she did so with gusto, and her efforts contributed to the improving stature of blacks at the national level in the Democratic party coalition. Repeatedly she told blacks that though the doors of opportunity were not open wide enough, the New Deal, with its wide-ranging programs for the economically disadvantaged, signaled the dawn of a new day. She exhorted blacks to join the military without reservation to defeat the Axis powers. Bethune did not just push administration positions, she wholeheartedly backed Roosevelt's reelection campaigns, especially in 1940. Beyond expounding the virtues of the candidate and his programs, Bethune advised Democratic insiders on strategies for appealing to black voters. Invariably she pressed for concrete civil rights initiatives. She saw this as desirable in itself and as a shield against the administration's vulnerability in that area. Moreover, she called upon the Democratic Women's Committee to at least equal its Republican counterpart in sanctioning within the party both structures and visibility for black women—a recommendation subsequently realized.

Bethune promoted the administration in the glow of her cordial ties to Franklin and Eleanor Roosevelt. Exhibiting the full force of his genial personality with Bethune, the president supported her NYA directorship, saw her when she deemed circumstances warranted it, on occasion called her in to visit, extended messages to black organizations when she requested them, and within very narrow limits beyond NYA business acquiesced to her requests as a race leader. Eleanor Roosevelt associated with Bethune in a much closer way both politically and personally. She gained from the black leader a sensitive understanding of the country's racial problems and expert counsel on them. In addition to bringing Bethune into government, Roosevelt championed all her priority causes—her college, the NCNW, the NYA, and civil rights in general. And unlike scores of white female appointees in government who excluded Bethune from their informal support network, the First Lady consistently accorded her every consideration.

Bethune's unrestricted access to the White House, her standing in black America, and the security of her NYA bailiwick augured promisingly for her becoming race representative-at-large in the administration. In its broader context such a position required an individual to keep track of proliferating federal programs, to devise strategies by which black Americans could best obtain a fair share from them, and to work towards implementing them. Though Bethune enjoyed no government authorization for at-large activity, she confidently took this responsibility upon herself.

Bethune understood that at-large effectiveness necessitated competent staff. For this reason, on August 7, 1936, she organized, with the assistance of the U.S. Housing Authority's Robert Weaver, the Federal Council on Negro Affairs, popularly acclaimed as the Black Cabinet. This council was made possible through the New Deal's recruitment into government of more than one hundred black advisers. These professionals embodied the regeneration of a black American political presence lacking in the nation's capital since the demise of Reconstruction. According to Bethune's plan, the cabinet did in fact effect a loose coordination of government programs for blacks. Leaders from the National Urban League, the NAACP, the black press, and other race institutions as individuals and groups often took part it.

The Black Cabinet's most publicly acknowledged service was as facilitator to two precedent-setting national black conferences held in Washington at the Labor Department in January 1937 and January 1939. Though Bethune had prevailed upon the NYA to sponsor them, they focused not so much on youth as on a comprehensive consideration of Negro problems. In these forums, blacks prioritized their needs and recommended policy responses to the government. Bethune not only presided over the proceedings but also the process through which the findings of the conferences were disseminated throughout official Washington from the president on down.

The Black Cabinet's unpublicized work, however, contributed the edge to Bethune's at-large status in government. Members of the black network notified Bethune on an ad hoc basis of any sticky situation that required action from higher-ups. Once alerted, Bethune usually contacted Eleanor Roosevelt, as she did in 1942 after influential whites had created a racial tinderbox in Detroit by attempting to transfer to whites a federally funded housing project built for blacks. Partly as a consequence of Bethune and Roosevelt meeting, word soon passed down to the appropriate parties that the Sojourner Truth Project would indeed house blacks. At regular cabinet meetings, Bethune's salient activity was often receiving information—frequently meticulous analyses and program proposals. Armed with them, she strode forth to interact authoritatively with white individuals and groups on particular aspects of black welfare.

In the early 1950s, Bethune handled with satisfaction the development of Bethune-Volusia Beach, a black resort on the Atlantic Ocean, and the establishment of the Mary McLeod Bethune Foundation, a corporation centered in her home. Moreover, she gloried in promoting Frank Buchman's Moral Re-Armament, an international movement espousing absolute values around which the world's peoples could unite. Beyond these things, Bethune functioned most importantly as a quintessential symbol of achievement and dignity—a status to which twelve honorary degrees attested. As a luminous symbol, she traveled to Haiti, Canada, Switzerland, and Liberia. During the Liberian visit in January 1952 she enjoyed the status of a U.S. delegate to the inauguration of President William Tubman. But on occasion rejection stared her in the face. During the McCarthy hysteria, the

Board of Education in Englewood, New Jersey, denied Bethune a school's platform because she had been labeled a Communist subversive. In response, Americans who knew the vision that had undergirded her life—a vision of a country eschewing segregation and discrimination so as to appreciate the value of individuals regardless of race, color, creed, or gender—rallied to her defense in a movement reversing the board's action. Honors and awards came to Bethune until her death from a heart attack on May 18, 1955.

Bethune wrote articles for several periodicals, including *Journal of Negro History*, *Ebony*, and *Who, The Magazine about People*. She authored chapters in two books, contributed regularly to Bethune-Cookman College's periodical, *The Advocate*, and wrote for NACW, and NCNW Publications. In addition, Bethune wrote a column for the *Pittsburgh Courier* in 1937-1938, and the *Chicago Defender* in the late 1940s and early 1950s, and a small collection of her writings appears in *Mary McLeod Bethune: Her Own Words of Inspiration*.

References

Bethune-Cookman College. *Travels through a Generation*. Daytona Beach, Fla.: 1975.

Bethune, Mary McLeod. NACW Presidential Address, August 2, 1926. Bethune Papers, Amistad Research Center.

———. National Council of Negro Women, Annual Report. October 1941. Bethune Foundation.

Daniel, Sadie Iola. *Women Builders*. Washington, D.C.: Associated Publishers, 1931.

Holt, Rackham. *Mary McLeod Bethune: A Biography*. Garden City, N.Y.: Doubleday, 1964.

Leffall, Dolores C., and Janet L. Sims. "Mary McLeod Bethune—The Educator." *Journal of Negro Education* 45 (Summer 1976): 342-59.

Ludlow, Helen W. "The Bethune School." *Southern Workman* 41 (March 1912): 144-54.

NYA Regional Conference Minutes, College Work Program, September 6, 1940. Bethune-Cookman Archives.

Peare, Owen. *Mary McLeod Bethune*. New York: Vanguard Press, 1951.

Ross, B. Joyce. "Mary McLeod Bethune and the National Youth Administration: A Case Study of Power Relationships in the Black Cabinet of Franklin D. Roosevelt." *Journal of Negro History* 60 (January 1975): 1-28.

Smith, Elaine M. "Mary McLeod Bethune and the National Youth Administration." In Mabel E. Deutrich and Virginia C. Purdy, eds. *Clio Was a Woman: Studies in the History of American Women*. Washington, D.C.: Howard University Press, 1980.

———. "Mary McLeod Bethune." *Notable American Women: The Modern Period*. Vol. I. Cambridge, Harvard University Press, 1980.

Collections

The Mary McLeod Bethune Papers at the Bethune Foundation, Bethune-Cookman College, consist of materials dating from about 1915, covering all phases of Bethune's life. The collection includes correspondence, articles, newspaper clippings, photographs, sound recordings, proceedings of meetings, speeches, and school records. Smaller and more narrowly focused Bethune papers are housed in the college archives, the Amistad Research Center in New Orleans, and the headquarters of the NACW in Washington, D.C. Bethune correspondence and other materials from 1935 to 1955 are located in the National Council of Negro Women Papers, National Archives for Black Women's History, Washington, D.C. Bethune papers are found also in the National Youth Administration records, Record Group 119, National Archives. The most relevant manuscript collections for Bethune's life, other than those cited, are the Mary Church Terrell Papers at the Library of Congress and the Eleanor Roosevelt Papers at the Franklin D. Roosevelt Library, Hyde Park, N.Y.

Copies of *The Advocate* and a number of bulletins are in the P. K. Younge Library of Florida History, University of Florida. Copies of *Aframerican Women's Journal* and *National Notes* are found respectively in the National Archives for Black Women's History and the Tuskegee University Library.

Vertical files containing contemporary newspaper clippings about Bethune are in the Woodruff Library of Atlanta University Center, the Moorland-Spingarn Research Center at Howard University, and the Schomburg Center for Research on Black Culture.

Elaine M. Smith

Camille Billops

(1933-)

Sculptor, printmaker, educator, research collection founder

Known primarily for her unique postmodern ceramic sculptures, Camille Billops's multifaceted artistic talents include printmaking, poetry, book illustration, pottery, drawing, jewelry-making, and most recently, film. Now living and working in New York City, Billops was born on August 12, 1933, in Los Angeles, California, the daughter of Lucious Billops and Alma (Gilmore) Billops. Her parents were maid and cook for wealthy employers until World War II, when they went to work in a defense plant to make more money to send their two daughters to private school. In October 1963 she married James Hatch and they have one daughter, Christa Victoria Billops Hatch Richards.

After graduating from California State College in Los Angeles in 1960 with a B.A., Billops studied sculpture on the West Coast with a Huntington Hartford Foundation grant. In 1973 she received the M.F.A. from the City College of New York. She also studied toward the Doctorat D'Université at the Sorbonne.

Billops has an extensive exhibition, teaching, and academic career. In 1960 she had her first exhibition at the African Art Exhibition in Los Angeles; then in 1963, an exhibit at the Valley Cities Jewish Community Center in Los Angeles. Beginning in 1965 with her one-woman show at the Gallerie Akhenaton in Cairo, Egypt, Billops has exhibited internationally in Hamburg, West Germany, Pakistan, and Taiwan, as well as extensively within the United States. Her most notable recent group exhibits include: ''1938-1988: The Work of Five Black Women Artists'' at the Atlanta College of Art Gallery, with art by Lois Mailou Jones, Howardena Pindell, Faith Ringgold, and Margo Humphrey (1989); and ''The Blues Aesthetic: Black Culture and Modernism'' at the Washington Project for the Arts (1989).

Billops has been a member of the faculty of the art department of Rutgers University, New Jersey; she has also taught at the City University of New York, the New York City Jail (the Tombs), and for the United States Information Service in India. She was artist in residence at the Asilah First World Festival in Morocco in 1978. In another academic capacity, since 1986 Billops has been the art editor of Indiana State University's *Black American Literature Forum*. In 1985 she guest edited a special art issue of the *Black American Literature Forum* and in 1991 she will guest edit a special film issue of the journal.

Black Cultural Research Center Founded

In addition to her academic and teaching activities, Billops cofounded the Hatch-Billops Collection in 1975 with her husband, James Hatch. Possessing more than ten thousand slides and more than one thousand oral histories, thousands of books, photographs, and reference materials, the Hatch-Billops Collection is an extensive archive of black American cultural history. She took primary responsibility for developing the slide collection and for making extensive contributions to the oral history library and the bio-data archives. Hatch-Billops also publishes a journal of interviews with artists, *Artist and Influence,* which features many of Billops's interviews.

Among Billops's most-mentioned works are *The Harlem Book of the Dead* (Dobbs Ferry, N.Y.: Morgan and Morgan, 1978), an anthology in conjunction with poet Owen Dodson, photographer James Van Der Zee, and writer Toni Morrison. Billops's ''signature'' sculpture is the ceramic series, ''Remembering Vienna'' (1986), a set of blocky puzzle pieces, often described as ''funky, folksy and funny.'' Completed after a lengthy stay in Taiwan, ''Remembering Vienna,'' reflects Billops's multicultural aesthetic with its Berlin-style decadence, Argentine-style dance, Chinese-style setting, and African-style geometric outlines. As does much of her work, it deals with tensions and love-hate feelings between man and woman. In a weird, comic, kinetic dynamic, her figures face one another, the male leering with a gold tooth at a woman who scowls and glares, creating a dialogic, interactive mode.

In her recent films, Billops continues her male-female themes, yoking them to family history in an interweaving of personal and private memories. She says, all of her work is about ''the celebration of family . . . private stories and personal vision'' (Wolfe, 26). *Suzanne Suzanne* (1938), a semi-documentary with an interview format, is about Billops's niece, a beautiful young black woman who is a former drug addict. Suzanne struggles to come to terms with her addiction, her memories of child abuse, and her family history. Suzanne's mother, the still-beautiful Billy, was a contestant in the 1976 Mrs. America contest. The two women try to come to terms with each other and with a troubled past. As they are interviewed separately and together, and as they talk with other members of what appears to be a loving family, there emerges the story of the family's domination by Suzanne's handsome alcoholic father, ''who beat her and her mother and asked of them a perfection that eluded him up to his death in 1967'' (Canby, *New York Times,* 27 March 1983). Billops's second film, *Older Women and Love* (1987), is a series of interviews with older women who talk about their relationships. It has been screened at film festivals in West Germany, Quebec, Rotterdam, and Atlanta. In progress is a third color documentary, *Finding Christa.*

Billops's work has been published in *Hamburger Abendblatt Daily, Encore, Essence, Black Enterprise, Yale Theatre,* and *Rasegna* magazines.

Camille Billops often dresses in a style as bold, imaginative, and whimsical as her art. Her long, native-American style braids, western-style hat, many necklaces and charms, and warm, easy smile show the ready humor of this self-styled ''sorceress'' of art.

References

Biography File, Fisk University Library.

Canby, Victor. ''New Directors/Films.'' *New York Times* (27 March 1983).

''Hatch-Billops Collection.'' Archives of Black American Cultural History. Flier.

Hatch, James V. ''The Sorceress of Brooke Street.'' *Black American Literature Forum* 19 (Spring 1985): 3-6. Includes photograph.

''My Life in Art: An Autobiographical Essay.'' *Black Art Quarterly* 1 (Summer 1977): 31-51.

Ploski, Harry A., and James Williams. *The Negro Almanac*. 5th ed. Detroit: Gale Research, 1989. Includes photograph.

Questionnaire, Fisk University Library.

Wolfe, George C. "Camille Billops." *Issue: A Journal for Artists* (Spring 1986): 26-29.

Photographs of Camille Billops are also available from the Hatch-Billops Collection, 491 Broadway, 7th Floor, New York, NY 10012.

Maria K. Mootry

Jane M. Bolin

(1908-)

Judge

When she was thirty-one years old, Jane Matilda Bolin became a judge in the Domestic Relations Court of the City of New York. She became widely known in her position as the first black American woman appointed judge in the United States, and she served on the bench for forty years.

Jane Matilda Bolin was born on April 11, 1908, in Poughkeepsie, New York, one of four children. Her father, Gaius C. Bolin, was born in Poughkeepsie of a Native American mother and a black American father, who was in the wholesale produce business. Gaius C. Bolin was the first black American graduate of Williams College in 1889. He read law in Poughkeepsie with a retired judge, was admitted to the bar, and for more than fifty years practiced law in that city. He was president of the Dutchess County Bar Association. Jane M. Bolin's mother, Matilda (Emery) Bolin, was born in England, immigrated to the United States with her parents who settled in Poughkeepsie.

Jane M. Bolin is an honors graduate of both Poughkeepsie high school in 1924 and Wellesley College, where in 1928 she received an A.B. degree. In 1931 she graduated from Yale University School of Law with an LL.B. To fulfill a requirement of the state of New York, she clerked in her father's law office for six months before taking the New York State Bar examination. She was admitted to the New York Bar and practiced in Poughkeepsie for a brief time. She then moved to New York City, married, and practiced with her attorney husband, Ralph E. Mizelle.

Her rise to success in the legal profession came swiftly. She was appointed an assistant corporation counsel for New York City, a position which she held from 1937 to 1939. Mayor Fiorello La Guardia appointed Bolin to a ten-year term as judge of the Domestic Relations Court of the City of New York on July 22, 1939, making her the first black American woman judge in the United States. The court was subsequently renamed Family Court of the State of New York. She was reappointed for successive ten-year terms by mayors William O'Dwyer, John Lindsay, and Robert F. Wagner, Jr. When retirement became mandatory, she left the bench after forty years on January 1, 1979.

Bolin's retirement was recognized at two retirement dinners, one by the judges of the Family Court of the State of New York, followed by a public symposium held in December 1978. Among the speakers at the symposium were Judge Leon Higginbotham of the United States Court of Appeals and Thomas Emerson, a Yale Law School professor, who in 1931 graduated with Bolin from the law school.

During her career and after retirement as well, Bolin has been involved in professional activities, having joined the Bar Association of the City of New York, the Harlem Lawyers Association, and the New York State Association of Family Court Judges. Bolin also devoted considerable time to community activities, serving on numerous boards, including those of Wiltwyck School for Boys, Dalton School, Child Welfare League of America, New Lincoln School, United Neighborhood Houses, Neighborhood Children's Center, and the local and national NAACP. Expanding her interest and talent in other areas, she became a member of the Committee on Children of New York City, the Scholarship and Service Fund for Negro Students, the Urban League of Greater New York, and the Committee Against Discrimination in Housing.

Bolin has traveled extensively to all the continents except Antarctica, and she has met several heads of state in Africa. She has known several presidents of the United States and was entertained by Eleanor Roosevelt, wife of President Franklin D. Roosevelt, both in New York and in her Hyde Park home. Among her host of friends and associates were noted educator Mary McLeod Bethune and Judge and Mrs. J. Waties Waring of South Carolina. Waring was the judge in the first public school desegregation case.

Retirement for Bolin meant primarily a change in positions. She was a volunteer reading teacher in the New York City public schools for two years. Then she was appointed to the Regents Review Committee of the New York State Board of Regents, which holds hearings involving professional discipline of over thirty-two professions licensed by the New York State Board of Regents. She continues in that capacity.

Jane M. Bolin's intellect, personality, and beauty have been acknowledged by organizations and officials who appointed her to positions as well as by those such as John Powers, head of one of the largest and best-known modeling agencies in the world, whose name for many years has been identified with models and cover girls. He selected among the group of "Powers Girls" of 1949 Bolin. Powers said of Jane Bolin:

> Her regal dignity is compelling indeed. She has admirable control and wonderful capacity for relaxation. Her face shows great qualities of patience and repose (43).

Her many other recognitions include the receipt of LL.D. degrees from Morgan State University, Western College for Women, Tuskegee University, Hampton University, and Williams College.

In 1933 Jane M. Bolin married Ralph E. Mizelle, who died in 1943. Then in 1950 she married Walter P. Offutt, Jr., a minister, who died in 1974. She has one son, Yorke Bolin Mizelle, and one grandchild, Natascha M. Mizelle. She lives in Long Island, New York.

References

Bolin, Jane M. Interview with the author. 30 April 1991; May 1991.

"Lady Lawyers." *Ebony* 2 (August 1947): 18. Cover photograph; others with article.

Powers, John. "The Most Beautiful Negro Women in America." *Ebony* 5 (November 1949): 42-44. Photograph, p. 43.

Robinson, Wilhelmena S. *Historical Negro Biographies.* New York: Publishers Company, 1967. 164.

Who's Who in Colored America. 7th ed. Yonkers, N.Y.: Christian E. Burckel, 1950. 38.

Jessie Carney Smith

Margaret Bonds

(1913-1972)

Composer, musician, educator

A skilled composer who helped reawaken public appreciation of spirituals, among her many musical and creative achievements, Chicagoan Margaret Allison Bonds (Richardson) was born on March 3, 1913. She came from a musical family. Her mother, Estella, was a church organist and music teacher whose home was a gathering place for young black writers, artists, and musicians. Among them were composers Will Marion Cook and Florence Price. Margaret Bonds began to write music at the age of five, a piano piece entitled "Marquette Street Blues." Beginning at that age she studied piano with local teachers Martha Anderson and T. Theodore Taylor. While in high school she studied piano and composition with Price and later with William Dawson.

Bonds first received notice outside the black community in 1932, when, at the age of nineteen, she won the Wanamaker Foundation Prize for her song "Sea Ghost." She became the first black American soloist to appear with the Chicago Symphony Orchestra when she performed Price's Piano Concerto in F minor at the 1933 World's Fair. Inspired by Price's success as a composer, she became determined to focus as much as possible on composition. She received her B.M. (1933) and M.M. (1934) degrees from Northwestern University, where she studied with Emily Boettscher Bogue. Throughout the interwar years she continued to be active as a concert musician, appearing with orchestras and giving solo recitals. She also worked as an accompanist for Abbie Mitchell and Etta Moten, among others. It was also at this time that she opened the Allied Arts Academy of ballet and music for black children in Chicago. Greater scope for her compositional activities, however, did not come until she made a big move.

About 1939 Bonds went to New York City, where she served for a time as editor in the Clarence Williams music publishing firm. One of the few oldtime New Orleans jazzmen to be a success at the business side of music, Williams already was well past his biggest hits. His company, however, offered Bonds an entrée to the New York pop music scene. She wrote a few popular songs, including a successful one, "Peachtree Street," with Andy Razafar in 1939. In 1940 she married Lawrence Richardson. In 1941, with Harold "Hal" Dickinson, she wrote "Spring Will Be So Sad (When She Comes This Year)." Dickinson was founder and leader of the Modernaires vocal quartet, which sang this song with Ray Eberle on a 1941 record by the Glen Miller Orchestra. Some will know it as the flip side of "Perfida," which was a top ten hit. Like many other ballads of the era, "Spring Will Be So Sad" captures the feelings of loss or longing engendered by the World War II.

It was the concert music side, however, rather than the pop, that eventually took precedence in Bonds's career. She studied piano with Djane Herz and composition with Robert Starer at Juilliard. She also received a Rosenwald Fellowship and an award for studying composition with Roy Harris. She then toured, and sometimes performed a piano duet with Gerald Cook on radio broadcasts, in the United States and Canada. In 1944 the duo played an entire series on WNYC. In addition to her own works and those of other contemporary black American composers, her repertoire included black spirituals, the appreciation of which she promoted through her fine arrangements.

In later life Bonds taught in New York at the American Music Wing and served as music director for several of the city's theaters, including the Stage of Youth, the East Side Settlement House, and the White Barn Theater. Before moving to Los Angeles in the 1960s, she also organized a chamber music society to foster the work of black American musicians and composers and established a sight-singing program at Mount Calvary Baptist Church in Harlem. She worked with the Inner City Institute and Repertory Theater and wrote arrangements for the Los Angeles Jubilee Singers.

Greatest Contribution Seen as Composer

Bonds made her greatest contribution as a composer. Her output consists largely of vocal music. In addition to the pop songs, her best-known works are arrangements of spirituals for solo voice or chorus. Some of her arrangements were commissioned and recorded by Leontyne Price in the 1960s. Bonds's arrangement of "He's Got the Whole World in His Hands" is among her best-known. John Lovell, Jr., in his exhaustive *Black Song: The Forge and the Flame*, lists Bonds, along with Cook and Harry T. Burleigh, among twentieth-century composers whose arrangements contributed significantly to widening public enjoyment and appreciation of spirituals.

Among Bonds's other vocal works, the most important are settings of contemporary writers such as John Dos Passos, Robert Frost, and Langston Hughes. Several of her major works are settings of Hughes, including her most popular song, "The Negro Speaks of Rivers"(1941). A worthy alternative to the setting by Howard Swanson, it entered into the repertoire of Rawn Spearman and Lawrence Winter as well as that of Etta Moten. With Hughes she wrote *The Ballad of the Brown King* for vocal soloists, chorus, and orchestra (1954), which at one time was part of the annual musical calender of many black American churches. Other Hughes-inspired works are *Three Dream Portraits* for voice and piano (1959), perhaps the finest of all these Hughes settings, *To a Brown Girl Dead* (1956), the stage work for *Shakespeare in Harlem* (1959), and *Fields of Wonder* for male chorus and piano (1964). Her theater pieces on other texts are *Julie, U.S.A.*, and *Wings over Broadway*. She also wrote a ballet entitled *The Migration* (1964).

Bonds's instrumental music, both piano pieces and orchestral works, tends to be programmatic. Among her more ambitious piano works is, appropriately, the *Spiritual Suite*. *Troubled Water,* based on the spiritual "Wade in the Water," exists in a 1964 version for cello as well as the piano original often programmed by Frances Walker. The best-received of her small handful of orchestral works has been the *Montgomery Variations,* which she wrote in 1965 during the march on Montgomery and dedicated to Martin Luther King, Jr. Among her liturgically-inspired pieces is the Mass in D minor for chorus and orchestra or, alternately, for chorus and organ (1959). Her last major piece is *Credo* for baritone, chorus, and orchestra (1972), which one month after her death was performed by the Los Angeles Philharmonic Orchestra under Zubin Mehta.

Bonds's style was not a highly original one. As an arranger, she was influenced by Cook and Burleigh. "I came to realize," she said, "that most composers at one time or another reflect their friends" (Unpublished reminiscence, 1967, quoted in Abdul, 55). She was comfortable, too, with the received tenets of musical Romanticism, acknowledging Tchaikovsky as a model. At the same time, however, her arrangements of spirituals, with their jazz chords and strong syncopated basses, are among the most ragtime-influenced of all such arrangements. The vitality of her treatments is especially pleasing in uptempo spirituals.

Among Bonds's honors are awards from ASCAP, Alpha Kappa Alpha Sorority, the National Association of Negro Musicians, the National Council of Negro Women, and the Northwestern University Alumni Association.

References

Abdul, Raoul. *Blacks in Classical Music*. New York: Dodd, Mead, 1977.

Contributions of Black Women to America. Vol. 1. Ed. Marianna W. Davis. Columbia, S.C.: Kenday Press, 1982.

Green, Mildred D. "A Study of the Lives and Works of Five Black Composers in America." Ph.D. dissertation, University of Oklahoma, 1975.

Hitchcock, H. Wiley, and Stanley Sadie, eds. *The New Grove Dictionary of American Music*. Vol. 1. New York: Stockton Press, 1986.

Lovell, John, Jr. *Black Song: The Forge and the Flame*. New York, Macmillan, 1972.

Roach, Hildred. *Black American Music: Past and Present*. Vol. 1. Malabar, Fla.: R. E. Krieger Pub. Co., 1985.

Southern Eileen. *Biographical Dictionary of Afro-American and African Musicians*. Westport, Conn.: Greenwood Press, 1982.

Thomas, A. J. "A Study of the Selected Masses of Twentieth-Century Black Composers: Margaret Bonds, Robert Ray, George Walker, and David Baker." Ph.D. dissertation, University of Illinois, 1983.

Variety 266 (10 May 1972): 86.

Lester Sullivan

Matilda Booker

(1887-1957)

Educator

A Jeanes supervisor of "colored" schools in two Virginia counties, Matilda Booker worked tirelessly to improve educational facilities and opportunities for black students and teachers. Her eloquence and fund-raising capabilities were instrumental in opening the first high school for black children in Mecklenburg County.

Matilda Moseley Booker was born in Halifax County,

Virginia. She was raised by her mother and father with assistance from her grandfather. Booker's grandfather had been a slave and had witnessed his owner's efforts to educate her children. He wanted the same education for Booker. His aspirations for his granddaughter were matched by her eagerness to learn.

Booker received her early education at the Staunton River School in Halifax County, Virginia. Her parents then sent her to a United Presbyterian school, Thyne Institute, in Chase City. Here she lived with a cousin whose husband was a janitor for Thyne Institute. In payment for her keep, she did the housework and helped with the janitorial duties at Thyne Institute.

Upon leaving the institute, she began her teaching career with a third-class teaching certificate. She taught for two years for fifteen dollars a month. She advanced her contributions in education by assuming the position of principal of Little Bethel School in Henrico County in 1911.

In 1913 Booker was asked to work as a Jeanes supervisor for twenty-three colored schools in Cumberland County. The position was to be funded by the Anna T. Jeanes Foundation. Having watched Virginia Randolph's work as a Jeanes teacher, Booker was familiar with the demands made upon supervisors' personal and educational resources. This job required twelve months of continuous travel and work in schools, communities, and homes. Money had to be raised for blackboards, chalk, fuel, textbooks, repairs of old buildings, and increases in teachers' salaries. Schools were already closed when Booker arrived on her new job. The school term was short—two to five months depending on the crops in the area. Therefore, she had to campaign in the churches and communities to round up support for the schools.

She later found out that all but two of the twenty-three schools were in need of major repair. She also learned that many of her teachers had not gone beyond the fifth grade and only a few had teaching certificates. Although she faced these and many other challenges, Booker began with prayer and a zest for success. She immediately set out to improve the community and schools. She taught the women and girls how to preserve food. She conducted gardening and canning exhibits.

By the end of her seven-year tenure in the county, Booker had brought about many significant changes and improvements. She convinced parents to support a seven-month school term, which was the same as for white students. Eight new schools were built and thirteen old buildings were remodeled, using monies from the Julius Rosenwald Fund. She sent her teachers to summer school to improve their credentials; when she left, only three did not hold at least an elementary certificate. Booker herself also attended Virginia Normal and Industrial Institute, now Virginia State University, in Petersburg.

Booker increased the teachers' salaries by more than two-fold—up to twenty-seven dollars a month. Her extensive work in the community and at home was useful in raising the money needed for these improvements. In addition, she contributed a large part of her salary to implementing these changes.

In 1916 she married Samuel G. Booker (born in Cumberland County, Virginia, on August 22, 1892), who started a general store with a gas station. While Matilda and Samuel Booker had no children of their own, "their home became the home of a number of boys and girls who for one reason or another needed a "good" home where love, kindness, hard work, learning, going to school, strict discipline, and Christian reverence were the orders of each day" (*Cumberland County Virginia and Its People*, 79). These young people went on to become teachers, registered nurses, and entered other professions. The Booker home became the center of the neighborhood.

Booker's next call was to work in Mecklenburg County as supervisor of the colored schools. She worked there from 1920 to 1935. As with her previous position, she inherited numerous challenges, many of which were familiar to her. The teaching staff was even less qualified: Only five of the seventy-nine teachers even held elementary certificates and further, fifty-one of them held local permits. Once again Matilda Booker arranged for summer classes and extension courses for her teachers. Fifteen years later, almost three-fourths of the one hundred nineteen teachers in the fifty-six colored schools had certificates higher than elementary, many teachers had training beyond high school, eighteen had earned college degrees, and the principal of the county training school had earned a master's degree.

After the elementary schools were firmly established, Booker turned to the establishment of higher levels of training. Matilda Moseley Booker was instrumental in building the first high school for black children in Mecklenburg County. Again, after visiting homes and churches, holding numerous conferences with officials in county and state agencies, and sponsoring many fund-raising activities, she realized her dream. Mecklenburg County Training School at South Hill opened in 1926. In 1930 the first black children received high school diplomas from a Mecklenburg County public high school. Not satisfied with one school for black youth, Booker went on to initiate a fund-raising campaign and to build and open a second high school, West End School, at Clarksville, in 1935.

Matilda Moseley Booker discussed her success in this manner:

> So we gave programs and parties and raised money enough to paint our school on the inside and whitewash it on the outside. . . . We gave our whole life and time to the service of our people. They soon found out that four o'clock and pay-day were not our only objectives, and we found out that where there was a will there was a way. We were with the children at school five days, at the homes of our patrons in the late

afternoons and on Saturdays, and in Sunday school and church services every Sunday (Jenness, 26).

As a part of the Jeanes teacher movement, Matilda Moseley Booker contributed substantially to the education of rural black children in Virginia. Dorothy J. Harris, principal of West End High School in 1956, wrote a fitting tribute to Booker:

> Mrs. Booker did not accomplish all of this alone. Many of the ideas for the improvement of Mecklenburg's schools did not even originate with her—but so strong was her support of every progressive trend, so widespread was her influence with teachers, parents, pupils and community groups, so tirelessly did she work to reach the goal which she and the people of Mecklenburg County had set up—Matilda Moseley Booker and Mecklenburg's progress in public education cannot be separated. We, in Mecklenburg are happy to salute her, proud to acknowledge her contribution to Virginia's public school system—pleased to make it known that this part of the world is better because she lived and worked in it (Harris, 97).

An eloquent speaker, Booker could attract and hold the interest of people from all walks of life—the learned and the unlearned, the affluent and the needy, the Christian and the non-Christian. As she carried her message to the black churches and communities, the message was essentially the same: the importance of good home life, education, the acquisition of land, the importance of voting, and the value of hard work. Her concern was with helping black people develop into first-class citizens and she gave her time and efforts unselfishly to these causes.

References

Cumberland County Virginia and Its People. Marceline, Mo.: Cumberland County Historical Society, 1983.

Harris, Dorothy J. "Matilda Booker." *Virginia Education Bulletin* 37 (March-April 1956): 96-97. A photograph of Matilda Moseley Booker is printed on the cover of this issue.

Jenness, Mary. *Twelve Negro Americans*. New York: Friendship Press, 1936.

Elaine P. Witty

Eva del Vakia Bowles

(1875-1943)

Organization worker

Eva del Vakia Bowles, whose most notable work was done for and with the Young Women's Christian Association and who believed that the YWCA could be the best proving-ground for interracial cooperation, was born in Albany, Athens County, Ohio, to John Hawes Bowles and Mary Jane (Porter) Bowles. The Bowles family was quite distinguished and well-educated. Her father was the first black schoolteacher-principal in Marietta, Ohio. Upon learning that his school was the only segregated school in the area and that it was being kept open only to give him a position, he resigned. Though he had no other job opportunities in sight at the time of his resignation, he followed his family's tradition and was soon one of the first black railway postal clerks in Ohio, possibly in the nation. Her paternal grandfather, the Reverend John Randolph Bowles, a Baptist minister, is believed to be the first black teacher to receive a salary from the public school fund in Ohio. He had also served as chaplain of the Fifty-fifth Massachusetts Regiment during the Civil War. This environment of familial success set the standard that Eva Bowles upheld throughout her lifetime.

In 1883 the Bowles family moved to Columbus, Ohio, and

Eva del Vakia Bowles

Eva Bowles attended public schools there. After graduating, she attended Ohio State and Columbia universities, where she studied music and prepared herself to teach music to the blind. Her first position was at Chandler Normal School, an American Missionary Association institution in Lexington, Kentucky, where she became the first black teacher to be a member of that faculty. Later, Bowles taught in Saint Augustine, Florida; Raleigh, North Carolina; and also at Saint Paul's Normal and Industrial Institute in Lawrenceville, Virginia.

While in Virginia, Bowles met Addie W. Hunton, whose husband, William, was the secretary for "colored work" of the Young Men's Christian Association (YMCA) in New York City. Upon Addie Hunton's recommendation, Bowles was appointed to direct a project for black women under the auspices of the Young Women's Christian Association (YWCA). This project had small beginnings, having been started by a few churchwomen, but it became the 137th Street Branch YWCA, which was for many years the largest black branch in America. As the director of this project, Bowles became the first salaried black YWCA secretary in America.

In 1908, Bowles was called back to Columbus, Ohio, to become the first black caseworker in the Associated Charities of that city. In 1913, she was asked to return to New York to become the secretary of a subcommittee on colored work for the National Board of the YWCA. In 1917, this became a full-fledged committee. She was now in charge of the YWCA's work in the cities for black girls and women. She held this position and some others until her retirement.

In 1917 Bowles was appointed director of the Colored Work Committee of the YWCA's War Work Council. With this appointment she was given an appropriation of two hundred thousand dollars to use in improving the recreational opportunities of black girls and women who were entering industry, most of them for the first time. She began by setting up numerous recreational facilities in industrial centers throughout the nation and in communities where army camps had been placed. As part of her program, she employed an impressive number of outstanding black women as full-time workers and also as lecturers. Among this selected group were May Belcher, Crystal Bird, Sara W. Brown, Myra H. Colson, Ruth Anna Fisher, Josephine Pinyon, Ionia Whipper, and Cordella A. Winn. The establishment of fifteen hostess houses in various army camps, especially the one at Camp Upton, Yaphank, New York, so impressed Theodore Roosevelt that he assigned four thousand dollars of his Nobel Peace Prize to be disbursed as Bowles directed (Davis, 55).

In her 1919 report, Bowles said that "All the problems that face any girl in war times were ours, together with the more serious problem of race relationship and understanding" (Hutson, 214).

Due to the heavy wartime emigration of blacks to the North, there was a sharp rise in the YWCA work among urban black women. This rise was reflected at both the local and national levels. In 1920 the Committee on Colored Work became the Bureau of Colored Work, and in 1922 it became the Council on Colored Work. Bowles, in reporting on the accomplishments of the Colored Work Committee of the War Work Council, says that the war had given colored women the opportunity to prove their leadership ability. She also states that:

> The time is past for white leadership for colored people. As white and colored women, we must understand each other, we must think and plan together for upon all of us rests the responsibility of the girlhood of our nation (*The Work of Colored Women*, quoted in Davis, 55).

Bowles did not want an all-black YWCA, and she fought against those who wanted to create a permanent "colored department." Neither did she want a program where all of the decisions were made by white leadership. Either of these choices would have defeated her basic purpose. Bowles called what she wanted a "branch-relationship," which would allow black women to share fully and equally in all activities of the YWCA, whether as members or workers (*The Work of Colored Women*, quoted in Davis, 55).

It was Bowles's belief that the YWCA was "the pioneer in interracial experimentation" (*New York World*, 8 June 1930, quoted in Davis, 55), and she wanted to continue in this tradition. As a guest speaker on both Negro and white college campuses throughout the United States, at many regional YWCA conferences, and before numerous local boards of city branches, she presented her views concerning this issue. In 1931, when the Council on Colored Work was discontinued as an administrative entity, Bowles and her supporters believed a major battle had been won. However, in April 1932, when she felt the national board's reorganization plan would diminish "participation of Negroes in the policy making" of the association, she resigned, protesting their decision. (Davis, 55). Later, an article in the July 1932 *Woman's Press* stated that "she had the vision of a truly interracial movement in the Y.W.C.A. and has never deviated from it" (Davis, 55).

For a short time after her resignation from the YWCA, Bowles became an executive of the National Colored Merchants Association (CMA stores). However, she was still very interested in the YWCA, and from January 1934 to June 1935, she served as acting secretary of the West End Branch of the Cincinnati YWCA. Her many years of holding important positions had given her a keen insight into political methods, and in the 1940 presidential campaign she served as a Harlem organizer for the Wendell Willkie Republicans.

On June 14, 1943, while visiting her niece, Mrs. Arthur P. Davis, Eva Bowles died of inanition fever caused by gastric necrosis, in Richmond, Virginia. She was buried in the Bowles family plot in Columbus, Ohio.

A glance at the present-day growth of the YWCA gives one an immediate appreciation for the work that Eva Bowles did; however, as this organization expands its horizons to meet future needs, the value and success of Bowles's work will continue to grow and be remembered.

Among Eva del Vakia Bowles's writings are "The Colored Girls in Our Midst," (*Association Monthly*, December 1917), "Race Relations in the Light of Social Research," (*Woman's Press*, February 1929), and "The Y.W.C.A. and Racial Understanding" (*Woman's Press*, September 1929).

References

Bowles, Eva D. "Opportunities For The Educated Colored Woman." In *Black Women in White America: A Documentary History*. Edited by Gerda Lerner, New York: Pantheon Books, 1972.

Davis, Clarice Winn. "Eva del Vakia Bowles." *Dictionary of American Negro Biography*. Edited by Rayford W. Logan and Michael R. Winston. New York: Norton, 1982.

Hutson, Jean Blackwell. "Eva del Vakia Bowles." *Notable American Women: 1607-1950*. Vol. 1. Cambridge: Harvard University Press, 1971.

Norfolk Journal and Guide, 19 June 1943.

Who's Who in Colored America. 4th ed. Brooklyn: Thomas Yenser, 1937.

Woman's Press, September 1943.

Collections

The Moorland-Spingarn Research Center, Howard University, has a mimeographed copy of "Colored Work 1907-1920," which gives an account of Bowles's early years in the YWCA. Clarice Winn Davis has a carbon copy of her letter of resignation from the National Board of the YWCA dated April 1, 1932. Bowles's official reports are in the office of the National Board of the YWCA, New York City.

Phyllis Wood

Mary Elizabeth Bowser

(1839-?)

Union spy

Mary Elizabeth Bowser, whose real-life espionage activities rival anything seen in modern-day films, was born a slave in 1839 on the Van Lew Plantation outside Richmond, Virginia. She was freed after her master John Van Lew's death in 1851, along with the rest of the Van Lew slaves (Bowser, 369). Mary Elizabeth Bowser and another former slave named Nelson remained servants in the Van Lew home. Nelson may have been her father, and, as the story goes, she took him north with her when Richmond fell to Union soldiers.

John Van Lew was a prominent Whig and often entertained Virginia's leading society and distinguished visitors at his Church Hill mansion. His daughter, Elizabeth Van Lew, whose maternal grandfather had at one time been mayor of Philadelphia, received her education in that city and her intellectual stimulation from the Van Lew family. Elizabeth Van Lew's strong antislavery sentiments were public knowledge long before the Civil War. Richmond's townspeople assumed that her antislavery views developed while she was in school in Philadelphia and that her quiet mother, with whom Elizabeth Van Lew had a close relationship, shared her views. "When the war came . . . [she] remained openly loyal to the Union" (Trefousse, 509). Both mother and daughter carried food, books, and clothing to federal officers who were in Libby Prison. Elizabeth Van Lew is said to have helped prisoners escape and provided refuge for them in a secret chamber in the Van Lew home. Much of what was accomplished came because her social standing in Richmond left her free to carry on her work without interference.

Little is known about the private life of Mary Elizabeth Bowser. After the Van Lews freed their house servants, one of them, Mary Elizabeth Bowser, was sent north for education. The Van Lews had also purchased and freed family members of servants who worked in other family households.

Union Spy Activities Begin

Bowser returned to Richmond after the outbreak of the Civil War at the request of Elizabeth Van Lew, who sought her assistance on behalf of the Union war effort (*Afro-American Encyclopedia*, 369). It was recognized that Virginia's most noteworthy female spies for the Union side were the team of Elizabeth Van Lew and Mary Elizabeth Bowser of Richmond (Lebsock, 81). These two brave women, dedicated to the cause, prepared themselves for the task. Elizabeth Van Lew, educated, wealthy, and of a highly-respected family, affected a change in behavior to the extent that she came to be recognized as "Crazy Bet" (Bailey, 81). Mary Elizabeth Bowser, a former slave who became educated, "pretended to be a bit dull" (Alpha Kappa Alpha, 2). These postures enabled the two women to gain entry to places and have freedom of movement that otherwise might have proven difficult, if not impossible.

The Van Lew mansion, located in the Church Hill section outside Richmond, was in close proximity to Libby Prison, where federal officers and Yankee prisoners were kept. The prison stood practically at the base of Church Hill. Some accounts indicate that Elizabeth Van Lew gained entrance to the prison in the capacity as a nurse for the wounded prisoners while, as noted earlier, she was said to have been permitted freely to enter the prison with rations. Her dispatches to the Federal government gained in accuracy and value after she obtained permission to visit the prisoners (Bailey, 15).

The Van Lew mansion, formerly used as an Underground Railroad stop, became under Elizabeth Van Lew's administration a center of Union espionage activities. Elizabeth Van Lew's contacts enabled her to place Bowser as a domestic in the White House of the Confederacy. From here Bowser funneled everything she could learn to Van Lew (Lebsock, 81). She listened to the conversations as she served the Jefferson Davis table and read dispatches as she dusted. She is said to have stolen away each night to the Van Lew mansion, where she recited from memory the military plans discussed at Davis's dinner table (Dannett, 164). Utilizing trusted servants, the information was conveyed by Van Lew to an agent who then relayed it to Ulysses S. Grant, and in return brought her work from Grant and other Union officers (Dannett, 164).

Mary Bowser demonstrated qualities of bravery, high intellect, and trustworthiness. She perfected the role of a dullard while gathering military secrets from the head of state. Her life, as well as that of Elizabeth Van Lew, was at stake, yet she continued to work at this secret mission without detection. There is no doubt that her intelligence activities had an impact on the course of the war (*Afro-American Encyclopedia*, 369).

Bowser recorded her efforts in the war cause in a diary that never reached public view. The precise location of the diary was unknown, but it has been said that a prominent black family in Richmond, Virginia, owned it. Secrecy was allegedly maintained due to a fear that it might arouse "anti-Negro" feeling among the people in Richmond. McEva Bowser of Richmond indicated in telephone interviews with the author on 16 December 1989 and 25 March 1990 that the diary was once in the possession of Rosa Bowser, mother-in-law of Alice Bowser. McEva Bowser discovered the diary in 1952 as she examined the personal effects of her late mother-in-law for the purpose of disposing materials. She thumbed through the document, noting its content, and laid it aside. At that time she considered that it had no particular value. Later she recalled stories about the diary from her in-laws, but that information eluded her at the time. The diary was discarded during the disposal of the personal effects of Alice Smith Bowser (1884-1952) of Richmond.

Mary Elizabeth Bowser rendered an invaluable service to the Union cause through her espionage activities. Recognition was given for this service on October 16, 1977, as reported in the Richmond *News Leader*:

> A tree was dedicated yesterday at West Farms Soldiers Cemetery in the Bronx, in honor of Mary Elizabeth Bowser. Organizers of the tribute hope to trigger national recognition for Miss Bowser, who they say played a vital role in the Union's victory at Richmond, Va., in 1864.

References

Afro-American Encyclopedia. Vol. 2. North Miami, Fla., 1974.

Alpha Kappa Alpha Sorority, Richmond Chapters. Heritage Committee. "Mary Elizabeth Browser [sic]." In *Black Women and Richmond*. Richmond, Va., 1982.

Bailey, James H. "Crazy Bet, Union Spy." *Virginia Calvacade* 1 (Spring 1952): 14.

Bowser, McEva. Interview with Harriette A. Peterson. 16 December 1989; 27 March 1990.

Dannett, Sylvia G. L. *Profiles of Negro Womanhood*. Vol I. Yonkers: Educational Heritage, 1964. 164.

Lebsock, Suzanne. *A Share of Honor: Virginia Women 1600-1945*. Richmond: Virginia State Library, 1987.

News Leader (Richmond), 16 October 1977.

Trefousse, H. L. "Elizabeth L. Van Lew." *Notable American Women 1607-1950*. Vol. III. Cambridge: Harvard University Press, 1971.

Collections

The Van Lew Papers are in the New York Public Library and include information on "Crazy Bet, Union Spy" and activities of women spies of the Van Lew period.

Harriette A. Peterson

Mary E. Branch

(1881-1944)

Educator, social activist

From a humble beginning as a maintenance worker who also helped her washerwoman mother by picking up and delivering clothes to white students and educators, Mary Elizabeth Branch climbed the ranks to become president of a college. Her early exposure to books at home and in her workplace doubtless gave her a lasting appreciation for them, for one of her prime concerns as a college president was the development of the school's library. Her concern also for providing for the educational development of young black students led to the development of a self-help plan through which nearly all of her students worked to support their education. She was the first woman president of Tillotson College in Austin, Texas.

Mary Elizabeth Branch was born May 20, 1881, in

Mary E. Branch

Farmville, Virginia, one of six children born to Tazewell Branch and Harriet (Lacey) Branch. A former slave, Tazewell Branch was the town's shoemaker at the time of Mary Branch's birth. During the Reconstruction period, he was elected to the Virginia State Legislature. Mary Branch reminisced about her father's reading aloud each night for an hour or more from newspapers, magazines, and books. In fact, while the parents had no formal education, they could read and write, and they passed on to their children the knowledge that they had. The parents and children took turns reading good books, magazines, and newspapers and discussed and interpreted the readings in the family setting. Branch would later point out that her father knew the facts of history and could interpret history better than many college graduates.

Farmville, Virginia, was the home of State College, a school for white girls. Mary Elizabeth Branch was thirteen years old when she began to "attend" State College, not that she was admitted to a college for whites, for that would have been illegal under Virginia's segregation laws. Branch stated, "I attended State College in Farmville, for my mother washed the clothes for many of the teachers and the girls and I attended regularly to pick up and deliver the clothes" (Jenness, 89). She also helped in cleaning the floors and walls of the institution. She was assigned to clean the library and often she would pick up books quietly and read them. This act, too, was forbidden.

After completing the eighth grade in Farmville, Branch went off to continue her education at Virginia State College, Petersburg, Virginia. As was the general practice of black colleges at that time, the newly installed land grant college for blacks also contained a high school. Branch completed the high school courses and pursued course work of the normal school, studying teacher education to qualify her to become a teacher.

She and her five siblings worked their way through college. She graduated with honors at an early age. The year following her graduation, Branch began her teaching career in Blackstone, Virginia, as an elementary school teacher. Her salary was twenty-seven dollars and fifty cents a month. Teaching was the main profession open to an educated black American woman in the late nineteenth and early twentieth centuries. In Branch's case, teaching proved to be the perfect occupation.

Early in her teaching career, Branch was called to return to her alma mater in Petersburg to teach English. She remained on the faculty there for several years. Almost immediately "Branch's English," as it was known, became the most popular course on the campus, not because it was the easiest but because it was considered one of the hardest, most interesting, and most beneficial to students. Branch also served as a dormitory director for men and women at different times. Additionally, disciplinary problems and student management became her responsibilities.

Later she continued her studies at the University of Pennsylvania and Columbia University. In 1922 she earned the bachelor of philosophy degree from Columbia University and the master of arts in English in 1925. She also studied toward the doctoral degree in the school of education. With this additional education, she was sought out and appointed dean of women of Vashon High School in St. Louis, Missouri. Vashon High School was the largest school for black American girls in the country. Branch arrived at her highest point in secondary education. She stated that, considering her position at Vashon, the salary was good. "I enjoy the work here even though it is one of the poorest negro neighborhoods" (Jenness, 92). Because of her outstanding work, the school board transferred her to a better-paying position in the normal school. She asked to be transferred back to the high school. There she felt she could be of greater service to those who were most needy and where education was highly respected.

Tillotson College Appoints Its First Woman President

To Branch's great surprise, there came a call from the American Missionary Association for her to become president of Tillotson College in Austin, Texas. The college was one of six black colleges founded and supported by the American Missionary Association (AMA). Tillotson was at a critical point in its history, and a strong leader would be needed. Since the school was now a woman's college, the AMA decided that a woman should be appointed president. The United States Department of Education had just surveyed the black colleges and as result of its findings recommended that Tillotson should be closed. The association looked for someone in the field of public education. On two different occasions, Branch refused to accept the position. The career would mean giving up an excellent salary as well as turning down an offer at the St. Louis City College to teach summer school. She could earn twice the salary the American Missionary Association could afford to pay the president of Tillotson. She reassessed the matter and found a compelling reason to accept the presidency. "I thought of the number of white teachers who had gone south for years since the Civil War." Branch also "prayed over the matter and finally got a definite feeling that I should go" (Jenness, 93-94). There were those, however, who doubted a woman's ability to serve effectively as president of a college. One of these was a prominent Baptist minister who "felt that the School was doomed for failure in choosing a Woman Executive but this minister lived to see the mistake which he made" (Shackles, 24).

The school was in a terrible condition, and the AMA had no money to give to support the budget. However, Branch was given a free hand. Working with nine new professors, the rebuilding process was begun with the development of a five-year plan. The new president gave her first attention to the sad condition of the library, which contained 3,000 volumes, many dilapidated. She wrote to thousands of her friends and acquaintances requesting books—new and used. She besieged second-hand bookstores of Austin, Texas, to help the college's library. Steadily the volumes were brought up to 12,000, as required by the Southern Association of Colleges and Schools, the regional accrediting agency. Branch supported the interest of the school's graduates, who expressed a desire for the institution to return to coeducational status. She felt that money could be used to educate young black men and women as well, and concluded that "it is more realistic to have the boys and girls trained together" (Shackles, 25).

The physical plant was upgraded through a difficult and long fund-raising program. The primary problem now was how to persuade more academically talented students to study at the college. A plan of self-help for students was developed through which ninety percent of the college expenses could be earned while working on campus. In this instance a student would not have to leave every other year to find employment to earn the required one hundred eighty dollars in annual fees.

Before Branch arrived in 1930, only one faculty member at the college had earned a master's degree. By 1933, under her spirited leadership, the entire faculty had master's degrees and many were planning for advanced graduate study. Viewing all the progress, a visitor once asked, "How did you get the money to do all of this?" The answer the faculty member gave was, "Our President knows how to make a little go a very long way" (Jenness, 100).

In recognition of her outstanding contribution to higher education, Mary Elizabeth Branch was awarded two honorary degrees, the LL.D. degree from Howard University—of which she was the first recipient—and the Doctor of Pedagogy awarded by Virginia State College. "The crowning achievement of Miss Branch's administration was the securing in December of 1943 of the class 'A' rating for Tillotson College from the Southern Association of Colleges and Secondary Schools," the regional accrediting agency ("The Life and Work of the late Mary E. Branch," 3). She was the only black woman president of a senior college accredited by SACS at that time.

Mary Branch became president of the local NAACP and joined various clubs. Her love for books led her to assist in organizing a book-a-month club. Branch and Mary McLeod Bethune were good friends, and the close relationship between Bethune and Eleanor Roosevelt often meant that Branch would join Bethune in her many conferences with President Franklin Roosevelt and his wife, Eleanor.

Mary Branch was an attractive, charming woman who was always well-groomed. "Although she never married . . . she encouraged those around her to marry and develop wholesome families. She was called a 'matchmaker.'" She used home economics training in the school to achieve her goals for young women: "We do our best to make out girls scientifically domestic for its helps them both to get a job and keep a husband" (Shackles, 25). Tillotson's young women were on the average very attractive and they were highly respected in the community. Branch often expressed pride in them, and she adopted one young lady, La Flourah Bledsoe, as her own daughter.

Mary Elizabeth Branch died on July 6, 1944, in a Camden, New Jersey, hospital from an unsuccessful operation on an internal goiter. The college and the educational community mourned the loss of a woman with a big sympathetic heart who left ambitions that would spur, inspire, and challenge black youth. She was a forceful and efficient executive, yet gentle and kind in the educational, civic, and religious circles in which she moved.

References

Jet 25 (11 August 1963): 11.

Jenness, Mary. "Making Bricks without Straw." In *Twelve Negro Americans*. New York: Friendship Press, 1936.

"The Life and Work of the Late Mary E. Branch." Tillotson College *Bulletin*. (January 1945): 3-4.

Shackles, Chrystine I. *Reminiscences of Houston Tillotson College*. Austin, Tex.: privately printed, 1973.

Who's Who in Colored America. 4th ed. Brooklyn: Who's Who in Colored America, 1937.

Collections

Archives of the Downs-Jones Library at Houston-Tillotson College, Austin, Texas, contain correspondence, memoranda, ledgers, photographs, and a portrait of Mary Elizabeth Branch.

Reavis L. Mitchell, Jr.

Carol Brice

(1918-1985)

Singer

Carol Lovette Hawkins Brice, a contralto concert singer, was born April 16, 1918, in Sedalia, North Carolina. Her father, John Brice, was a Presbyterian minister and schoolteacher from Indianapolis, Indiana. The Reverend Mr. Brice served as a chaplain in World War I, and because his absence from the family subjected his young wife, Ella (Hawkins) Brice, to great strain, the one-year-old Carol, youngest of four children, was placed with her aunt, Charlotte Hawkins Brown, who had founded Palmer Memorial Institute, a school for black children in Sedalia. She attended school at Palmer, and after finishing a junior college course there, enrolled at Talladega College in Talladega, Alabama.

Her unusual vocal talent became apparent early in life, when she was about three years old. As a child alto prodigy, she traveled with her school's Glee Club. At age fourteen, Carol Brice toured as soloist with the Palmer Institute Singers, and she continued to win admiration for her singing while in college. She took her bachelor of music degree from Talladega College in 1939 and enrolled that same year at Juilliard School of Music in New York City. At Juilliard she studied with Francis Rogers and served as a soloist at St. George's Episcopal Church in New York, where she worked with Harry T. Burleigh, a noted black American baritone, for five consecutive years, 1939-1943. Brice auditioned for and won a fellowship at the Juilliard School. In 1941 she sang at a concert celebration of the third inauguration of Franklin D. Roosevelt as president of the United States. While still a student, she appeared in Mike Todd's production of *The Hot Mikado*, starring Bill "Bojangles" Robinson, at the New York World's Fair of 1939. It was during the run of the Mikado that she met Thomas Carey, a fellow member of the chorus, who was from Louisiana. They were married at Christmas time, 1942, and a son was born in 1944.

In 1944 Carol Brice won the Walter W. Naumberg Award for laudable performance as a singer, becoming the first black American to do so. That award made possible a Town Hall debut, which took place on March 13, 1945, and drew high praise from the New York critics. Soon after the Town Hall concert, Brice presented a televised recital for the Columbia Broadcasting System and later that year performed as a soloist with the Pittsburgh Symphony orchestra. She subsequently sang with the Boston Symphony in 1946 and with the San Francisco Symphony in 1948.

Brice Takes Stage Roles

On stage, Carol Brice performed the role of the Voodoo Princess in Clarence Cameron White's *Ouanga*, which was staged at the Metropolitan Opera in 1956 and at Carnegie Hall as well. She played Addie in Blitzstein's *Regina*, Kakou in Arlen's *Saratoga*, Maude in *Finian's Rainbow* (1960), Queenie in Jerome Kern's *Show Boat*, and Maria in Gershwin's *Porgy and Bess* (1961, 1976). She was Harriet Tubman in *Gentlemen, Be Seated* (1963), and from 1967 to 1971 appeared in *Carousel*, *Show Boat*, and *Porgy and Bess* at the Vienna Volksoper.

Carol Brice toured extensively with her brothers Eugene and Jonathan, who served as her accompanist. Eugene Brice was a graduate of Juilliard and sang in numerous Broadway musical productions. Jonathan had served during World War II with General Patton's Third Army. He also sang with the Robert Shaw Chorale and the New York City Opera. Loelita Brice, their sister, married and moved to Philadelphia. In 1958 Carol Brice and her brothers were presented in concert at New York's Town Hall.

Carol Brice recorded extensively. Her best-known recordings, produced on the Columbia label, include Gustav Mahler's "Songs of a Wayfarer," with Fritz Reiner and the Pittsburgh Philharonic Orchestra; Falla's *El Amor Brujo*; R. Nathaniel Dett's *The Ordering of Moses*; and *The Grass Harp*, by Richardson. She won a Grammy for her recording of *Porgy and Bess*.

In 1974 Carol Brice joined the music faculty of the University of Oklahoma at Norman, where she and her husband, also a member of the music department, established the Cimarron Circuit Opera Company. She continued to give recitals and to sing in various oratorios and operatic productions concurrently with the discharge of her teaching duties. She often performed jointly with her husband. In 1977, Brice and Carey were named Oklahoma Musicians of the Year.

Critics Praise Brice's Singing Qualities

The voice of Carol Brice has been described as one of the most outstanding voices of the twentieth century. Serge Koussevitsky called hers a "universal" voice, one that embodied the best characteristics of her predecessors and appealed to audiences of widely-differing cultures. But, said Neil Scott, writing in the Winter 1947 issue of *Opportunity* magazine, "it would be wrong to say that Miss Brice is like everybody else, because what she really is and hopes to be is the 'First Carol Brice,' for out of a soul keenly tuned to the feelings of life, pain, hope, anger and despair of people great and small, she takes her golden voice and expresses through it the composer's basic emotions of humanity. Therefore, when you hear a Brice concert, you, too, will get that feeling of universality" (94). Her voice has been compared to those of Schumann-Heink, Sophie Braslau, and Marian Anderson. One critic noted that her voice seemed "to have a soprano quality as well as one of the most velvety of deep contralto timbers," while an eminent English conductor declared, "I would unhesitatingly put Carol Brice in the category of genius."

Carol Brice died in Norman, Oklahoma, on February 15, 1985.

References

De Lerma, Dominique-René. "Carol (Lovette Hawkins) Brice." *New Grove's Dictionary of American Music*. Edited by H. Wiley Hitchcock and Stanley Sudie. New York: Macmillan, 1986.

Ewen, David. *Living Musicians*. New York: Wilson, 1940.

Guzman, Jessie Parkhurst, et al., eds. *Negro Yearbook*. New York: Wise, 1952.

Scott, Neil. "Carol Brice Is Just a Typical American Girl." *Opportunity* 25 (Winter 1947): 93-94.

Southern, Eileen. *Biographical Dictionary of Afro-American and African Musicians*. Westport, Conn.: Greenwood Press, 1982.

Turner, Patricia. *Afro-American Singers*. Minneapolis: Challenge Productions, 1977.

Who's Who of American Women. 8th ed. Chicago: Marquis, 1973.

Lois L. Dunn

Gwendolyn Brooks

(1917-)

Poet, writer, lecturer

Poet Gwendolyn Elizabeth Brooks was born June 7, 1917, in Topeka, Kansas, the daughter of David Anderson Brooks and Keziah Corinne (Wims) Brooks. She graduated from Wilson Junior College in 1936. Over the years she has been the recipient of numerous honorary doctorates—more than fifty of them; she is a member of the American Academy of Arts and Letters, and, in Chicago, a member of the Society of Midland Authors. Her poetry has been celebrated and criticized by both black and white audiences; her writing has reflected changes in her life and in society, but her talent and skill with language have made her voice impossible to ignore.

There was one other child in the family, Raymond (now deceased), who was sixteen months younger and whose photographs as a child and grown man are in Brooks's

Gwendolyn Brooks

autobiography, *Report From Part One* (1972) (hereafter referred to as *RPO*) It is in this book, also, that one finds a joyful accounting of the poet's youth, which helps to explain Gwendolyn Brooks's attitudes about family, race, friendship, teaching, learning, and all that has gone into the making of an American poet of Brooks's talent and stature. She had a happy and secure childhood, surrounded by loving and supportive parents. Her mother went back to her home in Topeka to give birth to Brooks, but both returned five weeks later; thus, Brooks is (and considers herself) a native Chicagoan. As she said in a 1967 interview with Paul M. Angle, "I intend to live in Chicago for *my* forever" (*RPO*, 136: the emphasis on "*my* forever" probably refers to the sentiments in her poem "Friend," in *Beckonings*).

According to Brooks's mother, the poet started writing at age seven, and Brooks writes, "I have notebooks dating from the time I was 11, when I started to keep my poems in composition books. My mother decided that I was to be the female Paul Laurence Dunbar" (*RPO*, 169). Thus, the habit of writing as well as reading was established early. Her mother had been a teacher; her father, a janitor and a man of character and impressive intelligence who had wanted to be a doctor and had studied premedicine for a year and a half at Fisk University, read stories and sang songs to the children. Thus, the habits of literature and learning were an early part of Gwendolyn Brooks's life.

Brooks's high school years were punctuated with easily-remembered highs and lows, some of which were recorded in her 1971 interview with Ida Lewis: "No blacks were teaching in that school, which was Englewood High. I'd gone to several high schools previously. I'd spent one year at Hyde Park Branch, which I hated. It was my first experience with many whites around. I wasn't much injured, just left alone. I realized that they were a society apart, and they really made you feel it. Then I left and went to Englewood, and graduated from it. Englewood was a mixed school; I seemed to get along better there, though I still wasn't popular. There, all blacks were somewhat alone (*RPO*, 172). (She had spent her second year at Wendell Phillips High.) She knew her darker color was a barrier to great popularity among the other students, and she was quieter and shyer than most, but as she also said to Lewis: "I wasn't willing even to try to become so [more popular]. It seemed impossible to change myself entirely . . . " (*RPO*, 172).

This was the social creature speaking, for the poet was reading and learning about newer poets such as T. S. Eliot, Ezra Pound, e. e. cummings, William Carlos Williams, and Wallace Stevens. James Weldon Johnson, to whom she sent poems, wrote that she had talent but should read modern poetry. (Her actual meeting with Johnson later was a disappointment, for he could not recall having written to her with encouragement—"I get so many of them [poems], you know," he said to her, *RPO*, 173.) She received enthusiastic encouragement from Langston Hughes, who read her poems right away upon meeting her when she was sixteen. His enthusiasm served as inspiration to the young Brooks, and years later, she and her husband gave him a party in their two-room kitchenette (*RPO*, 70-1).

The September following her high school graduation, Brooks attended the newly opened Woodrow Wilson Junior College, which, she said, opened just at the right time, for "if it hadn't opened its doors right then, perhaps I would not have had those two years of college I did get." Since that time, Gwendolyn Brooks has garnered so many honorary doctorates that the length of her "official" education becomes less important in relation to knowledge.

It was two years after she graduated from Wilson that Gwendolyn Brooks met her future husband, her "first lover," Henry Lowington Blakely II. He and she give the same accounting of how they met when both were twenty-one: Blakely, a writer and one of two blacks who worked on the student newspaper, the *Wilson Press*, was told by more than one person that there was "a shy brown girl who attended Junior NAACP meetings and wrote poetry" (*Say That*, 6). He went to a meeting where Brooks and her friend, Margaret Taylor (later Burroughs, of the DuSable Museum), were seated and Taylor, espying the young man called out: "Hey Boy . . . This girl wants to meet you." Brooks later told Blakely that on seeing him she confided to Margaret, "That's the man I'm going to marry" (*Say That*, 6). And marry they did, sharing the good and the bad for thirty years until they separated in 1969: "We understood that our separation was best for the involved. (That won't be enough for the reader but it is enough for me.) The reasons for the failure of a marriage are the proverbial legion. But is 'failure' always quite the word? The relationship between a man and a woman properly develops from one stage to another, and it sometimes properly occurs that the last stage, to somebody's or nobody's surprise, is a dignified separation" (*RPO*, 58). In 1973 the Blakelys, nevertheless, reunited,and they celebrated their golden anniversary by going out to dinner on September 17, 1989.

During the 1940s and 1950s Gwendolyn Brooks lived the life of a learner and achiever in the world of poetry. In 1941, Inez Cunningham Stark, who can be described as a fugitive from the "Gold Coast" (a rich and fashionable area of Chicago), came to the South Side Community Art Center to present a class on modern poetry. "This class of hers was very alive. We were encouraged to tear each other to pieces. . . . It helped me to have somebody tell me what he thought was wrong with my work, and then bounce the analysis back and forth" (*RPO*, 174). Many of the members of this group became distinguished in their chosen fields, for example, Margaret Burroughs and poet Margaret Danner Cunningham, who for a brief time was an editor on the staff of *Poetry*. It was a time when Brooks believed integration was the answer to the racial problems that plagued the United States. As she expressed it: "1941 through 1949 was a party era" (*RPO*, 68). Brooks has recently described that time to this biographer: "These were talking parties. We discussed what was happening in the world and what *we* could do to correct it."

It was also a stimulating time for her writing. She received her first public award in 1943 from the Midwestern Writers' Conference and was asked subsequently by Emily Morison of Knopf if she had enough poems for a book. She sent forty to the editor, who liked the "Negro poems," and she asked Brooks to submit a bookful of those sorts of poems. Brooks revised her manuscript with an emphasis towards presenting her "Negro poems," and rather than try Knopf a second time Brooks sent them to Harper and Brothers. Although there were some reservations about the poem "Ballad of Pearl May Lee,"—the senior editor had received enthusiastic comments from Richard Wright—her book, entitled *A Street in Bronzeville*, was accepted and appeared in 1945. Brooks, in *Report From Part One*, abandons the reader at the point where she has the joy of receiving the author's copies of this first book, but *A Street in Bronzeville* launched her career. The reviewer in the *New Yorker* wrote: "She writes with style, sincerity, and a minimum of sentimentality" (88). And in *Poetry*, the reviewers noted: " . . . she shows a capacity to marry the special quality of her racial experience with the best attainments of our contemporary poetry tradition" (164). She also received friendly and encouraging letters from Claude McKay and Countee Cullen (*RPO*, 201). Indeed, Gwendolyn Brooks had arrived in the world of poetry.

In 1945 she was one of the ten women to receive the *Mademoiselle* Merit Award for Distinguished Achievement. This was, indeed, a heady time, for she went to New York where she met Richard Wright and Ralph Ellison, among others. This was a time when she was a strong admirer of such contemporary poets as John Crowe Ransom, Wallace Stevens (who later asked "Why did they let the *coon* in to Pulitzerland?"), Joyce, Eliot, Langston Hughes, and Merrill Moore, as well as older writers within the accepted canon of universal expression, such as Chekov, and Dickinson. The concerns in the poetry of her first book, to be sure, were of the black community, but the style of her writing was "white," steeped as she was in "serious" literature by such poets as Shakespeare, Milton, and Donne. Houston Baker remarks on this when he observes some of her writing possesses "the metaphysical complexities of Apollinaire, Eliot, and Pound" (Baker, 23).

Annie Allen (1949) appeared at a time when Brooks had been working hard on both poetry and prose. A proposed novel, *American Family Brown*, was rejected by her publisher in 1947, and thereafter she concentrated on the poetry that appeared in *Annie Allen*, including the long piece, "The Anniad." The promise of her book was fulfilled, although there were critics who took Brooks to task for the high tone of her language and some obscurities resulting from this. Rolfe Humphries, while praising Brooks, believed her stress on style and language was too pronounced. He complained of being distressed "when she seems to be carried away by the big word or the spectacular rhyme; when her ear, of a sudden, goes all to pieces" (*Nation*, 306).

Pulitzer Prize Awarded for Poetry

The more serious criticisms of *Annie Allen* (her friend don l. lee wrote in the preface of *Report From Part One* that the book "seems to have been written for whites," (*RPO*, 17) did nothing to repel the awarders of the Pulitzer Prize in 1950. Gwendolyn Brooks was the first black, female or male, to receive a Pulitzer Prize of any sort for her book of poetry, *Annie Allen*, a book don l. lee proclaimed to have been "unread by blacks" (RPO, 17).

Maud Martha (1953) is an autobiographical novel and, in the author's belief, this form "is a better testament, a better thermometer, than memory can be" (RPO, 190). But the novel remains a manipulation of Brooks's experiences and the people she had known or shared deep moments with, not a record of absolutely true happenings. In a rereading of this book, scholar Mary Helen Washington suggests deep feminist values that were not acknowledged when the book was first published, saying:

> Current feminist theories which insist that we have to learn how to read the coded messages in women's texts—the silences, the evasions, the repression of female creativity—have helped me to reread *Maud Martha*, to read interiority in this text as one of the masks Maud uses to defend herself against rage. But if she cannot rely on the spoken word for help, she certainly appropriates power in more concealed ways—she writes her husband out of the text midway, she reduces her mother to a vain, pretentious fool, and she assigns her beautiful sister to a static end in a compromising marriage (Washington, 260).

Brooks's opinion of such an interpretation of her work consists of one word—"BUNK."

Brook's first of four books of children's poetry was published in 1956; adult collections followed: *The Bean Eaters* (1960), *Selected Poems* (1963), and *Riot* (1969). Ezekiel Mphahlele has pointed out, "Miss Brooks is essentially a dramatic poet, who is interested in setting and character and movement. . . . She is interested in bringing out in its subtlest nuances the color of life that conflict eventually creates" (Mphahlele, 26). *The Bean Eaters* allowed Brooks the full range of her poetic involvement in the lives of black folk. She writes of the murder of Emmett Till, she cuts through the bravura of young black boys in "We Real Cool," she is biting and sardonic in "Lovers of the Poor," and she describes, ironically, the visit of a black reporter to Little Rock in 1957, ending the poem with a line she now rejects, "The loveliest lynchee was our Lord." (She has explained recently to this biographer, "So many 'lynchees' today—body and spirit—I feel it's *foolish* to pick out one as having suffered more exquisitely than any other, even though we're citing *The Lord*!") This last book before her spectacular and surprising new direction book, *In the Mecca*, was seen by one critic as "Brooks's ascent to the foothills of her grand heroic style. From the new level, we see the power of skill and commitment combining with her narrative gift. We note the inclusion of more types of characters, white as well as black; the use of satire along with irony; and projection into white consciousness" (Melhem, 131).

She had reached a high point in her writing career, but she was to change soon and follow the moods of her own people more closely in the poetry she produced.

Black Writers' Conference Influences Work

In the Mecca (1968) seemed to burst upon the scene after a 1967 visit Brooks made to the Second Black Writers' Conference at Fisk University, which she described in 1971 as discovering "what has stimulated my life these past few years: young people, full of a new spirit. They seemed stronger and taller, really ready to take on the challenges. . . . I was still saying 'Negro,' for instance" (RPO, 167).

It has been noted that *In the Mecca* started out as a novel, and it had various revisions before appearing as it stands now—a book of poems that presents a microcosm of black life in an all-too-crowded urban setting. The title poem is long (807 lines) and poignant, detailing the search for Pepita, the young daughter of Mrs. Sallie Smith, who has just come home from working in some white person's fine house:

> SUDDENLY, COUNTING NOSES, MRS. SALLIE SEES NO PEPITA! 'WHERE PEPITA BE?' (*World*, 385).

The reader is introduced, bit by bit, to certain types of characters who inhabit the Mecca, that teeming crowded building that maintains not only poverty and failed dreams, but violence. In search of Pepita, then, black life and thought are explored in vignettes of real-life situations of the city black during the mid-1960s.

Poems in the second section of the book are short and include the ones dedicated to Medgar Evers and Malcolm X.

Gwendolyn Brooks was moving more deeply and inextricably into her native black world. As she wrote: "Until 1967 my own blackness did not confront me with a shrill spelling of itself. I knew that I was what most people were calling 'a Negro'; I called myself that, although always the word fell awkwardly on a poet's ear; I had never liked the sound of it" (*RPO* 83). And in the interview with Claudia Tate, Brooks stated emphatically: "[Before that time] I wasn't writing consciously with the idea that blacks *must address* blacks, *must write* about blacks. . . . I'm trying [now] to create new forms, trying to do something that could be presented in a tavern atmosphere" (Tate, 40, 41). *In the Mecca* was Brooks's declaration of independence from integration, because by 1969 she had changed her relationships with Harper's and was publishing exclusively with blacks. (Her last book published by Harper's came out in 1971—*The World of Gwendolyn Brooks*.) As she told one interviewer, "I have no intention of ever giving my books to another white publisher" (Tate, 45). In 1969 Brooks was nominated for but did not receive a National Book Award for *In the Mecca*.

Brooks's post-1969 books reflect her reaching out to her ordinary black readers in language as well as subject matter, although she has been careful to stress: "I don't want to say these poems have to be simple, but I want to *clarify* my language. I want these poems to be free. I want them to be direct without sacrificing the kinds of music, the picturemaking I've always been interested in" (Tate, 44).

Riot (1969), *Aloneness* (1971), *Broadside Treasury* (1971), *Jump Bad* (1971), *Report From Part One* (1972), and *Beckonings* (1975) were published by Broadside, the Detroit-based press started by Dudley Randall (black poet, librarian, and Poet Laureate of Detroit). *Blacks*, published in 1987 by the David Company (Brooks's own company), is an anthology of her published works from the beginning to 1987. This collection contains many poems that are not in *The World of Gwendolyn Brooks*, such as "A Catch of Shy Fish," "The Life of Lincoln West," and "The Near-Johannesburg Boy."

The pilgrimage to one's past is a journey many writers make, and Gwendolyn Brooks took hers to Africa in 1971, where she discovered the ambivalences of connecting with a culture that was her own, but not quite. As she observed in her hotel—" . . . a wastebasket with 'leopard' cloth. A 'Renoir' on a wall. (White women. Pensive white women, plumply sitting.) There is a fat elephant on my key" (*RPO* 87). She meets with courtesy and indifference; she scrapes what she can to bring her together with her past. She will go again.

Poetry Spans Two Periods

The poetry of Brooks spans two distinct periods, pre-1967 and post-1967, or to quote Brooks: "The forties and fifties were years of high poet-incense; the language-flowers were thickly sweet. Those flowers whined and begged white folks to pick them, to find them lovable. Then—the sixties: independent fire!" (*Say That*, 1). Some might also say she is currently in stage three, which is an amalgam of the previous ones with a widening of both form and content. Despite what seems a stated philosophical dichotomy in Brooks's work, her friend Lerone Bennett has aptly pointed out: " . . . she has always written about the sounds, sights and flavors of the Black community" (*Say That*, 14). And another close friend, fellow-poet, and editor of two of her books, Haki R. Madhubuti (formerly don l. lee) has stated: " . . . her greatest impact has been as key player in the literature of African-American people" (*Say That*, xi). What is important, then, is an understanding that the writings of Gwendolyn Brooks, whether poetry or prose, have been directly involved around the ethos of blacks.

There is richness and an erudite adherence to form and language in Brooks's early poetry. She demonstrated her deep knowledge of the sonnet form (Petrarchan, Spenserian, Shakespearean, and variations of them), used alliteration with rich vocabulary, grace, wit, and slanting rhyme. Houston A. Baker, Jr., has observed: "Her ability to dislocate and mold language into complex patterns of meaning can be observed in her earliest poems and in her latest volumes. . . ." (Baker, 28).

But Brooks herself would not like to have her poetry discussed in relationship only to her early poems, for she is a pure poet in whatever stage of development one might discover her. She tours a great deal, having forty years ago overcome her shyness to speak before her audiences, and she is a generous poet who has continued to work with children and prisoners. She uses her own money to pay winners in her poetry contest (*Chicago Tribune*, 27 June 1989, 1:15). On June 11, 1989, she was feted at Navy Pier in Chicago by fifty poets reading to her in celebration, inexplicably, of her seventieth birthday two years after it had occurred, and she was given a $48,000 lifetime achievement award in 1989 from the National Endowment for the Arts, which was announced at the June 11 festival. In 1990 she became the first scholar to hold the newly-established Gwendolyn Brooks Distinguished Chair of Creative Writing at Chicago State University.

During April of 1989, Gwendolyn Brooks participated in the celebration of National Library Week in her neighboring towns of Hammond and Gary, Indiana. She was scheduled to visit Gary after her session in Hammond, but she was nearly an hour late. The crowded room of children and others was warm, and the library board members, as well as the director, valiantly filled the time with information and shared concern about the importance of libraries and literature. Brooks finally arrived and came down a side aisle, smilingly, even though she had been kept overlong by her previous host (Brooks is a punctual person), and she said to her anxious audience: "Believe me, I'll stay as long as you want me. I'll sign each slip of paper, or book. . . ." And she did, with grace and charm and open good humor. And love.

One of her earliest remarks was to ask for Darlwin Carlisle, a young girl who had lost both legs to her knees when her mother left her abandoned in a freezing room, who was there with classmates. Brooks wanted to celebrate the spirit of that brave and lovely girl who scampers about on artificial legs like any other child, and she was photographed with the children after her presentation. The instant Brooks entered the room there was an aura of joy and goodwill and love for the truth about life, even its bad aspects, through the medium of poetry. Her presence is a talisman of hope and "can do" for young people, both black and white; but especially for the young black, she represents accomplishment coupled with extraordinary humanism. "Waiting for the Paladin" ("The Anniad")—Gwendolyn Brooks is always worth the wait, as the unspoken endorsments demonstrate the moment she steps into a room.

References

Baker, Houston A., Jr. "The Achievement of Gwendolyn Brooks." *CLA Journal* (September 1972): 23-31.

"Books." *New Yorker* 21 (22 September 1945): 88.

Brooks, Gwendolyn. *Report From Part One*. Detroit: Broadside Press, 1972.

———. *The World of Gwendolyn Brooks*. New York: Harper & Row, 1971.

Humphries, Rolfe. "Verse Chronicle." *Nation* (24 September 1949): 306.

Kent, George E. *A Life of Gwendolyn Brooks*. Lexington: University Press of Kentucky, 1989.

Melhem, D. H. *Gwendolyn Brooks: Poetry and The Heroic Voice*. Lexington: University Press of Kentucky, 1987.

Mphahlele, Ezekiel. *Voices in the Whirlwind, and Other Essays*. New York: Hill and Wang, 1972.

Say That the River Turns: The Impact of Gwendolyn Brooks. Edited by Haki Madhubuti. Chicago: Third World Press, 1987.

Tate, Claudia, ed. *Black Women Writers at Work*. New York: Continuum, 1983.

Washington, Mary Helen. "'Taming all that anger down': Rage and silence in Gwendolyn Brooks's *Maud Martha*." *Black Literature and Literary Theory*. Edited by Henry Louis Gates, Jr. New York: Metheun, 1984.

Wilder, Amos N. "Sketches from Life." *Poetry* 67 (December 1945): 164-66.

Collections

The papers and literary effects of Gwendolyn Brooks are scheduled to go to Chicago State University, where the world center for the study of Brooks is to be established. Additional papers and letters by Brooks are in the Woodruff Library at Clark-Atlanta University. The typescript for *Annie Allen* is located in the library of the State University of New York at Buffalo.

Margaret Perry

Charlotte Hawkins Brown

(1883-1961)

Educator, school founder, author, civic leader

As the distinguished founder of the Palmer Memorial Institute, Charlotte Hawkins Brown served for more than half a century as one of the pioneering and driving forces in American preparatory education for black youths. Unafraid of new ideas and experiment, she did much to foster equality of educational opportunity in the South by the power of her vision and the force of her conviction in setting high standards of educational excellence both for her faculty and her students.

The granddaughter of slaves, Charlotte Hawkins Brown was born Lottie Hawkins on June 11, 1883, in Henderson, North Carolina. She and her brother, Mingo, were the

Charlotte Hawkins Brown

children of Caroline Frances Hawkins and a father whose identity has not been established. Lottie's grandmother, Rebecca Hawkins, was a direct descendant of the English navigator, Sir John D. Hawkins, and was a favored slave on the plantation of his descendants in central North Carolina. Raised in an attractive home on land that was part of the former Hawkins plantation, Lottie Hawkins grasped in her early years the educational and cultural aspirations of her mother and grandmother.

In 1888, Lottie Hawkins moved to Cambridge, Massachusetts, with eighteen other members of her family, who were looking for better social and educational opportunities in the North. Her mother had married Nelson Willis, and together they operated a hand laundry and provided a good home for the family near Harvard University. Mrs. Willis boarded young men who were students at Harvard and also cared for infants in her home. Lottie Hawkins attended the Allston Grammar School and as a child developed a friendship with Alice and Edith Longfellow, the children of Henry Wadsworth Longfellow, who lived in her neighborhood. The family usually journeyed at Christmas time back to Henderson, North Carolina, where Hawkins kept in touch with her southern heritage.

Lottie Hawkins showed an early talent for leadership and oratory, which became evident when at twelve she organized the kindergarten department in the Sunday school of the Union Baptist Church in Cambridge, and at fourteen was chosen orator for a church anniversary that was attended by the governor and his council. At Cambridge English High School she was an exceptional scholar. She also developed her talent in art there by sketching crayon portraits of her classmates. As she prepared to graduate in 1900, she found a job caring for two infants after school in order to earn money for a silk slip to wear with her white organdy graduation dress. Alice Freeman Palmer, the educator, humanitarian, and second president of Wellesley College, observed Hawkins one day as she was pushing the baby carriage and reading the Roman author Virgil from her Latin book. The girl's intelligence and desire for knowledge impressed Palmer, who later became her benefactor and had an enduring influence on the her life.

Believing that "Lottie" sounded too ordinary to be put on her diploma, Hawkins changed her name to Charlotte Eugenia Hawkins. Having been inspired by Booker T. Washington to use her northern education to teach black people in the South, she had a strong desire to attend Radcliffe College in Cambridge in order to get a superior education. Her mother was adamant against it, believing that with a high school education she could get a teaching appointment in the Massachusetts schools, which at that time did not require teachers to have a normal school diploma. Charlotte Hawkins compromised with her mother and agreed to attend a two-year normal school. In looking through the catalogue of the State Normal School, she saw the name of Alice Freeman Palmer, who was a member of the board of education that governed the normal schools of the state. Hawkins wrote to Palmer for a recommendation, and Palmer responded by voluntarily paying her expenses to attend the State Normal School at Salem, Massachusetts, where she enrolled in the fall of 1900.

As she rode home on the train at the beginning of her second year at Salem, Hawkins happened to meet a field secretary of the American Missionary Association, a group of white advocates in New York who financed and administered schools for blacks in the South. The representative offered Hawkins a job as a teacher, with a choice of a well developed school in Orlando, Florida, or a rural school near McLeansville, North Carolina. Excited by the opportunity to return to her native state to teach less fortunate members of her own race, she accepted the job, left Salem Normal School a year earlier than her class, and traveled to North Carolina in October 1901. The diminutive eighteen-year-old, well dressed in a tailored suit, stepped off the train at McLeansville, a small town four miles from the Bethany Institute where she was to teach. After questioning, walking, and then riding in a wagon pulled by a mule, Hawkins arrived at a run-down country church that also served as the school. Disappointed but still eager, she settled in her attic room over the parsonage of the Bethany Congregational Church and on October 12, 1901, held her first class for fifty children who came from miles around. She used most of her salary of thirty dollars per month to buy clothes and supplies for the school children.

At the end of the school year the American Missionary Association closed its one- and two-teacher schools for lack of funds. The association closed Bethany Institute and offered Hawkins a position elsewhere, but the Sedalia community was anxious to have her remain there and teach. She put off her plans to further her education, feeling a strong responsibility to the people of Sedalia, and decided to stay there and build a school for her people.

Alice Freeman Palmer Memorial Institute Founded

Charlotte Hawkins returned to Cambridge, Massachusetts, in June 1902 and discussed with Alice Freeman Palmer her plan to start a school. Mrs. Palmer promised to help Hawkins in the fall, after she returned from Europe, by calling on her friends for their interest and financial support. Hawkins spent the summer of 1902 in New England giving recitations and musical recitals to raise money to open her school. When she returned to Sedalia, the people of the community gave fifteen acres of land for the school, and the minister of Bethany Congregational Church donated an old blacksmith shop, which she made into classrooms with the money she had raised from northern philanthropists. With meager facilities but great enthusiasm, Hawkins opened her school on October 10, 1902, naming it the Alice Freeman Palmer Institute, in honor of her friend and benefactor. Along with the academic subjects, Hawkins emphasized industrial and vocational education. Palmer died that fall before she was able to promote Hawkins's work with the people of Cambridge, but Hawkins was able to get financial backing later from many of Palmer's acquaintances. Upon Palmer's death, Hawkins added "Memorial" to the name of the school.

In 1905, Hawkins used the money that she received from a letter-writing campaign to build Memorial Hall, the first new building on the Palmer campus. During the next several years, the school grew steadily, with Hawkins running the school, teaching, and raising money from philanthropists in New England, New York, and in the South. At the same time that she fulfilled all of these responsibilities, Hawkins furthered her own education. In addition to receiving a diploma from Salem Normal School in 1901, she studied at Harvard University and at Wellesley and Simmons Colleges.

On November 23, 1907, the Palmer Memorial Institute was incorporated and a board was appointed. With the purchase of more land, the school was able to offer students who were unable to pay their expenses the opportunity to grow their food. The number of faculty members increased, as did the number of cultural and academic courses, and classes in agriculture, industrial arts, and home economics.

While in Cambridge attending summer school at Harvard University in 1909, Charlotte Hawkins met Edward Sumner Brown, a student at Harvard who had rented a room in her mother's house. After a two-year romance, Charlotte Hawkins and Ed Brown were married on June 12, 1911. Brown, who had finished Harvard that year, went with his wife to Sedalia, where he taught at Palmer Institute and was responsible for the boys' dormitory. After one year, however, he left Sedalia to teach at a school in South Carolina. He and his wife continued to correspond and visit, but he did not return to Sedalia to live, and their marriage, which had been so happy in the beginning, ended in divorce in 1915.

About this time Charlotte Hawkins Brown took the three daughters of her brother, Mingo, to raise after their mother died. In addition, she accepted the responsibility for the four children of her youngest aunt, Ella Brice, whose musical career kept her away from her home in Sedalia. With these seven children to care for, Brown needed more than dormitory space, so she built her own home on the campus, a frame house that she called Canary Cottage. All of these children graduated from Palmer Memorial Institute and went on to well-known institutions of higher education. One of the Hawkins children, Maria, pursued a musical career in Hollywood, where she met and married a prominent vocalist, the late Nat "King" Cole.

By 1916, the Palmer Memorial Institute had built four buildings, and the school had begun to make its presence known all across the South. Two fires, in 1917 and 1922, resulted in the loss of the Industrial Building and Memorial Hall. Through help from citizens in the Sedalia and nearby Greensboro communities, as well as the contributions of various northern philanthropists, Brown was able to replace Memorial Hall in 1922 with the Alice Freeman Palmer Building, the school's first brick building and the center of campus activity.

In 1919, Charlotte Hawkins Brown published her first book, an eighteen-page short story that is sometimes listed as a novel, *Mammy: An Appeal to the Heart of the South*. Based on the life of a slave in the Sedalia area whose faithful service was not appreciated by the wealthy spinster for whom she had worked, the work is an indictment of southern slaveholding families who failed to reward their slaves' loyalty and left them destitute in old age. This fiction, along with her artistic and musical pursuits, illustrates the creative artistry that characterized Brown's diverse and outstanding contributions as an educator and leader.

By 1922, when the Palmer Memorial Institute graduated its first accredited high school class, Brown had built Palmer into one of the nation's leading preparatory schools for black students. After she introduced a junior-college academic program in the mid-1920s, the school began a transition away from its primary emphasis on agricultural and vocational training and began to focus on its secondary and postsecondary components, attracting students from around the country.

Through the years, Charlotte Hawkins Brown became ever more important to the rural Sedalia community. Constance H. Marteena describes her influence there: "Year by year, Charlotte Hawkins Brown became a more vital source of their inspiration and their guiding spirit. . . . Often the citizens of Greensboro referred to Palmer as 'Sedalia,' so close were its ties to the community" (55). Her community leadership manifested itself in the active participation of the Palmer students in the life of the community as well as in the betterment of the lives of the local citizens, whom Brown encouraged to improve their health care, farm methods, political action, and general knowledge, and to seek independent home ownership. Believing that interracial contacts were necessary for the education of black students, she sponsored cultural exchange programs with the North Carolina State College for Women at Greensboro. Brown also was responsible for bringing together the people in the Sedalia community with the national leaders who took part in the formal programs at Palmer and with the northern philanthropists who supported the school. Her associates included Mary McLeod Bethune, who founded Bethune-Cookman College; Eleanor Roosevelt; and Booker T. Washington and his wife, Margaret Murray Washington, who was also an educator.

Brown's National Leadership Emerges

Brown's personal diplomacy and strong resolve were special strengths in notably advancing the understanding of black American life among people across the country. In the 1920s, she opposed racial discrimination by bringing lawsuits whenever she was insulted or forced to follow the Jim Crow laws and by speaking about these experiences at large gatherings. In 1921 the YWCA national board appointed Brown to its membership, the first such appointment for a black person. Brown also campaigned openly against lynching, a dangerous position to take in the South at the time. Her leadership on these matters combined a capacity to inspire with practical wisdom.

For her work as an educator, Brown was inducted into the

North Carolina Board of Education's Hall of Fame in 1926, but her contribution to the state of North Carolina went far beyond her work at the Palmer Memorial Institute. As one of the organizers in 1909 and later president of the North Carolina State Federation of Negro Women's Clubs, she worked for the betterment of black women, establishing the Efland Home for Wayward Girls. When continuation of this institution became prohibitively expensive for Brown's organization, she persuaded the North Carolina General Assembly to establish a new facility, the Dobbs School for Girls, located first in Rocky Mount and then in Kinston, North Carolina, to continue its work. Her leadership in this organization led to the establishment of a scholarship fund for black female college students and to the publication of *Negro Braille Magazine*, among other projects. Her support of a training school for unfortunate boys in the state was significant in the establishment of the Morrison Training School, which was later under the direction of a graduate of the Palmer Memorial Institute. In 1928, Brown was elected a member of the Twentieth Century Club of Boston, which honored persons of distinction in the fields of education, art, science, and religion. She was the first black woman to gain this distinction. Her influence as a club administrator and as a leader in many worthwhile causes spread to other areas of the country through Palmer's graduates, who carried Brown's zeal to their home communities.

The Palmer Institute gained a far-reaching reputation for excellence in music through the Sedalia Singers, a musical group organized and often directed by Brown. Performing at the White House, New York's Town Hall, and Boston's Symphony Hall, this group attracted many of the Palmer students to the study of music. Local performances by the Sedalia Singers sparked the interest of many prominent citizens from nearby Greensboro in the Palmer Memorial Institute and in Sedalia.

When the Palmer Institute reached its thirty-third anniversary in 1934, the distinguished speakers at the ceremony celebrated the growth of the institution and praised Brown for her wisdom, vision, and contribution to the improvement of racial understanding. A decade later Brown received the Second Annual Award for Racial Understanding from the Council of Fair Play, which recognized her lifelong activities to improve interracial understanding nationally and internationally.

As president of the North Carolina Teachers Association from 1935 to 1937, Brown was able to effect changes in the education of black Americans in the state, with goals to improve educational facilities, increase salaries for teachers, and encourage teachers to develop each child's greatest creative potential. Looking beyond the secondary level, Brown also worked to persuade the North Carolina Negro College Conference to raise admission standards. Recognizing Brown's numerous educational and civic services, Lincoln University in Pennsylvania awarded her an honorary doctorate in 1937. Subsequently, she was honored with several honorary master's degrees and with additional honorary doctorates from Wilberforce University, Howard University, and Tuskegee Institute.

In 1937 Brown faced a reorganization of the school when the county opened a public high school at Sedalia and the state withdrew its subsidies from the Palmer Institute, which had been educating the community children through the high school level. At the same time she also led the way in changing the curriculum to improve her students' general knowledge and to emphasize the acquisition of good manners and social graces in preparing each student to be a member of American society.

In 1940 North Carolina's Governor Clyde R. Hoey recognized Brown's service to the state by naming her a member of the State Council of Defense, whose exclusive membership prior to this appointment had included the state's most respected white citizens. As the reputations of Charlotte Hawkins Brown and the Palmer Memorial Institute grew nationally in the 1940s, Brown was in great demand as a lecturer and speaker at college commencements, church meetings, and interracial club groups. She addressed the students at Mount Holyoke, Smith, Radcliffe, and Wellesley Colleges on an annual basis for more than ten years. Always advocating interracial understanding, she spoke on a wide range of topics, from education to the place of blacks in American life. With the publication in 1941 of her second book, *The Correct Thing to Do, to Say and to Wear*, in which she discussed the principles of social decorum, she also became known as "The First Lady of Social Graces," and she received numerous invitations to lecture on fine manners and decorum. This book, which was used originally as a guide for the students at Palmer, went through five printings and was revised in 1948 for current use. Many young people in schools across the country later commented on the book's lasting influence in their lives.

As the Alice Freeman Palmer Memorial Institute celebrated its forty-fifth anniversary in 1947, Brown announced plans for a fund-raising campaign for an endowment fund for the school. Her concern was not for immediate funding but for the time after her tenure would be complete. On that occasion she summed up the accomplishments of her school: "I should like to live at least five more years to celebrate half a century of progress in the education of the Negro and in the establishment of better relations between the white and colored races" (Marteena, 95). Gifts of appreciation were coming in from local businessmen and others, but the campaign was postponed because of a fire that destroyed the girls' dormitory in February 1950. While Brown, at sixty-seven years of age, watched an important part of her life's work go up in flames, she relied on the spiritual faith that had brought her through a number of crises. "So long as I have faith in God," she said at the time, "He will send friends to help us" (Dannett, 62). The money in hand and additional gifts enabled the school to have the dormitory rebuilt before the beginning of the next school year.

Brown Retires from Palmer Memorial Institute

On October 5, 1952, after fifty years of service, Brown retired as president of the Palmer Memorial Institute. Regarding retirement she commented, "Retire, yes—rest, *never*!" (Marteena, 97). Brown remained on campus as vice-chairman of the board of trustees and as director of finances until 1955. Her successor, Wilhelmina Marguerita Crosson, shared Canary Cottage with her and was able to draw on her knowledge and inspiration. At the end of the 1950s, the Palmer Memorial Institute was enrolling annually about two hundred junior and senior high students who came from across the nation, from the Caribbean, and from Africa.

Suffering from diabetes, Brown died in a hospital in Greensboro, North Carolina, on January 11, 1961. Mourners at the memorial service held in the chapel at the Palmer Memorial Institute crowded every available space inside and outside the building. After the service, at which Mordecai Johnson, the president of Howard University, delivered the eulogy, Brown was buried at the front of the campus of the Palmer Memorial Institute. The grave is marked by a bronze plaque that enumerates both her personal accomplishments and those related to the founding and development of the institute.

The spirit and ideals of Charlotte Hawkins Brown continued after her death to guide those charged with the administration of the Palmer Memorial Institute. The numbers of students who applied to Palmer Memorial Institute diminished, however, perhaps because the times had changed, public education for black children had improved, and the need for private secondary education was not as great. In addition, financial difficulties plagued the school—difficulties brought on by the withdrawal of support from many of Palmer's supporters after Brown's death, and by the rising costs of maintaining the program.

On February 14, 1971, the Alice Freeman Palmer Building was completely destroyed by fire. Some observers point to the loss of this building as the tragedy that made continuation of the school financially impossible. Historian Charles W. Wadelington, however, confirms that Robert Gregg Stone of Boston, Massachusetts, had, in fact, pledged sufficient funds for the school to continue, and that a record number of students, both black and white, had enrolled at Palmer for the fall of 1971. He suggests that a number of Palmer board members influenced the closing of Palmer so that it could become a part of Bennett College, which is located in Greensboro. In November 1971, Bennett College assumed the debts of the Palmer Institute and took over the site. This college did not use the Institute facilities, however, and the school and property later changed ownership and continued to lie dormant except for a brief period in which an elementary school was operated there.

Charlotte Hawkins Brown Historical Foundation Established

In 1983 the Charlotte Hawkins Brown Historical Foundation was incorporated to assist the state of North Carolina in establishing the state's first historic site in honor of a black person and a woman. In 1987, the former campus of the Palmer Memorial Institute was designated a state historic site. The former Carrie M. Stone Teachers' Cottage now houses the foundation and a state visitors' center, which features exhibits honoring Brown and the Palmer Memorial Institute. Canary Cottage is currently under restoration, and the state has plans to restore other buildings on the site. In addition, a black American history resource center will be established to emphasize the contributions to education and society made since 1865 by other outstanding black Americans and will promote scholarly research in black American history and culture.

From the inception of the Palmer Memorial Institute in 1902, the history of the institution was inextricably tied to the life of its founder. In developing this school into one of the most important fountains of educational opportunity for blacks in the South, Charlotte Hawkins Brown combined qualities of leadership and appreciation of academic ideals with profound understanding of national and regional needs, as well as appreciation of local community aspirations. The presence of her institute, on the local, state, and national levels, made a certain and visible difference in the character development, educational attainments, and daily lives of numbers of black students and many non-students as well.

Throughout her career Brown never lost the tough and resourceful spirit of her native North Carolina. Her remarkable tenacity, sustained for more than half a century as she taught the young, raised seven children of relatives, and helped lead North Carolina through important and necessary changes in interracial understanding, contributed to the diversified and outstanding achievements that brought distinction to her and to her region. In accord with the supplication on the plaque at her gravesite, Charlotte Hawkins Brown's memory, indeed, continues to "lend inspiration always to this place and its people."

References

Brown, Charlotte Hawkins. *Mammy: An Appeal to the Heart of the South*. Boston: The Pilgrim Press, 1919.

———. *The Correct Thing To Do, To Say, To Wear*. Boston: The Christopher Publishing House, 1941.

Daniel, Sadie Iola. *Woman Builders*. Washington, D.C.: Associated Publishers, 1970.

Dannett, Sylvia G. L. "Charlotte Hawkins Brown." *Profiles of Negro Womanhood*. Vol. II. Yonkers, N.Y.: Educational Heritage, 1966.

Marteena, Constance Hill. *The Lengthening Shadow of a*

Woman: A Biography of Charlotte Hawkins Brown. Hicksville, N.Y.: Exposition Press, 1977.

Stewart, Ruth Ann. "Charlotte Eugenia Hawkins Brown." *Notable American Women: The Modern Period*. Cambridge, Massachusetts: Harvard University Press, 1980.

Tillman, Elvena. "Charlotte Hawkins Brown." *Dictionary of American Negro Biography*. Eds. Rayford W. Logan and Michael R. Winston. New York: Norton, 1982. 65-67.

Wadelington, Charles W. Interview with author, 8 November 8, 1990. (Wadelington is minority interpretation specialist at the Division of Archives and History, North Carolina Department of Cultural Resources, Raleigh, North Carolina.)

Collections

The Charlotte Hawkins Brown Papers are located in the Schlesinger Library, Radcliffe College, Cambridge, Massachusetts. The collection contains correspondence, speeches, memorabilia, materials related to the Palmer Memorial Institute, and biographical material, including a fragmentary autobiography by Brown and an incomplete, unpublished biography, *The Twig Bender*, by Cecie R. Jenkins.

The most complete collection of materials on Charlotte Hawkins Brown is located in the Charlotte Hawkins Brown Collection, Division of Archives and History, North Carolina Department of Cultural Resources, Historic Sites Section, Raleigh, North Carolina.

Papers on Charlotte Hawkins Brown's work with the National Council of Negro Women are in the National Council of Negro Women's National Archives for Black Women's History, Washington, D.C.

Collections of materials on Charlotte Hawkins Brown and the Palmer Memorial Institute are located at the Schomburg Center for Research in Black Culture, the New York Public Library, New York City; in the North Carolina Historical Room at the Greensboro Public Library, Greensboro, North Carolina; in the collection of Afro-American Women's materials in the Thomas F. Holgate Library at Bennett College, Greensboro, North Carolina; in the W.C. Jackson Library at the University of North Carolina at Greensboro, Greensboro, North Carolina; and in the Amistad Research Center at Tulane University, New Orleans, Louisiana.

There are photographs of Charlotte Hawkins Brown in the Griffith J. Davis Collection, Duke University Library, Durham, North Carolina.

Marsha C. Vick

Dorothy Brown ("D." Brown)

(1919-)

Surgeon, humanitarian

Dorothy Lavinia Brown, a woman who single-mindedly pursued her dream to practice medicine and became the first black surgeon in the South, was born on January 7, 1919, in Philadelphia, Pennsylvania. Her young, unmarried mother took her to Troy, New York, when she was only two weeks old. The mother soon found that she was unable to give her daughter proper care. She therefore placed the five-month old Dorothy in Troy Orphanage (later named Vanderhyden Hall), where she remained until she was thirteen years old. Herbert Hunn, superintendent of the orphanage, was a good, humane person, and he liked Brown very much. He was one of her very first friends and allies, and he recognized and encouraged her earliest scholastic achievement. Each year Dorothy Brown took the prize as the best student at the orphanage.

When she was five years old, Dorothy Brown underwent surgery to remove her tonsils and adenoids. Brown recalls that she was excited and also very curious about what was happening to her and as a result of the experience formed a strong decision to become a physician. Although the adults around her tended to dismiss her stated resolution to study medicine as a child's impractical dream, highly unlikely of attainment, she never once after her youthful decision doubted that she would someday become a doctor.

Although Dorothy Brown had known almost no other life except that of the orphanage, and that a fairly agreeable life, she nevertheless became somewhat concerned and saddened, during her ninth year there, that she never had any visitors as the other children did. She forthwith went to see Superintendent Hunn and discussed her problem with him. Within a few days after their brief interview, the Frank Coffeens and their daughter, members of a local Presbyterian church, came to visit with her, and after that, again and often, thus filling a part of the lonely void that she had felt in her life.

When Dorothy Brown was thirteen years old, her mother took her out of the orphanage to live with her. But the years of separation were not to be quickly overcome, and mother and daughter were never to form a familial bond. Four times the daughter ran away from her mother. Finally her mother decided that Dorothy Brown, at thirteen, was old enough to go into domestic service and placed her as a mother's helper in the home of Mrs. W. F. Jarrett of Albany, New York. When Jarrett inquired of Dorothy Brown what she wanted to be when she grew up, the girl told her that she was going to become a doctor. Realizing that her young helper was already very seriously committed to her vocation, Jarrett promised to help her to return to Troy and complete her high school course. During a period of about a year and a half as an employee in the Jarrett home, Dorothy Brown, now sixteen, was able to save four or five hundred dollars, which would see her through high school. During her stay in Albany she had read a great deal, especially in textbooks of Latin, algebra, and chemistry, having determined that these subjects would furnish her with good background for the college studies and medical course that she would later pursue.

On her return to Troy, Dorothy Brown found herself without a permanent address. The school principal, upon becoming aware of her situation, began efforts to find her a place to live. Samuel Wesley Redmon and his wife, Lola Cannon Redmon, came forward and provided for the young woman a place in their home and became her foster parents. Dorothy Brown was happy with the Redmons. They secured a double bass violin for her, and she played in the high school orchestra. She was often encouraged to relinquish her dream of becoming a doctor, but she was steadfast in her decision.

After graduating from high school, Brown went to work for a family in Troy. She learned through Mrs. Charles E. Smart, a local churchwoman, that the Women's Division of Christian Service of the Methodist Church in Troy wanted to send a qualified black female student to Bennett College in Greensboro, North Carolina. This group helped her to obtain a scholarship to Bennett, and she was soon enrolled there. At college she was advised to prepare for a career as a schoolteacher, but she carefully chose courses that would lead to medical school. She graduated second in her class at Bennett, receiving the B.A. degree in 1941. When the Methodist women asked her what she planned to do after having completed her college studies, she replied that she intended to work and save money to pay her expenses at medical school.

By 1942 the United States was involved in World War II. Dorothy Brown qualified through study at Cornell University, in Ithaca, New York, for employment by the Army Ordnance Department and worked nine months in Rochester, New York, as a civilian inspector of gauges and target and practice bombs. She then returned to Troy and worked as an inspector at a defense plant.

In 1944 she met once again with the Methodist women, who were so impressed that she had been able to save a significant sum of money towards attending medical school that they urged her to enroll as soon as possible and promised that they would help her. She was subsequently accepted at Meharry Medical College, Nashville, Tennessee. Each summer she returned to work in Troy. Hunn, her old friend at the orphanage, helped her to obtain an additional $700 to support her studies, and the church women maintained their interest in her scholastic efforts and her financial need. She graduated from Meharry in 1948, in the upper third of her class.

Brown Becomes Surgeon

Dorothy Brown spent a year as an intern at Harlem Hospital in New York City. She also applied for a surgical residency at that institution but was denied an appointment. The bias against women as surgeons was very strong, the predominant opinion among medical experts being that women were not physically or emotionally strong enough for such work. But she would not be deterred. She returned to Meharry and persuaded Matthew Walker, then chief of surgery, to admit her to a residency there. Since completing the residency in 1954, she has continued to practice medicine in Nashville. She was the first black American female surgeon in the South, and she is a fellow of the American College of Surgery. Until Riverside Hospital, a medical facility operated in Nashville by the Seventh Day Adventist Church, was closed in 1983, Brown was educational director of the Riverside-Meharry Clinical Rotation Program and chief of surgery at Riverside. She has served on the National Advisory Board of the National Institutes of Health and is now attending surgeon at George W. Hubbard Hospital and professor of surgery at Meharry Medical College.

Dorothy Brown's life has been punctuated by a number of firsts, among which is her distinction as the first single woman in modern times to adopt a child in the state of Tennessee. When she reached the age of forty without having married, she began to consider the possibility and desirability of raising a child. It would satisfy her urge to nurture another person into adulthood, a person with whom she could share her philosophy of life. A local woman came to her one day, told her she was unmarried and expecting a baby, and offered her the child for adoption. Dorothy Brown's attorney checked Tennessee adoption laws and determined that she would be able to adopt the child. She named her new daughter Lola Redmon in honor of Lola Cannon Redmon, her own foster mother.

Her strong interest in helping people in every way available to her prompted Brown's interest in political service. In 1966 she was elected from the fifth district to the lower house of the Tennessee State Legislature for a two-year term. She was the first black woman to serve in that body. In 1968 she ran unsuccessfully for a seat in the Tennessee Senate. Much of the controversy of the campaign centered on her authorship and sponsorship of a bill to liberalize Tennessee's abortion law, a bill that now seems quite conservative in light of some current attitudes regarding abortion and women's rights. However, public sentiment at the time was unfavorable to the consideration and passage of such a law, and Brown was defeated.

Dorothy Brown is a past member of the board of trustees at Bennett College. She is a member of the United Methodist church and Delta Sigma Theta Sorority. She has received many awards and honors, including honorary doctoral degrees in humanities from Bennett College and Cumberland University, Lebanon, Tennessee. She is a frequent speaker and panelist on a variety of scientific, religious, medical, political, and other topics of general nature. She has written numerous articles for professional publications as well as for inspirational guides. In August 1982, she wrote the narrative essay, "My Journey Through Reason in Search of an Answer" for the Fifteenth Quadrennial Assembly, United Methodist Women, in Philadelphia, Pennsylvania. *Run to Life—A Day in the Life of Dr. "D" Brown*, a film produced by the Board of Higher Education of the United Methodist Church, premiered in Nashville and was used for several years in raising funds for the support of the twelve historically black colleges and universities maintained by that denomination.

Asked for a statement of her basic beliefs and attitudes, Dorothy Lavinia Brown wrote for the Fisk University Library:

> My basic philosophy of life is the belief that we are here for a purpose—each of us being endowed with multiple talents; our charge is to develop one or as many of these talents as possible and to use these talents and the days of our living to glorify God. Therefore I must "Run to Live," and I must seek to serve in as many different areas of endeavor as I can.

In her essay "Thus Would I Live" she states, "My favorite Bible text is 'Whatsoever ye would that men should do to you, do ye even so to them.' . . . I want to so order my life that its impression, its impact, might always be positive and spiritually constructive."

References

Brown, Dorothy. "History and Evolution of Abortion Laws in the United States." *Southern Medicine* 61 (August 1973): 11-14.

———. "Thus Would I Live." Papers of Dorothy L. Brown, Fisk University Library.

Miller, Ronnie. "Spotlight: Dorothy Brown; Strong will overcomes obstacles to career." *Nashville Banner* (28 July 1986).

Peale, Norman Vincent. *The Power of the Plus Factor*. New York: Fawcett, 1987.

Who's Who of American Women. 8th ed. Chicago: Marquis, 1978.

Who's Who Among Black Americans 1990-91. 6th ed. Detroit: Gale, 1991.

Collections

Papers and photographs of Dorothy Lavinia Brown are in the Special Collections at Fisk University Library. She is also included in the Black Oral History Project of the Fisk library.

Lois L. Dunn

Hallie Brown

(c. 1845-1949)

Educator, writer, elocutionist, civil rights leader

One of the most important black leaders ever to emerge, teacher, writer, librarian, and elocutionist Hallie Quinn Brown was born March 10, circa 1845, in Pittsburgh, Pennsylvania. She died September 16, 1949, of coronary thrombosis in Wilberforce, Ohio. (The exact date of her birth is not known. Some published reports put the year as 1845, others 1849, 1850, and as late as 1855. She was thought to be at least one hundred years old when she died.) Brown spent a lifetime working for equal rights, women's rights, and human rights. She was internationally-known as a speaker who campaigned for a better life for black Americans, and thus for all Americans. The rich text of her life ensures her place in American history.

Hallie Brown's parents, Thomas Arthur Brown and Frances Jane (Scroggins) Brown, were former slaves. She was the fifth of their six children. Thomas Brown was the son of a Scottish woman who owned a plantation in Frederick County, Maryland, and her black overseer. He was allowed to purchase his freedom and that of his sister, brother, and father. Frances Scroggins Brown was born in Virginia and was later freed by her grandfather, a white Revolutionary

Hallie Brown

War officer and planter. Thomas Brown and Frances Scroggins married around 1840 and made their home in Pittsburgh. Thomas Brown became a steward and express agent on riverboats that sailed between Pittsburgh and New Orleans. The Browns accumulated considerable real estate before the Civil War and sought to provide their children with the opportunity to acquire an education.

The Brown's Pittsburgh home became a station for the Underground Railroad and weary travelers. Leading a life of relative privilege, Hallie Brown was exposed at an early age to concern for education and human rights. This concern for humanity would carry over into her adult life.

In 1865 Hallie Brown moved with her family to Ontario, Canada, where the father engaged in farming. In 1870 the family moved again, this time to Wilberforce, Ohio. Brown and her younger brother enrolled in Wilberforce University, where Hallie Brown was one of seven graduates and salutatorian in 1873. She received the B.S. degree, completing the classical scientific course. She received an honorary master of science degree in 1890 and an honorary doctorate of laws in 1936 from Wilberforce.

Hallie Brown led a varied and interesting life. Upon graduating from Wilberforce, she began her teaching career at plantation schools in the South. Initially, she went to South Carolina, where she had to endure a rough life. She taught a large number of children from surrounding plantations as well as a class of older adults. Consistent with her background, Brown taught her students how to read the Bible. She also taught in the public schools of Columbia, South Carolina.

Brown later moved to the Sonora Plantation in Mississippi. Like most schools for blacks, the plantation school had no windows, but it had many cracks and open spaces that caused students to be exposed to the elements. Brown was unsuccessful in getting local authorities to make repairs to the building, but with her missionary spirit and devotion to duty, she and two of her larger male students took cotton seed, mixed the seed with soil, and made a plastic-type mortar. With her own hands, Brown took the mortar and filled all the cracks, protecting her students from inclement weather.

Brown's success as a teacher spread far and wide. She left the Sonora Plantation to teach second grade in the Yazoo City, Mississippi, public schools. Her pupils included children as well as adults. She declined a reappointment at the insistence of her mother, who was concerned about the tense and unsettled political conditions in Mississippi as Reconstruction drew to a close in the mid-1870s. From 1875 to 1887 Hallie Quinn Brown taught at Allen University in Columbia, South Carolina, serving also as dean. She returned to Ohio and to public school teaching in 1887. She taught in the Dayton public schools for four years. During this time she also showed concern for the increasing number of migrant workers from the South by establishing an adult night school.

Tuskegee Appoints Brown Lady Principal

During the 1892-1893 academic year, Brown accepted the position of lady principal at Tuskegee Institute in Alabama. In 1893 she was appointed professor of elocution at her alma mater, Wilberforce. However, due to her extensive travels, she did not accept the position until 1906. Because she was connected to Wilberforce, her path crossed that of two other prominent blacks who taught at Wilberforce: Elizabeth Keckley, former modiste to Mary Todd Lincoln, who taught domestic arts from 1892 to 1896, and W. E. B. Du Bois, who taught Latin and Greek from 1894 to 1896.

Brown had enrolled in summer courses at the Chautauqua Lecture School, where she graduated in 1886. She had also been influenced by a Professor Robertson of the Boston School of Oratory, whom she met while teaching in Dayton. After taking one of his courses, the art of speech and oratory, her brilliant career as an elocutionist began. In an effort to raise money for Wilberforce, Brown was sent on a lecture tour and was very well received. In 1881 President Benjamin F. Lee of Wilberforce formed the Wilberforce Grand Concert Company (later known as Stewart Concert Company), an organization developed to benefit the university. Brown became a member of the group, serving as a reader (elocutionist). She traveled with the group for four years. Tours of the company were well-organized and concerts were well-executed; however, the tours failed to collect any substantial money for the college, and the group was disbanded in 1887.

Brown began to travel extensively, nationally and internationally, as a lecturer and elocutionist. She used Ohio and Indiana as testing grounds, and later traveled throughout the United States. She was well received wherever she went. The Red Oak, Iowa, *Express* reported that:

> Miss Hallie Q. Brown has but few equals as an elocutionist. She has a sweet, flexible voice. Her enunciation is distinct, her manner graceful and her gesticulations eminently appropriate to the character of her selections. Some of her humorous selections caused wave after wave of laughter to roll over the audience and were most heartily encored (Majors, 234).

The *Daily News* of Urbana, Ohio, reported that "Miss H. Q. Brown, the elocutionist, ranks as one of the finest in the country" (Majors, 234). Further the Newport, Rhode Island, *News* reported that Hallie Quinn Brown "displayed remarkable powers of pathos and dramatic elocution. . . . The audience was the largest ever gathered at a public entertainment in that place" (Majors, 234)

The Marion, Illinois, *Monitor* declared:

> The select reading of Miss Hallie Q. Brown was very fine. From grave to gay, from tragic to comic, with great variation of themes and humors, she seemed to succeed in all, and her renderings

were the spice of the night's performance (Wesley, 15).

Between 1894 and 1899 she toured Europe, spending considerable time in Switzerland, France, Germany, and England. She spent the majority of her time in England touring major cities. On her second trip to Europe in 1894, she was sponsored by Frederick Douglass, whom she had met the previous year at the Chicago World's Fair. Douglass gave her a letter of introduction to his friends in England, asking their support in her fund-raising efforts.

Hallie Quinn Brown's recitations revolved around life among blacks in the United States, black songs, and folklore. Temperance was another topic of great concern to her and one that was the subject of many of her lectures. She spoke on behalf of the British Women's Temperance Association. In 1895 she spoke before the World's Women's Christian Temperance Union in London.

During her extensive stay in England, Brown had the opportunity to speak before British royalty. In 1899 she was entertained by Queen Victoria at tea in Windsor Castle. She spoke at an entertainment for Alexandra, the Princess of Wales. The lord mayor of London invited Brown to Queen Victoria's Jubilee as his guest. Thus, Brown appeared before the queen on two separate occasions. She also appeared in a command performance before King George V and Queen Mary of England. A member of Parliament provided Brown admission to the funeral of William E. Gladstone.

On many of her trips abroad Brown sought funds on behalf of Wilberforce University. On the 1894 trip, when she was sponsored by Frederick Douglass, she raised funds for a library. In 1910 she again traveled to Europe and succeeded in acquiring funds that led to the construction of a new dormitory, Kezia Emery Hall, which was dedicated in 1913. The building was named for the mother of the benefactor, E. Julia Emery, a London philanthropist. Brown's contribution to the raising of funds for a dormitory was indeed significant. President William Scarborough of Wilberforce had initiated a campaign to raise funds for a much-needed girls' dormitory. Andrew Carnegie had indicated his intention to give half of the funds needed for construction of the building, provided the other half could be raised from other sources. Despite an intensified effort to raise the money in the United States, little was received. Brown was able to interest E. Julia Emery in the project, and she gave the other half needed to erect the building—sixteen thousand dollars.

Hallie Quinn Brown curtailed her speaking engagements in 1906, when she resumed teaching full-time as a professor of elocution at Wilberforce. She remained in the department of English for several years. She was also a member of the Wilberforce Board of Trustees. Brown was dedicated and committed to the cause of education, especially for her race.

Brown distinguished herself and made significant contributions in many other areas: religion, political issues, women's issues, and racial uplift. Her trip to Europe in 1910 was to attend the World Missionary Conference in Edinburgh, Scotland. Brown was sent as a representative of the Women's Parent Missionary Society of the African Methodist Episcopal (AME) church. She remained in England for seven months and lectured widely on a number of issues. The *Sheffield Daily Telegram* called her "one of the finest female elocutionists in the world" (Wesley, 16).

Wilberforce was affiliated with the AME church and Brown was heavily influenced by Bishop Daniel A. Payne, founder of the college. She was also active in the AME church. In 1900 she was the first woman to actively campaign for an office at the church's General Conference. She was unsuccessful in her bid to become the secretary of education. She continued to fight for the equal rights of women in the church with much the same zeal as she had for temperance. While teaching in Mississippi earlier, Brown felt that her efforts at giving many the privilege of reading the Bible were thwarted by the twin vices of tobacco and alcohol. She continued to teach a Sunday school class of college students until a few years before her death.

Brown Supports Women's Rights

When she was a student at Wilberforce, Brown heard Susan B. Anthony speak. This encounter would have a lasting impression on her, as Brown became an active and vocal advocate of women's rights in general. This crusade was evident in her efforts in the AME church. She was one of the first black women to become interested in forming women's clubs. She started the Neighborhood Club for black women in Wilberforce. In 1893 her efforts went beyond the local level as she stimulated national interest in black women's organizations.

Concern for the development of black women's organizations stemmed from Brown's experiences of the racial and social inequality prevalent in American society. The organizations that black women created were primarily engaged in helping the poor, caring for the aged and sick, and supporting and contributing to churches. The actual impetus for Brown's founding the first organization for black women was the exclusion of a black representative from the board of the 1893 Columbian Exposition. Brown wanted blacks to be involved in the planning stages of the exposition. When she requested that a black representative be appointed to the Board of Lady Managers, she was informed that representation could only come from national organizations. As a result, the Colored Women's League in Washington, D.C., a forerunner of the National Association of Colored Women, was formed. Established in 1894, some of the objectives of the Colored Women's League were racial and social progress, industrial and educational development, and educational improvement of black women. Several prominent women signed the document organizing the group, including Mary Church Terrell, Anna J. Cooper, Charlotte Grimké, and Josephine Bruce. Although Brown was not a part of the organization, its existence stemmed from her request to the Columbian Exposition.

The National Federation of Afro-American Women

(NFAAW) was formed in 1895 through the initiative of Josephine St. Pierre Ruffin, with Margaret Murray Washington as its first president. It was the merger of the NFAAW and the Colored Women's League that led to the development of the National Association of Colored Women (NACW). Mary Church Terrell, who had taught for a short time at Wilberforce, was the first president of this new national organization.

Hallie Quinn Brown held leadership positions in the Ohio State Federation of Women's Clubs (president, 1905-1912) and the National Association of Colored Women (president, 1920-1924). While president of the national group, she launched two significant programs—a scholarship fund for qualifying black girls to be used for higher education and the renovation and preservation of the Frederick Douglass home in Washington, D.C.

In 1924 Brown encountered a slight problem. Margaret Murray Washington, widow of Booker T. Washington, was concerned about what she perceived as internal conflict among the NACW's national leaders. She expressed those concerns in a letter to Nannie Helen Burroughs and sought her assistance in keeping the organization free of internal dissension, lest the gains they had made would be lost. Her concerns stemmed in part from a meeting called by Brown prior to the NACW's national convention held in Chicago in 1924. Brown had selected certain women to attend the meeting, excluding Margaret Murray Washington. Much of the conflict was resolved with the election of Mary McLeod Bethune as president in 1924. Brown remained honorary president until her death.

Brown was also active in political activities and organizations. In the 1920s, while active in the NACW, she was vice-president of the Ohio Council of Republican Women, member of the Advisory Committee of the National League of Women Voters, member of the Colored Women's Department of the Republican National Committee, and chairperson of the executive committee, Negro Women's National Republican League. She was equally active in the presidential campaigns of Warren G. Harding and Herbert Hoover. In 1921 she complained in a letter to President Harding about the opposition of white women employees to the appointment of a black as the Registrar of the Treasury. She indicated in her letter the willingness of black women to fill the places of white women if they could not accept the black department chief.

Brown spoke before the Republication National Convention in Cleveland in 1924. Following the convention she served as director of Colored Women's Activities in Chicago.

Hallie Quinn Brown was a strong advocate of civil rights for blacks. She often spoke out against discrimination. In 1922 she met with Senators Shortbridge, Lodge, and McCormick and President Harding to appeal for a national antilynching bill. She was spurred to action by Ida Wells Barnett, who felt that the NACW was not adequately responding to its constituency. In an editorial in *The Woman's Forum*, Barnett noted the lack of substantive support by the organization for the Dyer Anti-Lynching Bill. Brown called upon NACW members to demand that the federal government eliminate lynching by passing the needed legislation.

In 1925 at the All-American Musical Festival, sponsored by the International Council of Women, Brown harshly criticized the segregated seating in the Memorial Continental Hall in Washington, D.C. Initially, the Daughters of the American Revolution (in which Brown's mother qualified for membership) refused to let the International Council use the hall. They worked out a plan that would seat blacks in a segregated section. As a part of the program, a number of black groups were scheduled to perform, including the Hampton Institute and Howard University glee clubs. Brown warned that unless the segregation policy was changed the groups would not participate. The DAR insisted on segregated seating. The groups refused to perform before the international audience, and the black audience left the event. Members of the NACW and other blacks walked out rather than be subjected to such blatant discrimination. The actions of Brown and others were reported in the 6 May 1925 issue of the *New York Times*. The headline read "Feeling that they had been discriminated against, a group of black women walk out of the International Council of Women's Conference."

Black men and women worked together on issues of concern to the black community. Brown lent her support to the efforts of the NAACP to defeat a national bill and a Wisconsin bill designed to prohibit interracial marriages. Brown, then president of the NACW, responded to a telegram from James Weldon Johnson, national secretary of the NAACP. Despite the fact that most interracial marriages were between black men and white women, Johnson had indicated to Brown that the bill demeaned black women by implication. Brown garnered the support of officers of state chapters of the NACW to aid in the defeat of the legislation. The state and national bills were eventually defeated.

Among her many other accomplishments, Hallie Quinn Brown was also an author. She penned a number of books and pamphlets, including *Pen Pictures of Pioneers of Wilberforce* (1937) and *First Lessons in Public Speaking* (1920), the first speech text written by a black American. Her most noted work was produced when she was about seventy-five years old. *Homespun Heroines and Other Women of Distinction*, published in 1926, contains the biographies of sixty black women born in the United States or Canada between 1745 and 1900. It is a valuable source of biographical information and photographs of a number of black women who may otherwise have remained obscure. Included among the biographies are those of Brown's mother, Frances Jane Scroggins Brown, and aunt, Eliza Anna Scroggins.

Hallie Quinn Brown never married and lived in her family home, Homewood Cottage, until her death in 1949. The Hallie Quinn Brown Memorial Library of Central State

University and the Hallie Q. Brown Community House in Saint Paul, Minnesota, are named in her honor.

References

Afro-American Encyclopedia. Vol. 2. North Miami, Fla.: Educational Book Publishers, 1974.

Brown, Hallie Q. *Homespun Heroines and Other Women of Distinction.* Xenia, Ohio: Aldine Pub. Co., 1926. Reprint-ed. New York: Oxford University Press, 1988.

Daniels, Sadie Iola. *Women Builders.* Washington, D.C.: Associated Publishers, 1970.

Dannett, Sylvia G. L. *Profiles of Negro Womanhood.* Vol. I: 1619-1900. Yonkers, N.Y.: Educational Heritage, 1964.

Davis, John P. *The American Negro Reference Book.* Englewood Cliffs, N.J.: Prentice-Hall, 1966.

Johnson, George T. "Hallie Quinn Brown." *Dictionary of American Negro Biography.* Edited by Rayford W. Logan and Michael R. Winston. New York: Norton, 1982.

Majors, M. A. *Noted Negro Women: Their Triumphs and Activities.* Chicago: Donohue and Henneberry, 1893.

McFarlin, Annjennette S. "Hallie Quinn Brown: Black Woman Elocutionist." *Southern Speech Communication Journal* 46 (Fall 1980): 72-82.

McGinnis, Frederick A. *A History and Interpretation of Wilberforce University.* Blanchard, Ohio: Brown Pub. Co., 1941.

Neverdon-Morton, Cynthia. *Afro-American Women of the South and the Advancement of the Race, 1895-1925.* Knoxville: University of Tennessee Press, 1989.

New York Times, 6 May 1935.

Wesley, Charles H. "Hallie Quinn Brown." *Notable American Women, 1607-1950.* Vol. I. Cambridge: Harvard University Press, 1971.

———. *The History of the National Association of Colored Women's Clubs.* Washington, D.C.: NACW, 1984.

Collections

The papers, photographs, and memorabilia of Hallie Quinn Brown are in the library named in her honor at Central State University. A photograph of Brown is also published on the frontispiece of her book *Homespun Heroines.*

Mamie E. Locke

Letitia Brown

(1915-1976)

Educator, historian

Letitia Woods Brown, a historian who has helped preserve black history, both on paper and at historic sites, was born October 24, 1915, in Tuskegee, Alabama, the daughter of Matthew Woods and Evadne (Adam) Woods. Both parents were members of the faculty at Tuskegee Institute (now University). In 1947 she married Theodore E. Brown, an economist with the United States Department of State, and they became the parents of Lucy and Theodore, Jr. She died on August 4, 1976, of cancer at her home in Washington, D.C.

Letitia Brown graduated from Tuskegee Institute in 1935 with a bachelor of science degree. She received a master of arts degree from Ohio State University in 1937, and the Ph.D. degree from Harvard University in 1966.

Brown was a teacher in Macon County, Alabama, 1935-1936; instructor in history, Tuskegee Institute, 1937-1940; tutor, LeMoyne-Owen College, Memphis, Tennessee, 1940-1945; and associate professor of history and American civilization, Georgetown University, 1971-1976. In 1968 she was senior Fulbright lecturer at Monash University and Australia National University. She was consultant to the Federal Executive Institute, 1971-1973.

Letitia Brown was a member of the Committee on Objectives for National Assessment of Educational Progress, 1972-1973. Other professional memberships included the American Historical Association, Organization of American Historians, Association for the Study of Afro-American Life and History, Southern Historical Association, and African Heritage Studies Association of Afro-Americans. In 1961, Letitia Woods Brown and her husband helped train the first group of Peace Corp volunteers at the University of California, Berkeley.

At her death in 1976, she was the only full-time black faculty member at George Washington University, Washington, D.C., a leader in the development of the District of Columbia studies, and a forceful voice in the field of historic preservation in the nation's capital. As a member of the Committee on Landmarks of the National Capital, she was instrumental in preserving sites relevant to the history of the black community in Washington.

A scholarly writer, Letitia Woods Brown used an unusual approach in her historical works. She successfully made the history of free blacks come alive, and she emphasized the progress of free blacks, particularly in Washington, D.C.

Among her works are: *Washington from Banneker to Douglass, 1791-1870*, co-authored with Elsie M. Lewis (Washington, D.C.: National Portrait Gallery, Smithsonian Institution, November 1971); *Washington in the New Era, 1870-1970*, co-authored with Elsie M. Lewis (Washington, D.C.: National Portrait Gallery, Smithsonian Institution, 1972); and *Free Negroes in the District of Columbia, 1790-1846*, coauthored with Richard Wade (New York: Oxford University Press, 1972). In the foreword to *Free Negroes*, Wade summarizes Brown's attention to blacks in the District of Columbia:

> Letitia Woods Brown . . . adds new dimension to these topics [blacks in Washington]. She carefully examines the development of the free Negro population in the nation's capital, from its establishment to the decade prior to Emancipation. The number grew from 783 in 1800 to over 11,000 in 1860. By the Civil War, free Blacks comprised 78% of the Negro residents, while at the beginning slaves outnumbered them five to one (viii).

Brown traces blacks from bondage to freedom, through descent from free mothers, by sale, by petition, or by the will of the master. She documents her writings with concrete evidence drawn from court records, real estate conveyances, newspapers, and diaries, and presents the information in contemporary vocabulary.

In describing the life of free Negroes in Washington, she notes that although there were discrimination and racial barriers and most were confined to manual labor and domestic service, there were also doctors, schoolteachers, and ministers. Free Negroes owned homes and property, paid taxes, and had a social life that was unheard of by slaves.

Historian Benjamin Quarles called her book ''a real breakthrough'' in black history:

> It concentrates on urban Blacks when most Blacks still lived in a rural setting, and [it] was equally significant because of Washington, D.C.'s role as the Capital city. I was always impressed not only by her grasp of Black history and American history but by her realism and toughness. She has the ability to make history come alive (238).

References

Brown, Letitia Woods, and Richard Wade. *Free Negroes in the District of Columbia*. New York: Oxford University Press, 1972.

Contemporary Authors. 69-72 Detroit: Gale Research, 1978.

Contributions of Black Women to America. Vol. 2. Edited by Marianna W. Davis. Columbia, S.C.: Kenday Press, 1981.

New York Times, 5 August 1976.

Guy C. Craft

Josephine Beall Bruce

(18?-1923)

Clubwoman, educator

Josephine Beall Wilson Bruce, a native of Cleveland, Ohio, is known primarily for her work as a college administrator, her prominence in the black woman's club movement, and her activities in Washington, D.C.'s social circles, where she moved freely, first due to her husband's position as U.S. senator and later as result of her own popularity.

Born probably in Philadelphia, Bruce was the oldest daughter of five children born to socially prominent Harriet and Joseph Willson. (In time, either the family or the press dropped one ''l'' in the spelling of Willson.) Her family moved to Cleveland, Ohio, when Josephine was about one year old. The children attended racially integrated schools in the city. Willson, a dentist, was born in Augusta, Georgia, February 22, 1817, and educated in Philadelphia and Boston. Nothing is known yet about Harriet Willson's background.

Josephine Beall Bruce

After being an invalid for several years, Joseph Willson died in late August or early September 1895 of diabetes at home at 449 College Avenue in Indianapolis, where the family had moved. According to the *Washington Bee,* he was survived by his widow and five children: Leonidas S., Cleveland, Ohio; Emily F. Harang, La Forche Parish, Louisiana; Josephine Beall Bruce, Washington, D.C.; and two unmarried daughters—Mary A. and Victoria A., both of whom taught school in Cleveland for several years. Both the mother and Josephine Bruce loved literature and classical music. The parents were keenly interested in education. It follows, then, that the Willson children would be educated also, and not unlikely that Josephine, Mary, and Victoria would become teachers or enter a highly visible profession.

Bruce graduated from Cleveland's Central High School in 1871, then completed a short course for teachers that led her to a teaching position at Mayflower School. It has been said that she was the first black teacher in Cleveland's public schools. She also became an accomplished linguist. She and politician, planter, entrepreneur, and lecturer Blanche Kelso Bruce met sometime in 1876, and they were married on June 24, 1878. The private ceremony was performed at the Willson residence, 228 Perry Street, in Cleveland. She was elegantly dressed in a white silk gown trimmed in satin that a New York designer made especially for her. Their four-month wedding trip has been described: They made "a bridal tour through the principal cities of Europe, where marked attentions were shown the young couple from foreign nobility and distinguished residents, among whom were Minister Welsh at London, and Minister Noyes at Paris" (Simmons, 702). They also toured historic sites, and visited art galleries and the theater. While in Paris for two weeks, Bruce purchased an extensive wardrobe, including gowns, that were no doubt the subject of various news articles later describing her exquisite attire. In Europe the Bruces found less discrimination against the black race than existed in the United States, and Blanche K. Bruce said "he thought European countries far in advance of his own" (*New York Times,* 7 December 1878, quoted in St. Clair, 127).

When they returned to Washington, the Bruces lived temporarily in "Hillside Cottage," the home of John Mercer Langston, who at the time was serving as United States minister to Haiti. The center of Washington's black elite social life when Caroline Wall Langston lived there, the home was once again a social magnet when Bruce became a grand hostess. Simmons said that "Mrs. Bruce is a remarkable woman, wonderfully fitted to command the dignity and respect of her position, and she presides over her capital residence with true womanly grace, making it a fit rendezvous for the distinguished circle of friends with which she and her husband have been so closely identified" (702). Thursdays were set aside as "reception days"—a time for Bruce to entertain women from the Republican circles as well as wives of cabinet members and congressmen (Gatewood, 6, 34). The grand style of entertainment continued in their M Street home. Like other prominent black and white women of the day, Bruce managed the servants in the household and recognized the problem in locating and retaining well-trained cooks and maids.

Blanche Kelso Bruce was born a slave of mixed ancestry near Farmville, Prince Edward County, Virginia, the youngest of eleven children of Polly, a slave owned by Pettus Perkinson. We know nothing of the origin of his given name; however, his surname was that of his mother's owner prior to Perkinson. Moved between 1844 and 1850 to Missouri, to Mississippi, and back to Missouri, Blanche Kelso Bruce later escaped to the free state of Kansas. Having been tutored early by young William Perkinson, he built on that training in Kansas, where he received additional tutoring from a minister. He also opened the first elementary school in the state for blacks and taught there for a while. Although a number of published sources state that he studied at Oberlin College, the college has never been able to establish his attendance.

Hearing Bruce speak in Memphis, Tennessee, Mississippi governor John Lusk Alcorn encouraged him to move to Mississippi, and soon after his arrival there in February 1869 he moved swiftly into political positions, resulting in 1874 in his election to the United States Senate. He served a full term (1874-1881) and was the second African-American from the state, after Hiram R. Revels, to hold such a position.

The Bruces remained keenly interested in education. Josephine Bruce and clubwomen Mary Church Terrell and Josephine St. Pierre Ruffin were proponents of Booker T. Washington's industrial education for the masses. For their children, however, such a training was untenable.

Blanche Kelso and Josephine Beall Bruce "enjoyed the good life of elite Negroes during late-nineteenth-century Washington" (Shapiro, 75). Apparently wealthy by some standards, Blanche Kelso Bruce had acquired some three thousand acres of Delta land and owned two plantations in Bolivar County, Mississippi—both profitable enterprises. To serve his plantations he influenced the establishment of a post office in Bolivar County and named it Josephine, Mississippi, in honor of his wife. For additional income, he received substantial fees for speaking engagements and operated a successful investment, claims, insurance, and real estate business in Washington. He also had been register of the treasury (1881-1885 and 1889-1893) and recorder of deeds for the District of Columbia (1889-1893).

The Bruces were an attractive, polished, poised, and well-dressed couple who obviously attracted the attention of even the most unobservant bystander: he was of café-au-lait complexion, had curly hair, was graceful, well built, exquisitely groomed (Shapiro, 75); she has been described as having "Caucasian features, large, beautiful eyes, a somewhat brunette complexion, and long, slightly wavy hair. Her form is slender and shapely, and she dresses in elegant taste" (Frank G. Carpenter, quoted in Shapiro, 75). The press made it known the difficulty one would have in detecting evidence of Josephine Bruce's African ancestry. Further notice of Josephine Bruce's appearance was made by a reporter who observed her during a visit to the White House in 1880, when blacks had such a privilege for a while. Called "one of the most notable features" of a presidential reception, the reporter wrote:

> The tall, graceful figure of Mrs. Bruce was displayed in a black velvet princess dress, elaborately trimmed with gold-colored satin, richly embroidered, and drapings of pointed duchess lace, studded with butter-cups at her waist and throat. Her soft brown hair was simply and becomingly arranged, the only ornament worn being a cluster of tiny rosebuds embedded in lace. Her jewels consisted of solitaire diamonds worn in the ears and around the neck. Mrs. Bruce's toilette was considered one of the most tasteful and magnificent of the evening (quoted in Sterling, 427-28).

During Blanche K. Bruce's first term as register of the treasury, the Bruces participated in functions on Capitol Hill and aroused some hostility. According to the *Cleveland Gazette*:

> The ladies who assisted the President to receive on January 1st seemed to ignore Mrs. Bruce, the colored wife of ex-Senator Bruce, and the poor lady sat in a corner like a bronze statue. Mrs. [John A.] Logan took her by the hand and led her up to the thirty-five ladies and introduced her to all of them in a manner so sweet and at the same time so sarcastic that they all smiled upon the colored woman (29 November 1884, 3).

In 1886 Joseph Willson moved his family from Cleveland to 449 College Avenue, Indianapolis, Indiana. The Bruces and their son, Roscoe, joined them later in 1887 for about eight months while Blanche Bruce was on an eighteen-month lecture circuit. They returned to Washington in the spring of 1888 and established their residence at 2010 R Street Northwest. In spite of their social popularity, they drew local criticism in Indianapolis and in Washington for their "detachment from their race." They even attended white churches—the Protestant Episcopal Church in Indianapolis and the First Congregational Church in Washington (St. Clair, 199). Joseph Willson also attended the Protestant Episcopal Church in Indianapolis and his funeral was held there in 1895.

The Bruces' son, Roscoe Conklin Bruce (1879-1952), attended Phillips Exter Academy from 1896 to 1898 and graduated magna cum laude and Phi Beta Kappa from Harvard University in 1902. In the fall of that year he was appointed head of the academic department at Tuskegee Institute and his charge was to "correlate" or "dovetail" the curriculums in the academic and industrial departments. Feeling that the academic program was being eroded and having differences with Booker T. Washington, he resigned and moved to Washington, D.C., in 1906 to become supervising principal of the black public schools. The next year, with Washington's influence, he became assistant superintendent in charge of black schools—a position that he held for fifteen years. Influenced by Booker T. Washington, he is said to have established trade schools for black youth and recommended the founding of an agricultural school. Through his efforts the city established the first black junior high school and a black teacher's college. According to Harlan, "his emphasis on vocational and industrial education and his frequent dogmatic personnel policies aroused these black citizens to organize the Parents' League and seek Bruce's removal from office" (*Booker T. Washington Papers,* Vol. 4, 391; hereafter *B.T.W. Papers*). Another allegation was that Bruce was "morally delinquent" (Gatewood, 326). Later, after resigning under pressure from the school system, he was engaged in several real estate ventures and held other positions, such as principal of a black high school in Kendall, West Virginia.

Josephine Bruce Undertakes Club Activities

At some point during her years in Washington, Bruce had been president of the Booklovers Club, among whose presidents had been also M. E. Hilyer, Mary Church Terrell, and Coralie Franklin Cook. Little else on Bruce and her club activities appears in known sources until 1892, when she joined Helen A. Cook, Charlotte Forten Grimké, Anna Julia Cooper, Mary Church Terrell, Mary J. Peterson, Evelyn Shaw, and Ida B. Bailey in organizing the Colored Women's League, which they incorporated in 1894. The league was to identify the social progress of blacks, promote unity among the race, and develop ways to promote the best interests of black people. When the Cotton States Exposition was held in Atlanta, Georgia, in 1895, the Ladies Auxiliary Committee proposed the idea of a woman's congress to be held there. In December 1895 the Atlanta Congress of Colored Women met, becoming the second national convention of black American women ever held, the first being the National Federation of Afro-American women held in Boston, Massachusetts, in 1895. Bruce was president of the congress, where the women resolved to work to advance social purity, improve their homes and child culture, establish more clubs, and form children's clubs. When the National Federation of Afro-American Women held its convention at Nineteenth Street Baptist Church in Washington, D.C., on July 20, 21, and 22, 1896, with Margaret Murray Washington as president, Josephine Bruce gave an address on "Women's Work" and noted: "It is only as we keep abreast in the restless march of progress that we can expect recognition as a factor in that progress" (Wesley, 38).

Apparently Margaret Murray Washington and Bruce became friends—certainly they knew each other well from their club activities. Booker T. Washington knew of Bruce's oratorical skills and sense of purpose as exhibited in club activities. Washington wrote to Hollis Burke Frissell of Hampton Institute on October 23, 1896, with favorable comments about Bruce's visit to Tuskegee during that week, where she spoke to students as a group, lectured in classes, and gave a separate lecture to the faculty. "We are finding her visit very helpful in every way," he said. "She is a woman of fine sense and refinement, there is no nonsense about her. I thought perhaps you might like to have her visit Hampton and speak to the students as a whole or to the girls alone'' (*B.T.W. Papers*, Vol. 4, 226-27).

The Colored Women's League and the Federation of Afro-American Women merged in 1896 to form the National Association of Colored Women (NACW). The third annual meeting of the NACW was held in Howard Congregational Church in Nashville, Tennessee. Blanche Kelso Bruce wrote to Booker T. Washington on September 8, 1897, about the impending meeting and said:

> Mrs. B. starts to Nashvill[e] Saturday, 12 inst. where she will meet Mrs. Washington. I trust our ladies may accomplish more in their conventions than we men have thus far done in ours (*B.T.W. Papers,* Vol. 4, 327).

Washington gave a short speech before the convention on the second day; Margaret Murray Washington chaired the executive committee and Bruce was on the resolutions committee.

The first biennial meeting of the NACW was held in Chicago in Quinn Chapel African Methodist Episcopal (AME) Church on August 14-16, 1899. On Sunday morning pulpits in local churches were opened to the clubwomen and several of the women spoke from these pulpits. Among them were Fannie Barrier Williams in the All Souls Church, NACW president Mary Church Terrell in Grace Presbyterian Church, and Bruce in Quinn Chapel AME Church. At the convention Bruce read a powerful paper on labor problems, which prompted the convention members to adopt the following resolution:

> Resolved, that the attitude of trade unions in nearly all forms of organized labor toward Negro working men is both shortsighted and cruel. The divine right to work ought not to be taken from a people who have already had so many rights stripped from them (Wesley, 47).

A committee was appointed to monitor the work of labor leaders and the National Industrial Commission and to bring about cooperation between black and white workers.

If she had not done so already, Bruce won the support of some club members as the convention continued, and she became a candidate for president. Also in the running were Margaret Murray Washington, Lucy Thurman, Josephine St. Pierre Ruffin, and Josephine Silone Yates. Mary Church Terrell, however, was reelected for the 1899-1901 biennium.

Bruce Becomes Tuskegee's Lady Principal

Blanche Kelso Bruce had died on March 17, 1898 of diabetes and chronic nephritis as the primary cause and glycohemia as the immediate cause. Josephine Bruce moved to Indianapolis, where she lived with her sisters Victoria and Mary Willson for a little more than a year. Apparently Bruce found an offer from Booker T. Washington appealing—and from 1899 to 1902 she was lady principal at Tuskegee Institute. While some called the financially secure Bruce brave for accepting the challenge to help her race, others condemned her for ''cutting a poor deserving woman out of a job'' (Indianapolis *Freeman*, 23 September 1889; quoted in Gatewood, 38). In negotiating the offer, she asked for a salary of ninety dollars a month but accepted Washington's offer of eighty dollars per month and board and all expenses except traveling. By 1901, however, her salary of ninety dollars per month was the seventh highest the institute offered.

Bruce's presence on the Tuskegee campus was not unnoticed. Here she was the epitome of a genteel lady and served a much-needed role for many rural Tuskegee students. Portia Marshall Washington, daughter of Booker T. Washington and his first wife, Fannie Virginia Norton Smith Washington, observed Bruce's strong convictions and high principles in an interview in the *Birmingham Age-Herald*:

> Direct teaching in manners and morals, like that given by Mrs. Bruce, our dean,. . .is also a very important factor in the uplifting of the people. The conditions out of which these students have, many of them, come are squalid and miserable beyond the imagination of Northerners. A large number of the girls have never known in their poor homes any of the refining influences. Perhaps their parents are living in sin. And the climatic conditions in the South, added to the temperamental laxity in manners that is undoubtedly a characteristic of the submerged negro woman, all tend to make the labors of Mrs. Bruce exceedingly valuable.
>
> Very often when the girls come to Tuskegee they lie atrociously. But Mrs. Bruce is especially stern about falsehoods, and the girl who does not very soon evince a desire to be truthful is sent back to her home (Quoted in *B.T.W. Papers,* vol. 6, 323-24).

Harlan draws on an article in the *Washington Colored American*, July 27, 1901, which states that there was a curious turn of events in the position that Bruce and Margaret Murray Washington held among NACW members. At the convention held in Buffalo, New York, on July 9-12, 1901, both women were candidates for the presidency:

> When they both attended a white club meeting during the convention instead of one held for the candidates by the Phillis Wheatley Club of Buffalo, on the ground that they had already accepted the white club's invitation, so much bitter feeling was aroused that both were defeated by Mrs. J. S. Yates [Josephine Silone Yates] of Kansas City, Mo. (*Washington Colored American*, 27 July 1901, 1, 5, cited in *B.T.W. Papers,* Vol. 6, 179).

Bruce, however, was elected to serve as chair of the executive board. Her address was listed as Josephine, Mississippi—the post office address founded by her husband—although she was still on the Tuskegee administrative staff, which she left in 1902.

In June 1904 when the fourth biennial meeting of the NACW was held in Saint Louis, Missouri, Bruce had already been selected one of the five women to attend the International Congress of Women to be held in Germany that year. The others were Mary Church Terrell, Coralie Franklin Cook, NACW president Josephine Silone Yates, and Margaret Murray Washington. When the Saint Louis convention elected officers to serve from 1904 to 1906, Bruce was once again elected to chair the executive board, and she was still living in Josephine, Mississippi.

Writing about the fourth biennial meeting in 1904 in an article titled "The Afterglow of the Women's Convention," Bruce noted that the meeting was well attended, with nearly two hundred delegates presenting their credentials. Alternates and guests swelled the size of the sessions, thus attesting to the general interest aroused by the meeting. Those in attendance saw great changes in the women's work. They had defined their purpose more clearly, developed greater insight and were more discriminating in the conduct of business and in the nature of the propositions submitted. "Purpose" had become the watchword of the clubs and the groups had joined hands for service. Bruce found that such union produced strength—both a surprise and pleasure for those in attendance. "The consciousness of new and growing strength becomes the moving force and numerous are the ways that open to the willing minds for the exercise of the new-found power," she said (541).

In 1906 she returned to Washington, D.C.—the same year in which her son, Roscoe, left Tuskegee to become high school principal in Washington. She returned to her social position in the city and she managed the family's real estate holdings in Mississippi and in Washington, D.C.

The Detroit convention in 1906—the fifth biennial session—saw a significant increase in club membership as result of the work of the NACW organizers. Bruce sought the presidency of the NACW but the matter of color disrupted an "otherwise harmonious convention." Many delegates actually regarded her as a white woman; some said that she was not altogether a Negro, and some felt that the light-skinned women had been running the association and it was now time "to demonstrate that the African is as talented." The press said the difficulty came "not because she was too black, but because she was too white." The embarrassed Bruce withdrew from candidacy (*Mary Church Terrell Papers,* Library of Congress, quoted in Gatewood, 142). Lucy Thurman of Jackson, Michigan, was elected. Notwithstanding this situation, Bruce remained active at the convention. Issues then timely—the convict lease system, lynching, education, improved home life—were presented through the usual method of papers read by officers or other notable persons. Bruce, Mary Church Terrell, Margaret Murray Washington, and Nannie Helen Burroughs were among those presenting papers.

Bruce's activities with the club movement lessened; in 1915 she is known to have attended the meeting of the World Purity Federation in San Francisco with her good friends, George and Coralie Franklin Cook.

After Bruce's son moved to Kendall, West Virginia, about 1921, "he left his mother, wife, and three children at Kelso Farm, the family's summer home outside the District of Columbia in Maryland" (Gatewood, 326). Apparently Bruce was a strong influence in her son's life and advised him in professional and business matters. Certainly after his move to West Virginia and some financial difficulties, he relied on her financial aid. She died at Kendall, West Virginia, on February 23, 1923. "She asked that he devote the rest of his life to law and literature, and made ample provision in her will for that purpose" (*Cleveland Gazette,* 26 May 1923, 1). He never pursued law.

During the active years of her club work, Josephine Beall Bruce published a number of articles—some, though not all, as a result of her office as editor of *National Notes*, the official organ of the NACW. She assesses the impact of education on black women in an article, "What Has Education Done for Colored Women":

> Evidence is not wanting to show that our educated colored women have risen to some eminence in the world. In any considerable community into which one may go, will be found colored women of education who have gained distinction as teachers, as leaders in philanthropic work, as temperance advocates, as church workers, and in many other lines of activity which require ability, endurance, education, and character (294-95.)

She calls for the need to see "evidences of general growth due to education below the exceptional woman." Her study examines what was happening to the black population in Farmville, Virginia; Calumet, Louisiana; Xenia, Ohio; and Saint Louis, Missouri—all with starkly contrasting black lifestyles. She concludes:

> Much more might be added to the credit of the educated colored woman. The achievements of numberless individual women of noble useful lives all over the country might be cited, but to bring to light the results of community improvement due to the influence of the educated women, working together with their educated brothers, is perhaps an effective method of proving the case of the educated colored woman (298).

Bruce's other writings include "They Entertained the Federation and Promoted the Success at the Convention," *Women's Era* (August 1896): 5-6; "The Ladies Auxiliary," *Woman's Era* (October-November 1896): 9; and "The Farmer and the City Folk," *Voice of the Negro* (June 1904): 237. We know little else of Bruce's writings until 1915, when her essay on "Colored Women's Clubs" was published in a special section titled "Votes for Women," in which she gave an overview of the NACW's history in *Crisis*, (10 August 1915): 178-92.

References

Bauman, Roland M. Letter to Jessie Carney Smith, 23 January 1991.

Bruce, Josephine B. "The Afterglow of the Women's Convention." *Voice of the Negro* (November 1904): 541-43.

——. "What Has Education Done for Colored Women." *Voice of the Negro* (July 1904): 294-98.

Cleveland Gazette, 26 May 1923.

"Dr. Joseph Wilson's Death." *Washington Bee*, 7 September 1895.

Gatewood, Willard B. *Aristocrats of Color: The Black Elite, 1880-1920*. Bloomington: Indiana University Press, 1990.

Harlan, Louis R., and others, eds. *Booker T. Washington Papers*, Vol. 4, 1894-1898; Vol. 5, 1899-1900; Vol. 6, 1901-1902. Urbana University of Illinois Press, 1975.

Low, W. Augustus, and Virgil A. Clift. *Encyclopedia of Black America*. New York: McGraw-Hill, 1981.

"Notes and Comments." *Cleveland Gazette*, 29 November 1884. 3, col. 2.

Salem, Dorothy. *To Better Our World*. Brooklyn: Carlson Publishers, 1990.

Shapiro, Samuel L. "Blanche Kelso Bruce." *Dictionary of American Negro Biography*. Edited by Rayford W. Logan and Michael R. Winston. New York: Norton, 1982.

Simmons, William J. "Blanche K. Bruce." *Men of Mark*. Cleveland: George M. Rewell, 1887.

Sterling, Dorothy, ed. *We Are Your Sisters*. New York: Norton, 1984. Includes photograph.

Wesley, Charles Harris. *The History of the National Association of Colored Women's Clubs*. Washington, D.C.: NACW, 1984. Includes photograph.

Jessie Carney Smith

Grace Ann Bumbry

(1937-)

Singer

Grace Ann Bumbry, one of the brightest stars of twrntieth-century opera, was born January 4, 1937, in Saint Louis, Missouri. She was the youngest child of James Bumbry, a freight worker for the Cotton Belt Route Railroad, and Meliza Bumbry, a schoolteacher who came from the Mississippi Delta. The family was musical. Her two older brothers, Benjamin and Charles, were members of the Young People's Choir of Union Memorial Methodist Church, while her mother and father were members of the church's choir. Grace Bumbry also became a member of the Young People's Choir by the age of eleven, having learned all of the songs earlier. Having also studied piano with her mother from the age of seven, Bumbry brought to the choir an ability to read music as well as a full repertoire and a phenomenal emerging voice and talent.

Music was always a part of Bumbry's home and school life. The Bumbry household was a gathering place for the young neighborhood musicians. At such gatherings Bumbry's brothers played instruments while she played the piano and sang along with others of the group.

Grace Ann Bumbry

Bumbry came under the influence of Kenneth Brown Billups when she entered Sumner High School in Saint Louis. Billups was a nationally recognized choral director and musician, who was later to become the president of the National Association of Negro Musicians. He was known as a stern teacher and a demanding choir director. Bumbry became a member of the prestigious A Cappella Choir, and Billups, recognizing an unusual vocal instrument and talent, encouraged her to study voice. Marian Anderson, the great contralto, heard Bumbry sing "O don fatale" from *Don Carlos* at seventeen. Anderson brought Bumbry to the attention of the renowned Sol Hurok, the impresario who had guided Anderson's career. Hurok kept in touch.

Bumbry graduated from Sumner High School in January 1954 and later appeared in a teenage talent contest on Saint Louis's KMOX, where she won a one-thousand-dollar United States war bond, a New York trip, and a one-thousand-dollar scholarship to Saint Louis Institute of Music. The institute's trustees did not wish to admit a black American and offered Bumbry private lessons on a segregated basis. Her family refused. When Bumbry appeared on Arthur Godfrey's national "Talent Scouts" through the efforts of the executive of KMOX, scholarship offers came from several major schools of music. Bumbry chose Boston, but subsequently transferred to Northwestern University, where her mentor, Billups, had received a master's degree in music. Although Bumbry was welcomed at Northwestern, she was not encouraged to become a member of the famous Northwestern Choir, presumably because it would be difficult to find housing for a black student as the choir made its national tours.

It was at Northwestern, however, that Bumbry began her association with the revered Lotte Lehmann. After her retirement from an active performing career, Lehmann had become one of the most outstanding discoverers and developers of vocal talent in the country. Bumbry attended the master classes of the great former star of the operatic and concert stage. When she heard Bumbry sing, Lehmann persuaded the young singer to study with her for the summer at the Music Academy of the West in Santa Barbara, California. Thus, Bumbry became a protégée of Lehmann and continued to study with her and Armand Tokatyan for more than three years. There was tension between the two, however. Lehmann envisioned an opera career for Bumbry while Bumbry, being shy and somewhat reserved, wanted a concert stage career. Lehmann coached Bumbry into dramatic gestures and operatic scenes and eventually won the young singer over to her way of thinking. It was also at this time that the controversy over Bumbry's voice classification began. Lehmann insisted that the young student was a mezzo-soprano while Tokatyan felt that she was a soprano. The dispute was temporarily settled after Tokatyan's death when Bumbry decided for herself that she was a mezzo. As she was offered more soprano roles, Bumbry was to decide quite some time later that she was indeed a soprano.

While studying with Lehmann and Tokatyan, Bumbry won several awards. In 1957 she won both the Marian Anderson Award and the John Hay Whitney Award. In 1958 Bumbry became a semifinalist in the Metropolitan Opera Auditions of the Air and won a one-thousand-dollar prize.

Europe seemed to offer more opportunities for young singers, and Bumbry made her European debut in June 1959 at Wigmore Hall in London. In the fall she went to Paris, where she sang with the Paris Philharmonic Chorus in Bach's *Actus Tragicus* cantata and Handel's *Messiah* with the Colonne Orchestra. She made her debut as Amneris in *Aida* in March 1960 with the Paris Opera. Subsequently, she signed a three-year contract with the Basel, Switzerland, Opera where she gained further experience on the operatic stage and more familiarity with the repertoire. When the Paris Opera toured Japan in 1962, Bumbry sang the lead role in *Carmen*.

Black Venus Stirs Controversy

Bumbry came more fully into the international spotlight when she debuted as Venus in *Tannhäuser* on July 23, 1961, at the Wagner Bayreuth Festival. Her selection by Wieland Wagner, the grandson of the composer, caused a controversy in the musical world. Many could not accept the fact that Venus would be black. Many members of the cast protested, and the press fed the controversy by insisting that a black Venus was against Richard Wagner's intention. Bumbry reacted to the storm quietly and went about learning the music. On the night of the performance, however, Bumbry received forty-two curtain calls. The press, which had so recently denounced her selection, showered praise upon her. News of Bumbry's triumph reached America. *Newsweek* of August 7, 1961, reported that Wieland Wagner stated, "When I heard Grace Bumbry I knew she was the perfect Venus. Grandfather would have been delighted" (36). Wieland made such a statement despite the fact that his grandfather, Richard, was considered by many to be a notorious anti-Semite and racist. *Newsweek* went on to say:

> For a sometime choir girl whose mother was a Mississippi schoolteacher and whose father is a railroad freight handler, Miss Bumbry's triumph was the greatest yet in an operatic career launched in Europe earlier this year. . . . Now Grace Bumbry, newly traveling the road to fame, could note that of the 42 curtain calls in the 30-minute Bayreuth ovation, her returns brought the sharpest applause (36).

The Bayreuth *Tannhauser* Venus was followed by her American debut in the role in 1963 with the Chicago Lyric Opera. Her American presence had previously been established, however, on the concert stage. In November 1962 Bumbry made her Carnegie Hall debut in which she featured the artistically demanding lieder of Strauss, Schubert, Brahms, and Liszt. The November 19, 1962, *Newsweek* reported:

> Though some purists felt that classics like Schubert's "Der Doppelgänger" had eluded her, the audience at Carnegie reveled in hearing such a program sung with so much vocal splendor. Her

voice is big, its range is wide, and its color gloriously rich (73).

Also in 1963, Bumbry made her debut at Covent Garden. This was followed by roles as Lady Macbeth (1965-1966) and Carmen (1966-1967) at Salzburg. She later sang Stantuzza at La Scala, the Rome Opera, and the Vienna Saatsoper in 1970. Her return to the soprano repertoire began with the role of Salome, which brought her back to Covent Garden in 1970. In 1973 she sang the role at the Metropolitan Opera in New York. This appearance at the Metropolitan had been preceded by her debut there in the role of Eboli in Verdi's *Don Carlos* on October 7, 1965, when she was given three curtain calls. Abdul writes:

> It was apparent from her entrance that Miss Bumbry was star material. She swept in on cue and paused majestically for that extra split second that marks a star from a run of the mill debutante. The audience burst into a stormy ovation before she had sung one note.
>
> And when she sang the fiendishly difficult aria "Canzone de Velo," which requires the mezzo to sing with the flexibility of a coloratura, Miss Bumbry tossed it off as if it were the easiest task in the world for her. This only served to whet the audience's appetite for what was to come in (110).

Although she chose to live in Europe, Bumbry maintained an American presence. When Beverly Sills decided to boost the New York City Opera's image with major artists, she chose Bumbry to play Medea as well as to play Abigaille in *Nabucco*. In 1985 she played the role of Bess in the Metropolitan's *Porgy and Bess* under James Levine. The opera played to full houses for three years.

When Bumbry married Polish-German tenor Erwin Jackel on July 6, 1963, he gave up his career as a singer to be her manager. The old dispute arose again as she began to explore more of the soprano literature. Her husband disagreed and eventually they were divorced. Bumbry, however, continued to perform both the mezzo and soprano repertoires.

A partial discography of Bumbry's works includes the following: *Aida* (ANG M-63229, RCA, LSC-6198); *Aida Highlights* (ANG 4AV-3490, RCA RK-1237); *Carmen Highlights* (ANG 4AV-34005); *Le Cid* (Col M2K-34211); *Messiah Highlights* (LON-421212-4); *100 Singers—100 Years* (RCA-CRM8-5177); *Operatic Arias* (ORF-S-0818141);*Requiem* (Mozart) (ANG-AE 34461); and *Tannhäuser* (PHI (CD) 420122-2).

References

Abdul, Raoul. *Blacks in Classical Music*. New York: Dodd, Mead, 1977. 110-11.

Current Biography. New York: H. W. Wilson, 1964. 60-62. Photograph, p. 61.

Newsweek 58 (7 August 1961): 36. Includes photograph.

"Test by Lieder." *Newsweek* (19 November 1962): 73. Includes photograph.

Tudor, Dean, and Nancy Tudor. *Black Music*. Littleton, Colo.: Libraries Unlimited, 1979. 454.

Southern Eileen. *Biographical Dictionary of Afro-American and African Musicians*. Westport, Conn.: Greenwood Press, 1982. 55.

Story, Rosalyn. *And So I Sing: African American Divas of Opera and Concert*. New York: Warner Books, 1990. 141-56. Photograph, p. 143.

Ben E. Bailey

Selma Hortense Burke

(1900-)

Sculptor, educator, school founder

Selma Burke is one of America's most gifted and distinguished artists, "and I have paid my dues," she said recently in an interview (3 September 1990). Her long career spans the Harlem Renaissance, the Great Depression, and two world wars. At the age of ninety-one, she may be one of America's most active artists. This is at least the opinion of her publicist, Ron Asby. "Even now, this exuberant artist works on three or four works at a time. Her strong personality rubs off on people. Being around her has been both encouraging and stimulating. I work in wood and know how hard it is to work in the medium of stone. I wish I could keep up with her, but I can't" (Interview with Rob Asby, 12 September 1990).

Selma Hortense Burke was born in Mooresville, North Carolina, in 1900, the seventh of ten children of a railroad brakeman and African Methodist Episcopal (AME) Zion minister and his wife. Mary L. Burke Cofield, her mother, was twelve years old at the end of slavery. Her great-grandfather, Samuel S. Jackson (who fought in the Civil War), was owned, according to Burke, by the family of Stonewall Jackson (Interview with Selma Burke, 10 September 1990). Her great-grandmother was "owned by the family of Harriet Beecher Stowe" (Schlegel, 21). Although her father died when Selma Burke was twelve, her mother in 1970 was already one hundred one years old. At the time of this writing Burke's two sisters, aged ninety-four and eighty-five, still survive.

Because of her mother, Selma Burke began her professional career in medicine rather than art. "You can't make a living at that,'' Burke recalls her mother saying about her desire to study art (Schlegel, 21). Her postsecondary education began at Slater Industrial and State Normal School (now Winston-Salem State University), where she met Simon Green Atkins, the school's founder, who encouraged her ''to do something with her life'' (Daniels, 16). She continued her studies at Saint Agnes Training School for Nurses at Saint Augustine College, Raleigh, North Carolina, in 1924. This was followed by additional studies at Women's Medical College in Philadelphia, Pennsylvania.

Selma Burke's work as a nurse eventually was to lead her back to art. She began working for a wealthy New York dowager who urged her to continue her interest in art. She moved to Philadelphia, where she started lessons in sculpture at the Leonardo da Vinci School. While studying at New York's Cooper Union, she met Augusta Savage, another noted black American sculptor. With the aid of scholarships, Burke studied art at Sarah Lawrence College and took a MFA at Columbia College in 1941.

As many black American artists before her, Selma Burke made the obligatory journey to Europe, notably to France and Austria. In Vienna, Austria, she studied ceramics with Polvoney, and in Paris she studied sculpture with Aristide Maillol. She also studied architecture with Frank Lloyd Wright and Josef Hoffman, who is considered the ''father of modern architecture'' (Boar, 28). Selma Burke talks passionately about her trips to Montparnasse in Paris where there were many private consultations with the painter Henri Matisse concerning her work. ''He told me to loosen up and stay free to be open and honest. He said that I had a big talent and he wanted me to add size and volume to my drawings. He wanted me to open up as a person'' (Interview with Selma Burke, 10 September 1990). When asked about Matisse's influence on her work, she cited the composition *Female Torso,* which she described as a drawing in charcoal on yellow paper. She cited the composition *Temptation* as one that resulted from her work with Maillol.

Selma Burke speaks with pride when she talks of her family members who finished college; namely, from Livingstone College in Salisbury, North Carolina, and Johnson C. Smith University in Charlotte, North Carolina (among them Geneva Miller Burke, the Reverend S. J. Burke, and Granville Burke). She speaks with greater pride when she talks of her great-grandfather, Samuel S. Jackson, who ''exchanged his chains for an education.'' He earned his degree at Berea College in Berea, Kentucky. Her mother, who wanted all of her children to be professionally trained, herself entered college at Winston-Salem State University at the age of seventy-five. (Interview with Selma Burke, 10 September 1990).

The more famous of her two marriages was to Claude McKay, Harlem Renaissance poet extraordinaire, whom she met in 1935. She ''respected McKay's accomplishments and his wide knowledge of European art and sculpture. She was herself studying to become a sculptor, and she learned much from McKay's intimate knowledge of European and African art'' (Cooper, 305). The marriage ended in divorce after her return from Europe. After a reconciliation and another divorce, she married Herman Kobbe, an architect, in the 1940s. This marriage ended with his death in the early 1950s. To neither union were born children. ''Art was enough'' declared Burke during an interview with Sharon Schlegel of the *Trenton Times* (9 October 1983, 21).

Sculptor Creates Design for Coin

At the age of five, Selma Burke's sister's nursery rhymes and the clay of a white dried-up riverbed excited her artistic imagination. ''I would create from them butterflies and other forms out of that clay'' (Schlegel, 21). And this five-year-old would later create a sculpture that would lead to national and international fame. She won a 1943 competition over eleven other competitors, three of whom were black, to design the portrait of President Franklin Roosevelt that appears on the dime. Burke remembers vividly her February meeting with President Roosevelt and her conversations with Eleanor Roosevelt, who criticized Burke's image of her husband, which she found too young.

After a life of art, sculpture, and teaching, one of Burke's dreams came true. At the age of eighty-three, the Selma Burke Gallery opened in 1983 at Winston-Salem State University. The seed for the gallery seems to have been planted in 1972 when her works were exhibited at the Benton Convention Hall on the campus. The graduate chapter of the Delta Sigma Theta Sorority was granted funds by the Urban Arts of the Winston-Salem Arts Council to inventory the Burke collection. The more than one hundred works, valued at more than $250,000, all come from Selma Burke's private collection. Other prominent artists such as Romare Bearden, Richard Satterwhite, and Claude Ward, are represented in the collection. According to the first curator of the Burke gallery, this is the first time a gallery has been named in honor of an African-American woman artist (Interview with Hayward Oubre, 16 September 1990). In the summer of 1990, amid some apparent controversy, the gallery was moved to Johnson C. Smith University in Charlotte, North Carolina.

Selma Burke's life has been dedicated to teaching others about sculpture and art. She has taught at Livingstone College, Swarthmore College, and Harvard University, as well as Friends Charter School in Pennsylvania and Harlem Center in New York. From 1967 to 1976 she worked at the Mellon Foundation as a consultant and as education coordinator at the Carnegie Institute. Students all over the country have had the opportunity to hear Burke. Private students are taught in her studio in New Hope, Pennsylvania. New teaching duties began in October 1990 in the Honors College at Johnson C. Smith University. She founded the Selma Burke Art Center in Pittsburgh. She is also founder of the Selma Burke School of Sculpture in New York.

In addition to the works on display at the Selma Burke Gallery at Johnson C. Smith University, other works can be viewed at the Metropolitan Museum of Art, Whitney Museum, and Philadelphia Art Museum. Burke's statue of Martin Luther King, Jr., stands in Marshall Park in Charlotte, North Carolina. Presently she is working on an autobiography "in order to set the record straight," and a coffee-table collection of her sculpture. In fall 1990 the artist attended exhibits of her work at the Kingsley Center, Pittsburgh, Pennsylvania, and at the Lyndon Baines Johnson Library in Austin, Texas.

Numerous awards have distinguished the career of Selma Burke. The most recent awards include the Candace Award for extraordinary achievements by black women (1983), the Pearl Buck Award (1988), and the *Essence* Magazine Award (1989). She has been awarded honorary degrees from Livingstone College, North Carolina Central University, the James Teamer School of Religion, Moore College of Art, Winston-Salem State University, Wake Forest University, Spelman College, and Johnson C. Smith University.

Selma H. Burke, the American artist (for she refused to be categorized throughout her career in any other way), summed up her life as an artist: "I really live and move in the atmosphere in which I am creating" (Interview with Selma Burke, 3 September 1990).

References

Asby, Ron. Interview with the author, 12 September 1990.

Blue, Greenberg. "Mooresville Sculptor Keeps Promise." *Winston-Salem Magazine* (June 1984).

Boar, Harriet. "Black Sculptress Has Come a Long Way." *Charlotte Observer*, 9 April 1970. 28.

Burke, Selma. Interview with the author, 3 September and 10 September 1990.

Cederholm, Theresa Dickason, ed. *Afro-American Artists: A Bio-bibliographical Directory*. Boston: Boston Public Library, 1973. 91.

Cooper, Wayne F. *Claude McKay: Rebel Sojourner in the Harlem Renaissance; A Biography*. Baton Rouge: Louisiana State University Press, 1987. 305-306.

Driskell, David. *Hidden Heritage: Afro-American Art, 1800-1950*. Bellevue Art Museum, Art Museum Association of America. Bellevue, Wash., 1985. 57, 59, 61, 94.

———. *Two Centuries of Black American Art*. Los Angeles: County Museum of Art. New York: Alfred A. Knopf 1976. 160-61, 177.

Igoe, Lynn Moody, with James Igoe. *250 Years of Afro-American Art: An Annotated Bibliography*. New York: Bowker, 1981. 525-27.

Nell, Daniels. "WSSU's Selma Burke Gallery." *Winston-Salem* [Magazine] (July/August 1989): 16.

Oubre, Hayword. Interview with the author, 16 September 1990.

Pendergraft, Norman E. *Heralds of Life: Artis, Bearden, Burke*. Durham: Museum of Art, North Carolina Central University, November 1977. 15-16.

Schlegel, Sharon. "Selma Burke: The Artist is Honored." *Trenton Times*, (9 October 1983): 21.

Slade, John. "Selma Burke Art Gallery Now Open." *Inside WSSU* 1 (1 November 1983).

Twardy, Charles. "A Lasting Impression." Columbia: South Carolina, March 13, 1987.

Rosa Bobia

Yvonne Braithwaite Burke

(1932-)

Lawyer, politician

Yvonne Braithwaite Burke has been a formidable power both as a lawyer and as a politician from the state of California. Her salient contributions, both political and legislative, to California and to the nation have had significant

Yvonne Braithwaite Burke

positive consequences for the quality of life for minorities, women, and the poor.

The only child of James T. Watson and Lola (Moore) Watson was named Pearl Yvonne Watson at birth on October 5, 1932, in Los Angeles, California. Watson was a janitor at the MGM Film Studios and his wife was a real estate agent. Because Yvonne disliked Pearl as a first name, she dropped it while a youngster growing up on the east side of Los Angeles.

Yvonne Watson's elementary school educators recognized her exceptional intellectual prowess very soon after her enrollment, and she was transferred to a private school associated with the University of Southern California. She attended Manual Arts High School and became vice-president of the student body.

Her college education began at the University of California, Berkeley, in 1949. This was made possible by the help of a scholarship from her father's building services union. In her junior year, she transferred to the Los Angeles campus of the University of California. She received her juris doctor degree from the University of Southern California Law School in 1956, graduating in the top third of her class. While in law school, she was refused admission to the campus women's law society. To counteract this overt act of bigotry, Burke and two Jewish students started a rival professional sorority. During this period of her life as an aspiring young attorney, she paid part of her tuition by modeling for *Ebony* magazine and by working in a garment factory and in campus libraries.

After graduating she went into private law practice, specializing in civil, probate, and real estate law. During the fifties, she was acutely aware of the pervasive discriminatory practice of denying blacks, women, and sometimes Jews the opportunity to join established law firms, regardless of their academic achievement.

Yvonne Watson married Louis Braithwaite, a mathematician, in 1957, a marriage that ended in divorce seven years later.

During the Watts riots in 1965, she organized a legal defense team for rioters, and Governor Edmond G. Brown appointed her attorney for the McCone Commission to investigate the causes of this major social disturbance.

Arenas in the Political World Opened

Her victorious campaign in 1966 as the first black assemblywoman, representing the Sixty-third Assembly District of California, was the beginning of a meteoric ascendancy in the political world. She was reelected in 1968 and again in 1970. These political triumphs were not easily achieved because Burke was the victim of scurrilous attacks and accusations of being a black militant and a Communist. During her tenure in the California legislature, she was a diligent supporter of such progressive programs as prison reform, child care, equal job opportunities for women, and increased aid for education. During her three terms in office, Burke introduced legislation to prohibit racial discrimination in state construction contracts and to provide free day-care centers on college campuses.

Although Yvonne Burke had a fairly easy campaign in both the primary and general election for the California Assembly in 1968, it was a particularly difficult year for her. In her oral history she describes her experience of that eventful and traumatic year:

> I was a [Robert F.] Kennedy delegate. Kennedy came in very late to the state of California. I worked very hard in his primary campaign. Of course, '68 was a very difficult year for me, because I sort of lived in a life of tragedy. I had been very active . . . in the civil rights movement; I had gone down to the South with Martin Luther King, [Jr.]—I had been down there while I was a state legislator. Then he was killed in April. I went down to assist with the funeral, and I did the protocol for the funeral. Then shortly after that, I came right back here [California]. It was May, and the Kennedy campaign started. I worked very hard on the Kennedy campaign. Robert Kennedy was killed the day of the election. Then it was a summer [when] the Vietnam War was starting to escalate. I was a delegate to the Democratic Convention on the platform committee. I had a personal tragedy in my life; my mother [Lola (Moore) Watson] died in the middle of it. I was involved in the platform committee there; for two weeks I was in Chicago, where the police did everything but put me in jail. I mean I was harassed and subject to just tremendous pressures. . . . It was terrible, it was terrible. The whole experience, the whole year, was just one that I just hardly got through (Burke, "New Arenas of Black Influence," oral history 1982, transcript, 23).

Yvonne Burke became disenchanted and frustrated at the unresponsiveness of the state legislature concerning what she believed to be critical social problems. When a court-ordered reapportionment of California created the Thirty-seventh Congressional District, she decided to enter the Democratic primary for the new seat, which encompassed a predominantly black population in southwest Los Angeles. A formidable opponent was Billy Mills, a black Los Angeles city councilman. She defeated Mills and three other candidates by winning fifty-four percent of the votes to become the Democratic nominee for this congressional seat. On June 14, 1972, several days after her victory, she married William A. Burke, a Los Angeles businessman and former aide to her opponent, Mills.

Burke Gains National Prominence in Politics

At the Democratic National Convention in Miami Beach, Florida, in July 1972, Burke served as vice-chairperson of a meeting convened to determine the Democratic party political platform and consider rule change. The meeting soon became quite disorderly due to strong disagreements over proposed rule changes. Though the meeting became the longest in history for a Democratic platform committee, Burke's competence and deftness guided the session to a successful conclusion. After a record-setting twenty-one votes, she finally gained approval of extensive changes in the Democratic party's rules. The result was that the convention permitted greater participation by minority groups in the political process of the Democratic party. Her performance at the convention catapulted her to national prominence in American politics.

On November 23, 1973, Yvonne Burke gave birth to a daughter, Autumn Roxanne, becoming the first member of Congress to give birth while serving in office. She also has one stepdaughter, Christine.

Yvonne Burke was reelected in 1976 to the House, but resigned in 1978 to run for the office of California state attorney general. She successfully garnered the nomination of the Democratic party, but was defeated by George Deukmejian in the general election.

In June 1979 Governor Jerry Brown appointed Yvonne Braithwaite Burke to fill a vacancy for the Los Angeles County Board of Supervisors. She served as a member of this powerful five-member board until her election defeat in 1980.

In an article for *Ebony* magazine (March 1974), Burke outlined the kind of world she envisioned for her infant daughter: "I visualize a time within the next ten years when we should have fifty Black Congressmen because right now there are at least that many districts with 35 per cent or more blacks. It's just a matter of time until we have a Black governor and, yes, a Black President (Burke, "The Kind of World I Want for My Child," 149).

Among the numerous prestigious and influential memberships she holds are: trusteeship, Urban League; Women Lawyer's Association; Coalition of 100 Black Women; University of California Board of Regents; director, Los Angeles Branch Federal Reserve Bank of San Francisco; and board of directors, United Negro College Fund. In 1984 she was vice-chairperson of the Olympics Organizing Committee.

Honors and awards include: Professional Achievement Award, UCLA, 1974; designation as one of two hundred future leaders, *Time* magazine, 1974; Chubb Fellow, Yale University, 1972; Fellow, Institute of Politics, John F. Kennedy School of Government, Harvard University, 1971-1972; and numerous awards from the Los Angeles City Council and the Los Angeles Board of Supervisors.

Presently, Yvonne Braithwaite Burke is a partner in the firm of Jones, Day, Reavis and Pogue, in Los Angeles.

References

The Almanac of American Politics, 1978 New York: E. P. Dutton, 1978.

Burke, Yvonne Braithwaite. "The Kind of World I Want for My Child." *Ebony* 29 (March 1974): 146-53.

———. "New Arenas of Black Influence." Transcript of interview by Steven Edginton, 1982. Oral History Program, Powell Library, University of California, Los Angeles.

Current Biography Yearbook. New York: H. W. Wilson, 1975.

The Current Black Man, Decade '70. Vol 1, Part 1. Los Angeles: Record Publishing Co., 1970.

Encyclopedia of Black America. Edited by August D. Low and Virgil A. Clift. New York: McGraw-Hill, 1981. Page 680 shows a photograph of the Congressional Black Caucus for 1974, which includes Burke as a member.

Lanker, Brian. *I Dream a World:* New York: Tabori and Chang, 1989. Page 130 contains a photograph of Burke.

The Negro Almanac. 4th ed. New York: Wiley, 1983. 379.

Robinson, Louie. "Women Lawmakers on the Move." *Ebony* 27 (October 1972): 48-56.

Who's Who Among Black Americans, 6th ed. Detroit: Gale Research Inc., 1990.

Who's Who in America, 45th ed. Chicago: Marquis, 1989.

Who's Who in American Politics, 8th ed. New York: Bowker, 1982.

Collections

The oral history interview of Yvonne Braithwaite Burke by Steven Edgington is on deposit in the Oral History Program, Powell Library Building, University of California, Los Angeles. Photographs of Burke are available from the Department of Special Collections, University Research Library, UCLA.

Oscar L. Sims

Margaret Taylor Burroughs

(1917-)

Artist, arts administrator, educator, lecturer, museum director, writer

Margaret Burrough's contributions to education, art, literature and the preservation of black American history and heritage seem almost limitless. In 1961 she and her husband, Charles, opened the Du Sable Museum of African-American History in their home in Chicago. She has worked both at home and abroad to expand global consciousness and to promote human rights and awareness of the beauty and durability of black art and culture.

Margaret Burroughs was born to Octavia Pierre Taylor and Alexander Taylor on November 1, 1917, in Saint Rose Parish, Louisiana, a small town near New Orleans. Three years later, as part of the great migration, the family moved to Chicago hoping for improved living conditions. Burroughs's father exchanged his background as a farmer for labor in a railroad roundhouse. Her mother, however, continued working as a domestic servant.

While the family's economic circumstances did not change dramatically, the Taylors and other southern émigrés did gain access to greater educational and cultural opportunities in the North. In 1933 Burroughs graduated from Englewood High School and began exhibiting her work in local art fairs. Two years later she participated in the production of Langston Hughes's *Don't You Want To Be Free?* by the Negro People's Theatre at the South Side Abraham Lincoln Center. In 1937 she graduated with a teaching certificate for elementary grades from Chicago Normal College. Two years later she obtained an Upper Grades Art Certificate from the same institution, which was by then called the Chicago Teacher's College (now Chicago State University). During the same year (1939), at the age of twenty-two, Burroughs married artist Bernard Goss. From this union was born their daughter, Gayle Goss Toller.

During the following decade, Burroughs embarked on her lifelong career as an artist, educator, and community worker. In 1940 she became a charter member of the Chicago South Side Community Art Center, which was dedicated by Alain Locke and Eleanor Roosevelt. She has worked with this center for twenty years as an officer and a trustee. The center provided a place for black Americans to take art classes and exhibit their work. Burroughs's own prints and watercolors were exhibited there in 1941 and 1945 and one of her pieces won a citation in 1953.

Throughout the early 1940s, Burroughs's work was displayed in cities across the nation, including Chicago at the American Negro Exhibition (1940), New York at the McMillen Inc. Galleries (1941), and Atlanta at Atlanta University (1941, 1943, and 1945). The latter exhibit proved to be most significant for Burroughs. It was one of a series of annual events initiated by Hale Woodruff in 1942 for the promotion of African-American art on a national level. They offered both young and older artists a chance to exhibit and opportunities to win purchase prizes, and they formed the basis of a permanent collection of African-American art at Atlanta University. Burroughs, who had won the third print award in the 1947 Annual, recalled what the occasion meant to her:

> But for the Atlanta Show, I might not be here. I never would have seen the creative light of day. For most of us, the Atlanta Show provided the first memory, the first mention, and the first knowledge of the black arts presence. I saw in those catalogs the works of black artists like Jacob Lawrence, John Wilson, Elizabeth Catlett, Charles White, Aaron Douglas, William Artis, and many others. This Exhibition vehicle, was founded by Hale Woodruff and nurtured by Atlanta University. Because of this Annual, Atlanta University became an oasis in the Southern desert, not only for the Black artist of the South, but for those also in the North, East and West as well. . . . To many of us coming up in the 40s . . . acceptance in the Atlanta Show, helped to bring us Negro artists together from all over the country (Stoelting, 24).

Much to her delight, Burroughs later won the Watercolor Purchase Award at the Atlanta University Art Annual in 1955.

With a growing concern for the education of youth, Burroughs elected to increase her knowledge and skills toward that end. She graduated from Chicago Normal College in 1937 with an elementary teacher's certificate. In 1946 she received her bachelor's degree in art education from the Art Institute of Chicago. In the same year she began her first job as an art instructor at DuSable High School in Chicago, a position she was to hold for the next twenty-two years until 1968. In time, Burroughs and Goss realized that their relationship was no longer working, and they divorced. Burroughs then moved into a coach-house studio across from the Art Center on Michigan Avenue. Within a few short years, she published her first book, secured a graduate degree, and remarried.

In 1947 she wrote and illustrated a children's book, *Jasper, the Drummin' Boy*. The same year Burroughs received an honorable mention for printmaking at the annual Negro Art Exhibition. In 1948 she not only received her master's degree in art education from the Chicago Art Institute, but also exhibited her work at the San Francisco Civic Museum at the Illinois State Fair. On December 23, 1949, she married Charles Gordon Burroughs, a poet and writer who had lived for seventeen years in the Soviet Union. They later adopted their son, Paul.

The 1950s brought international recognition to Burroughs's art. After being included in a group exhibition at the Market Place Gallery in New York in 1950, Burroughs had a one-woman show in Mexico City, 1952-1953. On sabbatical leave from teaching, she and her husband lived in Mexico, where she studied at the Esmerelda Art School and the Taller de Grafica (School of Graphic Arts). Others who studied at the institution were Hale Woodruff, John Wilson, Lawrence Jones, and Charles White. It was there that Burroughs, like her friend Elizabeth Catlett, studied the theory of art as a vehicle of social commentary. She was greatly influenced by the way the muralists Rivera and Orozco merged art with politics. Responding to the call for art for the masses, Burroughs developed her style of figurative imagery using the "democratic" media of linoleum cuts and woodblock prints. With this medium, multiple images can be made and sold inexpensively to working people. An example from this period is her *Moses* (1954), a determined portrait of the abolitionist Harriet Tubman (illustrated in Dover, p. 20). By the early 1960s Burroughs had depicted many other great African-Americans such as Crispus Attucks, Frederick Douglass, and Sojourner Truth. Burroughs wrote a poem that appeared in her first volume of poetry to her grandson, Eric Toller, to explain the responsibility she felt in creating these images. *What Shall I Tell My Children Who Are Black?* (1968), refers back to the collection of African-American folk expressions she had published in 1955, *Did You Feed My Cow? Rhymes and Tales from City Streets and Country Lanes*. Burroughs intended to develop herself and her students as fully as possible by preserving and contributing to their common heritage.

Thereafter the artist's work increasingly merited attention. She began to expand her repertoire of oils, acrylics, and prints to include sculpture and batik. Her art was exhibited in Mexico City again in 1955. Burroughs's pieces also were hung at the Kenosha Museum in 1953 and the Hull House in Chicago in 1955. That same year, Burroughs won a citation from the Commission for the Negro in Arts. Two years later her art was displayed at the Annual Lake Meadows Outdoor Arts and Crafts Fair, which she founded along with Bernard Goss, Marion Perkins, and others. Additionally, in 1957 Burroughs received the First Annual Art Festival Citation from the Beaux Arts Guild of Tuskegee Institute (now University). Her prints were next exhibited at Howard University in 1961, the National Conference of Artists at Lincoln University in Jefferson City, Missouri, in 1962 (where she won the Hallmark Prize for the "best in the show"), and at Xavier University in New Orleans in 1963.

Committed to her role as an educator, Burroughs did postgraduate work during the summers at Teachers College, Columbia University, 1958-1960. She became increasingly disappointed with school texts, however, which ignored or trivialized the significant achievements of black people:

> There was nothing about our glorious past in Africa and very little about our immense contributions to the growth of this country. . . . Africans were portrayed in the crudest of manners. . . . "How could we expect to develop healthy concepts about ourselves if we kept getting force-fed that inaccurate, racist material?" I asked myself (quoted in Dickerson, 49).

Burroughs was determined to enact concrete changes immediately. In 1959 she helped found the National Conference of Artists (NCA) and remained its chairperson until 1963. The NCA furnished a networking system to encourage black American artists throughout the United States. From 1960 until 1962 Burroughs was the art director and assistant in research for the Negro History Hall of Fame, which was presented at the Chicago Coliseum by the *New Crusader* newspaper.

DuSable Museum Opens

While the Negro History Hall of Fame gave much-needed recognition to black peoples, Burroughs envisioned a permanent institution that would be "dedicated to preserving, interpreting and displaying our heritage" (quoted in Dickerson, 49). Thus, she and eleven others formed the National Negro Museum and Historical Foundation, which presented annual Negro history programs and exhibitions. In 1961 Charles and Margaret Burroughs opened the Ebony Museum of Negro History in their home on Michigan Avenue. Inspired by the positive community response, Margaret Burroughs labored to raise funds for expansion of the museum's facilities and programs. By way of acknowledging Chicago's founding father and encouraging economic support from the city, the institution changed its name in 1968 to the DuSable Museum of African-American History in Chicago. Jean Baptiste Pointe DuSable, a man of African descent, received public recognition as one of the first settlers in northern Illinois in the 1700s. The appellation achieved its goal; Chicago donated to the DuSable Museum an old administration building in Washington Park on the South Side. Today, the museum encompasses more than 60,000 square feet of space. From a small group of volunteers, Burroughs has developed the institution into one with a staff of twenty-one. The museum has over one thousand members and is funded by membership fees, operational grants, and contributions from foundations and businesses. The museum is also supported in part by a state tax levy.

The DuSable houses a fifty-thousand item collection of art, papers, artifacts, and memorabilia, including more than ten thousand books related to black history and culture, as well as objects once owned by notable African-Americans. Burroughs states, "We try to get personal items because they mean a lot more to children" (Edwards, 35). Highlights include the academic robe worn by W. E. B. Du Bois when he received an honorary degree from the University of Ghana; Joe Louis's Golden Glove Championship gloves, paintings, sculptures, and books from the collection of Langston Hughes, as well as other rare artifacts.

Indebted to Burroughs for her devotion to art and education, the Illinois community graciously thanked the educator in numerous ways. She has received numerous awards, citations, and honors. For her participation in the State of Illinois Centennial of Emancipation Committee she was given a Centennial Award in 1963. The same year she accepted a National Conference of Artists Trophy. Three years later Burroughs won the Volunteer for Community Improvement Award, and in 1968, the Prospair Girls Social and Charitable Club Award. The recipient of more than a dozen honorary doctorates, Burroughs was honored in 1908 by President Carter at the White House.

Throughout her life, Burroughs has been recognized as an enthusiastic, tireless teacher. After giving art classes for twenty-seven years at DuSable High School, she was invited to teach African and African-American art history at the Chicago Art Institute for one year (1968-1969). Burroughs then accepted a position as professor of humanities at Kennedy-King City College, a position that she held from 1968 to 1979, when she officially retired from teaching. She also persevered in educating the public by lecturing throughout the United States and serving as a member of the Governor's Commission on the Financing of the Arts in the State of Illinois in 1971. That same year Burroughs received a New City Award from the Better Boys Foundation.

In 1972 Burroughs's lifelong commitment to art education was formally recognized in the academic world; she received an honorary doctoral degree (DLH) from Lewis University in Lockport, Illinois, although *Black American Writers* says 1972; Dickerson, Tibbs, and *Contemporary Authors* say 1973; and *Who's Who in Black America* says 1974. Additional tributes quickly followed, including an Urban Gateways Honor Award, a leadership award for excellence in art from the YWCA, and a Rockefeller Family Foundation Award.

Burroughs proceeded to give tirelessly to her community, and she served as director of the DuSable Museum from 1961 to 1985, when she became emerita. Further, from 1976 until 1980 she served on the Chicago Council on Fine Arts. In 1983 the educator received her second doctorate of humane letters degree, this time from Chicago State University. In 1988 her alma mater, the Art Institute of Chicago, awarded her a doctorate of fine arts, its highest award.

Although Burroughs's art had first been seen in another country in 1952, it was not until 1965 that her work again gained similar attention. This time she achieved two one-woman shows in Eastern Europe; her solo exhibitions took place in Poland and the USSR, and her work was also included in the International Kook Art Exhibit in Leipzig, Germany. Burroughs saw her art displayed abroad as she traveled throughout Europe and the Soviet Union that year. The following year she returned to Russia leading a delegation of African-American artists. The USSR responded by displaying Burroughs's art at the House of Friendship in Moscow in 1967. Profoundly moved by her journeys, Burroughs declared, "I wish my art to speak not only for my people, but for all humanity . . . my subject matter is social commentary and seeks to improve the condition of life for all people" (Bontemps, 64).

With an increasing global consciousness, Burroughs worked actively on many international committees in the late 1960s, particularly those concerned with the African diaspora. In 1968 she served on the American Forum of African Studies Program and was part of the staff of the American Forum for International Study at the University of Ghana the following year. In 1970 she advised two groups—the staff of the American Forum for International Study at the University of the West Indies in Jamaica and the Chicago Council of Foreign Relations.

In 1968 Burroughs received a National Endowment for the Humanities grant to study museology at the Field Museum of Chicago. That same year she took additional courses at the Institute of African Studies at Northwestern University. She continued her formal education at Illinois State University in 1970.

Since Burroughs's initial sojourns to West Africa in 1968 and the Caribbean in 1970, she has returned many times to those areas, traveling in Egypt, Ethiopia, Kenya, Tanzania, Dahomey, Togo, Nigeria, and Morocco, as well as Haiti, Jamaica, and Trinidad. Further, in 1977 she was one of sixteen women selected to tour China. These journeys have reaffirmed Burroughs's commitments to ending oppression of people of color everywhere and contributing to "the betterment of life for all mankind and especially my people" in all aspects of her life (Dickerson, 52).

Burroughs Writes Poetry and Short Stories

Burroughs's growing belief in global citizenship affirmed multiple forms of expressions. Joining with active nationalists and Pan-Africanists throughout her country, she began to write poetry focusing on the legacies of Africans and African-Americans. During the 1960s Burroughs held public readings of her prose poems at the DuSable Museum, messages that were "statements which the time I live in compelled me to make" (Dickerson, 50). Drawing on folk traditions and contemporary events, Burroughs wrote in simple, direct language for a broad audience. Her themes concentrated on the historical and cultural accomplishments of black peoples, particularly African-American freedom fighters. "Brother Freedom" was her first significant published poem in this vein. It appeared in the 1967 anthology dedicated to Malcolm X (El-Hajj Malik El-Shabazz), *For Malcolm; Poems on the Life and Death of Malcolm X*. The publication was significant for Burroughs; it placed her work on a par with that of forty-two other poets, among them such distinguished writers as Amiri Baraka, Gwendolyn Brooks, Robert Hayden, and Margaret Walker.

The following year Burroughs published her first volume of poetry, *What Shall I Tell My Children Who Are Black?* (1968). The title poem has become famous throughout the United States.

Another notable piece of hers is the proselike "Everybody

But Me,'' which concerns the lack of citizenship accorded to African-Americans in a supposed democracy. The extended monologue lists United States symbols of liberty such as Washington and Lincoln, the Declaration of Independence, the Constitution, and the Bill of Rights, commenting on their exclusion of African-Americans.

Seeking a greater knowledge of black culture and inspired by her initial journeys abroad, Burroughs next secured a travel grant to West Africa from the American Forum for International Study in 1968. That summer in Ghana provided imagery for her second volume of poetry, *Africa, My Africa* (1970). In eighteen poems, Burroughs explored the meaning of her personal background and African heritage in the larger context of the African-American experience as both a continuation and division of Africa's history.

While Burroughs actively pursued writing in the 1960s and 1970s, she by no means abandoned the visual arts. In 1969 her work was exhibited at three locations in the United States—Fox Valley Presbyterian Church in Geneva, Wisconsin, Ball State Teacher's College, and Atlanta University, where she won third place in sculpture. Her art was also included in a group show at Elmhurst College the following year. Burroughs's work continued to be acclaimed in Chicago; it was shown at the YWCA in 1973 and in a series of solo exhibitions at the Southside Community Art Center in 1972, 1974, and 1978. Additionally, Burroughs was represented in the major traveling exhibition, ''Two Centuries of African-American Art'' in 1976. Her first retrospective then occurred in 1982; she was honored along with the sculptor Marion Perkins at the Evans-Tibbs Gallery in Washington, D.C. In the late 1980s, Burroughs's work could be seen in the following group shows: Nicole Gallery in Chicago, 1986; the South Side Community Art Center, 1987; and the Museum of Fine Arts in Houston, 1988.

There was scarcely a year in the 1980s that Burroughs did not receive a well-deserved award. In 1980 she was one of the ten black artists honored by President and Mrs. Carter at the White House. At the same time her art was shown in the ''Ten Black American Artists'' exhibition at the Corcoran Art Galleries. Also in 1980, Burroughs was named Senior Citizen of the Year by the Chicago Park District. The following year Burroughs was invited to be a member of the National Commission on Negro History and Culture.

In 1982 she was the recipient of three notable commendations; Burroughs was named an outstanding alumnus of Chicago State University; she secured an honorarium from the Friends of the Anne Spencer Foundation in Lynchburg, Virginia, and she was given an Excellence in Art Award from the National Association of Negro Museums.

Another banner year for Burroughs was 1986. She was saluted by the Illinois State Legislature, cited for outstanding service in the arts and humanities by the Chicago, DuSable, Fort Dearborn Historical Commission, Inc., and February 1 of the year was proclaimed ''Dr. Margaret Burroughs Day in Chicago'' by Mayor Harold Washington.

The following year brought even more tributes. Burroughs's accolades were a certificate of appreciation from the United States Postal Service, Chicago Branch; the Progressive Black Women's Award; an Enverite Charity Club Distinguished Woman Award; Paul Robeson High School Award; Recognition of Excellence Award; I'R Electrical Organization Award; Chicago Youth Center Award; and a Community Service Award from the Black Law Students Association of John Marshall Law School.

Burroughs next earned a senior achievement in the arts citation and a Woman's Caucus for Art Award from Houston Museum of Fine Art in 1988.

In her emerita status since 1985, Burroughs serves as a commissioner of the Chicago Park District appointed by Mayor Harold Washington in 1986 and reappointed by Mayor Eugene Sawyer in 1988 for a full five-year term. She lectures and makes presentations to schools, colleges, and universities. She also perseveres as a valued member of her brainchild, the DuSable Museum of African-American History. Ever devoted to safeguarding and enriching black culture, Burroughs's recent projects include collecting African games and compiling a volume of poems in honor of Paul Robeson. Skilled in many fields in the humanities, as well as in business and diplomatic relations, Burroughs is truly a renaissance woman.

Selected writings of Margaret Burroughs are in the following works: Floyd Barbour, ed., *The Black Seventies* (Boston: Sargeant, 1970); Simmons and Hutchinson, eds., *Black Culture;* Erlene Stetson, ed. *Black Sister: Poetry by Black American Women, 1746-1980* (Bloomington: Indiana University Press, 1981); and in a variety of periodicals, such as *Art Gallery, Freedomways, Negro Digest, Phi Delta Kappa Magazine,* and *Arts Magazine.* Books by Margaret Burroughs are *Africa, My Africa* (Chicago: DuSable Museum, 1970); *Did You Feed My Cow?* (New York: Crowell, 1955; also revised edition under the name Margaret Taylor Burroughs, Chicago: Follett, 1969); and *Jasper, the Drummin' Boy* (New York: Viking, 1947; Chicago: Follett, 1970).

References

Atkinson, Edward J. *Black Dimensions in Contemporary Art.* New York: New American Library, 1979.

Barbour, Floyd, ed. *The Black Seventies.* Boston: Sargent, 1970.

Bontemps, Jacqueline Fonvielle. *Forever Free: Art by African American Women 1862-1980.* Alexandria, Va.: Stephenson, 1980.

Burroughs, Margaret T. *What Shall I Tell My Children Who Are Black?* Chicago: MAAH Press, 1968. 29.

Celebrating Negro History and Brotherhood: A Folio of Prints by Chicago Artists. Chicago: Seven Arts Workshop, 1956.

Contemporary Authors. Detroit: Gale, 1977.

Dickinson, Mary Jane. "Margaret T. G. Burroughs." In *Dictionary of Literary Biography*. Vol. 41: *Afro-American Poets Since 1985*. Eds. Trudier Harris and Thadious M. Davis. Detroit: Gale, 1985. Fine, detailed analysis of Burroughs's poetry. Also provides two photographs of the poet and a lithograph by Burroughs.

Dover, Cedric. *American Negro Art*. Greenwich, Conn.: New York Graphic Society, 1969. Reproduction of Burrough's print, *Moses*, p. 20.

Editors of Ebony. *Ebony Success Library*. Vol. 1. *1,000 Successful Blacks*. Chicago: Johnson Pub. Co., 1973.

Edwards, Audrey. "They Made It Happen." *Black Enterprise* (May 1980): 33-40. Discusses Burroughs as one of four women of achievement and focuses on her development of the DuSable Museum in Chicago.

Lewis, Samella S., and Ruth G. Waddy. *Black Artists on Art*. Vol. 2. Los Angeles: Contemporary Crafts, 1971. This work provides a brief artist's statement, Burroughs's photograph, and illustrations of two bronze sculptures from 1968, *Black Queen* and *Head*.

"Prints by Margaret G. Burroughs." *Freedomways* 1 (Spring 1961): 107-109.

Rush, Theresa Gonnels, Carol Fairbanks Myers, and Esther Spring Arata. *Black American Writers Past and Present*. Metuchen, N.J.: Scarecrow Press, 1975. Provides a contemporary photograph of the writer.

Stoelting, Winifred. *Hale Woodruff: 50 Years of His Art*. New York: Studio Museum of Harlem, April 29-June 24, 1979.

Tibbs, Thurlow E., Jr. *Margaret Burroughs/Marion Perkins: A Retrospective*. Washington, D.C.: Evans-Tibbs Collection, 1980s.

Who's Who Among Black Americans. 6th ed. Detroit: Gale, 1990.

Who's Who in American Art. New York: Bowker, 1978. 1980.

Collections

Art by Margaret Burroughs is in the following collections: Alabama Agricultural and Mechanical University Print Collection (Huntsville, Alabama); Alabama State University (Montgomery, Alabama); Clark-Atlanta University (Atlanta, Georgia); DuSable Museum of African-American History (Chicago, Illinois); Howard University (Washington, D.C.); Jackson State University Art Collection (Jackson, Mississippi); Johnson Publishing Company (Chicago); and Oakland Museum (Oakland, California).

Theresa A. Leininger

Nannie Helen Burroughs

(1879-1961)

School founder, educator, civil rights activist, feminist, religious leader

Nannie Helen Burroughs was a majestic, dark-skinned woman. Her voice was commanding, and she was a spellbinding, outspoken orator. She belonged to the network of southern black female activists who emerged regionally as the leaders and members of national organizations—groups that included Mary McLeod Bethune, Lugenia Burns Hope of Atlanta, Lucy Laney and Florence Hunt of Georgia, Nettie Napier and M. L. Crosthwait of Tennessee, Jennie Moton and Margaret Murray Washington of Alabama, Maggie Lena Walker of Virginia, and Charlotte Hawkins Brown and Mary Jackson McCrorey of North Carolina. William Pickens, a pioneer NAACP administrator and writer, stated: "No other person in America has so large a hold on the loyalty and esteem of the colored masses as Nannie H. Burroughs. She is regarded all over the broad land as a combination of brains, courage, and incorruptibleness" (Flyer, n.d.)

Nannie Helen Burroughs, educator, civil rights activist,

Nannie Helen Burroughs

feminist, and religious leader, was born in Orange, Virginia, May 2, 1879, the daughter of John Burroughs and Jennie (Poindexter) Burroughs. Her parents belonged to that small and fortunate class of ex-slaves whose energy and ability enabled them to start towards prosperity almost as soon as the war that freed them was over. Young Nannie moved with her mother to Washington, D.C., in 1883. She was educated through the high school level at the M Street High School in the nation's capital and graduated with honors in 1896. She studied business in 1902 and received an honorary A.M. degree from Eckstein-Norton University in Kentucky in 1907.

Burroughs was employed in Louisville, Kentucky, from 1898 to 1909 as bookkeeper and editorial secretary of the Foreign Mission Board of the National Baptist Convention. While in Louisville, she organized the Women's Industrial Club, which conducted domestic science and secretarial courses. Nannie Burroughs was one of the founders of the Women's Convention, auxiliary to the National Baptist Convention USA, and served efficiently as its corresponding secretary for almost a half century (1900-1947). From 1948 until her death in 1961 she was president of the Women's Convention. The convention comprised the largest group of African-Americans in the world, and its auxiliary was a potent force in black religious groups.

Her childhood dream of establishing an industrial school for girls resulted in her mobilizing the initiative of the Women's Convention to underwrite such a venture. On October 19, 1901, the National Training School for Women and Girls opened at Fiftieth and Grant streets Northwest, Washington, D.C., with Nannie Burroughs as president. By the end of the first year the school had enrolled thirty-one students. Twenty-five years later it boasted of more than two thousand women trained at the secondary and junior college level. Housed in the campus dormitory, the girls came from all over the United States, Africa, and the Caribbean Basin. Burroughs placed great significance in training for spiritual values and thus dubbed her school the "School of the 3 B's—the Bible, bath, and broom." These were indispensable tools for racial progress. In 1934 the school was named the National Trades and Professional School for Women. The school was inactive for a period during the Great Depression of the 1930s; Burroughs reopened it and continued to direct the school until her death in 1961. In 1964 the board of trustees abandoned the old trade school curriculum and reestablished it as the Nannie Helen Burroughs School for students at the elementary school level.

Burroughs's sensitivity for the African-American working woman was expressed during her participation in the club movement among women of color during the late decades of the nineteenth century and the early decades of the twentieth century. Black women organized first on a local level and then nationally to shoulder educational, philanthropic, and welfare activities. Urbanization, the urgent needs of the poor in a period of rapid industrialization, and the presence of a sizeable group of educated women with leisure time led to the emergence of a national club movement. In the 1890s local clubs in a number of cities began almost simultaneously to form federations. In 1896 the newly formed National Association of Colored Women (NACW) united the three largest of these and more than a hundred local women's clubs.

In addition to her laudable contribution to the NACW, Burroughs also founded the National Association of Wage Earners in order to draw public attention to the dilemma of Negro women. Its national board included Nannie Burroughs as president, with well-known clubwomen Mary McLeod Bethune as vice-president and Richmond, Virginia, banker Maggie Lena Walker as treasurer. The women placed more significance on educational forums of public interest than on trade-union activities. Burroughs was a member of the Louisville, Kentucky, Ladies' Union Band; she was also a member of Saint Lukes, a fraternal order, Saturday Evening, and Daughters of the Round Table clubs.

Close examination of women's clubs in several communities suggests that the importance of their work has been seriously underestimated. Black American communities have a continuous record of self-help, institution-building, and strong organization, to which black women have made a continuous contribution. The stimulus for organizing arose wherever a compelling social need remained unmet. Most frequently, women's clubs were formed in order to provide caring facilities for black children. The virtual dearth of social welfare institutions in many southern communities and the recurrent exclusion of blacks from those that existed led black women to found orphanages, day-care facilities, homes for the aged, and similar services. The founding and support of educational institutions had been an unbroken activity in the black American community since the days of slavery, but the extent to which women contributed and often sustained them has yet to be recorded. In the case of the most prominent female founders of black educational institutions—Lucy Craft Laney, Charlotte Hawkins Brown, Mary McLeod Bethune, and Nannie Burroughs—the schools became centers for community organizations, women's activities, and a network of supporting institutions.

Equal Rights for Black Women Advocated

Nannie Burroughs, along with several members of the network of clubwomen, believed that black women should not take a passive position or one subordinate to men, and criticized those black males who refused to support efforts toward equal rights. These reformers differed from their white sisters in that they did not define feminism as a response to black male exploitation. Black men were not held exclusively accountable for the sexual discrimination practiced by whites of both genders. Burroughs was a vocal supporter of racial and sexual consciousness.

Burroughs was an unyielding advocate of racial pride and African-American heritage, and she was a life member of the Association for the Study of Negro Life and History. When the association met at its twelfth annual conference in Pittsburgh in 1927, Burroughs shared the platform on the final day with the association's illustrious founder, Carter Godwin

Woodson, and the distinguished Howard University scholar and writer Alain LeRoy Locke. Her paper, "The Social Value of Negro History," was described in the *Journal of Negro History* (January 1928): "By a forceful address Miss Nannie Burroughs emphasized the duty the Negro owes to himself to learn his own story and the duty the white man owes to himself to learn of the spiritual strivings . . . of a despised but not an inferior person" (6).

Burroughs, along with other clubwomen, labored resolutely to memorialize the home of Frederick Douglass in Anacostia, a section of the District of Columbia, that was officially dedicated by them on August 12, 1922. Burroughs served as secretary of the Frederick Douglass Memorial Association.

Nannie Burroughs was a steadfast supporter of the religious and secular program advanced by Walter Henderson Brooks and the Nineteenth Street Baptist Church in the District of Columbia. Brooks was a prominent clergyman, scholar, and temperance advocator. He pastored the eminent Nineteenth Street Baptist Church for a number of years. He denounced not only drunkenness but gambling, fornication, and adultery. But he also preached and advocated the social gospel. The NACW was founded at his church in 1896. Brooks served as a trustee of Nannie Burrough's National Training School for Women and Girls. Burroughs was a devout and steadfast Baptist and worked for almost fifty years with the Baptist World Alliance; she attended the first meeting in London in 1905. And from 1950 to 1955 she was elected member-at-large of the Executive Committee. She addressed the 1950 alliance meeting in Cleveland, Ohio, on the subject "On Him Alone We Build." As a young woman she addressed the historic Negro Young People's Christian and Educational Congress held in Atlanta, Georgia, August 6-11, 1902. As the corresponding secretary of the Women's Convention of the National Baptist Convention, Burroughs's address was "The Colored Woman and Her Relation to the Domestic Problem." In the address she stressed:

> The training of Negro women is absolutely necessary, not only for their own salvation and the salvation of the race, but because the hour in which we live demands it. If we lose sight of the demands of the hour we blight our hope of progress. The subject of domestic science has crowded itself upon us, and unless we receive it, master it and be wise, the next ten years will so revolutionize things that we find our women without the wherewith to support themselves (Penn, 324-29).

Burroughs was active in the antilynching campaign and supported federal intervention to prevent lynching and backed antilynching bills introduced in Congress. She was a member of the Women's Division of the Commission on Interracial Cooperation (CIC) and disagreed with CIC's Association of Southern Women for the Prevention of Lynching. Burroughs met with representatives of the association in 1935 in Atlanta to resolve the question of the association's continued opposition to federal intervention. Burroughs noted that she expected the passage of antilynching laws whether the association lent its support or not.

She was a much sought-after speaker and writer. Burroughs was considered one of the most stirring platform orators in the country and one of the pioneers in exalting the status of women. The writings of Nannie Burroughs reflect both strong religious convictions and the belief in racial self-help and self-reliance. In her article "Not Color but Character" (*The Voice,* July 1904, pp. 277-78), she castigates black women who failed to value their natural beauty. In an article in the *Southern Workman* (July 1927), "With All Thy Getting," Burroughs prophetically wrote, "No race is richer in soul quality and color than the Negro. Some day he will realize it and glorify them. He will popularize black" (301). She was highly influenced by a very deep belief in God and she felt that racial equality was an ethical priority—a spiritual mandate from heaven. She condemned segregation and also such concepts as individualism and race deliverers. In the article "Nannie Burroughs Says Hound Dogs are Kicked but Not Bulldogs" (*Afro-American,* 17 February 1934), she told her readers to use "ballots and dollars" to fight racism instead of "wasting time begging the white race for mercy." She noted the great moral, spiritual, and economic asset of the black woman. The black woman "carries the moral destiny of the two races in her hand," she said:

> Had she not been the woman of unusual moral stamina that she is, the black race would have been made a great deal whiter, and the white race a great deal blacker during the past fifty years. She has been left a prey for the man of every race, but in spite of this, she has held the enemies of Negro female chastity at law (Burroughs, "Black Women and Reform," 187).

"Chloroform Uncle Tom" Mandate Issued

Speaking in Baltimore, Maryland, in December 1932, Burroughs secured a headline in the *Pittsburgh Courier:* "Fighting Woman Educator Tells What Race Needs." The article continued:

> "Chloroform your Uncle Toms" said Miss Nannie H. Burroughs of the National Training School for Girls, Washington, D.C. to an applauding crowd of 2500 that overflowed the City-Wide Young People's Forum, at Bethel A.M.E. Church Friday night.
>
> Speaking on the subject "What Must the Negro Do to Be Saved?" Miss Burroughs said, "The Negro must unload the leeches and parasitic leaders who are absolutely eating the life out of the struggling, desiring mass of people."

The *Afro-American*, a Washington, D.C., weekly newspaper, in the week of April 14, 1934, carried an article written by Burroughs concerning "Eating in Public Places." She stated:

> There is confusion on Capitol Hill! A Congressman for North Carolina does not know the difference between public, social rights and private social equality. Admission to eating, or patronizing public places, operated under license or franchise, is a public privilege—a legal or civil right for which the taxpayer and patrons pay.

In 1934 the intrepid Nannie Burroughs took W. E. B. Du Bois of the NAACP to task. The headline in the *Afro-American*, April 28, 1934, screamed "Nannie Burroughs Says the Doctor is Tired, Fought a Good Fight, but Did Not Keep the Faith on the Segregation Issue." Du Bois had suggested to black Americans that they submit to segregation. Burroughs stated, "You would think that the world is coming to an end because one man 'does not choose to fight' segregation any longer. . . . Any man who is hired can quit when he pleases. A person who is getting paid to solve the Negro problem is no exception to the rule. . . . Du Bois is at least or at last honest. He could have kept his mouth shut and continued to draw his decreasing stipend from the NAACP. . . . Dr. Du Bois is tired. He has fought a good fight. It is too bad that he did not keep the faith and finish his course."

Self-Help Project Launched

Nannie Burroughs in July 1934 launched Washington's first "Negro self-help project." A laundry, formerly owned by the training school, was turned over to the federal government by Burroughs. The Federal Emergency Relief Authority renovated the building, which included a laundry and dry-cleaning plant, a barber shop, a sewing and canning center, a commissary, a garment-making and upholstery shop, and a shoe-repair shop. Nationwide interest was kindled in the project as it performed as a model for other projects that were inaugurated during the Great Depression in other parts of the United States.

In 1944 the Baptist Woman's Auxiliary initiated a quarterly journal, *The Worker*, under the editorship of Nannie Burroughs. She also wrote works of a religious nature: *Grow: A Handy Guide for Progressive Church Women* (n.d.), *Making Your Community Christian* (n.d.), and *Words of Light and Life Found Here and There* (1948). For a number of years she wrote a syndicated column, "Nannie Burroughs Says," which was carried by several black newspapers in a prominent position. In a lighter vein, she authored *The Slabtown District Convention: A Comedy in One Act*, which had a number of editions (the 11th dated 1942). It was a popular church fund-raiser similar to "Tom Thumb Wedding" and "Battle of the Roses" efforts.

Nannie Helen Burroughs died of natural causes in Washington, D.C., in May 1961. Funeral rites were held in the Nineteenth Street Baptist Church with interment in Lincoln Memorial Cemetery, Suitland, Maryland. There were no immediate survivors.

A photograph of Charlotte Hawkins Brown, Mary McLeod Bethune, and Nannie Helen Burroughs is on view at the Brown historic site in Sedalia, North Carolina. Her circle of friends was immense because of her women's club, religious, civil rights, and educational affiliations. Burroughs carried the virtues of Victorian America to the masses and taught them to the young black women in Washington, D.C.

References

Afro-American (28 April 1934). Includes photograph.

Barnett, Evelyn Brooks. "Nannie Helen Burroughs." *Dictionary of American Negro Biography*. Eds. Rayford W. Logan and Michael R. Winston. New York: Norton, 1982.

———. "Nannie Helen Burroughs and the Education of Black Women." In *The Afro-American Woman*. Eds. Sharon Harley and Rosalyn Terborg-Penn. Port Washington, N.Y.: Kennikat Press, 1978.

Burroughs, Nannie Helen. "Black Women and Reform." In "Votes for Women." *Crisis* 10 (August 1915): 187. Photograph, p. 182.

———. "Eating in Public Places." Washington *Afro-American* (14 April 1934).

———. "Not Color but Character." *The Voice of the Negro* 1 (July 1904): 277-78.

———. "With All Thy Getting." *Southern Workman* 56 (July 1927): 301.

Daniels, Sadie I. *Women Builders*. Washington, D.C.: Associated Publishers, 1931.

"Fighting Woman Educator Tells What Race Needs." *Pittsburgh Courier* (23 December 1932).

Harrison, Earl L. *The Dream and the Dreamer*. Washington, D.C.: Nannie H. Burroughs Literary Foundation, 1956.

Mather, Frank Lincoln. *Who's Who of the Colored Race*. Chicago: Mather, 1915.

"Nannie Helen Burroughs Says Hound Dogs are Kicked but Not Bulldogs." *Afro-American* (17 February 1934). Includes photograph.

Obituary. *Washington Post* (21 May 1961), (22 May 1961).

Penn, I. Garland, ed. *The United Negro: His Problems and His Progress*. Atlanta: D. E. Luther, 1902.

Pickens, William. *Nannie Burroughs and the School of the 3B's*. n.p., 1921.

Who's Who in Colored America. 7th ed. Yonkers-on-Hudson, N.Y.: Christian Burckel, 1950.

Collections

A comprehensive collection of materials related to her life and activities can be found in the Nannie H. Burroughs Papers in the Library of Congress.

Casper LeRoy Jordan

Vinie Burrows

(1928-)

Actress, director, radio producer

Born November 15, 1928, in New York City and educated there with a B.A. degree from New York University, Vinie Burrows is a performing actress, director, and producer. During her career she has been adjunct professor, Saint Peters College; lecturer, New School of Social Research; and drama director, Franklin Marshall College.

While still a student at New York University, she made her acting debut with Helen Hayes in the stage production of *The Wisteria Trees* (1950). Other stage production appearances include *The Green Pastures* (1951), *Mrs. Patterson* (1954), *The Skin of Our Teeth* (1955), *The Ponder Heart* (1956), *Come Share My House, Nat Turner* (1960), *Mandingo* (1961), *The World of Shakespeare* (1953), and *Black Medea* (1978). Burrows has appeared on and off Broadway with such stars as Cicely Tyson, Mary Martin, Ossie Davis, and James Earl Jones. She is an affilate member of the New York Black Theatre Alliance (BTA). In 1969 she performed at the First African Cultural Festival in Algiers.

While Vinie Burrows has made television appearances in such shows as "Christopher Closeup," "Camera Three," "The Merv Griffin Show," and "The Tonight Show," she is best known for the artistry of her one-woman shows. She adapts, arranges, and performs these representative dramatic works. The most successful of these shows was *Walk Together Children,* a program of poetry, prose, and songs by black authors dramatizing the black experience in America. First produced off-Broadway by Robert Hooks, with Burrows as the sole star and performer, at the Greenwich Mews Theater November 11-December 1, 1968, it toured more than nine hundred colleges to wide acclaim in the United States, Holland, Switzerland, Nigeria, Algeria, and Vietnam. In 1972 it was revived off-Broadway at the Mercer-Brecht Theater for eighty-nine shows. In explaining her reason for doing a one-woman show, she said:

Vinie Burrows

> As a Black actress, whose talents have never been fully used in our theater, I have turned to solo performances, not merely to find employment but also to gain a greater measure of artistic fulfillment and personal satisfaction. . . . I have tapped a rich vein from my own Black culture and heritage (*Essence,* 77).

A second popular show, *Phillis Wheatley, Gentle Poet, Child of Africa,* (1973), presented dramatic readings of Wheatley's poetry and letters with the assistance of renowned dancer Pearl Primus. Other dramatic one-woman shows include: *Shout Freedom* (1963), dealing with women's and children's liberation; *Dark Fire* (1965), African legends, myths, folktales, and proverbs; *Sister! Sister!* (early 1970s), a women's performance presented in Los Angeles and Martha's Vineyard, Massachusetts; *Echoes of Africa* (early 1970s), readings from contemporary African writers in French and English; *The Female of the Species* (1966), a poetic collage portraying seven women based on the writings of William Shakespeare, Oscar Wilde, Edgar Allan Poe, Lewis Carroll, and Langston Hughes; and *From Swords to Plowshares* (early 1970s), dealing with war and peace.

Need for Realistic Portrayal of Blacks in Films Cited

Writing on the need to change black films produced in the 1970s, Vinie Burrows said that the films were spurred by the "greed and zeal of White producers seeking to shore up sagging industry profits." On the screen blacks were "superstuds" and then blacks became "not only beautiful, but bountiful" for the white producers. She continued:

> Black was beautiful to a Black audience who seven decades of popular filmmaking had ignored; whose existence as other than maids and mammies, sambos and shufflers had been denied. The hunger of the Black community to see Blackness triumph over Whiteness in celluloid fantasy is a psychological mechanism social scientists might contend is a necessary emotional cathartic. Nevertheless, it is a damaging misdirection of energies born of oppression and frustration (*Encore,* 48).

She called for the black artist, filmmaker, writer, editor,

producer, and performer to recognize the power of the film medium in helping to clarify the thinking and aspirations of more than thirty million blacks. She felt that up to that time films had presented unrealistic portrayals of black life, and these persons were the ones to portray accurately the reality of black life. She sees "a vast reservoir of story ideas from Black history in America and elsewhere in the diaspora . . . waiting to be tapped. And, with a splendor and majesty of material to surpass any previous film epics or spectacles" (*Encore*, 48).

Vinie Burrows is a member of the American Educational Theatre Association, American Federation of Television and Radio Artists, Black Theater Alliance, and the Committee for the Negro in the Arts of the Screen Actors Guild. Also a founding member of Women for Racial and Economic Equality, Vinie Burrows's interest in women's rights, disarmament, and the anti-apartheid struggle has led her to be extremely active in civil affairs. As an NGO (Nongovernmental Organization) permanent representative to the United Nations, Burrows is actively influential in political, social, and economic issues, especially where they focus on women. She has produced a weekly live radio show to address these concerns. She currently resides in New York City.

References

Burrows, Vinie. "Black Films: Time for a Change." *Encore* 4 (August 1975): 3, 48. Includes photographs.

Essence (New Directions Section) 3 (May 1972): 76-77. Photograph, p. 77.

Mapp, Edward. *Directory of Blacks in the Performing Arts*. 2nd ed. Metuchen, N.J.: Scarecrow Press, 1990.

Peterson, Bernard L., Jr., ed. *Contemporary Black American Playwrights and Their Plays*. Westport, Conn.: Greenwood Press, 1988.

Ploski, Harry A., and James Williams. *The Negro Almanac*. 5th ed. Detroit: Gale Research, 1989. Photograph, p. 1376.

Smythe, Mabel M., ed. *The Black American Reference Book*. Englewood Cliffs, N.J.: Prentice-Hall, 1976.

Woll, Allen L., ed. *Dictionary of the Black Theatre*. Westport, Conn.: Greenwood Press, 1983.

Maria K. Mootry

Anita Bush

(1883-1974)

Dancer, actress, stock company founder

As is the case with many early performers, the life of Anita Bush is imperfectly known. Fortunately, we can sketch in her early life, and we know the circumstances surrounding the Anita Bush Players, the first major professional black dramatic company in the United States, in some detail thanks to the research of Sister M. Francesca Thompson, OSF, who conducted oral interviews with her and with Clarence Muse in 1969-1970.

Anita Bush grew up in Brooklyn. Her father was a tailor with clients from the theater. She had at least one sister. The two girls were stagestruck from the time they had extra roles in a production of *Anthony and Cleopatra*. At that time there were no openings for blacks on the regular professional stage. When she was sixteen, Anita Bush was allowed to join the very successful Williams and Walker Company as a dancer. She was with the company when it toured England with its smash hit, *In Dahomey*. In 1909 Walker was forced to break up the company due to his illness. Anita Bush formed her own dance group with four or five other women and toured successfully until 1913 when a serious accident incapacitated her and cut short her career as a dancer.

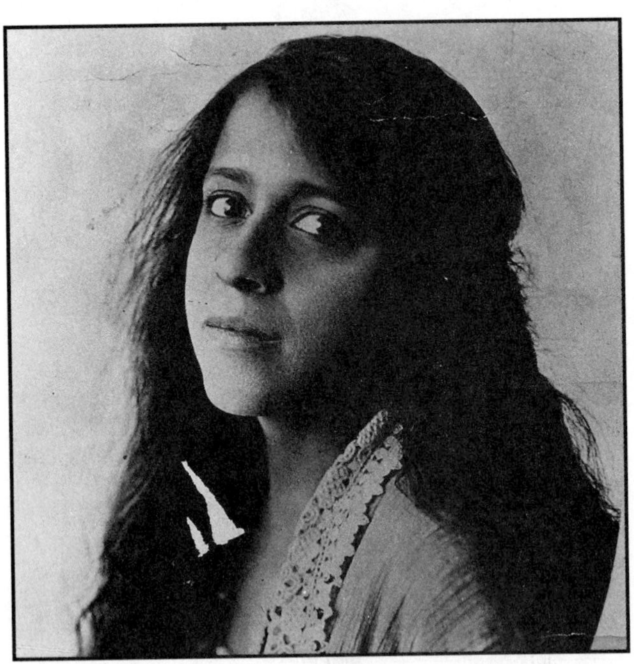

Anita Bush

Spending months on crutches, she did not recover her health for more than a year.

Anita Bush Players Formed

In 1915 there were two major theaters in Harlem open freely to black audiences, the Lincoln and the Lafayette. Both needed shows to attract an audience and pay their way. Backed with only cheek and an idea, Anita Bush approached Eugene "Frenchy" Elmore, the manager of the Lincoln Theatre, with the offer to fill his theater with the offerings of the Anita Bush Players, a stock company offering legitimate plays. When he accepted her offer and proposed the company open in two weeks, she had to scramble frantically to form her troupe. She got in touch with Billie Burke, a white director who was known in Harlem, and selected a play. She also ran into an old friend, Jesse Shipp, a well-known vaudevillian and director. His verdict on the enterprise was frank. "[He] promptly assured her that she was crazy and that the time was not ripe for such a venture. He felt that there weren't enough Black actors proficient in straight drama to provide a competent cast" (Thompson, 16). Bush persevered, recruiting Charles Gilpin, Dooley Wilson, Carlotta Freeman, and Andrew Bishop. With these forces, the Anita Bush Players opened at the Lincoln on November 15, 1915, with *The Girl at the Fort*, a light comedy. The success of the company was such that the players made the transfer to the larger Lafayette Theatre, where they opened on December 27, 1915.

The life of the Anita Bush Players was short. On March 2, 1916, the *New York Age* advertised a play starring Charles Gilpin supported by the Lafayette Players (Thompson, 19). Despite the change of name, Anita Bush remained with the troupe until 1920. She helped form a touring Lafayette Players Company in Chicago in 1916; a third company was formed in Baltimore. After beginning well in the early years, all three companies continued with diminishing success through the mid-1920s. In 1928 the New York Company transferred its base to Los Angeles, where it lasted until it officially closed on January 23, 1932.

In 1921 Anita Bush appeared in the all-black film *The Crimson Skull*, a mystery western shot in the all-black town of Boley, Oklahoma. Her costars were Bill Pickett, a champion rodeo rider, and Lawrence Chenault, a Lafayette Players alumnus who played in numerous black films in the 1920s. Presumably, the film was made by the same Norman Film Manufacturing Company that released *The Bull Doggers* in 1923 with Anita Bush and Bill Pickett. This film demonstrated Pickett's skills and also featured trick riding by black cowboys and cowgirls (Klotman, 84). After these movies, Bush's activities are at present unknown until the late 1930s, when she appeared in the black musical *Swing It* in 1938 and *Androclės and the Lion* in 1939. The Federal Theatre Project produced both plays. Anita Bush was also for many years executive secretary in the Negro Actors' Guild. She made a television appearance in "Free Time" in 1971.

Anita Bush is best known today for her part in founding the Anita Bush Players, which was a stock company putting on a new play every week, rehearsing by day and playing in the evenings. The stock of plays was made up of plays by white authors that had already proven their appeal downtown. Its successor, the Lafayette Players continued this tradition for the most part. Still, the players gave black audiences in Harlem access to legitimate drama and allowed black actors and actresses to gain stage experience in straight plays. Four actors associated with the troupe's early days did go on to wider fame. Lawrence Chenault appeared in some eighteen black films between 1920 and 1934. Dooley Wilson is remembered best for a bit part in the film *Casablanca*. Charles Gilpin starred in Eugene O'Neill's *The Emperor Jones* in 1920, in which he scored such a signal triumph that he was invited to the White House and received the Spingarn medal the following year. Clarence Muse, who lived to be ninety, dying in 1979, had a long and varied career in show business as a singer, producer, and actor, to mention only his most important activities; he made more than 150 films. It is fitting that he sum up the importance of the Anita Bush Players:

> Our aim was to give vent to the talent and to prove to everybody who was willing to look, to watch, to listen, that we were as good at drama as anybody else had been or could be. The door was opened a tiny bit to us, and, as always, the Black man when faced with an open door, no matter how small the wedge might be, eased in (Thompson, 18).

Anita Bush died on February 16, 1974. She deserves recognition for opening the door a tiny bit.

References

Klotman, Phyllis Rauch. *Frame by Frame—A Black Filmography*. Bloomington: Indiana University Press, 1979.

Oppenheimer, Priscilla. "Anita Bush." In *The Harlem Renaissance: A Historical Dictionary of the Era*. Edited by Bruce Kellner. New York: Methuen, 1984.

Thompson, Sister M. Francesca, OSF. "The Lafayette Players, 1917-1932." In *The Theater of Black Americans*. Edited by Errol Hill. Vol. 2. Englewood Cliffs, N.J.: Prentice-Hall, 1980.

Robert L. Johns

Octavia E. Butler

(1947-)

Writer

One of the most intriguing writers in the science fiction genre, Octavia Butler began writing as a child and never looked back. Her fertile imagination shows no sign of waning, and critics and fans alike see subtleties in her work that go beyond the boundaries of science fiction.

Octavia Estelle Butler was born June 22, 1947, in Pasadena, California. She was the only child that her mother, Octavia Margaret (Guy) Butler, successfully carried to term, having lost four children before Butler's birth. Octavia Butler's father, Laurice Butler, died when Butler was still very young; in fact, "memories" of her father consist more of stories told about him by her mother and grandmother than actual recollections. (Unless otherwise indicated, all personal information about Butler is derived from two telephone interviews, 18 May 1990 and 5 June 1990.)

The Pasadena community that nurtured Octavia Estelle Butler was a racially mixed and culturally integrated community where African-American, Asian and Asian-American, Hispanic, and white peoples resided together. Although Butler knew something about the detrimental effects of racial discrimination from occasionally accompanying her mother to her job as a domestic worker, witnessing how she was treated by her employers, and also from listening to her grandmother's stories about life on a Louisiana sugar plantation, she never personally experienced the more rigid forms of a segregated society. "I never," she said, "lived in a segregated neighborhood nor went to segregated school; the whole community was an economic ghetto." Her family struggled to make ends meet but so did other families around them. One way Octavia M. Butler supplemented the family income was to take older boarders or pensioners into the home. These were people who "were not in the best of health," but their problems were not severe enough to require hospitalization. Butler recalls three such boarders, a diverse group but all "nice," from whom she learned "other versions of being human and an adult."

Because she grew up in a setting surrounded largely by adults, Butler has described herself in childhood as a "very solitary individual." As an isolated only child, she never really learned how to interact with other children in the neighborhood nor how to cope with them at school. As a consequence, she found it much easier to stay to herself and use the time she spent alone reading. She was an "avid and indiscriminate reader" who read whatever was available.

Six feet tall, with strong features and a dark brown complexion, Butler wears a neatly shaped Afro haircut. She had grown "very tall, very quickly" as a child—something women were not supposed to do. She had also been a daydreamer and extraordinarily shy. This shyness prevented her from full participation in such customary childhood enterprises as singing in church choirs—"I was far too shy to do anything like singing"—or reciting poems for Sunday school programs or participating in school activities, even though she faithfully and responsibly memorized the poems. Standing up to give reports in school terrified her, and oral recitations took more emotional energy than the child could manage; these tasks were simply, in her words, "a lost cause."

Because she suffered from an unrecognized dyslexia, a disorder affecting the perception of words and letters, Butler did not perform well in school, making "mediocre to bad grades," nor did she realize that she was actually a very bright young woman until the eighth grade. Then she and a classmate, a Hispanic youth she had known since the sixth grade, staged a contest to see who could earn the better grades.

They had both recently transferred to Washington Junior High, a school outside of their neighborhood. This classmate was a "nice and smart" young man who unfortunately suffered from Tourette's Syndrome, a neurological disorder that causes uncontrollable vocalizations, usually profane. As Butler explained, "He was a nice boy who sometimes called me dirty names. I knew he was bright; I just did not know I was." To her surprise, Butler won their competition and had a revelation. It was, as she described it, "the first time I'd ever done anything to impress myself." She also discovered that when she was prepared, she could manage an oral report before a class despite the difficulty. Here again, her ability to perform surprised her.

From grade school to junior high through high school and college, Butler's terror of speaking publicly before a class or groups caused her great difficulties. And, as a sad commentary on how the education system mistreats and scars some children, rather than offer such a painfully shy student real assistance or understanding, most of her teachers were insensitive individuals who were sometimes bigoted or who humiliated her in front of the class, even when she had done nothing wrong. As Butler recollected, these teachers tended to be "very contemptuous" of her and simply assumed that she had not done her homework. In the twelfth grade, still terribly anxious about oral presentations, Butler went so far as to record a class project at home on a tape recorder and then bring the tape to play in the classroom rather than face the overwhelming obstacle of reciting before the class.

There were, however, three junior high and high school teachers who made a critical difference in Butler's development. The first of these was Miss Peters, a seventh grade home economics teacher at McKinley Junior High, who took the time to read Butler's stories. She had begun to write at age ten, but Peters was the first teacher to read her stories and to offer encouragement. The second teacher was Mr. Pfaff, a stimulating and generous eighth grade science teacher at Washington Junior High. He was able to communicate effectively his own love of the field to his students, and as a result, Butler, who already loved and found science fascinating, had a wonderful time in his class. The "nonsense" she had absorbed as a child—"if you swallow a hair it will turn into a worm"—was replaced by scientific facts. Pfaff also allowed Butler to share with the class her book on astronomy, the second brand new book she had ever bought for herself. (The very first book she purchased had been about wild horses.)

In addition, and more critically important, it was Pfaff who took the time to type for Butler the first story she ever submitted to a science fiction magazine for publication. He took the poorly-prepared copy the thirteen year old novice writer had given him, corrected the spelling, made a few changes in the punctuation to "make the story readable," then retyped it, albeit single-spaced and without regard to proper submission format. Butler recalls his action fondly, ruefully acknowledging that rarely do teachers go to such an extreme for their students.

Both Peters and Pfaff were white. Butler did not have a class with a black teacher until the ninth grade. Ms. Buggs taught ninth grade English, social studies, and drama. Butler remembers her as the only teacher who truly understood how much presenting material orally terrified the young student. Instead of failing Butler for either refusing to recite or for doing it poorly, Buggs allowed her to substitute written reports. It was not until Butler graduated from college that she realized she must, if she wanted to successfully promote her books, discover how to speak in public comfortably. Then she paid for a self-help public speaking course and with the assistance of other individuals in the group, learned how to overcome the fear of public presentations.

In 1965, Butler graduated from Pasadena's John Muir High School. The idea of going to college frightened her, but she knew her mother expected her to continue her education. As a compromise, she worked during the day and enrolled in night classes, taking course work in fiction writing at Pasadena City College. By the second semester, she signed up for a full course load, having proved to herself that her fears were groundless. She finished the two-year degree program, graduating in 1968. She then attended California State College, Los Angeles, studying anthropology and history, English, speech, and other social sciences; but her dissatisfaction with the lack of creative writing courses at Cal State led her to withdraw from the college. Subsequently, while working at a variety of odd jobs—which the protagonist in her fourth published novel *Kindred* (1979) describes—she took evening writing courses at the University of California at Los Angeles (UCLA) and began attending writing workshops sponsored by the Writers Guild of America West in 1969-1970. These "open door" or integrated workshops, taught by Harlan Ellison and Sid Stebel, gave Butler the best instruction in writing for a specific genre. Harlan Ellison, a highly regarded science fiction writer and an editor, was very influential, and Butler described him as her "first honest critic." To Stebel, Butler attributes her developing ability to structure a story and to summarize its substance using one active sentence. Ellison was also responsible for Butler's invitation, in the summer of 1970, to participate in the Clarion Writers Workshop in Clarion, Pennsylvania—a six-week course for prospective science fiction writers. Each week, different writers, each well-established and successful in the field, instructed participants on shaping their material, sharpening their craft, and selling their stories.

The various jobs Butler held to support herself while she studied illustrate both the difficulties she surmounted and her commitment to the goal of becoming a writer. At one time she was a clerk typist for an aerospace firm and at another, a telephone solicitor; in addition, several other "temporary" work experiences are summarized in the following catalog by Edana Franklin, called Dana, the black narrator and heroine of *Kindred:*

> I was working out of a casual labor agency—we regulars called it a slave market.
>
> You sat and sat until the dispatcher either sent you out on a job or sent you home. Home meant no money. Put another potato in the oven. Or in desperation, sell some blood at one of the store fronts down the street from the agency. I had only done that once.
>
> Getting sent out meant the minimum wage—minus Uncle Sam's share—for as many hours as you were needed. You swept floors, stuffed envelopes, took inventory, washed dishes, sorted potato chips (really!), cleaned toilets, marked prices on merchandise . . . you did whatever you were sent out to do. It was nearly always mindless work, and as far as most employers were concerned, it was done by mindless people. Nonpeople rented for a few hours, a few days, a few weeks.
>
> I did the work, I went home, I ate, and then slept for a few hours. Finally, I got up and wrote. At one or two in the morning, I was fully alive, and busy working on my novel. (*Kindred*, 52-53)

Though often menial, these makeshift jobs permitted Butler, a single woman, to survive until the sale of her first published novel allowed her to turn full-time to writing.

She had known since childhood that she would become a writer. At age ten, she had written fantasy stories; at eleven, she wrote romances; at twelve, she discovered science fiction and liked the genre especially well because of the freedom it offered and its release from the realities of the everyday life around her. At thirteen Butler began to submit stories to the pulp magazines in the field. In a 1986 interview in *Black Scholar*, Butler described science fiction as "potentially the freest genre in existence," maintaining that its only limitations are "what people think should be done with it and what editors think should be done with it, although less now then in the past'' (14). Without pause or qualification, when Octavia E. Butler is asked what she thinks her most significant contributions to the community or her most important accomplishments have been, she replies ''my work.'' Most of the friends Butler identifies are also related to her work and are science fiction writers themselves. Apart from Harlan Ellison, Butler counts among her friends Theodore Sturgeon (now deceased), Steve Barnes, and Samuel R. Delany.

Butler Wins Hugo

Butler's work, her science or speculative fiction, whether in the novel form or the short story, has been critically admired and acclaimed as inventive, engaging, provocative, daring, terrifying, thrilling, spellbinding, and challenging. Her ''Speech Sounds,'' published originally in *Isaac Asimov's Science Fiction Magazine* (December 1983) won both the Hugo and the Nebula Awards, science fiction's highest awards conferred by fans and other science fiction writers. Other short stories include ''Crossover'' (1971), ''Next of Kin'' (1979),'' and ''The Evening and the Morning and the Night'' (1987). ''Next of Kin'' is not science fiction at all but a story that focuses on two odd, lonely people who share a unity of spirit. Butler's ''Bloodchild,'' depending on the reader's gender, is either a story of enslavement or a ''pregnant man'' story. ''The Evening and the Morning and the Night'' illustrates Butler's continued fascination with issues of ''personal responsibility'' regardless of the difficulty; and ''Crossover,'' the first story for which Butler was paid, is another story of an odd and lonely woman—who fantasizes a boyfriend, and then the fantasy ''gets out of hand.''

Five novels comprise Butler's Patternist saga, a complex detailed narrative featuring the birth of Homosuperior and stretching from precolonial Africa to a far distant and grim future where technology is virtually absent and humankind has mutated radically. The idea for the Patternist novels actually developed from some of the early stories that Butler wrote while still a teenager. For the science fiction pulp magazines she had labored to write the kinds of stories she thought they wanted, ''stories about thirty-year old white men who drank and smoked too much.'' But for her own amusement, she wrote stories about an Earth girl carried off to Mars. Eventually, these tales became the framework for that part of the Patternist saga set in the far future and on a different world. Still in high school, Butler began to write the stories that would serve as the basis for illustrating the Patternist's origins on Earth. As a consequence of her fascination with the varied stages of Patternist development, Butler found these novels relatively ''easy to write'' because they had been resonating in her mind for many years.

In order of publication, the novels in the series as *Patternmaster* (1976), *Mind of my Mind* (1977), *Survivor* (1978), *Wild Seed* (1980), and *Clay's Ark* (1984). Despite their publication chronology, readers interested in the actual sequential development should read the novels in the following order: *Wild Seed*, *Mind of My Mind*, *Clay's Ark*, *Survivor*, and *Patternmaster*. Butler has said that she rejects the notion of an ideal society, stipulating that ''I don't write utopian science fiction because I don't believe that imperfect humans can form a perfect society. I write what I write and when I finish, I send it off to my publisher and they worry about what genre it falls into'' (*Black Scholar*, 14).

The only published novel standing outside of a series, and the most successful of all the novels, is *Kindred*. This tale, originally entitled ''To Keep Thee in All Thy Ways'' and called by Butler a ''grim fantasy'' rather than outright science fiction because ''it has no science in it,'' speculates about what it would be like for a modern African-American woman to endure the ordeal of slavery as her ancestors knew it. Her heroine, Dana Franklin, is mysteriously transported from her 1975 Los Angeles home across time and space to emerge in 1830s Maryland—a free black woman in a slave state. How Dana Franklin ''travels'' is not as important as what she experiences. And the fact that Dana is involved in an interracial marriage is a deliberate attempt to illustrate the ''complications'' of race relations. In the introduction to the reissued *Kindred* (1988), Robert Crossley notes that Butler has been ''more consistent'' than other writers employing the genre in her use of science fiction's ''conventions to tell stories with a political and sociological edge to them, stories that speak to issues, feelings and historical truths rising out of Afro-American experience'' (xi).

With the publication of *Imago* (1989), Octavia Butler completed the last novel in her xenogenesis trilogy. These three novels, *Dawn* (1987), *Adulthood Rites* (1988), and *Imago*, recount humankind's near total destruction because of nuclear war and how the remnants of humanity are salvaged by a wandering race of aliens, the Oankali. In *Dawn*, readers first meet the Oankali, inveterate genetic engineers who must trade their genes with other species they meet. They are, in fact, ''committed to the trade'' because such trading ''renews us, enables us to survive as an evolving species instead of specializing ourselves into extinction or stagnation.'' *Dawn* also introduces Lilith, possibly the most intriguing of Butler's black heroines, embodying strength, compassion, and the judicious use of power in order to survive and to teach other survivors how to adapt. The subsequent novels explore the range and ramifications of human/alien interaction, the human and Oankali responses to that interaction as each species learns (or refuses to learn) about the other, and the birth of a new species, carrying the genes of both.

The three novels in the trilogy permit Butler to continue her exploration of several important themes: the responsible exercise of power and the workings of power relationships among the strong and the weak; change; the outsider; the recognition of a global community made up of various peoples; the validity of difference, and concomitantly, the human capacity to fear difference, to fear change; and society's need to transcend such fears. A major theme of the xenogenesis trilogy is the necessity for humankind to surmount what is called in the novels the ''Human Contradiction,'' that is, the idea that humankind is both hierarchical and intelligent; these characteristics, taken together, are considered a lethal combination. Butler does not see her fiction as having any hidden agenda or advocating any covert political bias. While her basic message may be "live and let live," below that the careful reader may note something akin to a biological determinism and an environmental concern, perhaps recognizing Butler's sense that humanity is on the track to "using up our environment" and that our "ability to misuse technology" is leading to the ultimate "crash" of our species.

The primary audience supporting Butler's speculative fiction is composed of three distinct groups. First is the science fiction audience—readers who follow writers and developments in the genre avidly. The second group is the feminist audience—generally white women—and others intrigued by the feminist angle in Butler's tales. And last is a developing black American audience—growing as more black readers discover Butler as a black woman writer who, although working in a genre outside the customary realistic tradition, nevertheless uses many of the same social or racial touchstones as other, more recognized, black American writers. Occasionally, a fan might hold simultaneous membership in all three groups—a science fiction reader, a feminist, and a black American.

Presently, Octavia Butler lives and works in Pasadena, California, having returned to her hometown after spending several years in Los Angeles. Rather than use a word processor or computer, she continues to draft her manuscripts on a large, office model, manual typewriter. The 1990s will usher in her newest series of science fiction novels; in this set of projected novels, humanity will be going out into space—much sooner than we think. The working title for the first book in this envisioned series is *God of Clay*; subsequent novels will take readers forward well into the twenty-first century, almost to the twenty-second. Although planned as a series, Butler intends to structure these novels so that chronological publication order will not matter. Except for the first volume, the sequence for reading the novels will not be a relevant factor.

References

Banfield, Bever-leigh. "Octavia Butler: A Wild Seed." *Hip* 5 (1981): 48-50, 72, 74, 77.

Beal, Frances M. "*Black Scholar* interview with Octavia Butler: Black Women and the Science Fiction Genre." *Black Scholar* 17 (March/April 1986): 14-18.

Butler, Octavia M. Interviews with Sandra Y. Govan. 18 May 1990; 5 June 1990.

Butler, Octavia M. *Kindred*. Boston, Mass.: Beacon Press, 1988.

Davidson, Carolyn S. "The Science Fiction of Octavia Butler." *Sagala* 2 (1981): 35.

Elliot, Jeffery. "Interview with Octavia Butler." *Thrust* No. 12 (Summer 1979): 19-22.

Harrison, Rosalie G. "Sci Fi Visions: An Interview with Octavia Butler." *Equal Opportunity Forum Magazine* 8 (1980): 30-34.

Mixon, Veronica. "Futurist Woman: Octavia Butler." *Essence* 9 (April 1979): 12, 15.

Norwood, Chico C. "Science Fiction Writer Comes of Age." *Los Angeles Sentinel*, 16 April 1981.

O'Connor, Margaret Anne. "Octavia E. Butler." *Dictionary of Literary Biography*. Boston: Beacon Press, 1988.

Peck, Claudia. "Interview: Octavia Butler." *Skewed: The Magazine of Fantasy Science Fiction, and Horror* 1 [n.d]: 18-27.

Warga, Wayne. "Corn Chips Yield Grist for Her Mill." *Los Angeles Times*, 30 January 1981.

Collections

At present, Butler has all of her papers and manuscripts in her possession.

Sandra Y. Govan

Selena Sloan Butler

(1872?-1964)

Community leader, child welfare activist, organization leader

Selena Sloan Butler, community and child welfare leader and parent-teacher organization leader, was born January 4, 1872(?) (she was never forthcoming about her age), in Thomasville, Georgia, the daughter of Winnie Williams, a woman of African and Indian descent, and William Sloan, a white man. William Sloan is reported to have supported the family, but he did not live with them. The early household consisted of Butler, an older sister, and Winnie Williams. From all sources, Selena Sloan's mother died young, and Butler lost contact with her older married sister. She could not publicly acknowledge her white father, leaving her bereft of any ties or contacts with her family or birthplace.

Butler received elementary education training from Thomas County missionaries. She was endorsed for admission to the Spelman Seminary by her mother's minister. The Atlanta Baptist Female Seminary, now Spelman College, had been founded in Atlanta in the basement of Friendship Baptist Church by two New Englanders: Sophia Packard and Harriet Giles. The seminary opened in 1881. The Rockefeller family became interested in the project and John D. Rockefeller made a significant contribution, whereupon the name was changed to Spelman Seminary in honor of Rockefeller's mother. Butler was one of the one hundred boarders among nearly five hundred enrolled students. Butler profited from her six years of education at Spelman, studying the higher normal and scientific course and working on the school magazine. She received her high school diploma with Spelman's second graduating class in 1888. At the age of sixteen, Butler began her public life of service to her fellow beings.

For the next five years, Butler eked out an existence as an English and elocution teacher in Atlanta. She organized and taught kindergarten at Morris Brown College. Perhaps in 1891, Butler moved to Tallahassee, Florida, where she continued teaching and served as lady preceptress at the State Normal School (now Florida Agricultural and Mechanical State University).

On May 3, 1893, Selena Sloan married Henry Rutherford Butler (1864-1931). Henry Butler was born in Cumberland County, North Carolina, the son of William T. and Caroline Butler. He entered Lincoln University in Pennsylvania in 1881 and received a B.A. in 1887 and an M.A. degree in 1890. He received medical training from Nashville's Meharry College of Medicine, receiving his M.D. degree in 1890 (having entered Meharry in 1887). He took further courses at Harvard Medical School in ensuing years. One child, Henry Rutherford Butler, Jr., was born of this union on November 1, 1899.

Both cordial and brilliant leaders, the Butlers shared nearly forty years of professional interests and common values, European travel, and a commitment to improve the citizenry and the black American community. In 1894 the Butlers traveled to Cambridge, Massachusetts, where Selena Butler attended the Emerson School of Oratory while her husband pursued special courses in the diseases of children and surgery at Harvard University (for most of his professional life, Henry Butler specialized in juvenile diseases). Selena Butler took time from her studies to represent the Atlanta Women's Club (she was a charter member) at the organization meeting of the National Federation of Colored Women's Clubs in Boston. The young couple returned to Atlanta in 1895, and Henry Butler practiced medicine while Selena Butler taught school. She was a pioneer night school teacher selected by the board of education to staff its first night school at Yonge Street School. She did private tutoring in elocution and public speaking. Selena Butler established, edited, and published for several years the *Woman's Advocate*, a monthly paper devoted to news and problems of particular interest to black American women.

During the First World War, Selena Butler was active with the entertainment group working with black enlistees at Camp Gordon near Atlanta. She also worked in the Auburn Avenue Branch of the Atlanta office in charge of the sale and distribution of war savings stamps and certificates. At the close of hostilities, she was cited by the American Red Cross for her outstanding work and leadership.

Selena Butler's dedication to parent-teacher associations grew out of her efforts to educate her son, Henry, Jr. The Butlers maintained a substantial home at 20 Boulevard Street N.E., in a fashionable black American neighborhood in the "Old Fourth Ward." The elite of black Atlanta lived on the street, and the fairly new campus of Morris Brown University (now Morris Brown College) was nearby. In addition to Henry Butler's practice, he became a partner in the first black-owned drugstore in Georgia. However, the family was still thwarted by Atlanta's restrictive programs as they related to people of color, especially in education. Selena Butler set up a kindergarten program in her own home when she and neighboring mothers could not find a preschool teacher for their children.

First Black Parent-Teacher Association Founded

One early spring afternoon, Selena Butler sat in a rocking chair in her backyard and was lulled into a deep sleep. In a dream she wrestled with the problems of her race; and in this semiconscious state Butler had a vision of sobbing black children with outstretched hands imploring her help. Butler awoke and accepted the task of enhancing the lives of children and dedicated her life to it. She followed the children of her kindergarten to their neighborhood public grammar school on Yonge Street. She called on like-minded women who would be interested in the formation of an organization that would have the same objective as the National Congress of Parents and Teachers. The problems were the same, and in some instances more intense. It was at Yonge Street School in 1911 that she established the first black parent-teacher association in the country.

From this foundation Butler developed in 1919 the Georgia Colored Parent-Teacher Association (GCPTA) and acted as its president for a number of years. The call for a meeting brought people from every major city in the state of Georgia together in Atlanta. The meeting was held at the war camp community center on Edgewood Avenue. In the lecture room of Big Bethel African Methodist Episcopal Church in 1921, after two years of organizational activities, the organization became permanent. Butler founded the congress's organ, *Our National Family*.

Butler expanded her efforts resolutely beyond the state level on May 7, 1926, when the National Congress of Colored Parents and Teachers (NCCPT) was constituted at a meeting in Atlanta, under the aegis of the Sixth Annual Convention of the Georgia Colored PTA and the Thirtieth Annual Convention of the National Congress of Parents and Teachers. As the founding president of the new organization, Butler created a successful working link with the white National Congress. The NCCPT adopted the congress's policies and programs and in return it received assistance and encouragement through an integrated advisory committee. Although the black group served principally in those states maintaining segregated schools, the arrangement with its sister organization advanced greater cooperation between black and white groups in school systems, especially at the local level, where such communication was atypical. Butler received the support of several white Georgian leaders and the organization became, in her words, a conduit for "effecting interracial education work." The organization adopted the "Seven Cardinal Principles" that the white group had propounded:

1. Health and safety;
2. Worthy home membership;
3. Mastery of tools, technique, and spirit of learning;
4. Citizenship and world goodwill;
5. Vocation and economics effectiveness;
6. Wise use of leisure;
7. Ethical character (*History of the Georgia Conference of Colored Parents and Teachers*, 22).

The congress further adopted the objectives of the National Congress:

> To promote the welfare of children and young, in home, school, church and community.
>
> To raise the standards of home life.
>
> To secure adequate laws for the care and protection of children and youth.
>
> To bring into closer relation the home and the school, that the parents and teachers, may cooperate intelligently in the training of the child (22).

Committee Activities Address Social Ills

Butler was principally occupied with the work of the black National Congress, but she performed an important role in several bodies in her city and state. She was a delegate at the founding convention of the National Association of Colored Women held in Boston. Her paper on "Convict Lease System," read before the first annual convention of NACW held in Nashville, Tennessee, September 15-17, was printed in pamphlet form and distributed. Butler was first president of the Georgia Federation of Colored Women's Clubs. Both Selena and Henry Butler were members of the Georgia Commission on Interracial Cooperation (CIC), which laid the groundwork for much of the improvement in race relations experienced in the years between the two world wars. The CIC was founded in Atlanta in 1919 in an effort to ameliorate racial tensions growing out of World War I. Seeking to bring "the best" whites and blacks together, CIC organized some eight hundred state and local interracial committees throughout the southern states. In 1930 Selena Butler was part of the group of southern women to form the Southern Women for the Prevention of Lynching. But the CIC and Southern Women for the Prevention of Lynching were absorbed in the newly formed Southern Regional Council in 1943. She was a member of Atlanta's top women's literary and social club, The Chautauqua Circle, and was both an organizer of the Ruth Chapter of the Order of the Eastern Star in Atlanta and for many years Grand Lecturer of the lodge in Georgia. Butler was an early worker in the Phyllis Wheatley Young Women's Christian Association; she served for many years as chairperson of its board of trustees and aided in the fundraising activities for its building committee.

In 1931 Henry Butler died, and a few years later Selena Butler traveled to Europe with her son, Henry Butler, Jr., a graduate of Harvard Medical School. Residing in London, she maintained her child welfare activities by working in the Nursery School Association of Great Britain, the British counterpart of the PTA. She was also active in the work of the Cancer Association and was among those workers invited to tea by the Lord Mayor of London.

At the onset of the Second World War, Selena Butler returned to America. She followed her son to Arizona—Fort Huachuca had been organized to provide a base for the training of black American armed forces officers, and her son was attached to the medical services at the hospital. She established a Gray Lady Corps there. She was affectionately known as "Mother Butler" and several units in training at the fort gave a testimonial program in her honor before leaving.

In 1947 Butler returned to her home in Atlanta. In 1953 she moved for the last time to live with her son and daughter-in-law in Los Angeles. She remained active there in the Congregational church (she was a deaconess emerita), and in several welfare organizations, including the board of the Sojourner Truth Home, a member of the Charles R. Drew Medical Society Auxiliary, and a member of Las Madrinas (Alpha Kappa Alpha Sorority mothers' organization).

Death came to Butler in October 1964 of congestive heart failure; her body was returned to Atlanta for burial next to her husband in Oakland Cemetery on Monday, October 12. Last rites were conducted at First Congregational Church, where she maintained her membership. She received full fraternal rites of the Prince Hall Grand Lodge of Georgia, of which her husband was grand master before his death. The Order of the Eastern Star honored her with full rites, since she was organizer of Atlanta's Ruth Chapter and a former Grand Lecturer of the order.

Selena Sloan Butler's attachment to interracial cooperation and child welfare earned her many tributes in her lifetime: from the Lord Mayor of London, the American Red Cross, and Spelman College; and an appointment from President Herbert Hoover to the White House Conference on Child Welfare and Protection. This appointment made her a representative of the National Congress of Colored Parents and Teachers; she served on the Infant and Pre-School Child Committee, whose work contributed to the writing of the landmark Children's Charter. Honors continued posthumously; the black and white PTAs, after their integration in 1970, elevated Butler to national founder status alongside Alice McClellan Birney and Phoebe Hearst, the founders of the National Congress of Parents and Teachers. Atlanta renamed the Yonge Street School after her husband and a historic marker was unveiled noting that the school was the site where the CPTA was founded. The adjacent park was named the Selena Sloan Butler Park in her honor on February 13, 1966. In 1976 the Georgia State Department of Education commissioned a portrait to hang in its Hall of Fame at the capitol in acknowledgment of Selena Sloan Butler as one of Georgia's renowned educator citizens.

Contemporaries of Butler remember her as a very light-skinned woman with a foreboding mien. Her training in elocution was evident in her precise speech. However, she was very amiable and sociable with her peers. She was a devoted member of the First Congregational Church of Atlanta. Of her varied activities extending over many years, Butler always felt that her work and duties as wife, mother, and homemaker, which she never once neglected, were closest to her heart. She was associated with and friends to many: Mary McLeod Bethune, Nannie Helen Burroughs, and Mary Church Terrell in the women's club movement; educators at the Atlanta University complex and especially with the wife of president John Hope of Morehouse College, Lugenia Burns Hope, and the Neighborhood Union's mission of giving social service to the needy; black and white members of the Georgia Commission on Interracial Cooperation, which included the renowned educator, Lucy Laney. She was also a correspondent of Eleanor Roosevelt, the wife of United States President Franklin Delano Roosevelt.

References

Atlanta Daily World, 8 October 1964; 10 October 1964.

Atlanta Journal and Constitution, 7 October 1964; 8 October 1964; 9 October 1964.

History of the Georgia Congress of Colored Parents and Teachers. Atlanta: The Congress, 1970.

Roth, Darlene R. "Serena Sloan Butler." *Notable American Women: The Modern Period. Cambridge: Harvard University Press, 1980.*

Wesley, Charles Harris. *The History of the National Association of Colored Women's Clubs. Washington: NACW, 1984.*

Collections

As of 1980 Selena Sloan Butler's papers were in the possession of her family. Manuscript sources include collections housed in the Special Collections of the Atlanta University Center's Robert W. Woodruff Library and contain a Butler file, a Chautauqua Circle file, a Neighborhood Union file, and the Georgia Commission on Interracial Cooperation file. The collections contain a number of photographs of Butler.

Casper LeRoy Jordan

C

Shirley Caesar

(1938-)

Singer, religious leader

Shirley Caesar was born October 13, 1938, in Durham, North Carolina, one of twelve children of "Big Jim" and Hallie Caesar. She grew up in a strict Holiness family under the teachings of Mt. Calvary Holy Church. Her early singing experiences began in the church with family members, where she was known as "Baby Shirley." Her father was a quartet singer with the Just Come Four of North Carolina. It has been observed that Shirley Caesar's singing has been greatly influenced by Big Jim Caesar's "blue notes and slurs." After her father's death when she was twelve years old, Shirley Caesar began a career as a gospel singer to help support her invalid mother, and to spread the word of gospel, she worked later as an evangelist as well. Her early career was also influenced by gospel preacher Leroy Johnson.

Shirley Caesar completed secondary school in the public schools of Durham, North Carolina, and studied business education at North Carolina State College (now North Carolina Central University). The December 1986 issue of *Totally Gospel Magazine* states that she holds a bachelor's degree in business administration. She studied at Shaw University in Raleigh, North Carolina, with plans to pursue a master's degree in divinity at Duke University. Her studies at North Carolina State College were interrupted after two years so that she could expand her growing gospel career as a member of Albertina Walker's Caravans of Chicago, Illinois, in 1958.

Queen of Evangelistic Gospel Singing Reigns

Shirley Caesar has been called "the reigning queen of evangelistic gospel singing" in Viv Broughton's book, *Black Gospel*. She is noted as much for her preaching as gospel singing, which, in black American culture, is not unusual. Rhythmic timing, vocal power, and a charismatic delivery style are practically inseparable from and are an integral part of black-style singing or preaching. Evangelistic Caesar, as she is referred to, integrates singing and preaching with such seamlessness that it sometimes becomes difficult to know when one begins and the other ends. It has been said that Shirley Caesar is particularly gifted in her ability to take a cliché and infuse it with an original flavor. She became an evangelist in 1961 prior to leaving the famous Caravans in 1966. According to Southern, she was "the leading gospel singer of her generation," with a "rock-gospel" style. Her repertoire differed from that of her contemporaries in that she sang sacred music only (Southern, 61).

Caesar refers to herself as a "traditional" gospel singer, presumably meaning her identification with the pre-1960s style urban gospel. She is a part of the Rosetta Tharpe, Mahalia Jackson era—two early great gospel soloists from the 1930s and 1950s. It was as a member of the Caravans from that cradle of traditional gospel music, Chicago, that Caesar gained her first national exposure and experience as recording artist. Albertina Walker "discovered" Caesar during one of the Caravans's concerts in Raleigh, North Carolina. She was invited to join the group that contained the noted singers Inez Andrews, Cassietta George, Delores Washington, and Dorothy Norwood. She remained in the Caravans, singing some of her biggest hits, such as "Sweeping Through the City," and "Running for Jesus." Her sermonette songs include "Don't Drive Your Mama Away," "Faded Rose," and "No Charge." She recently made a bow to a more contemporary style with the Reverend Al Green, "Sailing on the Sea of Your Love," "Put Your Hand in the Hand of the Man From Galilee," "Hold My Mule," and "Martin," a special dedication to the Reverend Martin Luther King., Jr. Caesar says this song has special meaning for her.

Her career has escalated since she formed own group, the Caesar Singers, after eight years as a member of the Caravans. Today she is among the most sought-after and commercially successful of all professional gospel singers. She has appeared at colleges, universities, festivals, churches, and auditoriums in the United States and Europe.

Shirley Caesar has been elected a member of the Durham, North Carolina, City Council. She is copastor, with her husband, Bishop Harold Ivory Williams, of the Mt. Calvary Holy Church in Winston-Salem, North Carolina. She founded and directs the Calvary and Shirley Caesar Outreach Ministries, a goods and clothing program for needy families.

Loved by the community of gospel artists, Shirley Caesar counts among her many friends and colleagues the Reverend James Cleveland and members of the Martin Luther King family, with whom she traveled singing "Martin,"

Descriptions of Shirley Caesar invariably call attention to her diminutive size, suggesting a petite ball of moving energy. Heilbut says that Caesar is "aggressive . . . small, pretty and gifted with great muscular control. . . . Her career is a model of sheer energy and spunk"(266).

Her career and accomplishments have led to many awards and honors. Shirley Caesar was named best female gospel singer three times in *Ebony* magazine. She received the 1972 Grammy Award for "Put Your Hand in the Hand of the Man From Galilee," and she has received six Grammy awards—more than any other gospel singer. In 1975 and 1977 she received the Peoples' Choice Award. In 1982 she received the Dove Award. In 1985 she received the NAACP Image Award for her positive influence on the black community. SESAC music publishers gave her the Lifetime Achievement Award in 1986. *Billboard Magazine* lists Shirley Caesar as the number one artist for 1989, and her album *Live in Chicago* as number one for the same year.

Shirley Caesar has appeared on a number of television shows, including "Musical Chairs," "The Today Show," "Merv Griffin Show," "Positively Black" (1975), "Ebony Music Awards" (1975), and "Late Night with David Letterman" (1987).

Caesar's recordings include: *Best of Shirley Caesar* (Savoy 14202); *Celebration.* (Rejoice 7-01-500128-4); *Go.* (Myrrh WR-8107); *Her Very Best.* (Word WR-8365) (CD 8365); *Live in Chicago.* (Word WR-8385); and *Sailin'* (Myrrh WR-8106).

References

Boyer, Horace. "Shirley Caesar." *New Grove Dictionary of American Music.* Vol. I. Edited by H. Wiley Hitchcock and Stanley Sadie. New York: Macmillan, 1986.

Broughton, Viv. *Black Gospel: An Illustrated History of the Gospel Sound.* New York: Sterling Publishing Co., 1985.

"First Lady of Gospel," *Ebony* 37 (November 1977): 98.

Heilbut, Tony. *The Gospel Sound.* New York: Limelight Editions, 1982.

Mapp, Edward. *Directory of Blacks in the Performing Arts.* 2nd ed. Metuchen, N.J.: Scarecrow Press, 1990.

"The Queen of Gospel Music." *Totally Gospel* (December 1986):

Southern, Eileen. *Biographical Dictionary of Afro-American and African Musicians.* Westport, Conn.: Greenwood Press, 1982.

Pearl Williams-Jones

Blanche Calloway

(1902-1973)

Singer, entrepreneur

Blanche Calloway (Jones), one of the most successful bandleaders of the 1930s and the only woman to lead an all-male band, was born on February 2, 1902, in Baltimore, Maryland, and died December 16, 1973, in Baltimore. She was one of four children born to Cabell Calloway and Martha Eulalia (Reed) Calloway. The family lived in Rochester, New York, from 1906 to around 1918, then moved back to Baltimore when Blanche Calloway was about sixteen years old. Her father attended Lincoln University in Pennsylvania and became a lawyer. While in Rochester, however, he had been in the real estate business. Her mother had attended Morgan State College and became a teacher in the local Baltimore schools.

About two years after the return to Baltimore, Cabell Calloway, Sr., died. Some time later, Martha Calloway married John Nelson Fortune, and they had two children. The Calloway family was very religious, active in Grace Presbyterian Church, and well-respected in the black community. The family was also musically-oriented, for her mother was a church organist and two of her brothers became professional musicians, Cabell (Cab) and Elmer. Cab, named for his father, emerged toward the end of the Harlem Renaissance of the 1920s as a bandleader and entertainer and was to become nationally and internationally known.

Calloway Forms Jazz Band

In her childhood, Blanche Calloway studied piano and voice with Llewelyn Wilson. During her teens she sang in a church choir. As a serious developing music student, she studied at Morgan State College. She dropped out of college because of her interest in show business. At first she performed in local revues, stage shows, and nightclubs. Her professional career blossomed, and she joined the 1923 touring companies of Noble Sissle and Eubie Blake's musical *Shuffle Along* and the James P. Johnson show, *Plantation Days.* When *Plantation Days* ran its course in Chicago, Illinois, in 1927, she took up residency in Chicago and became a nightclub entertainer. Subsequently she and her brother, Cab Calloway, had their own act: he as the bandleader and she as the featured vocalist. In 1931 she fronted for Andy Kirk's band in a residency at Philadelphia's Pearl Theatre.

Between 1931 and 1938 she formed, led, and directed her own orchestra, becoming the first black woman to lead an all-male band. She preceded her brother Cab in show business and for many years was known to have an excellent band act.

At this time her band included, periodically, William "Cozy" Cole on drums, Victor "Vic" Dickinson on trombone, and Albert "Andy" Gibson and Ben Webster on tenor saxophone, to name a few. Research reveals that Blanche Calloway's all-male band appeared at New York City's Lafayette Theatre in 1931-1932 and 1934, the Harlem Opera House in 1934 and 1935, and the Apollo Theatre in 1935-1938 and 1941. In the early 1930s she named her orchestra Blanche Calloway and Her Joy Boys; eventually she called the band Blanche Calloway and Her Orchestra.

Calloway's band once made a five-band tour with Bennie Moten, Andy Kirk, Chick Webb, and Zack Whyte's bands. In 1931, 1934, and 1935, she and her band recorded frequently for Victor. Her band performed extensively across the United States, including such cities as New York City, Baltimore, Boston, Atlantic City, Indianapolis, Cleveland, Cincinnati, St. Louis, Kansas City, and Pittsburgh. Her band's theme song became "Growlin Dan," while her best-known song was "I Need Loving."

At the height of her career, Cab Calloway was known as "Blanche's younger brother." She was the one who introduced her brother to the world of entertainment when he was about eighteen years old, although she pointed out to him the negative elements in such a business. Cab Calloway dedicated his book, *Of Minnie the Moocher and Me*, published in 1976, to his wife and family and "sister Blanche who introduced me to the wonderful world of entertainment."

In 1931 the *Pittsburgh Courier* made a survey of thirty-eight outstanding national black orchestras. Calloway's band ranked ninth, only five points behind Louis Armstrong and well ahead of such bands as those of Jimmie Lunceford, Chick Webb, Bennie Moten, and Claude Hopkins, who became part of jazz history. This was quite a feat, since as a female bandleader she had to cope with sexism and male chauvinism. On January 16, 1932, the *Pittsburgh Courier* published an article in which the reviewer considered Calloway as "one of the most progressive performers in the profession" and acknowledged her for her ownership, management, and directorship of her popular band. During the later thirties to the mid-forties she performed as a soloist, except when she put together an all-girl band in 1940. She made an appearance with an all-girl orchestra at Club Harlem in Atlantic City. The group never became successful. By 1944, she gave up the harsh life of one-night stands, compounded by segregated hotels, restaurants, and other public accommodations. She settled in Philadelphia, participated in community and political affairs, and was elected as a Democratic Committee Woman. Around 1953 she moved to Florida.

During the 1950s Calloway was employed as a disc jockey on radio station WMEM in Miami, Florida. After her stint as a disc jockey in Miami, she founded and served as president of Afram House, Inc., a firm specializing in cosmetics and hair preparations for blacks. In Miami she continued her interest in politics and became the first black woman to vote in 1958.

In "Dance Bands That Made History," an article published in *International Musician* in 1950, Blanche Calloway was singled out with seven female orchestra leaders for recognition. She was the only black orchestra leader on the list.

References

AKA Sorority Heritage Series. Chicago: Alpha Kappa Alpha Sorority, 1940.

Allen, Walter C. *Hendersonia: The Music of Fletcher Henderson and His Musicians: A Bio-Discography*. Highland Park, N.J.: Walter C. Allen, 1973.

"Band/Orchestra Survey." *Pittsburgh Courier* 16 January 1932.

Black Stars (September 1973): 50.

Calloway, Cab, and Bryant Rollins. *Of Minnie the Moocher and Me*. New York: Crowell, 1976.

Chicago Defender, 20 July 1940.

Chilton, John. *Who's Who of Jazz: Storyville of Jazz to Swing Street*. 1970. Reprinted. Chicago: Time-Life Records Special Edition, 1978.

"Dance Bands that Made History." *International Musician* (October 1950).

Dawn Magazine, April 1979.

Encyclopedia of Black America. Edited by W. Augustus Low and Virgil A. Clift. New York: McGraw-Hill, 1981.

Handy, D. Antoinette. *Black Women in American Bands & Orchestras*. Metuchen, N.J.: Scarecrow Press, 1981.

Jet (4 January 1979): 60.

"Remembering Blanche Calloway." *Afro-American* (Richmond), 30 December 1978.

Sepia (March 1979): 10.

Southern, Eileen. *Biographical Dictionary of Afro-American and African Musicians*. Westport, Conn.: Greenwood Press, 1982.

Washington Post, 19 December 1978.

Joan Curl Elliott

Lucie (Lucy) Campbell Williams

(1885-1962)

Composer, educator, evangelist

"Mrs. Lucie Campbell Williams, character of the past, present and future, we salute you. Your colorful career lives forever. You are more than a woman of stately stature—you are a legend woven into the fabric of human endeavor" (*Miss Lucie Speaks,* 43). This tribute to "Miss Lucie" was given before the National Sunday School and Baptist Training Union Congress in June of 1962, just six months before her death. Lucie Campbell was being honored by the National Baptist Convention for her service that spanned over five decades. She was the author of many of her denomination's best-loved hymns. She was a professional educator whose accomplishments brought her national recognition. She was a Christian whose life added much to the world. Her life is indeed a legend.

Lucie Eddie Campbell was born in 1885 in Duck Hill, Mississippi, to Burrell and Isabelle Campbell. Her birth was untimely: she was born in the caboose of a train just as it neared their home. She was the seventh and youngest child in her family, though her family was to change tragically on the day she was born. Her father, a railroad worker, was killed in an accident on his way to see his newborn daughter. Before her second birthday the family moved in hopes of finding an easier life. They settled in Memphis, Tennessee, near the famed Beale Street.

Campbell's education began in the public schools of Memphis. As an elementary school student, she won state penmanship awards and in high school graduated as valedictorian of her class. Her education extended outside the classroom to the streets of her neighborhood and the influences of Beale Street. She says that it was here that she learned to master her environment (*Miss Lucie Speaks,* 32).

Campbell's formal music education is an example of her lifelong determination to succeed, no matter what the odds. Her mother could only afford to send one child for music lessons and chose Lucie's sister Lora. Lucie, undaunted, would eavesdrop on her sister's lessons, learning everything she could. When Lora wanted to stop taking lessons, Lucie promptly volunteered. For most children, having no piano on which to practice would have been the perfect excuse for slacking off, but not for Lucie. On the long walk to school she would practice the piano fingerings in the air. The practice paid off. As Lucie's musical proficiency increased, her popularity as a performer increased; she often entertained visiting guests with her music. At age nineteen, Campbell organized a group of talented Beale Street musicians into The Music Club, a group that "provided means of development and expression through public concerts" (*Beale Street,* 157). Though the group was generally much smaller, Lucie Campbell organized this group and brought in others to form a thousand-voice choir that sang at the National Baptist Convention.

Campbell Becomes Teacher

While Campbell's work in music flourished, she continued her education. In her sixteenth year of school she was called to begin teaching in the Memphis public schools. This was the beginning of a forty-three year career teaching American history and English at Booker T. Washington High School. Campbell later received her baccalaureate degree from Rust College, Holly Springs, Mississippi, and a master's degree from Tennessee Agricultural and Industrial State University, Nashville.

As Campbell became known as a professional educator and a professional musician, she was often asked about her career choice as a history and English teacher. In reply she stated, "Teaching is my vocation, music is my avocation" (*Miss Lucie Speaks,* 13). However, she gained her fame from both her vocation and her avocation. As an educator she was widely respected by both her students and her peers, being elected to the vice-presidency of the American Teachers Association. Her colleagues from Tennessee chose her as the president of the Tennessee Teachers Association.

Campbell's proclaimed avocation of musician and composer was certainly as noteworthy as her vocation of educator. In 1919 her first song was published: "Something Within." The song was written for a blind boy because, in the words of Campbell, "He couldn't see and he wanted to sing but refused to sing the blues" (*Miss Lucie Speaks,* 14). This song was followed by more than a hundred others in her lifetime. Her best-known songs include "The Lord is My Shepherd," "Heavenly Sunshine," "I Need Thee Every Hour," and "He Understands, He'll Say Well Done" (Southern, 62). Her involvement in music was not limited to hymn writing. It was in 1919, the same year her first song was published, that she introduced to the National Baptist Convention a young woman by the name of Marian Anderson. Lucie Campbell was her accompanist on this occasion.

Campbell was actively involved in directing the music programs of both her local church and her denomination. She served as music director of her church—Tabernacle Baptist Church in Memphis, Tennessee—and as music director of the National Baptist Sunday School and Baptist Training Union Congress, a position she held for more than thirty years. Her contribution to her denomination was truly significant, guiding the members through three decades of worship through music. The National Sunday School and Baptist Training Union Congress showed its appreciation of Campbell when it declared June 20, 1962, Lucie E. Campbell Appreciation Day. The celebration was held in the

Denver, Colorado, Municipal Auditorium and tens of thousands were on hand for the celebration.

Campbell's accomplishments reached beyond the realm of her vocation and avocation and included national recognition when she was called to take part in two presidential conferences in Washington, D.C. In 1946 she was appointed to the National Policy Planning Commission of the National Education Association. She also became the first woman of any race to serve on the federal grand jury in Memphis. She was in demand as a speaker and traveled frequently. Her messages were primarily religious in nature, most often uplifting, and always inspiring, as seen in these excerpts from her speeches published in *Miss Lucy Speaks:*

> To win, one must be big enough to see the worth in others, big enough to cheer when others score (11).
>
> We need women in times like these who have and can weather the storm. Women like you who have faith in God's promises. God has not promised us a smooth journey, but He has promised us a safe landing. We need women who pray and ask God for what they want, believing and trusting Him who is the author and finisher of our faith. Women who can get a prayer through (29).
>
> Life is a sea. We are the ships. Let us go straight to harbor (36).

Lucie Campbell married C. R. Williams relatively late in life, though little is known about the marriage.

Perhaps Lucie Campbell's greatest accomplishments were in the lives that she reached, both in her teaching, by her extensive speaking, and through her music. Those who speak out to praise her are numerous, but of all the long, eloquent speeches given about her, this simple statement may be the most telling: "But all Miss Lucie wanted was to help the world see Jesus—and she did that with remarkable distinction" (*Miss Lucie Speaks,* 44).

References

Ebony 30 (November 1974): 104. Photograph.

Lee, George W. *Beale Street.* New York: R. O. Ballou, 1934.

Southern, Eileen. *Biographical Dictionary of Afro-American and African Musicians.* Westport, Connecticut: Greenwood Press, 1982.

Washington, Wiliam M., Ed. *Miss Lucie Speaks.* Nashville, Tennessee: n.p., 1971.

Elizabeth Patrick

Alexa Canady

(1950-)

Neurosurgeon

> As one of the first of the new generation of black women neurosurgeons, I have a responsibility to seize hold of the opportunities created by the movement of the sixties as well as the generations before. Those of us in small, highly specialized fields have an opportunity to reaffirm the equality of black people in the entire gamut of study.

Alexa Irene Canady wrote this in 1977 soon after becoming the first woman and first black neurosurgical resident at the University of Minnesota.

Alexa Irene Canady was born in Lansing, Michigan, on November 7, 1950, to Elizabeth Hortense (Golden) Canady and Clinton Canady, Jr. Her father, a highly-respected dentist in Lansing, was a graduate of the School of Dentistry of Meharry Medical College. Her mother, a graduate of Fisk University, was active in civic affairs of Lansing and also served as national president of Delta Sigma Theta Sorority. She was a role model for her daughter, who said of her, "She's bright, energetic, and committed, and has a sense that getting up each day is an adventure. My grandmother is also a role model because she always treated me like I was a person who was worth listening to even when I was a little person and not worth listening to" (Lanker, 128).

The family lived outside the city of Lansing, and Canady and her brother attended the local elementary school, the only two black students in the school. Some of her precollege school years coincided with the civil rights struggles of the 1960s, a time of inspiration and striving and pride for many young blacks. For her academic accomplishments in high school, Alexa Canady was named a National Achievement Scholar in 1967.

She enrolled in the University of Michigan and received the B.S. degree in 1971. She was admitted to its College of Medicine, where she further distinguished herself by being elected to Alpha Omega Alpha Honorary Medical Society. In 1975 she received the M.D. degree cum laude and a citation from the American Medical Women's Association.

Her graduate medical education began with an internship

at New Haven Hospital—Yale, 1975-76. This was followed by the historic appointment as the first female and first black to a residency in neurosurgery at the University of Minnesota from 1976 to 1981. She viewed this attainment as a juxtaposition of personal qualifications and socio-political change in America at that time. She wrote: "When I got a residency in neurosurgery, I got it not because I'm smarter than somebody forty years ago, but because the politics were such that they needed a black woman and I was there and qualified. I had impeccable credentials coming out of medical school, but there was an undercurrent of, 'How can you, a black woman, have the audacity to want to do this? Don't you know that you've got a double whammy?' Well, I came along at a time when it offered them a double positive. They could fulfill the quotas and say, 'I finished woman. I finished black, and all it took was one person instead of two.' So that became a positive for me" (Lanker, 128).

After successful completion of her residency, she did a fellowship in pediatric neurosurgery at Children's Hospital in Philadelphia in 1981-1982. At the same time she was instructor in neurosurgery at the University of Pennsylvania College of Medicine. She moved to Detroit in 1982 and joined the neurosurgery department of Henry Ford Hospital and in 1983 took a position as pediatric neurosurgeon at Children's Hospital of Michigan and became head of the department. Canady was also affiliated with the William Beaumont Hospital in Royal Oak, Michigan. Certified by the American Board of Neurological Surgery in 1984, she is clinical associate professor at Wayne State University in Detroit.

Her commitment to the important caring aspect of medicine is evident in her statement about the nature of her profession: "One of the things I think surgeons have to do is shift emphasis. My job is really not to cut. My job is to help people, which often included cutting, and that's a very different focus" (Lanker, 128).

References

Canady, Alexa Irene. Questionnaire to Jessie Carney Smith, 1977.

Lanker, Brian. *I Dream a World: Portraits of Black Women Who Changed the World.* New York: Stewart, Tabori & Chang, 1989. Photograph, p. 129.

Directory of Medical Specialists. 22nd ed. Detroit: Marquis, 1986.

Ralph J. Cazort

Mary Elizabeth Carnegie

(1916-)

Nurse, educator, nursing administrator, author

Mary Elizabeth Lancaster Carnegie is a highly respected leader in nursing of national and international prominence. Her career in nursing presently spans more than a period of fifty-three years, during which time she has been and continues to be a leader and an agent for change in the nursing profession. Carnegie has an impressive career that encompasses bedside nursing, nurse education, educational nursing administration, consultation, nursing research, editorial positions on various prestigious nursing journals, distinguished visiting professorships and endowed chairs, and numerous publications and professional presentations. Carnegie has championed the cause of equality for black women in nursing and written about the history of inequality black women experienced. Carnegie's concerns for equality include women of all races.

Mary Elizabeth Lancaster Carnegie was born on April 19, 1916, in Baltimore, Maryland. She was the fourth child born to John Oliver Lancaster and Adeline Beatrice (Swann)

Mary Elizabeth Carnegie

Lancaster. She had two older sisters and a brother, and one younger brother. She grew up in Washington, D.C., with her aunt and uncle, Rosa and Thomas Robison, and her primary and secondary education was obtained in the District of Columbia. She was reared in the Catholic religion and her hobbies were playing the organ for children's mass and singing in the choir. During her early years, Carnegie considered becoming a nun.

Carnegie attended Dunbar High School, an all-black school in Washington, D.C. She worked after school and on weekends preparing fruits at Allies Inn in order to complete her high school education. Allies Inn was a cafeteria that hired black workers but only catered to whites. Carnegie graduated from high school at the age of sixteen and thereafter went to spend some time with family living in New York. While in New York, a relative who had attended Lincoln School for Nurses encouraged her to consider nursing as a career. She applied to the Lincoln School for Nurses, took the aptitude test, returned to Washington, D.C., and for the time being gave the application no additional thought.

Carnegie was notified in July 1934 that she was accepted to the privately-owned Lincoln School for Nurses, and in September of that year she began her nursing education. Carnegie liked nursing and enjoyed her student years at Lincoln School. A tall, light skinned black woman, Carnegie was nicknamed "Lanky," by her peers at Lincoln, short for Lancaster and describing her tall frame. This nickname stuck with her throughout the years.

In 1936, during Carnegie's student years at Lincoln, she had the opportunity to hear Mabel Keaton Staupers, executive secretary of the National Association of Colored Graduate Nurses (NACGN), tell the story of the association and the struggle black nurses were having in obtaining recognition by all members of the nursing profession, in gaining admission to nursing schools, and in obtaining employment in hospitals and public health agencies throughout the country. It was from this encounter with Staupers, a feisty black nursing leader, that Lancaster's interest in and concern for equal opportunities for black nurses was stimulated.

The Lincoln School for Nurses was one of the few schools in New York City that accepted black students, and Carnegie graduated from it in 1937. Since the economic depression was not over, the class of thirty graduates was, as described by Carnegie, faced with the problem of getting a job, a task that was a difficult prospect at that time. This undertaking was made more difficult because only four of the two hundred hospitals located in New York City employed black nurses. However, Carnegie and a few of her colleagues found immediate employment as staff nurses at Lincoln Hospital, one of those four institutions. The monthly salary of $75 plus maintenance was considered a princely sum at that time.

New graduate nurse Lancaster immediately took the state board and the civil service examination for junior graduate nurses. After passing both examinations, she was appointed to the Veterans Administration Hospital in Tuskegee, Alabama, one of the two federal hospitals in the United States that employed black nurses. (The other was Freedmen's Hospital in Washington, D.C., but assignment there depended upon the successful completion of one year's probation at the Veterans Administration Hospital in Tuskegee.) It was in traveling to her new job that Mary Elizabeth Lancaster first encountered the dreadful segregation practiced on the public transportation of the South when she was forced to travel in a small coach next to the engine.

With her goal of obtaining the best possible education, she attended West Virginia State College full-time in return for giving professional service in the school health program. This allowed her to graduate in 1942 with a bachelor of arts degree and an offer of a job as clinical instructor at the segregated Saint Philip Hospital School of Nursing, the black wing of the Medical College of Virginia.

At that time in the South, black nurses were addressed as Nurse and white nurses as "Miss," but Carnegie and her colleagues instructed their students to address each other as Miss and also to refrain from calling their black patients by their first names, even though the white nurses and doctors did.

Like many other black nurses during World War II, Carnegie wished to serve her country. However, in 1944 her application to the Navy Nurse Corps was rejected with the explanation that black nurses were not being assigned to the Navy. It was not until spring 1945 that black nurses were accepted into the United States Navy, and in 1948 discrimination in the armed forces was eliminated by President Harry S. Truman.

Black College Provides Education for Black Nurses

During the 1940s and 1950s few black American nurses had bachelor's degrees and even fewer had master's degrees. Therefore, relatively few black nurses occupied leadership positions, and the administrators of many schools for black nursing students were white. Carnegie felt that these directors manifested little personal interest in the further development of their former black students, and the indifferent attitude she noted was reflected not only in the programs but in the community's reaction to the black nurse. Carnegie believed that if this invidious position was to be changed, it was necessary to develop college programs to train high-caliber educators and administrators capable of preparing quality black nursing professionals. The black unit of the National Council for War Service was able to encourage Hampton Institute (now University), a college for blacks, to establish in 1943 a collegiate nursing program. Carnegie was released from Saint Philip's through the efforts of the NACGN to serve as assistant director of this new program. Since some time passed before a white director was appointed, Lancaster sought assistance from consultants from the National Nursing Council for War Service and the United States Public Health Service. She initiated the groundwork to establish the school and admitted the first group of nursing students to the program. She is credited for initiating the nursing program at Hampton, which was the first baccalaureate program in the state of Virginia.

Before the end of that first year at Hampton, Mary Elizabeth Carnegie was awarded a fellowship by the Rockefeller Foundation, and in 1944 she enrolled at the University of Toronto, Canada, as a student in nursing school administration. Uncertain about housing accommodations on campus, she contacted a former student, Bernice Carnegie, who arranged housing with her sister. While studying in Toronto, she met and married Bernice's brother, Eric Carnegie, in December 1944.

On completion of this course, she accepted an offer to become dean of the nursing program at Florida Agricultural and Mechanical College in Tallahassee. This was considered a major challenge because the School of Nursing was one of two for blacks in the state and the only one administered by blacks. The challenge was accepted, and Carnegie set out to develop a high-quality nursing education program. Although the college was in Florida, students traveled one thousand miles to a hospital in Baltimore, Maryland, to obtain a one-year period of clinical experience in medical, surgical, pediatric, and obstetrical nursing because of Florida's segregation polices. This separation almost completely removed students from the supervision and control of the college.

One of the first tasks Carnegie undertook was to seek affiliation with hospitals closer to home; however, she met with racial discrimination. Although the nursing directors in the state accepted her request to visit, on her arrival, discovering that she was black, every one refused to shake the hand she extended in greeting. This ill-mannered rebuff confirmed Carnegie's concern that students should not be exposed unnecessarily to discriminatory practices, and therefore clinical facilities had to be found. Carnegie's continued faith in the human race, which at this point was badly shaken, was rewarded when the director of nurses at a large county hospital, Duval Medical Center in Jacksonville, Florida, agreed to the use of the hospital wards as a clinical facility for the black students. This agreement was later confirmed by the board of directors of the hospital, the college, and the Florida State Board of Nurse Examiners. However, this matter was not so easily settled, and the white nurses threatened to walk out if the black students were placed there. The walkout did not occur, a relief for the frightened students and others concerned.

Mary Elizabeth Lancaster Carnegie's involvement in and contributions to professional associations are significant. Although the American Nurses' Association (ANA) had never prohibited black nurses from membership, in Florida they could not belong because the Florida State Nurses Association (FSNA), which was the avenue for entry to the ANA, denied them full membership even though they had paid full dues. As the dean of the only collegiate school in the state whose immediate superior, President William H. Gray, was also black and supportive of her, Carnegie was able to fight the cause for black nurses. It was through her efforts that the president of the Florida State Association of Colored Graduate Nurses (FSACGN) was made a courtesy member by the board of directors of FSNA, but without voting privileges.

It was while serving as president of the FSACGN in 1948, and therefore as a courtesy member of the FSNA board of directors, that Carnegie was made a full member of the FSNA board. Later, through the fund-raising activities of the FSACGN and contributions from the FSNA, she was able to attend the fiftieth anniversary of the International Council of Nurses, which was held in Stockholm, Sweden, in 1949. Shortly after her return to Florida the decision was made in May 1950 to dissolve the FSACGN. In 1949 Carnegie sought and won election to the board of directors of the FSNA, becoming the first black nurse to hold this elected position in Florida. She was reelected in 1950 for a two-year term. Her election and reelection to the board of directors of the FSNA was an indication of the high regard in which she was held. The dissolution of the FSACGN meant that black nurses had to be accommodated at both district and state levels. Although this called for a major change in attitude by white nurses, integration of the FSNA was well on the way by 1952.

Even though the struggle for lowering the segregation barriers was taking place, Mary Carnegie never lost sight of her goal of continuing her own education. She obtained a master of arts in administration in higher education from Syracuse University in 1952. On her return to Florida she was again instrumental in getting an extension program for black graduate nurses started at Florida Agricultural and Mechanical College, Jacksonville, and in Miami.

Nursing Journalism Career Begins

The year 1953 marked the beginning of a new role and career—nursing journalism. The American Journal of Nursing Company in New York, which publishes the *American Journal of Nursing* (AJN) and other prestigious nursing journals and is owned by the American Nurses' Association, offered Mary Elizabeth Lancaster Carnegie a post as assistant editor of *AJN*, the official organ of the ANA. She remained in this position for three years before becoming associate editor and then senior editor of *Nursing Outlook*.

In 1972 Carnegie earned a doctorate in public administration from New York University. Thereafter she became editor of the premier journal, *Nursing Research*, and continued in that capacity from 1973 to 1978, when she retired. She remains editor emeritus for *Nursing Research*, and her interest in research, particularly historical research, is well-known.

Retirement has not diminished her interest in or commitment to the nursing profession. Carnegie has accepted numerous distinguished visiting professor appointments and occupied various endowed chairs at prestigious universities. During the 1989-1990 academic year she occupied the Loewenberg Chair of Excellence at Memphis State University, Memphis, Tennessee. Since the 1990-1991 academic year, Carnegie has served as distinguished visiting professor at Indiana University School of Nursing. While there, she continued work on the second edition of *The Path We Tread: Blacks in Nursing*.

Mary Elizabeth Lancaster Carnegie is the recipient of numerous awards and honors. In addition to her Rockefeller Foundation study fellowship, in 1951-1952 she received a study fellowship to complete her work at Syracuse University. Her legacy of awards includes the Mary Mahoney Award in 1980 from the American Nurses' Association and doctor of science in 1989 from State University of New York's Downstate Medical Center. She is a member of Pi Lambda Theta honor society on education (1952), Alpha Kappa Delta honor society in sociology (1965), honorary member of Chi Eta Phi national nursing sorority (1960), and was made honorary member of Sigma Theta Tau and the Association of Black Nursing Faculty in Higher Education. In 1975 she received the Mabel K. Staupers Award given by Chi Eta Phi, Omicron Chapter, for distinguished and remarkable service to New York City. In 1972 she received honors from New York University and a citation from Lincoln School for Nurses. She received the New York University Alumni Award in 1973.

In 1966 the Student Conference and Study Center at Mississippi Valley State College, Department of Nursing, was named the Mary Elizabeth Lancaster Carnegie Student Conference Study Center. The nursing archives at Hampton University were dedicated in 1977 and named the Elizabeth Lancaster Carnegie Archives. At present a fund is under way to establish the Mary Elizabeth Carnegie Endowed Chair at Howard University in Washington, D.C.

Mary Elizabeth Lancaster Carnegie has had wide consultative experience, including the Allstate Foundation Project on Recruitment of Minorities in Nursing in 1973 and a long list of colleges and schools of nursing. Since June 1943 she has lectured widely and participated in workshops and seminars. Many of her lectures are on the concerns of women in education, the state of nursing, women in the community, and women in the church. Her professional activities have taken her through the United States and to Ghana, Zimbabwe, Kenya, North, Central, and South America, Europe, and Asia. She is often the keynote speaker at professional gatherings and commencement programs.

Some of the professional and community activities in which Carnegie has been involved are the Advisory Committee of the New York City Correctional Institution for Women at Riker's Island, board of directors of the Nurses Educational Funds (for which she initiated the Carnegie Scholarship for black doctoral candidates and the Massey Scholarship for black master's degree candidates), and the Minority Doctoral Fellowship program. Carnegie is a member of the American Nurses' Association, National League for Nursing, a fellow in the American Academy of Nursing, and a member of numerous other professional nursing organizations. She is a member of the American Society for Public Administration, American Academy of Political and Social Science, American Writers Association, and the American Society of Magazine Editors.

Mary Elizabeth Lancaster Carnegie's publications are numerous. She is author or editor of many books, numerous periodicals, and articles. Some notable works she has written or edited are *Women in Education*, in *Education Synopisis* (New York: New York University Press, 1964); *Disadvantaged Students in R. N. Programs* (New York: National League for Nursing, 1974); and "The Minority Practitioner in Nursing," in *Current Issues in Nursing Education* (New York: National League for Nursing, 1974). Her periodical publications began in 1945, one of which is "How a Nursing Program was Developed in a Negro College," *American Journal of Nursing* (February 1945). Her contributions to the literature in the nursing profession are remarkable. While Distinguished Visiting Professor at the University of North Carolina at Greensboro, she wrote *The Path We Tread: Blacks in Nursing 1854-1984,* which Carnegie describes as her greatest contribution to nursing. While occupying the Vera C. Bender Endowed Chair at Adelphi University, Garden City, New York, Carnegie wrote her autobiography in *Making Choices; Taking Chances: Nursing Leaders Tell Their Stories*.

Mary Elizabeth Lancaster Carnegie is articulate, and she has a congenial personality. She likes to play her piano and sing, and does so spontaneously for social gatherings. She has created an impact on the nursing profession in general, and specifically in areas of research, publication, and in the struggle for equality of black nurses. Her impact is so tremendous that she has, in fact, already received honors generally bestowed upon the deceased, such as historical nursing archives, a nursing study room, and a forthcoming endowed chair named in her honor. Her belief is that nursing is leading the other professions in its commitment to equality for all its members. She is one of those remarkable women who have overcome tremendous obstacles through her courage, integrity, and intellectual ability. She has mentored many nurses, her career serves as a beacon, and she is an exceptional role model for black nurses and women.

References

Carnegie, M. E. *Contemporary Minority Leaders in Nursing*. Kansas City, Mo.: American Nurses' Association, 1983.

———. *Making Choices; Taking Chances*. Edited by T. Schorr and A. Zimmerman. St. Louis: C. V. Mosby, 1988.

———. *The Path We Tread: Blacks in Nursing, 1854-1984*. Philadelphia: Lippincott, 1986. Includes photographs of Mary Elizabeth Carnegie.

———. "The Path We Tread." *International Nursing Review* 9 (October 1962).

———. Curriculum Vitae. 1990.

———. Interview with Althea Davis, June 1990.

Davis, A., and Grayson. "Mary Elizabeth Carnegie: A Black Nursing Leader." Unpublished paper, 1984.

Dannett, Sylvia G. L. *Profiles of Negro Womanhood.* Vol. 2. Yonkers, N.Y.: Educational Heritage, 1966.

Staupers, Mabel K. *No Time for Prejudices.* New York: Macmillan, 1961.

Althea T. Davis

Diahann Carroll

(1935-)

Singer, actress

Diahann Carroll (Carol Diahann Johnson), celebrated singer and actress, was born July 17, 1935, in the Bronx, New York City. The daughter of John Johnson and Mabel (Faulk) Johnson, she has a sister, Lydia, thirteen years her junior. Diahann Carroll attended New York Public School Number 46 and Stritt Junior High School in Harlem before entering a phase of her formal education that was to have a major impact on her future. At the urging of a guidance counselor at Stritt, her mother enrolled her in the High School of Music and Art, where as noted in her autobiography *Diahann!*, she experienced "a whole new world, unlike anything I had ever seen or imagined possible" (27). The tough academic curriculum, in addition to the demanding requirements of voice and music theory classes, opened her eyes to ideas and possibilities she had not before considered.

Her formal training there, combined with insights gained in "show business school," the dressing rooms shared with nightclub chorus and show girls, were essential elements in her budding singing career, which grew steadily after she graduated from high school. Both her father, a subway conductor for the New York Department of Transportation, and her mother, a trained nurse who stayed at home to care for her family, insisted that her enrollment in college be the condition on which she would be allowed to continue to perform. She enrolled in New York University, but her parents' dream of her becoming a teacher or doctor soon faded as she became more and more involved in show business. Because Carroll yielded increasingly to the demanding schedule and lucrative rewards of nightclub engagements, her parents agreed to allow her to leave school at the end of the first year and take two years to establish her career in entertainment. If unsuccessful, she would return to school; her decision to leave was never to be revoked.

Diahann Carroll as Chanteuse

In the preface to her autobiography, written with Ross Firestone and published in 1986, she describes herself accordingly:

> I am forty-nine years old. I have been a singer, an actress, a daughter, a mother, a wife, a lover, a friend. I have had my ups, a lot of downs, and now I am at the highest point of my career, at the top of my life. . . . All I ever wanted to do was sing. What happened was more. (4)

Her success has been wide-ranging, not only in terms of the diverse fields of entertainment in which she has worked, including nightclubs, stage, screen, and television, but also with regard to her international fame, which has netted her numerous prestigious awards and continues to attract large audiences. Carroll's ability to adapt and succeed in a variety of media and roles results from a distinctive combination of talent, sophistication, and beauty. Of average height—approximately five feet six inches—and slim, her combination of looks, dress, and demeanor embodies a striking presence that has evoked such adjectives as regal, alluring, and elegant, and that has won her a place on the Ten International Best Dressed List.

It was at the age of fifteen that she was first seriously introduced to high fashion and stylish flair in her job as a model with *Ebony*. She once reported in *Jet* magazine that the modeling job with Johnson publications was where she "learned to wear clothes and slink around like a gorgeous model and stand right and walk. I think that may have been one of the things that attracted Richard Rodgers to call me when he wanted to write *No Strings*" (1985, 58). She used what she learned to her advantage as her career in singing as well as in acting developed. It was her singing, however, her first love, which propelled her into her immensely successful career.

Her first opportunity to sing in public was at the age of six, when she was a member of the Tiny Tots Choir in Adam Clayton Powell's Abyssinian Baptist Church. From that point on, her passion for performing flourished as she took piano and voice lessons, performed in school plays, and, prompted by her mother, became an avid theatergoer. Although it was her mother who introduced her to the performing arts and devotedly persisted in her music training, it was Carroll, very early grasping a sense of her own talent, who helped herself by seeking out contests and winning in a number of competitions. When she was ten years old, the scholarship she won after auditioning for an organization affiliated with the Metropolitan Opera granted her special piano and voice lessons. While in high school, the sixteen-year-old Carol Diahann Johnson auditioned as "Diahann Carroll" and won the opportunity to be a contestant on the popular television show, "Arthur Godfrey's Talent Scouts." Her singing won first prize, which entitled her to appear on Godfrey's radio program; he asked her to return for three weeks.

Her first major booking, for which she earned a considerable sum, came about early in her year at New York University. After winning a talent contest on the television show "Chance of A Lifetime" for three consecutive weeks, she received three thousand dollars and a one-week engagement at the lavish Latin Quarter. She acquired an agent, showman Lou Walters, and a personal manager, and from then on worked her way up to grand clubs and hotels, several of which she has returned to again and again over the years. Among the many well-known places in which she performed are the Persian Room (Plaza Hotel, New York), the Sands Hotel (Las Vegas), the Palmer House (Chicago), and the Ambassador (Los Angeles).

Diahann Carroll has also been featured in concerts in Philharmonic Hall at the Lincoln Center for the Performing Arts (1962) and at the Kennedy Center in Washington, D.C. (1971). She has starred in numerous television specials of her own as well as in specials with such headliners as Judy Garland, Danny Kaye, and Harry Belafonte. Many of the memorable tunes sung in those performances have been recorded on best-selling albums. Her talent as a vocalist also earned her a Grammy Award nomination.

Carroll Emerges As Stage and Screen Star

Diahann Carroll's commitment and dedication to her work is so strong that it has at times seemed to her to be a "'sickness' which I have which makes me want to perform as much and as often as possible" (Carroll, 134). She did just that—performed frequently and intensely on stage and in films in the nearly thirty years spanning 1954 and 1982. Her early success as a nightclub performer whetted her appetite for more extensive involvement in show business. A brief part in a movie, *Carmen Jones*, led her that same year to her stage debut on Broadway. At the age of nineteen she appeared in the role of Ottilie, the naive protégée of a West Indian bordello proprietress, at the Alvin Theater in *House of Flowers*, Harold Arlen's adaptation of a Truman Capote story. The short-running play, starring Pearl Bailey, won Carroll a nomination for a Tony Award as well as the attention of Richard Rodgers, who subsequently cast her in the starring role of her next Broadway play. Particularly memorable highlights of her performance were her renditions of the songs "A Sleepin' Bee" and "House of Flowers," which have been prominently featured among her album recordings. The casting director of *House of Flowers*, Monte Kay (Fremont Kaplan), married Diahann Carroll in September 1956. In 1960 their daughter, Suzanne Patricia Ottilie, was born.

Spurred on by her growing popularity as a singer, by attaining roles in three films between 1959 and 1961 (*Porgy and Bess*, *Paris Blues*, *Goodbye Again*), and by being selected for the *Cue* magazine Entertainer of the Year award (1961), she appeared once again on Broadway at the Fifty-fourth Street Theater and scored a major triumph in the musical comedy *No Strings*. She won the coveted Tony Award for best female performance in a musical. Playing the role of Barbara Woodruff, a role specially created for her by Richard Rodgers, Carroll was cast opposite Richard Kiley in a story about a black high-fashion model who falls in love with a white Pulitzer Prize-winning novelist. Her elation at her success in the play suddenly turned to disappointment when she learned that she would not be cast in the movie version. She nevertheless took the show on the road and then turned her attention to film.

After appearing in several movies, she returned to the stage in 1978 for a brief run opposite Cleavon Little in *Same Time Next Year* at the Huntington Hartford Theatre. Five years later, in 1983, she was on Broadway once again, this time as the first black actress to replace a white actress in a leading role. Producer Ken Weisman asked her to replace the vacationing Elisabeth Ashley in *Agnes of God*. Playing the demanding role of Dr. Livingston, a psychiatrist, was one of her most formidable tasks. Both drained and excited by the demands of the assignment, she felt that "the public reaction to my performance was so gratifying, and I was so happy performing this difficult and challenging role that when the week ended, I didn't want to give it up!" (Carroll, 235-236).

Diahann Carroll appeared in a steady succession of movies in the twenty years between 1954 and 1974. In her first film, *Carmen Jones* (Twentieth Century Fox), starring Dorothy Dandridge, she had a minor role as Myrt, Carmen's sidekick. Her next film was in 1959, in the part of Clara in *Porgy and Bess* (Columbia). She then made two films produced by United Artists in 1961: *Paris Blues*, starring Sidney Poitier, and *Goodbye Again*, in which she sang two songs by Dore Previn. The filming of *Paris Blues* coincided with one of the high points of her long, tormented relationship with Sidney Poitier, who was married. The relationship, which had precipitated the end of her already failing marriage with Monte Kay, had finally ended by the time she completed her next two films, *The Split* (1967, Paramount) and *Hurry Sundown* (1968, MGM). A brief engagement in 1972 to talk show host David Frost, whom she did not marry, was followed by her marriage in 1972 to Freddie Glusman, owner of several women's hotel shops. That marriage also ended in divorce three months later.

Despite disappointments in her personal life, Diahann Carroll was undaunted in pursuit of continued career success. She had already achieved highest accolades for a number of television appearances, most notably for her own weekly series "Julia." The opportunity for a major role in a film came in 1974, when she was called to play the lead in *Claudine* (Twentieth Century Fox) to replace the dying Diana Sands, who had been diagnosed with terminal cancer. It was a bittersweet triumph for Carroll, a long-time admirer and friend of Sands, with whom she had attended elementary school. In the role, a direct contrast to that of her very popular television character Julia, she portrayed a poor, single mother in Harlem struggling to raise her children. Reflecting on the experience of filming that movie, Diahann Carroll wrote:

> I couldn't see anyone else in the world playing her. I felt I could give life to her humanity. I felt I could make people care about her. And I knew it

> was an incredible opportunity to test my skill as an actress . . . I couldn't wait to put aside the couture gowns and to work without glamorous make-up. I looked forward to the challenge: I wanted to let my talent out, to expose it, to test it (200).

Although Carroll made no money on the low-budget film, she was more than well compensated by the chance to work with James Earl Jones and by her growth as an actress in the role, for which she won an Oscar nomination as best actress.

Television Appearances Begin

Perhaps the greatest number of her admiring fans have been attracted through television, a medium with she has been associated almost as long as with nightclub performances. In addition to performances in many television specials and appearances on talk shows with hosts such as Jack Paar and David Frost, featured roles in dramatic television movies and series have figured prominently in her career. She achieved an important first in 1968 as the first black woman to have her own weekly television series, "Julia." In the popular NBC series, Carroll starred as Julia Baker, a middle-class Vietnam War widow raising a five-year-old son. The enormously popular show, conceived by Hal Kanter as an attempt to forward the cause of mutual understanding and good will in the highly charged, racially tense atmosphere of the time, was, ironically, fraught with problems surrounding its impact on its black audience. Criticism and controversy focused on the authenticity of Julia's character (she was not supposed to be glamorous but had an opulent wardrobe and plush apartment), the lack of a strong black male role model, instances of blatant racism in the script, and inaccurate depictions of the black family. Carroll and her producers struggled to come to terms with the social implications of portraying a type, represented earlier in films such as *Paris Blues* and *Hurry Sundown*, which was quickly attacked from the point of view of social relevance. For some, Julia was "an exquisite bronze Barbie doll," a "Doris-Day-in-blackface," whose "speech, dress, mannerism, looks, and life style [represented] the great white ideal" (Bogle, 210-11). The pressures and demands of time, which kept her away from her daughter, and the constant requests to respond to the various critics made the starring role less and less appealing for Carroll, who asked to be released from her contract in 1970.

Because of her inspiration to other black actresses and actors, however, Carroll was lauded for her contribution by induction into the Black Filmmaker's Hall of Fame (1976) and selection for the NAACP Eighth Image Award for Best Actress. Among the numerous other dramatic television movies and series in which she appeared are "Naked City," for which she received two Emmy nominations, "Peter Gunn," "I Know Why the Caged Bird Sings," "Sister, Sister," "From the Dead of Night," and "Roots, the Next Generation." Shortly after the Oscar nomination for *Claudine*, Carroll was interviewed in 1975 by Robert DeLeon, then managing editor for *Jet* magazine. A three-month courtship between the editor, who was twenty-six, and Carroll, who was forty, was followed by marriage; that union was abruptly ended two years later by the tragic death of her husband in a car accident.

Diahann Carroll continued to pave the way for blacks in entertainment by attaining another first in 1984: the first black woman to star in a nighttime soap opera. She took the role of the notorious Dominique Devereaux on "Dynasty." In her role as the flamboyant, demanding, and villainous arch-competitor of Alexis Carrington (played by Joan Collins), Carroll succeeded in boosting the ratings of the show as well as her own popularity. She found the experience to be "entirely different" and "a dream come true," a tremendously rewarding culmination to a long and successful career (244).

Since the end of that series, she has continued to perform in hotels and nightclubs, not only in solo concerts, but at times with her fourth and current husband, Vic Damone, whom she married in 1987. The professional organizations to which she belongs include the Actors' Equity Association, the American Federation of Television and Radio Artists, and the Screen Actors' Guild. Her enduring success reflects a personal philosophy that she expressed two decades ago, when she stated:

> This is one of the most difficult careers you can choose, and you have to be prepared to give everything you have. When you have to sacrifice so much, the only satisfaction that makes it worthwhile is your own sense of dedication. The more you give, the stronger that sense becomes, and this is your best reward (Wormley and Fenderson, 139-140).

References

Bogle, Donald. *Toms, Coons, Mulattos, Mammies, and Bucks: An Interpretive History of Blacks in American Films*. New York: Viking, 1973.

Carroll, Diahann, and Ross Firestone. *Diahann! An Autobiography*. Boston: Little, Brown, 1986. Contains portraits of family and friends taken over several years and photographs of selected scenes from movies.

Current Biography Yearbook. New York: H. W. Wilson, 1962. Includes photograph.

"Diahann Carroll and Joan Collins Renew Their Feud in 'Dynasty' Roles." *Jet* (29 September 1986): 58-60.

"Diahann Carroll and Vic Damone Marry at Golden Nugget Casino." *Jet* (19 January 1987): 12-14.

"Diahann Carroll and Vic Damone: New Marriage and New Career on Stage." *Jet* (26 January 1987): 57-58.

"Diahann Carroll Talks about Her Life, Loves, and Career in a Revealing Interview." *Jet* (23 December 1985): 56-58.

The Ebony Success Library. Vol. I. *1,000 Successful Blacks*. Chicago: Johnson Pub. Co., 1973.

International Motion Picture Almanac. 61st ed. New York: Quigley Publishing Co., 1990.

Toppin, Edgar. *A Biographical History of Blacks in America Since 1528*. New York: David McKay, 1971.

Who's Who Among Black Americans. 6th ed. Detroit: Gale Research, 1990.

Who's Who of American Women. 16th ed. Chicago: Marquis, 1990.

Wormley, Stanton, and Lewis Fenderson, eds. *Many Shades of Black*. New York: William Morrow, 1969.

Carolyn R. Hodges

Betty Carter

(1929-)

Singer

Betty Carter is acknowledged by her peers as one of the greatest jazz singers of this age, a consummate musician, and an uncompromising critic with high artistic standards and ideals. She excels in presenting jazz in its purest form: the small acoustic ensemble where she is backed up by piano, drums, and bass, which has become standard for her. Although typical for small instrumental ensembles fronted by an instrumental soloist, this grouping is somewhat unusual for a jazz vocalist, especially as she presents a full concert in this format. Featuring bebop and modern jazz stylizations of new songs and standard repertoire, her performances emphasize melodic virtuosity, improvisation, individual freedom, and group cohesion in a very tight and well-balanced rhythmic context.

Twice previously a nominee, she won the coveted Grammy Award in 1989 for her outstanding album *Look What I Got!* (Polygram/Verve Records) and stands today in the front rank of jazz performing artists. Over the course of forty years as a professional jazz artist, she has maintained the highest of personal standards. In fact, she has a well-known reputation as something of a "prima donna" for requiring the strictest control of her concerts and demanding excellence at all levels affecting the musical integrity of her performance.

Betty Carter was born Lillie Mae Jones, in Flint, Michigan, on May 16, 1929. She has a sister, Vivian, and a brother, James, and two sons, Myles and Kagle, both college graduates. She came up through some hard times, including being on welfare during the depression. After her family moved to Detroit, there was work for both parents in defense plants. Her father also became director of the senior choir at Chapel Hill Baptist Church, and her schooling continued in Detroit area schools, including piano studies at the Detroit Conservatory of Music.

She became interested in jazz while at Northwestern High School in Detroit. At a local soda shop with a juke box, she and her friends used to listen to what was then "hot": bebop, the new jazz genre introduced by Charlie Parker and Dizzie Gillespie. She listened to most of the mainstays of jazz of her day, including Parker, Gillespie, Louis Armstrong, Billie Holiday, Duke Ellington, and others at various local clubs. Her first award came when she was sixteen. She won second prize at black amateur night at the Paradise Theatre, accompanying herself on piano and singing "The Man I Love," which remains one of her favorite songs.

While in high school, she was often called on to play the piano before assemblies and gained some experience as a result. Also, she frequently took on engagements with a local trio at small clubs in various nearby cities: Cincinnati, Dayton, Lima, and Toledo, using the stage name of Lorene Carter. She frequently sat in with visiting groups led by Parker, Gillespie, Miles Davis, and Max Roach, and her favorite band was Gillespie's. After singing with Lionel Hampton's band at a local dance, she was later hired as his vocalist. Hampton, in fact, gave her the nickname of "Betty Bebop" after she told him that Gillespie's band, not his, was her favorite. She subsequently adopted the "Betty," and Betty Carter became her stage name.

Her professional career had its beginnings at this time, when she was nineteen years old, with her performances at club dates and then the regular engagements with Lionel Hampton's band in 1948. As with many artists in this genre, her subsequent career took many turns. She performed club dates at numerous prominent jazz clubs throughout the country, including the Apollo Theatre, Apollo Bar, and Village Vanguard in New York, the Showboat in Philadelphia, and Blues Alley in Washington, D.C. She has performed live concerts at the Newport Jazz Festival, in major cities, and on many college campuses across America.

With the advent and increasing popularity of the rock and roll and rhythm and blues movements, record companies gave less production emphasis to jazz releases, preferring to make quick money with the rising stars of our country's youth who offered an easily-marketable diet of renditions in these genres. This situation has prevailed into the 1990s, and jazz purists have had to look elsewhere for support. In Carter's case, she opted to maintain personal control of her career, launching her own record company (Lil-Jay Productions and Bet-Car Records), seeking dates before college audiences and at small clubs, but always keeping true to her ideals of presenting fresh, vibrant interpretations of jazz in a chamber music format.

Writers who have described her art include three of the

country's most discerning music critics: John S. Wilson, Whitney Balliett, and John Dreyfuss. Together these three writers aptly summarize her art, showing several diverse facets of her style and presentation. Writing in *The New York Times* (2 August 1972 and 24 November 1978), Wilson takes a classic musician's stance, critiquing performance aspects. He said:

> Miss Carter's singing concept has mellowed. Many of the rougher, raspier edges have been honed down. . . . She has a rich, vibrant, and very flexible voice . . . [and] she moved from ballads delivered with a deliberateness and intensity that were sustained by rich colors and the seamless continuity of her voice to wildly inventive scat singing and vocalizing, from dazzling dashes that took her careening through tongue-twisting lyrics to the buoyant, rhythmic exuberance in which she brought all these factors together.

Writing in the *New Yorker* (20 September 1982), Balliett skillfully paints a verbal portrait of her vibrant stage presence, movement, and the visual aspects of her art:

> Her eyes close suddenly and her eyebrows shoot up. Her lips pout and her chin sinks stubbornly into her neck—naughty-child fashion. . . . She begins a song standing slightly stooped, with the microphone in her right hand, and her right leg slightly crooked. Her left arm is horizontal, and her left hand is just so—the thumb cocked, the index finger and the little finger out straight, and the middle fingers folded flat. . . . The bridge of the song begins, and she swings her head back and forth to emphasize the words, Her brow furrows, her eyes shut, then open, and she looks sharply over her left shoulder. She shifts the microphone to her left hand, puts her right hand on her right hip, and swings her head until it is directly over her right arm—Egyptian queen.

Dreyfuss, in *Rolling Stone* (7 October 1976) writes of her total devotion to bebop and jazz as an art form, of her demanding, uncompromising nature that often does not endear her to club managers and promoters, and of her constant striving for perfection and recognition, particularly by her peers and followers in the jazz field. Mark Jacobsen's *Village Voice* review (18 August 1975) of her performance in a stage show, "Don't Call Me Man," is credited with calling attention to her anew at a point where her career was struggling but, as always, she refused to commercialize or lower her standards. Of her stage performance, he wrote: "As an actress she proved to be as earthy as her singing is exotic. . . . It could have been the debut of a major musical personality, in Brooklyn and without significant publicity." He continued:

> Years back she realized she would rather play with a combo than stand in front of it. She's wary of the syndrome which makes millionaires of singers and leaves musicians in the pits. She decided it was, for the most part, musicians who are responsible for creation in jazz, and resolved to take her lumps with them rather than go to Vegas and wear chiffon.

Another reviewer, Linda Prince (*Down Beat*, 3 May 1979) waxes almost poetic: "Dark and smoky, Carter's voice becomes crystal clear as it careens to her upper register. Dramatic, unexpected forays to her lower register are as startling as the deep blasts of a foghorn on a summer day."

Typically, her group stresses youth, as do her audiences. She prefers to select young musicians for her trio. For example, her recent trio included pianist Darrell Grant, drummer Troy Davis, and bassist Tarus Martin, all in their twenties. She finds the energy level and fresh ideas of young players stimulating and revitalizing. Further, she seeks to make every performance new and unique in the purist tradition of jazz. Her audiences, by their makeup, respond positively to youth and the constant striving for fresh and novel statements. Nobody wants a second Sarah Vaughan, Lester Young, or Billie Holiday; a repeat is not a positive achievement in jazz by her ethics. And so, Carter continues to perform, create, improvise, and expand our horizons.

References

Balliett, Whitney. "Jazz; Betty Bebop." *New Yorker* 66 (20 September 1982): 110-117, 120, 122.

Carter, David. "Betty Carter: Blue Chip Performance." *Down Beat* 44 (21 April 1977): 44-45.

Crouch, Stanley. "Audience with Betty Carter." Record review. *Village Voice* (31 December 1980): 30.

Current Biography. New York: H. W. Wilson, 1982.

Dreyfuss, Joel. "Betty Carter." *Rolling Stone* (7 October 1976): 18.

Feather, Leonard. *Encyclopedia of Jazz in the 70's*. New York: Horizon Press, 1976.

———. *New Edition of the Encyclopedia of Jazz*. New York: Horizon Press, 1960.

Jacobson, Mark. "Don't Call Me Man." Review. *Village Voice* (18 August 1975): 100.

Jones, James T., IV. "Look What We've Got!." *Down Beat* 56 (August 1989): 24-26.

New York Times, 2 August 1972. 24 November 1978.

Nolan, Herb. "Betty Carter's Declaration of Independence." *Down Beat* 43 (12 August 1976): 23-24, 54.

Prince, Linda. "Bebopper Breathes Fire." *Down Beat* 46 (3 May 1979): 12-14, 43.

Southern, Eileen. *Biographical Dictionary of Afro-*

American and African Musicians. Westport, Conn.: Greenwood Press, 1982.

Darius L. Thieme

Eunice Hunton Carter

(1899-1970)

Lawyer, community leader

To be a success in one major area of work is usually the dream and highest goal of one's life; however, for Eunice Hunton Carter this was not enough. She achieved much more. She was born in Atlanta, the third child of William Alphaeus Hunton and Addie (Waites) Hunton. Of the four Hunton children, only she and a younger brother survived infancy. After the 1906 race riots, she moved with her family to Brooklyn, New York. As a national executive with the Young Men's Christian Association (YMCA), William Hunton was quite well-known and successful. After leaving his native Canada, he had pioneered in establishing YMCA services for blacks in Virginia, as well as other states. Addie (Waites) Hunton, a teacher, clubwoman, and an active participant in the work of the Young Women's Christian Association (YWCA), was the daughter of a middle-class family from Norfolk, Virginia. Under the auspices of the YWCA, she did field service in France during World War I. Growing up in this enlightened atmosphere of educational and personal commitment to public service provided the basic framework for Eunice Hunton Carter's successful careers.

Carter attended public schools in Brooklyn and in Strassburg in 1909-1910 while her mother studied at Kaiser Wilhelm University. In 1917, she enrolled at Smith College, graduating in 1921 with both an A.B. and an A.M. degree. Her master's thesis was on reform in state government, with special attention given to the state of Massachusetts. For the next eleven years, she worked with many family service agencies and also took courses at Columbia University.

In 1924, Eunice Hunton married Lisle Carter, a dentist who had been born in Barbados and who practiced in New York. Lisle Carter, Jr., their only child, was born the next year. By this time Eunice Hunton Carter's unusual talents in the social work field had already brought her recognition. However, Carter's devout Episcopalian beliefs and her commitment to the improvement of society were guiding her toward a more active public life. In 1927, she began taking evening law classes at Fordham University, where she received her LL.B in October 1932; she was admitted to the New York bar in 1934. She opened a private practice and also continued to be very active in civic organizations and Republican politics.

Following the Harlem riots in the spring of 1935, Mayor Fiorello La Guardia appointed Carter secretary of the Committee on Conditions in Harlem. In August 1935, she was named by special prosecutor Thomas E. Dewey as the only woman and the only black on his ten-member staff for an extraordinary grand jury investigation into rackets and organized crime. According to newspaper accounts, Dewey was focusing special emphasis on the Harlem policy rackets dominated by Dutch Schultz (Arthur Flegenheimer). Carter's knowledge of conditions in Harlem made her a valuable asset to this staff. She is credited with bringing forth the crucial evidence that sealed the case against Lucky Luciano. Later that same year, Dewey, who was now district attorney, named her deputy assistant district attorney for New York County. Greatly distinguishing herself as a trial prosecutor in this position, she served until 1945, when she returned to private practice.

A staunch Republican, Carter was prominent in New York Republican politics for many years. In 1934 she campaigned unsuccessfully to win a seat in the New York state assembly; however, she remained a close associate of both Thomas Dewey and Nelson Rockefeller.

Being a first in many areas seemed to be a part of Carter's destiny, and when her good friend, Mary McLeod Bethune, organized the National Council of Negro Women (NCNW), she became a charter member. She served as its legal advisor and was both a member and the chairman of the board of trustees. She and Bethune were representatives of the NCNW at the founding conference of the United Nations in San Francisco in 1945. Carter remained the accredited NCNW observer at the UN until 1952.

In 1947, she was made a consultant to the Economic and Social Council of the United Nations for the International Council of Women and served as chairman of its Committee of Laws. At the United Nations conference in Geneva, 1955, Carter was elected as chairman of the International Conference of Non-Governmental Organizations. Being a frequent traveler to Europe, she served as an advisor to women in public life for the German government in 1954.

With her parents being so active in both the YMCA and the YWCA, it was only natural that Carter followed their tradition. She served the YWCA as a member of its national board, a member of the Administrative Committee for the Foreign Division, and as cochair of its Committee on Development of Leadership in Other Countries. She was also very active in the Upper Manhattan YWCA, formerly the Harlem branch.

In 1952, Carter retired from an active law practice, but her interest in women's organizations and equal rights for women continued. After her retirement, she volunteered her services to many of the organizations with which she had been associated. In 1963, eleven years after her retirement, her husband died. Jean Hutson has characterized Carter as a "charming and strong-willed woman . . . a stimulating conversationalist who was at ease with people from all walks of life" (142).

On January 25, 1970, Eunice Hunton Carter died in Knickerbocker Hospital, New York City, after an illness of a few months. The many good things that Eunice Carter fought for and helped to bring about will long be remembered, for she spent her life working for the betterment of mankind.

References

Hutson, Jean Blackwell. "Eunice Hunton Carter." *Notable American Women: The Modern Period.* Cambridge: Harvard University Press, 1980.

New York Age, 5 November 1955.

New York Amsterdam News, 31 January 1970.

New York Herald-Tribune, 6 August 1935.

New York Times, 26 January 1980.

Collections

The Woodruff Library of the Atlanta University Center has a biography file, a file on women, and an NCNW file, each containing information on Eunice Hunton Carter. The National Archives for Black Women's History, National Council of Negro Women, in Washington, D.C., and the Schomburg Center for Research in Black Culture are other repositories of materials on Carter.

Phyllis Wood

Elizabeth Carter Brooks

(1867-1951)

Educator, clubwoman, civic activist

Elizabeth Carter Brooks, teacher, clubwoman, and civic activist, was born in New Bedford, Massachusetts. Her mother, Martha D. Webb, was born in slavery in Virginia and sent north to be educated. She lived in New Bedford seventy-six years until she died in 1939 at the age of ninety-two. Brooks was educated in the New Bedford public schools, Swain School of Design, Harrington Normal Training School, and she earned the LL.D. from Wilberforce University in Ohio. After graduating from the New Bedford High School, she taught at the Howard Colored Orphanage in Brooklyn, New York, for a few years in the 1880s. She was elected secretary of the Brooklyn Literary Union at its inception in 1883. She was a leader in the vanguard against social injustice. Upon returning to her hometown, she became the first black woman to graduate from the Harrington Normal School and the first of her race hired as a public school teacher in New Bedford. After a long career as a teacher, she retired in 1929 from the William H. Taylor School and a New Bedford public school was later named in her honor.

Interested in community services from an early age, Brooks's most outstanding achievement was the establishment of the New Bedford Home for the Aged. She envisioned founding a home for the elderly while still a student at the Harrington Normal School. She began planning for the institution, and in 1897 the New Bedford Home for the Aged opened. Beginning without funds, Brooks contributed the rent for the first six months from her personal funds, and the home prospered over the years under her guidance. The home, which accommodated both black and white elderly persons, was erected at 396 West Middle Street. A permanent structure for the home was built in 1907 and dedicated in 1908. Elizabeth Brooks was president of the New Bedford Home until 1930 and also president of the Woman's Loyal Union, the local women's club that sponsored the home for the aged. She received a gold pin in 1947 on the fiftieth anniversary of the home.

Elizabeth Carter Brooks was a leader in the organization of black women's clubs and inspirational in the movement to develop strong federations. She accepted the office of recording secretary for the National Federation of Afro-American Women in 1895. She was the first recording secretary of the National Association of Colored Women (NACW) in 1896 and vice-president-at-large of the association in 1906. Thus, Brooks was an experienced clubwoman by the time she assumed the presidency of the NACW in 1908. She was the fourth president of the national association, following Mary Church Terrell, Josephine Yates, and Lucy Thurman. Her vast knowledge of club work enabled her to make financial and other administrative improvements while in office. She traveled extensively, making personal contacts and inspecting the clubs, societies, and circles of the national association. Through her efforts, an annual scholarship was established for worthy students at Mary McLeod Bethune's Normal and Industrial School for Girls (later Bethune-Cookman College) at Daytona Beach, Florida, and the first national songbook for the National Association of Colored Women was published by its department of music. Brooks's influence was widespread on a local and national level. She declared, " . . . we raise our banners and hail the New Era of Expansion; we must organize more and more" (Minutes of the Seventh Biennial Convention, NACW, 23 July 1912).

Brooks Helps Organize Black Women's Federation

Brooks, Josephine St. Pierre Ruffin, and Mary H. Dickerson were among the eleven women who organized the Northeastern Federation of Women's Clubs in Ruffin's home on June 3, 1896. Incorporated as the New England Federation of Women's Clubs, the name was changed at its 1908 convention in Boston to the Northeastern Federation. As a result of Brooks's persistent dedication to club work, she was president of the federation for twenty-seven years. The clubs of the Northeastern Federation adopted the motto, "For God and Humanity." Over the years the federation supported community centers, day-care centers, scholarship funds, and other worthy causes. Leaders of the local black women's clubs in Massachusetts organized the Massachusetts State Union of Women's Clubs in April 1914. This union established and maintained the Harriet Tubman House in Boston. The official news organ of the Northeastern Federation of Women's Clubs, to which each state association contributed, was the *Northeastern Journal.*

Brooks was a charming woman with a warm personality. She was scholarly in appearance, with medium-length hair and brown complexion. She was described by friends as "a woman of good deeds" who spent her entire life helping others (New Bedford *Standard Times*, 20 June 1948). She reflected the NACW motto, "Lifting As We Climb." Dedicated to social and political improvement, Brooks was a motivating force in the NAACP, joining the association soon after its founding in 1909. She was a founder of the New Bedford Branch of the NAACP and served as president of the New England Regional Conference. She was honored in 1948 as president emeritus of both the New Bedford NAACP and the regional conference. Like other black women civic and club leaders, Brooks was patriotic. During World War I, she became involved with the War Work Council under Eva D. Bowles of the National Board of the YWCA. Taking a leave of absence from teaching, she went to Washington, D.C., to supervise the building of the Phillis Wheatley YWCA at Rhode Island Avenue and Ninth Street, N.W.

Elizabeth Carter Brooks was deeply involved in religious activities. Through her work she met William Sampson Brooks, bishop of the African Methodist Episcopal (AME) church, whom she married on May 12, 1930. The couple moved to San Antonio, Texas, where Brooks was presiding bishop of Texas. After his death in 1934, Elizabeth Carter Brooks returned to New Bedford and continued her work in the AME church. Religion was the foundation of her life. She was elected president of the New England Conference Branch Women's Mite Missionary Society. The New Bedford Bethel AME Church later dedicated two windows in her honor.

An outstanding woman, Elizabeth Brooks combined compassion and understanding with the ability to work effectively for social and civic improvement. She was a founder and dependable member of the executive committee of the Interchurch Council of Greater New Bedford. She made a special contribution to local history and black history when, in 1939, she purchased the home of Sergeant William H. Carney, a Civil War hero with the Fifty-fourth Colored Regiment of Massachusetts and the first black soldier awarded the Congressional Medal of Honor for his heroic efforts at Fort Wagner. Located at 128 Mill Street, the home was preserved as a memorial and later owned and maintained by the Martha Briggs Educational Club.

Elizabeth Carter Brooks, an honored and valued resident of New Bedford, resided at 211 Park Street for many years. In July 1951, at the age of eighty-four, she was stricken with a cerebral hemorrhage and taken to St. Luke's Hospital, where she died four hours later. Brooks is remembered for her impressive accomplishments in club work, social welfare work, and community affairs. She exerted leadership during the most productive periods of the NACW. She devoted her life to public service and activism based upon an intelligent, common-sense view of conditions during her lifetime.

References

Afro-American (Baltimore), 14 April 1926.

Dannett, Sylvia G. L. *Profiles of Negro Womanhood.* Vol. 1. Yonkers, N.Y.: Educational Heritage, 1964.

Davis, Elizabeth Lindsay. *Lifting As They Climb:* Washington, D.C.: National Association of Colored Women, 1933.

National Association of Colored Women. Minutes of the Seventh Biennial Convention. Hampton, Va.: NACW, 23 July 1912. Moorland-Spingarn Research Center, Howard University.

Standard Times (New Bedford) 20 June 1948; 13 July 1951.

Floris Barnett Cash

Alice Dugged Cary "Mother Cary"

(?-1941)

Educator, social worker, clubwoman

Alice Dugged Cary was an educator, social worker, and pioneer clubwoman whose influence and care touched the lives of students, peers, soldiers, urchins, delinquent girls, fellow clubwomen and community workers, and the black population of Atlanta. Cary was born in New London, Indiana, and died in Atlanta, Georgia, September 25, 1941, of a severe heart attack. Her father was John Richard Dugged and her mother Josie A. (Gilliam) Dugged. Alice Dugged was one of three children.

She married the Reverend Jefferson Alexander Cary on June 15, 1888, in Atlanta, Georgia. Cary was a trustee of Wilberforce University and an African Methodist Episcopal (AME) church minister and was the father, by a previous marriage, of Archibald J. Carey (1868-1920), a bishop of the

African Methodist Episcopal Church elected in 1920 (the "e" is used when referring to the bishop and his issue). Reverend Jefferson Cary had a parish in Athens, Georgia, where a son was born and died in infancy. The young couple had met at Wilberforce University in Ohio where Dugged was attending college.

Alice Dugged had been educated in the public schools of Marshall, Michigan, and at Wilberforce University, graduating in 1881 with an M.Pd. degree. She studied at summer school at the University of Chicago and Harvard University and the Detroit School of Expression. She received an honorary A.M. degree from Morris Brown College. She studied art under the distinguished artist Henry Osawa Tanner at Clark College in Atlanta.

While enrolled as an undergraduate, she served as teacher of foreign languages at Wilberforce University. After graduation she taught in the public schools of Kansas City, Kansas, for one year. She was first assistant principal of New Lincoln High School in Kansas City, Missouri, for four years. In Atlanta, Alice Dugged Cary taught in the public schools for seven years as the first female principal of West Mitchell Street School. She was also an instructor in the summer schools of Georgia for eighteen summers under State School Commissioners. For seven summers she was the director of summer playgrounds in Atlanta.

Cary Pioneers in Education

It was in Atlanta that Cary carved for herself an indelible niche as a pioneer in the education of black American youth and in fostering activities to promote good community relations. In 1886 she was elected the second principal of Morris Brown College and was the first woman to hold this position. She was known as a strong principal. This was the beginning of her lifelong association with the college; she served as principal of the normal department for three years, chair of the education department for four years, and when the school became a college she chaired the English department until 1921. George A. Sewell notes that "Mrs. Carey was the first woman to be principal of Morris Brown's Normal Department and assumed in addition many academic and extra classroom duties." The faculty during Cary's administration consisted of one coworker, Annie B. Thomas. She was a strict disciplinarian and was highly respected.

Cary secured playgrounds for children in Atlanta and directed them for seven summers. She was probation officer in the city for several years and accomplished much along civic lines for the benefit of the youth. As a probation officer, visiting courts and obtaining custody of boys and girls, she secured many pardons for offenders. She was instrumental in having a modern industrial school built in Fulton County for juvenile offenders.

Perhaps her earliest impact in the field of education was, as noted earlier, in her position as first principal of West Mitchell Street School. Almost simultaneously (1881) she began a lifetime affiliation with Morris Brown College. It is doubtful that the tremendous influence of her personality in the formative years of the college will ever be fully realized. Although she served only one year as principal, she remained on the faculty and helped to influence the lives of many generations of students. Cary's special training in foreign languages made her a versatile teacher. Annie B. Thomas, in her history of Morris Brown, states that Cary served as registrar during the presidency of E. W. Lee.

During World War I, Cary was head of the Red Cross and captain of Canteen Atlanta. Her visits to Fort McPherson in Atlanta, where she read to the soldiers, told stories, and carried students from Morris Brown College to provide musical programs, made her a dynamic factor in the soldier's lives. After the Armistice was signed, she continued to cheer the injured who had returned from overseas. In 1918 she was a traveling advisor for the U. S. Labor Department.

Club Activities Strengthened for Women

Despite the weight of her duties as a Morris Brown faculty member, Cary always found time to engage in community activities. She was active in the area of club work among black American women. After organizing Atlanta clubs, she sought to organize the state and served as president of the Georgia Federation of Women's Clubs. She was statistician of the National Federation of Colored Women's Clubs for four years and auditor for two years. At her own expense she traveled widely to keep abreast of the activities of the national club movement. Cary served on the YWCA Board of Atlanta for six years. Active in the African Methodist Episcopal church, for two years she was president of its Women's Home and Foreign Mission Society for North Georgia and participated in the church's annual conferences for fourteen years. She presided over the State Temperance Union for two years, was an active member of the Zeta Phi Beta Sorority, and served as the national president of the sorority. In 1925-1926, she also was president of the Epsilon Zeta Chapter of Zeta Phi Beta in Atlanta, of which she was a charter member.

Alice Cary served as the first librarian of the Auburn Avenue Branch of the Atlanta Public Library, which provided blacks with an access previously denied them. This was the first branch for black patrons in Atlanta and offered excellent and innovative services to the black population. She was chosen in 1921 and served for a number of years, spending some of her time at the system's Central Branch.

Each Christmas she cheered the needy street urchins and newsboys by decorating a tree at various sites in the city. She was known as "Mother Cary" and bore the distinction of being the guiding light in lives of college women all over the world.

Cary had an abiding interest in the care of delinquent black girls and was to see her dream to attend to their needs realized. From the *Wagon Wheel*, a campus publication from Morris Brown, comes this tribute:

> There are many achievements which distinguished this noble tutor from others of her rank. . . .

> Through her zeal and intelligence, through her years of sacrificial toil as head of the Women's Federation of Clubs and her interest in humanity at large, her dream has been fulfilled—a home for delinquent girls, which recently was dedicated on a beautiful site near Macon, Georgia. . . . Through her influence many have received a higher education and now stand as a tribute to her guidance.

Alice Dugged Cary was awarded the letter "B" at a formal program held during the 1939 football season at Morris Brown, which occasion also distinguished her as the only woman to win such an honor. After a long and fruitful career, Cary died on September 25, 1941, in Gaines Hall on the campus she had loved so well. Many of the bishops of the African Methodist Episcopal Church were her friends, as were presidents of Morris Brown College. She was well-known in the women's club circuit and was friendly with Mary McLeod Bethune, Charlotte Hawkins Brown, and Mary Church Terrell. At the time of her death, obituary notices stated that she had written a history of Morris Brown College, and the manuscript was ready for publication.

References

Atlanta Daily World, 26 September 1941.

Sewell, George A., and Cornelius V. Troupe. *Morris Brown College, the First Hundred Years, 1881-1981*. c. 1982.

Who's Who in Colored America. New York: Who's Who Corp., 1927-1940.

Casper LeRoy Jordan

Melnea Cass
"First Lady of Roxbury"
(1896-1978)
Community leader, civil rights activist

The life of Melnea Jones Cass was a whirlwind of work for and service to others. Her achievements, struggles, and awards—when summarized—are astonishing in their scope and seem endless. Her profound affect on the lives she touched is incalculable. Cass, simply and without fanfare, best described herself and her work: "Life is no brief candle for me! It is a sort of splendid torch which I got hold of for a moment, and I want to make it burn as brightly as possible . . ."

Melnea Agnes Jones Cass was born in Richmond, Virginia, on June 16, 1896, the eldest of three daughters of Mary (Drew) Jones and Albert Jones, who both grew up in Richmond and had perhaps a fourth- or fifth-grade education. Her father was a janitor and her mother a domestic worker. As her father wished to improve the family's economic and educational opportunities, he moved them to Boston, Massachusetts, to the South End, when Cass was five years old. Ella Drew, an older sister of her mother, was already in Boston and had encouraged them to make the move. In Boston both parents continued the type of work they had been doing in Richmond. Cass was eight years old when her mother died; thereafter, she and her sisters were raised by their father and their Aunt Ella, who, as Cass said, "stepped in like a second mother" (*Black Women AOral History Project Interview*, 7). After a few years their aunt moved the girls to Newburyport, Massachusetts, and placed them in the care of Amy Smith.

Melnea Jones Cass began her education in the public schools of Boston. After graduating from grammar school in Newburyport, she attended Girls' High School in Boston for one year. Her Aunt Ella heard about St. Francis de Sales Convent School, a Catholic school for black and Indian girls in Rock Castle, Virginia, and decided to enroll Melnea in the school. The students had courses in household management in addition to their academic curriculum. Cass graduated in 1914 as valedictorian of her class. She returned to Boston to the home that her Aunt Ella had established for the girls.

Cass looked for work as a salesgirl in Boston, but found that there were no opportunities for blacks. Since she did not want to work as a maid in a beauty parlor or in a restaurant, she finally decided that, with her training, she would become a domestic worker. She did this type of work until her marriage in December 1917.

Melnea Jones's financé, Marshall Cass, was going to war and married her before he left. She moved in with her mother-in-law, Rosa Brown, and took care of the cooking and the house. While her husband was in the service, the first child, Marshall, was born. After his return the family moved into their own home. They later became the parents of two daughters, Marianne and Melanie. Although it was not necessary financially except during the depression, and even though her husband did not wish her to work, Melnea Cass occasionally went out as a domestic worker. Her husband died in 1958.

Cass Becomes a Suffragist

It was through her mother-in-law, who was widely known for her civic work in Boston, that Melnea Cass became involved in community and church activities. Rosa Brown was the one who persuaded her of the importance of voting. After the Nineteenth Amendment to the Constitution was passed in 1920, Cass organized black women in her community to cast their first vote. She was involved in women's suffrage activities for the rest of her life.

As a young woman, she attended William Monroe Trotter's lectures and protest meetings and was a faithful reader of *The Guardian*, which he had established in 1901. Soon after her marriage she joined the National Association for the Advancement of Colored People (NAACP). She attended meetings whenever she could, and became more active as her children grew.

It was in the 1920s that Melnea Cass began a lifetime of volunteer work on the local, state, and national level. She first contributed her services to the Robert Gould Shaw House, a settlement house and community center. She was the founder of the Kindergarten Mothers. They later helped establish a nursery school at Shaw House and changed the name of their club to the Friendship Club. The membership consisted of mothers who lived in the community; they raised money for Shaw House, gave parties for the children, and helped wherever they were needed. She served as president twice and as secretary, and chaired several committees. She selected the club motto: "If we cannot do great things, we can do small things in a great way."

Her community activities over the years were numerous and varied and can be only briefly described. She joined the Pansy Embroidery Club in 1917 and was also a member of the Harriet Tubman Mothers' Club and the Sojourner Truth Club, all clubs in the Massachusetts State Union of Women's Clubs. Through the years, she was president of all three clubs and held other offices. She worked in the Northeastern Region of the National Association of Colored Women's Clubs (NACW) as secretary, chairman of the board, vice-president, and president, and in the 1960s was vice-president of the national organization. In the 1920s she helped in forming the Boston local of the Brotherhood of Sleeping Car Porters. For twenty years she was vice-president of the Harriet Tubman House. She was a member of the Women's Service Club and was for seventeen years its president. This club set up a dormitory for young black women, mainly from the South, and organized training programs to help them get work. Melnea Cass felt that one of her most important achievements was in getting legislation passed in the state of Massachusetts to improve compensation and benefits for domestic workers. During World War II she was one of the organizers of Women in Community Service, which later became Boston's sponsor of the Job Corps.

In 1949 she was a founder and charter member of Freedom House, which was conceived by two local residents and social workers, Muriel and Otto Snowden. It remains a private advocacy and social service agency set up for the improvement of the black community. In the 1950s Mayor John Collins appointed her the only female charter member and community member of Action for Boston Community Development (ABCD), an agency to help people who were losing housing because of urban renewal. It later became a permanent advocacy agency working on behalf of the poor. For ten years she was a member of the Board of Overseers of Public Welfare for the city of Boston, to advise the mayor and to help the Welfare Department administer its services and money.

Cass Promotes Rights of Blacks and the Elderly

Melnea Cass held a life membership in the NAACP and served in many capacities in the Boston branch, from committee member to board member. She was president of the Boston branch of the NAACP from 1962 to 1964. It was during her term that the NAACP organized demonstrations against the Boston School Committee and held sit-ins at their offices to support desegregation and improved educational opportunities in the schools. In 1933 she participated in demonstrations led by William Monroe Trotter to get Boston department stores to hire blacks, and in 1934 she demonstrated to get Boston City Hospital to hire black doctors and nurses. She was a lifetime member of the Boston Equal Rights League, founded by William Monroe Trotter. In 1901 he started a wreath-laying ceremony which, annually on March 5, honors Crispus Attucks, a former slave, who was among the first men to be killed in the Boston Massacre in 1770. After Trotter's death in 1934, Melnea Cass continued the tradition. And it is because of her efforts that Boston annually celebrates the birthday of Frederick Douglass.

Cass's concern for the elderly was recognized by both the state of Massachusetts and the city of Boston. Governor Francis Sargent appointed her chairperson of the state Advisory Committee for the Elderly, where she served in 1975 and 1976, and in 1975 Mayor Kevin White appointed her chairperson of the Mayor's Advisory Committee for Affairs of the Elderly. She was also a member of the Mayor's Citizens' Advisory Committee on Minority Housing. She was president of the Roxbury Council of Elders; one of its special concerns was preparing and serving meals for the elderly. In 1973 she was appointed by Elliott Richardson, then United States secretary of Health, Education and Welfare, to represent the consumer's Medicare interests on the National Health Insurance Benefits Advisory Council.

Melnea Cass was one of the founders of Chapter Seven of United War Mothers in Roxbury, Massachusetts. She was also the first black woman elected state president of a national patriotic organization—United War Mothers of America. Other similar activities included membership in Chapter Twelve, Gold Star and War Parents of America, where she was elected the first woman president. For more than twenty-nine years she was treasurer of the William E. Carter Auxiliary Sixteen of the American Legion.

For many years she was a member of the Boston YWCA, also on their board and involved in committee work. She left the organization in 1951 because of its discriminatory practices. Both the national and the local YWCA made many changes through the years. She returned in 1976, honored by their Women '76 program, when the main branch of the Boston YWCA was renamed the Melnea A. Cass Clarendon Street Branch of the YWCA.

For most of her adult life, Cass attended St. Mark

Congregational Church. She was a charter member of the Mothers' Club, chairman of the Social Action Committee, and belonged to the Pastor's Aid Club and the Missionary Guild for more than thirty years. She was on the Race and Religion Committee of the United Church Women and occasionally lectured on their behalf.

Melnea Cass's battles for civil rights and equal opportunities were difficult and uphill; it was only in the last fifteen years of her life that she received numerous honors and awards. Mayor John Collins of Boston proclaimed "Melnea Cass Day" on May 22, 1966, with a community salute to the "First Lady of Roxbury" attended by overmore than two thousand people; on May 26, 1968, the city of Newton also proclaimed "Melnea Cass Day." She was often called "Roxbury's First Lady." On June 19, 1968, the Melnea A. Cass Metropolitan District Commission (MDC) Swimming Pool and Skating Rink complex was dedicated by Governor John Volpe. In 1973 the Boston Juvenile Court conferred an award for her distinguished service on behalf of young boys and girls on probation. In 1974 she was named Massachusetts Mother of the Year; Harvard University also recognized this honor by sending her a Harvard chair and the NAACP gave her a special tribute. On May 18, 1977, she was honored as one of seven "Grand Bostonians." Melnea A. Cass Boulevard opened in Boston in 1981, and in 1989 a mixed-income apartment development was dedicated and named Cass House.

She received awards for her community service from many organizations, including Action for Boston Community Development, Freedom House, Massachusetts State Federation of Women's Clubs, the NAACP, National Association of Colored Women's Clubs, Eastern Chapter of the National Association of Social Workers, National Conference of Christians and Jews, Negro Business and Professional Women, Northeastern Federation of Women's Clubs, and Zeta Phi Beta Sorority. She was recipient of honorary degrees in the humanities from Boston College (1976), Northeastern University (1969), and Simmons College (1971).

Melnea Cass's friends and acquaintances were wide-ranging, representing all walks of life. Among them were Boston mayors John Collins and Kevin H. White (whom she often reprimanded); Massachusetts governors Michael S. Dukakis, Endicott Peabody, Francis Sargent, and John Volpe; senators Edward M. Kennedy and Edward W. Brooke (whom she described as being "just like one of her children") (*Sunday Herald Advertisement*, 20 June 1976, Magazine, 18); House Speaker Thomas P. O'Neill, Jr.; State Representative Royal Bolling; Judge Arthur Garrity, who was assigned by the United States Supreme Court to oversee Boston's school desegregation; Humberto Cardinal Medeiros of the Archdiocese of Boston; singer Roland Hayes; Melvin Miller, publisher of the *Bay State Banner*, for which she wrote a weekly column; A. Philip Randolph; Muriel and Otto Snowden; and William Monroe Trotter. Community leaders sought her counsel, but she never forgot her neighbors. Many can testify to the help given them by Melnea Cass. In 1975 she wrote her credo:

> I am convinced that my life belongs to the whole community, and as long as I live, it is my privilege to do for it whatever I can, for the harder I work the more I live. I rejoice in life for its own sake! Life is no brief candle for me! It is a sort of splendid torch which I got hold of for a moment, and I want to make it burn as brightly as possible before turning it over to the future generation (Funeral Service Program, 19 December 1978).

Melnea Cass died on December 16, 1978, after a long illness. St. Mark Congregational Church, her home church, was filled for her funeral; an overflow crowd watched via telecast in the church basement and at a nearby church. Among the speakers at the funeral were Senator Edward Brooke, Governor Michael Dukakis, and Mayor Kevin White. She was known for her selflessness, goodwill, common sense, humility, and enthusiasm.

In his eulogy, the Reverend Michael E. Haynes, pastor of the Twelfth Baptist Church, said:

> In an age when divorce, separation and child abandonment seem to doom the basic and fundamental unit of an effective society—the home—Melnea Cass implemented the Biblical formula for a Godly and rich family life and a stable society. . . . The Holy Word asked, "Who can find a virtuous woman?" We have found her—in a modestly furnished third-floor walk-up tenement flat on Harold Street in Roxbury, Massachusetts, where a beautiful, radiant, strong, courageous, generous, God-loving Christian black woman named Melnea A. Cass held court around a quaint, old-fashioned dining room table (*Bay State Banner*, 21 December 1978).

References

Bay State Banner, 21 December 1978; 28 December 1978; 1 March 1979.

Black Women Oral History Project Interview with Melnea A. Cass. Cambridge: Schlesinger Library, Radcliffe College, 1982.

Boston Globe, 18 April 1974; 24 April 1974; 20 December 1978; 19 February 1989.

Community Salute Booklet. Boston, Mass., May 22, 1966.

Equal Times 3 (January 9-22 1979): 5.

St. Mark Congregational Church, Roxbury, Mass. Funeral Service Program for Melnea Jones Cass. December 18, 1978.

Sojourner 8 (February 1983): 6.

Sunday Herald Advertiser (Boston) 20 June 1976.

Collections

Tapes and transcripts of an interview for the Black Women Oral History Project, as well as photographs and newsclippings, are available at the Schlesinger Library, Radcliffe College.

Ruth Edmonds Hill

Elizabeth Catlett

(1915-)

Sculptor, painter, printmaker

Celebrated internationally for her figurative sculpture and prints, Elizabeth Catlett is one of the premier black American artists of the twentieth century. Catlett is also known, however, as a cultural nationalist and civil rights activist. Her left of center political beliefs have led her to become an expatriate, living in Mexico as a citizen of that country since 1962.

The grandchild of slaves, Elizabeth Catlett was born in Washington, D.C., on April 15, 1915, and grew up in a middle-class home built by her father's family. Catlett's father, a mathematics professor at Tuskegee Institute, died before she was born. Encouraged by her mother and a high school teacher impressed with Catlett's skills in drawing and carving, she decided to go to school in Pittsburgh where a cousin was living. She wanted to go to the Carnegie Institute of Technology but knew that blacks had never been admitted to the art school. Although well aware of discriminatory practices in Washington, D.C., and the South, Catlett believed that things would be different in the North, especially when the school saw how well she did on the entrance examination. It was a gravely disappointing experience when she was turned down.

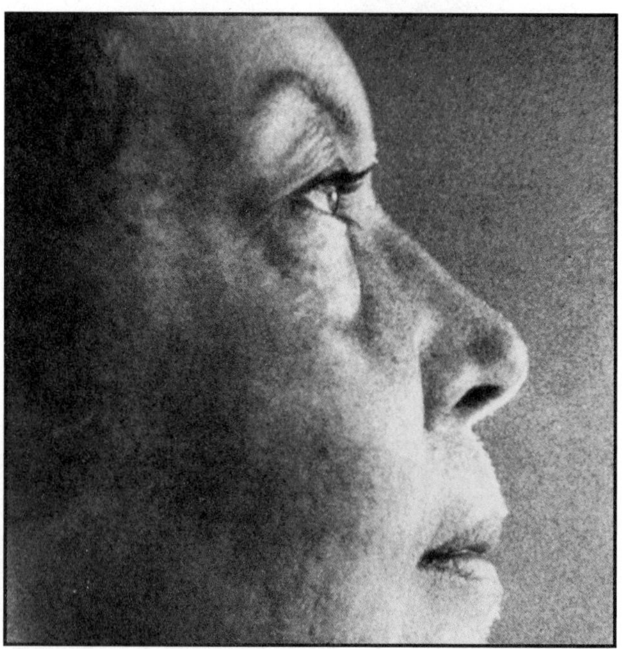

Elizabeth Catlett

Instead, Catlett entered Howard University in 1933. She chose the university because it was the first black college to establish an art department. There she began to major in design under the tutelage of Lois Mailou Jones. She also studied printmaking with graphic artist James Lesene Wells and drawing with artist and art historian James A. Porter. Porter, as author of one of the first books on black American art, knew well the obstacles Catlett would face in her artistic career. He urged her to gain professional experience by working for the government-sponsored Works Progress Administration (WPA)/Public Works of Art Project (called the Federal Art Project in 1934). Catlett maintained a position in the mural division for two months at the rate of $23.50 a week. There she became aware of the Mexican muralists Diego Rivera and Miguel Covarrubias, whose political beliefs about the purpose of art would significantly influence her later work. Catlett's experience on the federal relief program profoundly affected both her art and her life. She declared her new major to be painting and gradually began her lifelong commitment to social change for the betterment of those less fortunate than herself.

When Catlett graduated cum laude with her B.S. in art in 1936, the United States was still recovering from the Great Depression. Few jobs in the arts were available, but she secured a position teaching high school in Durham, North Carolina, at fifty-nine dollars a month. Frustrated with a year of earning a wage less than that of white instructors, Catlett joined the North Carolina Teachers Association in an effort to equalize salaries for black faculty members. She was joined in this campaign by an NAACP attorney, Thurgood Marshall. Realizing the grim situation of the segregated South, Catlett returned to Washington, D.C., to earn money for graduate school.

Catlett chose to study at the University of Iowa partially because it was one of the few state institutions that did not charge out-of-state student tuition. However, the school also did not permit black Americans to live in the dormitory, so she commuted from the black ghetto in Iowa City. Catlett worked diligently at her education and first exhibited her work at the university in 1939. For her efforts, she was the first student ever to earn an M.F.A. in sculpture at the University of Iowa (1940). Although economics played a role in Catlett's choice of a graduate program, she was also drawn to the university because of the teacher Grant Wood, an American Realist painter. Wood advised Catlett to depict her race and influenced her later decision to work primarily in sculpture. A limestone sculpture of a black American mother and child was Catlett's M.F.A. thesis and won her first prize in sculpture from the American Negro exposition in Chicago in the summer of 1940. The latter exhibition was assembled by Alonzo Aden with aid from the Harmon Foundation and the WPA. Among the notable artists represented in the show were Catlett's future husband, Charles White, as well as Robert Blackburn, Selma Burke, Eldzier Cortor, William Jennings, Lois Mailou Jones, Jacob Lawrence, and Hughie-Lee Smith.

After graduation Catlett taught at Prairie View College in Texas during the summer of 1940. That same year she won first prize in sculpture in the Golden Jubilee National Exposition in Chicago. She then worked as head of the art department at Dillard University in New Orleans for two years. There Catlett continued to campaign for higher wages for the faculty. Though not successful, she did win two other victories. Nude models were permitted in her life classes, and she persuaded a local museum to admit black students for the first time ever to see an exhibition of Picasso's works.

During the summer of 1941 Catlett took a ceramics class at the Art Institute of Chicago and while in Illinois met and married artist Charles White. In 1942 the couple moved to Hampton, Virginia, where Catlett taught at Hampton Institute and White executed a mural commission. The same year Catlett's work was exhibited at Atlanta University; she would be represented there again the next year and would win prizes later. The pair then moved to Harlem, New York.

Like many other artists, Catlett and White thrived on the rich cultural atmosphere that had developed during the Harlem Renaissance in the 1920s. In the following decades the city continued to be a magnet for black Americans in the humanities; they met artists Charles Alston, Ernest Crichlow, Jacob and Gwendolyn Lawrence, and Norman Lewis; poet Langston Hughes; performers Jon White and Leadbelly; and actor/activist Paul Robeson.

Catlett supported herself in New York by teaching at a community institution for adult education, the George Washington Carver School. With her salary she continued her studies in several media, working privately with the French sculptor, Ossip Zadkine, in Greenwich Village and learning lithography at the Art Students League. She also continued to show her work around the country, at the Institute of Contemporary Art in Boston in 1943; the Baltimore Museum of Art, the University of Chicago, the Renaissance Society, and the Newark Museum in New Jersey, all in 1944; and at the Albany Institute of History and Art in 1945.

Works Honoring Black Women Produced

In recognition of Catlett's achievements, including winning second prize in sculpture at the Atlanta University Annual in 1946, the Julius Rosenwald Foundation awarded Catlett a fellowship to do a series of works honoring black women. At that time the Whites were having marital problems but accepted an invitation to work in Mexico City. At the Taller de Grafica Popular (TGP), they worked together with other artists on a volume of prints portraying life throughout the Mexican republic. The TGP was a graphic arts and mural workshop where artists collaboratively created art to aid socio-political change. It was founded in 1937 by Leopoldo Mendez, Luis Arenal, and Pabio Higgins. Catlett recalls what the institution meant to her:

> The search for learning took me to Mexico, to the Taller de Grafica Popular, where we worked collectively, where we had strong artists and weak artists, and each one learned from the other. Everybody offered something—and when you saw the product, even if you were weak, you saw a collective product that you had helped form. It makes a difference in your desire to work and your understanding of what you're doing. At the same time we did individual work. I would say it was a great social experience, because I learned how you use your art for the service of people, struggling people, to whom only realism is meaningful (Lewis, *Art: African American,* 126).

It was at the TGP with the sponsorship of the Rosenwald grant that Catlett produced a significant portfolio of linocuts depicting black laborers, artists, and farmers. "The Negro Woman" earned Catlett her first solo show; the exhibition was held at the Barnett-Aden Gallery in Washington, D.C., 1947-48.

Although the sojourn in Mexico proved artistically beneficial for both Catlett and White, their relationship floundered and upon their return to New York City, they separated. Catlett then went back to work at the TGP and continued her studies with Francisco Zuniga. She also developed her wood carving at *la Esmerelda, La Escuela de Pintura y Escultura* in Mexico in 1948.

Among the members who joined the TGP in the 1940s was Francisco Mora, Catlett's second husband. Born in Uruapan, Michoacan, Mexico, in 1922 to an urban working-class family, Mora sympathized with the lower class, especially miners who were exposed to dangerous working conditions and poor wages. In oil painting, lithographs, and murals Mora depicted the life of the Mexican people and made a firm commitment to the practice of social art.

In 1947 when Catlett and Mora married, both of their countries were in political and social turmoil. In the United States leftist-oriented people in the arts continually battled the House of Representatives Un-American Activities (HUAAC) Committee and Senator Joseph McCarthy. Despite the oppressive atmosphere during the following decade, the couple persevered in creating work with political content. Catlett won second prize again at the Atlanta University Annual in 1956 and received a diploma in printmaking from the First National Painting and Printmaking Exhibition in Mexico City in 1959. Mora executed three murals commissioned between 1950 and 1958: "Freedom of the Press" at the *El Sol de Toluca* newspaper office, "Folklore Map of Mexico" at the Hotel de Prado, and "Education for the

People'' at a primary school in Santa Maria Tarasquillo, Mexico. Because their art and their association with the TGP were deemed radical, Catlett and Mora were suspected of being Communists. The charge became explicit in 1959. Accused of belonging to the Communist party, Catlett was arrested as an undesirable alien. Three years later she left the United States to become a Mexican citizen. Like Barbara Chase-Riboud, another black American sculptor who has made her permanent home abroad (in Paris, France), Catlett insists that her decision was not a condemnation of the United States, but instead a dedication to her adopted country where she could live as a responsible, active member of society: ''I changed my citizenship because I have been living in Mexico since 1946, and I'm a political person. . . . I couldn't do anything political in Mexico unless I was a citizen'' (Oliver, 88). Not pleased with her political statements, the United States government banned Catlett from traveling in the United States for nine years.

Nonetheless, Catlett thrived in her new environment. She had been hired in 1959 as the first woman professor of sculpture at the National School of Fine Arts in San Carlos, Mexico. Catlett served there as chair of the department and taught classes until her retirement in 1973. During the first year of her Mexican citizenship (1962), she not only had a solo exhibition of sculpture and prints at the place of her employment but also won the Tlatilco Prize in the First Sculpture Biannual in Mexico. Catlett won a major prize each ensuing year in the 1960s. In 1963 she received an honorable mention from the Second Latin American Print Exhibition in Havanna, Cuba. She next was recognized with the Xipe Totec Prize in the Second Sculpture Biannual in 1964. Then in 1965 she won first prize in sculpture from the Atlanta University Annual.

Impressed with her prestigious commendations, the National Polytechnic Institute in Mexico commissioned Catlett to create a ten-foot high bronze statue in 1966. *Olmec Bather* demonstrates Catlett's appreciation for Mexico's great historical civilizations. The country's heritage, as well as that of the United States, continued to inspire Catlett. She states:

> I am inspired by black people and Mexico people, my two peoples. Neither the masses of black people nor Mexican people have the time or the money to develop formal aesthetic appreciation. And so I try to reach them intuitively because they have an intuitive appreciation and thus help, if I can, their aesthetic development. I'm certainly not going to do calendar art. But if in sculpture I can do a subject that is clear and at the same time a sculpture of form which they will understand intuitively, then I feel I have accomplished something (*Ebony,* 94).

Traditional figurative Hispanic and African sculpture provided Catlett rich source material to reach both her peoples throughout her life.

In 1967 Catlett's art was included in a group exhibition at the City College in New York. The following year her work was displayed at the Cultural Program of the XIX Olympics in the Stone Carving Exhibition, the Solar Exhibition, and the Olympic Villa Exhibition.

While Catlett is perhaps best known as a sculptor, she is also well-recognized for her prints. She appreciates the medium primarily because many originals can be made at relatively low cost and sold to people with low incomes. Catlett explains:

> I believe that art should be available to all people. Non-objective art, for me, has many valuable aesthetic qualities, but has been used to create a snob group in the arts, both of creators and observers. Magazine cover and calendar art, on the other hand, has been used to dull the natural aesthetic feelings of ordinary people. Here, in Mexico, it is different. There is a rich historical tradition in art; the poorer people, who are great creators in the popular arts, regularly visit the murals and museums. Their appreciation extends to all art forms that do not require special and formal education to be understood (Dover, 54).

Catlett excelled in lithography and linoleum prints. In 1969 she won the first purchase prize from the National Print Salon in Mexico. The following year she received a prize to study and travel in the German Democratic Republic and showed her work at the Intergrafic Exhibition in Berlin.

Inspired by her sojourn abroad, Catlett applied for and received a grant from the British Council to visit art schools in Britain in 1970. Her travels made her more firmly committed to what she termed the ''worldwide drive for national liberation.'' While Catlett deeply appreciated the chance to see artistic developments in other countries, she emphatically stated that art must address the needs of people around the world. ''I don't think we can still keep going to Paris and Rome to see what the last word is in art and come back to our desperate nations and live in intellectual isolation from what's going on in our countries and ghettos'' (*Ebony,* 95).

As Catlett's artistic reputation grew, so did demands for solo exhibitions of her work. She achieved seventeen one-woman shows in the 1970s alone, most of them in the United States. They took place at: The Studio Museum in Harlem, New York (1971-72); Howard University Galleries in Washington, D.C., Museum of the National Center of Afro-American Artists in Boston, Atlanta Center for Black Arts, and the Rainbow Sign Gallery in Berkeley (all 1972); Saxon Princes' Summer Palace in Dresden, German Democratic Republic, The Carl Van Vechten Gallery of Fine Arts at Fisk University in Nashville, and Jackson State College in Mississippi (all 1973); Southern University in Baton Rouge, Louisiana (1974); Scripps College in Claremont, California (1975); The Gallery in Los Angeles (1976); Alabama Agricultural and Mechanical University (which traveled to seven universities in Alabama) and the Nexus Gallery in New Orleans (both in 1978); as well as the Main Public Library in Las Vegas, the Pyramid Gallery, and Your Heritage House in Detroit (all in 1979).

Catlett developed a figurative style early on in her career. She was drawn to the human body for its beauty and expressive qualities, as well as its immediate accessibility to a wide audience. She strove to attain perfection in realism, technique, and finish with each work. The artist declared:

> Art must be realistic for me, whether sculpture or printmaking. I have always wanted my art to service Black people—to reflect us, to relate to us, to stimulate us, to make us aware of our potential. . . . Learning how to do this and passing that learning on to other people have been my goals. I have learned from many people, from the restlessness and inquisitiveness of the young, from my mother, from other Black people who have struggled to better themselves—from childhood right on up to now. It has taken a long time to find out that technique was the main thing to learn from art schools. It's so important—technique—how to do things well. It's the difference between offering our beautiful people art and offering them ineptitude. They deserve the very best and we have to equip ourselves to give them our very best. You can't make a statement if you don't speak the language (Lewis, 125-26).

Great Historical Black Figures Portrayed

Joining many other black American artists in the 1960s and 1970s, Catlett sought to educate the public with her portrayals of great figures in black history. Her depictions ranged from abolitionists in the nineteenth century, such as Harriet Tubman, to contemporary heroes, as evidenced in *Homage to the Panthers* (linoleum cut, 1970) and *Malcolm Speaks for Us* (linoleum cut, 1969). The latter work won a top purchase prize, was bought by the National Institute of Fine Arts, and now belongs to the Mexican government. Catlett explained the purpose of her portraiture in 1971 when she wrote, "I have gradually reached the conclusion that art is important only to the extent that it aids in the liberation of our people. . . . I have now rejected 'International Art' except to use those if its techniques may help me make the message clearer to my folks" (Rubenstein, 320).

Internationally recognized for her well-researched and sensitive renderings of black heroes, Catlett was commissioned to depict two historical black Americans in the land of her birth. In 1973 she produced a life-size bronze bust of Phillis Wheatley for Jackson State College in Mississippi. Two years later she created a ten-foot-tall bronze sculpture of Louis Armstrong for the City Park of New Orleans. The work was unveiled in the Bicentennial Celebration of 1976.

In addition to portrait studies, Catlett produced more abstract works with symbolic content and titles, such as *Black Flag* (cedar, 1970) and *Magic Mask* (mahogany, 1971). Works in this vein are powerful acknowledgements of a history of oppression, but also expressions of black pride. *Target Practice* (bronze, 1970) is the head of a black man framed by a large rifle sight and mounted trophy-like on a wooden pedestal; *Black Unity* (walnut, 1968) depicts two calmly dignified heads reminiscent of certain West African masks. Seen from the other side, however, the sculpture reveals a large clenched fist, symbol of black power. Catlett affirms her heritage artistically in formal terms as well as in content. Rather than work in the Western medium of white marble, she seeks materials that reflect the beauty and diversity of skin tones among black peoples. She sculpts wood such as walnut, Spanish cedar, and mahogany, stones such as black marble and onyx, and she shapes terra-cotta and bronze.

While Catlett's sculpture became increasingly abstract in the biomorphic postwar manner of sculptors Henry Moore and Constantin Brancusi in her later years, she continued to focus on the human figure, and specifically the black female body. Her sculptures are exquisitely shaped expressions of dignity, pride, and power. Catlett explained:

> I don't have anything against men but since I am a woman, I know more about women and I know how they feel. . . . Artists do work with women, with the beauty of their bodies and the refinement of middle-class women, but I think there is a need to express something about the working-class Black woman and that's what I do.
>
> I'm interested in women's liberation for the fulfillment of women, not just for jobs and equality with men and so on, but for what they can contribute to enrich the world, humanity. Their contributions have been denied them. It's the same thing that happens to Black people (Lewis, *The Art of Elizabeth Catlett,* 102).

Catlett's images of women focus on three themes—nobility, action, and motherhood. In the first group are portrait busts and idealized heads, such as *Bronze Head* (1976). Each face contains classic qualities of traditional, representational West African sculpture—alert, open eyes symbolizing knowledge, closed lips indicating discretion, and smooth skin in praise of youthful energy. In the second group are Catlett's depictions of ordinary workers, such as *Negro Woman* (in terra-cotta, before 1960), as well as idealized portrayals of women poised for action, such as *Black Woman Speaks* (Spanish cedar with polychromed eyes and ears, 1970), and *Homage to My Young Black Sisters* (mahogany, 1968). These works are political statements about the position of black American women in society and their determination to elevate themselves.

By far Catlett's favorite theme, however, is motherhood. Beginning with her master's thesis depiction of a mother and child, Catlett has spent years exploring the topic. She executed many pieces with the same title in terra-cotta and wood, as well as variations on the motif in lithography (*Black Maternity,* 1959) and marble (*Negro Mother and Child,* 1940). *Maternity* (1980) in black marble is a strong expression of that special bond. Catlett abstracts a woman's bust into a hollow shape reminiscent of West African heddle pulleys. Although the mother's uplifted head looks to the side, her arms cradle the fetus/child in a firm, but open embrace. The small figure reaches towards life-sustaining breasts. Situated in this cavity, the baby is symbolically at once in the uterus, and always in the mother's heart. Catlett finds special pleasures in portraying motherhood for personal reasons. For ten years after her marriage to Mora and the birth of their three children, Catlett had no time to sculpt. However, she believes that being a mother gave her work "immeasurably more depth." She maintained, "raising children is the most creative thing I can think of" (*Ebony,* 1970, 101). Other women concurred with Catlett's statement and held both her parental care and artistic creativity in high esteem. Women's groups on both coasts of the United States showed their appreciation of Catlett's work by giving her awards in the early 1980s. In 1981 she received an award from the Women's Caucus for Art at the national congress in San Francisco. And in 1985 she achieved a bronze sculpture award from the National Council of Negro Women in New York.

Catlett's art continued to merit attention from other groups as well. In 1976 Howard University commissioned her to create a twenty-four-foot-high bronze relief for the Chemical Engineering Building. The following year she was given an Alumni Award by that same institution, her alma mater. The next commission came from the Secretary of Education in Mexico City; in 1981 Catlett completed two life-size bronze sculptures, *Torres Bodet* and *Vasconcelos.*

The last decade brought Catlett more well-deserved solo exhibitions. Her one-woman shows were held at the Chi-Wara Gallery in Atlanta; the Malcolm Brown Gallery in Shaker Heights, Ohio (1981); The Gallery Tanner in Los Angeles (1982); New Orleans Museum of Art (1983); Main Public Library in Miami, Southeast Arkansas Art and Science Center in Pine Bluff, Kilcawley Center Art Gallery at Youngstown State University in Ohio, Arkansas Art Center in Little Rock, African American Museum in Dallas, University of Mississippi, and Masur Museum of Art in Monroe, Louisiana (all in 1984); Spelman College in Atlanta and Norfolk State University in Virginia (both in 1985); Winston-Salem Urban League in North Carolina, Women's Building in Los Angeles, and Mississippi Museum of Art in Jackson (all in 1986); and the Jamaica Arts Center in New York (1990).

Work by Catlett was also included in the following traveling survey exhibitions: "Amistad II: Afro-American Exhibition (1975-77)," "Two Centuries of Black American Art (1976-77)," "Forever Free: Art by African-American Women (1981)," and "The Art of Black America, Art Museum Association (1985-86)."

Catlett's artistic honors in the 1980s include the Brandywine Workshop Award from the Philadelphia Museum of Art (1982), the purchase prize in drawing from the *Salon de la Plastica Mexicana* (1985), and the purchase prize in printmaking from the same institution in 1986.

Aptly called "La Maestra" by her students, Catlett continues to enrich our vision of the world with her art. Still residing in Mexico, she and her husband now devote their time to traveling and creating "art for liberation and for life" (Lewis, *Art: African American,* 127). Catlett's credo is that:

> Art can't be the exclusive domain of the elect. It has to belong to everyone. Otherwise it will continue to divide the privileged from the underprivileged, Blacks from Chicanos, and both rural, ghetto, and middle-class whites. Artists should work to the end that love, peace, justice, and equal opportunity prevail all over the world; to the end that all people take joy in full participation in the rich material, intellectual, and spiritual resources of this world's lands, peoples, and goods" (Lewis, *The Art of Elizabeth Catlett,* 26).

References

Bontemps, Jacqueline Fonville. *Forever Free: Art by African-American Women 1862-1980.* Alexandria, Va.: Stephenson, 1980. 68-69, 174-76.

Brown, B. A. "Expressing Social Concerns." *Artweek* 17 (March 1986): 5.

Cotter, Holland. "Black Artists: Three Shows." *Art in America* (March 1990): 165-71, 217.

de la Cuesta, M. Durand. "Elizabeth Catlett, Outstanding Sculptor of Our Epoch." *Nosotros* (Mexico) (July 1962).

Dover, Cedric. *American Negro Art.* Greenwich, Connecticut: New York Graphic Society, 1960.

Driskell, David C., and Fred F. Bond. *An Exhibition of Sculptures and Prints by Elizabeth Catlett.* Nashville: The Carl Van Vechten Gallery of Fine Arts, Fisk University, 1973.

Fax, Elton Clay. *Seventeen Black Artists.* New York: Dodd, Mead, 1971.

Gedeon, Lucinda. *Sculpture, Elizabeth Catlett / Francisco Mora, Watercolors.* Tempe, Ariz.: University Art Museum, January 11-February 15, 1987.

Goldman, Shifra M. "Six Women Artists of Mexico." *Women's Art Journal* 3 (Fall-Winter 1982-1983): 1-9.

Gouma-Peterson, Thalia. "Elizabeth Catlett: 'The Power of Human Feeling and of Art.'" *Woman's Art Journal* 4 (Spring/Summer 1983): 48-56. Also in *Arts Quarterly* 5 (October-December 1983): 26-31.

Hewitt, Mary Jane. "Elizabeth Catlett." *The International Review of African-American Art* 7 (1987).

Lewis, Samella. *Art: African-American.* New York: Harcourt Brace Jovanovich, 1978.

———. *The Art of Elizabeth Catlett.* Claremont, Calif: Hancraft Studios, 1984.

"My Art Speaks for Both My Peoples." *Ebony* 54 (February 1970): 94-96.

Oliver, Stephanie Stokes. "Elizabeth Catlett: Portrait of a Master Sculptor." *Essence* 16 (June 1985): 85-88..

Paintings, Sculpture, and Prints of the Negro Woman by Elizabeth Catlett. Introduction by Gwendolyn Bennett. Washington, D.C.: Barnett Aden Gallery, December 1947-January 1948.

Rodilles, Ignacio Marques. "Betty Catlett: Artists de un Mondo Anhelante." *El Sol de Mexico* (Sunday supplement) 9 March 1975.

Rubenstein, Charlotte Streifer. *American Women Artists.* Boston: G. K. Hall, 1982.

Who's Who in American Art. New York: Bowker, 1976, 1978, 1989-1990.

Film

Mora, June. *Elizabeth Catlett.* Los Angeles: Contemporary Crafts.

Collections

Printed material (circa 1978) concerning Elizabeth Catlett is in the Archives of American Art, Smithsonian Institution, Washington, D.C.: Art by Elizabeth Catlett is in the following collections: Barnett-Aden Collection (Boca-Raton, Florida); Clark-Atlanta University (Atlanta); Cleveland Museum of Art (Cleveland); DuSable Museum of African-American Art and History (Chicago); Fisk University (Nashville); Hampton University (Hampton, Virginia); The High Museum of Art (Atlanta); Howard University (Washington, D.C.); Instituto Nacional de Bellas Artes (Mexico); Jackson State University (Jackson, Mississippi); Library of Congress (Washington, D.C.); Metropolitan Museum of Art (New York); Museo de Arte Moderno (Mexico); Museum of Modern Art (Chicago); National Institute of Fine Arts (Mexico); Narodrniko Musea (National Museum, Prague, Czechoslovakia); National Museum of American Art (Washington, D.C.); National Polytechnic Institute (Mexico City); New Orleans Museum of Art (New Orleans); Schomburg Center for Research in Black Culture New York Public Library; State University of Iowa (Iowa City); and The Studio Museum in Harlem (New York). Private collections of Catlett's works are in New York, Washington, D.C., Paris, Buenos Aires, Havanna, Tokyo, Moscow, and Prague.

Theresa A. Leininger

Barbara Chase-Riboud

(1939-)

Sculptor, writer, poet

Living in Paris since 1961, Barbara Chase-Riboud has achieved international recognition for her remarkable contributions to the humanities. She first distinguished herself in the art world with printmaking, and then became known for her distinctive abstract metal-and-fiber sculptures, black-chalk drawings, and jewelry. Next, Chase-Riboud moved into the field of literature and won awards both for her fiction and poetry; since 1974 she has published three novels, two volumes of poetry, and several essays.

Chase-Riboud was born on June 26, 1939, in Philadelphia, Pennsylvania, to Vivian May (West) Chase, a histology technician, and Charles Edward Chase, a contractor; she was an only child. Her mother's ancestors were slaves who had escaped to Montreal, Canada, on the Underground Railroad. Chase-Riboud's talent in the arts was recognized at an early age; at five years of age she was taking dance lessons, at six there were piano lessons, and at seven art lessons. She began working in sculpture and ceramics at Fletcher Art Memorial School in Philadelphia in 1946 and won her first prize at the age of eight. Chase-Riboud continued her studies at the Philadelphia Museum School of Art (1947-1954). By the time she was fifteen years old she won a *Seventeen* magazine award for one of her prints, which was purchased by the Museum of Modern Art from the exhibition organized by the ACA Gallery in New York.

The artist received a strong classical education, achieving her B.F.A. in 1957 from Tyler School at Temple University. The same year Chase-Riboud first exhibited her work at the Philadelphia Art Alliance and won its Purchase Prize. She also won first prize in the National College Board Art Contest from *Mademoiselle*. She then studied at the American Academy in Rome for a year (1957-1958) under the sponsorship of a John Hay Whitney Foundation Fellowship. There she executed her first works in bronze and established her first contacts in Europe. Her exhibitions in Italy included those at the Spoleto Festival (with Ben Shahn, Dominico Gnoli, and Jerome Robbins) in 1957, and the American Academy in Rome and the Gallery L'Obeliso, both in 1958.

On Christmas 1957, Chase-Riboud's friends left her stranded on a dare in Egypt. Abandoned by them, she found herself rescued by the black American cultural attaché in Cairo. He befriended the artist and invited her to stay with his family. This three-month sojourn promoted a turning point in Chase-Riboud's traditionally academic art. She states:

> I grew up that year. It was the first time I realized there was such a thing as non-European art. For someone exposed only to the Greco-Roman tradition, it was a revelation. I suddenly saw how insular the Western world was vis-a-vis the nonwhite, non-Christian world. The blast of Egyptian culture was irreversible. The sheer magnificence of it. The elegance and perfection, the timelessness, the depth. After that, Greek and Roman art looked like pastry to me. From an artistic point of view, that trip was historic for me. Though I didn't know it at the time, my own transformation was part of the historical transformation of the blacks that began in the 60s (Munro, 372).

After her study abroad, Chase-Riboud continued her education at Yale University under the direction of Josef Albers and Paul Rudolph and received her M.F.A. in 1960. The same year she completed an architectural commission, a monumental fountain for the Wheaton Plaza, near Washington, D.C.

The first five years of the 1960s were a time of diminished artistic output for Chase-Riboud. After graduation from Yale, she went to London, England, to marry her former professor. Disenchanted with the country, the climate, and the fiancé, she traveled to Paris for the weekend, then made the city her permanent home. At an exhibition of Yves Klein, she met the art director of the *New York Times,* who offered her the job of Paris art director. This ended when she married French photographer Marc Riboud on December 25, 1961, in Mexico. The next years were spent traveling with her husband on his assignments to Russia, India, Greece, and North Africa. Chase-Riboud was the first American woman to visit the People's Republic of China after the Revolution in 1949, including Inner Mongolia and Nepal. During these journeys, she became fascinated with Asian art and made mental notes for later work.

In the second half of the 1960s, Chase-Riboud resumed her artistic activity. Echoes of yin and yang symbolism appeared in the solo exhibition of her drawings and sculpture in Paris in November 1960; these works dealt with the union of opposites—male/female, negative/positive, black/white. Chase Riboud's sculpture quickly gained more notice and was exhibited in the New York Architectural League Show, 1965; the Festival of Negro Art in Dakar, 1966; L'Oeil Ecoute Festival of Avignon, 1969; and Americans of Paris, Air France, 1969. During this time Chase-Riboud also gave birth to two sons, David Charles and Alexei Karol.

African Influence Seen in Sculpture

Chase-Riboud's early sculptures are characterized by abstract organic shapes and poetic literary figurative compositions reminiscent of Germain Richier and Alberto Giacometti (for whom she wrote a poem after meeting him). She created compositions from two materials strongly contrasting in texture and finish—bronze and wool, steel and synthetics, or bronze and silk (see, for example, *Black Zanzibar Table* in *Forever Free,* p. 73, and *She #1* in *Art: African American,* p. 183). These sculptural compositions were constructed initially to hide the support system underneath the fibers. However, her expressive abstractions soon came to refer to certain West African dancing masks with their combination of diverse materials, such as wood, raffia, hemp, leather, feathers, and metal. Journeys to Africa, beginning with participation in the Pan-African festival in Algeria in 1966, strongly affected Chase-Riboud's artistic development. "I found myself there," she says of the Pan-African festival in Nigeria of 1969, "with all the freedom fighters and liberation groups—the Algerians, the South Africans, the Black Panthers from America. A kind of historical current brought all of these people together in a context that was not only political but artistic" (Richardson, 48).

Chase-Riboud began to employ bricolage as well as ancient lost-wax casting techniques and African symbols in her work. The combination of these formal concerns with modern materials and contemporary events was developed in her *Malcolm X* series of 1969-1970 and expanded exhibition at the Massachusetts Institute of Technology, "Four Monuments to Malcolm X" in 1970. Rather than make political art, Chase-Riboud pays tribute to the struggle of the 1960s with elegiac elegance. She declares, "Sculpture should be beautiful, each element has an aesthetic as well as a symbolic and spiritual function. My idea is to reinterpret the aesthetic function in contemporary terms, using modern materials" (Nora, 62). Her sculptures are powerful studies in contrasts—unyielding metals supported by braided, knotted, and wrapped fibers that interchange functions. The soft wool and silk become hard and the rigid bronze and steel seem to dissolve into softness.

Chase-Riboud was influenced by Albers's color studies at Yale as well as Minimalist approaches prompted by the New York School, such as the work of Eva Hesse, Robert Graves, and Robert Morris (the artist was also friends with Ken Nordland). However, she developed a unique style in the 1960s and 1970s that she described as "maximal" (Nora, 62). Her insistence on beauty and finish alienated her from contemporary trends in American art. Still, Chase-Riboud's revolt against styles such as Pop (and its concern with white mass culture) freed her to explore other possibilities in sculpture. She found her art more analogous to the density and complexity in avant-garde music of the 1960s. John and Alice Coltrane, Steve Reich, Terry Riley, and John Cage, like Chase-Riboud, incorporated African and Asian elements in their work, paying careful attention to texture and evocative qualities. Chase-Riboud found that such art approached the power of classical West African sculpture. According to the artist:

> If "beauty" can be called "black" in the same way that honor can be called "black," then *Zanzibar* [one of Chase-Riboud's sculptures] can be described as such. There is a mysterious

> and not far from threatening underbelly to this "beautiful" surface which has the same emotional effect as some African sculptures have on Westerners—and for the same reasons; displaced in time and space, taken out of their real environment, they assume a certain impenetrability that can disconcert and repel as well as please and attract (*Contemporary Artists,* 185).

Chase-Riboud's art continued to win her recognition through the 1970s, with a National Endowment for the Humanities fellowship in 1973 followed by an Outstanding Alumni Award from Temple University in 1975. Her one-woman exhibitions during this time include those at the Betty Persons Gallery in New York in 1972; Berkeley (California) Museum, 1973; Massachusetts Institute of Technology, 1973; Indianapolis Art Museum, 1973; Detroit Art Institute, 1973; Leslie Rankow Gallery in New York (jewelry), 1973; Betty Persons Gallery in New York; Museum of Modern Art, Paris, 1974; and the Kunstmuseum in Dusseldorf, and the Kunsthalle in Baden-Baden, both in 1974.

Group shows include those at the Museum of Fine Arts in Boston, 1970; Whitney Museum of American Art (New York), 1971; National Gallery of Art, Smithsonian Institute (Washington, D.C.), 1971; National Gallery of Art (Toronto, Canada), 1971; Hudson River Museum, 1971; Museum of Modern Art (New York); Carnegie Institute (Pittsburgh); the Centre Pompidou (Paris); Newark Museum, 1971; Salon de la Jeune Sculpteur, 1971; Salon de Mai, 1971-1972; the Salon des Nouvelles Realités, 1972; and Dokumenta (Kassel, Germany), 1977.

Chase-Riboud's achievements in the visual arts continued to earn her international recognition. At the invitation of the United States Department of State in 1975, she gave poetry readings and slide lectures of her art in Senegal, Mali, Ghana, the Ivory Coast, Tunisia, and Sierra Leone. Her work also merited attention in the form of solo exhibitions at the Musée Reattu in Arles (1976); the Kunstmuseum in Freiburg (1976); the Bronx Museum in New York (1980); the Museum of Modern Art in Sydney (1980-1981); and the Studio Museum in Harlem (1981). For her many contributions to the arts, including her first novel, *Sally Hemings,* Chase-Riboud was awarded an honorary doctorate of arts and humanities from Temple University in 1981. After her divorce from Riboud that same year, on July 4, she married Sergio G. Tosi, an Italian art dealer and publisher.

Recent Creativity Focused on Writing

In recent years Chase-Riboud's creative output has centered more on writing than the visual arts. Her first book of poems, *From Memphis to Peking,* published in 1974, was inspired both by her visits to Egypt and to the People's Republic of China. With the unifying theme of physical and spiritual journeys, it focuses on the writer's family origins and the quest for mystical knowledge.

Chase-Riboud produced her first novel, *Sally Hemings*, in 1979. Well researched and written, it concerns the alleged slave mistress of President Thomas Jefferson. The author was captivated by the mystery surrounding the Jefferson-Hemings relationship upon reading Fawn Brodie's biography of Jefferson. She tried to convince numerous friends to write the novel, then finally did it herself at the suggestion of Toni Morrison, her poetry editor at Random House. *Sally Hemings* won Chase-Riboud the Janet Heidinger Kafka Prize as best novel written by an American woman and was subsequently translated into French, German, Italian, Spanish, Swedish, Danish, Finnish, and Slavonic. Chase-Riboud was also honored with a gold medal by one of the Italian academies in 1979.

Her second book of poems, *Love Perfecting,* appeared in 1980. Although the volume received less notice than *From Memphis to Peking,* Chase-Riboud continued to write poetry for herself. The genre, she says, "is very close to a discipline both familiar and dear to me: drawing. Both are dangerous searches for perfection . . . drawing prepared me for the demands of poetry" (Richardson, 45). Chase-Riboud's perseverance paid off. In 1988 she won the Carl Sandburg Poetry Prize as the best poet for her book, *Portrait of a Nude Woman as Cleopatra, a Meloloque.* The writer won more acclaim, however, for her novels and sculpture, than for her poetry and drawings.

Chase-Riboud continued her exploration of slavery in her second novel, *Valide,* which was promptly translated into all the major European languages, adding Dutch to her list of publishers. The piece focuses on a Martiniquian slave who became the most powerful woman in the Ottoman Empire during the late eighteenth and early nineteenth centuries. The protagonist, as mother of the sultan, directs his harem. Issues that predominate in this novel and Chase-Riboud's other writings include constructions of power involving race and gender, liberty, history, and myth-making. In 1980, a year after the publication of *Valide,* Chase-Riboud carried on those themes with her third novel, *Echo of Lions.* This work is based on the true story of an extraordinary West African called Cinque who led a successful rebellion on board the Spanish slave ship *Amistad* in the early nineteenth century. After killing the captain and his crew, these men attempted to sail back to Sierra Leone but landed on the East Coast of the United States and subsequently endured four years of trials before being declared free. Coming full circle, Chase-Riboud wrote about a fight for liberty that occurred in the town where she received her graduate education, New Haven, Connecticut. For this book she was cited by the Connecticut State Legislature and the governor for excellence and achievement in literature in 1989. Additionally, both *Echo of Lions* and *Sally Hemings* have been optioned by movie companies.

Chase-Riboud has authored several other novels that are pending publication and she continues to write. Throughout the last decade, she has also continued to produce visual art. In the spring of 1990, she was the fourth annual Artist-in-Residence at Pasadena City College in California and had a solo exhibition in April at the University Museum. At the college she lectured, conducted studio courses, and worked in wax and clay using a propane torch, a hot plate, sculpting tools, and ordinary implements such as kitchen knives. While Chase-Riboud still makes metal and fiber sculptures, she has also begun to create multimedia compositions embellished with automatic writing. The artist is now planning an exhibition of recent works that will open at the Art for Architecture Gallery in New York in 1991, and will travel to Paris, Milan, and Madrid.

Chase-Riboud and her husband now divide their time between Paris and Rome. In the latter city, , her studio in the Palazzo Ricci was reputedly also used by the sixteenth-century goldsmith Benvenuto Cellini. The artist does not believe in expatriatism, however, and does not see herself as one who lives in another country because she does not love her own. Instead, she declares of the City of Lights:

> Paradise it is not, but a view from another country is a precious gift, and I have always taken advantage of it. I detest criticism of America from Parisians, yet I accept my own critical view of the United States from this side of the ocean (''Why Paris?,'' 66).

Chase-Riboud continues to contribute to the rich legacy of African-American culture in Paris, in the tradition of such artists as painter Henry O. Tanner, sculptors Augusta Savage and Nancy Elizabeth Prophet, and writers such as Countee Cullen, Langston Hughes, Richard Wright, and James Baldwin. She explains, ''for me, the mystique, the verve, the sense of liberation persist here'' (''Why Paris?,'' 66).

References

Barbara Chase-Riboud. New York: Bertha Schaefer Gallery, February 1970.

Bontemps, Arna Alexander, and Jacqueline Fonveille-Bontemps. *Forever Free: Art by African-American Women 1882-1980.* Alexandria, Virginia: Stephenson, 1980. Includes illustrations of the artist and her sculpture, *Black Zanzibar Table* (1974), pp. 72-73, as well as a bibliography and essay relating her work to that by other African-American women artists.

Chase-Riboud, Barbara. *Echo of Lions.* New York: William Morrow, 1989.

———. *From Memphis to Peking.* New York: Random House, 1974.

———. ''The Life and Death of Josephine Baker.'' *Essence* 6 (February 1976): 36-37.

———. *Sally Hemings, a Novel.* New York: Viking, 1979.

———. *Portrait of a Nude Woman as Cleopatra, a Melologue.* New York: William Morrow, 1988.

———. *Echo of Lions.* New York: William Morrow, 1989.

———. ''Le Plaisir d'Etre Étrangère.'' *Le Monde* (23 January 1983).

———. *Valide: A Novel of the Harem.* New York: William Morrow, 1986.

———. ''Why Paris?'' *Essence* 18 (October 1987): 65-66. This short essay explains the author's reasons for living abroad and gives a brief history of African-Americans in Paris. This issue of *Essence* also profiles other African-Americans now living there and offers tips on tourism and fashion.

Contemporary Artists. London: St. James Press, 1975.

Dover, Cedric. *American Negro Art.* Greenwich, Conn.: New York Graphic Society, 1960. Includes reproductions of the sculptures *Adam and Eve* (1958), *Mother and Child* (1956), and *The Last Supper* (1958), all on plate 66.

Fine, Elsa Honig. ''Mainstream, Blackstream and the Black Art Movement.'' *Art Journal* (Spring 1971).

Heller, Nancy G. *Women Artists: An Illustrated History.* New York: Abbeville Press, 1987.

Igoe, Lynn M. *Two-Hundred Fifty Years of Afro-American Art: An Annotated Bibliography.* New York: Bowker, 1961. Provides excellent bibliography on Chase-Riboud through 1976.

Kisselgoff, A. ''Watching China from the Inside.'' *New York Times* (4 April 1967).

Lewis, I. ''People: Barbara Chase-Riboud.'' *Essence* 1 (June 1970): 62, 71.

Lewis, Samella. *Art: African American.* New York: Harcourt Brace Jovanovich, 1978. With a reproduction of the bronze and silk sculpture *She #1* (1972).

Munro, Eleanor. *Originals: American Women Artists.* New York: Simon and Schuster, 1979. Contains candid interviews with the artist.

Naylor, Colin, and Genesis P-Orridge, eds. *Contemporary Artists.* New York: St. Martin's Press, 1977. Chronological biographical listing and artist's statement. Black-and-white illustrations of the sculpture, *Malcolm III,* 1970, p. 185.

Newton, Edmund. ''Now Showing: The Artist at Work.'' *Los Angeles Times* (3 May 1990).

Nora, Francoise. ''From Another Country.'' *Art News* 71 (March 1972): 60-64. Fine analysis of Chase-Riboud's art in its historical context.

Nora-Cachin, Francoise, Pol Bury, and Barbara Chase-Riboud. *Barbara Chase-Riboud.* Paris: Musée d'art moderne de la ville Paris, 25 avril-2 juin, 1974. Catalog with little text, but twenty black-and-white illustrations of the artist's sculptures and drawings.

Palmer, A. "Jewelry Mirrors Her Sculpture." *New York Times* (29 April 1972).

Richardson, Marilyn. "Barbara Chase-Riboud." In Thadious M. Davis and Trudier Harris, eds. *Dictionary of Literary Biography*, Vol. 33: *Afro-American Fiction Writers After 1955*. Detroit: Gale Research, 1984. Includes photographs of Chase-Riboud alone and with her two sons as well as reproductions of the covers of *From Memphis to Peking* and *Sally Hemings*.

Rubenstein, Charlotte Streifer. *American Women Artists: From Early Indian Times to the Present*. New York: Avon, 1982.

———. *Barbara Chase-Riboud* (exhibition catalogue). Pasadena: Pasadena City College, April 1-28, 1990.

University Art Museum, Berkeley. *Chase-Riboud*. Berkeley, Calif: January 17-February 25, 1973. One of the most extensive catalogues on Chase-Riboud, including fifteen full-page black-and-white reproductions of her sculpture and drawings.

Who's Who Among Black Americans. 4th ed. Lake Forest, Ill.: Ann Wolk Knouse, Publisher, 1985.

Who's Who in America. Wilmette, Ill.: Marquis, 1978-1980; 45th ed, Vol. 1, 1988-1989. 534..

Who's Who in American Art. 1973, 1976, 1978, 1980, 1983, 1989-90 (p. 180).

Who's Who of American Women. Chicago: Marquis, 1976-81.

Wilson, Judith. "Barbara Chase-Riboud: Sculpting Our History." *Essence* (December 1979): 12-13.

World Who's Who. Chicago: Marquis, 1977-89.

World Who's Who of Women. Cambridge, Eng.: International Biographical Center, 1987.

Selected Films, Videotapes, and Television Specials

Barbara Chase-Riboud. School of Design, Minneapolis. Videotape. New York: Dorothy Beskind, October 1973.

Connecticut Public Television Special with Nancy Savin, March 2, 1989.

Femme á Femme. The French Broadcasting Company, Channel 3, December 20, 1989.

Five. Film produced by Alvin Yudkff for the Seagram Company. New York: Silvermine Films, 1971. Includes Romare Bearden, Betty Blayton, Barbara Chase-Riboud, Richard Hunt, and Charles White.

Like It Is. Televised documentary film and interview on the sculptures *Malcolm X Monuments*. Produced by Charles Hobson and Margarite Jones. WABC-TV, April 1970.

McNeil/Lehrer News Hours. Interview with Charlayne Hunter-Gault on WNET-TV, March 6, 1989.

Scully Recontre. The Canadian Broadcasting Company. Interview with Robert Scully, January 18, 1990.

Sixty Minutes. CBS, May 1979.

Twentieth Century American Art. Documentary by Sunrise Semester presented by Ruth Bowman and produced by Patricia Myers, 1972.

Collections

Art by Chase-Riboud is in the following selected collections: Acquisitions des Musées Nationaux (Paris); The University Museum, (University of California, Berkeley); Bertha Schaefer Gallery (New York); Centre National des Arts Contemporaines, National Museum of Modern Art (Paris); The Geigy Foundation (New York); The Kenton Corporation (New York); Lannan Foundation (New York State); The Metropolitan Museum of Art (New York); The Museum of Modern Art (New York); The Newark Museum (Newark); The New York Public Library; New York State Office Building; Pasadena, University Collection (California); The Philadelphia Art Alliance (Philadelphia), and Saint John's University (New York).

Theresa A. Leininger

Alice Childress

(1920-)

Writer, actress, and director

Alice Childress is a multitalented writer, actor, and director who has been on the cutting edge of black American cultural activity for more than half a century. Born into a poor, uneducated family on October 12, 1920, in Charleston, South Carolina, Alice Childress "never planned to become a writer" ("A Candle," 112). Her great-grandmother, Annie, was a slave who, after the Civil War, was taken by her owners to Charleston and abandoned at the age of thirteen, without family, money, or even decent clothes. She was rescued by a white woman, Anna Campbell, who invited her to live in her home. Campbell's son was a sailor who impregnated Annie and then disappeared. Campbell accepted Annie's child, Eliza, as her son's and intended to make Annie and Eliza her heirs. However, after her death, Campbell's cousins claimed all of the property and forced Annie and Eliza into destitution.

Eliza Campbell, Alice Childress's grandmother, married "a mill-hand slave descendant and they raised seven children in abject poverty." Eliza Campbell also raised Childress. Although Childress was encouraged by teachers to write, she was not able to finish high school. As she began to write, she resisted advice to write about the few blacks who "win prizes and honors by overcoming cruel odds." Rather, she chose "to write about those who come in second, or not at all . . . the intricate and magnificent patterns of a loser's life." Unimpressed by capitalistic American propaganda about how everyone can attain the American Dream, Childress observes that, "No matter how many celebrities we may accrue, they cannot substitute for the masses of human beings. My writing attempts to interpret the 'ordinary' because they are not ordinary" ("A Candle," 112).

Childress began her career as an actor in New York in 1940. She worked as an actor and director with the American Negro Theatre for twelve years. Later she performed on Broadway and on television. In 1955 her play, *Trouble in Mind,* was produced off-Broadway to mixed reviews. An exposé of the racist treatment of black actors in white plays, *Trouble in Mind* won the 1956 Obie Award for the best original off-Broadway play, but "it was never performed on Broadway due to disputes over theme and interpretation which caused Childress to withdraw it" (*Contemporary Literary Criticism,* 104). In fact, Childress:

> has been, from the beginning, a crusader and a writer who resists compromise. She tries to write about Negro problems as honestly as she can, and she refuses production of her plays if the producer wants to change them in a way which distorts her intentions (Abramson, 190).

If Childress's integrity has lessened her appeal to some producers, many members of her audience are grateful that she has portrayed the world honestly as she sees it. The playwright-novelist John Killens recalls being inspired in the 1940s and 1950s by Childress's "exuberant celebration of the Black experience . . . . One left the theater after an evening with Alice Childress imbued with pride and with the spirit to struggle" ("The Literary Genius," 129). In particular, Killens was uplifted by Childress's compassion and her "power as a great humorist": "Love of life and people, accent on struggle, humor as a cultural weapon. *Love, struggle, humor.* These are the hallmarks of her craft, of her artistry" ("The Literary Genius," 129).

Controversial Works Bring Mixed Reactions

In 1966 another controversial Childress play, *Wedding Band: A Love/Hate Story in Black and White,* was produced at the University of Michigan in Ann Arbor. In 1972 it was produced off-Broadway at the New York Shakespeare Festival Theatre, directed by Childress and Joseph Papp. Set in 1918, *Wedding Band* represents love between a white man and a black woman amidst the realities of white bigotry in South Carolina. Like much of Childress's work in the theater, this play received mixed reviews; critics praised its compassion, honesty, humor, and pathos, but generally found the plot uneven and some of the scenes propagandistic.

In 1973 Childress's first of many novels, *A Hero Ain't Nothin' but a Sandwich,* was published. This novel was enthusiastically praised, and it received multiple national awards, including being named one of the Outstanding Books of the Year by the *New York Times Book Review.* The fact that the novel was banned in a Savannah, Georgia, school library is perhaps further testament to its power. (The entire state of Alabama had banned broadcast of Childress's play, *Wine in the Wilderness,* in 1969.) In *A Hero* Childress:

> intimately portrays the oppression of the working class people living in Afro-American communities. With fine perception, she tells about thirteen year old Benjie Johnson, a victim of drug addiction, his family, friends and neighbors living in the Harlem ghetto (Rogers, 72-73).

In 1987 Childress's play, *Moms,* was produced at the Hudson Guild in New York. A celebration of the black actor-comedian Jackie (Moms) Mabley (1894-1975), the play received warm reviews; Edith Oliver wrote in the *New Yorker* that it was "very funny" and "written with considerable tact, with just enough story to keep things moving and varied and to display the best of Moms' wares" (105). Childress's fascination with Moms is part of her ongoing interest in the lives of black Americans, particularly black women, who must fight against multiple oppressive forces in their struggles to find a voice. Childress believes that "being a woman adds difficulty to self expression, but being Black is the larger factor of struggle against odds" ("A Candle," 115).

In addition to her remarkable theatrical and literary achievements, Childress has lectured at several colleges and universities, including Fisk University and the Radcliffe Institute for Independent Study in Cambridge, Massachusetts. She has been married since 1957 to her second husband, Nathan Woodard, a musician who frequently composes music for her plays. She has one daughter, Jean, from her first marriage. Childress resides in New York.

References

Abramson, Doris E. *Negro Playwrights in the American Theatre: 1925-1959.* New York: Columbia University Press, 1969.

Black Writers. Detroit: Gale Research, 1989. 100-103.

Childress, Alice. "A Candle in a Gale Wind." *Black Women Writers (1950-1980): A Critical Evaluation.* Ed. Mari Evans. New York: Doubleday, 1984. 111-16.

———. *A Hero Ain't Nothing' but a Sandwich.* New York: Coward, 1973.

———. *Moms: A Praise Play for a Black Comedienne.* Produced off-Broadway at Hudson Guild Theatre, 4 February 1987.

———. *Trouble in Mind.* In *Black Theatre: A Twentieth-*

Century Collection of the Work of Its Best Playwrights. Ed. Lindsay Patterson. New York: Dodd, Mead, 1971.

———. *Wedding Band: A Love/Hate Story in Black and White.* New York: Samuel French, 1973.

———. *Wine in the Wilderness: A Comedy-Drama.* First produced in Boston by WGBH-TV, 4 March 1969. In *Black Theatre: A Twentieth-Century Collection of the Work of Its Best Playwrights.* Ed. Lindsay Patterson. New York: Dodd, Mead, 1971.

Contemporary Authors. Vols. 45-48. Detroit: Gale Research, 1974. 93.

Contemporary Literary Criticism. Vol. 12. Detroit: Gale Research, 1980. 104-09.

Killens, John O. "The Literary Genius of Alice Childress." *Black Women Writers (1950-1980): A Critical Evaluation.* Ed. Mari Evans. New York: Doubleday, 1984. 129-33.

Miller, Jeanne-Marie A. "Black Women Playwrights from Grimké to Shange: Selected Synopses of Their Works." *But Some of Us Are Brave.* Eds. Gloria T. Hull, Patricia Bell Scott, and Barbara Smith. New York: Feminist Press, 1982. 280-96.

Oliver, Edith. "Moms." *New Yorker* 65 (23 February 1987): 105.

Rogers, Norma. "To Destroy Life." *Freedomways* 14 (1974): 72-75.

Kari Winter

May Edward Chinn

(1896-1980)

Physician, scholar

In 1926, when few blacks considered higher education a viable option, May Edward Chinn was completing her work for the M.D. degree at the University of Bellevue Medical Center. The first black woman to graduate from that institution and the first, in 1926, to intern at the then predominantly white Harlem Hospital, Chinn would go on to make a significant contribution to society in general and the black community in particular.

May Edward Chinn, an only child, was born April 15, 1896, in Great Barrington, Massachusetts. Her father, William Layfette Chinn, an African-American, was born a slave in 1852 in Manassas, Virginia. Her mother, Lula Ann (Evans) Chinn, an African-American/American Indian, was born in 1876 in Norfolk, Virginia. Her mother was, in part, a descendant of the Chickahominy Indians, a smaller tribe within the large Algonquin tribe.

Although May Edward Chinn did not complete high school, she passed tests and was accepted for enrollment at Teachers College of Columbia University, where she obtained a bachelor of science degree in 1921. During an interview with Charlayne Hunter-Gault, Chinn "recalled that her father, who had been a slave, opposed her even going to college. But her mother, who 'scrubbed floors and hired out as a cook,' became the driving force behind her educational effort." (*New York Times*, 16 November 1977). She enrolled in Teachers College at Columbia University as a music major, but was persuaded by one of her teachers, Jean Broadhurst, to change her major to science.

Chinn obtained the doctor of medicine degree from the University of Bellevue Medical Center (now University Medical College, New York University) in 1926. She also obtained a master of science degree in public health from Columbia University in 1933. During 1928-1933, Chinn studied with George Papanicolaou, the father of cytological methods for diagnosis of cancer—the "Pap" smear. Between 1948 and 1955, she studied exfoliative cytology at Cornell University Medical College, again with George Papanicolaou. Additionally, she attended post-graduate seminars in medicine and related fields in many colleges in America, Europe, and Japan between 1930 and 1977. Clearly, Chinn was well-prepared for her career in medicine.

It is not surprising then that she held numerous positions, many simultaneously, during her illustrious career in the field of medicine. She was a physician to a Catholic convent—Francian Handmaids of Mary, a group of black nuns in New York City, from 1928 to 1976. Her interest in cancer began during her second year of practice, and she worked in the field of cancer research from 1930 to 1977, while at the same time engaged in her own private practice. In 1937, she was an examining physician for the Juvenile Aid Bureau in New York City. She served as a staff member at the Strang Clinic of Memorial Hospital in New York City from 1945-1974, as well as a staff member at the New York Infirmary for Women and Children for one year in 1945, and again from 1960 to 1965. Additionally, she served as a clinician with the Department of Health Day Care Centers in New York City from 1960 to 1977. After retiring in 1977, Chinn became a consultant to the Phelps-Stokes Fund, an educational foundation that, among other activities, brings medical students from Africa and other parts of the world to the United States.

Commitment to Medical Care Brings Awards

Chinn's numerous awards and honors provide evidence of her dedication and commitment to using her talents to assist those in need of medical care. Indeed, these honors and awards are merely reflections of her many years of activity in service to her community. As early as 1957, she received a citation from the New York City Cancer Committee of the

American Cancer Society. In October 1977, Chinn, along with five other black female physicians, was honored in New York City by the Susan Smith McKinney Steward, M.D. Society for "devoted services to their communities for more than fifty years." It is worthy of note that Chinn was one of the founders of that society, founded in 1975 for the "express purpose of aiding Negro women in medical school and to document the achievements of Negro women in medicine over the years."

She was honored by the Long Island Council N.C.N. in 1961 "for many years of meritorious service in promoting high health standards for women and girls in the community and her recent contribution to the medical profession in the field of cancer research." In 1960, the Harriet Beecher Stowe Junior High School in New York City named her "Our Lady Of The Year," for, in the words of the citation, "your dedication as a physician; your determination to conquer cancer through research and lectures to the public; your devotion to the welfare of others regardless of race, creed or color serves as an inspiration to others. It is due to the efforts of such people as you that we entrust our hopes for a better world."

In May 1979 Chinn was awarded an honorary doctor of science degree by Columbia University, as well as receiving the Distinguished Alumnus Award from Teachers College. Columbia's citation called her a "brave warrior in the fight against sickness, poverty, and injustice." In June 1980, New York University honored her with a doctor of science degree for "long life service" to Harlem patients and pioneer work in early cancer detection. The Manhattan branch of the New York Urban League named her guest of honor at its annual New Year's reception held at the Time-Life Building in New York City in January 1980.

Even though Chinn was engaged in numerous activities directly related to her medical practice, she somehow found time to participate in professional organizations. She held elected memberships in several prestigious professional organizations, including the American Academy of Family Physicians (1977, life member); the Society of Surgical Oncology, Memorial Hospital in New York City (1974); and the New York Academy of Science (1954). In 1959, she was declared a fellow in the American Geriatrics Society. She also held memberships in many other professional organizations, such as the American Society of Cytology (1972), the American Academy of General Practice (1970), the American Cancer Society (1968), the American Academy of Family Practice (1954), and the Medical Society of New York City.

Additionally, she held memberships in such noted nonprofessional organizations as the American Museum of Natural History, the Smithsonian Associates, the NAACP Educational Fund, the National Urban League, the Foreign Policy Association, and the National Council of Women of the United States.

Perhaps the most notable persons among her friends and associates were Paul Robeson and his wife. In the manuscript of her autobiography (Special Collections, Fisk University Library), Chinn recalled that the first thing the assistant dean said to her during her interview for medical school was, "Do you know Paul Robeson?" She replied, "Yes, I was his accompanist for several years before he became famous." Most of the interview time was consumed with conversation about Paul Robeson. After she was notified of her acceptance into the 1922 class of medicine, she later told Robeson, "Because I know you, I have been accepted into medical school at New York University, Class of 1922."

May Edward Chinn practiced medicine in New York City for more than fifty years before she retired in 1977. Though Chinn had a distinguished career in medicine, many years of her practice occurred during a time when black doctors were not afforded the same respect and privileges as their white counterparts. Excerpts from her autobiography provide some insight into the problem:

> We doctors in Harlem had many problems in common in the late 30's and early 40's. This was before the founding of Doctor Crump's "International Hospital" in Harlem.
>
> Chief among them was that Negro doctors were denied any hospital connection whatever. There was no City Hospital in New York City where we could attend an Out-patient Clinic or their Ward Service for study and observation of the newer diseases and the effects of the newer drugs.
>
> So it was that the Negro doctor, including myself, was forced to practice medicine, surgery and obstetrics as the old-fashioned "family doctor" did one-hundred years ago in the deep rural South—in Appalachia—with the nearest hospital being not fifty miles away; for us, so far away that we did not know "how far." Even if a hospital was around the "bend of the road"—it was useless to us who were denied any privilege whatsoever of its facilities. So we managed the best we could.

Indeed, Chinn and her black counterparts managed well. She continues in her autobiography:

> I have practiced 'family medicine' in Harlem, New York City for more than fifty years. 'Family Medicine' is really the treatment of all members of the family.
>
> I never had a 'speciality' per se. I preferred managing the care of babies, children, and women of all ages. The first years of my practice consisted of persons 'apparently' well and the very ill. My interest in cancer began in my second year of practice.
>
> After seeing such misery in suspected cancer

> patients, I kept saying to myself—there must be some way of having this disease diagnosed earlier. Certainly there must be some way of slowing its process down until newer methods are found to control it, or, I thought wistfully, perhaps to cure it.
>
> Throughout my years of practice I have always maintained one clinic for children. After 1974, I continued my private practice and increased my children's clinics to three.
>
> Under the Department of Health, New York City, I was Clinician to three Day Care Centers. Our children ranged from three to six years of age. I worked with them until August 1, 1977.
>
> Since retirement from active practice, I have continued to work on different medical committees for the County of New York City Medical society and the American Cancer Society, New York City Division.

Although she spent many hours in her practice, Chinn did not accumulate much wealth as a physician because in many cases she did not charge her patients for her services. As a result, in her final years she did not travel much beyond her Harlem apartment because she did not have the money. On December 1, 1980, she collapsed and died at age 84 while attending a reception at Columbia University, honoring one of her friends, John Wilson, an architect.

May Edward Chinn was an outstanding woman whose religious doctrine was simple: "Without Brotherhood and the Practice of Brotherhood, our religion means nothing." Her philosophy was also simple: "Become involved with the problems of your Nation, your state, your city, and especially with your immediate neighborhood. Help those with problems—Help them to take the next step—UPWARDS."

References

Ennis, Thomas W. "Dr. May Edward Chinn, 84, Long a Harlem Physician." *New York Times*, 3 December 1980.

"Her Heart Is Strong." *New York Times*, 6 January 1980.

Hunter-Gault, Charlayne. "Black Women M.D.'s. *New York Times*, 16 November 1977.

"*Medical Profession in Harlem Gets New Addition.*" *New York Amsterdam News*, 16 June 1926.

Haynes, Olyve Jeter. "*1919-1930—Over the Years with Dr. May E. Chinn.*" Letter to May Edward Chinn, exerpted in Chinn's autobiography. Special Collections, Fisk University Library.

"Three Of Our Finest." *Interstate Tattler*, 21 March 1930.

The 2,000 Women of America. Chicago: Marquis, 1970.

Who's Who of Americans with World Notables. Chicago: Marquis, 1970-71.

Collections

The papers of Mae Edward Chinn consist of certificates, honorary letters from the 1960s and 1970s, photographs, papers relating to the death of her parents, résumé, and other materials and are in the Schomburg Center for Research in Black Culture. A manuscript of her autobiography and other personal notes are in the Special Collections of Fisk University Library.

Gloria Long Anderson

Shirley Chisholm

(1924-)

Politician, author

Shirley Anita St. Hill Chisholm was elected to the House of Representatives in 1968. Her election was noteworthy because of the disadvantages that she overcame to secure victory. In her own words, she was "the first American citizen to be elected to Congress in spite of the double drawbacks of being female and having skin darkened by

Shirley Chisholm

melanin'' (Chisholm, *Unbought and Unbossed,* xi). Chisholm is a driven person, so this accomplishment and her legislative acts were not sufficient to satisfy her. In 1972 she became the first woman as well as the first black to seek a major party nomination for President. Furthermore, she has authored a pair of autobiographical works entitled *Unbought and Unbossed* and *The Good Fight.* Her auspicious accomplishments are rooted in modest but remarkably efficient beginnings.

Shirley Anita St. Hill Chisholm was born in Brooklyn on November 20, 1924, to Charles and Ruby St. Hill. At the age of three, she and her two younger sisters, Muriel and Odessa, were sent to Barbados to live with their grandmother, Emily Seale, to allow the St. Hills to save some money. Her grandmother was assisted in caring for the children by Chisholm's Aunt Myrtle and Uncle Lincoln. The children stayed there seven years. It was here that Shirley Chisholm received the foundation for her further learning. ''Years later I would know what an important gift my parents had given me by seeing to it that I had my early education in the strict, traditional, British-style schools of Barbados. If I speak and write easily now, that early education is the main reason'' (Chisholm, *Unbought,* 8). It was not all work on the island. The St. Hill girls and their four cousins who lived there explored the farm and village. Eventually, all things had to come to an end, and the St. Hill girls had to return to Brooklyn with their mother.

In Brooklyn the depression had kept the St. Hills from realizing their financial goals. However, in 1934, after seven years, Ruby St. Hill went back to Barbados to retrieve her children. When the children returned to Brooklyn, they were introduced to their baby sister, Selma, born while they were in Barbados. Returning to New York was hard. After years of living in warm and beautiful Barbados, the transition to New York was difficult. ''That first winter, they shivered in a cold-water apartment. Its only heat came from the kitchen coal stove'' (Scheader, 13).

The return was made easier by caring and stimulating parents. Charles, the father, was an impressive man who, despite only finishing the equivalent of the fifth grade, read voraciously. He read several newspapers a day in addition to anything else he could get his hands on; in later years, Shirley Chisholm recalled that ''if he saw a man passing out handbills, he would cross the street to get one and read it'' (*Unbought,* 13). During these early years, his daughter grew to idolize him and his effect upon her was lifelong. His influence surely was the beginning of her interest in black rights, for her father was a follower of Marcus Garvey. Garvey was an early black leader who believed that ''black is beautiful'' and sought to maintain racial purity, uplift, and solidarity. Her mother also had a profound impact upon her life; she worked to make her daughters renaissance women: ''We were to become young ladies—poised, modest, accomplished, educated, and graceful, prepared to take our places in the world'' (*Unbought,* 13). Although living in the depression, her parents sought to provide the best they could for their daughters. They paid for lessons and bought a new piano on time. An environment such as this could not help but stimulate the children toward greatness.

Chisholm's initial experience in New York schools was opposite to the positive situation in Barbados. A sixth grader in Barbados, Chisholm was placed in grade Three-B with children two years her junior due to a deficiency in her knowledge of American history and geography. However, she eventually was provided with a tutor and in a year and a half, she caught up to her peers. During her high school years, her mother kept a tight rein on her, forcing her to develop good study habits. This allowed her to graduate with a high enough grade point average to draw several scholarship offers, including ones from Vassar and Oberlin. However, finances forced her to enroll in Brooklyn College.

Living in the black community of Barbados insulated young Shirley from the growing racial tensions of the United States. Even upon her return to Brooklyn, she was not in a racially charged situation. She grew up in a primarily white, Jewish neighborhood, with a small minority population thatwas well integrated into the community. In 1936 the family moved to Bedford-Stuyvesant. The new area contained a more racially balanced community. Approximately half of the area residents were black. However, with a greater potential for black strength, tensions ran higher; here Chisholm first began to hear racial slurs and become cognizant of the race lines. These developments continued to lead her toward a sense of black consciousness.

Brooklyn College was a period of immense growth for Shirley Chisholm. She chose to become a teacher, believing there was no other career option for a young black woman. She, however, majored in psychology and minored in Spanish. During her sophomore year, she joined the Harriet Tubman Society. This group had a profound impact on Shirley Chisholm's ideas; she says, ''There I first heard people other than my father talk about white oppression, black racial consciousness, and black pride'' (*Unbought,* 23). As her college career progressed, her immense abilities became evident. Shirley Chisholm later recalled, ''More and more people, white and black, began to tell me things like, 'Shirley, you have potential. You should do something with your life''' (*Unbought,* 25). Her belief that she needed to do something important strengthened, not changed, her resolve to become a teacher. She believed she could better society by helping children; however, she also had a growing desire to assist in altering the treatment of her race. It was during this period that the seed for a political career was first planted. It was done by a blind, white political science professor, Louis Warsoff. He was one of Chisholm's favorite teachers and suggested she ought to go into politics. At the time, however, this seemed impossible to her, for she responded, ''You forget two things. I'm black—and I'm a woman'' (*Unbought,* 26). But the seed, not yet ready to sprout, was planted.

Upon receiving her diploma, Chisholm began looking for a job. Despite her graduation cum laude from hunting was difficult. Small and young-looking, she did not look old enough to be a teacher and was repeatedly told so. Ella

Hodges, of the Mount Calvary Child Care Center in Harlem, hired her on probation, and she then ended up staying seven years. During this time, she also enrolled in Columbia University night school to seek her master's degree in early childhood education. At Columbia she met a graduate student who had recently migrated from Jamaica. His name was Conrad Chisholm. During their early conversations, he attempted to convince her there was more to life than work. "The one attribute of Conrad's that particularly caught Shirley's fancy was his ability to get her to give up her day-to-day plans in order to be with him" (Flynn, 203). The following year they were married. This was to be a strong and happy marriage. Conrad was a perfect match for the outgoing, ambitious, driven Shirley. "A compactly built, easy going West Indian, he has said he is quite willing to work behind the scenes and let his wife be 'the star in our family'" (Christopher, 256). Conrad was a private investigator; because Shirley feared for his safety in this line of work, she encouraged him to obtain employment from New York City as a Medicaid claims investigator.

In contrast with her later success, Shirley Chisholm's entrance into politics was decidedly unspectacular. During her college years, she attended a few meetings of the Seventeenth Assembly District Democratic Club. She remained a member of this organization for a number of years, performing minor but important tasks. During her senior year, she was introduced to Wesley Holder. He was a black man from Guiana who worked to elect black candidates from black districts. It was with him that she first received a taste of political success—even if vicariously. "In 1953 Mac Holder formed a group he called the Committee for the Election of Lewis S. Flagg, Jr. Flagg, an outstanding black lawyer, was running for the district seat on the municipal court bench " (Chisholm, *Unbought*, 34). Against all odds, this campaign succeeded. Holder was not satisfied but hoped to go on to greater achievements. To this aim, he formed a new political club. "He tried to hold the Flagg Committee together by turning it into the Bedford-Stuyvesant Political League" (*Unbought*, 35). Unfortunately, this was not meant to be. The organization, after only marginal success, was riddled by strife over a hard-fought campaign for the presidency between Holder and Chisholm. Holder won, creating a rift between him and Chisholm and forcing her out of the league. His success was short-lived, marred by the dissolution of the league several months later. Temporarily, and for the first time in many years, Shirley Chisholm was out of the political arena.

Her hiatus, however, lasted only a few years. In 1960 she helped to form the Unity Democratic Club. Its plan was to defeat the Seventeenth Assembly District political machine and take over the district. While pushing for reform, the Unity Democratic Club teamed with the Nostrand Democratic Club to push for the election of two committee members. Despite good showings, both men were defeated. With long-range planning, the groups were more successful in 1962. Both their candidates were elected and control of the Seventeenth Assembly District fell to them. This victory would be particularly important when in 1964 their candidate was appointed to the bench. A new candidate for assemblyman had to be chosen. Shirley Chisholm immediately began campaigning for herself. Despite opposition, she was selected to replace him as their candidate in the upcoming election. The campaign was difficult. She recalls that "it was a long, hard summer and fall. I won by a satisfying margin, in a three-way contest, with 18,151 votes to 1,893 votes for the Republican, Charles Lewis, and 913 votes for the Liberal, Simon Golar" (*Unbought*, 54). As a result of her victory, Shirley Chisholm spent the next four years in the New York State Assembly. Her baptism in public life began.

Career as Public Servant Begins

Shirley Chisholm began her service in the New York State Assembly with flare, quickly establishing her own independence from the state party structure. At the beginning of her first term, there was a highly-contested race for party leader between Anthony Travia, the former minority leader, and Stanley Steingut. Bucking expectation, Shirley Chisholm sided with Travia, one of only two Brooklyn assemblypersons to do so. She also was an active legislator. Two of her bills are particularly noteworthy. The first created a SEEK program, which made it possible for disadvantaged young people to go to college. Her other bill created unemployment insurance for domestic and personal employees. During her tenure, she won acclaim. "The Associated Press called us [her and Percy Sutton] two of the most militant and effective black members of the Assembly" (*Unbought*, 61). With this experience behind her, she was ready to move on to the next challenge.

The Congressional campaign was made possible by the correction of an old evil. When the Supreme Court ordered redistricting because of previous gerrymandering, a primarily black Twelfth District of New York was created. Shirley Chisholm was the choice of a citizens committee, which interviewed many candidates. She was chosen for her independent and indomitable spirit. She entered into a primary race with William Thompson, the party machine candidate, and Dolly Robinson. Facing odds like these, she needed a miracle and she got Mac Holder. Her former mentor called and offered his assistance. With his assistance as well as that of others, and with hard work, she began campaigning; "I didn't have the money for a conventional congressional campaign; I had to make up for it with hard work" (*Unbought*, 69). The rigorous schedule paid high dividends. She won by about one thousand votes following a small voter turnout. The Republican candidate was James Farmer, the former national chairman of CORE, the Congress of Racial Equality. His campaign was well staffed and financed. About the time his nomination was announced, Shirley Chisholm became seriously ill. She was diagnosed as having a massive tumor. It was benign, but surgery was still necessary. In late July, she underwent surgery for removal of the tumor. After a short convalescence and with Conrad's help, she began campaigning again. Assistance was offered by many women's organizations, particularly after Farmer began to turn the campaign into a gender issue. Despite Farmer's money and his attempt to use her sex against her, Chisholm was too powerful. In the November election, Shirley Chisholm beat him decisively. "He had the Liberal endorsement, but even so I drew 34,885 votes to his 13,777 combined" (*Unbought,* 77). Washington was the next stop for Congressman Chisholm.

Chisholm quickly demonstrated that the rebelliousness that she displayed in the New York State Assembly was still prevalent. "Her House tenure started in controversy in 1969 when House leaders put her on the Agricultural Committee, believing they were doing her a favor because of the committee's jurisdiction over food stamps" (Ehrenhalt, 827). She demanded to be taken off this committee, feeling that it was not where she could best serve her constituency. Surprisingly, she was successful in her attempt and was switched to the Veterans' Affairs Committee. She stayed on this committee for only two years, for in 1971 she switched to the Education and Labor Committee, which is where she wished to be. Here is an example of Shirley Chisholm learning to work within the system, for the appointment may have been part of a deal. "She was widely believed to have won that assignment by supporting Hale Boggs of Louisiana in his successful campaign for majority leader against the more liberal Morris K. Udall of Arizona" (Ehrenhalt, 827). On that committee she campaigned for the poor, working for minimum wage increases and federal subsidies for day care centers, a bill that President Ford vetoed. Even before this, Congresswoman Chisholm had decided it was necessary to change the power structure from the top. Thus, she had campaigned for the United States presidency.

She was the first black and the first woman to seek a major party nomination for President. She ran for the nomination in 1972. She began the race like all her previous political ventures, as a poorly-funded and hard-working underdog. This time, however, her work ethic and drive were not enough to succeed. She attempted to put together a coalition of blacks, feminists, and other minority groups, but this effort failed. She failed even to win the support of the Congressional Black Caucus, creating a rift between her and them. By the time the convention rolled around, a loss was already assured. Chisholm went to the 1972 convention with 24 delegates.

In the end she got 151 votes, released to her by Hubert H. Humphrey and other candidates who had given up on the "stop George McGovern" campaign (Ehrenhalt, 827). Her campaign cannot be deemed a true failure because of the ground-breaking nature of the endeavor. "In terms of black politics, I think an effect of my campaign has been to increase the independence and self-reliance of many local elected black officials and black political activists from the domination of the political 'superstars'" (Chisholm, *The Good Fight,* 162). Never shy to suggest her own importance or the importance of her actions, Shirley Chisholm spoke on the further impact of her campaign:

> The United States was said not to be ready to elect a Catholic to the Presidency when Al Smith ran in the 1920's. But Smith's nomination may have helped pave the way for the successful campaign John F. Kennedy waged in 1960. Who can tell? What I hope most is that now there will be others who will feel themselves as capable of running for high political office as any wealthy, good-looking white male (Chisholm, *Good Fight,* 12).

Despite whatever future political ramifications the campaign had, it was ultimately unsuccessful.

She remained in Congress, moving up the seniority ladder. In 1977 she moved to the powerful House Rules Committee. Furthermore, she was elected secretary of the Democratic Caucus, a largely honorific post. In 1980 she went against tradition, and she and two Democrats joined the committee's Republican members to force a floor vote on a bill calling for twice-yearly cost-of-living raises for federal retirees. She voted this way despite intense lobbying from Speaker Thomas "Tip" O'Neal. A more important disappointment to her party is her failure to support strict environmental laws that she feels would cost people jobs. However, as the years have passed, she has gradually become a more loyal party member. In her first two years in Congress, she only supported the party on 97 of 127 bills. In 1979 and 1980, she voted the party way on 154 of 163 bills. Both ways, this proud woman fought for what she thought was best.

The years passed and Shirley Chisholm gained more power in Congress. Her increasing length of tenure moved her up in the seniority system. Also, her position in the House of Representatives was safe. Even during the late seventies, when the conservatives were beginning to win elections, her power base in the Twelfth District remained secure. Her personal life was not as uniformly successful: "In February 1977 Shirley St. Hill Chisholm surprised the public again when she and Conrad Chisholm were divorced. Drifting apart for a long time, they agreed to end their almost thirty-year marriage" (Scheader, 113-114). She, however, did not remain single for long. Later that same year she remarried. This time she wed Arthur Hardwick, Jr., a black businessman she had first met ten years earlier when both of them were in the New York State Assembly. In 1979 he was almost killed in a car accident. During his convalescence, she was regularly called away to perform her Congressional duties. However, these demands began to weigh heavily upon her. "Her husband's accident and the new conservative climate in Washington prompted Shirley to think about her own goals" (Scheader, 116). On February 10, 1982, Shirley Chisholm announced her retirement.

Upon retirement, she still remained active. She remained an active participant of the lecture circuit. Furthermore, she became the Purington Professor at Mount Holyoke College. There she quickly became at home in her new surroundings. She taught classes in political science and women's studies. In 1985 she was visiting scholar at Spelman College. In 1986 Arther Hardwick died of cancer. Following the 1987 spring semester, she retired from teaching. This is not the end of her story.

When Jesse Jackson started his campaign for the presidency in 1984, Shirley Chisholm began working for him. With more time available, her support increased for his 1988 campaign. In the eyes of many, his campaigns were a direct result of her earlier attempt. "His [Jackson's] New Jersey chairman, Newark Mayor Sharpe James, credited Shirley for paving the way. 'If there had been no Shirley Chisholm, there would have been no 'Run, Jesse, run,' in 1984 and no 'Win, Jesse, win' in 1988, said James" (Scheader, 121). Working for the Jackson campaign was not the extent of her political activities.

National Political Congress of Black Women Formed

Following several disappointments at the 1984 Democratic Convention, Shirley Chisholm was determined to continue the struggle. She gathered nine black women together. This led to a major four-day convention of five hundred black women. They created a new organization, the National Political Congress of Black Women (NPCBW). Shirley Chisholm was chosen as its first leader. The group grew fast, with 8,500 members in thirty-six states by 1988. By this point, it was beginning to wield some real political power. "The group sent a delegation of 100 women to the 1988 Democratic National Convention to present demands for promoting civil rights and social programs" (Scheader, 123). Thus, Chisholm has remained a potent force in politics.

Who's Who Among Black Americans lists many of her affiliations and honors. Shirley Chisholm has been active in the League of Women Voters, the Brooklyn Branch of the NAACP, the National Board of Americans for Democratic Action, and Delta Sigma Theta Sorority. She has been on the advisory council of the National Organization of Women and an honorary committee member of the United Negro College Fund. Among her many awards are numerous honorary degrees, a listing on the Gallup Poll of Ten Most Admired Women in the World for three years, and recognition by Clairol in its 1973 "Woman of the Year" Award for Outstanding Achievement in Public Affairs (236).

Among her many achievements, her most lasting may be her books. She has written two autobiographical works. The first, *Unbought and Unbossed,* details her early life and her rise, culminating in her election to the House of Representatives. The second book, *The Good Fight,* details her unsuccessful run for the 1972 Democratic party nomination. Both works express her self-confidence in her ability and her beliefs and hopes for the future of blacks and women.

Shirley Chisholm has been a maverick her entire life. She has never accepted the role society created for her. By rebelling, she has achieved many great things. She has been elected to offices and honored with awards and degrees. But they are not what she feels is important:

> I do not want to be remembered as the first black woman to be elected to the United States Congress, even though I am. I do not want to be remembered as the first woman who happened to be black to make a serious bid for the presidency. I'd like to be known as a catalyst for change, a woman who had the determination and a woman who had the perseverance to fight on behalf of the female population and the black population, because I'm a product of both, being black and a woman (Scheader, 124).

References

Brownmiller, Susan. *Shirley Chisholm, A Biography.* Garden City, N.Y.: Doubleday, 1970.

Chisholm, Shirley. *The Good Fight.* New York: Harper and Row, 1973.

———. *Unbought and Unbossed.* Boston: Houghton Mifflin, 1970.

Christopher, Maurine. *America's Black Congressmen.* New York: Crowell, 1971.

Ehrenhalt, Alan, ed. *Politics in America: Members of Congress in Washington and At Home.* Washington, D.C.: Congressional Quarterly, 1981.

Flynn, James J. *Negroes of Achievement in Modern America.* New York: Dodd, Mead, 1970.

Scheader, Catherine. *Shirley Chisholm: Teacher and Congresswoman.* Hillside, N.J.: Enslow Publishers, 1990.

Who's Who Among Black Americans, 1990/1991. 6th ed. Detroit: Gale Research, 1990. 236.

Alan Duckworth

Septima Clark

(1898-1987)

Educator, humanitarian, civil rights activist

Septima Poinsette Clark was born on May 3, 1898, in Charleston, South Carolina, the second of eight children of Peter Porcher Poinsette and Victoria Warren (Anderson) Poinsette. For her years of dedication to the cause of black literacy, black voter registration, and women's and civil rights, Clark was to become known as the "queen mother" of the civil rights movement.

Clarks father, Peter Poinsette, was born a slave on the plantation of Joel Poinsette, who brought the poinsettia plant

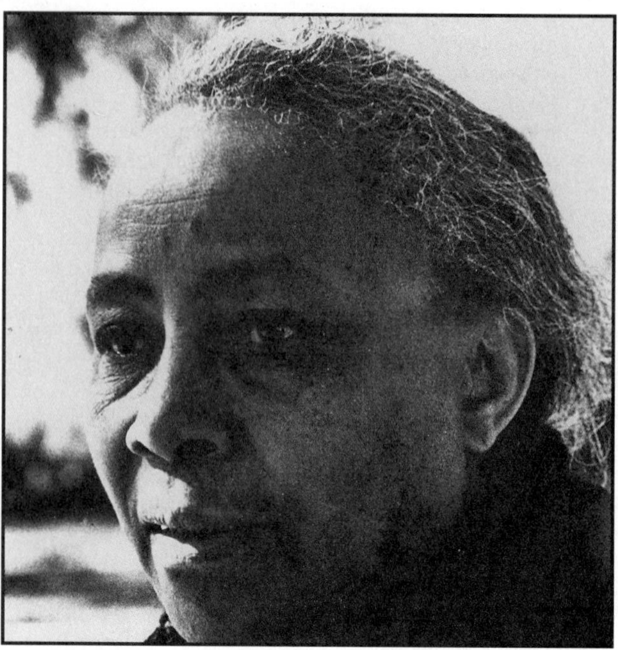

Septima Clark

from Mexico when he was United States ambassador there. Peter Poinsette worked in the plantation house and came out of slavery at the end of the Civil War, when he was about eighteen, a tolerant, non-embittered person. He became a cook on ships with the Clyde Line that plied from New York to Miami. Clark's mother, Victoria Warren Anderson, was born in Charleston, but raised in Haiti by older brothers who were cigar makers. There she learned to read and write from English teachers, which made her a fiercely proud person. Her family moved to Jacksonville, Florida, when she was eighteen; she married Poinsette and moved with him to Charleston, where he became a caterer while she took in laundry at home.

Peter and Victoria Poinsette named their second child Septima after a sister of Victoria's, Septima Peace. Although *septima* is the Latin word for seventh, in Haiti it means sufficient, hence her aunt's name meant "sufficient peace." People always had difficulty pronouncing "Septima"; sometimes they placed accent on the first syllable, sometimes on the second. Even as a child, Septima gathered younger children together for outings, so she gained the nickname "Little Ma" or "Le Ma." As an adult, she was often known as "Miss Seppie."

Clark was sent to private school from first to third grade, then to public school from fourth to sixth, then to Avery Normal School, a private school for educating black teachers operated by the American Missionary Association. After she finished ninth through twelfth grade there, her teachers wanted her to attend Fisk University, but her parents were unable to afford it.

Clark Begins to Teach

Since black teachers were forbidden to teach in the public schools of Charleston and worked only in the surrounding communities, Clark began her teaching career at Promise Land School on Johns Island in 1916. For three years she taught one room of fourth through eighth graders how to read and write, using no materials except pencils and paper for the children, brown-paper dry-cleaners bags (in place of a blackboard), and single copies of books from the Charleston Library. Evenings she taught adults who wanted to read the Bible or organizational handbooks, and she joined the National Association for the Advancement of Colored People (NAACP).

For a year Clark returned to teach in Charleston at Avery Institute; that year the local NAACP chapter decided to try to change the state law to permit black teachers in public city schools. Clark, with her private school class, went door to door collecting signatures from parents who wanted black teachers; legislators were convinced and changed the law in 1920.

On May 23, 1920, the young teacher married Nerie Clark, a sailor she met in Charleston. He had grown up in the mountains of eastern North Carolina and worked in the navy as a cook. She married against the wishes of her mother, who objected to Clark's darker color and to not knowing enough about him. Clark had two babies, one who died after twenty-three days and one healthy boy named Nerie. The marriage ended with the husband's death from kidney failure about 1924. Clark never married again, feeling that no other man would treat her son properly.

Leaving the baby with her parents-in-law in Hickory, North Carolina, Clark returned to Johns Island to teach for three more years, then moved to Columbia, South Carolina, which offered better income and opportunities. In the seventeen years she stayed in Columbia, she took summer courses at Columbia University in New York City and Atlanta University under W. E. B. Du Bois, and received her bachelor's degree from Benedict College and her master's from Hampton Institute (now University) in Hampton, Virginia. In addition, she was active in many clubs and civic groups, learning to organize programs of all kinds in an atmosphere more democratic than Charleston had been, with its rigid caste patterns that did not permit Clark to associate with lighter, upperclass blacks because of her lowly origin. In Columbia she worked with the NAACP to secure equal pay for black teachers; usually they received about half of what white teachers were paid. The NAACP sent attorney Thurgood Marshall, who took the case put together by the local chapter to federal court and won.

In 1947 Clark returned to Charleston to care for her mother, who had suffered a stroke. During the ensuing years she taught remedial reading in grades four through seven and worked in civic organizations, including Alpha Kappa Alpha sorority, Centenary United Methodist Church, and the black YWCA. In 1947 a local white judge of the federal district court, Julius Waties Waring, ruled that blacks must be permitted to vote in the Democratic primary. Admiring this stand, Clark invited Waring's wife to speak at the YWCA and began to attend dinners at their home. Her courage was greatly tested, for white society completely ostracized the Warings, and blacks began to shun Clark for stirring up trouble.

Highlander Folk School Provides New Outlet

About 1950, a coordinated legislative attack by white southerners against the NAACP began throughout the South. In 1954 the South Carolina legislature barred teachers from belonging to the NAACP. Clark tried unsuccessfully to fight this law and, refusing to deny her membership, lost her job just four years short of retirement. Unable to find employment anywhere in South Carolina, she moved in June 1956 to Highlander Folk School, fifty miles northeast of Chattanooga, Tennessee, as director of education.

Highlander Folk School had been in operation for twenty-four years as a retreat and planning center for community activists. Founded by Myles Horton, it focused during the thirties and early forties on serving labor unions, especially in the textile industries. Highlander refused to obey segregation laws and customs, not even for unions; it became one of the few places in the South where blacks and whites could meet, eat, and sleep under one roof.

Clark began going to Highlander Folk School in 1954. By the summer of 1955 she was directing the workshop on the United Nations, which was attended by Rosa Parks of Montgomery, Alabama. Parks, secretary to the Montgomery chapter of the NAACP and mother figure to the teenagers of the NAACP Youth Council, had never been in a situation of racial equality before going to Highlander. Clark made a powerful impression on her:

> I am always very respectful and very much in awe of the presence of Septima Clark because her life story makes the effort that I have made very minute. I only hope that there is a possible chance that some of her great courage and dignity and wisdom has rubbed off on me. When I first met her in 1955 at Highlander, when I saw how well she could organize and hold things together in this very informal setting of interracial living, I had to admire this great woman. She just moved through the different workshops and groups as though it was just what she was made to do, in spite of the fact that she had to face so much opposition in her home state and lost her job and all of that. She seemed to be just a beautiful person, and it didn't seem to shake her (Brown, *Ready From Within*, 16-17).

Among the people Clark had been taking to Highlander from Johns Island was Esau Jenkins, who wanted to help black islanders learn to read so they could register and elect him to office. Clark, Jenkins, and Horton collaborated on resolving the problem and in January 1957 opened a citizenship school on Johns Island, which later served as the prototype for such schools all over the South. The "school" met in rooms behind a community-owned grocery store in the evenings; it used no textbooks, only materials that adults wanted to read, such as order forms from Sears Roebuck and selections from the state constitution required for registration. Perhaps most important, the citizenship school hired as its teacher a beautician, Bernice Johnson, rather than a professional educator. Within three months all fourteen members of the first class had registered to vote, and soon five schools, all supervised by Johnson, were operating on the off-shore islands.

Clark coordinated the citizenship schools program from Highlander, going out to contact ministers and other local leaders all over the South to persuade them to establish citizenship schools. She brought prospective teachers to Highlander, where she taught them the methods of listening to people's concerns, using materials as texts, analyzing community problems, and discussing how blacks could assume more local power. By the spring of 1961, eighty-two teachers who had been trained at Highlander were holding classes in Alabama, Georgia, South Carolina, and Tennessee.

A crisis occurred on July 31, 1959, when Tennessee state police made a raid on Highlander while Clark was in charge, attempting to find evidence they could use to revoke Highlander's charter and close it down. After a trial in which Clark was harassed while on the witness stand, the state closed Highlander and in December 1961 auctioned off all its property without compensation.

Horton had anticipated the closing of the school and had negotiated with Martin Luther King, Jr., to transfer the sponsorship of citizenship program from Highlander to the Southern Christian Leadership Conference (SCLC), founded in March 1957. Clark moved to Atlanta and set up her training sessions at the Dorchester Cooperative Community Center in McIntosh, Georgia. She and two other SCLC staff-members—Dorothy Cotton and Andrew Young—drove all over southern states bringing busloads of students to the Dorchester Center. Many of the South's black leaders, such as Fannie Lou Hamer and Hosea Williams, became aware of the political situation in their area through their experience at the Dorchester Center and with the citizenship schools.

At the Dorchester Center, Clark used the practical methods she had been developing for more than forty years. In mathematics class, she taught how to figure out seed and fertilizer allotments. In literacy classes she worked upward from street signs and newspapers to the portions of the state constitutions required for voter registration. Her great gift lay in recognizing natural leaders among the poorly educated masses—midwives, old farmers and draymen, grandmothers who had pushed children and grandchildren through school—and imparting to them her unshakable confidence and respect.

In 1962 the SCLC joined four other groups—the Congress

of Racial Equality (CORE), the NAACP, the Urban League, and the Student Non-Violent Coordinating Committee (SNCC)—to form the Voter Education Project. In the next four years, all these groups together trained about ten thousand teachers for citizenship schools. During this period almost seventy thousand black voters registered across the South. After the Voting Rights Act passed in 1965, registration increased rapidly and at least one million more black people registered by 1970. Two years later they elected the first two blacks since Reconstruction to the U. S. Congress—Barbara Jordan from Texas and Andrew Young, who helped Clark set up all those citizenship schools.

Clark Leads in the Women's Movement

Clark realized that discrimination occurred not only between blacks and whites, but between rich and poor, old and young, men and women. All her life she defended the rights of women, encouraging them on Johns Island and in black churches in Montgomery and elsewhere, criticizing the ministers of the SCLC for their lordliness, speaking at the first national meeting of the National Organization of Women (NOW).

Clark was emphatic in her belief that the civil rights movement grew out of the women's movement, not the other way around, as is commonly interpreted:

> Many people think that the women's liberation movement came out of the civil rights movement, but the women's movement started quite a number of years before the civil rights movement. In stories about the movement you hear mostly about the black ministers. But if you talk to the women who were there, you'll hear another story. I think the movement would never have taken off if some women hadn't started to speak up. A lot more are just getting to the place where they can speak out. This country was built up from women keeping their mouths shut. It took fifty years for women, black and white, to learn to speak up. I had to learn myself, so I know what a struggle it was (Brown, 82-83).

When Clark retired from active SCLC work in the summer of 1970, she was presented with the Martin Luther King, Jr., Award, "for Great Service to Humanity." Other honors included a Race Relations Award from the National Education Association in 1976, a Living Legacy Award from President Jimmy Carter in 1979, and South Carolina's highest civilian award, the Order of the Palmetto, in 1982.

After she retired, Clark had to fight for her pension and back pay. When she was fired in 1956, all her retirement funds in the state pension were canceled. By 1976 the National Education Association was airing her case all over the United States, and soon the state legislature decided to pay her an annual pension of $3,600. Lawyers advised Clark that the state still owed her a salary from 1956 to 1964, what she would have earned if she had not been unjustly fired. She refused to press legal charges, although she sent letters to most of the legislators and to NAACP attorneys. In July 1981 the state legislature approved paying her back salary.

Clark celebrated her seventy-eighth birthday by winning election to the Charleston School Board; she served two terms before turning it over to younger leadership. She had many friends all over the United States from her days traveling to raise funds for Highlander Center. In 1980, 1984, and 1986 she flew to California to be honored, and in 1987 she was driven to Philadelphia to receive an American Book Award for her second autobiography, *Ready from Within: Septima Clark and the Civil Rights Movement*. A few months before her death on December 15, 1987, a photograph was taken of her that became the cover for the book *I Dream a World: Portraits of Black Women Who Changed America* by Brian Lanker.

Clark Called "Queen Mother" of the Civil Rights Movement

At her funeral many leaders testified to the significance of Clark's life. The mayor of Charleston, Joseph P. Riley, Jr., said that "her purity is everlasting and universal; her legacy is everywhere." Sometimes known as "Mother Conscience," she was also known and loved as the "queen mother" of the civil rights movement. Reverend Joseph E. Lowery, president of the SCLC, testified: "Like Harriet Tubman, who led her people to freedom through territorial pilgrimages, Septima Clark led her people to freedom through journeys from the darkness of illiteracy to the shining light of literacy" (Barney Blakeney, 1)

Taylor Branch, author of *Parting the Waters: America in the King Years 1954-1963*, dedicated that book to the memory of Septima Clark, whom he considered "one of the most powerful impacts on the whole scene" "Writing an American Epic," *Christian Science Monitor*, 3 February 1989). Branch saw Clark's character as:

> a miraculous balance between leathery zeal and infinite patience. Clark was a saint even to many of the learned critics who predicted she would fail. A professor visiting Highlander complained that John Lewis was not a suitable leader—he stuttered, split his infinitives, had poor reading patterns. 'What difference does that make?' she asked. All that would come, she said. Besides, the people he needed to lead already understood him. . . . As always, she worked both sides of the gaping class divide without letting the friction ruin her spirits (Branch, 264).

Clark faced class and caste discrimination all her life, even within the black community. As the daughter of a slave and a washerwoman, she was not invited to the homes of the mulatto community of Charleston, nor was she ever invited to the King's Atlanta home. Furthermore, most of Clark's family, neighbors, and colleagues believed that she was causing trouble and considered her way ahead of her time. When she was fired, her sorority, Alpha Kappa Alpha, gave her a testimonial dinner to honor her work, but no sorority sister stood beside her for a photograph for fear of losing her job by being associated with Clark.

In physical appearance Clark reflected her mixed ancestry. Her father was pure African, since his mother was pregnant with him when she was brought over on a slave ship. Her mother was medium brown with soft straight black hair, since her father was a Muskhogean native American from the sea islands. Medium dark brown in color, Clark's hair was partly kinky, incurring the disapproval of her mother. As an adult, Clark usually wore a wig. A sturdy, active person accustomed to working hard all her life, she suffered arthritis during her last years, but became frail and ethereal only during her last months after a series of strokes.

Clark's influence has even now not been fully recognized. With her combination of zeal and patience, she bridged the chasm between poor and middle-class African-Americans. She served as a crucial link between King and the grassroot; while King and the SCLC preachers preached, she translated their ideas into action. With her quick understanding, acceptance of frailty, and identification of strength, she learned to bridge every human chasm.

References

Blakeney, Barney. "Mourners Recall Extraordinary Life of Septima Clark." *Charlston Post and Courrier* (20 December 1987) 1.

———. "Literacy and Liberation," *Freedomways* (First Quarter, 1964): 113-24.

Branch, Taylor. *Parting the Waters: America in the King Years 1954-1963*. New York: Simon and Schuster, 1989.

———. "Writing an American Epic." *Christian Science Monitor* (3 February 1989).

Brown, Cynthia S., ed. *Ready from Within: Septima Clark and the Civil Rights Movement*. Navarro, Calif.: Wild Trees Press, 1986.

Clark, Septima P. *Echo in My Soul*. New York: E. P. Dutton, 1962.

Derkes, Scott. "Dat Not Be My Echo," *South Carolina Wildlife* 26, 4 (July/August 1979): 44-49.

Gallman, Vanessa. "Septima Clark: On Life, Courage, Dedication." *View South* 1, 4 (July/August 1979): 13-16.

Glen, John. *Highlander, No Ordinary School*. Lexington, Ky.: University of Kentucky Press, 1989.

Lanker, Brian. *I Dream a World:* New York: Stewart, Tabori and Chang, 1988.

Tjerandsen, Carl. *Education for Citizenship: A Foundation's Experience*. Santa Cruz, Calif.: Schwarzhaupt Foundation, 1980.

Collections

Clark's papers are held in the College of Charleston, Charleston, South Carolina. Also helpful are the Papers of Highlander Research and Education Center, State Historical Society of Wisconsin, Madison. Interviews with Clark are: Eugene Walker, July 30, 1976, and Jacqueline Hall, June 25, 1981, Southern Oral History Program Collection, Southern Historical Collection, University of North Carolina, Chapel Hill; and Peter Wood, February 3, 1981, and Eliot Wigginton, June 29, 1981, Highlander Center Archives, Newmarket, Tennessee.

Cynthia Stokes Brown

Alice Coachman

(1923-)

Athlete

"I've always believed that I could do whatever I set my mind to do," Alice Coachman told an *Essence* magazine reporter. "I've had that strong will, that oneness of purpose, all my life. . . . I just called upon myself and the Lord to let the best come through." And come through it she did. Coachman became the first black woman to win an Olympic gold medal in track and field.

Coachman was born on November 9, 1923, in Albany, Georgia. She discovered her love for sports while in the Monroe Street Elementary School, when she and her friends tied strings of rope together and practiced seeing how high they could jump. When she wasn't challenged enough, though Coachman took on the boys at a local playground. "They'd challenge me at jumping high. They never could beat me." Such play worried her parents, who wished their daughter to be more ladylike; but Coachman loved the rough-and-tumble and paid no attention. Despite the spankings her parents occasionally administered to discourage her wild ways, Coachman kept running off to the competition of the playground. "It was a rough time in my life," she told *Essence*. "It was a time when it wasn't fashionable for women to become athletes, and my life was wrapped up in sports. I was good at three things: running, jumping, and fighting."

Fortunately, Coachman's fifth-grade teacher, Cora Bailey, recognized the young athlete's potential and began to encourage it in a more formal way. When Coachman entered Madison High School in 1938, she easily made the track team under coach Harry E. Lash. Her remarkable abilities soon attracted the attention of Tuskegee Institute recruiters, and both of her former coaches encouraged her to enroll there for the coming academic year. The next summer, when she was only sixteen, she was invited to compete for Tuskegee in the women's track and field national championship, even before attending her first class.

In her childhood, Coachman had dreamed her fame might come on the stage, for she had been strongly influenced by her two favorite entertainers—the white movie star Shirley Temple and the black jazz saxophonist Coleman Hawkins. But after she won a first place in the AAU high jump in 1939, she understood she could find celebrity in the sports she had so long loved and nurtured: "The Lord saw that he wanted me to be known by the abilities he gave me . . . through jumping" (Albany *Herald*), She later recalled that this first national competition in Waterbury, Connecticut, was her biggest thrill: "That first medal, in Connecticut, was probably the greatest. I'd never been anywhere, and I just loved the sights along the way. It was all so new" (Albany *Herald*).

In 1940 Coachman entered Tuskegee Institute High School, where her skills could be nurtured under the guidance of women's track coach Christine Evans Petty and coach Cleve Abbitt. By the time Coachman graduated in 1943, she had already won national fame; in that year alone she won the AAU nationals in both the running high jump and the fifty-yard dash. She continued at Tuskegee Institute working toward a trade degree in dressmaking, which she received in 1946. By that time, she held four national track and field championships: the fifty and hundred-meter dashes, the four-hundred-meter relay, and the running high jump. While at Tuskegee she also played basketball—so tenaciously, in fact, that as an all-conference guard she led her team to three straight SIAC women's basketball championships.

Coachman's six years at Tuskegee were marked by great national honors, but with World War II raging in Europe she was denied the chance to prove herself in international competitions. When she transferred to Albany State College in 1947, it was to continue both her education and her athletic career in American track and field. Two years later, in August 1949, she graduated from Albany State with a bachelor's degree in home economics.

By the time she entered Albany State, Coachman was a national figure in women's track and field. She had become the one to beat during the women's national championships of 1945, when she had finally overcame her chief rival, the Polish-American superstar Stella Walsh, by winning both the hundred-meter dash and the high points trophy. At the same meet Coachman again won in her specialty—the running high jump—using her unique form of jumping that she called neither western roll nor straight jumping but rather "half and half." She did not attribute her accomplishments to superior style, however. "I trained hard," she told the Albany *Herald*. "I was sincere about my work. As I look back I wonder why I worked so hard, put so much time into it—but I guess it's just I wanted to win. And competition was very tough. You had to be in shape to win" (Albany *Herald*).

Since the last Olympiad had been held years before in 1936, Coachman was not thinking particularly about international competition, but the officials for the U.S. women's team were. They invited her to join the American team for the London Olympics of 1948. Although her back was sore and even the thought of overseas travel made her homesick, she decided to compete: "I was the country's best prospect, and I couldn't let my country down." For the five previous years she had been the only black on the All-American Women's Team, and while several other black women represented the United States in 1948 (including two-hundred-meter specialist Audrey Patterson, whose third place finish would make her the first black woman to become an Olympic medalist), Coachman remained something of a loner on the trip over.

Coachman recalled in an *Essence* magazine article that she was shocked when she arrived in England to discover "my picture was everywhere and everyone seemed to know all about me. All those people were waiting to see the American girl run, and I gave them something to remember me by."

Coachman Wins Olympic Medal

The young woman who took the field in London was five feet eight inches tall, weighed 130 pounds, and was pretty enough that the Baltimore *Afro-American* described her as a comely girl "with a gracious and pleasing personality" (Baltimore *Afro-American*). But more to the point, she was a superior athlete with a fighting heart that proved its worth after she injured her hip in the high jump preliminaries: "That was the toughest victory I ever won. Those girls from Europe jumped from odd angles. Every time I jumped a distance they came back and matched it." Finally, in the finals, on her first jump, Coachman soared over the bar set at five feet six and one-eighth inches. The jump was a new Olympic record and gave her the American women's team's only gold medal of the competition.

Returning to America in triumph, Coachman was introduced to President Harry S. Truman. As she told a reporter for the *Afro-American* "I felt good for my family, for my Albany, Georgia, home, for my school, and for my fellow Americans who are privileged to live in this land of opportunity" (Baltimore *Afro-American*; reprinted, Albany *Times*). The major American newspapers had failed to notice her achievements, but in Georgia she was given a motorcade ride from Atlanta to Macon, where she was welcomed by the chief of police, who was standing in for the mayor. She was happy to be home, and she knew that her own people, at least, appreciated her accomplishments.

The Olympics over, Coachman left athletics at the pinnacle of her career. She took up teaching high school physical education in Albany, Georgia, and married N. F. Davis (whom she later divorced). As the mother of two children, son Richmond and daughter Diane, she continued to coach young athletes who were probably only dimly aware of her trailblazing accomplishments: twenty-five AAU national titles, twelve straight years as national high jump champion, the first black female Olympic gold medalist, and member of the National Track and Field Hall of Fame (1975).

In an era when too many American women held an ideal of femininity antithetical to hard work and fierce competitiveness, Coachman was different. When she was asked by a reporter for the Macon *Telegraph* why European women outperformed American women at the Olympics, Coachman replied that they were "just better athletes, that's all." But on reflection, she added that she also supposed they worked harder than American women. She could have been speaking about herself, for that was Coachman—a combination of talent and hard work—who attempted to "Let the best come through."

References

Afro-American, Baltimore, n.d.

Bernstein, Margaret. "That Championship Season." *Essence* 15 (July 1984): 59, 124, 128.

Herald (Albany), 13 March 1974; 16 August 1984.

Jackson, Tenley-Ann. "Olympic Mind Power." *Essence* 15 (July 1984): 63.

Telegraph, (Macon) 2 September 1948.

Times, Albany, 28 March 1979.

Collections

Photographs and news clippings of Alice Coachman (Davis) are available in the Fisk University Library Special Collections.

William D. Piersen

Jewell Plummer Cobb

(1924-)

Biologist, educator

Jewell Plummer Cobb's contributions as scientist, educator, and administrator have been immortalized by the hanging of her photograph in the National Academy of Sciences in Washington, D.C., and by the naming of residence halls for her at Douglass College, Rutgers University, and at California State University, Fullerton.

Cobb was born in Chicago, where she grew up as an only child in an upper middle-class home where the emphasis was on the concerns and accomplishments of black people nationwide. Her father, Frank V. Plummer, was born in Washington, D.C. He graduated from Cornell University, where he was one of the founders of Alpha Phi Alpha Fraternity. After he completed medical training at Rush Medical School in Chicago in 1923, he began practicing in that city, serving the great wave of newly-arrived black migrants from the South. He set up an office at Fifty-ninth and State streets, a streetcar transfer point for commuting stockyard workers. This made it convenient for them to use the transfer time allowance to visit the doctor without paying an additional transportation fare and without a special trip into town.

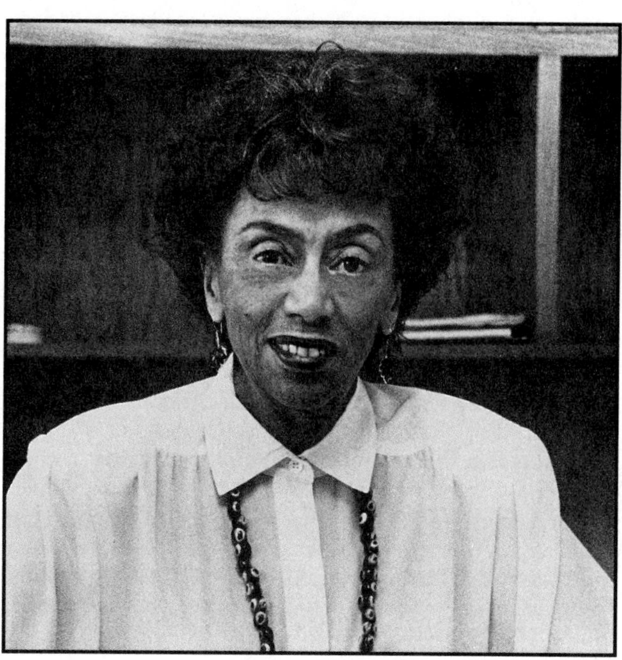

Jewell Plummer Cobb

Cobb's mother, Carriebel (Cole) Plummer, moved with her family as a child of three from Augusta, Georgia, to Washington, D.C. She studied interpretive dancing, which had been made famous by Isadora Duncan, at Sargeants, a physical education college affiliated with Harvard University. After she and her husband settled in Chicago she worked as a teacher of dance in the public schools and in Works Projects Administration (WPA) projects. She later enrolled in the Central YMCA College (which became Roosevelt University) and received a bachelor's degree the same year that her daughter graduated from Talladega College.

Cobb has enjoyed an upper middle-class status but is aware of the limitations that are placed on black people in the United States. From her earliest memory she heard discussions of racial matters—the hopes and frustrations of her family and their associates. She became familiar with the aspirations, successes, and talents of black people. Her mother was a friend of historian Carter G. Woodson and writer/librarian Arna Bontemps, and her uncle, Bob Cole, was a musician, a well-known producer of musicals in New York. Allison Davis, the famous black anthropologist, lived in their apartment building in Chicago, as did Alpha White, the director of the YWCA. Other important black American artists and professional people lived in the vicinity. Cobb never lost sight of the fact that she was a black person living in a white-dominated society. Through the years the Plummer family changed their place of residence more than once, always to a better location, and always after the white population had fled, thereby making a choice part of the city available to minorities for the first time.

As a young person Cobb had the advantage of her father's home library, a comprehensive collection of material about black Americans, scientific journals and magazines, and periodicals of current events. Her mother took her to the ballet and to see *Porgy and Bess* in New York City when she was four. For the summer months Cobb went with her parents to Idle Wild, a resort in northern Michigan, where black people who were financially comfortable maintained homes around a scenic lake. Year after year, at the end of the school session, she met friends there, peers who were sons and daughters of the privileged class of black Americans. These friends were typical of the young people who were her friends in public school and in college. Although Cobb had white friends in the somewhat racially mixed public schools, the focus of her social life was Saint Edmunds Episcopal Church in Chicago, where she was confirmed, took communion, and sang in the choir.

Decades later Cobb learned about the gerrymandering of the school districts in Chicago to prevent extensive integration by black children. In one instance the removal of the non-white students resulted in enough space to found a community college in the building. Cobb's friends, like her, were well-motivated young people who took their studies seriously. There were black students in her school who studied science, but none among her close circle of friends. Some were attracted to economics and other social sciences, and a number wanted to become teachers.

In spite of the covert racial segregation that was apparent in her schools, Cobb felt that her pre-college education was good and that it gave sufficient preparation for the demanding studies that lay before her. All through public school she was a member of the honor society. There was no question about her continuing on to college; the only decision to be made was which college. Based on her excitement and exhilaration when she first looked into the lens of a microscope, she had chosen a career as a biologist in her sophomore year of high school. She was further stimulated by Paul Dekruif's intriguing book, *Microbe Hunters* (Blue Ribbon Books, 1926). Consequently she added a year of biology to the mandatory graduation requirement.

After high school Cobb decided to attend the University of Michigan because she had many friends from Idle Wild who were going there, and she was attracted to the glamour of the Michigan football team led by Tom Harmon. At that time, in 1941, the dormitories were segregated so that all black students, undergraduate as well as graduate, were required to live in one house.

At the end of the third semester, with the encouragement of Hilda Davis, dean of women, Cobb transferred to Talladega College, Talladega, Alabama. Talladega did not accept transfer credits, but students were allowed to take examinations for completion of a course whenever they felt prepared to satisfy course requirements. Cobb entered an accelerated program in which she took summer classes, had private sessions, and took examinations. She graduated three and a half years afterward, in 1944, with a major in biology. Because of the wartime call for college-age men into the armed forces, of the thirty-two graduates only four were men.

Having been awarded the baccalaureate degree, Cobb accepted the advice of a Talladega professor and enrolled in New York University. Before she left Talladega she had applied to New York University unsuccessfully for a teaching fellowship there. However, when she appeared at the institution, armed with her excellent credentials and poise, she was offered a fellowship that she held for the next five years. From 1944 to 1950 she continued as graduate student and teaching fellow, working toward the master's (completed in 1947) and doctorate (completed in 1950), both in cell physiology. With the Ph.D. in physiology from New York University, Cobb was ready to begin her career in science, education, and administration.

Cell Biologist Begins Research

Rather than going into a medical career, Cobb elected to work in biology because of her preference for the theoretical research approach to biology as opposed to the pathological approach. She considers herself primarily a cell biologist and not a molecular biologist. While the major concerns of the molecular biologist are atoms and molecules that are minute in size when compared with a cell, the cell biologist observes the action and interaction of living cells that are the components of our living bodies.

Cobb is most interested in tissue culture of cell biology; cells are grown outside of their native habitats—in test tubes or flasks—and studied under microscope. The research project that she is most proud of in her scientific career involved growing human tumors in culture at the Cancer Research Foundation. With Dorothy Walker Jones (then Cobbs's research assistant, and now a professor in the graduate school at Howard University in biology) Cobb studied the effects of newly discovered cancer chemotherapy drugs on human cancer cells. The results of this work are still valued in medical research. In addition, Cobb has conducted pioneering laboratory work in the study of drugs used with cancer treatment.

Within cell biology, Cobb's concentration is pigment cell research, specifically, melanin, a brown or black pigment that colors skin. She was interested in melanin's ability to shield human skin from ultraviolet rays, and the possibility that it evolved in Africa. All of Cobb's investigative work after the doctorate had some involvement with melanin, mostly with melanoma, a usually malignant tumor on the skin. Her research included work on mouse melanoma at Sarah Lawrence and Connecticut colleges.

Because of Cobb's love of things scientific, she continued her research for many years after entering college administration. She found teaching satisfying, but preferred the laboratory. She was able to do research, teach, and perform the duties of dean concurrently at Sarah Lawrence College and at Connecticut College. Cobb would spend the first morning hours in the laboratory. From there she went to the administrative office, and then devoted the remaining hours of the work day to the classroom. At Douglass College, the rigors of being dean of the college forced her to give up the investigative work, but she taught tissue culture for three of the five years of her tenure there.

While Cobb has done no research work since she went to Douglass College in 1976, she reads research literature regularly and is committed to the advancement of the study of the sciences by groups that are underrepresented in those fields: women and minorities. She has seriously considered the "reasons behind the fact that women, who constitute 52 percent of the population, make up only 20 percent of the scientists but less than one percent of the engineers" (Cobb, 236). In the article, "Filters for Women in Science," which appeared in the *Annals of the New York Academy of Sciences* in 1979, Cobb likened the situation of women to a filter, a familiar tool in the research laboratory, through which a filtrate passes according to the filter's pore size. She spoke of women as the filtrate that must pass through filters that have smaller pores than those for men.

In the article, Cobb called for a meaningful change in the well-ingrained assumptions about the role of women in society and their ability to successfully complete a course of study in the sciences. She listed a number of remedies—her own, and those of others—starting with support for girls in elementary through high school to broaden their interest and guide them into the sciences. Among the steps that can be taken providing positive information about the study of science.

For women who are already in college, Cobb endorses the informal meetings for discussion between established women scientists and women undergraduates and graduates. Other suggestions involve special funding for the needs of women in graduate study, such as assistance for young mothers who want to teach part-time.

Cobb is saddened by the knowledge that in one recent year, in all of the universities in the United States, there were only four doctorates in mathematics awarded to black American candidates. But she is very proud of the privately funded pre-medical and pre-dental programs for minority students, which she founded at Connecticut College. It served approximately forty students, with about ninety percent being accepted into medical or dental schools. Unfortunately it was dropped by the president of the college after Cobb left Connecticut. However, this model program has been duplicated at more than twenty colleges across the country.

As Trustee Professor at California State College, Los Angeles, Cobb is involved in the consortium of six colleges in the Long Beach Basin, financed by a grant from the National Science Foundation, to motivate minorities to study science and engineering. The strategy is to obtain corporate support to replace federal money, which is not expected to last much longer. At the same time Cobb is wrestling with how best to bring about an increase in the number of minority students in mathematics and science. The college faculty has volunteered time for one-on-one tutoring and for personal relationships with the students. The administration knows that the students must have a firm foundation in mathematics, a crucial prerequisite for entry into the scences.

Cobb's pleasure in football is tempered by a longing to see a number of young black men in the laboratories equal to that on the football field. She is sure that the disparity is not due to a lack of ability. On the contrary, it requires considerable discipline and brainpower to learn, retain, and execute the intricate football or basketball plays—to think in split-second increments of time. The tragedy is that there has not been a proportional commitment to use these skills outside the world of sports.

Scholar/Researcher Named College President

Of all of her professional appointments, the most rewarding to Cobb was the presidency of California State University, Fullerton. There she established the first privately-funded gerontology center in Orange County, lobbied the state legislature for the construction of a new engineering and computer science building and a new science building, installed the first president's opportunity program for students from ethnic groups that are not fully represented on campus, and made the change from a strictly commuter campus to one with an apartment complex for student residences, named in honor of Cobb.

Jewel Plummer Cobb was married in 1954 to Roy Raul Cobb of New York and divorced in 1967. They had one son, Roy Jonathan Cobb, who was born in 1957. By the time her son was fourteen, Cobb had given him her father's stethoscope and the collapsible field microscope that he had used as a medic in World War I. The young man kept the microscope in his room examining such things as grass and dirt, and used the stethoscope to listen to the heartbeats of living things. On Saturday mornings he would go to his mother's laboratory at Sarah Lawrence College. From Phillips Exeter prep school Ray went to Wesleyan College, graduated with a major in biology, and then went to Cornell Medical School for the M.D.

There is a strong history of medical and scientific study in Cobb's family, beginning with her paternal grandfather, Robert Francis Plummer, who graduated from Howard University in 1898 as a pharmacist, followed by her father, Frank V. Plummer, the medical doctor. Cobb represents the third generation. The fourth generation is Cobb's son, Roy, a New Jersey radiologist who specializes in magnetic resonance images.

Among Cobb's prestigious appointments are: post-doctorate fellow, National Cancer Institute, 1950-1952; instructor, Anatomy Department, University of Illinois College of Medicine, 1952-1954; professor, biology department, Sarah Lawrence College, Bronxville, New York, 1960-1969; dean of Connecticut College and professor of Zoology, 1969-1976; dean of Douglass College and professor of Biological Sciences, 1976-1981; president, California State University, Fullerton, October 1981-July 1990; president emeritus, California State University, Fullerton, and Trustee Professor, California State University system, July 1990 to the present.

Cobb's research experience has been in cancer cell biology, with human tumors and cancer chemotherapeutic agents. Her studies were concentrated on human and other mammalian melanomas, and the effects of cancer chemotherapeutic agents and hormones on human and mouse melanomas in tissue cultures. She spent a research sabbatical in 1967 at Laboratorio Internazionale di Genetica e Biofisica, Naples, Italy.

Awards and citations include: Key Pin Award for scholarship, outstanding woman alumna of 1952, Graduate School of Arts and Science, New York University; member, Sigma Xi National Honorary Science Society; member, the Institute of Medicine of the National Academy of Sciences; and holder of the Douglass Medal of Douglass College Rutgers University. Two other distinguished honors are the naming of the Bunting-Cobb Mathematics and Science Hall for Women, Douglass College, and the naming of the Jewel Plummer Cobb Residence Halls, California State University, Fullerton. The selection of her photograph to hang in the National Academy of Sciences as a distinguished black scientist is a tribute to Cobb and her scholarship. Ten honorary doctorates have been awarded to Cobb.

Cobb is the author of forty-six publications, thirty-seven of scientific content, and nine dealing with issues associated with minorities and/or women.

References

Cobb, Jewel Plummer. "Filters for Women in Science." *Annals of the New York Academy of Sciences.* Vol. 323, 1979.

Cobb, Jewell Plumber. Interview with author, 9 January 1991.

Collections

The personal papers of Jewell Plummer Cobb are housed in the Schomburg Center for Research in Black Culture, New York City.

Dona L. Irvin

Johnnetta Betsch Cole

(1936-)

Educator, anthropologist

Johnnetta Betsch Cole, educator, anthropologist, and the first black woman president of Spelman College, was born October 19, 1936, in Jacksonville, Florida. In the community of higher education administrators, Cole is seen as an effective advocate for the liberal arts curriculum and knowledgeable about keeping it rigorous and relevant to a changing world. She is also known as a magnetic and affirmative force in the lives of her students. In her first interview with Johnnetta Cole after the announcement about her assuming the presidency at Spelman College, Paula Giddings indicated that Cole "has a sensibility born of an affectionate middle-class family, a supportive Black community and the unforgotten pain of the segregated South of the 1940s" (Giddings, 35).

Cole's maternal great-grandfather, Abraham Lincoln Lewis, cofounded the Afro-American Life Insurance Company of Jacksonville in 1901. Her father, John Betsch, Sr., worked with Atlanta Life Insurance Company but later joined his wife's family business, Afro-American Life. Mary Frances (Lewis) Betsch, Johnnetta Betsch's mother, an educator and graduate of Wilberforce, taught English and was registrar at Edward Waters College before joining the

Johnnetta Betsch Cole

family insurance business after her husband's death. Johnnetta Betsch Cole has an older sister, Marvyne Betsch, an Oberlin graduate, and a younger brother, John Thomas Betsch, Jr., a jazz musician living in Paris, France.

Cole spent her formative years in Jacksonville and entered Fisk University in the summer of 1952 at age fifteen under the school's early admissions program. She went to Fisk because of strong encouragement from her parents and high grades on the entrance examinations. It was here that she met Arna Bontemps, librarian, which was her first daily contact with someone who wrote books. It was here also, she recalls, that "the world of the intellectual is what Fisk really did trigger for me" (Giddings, 56). After only one year at Fisk, however, she left and joined her older sister, who was a student at Oberlin College. During her first year at Oberlin (1953) she took an anthropology class on racial and cultural minorities taught by George Eaton Simpson, which inspired her to major in sociology and pursue a career in anthropology. Simpson's discussion of the retention of African culture in the New World was to have a profound impact on Cole's intellectual development and subsequent academic interests.

Her interest in anthropology was sparked in part because it was new and unfamiliar. "I became an anthropologist in a sense because then I was *exposed* to a possibility, because there was an option out there that I had never dreamed of" (Giddings, 57). Later when she went home and informed her grandfather that she wanted to be an anthropologist, a most unusual professional aspiration for an African-American woman during the 1950s, he was startled and looked at her and exclaimed, "What's THAT!" He was really saying "Why that?" because he had every expectation that she would join the family insurance business. Cole stood her ground because she really wanted to become an anthropologist who "studies people and understands us and goes away and lives with these people—and in my case it would be to go to Africa, and understand Africa. And then to finally understand what happened to us here" (Giddings, 57). She also attributes her earlier love of learning to her first grade teacher, Bunny Vance, and to Olga Bradham, her mother's closest friend and head librarian of the "colored" branch of the Jacksonville public library. Other black women who influenced her when she was young were Martha Berhel, librarian at Bethune-Cookman College, and Marian Speight, a romance languages professor at Bethune-Cookman. She also knew Mary McLeod Bethune, president of Bethune-Cookman College, and actually heard her tell the story of how she founded the institution and became its president. Her earliest role models were clearly black women schoolteachers, librarians, a college president, and her own mother, also an educator.

After graduation from Oberlin in 1957, Johnnetta Cole went to Northwestern University to pursue a master's degree in anthropology, which she earned in 1959. She continued her graduate study as a doctoral student there and also met Robert Cole, a fellow graduate student and the white son of a dairy farmer from Iowa. They married in 1960 and when he came to Jacksonville to meet Cole's parents, threats from the white community indicated that the family's insurance company would be bombed, and the family would suffer. The first two years of Cole's marriage to economist Robert Cole were spent in Liberia, where they worked together on research for their respective dissertations. He conducted economic surveys and she engaged in fieldwork in the villages and towns of that West African nation. In 1962 their first son, David, was born in Monrovia. Johnnetta and Robert Cole returned to the United States in 1962, and Robert took a teaching job at Washington State University. Johnnetta Cole worked part-time, had a second son, Aaron (1966), and completed her dissertation on "Traditional and Wage Earning Labor in Liberia." In 1965 she was named Outstanding Faculty Member of the year at Washington State.

She was awarded the Ph.D. in anthropology in 1967 from Northwestern University, where she studied under the noted anthropologists Melville J. Herskovits and Paul J. Bohannan. Later she joined the faculty at Washington State, where she was assistant professor of anthropology and director of black studies, a program that she helped to create. She stayed at Washington State until 1970, when she was offered a tenured faculty position at the University of Massachusetts, Amherst, where she was also invited to play a critical role in the ongoing development of their Afro-American Studies program. Robert taught economics at Amherst College and the University of Massachusetts; a third son, Che, was born in 1970; finally, after twenty-two years of marriage, Robert and Johnnetta Cole divorced in 1982.

For thirteen years, Cole remained at the University of Massachusetts, Amherst, where she was assistant professor of Afro-American Studies, later full professor of both Afro-American Studies and anthropology, and later provost of undergraduate education (1981-1983). When the full history of the development of black studies in the American academy is written, Johnnetta Cole's important role in its evolution will surely be mentioned. Her association with *Black Scholar* during this same period is an important manifestation of her interest in the development of the new discipline of black studies as well.

After a distinguished career at the University of Massachusetts at Amherst, Cole was named 1983 Russell Sage Visiting Professor of Anthropology at Hunter College of the City University of New York. From 1983 to 1987 she was a full professor in the anthropology department and from 1984 to 1987 she was director of the Latin American and Caribbean studies program. In 1986 she was appointed to the graduate faculty of the City University of New York. Previously, she held two visiting posts—one at Williams College during the winter study term, 1984 and 1985, as Luce Visiting Professor, and in 1986 as visiting professor of women's studies at Oberlin College. Speaking about her achievements at the University of Massachusetts before going to Hunter, she sums up by alluding to an "opening up of the college" through "increased interchange with other institutions in the Pioneer Valley—opening up the exclusive club of the faculty to other groups; opening up the curriculum to include a broader spectrum of the human experience'' (Bateson, 71).

While at Hunter College, her landmark book, *All American Women* (1986) was published, breaking new ground in women's studies because of its sensitivity to the intersections of race, ethnicity, class, and gender. Cole started thinking seriously about gender on her first visit to Cuba with a delegation of African-Americans. Widely published during her outstanding academic career, her scholarship focuses on cultural anthropology, Afro-American studies, and women's studies. Her fieldwork includes studies of a South Side Chicago black church, labor in Liberia, racial and gender inequality in Cuba, Caribbean women, female-headed households, the ways women age, and Cape Verdean culture in the United States. A rich source of biographical information on Cole can be found in *Composing a Life,* written by her friend and colleague, Mary Catherine Bateson, the anthropologist and daughter of Margaret Mead. Bateson and Cole were faculty colleagues at the University of Massachusetts, Amherst. The text is an analysis of Bateson's own life and those of four friends, all of whom faced ''discontinuities and divided energies, yet each has been rich in professional achievement and in personal relationships—in love and work'' (Bateson 15-16). The portrait that emerges is the result of Bateson's ten-day stay at Reynolds Cottage, the president's residence, shortly after Cole was named president of Spelman College in 1987.

Spelman Names First Black Woman President

On April 5, 1987, Johnnetta Betsch Cole was named the first black woman president of Spelman College, the oldest institution of higher learning for black women in the United States. Shortly thereafter, she gained the affectionate title of ''sister president,'' a label she gave herself in the first published interview during her presidency that appeared in *Ms.* magazine in October 1987. She came to the presidency at midpoint in a career that spanned significant scholarship and distinguished administration. William Strickland, director of the W. E. B. Du Bois Collection and assistant professor of political science at the University of Massachusetts, Amherst, where Cole had spent thirteen years, asserted that she would bring a new style of leadership. ''Her gift is her vision, which is non-narrow, nonchauvinistic, and internationally humane.'' She represents much more hope than is common in most leaders. The students at Spelman describe her as ''approachable, accessible, visible, and a real sister who cares about us'' (Edwards, 74).

In 1987 when Cole assumed the leadership of Spelman College, the 107-year-old liberal arts college for black women, it was her hope that scholars, teachers, artists, policy analysts, and community leaders would turn to Spelman for comprehensive information on the rich and diverse history, struggles, conditions, and accomplishments of black women. In fact, she intended to help Spelman become a renowned center for scholarship by and about black women and also the premier institution for educating and nurturing black women leaders from around the world.

In December 1988, Cole married a childhood friend, Arthur Robinson, Jr., in Reynolds Cottage. A public health administrator, Robinson brought to their new family two sons, Arthur J. III, and Michael. Johnnetta Cole Robinson is now the mother of five sons and the surrogate mother of 1700 Spelman daughters.

Widely recognized as a leader, Johnnetta Betsch Cole is former president of the Association of Black Anthropology and the International Women's Anthropology Conference. She has been included in *Who's Who in Black America* and *Who's Who of American Women.*

Johnnetta Cole holds board of directors' appointments with the following organizations: American Council on Education, Association of American Colleges, Atlanta Chamber of Commerce, Citizens and Southern Georgia Corporation, Council on International Educational Exchange, The Feminist Press, The Global Fund for Women, The Points of Light Initiative Foundation, and The Study Hall and Emmaus House. She is a member of the board of trustees of her alma mater, Oberlin College, and is a member of the executive board of the Fulton County Blue Ribbon Commission on Teenage Pregnancy. She is a member of the advisory boards of Atlanta Women's Network, Center on Violence and Human Survival, Sisterhood in Support of Sisters in South Africa, and she is on the executive committee for Campus Compact. Her editorial board appointments are with *Anthropology and Humanism Quarterly, Black Scholar* (advisory and contributing editor), *Emerge* magazine (editorial advisory board), and *SAGE: A Scholarly Journal on Black Women.* She is also a columnist for *McCall's* magazine.

She is a member of the Atlanta Rotary Club; Coalition of 100 Black Women, Atlanta Chapter; Council on Foreign Relations; Delta Sigma Theta Sorority; National Council of Negro Women; National Political Congress of Black Women; Smithsonian Council; the Utopian Literary Club; and the Women's Foreign Policy Council. She is a fellow of the American Anthropological Association.

Cole's academic and professional honors include: The American Woman Award from the Women's Research and Education Institute, 1990; the Jessie Bernard Wise Woman Award, Women's Policy Institute, 1990; Essence Award, Education, 1989; Working Woman Hall of Fame, 1989; Candace Award, Education, National Coalition of 100 Black Women, 1988; Elizabeth Boyer Award, Women's Equity Action League (WEAL), 1988; and Woman of the Decade Award, The Women's Leadership Institute of Avila College, 1988. She has received honorary degrees from the following institutions: Bates College, Dennison University, Fisk University, Grinnell College, Macalester College, New York University, Princeton University, Southeastern Massachusetts University, The College of Wooster, and the University of Massachusetts.

Johnnetta Betsch Cole edited *Anthropology for the Nineties: Introductory Readings* (Free Press, 1988) and *Anthropology for the Eighties: Introductory Readings* (New York:

Free Press, 1982). She is author of the following articles and publications: "What If We Make Racism a Woman's Issue," *McCall's* 118 (October 1990), pp. 39-40; "The Making of the Cuban Nationality," *In Cuba: A View From Inside* (New York: Center for Cuban Studies, 1985); "On Racism and Ethnocentricism," with Elizabeth H. Oakes, an Afterword to *The Changelings*, by Jo Sinclair (New York: The Feminist Press, 1985), pp. 339-47; Foreword, *Student Culture and Activism in Black South African Universities*, by Mokubung O. Nkoma (Westport, Conn.: Greenwood Press, 1985); "Vera Mae Green (1928-1982)," *American Anthropologist*, 84 (1982), pp. 633-35; guest coeditor with Sheila S. Walker, Fall and Winter 1980 issues of the *Black Scholar* on Afro-American Anthropology (included in the issues are "An Introductory Essay," with Walker, and "Race and Equality: The Impact of the Cuban Revolution on Racism," 1980); "Militant Black Women in Early U. S. History," *Black Scholar*, (1978), 38-44; "Soul and Style," in *Festac '77* (official book of the Festival of African Arts and Culture, Nigeria, 1977, African Journal, Limited, Kirkman House, London, England, and the International Festival, Tkoyi, Lagos, Nigeria); "The Black Bourgeoisie," in *Through Different Eyes*, Peter I. Rose, Stanley Rothman and William J. Wilson, eds. (New York: Oxford University Press, 1973), pp. 25-43; "Black Women in America: An Annotated Bibliography," *Black Scholar*, 3 (1971), pp. 42-43; "Culture Negro, Black and Nigger," *Black Scholar*, 1 (1970), pp. 40-44; and "Growth Without Development," with Robert W. Clower and others, (Evanston: Northwestern University Press, 1966).

References

Bateson, Catherine. *Composing A Life*, New York: The Atlanta Monthly Press, 1989.

Bernstein, Alison. "Johnnetta Cole: Serving By Example." *Change Magazine* 19 (September/October 1987): 45-55.

Edwards, Audrey. "The Inspiring Leader of Scholars and Dollars." *Working Women* 14 (June 1989): 68-74.

Giddings, Paula. "A Conversation with Johnnetta Betsch Cole." *SAGE: A Scholarly Journal on Black Women* 5 (Fall 1988): 56-59.

———. "Johnnetta B. Cole, 'Sister President.'" *Essence* 18 (November 1987): 35.

McHenry, Susan. "Sister President." *Ms.* 16 (October 1987): 58-61.

McKinney, Rhoda E. "'Sister' Presidents." *Ebony* 43 (February 1988): 82-88.

Collections

Numerous newspaper articles have appeared throughout the country on the presidency of Johnnetta Betsch Cole. In addition, the Spelman *Messenger*, the official publication of the college, contains information on her presidency since 1987. Photographs are available from Spelman College as well as copies of her speeches, papers, and other items

Beverly Guy-Sheftall

Rebecca J. Cole

(1846-1922)

Physician

For blacks in the 1860s, the outlook for a career in the medical profession was anything but bright. Black women who went into medicine, however, did not let gender or race deter them from their quest for knowledge. They met the tests, confronted the prejudices, and prevailed. Rebecca J. Cole was one who dared to enter the white, male-dominated medical field.

Born on March 16, 1846, in Philadelphia, Pennsylvania, Cole was the second of five children. According to the 1880 census records, all the members of her family were listed as mulattos. The oldest sister, Sallie E. married Henry L. Phillips, a clergyman from the West Indies, and they had a son and a daughter, Harry L. and Rebba, both born in the West Indies. Cole's other siblings were Hamilton, an upholsterer, Dora J., a schoolteacher, and Joseph W., a government clerk. The Cole children occupations indicate that each received a good education, which enabled them to be more than domestic manual laborers.

In 1863 Cole graduated from the Institute for Colored Youth, which was located in Philadelphia. Richard Humphreys, a Quaker, had provided ten-thousand dollars in his will to begin this school for blacks, which was chartered by the state of Pennsylvania in 1842. Its purpose was to educate and improve "colored youth of both sexes, to qualify them to act as teachers and instructors of their own people" (Report of the Board of Managers). While at the institute, Cole received a ten-dollar prize "for excellence in classics and mathematics, and for diligence in study, punctuality of attendance, and good conduct" (*Annual Report*, 1862, 15). After graduation, she taught for a short time before matriculating, in 1864, at the Female Medical College of Pennsylvania (now known as The Medical College of Pennsylvania). Little is known about her life as a medical student, except that to fulfill a graduation requirement she wrote a thesis titled *The Eye and Its Appendages*.

In 1867, the fifteenth annual commencement of the medical college. was held. When Cole received her medical degree at this time, she became the second black female physician in America and the first black woman to graduate from the Female Medical College of Pennsylvania. Cole then went to New York, where she was appointed resident physician at the New York Infirmary for Women and Children.

Cole Addresses Needs of the Poor

Elizabeth Blackwell, the first American woman to receive a medical degree, had established the first hospital owned and run by women physicians. The New York Infirmary for Women and Children had opened its doors on May 7, 1857. In addition to the usual departments and dispensary practices, Blackwell started a sanitary visitor program in her hospital. The physician assigned to the duty of sanitary visitor was to give simple and practical instructions to poor mothers on the management of infants and the preservation of the health of their families. Cole, a valued member of the staff who had been providing her services to patients in the slum area, was assigned to fill this post.

Cole later practiced for a short while in Columbia, South Carolina, and was a superintendent of the Government House for Children and Old Women in Washington, D.C., before returning and settling in Philadelphia. There she established an office, served as superintendent of a home for the homeless, and with fellow physician Charlotte Abby, conducted a Woman's Directory that gave medical and legal aid to women. Cole had practiced medicine for more than fifty years, when she died in Philadelphia on August 14, 1922.

References

Institute for Colored Youth. *Report of the Board of Managers*, 1859.

———. *Annual Report. 1862.*

Kerr, Laura. *Doctor Elizabeth*. New York: Thomas Nelson and Sons, 1946.

Lerner, Gerda, ed. *Black Women in White America*. New York: Random House, 1972.

Collections

The Archives and Special Collections on Women in Medicine, The Medical College of Pennsylvania, contains information on Rebecca J. Cole. Census information is available in the National Archives and in the federal branch in Philadelphia. Data in this biography were selected from the 1880 census, roll no. 1170, Supervisor District no. 1, Enumeration District no. 116.

Margaret Jerrido

Bessie Coleman

(1893-1926)

Aviator

Bessie Coleman, an early aviator, proved and continues to be an inspiration for black aviators—men and women alike. Coleman was born in Atlanta, Texas, on January 26, 1893. Her family moved to Waxahachie, near Dallas while she was still a toddler. When she was seven years old her father, who was three-fourths Indian, moved back to Indian territory, leaving her mother to rear four daughters and a son. Susan Coleman supported her family by picking cotton and taking in laundry, and the children helped her in her work. She could not read or write at that time, but she encouraged her children to learn as much as they possibly could.

When Bessie Coleman finished high school, she wanted to go to college. Her mother let her keep the money she earned from washing and ironing for her college expenses. Coleman enrolled in Langston Industrial College (now Langston University) in Oklahoma. Her money lasted for only one semester, when she had to drop out of school. She then moved to Chicago, where she took a course in manicuring and started working at the White Sox Barber Shop on Thirty-fifth Street near State Street. Later Coleman managed a chili restaurant on Thirty-fifth Street.

Coleman continued to be an avid reader, and she kept abreast of current events and developments. She became interested in the fledgling field of aviation. Always ambitious for new challenges, she decided to pursue a career in aviation and set three goals for herself.

Coleman's first goal was to learn to fly and earn a pilot's license. She became discouraged, though, when all of her applications for admission to aviation schools were rejected. But she was encouraged by Robert S. Abbott, founder and editor of the *Chicago Defender* newspaper, who became her staunch supporter and promoter. At his suggestion, she learned French and went abroad to study aviation. Coleman took flying lessons from French and German aviators. She studied under the chief pilot for Anthony Fokker's aircraft corporation and learned to fly the German Fokker airplane.

When Coleman returned to the United States in 1921, she had earned her pilot's license. After another trip to Europe, she returned in 1922 with her international pilot's license. She was the first black woman to earn pilot's licenses, only ten years after the first American woman had earned a license and less than twenty years after Orville and Wilbur Wright had made the first successful flight in 1903.

Coleman's second goal was to become a recognized stunt

and exhibition flier. Barnstorming was, in fact, the main area of aviation open to women in the United States. This goal she began to achieve immediately. During the Labor Day weekend of 1922 Coleman made her first appearance in the United States in an air show. This event, which took place at Curtiss Field near New York City, was sponsored by Abbott and the *Chicago Defender*. Six weeks later she repeated her performance in Chicago at the Checkerboard Airdrome (now Midway Airport), again under the sponsorship of Abbott. Her manager was David L. Behncke, founder and president of the International Airline Pilots Association.

Coleman Demonstrates Talent in Air Shows

The two air shows were attended by thousands of spectators, who marveled at the daring stunts performed by this petite and attractive young lady. Coleman soon came to be known as "Brave Bessie." She participated in air shows in many cities throughout the United States, including her hometown of Waxahachie, Texas. While in California, she did some aerial advertising for the Firestone Rubber Company. She also gave lectures on the opportunities in aviation at schools and churches wherever she went.

Coleman did not live long enough to achieve her third goal, which was to establish an aviation school where young black Americans could learn to fly and prepare for careers in aviation. The main sources of funds for this endeavor were her barnstorming and lecturing activities. Early in 1926 she wrote to her sister Elois that she was on the threshold of opening this school. But she was not to realize these plans. Coleman met an untimely death on April 30, 1926, at the age of thirty-three.

Coleman was in Jacksonville, Florida, at the invitation of the local Negro Welfare League to perform in an air show for the Memorial Day celebration. On the evening of April 30, she and her mechanic were making a practice run, with her mechanic piloting the plane. During one of the maneuvers the controls of the plane jammed. Bessie Coleman was catapulted out of the plane and fell to her death. One of the last friends she had seen in Jacksonville was Robert S. Abbott, the Chicago newspaper publisher and her supporter. She had chanced to meet him in a restaurant, and they had a happy reunion the day before her death. After services in Jacksonville, Coleman's body was flown to Chicago. Last rites were held at the Pilgrim Baptist Church at 33rd Street and Indiana Avenue, with the burial at the Lincoln Cemetery in southwest Chicago.

Although Coleman did not achieve all of her goals, her pioneering accomplishments were an inspiration to other black men and women who became active in aviation. Within a few years after her death, black fliers were perpetuating her memory through the Bessie Coleman Aero Clubs and the *Bessie Coleman Aero News*, a monthly periodical first issued by these clubs in May 1930, with William J. Powell as the editor. Powell was also the author of a book about black Americans in aviation, *Black Wings* (1934), which had as its frontispiece a photograph of Coleman in her flying uniform. Powell dedicated this book to "the memory of Bessie Coleman . . . who although possessed of all the feminine charms that man admires in the opposite sex, also displayed courage equal to that of the most daring men" (n.p.).

Black men and women aviators also remembered Bessie Coleman every Memorial Day by flying in formation over Lincoln Cemetery and dropping flowers on her grave. In 1975 the Bessie Coleman Aviators organization was formed in the Chicago area by young black American women who were actively interested in aviation and aerospace.

The first monument recognizing black Americans' achievement in aviation from 1917 to 1990 was unveiled in 1990 at Lambert-Saint Louis International Airport. The 51-foot-long mural was done by Spencer Taylor and titled "Black Americans in Flight." It features 75 men and women pioneers in aviation, including Bessie Coleman and Mae Jemison, the first black woman astronaut.

References

Chicago Defender. Various issues published during her career include information on Coleman.

"First Monument Recognizing Black Aviators is Unveiled." *Jet* 78 (3 September 1990): 34.

Goodrich, James. "Salute to Bessie Coleman." *Negro Digest* 8 (May 1950): 82-83.

Holden, Henry M. "Brave Bessie, the Barnstormer." *Sisters* 2 (Spring 1989): 6-8.

King, Anita. "Brave Bessie; First Black Pilot." *Essence* 7 (May 1976): 36; 7 (June 1976): 48.

Patterson, Elois. *Memoirs of the Late Bessie Coleman, Aviatrix (Pioneer of the Negro People in Aviation)*. Privately published, 1969.

Powell, William J. *Black Wings*. Los Angeles: Ivan Deach, Jr., Publisher, 1934.

Robinson, Nancy. "Black Wings Made to Fly." *Sepia* 30 (June 1981): 56-57.

St. Laurent, Philip. "Bessie Coleman, Aviator." *Tuesday* (9 January 1973): 10, 12.

"They Take to the Sky." *Ebony* 32 (May 1977): 88-90.

Penelope L. Bullock

Cardiss Collins

(1931-)
Politician

When Cardiss Hortense Robertson Collins was a little girl, she ran away from home—as far as the front steps, just until evening. Even then, she was beginning to develop the independent yet sensitive spirit that would help her to face the challenges of her life. As she climbed the stairway home, she probably did not dream of walking the steps of Capitol Hill. Yet, as an adult, the streets of Washington and the corridors of its federal buildings have become very familiar to her. One of the major challenges that she has accepted is the task of representing Chicago's Seventh District in Congress. First taking that office in 1973, she became the "first black congresswoman from the state of Illinois" (Harris, 20) and "the fourth black woman to serve in Congress" (*Congressional Quarterly's Guide,* 649). For some time she served alone; "for nearly a decade [she] was the only Black woman in Congress" ("A Black Woman's Place," 104). In her various roles as congresswoman, she has emerged as "a national leader inner-directed enough to move on her own agendas rather than to be buffeted about by the world's agendas" (Poinsett, 64).

Cardiss Hortense Robertson Collins was born in Saint Louis, Missouri, on September 24, 1931. Her father, Finley Robertson, worked as a laborer and her mother, Rosia Mae (Cardiss) Robertson, was a nurse. Cardiss was their only child. She spent part of her childhood in Saint Louis but moved to Detroit, Michigan, when she was ten years old (*Biographical Directory,* 810). There she attended Bishop and Lincoln Elementary Schools and graduated from Detroit's High School of Commerce.

Cardiss Collins

Unable to find a good job in Detroit, Collins moved to Chicago when she was eighteen. She lived with her maternal grandmother and worked first at hand-tying mattress springs in a factory, next as a stenographer with a carnival equipment company, and then as a secretary with the Illinois Department of Revenue. Seeking to advance in her job, she enrolled in evening school at Evanston's Northwestern University, studying accounting. As a result of her efforts, she eventually became an accountant and then an auditor with the department.

But her life did not consist entirely of work and study. Sometime during her career, she met and grew to love George Washington Collins. The two were married in 1958. Collins was a politician, and Cardiss Collins actively supported his endeavors. While retaining her own career and raising their son, Kevin, she helped organize and took part in her husband's campaigns for Democratic committeeman and then alderman in Chicago. Enjoying the involvement in politics, Cardiss Collins eventually added to her other responsibilities the task of representing the Democratic party as committeewoman in Chicago's Twenty-fourth Ward.

George Collins also enjoyed his political responsibility and decided to wage a bigger campaign. Again, his wife supported and assisted him as he campaigned for and carried out the duties of congressman from Illinois' Sixth District, and then the Seventh, in the United States Congress. As a representative, he placed his emphasis on helping people rather than on acquiring distinction for himself. "In Congress, Collins said his aim was to be of service 'in any way' possible to the voters. He kept his district office open six days a week and tried to get back to Chicago every weekend. He spent hours listening to people who lined up to see him about their troubles with poor housing, unemployment, and the spreading drug traffic" (Christopher, 266).

But on December 8, 1972, life ended abruptly for George Collins and changed drastically for Cardiss Collins and her son. On that "rainy, foggy night" Congressman Collins "was hurrying back [to Chicago] to plan the annual Christmas party for the district children. While approaching the airport, his plane [a United Airlines flight] crashed without warning into a residential section and burst into flames. The forty-seven-year-old congressman was killed along with forty-four others" (Christopher, 267-68).

Amidst her grief and the many adjustments to be made following her husband's death, Cardiss Collins had a major decision to make. Chicago's Mayor Richard Daley offered to back her if she would seek to fill the remainder of her husband's term. In some respects, "it seemed natural that she should run for the political office herself after his death" (Harris, 20). But the decision was not an easy one, and she did not have long to deliberate. Still, the idea was difficult for her even to contemplate. She later recalled, "I never gave politics a thought for myself. When people started proposing my candidacy right after the crash, I was in too much of a daze to think seriously about running" (Trescott, "Another," G-4).

She did like the thought of carrying out the work that her husband had begun. She also "felt a commitment to the Democratic party" (Edwards, 85) for its part in her husband's election campaigns. However, her concern for Kevin's welfare overshadowed other considerations: "He was a father's boy; they were very close and talked on the phone every day" (Trescott, "Another," G-4). She talked with Kevin about the decision and discovered that her son was developing his own ability to face challenges. Later, he told a reporter, "When we discussed her coming to Washington, I told her, 'I want you to take his place, to keep the Collins name going.'" Still, Collins was concerned. "Kevin's security was foremost. Kevin knew the sacrifices; I knew the pitfalls. And Kevin didn't want to leave Chicago. So first I had to deal with his stability," she said (Trescott, "Coming," C-3). That stability was provided by Kevin's grandmother. Cardiss Collins stated, "My mother came out of retirement to take care of him for me. She knew she was needed, and I knew he was being well taken care of, and he got a chance to be spoiled by his grandmother" (Edwards, 85).

Congressional Seat Easily Won

In January 1973 Cardiss Collins resigned from the Illinois Department of Revenue, where she had worked for twenty-two years, to embark upon her own campaign for Congress. She won the race, capturing a large majority of the votes, a trend that would continue in future elections. No time elapsed for simply enjoying the thrill of victory. The work began "two days after her election" (Trescott, "Another," G-4). On June 6, 1973, Cardiss Collins began to take action on the kinds of issues that would characterize her stand throughout her terms of office. She "quickly organized her office and started working on a bill to combat credit discrimination against women." Her "first congressional vote was against an amendment disapproving the reorganization of drug-oriented bureaus" (Trescott, "Another," G-4).

Those first days, even the first years, were especially difficult ones. She was learning to live with her grief in a setting that readily prompted memories. "I walk down the corridors of Congress and I'll pass something that reminds me of the past. The conversations will come back. Coming to Congress has been a learning experience, publicly and privately" (Trescott, "Another," G-4). She was adjusting to being away from her son. At one point she stated that if she had to make the decision again, she would not choose the same path: "I was lonely and alone. My son was alone. I regret that lost time." Even after she had survived those first years, she still regretted the separation: "The worst thing was suddenly looking around and discovering Kevin was a man. He had grown up without me. . . . When I returned to my district on weekends, I only saw him asleep. Then when he started dating I saw him at the doorway—he was going out when I was coming in" (Trescott, "Coming," C-3).

Adjusting to life in Congress was no small challenge in itself. Helping her husband in his career had given her some exposure to the system: "My greatest impression of politics before George died was that it was hard work. Now I realize that I learned a great deal just by being around" (Trescott, "Another," G-4). But she still had much to learn: "I guess I must have been a member of Congress all of 24 hours when I realized that, as the wife of a politician, I had just been a political spectator—not really playing the game. The difference started rolling in, like a sledgehammer, believe me'" (Edwards, 102).

Congressional procedures were a mystery to her. "Entering office during the middle of term, Collins missed the orientation given freshmen members of Congress and had to learn the ropes by trial and trauma. 'I had to learn just the elementary things of how to get attention from the chair so I could get up on the floor to talk. . . . I had to learn what was meant by an "open rule" and a "closed rule." Ultimately I'd find myself whispering to the congressmen next to me, 'Now what do you do if you want to do so-and-so?'" Her hardest lesson, she says, was realizing "that I was not in the city of Chicago, which was controlled by a master politician" (Edwards, 102). But having accepted the challenge, Congresswoman Collins conscientiously worked at overcoming the difficulties. In 1979 she reflected, "In the last six years my biggest roadblock has been shyness. I was basically an introvert, but once people learned I had something to say, I gained confidence. But it took a long time to come out of my shell and realize I was here, doing this alone" (Trescott, "Coming," C-3).

Pain was followed by the joy of growth and seeing the results of hard work produced a sense of accomplishment. "To her surprise and delight she found that she loved politics. At the end of her term she told Mayor Daley she'd like to stay on, and she's been in Congress ever since" (Edwards, 85, 102). She has taken seriously her role as representative of the people, and has served in Congress with a clear sense of purpose. In 1977, she stated that her primary objective was "to provide better living and working conditions for people of the Seventh District and other low and moderate income people throughout the country" ("Women in Government," 91). Her commitment to working toward these goals through the political system stems from her belief that her daily tasks are not remote from the lives of people in Chicago or San Francisco or Boston. "'Government,' she says quite simply, 'permeates every aspect of our lives. Once you realize that, you also realize the necessity to participate in a system that is dictating every step you take, every movement you make up or down the ladder'" (Edwards, 85).

Collins Heads Congressional Black Caucus

Perhaps that commitment explains why Collins has been described as "a woman who has traded in her shyness for a more forceful voice and leadership role" (Trescott, "Coming," C-1). She has been unafraid to venture into roles that were new not only to her personally but also to black women. Just two years after beginning her service in Congress, "she was appointed Democratic whip-at-large, the first black and the first woman to hold that party leadership rank" (Glaser, 162). Later, she was elected chairwoman of the House Government Operations Subcommittee on Manpower and Housing—again the first black and the first woman to serve in that capacity. One of her biggest challenges came when her colleagues in the Congressional Black Caucus unanimously elected her to be the first woman ever to lead that group. Such a visible position allowed no room for shyness; as one writer noted: "Rep. Cardiss Collins boldly took the risk of clashing with the Chicago Machine that had elected her to assume the chair of the powerful seventeen member Congressional Black Caucus, whose past leaders have been aggressive in their demands on behalf of the nation's 30 million Blacks" (Reynolds, 36).

"Quietly determined" (Trescott, "Coming," C-3), Chairwoman Collins immediately set about the new task that was before her. "In a matter of days, the Chicago lady, whose hobby is papering the walls and laying tile on the floors of her home, had refurbished the Caucus scenery. She lobbied for a new position of vice-chairperson to reduce 'the enormous load' of the chairperson. . . . She [formed] . . . a new committee to revise the constitution and make provisions for a policy and steering committee to further expand involvement of more members in decision making" (Booker, 30).

Again Collins had specific goals. She thought that the caucus should be "Black people-oriented" (Booker, 30) and that it should be unified in its efforts. Near the end of her two years as leader, one writer reported, "Cardiss says she has been proudest of her ability to help shape the 17 individual caucus members into a more unified body. 'We now speak as a group,' she says" (Edwards, 105). In guiding the group, she carefully avoided singling out her own voice. "Her togetherness theory . . . exploded any prevailing thought that she had a desire to use the position to skyrocket into national prominence. She could do so if she wanted, but Rep. Collins is not that type. She feels that what counts is not notoriety but results" (Booker, 30).

Collins's leadership style helped to create unity. Caucus members appreciated her respect for each person and her ability to give the issues an open hearing. Early in her term of office, one writer emphasized, "Insiders say she has already distinguished herself as a moderator in the group's often-raucous meetings, presiding over debates rather than arguments" (Poinsett, 66). Colleagues praised her sense of balance: "'One of the things that I admire most about her as chairperson is that she is completely democratic,' reports Rep. Parren J. Mitchell (D., Md.), her immediate predecessor. 'Very often chairpersons tend to become kind of autocratic. She almost bends over backwards not to do that. That doesn't mean she can't be tough when she wants to be, but it's a fair hearing always, even though she may have a very firm position on something'" (Poinsett, 66).

Representative Charles Diggs (D., Mich.), who founded the caucus, also gave her a high recommendation. "She is always properly assertive. . . . She uses a general forcefulness but with a degree of sophistication that helps her recognize the personalities and views of the caucus. That's no easy feat!" (Trescott, "Coming," C-3). Her sense of fairness is appreciated outside the caucus, as well. Wayne Grisham, (R., Calif.), who served with her on the Manpower Subcommittee, observed, "During the Community Services Administration hearings, Collins said frankly that these were programs she cared about and that affected her constituents. But at the same time she looked very closely for areas where the government wasn't getting it's money's worth" (Trescott, "Coming," C-3).

As leader of the Black Caucus, Collins did have "a broker's seat at the table of Washington power" (Edwards, 85), and she was unafraid to be "a valuable and independent" leader when necessary (Barone, 362). On behalf of the caucus and the people it represents, she aggressively attacked President Jimmy Carter's proposal for significant budget cuts in social welfare programs. She even threatened the withdrawal of black support. One article reported, "In no previous election season has so formidable a Black leader issued such an ultimatum" ("Rep. Collins Delivers," 6).

In her early days as chairwoman, she had also issued an ultimatum to her colleagues: "We're going to have to be in there fighting for butter, because they're going to give everything to guns. . . . We're likely to lose many of the civil rights gains we made. To the extent that we sit down and accept this, our cause is lost. To the extent that we are vigilant and keep a very watchful eye across the board, we can salvage something." ("Our New Men," 40). Under her vigilant leadership, the caucus let its voice be heard. Due to their efforts, an anti-busing amendment to the Constitution was defeated (Poinsett, 66). Pressure from the Black Caucus forced the cancellation of "Mr. Dugan," a television show they deemed uncomplimentary to blacks (Fleming, 20). They also worked to gain the "District of Columbia full representation in the House and Senate and monitor the 1980 census to see that minorities are not undercounted, . . . hold the Social Security taxes at current levels and press for economic sanctions on South Africa and Rhodesia" (Poinsett, 66).

In addition to chairing the Black Caucus, Collins has also served on a number of important committees in Congress. Speaker Thomas "Tip" O'Neill appointed her to the House Democratic Steering and Policy Committee, "the most powerful of internal House organizations." This organization "determines members assignments, makes nominations for committee chairpersons, makes recommendations concerning party policy and legislative priorities and schedules matters for House action" ("Cardiss Collins Named," 4). She has chaired the Government Operations Subcommittee on Manpower and Housing and has actively taken part in the House Select Committee on Drug Abuse and Control and the House Committee on International Affairs Subcommittee on Africa. Other committee activities include terms on the Government Operations Subcommittee on Government Activities and Transportation and on the Energy and Commerce Committee, "the most sought after assignment for House Democrats" (Barone, 362).

Throughout her terms in Congress, Collins has been careful to do what she asked of the members of the Black Caucus. She has consistently exercised vigilance in watching after the concerns of black Americans and of other minorities as well. She strongly criticized the Reagan Administration for its civil rights policies. She refused to look aside quietly when the United States Justice Department, the Federal Trade Commission, and the National Endowment for the Humanities failed to submit required goals and timetables for hiring women and members of minority groups. Nor has she allowed discriminatory hiring practices among private agencies, such as airlines, and the broadcasting industry to be overlooked. She has sponsored legislation to help small and minority-owned businesses. She has also spoken for a greater awareness of Sickle Cell Anemia and against toothpaste packaging that is uncomplimentary to blacks.

Collins expressed her concern personally in a 1981 *Ebony* article directed specifically to black men and women. Acknowledging the tensions existing between them, she speaks openly about the causes of division and suggests ways to begin working toward a new unity. She states, "If the deterioration of the Black family unit is to be reversed, there must be a return to the mutual love, respect and strong support Black men and women had for each other in former years—the kind of love and trust that held so many Black families together in the most difficult times" (Collins, "Plea," 78). In a 1990 *Ebony* article, she stressed her concern for all American households, stating that the most significant task for the future is to "take responsibility for our families before we have lost them forever" ("45 Years," 68). Once family unity is achieved, she advocates national unity. Blacks must be concerned not only about the welfare of their own families but also about the well-being of people throughout the nation. They can express their concern by exercising their right and responsibility to vote.

Collins sets an example by her own participation in politics. One writer remarks, "Collins is uncompromising when it comes to seeing that the needs of the poor, the elderly, and women be met adequately by government programs. Social legislation has become her major concern" (Stineman, 32). In Chicago "she has used her influence to help establish the first black bank, to bring in funds for more health centers and to provide several thousand new housing units" (Reynolds, 36). Her concern extends, however, beyond the boundaries of her own district to include the whole nation.

Needs of the Poor and Elderly Addressed

One of Collins's top priorities is meeting the needs of the poor. "Addressing hard social policy issues is a must for her if she is to service her district successfully. With a large mass of urban poor in Chicago she must be sensitive to AFDC (Aid to Families with Dependent Children) issues, welfare reform, day care services, supplemental security income, and a host of other social concerns" (Cummings, 40-41).

On behalf of the elderly, Collins has worked for legislation to include the expense of cancer tests as a part of Medicare coverage. She has also supported laws to help protect older Americans against violent crimes. Because of her excellent voting record on issues affecting the elderly, she received a one hundred percent rating from the National Organization of Senior Citizens.

Collins's voting record has also merited a hundred percent "political accountability" rating from the League of Women Voters ("Seven Caucus," 6). She has sought to provide convenient daycare services in government buildings. She introduced a bill to bring the cost of postmastectomy breast prosthesis under Medicare for patients who couldn't afford to pay. She has joined forces with other black congresswomen "on demands for clear, consistent Health, Education and Welfare guidelines for sterilization and for federal curbs on the use of dangerous birth control drugs whose side effects have included sterility" ("Women on Government," 91). She not only does her own part but also encourages other women to be active in politics. "Mrs. Collins appeals to black women to take the lead in melding the forces of the black-led civil rights movement and women's liberation. Negro women, she suggests, can serve as a bridge between the two groups, thereby helping to overcome the white and black males' fear of the aggressive, insistent feminists" (Christopher, 283).

As a woman in Congress, Collins has consistently demonstrated concern for the health and safety of all Americans. In addition to the efforts already mentioned, she has sought to encourage the use of cancer-screening tests and has worked for safe travel on airlines and trains and for international controls on drug trafficking.

Even while encouraging black Americans to vote on issues affecting their own lives, Collins also encourages them to look beyond the boundaries of America. As chairwoman of the Black Caucus, she spoke to an audience of some seven thousand people at an annual fund-raising dinner—an audience that included the notable absence of President Carter, who had not been invited. "Her language alternated between mildness and militance as she defended the citizenship right and responsibility of Blacks to move beyond ghetto politics—as had Martin Luther King, Jr.—toward participation in U. S. foreign policymaking which impacts heavily on their lives" (Poinsett, 63).

Her words and her emphasis became even stronger when people questioned the appropriateness of "Black participation in foreign affairs." She unhesitatingly declared:

> No other ethnically or nationally identifiable group has more right to be involved in foreign decision making than we do. Our history, if nothing else, sets the precedent. We as Blacks are a foreign affair!. . . . There is a definite interrelation between events and actions in the international arena and what happens here at home through our legislative process. Either all Americans pursue the common interests of this nation together as one; or we will each separately help to sink it (Edwards, 105).

Her own involvement in international issues is apparent. Along with Representative William H. Gray (D., Pa.), she initiated a day-long workshop to discuss United States policy in the Caribbean during the 1980s. She has visited China and has surveyed "the coca and marijuana fields of Mexico, Peru, Columbia, and Bolivia" (Malone, B-1). When her mother died in 1988, she flew home from a conference in Germany. Earlier, she had visited Israel and through her account of that visit encouraged compromise on both sides. Collins was "one of two Congresspeople" (Reynolds, 36) who "toured the six-nation, drought-ravaged Sahel region of Africa with Mrs. Lillian (Miz Lillian) Carter, the President's 80-year-old mother," who gave her the nickname "Disco" (Poinsett, 66).

To nurture her own personhood and to maintain a sense of humor in the midst of helping to establish national and international governmental policy does require an energetic personality. Along with her interest in foreign affairs, Collins has continued to enjoy "reading, . . . jazz . . . and live acts at the Pigfoot and Blues Alley" (Trescott, "Coming," C-3). She also likes to bowl with her son and to play poker. While one person describes her as "thoughtful and serious" (Glaser, 162), another speaks of "the hip idiom and infectious laughter that laces much of her conversation" (Poinsett, 68). As a Congresswoman, she must sometimes be tough, but as a woman, she "displays a strong combination of wit, candor, confidence and homespun charm" (Trescott, "Another," G-4).

Cardiss Collins "believes and has proven that 'any woman can overcome obstacles if she possesses a healthy dose of faith in her own abilities" (Reynolds, 37). She has overcome the shyness that she once felt so strongly and the uncertainties of those first days in Congress. She now "seems to have learned her lessons well and moves with the easy assurance of one who has found the cloak of office a comfortable fit" (Edwards, 102).

One writer suggests a possible key to her success:

> Someone who dares step directly into the Congressional arena without a history of deep entrenchment in state politics, or without immersion in the field of law or government, or without an education in one of the finest private or state colleges or universities in the country is courageous and merits the plaudits of the less daring. Somehow, though, applause for Cardiss Collins seems inappropriate because she is best viewed as a natural politician. This is true not only because she apparently has a set of specific, people-oriented goals but also because she keeps an ear close to the ground of her constituency" (Cummings, 40).

Collins is aware of the needs of her constituents because she is dedicated to making herself available to the people she serves. One writer mentions that she "walks the streets visiting with her constituents" and that she "attended fourteen block parties" one Saturday (Malone, B-1). Another reports that "Mrs. Collins feels compelled to visit her district nearly every weekend to keep in touch with the voters" (Christopher, 283). Her schedule focuses on people:

> Up at 5:30 every morning, she spends the first hours briefing herself on the day's work, boning up on legislation, and planning strategies. When Congress is in session, she attends at least two social functions daily. . . . Each month she faithfully reserves eight days for a visit to her home district. . . . It is this contact that keeps her sensitive to the Black viewpoint (Booker, 30).

Collins has a reason for continuing her hectic schedule and a reason for her continued dedication. She considers the challenges she faces to be worth the effort they require.

> There are very few Blacks who can do something about the plight of the 25 or 30 million Blacks in this country. There are only 17 of us in Congress [in 1979], relatively few Black judges, few Blacks in high places. So whenever the highest elected tribunal in the nation can help write the last word on issues affecting minorities—well that's tremendous satisfaction. It's worth whatever sacrifice, whatever suffering, whatever self-denial. Victory like that is sweet (Poinsett, 68).

References

Barone, Michael and Grant Ujifusa. *The Almanac of American Politics, 1990.* Washington, D.C.: National Journal, 1989. Includes photograph.

Biographical Directory of the United States Congress, 1774-1989. Bicentennial ed. Washington: Government Printing Office, 1989. Includes photograph.

"Black Caucus Examines U.S. Relations With Caribbean." *Jet* 59 (25 December 1980): 38.

"A Black Woman's Place is in the . . . House of Representatives." *Ebony* 46 (January 1991): 104-105, 108, 110.

Booker, Simeon. "Washington Notebook." *Ebony* 34 (April 1979): 30.

"Cardiss Collins Named to Powerful House Panel." *Jet* 67 (14 January 1985): 4. Includes photograph.

Christopher, Maurine. *Black Americans in Congress.* Rev. ed. New York: Crowell, 1976.

Collins, Cardiss. "A Plea for Respect." *Ebony* 36 (July 1981): 78. Includes photograph.

———. "U.S. Support for Israel." *Encore* 4 (August 1975): 52. Includes photograph.

"Collins: United Airlines Must Hire More Blacks." *Jet* 71 (23 March 1987): 8.

Congressional Directory, 1989-90. 101st Congress. Washington, D.C.: Government Printing Office, 1989.

Congressional Quarterly's Guide to Congress. 3rd ed. Washington, D.C.: Congressional Quarterly Service, 1982.

Cummings, Bernice and Victoria Schuck. *Women Organizing: An Anthology.* Metuchen, N.J.: Scarecrow Press, 1979.

Duncan, Phil, ed. *Congressional Quarterly's Politics in America, 1990.* 101st Congress. Washington, D.C.: Congressional Quarterly Service, 1989. Includes photograph.

Edwards, Audrey. "Cardiss Collins: Do Your Votes Count?" *Essence Magazine* 11 (November 1980): 84-85, 102, 105, 107. Includes photograph.

Fleming, Robert. "Congressional Black Caucus: Cardiss Collins Promises More Clout." *Encore* 8 (April 1979): 20-21. Includes photograph.

"45 Years From Today: What's Ahead for Blacks and Whites." *Ebony* 46 (November 1990): 54-77.

Glaser, Vera and Laura Elliott. "Woman Power." *Washingtonian* 18 (May 1983): 156-164. Includes photograph.

Harris, Jessica B. "More Political Victories for Black Women." *Encore* 2 (August 1973): 20. Includes photograph.

Kurtz, Howard. "Hill Hearing on Amtrak is Cancelled." *Washington Post,* 8 March 1985. A-5. Includes photograph.

Malone, Julia. "Folks Back Home Speak Their Piece to Representatives." *Christian Science Monitor,* 8 September 1983. 1, 12. Includes photograph.

"Our New Men in the House: Congressional Black Caucus Picks Up Four New Members, Loses One in General Election." *Ebony* 36 (January 1981): 40-42.

Parker, Laura. "Hijack Alert Issued Before Lockerbie." *Washington Post* 20 March 1989. Includes photograph.

Poinsett, Alex. "The New Cardiss Collins." *Ebony* 35 (December 1979): 63-68. Includes photograph.

Ragsdale, Bruce A. and Joel D. Treese. *Black Americans in Congress, 1870-1989.* Washington, D.C.: Government Printing Office, 1990. Includes photograph.

"Rep. Collins Delivers Ultimatum to Carter: Change Jobs Policies." *Jet* 58 (26 June 1980): 6. Includes photograph.

"Rep. Collins Urges More Access for Blacks in Media." *Jet* 60 (19 March 1981): 29.

Reynolds, Barbara. "Cardiss Collins Chairperson." *Black Collegian* 9 (May-June 1979): 36-37. Includes photograph.

"Seven Caucus Members are Perfect to Women's League." *Jet* 60 (2 April 1981): 6.

Stineman, Esther. *American Political Women: Contemporary and Historical Profiles.* Littleton, Colo.: Libraries Unlimited, 1980.

Tolchin, Martin. "Congressional Blacks Vow to Stir Campaign Against Budget Cuts." *New York Times,* 1 March 1979.

Trescott, Jacqueline. "Another Widow in the House: Mrs. George Collins Takes Over Husband's Seat in Congress." *Sunday Star and Daily News,* 1 July 1973. Includes photograph.

———. "The Coming Out of Cardiss Collins." *Washington Post,* 21 September 1979. Includes photograph.

"3 U.S. Agencies Facing Action Over Hiring Goals." *New York Times,* 22 August 1984.

"2 House Members Call for Outside Inquiry on F.A.A. Doctor." *New York Times,* 21 December 1986.

"U.S. Rep. Collins' Mother Dies After Brief Illness." *Jet* 75 (12 December 1988): 12.

"Women in Government." *Ebony* 32 (August 1977): 91. Includes photograph.

Wynter, Leon E. "Can Colgate Ward Off a Threatened Boycott?" *Wall Street Journal,* 29 March 1990.

"Young Saves Face for Carter At China Dinner." *Jet* 55 (15 February 1979): 5. Includes photograph.

Marie Garrett

Janet Collins

(1917-)

Dancer, Choreographer, Educator

Recognized at an early age as a gifted artist, Janet Faye Collins went on to become one of the most versatile and highly-acclaimed dancers of her time; she has been recognized as well for her impressive talent in choreography and dance instruction. Born on March 2, 1917, in New Orleans, Louisiana, Collins was one of six siblings (five girls and one boy) in a large family of modest means. Like her hard-working father and mother, a tailor and seamstress who managed to provide each of their children a college education, Collins combined supreme talent with utmost effort in building a career filled with accomplishments that were anything but modest.

When Collins was four years old, her family settled in Los Angeles, California, where she was to spend her formative years attending school and training in both classical ballet and modern dance. She began toe-dancing at the age of ten at a Catholic community center near her home. With amusement she describes this early start in dancing as a matter of "'butterflies, bees, and flowers. Little tots bobbing around to the thump of an exaggerated piano beat'" (Gilbert, 44). Serious ballet studies began when she was twelve. Her mother would sew costumes for dance pupils preparing for dance recitals so that she could acquire training in ballet technique under the guidance of famed instructors Louise Beverly and Charlotte Tamon. This was but the beginning of study under a succession of illustrious teachers who trained her in ballet, modern dance, and choreography. Among the notables who followed Beverly and Tamon were: in ballet, Carmelita Maracchi, Maria Slavenska, Adolf Bolm, Madam Toscanini, and Dorothy Lyndall; in modern dance, Lester Horton; in Spanish forms, Angel Casino; and in choreography, Doris Humphrey and Hanya Holm.

Making her professional debut in vaudeville shows while she was still in junior high school, Collins gradually achieved recognition and opportunities for work. After high school, she completed her formal education at the Los Angeles City College and Arts Center School, while continuing her dance training under established professionals. Her career as a concert and theatrical dancer gained momentum in 1940, when she worked as a principal dancer for Los Angeles Musical Productions. Her appearances included *Run Little Chillun* and *Mikado in Swing*. In 1941, while touring the West Coast for a production of *Cabin in the Sky*, Collins auditioned for and was immediately hired as a principal dancer for the then three-year-old, world-famous black dance troupe formed and directed by Katherine Dunham. Collins remained with the group for two years, after which she left with another of Dunham's premier dancers, Talley Beatty, in order to form a dance duo. The duo performed for one year in California before separating to follow individual pursuits.

All the while Collins was gaining experience as a theatrical and concert dancer, she continued to become more and more versatile by working on expanding her repertoire. In 1945 she won a Julius Rosenwald Fellowship, which allowed her time to develop her own dance compositions. For one of her several projects she conducted research on Hebraic dances, in which she received the assistance of Ernest Bloch, eminent Swiss-born composer of Hebrew music. Spirituals constituted another area of her studies, which she later rendered, along with her marvelous Biblical portrayals (*Three Psalms of David*, for instance) into many inspired interpretations. In 1946 Collins had a role in a film produced by Jack Cole, *The Thrill of Brazil* (Columbia), but national recognition was to come when she migrated from California to New York.

The break that propelled Collins to the zenith of her career came in 1947, when she had her first solo recital at Las Palmas Theater in Los Angeles. As a result of her performance, she received a scholarship to study composition under Doris Humphrey in New York, where she made her debut, in 1949, in a performance at the Young Men's and Young Women's Hebrew Association (92nd Street "Y"). On the basis of two solos during that performance, she was propelled to stardom, with reviewers touting her as "the most highly acclaimed gifted newcomer in many a season," and "the most exciting dancer in a long time" (Stahl, 29).

Collins was subsequently sought out increasingly for lead roles in theatrical productions and solo concert performances. She performed in a concert for the Young Men's Hebrew Association and was selected as the principal dancer in the Cole Porter musical *Out of This World* (1950). That performance earned her the prestigious Donaldson Award for the best dancer of the theater season (1950-51), an award she was able to place alongside the Dance Magazine Award (1949) and the Mademoiselle Magazine Award for "Woman of the Year" (1950). She also received scholarships for ballet, to work under Madam Toscanini, daughter of the famed Italian conductor Arturo Toscanini, and one for modern dance, to work under Hanya Holm, who choreographed her role in *Out of This World*. Collins's vastly growing repertoire was further spread through the medium of television, where she appeared regularly on variety shows such as "The Admiral Broadway Review" (NBC and Dumont), "This is Show Business" (CBS), and the "Paul Draper" and "Jack Haley" shows.

Metropolitan Opera Hires Its First Black Prima Ballerina

In 1953, when she was at the height of her career, it was said that Collins "broke down more barriers than any dancer of her color" ("Dunham Dance Graduates," 50). She had, indeed, done so in being hired in 1951 as the first black prima ballerina of the Metropolitan Opera, a position that she retained for three years (1951-54). In 1954, while reminiscing on her early days as a ballet dancer, Collins remembered her disappointment and dejection when the director of the Ballet Russe of Monte Carlo, on tour in Los Angeles, declined to hire her despite an impressive audition, because "they couldn't take me along for specialty roles. It would have been too expensive. And for the *corps de ballet* he said he'd have to paint me white" (Stahl, 28). Briefly disappointed, she returned, undaunted and more determined, to practicing and performing. Years later, when Zachary Zolov, choreographer for the Metropolitan Opera, approached Rudolph Bing, the Metropolitan's general manager, with the proposal to hire her for lead dancer in *Aida*, skill was the single consideration and she was immediately hired. Her fame rapidly spread as audiences marveled at her technique. Again and again, audiences and reviewers alike cheered and rhapsodized about her outstanding performances. She is particularly noted for her memorable appearances in *Aida*, in *Carmen*, in *La Gioconda*, and in *Sampson and Delilah*.

Concurrent with her position with the Metropolitan Opera, Collins performed between 1952 and 1955 under Columbia Artists Management in a number of solo concert dance tours in the United States and Canada. She then abandoned stage and concert tours and rejected offers to tour Europe in order to devote full time to teaching and developing plans for her own dance troupe. Always the perfectionist, Collins was very demanding of the students with whom she worked, expecting no less of them than she would of herself. She insisted that they study human anatomy, that they undergo rigorous physical conditioning, and that they devote the utmost concentration to every movement. The benefit of her expertise has been enjoyed by students at a number of schools where she taught. They include: the Modern Dance School of American Ballet (1949-52); Saint Joseph School for the Deaf (1959-61); Marymount Manhattan College (1959-69); Manhattanville College of Sacred Heart (1961-65); and Mother Butler Memorial High School (1966). Collins's abilities as a dancer and teacher were further augmented by her considerable talent as a costume designer and choreographer. From her work with Doris Humphrey and Hanya Holm she developed her own style and choreographed operas and the following concert works in many of which she performed: in 1947, *Blackamoor, Eine Kleine Nachtmusik, Spirituals, Protest, Après le Mardi Gras*; in 1949, *Juba, Three Psalms of David*; in 1951, *Moi l'Aimé Toi, Chère*; in 1960, *The Satin Slipper*; in 1965, *Genesis*; in 1972, *Cockfight*, in 1973, *Birds of Peace and Pride, Song, Fire Weaver*, and *Sunday and Sister Jones*.

Characterizations of Collins's dance technique are filled with superlatives that emphasized her seldom-matched "incredible artistry and breathtaking movements" ("Janet Collins," 53). Descriptions of her appearance and carriage, too, are equally exalting, depicting a presence that exemplifies physical perfection, a "miniature of the physical perfection taught by the Greeks, which seems to fit any age, as long as the proportions are harmonious" (Gilbert, 44). She is a slender, nymph-like, yet strong, "little elfin brown woman" ("Janet Collins," 53) of perfect proportions with sleek black hair and striking cheekbones, further emphasized by her regal carriage. Her beautiful body is a product of rigorous discipline in practice and physical training, and her precise, seemingly effortless movement is a result of thorough knowledge of human anatomy and thorough grounding in dance technique.

At once cool and exotic, a study in perfectly-controlled power and tension, she exudes a harmony of spirit in the manner in which she achieves a perfect marriage of art and science, of precise technique and creativity in dance. Questioned about her formula for keeping separate the presumably conflicting techniques of ballet and modern dance, Collins denied there was such a conflict and insisted instead that knowledge of both were essential:

> to extend the range of the body . . . the illusion you communicate while dancing depends on what you feel about your dance. For instance, I love Mozart. For that I need elevation and lightness, which I've learned from ballet. I love spirituals, too, and for that there is modern dance and a feeling of the earth (Gilbert, 28).

Collins's ability to magnetize her audiences and to convey powerfully the emotional content of her works so as to move people to tears, as with her performance of the spiritual "Nobody Knows the Trouble I've Seen," has not only been rewarded by many awards, but lauded in verse. One admirer, in a tribute to her in *The Negro History Bulletin*, reflecting on Collins's ability to use her art form to support truth, writes in a poem entitled "to a Dancer" that upon seeing the magic, overwhelming beauty expressed in her dance: "Then even those who doubt / Would see a symphony, enriched by / Truth" (Milton, 69). The verse goes on, proposing that Collins's artistry inspires not only pride in race but draws universal appeal that, by its magnificence, must force one to abandon bigotry and hatred. Another admirer, Joseph Clancy, lauds the universal, timeless, and awe-inspiring quality of her art in "The Dancer," published in *Commonweal*.

References

Biographical Dictionary of Dance. London: Schirmer Books, 1982.

The Concise Oxford Dictionary of Ballet. 2nd ed. London: Oxford University Press, 1982.

Clancy, Joseph P. "The Dancer." *Commonweal* 75 (February 1962): 516.

The Dance Encyclopedia. New York: Simon and Schuster, 1967.

"Dunham Dance Graduates." *Ebony* 78 (June 1953): 48-53.

Gilbert, Morris. "Up and Coming." *New York Times Magazine* 1 February 1953. Photograph, p. 44.

"Janet Collins." *Ebony* 4 (September 1949): 43-54. Includes photographs.

"Janet Collins' Dance School." *Ebony* 11 (January 1956): 28-30. Includes photographs.

Milton, Nerissa. "The Young People's Corner." *Negro History Bulletin* 18 (December 1954): 68-69. Photograph, p. 68.

Stahl, Norma. "The First Lady of the Metropolitan Opera Ballet." *Dance Magazine* 28 (February 1954): 27-29. Includes photographs.

"U.S. Progress Inspires Gains Abroad." *Ebony* 11 (November 1955): 138. Includes photograph.

Who's Who Among Black Americans, 1990/91. 6th ed. Detroit: Gale Research, 1991.

"Women in Arts." *Ebony* 21 (August 1966): 93-95. Photograph, p. 94.

Collections

Biographical material on Janet (Fay) Collins is in the Julius Rosenwald Collection, Fisk University Library, Nashville, Tennessee.

Carolyn R. Hodges

Marva Collins

(1936-)

School founder

Marva Collins

In 1983 the first of a plethora of national educational reform reports was issued. Entitled "A Nation at Risk: The Imperative for Educational Reform," this report was published by the National Commission on Excellence in Education. "A rising tide of mediocrity" was used to characterize the state of education in the United States of America. This, and subsequent reports, recommended changes in preparing teachers and improving elementary and secondary education in the nation's public schools. The more than thirty national reform reports have sparked widespread state implementation of assessment measures, the main one being competency testing for teachers and students. The results have been both consistent and disturbing, for test data analyses have shown that prospective and practicing teachers and students of color score lower than their white and Asian counterparts.

One can be fairly safe in surmising that all the educational reform hoopla and the resulting negative fallout were not surprising to a prominent Chicago educator who had long and loudly complained about the level of preparedness and fitness of teachers, especially in the Chicago public and private school systems. In the early 1960s Marva Collins was well aware of serious problems in the nation's schools, particularly in Chicago. By 1975 she had had enough and would make a decision that would forever change not only her life but also the lives of thousands of Chicago school children. The field of education would never be the same after the opening of Westside Preparatory School, a haven for children considered as rejects from the Chicago public and private schools, places of dismal failure both academically and emotionally for too many children.

In the late 1970s Collins became the darling of the media, particularly the white media, according to her detractors. The editor of *Substance* magazine, a substitute teacher publication, expressed the sentiments of a substantial number of Chicago teachers thus: "The whole Marva myth was racist. . . . The white press decided that this must be a miracle teacher if these children were learning" (Adler and Foote, 65). Collins has been labeled a miracle worker by prominent people in and out of the teaching profession, not just by those in the media. Morley Safer, the reporter for "60 Minutes," continues to support her despite reports that chip away at her professional and personal integrity.

The idea of a "Marva Myth" is an intriguing one, however, for Collins's personal history is as interesting as the ongoing real-life saga of her school. Although her adult life has certainly been no fairy tale, her own and others' accounts of her formative years, especially her childhood, read like one and could easily begin with: Once upon a time, there was a little girl named Marva who lived in a big, pretty house and wore expensive, pretty, sashed and ruffled dresses and had a rich, smart, and prosperous daddy whom she loved very, very much.

According to Collins's autobiography, this is all true and bears out the adage that "Truth is indeed stranger than fiction!" Collins always cites her father as being the most important role model in her life and her formative years in Monroeville, Alabama, as the crucible for shaping and making her the woman she is today. *Marva Collins' Way,* the 1982 autobiography, lists her parents as Bessie (Nettles) Knight and Henry Knight, Jr., as does the biographical sketch in the 1986 *Current Biography Yearbook.* Therefore, it is puzzling and interesting to read that her maiden name is Nettles in other biographical sources, especially the 1989 Brian Lanker publication *I Dream a World.* One could surmise that these latter discrepancies were due to careless editorial proofreading, but the 1948 divorce of Collins's parents and her mother's subsequent remarriage may have left some psychic wound as the causal factor in the inconsistent listing of her maiden name. The divorce was traumatic because Collins was definitely a "daddy's girl" and an only child until adolescence; she gained a sister, Cynthia, after her mother's remarriage.

Born on August 31, 1936, Marva Collins lived in Monroeville, Alabama, until she and her mother moved to Atmore, a nearby town, after the divorce. As a child, Collins apparently spent most of her time with her father and less with her mother and her peers. Although Brian Lanker quotes her as saying "I don't want to be wealthy. I don't need that kind of power" (Lanker, 75), Collins's autobiography is a paean to her family's status in the community due to the accumulated wealth of her grandfathers and father. Henry Knight, Sr., was a grocery store proprietor and owner of rental properties, who always "wore Sunday clothes"; William Nettles, her maternal grandfather, was a successful farmer and meat peddler who was the first black man in town to own a car, a Model-T Ford. Collins's father inherited the store and increased the family wealth through ownership of a thousand-acre cattle ranch and a funeral parlor. The visible signs of the Knight family's status, according to Collins, were: "a six-bedroom white clapboard house that had polished wood floors, store-bought furniture, and oriental rugs" (Collins, 32), being dressed like a doll, which made her stand out from the other children, her father's ability to be respected by white businessmen and envious blacks, and the yearly purchase of a black Cadillac for Henry Knight's funeral business.

Henry Knight, Jr., treated his daughter as an equal because of her consuming interest in his business affairs, her quick, intelligent grasp of finance, and her absorption of his philosophical attitudes about life. When girls her age were playing with dolls and tea sets, Collins was working in her father's grocery store and accompanying him on cattle-buying trips across the state of Alabama. Citing him as "the greatest man who ever lived," Collins quite apparently derived much of her personal and professional attitudes and beliefs from her father. He was always supportive of and patient with the young girl, but her respect for him was rooted in his astute business sense, especially since he had only a fourth-grade education. The fact that he was financially well-off ranked on a par with the obvious respect accorded him, especially by white people. Any black Southerner born in the 1930s or 1940s will instinctively understand this because of having grown up during the era of rampant segregation when black males were routinely and systematically destroyed for being "uppity" and "forgetting their place." Knight's determination and absolute lack of fear when he believed in himself made a lasting impression on a young girl who watched her father quietly, but persistently, deal with hostile whites who physically threatened his life in her presence. From her father, Collins shaped her personality to reflect his major characteristics of self-pride, nonconformity, strong values, uncompromising beliefs, and strength.

Bessie Nettles Knight was respected and loved by her daughter, but she was never in the same league as Henry Knight, Jr. Although she was the one who dressed Collins in the pretty, store-bought dresses, it was the father who purchased them, as well as all the family's clothing. This was his method of preventing his wife from being insulted by white department store salesclerks who routinely called black women by their first names and refused to allow them to try on clothes they intended to buy. Collins considered her mother to be rather emotionally cold and more concerned with living up to and meeting societal social standards. The young girl learned virtually no housekeeping skills and was constantly chided for being clumsy. Yet, it is Bessie Knight who is given credit, albeit in the form of a left-handed compliment, for Collins's being an overachiever and an immaculate housekeeper. Ironically, the impetus was the constant maternal rejoinder that the young girl would never amount to much.

Marva Collins could read before she entered Bethlehem Academy. After finishing elementary school, she went to high school in Atmore to Escambia County Training School. Here she began to show traits of a feisty, strong-willed spirit by refusing to take a home economics course required of all female students. Instead, she enrolled in a typing class since she considered it more useful. Although Collins was threatened with the possibility of not being eligible to graduate, the teenager refused to give in. She strongly believed that black girls taking home economics bore out white people's expectations that they could only be domestics or homemakers. In 1953 Collins graduated as the only female ever who did not take that required course at her high school. As the first person in her family to go to college, Collins chose Clark College in Atlanta, Georgia, even though she had no notion about her future. College, therefore, was not an altogether positive learning experience, but she graduated with a bachelor's degree in secretarial science, since that seemed a sensible choice.

Being Henry Knight, Jr.'s daughter may have accorded Collins first-class status when she was growing up, but as an adult looking for a job, it meant nothing in segregated Alabama. Finding no suitable secretarial position open to blacks, Collins turned to the one profession she never planned to enter—that of teaching. At Monroe County Training School, she taught four business courses and got her basic teacher-training from her principal, who stressed knowing one's students and their capabilities. After a two-year teaching stint, Collins went to Chicago for a visit and decided to remain there. This was where she really began to live life as an independent adult.

Collins Begins Teaching in Chicago Schools

Out on her own at last, Marva Collins began a new life as a single adult with an apartment of her own, a new job as a medical secretary, and a new boyfriend. This was a great contrast to her life in Alabama, where she had lived with her grandparents and accepted financial gifts from her father even though she was teaching full-time. Within a year of her arrival, she was Mrs. Clarence Collins, wife of a draftsman. His main attractions were his love of children, devotion to his family, and a sense of level-headed calmness, although he was not college educated as was his new bride. After the marriage, she found that she missed teaching and applied for a position in the Chicago public school system. Due to a teacher shortage, Collins was immediately hired despite not having taken any education methodology courses. As a full-time substitute teacher, she was assigned to Calhoun South Elementary School to teach second grade. Here, without any prior teaching experience at that level, Collins began to come into her own as an innovative, creative teacher, who planned and taught according to learner needs rather than slavishly adhering to a preplanned curriculum guide. And here was where she began to run afoul of the "system", one she believed insensitive to black children, particularly those of low socioeconomic background in inferior schools. The epitome of the system was the poor quality of teaching and the negative attitudes of so many of her coworkers. Collins became known as a maverick and a troublemaker and soon became the target of emotional abuse from other teachers. Collins stayed at Calhoun for only a year. By that time she and her husband were beginning a family and adjusting to life in an interracial neighborhood, Garfield Park, which would become a black ghetto within seven years.

After the birth of Eric, the Collins's first child, Marva Collins returned to teaching with an assignment to Delano Elementary School, where she remained until leaving the school system. This school was to be her trial by fire.

In *Marva Collins' Way,* the third chapter could be subtitled either "From Better to Worse" or "Things Fall Apart." Collins describes her initial satisfaction with a school headed by a strong principal, one of the major criteria for an effective learning environment. To her, he was an excellent role model who espoused knowledge and understanding of classical literature and poetry as well as the need always to continue learning. There were also effective teachers with whom Collins interacted positively and from whom she gained expertise in teaching strategies. But the inevitable changes came, and in Collins's estimation, they were all negative: a principal who espoused going by the book, administrative fiats demanding and relying on standardized testing, the exclusive utilization of the "look-say" method of teaching reading, internecine bickering, uncaring teachers who were apathetic and disrespectful to children, and professional jealousy. This last factor would prove to be the most damaging to Collins because it has followed her and resulted in slanderous and vicious attacks on her character. "You think you're so great We think you're nothing [signed] a colleague" (Collins, 70); "Marva, you can't go . . . you have to bring your class back to the building. I've got a lot of trouble with the other teachers. They're giving me a hard time about letting you go" (Collins, 69). Collegial envy and little or no support from a weak principal led to dizzy spells, insomnia, self-pity, doubt, and even guilt. All these negative feelings were the fallout from Collins's attempts to provide a quality education for poor, inner-city children she believed were being shortchanged by an educational system that left their needs unfulfilled. Her own words shed light on a situation that could be considered from her own and her colleagues' point of view: "Was I self-righteous? Too rigid? All my life I had been serious, too serious. I wished I could be more like everybody else. . . . When I was sure I was right about something, I just couldn't back down or even compromise. As a teacher, my sympathies were only with my students. Could I have done more to understand my colleagues?" (Collins, 71).

Collins cites envy over her style of dress as a primal factor in the jealousy of colleagues, but many teachers are extremely well dressed; that was not enough to engender the depth of hostility described by Collins. The key might be in one's interpretation of the term "compromise." The traditional meaning focuses on making concessions, each side giving up something to get something, adjusting opposing principles; it is a meaning with which most people would agree. Collins, however, seemed to view the art of compromise as a total surrender of one's principles, beliefs, and singular point of view.

Preparatory School for Alternative Learning Founded

In 1975 Collins left the Chicago public school system and opened her own school, the Daniel Hale Williams Westside Preparatory School, in the basement of Daniel Hale Williams University, a Chicago community college. She and some neighbors received advice from the Alternative Schools Network, which also paid Collins's salary as director and curriculum developer. The college provided free space and equipment. Collins made appeals to any and everybody who could donate books and supplies, no matter the condition, age, or appearance. She even foraged in the Delano School garbage dump and found discarded books that were, most ironically, the Open Court Reading Series she had long favored for its phonics approach to reading. Beginning with only four children, including her own daughter, Collins gained only one more within a month and then, four months later, nearly twenty children were in her school. Although small in number, they were too many for such cramped quarters. Collins was indeed a miracle worker, but the real miracle was that they did not all develop claustrophobia. At the end of the school year, the decision was made to be totally independent but the problem was where the new school would be located. With only a five-thousand-dollar nest egg from her pension fund as collateral, Collins finally decided to use the top floor of her own home, a two-flat structure with a vacant upstairs apartment. Her faithful supporter, Clarence Collins, completely renovated the space over the summer of 1976. That September, eighteen children were enrolled in Westside Preparatory School. Why did the parents of those eighteen children trust Marva Collins to teach their children, especially since they had to scrape, borrow, and literally beg the money to pay the tuition? What was she able to do that one of America's largest public school systems could not do? What was she going to do that was better than Chicago's private schools?

First and foremost, Collins instilled confidence, pride, and self-esteem in children who had never had or who had lost these vital self-determinants of character. Some had been systematically ignored, some mislabeled as "slow" and "retarded," and some verbally and emotionally abused. Collins constantly assured them that she loved them and demanded that they live up to and fulfill her high expectations of them. She did this via the hands-on approach. Known as a teacher who never sat down, Collins walked the aisles, hugged, cajoled, and kept up a running commentary of maxims designed to encourage and uplift the spirits of children broken and defeated by the very institutions meant to do just the opposite.

What Collins actually taught was based on her own philosophy of education and a personal synthesis of the art of teaching. She always espoused the basics of learning and expected and demanded that learners meet her high expectations. Her characteristic technique has always been: "a blackboard, books, and a good pair of legs that will last through the day" (*Current Biography Yearbook,* 96). Because the media has always been obsessed with what they saw—for example, children reading Shakespeare and writing letters to Clytemnestra—how Collins taught was harder to pull together. Then too, one always had to wade through her diatribes and generalized criticisms of the American public school system to discover what she did as opposed to what she did not like—what every other teacher supposedly did in the classrooms across the nation. The components that do stand out are these: self-respect, with herself as the model for what a teacher should act and look like in demeanor and personal appearance; success, the promise to children that she would not allow them to fail despite their previous school failures; and self-reliance, belief in one's self and one's abilities. As children look at Marva Collins, they see the epitome of these first three global aspects of what an educated person can and should be; that is just what she intends. Next, teach the whole child: not just the mechanics of learning the three R's but character-building, morals, ethics, values, attitudes. Collins modeled her teaching methodology on her own elementary teachers' methods, especially the way they taught reading. As a child she loved to read and this became the bedrock of her teaching—helping children to see the value and beauty in loving to read, not just for the sake of gaining knowledge, but for pleasure as well. Next, application of learning to real life; showing that nothing exists in isolation; challenging by utilizing a wide variety of learning materials to enable students to improve their higher-order thinking skills; creativity, wracking one's brains to make learning both palatable and enjoyable; the best in literature and poetry; the classics; a Collins maxim: "The book you give to a child who is learning to read determines what he or she will read later on" (Collins, 66). Read. Read. Read. The key to all learning is read . . . and then read some more.

Of course Collins was not surprised by the educational reform reports of the 1980s; they simply bore out what she had been incessantly complaining about and justified her leaving the public school system to do it her way. Two years after relocating her school, the media discovered Marva Collins. The *Chicago Sun-Times* featured a story based on her claims that the Westside Preparatory students' standardized test scores in reading and language skills had jumped from below to as much as four years above grade level. Subsequently, *Time, Good Housekeeping, People, Jet, Newsweek, Black Enterprise, Ebony,* and a variety of educational journals ran feature stories on the "miracle teacher." The clincher, though, was a 1981 Hallmark Hall of Fame CBS television special entitled "The Marva Collins Story." The commitment to quality in the production was exemplified by the casting of Cicely Tyson and Morgan Freeman to portray Marva and Clarence Collins, respectively.

The first really important coverage was the 1979 "60 Minutes" story with Morley Safer, one of Collins's greatest defenders, as interviewer. Both exposures provided Collins with funds to move the school from cramped quarters in her home to a more permanent and substantial location. On the edge of Garfield Park, Collins found two office buildings suitable for Westside Preparatory School. A fifty-thousand-dollar grant was awarded by W. Clement Stone and the television movie paid a fee of one hundred thousand dollars. Collins also was by then commanding a ten-thousand-dollar fee for speaking engagements, and she used all the monies awarded and earned to purchase space for the new school. Now, Westside Preparatory School had more spacious quarters and became home to a five-member teaching staff, and two hundred students, with a waiting list of more than eight hundred, with Collins functioning as an administrator and teacher of teachers to do it her way.

With all the new-found prestige, the miracle teacher became a candidate for jobs with high visibility. After the airing of the 1979 "60 Minutes" show, Collins was offered positions as Secretary of Education in the Ronald Reagan administration, Chicago School Board member, and Los Angeles County School System superintendent. She declined all nominations to remain with her children. By 1982, instead of continuing to bask in her new-found glory, Collins discovered that the wounds from old jealousies were still festering, that her detractors had not forgotten the one who, in their eyes, was still acting like "some kind of god." *Substance* magazine, a publication of substitute teachers, published the findings of George Schmidt, a teacher recently released from his position. He claimed that Collins, from 1975 to 1979, had received $69,000 in CETA funds through the Alternative Schools Network, the same organization that had guided her efforts in opening the first school. This was newsworthy, because Collins had long insisted that she would never resort to accepting federal monies that would allow the government to mandate rules and regulations for her to follow. This stance had attracted politicians who were tired of "beggars for federal dollars" and caused the media as well to lionize Collins,.

As if this were not enough, an apparently disgruntled former Westside Preparatory teacher accused Collins of inflating standardized test scores, an accusation harder to prove since private schools were not required to give those tests nor report scores. Collins was also accused of plagiarism and pressuring parents who were delinquent with tuition payments. She appeared on the "Donahue Show" twice to answer these charges, once with her attorney as indication of the severity of claims against her. A prevailing perception by some Chicago teachers and local media persons was that they had been deceived by a larger-than-life persona who, after all the hoopla had died down, was a human being with the same human frailties as everybody else. But her defenders were still behind Collins one hundred percent. Prince, the Minneapolis-based rock, video, and movie star, has long supported Collins's National Teacher Training Institute. Kevin Ross, who left Seton Hall University as an illiterate basketball star, is one of her biggest boosters because Collins taught him to read when he was twenty-three years old; he went from second to twelfth grade reading levels. Mr. T. of "A-Team" fame paid tuition costs for sixty students from a Chicago housing project to attend the school. In defense of her claims about Westside Preparatory student test results, the admissions director of a noted Chicago private school verified those claims for forty-five students he tested over a four-year period, all Westside students.

Marva Collins's success in educating children who had gotten lost and trapped in the "cracks" of public and private schools cannot be denied. There are too many satisfied parents who had suffered too many sleepless nights worrying about the academic and emotional toll taken on their children prior to their enrollment in Westside Preparatory. There are too many donors who have given in the high five figures to underwrite educational activities at Westside Preparatory. There have been too many valid offers for consultancies to reputable and prestigious professional organizations. There are all the visits to Westside Preparatory from teachers and administrators the world over who come to sit at the feet of the miracle teacher and learn the Collins way of doing things.

Marva Collins is active in service and professional organizations. Her affiliations include member of the President's Commission on White House Fellowships, council of the National Institute of Health, National Advisory Board on Private Education, and National Department of Children, Youth, and Family Services. Her awards, honors and achievements include Educator of the Year awards from Phi Delta Kappa and the Chicago Urban League, United Negro College Fund Award, Fred Hampton Image Award, Sojourner Truth Award, Jefferson Award of the American Institute for Public Service, Legendary Woman of the World—City of Birmingham, Alabama, Watson Washburne Award, Reading Reform Foundation Award, and Endow a Dream Award. She is director and founder of Right to Read and a member of the NAACP and the Alpha Kappa Alpha Sorority. Institutions conferring honorary degrees on Marva Collins are Howard University, Amherst College, Dartmouth College, Washington University, Chicago State University, Central State University, and Wilberforce University. Founder of Westside Preparatory School and Westside Preparatory National Teacher Training Institute, she has written over thirty-five articles for publication in magazines, newspapers, and professional journals.

Collins envisions extending Westside Preparatory to meet her students' educational and personal needs. Brian Lanker quotes her thus: "Our children have problems when they leave here. They learn to shut up, they learn to fake it. Here they are free to disagree, free to disagree with me" (75). Not only a high school, but also a day-care center and an adult-education facility for the Garfield Park citizens are in the plans for an educational complex. Will she succeed? Probably so. Nothing has stopped her yet and she still has her greatest supporters, Clarence, her husband, and their three children—Eric, Patrick, and Cynthia. Collins will always have the support of hard-core inner-city residents who know that her life is living proof of her intentions. The Collins family has remained in Garfield Park despite the fact that they could have long since moved to suburbia. It is in the Collins household that one sees a flesh and blood Marva Collins: wife, mother, homemaker. *Essence* and *Ebony* magazines are among the few publications to show this side of the miracle teacher. Collins collects antiques, snuff boxes, and miniature rocking horses. During her travels abroad, she has bought artifacts, souvenirs, and home furnishings that reflect her diverse tastes and flair for decorating her home. Also in evidence are books, especially first editions. It is commonplace for her to read five hundred books annually, so an abundance of bookcases is not out of the ordinary in the Collins household. In an article in *Essence* magazine Collins stated that there was no need to leave Chicago's West Side: "For what? Now all the cab drivers knew me . . . [and] they are honking and blowing even when I don't need them. Leave the West Side—why? Something good is happening here" (Reynolds, 167). Since she fervently believes that there is good wherever one chooses to make it so, Marva Collins will succeed, on her terms, in her own way—Marva Collins's way.

References

Adler, Jerry, and Donna Foote. "The Marva Collins Story." *Newsweek* (8 March 1982): 64-65.

Collins, Marva and Civia Tamarkin. *Marva Collins' Way.* Los Angeles: J. P. Tarcher, 1982.

Current Biography Yearbook. New York: H. W. Wilson, 1987. 95. Includes photograph.

Keerdoja, Eileen, and others. "Report Card on Marva Collins." *Newsweek* (27 June 1983): 13.

Lanker, Brian. *I Dream a World.* New York: Stewart, Tabori, and Chang, 1989. 74-75. Photograph, p. 75.

Marshall, Marilyn. "Marva Collins: Weathering the Story." *Ebony* 40 (February 1985): 77-78, 82. Photograph, p. 82.

Reynolds, Barbara A. "Something Good is Happening Here." *Essence* 12 (October 1981): 106-108, 162, 167.

Smikle, Ken. "Trashing Marva Collins." *Black Enterprise* 12 (June 1982): 46.

Who's Who Among Black Americans, 1990/91. Detroit: Gale Research, 1991.

Who's Who in America. 44th ed. Vol. 1. Wilmette, Ill.: Marquis, 1987.

Dolores Nicholson

Coralie Cook

(18?-1942)

Civic worker, educator, activist

Coralie Franklin Cook was born in Lexington, Virginia, the daughter of Albert Franklin and Mary E. Franklin. Her date of birth is unknown. One of the founders of Storer College in Harper's Ferry, West Virginia, Cook graduated from that school and also from Emerson College, Boston, Massachusetts. She received further instruction from Martha's Vineyard Summer Institute and the Shoemaker School of Oratory. From 1882 to 1893 she taught at Storer College, and she moved to the position as superintendent of the Home for Destitute Colored Women and Children, Washington, D.C., where she remained from 1893 to 1898. Cook was professor of English and later held the chair of oratory at Howard University.

Coralie Franklin was married to George William Cook, who was born a slave in Winchester, Virginia, in a family of seven children. The family fled when the Union army captured the town and traveled north to Chambersburg, Pennsylvania, and on to Harrisburg, where they settled. While working for a Pennsylvania Dutch family, George

Coralie Cook

Cook's interest in seeking a higher education was fired. Later while working in New York City, he met the well-known abolitionist and religious leader, Henry Highland Garnet, who encouraged him to study at Howard University. George Cook entered Howard's Preparatory Department in 1874 and graduated in 1877. He received his B.A. degree from the College Department in 1881 and was valedictorian of his class. He received an M.A. degree from Howard in 1886, an LL.B. in 1898, and an LL.M. in 1899. George Cook was associated with Howard University for nearly fifty-eight years as an educator and later as secretary-treasurer, and he became the highest-ranking black official of the university. He was also a member of Howard's board of trustees. Among the friends of this noteworthy civic worker were "Frederick Douglass, John Mercer Langston, Blanche K. Bruce, John R. Lynch, Alexander Crummell, Archibald Grimké," and other black luminaries in Washington at the time (Winston, 124). He died on August 20, 1931.

In addition to her outstanding work as an educator, Coralie Franklin Cook was well-known for her civic activities, including her early work with the black women's club movement. In 1896 the two national organizations of black women—the Colored Women's League and the National Federation of Afro-American Women—met in Washington, D.C., July 14-16 and July 20-22 respectively. The two groups appointed a joint committee to consider a plan for merging the organizations. Representing the Colored Women's League were Fannie Jackson Coppin, A. V. Tomkins, Anna Jones, Julia F. Jones, Florence A. Barber, Emma F. G. Merrit, and Coralie Cook. The joint committee, consisting of seven members from each group, reached a consensus on the merger and elected Mary Church Terrell as chairperson of the new organization, the National Association of Colored Women (NACW). The first NACW convention was held in Nashville, Tennessee, the following year. Cook's involvement in NACW activities continued and when the association held its convention in Saint Louis in 1904, with Josephine Silone Yates as president, four black women were selected to attend the International Congress of Women held in Berlin—three from NACW and one from the outside. Mary Church Terrell was selected for her oratory skills and she addressed the group. Others attending were Margaret Murray Washington, Josephine B. Bruce, and Coralie Cook.

With her husband, Coralie Cook worked out the cottage system of the Government Training School at Blue Plains and received a commendation from the District Commissioners. She was a member of the District of Columbia Board of Education from 1914 to 1926. She was active in interracial affairs, and she served on the Board of Public Welfare. Cook was a member of the National District Social Hygiene Association. She had a special interest in children, as demonstrated through her membership in the Juvenile Protective Association and in her concern for children's playgrounds in the city. She belonged to the American Red Cross, the Book Lovers Club, and the Delta Sigma Theta sorority.

Drawing on her expertise in oratory, Cook addressed the Atlanta and Panama Pacific Exhibitions. She was a delegate to the Susan B. Anthony Seventieth Anniversary Mass Meeting held in Washington, D.C. Cook, a close friend of Susan B. Anthony, was also an activist and attended Anthony's eightieth birthday celebration, praised her, and called for greater interracial cooperation. In time, however, Cook's views changed, and she questioned the wisdom of black and white activists working cooperatively. When Mary White Ovington and the NAACP tried to recruit black women to attend the Woman's Party convention, Ovington asked Cook to join the team. But Cook answered:

> I have never been able to join the National Women's Party. [I am] heartily in sympathy with is object, [but] I do not subscribe to its methods. I regret also to have to say that I am not an "active" suffragist. The old Nat'l W.S.A. of which I was once an ardent supporter and member, turned its back on the woman of color . . . so I have not been "active" although I was born a suffragist (Giddings, 170).

While the extent of Cook's publications is not fully known, a known publication is an article in *Opportunity* magazine (June 1919, pp. 183-87) called "A Slave for Life: A Story of the Long Ago." She writes of Ephraim, a slave born of a black mother and white father, who lived near the Chesapeake.

Before her death, on Tuesday, August 25, 1942, Coralie Cook, who had been a quiet, tactful, high-minded woman of culture and public spirit, lived at 1231 Girard Street N.W. in Washington. Funeral services were held there. She was survived by her son, George William, Jr.; nieces Helen C. Jackson and Jessie Burrill; nephews J. Paul Clifford and John R. Clifford; and several grandnieces and grandnephews. The Washington, D.C., community had lost one of its great civic leaders.

References

Cook, Coralie Franklin. "A Slave for Life." *Opportunity* 7 (June 1929): 183-87.

Crisis 15 (November 1917): 24. Photograph.

Cropp, Dwight S. To Gail A. Kostinko, 1 July 1976. Moorland-Spingarn Research Center, Howard University, Washington, D.C.

Evening Star, 27 August 1942.

Giddings, Paula. *When and Where I Enter*. New York: Morrow, 1984.

Wesley, Charles Harris. *The History of the National Association of Colored Women's Clubs*. Washington, NACW, 1984.

Who's Who in Colored America, 1938-40. Brooklyn: Thomas Yenser, 1940. 131-32. Photograph, p. 132.

Winston, Michael R. "George William Cook." *Dictionary of American Negro Biography*. Edited by Rayford W. Logan and Michael R. Winston. New York: Norton, 1982.

Jessie Carney Smith

Anna "Annie" J. Cooper

(1858/59-1964)

Educator, scholar, writer, feminist, Pan-Africanist, activist

Throughout her life, Anna Cooper expressed strong concerns for justice and right conduct, equality for women, racial uplift and pride, and for fairness in social matters. Her thinking was global and thoroughly modern. Her life spanned slavery, the Civil War, Reconstruction, segregation, two world wars, a great depression, and an era of civil rights struggle. As an educator, writer, and scholar, she did not make headlines, but, perhaps more importantly, as a teacher and thinker who had known and learned from some of the greatest thinkers of her times, she affected untold numbers of young developing minds in ways that headlines cannot.

Annie Julia Haywood Cooper was born on August 10,

Anna "Annie" J. Cooper

1858 or 1859, in Raleigh, North Carolina, and died in Washington, D.C., on February 27, 1964. Her mother was Hannah Stanley (Haywood), a slave, and her father was most likely George Washington Haywood, the owner. A precocious child, Cooper was admitted to Saint Augustine's Normal School and Collegiate Institute (now Saint Augustine's College), an Episcopalian establishment that opened in Raleigh in 1868. There she soon distinguished herself and even became a tutor in those important years that followed Emancipation. When she finished her studies, she became a teacher at that same institution, where she met and in 1877 married a fellow teacher. Her husband, George A. C. Cooper, was a thirty-three-year-old former tailor from Nassau who had entered Saint Augustine's in 1873 to study theology; he died prematurely in 1879 just three months after his ordination, and Anna Cooper never remarried.

In 1881 the young widow entered Oberlin College, one of the few institutions accepting blacks and women at the time. She earned her A.B. degree in 1884 and taught modern languages at Wilberforce University (1884-1885). She returned to Raleigh the following year to teach mathematics, Latin, and German at Saint Augustine's. Oberlin awarded Anna Cooper an M.A. degree in mathematics in 1887, and that same year she accepted a position in Washington, D.C., at the Preparatory High School for Colored Youth, which in 1891 became the M Street High School and in 1916 was renamed the Paul Laurence Dunbar High School. Most of her career as an educator would be at this distinguished institution.

Cooper's first important work, *A Voice from the South: By a Black Woman from the South* (1892) consists mainly of essays and papers that she had delivered at various meetings and conferences. It demonstrates clearly the concerns that were to preoccupy her throughout life: women's rights and the uplifting of African-Americans—who at that time were just one generation removed from bondage.

The 1890s were peak years of experience and achievement for Cooper; while racist terrorism escalated, she and other black intellectuals organized and mobilized both to arouse public opinion and provide direction. During this decade Cooper attended numerous conferences, making addresses and presenting papers to such diverse groups and organizations as the American Conference of Educators (1890), the Congress of Representative Women (1893), the Second Hampton Negro Conference (1894), the National Conference of Colored Women (1895), and the National Federation of Afro-American Women (1896). In addition to her full-time teaching duties at the M Street School, Cooper also found time to do her first foreign travel: Early in the decade she went to Toronto on a summer exchange program for teachers, and in 1896 she visited Nassau. Cooper traveled to London in July 1900 to attend the first Pan-African Conference, where she presented a paper on "The Negro Problem in America"—the text of which has apparently not survived. Her London stay was followed by a tour of Europe, including a visit to the Paris Exposition, a stop at Oberammergau for the Passion Play, and a journey through the Italian cities of Milan, Florence, Naples, Rome, Pisa, and Pompeii.

Cooper was principal of the M Street School from 1902 until 1906. When she disputed the board of education's design to dilute the curriculum of "colored" schools, she was dropped from her position. She served as chair of languages at Lincoln University in Jefferson City, Missouri, from 1906 to 1910, then returned to the M Street School as a teacher of Latin.

In 1904, during her stint as principal, Cooper had impressed a visiting French educator, the abbé Félix Klein, who would later serve as an important contact when she decided to pursue the doctorate in France. Study at the Guilde Internationale in Paris during the summers of 1911, 1912, and 1913, then at Columbia University in the summers of 1914 through 1917, allowed Cooper to finish her course requirements for the Ph.D. With credits transferred, and two theses completed—an edited version of the medieval tale, *Le Pèlerinage de Charlemagne*, and an important historical study of French racial attitudes, *L'Attitude de la France à l'égard de l'esclavage pendant la Révolution*, Cooper successfully defended her dissertation at the Sorbonne on March 23, 1925. At age sixty-six she was only the fourth known African-American woman to earn the doctorate degree and among the first women to do so in France. This feat is all the more admirable when one considers the obstacles that Cooper had to overcome: Born in slavery, reared in a sexist and racist country, worked her way through school, she had taken in and raised two foster children while in her forties, and then adopted her half brother's five orphaned grandchildren (ages six months to twelve years) when she was in her late fifties.

In the latter years of her life, Anna Cooper retained a lively interest in education, and even before her retirement became involved with Frelinghuysen University in Washington, of which she served for a short while as president. Named for a senator who had been sympathetic to the struggle for equal rights, Frelinghuysen was a unique institution that only briefly became a university before socio-economic conditions and accrediting requirements combined to close it. Frelinghuysen was intended primarily for adult education and offered evening classes at several centers, providing academic, religious, and trade programs. These were particularly important for the many adult working people in the Washington, D.C., area who had moved in from points south where educational opportunities for blacks were limited.

Anna Julia Cooper died in her 105th year, on February 27, 1964. She was interred in the Hargett Street Cemetery in Raleigh next to her husband, whom she had outlived by 85 years.

Gender and Race Issues Viewed in Writings

Cooper's earliest writings, collected in *A Voice from the South,* mark her both as a dedicated feminist and an advocate of the race, with a firm position clearly and logically thought out. Her concern for women's rights grew out of her own experiences. As a student she was not encouraged in her schoolwork in the way that male students were, and her announced intention of going to college "was received with . . . incredulity and dismay" (Cooper, *Voice,* 77-78). "A boy," she wrote in later years, "however meager his equipment and shallow his pretentions, had only to declare a floating intention to study theology and he could get all the support, encouragement and stimulus he needed" (77). Not all colleges would admit women in those days, and of those that did, only a handful had ever graduated any African-American women—Fisk leading the way with twelve (73-74). When the British writer Matthew Arnold visited the United States in the early 1900s and spoke at an American college, he expressed surprise "that the young women in his audience . . . [had] paid as close attention as the men *all the way through*"; he suggested that too much education spoiled a woman's chances for marriage (67-68).

"I grant you" retorts Cooper, "that intellectual development, with the self-reliance and capacity for earning a livelihood which it gives, renders woman less dependent on the marriage relation for physical support (which, by the way, does not always accompany it)" (68). But—and here Cooper's deep conviction brings a lyricism bubbling to the surface—"Her horizon is extended. Her sympathies are broadened and deepened and multiplied. She is in closer touch with nature. Not a bud that opens, not a dew drop, not a ray of light, not a cloud-burst or a thunderbolt, but adds to the expansiveness and zest of her soul" (69). Learning enhances woman's appreciation of herself and others, and in no way diminishes her capacity for loving. "The question is not now with the woman 'How shall I so cramp, stunt, simplify and nullify myself to make me [eligible] to the honor of being swallowed up into some little man?' but the problem . . . now rests with the man as to how he can so develop his God-given powers as to reach the ideal of a generation of women who demand the noblest, grandest and best achievements of which he is capable" (70-71).

Thus the man, too, is a beneficiary from this fuller development of woman:

> The cause of freedom is not the cause of a race or a sect, a party or a class—it is the cause of human kind, the very birthright of humanity. . . . The Women's Movement, is essentially . . . an embodiment [of that cause]. It is not the intelligent woman vs. the ignorant woman; not the white woman vs. the black, the brown, and the red,—it is not even the cause of woman vs. man. . . . Woman's strongest vindication for speaking [is] that *the world needs to hear her voice.* It would be subversive of every human interest that the cry of one-half of the human family be stifled ("Woman versus the Indian," *Voice,* 120-21).

By undertaking to "help shape, mold, and direct the thought of her age, [woman] is merely completing the circle of the world's vision" (122).

Issues of woman's rights, uplifting the race, and social justice are closely related to intellectual development, which in turn depends greatly on education. Cooper's vocation as an educator was a lifelong commitment. She was nearing retirement, researching her doctoral dissertation in the French National Archives, when she told a reporter from the *Chicago Tribune:* "I am soundly convinced that every scrap of information I may gain in the way of broadening horizons and deepening human understanding and sympathies, means true culture, and will redound to the educational values of my work in the school room" (*The Third Step,* 10). In "What Are We Worth?" she wrote:

> The life that serves to develop another, the mother who toils to educate her boy, the father who invests his stored-up capital in education, giving to the world the energies and usefulness of his children trained into a well disciplined manhood and womanhood has paid his debt in the very richest coin. . . . And we may be sure, if we can give no more than a symmetric life, an inspiring thought, a spark caught from a noble endeavor, its value will not be lost (*Voice,* 266).

In an 1893 address to the Congress of Representative Women, she noted how in the less than thirty years since Emancipation, "Our girls as well as our boys flocked in and battled for an education" while many a "slave-mother" had to "eke out enough from her poverty to send her young folks to school" (Loewenberg and Bogin, 330). "This education," asserted Cooper, "has been like the little leaven hid in the measure of meal, permeating life throughout the length and breadth of the Southland, lifting up ideals of home and of womanhood; diffusing a contagious longing for higher living and purer thinking, inspiring woman herself with a new sense of her dignity in the eternal purposes of nature'' (330). So one should insist on ''encouragement for the education of our women and special care in their training,'' and ''if there is an ambitious girl with pluck and brain to take the higher education, encourage her. . . . Let there be the same flourish of trumpets and clapping of hands as when a boy announces his determination to enter the lists'' (''Higher Education of Women,'' *Voice,* 78-79). After all, not only is the black woman vital to the regeneration of the race, she is a vital part of the human equation. ''If one link of the chain be broken,'' Cooper assures us, ''the chain is broken. A bridge is no stronger than its weakest part, and a cause is not worthier than its weakest element'' (Loewenberg and Bogin, 330).

Throughout the years, Cooper's commitment endured, but her vision expanded from the obvious signs of inequality and injustice to the overall situation that created and maintained those conditions in the first place. By the time she did what should be considered her major work—her doctoral thesis at the Sorbonne—Cooper had matured and broadened her perspective considerably. *L'Attitude de la France à l'égard de l'esclavage pendant la Révolution* (Paris: Imprimerie de la Cour d'Appel, 1925) incorporates both sides of the Atlantic and studies the social and racial complexities of the Americas in a global and historical framework. Her opening lines reflect sentiments she had expressed before: ''Slavery in the European colonies of the Americas was an institution based solely upon an abuse of force. Created by a short-sighted and barbarous policy and maintained by violence, we shall see that it could be quickly abolished by a simple legislative measure when the people whom it dishonored realized that they could no longer violate moral law'' (7; translations by Pellow). The immorality of the abuse of force is a recurring theme in Cooper, as is the view that slavery could have been very easily ended if only the will had been present. As she noted in her dissertation defense, ''The custom soon disappeared in Massachusetts without opposition or discussion. They said quite simply that slavery was irreconcilable with their state constitution'' (*Third Step,* 18). And in *L'Attitude,* when the French government in 1794 ''declared slavery abolished . . . [and] decreed that all men without distinction of color . . . would enjoy . . . all the rights guaranteed by the French Constitution. . . . The vote, which was taken standing, was not even debated'' (108).

Although her dissertation at the Sorbonne is labeled as a study of French racial attitudes, it is equally a study of the successful struggle of slaves to throw off an oppressive system and to attempt the creation of a new order. And although this work centers on Haiti and France, Cooper shows that it is not limited geographically or historically, because the whole phenomenon of colonial plantation slavery impacted both sides of the Atlantic over a period of several centuries. In a word, events that took place in antebellum North Carolina, in pre-1843 Bahamas, and in revolutionary Saint Domingue/Haiti were all chapters in the same book of history.

Cooper's *L'Attitude* may at first glance appear to be a very ordinary work, one among many of the studies of events in Saint Domingue that led to the establishment of a black state by slaves who revolted. Indeed, her sources are far from extraordinary; official documents in the Archives de la Guerre and the Archives Nationales, contemporary journals, memoirs, polemic works on slavery, travelogues, and histories. Yet Cooper's work, if it does not make major discoveries or revelations, does possess the unique characteristic of its point of view: it is the work of an African-American scholar who was born a slave, and as such benefits from an insight and sensitivity that elude most histories. For one thing, she holds up positive African images and she praises black achievements; she emphasizes the fact that Toussaint L'Ouverture—the brilliant military strategist and leader of the slaves—was of pure and unmixed African descent, as she had remarked elsewhere that Martin Delany was an ''unadulterated black man'' of whom ''there was no discounting his race identity and attributing his achievements to some admixture of Saxon blood'' (*Voice,* 30). Similarly, in ''What Are We Worth?'' she used a positive metaphor when she wrote ''Certainly the original timber as it came from the African forests was good enough'' (*Voice,* 238).

Black courage in fighting for freedom was amply demonstrated during the United States Civil War, observed Cooper in ''What Are We Worth?'' (*Voice,* 278-80), and again in Saint Domingue when blacks, quoted in an archival document, berate mulattoes who had taken sides with the whites: ''You cowards! Have you forgotten that you were born into our community?. . . . Go tell the Barbarians who command you that we will never surrender; that liberty is for all men; that we are not animals and that we will die fighting!'' (*L'Attitude,* 161). And, if during the United States Civil War, blacks did not pillage and burn undefended areas, it was not because of cowardice but because they ''prefer the judicial awards of peace and have an eternal patience to abide the bloodless triumph of right'' (''The Negro as Presented in American Literature,'' *Voice,* 198).

In a word, Cooper's position is that of sympathy and direct identification with the oppressed, whom she sees as victims of Western civilizations—a phenomenon she often describes as ''barbarian.'' One of her most memorable references is her quote from Taine:

> Huge white bodies, cool-blooded, with fierce blue eyes, reddish flaxen hair; ravenous stomachs, filled with meat and cheese, heated by strong drinks. Brutal drunken pirates and robbers, they dashed to sea in their two-sailed barks, landed anywhere, killed everything; and, having sacrificed in honor of their gods the tithe of all their prisoners, leaving behind the red light of burning, went farther on to begin again (''Race Problem,'' *Voice,* 157).

In ''The Negro as Presented in American Literature'' she admits ''I have not enough of the spirit that comes with the blood of those grand old *sea kings* (I believe you call them) who shot out in their trusty barks speeding over unknown seas and, like a death-dealing genius, with the piercing eye and bloodthirsty heart of hawk or vulture killed and harried, burned and caroused. . . . I haven't it. I frankly admit my limitations'' (*Voice*, 196). And again, in reference to *Harold*, an anonymous novel that pits a refined and cultured black Englishman in a losing situation against American racism, Cooper observes, ''If the cultivated black man cannot endure the white man's barbarity—the cure, it would seem to me, would be to cultivate the white man'' (*Voice*, 210).

Having distanced herself from the barbarity of Western civilization, Cooper preferred to identify with a totally different tradition, to:

> kinship with a very tame and unsanguinary individual who, a long time ago . . . help[ed] a pale sorrow-marked man as he was toiling up a certain hill at Jerusalem bearing his own cross. . . . This Cyrenian fellow was used to bearing burdens and he didn't mind giving a lift over a hard place now and them. . . . And . . . by a rather strange coincidence this unwarlike and insignificant kinsman of ours had his home in a country (the fatherland of all the family) which had afforded kindly shelter to that same mysterious Stranger, when, a babe and persecuted by bloody power and heartless jealousy, He had to flee the land of his birth (''The Negro as Presented in American Literature,'' *Voice*, 196-97).

Cooper is never slow to attack racism as an obstacle to human happiness. Racism breeds barbarity and feeds upon it, afflicting both its practitioners and its victims. ''There can be no true test of national courtesy without travel,'' she writes in ''Woman versus the Indian'' (*Voice*, 93), deploring the rudeness and lack of civility of many white Americans toward blacks. As for segregated cars, Cooper refers to ''laws . . . in certain states requiring persons known to be colored to ride in one car, and persons supposed to be white in another'' (94), and elsewhere observes, ''Surely we are intelligent enough to ride in common buses without flying into one another's arms for a mongrel progeny'' (*Third Step*, 33). It was this obsession with race and color that lost Saint Domingue (which became Haiti) for France. Although black and brown did unite briefly to defeat the invading English in 1795, the general rule in that colony was civil war and strife between competing communities.

Cooper rejected the idea advanced by Bouglé, one of her French professors, that ''Human equality is a man-made concept resulting as a natural product of the transformations in Nordic Society'' (*Third Step*, 28). There are too many contradictions in that concept, not the least of which are lynchings, peonage, and systematic exclusion from public facilities. No, a ''better hypothesis,'' says Cooper, ''would be the postulate that progress in the democratic sense is an inborn human endowment—a shadow mark of the Creator's image, or if you will an urge-cell of the universal and unmistakable hallmark traceable to the Father of all'' (*Third Step*, 29-30). ''Thus far,'' she said, ''the civilization called occidental has attained partial equilibrium only by the physical and perhaps the intellectual forces'' (34). Equality should not be the equilibrium of force, conceded only when one cannot crush or exploit the other, but the equilibrium that comes when ''the big fellow with all the power and all the controls'' stops to consider and respects others as being as good as he is (35). Had that equilibrium been attained by Western civilization there might perhaps never have been such a thing as slavery, which was, wrote Cooper, ''l'exploitation de l'homme par l'homme, sans prétexte comme sans excuse, et seulement au nom du droit du plus puissant (the exploitation of man by man, without pretext or excuse, and solely in the name of the right of the most powerful) (*L'Attitude*, 7).

The selective ''equality'' described in Bryce's *Modern Democracies* (1921), one of the works that Cooper read to prepare her dissertation defense, ''proves conclusively'' she insisted, ''that a truly democratic government exists nowhere''; Bryce's ideal was simply a version of ''the White Man's Burden,'' keeping the right to rule exclusively in white hands. ''But let the Ruler bear in mind,'' warns Cooper, ''that the Right to Rule entails the duty and the inescapable responsibility to Rule Right. Let him recognize the differences among men . . . not as obstacles to fulfillment of destiny . . . [but differences] indicating precisely the providential contribution to that heterogeneity which offers the final test of our civilization, harmony in variety'' (*Third Step*, 35).

Intellectual Evolution Mirrors Social Development

Anna Cooper's intellectual evolution mirrored her social development. From the confined environment of a small, newly-emancipated rural community, she grew to become a broadly educated and knowledgeable scholar and teacher. From a young woman concerned with sexism and racism, she expanded her horizons to international proportions where her concerns could be viewed and addressed in a much broader context.

This process must have begun with her education at Saint Augustine's, particularly in the classics, when she studied the history of ancient Greece and Rome. Later she would have read some of the more recent European writers and thinkers, particularly those in France and Germany, which she was able to read in the original—as she did also the classics. But her personal contacts appear to have been particularly fruitful, beginning with her husband, George Cooper, who was born a free man in Nassau in 1843 or 1844 (emancipation in the British colonies occurred beginning in 1834). His experiences must have provided new perspectives to the curious and intelligent young Anna Cooper, who later went to see Nassau for herself.

Another important contact was the Reverend Alexander Crummell, founder of the American Negro Academy, with whom Anna Cooper had a long acquaintance. A former missionary in Liberia for twenty years (1853-1873), Crummell was the American grandson of an African dignitary and a graduate of Queen's College, Cambridge. His positive views on Africa and on the importance of education find echoes in Cooper's writings. Other significant contacts in Washington were made through Cooper's circle of friends, which, besides the Crummells, included the Grimkés—brothers Archibald and Francis, and the latter's wife, Charlotte Forten Grimké. The Reverend Francis James Grimké, a former slave and graduate of Princeton Theological Seminary, was active in civic affairs in the capital; his wife, Charlotte, the granddaughter of Philadelphia free black abolitionist James Forten (1766-1842) was an activist and a teacher; Archibald Grimké—also a former slave—was a graduate of the Harvard Law School, and served as United States consul to Santo Domingo from 1894 to 1898. These, and others—like W. E. B. Du Bois, Sylvester Williams, and Edward Wilmot Blyden—were individuals with international connections and interests.

It is not surprising, therefore, that Cooper would take the opportunity to travel when she had the chance. Her summer's stay in Canada had a positive impact on her; a glowing letter to her mother speaks of the beauty of Toronto and of the kindness of her hosts, while in *Voice* she refers to a "uniform matter-of-fact courtesy, a genial kindness, quick perception of opportunities for rendering any little manly assistance," which caused her to feel "shame for her country and mortification that her countrymen offered such an unfavorable contrast" (*Voice,* 88-89). Some years later, Cooper would be similarly impressed and pleasantly surprised by public civility in France, when she visited the Chambre des Députés, where it was customary in the public gallery for gentlemen to rise when a lady entered, and to remain standing until she was seated (*Third Step,* 42-43).

These examples of civility contrast with the ugly lack of it in the United States when Cooper describes train conductors who help white passengers descend but who "deliberately fold their arms and turn around when the Black Woman's turn came to alight. . . . The feeling of slighted womanhood," she observes, "is unlike every other emotion of the soul. . . . Its poignancy . . . is holier than that of jealousy, deeper than indignation, tenderer than rage" (90-91).

The 1900 Pan-African Conference in London must have been another important event in Cooper's formation. Arranged by the Trinidadian barrister, Henry Sylvester Williams, and attended by W. E. B. Du Bois, the composer Samuel Coleridge-Taylor, bishop Alexander Walters of Jersey City, former attorney general of Liberia F. S. R. Johnson, and the bishop of London, among others, the conference was held at the Westminster Town Hall and attracted considerable interest. Participants from the Caribbean, Africa, Europe, and the United States—Cooper among them—spoke on a variety of topics relating to peoples everywhere of African descent. The conference ended—after electing to honorary membership Emperor Menelek of Ethiopia and the presidents of Haiti and Liberia—with an address to the governments of all nations to respect the rights of colonized peoples everywhere.

Such exposure on an international scale surely gave Cooper an impetus to undertake the research necessary for her important work that was to earn her the Ph.D. degree. Cooper's great achievement is that she came to understand the importance of these wider, international dimensions, and, as a teacher, to communicate them to her students.

References

Bogin, Ruth, and Bert Loewenberg, eds. *Black Women in Nineteenth-Century American Life: Their Words, Their Thoughts, Their Feelings.* University Park: Pennsylvania State University Press, 1985.

Cooper, Anna Julia. *L'Attitude de la France à l'égard de l'esclavage pendant la Révolution.* Paris: Imprimerie de la Cour d'Appel, 1925. This was Cooper's main doctoral thesis, and has been translated by Frances Richardson Keller as *Slavery and the French Revolutionists (1788-1805).* Lewiston, N.Y.: Edwin Mellen Press, 1988.

———. *Life and Writings of the Grimké Family.* 2 vols. in 1. The Author, 1951.

———. *Le Pèlerinage de Charlemagne.* Paris: A. Lahure, Imprimeur-Editeur, 1925. Introduction by the Abbé Félix Klein. This is Cooper's secondary thesis for the doctorate at the Sorbonne.

———. *The Third Step.* n.p., n.d. (1950?). Autobiographical.

———. *A Voice from the South. By a Black Woman from the South.* New York: Oxford University Press, 1988. This is a reprint of the original 1892 edition with a foreword by Henry Louis Gates, Jr., and an introduction by Mary Helen Washington.

Gabel, Leona Christine. *From Slavery to the Sorbonne and Beyond: The Life and Writings of Anna J. Cooper.* Introduction by Sidney Kaplan. Northampton, Mass.: Department of History of Smith College, 1982. Excellent biography.

Giddings, Paula. *When and Where I Enter.* New York: Morrow, 1984.

Harley, Sharon. "Anna J. Cooper: A Voice for Black Women." In *The Afro-American Woman: Struggles and Images.* Eds. Sharon Harley and Rosalyn Terborg-Penn. Port Washington, N.Y.: Kennikat Press, 1978.

Hooks, Bell. *Ain't I A Woman?: Black Women and Feminism.* Boston: South End Press, 1981.

Hutchinson, Louise Daniel. *Anna J. Cooper, a Voice from the South.* Washington, D.C.: Smithsonian Press, 1981. Prepared in conjunction with an exhibit at the Anacostia Neighborhood Museum, Washington, D.C. This work is a rich mine of visual documentation with some sixteen photographs of Cooper (pp. 2, 18, 28, 40, 44, 72, 84, 102, 130, 154, 170-71, 174, 179, 187) from perhaps around 1877 onwards; photographs of her mother (p. 5), brothers (pp. 26-

27), and grand-niece (p. 173); photographs of people whom Cooper knew, of buildings where she lived, studied or worked; copies of her correspondence, notes, diploma, marriage certificate; pictures of the Haywoods and their various plantations; and reproductions of census reports, bills of sale, and various other archival documents.

Klein, Félix (Abbé). *Au pays de "La Vie intense."* Paris: Plon, Nourrit et Cie., 1907. There are several editions of this work, which describes Klein's visit to and impressions of the United States.

Sewall, May Wright. *World's Congress of Representative Women.* Chicago, 1893. Contains Cooper's "Remarks" following an address by Fannie Barrier Williams on "The Intellectual Progress of the Colored Women of the United States Since the Emancipation Proclamation."

Shockley, Ann Allen. *Afro-American Women Writers, 1746-1933.* Boston: G. K. Hall, 1988.

Who's Who in Colored America. 6th ed. Brooklyn: Thomas Yenser, 1942.

Collections

The papers of Anna J. Cooper, consisting of articles, clippings, letters, and speeches, are in the Moorland-Spingarn Research Center, Howard University.

David W. H. Pellow

Fanny Jackson Coppin (1837-1913)

Educator, civic and religious activist, feminist

Although Fanny Jackson Coppin was born a slave in 1837 in Washington, D. C., from her early childhood on she worked tirelessly to educate herself and her people. A champion of women, the homeless, and the poor, Coppin was honored both in life and in death; thousands of people from across the country attended her funeral in 1913.

Coppin's maternal grandfather was a mulatto named John Orr, a prominent caterer and waiter with substantial property holdings in Washington. Orr purchased his freedom in 1825, and, by 1828, had bought the freedom of his three sons. Later, in 1840, he purchased his eldest daughter, Sarah, who was then thirty years old and about to be married. And, upon his death in 1845, Orr freed his daughter Rebecca by will. However, in Fanny Coppin's words, he refused to free her

Fanny Jackson Coppin

mother, Lucy, "on account of my birth." In her autobiography, published in 1913, Coppin mentions her mother, Lucy, only once and makes no mention of her father (*Reminiscences*, 17). In 1953 Alfred Vance Churchill, with whose parents Fanny Coppin had lived while a student at Oberlin College from 1860 to 1865, suggested that she was the daughter of a slave woman and "a Carolina Senator."

Despite her slave status, Coppin maintained a close relationship with the free members of her family. Her free aunt, Sarah Orr Clark, earned only $6 a month, yet saved enough to purchase Coppin's freedom at the cost of $125. In 1850, due to the stringent resident requirements imposed after the recently passed Fugitive Slave Act and because of better educational opportunities, Coppin moved to New Bedford, Massachusetts, to live with Elizabeth Orr, wife of her uncle, John Orr. There she secured a job as a domestic. Due to her long work hours, Coppin was unable to attend school regularly. In 1851, she and her guardians moved to Newport, Rhode Island, again for better educational opportunities. Not wanting to become a financial burden to her relatives, Coppin secured a position as a servant in the home of the aristocratic author George Henry Calvert, the great-grandson of Lord Baltimore, who settled Maryland. Calvert's wife, Mary Stuart, was a descendant of Mary, Queen of Scots.

The Calverts' household served to nurture Coppin's love of the literary arts. With literary persons from Boston often visiting the Calverts, Coppin described the home as one of "refinement and education." In addition to the education she received through personal contact with such persons, she was able to hire a tutor at the Calverts' for one hour a day, three days a week, from her earnings of seven dollars a month.

Near the end of her six-year stay with the Calverts, she briefly attended the segregated public schools of Newport to prepare for the entrance examination for the Rhode Island State Normal School, which had recently moved from Providence to Bristol. Coppin's educational aspirations were always extremely high, and she refused to allow her race or gender to be deterrents in her quest for intellectual advancement.

Coppin's life in Newport was active and pleasant. She learned to play the piano and guitar and was the organist for the Colored Union Church there. The Calverts were childless, and Coppin remembered that Mrs. Calvert took a special interest in her and taught her sewing, darning, and needlepoint. Despite her seemingly uncomplicated life with the Calverts, it was her goal "to get an education and to teach my people." These goals were ones that she described as being "deep in [her] soul."

As planned, Coppin enrolled in the Rhode Island State Normal School, probably in 1859. In addition to the standard coursework, she studied French privately. While at the normal school, her desire to teach grew, and upon finishing the course, she stated that she still had much to learn. Had Harvard accepted blacks and women in 1860, Coppin very likely would have been listed among its graduates. While disappointed that she could not enroll there, Coppin learned that the Oberlin College curriculum was the same as Harvard, and, more importantly, it accepted blacks and women. In 1860 Coppin enrolled in the ladies department to prepare for the entrance examination of the collegiate department. In 1861 she entered the freshman class of the collegiate department. That year, only 199 out of 1,311 students were enrolled in the Collegiate Department. Also, at that time, no black woman had graduated from that department. Nevertheless, Coppin, with a tremendous amount of self-confidence, was not discouraged from pursuing and obtaining a college degree. She was assisted financially at Oberlin by a variety of sources. Her aunt Sarah Orr Clark provided some assistance, and Bishop Daniel A. Payne, a bishop of the African Methodist Episcopal Church, was so impressed by her determination and ambition that he provided her with a scholarship. In addition, she received a one hundred dollar grant from the Avery Fund of Oberlin College.

Always conscious of her race and gender, Coppin noted that although the collegiate department was opened to women in principle, its administrators " did not advise it." She recognized the challenge and the significance of her pursuit of a college degree and recalled:

> I never rose to recite in my classes at Oberlin but I felt that I had the honor of the whole African race upon my shoulders. I felt that, should I fail, it would be ascribed to the fact that I was colored (Coppin, *Reminiscences*, 15).

Far from failing, Coppin earned an impressive academic record and involved herself in nearly every facet of life at Oberlin. In addition to her classes, she continued to take private French lessons (the subject was not part of the Oberlin curriculum). She sang in the First Church Choir of Oberlin and, in order to supplement her income, gave piano lessons to sixteen children of Oberlin faculty members.

Coppin was a noted scholar in all of her classes and in her second year was elected a member of the prestigious Young Ladies Literary Society. The society was founded at Oberlin in 1835 and is considered the oldest women's club in America. The group debated many questions that were foremost during the Civil War years and sponsored programs that included the reading of poems, essays, and prepared orations. The largest of these programs took place during commencement week and was open to the public. Coppin appeared in these programs throughout her years at Oberlin. In 1862 she composed a poem and in 1864 she gave an oration titled "The Hero of Gettysburg" and appeared in a colloquy in which she depicted the continent of Africa. In her senior year she gave yet another oration, titled "Lorain News—August 30, 1865."

In addition to the experience the society afforded Coppin in public speaking and literary creativity, as a member of Oberlin's collegiate department she was responsible for "compositions, declamations and extemporaneous discussions weekly; and public original declamations, monthly" (*Catalogue of Oberlin College 1863-1864*, 38). These combined experiences were to provide her with a foundation in public speaking that enabled her to become an elocutionist of prominence.

During the Civil War years, when Coppin attended Oberlin, she was able to have one of her life's goals realized—to become a teacher of her race. When the freedmen began to pour into the city of Oberlin in 1863, she voluntarily established an evening class that met four nights a week. Although the class was open to blacks of all ages, most were adults who came to class after working all day. Virtually all of the adults were illiterate and Coppin taught them the rudiments of reading and writing. Despite her academic demands and the large number of music pupils she taught, Coppin was extremely conscientious with her evening class and often conducted public exhibitions to display the work of her students. The evening school drew many visitors, and the local newspaper, as well as abolitionist newspapers, carried accounts of its progress. The class continued until Coppin graduated in 1865. The success of her evening class resulted in her being chosen as the first black teacher in the preparatory department at Oberlin College. In 1865 she was elected class poet and graduated with a baccalaureate degree.

Leadership at the Institute for Colored Youth Begins

After graduation, Coppin was appointed principal of the female department of the Institute for Colored Youth in Philadelphia, a high school for blacks founded by the Society of Friends in 1837. Because of the publicity she had received for her evening school at Oberlin and for her outstanding academic accomplishments, Coppin was well known to the Philadelphia black community.

The Institute for Colored Youth was a prestigious school. It included a preparatory department, girls and boys high school departments, and a teacher-training course. The school's faculty included the most highly educated blacks of the period. Coppin was a huge success at the institute, and when principal Ebenezer Bassett was appointed to the position of U. S. Minister of Haiti in 1869, she was immediately promoted to principal of the entire school.

Coppins' promotion was of great significance for a woman. Rarely, if ever, did women head a coeducational high school with male faculty members. Although one male member of the faculty protested the appointment, the all-male Quaker Board of Managers stated that Coppin was even more qualified to lead the institute than the previous principal. In her four years at the institute prior to being appointed principal, Coppin had frequently been singled out for her outstanding teaching and leadership. Her ability to make learning easy and enjoyable became a trademark of her teaching style.

The Institute for Colored Youth was located within the heart of the Philadelphia black community, near the historic Mother Bethel African Methodist Episcopal Church. The *Christian Recorder*, the newspaper of the AME Church, carried news of the institute's and Coppin's activities, and she frequently wrote children's stories for the paper. In 1878 Coppin began writing a regular column titled "Women's Department' for the *Christian Recorder*. Through this column she was able to reach blacks on a nationwide basis—particularly black women. Her articles reported the achievements of women in education, employment, and other areas, and also reported cases of discrimination against black women. Always a staunch feminist, Coppin stressed in her column that women should pursue the same professions as men and not simply enter the traditional "women's" fields.

Coppin was active in many facets of the Philadelphia black community. She stressed self-determination and self-help. When the *Christian Recorder* was threatened with termination due to financial difficulty, Coppin organized a World's Fair to assist the paper financially. Although Coppin was Episcopal and the paper was a publication of the AME Church, she stressed to the black community that the termination of the paper should be a concern of all blacks, not just those of the AME denomination, since the paper employed blacks. She pointed out that the *Christian Recorder* "finds its way into many a dark hamlet in the South where no one has ever heard of the Philadelphia *Bulletin* or the New York *Tribune*" (Coppin, *Reminiscences*, 29).

The 1879 fair was a success and cleared the debt of the paper; in addition, the forty-two-year-old educator met her husband, Levi Coppin there. Coppin, at least fifteen years his wife's junior, was a native of Maryland and a minister of the AME church. The couple was married during the Christmas holidays of 1881 in Washington, D.C., and shortly after their marriage, the reverend was transferred to Bethel AME Church in Baltimore. While it was expected that Coppin would resign her position at the institute and move to Baltimore at the end of the 1881-82 school year, she remained at the institute. But, by 1884, Levi Coppin had obtained a transfer to the small Allen Chapel AME Church in Philadelphia, where he could be with his wife as well as study theology at the Protestant Episcopal Divinity School. Although the minister wanted his wife to give up her position as principal after their marriage, he saw that she was devoted to her work and "had a fixed course in life, and stubbornly maintained it until it became a fixed habit" (Coppin, *Unwritten History*, 356).

Coppin was reluctant to leave the Institute for Colored Youth at the time of her marriage because she was in the midst of a campaign to establish an industrial department at the school. Because blacks were shut out of the growing technical and industrial jobs of Philadelphia, Coppin decided that they should open their own industrial school. Her enthusiasm for the project was spurred "as I saw building after building going up in the city, and not a single colored hand employed in the constructions" (Coppin, *Reminiscences*, 28).

After a decade of speeches and fund-raising, the industrial department of the institute opened in January 1889. Although the department fell far short of the advanced technical classes Coppin had hoped for—it offered only courses in carpentry, bricklaying, shoemaking, printing, plastering, millinery, dressmaking, and cooking—the school was flooded with applications and a waiting list of hundreds was maintained. It was the first trade school for blacks in Philadelphia.

Coppin Addresses Women's Issues

In addition to raising funds for the Institute for Colored Youth during the 1880s, Coppin attempted to improve the employment situation of black women. With a committee of women from Mother Bethel Church, she opened a home for destitute young women in 1888. The three-story home included a matron and a visiting physician and offered courses in nurses training. In 1894 Coppin established a Women's Exchange and Girls' Home next door to her own house. In addition to providing housing for students and working females, the Women's Exchange gave instruction in cooking, dressmaking, and domestic economy. Periodic exhibitions of the industrial work were mounted and various articles made there were also sold.

After her marriage in 1881, Coppin became active in the AME Church. Combining her interests in women's and religious issues, she was elected president of the local Women's Mite Missionary Society and subsequently became national president of the Women's Home and Foreign Missionary Society of the AME Church. In 1888 she represented the organization at the Centenary of Missions Conference in London.

Coppin was politically active throughout her life and although women could not vote during her lifetime, she viewed the franchise as important not only for men but for women as well. She frequently spoke at political rallies and most often was the only woman on the program. When the

National Association of Colored Women was established in 1897, she became one of the organization's vice-presidents.

By the turn of the century, the years of activity began to take a toll on Coppin's health. She had spent endless hours working at the institute and had earnestly tried to find employment and housing for her students and other blacks in Philadelphia. Her speaking engagements had been voluminous, as had her involvement with civic and religious activities. In 1896 she became ill with pleurisy, which confined her to her home. She never fully recovered, and in 1901 she announced her retirement as principal of the Institute for Colored Youth effective in June 1902.

Although Coppin was extremely private concerning her personal affairs and made but one brief mention of her marriage to Levi Coppin in her autobiography *Reminiscences of School Life, and Hints on Teaching*, from all indications, the Coppins' marriage was a close one and Levi appeared very proud to be the husband of such a distinguished woman. He often spoke and wrote of her with deep respect, admiration, and appreciation. Although the school year was devoted to the institute, during the summers, Fanny Coppin often traveled with her husband on behalf of the AME Church. The year after Levi Coppin graduated from the Philadelphia Episcopal Divinity School, in 1887, he was appointed editor of the *AME Review*, a prestigious position within the church. He maintained this post until 1896, when he was appointed pastor of Mother Bethel. He remained there until 1900, when he was elected bishop of the Fourteenth Episcopal District in South Africa.

After her retirement from the institute in 1902, Fanny Coppin accompanied her husband to Capetown, South Africa. Because of her poor health and her age, many in the black community feared that she would not survive the trip. Prior to the Coppins' departure, a series of testimonials were given in Fanny Coppin's honor. Newspapers reported the audiences were overflowing at each occasion. Gifts and money were given to Coppin and, despite her great modesty, she was deeply touched by the outpouring of affection from the community and her former students. Making closing remarks at one of the testimonial dinners given on her behalf, she reflected on her life in Philadelphia and her connection with the institute. She told the audience of her great love for the institute and how her husband had understood her attachment to the school, allowing her to remain in her post as principal after their marriage. She stated that she had striven to do her best, considering each student individually and making each one important. She recalled her struggles to obtain the industrial department and to combine this training with an intellectual education. In closing, Coppin said that she had always had two schools—the institute and the Philadelphia black community. This statement summed up the educator's revelation that her life's dream had been realized —"to get an education and to teach my people." And the many who had come under her influence responded gratefully. On the day of the Coppins' departure, scores of friends from throughout the nation traveled to New York to see the couple sail to South Africa. The press reported the scene as one of "deep interest and a degree of sadness" (*Christian Recorder*).

The Coppins arrived in Capetown in December 1902, then traveled into the interior of the country. As many feared, the trip affected the health of Coppin, and she experienced fainting spells. She soon recovered, however, and devoted her time to developing missions among the women of the country. Her impact on the women of South Africa was great; the African missions raised ten thousand dollars to erect the Fanny Jackson Coppin Girls Hall at Wilberforce Institute the AME school in Capetown, as a symbol of their appreciation of the missionary-educator.

Spending only a year in South Africa, the Coppins left in December 1903. After visiting several European countries, they arrived in the United States in the spring of 1904. Bishop Coppin was then appointed to the Seventh Episcopal District of the AME Church encompassing South Carolina and Alabama. Fanny Coppin traveled to South Carolina with her husband; however, the South Africa trip had exacerbated her health problems, and by 1905 she was so physically weak that she spent the remaining eight years of her life confined primarily to her Philadelphia home.

Despite Coppin's confinement, her mind and memory were intact. In her final years, she devoted her time to reading books and conversing with the many friends and former students who visited her. In the year of her death, 1913, she began writing her autobiography and a book on pedagogy, *Reminiscences of School Life, and Hints on Teaching*. Although she completed the major portion of the book, a former student, William C. Bolivar, compiled the section concerning the Institute for Colored Youth faculty and students, which was still in manuscript form at the time of her death.

On January 21, 1913, Coppin died at her Philadelphia home. Hundreds of condolences poured in to her husband from across the nation and abroad. Seemingly reflecting the sadness of the occasion, a day of heavy rain accompanied Coppin's funeral services. Thousands, many of whom traveled from different cities and towns from around the country, filled Mother Bethel AME Church. Others, unable to obtain seats, stood outside in the inclement weather during the impressive four-hour ceremony. Testimonies were given by members of the many missionary and religious organizations with which Coppin had been affiliated, the graduates of the Institute for Colored Youth, and by a member of the Society of Friends. Of the day, the Philadelphia *Tribune* noted:

> The lowering clouds and heavy rain on Monday was a fitting prototype of the sorrow that saddened the hearts of several thousand souls who gathered at Bethel AME at 11 o'clock to attend the funeral services held over the remains of the late Mrs. Fanny Jackson Coppin, wife of Bishop L. J. Coppin.

Following the funeral, memorial services were conducted for

the deceased educator in Washington, D.C., Baltimore, and Philadelphia.

Known throughout her life as a champion of the poor, Coppin was an extremely modest and unassuming individual. A tall woman who dressed simply, she was a captivating speaker who never used notes. Throughout her life she attempted to make education available to blacks, whether wealthy or poor. During her tenure at the Institute for Colored Youth, she had tuition abolished so that the college preparatory school would be accessible to the children of the poor as well as the black middle class. Her concern for all endeared her to the many poor blacks of Philadelphia. As a Philadelphia journalist who had attended the institute commented: "Even with [Coppin's] rare learning, she never made even the humblest appear uncomfortable" (Philadelphia *Tribune*).

Coppin State College in Baltimore, Maryland, is named in honor of Fanny Jackson Coppin.

References

Catalogue of Oberlin College, 1863-1864.

Christian Recorder, 22 October 1902.

Coppin, Fanny Jackson. *Reminiscences of School Life, and Hints on Teaching*. Philadelphia: AME Book Concern, 1913.

Coppin, Levi Jenkins. *Unwritten History*. 1919. Reprint. New York: Negro Universities Press, 1968.

Drinkard-Hawshawe, Dorothy. "Fannie Jackson Coppin." *Dictionary of American Negro Biography*. Edited by Rayford W. Logan and Michael R. Winston. New York: Norton, 1982. 130-32.

Fishel, Leslie H., Jr. "Fanny Jackson Coppin." *Notable American Women: 1607-1950*. Vol. I. Cambridge: Harvard University Press, 1971. 383-84.

New York Age, 8 November 1890.

Perkins, Linda M. *Fanny Jackson Coppin and the Institute for Colored Youth, 1865-1902*. New York: Garland, 1987.

Tribune, (Philadelphia) 1 February 1913.

Collections

Documents concerning Fanny Jackson Coppin's Oberlin years are available in the Oberlin College Archives. Documents of her years as principal at the Institute for Colored Youth are available at the Friend's Historical Library, Swarthmore College. The *Christian Recorder* carried articles by and about Coppin from 1865 until her death in 1913.

Linda M. Perkins

Camille Cosby

(1945-)

Philanthropist, entrepreneur, foundation executive

Camille Olivia Hanks Cosby is a philanthropist, entrepreneur, and chief executive of Cosby Enterprises, whose primary interests are the support of black colleges and the education of black youth. Convinced that these institutions still graduate more blacks from middle-income families and that they build foundations of excellence, she challenges all blacks to come to the aid of black institutions.

Camille Hanks Cosby was born in 1945 to Guy and Catherine Hanks in Washington, D.C., the oldest of four children. Her father attended Southern University in Baton Rouge and then Fisk University in Nashville, Tennessee, where he received his master's degree. Her mother attended Howard University, Washington, D.C. Camille Cosby attended parochial schools and was reared in rather genteel surroundings. Her parents encouraged her in music, although she never became seriously interested in it.

After completing high school, she studied psychology at the University of Maryland, where she was introduced to Bill Cosby on a blind date. It was "love at first sight" for Bill Cosby and a marriage proposal on the second date (Norment, 150). Their first date was at a club where he was performing. The courtship did not flow smoothly at first. Although Bill Cosby asked Camille Hanks to marry him, her father opposed on the grounds that she was too young and should concentrate on her studies. Despite the opposition, they were married on January 25, 1964, at the starting point of Bill Cosby's illustrious career.

She dropped out of the University of Maryland at nineteen, when she married, and traveled to cities where Bill Cosby was trying to make his start. "Then he made an appearance on 'The Tonight Show' and came to the attention of the producer of 'I Spy' and the rest is history," said Camille Cosby (Oliver, 114). The Cosbys moved to California and suddenly became very successful people. Bill Cosby's rapid rise as a comedian also brought a rapid increase in the family's income and a drastic change in their lives. Both were inexperienced in financial management and in dealing with people who asked for their financial assistance. After Bill Cosby's manager apparently mishandled their money, the Cosbys decided that the two of them would manage his career and their finances as well.

They established a high-powered family business in Los Angeles. Camille Cosby, whom Bill Cosby describes as a shrewd businesswoman and "rough to deal with when it comes to my business," manages the enterprises (Norment, 152). The family enterprises include television's "The Cosby Show" and "A Different World," movies, comedies, videos, recordings, television commercials, books, and philanthropic gifts. She hires and fires the attorneys, accountants, private pilots, and the clerical and maintenance staff, including those in their homes in California, Massachusetts, Pennsylvania, and New York.

As Bill Cosby became a multimillionaire and a multimedia megastar and the family enterprises prospered, the Cosbys searched for meaningful ways to support the black community. Camille Cosby's interest in black colleges was inspired partly because her parents had attended them and partly because of the research that she had conducted to identify their problems. She visited eight black colleges, interviewed their presidents, and came away with a clear view of a uniform problem—their alumni were not supporting the colleges. Many were receiving first-generation college students, indicating that their graduates who had college-age students were sending them to white colleges. "It was a real eye-opener. I was stunned to know that the graduates of these institutions were not supporting them and that was because, perhaps, we as a people had bought into the idea that 'White is better'" (Johnson, "Bill and Camille Cosby," 34).

Refuting the idea of "white is better," since 1986 the Cosbys have donated more than $24.1 million to black colleges. Their largest gift, $20 million, was given to Spelman College in Atlanta, Georgia, at the May 1989 commencement—the largest personal gift ever in the history of black institutions. The funds are to be used to build the Camille Olivia Hanks Cosby Academic Center, to endow three chairs in the fine arts, social sciences, and humanities, and to support a library and archives in international African women research. "This $20 million gift to Spelman is many-fold, carrying many, many messages. Mostly, it is a gift to the world," said Bill Cosby (Johnson, "Bill and Camille Cosby," 30). The Cosbys are firm believers in education. On this issue Camille Cosby said:

> Once you educate someone, then you are allowing them to enter the mainstream of society, which means that they can then afford decent housing. First of all, they can get a decent job. They can buy good food, but most important is that they can start another generation cycle of educated African-Americans. The cycle can continue for generations to come (Johnson, "Bill and Camille Cosby," 34).

Her commitment to the black community is deep and sincere. "None of us can be strong unless we have the support of the community," she said. "And unless the community is strong, it's impossible for us to be strong. No matter how big we become" (Oliver, 114).

Camille and Bill Cosby started their humanitarianism by giving $1.3 million to Fisk University in 1986. In 1987 the Cosbys gave another $1.3 million to be divided equally among Central State University (Wilberforce, Ohio), Howard University, Florida Agricultural and Mechanical University (Tallahassee), and Shaw University (Raleigh, North Carolina). In 1988 they donated $1.5 million to be divided between Meharry Medical College (Nashville, Tennessee) and Bethune-Cookman College (Daytona Beach, Florida).

Camille Cosby has been involved in a number of philanthropic activities, including the key role in helping raise $337,000 for the Reverend Jesse Jackson's Operation Push. Even though Camille Cosby has aided such organizations as the NAACP and the Student Christian Leadership Conference (SCLC), her longest involvement has been with the United Negro College Fund.

According to Camille Cosby, she and her husband also send about twenty-eight students to various colleges and universities, and most of the colleges are black. Beyond the world of philanthropy, Camille Cosby is a producer of albums and videos. With her coproducer, Judith Rutherford James, she is in the preproduction phase of a film based on the life of Nomzamo Winifred "Winnie" Mandela.

Even though she enjoys her work as a philanthropist, Camille Cosby prefers her role as mother to four daughters and one son. She also enjoys doing her own cooking, which entails some mouth-watering soul-food dishes.

Continuing in the educational tradition, Camille and Bill Cosby sent their son, Ennis, to Morehouse College in Atlanta, and daughter Erinn to Spelman; they wanted the other children, Erika, Evin, and Ensa, to attend black colleges. Now that her home nest is virtually emptied of children, Camille Cosby is becoming more visible in the business affairs of the family in her position as partner in all of the Cosby enterprises.

While it is clear that Camille Cosby neither seeks or requires glory and honor for her achievements, she has received some, though not enough, recognition. In 1961 she was Omega Psi Phi beauty queen at Howard University, where in 1987, after delivering the Commencement address, she received an honorary doctorate. She received another honorary doctorate from Spelman on "Camille Cosby Day," or commencement day in May 1989. In her spirited commencement address entitled "Victory," she said:

> Despite all the [adversity] we have known in this country, we have had our victories. . . . Given the odds, we weren't supposed to stop being slaves. Given the opposition, we weren't supposed to have an education. Given the history, we weren't supposed to have families. Given the blues, we weren't supposed to have spirit. Given the power of the enemy, we weren't supposed to fight back. Not only have we achieved victories, we have—despite the powers against us—become our own victories" (Oliver, 64).

She holds honorary membership in Delta Sigma Theta Sorority. The group appealed to her because she found the Delta sisters "self-defining." The members have gone beyond themselves "to projects of community in our ghettos, in the courts, our schools, and, most important, in the African Diaspora," she said (Johnson, "Bill and Camille Cosby Discuss Secrets," 60). Camille Cosby is active in other groups with a national concern. She is a member of the board of directors of Essence Communications, the National Council of Negro Women, and the National Rainbow Coalition. She keeps well informed on pressing social issues.

The attractive, poised, Camille Cosby has been described as "classy, reserved and stubborn" (Norment, 154) and "a stunning woman with an earthy personality and a ready smile" (Oliver, 114). She is concerned with self-image and obedient to the laws of health—proper diet and exercise. Faced with the issue of whether or not to allow her gray hair to go without the color rinse that she used since she started graying while in her twenties, she decided to let the beauty of nature take its course. "I began to realize how imprisoned I had been to the [dye] bottle, and how wonderful it was to deal with my hair as it really is—and how wonderful it was to acknowledge my age" (Oliver, 114). On this issue she said also: "I needed the freedom. I need the freedom to define myself" (Johnson, "Bill and Camille Cosby Discuss Secrets," 58).

A doctoral candidate on leave-of-absence from the University of Massachusetts School of Education, where she received her M.Ed. degree in 1980, Camille Cosby doubts that she will actively use the degree. "But psychologically it will make me feel great," she said in an interview with Frances Lear ("Bill and Camille Cosby," 16). She and her family now reside in the state of Massachusetts.

References

'Biography. Camille O. Cosby." Camille O. Cosby office, Santa Monica, California.

"Bill and Camille Cosby." *Lear's* 4 (April 1991): 15-16. Photographs on cover and in text.

Johnson, Robert E. "Bill and Camille Cosby Discuss the Secrets of Living a Better Life." *Jet* (2 October 1989). 58-62. Includes photographs.

———. "Bill and Camille Cosby: First Family of Philanthropy." *Ebony* 44 (May 1989): 25-34. Includes photographs.

Norment, Lynn. "Three Great Love Stories." *Ebony* 43 (February 1988): 150-156. Photograph, p. 150.

Oliver, Stephanie Stokes. "Camille Cosby: An Intimate Portrait." *Essence* 20 (December 1989): 63-64. Includes family photographs.

Jessie Carney Smith

Julia Ringwood Coston

(18?- ?)

Publisher, journalist

In the decades following Reconstruction, the black American press evolved to include many specialized journals. Among the pioneers of the black periodical press in the United States was Julia Ringwood Coston, who published two magazines for black women in the 1890s.

Coston was born on Ringwood Farm in Warrenton, Virginia, and brought to Washington, D.C., at an early age. She attended public school, where she reached "the highest grade." Her education continued after she became governess to the family of a Union general. In 1886 she married William Hilary Coston, a student at Yale. William Coston had published a pamphlet, *A Free Man and Yet a Slave* (1884), which was later expanded and published as a book in Chatham, Ontario, in 1888.

William Coston was an AME minister. During their years in Cleveland, Ohio, where he was pastor of St. Andrew's Church, Julia Coston began publishing *Ringwood's Afro-American Journal of Fashion*. Though the magazine was much more than a fashion journal, it was widely complimented for coverage of the latest trends from Paris. Monroe Majors described *Ringwood's Afro-American Journal of Fashion* as a beautifully made and unique publication. Majors includes a statement from Coston, which may have been one of her editorials, that indicates how touched she was by the struggle of black women in the South and how much she wanted to "secure for Afro-American women and children all the blessings of this great country" (Majors, 252-53). Believing in the virtues of a strong yet soft and refined type of femininity, Coston felt that "in every situation in life, at home surrounded by luxury, or in the world struggling for preference, a woman's womanhood is her surest, strongest shield" (Majors, 254).

The staff of *Ringwood's Afro-American Journal of Fashion* included Sarah Mitchell (home department), Earnestine Clark Nesbitt ("Mother's Corner"), Susie I. Shorter ("Plain Talk to Our Girls"), Adina E. White (art department), Molly E. Lambert (literary department), and Mary Church Terrell (biographical sketches). The Philadelphia *Times* described the journal as

> especially designed to be an Afro-American magazine . . . edited in its different departments by colored women, but the pleasing fashion

> articles, instructive talks with girls and mothers and witty all-around paragraphs and interesting love stories make Ringwood's *Magazine* a welcome addition to any home, whether its occupants be black or white (Majors, 256).

The new fashion magazine was praised for its pleasing appearance, its many illustrations, and its variety in a number of newspapers, including the Philadelphia *State Journal,* which noted "it is the first publication of the kind, and should have the support of the Afro-American women of the land, as it is published by an Afro-American woman, and fully represents them as they are intelligent, virtuous and beautiful" (Majors, 257). A subscriber writing to Coston in 1892 expressed her delight with the magazine, which she felt was "so pure, so womanly—positively agreeable in its every feature as reading for private home, instruction and guidance" (Majors, 256).

Coston published two magazines while the couple lived in Cleveland. According to information in the *Ayer Directory of Newspapers and Periodicals*, she may have published *Ringwood's Afro-American Journal of Fashion* for a year or more before publishing *Ringwood's Home Magazine* (circa 1893-circa 1895). These periodicals appeared monthly; a year's subscription to *Ringwood's Afro-American Journal of Fashion* cost $1.25 in 1892. Though thousands of copies of each monthly issue were circulated, regrettably copies of neither title have been located.

Little else is known about Julia Ringwood Coston's life. She had two children, a daughter, Julia R., and a son, W. H. Her husband, William H., published a number of books and pamphlets in the 1890s.

References

Ayers Directory of Newspapers and Periodicals. Fort Washington, Pennsylvania: IMS Press, 1892, 1893/94, 1895.

Bullock, Penelope L. *The Afro-American Periodical Press, 1838-1909*. Baton Rouge: Louisiana State University Press, 1981.

Logan, Rayford W. "Julia Ringwood Coston." *Dictionary of American Negro Biography*. Edited by Rayford W. Logan and Michael R. Winston. New York: Norton, 1982.

Majors, Monroe A. *Noted Negro Women*. 1893. Reprinted. Chicago: Donohue & Henneberry, 1971.

Susanna Bartmann Pathak

Elizabeth "Libba" Cotten

(1892-1987)

Singer, musician

Although Elizabeth Cotten did not make her professional debut as a folk singer until she was sixty-seven years old, the self-taught musician had a great influence on many folk artists. The composer of such classics as "Freight Train" and "Washington Blues," whose unique style of guitar playing was imitated by many, worked many years as a domestic servant before being discovered by Pete Seeger and hailed as an important artist of the folk revival.

Cotten, frequently called Libba, was born in January 1892 in Chapel Hill, Orange County, North Carolina. She was the youngest of five children of George Nevills and Louisa (Price) Nevills. Her father, a dynamite setter in an iron mine, who made liquor to supplement the family income, was the son of a slave. Her mother was a midwife, the daughter of a farmer landholder from Siler City, North Carolina. Louisa Nevills was ten years old when the slaves were freed, and her family reacted to the Emancipation Proclamation with concern for protecting their horses from the Union Army.

Elizabeth "Libba" Cotten

Cotten was raised in Chapel Hill in the North Carolina Piedmont, an area that Bruce Bastin describes as having a strong blues and pre-blues tradition. He noted in *Red River Blues* that her "repertoire reflects the pre-blues dance pieces and tunes that were common in her girlhood" (282). Willie Trice, one of Bastin's informants, explained that the blues and rags played in the Orange County area at the time, when performed by banjo players, were called reels rather than blues. The music from her youth informed Cotten's later style.

Cotten's was also influenced by church music. She explained to Alice Gerrard in *Frets*:

> I was raised up goin' to Sunday School and singing. Everybody'd get a book and get up there and sing the songs. If there was notes, there was somebody always who would know the notes. And he'd sing it for you and then you'd follow him. We didn't know no notes. He'd know when to tell you to sing or what. "Now, if I'm an alto and you're a soprano, here's the lead. All right, you sing your part, now you sing your part, you sing yours." Well, if you weren't singing it right, he'd say, "You don't go up on that, you go down," or something for you to know what you were doing (27).

Cotten's was a musical family. She sang at home with her mother, and her uncles played fiddle and banjo. Although she would have preferred to learn to play the organ and piano, the first instrument she learned to play was the banjo, because her brother owned one. She recalled learning to play it when he was at work:

> Times when my brother'd go to work, I'd grab his banjo and turn the pegs and try to play it. Always ended up breakin' the strings. After dinner that night he'd roll a cigarette and go to get his banjo. I'd head for the bedroom and hide under the bed. There'd be a silence, then I'd hear him say, very quietly to himself, "She done it again." But he never would get after me to my face (Chalmers, 65).

Cotten quit school when she was eleven years old to earn money to buy a guitar. She went door to door, looking for work, and she developed a sales pitch. As she put it, she stood on the doorstep of each prospective employer and listed her capabilities: "I can scrub the floor and wash clothes and dust the furniture and carry in the wood and chips" (Chalmers, 65). She was hired by Miss Ada Copeland, who at first paid her seventy-five cents a month and later one dollar a month. When she had saved enough money, she bought a demonstrator Sears and Roebuck Stella for $3.75. Although Cotten's two brothers played and her sister chorded, none of them knew formal music:

> They didn't know nothin' about no music. They just played, like all country people get together and play songs. I learn yours and you learn mine and just keep on like that. But I didn't even have that much chance when I was learning. Nobody to help me to play (Gerrard, 28).

"Cotton Picking" Guitar Style Developed

What distinguished Cotten's guitar-style is that she played left-handed on a guitar strung for right-handers. According to Eileen Southern, Cotten "did not reverse the strings but turned the guitar upside down with the bass strings on the bottom" (86). Her upside-down style of playing the banjo and guitar "brings the rhythmic effect and emphasis inherent in the thumb to the middle and upper strings, while sustaining the traditional alternating bass with the fingers" (*Elizabeth Cotton Live!*). Stephen Michelson observes that the style is frequently imitated and "is often called 'Cotton [sic] picking' after Elizabeth Cotten who actually plays a right-handed guitar left-handed, playing the bass with her fingers, the treble with her thumb" (*Music from the Hills of Caldwell County*).

Cotten explained how she acquired this "Cotten" style:

> I had learned a banjo upside down and I couldn't change [the strings] because it belonged to my brother. Then when I bought the guitar, so much was said like, "You better change the strings, you can't play it left-handed," that they was changed as much as two or three times. And I could not play it. I couldn't play it, I couldn't tune it, I couldn't do anything with it. So I just sat down and took all the strings off, then I put 'em back on the old way and I stopped askin'. I started playing, learning different little tunes on it. I'd get one little string and then add another little string to it and get a little sound, then start playing.

"I banged that guitar all day and I banged it all night so nobody could sleep." Cotten recalled. "Nobody helped me. I give myself credit for everything I learned" (Chalmers, 65). What she developed from her self-instruction was, according to Kristin Baggelaar and Donald Milton, "two-finger and 'banjo' stylings for which her name is most famous. In addition to this 'Cotten style' of guitar picking, she plays a broken rhythm style, using three or four fingers and chording up the neck" (87).

Cotten's early musical career was by no means professional. Although she composed the classic "Freight Train" when she was only eleven and had a great future in music before her, two factors stifled her musical development. One was her marriage to Frank Cotten, and the other was the religious community. After their first date, they eloped and subsequently lived in her mother's home until they could afford to rent a house. Married at fifteen and a mother at sixteen—to a daughter, Lillie—Cotten could no longer devote herself to music. Cotten's musical development yielded to her religious experiences.

Thus, as a result of persuasive church officers and marriage and parenthood, Cotten left off her early music interests.

For the next fifty years, until she began to perform professionally in 1959, Cotten lived in various places and held several jobs. She moved with her husband and daughter between New York and Chapel Hill until her husband, a chauffeur, opened his own business in New York. Cotten worked as a domestic servant. In about 1947, the Cotten's divorced, and she moved to Washington, D.C., where her daughter was living. There, Cotten worked during the holiday season at Lansburgh's Department Store, on the fifth floor where dolls were sold.

In Lansburgh's, Cotten found a young girl who had wandered away from her mother. The girl's mother, Ruth Crawford Seeger was a composer and music teacher and wife of the ethnomusicologist Charles Seeger. Serendipitously, Ruth Seeger proposed that if Cotten chose to stop working at the store, she could come work for the Seeger's in Chevy Chase, Maryland. Cotten accepted her offer. At the Seeger home, Ruth Seeger was compiling a folksong collection for children, and her own children were learning music. Mike Seeger recalls that Cotten would use the young Peggy's guitar and practice in the kitchen, which she was doing when they first heard her play. Thus, Ruth Seeger "collected a few songs from Libba" for her compilation (Gerrard, 29).

Libba Cotten Becomes Professional Folk Artist

Cotten made her professional debut with Mike Seeger at a concert at Pennsylvania's Swarthmore College in 1959. She was sixty-seven years old. From that time to her death, Cotten was a professional folk artist and a part of a steadily increasing movement toward folk music appreciation. Bob Groom notes that by 1964, Cotten had appeared at the Newport Folk Festival with such notables as John Hurt, Skip James, John Estes, Muddy Waters, and Otis Spann. She appeared there again in 1968. From 1968 to 1971 and again in 1975, she performed at the American Folklife Festival in Washington, D.C. In 1968, according to Pete Seeger, "Libba Cotten, seventy-two years old and black, got a standing ovation from 3,000 white students at Duke University in March" (308). In 1969, she performed at the Smokey Mountain Folk Festival in Gatlinburg, Tennessee, and at Washington Square Church in New York City.

In November 1978, Cotten performed at the first Washington Blues Festival, a benefit for black blues musicians held at Howard University, where she was listed among such blues luminaries as Furry Lewis, John Estes, and Hammie Nixon. Also during the 1970s Cotten performed at Canada's Mariposa Folk Festival, the Philadelphia Folk Festival, McCabe's in Santa Monica, California, Washington's Kennedy Center, and at the Folklife Festival on the Eno River in Durham, North Carolina. In 1978, she played New York City's Carnegie Hall.

During the 1980s Cotten continued to perform steadily, and at age ninety toured Europe and America with Taj Mahal. Later she toured on her own, traveling roughly four months of the year.

Besides her performances at coffee houses, folk festivals, universities, and concert halls, Cotten developed a full recording career. She cut her first solo album, *Negro Folk Songs and Tunes*, in 1957, for Folkways. She also recorded on Folkways *Elizabeth Cotten, Volume II: Shake Sugaree*, 1967, *Elizabeth Cotten, Volume III: When I'm Gone*, 1975, and *Elizabeth Cotten Live!*, 1983. She also appeared in Pete Seeger's videotape "Rainbow Quest" as well as in the Grass Roots Series videotape "Old Time Music," 1974, and on PBS-TV's "Me and Stella," 1977.

Cotten's accomplishments have not been ignored. On July 29, 1972, she received the Burl Ives Award, presented to her at the Wolftrap Theater in Vienna, Virginia. This was a cash prize presented by the National Folk Festival Association to commemorate her "unique contribution to folk music." In 1984, she received a National Heritage Fellowship from the National Endowment for the Arts. More recently, she received a Grammy.

Chalmers described Cotten on stage as "a handsome, lean black woman" with "slim, dark hands," "a radiant face," "bright, searching eyes," and a "soft, untroubled voice," who sang "in a soft, raspy voice" (64). Gerrard describes her at eighty-seven as a "strong and determined person . . . proud of herself and her accomplishments" (26).

Cotten's performing style and her music reflect her uniqueness in the folk art genre. Like most folk performers, Cotten concerned herself with establishing between herself and her audience a common bond. In a 1968 observation, Pete Seeger stated:

> She walked gravely to the microphone, sat down, and started picking the guitar. It was a simple tune, and repeated itself over and over with only a few modest variations . . . Then she talked for a while, still strumming lightly. She told how, as a teenager, she had sneaked in to play her older brother's guitar (308).

Seeger notes Cotten's interest in getting the audience involved in the performance; she delivers tunes plainly and shares her own personal experiences.

Chalmers notes that audience participation is an important part of Cotten's performance: "Libba, after a few verses, demands of the audience 'Now you-all sing'" (64). He added, "the soul of her music is inseparable from the audience, for whom it is recreated in each time and space." She attempted to respond to her audiences' expectations of her and included facts about her own life. Indeed, her album *Elizabeth Cotten Live!* illustrates this stylistic point: each side contains a personal story relating to Cotten's experiences. Side A contains "Banjo Story" and side B contains "Guitar Story" and "Elizabeth Story." The album ends with "'Til We Meet Again," described as "a traditional hymn which Elizabeth always includes as an expression of her deep religious faith and her love for her audience" (*Libba Cotten Live!*). Appropriately, it is a traditional benedictory hymn of some black church services. Cotten's music reflects a deep spiritual interest while sustaining her reputation as a blues artist. When she entered the world of professional song, she was "convinced that the Lord loved folk music" (Chalmers, 66). It seems to be such love that provides for Cotten the joy of performing.

Cotten's technique is well-described by Gerrard, who observes "basically five styles": "her rag-time or two-finger style, for which she is best known"; a banjo style; a third style in which "she utilizes clusters of notes"; a banjo-like roll; and "a fifth style for backing songs that don't particularly lend themselves to melody picking" (26). Gerrard observes, furthermore, that her two-finger style can be heard in "Freight Train," and her banjo style in "Rattler" and "Georgia Buck," all on her first album; her use of clusters of notes "playing with her thumb and two or three fingers, often in arpeggios" is observable in "Buck Dance" and "Washington Blues," and her banjo-like roll in "Fox Chase," all on Volume II; and her fifth style shows in "Time to Stop Your Idling," sung by her granddaughter, Johnine Rankin, on Volume III (Gerrard, 26). Gerrard also notes that, "In general, her guitar style is a synthesis of turn-of-the-century parlor music, blues, church songs, and a little ragtime, and is heavily influenced by the piano" (26).

Like many folk artists, Cotten was a master of improvisation and rarely repeated a song in a rendition identical to an early one. Cotten, reporting that she did not know notes and could not read music, stated, "You just get a song and know it and just keep fooling around with it until you get it to sound like you want it to sound" (Gerrard, 28).

Cotten's guitar was "an 000-18 Martin from the late 1940's," and she used "three tunings: the standard E-A-D-G-B-E, bottom to top; another tuning two whole steps lower, D-A-D-F#-A-D, which she calls her 'Vastopol' tuning, and D-G-D-G-B-D, which she calls her 'Flang Dang' tuning" (Gerrard, 26). Likewise, Cotten's repertoire is varied. It includes songs and styles both original and borrowed, both old and new.

Cotten's most famous song, "Freight Train," has an interesting history. Composed by Cotten at the age of eleven, it has, according to Pete Seeger, "gone around the world" (308). The song, often attributed to other performers, was first recorded by Peter, Paul, and Mary in the early 1960s. Peggy Seeger also performed the song, and according to Groom, the version The Vipers and the Chas. McDermitt Skiffle Group performed as "Freight Train Blues" they received through Peggy Seeger (28). Court action was required in order for Cotten to secure the copyright for the song, and it was not until 1957 that she was granted the rights.

Cotten's songs are in the "tonality and feeling of Mississippi John Hurt, John Jackson of Virginia, and John Spence of the Bahamas, but her guitar and banjo styles are unique" (*Elizabeth Cotten Live!*). Her "Vastopol" resembles the style of Furry Lewis and groups as various as The Grateful Dead and the Seegers have adopted it. Baggelaar and Milton state that "Libba's bass runs are used frequently by other guitarists, and her basic picking styles have become standard patterns for folk guitar" (87).

Besides the influential "Freight Train," Cotten is also well-known for her instrumental "Washington Blues," transcribed and commented on by Janet Smith. Smith contends that "Washington Blues" is a ragtime piece that rivals "Freight Train" for its exemplification of the range of Cotten's playing style. Observing that Cotten "literally invents all of her hand-positioning techniques," Smith suggests that the skill revealed in "Washington Blues" goes "far beyond the ever-familiar 'Freight Train'" (30). "Washington Blues" was one of the early compositions of Cotten's professional career and was performed on various occasions in and around Washington, D.C., in the 1960s. Cotten died on June 29, 1987, at age ninety-five.

References

Baggelaar, Kristin, and Donald Milton. *Folk Music: More Than a Song*. New York: Crowell, 1976.

Bastin, Bruce. *Red River Blues: The Blues Tradition in the Southeast*. Urbana: University of Illinois Press, 1986.

Chalmers, Wilma Grand. *$2 at the Door: Folk, Ethnic and Bluegrass Music in the Northwest*. McMinnville, Oregon: Broadsheet Publications, 1981.

Cotten, Elizabeth. *Elizabeth Cotten Live!* Arhoolie. 1983.

"For These 'Youngsters' Life Begins at 80." *Ebony* 36 (February 1981): 60.

Funaro, Arti, and Artie Tatum. *Chicago Blues Guitar*. New York: Oak, 1983.

Gerrard, Alice. "Libba Cotten." *Frets* 2 (January 1980): 26-29.

Groom, Bob. *The Blues Revival*. London: Studio Vista Limited, 1971.

Harris, Sheldon. *Blues Who's Who:* New York: Da Capo Press, 1979.

Lanker, Brian. *I Dream a World*. New York: Stewart, Tabori, and Chang, 1989. 156-57

Michelson, Stephen. Liner notes to *Music from the Hills of Caldwell County*. Physical. Silver Spring, Md.

The New Grove Dictionary of American Music. Edited by H. Wiley Hitchcock and Stanley Sudie. New York: Macmillan, 1986.

"Ordinary Women of Grace: Subjects of the I Dream a World Photography Exhibit." *U.S. News and World Report* 106 (13 February 1989).

Seeger, Pete. *The Incompleat Folksinger*. New York: Simon and Schuster, 1972.

Smith, Janet. "The Music of Libba Cotten." *Frets* 2 (January 1980): 30-31.

Southern, Eileen. *Biographical Dictionary of Afro-American and African Musicians*. Westport, Conn.: Greenwood Press, 1982.

Laura C. Jarmon

Marie Bernard Couvent (Madame Bernard Couvent)

(c. 1757-1837)

School founder

Marie Couvent (Madame Bernard Couvent) holds a unique position in history as the founder of the "Institution Catholique des Orphelins Indigents," a school for indigent Negro orphans in New Orleans. When her husband, Gabriel Bernard Couvent, died on May 22, 1829, at the age of seventy-one, Marie Couvent inherited his entire estate. Known by her maiden name of Justine Fervin [Firvin], as well as by the name of Maria Gabriel Bernard Couvent, she had long nourished the dream of providing education for poor black Catholic orphans, many of whom had white fathers. After her husband's death, Marie Couvent began to consider making her dream a reality by donating a substantial part of her inheritance to establish a school for underprivileged free black orphans in New Orleans.

Marie Couvent's sympathy for the less privileged was probably a result of her own early life experiences. It is believed that she was born in Africa and conveyed as a slave to New Orleans, where her freedom was either granted by her master or purchased by her husband. Illiterate herself, Marie Couvent received no formal education. In fact, such an education would have been difficult to obtain in Louisiana, as H. E. Sterkx explains: "Education played a large role in the social life of free Negroes, but at no time were they permitted to enroll in White schools of the state" (268). Before Reconstruction, free blacks in New Orleans were educated in private schools or by private tutors. Alternatively, wealthy people of color could send their children to New England or Europe for an education (Desdunes, 106). For the impoverished free black, however, formal education was neither a possibility nor a reality until the Couvent school was opened. Indeed, Alice Dunbar-Nelson identified the Couvent school as the first free school for Negroes in the United States (Roussève, 43).

Marie Couvent firmly believed in education as the primary tool for the promotion of colored people. Rodolphe Desdunes affirms, "She had a deep compassion for little children condemned to live without the advantages of education in the midst of so much indifference and even hostility toward a class of people sorely tried" (104). As free Negroes, Marie Couvent and her carpenter husband had been able to amass considerable savings and property. They even owned several slaves themselves. Nevertheless, as free blacks, they were relegated to a social position hardly better than that of slaves: "Although Louisiana's free Negroes enjoyed exceptional legal and economic privileges, their social status was just above the slave level. At every turn they were victims of social discrimination imposed on them by custom as well as law" (Sterkx, 240). In the words of Doris Dorcas Carter, "Slaves were victimized by free blacks; free blacks were victimized by whites" (172). It was not unusual for wealthy free blacks to own slaves, as did the Couvents; it was, however, unusual for a well-to-do free black woman to provide generously for the education of poor free blacks. As Rodolphe Desdunes remarks, "Her [Marie Couvent's] attitude on the question of education has been a genuine reproach to the wealthy people of her era" (102). By envisaging and promoting education for all free blacks, Marie Couvent was clearing the path for a period in which black children would be permitted to attend free public schools along with white children.

Such an integrated period was quite a few years away, however, as evinced by the probate of Marie Couvent's will. The will was actually drawn up as early as 1832 with the guidance and encouragement of Marie Couvent's spiritual advisor, Father Manehault. In the will, Marie Couvent left land and several small houses on the corner of Union and Grands Hommes [Great Men] Streets to be used for the building of her school. She died five years later on June 28, 1837, at the age of eighty. However, her will was not properly executed until 1848, when the school was finally built. The delays in establishing the school were, in fact, a direct result of the prejudices of city authorities:

> The difficulty centered in the category of the school, for although private schools existed for whites and for blacks, nonmixed and sometimes mixed, education by and through an established institution for free people of color was not favored by city authorities, even when under the auspices of the community's leading Catholic church (Desdunes, 103).

Consequently, Marie Couvent's will was inoperative for nearly a dozen years until Father Manehault intervened to ensure its implementation.

Free School for Black Orphans Founded

In her will, Marie Couvent had placed the proposed school under the supervision of the Catholic clergy. It was Father Manehault who took responsibility for seeing that her wishes were fulfilled, a risky procedure in the face of the continuous prejudice that impeded the school's establishment. The free public school system had been organized for whites in 1841; however, free people of color were barred from these schools. To realize Marie Couvent's dream of a school for free indigent Negroes, Father Manehault therefore solicited aid from François Lacroix, a prominent citizen who organized the Society for the Instruction of Indigent Orphans. The society, formed in 1848, was dedicated to the execution of Marie Couvent's will. The members demanded that the executor of her will account for her property and turn it over to their society. Their settlement with the executor resulted in the establishment of a primary school for orphans of color in the third district of New Orleans, thus fulfilling Marie Couvent's dream.

The Couvent School offered a solid education without the burden of tuition. The school was liberally endowed by François Lacroix and his friends as well as by prominent free Negro benefactors. For example, Aristide Mary, a wealthy free man of color, bequeathed five thousand dollars to the school. Another wealthy free Negro of New Orleans, Thomy Lafon, made considerable donations to the school. The state of Louisiana even donated funds. For instance, in 1854, two thousand dollars from public funds was appropriated for the school. This money was allocated after a committee of the General Assembly observed and evaluated the school to make sure it was operating properly.

The school provided "a well-rounded education, intellectually, morally, physically, and spiritually" (Desdunes, 104), and boasted five or six talented teachers who taught in both French and English. All of the faculty members were people of color and therefore could develop sympathetic relationships with their pupils. Félicie Cailloux, a highly intelligent and pious black woman, was the first teacher and principal of the school. After her term, the location and size of the school changed, and in 1852, Armand Lanusse was named principal. He was succeeded by other prominent black leaders of the time, including Mesdames Thézan and Populus.

The program of study at the coeducational school included the classics. La Fontaine, Boileau, Fénelon, and Corneille were also studied in special classes offered in French as well as Spanish. The instructors at the Couvent school were dedicated and reputed to be the best in their field (McCants, 139). In addition, the school's importance rested on the fact that, "it was the best attended school during the time of slavery" (Desdunes, 104). Not only were the teachers distinguished, but the students also went on to distinguish themselves: "Numerous writers, poets, artists, who displayed exemplary conduct and superior intellects went forth from the doors of the institute for indigent orphans" (Desdunes, 105).

After the Reconstruction began, many of the black children in New Orleans began to attend free public schools with white children. By 1884, attendance at the Couvent School had declined so drastically that the school was in danger of closing. Thanks to the efforts of twelve concerned men, the school was saved. According to Dorothea McCants, it stands on Dauphine Street and is administered by the Catholic church under the name of the Holy Redeemer School (139). The school is a visible reminder of Marie Couvent's foresight and charity. Her dream of providing an education for poor free Negroes was ultimately realized with the support and persistence of Father Manehault, François Lacroix and friends, other benefactors, and the dedicated faculty who distinguished the Bernard Couvent School as one of the best in New Orleans.

References

Carter, Doris Dorcas. "Refusing to Relinquish the Struggle: The Social Role of the Black Woman in Louisiana History." *Louisiana's Black Heritage*. Eds. Robert R. MacDonald, John R. Kemp, and Edward F. Haas. New Orleans: Louisiana State Museum, 1979. 163-189.

Desdunes, Rodolphe Lucien. *Our People and Our History*. Baton Rouge: Louisiana State University Press, 1973. 97-108.

Fischer, Roger A. *The Segregation Struggle in Louisiana: 1862-1877*. Urbana: University of Illinois Press, 1974. 13-14.

Handy, W. C., ed. *Unsung Americans Sung*. American Society of Composers, Authors, Publishers, 1944. 138-39.

McCants, Dorothea Olga. "Madame Bernard Couvent." *Dictionary of American Negro Biography*. Eds. Rayford W. Logan and Michael R. Winston. New York: Norton, 1982.

Robinson, Wilhelmena S. "Mme. Bernard Couvent." *Historical Negro Biographies*. New York: Publisher's Company, 1969.

Roussève, Charles Barthelemy. *The Negro in Louisiana: Aspects of His History and His Literature*. New Orleans: Xavier University Press, 1937.

Sterkx, H. E. *The Free Negro in Ante-Bellum Louisiana*. Madison, N.J.: Fairleigh Dickinson University Press, 1972.

Barnsley Brown

Ida Cox
"Queen of the Blues"
(1896-1967)
Singer

The "Uncrowned Queen of the Blues," Ida Cox sang for twenty-five years on the vaudeville circuit. Born Ida Prather in 1896 in Toccoa, Georgia, and raised in Cedartown, Cox left home while a teenager to tour with a minstrel show. "I began my theatrical career as a comedienne back in 1915," she stated in a 1940 interview," " The next year, I was taught how to sing torch songs. . . . We called them blues back in those days" (Cobb, *Chicago Defender*) She met and married one of the trumpters traveling with the show, Alter Cox, but the marriage ended with his death in World War I. (Her second marriage, to Eugene Williams, produced a daughter, Helen.) Cox continued to tour the vaudeville circuit with various acts: the Florida Orange Blossom Minstrels, the Silas Green Show, and the Rabbit Foot Minstrels (the stepping stone to fame for Ma Rainey, the "Mother of the Blues,"and Bessie Smith, the "Empress of the Blues"). By 1922 Cox was an established solo performer. A WMC radio broadcast of her March 1922 performance at Memphis's Beale Street Palace prompted a *Memphis Commercial Appeal* critic to comment that: "Ida sang in most azure fashion" (*Chicago Defender*). The airing of that show may have been heard by Paramount scouts and led to a contract that eventually produced seventy-eight titles from September 1923 to October 1929.

Although Paramount claimed to have Cox under exclusive contract, she recorded for both the Harmograph and Silvertone labels simultaneously, using pseudonyms Julia [sic] Julius Powers and Jane Smith. Lovie Austin and her Serenaders accompanied her on the early recordings, producing some excellent music examples of the period. Cox's third husband, Jesse Crump, also played piano on some of her recordings and later became her music director. For her first release, the Paramount advertisement featured two photographs of Cox and hailed her as "The Uncrowned Queen of the Blues" and "The Blues Singer with a Feeling."

Paramount provided outstanding musicians to play for Cox's recording sessions, thus creating music with lasting quality and appeal. Unfortunately, these early recordings are technically inferior. Nevertheless, "Graveyard Dream Blues" with Tom Ladnier, Austin, and Jim Bryant is one of Cox's masterpieces; in it she proves that the title "The Blues Singer with a Feeling" is a worthy one. "Graveyard" typifies the subject matter frequently used by Cox when she was singing serious blues. Her voice was less powerful than Rainey's and Smith's, but it was as penetrating and convincing.

The release of some of Cox's best sides came in 1924. "Chicago Monkey Man Blues," "Mama Doo Shee Blues," "Kentucky Man Blues," "Death Letter Blues," and "Wild Women Don't Have the Blues" are characteristic of the style and subject matter that made her a favorite in the South and Midwest. Cox had a peculiar way of placing stress or emphasis on the verb, article, adjective, or conjunction in a phrase rather than on a noun. This gave her phrasing unusual rhythmic pulse, added an expressive flavor to simple melodies, and allowed her to milk each line of its fullest meaning.

> I followed my daddy to *the* burying ground,
> I followed my daddy to *the* burying ground,
> *I* watched the pallbearers slowly let him down
> ("Death Letter Blues").

Cox used what in many circles would be considered a dry, colorless voice to convey audacity and intensity equally well. Her voice could draw the listener into the situation with a heavy mournful sound that riveted the attention until the final melancholy note faded, or the sauciness in her words was conveyed with verve and a devil-may-care attitude.

Cox could swing with Fletcher Henderson, Austin, and Coleman Hawkins as well as moan with Tommy Ladnier's "prayerful" cornet. And musicians enjoyed working with a singer whose artistry surpassed that of many of her peers. J. C. Hillman, critic writing in *Jazz Journal*, confirms this point:

> Ladnier's collaboration . . . is everything that could be required, and Cox's integration into this and later groups is as much a result of her own artistry as of the . . . organization of the sessions. It is also evidence of the strength of her voice and personality that she sounds perfectly at home beside Ladnier's intense playing (Hillman, 9).

Cox Peaks as Blues Artist

Cox reached her artistic peak in 1925 and 1926 with such songs as "Mississippi River Blues," "Coffin Blues," and "Rambling Blues." Paramount, claiming that she had recently been crowned "Queen of the Blues," promoted her records with a photo of Cox's crowned head surrounded by genuflecting admirers.

Cox's act was praised highly for her singing, humorous repartee, beauty, and attire. She continued to tour Florida, Alabama, Tennessee, Texas, Missouri, and Oklahoma, often making return engagements in a matter of weeks. The Cox-Crump duo seemed to be an unbeatable combination at every theater in which they performed. This was an act that clicked, with both artists receiving acclaim for their individual talents. Charles O'Neal, Kansas City critic for the *Chicago Defender*, wrote:

As the curtain lifted, the house orchestra, against a background of black hangings, held the full stage. The saxophone began to moan; the drummer tossed his sticks. One was transported involuntarily . . . to a Harlem cabaret . . . [as] the orchestra struck up a slower . . . still more mournful strain.

The hangings parted and a great brown woman emerged, stunning in white satin, studded with rhinestones. Her face was beautiful, with the rich, ripe beauty of southern darkness, a deep bronze brown. . . . She walked to the footlights; then to the accompaniment of the wailing, muted brasses, the monotonous African beat . . . the dromedary glide of Jesse Crump . . . fingers over the . . . keys, she began her strange rites in a "voice full of moanin' and prayin' and sufferin'" . . . the singer swaying slightly to the rhythm (O'Neal, 11 June 1927).

Undoubtedly a queen of the blues, with regal bearing, dignity, and beauty befitting her position, Cox mesmerized and bewitched her audiences with her compelling rhythms. It was this sense of self, understanding of her art, and awareness of her audiences' needs and desires that propelled Cox to such a high level of appreciation. She knew that her folk thrilled to the suspense of her dramatic opening number, so she transported them on the drone of the drums, groans of the horns, and the moans of her voice to another time, place, mood. She knew they desired relief and release and needed uplifting, so she crooned the blues and, with tongue-in-cheek, offered advice. Audiences understood that Cox was able to take the substance of their pain, elevate it, and transform it to match their feelings.

Cox's Raisin' Cain Revue proved so popular on the Theatre Owners Booking Circuit (TOBA) that it was chosen to be the first TOBA show to open at New York's famed Apollo Theater. Surgery sidelined the star for a few weeks, but she returned in the fall of 1929 to continue through the difficult days of the Wall Street crash and its aftermath. A showwoman worthy of her profession, Cox endured the layoffs and pressed on, keeping the company on TOBA, traveling mainly on the southern route. She and Crump managed to obtain engagements that which lasted two to four weeks, enabling them to survive, but reviews appeared less frequently and contained little more than the information on location, members of the company, and length of run.

Shifting tastes and a weak economy forced Cox to reorganize the show. Personnel changes occurred frequently, because the money was often short or the company had long layoffs. Nevertheless, the midnight rambles were usually a success, and whenever possible Crump and the band played for dances in hotels, ballrooms, and nightclubs following the floor show. Renamed the Dark Town Scandals, the show moved to the interstate circuit for a brief period, but Cox and Crump broke it up and moved to the West Coast seeking a fresh start. A new show at Los Angeles's Lincoln Theatre lasted only a few weeks. The Dark Town Scandals were reorganized in 1935 and played to small houses in the Midwest. Cox would not acknowledge the inevitable—the decline of vaudeville with its high-stepping hoofers, slapstick comedy, and singers.

Like any good trouper Cox kept busy in the 1930s barnstorming throughout the South, drumming up business in Newbern, Hickory, and Charlotte, North Carolina; along the red, dusty clay roads of Milledgeville and Macon, Georgia; through hills and mountains of Alabama and Tennessee; along the route of the Mississippi to Natchez, Memphis, and New Orleans. And when she was lucky, she would hit Dallas's Ella Moore Theater, where they had clamored for tickets just a few years earlier

Ironically, a radio broadcast of the Hobby Lobby show in early 1940 prompted a feature story on Cox, heralding her comeback. Columbia Records had scheduled sessions for her reentry into the record market but for unknown reasons never released them. She later cut several sides for Vocalian with an all-star ensemble that included Hot Lips Page, J. C. Higginbotham, James P. Johnson, Charlie Christian, and Lionel Hampton.

John Hammond, whose love for blues and jazz carried him all over the eastern seaboard listening to and scouting for talent, spotlighted Cox in his 1939 "Spirituals to Swing Concert" at Carnegie Hall. His admiration for Cox led him to search for her to return to the recording studio several years later. She had suffered a disabling stroke that forced her into retirement and was reluctant to leave Knoxville, where she was actively involved with her church. Fortunately, after repeatedly protesting that "she was a regular church-goer and she didn't feel that it would be right for her to sing the blues again," Cox relented and recorded *Jazz Report*, her final album, in 1961 for the Riverside label. An updated version of "Death Letter Blues" proved that Cox still had the artistry to deliver the blues in spite of her poor health. Noted boogie woogie and blues pianist Sammy Price counted Cox as one of his favorites and considered himself honored to have been selected to play with the trio that recorded her final release. He said in an interview:

I liked her sound. I like that flowing blues sound . . . [the] good melodic lines, words that make sense, decent diction, or decent diction colloquially, you know. I'm speaking now about colored diction . . . . You didn't miss anything that Ida sang. When she said, "Way down yonder in Atlanta, G.A.," she said it so-ooo plain, and so clear, that you had to be affected by it in some way (26 April 1977).

Price's sentiments were expressed by John Wilson in his *New York Times* review of the album. Of the old singer's voice he said, "the artfulness of her phrasing is just as entrancing as it ever was. The personal quality of her singing immediately identifiable in a crowded field in her young days remain so."

The Uncrowned Queen of the Blues died of cancer in mid-

October 1967, leaving a legacy of fine showmanship, tireless dedication to her art and her audience, and a body of blues work that reveals her deeply personal view of life. She had outlived her esteemed colleagues—Smith and Ma Rainey, and kept alive the tradition of vaudeville and the blues as she barnstormed across the country. Cox proved to all that she was indeed a queen of the blues.

References

Chicago Defender, 27 May 1922; 10 March 1923; 4 August 1923; 15 March 1924; 29 March 1924; 4 April 1925; 11 April 1925; 9 May 1925; 30 May 1925; 5 September 1925; 21 November 1925; 5 January 1929; 17 February 1934; 31 March 1934; 19 May 1934.

Cobb, Ivorey. "Ida Cox Famed Blues Singer, Headed for New Comeback." *Chicago Defender*, 20 January 1940.

Godrich, John, and R. M. W. Dixon. *Blues and Gospel Records, 1902-1942*. London: Storyville Publications, 1969.

Hillman, J. C. "Ida Cox—Last Mile." *Jazz Journal* No. 21 (June 1968): 9.

"Ida Cox Goes Big in South." *Chicago Defender*, 1 April 1933.

O'Neal, Charles. "In Old Kaysee." *Chicago Defender*, 11 June 1927.

Pittsburgh Courier, 14 June 1924.

Price, Sammy. Interview with Daphne D. Harrison, 26 April 1977.

Riverside Record review for *Jazz Report*, May 1961.

Wilson, John S. "Surviving Stylist: Ida Cox Sings Blues in 'Classic Ways.'" *New York Times*, 10 September 1961.

Daphne D. Harrison

Ellen Craft

(c. 1826-c. 1897)

Abolitionist, school founder

Ellen Craft was born about 1826 in Clinton, Georgia, the daughter of a slave named Maria. Her father was Major James Smith, the mother's owner. Often mistaken for a member of her father/master's family, Craft especially incurred the displeasure of her mistress. When she was eleven, Craft was removed from the household and taken to Macon, Georgia, having been made a wedding gift for a

Ellen Craft

Smith daughter. In Macon, she met her future husband, William Craft, also a slave.

William and Ellen Craft are most famous for their remarkable escape from slavery, narrated in *Running a Thousand Miles for Freedom* (1860). In a daring journey, Ellen posed as a young male slaveowner and William as "his" slave. The determination to flee came from Ellen. She was particularly adamant about not wanting to bear children into slavery. William noted that being separated from her own mother at an early age had strengthened Ellen's resolve: "She had seen so many other children separated from their parents in this cruel manner, that the mere thought of her ever becoming the mother of a child, to linger out a miserable existence under the wretched system of American slavery, appeared to fill her very soul with horror" (Craft, 285).

At first, the Crafts hoped to avoid the potentiality of such a horror by not marrying until they could escape, but they could devise no plan to flee. They then received their owners' permission to marry and "toiled on" until December 1848. William stated that it was he who thought of a plan and together they worked out the details. According to another contemporary account, however, Ellen herself proposed the plan of her traveling as white, along with the details of the disguise. In the latter account, it was William who hesitated, with Ellen admonishing him not to be a coward. Whatever the origin of the ideas, Ellen's role was clearly the more difficult one, for she had both to impersonate someone of a different gender and to appear educated. William, on the other hand, was not stepping out of his familiar role, that of a slave.

The plan was as follows: Given the great distance they

would have to cover, they could not hope to make a successful journey on foot. Since Ellen looked white, however, they might be able to travel by train and other public transportation with William posing as Ellen's slave. She needed to play the role of a male because a white woman would not be traveling alone with a male slave. Suspicion would be aroused in that Ellen would be beardless. She would also be expected to sign in at hotels, something she could not do since she could not write. Her disguise was thus that of a sickly young man whose face was almost completely covered in a poultice of handkerchiefs and whose writing arm was in a cast. She also wore eyeglasses with green shades. With her hair cut short, and wearing men's clothing, she became "a most respectable looking gentleman" (Craft, 290).

The plan succeeded. Traveling primarily by train but with steamer and ferry connections, they went through parts of Georgia, South Carolina, North Carolina, and Virginia. Baltimore, Maryland, was their last stop in slave territory. They reached Philadelphia on Christmas Day 1848. From plan to completion, the trip took eight days.

Despite understandable fears, Ellen carried out her part with fortitude and quick thinking. William states that several times alone with him she burst into tears at the thought of the difficulty of the endeavor. Yet she did not falter when faced with the challenges of maintaining her disguise. For example, when she boarded the train in Georgia, she was "terror stricken" to see sitting beside her an old white man who knew her well and who had in fact dined at Ellen's owners' home the previous day. Rather than have him recognize her or her voice, she gazed out the window, pretending to be deaf. Forced to say something when the old man talked louder and louder, she answered in a single word, lessening the chances of her voice being recognized.

In Baltimore, threatened with detainment for being without documentation of William's ownership, Ellen questioned the official "with more firmness than could be expected" (309). Once they reached the safety of Philadelphia, William remembered Ellen's weeping "like a child"; he also remembered that she "had from the commencement of the journey borne up in a manner that much surprised us both" (314).

In Philadelphia, the Crafts were befriended by Quakers and free blacks. At first, Ellen Craft was distrustful of all whites. She did not believe that the Barkley Ivens family, white Quakers, could mean them any good. But the Ivens's generosity and gentle ways convinced her otherwise during the three weeks she and William spent with them recuperating from the strain of the journey. While regaining their strength, the Crafts received tutoring in reading and writing. William noted that both he and Ellen had learned the alphabet "by stratagem" while enslaved. In their time at the Ivens's home, they began to learn to read and they learned to write their names (Craft, 315-17).

The Crafts then moved on to Boston. They were assisted by abolitionists, including William Lloyd Garrison, Theodore Parker, and William Welles Brown. Brown arranged appearances for them, "sometimes charging an admission fee, an almost unprecedented practice in abolitionist circles" (Quarles, 62-63). Continuing to develop her skills as a seamstress, Ellen Craft studied with an upholsterer. (She had already made good use of her ability to sew by making the trousers she wore in the escape from Georgia.)

Fugitive Slaves Flee to England

The Crafts remained in Boston two years. They became the center of highly publicized events once again in 1850. They were forced to flee to England because of attempts to return them to slavery by means of the Fugitive Slave Law. Their former owners sent two slavecatchers with warrants for their arrest. William was ready to resist with force if necessary. Abolitionists in the Vigilance Committee of Boston played a strong role in sheltering the Crafts and in helping them get out of the city.

Once again, Ellen Craft showed firm resolve even as she recognized the depth of the danger. Mrs. George Hilliard, who informed Craft of the new threat, wrote: "My manner, which I suppose to be indifferent and calm, *betrayed* me, and she threw herself into my arms, sobbing and weeping. She, however, recovered her composure as soon as we reached the street, and was *very firm* ever after" (quoted in Still, 373).

Before fleeing Boston, the Crafts were married for a second time. Theodore Parker performed this ceremony on November 7, 1850. Because the ports in the Boston area were being watched, the couple went by land to Portland, Maine, and then on to Nova Scotia before they were able to book passage on a steamer from Halifax to Liverpool. They encountered racial prejudice and delays on the journey from Boston to Halifax, but they were finally able to leave American shores.

In England by December 1850, the Crafts continued to evoke interest. An interviewer for *Chambers' Edinburgh Journal* retold the story of their escape. Although the Crafts were clearly "on really free soil" for the first time, as the interviewer stated, attitudes toward skin color showed consistency with American views. The interviewer described Ellen Craft as "a gentle, refined-looking young creature of twenty-four years, as fair as most of her British sisters, and in mental qualifications their equal too." William, on the other hand, was described as "very dark, *but* of a reflective, intelligent countenance, and of manly and dignified deportment" (*Slave Testimony*, 273-74; emphasis added).

For six months after their arrival in England, the Crafts and William Welles Brown (who had gone to England in 1849), gave immediacy to the antislavery cause in travels within England as well as in Scotland. When they attended the Crystal Palace Exhibit in London with Brown several times during the summer of 1851, the ex-slaves were something of an exhibit themselves. White abolitionists made a point of promenading with them "in order that the world might form its opinion of the alleged mental inferiority of the African race, and their fitness or unfitness for freedom" (Still, 374).

In the fall of 1851, the Crafts continued their education at the Ockham School near Ripley, Surrey. This was "a trade school for rural youth founded by Lady Noel Byron, widow of the poet." The Crafts were able to teach others manual skills as they themselves improved their literacy (Gara, 397).

In October 1852, Ellen Craft gave birth to Charles Estlin Phillips. The Crafts had four other children, all born in England: Brougham, William, Ellen, and Alfred. True to her resolve, Ellen Craft bore no children into slavery. And if there were any question about her continued determination to be free, she spoke clearly in a letter published shortly after Charles's birth. In response to rumors that she was homesick for family still enslaved and would like to return to that life, Ellen Craft wrote that she would "much rather starve in England, a free woman, than be a slave for the best man that ever breathed upon the American continent" (*Liberator*, 17 December 1852, quoted by Gara, 397; Nichols, 152; Woodson, 265).

Running a Thousand Miles for Freedom was published in London, where the Crafts made their home beginning about 1852. William Craft remained a primary spokesman and the more public figure of the two. During the American Civil War, he was active in working against support for the Confederacy, and between 1862 and 1867, he made two trips to Dahomey. Ellen "was active in the British and Foreign Freed-men's Aid Society." In November 1865, the Lushingtons, English abolitionists who had helped the Crafts attend the Ockham School, brought Ellen Craft's mother to London (Gara, 397).

In 1868 the Crafts returned "with two of their children" to the United States (Still, 377). After working for a while in Boston, they returned to Georgia, where they purchased land in Bryan County, near Savannah. They opened an industrial school for colored youth. Ellen Craft must have had a major role to play, for "she forbade whippings in her school and 'made the plan that when the parents wanted to whip their children, they should take them into the grave yard, and when they got there to kneel down and pray'" (quoted in Sterling, 343).

In the 1890s Ellen Craft made her home with her daughter, who had married "William Demos Crum, a physician and later United States minister to Liberia. . . . By her request, [Ellen Craft] was buried under a favorite tree on her Georgia plantation. (She died about 1897.) William Craft survived her by several years, dying in Charleston in 1900" (Gara, 397).

The Crafts' achievements as a couple stand out against the backdrop of more typical examples of the fragmented families in slavery. At the same time, Ellen Craft stands out on her own as a talented, determined, intelligent, resourceful woman.

References

Blassingame, John, ed. *Slave Testimony: Two Centuries of Letters, Speeches, Interviews, and Autobiographies.* Baton Rouge: Louisiana State University Press, 1977.

Craft, William, and Ellen Craft. *Running a Thousand Miles for Freedom.* London: Tweedie, 1860. Reprinted. *Great Slave Narratives.* Ed. Arna Bontemps. Boston: Beacon Press, 1969.

Dannett, Sylvia G. L. *Profiles of Negro Womanhood, 1916-1900.* Vol. 1. Yonkers, N.Y.: Educational Heritage, 1964.

Gara, Larry. "Ellen Craft." *Notable American Women.* Vol. 1. Cambridge: Harvard University Press, 1971.

Nichols, Charles H. *Many Thousand Gone: The Ex-Slaves' Account of Their Bondage and Freedom.* Bloomington: Indiana University Press, 1963.

Quarles, Benjamin. *Black Abolitionists.* New York: Oxford University Press, 1969. 62-63, 134, 137, 150, 202-204.

Starling, Marion Wilson. *The Slave Narrative: Its Place in American History.* 2nd ed. Washington, D.C.: Howard University Press, 1988.

Sterling, Dorothy, ed. *We Are Your Sisters: Black Women in the Nineteenth Century.* New York: Norton, 1984. 62-64.

Still, William. *Underground Railroad Records.* Rev. ed. Philadelphia: William Still, 1886.

Woodson, Carter G., ed. *The Mind of the Negro as Reflected in Letters Written During the Crisis, 1800-1860.* Washington, D.C.: Association for the Study of Negro Life and History, 1926.

Arlene Clift-Pellow

Otelia Cromwell

(1874-1972)

Educator, author

Scholar, educator, and author, Otelia Cromwell was born on April 8, 1874, in Washington, D.C., to John Wesley and Lucy A. (McGuinn) Cromwell. Her father was born in Virginia of slave parents who purchased their freedom and moved to Philadelphia in 1851. He became a distinguished editor, scholar, lawyer, and educator in Washington, D.C. Lucy McGuinn Cromwell was also born in Virginia and died when Otelia Cromwell was only twelve years old, leaving her with five younger siblings and a sense of responsibility for their welfare. Except for Fanny, the youngest, who lived with their father and stepmother, and Martha, who married, Cromwell and her siblings Mary, Lucy, and John remained in the same household at 1815 Thirteenth Street N.W., Washington, D.C., until their deaths. Otelia had outlived them all when she died at the family home on April 25, 1972.

Cromwell received her early education in the public schools of Washington, D.C., including the M Street High School, the predecessor of the well-known Dunbar High School. After graduating from Miner Normal School, she taught for six years in the Washington public school system before entering Smith College in Northampton, Massachusetts, from which she was graduated in 1900 as the first black.

Upon returning to Washington, Cromwell once again taught in the public schools—briefly at the elementary level, later at the high school level at M Street and then Armstrong High School until 1922. At this point began the conflict with the school system that would plague her off and on for the rest of her life. Cromwell was attempting to perform in a segregated system as a black woman with more education than any of her black male supervisors and probably more than the whites. This did not bode well for her popularity, given her disposition towards forthrightness. Her first difficulty was in not quietly accepting the transfer from M Street, the classical high school, to Armstrong, the trade and technical high school. Cromwell objected but nevertheless was transferred, and records show she was a popular and respected teacher as long as she remained at Armstrong.

After receiving her M.A. in English from Columbia University in 1910, Cromwell spent a summer studying at the Wahrendorf Tochterschule in Rostock, Germany, and later two semesters at the University of Pennsylvania. She then decided to pursue graduate work in English literature at Yale.

During this period, either in late 1921 or early January 1922, Cromwell was offered a promotion from English teacher at Armstrong to head of the English and history department in the junior and senior high schools. Apparently, she refused this offer in order to pursue her graduate studies at Yale, for on January 22, 1922, the black assistant superintendent Garnet C. Wilkerson wrote her that he "could not subscribe to the policy of allowing the interests of the school system to suffer for the mere gratification of an employee's personal desire. . . . [It is] in the interests of the public school children of Washington that you postpone the date of the completion of the work leading to that degree. . . . This office is convinced that it is your duty to rely upon the combined judgement of your superior officers with respect to the Head of Department of English and History." Cromwell was undoubtedly the best-qualified candidate available since a compromise must have been reached; she continued to pursue her graduate study at Yale but accepted the position when offered it again in January 1923.

In 1926 she was awarded the Ph.D. in English from Yale and her dissertation, *Thomas Heywood, Dramatist: A Study in the Elizabethan Drama of Everyday Life*, was published by the Yale University Press two years later.

In 1930, after the Miner Normal School had been upgraded to a four-year college, Cromwell was appointed professor in the division of English language and literature, where she remained until her retirement in 1944.

Cromwell was a consummate scholar as well as an extraordinary teacher. After her first trip to Germany to broaden her knowledge, she made two additional trips to continental Europe and England. In 1931, along with Eva B. Dykes and Lorenzo Dow Turner, then the only other blacks in the country with a Ph.D. in English, Cromwell edited *Readings from Negro Authors for Schools and Colleges*, one of the first collections of its kind published in this country. In 1932 Cromwell was invited to be a member of the board of directors of the *Encyclopedia of the Negro*, under the chairmanship of Anson Phelps Stokes, which included among its nineteen members only one other woman, Florence Read, president of Spelman College in Atlanta, Georgia.

Cromwell published four articles in outstanding journals: "A Question of Motif" *English Journal* 9 (November 1928): 508-18; "Preparation for Freshmen Composition" *English Journal* 25 (September 1936): 551-56; "Essential Values in Education" *Harvard Educational Review* 10, (May 1940): 289-99; and "Democracy and the Negro" *American Scholar* 13, (Spring 1944). She reviewed Michel Grivelet's "Thomas Heywood et Le Drame Domestique Elizabethan" in *Shakespeare Association of America* 10 (Winter 1959): 120.

After Cromwell retireed in 1944 the following statement appeared in the Minutes of the Board of Education of the District of Columbia:

> The excellence of Professor Cromwell's training was reflected in her teaching . . . she developed among her students a keen appreciation of beauty and truth . . . she daily emphasized the value of thoroughness and openmindedness in her own classroom preparation. . . . The influence she exerted in her position cannot be easily estimated. Encouraging students to pursue graduate work in leading universities, stimulating them to write, she was still never too busy to listen to their problems, or to entertain them in small groups in her home.

In addition, a former student, Isadore W. Miles, then a teacher herself, wrote:

> Dr. Cromwell guided her pupils in the direction of their abilities and awakened them to their potentialities long before guidance, as a term, found its way into educational parlance. Through the years pupils and former pupils have continued to turn to Dr. Cromwell for the spiritual and intellectual guidance begun in this fine pupil-teacher relationship. . . . Pupils of a generation ago paid tribute to the living memory of Dr. Cromwell's outstanding success as a teacher. Her influence was the only tie that bound this group of persons, but it was enough to call them

from all walks of life to do her honor. No words could recapture the *elan vital* of that meeting.

Immediately upon her retirement, Cromwell embarked on what was to be her major scholarly work, *The Life of Lucretia Mott*, which was published by the Harvard University Press in 1958. The years she devoted to this research reveal her penchant for thoroughness. No stone was left unturned as she searched for material on every facet of her subject's life—family, the Quaker religion, the abolition movement in this country and abroad.

Reminiscent of the strain between this highly educated black woman scholar and the less well-trained black administrators is one final episode. Three-and-a-half years after Cromwell's retirement, the Federation of Teachers Local 27, which included in its membership and leadership some of her former students, wrote the Board of Education requesting that she be awarded the title professor emeritus. The board complied with that request and accordingly informed Cromwell of their decision. She, however, after writing the teachers' union thanking them for their intercession, wrote the board itself a refusal, reminding them of the passage of time since her retirement and the obligation of the board, not the union, to bestow such status.

In 1950, at the seventy-fifth anniversary of the founding of Smith College, Cromwell was one of the ten recipients of honorary degrees. She was a member of the Smith College Alumnae Association, College Club, American Association of University Women, NAACP, Modern Language Association, Writers Club, and St. Luke's Episcopal Church in Washington, D.C.

She was a most distinguished person, tall and gray-haired most of her adult life. Although she was soft-spoken, she had a great presence and abided by a strict code of ethics and principles. While others were more vocal in their reactions against the discriminatory practices of the day, Cromwell responded by refusing to patronize the stores in Washington because of their treatment of black customers and by not riding the public transportation—she walked or took taxis—because blacks were not employed as conductors or motormen.

Cromwell was unpretentious and avoided fanfare and publicity. She preferred to be called Miss rather than Dr. Cromwell.

References

Miles, Isadore W. Open letter, 23 May 1944, Otelia Cromwell Papers.

Minutes of the Board of Education, District of Columbia, February 16, 1944.

Wilkerson, Garnet C. Letter to Otelia Cromwell, 2 January 1922, Otelia Cromwell Papers.

Collections

Photographs of Otelia Cromwell are in the Smith College Archives.

Adelaide M. Cromwell

Maud Cuney Hare

(1874-1936)

Musician, folklorist, author

Musician, folklorist, and author Maud Cuney Hare was born on February 16, 1874, in Galveston, Texas, to Norris Wright Cuney and Adelina Dowdy Cuney. Her father, of Negro, Indian, and Swiss descent, was a well-known figure in Texas political life from the 1870s to the mid-1890s. Active in the affairs of the Republican Party of Texas, he served as secretary to the party's executive committee, was twice a delegate to the Republican National Convention, and was the recognized leader of the state's black vote. Wishing to be financially independent of public office, Norris Cuney established his own stevedoring business, employing some five hundred black men to load and unload vessels passing through the port of Galveston. Maud Cuney's mother, Adelina Dowdy, the youngest of six sisters known as "the handsome Dowdy girls," was the daughter of a white planter and a mulatto slave.

The Cuney home was a cultivated one. The mother who had a fine soprano voice and often sang publicly played the piano and sang, while the father enjoyed old Irish songs, martial airs, and melodies from Italian opera. In addition, he liked to read Hebrew, Greek, and Roman history and enjoyed Byron and Shakespeare. Into this setting were born Maud and a brother, Lloyd Garrison Cuney. Growing up in Galveston, Cuney Hare completed Central High School and looked forward to continuing her musical studies at the New England Conservatory of Music.

Cuney Hare Experiences Racism

Cuney Hare and her mother spent the summer of 1890 in Newport, Rhode Island, where arrangements were made for her, then sixteen, to enter the conservatory. She and another black student occupied a room in the Conservatory Home and for a short while there was no unpleasantness on account of race. In late October, however, the school informed Norris Cuney that a problem had arisen and that in order to insure the and satisfaction of the larger number of students, the parents of the "colored" pupils were requested to provide them with off-campus housing "for their own comfort, for the stability and welfare of the institutions whose advantages they covet and enjoy, and for the advantage of all concerned" (Cuney Hare, *Norris Wright Cuney*, 132). Although the other student readily consented, Cuney Hare's father emphatically refused. In a letter to the school, he cited the names of Massachusetts sons William Lloyd Garrison, Wendell Phillips, and Charles Sumner and continued: "Publications and catalogues attracted my attention to your institution. I accepted your invitation to the world to embrace its advantages for my child. I believed that your principles were fixed in the foundations of humanity, justice, and honor, and not subject to the control of a few misguided girls or parents. . . . I thought you had counted all the trifling costs and were braced for them. Judge, then, how greatly I have been deceived by your attitude in printed solicitations for patronage. . . . You request my cooperation in surrendering to the demands of prejudice by withdrawing my daughter; I cannot help you. Ask Massachusetts; ask her mighty dead; ask her living sons and daughters. They will cooperate with you, if you cannot solve the problem, and render your institution illustrious throughout all the ages" (Cuney Hare, *Norris Wright Cuney*, 133). To his daughter he wrote at the same time: "You were quite right, darling, when you said that you knew your father would tell you to stay. I can safely trust that my good name is in your hands. . . . Your conduct, dear, in this case meets my entire approval and makes me doubly proud of you. I only hope to see you pull through in your studies. I know you will make no mistakes as to your conduct in the school, knowing so well who you are. . . . I was preparing to sue the institution if they dared force you out of the building" (Cuney Hare, *Norris Wright Cuney*, 133-34). Cuney Hare refused to leave the dormitory, and as a result was subject to many petty indignities. "I insisted upon proper treatment. The attitude of myself and my parents was displeasing to the Conservatory management, but the instructors were just and the matter was finely adjusted by my remaining in the 'Home'" (Cuney Hare, *Norris Wright Cuney*, 134).

Upon completion of her studies, Cuney Hare returned to Texas to become director of music at the Texas Deaf, Dumb, and Blind Institute in Austin for two years, beginning in 1897. She subsequently joined the faculty of the Settlement Program of the Institutional Church of Chicago and later the Prairie View State Normal and Industrial College for Negroes in Prairie View, Texas. In 1906 she returned to Boston, where she married William P. Hare, of an old and well-known Boston family, and remained there for the rest of her life.

For many years, beginning about 1910, Cuney Hare edited the music column in *Crisis*, magazine and was a contributor of articles to such publications as *Musical America*, *Musical Quarterly*, and *Christian Science Monitor*. In 1913 she published a biography of her father: *Norris Wright Cuney; A Tribune of the Black People*, and in 1918 an anthology of poetry, *The Message of the Trees*, with an introduction by William Stanley Braithwaite.

In 1927 Cuney Hare founded the Allied Arts Centre and served as its director. The Centre's purpose was "to discover and encourage musical, literary, and dramatic talent, and to arouse interest in the artistic capabilities of the Negro child." In a letter to the theatrical editor of the *New York Age*, she outlined the Centre's intention. "The Allied Arts Centre plans to work along the lines of the new art movement in America. Our interest in the Little Theatre is not expressed in an edifice of endeavor and creative work. . . . Through our art classes we aim to cultivate friendliness with all racial groups. Two Japanese boys are registered in a Saturday class. We are opposed, you see, to the idea of separateness and hope, through conscientious work, to become one of the noteworthy streams in the making of an ideal New England and American spirit. . . . I am giving my services as unsalaried director in order to establish this cultural center for our youth." The Allied Arts Players flourished for several years, presenting romantic and historical plays, including one for which Cuney Hare wrote the music, *Antar, Negro Poet of Arabia*.

Cuney Hare Best Known as Music Historian

It is as a musical historian that Maud Cuney Hare is best known. "She collected songs from far off beaten paths in Mexico, the Virgin Islands, Puerto Rico, and Cuba," Clarence Campbell White would write of her in 1936. She was the first to collect and bring to the attention of the American concert public the beauties of New Orleans creole music"; (Introduction *Negro Musicians*). Cuney Hare's *Creole Songs* with introduction and notes, was published by Carl Fischer Company of New York in 1921.

The culmination of her years spent traveling and researching folk material however, was the publication, in 1936, of *Negro Musicians and Their Music*. It is a source book of great value, and an indispensable body of information. In the preface Cuney Hare notes that "the Negro, a musical force, through his own distinct racial characteristics has made an artistic contribution which is racial but not yet national." As the influence of stylistic traits termed "Negro" have become widespread, these expressions—primarily melody and rhythm—have become a compelling force not only in American music, but worldwide. However, Cuney Hare maintains, now that the Negro is essentially an American rather than an African Negro, he is "influenced by like social environment and governed by the same political system; thus we may expect the ultimate result of his musical endeavor to be an art-music which embodies national characteristics exercised upon by his soul's expression" (Cuney Hare, *Negro Musicians*, vi).

Negro Musicians and Their Music deals with African music from its earliest traces, African influences in America, folk song, and Negro idiom and it provides many musical illustrations. There are chapters on musical pioneers, music in war service, and musical progress, along with hard-to-find photographs. The chapter "World Musicians of Color" rescues from obscurity the contributions of little-known Negro musicians of other times and other places. Included are Ibrahim-al-Mahdi, Chevalier de Saint Georges, and violinist George Bridgetower, violinist, who was the first interpreter of Beethoven's Kreutzer Sonata. Cuney Hare's career was full and varied. She was additionally a concert and lecture-pianist and toured widely. In later years, she appeared with noted baritone William Howard Richardson in lecture-recitals on black folk song. One of their highly acclaimed performances was accompanied by a string quartet from the Boston Symphony Orchestra with Arthur Fiedler playing viola. Other appearances with Richardson took place at the Brooklyn Academy of Music, Syracuse University, Albany Historical and Art Association, and the Harvard Music Association. Their working relationship was so satisfying, Cuney Hare dedicated *Negro Musicians and Their Music* to Richardson, "In Remembrance pf Twenty Happy Years of Musical Partnership."

Cuney Hare died on February 13, 1936, and was buried in Galveston's Lake View cemetery between her mother and father.

References

Cuney Hare, Maud. *Negro Musicians and Their Music.* Washington: Associated Publishers, 1936.

———. *Norris Wright Cuney; A Tribune of the Black People.* New York: The Crisis Publishing Co., 1913.

Logan, Rayford W. "Maude Cuney-Hare." *Dictionary of American Negro Biography.* Edited by Rayford W. Logan and Michael R. Winston. New York: Norton, 1982.

New York Age, 15 November 1890; 26 March 1937.

Southern, Eileen. *Biographical Dictionary of Afro-American and African Musicians.* Westport, Conn.: Greenwood Press, 1982.

Jean Elder Cazort

Marion Vera Cuthbert

(1896-1989)

Educator, organization leader, writer

A pioneer in the study of black women, an advocate of interracial cooperation, and an accomplished writer in several genres, Marion Vera Cuthbert was one of the most progressive thinkers of her day. From her experiences as a teacher and administrator in the segregated South and as a professional woman in the North, she gained an understanding of the unique position of black American women in the twentieth century. It is this position, circumscribed by race and sex prejudice, that provided the framework for a lifelong commitment to equality and interracial harmony.

Marion Vera Cuthbert

Cuthbert was born to Victoria Means and Thomas Cornelius Cuthbert on March 15, 1896, in Saint Paul, Minnesota, and attended grammar and secondary schools there. She began her undergraduate study at the University of Minnesota but transferred to Boston University, where she earned the baccalaureate from the college of liberal arts in 1920. That year she received a Charles Foster Kent Fellowship from the National Council on Religion in Higher Education. She continued her formal education at Columbia University, earning a master's degree in psychology in 1931 and a doctorate in higher education from its Teachers College in 1942.

Cuthbert's career began in 1920 as a English teacher and assistant principal at Burrell Normal School in Florence, Alabama. Revered by her students and the community, she became principal in 1925. Louis Beasley, a former pupil, recounted her insistence that he finish school and "measure up." He also recalls how she broke with tradition, inviting the school's unlettered cook to join the faculty procession at the graduation ceremony (Beasley, "Tribute")

Cuthbert left Burrell in 1927 to become dean of women at Talladega College in Talladega, Alabama. As one of the earliest deans, she helped to formulate the philosophy and practice of this position in a 1928 essay "The Dean of Women at Work." She identified the "non-recognition" of the administrative authority of the dean of women (and implicit sexism) as a major obstacle in the black college setting (*Journal of the National Association of College Women*, 39-44).

During the summers of 1928 and 1929 and the 1930-31 academic year, Cuthbert studied in psychology at Columbia.

After completing her master's, she joined the leadership division of the national office of the Young Women's Christian Association (YWCA) in 1932. Among the first blacks hired in this division, she had responsibility for "education, personnel, and developing Negro leadership" (*Who's Who on the Staff of the National Boards*). Here she played a pivotal role in staff development and interracial relations education. Among her early projects were the YWCA Summer Training Institutes that began at Oberlin College in 1938. These four-week training sessions were designed to increase: "(1) the nature . . . and the growth of the YWCA; (2) the growth and changes in the field of public agency work; and (3) professional advances in related fields" among new professional staff (Cuthbert personal papers, "The YWCA Summer Training Institutes"). In addition to conducting workshops on interracial relations, international development, volunteer education, student development, and administration in the United States, Germany, Switzerland, and England, Cuthbert was liaison to the National Conference on Social Work and the Urban League. She was also affiliated with the United Council of Church Women and the NAACP, for which she served as vice-president of the board of directors.

Pivotal Role Played in YWCA Conference

Cuthbert made an especially important contribution as executive for the YWCA's National Negro Leadership Conference at West Virginia State College, on June 20-23, 1942. To this meeting came ninety-four delegates from twenty-four states and fifty-two cities. Major areas of concerns were: "(1) the problems of the Negro people; (2) the problems of [interracial] groups of people; (3) the problems of administration; [and] (4) the problems of the YWCA as a social force in [the] community and [the] world" ("The Negro Leadership Conference"). Among the speakers were civil rights leaders and educators such as Roy Wilkins, editor of the *Crisis*, and anthropologist Hortense Powdermaker. After several days of fellowship and debate, the delegates unanimously endorsed a motion calling for a "national human relations conference, interracial in character, with common problems emphasized rather than differences." This motion, consistent with Cuthbert's commitment to interracial work, represented a philosophical shift away from separate black constituency conferences toward conferences that were interracial in character and content (Bell and Wilkins, 7).

Though Cuthbert published in the 1920s, she blossomed as a writer during her twelve-year tenure at the YWCA. Frequently published in the *Womans Press*—the association's official publication arm from 1918 to 1953—and the *YWCA Magazine*, she also wrote or collaborated on numerous conference proceedings, pamphlets, and training materials. Among her notable publications are those that appealed to an audience broader than the YWCA's membership. These include *Juliette Derricotte* (*Womans Press* 1933), a brief biography written in tribute to a black YWCA activist; *We Sing America* (*Friendship Press*, 1936), a book of children's stories; *April Grasses* (*Womans Press*, 1936), a book of poetry; and *Songs of Creation* (*Womans Press, 1949*), a collection of inspirational prose.

From the 1930s to the 1960s, Cuthbert's essays, poetry, short stories, and book reviews regularly appeared in an array of periodicals. YWCA matters, education, black women, race relations, the concerns of youth, and religion are persistent themes in her nonfiction. By contrast, her poetry departs from social issues; instead, she draws from nature and her own spirituality as primary sources. Perhaps these contrasting themes suggest her need to confront—and retreat at times from—the multiple oppressions of daily life.

Cuthbert's 1942 doctoral dissertation—*Education and Marginality: A Study of the Negro Woman College Graduate*—deserves special mention. Widely regarded as a pioneering effort, it is an exploratory study of the effect of college experience on black women. She devoted chapters to the Negro woman in American society, the background of the Negro college woman, the graduates participating in the questionnaire study, motives for going to college, relationships with family after college, work life and personal living after college, major problems in social relationships, graduate women and the problem of leadership, and the evaluation of the college experience. She concluded that the college experience had a marginalizing effect on black women; moreover, this effect was sometimes exemplified by aloofness and indifference toward blacks generally, heightened personal isolation, race and gender discrimination in the workplace, and conflict with black men.

In 1944 Cuthbert returned to academia, joining the Brooklyn College Department of Personnel Services, probably its first black staff member. Her duties included counseling women and teaching in the department of sociology and anthropology, to which she transferred full-time two years later to become the first black faculty member. In addition to academic responsibilities, Cuthbert continued her affiliation with the YWCA, working on the leadership services, national student administration, local personnel, business and professional women's program, Y-teen, national intercollegiate Christian council executive officers, and administration committees.

Cuthbert retired from Brooklyn College as an associate professor in 1961, leaving New York City to begin a new life in Plainfield, New Hampshire. There she was welcomed with open arms by a community of friends who were amused by her desire to learn country ways. Despite the fact that she was one of few blacks, she became an integral member of this community—regularly attending the Plainfield Community Baptist Church; serving as Plainfield Library Trustee and incorporator of the Sullivan County Mental Health Association; affiliating with the Plain-Meri Home-makers Group, the College Club of Windsor, and the Mothers and Daughters Club; and speaking to numerous groups about social issues and new books. She also remained active with the YWCA as an honorary national board member and participant in international training projects.

Cuthbert lived in Plainfield until 1968, later moving to Concord, Hew Hampshire, and then to Windsor, Vermont and Claremont, New Hampshire, due to failing health. She died on May 5, 1989. At the close of a memorial service in Plainfield a week after her death her ashes were scattered from the top of Mount Ascutney in Vermont.

References

Beasley, Louis. "Tribute." Memorial Service for Marion Vera Cuthbert, 1896-1989. Plainfield Community Baptist Church, Plainfield, New Hampshire, 12 June 1989.

Bell, Juliet O., and Helen J. Wilkins. *Interracial Practices in Community Y.W.C.A.'s: A Study under the Auspices of the Commission to Gather Interracial Experiences as Requested by the Sixteenth National Convention of the Y.W.C.A.'s of the U.S.A.* New York: YWCA, 1944.

Cuthbert, Marion. "The Dean of Women at Work." *Journal of the National Association of College Women* 13-14 (April 1928): 39-44.

———. *Education and Marginality: A Study of the Negro Woman College Graduate.* Ph. D. dissertation. Teachers College, Columbia University, 1942. New York: Garland Publishing, 1987.

Kitch, Laura. Letter to Patricia Bell-Scott, 2 September 1989.

Norris, Elizabeth. Interview with Patricia Bell-Scott, 14 February 1989.

Rome, Joan V. Letter to Patricia Bell-Scott, 21 September 1989.

YWCA of the U.S.A., National Board Archives, New York, Records Files, "The Negro Leadership Conference, Statistical Report of the Leadership Conference." West Virginia State College, Institute, West Va., 23-30 June, 1942.

Who's Who on the Staff of the National Boards, circa 1932.

Woodward, Bertha. Interview with Patricia Bell-Scott, 6 June 1989.

Collections

Marion Vera Cuthbert's personal papers are in the Spelman College Archives, Atlanta, Georgia, and include information on the YWCA Summer Training Institutes, and annual reports, 1932-80. Reports and other information on Cuthbert are in the Records Files Collection, YWCA of the U.S.A., National Board Archives, New York City; Mugar Memorial Library, Boston University; Brooklyn College Archives; and Talladega College Archives.

Patricia Bell-Scott

D

Dorothy Dandridge

(1922-1965)

Actress

One of Hollywood's legendary beauties, Dorothy Dandridge was a multitalented woman who set several precedents in the motion picture industry. A child actress who went on to star in such films as *Carmen Jones* and *Island in the Sun* and such television series as "Beulah" and "Father of the Bride" (1961-1962), she was the first black woman to be nominated for an Oscar and the first to be held in the arms of a white man on the silver screen.

Dandridge was born on November 9, 1922, to Cyril and Ruby Dandridge. As a child, she performed with her older sister and only sibling, Vivian. Billed as the Wonder Kids, the sisters toured Baptist churches around the country with a two-act show scripted by their mother. In 1934, after moving to Chicago and subsequently Los Angeles, the Wonder Kids changed their stage name to the Dandridge Sisters and added the talents of thirteen-year-old Etta Jones. Together the trio triumphed in an amateur competition on radio station KNX, Los Angeles, defeating twenty-five white contestants.

Two years later the Dandridge Sisters were invited to perform at New York's famed Cotton Club, a nightclub that featured black talent and catered to white audiences. The act was so successful that they were given a spot in the regular program, performing on the same bill as the legendary artists Cab Calloway and W. C. Handy. Another prominent act found regularly in the line-up was the dynamic dance team of Harold and Fayard Nicholas, the Nicholas Brothers.

In 1937 the Dandridge Sisters made their Hollywood debut, with minor roles in the Marx Brothers classic film *A Day at the Races*. But after several one-night stands and recording dates with Jimmie Lunceford and his Orchestra, the trio dissolved. In 1941 and 1942 Dandridge performed solo in several musical film shorts: *Yes Indeed*, *Sing for My Supper*, *Jungle Jig*, *Easy Street*, *Cow Cow Boogie*, and *Paper Doll*.

Dandridge married Harold Nicholas in 1942 and settled with him in Los Angeles as he pursued a career in motion pictures. Three months later Dandridge was pregnant with her daughter Harolyn, born in 1943. Several years later, after institutionalizing her daughter, who was diagnosed as severely retarded, and divorcing her adulterous husband, Dandridge pursued a career as a nightclub singer, traveling the globe. In 1951 she appeared with the Desi Arnez Band at the Macombo, and, in that same year, became the first black to perform in the Empire Room of New York's Waldorf-Astoria Hotel.

Dandridge continued to work in Hollywood films and in 1954 obtained the role that would launch her career, the lead in Otto Preminger's all-black musical extravaganza *Carmen Jones*. The film, which featured Harry Belafonte, as well as Pearl Bailey and Diahann Carroll in supporting roles, was a critical success, winning a Golden Globe Award for the Best Musical Motion Picture of 1954, an Audience Award from the Berlin Film Festival in 1955, and an Oscar nomination for best actress for Dandridge, the first ever received by a black woman.

Time magazine thought that the success of the film would create more opportunities for blacks in the film industry, but that was not the case. Rather than being offered a wide variety of roles, Dandridge was typecast into the stereotypical roles commonly given to black actresses. As Dandridge explained, "I consider myself an actress, and I have always worked to be a confident one. I interpret a role to the best of my ability, and more often than not, and more often than I'd like, the role calls for a creature of abandon whose desires are stronger than their sense of morality" (*Ebony*, 1966).

In 1957 Dandridge again broke ground, this time as the first black woman to be held in the arms of a white man in a Hollywood motion picture. *Island in the Sun*, a highly controversial film, not only paired Dandridge and white actor John Justin, it also offered the reverse with the pairing of Belafonte and Joan Fontaine. The trend of interracial romance continued with Dandridge in such features as *The Decks Ran Red* (1958) and *Tamango* (1960).

Unable to find enough opportunities to work in feature films, Dandridge returned to nightclub performing. During her tour she met Las Vegas restaurateur Jack Dennison, whom she married in 1959. Three years later Dandridge divorced him and found herself bankrupt after a series of bad investments. She then tried to resurrect her failing career, but found little opportunity, making only a few television appearances. She died in her West Hollywood apartment on September 8, 1965, of an overdose of an antidepressant drug.

Dandridge appeared in the following films: *A Day at the*

Races (1937); *Going Places* (1938); *Bahama Passage, Lady from Louisiana, Sundown, Sun Valley Serenade* (1941); *Drums of the Congo, Lucky Jordan* (1942); *Hit Parade of 1943* (1943); *Atlantic City, Since You Went Away* (1944); *Pillow to Post* (1945); *Four Shall Die* (1946); *Ebony Parade, Flamingo* (1947); *The Harlem Globe Trotters, Tarzan's Peril* (also known as *Tarzan and the Jungle Queen*) (1951); *Bright Road, Remains to Be Seen* (1953); *Carmen Jones* (1954); *The Happy Road* (1956); *Island in the Sun* (1957); *The Decks Ran Red* (1958); *Porgy and Bess, Tamango* (1959); *Moment of Danger* (also known as *Malaga*) (1960); *Cain's Hundred, The Murder Men* (1962); and *Light's Diamond Jubilee* (1964).

References

Bogle, Donald. *Blacks in American Films and Television: An Encyclopedia*. New York: Garland, 1988.

———. *Brown Sugar: Eighty Years of America's Black Female Superstars*. New York: Harmony Books, 1980.

———. "The Dorothy Dandridge Story." *Essence* 15 (October 1984): 100-102, 146-148.

———. *Toms, Coons, Mulattoes, Mammies, and Bucks*. New York: Continuum Publishing, 1989.

Dandridge, Dorothy, and E. Conrad. *Everything and Nothing*. New York: Abeland-Schuman, 1970.

"Dorothy Dandridge-Hollywood's Tragic Enigma." *Ebony* 21 (March 1966): 171-182.

Leavy, W. 'The Real-Life Tragedy of Dorothy Dandridge." *Ebony* 41 (September 1986): 136-37, 140-46.

Frances K. Gateward

Margaret Danner

(1915-)

Poet

Poet Margaret Essie Danner was born to Caleb and Naomi Danner of Pryorsburg, Kentucky, on January 12, 1915. Personal information about the life of the writer is scant; however, it is known that she was married to Cordell Strickland and became the mother of Naomi (Mrs. Sterling Montrose Washington). Her grandchild, Sterling Washington, Jr., inspired her "Muffin poems." Danner later married Otto Cunningham. She attended Englewood High School in Chicago, and Loyola, Roosevelt, and Northwestern universities and the YMCA College. She also studied under Karl Shapiro and Paul Engle.

Even though Danner began writing poetry in junior high school (she won a prize for her poem "The Violin" when she was in the eighth grade), she first attracted cru¡tical attention in 1945, when she won second place in the Poetry Workshop of the Midwestern Writers Conference held at Northwestern University." In 1951 Danner became editorial assistant to *Poetry: The Magazine in Verse* and five years later was named assistant editor, the first black to hold that position. In 1961 she became poet-in-residence at Wayne State University in Detroit. While there, she became involved in community life. One of the results of this was the establishment of a community art center, Boone House, named for Dr. Boone, the minister of King Solomon Church, who allowed her the use of the empty parish house. A work by Danner entitled "Boone House" appears in a 1962 issue of *Negro History Bulletin*. A number of poets helped Danner in various ways at Boone House, including Dudley Randall, Robert Hayden, Hoyt Fuller, Owen Dodson, and Naomi Long Madgett.

First Collection of Poetry Published

In 1960 Danner published her first collection of poetry, *Impressions of African Art Forms*, which won high critical acclaim. With *Impressions* Danner introduced a frequent theme of her writing—Africa. "I have for many years been involved in the study of Africana, especially African Art," Danner said, "because I feel that man reveals a sensitivity through his creative work that is a clue to his present day reactions to problems and pleasures" (*Black Writers*, 134). It was not until 1966 that Danner was able to visit Africa, when she read her poetry in Dakar, Senegal, at the World Exposition of Negro Arts.

Poem Counterpoem was published in 1966. The volume comprises twenty poems by Danner and fellow Detroit poet Dudley Randall (ten each on alternating pages) that treat the same or similar subjects. Other collections of Danner's poetry include *To Flower Poems* (Hemphill Press, 1963; revised edition 1969) and *Iron Lace* (Kriya Press, 1968). The collection *The Down of a Thistle* (Country Beautiful, 1976) contains selected poems, prose poems, and songs. June M. Aldridge, writing in the *Dictionary of Literary Biography*, noted that several of Danner's poems make use of African images and symbols, for instance the thistle, as representative of black people. According to Aldridge, Danner's most anthologized poems,"The Elevator Man", speaks out against the actions of both white American society and the black man's apparent acquiescence and is so popular "because of the tremendous impact created by a very effective blending of tone, theme, and rhythm" (*DLB*, 88).

In summing up Danner's work, Aldridge says that her poetry does celebrate black people rather than protest their plight:

> As a group, the African poems are superior to Danner's other poems, and they will undoubtedly form the basis for her future reputation. . . .

Though Danner now finds it difficult to write poetry because of encroaching blindness, her perseverance is just as strong as her links to Africa. As a contributor to Afro-American literature and especially to the black arts movement, and as a poet who clearly understood the ties of African heritage, Danner will be remembered not only as a writer but as a guardian of culture (*DLB*, 89).

Danner edited two anthologies of poetry by students at Virginia Union University which were published by the university: *Brass Horses* and *Regroup*. She has won "the Harriet Tubman Award (1951), the Native Chicago Literary Prize (1957), was chosen one of the ten top poets by the University of Michigan (summer 1956), has received grants from the Women's Auxiliary of the Chicago Urban League, the African Studies Association, and the American Society for African Culture (1960), and a John Hay Whitney Fellowship (1959).

References

Aldridge, June M. "Margaret Danner." *Dictionary of Literary Biography*. Vol. 42. Detroit: Gale Research, 1985.

Black Writers. Detroit: Gale Research, 1989.

Gilin, Ronda. *Black American Women in Literature. A Bilbliography, 1976-1987*. Jefferson, N. C.: McFarland, 1989.

"Margaret Danner." *Negro History Bulletin* 26 (October 1962): 53-54.

Who's Who Among Black Americans, 1990/91. Detroit: Gale Research, 1991.

Helen Houston

Angela Davis

(1944-)

Social activist, educator

A sensitive child of the 1950s who became a militant revolutionary in the 1960s, Angela Davis fought for women's and civil rights and against poverty and racism with a passion that inspired millions.

Davis became acquainted with the techniques of nonviolence through the leadership of Martin Luther King, Jr., and with those of violence through the racism of Bull Connor. Introduced to socialism while in high school and communism

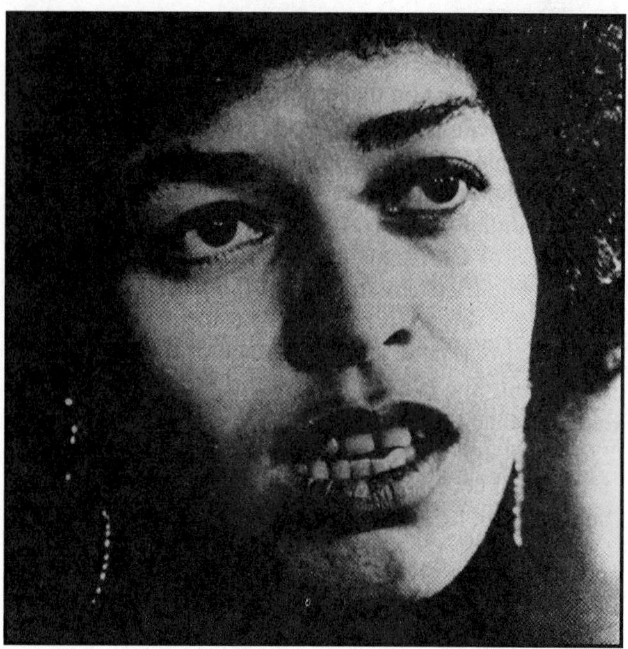

Angela Davis

while in college, her contact with third world students in France gradually influenced her own philosophy of life. In Los Angeles, her disillusionment with several civil rights groups moved her further to the radical left, until finally, her decision to join the Communist party completed her radicalization.

Davis was born on January 26, 1944, in Birmingham, Alabama, the oldest of four children. Her father, B. Frank, was an automobile mechanic who owned a gas station. He had been a teacher, but gave up the profession because of the meager salary. Davis's mother, Sallye E., was a schoolteacher, who taught her to read, write, and calculate before she began the first grade. As a child, Davis studied piano, dance, and clarinet and was highly regarded in her Girl Scout troop. The family lived in a middle-class section of Birmingham that was eventually referred to as Dynamite Hill because the area has been bombed frequently by the Ku Klux Klan.

At an early age, Davis became aware of school children having no lunches, warm clothing, or medicine. She was so moved, in fact, that she stole money from her father's change and gave it to her hungry friends. Since she had seen her mother give her sister's and brothers' old clothing to poor children, she rationalized her stealing as a good act. She felt if hungry children existed in the world, she had to do something about it. For the first time in her life she became conscious of social differences, especially between the rich and the poor.

Since black children were victims of a class-conscious Birmingham, they had poor self-images, Davis decided. The school system taught that blacks were poor because they were lazy. She heard the teachers say that they could pull themselves up by the bootstraps if they worked hard and diligently. Davis also resented the derogatory names she heard whites call blacks. Her mother tried to explain these verbal assaults to her children, even though it was difficult for her and for other black parents to explain a racist environment to their young.

At Carrie A. Tuggle Elementary School, where Davis attended, she experienced the disadvantages and advantages of a segregated school system. Disadvantages included attending old, dilapidated school buildings, using outdated textbooks discarded by white schools, and not having a gymnasium for sports activities. Although the advantages of segregated schools were few, blacks could run the schools the way they wanted except when the superintendent for "colored" schools visited. Davis and her classmates learned about black history—about the lives of Frederick Douglass, Sojourner Truth, Harriet Tubman, Denmark Vesey, and Nat Turner—and learned "traditional" Negro material, such as James Weldon Johnson's "Lift Ev'ry Voice and Sing" (often referred to as the Negro National Anthem). These cultural activities instilled in her a sense of pride. Nevertheless, Davis eventually realized that segregated schools provided few opportunities for the total development and growth of black children. Besides, many black teachers taught the official line of the white establishment—that the children would not amount to too much unless they were prepared to work extremely hard. The teachers seldom mentioned the fact that racism was the barrier that the children had to overcome.

Davis found Parker High School unstimulating academically, which contributed to her dissatisfaction with life. She was an "A" student at Parker, played in the band, and found pleasure in reading books. Although Birmingham had a "whites only" policy at the public library, blacks were able to withdraw books from a door in the back of the downtown branch.

Political Activism Begins Early

Davis's mother was politically involved and influenced her daughter considerably. In college Sallye Davis protested against the imprisonment of the Scottsboro boys and participated in the activities of the NAACP, even though the organization was outlawed in Birmingham in the mid-fifties. Davis learned from her mother's activism that she could protest against the system and count on her mother's moral support. Her grandmother, who constantly talked of slavery so that her grandchildren "would not forget about it," also influenced Davis. In the mid-fifties Davis and her mother took part in civil rights demonstrations in Birmingham, and in high school she assisted in the organization of interracial study groups that the police disbanded.

During her childhood, Davis spent several summers in New York City with her mother, who at that time was studying for a master's at New York University. At the age of fifteen, when she was in her junior year at Parker High School, Davis moved to New York to enter the Elizabeth Irwin High School, a progressive private school in Greenwich Village, on a scholarship from the American Friends Service Committee. Many teachers at this school had been blacklisted by the public schools because of their political ideology. Her parents had made arrangements for Davis to live in Brooklyn with the family of William Howard Melish, an active Episcopalian minister and winner of the 1956 Stockholm peace prize. While in New York Davis was introduced to socialist ideology and consequently joined Advance, a Marxist-Leninist group.

Her high school studies made Davis aware of her inadequate preparation in mathematics, science, and foreign languages. In Birmingham she was an "A" student, but here in New York she was average. In the summer she reenrolled in junior year courses and gradually rose to her normal level of performance. French was her most difficult subject in high school, yet, determined, she overcame this obstacle and graduated with honors in French from Brandeis University in Waltham, Massachusetts.

In 1961 she entered Brandeis and developed into an excellent student. She spent her junior year at the Sorbonne in Paris, where she made a glamorous impression on the other students, but devoted herself to her studies.

It was in Paris, in conversations with students from Algeria, that Davis became aware of revolutions against French colonialism and struggles for first-class citizenship among oppressed people. Her sensitivity to oppression was further ignited in September 1963, when four girls Davis knew were killed during the bombing of a church in Birmingham. Davis's philosophy of life also altered considerably as she began to study under the philosopher Herbert Marcuse at Brandeis in 1964-1965. She was sensitized by this philosopher's interpretation of the contemporary industrial society of the West, where the lower economic groups were oppressed and repressed. Marcuse felt that it was the duty of the individual to resist and rebel against the system—an idea that influenced Davis profoundly. Despite her sensitivity to mankind, however, she appeared aloof and distant.

A magna cum laude graduate of Brandeis with Phi Beta Kappa membership, Davis finished her undergraduate degree after the acceptance of her thesis on the novels of Alain Robbe-Grillet. After graduation, from 1965 to 1967, she studied with the faculty of philosophy at the Johann Wolfgang von Goethe University in Frankfurt, West Germany, and with Oskar Negt and Theodore Adorno. Both men admired her mind and acknowledged that she was by far the best student that they had taught. By now she not only spoke French exceptionally well but had mastered the German language.

Davis's Radical Activism Ignites

In 1967 Davis could no longer tolerate the deteriorating racist situation in the United States from a distance. Anxious to become involved, she enrolled at the University of California at San Diego, where Marcuse was teaching after his retirement from Brandeis. Under his direction she obtained her master's degree in philosophy in 1969, and, by the end of the following year, had completed all requirements for her doctorate except for her dissertation. At the university she began her active involvement with the civil rights movement, assisting in the development of the Black Students Council, developing a program for an experimental college for minorities, and supporting the San Diego Black Conference, an organization dominated by Ron Kerenga's rebellious group "Us."

In 1967 she attended a workshop in Los Angeles, "Economics and the Community," sponsored by the Student Nonviolent Coordinating Committee (SNCC). Attending this workshop changed her life radically. There she met Franklin Alexander and his wife, Kendra. Alexander was involved with SNCC, the Black Panthers, and the Communist party, while his sister, Charlene, was the leader of the Che-Lumumba Club, an all-black community cell in the black community of Los Angeles.

In 1968 Davis moved to Los Angeles and became totally involved with the Alexanders, who influenced her considerably. She became deeply involved with radical protests and rallies, although she eventually grew disillusioned with the SNCC and especially Stokely Carmichael, "Us," and the Black Panthers. Davis complained about the male chauvinism in these groups: women did all the work when a protest was organized, only to have the men complain that the women were taking over. After reflecting about the groups who were in tune with her political and social philosophy—her sensitivity for oppressed and repressed people and her distaste for racism and discrimination—she decided to join the Communist party on June 22, 1968. The radicalization was complete.

In the spring of 1969, Davis joined the faculty of the department of philosophy at the University of California at Los Angeles and developed four courses: "Dialectical Materialism," "Kant," "Existentialism," and "Recurring Political Themes in Black Literature." In spite of the popularity of her courses, Davis ran into conflict with the board of regents because of her membership in the Communist party. On July 1, 1969, William Divale, an ex-FBI informer, revealed in a letter published in the UCLA *Daily Bruin* that a communist was on the faculty. Eight days later a Los Angeles *Examiner* reporter identified Davis as the person. In spite of the recommendations of the department of philosophy and the chancellor of the university, the board of regents, under pressure from the governor of California, Ronald Reagan, fired her. Eventually, the courts reinstated her since the dismissal violated her constitutional rights, mainly the right to teach regardless of one's political affiliation.

Although the administration of UCLA continued to monitor and evaluate Davis's courses, students found the instruction excellent and unbiased. The board of regents was determined to terminate her contract, however. At the end of the academic year of 1969-70, the board denied her a new contract because she lacked a doctorate and because of her allegedly inflammatory rhetoric in the community.

The Soledad Prison Incident Spurs More Radicalism

Davis outraged the UCLA Board of Regents with her speeches made in the defense of the "Soledad Brothers." George Jackson and W. L. Nolen were two inmates at Soledad Prison in California who organized a Marxist-Fanonist revolutionary cell. In January 1970 Nolen and two other prisoners got into a fistfight and were killed by shots from the guard tower. When a white guard was found murdered, Jackson and two other prisoners were indicted for his murder.

Davis reacted emotionally to the event and threw herself energetically into the cause, organizing, picketed, and making speeches to raise defense funds. Without ever having seen Jackson, she fell in love with him—through a secret correspondence. He was killed by the guards during an alleged escape attempt, although charges had been dropped against him.

By now Davis symbolized the radical outlaw. Then she was indicted because she owned several guns that were used in a murder. Davis had bought the guns because of threats on her life, but, on August 7, 1970, Jonathan Jackson, George's brother, took the guns to the Marion County Courthouse in San Rafad, where prisoner James McClain was on trial for stabbing an inmate at San Quentin. Jackson pulled out the guns, took hostages, and made a run for a van in the parking lot. Before the van could pull away, Jackson, a judge, and two prisoners were killed. Since the guns found in the van were registered in Davis's name, a federal warrant was issued for her arrest. Rather than accept the warrant, Davis went into hiding. On August 18, 1970, the FBI placed her on the ten-most-wanted fugitive list, charged by the State of California with kidnapping, conspiracy, and murder. The FBI's hunt for Davis became high drama across the world. After a two-month search, the FBI found her in a motel in New York. Extradited to California, she remained in jail without bail until the movement for her release boomed into a world-wide protest. "Free Angela" rallies took place everywhere from Los Angeles to Paris to Sri Lanka. The slogan "Free Angela" appeared on billboards, in newspapers, and on posters everywhere. Protests took place outside of her jail cell. On February 23, 1972, a judge released Davis on $102,000 bail. The subsequent trial won international attention.

Since Davis was not at the scene of the murder, her lawyer argued that there was insufficient evidence to prove she was part of the murders plans. After thirteen hours of deliberation, the jury of eleven whites and one Mexican-American acquitted her on all counts. After the acquittal she had a mass benefit in New York to defray her legal expenses. She also became involved in efforts to consolidate this sentiment into one organization to fight racism and sexism. The National Alliance Against Racist and Political Repression grew out of the "Free Angela" movement. She has spoken on behalf of the organization and has led demonstrations on various issues since 1972.

Because of her militant activities, the California state Board of Regents and Governor Reagan voted in 1972 that Davis would never teach at a state-supported university. The American Association of University Professors censured UCLA at the time for lack of due process in its failure to renew Davis's contract. Although the university's department of philosophy requested her services, the board refused. For a year, beginning in 1975, Davis was a lecturer in black studies at Claremont College in Claremont, California; in 1967 she lectured in philosophy and political science at Stanford University; from 1983 to 1985 she lectured in ethnic studies at California College of the Arts and Crafts in Oakland; and in 1984 she lectured in history of consciousness at the University of California at Santa Cruz. From 1978 to the present, she has been a lecturer in women's and ethnic studies at San Francisco State University, and in the humanities at San Francisco Art Institute.

Davis received several honorary degrees in 1972, including the Doctor of Philosophy from Lenin University in the Soviet Union and the Doctor of Political Science from the University of Leipzig, in Germany. In 1979 she was awarded the Lenin Peace Prize. She has been a professor of philosophy at Moscow University and of political science at Havana University.

In 1980 and again in 1984, the Communist Party, U.S.A., nominated her as its vice-presidential candidate. From 1985 Davis has been a member of the executive board of the National Political Caucus of Black Women. She has served on the board of directors for the National Black Women's Health Project since 1986.

Davis has written numerous essays on political and judicial reform, rights of women, sexism, violence against women, and the rights of prisoners and mental health patients. Her book *If They Come in the Morning* and her best-selling *Angela Davis: An Autobiography* provide insights into her life and ideas. In *Women, Race and Class* and *Women, Culture and Politics* she leaves the reader with an understanding of the economic, racial, and class situation with which women must struggle. She has also written *Ma Rainey, Bessie Smith and Billie Holiday: Black Women's Music and the Shaping of Social Consciousness*. A documentary on Davis, "Portrait of a Revolutionary," has been produced by one of her students at UCLA. Because she is constantly in demand as a speaker and she publishes extensively in journals and books, she has never finished her dissertation on eighteenth-century German philosopher Immanuel Kent. She remains in the doctoral program in the department of philosophy of Berlin's Humboldt University.

References

Abbott, D. "Revolution by Other Means." Interview with Angela Davis. *New Statesman* 114 (14 August 1987): 16-17.

"Angela Davis: Radical of the 60's Changes with the Times." *Ebony* 45 (July 1990): 56.

Davis, Angela. *Angela Davis: An Autobiography*. New York: Random House, 1974.

———. *If They Come in the Morning: Voices of Resistance*. New York: Third Press, 1971.

———. "Lifting As We Climb: Radical Perspectives on the Empowerment of Afro-American Women." *Harvard Educational Review* (Summer 1988).

———. *Women, Culture and Politics*. New York: Random House, 1988.

———. *Women, Race and Class*. New York: Random House, 1982.

Giddings, Paula. *When and Where I Enter: The Impact of Black Women on Race and Sex in America*. New York: William Morrow, 1984.

Jackson, George. *Soledad Brother: The Prison Letters of George Jackson*. New York: Coward-McCann, 1970.

"Making of a Revolutionary." *Sepia* 19 (December 1970): 9-11.

Collections

A taped interview with Angela Davis in the Black Oral History Collection, Special Collections, Fisk University Library.

Joan Curl Elliott

Elizabeth Lindsay Davis

(1855- ?)

Educator, writer, club organizer

The success and popularity of the National Association of Colored Women (NACW) is due in part to the organizational talent and writing skills of Elizabeth Lindsay Davis. She became well known as national organizer of the NACW and author of *Story of the Illinois Federation of Women's Clubs*—the first known history of women's clubs published in any state. She wrote the equally historic work, *Lifting As They Climb*, which recounts the association's history from its beginning until 1933. In addition to her club work, she traveled extensively throughout the United States and lectured to churches and other organizations. Her articles in newspapers and magazines were well received.

Born in Peoria County, Illinois, in 1855, Elizabeth Lindsay Davis was the oldest daughter of Thomas H. Lindsay and Sophia Jane Lindsay, pioneer citizens of the state. She attended a one-room segregated school, and at age ten she was sent to Princeton, Illinois, to attend Bureau County High School, the first township high school in the state. She graduated with high honors, becoming one of the first three black Americans to graduate from the school. The other two were her brother-in-law, Henry Clay Gibon of Peoria, and Arminta Low Thomas of Princeton. Through the efforts of Robert G. Ingersoll, a friend of the Lindsay family, the township schools were integrated a few years after her graduation.

After graduation Davis continued to study, specializing in sociology, psychology, African-American history, and social service. She read widely and knew world events and the best ancient and modern literature. She taught school until 1885, when she married William H. Davis from Frederick, Maryland. Elizabeth Davis became an active worker in Saint Mark's Methodist Episcopal Church, where she held every office in the church except that of licensed minister. She also became an active clubwoman and social organizer. In March 1896 she organized the Phillis Wheatley Women's Club and served as president for twenty-eight years, leaving that office in 1924. From the time the National Association of Colored Women was organized in Washington, D.C., in July 1896, for many years she never missed its meetings. She was state organizer for Illinois clubs for six years, and beginning with the NACW election of officers in 1901, she was national organizer for nine years. She was honored on May 14, 1904, when the women of Johnstown, Pennsylvania, named their new affiliate, for which she served as organizer, in her honor. She became widely known in her position as national organizer and at each national meeting she reported on the growth of the membership both in number of clubs added and in women who joined. She also reported on the number of miles she had traveled. The women thanked her publicly for her organizational skills and her success with the membership drive. From 1910 to 1912 Davis was Illinois state president of the NACW.

Davis Writes Club Histories

By 1933 Elizabeth Lindsay Davis had become national and state historian. She wrote *Story of the Illinois Federation of Colored Women's Clubs, 1900-1922*, a valuable reference for club members in Illinois and for scholars interested in their history. The work is the first known record of women's clubs published in the United States. In addition to serving as a valuable reference work for Illinois women, it was a model for other such histories that followed. In 1933 she completed *Lifting As They Climb*, the history of the NACW. Despite its popularity, the history contained numerous printing errors, photographs were improperly placed, and it lacked an index. Davis had worked on the history for ten years and had gathered material found nowhere else, but she had rushed to have it ready for the Chicago Convention of 1933 under Sallie W. Stewart's administration. At the Nineteenth Biennial Convention held in Cleveland, Ohio, in 1935, national president Mary Fitzbutler Waring announced a threatened court proceeding against the association for publication costs of the history. To retrieve some of the money spent for publication, members were encouraged to buy the book at a reduced price. "The history is a wonderful book, and you can each read it with benefit," she said (Wesley, 109-110). Davis explained that the rush to complete the book prevented the proofs from being sent to her for review. "Yet, if you will take fondly therewith, in this book you will find some pith," she said (Wesley, 110). The court suit was averted after Waring paid the balance due. By 1946, NACW president Christine Smith spoke of Davis's "unfinished history," calling it "the only permanent record we have of the personnel and events of the National Association up to the date of its publication" (Wesley, 119). The supply of that edition had been exhausted, and Smith spoke of a need for a new edition.

During World War I, Davis was a worker devoted to the state council of national defense. When the war ended, she received an honorable discharge in recognition of valuable service to the federal government. Her work with the Liberty Loan Department during the war years was recognized also, and she was awarded a certificate of appreciation for selling war bonds.

Elizabeth Lindsay Davis was especially fond of youth, particularly young ladies, and her work with them throughout the country led them to claim her as their adopted mother. She traveled widely in all regions of the country and addressed clubs, churches, and other organizations. Her work as a writer became known and widely received through the newspaper articles that she wrote.

In addition to the Phillis Wheatley Club, she was a member of numerous organizations, including the Women's City Club, and was one of the twenty-seven graduates of its initial citizenship training class of 1923. She was active with the Chicago Forum League of Women Voters, the Woman's Aid, Giles Charity Club, E. L. D. Study Club, and the Service Club. She and her husband were active in most of the civic, social, religious, educational, and political affairs of the Chicago community.

Davis was particularly concerned with the woman's right to vote and the power of the vote in philanthropic work. She believed that the most successful philanthropic projects depended "absolutely upon the control of political influence by the best American citizenship, men and women working in unity and cooperation at the polls." She noted the need for systematic philanthropy to address the needs of social service and called for the use of the ballot "upon the heads of the great corporations and private individuals to direct their attention to the serious consequences of . . . industrial and social unrest, the crime, disease, and poverty emanating from bad housing and unwholesome environment" to persuade them to support social uplift ("Votes for Philanthropy," 14). She saw women in a pivotal role here:

> Woman is a pioneer in the forward movement for [s]ocial uplift, racial and community development, whether for the abandoned wife, the wage

earning girl, the dependent and delinquent child
of the countless hordes of the unemployed (14).

When the National YWCA invited two hundred prominent women to take part of a historic processional march down the aisle of the University of Chicago chapel in recognition of Leadership of Women, she was one of the participants (Davis, *Lifting As They Climb,* 204).

References

Dannett, Sylvia G. L. *Profiles of Negro Womanhood.* Vol. 1. Chicago: Educational Heritage, 1964. 248-49.

Davis, Elizabeth Lindsay. *Lifting As They Climb.* Washington, D.C.: National Association of Colored Women, 1933. 203-205.

———. "Votes for Philanthropy." In "Votes for Women." *Crisis* 10 (August 1915): 191. Photograph, p. 182.

Wesley, Charles Harris. *The History of the National Association of Colored Women's Clubs.* Washington, D.C.: NACW, 1984. Photograph, p. 110.

Who's Who in Colored America. 5th ed. Brooklyn: Thomas Yenser, 1940.

Jessie Carney Smith

Henrietta Vinton Davis

(1860-1941)

Elocutionist, actress, political organizer

Henrietta Vinton Davis, elocutionist, actress, and political organizer, was born in Baltimore, Maryland, in 1860. The daughter of Mansfield Vinton Davis and Mary Ann (Johnson) Davis, Henrietta Davis inherited her artistic talents from her father, a distinguished musician. From her stepfather, George A. Hackett, she acquired a revolutionary and radical zeal that would later be incorporated into her work with Marcus Garvey and the Universal Negro Improvement Association (UNIA).

At the age of fifteen, Davis began her career in the Maryland public schools. In 1878, after teaching in Maryland and in Louisiana, she returned to Washington, D.C., where she was employed as a copyist in the Office of the Recorder of Deeds, first under George A. Sheridan, and afterward under Frederick Douglass. Douglass, the celebrated abolitionist, newspaper editor, and leader, encouraged Davis to study drama.

As an African-American pioneer in the legitimate drama, Davis achieved recognition as an actress and a dramatic reader. In 1880, studying under the direction of Marguerite E. Saxon of Washington, D.C., she developed the techniques required for a career in theatrical arts. She also received training under Edwin Lawrence of New York City and Rachel Noah of Boston, where she attended the Boston School of Oratory. On April 25, 1883, she made her debut in the District of Columbia as an elocutionist introduced by Frederick Douglass.

Within four months of her debut, under the management of James Monroe Trotter and William H. Dupree, Davis toured the East Coast, performing in New York City, New Haven, Hartford, and Boston. In the fall of 1883 she appeared on the program of the Colored National Convention in Washington, D.C., and was acclaimed for her performance. In 1884 Davis resigned her position as copyist to pursue a stage career. She married Thomas T. Symmons, who became her manager.

From 1884 to 1915, Davis toured principal cities in the United States, the West Indies, and in Central and South America. Her recitals included Negro dialect selections from Paul Laurence Dunbar's works, classical selections from William Shakespeare's *As You Like It,* and Mark Twain's "How Tom Sawyer Got His Fence Whitewashed." By 1893 Davis had established her own dramatic company in Chicago, which produced the play *Dessalines* by William Edgar Easton, a black American playwright.

In addition to a career as an actress, Davis became an organizer for Marcus Garvey's Universal Negro Improvement Association. Davis first saw Garvey in the West Indies during her earlier travels. However, their first meeting did not occur until 1919, when she accepted his invitation to speak in Harlem at the Palace Casino. Davis's association with the Universal Negro Improvement Association, beginning in 1919, lasted until her death in 1941. In 1919 she became one of the original thirteen members of the UNIA of New York City.

Davis was at the pinnacle of her career at the time she decided to affiliate with the UNIA. Giving up her career to work with Garvey and the UNIA isolated her from many of her friends and longtime acquaintances, who were staunch members of the black elite. While some members of this class chose to support Garvey, most viewed him as a charlatan who was dangerous to the interests of African-Americans. Moreover, Garvey expressed a special dislike for mulattoes, many of whom were members of the black elite. Even though Davis, a woman of very fair complexion, was born into this class, she was heir to the philosophy of her stepfather, Captain George A. Hackett. During the antebellum period, advocating and protesting for the rights of African-Americans, Hackett was one of the most radical blacks in Maryland.

Prior to her involvement with the UNIA, Davis received extensive press coverage. After 1919 her work was cited primarily in the *Negro World*, the official organ of the UNIA. In spite of her celebrated status and extensive national and international work with the UNIA, there was no mention of her death in the leading black or white newspapers. Garvey had become persona non grata and so had Henrietta Vinton Davis.

Racial Pride Advocated

Davis was an ardent nationalist who fervently believed in African redemption. In the 1890s she was a supporter of the Populist party; later she backed the Socialist party. Pride of race and reverence for Africa were the cornerstones of her philosophy. She told African-Americans that they were superior to whites. She urged them to emigrate to Africa; to fight for African freedom from colonization; to take pride in using ''Negro'' instead of ''colored'' as the race designation; to fight segregation and never bow to suppression; and to teach their children to love their race, their blackness, and their African heritage. Davis was fierce, forceful, and uncompromising in her rhetoric. By all accounts her oratorical abilities were exceptional. The force of her conviction, combined with the eloquence of her speech, were major elements in her ability to sell the UNIA philosophy.

Garvey viewed Davis as an important and extremely loyal ally and a unique and valuable spokesperson for the UNIA. Dubbed Lady Davis, she was acclaimed wherever she spoke. Her speeches were highly laudatory of Garvey. After 1922, following the arrest and indictment of Garvey for mail fraud, she spent a great deal of her time defending him against the charges. After the trial and his conviction, she traveled and spoke extensively in an effort to save the organization.

Davis's loyalty to Garvey and service to the UNIA were rewarded in several ways. In 1919 she was appointed the first international organizer for the UNIA; she was one of the original directors of the Black Star Line as well as the second vice-president of the corporation. In 1924 Garvey sent her as part of the UNIA delegation to Africa to obtain consent for UNIA members to establish a colony in Liberia. Davis also traveled to Cuba in the 1920s to advance Garvey's cause, advocating black unity and nationalism.

Throughout the 1920s and the 1930s Davis was among the top leadership in the UNIA. Garvey felt women, rather than men, could better serve the cause of the movement, since women were more loyal to him. Davis's loyalty was evident throughout her involvement with the organization, particularly during the period of Garvey's imprisonment, when she assumed the responsibility of operating the UNIA from Jamaica. In 1929 Davis was promoted to the position of Secretary General, and in 1934 she was elected president of the organization. Little is known of Davis's activities after 1934. On November 23, 1941, she died in obscurity, a patient at Saint Elizabeth's Hospital in Washington, D.C.

References

Collier-Thomas, Bettye. ''Henrietta Vinton Davis, 1860-1941.'' *Black Women in America: Contributions to Our Heritage*. Booklet. Washington, D.C.: Bethune Museum and Archives, 1984.

Hill, Robert, et al.*The Marcus Garvey and Universal Negro Improvement Association Papers*. 6 vols. Berkeley: University of California Press, 1983-1989.

Majors, Monroe A. *Noted Negro Women*. Chicago: Donohue and Henneberry, 1893. 102-108. Photograph, p. 102.

Scruggs, Lawson A. *Women of Distinction*. Raleigh, N.C.: The Author, 1893. 85-88.

Seraile, William. ''Henrietta Vinton Davis and the Garvey Movement.'' *Afro-Americans in New York Life and History*, 7 (July 1983): 7-24.

Collections

While the papers of Henrietta Vinton Davis are uncollected, they are indispensable to the discussion of her relationship to Marcus Garvey and her role in the UNIA. Files of the newspaper *Negro World* and FBI files include additional information on Davis. The Schomburg Center for Research on Black Culture has a Marcus Garvey clipping file from *Negro World*.

Bettye Collier-Thomas

Hilda Davis

(1905-)

Educator, organizational leader

Hilda Andrea Davis, dean of women in historically black colleges for nearly thirty years, has been a leader in national black educational, religious, civic, and women's organizations throughout the twentieth century. She was born to Louis Alexander Davis and Ruth Gertrude (Cooke) Davis on May 24, 1905, at home on Seventeenth and Florida Avenue in Washington, D.C. She was the fourth child in a family of eight daughters and one son, and the family included a white foster child, Virginia, for about two years. Davis's childhood was filled with rich sibling and extended family relationships. Both sets of grandparents—the Davises and the Cookes—lived nearby on Eleventh Street; and among her six uncles was Benjamin Oliver Davis, Sr., who became the nation's first black general in the U.S. Army.

Davis, always a good student, attended public schools in the District of Columbia. At Garnett-Patterson Grammar School, a mischievous Charles Drew sat behind her—frequently dipping her pigtails in an inkwell. At Dunbar High School she fell in love with Latin and English. She also developed an inclination for talking in class—a practice that resulted in her removal from a study hall. Because her mother would not allow any subsequent study hall assignments, Davis took extra classes. For this reason, she graduated from high school at age sixteen in the summer of 1921, valedictorian of her class.

Davis had always wanted to be a nurse, but her father forbade this choice, arguing that nurses were generally licentious. She also wanted to go to a four-year college rather than to Miner Normal, the local two-year school that her elder sister Ruth Olivette attended. With the assistance of Elsie Brown, a high school teacher, she enrolled in Howard University in 1921 with a full-year scholarship that was renewed each year. At Howard, Davis majored in Latin and English. She also studied with such noted professors as William Leo Hansberry, historian and originator of early courses on Africa; Dwight O. W. Holmes, specialist in black higher education and later college president; Ernest E. Just, zoologist and research scientist; Kelly Miller, sociologist and administrator; and Lorenzo Dow Turner, linguist and sociologist. The student body included interesting personalities, among them Zora Neale Hurston, whom Davis remembered as an oddly dressed eccentric close to noted philosopher Alain LeRoy Locke.

The Howard experience was clearly a broadening one; here Davis began a pattern of organizational commitment and leadership. An outstanding student and campus leader, she was respected by her peers. She served as class secretary several terms; treasurer and president of the Alpha chapter of Delta Sigma Theta Sorority; member of the student council, editorial staff of a student newspaper, and Kappa Mu Honorary Society; and alumni secretary for the class of 1925. Not surprisingly, she was dubbed "prexy," "class politician," and "class grind" in the 1925 *Howard University Bison* yearbook.

Of great import to Davis and the women students at Howard was the appointment of Lucy Diggs Slowe as the first dean of women and associate professor of English in 1922. In this role, and as president of the National Association of College Women and founding president of the Association of Deans of Women and Advisers to Girls in Negro Schools, Slowe was an advocate of women's concerns in academe. She was also a role model for Davis, who would later become a dean of women, professor of English, and president of both the Association of Deans of Women and the National Association of College Women.

The college experience for Davis was not, however, without disappointments. She was deeply hurt by Professor William J. Bauduit's treatment of women in his mathematics courses. Believing women to be inferior to men, Bauduit taunted coeds. Though Davis graduated magna cum laude and was class salutatorian, she felt her record was permanently tarnished by an unfair "D" she received from Bauduit.

After graduation from Howard in 1925, Davis took a position at Palmer Memorial Institute in Sedalia, North Carolina. This was an outstanding preparatory school for blacks founded in 1902 by Charlotte Hawkins Brown. Though Davis had never heard of the school, jobs were hard to find, so she agreed to a one-year contract that provided room, board, and a salary of sixty-five dollars a month. During her five-year tenure, she served as a Latin and English teacher, director of girls' activities, and registrar and also helped develop the junior college curriculum.

Davis worked closely with Brown, affectionately known as "The Big Wheel" among the students. Greatly impressed by Brown's religious and assertive personality, Davis developed a keen sense of the psychological costs of racial segregation. She also had her first encounter with salary discrimination and protested to the American Missionary Association—the philanthropic organization that partially supported the school—after learning that women were paid less than men for equivalent work (Interview with Hilda A. Davis, 20 May 1989).

Desiring to advance her education and increase her earning power, Davis decided to pursue a master's degree. With Brown's assistance, she went to Radcliffe College in 1929 on a Marion A. Curtis Scholarship to major in English. She also arranged to room with Brown's mother, Caroline Willis, as blacks were not allowed to live on campus. Though she arrived at Radcliffe eager to begin her studies, events took a dramatic turn. After only eleven days in Cambridge, she was mugged near Radcliffe yard by a white man. She suffered a broken ankle and lay helpless on the sidewalk in the rain for more than a half hour. Despite being hospitalized for two months and out of class for nine weeks, she completed all courses with a "B" grade except one. Because of the one unsatisfactory "C" ("B" being the minimum required for graduate credit), she did not graduate in 1930. She worked the next year at Palmer and returned to Radcliffe in 1931 for an additional semester.

This final semester at Radcliffe proved to be eventful. When Davis expressed an interest in student personnel work, Bernice Brown, dean of the Radcliffe graduate school, arranged for her admission to the Alice Freeman Palmer course for Deans of Women taught by Lucy Jenkins Franklin at Boston University. Brown also encouraged her to pursue a doctorate at the University of Chicago. The Palmer course predictably set the stage for a career in student affairs. Years later Davis earned a doctorate in human development at the University of Chicago.

Davis Becomes Dean of Women

After earning the master of arts degree in 1932, Davis left Palmer for an appointment as dean of women and assistant professor of English at Shaw University—a liberal arts college founded for blacks in 1865 in Raleigh, North Carolina. In this position she was the only woman administrator and worked closely with William Stuart Nelson, Shaw's dynamic first black president. In addition to teaching, she had general responsibility for women students and was a member of the administrative council. She was also a member of committees on scholarship, personnel, discipline, student services, concerts and lectures, and social activities. Like most institutions of the day, Shaw's conduct codes were strict and unfair to women students; for example, women had curfews, but men did not. Despite this fact, Davis was remembered as a fair and generous dean, who frequently lent students money and sent them to conferences.

Davis left Shaw in 1936 to become director of women's activities and associate professor of English at Talladega College in Talladega, Alabama, a notable liberal arts college for blacks founded in 1867. Davis joined the administration of Buell G. Gallagher, a scholar, minister, and perhaps Talladega's most progressive white president. Over the next decade and a half Davis blossomed at Talladega. Within a few years she was named dean of women, responsible for the residential life, counseling, and discipline for women students. Revered by students and colleagues, she came to be regarded as "one of the most outstanding Deans" and "the best in the South" (Wilhelmena Hawkins to Hilda A. Davis, 10 November 1945, Talladega College Archives). She was especially remembered for her compassionate and courageous manner: she challenged college policy (for example, no smoking rules for women and salary inequities) that discriminated against women, as well as the local religious custom that forbade blacks from sitting with whites during worship.

Davis Heads National Organizations

Of particular significance is the leadership role Davis assumed in several organizations during this time. Becoming the second elected president of the Association of Deans of Women and Advisers to Girls in Negro Schools after Slowe's death in 1937, she provided much-needed stability in a time of crisis. She became the only person to serve two separate, nonconsecutive terms as president of the National Association of College Women, later known as the National Association of University Women (1939-1945 and 1957-1961); and during both periods she encouraged the association to address such issues as black women's role in the war effort, the space age, and the challenges of youth and aging. She chaired or served on major committees for the Association of Teachers of Language in Negro Colleges, later known as the College Language Association; the National Association of Deans of Women, later known as the National Association for Women Deans, Administrators, and Counselors; the American Association of University Women; and the Young Women's Christian Association. She became one of the few black members of the Society of Companions of the Holy Cross, an Episcopalian women's organization, and eventually became the first female senior warden of the Episcopal Diocese of Delaware.

Davis continued as dean of women through the administration of Adam D. Beittel (1945-1953), Talladega's last white president. However, when Arthur Douglass Gray, became the first black president in 1953, he was given the freedom to appoint his own dean of women, and Davis was offered a new position. It is likely that the move to displace Davis was motivated by concern for her influence among students, as there had been a strike before Gray's appointment. Rather than accept the reassignment, Davis resigned, and so ended her career in the black academe.

Having begun graduate study at the University of Chicago in 1933, Davis completed the Ph.D. in human development in 1953—the first black graduate of this program. After a series of temporary jobs, she accepted a position at the Governor Bacon Health Center in Delaware City, Delaware, in 1954. Her initial responsibility was to coordinate research at this residential facility for emotionally disturbed children. She eventually became chief of medical records and administrative assistant to Mesrop A. Tarumianz, state psychiatrist and superintendent of the Delaware Psychiatric Institutions and Agencies. Tarumianz was a fair and supportive supervisor who entrusted Davis with the responsibility of writing many of his reports. White colleagues, on the other hand, resented her ability and authority, and harsh treatment ensued after Tarumianz retired.

Seeking once again an equitable work environment, Davis accepted a position at the University of Delaware in 1965 as a special lecturer in the English department. In doing so, she broke the color barrier—becoming the first black with a full-time faculty contract. Though overt racism was not evident, women faculty—there were only three in the English department including Davis—were ignored and consistently not promoted. Despite the fact that she set up the university's first writing center, she was never named director. Instead, she served as associate director under two white men, both inferior in credentials and experience.

The University of Delaware mandated retirement at age sixty-five and Davis "retired" in 1970, accepting a faculty appointment at Wilmington College in New Castle, Delaware. As associate and later professor of English, she developed a writing program and taught an array of courses. She retired from this college in 1977.

The list of honors that Davis has received is long and impressive. Among these are induction into the Delaware Women Hall of Fame (1986), the Medal of Distinction from the University of Delaware (1987), and an honorary doctorate from Trinity College of Washington, D.C. (1989). She was appointed to commissions on the needs of black women and school finance by presidents Lyndon B. Johnson and Richard M. Nixon, respectively. She has also been cited for outstanding service by the Talladega College Alumni (1981) and the Wilmington Alumnae Chapter of Delta Sigma Theta Sorority (1981). While Wilmington College, the National Association of Deans, Administrators and Counselors, *SAGE: A Scholarly Journal on Black Women*, and the Long Island branch and Northeast section of the National Association of University Women have established awards and fellowships in her honor, the YWCA of New Castle County, Delaware, dedicated the new Hilda A. Davis Residence in 1988. Davis, is still active in many organizations, and currently resides in Newark, Delaware.

References

Howard University Bison, 1925. Washington, D.C.: Howard University, 1925.

Brett, Ruth. Interview with Patricia Bell-Scott, 1 June 1989.

Davis, Hilda A. Interview with Patricia Bell-Scott, 2 June 1988; 3 March 1989; 20 May 1989; 1 September 1989; 3 November 1989; 15 January 1990; 22 March 1990; 2 June 1990.

Cater, J. T. Letter to Hilda A. Davis, 1 June 1936. Hilda A. Davis Papers.

Shaw Bulletin. Catalogue 1932-33. Raleigh, N.C.: Shaw University, 1932.

Hawkins, Wilhelmena. Letter to Hilda A. Davis, 10 November 1945. Talladega College Archives, Talladega, Alabama.

Collections

The personal papers of Hilda A. Davis are to be deposited in the Spelman College Archives, Atlanta, Georgia. The Schomburg Center for Research in Black Culture contains Christene J. Sumpter and Lucinda F. Ward's National Association of University Women, Bicentennial Convention History, which outlines conference themes during Davis's tenure as president of the National Association of College Women. Institutional records are located at Bennett College, the Charlotte Hawkins Brown Memorial Historic Site, Shaw University, Schlesinger Library at Radcliffe College, and Talladega College.

* Note: A history of the black deans of women's association and Davis's role in it is in Hilda A. Davis and Patricia Bell-Scott, "The Association of Deans of Women and Advisers to Girls in Negro Schools, 1929-1954: A Brief Oral History," *SAGE: A Scholarly Journal on Black Women* 6 (1990), Ruth Brett, Edna M. Calhoun, Lucille J. Piggott, Hilda A. Davis, and Patricia Bell-Scott's "Our Living History: Reminiscences of Black Participation in NAWDAC," *Journal of the National Association for Women Deans, Administrators, and Counselors* 43 (1979), describes Davis's experiences as an early member of this historically white deans of women group.

Patricia Bell-Scott

Jennie Dean

(1852-1913)

Missionary, school founder, community leader

Pioneering educator and community leader Jennie Dean was born to slave parents in 1852 in Prince William County, Virginia. Information on Dean's early life is scant. It appears that her father, Charles, taught her to read and write and that she spent a few months at a country school. Later she moved to Washington, D.C., where she worked and sent her earnings back home, to help pay for the family farm near Sudley Springs, Virginia, where her father settled after the Civil War. Her parents, Charles and Annie Dean, were owned by the Cushing and Newsom families.

After establishing herself in Washington, Dean began to make weekend trips home. During those trips she went about the community establishing Sunday schools or missions and providing industrial training for children of the community. Soon she resettled in Prince William County and continued her missionary work among blacks.

Dean was particularly concerned about the exodus of black boys and girls to the cities. She urged parents to buy land and keep their children home. Her concern for the social development of boys and girls was reflected in a pamphlet that she wrote in 1896. Titled "Jennie Dean's Rules for Good Behavior among Her People," the pamphlet provided simple admonitions such as "Politeness Home and Abroad," "Don't Be Late in Going to Church; If You Are Late, Take a Seat Nearest the Door," "Don't Address an Audience with Your Hands in Your Pockets," and "Don't Turn Your Back on the Speaker." Dean taught these values to people everywhere she worked.

Dean's leadership and zeal led to the establishment of Mount Calvary Church. The congregation first met in the house that her father erected, but through her efforts a building fund prospered and the church was built and consecrated in 1880.

In his biography of Dean, *Undaunted Faith,* Stephen Johnson Lewis repeated Dean's masterful plea to the people of the community when they were trying to build a church:

> You can each give something if only a day's work. . . . Whenever you sell something, lay aside a small sum, if only a few pennies, for the building fund. Those who have nothing to sell, come and give your labor when we raise the building. After my day's work, I will go out and try to collect money for the fund (27).

Lewis also recalled that Dean lived by a guiding philosophy: "You do your part and I'll do mine."

Industrial School Founded

After twelve years of mission work, Dean devoted herself primarily to industrial education for blacks in northern Virginia and established the Manassas Colored Industrial School in 1894. She called upon black and white locals and a network of friends in Virginia, New England, and New York City to help raise funds for establishing the school. Men and women in various local communities donated their time and labor to construct the school building. In September 1894, the building was completed and a dedication ceremony was held, with Frederick Douglass addressing the audience. Seventy-five students were enrolled during the first year. By 1911 the school had eleven teachers, 150 pupils, a farm of 215 acres, and nine buildings. By 1915 a new library and a trades building had been added. Half of the funds needed for these additions came from friends in the North and half of the funds came from Andrew Carnegie. The Manassas Industrial School became a part of the public school system in 1933.

The curriculum of the school was vocational. In addition to the academic instruction provided for all of the students, the boys were trained in carpentry, masonry, blacksmithing, wheelwrighting, machinery, and agriculture and the girls in cooking, housekeeping, laundry work, and sewing. Many scholarships and part-time jobs were provided to assist students in paying the modest tuition fee that was charged. Through the years of the school's struggles and growth, Dean's direct involvement with its management and program decreased, but her interest in the progress of the school continued until her death.

Dean was not schooled in the social graces or in any more than the rudiments of reading and writing. Yet she was a leader in organizing Sunday schools and she founded a church and the Manassas Industrial School. Dean died in 1913 after several years of illness. She was buried in the cemetery of Mount Calvary Church. A stone marker with a bronze plaque stands on the Charter Cottage site where her family's original farmhouse stood.

References

Lewis, Stephen Johnson. *Undaunted Faith: The Story of Jennie Dean, Missionary, Crusader, Builder*. Catlett, Virginia: Circuit Press, 1942.

Prince William: The Story of Its People and Its Place. Compiled by Workers of the Writers' Project of Work Projects Administration in the State of Virginia. American Guide Series. Sponsored by the Bethlehem Good Housekeeping Club, 1941.

Elaine P. Witty

Ruby Dee

(1924-)

Actress, social activist

Ruby Dee is an actress known for her work on stage, screen, television, and radio, as well as her PBS appearances, recitals, and recordings with her husaband, actor and playwright Ossie Davis. Born Ruby Ann Wallace on October 27, 1924, in Cleveland, Ohio, she is the daughter of Marshall Edward Wallace and Emma (Benson) Wallace. She has two sisters and a brother. Her father was a porter and waiter on the Pennsylvania Railroad and her mother was a schoolteacher. When Dee was still a baby the family moved to New York City and settled in Harlem. Dee's mother insisted that her children study literature and music instead of spending their time on movies or listening to the radio. In the evenings members of the family read aloud to one another from the poetry of Longfellow, Wordsworth, and Paul Laurence Dunbar, a practice that stood her in good stead for her chosen profession.

In an interview with Patricia Bosworth in the *New York Times,* Dee said that as a child she was "painfully shy and not aggressive at all" (22 July 1970). She attended Hunter High School in New York City, where she made her decision to become an actress after being applauded by her classmates for having read aloud from a play.

After graduating from high school, Ruby Dee attended Hunter College to study Romance languages. From 1941 to 1944 she was an apprentice with the American Negro Theatre, which was located in the basement of the West 135th Street Branch of the New York Public Library. Among its members at the time were Hilda Simms, Harry Belafonte, and Sidney Poitier. She mopped floors, ushered, sold tickets, and painted scenery between appearances in such plays as *Natural Man, Starlight, Three's a Family, Hard Walk,* and *On Striver's Row.* In December 1943 she performed in the production of a World War II drama by Howard Rigsby and Dorothy Hayward entitled *South Pacific,* in which she worked with Wine Johnson in a walk-on part as a native girl named Ruth. During her student years, Dee also appeared in radio plays. After obtaining her B.A. from Hunter College in 1945, she worked briefly as a French and Spanish translator for an import business.

In February 1946 Dee appeared with Ossie Davis on Broadway in the role of Libby George in *Jeb,* Robert Ardrey's drama about the trials and frustrations faced by a returning black war hero. A few months later she was in the title role of the Broadway production of Philip Yorday's play *Anna Lucasta,* with Yvonne Machen and Isabelle Cooley.

She also starred in the show on its national tour, with Ossie Davis costarring in the role of Rudolph. She also played the role of Marcy, "a girl bewildered by the evil that surrounds her," in the all-black production *A Long Way from Home*. Dee and Ossie Davis were married on December 9, 1948, during a break in the rehearsals of Garson Kanin's *Smile of the World,* in which they played Evelyn and Stewart.

Dee appeared in the motion picture *The Jackie Robinson Story* in 1950 as the female lead opposite the black baseball star. Her performance as Sidney Poitier's wife in *Edge of the City* (1957) was rated as excellent by reviewers, and she was also commended for her portrayal of a family maid who confronts a seventeen-year-old black boy in *Take a Giant Step* (1959). Other films in which she appeared include *No Way Out* (1950); *The Tall Target* (1951); *Go, Man, Go!* (1954); *St. Louis Blues* (1958); *Virgin Island* (1960), *The Incident* (1967); and *Boesman and Lena* (1970).

Dee appeared in numerous plays including her husband's one-act play *Alice in Wonder* (1952). In *Purlie Victorious,* also written by Ossie Davis, Dee costarred as the ingenuous Lutiebelle Gussie Mae Jenkins, who helps preacher Purlie, played by Davis, to outsmart a white plantation owner. The show opened at the Cort Theatre on September 28, 1961, and ran for 261 performances. A film version, also starring Davis and Dee, was released by Trans Lux in 1963, with the title *Gone Are the Days*. She also appeared in Jean Genet's play, *The Balcony* (1963). She performed as Ruth Younger in Lorraine Hansberry's prize-winning play, *A Raisin in the Sun,* which was presented at the Ethel Barrymore Theatre from March 11, 1959, to June 25, 1960. She also appeared in *Bontche Schweig* and *The World of Sholm Aleichem*. In 1955 Dee took the title role in "This is Norah Drake," a daytime radio serial. As a member of Lyn Ely's touring company in 1958, she presented excerpts from *Anthony and Cleopatra* at New York and Connecticut schools.

In 1965 Dee became the first black actress to appear in major roles at the American Shakespeare Festival at Stratford, Connecticut, when she played Kate in *The Taming of the Shrew* and Cordelia in *King Lear*. Dee starred in productions of the Ypsilanti Greek Theatre and the University of Michigan's professional theater program. She appeared with Bert Lahr in Aristophanes's *The Birds* and played in off-Broadway productions of *The Cherry Orchard* and *The Would-Be Gentlemen*.

Actress Makes Television Debut

Dee made her television debut in October 1960 when she appeared in "Actor's Choice," on "Camera Three," presented on CBS. That same month she was seen in "Seven Times Monday," a "Play of the Week" on WNTA. In January 1961 she was in "Black Monday." Over the years she has been a guest in such television series as "The Fugitive" (ABC), "The Defenders" (CBS), "The Great Adventure" (CBS), and "The Nurses," (CBS). She received an Emmy nomination for her performance in one of the episodes of the "East Side, West Side" series, and won one in 1991 for her performance in "Decoration Day" (NBC). Dee has also appeared with her husband on National Educational Television programs, including the "History of the Negro People" series. In 1968 she became the first black actress to be featured in the popular ABC-TV serial "Peyton Place," in which she played Alma Miles, the wife of a neurosurgeon.

Dee has also played major parts in helping others. For more than twenty years she has devoted herself to racial equality, giving much of her time to serve on national committees and perform in benefit shows to raise money for the legal defense of civil rights workers arrested in demonstrations and for other related activities. Among the organizations with which she has been affiliated are the NAACP, the Congress of Racial Equality (CORE), the Student Nonviolent Coordinating Committee (SNCC), the Southern Christian Leadership Conference (SCLC), and she has given benefits for the Black Panthers and the Young Lords. To help talented young black women become established in the acting profession she has instituted the Ruby Dee Scholarship in Dramatic Art. Some other activities include making recordings for the blind, raising money to combat drug addition, and speaking out against United States military involvement in Southeast Asia.

As a team, Dee and Ossie Davis have many accomplishments. They have recorded *The Poetry of Langston Hughes* for Caedmon Records, and they have toured the United States together, giving recitals of dramatic scenes, poems, and stories. In 1964 they presented poetry readings against a jazz background at the Village Vanguard in New York City. As a team they recorded several talking albums for Caedmon. In 1974 they produced "The Ruby Dee/Ossie Davis Story Hour," which was sponsored by Kraft Foods on more than sixty stations of the National Black Network. Together they founded the Institute of New Cinema Artists to train selected youths for jobs in films and television and then founded the Recording Industry Training Program to develop jobs in the music industry for disadvantaged youths.

In May 1970 Dee and Ossie Davis were presented the Frederick Douglass Award by the New York Urban League for bringing "a sense of fervor and pride to countless millions." In 1975 Actors Equity presented them with the Paul Robeson Citation "for outstanding creative contributions both in the performing arts and in society at large." In 1981 Alcoa funded a television series on the Public Broadcasting System titled "With Ossie and Ruby," using guests to provide an anthology of the arts. The show began its second season in the spring of 1982. Other achievements include Operation PUSH Award, 1972, and the Drama Desk Award, 1974. Ossie Davis and Dee also starred together in Spike Lee's *Do the Right Thing* (1989)—Davis as the boozer and Dee as a fine actress with an unfulfilled career in white America. They were presented as older blacks unable to diffuse rising racial tensions.

Dee and Ossie Davis have two daughters, Nora and LaVerne, and a son, Guy. Her hobbies include painting, playing the piano, and studying world religions. Of her many successes, Dee recalled:

> One of the happiest moments in my life was when I wrote a play called *Take It from the Top*. I walked up to the Henry Street Settlement New Federal Theatre in Manhattan and saw people lined up three-deep around the block. We couldn't get everybody in. If that wasn't happy, that was frustrating (Turner, 90).

During the forty-years of their marriage, Dee and Ossie Davis have shared career ups and downs, rearing a family, and civil rights involvements. "The ratio of the good times to the bad times is better than 50-50, and that helps a lot," said Dee (Norment, 154). Ruby Dee and Ossie Davis live in a large house in New Rochelle, in New York's Westchester County.

References

"Black Poetry." *Washington Post*, 5 November 1969. C-1, 2.

Current Biography. New York: H. W. Wilson, 1970.

Dannett, Sylvia G. L. *Profiles of Negro Womanhood*. Vol. 2. Chicago: Educational Heritage, 1966.

"Facts of (Ghetto) Life." *Commonweal* 116 (July 1989): 402-403.

Kaufmann, Stanley. "Books and the Arts." *New Republic* 201 (3 July 1989): 24-26.

Landay, Eileen. "Ruby Dee." *Black Film Stars*. New York: Drake Publishers, 1973.

Norment, Lynn. "Three Great Love Stories." *Ebony* 43 (February 1988): 150, 152, 154, 156.

Rywell, Martin, comp. and ed. *Afro-American Encyclopedia*. Vol. 3. North Miami: Educational Book Publishers, 1974.

Smythe, Mabel M. "Black Influences in American Theater: Part II, 1960 and After." In *Black American Reference Book*. Englewood Cliffs, N.J.: Prentice-Hall, 1976.

Turner, Renee. "My Happiest Moment." *Ebony* 43 (March 1988): 86, 88, 90. Includes photographs.

Walker, Alice. "Black Sorority Bankrolls Action Film." *Ms*. 4 (June 1976): 45.

Who's Who Among Black Americans, 1990/91. Detroit: Gale Research, 1990.

Jo Ann Lahmon

Lucy A. Delaney

(1830-?)

Slave, author

"Those who were with me in the days of slavery will appreciate these pages, for though they cannot recur with any happiness to the now 'shadowy past, or renew the unrenewable,' the unaccountable longing for the aged to look backward and review the events of their youth will find an answering chord in this little book," wrote Lucy Ann Berry Turner Delaney in her autobiography, *From the Darkness Cometh the Light; or, Struggles for Freedom* (vii). Her friends, inspired by the strength, defiance, and fight for freedom that characterized this former slave, persuaded Delaney to publish her story so that others might share in the glory of her successful struggle. But Delaney's character had been set by her own defiant mother, who obtained her freedom through legal battle and who looked for ways for two daughters to escape bondage forever.

Delaney was born around 1830, one of two daughters of slaves. Her mother, Polly Berry, originally a free black, lived in the home of two families in Illinois. But Berry and four other blacks were kidnapped, bound and gagged, and carried across the Mississippi River to St. Louis, where they were sold into slavery. Berry's first owner, Thomas Botts, later sold his possessions, including his Negroes. A Major Taylor Berry, of Franklin County, purchased Berry to be a servant girl to his wife. Fanny Berry was pleased with her new servant's manners and appearance and decided to train her to become a seamstress. Major Berry's mulatto male servant met and was attracted to Polly Berry, and in a short time they married. Delaney and her sister, Nancy, were the offspring of that marriage. Major Berry became involved in a quarrel with another man, and they agreed to settle the disagreement by duel. Realizing the potential consequence of the event, Major Berry arranged a will that left his Negroes to his wife and stipulated that they were to be freed at her death. He was killed in the duel.

A few years later Major Berry's widow married Robert Wash, an eminent lawyer who later became a Supreme Court judge. The Washes lived with the slaves in the old Wash mansion, and apparently the Berrys enjoyed the living arrangements and conditions. Upon Mrs. Wash's death, however, trouble began for the Berrys. In direct opposition to Major Berry's will, Delaney's father was sold into slavery in the South. Her sister became a waiting-maid for Major Berry's daughter Mary Cox. In the meantime, Berry impressed on her daughters the urgency with which they must become free and worked with Nancy to design her route of escape from slavery. She instructed Nancy not to return to the

Cox family and to run away as soon as possible. She was to go to Canada, where her mother's friend, also a runaway slave, lived. The escape was realized; Nancy reached Canada and later married a prosperous farmer, bore children, and lived in freedom.

Polly Berry learned of the escape from Mrs. Cox, feigned disappointment, but rejoiced when she was alone with her daughter. Delaney, then twelve years old, and her mother began to plan their escape. A dispute with Mrs. Cox, which prompted Berry to become bold and defiant, led to her trip to the auction room and she was sold for five hundred dollars. On her return home to gather her belongings, she pledged to Delaney that one day she would buy her freedom. Three weeks later Delaney learned that her mother had escaped: a large reward was set, and she was tracked by bloodhounds. She arrived safely in Chicago only to be arrested by Negro-catchers and returned to St. Louis. She decided to sue for her freedom on the grounds that she had been kidnapped earlier, and a lawyer was hired to handle her case. She won her suit.

Delaney was sent to live with Martha Berry Mitchell, to whom Delaney was bold and defiant. "You have no business to whip me, I don't belong to you," she once said to her mistress (Berry, 26). Delaney remembered also her mother's encouraging words:

> My mother had so often told me that she was a free woman and that I should not die a slave. I always had a feeling of independence, which would invariably crop out in these encounters with my mistress. . . . I rebelled against such government, and would not permit her to strike me; she used shovel, tongs and broomstick in vain, as I disarmed her as fast as she picked up each weapon (Berry, 26-27).

Upon hearing complaints against Delaney from his wife, D. D. Mitchell expressed his disbelief in slavery. Martha Mitchell suggested that they sell Lucy, and they proposed to make arrangements for the sale. Hearing this, and remembering her mother's advice "never go out of the city," Delaney ran to her mother's house: Berry later took her to a friend's home for concealment.

Enslaved Daughter Becomes Free

On September 8, 1842, Berry sued Mitchell for possession of her child. While the case was pending, Delaney was jailed for seventeen months to prevent her from running away. In time, her mother secured the services of Judge Edward Bates, an abolitionist who ran unsuccessfully against Abraham Lincoln at the National Republican Convention. The suit for Delaney's freedom began on February 7, 1844. Judge Robert Wash, Harry Douglas, an overseer on the Wash farm, and a MacKeon, who had bought Berry from H. S. Cox prior to her escape, testified to convince the court that Lucy was Berry's child. The court ruled in favor of the Berrys and set the girl free.

Mother and daughter, now reunited and living in St. Louis, worked to secure funds sufficient to enable Berry to visit Nancy and her children in Canada. Since Berry was a fine laundress and Delaney an expert seamstress, they easily obtained work and commanded their own prices. While Berry was visiting in Canada, Delaney continued her work. Her love for fine sewing was impressive, and she made sure that "each stitch looked as if it were a part of the cloth." She lamented the advent of the sewing machine. "The art of fine sewing was lost when sewing machines were invented, and though doubtless they have given women more leisure, they have destroyed that extreme neatness in the craft, which obtained in the days of long ago" (Berry, 55).

In 1845 Delaney met and soon married Frederick Turner. The marriage ended quickly when Turner was killed in a steamboat explosion. Distressed over the loss, Delaney sought the comfort of her mother who "never believed in fretting about anything that could not be helped." She said: "*My* husband is down South, and I don't know where he is; he may be dead; he may be happy and comfortable; he may be kicked, abused and half-starved. *Your* husband, honey, is in heaven; and mine—God only knows where he is" (Berry, 56).

Four years later she married Zachariah Delaney of Cincinnati, and the union continued for forty-two years. They had four children—three girls and a boy. Two of the girls died while in childhood, the third died when she was twenty-two years old, and the son at twenty-four. But Delaney rejoiced that they were born free and died free. Berry lived with her daughter until she died. Longing to know about her father, Delaney made a long and persistent search and learned that he had lived on the same plantation for forty-five years, located fifteen miles from Vicksburg. He visited her in St. Louis, old, grizzled and gray, reflecting all of the hardships that slavery had inflicted upon him. The reunion with daughters Lucy and Nancy, who came from Canada, was rewarding, yet the father chose to return, without Berry, to his old associations that he knew well.

Delaney became active in religious, social, and civic activities in St. Louis. She became a member of the Methodist Episcopal Church in 1855. She was elected president of the first "colored society" organized for black women, called the Female Union, and was president of the Daughters of Zion. For three successive years she was matron of Siloam Court, Number Two, and was most ancient matron of the Grand Court of Missouri, in which only wives of masons are allowed membership. She was grand chief preceptress of the Daughters of the Tabernacle and Knights of Tabor, and secretary and member of the Colonel Shaw Women's Relief Corps, Number 34, of the Grand Army of the Republic.

The story of Polly and Nancy Berry and Lucy Delaney illustrates the refusal of slaves to accept their status, and their struggle to win freedom. More fortunate than most of their contemporaries, Berry and Delaney were able to vindicate their freedom in the courts while Nancy achieved hers by running away. Under the most extreme pressure, they strove to maintain their family connections and assert their autonomy. We know their study through Delaney's decision to preserve her heritage by writing it down. Although it is certain that Delaney was still living in 1887 when she would have been approximately fifty-seven years old, the date of her death is not yet known.

References

Delaney, Lucy A. *From the Darkness Cometh the Light; or, Struggles for Freedom*. St. Louis: Publishing House of J. T. Smith, n.d.

Jessie Carney Smith

Sara "Sadie" P. Delaney

(1889-1958)

Librarian, bibliotherapist

Sara Marie Johnson Peterson Delaney was chief librarian of the U.S. Veterans Administration Hospital in Tuskegee, Alabama, for thirty-four years. In this capacity she not only provided library service to thousands of physically and mentally disabled patients but also developed the art of bibliotherapy to the extent that her methods received world-wide recognition.

Sara "Sadie" P. Delaney

Delaney was born February 26, 1889, in Rochester, New York, the third of seven children of James Johnson and Julia Frances (Hawkins) Johnson. James Johnson's great-grand-mother escaped from slavery in Georgia on the Underground Railroad to live free in Canada. He worked as a valet or "gentlemen's gentleman" in his youth and forever after carried an air of dignity and pride, as well as a gold-headed cane. Julia Hawkins's forebears were Iroquois Indians. The family moved to Poughkeepsie, New York, for economic reasons, and lived at 33 Fall Kill Avenue. After Delaney completed high school, she attended Miss McGovern's School of Social Work for one year. She married Edward Louis Peterson in 1906 and had one daughter, Grace Peterson Hooks, in 1907; the marriage ended in 1921. Her second marriage was to Rudicel A. Delaney, of Jetersville, Virginia, in 1928.

Delaney Nurtures the Harlem Renaissance

Delaney began her professional career at the 135th Street Branch of the New York Public Library, training at its library school prior to her 1920 appointment. While at the 135th Street Branch, in the heart of Harlem at the beginning of the Harlem Renaissance, Delaney lived with William and Minnie Pickens at 260 West 139th Street. William Pickens was field secretary of the National Association for the Advancement of Colored People (NAACP). Minnie Pickens was also active in the NAACP and on the management board of the YWCA on 135th Street. This active, intellectual, socially responsible household, which included the three young Pickens children, reflected the excitement of the entire Harlem area as it shifted from a neighborhood of Irishmen, Jews, and Italians to a black one.

The Harlem library and its staff were deeply committed to meeting the needs of this changing population, which had a growing interest in African and diasporic cultures. The library director's annual report for 1920 notes: "Special attention has been given this year to the development of the 135th Street branch. Two interesting and significant features are the progress in children's work and the employment of colored assistants." The report further states that use of the children's reading room had greatly increased and that both circulation of books and registration of new readers had gone up. Delaney worked with children from public and parochial schools and with juvenile delinquents and boy scouts and she was cited for exceptional work. While working with special groups, Delaney became interested in the blind and so learned not only Braille, but also Moonpoint, another system of embossed reading invented in England by William Moon in 1847. (Moonpoint, a simpler system than Braille with fewer characters and none for technical or mathematical symbols, is still in use in England, Australia, Zimbabwe, and South Africa.)

Delaney often organized some of the library's weekly forums, which, from 1921 to 1923, included W. E. B.

Du Bois on Negro creative literature, James Weldon Johnson on Haiti, and other scholars and community leaders such as William H. Ferris, George Edmund Haynes, Hubert Harrison, and Fred Moore, editor of *New York Age*. An art exhibition was held in 1921, and programs featured African music and concerts by black musicians. During this time, Delaney was corresponding with L. Hollingsworth Wood about a scenario she was planning to write about Booker T. Washington, and she also belonged to a writers' club. A year after she left, Charles S. Johnson, the editor of *Opportunity*, wrote saying they missed her at their meetings, and he encouraged her to enter their next contest and "take off a prize" (Sadie P. Delaney Papers). Delaney, known for her tireless energy and creativity, seemed perfectly matched to this stimulating branch library in the vibrant Harlem community, yet when the offer came to serve at the Veteran's Hospital in Tuskegee, she accepted.

Delaney Takes Charge of Veterans Hospital Library

Delaney arrived in Alabama on January 1, 1924, and on January 3 the library—with one table and two hundred books—opened. In an article written a year later, Delaney detailed her experiences and accomplishments. In two weeks the library moved to a large room with space for an office. Peterson decorated with plants and flowers, wall maps, bulletins, and posters for positive psychological effect. She borrowed fairy tales from Tuskegee Institute because "there seemed no books suitable for mental patients." Books and magazines in wire paper-carriers were brought to men confined to bed. Circulation rose with these efforts as well as when atlases, dictionaries, newspapers, and encyclopedias were added. Gifts of pictures of eminent Negroes (Douglass, Washington, DuBois, Moton) and an autographed photograph of President Calvin Coolidge adorned the walls. Monthly programs and book talks were instituted, as was a weekly story hour in the psychiatric wards. The doctors and nurses were not overlooked. By January 15 they too had a library of books and journals. At the end of the year, the library had four thousand volumes for five hundred patients, and the medical library had eighty-five volumes for three hundred staff members. Delaney also established the Disabled Veterans' Literary Society to raise the reading standard and create a cultural atmosphere. An official letter informed her that it was the only veterans hospital library with such a group, and that the class of reading was higher than that of any other such library. Delaney wrote that she hoped to do greater and better work in the future and concluded: "Though in the extreme South, we try to bring to these veterans new material, recent current events, popular and helpful reading" (*Crisis*).

Delaney Pioneers Bibliotherapy

Delaney was to fulfill this hope during her lifetime. The "greater and better work" she did as a pioneer in bibliotherapy brought her recognition both nationally and internationally, from the general public, colleagues in the library profession, and black organizations. Although the term "bibliotherapy" was coined in 1916, the American Library Association's first committee to study this subject was not formed until 1939. Defined as "the treatment of a patient through selected reading" (Cantrell, 106), bibliotherapy's aim, whether practiced by librarians, social workers, or psychiatrists, is to enable patients to connect or reconnect themselves with a broad community of ideas and to add significance to their experience. The hospital's patients were greatly in need of assistance, as they had experienced the horrors of World War I with an attendant loss of values likely to produce antisocial, impulsive, or regressive behavior. Many were alcoholics, and many had lost limbs or had been blinded and did not know how to return to "normal life." And normal life for these black patients included the racial prejudice that was particularly virulent after the first world war.

Bibliotherapy seeks to reduce internal pressures such as aggression, guilt, or anxiety by using catharsis or sublimation and attempts to substitute verbalization for physical reaction. It aims to alleviate boredom or a sense of futility by developing new interests to promote personal growth and new ways to behave, decrease loneliness through a sense of a shared fate with others, reduce self-absorption by investment in people and ideas, stimulate aesthetic awareness, and promote socialization and group identity. Delaney, by design, instinct, and deeply held religious and social beliefs, promoted a full range of activities to accomplish these aims. Besides the literary clubs, monthly programs, and story hours, she started clubs for stamp and coin collecting, debating, bookbinding, and nature study. All of these activities led the men to communicate with each other where before they had stared blankly, in silence. In a February 1938 article in *Opportunity*, Delaney noted that the library became a laboratory and a workshop for the improvement and development of the whole individual. "Here minds long imprisoned in lethargy are awakened . . . and once again he is alive with the enthusiasm and joy derived from activity" (53). She and the patients participated in book discussions on radio. Delaney started a special department for the blind in 1934 and taught Braille to some patients, who in turn taught the system to others.

Delaney also brought in talking books and equipment that projected books on film on the ceiling or wall for patients who were immobilized. The Braille department of the Lions Club of Orlando, Florida, wrote to her on October 19, 1936: "You are the FIRST one in connection with Vets 'Homes,' 'Hospitals,' 'Facilities' and what-not who have [sic] carried even one pupil through to success." More than six hundred veterans were taught Braille by Delaney during her career.

Delaney Discovers Black Veterans' Literary Tastes

All of world literature was used by this librarian, regardless of the genre or the nationality or color of the author. But in 1932 in an article in the *Wilson Library Bulletin*, she addressed the reading interests of black veterans. She noted that interest and enthusiasm are displayed at any "mention (favorable or not) of the Negro." She added that they are trying to fit themselves for life and that their preferred reading includes biographies, history, anything about Negro soldiers, songs, poems, and books about Africa. The library "is aiding him in his upward struggle to lay aside prejudice, all sense of defeat, and to take in that which is helpful and inspiring by the means of books." The novels of Jessie Fauset were admired because "they depict the higher type of Negro life." *Dark Princess* by W. E. B. DuBois was popular because "it depicts international interest in the darker races." Although the veterans read race books, they also asked for literary classics, and they posed reference questions on every subject. In conclusion, however, Delaney pointed out: "Books about the Negro cannot be written fast enough to satisfy the insatiate desire of these veterans. Nothing can beat back this longing to know race history and facts . . . his great happiness will be in chanting his verse and singing his songs and knowing more about his people."

Working and writing did not keep Delaney from being an active participant in professional organizations and training other librarians for hospital library work. She was selected to represent American hospital librarians at a conference in Rome in 1934. While there she planned to do research on St. Augustine at the Vatican library. She also instructed students sent from the library schools of the universities of Illinois, North Carolina, and Atlanta to learn her methods. The Veterans Administration, too, adopted the practice of having its hospital librarians study the policies and practices of Delaney. Librarians from England and South Africa also came under her influence.

The professional organizations Delaney belonged to included American Library Association, where she was elected councillor for its Hospital Library Division (1946-1951), International Library Association, International Hospital Library Guild, League of Nations Library Committee, Neuropsychiatric Journal Club (VA Hospital, Tuskegee Institute), and Mental Hygiene Society (Tuskegee). Delaney also belonged to groups outside her profession, such as the National Council of Colored Women, Tuskegee Women's Club, Women of Darker Races of America, and the NAACP, where she served seven years on the advisory board in New York. She was a founder of the Friendship League of America, Negro Professional Women's Club (New York), Lambda chapter of Iota Phi Lambda Sorority (Tuskegee), and the first philatelic club in Tuskegee. She instituted the first State Conference for the Blind in Alabama, and after work she volunteered in the community to help blind white people.

Delaney not only collected stamps and coins but she also collected decorative art objects, such as rare porcelain, glass, silver, and antique clocks. Many writers have attested to the loveliness of her home and her graciousness as a hostess. In 1951, Georgia Douglas Johnson recommended her as a consultant for the project of two women from New York, Sara Lee Creech and Maxeda von Hesse, to develop a black doll that would "be as pretty and attractive as a white doll and liked for its beauty and not for its color." The quoted words are Eleanor Roosevelt's, then ambassador to the United Nations and a supporter of the project, in a letter to Delaney, who advised on the sculpture of the features. The letter invited her to a press conference at the Park Sheraton Hotel on October 22. Delaney was not able to attend, but the doll mailed to Delaney is still in her daughter's home in Tuskegee. After Delaney's death, some of her collection had to be sold, parts were donated to the George Washington Carver Museum at Tuskegee, and parts remain in the home.

For her pioneering work as a bibliotherapist, humanitarian, and leader in professional and social circles, Delaney received numerous awards and honors. There are well over fifty citations to her work in library, medical, psychological, and black journals. In 1934 she was included in *Professional Women of America*. Soon after, she was cited for exceptional work in hospital libraries by the Carnegie Corporation in Pretoria, South Africa. She was honored at both her twenty-fifth and thirtieth anniversaries at Tuskegee. She was selected "Woman of the Year" by the Iota Phi Lambda Sorority and the Zeta Phi Beta Sorority in 1948 and 1949 respectively. The following year, 1950, saw two more important honors. She was selected as "Woman of the Year" by the National Urban League and she received an honorary doctorate from Atlanta University. Some excerpts from her acceptance speech describe her feelings and philosophy:

> There has been a tremendous satisfaction in aiding hundreds of individuals to return to normal living. Thought of compensation has been obliterated for there is soul compensation in helping those who are ill. . . . Another lesson learned is the value of a busy life, the utilization of every minute of the day for something worthwhile. . . . Tonight I know more than I shall be able to express, if I live to be a hundred, of the contentment one gains through service to humanity. If I have contributed any thing at all, it has been in exploring new fields in hospital library service by using empirical methods until perfection could be attained. . . . I have tried to share my discoveries with other libraries (Delaney Papers).

Delaney concluded with a favorite poem:

> There is a destiny that makes men brothers None walks his way aloneAll that we send into the lives of othersComes back into our own (Delaney Papers).

A Veteran Pays Tribute to Delaney

At her thirty-year celebration in 1954, Clarence L. McKenzie, first president of the Disabled Veterans Literary Club, remembered Delaney's arrival late in 1923, before the new Veterans Hospital had been completed, before debris had been cleared away or trees planted. She informed them she was on six-months leave from the New York Public Library to organize a library. "We had been lonely and had suffered from some racial tension but this little lady brought with her a new type of friendship we had not experienced before. She was understanding, sincere and enthusiastic. She was as concerned about our minds as well as our desire to recover. She brought to us a new inspiration through books, and injected culture and real thoughts into our lives . . . . She said, 'Meet me tomorrow morning after breakfast and we shall organize a literary club.' " They met in the hall for weeks because there were no chairs, table or a room. She lent them her own books and magazines, and by January 1, the veterans "were on our way to a new way of life . . . it was with pride we packed [the library] daily to use the few books which began coming. Our meeting became so interesting that we actually forgot our ills. . . . Years have passed, thirty, but . . . she seems always young in spirit and I believe this library stands as beacon to the world of Veterans who have caught the Delaney Spirit to live through Books" (Delaney Papers). Sadie Delaney died three years later, and after her death on May 4, 1958, family and friends established the Sadie Peterson Delaney Memorial Scholarship Loan Fund at the Atlanta University School of Library Science. This tribute reflects her vital and life-long interest in training others in the library profession.

Another posthumous tribute came in 1982 when Delaney was inducted into the Alabama Library Association Roll of Honor for 1981-1982, with her name to be engraved on a copper plate and added to the permanent plaque on display in the Alabama Archives and History Department in Montgomery. Perhaps this award would have pleased Delaney most of all, because in 1952 and 1954 there was turmoil in the Alabama Library Association over the admission of blacks. In 1952 the Bi-Racial Committee recommended that the cause of librarianship in Alabama would be best served by the creation of a separate Alabama Negro Library Association. Angered by this presumptuous suggestion, Delaney sent copies to her friends Clyde Cantrell, director of libraries at Alabama Polytechnic Institute, and Helen Wessells, editor of *Library Journal*. Wessells agreed to publish the statement and assured Delaney that she would "be glad to pound away whenever possible on the whole basic problem of discrimination."

In 1954 the Alabama Library Association's membership was still divided on the question of black membership. In a letter dated April 7, 1954, the secretary wrote, "any insistence at this time on Negro membership, or even Negro visitation at the meeting, would result in more friction than it would be worth, would be embarrassing to both races, and it would serve only to set back such progress toward integration as has already been made." One wonders if Delaney, after nearly thirty years of service and honors, associated this rebuff with a much earlier one. When she was a child, her class was to present on stage a living American flag. She was excited and proud. When they were all lined up, reds with reds, blues with blues, and whites together, her teacher took her to the back of the room and said, "See, Sadie, you would make a hole in the flag. I can't let you be in it, but you can sing from behind the curtain" (Grace P. Hooks to Betty K. Gubert). In a memoir Delaney wrote, "I felt as though someone had struck me. When I regained my voice I said 'No Miss T. I will never sing behind the curtain.' I left the stage sobbing when I realized that my brown face had made a hole in my flag of the free. I soon dried my eyes and decided that I would still be part of the audience" (Grace P. Hooks collection of Delaney Papers). Delaney showed her strength, courage and determination early on.

Delaney's writings include "Bibliotherapy as an Aid to Rehabilitation," *Journal of the National Association of College Women* (1953); "Bibliography on Bibliotherapy," *Bulletin of Bibliography* (September-December 1951); "Bibliotherapy in a Hospital," *Opportunity* (February 1938); "Bibliotherapy for Patients in a Drug Antabuse Clinic," *Hospital Books Guide* (October 1955); "Library Activities at Tuskegee," U.S. Veterans Administration *Medical Bulletin* (October 1940); "The Library: A Factor in Negro Education," *Messenger* (July 1923); "The Library—A Factor in Veterans Bureau Hospitals," U.S. Veterans Bureau *Medical Bulletin* (April 1930); "The Negro and His Books," *Wilson Library Bulletin* (June 1932); "Place of Bibliotherapy in a Hospital," *Library Journal* (15 April 1938); "Time's Telling," *Wilson Library Bulletin* (February 1955); and "U. S. V. Hospital, Library No. 91, Tuskegee, Ala.," *Crisis* (January 1925).

References

Bauer, Henry C. "Seasoned to Taste." *Wilson Library Bulletin* (February 1955): 404.

Braille Department, Lions Club, Orlando, Florida. Letter to Sadie P. Delaney, 19 October 1936. In Sadie P. Delaney Papers.

Cantrell, Clyde H. "Sadie P. Delaney: Bibliotherapist and Librarian." *Southeastern Librarian* (Fall 1956): 105-109. Reprinted, *Congressional Record*, Appendix, January 17, 1957.

Crisis 29 (January 1925): 116-17.

Frydman, Gusta. Interview with Betty K. Gubert, 20 Februay 1990.

Hewitt, Vivian D. Interview with Betty K. Gubert, 6 April 1990.

Hooks, Grace P. Interview with Betty K. Gubert, 26 February 1990; 17 March 1990; 15 April 1990.

——. Letter to Betty K. Gubert, 17 April 1990.

Jones, Virginia Lacy. "Sadie Peterson Delaney." *Dictionary of American Library Biography*. Littleton, Colo: Libraries Unlimited, 1978.

"Library Group Cites Delaney." Undated and unknown newspaper article reporting Delaney's induction into the Alabama Library Assocation Roll of Honor for 1981-82.

"Librarian Hailed as Pioneer." *Christian Science Monitor* (28 August 1957).

"*Look* Applauds." *Look Magazine* (26 September 1950).

New York Public Library. *Annual Report of the Director*. New York: 1920.

Oppenheim, Gladys. "Bibliotherapy—A New Word for Your Vocabulary." Bloemfontein, South Africa, *Cape Times* (15 January 1938).

Professional Women of America. London: Mitre Chambers, 1934.

Roosevelt, Eleanor. Letter to Sadie P. Delaney, 16 October 1951.

——. "My Day." *New York Post* (January 18-22, 1957).

Sprague, Morteza D. "Dr. Sadie Peterson Delaney: Great Humanitarian." *Service* 15 (June 1951): 17-18.

Collections

Delaney's seven bound volumes of letters, clippings, and photographs were donated to the Schomburg Center for Research in Black Culture, New York Public Library, by her daughter, Grace P. Hooks, in 1983. Grace Hooks has retained an eighth scrapbook. There are letters from people as diverse as J. E. K. Aggrey, Franz Boas, Countee Cullen, Bette Davis, W. E. B. Du Bois, Luther Evans, Matthew Henson, Keyes Metcalf, Mary White Ovington, and Emmett J. Scott. There many other letters from equally known people and from other less well known, whose lives were touched at some point by this dynamic, indefatigable woman.

Betty K. Gubert

Clarissa Scott Delany

(1901-1927)

Poet, essayist, educator, social researcher

Clarissa Mae Scott Delany, poet, essayist, social researcher, and educator, was born in 1901 in Tuskagee, Alabama. She was one of five children born to the Emmett Jay Scotts. Her father served as Booker T. Washington's secretary at Tuskegee Institute from 1897 to 1915 and later became secretary-treasurer of Howard University in Washington, D.C., and Woodrow Wilson's special advisor on African-American affairs.

After spending her early years in Alabama, Delany entered New England's Bradford Academy in 1916. After three years at Bradford, she matriculated at Wellesley College. Her graduation in 1923 was an event of sufficient magnitude to warrant coverage inside the pages of the June 1923 *Crisis* magazine as well as a full-face photograph of her on the cover. Among her accomplishments at Wellesley were scholarship honors each year; participation in varsity hockey, which resulted in her earning an athletic letter in 1922; induction into Phi Beta Kappa; and membership in Delta Sigma Theta sorority. After she graduated from Wellesley, Scott taught at Dunbar High School in Washington, D.C., for three years, leaving after she determined that teaching was not her métier.

In 1926 Delany became the director of the Joint Committee on Negro Child Study in New York City. The committee's task was to engage in research on delinquency among black children for the purpose of determining the causes of and solutions to this social ill. The committee's research project was conducted in cooperation with the Department of Research of the National Urban League and the Women's City Club of New York.

In the fall of 1926, she wed Hubert Delany, a young attorney who in 1923 graduated from the City College of New York and in 1926 graduated from the New York University Law School and was admitted to the New York State bar. In later years Hubert Delany was to become an assistant state district attorney, a member of the New York City Tax Commission, a member of the national board of directors of the USO, and vice-president of the National Urban League. In 1942, New York City Mayor F. H. LaGuardia appointed him justice of the city's domestic relations court.

After her wedding in 1926, Delany became a homemaker, a career she herself described as interesting and absorbing. In poor health during much of her marriage, she was gravely ill in 1927 when she returned to her parents' home in Washington, D.C., where she died of a lung infection, probably tuberculosis.

Shortly after her death Delany was eulogized by Angelina Weld Grimké in the poem "To Clarissa Scott Delany," which appeared in Charles S. Johnson's 1927 collection *Ebony and Topaz* and in the tribute in the November 1927 *Opportunity* magazine. In *Opportunity*, the official organ of the National Urban League, Delany is described as a member of "the buoyant, newly hopeful ranks of the younger Negro group" and as someone with a "well-trained and relentlessly searching mind, a magnificent and sturdy idealism and all of the impetuous zeal of youth." The last line of the tribute expresses her contemporaries' perception of her: "She was superbly poised for life; and quietly she left it."

Delany Leaves Literary Legacy

Delany's literary legacy consists of a single published essay and four published poems. (Her unpublished writings were lost as members of her immediate family died.) Her essay "A Golden Afternoon in Germany" was published first in the December 1925 issue of *Opportunity* and reprinted in 1931 in *Readings from Negro Authors for Schools and Colleges*, edited by Otelia Cromwell, Lorenzo Dow Turner, and Eva B. Dykes (New York: Harcourt, 1931). Her first nationally published poem appeared in *Opportunity* as well. Printed in the June 1925 issue of the periodical, this poem, "Solace," tied with Joseph Seamon Cotter's "The Wayside Well" for fourth prize in the 1925 *Opportunity* poetry contest. In 1926 two more of Delany's poems appeared in national publications—"Joy" in *Opportunity* and "The Mask" in *Palms*. In 1927 these three poems and "Interim" were included in Countee Cullen's *Caroling Dusk: An Anthology of Verse by Negro Poets* (New York: Harper).

Delany's essay "A Golden Afternoon in Germany" is a clearly expressed, straightforward narrative in which she provides glimpses into the life of a young, genteel black woman in the early twentieth century. On the subject of race, two of the essay's revelations are that the writer needed to believe that in the western world there are places where racism does not exist and that the writer accepted the romantic myth of an unspoiled African Eden—a myth that had great currency during the Harlem Renaissance.

In her poems, Delany reveals herself to be a transitional poet whose works connect nineteenth-century and early twentieth-century black American women poets with their literary daughters. In the poetic continuum, she follows immediately on the thematic and stylistic heels of black American writers Angelina Weld Grimké, Jessie Redmon Fauset, and Georgia Douglas Johnson. Like most of theirs, her poems rely upon traditional rhythmic devices and contain conventional poetic diction; treat ladylike subjects such as joy and despair—subjects that place her poems solidly in the tradition of American women's poetry; and employ decorous images. In the continuum after Delany stand black American writers Gwendolyn Bennett and Helene Johnson, both of whom yielded more than did Delany to the lure of the new poetry's increasingly colloquial language, its broadened definition of appropriate poetic subjects, and its freer verse. Delany is one of a host of literary foremothers whose works are testimonies to sustained collective literary achievement by black American women.

In addition to the Cromwell and Cullen anthologies, Delany's works are included in *The Poetry of Black America*, edited by Arnold Adoff (New York: Harper 1973), and *Shadowed Dreams: Women's Poetry of the Harlem Renaissance* edited by Maureen Honey (New Brunswick, N.J.: Rutgers University Press, 1989).

References

"Clarissa Scott Delany." *Opportunity* 5 (November 1927): 321.

"Colored Students and Graduates of 1923." *Crisis* 1 (June 1923): 108-16.

Delany, Clarissa Scott. In *Caroling Dusk: An Anthology of Verse by Negro Poets*. Edited by Countee Cullen. New York: Harper, 1927.

Delany, Willetta. Interview with T. J. Bryan, 20 April 1989.

"The Prize Winners." *Opportunity* 3 (June 1925): 186.

"Survey of the Month." *Opportunity* 4 (August 1926): 262-66.

"Who's Who." *Opportunity* 4 (January 1926): 28.

T. J. Bryan

Wilhelmina R. Delco

(1929-)

Politician

Texas state representative Wilhelmina Ruth Fitzgerald Delco was born on July 16, 1929, in Chicago, Illinois, the oldest of five children of Juanita Fitzgerald Watson and William P. Fitzgerald, Sr. Her mother was a Chicago adult probation officer while her father was a court deputy to a Chicago judge. Being the oldest child, Delco was very close to her mother, who was her role model. Both parents instilled in her a sense of responsibility and a sense of public service, qualities which she has utilized in a life dedicated to the promotion of better education for people across the country.

As a Wendell Phillips High School student, Delco was active in student government organizations. In her senior year she served as president of her class and graduated salutatorian. Delco continued her education at Fisk University in Nashville, Tennessee, where she was involved in dramatics and sociology projects. She was a student during the early tenure of Fisk's first black president, Charles Spurgeon Johnson, internationally renowned sociologist, when Johnson's Race Relations Institute was in its heyday. Any student at Fisk during the 1940s must have been positively influenced by the university leadership to seek social and racial justice. In June 1950 Delco received a B.A. with a major in sociology and minor in economics and business administration.

It was at Fisk that she met her husband, Exalton Alfonso Delco, Jr., a native of Houston, Texas, and currently vice president for academic affairs at Austin Community College. To the Delcos were born four children: Deborah Diane Agbottah, Exalton Alfonso Delco III, Loretta Elmirle Edelin, and Cheryl Pauline Sawyer. As a nurturing parent, Delco was president of an elementary school Parent-Teachers Association (PTA), a junior high school PTA, and a county PTA council. She is a life member of the Texas Congress PTA and was the first black elected to the Travis County, Texas, school board.

Additionally, Delco's civic involvement is extensive, and primarily focuses on education. Among her involvements with educational committees and boards, Delco has held membership on the Education Commission of the State's Task Force on Education for Economic Growth; she is a current board member of the Southern Education Foundation; and she is former chairman of the Educational Testing Service Board in Princeton, New Jersey.

Delco Becomes Politically Active

A Democratic Texas legislator, Delco is serving her eighth term as state representative of Texas, District Fifty, Travis County. She was the first black legislator from District Fifty. Her commitment to education resounds through her legislative committee appointments. She served at least five consecutive legislative sessions as chairman of the House Higher Education Committee. She also served on the State, Federal, and International Relations committees. As a legislative, education, and community activist, Delco has received much recognition. The *Texas Observer* cited her as one of the "brightest spots in the House" and "a dedicated and forthright leader" during the sixty-eighth legislative session, when she campaigned for the creation of a comprehensive Constitutional construction fund. She was named Distinguished Professional Woman for 1987 by the Committee on the Status of Women at the University of Texas Health Science Center at Houston.

In 1986 Delco was inducted into the Texas Women's Hall of Fame in Austin. When she received this honor from Governor Mark White, Delco said, "Education is the key to coping with technological change and building a diversified economy in Texas." At that time she chaired the state legislative committee on higher education and received recognition for providing permanent funding for public state universities, particularly Prairie View A.& M. and Texas Southern, two historically black institutions.

To further attest to her recognition as a champion for higher education, Delco has received five honorary degrees, from St. Edward University, Lee College, Southwestern University, Houston-Tillotson College, and Wiley College.

An energetic speaker in great demand, Delco captures many audiences with her dramatic style. On October 6, 1988, she was invited by her alma mater to deliver Fisk University's Jubilee Day Convocation message. This is one of the university's most prestigious honors bestowed upon its graduates.

References

Delco, Wilhelmina. Interview with Mavis Donnelly, 27 February 1990.

———. Resume. 1988.

"Edelen Communications News Release," 23 September 1986.

Fisk News 49, no.1 (Winter 1989): 19-20.

Informer, Texas, 10 October 1987.

Who's Who Among Black American, 1990/91. 6th ed. Detroit: Gale Research, 1990.

Joan Adams Bahner

Henriette Delille and the Sisters of the Holy Family

(1813-1862)

Religious leader

Henriette Delille, the founder of the Roman Catholic Sisters of the Holy Family, was born a free Creole of color in New Orleans early in the year of 1813. She was the youngest of three natural children of Jean Baptiste Delille-Sarpy, a white Creole, and his *placée*, or mistress, Marie Joseph "Pouponne" Dias, a free woman of color. Delille's free black relatives were Creole, that is, Roman Catholic and French-speaking ex-colonials, and some owned large agricultural properties. Although she was too young to remember it, she always boasted that several of her free black uncles and cousins, including the celebrated swordsman Basile Crocker, served in the Battle of New Orleans. Her uncles Narcisse Labeau and Raphael Roig owned the plantations flanking that of white philanthropist John McDonogh, whose bequest built most of the pre-World War I public schools of New Orleans. The three were good friends. In addition to having prominent white friends, Henriette Delille and other members of her family were themselves so fair-skinned as to be mistaken for white on census records.

Henriette Delille appears to have been reared for *plaçage*, or for being the kept woman of a wealthy man. She studied music, dance, and French literature and was encouraged to cultivate every charm and accomplishment with which to attract a well-to-do white patron. Her mother also instructed her in nursing and in the preparation of folk remedies from local roots and herbs. When Dellile was about eleven and her sister Cecilia was seventeen, something happened to turn the little girl away from the path ordained by her family. Cecilia had met and formed a liaison with a wealthy Austrian-born commission merchant at a public ball—white men often sought black partners at these glittering parties for pay. At the same time, Delille met Sister Saint Marthe Fontier, a French nun. The only member of the French religious order of the Dames Hospitalier then living in New Orleans, Sister Saint Marthe bought a lot on Barracks Street in 1823 and, with the financial assistance of the free people of color, opened a school for young girls of that class. The little school became a nucleus for Catholic missionary activities among black people, slave as well as free. Having more to do than she could handle, Sister Saint Marthe instructed her free black students to teach religion to those slaves whose masters permitted it. By the time that Delille was about fourteen, she had entered wholeheartedly into the work, soon becoming actively engaged in visiting and nursing the sick and aged, feeding indigent people, and praying.

In 1826 Sister Saint Marthe began an effort to establish a branch of her order dedicated to apostolic work among the black people of New Orleans. She had two young women in training, one white and the other, Juliette Gaudin, a free woman of color. Gaudin was the Cuban-born natural daughter of Marie Therese Sainte La Cardonie, also free, and Pierre Gaudin, a white Creole. Her family moved to New Orleans when she was only nine. She became a close friend of Henriette Delille. After about a year, the fledgling religious community, perhaps because of white opposition to its interracialism, failed. Nevertheless, Henriette Delille and Juliette Gaudin retained their interest in the religious life. During the 1830s, Delille's continuing deep involvement in works of charity to the poor of her race must have become troubling to the family.

Even more important, Henriette Delille refused to go to the balls, exclaiming that "one hour with God in church is sweeter than the vanities found in the ballroom" (Detiege, 23). She offended her older relatives by condemning their lifestyle, with its extramarital alliances, as sinful. Her mother, Pouponne Dias, became even more worried about Henriette Delille's future. Without the economic security of a wealthy protector, what was her daughter to do for a living? Henriette Delille wanted only to be a nun and minister to the poor. Finally, in desperation, her mother encouraged her to enter a convent in France. There, Henriette Delille could escape the deprivation and discrimination that, Pouponne Dias felt, must come to anyone seeking to work among the bondsmen and the poorest of New Orleans. Henriette Delille, however, refused to leave New Orleans. Her focus remained entirely local.

Then, in 1832, Pouponne Dias had a nervous breakdown. Her affairs and those of her minor daughter were turned over to the courts. It was not until 1835, when she was declared of legal age, that Henriette Delille was able to sell her property. She and Juliette Gaudin had become close friends with Marie Jeanne Aliquot, a French-born woman twice their age. Aliquot was one of three blood sisters who moved to New Orleans to work in Catholic missions. One of Aliquot's sisters became an Ursuline nun in 1828, and in 1831 the other joined the staff of the Barracks Street school founded by Sister Saint Marthe. The day Marie Jeanne Aliquot arrived in the Crescent City in 1832, she was rescued by a black man after having fallen into the Mississippi River. From that time forward she dedicated herself to working with black people. In 1834 she took over the leadership of the girls' school established by Sister Saint Marthe. In 1836 she attempted to establish the Sisters of the Presentation, a religious community, with Henriette Delille, Juliette Gaudin, Josephine Charles, and six other young Creole women of color. To the people who saw her enthusiastically teaching the word of God to the slaves and anyone who would listen to her along the streets, Marie Jeanne Aliquot seemed eccentric, and many laughed at her. Both the local Catholic hierarchy and the civil government responded unfavorably to her new order because its membership was interracial. The experiment was soon squelched.

Sisters of the Holy Family Founded

At a time when males totally dominated Catholic and most other Christian missionary organizations, what the proposed community needed was a male clerical patron. This it found in the person of Father Etienne Jean François Rousselon, a French priest who arrived in New Orleans in 1837. By that time, the growing English-speaking Protestant American population was becoming more influential. City and state officials, often reflecting the influence of American race relations, were incensed by reports of Catholic missionary activity among black people, which they feared would lead to discontent among the free black population and insubordination among the slaves. Rousselon advised Aliquot to concentrate her missionary activities, at least for a while, among black people on the rural plantations, where invited, instead of in the city. The rural plantation country of southern Louisiana was still mostly Creole. He also became pastor-designate of Saint Augustine's, a new church under construction in the Tremé neighborhood, a Creole suburb of New Orleans with a large free black population. He secured from his superior, Bishop Antoine Blanc, permission to found a society of free black women—no white member would be included—under Henriette Delille's leadership. When the church was finished in 1842, the group, quietly and unofficially, became a reality.

At first, only three members, Henriette Delille, Juliette Gaudin, and Josephine Charles, were left from the original group, along with Aliquot, who lived as a member, albeit secretly, for the rest of her life. Father Rousselon had originally planned for what came to be called the Sisters of the Holy Family to be a contemplative or cloistered order. However, long before they formed their society, Delille and the others already had become engaged in charitable work. In a city where black Americans were either enslaved or circumscribed in their freedom, the Catholic church continued to emphasize that the order existed for the purpose of teaching religion. However, the New Orleans community of free Creoles of color was determined not to allow this to be the only goal.

In 1847, when the state legislature passed an act requiring incorporation of nonprofit societies, a lay Association of the Holy Family was formed for the support of the sisters. Under the leadership of François Lacroix, a prosperous free black tailor and brother of the wholesale grocer Julien Lacroix, the wealthiest black person in the city, the association built a hospice on Saint Bernard Street in 1849 for Delille and the others to care for the sick, aged, and poor. In 1850, Delille opened the group's first convent and a school for pay for free black girls on Bayou Road near Saint Augustine. Nevertheless, these first few "sisters" were not allowed to wear religious garb in public, and when they were mentioned in the Catholic press, they were simply referred to as "a group of pious, colored females" (Detiege, 42).

As their field of activity widened, Rousselon determined that the free black women needed greater training to prepare to launch formally the Holy Family order. In 1852 Delille made her novitiate at Saint Michael's, a school for white girls in Saint James Parish, under the Madames of the Sacred Heart. Later that year, at Saint Augustine, she, Juliette Gaudin, and Josephine Charles made their final vows. Around the same time, the Incorporation Act was amended to annul all religious associations of people of color, but the city of New Orleans seems to have ignored the law as it related to the new sisters. This may have been in deference to Creole sensibilities. At the same time, under the same amended statute, Saint James African Methodist Episcopal Church was shut down. Saint James, however, was unlike the Holy Family in that it was Protestant (that is, "American") and had no white supervision. In any case, in the 1850s the order was well and truly launched. During a decade of the city's notorious yellow fever, cholera, and malaria epidemics, the order's missions grew so much that the sisters had to open an annex to their hospice in 1860. Children orphaned in the epidemics were cared for in the new asylum on Dauphine Street. White and black alike received nursing from the sisters during the epidemics. Deaths in one epidemic were so great and produced so many orphans that, for a while, children of both races had to be housed together in the sisters' care.

The era of Civil War and Reconstruction brought new challenge to the Sisters of the Holy Family. On November 16, 1862, Delille died. The sisters numbered only twelve. Several mothers withdrew their daughters from the convent, stating that without Mother Henriette the order was finished. Several other young Creole nuns of color left for convents in France. In the weeks that followed, the Union occupied New Orleans. The struggling little order appeared to have reached low ebb. In the spring of 1863, Aliquot, who had been very ill, recovered enough to sally forth on a mission to rescue a young black woman who had been kidnapped and taken for sex into a Union camp, a task that quickly led to the elderly Frenchwoman's death on April 12.

By the time that Rousselon died, in 1866, the order was facing an important turning point. Until that time the Holy Family sisters had been permitted to accept candidates only from among the privileged Creole free people of color. Now, with the war over and the slaves freed, former bondswomen sought entry into the order. Chloe Preval, who had been the slave cook of the local archbishop, became the first to join. In return for his permission, however, the archbishop gave the order responsibility for keeping house at his residence and the attached ecclesiastical seminary. In 1871 Josephine Charles, now mother superior, designed a religious habit for the order. After chastising the black sisters for being "too proud" in wanting to wear habits, the archbishop eventually relented and in 1872 permitted his former cook, on the occasion of her first vows, to be the first to wear the habit publicly. Thus, it had taken nearly four decades—from 1836, when the church squelched Aliquot's interracial order, until 1872—before the Sisters of the Holy Family were finally permitted to wear habits. It could be argued that they secured the archbishop's permission, in effect, by accepting the role of being servants to him. The Sisters of the Holy Family had to seek means by which to practice humility. Being women of African descent in a racist society, every day they had to embrace humility as their way of life. It could also be argued, however, that in refusing for decades to relent in their pursuit of the religious life, the sisters demonstrated spectacular, unshakable faith.

Gradually the sisters began to receive greater public acceptance as part of local Catholic missions. Membership grew. The order opened other convents and schools in New Orleans and in the rural Baton Rouge area. In 1876 the sisters received final approval from the archbishop for their Rule. In 1881 they purchased a larger home, the former Orleans Ballroom in the French Quarter. Ironically, the old dance floor, site of countless romantic alliances and a major focus of the old system of interracial *plaçage,* became the new convent chapel. The principal convent of the order remained in that location until 1964, when the sisters moved to a larger site in a post-World War II suburb of the city. The sister's outreach eventually extended as far to the west as California and to the south as British Honduras. Today the Sisters of the Holy Family still provide domestic service at the residence of the archbishop, but their principal work consists of parish ministry, programs of the Confraternity of Christian Doctrine for religious education of public school students, and conducting their own elementary and secondary schools, homes for the elderly, and a nursing home. They also have begun to gather data for presenting the cause of their founder, so that Henriette Delille may be regarded as Venerable, which is the first step in achieving sainthood.

References

Detiege, Sister Audrey Marie, S.S.F. *Henriette Delille, Free Woman of Color: Foundress of the Sisters of the Holy Family*. New Orleans: Sisters of the Holy Family, 1976.

Hart, Sister Mary Francis Borgia, S.S.F. *Violets in the King's Garden: A History of the Sisters of the Holy Family of New Orleans*. New Orleans: Sisters of the Holy Family, 1976.

Smith, S.B.S. Sister Roberta. Interview, 4 February 1991. Xavier University Archives, New Orleans, Lousiana.

Lester Sullivan

Bernadine Newsom Denning

(1930-)

Educator, government official

As a lifelong educator and administrator, Bernadine Denning has worked toward improving the quality of education in public schools, as well as the social and economic environment of students and their families. She has also tried to awaken communities and government to the realization that those goals canot be fully realized until discrimination based on race, gender, and age is overcome.

Born on August 17, 1930, in Detroit, Michigan, Bernadine Newsom Denning was one of three children (two girls and one boy) born to William Charles Newsom, a factory worker, and Evelyn Tyler (Pembrook) Newsom. Denning remembers her mother as a "Trojan" whose example and advice inspired her to have the "courage and determination to succeed." Evelyn Newsom told her three children to look for the larger cosmic purpose in life since "The Lord has a master plan for us all" (Brown, 8). The Newsom family lived in the Brewster projects, composed of inner-city low-income housing.

Denning learned to swim at age eight at the Brewster Center, a skill she continued to develop in her teens and young adulthood. Institutions in the black community played a vital role in helping Denning and others develop their skills and self-confidence and receive realistic perceptions of the possibilities for future development. For example, the Lucy Thurman branch YWCA was an important center of activities for the black community of Detroit. By age sixteen, Denning was a swimming instructor at the Thurman YWCA, developing her ability to teach and laying the foundation for her future profession. Treva Goings and other black professionals at the YWCA provided programs and activities to the community and also served as role models, inspiring Denning to go to college. So important was the Thurman YWCA to Denning's early development that even in the 1980s, years after the Y ceased operations, she said, "I get all choked up inside when I pass the building today" (Brown, 8). Additional encouragement and support came from the people in the Brewster project community who "took me under their wings [because] they saw something in me," she said (Spratling, 22).

Denning attended public schools in Detroit, graduating from Northeastern High School in 1947 and enrolling in Michigan State Normal College (later renamed Eastern Michigan University) that fall. Her academic ability brought her recognition as a Faculty Women's Scholar, Joseph Doyle Scholar, and State Board of Education Scholar, and also helped pay some of her college expenses. Still, she had to work to supplement the money she received from her family. Throughout her college and young adult years, swimming remained an important activity for personal fulfillment, income-earning, and professional development. In addition to working in the kitchen of her dormitory, Denning worked as a lifeguard and swimming instructor from the second semester of her freshman year to graduation. From 1947 to 1951 she worked as a water safety instructor for the American Red Cross and in 1951, at the age of twenty, she became assistant director of the Burt Shurly Camp in Chelsea, Michigan, continuing in that summertime position until 1958.

During her college years, she started a synchronized swimming team, named the Catalina Club, which traveled the country instructing other swimmers in the techniques. Even in college, Denning encountered racism. When the swim team traveled, "My coach would always have to check to see if I could stay at the hotel," she said, and the year she entered the National Synchronized Swim competition, she and two other black girl swimmers were required to practice at midnight so that no one would see them. In 1948 she encountered racism as a contestant in the homecoming queen contest. Chosen as the representative of her dormitory, she was considered a favorite, but remembers that one of the whites in charge, who admitted Denning was the frontrunner, asked her, "Can you imagine how many negroes would come to this school if you won?" Instead the committee chose a white girl (Brown, 8-9).

In 1951 she graduated from Michigan State Normal College with a B.S. in physical education and was hired to teach in the Detroit public schools. From 1951 to 1959 she taught physical education, swimming, home economics, and family living at Jefferson Junior High School. Her teacher's salary made the family income too high for low-income housing, so the family was required to leave the Brewster projects. Through much of her career with the public system, Denning took graduate school courses and sought advanced degrees. In 1956 she received her M.Ed. degree from Wayne State University in Detroit. On August 26, 1956, she married Blaine Denning, formerly a student athlete at Wilberforce University in Xenia, Ohio, and Lawrence Institute of Technology, Southfield, Michigan, who later played professional basketball with the Harlem Globetrotters and the Baltimore Bullets. For twenty-five years he co-owned and comanaged Homes and Denning, a distributor of dairy products and the only black wholesale milk distributing company in Detroit. Subsequently, Blaine Denning worked with Detroit's Summer Youth Employment program. The Dennings also became landlords, owning about sixteen "HUD homes" for rental purposes. For relaxation, the couple purchased a cottage on Duck Lake in the 1970s, about fifteen miles west of Pontiac, where Bernadine Denning enjoys spending weekends "reading 'trashy novels,' gardening and latch-hooking." "Blaine Denning has supported all aspects of his wife's career; Bernadine considers him 'the world's most patient man''' (*Who's Who in Government,* 147; Brown, 10). They have one son, Blaine Denning, Jr.

From 1959 to 1972 Bernadine Denning worked in a series of administrative positions with the Detroit public schools. She served as coordinator of the Great Cities School Improvement Project from 1959 to 1962, counselor at Winship Junior High School from 1962 to 1965, and intercultural coordinator for the Detroit school system from 1965 to 1968. Then she worked as assistant director of Parent-Teacher-Student Activities from 1968 to 1972 and director of the Department of School Volunteers in 1971. In the meantime, additional graduate study at Wayne State University resulted in her receiving the education specialist designation in secondary education in 1966 and the Ed.D. in curriculum development in 1970. Her doctoral dissertation, "Evolving a Plan for Significant Student Participation in Decision-Making in Urban High Schools," evaluated six schools representing both inner and outer city schools in Detroit as well as suburban schools. The study found no substantial differences in student perceptions or desires for involvement in decision-making between urban and suburban high schools and recommended greater student involvement in decision-making as a method of helping students become aware of their responsibilities in both high school and community and of promoting democratic procedures.

Denning Directs Revenue-Sharing Program

The 1970s found Bernadine Denning working in several interrelated positions at the University of Michigan in Ann Arbor. Some of these positions involved relating university programs to off-campus constituencies and resulted in concurrent titles and positions to designate the coordination of these activities. Thus, from 1970 to 1973 she directed the Urban Program in Education, and from 1972 to 1975 she was both director of special studies and projects and coordinator of the Shaw College-Lewis College of Business joint University of Michigan program. In addition, from 1974 to 1976 she was an assistant professor of education. In 1975 she resumed employment with the Detroit public schools as director of Title IV—Civil Rights Office. Her work in this office attracted the attention of officials in the federal government and resulted in President Jimmy Carter's appointing her in 1977 as director of the Office of Revenue Sharing for the United States Department of the Treasury. This office distributed a portion of federal taxes collected—nine billion dollars a year—to approximately 39,000 governmental units throughout the nation, including states, counties, cities, towns, and townships. Civil rights enforcement was an element of her work as her office was authorized to withhold funds from governments that practiced racial discrimination. Denning was the third person to serve as director and was considered a very effective administrator. Still, after two years, she decided to return to life and work in Detroit.

In 1979 she became executive director of the Department of School-Community Relations for the Detroit public schools. To her, education involved "a partnership between the schools and the community," and her department helped bring the two together and build stronger community support for the schools. Much of her time was spent meeting with parent-teacher associations, ministers, civic leaders, and representatives of community groups. She often explained and defended school policies as well as helping plan school activities. In 1984 the title of her position was upgraded to assistant superintendent and she left the position and retired from the school system in 1985.

In 1986-1987 she came out of retirement to serve as director of the Human Relations Department of the City of Detroit. Formerly known as the Civil Rights Commission, the office oversees civil rights laws as they affect all Detroit residents, including monitoring the city's compliance with affirmative action requirements and investigating housing complaints. After working as an individual consultant in education and leadership training from 1987 to 1989, Bernadine Denning formed and became president of DMP Associates, an interracial professional consulting firm whose three partners all have extensive experience as teachers and administrators in the Detroit public schools.

Over the years Bernadine Denning has been active in and a significant contributor to large numbers of organizations. Her chief concerns—improving the quality of education available in public schools, improving the social and economic environment of students and their families, and combating racism, sexism, and age discrimination—have often led to such leadership positions as chair of the Michigan Women's Commission, chair of the Downtown Detroit Branch YWCA, 1970-1973; vice-president of the YWCA of the United States of America, 1976-1979; founder and board member of Black Women's Agenda (a women's legislative lobby), 1977-1988; and cochair of Michigan ERA (Supporters of Equal Rights Amendment) in 1976. She has also served as a member of the executive board of the Detroit NAACP, the executive committee of the Michigan United Negro College Fund, a commissioner of the Detroit Library Board, and a member of the State of Michigan's Attorney Discipline Board and of the Michigan Supreme Court's Gender Bias Task Force. In addition, in the 1980s she has been a trustee of the University of Detroit and of Central Michigan University (CMU chairperson in 1982). Her longstanding service to Delta Sigma Theta Sorority has included positions as president of the Detroit Alumnae Chapter, 1971-1973, regional director, 1976-1977, national projects chairperson, 1975-1977, and national social action chairperson starting in 1983.

Her many other civic activities include serving as vice-chair of the Black United Fund of Michigan in 1984 and as a board member for the Homes for Black Children and the Delta Home for Girls. She is listed in *Who's Who in America,* 1978-1979 and was inducted into the Michigan Women's Hall of Fame in 1989. She has received numerous awards from many local, state, and national organizations.

In surveying her life and career, Bernadine Denning considers the encouragement and support of her family to have been crucial in obtaining her goals and in overcoming racial and sexual discrimination.

References

''Bernardine Newsom Denning'' and ''Blaine Denning.'' *Personalities of Detroit.* Detroit: Detroit Public Schools, [c1974]. Includes photographs.

Brown, Jocelyn. ''A Woman of Courage, Dr. Bernadine Denning.'' *City Style* 1 (August 1986): 7-10. Includes photographs.

Denning, Bernardine Newsom. ''Evolving a Plan for Significant Student Participation in Decision-Making in Urban High Schools.'' Ed.D. dissertation, Wayne State University, 1970.

''*DMP Associates, Inc.* A Professional Consulting Firm.'' Brochure, n.d.

''Dr. Bernadine Denning: Office of Revenue Sharing.'' *Ebony* 32 (August 1977): 96. Includes photograph.

Kornegay, Francis Albert. *They Made It So Can You.* Detroit: Detroit Urban League, 1977. Photograph, p. 119.

Spratling, Cassandra. ''Bernadine N. Denning.'' *Essence* 12 (June 1981): 20-22. Photograph, p. 20.

Who's Who Among Black Americans. First ed. Northbrook, Ill. Who's Who Among Black Americans, 1976. 4th ed. Lake Forest, Ill.: Educational Communications, 1985. 6th ed. Detroit: Gale Research, 1990.

Who's Who in America. 40th ed. Chicago: Marquis, 1978.

Who's Who in Government. 3rd ed. Chicago: Marquis, 1977.

Who's Who of American Women. 6th ed. Chicago: Marquis, 1970.

Who's Who in the Midwest. 16th ed. Chicago: Marquis, 1978.

World Who's Who of Women. 3rd ed. Cambridge, Eng.: International Biographical Centre, 1976.

De Witt S. Dykes, Jr.

Juliette Derricotte

(1897-1931)

Organization official, college dean of women

Dean of women at Fisk University and a member of the general committee of the Worlds Student Christian Federation, Juliette Aline Derricotte was born on April 1, 1897, in Athens, Georgia, the fifth of nine children of Isaac and Laura (Hardwick) Derricotte. Her father was a cobbler and her mother a seamstress, and they managed to provide a home that was warm, affectionate, and secure. The lively and sensitive Derricotte, growing up in Athens, soon became aware of the racial mores of a small southern town in the early 1900s, learning, for example, that her family would always be the last to be waited on in a store. Her desire to attend the Lucy Cobb Institute, located in a section of Athens with spacious homes and tree-lined streets, was dashed when her mother finally had to tell her that it would be impossible because of her color. The recognition of that limitation was traumatic for Derricote but critical in forging her determination to do whatever she could to fight discrimination.

After completing the public schools of Atlanta, Derricote hoped against all odds that she would be able to go to college. A recruiter was able to convince her parents to send her to Talladega College. They could just manage the fifteen dollars a month for tuition and room and board, and that fall Derricotte made the long, rumbling train ride across the red hills of Georgia and Alabama to the town of Talladega. It was love at first sight when she saw the campus, with its large trees and graceful buildings, but she was shocked almost to the point of returning home when she discovered that all of the professors were white.

At Talladega Derricotte was a popular student and her warm personality made her many friends. One of her professors, recognizing her potential, suggested that she try for a public-speaking prize that included tuition. ''Of course, I can't do it,'' she almost managed to convince herself. But with some coaching, she won the contest and self-confidence as well. Derricotte became the most important young woman on campus, always in charge of something. She joined the intercollegiate debating team, made speeches, became president of the YWCA, and helped to plan student activities. When disputes arose between students and faculty, as they often did, Derricotte would be the spokesperson for whichever side she felt to be correct, yet she maintained the goodwill of both. It was during her years at Talladega that she came to the realization that one should work for something bigger than oneself.

After graduation from Talladega in 1918, Derricotte went

Juliette Derricotte

to New York to enroll in a summer course at the National YWCA Training School and in the fall was made a secretary of the National Student Council of the YWCA. In this position she visited colleges, planned conferences, and worked with student groups, bringing ideas and building leadership. She is credited with pioneering the methods of work and organizational structure that made the council an interracial fellowship. Through the warmth and forcefulness of her personality, she succeeded in making people understand each other in the most practical manner. She remained in this post for eleven years.

World Student Christian Federation Offers New Experiences

Derricotte had become a member of the general committee of the World Student Christian Federation and in 1924 was sent to England—one of two black delegates—to represent American college students. Four years later she was sent to Mysore, India. In these international settings, among representatives from around the world, Derricotte was always a curiosity and the centre of attention, which gave way to respect. In India she learned first-hand from her fellow delegates of the worldwide extent of repression and discrimination in all forms. She learned from a young Indian woman who had been told upon entering church that all the whites must be seated before she could be seated; from a young Korean tentmate who kept her awake until two A.M. telling her that to know the meaning of prejudice, segregation, and discrimination, she would have to be a Korean under Japanese government. She remained in India for seven weeks, living in YWCAs, student hostels, mission schools, the furnished camp of a maharajah, a deserted military camp with five hundred students from India, Burma, and Ceylon, and in Indian homes. She gained valuable insights, for she came to realize that the general committee, with its ninety or so delegates from around the world, was prophetic in the sense that:

> This is what can happen to all the world. With all the differences and difficulties, with all the entanglements of international attitudes and policies, with all the bitterness and prejudice and hatred that are true between any two or more of these countries, you are here friends working, thinking, playing, living together in the finest sort of fellowship, fulfilling the dream of the World's Student Christian Federation ''That All May be One'' (Derricotte, 282).

Derricotte proceeded to China and Japan for meetings with students there, and returned home to share her experiences with American students. Summing it all up, she wrote:

> Of course it was most interesting, but how can I say that I am no longer free; that the wealth as well as the poverty of India haunts me; I ache with actual physical pain when I remember the struggles of all India today: religious, caste, economic, social, political; how can I tell of the control which oil and rubber and jute have in the relations of East and West, or explain how back of oil and rubber and jute are the more fundamental and eternal puzzles of economics, race, and religion? My head whirls but every now and again I remember ''that there is so much more to know than I am accustomed to knowing and so much more love than I am accustomed to loving'' (Derricotte, 282).

In 1927 she received a master's degree in religious education from Columbia University, and from 1929 to 1931 she was the only woman trustee of Talladega College. Feeling a special call to participate in black education in the South, Derricotte resigned from the YWCA in 1929 and went to Fisk University as its dean of women. She entered a campus roiling with the problems of change and in revolt against long-outdated rules, particularly for young women. She eventually gained the confidence of the female students and gradually began to introduce the idea of freedom of action and responsibility for oneself. The students were beginning to feel comfortable. In November 1931, almost fully recovered from illness that had troubled her all summer, Derricotte decided to go to Athens to visit her mother. Making the trip with her were three Fisk students from Georgia. One of them, a young man, was to do the driving. They stopped for lunch with friends in Chattanooga and headed south towards Atlanta with Derricotte driving. About a mile outside Dalton, Georgia, their car collided with that of a white couple. The details of the accident have never been known. Derricotte and a student were seriously injured. They were given emergency treatment in the offices of several white doctors in Dalton, and two students were released. As the local tax-supported hospital did not admit blacks, Derricotte and the seriously injured student were then removed to the home of a black woman who had beds available for the care of black patients. The student died during the night, and Derricotte was driven by ambulance to Chattanooga's Walden Hospital, where she died the next day, November 7, 1931.

Perhaps Derricotte is best remembered today for her death and the national outrage it caused. There was a series of investigations; the NAACP became involved; the Commission of Interracial Co-operation of Atlanta made an investigation at the request of Fisk University and other organizations. Memorial services were held all over the country, and her friend, noted theologian Howard Thurman, delivered the eulogy at the service held in her hometown, reading her haunting words from the Mysore Conference.

References

Cuthbert, Marion V. *Juliette Derricotte*. New York: Woman's Press, 1933.

Derricotte, Juliette. "The Student Conference at Mysore, India." *Crisis* 36 (August, 1929): 267, 280-83.

Du Bois, W. E. B., "Dalton, Georgia." *Crisis* (March 1932): 85-87.

Jeanness, Mary. *Twelve Negro Americans*. New York: Friendship Press, 1925.

Leffall, Dolores. "Juliette [Aline] Derricotte." *Dictionary of American Negro Biography*. Edited by Rayford Logan and Michael Winston. New York: Norton, 1982.

Richardson, Joe M. *A History of Fisk University, 1865-1946*. University, Alabama: University of Alabama Press, 1980.

White, Walter. *New York Herald Tribune*, 31 December 1931.

Wygal, Winifred. "Juliette Derricotte, Her Character and Martyrdom: An Interpretation." *Crisis* 39 (March, 1932): 84-85.

Collections

The Thomas Elsa Jones Papers at Fisk University contain materials on Juliette Derricotte during her tenure at Fisk and the circumstances of her death. Derricotte's student records are at Talladega College, Talladega, Alabama.

Jean Elder Cazort

Irene Diggs

(1906-)

Anthropologist

Noted anthropologist Ellen Irene Diggs was born in 1906 in Monmouth, Illinois, a small college town located in the state's agricultural belt near the Iowa border. One of five children, she was raised in the supportive environment of an industrious working-class family. Despite her family's modest comfort, at an early age Diggs became cognizant of and disturbed by incidences of poverty and inequitable wages in her community. (At that time, Monmouth had a population of about ten thousand, two to three hundred of whom were black.) Even as a child, it was clear to Diggs that economic inequality had little to do with the amount of hard work a person performed but was based on other factors such as race and class. Diggs devoted her life to studying race relations and cultural differences among blacks in North, South, and Latin America.

Like many black families of the era, the Diggses perceived education as the most significant way to become upwardly mobile in society. From her voracious reading as a youth, Diggs grew determined to visit and learn as much as she could about the distant lands she knew from books, magazines, and newspapers. She attended Monmouth College for one year, on a scholarship, given yearly by the city's chamber of commerce for the highest scholastic average in the local high school, then transferred to the University of Minnesota, which had more extensive course offerings. At Minnesota, Diggs majored in sociology and minored in psychology. She graduated in 1928 with a bachelor of science degree, then enrolled in Atlanta University (now Clark-Atlanta) to pursue a graduate degree in sociology. In 1933, she received the university's first master's degree. Ten years later, in 1944, Diggs earned her doctorate in anthropology at the University of Havana.

During Diggs's second semester as a graduate student at Atlanta University, the distinguished scholar and activist W. E. B. Du Bois returned to Atlanta as a professor of economics, history, and sociology. Diggs registered for Du Bois's courses and did so well that Du Bois asked her to become his research assistant that summer. Apparently Du Bois appreciated Diggs's intellectual ability, for she remained his assistant for eleven years. Over the course of those years, Diggs helped research five of Du Bois's books, including his social history *Black Folk Then and Now*, and founded with him the journal *Phylon: A Review of Race and Culture*.

African Cultures in Latin America Studied

By the early 1940s, Diggs was in search of an independent career. After traveling to Cuba for a holiday, she returned the following year for intensive language study as a Roosevelt Fellow of the Institute of International Education at the University of Havana. Diggs became a graduate student of the distinguished professor of ethnography, Fernando Ortiz, an authority on the African presence in Cuban culture. Diggs's ethnographic activities included collecting folklore, recording music, photographing festivals, and observing rituals and dance. She traveled throughout the island in both rural and urban areas, writing on the survival and continued practice of elements of African cultures functioning quite visibly among twentieth-century Afro-Cuban descendants of Yoruban and Dahomean people.

A critical concept formulated in those two years in Havana was the functional differences in race relations operating in Latin America and in the United States. "Basically, the differences between the 'problem of race' in the United States and Latin America," Diggs wrote in the *Negro History Bulletin*, "is their different definitions of who is white" (107). Following World War II, Diggs journeyed to South America, where she spent almost a year in Montevideo, Uruguay, as an exchange scholar under the auspices of the U.S. Department of State's Division of International Exchange of Persons. In Montevideo, she continued archival research and became a participant observer in the Afro-Uruguayan and Afro-Argentinean (Buenos Aires) communities. During her stay in the Platine region, Diggs developed an interest in fine art and would write articles on the subject for various publications, including "Negro Painters in Uruguay" for *Crisis* and "The Negro in the Viceroyalty of Rio de la Plata" for *Journal of Negro History*. Her research and expertise in Afro-Latin America also made Irene Diggs unique among her black United States-based colleagues.

Returning to the United States in 1947, Diggs was invited to join the faculty of Morgan State College (now University). She retired in 1976 after almost thirty years of service to the department of sociology and anthropology.

Due to classroom commitment, Diggs had difficulty preparing book-length manuscripts. Instead, her work appeared in a wide variety of periodicals. She wrote many articles for the *Journal of Negro History* and *Phylon* and for newspapers such as the *Baltimore Sun* and reviews for many academic journals. Selected works by Diggs are: "Zumbi and the Republic of Os Palmares" *Phylon* 14, (First Quarter 1953): 62-70; "Color in Colonial Spanish America" *Journal of Negro History* 38 (October 1953): 403-27; "Legacy" *Freedomways* 5 (Winter 1965): 18-19; "Cuba before and after Castro" *The New American* (15 July 1976); "The Biological and Cultural Impact of Blacks on the United States" *Phylon* 41 (Summer 1980): 152-66. Additionally, Diggs coedited the *Encyclopedia of the Negro*. 1945.

Over the years, Diggs excelled in her role as the committed scholar active in community affairs. Although she never sought to be an officer, Diggs served on numerous civic and state-wide fact-finding commissions that affected the general population or focused on issues relating to the black American community. She participated on commissions concerned with mental health, corrections, and family welfare. Diggs was a founding member of the Women's Committee of the Baltimore Art Museum and on the board of the Peabody Conservatory. She has been a member of the American Anthropological Association and the American Sociological Association. In 1978 the Association of Black Anthropologists presented Diggs with the Distinguished scholar Award for her outstanding achievement in the scholarship and research on peoples of African descent.

As a black American anthropologist, Diggs has contributed to the field in terms of her scholarship on Afro-Latin America, Afro-American history, African history, and black intellectual history. Her latest volume, *Black Chronology* (1983), illustrates her view of culture and the use of historical research to document cultural change. The book is an exceptionally fine example of an African diaspora perspective, for it looks at the African experience both in and outside of Africa and focuses on the accomplishments of black peoples. The obvious influences in her scholarship are her mentors, Du Bois and Ortiz. Diggs is convinced that anthropology—properly taught—is one of the most useful subjects one can study.

References

Bolles, A. Lynn. "E. Irene Diggs." *A Bibliographical Dictionary*. Edited by U. Graces and others. Westport, Conn.: Greenwood Press, 1988.

———. "Irene Diggs: A Biographical Sketch." *Outreach* 5 (1983): 1-2.

———. "Irene Diggs: Coming of Age in Atlanta, Havana and Baltimore." Paper presented at the Eightieth Annual Meeting of the American Anthropological Association, Los Angeles, 1981.

Diggs, Irene. "Attitudes Toward Color in South America. *Negro History Bulletin* 34 (1971): 107-108.

A. Lynn Bolles

Sharon Pratt Dixon

(1944-)

Politician

Sharon Pratt Dixon lives by a motto that is illustrative of her genuine character: "In order to be a good leader, one

Sharon Pratt Dixon

must have skillfully mastered the art of compassion'' (Interview with Sharon Pratt Dixon, 21 October 1990. Unless otherwise indicated, all quotations used were taken from that interview.) At five feet three inches, Sharon Pratt Dixon, Democratic mayor of Washington, D.C., may be short in height, but she is a giant in personality and charisma. She is warm, dedicated, and committed to service. She possesses an infinite strength and iron will and will give the city her heart.

Dixon was born January 30, 1944, in Washington, D.C., to Carlisle and Mildred ''Peggy''Pratt. Three years later, a sister, Benaree, was born. Peggy Pratt died when Dixon was four. Her grandmother, Hazel Pratt, and aunt, Aimee Elizabeth Pratt, served as mother figures to Dixon, teaching her invaluable life lessons. Her father, Carlisle Pratt, a former Washington, D.C., superior court judge, held high expectations for Dixon. ''He is the person who shaped my philosophies of life,'' Dixon recalls. Pratt emphasized family ethics, good character and morals. ''My father stressed developing the mind, hard work, and a commitment to public service,'' she says, and her life is exemplified by the early lessons imparted by him.

Dixon attended Washington, D.C., public schools, namely Gage and Rudolph elementary schools and MacFarland Junior High School. She enjoyed team sports and loved to play baseball. An all-boys baseball club even asked her to join, but she declined. ''I was at that adolescent stage when you worry about looking good,'' she jokes, ''so I turned them down.''

An average student at first, Dixon began to work feverishly in her studies after enrolling at Roosevelt High School. Her instructors did not take her seriously, which made her determined to excel and go to college. She disciplined herself and studied five hours every night, graduating in 1961 with honors.

Dixon loved the glitz of the silver screen and the seemingly glamorous life of its actors and actresses. But upon enrolling at Howard University in Washington, D.C., political science outweighed an acting career. ''I always wanted to be an actress,'' she says wistfully. ''But my commitment to public service steered me in a direction in which I could initiate change.''

While an undergraduate, Dixon became a member of the Alpha Chapter of Alpha Kappa Alpha Sorority in 1964. She was also the first woman to run for student council president. Losing did not deter her. Dixon became a member of Pi Sigma Alpha national political science honor society and a Falk Fellow in political science. In 1965 she graduated with a B.A. in political science. She continued at Howard University's School of Law and received a juris doctor in 1968. While in law school, Dixon found the time to date and marry Arrington Dixon in 1966, who later became Washington, D.C., council chairman. The same year she graduated, Aimee Arrington Dixon was born on November 27, 1968. On November 8, 1970, the Dixons were blessed with another baby girl, Drew Arrington Dixon. The Dixon household was filled with love and family activities and the girls developed and matured through the years. In 1982, however, the Dixons were divorced. Aimee is a graduate of the Rhode Island School of Design, and Drew is a junior at Howard University.

From 1970 to 1971 Dixon was house counsel for the Joint Center for Political Studies in Washington, D.C., and from 1971 to 1976 she was an associate with Pratt and Queen legal firm. While in private practice ''she fought for the rights of children involved in custody battles, provided juveniles with strong and competent legal representation, and protected the rights of families'' (''Sharon Pratt Dixon,'' 1).

In 1972 Dixon joined the faculty at the Antioch School of Law, a position she held for four years. During this time, former Speaker of the House Thomas ''Tip'' O'Neill appointed Dixon to the District of Columbia Law Revision Commission, ''which transferred the city's criminal code from Congress to the District'' (*Washington Times,* 17 April 1990).

In 1976 Dixon accepted a position in the general counsel's office at Potomac Electric Power Company (PEPCO). Seven years later she was promoted, and later appointed vice-president for public policy, the first black American and first woman vice-president of consumer affairs. During Dixon's term, many new programs were initiated and implemented for the improvement of low-income Washington, D.C., residents as well as for senior citizens. Dixon also created jobs with new satellite branches of PEPCO. ''I wanted PEPCO to adopt new policies and a general approach of how to deal with changing methods," she explains. "Ideas, concepts and policies drive me!"

That drive may be innate. Dixon's interest in politics stems from her early childhood. "I've always been fascinated by people who shape public policy, such as Franklin Delano Roosevelt and Martin Luther King. Mr. King had excellent communication skills. He took complex issues and made them simple for everyone else." Dixon also admires Malcolm X for his boldness, search for truth, and his willingness to share his knowledge with others. Mentors Patricia Roberts Harris, who served in the Carter Administration, and astute businesswoman Flaxie Pinkard were the female role models for Dixon. Dixon also served as campaign manager for Harris in her bid for the mayoral seat in Washington, D.C., in 1982.

For more than twenty years, Dixon has been actively involved in politics in the Democratic arena. She was elected to four terms as the Democratic National Committeewoman from the District of Columbia, 1977-1980. From 1980 to 1984 she served as the Democratic National Committee Eastern Regional Chairwoman. Already accustomed to breaking gender barriers, Dixon was the first woman to serve as the Democratic National Committee Treasurer from 1985 to 1989. She has also been a member of the American Bar Association, Unified Bar of the District of Columbia, and the District of Columbia Women's Bar Association. She has been active with the Legal Aid Society, the American Civil Liberties Union, the Howard University Board of Trustees, the United Negro College Fund, and the Ward Four Democratic Club. Organizations that recognized Dixon for her work include the Washington, D.C. chapter of the NAACP, the United Negro College Fund, and the Association of Black Women Attorneys. As result of losing her mother at an early age, she has remained deeply committed to children, community, and family. She is a member of the Holy Comforter Church.

Nation's Capitol Elects Its First Woman Mayor

On November 6, 1990, Dixon became the first black American woman (and the first woman) to win the mayoral race in the District of Columbia. Perturbed by the city's looming fiscal problems, its soaring crime statistics, record homicide rate, and drug addiction, Dixon believes she can help rectify these problems. "I set the goal to win the nomination, then I set the goal to serve. The key is to put yourself in a position to effect the changes you want to take place."

As mayor, Dixon wants to set a new trend of public service, responsibility, and leadership. Her main goal is to facilitate black and Hispanic ownership of business and community properties. She plans to create solid programs that will assist both the city's seniors and its youth. Appalled by the drug problem and other crimes in the city, she proposes to "implement a Fresh Start drug treatment program to be administered by local church and community groups; target seized drug capital for drug fighting units and treatment programs and establish a Neighborhood Orientated Policing program where churches, community groups, businesses and the police work together" ("Sharon Pratt Dixon: Fresh Alternative," 8). Concerned that women have been expected to derive influence from their proximity to men with power rather than be influential as power figures themselves, she notes: "We need a political genesis, a renaissance in which masculine politics and the 'dog eat dog' mentality that earmarked it, is replaced by a feminine kind of politics in which you do what is right, not what is expedient" ("Why Not a Ms. Mayor?," B-3).

Dixon will continue to move on, doing great things and inspiring many people. Of the mayor's position, she says: "The office is a means to an end, not the end."

References

Dixon, Sharon Pratt. Interview with author, 21 october 1990.

"Election Results: Blacks Make New Gains Across U.S." *Jet* 79 (26 November 1990): 12-15. Photograph, 13.

"Sharon Pratt Dixon." Publicity material, Sharon Pratt Dixon for Mayor, Washington, D.C., n.d. Includes photograph.

"Sharon Pratt-Dixon: Fresh Alternative." *Georgetowner* 35 (29 June-12 July, 1990): 1, 8, 17. Photograph, pp. 1, 17.

"Sharon Pratt Dixon for Mayor." News Clippings. Sharon Pratt Dixon for Mayor, Washington, D.C., 1990.

Washington Times, 17 April 1990.

Who's Who Among Black Americans, 1990/91. 6th ed. Detroit: Gale Research, 1990.

"Why Not a Ms. Mayor?" *Washington Post* 10 July 1990.

Monda Raquel Webb

Mattiwilda Dobbs

(1925-)

Singer, educator

Mattiwilda Dobbs, internationally-known as a concert and opera singer and the third black American to song at the Metropolitan Opera, was born the fifth of six daughters of a United States postal railway clerk on July 11, 1925, in Atlanta, Georgia. Her father, John Wesley Dobbs, worked the run between Atlanta and Nashville, Tennessee. In those

Mattiwilda Dobbs

days of Jim Crow, he used to borrow books from Fisk University and other libraries to take home for his children who, because they were black, could not borrow from the Atlanta public libraries. He also required that each of his daughters take ten years of musical training. A piano was the first thing that her father had bought after he married Irene Thompson.

Dobbs sang in her high school choir but did not think seriously about vocal training until she was in college. When her singing voice was noticed, "I already had a long musical training," Dobbs has said. "If I had had no training when my voice was discovered, it might have been too late to start" (*Press*). By this time her father had become a prominent person. After he had retired from the post office in 1935, he had organized the Georgia Voters League, which, even before the civil rights movement's heyday of the 1960s, increased black voter registration in the state tenfold. He was fast becoming the leading Prince Hall Mason of his day. He and his family took a major part, too, in the life of Spelman College. Rare is the issue of the school newspaper that does not mention at least one of them when Dobbs and her sisters attended there. Active in the college choir, Dobbs sang with the combined choruses of Atlanta University, Morehouse College, and Spelman College in national radio broadcasts. She studied voice with Naomi Maise and Willis Lawrence James. "I would never have been a singer," Dobbs says, "if it were not for my father. I was too shy" (*Look*). She graduated first in her class, with majors in music and Spanish, in 1946.

Although she made a few concert dates in the local black community, Dobbs focused instead on further training. She went to New York to study privately with Lottie Leonard, the noted Wagnerian and specialist in lieder. "She is really responsible for all my vocal technique," Dobbs said. "At first I trained as a lyric soprano, but the high notes were always very easy for me, and gradually the voice took on a more coloratura character" (Gardiner). Just in case a singing career should elude her, Dobbs also entered Columbia University Teachers College, majoring in Spanish, studying music by day and Spanish by night. In 1948 she summered at the University of Mexico and, after appearing as a soloist at Columbia University's annual music festival, received her M.A. That fall she became among the first to win a Marian Anderson Scholarship. The Mannes School of Music awarded her a scholarship to its opera workshop. In 1949 she also won a scholarship to the opera workshop of the Berkshire Music Center at Tanglewood. She continued to study with Leonard until 1950.

Then Dobbs got the chance to go to Europe. By winning a three-thousand-dollar John Hay Whitney scholarship, she was able to travel to Paris to study with Pierre Bernac from 1950 to 1952, thereby expanding her knowledge of the full range of French song from the baroque to Poulenc. She was also coached in Spanish repertoire by Lola Rodriguez de Aragon. More importantly, Dobbs was able to perform and compete in the European music arena. For an American operatic success, it was still necessary first for American singers, not least black American ones, to succeed in Europe. She got some work on French radio in 1950. Then, in 1951, despite a sprained ankle and not having slept for twenty-four hours, she won first prize in the International Music Competition in Geneva. Dobbs sang Constanze's aria from Mozart's *The Abduction From the Seraglio*. Teresa Stich-Randall won second that year. Victoria de los Angeles had placed first only a few years earlier. The prize launched Dobbs's career.

It was a time for firsts. Gifted with great beauty of person as well as voice, Dobbs was to cut a fine figure on the operatic stage. Soon after winning at Geneva, she sang the lead in Stravinsky's *Le Rossignol* at the Holland Festival. In the 1952-1953 season she undertook an extended concert tour of Europe, starting with the Scandinavian capitals and then proceeding to the Netherlands, Belgium, France, Italy, and Britain. At the same time she was experiencing change in her private life. She had been engaged almost since she met him in Paris to Luis Rodriguez, a Spanish playwright and journalist. They married in Genoa on April 4, 1953. That year, at the request of Herbert von Karajan, she became the first black to sing at La Scala, where she played Elvira in Rossini's *L'Italiana in Algieri*. Within the month she also sang at the Genoa Opera House as the Queen of the Night in Mozart's *The Magic Flute*. Dobbs's success as Zerbinetta in Richard Strauss's *Ariadne auf Naxos* at the 1953 Glyndebourne Festival resulted in her being engaged from 1953 through 1958 by the Royal Opera House, Covent Garden.

In March 1954 Dobbs made her debut at Town Hall in New York City in a concert performance of *Ariadne auf Naxos* under Thomas Scheerman. Then, two days before she was to debut at Covent Garden, on June 28, her husband died in London of a liver ailment. "We knew that he might not have a long time,'' said Dobbs, ''so our happiness was very precious'' (Gardiner). Dobbs kept her engagement, a command performance of Rimsky-Korsakov's *The Golden Cockerel* before Queen Elizabeth II, the first time since 1919 that the opera had been performed at the Royal Opera. Dobbs played the Queen opposite Hughes Cuenod and Geraint Evans; the performance was conducted by Igor Markevitch. At Covent Garden she also later sang Gilda in Verdi's *Rigoletto,* the title role in Donivetti's *Lucia di Lammermoor,* Olympia in Offenbach's *Tales of Hoffman,* and the Forest Bird in Wagner's *Siegfried.*

Dobbs Makes American Operatic Debut

By then Dobbs's agent in Paris had arranged for her to sing for Sol Hurok. The impresario told her that the same agent had brought Marian Anderson to sing for him in the same hall at the same time of the year some two decades before. Dobbs remained under Hurok's international management for several years. In summer 1955 she conducted a three-month tour of thirty-five recitals in Australia, Fiji, and Hawaii. In September she made her American operatic debut in the lead in the San Francisco Opera's *The Golden Cockerel*, becoming the first black person to play a major role in that company. She toured Mexico and South America. She made her first recordings. Among the small labels of the early LP era that recorded her were Polymusic and Renaissance. The latter made a notable recording of Bizet's *Pearl Fishers* with her, later reissued on Cetra Gold in the late 1960s. For Angel, a major label, Dobbs made a recording of duets from *Rigoletto* with Jan Peerce.

On November 9, 1956, Dobbs made her debut with the Metropolitan Opera opposite Peerce in *Rigoletto.* Thus, Dobbs, only the third black American ever to sing at the Met, became the first one to sing a romantic lead at the Met. Following this, she went on a six-month tour of Britain, Scandinavia, Australia, New Zealand, Ireland, Israel, and the Soviet Union. In Israel she toured with the Israel Philharmonic Orchestra. In the Soviet Union, as part of the cultural exchange program of the United States government, she became the first Met artist ever to perform at the Bolshoi, where she played in Rossini's *The Barber of Seville.* The part of Rosina allowed her to choose any song predating Rossini to be interpolated into the singing lessons in the third act. Dobbs went to the trouble to learn Alabieff's ''The Nightingale'' in Russian. Surprised by the gesture, the Moscow audience went wild.

Dobbs returned to the Met on December 22, 1957, to play the lead opposite Richard Tucker in *Lucia di Lammermoor.* The next day she married Swedish journalist Bengt Janzon, who was the director of public relations for the Royal Opera in Stockholm. She had met him during one of what became many appearances as a guest artist there. When she was not traveling, she had made her home in Madrid. Now she moved her base of operations to Stockholm. This enabled her to concentrate on performing in those smaller European houses where her poised, bell-like voice carried well. Recording flattered her silvery voice, but, in live performance, it did not always overcome large orchestras in extremely large halls, like the Met, which seats 4,400 persons. This eventually limited her appearances at the Met to performances in the late 1950s and early 1960s in *Ariadne auf Naxos,* Verdi's *Un Ballo in Maschera,* Mozart's *Don Giovanni,* and *Tales of Hoffman.* She recorded the roles of both Olympia and Antonia in *Tales of Hoffman* in 1958 for Epic, a record label of American Columbia. In Europe, halls like Glyndebourne, which seats only one thousand, were perfect for her Constanze in *The Abduction From the Seraglio,* but she also continued to play large halls for solo recitals.

Dobbs's choice of material for recitals was fairly adventurous. In her first Town Hall solo recital, she had performed contemporary songs by Egk, Milhaud, Rodrigo, and Roussel as well as older music. In the Royal Festival Hall in London, she sang songs by Stravinsky, Respighi, and Castelnuovo-Tedesco in addition to baroque arias. In other venues, she performed works by Villa-Lobos and by contemporary United States composers as well as Louisiana Creole slave songs arranged by Camille Nickerson and African-American spirituals. Black American repertoire always played a large part in the recitals that Hurok scheduled for her on historically black American college campuses

During the first seven years of their marriage, Janzon accompanied Dobbs as her press agent. Traveling constantly, she was constrained to develop her own method for practicing. Before leaving Stockholm, she would record her own accompaniment at the piano. She would then practice along with the tape and later play it to accompanists in order to show them how she wanted it to go in recital. In this way her piano training gave her an advantage on the road (Barry, 5). In later years, Dobbs has traveled with members of her American family and summered with Janzon in Sweden.

At the high point of her career, in January 1962, Dobbs returned triumphantly to her hometown. During the previous year, the Met, as usual, had visited the Fox Theater in Atlanta (but without her in the cast). Black patrons had been required, as usual, to sit separately and use side entrances and the fire escapes. Dobbs vowed not to sing under those circumstances. The next year she gave her first citywide concert, with no segregation in seating, at the Municipal Auditorium. She was also given the key to the city. In 1963 she gave another successful recital at the auditorium.

In Britain Dobbs performed at the Edinburgh Festival and in Ireland at the Wexford Festival. On the Continent, she became a regular at the Hamburg and Munich Operas and at the Comische Opera in Berlin. In Vienna, the critics hailed her as the ''queen of Schubert lieder,'' which she regarded as the highest musical compliment she had received up to that time. She also appeared in opera in Copenhagen, Oslo, and Helsinki as well as in Stockholm. King Gustav Adolf of Sweden decorated her with the Order of the North Star following a gala performance at Covent Garden before the British and Swedish royal families. She began an association in the early 1960s with the two-hundred-year-old Drottningholm Court Theater outside Stockholm that enabled her to play a significant role in the revival of authentic performance practice in baroque and classical music. Perhaps the most perfectly preserved eighteenth-century court theater anywhere, the 350-seat Drottningholm was an ideal venue for chamber opera, and Dobbs had the ideal voice for it. Dobbs became a great favorite there, appearing regularly in its summer productions. Her greatest success there was as Constanze in *The Abduction From the Seraglio,* which she recorded in an English-language version for Angel with Nicolai Gedda, conducted by Yehudi Menuhin. Other recordings from the 1960s include a recital of French and German songs accompanied by the great Gerald Moore, *Don Giovanni* for Columbia, and the part of Olympia in Deutsche Grammophon's *Tales of Hoffmann* excerpts. Her active repertoire included more than two hundred concert pieces and twenty operatic roles.

Dobbs's career at its peak was principally a European one. Since then she has become more associated with the American music scene. In 1967 she returned to Atlanta for two months, performing in the short-lived local opera company under Blanche Thebom. This was the first time that Dobbs had taken her white husband with her into the South. After making a Third World tour in 1968, she began to divide most of her performing between Sweden in the summer and the United States during the rest of the year. In the 1972-1973 school year, she appeared widely in recital on American college campuses. She taught at the University of Texas in Austin. With the New Jersey Schola Cantorum, she performed in Franz Xavier Brixi's *Missa Solemnis* in D and at Carnegie Hall in Charpentier's *Te Deum* under Abraham Kaplan.

In 1974, with the election of her nephew, Maynard Jackson, to be the first black mayor of Atlanta, Dobbs spent even more time in the United States. She sang at the inauguration. Starting in 1974, she served as artist-in-residence at Spelman College, and in 1979 she received an honorary doctor of fine arts degree from her alma mater. In 1976 she sang Villa-Lobos's *Bachianas Brasilieras No.5* and Richard Strauss's Brentano lieder with the Atlanta Symphony under Robert Shaw. She taught at the University of Illinois at Champaign-Urbana. In 1977, for two months, she returned for the fourth time to Australia, and she sang with Nicolai Gedda in *The Pearl Fishers* with Lyric Opera, the new permanent company in Atlanta. In 1978, she, who had been among the first recipients of the Anderson Scholarship, sang before President Jimmy Carter at the awarding of the Congressional Gold Medal to Marian Anderson. In 1979 she appeared in Haiti at Richard Long's Black Arts Festival. The next year she sang for the inauguration of an exhibition about her career at the Library of Congress. She sang at the Kennedy Center for Black History Month. The Atlanta NAACP awarded her the James Weldon Johnson Award in Fine Arts in 1983. In 1989 she was elected to the board of directors of the Metropolitan Opera. She has been teaching at Howard University, Washington, D.C., since the 1970s.

References

Amistad Research Center News 2 (September 1973). 1.

Barry, Naomi. "Practice a Problem for Soprano." *New York Herald-Tribune*, 13 August 1965.

Gardiner, Eunice. "Mattiwilda Means Charm and Great Dignity." (Sydney, Australia) *Daily Telegraph*, 17 July 1955.

Gramophone, June 1954.

Look 33 (2 December 1969).

Press (Christchurch, New Zealand), 14 May 1968.

Stage, 17 June 1954.

Collections

The Dobbs Family Papers, the principal source for this essay, are in the Amistad Research Center at Tulane University, New Orleans.

Lester Sullivan

Dorothy Donegan

(1922-)

Pianist

Dorothy Donegan is one of America's great piano virtuosos. Her interests range from classical music, which she studies and practices daily, to jazz performances in clubs with a piano, drums, and bass ensemble, which is how she earns her living. Although she performed the Grieg concerto in 1972 with the New Orleans Philharmonic and the Southeast Symphony in Los Angeles, only rarely does she perform straight classical music for an audience. Still, she is noted for borrowing from classical pieces. As Whitney Balliett explains, "She may flavor "The Man I Love," say, with bits and pieces of Chopin, Fats Waller, Rachmaninoff, and Nathaniel Dett" (40). Her career has been buffeted by the trends that have affected all of jazz: the decline of the relatively small audience for this type of music when rock and roll came in and the refusal of the major recording companies to record and support this music, along with a modest revival beginning in the seventies.

Donegan was born on April 6, 1922, in Chicago, the daughter of Donazell Donegan and Ella (Day) Donegan. This was a second marriage for Ella Donegan, and there was a younger brother, Leon, who died about 1987. Coming from Huntsville, Alabama, Donazell Donegan was a cook on the

Chicago, Burlington, and Quincy Railroad; he died of a stroke in 1958. The family lived in a large apartment, and the mother added to the family income by renting out rooms. She supported her daughter's music studies and served as her first business manager. Ella Donegan died in 1972.

Donegan began taking piano lessons when she was eight years old; for the first five years she studied with Alfred N. Simms, who also taught Cleo Brown. She then studied with Rudolph Gantz, the head of the Chicago Musical College, and during her high school years was also under the tutelage of Walter Dyett. At the age of ten, Dorothy Donegan was playing organ in a church; by the age of fourteen, she was earning money by playing in small clubs on the South Side, eventually denting the color barrier by working at Costello's Grill downtown. In January 1942, Dorothy Donegan cut *Piano Boogie* for Bluebird, her first recording and the only one on that label.

Her professional concert debut was in 1943 at Orchestral Hall in Chicago; she presented Grieg and Rachmaninoff in the first half of her program and jazz in the second half. (She may have been the first black musician to play in the hall.) The concert received a front page review by Claudia Cassidy in the *Chicago Tribune,* and her reputation brought her to the attention of Art Tatum, who served as a mentor, showing her how to do things on the piano. A story in *Ebony* claims the concert was the result of a $1,500 bet by Garrick Stage Bar owner Joe Sherman that she could outdraw Vladimir Horowitz at the hall: Sherman is said to have won (''Is Jazz Going Highbrow?'' 17). In 1944 she and her mother went to the West Coast, where Donegan appeared in a duet with Eugene Rodgers in the United Artists film, *Sensations of 1945*. In addition to appearing in clubs in Los Angeles and New York, she also traveled with a Moms Mabley show for a while about this time. In the mid-forties she cut a dozen or so records for Continental.

In 1946 Dorothy Donegan appeared in the New York show *Star Time* and the following year took a nondramatic role in a play that closed before reaching Broadway. She married John McClain in 1948; they had one son, John, born in 1954. The McClains ran their own club in Los Angeles for a year, and Dorothy Donegan recorded for several companies during the decade. In retirement when her son was born, she studied sociology at the University of Southern California. This first marriage ended in 1958, but she was to marry twice more, once to William Miles and once to Walter Eady, and give birth to another son, Donovan Eady. Her comment is, ''I married two more men after that [first marriage], and I think I've been married three times too many. Every time there were dry periods in the sixties and seventies, I'd marry again. Then, when I got work, I'd drift away'' (Balliett, 40).

Pianist Plays at Top Clubs

During the forties and fifties, Dorothy Donegan generally had work. According to Reitz, she had in the fifties ''a 10-year contract with the Embers, a posh supper club on East 54th Street, to play 16 weeks a year'' (8-9). *Time* magazine adds that the salary was $2,000 a week (''Wild But Polished,'' 78). Other top clubs in New York, Chicago, and Los Angeles sought her services. It was while she was working at the Garrick Stage Bar in the early forties that she met Alberta Hunter, who was also appearing there. Hunter would say to her, ''Life is beautiful if you save your money'' (Balliett, 40). Donegan's kind of playing and showmanship were well suited to intimate clubs. She tells a story of her performance style at a period when a twenty percent tax on entertainment was applied if a club had dancers or singers in addition to musicians:

> I was doing a lot of wiggling then, moving my derrière around and snapping my fingers and carrying on, and the I.R.S. decided I was entertainment and put the tax on. That hurt business, so I went to the musicians' union, and the union asked, can she wiggle as long as she's playing? And they said yes, and took the tax off. A wiggle never hurt anybody (Balliett, 40).

Time magazine included ''horrible grimaces and irrepressible feet'' in the opening sentence of its story it devoted to her in 1942 (''Hazel's Rival?'' 73). Her stated determination to eschew mugging during her performances earned her a cover story and s story in the July 1946 *Ebony*.

This promise was hardly kept—she is still ''an electric performer, and a transcendental clown'' (Balliett, 37)—but she achieved eminence among her peers. Of her style and opinion of her fellow jazz pianists, *Ebony* wrote in 1958:

> She was once known for her souped-up versions of the classics. Today she plays a modern, hard-driving style with overtones of Art Tatum. She has little respect for the current crop of male and female jazz pianists. Of the males, she says: ''I've snowed them all under except one (the late Art Tatum). Most of them play like women'' (''Queen of the Keys,'' 84).

With the sixties and the advent of rock, small rooms went into decline, and like many other musicians, Dorothy Donegan found it increasingly difficult to find work. At the time of the breakup of her marriage to Eady in 1974, her career began to pick up again as work once again became available. She made sensational appearances at the ''Women Blow Their Own Horns'' program of the Kool Jazz Festival in New York City in 1981 and at the *Festival Der Frauen* in Hamburg in 1988.

Whitney Balliett describes Donegan's current style and technique:

> On her fast numbers she swings as hard as any pianist who ever lived, and on slow ballads she is delicate as a rose. Her technique rivals Art Tatum's. She is completely ambidextrous, her runs plummet like mercury, and she can play so fast that the individual beats merge into a kind of rhythmic glissando. She can produce thunder in

her low registers and seconds later, that leggiero touch in her high registers (40).

Dorothy Donegan is still an active musician. She lives in west Los Angeles. The recent issue of a compact disc, *Dorothy Romps: A Piano Retrospective 1953-1979* (Rosetta Records: CD1318) in the *Foremothers* series, makes a selection of her recordings readily available.

References

Balliett, Whitney. "Wonder Woman." *New Yorker* 60 (18 February 1991): 37-38. 40-41.

"Dorothy Donegan Wins In Her Son's Custody Battle." *Jet* 46 (5 September 1974): 46.

"Hazel's Rival?" *Time* 40 (16 November 1942): 73. Includes photograph.

"Is Jazz Going Highbrow?" *Ebony* 1 (July 1946): 15-19. Cover photograph and photographs with story.

Kinkle, Roger D. *The Complete Encyclopedia of Popular Music and Jazz: 1900-1950*. Vol. 2. New Rochelle, N.Y.: Arlington House, 1974.

"Queen of the Keys." *Ebony* 13 (March 1958): 84-88.

"People Are Talking About." *Jet* 34 (27 June 1968): 43.

Reitz, Rosetta. Record notes for *Dorothy Romps: A Piano Retrospective 1953-1979*. Vol. 9 in *Foremothers, Women's Heritage Series*. CD 1318. 1991.

Southern, Eileen. *Biographical Dictionary of Afro-American and African Musicians*. Westport, Conn.: Greenwood Press, 1982.

"Wild But Polished." *Time* 72 (3 November 1958): 78. Includes photograph.

Robert L. Johns

Anna Murray Douglass

(1813-1882)

Activist

Renowned freedom-fighter and orator Frederick Douglass is so positioned in the annals of black and American history that he virtually overshadows the significance of the woman in his life who, as his silent partner, helped make possible his escape from slavery, provided the stability and balance needed to facilitate his work, and played an important role in the abolitionist movement from the 1840s to the end of slavery. Anna Murray Douglass was more than the faithful and dutiful wife depicted in some accounts of Frederick Douglass. She was the family accountant, giving detailed attention to their financial health when her husband scarcely had time to do so. She was a recognized worker in the antislavery societies of Lynn and Boston, Massachusetts, and above all, according to Spradling, she was guardian to more than four hundred runaways who traveled through the Underground Railroad station in their Rochester, New York, home whether or not Frederick Douglass was present. She made a position in history for herself by "creating the conditions favorable for Douglass's development into a great personality and powerful force in American life" (Render, 523).

Anna Murray Douglass

Anna Murray was one of twelve children born to slave parents Bambarra and Mary Murray, and the first of their five children to be freeborn. Born in 1813, she "escaped by one month the fate of her older brothers and sisters born in slavery" (Foner, 21). When she was seventeen years old, Anna Murray left the family's eastern shore home in Denton, Caroline County, Maryland, and went to work as a maid for the Montells, a well-to-do French family in Baltimore, where she remained for two years. She spent the next seven years with the Wells family. She moved in the small circle of the East Baltimore Improvement Society where free blacks were regularly seen, but slaves were excluded unless they found a way to penetrate the invisible boundaries of the society. Anna Murray was particularly interested in Frederick Augustus Washington Bailey, later Frederick Douglass, who had entered the choice circle. Bailey's freedom became essential to the young couple, who had fallen in love and planned to marry. Having saved her earnings for nine years, Anna Murray reasoned that the most appropriate use of the money would be to finance Frederick Bailey's escape to freedom. According to Rosetta Sprague Douglass, the Douglasses's daughter, Anna Murray "had previously sold one of her feather beds to assist in defraying the expenses of the flight from bondage" (Douglass, 95). He wanted to marry her as a free man, not as chattel.

Bailey escaped from Baltimore on Monday, September 3, 1838, with the assistance a seafaring friend named Stanley, who provided the appropriate clothing to disguise Bailey as a sailor and "protection" papers that allowed him to travel in the slave state of Maryland. He arrived in New York City on September 4, lonely, afraid, and unable to move about freely, since he was a fugitive slave. He hid in the home of David Ruggles, the black secretary of the New York Vigilance Committee, and within a few days Anna Murray joined him. The Reverend James W. C. Pennington, an escaped slave from Maryland, married the couple on September 15, twelve days after Bailey's escape. Rosetta Douglass Sprague said that "a new plum colored silk dress was her wedding gown" (95). The couple were sent to New Bedford, Massachusetts, two days later, where Bailey hoped his skills as a caulker in the shipyards would provide their livelihood. The couple first assumed the name Johnson, as did most escaped slaves from the Baltimore area. In New Bedford, according to plan, they were to meet a prosperous family, the Nathan Johnsons. It was Johnson who introduced the couple as Douglass, not Johnson or Bailey—Frederick had already dropped his two middle names. Thus, Frederick and Anna Douglass began a new life in freedom. A graphic account of their journey to New Bedford is given in Douglass's autobiography, *My Bondage and My Freedom.*

Anna Douglass lacked the advantages of a good education in her youth, but she was a woman of strong character and much natural intelligence. In the new marriage she found it essential to continue work as a washerwoman to supplement the family's income. She brought to their New Bedford home the clothing, bed linen, kitchen essentials, and other furnishings from her Baltimore residence and made their two rooms on Elm Street overlooking Buzzards Bay as comfortable as possible. Once they were fairly well settled, Frederick Douglass became involved in community activities. His church involvement led him to become a local preacher. He also renewed his abolitionist activities and joined the New Bedford blacks in their abolitionist efforts. Anna Murray Douglass devoted herself to her husband and family, and also continued activities that were essential to her—activities for the advancement of the black race. Of her value to their early life, Frederick Douglass wrote to Thomas Auld, his former master:

> Instead of finding my companion a burden, she was truly a helpmeet. She went to live at service, and I to work on the wharf, and though we toiled hard the first winter, we never lived more happily (Letter to Thomas Auld, cited in Foner, 340).

References to Anna Douglass's life are in scattered sources, the fullest account having been prepared by her daughter Rosetta Douglass Sprague in "Anna Murray-Douglass—My mother As I Recall Her," published in the *Journal of Negro History,* 8 January 1923. According to Sprague, Frederick Douglass was absent from the home much of 1845 and 1846. During her husband's absence, Anna Douglass sustained the family by binding shoes. She also moved in the antislavery circles of Lynn and Boston, Massachusetts, and was recognized for her "sterling qualities." "No circle was felt to be complete without her presence." Women gathered weekly to prepare for the annual Antislavery Fair held at Boston's Faneuil Hall, where Anna Douglass was in charge of refreshments. She saved money from her shoe-binding business to donate to the antislavery cause, yet she always set aside some funds for hard times. Her skill as a financial manager was not unnoticed by her husband:

> I have often heard my father speak in admiration of mother's executive ability. During his absence abroad, he sent, as he could, support for his family, and on his coming home he supposed there would be some bills to settle. One day while talking over their affairs, mother arose and quietly going to the bureau drawer produced a Bank [sic] book with the sums deposited just in the proportion father had sent, the book also containing deposit of her own earnings—and not a debt had been contracted during his absence (Sprague, 96).

For a woman with no formal education and little earning power, Anna Douglass showed unusual capability for financial management.

While living in Massachusetts, the Douglasses had four children. Rosetta, the oldest, was born in New Bedford on June 24, 1839, and on December 24, 1863, married Nathan Sprague. Lewis H., the eldest son, was born on October 9, 1840, and on October 7, 1869, married Helen Amelia Loguen, daughter of Joshua W. Loguen, bishop of the AME Zion church. Frederick, Jr., the second son, was born in New Bedford on March 3, 1842, and in 1871 married Virginia L. Hewlett of Cambridge. Charles Remond Douglass was born in Lynn, Massachusetts, October 21, 1844, and on September 21, 1866, married at Rochester, New York. His first wife died in 1878, and on December 30, 1888, he married Laura A. Haley of Canandaigua, New York. The youngest child, Annie, was born in 1849 after their move to Rochester and died there when she was eleven years old. The children were educated in the Rochester schools but not without their father's fight for their admission.

In 1847 the Douglasses moved to Rochester, New York, where Frederick Douglass continued his speaking engagements and established his newspaper, the *Frederick Douglass Paper,* later known as the *North Star.* Anna Douglass regretted the move and the necessity for leaving her old friends, but she did see them on occasion, such as in Syracuse when the Douglasses were the guests of Unitarian minister Samuel J. May. Wendell Phillips, William Lloyd Garrison, Sydney Howard Gay, and others were in the parlor to greet them. In Rochester she continued her antislavery activities and faced the rampant prejudice in the 1840s. She accompanied her husband on very few of his short trips, preferring instead to attend to her own antislavery interests, maintain the home, and tend to her husband's needs. Although by this time they had a "home laundress," Anna Douglass was still a dedicated home manager who relieved her husband of all responsibilities of management, particularly as the home was "increased in size and in its appointments." On the matter of the mother's care of the father, Sprague said:

> It was her pleasure to know that when he stood up before an audience that his linen was immaculate and that she had made it so, for, no matter how well the laundry was done for the family, she must with her own hands smooth the tucks in father's linen and when he was on a long journey she would forward at a given point a fresh supply (97).

Underground Railroad Station Established

At an early age, the Douglasses's sons "aided in piloting runaway slaves to Canada through the Underground Railroad" (Gregory, 200). The Douglass home had become a vital link in the Underground Railroad for many slaves who traveled northward to freedom. Their nine-room home in Rochester included a suite of rooms that could easily be turned over to guests who came swiftly, quietly, and secretly in the night. Located on the outskirts of Rochester, the home was easily accessible to escaping slaves who in 1849 came in great numbers. History has yet to emphasize the value of Anna Douglass to the Underground Railroad and her role in aiding runaway slaves. Her first role in this venture came in 1838 when she financed Frederick Douglass's escape. In Rochester she provided for the comfort of many more runaways who sought refuge in the Douglass station. Rosetta Douglass Sprague observed: "It was no unusual occurrence for mother to be called up at all hours of the night, cold and hot as the case may be, to prepare supper for a hungry lot of fleeing humanity" (98). Since Frederick Douglass was away often, doubtless the primary responsibility for the fugitives' care and protection fell on Anna Douglass. In recognition of her work, Dannett called her an "abolitionist hostess" (252). But she was more than a hostess: she was an active agent on the Underground Railroad, and she was active in work to advance the race throughout her lifetime. In 1872 fire destroyed the well-appointed Rochester home and the memorabilia from the early days of housekeeping.

Although she could not read then, Anna Douglass was keenly interested in the *North Star* and encouraged Frederick Douglass to teach the business to their sons at an early age. At ages nine and eleven, the boys learned to do printing and also were employed to carry and mail papers.

The life of Anna Douglass was what she chose to make it, and she was unconcerned with the dictates of society. The protection of Frederick Douglass's interests was one of her primary goals. Of her mother's care of the father, Rosetta Douglass Sprague said:

> Father was mother's honored guest. He was from home so often that his home comings were events that she thought worthy of extra notice, and caused renewed activity. Every thing was done that could be to add to his comfort (98).

Frederick Douglass and his wife were at different intellectual poles. Arna Bontemps noted that, although early in their married life she got along well in Douglass's absence, "she welcomed him home with a kind of homage usually reserved for visiting Princes. She was neither proud nor ashamed of her literacy, her lack of interest in intellectual subjects" (90). While he appreciated her housewifely qualities and financial acumen, and apparently relied on her for providing such stability in their life, Frederick Douglass climbed to literary and oratorical heights while Anna Douglass chose to remain unlettered. A hired tutor was not able to change her attitude toward formal training, and in time, she barely learned to read. Instead, she chose to have daughter Rosetta read to her. The requirements for social graces often displayed at teas and other gatherings were of little concern to Anna Douglass—she did things her way in Rochester and continued to do so after the move to Washington, D.C., in 1872. The Douglass family lived at 316 A Street, N.E. until 1877, when for $6,700 they purchased a hilltop house that they called Cedar Hill, located across the Anacostia River and overlooking the Capitol.

Anna Douglass was a woman of quiet reserve, retiring disposition, and grim humor. She was also a strict disciplinarian. Through the years, the Douglass home was often filled with guests who ranged from runaway slaves to the highest dignitaries, such as Elizabeth Cady Stanton, Fredrika Bremer, and James Russell Lowell, yet Anna Douglass would accommodate each and make them welcome. But her reaction to white people, particularly after the move to Rochester, was unrelaxed, and she had little capacity for interracial mingling. No doubt she was easily misunderstood, for "she could not be known all at once, she had to be studied" (Sprague, 99). She was strong in her likes and dislikes (she disliked small talk and opposed drinking alcohol). She was discerning in her appraisal of character. In physical appearance, she was called "undistinguished." She was described by Fredrika Bremer, as "dark, stout and plain" (Bremer, *The Homes of the New World,* quoted in Quarles, 101). "Her straight black hair and her inexpressive features gave her face an Indian cast," said Quarles (101), and Minnie Blackall noted that invariably she would wear a "dark cotton dress and a red bandanna on her head" (Minnie Blackall Bishop to Charles H. Wiltsie, 25 February 1919, manuscript). She addressed her husband as "Mr. Douglass" and he referred to her affectionately as "Mother" (Render, 526).

In 1882 Anna Douglass, stricken with paralysis for four weeks, still directed the management of the home in Washington, D.C. ''The orders were given with precision and they were obeyed with alacrity. Her fortitude and patience up to ten days of her death were very great'' (Sprague, 100). Her strength in those final days of her life helped the family to bear the burden of her death.

References

Bishop, Minnie Blackall. Interview with Charles H. Wiltsie. Rochester Public Library. Manuscript.

Bontemps, Arna. *Free at Last: The Life of Frederick Douglass.* New York: Dodd, Mead, 1971.

Douglass, Frederick. *My Bondage and My Freedom.* New York: Miller, Orton and Mulligan, 1855.

Foner, Philip. *The Life and Writings of Frederick Douglass: Early Years, 1817-1849.* New York: International Publishers, 1950.

''Frederick Douglass.'' National Historic Site. Washington, D.C.: National Park Service, U.S. Department of the Interior, n.d.

Gregory, James M. *Frederick Douglass, the Orator.* Springfield, Mass.: Willey, 1893. 199-206.

Quarles, Benjamin. *Frederick Douglass.* New York: Atheneum, 1968.

Render, Sylvia Lyons. ''Afro-American Women: The Outstanding and the Obscure.'' *Quarterly Journal of the Library of Congress* 32 (October 1975): 307-21. Reprinted in *Black Women's History: Theory and Practice.* Vol. 1. Edited by Darlene Clark Hine. Brooklyn: Carlson Publishing, 1990. Portrait, p. 524.

Spradling, Mary Mace. *In Black and White.* 3rd ed. Supplement. Detroit: Gale Research, 1985.

Sprague, Rosetta Douglass. ''Anna Murray-Douglass—My Mother As I Recall Her.'' *Journal of Negro History* 8 (January 1923): 93-101.

Sterling, Dorothy, ed. *We Are Your Sisters: Black Women in the Nineteenth Century.* New York: Norton, 1984. Portrait, p. 136.

Jessie Carney Smith

Sarah Mapps Douglass

(1806-1882)

Educator, activist

Born in Philadelphia in 1806, abolitionist and educator Sarah Mapps Douglass was the daughter of Robert Douglass and Grace Bustill Douglass. From the turn of the century, the Bustill, Mapps, and Douglass families were prominent in Philadelphia circles. Douglass's maternal grandfather, Cyrus Bustill, a Quaker, who owned a bakery, operated a school and was one of the early members of the Free African Society, the first Afro-American benevolent organization. Her mother operated a Quaker millinery store next to the family bakery. Douglass's only brother, Robert, Jr., was a talented artist educated at the Philadelphia Academy of the Fine Arts.

Douglass received an unusually fine education at a time when all women were denied admission to any college and black women had difficulty obtaining an adequate secondary school education. She was privately tutored for several years; later, she entered the ''colored'' school that her mother and the wealthy Negro shipbuilder James Forten established in 1819 to provide their children with a better education than they could obtain in any of the other schools open to them.

Douglass Founds School for Black Youth

During the 1820s Douglass established a school for black children, one of ten such schools available in Philadelphia at that time. While the school was to be self-supporting, by 1838 the level of funding was insufficient to continue as Douglass wished. In March of that year the Philadelphia Female Anti-Slavery Society assumed its financial support. Douglass's mother had helped found that society in 1833, and Douglass probably joined soon after its inception. She attended a number of conventions, and by 1938 she had served the group as member of the board of directors, of the committee on annual fairs, of the education committee, librarian, and corresponding secretary. Her work in the society led to friendships with other members: Lucretia Mott, the wife of Robert Purvis; Charlotte Forten Grimké and her sisters Margaretta and Sarah, whose father was James Forten; and Sarah and Angelina Grimké, white abolitionists and daughters of Judge John F. Grimké, a prominent slaveowner in South Carolina. Douglass and the Grimké sisters came to be lifelong friends.

Patterns of racial segregation in Philadelphia were deep-seated and even involved the Quakers, the religious affiliation of Douglass, her mother, and her maternal grandmother. In Quaker meeting houses were special "Negro seats," or Negro pews, placed under the stairs or in a corner and guarded to keep the interracial membership from mixing. The Grimkés, also Quakers, and Douglass were appalled by the segregation. During the 1830s, some of the Quakers challenged the city's segregation practices, and Douglass's efforts in this cause were significant. When William Bassett of Lynn, Massachusetts, undertook a plan to bring his fellow New England Quakers into the antislavery movement, Douglass provided him with important information on the Arch Street Meeting's segregated seating practices. She also supplied Sarah Grimké with information that Grimké used in writing her 1837 statement "The subject of prejudice against color amongst the Society of Friends in the United States," written in response to her censure by the Quakers for insisting on sitting beside Douglass and her mother at services.

When Angelina Grimké and Theodore Weld, a prominent abolitionist, were married in May 1838, Douglass and her mother were among the Negro guests at the wedding. The Philadelphia press called the incident an intolerable act of abolitionists' "amalgamated" practices. Two days later, an angry mob burned down Pennsylvania Hall, the state antislavery society's newly built headquarters, and set fire to the Shelter for Colored Orphans. There were other riotous acts in Philadelphia, and the decade of the 1830s for the Douglass family was marked by various incidents of subtle and overt racial oppression and discrimination. Nonetheless, the friendship between the Welds and Douglass continued, and she became a frequent visitor in their home. She also regularly attended Quaker meetings, though decades passed before the Quakers altered their discriminatory practices.

Meanwhile, Douglass continued her teaching career. In 1853, when the Institute of Colored Youth opened in a wealthy Negro neighborhood, she was appointed head of the girls' primary department. The institute was a Quaker-supported school and the forerunner of Cheney (Pennsylvania) State College; it became known as a teacher-training institute for many public school teachers. Douglass remained there until her retirement in 1877. The quality of her teaching was exemplary, and her scholastic standards were so high that her students often received academic recognition at the end of the year. When the twelfth annual commencement was held on May 5, 1864, four of her students received cash awards—one for excellence in mathematics, one for superiority in Greek and Latin, one for good grades, and the other for diligence and good conduct.

On July 23, 1855, she married William Douglass, rector of St. Thomas Protestant Episcopal Church, a widower with several children. After her husband's death in 1861, Douglass devoted her time to antislavery activities and continued her teaching. She wrote articles and regularly contributed to *The Anglo-African*. When the Civil War ended, freedmen's aid groups developed all over the North. Douglass became vice-chairman of the Woman's Pennsylvania Branch of the American Freedmen's Aid Commission.

Douglass's prime contribution to society was in the training of black youth of Philadelphia and guiding them to instruct others who followed. She lived her life according to her convictions that education would shape a better world for her race and that racism in society had to be eliminated. She died in Philadelphia on September 8, 1882.

References

Dannett, Sylvia G. L. *Profiles of Negro Womanhood*. Vol. I. Chicago: Educational Heritage, 1964.

Lerner, Gerda. *Black Women in White America*. New York: Random House, 1972.

———."Sarah Mapps Douglass." *Notable American Women*. Vol. I. Cambridge: Belknap Press, 1971.

Logan, Rayford W. "Sarah Mapps Douglass Douglass." *Dictionary of American Negro Biography*. Edited by Rayford W. Logan and Michael R. Winston. New York: Norton, 1982.

Jessie Carney Smith

Rita Dove

(1952 -)

Poet, writer

Awarded the Pulitzer Prize for poetry in 1987, Rita Dove is widely considered one of the best contemporary American poets. Rita Dove was born on August 28, 1952, in Akron, Ohio, the daughter of Ray Dove, a chemist, and Elvira (Hord) Dove. She graduated summa cum laude from Miami University in Oxford, Ohio, in 1973 and received an M.F.A. in creative writing from the Iowa Writers Workshop at the University of Iowa in 1977. In addition to the Pulitzer, Dove has received numerous major awards, including fellowships from the National Endowment for the Arts and the Guggenheim Foundation and honorary doctorates from Miami University and Knox College in Illinois.

Rita Dove's first volume of poetry, *The Yellow House on the Corner* (Pittsburgh: Carnegie Mellon University Press, 1980), was published when she was twenty-seven years old. Her second volume, *Museum* (Carnegie Mellon University Press), was published in 1983. Both collections "won praise from reviewers for their technical excellence and unusual breadth of subject matter" (*Contemporary Literary Criticism*, 152).

Thomas and Beulah (Carnegie Mellon University Press, 1986), Dove's third and Pulitzer Prize-winning collection, interweaves personal and social history in a series of short lyric poems. Dove describes Thomas and Beulah as characters "based very loosely on my grandparents' lives" (152). The book, which spans the years 1919-1968 in Akron, Ohio, is divided into two parts. The first is written from Thomas's perspective and the second from Beulah's perspective. Although Thomas and Beulah share thirty-nine years of marriage and raise four children, their inner lives rarely intersect. Critics have praised Dove's ability to represent "the opposing sides of conflicts she deals with" (McDowell, 61). In her poetry she "gathers the various facts of this life and presents them in ways that jar our lazy assumptions. She gives voice to many positions and many characters" (McDowell, 61).

Dove describes herself as committed to combining "historical occurrences with the epiphanal quality of the lyric poem" (*Contemporary Authors,* 115). If her dramatization of characters, personal relationships, and social events is powerful, "wise and affectionate," her mastery of lyrical verse is brilliant. Critic Emily Grosholz observes that "Dove can turn her poetic sights on just about anything and make the language shimmer" (160-61). Dove typically focuses on the tragedies, joys, and dreams of "ordinary" black people in the Midwest. However, her fourth collection of poetry, *Grace Notes* (New York: Norton, 1989), contains a variety of short poems ranging in topics from intimate reflections on sexuality, motherhood, and aging to meditations on history, art, and international politics. As in her earlier poetry, Dove communicates powerfully through her incisive use of concrete details. She expresses her philosophy of poetry in the final stanza of a brief poem entitled "Ars Poetica:"

> What I want is this poem to be small,
> a ghost town
> on the larger map of wills.
> Then you can pencil me in as a hawk:
> a traveling x-marks-the-spot (48).

In addition to her volumes of poetry, Dove has published a collection of short stories, *Fifth Sunday* (Baltimore: Callaloo Fiction Series, 1985), and has a novel forthcoming. Her work has appeared in dozens of magazines and anthologies. A prolific and highly-disciplined writer, Rita Dove also has taught creative writing for more than a decade at various universities, including Arizona State and Tuskegee. She travels widely, believing that travel is "a good way to gain different perspectives and to avoid becoming complacent" (*Contemporary Authors,* 115). She was awarded a fellowship to write in Germany in 1980 and has also traveled in Israel and southern Europe.

Currently a professor of English at the University of Virginia, Dove lives in Charlottesville with her husband, Fred Viebahn (a novelist), and their daughter, Aviva.

References

Contemporary Authors. Vol. 109. Detroit: Gale Research, 1983.

Contemporary Literary Criticism. Vol. 50. Detroit: Gale Research, 1987. Photograph, p. 152.

Dove, Rita. *Fifth Sunday.* Baltimore: Callaloo Fiction Series, 1985.

———. *Grace Notes.* New York: Norton, 1989. Photograph on jacket.

———. *Museum.* Pittsburgh: Carnegie Mellon University Press, 1983.

———. *Thomas and Beulah.* Pittsburgh: Carnegie Mellon University Press, 1986. Photograph on back cover.

———. *The Yellow House on the Corner.* Pittsburgh: Carnegie Mellon University Press, 1980. Photograph on back cover.

Grosholz, Emily. "Marriages and Partings." *Hudson Review* 40 (Spring 1987): 157-64.

McDowell, Robert. "The Assembling Vision of Rita Dove." *Callaloo* 9 (Winter 1986): 61-70.

Kari Winter

Shirley Graham Du Bois

(1904-1977)

Political activist, writer, playwright, composer, stage director

Though Shirley Graham Du Bois may be known best as the second wife of prominent scholar, author, editor and activist W. E. B. Du Bois, her own accomplishments should not be overlooked. Shirley Graham was already in her forties when she married Du Bois and a well-known writer in her own right. By the time of the marriage in 1951, she had written a music drama, *Tom-Tom,* been active in the Negro Unit of the Chicago Federal Theater, written five biographies, and received three literary awards. An ardent supporter of Du Bois's work and vision, she would go on to produce eight more books and numerous articles and speeches after their marriage.

Shirley Lola Graham was the daughter of David A. Graham and Etta (Bell) Graham. She was born on November 11, 1904, in Indianapolis, Indiana, the only daughter and the oldest of five children. This date, furnished by the digests of her application for Julius Rosenwald Fund grants in 1938 and 1939, resolves some apparent difficulties with the date of

1907 in *Current Biography* (1946) and *More Junior Authors* (1963), and the date of 1906 implied by the account in her memoir of Du Bois, *His Day is Marching On* (1971), and commonly given in later sources. The statement in *Current Biography* (946) that Shirley Graham was born on a farm near Evansville, Indiana, appears to be an invention foreshadowing her efforts to seek freedom for black Americans. The farm is connected to her great-grandfather and served as a stopping place on the Underground Railroad. This great-grandfather was freed before the Civil War and purchased the farm as a result of his industry as a blacksmith. In 1963 Graham wrote that her "maternal grandfather was a Cheyenne Indian who had crossed the Mississippi River to settle in Illinois" (*More Juvenile Authors,* 103). She amplifies in *His Day is Marching On;* "Back in the late 1870s my mother's father had moved his small family from Missouri northward across open plains and settled in what was then hardly more than a farming outpost called Saint Paul."

Shirley Graham's father was an African Methodist Episcopal minister. She speaks of her and her brothers attending schools in Detroit, Chicago, Nashville, Colorado Springs, Spokane, and Seattle. She states that her earliest memories are of New Orleans and that she graduated from Lewis and Clark High School in Spokane, Washington.

In *His Day is Marching On* Shirley Graham places two important events of her youth in Colorado Springs, Colorado. In 1920, when she was thirteen, W. E. B. Du Bois came to give an address. He stayed with the family and made a tremendous impression on her. Subsequently, during her first year of high school, she wrote an editorial dealing with the YWCA's refusal to accept her for swimming classes because of her race. This classroom assignment was published in the local evening paper. It is possible that the Du Bois visit should be assigned to 1918, when she really was thirteen; otherwise, her first son would seem to be born before she normally would have finished high school.

If this change of date is correct, Graham's account of he first marriage poses no problems. "I married a year after finishing high school. In quick succession I knew the glory of motherhood and the pain of deep sorrow. Within three years I was a widow with two small sons, the younger still a baby" (*His Day is Marching On,* 37). The husband is only a name, Shadrack T. McCanns; Graham never used the name for professional purposes. The oldest son, Robert, was born on February 27, 1924, and the second, David, in May 1925. Robert died under harrowing circumstances in 1943 shortly after being rejected by the army as unfit.

From 1927 to 1928 Graham attended the Howard School of Music in Washington, D.C. Then from 1928 to 1931 she taught music at Morgan College (now Morgan State University) in Baltimore, Maryland. According to her application to the Rosenwald Fund, she earned a Certificate in French at the University of Paris in 1930; some later accounts have erroneously inflated this experience to two full years of study of music in Paris before she entered Oberlin. In 1931 she entered Oberlin College, where she obtained a bachelor's degree in 1934 and a master's degree in music history and criticism and fine arts in 1935 with a thesis on "Survivals of Africanism in Modern Music."

At first it seemed that music would be the field in which Graham made her mark. Her mother was her first teacher, but she wrote, "I came into consciousness with 'an ear for music' and soon I was able to accompany anything on the piano" (Complete Statement of Project . . . , p. 3). Her instruments were piano, pipe organ, and voice. At Oberlin she wrote a play depicting the history of black Americans from seventeenth-century Africa to present-day Harlem. The play was under consideration by the Cleveland-based Gilpin Players, when Ernst Lert, an Austrian conductor and opera director, spotted its potential as a libretto for a music drama for the Cleveland summer opera season. Graham wrote the music and *Tom-Tom* was performed at Cleveland Stadium from June 29 to July 6, 1932. An abridged version had been broadcast by NBC Radio on June 26.

After obtaining the M.A. from Oberlin in 1935, Graham spent a difficult year at Tennessee Agricultural and Industrial State College (now Tennessee State University) in Nashville. She met Du Bois again when he invited her to travel with him by car from Nashville to Lexington, Kentucky, to attend a teachers' conference. In 1936 she became supervisor of the Negro Unit of the Federal Theater in Chicago, where she gained more experience in the theater. She adapted Eugene O'Neill's *The Hairy Ape* for a black cast, worked on a black version of the *Mikado,* which became the *Swing Mikado,* and produced and wrote the music for *Little Black Sambo,* a well-received children's play. In 1938 she made a successful application for a Julius Rosenwald Fund grant; her project was to spend a year at the Yale School of Drama and to rework *Tom-Tom.*

The grant was renewed for a second year, and Graham moved in the direction of writing and directing plays: the last music we hear from Graham is the incidental music for Owen Dodson's *Garden of Time,* produced at Yale in 1939. *Coal Dust,* a three act tragedy about the struggle between management and labor, was first produced by the Gilpin Players in Cleveland in 1938 and, under the title *Dust to Earth,* by the Yale University Theater in 1941. The Gilpin Players also produced *I Gotta Home* (1940) and *Elijah's Ravens,* a three act comedy (1941). At Yale were produced *Deep Rivers,* a music-fantasy broadcast on the Mutual network (1939); *It's Morning,* a one-act comedy directed by Otto Preminger (1940); and *Track Thirteen,* a one act radio comedy broadcast on the Mutual Network (1940).

In the summer of 1940, Graham found a summer job with the Indianapolis YWCA, doing drama with classes of students. She stayed on as director of adult activities in the fall, and she had a three act comedy, *Mississippi Rainbow,* in production in Indianapolis in the spring of 1941. As the activities preceding the outbreak of the Second World War heated up, that summer she found herself doing USO work at Fort Huachuca in Arizona. This fort was beginning to have one of the largest concentrations of black soldiers in the country in a state which had practically no young black women. In late 1942 she was back in New York struggling to keep on her feet: a job working for the magazine *Common Sense*, for which she wrote the first political articles we know of from her, was only a stopgap. The overseas work for the USO she had planned on fell through. Fortunately, she had an almost unprecedented emergency two-month grant from the Rosenwald Fund, ostensibly to let her work on a play about the plight of the black soldier. She was able to find work as a field secretary for the NAACP in early 1943. Graham settled in New York, finding an apartment near Columbia University that she shared with Norma Jensen, a young white woman who also worked for the NAACP. They shared the apartment for three years, until Jensen's marriage. Then with the $6,500 Messner Award for *There Once Was a Slave* Graham was able to purchase a small house in Saint Albans on Long Island. This would be her headquarters until her marriage to Du Bois.

Author Published Series of Biographies

A Guggenheim fellowship apparently allowed her to concentrate on her writing and attend classes for two years at New York University from 1945 to 1947. With George D. Lipscomb, she had published *Dr. George Washington Carver, Scientist* in 1944, inaugurating a successful series of biographies aimed at young audiences. She would go on to write *Paul Robeson: Citizen of the World* (1946); *There Once Was a Slave*, a historical novel about Frederick Douglass which received the Messner prize (1947); *Your Most Humble Servant*, a biography of Benjamin Banister which received the Anisfield-Wolf prize (1949); *The Story of Phyllis Wheatley* (1949); *The Story of Pocahantas* (1953); *Jean Baptiste Pointe de Sable: Founder of Chicago* (1953); and *Booker T. Washington: Educator of Hand, Head, and Heart* (1955). Graham was also active in journalism and wrote at least one produced radio script. By 1950 she was established enough as an author to receive an award recognizing her achievements from the National Academy of Arts and Letters.

Graham was becoming more closely involved in politics, working for Roosevelt in 1944 and becoming a speaker at the organizing convention of the Progressive Party. The overwhelming defeat of this effort in the 1948 elections was a grave disappointment. In her opinion "democracy received a death blow in the United States in the year 1948" (*His Day is Marching On*, 105). She was to become increasingly involved in the peace movement and in other organizations which were labeled subversive during the national hysteria whipped up by the Cold War. It was this political activity that brought her into close contact with W. E. B. Du Bois.

Graham had found an apartment for Du Bois in New York when he returned to work with the NAACP after his forced retirement from Atlanta University at the age of seventy-five in 1943. The relations between the autocratic and militant Du Bois and the conservative and pragmatic leadership of the NAACP were never easy, and in 1948 the final break came. Graham and Du Bois found themselves sharing similar political views and working together in the same organizations. Nina Du Bois, his wife for fifty-five years, died early in 1950 in her Baltimore home, where she had lived since Du Bois returned to Atlanta University in 1934. By the end of the year Graham and Du Bois had decided to marry, setting the date as February 27. When Graham learned that Du Bois was to be indicted on the charge of being the agent of a foreign government, she insisted that they be married before the indictment was handed down and the marriage took place on February 14. After the ceremony was repeated on the twenty-seventh and they had honeymooned in Nassau, they engaged in extensive fundraising trips for the legal expenses of the defense. The trial later in the year ended in a judgement of acquittal from the judge.

The Du Boises bought from playwright Arthur Miller a divided house in a pleasant neighborhood in Brooklyn—this was to be their home until they left the United States permanently. There, for the most part, Shirley Graham Du Bois lent support to her husband during the difficult years of the McCarthy era. She later said:

> One of the reasons I married him . . . was because I knew he needed help. He needed somebody beside him who was in sympathy with what he was trying to do. So I married him with the intention of helping him carry on the work he was doing.
>
> At the time, I gave up all my own work: whatever I was doing seemed so insignificant compared to what he was doing that I let it all go so I could devote myself to him and his needs. He'd want a cup of coffee; I'd be there with coffee. He'd need a special book; off I'd go and find it for him (Mason, 51).

The State Department finally granted them passports again so that they could travel abroad in 1958. They spent five months in the Soviet Union and two months in China.

It was the threat of having their passports revoked that sent the Du Boises to Ghana in 1961, six months ahead of the scheduled date; the Supreme Court was to rule that Communists had to register under the Subversive Control Act, and it seemed likely that their passports would again be revoked. Fearing that they would soon be unable to leave the country, they hastened their departure even though W. E. B. Du Bois did not actually join the Communist Party until just before their departure. In Ghana W. E. B. Du Bois continued to work on the *Encyclopedia Africana* until ill-health forced his reluctant retirement in March 1963. He died on August 27, 1963, just two days before the March on Washington. He had become a citizen of Ghana on February 17 after the United States State Department refused to issue a new passport on the grounds that he was a Communist.

After Du Bois's death Shirley Graham Du Bois lived in Ghana until 1967 and then established her home in Cairo. Always working to forward the work of her husband, she continued to speak and write. In 1971, she published *His Day is Marching On*, a memoir of her husband. She then wrote

Gamal Abdel Nasser, Son of the Nile (1972); *Zulu Heart*, a novel set in South Africa (1974); *Julius K. Nyerere: Teacher of Africa* (1975); and *A Pictorial History of W. E. B. Du Bois* (1976). She traveled extensively but was barred from the United States until 1971 when she was allowed to visit for two months. During a more extensive visit in 1975, the University of Massachusetts at Amherst awarded her an honorary doctoral degree. Shirley Graham Du Bois died in Peking, China, where she had gone for cancer treatment, on March 27, 1977.

References

Black Writers. Detroit: Gale Research, 1989-. 157.

Current Biography. New York: H. W. Wilson, 1946. 221-22.

Fuller, Muriel, ed. *More Junior Authors*. New York: H. W. Wilson, 1963. Photograph, p. 103.

Graham, Shirley. Complete Statement of Project Presented to the Julius Rosenwald Foundation. Julius Rosenwald Archives, Fisk University.

———. *His Day is Marching On: A Memoir of W. E. B. Du Bois*. Philadelphia: Lippincott, 1971.

Graham, Shirley. To William Haygood, 23 November 1942. Julius Rosenwald Archives, Fisk University.

Marable, Manning. *W. E. B. Du Bois: Black Radical Democrat*. Boston: Twayne, 1986.

Mason, Deborah. "The Du Bois Legend Carries On in Cairo." *Sepia* 24 (January 1975): 45-53. Photographs.

Peterson, Bernard L., Jr. *Early Black American Playwrights and Dramatic Writers*. New York: Greenwood Press, 1990. 64-66.

———. "Shirley Graham Du Bois: Composer and Playwright." *Crisis* 84 (May 1977): 177-79.

Review of *Tom-Tom*. *Crisis* 39 (August 1932): 258. Photograph.

Southern, Eileen. *Biographical Dictionary of Afro-American and African Musicians*. Westport, Conn.: Greenwood Press, 1982. 152.

Collections

The Julius Rosenwald Archives at Fisk University contain materials dating from her 1938 grant application until the end of 1946. The Black Oral History Collection in the Fisk library includes an oral history interview with Shirley Graham Du Bois.

Robert L. Johns

Alice Dunbar-Nelson

(1875-1935)

Educator, author, journalist, social and political activist

Educator, author, and social and political activist Alice Ruth Moore Dunbar-Nelson won fame as a Harlem Renaissance poet and as the wife of Paul Laurence Dunbar. Ironically, however, she wrote far more prose than poetry and was married to Dunbar for only four years.

Dunbar-Nelson was born in New Orleans, Louisiana, on July 19, 1875. She was the younger of two daughters of Joseph Moore, a Creole seaman, and Patricia (Wright) Moore. Following her husband's disappearance, Patricia Moore continued to live in New Orleans, supporting her daughters on her earnings as a seamstress. Dunbar-Nelson received her basic education in New Orleans, graduating from high school and from the two-year teacher-training program at Straight College (now Dillard University). She later studied at Cornell University, Columbia University, the School of Industrial Art in Philadelphia, and the University of Pennsylvania, where she specialized in psychology and English educational testing. She began her teaching career in New Orleans in 1892 and, except for brief interruptions, continued teaching until 1931. In 1896, Dunbar-Nelson

Alice Dunbar-Nelson

moved to Medford, Massachusetts, with her mother, sister, and brother-in-law, James Young. Maintaining a joint home with her mother, sister, and herself as the nucleus was a practice that she observed throughout her life.

Dunbar-Nelson completed her first book, *Violets and Other Tales*, in 1895, the year that also marks the beginning of her romantic and literary relationship with Paul Laurence Dunbar. When one of her poems appeared in the Boston *Monthly Review* along with her photograph, Dunbar was so impressed that "he wrote to Miss Moore in care of the magazine, enclosing the poem 'Phyllis' dedicated to her picture" (Brawley, 62). They exchanged letters over a two-year period before finally meeting at a New York reception that a mutual friend, Victoria Earle Matthews, held for Dunbar. Already widely known in America and anticipating even greater literary fame through his scheduled readings in England, Dunbar made a commitment on their first meeting; he removed from his finger and presented to Dunbar-Nelson as symbol of their engagement—a gold ring that had belonged to his mother. The next day, February 6, 1897, Dunbar left on his reading tour. Dunbar-Nelson remained in New York City, where she accepted a public school teaching position and assisted Victoria Matthews in establishing in Harlem the White Rose Mission (later called the White Rose Home for Girls).

Dunbar Union Enhances Moore's Literary Career

On March 6, 1898, the couple were married by Bishop W. B. Derrick in New York City. Very soon after, Dunbar-Nelson left New York and joined her husband in Washington, D.C., where they enjoyed celebrity status as that city's Robert and Elizabeth Barrett Browning. Certainly, Dunbar-Nelson's literary fortunes increased during her marriage to Dunbar. They discussed and perhaps shared ideas for stories; moreover, her second book of short fiction, *The Goodness of St. Rocque* (1899), was advertised as a companion volume to Dunbar's *Poems of Cabin and Field* and published by his agent and publisher, Dodd, Mead and Company. Their happiness was soon marred, however, by Dunbar's tubercular condition and addiction to medicinal alcohol and by mutual accusations of selfishness and cruelty. Early in 1902 the Dunbars separated, thus ending both their marriage and their literary collaboration.

Following the separation, a somewhat liberated, independent Dunbar-Nelson moved to Wilmington, Delaware, where she worked at the Howard High School, first as an English and drawing instructor and subsequently as head of the English department. Her school assignments and related activities were varied and stimulating; she taught, supervised, administered programs, staged dramas, studied at universities, and published essays in professional journals. She also developed a series of intimate relationships with both women and men, including her female principal, Edwina B. Kruse; a retired U.S. Army sergeant, C. A. Fleetwood; and a fellow teacher, Henry Arthur Callis, whom she secretly married on January 19, 1910, and divorced a year later. Her third marriage in 1916, one in which she found some stability, was to Robert J. Nelson, a journalist. Unfortunately, however, a truly serene and stable life eluded Dunbar-Nelson. Opposite, warring elements within her, which operated in her bisexuality, also surfaced and can be documented in her personal and literary responses to race and to women's roles.

Dunbar-Nelson was perennially chastened and tormented by intra- and interracial difficulties. In an autobiographical essay, "Brass Ankles Speaks," she draws upon her childhood experiences of being rejected by dark girls who called her "half white nigger!" Nor did the persecution end with childhood; in high school, college, and various work assignments, "Brass Ankles" experienced rejection by whites because she was "'too white,' and not typically racial enough" and by brown-skinned coworkers who insisted that she was too white to work among her own people. During one particularly harrowing trip South, she was twice mistaken for a white woman and removed from Jim Crow cars but three times refused dining car service when black waiters "tipped off" the stewards. In short, according to Dunbar-Nelson, "The 'yaller niggers,' the 'Brass Ankles' must bear the hatred of their own and the prejudice of the white race." In her short story "Stones of the Village," Dunbar-Nelson develops a parallel dilemma for Victor Grabért who, as a child, endures social and cultural isolation. His Grandmére Grabért will not permit him to play with the black and yellow boys and, though he looks white, the white boys will not allow him to join their games. Instead, they echo the black boys' cruel taunts of "White Nigger!" While Dunbar-Nelson's fictional Grabért succumbs to the temptation of an easier life afforded those who "pass," "Brass Ankles" is proud to belong to the class characterized by E. C. Adams as "white enough to pass for white, but with a darker family background, a real love for the mother race, and no desire to be numbered among the white race." (Dunbar-Nelson, *Works*, Vol. 2, 311). On occasion, however, Dunbar-Nelson took advantage of her light complexion and passed for white, especially for convenience in traveling and in attending various events at theaters and opera houses.

Diary Records Gender and Racial Discrimination

Perhaps Dunbar-Nelson's *Diary*, a scintillating report of the years 1921 and 1926 through 1931, best summarizes her position in an era during which law and custom limited access, expectations, and opportunities for black women. In 1927, for example, she was denied a public school teaching position in Washington, D.C., after her physical examination revealed trace amounts of albumin and a fluctuating blood pressure. Dunbar-Nelson protested the control of her fate by white male physicians but to no avail. Later, reviewing "lovely letters" from four men to whom she had submitted work applications, she associates her unemployment—her condition—with slavery. "[W]here," she asks, "is the deliverance from my House of Bondage?" (*Diary*, 197).

Despite numerous rebuffs, Dunbar-Nelson nevertheless entered the field of journalism and made outstanding contributions in what was perhaps the least hospitable area of employment for a female during the early 1900s. And, as might be expected, she had trouble getting proper recognition and payment for her work. When Ira F. Lewis of the *Pittsburgh Courier* denied that paper's promised ten-dollar-per-column fee, Dunbar-Nelson reacted, using mild but uncharacteristic profanity: "Damn bad luck I have with my pen. Some fate has decreed I shall never make money by it" (*Diary*, 366). Even when employed at a school, the setting in which women have traditionally served in many roles, Dunbar-Nelson was undervalued. In October 1920, after eighteen years at Howard High School, he lost her position as English department head following her unsanctioned trip to Marion, Ohio, for Social Justice Day. When she worked as executive secretary of the American Inter-Racial Peace Committee, white male managers and her self-appointed black male advisor, Leslie P. Hill, monitored her office dress, her jewelry, and even her lipstick, for propriety. As a final devastating blow, her husband, Robert J. Nelson, with whom she published *The Advocate* from 1920 until 1922, expected her to maintain their home and the newspaper office, an expectation that she understood but successfully withstood, observing, "Men do like to keep women's personalities swallowed!" (*Diary*, 56).

It is not surprising that Dunbar-Nelson reveals such great insight and sophistication concerning women's roles, for in addition to her own varied experiences, she had published stories about male/female relationships since 1895 in *Violets and Other Tales*. Both "A Story of Vengeance" and "At Eventide" question ambition for women, and "The Woman" asks whether "chances for matrimony are increased or decreased when [woman] becomes man's equal as a wage earner." Dunbar-Nelson's personal ambition, economic necessity, attitudes, and experiences clearly place her among those who insist upon careers outside the home without loss of family life.

In January 1932, after Robert Nelson was appointed to the Pennsylvania Athletic Commission, the entire family moved to Philadelphia and enjoyed both prosperity and a circle of friends active in social, political, and literary organizations. Indeed, Dunbar-Nelson's family, naturally extended by her mother (until her death in 1931), sister, and sister's children, was further expanded and enriched through her literary and professional associations. Dunbar-Nelson lived in the company of a large network of black people with whom, philosophically, she shared ideas and civic and political activities. Moreover, on a practical level, she shared a common heritage and status as well as a deeply felt obligation to provide for visiting blacks all the basic needs of bed, board, intellectual stimulation, and relaxation—accommodations that she felt were systematically denied to people of color in Jim Crow America. Her circle of friends and associates was an enviably close-knit, nationwide society of intellectuals; it included poets Langston Hughes, James Weldon Johnson, Georgia Douglas Johnson, and Leslie Pinckney Hill; noted historian Carter G. Woodson; authors and professors W. E. B. Du Bois and Alain Locke; author and NAACP executive secretary Walter White; clubwoman and activist Mary Church Terrell; and educators Nannie Helen Burroughs, Mary McLeod Bethune, and Charlotte Hawkins Brown. On May 7, 1927, Dunbar-Nelson recorded her excitement in being "welcomed effusively" by Countee Cullen, James Weldon Johnson, and Carl Van Vechten at the *Opportunity* magazine literary awards dinner in New York City (*Diary*, 177); on December 9, 1927, while attending the "Fact-Finding and Stock-Taking Conference on Blacks in America" in Durham, North Carolina, she reports: "Du Bois and I sit back and observe youth . . . being radical"; on December 10, 1927, back in Washington, D.C., at Georgia Douglas Johnson's home, Dunbar-Nelson and Du Bois "get together a breakfast fit for the gods" (*Diary*, 207). Surely, Dunbar-Nelson's life was enhanced through these and other familial interactions with her contemporaries during one of the richest periods in the literary and cultural history of black Americans, and her own outstanding achievements constitute a significant, indelible part of that history. On September 18, 1935, Dunbar-Nelson died of a heart ailment at the University of Pennsylvania Hospital. Following cremation of her body, Robert Nelson scattered her ashes over the Delaware River.

Besides her poems, which were widely circulated in journals and anthologies, Dunbar-Nelson published two collections of essays, reviews, poems, and short stories featuring Creole culture. Though she never found a publisher for her longer fiction, she brought four novels to various stages of completion: *The Confession of a Lazy Woman* (1899), *A Modern Undine* (1901-1903), *Uplift* (1930-31), and *This Lofty Oak* (1932-33). Dunbar-Nelson also edited two volumes of oratory, *Masterpieces of Negro Eloquence* (1914) and *The Dunbar Speaker and Entertainer* (1920). Moreover, she wrote dramas, and hundreds of newspaper columns, including "From A Woman's Point of View" (later "Une Femme Dit," 1926), "So It Seems—to Alice Dunbar-Nelson" (1930) for the *Pittsburgh Courier*, and "As In a Looking Glass" (1926) for the *Washington Eagle*. In her essays, diary, and newspaper columns, Dunbar-Nelson displays the full range of her powers, both as a skilled reviewer of books, dramatic productions, musical performances, art, and film and as an astute judge of American political, social, and cultural mores. These selections, along with her poetry and fiction, make her a forceful and respected voice of the Harlem Renaissance and beyond.

References

Brawley, Benjamin. *The Negro Genius*. New York: Dodd, Mead, 1937.

———. *Paul Laurence Dunbar: Poet of His People*. Chapel Hill: University of North Carolina Press, 1935-6.

Bruce, Dickson D., Jr. *Black Writing from the Nadir: The Evolution of a Literary Tradition, 1877-1915*. Baton Rouge: Louisiana State University Press, 1989.

Dunbar-Nelson, Alice. *Give Us Each Day: The Diary of Alice Dunbar-Nelson*. Edited by Gloria T. Hull. New York: Norton, 1984.

———. *The Works of Alice Dunbar-Nelson*. Edited by Gloria T. Hull. 3 vols. New York: Oxford University Press, 1988.

Ford, Nick Aaron. "Alice Dunbar-Nelson." *Notable American Women, 1660-1950*. Vol. 2. Cambridge: Harvard University Press, 1970.

Gayle, Addison, Jr. *Oak and Ivy*. New York: Doubleday, 1971.

Hull, Gloria T. *Color, Sex, and Poetry*. Bloomington: Indiana University Press, 1987.

Kerlin, Robert Thomas, *Negro Poets and Their Poems*. 3rd ed. Rev. and enl. Washington, D.C.: Associated Publishers, 1925.

Loggins, Vernon. *The Negro Author: His Development in America to 1900*. New York: Columbia University Press, 1931.

Perry, Patsy. Review of *Give Us This Day: The Diary of Alice Dunbar-Nelson*. *Signs* 12 (Autumn 1986): 174-76.

Shockley, Ann Allen. "Alice Ruth Moore Dunbar-Nelson, 1875-1935." *Afro-American Women Writers, 1746-1933: An Anthology and Critical Guide*. Boston: G. K. Hall, 1988.

"The Soul's Forgotten Gleam." *Negro History Bulletin* 31 (April 1968); 4-5.

Wagner, Jean. *Black Poets of the United States*. Urbana: University of Illinois Press, 1973.

Williams, Ora. "Works By and About Alice Ruth (Moore) Dunbar-Nelson: A Bibliography." *CLA Journal* 19 (March 1976): 322-26.

Woodson, Carter G. "Notes: Alice Dunbar-Nelson." *Journal of Negro History* 21 (January 1936): 94-96.

Collections

Unpublished Dunbar-Nelson manuscripts are located in Special Collections, Morris Library, University of Delaware, Newark, Delaware.

Patsy B. Perry

Katherine Dunham

(1909-)

Dancer, choreographer, school founder, anthropologist

Taking a bow to a standing ovation for her leadership of *Treemonisha,* performed at Southern Illinois University's Carbondale campus in 1972, Katherine Dunham had again lived up to her title as the "Grand Dame of American Dance." Today, at eighty-one years of age, Dunham is still taking bows. She has traveled the world, been the guest of kings and rulers, performing not only her brilliant dances but also teaching through them the universal truths that intermingle and bind together the many cultures of the world.

Her path has carried her far from Glen Ellyn, Illinois, where she was born on June 22, 1909, to Albert Dunham and Fanny June (Taylor) Dunham. Her brother, Albert Dunham, Jr., whom Katherine Dunham always loved and adored, was four years old when "Kitty" was born. Through her ancestral heritage of African, Madagascan, Canadian-French, and American Indian, she was a "small League of Nations—largely black" (Harnan, 10). Fanny Dunham died when Albert, Jr., and Katherine were quite young, and the children lived with their aunt Lulu in the poverty-stricken south side

Katherine Dunham

of Chicago. Their father was working as a traveling salesman and was away for extended periods of time.

It was while living here that Katherine Dunham's interest in the theater began. Her uncle Arthur Dunham was a voice coach and choral leader, and he and other members of the Dunham family were rehearsing with the hopes of producing the musical drama, *Minnehaha*. Katherine, four years old at this time, wanted to participate too, but her aunt Clara said she was too young. These early experiences were ended when the children were removed by an older stepsister, Fanny Weir, because of the very poor conditions in which they were living. Carrying them to her own very comfortable apartment, she and her husband gave the children a regular schedule that included nourishing meals, daily baths, and plenty of rest. The court granted the Weir's custody until such time that their father could prove to the court that he could properly provide for them. Katherine was five and her brother nine when their father regained custody of them. Albert Dunham, Sr., had, by this time, married Annette Poindexter, a former schoolteacher from Iowa, and saved up enough money to buy a dry-cleaning store in Joliet, Illinois. To the children, their father was much changed from the happy, affectionate man they had known before their mother's illness and death. His deep grief over Fanny June's death had turned to bitterness as he had later watched all of his wife's holdings, including their home in Glen Ellyn, sold to cover debts incurred by the children of her former marriage. His drive for accomplishment drove him to work both himself and his family relentlessly.

Remembering her early days in Chicago, fifteen-year-old Katherine Dunham organized a cabaret party to raise funds for her church's annual rally. Some of the members boycotted the affair, but it was successful, raising the sum of thirty-two dollars. After high school Katherine Dunham entered Joliet Township Junior College, transferring after graduation to the University of Chicago. Albert, Jr., having earned a full academic scholarship, was already at the university, and his guidance, love, and support helped her adapt to university life very quickly.

At the university, Katherine Dunham met and became very good friends with Frances Taylor, who lived with her married sister, Mrs. Wilfred Bell. Dunham was invited to move into their home and she became Taylor's roommate. Dunham had a part-time job at the library, but she longed to teach dancing for her living; however, she had no studio and no money. Meanwhile, Albert had graduated with honors and stayed to do postgraduate work at the University of Chicago, while applying for a Rockefeller grant to study under philosopher Alfred North Whitehead at Harvard. Perhaps the first real financial security he had ever known broke his reserve not to marry, because he very soon asked Frances Taylor to be his wife. The wedding took place on September 13, 1929. The happy pair went off to live in Cambridge, where he would attend Harvard and she would finish college at Boston University. For Dunham this was a big jolt; she lost both her brother and her best friend at the same time.

One month later, on October 29, 1929, the Wall Street crash occurred, and the years of the Great Depression began. During this time Katherine Dunham worked at the library, babysat, and with the help of friends and her Russian dance teacher, Madame Ludmila Speranzeva, she started a dance school. For the first time, she began to work seriously on choreography. In 1931 Katherine Dunham's dancers put on "Negro Rhapsody" as the first act at the Chicago Beaux Arts Ball and received hearty applause from the audience. However, the good friends who had helped finance the studio were soon out of money, and it was closed. Feeling lonely and perhaps bereft, Dunham married Jordis McCoo, a fellow dancer. In a very short time she realized that she really was unready to forget her dreams and settle down. Fortunately, the marriage demanded very little since she went to school in the daytime and her husband worked nights at the post office. After school she and her friend Ruth Attaway, a drama teacher, looked for an inexpensive place to rent for a studio. They found an old stable with large, open spaces for their classes. It became a gathering place for such personages as Charles Sebree, Charles White, Langston Hughes, Sterling North, Arna Bontemps, Horace Mann, and others. All went well until winter came, lacking fuel to heat the stable properly, they were forced to close.

Dunham's next school, the Negro Dance Group, was a good stepping-stone, mainly because Madame Speranzeva allowed Dunham the use of her studio for pupils, and she coached Dunham privately in ballet and mime. Through Speranzeva, Dunham was introduced to the Isadora Duncan Dance Company and Fokine. She met Argentina, the famous Spanish dancer, and her partner Escudero. Though the school appeared to flourish, the parents of her black students wanted their daughters to study ballet for the sake of social graces and were concerned that the name of the school meant that they would be taught African dances. Though Dunham knew that the basic steps of the popular lindy hop, cakewalk, and black bottom had their origins in African tribal dances, she was also aware that she was unable to explain this easily to these parents. However, this whole dilemma worked out for her benefit, for through a presentation of Robert Redfield, a professor in ethnology, Dunham decided on anthropology as her college major. Through this door perhaps she could teach blacks not to be satisfied only with imitating others but rather to develop their own natural talents through hard work and technical training.

African and West Indian Dances Studied

In 1933 Katherine Dunham was chosen to hire and train 150 young blacks to present a program for the 1934 Chicago Century of Progress Exposition. From this honor came an invitation to a Julius Rosenwald Foundation reception. At this reception, she met Eric Fromm, a prominent psychiatrist, and the two became lifelong friends. After later seeing a performance by Dunham's dance group, Mrs. Alfred Rosenwald Stern invited her to appear before the foundation's board of judges to present her views on black dance. If they approved, she would receive a scholarship that would enable her to further her studies. On the appointed day,

Dunham met the board. After the necessary preliminaries, the chairman asked: "Now, Miss Dunham, just what sort of dance study would you like this committee to finance for you?" (Dannett, 173). Dunham asked if she might demonstrate some of the dance forms, since they were difficult to verbally describe, and the committee assented. Dunham started unsnapping hidden hooks on her primly tailored suit, and momentarily stood before them in dancing tights. She began to dance. When she had finished, she explained both the need and the cultural significance of studying the dances of Africa and the West Indies in their native environments. On February 15, 1935, Dunham received her Rosenwald Foundation travel grant. As part of her grant, she was to study for approximately three months with Melville Herskovits, head of Northwestern University's African studies, before beginning her travels. This time was invaluable to her, and Dunham later called Herskovits "a fantastic guide for getting to the bottom of things, the heart of the matter" (Harnan, 58). At twenty-five years of age she began a career that would take her many times to Europe, Mexico, South America, Africa, Australia, and Japan. This first journey was to take her to Jamaica, Martinique, Trinidad, and Haiti.

Accompong, a small, isolated village in the mountainous northeast part of Jamaica, was her first stop. She brought a letter of introduction to the chief, known as the Colonel, from Herskovits, one of a very few who had ever visited Accompong for any extended length of time. The natives of this village were originally members of the African Koromantee tribe. In the islands they are known as the Maroons, and they live high in the hills, away from local villages. Dunham was accepted by the Maroons and asked to join in all their dances and festivities, but they, though knowing her interest in the ancient dances, did not perform them. Three nights before she was to leave, the Colonel went into the city; in the stillness, Dunham heard the drum. That night the villagers performed the Koromantee war dance she had so longed to see and several other ancient dances for her pleasure. On this night she realized that the Colonel was not the only one who wished the old rituals forgotten; the young people of this village also desired the modernity they had found in the more progressive cities and villages.

As Dunham moved on to the other islands, she continued her anthropological probings into the origins of both the people and their dances. In Trinidad she was allowed to be an onlooker-participant in the ancient Shango rites. In Haiti, where she had her longest visit, there were neither leaders nor chiefs to either hinder or forbid the practice of the old religious rites. Establishing herself at the Hotel Excelsior in Port-au-Prince, Dunham made many friends among the government officials. These friendships allowed her to go into the back section of the country. Her mulatto, or "griffon," coloring also helped, since the Haitian social system was based on color, the lightest—though not white—being the most preferred (Harnan, 81). Her acceptance by the people of the back country was genuine, and she was invited to be an initiate into voodoo.

After the experience with voodoo, Dunham returned to Port-au-Prince to prepare for a dance concert she had promised to put on at the Rex Theatre. She had been told by the manager: "No country performers, no Voodoo dances, none of that kind of thing at the Rex" (Harnan 93). For her program she did a classical ballet, a gypsy dance from the operetta *Countess Maritza,* and for the grand finale, a Spanish dance in full costume. After this performance she received accolades of applause, flowers, phone calls, invitations, and her treks to the bush were excused by her charmed public as "artistic temperament." Dunham's acceptance by all classes of Haitians was a wonderful respite from the prejudices she had often encountered in her own country. Shortly before she left Haiti, Dunham decided that if she ever had enough money, she would return and buy the neglected, thought-to-be-haunted Habitation Leclerc.

Upon returning home, Dunham appeared again before the Julius Rosenwald Foundation and reported with music, dancing, pictures, and speech the many experiences of her trip. "It was a fascinating evening and got an enthusiastic write-up in the June 5, 1936, *Chicago Daily News*" (Harnan, 97). A short time after this evening, the Rockefeller Foundation granted her a fellowship for further studies toward her master's degree under the direction of Herskovits. In August of 1936, Dunham graduated from the University of Chicago with a bachelor's degree in anthropology. She later earned an M.S. from the University of Chicago and a Ph.D. from Northwestern University.

In Chicago, Madame Speranzeva and other friends had kept Dunham's dance troupe alive, and she immediately began rehearsing. An invitation was issued to her and the group to perform in a March 7, 1937, program titled "Negro Dance Evening," at the Young Men's Hebrew Association auditorium in New York. This was quickly accepted, and though it was a long distance to travel, it was the Katherine Dunham company's first chance to appear before a New York audience. Their performance was well received and Dunham and the group were exuberant. Now, more than ever, Dunham wanted to continue her anthropological exploration of dance, this time in Europe. The Rockefeller General Foundation Board rejected her proposal for the trip, so Dunham suspended her fellowship in June, with the possibility of taking it up again in October. She then applied for and was granted a Guggenheim Fellowship to pursue her dance studies.

On the evening of January 27, 1938, Dunham, as dance director of the Federal Theatre Project in Chicago, opened the program with *Ballet Fedre*. The next morning's newspapers praised all of the program, but were wild about "a firey folk ballet with choreography by Katherine Dunham," saying that *L'Ag'Ya* was "danced with enough abandon to make some of the preceding events seem pallid by comparison" (Harnan, 101). Dunham's artistry was beginning to be seen and appreciated. The teachings of Madame Speranzeva with their emphasis on acting and story line as well as the dancing skill, and the work that Dunham had done in Martinique where she had first seen *L'Ag'Ya*, the fighting dance, were very important background influences.

On this same evening came honors for the man who designed the sets and costumes, John Pratt. They wrote, "John Pratt's handsome tropical costumes . . . shared distinction of Miss Dunham's choreography" (Harnan, 102). This 1938 presentation was the first time Pratt and Dunham had worked together as a team, but they were to become known throughout the world. Born in Canada, John Pratt was a very tall, handsome white man who was then twenty-four years old. He had designed sets and costumes while studying at the University of Chicago, as well as having his art work exhibited at a Chicago gallery and university shows. Working together for many months strengthened the ties between Dunham and Pratt. After Dunham received her divorce, she and John Pratt were married in a private ceremony July 10, 1939, in Tecade, Mexico. In the world of artists in which they moved, color, creed, and nationality mattered little, if at all.

Dunham Launches Dance Career

In February 1940 the Katherine Dunham Dance Company opened at the Windsor Theatre, West 48th Street, with Dunham's own *Tropics and Le Jazz Hot*. The show was a phenomenal success. One critic said, "Katherine Dunham flared into unsuspecting New York last night like a comet. Unknown before her debut, she is today one of the most talked-about dancers" (Harnan, 105). John Martin of *The New York Times* said, "With the arrival of Katherine Dunham on the scene the development of a substantial Negro dance art begins to look decidedly bright. Her performance with her group at the Windsor Theatre may very well become a historic occasion, for certainly never before in all the efforts of recent years to establish the Negro dance as a serious medium has there been so convincing and authoritative an approach" (Harnan, 106). Martin also found "the absence of all sense of self-importance" one of the "most notable aspects" of Dunham's program. He further noted that there was "nothing pretentious about it." The Negro dance was designed to "externalize the impulses of a high spirited, rhythmic and gracious race," and Katherine Dunham's dances, as then introduced, "accomplished this end so beautifully." She actually "isolated the element of a folk art upon which more consciously creative and sophisticated forms can be built as time goes on. This is cultural pioneering of a unique sort" (Dannett, 175). Dan Burley wrote that the formula for her success was simply "the use to fullest advantage of the natural dancing technique of the Negro instead of the copied ideas of the whites" (Dannett, 176). Katherine Dunham was, indeed, on her way. From this night her name and her dances took her behind the footlights of the world's greatest stages. Her unique technique and stylistic perfection were the forces that propelled her toward that magic moment where the dancer, the dance, and the cultural story become one.

Soon after this success, an offer came for the Dunham Dance Company to take part in an all-Negro musical entitled *Cabin in the Sky*. The salary was three thousand dollars a week, more than any of them had ever dreamed of earning as dancers. Dunham's role was Georgia Brown, and for the first time she had the opportunity not only to dance, but to sing and act as well. The drama had a long and successful run. During this time, Dunham, in one of her interviews, revealed that those terrible aches she had felt years earlier during her voodoo initiation had later been diagnosed as arthritis. She also stated that she "would like to live in Haiti for maybe four or five months of every year" so that she and her troupe "could rest and rehearse between shows. We might start a dancing school in Port-au-Prince. All the Haitian children could come free. No one would ever be cold" (Harnan, 107).

Soon after her first trip to Haiti, Dunham had been also asked to serve as a committee member of the Illinois Project of the Federal Writer's Project, 1935-1943. Mangione says:

> One of the most renowned graduates of the Illinois Project was the dancer and choreographer, Katherine Dunham. On the Project she applied her University of Chicago training in anthropology to initiate several valuable black studies, one of which investigated Chicago's Negro Cults (one of them later became widely known as the Black Muslim movement). . . . Frederick [the Illinois director] considered her one of his most capable staff members and a promising author. He was impressed with the early draft of *Journey to Accompong*, which she was then writing in her spare time (Mangione 127).

In 1946, *Katherine Dunham's Journey to Accompong*, an autobiography, was published in New York.

Near the end of a most rewarding and successful tour of Mexico and Europe, 1947-1949, Dunham, Pratt, and the members of the troupe welcomed an opportunity to return to Haiti through an invitation from her old friend, Dumarsais Estimé, now president of the island. The warmth and blue water offered a much-needed rest. Before Dunham's first trip to the islands in 1935, she had received the sad news that her brother, Arthur, Jr. had apparently suffered a mental breakdown. He was under the care of the best doctors available, and it was believed that given time, rest, and treatment, he would recover completely. However, in May 1949 she received the news in Europe that her beloved brother had died. Ironically, his long recovery was practically complete, and he was to have resumed life outside the hospital in just a matter of weeks. Katherine Dunham, years later, referred to her brother's illness and death as the "supreme tragedy" of her life (Harnan, 139). On this return visit to Haiti, she and John Pratt had a friend investigate the possibility of purchasing Habitation Leclerc, and a short time later they did. As the year 1949, filled with both joy and sorrow, closed, Katherine Dunham received the sad news of her father's death, and also learned that her friend, President Estimé, had been forced to resign and was now exiled from Haiti. Katherine Dunham and John Pratt returned to the United States, and in 1950 she was dancing again to Broadway fans.

In December 1952 Pratt and Dunham adopted Marie Christine Columbier, a five-year-old French Martinique girl of mixed heritage. For awhile she accompanied her new parents on their travels but was eventually sent to school in Switzerland. In the succeeding years, Dunham choreographed several movies, choreographed the opera *Aida*, performed all over the United States, toured Europe, Australia, South America, the Orient, and opened a medical clinic in Haiti. In 1959 *A Touch of Innocence*, the painful story of the first eighteen years of her life, was published.

Katherine Dunham, at the request of President Leopold Sedar Senghor, went to Africa to help train the Senegalese National Ballet and serve as technical cultural advisor to him in preparation for the First World Festival of Negro Arts at Dakar, Senegal, in 1965 and 1966. Here, in Africa, the mother country of all of the dance studies Dunham had made, she felt quite at home. It was in Dakar, in a house that she and Pratt rented, that she finished her frank, captivating, personal narrative, *Island Possessed*, about Haiti and its people. In 1969 she and Pratt gave up their house in Dakar to return to the United States. The political unrest was one factor in this decision, but a proposal, the East Saint Louis project, which Dunham had presented to Sargent Shriver in March 1965, was the main impetus of their return.

In the earlier presentation of her thesis to Shriver, Dunham had stated that: "The need for objectives to replace crime and delinquency, for disciplines for the leisure time of the young, the necessity in the face of increasing poverty to provide the essentials of human sustenance . . . are grave preoccupations." She proposed that her kind of dance school, which also taught such subjects as psychology, anthropology, and languages, would do this kind of neighborhood a lot of good. "The project presented reaches far beyond dance in the popular definition. . . . Dance as it would serve the East Saint Louis project is concerned with the fundamentals of human society" (Harnan, 200).

With this project, Dunham, whose title was Visiting Artist in the Fine Arts Division of Southern Illinois University's Edwardsville campus, faced one of the biggest challenges of her life. The funding problem was solved by several philanthropic organizations who were willing to support the work of Southern Illinois University, but getting to those students she wanted to help was still an unsolved problem in her mind. Through her daughter, Marie Christine, now nineteen years old, and Jeanelle Stovall, a vacationing United Nations interpreter, Katherine Dunham's door to the students was opened. By December 1967 Katherine Dunham had become cultural affairs consultant to the Edwardsville campus of Southern Illinois University. She was also named director of the Performing Arts Training Center and the Dynamic Museum. Her home was located in the East Saint Louis ghetto among the people with whom she expected to work.

The Dynamic Museum was a wonderful teaching aid, for here the objects that the Dunham Dance Company had collected all over the world were displayed, touched, and used. John Pratt was the curator of the museum and his own artistic costumes were on display, along with books, foreign theater posters, programs, records, and films of the dancers at the zenith of their fame. Having started schools of dance, theater, and cultural arts in Chicago, New York, Saint Louis, Haiti, Stockholm, Paris, and Italy, Dunham knew both the rewards and the difficulties that a school can bring; this one offered specific knowledge to students that could not be found elsewhere.

In 1968 Dunham received the Professional Achievement Award from the University of Chicago Alumni Association honoring her for having brought distinction to herself in her vocational field as well as "credit to the University and real benefit to her fellow citizens" (Harnan, 210). Other awards given during her period of residency in East Saint Louis were the Distinguished Service Award from Southern Illinois University, the Eight Lively Arts Award, and the Contribution to the Arts Award from the Black Academy of Arts and Letters.

After Dunham retired, she opened the Katherine Dunham Center in East Saint Louis. Here she has her school and museum. The two main features that she directs each year are the Children's Workshop and the Dunham Technique Seminar and Institute for Interculture Communication. Her husband, John Pratt, died March 3, 1986. Their daughter, Marie Christine, lives in Rome, Italy. Dunham, now eighty years old, divides her time between East Saint Louis and Haiti, avoiding the cold winter months that increase the pain of her arthritic condition.

Wherever she went, Dunham made a worthy contribution toward the cultural development of mankind. Her many honors and awards include: the Rosenwald and Guggenheim fellowships; Artist-in-Residence, Southern Illinois University, Edwardsville; Visiting Mather Scholar, Case Western Reserve University; Honorary Women's Scientific Fraternity, University of Chicago, 1937; Chevalier of Haitian Legion of Honor and Merit, 1952; Commander, Haitian Legion of Honor and Merit, 1958; grand officer, Haitian Legion of Honor and Merit, 1968; honorary citizen, Port-au-Prince, Haiti, 1957; laureate and member, Lincoln Academy, 1968; key to the city of East Saint Louis, 1968; Dance Magazine Award, 1969; Certificate of Merit, Improved Benevolent and Protective Order of Elks of the World, 1969; Saint Louis Argus Award, 1970; East Saint Louis Monitor Award, 1970; Katherine Dunham Day Award, Detroit, 1970; Certificate of Merit, International Who's Who in Poetry, 1970-71; Dance Division Heritage Award, American Association of Health, Physical Education, and Recreation, Detroit, 1971; East Saint Louis Pro-8 Award, 1971; National Center of Afro-American Artists Award, Elma Lewis School of Fine Arts, 1972; doctor of humane letters degree, MacMurray College, Jacksonville, Illinois, May 1972; Ph.D.L., Atlanta University, 1977; Black Merit Academy Award, 1972; and Woman for a Day, radio station WRTH, 1973. She is founder of the Foundation for the Development and Preservation of Cultural Arts and the Dunham Fund for Research and Development of Cultural Arts.

Early in her career Katherine Dunham said: "I would feel I'd failed miserably if I were doing dance confined to race, color or creed. I don't think that would be art, which has to do with universal truths" (Harnan, 212). Her life is a testimonial to those universal truths and she surely has not failed. She has not only distinguished her own race, but has also enriched every other race through the deeply moving, exquisite message of her dance.

The dancer and her dance are yet so closely entwined that one can best describe Katherine Dunham with the following words of Yeats:

> O body swayed to music, O brightening glance,
> How can we know the dancer from the dance?

References

Dannett, Sylvia G. L. *Profiles of Negro Womanhood.* Vol. 2. Yonkers, N.Y.: Educational Heritage, 1966.

Harnan, Terry. *African Rhythm-American Dance.* New York: Knopf, 1974.

Mangione, Jerre. *The Dream and The Deal: The Federal Writers' Project, 1935-1943.* Boston: Little, Brown and Co., 1972.

Rush, Theressa Gunnels, Carol Fairbanks, and Esther Spring Arata. *Black American Writers, Past and Present.* Vol. 1. Metuchen, N.J.: Scarecrow Press, 1975.

Stovall, Jeanelle. Interview with author, 27 October 1990.

Yeats, William Butler. "Among School Children." *Selected Poems and Three Plays.* Ed. M. L. Rosenthal. 3rd. ed. New York: MacMillan, 1986.

Collections

Information on Katherine Dunham is available in the University Archives of Southern Illinois University at Carbondale. Biographical material may be found in the Rosenwald Collection and portraits are in the Gershwin Memorial Collection, Fisk University, Nashville, Tennessee. Correspondence should be addressed to: The Katherine Dunham Center, 532 North 10th Street, East Saint Louis, Illinois 60001.

Phyllis Wood

Alice Dunnigan

(1906-1983)

Journalist

Alice Allison Dunnigan was the first black American woman reporter to gain access to the press galleries of the United States Capitol and be accredited to the White House and the State Department. She served as chief of the Washington bureau of the Associated Negro Press for fourteen years from 1947 to 1961. This pioneering journalist was born on a farm outside Russellville, Kentucky, on April 27, 1906, to Willie Allison and Lena (Pittman) Allison. Dunnigan had one half-brother, Russell, who was seven years older. Her father was a sharecropper who raised tobacco, and her mother took in laundry. Her family was very strict and instilled in her the importance of work; she had few playmates, and as a teenager she was not allowed to have boyfriends. From an early age Dunnigan loved school, beginning to go informally one day a week when she was four and learning to read before she entered the first grade.

When Dunnigan completed, as valedictorian, the ten years of education available to blacks in the segregated Russellville schools, she wanted to continue her schooling, but her parents did not concur. The last-minute intervention of her Sunday school superintendent, William Russell, the only black dentist in the town, made it possible for Dunnigan to attend Kentucky State College in Frankfort, where in 1926 she earned her two-year elementary teachers' certificate in one year through her diligent work. That year she began her teaching career in a one-room rural school and married Walter Dickenson of Mount Pisgah. They divorced in 1930 and the following year she married Charles Dunnigan, who had been a childhood friend; they separated in 1953. This marriage produced one child, Robert William, father of Dunnigan's four grandchildren. Teaching and going to school as the opportunity arose, Alice Dunnigan finally graduated from West Kentucky Industrial College in 1932.

By the time a call for government workers went out in 1942, Dunnigan was tired of teaching and of the menial jobs it was necessary for a black teacher to take in order to eke out a living during the five months when schools were not in session. One summer, one of her jobs—two days a week courtesy of the Works Progress Administration (WPA)—involved washing the tombstones in the white cemetery. At the same time, she was also working four hours a day in a dairy, cleaning house for a family, and doing washing at night for another family, earning in all about seven dollars a week. In pursuit of a government job she took the examination for civil service grade two—the highest available to her at the location in Kentucky—and went to work for the War

Labor Board in Washington, D.C. By the end of the war and after a year of night courses at Howard University, she had reached the level of economist in the Office of Price Administration. Although efforts were made to place workers in other governmental positions after the abolition of this agency, Dunnigan faced great difficulty in finding work due to discrimination against hiring blacks in positions at the level she had attained.

Dunnigan had been interested in writing since she was a child. About the time she was in the eighth grade, she began writing a local news column for the black-run *Owenborough Enterprise*. She continued to write articles, poems, and little stories for newspapers all during her time in Kentucky. This interest eventually led to her appointment as chief of the Washington Bureau of the Associated Negro Press in 1947. Her first act was to get press credentials, starting with access to the press galleries of the House of Representatives and the Senate. Her request was initially denied on the grounds that she did not represent a daily paper—all newspapers using the services of the Associated Negro Press were weeklies. After a persistent effort of about six months, she succeeded and gained her accreditation about a week after the first black man, Louis Lautier, received his. Her further credentials from the White House Press Association and the State Department Press Association followed without difficulty; only obtaining a Metropolitan Police Pass for Washington, D.C., caused further problems.

Dunnigan's early newspaper work in Washington did not mean immediate affluence. Not only was she badly paid to start with, but the checks often arrived late. Even though she stoked the furnace to defray expenses in the house in which she had a one-room basement apartment, paying her rent was a continuing problem. After exploring ways to supplement her income, she began to write for magazines and also found other writing jobs.

Dunnigan Becomes White House Correspondent

Dunnigan was the first black woman to be an accredited White House correspondent. As such she was one of two women in the press pool that accompanied President Harry S. Truman on a 1948 campaign trip by train to California. She was active in the Women's National Press Club, which became the Washington Press Club when men were allowed to join. Although she did not seek office in the many organizations in which she was active, such as the Capital Press Club, preferring a background role, her association with the Women's National Press Club allowed her the opportunity to travel to Canada for Expo '67 and to Israel for the country's tenth anniversary celebration. Her overseas trips also included visits to South America, Africa, Mexico, and the Caribbean. Haitian President François Duvalier honored her for articles she wrote on Haiti. Both her press work and government service led to extensive travel in the United States.

In 1960 Dunnigan worked in Lyndon B. Johnson's campaign for the Democratic nomination, traveling on his private plane to the convention in Los Angeles; Johnson became John F. Kennedy's vice-presidential running mate. When Kennedy set up by executive order the President's Committee on Equal Employment Opportunity, the committee's chair, Johnson, appointed Dunnigan education consultant. She worked with great diligence and success with this committee until the Civil Rights Act of 1964 established a permanent committee, and she was fortunate enough to be able to stay on for another year as the presidential committee wound up its work. In 1966-1967 she served as information specialist for the Department of Labor, and then she became editorial assistant for the President's Council of Youth Opportunity. With the election of Richard M. Nixon in 1968, Democratic staff members were replaced by Republicans, but she managed to remain in the position although frozen out of the operations of the council until the appropriation for her job was terminated. Dunnigan was finally out in 1970 with entitlement to a full year of severance pay.

Dunnigan then turned to writing projects. The first was her autobiography, *A Black Woman's Experience—From Schoolhouse to White House,* published in 1974. This is a lengthy work of considerable interest. The first 187 pages are a vivid account of growing up black in rural Kentucky. The more than 450 pages remaining, based largely on her clipping files, supplemented by her later discoveries, are a fascinating picture of her work in government, politics, and journalism and are designed to be very much a historical document offering insight into the period from the forties through the sixties. Dunnigran's second book was *The Fascinating Story of Black Kentuckians: Their Heritage and History*. It grew from her experiences as a teacher: discovering that there were no references to blacks in local school history books, she began to prepare fact sheets and eventually presented the materials she was assembling in a weekly column for the *Louisville Defender*. The interest generated was great enough that she tried to compile the materials into a book, but in the 1930s no publisher could be found.

Over the years Dunnigan received numerous awards, including the Newsman's Trophy from the Capital Press Club (1951), a Kentucky Colonel commission (1962), an honorary degree from Colorado State Christian College (1973), a plaque from the National Newspaper Publishers Association (1975), and induction into the Journalism Hall of Fame at the University of Kentucky (1982).

Dunnigan was most proud of the work she did in journalism. In response to a 1977 questionnaire she wrote:

> I feel that one of my most significant accomplishments was the leading role I played in the demands for equal opportunities for Black reporters in the Nation's Capital. . . . [T]he role of the Black press, like all other newspapers, is that of objectively reporting the news as it happens, but it has another function equally as important—that of fighting oppression. Without Black reporters constantly on the national scene to record contemporary history of the Negro's

role in the fight for civil rights, equality and justice, and without authors and historians to compile these facts into a permanent record, the deeds, efforts and struggles of the Black man in his progressive fight for security and recognition would forever be lost to history (Biography file).

Alice Allison Dunnigan died of an abdominal disease in Washington, D.C., in 1983.

References

"Alice Dunnigan, Noted News Woman, Dies At 77." *Jet* (23 May 1983): 42.

Black Women Oral History Project Interview with Alice Allison Dunnigan. Cambridge: Schlesinger Library, Radcliffe College, 1977.

Dunnigan, Alice Allison. *A Black Woman's Experience—From Schoolhouse to White House*. Philadelphia: Dorrance and Company, 1974.

———. *The Fascinating Story of Black Kentuckians: Their Heritage and Tradition*. Washington, D.C.: Association for the Study of Afro-American Life and History, 1979.

"White House Reporter," *Opportunity* 26 (Spring 1948): 52, 56-67.

Collections

The papers of Alice Dunnigan are in the Moorland-Spingarn Research Center, Howard University, Washington, D.C. Information on Dunnigan can also be found in the Biography File of Fisk University Library, Nashville, Tennessee.

Robert L. Johns

Alfreda M. Duster

(1904-1983)

Civic leader, activist, social worker

Alfreda M. Barnett Duster was an important civic leader in Chicago, Illinois, and an activist and social worker committed to black youth. She was born in Chicago on September 3, 1904, the youngest of six children born to Ferdinand L. Barnett and Ida B. Wells Barnett. Her father, born a freeman in Nashville, Tennessee, was a lawyer and publisher of the first black Chicago weekly, *The Conservator*, which was established in 1878. Barnett was also the first black American to be an assistant state's attorney for Cook County, Illinois, a position to which he was appointed in 1896. In 1906 he ran, unsuccessfully, for a municipal court judgeship.

Duster's mother, born in slavery in Holly Springs, Mississippi, was a cofounder of the NAACP, the founder of the Alpha Suffrage Club—the first such organization for black women in Illinois—and was active in both the black and interracial women's club movement. She is best known, however, as the journalist who launched the nation's first anti-lynching campaign from Memphis, Tennessee. After three black men were murdered there in 1892, Wells Barnett investigated the circumstances behind 728 other lynchings over the previous decade and concluded that black men were being killed because of their political and economic progress in the South. Her views, published in the newspaper the *Free Speech*, resulted in her office being burned down and Wells Barnett herself being exiled from the South on the threat of death. In 1893, she met Ferdinand Barnett, a widower with two sons, at the World's Columbian Exposition in Chicago. The two activists married in a large wedding in Chicago on June 27, 1895.

Alfreda Duster was born nine years later. As the youngest child, she recalled that her primary household chore was to have the potatoes cooked and the hot water boiling for the corn pone by the time her father got home from work in the evening. She was sometimes late because of her preference for skating, which she did nearly ever day. Her father was a quiet, mild-mannered man who did not allow liquor or smoking in the house. Duster said that the tasks of disciplining the children fell on her mother, who was "very, very firm" yet "kind in her firmness." The household virtually hummed with visitors, who would begin coming to the house soon after dinner to see her father, who had a a law office in downtown Chicago. In addition, fellow activists such as Monroe Trotter, Carter G. Woodson, and Hallie Q. Brown were frequent visitors to the large house on Grand Boulevard, which is now a national historic site.

Duster was educated in the public schools of Chicago and in 1921 entered the University of Chicago, where she earned a Ph.B. degree in three-and-a-half years because of advanced standing. In 1924, the year she graduated from college, she married Benjamin Duster, a law clerk in her father's office. For the next twenty years, she reared five children and was a volunteer in the Chicago community. Duster was active in the Hartzell Methodist Church, the Southside Community Committee, and the Douglas School PTA. She also worked with children in after-school and Saturday academic sessions to supplement inadequate curriculums and assisted her husband in his duties as precinct captain and secretary of the Second Ward Regular Republican Organization. Among the couple's closest friends were other political and civic activists, including U.S. representative William Dawson, Illinois congressman Charles Jenkins, and Supreme Life Insurance president Earl B. Dickerson.

The death of Duster's husband in 1945 prompted her to utilize her skills in the workplace. She became a social worker for the Division of Community Services of the

Illinois Youth Commission, concentrating on the then newly developing field of community organization, which focused on means of eliminating negative influences in community setting. Focusing on adolescents, Duster was a juvenile delinquency prevention coordinator assigned to the Southside Community Committee, one of the affiliates of the Chicago Area Project. For ten years she also administered the girls program at Camp Illini, a resident camp for the underprivileged, until she resigned in 1965. Subsequently, she worked part-time for the Woodlawn Community Service Agency and the Catalyst for Youth program—a talent search project that recruited and counseled high school students prior to entering college.

Throughout these years, Duster continued her volunteer activities. She remained active in the PTA and also became involved in the Citizens' School Committee—a group formed to keep the school system free from political influence. Additionally, Duster was a member of the University of Chicago Women's Board and Steering Committee, the cabinet of the University of Chicago Alumni Association, the United Methodist Church Women, and the Ida B. Wells Club of the National Association of Colored Women—an organization that her mother helped establish.

Her dedication to both the community and her children—all five of whom earned graduate degrees and are outstanding professionals—earned Duster many awards. She won mother of the year awards from the Welfare Council of Metropolitan Chicago, the State Street Council, and the Harriet M. Harris YWCA. Other awards include the University of Chicago Alumni Association's citation for public service and the Opportunity Center's Bootstrap Award in Chicago. In 1970, after almost forty years of effort to edit and find a publisher for her mother's autobiography, *Crusade for Justice* was issued by the University of Chicago Press, for which she received a National Council of Negro Women Award for Literary Excellence and Outstanding Humanitarian Contributions.

On April 2, 1983, Duster died of a cerebral hemorrhage in Chicago. She was seventy-nine years old.

References

Chicago Defender, 15 June 1974.

Duster, Alfreda M. Black Women Oral History Interview. Cambridge: Schlesinger Library, Radcliffe College, 1978.

Hill, Ruth Edmonds. *Women of Courage*. Radcliffe College, 1984.

Paula Giddings

Eva B. Dykes

(1893-1986)

Educator, writer

One of the first three black American women to earn a Ph. D. in 1921, Eva Dykes displayed an unswerving commitment to education and excellence throughout her life and career. She was honored in 1976 as a pioneer in the full intellectual development of black women by the National Association of Black Professional Women in Higher Education.

Eva Beatrice Dykes was born in Washington, D.C., on August 13, 1893, the second daughter of James Stanley Dykes and Martha Ann (Howard) Dykes. There was an older sister, Florence "Flossie," and a younger, Anita. Her maternal grandparents were slaves on a plantation in Howard County, Maryland. In her background was a strong family tie to Howard University in Washington. Her father, two uncles, and one of her sisters were graduates of the university, and the other sister graduated from its training school. Her mother attended Howard's preparatory school but had to leave because of poor health. James Dykes and his wife were divorced when the children were young, but Martha Dykes managed to keep the family together with the assistance of her brother, James C. Howard, a physician who became a prominent Seventh Day Adventist. Florence Dykes graduated from Howard and taught in its commercial college until her death after a brief illness on October 5, 1917. Anita Dykes married, and it is through Anita Dykes Simms that the closest living relatives of Eva Dykes descend.

Eva Beatrice Dykes studied at Howard University Training School for grades one through four and completed her primary education at the Lucretia Mott Elementary School. She then attended the M Street High School before entering Howard University, from which she graduated summa cum laude in 1914. After her graduation she taught English and Latin for a year at Walden University in Nashville, Tennessee. (The school no longer exists.) She then undertook further study at Radcliffe College, which did not accept the validity of her undergraduate degree and enrolled her as an unclassified student. In 1917 Radcliffe awarded her the A.B. degree in English magna cum laude, with honors in English, and she was elected to Phi Beta Kappa. The following year she received the A.M. According to the *Howard University Record,* she had a grade of A in eighteen of the twenty-three courses she took at Radcliffe and a B in the others (467). She completed the requirements for the Ph.D. on March 21, 1921, when she defended her dissertation on "Pope and His Influence in America from 1715 to 1850." She was one of the first three black American women to earn a Ph.D., all of whom were awarded their degrees that year, and she was the first to complete the requirements, although her commencement on June 22 was the latest. The other two to earn their degrees that year are Sadie T. Mossell Alexander, economics at the University of Pennsylvania, and Georgianna R. Simpson, German at the University of Chicago.

Eva B. Dykes's commitment to learning and teaching is clear; equally important was her commitment to her church. In December 1920 she joined the Seventh Day Adventist Church. She undertook this engagement with the utmost seriousness; she spoke to friends of a marriage offer from a physician, which she turned down regretfully because the man did not share her faith (Reynolds, 17). An accomplished pianist, Dykes also had a strong avocation in music that she placed at the service of her church work. She was not ashamed to perform on a portable organ in the streets with evangelizing groups. She also gave Bible lessons and worked for the conversion of others. The most famous example of her devotion to her church is the warning she made to the dean of Howard University that she could not give service to the university between sundown Friday and sundown Saturday because of her allegiance. It is to President Mordecai Johnson's credit that he recognized that this devotion to her church was a positive reason to hire her.

It was in 1929 that Eva B. Dykes joined the faculty of Howard University; previously she had taught for nine years at the former M Street High School, which had become the Paul Laurence Dunbar High School. She taught until 1944 at Howard, where the faculty of the College of Liberal Arts honored her by naming her the best all-around teacher in the university in 1930. The university honored her with the Alumni Award for Distinguished Postgraduate Achievement in 1945. In addition to her teaching, committee work, and service as associate editor of the *Howard University Record*, she also engaged in scholarly work and other writing. She was coeditor, with Otelia Cromwell and Lorenzo Dow Turner, of *Readings From Negro Authors for Schools and Colleges* (New York: Harcourt, Brace, 1931), and she wrote *The Negro in English Romantic Thought* (Washington, D.C.: Associated Publishers, 1942), and articles for learned journals, as well as many articles for church publications. In 1934 she began a column for *Message Magazine* and continued it for fifty years.

In 1944 Eva B. Dykes accepted the invitation of James Lewis Moran to go to Oakwood College in Huntsville, Alabama. This Adventist school had begun as an industrial school in 1896 and was currently a junior college; Moran's ambition was to create a four-year school. Dykes was the first Ph.D. to join the faculty—the only one for more than ten years—and was immediately made head of the department of English. There is some question whether her salary was forty-two dollars a week, equal to that of the president, or forty-one, because the board of trustees insisted that the president be paid at least one dollar more. The remainder of her life was to be in service to the school as a teacher and leader. She retired in 1968 but was called back in 1970 for three more years until she asked for a reduced load in 1973, leaving the classroom for good in 1975.

Louis B. Reynolds remembers her leadership abilities when Oakwood was seeking the accreditation it gained in 1958 and Eva B. Dykes headed the faculty accreditation committee:

> When she talked of money for much-needed facilities at Oakwood, it seemed to her the board members were dragging their feet. At the time of the annual meeting she invited three or four of us whom she knew well to breakfast, and while we ate, she lectured us from prepared notes on the need for immediate action and she outlined in one-two-three order what she felt we ought to do (17).

Mrs. C. B. Rock, a former student and wife of one of Oakwood's presidents, remembers her as a "caring, yet disciplined teacher: Every 't' had to be crossed and every 'i' dotted and, if not, an 'F'. . . . And if you answered (a question in class), and she didn't hear, 'F'" (Hollon, A-6). She would often end her class with the words "audibility" and "minimum standards" (Swann, 16). She also insisted on eight or nine textbooks for her courses—including works like *Five Thousand Words You Should Know*—even though she was amused when freshmen students borrowed children's wagons one day to haul their books to class (Hollon, A-6). At the same time, she was generous to students in her private help. Her outstanding contributions to the college were recognized when the library was named the Eva B. Dykes Library on April 22, 1973.

Black Adventist Conferences Established

There was further service to the college in her direction of the Oakwood College Church Choir, of the Oakwood College Choir, and of the Faculty Women's Chorus, as well as her sponsorship of other college groups. In addition to the offices she filled in her church, she extended her musical work to direct camp meeting choirs for the various conferences. According to Carlos Medley, she was also a leader in the movement to establish "colored" conferences in the denomination. Churches both in the North and in the South had been basically segregated since 1909. In the face of continuing discrimination, she joined the movement that resulted in the formation of the seven "colored" conferences of the Adventists in 1941 (5).

A small woman, Eva B. Dykes was also humble. She often said "I am so very ordinary" (Warren, 13). Louis B. Reynolds tell us:

> There are about her no put-on or professional airs. Dignity, she raised us to understand, had nothing to do with one's social station: character, conduct, were everything. Attitudes of class superiority she considers not only in excess of her credentials but distasteful in themselves. She tells her students the doctorate is purely an

> academic title and it is not necessary for people to call her doctor (17).

He also tells us that one of her most decided traits was a dislike of having people fail to live up to their promises. "Failing to fulfill a promise was to her a kind of falling from grace. She never put herself in the position of being disappointed a second time" (17).

It is fitting that she was able to attend the charter meeting of the National Association of Black Professional Women in Higher Education in Racine, Wisconsin, on April 5, 1976—Georgianna R. Simpson had died and Sadie T. Mossell Alexander was unable to be present. There Geraldine Rickman said:

> We have in our midst a pioneer. Pioneers are special people. "Firsts" are always difficult. We don't know that things can be done, that dreams can be fulfilled, that great accomplishments can be realized, until somebody takes that first step and shows the way. Black women had never realized the full intellectual development and potential until this pioneer, Dr. Eva. B. Dykes, 55 years ago dared to take the first step and show the way (Williams, 12).

Eva B. Dykes died on October 29, 1986, at the age of ninety-three. Her funeral was held on Sunday, November 2, 1986, in the Oakwood College Campus Church.

References

Alexander, Sadie T. M., Ph.D., J.D., and Eva B. Dykes, Ph.D., Reception and Dinner in Honor of National Association of Black Professional Women in Higher Education, 4 April 1976.

"An Era Ends: Eva B. Dykes 1893-1986." *The Spreading Oak*, 13 November 1986. 1. Includes photograph.

"Eva B. Dykes." *Howard University Record* 15 (June 1921): 467-68. Photograph, p. 467.

Ford, H. E. "A Modern Educator." *Message Magazine* (July-August 1938): 2. Photograph on cover.

Hill, Ruth Edmond, ed. *Women of Courage*. Based on the Black Women Oral History Project. Sponsored by the Arthur and Elizabeth Schlesinger Library on the History of Women in America. [Cambridge, Mass.]: Radcliffe College, 1984. 26. Includes photograph.

Hollon, Marian. "At 90, Dr. Dykes Remains an Inspiration." *Huntsville Times*, 27 May 1984. A-6.

Medley, Carlos. "Laced with Grace." *Adventist Review* (1 February 1990): 5.

"Negro Adventists." *Ebony* 6 (May 1951): 96-98. Photograph, p. 96.

Obsequies for Dr. Eva Beatrice Dykes. (2 November 1986).

Peterson, Frank L. *Climbing High Mountains*. Washington, D.C.: Review and Herald Publishing Association, 1962.

Reynolds, Louis B. "She Fulfills the Impossible Dream." *Review and Herald* (4 January 1973): 15-17.

Swann, Retha Lockett. "Dr. Dykes, On America and the Church." *Insight* (16 November 1976): 13-16.

Warren, Mervyn A. "I Am So Ordinary." *Vibrant Life* 1986 (Special Report Issue): 14-14. Photographs, pp. 12, 14.

Who's Who in Colored America. 3rd ed. Brooklyn, N.Y.: Who's Who in Colored America, 1932. 139-40.

Who's Who in Colored America. 7th ed. Yonkers-on-Hudson, N.Y.: Christian E. Burkel, 1950. 171.

Who's Who in Colored America. Vol. 1. New York: Who's Who in Colored America, 1927.

Williams, Dewitt S. "The Impossible Dream." *Message Magazine* (July/August 1987): 10-12. Photograph, p. 10.

Collections

Papers and memorabilia are in the Eva B. Dykes Library, Oakwood College, Huntsville, Alabama, and in the Moorland-Spingarn Research Center, Howard University, Washington, D.C. An interview with Eva B. Dykes is in the Radcliffe College Black Oral History Collection.

Robert L. Johns

E

Ramona Hoage Edelin

(1945-)

Organization executive

As a consequence of the work of her parents, her mother in particular, Ramona Hoage Edelin's life, character, and deepest and longest-held commitments were shaped in the context of values and experiences that form the core of institutions devoted to higher education. The only child of George Hoage and Annette (Lewis) Hoage (later Annette Lewis Phinazee), Edelin was born on September 4, 1945, in Los Angeles, California. Edelin grew up in the academic settings of South Carolina State College (Orangeburg, South Carolina), Atlanta University (Atlanta, Georgia), and Southern Illinois University (Carbondale, Illinois). Her formal education began with her enrollment in the Oglethope Elementary School, the laboratory school of Atlanta University, and continued in Lincoln Junior High School in Carbondale, Illinois, and the Stockbridge School in Stockbridge, Massachusetts, from which she graduated in 1963.

Ramona Hoage Edelin

During the next four years Edelin literally blazed her way through Fisk University, starting with her reception of the Sarah McKim Maloney Award in 1964, and continuing through her graduation in 1967 with a collection of major distinctions: a B.A. magna cum laude in philosophy, with departmental honors; election to Phi Beta Kappa and Gold Key Honor Society; general university honors; a listing in *Who's Who Among Students in American Colleges and Universities;* and contributing editor to the Fisk *Herald,* the student literary magazine, and editor of the *Fisk Forum,* the campus newspaper. On the dean's list for outstanding academic achievement virtually every semester, Edelin was also a regular participant in the university's honors program. In addition, she was also responsible for conceiving and helping to implement a voluntary honor code that allowed those students who signed a pledge to be bound by their honor while taking unproctored examinations, an option available at few other institutions of higher education in the country at the time. Without question, Edelin was among the most stellar minds and talents that passed through Fisk University during the mid-1960s. Both her peers and faculty were astounded by her brilliance. All the more so since she was, as well, "one of the finest things on the yard," recognized, in part, in her being chosen as a campus queen several times, including Miss Sophomore and Miss Alpha Phi Alpha.

However, the Fisk yard was neither sufficient nor intended to contain her prodigious capabilities. Between her junior and senior years she was one of a small number of persons from around the country selected for intensive studies at Harvard University. Married to (and many years later divorced from) Kenneth Edelin, a medical doctor, after her graduation from Fisk University, she went on to earn an M.A. in philosophy from the University of East Anglia in Norwich, England, in 1969 while the family (a son, Kenneth, Jr., had been born) was in England as Kenneth Edelin, Sr., completed a tour of military service. After the family returned to the United States, Ramona Hoage Edelin entered the doctoral program in philosophy at Boston University, receiving the Ph.D. in 1981 after completing her studies with a dissertation on W. E. B. Du Bois.

A daughter, Kimberley, was born during these years. This enlargement of her family, to which she continues to be deeply dedicated, brought additional joys and responsibilities but did not prevent Edelin from building a noteworthy career in education as teacher and administrator. She taught in the European division of the University of Maryland while in England and at Emerson College, Brandeis University, and Northeastern University during her years in Boston. While at Northeastern she was founder and chair of the department of African American Studies.

From this brief survey of the life of Ramona Hoage Edelin several things stand out. First, education—serious, demanding education—has been a consistent, nurturing, and central factor in her life, as both student and teacher. Second, Edelin's own educational experiences, and those she has provided for others, have been guided by an unwavering commitment to excellence. Third, from her undergraduate years through her doctoral dissertation, and continuing today, Edelin has been devoted to achieving the most insightful and impassioned understanding possible of the histories and lives of African people, which she puts to work to help realize their potential for, in her words, "mastery" and "greatness." These elements of her life, long in the making, come together to form the woman who is now devoted to shaping and institutionalizing agendas to secure the lives and well-being of black Americans into the next century:

> A certain quickening of the will is moving through the African-American group as the dawn of the new millennium approaches. This quickening heralds a process of cultural renewal, development, and the rebirth of mastery, greatness, and perfect equality for a people whose humanity itself has, by grace, survived what might have been utter devastation. The job of the 1990s is to leave four hundred-plus years of bare survival behind so that a new African being—in the United States and throughout the world—will cross the threshold into the year 2000 (Edelin, "African America in the Year 2000," 559.)

Edelin Heads National Urban Coalition

Ramona Hoage Edelin is currently president and chief executive officer of the National Urban Coalition, an action and advocacy organization founded in 1967 and based in Silver Spring, Maryland. Since joining the coalition in 1977 as executive assistant to the president, she has held the positions of director of operations, vice president of operations, senior vice president of program and policy (during which time she directed programs in housing and economic development, health and urban education, and advocacy), and chief executive officer. She became respected for her insight into a broad range of urban issues and has been especially identified for her contributions to the development and implementation of the coalition's "Say YES to a Youngster's Future" program, an early intervention, family-learning program aimed at exposing black American, Latino, native American, and female children, ages four to nineteen, to mathematics, science, and computer technology to help prepare them for high technology jobs of the next century. Under Edelin's guidance as president and chief executive officer, the National Urban Coalition has instituted a Leadership Strategy Series, named in honor of M. Carl Holman (deceased), past president of the coalition, which assembles leaders from national organizations, business, labor, Capitol Hill, foundations, educational institutions, and community-based and youth groups for strategic sessions on pertinent issues of public policy and organizational development. It is from this important organizational position, drawing on her wealth of experience and considerable intellectual capabilities, that Edelin has sounded the call-to-arms for, and taken a front-line position in, what she has termed the "cultural offensive": a national effort to bring about cultural renewal as a crucial endeavor devoted to community and economic development and political empowerment for black Americans.

Why a "cultural" offensive? It is necessary, according to Edelin, because black Americans, at present, are, on the whole, without cultural integrity, that is to say, are without a harmonious group identity that insures wholeness and self-sufficiency. Drawing insights from her chief intellectual mentor, W. E. B. Du Bois, Edelin is convinced that black Americans still must resolve the dilemma of "twoness":

> an American, a Negro; two souls, two thoughts, two unreconciled strivings; two warring ideals in one dark body, whose dogged strength alone keeps it from being torn asunder. . . . This waste of double aims, this seeking to satisfy two unreconciled ideals, has wrought sad havoc with the courage and faith and deeds of ten thousand people, has sent them often wooing false gods and invoking false means of salvation, and at times has even seemed about to make them ashamed of themselves (Du Bois, *The Souls of Black Folk,* 3, 5).

Cultural integrity will, Edelin argues, provide the foundation with the formation of a "profound new identity" that will incorporate, among other things, a recovery of African legacies crucial to black's understanding of themselves. Only on this foundation will black Americans be able to move from bare survival to the rebirth and development that will bring mastery and greatness. And only in the context of an appropriate culture, "the vehicle that moves . . . human groups forward" will this be possible (Edelin, "African America in the Year 2000"). Without it, she argues, "we will never sit at the table of cultures as equals with the rest of the world's people" (Edelin, "Toward An African-American Agenda," 175).

Edelin has assumed a leading role in assembling key persons from around the nation to carry out the cultural offensive. The coalition's "Say YES to a Youngster's Future" family development program, through its educational agenda, is devoted to arresting the decimation of young people by helping to create an environment more conducive to their forming wholesome self-perceptions. The program substitutes new programs for educational programs that are inadequate for either group advancement or participation in the economic mainstream. One of Edelin's major concerns is to analyze successful approaches to education—identified, tested, and certified by successful educators of black American youth—and assess them for their value for facilitating the shift from survival to the appropriation of a new identity, cultural integrity, mastery, greatness, and equality. Through the Coalition's Leadership Strategy Series, Edelin is committed to countering the lack of unity in leadership and in resource accumulation and utilization by promoting forms of leadership that have sufficient will to achieve unity and consensus on an agenda for the cultural offensive that will include such an educational program as an item of first priority.

These concerns were prominent during Edelin's participation in the 1989 African American Summit, which she had a significant hand in organizing as program chairperson. The major focus of the summit was the development of a unified agenda for political and economic development. She has other concerns pertinent to the national black American community, as well, among them those having to do with: the condition of family life, health and health care, economic development, politics, criminal justice, foreign policy, housing and urban policy, entertainment and information media, and the continuing struggle for maintaining and acquiring civil rights.

Edelin has been and continues to be actively involved in numerous agencies and organizations: a member of the District of Columbia Humanities Council; a member of the boards of directors of the Boston Black Repertory Company, WINNERS, The Bridge, and the Association for Better Living; a member of the Board of Elders of the African Heritage Institute; an active alumna and supporter, financially and otherwise, of her alma mater, Fisk University; a member of Delta Sigma Theta and Women in Politics.

Her contributions and achievements continue to bring her significant honors and distinctions: recognition as one of the Outstanding Young Women of America (1975) and identification by *Ebony* magazine as one of the "Women to Watch" (1982); the Roxbury [Massachusetts] Action Program Distinguished Service Award (1975); 1986 YWCA Academy of Women Achievers (1987); the IBM Community Executive Program (1983); Southern Christian Leadership Conference Leadership Award for Progressive Leadership (1989); and being named one of the "100 Most Influential Black Americans." She is the author of a number of publications including, in addition to those mentioned previously, "Revolutionary Aspects of Acquiring Skills," (Atlanta University, Center for African and African-American Studies position paper); "Kenneth C. Edelin: A Living Sacrifice?" (*Encore*, 4, May 1975); "Has Anyone Read *The Crisis of the Negro Intellectual* Lately?" (*Black World*, 25, March 1976); "Shirley Graham Du Bois" (*First World*, May/June, 1977); review of W. E. B. Du Bois, *The Education of Black People: Ten Critiques 1906-1960* (*Urban League Review*, Winter 1976); "Role of the African Woman Since Slavery: Culture Bearer" (excerpted in *Encore*, 4, Special Issue, 23 June 1975); and coauthor of "Women at Work" (Wellesley College Center for Research on Women, Winter 1978). Edelin is a regular contributor to the commentary page of the *Afro-American* newspaper chain through her weekly column, "On the Cultural Offensive."

Through these efforts and her leadership of the National Urban Coalition, this nation, and black Americans in particular, are beneficiaries of one of the most capable and devoted, thus one of the most notable, black American women—or men—in this nation.

References

Campbell, Gail A. "Targeting Urban Ills: The First Woman Chief of the National Urban Coalition." *Washington Times*, 13 July 1988.

Du Bois, W. E. B. *The Souls of Black Folk*. Fisk University Diamond Jubilee Edition. Nashville: Fisk University Press, 1979.

Edelin, Ramona. "African America in the Year 2000." *The World & I* (January 1990): 558-69.

———. "Toward An African-American Agenda: An Inward Look." In *The State of Black America 1990*. New York: National Urban League, 1990.

Who's Who Among Black Americans, 1990/91. Detroit: Gale Research, 1990.

Lucius Outlaw

Marian Wright Edelman

(1939-)

Lawyer, organization founder, children's rights activist

Marian Wright Edelman, attorney and founding president of the Children's Defense Fund (CDF), has been an advocate for disadvantaged Americans for her entire professional career and is primarily known as a children's rights crusader.

Edelman was born the youngest of five children on June 6, 1939, the daughter of Arthur Jerome Wright and Maggie Leola (Bowen) Wright in Bennettsville, South Carolina. Her father was the minister of Shiloh Baptist Church and had been influenced by Booker T. Washington's self-help philosophy. He expected his children to get an education and to serve their community. "The only bad thing about that is that none of us learned how to relax," Edelman recalled in an interview for a lengthy profile that appeared in a 1989 issue of the *New Yorker*. "Working for the community was as

Marian Wright Edelman

much a part of our existence as eating and sleeping and church." Arthur Wright established the Wright Home for the Aged in the segregated town of Bennettsville and his wife, Maggie, ran it. Edelman recalls that her father probably never made more than two hundred dollars a month, "but none of us ever felt poor, and compared to the people around us, we weren't" (Tomkins, 54). Her father also believed in black role models and whenever prominent blacks came to town, the Wright children were taken to hear them. Marian was named for Marian Anderson, whom she was taken to hear as a child. Her father, who had a profound impact on her development and her priorities, died when Edelman was only fourteen.

After graduating from Marlboro Training High School, Edelman was persuaded by her mother and brother, Harry, to attend Spelman College in Atlanta, Georgia, though her first choice was Fisk University in Nashville, Tennessee. "I hated the idea of going to a staid women's college," she observed, "but it turned out to be the right place for me after all" (Tomkins, 56). She entered Spelman in 1956. Because of her outstanding scholarship, she won a Charles Merrill study/travel grant for study abroad during her junior year. She spent the first summer at the Sorbonne University studying French civilization but decided to spend the remainder of the academic year at the University of Geneva in Switzerland.

During the second semester, Edelman studied for two months in the Soviet Union under a Lisle Fellowship; because of her interest in Tolstoy, she had always wanted to go to Russia. After her travels in Europe over the course of a year and two summers, she returned to Spelman a different person: "It was a great liberating experience. After a year's freedom as a person, I wasn't prepared to go back to a segregated existence," she recalled. In 1959, the year of sit-ins and the first student protests in the South, she returned to Atlanta for her senior year and became active in the embryonic civil rights movement that was to alter profoundly United States race relations in the South. During her senior year (1960) she participated in one of the largest sit-ins in Atlanta at City Hall. Fourteen students were arrested, including Edelman. It was during this time that she decided to go to law school instead of pursuing graduate study in Russian studies at Georgetown University, which would have prepared her for a career in foreign service. During this time she also became aware of the fact that civil rights lawyers were scarce and sorely needed.

After graduating valedictorian of her Spelman class in 1960, she applied to Yale University Law School and entered as a John Hay Whitney Fellow. During spring break of her last year in law school (1963), she went to Mississippi and got involved in the voter registration drive, which her friend, Robert Moses, led as a field secretary for the Student Nonviolent Coordinating Committee (SNCC). She returned to New Haven, graduated from Yale in 1963, and after a year's training in New York went to Jackson, Mississippi, as one of the first two NAACP Legal Defense and Educational Fund interns. In the spring of 1964 she opened a law office and continued civil rights work, which consisted largely of getting students out of jail. During this time she was threatened by dogs, thrown into jail, and before taking the Mississippi bar, was refused entry into a state courthouse. Asked if at that time she despaired about the law as a viable instrument of social change, she replied, "Sure, like every morning. But one keeps plugging, trying to make our institutional processes work." At age twenty-six, she became the first black woman to pass the bar in Mississippi. Her civil rights crusading continued when she headed the NAACP Legal Defense and Education Fund in Mississippi from 1964 to 1968. Edelman wrote about her intense commitment to liberation and struggle after her return from a year abroad in an article that appeared in the Spelman *Messenger:*

> I realize that I am not fighting just for myself and my people in the South, when I fight for freedom and equality. I realize now that I fight for the moral and political health of America as a whole and for her position in the world at large. . . . as I push the cause for freedom a step further, by gaining my own. . . .I know that I, in my individual struggle for improvement, help the world. I am no longer an isolated being—I belong. Europe helped me to see this (6).

While in Mississippi, she met Peter Edelman, a Harvard law school graduate and one of Robert Kennedy's legislative assistants, who was working in 1967 on the Senate's Subcommittee on Employment, Manpower, and Poverty. She was going through a transition realizing that in order to change things in Mississippi, she had to impact federal policy. After receiving a Field Foundation grant to study how to make laws work for the poor, she moved to Washington,

D.C., in March 1968 and started the Washington Research Project. This was a difficult time for the nation and the movement. Martin Luther King, Jr., had been assassinated in April and Robert Kennedy was shot two months later. In July Marian Wright married Peter Edelman, who was among the group of Kennedy aides who, after Kennedy's death, received Ford Foundation grants to help them make the transition to other careers.

In 1971 the Edelmans left Washington and moved to Boston, where he became vice-president of the University of Massachusetts, and she became director of the Harvard University Center for Law and Education. She flew to Washington weekly to oversee the activities of the Washington Research Project. By this time their interracial marriage had produced two sons—Joshua and Jonah. Ezra was born in 1974.

Children's Defense Fund Founded

In 1973 Marian Edelman founded the Children's Defense Fund (CDF), a nonprofit child advocacy organization that was based in Washington, D.C. Its mission was to provide systematic and long-range assistance to children and to make their needs an important matter of public policy. Her work with the CDF and her passionate devotion to the rights of children have brought her national recognition as "the children's crusader." The Edelmans returned to Washington in 1979, where Peter Edelman obtained a teaching post at the Georgetown University Law Center.

Teen pregnancy, especially in the black community, became a major issue in 1983. "I saw from our own statistics that fifty-five and a half percent of all black babies were born out of wedlock, a great many of them to teen-age girls. It just hit me over the head—that situation insured black child poverty for the next generation" (Tomkins, 70). In 1983 CDF launched a major long-term national campaign to prevent teenage pregnancy and provide positive life options for youth. It included a multimedia campaign that consisted of transit advertisements, poster, television, and radio public service announcements, a national prenatal care campaign, and local volunteer Child Watch coalitions in more than seventy local communities in thirty states around the country. CDF was also largely responsible for the Act for Better Child Care, which was introduced in the Senate by Alan Cranston, a liberal Democrat from California, in November 1987.

Under Edelman's leadership, CDF has become one of the nation's most active and effective organizations concerned with a wide range of children's and family issues, particularly those that most affect America's poorest: children. CDF's mission is to teach the nation about the needs of children and encourage preventive investments in children before they get sick, drop out of school, suffer too-early pregnancy or family breakdown, or get into trouble. CDF has become an effective voice nationwide in the areas of adolescent pregnancy prevention, child health, education, child care, youth employment, child welfare and mental health, and family support systems.

In 1980 Edelman became the first black and second woman to chair the Board of Trustees of Spelman College, her alma mater. In 1971 *Time* magazine named her one of America's two hundred young leaders. She was the first black woman elected to the Yale University Corporation (1971-1977). From 1972 to 1977 she was on the board of the Carnegie Council on Children. Currently she serves on the boards of the NAACP Legal Defense and Education Fund, the Aetna Life and Casualty Foundation, the March of Dimes, Citizens for Constitutional Concerns, Joint Center for Political Studies, United States Committee for UNICEF, Center for Budget and Policy Priorities, and the Board of Trustees of Spelman College. She is also a member of the Council of Foreign Relations. In 1983 she was named one of the one hundred most influential women in America by the *Ladies Home Journal*. In 1985 she became the recipient of the prestigious MacArthur Foundation Prize Fellowship.

Edelman was a member of the Presidential Commission on Americans Missing and Unaccounted for in Southeast Asia (1977); United States-South Africa Leadership Exchange Program to explore the role of women leaders in South Africa (1977); National Commission on the International Year of the Child (1979); and President's Commission for a National Agenda for the Eighties (1979). She is also a member of the District of Columbia Bar; the state of Mississippi Bar; and the Commonwealth of Massachusetts Bar. A 1987 *Time* magazine article called Marian Wright Edelman "one of Washington's most unusual lobbyists" whose "effectiveness depends as much on her adroit use of statistics as on moral persuasion" (Traver, 27). In the same year Harvard University Press published *Families in Peril: An Agenda for Social Change*, based on Edelman's William E. B. Du Bois lectures delivered at Harvard in 1986. In this pioneering book Edelman states that "the tide of misery that poverty breeds and that Blacks have borne disproportionately throughout history has now spread to a critical mass of white American families and children."

Edelman's awards are numerous: Louis Waterman Wise Award (1970); Outstanding Leadership Award of National Alliance of Black School Educators (1979); Distinguished Service Award of the National Association of Black Women Attorneys (1979); National Award of Merit of the National Council on Crime and Delinquency (1979); and Washingtonian of the Year (1979). In 1980 Edelman received the following awards: Whitney M. Young Memorial Award (Washington Urban League); *Black Enterprise* Magazine Professional Achievement Award; National Women's Political Caucus/Black Caucus Outstanding Leadership Achievement Award; National Hookup of Black Women's Outstanding Community Service Award; and Big Sisters' Women of the Year Award. In 1981: American Academy of Pedodontics, Award of Recognition; honorary membership, Delta Sigma Theta Sorority; Rockefeller Public Service Award. In 1982: Gertrude Zimand Award (National Child Labor Committee); and Florine Lasker Award (New York Civil Liberties Union). In

1984: Anne Roe Award (Harvard University Graduate School of Education); Roy Wilkins Civil Rights Award (NAACP Image Awards); Women's Legal Defense Fund Award; and Hubert H. Humphrey Award (Leadership Conference on Civil Rights). In 1985 there was the Barnard College Medal of Distinction and in 1986 the Grenville Clark Prize, Dartmouth College. In 1987: Compostela Award (The Cathedral of Saint James); A. Philip Randolph Award (The National Urban Coalition); The Achievement Award (The American Association of University Women); The William P. Dawson Award (The Congressional Black Caucus); The Trumpeter Award (National Consumer League); Colleague, Saint John the Divine; Catherine Dunfey Award: New England Circle; and an honorary membership in the American Society of Dentistry for Children. Finally, in 1988: the Albert Schweitzer Humanitarian Prize, Johns Hopkins University.

Edelman has received honorary degrees from the following institutions: Smith College (1969); Lesley College (1975); Lowell Technological Institute (1975); Russell Sage College (1978); Williams College (1978); College of New Rochelle (1979); Syracuse University (1979); Swarthmore College (1980); State University of New York at Old Westbury (1981); Marymount Manhattan College (1981); Bard College (1982); University of Massachusetts (1982); St. Mary's College (1983); Hunter College (1983); William and Hobart College (1984); Mount Vernon College (1984); Saint Joseph College (Hartford, 1985); Columbia University (1985); Amherst College (1985); University of Pennsylvania (1985); Yale University (1985); New York University (1986); Rutgers University (1986); Bates College (1986); Maryville College (1986); Bank Street (1986); Georgetown University (1987); Chicago Theological Seminary (1987); Wheelock College (1988); Wheaton College (1988); University of North Carolina (1988); Tulane University (1988); Northwestern University (1988); Graduate Center of City University (1988); Grinnell College (1988); and Brandeis University (1988).

An extensive writer, Edelman is author of *Children Out of School in America* (Washington, D.C.: Children's Defense Fund, 1974); *School Suspensions: Are They Helping Children?* (Washington, D.C.: Children's Defense Fund, 1975); *Portrait of Inequality: Black and White Children in America* (Washington, D.C.: Children's Defense Fund, 1980); and *Families in Peril: An Agenda for Social Change* (Harvard University Press, 1987). Published articles include: "Southern School Desegregation, 1954: A Judicial-Political Overview," *The Annals of the American Academy of Political and Social Science*, (May 1973); "Twenty Years After Brown: Where Are We Now?," *New York University Education Quarterly*, (Summer 1974); "Winston and Dovie Hudson's Dream,"(an analysis of the status of school desegregation and myths of resistance), *Harvard Educational Review*, (November 1975); "In Defense of Children's Rights," *Yale Alumni Magazine*, (February 1978); "Today's Promises—Tomorrow's Children: Putting Children First on the National Agenda," *Young Children*, (March 1978); and "Who Is For Children?," *American Psychologist*, (February 1981).

References

"By Marian Wright." *Spelman Messenger* 76 (May 1960): 5-6.

"Letters from Two Merrill Scholars." *Spelman Messenger* 75 (November 1958): 18-19.

Tomkins, Calvin. "Profiles: A Sense of Urgency." *New Yorker* (March 1989): 48-74.

Traver, N. "They Cannot Fend for Themselves." *Time* 129 (23 March 1987): 27.

Collections

Information on Marian Wright Edelman can be found in the Spelman College Archives and the offices of the Children's Defense Fund, 122 C Street, N.W., Washington, D.C., 20001. An extensive photograph collection of Edelman is also stored there.

Beverly Guy-Sheftall

Helen G. Edmonds

(1911-)

Educator, historian, civic worker

An educator for more than forty years, Helen Grey Edmonds has been celebrated nationwide for her academic and civic achievements. She was born on December 3, 1911, in Lawrenceville, Virginia, to John Edward Edmonds and Ann (Williams) Edmonds. Her father was a contractor in the building trades who, at the height of his career, employed a work crew of twenty-two men. Her mother was a homemaker who cared for the four Edmonds children, all of whom became college graduates.

The attainment of higher education was something that was simply expected in the Edmonds home. Saint Paul's School, founded and supported by the Episcopal Church and patterned after Hampton and Tuskegee institutes, was located in Lawrenceville and served as an inspiration to the majority of the black population there. Although the school was located in a "plantation county" and sat on sixteen hundred acres of farm land, the curriculum was demanding.

After completing the academy, Edmonds remained in Lawrenceville for junior college before transferring in 1931 to Morgan State College (now University) in Maryland. At Morgan State she wanted to major in Latin, but, because it was "fading out of the high school curriculum," she added English and history to her concentration in Latin. After

Helen G. Edmonds

receiving a bachelor's degree from Morgan State in 1933, Edmonds began teaching Latin, Greek, and history at the Virginia Theological Seminary and College in Lynchburg. After one year at Virginia Theological, she returned to Saint Paul's as an instructor in history. Meanwhile, she pursued as master's degree in history at Ohio State University.

In 1938 Edmonds was awarded the M.A. at Ohio State while still on the faculty at Saint Paul's. She left her alma mater in 1940 and assumed a position on the history faculty at North Carolina College (now North Carolina Central University) in Durham the following year. She was to remain an active member of the faculty at North Carolina for thirty-six years. Meanwhile, in 1946, she earned a doctorate in history from Ohio State, becoming the first black American woman to be awarded that degree in the history of the university. Inspired by W. E. B. Du Bois's study at the University of Berlin, Edmonds attended the University of Heidelberg (Germany) in 1954 and 1955.

During her long career at North Carolina, Edmonds rose from an instructor in history in 1941 to graduate professor of history in 1946, chair of the department of history (1963-64), dean of the graduate school of arts and sciences (1964-71), member of the interim committee for the administration of the university (1966-67), and university distinguished professor (1971-77).

Concurrently with her tenure at North Carolina Central and since her retirement from the university, Edmonds has been a visiting professor or scholar at several other colleges and universities, including Portland State University (summers 1968-74), Rochester State University (1982), Ohio State University (1984), Massachusetts Institute of Technology (1984-85), Harvard University (1985-86), and Radcliffe College (1986-88).

Edmonds has authored at least ten articles and books. The more noted of these are *The Negro and Fusion Politics in North Carolina* (1951), a classic study of post-Reconstruction political developments in the Tarheel state, and *Black Faces in High Places* (1971), a biographical compilation. *The Negro and Fusion Politics* was included among the one hundred outstanding books about North Carolina in a 1956 publication compiled by Richard Walsen and Hugh T. Lefler.

In addition to her writings, Edmonds has achieved considerable distinction as an orator. She has been principal or keynote speaker at more than one hundred American and foreign universities, including Duke, Fisk, Howard, Rutgers, and Stanford, and the universities of South Carolina, Stockholm, and Monrovia. In March 1983 she delivered the commencement address to 1,428 graduates of Ohio State University at the end of the winter quarter. In her speech before the predominantly white audience, she declared that "racism in our land is all pervasive, and it is practiced by and in all ethnic groups in our pluralistic society."

Despite a full academic life, Edmonds has held important leadership positions in both scholarly and civic organizations, including the Southern Fellowships Fund, the United Negro College Fund, the NAACP Legal Defense Fund, the Robert R. Moton Memorial Institute, and the United Research and Development Corporation. Between 1970 and 1974 she was national president of the Links, a women's public service organization. During this period the group raised one million dollars in support of the United Negro College Fund For a year, Edmonds served as national chair of the humanities bicentennial celebration of the Association for the Study of Negro Life and History. In this capacity she coordinated celebrations of the bicentennial of the American Revolution in dozens of black communities throughout the United States as well as a national conference on the bicentennial.

Political Involvement Brings National Distinction

In the public sector, Edmonds has received appointments to numerous advisory committees in the state of North Carolina, including Governor James Martin's Task Force on Minority Concerns and Issues in 1985. But her most distinguished service has come at the federal level. A lifelong Republican, she became the first black woman in American history to second the nomination of a candidate for president of the United States in 1956. At the Republican National Convention in San Francisco that year, she gave a nominating speech on behalf of General Dwight D. Eisenhower. After Eisenhower won the nomination and the presidency, he sent Edmonds as his personal representative to the dedication ceremonies of the new capitol building in Monrovia, Liberia. She not only addressed the audience at the ceremonies, but while in the west African nation gave seven other major addresses to schools, colleges, and civic groups. Later, the

U.S. Department of State enlisted her services for an international education exchange program to western Europe in 1957. Later, in 1976, the U.S. Department of Defense named her a member of its Advisory Committee on Women in the Armed Services.

Although it was Eisenhower who first solicited Edmonds's services to the federal government, her major activities occurred during the administration of President Richard M. Nixon. In 1970 Nixon named her an alternate delegate to the General Assembly of the United Nations. In this capacity she also chaired the U.S. delegation to the third committee during the celebration of the twenty-fifth anniversary of the founding of the United Nations. During that year, Nixon also appointed Edmonds to the National Advisory Council of the Peace Corps. Other appointments included member of the Social Science Advisory Council to the U.S. Arms Control and Disarmament Agency (1971) and member and vice-chair of the National Advisory Council to Education Professional Development (1973, 1975-76).

Because of her distinguished contributions to the people of North Carolina and the nation in education and in civic and social service, Edmonds has been honored by hundreds of schools, colleges, and social and professional organizations and by the local, state, and federal government. Among these recognitions are the Oliver Max Gardner Award of the University of North Carolina (for the "greatest contribution to the welfare of the human race," 1975), the Candace Award of the Coalition of 100 Black Women (1982, of which she was the first recipient), Helen Grey Edmonds Day in Durham, North Carolina (March 1, 1982), the Hugh McEniry Award of the North Carolina Association of Colleges and Universities (for her "principles of dedication and commitment to the education and advancement of the state [of North Carolina]," 1982), and the Distinguished Achievement Award of the Radcliffe College Alumni Association (1989). Additionally she was named Distinguished Woman of North Carolina (1986), and Percy L. Julian Memorial Lecturer, DePauw University (1989). At least three organizations, including the Bachelors-Benedict Club, Norfolk, Virginia (1958), the Southern Area of the Links (1963, 1973), and the Daughter Elks of IBPOE (1977) have selected Edmonds as their "Woman of the Year."

In addition to citations by the city of Durham and the state of North Carolina, Edmonds has been cited by the cities of Columbus, Los Angeles, and New Orleans and the state of Michigan, among others.

Colleges and universities recognizing the work of Helen Grey Edmonds with honorary degrees have included Morgan State University (1958), Saint Paul's College (1977), North Carolina Central University (1978), Ohio State University (1983), Duke University (1983), and Virginia Union University (1986).

It is perhaps safe to assert that few, if any, of Edmonds's recognitions were more personally satisfying than the establishment of the Helen G. Edmonds Graduate Colloquium of History at North Carolina Central University in 1977. This scholarly symposium, which also features an annual luncheon, was created by the twenty-five persons holding a Ph.D. in history and the social sciences who completed their studies in the undergraduate and graduate departments of North Carolina Central University under the mentorship of Edmonds.

Although, Edmonds is approaching the eighth decade of her very active life, she remains devoted to a full schedule of academic and civic pursuits. In addition to researching and writing a history of black women in politics, Edmonds holds visiting professorships, gives lectures, and sits on various trustee and advisory boards.

References

Bunting Institute Newsletter, Spring 1987.

Burlington Free Press (Vermont), 26 February 1986.

Chicago Tribune, 25 February 1981.

Cleveland Call and Post, 3 March 1983.

Columbus Citizen-Journal (Ohio), 29 May 1984.

Durham Morning Herald, 5 April 1981; 24 March 1986.

Durham Sun, 18 April 1985; 21 March 1986.

Hale, Frank W., Jr., comp. "Helen G. Edmonds and Eternal Verities." In *They Came and They Conquered*. Columbus, Ohio: Ohio State University Graduate School, 1983.

Harvard Crimson, 5 April 1989.

Harvard Gazette, 7 April 1989.

Miller, Carroll L. "Profile: Dr. Helen Grey Edmonds." In *Role Model Blacks*. Muncie, Ind., Accelerated Development, 1982.

Negro History Bulletin 40 (September-October 1977).

Radcliffe News, April 1986.

Who's Who in America. 39th edition. Chicago: Marquis, 1980.

Who's Who in the World. 3rd ed. Chicago: Marquis, 1977.

Wilson, Emily. "You Follow Me? Helen G. Edmonds." In *Hope and Dignity—Older Black Women of the South*. Philadelphia: Temple University Press, 1983.

Alton Hornsby, Jr.

Ophelia Settle Egypt

(1903-1984)

Social worker, educator, writer

It was through her research on former slaves and the current status of black sharecroppers in Georgia, accomplished in conjunction with the Social Science Research Institute at Fisk University, that Ophelia Settle Egypt's work first became well known, and her studies provided a solid basis for new scholarship. But her work in the area of social service met an important need in the black community. It enabled her to provide social and emotional relief to black youth, unmarried mothers, and needy blacks throughout the several communities in which she unstintingly gave her expertise and time.

Ophelia Settle Egypt was born February 20, 1903, in Clarksville, Texas, the daughter of Green Wilson Settle and Sarah (Garth) Settle. Egypt died in Washington, D.C., on May 25, 1984. She grew up in a family of seven children—three were born to her parents and four were born to her father by a previous marriage. Her mother died when Egypt was five. Her maternal grandmother had lived in Decatur, Alabama, her maternal grandfather in Alabama and later North Carolina. Her paternal grandparents had lived in Corinth, Mississippi. Both sets of grandparents had lived in slavery and her maternal grandparents, in particular, who raised Egypt after her mother died, often gave accounts of slave life.

She was sent to live with an aunt in Denver, Colorado, to survive the serious asthma condition that she had developed. A young black dentist persuaded her to attend Howard University in Washington, D.C., where she received the B.A. degree in 1925. From 1925 to 1926 she taught in Orange County Training School in the rural area near Chapel Hill, North Carolina. She entered the University of Pennsylvania but was disheartened over the rudeness of fellow black students, who ignored her until she began associating with writer Arthur Huff Fauset. After that, all blacks on campus sought out Egypt. In 1928 she received her M.A. degree from the University of Pennsylvania.

Just before her her graduation, Charles Spurgeon Johnson, who was leaving his post as editor of the National Urban League's *Opportunity* magazine to establish and head the social science department at Fisk University in Nashville, Tennessee, wrote to the University of Pennsylvania and other institutions to identify black sociology graduates who might be asked to join his faculty. He wrote to Ophelia Egypt; she accepted his offer to become instructor and research assistant, and together they built the department and recruited other staff. She found Johnson a "complicated, wonderful person," with a "poker face." "He was quiet," a deep thinker with "great ideas. He could always get money and get people to work for him." Many people criticized Johnson and accused him of "using people, then . . . go on and get someone else" (Ann A. Shockley interview with Ophelia Settle Egypt, 12 December, 1972. Unless otherwise indicated, all quoted information was taken from that interview). But Ophelia Egypt disagreed with this view, saying that he was a very helpful person who always gave his staff credit for their work, and that he helped her tremendously in her own research interests. She spoke of the research staff's meeting at Mau Mee's, a black soul-food restaurant near Fisk where Johnson took the staff for meals during their local research. "Mau Mee's helped more students through Fisk," she said, and "Roland Hayes was one of the people she helped." On such occasions as their visits to Mau Mee's, Johnson often told jokes. "He had a wonderful collection of jokes, He would tell us these jokes . . . [and] never crack a smile." Secretly the staff called him "Mister Charlie."

Former Slaves Interviewed

Egypt assisted Johnson in several research projects as chief field researcher. Notable among her projects were a study on the Negro in Tennessee and research that resulted in the publication of *Shadow of the Plantation* and *The Negro College Graduate*. She became involved in research on former slaves quite by accident. While researching the Negro in Tennessee, she ran across a number of former slaves. "Remembering my grandmother and grandfather's stories [on slavery], I was more interested in the slavery part than I was in some of the other material I was supposed to get. So when I called this to his [Johnson's] attention he saw one of these interviews and said, 'This is a gold mine!; get on out there and get as many of these as you can.'" He assigned a secretary to assist with the interview project.

The interview project with more than one hundred former slaves in Tennessee and Kentucky was a vital work that resulted in the compiling of essential information to provide missing links in black and American history. Since Egypt initiated the work, Johnson always considered it her project. Former slaves in Tennessee were interviewed in 1929-1930 and others in 1932. Initially in the process, the subjects were encouraged to recount their slave experiences as they wished, without attention to structure. After that, Egypt and her secretary prepared a list of questions to ask the former slaves so that they might determine the slaves' views on some issue, determine if any patterns were set, and verify information that other subjects gave. If the interviewee mentioned something that another former slave had already said, more probing questions on that subject were asked. Among the interviews was one with a member of the Fisk Jubilee Singers and another involving East Grissard, around which a folk legend developed, although some of the facts are correct. On a few occasions the former slaves were reluctant to talk, but in time all talked freely. Egypt published the interviews in *Unwritten History of Slavery* (Social Science Source Documents Number 1, Fisk University, 1945; they were subsequently republished as *God Struck Me Dead* (Philadelphia: Pilgrim Press, 1969). While the names of the former slaves are recorded on the interview transcripts, fictitious names are given in the published works.

Egypt's research on *Shadow of the Plantation* resulted in interviews with black sharecroppers in Macon County, Alabama, near Tuskegee Institute (now University), whose pathetic conditions were hardly removed from slavery. The Fisk team found that Macon County was the worst area in that part of the country, with conditions far inferior to those in south Georgia, where they also conducted research. Settle and the team visited churches and lodge meetings to talk with the sharecroppers and persuade them to take advantage of training experiences at Tuskegee Institute. There they would be taught survival techniques for dealing with plantation owners who kept them in slave-like conditions. It was in Macon County also that in 1932 the U.S. Public Health Service undertook the noted syphilis study, known as the Tuskeegee Study, using 431 black men as guinea pigs. The Fisk researchers knew of the study and were erroneously told that blacks with "bad blood" (or syphilis) were being given injections for treatment. Little did the researchers or the men in the experiment know that this was untrue. The subjects continued to spread the dreaded disease. Less than a fourth of the men survived while the others lived in prolonged misery and died slow painful deaths.

Egypt left Fisk in 1933 to become a social worker for a relief agency in Saint Louis. The nation was in the Great Depression, and the agency sought sociologists and social workers to work with the black poor. Since she was asked to come to Saint Louis and could address her special concern for helping people, she accepted the challenge. Meanwhile, Charles S. Johnson, though regretful at her leaving, persuaded Egypt to take the slave narrative material with her and encouraged her to continue the work. In Saint Louis, Egypt became a dedicated social worker. She tells of difficulties experienced in persuading some needy families to accept relief.

After a brief stay in Saint Louis, Ophelia Egypt moved to New Orleans, where she became head of social services at Flint Goodridge Hospital. Her salary was less than she had received in Saint Louis, but she liked the more prestigious position. She enrolled in social work courses offered through the hospital and strengthened significantly her educational background in the field. She remained at Flint Goodridge for five years, until 1939. At that time Inabel Burns Lindsay, who had been her supervisor in Saint Louis, moved to Howard University to work with E. Franklin Frazier; Ophelia Egypt also went there. Frazier was known for his research on the black family. "I had worked with him at Fisk in the department—doing his own projects, but he worked closely with the staff," she said. She was assistant professor in the School of Social Work at Howard for ten years (1939-1949).

While she was at Howard, Ophelia Settle met and then married in June 1940 Ivory L. Egypt, a dining car waiter. On October 16, 1942, their son, Ivory Lester, Jr., was born. Ophelia Egypt also had a stepson, Thurman Lee Egypt. Ivory Lester, Sr., died in 1953.

During these years also she obtained the M.S. degree from Columbia University School of Social Work (1944). By this time she had become intrigued with the developments in social work. Rather than return to Howard after obtaining her degree, Ophelia Settle Egypt decided to return to the field. She also continued to study and received an Advanced Curriculum Certificate from the University of Pennsylvania School of Social Work in 1950.

Egypt Works with Unmarried Mothers

Ophelia Egypt spent the next two years (1950-1952) as a probation officer in the Juvenile Court of Washington, D.C. From 1952 to 1954 she was executive director of the Iona R. Whipper Home for unmarried black mothers in the District of Columbia. She found the work there fascinating. Some of the young mothers "were unloved . . . and unwanted by their parents." When the land and facility were taken for a public housing project, Egypt stayed on until the young women gave birth and arrangements were made for them.

Continuing her career in social work, Egypt was a caseworker for the Family and Child Services from 1954 to 1956. There she worked on a special project for unmarried mothers. She had some contact with the agency while she was still with the Whipper Home. Changing positions again, she moved to Planned Parenthood as education director. In this position she taught the community residents about planning for parenting. To reach the residents, she held tea parties in the homes of members of the board. Soon the need for a community clinic was seen. She also broadened her work to include sex education for teenagers. She founded the Parklands Neighborhood Clinic, Planned Parenthood of Metropolitan Washington, D.C., and was its director for the next twelve years (1956-1968), and from 1968 to 1970 she was family planning consultant, Office of Economic Opportunity, United States Department of Health, Education, and Welfare and continued her work for Planned Parenthood. Retiring in 1968, Egypt became a writer of children's books.

Ophelia Settle Egypt describes her chief community interest after retirement:

> [I] work with school children, acquainting them, through reading, discussions, and visual aids, with the rich heritage left by their ancestors who were slaves. Stressing the positive aspects of the slave family and its efforts to hold together in spite of hardships and forced physical separations as well as their struggles, hopes and accomplishments during and following slavery, to stimulate the children to do their best to emulate them in spite of their own frustrations and difficulties (Questionnaire).

Egypt's interest in teaching children about slavery has been demonstrated also in her publication of a volume of *Unwrit-*

ten History of Slavery, with interviews added after the first volume and designed for children ages twelve and above.

Egypt was active in her professional association as a Gold Star member of the National Association of Social Workers. Her interest in writing led her to become a member of the Black Writers' Workshop of Washington, D.C., and to serve as a volunteer speaker and discussion leader for children in schools and libraries in an effort to stimulate interest in reading and in history. She joined the Garfield-Douglas Civic Association and for a while was its president. She served on the board of Health-Aide Service of Metropolitan Washington, D.C., and was also a member of the Speakers' Bureau, Anacostia Neighborhood Museum.

Ophelia Settle Egypt's work was recognized through honors and awards that she received. The Iota Phi Lambda Sorority, Alpha Gamma Chapter, honored her with the "Woman of the Year" Award in 1963. On May 25, 1975, she received the Club Twenty's International Women's Year Award. She received yet another award from the Men of Christ in her church—First Baptist Church in Highland Park, Maryland—for "outstanding service as a senior citizen."

Her writings were varied in focus: "Social Attitudes During the Slave Regime," *Publication of the American Sociological Society,* 28 (May 1934); also published in August Meier and Elliott Rudwick, eds., *The Making of Black America* (Atheneum, 1969); "Sight Saving in Young Adults Through Social Service," *The Sight Saving Review* 11 (December 1941); "One Little Boy Meets Prejudice," *Parents* magazine (February 1956); "Helping a Tuberculosis Patient Face Surgery," *Journal of Social Casework,* (March 1951); "Reaching and Keeping the Client," *Public Family Planning Clinics,* conference report (Searle Co., 1965); "Memories of Sterling Brown Walking the Campus Like a Natural Man," *Sterling Brown; A Umum Tribute,* (Black History Museum, UMUM Publishers, 1976); *Unwritten History of Slavery,* originally issued in 1945 by the Social Science Institute, Fisk University, as Social Science Document 1 (Microcard Editions, 1968); *James Weldon Johnson* (Crowell, 1974); Foreword, *Joy Cometh in the Morning,* by Annetta Elam Capdeville (The Author, 1979); and "Three Ex-Slave Interviews," *Indigne: An Anthology of Future Black Arts,* Black History Museum Committee, eds. (Philadelphia, 1980).

When asked how she became interested in writing children's books, particularly the work on James Weldon Johnson, Ophelia Settle Egypt gives credit to writer and editor Sharon Bell Mathis. Mathis, who at that time was an editor at the Thomas Y. Crowell publishing company, complained that most of the writers of children's books published by Crowell were white. She spoke before the Writers' Workshop of Washington, D.C., and persuaded members of the group to write on a black personality. Egypt chose James Weldon Johnson because he, too, had been at Fisk as professor of creative writing while she was there. After researching and writing on James Weldon Johnson, she said, "I think I know that man so much better than I knew him at Fisk."

Ophelia Settle Egypt's interview work with former slaves is noted in Stanley Feldstein, *Once a Slave* (Morrow, 1971); Bertram Wyatt-Brown, *The American People in the Antebellum South* (Pendulum Press, 1973); and Eugene Genovese, *Roll Jordan Roll* (Pantheon Books, 1974).

References

Brown, Warren. "A Shocking New Report on Black Syphilis Victims." *Jet* 43 (9 November 1972): 12-15.

Egypt, Ophelia Settle. Interview with Ann Allen Shockley, 2 December 1972.

Shockley, Ann A., and Sue P. Chandler. *Living Black American Authors.* New York: Bowker, 1973.

Collections

The Ophelia Settle Egypt Papers are in the Moorland-Spingarn Research Center, Howard University. A taped interview with Egypt as well as a biography file are in Special Collections, Fisk University Library.

Jessie Carney Smith

Zilpha Elaw

(1790?-?)

Religious leader, school founder

Zilpha Elaw is one of a growing number of nineteenth-century black American women who have recently been rediscovered. Nevertheless, the only information we have about her comes from her 1846 autobiography, *Memoirs of the Life, Religious Experience, Ministerial Travels and Labours of Mrs. Zilpha Elaw, An American Female of Color: Together with Some Account of the Great Religious Revivals in America [Written by Herself].*

Like many people writing spiritual autobiographies, Elaw focuses on her development as a Christian rather than on the particulars of her "worldly" existence. Elaw described her autobiography to people she met while serving as a minister in England, offering it to them in lieu of a keepsake, calling it:

> [a] more lively memento of my Christian esteem . . . a representation, not indeed, of the features of my outward person, drawn and coloured by the skill of the pencilling artist but of the lineaments of my inward man, as inscribed by the Holy

> Ghost, and according to my poor ability, copied off for your edification (51).

Details about Elaw's life are sparsely sprinkled throughout her fascinating accounts of prophetic dreams and visions and her courageous travels as a minister in England, New Jersey, New England, and the southern United States, where her faith in God and her commitment to preaching the Gospel overcame her fear of being enslaved. Though she centers her autobiography on her religious beliefs, Elaw vehemently speaks out against slavery and racial prejudice.

Elaw's *Memoirs* follows the established pattern for these types of narratives. In it she describes her own progress towards salvation, which, for her, as a Methodist, was a three-step process: first repentance, then justification, and finally the gift of sanctification. The visions and prophesies that led to her salvation and eventually to the ministry provide the most fascinating and dramatic moments in her narrative.

Her autobiography notes that Elaw was born in Pennsylvania to free parents who were also deeply religious. Andrews estimates Elaw's date of birth to be somewhere around 1790. She was, as she tells us, one of three surviving children; she had a brother about six years older than she and a younger sister, Hannah. Her brother went to live on the family farm with their grandparents, and Elaw did not see him for more than thirty years. When Elaw was twelve years old her mother died while giving birth to her twenty-second child. All except three died in infancy. Her father died a year and a half later, after his wife. (Unfortunately Elaw does not offer specific dates for any of these events, nor does she tell her parents' names or even her own maiden name.)

After her mother's death, Elaw's father sent her younger sister to live with an aunt. Elaw went to live with a Quaker couple, Pierson and Rebecca Mitchel, where she remained until she was eighteen. Apparently she and Rebecca Mitchel never got along, though Elaw says she and Mr. Mitchel shared a mutual faith in God. The Mitchels provided her with some financial assistance ten years after she left them. And she describes a warm and friendly reunion with William and Achsah Mitchel, the couple's sons, who came to Burlington, New Jersey, to give her the money.

Dreams of Salvation Lead to Conversion

The Mitchels were Quakers and therefore did not engage in overt demonstrations of their religious faith, something Elaw had grown accustomed to while still living with her parents. The absence of daily religious observances in the home, Elaw believed, caused her to give in to sinful impulses, including blasphemy. This particular sin troubled her a great deal and inspired the first of many dreams that began her progress towards salvation. Soon after one such dream, in which she found herself unprepared to meet God on the day of judgment, God manifested himself to her. At this time she was fourteen years old and had begun attending Methodist meetings. She writes:

> As I was milking a cow and singing, I turned my head, and saw a tall figure approaching, who came and stood by me. He had long hair which parted in the front and came down on his shoulders; he wore a long white robe down to the feet; and as he stood with open arms and smiled upon me, he disappeared (56).

This manifestation marks her conversion to God, told, she says, "in language unvarnished by the graces of educated eloquence, nor transcending the capacity of a child to understand" (57). In 1808 she joined the Methodist Episcopal Society and was received by the Reverend J. Polhemos. Six months after being accepted into this society, the Reverend Joseph Lybrand baptized her.

In 1810 she married Joseph Elaw, a fuller. For a time the couple lived about twenty miles from Philadelphia, then moved to Burlington, New Jersey, because of a job opportunity for Joseph. The marriage does not appear to have been a particularly happy one; Joseph Elaw did not share his wife's deep faith in God and, as she tells us, tried on one occasion to tempt his wife to stray from her religious beliefs by taking her to a ballroom in Philadelphia. Elaw expresses conventional beliefs about women's role in marriage, stating that the woman should be a helpmate to her husband. But she also warns female readers "against being thus unequally yoked with unbelievers." "In general," she cautions, "your lot would be better, if a millstone were hung about your necks and you were drowned in the depths of the sea, than that you should disobey the law of Jesus [Matt. 18:6]" (61). Without a shared faith in God, she says, the wife cannot perform the role prescribed for her in the Scriptures.

Elaw's career as a minister was brought about by an extraordinary series of events. Her sister, Hannah, had a deathbed vision in which Jesus instructed her to tell Elaw to preach the Gospel. Elaw was at first reluctant to do so, in part because she "continually endured such sore trials from my poor unconverted husband as powerfully operated to deter me from the thought of such an undertaking" (75). But after she suffered a near-fatal illness cured by a painful operation that "well nigh proved the breaking asunder of the slender thread of life," a messenger, whom she discovered to be "not really a human being but a supernatural appearance," told her to have faith in her recovery and to look forward to "another camp-meeting," where "thou shalt know the will of God concerning thee" (77). Elaw did indeed live to go to this camp meeting, and it was here that she received the commission to preach. At this time she would have been about twenty-eight years old. The other ministers in her society approved of her becoming a minister. Her husband, however, was another matter, though he did come to hear his wife preach, much to her surprise. Nevertheless, the idea of having his wife preaching in public caused him a great deal of grief. But she refused to give in to his request to stop preaching.

On January 27, 1823, Joseph Elaw died from "an intractable consumption," leaving Elaw to support herself and their daughter, then about eleven years old. Elaw never tells her daughter's name, though her *Memoirs* reveals that the daughter became a Christian, converted by her mother's preaching. She also blessed her mother with at least two grandchildren, both boys, the first one born on December 10, 1834.

Sometime after her husband's death, Elaw opened a much-needed school in Burlington. She kept her school open for about two years. Aided in part by the Society of Friends, who provided books and other needed supplies, the school was successful. But she felt restless and dissatisfied because she had not continued to preach as God had commissioned her to do. After overcoming her anxiety about her finances and leaving her daughter and her duties as a teacher, she eventually set out for Philadelphia. She remained away from home for seven months. In April 1828 she returned, though she stayed for only a few days before finding herself called back to preach in Philadelphia and in the South. Thus she began her travels as a minister.

In the remaining parts of *Memoirs*, Elaw describes her travels throughout the United States and in England, where she arrived on July 24, 1840. She remained in England for at least five years. In her dedication, written in 1845, she says she is ready to "rejoin my dear friends in the occidental land of my nativity." But what happened to her after this point remains unknown. The record of her life begins and ends with her *Memoirs*.

Role of Black Women in Methodism Noted

In spite of her reluctance to favor readers with specific information about herself, Elaw's *Memoirs* provides a wealth of information about the customs of the Methodist Episcopal Church, the tradition of the camp meeting, and the role of black women in Methodism and indeed in nineteenth-century America. Elaw understood how race, gender, and even class affects people's perceptions of each other. During the course of her ministry, she preached to whites and blacks, wealthy and poor alike. As she notes, "my ministry had been attended by persons of every rank in life" (104). While she was in Washington, D.C., she says, "my concern was desired by many of the great folks, even by the friends and associates of the President of the United States" (96). Anne McCarty Lee, the wife of General "Lighthorse" Harry Lee, once invited her to preach for a group of friends that included Minerva Denison Rodgers, who was married to U.S. Navy officer John Rodgers. Very much aware that her ministry frequently drew people who came simply "to hear the coloured female preacher," Elaw did not let other people's curiosity or prejudices deter her from preaching. In fact, her autobiography includes some direct challenges based on Scriptural evidence to those who maintain women should not be allowed to preach. Elaw notes that these curiosity-seekers sometimes found themselves moved to convert after hearing her sermons.

Elaw's *Memoirs* is a testimony to her courageous life as a traveling minister and, as an example of a spiritual autobiography, an early and important form of black American women's autobiography. Her autobiography lets us look not only at the profound effect religious faith can have on an individual but also gives us a glimpse into an intelligent and probing mind unwilling to bend simply to suit convention. Certainly Elaw is an excellent example of a woman who carved out her own identity and purpose in life. Though her culture would have restricted her solely to the roles of wife and mother, she transcended its narrowly prescribed definition of womanhood. Her newly rediscovered *Memoirs* testifies to a life wellspent following the course set by her own conscience.

References

Andrews, William L., ed. *Sisters of the Spirit: Three Black Women's Autobiographies of the Nineteenth Century*. Includes Zilpha Elaw's *Memoirs of the Life, Religious Experiences, Ministerial Travels and Labours of Mrs. Zilpha Elaw, An American Female of Color*. Bloomington: Indiana University Press, 1986.

Braxton, Joanne M. *Black Women Writing Autobiography: A Tradition within a Tradition*. Philadelphia: Temple University Press, 1989.

Shockley, Ann Allen. "Zilpha Elaw." *Afro-American Women Writers, 1746-1933: An Anthology and Critical Guide*. Boston: G. K. Hall, 1988.

Candis LaPrade

Elleanor Eldridge

(1785-1865)

Entrepreneur, businesswoman

Much of the information on the life of entrepreneur and tradeswoman Elleanor Eldridge comes from *The Memoirs of Elleanor Eldridge* (1838)—one of the few narratives about a free Negro woman. Although the authorship of Eldridge's *Memoirs* generally has been attributed to writer Frances Whipple Greene, uncertainty exists as to whether Eldridge actually lived or whether she was a product of Greene's literary imagination. However, early accounts, such as Louis Kaplan's *A Bibliography of American Autobiographies*, suggest that Eldridge wrote her own autobiography.

Elleanor Eldridge was born free March 26, 1785, in Warwick, Rhode Island, and died about 1865. Greene's rendition of Eldridge's memoirs report that she was the granddaughter of a native African trader who, along with his family, was kidnapped and sold into slavery. Tempted on board a ship by an American slaver under the pretense of making a potentially lucrative trade, the Congo chieftain did not realize his fate until the ship had set sail. Thereafter, he, his wife, and his four children were herded below deck and from that point on, were treated as chattel.

Eldridge's maternal grandmother was a native Indian named Mary Fuller, who purchased her slave husband Thomas Prophet by selling a portion of the numerous acres of land belonging to her family. Mary lived to age 102 and died in 1780. Her daughter, Hannah, was reportedly still of childbearing age when Mary died.

Eldridge's father, Robin Eldridge, and her two uncles won their freedom because they volunteered their services in the on-going American Revolution. They were granted their freedom and promised two hundred acres of land in the unsettled Mohawk country, now western New York. But the government reneged on the offer of a land grant, forcing Robin Eldridge to scrounge to earn and save enough money to purchase land and build a house in Warwick, Rhode Island. He married Hannah Prophet and they had nine children, five of whom lived to maturity.

Elleanor Eldridge, the last of seven daughters, was only ten when her mother died. Eventually she was taken under the wing of Elleanor Baker, one of her mother's laundry customers, who took great interest in the young girl. That Elleanor Eldridge was named after her suggested the level of friendship and respect that existed between the two women. Upon Hannah's death, Baker convinced Elleanor's father to allow the child to move in with her namesake. While living comfortably with Baker, Elleanor Eldridge learned many skills that proved beneficial when she moved out on her own and started her own money-making enterprises.

Through hard work, Eldridge accumulated capital enough to purchase a sizable amount of real estate and build a comfortable home for herself. After learning several useful trades, such as managing a dairy, weaving, whitewashing, and wallpapering, she contracted herself out to do local jobs and amassed impressive savings. Her clients spoke highly of her work and ultimately came to her defense when her property was extorted by a white opportunist disguised as her friend. Free, unwed, and living comfortably off her own wages, this black American woman was respected in her hometown.

Eldridge Swindled in Real Estate

Eldridge had already acquired considerable real estate in Warwick when she sought to purchase a parcel of land and buildings adjacent to her home. Yet foul play surrounded all of her efforts to secure this property. Despite having rented the property for some five years and expressing continued interest in possibly purchasing it, Eldridge was at first passed over when the white owner decided to sell the property to an acquaintance without so much as informing her. Since the property and its dwellings were so strategically positioned next to Eldridge's home, she did not hesitate when the original owner finally offered to sell it to her.

> She finally came to a bargain with Mr. C______ [the original owner who mortgaged the property in order to pay for the home on its premises], agreeing to give two thousand dollars for the house. She paid the five hundred dollars down; and then gave a mortgage on the house to Mr. Greenold [the new owner] for fifteen hundred dollars. This was to be paid in four years (Loewenberg, 83).

Pleased with the verbal agreement and unaware of pending deceit, Eldridge decided to take a trip to visit relatives in Adams, Massachusetts.

By anyone's standards, Elleanor Eldridge was a wealthy woman when she left Warwick en route to Adams; however, she was to return several months later to financial ruin. Despite lingering weakness from a recent bout with typhus fever, Eldridge insisted upon going through with her travel plans. A sudden relapse forced her and the brother who accompanied her to spend several days in a hotel in Hadley, where she was able to regain her strength. While there, Eldridge was recognized by several of her townspeople, who returned home to spread the news that Elleanor Eldridge was near death. This rumor, which eventually made its way to Greenold, precipitated the devastating loss of her property. Since Eldridge resumed her trip once she had regained her health, she was not able to stop the ruthless chain of events in Warwick that allowed Greenold to recoup his meager financial investment in the deal. Several months passed before she and her brother decided to return the following spring. What they discovered shocked them:

> Mr. ______ of Warwick, had attached and sold property, which a few months before had been valued at four thousand dollars.—Why he wished to attach so large a property, for so small a debt, is surprising enough; since Elleanor had then in her possession two house lots, and the little house and lot at Warwick; either of which would have been sufficient to liquidate the debt (Loewenberg, 86).

Equally shocking was the conspiracy among the white law officers to cover up the illegal acquisition of her land. When she took the matter to court with documented proof that the sale of her property had not been rightfully advertised and conducted, the judge threw out her evidence by insisting that due notice had been given.

Despite the numerous obstacles that blocked her efforts to retrieve her property, Eldridge persisted. She decided to go along with an even more unfair arrangement. Not only did the unrightful owner elevate the original price of the property, but he also added the cost of storing her personal items during the whole affair. Confident that she could raise the collateral, however, Eldridge signed an agreement that forced her to re-buy her own property for much more than it was originally worth. Eldridge accepted this final deal, worked off the debt, and finally regained the rewards of her life's work.

Through the entire ordeal, Eldridge had the support of numerous friends—white and black. As a result of her fine reputation in the town, she also gained help among Warwick's local residents in her lawsuit against Warwick's sheriff for improprieties in the sale of her property. Evidence of this support may be found in *The Memoirs of Elleanor Eldridge*, a work written to "render some small assistance to one who has been the subject of peculiar adversity and wrong" and to "[bring] forward, and [set] before the colored population, an example of industry and untiring perseverance, every way worthy their regard and earnest attention" (*Memoirs*, preface). One supporter wrote:

> Having employed Elleanor Eldridge to work for me, occasionally, during the last sixteen years, at white-washing, painting, papering, &c., I can recommend her, as an honest, industrious, and faithful woman, who has been peculiarly unfortunate in the loss of her property, which she obtained by thirty years of hard labor (9).

Several other allies wrote:

> We, the undersigned, having known and employed Elleanor Eldridge to work for us during many years, recommend her as an uncommonly industrious woman—honest and faithful. We think her deserving to hold the property so dearly bought, with the hard labor of thirty years; and worthy a PREMIUM for her untiring perseverance to make herself independent of charity, when sickness, or old age should disable her to pursue her accustomed avocations (10-11).

Based strictly upon popular support, Eldridge would have regained her property without incident. However, as the Rhode Island poet, journalist, and essayist Francis Greene observes, "the subject of this wrong, or rather of this accumulation of wrongs, was a woman, and therefore weak—a COLORED WOMAN—and therefore contemptible. No MAN ever would have been treated so; and if a WHITE WOMAN had been the subject of such wrongs, the whole town—nay, the whole country, would have been indignant: and the actors would have been held up to the contempt they deserve!" (Loewenberg, 88).

Kaplan classifies Eldridge's *Memoirs* as autobiography and includes it in *A Bibliography of American Autobiographies*. Here he registers data for its 1838 and 1839 publications. Neither entry mentions Greene as the author of *Memoirs*. The 1838 entry is described as "The story of Negro servant in Rhode Island," and the 1839 description provides more evidence that Eldridge is the author. The *Memoirs* are then described as including "her later career in which she describes her business activities."

But Bert Loewenberg and Ruth Bogin, in the book *Black Women in 19th Century American Life,* bring the issues of authenticity closer to resolution by examining the 1830 census of free blacks in Providence, Rhode Island:

> An Elleanor Eldridge . . . seems clearly to have been the person in question. There can be little doubt of her existence. The volume was certainly written about her, although some fictitious elements cling to the narrative (78).

References

Greene, Frances. *Memoirs of Elleanor Eldridge*. Providence: Albro, 1838, 1839.

Kaplan, Louis ed. "Eldridge, Elleanor." *Dictionary of American Negro Autobiographies*. Wisconsin, 1961.

Loewenberg, Bert, and Ruth Bogin, eds. *Black Women in 19th Century American Life*. University Park: Pennsylvania State University Press, 1976.

Logan, Rayford W. "Eldridge, Elleanor." *Dictionary of American Negro Biography*. Eds. Rayford W. Logan and Michael R. Winston. New York: Norton, 1982.

Sandra G. Shannon

Daisy Elliott

(1919-)

Politician, civil rights activist

One of the most powerful and effective legislators ever to come out of the state of Michigan, Daisy Elliot is perhaps best known for her co-authorship of the Elliot-Larsen Civil Rights Act of 1977, called the most comprehensive civil rights act adopted by any state up to that time.

Born November 26, 1919, in Filbert, West Virginia, Daisy Elizabeth Lenoir was the sixth of eight children (five girls, three boys) born to Robert Lenoir and Daisy (Dorum) Lenoir. Robert Lenoir was a coal miner remembered by his daughter, Daisy, as a hard-working father who provided steady and sufficient support for his family. Mother Daisy Lenoir was an educated person who, rather than seeking outside employment, concentrated upon housekeeping and child-rearing, as she and her husband had agreed.

Thus, Robert and Daisy Lenoir were able to provide an economically modest, stable, and loving home environment for their children. A short time after Daisy Elizabeth's birth, the Lenoir family moved to Beckley, West Virginia, where she grew up, attended public schools, and graduated from Stratton High School in 1936. At age seventeen, she married

Robert Elliott, a carpenter, on her birthday, November 26, 1936. One daughter, Doris Mae Elliott, was born in 1938. In 1940, Daisy Elliott began to care for a foster son, Robert Simmons, and later, a foster daughter, Angela Gibbs.

In 1941 or 1942, Daisy and Robert Elliott migrated to Detroit, seeking wartime factory jobs. They worked for the Murray Corporation in Detroit for a period of time in the 1940s. Daisy Elliott trained and worked as a riveter and became an inspector at Murray Corporation. In late 1944 or early 1945, the Elliotts moved their family to the Vallejo, California, area where Daisy Elliott worked as a shipfitter's helper and inspector in a Navy shipyard. After approximately two years in California, the family returned to Detroit. Shortly afterwards, the Elliotts received a divorce in June 1947. Daisy Elliott remained close to her parents and siblings. By the late 1940s, most of them had migrated to Detroit to be near Daisy. On June 12, 1964, she married Charles Bowers, an employee of the Detroit Department of Transportation, who was educated at Morristown College in Tennessee and Morris Brown College in Georgia.

On several occasions, Elliott sought to upgrade her job skills by acquiring additional education. Thus, she studied at Wayne State University in Detroit in 1944, then at Vallejo College in California, and completed a course of study and graduated from the Detroit Institute of Commerce in 1950. By the early 1950s she was selling real estate, working for the Hughes Realty Company in Detroit. In the late 1950s she worked for about four years in a secretary of state branch office, first as a title examiner and later as assistant manager. She had a long-standing interest in improving the social and economic standing of black Americans and in widening opportunities for women. Her wartime experiences showed that the pressure of civic organizations combined with governmental orders against job discrimination could accomplish a great deal. In the 1940s, the Fair Employment Practices Committee, established by the national government, was credited with opening up two million or more jobs for blacks in industry, some of them in Michigan. Daisy Elliott and others wanted the government to continue combating discrimination and broadening opportunities. Thus, she became active with civic organizations that emphasized programs of social improvement and political involvement. In addition to serving as president of the Progressive Civic Arts Club from 1959 to 1962 and being a member of the executive board and the Civil Rights Committee of the Trade Union Leadership Council in the 1950s, she was also a member of the NAACP and the League of Women Voters. She also became an active member of the Democratic party, eventually becoming a party official. She served as president of the Michigan Federated Democratic Clubs from 1957 to 1959 and as a Democratic Party Precinct Delegate in 1959.

By 1950 Elliott decided to concentrate on running for election to the Michigan House of Representatives, where one or more blacks had served on a regular basis since the 1930s. Thus in 1950 she entered the Democratic primary for the Michigan House of Representatives for the first time, losing but garnering a significant number of votes. As did several others who aspired to become state legislators, thereafter Elliott entered primaries regularly to increase her name recognition and support among voters. Starting in 1954, she entered the Democratic primary for the state legislature every two years through 1960, each time making a respectable showing but falling short of qualifying for the general election.

Daisy Elliott's opportunity to win an elective office for the first time came when Michigan chose delegates to a constitutional convention who were given the responsibility of revising the state constitution. Her previous campaigns had built a reservoir of voter support, but the decisive factor was her running as part of an interracial team that had strong union support. In both the primary in July 1961 and the general election in September 1961, team members were the top three votegetters, respectively: the Reverend Malcolm Dade, a black Episcopal priest, Daisy Elliott, and attorney Tom Downs, a white liberal activist and official of the Michigan State AFL-CIO. Elliott's work in the constitutional convention brought her recognition. Serving as a member of the committees on Executive Branch, Rules and Resolution, and Emerging Problems, she played a vital role in helping establish the Michigan Civil Rights Commission as part of the state constitution. She has been credited with writing the original language for Section 29 of Article V of the Michigan Constitution, which established a bipartisan civil rights commission authorized to investigate discrimination against any person because of religion, race, color, or national origin and to issue orders requiring compliance with antidiscrimination laws. Great significance was given to the work of the commission by defining it as a principal department of the executive branch of state government, not subordinate to any other department. Thus, Michigan became the first state to establish a civil rights commission by inclusion in its constitution, making its work perpetual. Daisy Elliott's work in the constitutional convention resulted in the State Bar of Michigan awarding her its Citation of Honor in 1962 and the Fifteenth District Democratic Party giving her its Distinguished Service Award in 1963.

Her success in the constitutional convention was crucial to her subsequent career as a state legislator. First, it gave her greater prominence with the voters, making her election more likely. Second, it heightened her desire to play a role in securing additional laws to make the work of the Civil Rights Commission as effective as possible. Elected to the Michigan House of Representatives for the first time in 1962, she was reelected every two years, serving continuously through 1978. One of ten black members, she was the fourth black woman elected to the Michigan State Legislature, but one of only two serving during her first term.

Legislator Sponsors More Than Eighty Bills

During the 1960s and 1970s, Elliott was an active and influential legislator who moved up in the leadership hierarchy of the House of Representatives. Three times, she was chair of the Constitutional Revisions Committee, including the 1973-1974 term when the committee's scope was expanded to include women's rights. She also chaired the Committee on Colleges and Universities before becoming the first woman appointed by the Speaker of the House of Representatives to chair the powerful Labor Committee, 1975-1978. As a frequent committee chair, Daisy Elliott was able to speed along proposed legislation she favored and to delay or block proposals she deemed undesirable to solve the state's problems. Thus, she sponsored or cosponsored more than eighty bills passed by the Michigan legislature affecting primarily the subjects of education, labor, senior citizens, women, juveniles, native Americans, and civil rights.

The Elliott-Larsen Civil Rights Act of 1977 is the best-known and probably the most far-reaching of these laws. After several years of attempting to develop legislative support to broaden the scope of the Michigan Civil Rights Commission and to strengthen its authority, Elliott and a white Republican legislator, Mel Larsen, introduced the bill into the House of Representatives in January 1975. They helped rewrite the bill seven times, adapted twenty-two of sixty proposed amendments, and secured passage by both houses of the Michigan legislature in the fall of 1976 and witnessed the governor's approval in January 1977. The law consolidated all previous civil rights laws, expanded the Civil Rights Commission's jurisdiction to include age, sex, height, weight, and marital status discrimination and authorized the commission to award a higher level of damages. For the first time the law granted women statutory protection against discrimination in educational facilities and public accommodations. The Elliott-Larsen Act was considered the most comprehensive civil rights act adopted by any state up to that time.

In the 1970s Daisy Elliott founded and authored some articles in a newsletter of considerable substance entitled *CAPITOL: Woman,* which reported on and analyzed women's issues. She also served as secretary of the Michigan Democratic Black Caucus, assistant chairperson of the Majority Caucus (Democratic) of the State Legislature, and a member of the Joint Legislative Liaison Committee of the Governor's Commission on Higher Education. In addition, she was a charter member of the National Society for State Legislators and a member of the Order of Women Legislators. Active with a variety of church, civic, and fraternal groups, she has received numerous awards, citations, and honors.

In 1978 Daisy Elliott sought election to a higher office—the state senate—rather than seeking reelection to the House of Representatives. Contesting for an open seat, Daisy Elliott lost in the primary to a hard-working and popular black male legislator, Jackie Vaughn. In 1980, after a two-year absence from the state legislature, she ran against her successor, defeated him in the primary, and regained her former seat in the legislature. In 1981 she was again appointed to chair the Labor Committee and was considered an influential legislator.

Nineteen eighty-two proved a momentous year for Daisy Elliott. First, redistricting forced her to seek reelection against another black state legislator, Carolyn Cheeks Kilpatrick. Second, in April 1982 she was charged with knowingly driving a stolen car. Daisy Elliott stated that her prosecution on theft charges was "politically and racially motivated" because "certain people" wanted her ousted as chair of the House Labor Committee. Newspaper stories reminding voters of the pending criminal charges against Daisy Elliott led to her defeat in the August 1982 primary, ending her legislative career. In the November 1982 trial, Daisy Elliott maintained her innocence of the charges, stating that she bought the car at a Cadillac dealership after being told it had been used as a demonstrator and receiving a document called "proof of sale." Courtroom analysis showed the proof of sale to have been falsified with Daisy Elliott claiming the car salesman must have falsified it. But the car salesman, Gary Strobbe, denied ever selling a car to Daisy Elliott and denied the signature on the document was his. Even though Don Massey, owner of the car dealership where Daisy Elliott claimed to have purchased the car, admitted that sometimes stolen cars are illegally sold at car dealerships, including his, and that Gary Strobbe was known to have served prison time for counterfeiting United States currency, on November 12, 1982, an all-white jury in a suburb of Lansing, Michigan, found Daisy Elliott guilty of knowingly possessing a stolen car. Elliott charged that she had been "set up" in order to get her out of the state legislature ("Rep. Elliott Faces Trial in Theft of Car," A-3; "A Battle of Two Incumbents," A-3; "Daisy Elliott Says She was 'Set Up,'" *Michigan Chronicle,* A-1).

Daisy Elliott was sentenced to one year in county jail, all but sixty days suspended, and a year's probation. She was also ordered to pay $5,300 in restitution and court costs. In 1984 the Michigan Court of Appeals refused to overturn the conviction, and (after additional appeals failed) she had to serve time in the Ingham County Jail in 1985 ("Court Turns Down Ex-Rep. Elliott's Appeal in Car Case," B-D08). In June 1985 Daisy Elliott returned to work as an administrative coordinator for the Detroit Housing Commission, a position she held into the 1990s ("Out of Jail—Back on the Job," A-3; "Daisy Elliott's Hiring Applauded," A-10).

References

"A Battle of Two Incumbents." *Detroit News*, 22 July 1982.

"Black Power in State Governments." *Ebony* 27 (April 1972): 94-103. Photograph, p. 102.

"Civil Rights Commission Turns 25." *Detroit Free Press*, 21 November 1989. Photograph, A-3.

"Court Turns Down Ex-Rep. Elliott's Appeal in Car Case." *Detroit News*, 8 May 1984. Photograph, p. B-D08.

"Daisy Elliott's Hiring Applauded." *Detroit News*, 20 June 1985. Photograph, p. A-10.

"Daisy Elliott Says She was 'Set-Up.'" *Michigan Chronicle*, 20 November 1982. Photograph, A-1.

Editors of Ebony. *Ebony Success Library*. Vol. 1. Chicago: Johnson Pub. Co., 1983. 106.

Interview with Daisy Elliott, 20 March 1991.

Lewis, Ferris E. *State and Local Government in Michigan*. 9th ed. Hillsdale, Mich.: Hillsdale Educational Publishers, 1984.

Michigan. *Constitutional Convention 1961 Official Record*. 2 vols. Lansing: State of Michigan, 1962. Photograph, Vol. 1, p. 20.

———. *Michigan Manual, 1961-1962*. Lansing: State of Michigan, 1961.

———. *Michigan Manual, 1963-1964*. Lansing: State of Michigan, 1963. Photograph in unnumbered section preceding page 1.

———. *Official Directory and Legislative Manual, 1951-1952*. Lansing: State of Michigan, 1951.

"Out of Jail—Back on the Job." *Detroit News*, 18 June 1985. Photograph, p. A-3.

"Rep. Elliott Faces Trial in Theft of Car." *Detroit News*, 18 June 1982. A-3.

"Rep. Elliott Loses Seats." *Detroit News*, 17 November 1982.

"Rights Bill is Daisy's Triumph." *Detroit News*, 10 March 1977. C-4.

"'Something for Daisy.'" *Michigan Chronicle*, 16 April 1983.

"States Boast Record Number of Negro Lawmakers." *Ebony* 20 (April 1965): 191-97. Photograph, p. 196.

Who's Who of American Women. 5th ed. Chicago: Marquis, 1969. 355.

Women in the Legislative Process. Lansing: Legislative Service Bureau, State Legislature, October 1977. Photograph, p. 18.

Women in the Michigan Legislature, 1921-1989. Lansing: Michigan State Legislature, 1989. Photograph, p. 19.

"Women Who Make State Laws." *Ebony* 22 (September 1967): 27-34. Photograph, p. 32.

De Witt S. Dykes, Jr.

Effie O'Neal Ellis

(1913-)

Physician, health administrator

A woman who has worn many hats in the medical field, some of them firsts for a black woman, Effie O'Neil Ellis has become a major national influence in the area of maternal and child care. Ellis was born in Hawkinsville, Georgia, on June 15, 1913, to Joshua P. O'Neal and Althea (Hamilton) O'Neal. Ellis is quoted in the *Atlanta Constitution* (6 August 1970) as being "the daughter of a successful builder of small homes."

Her primary education was obtained in Atlanta, Georgia. A conscientious and brilliant student, Ellis went through her undergraduate and graduate programs in a quiet and determined but spectacular manner. She received the A.B. degree with honors from Spelman College in 1933. She went on to Atlanta University and graduated with a master's degree in biology in 1935, the same year she married Arthur W. Ellis.

Because of her outstanding research work at Atlanta University, Ellis was awarded a study grant to go to Puerto Rico, where she studied diseases and parasites. Pleased with her work, she seriously considered specializing in parasitological research. Her work, however, gave Ellis an opportunity to observe the health care that was available for the poor. As a result of her observations, she changed her career plans and decided she could be of greater service to people by working in the medical field.

Ellis was admitted to the University of Illinois College of Medicine, where she showed outstanding abilities during her medical school years. She graduated from the University of Illinois College of Medicine on June 16, 1950. The commencement exercises were held at the university's undergraduate facilities at the Navy Pier. Out of the 160 medical graduates, Ellis was among 23 to graduate with honors. According to the *Evening Bulletin*, she ranked fifth in her class.

During the academic year 1950-51, Ellis served her internship at the University of Illinois Hospital. She did a residency in pediatrics at Massachusetts General Hospital in 1951-1952. In keeping with her outstanding achievements, Ellis was awarded a postdoctoral fellowship to study heart trouble in children at The Johns Hopkins University School of Medicine from July 1, 1952, through June 30, 1953. While at Johns Hopkins, Ellis was also hospital staff physician from July 1, 1952, through June 30, 1953, and again from July 1, 1956, through June 30, 1957. During the midst of her fellowship program, Ellis married James D. Solomon on March 23, 1953. The Solomons have one daughter.

James Solomon was born in 1913. He received his M.D. degree from Meharry Medical College in Nashville, Tennessee, in 1953 and later received a Ph.D. from the University of Illinois. Solomon went to Saint Elizabeth Hospital in Washington, D.C., in 1953. In 1958 he was appointed director of the laboratory at Saint Elizabeth's, a position he maintained until his retirement in 1983. Currently, Solomon is semiretired from his private practice and works as a consultant.

Maternal and Child Care Addressed

Ellis managed to juggle marriage, motherhood, and a demanding career. She was director of medical education and house pediatrician at Provident Hospital in Baltimore, Maryland, from 1953 to 1961. She then moved on to serve as director of maternal and child health for the Ohio State Department of Health in Columbus, Ohio, a post she held from 1961 to 1965. Always concerned about the welfare of children, Ellis felt she could have a positive impact on policy-making and decisions regarding the poor by serving in a number of capacities for the federal government. She was chairperson for a panel group at the 1969 White House Conference on Food and Nutrition. She served in the Department of Health, Education, and Welfare (HEW) as its first regional commissioner for social and rehabilitation service. She was also regional medical director of the HEW Children's Bureau. The highlight of her career, however, was being selected to serve in a newly-created post of special assistant for health services to the American Medical Association (AMA). Ellis became the first black woman to hold an administrative or executive office within the AMA. As the special assistant for health services, she was to be a special advisor on child and maternal health matters and health care of the poor. She served in this position from 1970 to 1975.

The tasks assigned to Ellis were well within her expertise. She had always stressed comprehensive services for maternal and child health. In addition, she believed in family planning as the greatest preventive tool in obtaining better maternal and child health care. She emphasized that family planning should be more than contraceptive measures. She traveled around the country speaking to community groups, medical organizations, health associations, and other educational audiences on the subject of prenatal care for mothers and health care for the poor.

One of her main concerns was preventive health before the baby was born. Ellis believed every mother should be taught family planning, prenatal and postnatal care, nutrition, sanitation, and be given advice on acute and preventive health care.

Ellis is a member of numerous organizations, including the National Medical Association, American Public Welfare Association, American Association on Mental Deficiency, American Association for Maternal and Child Health, Alpha Omega Alpha, and Delta Sigma Theta sorority. Among her awards and honors, Ellis is an honorary fellow of the School Health Association. She received the prestigious Trailblazer Award from the National Medical Association in 1970.

Effie O'Neal Ellis currently resides in Chicago.

References

Baltimore *Evening Bulletin*, 12 February 1952.

Who's Who of American Women. 8th ed. Chicago: Marquis, 1975.

Collections

Records and photographs of Effie O'Neal Ellis are in the Spelman College archives and in the School of Medicine archives, Johns Hopkins University, Baltimore, Maryland.

Margaret Jerrido

Evelyn Ellis

(1894-1958)

Actress

Evelyn Ellis, a stage, screen, and television actress whose successful career lasted more than thirty-five years, was born in Boston, Massachusetts, in 1894. While facts of her family life and educational background remain virtually obscured, and her name is not widely recognized among the host of black women who have achieved fame and recognition in the field of entertainment, Ellis's outstanding talent and performance as an actress remain indisputably documented in critics' reviews of her work both on and off Broadway.

Ellis made her professional stage debut in 1919 at the Harlem Lafayette Theatre in a production of *Othello*. This was followed by appearances on Broadway in Nan Bagby Stephen's production of *Roseanne*, and in a number of other Broadway plays before Ellis took roles in three major motion pictures. In 1927, she appeared as Lucy Bell Dorsey in the revival of *Goat Alley*, Ernest Howard Culbertson's 1921 drama about black life in the Washington, D.C., slums, and received praise for her "telling portrayal" (*New York Times Theatre Review*, 21 April 1927). This performance launched her later that same year to even greater success in her role as the tormented Bess in the hit drama *Porgy*, which was to become the basis of the libretto for George and Ira Gershwin's folk opera *Porgy and Bess*. After a ten-year period of relative inactivity during the financially beleaguered years following the 1929 stock market crash, Ellis returned to the stage, this time initially as a director. In 1937, under the auspices of the federal government's Negro Theatre program through the Works Projects Administration, Ellis staged Dorothy Hailparn's comedy *Horse Play*.

Her next major theatrical role, in 1941, was as Hannah Thomas, the mother of Bigger Thomas, in Orson Welles's highly acclaimed staging of Richard Wright and Paul Green's drama, *Native Son*. The next year Ellis played the same part in an equally successful revival of the play. Her roles as Bella Charles, a housekeeper in *Deep Are the Roots*, in 1945, and as Della in *The Royal Family*, 1951, in which Ossie Davis appeared, were eclipsed by her 1950 performance both as director and as actress in an all-black production of *Tobacco Road*, put on by members of the Negro Drama Group. In the lukewarm reception of the play staged by Ellis, her portrayal of a poor, starving mother was nevertheless singled out, along with that of John Tate, among the few "truthful elements that left a vivid impression" (*New York Times Theatre Review*, Vol. 5, 7 March 1950). Her last Broadway appearance, in 1953, was in William Stuckey's *Touchstone*. Her final roles on the stage were in a number of off Broadway productions, notable among which was her appearance at the Theater de Lys in Greenwich Village in *Supper for the Dead*, one of a trilogy of short plays by Paul Green.

Ellis's gradual withdrawal from the stage was accompanied by her appearance in television plays and, more conspicuously, in three major motion pictures. She made her screen debut in 1948 as Bessie in *The Lady from Shanghai*, produced by Orson Welles. In 1953 she assumed the role of Mrs. Barrow, the fighter's mother, in *The Joe Louis Story;* her final film was in 1955, in which she appeared as a maid in *Interrupted Melody*, which starred Glenn Ford and Eleanor Parker. After spending several months, beginning in December 1957, at the Variety Club's Will Rogers Memorial Hospital in Saranac Lake, New York, Ellis died of a heart ailment on June 5, 1958.

References

McGill, Raymond D., ed. *Notable Names in the American Theatre*. Clifton, N.J.: James T. White Co., 1976.

Nash, Jay Robert, and Stanley Ralph Ross. *The Motion Picture Guide: 1927-1983*. Chicago: Cinebooks, 1986.

New York Times, 6 June 1958.

New York Times Film Reviews. Reprinted. New York: The New York Times and Arno Press, 1970. Vol. 3, *Lady from Shanghai* (1948): 2259; Vol. 4, *The Joe Louis Story* (1949-58): 2736; Vol. 4, *Interrupted Melody* (1949-58): 2859-60.

New York Times Theatre Reviews. Reprinted. New York: The New York Times and Arno Press, 1920-70. Vol. 2, *Goat Alley* (21 April 1937); Vol. 4, *Horse Play* (28 August 1937); Brooks Atkinson, *Native Son* (25 March 1941, 24 October 1941); Vol. 5, Lewis Nichols, *Deep Are the Roots* (27 September 1945); Brooks Atkinson, *Tobacco Road* (7 March 1950); Brooks Atkinson, *The Royal Family* (11 June 1951); Vol. 6., Brooks Atkinson, *Touchstone* (4 February 1953); *Supper for the Dead* (7 July 1954).

Truitt, Evelyn Mack, ed. *Who Was Who on the Screen*. 3rd ed. New York: Bowker, 1983.

Variety, 11 June 1958.

Carolyn R. Hodges

Mari Evans

(1923-)

Writer

A much-awarded writer, Mari Evans has published many volumes of poetry, drama, and children's stories, written and produced several programs and plays for television and theater, and contributed essays and poems to more than two hundred anthologies. She has taught literature and creative writing for two decades at various American universities, including Purdue, Indiana, Northwestern, Cornell, and, most recently, Spelman.

Mari Evans was born in Toledo, Ohio. Her mother, a homemaker, died when she was seven years old, but she was well cared for by her father, an upholsterer. She credits her father with inspiring and nurturing her love of writing, beginning when she was a small child. Her first story was published in the school paper when she was in the fourth grade, and her father carefully saved it, thus "inscribing on an impressionable Black youngster both the importance of the written word and the accessibility of 'reward' for even a slight effort" (Evans, "My Father's Passage," 165).

At the age of ten Evans fell in love with the poetry of Langston Hughes. His work and his presence became a major force in her life and work. She observes that "what he gave me was not advice, but his concern, his interest, and, more importantly, he inspired a belief in myself and my ability to produce." As a friend and mentor, Hughes encouraged her to see writing as "a rigorous, demanding occupation" ("My Father's Passage" 166).

Evans's dedication to "great personal discipline" in writing was further enhanced when she accepted a position as an assistant editor at a predominantly white manufacturing plant. Evans recalls that although the white editor was hostile toward her, "he knew how to write. His first draft was as clean as my final copy, and I resented that so much that even his hassling became a minor annoyance. I revised and revised and revised" ("My Father's Passage," 167).

As an undergraduate Evans attended the University of Toledo. In 1979 she was awarded an honorary doctorate in humane letters by Marian College. Her much-celebrated poetry is "explicitly committed to specific political instruction" (Dorsey, 170). In 1970 she published her best-known collection of poems, *I Am a Black Woman*. This collection, which received the Black Academy of Arts and Letters First Poetry Award in 1975, powerfully articulates many of the politics, aesthetics, and sentiments of the civil rights and black power movements.

While many black feminists see the oppressions of race and gender as equally complex, severe, and pervasive, Evans has a clear sense of priorities: "I am Afrikan first, then woman, then writer" ("My Father's Passage," 168). She addresses a black audience, "reaching for what will nod Black heads over common denominators" ("My Father's Passage," 167).

Like Whitman's "Song of Myself," Evans's poems are often exhilarating in their celebration of life. She lovingly exults in being a member of the black community. Representing African-Americans as "a colonized nation" in an extraordinarily hostile world, Evans joyously affirms blackness (Dorsey, 170). She has continued to fight for social justice since the civil rights movement; indeed, she recently observed: "We've won no wars. The issues of '68 are still of paramount, even escalated, concern in 1991. All the current statistics support this" (Telephone interview with Mari Evans, 7 January 1991).

Evans's portrayal of white crimes against and inhumanity toward blacks is realistic and incisive, just as her celebration of blackness is inspirational. Some critics have noted (with no criticism intended) that Evans's poems not only "affirm blackness"; they also "reject whiteness" (Sedlack, 465; Dorsey 174-75). Evans sometimes represents blackness and whiteness as essences; one need only be black to be morally superior. This reversal of the valuations of the dominant ideology is usually a necessary part of liberation movements. However, the black American feminist Michele Wallace has noted the dangers of inverting racist values: "Not only does reversal, or the notion that blacks are more likeable, more compassionate, smarter, or even 'superior,' not substantially alter racist preconceptions, it also ties Afro-American cultural production to racist ideology in a way that makes the failure to alter it inevitable" (1).

From 1968 to 1973 Evans created and hosted a weekly issue-oriented television show that covered socio-political issues from a black American perspective. She was one of the first black American women to control her own television program. Although her work for theater is less well known than her poetry, her adaptation of Zora Neale Hurston's *Their Eyes Were Watching God* as a musical was introduced in New York by Hazel Bryant's RACCA theater and was later produced fully by the Karamu Theatre of Performing Arts in Cleveland. Performances followed at Cornell and Spelman. Her one-woman theater piece, Boochie, which focuses on child abuse, has been enthusiastically received in Indianapolis, Atlanta, and at the Billie Holiday Theatre in Brooklyn (Telephone interview with Mari Evans, 7 January 1991).

In 1984 Evans published a much-needed anthology of biographical and critical essays entitled *Black Women Writers (1950-1980): A Critical Evaluation*. This collection is an often-cited major contribution to literary studies.

Evans, divorced, has two sons. She has made her home for many years in Indianapolis, Indiana. In addition to maintaining a rigorous schedule of lectures around the country, she is currently working on a novel and a new volume of poetry.

References

Black Writers. Detroit: Gale Research, 1989. 188-91.

Contemporary Authors. Vols. 49-52. Detroit: Gale Research, 1975. 174.

Dorsey, David. "The Art of Mari Evans." In *Black Women Writers*. Ed. Mari Evans. New York: Doubleday, 1984. 170-89.

Edwards, Solomon. "Affirmation in the Works of Mari Evans." *Black Women Writers*. Ed. Mari Evans. New York: Doubleday, 1984. 190-200.

Evans, Mari, ed. *Black Women Writers (1950-1980): A Critical Evaluation*. New York: Doubleday, 1984.

———. *I Am a Black Woman*. New York: Morrow, 1970.

Sedlack, Robert. "Mari Evans: Consciousness and Craft." *CLA Journal* 15 (September 1971): 465-76.

Telephone interview with Mari Evans, 7 January 1991.

Wallace, Michele. *Invisibility Blues: From Pop to Theory*. New York: Verso, 1990.

Kari Winter

Matilda Arabella Evans

(1872-1935)

Physician, humanitarian, educator

During the nineteenth century, it was uncommon for a black woman to attend school at the college level and exceptionally rare for a black woman to attend and graduate from a medical school. But Matilda Arabella Evans was a pioneer, breaking new ground in the field of health care for blacks in South Carolina and across the country.

Matilda Arabella Evans was born to Anderson and Harriet Evans in Aiken, South Carolina, on May 13, 1872. She attended the Schofield Industrial School in Aiken, South Carolina, where she was one of the first students to enroll in the school for "colored" youth. Schofield Industrial School was established in 1868 by Martha Schofield of Philadelphia, Pennsylvania, under the auspices of the Pennsylvania Freedmen's Relief Association. Although the administrative office for the school was in Germantown, a section of Philadelphia, the school was located in Aiken, South Carolina. Young men and women from all parts of South Carolina were sent by various societies and church organizations to take advantage of the training available at the Schofield School. Reading, writing, arithmetic, and spelling were taught in the lower grades. In the upper grades, geography, history, grammar, philosophy, physiology, and botany were added. Lectures on the government of the United States were given, and instruction on the drawing of deeds, mortgages, and promissory notes was often included.

Thus Evans received an extensive education. With the encouragement of Martha Schofield, Matilda Evans enrolled in Oberlin College. Within three months, she had won a scholarship that took care of her tuition. Evans worked as a waitress in the dining hall during the school year and canned fruit during the summer months to help pay for other expenses. She attended Oberlin from 1887-1891; however, within a few months of completing the "classical course," she left college. Her dream was to become a medical missionary.

Evans taught for a short time at Haines Institute in Augusta, Georgia, and then at the Schofield School. Once again, Martha Schofield encouraged Evans and helped her to enroll at the Woman's Medical College of Pennsylvania. She matriculated in 1893, and during the 1894-1895 session she received assistance in the amount of one hundred dollars. Evans participated in the forty-fifth annual commencement of the Woman's Medical College of Pennsylvania held at the Academy of Music in 1897. Lucretia M. B. Mitchell, acting president of the Board of Corporators, conferred the degree of Doctor of Medicine on the twenty-eight candidates.

After graduating from the Woman's Medical College of Pennsylvania, Evans returned to Columbia, South Carolina, where she became the first black woman physician to practice in Columbia. Apparently her dream of becoming a medical missionary was no longer her primary concern as she realized the need for her services in the cities of the South.

Evans quickly established a private practice in Columbia, where she administered to black and white patients. She became a skillful and successful surgeon. An account in the *Palmetto Leader* (22 March 1930) describes Evans as giving herself "mind, soul, and body—so unreservedly to her profession that the demand for her services increasingly enlarged. . . ." While maintaining a thriving practice, Evans opened her home to serve as a hospital. Ideas to establish permanent health care facilities were being formulated in her mind.

Evans Founds Health Facilities

Evans was particularly interested in child welfare. In order to put her ideas into practice, she obtained permission from the school authorities to examine the "colored" children in the public schools of Columbia at her own expense. Her examinations revealed many children had bad tonsils and decayed teeth. Some of the children had enlarged hearts, skin eruptions, scabies, ringworm, and other diseases. After examination of the children, she knew she could demonstrate a need for health facilities for black people. As a result of her work, a permanent examination program was established in the public school system. During the course of her examinations, Evans continued her practice and conducted a baby clinic where poor families' babies could be brought in for advice and treatment.

One of the most important clinics Evans founded was the Columbia Clinic Association. She had visited Durham, Philadelphia, and New York City to see firsthand the latest and most scientific methods and practices in establishing clinics. Evans returned with ideas and suggestions for the Columbia Clinic Association. The clinic had originally been housed in the basement of the Zion Baptist Church. During the first day, seven hundred people came to the clinic for service. It was soon evident the clinic would outgrow its space, and with the assistance of friends, a permanent building was acquired within a short time. In the meantime, the Columbia Clinic Association had been approved by the State Board of Health. The aim of the clinic was to educate people in public health and to provide a variety of health services. The clinic had an eye, nose, and throat specialist and a dentist. In addition, free vaccinations were given to all the black children of the city. When the clinic was moved into larger quarters, mental health classes, taught by Evans, were added to the services. The services performed at the clinic were given free of charge.

In 1901 Evans founded the Taylor Lane Hospital and Training School for Nurses, later to be known as Saint Luke Hospital, in Columbia, South Carolina. According to the 1906 *Hospital and Training School for Nurses* bulletin, Columbia was a "growing city of over fifty thousand people, half of whom are colored." The Taylor Lane Hospital was the only facility for blacks. The founding of the institution was a pioneer endeavor. In order to maintain its stability and growth, Evans gave up her private practice and private sanitarium to act as superintendent of the Taylor Lane Hospital. Services were provided by several white physicians whom Evans said "willingly contributed their time and assistance at any hour, night or day, through storm, through sunshine to care for the afflicted poor of my people" (*Hospital and Training School for Nurses*). A number of Columbia's leading surgeons performed their first surgical work in this hospital under the guidance of Evans. The Nurses Training School provided nurses who were very much in demand and sought after by the doctors of the city. Through perseverance, hard work, and support from her white physician colleagues, Evans managed to found two hospitals and three clinics in Columbia, South Carolina.

In addition to founding health care facilities, Evans organized the Negro Health Association of South Carolina. The association was a vehicle through which she was able to spread her instructions on health and sanitation to every part of South Carolina.

Still another unselfish accomplishment of Evans was to open a pond located on land she owned to provide recreation to undernourished and underprivileged boys from eight to sixteen years of age. At the time she opened the pond, Evans could not swim. She proceeded to go through her journals and found an article written by an old sea captain. She followed his swimming instructions and taught herself to swim. As a result, she formed classes and taught hundreds of people to swim.

Her work did not go without recognition and reward. Evans was given a commission by the National Council of Defense. She was elected president of the Palmetto State Medical Society and was vice president of the National Medical Association. In 1930 Haines College in Augusta, Georgia, elected her trustee. During World War I, Evans was appointed a member of the volunteer Medical Service Corps. A religious person, Evans was a member of the Negro Civic and Religious Association. She was appointed by the Bishop of South Carolina to chair the Council of the Episcopal Church Upper Diocese.

Although Evans never married, she adopted the following children who bear her name: John B. Evans, Mattie O. Evans, Jessie Trottie Evans, Myrtle Evans Lee, Edward Evans Robinson, Gresham Evans, and Sydney Trottie Evans.

Evans found time to write articles and several larger works, one of which is *Martha Schofield: Pioneer Negro Educator* (Columbia, S.C.: DuPre Printing Co., 1916). Several of her articles appear in issues of the *Negro Health Journal* for 1916. According to a letter in her alumna folder in the Archives and Special Collections on Women in Medicine at The Medical College of Pennsylvania, a history of her life was written by G. S. Dickerman, M.D.

While attending the funeral of a former employee in Kershaw County, Evans became ill and was rushed back to Columbia. She died within a short time, at her home, on November 17, 1935.

Although she never realized her dream of becoming a medical missionary, Evans performed outstanding services among her own people in Columbia. She brought her services to people who may never have obtained any treatment. Matilda Arabella Evans, M.D., was more than a physician—she was a humanitarian, scholar, teacher, and friend to all people.

References

Caldwell, A. B., ed. *History of the American Negro*. South Carolina edition. Atlanta: A. B. Caldwell Co., 1919.

Davis, Marianna W., ed. *Contributions of Black Women to America*. Vol. II. Columbia, S.C.: Kenday Press, 1982.

Fourteenth Annual Report of the Schofield School of Aiken, South Carolina for the Year Ending July 1, 1882.

Hospital and Training School for Nurses, Aiken, South Carolina. 1906.

Jet (August 1964): 11.

Lerner, Gerder, ed. *Black Women in White America*. New York: Pantheon, 1972.

Palmetto Leader, 20 September 1930.

Woman's Medical College of Pennsylvania, "Faculty Minutes," 15 September 1895.

Collections

Materials on Evans are in the Oberlin College Archives and the Archives and Special Collections on Women in Medicine, The Medical College of Pennsylvania. A photograph from the Medical College collection has been published in *Contributions of Black Women to America*, Vol. 2, p. 379.

Margaret Jerrido

Lillian Evanti

(1890-1967)

Singer, composer

Although "every major cultural center in the world became familiar with the thrilling versatility of Evanti" (Lemieux, 215), one critic has said that Lillian Evanti is perhaps the most overlooked classical singer of the early twentieth century. She was the first black American to sing opera with an organized European opera company, and not only did she sing in five languages, she spoke them fluently (217).

Lillian Evanti was born Annie Lillian Evans on August 12, 1890, in Washington, D.C. She was privileged to be born into a well-educated, cultured, middle-class family. Her mother, formerly Anne Brooks, was a music teacher in the Washington public schools. Her father, W[ilson] Bruce Evans, an 1891 graduate of Howard University, was the organizer and first principal of Armstrong Technical High School in Washington, D.C., and devoted his life to education. Evanti had other relatives who were also memorable. Her great-uncle, Hiram Revels, was the first black United States senator, representing Mississippi. Two family members took part in abolitionist John Brown's raid on Harper's

Ferry, and Evanti is said to be a descendant of Nathaniel Green, who fought in the American Revolution.

Evanti began developing her musical talent early. She sang as a featured soloist as early as age four. She began to study piano at age five and was an accomplished performer by her teens. Her schooling included graduation from Washington's Armstrong Technical High School in 1908 and then from Miner Teachers College. She then taught kindergarten in the Washington public schools.

Lillian Evans enrolled in Howard University to pursue a degree in music. She was the protégée of Lulu Vere Childers and in 1915 first attracted public attention when she sang in concert with violinist Felix Weir and other assisting artists. She graduated in 1917 with a bachelor of music degree. After graduating from Howard University, she began touring as a concert artist. In 1918 she married one of her professors at Howard, Roy W. Tibbs. When she decided on a career in music, Lillian Evans took the advice of Harlem Renaissance poet Jessie Fauset and combined her last name and her husband's to make Evanti, a name she found more distinctive.

Lillian Evanti gave a debut recital in Washington and was in demand for local concerts, but she was determined to have a career in opera and to do so she realized she must travel abroad. In 1925 she left for France and within months was singing throughout France and Italy with the Nice Opera. She was awarded a contract with the Paris Opera in 1925 that would ultimately last three years. Her operatic debut came in 1925 when she sang the title role in Delibes's *Lakmé* at the Casino Theater in Nice, France. During the years 1925-1930 she studied voice under Madame Ritter-Ciampi and acting with M. Gaston Dupins.

When Evanti returned to the United States in late 1925, she was very well received. Her then-significant career was lauded in an editorial in the *Washington Daily American.* While known locally as Washington's own Mrs. Lillian Evans Tibbs, the editorial said the whole race should congratulate her "on her recent successes abroad in grand opera" (Lemieux, 216). The publication of her picture on the rotogravure page of a white newspaper meant Washington was also proud of her. Not uncharacteristic of the time—when a black had achieved so much—no mention was made of her race. "White papers are very careful, always, to indicate the race of a criminal . . . when that criminal is colored, but . . . if something worthwhile has been accomplished, the individual is merely an American" (Quoted in Lemieux, 216).

Evanti's popularity continued abroad with concerts throughout Europe in such cities as Paris, Monte Carlo, Menton, Montpelier, Nimes, Toulon, Milan, Turin, and Palermo in such works as Verdi's *La Traviata* and *Rigoletto,* in Donizetti's *Lucia di Lammermoor,* and Gounod's *Roméo et Juliette. La Traviata* was her favorite opera and she sang the entire opera in French, more than fifty times in Italian, and she learned it in English "to sing with a Negro company" (Greene, 176).

She spent most of her time in Europe until the rise of Hitler and Mussolini. Notable performances included *Lakmé* at the Opera Trianon Lyrique in Paris in 1927 and *The Barber of Seville* in Milan in 1930. Of the performance of *Lakmé* in Paris, one opera-goer was quoted as saying:

> So striking was her rendition of the "Bell Song" that the applause stopped the entire performance for several moments. That night Lillian Evanti made six or seven curtain calls to establish a precedent in that opera house. It was not only her brilliant musicianship, but her perfect language intonation and accent (Greene, 176).

In 1932 Gatti-Casazza, the director of the Metropolitan Opera, heard Evanti sing in Italy and asked her to audition for the Met, but even his influence as director could not overcome racial bias of the board members and she was not engaged.

Evanti continued concertizing throughout the United States and was popular with both segregated and unsegregated audiences. Her repertoire included twenty-four operas. A highlight for Evanti was a command performance for President and Mrs. Franklin D. Roosevelt on February 9, 1934. The *Washington Post*'s Paul Hume said, "Lillian Evanti showed that she still can cast a spell with the beauty of her voice" (Story, 96). Beginning in the late 1930s Evanti toured Latin American countries, including Cuba, Haiti, the Dominican Republic, and Venezuela. There, too, she was very popular. In Haiti she was awarded a diploma and medal with the rank of Chevalier, Ordre National de L'Honneur et Mérite. "One of the highlights of her career was a tour in Argentina and Brazil in 1940 sponsored by the State Department, with Toscanini and the NBC Orchestra" (Lemieux, 216). These tours included concerts and lectures. Evanti said of the tours:

> My Latin American audiences were enthusiastic. I sang in Spanish and French. Throughout my tour I gave lectures in Spanish—in Rio de Janeiro I had to speak in French.
>
> Astonishingly, the Latin American is delighted with the Negro spiritual and some of my lectures were centered around the spirituals (Greene, 176).

Throughout the 1940s and 1950s Evanti toured Latin America as a goodwill ambassador from the United States.

As a result of these Latin American tours, Evanti was inspired to compose "Himno Panamericano," which in 1945 was credited by the Inter-American conference as a significant contribution to Latin American Unity.

Lillian Evanti is sometimes credited as a founder of the National Negro Opera Company (NNOC), though some sources refer to her as instrumental in aiding Mary Caldwell Dawson in the founding of the opera company. At any rate, she was one of the significant contributors to the success of the NNOC. One of the NNOC's earliest productions was a 1943 production of *La Traviata*. Evanti not only sang the role of Violetta, but provided the translation of the original Italian text.

> Presented on an August evening, the production played to 15,000 people who packed into the amphitheater behind the Lincoln Memorial. The overflow was so great that another performance was scheduled for the next evening. The day after the first performance the *Washington Star* raved. "Poised and elegant in her delineation," wrote Alice Eversman, "she brings out, at the same time, the frivolity of Violetta's life in a way seldom emphasized by other interpreters. Her voice is brilliant with ringing high tones and sparkling smoothness in florid passages" (Story, 96).

During and after the war, Evanti remained in the United States. She was cited by General Eisenhower and others for her concerts at army and navy installations to the troops and was invited to sing at the White House by Presidents Eisenhower and Truman. She began her own publishing company, the Columbia Music Bureau, and wrote and published her own songs. One of those songs was a patriotic song, "Forward March to Victory," which was performed on a United States Army World Broadcast. During the 1948 Presidential campaign she wrote a campaign song for Thomas E. Dewey. In 1957 she wrote "Salute to Ghana," which was recorded by the United States Army Chorus and sent to Ghana.

Evanti's last years were spent singing, teaching voice, and being politically active. She worked to establish home rule in the District of Columbia, and along with Eleanor Roosevelt lobbied Congress for the creation of a national performing arts center in Washington.

Lillian Evanti was known for her beauty and grace. She was refined, had a great sense of pride, a flair for stylish dress, and an aura of grandness. She charmed her audiences both by her presence and her skill. Lillian Evanti died on December 6, 1967, at Ruth's Personal Care Home in Washington, D.C., after a long illness. She was survived by her son, Thurlow, and two grandchildren.

Evanti's motivation and style were legendary. Perhaps her most revealing statement, made to an interviewer in 1944, was, "All of this has taken hard work—and all that I plan to do will mean a lot of work, too, but if you have some place to go there is no other alternative" (*Opportunity*, 176). Though Madame Lillian Evanti was "a born diva" with "an instinctive temperament for opera" and was successful, especially for the times in which she lived, her career was called "tragically premature."

> Had she been born even ten years later, thus becoming a contemporary of Anderson's, she might have benefitted from the slow, painstaking broadening of horizons for black singers. Hers was the prototypical career of a black artist—a career of great promise truncated by the prejudice of the times (Story, 94, 97).

References

Berry, Lemuel. *Biographical Dictionary of Black Musicians and Music Educators*. Guthrie, Okla.: Educational Book Publishers, 1978. 67.

Cuney-Hare, Maud. *Negro Musicians and Their Music*. Washington, D.C., Associated Publishers, 1936. 247, 332, 357-358.

Greene, Marjorie. "Lillian Evanti." *Opportunity* 22 (Fall 1944): 176. Includes photograph.

Jet 34 (10 August 1968): 11. Includes photograph.

Lemieux, Raymond. "Lillian [Madame Evanti] Evanti." *Dictionary of American Negro Biography*. Eds. Rayford W. Logan and Michael R. Winston. New York: Norton, 1982. 215-217.

"Lillian Tibbs, First Famous Negro Opera Singer, Dies." *Jet* 33 (21 December 1967): 55. Includes photograph.

Southern, Eileen. *Biographical Dictionary of Afro-American and African Musicians*. Westport, Conn.: Greenwood Press, 1982. 129-130.

Story, Rosalyn M. *And So I Sing, African-American Divas of Opera and Concert*. New York: Warner Books, 1990. 94-97. Photograph, p. 95.

Who's Who in Colored America. 7th ed. Yonkers, N.Y.: Christian E. Burckel, 1950. 181. Includes photograph.

Collections

Information on Lillian Evanti is in the vertical files of the Schomburg Center for Research on Black Culture in New York.

Elizabeth Patrick

F

Sarah Webster Fabio

(1928-1979)

Poet, educator, critic

Sarah Webster Fabio, poet and literary critic who combined western metaphor with black "realism" in a significant contribution to the body of African-American literature, was born January 20, 1928, in Nashville, Tennessee, the daughter of Thomas Jefferson Webster and Mayme Louise (Storey) Webster. Thomas Webster worked as a Pullman porter on the Southern Illinois Railroad. Additionally, he earned extra money for his wife and six children by buying and selling real estate. Mayme Webster never worked outside the home, devoting herself instead to the full-time care of her three daughters, three sons, and husband. Apparently not in the best of health, Mayme died before Sarah completed college in 1946.

Fabio, a precocious young girl, graduated from Pearl High School in 1943 at fifteen and entered Spelman College in Atlanta, Georgia. Majoring in English and history, she remained at Spelman until 1945. She returned to Nashville during the summer of 1945 and decided not to return to Atlanta. Enrolling at Fisk University, she completed her degree in 1946. She was only eighteen years old. A handsome young dental student at Meharry Medical College's School of Dentistry might have influenced Sarah Webster not to return to Atlanta. She had fallen in love with Cyril Leslie Fabio II, and the two married in June following her graduation.

When her husband received his dental degree, the young couple moved to Florida, where Cyril was in the military. Their first child, Cyril Leslie Fabio III, was born January 30, 1947. A year later the family was stationed in Nashville when a second son, Thomas Albert, was born on January 25, 1948.

Soon after the birth of the second son, the family was again forced to move to Florida. On August 30, 1949, Sarah Fabio gave birth to her first daughter, Cheryl Elisa Louise. By age twenty-one, Sarah found herself the mother of three children under the age of five. Despite the strictures of being a military wife and mother of small children, Fabio, on one of their frequent moves back to Nashville, enrolled for courses at Tennessee State University, known in 1952 as Tennessee Agricultural and Industrial College. However, before she could complete a degree program, the family received an overseas assignment. In 1953 Sarah and her family moved to Germany. Here Fabio gave birth to a second daughter, Renee Angela, on September 20, 1955.

Returning to the United States, the family spent a brief tour of duty in Wichita, Kansas. Relentlessly pursuing a graduate education despite her pregnancy, Fabio enrolled in Wichita State University, where she took courses in English. Ronald Eric, Sarah's third son, arrived December 13, 1956.

After Cyril Fabio's military commitment was completed, the Fabio family moved to California, where they settled and where Cyril Fabio began to earn a living through the private practice of dentistry. After moving to Palo Alto, California, Sarah Fabio assumed the task of helping her husband establish his practice and settling her five children in schools and extracurricular activities. Not until 1963 was she able to return to her own education. Enrolling in San Francisco State College (University since 1975), she earned a master's degree in 1965. Degree in hand, she landed a teaching position at Merritt College in Oakland, where she taught from 1965 to 1968. Fabio also worked at the East Bay Skills Center from 1966 to 1967, helping inner-city youth improve their communication skills.

The middle and late 1960s proved to be an exciting and challenging time for Fabio. In 1966 she participated in the First World Festival of Negro Art in Dakar, Senegal. She was also affiliated with the University of California, Berkeley, and the California College of Arts and Crafts in 1968 as a poet and teacher of creative writing. She remained a frequent lecturer on these campuses until 1971.

In 1972 Fabio divorced her husband and took a position at Oberlin College in Ohio, where she remained until 1974. Lecturing and touring the country, she became a recognized critic and spokesperson for the black arts movement. In 1976, while teaching and pursuing graduate work at the University of Wisconsin, Fabio became ill. Returning to Meharry Medical College in Nashville, she was diagnosed with cancer of the colon. She took chemotherapy, which enervated her characteristic stamina but not her spirit. Fabio spent the last two years of her life with her oldest daughter, Cheryl, in Pinole, California. She died in November 1979, at the age of fifty-one.

Sarah Webster Fabio's stamina in dealing with five children, her wit, and her vision are what her children remember most (Telephone interview with Cheryl Fabio, 5 November 1990). But the world will remember her poetry, and African-

American literature benefits from her critical analysis. Those fortunate enough to have taken her classes will recall a brilliant, poetic woman, seasoned mother, and lover of knowledge.

Fabio's Works Published

Fabio began writing poetry during her many months of pregnancy and confinement, through moves that took her to strange and sometimes lonely places. Her first collection of poems appeared in 1968; entitled *Saga of a Black Man,* it was published by Turn Over Book Store. That same year she had articles published in *Black World, Journal of Black Renaissance,* and *Negro Digest.* Addison Gayle included her poetry in the popular anthology, *Black Expression,* which appeared in 1969. *A Mirror, A Soul* appeared in 1969, followed by *Black Talk: Shield, and Sword* in 1973, both published by Doubleday.

In 1972 Fabio recorded two albums for Folkways Records, *Boss Soul* and *Soul Ain't, Soul Is.* Fabio is anthologized in the following publications: *The Black Aesthetic,* ed. Addison Gayle, (Doubleday, 1971); *A Broadside Treasury,* ed. Gwendolyn Brooks, Broadside, 1971; *To Gwen With Love,* eds. Patricia L. Brown, Don Lee, and Francis Ward (Johnson Publishing Company, 1971); *Dices or Black Bones,* ed. Adam David Miller (Houghton Mifflin, 1970); *The Poetry of Black America,* ed. Arnold Adoff (Harper and Row, 1973); and *Understanding the New Black Poetry,* ed. Stephen Henderson (Morrow, 1973).

Fabio's books include *Dark Debut: Three Black Women Coming* (Harcourt Brace Jovanovich, 1966); *Return of Margaret Walker* (Broadside, 1966); *Double Dozens: An Anthology of Poets From Sterling Brown to Kali* (Broadside, 1966); and *No Crystal Stair: A Socio-Drama of the History of Black Women in the U.S.A.* (Broadside, 1967). *The Rainbow Sign* is a seven-volume collection of Fabio's poetry that she published in 1973. In 1976 Fabio's daughter Cheryl produced a film of her mother and set many of her poems to music. The film, *Rainbow Black* (1976), is currently being distributed by Cheryl Fabio from her home in California.

Fabio's poetry, while reflective of the black arts movement, with its emphasis on the black aesthetic, is somehow classic in its subtle blending of "soul" on the one hand and western literary metaphors on the other hand. "Evil is No Black Thing" is a case in point. The poem begins:

> Ahab's gaily clad fisherfriends,
> questing under the blue skies after
> the albino prize, find the green sea
> cold and dark at its deep center,
> but calm—unperturbed by the fates
> of men and whales (Henderson, 241).

This reference to *Moby Dick* is juxtaposed against a refrain that says, "Evil is no black thing." The poem concludes that "evil" is "a criss-crossed [sic] pile of / sun-bleached bones." "Tribute to Duke," which heralds Duke Ellington's musical genius, is one of Fabio's most popular poems.

When questioned about her politics, Fabio replied that she was a disillusioned Democrat, and on the subject of religion she reported that she was born Baptist, married Episcopalian, but respected Voodoo (81).

Fabio believed in saturating her work in the black experience and directed her works to a black audience. In 1968 she stated that a black writer's work "must seem 'real' to black people in order to have a validity distinguishing it from the 'realism' of the black experience as propounded in the works of American writers like Margaret Mitchell, William Faulkner, Eudora Welty, and Robert Penn Warren" (Fuller, 88). Fabio named Margaret Walker's *Jubilee* the most important novel since *Invisible Man.* As a critic and theorist, Sarah Webster Fabio was ahead of her time.

References

Contemporary Authors. Vol. 22. Detroit: Gale Research, 1988. 129.

Fuller, Hoyt. "Survey: Black Writers' Views on Literary Lions and Values." *Negro Digest* 3 (January 1968): 10-54, 88.

Henderson, Stephen, ed. *Understanding the New Black Poetry.* New York: Morrow, 1973. 241-42.

Page, James A., comp. *Selected Black American Authors: An Illustrated Bio-Bibliography.* Boston: G. K. Hall, 1977. 81-82.

Telephone interview with Cheryl Fabio, 5 November 1990.

Collections

The papers of Sarah Webster Fabio, including photographs, are held in the Special Collections of Fisk University Library, Nashville, Tennessee.

Nagueyalti Warren

Crystal Dreda Bird Fauset

(1893-1965)

State legislator, community leader, race relations specialist

One of the pioneers in the elective process was Crystal Fauset, the first black woman in America to be elected to a state legislature. Her election to this influential position seemed natural given her strong personality. One reporter wrote:

> Power surrounds the woman. It dwells within her, emanates from her, and yet, is very subtly hidden. Anyone who comes near Mrs. Fauset feels her greatness—in the sweep of her very alert glance, in the charm of her ready smile, in the warm sincerity of her hand clasp, and in her voice—like crisp staccato music, mellowed (*Chicago Defender,* 15 April 1939).

Crystal Dreda Bird Fauset, born on June 27, 1893, in Princess Anne, Maryland, was the youngest of nine children born to Portia E. (Lovett) Bird and Benjamin Bird. Her father served as the first principal of Princess Anne Academy, a school for young blacks, which later became part of the University of Maryland. Neither parent lived to witness the distinction that their daughter attained. Benjamin Bird, who had been born in Gettysburg, Pennsylvania, died in Maryland in 1897. Fauset's mother, Portia Bird, briefly succeeded her husband as principal of the school until her own death in 1900.

With the death of her mother, Fauset had to adjust not only to life without either of her parents but also to life in a new city. Her aunt, Portia Bird's sister, became her new guardian, and Boston became her new home. After completing the required curriculum in the city's integrated public school system, Fauset enrolled in Boston Normal School. Following her graduation in 1914, she taught school for three years. That first job marked the beginning of an active and varied career involving education, social work, and politics.

In 1918 Fauset became the first secretary for younger Negro girls with the national board of the Young Women's Christian Association (YWCA) in New York, and traveled into nearly all the States, Mexico, and Cuba studying Negro conditions in relationship to the general picture.'' She said that she learned from her experiences with the YWCA that humanity's ''problems cannot be segregated—wherever I went, they appeared as inter-racial problems'' (*Philadelphia Record*, 13 November 1938).

By 1927, when the American Friends Service Committee (AFSC) invited her to take part in ''an innovative program designed to communicate the human aspirations and longings of African-Americans,'' Fauset was already an accomplished speaker. In her 1928 report to the committee, she stated that ''her 210 speeches had reached almost 50,000 people in a single year.'' At the end of that year, she took much needed time for rest in Europe (Bogin, 224).

While educating other people about the concerns of the black American community, Fauset did not neglect her own education. In 1931 she received a bachelor's degree from Columbia University's Teachers College in New York. She did not neglect her interest in music either. Fauset was an accomplished singer and pianist and enjoyed lecturing on ''Music in the Life of America.''

In June 1931 she married Arthur Huff Fauset, principal of Philadelphia's Singerley School, and a man who was actively involved in community activities. The marriage was shortlived, but Arthur Fauset did not file for divorce until 1944.

Crystal Fauset's continuing commitment to educating the public about the concerns of black Americans led her to help found the Institute of Race Relations at Philadelphia's Swarthmore College. Beginning in 1933, she served as associate secretary. ''Three summers of that work impressed her with the necessity of 'reaching more people and going to the heart of the economic situation through political action''' (*Philadelphia Record*, 13 November 1938).

Having recognized a need, Fauset did not fail to take action. ''Her first real adventure into politics began when she became a member of the administrative staff of the W. P. A. [Works Progress Administration in Philadelphia] in 1935'' (*Philadelphia Tribune*, 2 June 1938). Around the same time, she organized the Philadelphia Democratic Women's League and then embarked on her venture into national politics. In 1936, Fauset became director of black women's activities for the National Democratic Committee and started ''selling 'Roosevelt humanitarianism' to Negro housewives'' (*Philadelphia Record,* 13 November 1938).

The decision to campaign for a position in the Pennsylvania legislature was not entirely her own idea. One newspaper reported:

> Her ability as a public speaker first caused the political powers that be to see Mrs. Crystal Bird Fauset as excellent timber for use in the Democratic Party. For she is one candidate for public office who had the unique distinction of having the leaders seek her out and urge her to run for the state legislature. (*Philadelphia Tribune*, 2 June 1938).

But she did have her own reasons for accepting the challenge that was presented to her. Another newspaper reported that the contrast ''of long, patient bread lines opposite swank Central Park apartments spurred [her] . . . into political activity.'' Seeing ''low economic status'' as ''the Negro's biggest problem,'' she determined ''to fight for three things in particular: more relief, more W. P. A. and better housing'' (*Philadelphia Record,* 13 November 1938).

Wisely, Fauset decided to base her campaign strategy more heavily on personal conversation than on public speaking engagements. She did make around twenty-five speeches, but ''other than that, she campaigned the modern way—by telephone. She talked with scores of persons between 8 A.M. and noon daily for weeks on end'' (*Philadelphia Record*, 13 November 1938). This strategy won her seven thousand more votes than her opponent in a district in which two-thirds of the population was white.

On November 8, 1938, Crystal Bird Fauset was elected Philadelphia's Democratic representative to the Assembly of the Commonwealth of Pennsylvania. At the time she took office "the number of women in State legislatures [had] dropped from a peak of 149 in 38 States in 1929 to 127 in 27 States for 1939" (*Washington Post*, 26 December 1938). She joined "a constituency three-fourths white," being "the only woman among six colored members in the Pennsylvania legislature" (*The Guardian*, 25 March 1939). Fauset was careful to emphasize, "My interest in people isn't in any sense limited to my race. . . . It is a universal interest in human beings" (*Philadelphia Record*, 13 November 1938). In 1939, Pennsylvania Governor George Earle recognized her efforts on behalf of all people by presenting to her the Meritorious Service Medal.

Newspaper accounts of Fauset's legislative activities focused on her superior ability as a public speaker. One reporter stated that she "charmed the huge audience with her fluent speech and ease of manner and it was with difficulty that she was able to leave" (*Pittsburgh Courier*, 1 April 1939). Another journalist remarked, "All of the women who listened to the magnetic legislator's well chosen, expertly delivered counsel, could only say, 'It's the best speech I've ever heard'" (*Chicago Defender*, 8 April 1939).

Through her speeches, Fauset sought to encourage all citizens, especially black women, to become involved in politics. She believed that "every woman should be consciously active in the improvement of the community in which she lives." To accomplish that involvement, "individual interests, except as they denote community progress, should be relegated into the background" (*Chicago Defender*, 15 April 1939). Fauset often cited past accomplishments of black women, but declared that it will be through "the use of the ballot that they can become conscious makers of history" (*New York Amsterdam News*, 8 November, 1938). On one occasion, she boldly proclaimed, "I do not care whether you like it, when I mention politics, for the salvation of our race, it must have a political tinge" (*The Guardian*, 25 March 1939).

Late in 1939, having served less than a year in her legislative post, Fauset resigned to join Pennsylvania's WPA. A part of her responsibility as assistant state director of the Education and Recreation Program was to act as consultant and adviser on all trade relations and problems in the Works Program in Pennsylvania. Always watchful for new ways to improve race relations, "she saw in this new work broader opportunity for developing a more progressive and liberal point of view among adults of both races" (*Afro-American*, 25 November 1939).

Fauset's next appointment resulted from her friendship with Eleanor Roosevelt and her leadership in Franklin Delano Roosevelt's election campaigns. On October 20, 1941, Fauset was named special consultant to the director of the Office of Civilian Defense. In this role, she became race relations adviser to New York's Mayor Fiorello LaGuardia, to Eleanor Roosevelt, and, indirectly, to the White House. She was described as "a consummate politician" and "a competent, friendly woman, with exceeding resiliency under pressure" (Ottley, 264).

Early in 1944, Fauset resigned from this position to take part in the Democratic election campaign. Late in the year, however, she withdrew from the Democratic National Committee because of disappointment in and lack of cooperation from party leadership. She described the chairman of the committee as a "dictator—a man not willing to deal democratically with Negroes" (*Los Angeles Tribune*, 16 October 1944). After so many years of active participation in the Democratic Party, she now declared her support for the Republican Party and its candidate for president, Governor Thomas E. Dewey.

In 1945 Fauset helped establish the United Nations Council of Philadelphia, forerunner of the World Affairs Council. As an officer of that organization until 1950, she was privileged to attend the founding of the United Nations in San Francisco. Concentrating her energies now on world politics, Fauset embarked on speaking tours in India, the Middle East, and Nigeria. She was present when India celebrated its independence. She even pursued a high-level diplomatic post in Africa.

On January 29, 1955, Fauset was awarded her second Meritorious Service Medal of the Commonwealth of Pennsylvania. The citation, presented by Governor John S. Fine, commended her for her "selfless devotion to the cause of furthering international amity by her able leadership in the American-Korean Foundation" (*Pittsburgh Courier*, 29 January 1955).

Political activities brought further disappointment, however. "In 1957 she protested in a telegram to the White House that the United States delegation to mark Ghana's independence should have included 'a woman like myself . . . to represent the millions of slave mothers' in America's past" (Bogin, 225).

Despite her disappointment, Fauset remained active in political and educational concerns until her death on March 28, 1965, in Philadelphia. In addition to her other activities, she had served as a trustee of Cheyney State Teachers College (later Cheyney State College), she had participated in a number of local and national organizations, and was an honorary member of the Lincoln Dames. This last group held a memorial service in her honor on May 23, 1965.

References

Berlack-Boozer, Thelma. "Crystal Bird Fauset is Guest at Local Banquet." New York *Amsterdam News*, 3 November 1938.

Bogin, Ruth. "Fauset, Crystal Dreda Bird." *Notable American Women. The Modern Period: A Biographical Dictionary*. Cambridge: Harvard University Press, 1980.

"Crystal B. Fauset, Former Legislator." *New York Times*, 30 March 1965. Includes photograph.

"Crystal B. Fauset Speaks in Boston." *Pittsburgh Courier*, 1 April 1939.

"Crystal Bird Fauset Due." *Los Angeles Tribune*, 16 October 1944.

"Crystal Bird Fauset's Ability as Public Speaker is Asset to Political Career." *Philadelphia Tribune*, 2 June 1938. Includes photograph.

"First Ladies of Colored America—No. 11" *Crisis* 50 (July 1943): 207. Includes photograph.

Galbreath, Elizabeth. "Typovision." *Chicago Defender*, 15 April 1939. Includes photograph.

Mason, Monroe. "Woman Legislator Stirs Large Crowd." *The Guardian*, 25 March 1939. Includes photograph.

"Medal Given to Crystal Fauset." *Pittsburgh Courier*, 29 January 1955.

"Mrs. Crystal Bird Fauset Tells Her Chief Interest." New York *Amsterdam News*, 3 December 1938.

Ottley, Roi. *New World A-Coming: Inside Black America*. Boston: Houghton Mifflin, 1943.

"Resigns Legislature Post." *Atlanta Daily World*, 9 November 1939. Includes photograph.

"Second Annual All Women's Dinner Held." *Chicago Defender*, 8 April 1939.

"She Found Political Honors Too Empty." *Afro-American*, National ed., Baltimore, 25 November 1939.

"Sight of Breadlines Drove Mrs. Fauset into Politics." *Philadelphia Record*, 13 November 1938.

"Women in Legislatures Show Drop." *Washington Post*, 26 December 1938.

Collections

Ruth Bogin's article in *Notable American Women* includes a survey of primary and secondary materials on Crystal Bird Fauset.

Marie Garrett

Jessie Redmon Fauset

(1882-1961)

Writer, educator, editor

Jessie Redmon Fauset had a career as a teacher, but she is best known for her writing and her contribution to the Harlem Renaissance as literary editor of the *Crisis*.

Fauset was born April 27, 1882, in Camden, New Jersey. She was the seventh child born to Redmon Fauset, an African Methodist Episcopal minister, and Annie Seamon Fauset. After the death of Annie Fauset, Redmon Fauset married Bella Huff, a widow with three children, and to this union three children were born, including writer Arthur Huff Fauset. Jessie Fauset grew up in cultured but economically poor circumstances in Philadelphia, graduating with honors from the High School for Girls in 1900 as the only black student. Officials at Bryn Mawr College, which Fauset sought to enter, obtained aid for her to go instead to Cornell University, from which she graduated in 1905 after a demanding course of study emphasizing languages (Latin, Greek, French, German, and English). She was the first black woman in the country elected to Phi Beta Kappa, and the only black graduate elected to that honor fraternity at Cornell before 1921.

Jessie Redmon Fauset

After being denied a teaching job in Philadelphia because of her race, Fauset taught one year at the Douglass High School in Baltimore before moving to Washington, D.C., where she successfully taught French at the M Street High School (after 1916 called the Dunbar High School) for fourteen years. Attractive, petite, light-skinned, pleasant, highly intelligent, highly educated, and well-read, yet exceedingly modest and even shy in social circumstances, Fauset was an impressive and effective teacher, according to her students. One of them recalled sixty years later that she was the first person he heard use the word "ubiquitous" in ordinary conversation, and it sent him scurrying to the dictionary.

Fauset completed two graduate degrees, a master of arts in French at the University of Pennsylvania in 1929, after summer courses in 1901 and 1912 and a year's work in 1918-19; and a certificate at the Sorbonne, Paris, France, after six months of study there in 1925-26. She returned to teaching French at DeWitt Clinton High School in New York City after her tenure as literary editor of the NAACP's publication, the *Crisis*, from 1919 to 1926.

Fauset Becomes Influential Literary Editor

Fauset's amiability, intelligence, education, and interactive teaching skills made her an exceptional and highly influential literary editor during the height of the Harlem Renaissance period. Poet Langston Hughes called Fauset one of the three "mid-wives" who guided the artistic development into life.

In 1919 Fauset was brought from Washington, D.C., to New York City and the offices of the NAACP and the *Crisis* by W. E. B. Du Bois, editor of the magazine from its inception in 1911. By that time, Fauset had published numerous short stories, poems, articles, and book reviews in the journal and had been fleetingly involved with various NAACP legal cases. She had also been an admirer of Du Bois, fourteen years her senior, from her college days at Cornell, beginning a correspondence with him just when her own father died and obtaining Du Bois's aid in locating summer teaching jobs as a college student.

From 1919 to 1926 Fauset took over much of Du Bois's work connected with the *Crisis* and with his international Pan-African Movement meetings (her facility in French in fact made her indispensable to some of this activity). She did much work for which Du Bois has been given credit by himself and others, including the short-lived but delightful children's publication *The Brownies' Book* (1920-21). For the twenty-four issues of this publication, Fauset wrote hundreds of signed and unsigned stories, poems, dialogues, biographies, and articles, as well as handling all of the correspondence with contributors and all of the editing.

As literary editor of the *Crisis*, Fauset discovered or published very early in their careers Langston Hughes, Jean Toomer, Claude McKay, and Countee Cullen, as well as many lesser-known women writers with views ranging from radical to conservative on racial and sexual issues, and with widely-differing writing styles.

Fauset included in the magazine many articles dealing with literary movements of the day, putting the *Crisis* at the center of the 1920s debates on how "the Negro" should be portrayed in art. Explanatory articles on the nature and structure of short stories and plays were designed for the wide audience reached by the *Crisis* and were successful in encouraging new writers to enter competitions sponsored by the NAACP, such as the Amy Spingarn awards for black writers of poetry, drama, essays, and short stories.

Fauset's own writing for the *Crisis* before and during her tenure as literary editor includes a large number of poems and stories, one rather lengthy novelette, translations from French and West Indian and African writers, many essays, book reviews, and articles on topics ranging from Egyptian nationalism and Brazilian emancipation to reports on the Second Pan-African Congress in Europe in 1921, which she attended as a delegate of Delta Sigma Theta sorority, of which she was a member.

This range of writing reveals a woman thoroughly aware of the American social and literary scene, as well as of the relationships of American life to what was being lived and written in other countries. Her reviews cover a wide range of material appearing in periodicals as well as books, and include evaluations of English and French works of fiction, drama, poetry, folklore, journalism, biography, criticism, and literary history, many of them dealing with Africa and African literature. Fauset's standards of form are invariably high even when she is strongly moved by content. Her negative criticism is kind and polite while nevertheless clearly stated. She attempts to find something to praise even when the sum of a review is negative. Her assessments of works that have since become well-known do not differ significantly from those of subsequent critics, as, for example, in her praising James Weldon Johnson's anonymously-published *The Autobiography of an Ex-Colored Man* in 1912.

Essays Less Recognized Than Fiction

Fauset is a very good—and heretofore unrecognized—essayist, with her intelligence, precise language skill, wide-ranging interests, and sensitivity suited more to this form than to that for which she is usually recognized, her fiction. Excellent examples are provided by five travel essays from France and Algeria in 1925-26, published in the *Crisis*. Fauset reveals deep interest in the lives and strengths of the poor in "Yarrow Revisited," contrasting the Paris she knew as a student in 1913 and the Paris of the Second Pan-African Congress in 1922 with the "workaday season" she knows in a cheap pension in 1925. "This Way to The Flea Market" describes in detail the lives of the extreme poor of all nationalities clinging to the fringes of the fortifications of Paris. Here and in "Dark Algiers and White" she concentrates on the women, looking beneath the "voluminous garments" of the Arabians, for example, to see "the misshapen bodies, broken and distorted by neglect, abuse and much beating of children."

Fauset's essays reveal a strong and gentle woman with happy childhood memories, an intense intellectual life, and wide social contacts as well as a deep awareness of the lives of the poor and of women. Her imagery and figurative language is suitably sparse and effective; she makes her points subtly and entertainingly. The personal essay form was particularly suited to her thought and writing skills. Fauset explores opinions and experiences in her essays that are invariably ignored when her fiction is cursorily examined.

Fauset's poems, neither simplistic nor innovative, reveal personal delights and pains behind her more public concerns, many seeking consolation in nature after love is gone. Most frequently anthologized is a lighthearted exploration of love and pain and irony called "La Vie C'est La Vie," first published in the *Crisis* in July 1922 (124). The poem's narrator sits "quiescent" in the park beside a man who loves her, idly watching the squirrels while his voice breaks "with love and pain."

Also anthologized, for example, in the Langston Hughes and Arna Bontemps anthology, *The Poetry of the Negro: 1746-1949* (1949) and in James Weldon Johnson's *The Book of American Negro Poetry* (1931), are Fauset's very good translations of French West Indian poets. She was aware, writing about translating Haitian writers in 1920, that "French poetry does not lend itself easily to our harsher, less flexible mould," making it difficult to convey the "charm" of the original, charm which nevertheless ranked, in her estimation, with the "charm of the poetry of France" (Sylvander, 129).

Fauset Most-Published Novelist of Harlem Renaissance

Fauset's short stories published in the *Crisis* lend some insight into themes of the fiction for which she is best known—she is, in fact, with her four novels, the most published novelist of the Harlem Renaissance period. "Emmy" shows her interest in the ironies of American discrimination based not only on skin color but on invisible "Black blood," and her more extensive concern with what characters do within the constraints of their heritage. "The Sleeper Wakes" presents some of the race and sex issues later developed in her novel *Plum Bun* in 1929. "Double Trouble" is an early version of the barely-avoided incest of her novel *The Chinaberry Tree* of 1931. In each case, the movement from the shorter to the longer exploitations of the themes shows conscious artistic development in Fauset's fiction.

In the early 1920s, Fauset was inspired to write her first novel by what she thought to be inaccurate or incomplete depictions of black life in fiction. *There Is Confusion* was published in 1924 by New York publishers Boni and Liveright (who also published Jean Toomer's *Cane* and Eric Walrond's *Tropic Death*, as well as white writers Theodore Dreiser, Ezra Pound, T. S. Eliot, Hilda Doolittle, H. L. Mencken, William Faulkner, Sherwood Anderson, and Hart Crane). Fauset's novel was well reviewed and sold well, even being issued in a second edition in 1928.

There is Confusion presents the story of two families through the marriage of Joanna Marshall from one family and Peter Bye from the other. Fauset traces the lives of the main characters from childhood and provides extensive information about their ancestry, leading to a plethora of characters, descriptions, and leaps in time that are often confusing. For its themes, however, the novel is a worthwhile read, depicting the kinds of racial discrimination faced by northern, urban blacks, and the kinds of responsive actions possible given American slave history, racially-mixed heritage, and various environments.

Many formal improvements by the time Fauset published her second novel, *Plum Bun*, in 1929, make it in many ways her best work. Time transitions are shorter and smoother than in her first novel, and the limitation of the point of view to one character, Angela Murray, gives the reader depth without confusion. The plot is structured by the nursery rhyme, "To Market, to Market, to buy a Plum Bun. Home again, Home again, Market is done." Angela is a young woman from a strong Philadelphia family of modest means. She and her mother can pass for white, her sister and her father cannot. In New York City as a struggling painter, Angela makes the choice to pass, becoming involved also with a rich white playboy (the "Plum Bun" section). "Home Again," the longest section of the novel, explores Angela's attempts to establish meaningful relationships with men and women she carefully evaluates. In the final "Market is Done" section, Angela sacrifices an award of a trip to France by revealing her racial identity in response to reporters' badgering of a black woman. In fitting nursery rhyme fashion, Angela is then rewarded not only by getting to France anyway but by a Paris reunion with her true love, Anthony Cross, who has lingered in the background throughout the novel in triple disguise—poor, black, looking white.

Fauset uses the plot freedom of the American romance while satirizing traditional romantic assumptions in *Plum Bun*. Black blood is customarily a "bar sinister" in American romance. Angela sees it just that way at the beginning of the book; her romantic ideal of adventure and love points directly toward being white and marrying white as well as rich. But it is only after Angela sees skin color, money, and marriage in a transformed light that Roger, the rich playboy, arrives at her door with a marriage proposal.

Stylistic Elements of Earlier Novels Return

Unfortunately Fauset's final two novels, *The Chinaberry Tree*, 1931, and *Comedy: American Style*, 1933, return to some of the stylistic defects of her first. The Frederick A. Stokes Company, which had published *Plum Bun*, balked a bit at her third, deciding to do it only after writer Zona Gale agreed with Fauset to write an introduction. The readers at Stokes, Fauset said, "declare plainly that there ain't no such colored people as these, who speak decent English, are self-supporting and have a few ideals'' (Jessie Fauset to Zona Gale, 20 October 1931). The Stokes company went on to publish Fauset's fourth novel as well as her third.

Despite weaknesses in form, the two novels are nevertheless worth reading for their thematic relevance. In her foreword to the 1931 book, Fauset said she wanted to explore ''the homelife of the colored American who is not being pressed too hard by the Furies of Prejudice, Ignorance, and Economic Injustice.'' This she does through a story set in a small New Jersey community named Red Brook, in which white townspeople appear only once, as onlookers to a skating party.

Both *The Chinaberry Tree* and *Comedy: American Style* use formal structures from analogues to drama, implicit in the former with its suggestions of classical Greek tragedy and Shakespearean festive comedy, explicit in the latter with its formal divisions using dramatic terms. Fauset had been extremely involved with drama in her New York City social life throughout the 1920s, naming theater-going as her favorite recreation. Her fourth and final published novel, in 1933, is divided into elements of a play: ''the Plot,'' ''The Characters,'' ''Teresa's Act,'' ''Oliver's Act,'' ''Phebe's Act,'' and ''Curtain,'' with each of the theatrical terms acting as *double entendre*.

At the age of forty-seven, in 1929, Fauset married Herbert Harris, an insurance broker somewhat incapacitated by World War I injuries, and they made their home with Fauset's sister Helen Lanning, an elementary school teacher, in a cooperative apartment on Seventh Avenue in Harlem until Lanning's death in 1936. Fauset and Harris were separated for a time in 1931 and 1932, during which time Herbert Harris was named corespondent in the divorce suit of Harold McDonald. In the early 1940s the Harrises moved to 247 Orange Road in Montclair, New Jersey, where they lived until Herbert Harris's death in 1958. Following his death, Fauset returned to Philadelphia, where she lived with her half-brother, Earl Huff, until her death.

Fauset's achievements in American literary history are significant and are particularly noteworthy when one recognizes the many ways in which she was a courageous and successful pioneer in education, in employment, in editing, in translating, and in writing. Her last two novels were published when the Harlem Renaissance she had helped spur was over, and the Great Depression was on. She attempted to write and publish more after her retirement from her second career in teaching in the 1930s, but by then it was too late. It often seems that great artists are less than admirable people. Jessie Fauset is an example of an extremely admirable person who made the most of her opportunities but whose modesty and selflessness prevented her from becoming a major American literary figure.

References

Baltimore Afro-American, 17 December 1932.

Lane, David K. Letter to Carolyn Wedin, 7 March 1976.

Fauset, Jessie Redmon. *The Chinaberry Tree*. New York: Frederick A. Stokes, 1931.

———. *Comedy: American Style*. New York: Frederick A. Stokes, 1933. Reprinted. New York: AMS Press, 1969.

———. ''Dark Algiers and White.'' *Crisis* 33 (April, May 1925): 255-58, 16-22.

———. ''Double Trouble.'' *Crisis* 26 (August, September 1923): 155-59, 205-209.

———. ''Emmy.'' *Crisis* 6 (December 1912): 79-87; (January 1913): 134-42.

———. ''La Vie C'est La Vie.'' *Crisis* 24 (July 1922): 124.

———. *Plum Bun*. New York: Frederick A. Stokes, 1929.

———. ''The Sleeper Wakes.'' *Crisis* 20 (August, September, October 1920): 168-73, 226-29, 267-74.

———. *There is Confusion*. New York: Boni and Liveright, 1924.

———. ''This Way to the Flea Market.'' *Crisis* 29 (February 1925): 161-63.

———. ''What to Read.'' Review of *The Autobiography of an Ex-Colored Man*. *Crisis* (November 1912): 38.

———. ''Yarrow Revisited.'' *Crisis* 36 (January 1929): 107-109.

Hughes, Langston. *The Big Sea*. New York: Hill and Wang, 1940. 72.

———, and Arna Bontemps, eds. *The Poetry of the Negro: 1746-1949*. Rev. ed. Garden City, N.Y.: Doubleday, 1970.

Jessie Fauset. Letter to Zona Gale, 20 October 1931, Portage, Wisconsin Public Library.

Johnson, James Weldon, ed. *The Book of American Negro Poetry*. New York: Harcourt, Brace, 1931.

Starkey, Marion. Interview with Jessie Fauset. *Southern Workman* 61 (May 1932): 217-20.

Sylvander, Carolyn Wedin. *Jessie Redmon Fauset, Black American Writer*. Troy, N.Y.: Whitson, 1981.

Collections

There is no comprehensive collection of Fauset papers. Significant material appears in the NAACP Papers at the Library of Congress, the W. E. B. Du Bois Papers at the University of Massachusetts, Amherst; the Amistad Research Center, Tulane University; the James Weldon Johnson Memorial Collection, Yale University; the Moorland-Spingarn Research Collection, Howard University; and the

Schomburg Center for Research in Black Culture, the New York Public Library. Photographs of Jessie Redmon Fauset can be found at the Library of Congress, Manuscript Division, and the Schomburg Center.

Carolyn Wedin

Dorothy Boulding Ferebee

(1890-1980)

Physician, educator

Dorothy Boulding Ferebee had a distinguished career as a physician and was a tireless promoter of medical education as a means of improving living conditions for women, for blacks, and for the poor.

Born in 1890 in Norfolk, Virginia, Dorothy Boulding Ferebee began her education at Armstrong Grammar School, and she graduated from English High School in Boston, Massachusetts, with the highest honors in a class of 329. Graduating from Tufts Medical School in 1924, she was again an honor student, as well as class historian. There she was elected to membership in Zeta Phi, an honorary medical society for women.

Growing up in Boston's fashionable Beacon Hill and coming from a family with eight lawyers, Dorothy Ferebee was the daughter of Benjamin Richard Boulding and Cornelia (Paige) Boulding. She was the niece of George Lewis Ruffin, the first black graduate of Harvard law school, who later became Massachusetts's first black judge. "All I heard at the table was 'your honor, I object,' or 'answer the question yes or no.' Yet all my life I wanted to be a doctor." These are the words of Dorothy Boulding Ferebee when she was interviewed at her home, in Washington, D.C., at the age of eighty. She continues:

> I would nurse and help the birds that fell out of trees, the dog that lost a fight. My grandmother would say "Do you need water, dolly?" and then say to my mother, "She's going to make a fine doctor." They weren't professional women but they gave me marvelous encouragement (*Washington Post*, 15 May 1978).

And marvelous encouragement was what she needed at the time this maverick entered medical school and started practice, for blacks in medicine were faced with great discrimination. However, Dorothy Ferebee the granddaughter of former slaves John and Cornelius Ruffin, was determined to keep her dream alive, bring it to reality, and become a trained physician.

After serving an internship in Freedmen's Hospital and moving to Washington, D.C., where she set up her medical practice in a poor, old section of Capitol Hill, Ferebee in 1919 started the Southeast Neighborhood House. It was a playground facility for black children to use while their mothers worked. Ferebee was familiar with this area, for she often drove her own patients across town to Freedmen's Hospital because the ambulance would not serve the neighborhood. She collected donations and persuaded the then all-white Friendship House board to provide a facility nearby. Forty-nine years later, Ferebee described what prompted her to start this greatly-needed facility:

> Georgie, a nine year old boy took his three year old brother to the babysitter each day. One day the babysitter couldn't work. Georgie's mother was across town at her job as a domestic and the ice box was empty, so Georgie stole a bottle of milk from a neighbor's porch and ended up in the Precinct.
>
> I went down and got him and paid for the milk and right then decided we needed a place for Black children of working mothers (*Washington Post,* 15 May 1978).

She served as president of the Southeast Neighborhood House for thirteen years. During that same time she was appointed instructor in obstetrics at the Howard University Medical School and appears to have served in this capacity for thirteen years.

Dorothy Boulding Ferebee married Claude Thurston Ferebee, a physician and medical educator at Howard University, in 1928, and later gave birth to twins—Claude, Jr., and Dorothy. Dorothy died from flu at the age of eighteen. She had been sick for only two days. Ferebee sought to combine marriage and family with her medical career. Unfortunately, it proved true that combining marriage with a medical career was difficult, for after being married for thirty years, the couple divorced.

Ferebee Addresses Medical Needs of Mississippi's Poor Blacks

For seven summers, 1935-1942, starting in the worst years of the depression, Ferebee directed gratis what came to be known as the Mississippi Health Project. Through her involvement with Alpha Kappa Alpha sorority, which included serving as basileus of the local chapter from 1936 to 1938, this became a national health project for all sorority chapters. Describing the Mississippi Health Project in an interview in the *Washington Post*, Ferebee told how she and a few coworkers from the sorority drove to Holmes and Bolivar counties in Mississippi. There they were greeted by blacks in infectious conditions: some suffered from malaria, many were not inoculated against diphtheria, smallpox, and other diseases, some suffered from woeful dental defects, and still others suffered from malnutrition caused by diets of meal, molasses, and fat meat. Ferebee, with the help of other sorority members, set up a stove outside and cooked prunes, raisins, other dried fruits, and rice. This project eventually grew into the Taborian Hospital, now the Mound Bayou Hospital. This became the first black hospital in Mississippi. Ferebee's work in Mississippi helped her to fulfill an aim that she had developed in childhood rivalry with her brother, Ruffin, who became an attorney—to help the poor, the old, the lonely, the young, the sick, the homeless, the hungry, and the disabled.

In 1939 Ferebee became supreme basileus of Alpha Kappa Alpha sorority. She was such an assiduous worker that she was asked to serve a second term. She declined, yet continued to speak before various chapters. At her speech before the Newport News, Virginia, chapter in 1944, "the church had no standing room. She was an excellent speaker, beautiful and charming" (Interview with Leah Kay Frazier, 5 April 1990).

On November 18, 1949, Ferebee became president of the National Council of Negro Women, having succeeded the noted educator and clubwoman Mary McLeod Bethune. Still serving as director of Howard University's health service, a position she held for twenty-seven years, she "sustained constructive dynamism," a phrase used to describe her in the *Journal of the National Medical Association* (March 1970). During this time she also continued her private practice. In 1950 she became a member of the executive board of the White House's Children and Youth Council and UNICEF. The United States Department of Labor sent her to Germany in 1951 to study the problems of women there. In 1959, for her contributions to the role of women in medical education and world improvement, she was awarded Tufts University's first alumni achievement award.

In the 1960s, President John F. Kennedy appointed Ferebee to the Council for Food for Peace. She made a five-month tour of Africa, lecturing on preventive medicine. Later she visited nineteen countries in Latin America, Africa, and the Middle East as a delegate to an international conference of women of African descent. On November 1, 1965, a Committee of Friends, in which ten organizations participated, sponsored a large appreciation dinner in her honor, at which the principal speaker was Ester Peterson, special assistant for consumer affairs in the Johnson administration. In 1967 Ferebee spoke before the three thousand delegates of the World Health Assembly in Geneva, Switzerland. After her official retirement in 1968, she was lecturer in preventive medicine at Tufts.

Like her aunt, Josephine St. Pierre Ruffin, a founder of the National Association of Colored Women's Clubs, Ferebee made a difference in others' lives. She received the Outstanding Service Award of the American Health Association in 1970. In 1975 she took a group of African and Caribbean women to tour Mound Bayou Hospital in Mississippi. During that time she had just broken her ankle at the Women's Conference in Mexico City. "She refused to go to the doctor and never slowed down. . . . On occasion she would lift her feet on the bus. . . . When we finally got her to the hospital, she rejected the crutches and came out of the hospital waving them" (Trescott, Interview with Nan Frederick).

Through her participation in over eighteen professional and civic organizations and through her service on over fourteen executive boards, Ferebee left her stamp upon her adopted city of Washington, D.C. She was president of the Medico-Chirurgical Society of the District of Columbia and of the Washington Urban League; a successful chairperson of fund-raising campaigns of the Washington Community Chest and the Women's Division of the United Negro College Fund; member of the board of trustees and executive committee of the Washington Community Chest; and on the board of directors of the District of Columbia Social Hygiene Society, the District of Columbia Commission on the Status of Women, the Washington Housing Association, and the Council on Social Agencies.

Dorothy Boulding Ferebee distinguished herself as physician medical consultant for the medical division, United States Department of State. She held memberships in several medical organizations, including the American College Health Association, the National Medical Association, and the Public Health Association. Ferebee established the Women's Institute. (No additional information is given on the institute.) She participated in the Meridian House Foundation for International Visitors, the YWCA, and the National Girl Scouts of America.

On September 14, 1980, America mourned the death of Dorothy Boulding Ferebee from congestive heart failure at Georgetown University Hospital.

References

"Black Female Doctors." *Ebony* 10 (February 1948): 22.

Bulletin of the Medical Chirurgical Society. 1948: 4.

Davis, Marianna W., ed. *Contributions of Black Women to America*. Vol. 2. Columbia, S.C.: Kenday Press, 1982.

Death, Ruth. *Washington Evening Star*, 16 January 1970.

"Dorothy Boulding Ferebee, M.D." *Journal of the National Medical Association* 62 (March 1970): 177.

Frazier, Leah Kay. Interview with author, 5 April 1990.

Howard University Magazine (November 1960).

Logan, Rayford W. *Howard University: The First Hundred Years, 1867-1967*. New York: New York University Press, 1967.

Parker, Marjorie. *Alpha Kappa Alpha: In the Eye of the Beholder*. Washington, D.C.: Alpha Kappa Alpha, 1978.

Ploski, Harry and Watten Marr, eds. *Negro Almanac*. 3rd rev. ed. New York: Bellwether, 1976.

Trescott, J. "Ferebee." *Washington Post*, 15 May 1978.

Tufts Medical College Alumni Bulletin. March 19, 1968.

Watson-Miller, Ingrid. Interview with author, 5 April 1990.

Collections

Files, correspondence, reports, publications, and photographs of Dorothy Boulding Ferebee are in the Moorland-Spingarn Collection, Howard University. The collection also contains information on the Mississippi Health Project.

Margaret Bernice Smith Bristow

Catherine "Katy" Ferguson

(1779?-1854)

Religious leader, social worker

Catherine Williams Ferguson was a pioneer in the Sunday school movement and a social worker. She was born around 1779 as her mother traveled by schooner from Virginia to New York. Apparently her mother was a house slave and was sold to "R. B.," an elder in a Presbyterian church there. Ferguson's mother rendered good service, as evidenced by her master's comment that "if she [Katy] was as good as her mother, she would do well" ("Catherine Ferguson," *New York Times* 20 July 1854). Ferguson had to do well at an early age, for her mother was sold again when the child was only seven. On Ferguson's deathbed, she described the separation by saying that, "before we were torn asunder, she (my mother) knelt down, laid her hand on my head, and gave me to God." This act by her mother and Ferguson's later acceptance of Jesus Christ shaped her life.

Ferguson joined the Old Scotch Presbyterian Church on Cedar Street in lower Manhattan around 1797. At age fourteen, with great trepidation, she approached the pastor, John Mitchell Mason, to "talk about her soul." Mason was a highly respected theologian as well as a strong believer in Jesus Christ, and Ferguson emerged from the interview "converted to God."

With the help of two women of the church, the new convert was freed from slavery by age seventeen. At age eighteen, Ferguson married. Nothing is known of her husband, and Katy Ferguson lost the two children born of the marriage. During this time, she earned her living by baking large cakes for weddings and other social affairs. When not baking these cakes for her select clientele, she would bake small cakes, place them in a long, narrow market-basket with a handle and carry them to her customers, who were always happy to see her. Ferguson invariably returned to her neat home with an empty basket.

In her daily travels, she observed many orphaned and abandoned children. On Sunday, she would call them in and see that they received Christian instruction. Because her mistress had not allowed it, Ferguson had not learned to read or write. Various people from her church taught the children. Then Ferguson would listen as they repeated what they had learned. Having heard the Scripture all her life and memorized large portions of it, she knew when they recited it correctly. When Mason heard of her school, he invited them to convene in the lecture hall of his church.

Ferguson Pioneers in Sunday School Movement

Various dates are given as to when the Sunday school moved into the Old Scotch Presbyterian Church. However, Mason left that church in 1814, so it was clearly before that date. Ferguson, probably without knowing it, was a pioneer in the Sunday school movement. The movement began in Gloucester, England, in 1780 and spread to America in the 1800s. An 1810 state law that required that slave masters teach Scripture to black children stimulated the effort. However, much of this teaching took place in the New York African Free School, which operated during Ferguson's lifetime.

In addition to organizing and overseeing Sunday school instruction, Ferguson took many children into her home. Some came from poor houses and others from destitute parents. She fed, cared, and prayed for them until they found homes. Over a forty-year period, she took in forty-eight children, both black and white. Every Friday she held a prayer meeting at her home and during the five years before she died, she held another on Sunday afternoons. At that time, she resided at Seventy-four Thompson Street. People remarked that, "where Katy lived, the whole aspect of the neighborhood was changed" ("Catherine Ferguson").

While she had to endure the loss of her mother, husband, and children, Ferguson also suffered at the hands of prejudiced whites within the church. The first time she took communion, the Reverend Mason personally escorted her to the Lord's table. But her kind spirit prevailed and she gave of herself to all. When asked whether she saved any of her money, she replied, "How could I, when I gave away all I earned" ("Catherine Ferguson").

The *New York Tribune* published the first account of Ferguson after her death on July ll, 1854, of cholera. The writer, who is unidentified, based this biography on an interview with the subject reportedly held on March 25, 1850. The biographer prefaced the report of the interview with the statement that "thousands in this community have heard of or known Katy Ferguson." She was described as a person of sensible conversation, eminent virtues, and extraordinary good deeds.

Early in 1900, another person wrote her recollections of

Ferguson upon learning that a memorial to her was planned. Katy Ferguson's "cheery look and talk, her devoted Christian spirit, and her benevolence could not but elicit respect" (Olcott, 463).

References

"Catherine Ferguson." *New York Tribune*, 20 July 1854.

Franklin, John Hope. *From Slavery to Freedom: A History of Negro Americans*. 4th ed. New York: Alfred A. Knopf, 1973.

Hartvik, Allen. "Catherine Ferguson, Black Founder of a Sunday-School." *Negro History Bulletin*, 35 (December, 1972): 176-177.

Latimer, Catherine A. "Catherine Ferguson." *Negro History Bulletin*, 5 (November 1941): 38-39.

Latourette, Kenneth S. *A History of Christianity*. Vol. 2. New York: Harper & Row, 1975.

Murray, Linda. "Katy Ferguson." *Narratives of Colored Americans*. Comps. Alexander Mott and M. S. Wood. 1877. Reprinted. Freeport, N.Y.: Books for Libraries, 1971.

"The Negro in New York." *Negro History Bulletin*, 5 (November 1941): 30. Contains a portrait of Catherine Ferguson.

New York Times, 13 July 1854.

Olcott, Mrs. John W. "Recollections of Katy Ferguson." *Southern Workman*, 52 (September 1923): 463.

Van Vechten, Jacob. *Memoirs of John M. Mason, D.D., S.T.P., with Portions of His Correspondence*. New York: Robert Carter and Brothers, 1856.

Margaret D. Pagan

Mary Fields "Black Mary" "Stagecoach Mary"

(1832?-1914)

Entrepreneur, stagecoach driver, mail carrier, pioneer, religious worker

They called her "Black Mary" or "Stagecoach Mary," but Mary Fields, the real name of this powerful and physically strong woman of unbelievable ability in her chosen professions, was a legend in her own time and one of the nation's most picturesque pioneers. Her biography reads like a folktale, and a glimpse of this six-foot-tall character who weighed well over two hundred pounds, striding the Rocky Mountain trails must have been startling. Actor Gary Cooper, who took an interest in Mary Fields when he was just nine years old, and who had vivid memories of her in Cascade, Montana, gives a revealing picture of Black Mary in the October 1959 issue of *Ebony*. Other published accounts of her career and character are also available.

Born a slave in a slave cabin somewhere in Tennessee around 1832, details of Fields's early life, like that of many who were born in slavery, are sketchy. By the time of her death in Cascade in 1914, however, she had tempered her fearsome behavior and was much loved by those who knew her. In fact, since she did not know her actual birth date and chose to honor herself whenever she wished, and so did the school system in Cascade by closing the school doors when Mary Fields needed a birthday celebration. She lived to become "one of the freest souls ever to draw a breath or a thirty-eight" (caliber Smith and Wesson pistol) (Cooper, 97). It has been said that for a brief time she lived on the Mississippi and had been a passenger on the riverboat Robert E. Lee when it raced Steamboat Bill's Natchez on June 30, 1870. It is conceivable that early on Fields had the wanderlust to go where life would be adventurous and where the freedom to do as she pleased was possible.

By 1884, Fields was living in Ohio, where she worked as a general handywoman at the convent run by the Ursulines—an order of Catholic nuns—in Toledo. Her status in the convent is disputed. One view is that she met Mother Amadeus, who headed the convent, and they became close friends. Another account is that Fields was a slave and the confidential secretary or servant of Judge Dunne, who has been identified as Mother Amadeus's father and again as her brother. Yet another source identified her as the personal servant of Mother Amadeus before her mistress took her vows.

Undisputedly, Mother Amadeus was the cause of Fields's move to Montana. Since 1866, Jesuit priests had worked among the Blackfeet Indians, thus paving the way for various church-supported activities. In 1884 Mother Amadeus went to the area and opened a school for Indian girls. Because she was unconditioned for the harsh climate, she became ill with pneumonia. Hearing about Mother Amadeus's illness, Fields rushed out West to her side and nursed her to good health. Without permanent ties in Ohio, Fields decided to remain at the mission and handle the odd jobs that needed attention. These included "everything from preparing the chapel altar to light construction work on the new convent building. Mary's primary duty . . . consisted of delivering foodstuffs and supplies to the mission" (King, 23). She also "did the freighting for the mission and often spent the prairie nights fighting her way through storms and braving great dangers," including fighting off animals to protect her cargo (Cooper, 98). The new convent was completed in eight years.

But for her terrible temper, fearlessness of man and beast, constant fighting with the hired men, and a gun duel with one of the men, Fields might have lived her remaining days working at the mission. She had spent ten years of her life in the nuns' service with little in exchange for her work. A barrage of complaints to the bishop in Helena, Montana, persuaded him to order the nuns to "send that black woman away." Fields's efforts to dissuade the Bishop were in vain. Disheartened, she left the mission. Her forced estrangement from Mother Armadeus was short-lived, for Mother Amadeus helped her open a restaurant in Cascade. Fields's demonstrated benevolence toward those who needed help was seen again in her business, where she extended credit to customers who promised to pay when they had money but never did. Thus, the restaurant did not succeed.

Fields Becomes Stagecoach Driver

Through Mother Amadeus's intervention again, Fields became a stagecoach driver for the United States government. Now in her sixties, she dressed in men's clothing—hat included—and puffed on a big black cigar, and for eight years carried mail and passengers between the mission and Cascade. She became known for prompt delivery regardless of the weather, and she was a familiar sight to those who observed her at work. She sat high atop the stagecoach seat and with expert skill managed the two teams of horses. For those who did not know, Fields appeared to be a big, tough black man.

In 1903, her stagecoach days over, Fields settled in Cascade and became the town's only black resident. Her popularity about town spread as she became involved in other activities that caused the residents to love and respect her. Although armed and tough—perhaps some residents feared her—she had a kind and gentle nature that could not be disguised. By this time Mother Amadeus had been transferred to Alaska to start new missions. Her successor, Mother Angela, tried hard but never replaced Mother Amadeus in the heart and soul of Mary Fields. Fields continued her efforts at entrepreneurship, took in washing, and soon expanded the business so that her entire home was turned into a laundry. When the business burned in 1912, local townspeople contributed the goods and services needed to rebuild it.

The esteem in which Fields was held was seen in the special privileges she received. An early mayor of Cascade allowed her to drink and smoke cigars in saloons with men—her favorite pastime and a privilege denied other women. When R. B. Glover leased the New Cascade Hotel to Kirk Huntley, he did so on condition that Fields receive her meals free. The townspeople honored her twice a year, or whenever she declared a birthday.

In her later life, Fields had tamed her temper. While rough, rowdy behavior was her regular manner, she had no tolerance for bad girls. She worked for $1.50 a day as a babysitter. She spent hours cultivating her flower garden. She became mascot and prime fan for the Cascade baseball team and honored the homerun hitters at each game with a large bouquet and the members of each team with a buttonhole bouquet of flowers from her garden. But most of all, she cared for the altar at Wedsworth Hall for the Catholic Society. She did not live to see the church completed. She died in 1914 and was mourned by the whole town. A simple wooden cross marks her grave in the Cascade Hillside Cemetery "at the foot of the mountains, by the winding road that leads to the old mission" (Cooper, 9). She is preserved in the annals of America's West and in the pen and ink drawings that in 1959 were hung in the Cascade bank.

References

Cooper, Gary. "Stage Coach Mary: Gun Toting Montanan Delivered U.S. Mail." As told to Marc Crawford. *Ebony* 14 (October 1959): 97-100.

"Cowboys and Minstrels: Aspects of Black Folk Culture." Brochure 38. Nashville, Tennessee: Fisk University Libray, n.d.

Katz, William Loren. *Black People Who Made the Old West*. New York: Crowell, 1977.

———. *The Black West*. 3rd ed., rev. and expanded. Garden City, N.Y.: Doubleday, 1971.

King, Anita. "Black Mary: A Westener with Style." *Essence* 4 (January 1974): 23, 91.

Jessie Carney Smith

Ada Fisher

(1924-)

Lawyer, educator, civil rights activist

A successful lawyer, educator and civil rights activist, Ada Lois Sipuel Fisher's desire to study law at the University of Oklahoma in 1946 played a major role in dismantling the system of segregated education in the United States and put her in the limelight.

Born in Chickasha, Oklahoma, in 1924, Fisher is the daughter of T. B. Sipuel, bishop of the Oklahoma Churches of God in Christ, and Martha B. (Smith) Sipuel, both from Dermott, Arkansas. She had an older brother, Lemuel T., an attorney who is now deceased; her sister, Helen Marie Sipuel Huggins, lives in Oklahoma. Growing up in Chickasha, Fisher graduated from Lincoln High School in 1941 and attended Langston University in Langston, Oklahoma, the only state-supported school open to black Americans under Oklahoma's legally mandated system of segregation. Her interest in the law developed during summers she spent in

Chicago with her first cousin, a lawyer, and his children. During her junior year, she married Warren W. Fisher, who in 1948 was working as a machinist in Providence, Rhode Island.

George Lynn Cross, president of the University of Oklahoma from 1942 to 1968, summarizes an article by Roy Parr in the *Daily Oklahoman* in January 1948, which throws further light on Fisher's decision to try to study law at the university:

> According to Parr, she said that she had decided to make her present fight for admission to the University of Oklahoma while she was a junior at Langston. Her decision was influenced, she said, by a state official who, when asked for better facilities for Langston, "just shrugged his shoulders and said we were lucky to have any school." She went on to say: "Six of us decided to apply for various departments at the University of Oklahoma. Everybody backed out, so I nominated myself chief guinea pig." She said that she did not plan to live on the campus, that she was interested only in learning, not socializing. She did say that she hoped, if admitted, to make friends with her fellow students and then added, somewhat forebodingly, "The few on the campus who might call me names—why, I won't even hear them" (49-50).

In 1946 the time appeared ripe to the national and state National Association for the Advancement of Colored People (NAACP) to challenge the State of Oklahoma's segregated education system, and the opening wedge was graduate education. The United States Supreme Court had decided in the Gaines case in 1938 that the State of Missouri must provide equal graduate education to all of its citizens; in effect the University of Missouri either had to admit Lloyd Gaines to its law school, or the state had to establish a law school for black Americans or abolish the law school for whites. In Oklahoma the failure of the obligation of the state to provide equal education to all its citizens was glaring at the graduate level, where there were no graduate programs at black institutions and some seventy different graduate programs offered at white institutions. The NAACP found in Ada Sipuel Fisher a well-qualified person with the desire to challenge the system, the perseverance to endure the delays of the law, the fortitude to stand up to the social pressures on her and her family, and the courage to face becoming the first black American in a potentially hostile environment. She could have chosen to have the state pay her tuition at an out-of-state school, but she refused this option.

Fisher Applies to Law School

Accompanied by her lawyers, Fisher applied to enter the University of Oklahoma law school on January 15, 1946. During a meeting with university president George Lynn Cross it was established that she was academically qualified to enter the school—Cross refused to complicate matters by raising the issue that Langston was not an accredited school—and he wrote the letter which stated that the sole reason she was denied admission was because of her race. This action established the base for legal action. The case was filed on April 6, 1946. After the final decision in the state courts in April 1947, the United State Supreme Court heard the appeal on January 8, 1948, and on January 13 issued an order that the state must provide a legal education for Fisher forthwith. It seemed to many that the unusual rapidity of the court's action was designed to ensure that she would be able to enroll for second semester classes at the University of Oklahoma beginning on January 29. On January 19 the State Regents for Higher Education voted to establish a law school at Langston University—three rooms in the state capitol were designated as classrooms, three faculty members were hired, and registration for the new school was set for January 26.

Fisher was not distracted from her goal; a petition was filed in state courts asking for an order to admit her to the University of Oklahoma on the grounds that the new law school did not provide an equal education. The petition was denied on August 2. Fisher's case was not appealed to Federal courts, as the NAACP lawyers now concentrated their efforts on the McLaurin case.

George W. McLaurin, a fifty-four year old professor of education at Langston, applied for admission to the doctoral program in education on January 28, 1948, just days after the Supreme Court decision in the Fisher case. (His wife, Peninah S. McLaurin, had been in 1923 the first black American to apply to the university and to be turned down.) Five other blacks applied for various graduate programs at the same time. The Federal District Court ruled on September 29 that the university must admit McLaurin. State laws requiring segregation were still in place, and there was room for uncertainty about whether other blacks could be immediately admitted upon application. On October 13 McLaurin registered for four classes. There was a hearing before the Federal court on October 25 seeking to overturn the policy of segregation; although the relief was denied, the process of going to the Supreme Court again was underway.

As more blacks applied for admission, the technical legal problems of determining which applications should be accepted became more and more burdensome to the school and to the state's attorney general, who had to rule on a case by case basis. Finally in 1949 the state legislature passed a law allowing the admission of all blacks to graduate courses on a segregated basis. This law was in place for the beginning of the summer session. Fisher was permitted to enroll in the university on June 17, although the Langston University law school was not to be officially suspended until June 30. (The school appears to have had only one student, who enrolled during the final semester of its existence.) The time between her first application and her first class was three-and-a-half years.

The United States Supreme Court ruled on June 5, 1950, to overturn all laws requiring segregation at the graduate level. Through their own efforts and the efforts of others on their behalf, Ada Lois Sipuel Fisher and George W. McLaurin had successfully dismantled the legal bases of segregated education at the graduate level. McLaurin was successful in his classes, but his health was not good and broke down just before he was to take the qualifying examinations. Fisher received her law degree in 1951.

She then practiced law with the firm of Bruce and Rowan in Oklahoma City until she accepted the position of instructor in American history and government at Langston in 1956. About the same time Fisher began working for an advanced degree in history during summer sessions at the University of Oklahoma. She received her master's degree in 1968. In 1974 she became chair of the social science department at Langston. Now retired, she is the mother of two children, Charlene Fisher Factory and Bruce.

Beginning with a 1949 National NAACP Youth Award, Fisher's achievements have been recognized. February 1, 1978, was designated as Ada Lois Sipuel day at the University of Oklahoma. In 1979 she received the Outstanding Alumnus Award from Langston University. The Smithsonian designated her as one of the 150 Outstanding Black Women who have most impacted the course and direction of American history in 1981. An anonymous donor gave the University of Oklahoma $100,000 to establish a scholarship in her name in 1991.

On May 11, 1991, the University of Oklahoma awarded Ada Lois Sipuel Fisher the honorary degree of Doctor of Humane Letters.

References

"Brown Guinea Pigs." *Ebony* 11 (June 1956): 93-96. Photograph, p. 94.

Cross, George Lynn. *Blacks in White Colleges: Oklahoma's Landmark Cases*. Norman, Okla.: University of Oklahoma Press, 1975.

Fisher, Ada Lois Sipuel. Interview with the author. 24 April 1991.

Hubbell, John T. "Some Reactions to the Desegregation to the University of Oklahoma, 1946-1950." *Phylon* 34 (March 1973): 187-96.

"Scholarship Honors Fisher." *OU People* 66 (Spring 1991): 9.

Robert L. Johns

Ella Fitzgerald
"First Lady of Song"

(1918-)

Singer, songwriter

Ella Fitzgerald, one of the most celebrated singers of this century, was born April 25, 1918, in Newport News, Virginia. Although Ella Fitzgerald can hardly recall her father, his memory was kept alive for by her mother, who spoke often of his guitar playing and singing. He filled their home with music. Her mother also sang soprano. When Fitzgerald's father died shortly after World War I, Ella Fitzgerald and her mother moved to Yonkers, New York. Mrs. Fitzgerald had a sister there and hoped to find a better life in the North, close to relatives.

Fitzgerald grew up just across the Hudson River from the Bronx and in the shadow of a Harlem that was then in vogue. Yonkers was a mixed neighborhood, and Fitzgerald had a variety of friends. She studied music in school, sang in the junior high school glee club, and took piano lessons. But the five dollars a month for lessons soon became too much for her mother to afford. Forced to quit, Fitzgerald soon forgot how to read music, a loss she recalls with regret.

Ella Fitzgerald

In her early teens, Fitzgerald discovered Harlem and its night magic firsthand. She and her girlfriends would go there on weekends to hear celebrities sing and to beg for autographs. On such an occasion, she found herself at the Harlem Opera House on Amateur Night. It was 1934; Ella Fitzgerald was sixteen, tall, and awkward. Her friends dared her to enter the talent contest. She accepted the challenge. In her hand-me-down dress and ill-fitting shoes, she entered the spotlight. She had intended to dance. On seeing her, the audience laughed. Because her knees were knocking together rapidly, she chose not to move from the spot where she stood rooted in fear. Since one must move in order to dance, Fitzgerald decided to sing instead. The audience ceased laughing as Fitzgerald sang "The Object of my Affection." She had learned the song from a Connie Boswell record, but the voice that emerged was a genuine talent of her own. She recalls three encores. She won first prize.

This was the first of many talent contests she was to win. Fitzgerald went on to appear at the Lafayette Theater on Seventh Avenue and 132nd Street. Her repertoire consisted of only three songs: "Believe It, Beloved," "The Object of my Affection," and "July." She sang these songs in every talent contest she entered in Harlem.

In 1935 Fitzgerald entered another competition at the Harlem Opera House. Winning first prize, she landed a week's work singing with Tiny Bradshaw and his band. As a result of this engagement, Fitzgerald was noticed, and an audition was arranged at the CBS Radio Network. She was offered a guest appearance on the radio show hosted by Arthur Tracy, one of her favorite singers. Her mother gave permission, as Fitzgerald was still underage, but before anything could come of it, Fitzgerald's mother died. Because she was now an orphan, the contract with CBS was no longer valid. Despite the fact that Fitzgerald went to live with her aunt, the authorities were dissatisfied, and she was forced into the Riverdale orphanage in Yonkers.

Institutional life was not enriching, and Fitzgerald continued to escape to Harlem, where she entered many amateur contests. Finally she made her way into the Apollo Theater. Nervous as usual, Fitzgerald walked on stage, sang her three songs, and won first prize. Her reward was fifty dollars. Appearing at the Apollo opened another door for her. The night of the amateur contest, Bardu Ali, who directed Chick Webb's band, had been in the audience. Hearing Fitzgerald sing, he is reported to have said, "This chick sings just like a horn." (Colin, 19). A few days later, he arranged for Fitzgerald to sing for Chick Webb. She sang for Webb, unaccompanied: she had perfect pitch. Despite the facts that she was not really physically attractive, that she wore boys' shoes, that "swing was really a man's thing" (*Brown Sugar*, 59), and that Webb already had a singer, Charlie Linton, and was not interested in a "girl singer" (Colin, 21), he was amazed at her vocal talent. He hired her, and she began her rise to stardom.

In the male-dominated world of jazz and swing, Ella Fitzgerald was a rare asset, one that many men could not seem to evaluate in other than physical terms. Donald Bogle writes in his book *Black Sugar: Eighty Years of America's Black Female Superstars* that if Fitzgerald had been "sexier" she might have developed into a "legendary public heroine" (139). He seems unaware that she did. Sid Colin seems impelled to continually comment on Fitzgerald's physical appearance in his book *Ella: The Life and Times of Ella Fitzgerald*. Of a later British performance he writes: "Ever since her film appearance in *Ride 'em Cowboy*, she had been putting on weight in quite an alarming fashion. Now, at the age of thirty, she must have appeared almost matronly. To the British, who were wont to think of American entertainers as resembling the frenetic Betty Hutton, it must have come as a profound shock" (89).

But at the beginning of her career, Webb, Fitzgerald's guardian and mentor, saw a jewel. Recognizing her for the rare talent she possessed, he told his manager, who had commented that Fitzgerald "looked incredible—her hair dishevelled, her clothes just terrible," "Gale, you'd be surprised what a beauty parlor and some make-up and nice clothes can do" (Colin, 28).

Fitzgerald Turns Professional

At age seventeen Fitzgerald turned professional, singing with Webb's band at the famed Savoy Ballroom. It was not long however, before her legal status became a problem. To solve this problem, Webb and his wife decided to adopt her, thus becoming her legal guardians. Webb groomed Fitzgerald for success slowly and carefully, telling her to relax, not to rush, and "go with the beat, always go with the beat" (Colin, 30). Under his tutelage Fitzgerald blossomed, and her confidence grew, but she never ever quite mastered her nervousness before a performance. Proud of his protégée, Webb demanded that band members and other jazz musicians treat Fitzgerald with respect. She responded by always acting like a lady.

Fitzgerald's first record was *Love and Kisses*, recorded with Chick Webb on June 12, 1935. It has since disappeared without a trace. Possessing a remarkable ear for music and the ability to imitate almost any musical instrument, Fitzgerald began "scat" singing. In October 1936 she recorded "If You Can't Sing It, You'll Have to Swing It" or "Paganini," using the unique style of improvising on syllables of no textual significance—scatting.

Although still a teenager, Fitzgerald's confidence had increased to the point where she began writing songs. On February 18, 1937, Billie Holiday recorded a song composed by Webb with lyrics by Fitzgerald. Titled "You Showed Me the Way," the song stands among Holiday's classic recordings of this period. The lyric is often described as "Tin Pan Alley love song conventions," but reveals Fitzgerald's subtle and genuine simplicity.

Continuing to write songs, in 1940 Fitzgerald wrote the lyrics to Duke Ellington's "In a Mellotone," and in 1945 Nat King Cole recorded "Oh, But I Do," for which she had written the lyrics. By 1943 she had written enough to gain membership in the American Society of Composers, Authors, and Publishers (ASCAP). She was the youngest person ever admitted to membership in this organization.

While in Boston during the spring of 1938, Fitzgerald was tinkling around on the piano singing the words to a nursery rhyme from her childhood days: "A-Tisket-A-Tasket, a brown and yellow basket." Al Feldman, a pianist and arranger for Webb, helped her, and together they came up with the song—a smash hit that by September of that year sold a million records. Excited by her sudden success, Fitzgerald momentarily lost her head. She got married to someone whose name, years later she has trouble recalling. Webb insisted that she have the marriage annulled, and she complied without argument.

On June 16, 1939, Chick Webb died of spinal tuberculosis. His death was a great loss to the jazz world and to Fitzgerald. Webb had been a good guardian and confidant, and Fitzgerald credits him for the positive influence he had on her musical technique. At age twenty-one, Fitzgerald found herself the leader of Chick Webb's band. She kept the band going on and off the road for three years. During this period, according to one unnamed source, she was married to Bernie Kornegay.

In 1942, with the beginning of World War II, the Chick Webb Band dissolved. Fitzgerald continued on her own, singing at various night spots. In 1944, Fitzgerald and the Ink Spots had a million-selling hit with "Into Each Life Some Rain Must Fall," and by 1945 they enjoyed another million seller, Duke Ellington's "I'm Beginning to See the Light."

In 1947, Ella Fitzgerald married Ray Brown, a bass player from Pittsburgh. On September 15th, the newlyweds sailed on the Queen Mary for London, where Fitzgerald was scheduled to open at the London Palladium. Fitzgerald was fast becoming an international cynosure. In 1949 the Browns purchased a house in Saint Albans, a borough of Queens, across the East River from Harlem. Fitzgerald expresses a profound love for children, although she had none of her own. In 1945, she was elected to the International Committee of the Foster Parents Plan for World Children. Other members of this committee included Bess Truman and Eleanor Roosevelt.

Deciding to rear a family, Fitzgerald and Brown adopted an infant. They named him Raymond Brown, Jr. When their marriage ended in 1953, Ray Brown, Jr., continued to reside with Fitzgerald. In 1967 they moved to California, and Fitzgerald purchased a home in Beverly Hills. Ray Brown remarried, and today Ray Brown, Jr., is also married and lives in Seattle, where he sings, plays guitar and drums, and leads a band. Fitzgerald never remarried. She lives with her two dogs, and Doreen, her housekeeper, and works forty weeks of every year.

Fitzgerald Wins Twelve Grammys

Fitzgerald's honors and awards are massive. She is the recipient of twelve Grammy awards; the Pied Piper Award presented by ASCAP; the George & Ira Gershwin Award for Outstanding Achievement; the American Music Award (1978); the National Medal of the Arts 1987 (presented at the White House); and innumerable popularity awards from *Downbeat Magazine*, *Metronome Magazine*, and *Jazz Award Poll*. She was named number one female singer in the sixteenth International Jazz Critics Poll (1968); Best Female Jazz vocalist 1981; and most recently Fitzgerald was honored on February 14, 1990, at a benefit concert at New York's Avery Fisher Hall for the American Heart Association. The New York Heart Association intends to establish the Ella Fitzgerald Research Fellowship with the money raised at the benefit.

In 1982, Fitzgerald was chosen by Harvard's Hasty Pudding Club as their "Woman of the Year." She also received the Whitney Young Award in 1984. On April 28, 1989, she became the first recipient of the Society of Singers Lifetime Achievement Award, named "Ella" in her honor. Awarded annually to one of the nation's finest singers, the Lifetime Achievement Award ranks in prestige with the Tony, Emmy, and Oscar. Among the honors Fitzgerald values most are the dedication at the University of Maryland of the Ella Fitzgerald Auditorium of Performing Arts, an honorary doctorate of humane letters from Dartmouth College, a doctorate of music from Howard University, and a doctorate of humane letters from Talladega College in Alabama.

Among Fitzgerald's greatest recordings are the famous *Gershwin Songbook*, a five-record set released in 1958, and the album *The Best Is Yet to Come*, which won the twelfth Grammy Award. Renowned jazz impresario Norman Granz has been Fitzgerald's close friend and personal manager since 1954. Buying out her long-term contract from Decca Records, Granz began to record her on Verve Records, his label (1956-60). Since 1972 she has recorded exclusively for Pablo, Granz's classic jazz label. To date she has twenty-five albums to her credit on this label.

Within the past decade Fitzgerald has made several television appearances, among them one with Frank Sinatra and another as part of the "Duke Ellington/Ella Fitzgerald Special" for Screen Gems Productions. A special with Andre Previn also aired on PBS. In 1955 she starred in *Pete Kelly's Blues*.

Ella Fitzgerald has performed all over the world. Granz capitalized on her international fame by capturing her performances live. He was the first producer to attempt this recording feat. Great works in this category include: *Ella in Berlin, Ella Fitzgerald/Newport Jazz Festival Live at Carnegie Hall,*" *Ella & Duke at the Cote d'Azur, Ella in London,*" *Montreux Ella, Ella Fitzgerald with the Tommy Flanagan Trio, Pablo Live-Montreux '77,* and *A Perfect Match, Ella-Basie, Montreux '79.*

What distinguishes Fitzgerald, setting her apart from all other vocalists, is her ability to sustain a unique style. Her voice has been described as sounding more like an instrument than has any other voice in this century. In more technical terms, she has an impeccable and sophisticated rhythmic sense, flawless intonation, and an extraordinary harmonic sensibility. Henry Pleasants in his book *The Great American Popular Singers* describes Ella Fitzgerald as "endlessly inventive," saying that "new melodic deviations and embellishments are as varied as they are invariably appropriate" (171). These facts, coupled with her classic simplicity and genuine humility, make Ella Fitzgerald a one-of-a-kind entertainer; a true legend in her own time.

Ella Fitzgerald's complete discography is available from Pablo Records, 451 North Canon Drive, Beverly Hills, California.

References

Bogle, Donald. Brown Sugar: Eighty Years of America's Black Female Superstars. New York: Harmony Books, 1980.

Colin, Sid. *Ella: The Life and Times of Ella Fitzgerald.* London: Elm Tree Brooks, 1986.

The Continuum Dictionary of Women's Biography. Ed. Jennifer S. Uglow. New York: Continuum, 1989.

"Ella Fitzgerald Saluted at New York City Gala." *Jet*, 7 (March 5, 1990): 56-67.

McHenry, Robert, ed. *Famous American Women.* New York: Dover, 1980. 133.

Nolden, R. *Ella Fitzgerald: ihre Leben, ihre Musik, ihre Schallplatten.* Gauting, Germany: 1986.

Pleasants, Henry. *The Great American Popular Singers.* New York: Simon & Schuster, 1974.

Who's Who of American Women 1980 ed. Wilmette, Ill.: Macmillan, 1980.

Nagueyalti Warren

Lethia C. Fleming

(1876-1963)

Organization executive, political worker, clubwoman

Lethia Cousins Fleming was a major force in city, state, and national Republican politics for more than three decades. She also was a leader in the colored women's club movement. Fleming, a contemporary of such women as Ida B. Wells Barnett and Mary Church Terrell, was born in Tazewell, Virginia, on May 13, 1876. She attended high school in Ironton, Ohio, and college at Morristown College, Morristown, Tennessee. For one year she taught school in Virginia before moving to West Virginia, where she taught for twenty years. She was also active in the women's suffrage movement. She married Thomas W. Fleming in 1912 and moved to Cleveland, Ohio.

Soon after arriving in Cleveland, Lethia C. Fleming became involved in the civic and social activities of the city. She became active with the women's suffrage movement in Cleveland and also was a founder of the Negro Welfare Association, later an affiliate of the National Urban League. In 1914 she was elected president of the Home for Aged Colored People. She also began working as a social worker, a position she held for eight years. Lethia Fleming became involved in local politics, most likely through her husband, who was a Cleveland city councilman. She worked as a ward leader, precinct committeewoman, and election officer. Her aspirations soon grew beyond Cleveland, and she became active on the state, regional, and national levels as well. In the late 1920s, Thomas W. Fleming was convicted of accepting a bribe from one of his constituents and sentenced to nearly three years in prison. After serving his sentence, he resumed his law practice and was not heavily involved in politics.

Lethia C. Fleming was quite an assertive and intuitive women and wasted no time in developing contacts and strong networks throughout the country. Her activities required extensive travel, during which she made speeches concerning women's rights, civil rights, education, racial harmony, and the uplift of the black race, particularly among women. For a short time during the 1930s she was national director of the *Woman's Voice,* a national magazine published in the interest of women in Republican politics. While in this position, Fleming encouraged Hollywood movie executives to produce a feature film about the story of the life of Booker T. Washington and Tuskegee Institute. She also was president of the National Association of Republican Women, an organization committed to the "integration of the Negro into full citizenship." Through this organization she was influential in many decisions, particularly in the mideastern and midwestern region of the country.

In the late 1920s Fleming was head of the Organization of Colored Women, Western Division, for the Republican National Committee. During this time she was located in Chicago. She also served on the powerful National Program Committee of the party.

Throughout the 1920s through at least 1950, Lethia C. Fleming maintained a close personal relationship with Claude Barnett, director of the National Negro Press Association and an influential player in Republican politics. She respected his opinion, and Barnett often advised Fleming about career moves, political strategies, and her club activities. The two maintained extensive correspondence, most heavily during the 1920s and 1930s. In 1940 Barnett encouraged Fleming to think about her position as a Republican, its meaning and significance for young black women, and the history of blacks' involvement with the party. From her thoughts a powerful article was created and run by Barnett's Associated Negro Press (ANP), which served black newspapers throughout the country.

It was through Barnett, who had entrees into various social, civic, and political circles, that Lethia Fleming met many of the people she came to know, work with, and depend on for support. Whenever she campaigned for an office within an organization or for a political figure, Barnett gave Fleming the proper connections as well as the publicity through the black press. Lethia Fleming was president of the Ohio Federation of Colored Women's Clubs (1928-1933), Grand Associate Matron of the Order of Eastern Star of Ohio and its jurisdiction, and a worker for racial justice through the Federated Churches of America. As she became more active in national political and social affairs, Fleming was valued for her ability to forge coalitions and reach the masses, both black and white. This influence was felt as she worked in the presidential campaigns of Calvin Coolidge, Herbert Hoover, and Alf Landon.

Fleming Heads National Organization of Negro Women

Like many of her contemporaries, Lethia Fleming was farsighted and proactive in gaining equal rights for blacks and women. In 1939, according to an ANP story written by Barnett, women from ten states met in Washington, D.C., to form the National Organization of Negro Women. The purpose of this group was to bring about the complete enfranchisement of blacks, to enroll as many black women as possible in the group, and to contribute to the financial support of the Republican party. Lethia Fleming was instrumental in developing the organization and setting its goals, and was elected to head the group. As further testament to her organizational ability and relative influence within the party, that same year she was appointed to serve on the Republican National Program Committee.

Lethia Fleming was president of the National Republican Women's Club in Washington, D.C., and Mary Church Terrell was treasurer. Fleming was also an officer in such groups as the League for Peace and Democracy and Negro Welfare Association, as well as a member of the Civic League of Cuyahoga County, Baha'i Movement on World Order and International Peace, National Negro History Association, American Association of Social Workers, and the NAACP.

Throughout the 1940s both Lethia and Thomas Fleming became ill, with Thomas Fleming finally becoming an invalid. Lethia Fleming took a leave without pay from her position with the Republican party. This leave caused a great financial strain, and as her husband's health stabilized, Lethia Fleming sought various political and government jobs through former contacts, one of whom was Mary McLeod Bethune. Throughout this period, Claude Barnett lent moral support and acted as a resource and liaison whenever possible.

Very little information exists about Lethia Fleming's life beyond the onset of World War II, although there is one letter to her from Barnett dated January 1950. She died on September 25, 1963.

References

Encyclopedia of Cleveland History. Eds. David D. Van Tassel and John J. Grabowski. Bloomington: Indiana University Press, published in association with Case Western Reserve University, 1987.

Lethia C. Fleming file, Box 11, Series 10, Folder 357, Claude Barnett Papers.

Thomas and Lethia C. Fleming Collection, Western Reserve Historical Society, Cleveland, Ohio.

Collections

The Claude Barnett Collection in the Chicago Historical Society, Manuscripts Division, contains biographical material and notes on Lethia C. Fleming as well as correspondence between Fleming and Barnett. Additional papers also are in the Western Reserve Historical Society, Cleveland, Ohio.

Karla Y. E. Frye

Kay Stewart Flippin

(1906-)

Educator

Kay Stewart Flippin, known for her work in atypical and early childhood education and as a socialite, was born Harriet Catherine Stewart on May 21, 1906. She was the only child of McCants Stewart and Mary (Weir) Stewart. McCants Stewart, son of the famed lawyer Thomas McCants Stewart, was the first black graduate of the University of Minnesota's law school in 1899. McCants Stewart met Mary Delia Weir, daughter of James and Victoria Frances Weir, at the campus of the University of Minnesota, where she and her sister, Harriet Anna Weir, were pursuing the teacher's training program. While they were undergraduates, McCants Stewart and Mary Weir became campus sweethearts and they married in August 1905 at the bride's home in Minneapolis.

After Mary Weir and McCants Stewart married, they moved to Portland, Oregon, where their daughter was born. As a black attorney, McCants Stewart experienced a life of hardship and tribulation and was unable to establish a law practice successful enough for him to support his young family. The pursuit of greener pastures was his chief motivation for moving to San Francisco in 1914, as he hoped this metropolis would afford a suitable work environment for his professional talents. He spent two years establishing himself enough in a practice with two other lawyers before calling for his family from Oregon in 1918.

Mary Weir Stewart suddenly found herself head of their small household in 1919, at the unexpected death of McCants Stewart. Mary Stewart, who had not worked outside the home except for an active role in organizing church activities, became involved in the War Camp Community Service, which provided recreational support services for enlisted black men. She managed the Victory Club, which was sponsored by the War Camp Community Service. Through her pragmatic management skills, she established the Booker T. Washington Community Center, which developed in 1921 from the residue funds of the Victory Club, as a community support to provide a platform for educational and social activities for the black community of San Francisco. Mary Stewart's involvement in these neighborhood activities was largely a labor of love for her, for she was often nonsalaried and eventually compelled by her financial circumstances to solicit a relatively dependable and steady employment at the Viavi Homeopathic Company, where she passed for white for occupational convenience. Flippin's grandmother had also passed for white for employment purposes in Minnesota, where she worked demonstrating cookware in department stores. Flippin's mother's sister, Harriet Weir, who was a teacher in Lead, Minnesota, also did so and was dismissed when her African-American heritage was discovered.

In spite of the family financial uncertainty, Flippin grew up in San Francisco in a sheltered and caring and oftentimes indulgent household that included, besides her mother, her grandmother, Victoria Frances Weir, and frequently her aunt, Harriet Weir, during summer months. The black community of San Francisco was relatively small and insular. Flippin attended Hamilton Grammar School and the Girls' High School—integrated schools in the neighborhood. Her transfer to the sociably more attractive Polytechnic High School, which was coeducational, was accomplished by a consistent pressure on a complaisant mother. Just a few short months prior to her graduation from high school, Flippin, upon advice from her mother (with a daunting history of teachers in both the Stewart and the Weir families), sought to enroll in the teacher's training program at San Francisco State College, when she encountered her first serious Jim Crow experience.

The registrar, Florence Vance, told her outright the futility of her proposed endeavor in teaching, since she would be unable to teach within the state school system because she was a "colored." Though Flippin was so seriously hurt by this snub that she gave up formal education and schooling for almost fifteen years, she was later inspired by this episode not only to complete her schooling but to complete a B.A. and a graduate degree in early childhood education and to return and perform as faculty on a staff where Florence Vance greeted her cheerfully and pretended to be a buddy. Flippin, much more mature and experienced, reciprocated tongue in cheek. Although Vance may not have remembered her disparaging remark to a stranger, Flippin is certain she must have heard of the episode since Flippin's return (Black Women Oral History Interview, 96).

Flippin's mother allowed her teenage daughter to accept employment with the Davis Schonwasser department store as an elevator operator, a job that paid twelve dollars a week, a prized wage. Within a span of almost fifteen years, she gradually progressed to a position where she was de facto buyer for the company. She was, however, denied this status officially—yet another expression of Jim Crow reality. She quit the company when another employee was sent from a different unit in the store for her to train for this position, which was justifiably hers. This incident made Flippin realize the importance of education to her (Kay Flippin to Esme Bhan, 28 January 1991).

While employed with the Schonwasser store, Kay Stewart in 1932 married Robert B. Flippin, son of George Albert Flippin. Robert Flippin was born on December 24, 1904, in Stromsburg, Nebraska, and had done most of his schooling in Nebraska. Mary Stewart heartily approved of her son-in-law, who was to become in 1937 the director of the Booker T. Washington Community Center, which she had founded in 1920. He was successful as a community activist, including prisoner rehabilitation work at San Quentin for Warden Clinton Duffy, who had established the first prison chapter of Alcoholics Anonymous in the United States. Robert Flippin continued the work of Duffy, who had to leave San Quentin upon his appointment to the Adult Authority, Sacramento, California.

Kay Flippin left the Schonwasser Company in 1939, completed her high school education and earned a bachelor's degree at San Francisco State College while simultaneously enrolling for an eighteen-week training course for child care teachers. This program resulted from an increased need for child care, as the times required around-the-clock shifts for the war industries. Kay Flippin worked under the tutelage of the noted pioneer in preschool education, Lynette Messer, who invited her to be a part of her trailblazer team for a demonstration school on the old campus of San Francisco State College. This was consistent with Flippin's "search for a non-violent employment in the war effort" (Kay Flippin to Esme Bhan, 28 January 1991).

The marital union of Robert and Kay Flippin produced no offspring. Robert Flippin's son, Stephen, born in 1949, was promised to the couple by the mother, Frances Burke, prior to his birth. Commenting on the son, Flippin said:

> I want to tell the many childless couples that it is not necessary to spend fortunes on drugs and surgeries to have a baby. I want to tell them that it is not necessary to be the biological parent of a child to love it. The baby promised to me by the mother was like waiting not nine months but six joyful gratefull [sic] ones and how when the phone rang in the early morning of Jan 15, 1949

> for Bob to come and take the mother to the hospital—I walked the floor until he called and said, "Bunch, we have a son," that [moment] the tears of joy flowed and preparation for his homecoming began (Kay Flippin to Esme Bhan, 28 January 1991.)

The natural mother, however, changed her mind once Stephen was born, though she allowed the child to spend summer vacations with the Flippins. Today, Stephen and Kay Flippin have a close relationship.

Kay Flippin expanded her teaching interests in studying the educational, medical, and psychological aspects of atypical children who could not be readily categorized in conventional standards of instruction. By 1955 she helped to establish the innovative and experimental program called Aid for Brain-Damaged Children, a project that aimed to determine systematically the requisite data on nonmotor-handicapped and brain-damaged children's relative competence in visual and auditory skills. Even though financial constraints caused this special unit to close, Kay Flippin was able to assimilate some of these techniques at the Northern California School for Cerebral Palsy.

Following her husband's death in 1963, Kay Flippin retired, only to be invited in 1966 to organize the Head Start program for the Laguna Salada School District in Pacifica, California. The program was very successful and widely adopted. An all-time professional high accomplishment was her appointment in 1968 as director of the new Cooper's Corner Child Care Center in Pacifica, from which she retired a second time in 1972.

Since her retirement, Kay Flippin has served as consultant for preschool education on an informal basis and devoted considerable time to collecting and organizing genealogical material on the Stewart, Flippin, Weir, and Jeffers families.

References

Black Women Oral History Project Interview with Katherine Stewart Flippin. Schlesinger Library, Radcliffe College, 1978.

Flippin, Kay to Esme Bhan, 28 January 1991. Author's personal papers.

Patterson, William L. *The Man Who Cried Genocide: Autobiography of William L. Patterson.* New York: International Publishers, 1971.

Women of Courage. Based on the Black Women Oral History Project. Ed. Ruth Edmonds Hill. Cambridge: Schlesinger Library, Radcliffe College, 1984. Includes photograph.

Collections

The papers of the Stewart, Flippin, Weir, and Jeffers families are housed in the Moorland-Spingarn Research Center, Howard University.

Esme E. Bhan

Ida Forsyne

(1883- ?)

Dancer

In March 1944, the in-house publication of the American Hotels Corporation carried the following item from Schenectady: "We have in our midst a movie star—Ida Forsyne Hubbard, our new elevator operator" (Stearns, 257). Forsyne did play the role of Mrs. Noah in the 1936 film *Green Pastures*, but earlier she had had a long career as a dancer—for a time a very successful one. Forsyne's life shows the pattern of a young dancer managing to establish herself, enjoying nine years of great acclaim in Europe, trying with diminishing success to rebuild a career upon her return to this country, and eventually failing.

Today the primary source for her life is Marshall and Jean Stearns's essential *Jazz Dance*; their account is based on interviews, conversations, and correspondence between 1960 and 1966.

Ida Forsyne was born in Chicago in 1883. In early billings the name is given as Forcen. It is not known if Hubbard is a married name or not; there is no information on the question of any marriage. Her mother worked as a domestic, and her father disappeared from their lives when Forsyne was two. By the time Forsyne was ten, she was dancing in the street for pennies, and during the summer of that year she was earning twenty-five cents a day for cakewalking with a ragtime band on a wagon which went about the Chicago World's Fair advertising a show. Forsyne actively sought out contact with show business, and when she was fourteen she ran away with a tab show, *The Black Bostonians*. This show went broke in Butte, Montana. Undaunted, Forsyne recruited a five-year-old boy, and they earned their way back to Chicago by singing and dancing in the aisles of the railway coaches.

Forsyne was then hired by Black Patti's Troubadours and worked with this troupe from 1898 to 1909, rising from fifteen dollars a week to twenty-five before the show shut down. Black Patti's Troubadours was formed to showcase the talents of Sissieretta Jones, an extraordinarily gifted classical singer who was barred from the operatic and concert stage by racial prejudice. A typical show is that of 1902: First came a farcial skit with eight musical numbers, *A Filipino Misfit*, then a quartet performed, then followed a tightrope act, a solo act, a grand cakewalk contest (Forsyne and her partner once won seven times in a row), another solo act, and finally an operatic medley featuring Sissieretta Jones. Forsyne had her solo number in the skit and joined the rest of the troupe in the chorus for the opera selections. In 1898 no one objected to her first specialty number; she appeared pushing a baby carriage and singing, "You're Just a Little Nigger, but You're Mine All Mine." During her time with the show, she received brief but complimentary reviews.

In the summers when the show was not touring, Forsyne sought and found work in one of the numerous shows in Atlantic City or on Coney Island. On Coney Island in 1899, a crucial event in her career occurred: she ruined a fine alto voice by the need to shout her songs to be heard over the band. She could still manage to sing somewhat "by sort of talking it" (Stearns, 252), but she was no longer primarily a singer-dancer but a dancer. This contributed to her later career difficulties.

In 1902, Forsyne joined the original cast of *Smart Set*. She was now a well-established and highly popular performer. In 1904 she appeared at the New York Roof Garden in Will Marion Cook's *Southerners*. Then in 1906 she joined Abbe Mitchell and *The Tennessee Students*, a seventeen-person troupe of professional New York musicians, who were traveling to London. There she was billed as "Topsy, the Famous Negro Dancer," and had a sensational success. She performed in a second London appearance, and for a solid year at the Moulin Rouge in Paris.

> "They Billed me as 'Topsy' in London," she says. Wearing a bandanna and a short gingham dress, she sang and talked "Lindy by the Watermelon Vine" and danced like a tiny tumbleweed. As she darted about the stage—"they described me as little, black and cute"—she filled the role of Topsy to perfection (Stearns, 253).

Forsyne accepted a long-term contract with the largest booking agency in Europe, the Marinelli Agency, when The Tennessee Students returned to the United States. For the next few years, she worked in Europe continuously without vacation, to great success and acclaim. In Moscow in 1911, she scored a triumph by introducing Russian dancing into her act. Forsyne defines kazotsky: "You know, you start from a squat, your arms on your chest, and kick out first one leg then the other." She then describes her act:

> "I just changed steps and traveled across the stage in a crouch, working out new combinations." She flung both legs out in front and touched her toes with her hands before she came down in time to the music. "Then I'd mix it up with down-steps, up-steps, and cross-ankle steps—I could never spin—and as a finale, kazotsky all the way across the stage and return, backwards" (Stearns, 248).

The outbreak of war in 1914 forced Forsyne to return to the United States. She could not have been prepared for the situation she faced: she found it extremely difficult to find work, and she would never reestablish herself as a headliner. Part of her problem was a professional pride that made it difficult to bend to the demands of her audience:

> I wanted to be a little different from the average colored performer. Perhaps my success in Europe made me feel that way. I lived a clean life—you can't spend all night in a gin mill and then do a Russian dance—and darned if I was going to learn (Stearns, 254).

Another part she ascribes to black prejudice: "I couldn't get a job because I was black, and my own people discriminate against me" (Stearns, 256). In addition, Topsy was no longer acceptable and Russian dancing bewildered black audiences. Forsyne remembered vividly the audience booing and catcalling at a performance of Russian dancing in Cleveland in 1920 and later performing to indifferent audiences while blues singer Bessie Smith called encouragement from the wings.

Forsyne worked again at Coney Island. In 1914 she did a "'Scay-a-Da-Hootch' dance in Flournoy Miller and Aubrey Lyle's *Darkdom* at the Lafayette Theatre" in Harlem. She tried the Theatre Owners Booking Association (TOBA) circuit with her own act, which folded in Richmond. In 1919 she had work in *They're Off* and *Over the Top* and in 1920 and 1921 *Strut Your Stuff*, *Town Top-Piks*, and *Holiday in Dixie*. For about two years, from about 1920 to 1922, Forsyne worked for singer Sophie Tucker, off-stage as a maid and on-stage as a dancer to build audience applause while Tucker took her bows. While this was an exploitative relationship, Tucker firmly refused to bend to the degrading rules a Washington, D.C., theater tried to impose: blacks could appear onstage only in blackface, and they could not watch the shows from backstage.

Forsyne tried to find work in nightclubs. She found that she could not endure working conditions, which included the requirement to mingle with the customers, and she had no success with the top-flight clubs. The nearest she came to success was to be hired and then informed on her first night that she would not be going on.

Dancer Returns to TOBA Circuit

In 1924, Forsyne was back on the TOBA circuit as one of six dancers backing Mamie Smith. There were small parts in the films *Darktown Strutters* (1925) and *Rainbow Chasers* was featured in *Malinda* (1929). A 1926 tour of the South in a late version of *Smart Set* appalled her because of the difficult conditions. In 1927 Forsyne was working for thirty-five dollars a week in Bessie Smith's show on the TOBA circuit. However, she resigned in 1928 when Smith decided to tour the South. Forsyne had a bit part in *Lily White* in 1930 and played the role of Mrs. Noah in the play (1932) and movie (1936) *Green Pastures*. Also in 1936, Forsyne appeared in a revival of *The Emperor Jones*. There was also a bit part in the 1935 film *The Underworld*. Except for work as a consultant to Ruthanna Boris on the choreography of *Cake Walk* for the New York City Ballet in 1951, Forsyne's theatrical career was over in 1936. Her attempts to be a full-time professional were basically over in 1928 when she left Bessie Smith, although she worked whenever possible. After working for some three-and-a-half years as a domestic, she became an elevator operator.

Forsyne was a small, dark-complexioned woman with an infectious grin. She wore a size two shoe and weighed less than one hundred pounds when she was dancing. The Stearnses tell us that Forsyne was still able to turn a cartwheel in 1962 when she was seventy-nine, but in 1966 at the age of eighty-three, she was living in a rest home.

References

Hughes, Langston and Milton Meltzer. *Black Magic*. Englewood Cliffs, N.J.: Prentice-Hall, 1967.

Oppenheimer, Priscilla. "Ida Forsyne." In *The Harlem Renaissance: A Historical Dictionary for the Era*. Edited by Bruce Kellner. New York: Metheun, 1984.

Sampson, Henry T. *The Ghost Walks: A Chronological History of Blacks in Show Business, 1865-1910*. Metuchen, N.J.: Scarecrow Press, 1988.

Stearns, Marshall and Jean Stearns. *Jazz Dance*. New York: Macmillan, 1968.

Robert L. Johns

Margaretta Forten
(1808-1875)
Abolitionist, educator, school administrator

Margaretta Forten, the eldest child of James Forten (1766-1842) and his second wife, Charlotte Vandine (1785-1884), was born in Philadelphia in 1808. She was named for her paternal grandmother, Margaret Forten, who had died two years earlier.

Both of Margaretta Forten's parents were freeborn. Little information is available about the background of Charlotte Vandine, other than that she was a free woman and a native of Pennsylvania. She was almost twenty-one when she married James Forten in December 1805. He was thirty-nine and had been widowed eighteen months earlier after a brief marriage.

James Forten's paternal great-grandfather had been brought to Pennsylvania from West Africa as a slave in the 1680s. His grandfather had secured his freedom, probably through self-purchase. Thomas Forten (d. 1773/4), James's father, was a skilled artisan. A sailmaker by trade, he fitted out small coasting vessels for at least one of colonial Philadelphia's great mercantile families. Thomas Forten passed on a basic knowledge of his craft to his son and also ensured that he received the elements of a formal education. For two years, James Forten was enrolled in the African School run by the Quaker abolitionist Anthony Benezet.

The family's precarious financial situation after the death of Thomas Forten obliged James Forten to leave school and find work. During the Revolutionary War he saw service on a privateer and endured several months as a prisoner of the British. After the war, he enlisted as a merchant seaman and set sail for England. Back in Philadelphia after a year abroad, he apprenticed himself to Robert Bridges, a white sailmaker who had once employed his father. Bridges placed great trust in the younger Forten, promoting him to foreman of the sail loft and even aiding him in purchasing a small house for himself, his widowed mother, and his sister's family. In 1796, when Bridges decided to retire, Forten took over the business.

With the help of Bridges and a member of the city's mercantile elite, Thomas Willing, Forten was soon well established in trade. The high quality of his workmanship, combined with his reputation for fair dealing, ensured that he had no shortage of customers. The only vessels he refused to fit out were those that he suspected were being used in the slave trade. As Philadelphia prospered from trade with China, India, the Caribbean, and Europe in the 1790s and early 1800s, Forten did well. Profits from his sailmaking business were invested in real estate, in moneylending, and eventually in bank and railroad stock.

By the time Margaretta was born, James Forten had moved his family from a cramped wood-frame house in Southwark, an area of wharves and workshops, to an elegant three-story brick house on Lombard Street, one of the city's main thoroughfares. That move not only announced to the world his entry into the commercial elite of Philadelphia, but it enabled him and his wife to raise their children in healthy surroundings. Less overcrowded than Southwark, with better sanitation and a more reliable water supply, Lombard Street escaped many of the epidemics that swept through Philadelphia's poorer districts. Even so, the household in which Margaretta Forten grew up was one in which privacy was at a premium. The house at ninety-two Lombard was home not only to her parents and siblings but to domestic servants and apprentices and journeymen from her father's sail loft. In 1810 the federal census recorded that there were fifteen members of the household; in 1820 there were eighteen and in 1830 twenty-two.

Margaretta Forten and her brothers and sisters were raised in a household that was always full of visitors. As James Forten's wealth grew, so did his standing within the black community. An officer of the African Masonic Lodge, a vestryman of St. Thomas's African Episcopal Church, and a leading voice in a host of organizations, he was often called upon to chair committees and speak for Philadelphia's black citizens on matters of importance. Other members of the city's black elite often called to consult with him. The young Fortens found many of their childhood companions within Philadelphia's black upper class. They also developed friendships with some of their white neighbors. Sea captain Daniel Brewton had been imprisoned with Forten during the Revolutionary War and that experience made the two men lifelong friends. Merchants like Thomas Ash, with whom James Forten did business, also called at the Forten home. Other ties developed simply because Forten was living in an area that was not segregated by race. Margaretta Forten's younger brother, Robert, was a childhood companion of a future congressman from Pennsylvania, William D. Kelley.

Other friends of the Forten children came from further afield. Robert and Joseph Purvis were natives of Charleston, South Carolina. Their father, a wealthy English cotton merchant William Purvis, moved his family to Philadelphia in an effort to ensure them a good education, and his sons socialized with the Fortens. (Both brothers eventually married into the Forten family.) James Forten's prominence as a businessman and abolitionist also brought into his family circle a young West African prince. In 1817 King Sherker, a powerful ruler in the Sierra Leone region and a man who had grown rich by participating in the slave trade, sent his grandson to a trusted business associate in Cuba with a request that he enroll the child in school. Unable to find a school for the boy in Havana, the merchant sent him to Philadelphia in care of a captain who knew James Forten and spoke highly of him. James Forten welcomed the unexpected visitor. As he told his old friend Paul Cuffe, the New England shipowner and advocate of African emigration, if abolitionists like himself could earn the gratitude of the child's grandfather, Sherker might be induced to forsake the slave trade.

Providing Margaretta Forten and her siblings with the companionship of children from many different backgrounds was one thing James Forten could do. However, the question of their formal education was not one that he could solve so easily. He wished to educate his children in a manner appropriate to his wealth and to the station in life he hoped they would one day occupy. He and his wife could teach them the elements of literacy at home, but the children needed to attend school. The schools that would admit black children were church and charity enterprises—adequate for instructing them in the basics, but hardly equipped to train them in the higher branches of education. The city's fashionable academies were completely closed to them.

James Forten and Grace Douglass Open School

As Forten's family grew, so did the challenge of finding suitable schools. By 1819 James and Charlotte Forten had six children. In addition to Margaretta, there were three daughters, Harriet, Sarah, and Mary, and two sons, James, Jr., and Robert. (The Fortens would eventually have two more sons—Thomas and William). Finally, the difficulties involved in securing a decent education for his children led Forten to open a school of his own, with the help of an old family friend, Grace Douglass. Grace Douglass was the daughter of community leader Cyrus Bustill. She had been born in Philadelphia, and it is likely that she and Forten had known each other since childhood. Douglass and her husband, Robert, a prosperous barber from the West Indies, faced many of the same problems as the Fortens. They had five children and they were determined to find some way that they "might be better taught than they could be in any of the schools then open to [them]." In 1819 the Fortens and the Douglasses hired a teacher, Britton E. Chamberlain, set up a school, and probably recruited more pupils from the wealthier families in the black community. When Chamberlain eventually left, the school was taken over by Grace Douglass's daughter, Sarah.

In addition to attending this school, Margaretta Forten and her sisters received some of their education at home. Charlotte Forten, Margaretta's niece, described how her grandfather "was obliged . . . to go to the expense of employing private teachers for his daughters"(Charlotte Forten Grimké, "Personal Recollections of Whittier," 468). James Forten was determined to educate them to become young women of refinement. Samuel J. May, a white abolitionist who visited the Forten home in 1833, was struck by how "lovely [and] accomplished" Forten's daughters were (May, 288). To the horror of some of his acquaintances, he insisted on escorting Margaretta Forten to an antislavery meeting.

That the education of Forten's daughters, as well as his sons, had been of a "superior kind" was clear not only to the sympathetic May but to other visitors to the Forten home. Margaretta, and probably her younger sisters, spoke and read French. Since her father had business contacts in Haiti, this was a distinct asset to him. Forten, as he was fond of telling friends like abolitionist William Lloyd Garrison, considered himself, first and foremost, "a man of business." He had too many demands on his time to acquire knowledge of a foreign language, but he could draw on the skills his children had acquired.

The affairs of the Haitian republic interested Forten for a number of reasons, personal and ideological, as well as commercial. His brother-in-law, Charles Vandine, had emigrated to Haiti in the 1820s and established himself as a merchant in Port-au-Prince. Forten also followed political events in Haiti and frequently cited the Haitian example to refute claims that black people could not govern themselves. On one occasion, Reverend Breckinridge, a leading member of the American Colonization Society and a man with whom James Forten had profound philosophical differences, was taking tea with the Forten family. He and Forten embarked on a discussion of Haitian politics. Eager to prove a point, Forten produced a letter from an acquaintance on Haiti and handed it to Breckinridge, who was obliged to confess that he could not read French. Forten then called upon Margaretta to translate it. The editor of an abolitionist journal, in recounting this incident, observed that Breckinridge went from the

Forten home to a meeting at which he argued that black people should leave the United States because they were intellectually inferior to whites.

Refinement could serve to refute notions of intellectual inferiority, but it could also bring an uncomfortable sense of being on display, as Margaretta Forten discovered to her chagrin. James Forten explained in a letter to the abolitionist Nathaniel P. Rogers that "the well meant, though injudicious, and sometimes really impolite notice which is taken, if any of us happen to do, or say any thing like other people" was "grating" to the feelings of black people. He described a visit paid to his family by a white abolitionist from Connecticut. The visitor "requested my Daughter to open the Piano, adding that he had never heard a colored Lady play." Forten added: "[H]e would not, I dare say, for the world have said this, had he thought it would have wounded her feelings, or that it conveyed to her mind the appearance of rudeness" (James Forten to Nathaniel P. Rogers, 28 March 1839). The daughter referred to by Forten was either Margaretta or Mary. By 1839 Harriet and Sarah had married and moved out of the Lombard Street home.

Margaretta Forten learned early in life that her father's wealth brought certain advantages, but could in no way purchase her or her family immunity from the affects of racism. In fact, Forten's business success sometimes provoked threats of violence, as did his articulation of such unpopular causes as abolition and racial equality, and his rejection of the policies of the American Colonization Society. In 1834 one of Margaretta Forten's younger brothers was attacked in the street by a mob of young white men. The child escaped the melee and a white neighbor who witnessed the assault supplied information that led to the arrest of the perpetrators. Some days later, as the city exploded in racial violence, a rumor circulated that the Forten home was to be attacked. Fortunately, Forten's standing was such that the mayor ordered his officers to patrol the neighborhood. There were further threats in 1838 when Pennsylvania Hall was destroyed, and in the summer after James Forten's death the house of his son-in-law, Robert Purvis, was singled out for attack.

There were other constant reminders that the situation of any black person was precarious in a nation where slavery had the sanction of law. In 1825 one of Margaretta Forten's cousins, Amos Dunbar, was apprenticed to a tailor by his parents so that he could learn a skilled trade. The "craftsman," who had apparently given an alias, promptly shipped the boy off to New Orleans and sold him as a slave. It took the intervention of James Forten and several members of the Pennsylvania Abolition Society to secure his release.

Abolitionist Fold Attracts Margaretta Forten

The influence of her parents, of the community in which she grew up, and of her own awareness of the injustices in American society drew Margaretta Forten into the abolitionist fold. Surrounded as she was from her earliest years by men and women dedicated to the eradication of slavery and prejudice, it could hardly have been otherwise. Many of those who visited the Forten home were committed opponents of slavery. Forten supplied much of the early funding for the antislavery journal the *Liberator* and its editor, William Lloyd Garrison, was always a welcome guest. Other antislavery supporters Margaretta met in her father's house included James and Lucretia Mott, Arthur and Lewis Tappan, George Thompson, Benjamin Lundy, Edward Abdy, and J. Miller McKim. In fact, any visitor to the city with any interest in abolition, from the United States or abroad, seemed to eventually find their way to Ninety-two Lombard Street.

Margaretta Forten, in common with the rest of her family, rejoiced in the creation of the American Anti-Slavery Society in Philadelphia in December 1833. She was moved to pour out her emotions in verse. Addressing the founders of the organization, who included her own brother-in-law, Robert Purvis, she wrote:

> Ye blessed few! who now have stood the storm
> Of persecution, in its direful form;
> Unmov'd have faced the foe in stern array
> Clad in bold armor for the dread affray;
> Your banner floats—its motto may be read,
> "DOWN WITH OPPRESSION! FREEDOM
> IN ITS STEAD!"
> Who are the great and good in this fair land?
> Ye who are foremost in this holy band;
> Ye blessed few! may God's protecting arm,
> O'er ye be spread, to shelter ye from harm;
> For though your foes maliciously do aim —
> To quash your ardor, and to brand your fame,
> Your course is onward! they cannot control,
> Nought *can* arrest the purpose of your soul.
> Ye have come forth the galling chain to sever,
> Ye have come forth the captive to deliver;
> A little while and then the chain shall fall,
> And they shall stand redeemed from every thrall.
> Ye blessed few! to ye shall still be given,
> The choicest blessings of a glorious heaven.
> Thrice blessed ye! to whom indeed belong
> The heart's warm tribute and the grateful song
> (*Emancipator*, 14 January 1834).

The poem is signed "M.T.F." The editor identified the author as "the daughter of a highly respected colored gentleman of Philadelphia." This is the only poem that can be attributed to Margaretta Forten with any degree of certainty. It is possible that she wrote other pieces under a pseudonym. Antislavery journals often contained poetry and prose by young black women from the Philadelphia community who chose to hide their identity behind such names as "Zoe," "Bera," "Ella," and "Zillah." Sarah Forten signed most of her pieces "Ada."

Initially denied full membership in the American Anti-Slavery Society, female abolitionists responded by forming their own societies. At the national level they organized their own conventions. With her sisters Sarah and Harriet,

Margaretta attended the Women's Anti-Slavery Convention in New York in 1837, as well as the two subsequent conventions in Philadelphia.

It was one thing to hold national conventions, but female antislavery advocates throughout the United States were also determined to give their activities a strong institutional base at the local level. It was, in fact, at this local level that some of their most effective work was done. The Philadelphia women were ahead of most of their sisters in this. In December 1833, Margaretta Forten helped to draw up the constitution that created the interracial Philadelphia Female Anti-Slavery Society. Her mother, two of her sisters, and her future sister-in-law joined in promoting the work of the organization. After her marriage, Sarah Forten moved away from Philadelphia, but Margaretta and Harriet Forten continued to be active in the society. Both sisters were frequently chosen to serve on the committee of management that organized the society's annual fair. As a teacher, Margaretta Forten took particular interest in the work of the society to promote the education of black children. As she had presided over the organization's birth, so she was present when it disbanded. On March 24, 1870, it was Margaretta Forten who moved the adoption of a preamble and resolution that dissolved the Philadelphia Female Anti-Slavery Society.

Unlike her sisters, Margaretta Forten did not marry. Seeking a career outside the home, she ran a successful private school for more than thirty years. From 1845 she was the principal of the Lombard Street Primary School. The school took boarders, some of whom lived in the Forten home. Students were sent to the school not only from Philadelphia but from much further away. For instance, in 1860 the wealthy mulatto businessman, William Ellison, Jr., arranged passage for his daughters, Elizabeth and Henrietta, from Charleston, South Carolina, to Philadelphia so that they could attend the Lombard Street school. Family contacts aided Margaretta Forten in recruiting wealthy Southern students. Her brother-in-law, Robert Purvis, kept up ties with his native city of Charleston, and her brother, Robert, took as his second wife a woman from that city's mulatto elite.

When she established her school, Margaretta Forten could draw on her extensive commercial and organizational experience. Her involvement in her father's business affairs began when she was a child. In 1817, at the age of nine, she witnessed a deed for him. In 1836, when he drew up his will, James Forten recognized her abilities: he appointed her to be one of his three executors. His was a complex estate to administer. He left real estate holdings to be managed, rents to be collected, promissory notes on which payment had to be demanded, and railroad and bank stock. As an executor, Margaretta Forten had to complete property deals begun by her father before his death and initiate several cases in the courts to protect the interests of herself and the other heirs.

Although she had no children of her own, Margaretta Forten exerted a profound influence on her young niece. Charlotte Forten was the daughter of Margaretta Forten's younger brother, Robert Bridges Forten. Mary Wood Forten, Charlotte's mother, died on July 9, 1840, when Charlotte was not quite three years old. After the death of his wife, Robert apparently entrusted his daughter to his mother and older sister. It was Margaretta Forten who was responsible for much of her niece's early education. Robert's move to Warminster township, Bucks County, some miles outside Philadelphia, and his subsequent remarriage did not estrange aunt and niece. When Charlotte went away to school in Salem, Massachusetts, she exchanged letters with her Aunt Margaretta. As Charlotte confessed in her journal: "Wrote a letter to my dear aunt. I can always write more freely to her than to any one else" (Stevenson, 19 November 1854). It was Margaretta Forten who identified Charlotte as the author of a poem published in the *Liberator* in 1855—to Charlotte's annoyance. Over the years, Margaretta Forten visited Charlotte in Salem and attended antislavery celebrations with her.

Through letters and conversations, Margaretta Forten shaped her niece's literary tastes, recommending to her such books as Gustave de Beaumont's novel, *Marie, ou L'Esclavage aux Etats-Unis*, Miss Mitford's *Recollections of a Literary Life*, and *John Halifax, Gentleman*, a work by the English author Dinah Maria Murlock (Stevenson, 14 April and 20 May 1857). Margaretta Forten also instilled in Charlotte a deep sense of pride in her family. In May 1857, for instance, Margaretta Forten forwarded to Charlotte a letter from Harriet Martineau to James Forten, Sr., that Martineau had written when she sent him a copy of her novel about the Haitian revolution, *The Hour and the Man*. When Charlotte was in Philadelphia, she and her aunt sewed together and discussed books they had read, as well as visiting Margaretta Forten's two married sisters. The close ties between Margaretta Forten and her niece endured when Charlotte went to the Sea Islands to teach at the Freedmen's School during the Civil War. Charlotte included in her letters to Margaretta Forten requests for clothing for the freedmen and toys for her younger pupils.

With the marriage of two of her sisters and the death of a third, Margaretta Forten took over the day-to-day running of the Lombard Street household for her aging mother and two bachelor brothers, Thomas and William. Visitors of all kinds were entertained in the Forten home, even if it was not the great social center it had been during James Forten's lifetime.

In an important respect, Margaretta Forten's role as a housekeeper facilitated the political career of her younger brother. William Forten carried on the family's tradition of activism. In the 1850s, he aided fugitives and gained notoriety by coordinating the defense of those charged with the death of a Southern slaveholder in the Christiana riot. During the Civil War, he helped to recruit black troops. For many years he was an officer of the Pennsylvania Equal Rights League. His ability to deliver the black vote for the Republican party proved crucial in Philadelphia politics in the 1870s. (It was probably because of his brother's work for the Republicans that Thomas Forten secured a patronage appointment as Clerk of Customs for Philadelphia. Federal Census 1880, Philadelphia, Fifth Ward.) William Forten never married, and the role of political hostess was played by his sister.

Illness forced Margaretta Forten to absent herself from her school on a number of occasions. Like her nieces and nephews, and two of her sisters, she evidently suffered from recurring respiratory problems, quite possibly due to tuberculosis. Nevertheless, she remained a dedicated and hard-working teacher and a tireless advocate of social reform until her death. Margaretta Forten died of pneumonia on January 14, 1875. She was buried beside her father, her brother, Robert, and her sister, Mary, in the cemetery of St. Thomas's African Episcopal Church. When the church sold its premises, her remains were moved to a lot owned by William Forten in the cemetery of the Episcopal Church of St. James the Less in Philadelphia. Her grave is unmarked.

References

Alonso B. Munoz to James Forten. Havana, 24 June 1817. *Pennsylvania Abolition Society Minutes*, 1800-24. Historical Society of Pennsylvania.

Anti-Slavery Reporter, June 1859.

Charlotte Forten Grimké. ''Personal Recollections of Whittier.'' *New England Magazine*, (1893).

Dannett, Sylvia G. L. *Profiles of Negro Womanhood*. Vol. 1. Yonkers, N.Y.: Educational Heritage, 1964.

Emancipator, 14 January 1834.

Federal Census, 1850, 1860.

Forten, James. Letter to Nathaniel R. Rogers, 29 March 1839. Nathaniel P. Rogers Collection, Treasure Room, Haverford College, Haverford, Penn.

Johnson, Michael P. and James L. Roark, eds. *No Chariot Let Down: Charleston's Free People of Color on the Eve of the Civil War*. Chapel Hill: University of North Carolina Press, 1984. 128-30.

Liberator, 10 May 1839. The story originally appeared in the *Herald of Freedom*.

May, Samuel J. *Recollections of Our Antislavery Conflict*. Boston: Fields, Osgood, 1869. Reprint. New York: Arno Press, 1969.

National Anti-Slavery Standard, 24 April 1844, 20 December 1849, 10 January 1857.

Pennsylvania Freeman, 17 March 1841.

Philadelphia County Deeds, M.R., Book 19, p. 655. City Archives, City Hall Annex, Philadelphia.

Philadelphia County Wills, 1768, #196, Book O, p. 258; 1842, #87, Book 15, p. 455. City Hall, Philadelphia.

Poulson's American Daily Advertiser, 31 May 1806.

Proceedings of the Anti-Slavery Convention of American Women, Held by Adjournment from the 9th to the 12th of May, 1837. New York: W. S. Dorr, 1837.

Proceedings of the Anti-Slavery Convention of American Women, Held in Philadelphia, May 15th, 16th, 17th and 18th, 1838. Philadelphia: Merrihew and Gunn, 1838.

Proceedings of the Third Anti-Slavery Convention of American Women, Held in Philadelphia, May 1st, 2d and 3d, 1839. Philadelphia: Merrihew and Gunn, 1839.

St. James the Less Episcopal Church, Philadelphia, Pennsylvania—Cemetery Records. Handwritten volume in the Collections of the Genealogical Society of Pennsylvania, Historical Society of Pennsylvania.

Stevenson, Brenda, ed. *Journals of Charlotte Forten Grimké*. New York: Oxford University Press, 1988. 26 July 1854, p. 91; 19 November 1854, p. 111; 28 March 1855, p. 132; 14 April, 20 May, 1857, pp. 211, 219; 12 May 1857, p. 218; 14 September 1862, p. 381; 20 November 1862, p. 400.

Winch, Julie. ''Philadelphia and the Other Underground Railroad.'' *Pennsylvania Magazine of History and Biography* 111 (January 1987): 5-6.

Collections

To date, no photographs or personal papers of Margaretta Forten have been located. The major sources for this biographical sketch were antislavery publications, Forten family deeds and wills, and the journals of Charlotte Forten Grimké.

Julie Winch

Charlotte L. Forten Grimké

(1837-1914)

Essayist, educator, translator, diarist

In the history of nineteenth-century America, few family names are more respected than that of the Fortens. A unique blend of political consciousness and social and economic privilege placed them at the forefront of the abolition movement in that era. According to legend, their American ancestry originated with an African slave brought to this country five generations before Charlotte Forten's birth. His son, the grandfather of James Forten, Sr.—the person most responsible for the family's fame and fortune—although born a slave, gained his freedom. Thus, there were four generations of free Fortens before the birth of Charlotte. Her

Charlotte L. Forten Grimké

family background provides the key to an understanding of the life of this nineteenth-century black American woman whose journals are the subject of literary and historical interest.

James Forten, Sr., (1766-1842) was born in Philadelphia where, for a while, he attended the school of Anthony Benezet, a well-known Quaker abolitionist. The death of his father, Thomas Forten, when James was seven years old, ended his formal education and forced him to find employment to support himself, his mother, and his sister. At the beginning of the Revolutionary War, James Forten volunteered for duty in the patriotic forces and became a powder boy on a Philadelphia ship, the *Royal Luis*. Unfortunately, the boat was captured by the British, and he spent seven months as a prisoner before he was released. Soon after his return to Philadelphia, disgusted with American slavery and the national treatment of blacks, he went to England for a year. Abroad, James Forten came into close contact with several abolitionists, including the well-known Granville Sharpe. These reformers sparked his interest in the antislavery movement.

Forten returned to America a confirmed abolitionist but also assuming responsibility for supporting his mother and his sister. Toward that end, he became an apprentice sailmaker to Robert Bridges. He learned the trade quickly and well, and by 1786, at the age of twenty, he was the foreman of the sail loft. In 1798, when Bridges retired, Forten bought the firm. Reportedly, his invention of a device for easier handling of the sails made his fortune. By the early 1830s he was a wealthy man employing many black and white workers. He was also on his way to becoming one of Philadelphia's most notable black citizens.

Financial security enabled James Forten to provide his family with material comforts then unusual for black people: a luxurious home at Ninety-two Lombard Street, travel, private education, and access to numerous social and cultural activities. At the same time, he gave a considerable portion of his energies and financial resources to social issues, often making his home the meeting place of black and white reformers across the eastern seaboard. In 1800, Forten signed a petition to Congress urging that body to modify the Fugitive Slave Act of 1793 and to take measures leading to the emancipation of the slaves. The petition was rejected. In 1813 he published a pamphlet of five letters against legislation to ban free blacks from settling in Pennsylvania. He was one of the most vociferous critics of the American Colonization Society, which advocated the relocation of free blacks in Liberia. Forten was a primary force behind the 1830 National Negro Convention in Philadelphia that condemned colonization, discussed the expansion of rights for free blacks, and advocated the abolition of slavery and equal rights for all black people in the country. He was a warm and respected friend of William Lloyd Garrison and an important adviser to, and the second largest financial supporter of Garrison's antislavery newspaper, the *Liberator*, first published in 1831. For several years Forten served on the Board of Managers for the American Anti-Slavery Society, organized in his home in 1833; and he was a founding member of the American Moral Reform Society, a group of black men dedicated to promoting education, temperance, economy, and universal liberty for all people. James Forten was also an equally generous supporter and financial contributor to causes for women's rights and world peace. Active almost to the end of his life, he died in 1842 at the age of seventy-six and had one of the largest funerals in the history of Philadelphia. White and black men and women paid glowing tribute to his life of struggle against moral evils of all kinds, but especially to his unfailing efforts to end slavery and to move the conscience of the country regarding the humanity of black people.

James Forten was one of the first people to speak to the speciousness of the argument for slavery and discrimination against black people on the basis of biology. As such, his ideology challenged all groups that supported forced migration of blacks to Africa. Initially, the Colonization Society had sought his support, suggesting that a man of his prestige could assume national leadership in Liberia. He rejected those arguments, holding firmly to the idea that the slaves should be freed and educated to take their place in American society. He was so persuasive on this issue that Garrison, who had been ambivalent toward colonization, came to agree with him. Forten was an outstanding man, but he was not alone in his beliefs. In the early nineteenth century, Philadelphia was a thriving center for reform-minded blacks and whites. In his civic efforts, Forten was closely linked to such black men as Richard Allen, Absalom Jones, and Robert Douglass, who also made enormous contributions of time, energy, and intellectual ideas to improve the lives of blacks in America.

Charlotte Forten, the granddaughter of James Forten, Sr., and daughter of Robert Bridges Forten and Mary Virginia (Woods) Forten, was born in the Forten family home on Lombard Street on August 17, 1837. If the figure of James Forten, who died five years later, loomed larger-than-life in her early years, other members of the family also shaped her life. Among those were her father, who followed his father's trade and political activism. Born in 1813, Robert Forten was educated privately, and family and friends praised him for talent and creativity. While still very young, he constructed a nine-foot telescope that was exhibited at the Franklin Institute in Philadelphia. Later he became a member of the Young Men's Anti-Slavery Society of Philadelphia and the Philadelphia Vigilance Committee of the New England Anti-Slavery Society. In the 1850s he moved to England and remained there until 1862 when, the Civil War in progress, he returned to America to enlist in the Union forces. Within a month he rose from private to sergeant-major and served as a recruiter for black troops in Maryland. Unfortunately, in 1864, illness resulting from his stay in Maryland forced his return in Philadelphia, where he died of typhoid fever soon after. He was the first black person to receive a military funeral in that city.

Other important influences in Charlotte Forten's life were her grandmother, Charlotte (for whom she was named), her three aunts: Margaretta, Sarah, and Harriet, and the husbands of the last-named two, Joseph and Robert Purvis. After her mother's death in 1840, Forten became very attached to them all, and remained so throughout their lifetimes. The elder Charlotte Forten was as civic-minded as her husband and insisted that her children assume responsibility for their own lives and consideration for the conditions of all black life in America.

Female Role Models Influence Young Charlotte Forten

Activist abolitionists and feminists, the Forten women gave young Charlotte Forten her most significant female role models. The elder Charlotte Forten, her daughters, and Mary Woods Forten were founding members of the Philadelphia Female Anti-Slavery Society (1833). The sisters, in particular, were so prominent in some public circles that New England poet John Greenleaf Whittier wrote a poem "To the Daughters of James Forten." In their daily lives, Margaretta, who never married, was a teacher and administrator in black segregated schools in Philadelphia; and Sarah, a writer, contributed poems and essays on civil rights issues to the pages of the *Liberator*. Sarah Forten served on the Female Anti-Slavery Society's Board of Managers in 1837, representing the group at the Philadelphia convention that year. Harriet Forten was a delegate to the 1837 and 1838 conventions.

The three sisters, their mother, and Charlotte's mother, were educated, hardworking women who held themselves and others to high moral standards. More importantly, they were part of a larger group of nineteenth-century black and white women committed to gender as well as race issues. Charlotte Forten met and knew many of the other women who shared ideas similar to those of her female relatives. After her father remarried in 1845, and she moved out of the family home with him, she maintained strong ties with Lombard Street and the homes of her aunts. Her first sixteen years of life passed amidst the ferment of three households of relatives. In addition to childhood experiences with cousins whom she adored, the enjoyment of nature and the fun of riding, reading, playing games, and engaging in flower- and berry-picking, there was an intricate but unmistakable interweaving in the fabric of her daily life of social reform addressing the abolition of slavery, women's roles, and the welfare of all black people in America.

The Purvises—two of three brothers—who married Sarah and Harriet Forten, were active, educated young black men, from a wealthy family. They arrived in Philadelphia from South Carolina with their parents in 1819. Their father intended to move them to England, but his premature death aborted that idea and the family settled permanently in Philadelphia. They were a welcome addition to the free black community in that city. Robert and Joseph Purvis devoted a great deal of their energies and wealth to the abolitionist movement and the welfare of free blacks.

Robert Purvis (1810-1898), for several years vice president of the American Anti-Slavery, was also a longtime member of the Pennsylvania Society for Promoting the Abolition of Slavery and its president from 1845 to 1850. In this capacity he worked as president during the life span (1839-1844) of the Vigilance Committee, an interracial group engaged with the daily activities of the Underground Railroad. He chaired its successor organization, the General Vigilance Committee, from 1852 to 1857. His home in Bucks County was a station on the Railroad. But Robert Purvis was also concerned with other issues, including the conditions of the lives of poor free blacks and the education of black youth. While he sent his own children to private Quaker schools, in 1853 he refused to pay taxes to his township until the authorities permitted black children to attend local pubic schools. Perhaps because of the substantial amount of the taxes on his vast property holdings, he won his case.

Like her father, Charlotte Forten did not attend Philadelphia's segregated schools. She had tutors at home, but when Robert Forten learned that there were integrated public schools in Salem, Massachusetts, he decided to send his daughter there to complete her education. Salem was a good choice because, as a progressive man, Forten wanted Charlotte to prepare for a career in teaching, and the town had a reputable Normal School. In Salem, where she arrived in 1853, Charlotte lived in the home of Charles Lenox Remond, his wife Amy Matilda Williams Cassey Remond, and their two children, Sarah Cassey Smith and Henry Cassey. The

Remond and Forten families were close friends in the struggle against slavery and other social ills. Charles Remond and his sister, Sarah Parker Remond, well educated, intelligent, and eloquent, were prominent early-nineteenth-century New England abolitionists. He was the first black to lecture for the Massachusetts Anti-Slavery Society and gained special notice when, in 1840, as an American delegate to the World's Anti-Slavery Convention in London, in a protest against gender-segregated seating, he gave up his seat on the floor of the meeting hall to sit in the gallery with the women delegates. He was still active in the abolitionist movement when Forten lived in his house (1853-1857).

In 1853, at the age of sixteen, Charlotte Forten enrolled at the Higginson Grammar School in Salem with its more than two hundred young women receiving instruction in spelling, reading, writing, English grammar, arithmetic, modern geography, and American history. In spite of occasionally encountering hurtful racism among her peers, which she documents in her journal, Forten graduated from Higginson in 1855 with "decided éclat." Her crowning success was having her poem, "A Parting Hymn," selected as the best from a group submitted by her classmates and sung by the students during the graduation ceremony. Forten was a hardworking student who enjoyed her studies. However, her relationship with the principal of the school, Mary Shephard, was the highlight of her school experience. Shephard was sympathetic to abolitionism and became Forten's lifelong friend. Following graduation from Higginson in 1855, Forten enrolled in the Salem Normal School, the same year she published her first poem, "To W. L. G. on Reading His 'Chosen Queen,' " in the antislavery journal the *Liberator*. She graduated from the Salem Normal School in 1856 and was immediately offered and accepted an opportunity to teach at the Epes Grammar School—making her the first person of her race to hold such a position in Salem. For her second graduation she wrote "Poem for Normal School Graduation." This appeared on the pages of the *Liberator* in 1856.

Biographies of Charlotte Forten indicate that during the following two years, in spite of bouts of ill health, she reported that she was happy in her new life. While doubts exist on how much she enjoyed teaching, there were other aspects of living in New England that she found very satisfying. From her childhood training, she believed it was her duty to serve her race, and she wanted to fulfill this responsibility. To this end, in 1856 she joined the Massachusetts Female Anti-Slavery Society and attended antislavery lectures and took part in related activities in Salem and other cities in the area. For personal development, she studied French, German, and Latin, read widely—as many as a hundred books per year—both from contemporary and great writers of the past, and indulged her passion for education and culture by attending lectures on literature and art and engaging in conversations with the people she most admired as bearers of the values she sought.

In November 1856, soon after she began to teach, Forten began to suffer from severe headaches. Over the following six months she was intermittently incapacitated, and in May 1857 she returned to Philadelphia to rest and recuperate over that summer in the home of her aunt and uncle, Harriet and Robert Purvis. Like many of the people in her family—some, like her mother, died of similar problems—she suffered from an ongoing respiratory ailment. Although she resumed teaching after this break, she was not well, and a year later she resigned her position at Epes and returned to Philadelphia.

For two years, Forten stayed with her family, but the idea of a life of uselessness and dependency was inimical to her self-image. In September 1859 she was back in Salem to work with her friend Mary Shephard at the Higginson Grammar School. Again, the effort was too great for her strength, and the following spring she resigned. She actively tried to get well and recovered sufficiently to resume her duties in the fall of that year, only to suffer another relapse that sent her back to Philadelphia in October 1860. While she rested, she maintained her interest in the abolition movement and taught with her Aunt Margaretta in a black segregated school. In the summer of 1862, she was back in New England to teach summer classes. It was then that John Greenleaf Whittier suggested to her that she might render a great service to her race by teaching among the former slaves. He told her of a "social experiment" recently begun by the Union on the South Carolina coast to prove the mass educability of blacks. The idea appealed to Forten, who also hoped that a warmer climate might be beneficial to her health. Interestingly, although by November 1862, hundreds of white teachers from the North, many of them women, were in the South to begin the work of preparing the former slaves for their roles as free people, the Boston Educational Commission denied Forten permission to participate in the project on the basis of her sex. Fortunately, the Philadelphia Port Royal Relief Association accepted her application.

Educator Teaches Newly-Freed Slaves

In late 1862, Charlotte Forten left Philadelphia for Port Royal, on Saint Helena Island off the South Carolina coast, which Union forces had captured in 1861. She was one of the first black teachers to arrive in the South in the wake of the Civil War, and the only one on Saint Helena Island during her stay there. Forten remained on Saint Helena Island from October 1862 until May 1864.

Charlotte Forten believed fervently in the value of her work among the former slaves. In a one-room schoolhouse attended by children of all ages, she did the best she could to teach her young charges the basics of elementary education: reading, writing, spelling, history, and mathematics. She also instructed children and adults in moral and social behavior. The job was physically and emotionally challenging for her, and she experienced tiredness and the loneliness of separation from life in Philadelphia and New England. Her early months on the island were especially difficult because she faced mixed responses from teachers, military personnel, and even the blacks she wanted to help. In spite of her good intentions, Forten's background, upbringing, and temperament did not help her to mediate her difficulties. She never developed social relationship with the former slaves, for while she grew to be fond of them as people and even came to know and feel deep admiration for some, including Harriet Tubman, she was often repelled by their crudeness and, to her, their unusual social and religious practices. Like her white contemporaries engaged in this and similar projects, she believed that the behavior of all blacks needed to be transformed to meet the standards of northern white middle-class mores before the group would be accepted on equal terms with the dominant society.

On the other hand, during the time spent on Saint Helena, Forten made new friendships and she was admired by many of those who, like her, had gone to help. She had high regard for Colonel Higginson, an abolitionist from Massachusetts, for his dedication to the black race, while he thought similarly of her for her intelligence, ladylike demeanor, and her desire to serve her people. She also praised General Rufus Saxton, commander of the Union forces in the Port Royal region, and Colonel Robert Gould Shaw, commander of the all-black Fifty-fourth Massachusetts Regiment for their gentlemanly qualities, intelligence, and willingness to face even death for the cause of the slaves. Others with whom she developed friendships included Ellen Murray of Milton, Massachusetts, and Laura Towne from Shoemarketown, Pennsylvania. These two were among the first to arrive on the island and set up a school there. In addition to serving as a teacher, Towne was a doctor whom Forten described as a "housekeeper . . . [and] everything . . . the most indispensable person on the place" (Stevenson, 31 October 1860, 392). Forten was also fond of Elizabeth Hunn and her father, John Hunn, from Philadelphia, who opened up a store for the ex-slaves on the island.

Forten wrote to William Lloyd Garrison of her experiences on Saint Helena in two letters that were published in the *Liberator* in 1862. More formal than the letters, her two-part essay, "Life on the Sea Islands" appeared in the *Atlantic Monthly* in 1864. On the whole, the time spent on Saint Helena was positive for her, and she expressed fulfillment in doing significant work for her race. Another bout with failing health and perhaps the death of her father in April 1864 led her to resign her post and return to Philadelphia in May of that year.

She was not there long. In the summer of 1865 she asked Whittier's help in securing a place in a sanatorium in Lexington, Massachusetts, but instead of going there, she took a position as secretary of the Teacher Committee of the New England Branch of the Freedmen's Union Commission in Boston. There she was the liaison between teachers in the South working with former slaves and those in the North who supported their efforts emotionally and financially. She held this job through October 1871. At that time she returned to South Carolina, to teach for a year at the Robert Gould Shaw Memorial School in Charleston. Following that, she moved to Washington, D.C. There, from 1871 to 1872, under Alexander Crummell, she taught at the M Street School (a black preparatory school), later renamed the Paul Laurence Dunbar High School. Her next appointment took her to the Fourth Auditor's Office of the United States Treasury department as a first-class clerk. She held this position until 1878, when she married Reverend Francis Grimké, minister of the Fifteenth Street Presbyterian Church in Washington. Charlotte Forten Grimké spent most of the rest of her life in Washington.

Through the Washington years, in spite of poor health, she reported in her journal that she was happy. Before her marriage she busied herself with work, making new friends, and renewing old relationships. Among the latter was her cousin, Charles Burleigh Purvis, a surgeon at the Freedmen's Hospital at Howard University.

On the surface, Charlotte Forten and Francis Grimké were very different from each other. Thirteen years his senior, she had been born into one of the nation's most respected black families, four generations removed from slavery. She was raised with wealth and privilege, surrounded by the elite of black Philadelphia society and some of the most well-known liberal white reformers of the time, while he and his brothers, illegitimate sons of a white plantation owner, had been slaves. Threatened once with being sold, Grimké had escaped for a time, was imprisoned when discovered, then sold to a Confederate soldier, and finally freed at the end of the Civil War. Subsequently, Francis Grimké and his brother, Archibald, traveled North and attended Lincoln University in Pennsylvania, where Francis Grimké graduated as class valedictorian in 1870. Two years later, he earned a master's degree and in 1874 studied law at Howard University. Giving up the idea of law as a career, he went to Princeton Theological Seminary and graduated in 1878, the year he married Charlotte Forten, and accepted the pastorship of the Fifteenth Street Presbyterian Church. The education of the Grimké brothers was partially paid for by their father's sister, Angelina Grimké Weld, a feminist abolitionist, who discovered her mulatto nephews and accepted them as equal members of her family in 1868. Archibald Grimké studied law at Harvard University and is best remembered for his association with the American Negro Academy, with W. E. B. Du Bois, and for his civil rights activities.

Beneath their surface dissimilarities, Francis Grimké and Charlotte Forten were well suited for each other. Like her, he was intelligent, educated, morally upright, and deeply concerned about matters of race. The Grimkés had one child, in 1880, a daughter, who died in infancy. After that, Forten Grimké turned her attention to working with her husband in his mission to the world: speaking out and writing against racism and oppression.

Between 1885 and 1890 the Grimkés lived in Jacksonville, Florida, where Francis Grimké was pastor of the Laura Street Presbyterian Church. Then they returned to Washington and to the Fifteenth Street Presbyterian Church. In addition to her church work, Charlotte Forten Grimké was deeply devoted to her niece, Angelina, Archibald Grimké's only child, who lived with them periodically.

In continuing poor health, but surrounded by good friends, who were mainly well-educated political activists, and a loving husband and niece, Charlotte Forten Grimké wrote that her last years were not sad. She enjoyed feeling at the center of the activity she most treasured. Although she spent her last thirteen months confined to bed, Francis Grimké's loving care made even this time less of a trial than it could have been. She died in her home in Washington on July 22, 1914, at the age of seventy-six.

Aside from her work for the betterment of the race, throughout her life Charlotte Forten Grimké nurtured literary aspirations. Between 1855 and the 1890s she wrote poems, essays, and at least one short story, some of which were published. Ironically, her reputation as a writer now rests on *The Journals of Charlotte Forten Grimké*, private records that have become public documents.

Life and Activities Preserved in Journal

Charlotte Forten Grimké began keeping a journal on May 24, 1854, six months after she moved to Salem. Four volumes record her thoughts and actions of the next ten years, covering much of her life from the time she went to Salem through her stay on Saint Helena Island, ending in May 1864. The fifth and final volume, with fewer entries than the earlier ones, begins in Jacksonville, in November 1885, more than twenty-one years after the close of the fourth. Periodic entries cover the period through March 1889, when she made her penultimate entry. The journal closes with a solitary entry written in Massachusetts in July 1892.

In the preface to the first volume of her journals, Charlotte Forten Grimké observed that this document represented her wish to capture in writing passing events of her life, which although of no interest to others, would provide her with pleasant memories at some future time. Specifically, she wished to record "thoughts of much-loved friends" from whom she might later be separated, and to note books she had read, places visited, and people met. In keeping with her goal for a lifetime of self-improvement, she wrote: "it will doubtless enable me to judge correctly of the growth and improvement of my mind from year to year" (Stevenson, May 1854, 58).

Charlotte Forten Grimké's first four journals convey a broad image of the first ten years (1854-1864) of the young black womanhood of one born and raised in a socially-conscious, elite black family. While the Fortens and their radical black friends also responded to their times in their own self-interests, these black men and women were at the moral center of the American tradition of social reform. Charlotte Forten's upbringing left her without ambivalence toward her duty and, in spite of her poor health, beginning in 1854, she carried it out unflinchingly.

At the same time, there were conflicts between Charlotte Forten Grimkeé's finely-developed middle-class sensibilities and her perceptions of her racial responsibility. Her reactions to the former slaves on Saint Helena Island underlie one such contested aspect of her life, and there were other symptoms as well. On the one hand, her cultural sensibilities were largely defined by her wide reading in the most genteel literature available to her and such activities as the many hours she spent in study, including learning foreign languages. Throughout her life she spared no efforts to improve her mind. In New England, the homes of the Remonds and later of the Putnams, black families with whom she lived, were as much meeting places for abolitionists and intellectuals as the Forten and Purvis homes in Philadelphia. Thus, her close associates in that crucial time in her development were largely black and white men and women of letters who were also committed to the abolitionist movement. In addition to abolitionist meetings and lectures, she regularly attended gatherings to hear speeches by such luminaries as Ralph Waldo Emerson, James Russell Lowell, Theodore Parker, and Henry Ward Beecher. Forten Grimké's journals make clear that these people gained her admiration because of their commitment to black freedom and their intellectual acumen.

On the other hand, except for a small handful of those from her own social class, the journals largely neglect the roles of black people, individually or collectively, in the reform movements. For instance, in comparison to her praise of white abolitionists, although she mentions some black activists like William Wells Brown and William Cooper Nell, she does little to highlight their historical significance. Frederick Douglass receives only two highly ambiguous passing mentions. In addition, even in the case of the Remonds, while she describes in some detail her social interactions with the family, she neglects to emphasize their full role in the movement, especially that of Sarah Parker Remond, a lecturer for the Massachusetts Anti-Slavery Society and a key political protest figure. Unfortunately, from the journals, contemporary readers learn nothing about the extent of black abolition activities at a time and in a place when they were rife.

Charlotte Forten Grimké had lifelong literary ambitions. In the mid-1850s, when she became ill, she thought seriously of writing as a way of financially supporting herself if she became an invalid. Given the reception of her work, the fulfillment of that goal would have been unlikely. Nevertheless, she persevered. *The Liberator*, which published her earliest poems in 1855 and 1856, also published "The Wind Among the Poplars" in 1859. Other poems appeared in *The National Anti-Slavery Standard*, *The Christian Recorder*, and *The Anglo-African Magazine*. Some poetry remains unpublished. In 1857, Charlotte Forten Grimké submitted the only short story she is known to have written, "The Lost Bride," to the *Ladies' Home Journal*. It was not published. But several of her essays were printed. Both *The Liberator* and the *Atlantic Monthly* published accounts of her experiences on the Sea Islands in the 1860s, and in 1893 her "Personal Recollections of Whittier" appeared in the *New England Magazine*. Her study of foreign languages gave her one success: her translation of Emil Erckmann and Alexander Chatrain's novel, *Madame Thérèse; or The Volunteers of '92*, published by Scribner's in 1869.

While Charlotte Forten Grimké did not achieve her goal of becoming a more recognized writer of the nineteenth century, her journals, one of the few such existing documents by black women of her time, are of great importance for the study of social and literary history of the period. They reveal interesting insights into the private thoughts of a representative of the group of middle-class black women who are often marginalized in the study of racial struggle and personal development. Race and how it affected her life and her collective responsibility to the group were always uppermost in Charlotte Forten Grimké's thoughts. Her insatiable drive to excel in whatever she did came from her identification with a people who, she felt, had to prove themselves to the rest of the world at all times. She demanded no less of other blacks than she did of herself, and she considered her achievements to be the proof of the capability of all blacks. Forten Grimké's journals inform us that even before W. E. B. Du Bois was born, the conflicts of double consciousness were a reality for educated activist black American women and men.

References

Billington, Ray Allen. *The Journal of Charlotte L. Forten.* New York: Norton, 1953.

Braxton, Joan M. *Black Women Writing Autobiography: A Tradition within a Tradition.* Philadelphia: Temple University Press, 1989. A study of the journals as autobiography.

Logan, Rayford W. "Charlotte L. Forten [Mrs. Francis J. Grimké]. Rayford W. Logan and Michael R. Winston, eds. *Dictionary of American Negro Biography*. New York: Norton, 1982.

———. "James Forten [Sr.]." Rayford W. Logan and Michael R. Winston, eds. *Dictionary of American Negro Biography*. New York: Norton, 1982.

Stevenson, Brenda, ed., *The Journals of Charlotte Forten Grimké.* New York: Oxford University Press, 1988. 58. Includes the complete journals.

Collections

The manuscript collection of Charlotte Forten Grimké's diaries, typescripts by her friend, Anna Julia Cooper, are at the Moorland-Spingarn Research Center.

Nellie Y. McKay

Aretha Franklin "Queen of Soul"

(1942-)

Singer

Aretha Franklin is the Queen of Soul, a title she won quickly in 1967 when the first five single records she issued on the Atlantic label each sold more than a million copies. These songs include "I Never Loved a Man," "Respect," and "Baby, I Love You." Her first album for the company, *I Never Loved a Man,* also sold more than a million, and her second did not fall far short. *Billboard, Cashbox,* and *Record World* all named her top female vocalist of 1967. The city of Detroit named February 16, 1968, Aretha Franklin Day, and the Southern Christian Leadership Conference (SCLC) gave her a special citation. One of the reasons for the award was her rendition of the Otis Redding song "Respect," which was labeled the new unofficial black national anthem, disputing the title given earlier to James W. and J. Rosamond Johnson's "Lift Every Voice and Sing." *Time* magazine gave her a cover on June 21, 1968, and rather condescendingly tried to define soul for its audience in an accompanying article. Although her career since this explosion into superstardom has had its peaks and valleys, she remains established as one of the world's greatest living singers.

Aretha Franklin's music is firmly rooted in the gospel music of the black church. Born March 25, 1942, in Memphis, Tennessee, Aretha Louise Franklin is the fourth of five children of the noted evangelist preacher and singer, Clarence La Vaughn Franklin and Barbara (Siggers) Franklin. The oldest sibling is Vaughn, the second is Erma, then Cecil—Aretha's manager for many years—then Aretha, then Carolyn, the youngest. When Aretha Franklin was two, the family moved to Detroit, where she has lived most of her life. She grew up in a substantial and comfortable residence, but when she was six, her mother left the family; she died when Aretha Franklin was ten. The housekeepers who had charge of the family while the father was touring did not adequately fill the child's need for parenting.

Among the mother substitutes were Mahalia Jackson, whose protégée she became, Clara Ward, and Dinah Washington, all famous singers and houseguests of her father's. Other musicians also stayed in the home: James Cleveland, Arthur Prysock, B. B. King, Dorothy Donegan, Lou Rawls, and Sam Cooke. James Cleveland had a particular influence on the family, helping Aretha Franklin on the piano and encouraging the girls in their formation of a gospel group that appeared in local churches and lasted eight months. Both of

Aretha Franklin

Franklin's parents were talented musicians, and her father cut many records of his singing and preaching. Mark Bego writes of him: "He rose from modest beginnings amid the cotton fields of rural Mississippi, to be heralded as 'The Man with the Million-Dollar Voice.' In the 1950s he is reputed to have commanded up to $4,000 per sermon" (11). Mahalia Jackson said Aretha Franklin's mother was one of the great gospel singers and continues, "After her mama died, the whole family wanted for love" (Bego, 13).

Of her childhood Aretha Franklin said, "We were very good kids. We roller-skated, sat on the back porch, and told jokes. I had a piano right off the back porch, and sometimes I'd sing all day, every day, with my sisters and my friends" (Bego, 16). She began playing the piano at age eight or nine, but rebelled at formal piano lessons. Clara Ward sang at Aretha's aunt's funeral so emotionally that Aretha recalls, "Clara knocked me out! From then on I knew what I wanted to do was sing" (Bego, 17).

At age twelve, Aretha Franklin sang her first solo in her father's church, New Bethel Baptist Church in Detroit, and parishioners were stunned by her expressive gospel singing. When she was fourteen, she began traveling with her father's revival. She was also widely exposed to drinking, carousing, all-night partying, and the prejudice of Southern whites. "When my father and I traveled in the South, we ran into it from time to time, usually in restaurants with separate black and white sections," Aretha Franklin recalls (Bego, 20). At age fourteen when she was strictly a gospel singer, she made her first solo recording with Chess Records. It was a startling set of hymns recorded at her father's church. (Sugar Hill reissued this recording in 1984, with the title *Aretha Gospel*.)

During this time also she joined a gospel quartet directed by Reverend James Cleveland, one of her first mentors; he taught her how to reach notes unknown to her and to sing what she felt. Her range reached five octaves, or forty notes. Traveling on gospel caravan extravaganzas with her father from age thirteen to sixteen provided Aretha Franklin with the experience for concert tours in the 1960s and 1970s. She sang with the real gospel giants.

At the age of fifteen she was a talented piano player and a teenage gospel-singing sensation, and she was just beginning to get over her childhood disappointments and the loss of her mother when she became pregnant. She named her son Clarence Franklin, after her father. Mark Bego comments, "What happened to Aretha as a teenager, set a pattern of victimization by the men in her life. At the age of fifteen, Aretha Franklin had already earned her right to sing the blues" (32).

Having dropped out of high school to have her baby in 1958, Aretha spent a lot of time at home listening to music and playing the piano. She was fascinated by the blues, especially by blues singer Dinah Washington. She began to plan how she was going to leave her family and try to succeed on her own. At age eighteen she decided to leave Detroit for New York City and to become a successful blues singer like Washington. She wanted to sing secular music. The break with gospel music did not mean a break with her father, who supported her career decision.

She possesses great vocal capabilities, characterized by Jim Miller: "[The] voice, a robust yet crystalline alto, is remarkable for its reliable intonation, expressive vibrato, and great range of pitch dynamics, and expression. She is able to execute changes of register, volume, and timbre with dexterity and fluency, often altering the entire color of her voice in successive verses of a song as the text demands" (163). When John Hammond of Columbia Records recalled his introduction to Aretha Franklin's singing through a demonstration record, he said, "This is the best voice I've heard in twenty years!" (Bego, 39). Hammond, who had also signed famous singers Billie Holiday and Bessie Smith, became Aretha Franklin's producer.

The five-year contract with Columbia that she signed in 1960 led to substantial but not spectacular success. The high point in this stage of her career came early, when she received the award as new star in the vocal division of *Down Beat* magazine's critics' poll in 1962, even though she does not characterize herself as a jazz singer. In July 1962 she was one of the headliners at the Newport Jazz Festival. According to Leonard Feather's *Encyclopedia of Jazz in the Sixties*, "Barbara Gardner of DB called her 'the most important female vocalist to come along in some years' and other jazz critics were equally enthusiastic. She was frequently compared with Ray Charles and Dinah Washington" (19).

The nightclub repertoire of pop songs with heavy orchestration that Columbia imposed on Aretha Franklin after the initial flirtation with jazz did not suit her and led to artistic and personal frustration. The dreary rounds of engagements in second-rate clubs did not improve matters. Her husband, Ted (Theodore Richard) White, replaced Hammond as her manager, and the pair waited out the expiration of the contract as Franklin continued to sell a modest number of records.

Aretha Franklin's move to Atlantic Records was well timed for her popularity and earning power. Al Bell of Stax explained to Phyl Garland about this time that between two hundred fifty and three hundred thousand sales represented the normal saturation point in the black market and to go beyond this figure needed the dollars of white consumers, basically teenagers and adults under twenty-five (*The Sound of Soul*, 128-29). For a decade the white consumer had been exposed to white performers, like Elvis Presley and many others, who had drawn upon (some would say ripped off) black music, and the white audience was now beginning to buy the records of black musicians. This was the discovery that made Motown and its stars giants in the music business, and Atlantic was actively working in the same vein. Franklin was now able to choose her own material and her own style. Thus, she was able to reach a wide audience without abandoning the qualities that made up her unique appeal to the black public. It was her enormous musical gift that ensured that her success was no flash in the pan.

As Jimmy Wexler, vice-president of Atlantic, gave Aretha Franklin the artistic freedom to choose her own materials, she drew upon her roots. Phyl Garland writes that a popular female contemporary said, "Aretha's still singing the same thing that she used to sing in church, except that now instead of saying 'My Lord,' she says, 'My man'" (24). (The great pioneer in this vein had been Ray Charles.) She also found a congenial way of working with the possibilities of recording technology: She first sings and plays the piano; then she is one of the backup voices as they are added; and finally, the rhythm and instrumental tracks are added. The results made music history.

Four Grammy Awards Won Early in Career

Between 1967 and 1969, Aretha Franklin won four Grammy awards: "Respect," the best rhythm and blues (R&B) recording for 1967; "Respect," the best R&B performance for a female in 1967; "Chain of Fools," the best R&B performance for a female in 1968; and "Share Your Love with Me," the best R&B performance for a female in 1969.

Her records selling more than a million copies include: "I Never Loved a Man (The Way I Love You)"/"Do Right Woman—Do Right Man" (Atlantic, 1967); "Respect"/"Dr. Feelgood" (Atlantic, 1967); "Lee Cross," "Until You Were Gone" (Columbia, 1967); "Baby, I Love You" (Atlantic, 1967); "Chain of Fools" (Atlantic, 1967); ("Sweet Sweet Baby) Since You've Been Gone"/"Ain't No Way" (Atlantic, 1968); "Think"/"You Send Me" (Atlantic, 1968); "The House that Jack Built"/"I Say a Little Prayer" (Atlantic, 1968); and "My Song" (Atlantic, 1968).

Her million-copy records in the decade 1970-1979 were: "Don't Play That Song for Me" (Atlantic, 1970); "Bridge Over Troubled Water"/"Brand New Me" (Atlantic, 1971); "Spanish Harlem" (Atlantic, 1971); "Rock Steady"/"Oh Me Oh My (I'm a Fool for You Baby)" (Atlantic, 1971); "Day Dreaming" (Atlantic, 1972); and "Until You Come Back to Me (That's What I'm Gonna Do)" (Atlantic, 1973).

There were six Grammy Awards for Aretha Franklin in the 1970s. They were "Don't Play That Song for Me" (Best R&B performance for a female in 1970); "Bridge Over Troubled Water" (Best R&B performance for a female in 1971); "Young, Gifted and Black" (Best R&B performance for a female in 1972); "Amazing Grace" (Best Soul Gospel performance in 1972); "Master of Eyes" (Best R&B performance for a female in 1973); and "Ain't Nothing Like the Real Thing" (Best R&B performance for a female in 1974). There were no million-copy records in the 1980s, but five Grammys: "Hold On, I'm Comin'"; "Freeway of Love," (Aretha album) (Best R&B performance for a female in 1985); "I Knew You Were Waiting (For Me)," and "One Lord, One Faith, One Baptism."

Aretha Franklin's life is as private as she can make it; as soon as it was feasible she arranged to spend two weeks out of every four at her Detroit home. Many people have perceived a discrepancy between the very shy person and the direct and uninhibited singer, a quality they remarked in the difference between her speaking voice and her singing voice. The directness of her singing is the quality the *Time* cover story, among others, emphasized:

> She does not seem to be performing so much as bearing witness to a reality so simple and compelling that she could not possibly fake it. In her selection of songs, whether written by others or by herself, she unfailingly opts for those that frame her own view of life. "If a song's about something I've experienced or that could have happened to me, it's good," she says. "But if it's alien to me, I couldn't lend anything to it. Because that's what soul is about—just living and having to get along" ("Lady Soul," 62).

The apparent directness of the songs has helped fuel the rumor mill. There were plenty of rumors and some public scenes in her first marriage to Ted White, who first met her in 1959. Aretha Franklin's marriage to Ted White lasted from 1961 to 1969 and produced two sons, Edward and Teddy, Jr. With the break from Ted White, she lost much of her confidence. According to Bego, "She really let loose after she left Ted" (128). It was hard for her to confront her problems head on, and she kept a low profile as she sorted out her personal life. She would cancel concerts at times of stress, a career-long habit.

Aretha Franklin's fourth son, Kecalf, born in 1970, was fathered by her new romance, Ken Cunningham. "Kecalf" combines Ken's name and Aretha's initials. Ken Cunningham had been her road manager in the late 1960s after her breakup with Ted White. Cunningham and Franklin had a six-year relationship, although they never married. He was responsible for the photography on her albums, and he helped her focus in a way that Ted White never had been able to do. Cunningham helped her to drink less and, in 1974, to shed some forty pounds she had put on in the late 1960s (Bego, 141). She broke up with him and found herself again free and single in 1977.

While appearing at a benefit for underprivileged children in the Los Angeles area, Aretha Franklin's son Clarence told actor Glynn Turman, "My mother just loves you." When asked, "Who's your mother?" Clarence said, "Aretha Franklin." Almost instantly, Aretha Franklin and Turman fell madly in love (Bego, 172). On April 12, 1978, they married at her father's New Bethel Baptist Church. In 1982 her storybook marriage suddenly and mysteriously ended, although she said that she moved back to Detroit because of her father's illness (Bego, 214). The Reverend C. L. Franklin had been shot by a burglar on June 11, 1979, and remained in a coma for five years. This tragedy deeply affected Franklin. She was at his bedside when he died on July 24, 1984. She gave two performances, in 1979 and 1981, as benefits to raise money for her father's hospitalization. Her sister Erma said, "She spent over a half million dollars on him, $1500 a week just for nurses. She and my dad were very, very, very close" (Bego, 221).

Aretha Franklin was always very generous and raised much money through benefit concerts. Causes that were worthwhile to her included the New Bethel Missionary Baptist Church's Relief Center and Mother Waddles's Perpetual Mission (*Jet,* 26 December 1989, 26). As Aretha Franklin said, "I do community work, donating to various organizations such as sickle-cell anemia and United Negro College Fund and the NAACP. I'm conscious of being a role model for children" (Bego, 289).

She also used her voice to raise funds at Carnegie Hall for the Joffrey Ballet in 1982, where tickets sold for one thousand dollars each. The Joffrey Ballet has honored Franklin by presenting a ballet that was choreographed using her music. In 1988 she did a public-service announcement against driving under the influence of drugs and liquor. Her hit record, "Think," was titled "Think . . . Don't Drive with Drugs or Drink!" (Bego, 279).

Singer Called Natural Resource

In 1986 Michigan legislators proclaimed Aretha Franklin's voice to be one of the state's natural resources because she had twenty-four gold records in the previous twenty years. In August 1989 Senator Carl Levin of Michigan presented Aretha Franklin with a plaque and a Senate resolution for her achievements in music and her contributions to the fight against drunk driving. Senator Lloyd Bentsen of Texas praised her continued appeal against drunk driving across generations and races, calling her "Our personal Dr. Feelgood." Levin said, "For this dedication to her craft, and her community, she earned what all of us covet—"R-E-S-P-E-C-T." Visibly moved, Aretha Franklin responded, "I'm overwhelmed. It is not every day that such a distinguished group of people presents such distinguished awards. I thank you so very much" (*Jet,* 7 August, 1989, 59).

Singing with her family was a lifelong venture. Franklin's brother and manager, Cecil Franklin, explained that Aretha Franklin's career began at age ten in his Baptist church, but it came to a halt after their father was shot. Cecil died at age forty-nine of a heart attack in 1990 (*Jet,* 15 January 1990, 14). Their sister Carolyn had died of cancer in May 1988. Carolyn had trained the background singers for her sister for many years. For thirty years, Cissy Houston, a close relative, recorded with Aretha Franklin. According to Bego, "in the 60s Cissy and The Sweet Inspirations began doing background vocals for everyone in the music business" (Bego, 117). Other members making it a family affair were two of Aretha Franklin's sons. As Bego relates, "One song, 'Giving In,' was written by Aretha's oldest son, Clarence, and another son, Teddy F. White, Jr., played the 'fill guitar' on the song" (Bego, 215).

Aretha Franklin has been in the record business for more than thirty years. She has had a career that other female vocalists can only dream of matching. She is to contemporary pop and soul music what Ella Fitzgerald is to jazz singing. Aretha Franklin's vast wealth of creative achievements is staggering. She has launched into the 1990s with her fame at an all-time high, and her fans await what the future holds.

References

"Aretha Gives Christmas Benefit Show for Needy." *Jet* 77 (26 December 1989): 26.

Bego, Mark. *Aretha Franklin.* New York: St. Martin's Press, 1989.

Current Biography Yearbook. New York: H. W. Wilson, 1968. 132-34.

Feather, Leonard. *The Encyclopedia of Jazz in the Sixties.* New York: Bonanza Books, 1966. 119.

Feather, Leonard and Ira Gitler. *The Encyclopedia of Jazz in the Seventies.* New York: Horizon, 1976. 138.

Garland, Phyl. *The Sound of Soul.* Chicago: Regnery, 1969. 24, 128-29, 191-203.

"Lady Soul: Singing It Like It Is." *Time* 91 (21 June 1968): 62-66. Cover portrait.

Low, W. Augustus, and Virgil A. Clift. *Encyclopedia of Black America.* New York: McGraw-Hill, 1981. 393.

Miller, Jim. "Cruising the Freeway of Love." *Newsweek* (26 August 1985): 69.

Miller, Jim. "Aretha Franklin." *New Grove Dictionary of American Music.* Edited by H. Wiley Hitchcock and Stanley Sadie. New York: Macmillan, 1986. 163-64.

Moses, Mark. *New Yorker* 63 (1 February 1988): 84-87.

"A Native of Detroit." *Jet* 76 (7 August 1989): 59.

Ploski, Harry A., and James Williams, comps. and eds. *Negro Almanac*. Detroit: Gale Research, 1989.

"Queen of Soul's Brother Rev. Cecil Franklin Dies of Heart Attack in Detroit." *Jet* 77 (15 January 1990): 14.

Southern, Eileen. *Biographical Dictionary of Afro-American and African Musicians*. Westport, Conn.: Greenwood Press, 1982. 137.

Who's Who Among Black Americans, 1990/1991. 6th ed. Detroit: Gale Research, 1990. 433.

Virginia Wilson Wallace

Charlotte White Franklin

(19?-)

Artist, educator

Renowned artist Charlotte White Franklin is a native of Philadelphia, Pennsylvania, and received her education in the Philadelphia schools. She is the daughter of Charles Fred White, a lawyer, real estate broker, civic figure, and the first black athletic commissioner of the Commonwealth of Pennsylvania, and Mary White.

Franklin has studied at the Tyler School of Art at Temple University in Philadelphia as well as San Fernando College of Art and the University of Madrid in Spain. She holds a B.A. (1945) and M.F.A. (1947) from the Tyler School of Art and also has taken postgraduate courses there. Franklin also holds a B.A. (1946) from the College of Education at Temple. She has studied further at the Instituto San Miguel de Allende at Guanajuato, Mexico (1947); Mexico City College (1958); the Escuela Nacional de Bellas Artes, Buenos Aires, Argentina (1960); the University of London (1960); and Temple University Abroad in Rome, Italy (1967). Franklin has received numerous honors and awards, that include a Fulbright Fellowship and a Philadelphia Board of Education Fellowship which enabled her to study at the universities of Madrid and Rome.

Franklin is an art teacher of renown and has served as chair of the art department in secondary education in the Philadelphia Public School System, as well as teacher at the Philadelphia Museum of Art. She has taught abroad in Surrey, England, and Buenos Aires, Argentina.

Exhibitions in which her works have been shown include the WCAU-TV studios; the Bi-Centennial Exhibition; Memorial Hall, Fairmont Park; Black Artists of Pennsylvania at Harrisburg; William Penn Memorial Museum; and the Exhibition of Monuments to Blacks in the American Revolution. She has exhibited one-woman shows in Cheam, Sutton, Charleston, and Surrey, England. She has also exhibited at Curitieva, Brazil (1960); Villa Jones, Mexico City (1964); Philadelphia Community College (1969); Drexel University (1969); Fine Arts Gallery, John Wanamaker Department Store (1970); Friends Select School (1971); Temple University (1971); Latin American Festival (1971); University of Pennsylvania (1974); Drexel University (1974); LaSalle College; Institute of Culture; Philomathean Literary Society Gallery; Women's University Club; and the Bi-National Gallery. Franklin also exhibited at sundry charities, civic centers, YMCAs and YWCAs, sorority houses, and other organizations from 1940 through 1960. Her work has been shown in California, Illinois, Pennsylvania, New York, Delaware, New Jersey, and other states.

Group shows in which Franklin has participated are Les Beaux Arts, Philadelphia (1940 and 1950); Rittenhouse Square Clothes Line exhibits (1940s-1950s); Atlanta University (1944); Philadelphia Festival (1967-1975); International Art Exhibit, American Association of University Women (1971); Focus (1974); ABC-TV Lounge (1974); Second World Art and Cultural Festival, Lagos, Nigeria (1974); University of Pennsylvania Press Museum (1974); Philadelphia's Art Alliance (1975); Philadelphia Museum Arts Council; Philadelphia Women in the Arts, Temple University; Philadelphia Board of Education, Afro-American Show, Civic Center; Association of Delaware Valley Arts Annual; American Exhibiting Artist Annual; Lee Cultural Center Annual; Free Library of Philadelphia; National Forums of Professional Artists Annual; Academy of Fine Arts; and Philadelphia Art Teachers Association.

Portraits of Black Women Executed

Franklin has executed portraits of fifteen distinguished black American women from Delta Sigma Theta Sorority that were exhibited at the Afro-American Historical and Cultural Museum of Philadelphia in 1976. Her portrait series of twenty-four black inventors commissioned by the Philadelphia Electric Company in 1977 is in the permanent collection of the Philadelphia Afro-American Historical and Cultural Museum.

The Three Martyrs Portraits hangs in Shaw Junior High School in Philadelphia. Franklin's other works include *Corner Boys*, *Cera del Mercado, Mexico City*, *Bahama Food Market*, *Nassau Straw Market*, *Los Andes, Huancayo, Peru*, *Carnival in Rio de Janiero*, *Listening to Dr. King's Dream*, *Half*, *The Rain God*, *Los Pabres*, *Street in Morocco*. *War Bride*, and *The Fishmonger*.

Franklin has appeared on several radio and television stations. She has presented demonstration lectures for art teachers and school assemblies as well as a demonstration lecture on ancient Africa.

Franklin holds memberships in the Secondary School Curriculum Committee for African and Afro-American Studies for the School District of Philadelphia Board of Education. She is a member of the Philadelphia Urban League, the NAACP, Common Cause, Public Citizen, Friends of the Free Library, Trustee of the Afro-American Historical and Cultural Museum, the Tafreta Gallery, Society of British Artists, National Forum of Professional Artists, Philadelphia Art Teacher's Association, Philadelphia Women's University Club, and Philadelphia North Art Council. Franklin has chaired the Wanamaker Junior High Bicentennial Committee and is a member of the National Society of Literature and the Arts as well as the Philadelphia Writers Club. She is listed in the *Crafts Directory U.S.A.* and the *International Registry of Profiles* in Cambridge, England.

Franklin's awards are numerous and include certificates of honor from 1975 through 1976 from the Philadelphia Afro-American Cultural and Historical Museum, Delta Sigma Theta Sorority, the Commemorative Bi-Centennial Print Series, Monuments to Blacks in the American Revolution, and the Federal Bar Association.

Her versatility is shown in her writings, which include an operetta, *Footnotes for Americans*, done for the Philadelphia public schools; "Fish and Chips," a television drama (1970); "Continental Construction, Africa" (1971), a portfolio; "Footnote of Blackfeet" (1973-74); and "Ancient African Continental Construction" (1975).

Charlotte White Franklin, who is divorced, has one daughter, Charma Leigha Franklin, who is also an artist and a secondary school art teacher. Both mother and daughter have participated in a tandem exhibition of their works in the inaugural show of the Women's Cultural Center Gallery of the Philadelphia Mid-City YWCA in 1974.

A skillful craftsman, Charlotte White Franklin works with flamboyant skills in cubist-oriented techniques. Her landscapes, markets, street scenes, carnivals, and workers are personalized documentations in disciplined and often muted color. Her canvases record her visual experiences in Central and South America, her Spanish and Italian travels, and American subjects.

References

Cederholm, Theresa Dickason. *Afro-American Artists: A Bio-Bibliographical Directory*. Boston: Boston Public Library, 1973.

Margaret Burroughs

J. E. Franklin

(1937-)

Playwright

Jennie Elizabeth Franklin, also called J. E. Franklin, is best known as the playwright of *Black Girl*, produced in 1971. However, she has had a varied career that includes writing additional plays and working as educator, analyst, and social service director. Franklin was born in Houston, Texas, on August 10, 1937, one of thirteen children in the family of Robert Franklin and Mathie (Robert) Franklin. While still a child, Franklin began recording her impressions of life in writing. In 1964 she received a B.A. degree from the University of Texas and in the same year married Lawrence Seigel, now deceased. She has one daughter, Malike N'Zinga.

In the summer of 1964 Franklin was a primary-school teacher in the Freedom School of Carthage, Mississippi. This job was followed by service as a youth director at the Neighborhood House in Buffalo, New York (1964-65); as an analyst in the United States Office of Economic Opportunity in New York City (1967-68); and as a lecturer in education at the Herbert N. Lehman College in the City University of New York (1969-75).

Franklin's playwriting began before the 1970s when the success of *Black Girl* brought her to the attention of theatergoers. Her first play to be performed, *First Step to Freedom* (1964), combined her interest in education and writing. This work was performed in Harmony, Mississippi, as part of the Congress of Racial Equality Student Nonviolent Coordinating Committee program to interest students in reading.

In 1971 Wooding King, Jr., produced *Black Girl* at the New Federal Theater before it was moved to the Theatre de Lys, where it ran for 234 performances. Franklin, King, and Shaunelle Perry, the director, proved to be a powerful trio, for audiences filled the theater and waited after each performance to congratulate members of the cast. For black theatergoers, *Black Girl* was the play to see. The play went on tour and also became a movie with Ossie Davis as director and Franklin as author of the screenplay. *Black Girl* involves the character, Billie Jean, a high school dropout who, in spite of being suppressed by both society and her matriarchal family, aspires to become a ballet dancer. Making choices is the underlying theme, which the playwright believes should be at the core of black theater and the arts.

In 1974 *The Prodigal Sister*, a musical with book and lyrics by Franklin and music and lyrics by Micki Grant, opened at the Theatre de Lys. This work was Franklin's second major New York production. The director was again Shaunelle Perry and the producer Woodie King, Jr. *The Prodigal Sister* concentrates on the experiences of a black girl, an unwed mother-to-be who leaves home to avoid her father's stern disapproval. Alone in the city, she has several bad experiences before returning home, this time to an understanding father. The scenes in the musical are divided into "beats," with a "Do Wah" musical group as an important ingredient.

In addition to dramatic works, Franklin has written other plays, including *The In-Crowd* (1965), *Mau Mau Room* (1972), and *Cut Out the Lights and Call the Law* (1972). In 1977 *In-Crowd* was produced as a musical in the New Federal Theatre.

Playwright Brings Feminine Voice to Theater

Franklin has brought a fresh, strong feminine voice to black theater. In her two major productions, she won the approval of audiences as well as many critics. Focusing her creative eye on black women, she has presented major characters who, in overcoming nearly insurmountable difficulties, give hints of continued progress.

Franklin is a member of the Authors League of America, Dramatics Guild, and Professional Staff Congress. Her awards include Media Women Award (1971), New York Drama Desk Most Promising Playwright Award (1971), Institute for the Arts and Humanities dramatic arts award from Howard University (1974), Ajabei Children's Theatre Annual Award (1978), Better Boys Foundation Playwriting Award (1978), and National Endowment of the Creative Arts Writing Fellowship (1979). In 1980 she was awarded a Rockefeller grant.

Franklin has also contributed articles to periodicals and has a work in progress: *Split the Atom: Theological Roots of Ontological Engineering*—research on the effects of metabiological engineering on the human species embodying art centered education in a unique approach to learning.

References

Black Writers. Detroit: Gale Research, 1989.

Wall, Ellen. *Dictionary of the Black Theatre*. Westport, Conn.: Greenwood Press, 1983.

Jean Blackwell Hutson

Martha Minerva Franklin

(1870-1968)

Nurse, civil rights activist, organization founder

Martha Minerva Franklin was one of the first nurses to campaign actively for racial equality for black nurses and the first to campaign nationally for such rights. Through her pioneering interest in improving the status of the black nurse, she was the founder and organizer of the National Association of Colored Graduate Nurses (NACGN).

Franklin was born on October 29, 1870, in New Milford, Connecticut. Her parents were Henry J. Franklin and Mary E. (Gauson) Franklin. Three children were born in the family: Martha was the middle child, having an older sister and a younger brother. The Franklin family resided in Meriden, Connecticut, and Martha attended Meriden Public High School, from which she graduated in 1890.

In 1895, at age twenty-five, Franklin entered the Woman's Hospital Training School for Nurses of Philadelphia. She graduated in December 1897 and was the only black graduate in her class. After graduation she returned to her home in Meriden, where she did private-duty nursing for a few years, later pursuing the same type of work in New Haven.

In the fall of 1906, Franklin began to study the status of the black graduate nurse in the United States. As a result of her two-year study, Franklin recognized that black nurses shared concerns and needed effective help that they must initiate themselves. She further believed that the organization of a national association of black American nurses would gain them recognition and would in time make it possible for them to serve the American public without racial bias. Thus, she sent out fifteen hundred handwritten letters asking nurses to consider a meeting in the near future.

Franklin Organizes National Association for Nurses

Adah Bell Samuels Thoms, president of Lincoln School of Nursing Alumnae Association, responded, inviting Franklin and interested nurses to meet in New York City as guests of the association. Fifty-two nurses attended the August 1908 meeting and Franklin set forth its purpose. She suggested that a permanent national organization of "colored" graduate nurses be formed to bring the nurses together to share and understand their problems. Her interests and goals were: to eradicate discrimination in the nursing profession, to develop leadership among black nurses, and to promote higher standards in administration and education. These goals were adopted as the goals of the NACGN.

Black physicians organized the National Medical Association (NMA) because they, too, experienced discrimination in practicing their profession. Their annual meeting was in New York City in 1908, at the same time the black nurses were holding their first meeting. Many doctors from the NMA attended the nurses' meeting to give encouragement and to pledge their support for this new endeavor.

In 1909 Franklin was unanimously elected president, thus serving for the first two years of this organization as its president. She was nominated and urged to serve a third term as president, but she declined. However, she was designated honorary president for life. Franklin remained involved with the organization and was permanently elected its historian. Through this national endeavor, Franklin developed a professional bond and personal friendship with Mary Mahoney, the first trained black nurse, and with Adah Belle Samuels Thoms. Although historical literature reveals very little about Franklin, it is known that she was slender, very fair in complexion, and often mischaracterized as a white nurse friend of ''colored'' nurses.

One of the first nursing leaders to recognize the NACGN was Lillian Wald of the Henry Street Settlement. Another leader and early friend was Lavinia Dock, secretary of the International Council of Nurses (ICN), who gave the officers of the NACGN advice on organization. Recognition by these two leaders was a valuable asset to the NACGN. Dock invited the NACGN to send a representative to the 1912 ICN meeting in Cologne, Germany. This was the first opportunity black nurses had to meet with other nurses at an international convention. The NACGN became internationally recognized, and this was the beginning for black nurses to join and participate in the ICN.

From its small beginnings, the NACGN grew to a membership of two thousand during World War I and over twelve thousand by 1940, with members from nearly every state. As membership increased, a national registry was established to aid black nurses in securing positions. The NACGN developed community and national support systems by establishing a local citizen's committee in New York State and an advisory council on the national level.

During the 1920s Franklin relocated to New York City. She enrolled in a six-month postgraduate course at Lincoln Hospital, became a registered nurse in New York State, and was employed as a school nurse in the New York City public school system. At the age of fifty-eight, still interested in continuing her education, she became a student at Teachers College, Columbia University, from 1928 to 1930, majoring in public health nursing.

Franklin never married. After living and working in New York for many years, she returned to New Haven and resided with her sister. At ninety years of age, Franklin was confined to her home and was unable to attend church regularly on Sundays due to her physical condition. Edwin Edmonds, past and present pastor of the Dixwell Congregational Church of Christ where Franklin was a member, knew her very well.

Edmonds visited Franklin at her home regularly for eight years prior to her death. He stated that ''she was a strong woman with character. Martha was a proud woman, and as an aged woman, Martha retained her dignity and polished mannerism.'' At times, he said, ''Martha reminisced about the Depression, a difficult time in which she maintained her dignity and refused to be made into a fieldhand'' (Interview with Edwin Edwards, 13 June 1986).

Franklin lived to the ripe age of ninety-eight and died of natural causes on September 26, 1968. Her gravesite is at Walnut Grove Cemetery in Meriden, Connecticut.

References

Carnegie, M. E. *The Path We Tread.* Philadelphia: Lippincott, 1986. Photograph, p. 93.

Davis, Althea T. ''Architects for Integration and Equality: Early Black American Leaders in Nursing.'' Ph.D dissertation. Teachers College, Columbia University, 1987.

Edmonds, Edwin. Interview with author. 13 June 1986.

Althea T. Davis

Elizabeth Freeman "Mum Bett" "Mumbet"

(c. 1744-1829)

Servant, nurse

During her lifetime and even after he death, she was known to the world as Mum Bett, a name apparently derived from Elizabeth. Lacking a surname, she sued for her freedom under the name of Bett, and she adopted the name Elizabeth Freeman upon winning her case in 1781. The proposed date of her birth is derived from the estimate on her gravestone that she was about eighty-five when she died on December 28, 1829. The stone further states that she was a slave ''for nearly thirty years,'' which would place the birth year around 1751 (Swan, 55). Theodore Sedgwick, Jr., a son in the family for whom she worked for many years, says that ''she supposed herself to be nearly a hundred years old'' (Sedgwick, 16). It is clear that Elizabeth Freeman was unsure of her age and that she lived long.

Elizabeth Freeman and her sister were born slaves of Pieter Hogeboom of Claverack, New York. It is asserted that both of her parents were born in Africa, but the only trace of them is her bequest to her daughter of "a 'black silk gown,' gift of her African father, and a 'short gown' that her African mother had worn" (Kaplan, 217). Pieter Hogeboom died in 1758. This may be the date that Elizabeth Freeman passed into the hands of the Ashley family, since Hogeboom's youngest daughter, Hannah, had married John Ashley of Sheffield, Massachusetts, in 1735. Ashley was a leading citizen of Sheffield and, eventually, a cautious revolutionary. From 1761 until he resigned in 1781, at the time when Elizabeth Freeman's suit came before his court, he was a judge of the Court of Common Pleas. He also held other state and local positions. In 1773 he was the chairman of the committee that drew up the Sheffield Declaration; the committee probably met at his house, and its clerk was twenty-six-year-old lawyer Theodore Sedgwick. The declaration contained a resolution stating: "Resolve that Mankind in a State of Nature are equal, free and independent of each other, and have a right to the undisturbed Enjoyment of their lives, their Liberty and Property" (Swan, 52).

This talk of liberty was not overlooked by Elizabeth Freeman. She never learned how to read and write, but she knew how to listen. According to Harriet Martineau's account, she learned:

> "By keepin' still and mindin' things." But what did she mean, she was asked, by keeping still and minding things? Why, for instance, when she was waiting a table, she heard gentlemen talking over the Bill of Rights and the new constitution of Massachusetts; and in all they said she never heard but that all people were born free and equal, and she thought long about it, and resolved she would try whether she did not come in among them (105).

It was in 1780 that Massachusetts approved its new constitution, and the following year a major incident occurred between Elizabeth Freeman and her mistress, Hannah Ashley. Theodore Sedgwick, Jr., says:

> In [the] state of familiar intercourse, instances of cruelty were uncommon, and the minds of the slaves were not so much subdued but that they caused a degree of indignation not much less than if committed upon a freeman.
>
> Under this condition of society, while Mum Bett resided in the family of Col. Ashley, she received a severe wound in a generous attempt to shield her sister. Her mistress in a fit of passion resorted to a degree and mode of violence very uncommon in this country: she struck at the weak and timid girl with a heated kitchen shovel; Mum Bett interposed her arm, and received the blow; and she bore the honorable scar it left to the day of her death. The spirit of Mum Bett had not been broken down by ill usage—she resented the insult and outrage as a white person would have done. She left the house, and neither commands nor entreaties could induce her to return (15).

Slave Sues for Freedom

Freeman sought legal help from Theodore Sedgwick, Sr., who undertook her case, which was heard in Great Barrington on August 21, 1781, as *Brom and Bett v. J. Ashley Esq.* All we know of Brom is that he was a black laborer of Sheffield, and Bett is identified as a spinster. The plaintiffs alleged that they were being illegally detained in bondage, and the jury found for them and ordered Ashley to pay thirty shillings damages and court costs. Ashley dropped his appeal of this ruling later after the Massachusetts Supreme Court ruled in another case that slavery was unconstitutional under the state constitution.

Elizabeth Freeman became a paid servant in the household of Theodore Sedgwick, who moved from Sheffield to Stockbridge in 1785. We know little of her own family. Theodore Sedgwick, Jr., says that she married at an early age and had one child. He adds that her husband died "in the continental service in the revolutionary war" and that she remained a widow for the rest of her life (16). Her will, signed with a cross on October 18, 1829, shows that she had a daughter, grandchildren, and great-grandchildren. W. E. B. Du Bois claims a family connection. In *Darkwater* (1920) he says that she was the cousin of his grandmother (173), but in *Dusk of Dawn* (1940), he identifies her as the second wife of his great-grandfather Jacob Burghardt, born about 1760; the direct line of descent is through Jacob's wife, Violet, with whom he had five sons and four daughters (110-114).

The Sedgwick connection, in contrast, is well documented: Four of the children of Theodore Sedgwick, Sr., left memorials of Elizabeth Freeman. In 1811 Susan Sedgwick painted in watercolors on ivory the portrait that is now in the possession of the Massachusetts Historical Society; Charles Sedgwick composed the long inscription on her gravestone; Theodore Sedgwick, Jr., used her as an exemplar in the antislavery lecture he delivered to the Stockbridge Lyceum in 1831; and Catharine Sedgwick, a novelist famous in her era, wrote about her in 1853. The family would have had need of her help: The younger Theodore, the second child and the oldest son, had been born in December 1780, and eight more children were to follow (two of the ten died young). The youngest, Catharine, was born on December 28, 1789. In addition, the mother, Pamela (Dwight) Sedgwick, suffered from several bouts of insanity, possibly severe depression, before her death in 1807. Catharine Sedgwick writes that Elizabeth Freeman was "the only person who could tranquilize my mother when her mind was disordered. . . . She treated her with the same respect she did when she was sane . . . her superior instincts hit upon the mode of treatment that has since been adopted" (cited in Swan, 55). Both Catharine and Theodore Sedgewick, Jr., attest to the high reputation Elizabeth Freeman had as a nurse.

Elizabeth Freeman's spirit is revealed in the family anecdotes about her behavior during Shay's Rebellion (1786). Theodore Sedgwick, Sr., was away, and she had to deal with the men who invaded the house. She is said to have hidden the family silver in her own chest of possessions and shamed the men into not searching it; the events are recounted with considerable elaboration by Harriet Martineau (106-109). Theodore Sedgwick, Jr., writes:

> She did not attempt to resist, by direct force, the rifling of property, which was one of the objects of the insurgents. She, however, assumed a degree of authority; told the plunderers that they "dare not strike a woman," and attended them in their exploring the house, to prevent wanton destruction. She escorted them into the cellar with a large kitchen shovel in her hand, which she intimated that she would use in case of necessity. One of the party broke off the neck of a bottle of porter. She told him that if he or his companions desired to drink porter, she would fetch a corkscrew, and draw a cork, as they might drink like gentlemen; but that, if another bottle should be broken, she would lay the man that broke it flat with her shovel. Upon tasting the liquor, the party decided that "if gentlemen loved such cursed bitter stuff, they might keep it" (17).

He concludes his praise of Elizabeth Freeman by stating:

> Having know this woman as familiarly as I knew either of my parents, I *cannot* believe in the moral of physical inferiority of the race to which she belonged. The degradation of the African must have been otherwise caused than by natural inferiority. Civilization has made slow progress, in every portion of the earth; where it has made progress, it proceeds in an accelerated ratio (18-19).

When Elizabeth Freeman finally retired she had enough money to buy a small house of her own. During her final illness she was visited daily by Catharine Sedgwick, who wrote, "I felt as awed as if I had entered the presence of Washington. Even protracted suffering and mortal sickness . . . could not break down her spirit" (cited in Swan, 5). After her death she was buried in the Sedgwick family plot in Stockbridge Cemetery—the only black and the only non-Sedgwick. Her gravestone reads:

> ELIZABETH FREEMAN, known by the name of MUMBET died Dec. 28 1829. Her supposed age was 85 years. She was born a slave and remained a slave for nearly thirty years. She could neither read nor write, yet in her own sphere she had no superior nor equal. She neither wasted time nor property. She never violated a trust, nor failed to perform a duty. In every situation of domestic trial, she was the most efficient helper, and the tenderest friend. Good mother fare well (Swan, 55).

Catharine Sedgwick recollected a sentence Elizabeth Freeman uttered:

> Anytime, anytime while I was a slave, if one minute's freedom had been offered to me, and I had been told I must die at the end of that minute, I would have taken it—just to stand one minute on God's earth a free woman—I would (cited in Swan, 54).

References

Chaffee, Zechariah, Jr. "Theodore Sedgwick." *Dictionary of American Biography*. Vol. 16. Ed. Dumas Malone. New York: Charles Scribner's Sons, 1935.

Dannett, Sylvia G. L. *Profiles of Negro Womanhood*. Vol. 1. Yonkers, N.Y.: Educational Heritage, 1964.

Du Bois, W. E. Burghardt. *Darkwater: Voices From Within the Veil*. New York: Harcourt, Brace and Howe, 1920.

———. *Dusk of Dawn: An Essay Toward an Autobiography of a Race Concept*. New York: Harcourt, Brace, 1940.

Kaplan, Sidney. *The Black Presence in the Era of the American Revolution 1770-1800*. New York: New York Graphic Society in association with the Smithsonian Institution Press, 1973. Portrait, plate 7 following p. 84.

Logan, Rayford W. "Elizabeth Freeman." *Dictionary of American Negro Biography*. Ed. Rayford W. Logan and Michael R. Winston. New York: Norton, 1982.

Martineau, Harriet. *Retrospect of Western Travel*. Vol. 2. London: Saunders and Otley, 1838.

Nell, William C. *The Colored Patriots of the American Revolution*. Boston: R. F. Wallcut, 1855. Reprinted. New York: Arno Press and the New York Times, 1968. Reprints portion of Theodore Sedgwick's pamphlet.

[Sedgwick, Theodore]. *The Practicability of the Abolition of Slavery*. New York: J. Seymour, 1831.

Swan, Jon. "The Slave Who Sued for Freedom." *American Heritage* 41 (March 1990): 51-52, 54-55. Portrait, p. 51; photograph of gravestone, p. 55.

Robert L. Johns

Meta Warrick Fuller

(1877-1968)

Sculptor

Meta Vaux Warrick Fuller has been characterized as "an elegant Victorian, deeply spiritual sculptor . . . [and] one of the most important precursors of the [Harlem] Renaissance" (Campbell, 25). The diminutive and strikingly beautiful artist was born in Philadelphia on June 9, 1877. Her parents, William and Emma Warrick, were considered well-to-do, since they owned and operated businesses in Philadelphia and Atlantic City. A great-grandmother was reputed to have been an Ethiopian princess brought to the American colonies as a slave. Emma Warrick, like her father, Henry Jones, served a mostly Caucasian clientele with the daughter owning and operating hairdressing parlors and the father operating a society catering business. William Warrick dabbled in real estate and owned a chain of barber shops. Meta Warrick was actually named for a favored client of her mother's, the daughter of a prominent senator. Two older siblings, William and Blanche, completed her immediate family. The two sisters learned the hairdressing trade and worked in their mother's shops with Blanche eventually becoming a full partner; William, the brother, became a physician.

Meta Warrick's artistic talents were not limited to just the visual arts. She also played the guitar, took private dancing lessons, and sang in a church choir. Fuller's father was her biggest booster and provided early art appreciation experiences by exposing her to the beauties of nature and museum art during her childhood. Fuller's first formal training was at J. Liberty Tadd Industrial Art School, after which she received a three-year scholarship to the Pennsylvania School of Industrial Art and a post-graduate scholarship to specialize in sculpture. In 1904 she won the top prize for ceramics from the Pennsylvania School of Industrial Art, and when she graduated, she received first prize for her metal crucifix of Christ as well as honorable mention for a clay model, *Procession of Arts and Crafts*. The highlight of her art education was the realization of her dream to study abroad.

Meta Warrick Fuller

At the turn of the century, Fuller sailed to Paris and met the two artists who would be great influences in refining her drawing and sculpting techniques, Augustus Saint-Gaudens and Auguste Rodin. Although it was an honor to have an audience with Rodin, Fuller instinctively knew that coming under his tutelage would be detrimental to the ongoing evolution of her own distinctive style. Despite her refusal of his offer, Rodin graciously offered to serve as mentor and critic. The Paris experience was also beneficial in that Fuller began to exhibit and sell her works at reputable galleries. Therefore, it was quite a "slap in the face" to return to America and meet prejudice head-on in the art world under the guise of her being considered a "domestic artist."

In exploring the influences on Fuller's life, racial prejudice on both personal and professional levels must be considered. During her childhood, the Warrick family spent summers in Atlantic City where Fuller first learned that her color would be a barrier to enjoying play activities with her white playmates. Years later, her introduction to Paris would be marred by prejudice in the form of a prospective landlady shocked to discover that the hopeful renter was not white. After her marriage to a Liberian physician, Solomon Carter Fuller, the newlyweds faced the hostility of neighbors who were convinced that a black couple moving into the neighborhood would lower property values. The fact that the newly constructed Fuller home surpassed all others in grandeur and cost was of no consequence.

A second influence on the evolution of Fuller's artistic style was the experience of meeting W. E. B. Du Bois in Paris. The American scholar, like Rodin, also functioned as a mentor by serving as her escort to social functions, introducing her to the "right people," and contributing to her knowledge of African and black American politics. Du Bois's Pan Africanist philosophy served as the inspiration for two of Fuller's most notable works, *Ethiopia Awakening* (1914) and *Mary Turner* (1919).

Coming into womanhood in the early twentieth century presented a challenge to Fuller as she was affected by the same societal expectations as were all women of that era. Any respectable young woman would certainly desire a proper marriage and Fuller was no different. Speaking of her mother and aunt, she said: "I was a disappointment to them because I wasn't making money hand-over-fist. I was eager to get out of that rut'' (Dannett, 37). After marrying Solomon Carter Fuller on February 3, 1909, and having three children, Fuller was pressured by her husband to remember that her first duty was to her family. One biographer expressed the belief that Fuller's domestic involvement curtailed opportunities to become an international artist (Ovington, 226). Yet another attributed the change in emphasis of subject matter to the times in which Fuller lived and the differences between Parisian and American appreciation of personal artistic style. Parisian art critics and connoisseurs raved over Fuller's choice of themes—horror, pain, and sorrow—and characteristics of masculinity and primitive power. Conversely, America was not ready to accept a black woman's portrayal of such subject matter: ''black persons were afraid to publicly verbalize the pain, sorrow, and despair of the black experience and a woman was seldom expected to voice any opinion at all'' (Hoover, 679). Once regarded as the ''sculptor of horrors,'' Fuller's later works were more often busts, medallions, and religious pieces of a tamer and more acceptable character. The ''sculptor of horrors'' appellation referred to her earlier depictions of suffering, death, and the afterlife in the works that the Parisian art world admired and purchased. As a child, Fuller's interest in the macabre was probably a result of hearing endless horror stories told by her brother and grandfather. As a sculptor, she used the themes to express with her hands what was not safe to verbalize. Her raw power, viewed as being masculine and primitive in her works, was Fuller's expression of the plight of her people.

An element of tragedy also figured into the quality and quantity of Fuller's works. In 1910 the Philadelphia warehouse where she stored her earliest and most promising works—those produced in Paris—burned, and sixteen years' work went up in smoke. Among these were *Man Eating His Heart, (Secret Sorrow),* the piece that caused Rodin to explain, ''Mademoiselle, you are a sculptor; you have the sense of form in your fingers'' (quoted in Dannett, 35). In later years, her husband, Solomon Fuller, became blind, and she gave up her beloved studio to tend to his needs. After his death in 1953, it was discovered that she had contracted tuberculosis and a two-year stay in a sanatorium was required to effect a cure. During this crisis, Fuller was forced to give up her studio forever.

A sense of community, in her role as an artist, is characteristic of Fuller, according to many of her biographers. It is probable that the Warrick family environment of her formative years heightened her need and desire to make her works accessible to those most likely to be receptive. Although Fuller designed and created many works for shows, exhibitions, and eventual sales, her community and the black colleges were the beneficiaries of specially commissioned works and outright gifts. In Framingham, Massachusetts, there are prominent works in the public library, the hospital where Solomon Fuller served as staff consultant, and the church she attended. The Howard University Art Museum owns a sculpture of Richard B. Harrison, ''De Lawd'' of *Green Pastures* fame. Livingstone College in Salisbury, North Carolina, was especially close to Fuller's heart as her husband, a native Liberian, was the first African graduate of the college division. Some years prior to receiving a Doctor of Letters degree from that institution, Fuller had presented the president, W. J. Trent, Sr., with a plaque that is still displayed in the library. Their close relationship was based on his having commissioned a sculpture when he was executive secretary of the Atlanta YMCA. Fuller also received a commission from Trent's successor, S. E. Duncan, to design and execute a medallion for a new campus building. The subjects of many busts have been relatives, friends, and people Fuller admired; for example, educator Charlotte Hawkins Brown, composer Samuel Coleridge Taylor, her husband, and her infant child. As a member of Framingham civic groups, Fuller was offered commissions and invitations to stage exhibitions and present lectures. On a more personal level, Fuller envisioned her studio as a salon and also utilized it to that end. She taught private lessons, entertained friends, held open houses, and staged annual Christmas exhibits there. With this quite active life, Fuller also raised three sons—Solomon C., Jr., Perry James, and William Thomas—only one of whom followed in her footsteps.

Despite the lack of concurrence among biographers as to the status of Fuller and the level of respect accorded her by her peers and the art world, she enjoyed an international reputation based on opinions of masters in the field. Although it was late coming, Fuller's reputation in America, especially in the Northeast and among Southern blacks, was well established. Despite perceived and real tragedies in her life, Fuller designed and created works that had significant meaning to her on both professional and personal levels. One can surmise that she would have preferred life on the Continent, but she was a product of the times and planned and lived her life accordingly. While her husband urged her to remember her familial duties, he still supported her endeavors and was the subject of one of her most famous works. When home life intruded on her work, she used an inheritance to build a studio away from her home. Yet, her life as wife, mother, and civic leader was as fulfilling as that of being a respected sculptor.

As a precursor of the Harlem Renaissance, Fuller was an exemplar whose works were ''among the earliest examples of American art to reflect the formal exigencies of an aesthetic based on African sculpture. . . . [She] memorialized the awakening defiance of her people'' (Campbell, 27). David C. Driskell said in *Harlem Rennaissance Art of Black America* that ''Fuller's art bridged the gap between a well established Black presence in European art circles and the gradual acceptance of the Black artists' work at home'' (154).

Fuller died on March 13, 1968, of natural causes. After her funeral in Framingham, her body was cremated and the ashes were dispersed in Vineyard Haven Sound, Massachusetts. Her three sons survived her.

Meta Fuller had expressed some characteristic thoughts:

> Art must be the quintessence of meaning. Creative art means you create for yourself. Inspirations can come from most anything. Tell the world how you feel . . . take the chance . . . try, try! (Dannett, 46).

She indeed created for herself first, and in being true to herself and her own convictions, she created timeless art.

References

Bontemps, Arna Alexander, and Jacqueline Fonvielle-Bontemps. *Forever Free: Art by African-American Women 1862-1980.* Alexandria, Va.: Stephenson, 1980. 76-77, 180-81. Photograph, p. 76.

Campbell, Mary S. Introduction to *Harlem Renaissance Art of Black America.* New York: The Studio Museum of Harlem, Harry Abrams Publishers, 1987. 11-55.

Dannett, Sylvia G. L. *Profiles of Negro Womanhood.* Vol. 2. Yonkers: Educational Heritage, 1966. 31-34.

Driskell, David. "The Flowering of the Harlem Renaissance: The Art of Aaron Douglas, Meta Warrick Fuller, Palmer Hayden, and William H. Johnson." *Harlem Renaissance Art of Black America.* New York: The Studio Museum of Harlem, Harry Abrams Publishers, 1987. 105-154.

Hayden, Robert C. "Meta Vaux Warrick Fuller." *Dictionary of American Negro Biography.* Eds. Rayford W. Logan and Michael R. Winston. New York: Norton, 1982. 245-47.

Hoover, Velma J. "Meta Warrick Fuller: Her Life and Art." *Negro History Bulletin* 40 (March-April 1977): 678-81. Includes illustrations.

"Meta Warrick Fuller: The Sculptor Rodin Admired." *Encore* (January 3, 1977): 3.

Ovington, Mary W. *Portraits in Color.* New York: Viking Press, 1927. 222-23, 226.

Rountree, Louise M. *The Brief International Story of Livingstone College.* Salisbury, N.C., 1980. 8, 26.

Lewis, Samella. *Art: African American.* New York: Harcourt Brace Jovanovich, 1978. 53-55.

Logan, Rayford W. "Meta Vaux Warrick Fuller." *Notable American Women: The Modern Period.* Cambridge: Harvard University Press, 1980. 255-56.

Who's Who in Colored America. 7th ed. Yonkers: Christian E. Burckel, 1950. 198. Entry under Solomon Carter Fuller.

Collections

Meta Warrick Fuller's works are in the following locations: Atlanta YMCA (Atlanta, Georgia); Business and Professional Women's Clubs (Washington, D.C.); Cleveland Art Museum (Cleveland, Ohio); Framingham Center Library (Massachusetts); Framingham Union Hospital (Massachusetts); Garfield School (Detroit, Michigan); Howard University (Washington, D.C.); Livingstone College Library (Salisbury, North Carolina); Mrs. Samuel Evans Collection (Chicago, Illinois); San Francisco Museum of Fine Arts (San Francisco, California); Schomburg Center for Research in Black Culture (New York City); and Saint Andrews Episcopal Church (Framingham, Massachusetts).

Dolores Nicholson

Mary Hatwood Futrell

(1940-)

Educator, political activist, reformer, organization leader

As Mary Hatwood Futrell finished her sixth year as president of the National Education Association (NEA), she made a number of observations. "We know that our responsibility is not just to the children of America, but to the children of the world. We know now that the destiny of the American family is intertwined with the destiny of the human family. And we know we can observe that misery or help halt that misery. Let us not be observers" (*NEA Today,* May 1989, 2). She challenged NEA members to bring about "a

Mary Hatwood Futrell

massive reduction of worldwide illiteracy by the year 2000'' (2). Futrell is a woman of her convictions—not just a talker, but a woman of action who was brought up to achieve.

''Teachers want to do more than simply teach facts. We want children to be equipped with 'stupidity detectors,' so they will know how to raise the questions and not simply accept what somebody tells them,'' said Mary Futrell (Blount, 13). She is committed to educational excellence and speaks out forcefully for teachers and other school employees on what is needed to improve America's schools. Her top priority is always to see that every child in America is guaranteed a quality education.

On August 31, 1989, Futrell stepped down from an unprecedented third term, or six years, as president of the NEA, the national organization that she has served in various capacities over the past twenty years, including three as its secretary-treasurer.

Born May 24, 1940, in Alta Vista, Virginia, Mary Hatwood Futrell is the second daughter of Josephine Hatwood (Austin). She lost her father, John Ed Calloway, at age four. Josephine Austin had left school to work after sixth grade, because her parents died, and she was determined her children would not have the same problem. When her husband died, she was determined that they would succeed through her love, attention, and discipline. Josephine Hatwood had wanted to be a nurse, but was forced to abandon this idea to support her children. She did domestic work for three families, in addition to cleaning churches to feed and clothe her children.

''Mama's toughness with me always left me feeling as if I pleased her less than her other children and that I could never entirely gain her good wishes,'' said Futrell (Futrell, ''Mama and Miss Jordan,'' 77). Her mother was harder on her than her sisters, because she had more gifts, more to give. It was more important for her to get all the schooling she could, because her mother knew many would be depending on her to do her best. At last she understood. (Futrell, ''Mama and Miss Jordan,'' 80). If ever a case had to be made for the importance of parental interest to a child's education, Josephine Hatwood would provide an excellent example.

Viewing her role in the future as ''staying close to education,'' Futrell hopes to provide children with the same sort of care and guidance that her own mother offered her years ago (Bender, 90). ''If I succeeded, a lot more kids can succeed,'' she affirms. ''But you have to give them an education, you have to nurture them, you have to hold on to them'' (Bender, 90).

Discipline and perfection were demanded of Futrell by her tenth grade teacher at Dunbar Public High School in Lynchburg, Virginia. As a punishment for too much talking, she had to write a thousand-word essay on education and its impact on the economy. She was forced to rewrite it with each paragraph beginning with a topic sentence. The second time she had to rewrite it to correct the grammar. The third time, the spelling. The fourth time, it was punctuation. The fifth time, it wasn't neat enough. The sixth time, it was accepted. Her teacher entered the final paper in an essay contest where the student won third prize. Futrell explained, ''Except for mama, she was the person I most wanted to please in this world'' (Futrell, ''Mama and Miss Jordan,'' 78).

Futrell's education continued at Virginia State University, where she received a B.A. in business education. To begin college, she received a scholarship of fifteen hundred dollars. ''My tenth grade teacher, Miss Jordan, nodded her head as if to say, 'See now, what you can do with discipline?''' (Futrell, ''Mama and Miss Jordan,'' 79). She earned her M.A. at George Washington University and did additional graduate work at the University of Maryland, the University of Virginia, and Virginia Polytechnic Institute and State University. She has received a number of honorary doctorates from such colleges as North Carolina Central University, Xavier University, Eastern Michigan University, and the University of Lowell in Massachusetts. The educator is married to Donald Futrell.

Mary Futrell is a twenty-year veteran classroom teacher of business education in the Alexandria, Virginia, schools. She moved through the ranks in the NEA to become president of the 1.9 million-member organization and was twice reelected, serving an unprecedented third term. She is regarded as a tireless educator who has spent almost all her adult professional life providing and attempting to assure quality education for the youngsters in the nation's schools.

In August 1989, Futrell became a senior fellow and doctoral student at George Washington University, where she is pursuing educational policy studies. She also assumed the post of Associate Director of the Center for the Study of Education and National Development, an organization she describes as ''a budding educational think tank, research center, and clearinghouse'' (Bender, 90).

NEA President Shares Views on Education

Mary Futrell was ''imbued with the impassioned belief that of all the forces that shape us into the people we are, none is more telling than education.'' She stated, ''The whole emphasis in the future is going to be on critical thinking skills, being able to use information in a highly technological society, and working in teams.'' She understood not only the immediate community but the global society as well. And all of that requires more education. Mary Futrell's message to young people is, ''Contrary to what they think, they're not going to be able to rely simply on hard work. They're going to have to rely on their gray cells'' (Bender, 85, 88).

Mary Futrell summarized her worldwide beliefs in her final column, ''President's Viewpoint,'' in *NEA Today*, as she stepped down from the NEA presidency. She ''thinks often of our tomorrows—of challenges that remain, of dreams still unrealized and hopes still unfulfilled. It is an exhilaration that comes of knowing that our journey must continue, because we have promises to keep'' (*NEA Today*, June 1989, 2).

She is pleased that UNESCO, UNICEF, the United Nations Development Program, and the World Bank formulated a four-year plan, at the heart of which is a tighter alliance among the world's educators. In her concluding address, she stated:

> Illiteracy prevents millions from participating in the life of our republic. It jeopardizes the American dream and threatens the very foundation of our democracy. We seek a more democratic world and the universalization of the ideals that have guided our Association for 132 years: quality education for all, human rights for all, economic justice for all. This goal eludes us until we can reach children who have neither books nor teachers. No nation has the right to deprive children of the best education that the teachers of the world, working together, can develop. All nations must affirm their interdependence. The United States has 25 million illiterate adults. The world is home to over 900 million. Failing to act perpetuates these tragedies. But if we act with the same devotion brought to the causes shared during my six years as your president, we can end these tragedies. We have promises to keep. (*NEA Today,* May 1989, 2).

In her monthly essay in *NEA Today,* there are seven categories of concerns on which Futrell focused during her six years as president of the organization. These concerns included: reduction of the dropout rate, improvement and expansion of the Head Start program, child care programs for young families, effective programs to deal with drugs in schools, adequacy of resources, expanded use of computers in teaching, and funds for college loans. She was concerned as well about NEA membership. The many issues raised by the report, *A Nation at Risk,* which highlighted the inadequacy of American education, had a major impact upon her thinking.

Dropouts are a pressing issue in Mary Futrell's mind. In March 1988, she addressed the topic of "National Dishonesty" regarding pushouts, a part of the dropout problem. She said, "The thousands of students pushed out of school by in-school discrimination demand and must have relief" (*NEA Today,* 2). The Robert F. Kennedy Memorial and the Southern Regional Council issued a call to action in 1973. She stated, "Their report, 'The Student Pushout: Victim of Continued Resistance to Desegregation,' charged that school districts had created a new category of classroom exile." She believed that pushouts include linguistic minority students, many of whom are learning English for the first time in high school. She elaborated on this issue:

> When these students can no longer endure messages that erode their self-esteem and demean their native heritage, they seek escape. We add these students to the dropout statistics. They don't belong there. They're pushouts. Only when we're honest enough to call them pushouts will we begin to solve their problem, which is our problem. (*NEA Today,* March 1988, 2).

With respect to educational quality and improving the effectiveness of the schools, Futrell believed that President George Bush and then Secretary of Education Lauro Cavazos were in agreement with her on many aspects of improving the schools. They favor the encouragement of minority teachers, and President Bush wants to be known as the Education President. Futrell states, "Secretary Cavazos and I share the belief that all children can learn. We agree on the importance of encouraging more minority young people to enter our profession. We agree that the federal government has a critical role to play in helping to battle drug abuse among our nation's young" (*NEA Today,* February 1989, 2). Cavazos's successor, Secretary of Education Lamar Alexander, apparently continues the same philosophy.

Futrell expresses concern, however, that cooperation from the nation's leaders is not always forthcoming. In March 1987, she complained that after presidents Eisenhower, Kennedy, Johnson, Nixon, Ford, and Carter had agreed that nothing matters more to the future of our country than education, President Reagan slashed the federal education budget by $5.4 billion, terminated all federal support for vocational education, sliced in half aid for college students, and reduced funds for handicapped students by $336 million. "For the seventh time in seven years," she said, "this President seeks to gut public education. Slashing federal education funds by 30 percent, says Senator Lawton Chiles (D-Fla.), is 'like cashing in your life insurance policy to take skydiving lessons.'" Futrell concludes, "The day we really long for is the day we are offered not skydiving lessons, but lessons that lift us toward the lofty ideals our six previous Presidents embraced" (*NEA Today,* March 1987, 2).

Another disappointment for her in lack of national cooperation was the Reagan Administration proposal to eliminate totally the federal program to help states educate homeless children. In July 1987, Congress recognized the need to educate homeless children by passing the Stewart B. McKinney Homeless Assistance Act and appropriating five million dollars to fund it. Under the act, state departments of education can apply for federal funds to develop programs to provide for the education of each homeless youth. If each of the estimated seven hundred thousand homeless children in America were given an equal portion of the five-million-dollar pie, each child's share would amount to $7.14, at best an amount for a six-month supply of paper, pencils, and pens. Futrell argued, "This is unconscionable; national security cannot rest on policies of child neglect" (*NEA Today,* April 1988, 2).

Child care for young families and Head Start are two examples of government programs that have many problems. Head Start, the successful federal preschool program for poor children, has never been adequately funded. Today it serves only 16 percent of those eligible. The other 84 percent often fall farther and farther behind as they age. Head Start and subsidized child care are programs that will help parents go back to work. The following facts speak for themselves, says Futrell:

> Six out of 10 American women with children under the age of six are employed outside the home. Over half of the mothers with children less than a year old are in the labor force. Two out of every three working women are either their families' sole providers or married to men who earn less than $15,000 a year. One-fifth of mothers of preschool children either aren't working at all or aren't working as much as they'd like, because they can't find good, affordable child care. Lack of child care is the major reason women on welfare don't have jobs. In 1986, our country spent $264 billion on education for children over six years of age, but only about $1 billion for educating younger children. And last but not least, every dollar invested in quality preschool programs saves nearly $5 in later costs for special and remedial education, welfare, and criminal justice (*NEA Today,* March 1989, 2).

Researchers now tell us that no more than half of all teachers stay in the teaching profession longer than five years. And as many as twenty percent exit at the end of their first year. Three factors drive men and women out of careers in education: inadequate pay, poor working conditions, and autocratic decision-making processes that mute the voice of the teacher. "Improved salaries must be priority number one," Futrell said in June 1987. "Today the average teacher salary has yet to reach $27,000. This average leaves teachers with less real buying power than we enjoyed a decade ago. Experienced teachers ought to be earning salaries in the $45,000 range and higher" (*NEA Today,* June 1987, 2).

Teachers also are driven from their positions due to the enormous amount of red tape required on the job and the lack of support personnel to enable them to complete a top-notch job. The motto of the Kentucky Education Support Personnel Association proclaims that support personnel are the backbone of education. Futrell believes that even a half hour spent with a student who has difficulty reading may make the difference between a child who grows up illiterate and a child who grows up to write literature. She observed, "Education Support Personnel membership within NEA has leaped from 10,000 to near 120,000 in eight short years" (*NEA Today,* November 1987, 2).

Mary Futrell is always impressed by the way support employees seem to understand instinctively the difference that even a few minutes of quality time, one on one, can make in a student's day, and a student's life. She knows of no school not in need of a more effective tutoring program.

Need for Drug Dependency Education Cited

Amid all the headlines about drug abuse, there is one piece of good news. The number of students using drugs, according to a new national survey, is dropping, because, as experts say, drug abuse education efforts are beginning to pay off. There is only so much one can do for young people already hooked on drugs, because adequate treatment programs simply do not exist. We can convince young people to try to kick their addiction, but there often is no place to send them for help. Mary Futrell observed, "Nationally, there are now more than six million Americans dependent on drugs, and only 250,000 slots in treatment programs" (*NEA Today,* April 1989, 2). Twenty-four times as many slots are needed.

Problems exposed by Futrell show that political leaders say they're for a national campaign against drug abuse, but they're just not willing to fully fund it. In February 1989, $441 million was proposed in spending for new education programs. Overall federal aid to education was not raised, even to keep up with inflation. Therefore, existing federal education efforts received almost half a billion dollars less than they need to operate at current levels.

Futrell continued, "The budget proposed for 1990 included what budget officials call a freeze on military spending, but it actually went up four percent, and the military budget lost no buying power." The education budget was increased with money for some new programs. Yet, Mary Futrell observed, "In real dollar terms, education ends up with less federal support. . . . The only true national security is a well-educated American people" (*NEA Today,* April 1989, 2). Less federal support will not solve the drug problem. With the reestablishment of the National Federation for the Improvement of Education as a major foundation, the primary issue is on dropout and literacy problems.

IBM is providing every school in the NEA's Mastery in Learning Project with a personal computer, a modem, a printer, and an experimental software package called People Sharing Information Network. All twenty-six Mastery in Learning schools nationwide will be electronically linked. Mary Futrell believes, "Our challenge now is to nurture and expand the relationship we've begun. Our challenge is to merge the traditional 3 R's with a new technological three R's. For whether as Resource tools, Research vehicles, or—most importantly—Restructuring mechanisms, computers offer our schools the promise of profound change" (*NEA Today,* December 1988, 2). Because of President Bush's election, Futrell felt she could count on his educational promise and was proud that the NEA cooperated with IBM to take the first steps toward the expanded use of computers in education.

George Bush and Michael Dukakis differed in their views on education. Although Futrell had preferred Dukakis for president, she worked well with Bush's support. Futrell was enthusiastic about the program of the Democratic candidates in the 1988 presidential election for the continuation and expansion of college loans. Thus, she expressed disappointment later that college loans were so drastically cut. She said in early November, 1988, before the election, "Senator Lloyd Bentsen, way back in 1971, proposed a program, called COSTEP that brought businesses and banks together to provide college loans to needy students. To date, the

COSTEP program has granted more than $100 million dollars in college loans to students in need. The cost to taxpayers: not one cent.'' She felt that the surest path to national security is support for programs that offer opportunity to youth. Futrell liked Bentsen's maxim: ''If you think education is expensive, try ignorance'' (*NEA Today*, 2).

Another issue on which Futrell experienced success was the phenomenal increase in NEA membership under her direction. In November 1989, the NEA announced its 1.98 millionth member. She built the NEA into the largest union in America. From September 1983 until September 1988, the NEA added two hundred fifty thousand members under her leadership. She succeeded in moving the staff from a position of traditionalism and from a go-slow attitude on reform to a position of leadership in that effort. Her successes have astounded even her most severe critics.

Mary Futrell believed, ''Each time NEA adds a new member, a new advocate is added for America's children, a new voice to speak on behalf of those who cannot vote, a new ally in our struggle for professional dignity and professional compensation.'' Her ambitious all-embracing goal was to open the NEA's ranks to all who contribute to the life of the schools and the welfare of students. She wished to include teacher assistants, nurses, counselors, librarians, bus drivers, cafeteria workers, clerical staff, maintenance workers, custodians, and higher education faculty. This idea, she believed, gives dignity and pride to all who are cogs in the wheel (*NEA Today*, September 88, 2).

In 1983 the landmark report, *A Nation at Risk*, called for a new commitment to education. The report spoke to all Americans and challenged the federal government. It bluntly urged the federal government to help make sure all schools had the resources they needed. Although that has not happened, attention has been focused on education. The share of the federal budget devoted to education has actually decreased to below two percent. Therefore, education reform is dying, Futrell said in May 1988. In July of the same year, she asked seven thousand NEA delegates to approve a bold initiative for education reform. She asked all NEA state affiliates to meet with their governors, state school officials, and state legislators and, with them, to designate at least one entire school district in every state as a living laboratory for restructuring America's schools. Working with school boards, parents, and civic leaders to develop programs to improve education, the NEA could have more clout for reform (*NEA Today*, May 1988, 2).

In an interview in October 1989, Mary Futrell reviewed her accomplishments:

> During the last six years one of my goals reached has been to help the NEA assume a more forceful and more positive position on teachers' union rights. Secondly, we increased union membership from 1.6 million to just under 2 million. Another has been our efforts to bring a higher visibility of teachers into the current talk about changing the curricula of today's schools. In addition, Operation Rescue, our dropout prevention and intervention program, implemented projects in 26 schools in 10 states engaging 15,000 students in enrichment and mastery projects (Howard, 30).

Josephine Hatwood Austin would undeniably be very proud that Futrell has obtained such influence in the national educational arena. She has had both the energy and the bravery to tackle any task. ''When you live in poverty you learn how to deal with an adversarial situation and survive . . . and prove them wrong,'' Futrell says (Blount, 13).

References

Bender, Steve. ''They Teach Our Children Well.'' *Southern Living* 25 (June 1990): 85-90.

Blount, Carolyne S. ''Initiating Qualitative Educational Issues.'' *About Time* 17 (November 1989): 13-16.

Futrell, Mary Hatwood. ''President's Viewpoint.'' *NEA Today* 7 (February, March, April, May 1989): 2. 7 (March, April, May, September, November, December 1988): 2. 6 (March, April, May 1988): 2. 6 (March, April 1988): 2. 5 (March, June , November 1987): 2.

———. ''Mama and Miss Jordan.'' *Reader's Digest* 135 (July 1989): 75-80.

Howard, Michael E. ''A Conversation with Mary Hatwood Futrell.'' *Black Enterprise* 20 (October 1989): 30.

Who's Who Among Black Americans, 1990-1991. 6th ed. Detroit: Gale Research, 1990.

Virginia Wilson Wallace

G

Marie D. Gadsden

(1919-)

Educator, government official, organization executive

Marie Davis Gadsden, a woman who has made giant strides toward bringing the global community closer together, was born on April 27, 1919, in Douglas, Georgia. Her father, Thomas Jethro Davis, obtained a B.S. degree from Morris Brown College in Atlanta, Georgia, an M.D. from Meharry Medical College in Nashville, Tennessee, and a D.D. from Turner Theological Seminary. Her mother, Louella Helen (Maryberry) Davis, received her credentials from Fisk University in Nashville, Tennessee, and Georgia State College (now Savannah State College) in Savannah, Georgia. After being threatened by a lynch mob, but warned and assisted by a white doctor, the family escaped from Douglas and moved to Savannah. Marie Davis married Robert Washington Gadsden, Jr., who was an aerial cartographer for the United States Department of Defense in the Map Service Division until his retirement.

Gadsden's parents expected her to excel and to serve in her community, and this she did. She financed her education through scholarships and fellowships. These full-time grants sustained her thirst for knowledge from junior high school in Georgia to graduate school. She received her B.S. degree in biological sciences from Savannah State College in 1938, an M.A. in English language and communication from Atlanta University, Atlanta, Georgia, in 1945, and her Ph.D. in language and literature with a minor in speech and drama from the University of Wisconsin, Madison, in 1951. As a Fulbright Scholar, Gadsden studied for two years at St. Anne's College, Oxford University, from 1951 to 1953, and pursued post-doctoral research at the University of Dublin in Ireland. During her studies at the University of Wisconsin, she was elected to the Student Government Association and was president of a women's housing cooperative (Groves Cooperative House). This house served as a cultural and ethnic institution for activities at the University of Wisconsin. She also served on the governor of Wisconsin's panel for human rights and spoke to groups around the state on human and civil rights. In 1982 the University of Wisconsin in Madison awarded her the doctor of humane letters degree for her outstanding service to communities on national and international levels. On May 6, 1988, the national office of the University of Wisconsin Alumni Association awarded her the Distinguished Alumni Award for outstanding professional achievement, distinguished alumni citizenship, loyalty, and service to the university.

Marie Davis Gadsden has held positions at Southern University in Baton Rouge, Louisiana; Texas Southern University in Houston; Atlanta University, Georgia State University, Morehouse and Spelman colleges in Atlanta; Alcorn College in Lorman, Mississippi; Dillard University in New Orleans; Howard, Georgetown, and American universities in Washington, D.C.; and Columbia University in New York City. During her tenure at these institutions she served as professor of English, chairperson of the humanities division, director of a college theater, coach of intercollegiate debate, and teacher of English as a foreign language. Other work experiences include registrar of admissions and records at Albany State College, Albany, Georgia; instructor of business and shorthand at Reid's Business College, Atlanta, Georgia; accountant at Atlanta Life Insurance Company; director of the Community Business Institute in Albany, Georgia; specialist, teaching English as a foreign language (TEFL) in the Anacostia section of Washington, D.C.; and professor in TEFL at the English Language Service, Washington, D.C. After sustaining a full academic career in the United States, she turned her attention to international education on a global level.

Gadsden Serves the Peace Corps

As a TEFL specialist from 1963 to 1965 with the Division of Training of the Peace Corps, Gadsden provided English services for the United States Department of State to foreign countries. For example, in Guinea she conducted tutorials in English for ministers in President Sekou Toure's cabinet, carried out English lessons for Radio Guinea, and provided TEFL library materials to the Guinean libraries. In addition, she observed and supervised Guinean TEFL teachers for the Ministry of Education. Her English lessons for Radio Guinea were beamed to countries in West Africa twice a week. She held daily classes at local teacher-training institutions—Ecole Normal des Jeunes Filles and the local Lycée Classique pour Garçons. As a resource person in TEFL, she served the British Embassy, the United States Missionary Programs, and the French Professional Institute. Other overseas TEFL activities include consultantships and workshops in Micronesia, Barbados, Guyana, and Casablanca, Morocco, and secondary school classes in Hanover, West Germany.

Leading staff training workshops from 1955 to 1970, Gadsden conducted language training instruction sessions, end-of-service evaluations, and general Peace Corps training and selection in Micronesia, the Philippines, Venezuela, Ecuador, Puerto Rico, and St. Croix and St. Thomas in the Virgin Islands.

From 1965 to 1967 while Gadsden was visiting professor at Columbia University, she supervised, coordinated, and trained Peace Corps volunteers who were to work with the ministries of education in Kenya and Uganda. Between 1968 and 1970 she served as training coordinator for the African region of the United States Peace Corps, which included twenty-four Francophone and Anglophone countries. Gadsden directed regional training centers in Puerto Rico and the Virgin Islands. In 1970 she was appointed country director of the Peace Corps in Togo. Working with all aspects of Peace Corps programs, she supervised 210 volunteers. In addition, she administered six United States programs in TEFL in such neighboring countries as Dahomey and Cameroon.

Speaking of her experiences with the Peace Corps, Gadsden said:

> The Peace Corps, perhaps the most significant international program sponsored by the United States government, taught a significant cadre of Americans about cultures by living within a culture. The Peace Corps also exposed volunteers to more than sixty-five languages of the world in which they were trained to master [sic] and established a network between Americans and citizens of other countries (Telephone interview).

Gadsden, the vice-president of the Phelps-Stokes Fund in the Washington Bureau from 1972 to 1984, designed and implemented an International Curriculum Development Program (ICDP) that aimed to bring an international aspect to the curricula of the historically black colleges and universities. She also increased awareness in the United States of the significance of these West African nations. "Though people lived thousands of miles apart, they all share something in common, man's humanity," she said (Telephone interview).

Through exchange programs, meetings of representatives, speaking tours, and other gestures of goodwill, Gadsden, under the auspices of the Phelps-Stokes Fund, worked to develop trust, knowledge, and sensitivity between black Americans and their West African counterparts. For example, the West African Ethnic Heritage Seminar arranged programs in Upper Volta, Sierra Leone, and the Ivory Coast in West Africa and provided black American college professors information and firsthand experiences in West Africa; in turn, they shared experiences on their campuses to dispel negative impressions of West Africa. Through this gentle but powerful program, reconciliation frequently replaced distrust. Under Gadsden's leadership, twelve ethnic heritage seminars took place in West Africa with administrators and college professors from forty-eight historically black colleges and universities.

During these ethnic heritage seminars, Gadsden and colleagues purchased, collected, and assembled realia and artifacts from the West African countries. Upon return to the United States, these art pieces were arranged into the West African Mobile Art Exhibit and lent to the participating historically black colleges and universities.

The Foreign Curriculum Consultant Program, another facet of the ICDP, worked to effect greater understanding between black America and West African nations. Gadsden selected knowledgeable young West Africans to come to the United States for speaking engagements and to serve as consultants for the black colleges that were engaged in revising their curricula with authentic materials on West Africa. West African and black American scholars wrote a book of modules that could be included in courses in the humanities, particularly art and music. This work, coedited by Ruth N'jiri and Marie D. Gadsden, was titled *A Book of Modules: Internationalizing the Curriculum*. Gadsden's work in international education with the historically black colleges and universities led to the development and implementation of a bachelor's program in African-American studies at many of these institutions.

While vice president of the Phelps-Stokes Fund's Washington office, Gadsden directed the American-Caribbean Scholars' Exchange Program. Again, this program provided opportunities for black American scholars to lecture at universities in the West Indies while the Caribbean scholars lectured and participated in home stays with faculty at historically black American colleges in the United States.

Gadsden, as a board member of the Phelps-Stokes Fund, assisted in fund-raising for the African Students' Aid Society. During the 1970s, for example, Nigeria went through several coups d'ètat that left their students stranded in the United States as a result of temporary collapse of the postal and financial systems. The aid program sustained many African students during a period of financial stress.

Continuing her leadership as an organizer and executive director of the Phelps-Stokes Fund, Gadsden gained a reputation for management and development programming. She organized a symposium to link black African college presidents and their post-secondary institutions with black American college presidents and historically black colleges and universities. Through her proposal, these representatives met at the Rockefeller International Center at Belaggio, Italy, on the outskirts of Milan. In addition, she created, implemented, and directed programs for refugees from Africa and the Caribbean; the African Paramedical Training Program for refugees from Ethiopa, Equatorial Guinea, Somalia, and Uganda for study in the United States; the Haitian Adult Development and Education Program in Florida; and the Southern African Scholarship Program for refugees from Namibia, South Africa, and Zimbabwe. Bureau programs during a ten-and-a-half-year tenure served more than two hundred postsecondary institutions in thirty-seven states; overseas administration involved programs in nine Caribbean countries and twenty-two African countries.

Understanding Between American Indians and Blacks Promoted

Gadsden was just as involved with the complex, pluralistic society of the United States as she was globally. Responding to the mission of the Phelps-Stokes Fund, she was equally sensitive to the native American Indian as she was to the poor black. Notwithstanding the same minority position held by native Americans and blacks in American society, both groups appeared to be insensitive to each other. The failure of both groups to identify with each other's problems was a major concern to her. She led workshops at the Navajo Community Junior College on the Navajo Reservation to bring about cultural understanding between native Americans and black Americans. Besides the program with the Navajo nation, she and her group of black scholars met on the Rosebud Reservation (Sioux) outside of Minot, North Dakota, to develop a degree of cultural congruence. At these week-long conferences she and ICDP members continued to devise curricula that encouraged students' familiarity with values and traditions of a multicultural society. In multicultural classrooms many problems in interaction arise. On this issue Gadsden stated:

> Teachers cannot rely solely on their own cultural knowledge and intuitions, but need the perspectives of individuals who come from these backgrounds. Training of teachers should consider cultural perspectives, styles, discourse patterns, body language and approaches which are effective bases for interaction with individuals who come from certain backgrounds. Living within another culture is the most effective stimulus for understanding and communication (Telephone interview).

Continuing its interest in Gadsden as a renowned international citizen, the Phelps-Stokes Foundation asked her to become a part of its delegation to the Republic of China, at which time the group became familiar with the fifty-six minority groups of mainland China.

After leaving her position at the Phelps-Stokes office, Gadsden became deputy director of the National Association for Equal Opportunity in Higher Education (NAFEO). Again, this organization reinforced her interest in West Africa and provided opportunities for black American college administrators and faculty to gain intensive experiences with African educators. She has led over fourteen groups to Senegal. Furthermore, NAFEO utilized her field experiences and her professional contacts in the United States, the Caribbean, Asia, and Latin America. She led six groups to Latin America and the Caribbean under the Group Study Abroad Program. As a guiding hand in NAFEO, Gadsden continued to deal with such global issues as health, hunger, human resources, and self-reliance.

Since her retirement, Gadsden has continued to receive calls for counsel or references or support of causes. Two events that merit mentioning are the visits to Gaberone, Botswana, in October 1990, and the receipt of the 1990 Presidential Award at the annual White House ceremony for vision, initiative, and leadership in the effort to achieve a world without hunger; a certificate of outstanding achievement was signed by President George Bush and presented on World Food Day at the White House. On the Botswana visit, she was part of the United States delegation as guests of the Botswana President and his wife, the Masires.

Gadsden's volunteer work includes memberships on boards of directors, advisory and executive committees for major organizations devoted to international development, the Academy for Educational Development, Aurora, Oxfam American, and the advisory committee on Voluntary Foreign Aid.

References

Christmas, Walter, ed. *Negroes in Public Affairs and Government*. Vol. 1. Yonkers, N.Y.: Educational Heritage, 1966.

Gadsden, Marie D. Interview with author. 26 June 1990.

N'jiri, Ruth and Marie D. Gadsden, eds. *A Book of Modules: Internationalizing the Curriculum*. New York: Phelps-Stokes Fund, 1978.

Collections

Correspondence, papers, photographs, and other materials on Marie Davis Gadsden are located at the Phelps-Stokes Fund office, Ten East Eighty-seventh Street, New York, NY, and in her private files.

Joan Curl Elliott

Irene McCoy Gaines

(1892-1964)

Civil rights activist, civic worker, clubwoman, social worker

The discrimination against blacks in employment, education, and cultural opportunities, particularly in Chicago, were key issues in the life and work of Irene McCoy Gaines. One means of addressing these issues was to work through the black women's club movement that was active in the latter part of the nineteenth century and well into the twentieth century. Political groups also provided an outlet to help find solutions to these social ills. Gaines devoted her life to the uplift of black women and youth. Through these means she established herself as a vital influence in black American life.

Irene McCoy Gaines was born in Ocala, Florida, on October 25, 1892. She was the younger daughter of Charles Vivien McCoy and Mamie (Ellis) McCoy and survived an older sister who died in childhood. When her parents divorced in 1903, Gaines and her mother moved to Chicago, Illinois. Gaines began her education in the Old Armour Mission Kindergarten, graduated from public elementary school and Wendell Phillips High School. She attended the Normal School of Fisk University, Nashville, Tennessee, from 1905 to 1910 and returned to Chicago. Her talent for written and oral expression was put to good use. Well-organized and assertive, Gaines won three oratorical essay contests between 1910 and 1914 and a popularity contest in 1914 at an NAACP carnival. In 1917-18 she directed the Girls Work Division, War Camp Community Service, in Chicago. From 1918 to 1921 she studied social work at the University of Chicago, and she studied at Loyola University's School of Social Administration from 1935 to 1937.

Gaines's life in Chicago immediately after she left Fisk was distressing. She wrote of her experiences:

> When I first left Fisk I felt all at sea! I did not know what to do. It was a dreadful struggle: I spent many days and nights seeking employment. I could not find anything clerical or suitable for my training. Whenever I answered an advertisement for work that I felt I could do, I was told colored help was not wanted. For a time I did very tiresome and unpleasant work, washing and dusting crockery, where I had to stand all day, and only received the small sum of $5 a week. There were times when I felt dreadfully discouraged (Irene McCoy Gaines to Dora Scribner, 10 June 1918).

She felt the importance of religion early in her life. She continued in her letter to Dora Scribner:

> "The Wonderful Invisible Helper" has greatly blessed me by giving me a few other fine friends like yourself, who have been wonderful inspiration to me: despite many handicaps and obstacles, which I have had to face, I now know that my unkind environment and obstacles were given me for a purpose, and that I have been made stronger by and through them.

Gaines became a typist in Chicago's Juvenile Court complaint department, where her experiences led to her awareness of the problems of blacks, particularly black women and children. She devoted her life to these causes. For fifteen years she worked in the area of social programs. In addition to the experiences in the Juvenile Court, she worked for the Urban League as recruiter and director of its Women's Division. From 1920 to 1922 she was industrial secretary of the YWCA's first black branch. Gaines was a caseworker for the Cook County Bureau of Public Welfare from 1940 to 1945 and from 1945 to 1947 she was executive director of Teenagers Group Work, a recreational program of the Parkway Community House and the YMCA.

Harris Barrett Gaines, a law student, and Irene McCoy were married in 1914. They had two sons, Harris Barrett, Jr., born in 1922, and Charles Ellis, born in 1924. Before the sons were born, Irene Gaines fought to end segregation and to open opportunities for black youth. Once her sons were in school, Gaines resumed a more active career in the community as a social worker. While with the Cook County Welfare Department she started clubs for young people. She criticized Chicago's public schools and the inferior conditions that existed. She spoke out against inequality that resulted from segregation. Her positions as a member of the Citizens Advisory Committee and president of the Chicago Council of Negro Organizations (CCNO) from 1939 to 1953 gave her a strong platform from which to launch her attacks.

Gaines addressed issues that are common social problems of today—teenage pregnancy and the care of pregnant youth. She was successful in her fight to improve facilities for the education of pregnant teenagers, and her efforts led to the establishment of Chicago's first integrated nursery schools.

Employment Opportunities for Blacks Sought

Blacks in Chicago at that time faced discrimination in employment. Gaines fought to improve employment conditions for black people. Her special concern for black women led her to investigate the working conditions of domestics, most of whom were black, and she encouraged them to organize and to strengthen their education. The first march on Washington was the result of Gaines's efforts. In 1941 she worked through the CCNO and led a group of fifty Chicagoans to the nation's capital, where protesters from states throughout the nation joined in the struggle. They organized into groups and visited governmental agencies to protest racial discrimination in employment. It has been said that Gaines's efforts paved the way for A. Philip Randolph's celebrated march on Washington scheduled for July of that year.

Before Randolph's march began, President Franklin D. Roosevelt issued Executive Order 8802 banning discrimination in federal and defense employment; thus, the pending march never occurred. But Gaines's protests continued and she testified before congressional committees on behalf of fair employment practices and legislation. While she was a Republican, she supported political candidates of any party who supported reform in employment.

Gaines became active in political affairs. From 1924 to 1935 she was president of the Illinois Federation of Republican Colored Women's Clubs, the first federation of Republicans in Illinois. She was Republican state central committeewoman for the first congressional district in 1928. In that same year and again in 1930, she was active in congressional campaigns for Ruth Hannah McCormick (Sims). Gaines was unsuccessful in her run for office during that period. From 1928 to 1936, Harris B. Gaines was a member of the state legislature. In 1940 Irene Gaines became the first black women to run for the legislature. She was the first black candidate in 1948 for the Republican nomination and election as member of the Board of County Commissioners from Chicago. In the general election, although her name was last on the ballot, she received nearly one million votes and led the ticket of Republican candidates who ran in Chicago.

Until she retired in 1947, Irene McCoy Gaines was employed as a social worker and held membership in the American Association of Social Workers. She was president of the Northern District Federation of Colored Women's Clubs and of the Illinois Association of Colored Women. When she retired as president of the Illinois association, the organization had served as the coordinating agency of nearly one hundred civic, educational, religious, labor, and social organizations. It was through the affiliation with these groups that Gaines led many causes and strengthened her political clout to effect the changes she sought. As a leader, she continued to fight segregation wherever it existed. In her position as chairperson of fine arts and literature, Northern District Association of Club Women (NACWC), she promoted the artistic and cultural development of black youth through a program called Negro in Art Week.

Involvement in Women's Clubs Accelerated

Gaines's work with the National Association of Colored Women (NACW) and the Illinois Federation of Republican Colored Women's Clubs, led to her national reputation as leader and advocate for social reform. She was the NACW's historian at first; in 1952, after being nominated from the floor of the national convention, she was elected president. She served two terms between 1952 and 1956 and led the club to a number of accomplishments, among them the establishment of a new clubhouse in Washington, D.C., and restoration of the home of noted abolitionist Frederick Douglass in Anacostia, Maryland, near Washington. Earlier, the national association had carried out its fundamental purpose of improving the quality of life for black families, enhancing working conditions for black women and children, and providing better educational opportunities for black youth. The various committees and departments integrated the association into all facets of community life. Under Gaines's leadership, the association continued its monumental work.

In 1954, Gaines noted the great work that had been done under the leadership of past presidents and expressed her view that "to live and work in today's world is a challenge to all women of goodwill." She called for women to participate more completely and directly in a "one world" program and make their influence felt in wider arenas so that the members would become "a part of a great sisterhood of all humanity" (*Negro History Bulletin*, 175). In her address to a regional group she stated:

> The National Association of Colored Women, Inc., does inspire Negro women of America to keep in step with the progress made by women of all other groups, and, through organized effort to win for themselves a greater and wider freedom. . . . Today's world is not the same in which our founders lived. They served in the horse and buggy era; these are the days of atomic energy. In our fifty-eight years of work there have been many changes and improvements: the telephone, radio and television; aerial flight; and the splitting of the atom (*Negro History Bulletin*, 175).

Gaines found that the new services of that period were often used destructively when they should have been used "for the constructive good of mankind." Black women were encouraged to work hand-in-hand with others to provide a richer life and benefit more fully from the social changes made by that time and from the new worlds available through scientific discovery.

The NACW, under the Gaines administration, was dedicated to harnessing the power of its 100,000 members who lived in forty-four states, the District of Columbia, Hawaii, and Haiti. They were challenged to continue the work begun earlier and to work more directly to help solve continuing problems of housing, health, unemployment, illiteracy, discrimination in all arenas, and youth and adult delinquency. The association's motto, "Lifting As We Climb," stood as their beacon, and Gaines offered to lead them to answer any call to improve the world's conditions and to enhance the quality of black life. Gaines ran for a third term in office in 1956 and won by a mere two votes in a highly contested election that was resolved only after legal aid was employed. In that year the Sears Roebuck Company gave the NACW fifty thousand dollars to sponsor a neighborhood improvement contest. Having a continuing interest in housing problems for blacks, Gaines was anxious to address this critical issue and to see that drastic changes were made in housing.

Gaines was a steward of Bethel African Methodist Episcopal Church, belonged to two other Protestant churches, and was active in the Theosophical Society and Moral Rearmament. She lectured for numerous activities in her affiliated churches as well as in other denominations. As president of NACW she was in great demand as a speaker and responded by lecturing extensively throughout the United States. Often as she spoke, Gaines, a very religious woman, drew on Biblical themes and quotations.

Her interests expanded to international arenas, especially where worldwide sisterhood was concerned. As vice president of the Chicago area's Congress of American Women in 1947 and as an officer in the NACW and CCNO, she read a statement before the United Nations Secretary General Trygve Lie condemning the "inferior status" of "colored women of America . . . [and] of the world" (Wheeler, 259).

Gaines received wide recognition for her notable work. Sigma Gamma Rho Sorority in 1951 elected her "Woman of the Year" and presented her with the Sigma Key. In that same year the Woman's Division of the AME Church, fourth district, elected Gaines "Woman of the Year" and presented her with a trophy. The Chicago and Northern District of Colored Women's Clubs elected her "Woman of the Year" in 1951 and presented her a plaque. In 1953 the Pekin Cleaners of Chicago named her "Woman of the Year," and she became an honorary member of Iota Phi Lambda Sorority—the national business woman's organization. In 1958 she was recognized for the NACW neighborhood improvement contest, for which she received the George Washington Honor Medal by the Freedoms Foundation at Valley Forge. Fisk University in 1959 honored Gaines with the Distinguished Alumni Service Award, and in 1962 she received an honorary degree from Wilberforce University in Xenia, Ohio.

After more than forty years of dedication to improving housing conditions the employment status of black women and youth, correcting inferior conditions in public schools, and the inequality imposed by segregation in numerous areas, Gaines died in Chicago of cancer in April 1964. For her humanitarian efforts, Fisk University's General Alumni Association honored Gaines at a meeting of the Chicago Fisk Club in March 1990.

References

Alumni Directory of Fisk University. Nashville: Office of Alumni Affairs, 1971.

Davis, Elizabeth Lindsay, comp. *Lifting As They Climb*. [Washington, D.C.]: National Association of Colored Women, 1933.

Gaines, Irene McCoy. Interview with B. S. Decker. *Christian Science Monitor*, 2 December 1957.

Gaines, Irene McCoy. Letter to Dora Scribner, 10 June 1918.

Negro History Bulletin, 17 (Summer 1954): 175-76.

Wheeler, Adade Mitchell. "Irene McCoy Gaines." *Notable American Women: The Modern Period*. Cambridge: Harvard University Press, 1980.

Who's Who in Colored America. 7th ed. Yonkers, N.Y.: Christian E. Burcel, 1950.

Who's Who of American Women. Vol. 2. Chicago: Marquis, 1950.

Collections

Papers of Irene McCoy Gaines, which contain memorabilia, clippings, and some speeches, are in the Chicago Historical Society.

Jessie Carney Smith

Phyllis "Phyl" T. Garland

(1935-)

Writer, music critic, journalist, editor, educator

Phyllis T. "Phyl" Garland was born on October 27, 1935, in McKeesport, Pennsylvania. Her father had been a professional jazz musician, and she studied piano as a child. Following her early schooling, she attended Northwestern University, receiving her B.S. degree in journalism in 1957. Her professional writing career has included working in reporting, feature writing, and editorial capacities for the Pittsburgh *Courier,* 1958-1965. Following this, she worked as a contributing editor, assistant, and associate editor for *Ebony,* 1965-1977, and editor, 1969-1971. She continues as a regular contributor to the magazine.

Garland's teaching career includes a position as assistant professor and acting chairman of the department of black studies at the State University of New York College at New Paltz, 1971-1973. She then moved to Columbia University in 1973, where she is now an associate professor in the School of Journalism. Her honors include the Golden Quill Award for Outstanding Features Writer (1962), the Headliner Award for Outstanding Women in the Country in the field of communications (1971) by Theta Sigma Phi, and the New Women in Communications Award (1974) by the New York Chapter of the Public Relations Society of America.

Garland is above all else a professional writer and journalist who includes a liberal sprinkling of teaching in her works. Her expertise ranges wide in the field of music, covering all bases: gospel, blues, jazz, soul, rock, pop, classical, and today's variety of crossovers. Besides her major contribution to music history, *The Sound of Soul,* she has written reviews and articles regularly for *Ebony* and *Stereo Review*. She has also done general and features articles for the Pittsburgh *Courier* and *Ebony,* serving in editorial capacities as well.

As a measure of her output, the computerized bibliographic aid *Info Trac's* recent "General Periodicals Index" listed no fewer than ninety-six reviews and articles by Garland in the period of October 1987 through August 1990. By another measure, in this period she produced a historical piece on Adam Clayton Powell, Jr., ("I Remember Adam") and a portrait of the sublime operatic star Jessye Norman ("Jessye Norman: Diva") for the March 1990 and March 1988 issues, respectively, of *Ebony,* in addition to reviews of such vastly divergent recording artists as Janet Jackson (January 1990, 103), the O-Jay's (November 1989, 138), the Brazilian pop artist Djavan (November 1990, 140), Miriam Makeba (July

1988, p. 86), Betty Carter (November 1988, p. 129), and Art Farmer playing the music of Billy Strayhorn (April 1988, 96), all for various issues of *Stereo Review*.

These listings are a brief sampling, showing a talented writer-critic with a very broad appreciation for all kinds of today's recorded output. Her comments are incisive in every sphere—appreciating the good jazz musician's use of improvisation or the velvety smooth vocal color of a pop artist crooning a love ballad, praising poignant touches of African sensibility and commenting on the vigorous bounce and drive of good pop-rock. She flavors her portraits of Jessye Norman and Adam Clayton Powell, Jr., with ample historic references and a warm appreciation of the personality she is describing. One can learn much from her depth and range of coverage. It is instructive to browse briefly through some of her recent writings and note her catholic tastes, ideals, high expectations, and the musical standards she champions.

Garland Writes on "Soul"

In *The Sound of Soul* we see Garland holding a protesting, squirming baby still so that it can be examined. She finds the child well and growing vigorously. The book comes as close as one can to solving the question of whether "soul" is an adjective or a noun and defining its many facets. The dimensions of feeling and emotive drive are dealt with, as are the roots and branches of this diverse genre. The book is used often as a text in courses that examine black music, its artists, and its various performance styles.

Her review of Shirley Caesar's album, *First Lady (Stereo Review),* instructs us concerning the shared heritage of gospel, blues, and rhythm and blues, mentioning numerous artists who represent phases of that heritage, including Thomas A. Dorsey, Ma Rainey, Clara Ward, and Rosetta Tharpe. She praises Caesar as a singer who "sings with all the fire-baptized fervor of an angel born, as she was, on Basin Street" (100).

In her review of a recent Millie Jackson album, *Feeling Bitchy, (Stereo Review,* December 1977), she chastises the artist for explicitly "potent raunch," noting the album's admonition to "please audition before airing," but at the same time, praises Jackson for "a voice that sounds like it has been soaked in whiskey overnight. Millie Jackson can transform even the simplest song into an intimate, compelling statement" (110).

What should we expect from an accomplished professional singer? Here are a few recommendations from Garland's recent reviews. She finds much to commend in Anita Baker's use of her vocal talents in her album *Compositions (Stereo Review,* December 1990). "First of all, Baker doesn't just sing. She embraces you with her voice, a lustrously textured contralto that she uses like an instrument, carefully shaping the contours and shadings of each note to produce a sculptured sound. She then bends these melodic fragments into fresh forms with absolute control and amazing fluidity" (118).

In Mark Murphy's album, *Kerouac: Then and Now,* he tries to recapture the 1950s blending of poetry and music, including many jazz standards of that era as well as a tribute to scat artist Eddie Jefferson *(Stereo Review,* August 1990). Garland appreciates his effort, praising his interpretation and delivery, and concludes "given his extraordinary talent and the consistent excellence of his recordings, it's odd that Mark Murphy isn't better known. Perhaps it's because he deals in subtlety in a raucous era when loud is equated with good. When the tumult subsides, as it eventually must, Murphy will be considered one of the major artists of our age" (75).

After chiding Betty Carter for singing flat in her album *Look What I Got (Stereo Review,* November 1988), she praises her rendition of "All I Got," "where she scats her vocals with the fleetness of a spirited horn player," and her interpretation of perhaps Carter's favorite song, "The Man I Love," where her vocal line blends "like an accompaniment to the splendid tenor sax of Don Braden" (129). Then, remarking that the combining of Carter and Carmen McRae in *The Carmen McRae-Betty Carter Duets* (*Stereo Review,* December 1988) amounts to a "vocal summit," she proceeds to instruct and inform us as to exactly what heights we can expect artists of this stature to soar:

> McRae reaches out assertively and grabs a song with her robust contralto, immediately imposing her imprint on lyrics and melody alike. Carter insinuates her way into the conceptual center of a piece, dissecting and reconstructing it with a cool, flat, almost vibratoless sound. And together they exemplify the art of jazz at its most exalted, the sort of inspired creation in motion that is at the heart of improvisation (135).

In Art Farmer's *Something to Live For—The Music of Billy Strayhorn (Stereo Review,* April 1988), she finds a jazz instrumentalist who exhibits "impeccable taste, making musical statements that are direct but eloquent, lean but expressive—music that swings with the deceptive ease that's the mark of a master." Also, in this review she reminds us of the close ties and "alter ego" relationship between Billy Strayhorn and Duke Ellington, reaching into their musical output as one of jazz history's greatest and most productive teams (96).

Garland shows breadth and insight in her reviews of Miriam Makeba's album *Sangoma (Stereo Review,* July 1988) and the Brazilian artist Djavan's *Puzzle of Hearts* album *(Stereo Review,* November 1990). In the latter, Garland sums up the quandary of a Brazilian competing in the United States market, noting that though his performance "retains the punch and directness of pop, it resonates with the rich rhythms and textures of his native land. The result is his most artistically satisfying effort since he emerged as a major figure in what is called World Music" (140). Makeba's return to the United States record market also shows an artist who stresses her deep heritage with an important album devoted to African song and folklore. Garland comments on the title's reference to the traditional healer, the *Sangoma,* and Makeba's personal belief in the power of spiritual healing, and concludes: "While the music itself is magically infectious throughout, appreciation of the songs is greatly enhanced by the liner notes, which explain their origins" (86).

As a creative and demanding critic, as well as a vastly talented and informative reporter, one sees readily that Garland has much to contribute to our knowledge of the music world and the figures who move on the forefront of today's stage. Her stature and importance are assured, as is her contribution to scholarship and to the education of those who are the appreciators and interpreters of art forms yet to come.

References

Ebony Editors. *1,000 Successful Blacks*. Vol. 1. *Ebony Success Library*. Nashville: Southwestern, 1973.

Garland, Phyllis T. "Anita Baker's Love Songs." *Stereo Review*. 55 (December 1990): 118.

———. "Art Farmer: Something to Live For—the Music of Billy Strayhorn." *Stereo Review* 53 (April 1988): 96.

———. "Betty Carter: Look What I Got." *Stereo Review* 53 (November 1988): 129.

———. "The Carmen McRae-Betty Carter Duets." *Stereo Review* 53 (December 1988): 135-36.

———. "Compelling Millie Jackson." *Stereo Review* 39 (December 1977): 110.

———. "Djavan: Puzzle of Hearts." *Stereo Review* 55 (November 1990): 140, 142.

———. "I Remember Adam." *Ebony* 45 (March 1990): 56, 58, 60, 62.

———. "Janet Jackson's Rhythm Nation 1814." *Stereo Review* 55 (January 1990): 103.

———. "Jessye Norman: Diva." *Ebony* 43 (March 1988): 52, 54, 56.

———. "Mark Murphy: Kerouac, Then and Now." *Stereo Review* 55 (August 1990): 75.

———. "Miriam Makeba: Sangoma." *Stereo Review* 53 (July 1988): 86, 88.

———. "The O-Jay's: Serious." *Stereo Review* 54 (November 1989): 138.

———. "Shirley Caesar: First Lady." *Stereo Review* 39 (October 1977): 100.

———. *The Sound of Soul*. Chicago: H. Regnery, 1969.

Ploski, Harry, and James Williams, eds. *The Negro Almanac*. 5th ed. Detroit: Gale Research, 1989.

Who's Who Among Black Americans, 1990/1991. 6th ed. Detroit: Gale Research, 1990. 452-53.

Shockley, Ann A. *Living Black American Authors*. Boston: G. K. Hall, 1988. 54.

Southern, Eileen. *Biographical Dictionary of Afro-American and African Musicians*. Westport, Conn.: Greenwood Press, 1982.

Darius L. Thieme

Sarah Garnet

(1831-1911)

Teacher, suffragist

Throughout her career in education, Minsarah J. Smith Tompkins Garnet was conscious of prejudice and discrimination and strove to improve the status both of black American teachers and of women. Garnet was born on August 31, 1831, in Queens County, New York, to Sylvanus Smith and Ann Eliza (Springsteel) Smith. She was known in later life as Sarah.

In 1831 the Smith family was living at 213 Pearl Street in what is now Brooklyn. Garnet's parents were of mixed

Sarah Garnet

Native American, white, and black descent, and she was the oldest of eleven children. One sister, Susan Maria Smith McKinney Steward (1847-1918), became a distinguished physician. Mary Smith was a hairdresser, Emma Smith Thomas was a schoolteacher, and Clara Smith Brown was a piano teacher. Two brothers were killed in the Civil War. Garnet's father is said to have received his early education from his grandmother, Sylvia Hobbs, who maintained a school in the attic of her home on Hempstead Plain, and he was a prosperous pig farmer. He died on July 19, 1875; her mother lived until November 4, 1896. At the time of Sarah Smith Garnet's death, there were three survivors among her brothers and sisters—Clara T. Brown, Mary Smith, and Susan Steward. (See the entry for Susan Maria Smith McKinney Steward for further details about the family background.)

All information about Garnet's own education is missing or vague, but she began teaching in 1845 at the age of fourteen in what one historian calls an African Free School in Williamsburg, which became a part of Brooklyn in 1855. An African Free School would have been established by the Manumission Society; if so, however, the connection by 1845 would have been extremely tenuous since the society turned all of its schools over to the Public School Society in 1834. (The Public School Society in turn handed over its schools to the Board of Education in 1853.) The school was probably a private school supported in part by public funds, a typical situation in New York State at the time when Protestant and Catholic differences were delaying the full implementation of a public school system. The school would almost certainly have been poor and struggling. Another historian tells of an unidentified man who walked fourteen miles every day as a child, crossing the river on the ferry, to attend a school in Manhattan because he felt that the Brooklyn schools for blacks he passed on his way were inferior. Garnet's beginning salary as a monitor was twenty dollars a year.

According to her obituary in the *New York Age* (21 September 1911), Garnet had married Samuel Tompkins, had had two children, and was a widow by the time she was scarcely twenty-one, which would place the death of her husband in late 1852. This information is in accord with statements made by Maritcha R. Lyons, a former student of Garnet's and later a personal friend and colleague, which say the husband's name was Tompkins and the marriage took place when Garnet was "in the first flush of womanhood" (114). (This version seems more reliable than that given by Leedell W. Neyland in *Notable American Women 1607-1950*, especially since the article is not completely accurate on other points (19). He identifies her husband as James Thompson, the Episcopal rector of Saint Matthew Free Church of Brooklyn, and places his death in the late 1860s. Rayford W. Logan in the *Dictionary of American Negro Biography* (253-54) generally follows Neyland.) The two children from this marriage died young.

Garnet was appointed principal of one of the colored schools in Manhattan in 1863. We currently know nothing about her teaching experience after her initial job when she was fourteen, nor do we know where she acquired additional training. (The Normal School at Albany was one of the few schools of higher learning in New York State open to blacks before the Civil War.) At the time Garnet began to teach in New York City, the state allowed but did not require separate school systems to be established by local communities, and the city maintained separate schools. In 1883 the Board of Education proposed closing three of the colored schools. Since the board did not appoint black teachers to white schools, several black teachers would have been dismissed. It is probably at this time that Garnet joined Bishop W. B. Derrick and lawyer T. McCants Stewart in testifying against the proposed change before the legislature. In a compromise in 1884, the law was changed to allow students of any race to attend either kind of school, although separate staffing was maintained. The law allowing the existence of separate schools was repealed in 1900, the year of Garnet's retirement. Thus, Garnet supervised a black staff during her entire career with the New York City Public Schools, although she would have had white students in the school after 1883. It was one of her former students, Susan Elizabeth Frazier, who was the first black appointed to a white-staffed school in 1896.

Garnet held the posts of principal at Grammar School Number Four, which became Public School Number Eighty-one, and at Public School Number Eighty for thirty-seven years from April 30, 1863, until she retired September 10, 1900, at the age of sixty-nine. During this period, the black population of New York City was relatively small—the 1860 census counted 12,574 blacks or 1.6 percent of the population; by 1900 in greater New York, there were 69,666 blacks or 1.8 percent. The beginning of Garnet's tenure was marked by an inauspicious event: the draft riots of July 13-16, 1863, when mobs of working class people vented their anger against blacks and abolitionists; there were approximately one thousand casualties, not all blacks, though they did suffer enormously, sixteen being hung by the mobs. A riot, albeit on a much smaller local scale, also marked her retirement. On August 15 and 16, 1900, police and gangs of white roughs beat blacks in the streets and station houses in retaliation for the death of a white policeman.

Garnet's second marriage was to the prominent abolitionist and Presbyterian minister Henry Highland Garnet about 1879. Born in 1815, he was sixty-four; she was forty-eight. The marriage was of short duration. Garnet died on February 12, 1882, almost immediately after his arrival in Liberia, to which he had been appointed United States minister.

In 1883, Sarah Garnet opened a seamstress shop on Hancock Street in Brooklyn; she maintained the shop until her death. Her residences before this date are uncertain, but the opening of the Brooklyn Bridge in that year would have made commuting from Brooklyn easier. At some point in her life as a widow, Lyons says that Garnet returned to her father's house "for an indefinite period" to take the role of "mother's helper" and "big sister" (114). We know that in 1900 Garnet was living at 205 DeKalb Avenue, the home of her sister Susan McKinney Steward before Susan's second marriage; it is not clear whether the address of the house where she died, 748 Hancock Street, is also that of the shop. Given her strong family ties to Brooklyn, not a part of New York City until 1898, it is possible that she had lived there almost continuously.

Garnet's career as a teacher saw the rise of professionalism and bureaucratization. Beginning as a fourteen-year-old teacher, she resolved to keep abreast of "the tide of progress. This entailed severe and exhausting hours of study and reflection. . . . She learned that much book knowledge, more culture and most executive ability should be included among the assets of the successful teacher" (Lyons, 113). Her obituary in the *New York Age* praises her ability: "She . . . won the fidelity of the teachers, the regard of the patrons and the ready obedience of the pupils by her reasonableness, her serenity of temper, her tact and her rare combination of affability and dignity" (21 September 1911).

Among her students were Walter F. Craig, a violinist and orchestra leader; Richard Robinson, a music director in public schools; Ferdinand L. Washington, a businessman; Harry A. Williamson, a podiatrist and author; and teachers Catherine Thompson, Mary E. Eato, Rosetta Wright, J. Imogen Howard, Florence T. Ray, Fanny Murray, S. Elizabeth Frazier, and Maritcha R. Lyons, the author of the sketch of her life in *Homespun Heroines*. The clustering of teachers is significant, for Garnet served as a powerful role model. From twenty dollars a year at the outset, Garnet's salary had reached twenty-five hundred dollars a year, a very respectable salary for the era though still less than a man's for a comparable position.

With her sister Susan Smith McKinney Steward, Victoria Earle Matthews, Maritcha R. Lyons, Gertrude Bustill Mossell, and Josephine St. Pierre Ruffin, in 1892 Garnet formed a committee of 250 women to raise money to replace the presses of Ida B. Wells's Memphis paper, which had been destroyed by mobs angered by her antilynching editorials. In the mid-nineties she was involved in the foundation of the Brooklyn Home for Aged Colored People.

Equal Suffrage Club Organized

In the late 1880s Garnet organized the Equal Suffrage Club with Lydia Smith, Verina Morton Jones, and others, and was its leading spirit. Though small, this Brooklyn-based black women's club worked for women's rights until after Garnet's death in 1911, and in 1907 the club pledged its support for the Niagara Movement (a forerunner of the NAACP). Garnet was an early member of the National Association of Colored Women, for which she was superintendent of the Suffrage Department for several years.

Some of her final acts were devoted to the cause of women's suffrage. In July 1911 Garnet had attended the first Universal Races Congress in London, where she had the opportunity of hearing her sister, Susan McKinney Steward, deliver a paper on "Colored American Women"—later published in the November 1911 issue of *Crisis* magazine. In conjunction with her sister, Garnet had arranged an exhibit of photographs of prominent American black women for the congress, and she took advantage of her stay in England to acquire suffrage literature. The welcome home reception, arranged on September 9 at her Hancock Street residence by the Equal Suffrage Club, included W. E. B. Du Bois's remarks on his impressions of the congress and drew other prominent guests, such as educator John Hope and his wife Lugenia (Burns). Sarah Smith Tompkins Garnet had celebrated her eightieth birthday while abroad and appeared in excellent health before her sudden death on September 17, 1911.

> The last day of the long consecrated life found her absorbed in her club work, her interest in general for amelioration and uplift. The last evening of that final day was spent by the fireside in her home, the place so long a Mecca for those who loved and admired her. She retired at the usual hours and she seemed in good health (*New York Age*, 21 September 1911).

References

Brown, Hallie Q. "Mrs. S. J. S. Garnett [sic]." In *Homespun Heroines and Other Women of Distinction*. Edited by Hallie Q. Brown. Xenia, Ohio: Aldine Pub. Co., 1926.

Dannett, Sylvia G. L. *Profiles of Negro Womanhood*. Vol. 1. Yonkers, N.Y.: Educational Heritage, 1964.

Hirsch, Leo H., Jr. "New York and the Negro 1783-1860." *Journal of Negro History*, 16 (October 1931): 382-473.

Logan, Rayford W. "Sarah J. (Smith) Thompson Garnet." *Dictionary of American Negro Biography*. Rayford W. Logan and Michael R. Winston, eds. New York: Norton, 1982.

Lyons, Maritcha R. "Sarah J. S. Garnet." In *Homespun Heroines and Other Women of Distinction*. Hallie Q. Brown, ed. Xenia, Ohio: The Author, 1926.

"Mrs. Garnet Dead." *New York Age*, 21 September 1911.

Ovington, Mary White. *Half A Man: the Status of the Negro in New York*. New York: Longmans, Green, 1911.

Neyland, Leedell W. "Sarah J. Smith Thompson Garnet." *Notable American Women 1607-1950*. Vol. 2. Cambridge: Harvard University Press, 1971.

Salem, Dorothy. *To Better Our World: Black Women in Organized Reform, 1890-1920*. New York: Carlson, 1990.

Seraile, William. "Susan McKinney Steward." *Afro-Americans in New York Life and History* 9 (July 1985): 27-44.

Wesley, Charles Harris. *The History of the National*

Association of Colored Women's Clubs. Washington, D.C.: NACWC, 1984. Photograph, 77.

Robert L. Johns

Frances Joseph Gaudet

(1861-1934)

Temperance leader, prison reformer, school founder

Frances A. Thomas Joseph Gaudet was a temperance leader, prison reformer, and founder of the Colored Industrial Home and School (later known as the Gaudet School) in New Orleans, Louisiana. She was born in Holmesville, Pike County, Mississippi. Her mother was the daughter of a slave preacher and an Indian. Her father, James Thomas, never returned from the Civil War. Frances, named for her Indian grandmother, had a brother, Eugene, two years her senior. The maternal grandparents provided a home for the children and their mother for Gaudet's first eight years.

Squire Yancey, her maternal grandfather, was one of the founders of the first church for blacks in nearby Summit, Mississippi. After the Civil War, this church became the site of the first school for black children of the area, with a northern missionary as the teacher. Gaudet began her schooling here, along with about twenty other children. The only student to have a book—her grandfather's old speller—she shared it with the others by tearing out a page for each child.

Gaudet's childhood in Mississippi was marked by poverty, love, and strong religious values. In her autobiography, she recalls the pleasure and excitement of the big monthly church meetings. People gathered from as far as thirty miles away to hear the preaching and then to share dinner. The children had no toys but amused themselves by catching butterflies, making mud pies and houses in the clay pile, and playing in the creek.

About the time that Gaudet was eight years old, her oldest uncle killed a man—a plantation overseer—for forcing his attentions on his wife, and thus became a fugitive. Squire Yancey believed it was time to leave the small Mississippi town, and the family moved to New Orleans.

At first, Squire Yancey sent Gaudet and Eugene to a private school near their home, but after he died some four years later, Gaudet began attending Clio Elementary School, a nearby public school for boys and girls. The mother remarried, and the new family moved to downtown New Orleans. Gaudet attended Straight University until her stepfather died, when she and her brother had to help their mother support the three children of the second marriage.

In her autobiography, *He Leadeth Me*, Gaudet tells how much it hurt her to leave school, and how she spent every spare penny she had for books. Her distress increased when her brother ran away to work as a cook on an Illinois Central freight train. However, he was able to make more money than in New Orleans, and he sent their mother rent money every month until she died some twenty years later.

On June 6, 1877, Gaudet married Charles Joseph. They had three children—Eugene, Edward, and Eva. Their marriage was happy for about ten years, then, as Gaudet puts it, "drink, the curse of America, gained a hold on him and destroyed our happiness and made a legal separation necessary" (Gaudet, 12).

In March 1894, about five years after her marriage to Charles Joseph ended, Gaudet found herself starting a prison ministry. On her way to visit a sick fellow-parishioner of Saint James African Methodist Episcopal (AME) Church of New Orleans, she met an elderly woman who was crying as a train left. Gaudet asked if she could help and walked the woman home. There she learned that the woman's son had been convicted of breaking into a store and robbing it and had been sentenced to five years of hard labor. That evening, the newspaper headlines told of more convictions and sentences. Gaudet then felt a call to go to the prisons and talk to the prisoners. She resisted at first, but then she said she "realized what my Master meant when He said that we must go into the highways and hedges, and compel . . . [sinners] to come by our kindly reasoning and Christian example" (Gaudet, 14). The next day she went to the mayor, and he granted her permission to visit the jails.

Prison Ministry Begins

Two days after receiving the mayor's approval, Gaudet made the first of many visits to the Orleans Parish Prison. A minister from Mississippi had asked her to help his son, whom he believed to be innocent of the charges against him. She and the minister visited the young man in the prison and talked with him. Then she asked if she could hold weekly prayer meetings in the cell area. Prison officials agreed, and two days later Gaudet and the minister returned to the jail. She spoke quietly with a condemned murderer about God's love and forgiveness; then she and the minister led the prisoners and their jailer in a simple prayer and hymn service.

Gaudet continued to talk and pray with the condemned man she had met at the first meeting, and he was able to face his execution with the dignity and calm that came from his conversion to Christ. During her eight years of prison ministry, Gaudet counted more than one hundred conversions and eleven hundred pledges to lead better lives.

Gaudet did not limit her prison ministry to prayer meetings, nor did she minister only to those of her race. She soon discovered that many prisoners had worldly needs also, such as clothing and the need for someone to serve as a contact with family and friends. Parish officials furnished no clothing to the prisoners, and Gaudet once found a man whose clothes had fallen apart during his four-month incarceration awaiting trial. Had she not discovered his needs and gone out to beg shoes and clothing for the man, he would have been unable to attend his own trial. Another time, the white widow of a United States senator from Alabama wrote to Gaudet asking her to help her son, in prison on a charge of being a pickpocket. When a white lawyer proved to be too expensive for the widow, Gaudet went out on her own, found evidence of the young man's innocence, and testified at his trial. Her intercessions with judges on behalf of repentant prisoners often resulted in more lenient sentences or even in sentences being set aside.

City officials, from the mayor on down, and newspapers recognized and respected the work Gaudet was doing and were almost always willing to listen to her. Those few people who criticized her were usually of her race; they objected to a woman visiting courts and prisons. However, Gaudet continued, secure in the knowledge that she was serving God by serving humanity.

The conditions at the workhouse and especially the treatment of women horrified Gaudet. The inmates desperately needed clothing, which she managed to obtain from both her white and black friends. There were no night matrons for the women's section, and men had charge of the keys to their cells. On a visit to the workhouse at the request of a Prison Reform Association officer to take custody of an infant, Gaudet learned that this baby had been conceived during a prior incarceration. The next day she spoke with the mayor, who arranged a meeting with the police commissioner. Together with the Prison Reform Association officer, she brought charges against the workhouse superintendent. Although she received threatening letters, Gaudet appeared at the hearing to testify against the superintendent. When the superintendent asked what right a Negro woman had to bring charges against a white man, Gaudet replied, "The right of a respectable, law-abiding citizen and property owner, whose taxes help to pay your salary and to whom you are amenable" (Gaudet, 42). The outcome of these charges, besides the removal of the superintendent, was the construction of a new prison; the city put the former workhouse to use to house stray animals.

Gaudet worked with both the Prison Reform Association and the Era Club of New Orleans. The latter group, which drew its membership from the leading white women of the city, offered its assistance in improving jail and court work. Their efforts helped bring a juvenile court into existence in July 1903. The Prison Reform Association, at Gaudet's behest, budgeted funds to help buy clothes for the indigent insane of New Orleans. Gaudet cut them out, then had women prisoners help her make them. A wealthy white woman, Ida Richardson, kept a cupboard of clothes available for indigent prisoners and other needy persons.

Soon after she began her prison ministry, Gaudet discovered what she considered the worst aspect of the parish prison and court system. Boys of all sizes and ages were put in the same prison as the men to await trial. Frequently, four or five weeks would go by before these boys came to trial, during which time they were exposed to all sorts of criminals. She vowed to save these children by building a home for them and having them committed to her care. She renewed this vow whenever she would come across a parentless child who had been released from jail only to return because, with no home, he went back to his old, evil companions.

Her proposed remedy was a good common school education, with manual training to learn a trade. Gaudet wanted to have a well-equipped agricultural and industrial school located in the suburbs of the city, so that there would be a market for the school's products. She also believed in compulsory Christian education.

All the time that she was helping prisoners, Gaudet was working as a seamstress to support herself and her three children. By the late 1890s she owned a house at 2611 Saint Ann Street, and she sometimes had people boarding with her. Her two sons were also working and living at home.

Gaudet was a strong believer in temperance. She was serving as Louisiana state president of the Frances Willard Woman's Christian Temperance Union (WCTU) in 1900 when the group sent a message to Queen Victoria, praising her stand with regard to human rights in Transvaal. In June of that year the National President of the WCTU appointed Gaudet as United States delegate to the international convention of the organization, to be held in Edinburgh, Scotland. Because she had to pay her own way, Gaudet mortgaged her house for the passage money but felt confident that once in Europe she would be able to live frugally and raise money by lectures.

Gaudet spent more than three months in Europe after the convention. She was the house guest of British nobility and had a private audience with Queen Victoria. She visited prisons and lectured in Scotland, Ireland, England, and France. When she returned to America in September, she spent three more months visiting prisons, giving lectures, and, as she puts it, "trying to make friends for the work to which I had given much labor, the building of the Colored Industrial Home and School for the colored boys and girls of Louisiana" (Gaudet, 117).

Her travels took her to Washington, D.C., for the national convention of the WCTU. As a convention delegate, she attended a reception hosted by President and Mrs. William McKinley in the White House and was introduced to the President. She returned, at long last, to New Orleans on December 23, 1900, and the next day she was visiting the prison again.

School for the Poor, Homeless, and Neglected Founded

On January 2, 1901, Gaudet was officially welcomed back

to New Orleans and honored at one of the largest black churches in the city. A resolution honoring her and recognizing her efforts "on behalf of the poor, homeless, and neglected boys and girls of her own race" called for "subscriptions and assurances of material aid for the Colored Industrial Home and School Association" (Gaudet, 9). With money she earned on her lecture tour and donations from friends and supporters, Gaudet purchased 105 acres of land on the outskirts of New Orleans. With the help of Ida Richardson and the *New Orleans Times-Democrat* newspaper, sufficient funds were raised to develop the property so that by 1912 the school had three main buildings, fifteen acres under cultivation, and a valuation of $75,000. Blacks as well as some of the most prominent white men in the community served on the advisory board for the school.

Adolph P. Gaudet, a Customs House employee, served as the first secretary of the board. He had been interested in the project from its inception and had given generously of his time and money. By 1905 he had persuaded her to abandon her vow to remain single, and they were married June 11 of that year. They lived at the school, where the new wife served as principal and supervised all aspects of the school's operations. In 1910 the school had forty-three resident children. The children were given love, a Christian education, and training in practical job skills. Gaudet often adopted children whose parents had died or were in prison or insane asylums. She continued to work with the courts for more humane treatment of juveniles and was joined in this effort by the Era Club of New Orleans and many other whites.

As time went by and some of Gaudet's leading supporters died, including her husband, Adolph, in January 1920, she came to the realization that, if the school were to continue, it would need a wider base of support and sponsorship. In addition, she was getting older, and her sight was beginning to fail. Since most of her support had come from New Orleans Episcopalians, in 1919 she decided to offer the entire facility to the Episcopal diocese of Louisiana. By 1921, a special committee recommended that the Diocese accept the offer, and the title to the property was transferred to the Episcopalians. Gaudet continued as principal until 1924, when she had to retire due to blindness. She received a pension, and went to live with relatives. On December 24, 1934, Gaudet died in Chicago.

The school, now known as the Gaudet Home and School, continued under the sponsorship of the Diocese of Louisiana, the New Orleans Community Chest, the American Church Institute for Negroes, and the Woman's Auxiliary of the Diocese. It became an accredited high school, and the site of a cooperative effort with Dillard University for the purpose of practice teaching. However, changing economic and educational conditions resulted in a slowly declining enrollment for the school. In 1952 the Orleans Parish school board bought most of the property for a black high school. The school became a group care home until 1963, when the state appropriated most of the remaining property for highway construction. The diocese was forced to close the home and find another way to serve black youth with income from the endowment created by the sale of property.

Today, Gaudet's work with young people of her race is carried on in Gaudet Hall, a recreational building that is part of Saint Luke Episcopal Church in New Orleans, and through various projects of Episcopal Community Services. A public elementary school has been named after her, and the name of Frances Gaudet is invariably included in lists of New Orleans women reformers of the early twentieth century.

References

Carter, Hodding, and Betty Werlein Carter. *So Great a Good: A History of the Episcopal Church in Louisiana and of Christ Church Cathedral, 1805-1955*. Sewanee, Tennessee: The University Press, 1955.

City Directories for New Orleans, Louisiana. 1895-1910. Tulane University, New Orleans, Louisiana.

Gaudet, Frances Joseph. *He Leadeth Me*. New Orleans: Louisiana Printing, 1913.

Jones, Girault M. *Some Personal Recollections of the Episcopal Church in Louisiana*. New Orleans: Churchwork Publication, 1980.

Sue Rowland

Zelma Watson George

(1903-)

Sociologist, educator, musicologist, government official, actress, singer, lecturer

Zelma Watson George has combined with little effort eight outstanding careers: sociologist, musicologist, educator, administrator, actress, singer, diplomat, and lecturer. Yet in characterizing these seemingly diverse careers, she says they are all different phases of the same life, not different careers. For her, the key is communication between people of all races and all countries. Thus, she defines her careers simply as communication.

Zelma Watson George was born December 8, 1903, in Hearne, Texas, the oldest of six children—Verta, Samuel, Jr., Vivian, Cathryn, and Jewell—of Samuel Elbert Watson, a minister and former school principal, and Lena (Thomas) Watson, a teacher. Both parents graduated from Bishop College in the same class. Her father later received a divinity degree from Virginia Union University in Richmond, Virginia. The Watson family lived first in Hearne, Texas, where her father was principal of a boarding school and her mother a

Zelma Watson George

teacher. Samuel Watson became a Baptist minister and moved about with his family to various pastorates.

Very early in her life, George had wanted to be an opera singer, but in the early 1900s she could not, as a black female, get into the operatic field as a singer. Both of her parents were trained musicians—her mother was an accomplished pianist and her father an accomplished cornetist and singer. Because they were educated, they wanted to be sure that their children received the best education possible. George did not attend public schools until she was in the sixth grade. She and the other children were taught at home by their mother, who included other children who were the same ages as her own so that there would be competition. It was a true one-room schoolhouse with one teacher, although George's father would come in and teach mathematics and a few other courses. When the family moved to Topeka, Kansas, George attended high school and also had her first integrated school experiences. It was a white counselor at the Topeka school who told her that she should not try to attend the University of Chicago. That advice made her more determined than ever to attend.

George's father said to her on her first day of classes as they sat in front of the University of Chicago, the university which had admitted her academically but had refused her dormitory housing because of her race:

> So, this is the college of your choice! This is where you feel you belong! Now, when you go in there, walk in like a bulldog. Don't go in there with your tail between your legs and your ears flopping on the floor. You'll be kicked and abused sure as you're born! Nobody kicks a bulldog! He doesn't go in barking or making any trouble for anybody. He knows where he's going and proceeeds without bothering anyone. Everybody lets him through. You walk in there like a bulldog! (George, "My Basic Beliefs").

No wiser words could have been spoken to her, for she has walked like a bulldog since then.

George auditioned for the choir but was refused; ironically, she was told her voice was 'too good' for the choir. When she appealed that decision, the chaplain cast the deciding negative vote and said that "to put [her] in the choir would be like putting a lame person in it. The people who came to worship would be distracted by [her] physical presence." However, being denied admittance to the choir was only one of several other denials she encountered while attending the university. When she tried out for the women's basketball team, the others decided to play football instead and tackled her, causing George a serious knee injury that has resulted in lasting damage. When she went to her first swimming class, which had been recommended as therapy for her knee, immediately, everybody got out of the pool with one young lady making a denigrating racial remark, "I don't swim with niggers." But the teacher quickly resolved this incident by stating that swimming is an elective whereupon everyone returned to the pool and class resumed (George, "My Basic Beliefs").

Fellowship of the World Experiences Gained

Each year while she was enrolled, George and her father reapplied for dormitory admisssion for her but were always refused. Yet, despite all of the negative racial experiences she encountered at the university, she says that her time there remains one of the greatest experiences of her life.

She was an avid student and flourished in the academic setting at the university. Claiming it as her own, "she loved the feel of the classroom, the give-and-take between teacher and student. She loved the library and its quiet study halls. She loved to sit leaning against a tree on its campus, with a book in hand, taking new ideas from its pages, pondering, projecting her own life" (Jelliffe, 11). At the university, she honed and broadened her research skills; she widened her circle of friends to include both men and women from every corner of the land and from many foreign countries. It was here that she first came to know the "fellowship of the world." Her skill in developing this feeling of world fellowship was to serve her well in her life's work of communication.

While the University of Chicago was key in her adult development, it was her family, and in particular her father whom she credits with having the first and greatest influence on her. George idolized her father, with whom she had a very special relationship. He was a well-educated man who had a close alliance with leaders—the thinkers, speakers, and doers of his time—as well as with non-leaders. He was involved in community and civic matters; he held forums at each of the churches he pastored, inviting prominent black speakers such as W. E. B. Du Bois, Booker T. Washington, Carter G. Woodson, James Weldon Johnson, A. Phillip Randolph, Mary Church Terrell, and Nannie Burroughs; many of these were also frequent guests in his home. He constantly encouraged people who came to his church to hear the speakers, to buy books for their children, and to let the children see them read. Her mother was a teacher, dean of women at Virginia Union University in Richmond, coordinator of religious activities at Tennessee Agricultural and Industrial State College in Nashville (now Tennessee State University), and on the staff as a teacher and matron for a men's dormitory.

Her father pastored churches in Palestine, Texas; Hot Springs, Arkansas; Dallas, Texas; Topeka, Kansas; and Chicago, Illinois. In 1918 the family was ordered out of Dallas by the Ku Klux Klan because of the father's suspected aid to a black prisoner who escaped from jail. Following her father's early death at the age of forty-seven, George, who had completed college and started work, began working two jobs to help her mother finance the education of her siblings. Each child completed college and held successful careers.

George's first job after graduating from the University of Chicago was as a social case worker for the Associated Charities of Evanston, Illinois. From that position she moved into work as a probation officer for the Juvenile Court in Chicago. In addition to her work, she was also enrolled in two institutions, studying music: first at Northwestern University for the study of organ and later at the American Conservatory of Music in Chicago, where she received a certificate for the study of voice. In addition to her work and study, George did volunteer work, particularly with the Girl Scouts. In 1932 she went to Tennessee Agricultural and Industrial State College as dean of women and director of personnel administration. She took her two college-age sisters and her mother with her. The sisters completed college there, and her mother later joined the staff at the request of the president. While performing her administrative duties, George also developed materials for the freshman orientation course she taught. She also continued with her volunteer work and established a Girl Scout troop, but because there were no black troops in the South at that time, she was unable to get them invested. So they functioned without national approval. George also began bringing about closer interaction between Fisk University and Tennessee State, developing between them healthy communication and the recognition of common cause. Continuing her heritage of community involvement, she became president of a chapter of the Fellowship of Reconciliation and saw this organization accomplish important social and civic education in the Nashville area.

After five years in Nashville, George married Baxter Duke, a young minister whom she had known when both were teenagers in Topeka, Kansas. The wedding was held in her father's former church in Chicago, and the couple moved to Los Angeles, where Duke had accepted a position as a minister at Avalon Christian Church. In addition to becoming a minister's wife, George accepted the role of developing the Avalon Community Center, a mission-type community center which provided in-service training and guidance of every sort. As the center's executive director, she had a staff of two hundred and worked with diverse age and racial groups of people, including teenagers, older adults, blacks, Asians, Hispanics, and whites. While working at the center, George began graduate study for her Ph.D. at the University of Southern California in the school of education. By the time she had completed one year of study, she had "confirmed her desire to make a comprehensive study of Negro music and to explore its sociological impact" (Jelliffe, 22). She applied for and received a two-year Rockefeller Foundation grant that enabled her to do extensive research all over the country on "Negro songs [and to] discover the purposes to which they had been put" (Jelliffe, 23).

It was during her research at the Cleveland Library that the members of her sorority, Alpha Kappa Alpha, entertained her and she met her next husband. (Her first marriage had failed after five years.) In 1944, she married Clayborne George, a well-known and respected lawyer and chairman of the Civil Service Commission, and she moved to Cleveland, Ohio, where she began an intense community, national, and international life of work and research. She combined several careers while actively giving of her time and skills to numerous volunteer groups. She also became an active member of Antioch Baptist Church, her husband's home church. She became a member and served on boards of such groups as the YWCA, Council of Church Women, Girl Scouts, Conference of Christians and Jews, the Council on Human Relations, the League of Women Voters, the Central Areas Community Council, Karamu, the Association of National Scholarships, the Phyllis Wheatley Association, the Cleveland Council on World Affairs, the American Society for African Culture, the NAACP, the National Council of Negro Women, the United Nations Board, the Urban League, the International Peace Academy, and many, many others.

George Continues Involvement with Music

In 1949 George fulfilled another aspect of her career when she sang with rave reviews the title role in Gian-Carlo Menotti's opera *The Medium* at the Karamu Theatre in Cleveland; the following year she repeated her performance in the same role on Broadway. In subsequent years, she sang the starring role in other operas: in 1951 at the Cleveland Play House, she performed the lead in Menotti's *The Consul* and in 1955 at the Karamu, she sang in Kurt Weill's *Threepenny Opera*.

George had received her master's degree in personnel administration in 1943 from New York University, and in 1947 and 1948 she had taken graduate courses in radio and television at Western Reserve University. In 1954, she received her Ph.D. in sociology and intercultural relations from New York University. Her dissertation, "A Guide to Negro Music: An Annotated Bibliography of Negro Folk Music and Art Music by Negro Composers or Based on Negro Thematic Material," was a seminal work in that it catalogs twelve thousand titles by or inspired by black Americans.

While she attended to her personal life and marriage to Clayborne George, which included very active social and community involvement, and while she pursued her research and singing, Zelma George was also gaining national and international recognition in the public service arena. In 1956, she was appointed by Secretary of Defense Charles E. Wilson for a three-year term to the Defense Advisory Committee on Women in the Armed Services. This led to extensive touring of military installations all over the country. In 1957, then Vice President Richard M. Nixon invited her to participate in the Minority Youth Training Incentives Conference, sponsored by the President's Committee on Government Contracts and the American Personnel and Guidance Association. In 1958, George was a participating member of the Washington Conference on the Community's Responsibility for the Development of Minority Potential. Also in 1958, President Dwight D. Eisenhower appointed George to membership on the President's Committee to plan the 1960 White House Conference on Children and Youth. In 1959, she received a United States State Department grant for a six-month lecture tour of thirteen countries in the Far East, Southeast Asia, Europe, and Africa. Because she went as a private citizen under the Educational Exchange Program, "the trip was arranged so that she was brought into contact with people of every social and economic level on informal as well as formal occasions." She spoke to large and small groups in schools and universities, to families in homes, to individuals, to clubs, to rotary organizations, and to Fulbright Alumni. This tour received favorable press coverage and resulted in high praise for George's ability to connect with her audiences in personal ways.

George Becomes Delegate to the United Nations

In 1960 Zelma Watson George was approved by the United States Senate as alternate to the United States Delegation to the Fifteenth General Assembly of the United Nations, where she represented this country on the Economics and Finance Committee. She received extensive press coverage when she rose in spontaneous applause when, despite an abstention vote by the United States, a resolution proposed by the African and Asian delegations recommending a "speedy and unconditional end of colonialism" passed. Although some in the press censured her actions, many applauded her (including some of her own delegation) for her courage. In reflecting on her action, George points out that it was not planned. "Your personal integrity is all you've got. . . . It was just something that, to be honest, I had to do" (Black Women Oral History Project Interview, 14-15).

Following her United Nations appointment, George became an even more highly-sought speaker and lecturer. Eventually, she became a full-time lecturer under the auspices of the Danforth Foundation and the W. Colston Leigh Bureau. Between 1964 and 1967, she visited fifty-nine colleges as a Danforth Visiting Lecturer.

In 1966 George was named executive director of the new Cleveland Jobs Corps Center for Women, a residential vocational training program for young women from low income backgrounds who have dropped out of school. She retired from this position in 1974. After retiring from the Jobs Corps Center, she continued to speak and lecture. She also taught at Cuyahoga Community College for a number of years in the 1980s.

George is the recipient of numerous awards and honors. These include the Dag Hammarskjold Award for Distinguished Service to the Cause of World Peace through World Law (1961); the Dahlberg Peace Award from the American Baptist Church (1969); Alumnus of the Year from the University of Chicago (1969); Alumnus of the Year from New York University (1973); the Mary Bethune Gold Medallion from Bethune-Cookman College(1973); United States Department of Labor Distinguished Citizen Award (1974); James Dodman Nobel Award in Human Relations (1985); Lifetime Achievement Award by the Black Professional Association of Cleveland (1985); a citation by the Greater Cleveland Women's History Week Committee as one of the "Women Who Shaped Cleveland;" and selection as one of a group of seventy-five contemporary black American women seventy years of age or older whose memoirs and biographies are included in the Black Women Oral History Project at Schlesinger Library, Radcliffe College.

George is still sought for speaking engagements and additional recognition. Recently, a shelter for homeless women and children was named in her honor. At the age of eighty-four and widowed, she still leads a very productive life, still serving on some community and national boards. She remains also a dedicated member of Antioch Baptist Church. Although George suffers from arthritis and uses an Amigo electric chair as a result of several operations on what she calls her "interracial knee," George still manages to do some of the things she wants to do. She still drives herself, often picking up friends to take them to meetings and other events. She is very warm and personable and receives even those she does not know well in a most gracious way. She willingly shares information about herself and remains a true inspiration.

George knew and was friends with many others who were great achievers, including sociologist E. Franklin Frazier, Charles S. Johnson, Angie Brooks (the first black woman president of the United Nations), Countee Cullen, and Langston Hughes. On her first trip to New York to do research for her master's degree, she relates that Langston Hughes and Countee Cullen took her out to lunch. This was during Prohibition, and she remembers being nervous about those around her who were "mixing" their coffee. She also remembers fondly that she and Langston Hughes spent time together when both attended the First World Festival of Negro Art in 1966 in Dakar, Senegal. After attending several sessions together, he suggested that they go to a local coffee house which, in addition to having the best French pastry, had been segregated when Senegal was a French colony.

Although she credits her father and mother with having a great influence on her life, she also gives special recognition to her husband, Clayborne George, who encouraged and provided her with loving and emotional support. For a woman like her, who enjoyed travel and communicating with people in different ways, whether speaking, singing, or entertaining, he was the ideal husband. Successful in his own career, he freely accepted her involvement in all her careers, which she characterizes as "different phases of the same life."

References

Abdul, Raoul. *Blacks in Classical Music*. New York: Dodd, Mead, 1977.

"Battissi Names 3 to Help Monitors." *Cleveland Plain Dealer*, 2 June 1985.

Bean, Don. "A Minority Report by Zelma George." *Cleveland Plain Dealer*, 25 May 1985.

Black Professional Association. "Life Achievement Award." Program. Cleveland, Ohio: Museum of National History, 24 November 1985.

The Council on Human Relations Conference. Cleveland, 12 June 1985.

Current Biography. New York: H. W. Wilson, 1961. 171-73.

Davis, Marianne W., ed. *Contributions of Black Women to America*. Vol. 1. Columbia, S.C.: Kenday Press, 1982. 88.

Eyman, Scott. "The Life and Times of the Determined and Gifted—and Indomitable Zelma George—Daddy Watson's Little Girl." *Cleveland Magazine* (1 March 1 1983): 68.

"5 Black Women 80+ Discuss Achievements." *Cleveland Plain Dealer*, 15 April 1986.

Gard, Connie Schultz. "It's a Wonderful Life." *Plain Dealer Magazine* (22 July 1990).

Garland, Phyl. "The Miracle on Ansel Road." *Ebony* 7 (May 1968): 90-100.

George, Zelma Watson. Biographical Sketch, April 18, 1990.

George, Zelma Watson. Interview with author. 18 April 1990.

George, Zelma Watson. Interview with Black Oral History Project. Schlesinger Library, Radcliffe College, 1978.

———. "My Basic Beliefs." Statement by Dr. Zelma Watson George on receiving The James Dodman Nobel 1984 Award in Human Relations. Cleveland, Ohio: The Council on Human Relations, June 12, 1985.

The Greater Cleveland Women's History Week Committee. "Women Who Shaped Cleveland—Honoring Dr. Zelma Watson George and Rowena Jelliffe." Program. Cleveland, Ohio: Cleveland State University, 7 March 1985.

Jelliffe, Rowena Woodham, and others. *Here's Zelma*. Cleveland: Job Corps Center Committee, 10 September 1971.

Keegan, Frank L. *Blacktown U.S.A.* "Two Black Women and a Newspaperman: Zelma George." Boston: Little, Brown, 1971.

Peery, Richard. "A Life's Work Honored." *Cleveland Plain Dealer*, 22 November 1985.

Ploski, Harry A. and James Williams, ed. *The Negro Almanac:* 4th ed. New York: Wiley 1983.

Robinson, Tracey L. "Zelma George: The Power of One." *Cleveland Plain Dealer*, 13 June 1985.

"Scholarship Named For Civic Leader Dr. Zelma George." *Cleveland Plain Dealer*, 28 February 1987.

"Two to be Honored During Women's Week." *Cleveland Plain Dealer*, 3 March 1985.

"Women of Courage." *Ebony* 16 (April 1961): 70-77.

"Zelma George Featured in History Exhibition." Coastal Communications News Release. Cleveland, Ohio: 29 November 1984.

Collections

Zelma Watson George retains control of all of her speeches, papers, pictures, collectibles, and publications; her papers and speeches ultimately will go to the Schomburg Center for Research in Black Culture in New York City. The Cleveland Public Library holds a clipping file on her.

Sandra E. Gibbs

Althea Gibson

(1927-)

Athlete

Althea Gibson once said: "Ain't that a blip" that a Harlem street rebel would go on to become a world tennis champion?" (Pizer, 191). Growing up on the streets of Harlem in the late 1930s and early 1940s was not easy, and Gibson was an incorrigible child, receiving punishments from both her father and her teachers. However, a talent for the game of tennis and a desire to be "somebody" provided the major

Althea Gibson

turning points in Gibson's life. She became the first black international tennis player in the world, winning at Wimbledon and Forest Hills. After a successful tennis career, she played professional golf and became the only black member of the Ladies Professional Golf Association (LPGA).

Gibson was born on August 25, 1927, in Silver, South Carolina. Her parents, Daniel and Annie Gibson, brought her to New York when she was still very young and reared her in the black belt of Harlem. The family lived in an apartment on West 143rd Street, and it was there that Gibson's three sisters, Millie, Annie, and Lillian, and her brother, Daniel, were born. Before coming to New York, Daniel Gibson was a sharecropper on a cotton farm. After bad weather ruined crops three years in succession, he moved to Harlem, where he obtained a job as a handyman in a garage. The Gibsons lived initially with their Aunt Sally but later moved to the apartment on West 143rd Street. "I don't remember anything about Carolina; all I remember is New York," Gibson says (Gibson, *I Always Wanted to Be Somebody*, 2).

As a twelve-year-old girl living in a congested Harlem tenement, Gibson learned to survive and to protect the rights of others. However, truancy permeated her teenage years. "I liked to play hooky and spend the day in the movies, especially on Fridays, when they had a big show at the Apollo Theatre on 125th Street," she says (16). Gibson graduated from junior high school in 1941, which was a surprise to her because of her low attendance. She rationalized that the teachers promoted her to the Yorkville Trade School for practical reasons rather than for academic ones. When Gibson requested a transfer to a downtown school because her friends went there, the school board denied the petition. This disappointment coupled with the logistical distance from familiar faces left Gibson embittered. Once again, truancy resurfaced, and Gibson found solace and comfort at the Society for the Prevention of Cruelty to Children, a place for troubled and homeless children. Compassion and understanding exemplified by the social workers made Gibson feel a peace and calm that had eluded her. A return to the home within a week alerted the social workers that Gibson had deep-seated problems. They told her that if her aberrant behavior continued, a girls' correctional facility would be her next home.

Gibson heeded this warning, but she preferred not to return to the trade school. She requested working papers, not usually given to children her age, on the condition that she attend night school for a designated number of hours per week. Gibson admits that she kept her promise for only two weeks. She worked, feeling for the first time a sense of importance, at several jobs ranging from counter girl at the Chamber Street branch of Choc Full O' Nuts restaurant chain to mail clerk at the New York School of Social Work. She liked the latter position best, but it lasted only six weeks. Instead of going to work as expected, Gibson went to the Paramount Theatre to see artists such as Sarah Vaughn. On Monday morning the supervisor inquired, "Where were you on Friday?" Gibson almost prevaricated but explained what happened. "I'm sorry," she apologized. "I won't do it again." Her supervisor commended her for honesty but dismissed her anyway, saying, "We can't have a girl who leaves an important job for foolish reasons" (Gibson, *I Always Wanted to Be Somebody*, 23). Gibson resented being penalized for honesty. Since she had met boxer Sugar Ray Robinson and his wife Edna while employed at the school, Gibson sought their council on many occasions. They encouraged her to complete her high school education in order to secure better employment and they later provided guidance in Gibson's tennis career. After the job loss at the school, she wanted to be "somebody," yet she felt "timid and lost inside herself" (Forsee, 61).

A period of restlessness and discontent followed, and Gibson lost numerous jobs in quick succession. Meanwhile, she loitered on the streets and came to the attention of the Welfare Department. Staff personnel made arrangements for Gibson to live in a less-crowded home and look for a job. "It was while I was living in a never-never land through the courtesy of the City of New York that I was introduced to tennis" (Gibson, *I Always Wanted to Be Somebody*, 25). Gibson also exemplified a talent for tennis in all of the games sponsored by the Police Athletic League on 143rd Street in her neighborhood. Although Gibson faced uncertainty about the future, it is evident that she had a flair for spirited competition. She played fast and pressing basketball on the neighborhood court. She hustled at stickball, a street version of baseball (using a broomstick and a rubber ball). She worked hard at paddleball (a form of conventional tennis with a court marked off similarly and played with a wooden paddle).

Buddy Walker, a musician who worked for the city recreation department in the summer, observed Gibson and said, "You are light-footed and have a lot of power. I wonder what you'd do with regular tennis." "How can I tell with no racket?" asked Gibson (Pizer, 169). She soon had her chance because Walker bought a second-hand racket that he had restrung. After she practiced batting balls at the handball court in Morris Park, Walker thought that her skills were sufficient to play a few sets at the New York Cosmopolitan Club with professional Fred Johnson. Gibson demonstrated above average skills; club members, impressed with her natural ability as a tennis player, provided a junior membership and financed her lessons. Gibson commented that the Cosmopolitan members were the "highest class of Harlem people and they had rigid ideas about what was socially acceptable behavior. . . . I'm ashamed to say I was still living pretty wild" (Gibson, *I Always Wanted to Be Somebody*, 29-30). Johnson taught Gibson the basic bread-and-butter strokes known as the backhand and forehand. In addition, Gibson learned not only to hit the ball indiscriminately across the court but to master footwork and court strategy. At the age of fourteen, Gibson met a well-to-do black woman, Rhoda Smith, whose daughter had died ten years previously. Smith befriended Gibson, bought her a tennis outfit, and "struggled to impart the polish the ghetto roughneck needed in tennis" (Toppin, 305).

Tennis Changes Defiant Gibson

The game of tennis changed Gibson's life dramatically and within a year, after lessons with Johnson, she won her first tournament, the girls' singles in the New York State Open Championship in 1942. Nina Irwin, the white runner-up in the tournament, had also taken tennis lessons from Fred Johnson. Still interested in Gibson's welfare and success, the Cosmopolitan Club members pooled their financial resources and sent Gibson to the American Tennis Association's national girls' championship, a predominantly black competition at Lincoln University in Pennsylvania. Gibson went to the finals but lost to Nina Davis. In later years, Davis recalls this 1942 match with humor: "Althea was a very crude creature. She had the idea she was better than anybody. I can remember her saying, 'Who's this Nina Davis? Let me at her.' And after I beat her, she headed straight for the grandstand without bothering to shake hands. Some kid had been laughing at her, and she was going to throw him out" (Gibson, 33). After this loss, Gibson practiced more fiercely on the Cosmopolitan courts; however, World War II caused the American Tennis Association national tournament to be canceled because of travel restrictions. The tournament resumed in 1944 and Gibson won the girls' singles in 1944 and 1945. It is at this point that Gibson met Sugar Ray and Edna Robinson again, and they not only provided encouragement for her on the tennis circuit, but they also bought a saxophone for Gibson, whose love of vocal and instrumental music was to play an integral role in her future.

In 1946, at the age of eighteen, Gibson became eligible for the women's singles and played at Wilberforce College in Ohio. She lost to Roumania Peters, a teacher at Tuskegee Institute. One critic believes that overconfidence defeated her, but not Peters. Despite the loss, Gibson attracted the attention of two black surgeons who were leaders in the American Tennis Association, Hubert Eaton of Wilmington, North Carolina, and Robert W. Johnson of Lynchburg, Virginia. Gibson comments that these two men "were getting ready to change my whole life" (Gibson, *I Always Wanted to Be Somebody*, 37). Eaton and Johnson recognized her potential and offered this proposal: they would feed, clothe, and educate her at their own expense. During the school year, Gibson lived with Eaton's family in Wilmington, attended high school, and practiced with him on his private court, the only one for blacks in the city. In the summer, Gibson received similar, though more intensive, instruction from Johnson and traveled with him to tournaments.

Although grateful for the doctors' generosity and attention, Gibson did not immediately accept their offer and saw it as a mixed blessing. On the one hand, she liked the idea of receiving further training, but on the other hand, the prospect of reentering high school at nineteen sounded bleak. Yet Sugar Ray Robinson and his wife counseled Gibson that an education was invaluable. As a result, she wrote Eaton in August 1946 and arrived in Wilmington a month later. In the summer of 1947 and for the next nine years Gibson won the American Tennis Association womens' championship. It was the decisiveness of her win that caught the eye of tennis enthusiasts who proclaimed her the best black woman tennis player in the United States.

Aside from tennis, Gibson realized that an education was the best avenue to be that "somebody" that had eluded her grasp as a child growing up in Harlem. She enjoyed school in Wilmington better than in New York and she graduated tenth in her class from Williston Industrial High School in June 1949. Before Gibson finished high school, Florida Agricultural and Mechanical College at Tallahassee offered her a tennis scholarship and encouraged her to spend the summer playing tennis on the campus. At twenty-two, Gibson entered college eager and mindful of what her mentors, Eaton and Johnson, had done: "Nobody could have been more grateful than I was to both doctors for everything . . . but it was good to feel a little bit independent again" (Gibson, *I Always Wanted to Be Somebody*, 57).

At Florida A & M, Gibson focused on her studies, which consisted of a full load of classes, tennis practice, playing on the basketball team, and working as a student assistant in the physical education department. Little time was left for anything else. Because of her love for music, Gibson found time to play in the school's marching band. She wanted to major in music but faculty advisors discouraged the disparate combination of tennis and music. Instead, Gibson pledged Alpha Kappa Alpha Sorority and juggled tennis and studies for the next four years.

Meanwhile, repeated attempts to compete in tennis caused Gibson to try harder, and she later accepted the invitation to play in Eastern and national indoor championships. She was not the first to break the color barrier in these matches; a black preceded her two years earlier—Reginald Weir. In both of Gibson's tournaments, Nancy Chaffee emerged the clear victor. Despite the loss, Gibson received a cheerful welcome from the Florida A & M marching band.

Gibson waited for an invitation from the United States Lawn Tennis Association to play in the prestigious summer grass court tournament at Forest Hills, Long Island. She waited and no invitation came. Alice Marble, a white tennis player, also waited for Gibson's invitation. When none came, "without any warning at all," Alice Marble wrote an editorial in the July 1950 issue of the *American Lawn Tennis* magazine that "kicked up a storm from one end of the tennis world to another" (Dannett, 220). Marble speaks her mind:

> I think it's time we faced a few factors. If tennis is a game for ladies and gentlemen, it's also time we acted like gentlepeople and less like sanctimonious hypocrites. If there is anything left in the name of sportsmanship, it's more than time to display what it means to us. If Althea Gibson represents a challenge to the present crop of women players, it's only fair that they should meet that challenge on the courts, where tennis is played. I know those girls, and I can't think of one who would refuse to meet Miss Gibson in competition. . . .
>
> The entrance of Negroes into national tennis is as inevitable as it has proven in baseball, in football, or in boxing; there is no denying so much talent. The committee at Forest Hills has the power to stifle the efforts of one Althea Gibson, who may or may not be succeeded by others of her race who have equal or superior ability. They will knock at the door as she has done. Eventually the tennis world will rise up en masse to protest the injustices perpetrated by our policymakers. Eventually—why not now? (Dannett, 220).

Gibson wrote that "all of a sudden, the dam broke" (Gibson, *I Always Wanted to Be Somebody*, 67). Her application to enter the New Jersey State Championship at the Maplewood Country Club was rejected; however, the Orange Lawn Tennis Club in South Orange, New Jersey, one of the outstanding clubs on the Eastern circuit, accepted Gibson's application to play in the Eastern Grass Court Championship, a tournament ranked second to the nationals in the tennis circles of the Atlantic seaboard. Gibson defeated one player but was eliminated by Helen Pastall in the second round. She reached the quarterfinals in the National Clay Courts Championships at Chicago, where Doris Hart beat her 6-2, 6-3. It was after this match that Harold Blair of the United States Lawn Tennis Association "passed the word to Mr. Baker (President of the USLTA) that if I applied for entrance into the Nationals, I would be accepted. I filled out the entry blank as fast as I could get hold of one" (Gibson, *I Always Wanted to Be Somebody*, 67).

Gibson Plays in Nationals

Gibson recounts the moment vividly when Lawrence Baker announced that "I was one of the fifty-two women whose entries had been accepted for the national championship tournament. . . . [H]e added meaningfully, [that] 'Miss Gibson has been accepted on her ability.' That was all I had ever asked" (68). Although Gibson won the first round match easily against Great Britain's Barbara Knapp in straight sets (6-2 and 6-2) in August 1950, she lost to Louise Brough, Wimbledon champion and former United States champion. Initially, Gibson felt good about her chances to win and built up a 7-6 lead in the third and deciding set. Throughout the match, Gibson fought Brough aggressively, but Brough emerged as the victor, 6-1, 3-6, and 9-7. Gibson attributes her loss to two disturbing factors: a "drenching thunderstorm," destroying one of the stadium's supports, delayed the game one day and the entourage of news reports following her movements unnerved Gibson to the point of distraction (71-73). Gibson became the first black to play major lawn tennis, but it would take seven years before returning to win the nation's tennis championship at Forest Hills.

Frustration and a lack of confidence characterize the next three years for Gibson because she saw her national ranking go from ninth in 1952 to seventieth in 1953. Although Gibson rose to thirteenth in 1954, during this dismal period she graduated from Florida A and M with a degree in physical education. She pushed tennis aside temporarily and joined the physical education department faculty of Lincoln University, Jefferson City, Missouri, teaching for two years and having a "wingding of a time with a wonderful man." While she was there, Gibson thought of joining the Women's Army Corps because her special young man headed the ROTC unit (82). It was while she was awaiting official word from the Army that Sydney Llewellyn, a Harlem tennis coach, persuaded Gibson to resume tennis and join the circuit.

The fact that Gibson played at Forest Hills was still of some significance, and it continued to open doors of opportunities for her, such as tours in Mexico and Southeast Asia. Winning tournament after tournament in quick succession, Gibson played in Sweden, Germany, France, England, Italy, and Egypt. She had won sixteen out of the eighteen tournaments. On the basis of this impressive record, she received a bid to play at Wimbledon. However, Gibson lost to Shirley Fry (4-6, 6-3, and 6-4) and lost to her again in the finals at Forest Hills (6-3 and 6-4).

In 1957 Gibson became the first black woman to compete and to win at Wimbledon and Forest Hills. Facing Darlene Hard at Wimbledon, Gibson won the singles match 6-3, 6-2 and teamed with Hard to win the doubles championship. At Forest Hills, Gibson emerged victoriously over Louise Brough, a former opponent, 6-3, 6-2. The following year, Gibson returned to Wimbledon and defeated Britain's Angela Mortimer 8-6, 6-2 in singles. Paired with Maria Bueno of Brazil in doubles, Gibson beat Margaret Gaborn du Pont and Margaret Varner 6-3, 7-5. In the decade after second victories at both Wimbledon and Forest Hills, Gibson admits having "so many prospects on the horizon that the future had no anxiety for me at all" (Gibson, *So Much to Live For*, 26). What she does not say is that new anxieties replaced old ones, and Gibson faced an uncertain future reminiscent of the Harlem years before tennis. What could a thirty-year-old tennis champion do with the rest of her life? Two basic needs colored Gibson's decision to retire from tennis. The need to secure a good living, referred to as "Old Devil Money," and to undertake a new profession contributed to Gibson's final decision as evidenced by these lines from the closing of her retirement announcement:

> I cannot make this statement without thanking everyone, as well as the game of tennis itself, for what it has done for me. In particular I should like to open my heart to all the people in the tennis world . . . who have offered me advice and criticism on my game, and my friends, all of whom collectively made it possible for me to become women's champion of the world. . . . I hope that I have accomplished just one thing: that I have been a credit to tennis and my country (Gibson, *So Much to Live For*, 27).

Gibson's retirement shocked fans and puzzled media reporters. Because the money was not in professional tennis, she undertook a number of activities such as: a singing career, appearing on the "Ed Sullivan Show" and recording albums on the Dot label; a series of tours with the Harlem Globetrotters; appearing in a tennis match prior to the game and during intermission with Karol Fageros (an old opponent in the 1950s); a Hollywood movie career, appearing in a John Ford Film, *The Horse Soldiers*, with John Wayne and William Holden; working as a community relations representative with Ward Baking Company; traveling to numerous cities to promote goodwill on behalf of Tip-Top Bread; and becoming a professional golfer, playing in several tournaments from 1963 to 1967. For Gibson, the golf game offered the best chance, not because it had been the exclusive sport of wealthy white women but because she had enough ability to compete on the tour. Gibson comments that "I was born too soon," meaning that now it is possible for women to earn a living at both tennis and golf if they had accomplished skills.

In recent years, Gibson, wife of New Jersey businessman William A. Darben, has been employed by the Essex County, New Jersey, Park Commission as a programmer of women's and girls' activities and as director of programs for the Valley View Racquet Club in North Vale, New Jersey. A firm believer in all sports, Gibson feels that no one succeeds without the help of others, as in the case of Alice Marble's trenchant editorial that opened the eyes and minds of the tennis world to reality. Elitism would no longer be tolerated in tennis.

Today, no one can rival Gibson's second serve except Steffi Graf. But more important, no black woman on the tennis circuit has achieved what Gibson did more than thirty years ago. Still interested in the game of tennis, Gibson attended the 1990 Wimbledon tournament and observed Zena Garrison, the first black woman to play in the finals since 1957-1958. Although Garrison lost to Czechoslovakian Martina Navratilova, she impressed the tennis world by eliminating Monica Seles in the finals and Steffi Graf in the semifinals, much as Gibson had done at Wimbledon and Forest Hills. Garrison may become the heir apparent to Gibson as the second black Wimbledon champion in the world. She has already superseded Gibson's record of being the only black woman to reach the finals. However, Gibson was the first black to capture titles in tennis and became one of the greatest athletes of her time, gathering and retaining world dominance in a sport that few blacks deemed a viable option for themselves. Althea Gibson wanted to be "somebody" and she succeeded *par excellence*.

References

Ashe, Arthur R., Jr. *A Hard Road to Glory: A History of the African-American Athlete Since 1946*. Vol. 3. New York: Warner Books, 1988.

"Althea Gibson Shares Her Knowledge with Collegians." *Jet* 58 (1980).

Baskin, Wade and Richard N. Runes. *Dictionary of Black Culture*. New York: Philosophical Library, 1973.

Bontemps, Arna. *Famous Negro Athletes*. New York: Dodd, Mead, 1964.

Casabona, Helen, and Alice Dawson. "Winners Circle: Outstanding Women Athletes of the Past 65 Years." *Women Sports and Fitness* 6 (1984): 5.

Dannett, Sylvia G. L. *Profiles of Negro Womanhood*. Vol. 2. Yonkers: Educational Heritage, 1966.

Davis, Lenwood G. *The Black Woman in American Society: A Selected Bibliography*. Boston: G. K. Hall, 1965.

Davis, Marianna W., ed. *Contributions of Black Women to America*. Vol. 1. Columbia, S.C.: Kenday Press, 1982. 503-509; 573, 575.

Dawson, Alice. "Matches to Remember: Women of the U.S. Open." *Women's Sports and Fitness* 7 (August 1985): 22-23, 45.

Drees, Jack, and James C. Mullen. *Where Is He Now?* Middle Village, N.Y.: Jonathan David Publishers, 1973.

Editors of *Ebony*. *1,000 Successful Blacks*. Vol. 1, *Ebony Success Library*. Chicago: Johnson Pub. Co., 1973. 123.

"First Black Wimbledon Champ, Althea Gibson, Recognized in England." *Jet* 66 (23 July 1984): 46-48.

"Former Wimbledon Tennis Champion Althea Gibson Interviewed." *San Francisco Chronicle*, 15 November 1984.

Forsee, Aylesa. *Women Who Reach for Tomorrow*. Philadelphia: Macrae Smith Company, 1960.

Garrett, Romeo B. *Famous First Facts About Negroes*. New York: Arno Press, 1972.

Gibson, Althea. *I Always Wanted to Be Somebody*. New York: Harper, 1958.

———. *So Much to Live For*. New York: Putnam, 1968.

Grimsley, Will. *Tennis: Its History, People and Events*. Englewood Cliffs, N.J.: Prentice-Hall, 1971.

Henderson, Edwin B., and others. *The Black Athlete: Emergence and Arrival*. Cornwell Heights, Pa.: Publishers Agency, 1976.

Low, W. Augustus, and Virgil A. Clift. *Encyclopedia of Black America*. New York: McGraw-Hill, 1981.

Lumpkin, Angela. *A Guide to the Literature of Tennis*. Westport, Conn.: Greenwood Press, 1985.

Orr, Jack. *The Black Athlete: His Story in American History*. New York: Lion Press, 1969.

Pizer, Vernon. *Glorious Triumphs: Athletes Who Conquered Adversity*. New York, Dodd, Mead, 1968.

Ploski, Harry A. and James Williams. *The Negro Almanac: A Reference Work on the Afro American*. New York: Wiley, 1983.

Reasons, George. *They Had a Dream*. Los Angeles: Los Angeles Times Syndicate, 1970.

Richardson, Ben. *Great American Negroes*. New York: Crowell, 1956.

Robinson, Wilhelmina S. *Historical Negro Biographies*. New York: Publishers Company, 1969.

Rywell, Martin. *Afro-American Encyclopedia*. Vol. 4. North Miami: Educational Books, 1974.

Smith, Margaret Chase. *Gallant Women*. New York: McGraw-Hill, 1968.

Smythe, Mabel M., ed. *The Black American Reference Book*. Englewood Cliffs, N.J.: Prentice-Hall, 1976.

Toppin, Edgar A. *A Biographical History of Blacks in American Since 1528*. New York: David McKay, 1969.

Who's Who Among Black Americans. 5th ed. Lake Forest, Ill.: Educational Communications, 1988. 256. 6th ed. Detroit: Gale Research, 1990.

Williams, Ora. *American Black Women in the Arts and Social Sciences: A Bibliographic Survey*. Metuchen, N.J.: Scarecrow Press, 1973.

Sharynn Owens Etheridge

Paula Giddings

(1947-)

Journalist, editor, author

Paula Giddings is a journalist, editor, and author. She uses her writing talent to analyze, present, and illuminate information and ideas in order to create change in society today.

Paula Giddings was born on November 16, 1947, in Yonkers, New York, and raised in its predominantly white residential section. Giddings's inspiration to make an effort toward change came from role models within her own family and the civil rights movement, which cranked into full force as she was coming of age.

Giddings's family went to Yonkers in 1888. Her paternal grandfather served on the board of education and was active in civil affairs. Her father, Curtis G. Giddings, a graduate of New York University, worked as a guidance counselor and school teacher in New York and later became the first black firefighter in Yonkers. He also established the Yonkers branch of the Congress of Racial Equality. Her mother, Virginia I. Giddings, was also a college graduate. She graduated from Virginia State University and worked as a guidance counselor in the New York school system as well. Giddings has a half brother and a half sister.

Before graduating from Gorton High School in Yonkers in 1965, Giddings had already begun to realize her desire to write by publishing her first work in the student literary magazine. She moved on to study at Howard University, graduating in 1969 with a B.A. in English.

Giddings went to Howard in order to learn from a black perspective and to be surrounded by a black community. Although she served as editor of the *Afro-American Review*, the Howard University literary magazine, she found that poetry was inadequate to satisfy her need for creative expression. Rather, she wanted to synthesize, analyze, and interpret information. In college Giddings began to believe that everything is interconnected. In line with a desire to travel, she began to explore foreign affairs. Special inspiration through her college years came from Professor Arthur P. Davis, who exposed her to black literature. She also admired Professor Jeane Marie Miller, who consistently was able to see things from a student's perspective and stood with students in their struggles.

After graduation in 1969, Giddings went to work for Random House in New York as an editorial secretary. She remained in this position until 1970, when she was promoted to copy editor. At this time Charles Harris at Random House was actively recruiting blacks to be editors, and he brought

Giddings into the ranks. Toni Morrison, another Howard graduate, was also an editor at Random House. During the early 1970s, Random House was publishing the works of many black American writers, including Angela Davis, Stokely Carmichael, and the Black Panthers. Through her position at Random House, Giddings had the opportunity to be at the forefront of the forces bringing these works in to be published.

When Charles Harris left Random House in 1972 to help establish the university press at Howard University, Giddings followed. At the Howard University Press, she worked as a book editor. Her job involved creating book ideas, and procuring and editing manuscripts. This allowed her to work closely with authors and gave her some decision-making power regarding the books to be published. She considered this opportunity of some significance, as the publishing industry and the media as a whole have been extremely influential in perpetuating racism in the United States.

After three years with the Howard University Press, Giddings left in 1975 to join the staff of *Encore America* and *Worldwide News*. Prompted to move by her desire to live abroad and a feeling of disillusionment as the civil rights movement wound down, she began to lose her drive and sought a position overseas to give her a new perspective.

She convinced publisher Ida Lewis to allow her to open a branch in Paris. There she worked as a journalist, reporting the news of the black community in France and traveling to such places as the Ivory Coast, South Africa, Uganda, and Kenya to report stories. Among prominent people Giddings interviewed were Winnie Mandela and President Idi Amin of Uganda. Far from home, Giddings began to feel pangs of homesickness. She returned to the United States in 1977, and until 1979 worked for *Encore* as an associate editor in New York City. There she was responsible for organizing the reporting of national and international stories about black and Third World communities.

Giddings Studies History of Black Women

In 1979, Giddings became part of a federally-funded project on black women's history. The project was designed to produce ten studies on the history of black women. She was given the responsibility of researching and writing two book-length manuscripts on "Black Women in the Arts" and "Black Women and the Resistance Struggle in America." From the project Giddings gained an intense interest in black women's history.

While searching for information, she became increasingly frustrated and intrigued. She began to see that black women did not fit well beneath the confusing categories of black (black men) and women's (white women) movements. As a result she applied for and received a Ford Foundation grant that led to her next project and most widely-known work to date: *When and Where I Enter: The Impact of Black Women on Race and Sex.*

Her book traces the history of black women from the late 1800s to the contemporary period, illuminating black women's achievements in the midst of their own reality. She identifies the conflicts and complexity of race and gender issues as well as the personal struggles that existed as background for their experiences and actions. Giddings believes that it is crucial for black women to know the contributions that other black women have made in the past. The book has been well received and is widely used in college courses across the country. It also has been translated into Dutch and Japanese.

In the years between 1984 and 1989, Giddings lectured at colleges all over the nation. She also helped coordinate and participated in conferences. Her writings have appeared in papers and magazines such as the *New York Times* and *Essence*. She was also appointed to the Governors Advisory Committee on Black Affairs in New York State and is a member of the Finance and Economic Committee.

In 1988, she published *In Search of Sisterhood: Delta Sigma Theta and the Challenge of the Black Sorority Movement.* She joined the sorority in college because she was impressed by its involvement in issues on campus. At that time she was looking for a community and found that she learned much about the positive and negative aspects of the workings of black women's organizations.

In 1988 Giddings became a fellow of the Barnard Center for Research on Women. She embarked on a five-year project in 1989 to write a biography of black American journalist Ida B. Wells. She is also teaching women's studies at Douglass College at Rutgers. Writing, however, is first and foremost for her. "I will write till I say good-bye to this world," she says (Interview with Paula Giddings, 12 March 1990). Giddings has never married.

In the future, Giddings anticipates further involvement with analytic, theoretical, and journalistic presentations of history and current affairs. In light of the emergence of Third World and black women's studies, she sees our next step as ensuring the smooth riding of coalitions between various minority groups. She also sees academia as the hotbed of the liberation movement in upcoming years and suspects that she will stay there in order to be at the forefront of events.

References

Contemporary Authors. Vol. 125. Detroit: Gale Research, 1989.

Giddings, Paula. Interview with author, 12 March 1990.

———. *In Search of Sisterhood: Delta Sigma Theta and the Challenge of the Black Sorority Movement.* New York: William Morrow, 1988.

———. *When and Where I Enter: The Impact of Black Women of Race and Sex.* New York: William Morrow, 1984.

Amanda Beth Zola with Adrienne Lash Jones

Nikki Giovanni

(1943-)

Poet, writer, commentator, activist, educator, publisher

Groundbreaking, prolific, and sometimes controversial poet Nikki Giovanni has been both lauded and criticized for her work. The guiding forces in her poetry and in her life have remained consistent, however: Her ability and willingness to change and grow, and her emphasis on a pride in her black heritage, which she shares with young people and adults alike.

Yolande Cornelia "Nikki" Giovanni, Jr., was born in Knoxville, Tennessee, on June 7, 1943, the daughter of Jones "Gus" Giovanni and Yolande (Watson) Giovanni. At age seventeen she entered Fisk University. After a break in her studies, she received her B.A. degree with honors in 1967. She majored in history. She did graduate work at the University of Pennsylvania School of Social Work in 1967 and undertook additional study at the Columbia University School of Fine Arts in 1968.

It is customary to discuss Giovanni's development in terms of decades. In the sixties, militancy characterizes her writing; in the seventies, greater introspection and attention to personal relationships; in the eighties, a global outlook with a greater concern for humanity in general. However, the various themes reflect changes in emphasis rather than wholesale abandonment of one concern for another.

Nikki Giovanni

Giovanni's overall approach—seeking and telling the truth, growing in the process—is grounded in her family heritage. Her strong grandmother, Luvenia Terrell Watson, was "terribly intolerant when it came to white people" (*Gemini*, 26). As a result of her outspokenness, Luvenia Watson was smuggled out of Albany, Georgia, under the cover of darkness by her husband, John "Book" Watson, and other family members. They had good reason to believe that her life was in danger. Luvenia and John Watson had hoped to reach the North, but settled in Knoxville, Tennessee, "the first reasonable-sized town" on their way (*Gemini*, 28). A teacher, John Watson returned to Albany to finish the school term—"Grandfather was like that." He then joined his wife in Knoxville, where they made their home.

Giovanni's mother, Yolande Watson, was the oldest of three daughters. Yolande met Jones "Gus" Giovanni at Knoxville College. From their subsequent marriage, two daughters were born. Jones Giovanni's roots were in Cincinnati, where Nikki Giovanni spent some of her formative years. Of the family surname, she has observed, "It just means that *our* slave masters were Italian instead of English or French" (Bailey, 49). Along with her grandparents, Giovanni's parents and her older sister, Gary, have been strong, positive influences on her development, even though Giovanni does not depict them (or herself) idealistically.

Giovanni has warned against reading her work—poetry or prose—as strictly autobiographical. Even so, because she assesses life from a personal perspective, her own experiences are essential starting points and often remain central themes for her writing. She states that *Gemini* (1971) merely "comes close" to being autobiography—truth being larger than merely what we remember (Tate, 68). Nevertheless, Giovanni's summary of the importance of her heritage in *Gemini* is illustrated in her work as a whole:

> Life/personality must be taken as a total entity. All of your life is all of your life, and no one incident stands alone. . . . My family on my grandmother's side are fighters. My family on my father's side are survivors. I'm a revolutionist. It's only logical (33).

Revolutionary Poet Attracts National Attention

It was as a revolutionary poet in the 1960s that Giovanni first came to national attention. During this period she became known as the "Princess of Black Poetry." The poetry in *Black Feeling, Black Talk* and in *Black Judgement* capture the spirit of the times. Other poets who became prominent during that period included Don L. Lee (later Haki Madhubuti) and Sonia Sanchez. Like her contemporaries, Giovanni found traditional poetic themes and techniques inadequate for the times.

Giovanni's activism revealed itself not only on paper. As a student at Fisk University in the mid-sixties, she had been a founding member of the university's Student Nonviolent Coordinating Committee (SNCC) chapter. Establishing the chapter was not an easy task, and her commitment is an example of her acting on principles rather than out of conformity.

Giovanni began her college studies at Fisk University in 1960, but she was "released" because she went home for Thanksgiving without asking permission of the dean of women. This incident is an example of her making decisions based on her values, in this case the primacy of family. Giovanni wanted to be with her grandparents, the Watsons, knowing that her grandfather was ill and that her grandmother needed her support. Looking back on the experience, Giovanni points out that she knew what the outcome would be, but if she had not gone to Knoxville, "the only change would have been that Fisk considered me an ideal student, which means little on a life scale" (*Gemini*, 7). When she returned to college it was because she felt ready. Her grandmother Watson said she would live to see Nikki finish college. Her grandmother died about one month after Giovanni graduated. (*Gemini*, 10-11, 148).

The significance of family and family-oriented themes deepened for Giovanni with the birth of her son, Thomas Watson, in August 1969. "Don't Have a Baby till You Read This" recounts the experience. Giovanni has noted: "I had a baby at 25 because I *wanted* to have a baby and I could *afford* to have a baby. I did not get married because I didn't *want* to get married and I could *afford* not to get married" (Bailey, 56).

As a mother, Giovanni had even more impetus to provide positive images for black children. Her response included establishing her own publishing company, Niktom, Limited, in 1970. At least in part, this endeavor can be read as an extension of the work she began in the sixties—to create literature that speaks directly to black people and that celebrates positive features of black life. In short, the concerns of the revolutionary were rechanneled rather than abandoned.

Throughout her work, Giovanni includes warm tributes to black women—famous and not famous. "Poems for Aretha," "The Geni[e] in the Jar (for Nina Simone)," and "Poem for a Retired Lady of Leisure I Know" are among these tributes. "Ego-Tripping" conveys Giovanni's exuberant celebration of the black woman: "For a birthday present when he was three / I gave my son hannibal an elephant / He gave me rome for mother's day."

The titles of many of Giovanni's books of poetry published in the 1970s—*Re-Creation, My House, The Women and the Men, Cotton Candy on a Rainy Day*—have an introspective, thoughtful focus. Paula Giddings finds *The Women and the Men* a "coming of age. For the first time, the woman-child is virtually absent," replaced by an adult (Evans, 214). Themes of relationships, of womanhood, and of motherhood are stressed. Again, Giovanni's themes are not readily summarized. The more personal themes are relevant to the wider world in that they suggest the values that should apply in making the world a better place. And Giovanni includes themes other than the personal. In *The Women and the Men*, the final section, "And Some Places," reflects her travel to Africa, which she visited with her friend Ida Lewis in 1971.

Giovanni Records Dialogues with Baldwin and Walker

Giovanni's interest in exploring others' ideas is illustrated in the books that transcribe her conversations with James Baldwin (1972) and Margaret Walker (1974). Both these dialogues demonstrate mutual respect even in the presence of clear generational differences. Topics are wide-ranging; both volumes include attention to black writing and to relationships between black men and women.

Record albums have served as another effective medium of expression for Giovanni. *Truth is on Its Way* (1972) helped launch Giovanni's lasting popularity as a speaker and reader of her own poetry. The album consists of Giovanni's reading her poems to background gospel accompaniment. For the most part the poems were written in the late sixties, the time of greater explicit militancy. Reading such poems as "The Great Pax Whitey" to "Peace Be Still" and "Second Rapp Poem" to "This Little Light of Mine" illustrated connections between the secular and the sacred in black art generally and made Giovanni's work more accessible to older generations.

The conversations and the albums underscore the importance of the spoken word for Giovanni. The Baldwin dialogues aired originally on "Soul," the television show produced by Ellis Haizlip. Haizlip also played a major part in the development of *Truth is on Its Way*. Giovanni and Walker's conversations resulted from their contact at the Paul Laurence Dunbar Centennial (University of Dayton, October 1972). In a postscript to her conversations with Walker, Giovanni sums up the importance of such an exchange: "I rather like the immediacy of talking . . . the mistakes . . . the insights . . . the risks inherent in hot conversation. Life is all about that balance between risk and inertia . . . that poetic equation" (148).

Her willingness to take risks continued to characterize Giovanni's work in the eighties. She deepened her perspectives, stressing respect for all people and the environment. "We are earthlings," Giovanni has noted (Tate, 71). Her poems and commentary of the eighties reflect her interest in space exploration as well as in anthropological studies. An example of the latter is "Hands" in *Those Who Ride the Night Winds* (1983). In a public reading, Giovanni has explained that her reading of anthropology led her to the conclusion (also the poem's conclusion) that the women of the species were the ones who most needed to stand and begin using hands, especially to hold the young and applaud the males, who need to have their egos stroked (Fisk University, 16 February 1990).

The reaction to *Night Winds* has varied. Paula Giddings,

who admires Giovanni's achievement and who wrote the introduction to *Cotton Candy on a Rainy Day*, characterizes the volume as "hollow, the thinking . . . fractious" (Evans, 215). Mozella Mitchell, on the other hand, finds that *Night Winds* "reflects [Giovanni's] heightened self-knowledge and imagination" (150).

Whatever the critical reading, it is clear that Giovanni is among those willing to take risks, to ride the night winds:

> A lot of people refuse to do things because they don't want to go naked. . . . But that's what's got to happen. You go naked until you die. . . . We as black people, we as people, we as the human species have got to get used to the fact we're not going to be right most of time, not even when our intentions are good. We've got to go naked and see what happens (Tate, 69).

The very title *Sacred Cows and Other Edibles* (1988) captures Giovanni's continued readiness to take on and devour society's myths, or to "go naked and see what happens." This collection of short prose pieces marks the twentieth anniversary of her first publication. *Sacred Cows* gives attention to sports, supplying special help to women in negotiating the terrain: "If they are in their underwear—it's Basketball; if they have on their pajamas—it's Baseball; if they wear helmets—it's Football" (93). Lighthearted without being trivial, insightful without being ponderous, Giovanni considers the implications of sports as an expression of culture. *Sacred Cows* covers a range of other topics, including selections on writing and on her relationship with her mother. Much of the book is centered on her time as a resident of Cincinnati, where she lived with her parents in 1978 after her father became ill.

Once she has written something, Giovanni moves on—no lack of inertia for her. She has acknowledged that she lacks discipline. On that point, William J. Harris observes: "She has the talent to create good, perhaps important, poetry, if only she has the will to discipline her craft" (Evans, 228). Finally, however, there can be no disagreement that Giovanni is a productive, talented writer. Her wit and candor as she stays "on the case," whatever the fundamental issues of the times may be, help explain why she remains consistently stimulating and significant.

Professional Activities, Awards, Achievements, and Publications

Giovanni has received honorary degrees from Wilberforce University, Worcester University, Ripon University, Smith College, College of Mount Saint Joseph on the Ohio, University of Maryland (Princess Anne campus), College of Mount Saint Mary (New York), and Fisk University.

Giovanni's academic appointments include assistant professor of black studies, Queens College of the City of New York (Flushing), 1968; associate professor of English, Rutgers University, Livingston College, New Brunswick, New Jersey, 1968-1972; visiting professor of English, Ohio State University, 1984-1985; professor of creative writing, Mount Saint Joseph on the Ohio, 1985-1987; Commonwealth Visiting Professor of English, Virginia Polytechnic Institute and State University at Blacksburg, Virginia, 1987-1989. Since 1989 she has been professor of English, Virginia Polytechnic Institute and State University.

As a columnist, Giovanni has authored "One Woman's Voice," for the Anderson-Moberg Syndicate of *The New York Times* and "The Root of the Matter," in *Encore American and World Wide News*. Her work has been published in *Negro Digest, Black World, Catalyst, Ebony, Essence, Journal of Black Poetry,* and *Newsday*. She has provided commentaries on National Public Radio and in many newspapers, including *USA Today* and *The Washington Post*. Her national and international television appearances have included Cable News Network (CNN), Black Entertainment Network, and participation in "Worldnet," United States Information Service-sponsored programs featuring satellite hookups to United States embassies around the world.

Her professional activity includes serving as judge in the Robert F. Kennedy Memorial Book Award selection, 1986-1987; member, The Ohio Humanities Council, 1987-1990; member, editorial board, *Artemis,* 1988-the present; and poetry editor, *Artemis,* 1989.

Giovanni is in constant demand to give poetry readings and lectures. Her writings appear in numerous anthologies, and she has been the subject of countless newspaper and magazine articles. In 1988, two awards were established in her honor: McDonald's Literary Achievement Award, a poetry award to be presented in the name of Nikki Giovanni in perpetuity; and the Nikki Giovanni Award for young African-American storytellers, sponsored by the National Festival of Black Storytelling. Other awards and honors include grants from the Ford Foundation, 1967; National Endowment for the Arts, 1968; Harlem Cultural Council, 1969; and National Council of the Arts, 1970.

Giovanni was named one of the ten most admired black women by the *Amsterdam News* in 1969. In 1970, *Ebony* magazine named her "Woman of the Year." In 1971, *Mademoiselle* magazine named her "Woman of the Year." In 1972, she was named *Ladies Home Journal* "Woman of the Year" (Youth Leadership Award), and she was recognized by Omega Psi Phi Fraternity for outstanding contribution to arts and letters.

Giovanni has clearly earned a prominent place in American life and letters. Since she first rose to national attention in the sixties, she has been consistently outspoken and charismatic. In great demand as a speaker, she is very generous with the time and consideration she gives to others, especially to young people. She has also been a prolific writer. Characteristically expressing her ideas with charm and good humor, she allows for opposite points of view as well: "I don't think everyone has to write the way I write nor think the way I think. There are plenty of ideas to go around'' (Evans, 207).

Giovanni's own thinking is subject to revision as well. She has observed:

> I like to think I've grown and changed in the last decade [the 1970s]. How else could I ask people to read my work or listen to me?. . . .Everything will change. The only question is growing up or decaying (Evans, 210; the same selection, ''An Answer to Some Questions on How I Write: In Three Parts'' is reprinted in *Sacred Cows*, 59-67).

Giovanni's books of poetry are: *Black Feeling, Black Talk* (Detroit: Broadside, 1968; 3rd ed., 1970); *Black Judgement* (Broadside, 1968); *Black Feeling, Black Talk/Black Judgement* (New York: William Morrow, 1970); *Re: Creation* (Broadside, 1970); *Spin a Soft Black Song: Poems for Children* (New York: Hill and Wang, 1971. Reprinted, New York: Lawrence Hill, 1985. Rev. ed. New York: Farrar, Straus, 1987); *My House: Poems* (William Morrow, 1972); *Ego-Tripping and Other Poems for Young People* (Lawrence Hill, 1973); *The Women and the Men* (William Morrow, 1975); *Cotton Candy on a Rainy Day* (William Morrow, 1978); *Vacation Time: Poems for Children* (William Morrow, 1980); and *Those Who Ride the Night Winds* (William Morrow, 1983). Also: a broadside: *Poem of Angela Yvonne Davis* (Detroit: Niktom, 1970).

Selected works of prose by Giovanni are: ''Black Poems, Poseurs and Power,'' *Negro Digest* 18 (June 1969): 30-34; *Gemini: An Extended Autobiographical Statement on My First Twenty-Five Years of Being a Black Poet* (Indianapolis: Bobbs-Merrill, 1971. Reprinted, New York: Viking, 1971); with James Baldwin, *A Dialogue: James Baldwin and Nikki Giovanni* (Philadelphia: Lippincott, 1973); *Sacred Cows . . . And Other Edibles* (William Morrow, 1988); and, with Margaret Walker, *A Poetic Equation: Conversations Between Nikki Giovanni and Margaret Walker* (Washington, D.C.: Howard University Press, 1974).

Recordings by Nikki Giovanni are: *Truth is on Its Way* (Right-on Records, 1972); *Like a Ripple On a Pond* (Niktom, 1973); *The Way I Feel* (Atlantic Records, 1974); *Legacies: The Poetry of Nikki Giovanni* (Folkways Records, 1976); *The Reason I Like Chocolate* (Folkways Records, 1976); and *Cotton Candy on a Rainy Day* (Folkways Records, 1978).

References

Bailey, Peter. ''Nikki Giovanni: 'I am Black, Female, Polite. . . .''' *Ebony* 27 (February 1972): 48-56.

Black Writers: A Selection of Sketches from Contemporary Authors. Detroit: Gale Research, 1989.

Collins, L. M. *Images of the Afro-American Woman: A Bibliographic Profile*. Introduction by Nikki Giovanni. Nashville: Fisk University Press, 1980.

Evans, Mari, ed. *Black Women Writers (1950-1980)*. Garden City, N.Y.: Doubleday, 1984.

Mitchell, Mozella G. ''Nikki Giovanni.'' *Dictionary of Literary Biography*. Vol. 41. *Afro-American Poets Since 1955*. Edited by Trudier Harris and Thadious M. Davis. Detroit: Gale Research, 1985.

Rush, Theresa Gunnels, Carol Fairbanks Myers, and Esther Spring Arata. *Black American Writers Past and Present*. Vol. 1. Metuchen, N.J.: Scarecrow Press, 1975.

Shockley, Ann Allen and Sue P. Chandler. *Living Black American Authors*. New York: Bowker, 1973.

Stetson, Erlene. *Black Sister: Poetry by Black American Women, 1746-1980*. Bloomington: Indiana University Press, 1981.

Tate, Claudia, ed. *Black Women Writers at Work*. New York: Continuum, 1984.

Who's Who Among Black Americans, 1990/91. 6th ed. Detroit: Gale Research, 1990.

Television Programs

''Spirit to Spirit: The Poetry of Nikki Giovanni.'' Public Broadcasting Corporation, the Corporation for Public Broadcasting and the Ohio Council on the Arts, 1986. Features Giovanni reading from her works.

Collections

Many of Giovanni's public papers are housed in the Mugar Memorial Library, Boston University, Boston, Massachusetts.

Arlene Clift-Pellow

Eliza Gleason

(1909-)

Librarian, library administrator, educator

When Eliza Atkins Gleason was awarded a Ph.D. from the Graduate Library School of the University of Chicago in 1940, she became the first black American to receive a doctorate in library science. Gleason's groundbreaking dissertation was entitled ''Government and Administration of Public Library Service to Negroes in the South'' and greatly influenced the future development of public library service to black Americans in that region. It was later published under the title *The Southern Negro and the Public Library; A Study of the Government and Administration of Public Library*

Service to Negroes in the South. In this study Gleason noted that public library service in the South was generally inadequate for all people, particularly blacks:

> The present status of public library service for the Negro in the thirteen southern states under consideration leaves much to be desired. While progress has been noted here and there, it is clear that public library facilities in the South are inadequate for all races—and much more inadequate for the Negro (187).

Eliza Atkins Gleason was born in Winston-Salem, North Carolina, on December 15, 1909, the youngest of seven children born to Simon Green Atkins and Oledna (Pegnam) Atkins. She had four brothers—Jasper Alston, Frank, Harvey, and Clarence—and two sisters—Ollie and Miriam. Her father founded Slater Industrial Academy, which later became Winston-Salem State University. He was president of this institution from 1892 to 1904 and from 1913 to 1934. His son Frank became president of the college in the 1930s.

A graduate of Fisk University in the class of 1930, Gleason received a bachelor of library science degree from the University of Illinois in 1931. Five years later in 1936, she earned a Master's of Library science from the University of California at Berkeley.

Gleason's career has been long and diverse. She began her career as assistant librarian, 1931-1932, at Louisville Municipal College. At Fisk University she headed the library's reference department from 1933 to 1937. For one year, 1936-1937, she was the library director at Talladega College.

Gleason Heads Library School

In 1940 Gleason was appointed the first dean of the new School of Library Service at Atlanta University. During that year she directed the setting up of the new library school, that opened in September 1941. The school was established to train professional black librarians, replacing the one at Hampton Institute which had closed. The Carnegie Corporation of New York, the General Education Board, and Atlanta University provided the financial support needed to initiate the program. The two full-time faculty members of the school were Wallace Van Jackson and Virginia Lacy Jones, who succeeded Gleason as dean. Twenty-five selected students were enrolled. Under Gleason's administration the School of Library Service at Atlanta in 1943 received its first accreditation from the American Library Association. This achievement was a genuine testimony to her excellent ability as a library educator.

Moving to Chicago in 1945 to be with her husband, noted heart surgeon Maurice F. Gleason, Eliza Gleason took a recess from her career to care for her adopted daughter, Joy Patricia. However, in 1953 her career resumed when she was guest lecturer at the Graduate Library School of the University of Chicago and head reference librarian at Wilson Junior College. From 1953 to 1967, she was associate professor and head of the reference department at Chicago Teachers College.

The Chicago Public Library was fortunate in 1970 to obtain Gleason's services as the assistant chief librarian in charge of regional centers. Under her direction the first regional center was opened in 1975: The Carter G. Woodson Regional Library Center. Gleason returned to library education in 1973 when she was invited to teach library science courses at an extension site of the library school of Northern Illinois University in Chicago. These courses were taught to capacity classes held at the central library of the Chicago Public Library.

In 1976 she accepted a joint appointment as assistant chief librarian at John Crerar Library, located on the campus of the Illinois Institute of Technology, as well as a professorship at the institution.

Because of her long career as an established authority on public libraries, Gleason was appointed by the mayor of Chicago to the board of directors of the Chicago Public Library in 1979. She served in this capacity for a year.

Throughout her career, Gleason has received many awards and held many important offices. From 1942 to 1946, she served on the council of the American Library Association. In 1964 she was elected to alumni membership in Phi Beta Kappa of Fisk University, and in 1964 she was appointed a board member of the Chicago Council of Foreign Relations.

References

Forde, Gladys I. Interview with Jessie Carney Smith, 2 April 1990.

Gleason, Eliza Atkins. ''Atlanta University School of Library Service.'' *Library Quarterly* 12 (July 1942): 504-10.

Gleason, Eliza Atkins. Interviewed, 8 January 1972.

———. *The Southern Negro and the Public Library; A Study of the Government and Administration of Public Library Service to Negroes in the South*. (Chicago: The University of Chicago Press, 1941).

Josey, E. J. and Ann Allen Shockley, eds. and comp. *Handbook of Black Librarianship*. Littleton, Colo.: Libraries Unlimited, 1977.

Josey, E. J., ed. *The Black Librarian in America*. Metuchen, N.J.: Scarecrow Press, 1970.

''Woman Quits High Library Job.'' *Chicago Tribune*, 5 May 1971.

Donald Franklin Joyce

Whoopi Goldberg

(1950-)

Actress, comedienne

Whoopi Goldberg is an actress who has emerged from a housing project in the Chelsea section of Manhattan, New York, to star in television and film and to win an Oscar, a Grammy, a Golden Globe award, and Oscar and Emmy nominations. She has striven to create and develop original material that exhibits her skill to present "believable individuals by virtuosic shifts in voice, body language and facial expression, in addition to narration" (*Current Biography,* 144). Her characterizations transform her into a variety of personalities, from a crippled girl to a tough-talking junkie with a Ph.D. in literature. One of Goldberg's most poignant and powerful characters is "a 9-year old street urchin who covers her tight braids with a white skirt that she pretends is long blond hair: 'I told my mother I don't want to be black no more. You have to have blond hair to be on *Love Boat*'" (Unterbrink, 206).

"Although her antic monologues contain elements of improvisational standup comedy, the pseudonymous Miss Goldberg is essentially a character actress [or actor, as she sometimes insists] whose original routines are really serio-comic plays, written in her head" (*Current Biography,* 144). Frustrated by the dearth of work for black character actors in the straight theater, several years ago Goldberg began to create her own varied repertoire and collection of offbeat social types whom she presented as believable individuals.

Goldberg was born Caryn Johnson in 1950 in New York City, where she and a younger brother, Clyde, lived with their mother, Emma Johnson, in a housing project in the Chelsea section of Manhattan. Goldberg notes that her father abandoned them early on and that her mother had to work a variety of jobs, including Head Start teacher and nurse, to take care of them. Goldberg claims that she is "half Jewish and half Catholic," and that one day she received her name by divine revelation: "One day I saw this burning bush and it said, 'Your name is boring, but have I got a name for you!'" (Unterbrink, 206). Of her invented name, Goldberg says,

> It was a joke. First it was Whoopi Cushion. Then it was French, like Whoopi Cushon. My mother said, "Nobody's gonna respect you with a name like that." So I put Goldberg on it. Goldberg's a part of my family somewhere and that's all I can say about it" (Current Biography, 145).

Goldberg attended the parish school of Saint Columbian Church on West Twenty-fifth Street, under the Congregation of Notre Dame. She demonstrated a propensity for acting at age eight, when she started acting at the Helena Rubenstein Children's Theatre at the Hudson Guild, having been influenced early by watching Gracie Allen, Carole Lombard, Claudette Colbert, and other established actresses in old movies on television. By age seventeen, she dropped out of high school, convinced that she was unable to grasp subject matter but unaware that she had dyslexia, which interfered with her performance. In the 1960s she joined the ruck of hippies but later asked herself if she was going to keep on doing drugs and kill herself or figure out what to do with her life. She decided that she wanted a better life: "I didn't stop altogether at once. It took many, many tries. . . . You fall a lot because it's hard" (Randolph, 111).

Goldberg became involved in "hippie politics" and was active in civil rights marches and student protests at Columbia University. She became a counselor at a summer camp on Ethical Culture held in Peekskill, New York. Since she had been born a mimic "with a natural, flawless eye and ear for details of character," her career was set to blossom when she found work on Broadway in the choruses of *Hair, Jesus Christ Superstar,* and *Pippin* (*Current Biography,* 144). From a brief marriage to her drug counselor in the 1970s during her drug rehabilitation period, she had one daughter, Alexandrea Martin.

Goldberg moved to the West Coast in 1974 to start over with her daughter and her childhood ambition: to act. "Acting is the one thing I always knew I could do," says Goldberg (Randolph, 111). She has held a series of jobs less glamorous than acting, such as bricklayer and styling hair at a mortuary. She was also a licensed beautician and a bank teller. She spent some time on relief—an experience that she finds disconcerting. "The welfare workers used to make these surprise visits because you weren't allowed to have friends," particularly if you gave them food, she recalls. If the welfare worker saw "a friend in the house with a plate of food in front of them, it would be deducted from your money the next month. . . . Getting off welfare, like getting off drugs, was a sweet triumph" (Randolph, 111).

Goldberg Moves from Theater to Film and Television

Goldberg wrote with Ellen Sebastian and performed a one-woman show in which she played the late comedienne Moms Mabley, whom she admired. She won a Bay Area Theatre Award for the performance. She continued to gain popularity as she moved from the theater to film. Goldberg made her debut in film when she appeared as Celie, a victim of spouse abuse in *The Color Purple.* Steven Spielberg's choice to cast Goldberg in a lead role made her an unforgettable face. For her performance in the film she won a Golden Globe Award, the NAACP Image Award, and an Academy Award nomination. This notoriety gave her sudden success that she maintains has not changed her life, claiming she works as hard as ever. Her other film credits include *Jumpin' Jack Flash, Burglar, Fatal Beauty, The Telephone, Homer and Eddie, Clara's Hero, Beverly Hills Brats, Ghost* (for which she won an Academy Award as best supporting actress), *The Long*

Walk Home, and *Soap Dish*. In October 1990, Following *Ghost*, Goldberg was named winner of the Excellence Award of the sixth annual Women in Film Festival. When the NAACP held its twenty-third annual Image Awards program in December 1990, she was named Black Entertainer of the Year.

Not limited to the theater and film, Goldberg joined Jean Stapleton on television in a new, short-lived situation comedy, "Bagdad Cafe," in which she played the hot-headed, softhearted cafe owner. She also appears on an irregular basis as a member of the crew of the starship *Enterprise* in "Star Trek: the Next Generation," and she was nominated for an Emmy for a guest appearance on *Moonlighting*. Goldberg, who sounds off on sex, drugs, race, and various other topics, has become one of the most sought-after black actresses. Basking in stardom and notoriety, Goldberg does not want to follow a traditional path for her career and or to be labeled a black actress. She readily says that "People have small minds. . . . I think of myself as an actor. I've said before, I can play a man—or a dog or a chair" (*Newsweek*, 60). Goldberg's special concerns are exhibited through her participation in Comic Relief, a fund-raiser for the homeless in which Billy Crystal and Robin Williams also appeared. In 1985 Goldberg had won a Grammy Award for best comedy album.

Life in the limelight has not always been easy for or kind to Goldberg. Some of her films, for example, *Jumpin' Jack Flash, Burglar,* and *Fatal Beauty,* were unsuccessful and put her movie career in jeopardy. In addition, some of the black community criticized her language, appearance, and role in *The Color Purple*. She has been criticized also for her Dutch husband, cameraman David Claessen, whom she married in 1986 but divorced less than two years later, and her current white male companion.

Known for her "Do-do braids," as she calls the locks of hair that she wears, Goldberg, whose main purpose for entertaining is to make people laugh, is a highly gifted performer who clearly achieves her purpose on stage. Short in stature and mild-mannered in appearance, she has been described as with "the face and personality of a wise child—with ingenuous eyes and a puckish smile" (*Current Biography,* 144). She admits, however, that she is temperamental—"Cranky as I wanna be," she said (Randolph, 110). A grandmother by the age of thirty-five, Goldberg is glad that her unmarried teenaged daughter made her own decision. "This baby was a choice and not a forced issue" (Randolph, 115). Whoopi Goldberg's triumph over dyslexia, drugs, welfare, and divorce is an example of the strength of her own determination and her will to succeed and excel—the mark of a survivor.

References

Current Biography. New York: Wilson, 1985. Photograph, p. 144.

Dworkin, Susan, "Whoopi Goldberg—in Performance." *Ms*. 12 (May 1984): 20.

Gill, Brendan. "The Theater." *New Yorker* 60 (5 November 1984): 155.

McGuigan, Cathleen. "Whoopee for Whoopi." *Newsweek* 106 (30 December 1985): 60.

Noel, Pamela. "Who is Whoopi Goldberg and What is She Doing on Broadway?" *Ebony* 40 (March 1985): 27-28, 30, 34.

Ploski, Harry A., and James Williams, comps. and eds. *The Negro Almanac*. New York: Gale Research, 1990.

Randolph, Laura B. "The Whoopi Goldberg Nobody Knows." *Ebony* 46 (March 1991): 110-12, 114-16. Includes photographs.

"23rd NAACP Awards Presented." *Tennessean,* 3 December 1990. Includes photograph.

Unterbrink, Mary. *Funny Women: American Comediennes, 1860-1985*. New York: McFarland, 1987.

"Whoopi and Jean Rap." *McCalls* (November 1990): 110-114. Includes photographs.

"Whoopi Goldberg and Jean Stapleton: Actresses Star in TV's New Bagdad Cafe." *Jet* 78 (23 April 1990): 58-60.

"Whoopi Goldberg Makes Her Funniest Film in 'Burglar.'" *Jet* 72 (20 April 1987): 56-57.

"Whoopi Wins Excellence Award." *Tennessean,* 28 October 1990.

Simmona E. Simmons

Nora Antonia Gordon

(1866-1901)

Religious worker, educator

Nora Antonia Gordon established a tradition at Spelman College, Atlanta, Georgia, in the training of young women to work as missionaries in Africa and in the education of African women at Spelman. Despite poor health and difficult living and working conditions in the Congo, she gave her brief life to the uplift of African people.

The parents of Nora Antonia Gordon once were slaves who belonged to General Gordon, who is said to have been well known. Like many other slaves, they took their name from their slave master. Nora Gordon was born in Columbus, Georgia, on August 25, 1866. She attended the public schools of La Grange, Georgia, and in fall 1882 she entered

Spelman Seminary in Atlanta. She is said to have brought with her many superstitions as well as mistaken ideas about religion. Her ideas soon changed, however, and she joined the Baptist church in Atlanta. Through her church work she organized temperance societies and Sunday schools and "caused family altars to be erected in the homes of her pupils" (Gibson and Crogman, 381). She completed her course in the industrial department of Spelman in 1885, and the next year the elementary normal. In 1888 Gordon graduated from the higher normal course, having written her graduation essay on "The Influence of Woman on National Character." Here she spoke in the intensity of her convictions:

> Let no woman feel that life to her means simply living; but let her rather feel that she has a special mission assigned her, which none other of God's creatures can perform. It may be that she is placed in some rude little hut as mother and wife; if so, she can dignify her position by turning every hut into a palace, and bringing not only her own household, but the whole community, into the sunlight of God's life. Such women are often unnoticed by the world in general, and do not receive the appreciation due them; yet we believe such may be called God's chosen agents. . . . We feel that woman is under a twofold obligation to consecrate her whole being to Christ. Our people are to be educated and christianized and the heathen brought home to God. Woman must take the lead in this great work (Brawley, 47).

Gordon Becomes Missionary to Africa

After graduating from Spelman, Gordon at once accepted a teaching position in the Atlanta public schools. Meanwhile, the secretary of the Society of the West wrote to Spelman in search of someone to assist the missionary already working in Palabala in the Congo. The board selected Nora Gordon's name from the four choices they had. In January 1889 Gordon received an offer to go to Africa immediately. On Sunday evening, February 17, a missionary service was held to acquaint Spelman's students with the slave trade in East Africa and efforts for its suppression, the spiritual awakening of the Zulus, the mission stations established on Congo, and other topics related to missionary work. In reference to her impending assignment, Nora Gordon said:

> Christ's preciousness to me makes me feel that I wish my feet had wings, that I might hasten to take the Bread of Life to the poor heathen. I have counted the cost of missionary service, and my love for Christ makes me willing to bear the many peculiar trials through which I am confident I must pass (Gibson and Crogman, 381).

The school held a farewell service for Nora Gordon on March 6, and on March 16, 1889, she sailed to London on her way to Africa.

In London Gordon visited the Missionary Training Institute under the direction of the Reverend H. Grattan Guinness and his wife. She wrote on April 11 that although the experience of waiting so long in London had been trying, she had profited from her stay. She had seen a number of flags flying above a local street and said: "Never before did the Stars and Stripes seem so beautiful. . . . I do praise God for every step I get nearer to my future home" (Brawley, 47). Gordon was given a flag to take with her on the remainder of the journey. If her schedule remained as established, Nora Gordon sailed on Wednesday, April 17, from Rotterdam on the steamer *African*, of the Dutch line. She would have arrived in the Congo about three weeks later.

Nora Antonia Gordon was active in missionary work in Palabala for about two years. She watched over children and taught school as well. She frequently sent home letters to her family and sent curios to Spelman. She commented on the local traditions followed when she first arrived. She found sad and amusing the local practice of sitting with backs to the preacher or teacher and yelling out in disbelief or dissatisfaction. She said: "One of the first workers, after speaking to a crowd of heathen, asked them all to close their eyes and bow their heads while he would pray to God. When the missionary had finished his prayer and opened his eyes, every person had stealthily left the place" (Brawley, 48). The atrocities in the Congo and the clashes between the Africans and the European officers led her to conclude: "The Congo Missionary's work is twofold. He must civilize, as well as Christianize, the people" (Brawley, 48).

In need of rest, Nora Gordon left Palabala in early 1891 and spent a short time in Lukungu, a station some two hundred twenty miles from the mouth of the Congo in an area heavily populated with people, churches, and schools. Clara A. Howard of Greenville, Georgia, a second missionary from Spelman College, was already there under the sponsorship of the Woman's Foreign Missionary Society of the East. Later that year, Gordon's move to Lukungu became permanent, and she had charge of the printing office. She remained there until 1893, when ill health compelled her to return to America. She brought with her two young women from Africa. Her plan was to return to Africa as soon as she could. Within two or three years of her return to America, no less than five young women from Africa had come to Spelman to study. Over the years, the college continued to attract African women as students.

After her health was restored in 1895, Nora Antonia Gordon married the Reverend S. C. Gordon, who worked at an affiliate of the English Baptist Mission at Stanley Pool. They sailed from Boston in July of that year, arrived in the Congo in August and settled in an old and well-established mission surrounded by other missions in the country. The mission, with its brick houses, broad avenues, fruit trees, and students with above-average intelligence, was far superior to those in her earlier assignment. Neither Nora Gordon nor the Africans were to enjoy the setting long, for officials of the Independent State of the Congo (later Belgian Congo) drove them out. The officials crossed over to the French Congo and prohibited the Protestants from preaching to Africans. Gordon, whose health was declining again, worked on to help the African people as best she could. She and her husband became disillusioned, however, by their restricted activity in missionary work.

In the summer of 1900, seven months after her second child died, Nora Gordon and her husband knew that they must return home. They spent two months in Belgium and England, then moved back to America. Nora Gordon died at Spelman on January 26, 1901, when she was only thirty-four.

References

Brawley, Benjamin. *Women of Achievement.* [Chicago]: Woman's American Baptist Home Mission Society, 1919. 43-56.

Dannett, Sylvia G. L. *Profiles of Negro Womanhood.* Vol. 1. Yonkers: Educational Heritage, 1964. 258-59. Line drawing, p. 258.

Gibson, J. W., and W. H. Crogman. *The Colored American.* Atlanta: J. L. Nichols, 1901. 380-81. Photograph, p. 380.

Jessie Carney Smith

Elizabeth Taylor Greenfield "The Black Swan"

(c. 1819-1876)

Singer, teacher

Elizabeth Taylor Greenfield's early life is partially recounted in her autobiography of 1855, *The Black Swan at Home and Abroad or, A Biographical Sketch of Miss Elizabeth Taylor Greenfield, the American Vocalist*. From other sources it is learned that she was born in Natchez, Mississippi, on the estate of her mistress, Mrs. Holliday Greenfield, a wealthy woman who was originally from Philadelphia, Pennsylvania. Because of advanced age, Mrs. Greenfield decided to move back to Philadelphia. However, according to the tenets of the Quaker sect, of which she was a member, she had to give up her slaves. She therefore manumitted some (and probably sold others), including Greenfield's mother and father, whom she sent to Liberia, the father being an African native.

Greenfield resided with Mrs. Holliday Greenfield until

Elizabeth Taylor Greenfield

she was about seven or eight years old. After that time she presumably went to live with her own relatives, namely her sister, Mary Parker. During this period she received no schooling and probably hired out to do day work. However, Mrs. Greenfield, being old and infirm, desired to have young Elizabeth as a companion (circa 1835-1836). Greenfield remained with her former mistress until about two months before Mrs. Greenfield's death in 1845, serving as both nurse and housekeeper. Elizabeth assumed the surname Greenfield, though her legal name was Taylor.

Mrs. Greenfield, in 1834, put her estate in the hands of four trustees and among items to be attended to was the sum of $1,500 to be set aside if Greenfield's mother, Anna, desired to return from Liberia. Another item required the sum of one hundred dollars to be paid to Elizabeth Greenfield yearly during her lifetime. She never received these funds, because Mrs. Holliday Greenfield's relatives contested the will, and the monies were consumed by lawyer's fees.

Greenfield had shown a propensity for singing and probably did so at her local church. Singing was frowned upon by the Quaker sect, but she was encouraged as much as possible by Mrs. Greenfield. After Mrs. Greenfield's death, Elizabeth Greenfield was virtually on her own and recounted that she had taught herself some of the rudiments of music. Later, a young white girl, a Miss Price, provided some additional instruction. Greenfield recounted that while singing at the home of Price, residents of the house heard her and encouraged her progress.

About 1849, Greenfield gained sufficient prominence that one of Philadelphia's leading musicians, William Appo, a friend and brother-in-law to the great bandmaster Francis

Johnson, secured her services for a performance in Baltimore, Maryland. At this time she advertised her services as a music teacher, leading to a presumption that she had a more active but a somewhat obscure role in musical affairs.

When great vocalists such as Theresa Parodi, Jenny Lind, "the Swedish Nightingale," and Catherine Hayes, the "Irish Swan," began touring in America, Greenfield was impressed. Upon discovering that Jenny Lind would be in Buffalo, New York, in 1851, Greenfield saved money and secured passage on the boat to hear this prima donna.

Success at Buffalo Leads to a Career

While aboard ship, Greenfield was heard by Mrs. H. B. Potter, a native of Buffalo, who invited her to her mansion. After hearing her sing, many prominent musical people decided Greenfield should be sponsored. Through the intervention of Mrs. H. G. Howard, a committee was organized to present her in recital before the Buffalo Musical Association on October 22, 1851. It was at this period that she was given the soubriquet "the Black Swan."

Although Greenfield made no mention of the fact in her autobiography, she was instructed by one of the local Buffalo musicians, who helped her shape her initial program. So successful was her appearance that she was invited to appear in such places as Rochester and Lockport, where she effected a managerial arrangement with Colonel J. H. Wood, former owner of Wood's Museum in Cincinnati. His role was to secure concerts in this country and Europe during the next three-year interval.

For the first tour, Colonel Wood mapped out a strategy for the remainder of 1851 and nearly all of 1852. Engagements were secured at Utica, Albany, and Troy in New York; Springfield, Boston, Lowell, Salem, and Worcester in Massachusetts; Providence in Rhode Island; Cleveland and Cincinnati in Ohio; Detroit, Jackson, and Niles in Michigan; and finally Milwaukee, Wisconsin, and Chicago in Illinois. At most places Greenfield received excellent coverage while demonstrating the wide scope of her vocal range—from C below middle C to A above the staff—which amazed most critics. In some instances her low voice was considered "deeper" than some of the male singers in those areas. Her pitch and diction were good, her repertoire acceptable, and her only apparent lacks were that her tones were not formed correctly according to the standards of the period, nor did she show familiarity with such vocal tricks as trills, runs, and scales.

One reviewer, journalist Benjamin Penhallow Shillaber, wrote of her recital in Boston:

> At the close of her first song, the enthusiasm of the highly respectable and very numerous assemblage seemed to know no bounds. It burst forth with an unappeasable furor, resulting in the reappearance of the songstress, who seated herself at the piano forte, and sang to her own simple accompaniment, a slow air, in full, round bass voice, that would have been envied by old Meridith himself—who used to sit under and sing "deeper and deeper still." Her tones probably reached down to G as represented by the open third strong of the violincello. No male voice could have given utterance to sounds more clearly and strikingly masculine; and people gazed in wonder, as though dubious of the sex of the performer—a doubt that was soon dispelled by the smooth sweetness of the next vocal piece from Norma, and by the astonishing height to which the "Swan" ascended, in surmounting and mastering the brilliant and beautiful cantata, "Like the Gloom of Night retiring" (LaBrew, *Elizabeth T. Greenfield*, I, 46f).

By May 1852 Greenfield returned to Buffalo, where its citizens witnessed more of her progress. However, Colonel Wood had arranged additional concerts at Toronto, Canada; Auburn, Utica, Watertown, and Ogdensburg in New York; and at Burlington and Battleboro in Vermont. Upon her return to Buffalo in late 1852, she rested while contemplating additional repertoire.

Meanwhile, Howard, acting as her protector, received a note in February 1853 that a promoter desired to exhibit Elizabeth Greenfield in New York after the opening of the World's Fair. He further desired to sponsor Greenfield on a three-month tour in the "interior of this, and adjoining states." Upon Howard's advice, a contract was drawn up in which Greenfield was to visit Europe after giving a few more concerts and making a debut in New York City.

Difficulties Encountered in New York Debut

In her autobiography Greenfield skimmed over her New York experiences, making mention that Madame Alboni, with whom she had become acquainted in Buffalo, was appearing at the Italian Opera House. She had hoped to hear her again but was refused a ticket. Her own scheduled debut was planned for Metropolitan Hall on Thursday, March 31, 1853, and the crowd estimated at four thousand, black citizens being excluded. There was also a threat to burn the house if a "colored woman" sang, and as a result police were stationed throughout the hall during the entire concert. Although somewhat frightened, Greenfield successfully acquitted herself, and the criticism ran, as it had elsewhere, "she needs more training."

The reviews from the New York press were most sympathetic, especially from the *New York Daily Tribune* which, after chastising the audience's poor conduct, said: "It is hardly necessary to say that we did not expect to find an artist on the occasion. She has a fine voice, but does not know how to use it. Her merit is purity and fullness, but not loudness of tone. Her notes are badly formed in the throat, but her intonation is excellent" (LaBrew, *ETG*, I, 79f).

The *National Anti-Slavery Standard* expressed an obvious concern: "A doubt very likely exists whether, being a negro, she can be a singer of any uncommon power; or, if it is conceded that she can be, then whether she ought, and should be permitted to exercise her genius before white people." It published a description from a correspondent which said:

> She possessed unquestionable power, though her skill was by no means extraordinary. Some of her notes were very sweet and clear. She showed great power and compass—the audience were [sic] pleased, amazed, gratified, overcome! For there were those who hoped for her success, those who were entirely incredulous, and those who would have hooted, if they dare. She was interrupted by applause, and at the end of the first piece, there was a genuine spontaneous uproar of clapping and stamping (LaBrew, *ETG*, I, 83).

Meanwhile, the black citizens were successful in approaching Greenfield who, after offering her sincere apologies for the proscription efforts of her managers, gave them a special concert to benefit the Home of Aged Colored Persons and the Colored Orphan Asylum. She then embarked for England.

Elizabeth Greenfield Visits England

Greenfield had signed a contract February 16, 1853, which was to cover a musical tour throughout England, Scotland, and Ireland, and upon her return, throughout the free states of America. It was to begin in March 1853 and continue through May 1, 1855. When she arrived in England she had difficulty with her promoter, whom she later dismissed, for failing to advance her payments from previous concerts.

Without guidance in England, Greenfield appealed to Lord Shaftsbury, a member of the antislavery society, who referred her to his lawyer. She was then directed to the residence of Harriet Beecher Stowe, then promoting her famous novel, *Uncle Tom's Cabin* (1852). Stowe recounted that she introduced Greenfield to the Duchess of Sutherland, also a member of the antislavery society and close companion to Queen Victoria, who thought she should be given the opportunity to perform (Stowe, I, 319). The Duchess of Sutherland allotted Greenfield funds to secure a piano for practice. Meanwhile, the duchess arranged to have Sir George Smart, the queen's musician, hear and accompany her. He remained her sole musical advisor for the remainder of her sojourn in England.

Greenfield made her debut at the Stafford House in April 1953. Upon hearing her, Samuel Ringgold Ward remarked: "I had the pleasure of hearing her sing at Stafford House. . . . What a sight for my poor eyes! Stafford House, British nobility, and a Negress! I saw the perfect respect with which Miss Greenfield was treated by all" (LaBrew, *ETG*, II, 111).

There were other performers assisting on the program, but all eyes were upon Greenfield. Some reviews were sympathetic, merely mentioning her musical selections, but the *London Times* spoke bluntly: "As a proficient in the vocal art, Miss Greenfield does not greatly shine, although her voice is one of the most extraordinary ever heard. . . . With such a voice, however, assiduous study under a competent professor might produce great results, and those who are interested in her welfare would do well to advise her to take advice in the proper quarter" (LaBrew, *ETG*, II, 112).

Other local arrangements included singing in the Hanover Square Rooms and a concert at Exeter Hall on June 15, 1853. By October Greenfield began touring in some of the provincial cities, such as Brighton, Dublin, Liverpool, Glasgow, Lynn, and Leeds in company with other performers.

By January 1854 Greenfield found it necessary to break relations with her manager and spend the remainder of her time studying with Sir George Smart and listening to concerts to which she was invited through the intervention of the duchess and her circle. By June it was thought necessary that she return to America. Therefore, her advisors, Sir George Smart, the Duchess of Sutherland, and others sought the aid of Queen Victoria, and Greenfield received a royal command to appear on May 10, 1853. For that appearance the queen gave her twenty pounds, which Greenfield undoubtedly saved for her return to America. The queen's remarks were judicious:

> I heard the negro singer, Miss Greenfield. . . . She has a most wonderful compass of voice, ranging over fully three octaves with fine, clear high notes, and then a perfect bass voice, powerful and strong like a man's. The two voices do not blend, which is a great disadvantage. . . . She was a slave—is very deserving and it is now thought best to send her back to America. The Duchess of Sutherland, who protects her very much, was there (LaBrew, *ETG*, II, 120).

Second and Third Tours Undertaken

Upon her return from England, Greenfield arranged a second tour that advertised not only her English engagements but placed special emphasis upon her compass of voice and vocal maturity. She decided to include the well-known Philadelphia tenor, Thomas J. Bowers, and began at Boston's Twelfth Street Baptist Church. At the Fifteenth Street Presbyterian Church, Washington, D.C., she "carried them all by storm" (LaBrew, *ETG*, II, 160). In New York City she gave a series of recitals and included Henry Fry's "Old Lady, Have I Sought Too Boldly." Fry, a music critic, did not think enough of her talents to review any of her performances. She then made tours to Baltimore, Maryland, and to the Midwest, Ohio, Michigan, and finally to the Canadian provinces.

In Hamilton, Ontario, Canada, the reviewer had only superlatives:

> The diffusion of knowledge continuously watches us our strength, and for our better encouragement to court her favours, invents many of her suitors with the attributes which point to the

> divinity of her origin—knowledge knows no partiality for colour, and in vindication of the immutable decree, gives us a pet child of song, Miss Greenfield. A vertical sun may have browned her complexion—warm latitudes may have nursed her, but the same gifts which rendered Jenny Lind, Catherine Hayes, and others conspicuous in the world's arena—are—in all, peculiarly her own (LaBrew, *ETG*, II, 160).

In fact, all the Canadian provinces, including Montreal, were both encouraging and sympathetic to Greenfield, especially in view of her command performance before their queen.

After this second tour, Greenfield began teaching in her home. Among those students were Lucy Adger, wife of the well-known musician and composer, Samuel P. Adger, and mother to other Philadelphia musicians.

Greenfield began her third tour in 1856. She visited New Jersey and New York (including Buffalo, Rochester, Utica, Troy, and Corning) and then proceeded to Canada (including Toronto, Montreal, Quebec, Hamilton, and Kingston). She then recrossed the border and appeared at Columbus and Cincinnati, Ohio; Jackson, Michigan; Milwaukee, Wisconsin; and worked her way back to Canada and New Jersey. Her reviews were excellent, showing that she had not lost touch with those who had heard her in previous years. This tour lasted approximately one year.

In Detroit the sentiment was expressed:

> The Black Swan sang last evening to a large and appreciative audience with entire satisfaction. Her vocal powers, improved by an experience of five years, surprised and delighted many who listened to her on the occasion of her first visit, and who then thought them unexcellable. She is indeed a prodigy, in the musical world (LaBrew, *ETG*, II, 188).

Greenfield did not tour again until 1863. Perhaps the increasing turmoil between the Dred Scott decision and the outbreak of the Civil War roused anti-black sentiment to a level that made her believe the touring would not be as easy as in former years.

By 1863 Greenfield decided she could wait no longer and prepared her final tour embracing the eastern and midwestern states. In places where she had already been heard, she was graciously received, for there were many who remembered her efforts prior to the war. However, new aspirants in the musical field had not heard of her, and some critical reviewers were more caustic in attempting to evaluate her career. Nonetheless, she gave vocally effective programs, a few of which were benefits for orphans, for whom she had always expressed a special concern. In Detroit, she appeared at the time of its second major riot, and though the news sources gave the riot much coverage, their anti-black sentiment did not affect their judgment about her recitals:

> Miss Greenfield's voice is remarkable for the wonderful facility with which she changes from the soprano to the baritone, or we should perhaps more strictly say, to the tenor register. We doubt whether there is another vocalist in the country who can approach her in this respect. We will not attempt to criticize her performance. It is enough to say that notwithstanding the prejudice of color, which is sometimes almost insurmountable with some people, and which evidently exhibited itself in the early part of the concert, there being faint applause and some laughter as the singer left the stage, yet, as the programs progressed, the appreciation of merit became more apparent, and the audience after the third piece, "Where Are Thou, Rudolph" by Wallace, burst forth in a hearty encore, which only closed on the reappearance of the singer (LaBrew, *ETG*, II, 205f).

Her final tour of 1863 included such places as Toronto, Ontario; Detroit, Ypsilanti, Ann Arbor, Jackson, Adrian, Monroe, Pontiac, and Saginaw, Michigan; Toledo, Ohio; and Milwaukee, Wisconsin. Upon returning to Philadelphia she was content to continue her teaching and curtailed any other long tours. But she was not idle.

As the war progressed, Greenfield lent her presence and talent to many social and religious events. By 1865 she sang appropriate songs on programs of the Social, Civil & Statistical Association of Philadelphia, which also presented such well-known speakers as the Reverend Stella Martin, Frederick Douglass, and Frances Ellen Watkins Harper.

Because of her important tours, Greenfield gained a national reputation. The novelty of a black woman singing socially acceptable music was a new concept to many musicians throughout the country. Throughout her entire career, she stood alone as a black aspirant in the vocal arts, for there was no black role model from which she could learn. Her success gives her a secure place in black American music history.

Greenfield Shows Her Generosity

Greenfield's character shows she was very generous in many ways. She gave benefits to help the orphans at Buffalo, New York City, and Detroit, and whenever possible, she gave to many black churches in time of need. She appeared in local recitals in Philadelphia, often not accepting her customary fees. Mary Ann Shadd, who had heard her as early as 1855 and who later edited her own newspaper, the *Provincial Freeman*, subsequently became one of her important champions.

A most important by-product of her activities was her attempt to organize a musical troupe, first named Black Swan Opera Troupe. This little-heralded group gave an initial program in Washington, D.C., "at the solicitation of many Eminent Statesmen and Citizens" on January 4, 1862, with the assistance of Madame Mary Brown, "the American

Nightingale,'' and Thomas J. Bowers, ''Signor Mario.'' Four years later her troupe, designated the Black Swan Troupe, gave a concert on May 16, 1866, in Philadelphia. Thus, Greenfield's operatic efforts foreshadowed new prospects for black singers.

Greenfield gave intermittent concerts in New York City (in 1859 for the Colonization Society), Cleveland, (1867 and 1868 for the Freedman's Aid Society), Saint Louis (1868), Chelsea, Massachusetts (1869), Chicago (1869), and Charleston, South Carolina (1874). At the latter place, it was erroneously reported that she had died.

In her later years, she was active in her church, Shiloh Baptist, and is reported to have directed the choir and given lessons. At the time of her death of apoplexy on March 31, 1876, she was deeply mourned by the community, and her death was reported in nearly all of the major papers of the time. Her death certificate is incorrect and in other instances cannot be trusted; for example, she is listed as ''white.'' Her last name is given as Greenfield, which clearly is an adopted or assumed name, and no evidence has been found of an adoption by her mistress, Mrs. Holliday Greenfield. In her will, she officially uses only Taylor as her last name.

Greenfield's career had been long and successful. She proved that black singers could succeed with much perseverance, even though there was great hostility among the ''genteel'' American white public against any great fine-arts movement among black musicians.

As to whether Greenfield was the best black singer of the period, Harriet Beecher Stowe's remarks noted that she was not the prettiest nor the best. Singers like Mary Kenton Augustus-Brown, ''niece'' to Francis Johnson, had been performing much more difficult works locally prior to Greenfield's attempts, but none desired to gain fame. Greenfield was therefore a pioneer whose efforts were not duplicated until the time of Madame Marie Selika.

Because of her pioneer musical activity, Greenfield reaped additional honors in 1879 when the Kansas City women organized the Greenfield Musical Club. In the late 1880s a trio known as the Black Swan Trio, featuring the singer Coralene Cushman, made appearances in minstrel-type programs and promoted their art in places such as England. Charles Pace and W. C. Handy named the Black Swan Recording Company in 1919 in another tribute.

As a singer, Greenfield endured much and broke new ground, for it was no easy feat to prove that Black Swans could sing.

References

Greenfield, Elizabeth Taylor. *The Black Swan at Home and Abroad, or a Biographical Sketch of Miss Elizabeth Taylor Greenfield, the American Vocalist.* Edited by William S. Young. Philadelphia: Privately printed, 1855.

Historical Society of Philadelphia. *Report of Evidence of Greenfield's Estate.*

LaBrew, Arthur R. *Elizabeth T. Greenfield.* 2 Vols. Detroit: Privately printed, 1969-84.

——. *Studies in Nineteenth Century Afro-American Music: The Underground Musical Traditions of Philadelphia, Pa. (1800-1900).* Detroit: Privately printed, 1983.

Philadelphia, County of. *Register of Wills In and For the County of Philadelphia, Pennsylvania.* No. 286, 1876.

Stowe, Harriet Beecher. *Sunny Memoirs of Foreign Lands.* 2 vols. Boston: Phillips, Sampson, 1855.

Trotter, James Monroe. *Music and Some Highly Musical People.* Boston: Lee and Shepard, 1878.

Ward, Samuel Ringgold. *Autobiography of a Fugitive of Toronto.* London: J. Snow, 1855.

Collections

Photographs of Elizabeth Taylor Greenfield are in the Harvard Theatre Collection, in Trotter between pages 66 and 67, and in the author's private collection.

Arthur R. LaBrew

Angelina Weld Grimké

(1880-1958)

Poet

Angelina Weld Grimké has received little more than a passing glance from literary scholars. Like most black female writers of the early twentieth-century, her life and her works have had very little visibility as compared to her more highly acclaimed male contemporaries. However, Grimké is a notable black American female writer, whose life and works span the tide between the nineteenth and twentieth centuries. Her friends included many important writers of the Harlem Renaissance. Her works include two dramas, several short stories, a few articles, and a great number of poems. Of these, her poems represent her best creative energies, even though they were primarily written as outlets for the pathos of her own being rather than for publication.

Being born into the distinguished biracial Grimké family gave Angelina Grimké a place of prominence in Bostonian society. The daughter of Archibald Grimké and Sarah (Stanley) Grimké, she had both abolitionists and slaveowners in her father's immediate family. Her white, paternal great-grandparents were John Faucheraud Grimké, a very wealthy

Angelina Weld Gremké

South Carolina slaveholder, Revolutionary War veteran, and extremely severe judge, and Mary Smith, the daughter of one of the wealthiest bankers in the Charleston area. Two of their children, Angelina and Sarah Moore Grimké, became Quaker abolitionists and moved to the North, eventually settling in the Boston area. Angelina married Theodore D. Weld, a leading abolitionist of the era.

Grimké's paternal grandfather was Henry Grimké, the brother of Sarah and Angelina, who owned a plantation, Cane-Acre, thirteen miles outside of Charleston, South Carolina. He and his wife had three children, and after her death he took one of his slaves, Nancy Weston, as his mistress and fathered three sons, Archibald Henry, Francis, and John. Dying while Weston was pregnant with John, Henry Grimké asked Montague, one of his white sons, to see that Nancy and her children were cared for as members of the family. His son did not honor his father's wishes. Francis, after escaping, being caught, and sold, was finally freed. Archibald escaped to the North. In 1868, while students at Lincoln University, Pennsylvania, Archibald and Francis attracted the attention of the two Grimké sisters when they saw an article in the *Anti-Slavery Standard* noting the remarkable achievement of the two young men. Angelina Weld immediately wrote and asked if they were by chance former slaves of her brother. They replied that they were indeed her nephews. She and her son Stuart visited the boys, and she openly acknowledged them as her nephews.

After the boys graduated, Francis became a minister and later married Charlotte Forten, a highly acclaimed black poet and essayist. Archibald continued his schooling at Harvard Law School, earned his LL.B. in 1874, and set up practice in Boston. In 1879, Archibald married Sarah E. Stanley, a white woman, who was the daughter of Mary Stanley and Methodist minister M. C. Stanley. During this same year, Archibald's Aunt Angelina died, and when a baby girl was born to him and Sarah the next year on February 27, they named her Angelina Weld Grimké, in memory of her.

It is known that Sarah Stanley Grimké's parents opposed her biracial marriage, and it is generally believed that their influence caused her to leave Archibald in 1883 and return to their home. She kept Angelina until 1887, at which time she returned her seven-year old daughter to her father. Though they corresponded often, Sarah Grimké never saw Angelina again. However, Sarah's sister, Emma Austin Tolles, did see and correspond with her niece. Tolles seems to have been very concerned that Grimké not forget her mother.

Despite the fact that her mother had abandoned her, Grimké, as a child, was surrounded by love and comfort. She loved her father intensely and sought always to please him. Being light-skinned and living in this social environment, she was sheltered from the poor living conditions and racial prejudice that most blacks experienced in the years following Reconstruction. However, by the time she wrote the drama *Rachel* (produced in 1916), and a short story, "The Closing Door" (published in 1919), she had become acutely aware of the racial problems and expresses her anger and her sense of helplessness in the dialogue of her characters.

Grimké attended several upper-class schools, liberal both educationally and politically, including Carlton Academy in Northfield, Minnesota, and Cushing Academy in Ashburnham, Massachusetts. Many times Grimké was the only black student in her classes. In 1902, she graduated from the Boston Normal School of Gymnastics and began teaching English in Washington, D. C., first at Armstrong Manual Training School, and then from 1916, at Dunbar High School. Her summers from 1906 to 1910 were spent as a student at Harvard. During the years in Washington, she produced most of her better-known writings. She retired from teaching June 30, 1926, because of ill health from a back injury sustained in a railway accident in July 1911.

Sadness Rules Grimké's Emotional Life

In the face of all the seeming advantages of Grimké's life, the sad tone of her work suggests that deep unhappiness and frustration were always present within her. In many poems and her diaries, she expresses the inner turmoil that her lesbianism created. Unfulfilled desire and thwarted longings are themes in much of her work. A note written to Mamie Burrill on October 27, 1896, seems to bear out the fact that she did have an adolescent relationship with her, for in it Grimké says: "Oh Mamie if you only knew how my heart beats when I think of you and yearns and pants to gaze, if only for one second upon your lovely face." In this same letter she asks Mamie to be her "wife" and ends it with: "Now may the Almighty Father bless thee little one and keep thee safe from all harm, Your passionate lover." After this relationship ended, it is not known if Grimké had others. It rather appears that as she matured she suppressed these desires and alluded to them only in her poetry.

Grimké was a small, light-skinned person, weighing only ninety-two pounds in 1899 and one hundred pounds in 1912, after she was a mature woman. Her demeanor was solemn and demure with a wistful sadness that was characteristic of her both as a child and as an adult. She had many acquaintances, but her father was seemingly the one person she considered to be her true friend. The following diary excerpt, written in 1912, emphasizes this:

> My father . . . is so much a part of me he is so all and all so absolutely necessary that I am taking him I find as a matter of course. This is wrong. I wonder, though, whether when some people are as one there may not be some little excuse. This I know now and I have always known it and felt. I have no desire absolutely for life without him.

Her father's final illness from 1928 until his death in 1930 was a decisive turning point in her life. Gloria Hull says:

> she became more irritable, litigious, and possibly neurotic . . . and the strain of nursing her father was complicated, too, by their extremely close relationship, which was . . . almost incestuous. Lacking a mother for balance, she was doubly . . . bound to him with the iron of affection and chastisement. . . . Lacking lovers, husband, her own family, these ties grew into an unhealthy lifetime dependency (149).

After her father died, Grimké moved to New York, supposedly for her writing, but she produced nothing. She spent the last years of her life almost a recluse in her New York City apartment. Her obituary in The *New York Times* on June 11, 1958, begins: "Miss Angelina Weld Grimké, poet and retired school teacher, died yesterday at her home, 208 West 151st Street, after a long illness. She was 78 years old."

Grimké's Poetry, Stories, and Plays Published

Though Grimké had been writing since her childhood, only a few of her works were published during her lifetime, a few short stories, her play *Rachel*, some nonfiction efforts, and a few of her poems and lyrics that appeared in the Norfolk *County Gazette* ("The Grave in the Corner," 1893; "To Theodore Weld on His Ninetieth Birthday," 1893), the Boston *Sunday Globe* ("Street Echoes," 1894), the *Boston Transcript* ("Longing," 1901; "El Beso," 1909), *Crisis* ("To Keep the Memory of Charlotte Forten Grimké," 1915; "To the Dunbar High School," 1917), and in *Opportunity* ("The Black Finger," 1923). Her poetry also appeared in anthologies by Alain Locke (*The New Negro*, 1925), Countee Cullen (*Caroling Dusk*, 1927), Otelia Cromwell and others (*Readings from Negro Authors*, 1931), and Robert T. Kerlin, (*Negro Poets and Their Poems*, 1935).

In Grimké's works the external forms are focused and orderly, while the internal meanings present themselves to the reader as distorted reflections evoking questions whose answers lead directly back to both her sad personal life and to the following explanation of her own creative process:

> I think most [poems] that I do are the reflections of moods. These appear to me in clearly defined forms and colors—remembered from what I have seen, felt. The mood is the spiritual atmosphere. Symbolic also. I love colors and contrasts. Suggestion. Whatever I have done it seems to me is a reflection of some mood which gives the spiritual atmosphere and significance. The mood has a physical counterpart in Nature in colors concrete imagery brought out by contrasts. Often to me the whole thing is not only a mood but symbolic as well. The more vivid the picture the more vivid the vibrations in the mind of the reader or listener. Each work has its different wavelength, vibration. Colors, trees flowers skies meadows. The more concrete, definite vivid the picture the more vivid the vibration of word in the reader or listener. And what is word? May it not be a sort of singing in the harp strings of the mind? Then on the principle of sympathetic vibration is there not in nature a harp singing also to be found (Incomplete holograph draft, Angelina Weld Grimké Collection).

Her definition of poetry is comparable to those of Coleridge and Wordsworth. Most of Grimké's poems bear greater similarities to those of the romantic and Victorian poets than to those of her contemporaries, in so far as her themes are more personal and traditional.

Grimké's major works focusing on a racial theme are her dramas, *Rachel* and *Mara*; however, in her poem "Tenebris" she subtly allows a tree's shadow to become at night a "huge and black" hand that quietly "plucks and plucks / At the bricks" whithat ch are " . . . the color of blood" of the white man's house. In another, "Beware Lest He Awakes," she warns the reader that one day the black man may awaken and avenge his wrongs. "At April," "Trees," and "Lullaby" are lyrics that touch what Grimké feels to be the sad future of black Americans ("At April," Stetson, 60-63; "Trees," and "Lullaby," Angelina Weld Grimké Collection). Her most radical work, in terms of her deep belief that black women should not bring children into this tormenting world, is "The Closing Door." In this short story a pregnant black woman hears of her brother's lynching, and the fear that her baby will be a male bears constantly on her mind. After her baby son is born, she goes totally insane and kills the child, thus saving him from the possible fate of all black men, and anticipating a prominent theme of Toni Morrison.

Much of Grimké's poetry portrays unconsummated, unrequited love. It is filled with isolation, hopeless longing, and rejection. Its tone is hushed and quiet with a subtle touch of delicate, mysterious fog covering the intensity of her double-edged images. In "El Beso" (Boston *Transcript*), the persona is lured to the lover's "eye and lip, / Yearning, yearning" for "Your mouth / And madness, madness / Tremulous, breathless, flaming, / The space of a sigh." However, the longed-for kiss is replaced by "awaking—remembrance, / Pain, regret—your sobbing; / and again quiet—the stars, / Twilight and you." Here Grimké uses twilight, stars, and quiet as natural, protective forces that gently, but surely, enfold both the joy and the pain. Grimké, in "Caprichosa" (Grimké Collection) oxymoronically calls her lover a "Cruel, dainty, little lady," who tempts her with teasing and flirting, "But, if my foot one step advances / . . . Lightly, swiftly, from me dances, / Darting at me mocking glances, / Cruel, dainty, little lady." "The Eyes of My Regret" (Cullen, 37) describes "the same tearless experience, / The same dragging of feet up the same well-worn path, / To the same well-worn rock," where twin stars become two eyes that watch and "draw me forth, against my will dusk after dusk; / The same two eyes that keep me sitting late into the night, chin on knees, / Keep me there lonely, rigid, tearless, numbly miserable, / The eyes of my regret." With vivid, piercing, imagistic irony, Grimké, in "The Puppet Player" (Cullen, 47), depicts conventional society's rejection of her lesbianism in an alliterative " . . . clenched claw cupping a craggy chin / [which] Sits just beyond the border of our seeing, / Twitching the strings with slow sardonic grin."

Grimké's greatest poetic tool is the juxtaposing of opposite images with such textual tension that they become parts of each other. The tensile strength thus created produces a force greater than either can ever have separately. In many of her poems the beauty of Nature, both in its dying and rebirth, becomes an integral matrix into which her subjects are placed or from which they are drawn. Death is often depicted as the only means of satisfaction and completion to Grimké's lesbian desires. In "A Mona Lisa" the speaker would like "to creep / Through the long brown grasses / That are your lashes . . . [and] poise / On the very brink/Of the leaf-brown pools / That are your shadowed eyes . . . [and] cleave / Without sound, / Their glimmering waters . . . [and] sink down / And down . . . / And deeply drown" (Cullen, 42-43).

"The Garden Seat" is the story of the persona revisiting a much loved, well-known place, alone now for the beloved is dead. Looking at the white stone that marks the grave, she says that those who are left alive "to follow upon the waiting shore" have the worst part because "The waters close again impenetrably: / Each one must make his way alone— / And this is Life!" With stark, vivid serenity, "Butterflies" (Grimké Collection), pictures death. The speaker, tired from watching someone dear dying, says: "Remembering you, forgetting you again; / . . . Nothing but weariness left: / . . . The silence of weariness; / The slow withdrawal of her who sat in that unresponsive body, / The young-soul-whiteness of her unloosening its shell, / And slipping out—and slipping out—and slipping out."

In "Grass Fingers" (Grimké Collection) the persona is lying in the grass, enjoying being touched and caressed by the tiny blades, but she says to the grass:

> You need not fear me
> Soon I shall be too far beneath you,
> For you to reach me, even,
> With your tiny, timorous toes.

In regards to imagery, some of Grimké's work bears similarity to that of T. S. Eliot in that a place, a character, or an object becomes the symbol of an emotion, and the circumstances become the framework in which the emotion shows its relation to other feelings and so acquires its individual significance. Grimké tells a story in "For The Candle Light" of a happy day when "The sky was blue, so blue . . . / And each daisy white, so white," that "I knew that no more could rains fall grey / And night again be night"; however, should that happen, she has, as a souvenir, " . . . in a book for the candle light, / A daisy dead and dry" (Cullen, 45). Eliot seems to express Grimké's thoughts of the future well when he states that "the future is a faded song, a Royal Rose or a lavender spray of wistful regret for those who are not . . . here. . . . Pressed between yellow leaves of a book that has never been opened" (134).

Best-Known Play Staged

Grimké's best-known work is *Rachel*, a three-act drama that was staged in Washington, D. C. at the Myrtilla Miner Normal School, March 3-4, 1916, at the Neighborhood Theater in New York City on April 26, 1917, and in Cambridge, Massachusetts on May 24, 1917, under the sponsorship of St. Bartholomew's Church. It was published in 1920. This work shows how prejudice in America demeans and almost destroys a very respectable black family. The play program for the Washington, D.C., premier performance advertised: "This is the first attempt to use the stage for race propaganda in order to enlighten the American people relative to the lamentable condition of ten million of colored citizens in this free Republic." The play received both positive and negative reactions. Criticism came at this time from some NAACP members who felt it to be propaganda, and later from Frederick Bond, who in *The Negro and the Drama* (1940), described it: "Lacking in the fundamental principles of drama, the piece is preposterous, and will hardly meet the approval of an audience." However, Alain Locke and Montgomery Gregory call it "apparently the first successful drama written by a Negro and interpreted by Negro actors," in *Plays of Negro Life* (1927). James V. Hatch included it in *Black Theater, U.S.A.: Forty-five Plays by Black Americans, 1847-1874* (1974).

As a drama, *Rachel* presents the social problem of racism and shows the emotional effects of the problem but offers no satisfactory solutions. The setting for all three acts is a tenement apartment in a "northern city" between the years 1900 and 1910. As the play opens, Mrs. Loving, a widowed seamstress, is worried because Rachel, her teenage daughter, is late getting home. Rachel rushes in and amid hugs and kisses tells her mother that she has a most wonderful reason for being late; she has met a little boy, Jimmy, on the stairs and just lost track of time as she talked and played with him. John Strong comes by to pick up some sewing for his mother;

he has a college degree, but must work as a waiter because no decent jobs are available to blacks. It is obvious that he is interested in Rachel. Tom Loving, Rachel's older brother, comes home and hands his paycheck to his mother, wishing he could give her more. Tom goes to school; he, too, has a low-paying job. The focal point of this act is Mrs. Loving's decision to tell her children about their father, a newspaper editor who had dared to speak out about the injustice done to an innocent black man who was hanged. Ten years earlier on this day, October 16, their father and half brother had been killed by a lynch mob of so-called Christians in the small southern town where they had lived. Tom reacts with anger and rage. Rachel cries out for the children:

> Then everywhere, everywhere, throughout the South, there are hundreds of dark mothers who live in fear, terrible, suffocating fear, whose rest by night is broken, and whose joy by day in their babies on their hearts is three parts—pain. . . . How horrible! Why—it would be more merciful—to strangle the little things at birth. And so this nation—this white, Christian nation—has deliberately set its curse upon the most beautiful—the most holy thing in life—motherhood! Why—it—makes—you doubt—God!

As the second act opens, it is four years later; both Tom and Rachel have college degrees. Tom is looking for a permanent job; Rachel, unable to find a teaching job, is staying at home helping her mother. John Strong has offered Tom a job as a waiter. As Tom broods over this unfairness, he says:

> I hear people talk about God's justice—and I wonder. . . . It seems our educations aren't of much use to us: we aren't allowed to make good—because our skins are dark. . . . Look at us—and look at them. We are destined to failure—they, to success. Their children shall grow up in hope; ours, in despair. Our hands are clean;—theirs are red with blood—red with blood of a noble man—and a boy. They're nothing but low, cowardly, bestial murderers. The scum of the earth shall succeed.—God's justice, I suppose.

Rachel, who adopted Jimmy after his parents died of smallpox, meets Mrs. Lane, who is looking for an apartment. She wants to move because of the terrible cruelties and embarrassments her little girl, Ethel, has had to suffer at school. Soon after this, Jimmy comes home and tells Rachel that some boys at school called him a "nigger" and threw stones at him; he asks her what this means. Rachel, in her anguish over not being able to change or eradicate these cruelties, takes the beautiful roses that John Strong has sent and crushes them under her feet, screaming:

> You God!—You terrible, laughing God! Listen! I swear—and may my soul be damned to all eternity, if I do break this oath—I swear—that no child of mine shall ever lie upon my breast, for I will not have it rise up, in the terrible days that are to be—and call me cursed. . . .If I kill, You Mighty God—I kill at once—I do not torture.

The act ends with Rachel collapsing on the floor. The last act takes place one week later. Rachel is recovering and playing with Jimmy, but suffering great mental anguish because she cannot stop Jimmy's terrible nightmares. She rejects John Strong's proposal, vowing to spend her life caring for black children, but she is not going to bring any into this world herself. The play ends with her running to comfort Jimmy. The last stage direction is: "The light in the lamp flickers and goes out. . . . It is black. The terrible, heart-broken weeping continues."

Today's theater audience might find the painful futility and sentimentality of the play tedious. Tom becomes angry over the situation but his anger serves no purpose. John tries to look at the circumstances with some objectivity, but in truth he cannot see anything better for himself than his head-waiter's job. Rachel, who is unable and unwilling to confront life and the prejudices it holds, withdraws into isolation. It was a generation later that leaders came forward to confront these issues and seek solutions to them.

Grimké's second and last drama, *Mara*, has four acts and its theme is also racial prejudice (Grimké Collection). A much-beloved only child, Mara, the daughter of retired black physician, Dr. Marston, is raped by a white man. Insanity, murder, and lynching are the sad results in this drama. As an epigraph, Grimké uses the Biblical text from Ruth 1: 20, "Call me Mara for the Almighty hath dealt bitterly with me." The setting is in the South, near the turn of the century, at the Cedars, the walled-in estate of Dr. Marston. Grimké has definitely matured as a writer in this drama. Her characters have more variety in their personalities, and the conversations between them are more engaging than those in *Rachel*. The plot, while having the same theme, does not contain superficial sentimentality, and the scenes fall into a more natural, rhythmic pattern without long lapses. Though *Mara* is definitely better than *Rachel*, there exists no record that Grimké ever attempted to have it published. The final version is a completely handwritten copy (no typed copy was ever made) of approximately 190 pages. Since much of the plot is written in the stage directions and sound effects, Grimké might have had more success had she written this as a novel.

Though she lived during a time when black writers were beginning to claim attention in the literary world, black female writers were not published often, nor were they usually given the attention that their male counterparts received. Nevertheless, Grimké was offered many opportunities to write articles and to deliver speeches. Her records show that she did not take advantage of many of these, possibly because of her rather quiet personality. As a poet Grimké is at her best with love and nature themes. The main criticism of most of her works is that almost all of them contain the same sad themes of unfulfilled longings and deep inner frustration. However, this must be seen and considered through the pathos of her life and social circumstances. Her family's prominent social position did not allow her the freedom to act on many of her deepest feelings, particularly to live openly as a lesbian. This unfulfilled desire drained her emotional well of creativity, and finally dried it up completely. What Grimké's success might have been had she lived later than June 10, 1958, can only be speculation. In her own life she rarely felt the rhythmic enchanting vibrations or heard the mystic sympathetic tones of Nature's aeolian harp; yet, through her beautiful, imagistic works she allows readers to become active participants in its ethereal performance.

References

Adolf, Arnold, ed. *Poetry of Black America: Anthology of the Twentieth Century*. New York: Harper, 1973.

Bond, Frederick. *The Negro and the Drama*. Washington, D.C.: Associated Publishers, 1940.

Cromwell, Otelia, Lorenzo Dow Turner, and Eva B. Dykes, eds. *Readings from Negro Authors*. New York: Harcourt, 1931.

Eliot, T. S.. *Four Quartets, III, The Complete Poems and Plays, 1909-1950*. New York: Harcourt, 1962.

Greene, Michael. ''Angelina Weld Grimké.'' *Dictionary of Literary Biography*. Vol. 50: Afro-American Writers vefore the Harlem Renaissance. Ed. Trudier Harris. Detroit: Gale Research, 1986.

Grimké, Angelina Weld. Poems anthologized in *Caroling Dusk*. Edited by Countee Cullen. New York: Harper, 1927.

———. ''A Biographical Sketch of Archibald H. Grimké.'' *Opportunity* 3 (February 1925): 44-47.

———. ''The Black Finger.'' *Opportunity* 1 (September 1923): 343.

———. ''The Closing Door.'' *Birth Control Review* 3 (September 1919): 10-14.

———. ''Death.'' *Opportunity* 3 (March 1925): 68.

———. ''Dusk.'' *Opportunity* 2 (July 1924): 196.

———. ''El Beso.'' *Boston Transcript*, 27 October 1909.

———. ''The Grave in the Corner.'' Norfolk *County Gazette*, 27 May 1893.

———. ''Little Grey Dreams.'' *Opportunity* 2 (January 1924): 20.

———. Manuscript Collection, Moorland-Spingarn Research Center, Howard University.

———. *Rachel: A Play in Three Acts*. Boston: Cornhill, 1920.

——— ''Street Echoes.'' Boston *Sunday Globe*, 22 July 1894.

———. ''To Keep the Memory of Charlotte Forten Grimké.'' *Crisis* 3 (January 1915): 134.

———. ''To the Dunbar High School.'' *Crisis* 13 (March 1917): 222.

Hatch, James V. *Black Theatre, U.S.A.: Forty-Five Plays by Black Americans, 1847-1874*. New York: Free Press, 1974.

Hull, Gloria. *Color, Sex, and Poetry*. Bloomington: Indiana University Press, 1987.

Kerlin, Robert T., ed. *Negro Poets and Their Poems*. Washington, D. C.: Associated, 1935.

Locke, Alain, and Gregory Montgomery. *Plays of Negro Life: 1886-1954*. 1927. Reprinted. Westport, Conn.: Negro Universities Press, 1970.

New York Times, 11 June 1958.

Stetson, Erlene, ed. *Black Sister: Poetry by Black American Women*. Bloomington: Indiana University Press, 1981.

Wood, Phyllis. ''Angelina Weld Grimké: Her Life and Her Works.'' Unpublished manuscript. 1988. Shephard Library, North Carolina Central University, Durham. Moorland-Spingarn Research Center Library, Howard University, Washington, D. C.

Collections

The Angelina Weld Grimké Collection is located in the Manuscript Division, Moorland-Spingarn Research Center, Howard University Library, Washington, D. C. Photographs are included.

Phyllis Wood

Verta Mae Grosvenor

(1938-)

Writer, culinary anthropologist

Verta Mae Grosvenor has assembled a colorful persona and career from a lifetime of activities that have been many and varied: She has been actress, dancer, clothing designer, and seamstress, but she is best known as a writer and ''culinary'' anthropologist.

She was born into the Smart family of Fairfax, South Carolina, on April 4, 1938, and grew up in Monk's Corner,

Fairfax, Allendale County, where she says she was related to most people there. She is the mother of two daughters, Kali and Chandra, and has been married twice. Former husbands are Robert S. Grosvenor and Ellensworth Ausby.

Grosvenor has traveled to or lived in many countries, notably Paris, where she attended the Sorbonne. In 1982, while serving as consulting editor for *Elan* magazine, she traveled to Brazil with a group of writers and editors. Then, in 1985, she was one of a group of nine writers to visit Cuba under the auspices of *Black Scholar* magazine. That same year, she made her first trip to Mississippi. Everywhere she has traveled she has added to her culinary treasury so that the recipes she gives in her traveling notes reflect great geographical diversity, yet have cultural connections.

According to the account of her early life given in her autobiographical work'' *Vibration Cooking,* Grosvenor was born a twin, prematurely, but her fraternal twin did not survive. She was told that she was a miracle child because with her birth weight she survived against odds. She used her infantile frailty to avoid picking cotton, and thus was able to observe family meal preparations closely. True to her heritage as a part of an extended family in which there was very strong bonding, she used her personal experiences as bases for the values, history, and myth included in her cooking recipes.

Grosvenor describes her maternal grandmother, Sula, as a superb cook and says she was of Indian descent, which was why she knew and cooked ''Indian food'' sometimes. Grosvenor rated her grandmother's crepes as superior to those in the Rue Gregoire des Tours, where she frequented restaurants and experimented with French cuisine, as she did at many other places while she lived in Paris.

When she was a teenager, Grosvenor's family moved to Philadelphia, Pennsylvania. The move is dated, not by calendar but, typically, by an incident; Grosvenor was kicked in the head by a mule but could not be treated at the nearest hospital—in Orangeburg, South Carolina—because it did not treat ''colored people.''

In Philadelphia, Grosvenor came to identify with the aunt for whom she was named—Verta. That aunt was said to ''be delicate boned but had the Smart strength . . . and was tribal'' (*Vibration Cooking,* 13). From her, Grosvenor says, she learned ''tribal love.'' It was such a connection to family that has spurred her to return to her roots at least once a year. Her grandmother, Estella Smart, joined the family in Philadelphia after the death of her husband, Cleveland Smart. From her, Grosvenor acquired much of her cooking skills and sewing ability as well as an individualistic sense of style. The extended Smart family lived on Norris Street in the house her grandmother purchased.

''Survival Cooking'' for Slaves Learned

Another relative who influenced Grosvenor and helped prepare her as a culinary anthropologist was her aunt, Rose Ritter Polite, who lived on 131st Street in Harlem and who specialized in an African dish, cow peas (called black-eyed peas in the United States) and red rice. From her Grosvenor learned about ''survival cooking'' that keeps people ''keeping on and gives them *la dolce vita* (*Vibration Cooking,* 24). It is this spirit that she inherited from a great-great-grandgrandfather, a former slave, whose story of rebellion and courage she was told.

Grosvenor credits her ancestors' longevity to their survival skills, having had an uncle who lived to be 112 and possessed an excellent memory; he used to recite poetry though he was uneducated. From him she heard about the Underground Railroad and the food prepared for Harriet Tubman and the runaway slaves. Grosvenor credits another great-uncle, Willis Ritter, with passing on family survival skills, for he lived to be 98 years old, had taught Latin and mathematics, and told her stories of slave deceptions that made survival and sometimes freedom possible.

As a youngster, Grosvenor engaged in creative activities, playing school, and ''acting and directing'' imaginary plays to amuse herself, for she was a latch-key child who spent much time alone. Her mother worked as a maid. Grosvenor also used her time to practice cooking. Sometimes she rode in the sidecar of her father's motorcycle during the time that he belonged to a cycle club. He, too, cooked and often competed with his brother, Alexander, who was a merchant seaman-cook, in cooking battles.

Her family had spread out: A cousin had married a person from India and moved to Madras; another had moved to the West Indies. From them Grosvenor learned recipes that she later incorporated into her own blends of African-American ones. Writing in 1986, she indicated the ''politics'' of such divulgences and explains that her kitchen is the world and that ''Afro-Americans could be associated with all foods,'' not just so-called ''soul food'' (*Vibration Cooking,* xv).

Enjoying exposure to diverse geographical locations while seeing kinships among cultures may explain Grosvenor's extensive travels and understanding of relationships. Similarly, her wide range of acquaintances makes her writing a compendium of names and networking, most often from kitchens, where she is most at home in relationships. She writes of dinners with people of diverse backgrounds and celebrity: writers, actors, politicians, and ordinary people. She even includes a recipe for White House barbecue that she attributes to an invitation to dine there during President Jimmy Carter's administration.

In recent years, Verta Mae Grosvenor has been a guest on several television shows, has catered many celebrity affairs, has been a commentator for National Public Radio, and was a guest at the 1990 New Orleans Jazz and Heritage Festival.

Her publications include *Vibration Cooking; or The Traveling Notes of a Geechee Girl* (Doubleday, 1976; Ballentine, 1986); *Thursdays and Every Other Sunday Off: A Domestic Rap* (Doubleday, 1972); and *Plain Brown Rapper* (Doubleday, 1975). She has also written columns for *Essence, Amsterdam News,* the *Chicago Courier, Ebony, Jet, McCalls, Publish-*

ers Weekly, and *Redbook*. She has contributed to *The Black Woman: An Anthology* and served as an editor for *Elan Magazine*.

References

Black Writers: A Selection of Sketches of Contemporary Authors. Detroit: Gale Research, 1989.

Garland, Phyl. "Vibes from Verta Mae." *Ebony* 26 (March 1971): 86-88.

Grosvenor, Verta Mae. "The Jogging Seventies." *Essence* 11 (December 1980).

———. "The Kitchen Crisis." In *The Black Woman: An Anthology*. Edited by Toni Cade. New York: New American Library, 1970.

———. *Vibration Cooking*. New York: Doubleday, 1986.

Rush, Theressa G., and others, eds. *Black American Writers, Past and Present: A Biographical and Bibliographical Dictionary*. Metuchen, N.J.: Scarecrow Press, 1975.

Shockley, Ann A., and Sue P. Chandler, eds. *Living Black American Writers*. New York: Bowker, 1973.

E. Delores B. Stephens

Lucille C. Gunning

(1922-)

Pediatrician, medical services administrator

Lucille C. Gunning considers herself first and foremost a pediatrician who benefited from the time when "teachers took you by the hand and molded you into the kind of doctor they wanted you to be or in their likeness" (Interview with Lucille C. Gunning, 27 October 1986). In retrospect she feels that she was molded in a positive way, and although she has grown in the profession, she never lost the lessons taught her by her role model teachers.

Gunning was born in New York City February 21, 1922. She was the oldest of two children born to Roland and Susan Gunning. Her brother died at seventeen. Her parents met in Jamaica, West Indies, where her father was a practicing pharmacist and her mother was a teacher. Seeking better opportunities, they came to New York City in the early 1920s. Instead of being able to secure a position as a druggist her father worked as a druggist's assistant. He supplemented his income by becoming the superintendent of the building where they were living in Harlem, while her mother taught school.

When Lucille Gunning was about thirteen months old, because of her poor health, she was taken to live with her paternal grandmother in Jamaica. When she was approximately five years old, her paternal aunt, a midwife of considerable repute in their community, took Gunning with her on a late-night delivery. Gunning waited as her aunt ministered to the patient, and heard considerable commotion and activity. She was to learn later that the baby died. What registered with her then was that, as the crying and screaming proceeded, a gentleman with a black bag arrived, driving his horse-drawn carriage. He was the doctor. She watched him as he entered the house carrying his black bag. She sensed that in everyone's mind was a given—had the doctor arrived earlier, the baby would not have died. The scene remains vivid in her memory. She realized later that sometimes there is nothing anyone can do, but she did not know that at the time. Gunning never discussed her perception of or reaction to that incident, but that point her determination to become a doctor was firmly established in her mind.

Her parents worked together tenaciously so her father could realize his dream of becoming a doctor. He was older than most applicants but he applied and was accepted to medical school in Edinburgh, Scotland. When he completed his studies he returned to New York with the intention of taking the family to Jamaica. However, he began his practice in New York City and remained there until his death.

Gunning completed high school in Jamaica and would have gone to college in England, but because of the war she came to live with her parents in New York City. She had told her family that she wanted to study medicine, but she met serious opposition from her grandmother and her father. They felt she should pursue nursing or teaching. At the time, a woman's femininity was questioned if she chose other than the traditional careers. But her mother was very supportive of her choice. When her father realized that she was determined, he gave her his complete support.

Lucille Gunning wanted to study premedicine at Barnard College in New York City and to attend Columbia University College of Physicians and Surgeons. But in her interview she was told that she could study nursing or teaching but not premedicine. She applied to and was accepted at New York University. After graduating with a B.A. in 1945, she went on to Woman's Medical College of Pennsylvania and graduated with an M.D. degree in 1949. She completed a rotating internship at the Harlem Hospital Center in New York City in 1950 and started a residency in infectious diseases at Herman Kiefer Hospital in Detroit, Michigan, in 1950. She served as chief resident in the department of pediatrics at Harlem Hospital from 1951 to 1952. From 1952 to 1953 she was pediatric chief resident at Woman's Medical College of Philadelphia Hospital. She was a fellow in pediatric cardiology at Grace New Haven Hospital at Yale University from 1953 to 1954.

In 1954 Gunning opened her private practice in pediatrics from offices in the Bronx and in New Rochelle, New York. During these years she also served as a child health physician for the Department of Health in New York City in the divisions of infant and preschool and child guidance. She was visiting attending physician in the pediatric departments of Harlem Hospital, Bronx Hospital, Parkchester General, and New Rochelle Hospital. In 1964 she took a fellowship in medicine at the Albert Einstein College of Medicine at Montefiore Hospital Medical Center. On completing this fellowship she became assistant attending at Morrisania, a city hospital, in the department of rehabilitation medicine. She is New York State and Ohio State licensed and board certified in physical medicine and rehabilitation. She was pediatric board eligible. In 1964, with the commitment to training at Montefiore Hospital, Gunning closed her general pediatric practice in the Bronx but kept her practice in New Rochelle.

As a specialist, her major areas of concern, commitment, and experience have been chronic illnesses in children—in particular handicapping conditions—and more recently mental retardation. Her dream has been to establish a pediatric hospital in the Harlem community with a pediatric rehabilitation service. Gunning believes that disabled children should be with other children and not with disabled adults. Their emotional and psychological needs are different from those of the disabled adult. It was this conviction that led her to establish and direct the division of pediatric rehabilitation at Montefiore Hospital and Medical Center in the Bronx from 1966 to 1971 and also led her to assume the job of chief of pediatric rehabilitation at the Harlem Hospital Center in New York Center in 1971.

While at Harlem Hospital, Gunning was an assistant professor in clinical rehabilitative medicine at Columbia University. This latter position gave her the opportunity to teach and discuss issues in pediatric rehabilitation. She was aware that this area of practice was not in the curriculum or a part of the rotating internship even of a pediatric residency. Despite the hardships, frustrations, and resistance at all levels, within this traditionally acute-care hospital that was committed to acute-care delivery, there emerged numbers of children with handicapping conditions. These children were the nucleus for the pediatric rehabilitation service. Getting her program started "was like breaking the ice, I was constantly on the defensive because this was a new field, it was not popular and had no prestige. Today it is an ever expanding field" (Interview with Lucille C. Gunning, 23 May 1990). She found that there were many children with handicapping conditions at Harlem Hospital. Children with developmental disabilities, a high incidence of mental retardation, and many who were thought to be mentally retarded were also suffering from sensory deprivation and mild cases of cerebral palsy, which tended to interfere with their learning. Through her observations, Gunning found that, although they had no major difficult disability, their function was impaired and they qualified for rehabilitation; therefore, she could be of assistance.

Disabilities of Children Given Attention

While she was at Harlem Hospital, Lucille Gunning gained experience working with children with Downs Syndrome. She established a developmental center where the parents could come. It gave them a place to play with their children while the parents and Gunning observed the children's development. The parents regarded the center as a school. She found that parents practiced the training techniques that they saw in an attempt to make their children as self-sufficient as possible. This reinforced another of her theories, that the parents had to be significantly involved in the treatment of the child and needed support in their efforts. Gunning feels that throughout her professional career parents and their children have been her most valuable mentors. She has learned more from them than from many studies.

Gunning served as field-work supervisor for the Sophie Davis School of Biomedical Education of the City College, City University of New York, from 1976 to 1979. This program provides for minority students' admission into any New York State medical school upon successful completion of the premedical college courses. Gunning is also one of the founders of the Susan Smith McKinney-Steward Medical Society of New York City, an organization of black American women physicians who, among other programs, provide counseling and mentoring to minority female students who have chosen medicine as a career. Her association with the Sophie Davis program and the Susan Smith medical society enabled Gunning to be of great value to aspiring medical students involved in both programs.

Gunning has published numerous articles on the subjects of childhood disabilities, pediatric rehabilitation, physical medicine and rehabilitation, child abuse, growth and development of the child with sickle-cell anemia, and mental retardation. In her study of and experience with disabled children, she has suggested that the person who cares for the chronically ill child should work with the psychologist or psychiatrist and take a much more active role in the habilitation of the child. "If the child is retarded we should review the whole issue of 'retardation' as well as the issue of retardation of the black child; rather than dealing with the intellectual impairment, deal with their asset profile and see what they are good at" (Interview with Lucille C. Gunning, 23 May 1990). While they may not be good in reading, writing, and mathematics initially, she has found the children to be extremely good at body mechanics, the arts, and music. However, she found it very difficult to secure funds to develop programs that could enhance these children's chances. In spite of these difficulties, through her developmental center Lucille Gunning was able to establish the first mothers' support group. Such groups have continued to function in the pediatrics department, especially in the sickle-cell program.

While she was at Harlem Hospital, Gunning also envisioned establishing an extended-care facility for children with chronic illnesses in the Harlem community, similar to Blythedale in Westchester. She believes that when chronically ill children are sent away from the community and the family is unable to visit the child, they become alienated from each other and from the community. As a result any gains from being at the facility (she does not want to call it a hospital) tend to be lost when the child goes home. This extended-care facility in the Harlem community would be the children's equivalent of a nursing home.

In 1981, after giving her opinions about pediatric rehabilitation at a conference for physiatrists, Gunning was approached by another participant. Gunning was advised that there was a position open for someone with her deep interest and expertise in pediatric rehabilitation and suggested that she was someone who could make a difference. After several months of careful and painful deliberation, she reluctantly resigned from Harlem Hospital and became the director of physical medicine and rehabilitation in the Children's Medical Center in Dayton, Ohio. There she would have the opportunity to validate her own conviction that a pediatric rehabilitation service could be developed in a children's hospital and that, for practical and philosophical reasons, it belonged there. She had attending privileges at the medical center in the pediatrics department and was appointed associate clinical professor of rehabilitative medicine at Wright State University Medical School.

Here was the challenge she had sought and awaited. She developed a program into which she incorporated her ideas of children with disabilities being with other children in the hospital, and being cared for in a collaborative effort by members of the various disciplines. Within her two-year contract Gunning developed a multidimensional pediatric rehabilitation service that was active, completely comprehensive, and professionally and personally validating and rewarding. She served on many committees in the position of physiatrist as well as a consultant to the Dayton Board of Education and physiatrist at the Wright Patterson Air Force Base.

Although her stay in Dayton was for only two years, she had realized her dream and was able to demonstrate that with the money and, above all, the commitment on the part of the hospital, her ideas could work.

Gunning has served on numerous committees and boards of directors for various organizations over the years. Among appointed positions, she has served as a physiatrist for the Juvenile Rheumatoid Arthritis Clinic at the Children's Medical Center in Dayton, Ohio, 1981; special consultant, Roy Littlejohn Associates, Washington, D.C., 1981; and physiatrist, Cerebral Palsy Clinic, Children's Medical Center, Dayton, Ohio, 1981.

Gunning's many honors and awards include the Charles Drew Pre-Medical Society of Columbia University Honorary Award, 1985; Physicians Recognition Award from the American Medical Association, 1983; and Harlem Hospital Pediatric Rehabilitation Clinic Citation, 1978 and 1979.

At present, Gunning is the deputy director of medical services for the New York State Office of Mental Retardation and Developmental Disabilities in Tarrytown, New York. Her responsibility is to insure the best care of developmentally disabled persons in various residences in which the state has placed them—in communal homes rather than in institutions. Her commitment is "to the art of medicine; you must go that extra step to provide quality care for the patient" (Interview with Lucille C. Gunning, 23 May 1990).

Gunning married in 1953 on completion of her pediatric residency. Her husband, Carlton E. Blackwood, also a native Jamaican, attended New York University where he received a Ph.D. in chemistry. He was a biochemical researcher at Columbia University. He accepted a post at Iona College in New York City, where he contributed to a successfully functioning department of chemistry. He died in 1974. In recognition of his achievements, Blackwood was awarded a full professorship, posthumously.

There were four children born to the marriage: Elaine Blackwood, J.D., M.B.A.; Alexander Blackwood, M.D. and Ph.D., pediatrician; Lydia Blackwood, Ph.D., clinical pediatric psychologist; and Ann Blackwood, M.D., in residency at Montefiore Hospital and Medical Center and research at Columbia Medical College of Physicians and Surgeons in New York City.

References

Gunning, Lucille C. Interview with author, 23 May 1990; 27 October 1990.

Juanita R. Howard

Rosa Guy

(1928-)

Writer

Traditionally, black American literature had meant literature that focused primarily on the South, urban inner-cities, or occasionally, the West or Southwest. Similarly, black literature for children has spotlighted the same people in the same geographic locations. Periodically, books would appear for children that depicted some vignettes of the lives of the African diaspora in the Caribbean or Central and South America. Rosa Cuthbert Guy is one of those authors who has broadened the scope of children's literature. Her books on the experiences of the African diaspora created a literary sensation when they were published. The books, for children and young adults, explore the alliances, entanglements, and cautions that exist between people of African descent born in the United States and people of African descent born in the

Caribbean. Additionally, her novels examine the day-to-day living of both groups.

Guy was born on September 1, 1928, in Trinidad, West Indies, to Henry Cuthbert and Audrey (Gonzales) Cuthbert. The family moved to the United States in 1932. Guy's mother died when she was nine, and her father died when she was fifteen. She speaks Creole and French in addition to English. She married Warner Guy (now deceased) and is the mother of one son, Warner Guy, Jr. She attended New York University and was a founding member and president of the Harlem Writers' Guild. She is an author and anthologist and currently resides in New York City.

Guy possesses an explicit literary and aesthetic philosophy that has a distinct political tone. She makes no apologies for the political aspect of her philosophy. Guy has argued that Western literature, instead of being a vehicle for uplifting the human spirit, has been a vehicle designed to celebrate and justify the subjugation of people of color, an insidious vehicle that omits or misrepresents the contributions of people color:

> The narcotic effect of the written work, as with all drugs, created to inhibit, must wear off. The need of systems to justify inglorious deeds of ancestors, to make plunderers and murderers into heroes in order to build self-esteem, can only make us pawns in our self-destruction by forcing us through the powerful injections of "words" to race haplessly toward the goal of total annihilation.
>
> Indeed, literature with its utopian intentions, meant to guarantee our spiritual and intellectual elevation, has succeeded in sealing us in myths that overestimate our collective intelligence ("Innocence, Betrayal, and History," 34).

Guy rejects these functions of literature, and the personal consciousness through which she filters her views, interpretations, and beliefs inoculates her against the negative and hegemonic functions of literature.

Guy characterizes herself as a teller of tales, albeit a gumbo of tales peppered by experiences in the Caribbean, United States, and Africa. This stew produces tales rich in myth, symbolism, and the voices of more than one culture. Guy appraises her work in this manner:

> I'm a storyteller. I write about people. I want my readers to know people, to laugh with them, to be glad with, to be angry with, to despair with people. And I want them to have hope with people. I want a reader of my work to work a bit more and to care ("Young Adult Books," 220).

In addition, Guy perceives herself as a chronicler of truth who desires to entertain readers, yet provide them with something of substance—knowledge—which will help them as they acquire responsibility for the future. Guy suggests that children and young adults exposed to war, environmental disasters, and violence are no longer innocent. This loss of innocence has the potential to breed a certain amount of insensitivity, cynicism, and jaded behavior about one's responsibilities to humankind. One solution she offers is to create literature that challenges the intellect and emotions, entertains, and leaves the reader hopeful:

> A novel to me is an emotional history of a people in time and place. If I have proven to be popular with young people, it is because when they have finished one of my books, they not only have a satisfying experience—they have also had an education ("Young Adult Books," 220-21).

Didacticism, however, does not pervade her work. Her books educate in the sense that the reader has acquired new knowledge and new interpretations and has undergone a variety of cognitive and affective experiences. In short, her books have an impact usually not encountered in children's and young adult fiction. Guy's literary canon is extensive and varied. She had written a one-act play, *Venetian Blinds* (1954), has contributed to magazines and journals such as *Cosmopolitan* and *Freedomways,* and has written one children's novel, *Paris, Pee Wee and Big Dog* (1984), one children's folk tale, *Mother Crocodile* (1981), eight young adult novels, *The Friends* (1974), *Ruby* (1976), *Edith Jackson* (1978), *The Disappearance* (1979), *Mirror of Her Own* (1981), *New Guys Around the Block* (1983), *And I Heard a Bird Sing* (1987), *The Ups and Downs of Carl Davis, III* (1989), and four adult novels, *Bird at My Window* (1985), *Children of Longing* (1971), *A Measure of Time* (1983), and *My Love, My Love* (1985). The bulk of critical attention accorded Guy relates to her young adult novels. She has won several awards for her novels: American Library Association Notable Book Award for *The Friends;* the American Library Association's Best Book for Young Adults Award for *Ruby, Edith Jackson,* and *The Disappearance.*

Some general comments are possible about the characters, themes, and settings of Guy's novels. Several character types appear in many. There are the young women from various Caribbean islands who experience a sense of dislocation and marginality as they are removed from their island paradises and placed in the dreariness of urban areas. There are the young women of Harlem and other urban areas, sometimes innocent, sometimes jaded, many times unloved or not loved in the manner that they crave. There are the smartly dressed, intelligent, efficient, and assertive middle-class mothers who can overwhelm or comfort. The young men are variously sophisticated, mature because of environmental necessity, hurt, loving, strong, weak, streetwise, and survivors. Many of the adult males are strong vocal types who care and attempt to guide younger charges through life. Her characters represent a range of types in Afro-Caribbean and African-American communities. Consider for example, the seemingly dissimilar characters of Phyllisia and Edith in the acclaimed novel, *The Friends:*

> Her name was Edith.

> I did not like her. Edith always came to school with her clothes unpressed, her stockings bagging about her legs with big holes, which she tried to hide by pulling them into her shoes but which kept slipping up, on each heel, to expose a round, brown circle of dry skin the size of a quarter. Of course there were many children in this class that were untidy and whom I did not like. Some were tough. So tough that I was afraid of them. But at least they did not have to sit right across the aisle from me. Nor did they try to be friendly as Edith did—whenever she happened to come to school (3).

Edith enters the class late and has an encounter with the teacher, who sarcastically dismisses her before the entire class. Edith ignores the comments, makes some sarcastic ones of her own, and puts the teacher "in her place" before the students:

> I pulled myself tall in my seat, made haughty little movements with my shoulders and head, adjusted the frills on the collar of my well-ironed blouse, touched my soft, neatly plaited hair and pointedly gave my attention to the blackboard (4).

Edith attempts to engage Phyllisia in conversation, but she ignores her. Meanwhile, the teacher has commenced with instruction, posed a question, and waits for an answer to the question. None is forthcoming voluntarily, so she turns to Phyllisia, dubbed monkey and teacher's pet by the other students. Phyllisia is forced to answer because it is expected and receives only praise from Edith, who states that her smartness did not emanate from attending their school, and hisses from the other students. During this encounter Phyllisia realizes that despite her efforts to conform, she is viewed only as a buffer between the insensitive and incompetent teacher and the students of whom she is frightened. Phyllisia begins to perceive that she has more in common with Edith than she thought. Most of Guy's characters are drawn in similar, complex ways.

Writing Themes Emerge from Characters' Experiences

Many young adult novels become "problem" novels simply because the authors construct a story around a problem, such as alcoholism. Guy wisely avoids the trap of the problem novel with a range of themes that emerge from the lives and experiences of the characters. For example, *Friends* offer a number of highly developed themes such as the relationships, often antagonistic, that exist among members of the African diaspora when they meet in Harlem and the need to develop a sense of identity not dependent upon one's family. Other novels such as *The Disappearance* (1979) explore the class antagonism that exists among some African-Americans. Whether or not the books succeed as literary products, Guy does not shy away from complex or controversial subject matter and themes. Consider *Ruby* (1976), the second in the trilogy comprised of *The Friends* (1974) *and Edith Jackson* (1978). Although not the central theme, *Ruby* explores the effects of a lesbian love affair on its teenaged participants, one a submissive, conforming, mousey type and the other a vibrant, intelligent, assertive, and independent type. *Edith Jackson*, in contrast, explores the effects of the sexual relationship a teenaged girl has with an older man, which has culminated in abandonment and pregnancy. Edith must decide whether she takes control of her life through an abortion and college or surrenders control of her life to single parenthood. Because of these and other controversial topics, some of Guy's books are censored. Many schools do not make the books available to students or place them on recommended book lists. Indeed, *Ruby* had to be published as an adult novel in England.

The settings Guy selects for her novels are crucial as well. She selects New York, mainly Harlem, as the setting to play out her characters' lives and to explore significant themes. Arguably, Harlem is a character because of the mythology that surrounds it: its immense potential, the legacies of the Garveyite and Harlem Renaissance movements, the convergence of the African diaspora in its neighborhoods, its poverty, and the myths and symbols that are evoked by its history. Many times the setting parallels the development of the character. For instance, Imamu Jones in the trilogy *The Disappearance* (1979), *New Guys Around the Block* (1983), and in *And I Heard a Bird Sing* (1987) assumes the persona of a streetwise Harlem manchild. He attempts to transport that persona to the clean, well-ordered middle-class home of the Aimsleys, his foster parents, or the Maldoon estate with its manorial specter. He finds that the persona does not work, generally, in these environments and that he must undergo subtle and overt changes as he interacts within them. The change is necessary if people are to perceive his goodness and intelligence and not believe the stereotype of the streetwise black American youth. Readers can perceive how Imamu's belief in himself increases as he changes environments:

> With the shower beating down on his head and shoulders, he gave himself over to a great feeling. Imamu had expected to miss his old Harlem neighborhood when he first moved to Brooklyn. He hadn't. Only good things had happened, and continued to happen, since they had come. He had liked the borough from the time the Aimsley family brought him there, two years before, as their foster child. Since then he had accomplished the impossible: He had brought his mother to this apartment; he had worked—was working—for the pleasure of living in a place that he had chosen, a good feeling. From a street cat to . . . Imamu laughed up into the jetting stream—no limits. He had a good job and the greatest boss a feller could have (*And I Heard a Bird Sing*, 4).

Imamu's elation does not last as he begins to doubt whether he belongs in the new environment when he becomes a murder suspect.

Guy is, above all, a meticulous craftsman. The care with which she shapes her characters, their language, and their environments is evident in each of her books. Critical response to Guy's work reflects upon that adherence to craft. In general, critics praise her vibrant characterizations, her spellbinding stories, and her ability to treat her readers as individuals capable of cognitive and affective growth. When they criticize Guy, critics generally cite what they perceive as Guy's dismal, dour, and hopeless settings, her use of vernacular language, overly-detailed and sometimes pretentious language, and her character types. Nevertheless, Guy manages to evoke considerable favorable critical response in the United States and England.

On the surface, England would seem an unlikely choice for Guy to have best-selling novels, but England has a significant number of people of West Indian descent, and school officials there have attempted to provide students with some knowledge of the Caribbean experience in the United States. Alice Walker's evaluation of *The Friends* is typical of positive responses:

> I am thinking of a young black girl who spent the first twenty years of her life without seeing a single book in which the heroine was a person like herself. . . . I do not know what damage being that girl has done me; I suspect a good deal. But now, with books like Rosa Guy's heart-slammer, *The Friends,* I relive those wretched, hungry-for-heroines years and am helped to verify the existence and previous condition of myself. . . . And so begins the struggle that is the heart of this very important book: the fight to gain perception of one's own real character; the grim struggle for self-knowledge and the almost killing internal upheaval that brings the necessary growth of compassion and humility *and courage*, so that friendship (of any kind, but especially between those of notable economic and social differences) can exist (Quoted in Senich, 78-79).

Occasionally Guy missteps, as in *Mirror of Her Own* (1981), a depiction of white middle and upper-class ennui, decline, deception, and disillusionment. The misstep is not because she focuses on white characters, but because the writing seems forced. Guy rebounds, however, with the bittersweet novel *Paris, Pee Wee and Big Dog* (1984) with its humor and portrayal of a day in the life of three young boys.

The achingly beautiful and haunting tale *My Love, My Love* (1985) reaffirms Guy's talents as a novelist. She manages to reinvent a folk tale set in the "jewel of the Antilles," a tale replete with Vodun gods, color castes, obsessive love, and death. Arguably, this is one of Guy's best works.

Guy takes risks with her novel's characters, themes, and settings. In the process she grows in her craft and redefines her personal style. She is a storyteller and she maintains the reader's attention through the artistic risks she takes.

References

Guy, Rosa. *And I Heard A Bird Sing*. New York: Delacorte, 1989.

———. *The Friends*. New York: Holt, 1974.

———. "Innocence, Betrayal, and History." *School Library Journal* 32 (November 1985): 32, 33-34.

———. "Young Adult Books: I Am a Storyteller." *The Horn Book Magazine* 61 (March/April 1985): 220-221.

Murray, E. Interview with Violet J. Harris, 30 July 1990.

Senich, G., ed. "Rosa Guy." *Children's Literature Review* 13 (1987): 74-89.

Something about the Author. Vol. 14. Detroit: Gale Research, 1978.

Who's Who among Black Americans. 6th ed. Detroit: Gale Research, 1990.

Violet J. Harris

H

E. Azalia Hackley
(1867-1922)
Artist, educator, philanthropist

From infancy, Azalia Smith Hackley's mother instilled in her daughter—who would become a champion of blacks in music—a love for learning and music. Emma Azalia Smith was born on June 29, 1867, in Murfreesboro, Tennessee. She was one of two children of Corilla (Beard) Smith and Henry Smith. Her mother was a schoolteacher and a native of Detroit. Henry Smith, originally from Tennessee, was trained as a blacksmith. After the family moved to Detroit, he maintained a curio shop and pursued various other occupations, including employment in the public library and a position as a church sexton. Azalia Smith's maternal grandfather, Wilson Beard, was a former slave who established a lucrative laundry business in Detroit in the 1830s. Her only sister, Marietta, was born in 1870.

During the early years of her marriage, Hackley's mother, Corilla Smith established a school in Murfreesboro for freed slaves and their children. The curriculum emphasized basic literacy skills and music. When hostility from the surrounding white community forced Smith to close her school in 1870, the family relocated to Detroit.

By the time Hackley entered school at the age of six, she could read and write. A precocious child, she began music lessons at the age of three under the tutelage of her mother. Hackley demonstrated a propensity for performance at an early age and often delighted visitors with her singing and piano playing.

The Smiths were the first black family to reside in their Detroit neighborhood, and when Hackley was enrolled in the nearby Miami Avenue Public School, she was its first black student. Her music education was expanded to include lessons in voice and violin. While in high school, she studied French privately and played piano in local dance orchestras during the evenings. She became a member of the prestigious Detroit Musical Society and on several occasions appeared in solo recitals. In 1883 she graduated with honors from Detroit Central High School. Her graduating class chose a composition written by Hackley to serve as its class march.

Sometime around 1883 the Smiths' marriage began to falter and they eventually separated. With her sister's poor health, additional contributions to the family finances became Hackley's responsibility. The result was an even stricter regiment, in part self-imposed, and in part the influence of her severely principled mother.

In the fall of 1883, Hackley entered Washington Normal School, an institution that specialized in training teachers. She was the first member of her race to gain admittance. To help finance her schooling, she played piano and gave music lessons. In January 1886 she graduated and immediately applied for a teaching position in the Detroit public schools. She was appointed to teach second grade at Clinton Elementary School beginning in September of that year.

Azalia Smith continued teaching until her resignation on January 29, 1894, the day she eloped with Edwin Henry Hackley. Edwin Hackley was a lawyer, journalist, poet, and a clerk in the Denver, Colorado, County Deeds Office. The couple had met about a year earlier at a concert given by the "Black Patti," Sissieretta Jones, while Edwin Hackley was vacationing with friends in Detroit. Their relationship was sustained through voluminous correspondence. Fearing the disapproval and wrath of her mother, Azalia Smith routed their letters through the hands of a sympathetic uncle. Azalia Smith and Hackley had a hasty and private marriage ceremony at the Episcopal Church of St. Matthew, with only one friend and the priest in attendance. After a brief honeymoon in Chicago, the couple settled in Denver.

The performance of Black Patti in Detroit held much more than simple sentimental significance for Azalia Hackley, for it was Jones's singing that inspired Hackley to pursue a musical career. In 1900 (or 1901) she was the first black American to graduate from the University of Denver School of Music, where she completed with honors the requirements for the degree of bachelor of music. Her debut recital in Denver in 1901 was also the beginning of her first concert tour. A review in the *Indianapolis Freeman* described her voice as "a high soprano of great range and sweetness" that was rapidly establishing her as "the most thoroughly artistic and cultured singer the race has yet produced."

Early notices were not altogether glowing, however. On one occasion a reviewer commented on a "lack of native melodiousness" in Hackley's performance (*Indianapolis Freeman,* 9 March 1901, 4). She was undaunted by such forthright appraisals, however, and in fact, welcomed constructive criticism. In a letter to the editor of the *Freeman* she expressed her gratitude to her critic: "I wish to thank you for the criticism in last week's *Freeman*. It is very refreshing as well as gratifying to have someone review the work I do whose criticism is based upon musical knowledge. I shall always treasure the item because of its 'uniqueness' in this respect.''

Hackley's physical appearance did not escape comment in the press, either. Her light skin and long, wavy, auburn hair caused some to think of her as a ''voluntary'' member of her race (Logan, 275; Love 2:107). ''During all of her professional life the color question played a tantalizing temptation,'' Hallie Q. Brown wrote. ''Offers have been made for our singer [Hackley] to cross the color fence and lose her identify with her race'' (Brown, 233). A writer for the *Freeman* suggested that for Hackley to succeed in her career, ''she may have to leave the race altogether as others have done, and, if so, a pardon in advance may well be granted for her; for God does not mean that such gifts shall be circumscribed, hampered, confined by mean circumstances'' (Woodbine, 4). No offer was lucrative enough, however, to motivate Hackley to abandon her people. She was, she observed, ''prenatally marked for everything black'' (Brown, 233).

Concert Artist Becomes Politically Active

When not on a recital tour, Hackley was engaged in numerous activities in the Denver area. She taught in the extension department of the University of Denver School of Music, sang in the Denver Choral Society, and conducted various choral concerts throughout the community. Her skill as a violinist was sought after, as well as praised by the press. She became a political activist, organizing a local branch of the Colored Women's League and serving as its secretary. With her husband, she founded a fraternal group, the Imperial Order of Libyans, which aimed to combat racial prejudice and promote patriotism. The primary organ of publicity for both these organizations was the struggling black newspaper, the *Denver Statesman,* edited by Edwin Hackley. Issues germane to the cause of black women were kept current in ''The Exponent,'' a page written and edited by Azalia Hackley. In one of her first articles she wrote:

> We have borne in mind the great need for thought and talk on the practical as well as the cultural side of woman's life. Our first work will be toward the education and improvement of our Colored women and the promotion of their interests (Davenport, 93).

Throughout her career, Hackley worked tirelessly for racial equality. She was an outspoken agitator for changes in the laws that permitted segregated public transportation. In April 1914, while en route from Texas by train, she was verbally insulted and humiliated by a railroad conductor who refused to hold a door for her. Hackley was so incensed by the incident that she felt compelled to alert the press and incite others to join her in undertaking retaliatory action. She vowed to begin legal proceedings. With the black citizenry rallying to the cause, she agreed to ''start the ball rolling as an example to others'' and she ''good naturedly consented to be the first martyr to the Jim Crow car agitation'' (*Chicago Defender*, 18 April 1914, 6). Hackley began a book recounting the incident and the fallacy of Jim Crowism, but the work was never published.

In spite of their collaboration in many civic endeavors, the Hackley marriage began to show signs of strain. Late in 1901, Azalia Hackley decided upon separation and left Denver for an extended concert tour. She settled in Philadelphia and became musical director at the Episcopal Church of the Crucifixion. In 1904 she organized the People's Chorus, comprised of one hundred of the finest voices in the black community.

Hackley Promotes Negro Spirituals

In carrying on the tradition begun by the Fisk Jubilee Singers in the 1860s, programming for the People's Chorus included a mixture of traditional classical works and black spirituals. The efforts of Hackley and others to showcase black music met with some resistance, however. Many black performers and critics still found ''the old plantation melodies repugnant'' because of their ''allusion to slavery'' and ''reminder of the misfortunes of a race'' (Cuney-Hare, 240). ''I rebelled whenever we had to sing spirituals,'' A. Merral Willis recalled of his days as a student at Howard University (Davenport, 153). In 1909 members of the choir at Howard University organized an official protest, refusing to sing spirituals. Hackley remained undaunted by negative attitudes toward spirituals, and she persisted in promoting the black musical genre as a vital component in the cultural and social development of her race. She succeeded not only in ''drawing attention to the melodic beauty of the music, but also gave the youth of the race a new respect for racial folk

E. Azalia Hackley

material, and an incentive to interpret it'' (Cuney-Hare, 242). Typical of Hackley's powers of persuasion was the reaction of A. Merral Willis to a speech given by Hackley in 1915: ''She talked so convincingly of the meaningfulness and deep heritage of the Negro's folk music that I was convinced'' (Davenport, 153).

The critical success of the People's Chorus performances of pieces from the standard classical repertoire was another of Hackley's crowning achievements. Traditionally, blacks were discouraged from performing classical music and from pursuing the training necessary to develop into successful classical artists (though a surprising number succeeded in the classical milieu as early as Elizabeth Taylor Greenfield [circa 1819-1876]). White audiences insisted on the programming of spirituals by black musicians almost to the exclusion of other music. The notion persisted that blacks should endeavor to perform only their own music because it relied solely on their natural gifts and required no training. Hackley set out to shatter these racial stereotypes. Years later she said of her philosophy: ''The masses of the colored people, if properly taught, can express the best music written. Of all the races the colored race could best express even Bach if they were taught to love Bach's music'' (Hackley, ''The Musical Progress of the Race During the Last Year'').

By 1905 it became increasingly apparent to Hackley that to continue succeeding as a conductor and teacher she should seek additional training. She decided to pursue study in Paris with Jean de Reszke (1850-1925), a well-known voice teacher and opera performer. Funding such a trip was her most immediate and compelling challenge. Even though her husband had recently joined her in Philadelphia, his business and publishing ventures in Denver had failed, depleting his finances. With the goal of raising enough money to travel to Europe, Hackley and several members of the People's Chorus presented an ambitious recital of solo works. The concert took place on October 19, 1905, at Philadelphia's Academy of Music and was a critical and financial success.

Hackley studied in Paris for the remainder of 1905 and returned to the United States late in 1906. Now a consummate artist, she presented another successful recital at the Philadelphia Academy of Music. The recital generated sufficient funds for to return to Paris the following year. She remained in Europe until the fall of 1907.

During her second trip abroad, Hackley began formulating a plan to fund other black musicians to study with well-known European teachers. Initially her scheme involved sponsoring one black artist every five years with money from her own concerts and other fundraising projects. To identify the most gifted and deserving black performers, she arranged a series of competitions. These were presented as recitals, the proceeds of which went to maintain the newly formed Hackley Foreign Scholarship Fund. The first such competition was held in 1908 with the prize money awarded to the violinist and composer Clarence Cameron White. White chose to study in London under the tutelage of the Afro-English composer Samuel Coleridge-Taylor. The next foreign scholarship was awarded to pianist and composer Carl Rossini Diton.

Fortified by White's success, Hackley decided to travel to London. (She financed her trip with yet another performance at the Philadelphia Academy of Music.) While in London, Hackley not only studied voice but also taught and performed several recitals. The trip marked a turning point in her marriage, for when she returned to the United States in 1909, she separated from her husband permanently. However, they were never divorced and their relationship remained amicable.

After her London trip, Hackley's efforts turned increasingly to voice pedagogy or what she referred to as ''voice culture.'' Her performances included a lecture on vocal production, general musicianship, and even tips on stage presence and poise. Demand for printed copies of her lectures became so great that in 1909 she published, at her own expense, *A Guide in Voice Culture*. Hackley intended this compendium of practical instruction to be readily accessible to readers with little or no previous musical training. It contains useful information on early twentieth-century vocal performance practice, for example: ''Vibrato is a different thing, one's very vitals are in sympathetic action. This should not be used often.''

In 1910, having chosen to abandon her concert career, Hackley began a series of farewell appearances. She continued to share the stage with her many protgés and included the requisite intermission lecture. Her talks sometimes became appeals for funds. Typical of this fund-raising format was the debut recital of the blind soprano Mary Fitzhugh, which took place in Chicago on November 7, 1910. Sylvester Russell, music critic for the *Defender*, described Hackley's lecture:

> During the intermission Mrs. Hackley made one of her famous speeches. She has improved in that direction since I heard her last in Philadelphia. She spoke of how she had undertaken the task of aiding Miss Fitzhugh, and the vicissitudes of life that go with a female argument, this time in favor of well earned sympathy. After her task of supererogation had been recited she stepped right up into the celestial abode of financial womanhood (Russell, 2).

One of the highlights of this recital was the duet performed by Hackley and Fitzhugh. In other works on the program Hackley was the piano accompanist.

Hackley's most celebrated farewell performance was given in Chicago's Orchestra Hall on October 19, 1911, to a capacity audience of 1,500. Her varied program included opera arias and spirituals. In addition, she continued her ongoing lecture series, this time concentrating on vocal pedagogy. Critic Minnie Adams wrote:

> Her voice demonstrations were marvels of art as she has acuteness enough to sing them and her

power of elucidating is exceedingly interesting. Very useful were the demonstrations of the fundamental principles of vocalization, much stress being laid on the all-important 'oo' as used in the Italian method of culture, this together with the diaphragmatic breathing were illustrated in the most unique, clear and pleasing manner (Adams, 21 October 1911, 5).

"Voice Culture" Among the Black Masses Promoted

Throughout her retirement tour, Hackley endeavored to "aid her race musically in the same spirit that Booker T. Washington is promoting industry" (Adams, 23 September 1911, 5). She visited dozens of college campuses and communities in various parts of the country, giving free lectures on voice pedagogy and organizing choruses. Her mission was to encourage and promote the serious study of music among her race. She was no longer satisfied with her previous philanthropic projects that placed a few talented black musicians in Europe to study. Instead she devoted her energy to reaching the masses through "musical social uplift" (Brown, 233).

Hackley continued to delight her audiences with her skill as a pianist, often accompanying herself: She played "without apparent effort, or detraction from her art as a vocal soloist" (Taylor, 1). In a performance in Pittsburgh, Pennsylvania, on July 22, 1912, she sang "'Thou Brilliant Bird,' by David, a composition that required great technique; she played the flute obligato upon the piano with exceptionally good effect and gave a splendid interpretation of this beautiful song" (Taylor, 1).

In each community she visited, Hackley amassed large choruses of local singers to demonstrate "voice culture." Her audiences became almost ungainly in size, often numbering in the thousands. By late 1913 Hackley had "instructed more students than the Boston Conservatory in its sixty years of existence. She instructed nearly 64,000 in her method of voice culture, in one day teaching 3,000 school children" (Aery 1). At Hampton Institute in Virginia, Hackley devoted the entire month of August 1913 to instruction in the art of oratorio performance and appreciation. Her lectures and demonstrations were innovative and compelling. She made "six-foot charts of the music and matter to be taught," which were effective and well received. Her series concluded with an "Oratorio Demonstration" that included "a musical 'Tug of War' between sopranos, altos, tenors and basses in oratorios, recitatives and solos, and a musical 'Spell Down' between boys and girls on the oratorios 'The Creation' and 'The Messiah'" (Aery 1).

In the Introduction to *A Guide in Voice Culture*, Hackley wrote: "If this little book proves helpful, an effort will be made to revise it and to add a second part" (Hackley 1909, n.p.). A sequel never appeared and instead Hackley published a series of articles in the *New York Age*. Beginning in late 1914, Hackley's eleven essays appeared weekly. Under the rubric "Hints to Young Colored Artists," the articles covered a broad range of topics. By way of continuing her publication of 1909, she included in this series two articles entitled "Demonstration in Voice Culture" (Hackley, 17 December 1914—4 March 1915). Another collection of her lectures, *The Colored Girl Beautiful*, was published in Kansas City in 1916.

In a 1914 interview, the conductor James Reese Europe noted that "great improvements in higher education for the Negro have not developed music as you might think. The schools and colleges for the Negro are all of an industrial character. The artistic side has naturally been neglected as of less importance. That is our great difficulty. The people of my race who love music must train themselves" (*Crisis*, May 1914, 17). Even with the overwhelming success of Hackley's lectures in voice culture, she too realized that there existed a grave shortage of well-trained black music teachers. To help rectify this situation, she decided to establish her own music school. Late in 1915, Hackley purchased a building in Chicago and opened the Normal Vocal Institute. Its curriculum was broad in scope and embraced instruction in piano, theory, voice culture, and languages. She chose as her assistant her protégé, the young contralto Pauline James Lee.

Hackley soon became restless and left Chicago to continue touring. The institute was run in her absence by Lee and Hackley's sister, Marietta Smith Johnson. With the assistance of church leaders and the local press, she organized huge Folk Song Festivals in dozens of communities from coast to coast. Her highly-acclaimed programs featured spirituals and classical pieces by such promising black composers as Harry T. Burleigh, Samuel Coleridge-Taylor, Will Marion Cook, R. Nathaniel Dett, Carl Rossini Diton, J. Rosamond Johnson, Clarence Cameron White, and others. Hackley's only published composition "Carola" was performed in these concerts.

The Normal Vocal Institute was plagued with financial difficulties, and early in 1917, instruction was discontinued. Hackley's frequent prolonged absences may have contributed to its demise. The black press blamed the residents of Chicago for failing to rally to her cause (*Chicago Broad Ax*, 30 December 1922, 1). Another project, The Azalia Hackley Music Publishing House, met the same fate. Advertisements indicated that this business venture flourished during 1916, but evidence of its existence vanished from the press late the following year.

The strain of Hackley's business failures took its toll on her health. In late 1916 she began suffering from a recurrent ear ailment that caused severe pain and dizziness and eventually impaired her hearing. She never completely regained her health, though she did enjoy intermittent periods of recovery sufficient to allow her to continue arranging Folk Song Festivals. Late in 1920 her strength returned briefly and she took advantage of the respite by undertaking a trip to Japan. She was hospitalized shortly after her return in 1921. In 1922 a planned tour in California met financial obstacles, precipitating Hackley's final emotional and physical collapse. She was brought back to Detroit by her sister. There she died of a cerebral hemorrhage on December 13, 1922. Burial took place in Detroit's Elmwood Cemetery beside her mother's body in the family plot.

In recognition of Hackley's immeasurable contributions to the cause of racial equality as performer, educator, philanthropist, and humanitarian, the E. Azalia Hackley Memorial Collection of Negro Music, Dance, and Drama was established in Detroit in 1943. Located in the Detroit Public Library, this immense and rich collection began under the auspices of the Detroit Musicians Association, the local affiliate of the National Association of Negro Musicians. Numerous other institutions have paid homage to Hackley as well. In the mid-1930s, Hackley's esteemed People's Chorus was renamed The Hackley Choral Society. The Detroit chapter of the National Association of Negro Musicians was named the Hackley Chapter in 1935. In 1939, A. Merral Willis founded a school in Hackley's name in New York. A building at Hampton Institute (now University) in Virginia was named Hackley Hall.

References

Adams, Minnie. "Daily and Weekly Papers Speak Highly of Mme. E. Azalia Hackley." *Chicago Defender* 23 September 1911.

———. "Retiring Song Recital of a Genius." *Chicago Defender* 21 October 1911.

Aery, A. W. "Mme. Hackley at Hampton." *Chicago Defender* 30 August 1913.

Brown, Hallie Q. "Madame Emma Azalia Hackley." In *Homespun Heroines and Other Women of Distinction*. Xenia, Ohio: Aldine Pub. Co., 1926. Reprinted. The Schomburg Library of 19th-Century Black Women Writers. New York: Oxford University Press, 1988.

Campbell, Gladys B. "The Vocal Teacher of Ten Thousand Negroes." *Half Century Magazine* 1 (September 1916): 6.

Chicago Broad Ax, 4 September 1915, 4; 30 December 1922.

Chicago Defender, 18 June 1910; 18 April 1914; 18 November 1916.

Crisis 8 (May 1914): 17.

Cuney-Hare, Maude. *Negro Musicians and Their Music*. Washington, D.C.: Associated Publishers, 1936. Reprinted. New York: Da Capo Press, 1972.

Davenport, M. Marguerite. *Azalia: The Life of Madame E. Azalia Hackley*. Boston: Chapman and Grimes, 1947.

Davis, Marianna W., ed. *Contributions of Black Women to America*. Vol. 1. Columbia, S.C.: Kenday Press, 1982.

Edwards, Vernon H. and Michael L. Mark. "In Retrospect: Clarence Cameron White." *The Black Perspective in Music* 6 (Spring 1981): 51-72.

Hackley, E. Azalia. "Carola: Spanish Serenade." Detroit: 1918.

———. *The Colored Girl Beautiful*. Kansas City, Mo.: Burton Publication Co., 1916.

———. *A Guide in Voice Culture*. Philadelphia: 1909.

———. "Hints to Young Colored Artists" series. *New York Age* IVarious issues, December 1914, January 1915, February 1915, March 1915).

———. Letter to Mr. W. Lewis. *Indianapolis Freeman*, 30 March 1901.

———. "The Musical Progress of the Race During the Last Year." *Indianapolis Freeman*, 25 December 1915.

Half-Century Magazine 1 (August 1916): 9.

Holly, Ellistine Perkins Lewis. "A Profile of Emma Azalia Smith Hackley." Chapter in "The E. Azalia Hackley Memorial Collection of Negro Music, Dance, and Drama: A Catalogue of Selected Afro-American Materials." Ph.d. dissertation, University of Michigan, 1978.

Indianapolis Freeman, 16 February 1901 9 March 1901 8 January 1916.

Knock, Booster. "Song Festival Big Success." *Baltimore Afro-American*, 24 March 1917.

Logan, Rayford W. "Emma Azalia (Smith) Hackley." *Dictionary of American Negro Biography*. Eds. Rayford W. Logan and Michael R. Winston. New York: Norton, 1981.

Love, Josephine Harreld. "E. Azalia Smith Hackley." *Notable American Women, 1607-1950*. Vol. 2. Cambridge: Harvard University Press, 1973.

McHenry, Robert, ed. "Emma Azalia Hackley." *Liberty's Women*. Springfield, Mass.: Merriam, 1980.

Musical America 29 (26 March 1919): 16.

Russell, Sylvester. "The Mary Fitzhugh Recital." *Chicago Defender*, 12 November 1910.

Southern, Eileen. "Emma Azalia Smith Hackley." *Biographical Dictionary of Afro-American and African Musicians*. Westport, Conn.: Greenwood Press, 1982.

Taylor, A. R. "Madame Hackley's Retiring Song Recital." *Chicago Broad Ax* 27 July 1912.

Washington [DC] Bee, 11 March 1916.

White, Lucien H. "Mme. E. Azalia Hackley is Dead After Months of Illness." *New York Age*, 23 December 1922.

Woodbine, Ed. "Stage." *Indianapolis Freeman*, 30 March 1901.

Collections

Materials pertaining to Hackley are housed in the following collections: the E. Azalia Hackley Memorial Collection of Negro Music, Dance, and Drama, Detroit Public Library, (clippings, a copy of *A Guide in Voice Culture*, several photographs, and personal artifacts). The Schomburg Center for Research on Black Culture, New York Public Library; Hampton University Library, Hampton, Virginia. The Black American West Museum and Heritage Center, Denver and The Robert W. Woodruff Library of Atlanta University Center (a copy of *The Colored Girl Beautiful*, memorabilia including special programs, biographical sketch, clippings, and photographs). Josephine Harreld Love, daughter of Hackley's protégé, Kemper Harreld, has in her possession a few letters, programs, and a photograph, in addition to her father's papers. Photographs of Hackley can be found in Davenport's biography, *Azalia: The Life of Madame E. Azalia Hackley.*

Juanita Karpf

Clara Hale "Mother Hale"

(1905-)

Institution founder

For fifty years Clara McBride Hale, known as "Mother Hale," has been the guardian of young children who were abandoned or born to addicted mothers. Hale House, located on 122nd Street in Harlem, has had more than eight hundred babies pass through its door. Hale's involvement with "mothering" young children began in 1932, when her husband died and she began to care for other people's children to earn extra money.

Hale, the youngest of four children, was born on April 1, 1905, in Philadelphia, Pennsylvania. Her father died when she was an infant, so her mother assumed the economic responsibility of rearing four children by providing board and meals to lodgers. She completed high school and married Thomas Hale. They moved to New York City, where he opened his own floor-waxing business. Since the income from the business was insufficient to cover all the expenses, Hale obtained employment as a domestic worker—cleaning theaters. Her husband died of cancer when she was twenty-seven, and she was left with the responsibility of rearing three small children: Lorraine, Nathan, and Kenneth. She doubled her domestic duties and cleaned homes during the day and theaters at night. She was not totally satisfied with this arrangement, for it meant leaving her children without adult supervision. Subsequently, she began to care for other people's children during the day. Regarding her child care role, Hale told Tom Seligson during an interview:

> The parents paid me. I didn't make a whole lot, but I wasn't starving. And the kids must've liked it because once they got there, they didn't want to go home. So what started as day care ended up being fulltime. The parents would see the children on weekends (*Current Biography*, 165).

Hale reared forty foster children until she retired in 1968. Initially, she began to care for children who were wards of the city. She was paid two dollars a week per child. All of her foster children, black and white, pursued a college education.

After Hale retired from foster care, Hale's daughter, Lorraine, in 1969 encountered a young woman who was a heroin addict nodding off in a Harlem park. She had a two-month-old baby girl falling from her arms. Lorraine gave the young woman her mother's address and said it was a place "where you can get help" (*Current Biography Yearbook,* 165).

Home for Drug-Addicted Babies Opened

The young woman took her child to Hale, and thereafter news spread that her home was for addicted babies. For a year and a half, Hale's three children provided the initial financial support for the addicted babies. In 1970 Percy Sutton, president of the Borough of New York City, began funding the project. Hale House assumed its present location at 154 West 122nd Street in 1975. The vacant five-story brownstone was rebuilt and has a floor for play and preschool activities, a nursery for detoxified babies, and a third floor where Hale keeps new arrivals during the withdrawal period.

The main objective of Hale House is to take drug-dependent children at birth, rear them until their mothers complete a drug treatment program, and reunite the mother and child when treatment ends. Clara Hale observes that during withdrawal the children suffer from stiff legs and backs, diarrhea, and vomiting. They also scratch themselves and cry constantly. Hale's cure is based on the healing power of love and positive reinforcement. For example, by 6:00 A.M. Mother Hale is up and giving bottles to several drug-addicted infants. She cleans and feeds the babies, and when they cry from the pains of withdrawal, she walks the floor with them, talks to them, but gives them no medicine, not even aspirin (*Current Biography Yearbook,* 167).

Hale notes:

> The children here know that someone loves them and they're happy. I make sure that they're always clean and well fed and comfortable. I tell them how pretty they are and what they can accomplish if they get an education. And I tell them to be proud of their Blackness, to be proud

of one another, and to pull together (Johnson, 58).

Her philosophy has a major positive effect: Hale House has been home to eight hundred unwanted babies since 1969.

Hale House receives referrals from the police, clergy, hospitals, and social workers. Children are admitted to Hale House regardless of ethnicity, religion, or gender. The age range is from ten days to four years.

Hale believes that color is not a factor in achieving one's goal. She contends:

> Being black does not stop you. You can sit out in the world and say, "Well, white people kept me back, and I can't do this." Not so. You can have anything you want if you make up your mind and you want it. You don't have to crack nobody across the head, don't have to steal or anything. Don't have to be smart like the men up high stealing all the money. We're good people and we try (Lanker, 55).

Hale's appearance is undoubtedly reassuring to her "children". She is short and slight and looks younger than her years. She has thin white hair, few facial wrinkles, and bright eyes. Her voice is warm and confident.

For Hale's unselfish commitment to babies who are born addicts, former President Ronald Reagan identified her as a "true American hero" during his State of the Union Address before Congress on February 6, 1985. Hale's response to this public adulation was that she did not feel like a hero; rather, she is involved in her life's work and likes it (Kastor, C-2). She contends that everyone has a role to assume in the world, and hers has been to love and care for children.

Hale was awarded an honorary doctorate of humane letters by John Jay College of Criminal Justice in June 1985. She received the Salvation Army's highest award, the Booth Community Service Award, on Wednesday, December 5, 1990.

References

"Chronicle-Clara Hale." *New York Times*, 5 December 1990. Includes photograph.

Current Biography Yearbook. New York: H. W. Wilson, 1985. Includes photograph.

Johnson, Herschel. "Clara (Mother) Hale: Healing Baby 'Junkies' With Love." *Ebony* 41 (May 1986): 84.

Kastor, Elizabeth. "The Hour of the Heroes." *Washington Post*, 8 February 1985.

Lanker, Brian. *I Dream a World*. New York: Stewart, Tabori and Chang, 1989. Includes photograph.

Stanley, Alessandra. "Hale House Fights City Hall for Babies' Fate." *New York Times*, 23 September 1990. Includes photograph.

Mary R. Holley

Millie E. Hale

(1881-1930)

Nurse, hospital founder, social activist, civic worker

Health care for blacks in the South is a long-standing problem, and Millie Essie Gibson Hale found no exception in Nashville, Tennessee, in the early 1900s. A nurse and the wife of a physician, she was acutely aware of the problems and the need for a hospital where the sick and injured could receive immediate care under the watchful eye of trained staff. On July 1, 1916, she opened the Millie E. Hale Hospital and Training School in Nashville. The facility became a place where black people with or without funds could be housed and treated for illnesses.

Hale was born February 27, 1881, in Nashville, Tennessee, to Henry and Nannie Gibson. According to the federal census report for 1900, Henry Gibson, a blacksmith, was

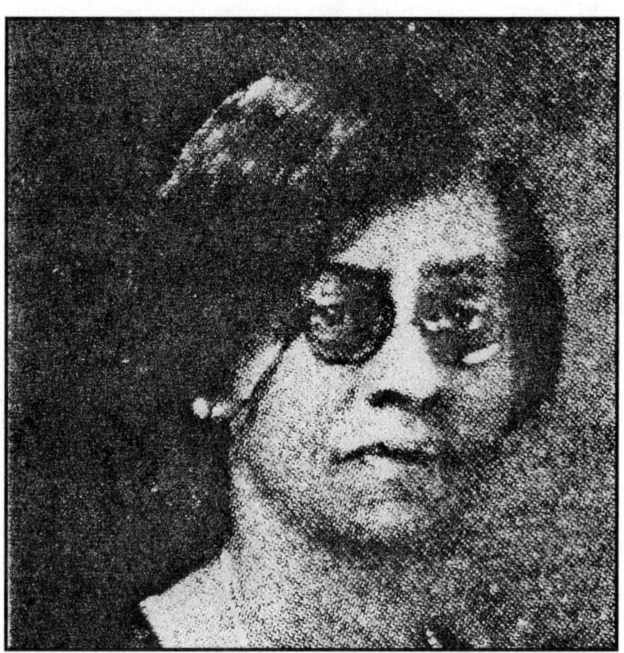

Millie E. Hale

born in July 1841; Nannie Gibson was born in August 1861. Hale had four siblings, Herbert H., W. B., G. W., and Katie.

Hale grew up in Nashville and graduated in 1901 from Fisk University's Normal School. She completed studies at the Graduate School for Nurses in New York City, and later, in 1927, she received a bachelor's degree from Fisk. Sometime in the early 1900s she married John Henry Hale. John Hale was born in Estill Springs, Tennessee, attended elementary school there and came to Nashville in the late 1890s. He graduated from Tennessee Central College in 1901 and in 1905 received his medical degree from Meharry Medical College. John Hale became a prominent physician and medical educator at Meharry Medical College, and after his wife's death, chief of surgery. They had two daughters, Mildred and Essie.

Millie E. Hale Hospital and Training School Established

As Nashvillians agonized over the health care of the city's residents, Hale provided partial relief for the problem. On July 1, 1916, she established the Millie E. Hale Hospital, located at 523 Seventh Avenue South, and served as nurse and superintendent. The first year-round hospital for blacks in the city, it was originally equipped to offer twelve beds and was staffed by Hale and two nurses in charge. By 1923 the hospital had a capacity of seventy-five beds and provided all modern conveniences for patient care. It was soon enlarged to provide one hundred beds and twenty-six nurses were on the payroll. By 1923 the hospital also had registered seven thousand patients; more than five thousand operations had been performed and the mortality rate was less than three percent (Ragland, 371). Assisting the surgeon-in-chief, John Hale, were four house physicians. The Hales lived at 419 Fourth Avenue South in Nashville. They converted their fourteen-room house into a community center for prenatal care and a baby welfare clinic. They also maintained a free dispensary and clinic for adults. The center was involved in numerous activities: It was a meeting place for black women who wanted to explore ways to uplift the black community; it offered facilities for women involved in club work; it provided a class in religious education; and it offered free health lectures.

According to the hospital's report for 1923, Hale purchased land and developed and maintained four large playgrounds for children's leisure activities. Under her administration, each June the hospital gave free picnics to youth, accommodating at least seven thousand in 1923, and a celebration called "Boys Week"—a reception for the black newscarriers of the day. Local support for the annual outings was noteworthy. The Nashville Electric Railway Company provided free transportation, while local residents donated the use of automobiles and also offered refreshments. The staff organized boys and girls into clubs and taught them healthful recreation. Hale had many "special" interests. One of them was in music, as seen in her Sunday school activities as well as in the free band concerts that she offered for youth three nights a week. Open air movies were held during on the same nights. Another was in assisting needy children. "She had an abiding interest in needy children and on Saturday before Easter each year she sponsored a city-wide Easter egg hunt in Greenwood Park. She solicited prizes from various businesses and individuals throughout the city to reward the children" (Interview with Sadie Galloway Johnson). Marcus Gunter added that Preston Taylor, noted black local businessman and founder and owner of Greenwood Amusement Park, cosponsored the egg hunt with Hale and offered a "golden egg" to the prime winner (Interview with Marcus Gunter, 1 April 1990). Hale also provided open air movies to youngsters three nights each week. Hale's interest in children was seen also in 1923 when she placed five infants, obviously orphaned, in good homes.

The 1923 report indicated further that 1,155 people were supplied free food, money, bedding, and coal for heating and cooking. An additional four hundred persons, who were ill, were sent free breakfasts and dinners from the hospital auxiliary. Free medical and surgical care was provided to the needy. While nurses visited 7,687 homes to minister to the bedside needs of the sick, much of this was without cost to the patients. When necessary, they prepared the family meals, cleaned their homes, and provided other relief for the family. Carfare was provided for these nurses. The auxiliary maintained a prenatal and baby welfare clinic and delivered more than one hundred lectures on health.

Hale, who also managed a community grocery store, had a keen interest in community activities and meeting community needs. The hospital Ladies' Auxiliary, which Hale headed, joined forces with the hospital staff and provided the human resources required to meet her community-oriented goals. Thus, black women of Nashville were important forces in development of social and cultural programs in the community. Together they offered educational programs, visited the needy, sick, and shut-in, and assisted with recreational programs and relief activities. The auxiliary and the hospital staff also published a monthly paper to carry to the black community health messages and hope for meeting their health needs.

The 1923 report also notes that one of the hospital staff attended to the needs of twenty neglected wives and saw that they received proper support. One needy widow's home was saved, perhaps from mortgage foreclosure.

Hale had visited most of the large hospitals in the North and East to gather information on hospital care and administration. Leading surgeons in the country commended her for the operation that she maintained. The hospital received favorable recognition from the American College of Surgeons and easily attracted nurses to its staff. Both the social service units of the hospitals and the Nurse Training Department grew. By 1925 twenty-four women had graduated, and twenty-five young women from Texas, Georgia, Alabama, Michigan, Kentucky, and Tennessee were enrolled in the program. The three-year nursing program included a course in social service and an internship program. "The problems in Nashville's black community made the need for a social service department essential, and it became one of the leading aspects of the hospital's programs. Clearly, the outreach to the needy in terms of relief as well as health care gave to the residents assistance that otherwise might not have been realized'' (Neverdon-Morton, 173). Neverdon-Morton found also that Meharry Medical College students provided some clinical work at the hospital's free outpatient clinic. The hospital was no longer listed in the *Nashville City Directory* after 1938, the year in which it officially closed. John Hale was at that time head of the department of surgery at Meharry and later the school physician at Tennessee Agricultural and State College.

Carrie Hale Ross, in a telephone interview on 24 March 1990, substantiated reports of the hospital given in the *Nashville Colored Directory* and reported by Neverdon-Morton. ''We would operate on people who had nothing to pay.'' Hale was an anesthetist nurse. Carrie Hale Ross, who under the tutelage of the Hales became an anesthetist nurse, recalls vividly the Hales and their careers in health care: ''As I talk about it I feel that I am reliving my life with Millie Hale.'' Ross recalls that Millie Hale's hospital became a ''Class A'' hospital under Hale's administration. That was an accomplishment to cherish in those days. About Millie's Hale's administration and the work of the hospital, Carrie Ross continued:

> She taught me in the hospital. The hospital staff and students did social service free. Senior nurses would stay with the sick free. If they had surgery, we would stay all night, and if they were having a child, we would stay until the doctor came. Sometimes nurses delivered the babies themselves. I delivered many babies, and I can still deliver babies.

Ross recalls that, as a nurse and hospital superintendent, Hale was the ''best in the business. A person would be successful if they followed Millie Hale's footsteps.'' She was also firm in her convictions and in her expectations of the nurses. ''I take no excuse,'' Ross quoted Hale. She and John Henry Hale were active in Saint Paul African Methodist Episcopal (AME) Church, then located on Fourth Avenue South in the vicinity of Hale Hospital. ''The Hales never missed a Sunday,'' Ross recalls. ''They spoke at some church nearly every Sunday afternoon. They were most sought after.'' Hale was superintendent of Sunday school and organized a Sunday school band.

Hale was active in community activities, including the YWCA. The national YWCA had been known to discriminate against black members and ignored the ''Christian'' responsibilities of the organization that the name embraced. Black women were not treated as equals, and the association readily accepted its segregated internal structure. Black members bitterly opposed these practices but chose to explore ways to influence the policies and practices of the national body. When the 1920 YWCA conference was held in Louisville, Kentucky, Lugenia Hope of Atlanta, Charlotte Hawkins Brown of North Carolina, and Hale ''were quite vocal during the meetings'' (Neverdon-Morton, 216). Hale's performance was characteristic of her approach to effecting change, whether administering the Hale Hospital or attending to other matters in the Nashville community.

Ross attests to Hale's position in the local community. She was exceptionally well-liked in Nashville. ''She had a beautiful sense of humor.'' Hale was active in many organizations, including the women's club movement. She worked with Frankie Pierce, who in 1925 was president of the Nashville Federation of Colored Women's Clubs. In addition to other organizations, she was a member of the Heliotrope Literary Circle and was president in 1925.

Hale had been ill for about three months in the spring of 1930. She died of nephritis on Friday, June 6, 1930, at 8:00 P.M. in the hospital that she founded. She was forty-nine years old. Funeral services were held on Monday, June 9, 1930, in Saint Paul AME Church. She was buried in Nashville's Greenwood Cemetery.

References

Alumni Directory of Fisk University. Nashville, Tennessee: Office of Alumni Affairs, 1971.

Gunter, Marcus. Interview with Jessie Carney Smith, 1 April 1990.

Johnson, Sadie Galloway. Interview with Jessie Carney Smith, 24 March 1990.

Nashville Colored Directory, Biographical, Statistical. Compiled by R. C. Grant. [Nashville], 1925. Includes photographs of Millie E. Hale and of the Millie E. Hale Hospital. The *Nashville Colored Directory* was reprinted in part, and with additions, under the title *The Black Yellow Pages*, [Nashville], 1990.

Neverdon-Morton, Cynthia. *Afro-American Women of the South and the Advancement of the Race, 1895-1925*. Knoxville: University of Tennessee Press, 1989.

Ragland, John Marshall. ''A Hospital for Negroes with a Social Service Program.'' *Opportunity* 1 (December 1923): 370-71. Includes photograph of Hale and the Hale hospital staff.

Ross, Carrie Hale. Interview with Jessie Carney Smith, 24 March 1990.

Collections

Miscellaneous clippings on Millie E. Hale, including a photograph of Hale and the hospital, a copy of the federal census record and certificate of death, and a few items on John Henry Hale are in the Special Collections, Fisk University Library. The Black Medical Archives of Meharry Medical College contain information on John Henry Hale.

Jessie Carney Smith

Adelaide Hall

(1904-)

Singer, actress

Adelaide Hall, jazz and stage singer and actress, was born on October 20, 1904, in Brooklyn, New York. Her father was a music teacher, and after his death in the early 1920s she began her professional stage career. Her career spanned more than a half century. She currently resides in London, England. There are presently no available published sources on Hall's family background, childhood, or musical training.

Hall was one of the multitalented black performers in the early black shows of the 1920s. Black stars appeared in musical revues, movies, and entertainment acts in Europe, on Broadway, and in black theaters across the United States. Among her contemporaries were Valaida Snow, Edith Wilson, Josephine Baker, Florence Mills, Eubie Blake, and Duke Ellington.

Married in 1925 to Bert Hicks, an ex-seaman from Trinidad, who became her manager, Hall and her husband eventually made Europe their permanent home about 1938. They operated several successful clubs in England and France: The Big Apple on the Rue Pigalle in Paris (circa 1935-1938), the Florida Club in the Mayfair section of London (1940s), and the Calypso Club, which opened in London after the war.

After moving to London, Hall costarred with Todd Duncan in *The Sun Never Sets* (1938) and was star of the musical *Keep Shufflin'* (1938). During the running of the show, Hall recorded two ballads with Fats Waller, "That Old Feeling" and "I Can't Give You Anything but Love." During the war years she entertained with the USO.

Two of Hall's contemporaries in the entertainment world were Ethel Waters and Alberta Hunter, and each provided some information about Hall in their biographies. While performing at Edmonds Cellar Club in New York City during the early 1920s, Waters remembers Hall:

> Adelaide Hall, who was then rehearsing for "Shuffle Along," came to see us almost nightly. She would do a number on the floor. Adelaide had a lovely soft voice, and after singing a sentimental song she'd go into a flatfoot-time buck with much beating and stomping (Waters, 149).

Alberta Hunter, an outstanding classic blues singer, remembered Hall as one of the most popular black singers on both sides of the Atlantic and also considered Hall as her protégé. Hunter spoke of events leading to Hall's final decision to move to Europe after being forced out of the home she purchased in 1932 in Larchmont, Westchester County, New York.

Actor/Singer Successful on Two Continents

Hall was one of the few black women entertainers to be successful in Europe and the United States. Her early appearances in Europe included *Chocolate Kiddies Revue* (1925) and *Blackbirds* (1927). In 1935-1936 she toured Europe with drummer Bennie Peyton and keyboard player Joe Turner. She worked with Willie Lewis and Ray Ventura in Paris (circa 1936-1937). After making England her home, she continued to tour throughout Europe.

As a solo singer, Hall worked with such musicians as Duke Ellington, Art Tatum, Fats Waller, Bennie Payne, Joe Turner, Bernard Addison, and Joe Loss. In 1927 Hall and Ellington recorded the immortal "Creole Love Call," with Hall singing a wordless instrumental solo, one of the many concepts pioneered by Ellington. She also became noted for her singing of "Diga, Diga, Doo" from the musical *Blackbirds*.

Art Tatum, jazz pianist, became her accompanist about 1931. Their collaboration resulted in the recording of several songs. In addition to world tours, Hall performed in famous clubs, including the Alhambra, Les Ambassadeurs, the Lido, and the Moulin Rouge (Paris); the Cotton Club and the Savoy (New York City); and the Savoy.

Hall continued her singing career into the sixties with recordings and tours in Europe and the United States. She participated in an anniversary concert for Paul Robeson at the Royal Festival Hall in London (1968) and a memorial service for Duke Ellington, also in London (1974).

In June 1979 Adelaide Hall, Edith Wilson, John W. Bubbles—all stars of the 1920s and 1930s—and Bobby Short, jazz pianist, performed at the Newport Jazz Festival. In a program of songs reminiscent of "Black Broadway" during the first half of the century, Hall joined in songs made famous by Ethel Waters and others. The same program was repeated in May 1980 at Town Hall in New York City.

Hall's theater credits include *Shuffle Along* (1922), *Runnin' Wild* (1923), *Chocolate Kiddies* (1925), *Desires of 1927* and *Blackbirds* (1927), *Blackbirds of 1928* (1928), *Brown Buddies* (1930), *The Sun Never Sets*, London, (1938), *Keep Shufflin'*, London (1938), *Kiss Me Kate*, London (1951), *Love From Judy*, London (1952), *Someone to Talk To*, London (1956), *Jamaica* (1957), and *Janie Jackson*, London (1958).

She appeared in the following films: *Dancers in the Dark* with Duke Ellington (1932), *All-Colored Vaudeville Show* with the Nicholas Brothers (1935), *Dixieland Jamboree* with Cab Calloway (1935), *The Thief of Bagdad* (1940), and *Night and the City* (1950).

Hall made three notable recordings: *I Can't Give You Anything But Love, That Old Feeling,* and *Creole Love Song.*

References

"Black Broadway." *New York Times,* 2 May 1980.

Chilton, John. *Who's Who of Jazz: Storyville to Swing Street.* New York: Da Capo Press, 1985.

Claghorn, Charles E. *Biographical Dictionary of Jazz.* Englewood Cliffs, N.J.: Prentice-Hall, 1982.

"Do You Remember Adelaide Hall?" *Negro Digest* 9 (May 1951): 73-74. Includes photograph.

Driggs, Frank, and Harris Lewine. *Black Beauty-White Heat: A Pictorial History of Classic Jazz, 1920-1950.* New York: William Morrow, 1982. Includes photograph.

Hughes, Langston, and Milton Meltzer. *Black Magic: A Pictorial History of the Negro in American Entertainment.* Englewood Cliffs, N.J.: Prentice-Hall, 1967.

Machlin, Paul S. *Stride: The Music of Fats Waller.* Boston: Twane Publishers, 1985.

Mapp, Edward. *Directory of Blacks in the Performing Arts.* Metuchen, N.J.: Scarecrow Press, 1978.

Meeker, David. *Jazz in the Movies: A Guide to Jazz Musicians 1917-1977.* New Rochelle, N.Y.: Arlington House, 1977.

Southern, Eileen. *Biographical Dictionary of Afro-Americans and African Musicians.* Westport, Conn.: Greenwood Press, 1982.

"Stage: Black Broadway." *New York Times,* 17 June 1979.

Taylor, Frank C. with Gerald Cook. *Alberta Hunter, a Celebration in Blues.* New York: McGraw-Hill, 1987.

Waters, Ethel, with Charles Samuels. *His Eye is on the Sparrow.* New York: Doubleday, 1951.

Ellistine P. Holly

Juanita Hall

(1901-1968)

Singer, actress, choral director

Juanita Long Hall was born November 6, 1901 (or 1902) in Keyport, New Jersey, and died February 29, 1968, in Bayshore, New York. This singer, actress, and choral director was best-known for her role as Bloody Mary in the 1949 Broadway stage production of *South Pacific.* She was the daughter of Abram Long and Mary (Richardson) Long. She had two siblings—a sister, Hilda Long Creed, and a brother, Horace Long. She received her primary and secondary schooling in Keyport and Bordentown, New Jersey.

Hall began singing very early in church choirs in her local communities with the encouragement of her maternal grandmother, who said that "she never knew how to do anything but sing." Hall's love of Negro spirituals began around the age of twelve, after hearing them sung at a revival meeting in New Jersey. In her words, "the whole quality of the singing grabbed hold of me" (*Ebony,* 30). By fourteen years of age, she had dreams of becoming a high dramatic soprano and was using her vocal talent to teach singing at Lincoln House in East Orange, New Jersey.

Little information has been found on the first twenty-five years of Hall's life. It is known that she married in her teens Clement Hall, an actor, who died in the 1920s. She never remarried and had no children. She attended Juilliard School of Music in New York City, taking courses in orchestration, harmony, theory, and voice. She also studied voice and acting with private teachers.

Hall spent more than forty years in the performing arts as choral conductor, stage and film singer, and actress. Her choral music activities brought her in contact with other black music pioneers, such as Hall Johnson, Eva Jessye, and William C. Handy. Hall's choral organizations were known for their high musical quality and discipline and many of her choir members went on to perform in Broadway stage productions. She also had a private voice studio.

Stage and Choir Careers Blossom

Hall was one of a few black stage performers to gain stardom on the New York stage and to be cast in leading roles in three successful Broadway musical productions. She spent more than twenty years playing minor parts and singing in choruses before her big break. It was during an audition for Talent 48, a revue put on privately by the New York City Stage Managers Club, that Richard Rodgers and Oscar Hammerstein II heard her sing. Their use of her talent came later. She was forty-nine at this point in her career and she continued to sing and act for the next nineteen years.

Hall's first professional stage experience was in the chorus of the Ziegfield production of *Show Boat* (1928), featuring Jules Bledsoe as "Joe," a role later made famous by Paul Robeson. She sang in the chorus of *Green Pastures* (1930) under the direction of Hall Johnson.

During the years 1931-1936 Hall sang as a soloist and was assistant director with the Hall Johnson Choir. She formed her own group in 1935, the Juanita Hall Choir, which remained together for five years as a Works Progress Administration (WPA) group. The choir appeared at park concerts, in schools, and at boys' clubs and was heard three times weekly over radio station WNYC. The Juanita Hall Choir was one of several groups that participated in the ASCAP Silver Jubilee at Carnegie Hall, New York City, October 2, 1939. At the World's Fair in New York City, 1939, Hall directed a three-hundred voice church choir.

During the forties Hall began appearing on stage in a series of dramatic and musical roles: *The Pirates* (1942); *Sing Out Sweet Land*, *The Secret Room* (1944); *Deep Are the Roots* (1945); *Mr. Peebles and Mr. Hooker* (1946); *S. S. Glencairn*, *Moon of the Caribees* (1948), and the film *Miracle in Harlem*.

Hall performed in one of the all-black musicals in the forties, *St. Louis Woman*, based on the novel *God Sends Sunday*, by Arna Bontemps and Countee Cullen. Pearl Bailey had the featured role with Juanita Hall, the Nicholas Brothers, Creighton Thompson, and others in supporting parts. Hall and Creighton Thompson appeared in minor parts in *Street Scene* (1947), with music by Kurt Weil and lyrics by Langston Hughes.

Hall was one of the leading black Broadway stars of the 1950s. In 1949 she was cast as Bloody Mary in the Pulitzer Prize-winning play, *South Pacific*, starring Mary Martin and Ezio Pinza. She went on to capture the role of Madame Tango in the 1954 musical, *House of Flowers*, starring Diahann Carroll. This was followed in 1958 with *Flower Drum Song*, where she played the principal role of Madame Liang, a mature Chinese lady.

It was in the musical *South Pacific* that Hall achieved her greatest fame as a singing actress. Her singing of "Bali H'ai" and "Happy Talk," two hits from the show, contributed to the success of the show and Hall's fame. She was personally selected for the roles in *South Pacific* and *Flower Drum Song* by the writing team of Rogers and Hammerstein. She went on to perform in the film versions of *South Pacific* and *Flower Drum Song* and the touring company of *Flower Drum Song*. Her honors included the Tony Award and the Donaldson Award for *South Pacific* (1950); Bill "Bojangles" Acting Award, 20th Century-Fox Appreciation Award, and Box Office Film Association Award for the film *South Pacific* (1958); and the Laurel Award as best actress (1962).

Hall performed in major nightclubs between 1950 and 1962: Cafe Society (New York City); Saint Moritz, Flamingo (Las Vegas); Black Orchid (Chicago); Elmwood Casino (Windsor, Canada); and The Flame (Detroit). Her television appearances included: *This Is Show Business*, *Philco Television Playhouse*, *The Ed Sullivan Show*, *Perry Como Show*, *Today Show*, *Coca Cola Hour*, *Mike Wallace P.M. East*, and *Schlitz Playhouse of Stars*.

As a concert artist, Hall sang Negro spirituals and songs written for her by Langston Hughes and Herbert Kingsley. She recorded four of Hughes's blues lyrics in 1949. In 1966 she scored a success in a Blues Recital at the East Seventy-Fourth Street Theater.

Hall is remembered by some of her choir members as a woman of immense talent and awesome firmness. She was an outspoken woman with a strong feeling about the rights of her people. On her death Richard Rodgers wrote in a tribute to Hall:

> I loved Juanita. I think everyone who had anything to do with her loved her. I don't remember her ever doing a thoughtless act or saying an unkind word. As an actress, she was a thorough professional, quick to grasp the essentials of a part, and a joy to work with. Everything she did on stage came across with such zestful spontaneity that many were surprised to learn of her classical voice training at Juilliard or her career as a concert singer. Juanita was also highly emotional. I recall that when I first played her song "Bali Ha'i," she was so overcome that she wept. For a composer, there's no nicer compliment.

References

"After 21 Years." *Time* 6 June 1949: 74-76. Contains photograph.

Hughes, Langston, and Milton Meltzer. *Black Magic: A Pictorial History of the Negro in American Entertainment*. Englewood Cliffs, N.J.: Prentice-Hall, 1967.

"Juanita Hall As Bloody Mary." *Ebony* (July 1950): 29-32. Contains photograph.

"Juanita Hall in 'Run Little Chillun.'" *Anthology of the American Negro in the Theatre—A Critical Approach*. Comp. and Ed. Linday Patterson. Cornell Heights, Pa.: Publishers Agency, 1976. 44, 238.

Lovell, John, Jr. "Sing in the Streets." *Crisis* 54 (June 1947): 172-74.

Mapp, Edward. *Directory of Blacks in the Performing Arts*. Metuchen, N.J.: Scarecrow Press, 1978. 149.

Nichols, Charles H., ed. *Arna Bontemps—Langston Hughes Letters, 1925-1967*. New York: Dodd, Mead, 1980. 291.

"'Richard Rogers Tribute to Juanita Hall, 1901-1968." *New York Times* 10 March 1968. Includes photograph.

Southern, Eileen. *Biographical Dictionary of Afro-American and African Musicians*. Westport, Conn.: Greenwood Press, 1982.

Ellistine P. Holly

Fannie Lou Hamer

(1917-1977)

Civil rights activist, sharecropper

The spirited civil rights activist Fannie Lou Townsend Hamer was born on October 6, 1917, in Montgomery county Mississippi, the twentieth child born to sharecropper parents. Hamer was deprived of many of the conveniences and benefits common to twentieth-century America: When her father was finally able to work the family out of abject poverty, an envious white neighbor poisoned the Townsend mules and cows, destroying the family's prospects.

Thus for Hamer, as for many black Americans oppressed by the sharecropper system, the firsthand experience of exploitation began at a very early age. At age six, she was entrapped into work by a plantation owner who enticed her to pick cotton with the promise of sweets—candies and cherries—things that were beyond the economic reach of black children. Week after week she was tasked to pick more and more cotton. By the time she was thirteen years old she was picking three to four hundred pounds. Yet she and her family were still poor. She reflected upon this experience in an interview with Robert Wright:

Fannie Lou Hamer

> I just wondered what in the world was wrong that all of the people that didn't work—they were people that had something that people that worked didn't have, as [it] still is . . . what's going on now.

Having been purposefully designed to maintain economic imbalance in favor of white people, the sharecropper system effectively kept blacks poor and whites economically secure. Of course, even the young eyes of children were able to see that there was a radical difference between the conditions of being white and being black, especially in the deep South—so much so that it was not uncommon for blacks, especially the young, to wish the whiteness for themselves. Even Hamer asked her mother, "Why weren't we white?" (Wright, 1). The question came out of her existential experience that whiteness meant plenty of good food to eat and plenty of good room to live in; and blackness sometimes meant nothing but hunger and inadequate housing.

In more ways than one, it was clear to the young that "to make it you had to be white." Hamer's mother responded, "No that's not it, don't ever let me [hear you] say that again. . . . Be grateful that you are black, because [if] God had wanted you to be white, you would have been white, so accept yourself for what you are" (Wright, 1-2).

For black sharecroppers, education was secondary to the needs of the plantation. Because of this, Hamer had only six years of school, for at that time the school period extended from December to March, the four months corresponding to the time black labor was not needed in the fields. Still, because of the lack of adequate clothing during the cold months, only about one month of schooling was possible.

Hamer's experience was not an exceptional one. Some blacks in the South, particularly in Mississippi, lived under the most inhumane conditions. It was not uncommon in the 1960s for a black person to work and be given three dollars per day. Hamer observed that in fact "a black man had no rights that a white man had to respect," for in Mississippi, as in other parts of the United States, "a white person could kill [a black person] without bothering to explain" ("Black Voices of the South," 51). In Sunflower County (Hamer's home), seventy percent of the black people were disenfranchised, and consequently the government was totally unrepresentative of the majority of the people. Blacks were at best second-class citizens, but most were actually treated as noncitizens. Still seeing the contradictions between black reality and white reality, in her prayers Hamer often asked God to give her a chance to just let me do something about what was going on in Mississippi.

In 1942 she married Perry "Pap" Hamer, a tractor driver from another plantation. Because they were unable to have children, they adopted two girls, one of whom died in 1967. Inheriting the impoverished tradition of her sharecropper family, she and her husband continued in the cycle of poverty. But Hamer was a hard worker, and eventually she was promoted from strenuous cotton-picking to the less strenuous but still low-paying job of timekeeper on the plantation.

Civil Rights Activities Attract Hamer

Because black life was cheap, blacks suffered many abuses. Hamer's life was a reflection of that continued abuse, pain, and suffering. L.C. Dorsey in the *Jackson Advocate* describes other dimensions of her suffering: "Mrs. Hamer knew about another kind of pain; the pain [of] watching your offspring die from poverty, related illnesses, and of suffering because of a handicap that had she not been poor, could have been corrected." Her life took a turn in 1962 when she met workers of the Southern Christian Leadership Conference (SCLC) and the Student Nonviolent Coordinating Committee (SNCC), who began mobilizing people to fight for freedom in Mississippi. As a result of this empowering encounter, Hamer became active in politics in Mississippi, especially in Ruleville. It all began at a rally led by the Reverend James Bevel of the SCLC and James Forman of SNCC held in August 1962. Hamer attended and vividly recalled the proceedings. The most effective communication mode in the black community, preaching was used to communicate the message at the rally. Bevel preached from Luke 12:54, "Discerning the Signs of Times," and challenged the people to look around them to see the signs of those times. Afterwards, James Foreman spoke specifically about voter registration, further challenging the people to action to effect change in their political leadership and thus causing positive change in their living conditions.

When the call was made for volunteers to challenge the unjust voting laws, Hamer was among the volunteers. At the appointed time, August 31, eighteen persons boarded an old school bus, owned and driven by a black man from another county, to go to Indianola to the courthouse to register to vote. There they were given a literacy test that required them to copy and interpret a portion of the Constitution of the State of Mississippi. Having failed the test, the eighteen reboarded the bus to return to Ruleville. En route home they were stopped by a highway patrolman, and the driver was arrested for driving a bus that was "too yellow," looking too much like a school bus, thereby creating potential confusion. When the group refused to be separated, the one-hundred-dollar fine was reduced to thirty dollars, which they as a group were able to collect among themselves.

Upon her return to the plantation, Hamer was met by the news that the plantation owner was very upset because she had registered to vote. Hamer said:

> The landowner said I would have to go back to withdraw or I would have to leave and so I told him I didn't go down there to register for him, I was down there to register for myself (Black Oral History Interview, Fisk University, 6 October 1962).

She left the plantation. The home to which she fled was riddled with gun shots. The entire family was subsequently dismissed from the plantation and suffered constantly from white backlash.

Returning to the courthouse in December 1962, and again failing the literacy test, Hamer left, declaring, "You'll see me every 30 days 'till I pass." It was on her third try in January 1963 that she became a registered voter (Sewell, 3). She became an SNCC supervisor in Sunflower County and actively engaged in teaching blacks to pass the literacy test. "I had to go off to take training where I could learn the different sections of the Constitution of Mississippi and then I could teach other people to write the different sections and then to give a reasonable interpretation," she said (Black Oral History Interview, Fisk University).

Life as a registered voter was not easy, for it became difficult for the Hamer family to get and maintain employment. Hamer then became a field worker in the civil rights movement. Following a civil rights workshop in Charleston, South Carolina, on their return trip to Ruleville on a Trailways bus, Fannie Lou Hamer and a group of nineteen stopped at a bus terminal in Winona, Mississippi, to get something to eat. Challenging the "white only" practice, they were attacked by state troopers, arrested, and charged with disorderly conduct. In that Winona jail, Hamer suffered one of the worst beatings of her life. She was taken to a cell with two black male prisoners who were given a black leather clutch loaded with metal and ordered to beat her or suffer severe consequences of refusing to follow the demands of the white prison guards. She was returned to her jail cell, where she and the other civil rights workers were released upon the intervention of James Bevel and Andrew Young. The incident left Hamer permanently injured.

Hamer Gains National Attention in Mississippi Freedom Democratic Party

Hamer came out of this experience more determined to change the unjust, oppressive, and racist system in Mississippi. She became more involved in political organizing. In the spring of 1964 the Mississippi Freedom Democratic Party (MFDP) was established after unsuccessful attempts to gain participation in the Mississippi Democratic party. Her work catapulted her to position of vice-chairperson of the Mississippi Freedom Democratic Party, under which she campaigned for Congress from the Second Congressional District of Mississippi. Even more importantly, it was as a leader of the MFDP that she gained national attention as the MFDP challenged the white Mississippi delegation to the 1964 National Democratic Convention in Atlantic City. The challenge resulted in the nation hearing her story as she testified before the credentials committee. Her story included atrocities such as the loss of employment because of her attempts to register to vote; the beatings such as the Winona, Mississippi, experience at the bus station; the arrest of the busload in Indianola for trying to register; and the many other brutalities perpetrated against blacks by whites.

The MFDP delegation did not obtain what it wanted; instead a so-called compromise was made. The compromise in effect gave two seats to the sixty-eight-member delegation. Some saw this as a moral victory. Hamer, along with other MFDP delegates, took exception to this interpretation of the compromise. Hamer was reported as saying, "We didn't come all this way for no two seats when all of us is tired."

As Hamer's horizons broadened and her involvement deepened, she became global in her interests and was able to see the injustices of the Vietnam War, becoming one of its early critics. Of that war she said, "We are sick and tired of our people having to go to Vietnam and other places to fight for something we don't have here." Consequently, she was able to draw a critical connection between war, racism, and poverty: "We want . . . to end the wrongs such as fighting a war in Vietnam and pouring billions over there, while people in Sunflower County, Mississippi and Harlem and Detroit are starving to death" (Hamer, "Sick and Tired," 24).

Hamer's life was not just about destroying racist and oppressive structures, but she was involved in much community building. She helped to bring to Ruleville the Head Start Program, the most successful of the War on Poverty programs. In actuality, because she felt that the War on Poverty programs were actually war on the poor—keeping them dependent—she concentrated on building alternative structures that would promote self-reliance. For workers displaced by mechanization, she organized the Freedom Farm Cooperative; two hundred units of low-income housing were built in Ruleville because of Hamer's fund-raising ability. She helped in starting a low-income day care center; and she was involved in bringing to Ruleville a garment factory that provided jobs.

Hamer's motivation was her deep-seated religious conviction. She spoke often of her Christian faith, which undergirded her commitment to the struggle for human dignity for black people. She constantly challenged those who professed to be Christian in their actions. She would say: "We serve God by serving our fellow [human beings]; kids are suffering from malnutrition. People are going to the fields hungry. If you are a Christian, we are tired of being mistreated." God in our lives could only be reflected through human beings' humanity to human beings. In a democracy, human dignity is insured through human and civil rights partially reflected in the exercise of the vote. Hamer was adept at relating the needs of oppressed people with the will of God (Hamer, "Sick and Tired," 26).

Hamer's understanding of God's will came out of her reading of the Bible. Often she would quote her favorite passage of scripture:

> The Spirit of the Lord is upon me, because he hath anointed me to preach the gospel to the poor; he hath sent me to heal the brokenhearted, to preach deliverance to the captives, and recovering sight to the blind to set at liberty them that are bruised (Luke 4:18).

This passage verified for her that God and Jesus Christ are on the side of the poor and oppressed. Ephesians 6:11-12 kept before her the fact that the problem keeping black people and poor people down was not of individual or personal nature, but structural, and therefore had to be dealt with as such:

> Put on the whole armour of God, that ye may be able to stand against the wiles of the devil. For we wrestle not against the flesh and blood, but against principalities, against powers, against the rulers of the darkness of this world, against spiritual wickedness in high places.

Her frequent references to Acts 17:23 informed her understanding that we are of one humanity:

> And hath made of one blood all nations of men for to dwell on all the face of the earth and hath determined the time before appointment and the bounds of their habitation.

Being one in humanity means that all peoples have a right to human dignity. This human dignity must include freedom from oppression. In fact, Hamer was known for her declaration that "We cannot separate Christ from freedom and freedom from Christ" (Hamer, "Sick and Tired," 25).

Hamer's views on a variety of social issues are given in her speeches and in published and unpublished oral interviews with her. She had a special interest in feeding, clothing, and housing the poor. In 1969 she founded Freedom Farm in Sunflower County, Mississippi, and fed 1,500 people with the food that was grown. She became involved with the Young World Developers, an organization that built homes for the poor. When a needy white man moved to the farm and sought food, clothing, and shelter for his family of five children, the family's needs were addressed. She was concerned about community health problems in Sunflower County and throughout the nation. She had an interest in education, and when Shaw University asked her to teach a course in black contemporary history, she agreed. When her class met, "sometimes parents would be there. Sometimes teachers would be there. It was a great experience for me," she said (Black Oral History Interview, Fisk University).

Hamer addressed the role and responsibility of black women: "To support whatever is right, and to bring in justice where we've had so much injustice" ("It's In Your Hands," 613). The special plight and role of the black woman had existed for 350 years, she noted, and she had seen it in her grandmother, a former slave who was 136 years old when she died in 1960. In reference to middle-class black women who a few years earlier failed to respect the work that she did, Hamer made a statement that was to become widely known and used frequently in other lectures:

> Whether you have a Ph.D., or no D, we're in this bag together. And whether you're from Morehouse or Nohouse, we're still in this bag together. Not to fight to try to liberate ourselves from the men—this is another trick to get us fighting among ourselves—but to work together

> with the black man, then we will have a better chance to just act as human beings, and to be treated as human beings in our sick society (Hamer, "It's In Your Hands," 613).

Her famous line, "I'm sick and tired of being sick and tired," was used in many of her lectures and has been reflected in the title of articles about her life.

For her devotion to the full cause of the civil rights movement and the uplift of black people, many colleges and universities awarded Hamer honorary doctoral degrees. These include Shaw University, Tougaloo College, Columbia College in Chicago, Howard University, and Morehouse College.

Though her life had been endangered and threatened many times over, her death actually came on March 15, 1977, from diabetes, heart trouble and breast cancer.

Hamer was not just a woman of words but a woman of deeds. In fact, it was her struggle against poverty that was the real war on poverty. She dedicated her life not only to challenging unjust political, social, and economic structures but to creating conditions that facilitated the development of self-reliance and self-determination among blacks and other poor people of the world. L. C. Dorsey's "Action Memorial" to Hamer not only makes this clear, but makes equally clear the challenge that Hamer left to us:

> A proper memorial would be one where all of us who loved her would dedicate and rededicate our lives to serving others and helping all of us achieve a greater measure of freedom, justice and love.

In Hamer's memory, Dorsey's plan called for the organization of registration drives, voter education programs, and campaigns against hunger, executions, police brutality, ignorance, poverty, and oppression. Her special love for young people also would be remembered in the memorial. By addressing these issues, Fannie Lou Hamer's life and contributions to humanity would be kept at the forefront.

References

"Black Voices of the South." *Ebony* 26 (August 1971): 51. Includes photograph.

Collum, Danny. "The Life of Fannie Lou Hamer." *Sojourners*, 2 December 1982.

Crawford, Vicki L., Jacqueline Anne Rouse, and Barbara Woods. *Women in the Civil Rights Movement*. Brooklyn: Carlson Publishing, 1990.

DeMuth, Jerry. "'Tired of Being Sick and Tired.'" *Nation* 198 (1 June 1964): 548-51. Drawing of Hamer, p. 549.

Dorsey, L. C. "An Action Memorial." Mississippi Council of Human Relations *Newsletter*, March 1977.

——. "Fannie Lou Hamer." *Jackson Advocate*, 31 August 1978): 8.

Hamer, Fannie Lou. Black Oral History Interview. Nashville: Fisk University Library, Fisk University, 6 October 1962.

——. "It's In Your Hands." Selection from "The Special Plight and the Role of Black Woman." Speech given at the NAACP Legal Defense Fund Institute, New York City, May 7, 1971. In *Black Women in White America*." Edited by Gerda Lerner. New York: Pantheon Books, 1972.

O'Dell, J. H. "Life in Mississippi: An Interview with Fannie Lou Hamer." *Freedomways* 5 (Second Quarter, 1965): 231-42.

Sewell, George. "Fannie Lou Hamer." *The Black Collegian* (May-June 1978): 20.

——. "Fannie Lou Hamer's Light Still Shines." *Encore American and Worldwide News* (18 July 1977): 3. Includes photograph.

Wright, Robert. "Interview with Fannie Lou Hamer," 9 August 1968. Civil Rights Documentation Project, Moorland-Spingarn Research Center, Howard University, Washington, D.C.

Collections

The Fannie Lou Hamer Collection of plaques, certificates, citations, photographs, and typescripts of some speeches is in Special Collections, Coleman Library, Tougaloo College. Her papers are also in the Amistad Research Center, Tulane University. In addition to the oral history interviews at Fisk and Howard universities, Hamer is included in the Mississippi Oral History Collection, University of Southern Mississippi.

Jacquelyn Grant

Grace Towns Hamilton

(1907-)

Politician, civic worker

Grace Towns Hamilton, controversial public figure and member of the Georgia legislature, was born on February 10, 1907, in Atlanta, Georgia, where she presently lives. She is the daughter of George Alexander Towns and Nellie Harriett (McNair) Towns, who had three other children. Grace Towns married Henry Cook Hamilton in June 1930. The couple had

Grace Towns Hamilton

one child, Eleanor Towns Hamilton Payne, born in 1931. Grace Towns Hamilton is grandmother to four children.

Hamilton's father, born in Albany, Georgia, was the oldest of five children of a former slave whose father was the half brother of Georgia Governor George W. Towns. Her mother, one of three children, was born in a comfortable setting in the Summerhill section of Atlanta.

Hamilton's parents had strong ties to Atlanta University. Her mother entered its Normal Department in 1893 and graduated in 1897; her father, having attended a private school run by one of the first graduates of Atlanta University, entered its grammar department in 1885 and graduated in 1894 in a class that included James Weldon Johnson. George Towns taught there for three years before earning a bachelor's degree from Howard University. In September 1902, during his second tenure at Atlanta University, he married Nellie McNair, his former student.

Hamilton grew up in the university environment and in an activist atmosphere, for her father was vocal on issues, especially racial injustice. While Hamilton's mother was a strong believer in family as her primary responsibility, when duties with four children permitted, she was active in the Atlanta community and was an organizer of the Gate City Free Kindergarten Association, "the first organized child care service center in Atlanta" (Mullins). Nellie McNair was active in the YWCA, and very active in her church. George Towns was active in the NAACP and in voter registration efforts. Due to the apparent privileges of the academic community many Atlantans saw the Towns family, and later, Grace, as aloof and elitist. She was privileged in her exposure to educational opportunities, in protection from hostilities in a city where racial conflicts occurred, and in opportunities to mingle with and be influenced by the influential persons who were her parents' acquaintances. She also was encouraged to be vocal in family discussions on topical matters.

Hamilton received her education at the Atlanta University high school (1919-1923) and Atlanta University, which she entered in 1923, receiving a bachelor of arts degree in 1927. While there, she was active in the Atlanta Interracial Student Forum, a project sponsored by the First Congregational Church to promote opportunities for exchange among students in the Atlanta area; she wrote for *The Scroll*, the student newspaper, which she edited during her senior year, and focused on the theme "Pioneers in Friendship." She was active in the YWCA and in 1926 attended one of its first interracial conferences—the biennial convention in Milwaukee, Wisconsin.

Hamilton's student experiences and the philosophy she developed through them, a belief in communication as a means to problem-solving, provided the direction that her professional life has followed. Her first position was Girls' Work Secretary at the Negro branch of the YWCA in Columbus, Ohio, while she pursued a master's degree at Ohio State University, from which she graduated in 1929. Returning to Atlanta, she began a teaching career, first at the Atlanta School of Social Work, then at Clark College.

After marrying Henry Hamilton in June 1930, Grace Towns Hamilton moved with him to Memphis, Tennessee, where he served as dean and professor of education at LeMoyne College and where she taught for four years. In 1931, their only child, Eleanor, was born. By now, Grace Towns Hamilton had discovered that teaching was not the field in which she wished to continue, and she turned her efforts to the public sector in 1935-36, conducting a survey of white-collar and skilled workers for the Works Progress Administration. Under the influence of Memphis figures Robert Church, Jr., whose father was called the "Boss of Beale Street," and Charles Houston, chief counsel for the NAACP, who often visited their Memphis home, Hamilton was introduced to the political process.

In 1941 the Hamilton family returned to Atlanta. Grace Hamilton became executive director of the Urban League in 1943; in her position she conducted "large-scale, fact-finding surveys concerning various problems plaguing Atlanta's black community" (Mullins, 107), focusing on education, voter registration, and citizenship, health, and housing. She organized a research committee on the public schools composed of prominent educators and social-work experts. The findings were published in 1944 as "Report on Public School Facilities for Negroes in Atlanta, Georgia" Through publicity and continued efforts, the committee's work led to revision of a bond proposal, originally focused on white schools only, to allocate four million of the nine million dollars to black schools. For her leadership, Hamilton was named the "Most Useful Citizen for 1945" by the Omega Psi Phi Fraternity. She worked with the All-Citizens

Registration Committee in an educator's role because her Urban League position constrained her from political activity. The committee's actions led to the election of the first black to the Atlanta Board of Education in 1953 and the first three to the City Democratic Executive Committee. The board of education member was the first black in municipal office since December 1870.

Hamilton also focused on the Urban League Health Committee to work to establish a hospital for non-indigent blacks and a training program for doctors and nurses. As a result, in September 1944 the West Side Health Center, "the first public health center for Negroes in Georgia," was opened. She was appointed to the interracial Advisory Board of Trustees of the Hughes Spaulding Hospital Authority by its head after pointing out to him that no women served on the board that developed the "116-bed 'teaching' hospital for private Negro patients" (Mullins). She was lauded for her continued work with those who wanted to see the hospital facilities and personnel developed, a group called the Foundation for the Advancement of Medical and Nursing Education.

Leadership Role in Improved Housing Noted

Between 1945 and 1956 Hamilton was working through the Urban League to assist various veterans in finding housing by conducting surveys and locating land. As a result, in 1950, the High Point Apartments were constructed; the Carver Public Housing Development followed in 1953 and the Perry Homes and 257 new single-family homes in 1955. The league, under her directorship, helped in changing the face of residential Atlanta. Such efforts did not go unnoted by hate groups and by critics who questioned her leadership style and her role as a woman in leadership. Some of those who knew and worked with her, such as Benjamin E. Mays, emphasized her ability to negotiate, persuade, and investigate.

While serving the Urban League, Hamilton was a member of the Committee for Georgia, a state affiliate of the Southern Conference for Human Welfare, on whose board she participated, and on the board of the Highlander Folk School in Monteagle, Tennessee. In 1954 she took a leave of absence from the league to become Assistant Director of Program Planning for the Southern Regional Council. She was also active in the NAACP, the Community Planning Council, the Fulton-Dekalb Interracial Committee, Partners for Progress, and the election efforts of Mayor Ivan Allen, Jr. In his autobiography, *Mayor: Notes on the Sixties*, Allen credits Hamilton with his "first awakening to the problems of the Negro" (quoted by Mullins, 202) through her work with the Urban League. In 1964 Mayor Allen appointed her to Atlanta's Fund Appeals Board. She later served on the Citizens Advisory Committee for Urban Renewal and on the board of Planned Parenthood in Atlanta.

From May to December 1966, Hamilton served as temporary director of the Atlanta Youth Council. In 1963 Georgia Governor Carl Sanders appointed her to his Commission on the Status of Women. She also served on the Citizen's Conference on Georgia's Judicial System and the Georgia Committee on Children and Youth. During the administration of presidents John F. Kennedy and Lyndon Johnson, she participated in a national conference entitled "To Fulfill These Rights." Other participants included James Baldwin, Senator Edward Brooke, Representative Shirley Chisolm, Charles Evers, Martin Luther King, Jr., and A. Philip Randolph. In 1966 she was one of three women appointed by President Lyndon Johnson to the Committee on Recreation and Natural Beauty, headed by Lawrence Rockefeller, to advise the president on beautification needs. From 1961 to 1967 she operated her own community relations firm.

Georgia Elects Its First Black Woman Legislator

Clearly, Hamilton's community work led to and paved the way for the position that she assumed next, for the reapportionment of the House in the Georgia legislature in the mid-1960s necessitated a special election in 1963. She decided to run for a seat in one of the newly created electoral districts, and she was one of eight blacks elected and the only one who ran against opposition. Thus, she became the first black woman elected to the Georgia legislature, where she became known as "The Lady from Fulton," the county in which her district lay.

During her nineteen years as representative, she served on several powerful committees: education, health, and appropriations in her first term—appointments made by the speaker, whom she had known previously—and succeeded in getting a few bills passed. She was overwhelmingly reelected for a second term, during which she focused on election reform, public health, and preschool education. She pushed for revision of Atlanta's charter to replace the aldermanic board with a strong-mayor system and for the creation of a new ward as the result of reapportionment after the census. The latter proposal passed in 1969; the first remained more controversial and continued to garner opposition. Other successes came for her proposals for school attendance laws, education for the deaf, mute, and blind, and state-wide kindergartens.

A heart attack in March 1969 slowed but did not stop Hamilton's work. On March 14, 1969, the House of Representatives showed its respect for her through a resolution (Atlanta Historical Society, MS 597). In 1970 she cosponsored a bill to redefine criminal abortion and to allow doctor and patient to make a decision, at least in the first twelve weeks of pregnancy (H.R. 1180); the bill was killed by the Hygiene and Sanitation Committee. During the remainder of her nineteen years (1965-1984) in the House, she sponsored bills for county consolidation and succeeded in getting a resolution passed that created an Atlanta-Fulton County Governmental Reorganizational Study Committee, on which she sat.

While many continued to applaud her, others pointed out flaws such as snobbery, arrogance, aloofness, stubbornness, single-mindedness, and inability to compromise. She was said by some to grow increasingly out of touch with the problems of black people. A colleague, who wished to remain anonymous, said that she disdained to serve as mentor to young people. As cochairperson of the House Legislative and Congressional Reapportionment Committee, she alienated members of the Black Legislative Caucus especially in her opposition to the 1981 redrawing of district lines to favor blacks. Thus, while some honored her with the title "Miss Grace," (*Atlanta Magazine*, 1986, 11), others worked to unseat her by supporting the young woman who successfully ran against her, Mable Thomas.

Since losing her seat in 1984, Hamilton has been engaged in limited activities because of her failing health, but has been assisting in compiling work on her life for a biographer, Loraine Spritzer.

In a recent interview, a current member of the Georgia House and a former colleague of hers, who wishes to remain anonymous, gave mixed views on Hamilton. According to the colleague, Hamilton was at once respected as a pioneer, known for her good relations with the Democratic leadership in Georgia, a strong leader of powerful committees such as the Policy Committee, a person of strong convictions, and a great "communicator," and at the same time, unsympathetic to the political aspirations of young blacks and to causes concerning blacks, a supporter of the speaker rather than a colleague to members of the Black Caucus, resented by the community in which she lives, and bitter in defeat (Interview by E. Delores Stephens, 26 May 1990).

In an article published in 1967, Grace Towns Hamilton at once acknowledges her privileged background:

> Yet my sheltered upbringing was a disadvantage, too. I had gone through high school and college in Atlanta University and didn't learn what the real world is like until. . .I got a job. . .at the YWCA in Columbus, Ohio. I had to learn after I was grown the barriers and limitations even in groups working for racial harmony (*Atlanta Magazine*, June 1967, 28).

She reveals what seemed to be the coda of her public work: she said to the interviewer, "I learned. . .that most people accept you on the terms you expect to be accepted." The article also recalls praise given her in 1960 by the *Atlanta Constitution* in an editorial that spotlighted her work for seventeen years with the Urban League.

Many other articles have been written about Hamilton's work. In failing health for the last few years, she lives quietly in the home she shared with her late husband in the Atlanta University community, attended by her sister, Harriett Jenkins, and visited by her minister, George Thomas, senior pastor at First Congregational Church (telephone interview with George Thomas, 26 September 1990), community leaders, researchers, and friends. According to her sister, Hamilton suffered a stroke in 1987 and has been plagued by other illnesses but has been able to make some public appearances, notably at the first in the lecture series named in her honor at Emory University and delivered by former United States Representative Yvonne Braithwaite Burke, and at the February 1990 unveiling of her portrait, which was commissioned by the Georgia legislature.

Hamilton's list of appointments and service is extensive and includes: Advisory Committee, Fulton County Democratic Party; Gate City Day Nursery Association; Board of Trustees, Meharry Medical College, Atlanta University, and Atlanta Arts Festival; board of the Multiple Sclerosis Society; vice chairperson, Atlanta Chamber of Commerce; Executive Board, Atlanta Landmarks, Inc.; member, New Order of Women Legislators, and Governor's Special Council on Family Planning.

Hamilton's honors and awards are similarly extensive and include: Towns Hamilton Award, Atlanta University Charter Day; Georgia Municipal Association Legislative Service Award; President's Award, Association of Private Colleges and Universities in Georgia; Liberty Bell Award, Law Day, Atlanta Bar Association; Good Neighbor Award, National Conference of Christians and Jews; Georgia Speaker of the Year, Barkley Forum, Emory University; WSB-TV Citation for Public Service; Community Service Award, Iota Phi Lambda Sorority; "Woman of the Year" of Atlanta, Inc.; Nonpartisan Community Service Award, Fulton County Republican Women; Alumna of the Year, Atlanta University; Achievement Award, New Jersey Chapter of the Links; Distinguished Achievements Award, Atlanta University; Life Fellow, Southern Regional Council; Black Women Pioneer Award, Black Women's Coalition of Atlanta; Atlanta Urban League Distinguished Community Service Award; Christian Council Community Service Award; and 1984 Southern Bell Calendar of Atlanta Black History. In recognition of her service also, Grace Towns Hamilton was awarded doctor of law degrees from the Woodrow Wilson School of Law and Emory University.

References

"Grace Hamilton: The Case for Commitment." *Atlanta Magazine* (June 1967): 28. Includes photograph.

"Hamilton Faces Tough Reelection Battle." *Atlanta Journal*, 3 August 1984.

Hamilton, Grace Towns. Interview with author, 26 May 1990.

Hamilton, Grace Towns. Interview with George Thomas, 26 September 1990; Harriett Jenkins, 26 September 1990.

"Legislature is Retirement Activity." *Atlanta Journal* 7 January 1972.

Levin, Rob. "Mrs. Hamilton Retires. . . ." *Atlanta Journal and Constitution*, 20 January 1985. B-14.

Mullins, Sharon Mitchell. "The Public Career of Grace Towns Hamilton: A Citizen Too Busy to Hate." Ph.D. dissertation. Emory University, 1976.

"Papers of First Black Woman in Legislature to be Unveiled." *Atlanta Constitution,* 28 September 1988.

Patureau, Alan. "Amazing Grace." *Atlanta Journal and Constitution,* 14 September 1986.

Sibley, Celestine. "Legislators Laud Grace Hamilton." *Atlanta Constitution,* 8 March 1985.

——. "Working to Keep Memories Alive." *Atlanta Constitution,* 27 April 1987.

Smith, Helen C. "Quiet Lasting Service: Grace Hamilton Devoted Career to the City She Loves." Georgia's Historic Mothers Series. *Atlanta Journal and Constitution,* 28 March 1976.

Collections

The Grace Towns Hamilton Papers are in the Atlanta Historical Society. Photographs are included.

E. Delores B. Stephens

Virginia Hamilton

(1936-)

Writer

Those who write for young people are often relegated to a type of literary ghetto, because writing for children has been marginalized. Often, the writers are perceived as vague, sexless persons who exist in life's shadow, rarely participating with any zest. Virginia Esther Hamilton defies these characterizations. She is not a marginalized author lurking in a literary inner-city. Critics have had to place Hamilton within the mainstream of literature because her inventive use of language, her complex weaving of theme, character, and form, and her use of various mythologies have raised children's literature to new heights of excellence.

At her best, Hamilton is a *griot*, a word sorcerer whose power is evident in her written texts and her oral presentations.

Her storytelling voice, undoubtedly, was acquired within the loving confines of her childhood home in Yellow Springs, Ohio, an area rich in mystery and history because of its role in the Underground Railroad. Here, Hamilton acquired a sense of "the known, the remembered, and the imagined," words she uses as the title of a 1987 article in *Children's Literature in Education.*

Hamilton was born March 12, 1936, the fifth and youngest child of Kenneth James Hamilton, a college graduate and musician, and Etta Belle (Perry) Hamilton, a homemaker. A "remembered" tale passed down through the generations of her family suggests that the Perry clan began when an ancestress, a leader of the Underground Railroad, guided her son through the maze of the Underground Railroad and deposited him in Yellow Springs, Ohio, only to disappear forever. His descendents, the Hamiltons, and her mother's family, the Perrys, nurtured and guided Virginia Hamilton through a happy childhood replete with music, tales, reading, and keeping company. That childhood finds its way in bits and pieces into her writing:

> My childhood was particularly fine if we allow for the fact that I had no concept of dollar poverty. We had land and plenty to eat. That my parents struggled for both was beyond the realm of my understanding. My childhood was rural and completely absorbing. And I don't remember as a child, ever wanting to be anything else. (Paul Robeson, x-xi).

The strong sense of self, family, community, and ethnicity Hamilton received from her family enabled her to withstand racial constraints as she grew up in the 1930s and 1940s.

Parental Talks Influence Writing Career

Although, as Hamilton writes, "In the public schools in the 1940s, we black children were taught little that might suggest that our people had contributed any lasting virtue to the American experience," she received *Knowledge* from home that contradicted this oppressive ideology (*Paul Robeson*, xii-xiii). Kenneth Hamilton provided the knowledge and race consciousness that was denied in school. Sitting on the porch and talking with and listening to her father as he played his mandolin, Hamilton reveled in her father's facts, memories, tales, and impressions of W. E. B. Du Bois, Paul Robeson, Florence Mills, Blind Lemon Jefferson, and other noteworthy black Americans. Paul Robeson was especially important. Her father recounted his uniqueness and Hamilton seized upon that as her goal:

> "Imagine," Kenneth Hamilton would begin, "that Mr. Paul Robeson woke up one morning to find there was more to the day than playing football. I know I did [Kenneth Hamilton played football for Iowa State]. I imagine he looked around him. He saw plenty of his people were preachers; there were enough morticians to reach from here to kingdom come. I imagine Mr. Robeson decided then and there he would be what there never had been before. And he was" (*Paul Robeson,* xiv).

This talk had a considerable amount of influence on Hamilton. She writes that the idea of uniqueness permeated her consciousness and caused her to seek uniqueness as a desired goal:

> Yet what came through clearly to me at the time was this: If one were to become anything, it

> would have to be not only the best but wholly original, a new idea. This concept sank deep into my consciousness. Imperceptibly, I grew up yearning for the unusual, seeking something unique in myself. I longed not just to write, but to newly write and like no one else. Kenneth Hamilton wanted no less for his youngest child (*Paul Robeson,* xiv).

Hamilton would later write a biography of Robeson for young people. Those summer evenings were the catalyst for a body of literature that is exceptional, decidedly unique, encompassing a variety of genres such as biography, folklore, and historical fiction, and unquestionably one of the largest bodies of literature created by a black American for children.

Living up to family expectations, Hamilton performed well in the small country school she attended although she lamented its limited curriculum. After graduating from high school, Hamilton received a five-year scholarship to attend college. She enrolled in Antioch College (1952-1955), a school noted for its academic and liberal reputation. Hamilton realized a long-cherished dream of travel to New York while enrolled in college: "Oh; how I wanted to leave the little town of Yellow Springs. Every night I lay in bed listening to the long, sad whistle of the train passing through from New York to Chicago. I wanted with all my soul to get to Manhattan, but is seemed I was trapped forever" (Commire, 64). The ache subsided as Hamilton spent her college summer years in New York working as a bookkeeper. Eventually, upon the advice of a college professor, Hamilton left school before taking a degree. She would later attend Ohio State University (1957-1958) and the New School for Social Research.

Hamilton lived in New York for fifteen years. While there, she worked in a number of occupations ranging from bookkeeper to singer. Her plan was "to find a cheap apartment, a part-time job, write, and have a good time. And it all came together" (*Something about the Author*). She lived in a community in the East Village among many creative people such as musicians, writers, and artists, a sort of modern-day Bohemia. During this period Hamilton met a kindred spirit, Arnold Adoff, a Jewish teacher, poet, graduate student, and manager of jazz musicians. They married on March 16, 1960. Adoff, too, has received critical praise for his poetry and a National Council of Teachers of English poetry award. In addition to his literary work, he serves as Hamilton's manager. Virginia and Arnold Adoff are the parents of a daughter, Leigh Adoff, and a son, Jamie Adoff. Hamilton currently resides in Ohio.

As most women writers are required to do, Hamilton combined familial and career responsibilities. While living in New York, she wrote constantly, sending manuscripts to magazines such as the *New Yorker*. In order to hone her writing skills, she enrolled in a writing course at the New School for Social Research taught by Hiriam Hayden, a founder of Atheneum Publishers. According to Hamilton, Hayden liked her writing and became a mentor of sorts. He desired to publish an adult novel she was writing, *Mayo,* but his publishing partners did not. By this chance of fate, Hamilton became available to children. A friend's encouragement would lead her to submit a manuscript she had written while attending Antioch College to a publisher.

That manuscript eventually became the published novel *Zeely*. *Zeely* was quite a departure from books that had depicted various aspects of the African-American experience. Heretofore, most books for children, with some notable exceptions such as *Hazel, Lonesome Boy,* and others, depicted African-Americans in stereotyped fashion. *Zeely* is the story of a sensitive, intelligent, and inquisitive girl named Elizabeth (who renames herself Geeder) who, along with her brother, goes to visit an uncle who lives on a farm. While rummaging in her uncle's attic, Elizabeth discovers some old magazines. One magazine contains pictures of African people that enthrall Elizabeth. Later, Elizabeth spies a gorgeous six-foot-tall African-American woman, Zeely, who bears an eerie resemblance to one of the women pictured in the magazine. Elizabeth is immediately attracted to Zeely and plots different ways of meeting her. The following excerpt describes their initial interaction:

> Geeder stood in amazement. Never had she seen Zeely dressed in such as way. She wore a length of varicolored silk wound around her delicate body and draped over her left shoulder. Around her head was a band of green silk, brilliant against her black hair. The long garment was beautiful and strange but the band around Zeely's hair was what held Geeder's attention. In her mind, she saw the picture of the Watutsi woman, the picture which right now she had hidden in her blouse. The Watutsi woman had worn such a headband.
>
> "I'm glad you've come," Zeely said. Her voice was quiet, hardly above a whisper, and yet, it was perfectly clear. She smiled, adding, "Please follow me." She turned and led the way into the forest. Geeder, still unable to speak, followed. . . . Zeely Tayber didn't seem to mind the silence between herself and Geeder. She was relaxed, serene. As she viewed Geeder from head to foot, her eyes were full of a strange light and dark.
>
> Geeder sat across from Zeely. When Zeely began to stare at her hard, she became watchful and held herself more like a lady. She could not read Zeely's eyes, nor could she fathom why Zeely was looking at her that way (91-93).

Thus began their friendship. Hamilton looks upon *Zeely* with special fondness, in part, because it was her first book and the major character resembled her at that age. Geeder represents the first of many loners Hamilton would depict in her novels.

Zeely is an important book because of its literary quality and its depiction of a "normal" black American family whose members were not beaten down by poverty and hopelessness and because of its authentic cultural images. *Zeely* garnered the Nancy Block Memorial Award from the Downtown (New York) Community School Awards Committee (1967), which was the beginning for Hamilton of a continuous trend of winning awards.

Hamilton Writes in Variety of Genres

Hamilton has written twenty-six books, including two biographies, six collections of folktales, and numerous works of fiction ranging from science fiction/fantasy to historical fiction. Most of these books have won multiple awards ranging from the Coretta Scott King Award for *Sweet Whispers, Brother Rush*, to the Edgar Allan Poe Award for *The House of Dies Drear*, to the Newbery Medal for *M. C. Higgins, the Great*. Few authors have won as many awards for literary excellence as has Hamilton; no author has won the Newbery Medal, the Boston-Globe Hornbook Award, the Lewis Carrol Shelf Award, the National Book Award, and the International Board on Books for Young People Award for a single book. Hamilton achieved this distinction with the publication of *M. C. Higgins, the Great*.

M. C. Higgins, the Great chronicles the quests of Mayo Cornelius Higgins as he attempts to forge his identity as a young man, share a friendship with an outcast neighbor, experience a bittersweet first love, and save his family from a possible disaster. The story, set in the mountains of Ohio, symbolizes a host of realities: love, freedom, community, heritage, and danger. Hamilton's portrayal of M. C.'s family—his mother, Banina, his father, Jones, his sister, and brothers, is arguably the best and most complex portrayal of a black American family in children's literature. For example, readers feel a kind of sweet anguish along with M. C., his father, and siblings as they wait for Banina's return from work. They greet her in a yodel-type song and she responds in turn; this family ritual is intimate, loving, and intense:

> Woven through his thoughts was the sound of Jones singing of courting. M. C. tried humming to himself, but he couldn't get rid of the sound. Nothing, not even his pole, could keep away the sad feeling, the lonesome blues of being grown, the way either his mother or his father could with their singing.
>
> Wistfully he wondered if he'd ever care about someone the way Jones cared about his mother. Jones's song was still in his mind when he conjured a picture of Banina, his mother. It was one of his favorite sights of her coming home from a far hill, late.
>
> It was M. C.'s birthday. They had known she would bring something for a present. They were all there on the side of Sarah's [Mountain on which their home was located] waiting. There were the kids. And there was Jones, trying to look as if he weren't waiting for her half of his life, but not trying too hard. Because Jones didn't mind waiting for Banina forever if he had to. But it was Macie Pearl who hurt most for her mother, who ached for her through every minute of every day without her (83-84).

Critics praise the novel for its richness and complexity in terms of theme, characterization, and form. But Hamilton admitted the book was almost a failed labor of love:

> No book of mine was ever in more danger of being a failed labor of love than was *M. C. Higgins, the Great*. None was to bring me more pleasure and pain writing. I had conceived the idea for it sometime after writing *The House of Dies Drear* (Macmillan) in 1968. I had worked through one chapter of *M. C.*, another, and another—when abruptly nothing more would come ("Newbery Award Acceptance," 340).

Her literary muse reinvigorated, Hamilton completed the novel. The rest is literary history. Few writers are willing to express in writing an aesthetic/literary or political philosophy. Hamilton hinted at hers during her Newbery Award acceptance speech:

> But no ones dies in *M. C. Higgins, the Great* or in any of my books. I have neither written demonstrable and classifiable truths; nor have my fictional black people become human sacrifices in the name of social accuracy. For young people reading *M. C.*, particularly the poor and the blacks, have got to realize that his effort with his bare hands to stay alive and save his way of life must be their effort as well. For too long, too many have suffered and died without a cause. I prefer to write about those who survive—such as old Sarah McHiggon of the mountain, Banina Higgins, and the Killburns, who have good cause for living (343).

Hamilton has found that it is difficult to be just a writer. One's gender, race, or political philosophy influences one's work. She once sought to assume the label of "writer," but has since recognized the role and function of gender, race, geographic location, and political ideology on her writing. Hamilton has labeled it a struggle, yet a struggle she willingly engages:

> I want my books read. I want an audience. I struggle daily with literary integrity, black cultural integrity, intellectual honesty, my desire for simplicity in the storytelling, and the wish for strong, original characterization, exceptional concepts for plots. . . . But when I sit down to write a story, I don't say to myself, now I'm going to write a black story. I've often said, much to the 'startlement' of white friends, that black people don't really think about the fact that they are black every waking moment, just as some of my friends don't think about being

> white. It happens that I know my tribe, as it were, better than any other tribe because I am one of them. I am at ease with being black. The constant in my books is that the characters are black and yet, the emotional content is simply human ("The Mind of a Novel," 12-13).

Hamilton does not sidestep controversial topics in her books. Two of her recent books, *A Little Love* and *White Romance*, broach subjects such as teenage sex, heavy metal music, drugs, and psychically disturbed youngsters. However, Hamilton cannot be classified as a writer of "problem" novels. The problems in her novels are a part of a multitextured narrative.

Similarly, Hamilton occasionally defies conventions in content in her novels such as *Sweet Whispers, Brother Rush*, *The Planet of Junior Brown*, and *Anthony Burns*. These novels contain complex stylistic features, for children's books, such as stream-of-consciousness ruminations, multiple settings, and shifting time periods, combinations of differing genres, and major characters in psychic and emotional distress. These books have challenged critics, who sometimes state that Hamilton is writing for adults or is too sophisticated for even the most advanced child reader. Hamilton responds to those criticisms thus:

> Books like my own, which are occasionally mildly experimental—with subject matter having to do with mental dissociation, graphic imagery of nuclear explosions, Amerindian and black survival in a hostile majority society, children alone and hungry for love and companionship—are said to be, and often by those who should know better, only for the especially gifted child. . . . These adults would keep the young at a safe and quasi-literate level, where their responses to life and the world remain predictable and manageable. The way I counteract such backwardness is by keeping fresh my awareness of young people's keen imaginations and by responding to their needs, fears, loves and hunger in as many new ways as possible ("The Mind of a Novel," 15-16).

Hamilton shares her knowledge with teachers, students, and writers as she makes presentations at conferences sponsored by the National Council of Teachers of English, the International Reading Association, and the Ohio State University Children's Literature Conference. In addition, she teaches occasionally at colleges and universities, most recently Queens College (1986-1987) and Ohio State University (1988-1989).

Essentially, Hamilton has accomplished what she dreamed about as she acquired the *knowledge* from her father. She is a unique writer who has a valuable and valued gift that she shares in unexpected, delightful, and intellectually challenging ways. She remains the storyteller and has become the knowledge-giver:

> Through character, time, and place, I've attempted to portray the essence of a race, its essential community, culture, history and traditions, which I know well, and its relation to the larger American society. I endeavor to demonstrate the nexus the black group has with all other groups, nationalities and races, the connection the American black child has with all children and to present the best of my heritage ("The Mind of a Novel," 15).

She does so in a triumphant manner which ultimately leaves the reader, not with a happily-ever-after ending but rather with a hopeful ending. Her audience eagerly awaits her next publications, an anthology of folk tales representing many of the world's cultures.

Books by Hamilton include *Zeely* (New York: Macmillan, 1967); *The Time-Ago Tales of Jadhu* (Macmillan, 1968); *Time-Ago Lost: More Tales of Jadhu* (Macmillan, 1969); *Paul Robeson: The life and Times of A Free Black Man* (New York: Harper, 1975); *The Writings of W. E. B. Du Bois* (New York: Crowell, 1976); *Arilla Sun Down* (New York: Greenwillow, 1976); *Justice and Her Brothers* (Greenwillow, 1978); *Jadhu* (Greenwillow, 1980); *Dustland* (Greenwillow, 1980); *The Gathering* (Greenwillow, 1981); *Sweet Whispers, Brother Rush* (New York: Philomel, 1982); *The Magical Adventures of Pretty Pearl* (Harper, 1983); *Willie Bea and the Time the Martians Landed* (Greenwillow, 1983); *Junius Over Far* (Philomel, 1985); *The People Could Fly: American Black Folktales* (New York: Knopf, 1985); *The Mystery of Drear House: Book Two of Dies Drear* (Greenwillow, 1987); *In the Beginning: Creation Stories from Around the World*; *The Bells of Christmas* (Knopf, 1989); *The Dark Way* (New York: Harcourt Brace, 1990; and *Cousins* (Harcourt Brace, 1990).

References

Hamilton, Virginia. "The Mind of a Novel: The Heart of the Book." *Children's Literature Quarterly* 8 (Winter 1983): 10-13.

———. "Newbery Award Acceptance." *Horn Book* 51 (August 1975): 337-343.

———. "On Being a Black Writer in America." *The Lion and the Unicorn* 10 (1986): 15-17.

———. *Paul Robeson: The Life and Times of a Free Black Man*. New York; Harper, 1975.

———. "The Known, the Remembered, and the Imagined: Celebrating Afro-American Folk Tales." *Children's Literature in Education* 18 (Summer): 67-75.

Something about the Author. Vol. 56. Detroit: Gale Research, 1989.

Collections

Virginia Esther Hamilton's papers are to be located at

Kent State University. Her photographs appear on book jackets and, in reference sources such as *Something about the Author*.

Violet J. Harris

Lorraine Hansberry

(1930-1965)

Playwright, activist

Lorraine Vivian Hansberry knew about making painful choices. She lived a life of commitment, conviction, and conflict. She deserves to be recognized as a revolutionary, as a political activist, and as an intellectual of uncompromising integrity. During her brief lifetime, she wrote insightful dramas about the most controversial issues of her day, one of them assured to be remembered and revived as a classic. She also left numerous newspaper articles and essays on such challenging topics as racism, homophobia, world peace, black art and history, existentialism, world literature and theater, the Civil Rights Movement, The House Un-American Activities Committee, the Cuban missile crisis, and her own work. She was one of the sharpest observers and most brilliant intellects, as well as one of the most talented theater artists, of her time. Hansberry is remembered as one of the most important black American writers of this century.

Lorraine Hansberry

Hansberry was born on the South Side of Chicago, May 19, 1930, to Carl A. Hansberry and Nanny Perry Hansberry. She was the youngest of four children by a margin of seven years. She felt somewhat alienated because of the distance she perceived between herself and the rest of her family, which led her to become independent and develop a tendency to introspection. She became comfortable spending time alone, although she could also be extremely gregarious and entertaining, and possessed an intense curiosity about people all her life. The Hansberrys were a very prominent family, not only in the black community of Chicago, but also in national black cultural and political circles. Hansberry was introduced to some of the most important black political and cultural figures of her time when she was still a little girl. She knew Paul Robeson, Duke Ellington, Walter White, Joe E. Louis, and Jesse Owens, who were visitors of her parents.

Hansberry's family had been involved in the struggle for black liberation for generations. Her maternal grandparents had been born into slavery, and her grandfather had attempted an escape. The family kept these memories alive, and as a child, Hansberry was taken on a trip to Tennessee to meet her grandmother, whose memories of slavery were nothing like *Gone With the Wind*, as Hansberry later observed in her posthumously published book, *To Be Young, Gifted And Black*. Her mother was a schoolteacher who left teaching and dedicated herself to the struggle for political and social reform by serving on a ward committee. Her uncle, William Leo Hansberry, was a distinguished professor of African history at Howard University. Because of his work in African culture and history, a college was named for him at the University of Nigeria, and he often brought African students and political exiles with him to visit the Hansberrys. Hansberry became aware of Pan-Africanism and the international dimension of black liberation at an early age.

Her father's efforts on behalf of the struggle for change became the focal point of Hansberry's political education when their family became a test cast for integrated housing in 1938. He felt that they must move into an all-white neighborhood so that he could challenge Chicago's restrictive real-estate covenants, which legally upheld discrimination in housing. Carl Hansberry had long been involved in politics as an active member of the NAACP and the Urban League. He was a philanthropist and had been a U. S. Marshall and run for Congress.

So, when Lorraine Hansberry was eight years old, the family moved into a previously segregated neighborhood, confronting mob violence while her father fought the battle in court. Angry whites threw bricks, and a concrete slab barely missed hitting her in the head. The Hansberrys bravely occupied the house until a lower court ordered them to leave. Her father fought this case all the way to the U. S. Supreme Court, which struck down restrictive covenants in the famous *Hansberry* v. *Lee* decision of 1940. But the practice of restrictive covenants went on in Chicago anyway, even though the law no longer supported them, and Carl Hansberry became bitter and disillusioned and wanted to move his family away from a country that would not enforce the laws it passed. He tried to relocate in Mexico, where he had purchased property, but he died in 1946 before he could carry out these plans.

Hansberry's two brothers were also active in the struggle for black liberation during World War II. Carl, Jr., served in a segregated unit, and Perry contested his draft because of discrimination against blacks in the armed services. All of these influences helped form Hansberry's lifelong commitment to the struggle for black liberation. Her family's attitudes and her early association with their famous visitors helped give her the confidence and the assurance she would later need to stand up to such powerful figures as Otto Preminger, Mike Wallace, and Robert Kennedy.

Interest in Writing for the Stage Develops

In 1948 Hansberry decided to attend the University of Wisconsin instead of Howard University, where her parents wanted her to go. One afternoon she wandered into a rehearsal of Sean O'Casey's play *Juno and the Paycock* and she was so struck by it that she became interested in writing for the stage. She grew increasingly dissatisfied with the curriculum at Wisconsin, feeling that most of her classes were irrelevant to her interests as a black intellectual, so she left in 1950 to pursue another kind of education in New York. She went to work as a reporter for Paul Robeson's radical black newspaper, *Freedom*, writing politically astute articles as well as book and drama reviews. She became an associate editor in 1952. That year she went to the International Peace Congress in Uruguay as Paul Robeson's representative because the State Department had denied him a passport. She was traumatized by poor flying conditions and barely made it back to the United States in one piece, but she was excited by the congress, which broadened her awareness of important issues such as poverty, dictatorships, the arms race, and United States interference with Latin American countries. Hansberry welcomed the opportunity to meet with women of color from other counties, and she used materials from this experience to write a remarkable essay (unpublished) "Simone De Beauvoir and *The Second Sex*: An American Commentary, 1957."

By the time she wrote that essay, Hansberry had also been coming out as a lesbian, although this fact was never made public. Her awareness of feminist issues was ahead of her time, as well as her realization that homophobia and racism were linked. She grasped the connections between the struggle for gay rights, rights for people of color, and rights for women long before such terms as homophobia and feminism had come into the vernacular.

Her marriage in 1953 to Robert Nemiroff, a white Jewish intellectual and member of the Communist party, had caused friction between her and the black nationalists whose cause she supported all her life. But the black nationalists and the Communist party, with which Hansberry also sympathized (though she never became a party member), both have strong lines against homosexuality. Partly because of these attitudes, and partly because her family would not have been supportive of Hansberry's sexual preference, she chose to keep her separation from Nemiroff in 1957 a secret. She and her former husband maintained the closest possible professional and personal relationship until her death, and Nemiroff still maintains control over her papers, as well as holding the rights to her published works. In a personal interview conducted with Nemiroff in San Francisco in 1986, he indicated that the reason for their separation had to do with Hansberry's sexuality, but it was clear that their commitment to each other never diminished in any other way. The fact that Hansberry trusted him with revisions of *Les Blancs* (her last play, left unfinished at the time of her death), and named him as her literary executor would seem to support this interpretation of their separation.

It would be a mistake to emphasize Hansberry's struggles with special interest groups over her struggle against the dominant culture. Her commitment to the fight against the white power elite remained her first priority, and that never lessened. Hansberry began to realize that the best contribution she could make to the causes she believed in was through creative writing, and so, with the support of Robert Nemiroff, she resigned the *Freedom* editorship in 1953 to concentrate on her own work. She held a variety of odd jobs until Nemiroff wrote a hit song ("Cindy, Oh Cindy") with Burt D' Lugoff in 1956. The money from this venture enabled her to quit working, and write full-time.

A Raisin in the Sun Impacts the American Public

In 1957 Hansberry completed a play whose title she had taken from Langston Hughes's poem "Harlem." The poet warns that a dream deferred will "dry up / like a raisin in the sun-" or it will explode. The title points out the hopeless social conditions that force the black family in her play to defer their dreams until their own strength and pride help them struggle toward opportunity. One of Nemiroff's associates in the music business, Philip Rose, was so impressed by the play that he wanted to produce it on Broadway, but he could not persuade any of the well-known producers in New York to take a chance on it. They thought that nobody would come to see a serious play about a black family. Rose was advised to make it a musical with some hot production numbers if he wanted to appeal to theater audiences. Undaunted, Rose raised the money by finding a large number of small inventors and, when he was refused bookings on Broadway, he took *A Raisin in the Sun* to New Haven and Philadelphia for trial runs. This gave Hansberry an opportunity to be near the play and to be able to rewrite and shape it into its final form. Sidney Poitier lent notoriety to the cast, but the rest of the outstanding performers, including Claudia McNeil, Ruby Dee, Diana Sands, Louis Gossett, Ivan Dixon, Glynn Thurman, Douglas Turner Ward, Lonnie Elder III, and director Lloyd Richards, were all virtually unknown to the dominant culture. After a brief but successful run in Chicago, the play finally opened at New York's Ethel Barrymore Theatre on March 11, 1959.

Nobody, not even the play's staunchest supporters nor the author herself, could have predicted what an impact *A Raisin in the Sun* was to make on the American public. Twenty-five years later, the play was revived across the country and given important productions at the Kennedy Center and on PBS, with Esther Rolle and Danny Glover in the leading roles. Its status as a classic is now assured.

The play, which was the first on Broadway by a black female playwright, received very good reviews from the seven most influential critics of the New York press and ran for 538 performances. Then, in May 1959, Lorraine Hansberry became the first black playwright and one of the few women to win the coveted New York Drama Critics Circle award for Best Play of the Year. Her formidable competition for this prize included Archibald MacLeish's existential verse play, *JB*, Tennessee Williams's *Sweet Bird of Youth*, and Eugene O'Neill's posthumously produced *A Touch of the Post*. Hansberry became famous within two months of the opening of her first produced play. And since the play dealt with the oppression of blacks, she also became a spokesperson for and symbol of American blacks. Perhaps because of her early familiarity with famous persons in her parents' home, her fame never went to her head. She refused to be seduced by it, just as she resisted attempts made by emissaries of the dominant culture to assimilate her and dilute her revolutionary stance.

Response to the play was overwhelmingly favorable from black and white audiences and critics. Theaters suddenly had to cope with racially mixed audiences, which led to demonstrations and theater boycotts in some cities. *A Raisin in the Sun* created unprecedented opportunities for black theater artists across the nation and was the first serious black drama to have real impact upon the dominant culture.

But because it did appeal to white audiences, militant black nationalists criticized the play, labeling it integrationist and, in extreme cases, assimilationist. Black playwrights such as Ed Bullins, who were interested in departing from realism, and in aesthetic experimentation by black authors for black audiences, called it "kitchen melodrama," and did not include it in black anthologies. At the time, Amiri Baraka did not consider it as true black art. But in 1987, on the occasion of its twenty-fifth anniversary, Baraka reversed that decision in an essay on *A Raisin in the Sun*, that appeared in the *Washington Post*. Study of the complete prose and plays of Hansberry reveals a writer whose concerns were clearly not commercial, and she remained a revolutionary throughout her life.

Hansberry's Life and Work Misinterpreted

One reason for misinterpretation of Hansberry's life and work is a quote attributed to her by Nan Robertson in a *New York Times* interview about her Broadway hit: "I told them this wasn't a 'negro play.' It was a play about honest-to-God, believable, many-sided people who happened to be Negroes." This statement, which distorted her real views, was twisted even further by Harold Cruse in his widely read book, *The Crisis of the Negro Intellectual*: "I'm not a Negro writer—but a writer who happens to be a Negro." Hansberry's real position on this question was articulated to interviewer Eleanor Fisher in an attempt to silence these infuriating misrepresentations. She said that "it is impossible to divorce the racial fact from any American Negro." Concerning the family in *A Raisin In the Sun*, she explained to the *New York Times*:

> From the moment the first curtain goes up until they make their decision at the end, the fact of racial oppression, unspoken and unalluded to, other than the fact of how they live, is through the play. It's inescapable. The reason these people are in the ghetto in America is because they are Negroes.

The conflict in *A Raisin in the Sun* at first centers upon what the Younger family will do with ten thousand dollars insurance money their father has left them. He has recently died from overwork and grief from the death of his third child. The eldest child, Walter Lee, wants to invest the money in a liquor store so he can leave his "nothing" job as a white man's chauffeur and go into business. He is obsessed by the idea of money. Walter feels trapped and desperate; Hansberry painted a haunting picture of manhood assaulted by social and economic pressures, and Sidney Poitier gave an electrifying performance that comes across in the film version. Walter Lee's sister, Beneatha, wants to use the money for medical school. In his desperation, Walter Lee has little sympathy for what he thinks is ambition inappropriate for a woman. Mama Lena Younger wishes she could stretch the money to satisfy everybody, but realizes she cannot, so she decides to make a down payment on a house for the family so they will no longer have to put up with high rent and overcrowding. The rest of the money she gives to her son for his business, hoping to alleviate his despair. She asks only that he save some of it for Beneatha's education.

Lena Younger's decision to buy a house in an all-white neighborhood enlarges the initial conflict and eventually unites the family against racism. An emissary from their new neighborhood, Lindner, visits the family and offers to buy their house at a profit for the Youngers if they will not move in. This brings up the theme of restrictive covenants, with which Hansberry was painfully familiar. They refuse his humiliating offer, but then Walter Lee loses all the money given him by Lena Younger to a con artist, and unbeknownst to the rest of the family, calls Lindner back to make the deal, which leads to the climax of the play. Instead of accepting the insulting offer of money, Walter Lee asserts his pride and his manhood by refusing Lindner's deal, and the play ends with the family moving out of the ghetto after all.

The critics and audiences interpreted this as a happy ending, amazing Hansberry. She did intend to show the triumph of the human spirit over obstacles, something she believed in and felt that black people were capable of, but the idea that the Youngers' problems were over because they had moved into a white neighborhood was ridiculous to her.

Hansberry was well aware of the problems they would be facing and had originally written a fourth act showing the Youngers sitting, armed, in their new house with an angry white mob outside. She cut this act for several reasons—some of them practical: the play ran too long with the extra act, and they needed to save money on the production. Hiring extras would have been an added expense. But the main reason was that she believed in the endurance and the heroism of black people in the face of oppression and that was what she wanted to emphasize. She wanted the audience to see that black Americans wanted change, and that they were brave enough to make it happen. She also wanted white Americans to understand black people, in the hope that fear and ignorance could be removed as obstacles to equal rights.

Hansberry was a Pan-Africanist, but she was never a separatist. She believed that black people should unite and support each other, but she also believed that the dominant culture had to change. She linked the black American struggle to the black African liberation movement in her play through the character of Joseph Asagai, Beneatha's Nigerian suitor. Asagai, who may have been inspired by African students she met through her uncle, Leo Hansberry, is committed to driving out the colonial government in his country. Beneathea decides to marry him and practice medicine in Nigeria. This theme of Pan-Africanism was revolutionary for a play of the time, particularly a Broadway hit, and it introduced these ideas to the American public. Hansberry's thinking on this issue was no doubt influenced by her uncle while she was very young, and she expanded upon it under W. E. B. Du Bois at the Jefferson School for Social Science. So close was her association with Du Bois that she was called upon to deliver the eulogy at his funeral.

There is no doubt that Hansberry's choice of themes for the play make it a drama about the black struggle for liberation. But the play also contains universal themes, among them marital and generational conflict, women's rights, idealism versus cynicism, the American Dream, the dangers of materialism, and Christianity versus atheistic humanism. The play is also very well-constructed, clear and direct, and full of wonderful roles for actors. All these things, including Hansberry's wit, flair for dialogue and stage business, and solid dramaturgy, help locate *A Raisin in the Sun* among the best plays of this century. It opened the door for black Americans in theater and paved the way for the black theater movement of the 1960s and beyond. When pressed in a personal interview, Ed Bullins admitted that, "Lorraine made a lot of things possible."

Ironically, the white press criticized the play for being a formula money-maker and tried to attribute its success to white liberal guilt over "the Negro question." Representatives from the dominant culture felt free to attack Hansberry for everything and anything related to the issue of racism. In an interview, Mike Wallace grilled her about "Negro anti-Semitism," and tried to blame blacks for the violence in Kenya. Keeping her composure, she replied that it was a mistake to "equalize the oppressed with the oppressor" (*Lorraine Hansberry Speaks Out*, Caedmon Records, 1972).

Hansberry took strong exception to Albert Camus's notion of universal guilt and was highly critical of Genet, Beckett, and the Beat Generation. She felt that their obsession with individual mortality and their idea that real progress is impossible were all luxuries that only self-indulgent intellectuals who were not oppressed could afford. She wrote a hilarious satire of Beckett's *Waiting for Godot* entitled *The Arrival of Mr. Todog* (unpublished), and numerous articles on the subject, including "Genet, Mailer, and the New Paternalism" for the *Village Voice*, and "The Negro Writer and His Roots: Toward a New Romanticism" for the *Black Scholar*. She considered existentialism and the Theatre of the Absurd socially irresponsible, intellectually valueless, and a spiritual dead end.

Alarmed at the vogue these ideas enjoyed among the intellectuals of her age, Hansberry created her second drama, *The Sign In Sidney Brustein's Window*, produced in 1964. It was not nearly the commercial success that her first play had been, for a number of reasons. The intellectual content of the piece was over the heads of most of her audience, and the critics lost patience with it. Even more significantly, critics were frustrated because they could not "type" this playwright. Here was a black woman writing a play about a white male Jewish intellectual. Hansberry disappointed all the people who expected a sequel to *A Raisin in The Sun*, and defied all attempts at classification. She could never limit herself to one issue, one form of expression, or one style of writing. Another reason for its lack of commercial appeal is that its plot is less clear than her first play's, and its structure is sometimes unwieldy. But by the time *Brustein* went into rehearsal, Hansberry was too ill to give her best energy to the arduous process of rewriting that the art of playwriting demands.

Activist Signaled Danger to the Dominant Culture

Hansberry signified several dangerous things to the dominant culture, particularly after her fame gave her national exposure. She was a lesbian, although never publicly, she was a Pan-Africanist, and in 1961 she donated money for the station wagon used by James Chaney, Andrew Goodman, and Michael Schwerner, who were Freedom Riders in Mississippi at the time of their murder. In 1962 she gathered support for the Student Nonviolent Coordinating Committee (SNCC) and was a vocal critic of the House Un-American Activities Committee and the Cuban missile crisis. She stood up to Otto Preminger in her criticism of *Porgy and Bess* as a racist play in a highly-publicized interview, and on May 24, 1953, she and several prominent blacks met with Attorney General Robert Kennedy.

The meeting did not go well. Kennedy seemed to expect these successful black artists and intellectuals to endorse America as a land of freedom and opportunity, while the participants had no such intention. Everything in America was not "all right," and Hansberry led the walk-out with the statement that she was not worried about the state of oppressed black people "who have done splendidly . . . all things considered,'' but about ''the state of the civilization which produced that photograph of the white cop standing on that Negro woman's neck in Birmingham'' (Baldwin, 269-72).

It is not clear exactly when the FBI opened their file on Hansberry, but she was classified as a member of ''black nationalist-hate groups.'' The dominant culture began to put pressure on her and to make it increasingly important that she maintain alliance with supportive groups such as SNCC, the black nationalists, and the Communist party. She was forced to prioritize her issues so that the issue of gay liberation took a back seat to black liberation and world peace. She also had her life cruelly curtailed by cancer at the age of thirty-four. Given her prolific output in such a short lifetime, we can only speculate what contributions she would have made to her many fields of interest had she lived.

Hansberry was a fighter. She suffered a paralyzing stroke six months before her death and lost her speech and eyesight. But she battled back and regained both, leaving her sickbed to raise money for SNCC, to meet with Robert Kennedy, to attend rehearsals for *The Sign In Sidney Brustein's Window*, and to deliver a speech on what it meant ''To be young, gifted and black,'' to winners of a United Negro College Fund writing contest. She went through two unsuccessful operations and had heavy treatments of radiation and chemotherapy, yet she continued to work for the causes that concerned her throughout 1964.

During that year she published a radical volume called *The Movement: Documentary of a Struggle for Equality*, with strong photographs of racist brutality including lynchings and an equally potent text. She continued work on two plays, *Les Blancs* and *The Sign In Sidney Brustein's Window*, and a play about the eighteenth-century feminist, Mary Wollstonecraft. On June 15 she left the hospital to participate in the famous Town Hall debate between black militant artists and white liberal intellectuals on ''The Black Revolution and the White Backlash.''

When it became clear that she would never be able to finish *Les Blancs*, she had many long conversations with her former husband so that he could finish it after her death. Though their divorce had become final on March 10, 1964, they continued to see each other daily until the end. Robert Nemiroff and influential friends of his and Hansberry's kept *The Sign In Sidney Brustein's Window* running for 101 performances, a remarkable achievement given its mixed reviews. It closed with the author's death on January 12, 1965.

Hansberry's Works Censored

Hansberry had many serious problems with censorship, which kept some of her best work from ever reaching the public. She wrote the screenplay for the film version of *A Raisin in the Sun*, including several interesting scenes that Columbia Pictures censored because they were too critical of the dominant culture. Hansberry had to be content with the film (which is basically a shortened version of the play with a few scenes shot on location outside the Youngers' apartment) because at least it did not distort the message of her work. Still, much of the philosophical discourse in the play was taken out, and the melodramatic musical score tends to sentimentalize it. In spite of these changes and omissions, the film won a nomination for Best Screenplay of the year from the Screenwriters Guild and a special award at the Cannes Film Festival in 1961.

In 1960 she was commissioned by NBC to write one screenplay for a series on the Civil War that was to include five episodes, hers being the first. Dore Schary was to produce and direct her piece, which is entitled, *The Drinking Gourd*. It is a scathingly brilliant denunciation of the slavocracy, showing the devastating effects of the slave system upon whites as well as blacks. In a scene reminiscent of *King Lear*, the slave, Hannibal, is blinded by a white overseer because he is caught learning to read. *The Drinking Gourd* is a powerful drama, tightly constructed, and representative of Hansberry at her best. Yet it was never produced. NBC paid Hansberry for the script, then shelved it and decided against producing the entire series. It was published in 1972, but has yet to be produced in its entirety. Scenes from it are included in Robert Nemiroff's play, a compilation of Hansberry's writings entitled (as is the book) *To Be Young, Gifted and Black*.

Unfinished Play Produced

Her unfinished play, *Les Blancs*, was not produced until 1970 at the Longacre Theatre in New York. It received violently mixed reviews and ran for only forty-seven performances. Revived in 1986 by The Lorraine Hansberry Theatre in San Francisco, it is Hansberry's most political play, set in Africa at the time of an impending revolution. The heroic protagonist, Tshembe Matoshe, must choose between his white wife and comfortable family life in England and leading his people in the fight against colonial oppression. Inspired by the vision of a female warrior figure, Tshembe decides in favor of the revolution, even though it means killing his own brother and accidentally causing the death of a white woman who has been like a mother to him. Her last published play, *What Use Are Flowers*?, shows a band of children struggling to survive after a nuclear holocaust, and a hermit's efforts to reawaken their capacity for knowledge and their appreciation of beauty.

Significant books by Hansberry include: *A Raisin in the Sun* (New York: Random House, 1959; London: Methuen, 1960); *The Movement: Documentary of a Struggle for Equality* (New York: Simon & Schuster, 1964); retitled *A Matter of Colour: Documentary of Struggles for Racial Equality in the USA* (London: Penguin, 1965); *The Sign in Sidney Brustein's Window* (New York: Random House, 1965); in *Three Negro Plays* (London: Penguin, 1969); *To Be Young, Gifted and Black: Lorraine Hansberry in Her Own Words*, adapted by Robert Nemiroff (Englewood Cliffs, N. J.: Prentice-Hall, 1969); *Les Blancs: The Collected Last Plays of Lorraine Hansberry*, ed. Robert Nemiroff (New York: Random House,

1972)— includes *Les Blancs*, *The Drinking Gourd*, and *What Use Are Flowers*?

Hansberry's play productions include: *A Raisin in the Sun*, New York, Ethel Barrymore Theatre, 11 March 1959; *The Sign in Sidney Brustein's Window*, New York, Longacre Theatre, 15 October 1964; *To Be Young Gifted and Black*, adapted by Robert Nemiroff, New York, Cherry Lane Theatre, 2 January 1969; and *Les Blancs*, adapted by Nemiroff, New York, Longacre Theatre, 15 November 1970. Her screenplay was *A Raisin in the Sun*, Columbia Pictures, 1961. The television production of Hansberry's work *To Be Young, Gifted and Black*, adapted from Nemiroff's play based on Hansberry's writings by Robert M. Fresco, NET, was presented in January 1972. In 1972 her recording was produced: *Lorraine Hansberry Speaks Out: Art and Black Revolution*, selected and edited by Nemiroff, Caedmon Records (TC 1352). Other works include "A Challenge to Artists," in *Voice of Black America: Major Speeches by Negroes in the United States 1787-1971*, ed. by Philip S. Foner (New York: Simon & Schuster, 1972), pp. 954-959.

Periodical articles by Hansberry are: "Willy Loman, Walter Lee Younger and He Who Must Live," *Village Voice* 12 August 1959; "On Summer," *Playbill* 27 June 1960; "This Complex of Womanhood"(*Ebony*, 15 August 1960: 40); "Genet, Mailer and the New Paternalism," *Village Voice* 1 June 1916; "A Challenge to Artists" (*Freedomways* 3, Winter 1963: 33-35); "The Black Revolution and the White Backlash," Transcript of Town Hall Forum (*National Guardian* 4 July 1964); "The Nation Needs Your Gifts" (*Negro Digest* 13, August 1964): 26-29; "The Legacy of W. E. B. Du Bois" (*Freedomways* 5, Winter 1965: 19-20); "Original Prospectus for the John Brown Memorial Theatre of Harlem" (*Black Scholar* 10, July/August 1979: 14-15); "The Negro Writer and His Roots: Toward a New Romanticism" (*Black Scholar* 12, March/April 1981: 2-12; and "All the Dark and Beautiful Warriors" (*Village Voice* 16 August 1983).

References

Abramson, Doris E. *Negro Playwrights in the American Theatre: 1925-1959*. New York: Columbia University Press, 1969.

Baldwin, James. "Lorraine Hansberry at the Summit." *Freedomways* 19 (1979): 269-72.

Baraka, Imamu Amiri. "Raisin in the Sun's Enduring Passion." The *Washington Post*, 16 November 1986.

Bigsby, C. W. E. *Confrontation and Commitment: A Study of Contemporary American Drama, 1959-1966*. London: MacGibbon & Kee, 1967.

Brown, Lloyd W. "Lorraine Hansberry as Ironist." *Journal of Black Studies* 4 (March 1974): 237-247.

Bullins, Ed. Interview. Berkely, Calif., November 1983.

Carter, Steven R. "Commitment Amid Complexity: Lorraine Hansberry's Life-in-Action." MELUS 7 (Fall 1980): 39-53.

Cruse, Harold. *The Crisis of the Negro Intellectual*. New York: William Morrow, 1967.

Haisteon, Loyle. "Lorraine Hansberry: Portrait of an Angry Young Writer." *Crisis* 86 (April 1979): 123-124, 126, 128.

Lorraine Hansberry Speaks Out: Art and the Black Revolution. Caedmon Records, 1972.

Marre, Diana. *Traditions and Departures: Lorraine Hansberry and Black Americans in Theatre*. Ph. D. dissertation. The University of California, Berkeley, 1987.

Ness, David E. "The Sign in Sidney Brustein's Window: A Black Playwright Looks at White America." *Freedomways* 11 (Fourth Quarter 1971): 359-366.

New York Times, March 1959.

Terkel, Studs. "An Interview with Lorraine Hansberry." WFMT Chicago Five Arts Guide, 10 (April 1961): 8-14.

Wilkerson, Margaret B., ed. *Nine Plays by Black Women*. New York: New American Library, 1986.

Collections

The Hansberry papers are held by Robert Nemiroff.

Diana Marre

Frances E. W. Harper

(1825-1911)

Writer, activist

Of Frances Ellen Watkins Harper, one scholar said:

> In an era full of extraordinary black women, Frances Watkins Harper, abolitionist and feminist, lecturer, poet and novelist, was one of the most extraordinary among them. If she had published nothing else, *Iola Leroy* would have been sufficient for her to claim a place among the intellectuals of her time. . . . Harper takes us to the heart of the most complex problems that faced black Americans in the post-Civil War era, and blazes a trail toward solutions" (Telephone interview with Nellie McKay, 11 April 1991).

Frances Ellen Watkins Harper was born in 1825 in Balti-

Frances E. W. Harper

more, Maryland. Born free and the only child of a mother who died when she was two years old, Harper was reared by an aunt and educated in a private school run by her uncle, William Watkins, a minister. Harper was a lonely child given to quiet musings and was profoundly affected by the abolitionist teachings of the school she attended.

Unable to attend school beyond her thirteenth year, she began working as a housekeeper. The family for whom she worked owned a bookstore. Thus, she spent her spare time reading in an effort to advance her education. By age fourteen she had written an essay and composed several poems.

In 1850 Harper left the slave state of Maryland and settled in Ohio, where she taught at Union Seminary, an African Methodist Episcopal (AME) church near Columbus. This seminary became a part of Wilberforce University. Frances Watkins became the first black American woman instructor in vocational education at the school. She taught domestic science.

In 1852 Harper left Ohio and moved to Little York, Pennsylvania. Responsible for teaching a class of "fifty-three untrained little urchins," she quickly resigned her post (Shockley, 57). She found herself becoming severely depressed, the result of being away from her home in Maryland and her increasing awareness of the atrocities of slavery. In 1853 Maryland passed a law forbidding free blacks from entering the state. Thus, she was forced into exile. To return would mean risking her freedom, as the law stated that free blacks could be imprisoned or remanded into slavery.

For several years Harper moved frequently, going to Philadelphia in 1854 and living in a station of the Underground Railroad. She visited the antislavery offices in Boston and New Bedford. In August 1854 she lectured in both cities on "Education and the Elevation of the Colored Race" (Shockley, 57). So moved was she by the horrors of slavery, she became a permanent lecturer for the Maine Anti-Slavery Society. She traveled throughout New England, Ohio, and New York. Her effectiveness as a lecturer led the Pennsylvania Anti-Slavery Society to hire her. Between 1854 and 1860, Harper traveled widely and lectured often, usually two or three times a day. "You would be amused," Harper wrote a friend, "to hear some of the remarks which my lecturers call forth. 'She is a man,' again 'She is not colored, she is white. She is painted'" (Brown, 102).

Often referred to as the "Bronze Muse," combining as she did her poetry with her lectures on the evils of slavery, Frances Harper was a petite, dignified woman whose sharp black eyes and attractive face reveal her sensitive nature (Brown, 102; Shockley, 51). Her musical voice underscored the sincerity of her speech. She was not reluctant to extend financial support to those in need and to support her causes. William Still, mentor, friend, and conductor on the Underground Railroad, wrote that she was "one of the most liberal contributors, as well as one of the ablest advocates for the Underground Railroad and the slave" (Still, 755).

Frances Ellen Watkins married a young widower named Fenton Harper on November 22, 1860, in Cincinnati, Ohio. The savings from her lectures and book sales enabled her to purchase a farm near Columbus, Ohio, where she and her husband settled down to married life. During her marriage, Harper gave birth to one daughter, whom she named Mary. Married life inhibited Harper's travel, but following the death of her husband on May 23, circa 1864, she again emerged as a political activist and traveling lecturer, now advocating equal rights for the newly liberated slaves.

Taking her daughter, Mary, and their few belongings, Harper set out on a grueling self-financed speaking tour in 1867. From 1867 to 1871 she gave daily lectures throughout the war-torn South, visiting thirteen southern states. Lecturing on the needs for racial uplift, moral reform, and women's rights, she addressed Sunday school audiences, women's groups, and anyone who would listen to her message. Some of her topics included "The Demands of the Colored Race in the Work of Reconstruction," "Enlightened Motherhood," and "Racial Literature." As women's clubs increased in popularity, Harper became a favored speaker for the women's movement. She addressed the International Council of Women in Washington, D.C., in 1888, and in Chicago she lectured on "Women's Political Future" for the Columbian Exposition (Shockley, 191).

A staunch supporter of the temperance movement, from 1875 to 1882 she served as superintendent of the "colored branch" of the Philadelphia and Pennsylvania chapters of the Woman's Christian Temperance Union. From 1883 to 1890, she directed the Northern United States Temperance Union. Finally, in 1922, her work was recognized posthumously and her name placed on the Red Letter Calendar of the World Women's Christian Temperance Union. Harper was also an active member of the National Council of Women, the American Women's Suffrage Association, and the American Association of Education of Colored Youth.

Confronting racism in the women's movement, Harper, accompanied by six colleagues—Fannie Barrier Williams, Anna Julia Cooper, Fannie Jackson Coppin, Sarah J. Earley, and Hallie Q. Brown—charged the international gathering of women at the World's Congress of Representative Women in Chicago (1893) with indifference to the needs and concerns of black American women. Harper, an astute political analyst, declared that women stood on the threshold of woman's era, and that the time was at hand for them to seize political and economic power. Frances Harper and other black American women intellectuals had depended on the suffrage movement to represent their feminist concerns. However, it was soon clear that black American women were to achieve sexual emancipation, they would have to organize themselves. Harper was active in establishing the National Association of Colored Women (NACW) and became its vice-president.

Harper's daughter never married. Becoming a Sunday school teacher, lecturer, and volunteer social worker, she accompanied her mother around the United States. She died in 1909. She and her mother were unusually close. Harper's only novel, *Iola Leroy,* is lovingly dedicated to Mary E. Harper.

Literary Career Launched

Harper's first volume of poems and prose appeared in 1851. A small collection titled *Forest Leaves* but also printed as *Autumn Leaves,* it appeared in Baltimore. At the time, Harper was but twenty-one years old. Copies of this work, unfortunately, are no longer extant. The book that actually launched Harper's literary career, however, is *Poems on Miscellaneous Subjects,* 1854. Published while she was in Boston, this work contains a preface by the renowned abolitionist, William Lloyd Garrison. Garrison praised her work, predicting her success as a poet. Her success was unprecedented. The book was reprinted four times in 1857, 1858, 1864, and 1871, rendering Harper the most popular black American poet of the times.

Harper did not limit herself to one genre. In 1859, trying her hand at the short story form, she became the first black American woman to publish in this genre. "The Two Offers" appeared in the *Anglo-African* (September/October 1859). In 1869 Harper published *Moses: A Story of the Nile,* a long narrative poem in blank verse. In 1889 a second edition of this poem was published. *Sketches of Southern Life* appeared in 1872 with an 1888 reprint. Three works, *Light Beyond Darkness, The Sparrow's Fall and Other Poems,* and *The Martyr of Alabama* were included in *Atlanta Offering,* which appeared in 1895.

Harper's one novel, written when she was sixty-seven years old, *Iola Leroy; or Shadows Uplifted,* appeared in 1892. In 1900 Harper published *Poems* and in 1901, *Idylls of the Bible.*

Unlike some of the poets of the period, who wrote sentimental verse with trite rhymes and hackneyed themes, often avoiding race and politics, Harper's verse and prose fiction are decidedly political. Many of her poems focus on the atrocities of slavery in general and the cruelties towards women in particular. "The Slave Mother" was the most popular of Harper's politically conscious work. A poignant poem, capturing the traumatic separation of mother and child and recreating the terror of the auction block, "The Slave Mother" is one of Harper's most frequently anthologized poems, appearing in *Afro-American Women Writers*:

> Heard you that shriek? It rose
> So wildly on the air,
> It seem'd as if a burden'd heart
> Was breaking in despair (Shockley, 59).

"The Slave Auction" and "Bury Me in a Free Land" were also popular poems; these two are included in Arthur P. Davis and J. Saunders Redding's *Cavalcade.* The importance of Harper's verse went unacknowledged until feminist scholars and researchers rediscovered her significance in this, another woman's era. Characteristic of the masculine dismissal of female letters, Davis and Redding write: "The best that can be said for her verse is that it was conventional and, by the popular standards of her time, competent" (101).

Harper's poetry withstands the test of time. The final stanza of "Bury Me in a Free Land" is perhaps unsurpassed by any writer, black or white, male or female, in the sentiments it expresses:

> I ask no monument, proud and high,
> To arrest the gaze of the passers-by;
> All that my yearning spirit craves,
> Is bury me not in a land of slaves (Davis, 104).

Harper's themes prove timeless as well. "A Double Standard" expresses well her disapproval of male privilege and supremacy condoned by society. She calls for the sexual liberation of women that is yet to be achieved.

Harper's short story, "The Two Offers," is an early feminist piece presenting an independent, intellectual woman, Janette Alston, juxtaposed against her rich and sheltered cousin, Laura Lagrange. Harper uses this story to make important statements about love, marriage, and the role of women in society. Fully aware of the stereotypic role of women in American fiction, Harper writes:

> You may paint her in poetry or fiction as a frail vine, clinging to her brother man for support and dying when deprived of it. And all of this may sound well enough to please the imagination of schoolgirls, or lovelorn maidens. But woman—the true woman—if you would render her happy, it needs more than the mere development of her affectional nature. Her conscience should be

> enlightened, her faith in the true and right established, and scope given to her heaven-endowed and God-given faculties. The true aim of female education should be, not a development of one or two, but all the faculties of the human soul, because no perfect womanhood is developed by imperfect culture (Shockley, 65).

Always concerned for the plight of women, Harper sought to destroy many sentimental notions about love and marriage. Of love she writes:

> Intense love is often akin to intense suffering, and to trust the whole wealth of a woman's nature on the frail bark of human love may often be like trusting a cargo of gold and precious gems to a bark that has never battled with the storm or buffeted the waves (Shockley, 65).

In the short story, Harper questions the Victorian concept of a woman's role as well as the term "old maid," for which there was no corresponding term for males who never married. Responding to Laura's fear of becoming an "old maid," Janette, who remains unmarried, says:

> Is there not more intense wretchedness in an ill-assorted marriage, more utter loneliness in a loveless home, than in the lot of the old maid who accepts her earthly mission as a gift from God and strives to walk the path of life with earnest and unfaltering steps? (Shockley, 61).

Novel Articulates Cultural History

Harper's novel, *Iola Leroy,* is best appreciated within the context of its times. During and after the Reconstruction, the plight of black Americans steadily increased. Dire poverty, ignorance, and the enactment of Black Codes against the newly emancipated slaves were contributing factors. Southern writers such as Thomas Nelson Page, George Washington Cable, and Joel Chandler Harris created stereotypes of blacks that needed to be refuted. Critic Frances Foster cogently argues that while biographies, autobiographies, and essays denied the stereotypes, these genres did not always reach the same readers on the same level as the fiction of the Plantation School.

Racial tension both in the South and in the North had intensified. Many whites who once sympathized with the plight of black Americans were now questioning their ability to live free. The emerging image of the black man was one of a shiftless, ignorant, oftentimes violent criminal and rapist. The black woman was portrayed as morally loose, unfaithful, and a spreader of sexually transmitted diseases. Finally, African-Americans were thought incapable of creating literature. Harper, faced with the pressure to speak for her people, reverse negative images, and create an aesthetically pleasing work, embarked upon a formidable task at a point in her life when many would have retired.

The nineteenth century aesthetic demanded a literature that was socially conscious. *Iola Leroy* was a novel committed to raising the social consciousness of its readers. As literary aesthetics changed, especially the African-American aesthetic, Harper received criticism for those very aspects of her novel for which she was once acclaimed. The novel, proclaimed by the *AME Church Review* as the crowning effort of Harper's life, was also praised by the Philadelphia *Public Ledger*, which said that the plot was natural and realistic, as were the characters (Foster, Introduction).

Iola Leroy reached a wide audience and was well received when it first appeared. But by 1911 it had lost its critical appeal. For the next several decades, although acknowledged as historically significant, the novel was criticized for its aesthetics. Hugh Gloster dismissed the book because he believed it imitated William Wells Brown's novel. Other critics, all male, attacked Harper's sentiment and idealism. Contemporary critics, mostly feminist, have criticized Harper's use of mulatto characters and questioned her female aesthetic. But among those—Barbara Christian and Vashti Lewis are two such critics—all seem to agree that the novel is not to be dismissed. Once thought of as the first novel written by a black American woman, Harper's novel, though not the first, is important for articulating the issues and concerns of its times. Many of the women's issues are pertinent today.

In 1987 Beacon Press reprinted *Iola Leroy*, edited by Deborah E. McDowell, for its Black Women Writers Series. In 1988, *Iola Leroy*, edited by Henry Louis Gates, Jr., was included in the Schomburg Library of Nineteenth-Century Black Women Writers. Since the reprinting of the novel, it has found its way into many women's studies and African-American literature courses in colleges and universities throughout the nation.

Iola Leroy not only offers insight into the period following the Civil War but chronicles the development of a young woman growing up during a time when women were restricted and when African-Americans were oppressed and abused despite their emancipation. Often compared to *Clotel* by William Wells Brown, the novel is actually better understood within the context of the sentimental woman's novel of the period. Hazel Carby's reference to Nina Baym's schemata of white women's fiction is appropriate for foregrounding Harper's novel (see "References" for Carby and Bayn). The general outline in these novels was the story of a young heroine, usually an orphan, forced to depend on her own resources for survival. After many trials and tribulations, the heroine successfully escapes the pitfalls of life, bypasses all suitors who are not financially well off, and concludes her life with a successful marriage. Marriage serves as the ultimate fulfillment for the heroine.

Harper uses this basic structure to her advantage but breaks new ground when the structure does not serve her purpose. Iola, the young heroine, is an orphan suddenly forced to survive in a world not of her own making. Reared to believe that she is white, she is not told until her white father dies of her complete heritage. Her mother is a mulatto whom her father educated, emancipated, and married. This revelation complicates the situation of the orphan. Iola goes immediately from being an orphan to being a slave. Although she escapes from slavery, she refuses to pass for white, a refusal that affirms her heritage but adds to the complications of her life. Iola's mother and brother are still alive; thus part of her quest is to locate her family. In a dimension peculiar to the African-American experience, Harper uses the quest within the form of the sentimental novel, thereby altering the formulaic woman's novel to suit her needs.

When Iola successfully locates her family, Harper again adds color to the form of the woman's novel. Iola refuses several marriage proposals. Clearly, marriage is not the ultimate solution for successful self-fulfullment. Nor is it necessary for the suitor to be rich. Harper articulates, through the character of Iola, the need for female economic independence. "I have a theory that every woman ought to know how to earn her own living," Iola tells her uncle, and adds, "I am going to join the great rank of bread-winners" (1987 ed., 205). Asserting this feminist line, the first to appear in black American women's fiction, Harper demonstrates two things. First, she is able to voice the need for independent womanhood, and second, she clearly demonstrates how that need is frustrated if the woman is a black. True, most black American women had no choice but to work, but it was not easy for them to obtain jobs, as the line from Uncle Robert indicates. "'When he advertises for help he means white women,' said Robert" (205).

Iola's refusal to marry in order to find happiness, her insistence upon working, and her abiding commitment to the uplift of her race, take the novel beyond the boundaries of the typical sentimental novel. Ultimately, the novel concludes with Iola's marriage to Dr. Latimer, an African-American who shares the same ideas of social uplift.

Harper's greatest hope was for black Americans to overcome the handicaps of their former condition. At the completion of her novel she says:

> The race has not had very long to straighten its hands from the hoe, to grasp the pen and wield it as a power for good, and to erect above the ruined auction-block and slave-pen institutions of learning" (282).

Of her own work, Harper writes in a note following *Iola Leroy:*

> From threads of fact and fiction I have woven a story whose mission will not be in vain if it awakens in the hearts of our countrymen a strong sense of justice and more Christlike humanity in behalf of those whom the fortunes of war threw, homeless, ignorant and poor, upon the threshold of a new era (282).

Harper's work is didactic and moralistic in the true sense and spirit of the Victorian period. Many of the issues that she addressed were indeed directed toward the newly emerging middle class. Because of their privilege, she felt they needed a sense of noblesse oblige. In fact, it was Harper, not Du Bois, who gave birth to the concept of "talented tenth." It was she who first articulated the need for those with education and training, both male and female, to commit themselves to the social betterment of the race. She of course was not alone in calling for social uplift. Another woman contemporary, Anna Julia Cooper, demanded the same effort from middle-class black American women and men. The irony is that when an assessment of the post-Civil War years was made, the names Harper and Cooper were not mentioned. Fortunately, the record is finally being set straight.

The poem that concludes *Iola Leroy* demonstrates Harper's faith in a new day. She wrote:

> There is light beyond the darkness,
> Joy beyond the present pain;
> There is hope in God's great justice
> And the negro's rising brain.
> Though the morning seems to linger
> O'er the hill-tops far away,
> Yet the shadows bear the promise
> Of a brighter coming day (282).

Frances Ellen Watkins Harper died in Philadelphia, Pennsylvania, of a heart ailment on February 20, 1911, when she was eighty-seven. Funeral services were held at the First Unitarian Church, and she was buried on February 24 in Eden Cemetery, Philadelphia.

References

Baym, Nina. *Woman's Fiction: A Guide to Novels by and about Women in America 1820-1870.* Ithaca, N.Y.: Cornell University Press, 1978.

Brown, Hallie Q. *Homespun Heroines and Other Women of Distinction.* Xenia, Ohio: Aldine Pub. Co., 1926. 97-103. Photograph between pp. 96-97.

Carby, Hazel. Introduction. *Iola Leroy.* Ed. Deborah E. McDowell. Boston: Beacon Press, 1987. 1-20.

Davis, Arthur P., and J. Saunders Redding, eds. *Cavalcade: Negro American Writing from 1760 to the Present.* Boston: Houghton Mifflin, 1971.

Foster, Frances Smith. Introduction. *Iola Leroy.* Ed. Henry Louis Gates, Jr. New York: Oxford University Press, 1988.

Harper, Frances E. W. *Iola Leroy.* Ed. Deboran E. McDowell. Boston: Beacon Press, 1987.

Lerner, Gerda, ed. "Black Women in the Reconstruction South." In *Black Women in White America.* New York: Pantheon, 1973.

McKay, Nellie. Interview with the author. 11 April 1991.

Sherman, Joan R. *Invisible Poets: Afro-Americans of the*

Nineteenth Century. 2nd ed. Urbana: University of Illinois Press, 1989. 62-74. Photograph, p. 64.

Shockley, Ann Allen. *Afro-American Women Writers 1746-1933*. Boston: G. K. Hall, 1988. 56-61.

Still, William. Introduction to the second edition. *Iola Leroy*. Philadelphia: Garigues Brothers, 1892.

Nagueyalti Warren

Barbara Harris

(1930-)

Religious leader

On Saturday, September 24, 1988, the Reverend Barbara Clementine Harris was elected suffragan bishop of the 110,000-member diocese of Massachusetts. She became the Right Reverend Barbara Clementine Harris on February 12, 1989, the 834th and first female bishop, thus breaking more than four hundred years of tradition of the Anglican Communion with her elevation to the episcopate, a two-thousand-year apostolic succession. History was made as this black American woman was transformed into a symbol for the 2.5-million-member Protestant Episcopal church and for Anglicans the world over.

Barbara Harris

When the bishop-elect's procession entered Hynes Veteran Center, spontaneous applause thundered throughout the auditorium as she came into view. Because the preceding processions had been so lengthy and slow-moving, the processional music was out of sequence; therefore, it was somewhat prophetic and fitting that the St. Paul African Methodist Episcopal (AME) Church Choir began the familiar "Ride on, King Jesus . . . no man can hinder me . . . " as Harris appeared. Once the choir segued into "In That Great Gittin' Up Mornin,'" the whole audience was clapping along in a completely spontaneous fashion, albeit *on* the beat. But the consecration of this new bishop had implications for others as well. As the first woman consecrated to the episcopate in any one of the three major branches of Christianity—Anglicanism, Roman Catholicism, and Eastern Orthodoxy—Harris "gives new hope . . . and new vision to hundreds of thousands who have felt alienated by the church"(*Tennessean*, 26 September 1988).

The August 1989 *Esquire* magazine featured a striking commemorative photograph of the new bishop attired in her Eucharistic vestments. The caption "Amazing Grace" was fitting for many see in her the hope of a renewed and revitalized Episcopal church led by the Holy Spirit. Philadelphia, Pennsylvania, the birthplace of this "Church of Presidents," is also the birthplace of the Right Reverend Harris. She, her older sister, Josephine, and younger brother, Thomas, were born to Walter Harris and Beatrice (Price) Harris. As lifelong Philadelphians, the Harris family has lived in the same Germantown home for more than seventy years. Harris, born on June 12, 1930, graduated from Philadelphia High School for Girls in 1948 and attended Villanova University (1977-1979) and Hobart and William Smith College STD (1981). At the latter two institutions, she completed college courses and special training designed for mid-career clergy recruits.

As a "cradle Episcopalian," Harris gave early notice of her intention to make the church the instrument of Jesus's dictate to "love the Lord your God with all your heart . . . soul, and with all your strength" and to "love your neighbor as yourself" (*Prayer Book and Hymnal*, 351). Baptized and confirmed at St. Barnabas Church in Germantown, as a teenager she played the piano for church school and started the Young Adults Group. At the time, it had between fifty and seventy members and was the largest such youth group in the city. It still exists, with some of the original members, as the Adult Fellowship. As an adult, Harris was an active volunteer with the St. Dismas Society and succeeded her rector, the Reverend Canon Charles L. L. Poindexter, as board member of the Pennsylvania Prison Society, the oldest such group in the nation. Poindexter's involvement stemmed from his concern over an embarrassing lack of black clergy in prison ministry. He recruited Harris, who carried on this volunteer ministry for some fifteen years, longer than anyone else. The racially mixed St. Dismas Society visited prisons on Sunday evenings and weekdays to hold services, provide counseling, and be special friends to the prisoners.

In 1968, St. Barnabas merged with St. Luke's, a predominantly white parish; it is now St. Luke's Church, the largest parish in Philadelphia and still the home church of Harris's family. According to Poindexter, Harris, feeling that St. Luke's was too staid, transferred her membership to the North Philadelphia Church of the Advocate with the blessings of her rector. Once the way was open for women's ordination, Harris began to fulfill a lifetime dream by studying for the ministry. She was ordained to the diaconate in 1979, served as deacon-in-training at the Church of the Advocate in 1979-1980, and was ordained to the priesthood in 1980. Harris's parish-based ministries were as priest-in-charge at St. Augustine-of-Hippo (Norristown, 1980-1984) and as interim rector at the Church of the Advocate, where she was serving when elected as suffragan bishop of the diocese of Massachusetts.

Controversy Stirs on Harris's Election

The controversy over Harris's election revolves around several basic issues. First, she is a divorced female, and it is ironic that a male competitor and her predecessor as suffragan are divorced males over whose marital status no such ruckus was raised. Secondly, traditionalists believe that because the apostles were men, the position of bishop must be reserved for men. Others criticized her educational background and experience. Harris's educational, theological, and ministerial qualifications differ from the more traditional and formal university and seminary-based training and parish-based ministry heretofore considered as prerequisites to the episcopate. Harris's tenure as executive director of the Episcopal Church Publishing Company (ECPC) and as frequent contributor to its liberal and highly controversial publication, *The Witness*, cause detractors to view her as a dangerous activist.

The issue of sex has no validity in light of the 1976 General Convention action opening all orders (deacon, priest, and bishop) to women. The issue of her educational qualifications and experience is likewise invalid, as Harris attended college and completed seminary requirements through an approved alternate route quite to the satisfaction of the diocese of Pennsylvania, by whose canons she was deemed fit for ordination. As an aside, it is rumored that Harris made the highest General Ordination Examination scores in her group after completing her studies. The new bishop also spent over ten years as senior staff consultant and as a chief public relations executive at Sun Oil Company; one can be fairly certain that this corporation, like others, carefully scrutinized the qualifications of those sitting in seats of upper-level management. Harris also had eight years of parish experience and according to the Reverend Paul Washington, "spent enough time in prisons ministering to prisoners and captives to have almost served a two-year sentence herself" (*Witness*, April 1989).

The Right Reverend J. Antonio Ramos spoke to this issue in terms of the emergence of alternative forms of education for ministry development; the Reverend Carter Heyward refered to Harris as "[not] having been educated in the halls of 'educated men' but rather in the course of living life among her people" (*Witness*, April 1989). The issue of social activism is one of consequence, for Harris is indeed a social activist and she is, in a sense, dangerous. Her social activism has been noted and accepted by some; for example, Paul Washington said "today, I am sending you one who burns when others are offended " (*Witness*, April 1989). As accused by those who fear and criticize her, Harris is guilty as charged in that she has promised to "bring sensitivity to the needs of different kinds of people, including minorities, women, the incarcerated, the poor and other marginalized groups" (*Tennessean*, 25 September 1988). Harris made this assertion in a statement distributed to the diocesan delegates who elected her to be their suffragan bishop.

The position of suffragan is that of an assisting bishop, one which is considered permanent at the time of election. The bishop coadjutor, however, is elected specifically to succeed the diocesan bishop at the latter's retirement—this gives rise to the tongue-in-cheek reference to the suffragan as "suffering bishop." This person may, indeed, succeed the diocesan bishop, but only if elected again by the diocesan convention to do that. Harris's main responsibilities will focus on pastoral care for a specific geographical area of the Massachusetts diocese. She will help people in local parishes in dealing with typical parish issues such as calling rectors and parish growth and development. One newspaper account of Harris's election referred to the position as a relatively minor and unimportant one, thus disparaging her role in the life of the diocese and the church at large. Jesus's dictate to his apostles to "feed my sheep" certainly is typified in this office that relates directly to the uplift and edification of "God's People." This position would seem to be tailor-made for one, like Harris, with a strong commitment to social justice and the professional acumen derived from years as a corporate executive.

In combining her spiritual quest for social justice and her editorial skills honed as a public relations executive, Harris has long utilized not only the pulpit but also the media to prophesy against social ills demanding attention and rectification by the church. As ECPC executive director, Harris regularly authored the controversial column "A LUTA CONTINUA: The Struggle Continues," which became the barometer for the rise and fall of subscription renewals and cancellations. Readers have never been lukewarm about Harris's views; they were, and are, either wholeheartedly supportive or rabidly indignant over her commentaries that spared no "sacred cows." Such columns as "Of Many Things" and "a double standard" tackled diverse issues ranging from the Consultation on Church Union (COCU) plan for implementing shared mission and unity to bombing of public facilities, especially those serving women seeking family planning and/or abortion counseling and services. She chided the federal government for labeling bombings by freedom fighters as acts of terrorism and conspiracies while dismissing bombings of the above facilities as "the work of 'fanatics' spurred on by . . . religious zeal" (*Witness*, February 1985). Since her elevation to the episcopate, Harris has continued to speak out on issues the church cannot ignore. A recent *Witness* article, "The Politics of AIDS," was excerpted from a keynote speech to the National Episcopal AIDS Coalition and focused on three paramount concerns: the politics of AIDS affecting medical breakthroughs, the legal and civil rights of AIDS sufferers and others for whom testing is required, and the rise of the AIDS epidemic among teenagers. Far from being a wild-eyed radical, Harris seeks solutions and concrete ways by which the church can lead and be the advocate for those unable to fend for themselves.

Because the new bishop has always been known as a staunch advocate for women's rights, it may surprise some to learn that all women were not ready for her election as bishop. There still exist many women who fervently believe in the male-only succession in the apostolic line, probably as an extension of their adherence to a preference for a male-dominated clergy and a clear-cut gender distinctive society. But not all. Many distaff Episcopalians long resented their status, or lack of it, especially since their United Thank Offering (UTO) contributions added millions to the church coffers. Foremost among their grievances was the long struggle to be approved as deputies to General Convention. Although a woman was provisionally seated in 1946, the approval for a constitutional change to allow women deputies was not forthcoming until 1967. With such a parochial attitude, it comes as no surprise to learn that constitutional changes to approve women's ordination to the diaconate and priesthood were not effected until 1970 and 1976, respectively.

The "Philadelphia 11" Force Action

But 1974 would prove to be the time of crisis for the Episcopal Church: That was the year of the infamous (or famous, depending on one's point of view) "Philadelphia 11." This was the group of eleven female deacons who sought ordination to the priesthood in spite of the church's stalling on the issue. Harris was there as a participant in the ordination service held at the now historic site of the Church of the Advocate, and the host rector was the Episcopal priest who would preach her consecration sermon fifteen years later. In that sermon, the Reverend Paul Washington mentioned that Harris had flown in from California to lead the procession as crucifer, not knowing that it was the beginning of the journey that would lead to an act of great consequence for the church.

Three retired bishops ordained the "Philadelphia 11," but the House of Bishops declared the ordinations invalid some two weeks later at an emergency meeting. In 1975, four additional female deacons were ordained to the priesthood at the Church of St. Stephen and the Incarnation in Washington, D.C. Both irregular ordinations were the focal point at the 1976 Minneapolis General Convention, but, at long last, the struggle was over. Both Houses endorsed the ordination of women to the priesthood and in 1977 the fifteen "irregulars" were regularized. The September 1984 *Witness* celebrated the Tenth Anniversary of Women Priests, and Harris authored the article "Celebrating a Dream Yet to Come True." An accompanying photograph shows her with other officiants at the Eucharist in the very church where she had led the procession for the "Philadelphia 11." The Right Reverend J. Antonio Ramos noted in the anniversary sermon that he preached, "I look forward to the day, soon, not 25 years from now, when a woman in Episcopal orders will preach the Word of God in a celebration like this" (*Witness*, September 1974). In 1974, Ramos was the only active diocesan bishop present at the irregular ordination but was not allowed to ordain women because of the danger in which he would have been placed, thus the utilization of retired bishops. In 1984, little did he know that his wait would be only five years, not twenty-five, and he would place the episcopal ring on Harris's finger and be the first to kneel and kiss the ring in the spirit of collegial friendship and respect.

Another strategy to urge the church to be more responsible to its diverse membership was the convening of the "Consultation" by the then Reverend Harris. This early 1980s group was comprised of nine Episcopal groups that formed a coalition to "raise concerns [to] shape the identity and mission of the Church at General Convention and beyond" (*Witness*, June 1985). Its Vision Statement focused on the need to address the four systemic ills of racism, sexism, class discrimination, and imperialism by challenging the church to recognize, define, and act on the inherent evil in systems allowing the continuation of deprivation and injustice. Perceived as the fringe element of the church, the nine groups were the Episcopal Peace Fellowship, Episcopal Urban Caucus, Integrity, Episcopal Women's Caucus, Union of Black Episcopalians, Appalachian People's Service Organization, Episcopal Church Publishing Company, Hispanic Concerns Group, and Asian-American Concerns Group.

Bishop Harris has also been a longtime active supporter and member of the Union of Black Episcopalians (UBE). Deborah Harmon Hines, past national UBE president, provided a mini-history of the group starting with the goals: to promote the participation of blacks throughout the church and to eradicate racism in the church and society. The UBE was founded in 1968 by seventeen black clergy at St. Phillip's parish in Harlem as the Union of Black Clergy. There being no female clergy at the time did not deter the wishes of women to become members, and a few black women asserted themselves, among them Harris and Mattie Hopkins of Chicago, and joined the "brothers." As more black women sought membership, the group became the Union of Black Clergy and Laity and, finally, the UBE as it is today. On the surface, males held the key positions, but the women were the glue holding the organization together with the specialized skills and talents that they had brought with them, especially Hopkins, an educator and community activist, and Harris, the public relations expert. Their efforts were largely undocumented because what happened was usually reported rather than who did what, but when oral histories are recounted, distaff efforts are always touted as being pertinent to the agenda. The UBE has long been another vehicle for Harris's exercising her social justice ministry and her continuous efforts to ensure non-exclusionary participation in the life of the church.

Bishop Shows Her Human Side

Harris has been described in terms of her effectiveness as a catalyst for social justice in the church and as a larger-than-life symbol for people who have long been marginal and impotent members of societal institutions, including the church. But Harris is a flesh-and-blood person, one who laughs when pleased, cries when saddened, scolds and chides when angered, bleeds when cut. She is many things to many people, all of whom see their own particular side of her many-faceted personality.

The Reverend Florence Li Tim-Oi, first ordained female Anglican priest, met Harris at the 1988 Lambeth Conference and described her as being neat and well-groomed, sharp featured with bright eyes and a radiant smile. A *U.S. News & World Report* writer described Harris as friends know her. Mentioned were the bishop's three-inch heel patent-leather pumps, her spiky mauve fingernails, a magnificent gold and diamond ring, and the signet ring of the episcopate. To those wanting to kiss the ring, the bishop replied, "Forget the ring, sweetie, kiss the bishop!" In reply to the very real concern of the Church of England's on-going refusal to recognize the status of female priests and bishops, Harris answered with a rejoinder displaying rapier-sharp wit rather than anger: "I could be a combination of the Virgin Mary, Lena Horne and Madame Curie and I would still get clobbered by some." Further described as "someone you'd like to invite down to the corner bar to dish the dirt over a beer," Harris is also the person who, during the summer of 1964, registered black voters in Mississippi in lieu of her summer vacation; in addition, she was a participant in the Selma, Alabama, march with Martin Luther King, Jr.

The 1948 Philadelphia High School for Girls yearbook described Barbara Harris as "slim, spirited, happy-go-lucky Bobby" (*Witness*, April 1989). Harrison DeShields, however, remembers another "Bobby." In the 1940s, DeShields attended Philadelphia's Central High School, one noted for its stringent entrance requirements and a black student population of around 50 out of a total of 1,700. He and his buddies, Robert Nix, Jr., Chief Justice of the Pennsylvania Supreme Court, and Billy Walker, a physician, now deceased, always timed their arrival at the subway station stop to coincide with that of Harris and her girlfriends, Mary Carter and Marilyn Baker, who attended junior high school. Because Central was so "tough," it was an honor to attend and a challenge to succeed, especially for the few minority students admitted at the time. DeShields's two distinct memories of her are that Harris was charming and attractive, thus making her fascinating to him, and that she was always concerned about the Central High boys, especially their academic welfare. He also noted that her first job after high school graduation was with Joe Baker Associates, a black public relations firm owned by the first black man hired as a permanent writer by the *Philadelphia Inquirer*. Harris edited a publication geared towards encouraging young blacks to attend historically black colleges. DeShields had not known what became of Harris until her election as bishop.

Myrtle Gordon of Atlanta, Georgia, national church consultant on aging and UBE consultant on clergy wives, in an interview with Aleathis Dolores Nicholson, characterized Bishop Harris as "a strong black woman, small in stature, fiercely strong in her beliefs, loyalties, and concern for people's welfare in relation to the witness of the church; a dynamo in her strong convictions; one motivated and propelled to rectify situations caused by the church's failure to perceive and attend to people's needs." Gordon spoke of Harris's fierce loyalty to the church, and her ability to recognize those weaknesses in need of strengthening so as to ensure that people be able to realize the true mission of the church and achieve wholeness.

References

Boston Globe, 12 February 1989.

Charlotte Observer, 26 September 1988.

Cincinnati Enquirer, 12 February 1989; 13 February 1989.

CLASS, May 1989.

Deshields, Harrison. Interview with Aleathia Dolores Nicholson, 2 March 1990.

Esquire, August 1989.

Gordon, Myrtle. Interview with Aleathia Dolores Nicholson, 4 March 1990.

Hines, Deborah Harmon. Interview with Aleathia Dolores Nicholson, 1 March, 1990.

Interchange, Diocese of Southern Ohio, October 1988, March 1989.

Jet, 13 February 1989; 29 February 1989.

Journal-News (Philadelphia), 12 February 1989.

Lexington Herald Leader, 12 February 1989.

Linkage, December 1985/January 1986.

Newsweek, 13 February 1989.

Poindexter, Charles L. L. Interview with Aleathia Dolores Nicholson, 5 March 1990.

Prayer Book and Hymnal: Containing the Book of Common Prayer and the Hymnal 1982. New York: Church Hymnal Corporation, 1986.

Reid, Videi. Interview with Aleathia Dolores Nicholson, 2 March 1990.

Tennessean, 25 September 1988; 26 September 1988; 5

February 1989; 13 February 1989; 17 February 1989; 25 February 1989.

Time, 26 December 1968.

"The Union of Black Episcopalians: An Opportunity for Christian Action." 1985-86 Fact Sheet.

U.S. News & World Report, 19 June 1989.

USA Today, 26 September 1988; 30 September 1988.

The Witness, 1974.

Collections

Files of nearly all urban newspapers and weekly and monthly magazines have coverage for September 1988 and February 1989 that include the election and consecration of Harris. The Diocesan Press Service is the major source of news articles for Diocesan Newsletters, such as *Interchange* for Southern Ohio, "Crossties" for Tennessee. Each diocese has its own newsletters.

Major photographs of Bishop Harris are included in *Esquire*, August 1989, where a full shot was taken at the cathedral site; the *Boston Sunday Globe*, 12 February 1989, has published the most striking shot, an overhead of the "laying on of hands" by twenty-five bishops. The commemorative issue of *Witness*, April 1989, is devoted to Harris and gives a color photograph, p. 25.

Aleathia Dolores Nicholson

Judia C. Jackson Harris

(1873-19?)

School founder, race relations advocate, land club founder

Judia C. Jackson Harris founded the Teacher Training and Industrial Institute, as well as land clubs that improved the quality of black social and economic life in Georgia. She was president of the Athens Women's Club, chair of the 8th District of Women in World War work, president of the Athens Branch of the Interracial Committee, and the second vice-president of the National Association of Teachers in Colored Schools. She also wrote articles, pageants, and *Race Relations*, in the hope that better understanding between blacks and whites could be achieved.

Harris was born on February 1, 1873, in Athens, Georgia, the daughter of Louise (Terrell) Jackson and Alfred Jackson. She received her education in the public schools of Athens, the Normal Department of Atlanta University (1890-1894), Harvard College (1904), the University of Chicago (1909), and the University of Pennsylvania (1915). On June 26, 1912, she married Samuel F. Harris. Very little is known about her personal life.

Harris was principal of the Athens, Georgia, city schools from 1901 to 1902. She gave up her principalship to cast her lot with a community at Helicon Springs, about five miles from Athens. This community was composed of very poor people; ignorance abounded, cabins were dilapidated, and the land was poorly cultivated. Her first task was to encourage land ownership among the people, and soon forty acres of land owned by ten different African-Americans was secured for school purposes. Since the county had no funds to erect a school building, the General Education Board, through its secretary, Wallace Buttrick, gave six-hundred dollars for this purpose provided that the necessary land be deeded to the county and that the county supply teachers for the school. After these conditions had been met, the Peabody Fund came forward with one-hundred dollars toward the building fund. As a result, a modern two-story Model and Training School was erected (later called the Teacher Training and Industrial Institute, Athens, Georgia).

The school was envied by the whites in the community, who expressed their jealousy by throwing a dead dog on the front porch of the school and by placing wagons across the road to make the approach to the school impossible. These insults, however, failed to deter Harris in her efforts to serve her people, and soon she gained the goodwill of all of the leading citizens of Clark County, as well as that of her immediate neighbors. Eventually there were three buildings on the campus, the main building being of brick with classrooms, office, and library. Harris's noble work attracted many visitors, both northern and southern, who were most generous in praise and contributions.

Land Clubs Founded

In 1901 Harris organized land clubs in the state of Georgia. The clubs fostered the development of black communities that allowed the acquisition of more than two thousand acres of land for homes. The organizations improved black home life and established schools as centers for activities. Harris stimulated the farmers for miles around to improve their farming methods, encouraged them to build neat and attractive homes, and insisted that their children attend school.

Harris's major writings included *Race Relations* (McGregor Company, 1925), and four pageants of racial, historical, and religious nature. *Race Relations* was written "to promote better race feelings." Harris sought expressions from a diverse group of people in a desire that the 16-page offering would "aid in bringing about a better understanding." She was a contributor of articles to magazines and newspapers of the day.

References

Bacote, Clarence A. *The Atlanta University Story*. Atlanta: 1969.

Harris, Judia C. Jackson. *Race Relations*. McGregory Company, 1925.

Who's Who in Colored America. 2nd ed., 1918-29. New York: Who's Who in Colored America Corporation, 1929. Photograph, p. 167.

Casper LeRoy Jordan

Marcelite J. Harris

(1943-)

Military officer

Marcelite Jordan Harris, a brigadier general, is vice-commander of the Oklahoma City Air Logistics Center at Tinker Air Force Base, Oklahoma. She was the U.S. Air Force's first woman aircraft maintenance officer and one of the first two women to be "air officers commanding" at the Air Force Academy in Colorado. Not only was she the first woman appointed maintenance squadron commander in Strategic Air Command, she also became Air Training Command's first woman wing commander. After setting other records as a woman "first," she reached the rank of brigadier general in 1990, thereby becoming the first black woman general in the Air Force.

Marcelite J. Harris

Born January 16, 1943, in Houston, Texas, Harris is the daughter of Cecil O'Neal Jordan, Sr., a postal supervisor, and Marcelite (Terrell) Jordan, a high school librarian. She has one sister, Elizabeth, and one brother, Cecil O'Neal, Jr. Her maternal great-great-grandfather, Pierre Landry, was the son of a slave woman and her master born on the Provost plantation in Ascension Parish, Louisiana. Although he lived the first thirteen years of his life virtually free, after being sold he opened a plantation store to sell approved items to other slaves and became head carpenter for the plantation. After the Civil War and freedom came, he moved to Donaldsonville, the parish seat, where he was elected mayor in 1868. Between 1870 and 1884 he served in the state house of representatives and in the state senate, and then left politics to practice law. Harris's maternal great-grandfather, I. M. Terrell, was an educator who founded the first school for blacks in Fort Worth, Texas.

Harris graduated in 1960 from Kashmere Gardens Junior-Senior High School and in 1964 from Spelman College in Atlanta, Georgia, with a bachelor of arts degree in speech and drama. Later she earned a bachelor of arts degree in business management at the University of Maryland, Asian Division. She completed the Air Force's Squadron Officer School by correspondence and Air War College by seminar. She also completed Harvard University's Senior Officers National Security in residence as well as the Defense Department's CAPSTONE course for general officers.

In September 1965 Harris entered the United States Air Force through the Office Training School at Lackland Air Force Base, Texas, and graduated in December of that year. She was then assigned to the position of assistant director for administration at the 60th Military Airlift Wing at Travis Air Force Base, California.

Harris became administrative officer for the 388th Tactical Missile Squadron in January 1967, based at Bitburg Air Base, West Germany. In May 1969 she was reassigned as the maintenance analysis officer with the 36th Tactical Fighter Wing at the same air base.

After completing her German tour, Harris was the first woman in the Air Force to become aircraft maintenance officer upon graduating from the Aircraft Maintenance Officer Course at Chanute Air Force Base, Illinois, in May 1971. Three months later she became the maintenance supervisor for the 469th Tactical Fighter Squadron located at Korat Air Base, Thailand.

After returning to the United States, Harris was assigned as the job control officer for the 916th Air Refueling Squadron located at Travis Air Force Base, California. She became the squadron's field maintenance supervisor in September 1973.

Two years later Harris was assigned as a personnel staff officer at Headquarters, United States Air Force, Washington, D.C. Among her assignments was that of White House social aide to President Jimmy Carter. In May 1978 she became commander of Cadet Squadron Thirty-nine at the United States Air Force Academy, Colorado, and thus was selected as one of the first two women to be "air officer commanding."

Returning to the maintenance career field, in July 1980 Harris became maintenance control officer for the 384th Air Refueling Wing at McConnell Air Force Base, Kansas. A year later she became the first woman maintenance squadron commander in Strategic Air Command, assuming command of the 384th Avionics Maintenance Squadron, McConnell Air Force Base. Eight months later Harris assumed command of McConnell's 384th Field Maintenance Squadron.

In November 1982, Harris was assigned to the Pacific Air Forces Logistic Support Center, Kadena Air Base, Japan. She became the Air Force's first woman deputy commander for maintenance when she assumed the position at Keesler Air Force Base, Mississippi, in March 1966. She served as commander of the 3300th Technical Training Wing, Keesler Technical Training Center, Keesler Air Force Base, Mississippi, assuming the position on December 3, 1988. At that time she became the first woman wing commander in Air Training Command. On September 8, 1990, Harris attained the rank of brigadier general, and is currently vice-commander of the Oklahoma City Air Logistics Center at Tinker Air Force Base, Oklahoma. According to *Jet* magazine, in her position she "helps oversee 26,000 workers in the maintenace of all types of military aircraft and missiles."

Among the numerous military honors Harris has received are the Bronze Star, Meritorious Service Medal with three oak leaf clusters, Air Force Commendation Medal with one oak leaf cluster, Presidential Unit Citation, Air Force Outstanding Unit Award with eight oak leaf clusters—one with valor, Air Force Organizational Excellence Award with one oak leaf cluster, National Defense Service Medal, Vietnam Service Medal, Air Force Overseas Ribbon—Short Tour, Air Force Overseas Ribbon—Long Tour with one oak leaf cluster, Air Force Longevity Service Award Ribbon with four oak leaf clusters, Republic of Vietnam Gallantry Cross with Palm, and the Republic of Vietnam Campaign Medal.

She married Maurice Anthony Harris, a native of Portsmouth, Virginia, and now a retired lieutenant colonel from the Air Force and a law student at Louisiana State University. They are the parents of a son, Steven, and a daughter, Tenecia.

References

"Brigadier General Marcelite J. Harris." Biography. United States Air Force. Office of Public Affairs, HQ Oklahoma City Air Logistics Center. Tinker Air Force Base, Oklahoma. Includes photograph.

"Dunn-Landry Papers." *Amistad* 2 (August 1984): 1, 3. Includes photographs.

"Harris 1st Black Female General in U.S. Air Force." *Jet* 79 (12 November 1990): 7.

Jessie Carney Smith

Patricia Harris

(1924-1985)

Lawyer, government official

Patricia Roberts Harris made history during her lifetime and achieved many firsts. American history will remember her as the first black woman to serve in a United States president's cabinet, as secretary of Housing and Urban Development and as secretary of Health Education and Welfare; she was also the first black woman to serve her nation as ambassador and to lead an American law school.

Harris was born on May 31, 1924, in Mattoon, Illinois, to Bert and Chiquita Roberts. Early in her life, Pat Harris's father, a dining car waiter for the Illinois Central Railroad, abandoned the family, leaving her and her brother, Malcolm, to be raised by their mother. In her formative years, Harris became aware of the importance of an education, saying, "we didn't have a lot of money [but] we believed in education and . . . in reading" (*Ambassador for Progress*,

Patricia Harris

3). As one of the few black families in Mattoon, Illinois, she also came to know about racism when one of her grade school classmates called her a nigger.

After receiving her secondary education in Chicago, Illinois, Harris entered the School of Liberal Arts at Howard University in 1941, from which she graduated summa cum laude in 1945 with an A.B. degree. Later she was elected into Phi Beta Kappa. It was during her college days at Howard that Pat Harris gained a social consciousness about the ramifications of segregation in the American society. In 1943 she joined other Howard students in one of the first student sit-ins at the Little Palace Cafeteria, which refused to serve blacks in the midst of the black community. This experience caused Harris to pay even closer attention to her studies, for she knew that without excelling in her academic work, her life would be more difficult.

Harris entered graduate school and worked several years at the Chicago YWCA before assuming the position of executive director of Delta Sigma Theta in 1953. She subsequently married William Beasley Harris, a lawyer who encouraged her to attend law school. In 1957 she enrolled in the George Washington University School of Law, where she excelled. She was a member of the law review and was elected to the Order of the Coif, a national legal honor society, and graduated first in her class of ninety-four students in 1960. After graduation, Harris joined the appeals and research staff of the criminal division of the United States Department of Justice, where she remained until she joined the Howard University Law School faculty on a part-time basis as a lecturer in law in 1961. The rest of her time was spent as associate dean of students at Howard University. The appointment of Harris to the law school faculty made her the fifth woman to teach at Howard's law school. Among the courses she taught were torts and international law.

Around 1963 Harris was appointed to Howard's law faculty on a full-time basis, one of two women on the law faculty. In June 1965 Harris, a Democrat, took leave from her teaching responsibilities to accept an appointment by President Lyndon B. Johnson as ambassador to Luxembourg, a position that she held until September 1967. While ambassador to Luxembourg, Harris received several awards, including the Alumni Achievement Award from George Washington University and the Distinguished Alumni Award from Howard University in 1966. In 1967 Harris was the recipient of the Order of Oaken Crown for her distinguished service in Luxembourg.

After retiring as ambassador, Harris returned to Howard's law school as a professor on a full-time basis, serving simultaneously as United States alternate delegate to the Twenty-first and Twenty-second General Assembly of the United Nations from 1966-1967 and as United States alternate to the Twentieth Plenary Meeting of the Economic Community of Europe in 1967.

Harris Receives Federal Appointments

In 1969 Harris, then a professor of law, was appointed dean of the Howard University School of Law, a position from which she resigned within thirty days after being appointed. Although her deanship was short because of a host of issues ranging from a student uprising and faculty disagreements to a disagreement with the president of Howard University, she was the first black woman to head a law school. She later joined the Washington, D.C., law firm of Fried, Frank, Harris, Shriver, and Kampelman, where she practiced corporate law until President Jimmy Carter appointed her as secretary of Housing and Urban Development in 1977. She served in this position for three years. In 1980, Carter appointed Harris as secretary of the Department of Health, Education and Welfare, a position in which she served until Carter was defeated in the presidential election of 1980.

In 1982 Harris ran for, but lost a bid to become the mayor of the District of Columbia. The campaign was tough and bitter. She lost the Democratic primary to Marion S. Barry, Jr., receiving only 36 percent of the vote. In 1983, twenty-three years after receiving her law degree from George Washington University, she was appointed as a full professor of law in its law school. She held this position until she died of cancer on March 23, 1985, shortly after the death of her husband.

From a very early age Harris never allowed her aspirations or personhood to be controlled by racism or sexism. After being called a nigger at age six, Harris said that she "never felt . . . that [she had] anything to prove to white people." Rather, her philosophy, one that carried her to extraordinary heights, was "to do . . . what I think I ought to be able to do" (Smith, 440).

Harris believed in education. She thought that if a child was inspired to read for pleasure, learning would follow. Books, not television, were her priority, for as she said, "It is in the world of books, the ability to read, that one finds out how similar men are from one age to another" (Smith, 441).

That blacks faced barriers of discrimination in America troubled Harris because segregation "limited . . . the experiences that they were permitted to have." She had faith that one day "racial segregation . . . in . . . American life [would become] unacceptable." Although a lawyer, Harris was "always . . . suspicious of those who believe[d] that the protector of minorities [was] in the courts" and that it took "a combination of action—the enactment of legislation and the courts—to protect the rights of minorities" in America (*Ambassador for Progress*, 7-8). She believed that social change could be influenced through corporate responsibility, a belief that she practiced as a member of the board of directors of several major corporations, including Chase Manhattan Bank, Scott Paper Company, IBM, and as a trustee of the Twentieth Century Fund.

Harris believed that blacks were obligated to speak out against injustice, for to keep silent was undemocratic. Speaking out was not limited to domestic issues. She asserted that it was the role of blacks to also communicate to "the nonwhite majorities of this world'' (''Ambassador Harris Cites Needs,'' 4).

Harris is best known for her response to Senator William Proxmire, who, during her Senate confirmation hearing in 1977 for secretary of Housing and Urban Development, questioned whether Harris was ''sympathetic to the problems of the poor.'' Harris's response made every major newspaper in the country. She said:

> You do not understand who I am. . . . I am a black woman, the daughter of a Pullman car waiter. I am a black woman who even eight years ago could not buy a house in parts of the District of Columbia. I didn't start out as a member of a prestigious law firm, but as a woman who needed a scholarship to go to school. If you think that I have forgotten that, you are wrong (Smith, 439).

Harris, who has been described as stunning, was petite and of medium height. She was opinionated and had a sharp tongue. Driven by the need to do well, once Harris found her principle, she could not be moved. Many viewed this as a admirable characteristic; others, as a flaw. Whatever people may have thought about her personality, no one can legitimately deny that her razor-sharp mind and abilities were extraordinary—characteristics that took her to the top of her profession.

Patricia Harris Expresses Her Views

Historians searching the record for the views of Harris will find them. Her interviews were informative; her speeches poignant and at times provocative and philosophical. Her views as a public official clearly demonstrate a concern for good government, racial harmony, and the elimination of racial and sex discrimination. As secretary of Housing and Urban Development, Harris's words speak for themselves. Speaking on the subject of the Federal government and the poor, Harris stated:

> In the past, the Federal Government has not adopted national policy which simultaneously addresses the weakening of older central cities' economies, the causes and negative effects of suburbanization, and the plight of central city minority groups. In many cases, it has inadvertently contributed to the problems . . . (Testimonial Speech).

On jobs for minorities and minority youth, Harris stated:

> It should not be new to you that the minority unemployment rate is consistently higher than the unemployment rate for whites, and it generally approaches a factor of two to one. For minority youths, conditions are even worse with unemployment in some areas reaching as high as 30% to 40%. . . . I am concerned that an entire generation may grow up without the opportunity to hold a decent job. We cannot allow that to happen (''Building Stronger Urban Economics'').

In a speech addressing racial discrimination in housing, Harris noted:

> If a Black person looking through newspaper advertisements for an apartment to rent or a house to purchase, were to select four apartments or brokers to visit, the probability of encountering discrimination would be 75 percent in the rental market and 62 percent in the sales market. There is clear probability that discrimination is even more prevalent, especially in view of the fact that the forms it takes have become more extensive and more sophisticated in recent years (Speech Before the National Committee Against Discrimination in Housing).

In a speech touching on her visions and the uniqueness of the American people as relates to the world, Harris stated:

> We are a unique nation and a unique people. We are more tied to all the nations and peoples of the world than any other nation in this world. That is why we are more concerned with what happens around the world than any other nation. . . . Because of this, Americans are concerned that the violence, the terrorism, the wars, the threats of war, the poverty, the ignorance, the disease—that all of these things could in time spill over to our own cities and neighborhoods, and threaten our way of life (Exporting American Ideals).

Finally, in a speech on the role of women in the future, Harris left a vision that women would assume their proper roles as leaders of America. She stated:

> I want to hear the Speaker of the House addressed as Madam Speaker and I want to listen as she introduces Madam President to the Congress assembled for the State of the Union. I want Madam President to look down from the podium at the women of the Supreme Court who will be indicative of the significant number of women judges throughout the Federal and State judicial systems (Speech before the National Women's Political Caucus Convention).

References

Ambassador for Progress: Black Americans in Government. Buckingham Learning Corp., 1969.

''Ambassador Harris Cites Needs for Racial Progress in Marketing 99th Anniversary of [Howard] University.'' *Howard University Magazine* (4 April 1966): 8.

''Black Woman Joins Three Boards.'' *Business Week* (29 May 1971): 22.

Greenfield, Meg. "The Brief Saga of Dean Harris." *Washington Post*, 23 March 1969.

Harris, Patricia Roberts. "Building Stronger Urban Economics." Speech Before Editors of Trade Union Publications, 4 May 1978.

———. "Exporting American Ideals." Speech Before the Conference Board, New York, 18 May 1978.

———. Speech Before the National Women's Political Caucus Convention, Cincinnati, Ohio, 14 June 1979.

———. Speech Before the National Committee Against Discrimination in Housing), Washington, D.C., 17 April 1978.

———. "Testimonial Speech for Honorable Henry S. Reuss, Milwaukee, Wisconsin, 13 October 1977.

"Honorable Patricia Roberts Harris." *Vogue* (May 1966): 202-203.

"Howard Says Farewell to Patricia Roberts Harris." *Capstone* 6 (April 1985): 1.

"Ladies Home Journal Woman of the Year 1974." *Ladies Home Journal* (April 1974): 83.

Murray, Pauli. *Song in a Weary Throat*. New York: Harper, 1987.

Principle Officers of Department of State and United States Chiefs of Mission. Washington, D.C.: U.S. Department of State, 1988.

"A $200 Billion Budget." *Dawn Magazine* (March 1980): 4.

Who's Who Among Black Americans, 1990-91. Detroit: Gale Research, 1991.

Other Sources

The source of much of Harris's life is in memorials written after her death. See for example, J. Clay Smith, Jr., "Patricia Roberts Harris: A Champion In Pursuit of Excellence," *Howard Law Journal* 29 (1986), p. 440, and Memorial Tributes, *George Washington Law Review* 53 (1985), p. 319. Patricia Harris was covered widely by the national press during her years in public office. Various news accounts, particulary those dealing with her short tenure as dean of the Howard University School of Law, may prove useful.

Collections

Patricia Roberts Harris left many of her private papers to the Library of Congress. Photographs of Harris are in the Moorland-Spingarn Research Center, Howard University.

J. Clay Smith, Jr.

Trudier Harris

(1948-)

Educator, folklorist

Trudier Harris, J. Carlyle Sitterson Professor of English and African-American Literature and chairperson of the African-American studies curriculum, University of North Carolina at Chapel Hill, is one of a growing number of leading African-American literature and folklore scholars today.

Born in Mantua, Alabama, on February 27, 1948, she is the sixth of nine children born to Terrell Harris and Unareed (Burton) Harris. In a distinguished career consisting of a long list of publications, teaching awards, and honors, Harris has contributed to the increased volume and availability of scholarship in the African-American literature and folklore canon in recent years and has aided in the profound growth and expansion these fields have undergone in colleges and universities.

Joseph Flora, University of North Carolina professor of English and department chairperson (1980-1991), says that the [endowed] J. Carlyle Sitterson Chair that Harris holds "is evidence that the University has recognized and values the place she has earned." Flora also recognizes Harris as "a leader in the field who helped set the canon for African-American Literature" (Interview with Joseph Flora, 28 June 1990).

Doctoral students like Keith Clark, who have studied under Trudier Harris, affirm an essential role that she plays in shaping and influencing students' academic careers. Harris's presence as a faculty member at the University of North Carolina, Chapel Hill, was a major factor in Clark's choosing to study American and African-American literature at the university. Clark, who has conducted extensive research on James Baldwin, says that Harris has provided a "fresh and provocative analysis," particularly of Baldwin's female characters (Interview with Keith Clark, 14 November 1990). In a review of Harris's *Women in the Fiction of James Baldwin* (University of Tennessee Press, 1985), Nellie McKay writes the following:

> Harris breaks new ground with this book. Cross-gender representations have been a problem for black writers and critics for some time, but no one before has systematically examined a writer's body of work to explore the topic. . . . The book is thorough and useful, and sets a model for further cross-gender explorations of black writers (*Signs*, 344).

In addition to *Women in the Fiction of James Baldwin*, Trudier Harris is the author of *Fiction and Folklore: The Novels of Toni Morrison, Exorcising Blackness: Historical and Literary Lynching and Burning Rituals* (Indiana University Press, 1984), and *From Mammies to Militants: Domestics in Black American Literature* (Philadelphia: Temple University Press, 1982). Harris has books in progress that include *Reflections on the Color Purple* and *Moms Mabley and American Humor*.

She is also the editor or coeditor of six books in the critically-acclaimed *Dictionary of Literary Biography* series, a colossal biographical study of leading African-American writers and a source study for scholars. The series that Harris coedited with Thadious Davis include *Afro-American Fiction Writers After 1955* (1984), *Afro-American Writers After 1955: Dramatists and Prose Writers* (1985), and *Afro-American Poets After 1955* (1985), all published by Gale Research Company in Detroit. Harris is the sole editor of the final three books in the series: *Afro-American Writers Before the Harlem Renaissance* (1986), *Afro-American Writers from the Harlem Renaissance to 1940* (1987), and *Afro-American Writers from 1940 to 1955* (1988). She is contributing writer for eleven additional books. Her more than twenty-five articles and book reviews span some fifteen years of publication.

In addition to her scholarship in English, African-American literature, and folklore, Harris is an award-winning professor in the teaching arena. She is particularly noted for her outstanding work in UNITAS, a cultural exchange program involving undergraduates in an environment that allows for direct instructor-to-student involvement. She has taught a UNITAS living/learning course with American and international students. And in 1988, she won the Roscoe B. Tanner Award for Excellence in Undergraduate Teaching.

As a child, Harris attended elementary school at the Thirty-second Avenue Elementary School, and she graduated from Druid High School in Tuscaloosa, Alabama, in 1966. At Stillman College in Tuscaloosa, she earned a bachelor of arts degree, graduating magna cum laude, in 1969. Harris then attended Ohio State University, where she completed an M.A. in English in 1972 and a Ph.D. in American literature and folklore in 1973.

Her dissertation, "The Tie That Binds: The Function of Folklore in the Fiction of Charles Waddell Chesnutt, Jean Toomer and Ralph Ellison," under the direction of Patrick B. Mullen, stands among a growing body of materials that has helped to enlarge the folkore canon as currently taught in numerous colleges and universities. Today, in addition to her recognition as a leading African-Americanist, Harris is recognized as one of the country's foremost folklore scholars. In 1989, she was the Woodrow Wilson Scholar-in-Residence at Spelman College in Atlanta, where she met with student and faculty groups, taught five classes, and gave a public lecture, "Beyond Broomsticks and Black Cats: The Conjuring Tradition in the Works of Contemporary Black Women Writers." At a December 1988 meeting of the Modern Language Association in New Orleans, she presented two papers, "Margaret Walker's and Eudora Welty's Differing Visions of the South" and "Folklore in Contemporary Afro-American Literature."

Prior to coming to work at the University of North Carolina, Chapel Hill, Harris worked as an assistant professor of English at the College of William and Mary in Williamsburg, Virginia, where she was honored with a Thomas Jefferson Teaching Award (1978), an Alumni Fellowship Award (1978), and a Summer Research Grant (1979). She also taught in the Poznan, Poland, School of English in the summers of 1981 and 1983 as a visiting professor. In addition, she was a visiting distinguished professor at Ohio State University in Columbus in the fall of 1988 and William Grant Cooper Visiting Distinguished Professor of English at the University of Arkansas in Little Rock in the spring of 1987.

She has received a host of grants and fellowships that include the National Endowment for the Humanities (in residence at Brown University) and a National Research Council Ford Foundation Fellowship. She was appointed Carnegie Faculty Fellow to the Mary Ingraham Bunting Institute at Radcliffe/Harvard University in 1981-1983, and was appointed research associate to the W. E. B. Du Bois Institute for Afro-American Research at Harvard University in 1982-1983.

An indefatigable researcher, Harris continues to widen her scholarly base, adopting bigger and more expansive projects. She cites becoming editor for the African-American section of the *Oxford Companion to Women's Writing in the United States* in the spring of 1990 among her most recent major activities. In addition, in 1989-1990, she was a fellow at the Stanford Center for Advanced Study in the Behavioral Sciences. Rather than spend a summer of relaxation following her work at Stanford, she toured Kenya on a fact-finding study mission with a group of educators. New challenges await Trudier Harris as she embarks on her newest career addition; chairing the African-American studies curriculum at the University of North Carolina, Chapel Hill, while remaining a J. Carlyle Sitterson Professor of English, an African-American Literature scholar, and a folklore specialist.

References

Clark, Keith. Interview with the author, 14 November 1990.

Flora, Joseph. Interview with the author, 28 June 1990.

McKay, Nellie. "Review of *Women in the Fiction of James Baldwin*." *Signs* 13 (Winter 1988): 344.

Helena Woodard

Hazel Harrison

(1883-1969)

Musician, educator

Known as "the dean of native pianists," Hazel Lucile Harrison's fifty-year career as a concert pianist brought her international recognition, though she was not well-known by white audiences in the United States, where her race barred her from acceptance on the major concert stages.

Born in La Porte, Indiana, on May 12, 1883, Harrison was the only child of Hiram Harrison and Olive (Wood) Harrison. Her father worked as a barber, eventually owning his own shop in downtown La Porte, while her mother operated a small beauty parlor in the family home on Clay Street. Hiram Harrison had a fine tenor voice and was a frequent soloist at the First Presbyterian Church, where he also played the piano for Sunday school. Harrison's musical gifts became apparent at an early age, and music lessons began when she was about five and had to be lifted onto the stool. Her first teacher was Richard Pellow, an Englishman who taught music in the La Porte schools and who served as organist for the First Presbyterian Church. He would tell her, "I will give you a penny for every perfect lesson that you have." "And I would always have them perfect," she recalled many years later (Cazort, 5).

By the time she was twelve Harrison had already acquired a significant local reputation and appeared often on musical programs. In addition, she was sought after to provide dance music for social occasions, which often lasted until two o'clock in the morning. She might easily have become a dance-hall pianist had it not been for her mother's determination that she pursue a serious music career. When she was in high school, she began study with Victor Heinze of Chicago, well-known pianist and teacher. It was Heinze who recognized her talent and nurtured her artistic development. While in her senior year in high school, Harrison played for dancing lessons given in La Porte by a Chicago dancing master and in the spring gave a recital at Studebaker Hall in Chicago. After graduation she became a full-time piano teacher in La Porte, attracting many pupils. At the same time she continued her studies with Heinze and maintained an arduous practice schedule.

Harrison Tours Germany

In Harrison's day, a European appearance was obligatory for any American musician aspiring to a concert career. Thus it was that Victor Heinze arranged a German tour for her in the fall of 1904 that would be climaxed by an appearance in Berlin with the Berlin Philharmonic Orchestra. On this occasion, on October 22 at Berlin's Singakademie, with the orchestra under the direction of August Scharrer, she played the Grieg A-minor and Chopin E-minor concertos. The reviews were complimentary, and for the most part, concerned themselves with her musicianship. They spoke of Harrison's "great talent and excellent technique," of her musical intelligence, her "unusually nice cantabile," and of the great promise for her future. However, a black performer of classical music in 1904 Berlin was an oddity. One reviewer noted, "Taken all in all, the little mulatto amounted to something of a sensation"; another said, "Is it the Caucasian blood in her veins that is doing the work, for she is not a full-blooded negress?" (Cazort, 20).

Returning to La Porte in 1905, Harrison continued her previous schedule of teaching and practicing and commuting to Chicago for lessons. She was attracting increasing critical notice. After a recital at Music Hall in Chicago in 1910, the reviewer for the *Chicago Tribune* wrote that she had "gifts and talents which make unquestionable her more than usual aptitude for the career of concert pianist. . . . Miss Harrison is studying under the most difficult and trying conditions. . . . It would certainly seem that a young woman so undeniably gifted as this one has proven to be should find the support and help of music lovers who have money to spare" (Cazort, 24). An anonymous cash gift from two Chicago women enabled her to make serious plans to return to Germany. By late 1911 she was booked by the Hermann Wolff concert agency for a series of recitals in Germany, opening in Berlin. Before leaving La Porte, she gave a farewell recital for the townspeople, in anticipation of which the merchants closed their shops early so that all could attend.

Towering over the Berlin musical scene at this time was Ferruccio Busoni, the great pianist and composer, who, upon hearing Harrison play, offered to direct her studies, even though he had previously decided to take no more pupils. This association with Busoni was the most significant of her musical development. She became a regular visitor in the Busoni household, where she came to know many of the leading musicians of the day. Accompanied by her mother, she remained in Germany as a pupil of Busoni, and later of his assistant, Egon Petri, until the outbreak of the war in 1914.

Returning home, Harrison was hailed in the black press as the "premiere pianiste of the colored race" and the "world's greatest pianist." She entered a U.S. musical scene that was rich with now-legendary performers and began her own concert career, with Chicago as her home base. For the remainder of the decade, and throughout the twenties and into the thirties, Harrison was a full-time concert pianist, covering much of the country in the course of her spring and fall recital tours. Her name was widely known, and she was the unrivaled pianist of the day for the nation's black classical music lovers. She emerged in the press as being in the front rank of American artists. After a recital in Chicago's Kimball Hall, one critic wrote that "she is the last word in musical artistry and belongs in the ranks of premiere virtuosos of today''; another said, ''Hazel Harrison is in a class by herself, and that a class at the head of all the others.''

In 1926 Harrison returned to Germany for a year's study with Egon Petri. The decade closed with Harrison being honored by the University of Chicago for leadership in the field of music. Her 1930-1931 concert season opened with a Town Hall recital, followed by one at Boston's Jordan Hall. At the season's end she received a scholarship for study with Percy Grainger.

In 1931 Harrison began a long career of teaching, first at Tuskegee Institute from 1931 to 1936, then at Howard University from 1936 to 1955, and finally at Alabama State College from 1958 to 1963. She continued to give recitals and to go on tour. At Tuskegee in 1932 she performed with the touring Minneapolis Symphony Orchestra under Eugene Ormandy. Later, on a three-year leave from Howard University, she made a concert tour of the United States, climaxed by an appearance with the Hollywood Bowl Symphony Orchestra, in conjunction with the annual meeting of the National Association of Negro Musicians. During her long tenure at Howard, she gave many Washington recitals and enjoyed a large local following. Now known as ''the dean of native pianists'' because she had been longer before the public than any of her compatriots, she made a final Washington appearance in 1954 at the National Gallery of Art.

Although her concert tours were fully booked and there were occasional concerts in major halls, Harrison performed for the most part in black churches, high school gymnasia, and on black college campuses. The pattern of segregated audiences and management systems rarely yielded to include her. Access to the mainstream of concert business—performances with symphony orchestras and recording contracts—was denied her because of her race. Harrison's appearances as a soloist with major orchestras took place under special circumstances and before special audiences. Her hopes to secure concert management with Sol Hurok were dashed when, after an audition with him, he told her, ''You play like the masters and there is none other out there that plays any better. But the public is not ready to accept a Negro pianist. You are ahead of your time'' (Cazort, 118).

After retiring from Howard University in 1955, Harrison lived for three years in New York City, where she maintained a studio and coached pupils for public performance. In 1958 she moved to Montgomery to begin teaching at Alabama State College. Her last major appearance was in 1959, when she was seventy-five years old, before a large audience in the campus auditorium. It was a memorable and moving occasion. Her career had now spanned fifty years. In 1963, at age eighty, she retired again, remaining in Montgomery and teaching privately. After a few years she moved to La Grange, Georgia, to live with relatives, and finally back to Washington, where she died on April 28, 1969, after a brief illness. Her funeral was held in Rankin Chapel on the Howard University campus, and she was buried on a hillside at Lincoln Memorial Cemetery, holding music in her hands.

Harrison was married twice: in 1918 to Walter Anderson, ending in divorce in 1929, and in the 1950s, for a short time, to Alan Moton, also ending in divorce.

References

Cazort, Jean E., and Constance Tibbs Hobson. *Born to Play: the Life and Career of Hazel Harrison.* Westport, Conn.: Greenwood Press, 1983.

Chicago Defender, 1910-1930.

La Porte Daily Herald, 1895-1912.

La Porte Herald-Argus, 26 June 1925; 1 April 1938.

Love, Josephine Harreld, ''Hazel Lucile Harrison.'' *Notable American Women, The Modern Period.* Cambridge, Mass.: Harvard University Press, 1980.

Musical Courier, 1904, 1926.

New York Age, 1910-1930.

Tuskegee Messenger, 1920-1936.

Collections

The Hazel Harrison Collection at the Moorland-Spingarn Research Center at Howard University contains photographs, letters, and taped interviews with pupils, colleagues, and friends.

Jean Elder Cazort

Vivian Harsh

(1890-1960)

Librarian

For twenty-six years Vivian Gordon Harsh, the first black American to head a branch library in the Chicago Public Library System, enriched the cultural life of the black community in Chicago by initiating many projects and public forums.

The George Cleveland Hall Branch Library was devised in the late 1920s by philanthropist Julius Rosenwald, who had constructed an apartment complex at Forty-seventh and Michigan avenues on Chicago's South Side for middle-class blacks. One of his advisors, George Cleveland Hall, who was chief of staff at Provident Hospital and a member of the Chicago Public Library Board of Directors, suggested to Rosenwald that he build a cultural center for the residents near the new complex. Rosenwald agreed to contribute land that he owned for a library if Hall would convince the board of directors of the Chicago Public Library System to erect a branch library. Hall was successful in persuading the board to build a library on the site. Construction began on the new branch library in early 1929. Unfortunately, Hall died before it was completed. The board of directors decided to name it in Hall's honor.

On January 16, 1932, when the George Cleveland Hall Branch Library was opened, Harsh was at its helm. She was ably assisted by Charlemae Hill Rollins, who would become a world-renowned children's librarian and author, and Marian Hadley, a specialist in black history. Finally, a branch library had been built in a black neighborhood for Chicago's black citizens.

Vivian Gordon Harsh was born in Chicago at Forty-fourth Place on the city's South Side on May 27, 1890. She was the older of two children in the family of Fenton G. Harsh, one of Chicago's pioneer families. Her mother was one of the earliest graduates of Fisk University. Fenton Harsh, Jr., her brother, became a successful Chicago realtor. A graduate of Chicago's Wendell Phillips High School, Harsh attended Simmons College, Columbia University, and the Graduate Library School of the University of Chicago.

Black Collection Built for Chicago

In 1934 Harsh, already director of the Hall library, received a Julius Rosenwald grant to travel to the major bookselling centers in the United States to purchase books by and about blacks. Among the cities visited were Boston, New York, Washington, D. C., Cleveland, Baltimore, Detroit, Nashville, and Atlanta. When she returned to Chicago, she housed the fruits of her trip in one wing of the branch and named the new collection the Special Negro Collection. Some of the first-edition works acquired were *Souls of Black Folk* by W. E. B. Du Bois, *History of the Negro Race in America, 1619-1880* by George Washington Williams, *Poems on Various Subjects, Religious and Moral* by Phillis Wheatley, and *Clotel; or, The President's Daughter* by William Wells Brown.

One of the most popular projects that Harsh started was the Public Forums. Outstanding black personalities visiting Chicago were invited to speak at the programs. They were always well-publicized and consequently well-attended. Among some of the speakers were Horace Cayton, Charles S. Johnson, Zora Neale Hurston, Claude McKay, Arthur S. Schomburg, and Carter G. Woodson.

Harsh established and developed lifelong friendships with many of the country's black writers. One of these writers was Richard Wright, who was a frequent visitor to the branch during his years in Chicago. It is reputed that Harsh introduced him to the works of Gertrude Stein. When Wright published *Native Son* in 1940, he gave the library an autographed copy of the work. A photograph of Wright presenting the copy to Harsh is on display in the collection. Langston Hughes always visited the library when he was in Chicago. He frequently presented poetry readings to standing-room crowds in the library. Both Wright and Hughes gave original manuscripts to the library. In the early 1940s Wright gave Harsh a short novella entitled "Big Boy Leave Home," which was published in *Uncle Tom's Children*. Hughes contributed four revisions of the typescript of *The Big Sea*.

The Great Books Program was another project initiated by Vivian Harsh at the library. Many of the community's black intellectuals, as well as average library patrons, attended these programs, which lasted for more than twenty years.

Harsh retired in 1958 and an era in Chicago's library history ended. She died on August 17, 1960, and was mourned by the library and the black community. In 1967 the curator of the Special Negro Collection suggested to Alex Ladenson, the commissioner of the Chicago Public Library, that the collection should be renamed the Vivian G. Harsh Collection of African-American History and Literature. The Board of Directors subsequently approved the new name for the collection that is housed in new quarters in the Carter G. Woodson Regional Library Center.

References

Joyce, Donald Franklin, "Research Notes, Resources for Scholars: Four Major Collection of Afro-Americana, Part 1: Two Public Library Collections, Vivian G. Harsh Collection of Afro-American History and Literature, Chicago Public Library." *Library Quarterly* 58 (January 1988): 70.

Encyclopedia of Black America. Edited by W. Augustus Low and Virgil A. Clift. New York: McGraw-Hill Book Co., 1981.

Slaughter, Adolph J., "The Vivian Harsh Story: Historian Who Never Wrote," *Chicago Daily Defender*, 29 August 1960.

The Wabash Avenue YMCA Pamphlet. Chicago, n.d. Contains obituary and photograph of Harsh.

Donald Franklin Joyce

Della Irving Hayden

(1851-1924)

Educator, school founder, community worker

Della Irving Hayden, an outstanding educator and community worker and founder of the Franklin Normal and Industrial Institute, was born in Tarboro, North Carolina, in 1851. She spent her first years in the care of her grandmother while her mother worked in Virginia. In 1865 she was reunited with her mother, Charlotte Irving, in Virginia.

After being taught some rudiments of spelling by a white friend, Hayden's thirst for education was persistent. Finding no free schools in her home county, Hayden's mother arranged for her to start in a school under the control of the Freedman's Bureau in Nansemond County, Virginia. Later they moved to Franklin, Virginia, and she attended public school there. In 1872 she entered Hampton Normal and Agricultural Institute. She graduated with high honors in 1877 and returned to her hometown of Franklin, where she became principal of a public school. While pioneering as a female school administrator, she also became a general leader and advisor for the community.

As a member of Cool Springs Baptist Church of Franklin, Hayden organized many Sunday school classes and societies. The pattern of community service started here was reflected throughout her life. She organized a large temperance society among the students and the State Teachers' Temperance Union. She also organized several Bible boards and a Young Women's Christian Association (YWCA).

In 1880 she married Lindsey Hayden, a gentleman whom she had met at Hampton. Sadly, he lived only five months after they married.

Hayden became lady principal of the Virginia Normal and Collegiate Institute in 1890. In 1904 she opened the Franklin Normal and Industrial Institute in Franklin. The school accommodated about forty boarding students, one hundred day students, and a thriving kindergarten. Hayden's work was assisted by support from a Mrs. Marriage Allen of London, England, a missionary.

Greatly admired for her generosity in assisting students financially with her own meager funds, Hayden was also loved for the message of self-help that she spread through the church, community, and school. She taught that the spirit of self-help was the root of all genuine growth in an individual. This attitude was reflected in Hayden's own words published in a 1938 article titled "A Graduate's Reminiscences" in the *Southern Workman:*

> Most of the money that I have used to run the school has been given by my own race. It has been taken up at Sunday Schools, churches, and conferences, and has come in small quantities. I have been trying to teach my people to help themselves.

Because of her love for people and her leadership over the years, many children called her "Mama Hayden."

In 1924, Hayden was described in the Suffolk *Daily Press* as "perhaps the best known woman educator of the Colored race in Virginia, having taught consistently for about 50 years." Her eminence as an educator grew from her diligent instruction for twelve years in Southampton County, thirteen years as lady principal of Virginia Normal and Industrial Institute at Petersburg (now Virginia State University), twenty-one years as leader at the Franklin Normal and Industrial Institute, which she founded, and four years at various other places.

Hayden's devotion to her race and her work is reflected in letters that she wrote to Hampton Institute for their alumni reports. Hampton's *Southern Workman* published some of these reports:

> My experiences of thirty-three years in the schoolroom have not always been smooth sailing, I cannot save the whole race, but every boy and girl that I can train in the right way will make the race stronger and the state better. It has been my privilege to urge thousands of my people to buy land, build homes, educate themselves, and become good citizens. Many have taken my advice and houses are being built in all parts of the country (690).

Hayden died from injuries sustained in an automobile accident on December 10, 1924, in Suffolk, Virginia.

References

Contributions of Black Women to America. Vol. 2. Edited by Marianna W. Davis. Columbia, S.C.: Kenday Press, 1982.

Daily Press (Suffolk), 14 December 1924.

Hayden, Della Irving. "A Graduate Reminiscences." *Southern Workman* 67 (March 1938): 89-96.

———. "My Life Work." *Southern Workman* 38 (December 1909): 688-91.

Majors, M. A. *Noted Negro Women*. Chicago: Donohue and Henneberry, 1893. Includes line engraving of Hayden.

Scruggs, L.A. *Women of Distinction: Remarkable in Works and Invincible in Character*. Raleigh, N.C.: Privately printed 1892.

Collections

Information on Della Irving Hayden is located in the University Archives, Hampton University, and provided the basis for much of the Hayden biography.

Elaine P. Witty

Elizabeth Ross Haynes

(1883-1953)

Sociologist, social worker, organization official, author

Elizabeth Ross Haynes, a pioneer social worker, sociologist, author, first black national secretary of the national YWCA, and a builder of the national YWCA movement, was born on July 30, 1883 in Lowndes County, Alabama, the daughter of former slaves Henry Ross and Mary (Carnes) Ross. She studied at State Normal School (now Alabama State University) from 1896 to 1900 and graduated as valedictorian of her class. From there she studied at Fisk University in Nashville, Tennessee, where in 1903 she received the A.B. degree. She taught school in Alabama and Missouri, and spent each summer from 1905 through 1907 in the graduate school of the University of Chicago. The 1922-1923 school year was spent in study at Columbia University, where in 1923 she received the A.M. degree in sociology.

Elizabeth Ross married George Edmund Haynes on December 14, 1910. A sociologist and later a founder and executive director of the National Urban League, George Edmund Haynes was born on May 11, 1880, in Pine Bluff, Arkansas, and was a student at Fisk from 1899 to 1903, when he graduated with the A.B. degree. He and Elizabeth Ross certainly knew each other at Fisk, since their Fisk years overlapped. He received an M.A. from Yale University in 1904 and a Ph.D. degree from Columbia University in 1912. He spent the summers of 1906 and 1907 in study at the University of Chicago, overlapping Elizabeth Ross's years there. He did additional study at the New York School of Social Work (1908-1909). After marriage, he was professor of social science at Fisk University from 1910 to 1920. On July 17, 1912, the Haynes's son, George Edmund, Jr., was born. George, Sr., was granted a leave-of-absence from Fisk to serve as special assistant to the Secretary of Labor, where he held the title Director of Negro Economics, United States Department of Labor, Washington, D.C., from 1918 to 1921.

Elizabeth Ross Haynes

Elizabeth Ross Haynes taught high school in Galveston, Texas, for two years. Prior to her marriage, the YWCA had appointed Elizabeth Ross Haynes as its first black national secretary, giving her responsibility for activities largely among the colleges as well as supervisory responsibility in cities where black YWCAs were established. She traveled over the major portions of the country organizing and directing the work of the association. After marriage, while George Haynes was teaching at Fisk, Elizabeth Haynes was a volunteer worker for the YWCA and remained active in this position until about 1925. While her husband worked for the Department of Labor during World War I, she was in Washington and served as a volunteer for the Women's Bureau of the United States Department of Labor. From 1920 to 1922 she served the United States Employment Service as domestic service secretary.

Elizabeth Ross Haynes was keenly interested in the plight of black women. After World War I considerable attention was given to women in the work force. But black women were the ones who ensured that the attention extend to their black sisters. For example, black women petitioned the First International Congress of Working Women at its meeting in Washington, D.C., in 1919, to offer programs that were more relevant to black women. According to Giddings, "The program of the congress included equal pay for equal work, inclusions in areas reserved for men, a forty-four-hour week, social insurance, maternity benefits, and job training. But black women, not to mention their special needs, were excluded." A message signed by "Representative Negro Women of the United States in behalf of Negro Women Laborers of the United States" was presented to the international congress. Mary Church Terrell, Nannie Helen Burroughs, Elizabeth C. Carter, and Elizabeth Ross Haynes were among those who signed the petition (Giddings, 154). When the Council for Interracial Cooperation (CIC), organized in Atlanta in 1920, it was to be the vehicle for interracial cooperation.

But there were reformers within the organization itself who found a need to create a splinter group. In October 1920, ninety-one women from Protestant denominations, women's clubs, and the YWCA met in Memphis, Tennessee, to explore issues not yet addressed by the larger body. The black delegates on the program were Margaret Murray

Washington, Charlotte Hawkins Brown, and Elizabeth Ross Haynes. Washington spoke on social achievements of rural Southern blacks, the work of Tuskegee Institute to enhance organized family life, and, to the distress of the other black speakers, Southern black women's debts to white women. Brown bitterly attacked this latter view of Washington, and raised a number of critical issues, particularly the failure to address black women as "Mrs." Haynes gave a low-keyed, analytical, and dramatic address that focused on life in a segregated society (Giddings, 171-74).

Employment Problems of Black Women Addressed

In 1922, while Haynes was with the Women's Bureau, she published "Two Million Negro Women at Work," which is often quoted in reference to black women and employment. She reported that the three types of occupations in which most black women were engaged at the time were domestic and personal service, agriculture, and manufacturing and mechanical industries. Their saddened plight was described further:

> To-day they are found in domestic service, nearly a million strong, with all their shortcomings—their lack of training in efficiency, in cleanliness of person, in honesty and truthfulness, and with all of the shortcomings of ordinary domestic service; namely basement living quarters, poor working conditions, too long hours, no Sundays off, no standards of efficiency, and the servant "brand" (Ross, 64).

Haynes found that white women were displacing black women in domestic and personal service, and, at the same time, wages for black women were falling. Most of the laundries in Washington, D.C., paid below minimum wage. Bonds between the mistress and the maid were weak, with no personal interest in the thoughts and problems of the other shown on either side. In fact, they generally disliked each other. Through direct contact with the workers, Haynes reported pathos, restlessness, ignorance, inefficiency, and an absolute need to standardize domestic service as an occupation or industry and to establish domestic-training schools as a part of public employment agencies. In agriculture she found rural black women traveling four and five-mile distances to work in hot fields, often staying late to work in the cool evenings. The only recreation or social contacts that many women had were the monthly church meeting, funerals, or annual trips to town at cotton-seed time. Haynes found women in manufacturing poorly paid, their wages ranging from six to ten dollars for a sixty-hour work week. Work conditions were deplorable. She reported that "the work is dirty, and most of the factories are poorly ventilated . . . the result is that the tobacco fumes and dust almost suffocate new workers" (68). Women were employed in other factories; for example, in Virginia and Maryland there were from five to eight thousand black women workers. But the employment situation was difficult for black women, especially those who sought even a day's work through agencies or friends and who were willing to clean, wash, sell goods, or do other jobs to earn a living. Again, because they were inefficient and untrained in simple tasks, they were restricted in opportunity.

In 1924 Elizabeth Ross Haynes was elected to membership on the national board of the YWCA and she remained on the board until 1934. Through her board membership and earlier work as national secretary, she helped build the national YWCA movement. She was the first black woman to hold this position. At the time of her election the YWCA was highly segregated and black women would not be integrated fully into association life and activities until 1946. White women had run the organization, set policies governing the black branches, determined whether or not a branch could be established, prevented black national secretaries from working in the south, and in general suppressed the opportunity for black leadership in the organization to flourish. In the fight to end the racist practices then were Lugenia Burns Hope, Lucy C. Laney, Mary Jackson McCrorey, Eva del Vakia Bowles, and Charlotte Hawkins Brown.

George and Elizabeth Haynes moved to New York City when George Haynes changed employment. Their employment and civic interests were similar. While he was secretary of the Commission on Race Relations, Federated Council of the Churches of Christ in America, she was active in interracial work for the council for a number of years. She also held membership on the New York Planning Commission and the Harlem Better Schools Committee. She also had a keen interest in the work of the black women's club movement, particularly the social service activities that related to her education and experience. She was chair of the Industry and Housing Department of the National Association of Colored Women. In 1935 she was elected coleader of the Twenty-first Assembly District, New York County. Her election crossed party and racial boundaries, and her work was ninety percent or more economic, social, and educational. In this administrative post she dealt with problems of unemployment, assistance to the elderly, soldiers' and widows' pensions, delinquency, zoning, and legislation, among other issues. She was also superintendent of the Junior Department of Abysinnian Baptist Church School in New York as well as secretary of the board of managers of the Adam Clayton Powell Home for the Aged.

Haynes published two important black biographical works. One of these, *Unsung Heroes* (New York: Du Bois and Dill, 1921), gives the life story of several celebrated blacks, including Sojourner Truth, Harriet Tubman, and Phillis Wheatley. The other, *The Black Boy of Atlanta* (Boston: House of Edinboro, 1952), is a study of Major R. R. Wright, the famous black educator and banker. Her master's thesis, "Negroes in Domestic Service in the United States," was published in the *Journal of Negro History*, 8 (October 1923), 384-442.

Elizabeth Ross Haynes was a member of the Alpha Kappa Alpha Sorority, a Republican, and a Baptist. She died in New York Medical Center on October 26, 1953, at age seventy.

Her funeral was held on Thursday, October 29 at 1:00 P.M. in Abyssinian Baptist Church.

References

Bogin, Ruth. "Elizabeth Ross Haynes." *Notable American Women: The Modern Period.* Cambridge: Harvard University Press, 1980. 324-25.

Fisk News (May 1923): 23.

Giddings, Paula. *When and Where I Enter.* New York: New York: Morrow, 1984. 145-46, 154, 158n, 173-74.

"Green Cross to Celebrate Anniversary." *Newark Herald,* 15 May 1937. Includes photograph.

Haynes, Elizabeth Ross. "Two Million Negro Women at Work." *Southern Workman* 51 (February 1922): 64-72.

Jet 23 (1 November 1962): 11. Includes photograph.

Lerner, Gerda, ed. *Black Women in White America.* New York: Pantheon Books, 1972. 255-60.

New York Amsterdam News 21 August 1937. Includes photograph.

Obituary. *Daily News* 27 October 1953; *Daily Worker* 27 October 1953; *New York Age* 31 October 1953, 1; *New York Amsterdam News* 31 October 1953, 2; *New York Times* 27 October 1953.

Richardson, Joe M. *A History of Fisk University, 1865-1946.* University, Ala.: University of Alabama Press, 1980. 174.

"Statement of the Career of Mrs. Elizabeth Ross Haynes." Typewritten document, n.d. Schomburg Center for Research in Black Culture.

Who's Who in Colored America. 2nd ed. New York: Who's Who in Colored America Corp., 1929. 173-75. Photograph, p. 175.

Collections

A biography file on Elizabeth Ross Haynes is in the Schomburg Center for Research in Black Culture, New York, and the Moorland-Spingarn Research Center, Howard University. A small collection of papers Elizabeth Ross Haynes's papers, including an unfinished novel, are in the James Weldon Johnson Memorial Collection, Yale University, and in the archives of the National Board of the YWCA, New York City.

Jessie Carney Smith

Eliza Healy (Sister Mary Magdalene)

(1846-1919)

Educator, religious leader

Eliza Healy, born December 23, 1846, in Macon, Jones County, Georgia, was a nun, teacher, and convent superior. Her parents were Michael Morris Healy, an Irish plantation owner, and Mary Eliza Clark (Healy), his mulatto slave concubine and wife, either common-law or legal. Her parents, siblings, and family life had a direct bearing on her choice of vocation and her achievements as a nun and administrator.

Michael Healy, a soldier who deserted his post while serving in Nova Scotia, during the War of 1812, eventually arrived in Jones County, Georgia, in 1818. After acquiring approximately 1,300 acres in the Georgia land lotteries, he developed his acreage into a plantation with the help of the forty slaves he subsequently purchased to work the land. Michael Healy also purchased from Sam Griswold of Clinton a sixteen-year-old mulatto named Mary Eliza Clark. Griswold was also the owner of her sister Nancy, whose freedom Healy's future children would purchase. Healy made Eliza Clark his common-law wife. To circumvent the Georgia laws against miscegenation, he took her abroad for a marriage ceremony. The sacrament of marriage was important because any taint of illegitimacy would jeopardize the future priesthood of the sons she was to bear. A marriage between Michael Healy and Eliza Clark was not recognized in Georgia because under Georgia law she was a slave, and any offspring produced by Eliza Clark Healy would be slaves. Through a special act of the Macon, Georgia, legislature, she could be emancipated, which would make her future children free citizens, but such an act was very unlikely.

She bore Michael Healy ten children, technically all slaves. They were James Augustine, Hugh, Alexander Sherwood, Patrick, Michael, Eugene, Martha, Eliza, Amanda Josephine, and one unamed. These children demonstrated their precociousness in no small way, as five of them became pillars in the Catholic church and one distinguished himself in the United States Navy. Michael Healy loved his children and did everything in his power to protect them from the bondage inherent in a slave society.

Apparently the Healy family lived together. There is no evidence of Michael Healy having shared his life with a white woman. He and Eliza Clark Healy, an intelligent woman, taught their children to read and write at home; thus, they ignored the laws that mandated that slaves were to be kept ignorant. Michael Healy decided to get his children out of Georgia and sent them to the North to be educated.

James was the first to go, followed by his two brothers and later Martha. Michael Healy, an Irish Catholic, confided his family problem to Bishop Fitzgerald of Boston on one of his trips North. Bishop Fitzgerald was instrumental in finding schools, surrogate parents, and homes for the children. He made the Healy sons his personal protégés. The Healy children never lacked friends in high places of the Roman Catholic church; respect for them reached all the way to the papal throne. Needless to say, their superior intellect was a primary factor in the considerations extended to them.

Michael Healy could not risk having his children come home during summer vacations; therefore, he hoped to sell his plantation and relocate North to be near his children. However, death claimed him and Eliza Clark Healy before he could bring his plans to fruition. Eliza Clark Healy died in May 1850 and Michael Healy soon after in August 1850. Their deaths made Eliza Healy an orphan at the age of three.

After the death of her parents, Healy and her remaining siblings were brought to New York and baptized at Saint Francis Xavier Church on June 13, 1851. Their brother Hugh, now assuming responsibility for the younger children, enrolled Healy and Amanda Josephine in Notre Dame, a boarding school in Saint Johns, Quebec, where Martha was a novice. The sisters of Notre Dame were now responsible for their care. Healy graduated from Villa Maria, Montreal, under Sister Nativity in 1860. At Villa Maria she met Elmira Drummond, who became her close friend. Healy and Amanda Josephine returned to Boston to the home of Mr. and Mrs. Thomas Hodges on East Springfield Street; the Hodges had been their foster parents. Healy completed her studies in Boston under the guardianship of Monsignor Williams, a close friend of Father James Healy, who purchased a home for the family in West Newton. Martha left the convent in 1864 to rejoin the family. Healy lived in the family home twelve years before entering the novitiate.

Four other Healy children distinguished themselves as black American Catholics. James Augustine Healy, D.D., the oldest, became the first black priest and bishop of Portland, Maine. Another brother, Alexander Sherwood Healy, D.D., J.C.D., became rector of the largest cathedral in Boston, and a third brother, Patrick Francis Healy, S.J., Ph.D., became the first black Jesuit and the second founder and president of Georgetown University in Washington, D. C. Amanda Josephine Healy became a nun.

Healy, James, Amanda Josephine, and Mrs. Hodges toured Europe and Asia Minor in January 1868. In 1874 Healy entered the novitiate of the Congregation of Notre Dame in Montreal to prepare for a career as a nun and teacher. She was twenty-eight years old. She took the basic vows of poverty, chastity, and obedience on July 19, 1876, and the vows of stability on August 30, 1882. She took her vows again in 1893 to replace the forms that had been burned in a fire. Her brother, Monsignor James, delivered in French the message at the original taking of her vows, which was the eve of the feast of Saint Mary Magdalene. She chose that name as her own. Healy became a practitioner of personal poverty, often repairing her clothes to the last thread. Many times she was heard to say, "Now I am doing this in a spirit of expiation and poverty" (Archives, n.p.).

Following the profession of her final vows, Healy was to be "employed for teaching children or for such other works, duties and functions that her superiors require of her" (Archives, S46J). In 1876 she was assigned to Saint Patrice School in Montreal as a teacher. In 1877 she was in the novitiate. In 1878-1881 she was assigned to Brockville. In 1881-1886 she was sent to Sherbrooke in Quebec. In 1886-1888 she was assigned to Saint Antoine Academy. In 1888-1890 she returned to Saint Patrice School. In 1890-1894 she went back to Saint Antoine Academy. In 1894-1895 she went to Ottawa in Ontario as an assistant. In 1895-1897 she became superior at Huntingdon. In 1897-1898 she was superior at Saint Denis Academy. In 1898-1890 she was director of English studies at the motherhouse in Montreal. In 1900-1903 she attended normal school. In 1903 she was named superior at Villa Barlow in Saint Albans, Vermont, where she remained for fifteen years. In 1918 she became superior at the Academy of Our Lady of the Blessed Sacrament, Staten Island.

Saint Albans School Prospers

At Saint Albans in Vermont, Healy showed herself as a superior businesswoman—shrewd, resourceful, and talented. She was sent to Saint Albans as a last resort. Operating in the red, Villa Barlow was burdened with debt and could no longer maintain itself. The community that was buying and restoring the school saw itself on the verge of losing its monetary investments and considered abandoning the project. Having disagreements with the parish and diocesan authorities, Healy fought hard in the beginning, but through her business sense, she overcame obstacles, paid debts, and got Saint Albans in the black. Saint Albans became one of the most prosperous houses in the United States. Because the community adored her, students from the families of prominent citizens enrolled there for an education.

Archives of the Congrégation de Notre Dame records that Healy:

> Was an uncharacteristic figure, a unique personality . . . of uncommon distinction. Her clear and well developed mind, multiplied tenfold . . . by an intensive education, practical as much as artistic, with extensive knowledge in all realms, putting her abreast of all situations and at ease with all types of minds . . . [with a] personality cast in a simple mold, thorough in her ideas, fair in its judgments and evaluations, energetic, [and] sincere in all her relationships [gained her the respect of all who came in contact with her.] As a

> superior, she had the talent to administrate with wisdom, tact and kindness, without violating the laws of her instinctively demanding nature (320).

Healy, a perfectionist, was often heard saying, "What is worth doing is worth doing well." She had little patience for imperfect work done in the name of God. At Saint Albans she established matters of taste, making it the first school to have works of art in the convent.

In 1918 Healy was asked to make a sacrifice for God and take the assignment as superior at the Academy of Our Lady of the Blessed Sacrament on Staten Island. She was seventy-one years old. The news came as a surprise. She was reluctant but obedient and proceeded in faith, uncomplaining. At Staten Island she labored with the industriousness and courage of a twenty-one-year-old. Her managerial skills were impressive, and within eight months the Academy of Our Lady of the Blessed Sacrament had a monetary surplus. She had hoped to have the same success that she experienced at Saint Albans, but it was not to be so. Her time on earth was expiring.

A sudden fainting spell revealed an advanced heart problem. Healy was relieved of her activities and sent to the infirmary. She left the Academy of Our Lady of the Blessed Sacrament in Staten Island and went to the motherhouse to recuperate. She remained there four months before succumbing to complications of a heart condition, an ailment that had also claimed the life of her oldest brother, James, eighteen years earlier.

On September 13, 1919, 8:50 p.m., the eve of the Exaltation of the Holy Cross, Healy died. This eve was symbolic because all her life she had a special devotion for the cross. She was probably in considerable pain but did not complain. It is likely she felt excessive dryness in her throat and chest but did not press the nurses for beverages; she drank only what was prescribed for her. The *Archives of the Congrégation de Notre Dame* state:

> Those who lived to gather round her bed in the infirmary were chiefly impressed by her uncomplaining patience, her childlike obedience, her touching gratitude for the care and kindness she received. Her spirit of faith shone out in her preparation for, and reception of the Last Sacraments. . . . Often she was heard to say with an accept of earnest conviction, "How happy I am to die in the Congrégation de Notre Dame!". . . . [T]he end came quickly, peacefully, and without struggle [or] agony.

Foley's account indicates Healy died from cancer brought on by an arm injury from a laundry wringer, for which she received twenty-eight stitches (302).

References

Afro-American Encyclopedia. Vol. 6. North Miami, Fla.: Educational Book Publishers, 1974.

Contributions of Black Women to America. Vol. 1. Ed. Marianna W. Davis. Columbia, S.C.: Kenday Press, 1982.

Foley, Albert S. *Bishop Healy: Beloved Outcast*. New York: Farrar, Straus and Young, 1954.

——. *Dictionary of American Negro Biography*. Edited by Rayford W. Logan and Michael R. Winston. New York: Norton, 1982.

Collections

Information on Eliza Healy (Sister Mary Magdalene) may be found in the Archives, Les Soeurs de la Congrégation de Notre Dame de Montréal.

Gerri Bates

Josephine D. Heard

(1861-1921?)

Poet

Poet Josephine Delphine Henderson Heard was born in Salisbury, North Carolina, on October 11, 1861. Her parents were slaves who were permitted to hire themselves out in Charlotte, North Carolina. Heard was able to read when she was five years old, and she took delight in reading the Bible to her aged neighbors. She attended school in Charlotte and then at Scotia Seminary in Concord, North Carolina, completing her education at Bethany Institute in New York. This pattern suggests that as at least semiskilled workers, her parents may have been able to contribute towards her education. She is credited with contributing poems published in several leading religious publications and with musical skills well enough developed to have composed and written a piece played at the New Orleans Exposition. With this background, Heard began to teach at Mayesville and Orangeburg in South Carolina, and then, rather surprisingly, in Covington, Tennessee, a town not far from the Mississippi on the western edge of the state. In 1821, at the age of twenty-one, she married William Henry Heard, who was some eleven years older and for whom this was a second marriage.

William Henry Heard was born in Elbert County, Georgia, on June 25, 1850. Put to the plow when he was so young that he had one specially adapted to his size, he began a quest for education as soon as he was free. He scrambled to learn, taking advantage of every opportunity to go to school, hiring himself out as a laborer and taking part of his pay in instruction, and hiring people to give him lessons. As soon as he felt himself competent, he began teach while continuing his own education. In 1872 he was Republican county chairman for Elbert County and a candidate for the state legislature. After losing a dramatic election involving theft of voting tickets, he moved across the river into Abbeville County in South Carolina, where he continued teaching and his involvement in politics. There were violent confrontations during the elections of 1876, and he was kidnapped and nearly lynched, but Heard managed to secure the county's votes for Rutherford B. Hayes, acquired a scholarship from the county to the University of South Carolina, and won a seat in the state legislature. Part of the bargain that gave Hayes the presidency was the repudiation of Reconstruction, and Heard was turned out of the university after a year and lost his seat. He then went to Athens, Georgia, where he taught in an African Methodist Episcopal (AME) school, managed a term at Clark University, and spent a year as a junior at Atlanta University. He had his conversion experience on May 16, 1879, and he was authorized first to exhort and then to preach by the end of that year. In 1880 Heard was appointed railway postal clerk on the recommendation of independent Democratic Congressman Emory Speare. His route included the run between Atlanta and Charlotte.

There is no indication of when and where William Henry Heard met and courted Josephine Henderson. The marriage of the thirty-one-year-old Heard and the twenty-one-year-old Henderson took place on January 22, 1882, the year he gave up the position of railway postal clerk and became a full-time minister, first in Aiken, South Carolina, and then in Charleston. There were no children from the marriage. In 1888 the couple moved north to Philadelphia, and in 1890 Heard published her first volume of poems, *Morning Glories*, with the support of her husband and Bishop Benjamin Tucker Tanner. After various postings in Pennsylvania, William Henry Heard accepted in February 1895 the post of minister resident and consul general in Liberia from Grover Cleveland, with the recommendation and assistance of Bishop Henry Neil Turner. William Henry Heard apparently traveled alone to London, where he spent less than a week before joining Turner in Liverpool. The two men traveled together to Liberia. In 1896 William Henry Heard returned home on leave from the consular service; Josephine Heard accompanied him as far as England on the return trip, and they visited France and Italy together. Heard went on to Liberia, and it was in 1899 that he returned to Philadelphia. In 1901 Josephine Heard published a second, augmented edition of *Morning Glories*.

William Henry Heard undertook the position of secretary-treasurer of the Connectional Preachers Aid and Mutual Relief Association in 1904. This meant that he was absent from home for four months every year for four years, traveling to forty-four states, often under very adverse circumstances. In 1908 he was elected bishop and assigned to West Africa. This time his wife accompanied him to Africa, along with eight other missionaries. In 1916 the war forced them home, and William Henry Heard was assigned to Louisiana and Mississippi; in 1920 he was assigned to the First Episcopal District. At some point during their stays in Philadelphia, the Heards established their residence at 1426 Rockland Street. William Henry Heard wrote his memoir in 1923, and he died in September 1937.

Historian Ann Shockley gives the date of Josephine Heard's death as 1921, but her husband writes in 1923 as if she were still alive:

> In 1882 I married my second wife, Miss Josie D. Henderson of Charlotte, North Carolina. She is scholarly and poetic, and her use of the English language, as well as the criticism of my sermons, have done much in making me the preacher they say I am (94).

As published in 1890, Heard's *Morning Glories* is a small book containing seventy-two pieces, divided into "Musings" (fifty-nine), "The Race Problem" (three), and "Obituaries" (ten). Citing her final poem, "An Epitaph," Joan R. Sherman, in *Collected Black Women's Poetry*, wrote that "Heard's verses lack originality of topic and execution; emotions never rise above sentimentality and religious piety; language is insipid and sometimes unintelligible . . . . It is difficult among these repetitive verses to find a fresh idea or imaginative phrase. 'She hath done what she could' " (xxix-xxx). It is difficult to disagree with this evaluation, and the interest the poems may have for feminist criticism does not lie in their poetic value according to traditional standards. In one major strand of her work, Heard is working in a poetic tradition that allied poetry closely to public speaking, and her verse aims at immediate comprehension during public recitation. For the contemporary reader, the sentiments are perhaps too predictable and the language too diluted to sustain interest over the ten stanzas of "They Are Coming," but delivered by a skilled speaker, these lines might sill move a sympathetic audience. The first stanza runs:

> They are coming, coming slowly—
> They are coming, surely, surely—
> In each avenue you hear the steady tread.
> From the depths of foul oppression,
> Comes a swarthy-hued procession,
> And victory perches on their banners' head.

References

Heard, Josephine D. *Morning Glories*. Philadelphia: Privately printed, 1890. Reprinted in *Collected Black Women's Poetry*. Vol. 4. New York: Oxford, 1988. Both contain a portrait of Heard opposite title page of *Morning Glories*.

Heard, William H. *From Slavery to Bishopric*. Philadelphia: The Author, 1924.

Majors, M. A. *Noted Negro Women*. Chicago: Donohue and Henneberry, 1893.

Sherman, Joan R. "Introduction." *Collected Black Women's Poetry*. Vol. 4. New York: Oxford, 1988.

Shockley, Ann Allen. *Afro-American Women Writers 1746-1933*. Boston: G. K. Hall, 1988.

Robert L. Johns

Anna Arnold Hedgeman

(1899-1990)

Lecturer, consultant, author, activist, social worker

Anna Arnold Hedgeman's concern for resolving national and global ethnic inequities has been manifest in her involvement with the first fair employment practices legislation, the 1963 March on Washington, the passage of the 1964 Civil Rights Bill, and the creation of African-American studies programs on many college campuses. She believed that the chaos seen in the sixties could give way to a world of freedom and that equality could emerge. She was an articulate, outspoken advocate and a warrior for social justice; women, minorities, and the world's poor have been the benefactors of Anna Arnold Hedgeman's decades of work.

Born July 5, 1899, in Marshalltown, Iowa, and reared in Anoka, Minnesota, Hedgeman was one of five children born to William James Arnold and Marie Ellen (Parker) Arnold. William Arnold, the son of slaves, was born in South Carolina and educated at Clark University in Atlanta, where he received both his high school and college training. He left the South almost immediately after graduating from college and moved to the Midwest at the turn of the century. Little is said of Marie Arnold's background, but she taught a young Hedgeman to read at home. At that time Hedgeman, then six years old and eagerly waiting to begin school, was the oldest of three girls and had to care for the mother when she became ill. She notes the beauty of her sisters, saying that "everyone said so." The blue eyes, golden hair, and blue vein in the cheek of one sister, and the long black silky curls and "an exquisitely wistful appeal" of the other meant that they viewed beauty by white standards. "I was plain and a bit solemn," she wrote in *The Trumpet Sounds* (9). To compensate for the difference between Hedgeman and her sisters, the mother complimented Anna on her disposition. At an early age Hedgeman felt that "there was something special" that she lacked.

Anna Arnold Hedgeman

The Methodist church and the school were vital parts of the Arnold family's life. As a young child Hedgeman felt the pain of racial insults and the impact of color on other people, especially when a three-year-old asked, "Anna, are you really a nigger?" After Hedgeman discussed the matter with the child's mother, the little girl never ran to meet Hedgeman again as she passed on her way to and from school. "This was the first time a child ever rejected me and the scar remains until this day," she said (*The Trumpet Sounds*, 10). So did the scar of the racial slur.

In 1918 Hedgeman graduated from high school and in the fall of that year entered Hamline University, a Methodist college in Saint Paul, Minnesota. She was the school's first African American student. Hedgeman wrote in a letter to Jessie Carney Smith that she no longer used "black" as her ethnic designation, but used "African (known as the Black Continent) American (no hyphen) to include many of the areas of the world to which we have also given leadership, (even if unrecognized)." During her sophomore year, 1919, she went to hear W. E. B. Du Bois, then with the NAACP, lecture in a local church. His impressive speech made her scurry to the library to read his *Souls of Black Folk*. Because of regular college routines, her interest in the scholar and his work at that time was short-lived. Hedgeman, Hamline's first African-American graduate, completed her bachelor's degree in 1922 with a major in English.

In September 1922 Hedgeman left for Rust College, a Methodist college for African Americans located in Holly Springs, Mississippi, where she taught ancient and modern history, logic and methodology, as well as English, her college major. The poverty of most students, and of the college as well, touched Hedgeman as she had never been touched before. Some of the students were older and worked in the fields to earn money to gain the grade school education that the college offered. Impressed by their dedication and the school's mission, she used her summer vacation for graduate study at the University of Minnesota. The overwhelming difficulties that the students and the college faced created in Hedgeman a deep hatred for all southern whites. She did not return to Rust after the second year.

Through the assistance of Eva D. Bowles and Cornella Winn, in fall 1924 Hedgeman obtained a position with the Negro branch of the YWCA in Springfield, Ohio. Soon she was in demand for lectures on race relations. After spending the summer of 1926 in New York, she decided to move to the East, where she became executive director of a Negro branch YWCA in Jersey City, New Jersey. By 1927 she had become secretary of the West 137th Street Branch of the YWCA in Harlem. Among the African American luminaries who participated in the Y's programs were Charlotte Hawkins Brown, Mary Church Terrell, Maggie Lena Walker, Annie Turnbo Malone, Mable Keaton Staupers, W. E. B. Du Bois, A. Philip Randolph, George Schuyler, and James Weldon Johnson. By 1929 when the Great Depression was beginning, Hedgeman organized employment efforts, established referral services to the Works Progress Administration (WPA) and the National Youth Administration, established workshops to train seamstresses and nurses' aides, assisted in manning soup kitchens, and provided other employment assistance.

By fall 1933 Hedgeman had accepted the position as executive director of the Catherine Street Branch of the YWCA in Philadelphia. Crystal Bird Fauset, formerly of the national YWCA staff, chaired the volunteer committee of this black branch. Meanwhile, after her two-year engagement to Merritt Hedgeman of the Music Division of the Civil Workers Administration and later a concert artist, the two married in New York City. With their families now in New York, Hedgeman soon resigned her post and returned to New York. In 1934 she became supervisor and consultant to the Emergency Relief Bureau (now known as the Department of Welfare). Four years later she resigned to become director of the Negro branch of the Brooklyn YWCA, but the segregation policies of the national body became so unacceptable to Hedgeman that she left the position.

Hedgeman joined the civilian defense of the Roosevelt administration and worked out of the New York office as assistant in race relations. In February 1944 she left for Washington, D.C., to become executive director of the National Council for a Permanent Fair Employment Practices Commission and initiated national legislative and educational programs. She remained in the post for two years, and on February 12, 1949, she was sworn in as assistant to the administrator of the Federal Security Agency (later known as Health, Education and Welfare). From 1954 to 1958 Anna Hedgeman was an assistant in the cabinet of Mayor Robert F. Wagner, Jr., of New York City. She had liaison responsibility for eight city departments and international guests of the city. In fall 1958, after she reached a professional crossroad, S. B. Fuller asked her to join his firm, Fuller Products Company, as public relations director. She accepted, made contacts with church and civic groups, and gave daily lectures for salespersons. When Fuller purchased the *New York Age*, he asked Hedgeman to work full-time as associate editor and columnist. She worked with the newspaper until it was discontinued in spring 1960.

After spending some time as coordinator of special events for the Commission on Religion and Race, Hedgeman became associate director of the Department of Social Justice and for two years served as director of Ecumenical Action, the National Churches of Christ. This took her into the planning stages of the March on Washington, then scheduled for August 28, 1963. A. Philip Randolph had called for the march as a way to create a new sense of dignity among young African Americans, but Martin Luther King, Jr., soon announced his call for a march to Washington in July 1963 to urge the passage of a strong civil rights bill. Randolph and King joined forces and scheduled a single march in which other civil rights leaders such as James Farmer and John Lewis would participate. Through her work with the National Council of the Churches of Christ, Hedgeman was asked to find thirty thousand white Protestants from across the nation to participate in the march.

Hedgeman Becomes Major Architect of Civil Rights March

Hedgeman was a major architect of the March on Washington movement of 1963. She assisted in the creation of the interfaith (Catholic, Protestant, and Jewish) leadership which made the final passage of the Civil Rights Bill of 1964-1965 a reality. One week before the march was to occur, she noted on the draft program that no woman was listed as speaker. Randolph was to ask several African American women to stand as he reviewed the historic role of such women in the movement, then they would bow at the end of his presentation. Hedgeman began her protest immediately, for she wished to avoid embarrassing the six African American men who were leaders in the movement and who would be on program. She wrote to Randolph and sent copies to each of the leaders involved. By the final meeting of the March Committee none of the men had responded. Hedgeman read from the floor a copy of her memorandum to Randolph:

> In light of the role of Negro women in the struggle for freedom and especially in light of the extra burden they have carried because of the castration of our Negro man in this culture, it is incredible that no woman should appear as a speaker at this historic March on Washington Meeting at the Lincoln Memorial. . . .
>
> Since the "Big Six" [Civil Rights leaders] have not given women the quality of participation which they have earned through the years, I would like to suggest . . . that a Negro woman make a brief statement and present the other Heroines just as you have suggested that the Chairman might do. . . . It occurred to me that pride in our Militant Younger Generation might make it possible for the older women to bow to youth and ask Mrs. Diane Nash Bevel to repre-

> sent women and all youth in one person. . . . She is a disciplined person . . . [and she] is in essence the consummation of the quality of the past of Negro woman and part of the hope of all of us for the future (*The Trumpet Sounds,* 179-80).

On the day of the march the problem was corrected, but Hedgeman and others were reminded by the initial plan that black women, as well as white women, were still treated as second-class citizens in American culture.

Hedgeman was involved in international as well as national activities. In 1953 she spent three months in India as an exchange leader for the Department of State. In 1956 she spent six weeks in the Middle East and Israel discussing current international problems with key governmental and nongovernment officials. She participated in two international conferences on social work in Munich, Germany (1956), and Tokyo, Japan (1958), discussing reciprocity for seamen of the world. She was keynote speaker for the first Conference of the Women of Africa and of African Descent held at Accra, Ghana, in 1960, and in 1973 she participated in the International Conference of Social Work at The Hague, Netherlands.

Hedgeman has served as teacher, lecturer, and consultant to numerous educational centers, boards, and colleges and universities, particularly in the area of African-American studies. She has presented courses in African-American studies and held inservice training series for public school teachers. In later years she owned Hedgeman Consultant Services in New York City.

Hedgeman held memberships in numerous organizations, such as the Child Study Association, Community Council of the City of New York, National Urban League, NAACP, United Nations Association, Advisory Committee on Alcoholism, Advisory Committee on Drug Addiction, and the National Conference of Christians and Jews (where she served on the board of directors).

Hedgeman's alma mater, Hamline University, inducted her into Phi Beta Kappa in 1976. Honorary doctoral degrees have been received from Hamline University (1948), Upsala College (1970), Benedict College (1978), Dowling College (1977), and Macalaster College (1980). Her other recognitions include the Alpha Kappa Alpha Sorority Meritorious Citation as a pioneer for human rights, 1953; Consumer Protective Committee Award, 1955; Outstanding Citizens' Award, Abyssinian Baptist Church, New York City, 1956; Zeta Phi Beta Sorority Award, 1956; Manhattan Arts and Educational Guild Award Certificate, 1957; Rust College Shield Award, 1971; Tenth Anniversary Award, Delta Ministry of Mississippi, 1974; and the Frederick Douglass Award in recognition of distinguished leadership toward equal opportunity, 1974.

Hedgeman is author of *The Trumpet Sounds* (New York: Holt, Rinehart, 1964), *The Gift of Chaos* (New York: Oxford University Press, 1977), and articles in numerous organizational publications, newspapers, and journals.

After nearly a lifetime of concern for justice in all aspects of national and world culture, Hedgeman, who had been a resident of the Greater Harlem Nursing Home, died on January 17, 1990, in Harlem Hospital.

References

Contemporary Authors. Vol. 15-16. Detroit: Gale Research, 1966.

Hedgeman, Anna Arnold, Biography File, Fisk University Library.

———. Letter to Jessie Carney Smith, 19 December 1980.

———. *The Trumpet Sounds.* New York: Holt, Rinehart and Winston, 1964.

Low, W. Augustus, and Virgil A. Clift. *Encyclopedia of Black America.* New York: McGraw-Hill, 1981.

New York Times, 26 January 1990.

Ploski, Harry A., and James Williams. *Negro Almanac.* 5th ed. Detroit: Gale Research, 1989. Photograph, p. 1381.

Who's Who of American Women. 8th ed., 1974-75. Chicago: Marquis, 1973.

Collections

Speeches, notes, correspondence, photographs, and other materials on Anna Arnold Hedgeman are in the Schomburg Center for Research on Black Culture and in the Fisk University Library. Oral history interviews are in the Black Women Oral History Collection, Schlesinger Library, Radcliffe College, the YMCA Oral History Collection, Moorland-Spingarn Research Center, and the Schomburg Center.

Jessie Carney Smith

Dorothy Height

(1912-)

Organization leader, social servant, civil and women's rights activist

Dorothy Irene Height has served as president of the National Council of Negro Women (NCNW) since 1957. Under her leadership the council has grown as a coalition of black women's organizations, focusing especially during her

Dorothy Height

tenure on global issues that affect the struggles of women. She also served as national president of Delta Sigma Theta sorority from 1947 until 1956, has served on numerous United States committees concerned with women's issues, won countless service awards, and has traveled extensively for the cause of women's issues worldwide. She spent the majority of her professional life as a staff member of the Young Women's Christian Association's (YWCA) National Board. Through her professional and voluntary responsibilities, Height has fought to improve the status of women and to empower women to speak in their own behalf.

Height was born on March 24, 1912, to James Edward Height and Fannie (Borroughs) Height. The family moved from Richmond, Virginia, to Rankin, Pennsylvania, a small mining town, in 1916. She has one sister, a half sister, and a half brother. Her father worked as a building contractor, and her mother was a private nurse to cancer patients. The family worshipped at a local, segregated Baptist church where James Height, a religious man, was choirmaster and Sunday school superintendent. Reminiscing about her earliest years, Height recalled that most of her life was spent in the church and related organizations, where she ''sort of followed [her mother] around and got into the idea of organizing clubs'' (*Current Biography Yearbook,* 216).

Height attended Rankin High School, where she was an exemplary student, both in academics and athletics. She won spelling, debate, and speech contests throughout high school while maintaining a straight ''A'' grade point average. After outgrowing childhood asthma and reaching a height of five-feet nine-and-a-half inches by age eleven, she played center on the basketball team. She also cowrote the school song and sang in a trio. Outside of school she became active in the YWCA, where her leadership skills and her basketball prowess were developed. By the age of fourteen, Height was elected president of the Pennsylvania State Federation of Girls Clubs.

Upon graduation from high school, Height applied to Barnard College in New York City. She was informed by the school, however, that they already had two black students and therefore she would have to wait a term or more. She chose instead to attend New York University, using a one-thousand-dollar scholarship she had won from an Elks Fraternal Society's national oratorical contest. While attending NYU, she lived with her sister and worked at odd jobs to support herself. Height finished her undergraduate course work in three years and in her fourth year worked to receive her master's degree in educational psychology. This course work was completed in 1933.

After completing her formal education, Height took a practice teaching position at Brownsville Community Center in Brooklyn. Also, following the founding of the United Christian Youth Movement in 1935, she became an active member and quickly became one of its leaders. This position enabled her to travel widely throughout the United States and to Europe. In 1937 she represented the organization at the International Church Youth Conference in Oxford, England, as well as serving as a youth delegate at the World Conference of Christian Youth in Amsterdam, Holland. In 1938 Height, acting as a representative of the Harlem Youth Council, became one of ten American youths to help Eleanor Roosevelt plan the 1938 World Youth Congress that met at Vassar College in Poughkeepsie, New York.

In 1935 Height became a case worker for the New York City Department of Welfare. To strengthen her background for this position, she began course work at the New York School of Social Work. Following the Harlem riots of 1935, she was promoted to an advisory position to examine the unrest.

Height accepted a position with the YWCA in 1938 after her return from Europe to the United States. By this time she had decided that she could use her skills more productively in an organization that was inclusive of the races and international in character. This new job took her from Brooklyn to Harlem where she became assistant director of the Emma Ransom House, a place of lodging for black women.

Plight of Domestic Workers Attacked

In her new capacity, Height was immediately confronted with the plight of large numbers of black American women in domestic service jobs working under deplorable conditions. She became their advocate, speaking up, for example, in 1938 when she testified before the New York City Council about the despicable practice occurring in Brooklyn and the Bronx daily. Here on the streets, in what she called a ''slave market,'' young black girls would bargain with passing motorists for a day's housework at substandard wages (*Current Biography Yearbook,* 217). The battle for fair wages for domestic workers is one that she maintains to this day, urging them to organize and form unions.

This period of her life set the course for much of her future work. In 1937 Height not only began working with the YWCA but she also met Mary McLeod Bethune, president and founder of the National Council of Negro Women (NCNW). This meeting was life-transforming, as she joined the organization that she was to lead for more than thirty years.

In 1939, Height relocated to Washington, D.C., to take a new position as executive secretary of the YWCA Phillis Wheatley Home. At this time she also became a member of Delta Sigma Theta sorority. She immediately made her presence and ideas known. At an executive committee meeting in June 1940, Height proposed that the Delta Sigma Theta Sorority adopt as a national project a job analysis program that would analyze the reasons that black women were excluded from so many of the jobs open to women, increase the number of positions for black women on jobs already accessible to other women, and improve conditions under which many unskilled workers were forced to work. The project was deemed of utmost importance because at that time many women over the age of fourteen were working, and most married black women held employment outside of their homes. Another major emphasis of the project was to achieve a substantial representation of leaders on labor policy boards and commissions. Height headed the project for the organization. During the same year she also directed the YWCA School for Professional Workers in Mt. Carroll, Illinois.

Height's professional career with the national board YWCA began full-time in 1944, when she became a staff member for leadership development at the board headquarters in New York City. In this capacity she was assigned to aid in the development of training programs for volunteers and staff of the YWCA. As a member of the staff, she played a key role in planning the organization's landmark convention in 1946, where the membership voted to support an interracial charter to mandate integration of facilities and activities to the limits of the law. At this convention, she became the national board's interracial education secretary.

During 1944 Height was also elected vice-president of Delta Sigma Theta. Three years later she became national president. During the nine years she held the position, according to Paula Giddings's history of the organization, "neither the direction nor the substance of the initiatives changed under [her] leadership, but the breadth and interest in them did" (Giddings, 219). She expanded the sorority into one more focused on the relationship between black women in America and in Third World countries. When she was invited by the World YWCA to teach for four months at the Delhi School of Social Work in India in 1952, for example, she relayed the similar conditions of women in India and convinced her sorority members to establish a scholarship for two Hindu women.

The creation of international Delta chapters can be directly attributed to Height. Following her participation in the bicentennial celebration of Haiti in Port-au-Prince in 1950, she organized the sorority's first international chapter. Further, the organization established a Haitian relief fund, which after only four years proved invaluable when the island was hit by the destructive Hurricane Hazel. Height also increased the board's international and political consciousness by taking them to meet members of the United Nations' Department of Information and the Political and Economic Committee on the Rights of Women.

Height also had plans for the Deltas on the home front. They started a bookmobile to serve the black people of Georgia and held a series of nationally broadcast town meetings. Height later recalled that she was "looking for ways in which we [could] make Delta stand out from day to day; to take a look at ourselves and see how we [could] have a stronger and better program; to see what to develop for Deltas; and to work together, play together, yet find a kind of unity which [could] make the organization live" (Giddings, 224). She was successful in just that. She made Delta run smoothly, stepping down from the presidency in 1956 after she felt she had accomplished her goals for the organization.

Height Heads National Council of Negro Women

After her term as sorority head ended, Height could not long remain outside of club politics. In 1957 she became president of the National Council of Negro Women. The council, created by Bethune, was conceived as a means of "uniting middle- and upper-class black women in humanitarian causes and social action programs . . . [through] policies and programs stressing inter-race and inter-class cooperation" (*Current Biography Yearbook*, 216). It is an umbrella group for local and national organizations engaged in "development and utilization and women in community, national and international life" (*Encyclopedia of Associations*, 1776). These goals are accomplished on economic, political, and social levels using the resources available to individual members and the unity of the groups.

Through the organization, Height became an integral part of the leadership of the civil rights movement in the United States and abroad. Beginning in 1948, when Governor Nelson Rockefeller of New York appointed her to the state Social Welfare Board, she has held a variety of official and unofficial positions, representing black American women's issues.

In 1960, in the wake of major changes in the African political scene, the Committee on Correspondence sent Height to study women's organizations in five African countries. As a result of that travel she acted as a consultant to the secretary of state. In this capacity, Height is said to have "used her influence to help win American aid for the new black African nations and foster a consciousness of identity between the struggles of blacks here and there" (*Current Biography Yearbook*, 217).

As the civil rights struggle expanded in the United States,

Dorothy Height was there. The NCNW held voter education drives in the North and voter registration drives in the South. Working with the Student Nonviolent Coordinating Committee (SNCC), the NCNW raised funds and paid students who postponed their college education to rally for the civil rights struggle.

Height was instrumental in getting the YWCA involved with the struggle as well. In 1963, as newly appointed secretary of the Department of Racial Justice, she was asked to plan strategies to overcome internal segregation in the association. Although the membership had committed to integration thirteen years before, the YWCA had never really achieved this goal; rather, they had concentrated on strengthening so-called equal black branches. Height was given the task of helping member associations to desegregate all facilities, branches, and local staff and to design training programs for volunteers and staff. One example of her work was the involvement of the YWCA in setting up a stable line of communication between black and white citizens in Alabama, where they arranged workshops to enlighten congressmen who had previously ignored the concerns of their few black constituents. Another example was a telephone registration project that was initiated through the YWCA's radio station in New York City, WMCA.

During these controversial years in America, Height offered her leadership in many arenas. She was chairperson of the Committee on the Status of Women, Equal Employment, and Employment of the Handicapped. As well, the NCNW was represented on the Council for United Civil Rights Leadership. Height also served as a member of the American Red Cross Board of Governors from 1964 to 1970 and on the Ad Hoc Committee on Public Welfare of the United States Department of Health, Education, and Welfare. She was a consultant to the New York State Social Welfare Board from 1958 to 1968. The degree of Height's visibility was apparent when an advertisement for American Airlines featured her in the November 1963 *Ebony* magazine.

During the early years of the civil rights movement, Height was known to take a rather moderate stance on matters of integration and civil rights. She did not support the call for black power as a means to attain the rights promised to all citizens of the United States. However, by 1972 she altered her position, stating that:

> White power in the system in which we live is a reality. . . . We have to see that we have been treating the symptoms instead of causes. I think this does call for the more direct approach to the societal conditions (*Current Biography Yearbook,* 218).

This change in attitude was evident in her activities in the council and the YWCA. The council was finally coming closer to "bringing all the fingers together in a mighty fist," which was the vision of Bethune at its inception (Noble, 140). According to author Jeanne Noble, Height was able to build a financial and administrative capability that positioned the NCNW to become eligible for large foundation grants; a first in the history of black women's organizations.

The Ford Foundation granted the council three hundred thousand dollars to begin Operation Woman Power, a project to help women open their own businesses and to provide funds for vocational training. During the same period, the United States Department of Health, Education, and Welfare supplied the means for a job training program for teenagers. The council spent time in areas where community needs were not being met, calling them to the attention of those in power. It went to rural areas and bought seed and feed for poor farmers and communities and started food cooperatives.

With the new influx of philanthropic and government dollars, Height led the organization into an era of phenomenal growth. With at least ninety workers in their staff, the work of the NCNW was critical to programs ranging from pig banks in the rural South to leadership training for African women. The YWCA also felt the impact of Height's mild radicalism. In 1970 at its triennial convention, Height was one of the principal architects of the now famous YWCA One Imperative, which affirmed for the organization the primary importance of "elimination of racism" as a means to cure oppression in society. She was adamant in her conviction that the pressures of being black and a woman in America deserved their deepest consideration. Height felt "the Y must get middle-class black and white liberals into the ghettos working not for, but with, minority groups" (Noble, 140). The YWCA released a public affairs statement confirming her projection of the devastation that would be wrought upon America if racism is not eradicated. In 1978 Height was lauded by Simeon Booker, in *Ebony* magazine, for her activism. In his column, "Washington Notebook," he told readers of her fight to gain approval for the first monument to a black person in the nation's capital. The statue of Mary McLeod Bethune is now located in Lincoln Park. He also informed readers about an educational campaign in South Africa that the council was operating under Height's leadership. According to Booker, she achieved great success in the 1960s despite her position as "a black female token on the male-dominated Civil Rights front" (Noble, 140).

During the past three decades the council has remained diligent in its role as a catalyst for effecting change in the position of black women. Currently, their focus has been on the revival of black family life, with annual celebrations that they call Black Family Reunions. These events are intended to encourage and renew the concept and admiration of the extended black family. This once-powerful barrier against racism and its attendant ills, such as juvenile delinquency, drug use, and unwanted teen pregnancy, is seen by Height and the NCNW to be the key to restoring the community. For example, in 1988 the council, along with the more than ninety thousand in attendance, gathered to lobby policy makers who continue to ignore the relationship between social and economic progress and family structure. The agenda focused on distortions of black family life perpetuated in the media and "promoting marriage and advocating the re-emphasis of traditional values in the black community," according to the *Wall Street Journal*. The *Journal* commended the council for the celebrations: "If its movement to reinforce black families gains momentum, it could be the best thing that ever happened to the black underclass" (*Current Biography Yearbook*, 218).

In addition, under Height's leadership the council publishes *Black Woman's Voice* and runs a Women's Center for Education and Career Advancement for minority women in nontraditional careers, an Information Center for and about black women, and the Bethune Museum and Archives for black women's history. It has offices in West and South Africa, working to improve the conditions of women in Third World countries. Height has spoken extensively on the responsibilities of the United States, United Nations, and local organizations in pursuit of these improvements.

Height has been central in the success of three influential women's organizations and they have been substantially affected by her leadership. As president and executive board member of Delta Sigma Theta, Height left the sorority more efficient and globally focused, with a centralized headquarters. Height's work with the Young Women's Christian Association led to integration and sincere and productive participation in the civil rights movement. The National Council of Negro Women is now a competent umbrella for 240 local groups and thirty-one national organizations. In different ways each organization has been striving toward the unified goal of equal rights for black women all over the world. Through diligence, excellent managerial skills, good use of contacts, and use of authority, she has left an undeniable mark in each endeavor she has undertaken. Height is the recipient of a multitude of awards and holds honorary degrees from Tuskegee University, Coppin State College in Maryland, Harvard University, and Pace College in New York.

References

"American Airlines Advertisement." *Ebony* 19 (November 1963): 118.

Black Women Oral History Project Interview. Schlesinger Library, Radcliffe College, 1974.

Booker, Simeon. "Washington Notebook." *Ebony* 33 (May 1978): 29.

Contributions of Black Women to America. Vol. 2. Ed. Marianna W. Davis. Columbia, S.C.: Kenday Press, 1982. Includes photograph.

Current Biography Yearbook. New York: H. W. Wilson, 1972. Includes photograph.

Encyclopedia of Associations. Vol. 1, Part 2. Eds. Deborah Burek, Karin E. Koek, and Annette Novallo. Detroit: Gale Research, 1990.

Encyclopedia of Black America. Edited by W. Augustus Low and Virgil A. Clift. New York: McGraw-Hill, 1981.

"Family Affair." *Wall Street Journal* 20 September 1988.

Giddings, Paula. *In Search of Sisterhood*. New York: William Morris, 1988.

Manning, Beverly. *We Shall Be Heard*. Metuchen, N.J.: Scarecrow Press, 1988.

Noble, Jeanne. *Beautiful, Also, Are the Souls of My Black Sisters*. Englewood Cliffs, N.J.: Prentice-Hall, 1978.

Rowan, Carl T. "Crusade of Hope." *Washington Post* (1 September 1987): A-23.

Collections

The papers of Dorothy Irene Height are in the office of the National Council of Negro Women, Washington, D.C.

Jenifer Lyn Grady and Maalik Edwards, with Adrienne Lash Jones

Sally Hemings

(1773-1836)

Slave companion

During the period of American slavery, the lives of millions of people of African descent were lost forever in irrecoverable silence; we will never know the stories of the vast majority of enslaved people because the dominant culture deprived slaves of their voices as well as their homelands, their languages, their labor, their bodies, and their children. Sally Hemings was more fortunate than most in the sense that at least legends about her have survived. However, the Sally Hemings legends are so entwined with political lies, secrets, and silences that it is very difficult for the modern scholar to ascertain much about her.

Whatever the agonies, joys, ideas, and experiences of the historical Sally Hemings may have been, her body has figuratively become the territory over which American racial and sexual battles have been waged for nearly two hundred years. Although we will never find the "true" Sally Hemings, the history of controversy surrounding her is deeply revealing of the American oppression of race and sex. In fact, very little has been written by scholars about Hemings herself; most of the controversy has centered on Thomas Jefferson. The historical evidence establishes convincingly that Jefferson owned a slave named Sally Hemings, and that she bore several mulatto children. The central question for traditional white male politicians and scholars is whether or not Jefferson, the author of the Declaration of Independence, was the father of those children. In other words, was Jefferson guilty of the crime of miscegenation? Did he enslave his own children?

Interesting as these questions are, African-American and feminist scholars may find themselves more interested in the historical erasure of black women's voices and lives. In 1979 the Viking Press published *Sally Hemings,* a novel in which author Barbara Chase Riboud attempts to reconstruct what the life of Sally Hemings may have been like, from Heming's perspective. The novel dramatizes the interconnections between slavery and the subjugation of women in the patriarchal American nation—interconnections that were powerfully analyzed by feminist-abolitionists in the nineteenth century. Chase Riboud portrays these interconnections through the eyes of a patriotic Southerner named Nathan Langdon, who thinks:

> That Sally Hemings was a victim was certain. Her submissiveness was what had made her the perfect slave, but, to his mind, the perfect woman as well. To misuse his moral or physical power over a woman, however, was abhorrent to him. A man's power over a woman was like the master's power over a slave. It came from an innate superiority (46).

Rather than question patriarchal values, Langdon is upset by a patriarch's "abuse" of his natural, God-given power. Patriarchy, after all, was supposed to be beneficent to all concerned.

Although Chase Riboud's *Sally Hemings* is a scholarly, thought-provoking work of fiction, it was mass-marketed in 1980 by Avon Books as a "historical romance" that attempts to eroticize the oppression of women under American slavery. The Avon edition's jacket features a close-up of a light-brown bosom. Between the large, exposed breasts hangs a miniature portrait of Thomas Jefferson encased in a locket. Hemings is described on the front and back covers as Jefferson's "mistress" who "loved him more than she loved her freedom." The realities of the sexual exploitation of slave women and white men's enslavement of their own children are clouded by the assertion that Jefferson and Hemings shared "a forbidden passion that endured almost four decades—a passion that shook the very foundations of America."

Sally Hemings was born in Virginia in 1773. She was the daughter of a white man named John Wayles (1715-1773) and a mulatto slave named Elizabeth Hemings (1735-1807). Elizabeth was the daughter of Captain Hemings, a white ship captain, and an African slave. According to Barbara Chase Riboud, by 1807 Elizabeth Hemings had 104 descendants: "Black. Brown. Yellow. White. All slaves" (40). Seven of these descendants may have been the offspring of Sally Hemings and Thomas Jefferson. Durey states that it is an "undeniable fact that 'white' slave children lived at Monticello" as well as neighboring estates, and that members of the Virginia gentry were well aware of the paternity of many of the slaves (160).

After piecing together the historical evidence, Chase Riboud suggests that Thomas Jefferson first seduced Sally Hemings in Paris when she was fifteen years old. As an enslaved daughter of John Wayles, Sally was the half-sister of Jefferson's deceased wife, Martha Wayles (1748-1782). Jefferson never remarried, and he may have maintained a thirty-eight year liaison with Sally Hemings—a liaison that ended only with his death in 1826.

The Jefferson-Hemings controversy was first placed before the public on September 1, 1802, by James Thomson Callender, a political enemy of Jefferson. It was an election year and Jefferson was in the middle of his first term as President of the United States. In his newspaper, the *Recorder,* Callender wrote:

> It is well known that the man, *whom it delighteth the people to honor,* keeps, and for many years past has kept, as his concubine, one of his own slaves. Her name is SALLY. The name of her eldest son is TOM. His features are said to bear a striking although sable resemblance to those of the president himself. . . . By this wench Sally, our president has had several children. . . . THE AFRICAN VENUS is said to officiate, as housekeeper at Monticello (Quoted in Durey, 158).

In the months that followed, Callender added more detailed information about Sally Hemings and her children in subsequent articles.

In his book on Callender, Michael Durey argues that although Callender was motivated by partisan politics and a desire for personal revenge against Jefferson, his facts were almost always correct. Indeed, "of the four major accusations [Callender] threw at Jefferson, only the Sally Hemings affair is in any doubt" (Durey, 160). Durey further points out that "Jefferson was present at Monticello nine months before the birth of each of Sally's children" (Durey, 161). Some defendants of Jefferson have asserted that one or both of Jefferson's nephews, Samuel and Peter Carr, were the father(s) of Hemings's children. In any case, all arguments appear to have been politically motivated. As Durey says, the controversy has:

> echoed down the years since Callender first publicized it. An ideal subject for partisan exposition, it was used by British visitors to denigrate American democratic society in the 1830s, by abolitionists in the period around the Civil War, and by blacks in the late 1950s as part of the early civil rights campaign (157).

Hemings-Jefferson Legends Told

Throughout the nineteenth century, legends and folk songs about Jefferson and "Black Sally" persisted; they were especially popular in Virginia. On March 13, 1873, "an obscure weekly newspaper in Waverly, Ohio, the *Pike County Republican,* published an autobiographical narrative of a former slave of Thomas Jefferson's named Madison Hemings" (Malone, 523). Madison may have been the sixth child of Sally Hemings and Jefferson, born in 1805. Madison left Virginia and settled in Ohio in 1836, where he worked as a skilled carpenter for many years. White southern historians have repeatedly attempted to discredit Madison's narrative, although it coincides remarkably well with evidence from other historical sources. Madison Hemings stated that he was Jefferson's son and that his mother, Sally Hemings, had been Jefferson's concubine for many years.

The controversy surrounding Madison Hemings's story reveals a great deal about the political situation in the United States. The white editor who interviewed Madison Hemings and published his story was a Republican activist who opposed the dominant Democratic party in Pike County, Ohio. He published a series of stories entitled "Life Among the Lowly" in order to expose the cruelties of slavery and to advocate granting blacks more than "nominal freedom" in the postbellum south (Quoted in Malone, 526). He described Madison Hemings as a "straightforward, "intelligent man" who "understands himself well" (526). The editor added that Madison was "sparely made, with sandy complexion and a mild grey eye"—in other words, very similar to Jefferson in appearance (527).

The Democratic editor of the Waverly *Watchman* published a scathingly racist reply on March 18, 1873. He asserted that "there are at least fifty negroes in this county who lay claim to illustrious parentage. This is a well known peculiarity of the colored race" (Quoted in Malone, 527). Rather than admitting the historical reality of the sexual exploitation of enslaved women, the editor repeated stereotypes about black women's uncontrollable sexuality:

> They want the world to think they are particular in their liaisons with the sterner sex, whether the truth will bear them out or not. This is a well-known fact to those who have been reared in those States where slavery existed, and with them, no attention whatever, is paid to these rumors.—If they were, the "master" would have to bear the odium of all the licentious practices that are developed on the plantation (527-28).

Clearly this editor has a personal as well as political stake in denying Madison's Hemings's story; he wants to believe that blacks are odious rather than facing the odiousness of slavery. He concludes his rebuttal by comparing Madison Hemings to a "stud-horse" whose owner publishes a ludicrous statement of pedigree.

In 1952 Ralph Ellison used the Sally Hemings story to make precisely the point that the editor of the Waverly *Watchman* feared. In *Invisible Man* a black, shell-shocked World War I veteran greets the white character, Norton, as his grandfather, Thomas Jefferson. As critic Bernard Bell observes, Ellison's satire:

> is double-edged. While reconstructing the legend that one of the fathers of the country, the principal author of the Declaration of Independence, also fathered three or more children by his slave mistress, Sally Hemings, Ellison simultaneously deconstructs the myth of white purity and the fear of miscegenation by illustrating that since the founding of the nation white men have been violating black women and fathering children by them (207).

The factual details of the Sally Hemings-Thomas Jefferson relationship probably will never be known. Yet, Sally Hemings remains an important, thought-provoking symbol. The legends surrounding her are revealing and worthy of study. However, her story has never truly been told. Whoever she may have been, she surely was more than a piece of Jefferson's property or a victim of sexual exploitation.

References

Bell, Bernard W. *The Afro-American Novel and Its Tradition.* Amherst: University of Massachusetts Press, 1987.

Chase-Riboud, Barbara. *Sally Hemings.* New York: Avon, 1979.

Durey, Michael. *"With the Hammer of Truth": James Thompson Callender and America's Early National Heroes.* Charlottesville: University of Virginia Press, 1990.

Ellison, Ralph. *Invisible Man.* New York: Random House, 1952.

Malone, Dumas, and Steven H. Hochman. "A Note on Evidence: The Personal History of Madison Hemings." *Journal of Southern History* 41 (November 1975): 523-28.

Kari Winter

Aileen Hernandez

(1926-)

Entrepreneur, labor relations specialist, women's rights advocate

Aileen Clark Hernandez is one of the most influential women of her time, especially in issues of labor relations, women's rights, and equal employment concerns. Aileen Clark is the middle child and only daughter of three children born to Charles and Ethel Clark, both of whom were of Jamaican descent. Her father worked for an art supply house and her mother worked in the garment industry during the Depression. All three children were taught that there would be no differences in their treatment because of gender. All were taught to cook, sew, and care for their personal belongings. Thus were sown the seeds that eventually blossomed into a working philosophy—the belief that there should be no difference in treatment in the world of employment due to one's race and/or gender—that has guided Hernandez's personal and professional life.

Aileen Clark Hernandez was born in Brooklyn, New York, on May 23, 1926. There she attended Bay Ridge Public School 176, graduating as class valedictorian, and Bay Ridge High School, graduating as class salutatorian in 1943. With a scholarship in hand, Hernandez pursued a college degree at Howard University in Washington, D.C. Majoring in political science and sociology, she participated in various extracurricular activities that reflected her personal interests and commitments toward solving racial problems. As a member of the campus branch of the NAACP, Hernandez picketed the National Theater, the Lesner Auditorium, and the Thompson restaurant chain. She wrote a column for the *Washington Tribune* that dealt with university activities, and during her junior and senior years served as editor of *The Hilltop,* Howard University's school paper.

After graduating from Howard University, Hernandez worked as a research assistant in the political science department there. During the years 1947-1959, she attended: the University of Oslo, where she studied comparative government and participated in the International Student Exchange Program; New York University, where she took classes in public administration (1947); the University of California at Los Angeles, where she studied adult and nursery education; and the University of Southern California. By 1959 she had obtained a master's degree in government from Los Angeles State College. In 1959 Hernandez was married to an African-American garment cutter from Los Angeles, but was divorced in 1961.

One of the many areas of interest and avocation pursued by Hernandez was that of labor relations. Such interest appears to have been sparked and/or generated early when she became an intern with the International Ladies Garment Workers Union (ILGWU). That was during the early 1950s, when the ILGWU was trying to expand educational programs for its membership by providing qualified staff to conduct classes in such diverse areas as languages, the fine arts, and government. Hernandez, after completing her internship, was assigned to work the West Coast office in Los Angeles. From 1951 to 1959 she helped organize the office and served as shop organizer and assistant educational director. From 1959 to 1961 she was director of public relations and education. Duties varied and put her in direct contact with the people being served:

> Her activities ranged from planning picnics and dances to organizing legislative mobilizations, political rallies, strikes, and picket lines. She also taught principles of unionism and pre-naturalization classes in English and citizenship to foreign-born union members at the University of California's adult education extension at Los Angeles (Christmas, 190).

During 1960, Hernandez represented the State Department as a specialist in labor education, and as such toured South American countries (Venezuela, Columbia, Chile, Peru, Argentina, Uruguay) discussing American trade unions, the position of minority groups in the United States, the status of women, and the American political system.

In 1961 Hernandez left ILGWU to serve as campaign coordinator for Democrat Alan Cranston in his bid for state comptroller. After Cranston was elected to the post, she was appointed assistant chief of the California Fair Employment Practice Commission (FEPC). Serving ably in this appointment, Hernandez supervised a staff of fifty, covering activities in the San Francisco, Los Angeles, Fresno, and San Diego field offices. She developed a technical advisory committee that studied the effects of industrial testing in hiring minority group members. As a result of her work with ILGWU, Hernandez was named "Woman of the Year" by the Community Relations Conference of Southern California.

Because of Hernandez's educational background and breadth of experience in both labor relations and fair-employment legislation and guidelines, Governor Edmond Brown recommended and President Lyndon B. Johnson appointed her to the Equal Employment Opportunity Commission (EEOC). The commission was charged under Title Seven of the 1964 Civil Rights Act, as amended, to enforce federal laws that prohibit employment discrimination because of race, color, religion, national origin, and sex. Hernandez's appointment was both logical and noteworthy, for she became the only woman on this five-member commission. Hernandez has been quoted as saying of her appointment:

> I think when people in politics make appointments to commissions they are always trying to balance out various parts of the community. So they sort of hit the jackpot when they get someone who's black, who is a woman, who has a Mexican-American last name, who comes from California, and who's been in the labor movement ("Conversation: Ida Lewis and Aileen Hernandez," 20).

Audrey Colom, then president of the National Women's Political Caucus (NWPC), states that when Hernandez was nominated, her group was forced to make a recommendation between two very capable persons—one, of course, being Hernandez, while the other was Ron Brown, who is now chairperson of the National Democratic party, the first black male to hold such a position.

Hernandez resigned her position with EEOC within eighteen months of her appointment. She believed in its purpose but felt the commission, because of lack of true enforcement powers, was hand-strapped and therefore could not implement its policies. During her tenure with the commission, a noteworthy policy change occurred in that the airlines reversed their standard policy of terminating women flight attendants whenever they married.

Public Relations and Management Firm Founded

In 1966, Hernandez started her own public relations and management firm, Hernandez and Associates. Through this vehicle, she is able to pool her knowledge, resources, and interests and advise private business, government, labor, and other organizations on programs that use minority groups and women.

Perhaps Hernandez is most noted for being the first black woman appointed to a position with the National Organization of Women (NOW). Initially appointed in 1967 as NOW's western vice-president, she was later appointed (1971) as president and succeeded Betty Freidan, NOW's founder and first president. The appointment came at a time when NOW and the women's liberation movement were regarded by black women as an unwelcome element of competition. Typical comments regarding the movement as it related to black women specifically and blacks in general include the following:

> We should stand behind our men, not against them. . . .
>
> This movement won't be any different from the Woman Suffrage theory: White women won the right to vote way back then but black people, including black women, didn't win this right until more than 100 years later. . . .
>
> Just a bunch of bored white women with nothing to do—they're just trying to attract attention away from the black liberation movement (King, 68-70, 75-76).

To Hernandez, NOW and its activities represented a natural extension of the civil rights movement. She spurned the idea that NOW was just for elitist white women who had nothing to do:

> In our Statement of Purpose, though, NOW is much broader. We say very clearly that we consider the women's movement as an extension of the civil rights movement, that is, a movement for all people. It's not in contradiction to the black movement or to any other effort that's trying for the inclusion of people in society. We see it as a natural outgrowth of the black movement. As a black woman, I particularly think that it is important to be involved in women's liberation, largely because black women are desperately needed in the total civil rights movement. Until women, black as well as others, gain a sense of their own identity and feel they have a real choice in the society, nothing is going to happen in civil rights. It's not going to happen for blacks; it's not going to happen for Mexican-Americans; it's not going to happen for women ("Conversation," 22).

Hernandez's involvement in community and national affairs is encompassing and represents a Who's Who compendium of organizations. She is or has been a member of: the Board of Directors of the National Committee Against Discrimination in Housing; the Executive Committee of Common Cause; the Steering Committee of the National Urban Coalition; Task Force on Employment of Women of the Twentieth Century Fund; American Civil Liberties Union; National Association for the Advancement of Colored People; Industrial Relations Research Association; American Academy of Political and Social Sciences; Board of Trustees for Working Assets Money Fund; Board of Overseers for Civil Justice, Rand Corporation; advisor for the National Institute for Women of Color; treasurer of Eleanor R. Spikes Memorial Fund; cofounder and member of Black Women Organized for Action; and the National Hook-up of Black Women.

Hernandez has been recipient of the Bay Area Alumni Club's Distinguished Post Graduate Achievement Award (1967); Charter Day Alumni Post Graduate Achievement in Labor and Public Services Award (1968); Ten Most Outstanding Women in the Bay Area Award (1968); recipient of the Doctor of Humane Letters, Southern Vermont College (1979); Equal Rights Advocate Award (1981); Friends of the Commission on the Status of Women Award (1984); and the San Francisco League of Women Voters Award (Ten Women Who Made a Difference—1985).

Aileen Clark Hernandez continues to lecture on civil rights, equal employment opportunity, trade unionism, and issues related to these themes. Her public relations agency, Hernandez and Associates, is located in San Francisco, and her clients have included United Airlines, Standard Oil, United Parcel Service, National Alliance of Businessmen, University of California, and the California cities of Richmond, Berkeley, and Los Angeles.

References

Afro-American Encyclopedia. Vol. 4. Miami: Educational Book Publishers, 1986.

Christmas, Walter. *Negroes in Public Affairs and Government.* Vol. 1. Yonkers, N.Y.: Educational Heritage Year, 1966.

"Conversation: Ida Lewis and Aileen Hernandez." *Essence* (February 1971): 20-25, 74-75.

Current Biography. New York: H. W. Wilson Co., 1971.

Dreyfurs, Joel. "Civil Rights and the Women's Movement." *Black Enterprise* 8 (September 1977): 36-37, 45.

King, Helen. "The Black Woman and Women's Lib." *Ebony* (March 1971): 68-70, 75-76.

Who's Who Among Black Americans, 1990/91. 6th ed. Detroit: Gale Research, 1990.

Marva Rudolph

Amanda Gray Hilyer

(1870-1957)

Entrepreneur, pharmacist, civic worker, civil rights leader

For more than sixty years Amanda Victoria Gray Hilyer was a resident of Washington, D.C., where her cultural, social, business, and political activities made her a well-known and respected member of the community. She was born in Atchison, Kansas, on March 24, 1870, and attended public schools there. Background information on her family and her life in Kansas is not yet known. In 1893 she married Arthur S. Gray, and they moved to Washington, D.C. She attended Howard University School of Pharmacy, from which she received the pharmaceutical graduate degree in 1903. The Grays opened a pharmacy at Twelfth and U Streets in northwest Washington—a location in the heart of the black business district of that time.

Hilyer devoted much of her life to the black community in Washington, D.C. She was president of the board of directors of the Ionia R. Whipper Home and helped to found the S. Coleridge Taylor Choral Society. She was a member of the Citizens Committee for Freedmen's Hospital Nurses, a life member of the NAACP, and served on Berean Baptist Church's board of trustees. She was secretary of the Treble Clef Club and president of the Howard University Women's Club.

Hilyer belonged to the Friends of Art of Howard University and was a life member of the Association for the Study of Negro Life and History (known later as the Association for the Study of Afro-American Life and History). Through her membership and work in the Booklovers Club, she helped to found the Phillis Wheatley YWCA. When it was incorporated in 1905, she became its first recording secretary.

Robert G. McGuire III, who has written the only known biographical sketch of Hilyer and who based much of his information on interviews with local residents, tells of other activities of Hilyer and the Booklovers Club. "In 1911 they protested to President Taft against the hanging of a woman, Mattie Lomas; in March 1913 they passed a resolution opposing the opening of five-cent theaters on Sunday; and later in the year they agitated for the appointment of a matron to oversee the activities of colored youth at the public beach in Washington" (313).

After Arthur S. Gray's death in 1917, Hilyer closed the pharmacy and, like many other black women of the time, became involved in the efforts of World War I. She directed U.S. army camps. In the *Encyclopedia of Black America* (439), Low and Clift place her with camps at Upton, Dix, and Taylor, while Robert G. McGuire III reports that the War Work Council sent her to Camp Sherman in Chillicothe, Ohio. For a while after the war she lived in St. Louis and was president of the Phillis Wheatley YWCA.

In 1923 she married Andrew F. Hilyer, a Washingtonian, who was born a slave in Georgia on August 14, 1858. He was an author, inventor, and civil rights leader who was educated at Howard University. Hilyer and his first wife had worked with the Grays in many civic and social activities. Two years after his marriage to Amanda Gray, Hilyer died.

Hilyer continued her civic activities in Washington as president and board member of the Ionia Whipper Home for Unwed Mothers. Ionia (Rollin) Whipper, 1872-1953, for whom the home was named, had graduated from Howard in the same year as Hilyer and became a moral reformer. Hilyer joined others who worked to restore the Frederick Douglass home in the Anacostia section of the city.

Hilyer suffered a stroke and died on June 29, 1957, at her home, 1833 Vermont Avenue Northwest in Washington. She was eighty-seven years old. Her funeral services were held in Berean Baptist Church, and she was buried in Harmony Cemetery.

In death Hilyer still provided support for the variety of educational, church, and civic interests to which she had made a notable contribution. Beneficiaries were the Berean Baptist Church, Eleventh and V streets, which received a cash contribution and window in memory of to her first husband, Arthur S. Gray. The Ionia Whipper Home received three thousand dollars to apply to a building loan. Howard University received five hundred dollars to support a student-aid fund and an additional five hundred dollars for the department of art. The Phillis Wheatley YWCA and Stoddard Baptist Home each received fifty dollars, and her collection of books was given to the Moorland Collection at Howard University. Niece Courtney Davis Scott was given sole control of the property at 1833 Vermont Avenue N.W., where Amanda Hilyer lived. Following the niece's death, the property was to be awarded to the Association for the Study of Negro Life and History. The former pharmacist further asked that funeral expenses not exceed $500 and that she be buried in Harmony Cemetery in the same lot and same grave as her first husband.

Hilyer dedicated her life to the educational, social, and moral uplift of black people, particularly those in Washington, D.C.

References

Afro-American (Washington), 16 July 1957.

Encyclopedia of Black America. Edited by W. Augustus Low and Virgil A. Clift. New York: McGraw-Hill, 1981.

Evening Star (Washington), 2 July 1957.

McGuire, Robert G., III. "Amanda V(ictoria) Gray Hilyer." *Dictionary of American Negro Biography*. Edited by Rayford W. Logan and Michael R. Winston. New York: Norton, 1982.

———. "Andrew Franklin Hilyer." *Dictionary of American Negro Biography*. Edited by Rayford W. Logan and Michael R. Winston. New York: Norton, 1982.

Collections

The Moorland-Spingarn Collection at Howard University contains brief information on Amanda Hilyer, primarily obituaries.

Jessie Carney Smith

Natalie Hinderas

(1927-1987)

Musician, educator

Natalie Hinderas, internationally acclaimed concert pianist, was one of the first black artists to gain prominence in the field of classical music. From the time of her debut in 1954 until her death in 1987, she was a frequent soloist with major orchestras and at recitals and music festivals across the country, as well as in Europe, Asia, and Africa. A dedicated teacher, she was a member of the music faculty at Philadelphia's Temple University and held piano master classes at many major music schools.

Hinderas was born Natalie Leota Henderson on June 15, 1927, in Oberlin, Ohio. Music was an integral part of family life. As Hinderas said in the *New York Times*, "I grew up with music. I listened to my mother practice. I still remember her playing Rubinstein's D minor Concerto and Franck's Prelude, Chorale and Fugue. . . . My mother was marvelous. She was understanding and never interfered with my studies." Both parents were gifted and successful musicians, as was her great-grandfather, a bandmaster. Her father, now deceased, was a professional jazzman with his own group that toured Europe for several years. Her mother, Leota Palmer, has been a prominent conservatory music teacher (piano), at the Cleveland Institute of Music and the Jenkintown Music School near Philadelphia. A child prodigy who began playing the piano at age three and began piano study at age six, Hinderas was admitted to the Oberlin School of Music when she was eight years old. She played her first full-length recital in public that year. At the age of twelve, she played Grieg's Piano Concerto with the Cleveland Women's Symphony. In 1945, she earned her bachelor of music degree from Oberlin, becoming their youngest graduate. She then went on to study with Olga Samaroff, who had a brilliant career as a concert pianist early in the century, at the Juilliard School of Music. It was at Samaroff's suggestion that she changed her name from Henderson to Hinderas. She later studied with Edward Steuermann, a proponent of the German school of piano playing, at the Philadelphia Conservatory of Music for five years. Her music education also includes composition study with Vincent Persichetti.

Pianist Gains Sensational Recognition

From her earliest performances, Hinderas had been recognized as a musician of outstanding talent. Her debut at New York City's Town Hall in 1954 with a program including Hindemith's Sonata No. 1, Mozart's Sonata in F, Ravel's *Alborado del Gracioso*, Berg's Piano Sonata, and Chopin's F-minor Ballade was praised in a *New York Times* review, which described her as having "imagination and personality, obviously a fine musical background, and a technique in good functioning order. . .[who with] a few years more experience should take her place as a first-class pianist" (14 November 1954, 83). However, the fifties, as well as the sixties, were difficult times for black instrumentalists to make a breakthrough, and it was not until 1972 that she attained the recognition her talents deserved. In that year she made sensational debuts with the Philadelphia Orchestra and the New York Philharmonic, performing the solo part in the Concerto for Piano and Orchestra by the Argentinean composer, Alberto Ginastera, which was described by the *New York Times* as a "blockbuster." Her performance as soloist with the Symphony of the New World performing Ravel's Piano Concerto in G was praised for its "crisp precision and wonderfully infectious spirit" (*New York Times*).

Thereafter, Hinderas toured widely in the United States, performing time and again with major orchestras, including the Philadelphia Orchestra, the New York Philharmonic, the Cleveland, Dallas, Atlanta, Detroit, Los Angeles, San Francisco, Florida, Toronto, and Chicago orchestras. Her best-known performances, besides the Ginastera, include Rachmaninoff's Concerto No. 2 In C Minor, the Schumann Piano Concerto, Gershwin's *Rhapsody in Blue*, and George Walker's Piano Concerto No. 1, which she commissioned in 1975 through a grant from the National Foundation for the Arts.

Over the years, Hinderas became known for her vitality, versatility, and technical virtuosity. The *Washington Post* applauded the "sense of ease and . . . careful attention to the music's dramatic overtones" with which she "negotiated the considerable technical demands" of George Walker's Piano Concerto at its premiere performance in 1976 by the National Symphony Orchestra. In 1981, the *San Francisco Chronicle*, reviewing a recital of a "super-bravura" performance of selections by Bach, Beethoven, Debussy, Chopin, Prokofiev, Gottschalk, and Grieg, called the event "an ideal model for what a great musical evening can achieve" and proclaimed her to be "one of the great pianists of our era." The *San Francisco Chronicle*'s review of her September 1986 appearance with the American Symphony Orchestra, a year before her death, said, "Musically, the significant success of the evening belonged to Natalie Hinderas, soloist in a performance of the Rachmaninoff Second Piano Concerto, which was exceptional in all appropriate ways."

Hinderas is also well-known for her support and performance of the music of black composers. Her recording in 1971 of a record set produced by Desto Records, entitled *Natalie Hinderas Plays Music by Black Composers*, was one of the first large-scale anthologies of the music of black composers and has been widely praised over the years. The album contains the works of nine composers: R. Nathaniel Dett, Thomas H. Kerr, Jr., William Grant Still, John W. Work, George Walker, Arthur Cunningham, Hale Smith, and Olly Wilson. A review in the *American Record Guide* in April 1971 said:

> Miss Hinderas studied with, among others, Olga Samaroff and Edward Steuermann. The influence of both shows in her playing: Samaroff in the rich tone and warmly romantic feeling she can produce, Steuermann in her ability to handle the most demanding technical and intellectual requirements of advanced compositional styles. Frankly, I can think of few pianists who could play all of the music in this set with such success, producing simple lyricism in one moment and rasping along the piano strings the next, and with equal conviction (476-78).

Other recordings include a Columbia Records release of a performance of the George Walker Concerto with the Detroit Symphony under the direction of Paul Freeman and an Orion release entitled *Natalie Hinderas Plays Sensuous Piano Music*.

Hinderas was also a frequently featured performer at music festivals, such as the Hollywood Bowl, California; Blossom Center, Ohio; Grant Park, Illinois; Chautauqua, New York; Ambler, Pennsylvania; and Temple Music Festival. She gave numerous recitals for the Washington Performing Arts Society, the Philadelphia All-Star Forum, Valley Forge Music Fair, and Today's Artists Series in San Francisco. She also performed in recitals and at summer festivals at colleges and universities across the country.

Hinderas Appointed Cultural Ambassador

Hinderas toured and concertized widely in Europe, Asia, and Africa. In 1959 and 1964 her tours were sponsored by the United States Department of State, which appointed her a United States Cultural Ambassador. As such, she performed, lectured, and appeared with American diplomats in Scandinavia, the Middle East, Indonesia, Singapore, Hong Kong, the Philippine Islands, Poland, and Yugoslavia. Other European appearances included London, Vienna, Melk, Eisenstadt, Munich, Stuttgart, Heidelberg, Darmstadt, Frankfurt, Milan, Amsterdam, the Hague, Stockholm, and Norrkoping.

This versatile performer also appeared on both network and public television while under contract with the National Broadcasting Company. She created and coproduced a Philadelphia public television program, called "Contrasts," which aired nationally. She also created and produced a video entitled *Footnotes on Gershwin* with Kay Swift, William Bolcom, and Joan Morris, on which she both performed and hosted. She was interviewed extensively on radio and television, notably on NBC's "Today Show" and WQXR's "Robert Sherman Show." Other radio highlights include the "Robin Hood Dell Previews" on WUHY-FM Philadelphia, interviews with prominent Dell conductors and soloists, which she coproduced and cohosted.

Throughout the years, Hinderas successfully combined her careers as performer and music educator. She joined the faculty of the College of Music, Temple University in Philadelphia, in the 1960s and was professor of piano there at the time of her death. Her master classes on college campuses across the country were in great demand. She was a frequent guest lecturer at colleges, universities, and music schools. She received many prestigious awards, including the Levintritt Award, "Musical America's" Musician of the Month award, an honorary doctorate of music from Swarthmore College, the Governors' Award for the Arts (Pennyslvania), and the Pro Arte Award. She was awarded fellowships from the Martha Baird Rockefeller, John Hay Whitney, and Julius Rosenwald foundations.

Hinderas was married to Lionel Monagas, a television producer. They have a daughter, Michele Monagas. Hinderas died of cancer in her home in Philadelphia in August 1987.

References

Abdul, Raoul. *Blacks in Classical Music*. New York: Dodd, Mead, 1977.

"American Symphony—Whirlwind Visit." *San Francisco Chronicle*, 29 September 1986.

"A Colored Girl Like You Can't Play in the Hollywood Bowl." *New York Times*, 19 November 1972. Includes photography.

Hinderas, Natalie. Biographical information courtesy of Joanne Rile Artists Representatives, 424 West Upsal Street, Philadelphia, Pa. 19119.

"In Praise of a Concerto." *Washington Post*, 15 January 1976. Includes photograph.

"Miss Hinderas Plays Debut Piano Recital." *New York Times*, 14 November 1954.

"Natalie Hinderas, A Fine Night With an Invincible Pianist." *San Francisco Chronicle,* 9 March 1981.

"Natalie Hinderas Plays Music by Black Composers." *American Record Guide* 37 (April 1971): 476-78.

"New World Delights in a Solid Program of Weber, Brahms." *New York Times,* 21 October 1974.

Southern Eileen. *Biographical Dictionary of Afro-American and African Musicians.* Westport, Conn.: Greenwood Press, 1982.

Robert W. Stephens

Billie Holiday "Lady Day"

(1915-1959)

Singer

Arguably one of the most influential jazz singers of our time, Billie Holiday's story is one characterized by triumph and tragedy. Her autobiography, *Lady Sings the Blues,* which in 1972 became a movie by the same title, chronicles a life that begins with a troubled childhood and spans a successful and lucrative singing career of some thirty years. Like most musicians whose music is the sum total of their life experiences, she was particularly sensitive to the sting of rejection by those who could not accept or identify with those life experiences that informed her unique musical style. Like black Americans throughout the entertainment world during that period, Holiday was also subjected to the overt and covert racism that pervaded the industry as much then as many would argue it does now.

As profound as these experiences were, her singing style was never sentimental in a weak way, as some might expect. Instead, her graceful phrasing and distinctively light timbre enabled her to render popular jazz tunes dealing with heartbreak, despair, and loneliness with a buoyancy that rose above the heavy sentimentality of the words. Although famous for her poignant renditions of her own life-based compositions such as "God Bless the Child," "Don't Explain," and "Fine and Mellow," her repertoire also included lighthearted Cole Porter and Irving Berlin tunes, such as "I Get a Kick Out of You" (Porter) and "Isn't This a Lovely Day" (Berlin).

In his album cover notes on *All or Nothing At All* (1978), jazz historian Stanley Crouch suggests that Holiday's success as a jazz singer had more to do with "her extraordinary musical talent" and the nature of the jazz genre than with the emotional impact of victimization. He argues that as a singer with a unique sound, whom some thought would have no commercial appeal, Holiday "personifies the reasons why jazz has become so significant, for it is the most democratic of Western musics; in the sense that it has been developed by every imaginable type of musician, from the most primitive to the most urbane." He points out as well that jazz is a music "in which the lyric content can be extremely melancholy while the rhythmic accompaniment can be exuberant, buoyant—swinging." Crouch contends that although most people conceive of "jazzing something up" as making it more complicated, in actuality, "it would be much better to say that, at its best, to jazz something up is to straighten it up, make it more humanly valuable rather than less." This description captures the essence of Billie Holiday's music.

In order to understand more fully the development of this gifted vocalist, it is important to examine the social and musical environment in which she grew up and to appreciate the combination of events that set the stage for her emergence as a jazz singer in the musical and cultural milieu that existed in the Harlem of the 1930s.

Billie Holiday was born Eleanora Fagan on April 7, 1915, in Baltimore, Maryland. Her parents, Sadie Fagan and Clarence Holiday, though unmarried at the time of her birth, did marry when she was three years old. The marriage failed, however, because of the frequent absences of her father, who as a guitarist and banjoist with some of the earliest jazz bands, often had to travel in order to perform. Indeed, he was a musician of some stature who worked with many leading bandleaders of the day, including Billy Fowler, Fletcher Henderson, and Don Redman, and also with the McKinney's Cotton Pickers.

Holiday's mother tried as best she could to support the family on wages earned as a domestic worker. But the earnings were much too small, and she was eventually forced to leave Holiday with relatives so that she could look for work in Philadelphia and New York, where the wage scale was higher. Although conditions were overcrowded and Holiday often had to endure a very contentious relationship with her cousin, Ida, her life did have its happy moments. She established a very close and loving relationship with her great-grandmother, a former slave on a Virginia plantation, who had given birth to sixteen children fathered by the white plantation owner by the name of Charles Fagan. This was also the time when Holiday decided to change her name to Billie, after one of her favorite movie stars, Billie Dove.

As a child, Holiday was a very enterprising young woman who earned money by babysitting, running errands, and scrubbing steps in the neighborhood. Whatever she did, nothing was more important to her than singing. And she took advantage of every opportunity available to sing and listen to music. One place she found music happened to be a neighborhood brothel, which had one of the few victrolas in the area. It was there she first heard the music of artists like Bessie Smith and Louis Armstrong, who were later to become her musical mentors. These recordings, and most recorded music in the black American community, were being developed for the booming "race market." This is a term developed by the recording industry and was used to describe the industry's targeting of black audiences in the 1920s. Record companies that previously had been slow to record black artists responded with great haste to the tastes of the black community after the overwhelming success of Mamie Smith's 1920 hit, "Crazy Blues," featuring her Jazz Hounds. That recording, which sold more than five hundred thousand copies, opened doors for and boosted the careers of such classic blues greats as Ma Rainey and her protégée, Bessie Smith, as well as Victoria Spivey and Alberta Hunter. But perhaps most important, Mamie Smith's success paved the way for the recordings of other black performers who followed her, including Billie Holiday.

It was during these formative years that Holiday developed an affinity for the recordings of Bessie Smith. Although Holiday later resisted being called a blues singer, her style was strongly grounded in the blues tradition—not in terms of musical structure, but in terms of feeling. She is often quoted as saying, "I got my manner from Bessie Smith and Louis Armstrong, honey. [I] wanted her [Bessie's] feeling and Louis' style." Although there would be a sharp contrast between the big sound of Bessie Smith and Holiday's light vibrato, this description, taken from Harrison's views of the Empress of the Blues, as Smith was known, could have been written about Billie Holiday as well:

> Jazz musicians, gospel singers, and popular song vocalists all acknowledge Bessie as a major influence because of her keen sense of timing, her expressiveness, and her flawless phrasing. . . . She drained each phrase of its substance and bathed each tone with warmth, anger, or pathos. . . . Although both [Ma] Rainey and Smith generally confined the melodic range of their songs within intervals of a fifth or a sixth, Smith employed more improvisation—rhythmic and melodic—which endowed the lyrics with added power and meaning. Her association with jazz musicians had a mutually beneficial effect and she developed vocal techniques as sophisticated as the techniques used by a horn player (52).

Horn Players and the Blues Tradition Influence Holiday's Style

Like Bessie Smith, Holiday was also deeply influenced by horn players. In those early days, it was the playing of the great Louis (Satchmo) Armstrong, whom she heard on many of Bessie Smith's albums. Well-known as a jazz composer, Armstrong was also the first to develop improvisation and scat singing and had a strong influence on many jazz artists. "Armstrong, like Bessie Smith," according to Crouch, "was a master of inflection, capable of coming down on a note in almost endless ways, to the extent that one tone could jab, bite, simmer, dissolve, swell, yelp, sizzle, or grind" (Album cover notes, *All or Nothing At All*). In later years, as an established performer, Holiday's association with some of the finest jazz musicians of the time, especially Count Basie's tenor saxist, Lester Young, would produce some of her best work. The horn-like qualities of her singing were often commented upon. In the *Illustrated Encyclopedia of Jazz* Brian Case and Stan Britt point out that:

> Her timing, for example, was as impeccable as the finest jazz instrumental players. She phrased in a definitely instrumental fashion, although her instrumental-like, horn-influenced singing never was less than music, distorting neither melodic line or interfering with the matchless way in which she lived a lyric. . . . With Lester Young, she established an almost unbelievable rapport, tenorist providing sublime intros, obbligatos, as well as solos of superlative quality, each complementing, enhancing vocal lines to perfection (99-100).

It is not surprising that on some of these recordings, her voice often took on the qualities of the instruments themselves. As Holiday herself put it, "I don't think I'm singing. I feel like I'm playing a horn. I try to improvise like Les Young, like Louis Armstrong or someone else I admire. What comes out is what I feel. I hate straight singing. I have to change a tune to my own way of doing it. That's all I know" (*Celebrating the Duke,* 78).

The impact of the blues cannot be ignored when examining the influences on Holiday's music. Holiday's songs, like the blues, are conceptually and in essence music that can be traced to African work songs, which were the legacy of generations of African slaves. Field hollers, a method of sung communication between slaves, as well as church hymns and spirituals, were all significant influences. Similarly, the blues is at its core a mode of expression in an estranged subculture where expression is censored. What the expression dealt with, very simply, was life and all of its vicissitudes, be it sorrow or joy, loneliness or celebration, poverty or plenty. Traveling minstrel shows spread the blues tradition throughout the United States, where it mirrored changing black sensitivities as well as the cultures of urban and country life. Like many other forms of popular music such as rhythm and blues, rock and roll, soul and gospel, jazz has it proponents, like Holiday, whose styles reverberate with the "tell it like it is" essence of the blues tradition.

When she was ten, an attempted rape by a neighbor led to Holiday's incarceration in a Catholic reformatory, a term meant to last until she reached the age of twenty-one. One night, as a punishment, she was locked in a room with the corpse of a child that had been killed in an accident. When Sadie Fagan learned of the incident, she pleaded with the authorities to allow her daughter to be released. Permission was granted and in 1927 Holiday joined her mother in Harlem. It was there in a Harlem brothel, where her mother had unwittingly boarded her, that she became a prostitute. However, this career was shortlived; she refused to succumb to the demands of a customer who later maneuvered her arrest. She was thirteen years old at the time. In order to avoid being sent to another reformatory, her mother told the judge that Billie was eighteen so that she could be sentenced as an adult. As a result, Holiday spent four months in an adult correctional institution on the East River.

As the 1920s drew to a close, Billie Holiday and her mother were living on 139th street in the heart of Harlem, which was in a depression even before the rest of the country was caught in the grip of the Great Depression. In Harlem, for every person who had a job there was one who was out of work. As Holiday recounts the story in her autobiography, the family was in dire straits when Sadie Fagan fell ill and could not work. They were on the brink of starvation and eviction when the fifteen-year-year old Holiday stormed the restaurants and speakeasies of Seventh Avenue desperately trying to find work. In a basement speakeasy called Pod's and Jerry's (also known as The Log Cabin), she was given a chance to sing after miserably failing a dance audition. She sang "Trav'lin' All Alone," a popular tune at the time. By the end of the song, she had won over the entire audience and the club's managers. She was hired on the spot.

Around the same time that Holiday began her career in a Harlem speakeasy, Harlem had reached the peak of an artistic, cultural, and economic revitalization that had been taking place since the mid-1920s. Harlem became a magnet for black performers who were being booked into Harlem clubs instead of their usual downtown venues. The ferment gave rise to an exotic nightlife that became an obsession for middle-class America. The fires of this obsession were fanned by the writers of the day, especially Carl Van Vechten, who wrote a bestseller called *Nigger Heaven*, depicting Harlem life. Musicians from across the country were drawn to the vibrant musical environment that became a microcosm of the latest sounds and styles from around the country—including jazz in all its forms. As Bud Kliment notes in his biography of Billie Holiday:

> Earthy blues, syncopated ragtime and jubilant gospel were already present in Harlem by 1920. But when itinerant musicians such as Fletcher Henderson and Duke Ellington arrived there in the early part of the decade, they brought something new with them: a form of music called jazz. An amalgam of blues, ragtime spirituals, folk music and marches, it quickly became an uptown favorite (37-38).

It was in this highly-charged musical and social environment that Holiday was first heard. Timme Rosenkrantz and Inez Cavanaugh describe a night at Pod's and Jerry's in 1934 when they first heard what they called "the Jazz Voice of our century," the unforgettable voice of Holiday:

> Billie lifted a voice that was the embodiment of her strange beauty—the heaven, the hell, the joy, the pain of being a Negro. Out came the music from the depths of her soul as if in constant struggle to reconcile the love in her heart with the hell in her life. . . . (Album notes, *Billie Holiday's Greatest Hits*).

Talented Lady Day in Great Demand

For the next seventeen years, Holiday (also known as "Lady Day") established herself as one of the most sought-after singers in the clubs of Harlem, Greenwich Village, and Manhattan's Fifty-second Street. Her earliest performances were in Harlem clubs with names like Monette's, Mexico's, the Hot Cha Cha Club, the Shim Sham Club. Many of the clubs had been speakeasies during Prohibition, selling illegal alcohol along with food and entertainment. After prohibition was repealed in 1933, many became legitimate clubs. It was at Monette's that she was discovered by music producer and promoter John Hammond. As Bud Klimert described in his book *Billie Holiday*:

> Hammond immediately recognized Holiday's enormous talent when she came out and sang "Wouldja for a Big Red Apple?" As she moved from table to table, he sat transfixed. "To my astonishment," he said, "she sang a completely different chorus to the same tune at each table. It was the first really improvising singer that I had heard." By the end of the evening, Hammond, who would later help launch the careers of such diversely talented artists as Benny Goodman, Count Basie, Bob Dylan, Aretha Franklin and Bruce Springsteen, thought that "she was the best jazz singer I had ever heard" (44-45).

Hammond wrote Holiday's first rave review in the *Melody Maker* and brought many influential people to hear her, including Joe Glaser, Louis Armstrong's manager, who agreed to manage her. John Hammond was also instrumental in the launching of Holiday's recording career in 1933 by introducing her to Benny Goodman, then a radio studio musician who dreamed of having his own orchestra. At that time vocalists were not featured performers on recordings, and Holiday sang just a few choruses of "Your Mother's Son-in-Law" and "Riffin' the Scotch." Shortly thereafter, Hammond organized another recording session that became the standard for Holiday for the next few years. Jazz pianist Teddy Wilson was brought in to conduct groups of seven or eight musicians, always the finest jazz musicians of the time, including Benny Goodman on clarinet, Roy Eldridge on trumpet, and Ben Webster on saxophone. Together they recorded such Holiday standards as "I Cried For You," "Mean to Me," "My Man," "I Cover the Waterfront," "I Only Have Eyes For You" and "Miss Brown to You." Although none of the tunes became hits at the time, they were initially very popular on the jukebox, a new innovation that allowed people to play records for just one nickel.

It was also at a Harlem nightspot called the Hot-Cha Bar and Grill that Holiday was discovered by the master of ceremonies of the Apollo Theatre, who booked her for a week starting in April of 1935. She was a tremendous success before a tough New York audience that had been known to "boo" performers off the stage. She was invited back for a second appearance that August. Her success on the stage of the most important black entertainment center in the country was a major stepping-stone to her commercial success.

During this period Holiday also appeared in clubs outside of New York, including a long run at Chicago's Downbeat Club in 1942, several years after an unsuccessful early attempt at the Grand Terrace in 1936. She became a favorite with movie personalities at the Red Colonna in the San Fernando Valley, the Plantation Club in Los Angeles, and at Billie Berg's, with Lester Young as accompanist. Road tours with Count Basie in 1937 and Artie Shaw in 1938 were less joyous occasions. Road shows were brutal affairs. Musicians traveled hundreds of miles by bus, with barely enough time to rehearse and dress between performances. The pay was so low and expenses so high that many did not break even. For black performers, especially a black singer in an all-white band, the road was a nightmare. The use of eating, sleeping, and bathroom facilities was severely restricted for all blacks. A performer on the road had no choice but to breach these barriers in order to survive. The result was often violent. After these experiences, Holiday decided to try her luck as a solo performer. This transition was made easier by the opening of Barney Josephson's Cafe Society in Greenwich Village.

Cafe Society was designed to be a truly multiracial nightclub, a unique concept in the Manhattan of the 1930s. Obviously, the music-loving public was ready for such a change, because the club was a huge success made possible in part by the enormous popularity of Holiday. Her two-year residence there firmly established her as a star. As described by Ralph Gleason in *Celebrating the Duke:*

> Billie Holiday, when she was in her prime . . . was simply the most magnetic and beautiful woman I have ever seen as well as the most emotionally moving singer I have ever heard. I remember when she opened at Cafe Society, in December 1939, for her first big nightclub break. She was simply shocking in her impact. Standing there with a spotlight on her great, sad, beautiful face, a white gardenia in her hair, she sang her songs, and the other singers were never the same thereafter (80).

Holiday's appearance there also marked another turning point in her career with her debut of an antilynching song called "Strange Fruit," based on a poem by Lewis Allan. Although many found the song objectionable, it was a huge hit. Holiday went on to record it on Milt Gabler's Commodore label with Frankie Newton's orchestra. Klimer contends that it was this song that established Holiday as a "serious dramatic singer," a style that was popular with her fans. "She gradually gained a reputation for being a torch singer, a performer of sentimental songs about heartbreak and unrequited love"(69).

Breaking into "Swing Street" (Manhattan's Fifty-second street) was a slower process. In the late 1930s and early 1940s, the clubs there were still largely segregated. Holiday and Teddy Wilson were virtually the only black performers there during that time and they were relegated to intermission performances. Both lost their first jobs at the Famous Door by fraternizing with the customers. The opening of the Cafe Society and the formation of integrated bands like Benny Goodman's worked to change that. Eventually Holiday was able to open as a headliner at a club called Kelly's Stables, where she appeared with Nat Cole, the Coleman Hawkins Band, the Ray Eldridge Band, and Una Mae Carlisle, among others.

Peak Years in Popularity Reached

The next few years following the Cafe Society appearances were probably Holiday's peak years in terms of popularity. As Ian Carr described her in *Jazz: The Essential Companion:*

> At her peak, in the swing-happy '30's, Billie Holiday was unquestionably the greatest jazz singer of them all, an avant-garde artist of her time who polished unremarkable popular songs into iridescent gems. She ecstatically recreated her songs' melodies in a small, worldly voice that, in Barney Josephson's words, "rang like a bell and went a mile" (237).

By this time, she was recording alone on the Vocalion label and with Teddy Wilson on Brunswick. Later she recorded on Decca and became one of the first jazz artists to use strings as an accompaniment. She also made her acting debut in radio soap operas and a short film called *Symphony in Black* with Duke Ellington's Orchestra. Her role was remarkably similar to the one Bessie Smith played in her first and only film appearance in *St. Louis Blues,* made in 1929. In the film, she played a prostitute who sings a poignant love song after being knocked to the floor. For Holiday, it was a disappointing introduction to the film industry, where white filmmakers often portrayed blacks in uncomplimentary roles.

Unfortunately, Holiday's professional success during this peak period was not accompanied by personal triumphs. Her marriage to Jimmy Monroe in 1941, a destructive relationship, marked the beginning of a heroin addiction that she fought for the rest of her life. Inspite of this, her singing career was still on the upswing. In 1943, she won the first of several music industry distinctions, an award for "Best Vocalist" in a jazz critics poll, followed by her first appearance on the stage of a New York City concert hall, the Metropolitan Opera House. She also appeared at New York City's Town Hall. Other awards during this time included several Esquire awards from 1944 to 1947 and the Metronome Award in 1945 and 1946. In 1946 she made her Hollywood acting debut with Louis Armstrong in a movie called *New Orleans*. Since the movie was about the music scene in New Orleans, she had hoped she would be playing herself. Both she and Armstrong were cast as domestics. This was the end of her acting attempts. In 1947, she was arrested for the first time on a narcotics charge. Ironically, she had just emerged from a New York sanatorium where she had gone in 1946 to kick the habit. Of course, this alerted the public, which included narcotics agents, to her addiction. During a performance at the Earle Theatre in Philadelphia, agents searched her room and came up with enough evidence to convict her of narcotics possession. She was sent to the Federal Reformatory for Women at Alderson, West Virginia, where she served a nine-month term.

Upon her release, Holiday was denied a cabaret card, which was needed in New York to work in any establishment that required a liquor license. Therefore, she could only play theaters and concert halls if she was to work in New York at all. Joe Glaser, her agent, booked her into Carnegie Hall immediately. She played to a sold-out house. Chairs were put on the stage behind her so that a few hundred additional people could hear her sing. Although the concert was a tremendous success, a subsequent Broadway revue at the Mansfield Theatre called "Holiday on Broadway," closed after just three weeks, probably because of advertising problems. She also appeared at the Strand Theatre with Count Basie's orchestra, which drew some of the biggest crowds in its history. At this time, she formed an association with John Levy, who as manager of the Ebony Club in New York, arranged for her to perform there even without a cabaret card. Even though Levy made it possible for her to perform again in a New York club, Holiday paid a heavy price. In 1949, while performing in a San Francisco club, she was arrested again for narcotics possession as a result of Levy's drug use. She was cleared of the charges after several months.

The 1950s are generally considered a period of decline for Holiday, due primarily to drug and alcohol-related problems. Yet she continued to record on Verve for Norman Granz, jazz promoter and producer, and made a variety of recordings with Ben Webster, Freddie Greene, and Harry Edison. Some critics thought that her voice had been ruined by the effects of her addictions. Others disagreed. A 1987 review of *The Billie Holiday Songbook* says:

> Nowhere is the disparity between the young, life-embracing singer of the '30's and '40's and the bruised, aged-before-her-time Billie Holiday of the '50's more apparent than in this collection of trademark songs she recorded for Verve. Better-or-worse judgments just don't apply here. The vocal timbre may have hardened, but these seasoned interpretations are so marked by divested emotion and hard-won insight that they are essentially different songs. Billie's artistry keeps them free of maudlin sentiment and self-pity (*High Fidelity,* 74).

In this last phase of Holiday's career, some of the happier moments included the realization of a long-awaited dream, which was to perform in Europe. She first appeared there in 1954 on a Leonard Feather Jazz Club U.S.A. tour stopping in Scandinavia, Germany, Holland, Belgium, France, Switzerland, and England, where she performed for a crowd of six thousand at London's Royal Albert Hall. At home, she appeared at the Newport Jazz Festival, the first jazz festival in the United States, and received a 1954 *Down Beat* award. On a personal note, her marriage to Louis McKay in 1956 provided a steadying influence. Through his encouragement, she collaborated with a friend at the *New York Post,* William Dufty, to write her life story. A few months after its publication in 1956, she was arrested for possession of drugs. Instead of going to prison, she was permitted to seek rehabilitation in a sanatorium. Although the treatment was successful, the underlying problems were not resolved and she later resorted to alcohol, which eventually destroyed her marriage and contributed to the continued decline of her health. Toward the end of the 1950s, heavy drinking and bad health made her an unreliable performer. She did work regularly from time to time, even appearing on a televised special in 1957 called "The Sound of Jazz" with Lester Young. In 1958 she recorded "Lady in Satin" with the Ray Ellis Orchestra, one of her biggest sellers. Her last performance was at the Phoenix Theatre in 1959, where she had to be led off the stage after completing two songs. Holiday died in Harlem's Metropolitan Hospital on July 17, 1959.

Today, Holiday is widely considered one of the most influential jazz singers of our time. As Ralph Gleason said in *Celebrating the Duke:*

> She was a singer of jazz, the greatest female jazz voice of all time, a great interpreter, a great actress and the creator of a style that, in its own way, is as unique and important to jazz as the styles of Louis Armstrong, Charlie Parker and Lester Young. . . . She did something no other woman has ever done in jazz. Today, if you sing jazz and you're a woman, you sing some of Billie Holiday. . . . No vocalist is without her influence (75).

References

Carr, Ian, Digby Fairweather, and Brian Priestley. *Jazz—The Essential Companion.* New York: Prentice Hall, 1987.

Case, Brian, and Stan Britt. *Illustrated Encyclopedia of Jazz.* New York: Harmony Books, 1978. Includes photograph.

Chilton, John. *Billie's Blues.* New York: Stein and Day, 1975.

——. *Who's Who of Jazz: Storyville to Swing.* Philadelphia: Chilton Book Co., 1972.

Crouch, Stanley. Album cover notes from *All or Nothing At All.* Billie Holiday. Verve. 1978.

Futterman, Steve. Review of *The Billie Holiday Songbook. High Fidelity* 37 (May 1987): 74.

Gleason, Ralph J. *Celebrating the Duke and Louis, Bes-*

sie, Billie, Bird, Carmen, Miles, Dizzy and Other Heroes. Little, Brown, 1975. Contains photographs.

Harrison, Daphne Duval. *Black Pearls: Blues Queens of the 1920's.* New Brunswick: Rutgers University Press, 1988.

Holiday, Billie, and William Dufty. *Lady Sings the Blues.* 1956. Reprinted. London: Penquin, 1988. Includes selected discography.

Kliment, Bud. *Billie Holiday: Singer.* New York: Chelsea House Publishers, 1990. Includes photograph and selected discography.

"The Paradox of Billie Holiday." *Variety* 5 (22 July 1959).

Rosencrantz, Timme, and Inez Cavanaugh. Album notes from *Billie Holiday's Greatest Hits.* Columbia Records.

"Swing. Best of the Big Bands. Vol. I." MCA Home Video. 1987. Includes Billie Holiday singing "God Bless the Child" and "Baby, Will You Fall in Love?"

Who Was Who in America. Vol. 4, 1961-1968. Chicago: Marquis, 1968.

Wintz, Carl D. *Black Culture and the Harlem Renaissance.* Houston: Rice University Press, 1988.

Robert W. Stephens

Annie Wealthy Holland

(1871-1934)

Educator, organization founder

In the early decades of the twentieth century when de jure segregation and intransigent poverty prevented most black Americans from acquiring even a basic education, Annie Wealthy Daughtry Holland, a tireless teacher and intrepid organizer, effectively mobilized rural black communities to support education and improve their living conditions. Moving from southeastern Virginia to neighboring North Carolina, Holland applied the concepts of industrial education and the principles of community cooperation and self-help to teach practical skills to thousands and to organize improvement clubs. Her thirty years of effort laid the foundations for the rural cooperative movement and parent-teacher associations among black Americans in North Carolina.

Annie Wealthy Holland

Holland was born in Virginia in 1871 on a farm adjacent to the wealthy plantation, where her grandfather and great-grandfather had both been slaves. In the 1860s the Wealthy family freed her grandfather, Friday Daughtry. He started his own farm with twenty acres, a mule, and a cow, and eventually acquired one hundred fifty acres and had a comfortable living. In 1869 his eldest son, John, married Margaret Hill, and when the first of their seven children was born, they named her Annie Wealthy Daughtry.

As the eldest child, Holland grew up shouldering responsibility. She helped care for her younger siblings and attended the Isle of Wight school for blacks. After a difficult marriage to Annie Daughtry's father, her mother married a second time and the family moved to Southampton County. Two years later Holland's grandfather, Friday Daughtry, brought her back to Isle of Wight, where she worked on the family farm and completed her studies at the county school. By now she had developed a lasting love for rural life and a consuming commitment to education.

At sixteen years of age, she enrolled at Hampton Institute as an eighth-grade industrial student. Her grandfather paid the first year's school expenses, but ill health curtailed his support. To earn money for the coming school year, Holland went to work in the summer for a wealthy white family in New York. She completed a second year at Hampton, but the following summer a bout with recurring malaria forced her to quit working before the summer was over and to spend what money she had earned on medical bills. Lacking funds to pay school fees, she finally dropped out of Hampton. Her grandfather helped her pay for room and board with an uncle in Washington, D.C., where she spent another term in school, but he was unable to continue providing even this modest support. She returned home to work as a teacher in the county elementary school.

During this era, an examination system allowed prospective teachers to acquire a certificate and secure a job without a college degree. Normal schools were established in the latter decades of the nineteenth century to provide teacher training. Holland ultimately completed a summer course at Virginia Normal Industrial Institute in Petersburg and passed the examination for a permanent teaching certificate.

After she began teaching, financial pressures and family responsibilities continued to mount. Her mother died, leaving three young children, one only a year old, to be cared for. In a letter she later wrote to the principal of Hampton Institute, she recalled, "I then gave up all hope of ever returning to Hampton, for I knew I had to be mother for these children. My grandparents were old and feeble, especially my grandmother. My stepfather was a drunkard and did not support his family at all" (Annie W. Holland to Hollis B. Frissell, 27 October 1914, Hampton University Archives).

She left teaching and went back to New York to work as a nurse and dressmaker, but her grandmother's rapidly failing health forced her to return home, where she resumed teaching. Just before her grandmother died, Annie Wealthy Daughtry married Willis B. Holland, a Hampton graduate, who was also a teacher. In 1897, she moved with him to Franklin, Virginia, where he was principal of a school, and worked as his assistant until 1899 when she asked to be transferred to the rural areas outside Franklin because of recurring illness. She recovered her health and discovered her life's work in the countryside.

Rural Community Assistance Programs Promoted

Severe problems emerged in her first term. Student attendance was erratic, and many came to class in tattered, inadequate clothing. Holland began to visit her students' homes and discovered that only two black families in the area owned their own land or homes. She was rooming with one of the two. The rest were impoverished tenant farmers who could not afford to send their children to school before they had harvested their crops. After they paid rent for their tools and houses and paid on the continually mounting debts for seed and supplies, they rarely had enough money left to buy books and clothing for school. Neither could they afford to buy land, because the owners would sell only in large lots they could not afford.

Persuading them to pool their funds, Holland patiently organized them into cooperative buying clubs. She raised money to buy shoes for children to wear to school in the cold winter months and bought flannel so they could make a change of clothing for the fall. These initial efforts to meet community needs prepared her for much greater organizing activity in North Carolina.

In 1903 she completed the teacher training course at the Normal Industrial Institute in Petersburg and passed the examination for a five-year certificate. In 1905 her husband resigned from Franklin school and permanently left teaching to sell insurance. She was appointed to the vacant principal's position and went to work to build enrollment. She and an assistant were the only teachers. Enrollment had mounted to 148 students by 1909 and continued to grow. Operations were hampered by a lack of funds, and the board of trustees shortened the school year from six to five months.

Such problems were common in school systems of that era. Public education in general received little government support and rural schools spent even less per student than city schools. At the turn of the century most of the population in the United States was rural. The rural majority was even greater in the South, which depended on agriculture for economic development. In North Carolina, where Holland spent the best of her working years, rural schools were not organized under a central admini-stration until 1900. Public elementary schools for black Americans did not receive regular financial support from public funds until 1910. Until 1918 there were no public secondary schools for any race in North Carolina.

In 1911 Holland moved to North Carolina to work at Gates Institute in Sunbury, where she was Gates County rural school supervisor, overseeing industrial classes in the twenty-two schools. In 1912 she moved to nearby Corapeake, where she expanded her work to include improving one and actually building another school.

In a letter from Corapeake she wrote:

> I have for the past two years been working hard to interest the people in improvement of school buildings. As a result we are having erected a nice school building that we feel will be a credit to the community. It is to cost $1,000. When completed, we think it will cost a little more than that. We have just completed a room that was added to one of our school buildings. That will cost a little over $300. The people gave $114 in cash, labor, and material; the county $112; and we have the promise of the balance from the Rosenwald Fund (Newbold, 76)

Philanthropy Aids Black Schools

The Julius Rosenwald Fund was established in 1910 by the major stockholder of the Sears Roebuck Company, then the major catalogue retailer in the country. The fund was used extensively to finance building programs for black schools by providing matching funds. Financial support from Rosenwald, the Slater Fund, and the Duke Foundation was crucial to the hard-pressed segregated schools. Private philanthropy was a major factor in the development of black education in North Carolina. Perhaps the most important of these foundations was the Anna T. Jeanes Fund for the Assistance of Negro Rural Schools in the South. The Jeanes Fund paid the salaries of rural supervisors of industrial education: sewing, cooking, gardening, agriculture, blacksmithing, carpentry, chair caning, hammock making, mat- making, canning, and other manual skills needed in rural communities. The fund was established in 1907 two years before its unusual benefactor died. Jeanes, a Philadelphia Quaker, had established a reputation for philanthropy and simplicity. In one of her acts of charity, she built a home for the aged and disabled. Although she was a millionaire, in her old age she lived in the boarding house herself in a plain room where she received no special attention.

In 1905 Anna T. Jeanes received a visit from Booker T. Washington, founder and principal of Tuskegee Institute, then the premier industrial school in the South, and Hollis B. Frissell, principal of Hampton Institute, the forerunner of Tuskegee and Washington's alma mater. The two men asked the reluctant donor to fund building programs for their respective schools. Apparently prodded by fellow philanthropist George Foster Peabody, she gave one hundred thousand dollars to each school. Two years later, just before her death, she established a one-million-dollar trust fund, the Anna T. Jeanes Foundation, and gave Frissell and Washington authority to create a board to administer the fund.

Washington had established a reputation for channeling money from white philanthropists to a variety of schools for African- Americans. He put together a board that included a future United States president, Howard Taft, and prominent industrialist Andrew Carnegie. Washington was named chairman of the executive committee and James H. Dillard, a liberal white southerner and former Tulane professor, its president and director.

Washington championed industrial education, the teaching of manual labor skills to rural blacks, instead of courses such as geography, history, algebra, and literature that were being taught elsewhere. He and his supporters considered manual education the kind that "would actually mean something to the people in the community where the school exists" (Harlan, 199). Most northern industrialists apparently agreed and the Jeanes teachers, as they became popularly known, used this concept to create a positive climate for later developments in black education.

Holland Becomes Jeanes Fund Supervisor

In 1914, three years after she had moved to Gates County, Holland returned to Hampton Institute to take a special ten-day summer normal course in agriculture. In 1915, she was appointed State Home Demonstration Agent for North Carolina, a position that made her the Jeanes Fund State Supervisor. Most Jeanes supervisors were women between thirty-five and fifty years of age who were experienced teachers with established reputations in public schools. About half were educated at Hampton, Tuskegee, or other normal and industrial schools. The first one was appointed in Georgia and another in Virginia before Holland was chosen for the job in North Carolina. Her family continued to live in Franklin, Virginia, while she apparently lived in rooming houses during the school term. She went home the remaining months and on weekends whenever possible. Holland gave birth to a daughter who married and remained in Franklin, where she raised her own family.

As state supervisor, Holland was responsible for the work of forty-five county supervisors. Traveling by train or catching a ride with local friends, Holland kept a rigorous schedule. In April 1916, N.C. Newbold, the director of the state's education program for blacks, set her itinerary for the next two weeks. He told her to visit ten eastern counties, from Bertie County in the north to Robeson County on the South Carolina border. He expected her to spend about two days in each county helping organize homemakers' clubs. In May, after she had returned from the tour, she reported "good results," adding, "to me the entire trip has been very pleasant. It has been full of inspiration and I hope I have given the same to those with whom I have been associated" (Annie W. Holland to N. C. Newbold, 16 May, 1916, North Carolina State Archives).

The following year she reported visiting the Piedmont counties: Mecklenburg, Gaston, Iredel, Buncombe, and Alamance. She traveled to the mountainous Wilkes County and beyond. Between May 29 and July 1, 1917, she visited twenty-one counties, teaching vegetable canning, chair caning, gardening, and other skills and encouraging the Homemakers Clubs to raise and sell poultry and pigs.

During the 1916-1917 school year, Jeanes teachers under Annie Wealthy Holland's supervision made 3,700 visits to thirty-five counties, covering more than 1400 schools. They reported organizing improvement leagues, getting buildings painted or whitewashed, outhouses built, and grounds improved. About ten percent of the schools extended their terms from four to five months that year.

Most rural schools had only one room and a single teacher for fifty to one hundred students. Often classes were held in a local church because there were no school buildings. Many schools lacked windows, stoves, or even tables and chairs. Often there were no books or tablets, blackboards, or chalk. The Jeanes teachers not only supervised classroom instruction and demonstrated how to teach canning and cooking, they also made frequent home visits, attended local churches, and helped teachers organize commencement exercises to rally public support for the schools. They put together improvement leagues and mothers clubs and helped sponsor concerts and other programs to raise money for education.

In the perspective of some observers, Jeanes teachers were unpaid county superintendents who trained black teachers without pay. In the 1920s Jeanes teachers reportedly earned between seventy and one hundred twenty dollars a month. In 1915, when Newbold appointed Holland North Carolina State Supervisor, half of her salary was paid by the Jeanes Fund and the rest by the North Carolina Negro Teachers' Association (NCTA), an organization of black teachers. The NCTA considered Holland a "full-time field agent to promote Negro education in the state and to voice the attitudes of the Negro people in-state in matters educational" (Murray, 30).

In addition to her role as industrial teacher, Holland had also become a leader, an advocate and spokesperson for black education.

In 1921, the North Carolina General Assembly passed legislation that established the Negro Division of Education. Newbold was named director. He changed Holland's title to State Supervisor of Negro Elementary Schools, and she was from then on paid in part with state funds.

Holland Promotes Educational Groups

Continuing her travels throughout the state, she organized reading circles and other clubs to promote black education. In 1923-1924, she started the movement to organize local parent-teacher associations that were founded from the Community Leagues that Jeanes teachers had helped originate. In 1925, her husband died. She continued to work with the PTA movement.

In 1927, under her leaderhip, the North Carolina Congress of Parents and Teachers was founded. In April 1928, the congress held its first annual meeting at Shaw University in Raleigh.

Seven hundred eighty-four local PTA's with a membership of 15,770 were represented at this first meeting, and that year the congress raised fifty thousand dollars to support black schools. Holland was elected president of the organization and held that position until she died.

The Congress of Parents and Teachers was a national organization founded by black Americans to promote child welfare, raise the living standards of black families, develop closer relations between parents and teachers, and "secure for every child the highest advantages in physical, mental, moral and spiritual education" (Newbold, 80-81).

Meanwhile, between 1926 and 1928, Jeanes supervisors under Holland's direction made more than six thousand visits and helped organize over nine hundred PTA's. They installed 205 libraries and built 44 new school buildings, raising more than $43,000. Holland helped expand the work of the Jeanes teachers to help health workers teach dental hygiene and good health habits in the schools.

The Jeanes Report for 1930-1931 listed more than 7,700 school visits and an increase in the school term from the previous four months fifteen years before to more than six months. Jeanes supervisors visited nearly every black elementary school that year as Holland led North Carolina's black educators in a steady effort to improve the overall life of black American communities despite the severe restrictions of the segregated school system.

In the 1930s the average southern state annually spent about forty-five dollars per capita to educate white children and about twelve dollars per capita for black children. North Carolina's average was only slightly higher. It spent about fifty dollars per white child and about sixteen dollars for each black child. The school term for black children in the state lasted 138 days, for white, 154. North Carolina, with a relatively small black population, had 260,135 black children enrolled in public schools, second only to Mississippi, which had a much greater black population. Although facilities for black children were seldom as good as state officials claimed they were, black education in North Carolina seems to have been slightly better than it was in other southern states. Holland felt that despite limitations, her job was a "service to my people."

Known as a peacemaker, Annie Wealthy Holland was one who lay her life "at the feet of Jesus." She had a cheerful disposition, ready, smile and greeted all with kindness. She made friends easily and was endowed with both persistence and tact. Her character undoubtedly helped her win support for the schools and for the ideal of mutual cooperation that she espoused.

The origin of the cooperative movement among black Americans in North Carolina lay in great part in the activities of the Jeanes supervisors who worked under Holland. The cooperative movement gained momentum in the 1930s and 1940s when the depression nearly devastated the already poor rural black communities and benefits from the wartime industrial boom rarely reached them.

On January 6, 1934, Annie Wealthy Holland collapsed while addressing a county-wide black teachers meeting at Louisburg, North Carolina, a small town north of Raleigh in Franklin county. She died minutes later in a doctor's office and was buried in her home state of Virginia. At a subsequent North Carolina Negro PTA meeting at Shaw University, a tree was planted in her memory. A women's residence hall at North Carolina Agricultural and State University, Greensboro, is named in her honor.

References

Brawley, Benjamin. *Doctor Dillard of the Jeanes Fund.* New York: Fleming H. Reuell Company, 1930.

Brown, Hugh Victor. *A History of the Education of Negroes in North Carolina.* Raleigh: Irving Swain Press, 1961.

Hampton University Archives. Student Record of Annie Wealthy Holland.

Harlan, Louis R. *Booker T. Washington: The Wizard of Tuskegee, 1901-1915.* New York: Oxford University Press, 1983.

Jones, Lance G.E. *The Jeanes Teacher in the United States, 1908-1933.* Chapel Hill: University of North Carolina Press, 1937.

Murray, Percy. *History of the North Carolina Teachers Association.* Washington, D.C.: National Education Association, 1984.

Newbold, Nathan C., ed. *Five North Carolina Negro Educators.* Chapel Hill: University of North Carolina Press, 1939.

North Carolina State Archives, Department of Public Instruction. Division of Negro Education. Correspondence between Annie W. Holland and N. C. Newbold and Jeanes Supervisory Reports for 1916-1917, 1926-1928, and 1930-1931.

Pitts, Nathan A. *The Cooperative Movement in Negro Communities of North Carolina*. Ph.D. dissertation. Catholic University of America, 1950.

Plummer, Owen York. "Rural Education in North Carolina." Master's Thesis, Howard University, 1937.

Shaber, Sarah R. "Annie Wealthy Holland." *Dictionary of North Carolina Biography*. Ed. William S. Powell. Chapel Hill: University of North Carolina Press, 1988.

Raleigh News and Observer (7 January 1934).

Wright, Arthur D. *The Negro Rural School Fund, Inc., Anna T. Jeanes Foundation, 1907-1933*. Washington, D.C.: Negro Rural School Fund, 1933.

Collections

Primary materials relating to Annie Wealth Holland are in the North Carolina State Archives, Department of Public Instruction, and in the archives of Hampton University, Hampton, Virginia.

Adrienne M. Israel

Jennifer Holliday

(1960-)

Singer

Jennifer Holliday, a Tony Award-winner for her performance in *Dreamgirls* and a Grammy Award-winner for her performance of one of the songs from that show, is a composer as well as a singer whose ability to bring life to her on-stage roles set her on a direct course to Broadway.

Jennifer-Yvette Holliday was born to Oil Holliday and Genevive (Eaton) Holliday on October 19, 1960, in Riverside, Texas, a suburb of Houston. Her father was a Baptist minister and her mother an elementary school teacher who had other positions, including seamstress, newspaper delivery person, and attendant in a senior citizen home. Holliday's parents divorced when she was a baby. She has a half-brother and sister.

When she was in the fifth grade, Holliday joined the choir of Gethsemane Baptist Church in Houston as a soloist. When she was in the eighth grade, the Pleasant Grove Missionary Baptist Church, the largest black church in Houston, hired her to sing gospel solos on their weekly televised services.

During her teen years, Holliday was employed at a fast-food counter and Sears Roebuck to earn extra money. Nevertheless, she maintained an A scholastic record at the High School of Engineering Professionals and served as student council president. She had ambitions to become a lawyer like her idol, Barbara Jordan, but this goal has been deferred.

When Holliday was eighteen, she was asked to assume a role in the production of Vinnette Carroll's musical *Don't Bother Me, I Can't Cope*. James Patterson, a young dancer with the national company of *A Chorus Line*, saw her performance in the show and convinced her to audition in New York City for the touring company of Vinnette Carroll's Broadway hit, *Your Arms Too Short to Box with God*. Initially, when she joined the show, she was not well received by members of the cast. She said in an *Ebony* interview in 1980 that Carroll encouraged her during the show's tour and was very supportive. After the Broadway debut of *Your Arms Too Short to Box with God*, she received praise for her performance, especially the songs: "Just a Little Bit of Jesus Goes a Long Way," and "I Love You So Much Jesus."

As a result of her performance on Broadway, Holliday signed a recording contract with Geffen Records for an album to be produced by Billy Preston. She requested Susan De Passe as her manager and was to write half of the tunes for the album. Subsequently, Tom Eyen, a playwright and lyricist, invited her to participate in the workshop of a tentative musical, *One Night Only*. This new musical was retitled *Dreamgirls* and was based on the singing group, the Supremes.

Holliday left the workshop in December 1981 because it was too demanding. She was still performing in *Your Arms Too Short to Box with God*. She had some disagreements with Michael Bennett over her role in *Dreamgirls*. When Bennett called Holliday to tell her that she was fired, Holliday told him that she had resigned. Unable to find another person to replace her, Bennett wrote the second act of *Dreamgirls* to Holliday's specifications.

Dreamgirls opened at the Imperial Theatre on Broadway on December 20, 1981. The song, "And I Am Telling You I'm Not Going," disclosed the range and intensity of Holliday's lusty voice. After the performance of this song, the audience would loudly applaud and emotionally sympathize with Effie's determination not to leave her man.

Holliday feels that her artistic abilities have not had as wide an exposure as she would like among blacks. "I have something that is universal, that is non-denominational and that has allowed me to go into all homes—Jewish, Catholic, Methodist, Baptist, black and white. But someday I hope to do something that my people can really appreciate" (*People*, Feb. 8, 1982, p. 90). Holliday feels that while *Dreamgirls* is about black entertainers, it was packaged for a general

Broadway audience, and "at forty dollars a ticket, few [blacks] can afford it" (90).

Professionally, she indicated that she had been influenced by a number of black rhythm and blues singers, including Patti LaBelle, D. J. Rogers, Aretha Franklin, and Gladys Knight. During high school she listened to their records and imitated them while ignoring the formal training offered by her high school music teacher.

Jennifer Holliday received a Tony award in 1982 for her performance in *Dreamgirls*. Also, she received a Grammy Award in 1981 for the song "And I Am Telling You I'm Not Going."

References

Bailey, Peter A. "Dreams Come True on Broadway for Young Stars in *Dreamgirls*." *Ebony* 37 (May 1982): 90.

——. "A Holliday Hit on Broadway." *Ebony* 35 (October 1980): 122.

Current Biography Yearbook. New York: H. W. Wilson, 1983.

Lawson, Carol. "She Fought Michael Bennett and Became His Star." *New York Times* (21 December 1981): C-5. Includes photograph.

People 17 (11 January 1982): 55; 17 (8 February 1982): 90. Includes photograph.

Who's Who Among Black Americans, 1990/1991. 6th ed. Detroit: Gale Research, 1990.

Mary R. Holley

Margaret Cardozo Holmes

(1898-)

Hairstylist, entrepreneur

When Margaret Cardozo Holmes and her sister opened Cardozo Sisters Hair Stylists in 1929 and turned it into one of the best and most popular shops in Washington, D.C., they were following two family traditions: the practice of hairdressing, and successful business entrepreneurship. By combining science with the artistry of their trade, the Cardozo Sisters were able to retire in 1971 from a flourishing business.

Margaret Cardozo Holmes was born in Washington, D.C., on July 5, 1898, the eldest of five daughters and one son of Blanche (Warrick) Cardozo and Francis Lewis Cardozo, Jr. At that time her father, a former teacher, was a supervising principal in the Washington public schools; her mother also was a schoolteacher. Her maternal grandparents, Emma and William Warrick (William was born a free black in Virginia), owned prosperous hairdressing and barbering establishments, catering to Quakers in Atlantic City and Philadelphia. On her father's side, she was descended from Isaac Nuñez Cardozo, a Spanish Sephardic Jew, and a woman of mixed blood. Their son, Francis Lewis Cardozo, Sr., became secretary of state in South Carolina during the Reconstruction period. One of her relatives was Eslanda Cardozo Goode Robeson, the wife of Paul Robeson.

During the summers, Holmes and her mother and sisters visited Emma Warrick in Atlantic City, New Jersey, and often helped in the shop. By the age of nine, Holmes was using a palmleaf fan to dry patrons' hair, and at the age of ten was setting hair and helping her grandmother weave hair for wigs. Emma Warrick also began teaching the girls how to make hair products, such as grower and brilliantine.

When Margaret Cardozo's mother became sick one summer, eleven-year-old Margaret was left in Atlantic City to take care of her. The other five children returned to Washington, D.C., and essentially were under the care of nine-year-old Elizabeth day and night, without any adult supervision. Francis Cardozo, Jr., who was supervising both day and night schools, had little time for his lively young girls. Margaret stayed out of school from September 1910 to February 1911 to nurse her mother. Before the mother died in 1911, she asked Margaret to go back to Washington to help Elizabeth take care of the younger children. Even though their paternal grandmother then looked after them, the children all regarded Elizabeth as their mother.

After his wife's death, Francis Cardozo made a decision to break up the family and in 1915 sent the three oldest girls, Margaret, Elizabeth, and Emmeta, to St. Francis DeSales Convent School in Rock Castle, Virginia. They completed school there, learning typing and stenography. Margaret Holmes later attended Armstrong High School in Washington, D.C., which was noted for its art department. The younger girls, Catherine and Frances, were sent to Mother House, Holy Providence, in Pennsylvania. Both schools had been founded by the heiress Catherine Drexel for the education of blacks and Indians, especially training them to be house servants. Under the care of the nuns, who in a way took the place of their mother, all of the girls became Catholics. Their father hoped that the girls would choose teaching as a career, as their mother and he had done, but the interests of the three older girls turned them eventually toward hairdressing.

In 1927 Holmes and her sister Emmeta went to Paris,

where Emmeta enrolled in a beauty school. The idea was for Emmeta to learn a trade with a little glamour to it; she later joined the Ziegfeld Follies.

Cardozos Establish Hairstylist Business

In September 1929 Elizabeth Cardozo Nicholas opened a hairdressing business in her home. She was separated from her husband, had two sons who needed her attention, and had to earn a living. In 1933 she invited her sister Margaret to join her. At the time, Holmes was living in Philadelphia and working as a milliner. The two sisters had little money but felt that they belonged together and that the hairdressing business was their destiny. Soon thereafter Elizabeth moved to a larger apartment to accommodate the business. In order to add another dimension, Margaret Cardozo studied the kinds of work that Elizabeth herself did not already do. In 1937 they moved the business out of Elizabeth's apartment and into its own shop, one of the best-equipped shops, black or white, in Washington. They used the name Cardozo Sisters Hair Stylists.

They learned by constant experimentation on their own hair. As children in their grandmother's shop, they had worked only with white clientele. In their own business they took techniques from black businesses, such as Poro or Apex, and combined them with skills learned from white hairdressers. They also developed some of their own products. As the sisters could pass, they visited the white trade shows and brought back information and techniques for their own business. They called it scouting. Their supplier knew that they were black, but since they would buy products through him, it was in his best interest to see that they were admitted to the shows. It was a while before others realized that they were black. By the 1950s they were so well accepted that they could insist that the operators in their shop had to be invited.

When Holmes joined the business she immediately started researching and studying about all kinds of hair. In the 1940s the trade show people began to be interested in hair from the scientific point of view in order to develop new products. Manufacturers were making many new products, but they were not developing them for the hair of black people, as there were few shops. Cardozo Sisters was approached by the Gillette Company, which was doing a study on hair. They were trying to develop the first chemical straightener for the hair of blacks. They were never successful. They asked Margaret Cardozo Holmes to work with them in developing the product. Holmes became the chemical specialist at Cardozo Sisters and was the one to train operators in the use of the different relaxants. She also wrote an article about chemical relaxation of hair, but it was never published.

Catherine Cardozo Lewis joined the business in 1949 and over a period of time became general manager. She resigned in 1965. In 1971 the Cardozo sisters sold the business to Camilla Bradford Fauntroy, who had worked with them for many years. This business, which had begun in an apartment, was then grossing more than $325,000 a year and had about twenty employees. Both Margaret Holmes and her sister Elizabeth Nicholas Barker then became consultants to the new owner.

In her adult life Margaret Cardozo Holmes left the Catholic church. In the convent school she had felt no prejudice and was prepared to be accepted in any Catholic church. In very segregated Washington, D.C., where she lived, this was not so. She once told one of the nuns from the school that if there was a Catholic church in Washington where she and her husband would be accepted and if they could sit wherever they pleased, she would return to Catholicism.

Margaret Holmes has been a member of the Business and Professional Women's Club in Washington, D.C., and the Howard Faculty Wives. She is a life member of the NAACP. Another organization to which she gives her attention is The Godmothers, which was formed about 1972, to raise money as an emergency fund for children.

In 1929 she married Eugene Clay Holmes, who became a professor of philosophy and head of the philosophy department at Howard University. He died in 1980. They had no children.

In her early years, Margaret Cardozo Holmes was taken under the wing of her aunt, the renowned sculptress Meta Warrick Fuller. Fuller wished to adopt her and train her as an artist. Although Holmes knew that she was artistic, this was not the route she wished to take. She eventually found her outlet in using her hands to creatively style hair.

Elizabeth Barker described her sister Margaret Holmes and her relationship with the operators in the shop in the following words:

> There wasn't any way to be but uplifted when she was around. Nobody resented that, but she walked around with her queenly air which nobody resented, and they seemed to love her because she had taught them all she knew and she never failed to make them good hairdressers. . . . She also taught them efficiency. She was one of the fastest operators we ever had (*Black Women Oral History Project Interview*, 22).

References

Black Women Oral History Project Interview with Elizabeth Barker. Cambridge: Schlesinger Library, Radcliffe College, 1979.

Black Women Oral History Project Interview with Catherine Cardozo Lewis. Cambridge: Schlesinger Library, Radcliffe College, 1981.

Boston Sunday Globe (16 March 1980).

Washington Post (25 October 1977).

Collections

Tapes and transcripts of interviews given by Margaret Cardozo Holmes and her sisters for the Black Women Oral History Project are available at the Schlesinger Library, Radcliffe College. Photographs are also in the collection.

Ruth Edmonds Hill

Nora Holt

(c. 1885-1974)

Association founder, music critic, educator

Nora Holt was a respected music critic, possibly the first black to earn a master of music degree, a principal mover in the foundation of the National Association of Negro Musicians, and an active promoter of classical music and black musicians through her radio programs in 1945-1964. Those who discover her through interest in the Harlem Renaissance are likely to remember her as "the scintillating Negro blonde entertainer de luxe" (Langston Hughes, *The Big Sea*, 254) singing bawdy songs at parties, the model for the rich, very elegant, and promiscuous Lasca Sartoris in Carl Van Vechten's *Nigger Heaven* (1926), and a principal in an eyebrow-raising divorce from her fourth (or fifth) husband, Joseph L. "Moe" Ray.

Holt was born Lena Douglas in either 1885 or 1890 in Kansas City, Kansas. Her parents were Gracie (Brown) Douglas and Calvin N. Douglas, a minister in the African Methodist Episcopal (AME) church and a presiding elder for more than forty years. Lena Douglas began taking piano lessons when she was four. Two sources (Priscilla Oppenheimer and Bruce Kellner) agree that there was a marriage at the age of fifteen to a musician, Sky James, and *Ebony* gives the name of Phillip Scoggins, a Kansas City politician ("Most Married Negroes," 51). Probability would favor the first account, since a brief marriage and a quick annulment or divorce seems compatible with the statement that Lena Douglas earned a B.A. at Western University, an AME school in Quindaro, Kansas, where she was valedictorian of her class (Dannett, 146). (Berry states that she "received her formal training from Kansas State College where she graduated in 1915" [99].) Phillip Scoggins is accepted by all as one of her Kansas City husbands. Eileen Southern states that Lena Douglas played the organ for several years in Saint Augustine's Episcopal Church in that city (*Biographical Dictionary*, 187). Lena Douglas moved to Chicago in about 1916. Before this change of residence, she had married Phillip Scoggins, and after his death, Bruce Jones, a barber. That marriage lasted for about a year. Jones may be the "Chicago husband" whom Joseph Ray asserted Holt had not properly divorced (*Chicago Defender*, 17 December 1927).

The year 1917 would turn out to be extremely important to Lena Douglas. She received a bachelor's degree in music from the Chicago Musical College, she married George Holt, a wealthy Chicago hotel owner some forty years her senior, and she became music critic for the *Chicago Defender*, a position she held until 1921. Before her marriage, she supported herself by entertaining in the "Gold Coast" homes of Chicago's white elite by, in her words as quoted by Dannett, "singing light songs, Noel Coward melodies, and spirituals at their elegant dinner parties" (146) and at the same time working in Chicago's red-light district in such notorious establishments as that of the Everleigh Sisters. (Holt's reference to Noel Coward is a reflection of her later repertoire; in 1917 Coward was only an aspiring star, eighteen years old.) Also, in addition to changing her last name to Holt through marriage, Lena adopted the first name Nora.

In 1918, Nora Holt may have become the first black American to earn a master's degree in music. At the Chicago School of Music, she studied with Felix Borowsky and took additional work in composition from Thorwald Olterstrom. A symphonic work, *Rhapsody on Negro Themes*, was her master's thesis. In addition to her work as music critic for the *Defender*, she published from 1919 to 1921 a magazine called *Music and Poetry*. Nora Holt was also instrumental in founding the National Association of Negro Musicians. The clearest outline of this event is an article entitled "The Chronological History of the NAMN," published in *Music and Poetry* in July 1921. The article is most accessible in its reprint in *The Black Perspective in Music* on the occasion of her death in 1974. The sequence of events is as follows.

Clarence Cameron White, a young violinist in Boston who later played at Nora Holt's marriage to Joseph Ray, had issued a call for such an association in 1916, and a meeting was planned to be held at the fiftieth anniversary of Hampton Institute, but the plans fell through because of the approach of the war. In October 1918 R. Nathaniel Dett of Hampton Institute sent out further letters on White's behalf explaining another postponement due to the influenza. In November 1918 Nora Holt, by that time music critic for the *Chicago Defender* and unaware of the previous initiatives, issued a call to form a national association in the newspaper and followed up her call by working with Chicago musicians to develop plans, an effort that culminated with a meeting at her home in Chicago on March 12, 1919, where plans for a national meeting in Chicago in July were drawn up. Persons attending the Second Annual Music Festival of Paul Lawrence Dunbar High School in Washington, D. C., formed a preliminary conference at the suggestion of Henry Grant. They learned of the Chicago plans and endorsed them. The National Association for Negro Musicians came into being at the meeting in Chicago on July 29-31. Nora Holt was elected vice-president of the association and served for three years.

George M. Holt died in 1921, leaving Nora Holt a wealthy widow at the age of thirty-five (or thirty). In 1923 she married Joseph L. Ray. Ray had used his position as personal attendant to Charles Schwab, the Pennsylvania steel magnate, to acquire the food concession at Schwab's Bethlehem Steel Works. The marriage was brief and acrimonious and furnished ample material for the front pages of papers like the *Chicago Defender* and scandal sheets like *Heebie Jeebies* and the *Inter-State Tatler*. It was a major social event. According to Oppenheimer and Kellner, the bride wore more than six carats of diamonds in each ear and had a black eye allegedly given by Dr. Gordon Jackson, with whom she was having an affair (172). The *Chicago Defender* gives a useful resume of the following events in recounting Nora Holt's final legal victory.

First Ray sued for divorce on the grounds that his private detectives had discovered his wife and Leroy Wilkins, brother of a Harlem cabaret owner, together in a boarding house in New York. On appeal Nora Holt won her countersuit. Then Ray sued for fraud to try to regain possession of thirty thousand dollars worth of real estate he had placed in his wife's name and twelve thousand dollars worth of jewels. In this suit he also alleged that his marriage was invalid in the first place because she was improperly divorced from a "Chicago husband." Although he was supported by the corporate lawyers of the Bethlehem Steel Corporation, Ray lost this suit also (17 December 1927).

All of these events were copiously covered on the front page of the *Chicago Defender*. Carl Van Vechten, who was her friend until the end of his life, gives us an example of the sort of gossip that was circulating: "Soon [after the marriage] she began to operate on so extensive a scale that Mr. Charlie Schwab became alarmed and demanded that her husband divorce her so that she could be removed from Bethlehem" (*Letters*, 87). In fairness to Nora Holt, it must be admitted that her statement to the *Chicago Defender* on February 6, 1926, is a model of decorum and injured innocence, alleging Ray was insanely jealous and reducing the legal battles to a dispute over property by implying that he was trying to gain control of her wealth. There had been another scandal in 1925 when detectives acting for Mrs. W. L. Patterson, wife of a Harlem lawyer, discovered that lawyer and Nora Holt in compromising circumstances (Oppenheimer and Kellner, 173).

After her separation from Ray, Nora Holt began to travel extensively and became noted for her appearances at parties in New York; she also developed a considerable reputation as an entertainer abroad. The details of the trips are somewhat hazy, but she spent long periods overseas until shortly before World War II. The *Chicago Defender* states that she took a trip abroad after the divorce and before the trial for fraud (17 December 1927). She and Carl Van Vechten were certainly acquainted by the summer of 1925, when she served as the model for Lasca Sartoris in his novel; in his novel, Lasca gives "a vivid impression of magnetism and distinction" (*Nigger Heaven*, 80), and she is presented as a person who "always raises hell here, without intending to . . . . She just can't help it. She's just naturally full o' pep and she bounces the papas off their rails" (85). From the Van Vechten letters she was certainly abroad in late 1928, and in September 1929 she was a hostess at a Coventry Street restaurant (Lewis, 264). Sylvia Dannett speaks of Nora Holt's experiences abroad and quotes from a columnist who describes her in performance in London:

> Nora Holt, a blond Creole . . . has a presence and manner similar to Sophie Tucker. Same mop of golden curly hair, the same perky good-humored lift of the head and the same appealing smile . . . but her voice is even more astonishing. She can produce sounds not comparable to orthodox singing, ranging from deepest low voice to a shrilling high, often unaccompanied by words (147).

Nora Holt learned French and spoke of entertaining at private parties in Paris every year for four years. In the 1930s before her permanent return to the United States, she worked for several years in Shanghai. It is during this period of travel and entertainment that a classic example of the failure of intercultural understanding occurred. During a bon voyage party in New York, Nora Holt sang "My Daddy Rocks Me With One Steady Roll." "As she ceased, a well-known New York matron cried ecstatically, with tears in her eyes: 'My dear! Oh, my dear! How beautifully you sing Negro spirituals!'" (Hughes, 254).

Nora Holt Becomes Music Critic

Upon her return to the United States, Nora Holt settled in California and turned to other lines of endeavor. She passed an examination to qualify to teach music in the public high schools by the summer of 1937 (Van Vechten, Letters, 154). She taught school and was connected with a beauty shop—either as owner or operator—during the period she was in California. In 1943 she returned to New York and became music critic and church editor for the *Amsterdam News*, a position she held until 1956. She became the first black American member of the Music Critics Circle in 1945.

The memories of her earlier marital experiences were perhaps revived when *Ebony* selected Nora Holt as the only woman in its article on "Most Married Negroes" in October 1949. Still, if there were people with negative feelings dating from the 1920s, the dislike had diminished by 1950, when a testimonial concert was held for her on July 17. Van Vechten was moved to exclaim: "Think of it! Nora and Ethel [Waters] are now highly respected women on the top of the heap" (*Letters*, 242). In 1956 Nora Holt became music critic for the *New York Courier*. Beginning in 1945, she staged an annual program, "American Negro Artists," for radio station WNYC. From 1953 until 1964 she was the producer of "Nora Holt's Concert Showcase" for radio station WLIB. The half-hour weekly program was devoted to classical music. Nora Holt retired to California in 1964, where she died on January 25, 1974.

Carl Van Vechten, her lifelong friend, wrote: "A fabulously amusing and talented person who deserves a biography of her own, she played the piano divinely and was a fine artist as an interpretive singer. Extremely chic, she had a long and notable career'' (*Keep A-Inchin' Along*, 184). Most of Holt's performing career involved private parties in the United States and both private parties and nightclubs abroad. As a result, her skills as a performer may be undervalued. She wrote some of her material and may have attempted extended compositions. The statement that she studied with Nadia Boulanger in 1931 (Southern, 187) should be treated with caution, but any remaining material appears not to have been located and examined. Much of the information about her life, especially the early portions, appears to come from her own statements and needs to be verified, not necessarily because she was lying but because she appears to be shading the picture to fit the expectations of her listener. However, the wide divergence in the accounts of her life seem to have a simple explanation: Nora Holt simply does not fit neatly into our paradigms. She was a talented performer of ''light'' music who devoted a substantial portion of her life to promoting ''classical'' music. In her sexual behavior, she violated gender rules. Nora Holt was a highly intelligent woman who loved fine clothes and parties, and she pushed against the limits society imposed on black Americans and on women in her quest for experience. It is to be hoped that this complex and interesting woman does one day have a full-scale biography.

It is fitting to close with Nora Holt's own words, which perhaps explain her gift for friendship and her indomitable spirit. She was speaking to a group of eight or ten-year-old children at the Lutheran Church on Convent Avenue and 145th Street:

> There's just one word in the English language you just never should use . . . a four-letter word. . . . You must never use the word ''HATE.'' If you don't like something, say ''I don't like it,'' ''I don't want it,'' ''I despise it,'' anything, but never the word HATE. The same with a friend, neighbor; just do not use the word to describe your emotion for anything (Dannett, 149).

References

Berry, Lemuel, Jr. *Biographical Dictionary of Black Musicians and Music Educators.* Vol. 1. Guthrie, Okla.: Educational Book Publisher, 1978.

Dannett, Sylvia G. L. *Profiles of Negro Womanhood.* Vol. 2. *The Twentieth Century* Yonkers, N.J.: Educational Heritage, 1964. Photograph page 144.

Hughes, Langston. *The Big Sea.* New York: Wang and Hill, 1963. Reprinted. New York: Thunder's Mouth Press, 1986.

Hughes, Langston, and Milton Meltzer. *Black Magic.* Englewood Cliffs, N.J.: Prentice-Hall, 1967. Photographs on pages 324, 347.

Kellner, Bruce, ed. *''Keep A-Inchin' Along'': Selected Writings of Carl Van Vechten about Black Art and Letters.* Westport, Connecticut: Greenwood, 1979.

———. *Letters of Carl Van Vechten.* New Haven: Yale University Press, 1987.

Lewis, David Levering. *When Harlem Was in Vogue.* New York: Knopf, 1981.

''Most Married Negroes.'' *Ebony* 4 (October 1949): 51, 53.

''Mrs. Nora Holt Ray Wins Again in Tilt With Husband.'' *Chicago Defender*, 17 December 1927.

''Mrs. Nora Holt Ray's Silence Ends; Tells Her Side of Married Life.'' *Chicago Defender,* 6 February 1926.

''The National Association of Negro Musicians and Nora Holt.'' *The Black Perspective in Music.* 2 (Fall 1974): 234-235.

Oppenheimer, Priscilla, and Bruce Kellner. ''Nora Holt.'' In *The Harlem Renaissance: A Historical Dictionary for the Era.* Ed. Bruce Kellner. New York: Methuen.

Southern, Eileen. *Biographical Dictionary of Afro-Americans and African Musicians.* Westport, Conn.: Greenwood Press, 1982.

Van Vechten, Carl. *Nigger Heaven.* New York: Knopf, 1926. Reprinted. New York: Octagon Books, 1973.

Robert L. Johns

Julia Hooks

(1852-1942)

Musician, educator

Julia Ann Amanda Morehead Britton Werles Hooks was a gifted musician and teacher who promoted the educational, social, and cultural advancement of blacks in Memphis, Tennessee. Born in Lexington, Kentucky, in 1852, Hooks died in Memphis in 1942, her life spanning the Civil War and two world wars.

Julia Hooks's father, Henry Harrison Britton, was a free man of color who had been hired to work on the Marshall plantation, where he met and was attracted to Laura Marshall, the daughter of the Honorable Thomas F. Marshall and his slave, Mary, who had died giving birth to Laura. One source indicates that the childless mistress of the house, Elizabeth Marshall, had not only treated her husband's black child well but had also, upon her deathbed, while her

Julia Hooks

husband was away in the Mexican War, arranged Laura's freedom and her marriage to Henry Britton. The couple continued to live on the plantation, where Julia Ann Amanda Morehead Britton was born and grew up the second of five children, including an older sister Mary, a younger sister Susan, an older brother Robert, and a younger brother Tommy.

With her dark skin and long straight hair, Hooks (who may well have been named for Amanda Morehead, the daughter of Governor Charles Morehead of Kentucky) resembled her father, who was of Indian descent. In an autobiographical sketch that appears at the end of the *Afro-American Encyclopedia of 1895*, Julia Hooks painfully recalls how as a young child she had to pass as her mother's slave when they traveled together to perform at musical engagements.

Her passage through a world that could require that she pass as a slave and her mother as a free woman was mitigated by music and by education. Julia Hooks would early reveal her gift for music to her mother, who also played the piano and was a talented singer. According to one account, the by now bereaved Tom Marshall, who may have privately, though never publicly, claimed Hooks as his grandchild, paid the English Madame Maud Worthington to give Hooks piano lesson, just as he had earlier made arrangements for Hooks and her sister Mary to attend the William Gibson School in Louisville, Kentucky.

Before the onset of the Civil War, Mary and Julia left the Gibson School and returned home to the plantation, where one report states that Hooks helped her mother surreptitiously teach blacks to read at a time when to do so was illegal. It is perhaps at this time that Hooks discovered her love for teaching. Around 1869, after the war, and after the death of the Marshalls, the Britton family moved to Berea, a community founded in central Kentucky by Reverend John Fee and based on the idea of integrated education. Here Hooks attended Berea Academy, becoming one of the first black women in the country to attend college. In addition to attending classes at Berea, Julia Hooks also held the position of instructor of instrumental music, thereby helping to support the family. Thanks to the efforts of Selma Lewis and Marjean Kremer, it is an established fact that while at the academy, Hooks was one of two black faculty members who "responded favorably" in 1872 to the Berea College Board of Trustees's official declaration that they were "not opposed to interracial dating."

In 1872 the "petite and elegant" but dynamic Julia Ann Britton married Samuel Augustus Werles, a native of Ohio, a graduate of Oberlin, and an African Methodist Episcopal (AME) pastor who had opened a free school in Greenville, Mississippi, where the couple made their home. Hooks assisted her husband at the school and continued to teach there after Werles died of yellow fever in 1873. She remained in Mississippi, in 1875 campaigning for the successful election of the black sheriff of Bolivar, Blanche K. Bruce, to the United States Senate from Mississippi.

In 1876 Hooks traveled to Memphis, where she taught in the public schools, made friends, and settled down, committing herself to life in this city, which was attracting many blacks during this time. In Memphis, Hooks met and became the friend of Robert C. Church, one of Memphis's most wealthy and influential black men, and Ida B. Wells, who wrote for and purchased an interest in the *Memphis Free Speech and Headlight*. When yellow fever struck Memphis in 1878, Julia Werles, who, the story goes, had gone to the Citizen Relief Office to get information for one of the fever's victims, met Charles Hooks, whom she would marry in April 1880. Shortly after the birth of their first child on July 22, 1881, Julia Hooks's father died on November 30; Laura Britton died four years later in 1885. Another son, Robert, was born to the Hookses on October 22, 1890.

Hooks Works for the Community

Though suffering the loss of her parents and raising a family, Julia Hooks's efforts for the welfare of her community never flagged. She continued as a teacher and also privately taught music lessons, one of her students being W. C. Handy, whom she coached on orchestration. She participated in, if indeed she did not help start, the Liszt-Mozart Club, and in 1891 she founded the Negro Old Folks and Orphans Home, raising money for the building by playing concerts. Though one report says that the city opened the Negro Juvenile Court Detention Home in 1902 and another says that Julia Hooks founded the home, the indisputable fact is that she had a hand in the establishment of the facility that was, like her home, located on Lauderdale Street; her husband, Charles Hooks, who was one of the truant officers at the home, was killed by one of its wards. Determined to advance the civil rights of blacks in Memphis, Hooks tried to integrate the only public library in the city, and she actually attended "a major cultural event at a white theater" (Chisenhall, 19).

Julia Hooks eventually opened her own school, the Hooks Cottage School, and operated the Hooks Conservatory of Music. Hooks Conservatory of Music was, according to George W. Lee, one of the first schools in the South attended by both white and black students (*Beale Street*, 153-54). She became a charter member of the Memphis Branch of the NAACP in 1917. Julia Hooks died when she was ninety years old and "according to her obituary was able to play the piano until a few weeks before she passed away" (Church and Walter, 44). Church and Walter best describe the humanitarian essence of Hooks: "A dignified, compassionate woman, her sincerity and gentle manner inspired confidence and trust" (43-44). This untiring woman, the grandmother of Benjamin Hooks, Jr., first black member of the Federal Communications Commission and executive director of the National Association for the Advancement of Colored People, truly merited her reputation as the Angel of Beale Street.

Hooks wrote on the welfare of black youth:

> Wisdom says and it is policy that the State should take the advantage of giving her subjects the proper training at the proper time. She should train the mind while it is capable of being easily trained. No need to argue about home training, that cannot be relied upon for securing a saving kind of citizenship, neither can this ever be the case until the young shall have been educated with some special reference to their parental vocation. . . . Justice demands that strength and nobility of character can only be secured by well-directed efforts in the schools where the masses must be educated. Justice says that it is better for to treble the school tax and legislate for compulsory education and inculcate good moral principles in the minds of the young, than to deprive them of the advantages of the necessary training (332-39).

References

Afro-American Encyclopedia of 1895. Comp. James T. Haley. Nashville: Haley and Florida, 1896.

Chisenhall, Fred, and Margaret McKee. *Beale Black & Blue: Life and Music on Black America's Main Street*. Baton Rouge: Louisiana State University Press, 1981.

Church, Roberta, and Walter, Ronald. *Nineteenth Century Memphis Families of Color: 1850-1990*. Memphis: Murdock Printing, 1987.

Hamilton, G. P. *The Bright Side of Memphis*. Memphis: Burke's Book Store and Frank and Gennie Myers, n.d. Reprinted 1908.

Hooks, Julia. "Duty of the Hour." *Afro-American Encyclopedia*. Comp. James T. Haley. Nashville: Haley and Florida, 1896.

Kremer, Marjean, and Lewis, Selma S. *The Angel of Beale Street: A Biography of Julia Ann Hooks*. Memphis: St. Luke's Press, 1987.

Lee, George W. *Beale Street: Where the Blues Began*. New York: Robert O. Ballou, 1934.

Collection

Photographs of Julia Hooks are in the Mississippi Valley Collection at Memphis State University, the Roberta Church Collection, and the Hooks Brothers Collection in Memphis. For access to the Roberta Church Collection, contact Sara Roberta Church, 99 North Mid-America Mall, Memphis, TN 38103. For access to the Hooks Brothers Collection, contact Julia Hooks Gordon, (901) 452-6470.

Vanessa D. Dickerson

Lugenia Burns Hope

(1871-1947)

Activist, clubwoman

As a "race woman," Lugenia D. Burns Hope worked tirelessly to bring equality to all Americans through the NAACP, the Urban League, and the Commission on Interracial Cooperation (later the Southern Regional Council); in conjunction with Jessie Daniel Ames, she also worked with the all-white Association of Southern Women for the Prevention of Lynching (ASWPL). She was a member and/or official of the National Association of Colored Women's Club, the National Council of Negro Women, and the International Council of Women of the Darker Races. The list of organizations goes on, but the effects of Hope's work are immeasurable.

Lugenia D. Burns Hope was born February 19, 1871, in St. Louis, Missouri, the youngest of seven children born to Ferdinand Burns and Louisa Bertha Burns of Natchez, Mississippi. Between 1890 and 1893, she attended the Chicago Art Institute, the Chicago School of Design, and the Chicago Business College. She married John Hope on December 27, 1897, and had two sons, Edward S. and John II. By the early 1930s her health began to decline. She died of heart failure in Nashville, Tennessee, on August 14, 1947, was cremated, and her ashes were scattered over the campus of Morehouse College in Atlanta.

Neighborhood Union Organized

Lugenia Burns Hope began early on the career of community activism that would eventually distinguish her as a black reformer. During her adolescent years in Chicago she worked with several charitable agencies, including Jane Addams's Hull House. She carried this involvement to Nashville, Tennessee, when as a new bride she accompanied her husband—leading black intellectual and eventually college president John Hope—to Roger Williams University, where he was then an instructor. There she conducted classes in arts and crafts and in physical education for the female students. Within a year the Hopes moved again, this time to Atlanta, where John Hope had accepted a position as classics instructor at Atlanta Baptist College, later Morehouse College.

In 1906 John Hope became Morehouse's first black American president. For thirty-three years the Hopes lived and worked at Morehouse College and later Atlanta University. Soon after arriving in Atlanta, Lugenia Hope became a member of the group of women who were working to provide day-care centers for the children of the West Fair community. This core group later became the founders of the Neighborhood Union, the first female social welfare agency for blacks in Atlanta. For twenty-five years she led this agency in providing medical, recreational, educational, and civic services in Atlanta's black communities. By 1930 the structure and policies of Hope's Neighborhood Union had been adopted by Haiti and Cape Verde in their efforts at community-building.

During World War I, Hope, like other southern black women, responded wholeheartedly to the war effort. She and the Neighborhood Union conducted the YWCA's Atlanta War Work Council for black soldiers. They petitioned for better police protection, access to public facilities, and the creation of more recreational centers. Hope's success at directing the Atlanta work led to her promotion to the position of national supervisor of the YWCA's black hostess-house program, which provided recreational facilities for soldiers and centers for their families.

As Hope rose on a national level because of her community, club, and settlement work, she was constantly in demand as a speaker. In 1927 she was a member of Herbert Hoover's Colored Commission, established to investigate the catastrophic flooding in Mississippi. Between 1920 and 1940 she served as an assistant to Mary McLeod Bethune in her capacity as director of the Negro Affairs Division of the National Youth Administration, helping to implement its programs in black communities. Hope also lectured nationally for the National Council of Negro Women and served as an organizer of the National Association of Colored Graduate Nurses.

Hope's appointments and elections include founder, president, and chairperson of the Board of Managers of the Neighborhood Union, 1908-1935; chairperson of the Women's Civic and Social Improvement Committee for better black schools in Atlanta, 1913; director of the Hostess House Program for Black Soldiers, YWCA, 1917; founding member of the Atlanta Branch of the National Association of Colored Women's Clubs, 1916; coordinator, Gate City Free Kindergarten Association, 1908; member of President Herbert Hoover's Colored Commission on the flooding in Mississippi, 1927; and first vice president, NAACP, Atlanta Chapter, 1932.

Hope interacted with many black luminaries of the time. In addition to Bethune, her work brought her in contact with Charlotte Hawkins Brown, Lucy Laney, Margaret Murray Washington, Jennie Moton, Maggie Lena Walker, Madame C. J. Walker, Mary Church Terrell, W. E. B. Du Bois, Paul Robeson, Jessie Daniel Ames, Nannie Helen Burroughs, Georgia Douglass Johnson, Mary Jackson McCrorey, Nettie Napier, Ida B. Wells Barnett, Booker T. Washington, Janie Porter Barrett, Daisy Lampkin, and Walter White.

Though Lugenia Burns Hope had a very complex personality, she was caring and nurturing, especially with the young men at Morehouse College. A domineering woman, she was aggressive and assertive in her organizations and agencies. She was strongly opinionated and a good executive. Her speeches addressed motherhood, community organization, feminism, segregation, interracial work, antilynching, education, and other topics. On the issue of racism, she challenged the white women of the Methodist Church to address the topic:

> It is difficult for me to understand why my white sisters so strenuously object to this honest expression of colored women as put forth in the discarded preamble. After all, when we yield to public opinion and make ourselves say only what we think the public can stand, is there not a danger that we may find ourselves with our larger view conceding what those with the narrow view demand? (Rouse, 112).

On teaching her son about racism after he was the recipient of a racial slight, she said:

> This raised problems in his mind . . . in spite of my effort to keep the truth from him. I did not want to burden his young life because I knew it would have to come all too soon anyway. The Negro mother has to pray for patience and insight lest she forget that above all her little ones must not become embittered (Rouse, 33).

Lugenia Burns Hope lived a life of activism, whether in civic service to the black community, attention to the needs of soldiers, or the quest for full equality for black Americans. Her aggressive, assertive style, balanced by her nurturing manner, doubtless resulted in the many accomplishments for which she is noted.

References

Beard, Anne. "Mrs. John Hope: Community Builder in

Atlanta, Georgia, 1900-1936.'' M.A. thesis, Atlanta University, 1975.

Giddings, Paula. *When and Where I Enter: The Impact of Black Women on Race and Sex in America.* New York: William Morrow, 1984.

Hall, Jacquelyn D. *Revolt Against Chivalry: Jessie Daniel Ames and the Women's Campaign Against Lynching.* New York: Columbia University Press, 1965.

Lerner, Gerda. ''Early Community Work of Black Club Women.'' *Journal of Negro History* 59 (April 1974): 158-67.

———, ed. *Black Women in White America.* New York: Pantheon Books, 1972.

Rouse, Jacqueline A. ''The Legacy of Community Organizing: Lugenia Burns Hope and the Neighborhood Union.'' *Journal of Negro History* 69 (Summer, Fall 1984): 114-33.

———. ''The Life and Times of Lugenia D. Burns Hope, 1871-1947.'' *Dictionary of Georgia Biography*, Vol. 1. Athens: University of Georgia Press, 1983.

———. *Lugenia Burns Hope: Black Southern Reformer.* Athens: University of Georgia Press, 1989. This is a major work on Hope and includes an extensive bibliographical listing and notes.

Neverdon-Morton, Cynthia. *The Afro-American Women of the South and the Advancement of the Race, 1895-1925.* Knoxville: University of Tennessee Press, 1989.

Collections

Personal papers of John and Lugenia Burns Hope, and papers of the Neighborhood Union Collection, the Association of Southern Women for the Prevention of Lynching, and the Commission on Interracial Cooperation are located in the archives of the Woodruff Library, Atlanta University Center. The Neighborhood Union Collection contains copies of her speeches on various topics. Additional information may be found in the Emma and Lloyd Lewis Collection, the University of Illinois, Chicago Circle. Hope's biographer has in her possession notes and interviews conducted with her sons, grandniece, and cousins. Photographs are in the biography, the Neighborhood Union, and the Lewis papers, and at Morehouse College, Atlanta, Georgia.

Jacqueline A. Rouse

Pauline Hopkins

(1859-1930)

Writer, editor, playwright, singer, actress

Pauline Elizabeth Hopkins, a writer born in 1859, began her literary contribution at fifteen when she was a recipient of a prize of ten dollars in gold for writing an essay, ''The Evils of Intemperance and Their Remedies.'' Born in Portland, Maine, Pauline Hopkins, an author of several short stories and a novel, is an interesting literary figure whose works were overlooked until recently. She served as editor of the *Colored American*, a monthly illustrated magazine that began publication in May 1900. *The Colored American* was the first black magazine established in the twentieth century. Strongly supported by her associates and peers, Hopkins stressed the need for the periodical because no other monthly serial was exclusively devoted to the interests of African-Americans. While the *AME Church Review* had a similar mission, *The Colored American* documented and disseminated information on the contributions of blacks in literature, art, science, music, religion, and other areas. Many of Hopkins's works were published in this forum.

For a long time Hopkins's name was missing from books on black literature. However, writer and scholar Ann A. Shockley has done significant research to highlight Pauline Hopkins. A playwright, orator, and literary editor, Hopkins established the ''Colored Troubadors,'' who presented recitals and concerts and received attention from the press. Shockley states that Hopkins's greatest desire was to become a playwright. She became a dramatist and troubadour with the writing of the musical drama *Slaves' Escape: or the Underground Railroad*, copyrighted by Hopkins in 1879. The play was also called *Peculiar Sam*, and the number of acts range from four to three. Embodied in this drama is the theme of slavery. Shockley states that:

> The drama relates the story of how the underground railroad assisted slaves in their flight to freedom. It was presented by the Hopkins' Colored Troubadors which included W. A. Hopkins (possibly Miss Hopkins's stepfather) as a mulatto overseer, her mother, S. A. Hopkins a mammy, and Pauline as the pet of the plantation. Jubilee songs were sung throughout the drama. When the play was presented at the Oakland Garden in Boston on July 5, 1880, it received good notices (Shockley, ''A Biographical Excursion into Obscurity,'' 23).

One particular program given at Arcanum Hall in Allston,

Massachusetts, on November 24, 1882, "listed Miss Hopkins as Boston's favorite Colored Soprano" (Shockley, 23).

A proponent of black history, Pauline Hopkins wrote a series of biographical sketches on "Famous Women of the Negro Race" and "Famous Men of the Negro Race" for the *Colored American*. In the article "Away from Accommodation: Radical Editors and Protest Journalism, 1900-1910" published in *Journal of Negro History* (October 1977, p. 326), the authors note that Pauline Hopkins talked about a renaissance of black literature long before writers commonly discussed such a movement. The biographical sketches of black men and women offer much information about them but give no sources of information, thus making it difficult for scholars and historians to verify the data. They are character sketches in which Hopkins praises particular men and women for their accomplishments and achievements.

In the *Dictionary of American Negro Biography*, Dorothy Porter reports that Hopkins, who repeatedly declared that history is biography, crafted twenty-one of these valuable sketches. The list included William Wells Brown, Frederick Douglass, Toussaint L'Ouverture, Harriet Tubman, Lewis Hayden, and Charles Lenox Remond. Porter claims that Hopkins also wrote biographies of prominent white men. While undocumented, Hopkins's biographies are written after much research; they are well illustrated with engravings from paintings and photographs (325).

Looking at the contributions of black women writers to literary history as a patchwork quilt where each person's works form an intricate patch of literary history, Hopkins emerges as a feminist, a strong voice and force making salient contributions to the patchwork of writers. Hopkins shares threads of feminist issues with other black women writers such as Alice Ruth Moore Dunbar Nelson (1875-1935), her near contemporary.

Hopkins wrote many literary works while serving as an editor of the women's section of the *Colored American*. Her protest novel, *Contending Forces: A Romance Illustrative of Negro Life North and South* (1900), is one of her most popular works. The novel is convoluted with many subplots of mulatto brother and sister. The main characters are Will and Dora Smith, and two boarders with the Smith family—Sappho Clark, a beautiful octoroon, and John Langley. Will pursues Sappho, loses her when she compromises with Langley, and is reunited with her by the novel's end. While heir to many of the novelistic features of the day, *Contending Forces* is nonetheless an ambitious endeavor (Campbell, *Dictionary of Literary Biography*, 184).

Hopkins has many other literary works to her credit, including a serial novel, *Of One Blood*, which appeared in several segments in the *Colored American*. The following synopsis from the *Colored American*, September 1903, captures the essence of the novel:

> Reuel Briggs, a young medical student, interested in mysticism, sees a face that haunts him. He attends a concert with his friend Aubrey Livingston, and there discovers in a negro concert-singer the owner of the mysterious face. He sees this woman again on Hallow Eve while playing at charms with a party of young people at Vance Hall, the home of Livingston's betrothed. Early the next morning he is called to attend victims of a railroad disaster at the hospital. He finds among them the girl whose face haunts him, in a cataleptic sleep which the doctors call death. He succeeds in restoring her to consciousness, but with a complete loss of memory. She loses her identity as a negress. Reuel falls deeply in love with her. He finally restores her to health and is determined to marry her, but finds his circumstances too straitened. Aubrey Livingston helps him out by offering to obtain for him a place in an expedition about to explore the ancient city of Meroe in Africa. Reuel accepts, but marries Dianthe. Later Dianthe finds that Livingston is in love with her and he acquires a power over her and she cannot resist (643).

It is also later revealed that Dianthe and the two men were of the same blood—the two men were her brothers. Hopkins's conclusion is:

> To our human intelligence these truths depicted in this feeble work may seem terrible,—even horrible. But who shall judge the handiwork of God, the Great Craftsman! Caste prejudice, race pride, boundless wealth, scintillating intellects refined by all the arts of the intellectual world, are but puppets in His hand, for His promises stand, and He will prove His words, "Of one blood have I made all races of men" (*Colored American*, December 1903, 807).

Although Hopkins's works appeared to be popular, there were negative responses to some of her writings, as demonstrated with the following comment from the *Colored American*, March 1903:

> I have seen beautiful home life and love in families altogether of Negro blood. . . . The stories of these tragic mixed loves will not commend themselves to your white readers and will not elevate the colored readers. I believe your novelists could do with a consecrated imagination and pen, more for the elevation of home life and love, than perhaps any other one class of writers. What Dickens did for the neglected working class of England, some writer could do for the neglected colored people of America (299).

Hopkins's reply was:

> My stories are definitely planned to show the obstacles persistently placed in our paths by a dominant race to subjugate us spiritually. Marriage is made illegal between the races and yet

> the mulattoes increase. Thus the shadow of corruption falls on the blacks and on the whites, without whose aid the mulattoes would not exist. . . . The home life of Negroes is beautiful in many instances; warm affection is there between husband and wife, and filial and paternal tenderness in them is not surpassed by any other race of the human family. But Dickens wrote not of the joys and beauties of English society; I believe he was the author of "Bleak House" and "David Copperfield." If he had been an American, and with his trenchant pen had exposed the abuses practiced by the Southern whites upon the blacks—had told the true story of how wealth, intelligence and femininity has stooped to choose for a partner in sin, the degraded. . .Negro whom they affect to despise, Dickens would have been advised to shut up or get out. . . . Let the good work go on. Opposition is the life of an enterprise; criticism tells you that you are doing something (*Colored American*, March 1903, 400).

Hopkins's contributions to the *Colored American* satisfied a void. She was constantly creating and sharing her works with her readers, but she was also responsive to the readers' views.

Hopkins Neglected in the Annals of Black Literature

The *Colored American* appeared to be the main forum for Pauline Hopkins's works, which for the most part have been critically neglected in the broad dimensions of black fiction. Ann Shockley's research has been crucial in illuminating Hopkins's contributions to the literary patchwork.

Jane Campbell's article in *Dictionary of Literary Biography* says "Pauline Elizabeth Hopkins, despite an impressive record of productivity and creativity as a novelist, playwright, short fiction writer, editor, actress, and singer, is another Afro-American writer who has essentially been consigned to the dustbins of American literary history" (182). She further declares that Hopkins is a skillful author, managing an adroit fusion of women's romance and black historical concerns. Campbell senses that in Hopkins's work, *Contending Forces,* one of the most important chapters fictionalizes the collective efforts of black American women to change history. In this chapter, a large group of women gather to make garments for a church fair. Mrs. Willis plays a significant role here; she embodies the black women's club movement that united its participants in the crusades against lynching and Jim Crow laws. This work charts the black woman's role in changing history through her solidarity with other women, forging a new vision of society that runs counter to the one white culture promulgates. According to Campbell, Hopkins turns to the ideal of domesticity, enshrining the possibilities inherent in the home where a sewing circle can become a political forum.

Not limited to one genre, Hopkins also wrote short stories and two lengthy serials in addition to *Of One Blood: Hagar's Daughters, A Story of Southern Caste Prejudice*, published under her mother's name; and *Winona, A Tale of Negro Life in the South and Southwest* (May 1902 to October 1902). The recurring idea of the short stories was that of interracial relationships; this theme fueled some negative feelings and led to the cancellation of subscriptions by some white readers.

September 1904 marked an interruption in her career aseditor because of ill health. The November issue praised her services and conveyed warm sentiments for her recovery. Subsequently the magazine assumed new ownership under Fred R. Moore, who had secretly received a subsidy from Booker T. Washington. Dorothy L. Porter in an article in a 1912 *Crisis* says that Hopkins had not been conciliatory enough for the new management (Porter, 326).

Her writing continued briefly as she contributed to *Voice of the Negro*, also an early twentieth-century magazine founded in January 1904. Her article in the December 1904 issue, "The New York Subway," gave detailed information regarding the building of the tunnel and the construction of trains. From February to July 1905 she wrote for the *Voice*.

Hopkins Establishes Publishing Company

Hopkins' literary career began to decline after her work for the *Voice of the Negro*. She later founded her own publishing company, P. E. Hopkins and Company. In 1905 she published in Cambridge *A Primer of Facts Pertaining to the Early Greatness of the Possibility of Restoration by Its Descendants with Epilogue*, a thirty-one page booklet. In February and March 1916 Hopkins contributed two articles to *New Era Magazine*.

Hopkins lived in obscurity after 1916. She died on August 13, 1930, at the Cambridge Relief Hospital after suffering on the previous day burns on her entire body when her dress caught on fire. She was buried on August 17 in the Hopkins family plot on Lilac Path in the Garden Cemetery, Chelsea, Massachusetts.

While present-day scholars give Pauline Hopkins far greater significance as an editor and journalist than did her contemporaries, many of her literary accomplishments still need to be brought to the forefront. But her contemporaries could not deny her significance as one who contributed to the artistic patchwork quilt of black women writers.

References

Campbell, Jane. *Mystic Black Fiction: The Transformation of History*. Knoxville: University of Tennessee Press, 1986.

——. "Pauline Elizabeth Hopkins." *Dictionary of Literary Biography*. Vol. 50. Detroit: Gale Research, 1986.

Carby, Hazel. *Reconstructing Womanhood: The Emergence of the Afro-American Woman Novelist.* New York: Oxford University, 1987.

Clark, Edward. *Black Writers in New England.* Boston: National Park Service, 1985.

Johnson, Abby Arthur. "Away from Accommodation: Radical Editors and Protest Journalism, 1900-1910." *Journal of Negro History* 62 (October 1977): 325-338.

Porter, Dorothy L. "Pauline Elizabeth Hopkins." *Dictionary of American Negro Biography.* Eds. Rayford W. Logan and Michael R. Winston. New York: Norton, 1982.

Mainiero, Lina. *American Women Writers.* New York: Frederick Ungar Publishing, 1980.

Page, James A. *Selected Black American, African, and Caribbean Authors: A BioBibliography.* Littleton, Colo.: Libraries Unlimited, 1985.

Shockley, Ann Allen. *Afro-American Women Writers: An Anthology and Critical Guide.* Boston: G. K. Hall, 1988.

——. "Pauline Elizabeth Hopkins: A Biographical Excursion into Obscurity." *Phylon* 33 (1972): 22-26.

Simmona E. Simmons

Lena Horne

(1917-)

Entertainer, singer, actress

If one sifts through the many clippings documenting world media coverage of Lena Horne's career, a chronological study of language, especially the adjectives, quite accurately reflects her gradual maturity as a person and performer—from the "sultry, sloe-eyed, alluring, exotic, luscious, dusky beauty," to a "scintillating voice" with "talent, poise, dignified charm," to "character and dignity, giving credit to race, sex, and country," to, ultimately, the "American Dream."

Lena Calhoun Horne, singer, entertainer, and actress, was born June 17, 1917, in the Bedford-Stuyvesant section of Brooklyn, New York, to Teddy Horne and Edna (Scottron) Horne. Even though both her parents belonged to respectable black middle-class families, Teddy, a numbers banker, and Edna, a struggling actress, were financially unable to maintain an independent household for themselves as a married couple and moved in with Teddy's parents at the Horne residence on Chauncey Street. The strained marriage of Edna and Teddy Horne ended within four years when Teddy left his wife. Though deprived of a natural father at age three, Lena Horne later benefited from her father's returning to play a protective role in her life at a time that was professionally crucial, and the two developed a closeness that was to last until his death.

Lena Horne

In the early twenties, soon after Teddy left his wife and daughter, Edna Scottron Horne also departed, leaving Lena with her paternal grandparents, to pursue her aspirations as an actress with the Lafayette Stock Company in Harlem.

Lena Horne's grandmother, Cora Calhoun Horne, was a domineering woman who had a formidable influence on Horne's early life. A detailed genealogical study of Lena Horne's paternal and maternal heritage has been prepared by her daughter, Gail Lumet Buckley in *The Hornes: An American Family.* Buckley credits Cora Calhoun Horne with helping Paul Robeson through college and says that she knew W. E. B. Du Bois when he was young "Willie." Extremely civic-minded, Cora Calhoun Horne was very active in the Urban League, the Women's Suffrage Movement, and the NAACP. In addition to starting Lena Horne's formal education at the Brooklyn Ethical School, she also registered the two-year-old Lena as a member of the NAACP.

Around 1924, Lena Horne moved in with her mother, who was generally in ill health, and during the next few years had nomadic experiences traveling with the struggling actress and living with relatives, acquaintances, and strangers in Philadelphia, Miami, Macon and Atlanta, Georgia. She returned to Brooklyn to stay with members and friends of the Horne family. This was the beginning of the several "extreme contrasts, conflicts and constant moving" that Lena Horne reflects on in her essay "Believing in Oneself," which she wrote for *Many Shades of Black*, a compilation of essays by successful black Americans edited by Stanton L. Wormley and Lewis H. Fenderson. While her mother was gone again, Lena Horne attended the Brooklyn public schools and the Girls High School until she was fourteen years old. Then her mother returned from a Cuban tour with a Cuban husband, Miguel ''Mike'' Roderiguez, to claim Lena again. These were difficult times during the Great Depression that followed the stock market crash of 1929. The Cuban immigrant with a strong Spanish accent and an ailing actress, who had never been very successful anyway, had an even more difficult time finding employment. Thus Horne's early teen years were spent in near poverty in the Bronx area of New York City, where the Rodriguezes had moved to avoid the snubs of a very insular black middle class of the Brooklyn area.

Lena Horne, who as a little girl aspired to be a teacher, out of necessity at age sixteen quit school and went to work for the famous, for-whites-only Cotton Club in Harlem. This arrangement materialized through the influence of the club's dance choreographer, Elida Webb, who knew Horne's mother. Lena Horne qualified easily, for she was light-skinned, tall, slim, with ''good'' long hair, young, and beautiful. (The one physical flaw in Lena Horne's beauty is her slightly bowed legs. Later she almost always appeared in long gowns to hide this imperfection.)

Fortunately for Lena Horne, a decision, in spite of the tremendous sacrifice it took, was made early to invest a portion of her twenty-five-dollar-a-week wages from the Cotton Club in music lessons—an investment that figuratively paid dividends in gold. Lena Horne had begun her long, very successful career in the entertainment business. At the Cotton Club, she worked with some established names of black entertainment, such as Cab Calloway, Ethel Waters, Billie Holiday, Count Basie, and Duke Ellington.

By 1934, much to the distress of the Cotton Club management, Lena Horne came to the attention of Lawrence Schwab, the producer of *Dance with Your Gods,* where she got her feet wet with brief exposure on Broadway. Soon afterward she left the Cotton Club to be a singer with Noble Sissle's Society Orchestra in Philadelphia in 1935—a move that helped heighten her image in the public eye. Up until this point in her life, Lena Horne's career had pivoted on her looks rather than on her talent as a singer.

Teddy Horne, Lena's father, reappeared in her life and remained a major influence until his death in 1970. Teddy Horne was now operating the Belmont Hotel in Pittsburgh.

During travels with the Noble Sissle Society Orchestra, Lena Horne once again faced not only the inconveniences of being without a regular home but the crude realities of the Jim Crow existence. These conditions pushed her to a kind of desperation that caused her literally to marry the first person she could. Her first husband was Louis Jones, a friend of her father's, who was nine years her senior.

Lena Horne wore black, which she considered a sophisticated color, when she married Louis Jones in her father's house on Wiley Avenue in Pittsburgh in January 1937. A difficult four-year marriage produced two offspring—Gail, and two years later, Teddy. Lena Horne's mother opposed her marriage to Louis Jones, and their relationship remained strained until the mother's death in 1981. She tried to sue Lena Horne at one point, but they settled out of court, and Lena Horne's attempts at peace-making after her father's death were unsuccessful.

Career in Show Business Opens

Lena Horne's tour with Noble Sissle's band led to a starring role in the revue *Blackbirds of 1939*—a show of short duration. By the fall of 1940, a twenty-three-year-old Lena Horne left her husband and children to return to New York City to renew her career. She wanted to arrange for a suitable place for her children so they could live with her. After an initial struggle, Lena Horne got a career break that she considers the ''real'' beginning of her show business profession. Charlie Barnett made her the chief vocalist with his all-white band in late 1940. While with this band, she recorded, under the Bluebird label, ''You're My Thrill,'' ''Haunted Town,'' and ''Good For Nothing Joe''; the latter soon became a hit. Lena Horne could now provide a comfortable home for her children, but in 1941 when she went to Pittsburgh, Louis Jones permitted her custody of Gail alone. She did not fight for Teddy and settled for sharing him during visits. In New York Lena Horne was now enjoying the stability she had struggled hard to achieve. She was in 1941 the featured singer at the Cafe Society Downtown, earning seventy-five dollars a week. Her fame was rising, and she was dating the world heavyweight champion, Joe Louis.

It was at Cafe Society in 1941 that she met Paul Robeson, the world-famous black American performer, and Walter White, the executive director of the NAACP, both in the same evening. Through their friendship and influence Lena Horne began to appreciate the strength of racial solidarity and developed a heightened awareness for the part her grandmother, Cora Calhoun Horne, played in that mission.

Lena Horne had been at the Cafe Society barely a few months when the offer came for her to perform at the Trocadero Club in Hollywood. As someone who had frequently experienced the harshness of the Jim Crow system and had found Hollywood, during her brief stay there for the filming of *The Duke is Tops,* just as racist, Lena Horne was reluctant. Walter White, however, counseled the young singer to accept the challenge and help break the traditional stereotyping of black Americans in films. In early 1942, Lena Horne moved to Hollywood with her daughter and cousin, Edwina, who had been taking care of Gail.

Lena Horne had been performing less than two months at the Little Troc Club when she came to the attention of Robert Edens of Metro-Goldwyn-Mayer (MGM), who arranged for her to audition for producer Arthur Freed. The audition was successful. She had the timely counsel of her father, who had joined her, and Walter White, who happened to be in Hollywood during this crucial time. (Lena Horne credits Roger Edens for ''discovering'' her; however, James Haskins and Kathleen Benson in chapter five of *Lena: A Person-*

al and Professional Biography of Lena Horne, have argued, with the support of interviews with Frances Williams, that it was Harold Gumm, her energetic agent who had followed Horne to Hollywood, who *made* Lena Horne.) In 1942, Lena Horne was the second black American woman to sign a contract with a motion picture company in Hollywood. (The first black woman was Madame Sul-Te-Wan, who was signed by D. W. Griffith in 1915.) The seven-year contract provided for an initial salary of two hundred dollars per week and clearly stipulated that Horne would not be asked to play any stereotypical roles.

Ironically, Lena Horne lost her first chance to play a speaking part in a mixed-cast movie as the wife of Eddie "Rochester" Anderson in *Thank Your Lucky Stars* to Ethel Waters because she was too light and a darker makeup made her seem to be in blackface. The next speaking role in a mixed film came almost thirty years later in *Meet Me in Las Vegas* in 1956. Her first movie at MGM was *Panama Hattie*, which featured her in a role that was to become MGM's typical presentation of her in many other films that she did in the next two years. Her performance was always limited to a guest-spot number that could be easily edited out during showings in Southern theaters. She was usually featured elegantly gowned, leaning against a pillar. In contrast, her television appearances in the 1960s and 1970s, which she fiercely controlled, usually portrayed her doing solos sitting on a stool or standing alone on the stage. (In their recent book, *Split Image: African-Americans in the Mass Media*, Jannette L. Dates and William Barlow discuss the politics and control by black entertainers of their television image, pp. 287-288.)

In the only all-black film that Lena Horne did for MGM (*Cabin in the Sky*, released in 1943), she played the major role as temptress Georgia Brown. This was the only major screen assignment MGM afforded her. Other films that featured Lena Horne in a guest spot were *As Thousands Cheer, Swing Fever, Broadway Rhythm, Two Girls and a Sailor, Ziegfeld Follies*, and *Till the Crowds Roll By*. Her last film with MGM was *The Duchess of Idaho* in 1950. Several factors contributed to the decline of offers to Lena Horne. Besides the "painful pragmatism" of sales and southern audiences, the managers at MGM felt they had done their duty toward Lena Horne's contract. Besides, the political changes and fear of communism and blacklistings by *Red Channels* publications all contributed negatively toward demands for several other black American performers as well. For details see *The Hornes* (208), *Lena* (135-38), and *Split Image* (287-89).

Star Excels in *Stormy Weather*

The managers at MGM obviously had no new major roles for Lena Horne after *Cabin* and loaned her to Twentieth Century Fox, where she did another all-black film, *Stormy Weather*, a musical on the thinly disguised life of Bill "Bojangles" Robinson. The title track of "Stormy Weather" is still her classic number.

It was during the filming of *Stormy Weather* that Lena Horne met Leonard "Lennie" George Hayton, her musical mentor, whom she secretly married in 1947. Married once before, Lennie Hayton, like Louis Jones, her first husband, whom she divorced in 1944, was nine years her senior. Hayton had joined MGM in 1941 as composer-conductor. He is most remembered for his music direction in *The Harvey Girls* with Judy Garland and *Singin' in the Rain* with Gene Kelly. In 1949 he won an Oscar for *On the Town* and an Academy Award in 1970 for the film version of *Hello, Dolly*. Lena and Lennie Hayton enjoyed their "easy" marriage for twenty-four years until Lennie died unexpectedly in 1971. Lena Horne admitted after Hayton's death that she grew to love him even though she initially married him for career reasons. (For violent reaction to the announcement of their marriage, see *Time*, 25 May 1981, 96; and *Lena*, 127.)

Lena Horne was the pinup girl for thousands of black American soldiers during World War II, and she performed on USO tours only when *all* soldiers were admitted to the auditorium.

In earning power, Lena Horne was one of the nation's top black entertainers by the mid-forties. MGM was paying her $1,000 a week for forty weeks a year. Her nightclub and theater appearances easily added up to $10,000 dollars a week, or $6,500 a week plus a percentage of the gate. She was getting royalties for her several recordings and charging up to $2,500 for radio appearances. Her record high was $60,000 a week in the fall of 1948 at Cibacabano in New York, where she returned in 1951 and grossed $175,000 in twenty weeks. By 1952 she was charging $12,500 weekly, which meant that tickets were generally beyond the reaches of most black audiences.

Lena Horne, now a consummate performer, had overlapping assignments in movies, theater, television, and recording studios in the 1950s and the 1960s. An international star, she was performing the world over. Her first Broadway show, *Jamaica*, premiered in 1957, and she frequented national television shows hosted by Ed Sullivan, Perry Como, Steve Allen, Milton Berle, and Frank Sinatra. She did a few benefits with Harry Belafonte and in September 1969 performed "Monsanto Night Presents Lena Horne" for NBC.

Lena Horne was increasingly active in the civil rights movements during these years. She was present at the March on Washington in August 1963. She supported unions and became an active honorary member of the Delta Sigma Theta Sorority.

Her father, who had been was a stabilizing factor since her move to Hollywood, died of emphysema during the summer of 1970, and within months, in September, her son, Teddy, died of kidney disease. She hardly had time to recover when in April 1971 her husband, Lennie, suddenly died. She lived a relatively quiet life in Santa Barbara during the early seventies, but by 1974 she was performing on Broadway with Tony Bennett. In 1978 Lena Horne played in the black movie version of the *Wizard of Oz,* directed by her son-in-law, Sidney Lumet. *The Wiz,* the most expensive of all-black-films ever produced, proved to be a box-office failure.

Even though Lena Horne did a farewell tour between June and August 1980, she was not ready to retire and triumphed beautifully on April 30, 1981, in *Lena Horne: The Lady and Her Music,* which has been the longest-running one-woman show on Broadway. Since then she has won many awards in music and the Kennedy Center Award for Lifetime Contribution to the Arts. In 1979 Howard University presented her with an honorary doctorate degree. Lena Horne declared:

> I had been offered doctorates earlier and had turned them down because I knew I hadn't been to college. But by the time Howard presented the doctorate to me, I knew I graduated from the School of Life, and I was ready to accept it ("Lena Horne: The Lady and Her Music").

Her honors continue. "Overcoming barriers of racial prejudice, you have always strived to be the best that you could be" said Rosaline Gorin, president of Radcliffe College Alumnae Association, while a giving medal to honor Lena Horne in 1987 (*Harvard Alumni Gazette*, 11). These honors are a superb finale for a career that started in the desperation of poverty.

Lena Horne wrote her autobiography with Richard Schickel in 1965, which Doubleday published. She currently resides in New York City.

References

Buckley, Gail Lumet. *The Hornes: An American Family.* New York: Knopf, 1986.

Dates, Jannette L., and William Barlow, eds. *Split Image: African-Americans in the Mass Media.* Washington, D.C.: Howard University Press, 1990.

Harvard University. *Alumni Gazette* (June 1987): 11.

Haskins, James, and Kathleen Benson. *Lena: A Personal and Professional Biography of Lena Horne.* New York: Stein and Day, 1984.

Horne, Lena. "Believing in Oneself." In *Many Shades of Black.* Eds. Stanton L. Wormley and Lewis H. Fenderson. New York: William and Co., 1969.

Horne, Lena, with Richard Schickel. *Lena.* New York: Doubleday, 1965. Includes photographs.

"Lena Horne: The Lady and Her Music." Program. Howard University, Washington, D.C., 1979.

Letters and interviews, Lena Horne, Gail Lumet Buckley, and Sherman Sneed with Esme Bhan, June-August 1990.

Collections

Lena Horne's personal memorabilia and papers will be deposited at the Schomburg Center for Research of the New York Public Library. In addition to the sources above, photographs of Lena Horne are in the Moorland-Spingarn Research Center, Howard University, and in the Carl Van Vechten Collection at Fisk University.

Esme E. Bhan

Anna Hudlun "Mother Hudlun"

(1819-1914)

Humanitarian, civic worker

Anna Elizabeth Lewis Hudlun's work through various social and civic organizations provided significantly to the uplift of blacks in Chicago, but history records her most outstanding work as that with the victims of Chicago's great fires of 1871 and 1874, for which she has earned the respectful titles "Fire Angel" and "Chicago's Grand Old Lady."

Shortly before Anna Hudlun was born in Uniontown, Pennsylvania, on February 6, 1840, her slave mother was freed by the Quaker family who owned her, and the happiness and joy the mother realized upon her emancipation was at once transferred to her newborn. The responsibility of a single parent with a little child to support was enormous. The mother was fortunate to find another Quaker family from Pennsylvania who was willing to take Anna to live with them while the mother traveled with one of the prominent families of the country.

As the years progressed, Hudlun's mother thought seriously of her daughter's future, so she joined her daughter and together they traveled west, stopping in Saint Louis, Missouri, and settling in Chicago in 1854. While in Saint Louis, Anna Elizabeth Lewis met a young man, Joseph Henry Hudlun, who was born a slave in Culpepper Court House, Virginia, October 4, 1839. The meeting seemed a casual one at the time, but in 1854 Hudlun also located in Chicago. After a brief courtship, Anna Elizabeth Lewis and Joseph Henry Hudlun were married in 1855.

The Hudluns realized early that they would need to acquire property if they were to become substantial citizens. The Hudlun house was a five-room cottage, one of the first in the area contracted for and built by black owners in 1857. Located at 279 Third Avenue, near Dearborn Station, their little home became the mecca of social and civic activities for old pioneers, and strangers as well. On February 14, 1864,

Anna Hudlun gave birth to their daughter, Joanna Cecilia, in Third Avenue home.

An act that endeared the Hudluns to Chicagoans occurred during the distressing Chicago fire of October 1871: The doors of the Hudlun home were thrown open to blacks and whites. The five-room cottage and shed-kitchen housed as many as five families of both races, and they lived in harmony. Their sustenance consisted of hardtack furnished by the city and water that Joseph Hudlun drew from Lake Michigan and transported to the house in his buggy. The arrangement sufficed until roomier quarters and better fare could be provided.

Joseph Hudlun was also active in community affairs. A conscientious and frugal man, he amassed considerable property during his lifetime. For forty years he served as a respected member on the Chicago Board of Trade. On the night of the fire of 1871, Joseph Hudlun left his family, went to the Board of Trade building during the most dangerous time of the fire, opened the vaults, and saved many of the valuable books and papers of the institution. As a testimonial to Joseph Hudlun's character and the regard that others had for him, upon death his younger son, Joseph Henry, Jr., was placed on the Board of Trade. Anna Hudlun would also feel protection for herself and her family through her son's position on the board. An oil portrait of Joseph Henry Hudlun, Sr., hangs in the Hall of Celebrities of the Chicago Board of Trade.

But Joseph Hudlun was not the only one to perform a great humanitarian deed that night of the Chicago fire; Anna Hudlun or "Mother Hudlun," as she was affectionately called, searched for the distressed and aided and comforted them either by providing shelter or ministering to their needs. As a result of her work, she became known as the "Fire Angel"—a title that she maintained until she died on November 21, 1914.

In 1874 Chicago witnessed a second major fire that destroyed the homes in black neighborhoods. Mother Hudlun again sought out the homeless and distressed and gave them food and clothing, and housed as many families as she could. This time, in love and respect for her work, she became known as "Chicago's Grand Old Lady" (Brown, 143).

While Anna Hudlun was busy rearing the family, she found time to participate in other worthwhile causes. She was Chicago's foremost humanitarian and community worker of her time. She was a respected member of the Chicago Board of Trade, and became active in the Quinn Chapel African Methodist Episcopal Church. (Her mother was among the earliest members of Quinn Chapel.) Beyond the church, Anna Hudlun worked to keep the mixed schools of Chicago open and ministered to the sick and needy of all groups in her neighborhood. While she gave unconditionally to the distressed fire victims, she gave also to the care of dependents of the Juvenile Court. She was active in the black women's movement—a part of the Federation of Women's Clubs. One of the goals of the women's clubs was to care for the needy and to find shelter for the aged and infirm. She helped place people in the Home for Aged and Infirm of which her daughter, Joanna, was cofounder and which was in existence from 1898 to 1908. Anna Hudlun was an early member of the Old Settlers Club, organized for the purpose of keeping alive "the memories of the work of the pioneers and the Negroes and to be of general help to the Colored people of the city" (*Intercollegian Wonder Book,* 196).

References

Brown, Hallie Quinn. *Homespun Heroines*. Xenia, Ohio: Aldine Pub. Co., 1926. 141-44. Photograph facing p. 141.

Davis, Elizabeth Lindsay. *The Story of the Illinois Federation of Colored Women's Clubs, 1900-1922*. Published by the Federation, 1922.

Robb, Frederick H., ed. *1927 Intercollegian Wonder Book or The Negro in Chicago 1779-1927*. Vol. 1. Chicago: Washington Intercollegiate Club of Chicago, 1927. Photographs, p. 128, p. 227.

Who's Who in Colored America, 1938-1940. 5th ed. Brooklyn, N.Y.: Thomas Yenser, 1940.

Dorothy E. Lyles

Gloria T. Hull

(1944-)

Educator, poet, feminist

An outstanding scholar and poet, Gloria Theresa Thompson Hull is changing the contours of African-American and feminist scholarship and criticism in the academy. Born December 6, 1944, to Jimmie (Williams) Thompson, Gloria Thompson grew up in her birthplace, Shreveport, Louisiana. Her mother migrated to Shreveport from East Texas, where she was born in 1914. Jimmie Williams was only able to complete an elementary education. However, Hull's mother relished the things she learned in school. Having a prediliction for dialect poetry, she committed it to memory and recited Paul Laurence Dunbar's poems to her children.

Quite early, Hull was recognized as one of those "smart kids" who earned good grades. She attended West Shreveport Elementary School where she was indeed a good student. Hull matriculated in Central Junior High School and later completed Clark Junior High School. A junior high school teacher, Mrs. Selcy S. Collins, recognized Hull's talent and potential and encouraged her to strive for excellence.

Hull graduated from Booker T. Washington High School in 1962. That fall she entered Southern University in Baton Rouge, Louisiana. During her college career she joined the Alpha Kappa Alpha Sorority. An excellent student majoring in English, she graduated summa cum laude in May 1966. On June 12, 1966, she married Prentice H. Hull, a fellow student at Southern University. The Hulls have one son, Adrian Prentice Hull, born August 5, 1968.

The fall of 1966 found Hull, the recipient of a National Defence Education Act Fellowship, enrolled at the University of Illinois, Urbana. She remained in Illinois for only one semester. In 1967 she began a degree program at Purdue University in Lafayette, Indiana. Gloria Hull assumed a faculty appointment at the University of Delaware in Newark. She completed her dissertation, ''Women in Byron's Poetry: A Biographical and Critical Study,'' and received her degree in June 1972. In 1977 Hull became an associate professor of English. Active with black American students and concerned about the issues affecting them, Hull received the Outstanding Service Award from the University of Delaware Black Student Union for the academic year 1975-1976. Hull was nominated for the Excellence in Teaching Award four times: 1977, 1981, 1984, and 1987.

Hull's scholarly writing reveals her real self. In ''Researching Alice Dunbar-Nelson: A Personal and Literary Perspective,'' she writes: ''Having painfully developed these convictions [to function as a black woman in space dominated by white males] and a modicum of courage to buttress them, I now include/visualize everybody (my department chair, the promotion and tenure committee, my mother and brother, my Black feminist sister, the chair of Afro-American Studies, lovers, colleagues, friends) for each organic article, rather than write sneaky, schizophrenic essays from under two or three different hats'' (*All the Women Are White*, 194).

Outlining her black feminist approach to scholarship, Hull lists the fundamental tenets: (1) Everything about the subject is important for a total understanding and analysis of her life and work; (2) the proper scholar stance is engaged rather than 'objective'; (3) the personal (both the subject's and the critic's) *is* political; (4) description must be accompanied by analysis; (5) consciously maintaining at all times the angle of vision of a person who is both Black and female is imperative, as is the necessity for a class-conscious, anticapitalist perspective; (6) being principled requires rigorous truthfulness and 'telling it all'; (7) research/criticism is not an academic/intellectual game, but a pursuit with social meanings rooted in the 'real world' (''Researching Alice Dunbar-Nelson, 193).

In 1986 Hull became full professor of English at the University of Delaware. While on the faculty at Delaware, Hull received a number of grants, fellowships, and post-doctoral awards. Among them are a National Endowment Fellowship Summer Stipend, 1979; Rockefeller Foundation Fellowship, 1979-1980; Humanities Semester Development Grant (Delaware), 1981, 1982; Fund for the Improvement of Post-Secondary Education, ''Black Women's Studies Faculty and Curriculum Development Project'' (with Barbara Smith and Patricia Bell Scott), 1982-1984; Mellon National Fellowship, Wellesley College Center for Research on Women, fall 1983; Fulbright Fellowship, 1984-1986 to the University of the West Indies in Jamaica; and Ford Foundation Postdoctoral Fellowship, 1987-1988. The Ford postdoctoral project took Hull to the Institute for Research on Women and Gender at Stanford University. As a visiting scholar of the institute, Hull was wooed away from the University of Delaware with its frigid winters by the California sun and a position as professor of women's studies/literature at the University of California, Santa Cruz. She accepted the position in the fall of 1988. In 1989 Hull became chairperson of women's studies.

When asked about future plans, Hull replied that she wants to perfect her teaching and test the demands of administration. She is the recent recipient of a 1991 grant from the American Association of University Women, which she will use to further investigate black women's poetry.

Women's Issues Addressed in Writings

Hull's book publications include: the award-winning *All the Women are White, All the Blacks are Men, But Some of Us are Brave: Black Women's Studies*, edited with Patricia Bell Scott and Barbara Smith (Old Westbury, N.Y.: The Feminist Press, 1982); Introduction by Smith-Hull reprinted as ''The Politics of Black Women's Studies'' in *Learning Our Way: Essays on Feminist Education*, eds. Charlotte Bunch and Sandra Pollack (Trumansburg, N.Y.: The Crossing Press, 1984); *Give Us Each Day: The Diary of Alice Dunbar-Nelson*, edited with a critical introduction and notes (New York: Norton, 1984; paperback edition, 1986); *Color, Sex, and Poetry: Three Women Writers of the Harlem Renaissance* (Bloomington: Indiana University Press, 1987); *The Works of Alice Dunbar-Nelson*, Vols. 1-3, edited with a critical introduction (New York: Oxford University Press, 1988); and *Healing Heart: Poems 1973-1988* (Latham, N.Y.: Kitchen Table Press, 1989).

Hull has given major addresses and poetry readings, and served on panels throughout the United States and the world. She serves as editorial consultant to *Feminist Studies*, and from 1978 to 1986 she was advisory editor to *Black American Literature Forum*. Listed in *Who's Who Among Black Americans, Contemporary Authors* and featured in *Women of Power: A Magazine of Feminism, Spirituality, and Politics*, 15 (1989), 50-53, Hull was named ''Outstanding Young Woman of America'' in 1977.

References

Contemporary Authors. Vol. 25. Detroit: Gale Research, 1989.

Hull, Gloria T. ''Curriculum Vitae,'' September 1989.

———. *Healing Heart: Poems 1973-1988*. Latham, N.Y.: Kitchen Table: Women of Color Press, 1989.

Hull, Gloria T., Patricia Bell Scott, and Barbara Smith, eds. *All the Women are White, All the Blacks are Men, But Some of Us are Brave*. Old Westbury, N.Y.: The Feminist Press, 1982.

Hull, Gloria T. Interview with the author, 14 November 1990.

Nagueyalti Warren

Alberta Hunter

(1895-1984)

Singer, composer, nurse

On January 11, 1977, licensed practical nurse Alberta Hunter called Goldwater Memorial Hospital on Welfare Island (now Roosevelt Island) to say that she would not be coming in because she was not feeling well. In the ensuing conversation she was informed that she faced mandatory retirement on her next birthday, April 1, and that she need not come in any more because of her accumulation of leave. The staff of the personnel office believed that she would be seventy on her birthday; in fact, she would be eighty-two. At the retirement party she reluctantly attended, she received recognition for twenty years service to the hospital—she had been hired on May 16, 1957. Few of her fellow workers knew that she had been a famed singer, and no one could have predicted the final turn in her life. About five months later, on October 10, she opened at Barney Josephson's restaurant, The Cookery, in Greenwich Village and launched a second singing career. For the remaining seven years of her life she was more famous than she had ever been before.

Alberta Hunter

Alberta Hunter was born on April 1, 1895, at 288 1/2 High Street in Memphis, Tennessee. She was the second child of Charles E. Hunter, a sleeping-car porter, and Laura (Peterson) Hunter. Her sister, La Tosca, was two years older. Charles Hunter abandoned the family soon after Alberta Hunter's birth—she was told and believed until her death that he had died. Her mother worked as a maid in a brothel. Since Laura Hunter was very prudish, she never talked of her job and in fact seems never to have discussed sex at all with her children. A strict disciplinarian who had no need to use physical force, she was also a very self-contained woman and spoke little of what she felt or thought. Her second daughter grew up to become like her in many ways; at the age of eighty-seven she told a correspondent for *Time* magazine, "I'm the image of my mother . . . exactly like her in every way" (Clarke, 82).

Until Alberta Hunter was eight, the primary child-rearing role in the family was filled by her maternal grandmother, Nancy Peterson. The family was not very religious—Laura Hunter did not go to church—but the children attended services at the Collins Chapel Colored Methodist Episcopal Church, a decidedly "refined" church for upward strivers. There the young Hunter heard many sermons on self-help and self-improvement.

About 1906 or 1907, Laura Hunter married Theodore "Dode" Beatty, who was very jealous and often struck her. Alberta Hunter hated him and was extremely jealous of her much younger stepsister and of her own older sister, a tall girl with "good" hair and features, whom she felt her mother favored. A further complication in her development was sexual molestation by adult men. Sometime beginning in 1909 she was subjected to a period of sexual abuse by the white boyfriend of her family's white landlady. Also, at an undetermined period, she was molested by a fat black school principal, whose parents she visited on weekends. She grew up a fiercely independent and aggressive child, whose nick-name was "Pig" because of her inability to keep herself and her clothes clean except for church on Sundays. Her mother's sole self-indulgence was the daily newspaper she always insisted on having and reading. Alberta Hunter shared her curiosity about the world and had an intense ambition to better herself and become somebody.

In July 1911 Floyd Lillian Cummings, "Miss Florida," one of Alberta Hunter's teachers, was going to Chicago with the man to whom she was secretly married. She had an unused child's pass and offered to take the sixteen-year-old along if her mother gave permission. Knowing what her mother's reaction would be, Alberta Hunter did not bother to ask, borrowed ten cents from a friend, and set off. Her character and personality had already been formed in large measure by her experiences in Memphis, She had known love and happiness, but she had also known the deep hurt she defined many years laster as the basic experience of the blues:

> Many people think a woman sings the blues only when she is in love with a man who treats her like a dog. . . . I've never had the blues about no man, never in my life, honey. If a man beats me, I'll take a broomstick and beat him to death.
>
> But that's not the blues. We sing the blues because our hearts have been hurt. Blues is when you're hungry and you don't have no money to buy food. Or you can't pay your rent at the end of the month. Blues is when you disappoint somebody else; if you owe some money to your best friend, and you know he needs it, but you don't have it to give it to him.
>
> But just plain ol' ordinary "I don't have some,"—that's not the blues. Most young people today don't have real needs. They just have a few worries. They have needs for things that maybe they could do without. That's not the blues (Taylor, 263).

Singer's Career Begins Early

In Chicago Alberta Hunter looked up a Memphis acquaintance, Helen (Ellen) Winston, who found her a job cleaning up and peeling potatoes in a Hyde Park boarding house for six dollars a week and room and board. Hunter's eye, however, was on the ten dollars a week that singers could make. In her time off she set out to look for a job. Her persistence at Dago Frank's, a semi-discreet brothel at Archer and South State streets, paid off after several months of asking. She learned on the job, since her initial repertoire consisted of two songs, one of which she had hurriedly learned after getting the job. (Hunter denied claims that she had already sung in Memphis.) She worked at the house until the place closed in the summer of 1913, learning new songs, avoiding the pimps, and receiving advice and help from the women. At her next job at Hugh Hoskins's, a club with a black clientele on Thirty-second and South State streets, she met some of Chicago's leading black pickpockets and confidence men. She stayed there for fourteen months. Her mother came to live with her, and the two women got on well by not confiding in each other—Hunter never learned of the circumstances of the breakup of her mother's marriage, and she never told her mother of her own attachments to women.

Hunter next worked at Teenan Jones's Elite Number One at Thirtieth and South State streets, another cabaret basically for blacks, and then in 1915 she went to the Panama Café at Thirty-fifth and South State streets, one of the top spots in Chicago, with a largely white clientele. Downstairs in the more refined room the elite of black women performers appeared—they included Cora Green, Mattie Hite, Nettie Compton, Florence Mills, and Ada "Bricktop" Smith. Upstairs were the barrelhouse singers, but Hunter herself did most of the singing there. She worked from eight to midnight and then performed in after-hours clubs. Her popularity became so great that composers paid her to introduce their songs. Maceo Walker made her one of the first to sing "Sweet Georgia Brown," and W. C. Handy had her plug "Saint Louis Blues."

After a shooting in 1917, the police closed the Panama Café, and Hunter moved next door to the De Luxe Café for a week and then across the street to the Dreamland Ballroom, the headquarters of Joseph "King" Oliver and his band. She spent five years there, starting at $17.50 a week and eventually rising to $35—plus the tips, which on a good night could be as much as four or five hundred dollars. She knew how to garner more than her share of the tips, which were supposed to be split among all the musicians. Once when she was working at the Burnham Inn on the outskirts of Chicago, the lights went out and a shot rang out. The lights came on to reveal a dead man on the floor and Alberta Hunter with her hand in the tip box. She, along with the other singers, also had less obvious and direct ways of increasing her share.

Hunter was also singing in other clubs whenever possible, after hours and during her time off. She knew and was working with some of the most talented musicians in the world, including Lillian Hardin. Her socializing with her fellow musicians was limited by her reserve, by the very fact that she was working, and the fact that she neither drank, smoked, nor took drugs. Male musicians felt obliged to apologize for using rough language in her presence. In her singing, she drew a firm line between suggestive lyrics, which she handled with gusto and which, moreover, earned money, and explicitness, which she rejected.

Hunter was just as firm in her private life; she maintained complete discretion about her lesbian relations—in Chicago she had a long-term relationship with Carrie Mae Ward and later in New York, with Lottie Tyler, Bert Williams's niece. She strongly disapproved of Ethel Waters's behavior both in using bad language and in publicly quarrelling with her girlfriends. Hunter's marriage to William Saxby Townsend in 1919 lasted two months. She had known him for two days when they crossed the river from Cincinnati to Covington, Kentucky, and married on January 27. Back in Chicago, Laura Hunter Beatty charged him nine dollars a week for his room and board, and Alberta Hunter refused to have sex with him and kicked him out after two months.

Dreamland was a large room, and although her voice was not as big as those of Bessie Smith or Ethel Waters, Hunter had no trouble filling it. She helped build her popularity by making a point of appearing in the latest fashions, and her popularity meant she could contribute to the launching of songs like "Beale Street Blues" and "A Good Man Is Hard to Find." She also began to seek ways to advance her career, looking first to the stage. From August to October 1929 she played in three shows—*Canary Cottage*, *Miss Nobody from Starland*, and *September Morn*—each in two-week runs at the Avenue Theater in Chicago; *Canary Cottage* ran for another two weeks at the Dunbar Theater in Philadelphia, but she left the cast after another week's run at the Lafayette Theater in Harlem. In May 1921, she made a quick trip to New York to cut her first record for the Black Swan label. The following year she switched to Paramount because she believed that Black Swan was promoting Ethel Waters and neglecting her. Among her earliest recordings for Paramount was her own song "Down Hearted Blues." She also recorded for another label under an assumed mane.

During part of 1922, Hunter was trying to establish herself in New York. She starred with Ethel Waters in *Dumb Luck,* a show so bad that it closed out of town, stranding the cast. Ethel Waters managed to sell the scenery and costumes and pay the cast but bought tickets back to New York only for herself and her girlfriend; Hunter came up with the money for the return tickets for the rest of the cast. That fall she returned to acclaim in Chicago, where she met Harry Watkins, a chorus-line dancer, who became one of her closest friends for sixty years. In April 1923 the boyfriend of singer Mae Alix became so upset about what he perceived as an overly close relationship between the two women that Hunter felt that a quick and permanent removal to New York was prudent.

Hunter left Chicago on Saturday, April 14; on Wednesday, April 18, she opened in Eddie Hunter's *How Come?* at the Apollo Theater at Forty-second Street and Broadway. The show had opened the previous Monday to bad reviews, and the addition was an attempt to bolster the show, which hung on in New York for five weeks and then went on the road, seldom making enough to pay Hunter her full salary of $140 a week. *How Come?* closed out of town in October. A show titled *Stars of How Come?,* with Alberta Hunter in the cast, opened at the Lincoln Theater in Harlem in November, closing in December. This year also included Bessie Smith's hit recording of Hunter's "Down Hearted Blues." (The two women never met.) As was often the case with early recordings, this one brought little money to her. Many early performers and composers, especially blacks, were regularly cheated out of their proper profits. In later years, a more experienced Hunter was vigilant in efforts to establish and maintain her copyrights.

Alberta Hunter was involved in Eddie Hunter's next effort, *Struttin' Time,* which opened at the Howard Theater in Washington, D.C., on May 18, 1924, for four weeks and then moved on to the Dunbar in Philadelphia, where it closed. She also was making further changes in her life. She bought a cooperative apartment at 133 West 138th Street, across from the Abyssinian Baptist Church. When her mother cut short her first visit to New York after one day, she rented it and found a cheaper apartment for herself and Lottie Tyler. She also began working in vaudeville on the Keith Circuit. There were disadvantages to this choice. The few black acts were placed early in the program to warm up the audience—if they were too successful the other acts complained and refused to follow them—and blacks could not wear the fine clothes they used in shows for their own people. Typically, the men were expected to wear overalls and the women bandannas and ragged dresses. In addition, press coverage of the circuit was so bad that the performers were practically invisible in New York theatrical circles.

Hunter could dance adequately, if necessary, and she is credited with introducing the Charleston to the white folk of West Virginia. There is controversy about whether she invented and introduced the black bottom. If she did, she was not eager to claim the credit for it in her later years. Her involvement with the Keith Circuit continued through April 1927 except for brief engagements at places like the Hot Feet Club in New York in late 1924. Many of her bookings were in New York State, and she could spend time in the city and continue to record. Paramount found out about her contract violations and dropped her in 1924. In late 1925 she began to record for Okeh, cutting some fourteen issued records by September 1926.

Hunter was not prominently involved in the Harlem Renaissance, although she came to know and admire Langston Hughes, whose aunt, Toy Brown, for many years did the alterations on the gowns she wore when performing. She also admired A'Lelia Walker's attitude toward Harlem society and attended some of her parties.

Performer Entertains in Europe

On August 5, 1927, Hunter sailed for Europe in the company of Lottie Tyler, ostensibly on vacation. Tyler soon fell in love with someone else and returned to the United States; this marked the end of the relationship, though not of the friendship. Hunter knew enough of the right people in Europe to be invited to very fashionable parties and like most black Americans, she found the lack of constant overt racism in France refreshing. By the beginning of November, she was working in a Paris club and in December moved to the Riveria. Her chance to get a work permit for England came when Noble Sissle organized a benefit performance by black entertainers for flood victims in London on January 29. After she had performed in various clubs and theaters in England, the duration of her work permit was extended. She also found a more prestigious role on the stage. On May 3, 1928, she opened in the part of Queenie in the London production of *Show Boat,* which also starred Paul Robeson. She won high praise for her performance in the show, which ran for 350 performances. Her headquarters in England at first was the room she rented from John Payne, the black American baritone, at 17 Regents Park Road. Payne and his protectress, Lady Mary Cook, were most helpful to black Americans in England. For a time Marian Anderson lived in the room next to Alberta Hunter's. When *Show Boat* closed, Alberta Hunter worked in Paris for a few weeks and then sailed for home on May 22, 1929.

Back in the United States, Hunter found it hard to get work despite her star status in Europe. She again worked on the Keith circuit, but vaudeville was dying because of the competition from the movies. She had a six-week engagement with Earl Hines and his orchestra at the Grand Terrace Café in Chicago, but after a good opening night, the audiences were not enthusiastic. Back in New York she got good reviews for her part in *Change Your Luck,* which opened on June 6, 1930; the musical, nonetheless, was a flop. In the fall of that year she had a run-in with Frank Shiffman, the white manager of the Lafayette Theater in Harlem, who was notorious for slashing performers' contracted salaries if audience reaction was poor, as it was to her performance.

A major change in her life was the establishment of Laura Hunter Beatty Fields in her Harlem apartment in early 1930. (Her mother had married a Jim Fields in Chicago; he was now dead.) In May 1931 Alberta Hunter moved into the apartment herself, and the two women fell into a way of life that would last as long as her mother lived. Laura Fields cooked—she could at least make good spaghetti, while her daughter's culinary skills extended only as far as heating the canned variety—and took care of the apartment, even insisting on making her daughter's bed. The mother seldom left the apartment; she had only two friends, and they visited her. She also read every newspaper she could get her hands on. When Alberta Hunter was going away, she stocked the spare room with food and saw to it that there was someone to bring more; very often this was Harry Watkins when he was in town. The downstairs neighbor, actress Rose McClendon, checked on the older woman every day until McClendon's illness and death in 1936. McClendon would pound on the door, which Laura Fields refused to open because she disapproved of McClendon's "salty" language (Taylor, 117).

In late May 1933 Hunter returned to Europe, where she had no difficulty in finding work. After stints in Paris, London, and Amsterdam, she was featured in the 1933-1934 Casion de Paris revue, *Vive Paris!* She used some of her free time to acquire a serviceable command of French. By July 1934 she was working in England. She appeared in the film *Radio Parade of 1935,* notable only as the first British film to use color, though only in the final sequence, in which she appeared. Her British work permit was lifted in January 1935. Since her mother was ill, she returned to New York for a short visit, but after the failure of *Connie's Hot Chocolates for 1935,* a Broadway night-club revue, she went back to Europe. She spent two months in Copenhagen, where she was always a favorite, and also worked in Egypt, as well as in London and Paris. In 1937 she was featured in a special short-wave program by NBC directed to the United States; this was the first time her mother heard her perform.

On the basis of this performance, Hunter was offered a chance to perform on radio in New York by NBC. The regular broadcasting began on October 15—five minutes quickly expanded to fifteen minutes, five days a week on a local station. One day a week the program went out nationally and another, internationally. When NBC's option expired early in 1938, she went back to Europe, returning reluctantly in September when the State Department advised Americans to leave because of the imminent danger of war.

After a brief run at El Morocco, Hunter landed a featured role in Dorothy and Dubose Heyward's *Mamba's Daughters,* which starred Ethel Waters and opened on January 3, 1939. During the play's break for the summer, Hunter's activities included recording six sides for Decca with Lillian Hardin Armstrong on the piano. She decided to return to the play when it began its road tour in October, even though Ethel Waters, sensing in her a rival, treated her very badly. The play stayed on the road until it returned to New York on March 23, 1939, where it ran for two weeks. Hunter was still hoping to be able to return to Europe.

The onset of World War II meant hard times for established black performers, as they were barred from Europe, nightclubs were closing, and a new wave of young black performers was coming into prominence. Hunter kept on working; she composed new songs, recorded them, sang on the air, performed in New York, and tried her luck out of town. She worked in Chicago, Detroit, and Cleveland. She went south to perform in nightclubs in Nashville, Dallas, and Fort Worth. She also converted her occasional letters to newspapers into a regular column "Alberta Hunter's Notebook," which ran from late May 1942 to August 1943 in the *Afro-American*. Her longest run was a full year at the Garrick Lounge in Chicago beginning in May 1943. There she was surprised one day to meet her nephew, La Tosca's son, Sam Sharp, Jr., then a member of the Harlem Globetrotters.

Both aunt and nephew were soon off to war. Dick Campbell had been appointed to coordinate black talent for the USO, and he made Hunter head of a small group to tour in the China-Burma-India theater. This tour, which involved considerable hardship and danger, lasted from August 1944 to March 31, 1945. After the war, she was one of forty persons selected to receive the Asiatic-Pacific Campaign Ribbon. Although the European war was over soon after her return, she was sent to entertain the troops still there. The highlight of the tour was the performance on June 11 at the party to celebrate the victory given by General Dwight D. Eisenhower for Soviet Marshall Georgi K. Zhukov.

Hunter was performing in Washington when she learned of her sister's death—she felt no great grief and did not attend the funeral. She did, however, go to Portland, Oregon, to receive her campaign ribbon and spent some time as house guest of Ethel Waters in Los Angeles—Waters was in New York at the time. Hunter may have begun to feel more keenly her status as a senior performer when the *Afro-American* asked her to write the obituary of Mamie Smith, which appeared on November 2, 1946. On December 6 she was a flop at the Apollo Theatre in Harlem and never worked in a black theater again. After another USO tour of the Far East from May to September 1947 and some club dates, she undertook a tour with the Veterans Hospitals Camp Shows in January 1948. This tour lasted most of the year. There was to be a second three-month tour beginning in January 1950. Touring conditions in the South for the black performers were nearly as bad as they had been on the Theatre Owners Booking Association (TOBA) circuit years before. It was difficult to secure decent housing and food, and on occasion they had to call Washington even to secure admittance to the bases.

Beginning in the spring of 1951, Hunter spent an entire year in New York, working at the Bon Soir and La Commedia. She was also continuing to write songs—these were now often religious, although she did not drop her repertoire of risqué songs she sang quietly to tables of customers willing to tip heavily enough. One of her religious songs caused a sharp tussle with an agent who put Mahalia Jackson's name on the record label as author. In 1952 she was elected to membership in ASCAP, a rare honor at the time for a woman and for a black American.

In July and August 1952, Hunter undertook a USO tour of Europe and then, beginning in October, spent fifty-seven days in Korea, followed by visits to Japan and Okinawa. She was the first black woman performer to visit the war zone, and she ensured that her performances were memorable by wearing nothing under her gowns in spite of the bitter cold.

In February 1953, Hunter was again in New York working at the Bon Soir. A little less than a year later, in January 1954, her mother died. She probably began contemplating withdrawing from show business about this time. She joined a church on April 4, 1953; it was the Williams Institutional Colored Methodist Episcopal Church, which met in the building that had housed the old Lafayette Theater. Still, that summer she acted again with Ethel Waters in a road version of *Mamba's Daughters*. In the fall she was understudy to Helen Dowdy in Charles Sebree and Greer Johnson's play *Mrs. Patterson*. After ten weeks of tryouts on the road, the play opened on Broadway on December 1, 1954, and ran for three months. Dowdy's health was excellent and Hunter never went on. The play is chiefly notable for the glowing reviews of the performance of Eartha Kitt, who later said that she did not even know Alberta Hunter was ever associated with the play. In January 1956, Alberta Hunter joined the cast of *Debut* by Mary Drayton. The play lasted five days after its opening on February 22, 1956. This comedy, set in the South, gave Hunter the role of a happy servant who opened each act with a spiritual. She never appeared on stage. At the age of nearly sixty-two, she was ready to change careers.

Hunter had begun volunteer work at the Joint Diseases Hospital in Harlem. As a result of putting in 1,958 hours in one year, she was named Volunteer of the Year by the hospital on May 24, 1956. She began to study and passed the city's elementary school equivalency examination on December 16, 1955. Turned down by the hospital's nursing program, she turned to that of the YWCA and persuaded its director, Phillis Utz, to accept her. To accomplish this, her age was put back twelve years in the records. Hunter completed the program on August 14, 1956. After finishing a six-month internship and passing the state board examination, she received her practical nurse's license on August 7, 1957. She had already been hired by Goldwater Memorial Hospital. She moved into the nurses' residence; she had invited her old friend Harry Watkins to move into her Harlem apartment after her mother's death, and she would visit him on her days off to eat his cooking and pick up the mail that came there. In 1965 after a dispute with the building managers, she sold that apartment and bought another at 139th Street and Riverside Drive. She dropped almost all connections with show business and stayed in touch with only a few friends. She was persuaded to do two recording sessions in 1961 and to appear on videotape for Danish television in 1971. That same year Chris Albertson paid her two thousand dollars for taped interviews for the Smithsonian Institution.

Hunter was a very good nurse; she followed regulations exactly, but more than that, she had an excellent rapport with her patients. Apart from a couple of accidents and her arthritis and osteoporosis, her health was good. She was miserly on what she spent on herself, exact in demanding repayment of loans by people who had the ability to repay, and generous to her friends and in her charity. Beyond her contributions to individuals, she regularly gave to organizations. She consistently gave one hundred dollars a year to the NAACP, and in 1976 she contributed five hundred dollars to become a life member. She also increasingly preferred to be alone when she was not on duty. Even at the age of eighty-two she was not ready to retire. On her application for welfare after the hospital retired her, she added to the usual required statement about actively seeking employment the sentence, "I would have continued working if I had not been forced to retire" (Taylor, 120).

Hunter Returns to Show Business

Hunter's return to show business was fortuitous. In late May 1977 Bobby Short was giving a farewell party for Mabel Mercer, who was going to Europe. She suggested that he invite Hunter, and a mutual friend undertook to see that Hunter attended the party. There she sang two of her songs for songwriters Alec Wilder and Charles Bourgeois. Bourgeois mentioned her name to restaurant and nightclub operator Barney Josephson, who was trying to rebuild a flourishing career that had been wrecked in the McCarthy era. Mary Lou Williams, the jazz pianist, had suggested back in 1970 that he hire former stars like herself. Satisfied that Alberta Hunter still had her teeth (according to him, artificial teeth caused a whistling in sound systems), he hired her on the spot without an audition and sent her to Gerald Cook to work on her music. In the event, the opening was postponed to October 10, and Cook was replaced by another pianist at the opening, though he very soon became her regular accompanist.

The opening was a sensation. Hunter received rave reviews and television played its part—she quickly appeared on the "Today" show in the first of many television appearances, and she was constantly written up in magazines from *Guideposts* to *Playboy* for the rest of her life. This publicity assured her a celebrity status that she had never known before. Her celebrity was supported by an artistry that continued to impress her audiences. Whitney Balliett described her voice:

> Her voice is steady and rich, and her vibrato betrays none of the quaveriness that often besets older singers. Her phrasing is legato, and once in

> a while she uses a high, almost falsetto cluster of notes which startlingly recalls Mildred Bailey, who must have heard Alberta Hunter records when she was coming up in the twenties. There is a burnished, accreted assurance and depth of color in Alberta Hunter's singing (100).

Hunter's base of operations remained The Cookery until 1978 when she led off the opening of the Newport Jazz Festival at Carnegie Hall on June 27. She received roses and the key to the city when she returned to Memphis for the premiere of *Remember My Name,* for which she had done the sound track—issued as an album by Columbia—but, nonetheless, at the gala opening she blasted the city for its lingering racism. On December 3 she was persuaded to sing at the Kennedy Center lifetime awards program—one of the honorees was Marian Anderson. And finally, on February 27, 1979, she sang at Jimmy Carter's White House.

In July 1979 Hunter went on the road again, accepting very well-paid engagements in many cities. The following year she recorded another album for Columbia and received the Handy Award as Traditional Female Blues Artist of the Year. In 1982 she traveled to Europe and appeared at several jazz festivals. In 1983 and again in May 1984 she made appearances in Brazil.

Although Hunter's health problems were increasing, she was loath to admit them. She fell and broke a wrist and hip in Chicago on June 11, 1980. On February 7, 1981, she broke her left leg in a fall at The Cookery. During the hospital stay, she had a pacemaker installed, although she denied this to her closest friends. On December 4, 1982, she was hospitalized for internal bleeding, and over her objections an exploratory operation was performed and a large portion of her intestines had to be removed. She was able to return to perform at The Cookery in late June 1983. Finally, she had to admit that she could not complete a performance during the summer of 1984 in Denver—this was her last public performance.

Her usual mode of dress during these years was casual; she would sometimes perform at The Cookery wearing a denim skirt, a cheap blouse, mismatched bedroom slippers, and the trademark large earrings. In her padded winter coat with her shopping bags, she looked like a bag lady—one of the homeless women on the streets of New York. She pointed out that this mode of dress offered protection against muggers, but she also carried an ice-pick close at hand in one of her shabby shopping bags. Her sole extravagance was the fur coat she bought and wore once, to the White House reception before the Kennedy Center gala in 1978. She became increasingly demanding as her frailties increased and quarreled, though not irrevocably, with even her oldest and most supportive friends. In her last hospital stay in 1984, her nurses found her a demanding but not unreasonable patient.

Hunter was able to return to her apartment for the last few weeks of her life. Very frail, she could wake up and see the sky in her window as she liked and be alone to think. Some of the time she spent telling her life story to Frank C. Taylor. The book he wrote with Gerald Cook, based on these interviews and the extensive material she had kept, is the essential starting point for all future biography.

Hunter was found dead in her apartment on October 17, 1984. Her burial befit this fiercely independent woman. In her will she stipulated that no more than seven hundred dollars be spent on her funeral—she did not approve of expensive ones. The mortician who initially removed the body had a higher minimum fee. Through the yellow pages, her attorney found an undertaker on Staten Island who agreed to pick up and cremate the body for her stipulated fee. Hunter is buried beside her mother in Ferncliff Cemetery in Hartsdale, New York.

References

Balliett, Whitney. "Let It Be Classy." *New Yorker* 53 (31 October 1977): 100-112.

Clarke, Gerald. "Good Tune from an Old Violin." *Time* 120 (13 December 1982): 82.

Gilbert, Lynn, and Gaylen Moore. *Particular Passions: Talks with Women Who Have Shaped Our Times.* New York: Clarkson N. Potter, 1981. 245-53. Photograph, p. 245.

Spradling, Mary Mace. *In Black and White.* 3rd ed. Vol. 1. Detroit: Gale Research, 1980.; 467-68.

———. *In Black and White.* Supplement. Detroit: Gale Research, 1985. 196.

Taylor, Frank C., with Gerald Cook. *Alberta: A Celebration in Blues.* New York: McGraw-Hill, 1987. Photographs, Discography, pp. 285-95.

Videotapes and Films

Alberta Hunter: Jazz at the Smithsonian. Video LP. Sony Corporation, 1982. Catalog no. J0065. Reissued on Keith label 1990.

Alberta Hunter: My Castle's Rocking. Directed by Stuart Goldman. Color. 60 minutes, 16mm film/video. The Cinema Guild. A look at the decades-long musical career of Alberta Hunter.

Robert L. Johns

Clementine Hunter

(1886-1988)

Folk artist

Like Grandma Moses, to whom she was often compared, Clementine Hunter began painting late in life, though she was a practicing folk artist long before that. The prolific Hunter, who became known as one of the century's leading "primitive" artists, stopped painting only one month before her death. The quality and importance of her work is still being studied and discovered by new generations of artists and art historians.

Clementine (pronounced "Clementeen") Reuben Hunter was born in late December 1886 at Hidden Hill, a cotton plantation near Cloutierville, Louisiana. Her mother, Antoinette Adams, was of Virginia slave ancestry. Her father, Janvier (John) Reuben was a Louisiana Creole of native American, African, French, and Irish descent. She was originally given a French name, "Clemence," which appears in United States census records. But her Roman Catholic baptismal record gives the Latin "Clementiam" (Miller, 6-11; Wilson, 19-20).

In Cloutierville, Hunter experienced her only taste of formal education at a small Catholic elementary school. She attended school only briefly, remaining illiterate all her life. After a few years, the family moved near Natchitoches, the oldest town in the state, to Melrose Plantation on the Cane River. Melrose, formerly called Yucca Plantation, had been owned by the Metoyers, the wealthiest free black family in the United States before the Civil War. By Hunter's day, however, Melrose was owned by a white family. The dynamic mistress of the plantation since 1898 was Carmelite "Cammie" Garrett Henry, who sought to restore the antebellum structures, revive local arts and crafts, and develop a library of Louisiana history.

Hunter had two children with Charlie Dupree, an eccentric Creole with a mechanical aptitude approaching genius. He died about 1914. She had five more children with Emanuel Hunter, a hardworking Christian whom she married in 1924. After first working in the fields, Clementine Hunter moved to full-time domestic duties in the main house sometime in the late 1920s. She developed a creative flair for cooking, decor, basketmaking, sewing, and quiltmaking.

At the same time, Hunter doubtless experienced the influence of the many prominent visitors to Melrose, including Lyle Saxon, Roark Bradford, and Richard Avedon. When François Mignon, the single most influential person in her artistic life, became a resident of Melrose in 1939, Clementine

Clementine Hunter

Hunter was ready for what would follow. A Frenchman whose career in foreign trade through New York City was disrupted by the outbreak of World War II, Mignon became curator of Cammie Henry's collections and a friend to Hunter. Sometime around 1940, one evening about seven o'clock, Hunter, then already in her late fifties, showed up at Mignon's door with some nearly empty tubes of paint discarded by an artist visiting Melrose. Hunter told him that she figured that she could "mark" a picture of her own if she set her mind to it. He cast about and came up with an old window shade, and the next morning at five o'clock she presented him with a completed picture. Although this was not the first picture that she had produced, it was the first that she had ever shown to another person. Indeed, one of her earliest recognized works is a quilt from 1938 depicting black life on the plantation. Field hands and boatmen surround a central panel in which the main house is depicted. The solid red, blue, and golden yellow pieces of fabric employed in this quilt strongly resemble the broad, flat areas of similar color that were soon to appear in her painting.

With Mignon's encouragement, Hunter began to paint untiringly on anything that she or he could scrounge—cardboard boxes, paper bags, scraps of wood, and eventually canvas. Mignon had little money himself, but somehow he managed to come up with enough for an occasional Sears and Roebuck mail order. Additionally, Hunter used bottles, an old chest, gourds, and even old iron pots—anything that could hold paint. She also continued to make a number of outstanding quilts. By the time of her death, her paintings numbered in the several thousands.

Over the years Hunter's technique changed little, and many regard her earliest works as her best. They are uncluttered and generally better-composed. Later works by comparison sometimes appear crowded, repetitive, or clumsy. She appears always to have used oils. Claims that she tried watercolor in some of her early pictures can be attributed to oil paint that was thinned in order to stretch scarce supplies. In time the subjects of her painting widened, but they rarely strayed from her own memories. She said that she always preferred to paint from memory or from dreams rather than from life.

Painter's Works Form Three Categories

Hunter's topics may be grouped into three categories. First and foremost, there are the memory pictures. They show people gathering and cooking food, washing, tending children, attending school, playing games, dancing and honky-tonking, and attending revival meetings, weddings, baptisms, funerals, and the like. In addition, there are scenes of birds, ducks, chickens, and cats and still lifes of flowers, most of these also apparently from memory. The second category, comprising what are perhaps her most poignant pictures, consists of the religious scenes of the Nativity, the Flight to Egypt, angels flying, and the Crucifixion. In these the figures are almost always depicted as black. The so-called *Cotton Crucifixion* remains probably the most provocative painting in this category. (Hunter did not name most of her works, so owners have assigned names that may or may not reflect the artist's original intentions.) In *Cotton Crucifixion,* Jesus is black, but the thieves are white, and at the foot of the cross black field hands drag full sacks through rows of cotton. The third category is difficult to define because it incorporates such dissimilar and atypical works. These pieces, including abstract paintings, all were presumably prompted by some sort of outside influence.

Hunter's reputation began to develop in the late 1940s and 1950s. In 1959 her work drew more attention than that of any other in the New Orleans Arts and Crafts Show. In *Look* magazine, art critic Charlotte Willard counted Hunter among the most notable "primitive" painters in the country:

> They all paint real things, but they paint them from memory. The significant detail is magnified, the trivial, however big, is ignored. Their real people, their real flowers, their real landscapes have the reality of a dream, the emotional force and directness of a vivid personal adventure. The world on their canvases seems more wondrous and newly born (103-105).

This aptly describes Hunter's art. In 1955, the Delgado Museum (now the New Orleans Museum of Art), gave her a solo exhibition, the first it offered to a black artist. At the same time, Northwestern State College in Natchitoches held its first all-Hunter show. However, she was not allowed to view her work with the white patrons and had to be slipped in by the back door when the gallery was closed.

In 1956 Hunter created one of her most important works, the African House Murals at Melrose. Mignon had the idea for her to paint nine large plywood panels, each four-by-eight feet, and several small connecting ones, to be installed in the circa 1800 African House, so-called because of its similarity to traditional buildings of central Africa, with a steep roof and a wide overhang unsupported by posts. Hunter's realization of Mignon's idea is an all-inclusive, knowing, and witty view of plantation life along the Cane River, a remarkable achievement for a self-taught sixty-eight-year-old. She also painted murals for Ghana House and Yucca House, two other buildings at Melrose.

Throughout the 1950s Hunter's subjects and their treatment developed very little. The exceptions are the few collage-like pieces that reflect continued influence from her quiltmaking. A good example is her 1958 *Going to Church,* which has multi-colored borders that look like applique on a quilt (*Clementine Hunter,* exhibition catalog). Collage did not entirely enter into her work, however, until the 1960s, when James Register moved to Natchitoches. Second only to Mignon as an early supporter of Hunter, Register was a writer, sometime artist, and teacher at the University of Oklahoma. After visiting Melrose in the early 1940s, he began sending Hunter small cash payments and art supplies. In 1944 he secured for her a Julius Rosenwald Foundation grant. When Emanuel Hunter died in August of that year, Register helped to pay the funeral costs. Register and Mignon both acted as agents for the sale of Clementine Hunter's work.

By the time that Register settled permanently in Natchitoches in 1962, he had decided to try an experiment to test the talent and broaden the scope of the elderly artist whom he regarded as "almost a genius." During a period of two years, he cut up color advertisements from old magazines and pasted them to cardboard to form collages. He would take the pasteups to Hunter, one at a time, along with art supplies, to see what sort of work they would inspire. "Sometimes the montage would be so difficult, being only a series of color patterns," said Register, "the outlines would have to be traced on the board for her" (Wilson, 37). On its face alone, the whole project constituted an interference with Hunter's own vision. Certainly, the names of these 1962-1963 paintings probably have more to do with Register than Hunter. The pictures eventually came to number about one hundred, including titles such as *Chanticleer and the Moon Bird, Alice in Wonderland, Uncle Tom,* and *Porte Bouquet.* (Many of the Register commissions are held by the Ouachita Parish Library in Monroe, Louisiana, where they once circulated to library patrons.) The Register experiment prompted new work, however, with new, splashier color and patterns that eventually influenced her other painting, especially her flower pictures. Although she readily admitted that she did not like painting Register's "abstract" commissions and happily quit after the two years, the influence of renewed color if not also the collage technique continued to spill over into her later work. This may be seen in the last decade of the artist's life in her *Chicken Hauling Flowers,* which she painted in 1980 at the age of ninety-four. All in all, the abstract period is the briefest and least-known of her career but one of the most influential. It deserves greater study.

It also raises the issue of profit in Hunter's art. In the late 1960s Mignon reported that Hunter still routinely sold pictures for as little as six dollars each (''Cane River Memo''). Early patrons do not appear to have made a big killing on her work. After Register died in 1970, his collection of 110 paintings were valued altogether at only ten thousand dollars (Flyer for an auction). By the mid-1970s Hunter's paintings were becoming so valuable that more than one artist was forging them (*New Orleans Times-Picayune*). Yet, as late as 1975, *Reader's Digest* reported that Clementine Hunter received only a fraction of the two-hundred to eight-hundred dollars that her more sought-after pieces brought in big-city galleries. ''Like many other folk artists, she has done most of her work for the people in her own area—and at prices they can afford. They love her for it'' (Rankin, 118-22). It was not until ten years later, only about three years before Hunter died, that one white patron could complain, ''She may give her friends a little discount, but she likes money. Clementine's favorite thing in the world is a hundred-dollar bill'' (''Clementine Hunter'').

How much the charm of Hunter's story contributed to her popularity among collectors may never be known. For white patrons, at least, she filled a niche in the art market, as the black Grandma Moses (Dowdy, ''Louisiana's Primitive Artist''). Very few of Hunter's patrons were black. Some black community leaders in Natchitoches suspected white patrons of finding virtue in her art because of her illiteracy. Her unwillingness to leave the neighborhood of her youth, coupled with her illiteracy, probably precluded her having direct relations with major galleries and direct participation in the larger profits for her art since the mid-1970s. By her late eighties, however, she was able at least to save enough to get a house trailer to replace her old cabin and buy space in a mausoleum with a fine coffin. In December 1987 she stopped painting and took to her bed. On January 1, 1988, at the age of 101, she died.

During her lifetime, Hunter had some two dozen solo exhibitions at galleries of such institutions as Fisk University (1974), Dillard University (1975), and the University of Texas at Arlington (1980). Among major group shows in which her art was represented are ''Louisiana Folk Painting,'' the Museum of American Folk Art, New York City (1973), ''Two Centuries of Black American Art,'' the Los Angeles County Museum of Art and the Brooklyn Museum (1976-77), ''The Afro-American Tradition in Decorative Arts,'' the Cleveland Museum of Art (1978) and traveling (1978-79), ''Southern Works on Paper,'' 1900-1950, the Montgomery Museum of Fine Arts (1981), ''Forever Free: An Exhibit of Art by African-American Women, 1862-1980,'' Illinois State University (1981) and traveling (1981-82), ''What It Is: Black American Folk Art from the Collection of Regina Perry,'' Virginia Commonwealth University (1982), ''Black Women Artists: Achievements Against the Odds,'' the Neighborhood Museum of the Smithsonian Institution (1984), and ''Twentieth-Century American Folk Art,'' the University of Santa Clara, California (1985). Hunter's work is part of more than a score of permanent collections, including those of the Amistad Research at Tulane University, the Birmingham Museum of Art, the Dallas Museum of Fine Art, the High Museum in Atlanta, Illinois State University, the Louisiana State Museum, the New York Historical Association, Radcliffe College, and Vassar College.

References

Bailey, Mildred H. *''Clementine Hunter.'' Four Women of Cane River—Their Contributions to the Cultural Life of the Area.* Natchitoches, Louisiana: Natchitoches Parish Library 1980.

Black Women Oral History Project Interview with Clementine Hunter. Cambridge: Schlesinger Library, Radcliffe College, 1979.

''Cane River Memo.'' *Natchitoches Times*, 20 February 1968.

Clementine Hunter, exhibition catalog. Shreveport, Louisiana: Louisiana State University Library, 1971.

Dowdy, Verdis. ''Louisiana's Primitive Artist is Like a Black Grandma Moses.'' (New Orleans) *Clarion Herald*, 14 August 1969.

Flyer for an auction, 8 November 1970, Art Vertical Files, Louisiana Collection, Tulane University Library.

Knight, Margaret R. ''On a Sunday Morning at Clementine Hunter's.'' (New Orleans) *Times Picayune Dixie-Roto* Magazine, 17 October 1976.

Lamothe, Eva. ''A Visit with Clementine Hunter: Painter of Visions and Dreams.'' New Orleans *Arts Quarterly* 7 April/May/June 1985): 32-34.

Miller, Herschel. ''Clementine Hunter—American Primitive.'' *New Orleans Magazine* (December 1968): 6-11.

New Orleans Times-Picayune, 3 April 1974.

Plantation Menu: Plantation Life in Louisiana, 1950-70, and Other Matters. Edited by Oral Garland Williams. Baton Rouge, 1972.

Rankin, Allen. ''The Hidden Genius of Melrose Plantation.'' *Reader's Digest* 107 (December 1975): 118-22.

Visit to Melrose Plantation with François Mignon. Louisiana Heritage Association, Alexandria, Louisiana. LP record No. S737, 1967.

Willard, Charlotte. ''Innocence Regained.'' *Look* 17 (16 June 1953): 102-105.

Wilson, James L. *Clementine Hunter: American Folk Artist.* Gretna, Louisiana.: Pelican Pub. Co., 1988.

Collections

Information on Clementine Hunter is located in the Melrose

Collection, François Mignon Collection, James Register Collection, and Thomas N. Whitehead Collection—all in the Northwestern State University Archives, Natchitoches, Louisiana.

Lester Sullivan

Jane Edna Hunter

(1882-1971)

Organization founder and director, nurse

Trained as both a nurse and a lawyer, Jane Hunter's greatest and most fulfilling work was as founder and director of the Phillis Wheatley Association in Cleveland and in her dedication to enhancing the quality of life for black women.

Jane Edna Harris Hunter was born in Pendleton, South Carolina, on December 15, 1882, to sharecropper parents, Harriet (Millner) Harris and Edward Harris, on the Woodburn plantation. Her father, the son of a plantation overseer and a black woman, in complexion and features looked white. Hunter, who resembled him, was named for her English grandmother, Jane McCrary. Thus the young Jane resented her dark-skinned mother, and at times, in spite of her own light-brown skin and coarser features, preferred to identify with her white heritage.

Jane Edna Hunter

Home life was filled with friction because of Edward Harris's violent temper. Nevertheless, Hunter adored her father and almost always took his side when there were conflicts in the household. To his credit, he was a hard worker who was determined to keep his family together, and he instilled in Hunter the desire for education. His death when Hunter was ten was devastating to her, especially since she considered him to be a buffer between her and her mother.

After her father's death, Hunter was forced to leave her family to work as a domestic servant until Presbyterian missionaries offered her an opportunity to work and attend school. At Ferguson and Williams College in Abbeville, South Carolina, Hunter completed the equivalent of secondary school.

After graduation Jane Harris entered a loveless marriage with Edward Hunter, a man many years her senior. However, she soon came to realize that a marriage of convenience was most unsatisfactory to her. She moved on to work in Charleston, and shortly thereafter enrolled in the nurses training program at the Cannon Street Hospital and Training School for Nurses.

Jane Hunter's interest in the nursing profession was most likely rooted in her admiration for her maternal Grandmother Millner, a mulatto nurse-midwife who was trained by her former master, Thomas Pickens, a physician. As a child, Hunter had spent many pleasant days with her grandparents, and she remembered the life of "usefulness and services" that nursing had provided. After completion of her nurses training she worked for a private physician for a few years before going on to Hampton Institute for further training.

After a year at Hampton, Jane Hunter moved to Cleveland, Ohio, when she decided to join friends from Virginia who were moving to the city. She arrived in 1905 in a city where there were no safe living quarters for single black women and few social services available to aid in the adjustment to urban life. Further, she found that in spite of her training, the color line extended to the health services. After working as a domestic servant once again to survive, she finally gained employment as a private duty nurse and masseuse in the homes of some of the city's wealthiest families.

In 1910, when Hunter was thirty years old, her mother died. Her death came before the two were able to reconcile their differences. This led to a spiritual crisis in Hunter's life and for thirteen months her despair led her to contemplate suicide. She also had been troubled by her racial mixture and believed that such mixtures caused psychological problems. Earlier she had considered denying her black heritage, since her complexion would enable her to pass and to obtain privileges denied blacks. Moreover, she recalled her contempt for the snobbery of the black church in Charleston, where "high yellows" on the one hand and "chocolate browns'' on the other created almost visible lines of separation of the congregation. Some time would pass before she leaned toward service to people of her mother's race. Her recovery came in the decision to devote her life to enhancing the quality of life for black women.

In 1911, Hunter called together a group of friends who had experienced similar difficulties after moving to Cleveland. The group organized to raise money to rent a home for single black women, calling themselves the Working Girls Home Association. Hunter was elected president of the group. By 1913 Hunter had convinced some of her clients to support the effort. Most of the women were active members of the Young Women's Christian Association, which provided similar services for white women. However, in return for their financial aid to the black group, the association was renamed the Phillis Wheatley Association, with a two-story, twenty-three room house and a charter that guaranteed control by the benefactors. Hunter was the only black American woman to be retained as a trustee of the new organization. She was also hired by the new board to become its director.

In spite of bitter opposition from many black leaders in the city, the home opened and prospered in the wake of the wave of new migration to the city just prior to and during the first world war. The first facility was replaced in 1917 with the purchase of a large apartment building that could accommodate seventy-five women, and in 1926, the association moved into a brand new eleven-story building that had been built at a cost of more than half a million dollars.

Over the years, in addition to living space, the Phillis Wheatley Association also became an important center for employment services and training for black women. As a loyal follower of the ideology of ''self-help'' in the tradition of Booker T. Washington, Hunter believed that black women should become well-trained for the jobs most readily available to them; namely, domestic service. While this mission was popular with white financial supporters and board members, blacks often expressed fear that by catering to their dictates, Hunter stood in the way of progress into other, more lucrative and dignified jobs.

Self-Help Activities Sponsored

Thousands of women were housed and trained at the Phillis Wheatley between 1913 and the early 1960s, when black women had become well integrated into the YWCA. As the largest independent institution of its kind, the Phillis Wheatley Association became a model for similar facilities and self-help organizations around the country, under the auspices of the National Association of Colored Women (NACW). Over time, its program included a beauty school, kindergarten, a music school, summer camp, a gymnasium, secretarial school, and countless clubs and outreach organizations for blacks in Cleveland.

During her lifetime, Hunter became well known for her ability to raise funds, her strict domination of the association, her work with the Republican party and as a trustee of Central State University, and her work in the upper ranks of the NACW as director of their Phillis Wheatley division. From the latter association she became friends with other women institution builders such as Mary McLeod Bethune, Charlotte Hawkins Brown, and Nannie Burroughs. The four frequently exchanged visits and corresponded about programs and funding sources.

Prior to desegregation of public facilities, the Phillis Wheatley hosted numerous national organization meetings and many of the nation's most illustrious black persons. Rooms in the residence were regularly set aside for black men and women who visited the city and were not welcome in its hotels. Locally, the institution's dining room also served as a popular meeting place for black professionals and was one of the few places where black and white politicians and leaders could meet and share a meal. Hunter presided with pride as the gracious hostess. Most importantly, she used her influence to press for neighborhood services and decent living conditions for blacks.

In the same year that she began the drive for funds for her new facility, Hunter completed the Cleveland Law School and passed the Ohio Bar (1925). This training was most valuable as she became involved in real estate and stocks, serving as a director of the black-owned Empire Savings and Loan Company and the Union Realty Company.

By the end of her career, Hunter had been nominated for the coveted Spingarn Award of the NAACP and had been honored with a master of arts degree by Wilberforce College and a master of science degree by Tuskegee Institute in recognition for her work, which served as the embodiment and essence of the industrial philosophy of Booker T. Washington. Her legacy of more than a half-million dollars was left in trust for the education of young women from Ohio and South Carolina. The trust is still active under the guardianship of the Ameritrust Bank in Cleveland. She died in 1971 and is buried in Lakeview Cemetery in Cleveland.

References

Barton, Rebecca Chalmers. ''A Nickel and a Prayer: Jane Edna Hunter.'' In *Witnesses for Freedom: Negro Americans in Autobiography*. New York: Harper, 1948.

Hunter, Jane Edna. *A Nickel and a Prayer*. Cleveland: 1940.

Jones, Adrienne Lash. *Jane Edna Hunter: A Case Study of Black Leadership, 1910-1950*. New York: Carlson Pub. Co., 1990.

Collections

The principal sources for this essay are from the Jane Edna Hunter and the Phillis Wheatley Association papers at the Western Reserve Historical Society in Cleveland, Ohio, as well the references listed above.

Adrienne Lash Jones

Charlayne Hunter-Gault

(1942-)

Journalist

Charlayne Hunter-Gault and Hamilton Holmes were the first two black American students to attend the University of Georgia in January 1961. Students rioted to protest their admission, and for their safety the university had to temporarily suspend Hunter-Gault and Holmes. Hunter-Gault remembers that when she passed a group of tearful Caucasian female students, one of them said, "Here Nigger—here's a quarter, go change my sheets!" (Dreifus, 16). What were her reactions to this intense hostility and overt discrimination? She said in Brian Lanker's *I Dream A World*, "If you've ever been in the middle of a riot or the eye of a hurricane, you know it's very calm. That is exactly how I felt the night of the riot" (62).

Charlayne Hunter-Gault was born to Charles S. H. Hunter, Jr., and Althea Hunter on February 27, 1947, in Due West, South Carolina. Her father was a Methodist chaplain in the United States Army, and in 1954 when the family moved to Atlanta her mother worked at a real estate firm. Due to her father's tours of duty abroad, Hunter-Gault and her two younger brothers were reared primarily by her mother and grandmother. Hunter-Gault feels that her grandmother was a positive role model for her. According to *Current Biography Yearbook*, Hunter-Gault's grandmother was an energetic, inquisitive woman whose formal education ended in the third grade, but she used to read three newspapers a day. Her curiosity and gentleness have been influential characteristics in Hunter-Gault's life. She said that she knew at the age of twelve that she wanted to be a journalist. Her childhood hero was Brenda Starr, the comic strip reporter. She attended Turner High School in Atlanta from 1954 to 1959 and was an honor student. She graduated third in her class and edited the student newspaper, the *Green Light*.

Academically, Charlayne Hunter-Gault felt that her high school experiences prepared her to compete. She notes in *I Dream A World:*

> Even in the best high school in Atlanta, we had hand-me-down textbooks and our labs were certainly not as well equipped. So the fact that we were prepared to compete in the way that we did was a minor miracle that black schools accomplished (62).

After completing high school, Hunter-Gault wanted to pursue her degree in journalism, but the University of Georgia was the only college in Georgia with a school of journalism, and it was not admitting black students at that time.

To address this issue, a number of prominent Atlanta civil rights activists filed for an integration order with the federal court. Meanwhile, Hunter-Gault enrolled at Wayne State University in Detroit, Michigan. When the federal court issued the integration order in January 1961, she and Holmes became the first black American students to enroll in the college's 175-year history. Why did she continue her educational pursuits, knowing the racial climate among students and faculty at the University of Georgia? She said in an article she wrote for the *New York Times Magazine*, January 25, 1970:

> And yet I stayed, partly because I knew the world was watching. I think that, at that time, such a commitment was necessary. But the need is greater now, precisely because the world isn't watching. The move of black students to black colleges is fine for those who can afford it. But Benny Roberson lives here in Athens where there is no black college, and he can't afford to go out of town. Things for blacks may improve now, not because the world is watching but because there are more Benny Robersons.

Charlayne Hunter-Gault graduated from the University of Georgia with a B.A. in journalism in 1963. She also married a fellow classmate and a Caucasian, Georgia-born Walter Stovall. Of their marriage, she comments in an article by Gerald C. Fraser published in the March 1987 issue of *Essence* magazine:

> The reason we got married was the reason that most people get married. They are in love with each other. We felt what we had to be very special if it could flourish under those stressful conditions, and in point of fact, it was very special (42).

Charlayne and Walter Stovall now divorced had one child from their marriage, a daughter named Susan Stovall.

Journalism Career Begins

After graduating from college, Charlayne Hunter-Gault accepted a position as a secretary at the *New Yorker* magazine. This acceptance was based on the condition that she eventually would be considered for writing assignments. From 1964 to 1967, she contributed to "Talk of the Town," a feature section for the *New Yorker*, and wrote short stories. In 1967 she received a Russell Sage Fellowship to study social science at Washington University in St. Louis, Missouri. During this time she edited articles for *Trans-Action* magazine, and later went to Washington, D.C., to cover the Poor People's Campaign. While in Washington, she joined the staff of WRC-TV as an investigative reporter and anchorwoman of the local evening news program.

She left WRC-TV and accepted a position with the *New York Times* in 1968. From 1968 to 1978, Charlayne Hunter-Gault specialized in covering stories in Harlem. She attributed her reportorial style to her experiences at the University of Georgia. She said to Claudia Dreifus in an interview for *Dial* magazine, February 1987:

> I saw how different journalists worked and also how I was treated as a story. There were journalists who were sensitive and I wanted to be like them. On the other hand, there was one reporter, whose name I won't mention, who pulled a mob together so that he could film them—he'd missed the real riot. . . . But him aside, if there's anything I carry with me from that time it's my interest in people. That's what all those integration cases were really about: people trying to make their way in society and people on the other side trying to prevent them from doing that. It seems to me that if there were a basic understanding on each side about the humanity of people, none of us would have been in the situation we were in (45).

Hunter-Gault feels that one has to carefully examine the social situation in which one finds oneself. She said in *I Dream A World,* "You have to assess every situation that you're in and have to decide, is this happening because I'm black? Is this happening because I'm a woman? Or is this happening because this is how it happens? (Lanker, 62)

Hunter-Gault combined career with marriage and parenthood. In 1971 she married Ronald Gault, a black Chicagoan, who is vice-president of First Boston Corporation and is a specialist in public finance. They have one son, Chuma Gault.

Over the years she has received numerous awards for her professional expertise. For example, in 1970 she and Joseph Lelyveld received the *New York Times* Publishers Award for the detailed portrayal of the life and death of a twelve-year old heroin addict. She received two additional Publishers Awards in 1974 and 1976 for urban reporting. She received the National Urban Coalition Award for Distinguished Urban Reporting, as well as the Lincoln University Unity Award for a report on teenage unemployment.

She has won two National News and Documentary Emmy Awards. One was for "Zumwalt: Agent Orange." This was a profile of Elmo Zumwalt III, who developed cancer as a result of being contaminated by Agent Orange in Vietnam. This spraying of the defoliant was authorized by his father, Admiral Elmo Zumwalt, Jr. Another Emmy was awarded for her report on the United States' invasion of Grenada in 1983. Her most prestigious award has been the George Foster Peabody Award, which she won in 1986. It was given by the H. W. Grady School of Journalism of the University of Georgia for the documentary "Apartheid's People." This documentary examined the effects of apartheid on South African whites and blacks.

Charlayne Hunter-Gault has been the recipient of numerous other honors, including: Journalist of the Year,1986, by the National Association of Black Journalists; the Good Housekeeping Broadcast Personality of the Year Award; the American Women in Radio and Television Award for Excellence in Journalism; and the Woman of Achievement Award given by the New York Chapter of the American Society of University Women. Presently, Charlayne Hunter-Gault is a journalist on PBS television, where she is seen regularly on "The MacNeil/Lehrer Newshour.".

References

Dreifus, Claudia. "A Talk with Charlayne Hunter-Gault." *Dial* 8 (February 1987): 15-17, 45.

Current Biography Yearbook. New York: H. W. Wilson, 1987. Photograph, p. 261.

Fraser, C. Gerald. "Charlayne Hunter-Gault: From Frontline to Firing Line." *Essence* 17 (March 1987): 40-42, 110. Includes photograph.

Hunter, Charlayne. "After Nine Years—A Homecoming for the First Black Girl at the University of Georgia." *New York Times Magazine* (25 January 1970): 24-25, 50.

Lanker, Brian. *I Dream A World: Portraits of Black Women Who Changed the World*. New York: Stewart, Tabori and Chang, 1989. Photograph, p. 63.

Ploski, Harry A., and James Williams, eds. *Negro Almanac*. Detroit: Gale Research, 1989.

Wexler, Alan. "The Lonely Years of Hamilton Holmes." *Ebony* 19 (November 1963): 101.

Mary R. Holley

Addie W. Hunton

(1875-1943)

Organization official, suffragist, educator, clubwoman, women's rights activist

A woman of many talents, who worked selflessly and excelled in numerous areas Addie D. Waites Hunton was primarily a crusader for the advancement of black Americans. Central to her work as an organization official, clubwoman, peace advocate, suffragist, teacher, and advocate of women's rights, was her concern that black Americans would be the beneficiaries of her work.

Born in Norfolk, Virginia, on July 11, 1875, Hunton was the eldest of two daughters and a son of Jesse and Adelina

Addie W. Hunton

(Lawton) Waites. Her father was a successful businessman and prominent resident of Norfolk, who owned a substantial wholesale oyster and shipping company and had a partnership in an amusement park for blacks. Jesse Waites helped found the black arm of the Elks (IBPOW) and was prominent in the African Methodist Episcopal church. Addie Waites began school in Norfolk, but while she was a young child her mother died, and she moved to Boston where she was reared by a maternal aunt. She received her high school education at Boston Latin School; then she went to Spencerian College of Commerce in Philadelphia, where in 1889 she became the first black American woman to graduate from the school. She taught school in Portsmouth, Virginia, for one year, then became lady principal at State Normal and Agricultural College in Alabama—now Alabama Agricultural and Mechanical University.

During this period Hunton spent little time in Norfolk; however, she met William Alphaeus Hunton, who had moved to the city. William Hunton was the son of Stanley Hunton, a former slave in Virginia who purchased his freedom in 1840 and emigrated to Chatham, Ontario, and Mary Ann (Conyer) Hunton, whom he met and married in Cincinnati, Ohio, and took to Chatham. The mother died when William Hunton was about four years old. "Billie" or "Willie," as he was called by his friends, had six brothers and two sisters. After high school, he graduated from the Wilberforce Institute of Ontario and in 1883 taught in a public school in Dresden, Canada. In 1885 he moved to Ottawa, where he worked as a government clerk for a while. Instead of preparing himself for the ministry as he had intended, he became active in the white YMCA. After chairing the Boys' Work Department, the International Committee of the YMCA persuaded him to go to Norfolk, Virginia, in 1888 to provide YMCA services for "colored men of the South." "I really had no choice. It was God's leading and I could but follow," he said (Hunton, *William Alphaeus Hunton,* 13, 17). Initially as founder and secretary of the Norfolk association for black youth,—the first to hold such a position in a black YMCA—he pioneered in establishing YMCA services for blacks in Virginia and around the country. In 1891 he became the first black secretary of the Colored Men's Department of the International Committee of the YMCA.

For at least three years William A. Hunton and Addie D. Waites developed a friendship that included separation from each other because of his travel schedule. They wrote almost daily, yet he was careful to let Addie Waites know that he was totally obligated to the work to which the Lord had committed to him. She resigned herself to make his life her own. The young, handsome, and cultured William Hunton married Addie D. Waites in her Norfolk home on July 19, 1893. She was described as "deep brown in color with a finely molded mouth, and large unfathomable eyes," and "a nobly beautiful woman" (Ovington, 59).

Addie Waites Hunton's commitment to her husband's work led her to new arenas of personal gratification and usefulness. For a time they remained in Norfolk, where she taught in the local schools and assisted her husband in his work. The Huntons then moved to Richmond, Virginia, and when William Hunton was transferred to the YMCA in Atlanta, Georgia, in 1899, the couple relocated again. Addie Waites Hunton was a secretary and the bursar at Clark College in Atlanta. For more than ten years—from the beginning of their marriage—she was also her husband's secretary, traveled with him to conferences, handled details, and gave him advice. She edited a little sheet called the *Messenger,* although the public recognized D. Webster Davis as the editor. Her long and close association with her husband in his work meant that she earned the reputation that she had later—pioneer in the organization for women that closely related to the YMCA.

While in Atlanta the couple began their family. Of the four children born to them, only the two younger, Eunice and William Alphaeus, Jr., lived beyond infancy. Eunice Hunton Carter (1899-1970) is also the subject of an essay in this book.

The Huntons had barely reached Atlanta in the spring of 1899, when a black man who lived in a nearby town was "accused of the usual crime;" his body was burned and some of its parts distributed for souvenirs. Eight years later violence erupted again—this time the Atlanta riot of 1906. Perhaps these two incidents stirred the militancy that some saw in Addie Waites Hunton. She had been called "cultured, soft-spoken and a great humanitarian," yet she "could be militant when necessary, particularly on the subject of Negroes." While in Atlanta and later in her Brooklyn home, "she spoke unequivocally against segregation" (Dannett, 200; Ovington, 59). The local trouble left the Hunton's anxious about the family's safety, particularly during William Hunton's absences from the city, and in December 1906 they moved to Brooklyn, New York.

Addie Waites Hunton's experiences in the YMCA were never unnoticed. Her work led the national board of the YWCA to appoint her secretary for work among black people in 1907. She toured the South and the Midwest in the winter of 1907-1908 while conducting a survey for the YWCA. She influenced a number of black women to enter YWCA work, including Eva Del Vakia Bowles, whom she recommended for city work with the YWCA, and Elizabeth Ross (Haynes) as first student secretary. From 1909 to 1910 she and her children studied in Europe while William Hunton continued his work at home. They spent several months in Switzerland and then Strasburg, where Addie Waites Hunton completed courses at the Kaiser Wilhelm University. When she returned home in 1910 she continued her YWCA activities and also enrolled in courses at the College of the City of New York. William Hunton, already plagued by health problems, had become seriously ill with tuberculosis. In June 1914, the family moved to Saranac Lake, New York, and in 1916 William Hunton died. In 1938, Addie Hunton's views of his life and contributions were published in her book, *William Alphaeus Hunton* (New York: Association Press, 1928).

YWCA Volunteer Serves Black Troops in France

When the First World War began, Addie Waites Hunton joined countless women who volunteered to assist in the war efforts. A widow with nearly adult children, she saw a need to reorder her life as well as continue service in an area of her interest. Hunton volunteered for YMCA services, but her initial request for overseas service was denied because she could not be easily released from her war work with the YWCA. Helen Curtis sailed alone, and three weeks later, in summer 1918, Kathryn Johnson of Chicago and Hunton sailed to France. Thus, they became the only three black women workers among two hundred thousand racially segregated black troops stationed there. Later, nearly a thousand black YMCA workers were assigned to France. Johnson had been adopted as the Daughter of the 370th Infantry Illinois Regiment, and Hunton felt responsible for the care of the "Fifteenth New York" and the "Buffaloes." They were disappointed, however, when Mrs. Theodore Roosevelt, Jr., assigned them to the Services of Supplies sector at Saint Nazaire, rather than to one of the fighting units.

Hunton offered a literacy course and a Sunday evening discussion program on race leaders, art, music, religion, and other subjects. Except when they came together for a special joint event, the three women volunteers each worked alone in a hut. They became morale-builders for the troops, particularly as the men prepared to move to front line activity. The segregated facilities and the shortage of staff meant that the women worked long hours, from nine in the morning until nine at night; they visited other camps as well. In October 1918 Hunton was desperately ill from influenza and exhaustion. Although the war had ended, there was still much for the YMCA women volunteers to do. At Christmas time Hunton was sent to a leave area in Southern France, Challes-les-Eaux, located near Aix-les-Bains, to become director at Chambery.

While she was in France, the Pan-African Congress met in Paris on February 19-21, 1919, to press for African causes. Hunton addressed the meeting, emphasized the importance of women in reconstructing and regenerating the world at that time, and called on women to seek the cooperation and counsel of the congress ("The Pan African Congress," 273).

In the spring of 1919 sixteen additional black women came to France as YWCA workers. These included concert pianist Helen Hagan and Mary V. Talbert, president of the National Association of Colored Women. Hunton continued her educational work and helped to organize religious, athletic, and cultural programs as well. In fact, she found that "the chief educational work to be done among the colored troops overseas was that of teaching them to read and write" (Hunton and Johnson, 199). The YWCA also worked with the American Library Association in establishing libraries to aid the educational programs, and large and valuable libraries were established for the black soldiers at Saint Nazaire, the leave area at Challes-les-Eaux, Camp Romagne, and elsewhere. In May Hunton was assigned to the military cemetery at Romagne, where for weeks she watched the men find the dead on the battlefield of the Meuse-Argonne and rebury them in the military cemetery. "It would be a gruesome, repulsive and unhealthful task, requiring weeks of incessant toil during the long heavy days of summer," she said (Hunton and Johnson, 235). Through it all the black soldiers faced "trials of discriminations and injustices that seared their souls like hot iron, inflicted as they were at a time when these soldiers were rendering the American army and nation a sacred service" (235). She returned to America in the autumn of 1919, after working in Brest among black troops waiting for transfer home. Hunton and Johnson wrote of their experiences with the troops in *Two Colored Women with the American Expeditionary Forces* (Brooklyn: Brooklyn Eagle Press, 1920).

Issues of Race and Gender Addressed

On her return home, Hunton devoted the rest of her life to matters of the race and black women. She had already established herself with the National Association of Colored Women during her Richmond years, and she became a member of the joint committee to bring the association and the Federation of Afro-American Women together in 1896 as the National Association of Colored Women. While living in Atlanta, she was state organizer for the Georgia Federation of Colored Women's Clubs. She wrote an essay, "Negro Womanhood Defended," which was published in the July 1904 issue of *Voice of the Negro.* Here she condemned the portrayal of the "moral weakness of Negro womanhood" as a part of the mysterious evil called the "race problem. . . . Unwarned, unmasked, with no sense of delicacy for her feelings, the Negro woman has been made the subject of an increasing and unmerciful criticism" (280). In addition, "the Negro woman was the subject of compulsory immorality'' as whites encouraged and fostered prostitution (281). The frailties of man since his inception were falsely charged to the Negro woman. From 1906 to 1910 Hunton was national organizer for NACW. She wrote ''The National Association of Colored Women: Its Real Significance,'' published with photographs of several NACW leaders in *The Colored American Magazine* (July 1908). In the May 1911 issue of *Crisis*, once again she wrote on ''The National Association of Colored Women.'' While president of the New York federation from 1926 to 1930, she added new departments and made the existing ones more efficient. During her administration the state was divided into regions, each with a president in charge. In 1927 she saw that the Empire State Federation of Women's Clubs, founded in 1908, was incorporated. She became parliamentarian and statistician in 1928.

Hunton's activities also embraced the Women's International League for Peace and Freedom. In 1926 she served on the six-woman league committee that visited Haiti to view the United States occupation. An articulate and outspoken member, she contributed a section on race relations to the committee's report, *Occupied Haiti*, edited by Emily Greene and published in 1927. The report condemned the intervention and advocated restoration of Haiti's independence. An advocate for peace, she became president of the Circle for Peace and Foreign Relations.

Her dedication to woman's causes was seen not only in her leadership roles with the NACW but in other areas as well. She was a member of the Girl Reserve Committee and Council on Colored Work of the national board of the YWCA and presided over the International Council of the Women of Darker Races. She belonged to the Brooklyn Woman's Club, and she became a staunch suffragist, leading her to join the Brooklyn Equal Suffrage League. In *When and Where I Enter* Paula Giddings notes Hunton's involvement in the suffrage movement around 1921 and the work of Mary Church Terrell, Verina Morton Jones, Addie Waites Hunton, and others who worked through the Suffrage Department of the NAACP and the NACW. They held voter-education programs and sought the help of white suffrage leaders to fight discrimination in the South.

After the Nineteenth Amendment was passed, granting women the right to vote, the Woman's Party, headed by Alice Paul, became the most vibrant feminist group for white women. The party also campaigned for an Equal Rights Amendment. Black women, on the other hand, wanted Paul and the Women's Party at the February 1921 national convention to support black women voters in the South, for discrimination at the polls was a ''race issue'' rather than a ''woman's issue.'' When the party's advisory council meeting of January 1921 rejected a motion to ask the convention to establish a permanent special committee to pressure Congress on this matter, Hunton wrote to Archibald H. Grimké of the NAACP that black women would ask for a hearing at the convention, picket the convention, and work out a secret strategy ''to give publicity to the wrongs inflicted upon the colored women of the South'' (Addie Hunton to A. H. Grimké, 29 January 1921, cited in Giddings, 167). Apparently Alice Paul then asked Hallie Q. Brown to read a resolution before the Resolution Committee at the convention with the idea that it would die there. Hunton and other black women were unrelenting in their struggle, and they realized that they had the National Woman's Party in a corner. A hostile meeting between Paul and sixty black women led to an apology from the party's officers, who talked with Hunton and apologized for Paul's behavior. Finally, the black women's resolution was read on the floor of the convention. It stated:

> We have come here as members of various organizations and from different sections representing five million colored women of this country. We are deeply appreciative of the heroic development of the National Woman's Suffrage Movement and of the tremendous sacrifice made under your leadership in securing the passage of the Nineteenth Amendment. . . .
>
> [Black women] have also come today to call your attention to the flagrant violations of the intent and purposes of the Susan B. Anthony Amendment in the elections of 1920. . . .
>
> Five million women in the United States can not be denied their rights without all the women of the United States feeling the effect of that denial. No women are free until all women are free.
>
> Therefore, we . . . ask that you will use your influence to have the convention of the National Woman's Party appoint a Special Committee to ask Congress for an investigation of the violations of the intent and purposes of the Susan B. Anthony Amendment in the elections of 1920 (Resolutions Re: National Woman's Party, February 15-18, 1921, quoted in Giddings, 169).

Although the resolution was rejected, Hunton wrote to clubwoman and banker Maggie Lena Walker expressing the women's important work: over the convention's objections, they brought the resolution to the floor, and a large contention of black women demonstrated that they were alert to the matter (Addie Hunton to Maggie Walker, 23 February 1921, cited in Giddings, 169).

Hunton was a vice-president and field secretary of the NAACP, and one of the principal organizers of the Fourth Pan-African Congress held in New York City in 1927. She was a member of the Civic Club of New York and the Alpha Kappa Alpha Sorority. Her last known public service was at a ceremony honoring outstanding black women at the New York World's Fair held in 1939. On June 21, 1943, Addie D. Waites Hunton died of diabetes in Brooklyn and was buried in Cypress Hills Cemetery there.

References

Dannett, Sylvia G. L. *Profiles of Negro Womanhood.*

Vol. 2. Yonkers: Educational Heritage, 1966. 199-206. Photograph, p. 198.

Davis, Elizabeth Lindsay. *Lifting as They Climb*. Washington, D.C.: National Association of Colored Women, 1933.

Giddings, Paula. *When and Where I Enter*. New York: Morrow, 1984. 87, 102, 166-69.

Hunton, Addie. "Negro Womanhood Defended." *Voice of the Negro* (July 1904): 280-82. Photograph, p. 281.

———. *William Alphaeus Hunton*. New York: Association Press, 1938.

Hutson, Jean Blackwell. "Addie D. Waites Hunton." *Dictionary of American Negro Biography*. Eds. Rayford W. Logan and Michael R. Winston. New York: Norton, 1982. 337-38.

———. "Addie D. Waites Hunton." *Notable American Women, 1607-1950*. Vol. 2. Cambridge: Harvard University Press, 1971. 240-41.

Hunton, Addie W., and Kathryn M. Johnson. *Two Colored Women with the American Expeditionary Forces*. Brooklyn: Brooklyn Eagle Press [1920].

Ovington, Mary White. *The Walls Came Tumbling Down*. New York: Harcourt, Brace, 1947. 59.

"The Pan African Congress." *Crisis* 17 (April 1919): 271-74.

Wesley, Charles Harris. *The History of the National Association of Colored Women's Clubs*. Washington: NACW, 1984. 38, 67, 88, 99, 202, 209, 292.

Who's Who in Colored America. 5th ed. Brooklyn: Thomas Yenser, 1940. 271.

Jessie Carney Smith

Ruby Hurley

(c. 1913-)

Civil rights activist, organization leader

Ruby Hurley, a native of Washington, D.C., exemplified the professional staff who led the NAACP's fight against segregation during the years of America's civil rights movement. After graduating from public school in Washington, where she had been taught by the son of the great abolitionist Frederick Douglass, Hurley attended Miner Teachers College and later Robert H. Terrell Law School. She went on to give thirty-nine years of service to the NAACP and to the bitter struggle for civil rights in America.

Hurley began National Association for the Advancement of Colored People (NAACP) work in 1939, helping to reorganize the Washington, D.C., local branch. Her success in developing a local youth council in that city brought her to the attention of the national association. "Young people today are aggressive, analytical, and even skeptical to the point of cynical . . . . They want to work in a movement of which they are an integral part" wrote NAACP Secretary Walter White in a letter about Hurley's appointment in 1943 as the new national youth secretary (Giddings, 257). Under Ruby Hurley's leadership as Youth Secretary, the number of NAACP youth councils and college chapters expanded at an unprecedented rate from 86 to more than 280 units with a total membership of 25,000.

In 1951 as the NAACP commenced an all-out legal attack on school segregation, Hurley was asked to go south to segregated Birmingham, Alabama, to coordinate NAACP campaigns for new branches in Alabama, Florida, Georgia, Mississippi, and Tennessee. The incipient organization of the southeastern states was established as the new Southeast Region of the association, and Hurley was named regional secretary and then regional director in 1952. As with the youth councils, her guidance proved especially fruitful, and the Southeast grew into the association's largest regional group—by 1969 the Southeast Region had 90,000 (including 13,000 in the youth councils), 431 adult branches, and 144 youth councils and college chapters.

At the time of her appointment as Southeast regional director, the Deep South was sharply divided by race and under the control of a white population deeply resentful of those who might challenge the established "southern way of life." Arriving as a tall, handsome, and reserved outsider from the North, Hurley found the total segregation of Birmingham far different from anything she had known in New York or Washington. Even something as inconsequential as playing checkers was illegal in the Birmingham of 1951 if the players were of different races; this was the city in which she was expected to establish the association's first permanent deep-south office.

As a field representative of the NAACP, Ruby Hurley was called upon to investigate the terrible racial crimes of the 1950s, sending her reports both to the FBI and to the association's *Crisis* magazine. In 1955 the Reverend George W. Lee encouraged thirty-one of his church people to register to vote in Belzoni, Mississippi, and then refused to obey local whites who demanded that he "get the niggers to take their names off the book"; for this affront to "southern standards," he was murdered in cold blood. Hurley was at that time the only full-time professional civil rights worker in the Deep South, so it was she who went into Mississippi to find out what had happened. What she saw was indelibly impressed on her memory: "I saw his body in the casket—I will not be able to forget how the whole lower half of his face had been shot away. A man killed because he, as a minister, said that God's children had rights as God's children and as American citizens'' (Raines, 132). Local authorities had reported the murder as a traffic accident. In August, Lamar Smith, a black man who had been active in voter registration, was gunned down on the courthouse lawn of Brookhaven, Mississippi, during a southern Saturday afternoon, a time traditionally devoted to gathering at the courthouse square—yet Hurley was told no one had seen or heard anything.

Later that same month Emmett Till, a fourteen-year-old Chicago boy visiting his southern relatives, was taken off and brutally beaten and lynched in Money, Mississippi, for allegedly whistling at a white woman. Ruby Hurley, joined by Mississippi NAACP officials Medgar Evers and Amzie Moore, began the inquiry and found witnesses despite the considerable dangers to anyone who talked about or investigated such crime. ''I really got a feeling of what the Underground Railroad during the days of slavery was all about,'' she said, ''how word would be passed by just the look in an eye, never the exact phraseology being used, never the clear language, always in some form that you have to sorta try to figure out what the people meant'' (Raines, 134). Local black men later told her that they had tried to protect her during the investigations by standing guard with shotguns in strategic locations in the piney woods; if so, she never saw them. Her faith in God alone comforted her as, disguised in old cotton-picking clothes, she went from plantation quarters to plantation quarters surreptitiously interviewing witnesses who would talk to no one but Hurley.

To ease his tensions, Medgar Evers had carried a gun hidden beneath the pillow on his car seat, but Hurley told him it wouldn't do any good:

> Medgar, that's not gon' do any good. If they're gon' get us, they're gon' get us. Because the way they behave, they're cowards. They're not gonna come and tell you, I'm gonna shoot you (Raines, 272).

When they finally did murder Medgar Evers one night in 1963, it was from ambush, a cowardly shot in the back, just as Ruby Hurley had feared. Hurley raced from Atlanta to Greenwood, knowing she was too late to say good-bye to her old friend. She recalled:

> Everybody was in such a state of shock that nobody had done anything about getting the blood cleaned up off the driveway or off his car or anything. So that was the first thing I did—get the blood up—before his wife sees it and before the children come back home (Raines, 272).

In her later years it angered her that young blacks often said older Negroes had sat passively by, ''taking it'' from white racists and their system of racial oppression, while the younger generation, who were fortunate enough not to have lived years with both property and life at constant risk, claimed that they alone had possessed the courage to act. The truth is that long before the radical young people of the Student Nonviolent Coordinating Committee (SNCC) brought in white volunteers to Mississippi to insure for the movement the interest and protection of the national media, a few brave souls like the NAACP's Ruby Hurley and Medgar Evers stood silhouetted alone against the white heat of racial hatred, knowingly exposing themselves as agitators in a country where the usual penalty for black radicalism was quick and ugly death.

> That was a period that wasn't easy, as much is said about what happened in the 1960s, but to me the fifties were much worse than the sixties. When I was out there by myself, for instance, there were no TV cameras with me to give me any protection. There were no reporters traveling with me to give me protection (Raines, 136).

Later practitioners of black power would disparage the conservative NAACP and its southern Negro allies as ''Uncle Toms,'' but none of those who spoke the loudest had ever been out there alone in Klan country like Ruby Hurley.

Alabama's Supremacy Laws for Education Challenged

In the winter of 1955-1956, Hurley became part of the NAACP drive to register Autherine Lucy as the first black student at the University of Alabama. When Lucy faced a mob of thousands of frenzied white zealots dedicated to protecting the state's white supremacy laws, there at Autherine Lucy's side, challenging segregation at the risk of her own life, stood Ruby Hurley.

The integration of the University of Alabama came at a time, it must be remembered, when after the battles and all their publicity ended, Hurley had to return to a home office in Birmingham, Alabama. Birmingham was a city whose black citizens were under the protection of the infamous police commissioner ''Bull'' Conner, whose defense of the local way of life was said to have included paying a Klansman to dynamite the church of a black minister who did not know his place. In Birmingham there was no one who could be counted on to defend effectively the regional director of the much-hated NAACP. Hurley remembers, ''I could be riding down the street and white men would drive by and say, 'We gon' get you.' Bombs were thrown at my home, and I've been kept awake at night with threatening phone calls [which came in on her unlisted number]'' (Raines, 134).

Her successes came at a great price to the organization and to Hurley herself. On the first of June, 1956, the State of Alabama struck back with an ex parte injunction that banned most NAACP activities in the state, including fund-raising, dues collection, and recruitment of new members. This was a delayed retribution for the NAACP'S support for the Montgomery bus boycott. The state argued that the NAACP had failed to comply with Alabama laws requiring ''foreign corporations'' to register with the state and turn over their membership roles. As Hurley says, ''We knew what would happen to our members if their names were made public'' (Raines, 135n). Ruby Hurley, as the association's agent in

Alabama, was forced to close her office. She never had the desire to return.

> At that point, [she recalls] I was just about sick of civil rights and sick of fighting the white folks and sick of the South and I said, "I've had it." Because every time I picked up the phone it was a threatening call, and when I'd go home, I never knew whether it was going to be a bomb. I had gotten down in weight; with my height I weighed about one hundred fifteen pounds. I couldn't eat, and days I'd go without food because I just could not eat in Jim Crow places. The only way I could get to a lot of places to fight for civil rights was by bus, and the bus stops, the places to eat, were all segregated, and I was not going to eat in a segregated place. So if I ran out of Hershey Bars, then I didn't eat until I got someplace where I could be fed. (Raines, 135).

She was ill, it seemed, nearly constantly; finally her doctor told her, "There isn't a thing wrong with you physically. It isn't a thing, but these niggers and white folks. That's all that's wrong with you" (Raines, 137). The source of her illness was a situational stress disorder, similar to those suffered by men in combat and by many others in the civil rights movement. Yet Hurley considered herself fortunate because unlike most southern blacks, she could take occasional short vacations in New York or Washington to recuperate. Still, she always returned again to the battlefield of the Deep South where the fight for human rights went on day after day in a painful combat for every inch of ground:

> It was a challenge, and I always emphasize, but for the grace of God, I couldn't have done it, because there were days when if I'd had any sense, I'da been scared. But I never let myself. I didn't get scared . . . I was mad. I got mad when we were put out of business and I had time to reflect on what had been going on. . . . (Raines, 137).

SNCC Challenges NAACP's Efforts

With the Birmingham office closed, Ruby Hurley opened a new regional office in Atlanta and again took up the battle. But the struggle, the movement, was becoming more complex. As the civil rights struggle grew into a revolution, the NAACP's efforts in both the courts and in recruitment were in danger of being overshadowed and overwhelmed by the far more exciting street actions of SNCC, the rapidly expanded Student Nonviolent Coordinating Committee. The nonviolent SNCC demonstrations of civil disobedience that provoked such violent reactions in the white authorities were better suited to the new visual and visceral media of television; the nation's attention was quickly diverted away from the slow-moving and methodical legalists of the NAACP and onto the helter-skelter young activists of SNCC.

Changes were exemplified in the Albany movement. Since the early sixties SNCC and the Southern Christian Leadership Conference, known as the SCLC, had been fighting a long, frustrating, and unsuccessful campaign for civil rights in Albany, Georgia. Local NAACP members feared that outsiders from SNCC, like activists Charles Sherrod and Cordell Reagon, were stealing their authority and moreover acting like pied pipers, leading local children into a series of suicidal demonstrations. An urgent distress call was sent to Atlanta, and Hurley and several other association officials rushed southward to try to restore discipline. Hurley drove down with Martin Luther King, Jr., Ralph Abernathy, and Wyatt Walker, SCLC leaders who were being called in to pull SNCC out of the fire after constant marches and jailings had burned out local morale.

The NAACP preferred negotiation to mass demonstrations like those of Albany, which led to incarceration with expensive bail bills and protracted court cases. The high costs of demonstrations in dollars and time weakened other fronts to which the national organization had given higher priority. Therefore, as James Forman head of the SNCC recalled, "Vernon Jordan and Ruby Hurley were furious with Sherrod for his activities in Albany" (Forman, 362). The internecine struggle that followed did no one in the movement any good. Bernice Reagon, the local secretary of the NAACP youth chapter in Albany, left the organization because of what seemed to her the association's unfeeling and petty antagonism toward SNCC organizers; she recalled being told that SNCC workers "come in and get you stirred up and leave you in jail and the NAACP has to pay the bills" (Williams, 165). And indeed, the NAACP's Roy Wilkins later complained, "We pay some of the expenses of the Albany movement, only to be insulted for being on the wrong side of the generation gap" (Wilkins, 286), while the SCLC's Martin Luther King, Jr., told his staff he needed more control over his activities so he would not be dragged into any new Albanys: "I don't want to be a foreman anymore." For her part, Ruby Hurley summed up SNCC's Albany successes with brutal frankness: "Albany was successful only if the objective was to go to jail" (Branch, 631).

The movement was changing, and although Hurley remained the dedicated Southeast regional director until her retirement on March 31, 1978, by which time she had given thirty-nine years of service to the NAACP, the many honors that came her way were more often from small and local groups. Nationally, the men of the movement garnered the lion's share of historical attention and public adulation, while the pioneers of the fifties fell into darkening shadows lost behind the blazing illumination with which television spotlighted the media-conscious activists of a new era.

From the late sixties onward, Hurley continued her labors outside the limelight. She was especially active in the Methodist church and many of its boards; and if she was often overlooked in the growing iconography of the freedom movement, she was not the kind of person who considered personal honors all that important anyway.

In the end, Hurley remained a private person. She knew that what she and her generation had accomplished was only part of the long, bloody, and continuing struggle of black people for their rights as Americans and as human beings. "I think," she said, "young people need to know, and some older people need to know, that it didn't all begin in 1960" (Raines, 137). Of her own work Ruby Hurley was modest, saying in her retirement speech that whatever she had been able to achieve was due to the support and cooperation of the board, officers, staff, and volunteers of the NAACP. What did she think she had achieved? Because she took the long view, her judgment was humble: "I was able to, I think, effect at least a climate for some change" (Raines, 137).

Ruby Hurley viewed herself in perspective to be only a small part in an old and long-standing struggle for human justice; but from our vantage point we can also recognize that she was in the vanguard of the greatest freedom movement in American history. Given the odds against her, and the power of the adversaries against whom she struggled, her achievements were clearly heroic rather than humble. She was among the bravest of the brave.

References

Branch, Taylor. *Parting the Waters*. New York: Simon and Schuster, 1988.

Forman, James. *The Making of Black Revolutionaries*. Washington, D.C.: Open Hand, 1985.

Giddings, Paula. *When and Where I Enter*. New York: Bantam Books, 1985.

Raines, Howell. *My Soul Is Rested*. New York: Penguin Books, 1977. This book contains two interviews with Ruby Hurley, one covering her work in the 1950s as Southeast regional director of the NAACP, and the other her reactions to the assassination of Medgar Evers.

Wilkins, Roy, and Tom Mathews. *Standing Fast: An Autobiography of the Civil Rights Movement*. New York: Viking Press, 1982.

Williams, Juan. *Eyes on the Prize*. New York: Viking Penguin Books, 1987.

Who's Who Among Black Americans, 1990/1991. Detroit: Gale Research.

Photographs of Ruby Hurley can be found in *Crisis*, Vol. 73 (January 1966), p. 40, and Vol. 76 (February 1969), p. 88; as well as in Williams, 1987, p. 210.

William D. Piersen

Zora Neale Hurston

(1891-1960)

Folklorist, writer

The list of words accurately describing the thirty-year career of Zora Neale Hurston includes anthropologist, dramatist, essayist, folklorist, novelist, short story writer, and autobiographer. She is noted as the first black American to collect and publish Afro-American and Afro-Caribbean folklore. Her interests in and study of black folklore throughout the African diaspora shaped her entire career as an essayist and creative writer in that she wrote numerous articles on various aspects of black culture—its dialect, religious rituals, and folk tales—and three of her four published novels deal with the common black folk of her native southern Florida.

Hurston was born on January 7, 1891, in Eatonville, Florida, to Reverend John Hurston and Lucy Ann (Potts) Hurston. Eatonville, the first incorporated black township in the United States, thrice elected John Hurston as mayor. Lucy Ann Hurston, a former country schoolteacher, taught Sunday school in her husband's Baptist church but worked primarily at home raising the eight Hurston children. Lucy Hurston's death when Zora was thirteen disrupted what had been an economically and emotionally stable childhood in an

Zora Neale Hurston

all-black, self-governing town. Fortunately, though forced to shift among the households of various relatives after her father remarried, the strong, fiercely independent sense of self that life in Eatonville fostered and nurtured in Zora Neale Hurston remained with her and influenced much of her writings.

In her autobiography, *Dust Tracks on a Road* (1942), Hurston credits the adult "lying sessions" (daily exchanges of folk tales) on Joe Clark's store porch in Eatonville for giving her important insights into the nature of human behavior. While many of the adults engaged in exchanging tales, singing songs, and "lying" were in fact unemployed at various times during Hurston's childhood, when Hurston described these sessions in various of her writings she studiously avoided protesting economic discrimination against blacks in America. She chose to demonstrate that black life in America was much more creative and vibrant than the surface poverty and one-dimensional acts of social protest. The poet and critic Arna Bontemps, one of Hurston's contemporaries during the Harlem Renaissance, correctly stated in his review of her autobiography that Hurston "deals very simply with the more serious aspects of Negro life in America—she ignores them" (Bontemps).

One of Hurston's earliest published essays, "How It Feels to Be Colored Me" (1928), states in no uncertain terms her refusal to spend her life lamenting the social plight of the black American:

> I do not belong to the sobbing school of Negrohood who hold that nature somehow has given them a lowdown dirty deal and whose feelings are all hurt about it. Even in the helter-skelter skirmish that is my life, I have seen that the world is to the strong regardless of a little pigmentation more or less. I do not weep at the world—I am too busy sharpening my oyster knife (215).

We can attribute this defiant confidence in her capabilities and in America's positive responses to her talents to her early life in Eatonville and her mother's encouragement to "jump at the sun" even if she did not always land there. Furthermore, her statement reflects her unwavering belief in the fundamental equality between the races: there were good and bad, strong and weak individuals among both races, and no one group was perfect.

Hurston left Eatonville at age fourteen to work as a maid and wardrobe assistant with a traveling Gilbert and Sullivan theatrical troupe. She left the troupe when it arrived in Baltimore, Maryland, and entered Morgan Academy, a predominantly black high school. She graduated from Morgan in June 1918 at age twenty-three, and in the fall of that year she entered Howard University, where she took courses intermittently until 1924. While at Howard, Hurston studied with distinguished black artists and scholars such as Georgia Douglas Johnson and the philosopher Alain Locke. Her first story, "John Redding Goes to Sea," was published in *Stylus*, Howard University's literary magazine, in 1921.

At age thirty in 1925, Zora Neale Hurston migrated to New York City and immediately became involved with the Harlem Renaissance, the black literary and cultural movement of the 1920s. During that time Harlem was the mecca for creative blacks from all over the United States and the Caribbean. Writers such as Claude McKay arrived from Jamaica, Eric Walrond from Barbados, Wallace Thurman from Salt Lake City, Jean Toomer and Sterling Brown from Washington, D.C., Rudolph Fisher from Rhode Island, and Langston Hughes from Kansas. Zora Neale Hurston, who befriended and worked along with all of these writers, was the only one to arrive in New York from the rural southeast—the cradle of black folk life that the renaissance celebrated. The sociologist Charles S. Johnson, who in 1925 founded *Opportunity: A Journal of Negro Life*, and Alain Locke, who edited *The New Negro* (1925), an anthology of writings by the renaissance writers, each admired and published Hurston's stories. She collaborated with Langston Hughes and a few other poets to publish *Fire!*, a one-issue literary magazine of black culture. Primarily because of the attention her stories attracted, Hurston received a scholarship in 1925 to attend Barnard College.

Black Folklore Collected

Awarded a B.A. from Barnard in 1928, Hurston continued her graduate studies at Columbia University under the direction of the anthropologist Franz Boas. It was Boas who encouraged Hurston to return to Eatonville to collect black folklore, which she did with the assistance of a private grant from a New York socialite, Mrs. Osgood Mason. *Mules and Men* (1935) is a collection of the folklore Hurston collected in Florida and Alabama between 1929 and 1931 and includes a revision of an essay on hoodoo she had written in 1931 for the *Journal of American Folklore*. *Mules and Men* is unique in that it is the first such collection of folklore published by a black American woman, and it is by a woman indigenous to the culture from which the stories arise.

The traditional practice among academicians in anthropology is to study cultures that are unfamiliar to the researcher to insure a scientific objectivity. Boas assumed that Hurston's familiarity with her native village, Eatonville, and the rural south in general would prove advantageous to collecting African-American lore. The manuscript Hurston produced after her trips south proved Boas correct. In his introduction to *Mules and Men*, Boas praised her work as invaluable because it "throws into relief the peculiar amalgamation of African and European tradition which is so important for understanding historically the character of American Negro life." Yet several black reviewers did not share Boas's enthusiasm for the affirmative, sometimes happy, side of black rural life represented in *Mules and Men*. The poet Sterling Brown argued that it should have included "a few slave anecdotes that turn the tables on old marster" or "a bit of grumbling about hard work" to present more closely the life of blacks working on a rural saw mill camp (Howard, 154). This type of complaint about the absence of bitterness over racism and economic exploitation in Hurston's works recurred throughout her career.

Hurston's first novel, *Jonah's Gourd Vine,* was published in 1934. It covers the life of John Buddy Pearson, a southern Baptist preacher, who during the week cannot resist adultery but who spends his Sundays in the pulpit as a holy man. When his parishioners voice their objections to his double life, Pearson refuses to change his behavior. The central conflict in this novel is within the man. He must accept the contradictions between the life of the cloth and the life of the flesh, between the spiritual and the material. It is a drama that, like the stories in *Mules and Men,* shows the amalgamation of African and Euro-American world views in the mind of a black American male. Traditional African tribal life interprets the expression of human sexuality as a spiritual act, whereas the Petrarchan ideal of love states that it never be expressed physically and the American Puritans echoed this view. Aspiring, middle-class black communities such as that in *Jonah's Gourd Vine* ascribed to the Puritanical view of human sexuality out of the desire to assimilate into mainstream American culture. John Pearson's defiance of the status quo cannot be sustained, because it is the conservative community's acceptance of him as its preacher that enabled him to realize financial success. The theme of a man's struggles with his conscience universalizes *Jonah's Gourd Vine.* The fact that it is rendered through Southern black American dialect localizes the novel but serves Hurston's purpose to study the basic humanity, not the race, of a man.

Their Eyes Were Watching God Called Hurston's Best Novel

Zora Neale Hurston published what critics agree is her best novel in 1937. Written in seven straight weeks in the Caribbean after a love affair ended, *Their Eyes Were Watching God* takes as its theme a black woman's search for an identity beyond that which prevailed in her small rural town. The main character Janie (Crawford) Killicks Starks Woods is a coffee-and-cream-colored quadroon. Raised by her maternal grandmother, a former slave, Janie rejects the community's expectations that she aspire to be the dutiful wife of a prosperous black farmer. From the onset of puberty, when Janie awakens under a blossoming pear tree, she yearns for an emotionally fulfilling union with another. This pear tree and Janie's expressed yearning to search beyond the horizon of her hometown symbolize her quest for a natural and unconstrained existence.

As evident in the best of Hurston's black love stories, for example, "The Gilded Six Bits" (1933), she believed that the institution of marriage could potentially fulfill the desires of a man and a woman if they shared a respect for one another. Women in Hurston's fiction desire husbands, but are not afraid to engage in verbal and physical confrontations when disagreements arise. *Their Eyes Were Watching God* satisfies the universal fantasy of an emotionally fulfilling marriage. The union between Janie and her third husband, Teacake Woods, has its problems, stemming from the many differences between them. Teacake is much younger, of darker complexion, and a migrant worker, but he respects Janie's integrity and her desires to participate in the folk life of the community. The novel insists on Janie's complete freedom to such an extent that she lives a feminist fantasy of expressing her sexual passion without facing its natural consequences of conception. This is a radical idea for the 1930s: that a beautiful black woman like Janie, left a widow living happily alone in her house at the end of the novel, can and should realize her fullest potential sexually and intellectually by and for herself.

Notwithstanding Hurston's suppression of the biological truisms of human sexuality in *Their Eyes Were Watching God,* the novel is a brilliant study of black folk and their language, their stories, and their mannerisms. All of this works symbolically as a measure of the characters' integrity and freedom, which in turn demonstrates a contrast to the image of the carefree, "happy darky" that prevailed in the fiction of many American novelists.

In spite of her beliefs in and advocacy of fulfilling relationships between men and women in her novels and short stories, the collection and study of Afro-American and Afro-Caribbean folklore was an all-consuming passion for Hurston. She pursued this with such intensity that she had difficulties maintaining long-term relationships with men. She was married twice, once in 1927 to Herbert Sheen, a musician, and again in 1939 to Albert Price III, with whom she had worked on Works Project Administration (WPA) projects. These marriages each ended in divorce, primarily because Hurston refused to give up her career as a folklorist to remain at home. According to Hurston's biographers, she was at first passionately in love with both of her husbands, but that love was not enough to replace her passion for studying the folkways of blacks and her desire to succeed as a creative writer. She used any money awarded to her (two Guggenheim Fellowships, 1936 and 1938, granted by Mrs. Osgood Mason, a wealthy white socialite) or earned through the sale of her novels to travel throughout the southern United States and the Caribbean.

Hurston's second collection of folklore, *Tell My Horse,* was published in 1938 following two trips to the Caribbean, specifically Haiti and Jamaica. On the one hand, *Tell My Horse* combines travel writing with transcriptions of folklore she gathered from the two islands. On the other, the book allows Hurston to make comparisons between the black cultures in the United States and the Caribbean. She is especially interested in intraracial color discrimination as the common denominator between the two worlds. The mulatto class of Jamaicans, fewer in number than the blacks, never ceased referring to the English or Scottish father from whom all personal refinements were inherited:

> It is as if one stepped back to the days of slavery or the generation immediately after surrender when [American] Negroes had little else to boast of except a left-hand kinship with the master. . . . Then, as in Jamaica at present, no shame was attached to a child born "in a carriage with no top"(126).

In the course of this analysis she does mention the emerging sense of race pride in the black (dark-complexioned) Jamaican population of the 1930s and applauds its representation in art. As in the case of *Mules and Men*, because Hurston felt a racial affinity with the culture, she discusses Afro-Caribbean folklore as though she were just another teller of the tales and proverbs. She tries to convey the rhythm of Caribbean speech.

African-American Religious Beliefs Reflected

Hurston published her third novel, *Moses, Man of the Mountain,* in 1939. It is a retelling of the Biblical legend of Moses from the Afro-American point of view. Hurston casts the Israelites as dialect-speaking southern blacks and Moses as a black voodoo doctor. The story blends fiction, folklore, religion, and comedy, and most critics assess it as a minor classic in Afro-American literature. The novel has its flaws, but Hurston's portrayal of Moses as a voodoo doctor is grounded in a truism of antebellum southern black culture. Historian Lawrence Levine explains in his *Black Culture, Black Consciousness* that the slaves' belief in Moses as a voodoo doctor was part of the way they Africanized the Christianity that the southern white planters tried to teach them. In traditional African cultures, the world from which African slaves were bought, a religious leader could perform magical acts in the course of a ceremony. Hence, stories about Moses turning his staff into a snake, changing wine to water, and parting the waters with a wave of his hand were comprehensible to African slaves, who accepted supernatural phenomena as coexisting with the everyday world. Though "converted" to Christianity, American slaves continued to practice voodoo as an alternative source of psychological enrichment. Subsequent generations of black Americans have continued this practice. *Moses, Man of the Mountain* may have its structural flaws, but the basic premise of the story reflects Hurston's extensive knowledge of Afro-American religious beliefs.

Given that by 1941 Hurston had written numerous anthropological articles, short stories, and plays, two collections of folklore, and three novels, her publisher J. P. Lippincott urged her to write her autobiography. Lippincott wanted a multivolume work that would chronicle her rise from southern rural obscurity to fame as an accomplished folklorist and novelist. According to Robert Hemenway in his *Zora Neale Hurston: A Literary Biography,* Hurston accepted a rich friend's invitation to vacation in California, where she completed the first draft of *Dust Tracks on a Road* by mid-July 1941 (275). It was published in 1942.

Notwithstanding the inaccuracies that her biographers warn us of, Hurston does offer a straight linear narration of her life, from her birth and early childhood nurturing among the black folk in Eatonville through her turbulent adolescence and her life as a vagabond after her mother's death and her father's remarriage. She outlines her pursuit of an education at Howard University and Barnard College and summarizes her ethnographic research and the writing of her novels. Hence Hurston does attempt to adhere to the conventional innocence-to-experience plot of autobiography, even though she demonstrates an aversion to specific dates and rigorously avoids mentioning many intimate details of her life, such as her two failed marriages.

Hurston's training as an anthropologist is evident in her narrative stance in *Dust Tracks* in that she positions herself as a mediator between her black American folk community and her white reading audience; she speaks in both the black folk idiom and the language of a graduate of Barnard College. She not only explains folk expressions, she incorporates folk narratives into her personal chronicle. In fact, *Dust Tracks on a Road* is as much a collection of folklore as Hurston's *Mules and Men* and *Tell My Horse.* She demonstrates a commitment to explaining herself in her memoirs as a product of the large body of black American folklore. Hence, unlike any other black American autobiography, *Dust Tracks* consists of an intricate interplay of the introspective personal engagement expected of an autobiography and the self-effacement expected of cultural descriptions and explications associated with ethnography.

Another important distinction of Hurston's *Dust Tracks on a Road* is that she seems obsessed with not appearing to complain about the social condition of the black American community. She does not lament, as does Richard Wright in his *Black Boy* (1945), the injustices white America inflicted on blacks. Rather, Hurston insists on a bicultural identity that allows her to pinpoint the contrasts and equivalences between the black folk community in which she was born and the larger world beyond Eatonville, Florida, where she was educated and eventually chose to reside. *Dust Tracks on a Road* was well received and won the Anisfield-Wolf Award in 1942 for its contribution to better race relations.

During the remainder of the 1940s Hurston was invited by several magazines, such as *American Mercury, Journal of American Folklore,* and *Saturday Evening Post,* to write articles and commentaries on various aspects of Afro-American culture. She reviewed books, plays, and musicals for the *New York Herald Tribune Weekly Book Review.* In most of these pieces Hurston maintained her anthropological interest in demonstrating how Afro-American culture fit in with the larger pattern of white American culture and did not engage in discussion of racial politics. However, in the articles Hurston wrote for *Negro Digest* during the 1940s, she began to voice some very pointed opinions on the mistreatment of blacks. In "My Most Humiliating Jim Crow Experiences" (1944), Hurston describes a visit she made to a white doctor in an exclusive section of Manhattan. While the reader can feel the humiliation Hurston must have felt when the doctor "went through some motions" of a superficial examination, she is careful not to rant over being mistreated. Instead, Hurston expresses pity for "the pathos of Anglo-Saxon civilization" with its "false foundation" that "cannot last" (*Negro Digest,* June 1944). The entire piece is a study in how to expose the inhumanity of Anglo-Saxons in a rational manner.

In 1945 Hurston published another article in *Negro Digest,* "Crazy for This Democracy," that seethes with cynicism over the exclusion of certain American ethnic groups from the democratic process. She realizes that the United States did not care to include the Third World in any of its international charters and agreements except to assist European nations to maintain colonies. "Our weapons, money, and the blood of millions of our men have been used to carry the English, French, and Dutch and lead them back on the millions of unwilling Asiatics" (*Negro Digest,* December 1945). Finally, in 1950 Hurston published a piece that revealed the extent to which she had to shape all of her writings to fit the stereotypes of blacks that prevailed in the minds of white publishing companies. In "What White Publishers Won't Print" Hurston, obviously speaking from twenty years of experience, insists that white publishers refuse any articles, short stories, or books that present images of blacks as fully assimilated into mainstream American culture. Hurston mentions two novels, both by white Americans, that she felt tried to present sincere portraits of "Negroes of wealth and culture:" Carl Van Vechten's *Nigger Heaven* and Worth Tuttle Hedden's *The Other Room.* She calls for a continuation of the stories begun in these books, especially from blacks themselves. The obvious problem at that time was to find a white publisher willing to accept such stories from black writers.

Hurston published her fourth and last novel in 1948. Unlike her three earlier novels, however, *Seraph on the Suwanee* was about southern white Americans. Hurston chose to write about a working-class southern white woman, Arvay Henson, in order to dispel the "old silly rule about Negroes not writing about white people" (Carl Van Vechten to Zora Neale Hurston, 2 November 1942). She depicts Arvay as a poor neurotic who believes that nothing good is ever going to happen to her because she does not deserve it. Arvay, like the central character in *Jonah's Gourd Vine,* must struggle with herself. She eventually resolves her inner conflicts and "grows" into a woman with a positive sense of self. The novel received mixed reviews at the time of its publication. Since the revival of interest in the life and writings of Hurston in the late 1970s, *Seraph on the Suwanee* is the only one of her published works that has not been reprinted. Contemporary critics do not see it as one of her best productions.

The 1950s marked the beginning of the end of Hurston's career; her income from her novels and folklore dropped significantly, forcing her to take on a series of menial jobs in various small towns in southern Florida. Moreover, Hurston published only a few articles and reviews during this time. None of her book-length manuscripts made its way into print. On October 29, 1959, after suffering a stroke, Hurston was forced to enter the Saint Lucie County Welfare Home in Fort Pierce, Florida. Her fiercely independent nature kept her from asking friends and family for shelter. She died in poverty at Saint Lucie on January 28, 1960, and was buried in an unmarked grave in a segregated cemetery. The novelist and poet Alice Walker, who identifies Zora Neale Hurston as her own literary foremother, traveled to the Fort Pierce, Florida, gravesite in August 1973 and placed a stone marker on the approximate spot of Hurston's grave.

According to the pictures of Zora Neale Hurston published in two biographies and the published comments of her literary contemporaries of the Harlem Renaissance, she was one of the most vivacious personalities of the era. Physical descriptions of her vary from that of a very fair-complexioned woman with freckles to a warm brown-complexioned woman with wide hips. Numerous photographs taken at various stages in her life, beginning with her student days at Howard University in the 1920s, show a woman with high cheekbones and sharp chin. Her aspect suggests the fearlessness she must have possessed in order to travel through the roughest parts of the South collecting Afro-American folklore. She admits to having carried a pearl-handled pistol that she was not afraid to use if the need had arisen. Yet she befriended both the poorest and the wealthiest black and white Americans with ease and believed there were no substantial differences between human beings at all.

References

Boas, Franz. Preface. *Mules and Men.* Bloomington: Indiana University Press, 1978.

Bontemps, Arna. "From Eatonville, Florida, to Harlem." *New York Herald Tribune* (22 November 1942).

Brown, Sterling. Review of *Mules and Men.* Unidentified clipping, James Weldon Johnson Collection, Yale University. Cited in Robert Hemenway. *Zora Neale Hurston: A Literary Biography.* Urbana: University of Illinois Press, 1977.

Hemenway, Robert. *Zora Neale Hurston: A Literary Biography.* Urbana: University of Illinois Press, 1977.

Howard, Lillie P. *Zora Neale Hurston.* Boston: Twayne Publishers, 1980.

Hurston, Zora Neale. "Crazy for This Democracy." *Negro Digest* 4 (December 1942): 45-48.

——. "How It Feels to be Colored Me." *World Tomorrow* 11 (May 1928): 215-16.

——. "My Most Humiliating Jim Crow Experience." *Negro Digest* 2 (June 1944): 25-26.

——. *Tell My Horse.* Philadelphia: Lippincott, 1938.

Levine, Lawrence. *Black Culture, Black Consciousness.* New York: Oxford University Press, 1977.

Van Vechten, Carl. To Zora Neale Hurston, 2 November 1942. James Waldon Johnson Collection, Yale University.

Walker, Alice, ed. *I Love Myself When I Am Laughing. . .: A Zora Neale Hurston Reader.* New York: The Feminist Press, 1979.

Collections

Zora Neale Hurston's papers are in the James Weldon Johnson Collection, Beinecke Library, Yale University; the Alain Locke Collections, Moorland-Spingarn Research Center, Howard University; the University of Florida, Gainesville, and Special Collections, Fisk University Library.

Alice A. Deck

Jean Blackwell Hutson

(1914-)

Library administrator and curator

For more than thirty years, Jean Blackwell Hutson guided the development of the world's leading public repository of materials that document the history and culture of peoples of African descent. In doing so, she became internationally recognized for her knowledge of resources on this subject. Known as the Schomburg Collection in 1948 when she came to the New York Public Library as curator, this repository is now the Schomburg Center for Research in Black Culture—a title more fitting to the library's history and purpose. Hutson processed acquisitions, publicized the collection widely, including the listing of its contents in a published book catalog, aided in the formation of a corporation to raise funds to support the center, and set the groundwork for the new research center facility. Her work at Schomburg aided in the preservation and promotion of scholarship on African-Americans worldwide.

Born Jean Blackwell on September 4, 1914, in Sommerfield, Florida, a small town south of Jacksonville, she was the only child of Paul O. Blackwell, a commission merchant who maintained a farm and bought and shipped produce, and Sarah (Myers) Blackwell, an elementary school teacher. When Hutson was four, she and her mother moved to her mother's home in Baltimore, Maryland; her father stayed in Florida to maintain his business and visited his wife and daughter over the years.

Hutson was a precocious child, frequently receiving extra books in school to read and to help her avoid boredom. She attended Douglass High School in Baltimore, graduating in 1931 as class valedictorian. The school was one of several great all-black high schools in segregated school systems where black history and literature were stressed and where many black luminaries had studied or taught. Yolande Du Bois, daughter of W. E. B. Du Bois and later the wife of Countee Cullen, and May Miller, daughter of sociologist, essayist, and educator Kelly Miller, were among Hutson's teachers. There she was also surrounded by well-known figures, such as Langston Hughes, who became her lifelong friend.

She enrolled at the University of Michigan immediately after graduating from high school, and three years later she transferred to Barnard College, where she graduated in 1935 with a B.A. degree in English. The next year she received the M.A. from Columbia University School of Library Science.

Hutson's library career began as soon as she completed her library education. She was librarian in the New York Public library branch libraries from 1936 to 1939. In 1939 she was school librarian and English teacher at Dunbar Junior High School in Baltimore. In that year, also, she married song lyricist Andy Razaf, but the marriage ended in divorce eight years later. In 1941 she was awarded a teacher's certificate from Columbia University. From 1942 to 1947 she returned to her position in the New York branch library system. The next year she was supervising librarian of the Woodstock branch of the New York Public Library, and from there she became curator of the Schomburg Collection, where she remained from 1948 to 1972.

On June 3, 1950, she married John Hutson, a coworker at the Countee Cullen Regional Library, and they had one daughter, Jean Frances. Continuing to develop her professional career, from 1962 to 1971 Jean Blackwell Hutson was lecturer and adjunct professor in the history department, Evening Division, City College of New York. Meanwhile, the 1960s had become turbulent years, both in race relations and in the demand for books and information on African-American themes. The well-developed Schomburg Collection was a mecca for research on African-American topics. About this time President Kwame Nkrumah of Ghana recognized Hutson's scholarship, extensive knowledge of books, reading, and research materials on African and African-American peoples and invited her to assist the University of Ghana in developing its Africana collection in the Balme Library. She accepted his offer and was assistant librarian at the University of Ghana for one year, 1964-1965.

Schomburg Library Names Hutson Head

After the Schomburg Collection was renamed the Schomburg Center for Research in Black Culture, New York Public Library, Jean Blackwell Hutson became chief and held that position from 1972 to 1980. She was also assistant director, collection management and development, black studies research librarian, New York Public Library, from 1980 until her retirement on February 29, 1984.

The Schomburg Collection was founded while Hutson was a student in the Baltimore public schools. The private library of Arthur Alphonzo Schomburg, a Puerto Rican of African descent, was purchased to form the nucleus of the library-museum. Schomburg had been around Harlem during the Renaissance and knew the importance of a center for the cultural and much of the political activity of central Harlem. The poets, writers, artists, and musicians of that era were very much a part of the community that visited the

Schomburg Collection and helped to establish a climate for research and for sharing ideas with the other cultural emissaries of the day. Their presence helped to attract students and laypersons as well.

During the Depression, various projects of the Works Projects Administration (WPA), such as the Negro in New York research projects, and the artists, writers, and theater projects, dramatized the significance of the library and helped to make it one of the most influential institutions in the community. Until the influence of Senator Joseph McCarthy discouraged free discussion of issues in the late forties and early fifties and other political trends took their toll, the Schomburg Collection and the library continued as a place for community activism, cultural development, and social interaction.

The Schomburg Center's historical significance resurged in the sixties and the library was positioned in an even more prominent place in the cultural development of black America. It continued as the center of great literary and artistic development in the black community, both in terms of its local geographical area and the broader community where its impact is also felt. Jean Blackwell Hutson contributed significantly to the center's development while she was in charge of the library. She witnessed the library-museum growth from a bookstock of approximately fifteen thousand volumes to seventy-five thousand volumes. She witnessed the appreciation of its holdings, as judged by its use, and saw its popularity grow from apathy to enthusiastic admiration with overflow crowds of student users, particularly in the turbulent sixties. On this issue Hutson said:

> Of course the Civil Rights movements in the United States and the success of the independence movements in Africa and the Caribbean were the powerful stimulants which brought about the identification of Black Americans with their African heritage and caused the terrific surge of interest in Black Studies. The Schomburg has been in the center of these surging tides (Biography file, Fisk University Library).

During Hutson's administration the library published its *Dictionary Catalog of the Schomburg Collection* (G. K. Hall, 1962), with supplements in 1967 and 1972, which caused the influence of the library to spread throughout the Americas, Europe, and Africa. Arthur Schomburg had collected works on blacks regardless of the subject or language in which they were written. That policy continued both under Schomburg's curatorship and under Hutson's administration. As a result, the collection had immediate international appeal. Hutson also expanded the collection of paintings in the library-museum by acquiring historically-significant paintings by black American artists that adorned the walls of the reading room. With the assistance of Mary Brady of the Harmon Foundation, the collection of paintings, sculpture, and other works of art grew.

In addition to fund-raising to support the library, Jean Blackwell Hutson spent her last years at Schomburg seeking funds to erect a new library building. Though the new library had been included in the New York City budget since 1970, a severe fiscal crisis in 1975 meant that the contract to erect the building was canceled. Before her retirement, however, construction on the building was begun. Hutson could retire in peace.

Long active in the community, Hutson has been a board member of the Harlem Associates of Neighborhood Agencies; Manhattan Advisory Council of New York Urban League; Municipal Art Society; and the Martin Luther King, Jr., Center for Social Change. She has been active with the American Library Association, NAACP, and National Urban League Guild. She was a fellow of the African Studies Association and a founding member of the Black Academy of Arts and Letters. She is a member of the Delta Sigma Theta Sorority. She was founding president and now vice-president of the Harlem Cultural Council.

Among her numerous awards, prizes, and special achievements are: Camp Minisink Award for meritorious service to the community, 1952; Who's Who Award of the Seventh Avenue Association, 1954; recognition by the New York Chapter of the Society for the Study of Negro Life and History, 1955, 1971; Annual Heritage Award of the Association for the Study of Negro Life and History, 1966; Black Heroes Memorial Award for Outstanding Community Service Commemorating the Lives of Malcolm X, Adam Clayton Powell, Whitney M. Young, Jr., and Martin Luther King, Jr., 1974; Lewis-Schuyler-Wheatley Arts and Letters Award, Delta Sigma Theta Sorority, 1976; Community Service Award, Kappa Omicron Chapter, Omega Psi Phi Fraternity, 1976; and Professional Service Award, Black Librarians Caucus of the American Library Association, 1980. She was honored along with other outstanding black women in the photographic exhibition, *I Dream A World.*

Writings by Jean Blackwell Hutson include "Choosing Books for Harlemites," *Opportunity* 17 (May 1939); preface, *Who's Who in Colored America,* 1952; "African Materials in the Schomburg Collection," *African Studies Bulletin* 3 (May 1960); "The Schomburg Collection," *Freedomways* (Summer 1963); preface, *Dictionary Catalog of the Schomburg Collection of Negro Literature and History* (Boston: G. K. Hall, 1962, 1967); preface, *Negro in New York* (New York: Oceana Publications, 1967); "Harlem, a Cultural History: Selected Bibliography," *Metropolitan Museum of Art Bulletin* (January 1969); and "The Schomburg Center for Research in Black Culture," *Encyclopedia of Library and Information Science* (New York: Marcel Dekker, 1978);

Jean Blackwell Hutson, consultant for many African-American collection development projects, will be remembered most for promoting study and research in the Schomburg Center through her years of dedicated service, particularly at a time when financing such resources was an unpopular idea, and later, when the multitude of research resources on African-American themes were all of a sudden "discovered." The retired librarian lives in New York City and continues to lecture and consult on various scholarly projects.

References

"Jean Blackwell Hutson: An Appreciation." New York Public Library. Schomburg Center for Research in Black Culture, March 29, 1984. Includes photographs.

Lanker, Brian. *I Dream a World.* New York: Stewart, Tabori, and Chang, 1989. Photograph, p. 88.

Who's Who Among Black Americans, 1990/1991. 6th ed. Detroit: Gale Research, 1991.

Who's Who in America, 1990/1991. 46th ed. Wilmette, Ill.: Macmillan, 1990.

Who's Who in Colored America. 7th ed. Yonkers, N.Y.: Christian E. Burckel, 1940. Photograph, p. 35.

Collections

Jean Blackwell Hutson is included in the Black Oral History Program, Fisk University Library, the Columbia University Oral History Collection, and the Schomburg Center Oral History Collection. A biography file on her is housed in Special Collections, Fisk University Library, Nashville, Tennessee.

Jessie Carney Smith

The Hyers Sisters
Anna Madah Hyers
(c. 1856-1930s)
Emma Louise Hyers
(c. 1858-c. 1899)
Singers

The Hyers Sisters, soprano Anna Madah and contralto Emma Louise, were musical pioneers. Among the first black women to enter the concert world in the post-Civil War period, they "formed a singing duo and toured the country, performing to great acclaim in the late nineteenth century" (Story, 33). Achieving national distinction on the American concert stage, the Misses Hyers, under the direction of their father, Sam B. Hyers, continued through the next decade with numerous triumphant successes, including the first black repertory company in the 1880s and bringing forth "one of the first musical shows to be produced by a black theatrical organization"(Sampson, *Blacks in Blackface,* 393). Lauded by critics as "among the great vocal artists of their generation" (Locke, 39), they enraptured audiences and the press throughout the nation with their phenomenal musicality. For the first four years of their career, the Hyerses toured extensively on the California circuit. Over the next decade, they rapidly forged a national reputation, gaining critical acclaim from the white press and discriminating audiences in major concert halls in the Eastern and Western states. Their repertoire was large and varied, ranging from plantation songs, popular ballads, drama, and musical comedy to operatic arias.

Born in Sacramento, California, in the 1850s, Anna and Emma Hyers revealed their precocious talents as children: "They possessed no small degree of lyrical talent; their voices, considering their tender years, were remarkably full, and resonant; and . . . they exhibited much fondness for music, and a spirit of great earnestness in all they undertook" (Trotter, 161). Beginning their basic music training with their parents. both amateur musicians, they later studied piano and voice formally with German professor Hugo Sank and former Italian opera singer Madame Josephine D'Ormy.

The Hyerses made their professional debut at the Metropolitan Theater in Sacramento on April 22, 1867: "On this occasion . . . their efforts were rewarded with grand success; the music critics and the press awarded them unstinted praise, and even pronounced them 'wonderful'" (Trotter, 162). Their concerts and versatility won glowing accolades. Covering their concert in that city, the *San Francisco Chronicle* predicted, "Their musical power is acknowledged; and those who heard them . . . were unanimous in their praises, saying that rare natural gifts would insure for them a leading position among the prime donne of the age. . . . Miss Madah has a pure, sweet soprano voice, very true, even, and flexible, of remarkable compass and smoothness. . . . Miss Louise is a natural wonder, being a fine alto-singer, and also the possessor of a pure tenor voice" (Trotter, 162-63).

They retired from the stage after their debut to continue study in preparation for making a national tour. On August 12, 1871, the Hyers Sisters returned to the concert stage and gave their first major recital at the Salt Lake Theater, accompanied by baritone Joseph LeCount; their father, tenor Sam Hyers; and an accompanist: "Their program included primarily operatic arias, duos, trios, and quartets" (Southern, 192). Reviewing the performance for the *Deseret News.* John Tullidge praised Anna's and Emma's ease, grace, and rapid execution in handling difficult selections of interpretation and intonation. "But notwithstanding these frequent changes, and intricate skipping intervals," he said, "Miss Anna accomplished the difficulty with ease, and perfectly in tune. The rapid cadence on the dominant was artistically rendered. . . . Miss Emma sang the alto in the 'Caro Ballato' with Miss Anna, in a duetto on the words, 'Qui si pria della partenza'. . . . This duet not only requires fine voices, but rapid execution also, or the rendition would be imperfect; but the sisters gave a charming interpretation to the piece. . . . The trio throughout was creditably performed, and was loudly applauded by the audience'' (Trotter, 164). In tribute to their excellent performance, the citizens of Salt Lake City extended the Hyerses a complimentary benefit performance, which they accepted.

A succession of highly successful concerts in principal cities throughout the West—Saint Louis, Chicago, and Cleveland—gained them widespread recognition: ''The Western press, particularly the daily papers of Missouri, Illinois, and Ohio praised the singers widely in their reviews. . . . Anna's singing E flat above the staff with the greatest ease, and her bird-like trills, caused her to be likened to Jenny Lind, while Emma's voice was said to be one of remarkable quality and richness 'rarely heard''' (Cuney-Hare, 216).

After their triumphant tour in the West, Sam Hyers, manager of the group, expanded it to include tenor Wallace King, baritone John Luca, and accompanist A. C. Taylor. Continuing the tour eastward, the troupe performed in New York City and in Brooklyn: ''Their performances in the city of New York and in other parts of the state drew large, cultivated, and enthusiastic audiences, and were . . . considered 'a revelation''' (Trotter, 172). The *Brooklyn Union* wrote, ''The young ladies are gifted with remarkable voices, and sing together with perfect harmony, displaying the full compass and beauty of their voices, which are clear and sweet'' (Trotter, 173).

Encouraged by their highly-acclaimed performances in New York, the Hyers Sisters continued the tour eastward with more engagements throughout principal New England cities. Aware of the barriers of racial discrimination on the American concert stage and of the lack of acceptance of black singers in prestigious music halls, with determination the Hyerses approached Boston, '''the Modern Athens,' that acknowledged centre of musical and general aesthetic culture . . . whose critical audiences ever received coldly, at first, all new comers, and who, guided by their own judgments and having their own standard of merit, never yield praise because it has been accorded in other sections'' (Trotter, 174). A '''brilliant' performance, their recital before this distinguished Boston audience . . . so delighted their audience that they decided to extend their stay for several months'' (Sampson, *The New Grove Dictionary*, 446). In a glowing review, one of the Boston newspapers wrote: ''We were invited . . . to hear the singing of two colored young ladies, named Anna and Emma Hyers, of San Francisco, at the Meionaon. They are aged respectively sixteen and fourteen years, and . . . may be called musical prodigies. They are, without doubt, destined to occupy a high position in the musical world'' (Trotter, 174).

Singing in concerts in Massachusetts, Rhode Island, and Connecticut, the Hyers sisters became celebrities. In 1872 they were invited to sing at Patrick S. Gilmore's World Peace Jubilee in Boston. By 1875 Sam Hyers formed the Hyers Sisters Concert Company and presented them in concert primarily in New England. Napier Lothian, director of the Boston Theater Orchestra, conducted a small symphony orchestra that supported the group during its Boston concerts. In 1875 the concert company also gave concerts of sacred music at the Boston Theater.

Concert Singers Stage Musical Comedies

During the mid-1870s the Hyerses, at the height of their popularity, continued to prosper and to add new attractions. By 1876, under the supervision of Sam Hyers, the concert company changed its format and became a musical comedy company: ''Over a period of a dozen or so years, they staged no fewer than seven musicals in repertory'' (Southern, *Music of Black America*, 240). Their first production, written especially for them and staged that same year, was *Out of Bondage* (1876), a story that traces the life of a freedman from slavery to education and refinement. The success of this musical production inspired the concert company to add other musicals and dramas to the repertoire: ''By the late 1870s the Hyers had staged *In and Out of Bondage* (1877), a three-act musical drama adapted by Sam Hyers; *Urlina: or, The African Princess* (1877; copyright notice filed in 1872 by E. J. Getchell); *Colored Aristocracy* (1877), a musical drama in three acts written by black novelist Pauline Hopkins . . . and *The Underground Railroad* (1879), a four-act musical drama also written by Hopkins'' (Southern, *Music of Black Americans*, 240).

During this period, the Hyers Company toured the United States under the Redpath Lyceum Bureau. As the first and only black repertory company, for more than a decade the Hyers Company was the most celebrated troupe in the country, acclaimed as ''one of the best opera bouffe troupes in America'' (251). According to Southern, all of the musical productions had racial themes and traced the characters from slavery to freedom and ''a more rewarding life'' (251). In 1883 the Hyerses joined the Callendar Consolidated Spectacular Minstrel Festival at the Grand Opera House in New York and later toured the nation with the minstrel troupe. This form of entertainment was popular then and was one of the few sources of consistent income for black musicians. By the 1880s the Hyers Sisters rejoined their own musical company, expanding it to include other notable talents—Billy Kersands, Celestine O. Brown, Don S. King, and pianist-composer Jacob Sawyer, among others. The company produced two musicals, *The Blackville Twins* (1887) and *Plum Pudding* (1887).

In the seasons immediately following, Anna and Emma Hyers appeared in separate ventures: ''Emma joined a company performing *Uncle Tom's Cabin* in 1894, and Anna joined John H. Isham's minstrel production 'Octoroons' to sing opera excerpts'' (Story, 35).

Emma Louise Hyers died shortly before 1900; Anna continued singing, joining the M. B. Curtis All-Star Afro-American Minstrels tour throughout the United States and Australia. After returning to the United States in the early 1900s, Anna Madah appeared with the John H. Isham's Oriental American Company until 1902. Anna became the wife of a Dr. Fletcher of Sacramento and retired from the stage. She remained active in music at church. According to Southern, she died in the 1930s (*Music of Black Americans)*, 240.

References

Cuney-Hare, Maude. *Negro Musicians and Their Music*. New York: Da Capo Press, 1974. 216.

Locke, Alain. *The Negro and His Music*. Washington, D.C.: Associates in Negro Folk Education, 1936. Reprinted. New York: Arno Press, 1969. 39.

Sampson, Henry T. *Blacks in Blackface*. Metuchen, N.J.: Scarecrow Press, 1980. 393.

———. "Hyers Sisters." *New Grove Dictionary of American Music*. Vol. 2. Eds. H. Wiley Hitchcock and Stanley Sadie. New York: Macmillan, 1986. 446.

Southern, Eileen. *Biographical Dictionary of Afro-American and African Music*. Westport, Conn.: Greenwood Press, 1982. 192.

———. *The Music of Black Americans*. 2nd ed. New York: Norton, 1983. 240, 251.

Story, Rosalyn M. *And So I Sing*. New York: Warner Books, 1990. 33, 35.

Toll, Robert C. *Blacking Up: The Minstrel Show in Nineteenth Century America*. New York: Oxford University Press, 1974. 210-211.

Trotter, James M. *Music and Some Highly Musical People*. Boston: Lee and Shepard Publishers, 1881. Reprinted: Chicago: Afro-Am Press, 1969. 161-63, 173-74.

Jacquelyn Jackson

I

Edith J. Ingram

(1942-)

Judge

Edith Jacqueline Ingram was born in Hancock County, Georgia, near the town of Sparta on January 16, 1942. She is the daughter of Robert T. Ingram and Katherine (Hunt) Ingram. Ingram received a bachelor of science degree in education from Fort Valley (Georgia) State College in 1963. Upon her graduation she taught in the elementary schools of Georgia from 1963 to 1968: Moore Elementary School, Griffin, Georgia, 1963 to 1967, and the Hancock Central Elementary School, Sparta, in the 1967-1968 academic year.

She has been a member of the National and International Association of Probate Judges, the Ordinaries' Association of Georgia, the Macedonia Baptist Church, the Delta Sigma Theta Sorority, the Hancock County Democratic Club, the Sheriffs' Association of Georgia, the Hancock County Women's Club, the National Association for the Advancement of Colored People, the Fort Valley State College Alumni Association, and the County Officers' Association of Georgia. Ingram has held board memberships on the East Central Committee for Opportunity, the Hancock Concerned Citizens Club, the State (Georgia) Democratic Executive Committee, and the Georgia Council on Human Relations. She has also served as president of the Ogeechee-Lakeview Management Company beginning in the early 1970s.

Ingram received the Outstanding Courage in Southern Political Arena Plaque from the NAACP in 1969, the Community Leaders American in 1971, and the Certificate of Merit from the Booker T. Washington Business College of Birmingham, Alabama, in 1971. She was included in the *World Who's Who of Women* in 1973 and was named "Women of the Year" by the *Mirror* newspaper of Augusta, Georgia, in 1972.

Hancock County Receives First Black Judge

Edith J. Ingram became the first black judge in Georgia. This was quite a development for the South, as noted by Ingram:

> "The law" in the South has been viewed for many years by blacks as the action arm of the oppressor. . . . The three standard qualifications for becoming a law enforcement officer were (l) to be white, (2) to be strong enough to carry a revolver, and (3) to be mean enough to utter Nigger! Nigger! Nigger! In the past when a black individual found himself in a confrontation with whites, there was never an opportunity to call "the law" for help because a call for help meant a call for hell ("Black Judges in the South," 31-32).

She was appointed Judge of the Court Ordinary of Hancock County, Georgia, in 1969. Since 1973 she has been Judge of the Probate Court of Hancock County. Judge Ingram hears cases involving probate, guardianship, traffic, lunacy, and the administration of estates, performs marriages, is custodian of the vital records, supervises county, state, and federal elections, and issues writs of habeas corpus.

References

"Black Judges in the South." *Ebony* (March 1971): 31-34; 36, 38, 40.

The Ebony Success Library. Vol. 1. Chicago: Johnson Publishing Co., 1973. Contains photographs and portraits, p. 164.

"The Distaff Side of Politics." *Ebony* (December 1973): 48-50; 52-54. A photograph of Ingram appears on page 50.

Low, W. Augustus, and Virgil A. Clift, eds. *Encyclopedia of Black America*. New York: McGraw-Hill Book Co., 1981.

Who's Who Among Black Americans. 1st ed., 1975-1976. Chicago: Who's Who Among Black Americans, 1976.

Who's Who in America. 39th ed., 1976-1977. Chicago: Marquis Who's Who, Inc., 1976.

Casper LeRoy Jordan

J

Jacquelyne Johnson Jackson

(1932-)

Sociologist, civil rights activist

"To thine own self be true"—Jacquelyne Johnson Jackson has *presence*, the kind born of the power of being completely oneself and willing to pay the price. Jackson was interviewed at her home in Durham, North Carolina, on March 5, 1990. The attractive, divorced mother of one lives alone. Her home reflects her unique character and interests. One wall of the room contains enlarged nineteenth-century photographs of relatives. On another wall are photographs of her daughter, Viola, at different ages.

Nearby are a photograph of Jackson's mother, still lovely in her eighties, and a beautiful paper silhouette portrait of her father, now deceased. Less conspicuously placed is a framed plaque presenting her with the key to the city of Tuskegee, Alabama, and photographs taken during her involvement with the civil rights movement. There is a vibrant abstract painting, purchased from a former student who sold her art to help pay her college tuition. Prominent in the room is a piano with an open hymnal. Jackson has played the piano since taking lessons with Portia Washington Pittman, Booker T. Washington's eldest child and only daughter. The phone rang more than once during the interview, people calling about papers and conferences. Jackson was also awaiting the return of a graduate student, whom she was helping with a dissertation, and the arrival of her daughter and son-in-law, whom she was expecting for dinner. The swirl of activity, the generosity of spirit, the love and appreciation of family and friends, and the ability to focus on more than one project at a time are typical of Jackson's life.

Jacquelyne Johnson Jackson and her fraternal twin, Jeanne, were born on February 4, 1932, in Winston-Salem, North Carolina. Their mother, Beulah Crosby Johnson, insisted on making the trip from Tuskegee Institute in Macon County, Alabama, to North Carolina so that her children could be delivered by the same physician who delivered her. This physician was the first black physician in Winston-Salem. Her father, James A. Johnson, did not object to his wife's decision. When asked to identify what in her family background contributed to her accomplishments, Jackson said: "Education was emphasized as part of child-rearing by my parents. . . . I was taught to think and to think independently. . . . In my early environment, I did not experience the negativity associated with being female."

Jackson's parents were solidly upper middle-class and part of an academic elite. Her mother had earned a bachelor's degree in English and Latin at Shaw University. Her father, a native of Eudora, Arkansas, majored in accounting, commerce, and finance at New York University, where he earned a bachelor's and a master's degree. Her mother also later earned a master's degree. Her parents moved from New York to Tuskegee in 1931 when her father was hired to establish and direct Tuskegee Institute's School of Business.

The Tuskegee of Jackson's formative years was populated by leaders in many areas. The Tuskegee Civic Association, led by the prominent black sociologist Charles Goode Gomillion, was a leader in the fight against institutional racism in Macon County, Alabama. Long before the Voter's Registration Act of 1964, Jackson's parents and other members of the Tuskegee Civic Association had campaigned successfully to become registered voters. Well-known acquaintances of Jackson's family included George Washington Carver and Benjamin O. Davis, Jr., who in 1954 became the first black general in the United States Air Force. Having been reared in such an atmosphere, it is not surprising that Jackson went on to add a list of firsts to her achievements.

Jackson earned her B.S. (1953) and M.S. (1955) in sociology from the University of Wisconsin, Madison. In 1960, Jackson went on to become the first black woman to earn a Ph.D. in sociology from Ohio State University. She became the first black postdoctoral fellow at Duke University's Center for the Study of Aging and Human Development (1966-1968); the first full-time black faculty member at Duke University Medical School (1968); and the first black on the medical school faculty to be tenured (1971). Jackson was also the first woman chair of what is now the Association of Black Sociologists and one of the primary architects and only woman among the founders of the National Caucus on Black Aged. Among the academic awards in recognition of excellence that Jackson has received during her lifetime are a John Hay Whitney Fellowship, a one-year fellowship in epidemiology at the University of North Carolina, Chapel Hill, School of Public Health, and a National Science Foundation fellowship in cultural anthropology. Other honors conferred upon Jackson are a President's Citation from the Association of Homes for the Aging (1972), the Solomon

Carter Fuller Award of the Committee of Black Psychiatrists of the American Psychiatric Association (1978), the key to the city of Nashville, Tennessee, the Du Bois Award of the American Society of Black Sociologists, and a Great Black Women of Achievement Award from Clark College.

Jackson's Concerns for People Leads to Involvement

Jackson's work has always been connected to real people and real issues. For example, her special interest in minority aging grew out of an experience with her godfather's brother while at Ohio state. This gentleman, a Mr. Nofles, was a middle-class home owner. His wife's health began to fail, and within one year, Nofles was forced to sell their home and move into public housing. Nofles was also in declining health and had to have a leg amputated. One of Nofles's two children by his first marriage moved them to Plaquimines, Louisiana, to live with her. The other daughter lived in New Orleans. Mrs. Nofles eventually wound up in a racially-segregated ward in New Orleans's Charity Hospital. Blood was "segregated" at that time. Jackson was instrumental in getting students to donate "black" blood on Mrs. Nofles's behalf (Jackson interview). Watching the lives of this prosperous, happy couple tragically unravel made Jackson aware of the particular vulnerability of minority aged.

Jackson was involved formally and informally in the civil rights movement. While teaching at Jackson State College in Jackson, Mississippi, Jackson's home was a haven for members of the Congress of Racial Equality (CORE). When, in 1964, the Association of Social Science Teachers was forbidden to hold a conference at Jackson State as planned, for fear of creating racial unrest, Jackson sought and obtained the support of Charles Evers (brother of Medgar Evers), the Mississippi field director for the NAACP, to hold the meeting at another site in Jackson. Jackson took part in the 1963 March on Washington. On February 7, 1964, a pregnant Jackson was present when three hundred policemen surrounded the Jackson State campus. When tense students began to hurl bricks and stones at the police, the police responded by firing into the crowd. Three blacks were shot during the "Jackson State Riot." In the late 1960s, Jackson and some students were working with a group of black American children from a Head Start program in Halifax County, North Carolina. Jackson noted that the Head Start facility was not suitable for a simple picnic. Although officially desegregated, a municipal park in nearby Durham was off limits to its black citizens. Jackson quietly arranged for the picnic to be held in the municipal park. She recalls that the whites present evacuated the park when her small group arrived (Jackson interview). The picnic, however, broke the invisible barrier and afterwards the park was truly desegregated.

Jackson has to her credit an impressive array of publications and other scholarly activities. She is a former editor of the *Journal of Health and Social Behavior* (1972-1975) and of the *Journal of Minority Aging*, a publication she helped found. She is the author of *These Rights They Seek*—a study of the Tuskegee Civic Association, the Montgomery Improvement Association, and the Alabama Christian Movement for Human Rights—and a classic work on the issues faced by the elderly in minority groups, *Minorities and Aging*. Jackson is also the author of "But Where Are the Men?," one of the first articles in recent years to address the status of American black women vis-a-vis American black men. Jackson has also contributed to such journals as the *Gerontologist* and *Journal of Health and Social Behavior* (as the first and still only black editor of an organ of the American Sociological Association), and popular publications such as *Ebony* and *Essence*. A more extensive listing of Jackson's work may be found in *Who's Who Among Black Americans*.

What has distinguished Jackson's life as an academician is her insistence that her work be applied to improve the quality of life of people. As noted by Ruppert A. Downing, "Responsible research, which goes beyond the concept of manufacturing knowledge through scholarly pursuits, is an advocacy service when findings are brought to the attention of agencies and decision-makers. The work of Black researchers such as Jacquelyne Jackson . . . illustrates advocacy through responsible research" (292).

Federal legislation and national, state, and local programs and policies have been influenced by advocacy through responsible research. At the same time, Jackson warns against "romanticizing the Black family" and the problems it faces. An example of this kind of romanticizing, according to Jackson, would be the critics of Alice Walker's *The Color Purple*, who vehemently deny that characters such as Mister ever existed. Jackson has found that "the truth is not our enemy and that the social problems facing us can best be solved by critical thinking, honesty, and activism" (Jackson interview).

References

Clarke, Jacquelyne Johnson. *These Rights They Seek*. Washington, D.C.: Public Affairs Press, 1962.

Downing, Ruppert A. "Human Services and the Black Adult Life Cycle." In *Black Adult Development and Aging*. Ed. Reginald A. Jones. Berkeley, Calif.: Cobb and Henry Publishers, 1989.

Jackson, Jacquelyne Johnson. "But Where Are the Men?" *Black Scholar* 2 (March 1977): 30-41.

———. Interview with the author, 5 March 1990. Durham, North Carolina.

———. *Minorities in Aging*. Belmont, Calif.: Wadsworth Publishing Co., 1980.

———. Unpublished manuscript.

Who's Who Among Black Americans, 1990/1991. Detroit: Gale Research, 1990.

Photographs of Dr. Jackson may be obtained at Duke

University Medical School, Wadsworth Press, and Prentice Hall Press.

Linda Anderson Smith

Mae Howard Jackson

(1877-1931)

Sculptor

An artist who stuck to her roots and used her own people as models, Mae Howard Jackson broke with the artistic and social traditions of the times, and, according to W. E. B. Du Bois, paid a price for her integrity. But her sculpture helped break down some of the existing stereotypes concerning black Americans and black artists.

Born in Philadelphia in 1877, Mae Howard Jackson was the daughter of Floarada Howard and Sallie Dunham. She grew up in Philadelphia, was educated in its public schools, and graduated from Professor J. Liberty-Tadd's Art School, also in Philadelphia. Afterwards she enrolled in the Pennsylvania Academy of Fine Arts, the first black woman to win a scholarship there, and studied at the Academy for four years. There she worked under professors Chase, Gerafly, and Boyle. Professor Boyle especially was a source of inspiration as well as a great practical help for her. She graduated in 1899.

In 1902 she married William T. S. Jackson, a mathematics teacher and high school principal of Washington, D.C. She moved to Washington and remained at her 1816 16th Street N. W. address for many years. Here she maintained a studio and quietly pursued her career as an artist. Contrary to the popular practice of the time, she did not do further study in Europe, preferring to rely on her United States training, in this regard being many years ahead of her time. In so doing she rejected the tastes of the day, which were based on European models, and pursued the representation of frank and deliberate racialism in her sculpture.

Sculpture Portrays Black Types

Mae Howard Jackson found the range and variety of blacks wonderfully in need of expression, and it was her portrayal and interpretation of these individual differences that helped to eliminate racial stereotypes in art, through which the black had been seen.

Jackson executed portrait busts of Kelly Miller, Paul Laurence Dunbar, W. E. B. Du Bois, Francis Grimké, and others. Her *Mulatto Mother and Her Child* and *Head of a Child* confirmed her ability to express complex themes as well. There was no doubt as to her talent. When the *Head of a Child* and *Mulatto Mother and Her Child* were on exhibition at the Veerhoff Gallery in Washington in 1916, the Washington *Star* said of the latter that it was "a very remarkable and dramatic work, touching upon the mysteries of heredity in a way which is exceedingly striking," and added: "Her work has always shown promise, but these pieces now on exhibit indicate exceptional gifts, for they are not merely well modeled but individual and significant" (*Crisis*, July 1916, 115). Earlier, at a 1912 exhibit in the Veerhoff Gallery, her bust of F. J. Grimké was praised by Washington critics as being "well-constructed and skillfully modelled" (*Crisis* June 1912, 67). She also exhibited at the Emancipation Exhibition in 1913, the Corcoran Art Gallery in 1915, and the National Academy of Design in 1916. Her "forthright portraits of forthright men" were always favorably received, for her technical proficiency, in addition to her lyricism, gave her art a special distinction.

In 1927 the establishment of the Harmon Foundation and its awards and exhibitions provided important opportunities for black artists of the day. Its goals to encourage the black artist, develop black art, and promote black themes and subjects as a vital phase of the artistic expression of American art provided a major impetus. Winners of its awards are now the great names of black American art. Mae Howard Jackson received the 1928 bronze award for sculpture for her bust of Kelly Miller.

Jackson devoted much of her time to teaching art to young black students. Possibly the best known of those whom she influenced is Sargent Johnson. The orphaned nephew of Jackson's husband, he spent part of his early life in the Jackson household, and it is quite possible that his initial introduction to sculpture was through her.

Active as an artist during an especially difficult time of race relations in America and enjoying only sporadic success, Jackson found that her career was severely restricted by the prejudice of the time which intensified her natural tendency to be withdrawn and reclusive. After her death on July 12, 1931, at Long Beach, Long Island, W. E. B. Du Bois wrote in the October issue of *Crisis*:

> The death of Mae Howard Jackson is a loss to art. She was a sculptor with peculiar natural gifts. With her sensitive soul she needed encouragement and contacts and delicate appreciation. Instead of this, she ran into the shadows of the Color Line. . . . Thus the questing, unhappy soul of the Artist beat battered wings at the gates of day and wept alone. She accomplished enough to make her name firm in our annals and yet one must with infinite sorrow, think how much more she might have done had her spirit been free!

References

Bontemps, Jacqueline F. *Forever Free: Art by African-American Women 1862-1980*. Alexandria, Va.: Stephenson Inc., 1980.

Chase, Judith W. *Afro-American Arts and Craft*. New York: Van Nostrand Reinhold, 1971.

Crisis 4 (June 1912): 67; 12 (July 1916): 115; 34 (September 1927): 231; 40 (October 1931): 351. The September 1927 issue contains a photograph of Jackson.

Lewis, Samella S. *Art: African American*. New York: Harcourt, Brace Jovanovich, 1978.

Locke, Alain. *Negro Art: Past and Present*. New York: Arno Press, 1969.

Jean Elder Cazort

Mahalia Jackson

(1911/12-1972)

Singer

Mahalia Jackson has been acclaimed America's greatest gospel singer by world press and publicity. She is certainly the best known, with a career that included television, radio, and concerts. Her early repertoire leaned heavily upon songs of her Baptist beginnings such as "Amazing Grace," and "The Day is Past and Gone." She recorded her first record in May 1937 for Decca, "God's Gonna Separate the Wheat from the Tares," and the Baptist hymn "Keep Me Every Day." From that point on, Jackson's talent and deep-rooted faith ensured that she had the whole world in her hands. Wilfred Mellers, in *Gospel Women of the Night*, says: "The magnificent voice and the fervent faith are almost inseparable; a voice of such vibrancy, over so wide a range, creates a sound that is as all-embracing, as secure as the womb, from which singer and listener may be reborn."

Mahalia Jackson

Mahalia Jackson was born in New Orleans, Louisiana, on October 26, 1911 or 1912, and died of heart failure in Chicago on January 27, 1972. She was the daughter of Charity Clark, a laundress and maid, and Johnny Jackson, a Baptist preacher, barber, and longshoreman. Mahalia Jackson was raised without the presence of her father. Her mother died when Jackson was five. She was raised by an extended family of one brother, six aunts, and several half-brothers and sisters—children of her father. Her grandparents had been born into slavery and were laborers on Louisiana rice cotton plantations. Some of her relatives were entertainers and played valses, quadrilles, polkas, and mazurkas at parties for white people. They also played blues and rags in Ma Rainey's Circus.

The strong musical life of New Orleans in the early 1900s made a profound impression upon the young Mahalia Jackson. She lived next door to a Holiness church whose rhythms and instruments appealed to her growing musical development. Jackson knew well the standard hymn tradition of the Mount Moriah Baptist Church where her family worshipped. In addition to the sacred music, she was surrounded by music of the Mardi Gras, street vendors, and the bars and dance halls of New Orleans's black community. These were the early days of the birth of jazz in Storyville—a place where Louis Armstrong, King Oliver, and Jelly Roll Morton got their start in the 1920s.

During childhood, Jackson had to work to help support her family, even while she attended grammar school. Biographical accounts differ concerning the time at which she left school—the fourth or the eighth grade. An autobiography written with Evan McLeod Wylie in 1966, *Movin' On Up*, states that Mahalia Jackson moved from New Orleans to Chicago in 1928 at sixteen years of age (41). There she joined the Greater Salem Baptist Church and its choir. At Salem, she also began a career in gospel singing as a member of the Johnson Gospel Singers.

Jackson's real ambition after arriving in Chicago was to become a nurse; however, she worked as a laundress and studied beauty culture at Madame C. J. Walker's and the Scott Institute of Beauty Culture. With that training, Jackson began the first of her several business ventures. She opened a beauty shop.

In 1936 Jackson married Isaac Hockenhull, a college-educated entrepreneur. He encouraged her business aspirations but realized the great potential of her developing musical talent as a bigger source of income. A moving chapter of Laurraine Goreau's book, *Just Mahalia, Baby*, tells how Hockenhull, or ''Ike'' as he was called, persuaded Jackson to audition for the Works Projects Administration (WPA) Federal Theatre production of *Hot Mikado* by Gilbert and Sullivan. In a well-known story, Ike told Mahalia Jackson, ''Halie, nobody can touch your voice. You've got a future in singing. It's not right for you to throw it away hollering in churches. Woman, you want to nickel and dime all your life?'' (78). Auditioning reluctantly, Jackson sang the old spiritual, ''Sometimes I Feel Like a Motherless Child.'' Even though she won the audition, she turned down the offer as from Decca records to sing the blues. It was Hockenhull's desire to see Jackson turn to the more lucrative world of blues and popular music. Her steadfast refusal to sing the blues throughout her long career is documented in an exchange with Louis Armstrong. Returning to Chicago from a European tour in 1937, he tried to persuade Jackson, saying: ''Got you a spot with the band, make you some real green, get to move around. You don't have to show me, I *know* what you can do with the blues.'' She replied, ''I know what I can do with it too, baby, and that's not sing it. Child, I been reborn!'' (Gorean, 75).

Just as a subsequent marriage in 1965 to musician Sigmond Galloway, Jackson's marriage to Ike Hockenhull ended in divorce.

A historic moment in gospel music brought together Jackson and the ''Father of Gospel Music,'' composer Thomas A. Dorsey, also of Chicago in 1929. He became her musical advisor and accompanist from 1937 to 1946. Jackson sang Dorsey's songs in church programs and at conventions to promote the new songwriter's compositions. Their association in fourteen years of travel was highly successful. Her signature performance of ''Precious Lord Take My Hand,'' composed by Dorsey, became one of the most requested songs in her growing repertoire.

Vocal Style, Delivery and Repertoire Gain Fame for Jackson

The Jackson swinging beat coupled with an intense, expressive, and emotional performance met with resistance in many black churches. Some felt the music to be too jazzy—too worldly for church worship. Viv Broughton commented in his book, *Black Gospel:*

> The more sophisticated and middle class black people in the northern cities weren't quite so taken with the idea of shouts and moans and Holiness excesses. It was all so retrogressive to them, a harking back to old indignities and to old African roots they would quite happily prefer to leave behind (53).

However, by 1947 Jackson had become the official soloist of the National Baptist Convention. Besides the traditional Baptist hymns and Dorsey songs, she excelled in, and became nationally known through the songs of the Baptist preacher, the Reverend W. Herbert Brewster of Memphis. Her recording on Apollo Records of ''Move On Up A Little Higher'' sold more than two million copies in 1946. She featured songs of other notable Chicago songwriters who were markedly increasing in number under the influence of Dorsey and the rising tide for gospel music in churches, in concert, and on record. Among them, Jackson recorded ''I Can Put my Trust in Jesus'' and ''Let the Power of the Holy Ghost Fall On Me'' by Kenneth Morris, a selection that earned her the French Grand Prix du Disque in 1949. During the 1950s she was featured on the noted Chicago journalist Studs Terkel's television program. By 1954 she had her own radio and television show while owning a flower shop in Chicago and traveling to perform concerts.

Signing her most lucrative record contract with Columbia Records in 1954, Jackson's concerts were increasingly heard in concert halls with fewer in the churches. Likewise, her repertoire expanded to include arrangements with orchestra in place of the piano and organ that she previously used. From the Columbia releases came ''Down By the Riverside,'' ''Didn't It Rain,'' ''Joshua Fought the Battle of Jericho,'' ''He's Got the Whole World in His Hands,'' and that New Orleans staple, ''When the Saints Go Marching In.''

Among the notable achievements of Jackson, many are ''firsts'' for those in the gospel music field. She appeared in concert at Carnegie Hall in 1950 and at the Newport Jazz Festival in 1958.

Author Tony Heilbut notes Jackson's political concerns:

> During the sixties, Mahalia was a loyal friend and supporter of Dr. Martin Luther King. . . . He loved her music. . . . She began featuring 'We Shall Overcome' at concerts. At King's funeral Mahalia sang his last request, ''Precious Lord'' (103).

Earlier, Jackson was featured at the 1963 March on Washington rally at which King made his famous speech, ''I Have a Dream.'' On that occasion, she rocked thousands on the grounds of the Lincoln Memorial with the Reverend Brewster's classic, ''How I Got Over.'' Jackson strongly supported the civil rights movement and was a militant supporter of King and his Southern Christian Leadership Conference (SCLC). She also supported Chicago's Mayor Richard Daley and sang at the 1961 inauguration of President John F. Kennedy.

Jackson Experiences European Success

Jackson first toured Europe in 1952. Music critics there heralded her as the world's greatest gospel singer, a rare artist with a wide range. Jackson's recordings had been introduced in Europe by the French jazz historian, Hugh Panassie, who was impressed by her voice and singing style. With a weekly radio program on ORTF (all-France radio), Panassie played Jackson's recordings regularly. The radio show was widely listened to in Great Britain and in other countries in Western Europe. In Paris she was called ''The Angel of Peace'' and became widely celebrated throughout the continent, singing to sold-out and standing-room-only crowds. At London's famed Royal Albert Hall, critic Max Jones spoke of her charm. "When she dances those little church steps at the end of a rocking number, you need a heart of stone to remain unsmiling" (Broughton, 54).

Jackson told Jones in one of hundreds of interviews for the press, "I don't work for money. I sing because I love to sing" (Broughton, 56). Her concerts consisted of seventeen to twenty selections even when a crowded schedule called for concerts on successive nights. She toured Europe in 1952, 1962, and 1963-1964. She also sang in Africa, Japan, and India in 1970. She met heads of state and royalty, including Prime Minister Indira Gandhi and members of the royal family in Japan.

The many historic accounts of Jackson's life usually speak of her generosity to family, friends, and young people. She received the Silver Dove Award "for work of quality doing the most good for international understanding." Jackson, according to biographer Laurraine Goreau, had an unfulfilled dream to build a temple where young people might study gospel music, religion, and academics. She established a Mahalia Jackson Scholarship Foundation for young people who wished to attend college.

Among the friends of Mahalia Jackson were most of her contemporaries in the gospel music field: Roberta Martin, Sallie Martin, Willie Mae Ford Smith, J. Robert Bradley, Robert Anderson, officials of Thomas A. Dorsey's gospel music convention, including the Ward Singers, and Rosetta Tharpe. Jackson encouraged the careers of Della Reese, Aretha Franklin, and James Cleveland. She had scores of friends throughout the country and around the world, among them radio and television personalities such as Ed Sullivan, Dinah Shore, Duke Ellington, Louis Armstrong, Percy Faith, Harry Belafonte, Albertina Walker, Brother John Sellers, and New York promoter Joe Bostic, who presented Jackson at Carnegie Hall and at his spectacularly successful gospel concerts at Randall's Island. She knew the Lyndon Johnsons, John F. Kennedys, and Harry S. Truman.

Tony Heilbut devotes a complete chapter in his book, *The Gospel Sound*, to "Mahalia the Queen." He calls her "the vocal, physical, spiritual symbol of gospel music. Her large (260 pounds), noble proportions, her face, contorted into something resembling the Mad Duchess, her soft speaking voice and hugh, rich contralto, all made her gospel's one superstar" (89). Henry Pleasants, author of *The Great American Popular Singers,* stated: "She would land on a note or a word she particularly liked, or wished to emphasize, and mouth it, or repeat it, or repeat parts of it, or shake it, or bite into it in a manner which often reminded me of a terrier puppy playing tug-o'-war with an old sock or shoe (201.) In a later entry in the *New Grove Dictionary of American Music*, which Pleasants coauthored with gospel music historian Horace C. Boyer, it was stated:

> Jackson was not the first, and possible not the finest, gospel singer, but it was largely through her compelling contralto voice and her personality that people of all races throughout the world came to respect gospel music as an idiom distinct from classical black spirituals (524).

Selected songs of Mahalia Jackson are published in *Favorites of Mahalia Jackson, the World's Greatest Gospel Singer* (New York: Hill and Range Songs, 1955). Some of her noted recordings include: *In the Upper Room with Mahalia Jackson,* EMI 335X 1753; *Mahalia Jackson Recorded Live in Europe* (1961), Columbia Records C88526 LP; *Mahalia Jackson—World's Greatest Gospel Singer and Falls-Jones Ensemble,* Columbia Records CL 2004, CS8759; *Mahalia Jackson's Latest Hits,* Columbia CL1473 CS 8264; and *Silent Night— Songs for Christmas,* Columbia CL1903, CS8703.

References

Broughton, Viv. *Black Gospel.* New York: Sterling, 1985.

Current Biography Yearbook. New York: H. W. Wilson, 1957. Includes photograph.

Dahl, Linda. *Stormy Weather.* New York: Pantheon, 1984.

Goreau, Laurraine. *Just Mahalia, Baby.* Gretna, La.: Pelican, 1975. Includes photographs.

Heilbut, Tony. *The Gospel Sound.* New York: Limelight Editions, 1971.

Jackson, Mahalia with Evan McLeod Wylie. *Movin' On Up.* New York: Hawthorne Books, 1966. Includes photographs.

Levine, Lawrence W. "Mahalia Jackson." *Notable American Women: The Modern Period.* Cambridge: Harvard University Press, 1980.

Low, W. Augustus, and Virgil A. Clift, eds. *Encyclopedia of Black America.* New York: McGraw-Hill, 1981.

Mellers, Wilfred. *Angels of the Night: Popular Female Singers of Our Time.* New York: Basil Blackwell, 1986.

Pleasants, Henry, *The Great American Popular Singers.* Saint Louis: Fireside Books, 1985.

Pleasants, Henry, and Horace Boyer. "Mahalia Jackson." *New Grove Dictionary of American Music.* London: Macmillan, 1986.

Southern, Eileen. *Biographical Dictionary of Afro-American and African Musicians.* Westport, Conn.: Greenwood Press, 1982.

Pearl Williams Jones

Nell Jackson

(1929-1988)

Athlete, coach, educator

At the age of fourteen, a young, talented black American girl was lured away from basketball, tennis, and swimming into track and field. She subsequently became an Olympic athlete in that sport, a national coach, an administrator, an educator, and a mentor. Nell Cecelia Jackson was born in Athens, Georgia, on July 1, 1929. Wilhemina G. Jackson and the late Burnette L. Jackson, Sr., had two other children—Burnette L. Jackson, Jr., and Thomas O. Jackson. Nell Jackson died on April 1, 1988, in Vestal, New York, after a short illness.

The Jackson family moved to Tuskegee, Alabama, where Jackson spent most of her early life. She graduated from Tuskegee High School and moved on in 1951 to earn her bachelor of science degree in physical education from Tuskegee University. Nell Jackson continued into graduate studies and in 1953 received her master of science degree in physical education from Springfield College. Jackson's next step on her education ladder involved 1955 summer study at the University of Oslo, Norway. She finally capped her journey into higher education in 1962 by receiving her doctor of philosophy degree in physical education from the University of Iowa.

As a young girl, Nell Jackson specialized in the 220-dash. As she explains:

> I was a 220 yard and 200 meter specialist. Some girls ran the 100 or long-jumped, in addition to running the 200. But I stayed with the 200 meters, or 220 yards, which is a few feet longer. There weren't really all that many choices at that time. The 220 was the longest event a woman could run then. There were a lot of so-called "studies" around then showing how "dangerous" it was for women to run longer distances, that they would upset their chemical and physical make up. It didn't make a great deal of sense to me, but there was nothing I could so about it. So I ran the 220 (Bortstein, 156).

Nell Jackson made the 1948 United States Olympic team to London, but did not place in her two events—the two-hundred meter and the four-hundred-meter relay. In 1949, however, she set an American record of 24.2 seconds in the two-hundred meter, a record that was to stand for six years. She was the National AAU champion in the two-hundred meter in 1949, 1950, and 1951. In the first Pan-American games held in 1951 in Buenos Aires, Nell Jackson won a silver medal in the two-hundred meter and a gold medal in the four-hundred-meter relay. From 1944 through 1952, Nell Jackson placed sixth or better in the two-hundred-meter events in which she participated.

Jackson's coaching career began at Tuskegee University, where she was head track and field coach from 1954 through 1962. Her outstanding work brought her to the attention of the Olympic organization, which in 1956 gave her the distinction of becoming the first black woman head coach of the women's Olympic track and field team. Nell Jackson went on to coach the 1969 United States women's track and field team, which participated in the World University Games. In 1972 she also coached the United States track and field team that participated in Martinique and the United States women's Olympic track and field team.

Nell Jackson had many talented students: Mildred McDaniels, gold medal winner, high jump, 1956 Olympics; Neomia Rodgers, high jump, member 1960 Olympic team; Maeoper West, Association for Intercollegiate Athletics for Women (AIAW) track and field champion and member of the 1973 World University Games; and Sue Latter, 1977 winner of the Athletic Congress (TAC) eight-hundred meter, third AIAW, and fifth World Cup.

Nell Jackson's career as a manager spanned twenty-three years. She began in 1964 as assistant manager of the United States women's national track and field team. She moved on to manager in 1965 and held this post in 1966, 1972, and 1977. In 1979 and 1982 she served as the manager of the Senior National Team.

From 1953 through 1960, Jackson was a physical education instructor at her alma mater, Tuskegee University. Upon completion of her doctoral work in 1962, she was rehired as an assistant professor. In 1960 she became a research assistant and in 1961 a graduate teaching assistant at the University of Iowa in Iowa City. She next worked, from 1963 through 1965, as an assistant professor of physical education at Illinois State University in Normal. In 1965 Nell Jackson moved to the University of Illinois in Urbana-Champaign and stayed there until 1973 as an associate professor. In 1973 she became the first black American assistant athletic director, women's track coach, and professor of physical education at Michigan State University. Jackson's last post, from 1981 through 1988, was as director of physical education and intercollegiate athletics at the State University of New York (SUNY) at Binghamton.

Nell Jackson left a legacy of research, scholarly publications, and creative endeavors. She published more than twenty articles, papers, and chapters in professional journals and books. Her 1968 textbook, *Track and Field for Girls and Women*, was a significant contribution to the literature of women's athletics. Jackson also produced the film *Grace in Motion* and was responsible for a number of widely-used National Collegiate Athletic Association (NCAA) instructional film loops.

Professional and public service involvement was an important part of Nell Jackson's life. In 1965, she organized the Illini Track Club for Girls and in 1963 and 1968 coordinated the track and field sections for the first and fifth National Institute on Girls Sports.

In the 1970s she was a member of the Urbana, Illinois, YWCA corporation board and the Lansing, Michigan, YWCA board of directors. This line of involvement continued until her death. From 1982 through 1988, she was a member of the Binghamton, New York, Urban League board of directors.

Nell Jackson served as chairperson of several important committees. From 1968 through 1971 she held this post on the AAU Women's Track and Field Committee. Jackson was also Division of Girls and Women in Sports (DGWS) liaison chairperson from 1966 through 1968 and the track and field Principles and Techniques of Officiating chairperson from 1964 through 1966.

Nell Jackson's committee involvement also was extensive. From 1969 through 1972 she was a member of the board of directors of the United States Olympic Committee. She was also, from 1964 through 1969, a member of the women's board of the United States Olympic Development Committee. From 1966 through 1968, she was an advisory member of the United States Olympic Games Planning Committee and from 1985 through 1988 a member of the International Relations Committee of the United States Olympic Committee.

Such an illustrious career seldom goes unrewarded. Nell Jackson received many awards and honors. Among the most outstanding were: Alumni Merit Award—Tuskegee University, 1973; Tuskegee University Athletic Hall of Fame, 1974; National Alumni Merit Award—Tuskegee University, 1977; National Association for Girls and Women in Sports (NAGWS) Presidential Citation, 1977; member of the Black Athletes Hall of Fame, 1977; one of five United States educators selected to attend the International Olympic Academy, Greece, 1980; AIAW Track and Field Sports Committee Chairperson, 1978-1981; vice-president of the Athletic Congress, 1979-1982; chairperson AIAW Ethics and Eligibility Committee, 1982; Department of Physical Education Alumni Merit Award, the University of Iowa, 1984; secretary of the Athletic Congress, 1985; National Track & Field Hall of Fame; 1989, Robert Giegengack Award, 1989 (the first to be given posthumously).

Nell Jackson was a member of the American Alliance of Health, Physical Education, Recreation and Dance, the American College of Sports Medicine, and the Athletic Congress.

Nell Jackson was teacher and mentor to many outstanding physical educators and administrators. These include: Dorothy L. Richey of Slippery Rock University; Barbara Jacket, 1992 United States Olympic coach; and Annie Croom of West Georgia College.

What has been published to date on Nell Jackson includes, almost exclusively, the stride chronologies found in award citations and obituaries. Nothing is yet available that touches on the salient fact that Nell Jackson was a black woman who successfully operated in a predominantly white, male-dominated sports environment.

References

Ashe, Arthur. *A Hard Road to Glory: A History of the Afro-American Athlete Since 1946*. New York: Warner, 1988.

Bortstein, Larry. *After Olympic Glory: The Lives of Ten Outstanding Medalists*. New York: F. Warne, 1987.

Contributions of Black Women in America. Vol. 1. Ed. Marianna W. Davis. Columbia, S.C.: Kenday Press, 1982.

Davenport, Joanna. "The Lady was a Sprinter—Nell C. Jackson." *TAC Women's Track & Field Newsletter* 4 (April, 1988).

Green, Tina Sloan, Carole A. Oglesby, Alpha Alexander, and Nikki Franke. *Black Women in Sport*. Reston, Va.: AAHPERD, 1981.

"Nell Jackson Inducted into Hall of Fame." *NAGWS News* 17 (Winter 1990). 1.

Iva Gloudon

Rebecca Cox Jackson

(1795-1871)

Religious visionary, religious leader, spiritual autobiographer

Rebecca Cox Jackson was a religious visionary, itinerant preacher, and spiritual autobiographer. A free-born African-American woman living in Philadelphia, she experienced a religious awakening in 1830 at the age of thirty-five that brought her to challenge the African Methodist Episcopal (AME) church of her upbringing. She was active initially in praying bands influenced by the early phase of the Holiness movement within Methodism. Eventually she joined and rose to leadership in the United Society of Believers in Christ's Second Appearing (Shakers), a religious socialism that embodied her own values. She founded a small, predominantly black and female Shaker family in Philadelphia on the eve of the Civil War.

Though Jackson died in 1871, this family lived on for another thirty or forty years. Remnants were still in existence when W. E. B. Du Bois studied the black churches in

Philadelphia's Seventh Ward between 1896 and 1898 (W. E. B. Du Bois, *The Philadelphia Negro,* 1899; reprinted, New York, Schocken Books, 1967). Shaker records indicate that the Philadelphia community was still in existence in some form as late as 1908, though in 1896 Rebecca Perot and several other elderly sisters rejoined the Watervliet, New York, Shaker community where Jackson and Perot had lived in the 1840s.

Jackson achieved a religious leadership role largely through visionary experience and her ability to communicate such experience to others. Like several other nineteenth-century African-American women preachers whose autobiographical writings have recently been reprinted, she moved from exhortation and prayer in private homes into a career of itinerant ministry, following an inner voice that she felt as direct contact with the divine. (For a selection of nineteenth-century African-American women preacher's autobiographies, see William Andrews, ed., *Sisters of the Spirit,* Bloomington: Indiana University Press, 1986.)

Jackson was unusual among this group of women preachers, however, in her intense concentration on inner reality over outer reality, and in her insistence that celibacy was an essential component of the "holy life" required by Christ's model. The Shakers attracted her initially because they also believed that celibacy and confession of sins were prerequisite to beginning a redeemed life on earth.

In confronting discriminatory treatment of blacks within Shakerism and seeing the necessity of black religious leadership, Jackson's career can be compared with that of Richard Allen, who founded African Methodism after rejecting segregationist practices within white Methodism. Though the religious institution Jackson founded has not survived, she has left as a permanent legacy a rich body of spiritual autobiography, published for the first time more than a hundred years after her death.

Jackson's writings, which were collected in 1980 in *Gifts of Power,* trace her inner life as a "new creature," from a dramatic awakening experience during a thunderstorm at age thirty-five through a thirty-year pilgrimage on which the major landmarks are "dreams and visions and revelations and gifts." She regarded her writings, as she did her life, as a medium through which the divine will express itself—"I am only a pen in His hand," she said (107).

Sketchy biographical information can be collected from allusions in Rebecca Cox Jackson's surviving spiritual writings. She was born on February 15, 1795, in Hornstown, Pennsylvania, about ten miles outside Philadelphia. Her mother, Jane Wisson or Wilson (maiden name unknown) was married at least twice, and probably three times, before her death in 1808. Nothing is known of Jackson's father. At the time of her mother's death, the thirteen-year-old Rebecca Cox was probably taken in by her elder brother, Joseph, a local pastor at the Philadelphia Bethel AME Church.

Public Career as Preacher and Shaker Eldress Develops

At the time of her conversion experience in 1830 she was married to Samuel S. Jackson, and the childless couple was living in Joseph Cox's household. Rebecca cared for Joseph's four children and earned her own living by taking in sewing. After her dramatic conversion and sanctification experiences, Jackson established herself as a spiritually talented member of a Covenant Meeting, composed primarily of AME church members who believed in the possibility of living a life of "Christian perfection."

Jackson and her spiritual sister, Mary Peterson, wife of AME preacher Daniel Peterson, started a small weekly meeting of their own. These meetings began to attract large crowds almost immediately, and they were visited by Morris Brown, Richard Allen's immediate successor as bishop of the AME church, in response to complaints that Rebecca Jackson was acting improperly as a woman "leading the men." (Because she refused to become a formal member of the church without receiving explicit divine instruction to do so, she was seen by AME authorities as intent on "chopping up the churches.") Bishop Brown was reportedly satisfied, after visiting Jackson's meeting, that "if ever the Holy Ghost was in any place it was in that meeting" (106).

Jackson experienced and recorded in her writings a great variety of spiritual gifts, including the ability to heal by prayer, prophetic dreams and semi-waking visions, and infallible guidance in her decisions by an audible inner voice. By 1833 her inner voice had assured her of her calling as a preacher, and she began her public career in the town of Marcus Hook, Pennsylvania, on the Delaware River, while on a visit there in 1833.

Increasingly frustrated by her dependence on her literate brother to help her with correspondence, Jackson prayed to God for the gift of reading and writing. Literacy had an especially important meaning to Jackson, because she was "the only child of my mother that had not learning" (107). Apparently her child-care responsibilities as the eldest surviving resident girl child in her mother's large and widely spaced family had made schooling impossible. Of her prayer for the gift of reading and writing, Jackson said:

> And when I looked on the word, I began to read. And when I found I was reading I was frightened—then I could not read one word. I closed my eyes again in prayer and then opened my eyes, began to read. So I done, until I read the chapter (108).

The achievement of literacy gave her the independent access to past revelations of the divine will that enabled her to defend her doctrine and practices of holy living against critical male clergy. Her spiritual autobiography records many instances of intense opposition to women preaching in general, and to her specific testimony against "the flesh." The opposition came from AME ministers, her husband, and even her once-idolized brother. She wrote of this period: "I had started to go to the promised land, and I wanted husband, brother and all the world to go with me, but my mind was made up to stop for none" (87).

When accusations that she preached a "false doctrine" reached epidemic proportions in Philadelphia in 1837, she demanded a formal trial for heresy from Methodist and Presbyterian ministers, in her own house, in the presence of "three or four of the mothers of the church." Apparently the ministers refused her request, and her final break with the AME church and Joseph Cox occurred at this time.

Throughout the later 1830s and early 1840s, Jackson traveled through Pennsylvania, northern Delaware, New Jersey, southern New England, and New York state, testifying to her own experience and urging others to lead a perfectly sin-free celibate life. She was attracted to the celibate, peaceable, spiritualistic Shaker community after first attending a meeting at the Watervliet community near Albany in 1836. She and her friend and disciple, Rebecca Perot, joined the society in June 1847. They lived in the South Family at Watervliet until July 1851, at which time they returned to Philadelphia.

Prior to her association with the Shakers, Jackson's image of her interior religious instructor and guide, like her image of God, was male. However, when first visiting the Watervliet Shakers in 1843, Jackson was impressed with a sequence of visions in which the Deity's female face appeared to her for the first time. The Shaker communities were settings in which such visions earned respect rather than ridicule or opposition.

Shakers believed that the Christ Spirit had descended twice in history into human form. The first incarnation, in Jesus of Nazareth, marked the beginning of the work of human redemption. The second incarnation, in Ann Lee of Manchester, completed the redemptive process and ushered in the promised millennium. This theology was originally developed in response to attacks on a religious society headed by a woman, Ann Lee (1736-1784).

According to the mid-century Shaker theology Jackson found so compelling, the godhead was actually composed of four aspects: the Almighty Father; a Holy Mother Wisdom who was the Almighty's coeternal female partner; the redeeming Son; and an equally necessary redeeming Daughter. Jackson's writings include impressive accounts of her visions of the Shaker's "mother in Divinity":

> At night we went to meeting and while they were worshipping God, I saw the head and wings of their blessed Mother in the center of the ceiling over their heads. She appeared in a glorious color. Her face was round like a full moon, with the glory of the sun reflecting from Her head. . . . And what a Mother's look she gave me. And at that look, my soul was filled with love and a motion was in my body, like one moving in the waves of the sea (168).

Throughout Jackson's first residence at Watervliet, her skills as a public speaker were recognized by the white Shaker leadership as very unusual. She preached frequently in the Sabbath meetings that were open to the non-Shaker public, and Shaker family records note her impressive performances: "Sister Rebecca Jackson rose up and spoke beautiful of the good way of God" (10 September 1848 entry, Watervliet Journal, V-B, 33).

But Jackson's writings also reveal that she came to develop a critical perspective on Shakerism's failure to take the gospel of Ann Lee to the African-American community. As sectional tensions heightened in the decade prior to the Civil War, Jackson seems to have felt the need to reestablish spiritual connections with the Philadelphia black community in particular. She noted in her diary in July 1848, "I dreamed that I was going south to feed the people." In February 1850:

> I received an encouraging work in confirmation to the word of God which He gave to me concerning my people, which work He has called me to do. And when the time arrives, no man can hinder me from doing it through the help of God (219).

Independent Shaker Family Established

Jackson and Rebecca Perot left Watervliet in 1851, and the Shakers believed she had turned her back on the Shaker way of life. Yet Jackson never doubted the essential truths of Shakerism as she understood it, and after several years in Philadelphia, during which time she and Perot experimented with seance spiritualism, she decided to return to the Watervliet community. During her second residence at Watervliet (1858-1859) she again negotiated with Shaker leadership about her mission to Philadelphia and successfully established her right to lead an independent Shaker "out family" there.

Little is known of Jackson's life after this time. In September 1862 her diary records her joy at the end of slavery:

> My cries to Almighty God, both day and night, were a continual prayer for the deliverance of my people from both spiritual and temporal bondage. I have now lived to hear the Proclamation of President Abraham Lincoln, framed in September in the year of our Lord 1862, that on the first of January 1863, all the slaves in the United States shall be set at liberty, and I say, "May God Almighty grant [a prosperous issue]" (282).

Nothing is recorded about how her small Shaker family fared during the Civil War or its immediate aftermath. The date of her last surviving diary entry is 1864. She died on May 24, 1871, and according to one Shaker historian, her body was taken to the New Lebanon, New York, Shaker community to be buried (Williams, 5).

A year after Jackson's death, Shakers from the Watervliet and New Lebanon communities made a missionary visit to the small surviving Philadelphia family. At that time the membership was predominantly black and predominantly female. A core group of the Sisters lived together in a single house and supported themselves by daywork, as laundresses or seamstresses in the city. Other nonresident Believers joined them in their evening religious meetings (New Lebanon Records, 1871-1905, 1916, Vol. 4, quoted in Williams, 5).

Regular visits between Watervliet and the Philadelphia family took place throughout the 1870s and 1880s, and it was through this renewed communication that Jackson's extant writings were gathered, copied, and preserved in Shaker manuscript archives. (The New Lebanon Shaker historian Alonzo Hollister gathered up all of Rebecca Jackson's surviving writings from Rebecca Perot, and copied them together into a manuscript anthology. See References.) In 1896 Rebecca Perot returned to Watervliet with three other aging Philadelphia Sisters. Perot died in 1901 and was buried in the Watervliet cemetery.

Jackson Known as Visionary Writer

> Friday morning, December 24, 1847, I received the following dream or vision. I thought I was in Philadelphia, at the corner of Race and 10th Streets, standing at the northeast. And at the southwest corner were two infants playing in the gutter. One was trying to destroy the other, by holding it under the mud and water. I stood and hallooed, and then ran and took up the child that was under. And it was lifeless. I restored it to life. Holding it in my left hand, I went south and then east, and came to my own door. Before entering, I looked up and saw a large body of stars in the heavens over my head. They were brilliant, and some were larger in size than any I had ever seen. I looked east, and saw a train coming from that direction to meet them. I looked north, and saw a body of them coming from the north, in the form of a diamond. They were large and bright. A company of horsemen moved before them, bearing their course south. On the southwest corner of the first rank rode a Great One on a large white horse, waving a banner or a sword. And he commanded the army. When these met the other two bodies of stars that were over the house where I was, they began to shower down out of themselves sparks of light upon the house and upon me. These sparks were like silver, when it reflects the sun from its surface. I then awoke (209-210).

As this sample visionary dream shows, Rebecca Jackson's spiritual writings describe an inner world to which few in the modern secular world have access. In her visions and dreams, laws of nature are violated with ease. She soars, lifts, leaps easily into the sky, flies through the air, looks down from a great height. She is given sudden, integrating flashes of understanding about the nature of the physical universe in visual form. She can leave the physical body behind, hold conversations with the angels, tour symbolic landscapes, and reenter the body again. Jackson's ability to record visionary experience was extraordinary. Her fidelity to the seemingly senseless or mysterious details of dream happenings must surely be related to her conviction that in writing, as in living, absolute loyalty to the guiding inner authority was required. As she asserts when describing one vision that she anticipates "may appear strange" to the reader, "I was told at the beginning to write the things which I seen and heard, and write them *as* I seen and heard" (170).

Rebecca Jackson's spiritual writing has received growing literary-critical recognition, beginning with Alice Walker's review of *Gifts of Power* in the *Black Scholar* in 1982:

> *Gifts of Power* is an extraordinary document. It tells us much about the spirituality of human beings, especially of the interior spiritual resources of our mothers, and, because of this, makes an invaluable contribution to what we know of ourselves" (Walker, "Gifts of Power," reprinted in *In Search of Our Mother's Gardens*, 78).

It has also been an important addition to texts used in broadening the definition of the "canon" of American literature to include women's personal and religious writings. Scholars in the fields of religion, church history, and African-American history have also begun to use Rebecca Jackson's writings as source material for a history of African-American women's spirituality and for developing new perspectives on Christian theology. Jackson's spirituality has been described as "worthy of consideration alongside classic works of female mystics such as Juliana of Norwich and Saint Teresa of Avila" (Foster, 109). Gloria T. Hull writes:

> One does not doubt that Jackson's Christianity is real. Nevertheless, her functional modes are reminiscent of the way Black/Third World people and women have practiced ancient, outlawed traditions behind more acceptable facades. That she was still called 'crazy' and 'witch' hints at the loneliness and ostracism which the keeping of her gifts entailed—an outsider status rendered even more acute by her race, sex, and class ("Review Essay: Rebecca Cox Jackson and the Uses of Power," 204).

References

Braxton, Joanne. *Black Women Writing Autobiography*. Philadelphia: Temple University Press, 1989.

Foster, Lawrence. Review Essay, *Church History* 53 (March 1984): 109-110.

Gates, Henry Louis. *The Signifying Monkey: A Theory of African-American Literary Criticism* (Oxford: Oxford University Press, 1988).

Hull, Gloria T. "Rebecca Cox Jackson and the Uses of

Power.'' *Tulsa Studies in Women's Literature* 1 (Fall 1982): 203-209.

Humez, Jean M. ''My Spirit Eye: Some Functions of Spiritual and Visionary Experience in the Lives of Five Black Women Preachers, 1810-1880.'' In *Women and the Structure of Society: Selected Research from the Fifth Berkshire Conference on the History of Women.* Eds. Barbara Harris and Jo Ann McNamara. Durham, North Carolina: Duke University Press, 1984.

———. ''Visionary Experience and Power: The Career of Rebecca Cox Jackson.'' In *Black Apostles At Home and Abroad.* Eds. David M. Wills and Richard Newman. Boston: G. K. Hall, 1982.

Humez, Jean M., ed. *Gifts of Power: The Writings of Rebecca Jackson, Black Visionary, Shaker Eldress.* Amherst: University of Massachusetts Press, 1980. Photograph, p. 63.

McKay, Nellie. ''Nineteenth-Century Black Women's Spiritual Autobiographies: Religious Faith and Self-Empowerment.'' In *Interpreting Women's Lives: Feminist Theory and Personal Narratives.* Ed. The Personal Narrative Group. Bloomington: Indiana University Press, 1989. 139-54.

New Lebanon Records, 1871-1905. Vol. 4, 1916. Manuscript in Shaker Museum, Old Chatham, N.Y. Quoted in Richard E. Williams. ''Mother Rebecca Jackson: One of the Black Shakers in Philadelphia.'' *Shaker Messenger* 1 (Spring 1979): 5.

Sasson, Diane. ''Life As Vision: The Autobiography of Mother Rebecca Jackson.'' *The Shaker Spiritual Narrative.* Knoxville: University of Tennessee Press, 1983. 158-88.

Setta, Suan M. ''When Christ is a Woman: Theology and Practice in the Shaker Tradition.'' In *Unspoken Worlds: Women's Religious Lives.* Eds. Nancy Auer Falk and Rita M. Gross. Belmont, Calif.: Wadsworth Pub. Co., 1989. 221-32.

Walker, Alice. ''Gifts of Power: The Writings of Rebecca Cox Jackson.'' *Black Scholar* 2 (September-October 1982): 64-67. Reprinted in *In Search of Our Mother's Gardens* (New York: Harcourt Brace Jovanovich, 1983): 71-82.

Watervliet Family Journal 10 September 1848 entry, V-B: 33. Shaker Manuscript Collection, Western Reserve Historical Society.

Williams, Richard E. *Called and Chosen: The Story of Mother Rebecca Jackson and the Philadelphia Shakers.* Metuchen, N.J.: Scarecrow Press, 1981.

———. ''Mother Rebecca Jackson: One of the Black Shakers in Philadelphia.'' *Shaker Messenger* 1 (Spring 1979).

Collections

The manuscripts from which *Gifts of Power* was edited include an autographed version of Jackson's incomplete autobiography, 146 pages long, unparagraphed and unpunctuated. This manuscript is owned by the Berkshire Athenaeum, in the Pittsfield Public Library, Pittsfield, Massachusetts. The other autographed manuscript located to date is a short booklet of Rebecca Perot's accounts of dreams along with a few of Rebecca Jackson's own dreams, in the Shaker Manuscript Collection of the Western Reserve Historical Society, Cleveland, Ohio.

The diary material in *Gifts of Power* has not been found in Jackson's handwriting, but only in edited transcriptions by Shaker historians based on writings that may not have survived. There is a rough draft anthology of Jackson's writings compiled by Alonzo Hollister in the Western Reserve Historical Society; and a ''fair copy'' produced by a later hand, in the Library of Congress Shaker Collection.

Jean McMahon Humez

Shirley Ann Jackson

(1946-)

Physicist

Shirley Ann Jackson is one of the most distinguished young black American scientists. She has made important theoretical contributions to several areas of physics; these include the three-body scattering problem, charge density waves in layered compounds, polaronic aspects of electrons in the surface of liquid helium films, and the optical and electronic properties of semiconductor strained layer superlattices.

Born in Washington, D.C., on August 5, 1946, Shirley Ann Jackson was the second daughter of Beatrice and George Jackson. She credits her continuing interest in science to the help provided by her father in the construction of science projects and the strong belief in education held by both parents. In addition, excellent mathematics teachers and an accelerated program in mathematics and science at Roosevelt High School provided a strong background that prepared her for the rigors of college. Of even more importance were the healthy environments of the home and secondary schools; they provided the necessary basis for the intellectual sharpness and psychological toughness needed to pursue a career in scientific research.

Graduating from Roosevelt High School in 1964 as valedictorian, she entered the Massachusetts Institute of Technology, where she received the S.B. degree in physics in 1968. In 1973 she became the first black woman to earn a Ph.D. from MIT; her research was in theoretical elementary particle physics and was directed by James Young, the first full-time tenured black professor in the physics department.

After earning her doctorate, she was a research associate (1973-1974, 1974-1976) at the Fermi National Accelerator Laboratory in Batavia, Illinois, and a visiting scientist (1974-1975) at the European Center for Nuclear Research in Geneva, Switzerland. At both places she worked on theories of strongly interacting elementary particles. Since 1976, Jackson has been at AT&T Bell Laboratories, Murray Hill, New Jersey, where she has done research on various topics relating to theoretical material sciences.

To date, Jackson has received ten scholarships, fellowships, and grants. They include: the Martin Marietta Aircraft Company Scholarship (1964-1968) and Fellowship (1972-1973); a Prince Hall Masons Scholarship (1964-1968); a National Science Foundation Traineeship (1968-1971); and Ford Foundation Advanced Study Fellowship (1971-1973) and Individual Grant (1974-1975). She has studied at the International School of Subnuclear Physics, "Ettore Majorana," in Erice, Sicily (August 1973), and the Ecole d'été de Physique Theorique, Les Houches, France (July-August 1978).

Shirley Jackson has received numerous honors, including election as a fellow of the American Physical Society (November 1986), selection as "Woman of the Year" by the Lenape (Monmouth County, N.J.) Professional and Business Women (October 1985), the CIBA-GEIGY "Exceptional Black Scientists" Poster Series (1981) and the Karl Taylor Compton Award of MIT (1970). Her professional society memberships include the American Physical Society, the American Association for the Advancement of Science, Sigma Xi, and the National Society of Black Physicists, of which she is a past president (1980-1982).

In 1985, New Jersey Governor Thomas Kean appointed Jackson to the New Jersey Commission on Science and Technology. She was re-appointed and confirmed for a five-year term in 1989. She has also served on committees of the National Academy of Sciences, American Association for the Advancement of Science, and the National Science Foundation, promoting science and research and women's roles in these fields. Jackson is a trustee of MIT, Rutgers University, Lincoln University (Pa.), and the Barnes Foundation. She is also a director for the Public Service Enterprise Group (Newark, N.J.), the New Jersey Resources Corporation (Wall, N.J.), and Core States/New Jersey National Bank (West Trenton, N.J.).

During her student years at MIT she did volunteer work at Boston City Hospital and tutoring at the Roxbury (Boston) YMCA. She is an active member of Delta Sigma Theta Sorority and was president, Iota Chapter, 1966-1968. She was vice president of the MIT Alumni Association during 1986-1988.

Shirley Jackson has published more than one hundred scientific articles and abstracts. Her papers have appeared in *Annuals of Physics*, *Nuovo Cimento*, *Physical Review*, *Solid State Communications*, *Applied Physics Letters*, and *Journal of Applied Physics*. A complete listing of her published scientific works may be found by consulting *Physics Abstracts*.

References

American Men and Women of Science. 13th ed. Vol. 3. New York: Bowker, 1976.

Shirley Ann Jackson. Résumé.

Who's Who Among Black Americans, 1990/1991. Detroit: Gale Research, 1990.

Ronald E. Mickens

Harriet Ann Jacobs

(1813-1897)

Writer

Published in 1861, Harriet Ann Jacobs's *Incidents in the Life of a Slave Girl, Written by Herself* (written under the pseudonym of Linda Brent and edited by L. Maria Child) is a unique narrative by a woman who recounts her life in slavery and her victorious struggle to win freedom.

A major contribution to the slave narrative genre, *Incidents* also shows to the reader the unique perspective of a black woman. Many feminist scholars recognize the difference in the male and female experiences of slavery and realize that many of the male-authored narratives, by Frederick Douglass and William Wells Brown, for example, are not wholly representative of slave life. Women in slavery found themselves operating and cooperating under different circumstances—meeting the demands of child care only to see their offspring sold as punishment, dealing with the jealousy of their mistresses, suffering the betrayal of their white "milk sisters" (Yellin, *Women and Sisters,* 89), and fending off the sexual advances of their masters only to capitulate in the end. These are some of the tribulations that Jacobs recounts in *Incidents* by transforming "herself into a literary subject in and through the creation of her narrator, Linda Brent" (*Incidents,* ed. Yellin, xiii-xiv).

Since Jacobs chose to recreate herself and the story of her life under the pseudonym of Linda Brent, then the story of Jacobs's real life experiences, or, at least, the incidents of her life, must be encapsulated or echoed in the autobiographical narrative told by Brent. For in the Preface by the Author,

Brent advises the reader to "be assured this narrative is no fiction. I am aware that some of my adventures may seem incredible; but they are, nevertheless, strictly true. . . . I have concealed the names of places, and given persons fictitious names. I had no motive for secrecy on my own account, but I deemed it kind and considerate toward others to pursue this course" (*Incidents,* ed. Gates, 1).

By tracing the correspondence between Jacobs and Amy Post, her white confidante, and Jacobs and Lydia Maria Child, her editor, the true authorship of *Incidents* has been verified and the pseudonymous people and places she writes about have been identified by Jean Fagan Yellin. Yellin chronicles Harriet Ann Jacobs's life and confirms she was born into slavery in autumn 1813 in Edenton, North Carolina. Her mother, Delilah, was the slave of Margaret and John Horniblow, an Edenton tavernkeeper; her father, Daniel Jacobs, was a skilled carpenter hired out at his trade and the slave of Dr. Andrew Knox and probably the son of Knox's neighbor Henry Jacobs; and her maternal grandmother, Molly Horniblow (called Aunt Martha in the book) was a slave freed in midlife who eventually owned a house on West King Street in Edenton, where she worked as a baker. Jacobs's younger brother, John S. Jacobs, was born in 1815.

Yellin confirms that when Jacobs's mother died, she and John were sent to the Horniblow estate, where they resided for six years. Margaret Horniblow was kind to Jacobs and taught her to read, spell, and sew. In 1825 Horniblow died and willed her slave girl to her three-year-old niece Mary Matilda Norcom (Miss Emily Flint in the book). A year later, Jacobs and her brother moved into the Norcom house, and one year after that, her father died.

Dr. James Norcom (Dr. Flint) made numerous sexual advances toward the fifteen-year-old mulatto girl, who successfully rebuffed him, and in retaliation Norcom forbade Jacobs's marriage to a free black man. Subsequently, the teenage Jacobs took on a young white lover, Samuel Tedwell Sawyer (Mr. Sands), both a neighbor and a lawyer, by whom she later had two children, Joseph and Louisa Matilda (Benjamin and Ellen). In 1835, when Jacobs was twenty-two, Norcom resolved to have a sexual liaison with her by building, four miles from the big house, a little home where she was expected to do light sewing work and return sexual favors.

Harassed by Dr. Norcom as well as Mrs. Norcom, Jacobs and her children moved in with her grandmother. Norcom finally resorted to sending Jacobs to a plantation in Auburn and threatened to send her children to be "broke in." Jacobs escaped, hiding with sympathetic white people and later in her grandmother's attic for seven years. These seemingly fantastic events are the reasons why many scholars, including historian John Blassingame, dismissed *Incidents* as a fictionalized narrative.

Jacobs Escapes to Freedom

Jacobs began a seven-year retreat "in a tiny crawlspace above a storeroom in her grandmother's house," where she could hear and see her children, unknown to them. Putting herself to good use, she passed the time reading, writing, and sewing. Eventually, she took a boat to New York, becoming a nursemaid in the home of Mary Stace Willis (Mrs. Bruce) and Nathaniel Parker Willis, according to Yellin.

The remaining events reported by Jacobs reveal her growing attraction to the antislavery movement. Jacobs travels while in the service of her employer, meets some famous abolitionists and reformers, and is persuaded to tell her story.

Yellin feels that the real impetus that lead Jacobs to write her autobiography at "irregular intervals" was a brief involvement with Harriet Beecher Stowe. Apparently, in 1852, Jacobs requested that Amy Post approach Stowe with the idea of having Stowe write about Jacobs's life. Jacobs also wanted to take her daughter to England in hopes that Louisa could persuade Stowe to introduce her to the English as the "good representative of a Southern Slave" and to meet with Jacobs (*Incidents,* Yellin, xviii-xix). However, Jacobs's correspondence with Post reveals that Beecher believed the English would fawn excessively over Louisa, and furthermore, Beecher wanted to verify Jacobs's story with Mrs. Willis. If the story were true, then Beecher would incorporate it in her forthcoming book, *Key to Uncle Tom's Cabin* (1853). Jacobs never revealed her sexual history to Mrs. Willis, and she felt that Stowe had betrayed her as a woman, denigrated her as a mother, and threatened her as a writer. She later expressed her racial outrage to Post: 'think dear Amy that a visit to Stafford House would spoil me as Mrs. Stowe thinks petting is more than my race can bear well what a pity we poor blacks cant [sic] have the firmness and stability of character that you white people have (Jacobs to Post, [Spring 1853?], *Incidents,* Yellin, xviii-xix).

Incidents first appeared in Horace Greeley's *New York Tribune* under the heading "Letter from a Fugitive Slave" (1855). The work not only narrated her slave experiences, but more significantly, addressed sexuality and the chauvinist attitudes of white men toward women in general and black women in particular. Still working as a domestic for the Willises, Jacobs wrote secretly. Once *Incidents* was finished, Jacobs had considerable difficulty getting the book published. She traveled to England with little success in finding a publisher, then signed with a Boston firm that later went bankrupt. The book was picked up by Thayer and Eldridge, who required a preface by L. Maria Child. Unfortunately, Thayer and Eldridge also went bankrupt. Having purchased the stereotyped plates, a Boston printer published *Incidents* in 1861, and in 1862 the London edition appeared under the title *The Deeper Wrong.* As stated in the preface, Jacobs intended "to arouse the women of the North to a realizing sense of the condition of two millions of women at the South, still in bondage, suffering what I suffered, and most of them far worse" (*Incidents,* Yellin, xviii-xix). Her book was intended to inspire women to participate in the political process and to realize that white women were not free until all women were free.

During the Civil War, Jacobs worked as a nurse and

teacher in the relief effort in Alexandria, Virginia. When the Emancipation Proclamation was issued, she wrote L. Maria Child (1 January 1863): "I have lived to hear the Proclamation of Freedom for my suffering people. All my wrongs are forgiven. I am more than repaid for all I have endured. Glory to God in the highest" (Child, *The Freedmen's Book*, 218). Harriet Jacobs lived the latter part of her life in Washington, D.C., where she and her daughter made their home. On March 7, 1897, she died and was buried in Mount Auburn Cemetery, Cambridge, Massachusetts.

References

Child, Lydia Maria. *The Freedmen's Book*. Boston: Ticknor and Fields, 1865.

Jacobs, Harriet Ann [Linda Brent]. *Incidents in the Life of Slave Girl, Written By Herself*. Ed. with a portrait and an introduction by Jean Fagan Yellin. Cambridge: Harvard University Press, 1987.

———. *Incidents in the Life of a Slave Girl, Written By Herself*. Ed. Lydia Maria Child. Boston: n.p., 1861.

Yellin, Jean Fagan. *Women & Sisters*. New Haven: Yale University Press, 1989.

Kelley Norman

Judith Jamison

(1944-)

Dancer, dance company director

Judith Jamison

While there are many black women who excel in those fields that are necessary to sustain life—law, medicine, and business—there are those who give us something to live for. They are called artists. One of the most dedicated artists in the field of dance is Judith Jamison. Her beauty and grace have been sweeping audiences off their feet since 1965. Joining the Alvin Ailey American Dance Theater in that year, she now extends the Alvin Ailey dance legacy from her position as artistic director of the company. "I dance basically for myself because I love doing it," she said in an interview for *Essence* magazine. "It's my best form of communication" (Harris, 64). She has been dancing since the age of six.

Judith Jamison was born on May 10, 1944, in Philadelphia, Pennsylvania, to John Jamison, a sheet metal worker, and Tessie Jamison, a teacher and former athlete. She took piano lessons from her father, who was once a part-time pianist and singer, and her parents enrolled her in the Judimar School of Dance in Philadelphia. She was six years old, tall and lanky, and full of energy. Instead of spending time on the playground, she poured her childhood energy into her dance lessons. At Judimar, she received instruction in tap, acrobatic, jazz, and primitive dance. Her teachers, Dolores Brown, John Jones, Melvin Brooms, and John Hines, nursed her until she burst out of her shell and prepared to take flight. Spending eleven years at Judimar, she also benefited from great and inspiring teachers such as Anthony Tudor, Vincenzo Celli, and Maria Swoboda. Her childhood was also enriched by the music, theater, and spiritual fervor of the historic Mother Bethel African Methodist Episcopal Church in Philadelphia.

After graduating from high school at seventeen, the young Jamison was awarded a scholarship to Fisk University in Nashville, Tennessee, where she began to work toward a degree in psychology. It took three semesters of study at Fisk before Jamison decided to return home and enroll at the Philadelphia Dance Academy (now the University of the Arts), where her ballet teachers were Nadia Chilkovsky, James Jamieson, and Juri Gottschalk. She supplemented their instruction with study of the history of the dance, its composition and art, and Labanotation (a system of dance symbols based on movements of parts of the body). In addition, she attended classes in the Lester Horton technique at Joan Kerr's Dance School.

In 1964 Jamison's talent was recognized by choreographer Agnes de Mille, who was teaching a master class at the Philadelphia Dance Academy. De Mille invited Jamison to dance in her new ballet The Four Marys, during its run in New York's Lincoln Center. After the ballet closed, Jamison took a job operating the Log-Flume Ride at the 1964 World's Fair until she landed another dancing gig.

In the fall of 1965 Jamison auditioned for Donald McKayle, who was directing dance sequences for a projected Harry Belafonte television special. Even though she did not get the part, she impressed Alvin Ailey, the founder of the Alvin Ailey Dance Company. She made her debut with the Ailey troupe in "Conga Tango Palace" at the Harper Festival in Chicago in 1965. Her association with the Ailey company changed her life dramatically, requiring her to travel almost ceaselessly. Her travels led to a tour of Western Europe in early 1966 and a side trip in April 1966 to the first World Festival of Negro Arts in Dakar, Senegal, at which the Ailey troupe was the only integrated modern dance company to perform. Later in the spring, the company collaborated with the Harkness Ballet in guest appearances and continued to perform at the Marais Festival in Paris.

In 1966, when Alvin Ailey's company temporarily dissolved because of lack of funds, Jamison joined the Harkness Ballet for several months. After an inspiring and rewarding American tour with the Harkness Ballet in 1967, her appearances ended when she fell on a slippery floor and injured her ankle.

After recuperating, Jamison rejoined the Alvin Ailey Dance Company for its 1967 European tour. From the late 1960s to 1980 the troupe toured the United States, Russia, France, India, Cuba, Sweden, and Japan. "One of her most notable roles was with Mikhail Baryshnikov in Alvin Ailey's *Pas de Duke*, set to the music of Duke Ellington" ("Judith Jamison: Extending the Alvin Ailey Dance Legacy," 136). Judith Jamison's two most prized awards are the one she received early in her career for her last performance at the Christmas Cotillion at Philadelphia's Convention Hall—an award of merit presented to her by Joan Crawford, and the Dance Magazine Award for 1972, which she shared with the Royal Ballet's Anthony Dowell. In August 1972 Jamison was appointed by President Nixon as an advisor to the National Council on the Arts.

Jamison left the company again in 1980 to perform in the Broadway musical *Sophisticated Ladies*. She also performed with the San Francisco Ballet and the Ballet of the Twentieth Century. By this time also she became interested in doing her own choreography. Alvin Ailey encouraged her to develop this talent and had his own company perform her first piece, *Divining*, in 1984. Her twelve-member company, the Jamison Project, made its debut in 1988.

Judith Jamison became the premier dancer for the Ailey Company. She gained fame as a "physically fabulous, deeply spiritual dancer" who engraved her image on the audience as she performed Ailey's fifteen-minute solo *Cry*, "a hymn to the sufferings and triumphant endurance of generations of black matriarchs," created especially for her. (Tobias, "Standing Tall," 106). This was her signature piece. According to Jamison, *Cry* was created as a birthday present for Alvin Ailey's mother "and it was dedicated to all black women, especially our mothers." Jamison found joy in teaching it to other women dancers, "watching them develop it as their own and seeing what they had to bring to it" ("Judith Jamison," *A Mind Is*, 7).

Ailey Protégée Heads Dance Company

That Judith Jamison was deeply influenced by Alvin Ailey is well known, and they had mutual respect for each other's talent. Alvin Ailey died in December 1989, leaving dance aficionados to worry about the future of the Alvin Ailey American Dance Theater. But his protégée, Judith Jamison, who clearly had earned the position of director by her stellar performances and experience as codirector and artistic associate over the years, was placed at the helm and immediately put to rest any anxieties about the company.

When the first season under her direction opened in 1991, Jamison told an audience at the City Center in New York about her vision for the company's identity and purpose. Except when a particular matter dictates, its familiar brassy showmanship will be replaced by a more contemplative simplicity (Tobias, "Rites of Passage," 55).

Ailey's legacy was evident in the repertoire for the 1990-1991 season as the dancers feature a revival of his *Hidden Rites*, created in 1973 and infused with modern, jazz, and classical dance techniques, and his *Revelations* and *Blues Suites*. Included also were Kris World's *Read Matthew 11:28*, which was created in 1988 for the Jamison Project and shows an African influence with Jamison at the pivotal center; Lar Lubovitch's *North Star*, created in 1978; and Jamison's own *Forgotten Time*. True to the company's historic mission, the preservation of works by pioneering black choreographers continues. Pearl Primus was asked to revive her 1952 *Impinyuza*, which shows a concentration of African influence.

Jamison asks her dancers to "luxuriate in the movement. Focus. Wrap yourself around the music" (Tobias, "Standing Tall," 106). Highly respected by the dancers because of her "personable style and dancer's intuition," Jamison sees as her goal "not to stand in Alvin's shadow, but on his shoulders" ("Extending the Legacy," 136; Tobias, "Standing Tall," 106).

The company is known for its major modern dance work, but it also has satellite enterprises, such as a school attended by some 3,200 students. Jamison plans to increase the company's exposure by establishing six-week residencies in various cities to provide classes to underprivileged youths in dance, creative writing, and stage production. Her concern is with fund-raising to support the company, the dance school, and the Alvin Ailey Repertory Ensemble. "I trust that corporations and other funders will realize that the Ailey company is an important part of the history of dance and that they will have faith in the growth and longevity of the company," she says ("Extending the Legacy" 136).

In December 1972 Jamison married fellow Ailey soloist Miguel Godreau. The marriage was unsuccessful, and since then her busy schedule has left her little time to do more than concentrate on dancing and managing the company. She is as commanding in her performances as she is in appearance. Fluid and spirited, the five-foot ten-inch Jamison, who wears a close-cropped hair-style, has "a low and soft voice, a beaming smile, and a warm manner that contrasts with her onstage awesomeness" (*Current Biography,* 205). What has worked for Jamison as a black American is regarded as an enhancement for the history of her race traced to the beginning of time. "I've got a million heartbeats in me," she said. "My folks have been dancing since the beginning of time, so I've got this advantage" ("Judith Jamison," *A Mind Is,* 7).

References

Allen, Zita. "Majesty in Motion: Judith Jamison." *Encore* 4 (December 22, 1975): cover, 27-28. Includes photographs.

"Creative Woman." *Ebony* 32 (August 1977): 135. Includes photograph.

Current Biography Yearbook. New York: H. W. Wilson, 1973. 202-205. Photograph, p. 203.

Editors of Ebony. *1,000 Successful Blacks.* Chicago: Johnson Pub. Co., 1973. 173. Includes photograph.

"Entertainment." *Connoisseur* 220 (December 1990): 52. Includes photograph.

Harris, Jessica. "Judith Jamison." *Essence* 9 (May 1978): cover, 62, 64. Includes photographs.

"Judith Jamison [Interview with Charlayne Hunter-Gault]." *A Mind Is.* 1 (Winter 1991): 4-8. Includes photographs.

"Judith Jamison: Extending the Alvin Ailey Dance Legacy." *Ebony* 46 (December 1990): 132-136. Includes photographs.

Ploski, Harry A., and James Williams. *The Negro Almanac.* 5th ed. Detroit: Gale Research, 1990. 1124, 1146-47. Photograph, p. 1124.

Sherman, Ellen. "Bringing Dance Home Again." *Essence* 4 (February 1975): 34-34, 72. Includes photographs.

Tobias, Tobi. "Rites of Passage." *New York* 24 (7 January 1991): 55-56.

———. "Standing Tall." *New York* (24 December 1990): 106. Includes photograph.

Roy L. Hill

Lucy C. Jefferson

(1866-1953)

Entrepreneur, clubwoman, civic leader, educator, philanthropist

Businesses owned and operated by blacks in Mississippi were said to be unknown until Lucy Crump Jefferson opened her funeral home in 1894. Her funeral home also changed the treatment of the black dead, as survivors had to be taught to use black funeral directors. Lucy Jefferson shared her wealth and her talent as an organizer with the black community by donating to various causes and working with women's groups and other organizations.

Lucy Crump Jefferson was born November 3, 1866, in Jackson, Mississippi, and died of cancer April 24, 1953, at Mercy Hospital in Vicksburg, Mississippi. Records give no mention of her father's first name but indicate that she was one of two children of Alice (Reynolds) Crump. Although the level of her schooling is unknown, she attended the public schools of Vicksburg. Lucy Crump married William Henry Jefferson, the son of a prosperous Virginia freedman, on June 20, 1889.

A cofounder of the W. H. Jefferson Funeral Home on December 1, 1894, and the Jefferson Burial Association in 1914, she became the sole owner of the businesses after the death of her husband in 1922. She continued her association with the funeral home business until her death in 1953. For a number of years she was a public school teacher in the city of Vicksburg.

The funeral home, the first established for blacks in Mississippi and reputed to be the first business in the state operated by and for blacks, has been in operation continuously since 1894. During its ninety-six years, it has been managed by three generations of the W. H. Jefferson family. It was first established in the eleven hundred block of Grove Street and was later moved to the nine hundred block of Main Street. The present structure, located at 800 Monroe Street, was dedicated on Sunday, April 1, 1965, and cited by the Vicksburg *Evening Post* as a monument to the courage and foresight of its founders.

Reflecting upon the hardships experienced during the early years of its establishment, Lucy Jefferson was quoted as saying that:

> Negroes had to be taught to use Negro funeral directors. They were just simply something the public was not used to. We were an oddity and doomed to early failure so thought many of our friends. W. H. Jefferson had to keep his job on

> the railroad to help pay expenses so that the late J. H. Jefferson, father of the present owners, took charge of the business. An embalmer from Memphis, Tennessee was hired to do the embalming. Within five years the firm was on the way to financial success. This was done through the support of many friends who have remained loyal to our business down through the years (Vicksburg *Evening Post*, 16 April 1965).

Charitable Contributions Gain Support

Jefferson's reputation as a philanthropist is well-documented by historians and was confirmed by interviews. In addition to supporting many worthwhile community causes, she gave generously in support of the establishment of the Margaret Murray Washington Home for delinquents, funded the Lucy C. Jefferson Scholarship, presented annually to a graduating high school student for more than forty years, and assisted countless other students in furthering their education.

A renowned civic, religious, and fraternal leader, she was affiliated with Camille Art and Literary Club, vice-president of the National Association of Colored Women's Clubs, and seventh president of the Mississippi State Federation of Colored Women's Clubs; she was a member of the first Interracial Council of Vicksburg, Southern Regional Council, and the National Association of Morticians; she was also high priestess of Love and Truth Tabernacle, Number One Hundred; Knights and Daughters of Tabor, president of the Vicksburg Ladies Union, Number Five, royal matron of Rose of Sharon, vice-president of the City Federation of Colored Women's Clubs, Chapter Twenty-four of Eastern Star; and finally she was member, steward, trustee, and president of the Missionary Society of Bethel AME Church, and trustee of Campbell College in Jackson, Mississippi.

During her presidency of the Mississippi Federation of Colored Women's Clubs (1928-1934), the Margaret Murray Washington Home for Delinquent Boys and Girls was dedicated and a full-time superintendent was employed.

Because of her profound interest in education of the young, she circulated a petition that caused a junior high school for black youth to be built in Vicksburg in 1966. Prior to that time, black students of junior high school level were educated at nearby McIntyre and Warren schools. For her efforts, an ultramodern high school was named in her honor in 1966.

Jefferson's closest friends, companions, and contemporaries included clubwomen, church leaders, and wives of funeral directors. Through her work in the Mississippi Federation of Colored Women's Clubs, she established ties with many Mississippi clubwomen.

Lucy Jefferson was a fair-complexioned, heavyset woman whose physical appearance was characterized by dignity and distinction. She was modest, well loved, and a highly respected businesswoman and community leader. Information on the contributions of Lucy Campbell Jefferson, a woman whose life was rich, rewarding, and vital in the black community of Vicksburg, is scant in published sources.

References

Interviews with Richard Bradford III, 21 February 1990; W. S. Denby, 24 February 1990; and W. H. Jefferson, Sr., 21 February 1990.

Mississippi Black Woman: A Pictorial Story of Their Contributions to the State and Nation. Eds. Geneva Brown Blalock and Eva Hunter Bishop. A bicentennial project of the Mississippi State Federation of Colored Women's Clubs. Jackson: 1976. Includes a photograph of Lucy Crump Jefferson.

Mosley, Mrs. Charles C., Sr. *The Negro in Mississippi History*. Jackson, Miss.: Hederman Brothers, 1969.

Sewell, George Alexander, and Margaret L. Dwight. *Mississippi Black History Makers*. Rev. and Enl. ed. Jackson: University Press of Mississippi, 1984.

Vicksburg *Evening Post* (16 April 1965).

Vicksburg *Weekly* (3 December 1937). Includes a photograph of Lucy Crump Jefferson.

Collections

Records of the Jefferson business, including photographs of Lucy Crump Jefferson, are located in the Jefferson Funeral Home, 800 Monroe Street, Vicksburg, Mississippi.

Cozetta W. Buckley

Mae C. Jemison

(1956-)

Astronaut, physician, government official

Mae C. Jemison, thus far this country's single black woman astronaut and scheduled for a shuttle flight in August 1992, is a versatile scholar whose primary interest is science and exploration of the universe. She has blended her skills in chemical engineering, medicine, and health care to become involved in one of the nation's leading experimental projects, survived the rigorous training programs necessary for space research, and emerged as a science mission specialist, which allows her to experiment with metals and new compounds and to study the effects of gravity on the human body.

One of three children, Jemison was born on October 17, 1956, in Decatur, Alabama, to Charlie Jemison, a mainte-

Mae C. Jemison

nance supervisor, and Dorothy Jemison, a schoolteacher. The family moved to Chicago when she was three to take advantage of educational opportunities. The Jemisons had a profound influence on their children's development and encouraged their talents and abilities. In addition, when she was four, Jemison's uncle, a social worker, helped to stimulate her interest in science. It drew her attention and she became especially interested in anthropology and archaeology. In school Jemison spent considerable time in the library reading and learning all she could about extinct animals, theories of evolution, science fiction, and particularly astronomy. Her family and friends constantly fostered her interest in these areas, and as result "I ended up being constantly aware of the world around me because of my own interest," she said (Johnson, B-5).

While she was in Morgan Park High School, one of Jemison's classes visited a local university, creating in her a curiosity about the biomedical engineering profession. She reasoned that such a position would require her to study biology, physics, and chemistry. Consistently on the honor roll, she graduated from high school in 1973 and entered Stanford University on a National Achievement Scholarship, later earning a degree in chemical engineering. Her versatility extended to nonscientific activities as demonstrated in her joining dance and theater productions and representing Stanford in Carifesta '76 in Jamaica; she also enrolled in courses in Afro-American studies and earned a second bachelor's degree in that field. Thus she has a firm knowledge of her own heritage and culture. Jemison's views on becoming a well-rounded person were firm then:

> Science is very important to me, but I also like to stress that you have to be well-rounded. One's love for science doesn't get rid of all the other areas. I truly feel someone interested in science is interested in understanding what's going on in the world. That means you have to find out about social science, art, and politics (Johnson, B-5).

After graduating from Stanford, Jemison entered Cornell University's medical school in fall 1977. Her interest in exploring the world and helping people led her to volunteer during medical school for a summer experience in a Thai refugee camp. "It's interesting to see new places and be involved in new things," she said (Johnson, B-5). She saw people who were malnourished, ill with tuberculosis, asthmatic, and who suffered from dysentery and other maladies. On a grant from the International Travelers Institute, she was engaged in health studies in Kenya in 1979. In that same year she organized the New York City-wide health and law fair for the National Student Medical Association.

After graduating from medical school in 1981, Jemison completed her internship at Los Angeles County/University of Southern California Medical Center in July 1982, and worked as general practitioner with INA/Ross Loos Medical Group in Los Angeles until December of that year. From January 1983 through July 1985 she was the area Peace Corps medical officer for Sierra Leone and Liberia in West Africa. There she was manager of health care for Peace Corps volunteers and United States Embassy personnel as well. In addition to handling medical administrative issues by supervising medical personnel and laboratories, she developed curricula and taught volunteer personnel, wrote manuals for self-care, and developed and implemented guidelines on public health and safety issues for volunteers. In conjunction with the National Institutes of Health and the Center for Disease Control, Jemison developed and participated in research projects on hepatitis B vaccine, schistosomaisis and rabies. In 1985 she returned to the United States and joined CIGNA Health Plans, a health maintenance organization in Los Angeles.

Jemison Joins Space Program

Jemison reached a decision early on that she wanted to be an astronaut. Here again she could "blend skills" and at the same time continue to develop her talents and abilities. The idea of space travel fascinated Jemison, who was already adventurous, inquisitive, and eager to learn and accomplish more. While working as a general practitioner in Los Angeles, she applied to the National Aeronautics and Space Administration (NASA) and enrolled in night courses in engineering at the University of California, Los Angeles. During this period an unfortunate turn of events occurred: Spaceship Challenger failed on January 28, 1986, and NASA temporarily suspended its astronaut selection process. Saddened but not deterred, Jemison said, "I thought about it because it was very sad because of the astronauts who were lost, but not in any way keeping me from being interested in it or changing my views" ("Space Is Her Destination," 98). Later, Jemison reapplied and NASA invited her to join the program. She was one of fifteen candidates chosen from a field of approximately two thousand qualified applicants.

Jemison joined NASA's space program in 1987, completing a one-year training and evaluation program in August 1988, which qualified her as a mission specialist. Her technical assignments included astronaut office representative to the Kennedy Space Center, Cape Canaveral, Florida, which involved processing space shuttles for launching by checking payloads, thermal protection system (tiles), launch countdown, and work in the Shuttle Avionics Integration Laboratory (SAIL) to verify shuttle computer software.

The United States and Japan have developed a joint mission to conduct experiments in life sciences and materials processing called Spacelab J, scheduled for launching in August 1992. Jemison has been selected as a mission specialist on the space team. As science mission specialist, she will experiment with new compounds and metals and at the same time study the effect of gravity on the human body.

Currently, there are 104 astronauts, of whom eighteen are women and five are black. She is the only black woman. Looked upon as a role model, Jemison says that "if I'm a role model, what I'd like to be is someone who says, 'No, don't try to . . . be like me or live your life or grow up to be an astronaut or a physician unless that's what you want to do'" ("Space Is Her Destination," 98). But she admits that she never had a role model. She is concerned about blacks and the NASA program. She readily acknowledges that blacks and other Americans have benefited from the space program, advances in communications, medicine, and the environment. "Some might say that the environment is not a Black issue, but I worked in Los Angeles and I saw more Black and Hispanic children with uncontrolled asthma as a result of pollution. Just as many of us get sick from those types of things, and, in fact, we have more problems with them because many of us don't have the availability of health care" (Marshall, 54).

Consistent with the pattern set by many who soar so high, Jemison took lessons from many different people. These were: "the college dance instructor who was full of energy and creativity; the 94-year-old woman, one of her patients in Los Angeles, who taught her to tango; her parents, who urged her to seek answers to her questions; and the Cambodian refugees she saw . . . in . . . a Thai refugee camp." It is important to take bits and pieces of influence by everyone you meet, she said (Johnson, B-5).

Jemison's distinguished career has brought recognition from many groups. In addition to her busy speaking engagement, particularly in colleges and schools, she was honored by *Essence* magazine in 1988 when she received the Essence Science and Technology Award. In 1989 she became Gamma Sigma's Gamma Woman of the Year. The mural *Black Americans in Flight* by Spencer Taylor, unveiled in the Lambert-Saint Louis International Airport, honors Jemison as the first black woman astronaut. She is a member of the American Medical Association, the American Chemical Society, and an honorary member of the Alpha Kappa Alpha Sorority. She spends her leisure time dancing, doing aerobics, traveling, and working in her yard. Jemison is now based at the Lyndon B. Johnson Space Center in Houston, Texas. For her concern with social needs of the community as well as with the space program, Jemison has been called a national asset.

References

Jemison, Mae C. "Biographical Data, M.D., Astronaut." Lyndon B. Johnson Space Center, Houston, Texas, October 1989; January 1991.

Johnson, Maria C. "Upward with Worldly Lessons." *Greensboro News and Record*, 28 January 1991. Includes photographs.

Marshall, Marilyn. "Child of the '60s Set to Become First Black Woman in Space." *Ebony* 44 (August 1989): 50, 52, 54-55.

The Missing Piece 3 (Summer/Fall 1990): 1. Includes photograph.

"Monument Recognizing Black Aviators is Unveiled." *Jet* 78 (September 1990): 34.

"1988 Essence Awards." *Essence* 19 (October 1988): 59-60. Includes photograph.

"Space Is Her Destination." *Ebony* 42 (October 1987): 93-98. Includes photographs.

Jessie Carney Smith

Eva Jessye

(1895-)

Composer, musician, choral director, educator, writer, actress

Eva Jessye, composer, choral director, educator, writer, actress, and lecturer, called "the dean of black female musicians, "has lived for nearly a century. She has the rare privilege not only of looking back on a remarkable sketch of history, but of knowing that she shaped a part of it.

Jessye was born in Coffeyville, Kansas, on January 20, 1895, to Al Jessye and Julia (Buckner) Jessye. When she was three years old, her parents were separated, and Eva Jessye lived most of her childhood with her mother's sisters and her grandmother. Her mother, Julia Jessye, moved to Seattle to work, and her father had little to do with her upbringing. Eva Jessye has strong, positive memories about her Buckner-

Knight family relatives. Some of her earliest recollections are of her great-grandmother Hill, who would come to visit from the "Nation," as Oklahoma was called before statehood. Grandma Hill was born in Indian country to the union of a slave mother and Cherokee father. Jessye attended public schools in Coffeyville and Iola, Kansas, Saint Louis, and Seattle.

At age nine, Jessye had an experience that she often says was the most powerful influence in her life. While recovering from typhoid, she had a dream—or a vision—in which she was a bannister of a staircase that led upward. Two hands—one of which was beautiful and glowing—were on the bannister. When she reached out to touch the hand, she heard a voice explaining that she was not yet worthy and that she must understand that there is something higher than the intellect. Jessye understood that although she would spend the rest of her life developing her brilliant mind and talent, she must never forget humanity—the need to help others. This has been the mandate that she has lived by. When she was thirteen, she was accepted by Western University in Quindaro, Kansas—a suburb of Kansas City. The school waived the usual admission age of fourteen, since public high schools in Coffeyville did not accept black students. While at Western, the precocious student was given many opportunities to work with the chorus and develop her writing skills.

After her graduation from the university in 1914, Jessye attended Langston University in Oklahoma for three summers. At Langston, she received a lifetime teaching certificate. She was also a protégée of the legendary Will Marion Cook, and she later studied with master theorist Percy Goetschius. Jessye taught in Oklahoma schools for several years. In 1920, she became director of the music department at Morgan State College in Baltimore, and in 1925 she was a reporter for the weekly *Baltimore Afro-American*. Jessye moved to New York in 1926. It was there that she established her outstanding fifty-year career as a choral director, composer, performer, writer, actress, educator, and lecturer. She was later called "the dean of black female musicians" and performed with many of the greatest musicians of the time—including maestros Leopold Stokowski, Eugene Ormandy, and Dimitri Mitropoulos.

Jessye joined a group called the Dixie Jubilee Singers. This ensemble eventually became the internationally-known Eva Jessye Choir. From 1926-1929, the choir performed regularly at the Capitol Theatre in New York, and in 1929 Jessye went to Hollywood to direct her choir in King Vidor's *Hallelujah*, a landmark motion picture—the first black musical. The choir continued to thrill audiences throughout America and Europe, and in 1934 Jessye was asked to become choral director for the experimental opera, *Four Saints in Three Acts*, by Virgil Thompson and Gertrude Stein. The renowned actor John Houseman commented extensively about *Four Saints* in his *Run-Through: A Memoir*.

Famed Choral Conductor Directs *Porgy and Bess*

Early in 1935, George Gershwin selected Jessye as the choral director of his new folk opera, *Porgy and Bess*. The Eva Jessye Choir performed on the opera's opening night—October 10, 1935. She would forever be associated with the story of *Porgy and Bess*—or more accurately, the many stories of rehearsals, performances, opening nights, and revivals in this country and abroad. Most of the great black singers of the day appeared in *Porgy and Bess* at one time or another. But Jessye had become known as the "Guardian of the Score" of *Porgy and Bess*. Indeed, she has a copy of the original 1935 score with handwritten instructions by Gershwin.

After the success of the opera, Jessye briefly returned to teaching as the choral director at Claflin College in Orangeburg, South Carolina. Later, however, she returned to her choir, and the group performed at the 1939 New York World's Fair. During World War II, Jessye helped with the war fund-raising effort with her Victory Concert tour. In 1944, she wrote the theme and directed the choir for the American-Soviet Friendship Day ceremonies held at Madison Square Garden in New York and the Watergate Theater in Washington, D.C. In 1963, Jessye directed the official choir for Martin Luther King, Jr.'s March on Washington.

Jessye appeared as an actress in New York and Hollywood. Other than her regular appearances in *Porgy and Bess*, she appeared on the stage in *Lost in the Stars* and in several movies, including *Slaves* and *Black Like Me*.

Jessye returned to the university campus in 1974 when she went to the University of Michigan. There she established the Eva Jessye Collection of Afro-American Music. In 1979, she went to Pittsburg State University in Kansas, where the remainder of her memorabilia is located. While in her beloved Kansas, she did much of her composing. Her outstanding *Chronicle of Job* and her oratorio, *Paradise Lost and Regained*, were both performed there, along with smaller works. During this time, she was named one of the six most outstanding women in Kansas history, and in 1978, the governor proclaimed "Eva Jessye Day" throughout the state.

Jessye left Kansas to return to Michigan, where she presently resides. She also spent a semester as artist-in-residence at Clark College in Atlanta, Georgia.

Jessye has honorary doctorates from the University of Michigan, Eastern Michigan University, and Wilberforce University; and she has been given numerous citations from government, educational, and musical organizations. She has been named to the Senior Hall of Fame in Everett, Washington, and named Kansas Ambassador of the Arts. She was honored for her contributions to the theater and to music when the historic Apollo Theatre in New York City reopened in 1985. Her photograph appears in the memorable collection *I Dream a World: Portraits of Black Women Who Changed America* by Brian Lanker.

Until recently, Jessye maintained her busy schedule of lecturing, composing, directing, writing, and making public appearances. It is possible that Jessye has known more black writers, musicians, artists, and actors than any one else alive: she is a living source of information. She is perhaps the leading expert on the Harlem Renaissance, in which she participated. Her long list of friends—including Langston Hughes, Hall Johnson, Augusta Savage, and many others—is synonymous with artistic achievement. She discovered and assisted countless young black artists whose names became household words. Jessye has material for two books that she is writing—one is an autobiography and the other an account of fifty years of *Porgy and Bess*. In recent years, she has also concentrated on her poetry. She sees a poem in many daily life experiences, and her poetry is frequently witty and usually has a moral. One of her best-known poems is "A Bag of Peanuts," a reminiscence of her childhood with her mother in Seattle many years ago.

A very attractive woman when she was younger, Jessye is still a striking, unforgettable figure in her nineties. While she is legendary, Jessye lives in the present. One of her favorite retorts whenever she is asked to delay something is, "What's the matter with *now?*"

Jessye has a reputation for demanding the best from those with whom she works. She demands no less from herself. She is an extraordinary woman—charming, intelligent, and warm. She can be unpredictable, a trait that adds to her multifaceted personality.

Deeply religious, Jessye is a lifelong member of the African Methodist Episcopal church. She is also a member of ASCAP, Songwriters Hall of Fame, Actors Guild, and Sigma Gamma Rho sorority.

On her ninety-second birthday, Eva Jessye wrote:

> Despite the trials that I've been through, I've reached the age of 92. I'm running not exactly scared, but I try to be prepared for what may come. Please, God, help me at the end to say, I've never failed a friend (Eva Jessye Collection, Florence Crim Robinson).

References

Abdul, Raoul. *Blacks in Classical Music*. New York: Dodd, Mead, 1977

Lanker, Brian. *I Dream a World*. New York: Stewart, Tabori and Chang, 1989. Photograph, p. 21.

Rush, Theressa G. *Black American Writers*. Vol. 2. Metuchen, N.J.: Scarecrow Press, 1975.

Southern, Eileen. *Music of Black Americans*. New York: Norton, 1971.

Collections

Numerous letters from Eva Jessye, unpublished materials, personal mementos, and hours of taped conversations with her are in the possession of the writer. Larger Eva Jessye collections are located at the University of Michigan and Kansas State University at Pittsburg (formerly Pittsburg State). Jessye has been the subject of several doctoral dissertations.

Florence Robinson

Beverly Johnson

(1952-)

Model, singer

Beverly Johnson (Potter Sims) splashed onto the Manhattan fashion scene in June 1971 when she was nineteen years old and she became an immediate star. Her search for a summer job in New York City had led her to *Glamour* magazine's office and to immediate employment as her extraordinary beauty, charm, physical appearance, graciousness, and innate talent were immediately noticeable. In four years her salary increased from sixty dollars an hour to one hundred dollars an hour. Johnson ascended rapidly and by age twenty-three she had become "a triple threat": She had been a runway model for Halston (parading the latest fashions at fashion shows); she had sung "Come Fly with Me" in a television advertisement for National Airlines and appeared in other commercials; and she had become the first black model to appear on the cover of *Vogue* magazine. By age twenty-five Johnson was a superstar and the top black model in the United States.

Born in 1952 to a middle class family in Buffalo, New York, Johnson comes from an interesting bloodline: her father, a machine operator, is part Blackfoot Indian and her mother, a surgical technician, is a Louisiana Creole. As a child, she was tall, awkward, and very interested in sports. She was attracted to the 1968 Olympics and barely missed qualifying in the 100-yard free-style in swimming. She won a full academic scholarship to Northeastern University in Boston, where she studied criminal justice with career plans to become a lawyer, until she was encouraged by friends to become a model. Without the essential portfolio Beverly Johnson, chaperoned by her mother, was still determined to try the rounds of agencies up and down Madison Avenue in New York. "When she did . . . some told her to go back to school, while others gave her the 'you're cute, but' routine" (Morgan, 14).

Johnson's friends knew that the five-feet eight-inch, 115-pound young woman, who has a classic nose, flawless skin, and well-kept, straight black hair, was noticeable wherever she went. A friend had given Johnson the name of a woman who operated a boutique and who knew an editor at *Glamour* magazine. Dressed in white knee socks and presenting a "student council" look, as she described herself, she entered *Glamour*'s offices, met with a panel of editors, and was asked to wait. Moments later she was called in and told the surprising news, "You're just what we are looking for" (Morgan, 14). Johnson was hired immediately and the next day she was on location.

High Fashion Model Shown on Women's Magazines

Johnson soon became known in the fashion industry as "B. J." During her five years with Ford modeling agency, she appeared on the August 1974 cover of *Vogue* magazine and won immediate international attention and praise. When she visited President-poet Léopold Sédar Senghor of Senegal, he said that "she reminded him of the Queen of Sheba, who came not from Africa but from Southern Arabia" (Morgan, 14). The American public knew the importance of Johnson's success. She had appeared on one of the most prestigious magazines in the world and the opportunity came not because she was black but because she was extraordinarily beautiful, talented, and appealed to wide numbers of women of all races. Johnson said of the *Vogue* appearance:

> It was history and I loved it. I'm not booked anymore as a Black model. I'm booked as a model. This means breaking into a new area and hopefully leaving the door open for more Blacks to do the same. To accomplish this is moving me as a person and moving my race because I am Black and I have that spirit, which is really so important for Black people, for Black women (30).

The editors of *Vogue* thought that Johnson had the "to-day" look—a fashion look that at that time might well have implied nudity. If so, it would not have applied to Johnson, "one of the few models who refuse to pose in the raw." For *Vogue,* the "'today' look . . . [meant] a natural look, a girl who is wholesome without being bland, strong without being tough, a girl who has character rather than a rigidly painted mask of beauty. It is the girl with great skin, great hair, great teeth, great eyes, a great figure and a great personality, the supergirl next door" (Morgan, 22). This is what the *Vogue* editors saw in Beverly Johnson, and they used famous photographer Scavullo to bring it out. Johnson appeared on *Vogue*'s cover first in August 1974 and again in June 1975 on the "American Woman" issue. Scavullo had been the photographer both times.

Johnson's popular appeal continued. In the early seventies she became the first black woman to appear on the cover of the French magazine *Elle*. By the mid-seventies she appeared on the cover of numerous magazines. When she first appeared on *Glamour* the magazine's circulation doubled and set a record. By 1977 Johnson had appeared on the covers of some twenty-five magazines, including fourteen for *Glamour* alone.

After ending five years with the Ford agency, Johnson signed with a rival company, the Elite agency, and continued to model high fashions. Her career also embraced other arenas. She began to talk of retirement when her career had fully blossomed. As much as she loved her work, Johnson wanted to pursue her other interests such as singing and acting. In 1977 she began to devote more time to her singing career. She was teamed with rock singer Phil Anastasia for two singles, and she also worked on an album. She had made a film debut in *Ashanti,* a movie filmed in Africa. She launched a line of skin care products called Farabee and wrote a beauty book.

When she was nineteen years old, Johnson married real estate agent Billy Potter. They divorced in 1974. She met Danny Sims, who was experienced in music publishing and theatrical management, owner of the Hemisphere agency and joint owner of Cayman Music. Their daughter, Anansa, was born in 1980. In 1987 Anansa posed with her mother for the AIDS Awareness Campaign print advertisements.

Johnson continues to model often for fashion magazines, catalogs, magazine editorials, and elsewhere. For example, in 1987 she appeared in an advertisement for *Essence* that shows how the busy, beautiful, and attractive model and mother meets her make-up demands, and in 1990 she appeared on a billboard advertisement for Capri cigarettes. The hard-working, outspoken model has had guest-host spots for Black Entertainment Television's "Video Soul," and she appeared in Freddy Jackson's video *Tasty Love.* In 1990 she made a number of television appearances on such shows as the "Oprah Winfrey Show" and the "Arsenio Hall Show."

References

"Couples." *People Weekly* 8 (10 October 1977): 98-102. Photographs, pp. 98, 99, 102.

Essence 4 (April 1975): 30-31. Photograph, p. 30.

"Model Make-Up Now." *Essence* 17 (January 1987): 58-59. Includes photographs.

Morgan, Ted. "I'm the Biggest Model, Period." *New York Times Magazine,* 17 August 1975: 12-15, 18, 20, 22, 24-24. Photographs, pp. 12, 13, 25.

Ploski, Harry A. and James Williams, eds. and comps. *The Negro Almanac.* 5th ed. Detroit: Gale Research, 1989. Includes photograph.

Jessie Carney Smith

Eunice Walker Johnson

(19? -)

Business executive, fashion show producer

Founded in 1958, one of the world's most elegant, elaborate, and popular fashion shows primarily for women, Ebony Fashion Fair, is making its usual dynamic splash in communities throughout the nation. With Eunice McAlpine Walker Johnson as producer and director, the show appeals to different races, ages, and genders, frequently giving the audience pulsating colors, opulent haute couture fashions by American and European designers, and exciting and attractive models not often seen by the public. The show makes a dramatic fashion statement, serves as a fund-raiser for sponsoring communities that sell subscriptions to *Jet* and *Ebony* magazines along with the admission ticket, and speaks to the imagination and expertise of Eunice Walker Johnson. During its history, the show has raised more than thirty-six million dollars for charities and community organizations. In addition to presenting the traveling fashion extravaganza, Eunice Johnson is fashion editor of *Ebony* magazine and secretary-treasurer of Johnson Publishing Company in Chicago, Illinois, where her husband, John H. Johnson, is publisher, chairman, and chief executive officer.

Born in Selma, Alabama, Eunice McAlpine Walker Johnson is the daughter of Nathaniel D. Walker and Ethel (McAlpine) Walker. Her grandfather, William H. McAlpine, who was born in slavery, was founder and second president of Selma University in Selma, Alabama. From 1880 to 1882 he was a founder and first president of the National Baptist Convention U.S.A. Nathaniel Walker was a prominent physician in Selma. At one time, Ethel McAlpine was a high school principal and a teacher at Selma University. The McAlpine and Walker families are featured in a section of Geri Major's book, *Black Society*.

Growing up in Selma, Eunice Johnson's favorite pastime was making elaborate costumes for her dolls. "I had the best collection of doll clothes of any of my peers," she said. Her craft enabled her to make her own clothes as well as shirts for her father ("Ebony Fashion Fair," 116).

Eunice Johnson graduated from Talladega College, Talladega, Alabama, with a B.A. in sociology. She had a minor in art. She received an M.A. degree in social services administration from Loyola University in Chicago. At the University of Chicago she completed studies of great books and also completed some graduate courses in journalism at Northwestern University. Her interest in interior decorating led her to study at the Ray Vogue School of Interior Design. Other courses she took to enrich her background and strengthen her expertise were sewing, tailoring, and fashion design.

In 1956, Jessie C. Dent, the wife of Dillard University's president, asked Johnson Publishing Company to sponsor a fund-raiser for the Women's Auxiliary of Flint-Goodrich Hospital in New Orleans. The highly-successful first show inspired John and Eunice Johnson to take it on tour as a benefit for other charities. Freda DeKnight, then food and fashion editor of *Ebony* magazine, organized the first national tour in 1958. Eunice Walker Johnson began to produce the Ebony Fashion Fair in 1963, and the show soon became well-known in the United States, as well as in fashion capitals in Europe, the sources of many of the garments modeled. The world's greatest designers create fashions for the annual Fashion Fair. Creations from the world's top black designers, such as Stephen Burrows, Jeffrey Banks, Patrick Kelly, and Willi Smith, have also been featured.

Each year the show centers around a specific theme; for example, in 1990 the theme was "Freedom Explosion." Johnson "conceives the Fair's themes each year, selects all garments that are shown, and supervises the selection and training of models" (*Ebony*, August 1977, 74). For thirty years, Johnson has traveled regularly to Florence, Milan, Rome, London, Paris, and New York to visit fashion houses and to select the "most dazzling fashions and to personally supervise photography of the fashions for *Ebony*" (Johnson, 185). From the start the show was a success and had widespread appeal. Eunice Johnson notes:

> In 1963, Emilio Pucci telephoned us from Florence, Italy, saying that he had just returned from a trip to Africa and had the inspiration to show his ready-to-wear fashions with fabric that he had designed featuring African masks. He wanted me to provide him with two "black models who look like Lena Horne." He later came to our office in Chicago, where we provided him with two models that he used in his ready-to-wear show at the Pitti Palace in Florence, Italy, in 1963.
>
> This was the first time Black models had ever paraded down the runways of Europe and the first time they had appeared at the Pitti Palace (Johnson, 185).

At a glance one assumes that the clothes are entirely high fashion; however, many are practical clothing appropriate for everyday wear. The show aims to offer options in styles. For example, the 1990 traveling show featured a full-figured model "whose clothing and personal flair [brought] the house down" (Johnson, 185). This versatility always helps the appeal to the black organizations that host the show each year in more than 160 cities. Through the sale of subscriptions for *Ebony* and *Jet* magazines, Fashion Fair has led to the raising of millions of dollars for churches, educational institutions, service organizations, and other sponsoring groups. At times models from the host cities have been invited to participate in the show. "I look for models that have a flair for fashion, a good natural stride, and an innate sense of confidence, for that self-assurance comes through on stage," Johnson says ("Ebony Fashion Fair," 114). The shows have been held in a variety of sites, such as coliseums, city auditoriums, country clubs, music halls, convention centers, and high school auditoriums or gymnasiums. Thus, through the vision of Eunice Walker Johnson, scholarships for black students have been raised, church building programs have been supported, and a host of other needy causes in the black community have been supported. At the same time, communities have had the pleasure of viewing the latest trends in the international fashion world.

Eunice Walker Johnson is a multitalented woman. When she is not traveling to fashion houses in New York and Europe to select designs or arranging the details of the annual show, she sits in her well-appointed office in the attractive Johnson Publishing House building at 820 South Michigan Avenue, handling the responsibilities of her other position with the publishing company. Her office displays foods from the *Ebony* kitchen—the section of the facility where foods are prepared and photographed for *Ebony* magazine as well as served to distinguished guests invited to the CEO's private dining room. A view of Eunice Johnson with Freda De Knight—who, until her death was home service director for *Ebony*—and her epicurean delights is shown in the September 1957 issue of *Ebony* (113). A founder of the company and the one who selected the name *Ebony* for the popular magazine when it was founded in 1945, has written articles for *Jet* and *Ebony*.

Johnson's contribution to America's cultural landscape has not gone unnoticed in high places. In 1972 President Richard M. Nixon named Eunice Walker Johnson a special ambassador to accompany Patricia Nixon to Liberia for the inauguration of William R. Tolbert, Jr., the country's new president. The entourage also visited Russia. When President Gerald Ford planned a visit to China, Japan, the Philippines, and Indonesia, he selected a blue-ribbon press corp of two hundred veteran members to accompany him. Eunice Johnson was the only black in the entourage. Other women in the group were United Press International's Helen Thomas, the then NBC-TV "Today Show" host Barbara Walters, and Naomi Nover of Nover News Service.

Civic, community, and professional organizations also appeal to Eunice Johnson, through which she devotes considerable time to social and economic uplift of the community. Her memberships and affiliations with such groups have been numerous and include the following: member of the women's board of the Art Institute of Chicago and the University of Chicago; board of directors, Selma University; advisory board, Harvard University School of Business; board of directors, United Negro College Fund; trustee board, Palm Springs (California) Desert Museum; and member of the Midwest Ballet and the National Foundation for the Fashion Industry. She has served as a trustee of Harvard Saint George School in Chicago, a director of the Adoptive Information Citizenry Committee, and on the board of the Hyde Park-Kenwood Women's Auxiliary of the Illinois Children's Home and Aid Society. She holds honorary degrees from Shaw University, Talladega College, and Selma University, and she is recipient of the Loyola University Alumni Award.

Personable, witty, attractive, and fashionable, Johnson is disciplined about nutrition and physical fitness, maintaining a size-eight figure.

John H. Johnson and Eunice McAlpine Johnson are the parents of Linda Johnson Rice, who at one time was fashion coordinator for the shows. She is now president of Johnson Publishing Company. John Johnson, Jr., died in 1981 of sickle-cell anemia.

References

Alpha Kappa Alpha Sorority. *Heritage Series*. Chicago: AKA, 1970.

"Ebony Fashion Fair Celebrates 33rd Anniversary." *Ebony* 46 (April 1991): 110-12, 114, 116. Includes photographs.

Ebony Success Library. Editors of Ebony. Chicago: Johnson Publishing Co., 1973. Includes photograph.

"Eunice W. Johnson." *Ebony* 32 (August 1977): 74, 76. Photographs, p. 74.

"Fried Ice Cream." *Ebony* 12 (September 1957): 110-114. Photograph, p. 110.

Johnson, Eunice. "Ebony Fashion Fair." *Ebony* 46 (November 1990): 185-86, 188, 190.

Major, Geri, with Doris Saunders. *Black Society*. Chicago: Johnson Publishing Co., 1976. Photograph, p. 316, 385.

"Publisher Johnson's Wife Only Black Press Corps Member In China with Ford." *Jet* 49 (18 December 1975): 8-9. Photographs, p. 8.

Jessie Carney Smith

Georgia Douglas Johnson

(1877-1966)

Poet, essayist, dramatist

Georgia Douglas Johnson wrote drama, novels, poetry, songs, short stories and other prose, much of which has been lost. Her literary reputation has traditionally been based solely on her verse. In 1922 James Weldon Johnson identified her as the first black woman after Phillis Wheatley and Frances Harper "to gain general recognition as a poet" (James Weldon Johnson, 181). In 1987 Gloria T. Hull concurs that Johnson was the "foremost" woman poet of the Harlem Renaissance in terms of productivity, reputation, and achievement. Still, she maintains that Johnson "could just as easily have come down through history known predominantly as a playwright rather than a poet" (Hull, 29, 168). In recent reexaminations of black women writers, critics like Gloria Hull and Erlene Stetson assert that a writer's stature must be based on her entire corpus (Stetson, 26; Hull 14-15). Johnson's literary contributions are currently being reassessed.

The Harlem Renaissance—the art movement that celebrated the New Negro's race consciousness—has traditionally been identified with male writers: Countee Cullen, Langston Hughes, Claude McKay, and Jean Toomer. Hull's study, *Color, Sex, and Poetry: Three Women Writers of the Harlem Renaissance*, documents how the sexual-literary politics of this era, along with broad social factors and patterns, excluded women from full participation in this movement. Cedric Dover's 1952 tribute to Georgia Douglas Johnson demonstrates this exclusion: "[Her] poems were published in the anthologies of this Renaissance, her books appeared in the decade that marked its beginning and end, and her home has always been a center for the writers and artists who gave it color and shape. She is definitely of it; but equally definitely not in it" (Dover, 633). Dover's assessment reveals how characteristics of a literary era are often determined without considering the women writers.

Georgia Douglas Johnson

Georgia Blanche Douglas Camp Johnson was born in Atlanta, Georgia, on September 10, 1877. The daughter of Laura (Jackson) Camp and George Camp, her paternal grandfather was English, her maternal grandmother was native American, and her maternal grandfather was black. In a 1927 autobiographical sketch, Johnson describes herself as a "little yellow girl in Atlanta, Georgia" (Cullen, 74). This heritage of mixed blood becomes a dominant theme in her writings.

Johnson grew up in Rome, sixty miles away from Atlanta. She describes her mother as having a "great big loving heart" and being very shy. (In 1931 Johnson talked with Theresa Scott Davis and Charles Y. Freeman about her youth; unless otherwise noted, the quotations in this paragraph and the next are her words from these conversations as quoted in Shockley). Johnson was a lonely child. Her mother worked during the day and resented the child's dominating personality. An aunt tried to give Johnson love and attention. Johnson began school in Rome and transferred to Atlanta. She did well in reading, recitation, and calisthenics but poorly in spelling and arithmetic. She continued to feel lonely at school and became withdrawn. At Atlanta University's Normal School she "experienced the first real homey sympathetic atmosphere" of her life, though she still felt isolated. "There were girls in school whom I would have liked to be associated with but I was too proud to seek them and I had no material offerings to make to attract superior girls." She cried the night before she graduated because she had to leave this "haven." An 1893 class photo shows her to be "a very mature-looking young girl in winter hat and furs" (Hull, 155).

Because of her loneliness at college, she had taught herself to play the violin and dreamed of becoming a composer. At the Oberlin Conservatory of Music and the Cleveland College of Music she studied harmony, piano, violin, and voice. While music was her "first and strongest passion, composition mainly,"she did not become a professional because "there seemed no outlets." While her training in music informs Johnson's poetry, critical attention has only recently focused on this "intricate weaving" (Stetson, 30).

Johnson Begins to Write Poetry and Drama

Returning to Georgia, she taught school in Marietta and then became an assistant principal in Atlanta. On September 28, 1903, she married Henry Lincoln Johnson, an Atlanta attorney and prominent member of the Republican party who had been delegate-at-large to the Republican National Convention since 1896. Georgia Douglas Johnson continued with her music and began to write stories and poems that she sent to newspapers and small magazines. She explains:

> I write because I love to write . . . . Long years ago when the world was new for me, I dreamed of being a composer—wrote songs, many of them. The words took fire and the music smoldered and so, following the lead of friends and critics, I turned my face toward poetry and put

> my songs away for a while. Then came drama. I was persuaded to try it and found it a living avenue—and yet—the thing left most unfinished, less exploited, first relinquished, is still nearest my heart and most dear (''The Contest Spotlight,'' 204).

Her poem ''Omnipresence'' appeared in the June 1905 *Voice of the Negro*. She and Henry Johnson had two sons: Henry Lincoln Johnson, Jr. (b. 1906) and Peter Douglas Johnson (1907-1957). In 1910 the family moved to Washington, D.C. William Howard Taft named Henry Johnson recorder of deeds in 1912, a post he held until 1916. From 1920-1925, he was Republican national committeeman from Georgia. While her husband tried to discourage her from writing, believing that her duties lay with him, the children, and caring for their home, others encouraged Georgia Johnson. Dean Kelly Miller at Howard University read Johnson's poems and put her in contact with William Stanley Braithwaite, whose poetry she had admired as a child. Johnson wrote that with their encouragement ''then began a quickening and a realization that she could do!'' (Cullen, 74).

Of her early work, Benjamin Brawley says that she ''cultivated especially the poignant, sharply chiselled lyric that became so popular with Sara Teasdale,'' the 1917 Pulitzer Prize winner for *Love Songs* (Brawley, 22). Indeed, the two were so frequently associated that Countee Cullen refers to Georgia Douglas Johnson ''in many instances bearing up bravely under comparison to Sara Teasdale'' (xiii). Winona Fletcher explains their similarities:

> Both poets wrote romantic, conventional verse, usually designated 'small poems' because of their length (four to eight lines with occasional poems of up to fourteen lines); both wrote lyrics that were drawn from simple introspection and instinct; neither concerned herself with religion or metaphysics'' (153).

As James Weldon Johnson notes, Johnson did not often experiment: ''She limits herself to the purely conventional forms, rhythms and rhymes, but through them she achieves striking effects'' (44). Like William Braithwaite, Countee Cullen, Alice Dunbar Nelson, and Angelina Grimké, she was a member of the Genteel School whose raceless or integrationist poetry portrayed universal themes in order to demonstrate competency within the Anglo-American tradition. Her poems began to appear in *Crisis* during 1916: ''Gossamer,'' ''Fame,'' and ''My Little One.''

Three Books of Poetry Set Johnson's Literary Reputation

Jessie Fauset helped Johnson select sixty-two lyric poems (composed mostly in quatrains) for her first book, *The Heart of a Woman* (Boston: Cornhill, 1918). In the introduction William Stanley Braithwaite wrote that these lyrics ''lifted the veil'' from what ''lies deeply hidden'' in a woman's heart (vii). Robert T. Kerlin commented on the ''[p]erfect lyrical notes, the most poignant pathos'' (148). Gloria T. Hull notes that Georgia Johnson's contemporaries ''failed to hear the irony, discontent, and quiet sedition that undercut some of [her poetry's] apparent sentimentality'' (21).

Bronze: A Book of Verse (1922) contains fifty-six poems in a variety of forms: sonnets, iambic heptameter lines, quatrains, and free verse. Dover says, ''The subject is still the heart of a woman, but now it is the heart of a colored woman aware of her social problem and the potentiality of the so-called hybrid'' (634). Georgia Douglas Johnson writes in the Author's Note: ''This book is the child of a bitter earth-wound. I sit on the earth and sing—sing out, and of, my sorrow. Yet, fully conscious of the potent agencies that silently work in their healing ministries, I know that God's sun shall one day shine upon a perfected and unhampered people.'' The volume becomes ''a sustained lyrical invocation'' with the nine sections moving from despair and entreaty to confidence and determination (Stetson, 31). The closing poems praise such individuals as John Brown, W. E. B. Du Bois, Emilie Bigelow Hapgood, Mary Church Terrell, and Henry Lincoln Johnson.

Fletcher says that Johnson's significance ''lies in her essence and development as a black poet whose writing reveals an awareness of the sociocultural and racial conditions of her own life that affected her creativity'' (153-54).

An Autumn Love Cycle (1928), Georgia Douglas Johnson's third collection, consists of fifty-eight poems, four to sixteen lines in length, which chronicle a woman's love affair, from beginning to end. In this work Johnson ''continues her mining of 'the heart of a woman' with . . . . a simple and straight-forward power that is not marred by self-conscious poeticizing'' (Hull, 175).

Stetson suggests that Johnson's first three works can be read as a whole:

> Over-all, all three volumes as musical lyrics form a sonata. The movement is from the intensely subjective world of the woman in the spring of life who is yet naive enough to shout her pain, to the summer of life, the red and fire of *Bronze* when motherhood, marriage and race exacts its toll on the female psyche and finally, to the autumnal season of realism and objectivity ''when love's triumphant day is done.'' (33)

These three books of poetry, which Georgia Douglas Johnson published between 1918 and 1928, have traditionally been the basis of her literary reputation.

Some contemporary reviewers lamented Johnson's return to raceless writing in *An Autumn Love Cycle*. Johnson identifies her predilection in a 1941 letter to Arna Bontemps:

> Whenever I can, I forget my special call to sorrow and live as happily as I may. Perhaps that is why I seldom elect to write racially. It seems to me an art to forget those things that make the heart heavy. If one can soar, he should soar,

> leaving his chains behind. But, lest we forget, we must now and then come down to earth, accept the yoke and help draw the load. (Hull, 179).

While she liked to soar especially when writing poetry, when she turned to drama Georgia Douglas Johnson took up the yoke and helped to draw the load. Like her contemporaries Angelina Grimké (*Rachel* 1916) and Mary Burrill (*Aftermath* 1919), she wrote dramas that protested lynching. Zona Gale, a popular white woman writer and critic, introduced Johnson to play writing sometime in the early 1920s. In two one-act plays (no longer extant) Johnson supports the Dyer Anti-Lynching Bill before its 1922 defeat; *A Bill to Be Passed* advocated its passage and *And Still They Paused* addressed the delay in its enactment. Another one-act play, *A Sunday Morning in the South* (circa 1925), opens in 1924 with a grandmother and her two grandsons having breakfast. Spirituals from the nearby church are heard in the background as a neighbor on her way to service tells them that the police are searching for a black man purported to have attacked a white woman. As they anticipate what will happen, Tom Griggs, the eldest grandson, says: ''They lynch you bout anything too, not jest women. They say Zeb Brooks was strung up because he and his boss had er argiment.'' Almost immediately the police arrive to arrest Tom, disregarding his protestations of innocence and the testimony of his family. Although the girl is uncertain about identifying him, the police insist that Tom ''fits'' the description of the man—''age around twenty, five feet five or six, brown skin''—''like a glove.'' Tom is taken away and lynched by the white mob—who ''wont gointer be cheated outen they Nigger this time''—before any appeals can be made. The grandmother dies when she hears the news. The play is effective because of its ''thorough and efficient exposition, swift but not hasty movement, variegated mix of mood and tone (from comic to pathetic), and tight construction'' (Hull, 172).

Blue Blood was Georgia Douglas Johnson's first drama to gain public attention, winning honorable mention in the 1926 *Opportunity* magazine competition. Produced that fall by the Krigwa Players in New York City with May Miller and Frank S. Horne, it was published by Appleton in 1927. The play addresses the rape of black women by white men after the Civil War. On the wedding day of their children, the mothers of the bride and groom begin bragging about their children's ''blue blood,'' only to discover that they have the same father—a wealthy white banker. The daughter is told, but the three women agree that the son must not discover the truth. Mrs. Bush, the bride's mother, says: ''Keep it from him. It's the black women that have got to protect their men from the white men by not telling on 'em.'' This comedy ends with the daughter running off to marry a former suitor, who still loves her, so that the secret can be kept. Still the serious subject underscores the happy ending, emphasizing how the pain of the past continues to haunt younger generations.

Plumes (submitted under the pseudonym of John Temple) won first prize in the 1927 *Opportunity* contest. Rachel France finds it one of the few American plays ''that proved itself a worthy heir to the 'universals' of folk drama'' (75). Set in the contemporary rural South, the drama opposes folk beliefs and modern medicine. A mother anguishes over her gravely ill daughter; she must decide whether to spend fifty dollars for a funeral or on an operation the doctor admits is just a ''last chance'' effort. After already losing two loved ones, Charity tells her friend: ''I made up my mind the time Bessie went that the next one of us what died would have a shore nuff funeral, everything grand,—with plumes!—I saved and saved and now. . . .'' Charity feels that the doctor cannot save her daughter. If she pays for the operation, she won't be able to show her love through a ''grand'' funeral ''with plumes'' on the horses that pull the hearse. Before she makes a decision, her daughter dies. Commenting on Georgia Douglas Johnson's ''authenticity,'' Hull says, ''In *Plumes*, she is as 'folk' as she is 'academic' in her poetry'' (170).

The play was presented by the Harlem Experimental Theatre, which sought to foster the development of the black folk play. *Plumes* also played as a trio with Eugene O'Neill's *All God's Chillun Got Wings* (1924) and Paul Green's *In Abraham's Bosom* (1926) at the Chicago Cube Theater and in other cities including Boston, New York, and Washington, D.C.. Patricia A. Young says of Johnson and her contemporaries—Burrill, Dunbar-Nelson, and Grimké:

> [T]hey wrote a number of plays presenting images of black life that were opposite to the exotic ones appearing in the commercial theater of the New Negro Renaissance. In their protest works, they make no attempt to disguise their political motives, and they address the realistic problems that Afro-Americans, especially Afro-American women, faced in their daily lives (152).

Even as her reputation was growing, Georgia Douglas Johnson was finding it more difficult economically to write. After her husband's death on September 10, 1925, she assumed financial responsibility for her sons' education. Henry Johnson, Jr., was then attending Bowdoin College and would continue at Howard University's law school. Peter Johnson was at Dartmouth College and would attend Howard University's medical school. In recognition of Henry Johnson's contributions, Calvin Coolidge appointed Georgia Douglas Johnson Commissioner of Conciliation for the Department of Labor, a post she held from 1925 to 1934. In 1928 Johnson identifies that her ''great fear'' is not to be able ''to do all of the work she has planned to do.'' She explains that though ''she works incessantly, her time is too much taken up with making a living to give very much of it to literary work'' (Calvin, *Pittsburgh Courier*, 1 July 1928). Hull documents the enormous courage it took for African-American women to dedicate themselves to writing during this time. ''Reared as proper, middle-class, almost Victorian black women who were trained to be proofs of black female morals and modesty,'' it was difficult for them to promote their own writings and to gain the financial and artistic support which was available to their male colleagues'' (Hull, 24). The lack of time for writing haunted Georgia Douglas

Johnson for the remainder of her life. In the July 1927 *Opportunity* she says:

> If I might ask of some fairy godmother special favors, one would sure be for a clearing space, elbow room in which to think and write and live beyond the reach of the Wolf's fingers. However, much that we do and write about comes just because of this daily struggle for bread and breath—so, perhaps it's just as well (204).

Johnson Provides Mecca for Black Artists and Intellectuals

Johnson's contributions to the New Negro movement extend beyond her writing. Her home at 1461 S Street N.W. became a mecca for black artists and intellectuals for four decades. She called it Half-Way House: "I'm half way between everybody and everything and I bring them together." Geraldyn Dismond, writer of the *Pittsburgh Courier* "Through the Lorgnette" column, describes Johnson in her October 29, 1927, column:

> She is very sensitive, retiring and absolutely feminine. Harlem has no hold on her and she is happiest when in her own home, surrounded by her flowers, pictures, books and two sons, or when presiding at her informal Saturday evenings at home for the young artists. She is almost timid and highly appreciative of any recognition that her people give her, and she rejoises [sic] in them. She is easily depressed, yet the simplest act of kindness sends her spirits soaring.

In *When Harlem was in Vogue*, David Levering Lewis describes the literary people who gathered to discuss art and to read their work: "In the living room of her S Street house behind the flourishing rose bushes, a freewheeling jumble of the gifted, famous, and odd came together on Saturday nights" (127). Among the guests were: Sterling Brown, Countee Cullen, W. E. B. Du Bois, Alice Dunbar-Nelson, Jessie Fauset, Angelina Grimké, Langston Hughes, James Weldon Johnson, Vachel Lindsay, Alain Locke, Richard Bruce Nugent, Anne Spencer, and Jean Toomer. Hull identifies Georgia Douglas Johnson's significance as hostess to the Renaissance: "[Her] role as cultural sponsor was all the more important because she played it outside of Harlem, New York, thus becoming a nexus for the intercity connections that helped to make the movement a truly national one" (6).

Georgia Douglas Johnson valued friendship. In her relationships with others lies "further evidence of her expansive, sensitive and life-giving sympathies" (Hull, 189). She "adopted" Langston Hughes, Glenn Carrington, and Harold Jackman as her "sons." Johnson says: "I take not only stray people in, but I try to see if somebody wants to live, and if they want to live, I do . . . my best to help them." Poet-playwright Owen Dodson elaborates:

> She took in anybody—old lame dogs, blind cats . . . any kind of limping animal. . . . Then she took in stray people—mostly artists who were out of money. People like Zora Neale Hurston who stayed there . . . or some artists who were a little berserk. And she was capable of giving them a soothing balm. She knew how to do for people. . . . When you entered the hallway, you knew that you were entering another country (Hull, 187).

The latter 1920s were Johnson's "brightest season in the public sun" (Hull, 167). In addition to writing and overseeing her literary salon, she traveled, speaking and reading in various cities. She was active in political and racial organizations, belonging to the American Society of African Culture, the (New York City) Civic Club, the District of Columbia Women's Party, the League for Abolition of Capital Punishment, the League of American Writers, the League of Neighbors, the (District of Columbia) Matrons, the National Song Writers Guild, the Poet's Council of the National Women's Party, the Poet Laureate League, the Poets League of Washington, the Republican Club of Washington, the Virginia White Speel Republican Club, and the Writers' League Against Lynching. She was also a member of the First Congregational church. Hull says, "Despite these affiliations, it is obvious that GDJ was not the clubwoman activist that some of her compeers were. Time, temperament, and interest led her in other directions. Unfortunately, this may have isolated her somewhat from other black women" (189).

Georgia Douglas Johnson was also a journalist. From 1926 to 1932 her "Homely Philosophy" weekly newspaper column was syndicated. In a June 30, 1928, column on conceit she writes in a typical vein: "Who of us has not looked about to find someone upon whom to fix the blame for our own vexations and troubles? Let us be fair and frank with ourselves at least and place the blame where it belongs—usually, upon our own heads. Always and ever, let us beware of ourselves." Hull says that in other aspects of her life Johnson also "relied heavily on inspirational cliches" which "were not so much platitudes as simplicities that living had brazened true" (186).

Under the pseudonym of Mary Strong, she organized a correspondence club, the "One World" Washington Social Letter Club, which began around 1930 and continued until at least 1965. She advertised with the slogan "One God One World One Hope" and encouraged: "If you can't travel—write! Your life is just what you make it, broad or narrow." She makes contact "with people all over the world and very specially, Africa. . . . The postage is quite a figure, but I consider this part of the offering I am happy to make to the dark Continent. I hope through the Club to bring to those who are eager for touch with the Western world, an avenue" (Hull, 206-07).

During the late thirties and forties after leaving the Department of Labor, she worked at temporary jobs and tried unsuccessfully to get published and to find support for her writing. In a March 1950 letter to Harold Jackman she wrote:

"You would be surprised to know how many foundations I have tried, and more surprised to learn that . . . each one, said 'no,' but most surprised to learn that I have still high hopes" (Shockley, 351). She continued to work on various writing projects. Between 1935 and 1939 she submitted at least five plays to the Federal Theatre Project: *Blue-eyed Black Boy*, in which the protagonist is saved from lynching when his mother reveals to the governor that he is his son; *Safe*, in which a mother who delivers a male child while hearing a lynching immediately strangles her baby in order to keep him "safe" from lynchers; *A Sunday Morning in the South*; and two historical dramatizations of escapes from slavery—those of Frederick Douglass and William and Ellen Craft. *Sunday Morning* was accepted but not performed.

Of the many short stories that Georgia Douglas Johnson wrote only three are extant today: "Free," "Gesture," and "Tramp Love." "Gesture" and "Tramp Love," were published in the summer 1936 and spring 1937 issues of *Challenge* magazine under the name Paul Tremaine.

During World War II Georgia Douglas Johnson "poured out a stream of effective poems and fighting songs," such as "To Gallant France" and "A Soldier's Letter" (Dover, 634). Her poem "Whose Son" accompanied a poster of a black soldier carrying a white comrade. "Tomorrow's World," which was set to music by Lillian Evanti, encouraged reflection upon the futility of war; it was read on the senate floor and published in the *Congressional Record*. Eighty poems collected as a *Bridge to Brotherhood* were meant "to foster and promote good feeling between the races" but were never published. After the war, she and Evanti collaborated on other pieces, three of which were published: "Dedication" (1948), "Beloved Mother" (1952), and "Hail to Fair Washington" (1953). Her trademark poem "I Want to Die While You Love Me" was also set to music and sung by Harry Burleigh on Victor Records.

In the 1950s she tried to publish *White Men's Children*—a novel dealing with the "interplay of bloods"—and the political biography of her husband entitled *The Black Cabinet* (Shockley, 351). In the December 1952 *Crisis* Cedric Dover wrote "The Importance of Georgia Douglas Johnson," which was the first time that her work had been discussed in a separate literary essay in an African-American magazine. Her poems continued to appear in such periodicals as the *Negro Digest* and the Baltimore *Afro-American* and her home remained "open to anyone at any time" (Hatch and Shine, 211). In her neighborhood she became known as "the old woman with the headband and the tablet around her neck." Georgia Douglas Johnson explained that she wore a notebook and pencil "so that when an idea, a word, a line for a poem comes, I jot it down." James V. Hatch describes her in the 1950s as "a beautiful, down-to-earth woman, who had no concern for appearances or material things. . . . Mrs. Johnson might have seemed eccentric to some, but to those who knew her she was a lovable old woman, and above all a true artist, who continued to write and publish her poetry until her death" (211).

In 1965 she received an honorary doctor of letters from Atlanta University and her last book of poetry was published—*Share My World*. This thirty-two-page collection contains poems from previous books as well as recent ones; most articulate her philosophy of life. In "Your World" she writes: "Your world is as big as you make it / I know, for I used to abide / In the narrowest nest in a corner / My wings pressing close to my side." The last stanza of the title poem reads: "And when I have rebuilt my world / Uncircumscribed and free / I shall invite all humankind / To share my world with me." In "One Lives Too Long" she writes of losing the desire to live forever: "But now I know the gift of death / Is merciful—when understood." In May 1966 she suffered a stroke and was taken to Freedman's Hospital in Washington, D.C. When she died on Saturday, May 14, May Miller was sitting with her, holding her hand while repeatedly saying, "Poet Georgia Douglas Johnson." Owen Dodson read "I Want To Die While You Love Me" and "Your World" at the funeral. She was buried in Lincoln Cemetery.

Only a portion of Georgia Douglas Johnson's work has been preserved. A 1944 letter to Jackman provides an insight into her productivity:

> Have about eight books here ready to get going—three new books of poetry, thirty plays both one and three act, thirty short stories, a novel, a book of philosophy, a book of exquisite sayings. . . . twenty songs . . . seems I must go to that last peaceful abode without getting them printed . . . but why should I worry. Balzac left forty unpublished books (Hull, 189).

Tragically, on the day of her funeral, the papers in her house—including manuscripts and correspondence—were simply thrown away. While her dream that the remainder of her corpus would be published was not realized, Georgia Douglas Johnson's legacy includes the encouragement to dream.

References

Brawley, Benjamin. *The Negro Genius*. New York: Dodd, Mead, 1937.

Calvin, Floyd. "Georgia Douglas Johnson Fears She Won't Have Time to Complete All of the Work She Has Planned." *Pittsburgh Courier* (7 July 1928).

"The Contest Spotlight." *Opportunity* 5 (July 1927): 204.

Cullen, Countee. *Caroling Dusk: An Anthology of Verse by Negro Poets*. New York: Harper, 1927.

Dismond, Geraldyn. "Through the Lorgnette." Pittsburgh *Courier* (29 October 1927).

Dover, Cedric. "The Importance of Georgia Douglas Johnson." *Crisis* 59 (December 1952): 633.

Fletcher, Winona. "Georgia Douglas Johnson." *Afro-American Writers from the Harlem Renaissance to 1940.*

Vol. 51 of *Dictionary of Literary Biography*. Eds. Trudier Harris and Thadious M. Davis. Detroit: Gale Research, 1987.

France, Rachel, ed. *A Century of Plays by American Women*. New York: Rosen, 1979.

Hatch, James V., and Ted Shine, eds. *Black Theatre, U.S.A.: Forty-Five Plays by Black Americans, 1847-1974*. New York: Free Press, 1974.

Hull, Gloria T. *Color, Sex, and Poetry: Three Women Writers of the Harlem Renaissance*. Bloomington: Indiana University Press, 1987.

Johnson, Georgia Douglas. ''Homely Philosophy.'' *Pittsburgh Courier* (30 June 1928).

Johnson, James Weldon, ed. *The Book of American Negro Poetry*. Rev. Ed. San Diego: Harvest, 1922.

Kerlin, Robert T. *Negro Poets and Their Poems*. Washington, D.C.: Associated Publishers, 1923.

Locke, Alain, and Jessie Redmon Fauset. ''Notes on New Books.'' Review of *Bronze*. *Crisis* 25 (February 1923): 161.

Shockley, Ann Allen. *Afro-American Women Writers 1746-1933*. Boston: G. K. Hall, 1988.

Stetson, Erlene. ''Rediscovering the Harlem Renaissance: Georgia Douglas Johnson, 'The New Negro Poet.''' *Obsidian* 5 (Spring/Summer 1979): 26-34.

Young, Patricia Alzatia. ''Female Pioneers in Afro-American Drama: Angelina Weld Grimké, Georgia Douglas Johnson, Alice Dunbar-Nelson, and Mary Powell Burrill.'' Dissertation. Bowling Green State University, 1986.

Collections

Georgia Douglas Johnson's papers are housed in the library of the Neighborhood Union Collection, Robert W. Woodruff Library, Atlanta University Center; Oberlin College Archives, Oberlin, Ohio; Harmon Foundation Records, Library of Congress Manuscript Division (information from Draft Register in Repository); correspondence in Miscellaneous Letters and Papers, Schomburg Center for Research in Black Culture, New York Public Library (photographs are also available); correspondence in the Countee Cullen Papers, Amistad Research Center, Tulane University, New Orleans; correspondence in various collections at the Moorland-Spingarn Research Center, Howard University (Thomas Montgomery Gregory, Angelina Weld Grimké, Francis J. Grimké, Rosey Pool, Arthur B. Spingarn, and Joel E. Spingarn).

Ann Trapasso

Halle Tanner Dillon Johnson

(1864-1901)

Physician

A black American woman who was to become known as a person of uncommon ability and the first black woman and first woman ever admitted on examination to practice medicine in Alabama, Halle (Hallie) Tanner Dillon Johnson was born on October 17, 1864, in Pittsburgh, Pennsylvania. She was the eldest daughter and one of nine children of Benjamin Tucker Tanner and Sarah Elizabeth (Miller) Tanner. (Her death certificate lists 1865 as her birth date and Gerri Major, *Black Society*, gives 1863.)

Johnson's parents married in 1858. Her father, who was born in 1835 of free black parents in Pittsburgh (his father's name was Hugh), received a college education before the Civil War, and supported his studies at Avery College by working as a barber. Her mother had been a teacher in Pittsburgh. After marriage, Benjamin Tanner became a successful minister, editor of the *Christian Recorder*, the *AME Church Review*, and finally a bishop in the African Methodist Episcopal (AME) church. Two of the Tanner

Halle Tanner Dillon Johnson

children died in infancy and the others lived into adulthood. Three of them attained more than ordinary distinction. Halle Tanner became a physician, Carlton Tanner became a minister in his mother's church, and Henry Ossawa Tanner (1859-1937) was a gifted and celebrated painter of landscapes, religious themes, and genre subjects. He was named in honor of abolitionist John Brown—given the middle name Ossawa, derived from Osawatomie, Kansas, where Brown fought proslavery men.

Benjamin and Sarah Elizabeth Tanner had a profound impact on the cultural development of their children. They also exposed them to the works of prominent black artists Edward M. Bannister and Edmonia Lewis. The family unit had always been strong, and Sarah Tanner devoted her time to the welfare of the family. Their residence, 2908 Diamond Street in Philadelphia, "was for over a quarter of a century a rest haven to the traveler and a solace to the family" (Brown). As president and treasurer of the Parent Mite Missionary Society of her church, she had to attend quarterly meetings of the group, which were great moments in the family's history. Her remarkable contribution to humanity caused Hallie Quinn Brown to recognize Sarah Elizabeth Tanner in a brief essay in *Homespun Heroines* (32-33). Indeed, the Tanner family had uncommon ability.

The details of Johnson's early life and education are unavailable in any known sources. She married Charles E. Dillon of Trenton, New Jersey, in 1886 and they had one child, Sadie, born in 1887. Nothing more is said of Dillon's life. According to Johnson's grandniece, Rae Alexander-Minter, Dillon died but his death date is unknown (Letter to Jessie Carney Smith, 17 August 1990). At the age of twenty-four, Johnson entered the Woman's Medical College in Philadelphia, completed a three-year course, and graduated in a class of thirty-six women on May 7, 1891, with high honor. Tuskegee Institute (now University) in Alabama had an opening for its first resident physician. Booker T. Washington, president of the school, had searched for four years to secure a black American resident physician to treat and minister to local health needs. White doctors in town had attended to the sick, charged moderate fees, and had been cordial and affable in their manners. But Washington felt "the growing need of broadening out its work and putting this responsible charge in the hands of one of the members of the race, if one could be found capable and venturesome enough to stand the rigorous examination which the State of Alabama gives to all applicants who desire to practice medicine within its borders" (Atlanta University *Bulletin*, n.p.).

Washington wrote to the dean of the Woman's Medical College in search of a black graduate for the position. Johnson responded and expressed interest in the position. In response, Washington wrote to Dillon:

> I am in receipt of yours of April 9 and in reply would say that we expect to have in the future a resident physician at the institution and prefer a lady. It is my intention to pass through Philadelphia either in May or June and at one of which times I shall like to see you, provided you think it well to consider our proposition. I will not make our offer binding until I have seen you. In the meantime I write the facts in reference to the position so that you will let me know whether or not you are inclined to consider the offer favorably.
>
> We will pay a salary of $600 a year with board for twelve months' work. . . . This is with the understanding that you would teach two classes a day, if necessary, and take full charge of the health department. We should expect you to compound your own medicine as far as possible. We are making our purchases of drugs at wholesale rates. Our greatest out-lay at present is for medicine. We are compelled to buy in small quantities at the local drug stores (Booker T. Washington to Halle Tanner Dillon, 16 April, 1891).

The *Booker T. Washington Papers* report conflicting dates of Halle Tanner's letter to Washington.

At that time Alabama was already requiring physicians who wished to practice in the state to pass either a local or state examination. Washington advised her that she could take either examination and expressed confidence that, although she was black, she would encounter no racial practices in the examinations. She would need to pass the examination and begin work at Tuskegee on September 1, 1891.

Washington described the city and noted the provisions that Johnson would have for additional income:

> Tuskegee is a town of about 3000 inhabitants, over half colored. In addition to the salary named. . .we have in connection with the institution 30 officers and teachers, seven or eight of these have families. This would have nothing to do with your school work and the compensation would be extra.
>
> We have never had a resident physician, I think you would like the work here as it is entirely in the hands of colored people. . . . (Booker T. Washington to Halle Tanner Dillon, 16 April 1891).

The salary would be modest, she was advised, but Tuskegee, like other black colleges of that era, attracted good faculty and administrators who were willing to come for the good of the cause. Tuskegee was supported by charity and workers who had a missionary spirit. "Halle and Mr. Washington met in Philadelphia in the spring of. . .1891, and he assured her and her father that Tuskegee would be the right place for a young black doctor to begin her career" (Rae Alexander-Minter to Jessie Carney Smith, 17 August 1990).

Tuskegee Appoints First Black Resident Physician

Dillon accepted the challenge and arrived at Tuskegee in August 1891. She became acquainted with the facilities, and several days later she left for Montgomery to prepare for the state examinations. "Mr. Washington had arranged for her to study for the strenuous exam with Dr. Cornelius Nathaniel Dorsette, who practiced medicine in Montgomery and was the first black physician to pass the Alabama medical examinations" (Rae Alexander-Minter to Jessie Carney Smith). Bishop Tanner was concerned over his daughter's success and wrote to Washington:

> Of course, we are all anxious about the Doctor. Not that we have any misgivings as to her ability to pass any reasonable and just examination. But we know that both her sex and her color will be against her (20 August 1891).

The Tuskegee Student, a campus publication, cited the appointment and gave an account of her examination by the state board—the examination that she elected to take. The fact that a black American woman was to sit for the examination and the record that she established caused quite a local and national stir. The examination was held in Montgomery without incident, and she was well received and courteously treated. As the examination was underway, there was public interest in seeing this person who, considering her color and gender and the race relations in Alabama at that time, dared sit for the test. The public was curious about such simple matters as "how she looked." She had been tested in ten subjects, each occupying a full day. The examination ended and the supervisor of the board was impressed with the neatness and cleanliness of her work. She returned to Tuskegee, expecting to hear the results of the examination within one week. Nearly three weeks passed before she was to learn that she had an average of 78.81—a grade that elated Johnson but led her to conclude that the "critical medical pen has been perhaps too rigorously applied to her papers" (Atlanta University *Bulletin*).

The conservatism of the medical profession in regard to black Americans notwithstanding, the press considered Johnson's record a signal victory. It must have made some change in southern white thought, especially among those who doubted the black American's ability to meet the challenges of various professions, particularly medicine. The passing of the examination meant that Dillon had become the first black American woman to practice medicine in Alabama. She also became "the first woman ever admitted on examination to practice medicine in Alabama." But the systematic discrimination against blacks had prevailed earlier when Anna M. Longshore, a white woman, failed the medical examination yet was admitted to practice medicine in Alabama before Dillon took the examination and passed. While at first Alabama newspapers "ridiculed the fact that a Negro was even to appear before the State board," once she became a qualified practitioner all major newspapers in the state noted her achievement.

Johnson remained as resident physician at Tuskegee from 1891 to 1894. During her stay she established a Nurses' Training School and the Lafayette Dispensary. In 1894 she married the Reverend John Quincy Johnson, who in 1893-1894 taught mathematics at the institute. In 1894-1895 John Quincy Johnson was president of Allen University, a private black college in Columbia, South Carolina. The Johnsons moved to Nashville, where he pastored Saint Paul AME Church from 1900 to 1903. They lived at 1010 South Cherry Street.

G. F. Ritchings, author of *Evidences of Progress Among Colored People,* reported that he visited Halle Johnson while the Johnsons were living in Princeton, New Jersey. He found her home "neatly kept" and she gave "every evidence of culture and refinement about the household." (412). The Johnsons had three sons—John Quincy, Jr., Benjamin T., and Henry Tanner. Halle Tanner Johnson died at home in Nashville during childbirth complicated by dysentery on April 26, 1901, when she was approximately thirty-seven years old. Her occupation at the time was listed as housekeeper. She is buried in Greenwood Cemetery. Family members known to be living today are the Johnsons' grandchildren, John Quincy Johnson of Sharon, Massachusetts; Joseph Johnson of Washington, D.C.; and Benjamin Tanner Johnson, Jr., of Berkeley, California. Two grandnieces—Rae Alexander-Minter, of the Bronx, New York, and Mary A. Brown, of Washington, D.C., also survive.

References

Alexander-Minter, Rae. "The Tanner Family: A Grandniece's Chronicle." *Henry Ossawa Tanner*. Exhibition catalog. Philadelphia: Philadelphia Museum of Art, 1991. Includes photograph of the Tanner family.

——. Telephone interview with author. 14 July, 1990, 17 August 1990. 20 August 1990.

——. Letter to author. 17 August 1990.

Atlanta University *Bulletin*. November 1891. Quotes article from *The Tuskegee Student*.

Bearden, Romare, and Harry Henderson. *Six Black Masters of American Art*. New York: Doubleday, 1972. Photograph of Halle Tanner Johnson's parents, p. 45.

Brown, Hallie Quinn. *Homespun Heroines and Other Women of Distinction*. Xenia, Ohio: Aldine Pub. Co., 1926. Includes a photograph and biographical sketch of Sarah Elizabeth Tanner, Halle Tanner Johnson's mother, and information on the Tanner family.

Contributions of Black Women to America. Vol. 2. Ed. Marianna W. Davis. Columbia, S.C.: Kenday Press,. 1982. Includes a photograph of the 1891 graduating class of the Woman's Medical College of Pennsylvania.

Dannett, Sylvia G. L. *Profiles of Negro Womanhood*. Vol. 1, 1619-1900. Yonkers, N.Y.: Educational Heritage, 1964.

Harlan, Louis, ed. *The Booker T. Washington Papers.* Vol. 3, 1889-95. Urbana: University of Illinois Press, 1972.

Major, Gerri, with Doris Saunders. *Black Society*. Chicago: Johnson Pub. Co., 1976. (Gives genealogical chart of the Richard Tanner family (free blacks in Pittsburgh on 19 August 1858, and Halle Tanner Johnson's paternal grandfather).

Mossell, Mrs. N. F.. *The Work of the Afro-American Woman.* Philadelphia: George S. Ferguson, 1908. Reprint-ed. Freeport, N.Y.: Books for Libraries, 1971.

Ritchings, G. F.. *Evidences of Progress Among Colored People.* 2nd ed. Philadelphia: George S. Ferguson Company, 1896. Photograph, p. 411.

Sterling, Dorothy, ed. *We Are Your Sisters: Black Women in the Nineteenth Century.* New York: Norton, 1984. Photograph with classmates, Woman's Medical College, p. 448.

Wright, R. R., Jr., ed. *Encyclopedia of African Methodism.* Philadelphia, AME Book Concern, 1916. Includes photograph of John Quincy Johnson.

Collections

Halle Tanner Johnson's papers are in the University of Pennsylvania archives. A small collection of clippings, photographs, and medical college records are in the Archives and Special Collections on Women in Medicine as a part of the Black Women Physicians Project, the Medical College of Pennsylvania. Some items are also in the Booker T. Washington Papers in the Library of Congress and published in *The Booker T. Washington Papers*, vol. 3, 1889-1899. Her death certificate is on file in the Tennessee State Library and Archives in Nashville.

Jessie Carney Smith

Helene Johnson

(1906-)

Poet

Helene Johnson (Helen Johnson Hubbell) was one of the youngest of the Harlem Renaissance poets. In African-American literary history, Helene Johnson's works are models for aspiring poets—especially for African-American women poets who have long been led to believe that no tradition of achievement exists among black American women in this genre prior to the 1960s. Additionally, in African-American literary history, Helene Johnson is a transitional poet whose works of the 1920s and 1930s signal a striking out in new directions among black American women poets, who began to abandon romantic themes and poetic conventions at this juncture.

She was born July 7, 1906, in Boston, Massachusetts, in New England Women's Hospital, the only child of Ella (Benson) Johnson and William Johnson. Born to a mother whose family had migrated from the southeastern United States to New England, Johnson counted among her ancestors Benjamin Benson and Helen (Pease) Benson.

Born a slave in Camden, South Carolina, located near the Sea Islands, the twice-married Benson was a carpenter by trade. Helen Pease Benson was his second wife and the mother of his three daughters—Ella, Rachel, and Minnie. Since Benson was a slave, Helene Johnson assumed that her grandmother was a slave as well. After his three daughters sought to improve their lots by moving north, Benjamin Benson followed them to Boston. Later he bought property in Oak Bluff on Martha's Vineyard, Massachusetts, and moved there, earning a living by building houses. While residing in Oak Bluff, Benson incurred the scorn of his neighbors—primarily because of his southern, non-Yankee origins and only secondarily because of his race. Unhappy in the North, Benson returned later in his life to his beloved South, where he lived out his final days. The family continues to own property in Oak Bluff, where black American writer Dorothy West, Helene Johnson's cousin, currently resides on land originally purchased by Benjamin Benson. (Most of the details of Johnson's life presented in this biographical sketch were provided by the poet herself during interviews conducted in 1986.)

Named in honor of her maternal grandmother, Helen Pease Benson, Helene Johnson felt parentless as a child. From her own perspective, she was a "Tennessee Williams child." She never knew her father; she had no idea what he looked like, having never seen a photograph of him. All she had been told was that he was a Greek, that he and her mother were incompatible, and that he probably lived in Chicago. She never determined whether he was actually of Greek origin or whether the designation "Greek" meant something else with regard to him. Neither she nor he seems to have attempted to locate the other.

Ella Benson Johnson was a domestic worker who was at her places of employment almost constantly. Among the families by whom Ella was employed were the Dwights, who lived at 14 Apian Way, Cambridge, Massachusetts, and the Badgers, who lived at 1688 Beacon Street, Boston, Massachusetts. Mr. Dwight was affiliated, Johnson recalled, with Harvard University, and the Badgers owned vast amounts of New Hampshire real estate. Respected by her employers for her forthrightness, Ella Johnson cooked for these wealthy families and performed other household tasks. Though she was not formally educated, she had an active mind and was interested in world happenings to such an extent that during their outings together, Ella and Helene Johnson attended events to which parents in the early twentieth century rarely took their children. Not only did her mother make sure that

Helene saw male newsmakers such as the Wright brothers but also, a feminist of sorts, she took pains to accompany her daughter to events that featured women prominently. In spite of Ella Johnson's native intelligence and curiosity, she was never able to improve dramatically her lot in life, largely because of color bias, her daughter believed.

During her childhood, Johnson lived primarily at 478 Brookline Avenue, Boston, Massachusetts, in a household that was largely female dominated. She remembered that her mother once had a male suitor who was a dentist but that the only male she normally encountered was Isaac Christopher West, Dorothy West's father, a produce dealer who was known during the early twentieth century as Boston's banana king. The other residents of 478 Brookline Avenue were Ella's sisters, Minnie and Rachel. Each of the sisters gave birth to a daughter within a single twelve-month period that spanned part of 1906 and 1907. Minnie gave birth to Jean; Rachel, to Dorothy; and Ella, to Helene.

Of her two aunts, Rachel was the one Johnson remembered more vividly. She recalled that Rachel disliked her and speculated that perhaps Rachel's disdain might have been a result of their similarity in personality. In spite of the friction between them, they occasionally conversed at length about the theater, which was Rachel's passion. Interestingly, Rachel dubbed the poet Helene, a name that appealed to Rachel because it had a fancy ring to it; the poet's legal name is Helen. Although the writer preferred Helen and used this name in most contexts, she signed the name Helene Johnson to all of her published poems, and she is known as Helene Johnson in literary circles.

During her childhood, Johnson's family went back and forth between Boston and Oak Bluff. She recalled that her Aunt Rachel was rather erratic and registered her and Dorothy in an Oak Bluff school at one point and then later enrolled them in a Boston school. In Boston, Johnson attended the Lafayette School, next the Martin School, and finally Girls' Latin High School. Additionally, she and her cousins took piano lessons at home and were tutored at home by Bessie Trotter—the daughter of Monroe Trotter, the politically active editor and founder of the black American newspaper *The Boston Guardian*—and Maude Stewart. Their tutoring was not like the tutoring that children of wealthy parents received but was instead supplemental to the education they received in school. In Johnson's view, she was bright in all subjects but was not ambitious enough to earn high grades consistently. She required challenges to excel. Without challenges she was, by her own admission, an indifferent student. Although she did not aspire to a degree, she enrolled in classes at Boston University after she graduated from high school.

Poetry Prize Brings National Recognition

In 1927 Johnson moved to New York City, ostensibly to attend Columbia University, where again she never seriously considered pursuing a degree. The chief reason she went to New York was that she believed that it was a more exciting place than Boston. She had first gained a sense of how thrilling the city could be during a brief visit in 1926, the year before she moved there. She had gone to the National Urban League's *Opportunity* dinner with acceptance speech in hand—a speech she prepared after having been informed that she had won a prize. The prize was First Honorable Mention for her poem "Fulfillment" in the *Opportunity* literary contest, a competition that attracted 1,276 submissions that year in its various categories. It is the young Helene Johnson of this period that Wallace Thurman describes in his 1932 roman à clef, *Infants of the Spring*, in which the young poet, fictionalized as Hazel Jamison, is depicted as a rarity in Harlem Renaissance literary circles: she had "a freshness and naivete which he [the protagonist Raymond Taylor] and his cronies had lost," and "surprisingly enough for Negro prodigies," she "actually gave promise of possessing literary talent" (231).

When Johnson returned to New York City in 1927, she was to remain in the city for more than half a century. Initially, she resided at the 137th Street YWCA. Later she moved to 43 West 66th Street in Manhattan off Central Park West. This building was at the time, Johnson recalled, the only apartment house in this section of Manhattan that allowed blacks to rent units. It was during this period that she became acquainted with a number of prominent Harlem Renaissance literary figures, some of whom resided in the same building. One of her fellow apartment dwellers was Zora Neale Hurston, who became a close friend who chastised Johnson for not exerting herself enough to reach her goals. Of all the Harlem Renaissance writers, Wallace Thurman was the one Johnson knew best. Brilliant and outspoken, Thurman, whom she loved dearly in a platonic sense, was always "Wally" to her. One of Johnson's earliest published poems, "A Southern Road," appeared in his short-lived *Fire!*; she is the only black American woman with a poem in the one and only issue of the periodical. Also, Johnson knew Langston Hughes, who always seemed Latin and not black to her. She met James Weldon Johnson, who seemed old and stern to her. And she knew Countee Cullen, who was a cultured individual who "fit in" in her perspective. His "fitting in" struck her because she sometimes felt like a misfit.

Johnson's first national recognition had come in 1925 when her poem "Trees at Night" won Honorable Mention in the *Opportunity* literary contest and when her poem "The Road" appeared in the landmark anthology *The New Negro*. By then Johnson, who was nineteen years old in 1925, had been writing for at least a decade. All her life she had aspired to be a writer, although whites such as the Dwights, her mother's employers, had encouraged Johnson to become a schoolteacher in the South—the chief vocation, the writer said, that whites recommended to intelligent blacks at the time. As a student at Girls' Latin High School, she remembered that when she was called upon to read one of her works, she habitually denied authorship and ascribed the pieces to her cousin, Dorothy. She attributed her denials to "some sort of psychotic thing." She recalled that it "almost killed" her "for somebody to recognize something" she wrote. When she wrote, she always wrote for herself—because she enjoyed writing. She was amazed that anyone ever read her poems. She credited her early interest in writing to her mother, who provided her with new experiences; to the supplemental education she received at home; and to her exploration of library books. She cited two literary influences on her writing: poet Richard Le Gallienne, the father of actress Eva Le Gallienne, and poet Edna St. Vincent Millay, who was extremely popular in the 1920s, especially with young women who saw her as symbolic of the period's "free woman." Neither of these writers is black. Johnson's identification with white role models is not surprising, given the dearth of black poets whose works were being published during her formative years.

From 1925 through the mid-1930s, Johnson's poems appeared regularly in periodicals. In some of her works, she conformed to literary conventions that governed black women writers of the early twentieth century. These poems are decorous lyrics in traditional forms that treat themes such as love, death, and nature. In the remainder of her published canon, Johnson experiments with free forms, uses black urban argot, and addresses topics such as race pride and female sensuality.

Most of her poems appeared in *Opportunity*, which published six of her poems in 1926 alone; also, her poems appeared in periodicals such as *The Messenger*, *Palms*, *Vanity Fair*, the *Boston Saturday Evening Quill*, *Harlem*, and *Challenge*. Additionally, Johnson's poems appeared in anthologies such as *Caroling Dusk* (1927) and James Weldon Johnson's revised edition of *The Book of American Negro Poetry* (1931). In his anthology, Johnson praised Helene Johnson's early poetry, that "bore the stamp of a genuine poet," he wrote (279). Granting that she possessed genuine lyric talent, he judged her best poems as those she wrote in the colloquial style, a style that many poets assumed, he indicated, to be easy but which Johnson realized required as much craftsmanship as conventional poetic forms.

A small number of Johnson's published poems do not belong to the group of colloquial poems that James Weldon Johnson applauds; rather this handful of poems adhere to traditional poetic standards. In the main these works are her least successful works. Among these poems, "Metamorphism" is a commentary on the vicissitudes in human affairs; the poem's stale images and jarring rhythmic devices are liabilities. Another poem, "Mother," is a melodramatic paean to a self-sacrificing madonna who loves her child so much that she would abandon Christianity to make her progeny happy. "Vers de Societe" is a love poem whose central image does not communicate a sense of passionate love.

Poet Writes of Love, Sensuality, and Race

In most of Helene Johnson's poems, she forsakes convention in part. In the works in which she abandons poetic tradition, she has recourse to sexually-charged language as the basis of metaphors. Among her themes is youthful sensuality. "Night," "What Do I Care for Morning," "Futility," and "Fulfillment" contain traces of these elements. The references in "Night" to the universally feminine moon's "pale bosom" and the "bower of her [the moon's] hair" suggest female sexuality. In "What Do I Care for Morning," the night is "yielding and tender." "Futility" suggests that society's laws prevent individuals from behaving naturally. Their natural desire is, the poem asserts, not for love in a parlor but for love that is "singing up and down the alley / Without a collar." "Fulfillment" is similar to the vibrant poems of Edna St. Vincent Millay; this poem is a catalog of experiences that sate the speaker's lust for life. These experiences include leaning "against a strong tree's bosom, sentient / And hushed" and melting "the still snow" with her "seething body" before kissing "the warm earth tremulous underneath." Interestingly, the catalog in this poem includes most of the themes that recur in Helene Johnson's *oeuvre*—nature's splendor; Western society's constraints, specifically on women and blacks; and her speakers' zest for life.

Joie de vivre is the theme of "Summer Matures," which placed second in the Holstein Poetry Section competition sponsored by *Opportunity* in 1927; the poem encourages love and mating in a mythological setting. "Invocation" and "Widow with a Moral Obligation" suggest a desire for life that transcends death. "Remember Not" encourages lovers to seize the day and love while they may.

Poems on youthful sensuality and joie de vivre constitute approximately one-third of Helene Johnson's published canon. Many of her other published poems are racial in theme. In the racial works, she took as James Weldon Johnson wrote in the revised edition of *The Book of American Negro Poetry*, "the very qualities and circumstances that have long called for apology or defense and extolled them in an unaffected manner"(279). Helene Johnson's racial poems show how blacks are attuned to rhythms and values that differ from those of Europeans and suggest that this dissimilarity causes displacement among blacks in the Western world.

Thematically, Helene Johnson's racial poems fall into three categories: protest poems, racial-pride poems, and poetic indictments of Western civilization. The poems in the last two groups repudiate literary exoticism, which flourished in the Western world during the early twentieth century.

In her protest poems, Helene Johnson—a member of the black bourgeoisie when she wrote her published works—is generally polite, even when she relates the horrors of a lynching, as in "A Southern Road," one of her most powerful poems, or when she tells of the whipping of a black woman in "Fiat Lux," a melodramatic poem that evokes thematically some of Frances Ellen Watkins Harper's racial poems. The politeness reflects not only the poetic limits imposed upon black American women writers who had little choice but to write ladylike protest poems but also the facts of Helene Johnson's life, which was characterized by relatively little overt racial discrimination and few economic hardships as she grew up in Boston.

Helene Johnson's racial-pride poems include "The Road," "Poem," "Sonnet to a Negro in Harlem," and "My Race." Largely because of her poems on this theme, she is viewed by some literary critics as the woman who wrote poems that most reflect the perspectives associated with the Harlem Renaissance. In the racial-pride poems, she celebrates the beauty of the collective black race and the inherent majesty of "ordinary" black individuals—who were not in the foreground in earlier black American literature, which tended to portray middle and upper-class achievers who were evidence of blacks' intellectual and moral strengths.

The poet's speakers indict Western civilization in "Magalu," "A Missionary Brings a Young Native to America," and "Bottled." These poems and others by Helene Johnson imply that blacks are closer to nature than whites and thus accept partially the myth of the noble savage. Further, these works suggest that Western society destroys blacks.

After the early 1930s, Helene Johnson's poems rarely appeared in periodicals, but anthologists—especially those who had been themselves participants in the Harlem Renaissance—sporadically included her works in their collections of black American literature. Among the anthologies in which her poems appear are Sterling A. Brown, Arthur P. Davis, and Ulysses Lee, *The Negro Caravan* (1941); Arna Bontemps, *Golden Slippers: An Anthology of Negro Poetry for Young Readers* (1941); Langston Hughes and Arna Bontemps, *The Poetry of the Negro: 1746-1970* (1970); and Arna Bontemps, *American Negro Poetry* (1974). Additionally, her poems are included in Arnold Adoff, *The Poetry of Black America*; Lindsay Patterson, *Rock Against the Wind* (1973); Nathan Huggins, *Voices from the Harlem Renaissance* (1976); Erlene Stetson, *Black Sister* (1981); and Maureen Honey, *Shadowed Dreams* (1989).

These anthologists have had only the poems published during the 1920s and 1930s to select from when they chose works by Helene Johnson for their collections. By the mid-1930s, she did not have "a certain laxity" she needed to write and to seek publication. On her silence since then, Helene Johnson explained, "It's very difficult for a poor person to be that unfastened. They have to eat. In order to eat, you have to be fastened and tightly." Helene Johnson became fastened partly as a consequence of her marriage during the 1930s to William Warner Hubbell, a motorman she met in New York City. Prior to marrying, she had beaux. Though she believed she was never pretty in the conventional sense, she was popular with men because she was attractive, she modestly indicated, "in a sort of ordinary way." William Hubbell liked her poems and tried to help her so that she could write. After a number of years of marriage, the couple separated, neither partner feeling the need to obtain a formal divorce. From this union was born Helene Johnson's only child, Abigail Calachaly Hubbell, on September 18, 1940. The baby was named "Abigail" because Helene liked the name. "Calachaly" is a name Helene's mother made up for a doll her daughter owned. A graduate of Bard College, Abigail Hubbell owns New York City's Off-Center Theater. Twice married, she is the mother of two sons—Jason Rosen, born to her and her first husband, Leonard Rosen, and Benson McGrath, born to her and her second husband, Anthony McGrath.

Not only did marriage and motherhood fasten Helene Johnson tightly from the mid-1930s on, but also the demands of full-time employment left her with little time to write as the years passed. Helene Johnson's succinct analysis of the impact that employment has on writers' creativity is based on her own experiences:

> Writing a little, we [writers] usually got jobs writing. . . . [Y]ou don't have too much time to go in another direction. And to write anything (it can be poetry or anything at all), you have to have time. You have to sit and rock like a fool or look out the window, and something will come by (Interview with Helene Johnson).

Following this employment pattern herself, Helene Johnson worked for a number of years as a correspondent at Consumers Union in Mount Vernon, New York, where she composed individual responses to subscribers' queries when form letters would not suffice. While at Consumers Union, she toiled alongside correspondent Gwendolyn Bennett, another Harlem Renaissance poet.

Impulsively, Helene Johnson left Consumers Union to pursue a lifelong dream of becoming an advertising copywriter—a dream that never became a reality. During the 1980s, after more than half a century in New York, she returned to the region of her birth—to New England—where she lived for a few years in a modest apartment in Onset, Massachusetts, a small town on Cape Cod. Although she suffered from osteoporosis and thyroid disease, her mental faculties remained unimpaired. Wise and alert, she still wrote poetry because writing was for her a necessity. In her view, her late poems are not, however, of the same caliber as her early poems; indeed, Helene Johnson referred to these late works as "inklings" or "trinkets." In the fall of 1986, she returned to New York City, where she lives with her daughter's family in Manhattan. She continues to write poetry, which she aspires to have published.

In spite of the merits of Helene Johnson's poems of the 1920s and 1930s, recent scholars and literary historians have generally tended to ignore her works. There seem to be two chief reasons for her obscurity. First, like most women poets of the Harlem Renaissance, Helene Johnson had no volume of poetry published. She attributed her failure to have a collection published to the racelessness of many of her poems. During the 1920s and 1930s, publishers were primarily interested, she believed, in racial works by black writers. Second, Helene Johnson and her contemporaneous black American women poets might have been forgotten because many of their works were grounded in the romantic tradition, which was passé even in the 1920s, a period during which

American poets were in the main rejecting traditional forms and themes.

Regardless of the reasons that critics and literary historians have forgotten Helene Johnson's poems, the result is that a poet whose works warrant reading is deprived of a place in African-American letters. As a racial poet, she is the best kind—a writer who uses the specific problems of a distinct group to make statements about the human condition in myriad contexts. One of the points she makes in these poems is that racial love and pride are crucial to the psychic health of members of oppressed groups.

Her raceless poems treat sensuality in such a manner that these works remain resonant. Vivid and immediate because of their images, these portraits of passion—which express their speakers' thirsts for life—transcend time and place.

For her poems' social messages, their universal statements about human desire to experience life fully, and their role as literary models, Helene Johnson's poems merit inclusion in chronicles of black American literature.

References

Bryan, T. J. "The Published Poems of Helene Johnson." *The Langston Hughes Review* 6 (Fall 1987): 11-21.

Hull, Gloria. "Black Women Poets from Wheatley to Walker." In *Sturdy Black Bridges: Visions of Black Women in Literature*. Ed. Roseann P. Bell and others. Garden City, N.Y.: Anchor-Doubleday, 1979.

Johnson, Helene. Interviews with the author, 18 January 1986; 27 August 1986; 28 August 1986. Telephone interview 29 June 1990.

Johnson, James Weldon. "Critical Notes." In *The Book of American Negro Poetry*. Rev. ed. New York: Harcourt, 1931.

Primeau, Ronald. "Frank Horne and the Second Echelon Poets of the Harlem Renaissance." In Arna Bontemps. *The Harlem Renaissance Remembered*. New York: Dodd, Mead, 1972.

Thurman, Wallace. *Infants of the Spring*. 1932. reprinted. New York: AMS Press, 1975.

T. J. Bryan

Norma Holloway Johnson

(19?-)

Federal judge

Norma L. Holloway Johnson has had many opportunities to celebrate life. One cause for celebration came on Monday, May 12, 1980. Official word from the White House confirmed that President Jimmy Carter had appointed her a judge on the United States District Court for the District of Columbia. The appointment by President Carter carried with it the distinction of being the first black woman appointed to a federal court in the District of Columbia.

Tuesday, July 8, 1980, is the day Norma Holloway Johnson joined the ranks of "the chosen few" men and women who reach this plateau in the judicial system. Since her appointment to the federal court, Judge Johnson has been assigned many significant cases as a trial judge and has sat from time to time, by designation, on the United States Court of Appeals for the District of Columbia Circuit. She has been appointed to two judicial conference committees as well as to several internal court committees concerned with judicial management. She has also served for five years (1985-1990) on the District of Columbia Judicial and Disability Commission, which monitors reappointment and conduct of District of Columbia judges.

Long before the landmark decision in the case of *Brown v. Board of Education* was decided by the United States Supreme Court, a little girl who would one day sit in one of the nation's highest courts of law was growing up in Lake Charles, Louisiana. This intelligent and talented child lived in a town that boasted of its pine and hardwood timber industry. Lake Charles considered itself the leading deep-water seaport for the exporting of rice. It was frequently referred to as the "city where the west begins" (Keyes, 114) and was best known for its lumber, oil, refineries, and gas wells. Although she spent most of her life in the District of Columbia, Lake Charles, Louisiana, boasts of being the birthplace of the Honorable Norma Holloway Johnson, judge, United States District Court for the District of Columbia.

For a young black female, growing up in a city like Lake Charles in the 1940s was no different from growing up in any other southern town. She could only look forward to attending separate but unequal public schools, matriculating at a predominately black college, and pursuing a "safe" career—becoming a nurse, a stenographer, a schoolteacher, a librarian, a social worker, a guidance counselor, a bookkeeper, or a dietician.

In those days, for girls like Norma Johnson to consider a career in medicine, engineering, business administration, or law was rare. Most females felt choosing a profession where the doors were open with opportunities to advance was a more productive option. Because of segregation in educational institutions and in the workplace, only a few women chose nontraditional careers.

Norma L. Holloway Johnson was born the only daughter of H. Lee Holloway and Beatrice (Williams) Holloway. At age fourteen, she discovered the real meaning of what it is like to have an extended family. She became a companion for her great-aunt, Bettie B. Henderson, her maternal grandmother's sister. Although it was an extremely difficult decision for both her and her parents to make, she left Lake Charles to go to live with her aunt in Washington, D.C., because Henderson was elderly and needed someone to help care for her. Besides, everyone was certain her "young legs" would be welcomed, and she was committed to doing all she could to help her aunt. Holloway's parents and younger brother remained in Lake Charles (Telephone interview with Norma Holloway Johnson, 25 April 1990).

It was there that Norma Johnson received a well-rounded education. Beginning with the ninth grade at Shaw Junior High School, she has only positive things to say about her learning experiences. She recalls, with almost photographic memory, courses she took at Paul Laurence Dunbar High School in the District of Columbia. "Dunbar High School was an exceptionally good high school for any student," she says. She sounded excited as she remembered those high school days (Telephone interview, 18 April 1990). She went on to tell about the unusual but challenging curriculum offered at Dunbar High School. She had an opportunity to select from such courses as biology, chemistry, physics, German, French, Greek, and Latin, which was her favorite subject.

To go to college or not to go to college was never an issue with Johnson. She grew up with the understanding that after she graduated from high school, she would indeed enroll in an institution of higher learning. Johnson planned to channel her energy and direct her enthusiasm toward improving the quality of life for the black race.

The training Johnson received at Dunbar High School prepared her for the rigorous course of study awaiting her at Miner Teachers College, now known as the University of the District of Columbia. Norma Holloway Johnson considers the old Miner Teachers College as one of the best schools in the nation. She proudly labels it "outstanding." "It was unusual in many ways. . . . For example, over fifty percent of the teachers at Miner had earned Ph.D. degrees," she recalled (Telephone interview, 18 April 1990). Norma Holloway graduated as valedictorian of her class in 1955.

Just a year before her graduation from Miner Teachers College, the Supreme Court handed down an unprecedented decision in the case of *Brown v. Board of Education*. "Considered the Supreme Court's most important decision of the twentieth century, the Court held that racial segregation of public school children, commanded or authorized by state law, violated the Fourteenth Amendment's guarantee of the equal protection of the laws. A companion decision, *Bolling v. Sharpe* (1954), held that school segregation in the District of Columbia violated the Fifth Amendment's guarantee of due process of law" (Levy 161). It was this historical decision that caused her to reevaluate her career goals and aspirations. She had grown up with the idea of becoming a dentist. However, she decided then and there that she could help achieve equal justice for her race by pursuing a career in law. Graduating magna cum laude from Miner Teachers College in 1955, Johnson enrolled in Georgetown University Law Center during the same time that she was teaching English in the District of Columbia Public School System. Many of her former students proudly recognize their English teacher as a distinguished jurist.

Legal Career Begins for Johnson

Only eighteen years after Johnson graduated from Georgetown University Law Center in 1962, she was appointed judge, United States District Court for the District of Columbia. She was the first black woman graduate from this prestigious law school, and she was the first woman graduate to be elevated to the bench—a far cry from her desire "to one day work as a lawyer for the NAACP Legal Defense Fund" (Telephone interview, 18 April 1990).

Her legal career began in the United States Department of Justice, where she served as a trial attorney in the civil division from 1963 to 1967. For the next three years, she served as an assistant corporation counselor in the Office of the Corporation Counsel for the District of Columbia. She ultimately became the chief of the Juvenile Division (Berry, 101). It was during this period also (June 18, 1964) that she married Julis A. Johnson, a native of Saint Louis.

Recognition of Norma Holloway Johnson's service to the community was recognized by President Richard M. Nixon. He appointed her in 1970 to the Court of General Sessions, which later became the Superior Court of the District of Columbia. She remained in this position for ten years (1970-1980).

As a leader in the legal profession, Johnson's community involvement has always been extensive and impressive. She remains active in many civic and professional organizations, of which she is a founding member for two: The National Association of Black Women Attorneys and the National Association of Women Judges, where she served as director from 1979 to 1981. She was elected treasurer of this association in 1989. For the past thirteen years, Johnson has served as historian for the NABWA, an office she still holds. Improving the way juveniles are treated in the justice system remains a top priority for Johnson. Since early 1970 she has devoted much time and energy to this issue and continues to address the entire issue of juvenile justice. One of her objectives is to prevent *any* child from spending time in a common jail. Having served several years on the executive committee of the National Association of Juvenile and Family Court Judges, Johnson is optimistic about reaching this goal. Much of her "spare time" is devoted to assisting with legal issues.

Despite her incredibly busy schedule, she continues to be active in many professional organizations. In recent years (1988-1990), she has served as president of the William Bryant American Inn of Court and as a trustee of the American Inns of Court Foundation. For the past eight years she has served as director of the Council for Court Excellence. From 1975 to 1984, she held the position of director for the National Institute for Citizen Education in Law. For this same organization, she chaired the advisory committee from 1978 to 1983. She is a life member of the National Bar Association, where she serves on the judicial council and as a fellow of the American Bar Foundation. She served as a director and secretary of the Washington Bar Association from 1969 to 1971. She holds memberships in the Judicial Administration Division of the American Bar Association, the Women's Bar Association, the District of Columbia Bar Association, and the American Judicature Society. For this society, she served as director from 1976 to 1981 and was a member of the executive committee for two years (1979-1981).

Norma Holloway Johnson's distinguished service to the legal community has been applauded many times. Most recently in May 1989, she was presented an honorary degree by the University of the District of Columbia.

As avid readers, both Johnson and her husband like to read works by Shakespeare. They are currently reading *Henry V*. Running a close second and third on Johnson's list of favorite authors are Paul Laurence Dunbar and Langston Hughes. She holds fond memories of her studies in literature and briefly mentioned two of her favorite poems by Hughes: "The Crystal Staircase" and "I've Known Rivers" (Telephone interview, 18 April 1990). Precious and few are the moments Norma Holloway Johnson gets to pursue another one of her favorite pastimes: drama. She also enjoys ballet and travel.

Johnson found her proximity to the seat of national government an inspiration that encouraged her conviction to devote her life to public service through law. She stands as a role model for women and minorities aspiring to the legal profession.

References

The American Bench. 4th ed. Sacramento, Calif.: Foster-Long, 1987-88.

Berry, B. "How to Keep Your Kids Out of Trouble: Keeping Kids Out of Trouble: The Judges Say Parents Who Are 'Busy' Are Frequently to Blame." *Ebony* 33 (October 1978): 100-106. Portrait, p. 106.

Congressional Directory. Washington, D.C.: U.S. Government Printing Office, 1989-1990.

Keyes, Frances Parkinson. *All This Is Louisiana: An Illustrated Story Book*. New York: Harper, 1950.

Levy, Leonard W. *Encyclopedia of the American Constitution*. New York: Macmillan, 1986.

Telephone Interview with Norma Holloway Johnson, 18 April 1990; 25 April 1990.

Who's Who Among Black Americans, 1990/1991. 6th ed. Detroit: Gale Research, 1990.

Who's Who in America. 45th ed. Wilmette, Ill.: Marquis, 1988-89.

Who's Who in American Law. 6th ed. Chicago: Marquis, 1990-91.

Who's Who in the South and Southwest, 1975-1976. Chicago: Marquis, 1975.

Felicia Harris (Felder) Hoehne

Clara Stanton Jones

(1913-)

Library administrator, educator, civic leader

Clara Stanton Jones, librarian, educator, and civic leader, was the first woman and first black American to serve as director of the Detroit Public Library. She was born on May 14, 1913, the daughter of Ralph Herbert Stanton and Etta (James) Stanton. Her father was an insurance supervisor, having served as the manager of the Saint Louis office of an insurance company and later as the supervisor of the Atlanta office of the Atlanta Life Insurance Company. Jones's mother, had been a school teacher until she married. She resumed teaching after her children grew up.

Ralph Stanton was a native of Natchez, Mississippi. He left Natchez as a young man and journeyed to Memphis, Nashville, Chicago, and then to Saint Louis. His father was the son of a slaveowner by the name of Stanton. Today the Stanton Mansion and Stanton College stand in Natchez, Mississippi. The former slave master, Stanton, had given Clara Stanton Jones's grandfather land, which enabled Jones's father to attend high school in Nashville, Tennessee.

Clara Stanton Jones's maternal grandparents were born in 1863 and 1861 respectively, and also knew slavery. They grew up in a small village, Saint Geneve—a French town in Missouri—and spent most of their early life on a farm. The couple moved to Saint Louis when they decided to marry. They were ordinary, hardworking folk who made their life on the farm, bartering with neighbors as the source of their income.

Jones's family life was warm and wholesome. She was the fourth of five children, having three older brothers and a younger sister, Etta Stanton Bullock, a librarian, who is now known as Essa Honono, following her marriage to the South African freedom fighter. All five of the Stanton children are college graduates. On June 25, 1938, Clara Stanton married Albert Jones, a social worker. They are the parents of three children—Stanton William, a budget analyst in California; Vinetta Claire, dean of the school of education and urban affairs, Morgan State University; and Kenneth Albert, an engineer with Westinghouse Company in Baltimore, Maryland. During the administration of President Jimmy Carter, Kenneth Albert Jones was a White House scholar.

Educated in Saint Louis public schools and a graduate of Summer High School in 1929, Jones matriculated at Milwaukee State Teachers College in 1929-30. She transferred to Spelman College in Atlanta and graduated with an A.B. degree in 1934. Continuing her education at the University of Michigan, she received an A.B. in library science in 1938. Because of her enormous contribution to the field of librarianship and her leadership in the profession, Jones has been awarded nine honorary doctoral degrees, from Shaw College, Ball State University, North Carolina Central University, Grand Valley State College, Saint John's University, Pratt Institute, Northern Michigan University, Wayne State University, and Spelman College.

Jones's professional career was distinguished, wide, varied, and productive. She held several preprofessional positions at Atlanta and Dillard universities. From 1938 to 1940 she was the reference librarian at Dillard University in New Orleans. From 1940 to 1941 she served as the associate librarian at Southern University, Baton Rouge, Louisiana. She spent thirty-four years at the Detroit Public Library, first joining the staff in 1944. From 1944 until 1949 she was classified as Librarian I; from 1949 to 1950 as Librarian II; and from 1950 to 1963 as Librarian III. She then became the library's neighborhood consultant for the Detroit Public Library system, serving in that capacity from 1968 to 1970. In 1970 Jones was named the first black American and first woman director of the Detroit Public Library. It was her experience in the Saint Louis Public Library that gave Jones the real appreciation and understanding of the importance of the public library: There were no black librarians on the staff of the Saint Louis Public Library during the early days of Jones's life. When she was employed at the Detroit Public Library in 1944, she was only the third black librarian to be hired by that library system.

Clara Stanton Jones

Jones contributed enormously to the development of branch library work at the Detroit Public Library. She pioneered in the coordination of programming. Later she became the library neighborhood consultant, a middle-management position responsible for bringing people from the inner city into the library and making the library a part of their lives. She traveled the city describing the library program and urging inner-city people to use libraries. She spoke to churches, community organizations, and schools. The inner-city people made no connection between the library and education. Jones considered this natural, for many black people came from the South to Detroit and during the days of slavery, teaching black people to read or write was a crime. One hundred years of segregation followed emancipation, and blacks were denied access to libraries. Her job was to help people participate in the public library. She went on radio and television programs to talk about basic services in public libraries and to encourage citizens to make use of this magnificent resource.

During Jones's tenure as director of the Detroit Public Library, she was faced with financial problems. Being politically astute, she appealed to the state to fund the Detroit Public Library, for it was the largest public library in Michigan and it was, in fact, a statewide resource. Because of her success in Detroit, Jones was invited to several state library associations to address those organizations on a variety of topics. One of her most notable addresses was "Survival Politics for Libraries," which she gave at the New York Library Association Conference in 1970. She urged librarians all across America to fight for financial support for public libraries. She also spoke on behalf of the disenfranchised. Another of her landmark speeches was "Reflections on Library Service to the Disadvantaged." This was a lecture she gave at the Annual Conference of the American Library Association (ALA) in 1974 and it was published as an ALA pamphlet. Jones supported special services to meet the information needs of the disadvantaged, showing that these services would assist the disadvantaged in becoming taxpayers who would later support the public library. Moreover, the public library, as a nonschool agency that educates, would provide the kind of education through reading that the schools sometimes overlook.

American Library Association Elects First Black President

Jones was invited to run for the presidency of the American Library Association in 1974. She was defeated by Allie Beth Martin, the director of the Tulsa Public Library. Martin, however, was unable to complete her full term due to illness, and she died on April 11, 1976. In the meantime, Jones had been nominated by petition in 1975 and was voted president-elect of the association, the first black American to hold this distinguished post. She was reluctant to run for president in 1975, for she had been defeated the previous year. But E. J. Josey, Annette Hoage Phinazee, and Samuel Morrison prevailed upon Jones to serve as the blacks' candidate. All black and women librarians in the fight for equal justice for minorities and women were thrilled about Jones's election to the presidency. Jones was inaugurated on July 22, 1976, as the association's president. It was a quirk of history that, during her term as acting president, the association celebrated its centennial anniversary (in 1976). No one ever thought that a black woman would be directing the association's affairs during this landmark year. Jones, who is a superb speaker and an elegant and eloquent woman, was a dynamic president.

Jones's ALA presidency was marred by the production of a racist film known as *The Speaker*. The Intellectual Freedom Committee had proposed a film on the First Amendment. Most members of the ALA thought that the film would be a library issue film, the ALA historically having been in the forefront for the protection of the First Amendment Bill of Rights as it relates to libraries. But the film was not a library film per se, since it focused on a racist person's right to speak. The ALA executive board at its spring meeting in 1977, voted to ban distribution of the IFC film until the ALA membership could view the film at its 1977 Annual Conference in Detroit. Black members of the association were appalled that the first black American president of the association had to be bogged down in a discussion of a film that demeaned the humanity and intelligence of black people. Following the showing of the film at the conference, a great debate ensued over the appropriateness of the association putting its name on such a film and distributing the film as an ALA product.

Twenty-five black members of the association prepared a document to be presented to the council and they declared:

> We, the undersigned members of the American Library Association, have requested this opportunity to make a statement because we believe that neither the Executive Board, the Council, nor the membership feels nor subscribes to what we perceive *The Speaker* to be representing in the name of the Association. . . . We maintain that *The Speaker* is fraudulent in nature because it rests upon a misrepresentation of the First Amendment; that the interpretation set forth is a manipulation of the First Amendment to deftly force the ordinary program-planning function choosing a speaker to conform to imaginary First Amendment strictures. This distortion completely discredits and invalidates *The Speaker* (ALA Council Document 1).

This was not the end of *The Speaker*, for many people wrote letters to the editors of the library press and several wrote articles. Clara Stanton Jones wrote an interesting article entitled "Reflections & Ruminations on *The Speaker*" which was published in the September 1977 issue of the *Wilson Library Bulletin*. Jones was unwavering in her protest and disgust with the film. She wrote in the *WLB*, "the importance of the overwhelming rejection of *The Speaker* by black ALA members should not be underestimated. This judgement indicates the film's score on a crucial test. The significance of this failure cannot be circumvented by characterizing the reaction as 'supersentive' or 'touchy' on the subject of race. These are responsible, concerned practitioners, many of whom have been outstanding leaders of the profession for many years. Racism is sometimes unintentional, as in this instance, but that can be likened to the plea of ignorance of the law—no excuse!"

Sanford Berman of the Hennepin County (Minnesota) Library saw the film and wrote his comments as follows:

> This movie is erroneously subtitled. It is less a "film about freedom" than a "film about foolishness" or—more gravely—about "bigotry and defamation." The "freedom" issue is phoney, the plot entirely contrived, the dialogue cliche-ridden. . . . The film promotes a vision of serious unreality concerning intellectual freedom problems in schools and libraries. . . . I had not thought it possible that a professional library association could produce a film about intellectual freedom that made the very concept seem dirty. Now I know better. Not recommended (19-20).

In spite of *The Speaker* fiasco, Clara Stanton Jones was not bitter, for she had a great presidency and history will never forget her yeoman contribution to the association.

Jones Addresses Issues in the Profession

The highlight of Jones's presidency was her program "Issues & Answers." The format was a conference within a conference that lasted an entire day and brought 1,500 librarians together. The program was designed to look at some of the problems and solutions as librarians move into the post-industrial society. Jones wrote in the forward to *Issues and Answers:*

> The "Issues & Answers" Program at the 1977 Annual American Library Association conference identified some major concerns and in-

> volved about fifteen hundred librarians in grappling with a few selected issues of primary importance of all. . . . [T]hus, the tripartite subject of the "issues and answers" program seems to choose itself—"the impact of technology, social and economic change on libraries." But, the subject was incomplete without practical application. It seemed logical to build the right to access to information into the framework of the "issues and answers. . . ." Hopefully, it contributed to a commitment to confront our professional problems and opportunities and to think our way through the demands of change (ix-x).

The Issues & Answers Conference allowed ALA participants the opportunity to engage in a dialogue and they were very satisfied. In their assessment of this format and the conference, Joseph Boisse and Carla J. Stoffler wrote, "There is little doubt that those individuals who participated in the program felt that it was extremely beneficial to them. They welcomed the opportunity to participate actively in the annual conference" ("Epilogue: Issues and Answers," 120).

Jones has a magmetic personality and is a "people person." Through her civic and community affiliations, she made an outstanding contribution to the city of Detroit. Having served on fifteen cultural, civic, and community boards in Detroit as well as on national boards, she knew the leaders of the NAACP, the National Council of Negro Women, the American Civil Liberties Union, the Women's International League for Peace and Freedom, the Historical Society of Michigan, and countless others. In addition to these boards, she served on the board of directors of the City National Bank of Detroit. In the library arena, she was a close friend of the late Virginia Lacy Jones. Her other close friends are Dorothy Porter Wesley, Eric Moon, Mohammed Aman, and many other nationally-known library leaders, both black and white. Jones spoke very fondly of her relationship with William E. B. Du Bois when she was at Atlanta University and Spelman University, especially when he returned to teach at Atlanta in the 1930s. She had the opportunity of knowing Howard Thurman, the great black mystic and theologian; Rayford Logan, historian; Langston Hughes, poet; James Weldon Johnson, poet, writer, and the first paid executive secretary of the NAACP; Hale Woodruff, artist; and many other eminent black scholars. Jones points with great pride to having been exposed to the great minds of black Americans, and she indicates that she is grateful and fortunate to have had the opportunity to study at a black college such as Spelman (Ann A. Shockley interview with Clara Stanton Jones, 1 August 1972). This background established for Jones a strong, positive image of black people's ability and accomplishments.

Following the 1943 riot in Detroit, the city was very conscious of developing good interracial relations in the community. Jones was drawn into a volunteer speaker's bureau for the mayor's Interracial Commission, which later became known as the Commission on Community Relations. Since she was already an outstanding and eloquent speaker and knew black American history, she was quite knowledgeable about the best ways to develop sound relationships among people, and so Jones was sought by the commission to go into white communities and talk about the aspirations and dreams of her people, and at the same time, listen to what those communities had to say. In most instances, Jones was the only black person in the lecture hall or room, but she was interested in human relations and worked very hard to bring the black and white citizens of Detroit together. She made a notable contribution to race relations in the city of Detroit. Jones was recognized for her community work in 1970, receiving an Achievement Award for Service to the Community from the Golden State Mutual Life Insurance Company.

The recipient of many awards for her contribution to the profession and her leadership of the Detroit Public Library, Jones received the award for Distinguished Service to Librarianship from the Black Caucus of the American Library Association in 1970; in 1971 she received the Distinguished Alumnus Award for Outstanding Service to the Library Profession from the University of Michigan School of Library Science. In 1975 Michigan honored her once again with the Athena Award for Humanitarian Service as a University of Michigan alumna. In 1978 Wayne County Community College in Detroit awarded her the Distinguished Service to the Community Award. In 1983 the American Library Association conferred upon her its most coveted award, the ALA Honorary Life Membership Award. She was cited as "Ambassador of Urban Librarianship and Creative Leader."

During her career, Jones wrote many articles that appeared in *Library Journal, Wilson Library Bulletin, American Libraries,* and other library publications. Her most notable book is *Public Library Information and Referral Service,* published by Gaylord Publications in 1978. Most of her major speeches have been published in proceedings or in collections. One of her outstanding addresses was given at North Carolina Central University on the occasion of the thirty-fifth anniversary of that university's School of Library Science. At that time she was awarded an honorary doctorate and her address was entitled "The Black Librarian." She said:

> Among black librarians there is a special intensity of "caring" about bringing books and information to people. "Solicitude and concern" help define the feeling. It is a quality beyond efficiency or even excellence of performance. It is a kind of persistence to the point of really touching people. It is an attitude that is unmistakable among Black Librarians, too common not to have deep roots. Throughout slavery in this country the law forbade the teaching of reading and writing to slaves. . . . Today's laws do not forbid anyone from learning to read and write, but poor educational and cultural programs and facilities are expressions of scorn for citizens' rights and well- being. We should

> reexamine our priorities in order to beware of continuing forms of enslavement in modern form. It is a bold claim but one that can be documented, that without libraries civilization as we know it could never have evolved; and without libraries civilization as we know it would perish (*The Black Librarian in the Southeast*, 18-19).

Most American librarians would consider Jones one of the foremost librarians in America. A woman of great energy and resourcefulness, Jones has had a very active community life. She was appointed to many boards in the community, and elected to many positions of leadership in her field. As the first black American president of the American Library Association, she had an extended presidency by having to serve as an acting president. She was appointed as a Regents Lecturer at the University of California, Berkeley, Graduate School of Library and Information Science in 1979 and 1980 and also as a member of the Advisory Committee for the SLIS. One of her most important appointments came when President Jimmy Carter appointed her to serve on the National Commission on Libraries and Information Science—a position that she held for four years, 1978-1982.

In assessing the importance of Jones, and in examining her many notable contributions, it is quite apparent that she is a person who is very proud of her black American heritage. During her lifetime she has done everything that she could—not only to support her people but also to support her profession. She is very supportive of the ALA Black Caucus, noting: "If black people don't nudge or point out or lay claim to and give support we will continue to be forgotten, so I think the Black Caucus is very necessary" (Ann Allen Shockley, interview with Clara Stanton Jones, 1 August 1972). Jones sees the Black Caucus as an opportunity for black librarians to come together for inspiration and development of strategy, for black librarians working individually are not as strong as they are working together for common goals. If black librarians did not have a Clara Stanton Jones, it would have been necessary to invent her.

References

ALA Yearbook. Chicago: American Library Association, 1976, 1979, 1984. Photograph, 1976, p. 19.

American Library Association. Council Document 11.1. 1977-78.

Berman, Sanford. "The Speaker: Not Recommended." *Interracial Books for Children* 8 (November 4-5) 1977.

Boisse, Joseph A. and Carla J. Stoffle. "Epilogue: Issues and Answers: The Participants' View." In *Issues and Answers*. Ed. E. J. Josey. Phoenix: Oryx Press, 1978.

Current Biography. New York: H. W. Wilson, 1977. Includes photograph.

Jones, Clara Stanton. "The Black Librarian." In *The Black Librarian in the Southeast*. Ed. Annette L. Phinazee. Durham: North Carolina Central University, 1980.

———. "Foreword." In *Issues and Answers*. Ed. E. J. Josey. Phoenix: Oryx Press, 1978.

Shockley, Ann A. Interview with Clara Stanton Jones, 1 August 1972. Black Oral History Project, Fisk University Library, Fisk University.

Who's Who in America. Chicago: Marquis, 1976.

Who's Who Among Black Americans, 1975-76. 1st ed. Detroit: Gale Research, 1976.

Who's Who of American Women. 9th ed. Chicago: Marquis, 1975.

Collections

The personal papers of Clara Stanton Jones are in the library of the School of Library Science, North Carolina Central University. An oral history record was made by Ann Allen Shockley in 1972 and is in the Black Oral History Collection, Fisk University Library.

E. J. Josey

Lois M. Jones (Madame Vergniaud Pierre-Noel)

(1905-)

Artist, educator

Lois Mailou Jones has been described as being "one of the few figures in American art to achieve a long, exciting, and inspiring career" (Driskell, 266). Unlike many of her predecessors and mentors, she has been acclaimed as a premier artist and art educator in American and abroad. Like her mentor, sculptor Meta Warrick Fuller, Jones, too, had to leave America to earn a living as an artist, for as Fuller and composer Harry Burleigh told her, "If you want a success in your career, you have to go to Paris" (LaDuke, 53).

Lois Jones, a native of Boston, was born on November 3, 1905, to Thomas Vreeland Jones, a lawyer, and Carolyn Dorinda Jones, a hairdresser and hat designer. Noticing her daughter's fascination with drawing, Carolyn Jones took her to clients' homes where she worked. This was Lois Jones's introduction to private art collections, an environment where she was free to entertain and amuse herself surrounded by priceless works of art. It was then that her mother began to propel her towards a career in art.

Jones attended Boston Normal Art School and studied drawing at the Boston Museum vocational drawing class in the afternoons and on Saturdays. She also served an apprenticeship with a Rhode Island School of Design teacher who was a costume designer. In 1923 Jones was awarded a four-year scholarship, the Susan Minot Lane Scholarship, to the Boston Museum School of Fine Arts and, after completing the diploma program, studied at the Designers' Art School of Boston in 1928. After a stint as a freelance designer, Jones traveled South to organize and head the art department at Palmer Memorial Institute. Located in Sedalia, North Carolina, a suburb of the more cosmopolitan city of Greensboro, the elite private school catered to the children of the "black bourgeoisie." Unaccustomed to blatant racism and discrimination, Jones was ill-prepared for the South's special treatment of its black citizenry. Lasting for two years, she left to accept a teaching position in the art department at Howard University, Washington, D.C., in 1930. Nearly fifty years of her life would be inextricably bound to this institution.

Prior to Jones's neophyte teaching experiences, she enjoyed success as a textile designer, but not the fact that it guaranteed anonymity. With the advice of Fuller, Burleigh, and Jonas Lie, president of the National Academy of Design, she began to concentrate exclusively on drawing and to make plans to study abroad. In 1937 Jones was awarded a Rockefeller Scholarship to study at the Academie Julian in Paris and subsequently got a renewal grant for summer study and travel to Italy.

Paris was the first great influence on the life and work of Lois Jones. For the first time in her life, she was free of America's stifling environment of racism and prejudice. Revelling in her new found freedom, Jones exclaimed: "Oh, my Lord, at last I'm living" (Striar, 70). While in Paris, Jones met distinguished French artist Emile Brenard who would serve as another mentor. She also met a fellow Academie student, Celine Tabary who would become a lifelong friend. Tabary and her family practically adopted Jones and provided a "home away from home" while she studied in Paris. A few years later, Tabary came to America for a short visit which stretched into a seven-year stay because of the war. She lived with Jones in Washington, D.C., and frequently interceded on her behalf by entering Jones's artwork in competitions not open to black artists. In the Parisian art galleries, Jones discovered African masks, which became prominent features in her works as her drawing style underwent a radical evolution that would be crystallized in the late twentieth century. But the most important experience was Jones's freedom to paint in the streets as well as in her own studio. Through the mid-1950s, Jones faithfully returned to the South Mediterranean region of France each summer to paint.

In 1938 Jones returned to America as an acclaimed artist in her own country. It was just as Meta Fuller predicted, for Jones's Paris output was received favorably, and she held her first solo exhibit at a prominent Boston art gallery. Throughout the 1940s and early 1950s, Jones grew professionally. Her collegiate education, begun in the 1920s and 1930s at Harvard and Columbia summer school sessions, culminated in an A.B. degree, with *magna cum laude* honors, from Howard University in 1945. Events were moving in a direction that would result in the second most important evolutionary period of Jones's life.

As she became more involved in her dual careers of teaching and creating art, the years passed and her mother reminded her that "paintings are rather quiet companions when one is lonely" (Striar, 72). Jones had been briefly engaged to a Hungarian artist, who had ardently wooed and pursued her. But she had been unable to forget a handsome Haitian art student with whom she had studied at Columbia summer school some years before. At that time, she had served as his guide to New York and had since inquired if he had married; to her delight, he had not, but they had lost contact. Then, in 1953, he suddenly reappeared and they were able to renew a friendship which culminated in a French wedding to which the mayor brought champagne to toast the newlyweds. As Madame Vergniaud Pierre-Noel, the Haitian culture of her husband became an integral part of her life. In 1954, Jones was invited to create a series of works on Haiti and was subsequently awarded the Order of Chevalier for Achievement in Art by then President Paul Magloire ("Artist on Sunlit Canvases," n.p.). With Jones's husband being a graphic artist, their careers complemented one another, as well as their shared love for his native country. Not only did they maintain a home in Haiti, Jones also traveled there nearly every summer to paint and carry out research projects on *The Black Visual Arts,* a Howard University-funded project (Gaither, n.p.). Before his death in 1982, Pierre-Noel had always been such a constant supporter of his wife's career that less was known about his artistic accomplishments. As a graphic artist, he had won international prizes for postage stamp designs and the Award of Excellence for a tribute to John F. Kennedy by the Associates of Industrial Arts.

In 1970 Jones was awarded a sabbatical leave, which gave her the opportunity to travel to the "Motherland" of Africa. There she was able to soak up the elements of native culture in eleven countries. This completed the third and last phase of the Black Visual Arts project, which also included black American artists and contemporary Haitian art. The year-long visit enabled Jones to recapture her heritage and transfer it to canvas, especially the constantly recurring African mask motif, Dahomean Appliques, collage art, the trompe-d'oeil faces, and the use of geometrical signs. Coupling Haitian influences of ritualistic voodoo symbols with an "angular cubistic" quality in her drawings and decorative and bright colors which reflect her background in design, Jones's later works are more striking and vibrant as she became more infused with the totality of the cultures of her native and adopted peoples.

As a black American woman artist, Jones had waged a never-ending battle to gain professional respect for the artistic works of all black American artists. Memories linger of the time she tried to apply for an assistantship at her *alma mater,* the Boston Museum of the Fine Arts School, only to be told to go South and help her own people (LaDuke, 54). Nearly twenty years later, her French companion, Celine Tabary, would have to enter Jones's oil painting in a prestigious competition closed to blacks. Although it was awarded a prize, Jones did not go to the Corcoran Gallery to claim her prize for a number of years since it was believed that a white artist had entered and won the competition. Much of her success is due to her lack of bitterness over such unfair and harsh treatment. Jones has never passively accepted this inhumanity, but she has steadfastly refused to allow old wounds or ill-treatment to fester and poison her soul and creative center. Even as a college professor, Jones met resistance in the form of sexism as her choice of the art medium of oil paint was challenged since a male colleague was the oil painter on the faculty and she was the designated water-colorist. Her determination was inherited from her father, a former building superintendent, who returned to school to become a lawyer at age forty. This quality of relentless persistence and perseverance enabled Jones to prevail despite the hurdles placed in her path and allowed her to excel in her field.

As one of the few teacher-artists to be successful in both fields, Jones has had an immeasurable influence on the training of fledgling artists because of her ongoing pursuit of excellence. Edmund Gaither says it best in *Reflective Moments: Lois Mailou Jones Retrospective: 1930-1972*: "Lois Mailou Jones has been a beacon of inspiration to generations of Afro-American artists, some of who were her students, and all of whom are her admirers." An example of her efforts to seek equity for her black sisters was the challenge she gave to an all-white audience at the first Conference of Women in the Visual Arts: "I would like to ask where are the black women artists? Where are they if you mean what you say about sisterhood?" She then repeated for the conference body a slide lecture that had been presented to a sparse crowd the day before to make sure that the attendees were conscious of the fact that black women artists were indeed producing art of excellent quality (Striar, 44).

Jones's students continually hail her a role model, one who exhibited commitment to one's work and to one's community. As an exemplar, Jones has virtually no peers. She has had over fifty one-person shows since 1937 and has been awarded at least three honorary doctorates. She received the Howard University Alumni Award in 1978. After serving as professor of design and watercolor painting from 1930 to 1977, Jones was granted emeritus status and a position as visiting artist-in-residence in the Howard University Graduate School of Arts and Sciences. Her research in Haiti and Africa resulted in priceless archival materials and a manuscript for publication in addition to numerous articles in professional journals. Jones's biographical data is listed in countless directories, journals, and books citing the contributions of black women artists and she has been featured in a number of technical art journals. Not only has she been honored by foreign heads of state, Jones was saluted, along with nine other black elders of art, by then President Jimmy Carter in 1980. Elected as a 1962 Fellow of the Royal Society of Arts in London, she has further secured international fame as the "Grand Dame of Afro-American art." Jones's personal statement reflects her primary concern: "The major focus is to achieve for Black artists their just and rightful place as American artists" (Resume, n.p.). The totality of Lois Mailou Jones's life is best summed up in the following:

> It was never enough for her to revel in her own joy and solid accomplishment as an artist. She also had to educate, to bring together, to sponsor and encourage, to act as an artist-ambassador between her people and the white majority; between Americans and people of other countries; between artists and viewers. This has been her goal and her life-style (Striar, 44).

It has also been said that

> She is, and has long been, a catalyst for artists, particularly black artists; but she has also never faltered in the creativity of her own work and in the generosity and humanity of her life. The measure of her gift is in the eternal giving of joy, color, and warmth which her paintings afford us, for behind the beauty of her designs and color is the love she bears for black people; and when the artist can make art the medium for a greater love, only triumph is possible (Gaither, n.p.).

Her works of art include *Les Fetiches* (oil, 1938); *Jennie* (oil, 1943); *Mob Victim (Meditation)* (oil, 1944); *Peasant Girl* (Haiti, 1954); *Bazar Du Quai Haiti* (1961); *Veve Voudou II* (oil collage, 1963); *Letitia and Patrick* (Haiti, oil, 1964); *Vendeuses de Tissues* (oil, 1964); *Moon Masque* (acrylic-collage, 1971); and *Ubi Girl from Tai Region* (acrylic, 1972).

References

"Artist of Sunlit Canvases." *Ebony* reprint, 1968. Includes photograph.

Bontemps, Jacqueline Fonvielle, and Arna Alexander Bontemps. *Forever Free: Art by African-American Women 1862-1980*. Alexandria, Va.: Stephenson, 1980. 94-94, 187-190. Photograph, p. 94.

Driskell, David C. *Two Centuries of Black American Art*. New York: Los Angeles County Museum of Art, Alfred A. Knopf, 1976. 266.

Gaither, Edmund B. *Reflective Moments: Lois Mailou Jones. Retrospective: 1930-1972*. Boston: The Museum of the National Center of Afro-American Arts. Museum of Fine Arts, March 11-April 15, 1973.

Jones, Lois M. Personal Resume. n.d.

LaDuke, Betty. "The Grande Dame of Afro-American Art: Lois Mailou Jones." *Sage* 4 (Spring 1987): 53-58.

Lewis, Samella. *Art: African American*. New York: Harcourt Brace Jovanovich, 1978. 67, 97-100.

Mutch, Susan. "Lois Mailou Jones: A Career with No End of Creativity." *Vineyard Gazette* (Martha's Vineyard, Massachusetts) 133 (29 August 1978): A-2.

"President Carter Salutes Artists." *The Capital Spotlight* 24 April 1980. 1.

Striar, Margurite M. "Artist in Transition." *Essence* 7 (November 1972): 44-45, 70, 72. Reproduction of Jones's self-portrait, p. 44.

Collections

Examples of works by Lois Mailou Jones are in the following selected locations: American Embassy (Luxembourg); Barnett Aden Gallery (Boca Raton, Florida); Brooklyn Museum (Brooklyn, New York); Clark-Atlanta University (Atlanta, Georgia); The Corcoran Gallery of Art (Washington, D.C.); Joseph Hirshhorn Collection, Smithsonian Institution (Washington, D.C.); Howard University Gallery of Art (Washington, D.C.); Johnson Publishing Company (Chicago, Illinois); Museum of Fine Arts (Boston, Massachusetts); Palais National (Port-au-Prince, Haiti); Schomburg Center for Research in Black Culture (New York City); University of Panjab (Panjab, Pakistan); Walker Art Museum (Bowdoin College, Brunswick, Maine); and Walter Reid Army Medical Center Museum (Washington, D.C.). An interview with Jones is in the Black Women Oral History Collection, Radcliffe College.

Dolores Nicholson

Sarah Garland Jones

(18?-1905)

Physician

Sarah Garland Jones, the first black woman to receive a medical certificate from the state of Virginia, was born soon after the close of the Civil War in Albemarle County, Virginia. Her parents were George W. Garland and Ellen (Boyd) Garland. Her father was the "leading colored contractor and builder of Richmond, Virginia."

Jones attended the public school system in Richmond and graduated in 1883 from the Richmond Normal School. She taught for five years and was regarded as one of the brightest "colored women" of the city. During her teaching years she married Miles Berkley Jones, a physician. Sarah Jones attended Howard Medical School in Washington, D.C., from 1890 to 1893, when she received her medical degree.

Upon returning to Richmond, Sarah Garland Jones was one of eighty-five candidates to take the state medical examination board in Virginia. Twenty-five of the white participants failed the examination. Jones received over 90 percent on the surgery portion of the examination. Passing the Virginia State Medical Examination Board gave her the distinction of becoming the first black woman to receive a medical certificate from the Virginia board.

Jones and her husband set up a practice in Richmond, where he would treat the men and she would treat the women. They maintained a lucrative practice for many years. Like several of their black physician colleagues, the Joneses founded a patient care facility in 1898. The hospital had about twenty-five beds and was mainly available for female patients. The hospital was called The Women's Central Hospital and Richmond Hospital. Incorporated in 1912, the hospital changed its name to Sarah G. Jones Memorial Hospital. In 1901 the Joneses began a training school for nurses affiliated with the hospital. The first nursing class graduated in 1901, and the school remained open until 1920.

At the time of her death in 1905, Sarah Garland Jones was the only black woman practicing medicine in the state of Virginia.

References

Brown, Hallie Q. *Homespun Herpoines and Other Women of Distinction*. Xenia, Ohio: Aldine Publishing Co., 1926.

Majors, Monroe A. *Noted Negro Women: Their Triumphs and Activities*. 1893. Reprint. Freeport, N.Y.: Books for Libraries, 1971.

Collections

Papers relating to Sarah Garland Jones are in the University of Virginia Archives and in the Moorland-Spingarn Research Center at Howard University. Photographs of Jones are in the archives of the Howard University School of Medicine.

Margaret Jerrido

Sissieretta Jones "Black Patti"

(1869-1933)

Singer

Madame Sissieretta Jones shared the stage with the best and brightest black composers, performers, and producers of

Sissieretta Jones

her time. She worked with and for some of the most powerful and influential white impresarios of her day. She was the toast of several continents, where an adoring public showered her with flowers, medals, gold, and gems of all descriptions. She gave private concerts for some of the royal families of Europe and command performances for four presidents of the United States. She did much to dispel the stereotypes of the minstrel tradition even when, in later years, she worked within it.

Maybe she broke too many barriers: She was successful on her own merits in one of the most male-dominated and unforgiving worlds—that of show business. Her trained, operatic voice—perhaps one in a million—was acclaimed by critics and huge numbers of black and white listeners. Though the press dubbed her "Black Patti"—the black answer to Italian prima donna Adelina Patti—"the musical world was not ready to accept black prima donnas" (Southern, 305).

It is difficult to explain why a role in a fully-mounted opera was denied to a talent of the caliber of Sissieretta Jones when, according to Orrin Clayton Suthern of the music department of Lincoln University in Pennsylvania, other black singers got the chance.

> May 11, 1903 marked the first of all-Negro performances of non-Negro operas. Verdi's "Aida" was sung by an all-Negro cast which included such competent artists as Mme. Estelle Pinckney Clough as "Aida"; George Ruffin as "Amonastro" and Theodore Drury as "Rhadames." The latter, according to James Weldon Johnson's account of the first decade of the 1900's, had formed the Theodore Drury Opera Company and annually performed grand operas, such as "Carmen," "Faust," and "Aida" at the Lexington Avenue Opera House in New York City (Suthern, 671).

Presumably, some in the audience were white and influential. At the time, Sissieretta Jones was touring with her Black Patti's Troubadours but would certainly have been available. Her physical appearance would not have denied her the role, and it is reasonably certain that she would not have objected to an all-black cast. She was then a member of an all-black troupe after all. In the mid-1890s, in fact, a *Philadelphia Times* writer observed, after a performance at the Academy of Music, "The thought was irresistible that she would make a superb Aida, whom her appearance, as well as her voice, suggested" (Story, 14). For the time being, at least, her non-appearance must remain a mystery. What is known is that it bothered her greatly: "Being excluded from opera because of her race was perhaps the biggest disappointment she had to face. She referred to it constantly" (Story, 14). Indeed, the seeming novelty—some would say anomaly—of blacks singing operas was often explained away by the white critics as being part of the "natural musical abilities of the Negro. . . . Being a 'natural' singer deprived (the Negro) of the discipline of his craft. It denied training, cultivation and an artistic use of the voice" (Petrie, 163).

Madame Sissieretta Jones's considerable achievements in the vocal performance arena were cheapened both by racial criticism of this type and by the decided mismatching of medium and material that characterized her performances for most of her final twenty years in show business. One of the more blatant examples of the "natural ability" type of criticism appeared at the height of her career in the *Chicago Tribune*, on January 8, 1893:

> She has been endowed by nature with a voice that in any throat would be remarkable for its great range and volume, but which, with her, possesses even greater attractiveness by reason of its having also the wonderful richness and fullness and peculiar timbre that lend the Negro singing voice its individuality. The tones in the lower and middle registers are of surpassing beauty, and those of the upper are remarkable for their clear, bell-like quality. Another striking element of the voice is its plaintiveness. . . . It is the heritage the singer has received from her race, and it alone tells not only of the sorrows of a single life, but the cruelly sad story of a whole people. It lends to her singing of ballads an irresistible charm, making her work in this kind of music as artistically satisfactory as it is enjoyable (Brawley, 141-42).

And this curious mixture of praise and condescension was about as good as Sissieretta Jones could ever get. Writer Rosalyn M. Story perhaps puts it best: "Though Jones was born with talent, it was her training and background that led her from an indigent upbringing as the daughter of an ex-slave to the most prestigious concert stages in the world'' (6).

She was born Matilda Sissieretta Joyner in Portsmouth, Virginia, on January 5, 1869. Jeremiah Malachi Joyner, her father, was pastor of the Afro-American Methodist Church there and also directed the choir, assisted by Matilda's mother, Henrietta, an accomplished soprano. Prior to his ministry, Jeremiah Joyner had been a body servant to his master through the Civil War. In 1876 Joyner was transferred to Providence, Rhode Island, and eagerly moved there, his wife and their only child following shortly thereafter. Providence was far more progressive in matters of race than most northern cities, let alone the South. It had a large, progressive black community, integrated public schools, and black men had voted there since 1842. It was, in short, a wonderful place for musically gifted parents to provide the best for their musically prodigious daughter.

From her earliest days, Matilda Joyner loved to sing. In her recollection of those early days, she admitted to being somewhat of a nuisance, as her mouth was open nearly all of the time. She would stand on the tops of furniture and perform for whoever would listen, and even in her preschool years she displayed a remarkable vocal prowess. ''She attended the Meeting Street and Thayer Street schools, both with integrated faculties and student populations. She sang at school functions and at festivals at the Bond Street Baptist Church. At fifteen, she entered the Providence Academy of Music and studied with M. Mauros and Ada Lacombe, a retired professional singer'' (Story, 6).

At age fourteen she married a ''handsome mulatto from Baltimore,'' David Richard Jones. They reportedly had one child who died in infancy. Before marrying, Richard Jones had been a newsdealer and bellman, but he soon showed himself to be a gambler (especially at the race tracks) and a spendthrift. ''Later, when he took over handling his wife's business affairs after a run-in with her professional manager, he showed himself to be a serious liability to his wife's career, spending her money flagrantly and failing to earn any of his own'' (Story, 7). But with the help of her proud parents, Sissieretta Jones became at age eighteen became a voice student at the New England Conservatory in Boston, coached by Luisiana Cappiani of New York. She was a quick study and soon developed a voice of considerable power and quality. Almost immediately thereafter, she found herself in great demand to give concerts in the churches of Providence.

Singer's First Professional Performance Leads to Fame

Even while still a student, Jones's first professional performance in 1887 at a concert before five thousand at Boston's Music Hall to benefit the Parnell Defense Fund won rave notices, and by 1888 she had achieved prominence for her work on the East Coast. Her first New York appearance was at the Bergen Star Concert at Steinway Hall. A month later she sang at Philadelphia's Academy of Music. Her concert at Wallack's Theatre in Boston (she was the first black artist ever to perform there) prompted a musical director from New York to telegraph impresario Henry Abbey that he had found a ''phenomenal singer.'' (Details of this critical period in Jones's life and career are disputed by many sources. What follows is a consensus.) Immediately, Abbey sent an agent to set up a tour of the West Indies, some sixty appearances in all. Before leaving, she performed for New York critics, who unanimously declared that she was destined to become one of the premier singers of the world. Jones's tour lasted eight months, played to packed houses that bestowed numerous medals and decorations. She returned to Providence for another year of study and a short tour of several eastern seaboard cities, and in December 1890 she performed in Haiti and the Virgin Islands. In Saint Thomas she was showered with pearls, rubies, and diamonds. In Cap Haitien she was given a purse of five hundred dollars in gold by the president of the Republic of Haiti.

Upon her return to the United States, Jones was selected to be the star attraction of the Grand Negro Jubilee at Madison Square Garden in April 1892. The *New York Clipper*, a show business publication, had already pronounced her the ''Black Patti,'' a name that stayed with her the length of her career. It was a sobriquet of mixed blessing, a name of dubious flattery at best, working as often against her as for her. Adelina Patti, the Italian-American prima donna, was universally acknowledged as the best at her craft, ''a diva 'to the manner born' and destined for deification'' (Story, 3). Though Jones's managers liked the name and the comparison, it struck some critics as pretentious, even exploitative. She had her own view:

> Jones adamantly disapproved of the title, no doubt realizing that comparison was inevitable and pointless. ''I do not think I can sing as Patti can,'' she told a *Detroit Tribune* reporter, ''and I have been anxious to drop the name. That is impossible almost, now it has become so identified with me.'' She feared audiences would think she considered herself Patti's equal. To a *Detroit Evening News* writer she insisted, ''I assure you I do not think so. But I have a voice and I am striving to win the favor of the public by honest merit and hard work. Perhaps some day I may be as great in my way, but that is a long way ahead'' (Story, 8).

The Jubilee appearance was a huge success, perhaps the turning point of Jones's career. Before the event, the *New York Times* announced the three-day extravaganza, featuring Jones, the Alabama Quartet, and 'a chorus of 400 colored people,' with instrumental music furnished by Jules Levy and his military band. Jones sang the cavatina from *Robert le Diable*, 'Swanee River,' Ettore Celli's vocal waltz 'Farfella,' and the aria 'Sempre libera' from *La Traviata*. Several papers singled out Jones for rave notices, and her career ascended rapidly from there. The more than 75,000 in attendance echoed the critical acclaim. Suddenly, Jones was famous.

After the Jubilee, her manager booked her into the Academy of Music in Philadelphia, after which there was talk of having her sing the "dark roles" in *Aida* and *L'Africaine* at the Metropolitan Opera House. She reportedly was even signed by Abbey, Schoffel, and Grau, then the managers of the Met. But "the world was not ready."

Still, 1892 was indeed a pivotal year for the young phenomenon. She had already performed in the Blue Room of the White House for President and Mrs. Harrison, the latter so delighted that she personally presented Jones with a bouquet of White House orchids. On the strength of that engagement she became a regular guest at events for Washington dignitaries, among whom were presidents Grover Cleveland, William McKinley, and Theodore Roosevelt.

At some time during this period Jones signed a three-year contract with Major J. B. Pond. This was a shrewd move, as Pond was himself a "shrewd, savvy businessman who managed the careers of sopranos Euphrosyn Parepa-Rosa and Clara Louise Kellogg, humorist Mark Twain, and clergyman and abolitionist Henry Ward Beecher" (Story, 9). He put together a program of popular and serious music that featured Jones, later hiring gifted pianist Alberta Wilson to accompany her. A black concert pianist and opera diva performing together was as rare as it was well-received. Eventually Pond added Paul Laurence Dunbar, Harry T. Burleigh, and Joseph Douglass, grandson of Frederick Douglass, to the program of what must have been the finest black entertainment of the day.

On the strength of Pond's management and savvy—and Madame Jones's prodigious talent—critics were unanimous in their praise of the show. They toured the Midwest and Northeast, stopping in such major venues as Chicago's Central Music Hall, Philadelphia's Academy of Music, Washington's National Theater, and New York's Carnegie Hall. At all of the latter, thousands were turned away. Pond succeeded in demanding two thousand dollars for Jones's week-long engagement at the Pittsburgh Exposition. At the time it was the highest salary ever paid a black artist. She had shared the stage with the greats of the era: Campannini, Materna, and Pat Gilmore. She certainly had all the tools to make it big. Poet, composer, and civil rights activist, James Weldon Johnson noted that "she had most of the qualities essential in a great singer: the natural voice, the physical figure, the grand air, and the engaging personality" (99).

By the time of her 1893 appearance at the Chicago World's Fair she was a bona fide box office attraction strictly on her own merits. Though the "Black Patti" label dogged her even then, the critics were using it as a starting point for discussing Jones's sensational performances and unique vocal gifts.

At this zenith of her career, trouble—almost entirely in the area of management—threatened to ruin everything. Details and versions of the story vary, but the picture that emerges points the finger of blame at her husband, who sought to manage his wife's career when her box office appeal was at its height. He made deals with smaller venues without consulting Pond, seeking to capitalize personally upon what looked like a guaranteed income. The lawsuits, countersuits, and injunctions that followed were a great embarrassment to all, and apparently a great strain on the marriage of Sissieretta and Richard Jones. It is clear that Richard Jones was not to blame for all the woes of Madame Jones experienced at this time, but it is universally agreed that he was little if any help. He was a large part of a complex and significant problem. The problem was greed of management coupled with overexposure (or attempted overexposure) of a bankable star.

Still, "though hard luck and the bad faith of those around her temporarily edged Jones' career off its track, she managed to carry on" (Story, 12). At some point between 1893 and approximately 1898 Jones and her husband divorced. Indications are that there was, at the very least, estrangement from 1893 onward, at least professionally. By then Morris Reno, president of the Carnegie Hall Association, managed most of her appearances. One of particular note was at the New York Conservatory with world-renowned composer Antonin Dvořák in 1894. Following soon after was a tour of England, Germany, and France, capped by a command performance for King Edward, then the Prince of Wales, and a stint at the Royal Opera House in Covent Garden that Jones said was "one of the most exalted triumphs of my career." Even there the "Black Patti" name followed, but the press declared her a "most worthy substitute" (Story, 12).

> It is not inconceivable that Sissieretta Jones used the period following her European tour and her divorce as a time for reflection and reassessment. She had survived unscrupulous management and a disappointing marriage, and escaped both relatively unscathed. She had been the toast of two continents; Europe and America both had praised her singing over the past eight years. On the stage she was a unique presence—intelligent, disarmingly attractive, and as an artist entirely professional. However, she was not white. And as a black woman in the nineteenth century, albeit a great artist, she was subjected to the same attitudes that beleaguered most blacks in nineteenth-century America (Story, 13).

Black Patti's Troubadours Formed

Indeed, as the list of appearances thus far makes obvious, Jones avoided southern cities, often noting that Louisville, Kentucky, was as far south as she would go. An appearance there in later years caused her some consternation when she noted that the black attendees were forced to crowd into the balcony while the orchestra level was only sparsely seated by whites. In addition, hotel accommodations—unless prearranged by a white manager—were difficult if not impossible to get. In later years she and her Troubadours would often tour in a private railroad car.

Social and professional discrimination were two realities

of living during those times that even a superstar could not overcome. All of her attempts at entering the legitimate opera world—whether with or without white help—would result finally in her exclusion because of race. Somewhere along the line someone decided that the public would not approve, and there were rumors that some of the white opera artists would refuse to share the stage with a black, however talented, especially in a subordinate role. If Sissieretta Jones were to sing operatic selections to mixed audiences, a more "acceptable" format would have to be found.

And thus it was that the Black Patti's Troubadours came to be:

> Finally, Jones found a way to satisfy her desire for the opera stage, and as a result, she turned a corner onto the path that would take her to the end of her career. The Black Patti's Troubadours, a multifaceted act organized by New York theatrical proprietors Voelkel and Nolan, occupied the next years of Jones' life and provided a forum for her operatic talent (Story, 14).

Managers Voelkel and John J. Nolan decided to build an all-black show around her, wishing to compete with Williams and Walker and other such shows. They brought in Bob Cole to write it and Billy Johnson to help with the songs, one of the earliest of which was "At Jolly Coon-ey Island." It went on the road in 1896 as "Black Patti's Troubadors." "While the operatic scenes were the drawing [card], the success of the Black Patti's Troubadours depended largely on its minstrel format." This is rather obvious in its advertisement:

> Better than a Circus
> Voelkel and Nolan's
> World Famous Incomparable
> BLACK PATTI'S TROUBADORS
> Greatest Colored Show on Earth
>
> Thirty of the Most Talented Singers, Dancers, Vaudevillists and Refined Colored Fun-Makers Under the Sun
>
> All New Features, The Very Incarnation of Mirth, Melody, Music and Darkey Fun.
>
> Black Patti
> (Mme. Sissieretta Jones)
>
> Whose marvelous voice and lyric triumphs are unparalleled. The most popular Prima Donna in the world with the people of all nations and all races. Countless millions in every part of the civilization have been charmed by her phenomenal voice. H.M. King Edward VII, the Duke of Cambridge, and other members of the Royal Family of England have honored her with their distinguished patronage (Reproduced in Bogle, 20).

There is but one official record of what Sissieretta thought of all this—to go from command performances for royalty to "darkey fun"—and it was characteristically restrained She said she much preferred to sing in concert, that "there are so many things in a vaudeville performance to distract the attention of the audience that they are not in a proper frame of mind to enjoy straight singing" (Story, 16). It was quite obvious to all right from the 1896 start that "Patti" was indeed the main attraction, the "great drawing card," in the words of James Weldon Johnson. But show after show was designed to begin with farcical sketches, burlesque, acrobatics, dances, and "hot stuff" unworthy of an operatic singer. A typical review was published in the Indianapolis *Freeman* on December 12, 1896, which describes this first part humorously as a "travesty," then goes on to delineate "Patti's" strange role in things:

> This travesty is followed by a great vaudeville olio [medley] and selections from the various grand and comic operas. In the operatic olio Black Patti has great opportunities to display her wonderful voice. She sustains the principal roles of "The Grand Duchess," "Carmen," "Bohemian Girl," "Trovatore," "Lucia," "Maritana," "Tar and Tartar," and "The Daughter of the Regiment." The rendition which she and the entire company give of this repertorical [sic] opera selections [sic] is said to be incomparably grand. Not only is the solo singing of the highest order, but the choruses are rendered with a spirit and musical finish which never fail to excite genuine enthusiasm. The work of Black Patti and the company has received the highest marks of public approval, and the forthcoming performances here will doubtless he highly appreciated (Quoted in Sampson, 387).

Incredibly enough, this mixed-format show that only after many years gave way to standard musical comedy was the vehicle for "Patti" for its entire duration. The Troubadours traveled and retraveled the country, sometimes pausing only for a month or two to remount a production in New York. Sometime around 1908, when audiences tired of the unsophisticated buffoonery of the minstrel "darkies," the group resurfaced as the Black Patti Musical Comedy Company with production of "A Trip to Africa," not without some satire and farce of its own.

Many performers built their careers with one or both of the Black Patti vehicles, from the early, struggling Aida Overton Walker to the solidly established Bob Cole and his "Willie Wayside" character. Earnest Hogan (Ruben Crowder), "the unbleached American," was a longtime favorite. Other career-builders included writer/performers Salem Tutt Whitney and Homer Tutt, "Happy" Julius Glenn, "the Wangdoodle Comedian," dancer Ida Forsyne, and countless others. A major reason for the long life of the show and the company was Black Patti's enormous drawing power in the South, which made the Troubadours "alone among the larger colored shows." (Johnson, 101). Apparently, vaudeville with opera on the side was more acceptable to southern audiences than "straight" opera and other classical performances by blacks.

Jones took a very proprietary role with her troupe, presiding with concern and tears over its inevitable demise in 1916. The final performance was in New York's Gibson Theater as payroll checks bounced everywhere. Minstrelsy—and the career of the Black Patti—were dead.

Sissieretta Jones then went home to her beloved Providence and devoted herself to church work and other causes. She cared for her mother until she died and then gave her last professional performance: a concert at the Grand Theater in Chicago. Occasionally she would sing at the local Baptist church. For a while she cared for two homeless boys. Without an income, she was, over time, forced to sell her real estate holdings and nearly all of the jewelry and precious gifts given her on her early West Indian tours. In her last years she was on relief.

A final irony occurred in 1927: A record company used her name, "Black Patti." It did not stay in business long, but was significant because it was only the second black-owned recording company. (The third is Berry Gordy's "Motown" labels, founded in the 1970s. Black Patti was operated by J. Mayo Williams, a former supervisor of race records for Paramount in Chicago. He knew a good name for a record company when he saw it:

> The records that bear her sobriquet offer fine jazz, blues, some sacred records (sermons, spirituals), a few examples of Negro humor, and even a few Wurlitzer organ solos played by Ralph Waldo Emerson. . . . The fact that the length of time between the first issue (8001) and the last (8054) was only some six months, and the absence of any star names in the catalog combine to suggest that Mayo Williams soon became disenchanted (Rust, 34).

What is even more disenchanting and disappointing is the fact that no one ever thought to record Sissieretta Jones. With the Black Patti label, the biggest star's name was on every one. With all the impresarios and managers she had in her career, not one of them semmed to realize that recording her would only broaden her already considerable appeal. The absolute lack of any commercial recording of the magnificent voice of Sissieretta Jones remains one of the great mysteries, ironies, and tragedies of her life.

Jones had survived a bad marriage and inept or corrupt management. She never was permitted to star—or even sing a supporting role—in a complete opera. But she was a woman of absolute dignity and refinement in a world that could not reconcile an operatically-trained voice with a woman of African descent. Her hard-won gains opened doors for many classically-trained black musicians who followed. Her status as a pioneer and role model is as undisputed as the superb quality of her voice.

In 1933 Jones became ill with cancer and was resigned to imminent death. At this point William Freeman and other—mostly local—friends helped to pay her bills and defray medical expenses. On June 24, 1933, in Providence's Rhode Island Hospital, Sissieretta Jones died penniless, and one of the greatest voices of perhaps all time was silenced permanently. Only intervention by Freeman and other friends prevented a burial in the town's "Potter's Field."

References

Bogle, Donald. *Brown Sugar: Eighty Years of America's Black Female Superstars.* New York: Harmony Books, 1980.

Brawley, Benjamin. *The Negro Genius.* New York: Dodd, Mead, 1937.

Cuney-Hare, Maude. *Negro Musicians and Their Music.* Washington, D.C.: Associated Publishers, 1936.

Fletcher, Tom. *100 Years of the Negro in Show Business.* New York: Da Capo Press, 1984.

Johnson, James Weldon. *Black Manhattan.* New York: Knopf, 1940. Reprinted. New York: Arno Press, 1968.

Kimball, Robert and William Bolcom. *Reminiscing with Sissle and Blake.* New York: Viking Press, 1973.

Petrie, Phil. "The Negro in Opera." In Lindsay Patterson, ed. *The Negro in Music and Art.* New York: Publishers Company, 1967.

Rust, Brian. *The Record Label Book: From the 19th Century Through 1942.* New Rochelle, N.Y.: Arlington House, 1978.

Sampson, Henry T. *Blacks in Blackface: A Sourcebook on Early Black Musical Shows.* Metuchen, N.J.: Scarecrow Press, 1980.

Southern, Eileen. *The Music of Black Americans: A History.* New York: Norton, 1971.

Story, Rosalyn M. *And So I Sing: African-American Divas of Opera and Concert.* New York: Warner Books, 1990.

Suthern, Orrin Clayton, III. "Minstrelsy and Popular Culture." *Journal of Popular Culture*, 4 (Winter 1971): 658-73.

Denis Mercier

Virginia Lacy Jones
(1912-1984)
Librarian, educator

Virginia Mae Lacy Jones, whose name is synonymous with black librarianship all over the world, was born in Cincinnati, Ohio, on June 25, 1912. Her parents were Edward Lacy and Ellen (Parker) Lacy. Her parents relocated to Clarksburg, West Virginia, in her early childhood, and she grew up in this mining town of about thirty-five thousand, situated in the northern part of the state. There were about twelve hundred blacks in the town, and the Lacys were hard-working, proud, poor, and ambitious. They lived in an integrated neighborhood; however, the schools that Jones first attended were segregated.

Fellow students belittled Jones because of her light complexion and long red hair and called her ''half-white nigger.'' Students stole her clothes and books. In spite of these dehumanizing experiences, Jones liked school and excelled in her studies. By the time she was ten years old, classmates stopped molesting her and she was popular in plays and musical events. There was no library at Kelly School, but the public library was open to all (not a common practice in many southern communities). Jones began her lifelong affair with books and libraries during these early years. In her high school days, she was in charge of developing a library for the school.

Virginia Lacy Jones

In the fall of 1927, Jones entered Sumner High School in St. Louis, Missouri, where she had moved to live with an aunt whose husband was on the faculty of the school. Jones had more distasteful racial experiences in St. Louis. Caste was a part of the social milieu at Sumner, and she was welcomed as a part of the light-skinned elite because of her hair and complexion and the professional position of her uncle. She was an honor-roll student and made friends with most of the students. She was a school cafeteria cashier and performed in musical and dramatic presentations. She also won a city-wide essay contest. Jones was greatly impressed with the reference librarians and their services at St. Louis Public Library, and she decided to become a librarian. She finished high school in 1929 and returned to West Virginia to earn funds in order to matriculate at Virginia's Hampton Institute, as it was called then, in the bleak, dark days of the Depression. She had three part-time jobs and with scholarship aid she completed three years in the School of Education and in the fourth year she entered the library school. She earned the bachelor of library science degree in June 1933 and in 1938 she earned a second bachelor's degree in education. Florence Rising Curtis, the director of the school, took a personal interest in Jones.

Jones Enters the Library Profession

Jones's first professional appointment was as assistant librarian of the Louisville Municipal College, the Negro branch of the University of Louisville. Eliza Atkins Gleason, the first black American recipient of the Ph.D. in librarianship, was the head librarian. Rufus E. Clement, later to become president of Atlanta University, was dean of the college. Jones was encouraged to seek a higher degree, and Florence Curtis encouraged her to return to Hampton.

During the period Jones was in Kentucky, she and the librarian at Kentucky State College organized the librarians' section of the Kentucky Negro Education Association. Librarians of color, like the black teachers, could not join the Kentucky Library Association. Jones was associated with Thomas Fountain Blue, the stalwart pioneer library administrator in charge of the Negro services at Louisville Public Library. Blue had inaugurated a series of in-service programs at the Western Branch for Negroes, which were attended by people beyond the boundaries of Kentucky. He is also reputed to have been the first black to address a session of the American Library Association (ALA). Jones planned and moved the library of the Louisville Municipal College into its new building.

It was during her second stint at Hampton that Jones faced racism in the American Library Association. In 1936, the association held its annual conference in Richmond, Virginia, and Curtis invited Jones to join her and a group of library school faculty and students to attend the conference. The presence of this group of blacks caused chaos at the conference. Special arrangements had to be made for the group to attend meetings, and special seating was provided. The exhibits were closed to them; however, because of her light skin color, Jones was admitted to the exhibits and stayed in the hotel. Protests were lodged with the leadership of ALA, and it was because of these protests that the association eschewed meeting in cities where all could not attend the meetings without humiliation. Jones later stated:

> I never liked the idea of passing for white, but I did it, nevertheless. . . . I had mixed feelings about doing so, felt a sense of shame for being dishonest and pretending to be what I was not, and for going where I was not wanted. . . . I felt a sense of triumph in outsmarting the blatant and cruel racial discrimination of whites (Jones, 26).

In 1936 Jones completed the B.S. in education degree with honors. There was a great need for trained black librarians in the South, and Hampton had the only library training program in the South that admitted blacks. Curtis had proposed to the General Education Board and the American Library Association the funding of a plan to offer courses for black school librarians at four regional centers in the South. After four consecutive summers the students would receive a degree in librarianship. These centers were located in Nashville, Tennessee; Atlanta, Georgia; Prairie View, Texas; and Hampton, Virginia. By Texas state law, a white person could not teach at Prairie View College, so Jones was named director of the Texas locale. This was the beginning of an exciting career in library education that would cover more than forty years of service. Traveling by train in the South, (sometimes as a white when things got perilous) was also the beginning of a long involvement with southern bigotry; but more importantly Jones said that the "journey was to lead me into the challenges, problems and gratifications of library education" (Jones, 27).

Curtis was interested in Jones's working toward an advanced degree in librarianship and looked forward to her continuing in library education. Jones approached the General Education Board, and she was given a fellowship under the condition that she would contribute "to library development for Negroes in the South." In the fall of 1937, Jones entered the library education program at the University of Illinois, Curtis's alma mater.

Racism Follows Jones

Racism was overt at Urbana-Champaign. Blacks could not live on campus, so Lacy roomed with a black couple near the campus. There were a little more than one hundred black the students in Illinois student body of thirteen thousand, most of whom had to live in hovels, and because food service was denied them in public places, they had great difficulties securing meals. Blacks could get lunch in the home economics building, but many times when a black sat at a table where whites were seated, the whites would leave. Many of the social events of the university were closed to black students. A number of the black students were engaged in protests against the racial climate at Illinois and expected all black students to participate. The burden of studies and Jones's urge to excel did not prevent her from being a part of the protest movement led by the Chicago chapter of the NAACP. After living under these stressful and threatening conditions, Jones finished the master's program with kudos from the dean on the quality of her work. (The dean was probably oblivious to the conditions under which she had studied at Illinois.)

President Rufus Clement of Atlanta University offered Jones a position as cataloger at Atlanta University's library. Clement had plans to open a library school and because of Jones's experiences at Texas and Louisville, he wanted her for the faculty. The Hampton library school had been closed in 1938, and the Atlanta library school opened in 1941. Jones visited a number of library education programs to observe their administration. Clement also promised to assist her in studying for the Ph.D. degree in librarianship. Eliza Atkins Gleason, a colleague at Louisville, was the dean of the newly-opened library school, and Jones was a faculty member. Thus, Virginia Lacy Jones, who married Morehouse College language professor Edward Allen Jones on Thanksgiving Day, 1941, embarked upon on her lengthy profession "to touch the lives of young people entering the Atlanta University School of Library Service" (Jones, 34). At first Jones taught the cataloging and classification, school library service, and children's literature courses.

Jones became concerned about demeaning images of blacks in children's literature, and along with Charlaemae Rollins of the Chicago Public Library and Mollie Houston Lee of the Raleigh, North Carolina, Public Library, protested to publishers about children's books, seeking, on behalf of black readers, changes in illustrations and stories.

In 1942, the Carnegie Corporation of New York financed the establishment of a Field Service Program at the library school to assist the school in contributing to the development and improvement of black schools in the South. Jones, along with the director of the project, Hallie Beachem Brooks, visited school libraries in Tennessee, Kentucky, Virginia, and North and South Carolina, offering to assist in the organization or reorganization of library service and the provision of bibliographical assistance in the area of collection development. While on the library tour, Brooks and Jones suffered sometimes hazardous conditions and physical discomfort in southern urban and rural settings.

In 1943, with the aid of another General Education Board fellowship, Jones entered the graduate library school of the University of Chicago to work toward the Ph.D. degree. The atmosphere at Chicago for minority students was a decidedly different one than that at Illinois and conducive to intense independent study at a high level. In 1945, Jones started a three-month visit to twenty-two southeastern cities to collect data for a study of "The Problems of Negro Public High Schools in Selected Southern Cities," and the resulting dissertation was completed and accepted. The newly minted Dr. Virginia Lacy Jones returned to Atlanta in the autumn of

1945. Jones was the second black to receive the doctoral degree in librarianship.

Library School Gains New Dean

Jones became the second dean of the School of Library Service at Atlanta University upon the resignation of Eliza Gleason. Jones was instrumental in broadening the curricular offerings of the school and inaugurating the annual trip to visit libraries in Baltimore and Washington, D.C., since many black students were often denied access to public libraries in the South and needed to observe excellent and accessible libraries in operation. The trip included visits to the Library of Congress and other federal libraries, the Folger Shakespeare Library, and Baltimore's Enoch Pratt Free Library.

With funds from a number of philanthropic groups, Jones and an innovative and motivated faculty sponsored a number of leadership conferences in the areas of public libraries, children's literature, black access to libraries, black American bibliography, and undergraduate library education. Jones and faculty members served as consultants to schools, colleges, and public libraries in the South in their efforts to improve services to their black users.

Jones was active in national library associations and was a member of the ALA Council and an officer in the Association of American Libraries. However, for many years she was completely isolated from contact with many southern white librarians. She was a charter member of the Georgia Chapter of the Special Libraries Association, but because of racial restrictions she could not belong to the Metropolitan Atlanta Library Association or the Georgia Library Association (her membership check was returned with a letter stating that GLA did not have provisions for her to become a member). It was ironic that a nationally known and acclaimed library educator and leader could not be considered for membership in regional library associations.

Jones served as chairperson of an ALA ad hoc committee on Opportunities for Negro Students in the Library Profession. The committee proposed ambitious projects to recruit more minorities to the profession, and although they were approved by the ALA Executive Committee, they were not funded.

In 1967 Jones was elected president of the Association of American Library Schools and President Lyndon B. Johnson appointed her as a member of the President's Advisory Committee on Library Research and Training Projects. Governor George Busbee appointed her to the Georgia State Board for the Certification of Librarians which she served from 1975 to 1980. Other honors include: a General Education Board Fellowship, 1937-38, 1943-45; the Hampton Institute Alumni Achievement Award in 1956; the Atlanta Bronze "Woman of the Year" Award in 1959; an honorary membership in the West Virginia Library Association in 1971; the Melvil Dewey Award of the ALA in 1973; an honorary membership in the American Library Association in 1976; a citation from the ALA Black Caucus for thirty years of service to black librarians, 1976; the Joseph W. Lippincott Award from the ALA in 1977; honorary degrees in 1979 from Bishop College and the University of Michigan; the Beta Phi Mu Award in 1980; and the Mary Rothrock Award from the Southeastern Library Association in 1982.

Virginia Lacy Jones served as dean of the library school at Atlanta until 1981. A pioneer in black library education, "Dean Jones," as she was affectionately known, was diminutive in stature, but a giant in library education and was known as the "dean of library school deans." Her affiliation with the school spanned four decades, and with the university, forty-two years.

In 1981 the Council of Presidents of the Atlanta University Center, a consortium of historically black colleges and universities, named Jones director of the Atlanta University Center's Robert W. Woodruff Library. The appointment served to crown her professional accomplishments. The center recognized her administrative, organizational, and planning skills and the wise, optimistic, dedicated, and humanitarian leadership she had demonstrated over the past forty-two years. She was also a scholarly and exacting person. Under Jones's leadership, the staffs and holdings of the six libraries of the center's institutions were merged into a new eighteen-million-dollar facility, inaugurating a new program of library service in the center. Despite her optimistic determination, Jones was not able to realize her vision for the Woodruff Library. Ill health forced her to resign her position in November 1983. At that time the Board of Trustees of Atlanta University named her Dean Emeritus. As an expression of their appreciation for years of service, the Atlanta University Center named the exhibition gallery in her honor as a fitting tribute to her life and labors. Illness prevented her from attending a proposed dedication ceremony, and on December 3, 1984, Jones died of cancer. Her husband, popularly known as "E. A.," and her "Aunt Lelia," who had lived with the Joneses in Atlanta for many years and was very dear to them, had preceded Virginia Jones in death. There were no children from the Jones marriage. On Sunday, May 19, 1985, a solemn celebration was held for a woman whose career in black librarianship was known throughout the world. Believing from her Virginia-ALA experiences that ethnic and racial barriers can and must be destroyed, she worked untiringly to make librarianship a better profession for all. The Beta Phi Mu award capsuled the professional character of Virginia Lacy Jones: "an excellent model of those who see professional education as encompassing administrative skill, leadership, adherence to principles of human rights, scholarship, and advanced thinking" (*ALA Yearbook*, 18). The esteem in which she was held by those who knew her was expressed in the University of Michigan's commendation when she was awarded an honorary degree:

> Dr. Jones is the personification of wise counsel, inspired teacher, patient mentor, and demanding scholar. In the library profession at large she is acknowledged as a courageous leader who has pointed the way to achievement and success

against barriers that most of us would have considered insurmountable (*ALA Yearbook*, 17).

Portraits of Virginia Lacy Jones hang in the reception area of the Atlanta School of Library and Information Studies, Trevor Arnett Hall, and the Virginia Lacy Jones Exhibition Hall of the AU Center's Woodruff Library.

References

ALA *Yearbook of Library and Information Service*. Chicago: American Library Association, 1985. Photograph pp. 17-18.

Jones, Virginia Lacy. "A Dean's Career." *The Black Librarian in America*, ed. E. J. Josey, Jr. Metuchen, N.J.: Scarecrow Press, 1970.

Who's Who Among Black Americans, 1977-78. 2d ed. Chicago: Who's Who Among Black Americans. Inc., 1978.

Who's Who in America, 1982-83. Vol. 1. Chicago: Marquis, 1983.

Who's Who in Colored America. 7th ed. Yonkers, N.Y.: Christian E. Burckel & Associates, 1950. This work gives Jones's birthdate as 1914. Photograph p. 318.

Who's Who in Library and Information Services. Chicago: American Library Association, 1982.

Women of Courage. An Exhibition of Photographs by Judith Sedwick. Based on the Black Women Oral History Project. Cambridge: Schlesinger Library, Radcliffe College, 1984. Includes biographical sketch and photograph, p. 55.

Collections

Personal papers of Virginia Lacy Jones are located in the Atlanta University Center's Robert W. Woodruff Library and in the School of Library and Information Studies of Clark Atlanta University. The Black Women Oral History Collection, Radcliffe College, contains an interview with Jones. Copies of the interviews are in selected libraries throughout the United States.

Casper LeRoy Jordan

Barbara Jordan

(1936-)

Politician, lawyer, educator

Barbara Charline Jordan gained national recognition as a politician, first in the Texas State Senate and then in the United States House of Representatives, where she had a nationwide television audience as the House Judiciary committee considered articles of impeachment against President Richard M. Nixon. Congressman Charles Wilson, a fellow member of the Texas delegation to Congress, said in 1975:

> In my view Barbara Jordan is the most influential member of Congress. I mean, if you're talking about the one person who is able to get to just *anybody*, I don't care who it is, and make them stop and listen to what she has to say and convince them that she is right. . . . Now it's obvious that Barbara is very smart, but don't forget that there are a lot of people here in Washington who are very smart. . . . So what makes Barbara so special? It's that along with all her superior intelligence and legislative skill she also has a certain *moral authority* and a . . . it's just presence, and it all comes together in a way that sort of grabs you, maybe you're kind of intimidated by it, and you have to listen when she speaks and you feel you must try and do what she wants. What Barbara has is not something you learn and develop, it's something that God gave her and it's something you can't really describe (Sanders, 141).

Jordan was born February 21, 1936, in Houston, Texas to Benjamin Meridieth Jordan, a warehouse clerk and part-time clergyman, and Arlyne (Patten) Jordan. Barbara had two older sisters, Bennie and Rose Marie. Houston was still a segregated city as Jordan was growing up, and the family was not affluent; nonetheless her immense strength comes from her background. She grew up in a house jointly owned and occupied by her father and her paternal grandfather, Charles Jordan, chairman of the deacon board of Good Hope Baptist Church. A special relationship developed between Jordan and her maternal grandfather, John Ed Patten, a former minister and the only non-church going member of the family. Patten had a horse and wagon junk business, and Jordan spent Sunday afternoons with him while her sisters were busy with the Baptist Young People's Union. He provided much direction to her, advising and training her to act and think independently and not fall into mediocrity. He thought of himself as above the average man and tried to instill the same sense of superior ability in Jordan. "Life," he would say, "is not a playground, but a schoolroom" (Jordan, 10). He tried to convince her that those who saw it that way would go on to learn from the experience which the world provided and succeed no matter what the obstacles. He was there for her until she went away to graduate school; then he died.

Barbara Jordan attended Phillis Wheatley High School in Houston and was an outstanding student there. She was at first a typical teenager, seeking to blend in with her friends—in the process building long enduring friendships. Influenced by a Career Day speech by Chicago attorney Edith Sampson, she decided to become a lawyer with no clear understanding of what that decision entailed. Beyond her studies and work

Barbara Jordan

in clubs she chose to make her mark in public speaking for which she soon showed great aptitude. In 1952 she became Girl of the Year, placed first in the state Ushers Oratorical Contest, and won a trip to Chicago, where she won the national contest.

After graduating from Phillis Wheatley High School in 1952, she attended Texas Southern University, living at home and commuting. She had an active social life and joined the Delta Sigma Theta sorority. When she decided to complete her degree rather than trying to go to law school after her junior year, she took a degree in government. Joining the debate team at Texas Southern, Jordan had a great deal of success. She was proud of tying Harvard in a debate; she was convinced that Harvard was the best college and later said that she considered a tie against them to be a win for Texas Southern. Her debate coach, Tom Freeman, was a major influence on her life. He coached her to many wins and to the tie against Harvard. When Jordan was looking for a law school, it was Tom Freeman who influenced her to go to Boston University Law School. Her father agreed "one way or another" to pay her costs, and she was off to Boston.

In Boston Jordan was competing with white students in a nonsegregated setting for the first time and the adjustment was not easy. She felt that she "learned at twenty-one that you just couldn't say a thing is so because it might not be so, and somebody brighter, smarter, and more thoughtful would come out and tell you it wasn't so. . . . I was doing sixteen years of remedial work in thinking" (Jordan, 93). She worked hard to overcome her perceived deficiencies. Her religious life began to change also from a focus on God's prohibitions to one on God's love under the influence of the sermons of Howard Thurman. In three years she graduated; she and Issie Shelton, also of Houston, were the only black women and the only women in a graduating class of 128. In that year, 1959, after taking the Massachusetts Bar examination, she went back to Houston and took the Texas Bar examination. She passed both.

Jordan was offered a job in Massachusetts, but it seemed to her to be far too anonymous, so she opted for a return to Texas. She opened a private law practice. Then, in the campaign for John F. Kennedy and Lyndon B. Johnson, she volunteered to develop a highly organized black-worker program for the forty predominantly black precincts of Harris County and managed to get an eighty percent voter turnout, the most successful get-out-the-vote campaign in Harris County that anyone could recall. That was her political beginning.

She became a speaker for the Harris County Democratic Party and deeply involved in politics. In 1962 she ran for the Texas House of Representatives and lost. She ran again for the same position in 1964 and lost again. Now facing family pressures to get married, she made a decision not to marry, "and it was a fairly conscious one, that I couldn't have it both ways. And that politics was the most important thing to me. I reasoned that this political thing was so total in terms of focus that, if I formed an attachment over here, this total commitment would become less than total" (Jordan, 119).

In 1965 Harris County was reapportioned and Jordan found herself in a newly created Eleventh State Senatorial District. In 1964, in her losing campaign, she had carried every polling place in this new Eleventh District. She ran a campaign against a popular liberal and won by a two-to-one margin. Two blacks were elected from the newly reapportioned Harris County—Barbara Jordan to the senate and Curtis Graves to the house.

When she went to Austin, Jordan made her biggest hit by trying her best to fit in, by being not different. As the first black elected to the Texas State Senate since 1883 and the first woman ever elected, she set her sights on being effective. She was honing her already finely developed political skills. One aspect of this was to know how things worked; she later said: "If you're going to play the game properly, you'd better know every rule" (Sanders, 142). This means also knowing the unwritten rules. In *Ebony* article "Barbara Jordan: Texan Is a New Power on Capitol Hill," Charles Sanders describes her skills at their full development:

> She not only dazzled [members of the Texas delegation] with her intellectual brilliance but also with her knowledge of their kind of rough-and-tumble politics. . . . [S]he never permitted the men of the "club" to feel uncomfortable around her. She could smoke and drink Scotch—just like them. She could tone down her Boston University kind of speech and talk Texas lingo—just like them. She knew as much as they did, or more, about such things as oil depletion allowances and cotton prices and the Dallas money

> market, but she never, says one member of the "club" made men "feel like we had a smart-aleck, know-it-all women on our hands." He explains: "Now Barbara doesn't try to play possum on you; she doesn't mind letting you know that she's got a very, very high I.Q. But she doesn't embarrass you by making you feel that you're nowhere close to being as smart as she is. It's an amazing thing how she can be standing there schooling you about something and still make you feel that you knew all that right along" (140).

She sought advice on what committee assignments she might get, dealing with both liberal and conservative people in the Texas Senate. She caught Lyndon B. Johnson's eye, and she was invited to the White House for a preview of his 1967 Civil Rights message.

In her six years in the Texas Senate, she "sponsored most of the state's environmental legislation, authored the first Texas minimum wage law, forced the state to place antidiscrimination clauses in all of its business contracts, and pushed the first package of urban legislation through a rural-minded state government dominated by white males" (*Ebony Success Library,* 149). She was in the Texas Senate until 1972. At that time she chose to run for the national House of Representatives and won. She took office in January of 1973, but before she left her position in the Texas Senate, she was elected president *pro tem,* and on a day when the governor and the lieutenant governor were supposedly out of the state she became governor for a day, June 10, 1972, adding to her list of "firsts." Her father lived to see this, going to the hospital in Austin on the 10th and dying from his heart problem the following day.

Defense of the Constitution Brings National Acclaim

When Jordan was elected to Congress, she asked Lyndon Johnson's advice on what committee assignments to request. This turned out to be a tremendously helpful approach. Johnson advised her to request the Judiciary Committee; he even made arrangements with the Ways and Means Committee and with the Judiciary Committee so that she was assured of that assignment. In retrospect, that assignment turned into a major task; after the Watergate Scandal erupted pressure built up in Congress until the Judiciary Committee went into the matter of impeachment of President Richard Nixon. Although she originally argued against public speeches on the subject, she got no support for that position and her fifteen-minute nationally-televised speech on the duty of elected officials to defend the Constitution and the way that those duties had been mishandled by the administration catapulted her into the public eye as nothing she had ever done before. Jordan disliked the idea of impeachment but felt that the evidence demanded that an indictment of Nixon be presented to the Senate. Her speech on July 25, 1974, in favor of impeachment used all her skill as a lawyer and as an orator to defend the constitutional issues that she felt were pertinent to her decision, and to persuade others of the rectitude of her position. *Newsweek* called her speech "the most memorable indictment of Richard Nixon to emerge from the House impeachment" (Cited in *Contemporary Authors,* Vol. 123, 195). She began by saying:

> "We the people"—it is a very eloquent beginning. But when the Constitution of the United States was completed on the seventeenth of September in 1787, I was not included in that "We the People." I felt for many years that somehow George Washington and Alexander Hamilton just left me out by mistake. But through the process of amendment, interpretation, and court decision, I have finally been included in "We the people."
>
> Today I am an inquisitor. I believe hyperbole would not be fictional and would not overstate the solemnness that I feel right now. My faith in the Constitution is whole. It is complete. It is total. I am not going to sit here and be an idle spectator in the diminution, the subversion, the destruction of the Constitution (Jordan, 186-87).

She then moved through the case against Nixon, concluding:

> Has the President committed offenses and planned and directed and acquiesced in a course of conduct which the Constitution will not tolerate? That is the question. We know that. We should now forthwith proceed to answer the question. It is reason and not passion which must guide our decision (191-92).

In the first session of her first term the Omnibus Crime Control and Safe Streets Act came up for renewal. Jordan proposed a civil rights amendment to mandate the use of federal funds in a nondiscriminatory fashion. She also introduced a bill proposing the repeal of the Fair Trade Laws, which allowed manufacturers to establish retail prices and to enforce them, a price-fixing mechanism which interfered with free competition.

Her reputation as one of the great orators of the twentieth century was sustained by her keynote address to the 1976 Democratic National Convention. As she prepared for it, she was forced to reveal that severe problems with the cartilage in one knee made it impossible for her to walk as far to the podium as the original plan envisaged. She said that "we cannot improve on the system of government handed down to us by the founders of the Republic, but we can find new ways to implement that system and realize our destiny" (*Contemporary Authors,* Vol. 23, 195). She went on to quote Abraham Lincoln, in terms of "a national community in which every last one of us participates; 'As I would not be a *slave,* so I would not be a *master.*' This expresses my idea of democracy. Whatever differs from this, to the extent of the difference, is no democracy" (Jordan, 231).

Newspapers picked up her speech at once. The Philadelphia *Evening Bulletin* (13 July 1976) said: "The Democrats were losing to boredom 1-0 last night when they had the good sense to bring Barbara Jordan to the bench. . . . [She] took it downtown . . . [a] Grand Slam. . . . Getting on the same podium with Miss Jordan is like singing along with Marian Anderson (Jordan, 232). The clamor was nationwide, and many were suggesting Barbara Jordan for vice president. She simply brushed that off with "It's not my turn. You'll know when it's my turn" (Jordan, 234). But Jimmy Carter did speak to her about a cabinet post. She seemed to want the post of attorney general; he seemed to have her in mind for the post of Health, Education, and Welfare secretary. The result of their differing views was that she was not included in the Carter cabinet. The position of attorney general went to Georgia attorney Griffin Bell.

In 1978 she decided not to run for Congress again and, in effect, retired into a teaching position at the Lyndon B. Johnson School of Public Affairs, University of Texas at Austin. In 1982 she was appointed to the Lyndon B. Johnson Centennial Chair in National Policy. She serves as a faculty advisor, as a minority recruiter, and as teacher at the University of Texas at Austin.

As for leaving Congress, Jordan said that she

> felt more of a responsibility to the country as a whole, as contrasted with the duty of representing the half-million people in the Eighteenth Congressional District. I felt some necessity to address national issues. I thought that my role now was to be one of the voices in the country defining where we were, where we were going, what the policies were that were being pursued, and where the holes in those policies were. I felt I was more in an instructive role than a legislative role (Jordan, 247).

An academic invitation was the catalyst which led her to the decision to leave political office. She received a letter from Harvard University stating that they had voted to give her an honorary doctorate at the next commencement. A month later another letter came from Harvard inviting her to speak at that commencement. Thinking about the speech at Harvard led her to the conclusion that she had to "leave elected politics . . . to free my time in such a way that it could be structured by the country's needs as I perceived them" (Jordan, 250).

Barbara Jordan has received more than twenty honorary doctorates from institutions such as Harvard, Princeton, and the University of Cincinnati. Her name appeared on many lists of most admired women and most influential women. She was the recipient of the Eleanor Roosevelt Humanities Award in 1984, voted "Best Living Orator" by the International Platform Association in 1984, was elected to the Texas Women's Hall of Fame in 1984, and for about ten years hosted a show on the Public Broadcasting System, "Crisis to Crisis with Barbara Jordan." Recently, Texas Governor Ann Richards appointed Jordan as her advisor on ethics in government.

References

Angelo, Bonnie. "An Ethical Guru Monitors Morality." *Time* 137 (3 June 1991): 9-10. Interview. Photograph, p. 9.

Brown, Ray B., ed. *Contemporary Heroes and Heroines.* Detroit: Gale Research, 1990. 225-29. Photograph, p. 225.

Contemporary Authors. Vol. 113. Detroit: Gale Research, 1985. Vol. 123, 1988.

Current Biography. New York: H. W. Wilson, 1974. 189-92.

Editors of Ebony. *Ebony Success Library.* Vol. 2, *Famous Blacks Give Secrets of Success.* Chicago: Johnson Pub. Co., 1973. 146-49.

Jordan, Barbara and Shelby Hearn. *Barbara Jordan: A Self Portrait.* Garden City, N.Y.: Doubleday, 1979.

Sanders, Charles L. "Barbara Jordan: Texan Is a New Power on Capitol Hill." *Ebony* 30 (February 1975): 136-42. Cover photograph, photographs.

United States House of Representatives. Commission on the Bicentenary. *Women in Congress.* Washington, D.C.: United States Government Printing Office, 1991. 117-18. Photograph, p. 117.

Who's Who Among Black Americans, 1990/91. 6th ed. Detroit: Gale Research, 1990. 718.

Collections

The Barbara Jordan Collection in the Heartman Collection at Texas Southern University contains books, photographs, speeches, correspondence, and other papers from her tenure in the Texas Senate as well as the United States Congress. It is regularly expanded.

James Duckworth

June Jordan

(1936-)

Poet, writer, educator

A prolific writer and a college professor, June Jordan writes in many genres but her poetic vision infuses all of her work and moves her one step away from the more militant poets who emerged in the 1960s. Born in Harlem on July 9, 1936, to Granville Ivanhoe Jordan and Mildred Maude

(Fisher) Jordan, June Jordan is the only child of West Indian immigrant parents. Granville and Mildred Jordan migrated to New York City from Jamaica. Granville Jordan worked as a postal clerk, mainly assigned to the night shift, and Mildred worked as a nurse. June Jordan was born in Harlem, but when she was five years old the family moved to Bedford-Stuyvesant in Brooklyn. Her parents purchased a brownstone on Hancock Street, where June Jordan grew up.

As a teenager, Jordan commuted to Midwood High School, where she was the only black in a student body of three thousand. After only one year in this environment, she transferred to one even less conducive to the development of her African-American psyche. Her parents' ambitions for her placed her in a "white universe,"—a New England preparatory school. The Northfield School for Girls in Massachusetts (now merged with Mount Hermon), is, however, where Jordan discovered her poetic voice. This voice was encumbered, nonetheless, by the white male poets to whom she was exposed, as their sensibilities were certainly not her own. Additionally, her parents opposed her efforts to become a poet. Beatings by an overly-authoritarian father, coupled with her mother's refusal or inability to defend her, led to a violent, confusing, and guilt-laden adolescence. Perhaps these experiences produced a heightened identity crisis, one that found resolution in the black consciousness movement of the 1960s.

Jordan graduated from preparatory school in the spring of 1953 and entered Barnard College in September. At nineteen she met and fell in love with Michael Meyer, a white student at Columbia University. They married in 1955. June withdrew from Barnard, interrupting her education to follow her husband to the University of Chicago, where he engaged in graduate study in anthropology. She attended the University of Chicago for one year from 1955 to 1956. In September 1956 she returned to Barnard, where she remained until February 1957.

Alexis Deveaux, writer for *Essence* magazine and also a friend of Jordan's, comments on her interracial marriage. "Interracial marriage was a felony in 43 states, including the ones they drove through on their way West. In Chicago, white people shouted 'nigger' and 'nigger bitch' at her [Jordan] when she and Michael walked the streets together" (quoted in Erickson, 148).

In 1958 a son and only child, Christopher David Meyer, was born. Jordan's marriage was unravelling, forcing her to assume full responsibility for their son. Thus, in 1963 Jordan accepted a position as an assistant to the producer of Frederick Wiseman's *The Cool World*, a film about Harlem. In 1965 she and Michael Meyer divorced. At twenty-nine, Jordan faced being a single parent, working mother who still fought with her parents and still needed to define her artistic self.

Despite the trauma of divorce, the hardship of single parenting, and working to earn a living, Jordan managed to find time to write. In 1969 Jordan's first book, *Who Look at Me*, published by Crowell, introduced her to the world as a poet. Dealing with African-American identity and depicting black life, Jordan's poems "struggle to determine and then preserve a particular, human voice . . . closely related to the historic struggling of black life in America" (*Soulscript*, xvii). Of the first poem in the book Erickson writes: "*Who Look At Me* is not only chronologically first but also logically first. The poem is a crucial starting point because its effort to contend with black-white relations is a necessary first step in self-definition for a black person and poet in a white society" (150).

In 1970, Jordan edited *Soulscript; Afro-American Poetry*. Defining poetry as technique for transforming language into voice, Jordan says, "Poems are voiceprints of language, or if you prefer, *soulscript*" (Introduction). *Soulscript* is a collection of poetry from children aged twelve to eighteen and of well-known poets of the 1960s. Other works by Jordan include: *The Voice of the Children*, (a reader) edited with Terri Bush (New York: Holt, 1970); *Some Changes* (poems) (New York: Dutton, 1971); *His Own Where* (young adult novel) (New York: Crowell, 1971); *Dry Victories* (juvenile and young adult) (New York: Holt, 1972); *Fannie Lou Hamer* (biography) (New York: Crowell, 1972); *New Days: Poems of Exile and Return* (New York: Emerson Hall, 1973); *New Room: New Life* (juvenile) (Crowell, 1975); *Things that I Do in the Dark: Selected Poetry* (New York: Random House, 1977); *Okay Now* (New York: Simon and Schuster, 1977); *Passion: New Poems, 1977-1980* (Boston: Beacon Press, 1980); *Civil Wars* (essays, articles, and lectures) (Boston: Beacon Press, 1981); *Kimako's Story* (juvenile) (Boston, Houghton Mifflin, 1981); *Living Room: New Poems, 1980-1984* (New York: Thunder Mouth Press, 1985); *On Call: New Political Essays, 1981-1985* (Boston: South End Press, 1985); and *High Tide—Marea Alta* (New York: Curbstone, 1987). In addition to books, Jordan has written a number of plays. Among them are *In the Spirit of Sojourner Truth*, produced in New York City at the Public Theater, May 1979, and *For the Arrow that Flies by Day*, a staged reading produced in New York at the Shakespeare Festival, April 1981. Jordan also composed the lyrics and libretto for *Bang Bang Ueber Alles* in 1985 (*Contemporary Authors*, 242).

To support herself and her son, Jordan worked in a number of places. Prior to the publication of her first book in 1969, she had published numerous short stories and poems in well-known periodicals including *Esquire*, *Nation*, *Partisan Review*, *Black World*, *Essence*, and the *New York Times Magazine*, under the name of June Meyer. In 1966 she began what would become her livelihood throughout the years. Jordan became an instructor in English and literature at the City University of New York. In 1968 she moved to Connecticut College in New London, where she taught English and directed the Search for Education, Elevation and Knowledge (SEEK) program. Jordan in 1968 joined Sarah Lawrence College in Bronxville, New York, as instructor in English and remained there until 1974. The City College of New York hired Jordan as assistant professor of English in

1975. In 1976 she moved to the State University of New York at Stony Brook and in 1982 was promoted to tenured full professor.

Writing Reflects Variety of Genres

Since the publication of her first book in 1969, Jordan has written prolifically in many genres. Her books for children utilize black English and promote what Jordan believes is "Black-survivor consciousness" (Erickson, 155). Her poetry matures from the lines in *Who Look At Me* that voice her concern for "white stares" to the declaration of her identity in *Some Changes*, where she proclaims, "I am black within / as is this skin" (Erickson, 155), to the ultimate realization that violence is a legitimate and logical response for self-defense.

Jordan's poetic vision is expansive and infuses all that she writes. The dramatic tension in her work emanates from the painful and poignant relationship Jordan endures with her parents. In 1966 her mother's suicide seemed to prompt a critical reexamination of her mother's life, not as mother of Jordan, but as woman with separate and distinct unfulfilled dreams. Jordan writes of her mother's sacrifice. In an address titled "Notes of a Barnard Dropout," delivered at the Reid Lecture at Barnard College in 1975, Jordan reveals her mother's life as split between the kitchen and "the little room." She tries to feel the rhythms of her mother's sacrifices and asks, "what had happened to you and your wish?" [To be an artist]. The "little room" is a metaphor for the suppressed space that would not allow for the development of the mother as artist.

Space is a recurring image in Jordan's work. Beginning with *The Voice of the Children*, where Jordan details the difficulty of finding a room for the workshop to meet, to the titles of her works, *New Life: New Room, Living Room*, and *His Own Where*, space is crucial to the development of self. Despite her work in other genres, Jordan is probably best known as a poet. She is often categorized with that group of militant poets that emerged during the 1960s. However, her poetry, while decidedly political and aesthetically black, is often uncharacteristic of the angry shrill of the "Black is Beautiful" decade. Jordan combines her personal, family pain with weltschmerz that results in arresting images.

The death of Jordan's father in 1974 works to deepen the biographical elements in her work. "Poems for Granville Ivanhoe Jordan" (*Things that I Do in the Dark*, 20) marks the omnipresence of the mother/father influence in her work.

A member of American Writers Congress (executive board member) and of PEN, Jordan is the recipient of many honors and awards. In 1969-1970 she received a Rockefeller grant for creative writing. That same year she was awarded the Prix de Rome in Environmental Design for 1970-1971. She also received the Nancy Bloch Award, 1971, for *The Voice of the Children*. The *New York Times* selected *His Own Where* as one of the year's outstanding young adult novels for 1971. This same novel was nominated for the National Book Award in 1971. Jordan received the Creative Artist Public Service Program poetry grant in 1978; a Yado fellowship in 1979; a National Endowment for the Arts fellowship in 1982; the achievement award for international reporting from the National Association of Black Journalists in 1984 and a New York Foundation for the Arts fellowship in poetry in 1985 (*Contemporary Authors*, 242).

References

Contemporary Authors. Vol. 25. Detroit: Gale Research, 1988.

Deveaux, Alexis. "Creating Soul Food: June Jordan." *Essence* 11 (April 1981): 82, 138-50.

Erickson, Peter B. "June Jordan." *Dictionary of Literary Biography*. Vol. 38. Eds. Thadious M. Davis and Trudier Harris. Detroit: Gale Research, 1985.

Jordan, June. "Notes of a Barnard Dropout." Reid Lecture, Barnard College, 1975.

———. *Things that I Do in the Dark*. New York: Random House, 1977.

———. *Soulscript: Afro-American Poetry*. Garden City, N.Y.: Doubleday, 1970. Introduction.

Nagueyalti Warren

Anna Johnson Julian

(19?-)

Educator, sociologist, entrepreneur

Anna J. Johnson Julian, educator, sociologist, and entrepreneur, is best known as an officer of Julian Associates, a chemical company, and of Julian Research Institute. Active in civic affairs in Chicago and the state of Illinois, she received distinction from several organizations for her contributions in these areas.

Julian was born in Baltimore, Maryland, the daughter of Adelaide (Scott) Johnson and Charles Speare Johnson. She earned three degrees from the University of Pennsylvania—a B.S. in 1923, with majors in sociology and English in 1923; an M.A. in sociology in 1925; and a Ph.D. in sociology (with honors) in 1937. She was the first black inducted into Phi Beta Kappa as well as the first black woman to receive a doctorate in sociology at the University of Pennsylvania. She had studied during summers at Columbia University and the University of Chicago. Julian was a case worker for Family Service in Washington, D.C., from 1925 to 1928, and an English teacher at the Bordentown Industrial Institute in

Bordentown, New Jersey, during the 1928-29 academic year. She then became an assistant in the department of research of the Washington, D.C., public schools, where she remained for ten years. On December 24, 1935, she married Percy Lavon Julian, a renowned chemist, civil rights leader, and researcher. They had two children, Percy Lavon, Jr., and Faith Roselle, and reared a nephew, Leon R. Ellis, as well. From 1948 to 1953 Julian was vice-president and treasurer of Suburban Chemical Company in Franklin Park, Illinois. In 1953 she became vice-president of Julian Associates and of Julian Research Institute in Franklin Park, a position she held until her retirement in 1962, when Julian Associates was purchased by Smith, Kline and French pharmaceutical company. After her husband died in 1975 Julian Research Institute was sold. She retained her office with the institute until 1976.

In addition to becoming well known in her position with Julian Associates, Julian was active in civic affairs. In 1963 Illinois governor Otto Kerner appointed her to the Commission on the Study of Birth Control. The report of this commission, completed after two years of study, was the basis for legislative action making it lawful to disseminate birth control information in the state. She was also a member of the Illinois Study Commission to the White House Conference on Children and Youth. British ambassador Nicholas Henderson appointed Julian to serve on the advisory council for the Marshall Scholarships, awarded annually by the British government to American scholars to study at British universities. She was a founding member of the board of directors of the Family Institute of Chicago, which later became affiliated with Northwestern University's department of psychiatry.

Julian serves on the women's board of the University of Chicago and has served on the board of governors of its International House. She served two terms as chair of the board of trustees of Rosary College, River Forest, Illinois, and is a life member of the trustee board of MacMurray College, Jacksonville, Illinois. She is on the board of Erickson Institute, which is associated with Loyola University in Chicago, and of the Boulé Foundation. In 1977 she was elected to the national board of the NAACP Legal Defense and Educational Fund. She has served on the boards of the United Nations Association and the Community Renewal Society, and on the Oak Park Board of Education.

Additionally, Julian has been a member of the World Service Council of the YWCA, has cochaired the United Negro College Fund in Oak Park and River Forest, and has served on the women's advisory board of the Chicago Foundation for Women. She is a member of the Oak Park-River Forest branch of the American Association of University Women. A fellow emeritus of the American Sociological Society, she is also a member of the American Academy of Political and Social Science and of the American Sociological Society. She serves on the advisory board of the Chicago area Phi Beta Kappa.

Julian has won a number of awards and honors. She is a member of Alpha Gamma Phi honor society. In 1958 she received the Brotherhood Award from the National Conference of Christians and Jews. She also received the Distinguished Service Award from the Community Renewal Society, 1972; the Chicago NAACP Legal Defense and Education Fund Award, 1973; Recognition Award for service to higher education, North Shore Chapter of the Links, 1978; Award of Merit, Women's Auxiliary of the NAACP; an award for humanitarian service from the National Council of Colored Women; and the Delta Sigma Theta Award of Distinction, 1979. In 1986 she was given the first Shalom Award from the Oak Park Community of Churches. In 1987 DePauw University conferred on her the degree Doctor of Humane Letters. In 1989 she received Rosary College's Certificate of Appreciation along with a gavel, in recognition of her long service on the board of trustees.

In 1976 Julian established the Percy L. Julian Scholarship Fund at DePauw University for science majors in honor of her husband, who died the previous year. In connection with the scholarship award at DePauw, she established the annual Percy L. Julian Memorial Lecture at which some of the country's most distinguished persons have spoken. She established the Percy L. Julian Scholarship at MacMurray College when the Julian Hall of Science was dedicated in 1976. She also awards an annual monetary prize to the highest ranking student in the graduating class at Percy L. Julian School in Phoenix, Arizona.

A member of the Links, she was chapter establishment officer for the term 1976-78. She is also past national treasurer and past national vice-president of the Links, and past national president of Delta Sigma Theta Sorority. A Congregationalist, she is a member of the First United Church in Oak Park, Illinois.

Julian's writings include: *Standards of Relief: A Study of One Hundred Allowance Families in Washington, D.C.*, 1937; "A Study of Juvenile Delinquency in Philadelphia, 1925-26," and "The Negro Social Worker in Washington, D.C.," both published in *Opportunity*; and numerous unpublished speeches. Now retired, Julian resides in Oak Park, Illinois.

References

Julian, Anna J. Johnson. Biography file, Special Collections, Fisk University Library.

Who's Who Among Black Americans, 1990/91. 6th ed. Detroit: Gale Research, 1990.

Who's Who of American Women. 8th ed. Chicago: Marquis, 1975.

A photo of Anna J. Julian is published in *Ebony* 30 (March 1975), p. 98, and in *Newsweek* (7 March 1988).

Jessie Carney Smith

K

Elizabeth Keckley

(c. 1824-1907)

Dressmaker, White House modiste

Tom Clark, deputy recorder of deeds for the District of Columbia, remembered Elizabeth (Hobbs) Keckley in vivid terms:

> She was a magnificent-looking woman, tall, stately and with an imperious-looking face and features of such distinction, that she would have been an outstanding personality at a social gathering of Louis the Fourteenth, when the Bourbons were at the peak of their power and still had an abundance of brains (Washington, 218).

He was describing a woman who had bought her freedom from slavery, established a sewing business, and became seamstress and friend to Mary Todd Lincoln. Another writer said of her, "Madam Keckley was the most celebrated colored person ever connected with the White House" (Washington, 205).

Elizabeth Keckley

Elizabeth (Hobbs) Keckley entered life as a slave in Dinwiddie, Virginia. The exact date of her birth is unknown. Many sources give the year 1818; others list 1820, 1824, 1825, and even 1840. In a document dated April 18, 1863, signed by Keckley, she stated that she was thirty-nine years old—which would suggest 1824 or 1825 may be accurate.

As with many slave families, Keckley's home was divided. Keckley and her mother, Agnes, belonged to the Burwell family. Her father, George Pleasant, belonged to "a man named Hobbs" (Washington, 205) and was allowed to visit his family only at Christmas and Easter. Just when Colonel Burwell was making plans for the family to be together, her father's master moved west. "The announcement fell like a thunder-bolt" on a family that had already endured painful separation. For some time Keckley's parents corresponded with each other, but they never were reunited. The letters from her father became special keepsakes for Elizabeth Keckley (Keckley, 25).

Early in life the young slave girl began to strive for specific goals and encountered the painful realization that the path would not be an easy one. When she was only four years old Keckley was entrusted with the keeping of the master's baby, Elizabeth. The experience became a lasting and vivid memory.

> My old mistress encouraged me in rocking the cradle, by telling me that if I would watch over the baby well, keep the flies out of its face, and not let it cry, I should be its little maid. This was a golden promise, and I required no better inducement for the faithful performance of my task. I began to rock the cradle most industriously, when lo! out pitched little pet on the floor. I instantly cried out, "Oh! the baby is on the floor," and not knowing what to do, I seized the fire-shovel in my perplexity, and was trying to shovel up my tender charge when my mistress called to me to let the child alone, and then ordered that I be taken out and lashed for my carelessness (Keckley, 20).

This episode is characteristic of the determination with which Keckley approached life and is also representative of the disappointments she faced.

That first thrashing was not the only one that Keckley

received at the hands of owners. Wounds to her self-esteem also were frequent. "I was repeatedly told, when even fourteen years old, that I should never be worth my salt," she remembered (Keckley, 21). Another especially painful memory was associated with her teenage years:

> I was regarded as fair-looking for one of my race, and for four years a white man—I spare the world his name—had base designs upon me. I do not care to dwell upon this subject, for it is one that is fraught with pain. Suffice it to say, that he persecuted me for four years, and I—I—became a mother (Keckley, 39).

The man was Alexander Kirkland. The son, named George, was Keckley's only child and was killed in battle while still a young man.

But Keckley met each challenge with the same industriousness with which she had rocked baby Elizabeth. As each problem presented itself, she sought—as she had done then—to find her own solution. The meeting of those challenges developed within her a sense of self-esteem that enabled her to endure the struggles and to conquer many of them. She said of her early life, "Notwithstanding all the wrongs that slavery heaped upon me, I can bless it for one thing—youth's important lesson of self-reliance" (Keckley, 19-20).

Throughout her life, Keckley not only relied upon her own resources but also served as a source of strength for others. Soon after George's birth, Anne Burwell Garland, daughter of the family whom Keckley's mother had served, took Keckley, George, and Agnes to St. Louis, Missouri. To meet the needs of his family, Mr. Garland considered hiring out Keckley's aged mother. Resolved to spare her parent such a burden, Keckley began her venture in the sewing business. Although her own health suffered, she "kept bread in the mouths of seventeen persons for two years and five months" (Keckley, 45).

While in St. Louis, Elizabeth Hobbs became reacquainted with James Keckley, who had moved from Virginia. He was a man whom she had "learned to regard with more than friendship" (Keckley, 46). But she declined his first offer of marriage because she was reluctant to bring children into slavery. Eventually, however, she accepted his proposal and married him in a brief ceremony in the home of the Garlands. Later she wrote:

> The day was a happy one, but it faded all too soon. Mr. Keckley—let me speak kindly of his faults—proved dissipated, and a burden instead of a helpmate. More than all, I learned that he was a slave instead of a free man, as he represented himself to be. With the simple explanation that I lived with him eight years, let charity draw around him the mantle of silence (Keckley, 50).

Longing to be free, Elizabeth Keckley spoke often to Mr. Garland about purchasing freedom for herself and her son George. Her master, tired of hearing her request, forbade her to ask again, but Keckley could not refrain from renewing her campaign. Garland petulantly offered to give her a quarter—fare for crossing the river—so that she might gain her freedom by escape. But Keckley refused her master's taunting challenge, declaring, "By the laws of the land I am your slave—you are my master, and I will only be free by such means as the laws of the country provide" (Keckley, 49).

Keckley Buys Freedom

Garland eventually set the price of freedom for Keckley and George at twelve hundred dollars. When Garland died and his estate was being settled, the need for Keckley to raise the twelve hundred dollars became immediate. Keckley decided to go to New York and appeal to the benevolence of the people. But Mrs. Le Bourgois, one of her patrons, told her, "It would be a shame to allow you to go North to *beg* for what we should *give you*" (Keckley, 54). Le Bourgois then raised the funds by petitioning other patrons. Keckley accepted the money as a loan, and on August 13, 1855, she and George became free citizens. Entitled now to the money that she earned, she began to save, and soon she repaid the loan that had enabled her to reach the goal of freedom.

In 1860 Keckley moved to Baltimore, where she attempted to earn a living by teaching young ladies to sew. After six weeks she abandoned the effort and moved to Washington, D.C. There she "sought and obtained work at two dollars and half per day" (Keckley, 64-65). To be able to stay more than ten days, however, she had to purchase a license and have someone affirm that she was free. One of her patrons, Miss Ringold, accompanied her to the mayor's office and helped her obtain a waiver of the license fee. With her usual industry, Keckley soon developed a clientele that included many of the most prominent ladies of the city: "Mrs. Jefferson Davis, Mrs. Stephen A. Douglas, and Mrs. E. M. Stanton" (Davis, 132).

Once again Keckley set a goal for herself and pursued it with conviction. "Ever since arriving in Washington I had a great desire to work for the ladies of the White House, and to accomplish this end I was ready to make almost any sacrifice consistent with propriety," she stated (Keckley, 76). The primary sacrifice was hard work. She patiently built the sewing business, which she operated from the rooms she rented at "first on Pennsylvania Avenue, then on 12th Street" (Washington, 226). Eventually, she employed as many as twenty young ladies, teaching them not only dressmaking but also charm and elegance:

> She was very particular and exacting and insisted that the young girls whom she was teaching to sew in her establishment sit erect at all times; and never allowed them to pin their sewing on their knees. This, of course, was to prevent them getting a stooping posture (Washington, 216).

Keckley's business success was derived not only from her sewing and teaching skills, but also from her bearing and personality. "She was imposing in stature, graceful in her every movement, with countenance sweet and intelligent" (Woodson, 56-57). People often admired "the beautiful and fitting way that she was gowned; refined and rich, but not gaudy." She also possessed "a conversational ability that would have done credit to . . . some of the best-educated persons who patronized her" (Washington, 218). In her dealings with others she was careful to show respect. One acquaintance recalled:

> There were certain rules of decorum she always observed. She never left a company of people or an individual with her back turned toward them or him. She would say "Good-bye means I am leaving so why continue to remain?" She considered it inelegant to cross the street except at the intersection. She was courteous to the "Nth" degree and to every favor requested she never failed to say, "I thank you" (Washington, 217).

These interpersonal skills, combined with Keckley's talent with a needle and thread, helped her to become "one of the most sought-after seamstresses in all of the capital" ("Black Woman's View," 98).

Keckley's White House Years Begin

Keckley's opportunities to fulfill her goal of sewing for the ladies of the White House came less than a year after she had started her business. The Lincolns moved to the capital, and "within two weeks after President Lincoln arrived in Washington in late February 1861, Mrs. Keckley had moved into the family orbit" (Quarles, 311). The haste was occasioned by Mary Todd Lincoln's having spilled coffee on her dress for the inaugural reception. Mrs. McClean, a friend of Mrs. Lincoln's, had assured Keckley that she could provide an opportunity for Keckley to work in the White House. And so, McClean recommended Keckley's abilities to the First Lady. Of the four seamstresses Mary Lincoln interviewed, she chose Keckley—with the provision that her services were not too expensive.

Keckley completed her first project in time for the reception, but not quite soon enough for the anxious new president's wife. When the seamstress arrived with the dress, Mrs. Lincoln had abandoned all hope of attending the reception. But Keckley offered to help her get ready, soothed her troubled spirit, and adorned her with appropriate accessories. Much pleased, the president complimented both ladies: "I declare you look charming in that dress. Mrs. Keckley has met with great success" (Keckley, 88). The president's wife was able to attend the reception and to do so with "grace and composure" (Keckley, 89). In time, both of the Lincolns came to depend on Keckley. Once accustomed to her services, "President Lincoln himself preferred not to make a public appearance unless 'Madame Keckley,' as he always referred to her had first tamed his unruly hair" (Sims, 57). He would turn to her and say, "Well, Madam Elizabeth, will you brush my bristles down tonight?" (Keckley, 203).

To Mary Lincoln especially, Keckley became more than just a "mantuamaker" (Keckley, 84). In the course of her years in the White House, she performed many roles. From the beginning she served not only as a dressmaker but also as a fashion designer and a personal maid. She became Mary Lincoln's traveling companion, accompanying her on trips to visit her son, Robert, or to meet her husband when he was away from the White House. She was often a nurse. When Mary Lincoln "was sick from her dreadful headaches, she wanted to see no one, nor have near her anyone but 'Lizabeth'" (Washington, 224). On some occasions, she was a protector. When a young actress approached Keckley in the hope of gaining admittance into the White House and its secrets, the loyal seamstress indignantly sent her away. "Sooner than betray the trust of a friend, I would throw myself into the Potomac river," she declared (Keckley, 94).

Keckley also fulfilled the role of comforter to Mary Lincoln in a way that no one else was able. Early in their acquaintance, Keckley suffered the loss of her only son. George had enlisted as a Union soldier and died on August 10, 1861, at Wilson's Creek, Missouri. Reserved and independent, Keckley bore her grief quietly. But she did admit, "It was a sad blow to me, and the kind womanly letter that Mrs. Lincoln wrote to me when she heard of my bereavement was full of golden words of comfort" (Keckley, 105). Just months later, in February 1862, Willie Lincoln, his mother's favorite son, caught a cold that developed into a fever. Keckley helped attend him during his illness and washed and dressed him when he died. Her own pain still fresh, she helped Mary Lincoln through the sorrow that threatened to overwhelm her. The experience of encountering grief together during those early days of their association strengthened their friendship.

Despite the distance between their positions, these two ladies developed a relationship that "prompted mutual growth and mutual support" (Lowenberg, 71). "For some unaccountable reason Mrs. Lincoln would yield to Mrs. Keckley when her husband could not get her to budge" (Washington, 224). One acquaintance even declared Keckley to be "the only person in Washington who could get along with Mrs. Lincoln, when she became mad with anybody for talking about her and criticizing her husband" (Washington, 225). Through Mary Lincoln, Keckley gained a wider perspective of the world. When Keckley founded and presided over the Contraband Relief Association "for the benefit of the unfortunate freedmen," Mary Lincoln not only offered moral support but also made a contribution of two hundred dollars (Keckley, 113-14).

The depth of the friendship between Keckley and Mary Lincoln was especially apparent on April 14, 1865, and in the days that followed. Hearing that Abraham Lincoln had been shot while attending a production at Ford's Theatre, Keckley unsuccessfully attempted to enter the heavily-guarded White House:

> I wanted to go to Mrs. Lincoln, as I pictured her wild with grief; but then I did not know where to find her, and I must wait until morning. Never

did the hours drag so slowly. Every moment seemed an age, and I could do nothing but walk about and hold my arms in mental agony (Keckley, 187).

The next day she learned that her mental picture of Mary Lincoln's grief mirrored reality and that Mary Lincoln had sent for her. However, three different messengers had failed in their attempts to locate her (Keckley, 189).

In recording her own sorrow as she witnessed the lifeless body of the president, Keckley observed, "Ah! never was man so widely mourned before. The whole world bowed their heads in grief when Abraham Lincoln died" (Keckley, 191). But Mary Lincoln, in her grief, refused the direct condolences of that world. She was unable to attend the funeral and then confined herself to her room for five weeks while she began to pack her belongings. Aside from the company of her own sons, the only person whose presence Mary Lincoln desired during those trying days was Keckley.

Keckley, the faithful seamstress helped Mary Lincoln with the packing, accompanied her to Chicago, helped her get settled there, and then returned to Washington to resume her business. Mary Lincoln said to her,

> Lizabeth, you are my best and kindest friend, and I love you as my best friend. I wish it were in my power to make you comfortable for the balance of your days. If Congress provides for me, depend upon it, I will provide for you (Keckley, 210).

But with a reputed debt of "seventy thousand dollars" (Keckley, 204) to be met, Mary Lincoln could not afford to retain Keckley.

The two ladies corresponded with each other, however, and when Mary Lincoln decided to secretly sell some of her clothes, she once again requested Keckley's assistance. In 1867 they met in New York, posing as Mrs. Clarke and a friend, and conducted an unsuccessful attempt to raise the needed money without attracting attention. Their identities were quickly discovered and highly publicized, and both women much criticized.

Keckley continued her sewing business for awhile in New York and then back in Washington. But she also entered into a new venture, hoping to solve the problems that she and Mary Lincoln faced. In 1868 G. W. Carlton and Company issued a book entitled *Behind the Scenes, Or, Thirty Years a Slave, and Four Years in the White House*. The title page described writer Elizabeth Keckley as "formerly a slave, but more recently modiste, a friend to Mrs. Abraham Lincoln." Keckley wrote the book in an effort to defend both Mary Lincoln and herself from the harsh criticism that was being heaped upon them. In the preface, she explained that people often judge others wrongly when they know only some of the events and none of the motives behind certain actions. She believed:

> The world have [sic] judged Mrs. Lincoln by the facts which float upon the surface, and through her have partially judged me, and the only way to convince them that wrong was not meditated is to explain the motives that actuated us (Keckley, xiv).

A desire to make money to help Mary Lincoln was also incentive for writing the book. In the preface, Keckley emphasized:

> I have written with the utmost frankness in regard to her [Mrs. Lincoln]—have exposed her faults as well as given her credit for honest motives. I wish the world to judge her as she is, free from the exaggeration of praise or scandal (Keckley, xv).

Exposed along with Mary Lincoln's faults were private matters of the Lincoln family life, a detailed account of the "old-clothes scandal" (James, 311), personal letters written by Mary Lincoln, and many of her private opinions about important people. Ruth Randall commented:

> There is no reason to doubt that Mrs. Keckley told the story with the idea of helping Mrs. Lincoln, and told it with what appears to be, with the testing of modern research, a high degree of accuracy. But the publication of the book, which stepped on a lot of prominent toes which were very much alive, resulted in another furor. A viciously clever parody called *Behind the Seams* by "Betsey Kickley," who was represented as a Negro woman who could sign her name only by making an X for her mark, was rushed into the print the same year (Randall, 414).

Keckley had prefaced her memoirs by stating, "In writing as I have done, I am well aware that I have invited criticism" (Keckley, xi). But she undoubtedly failed to foresee the effect that the criticism would have on the rest of her life. Robert Lincoln, humiliated by and enraged at the publication of his mother's private letters, refused to hear any explanations or apologies. According to some accounts, he persuaded the publisher to suppress the book. Although Keckley believed that Mary Lincoln bore her no grudge, she only heard from her "in a roundabout way" for the remainder of her life (Washington, 241). Two attempts to help Mary Lincoln financially had failed, and now no avenue existed for the giving or receiving of emotional support.

Ironically, in the final paragraph of her autobiography, Keckley had stated,

> Though poor in worldly goods, I am rich in friendships, and friends are a recompense for all the woes of the darkest pages of life. For sweet friendship's sake, I can bear more burdens than I have borne (Keckley, 330-31).

The rest of her life, she had few friendships and endured heavy burdens.

Keckley's sewing business declined, and she eventually abandoned the effort to keep it going. For a brief time (1892-93) she taught domestic art at Wilberforce University in Xenia, Ohio, and assisted the matron who had charge of the girls. While there, she prepared the university's exhibit for the 1893 World's Columbian Exposition. To many of the girls, she gave scraps of materials from which she had made dresses for Mary Lincoln so that they might make pincushions.

In her book Keckley stated that she had donated some treasured mementoes to Wilberforce University. The school, which her son, George, had attended, was "destroyed by fire on the night that the President was murdered" (Keckley, 203). In an effort to help the school be rebuilt, she wrote a letter in 1868 declaring her intention to donate the dress Mary Lincoln wore at the second inaugural address and the cloak and bonnet that she wore on the night of the assassination. Keckley also indicated that she would give to the university the president's brush and comb and a pair of his overshoes. But a footnote states that she decided to keep the right-hand glove that he wore at the second inaugural reception.

No records indicate that the authorship of Keckley's book was seriously questioned during her lifetime. However, in a November 11, 1935, *Washington Star* article, David Barbee attributed *Behind the Scenes* to Jane Swisshelm. He even seemed to question the existence of Elizabeth Keckley. John Washington quickly countered that assertion, stating in a November 15 article that Keckley had written the book. Investigating the issue further, Washington published his own book, *They Knew Lincoln*, in 1942. In it, he provided evidence to support his belief that James Redpath had helped Keckley to compile the book and had published Mary Lincoln's letters unedited, without Keckley's permission.

In a letter published in the *Journal of Negro History* in January 1936, Francis Grimké attested to the reality of Keckley's existence and as part of his description of her, certified her ability to have written the book. He stated, "She was not an educated woman, in the sense that she had passed through any educational institution, but she was a woman of marked intelligence and had made good use of the opportunities that she had of improving her mind" (Woodson, 57).

Researchers still question the authenticity of the work. In *Mary Lincoln, Biography of Marriage* (1953), Ruth Randall states:

> The Keckley book has the unsatisfactory status of a ghostwritten product; it has inaccuracies as all recollections have; it should be checked wherever possible; but when critically used it has considerable value for the careful scholar (Randall, 510).

As recently as 1982, Benjamin Quarles stated that the book was ghostwritten by James Redpath or Hamilton Busbey (311). Even if Keckley had help, or if the book was actually written by someone else, enough evidence exists to substantiate the information as memories of Keckley. Recognizing the value of those memories, Arno Press reprinted her book in 1968. In the beginning pages of the work, Keckley remarked, "I had been raised in a hardy school—had been taught to rely upon myself, and to prepare myself to render assistance to others" (Keckley, 19).

Little is known about Keckley's life following her sojourn at Wilberforce. She returned to Washington, D.C. Except for regular attendance and support of the Fifteenth Street Presbyterian Church, she seemed to retreat from the world. Pastor Francis Grimké recalled, "She used to come up the aisle, the very personification of grace and dignity, as she moved towards her pew. Often was heard: 'Here comes Madam Keckley,' All eyes were upon her" (Woodson, 57). Even though her presence in the congregation was noticeable, the love of conversation, so apparent in her earlier days, seemed to no longer exist.

Keckley's last years were spent in the Home for Destitute Women and Children in Washington, an institution that she had helped create. Loretta Simms, one of the residents, stated:

> She seemed sad and despondent all the time, talked to the inmates here very little, wrote very little if any, and read her Bible the greater part of the time. She seemed to have lost interest in everything, appeared worried, and really pined away (Washington, 219).

Except for a weekly ride, Keckley spent most of the time in her room, where a picture of Mary Lincoln hung on the wall above the dresser. One faithful friend, Eliza Williams, came to see Keckley daily. She remembered:

> Mrs. Keckley never liked to talk about her book, but would always say it was a "sad memory," and that she "wrote it to help Mrs. Lincoln," "what was in the book was true" and "Mrs. Lincoln knew it all," that "she tried many times to talk to Robert Lincoln, but he would never see her after he rebuked her for publishing his mother's letters" (Washington, 241).

During her final years, Keckley's only source of income was an eight-dollar-a-month (and later twelve-dollar-a-month pension) for which she had reluctantly applied after George's death. However, she was able to pay for her room and board at the home and "had enough left at her death to pay all of her bills, buy a grave and tombstone and then leave to the Home of Destitute Women and Children a neat sum of \$179.11" (Washington, 212-13). Financially and emotionally, Keckley maintained her self-reliance to the end.

Keckley died of a paralytic stroke at the home on May 26, 1907. She had been sick for only a brief time. Francis Grimké preached at her funeral, and Keckley was buried in Harmony Cemetery. Appropriate words from Psalm 127 were engraved on her tombstone: FOR SO HE GIVETH HIS BELOVED SLEEP. A portrait of Keckley, painted by a Mrs. Wilson, remained in the home for some time. Independence and service had characterized Keckley's life. The information contained in her autobiography will continue to serve research needs of Lincoln scholars for many generations.

References

"A Black Woman's View of Mary Todd Lincoln." *Ebony* 25 (March 1970): 98-100. Includes photographs.

Black Women in Nineteenth Century American Life. Eds. Bert James Loewenberg and Ruth Bogin. University Park: Pennsylvania State University Press, 1976. 70-77.

Brown, Hallie W. *Homespun Heroines and Other Women of Distinction*. Xenia, Ohio: Aldine Pub. Co., 1926. Reprinted. New York: Oxford University Press, 1974. 174-77. Includes portrait.

Dannett, Sylvia G. L. *Profiles of Negro Womanhood*. Vol. 1. Chicago: Educational Heritage, 1974. 174-77.

Davis, Arthur P. and J. Saunders Redding, eds. *Calvacade: Negro American Writing from 1760 to the Present*. Boston: Houghton Mifflin, 1971. 132.

First Annual Report of the Contraband Relief Association of D.C. 1863. Pamphlet.

Fry, Smith D, "Lincoln Liked Her." *Minneapolis Register* 6 July 1901.

Grimké, Francis J. *The Works of Frances J. Grimké*. Ed. Carter G. Woodson. Washington, D.C.: Associated Publishers, 1942. 544-49.

Keckley, Elizabeth. *Behind the Scenes: Thirty Years a Slave and Four Years in the White House*. New York: G. W. Carleton, 1868. Reprinted. New York: Arno Press and the *New York Times*, 1968.

Kickley, Betsey, pseud. *Behind the Seams, by a Nigger Woman who took in work from Mrs. Lincoln and Mrs. Davis*. New York: National News, 1868.

Logan, Rayford W. "Elizabeth Keckley." *Dictionary of American Negro Biography*. Edited by Rayford W. Logan and Michael R. Winston. New York: Norton, 1982. 375-76.

Loggins, Vernon. *The Negro Author: His Development in American to 1900*. Port Washington, N.Y.: Kennikat Press, 1964. 258-61.

Miers, Earl S. *Lincoln Day by Day: A Chronology, 1809-1865*. Vol. 3. Washington: Lincoln Sesquicentennial Commission, 1960. 148, 326-27.

Millstein, Beth and Jeanne Bodin. *We, The American Women: A Documentary History*. Chicago: Science Research Associates, 1977. 136-37.

Noble, Jeanne. *Beautiful, Also, Are the Souls of My Black Sisters: A History of the Black Women in America*. Englewood Cliffs, N.J.: Prentice-Hall, 1978. 50-54.

Quarles, Benjamin. "Elizabeth Keckley." *Notable American Women, 1607-1950: A Biographical Dictionary*. Vol. 2. Cambridge: Harvard University Press, 1971. 310-11.

Randall, Ruth Painter. *Mary Lincoln: Biography of a Marriage*. Boston: Little, Brown, 1953.

Sandburg, Carl. *Abraham Lincoln: The War Years*. New York: Scribners, 1939: Vol. 1, 457-58, 547-48; Vol. 2, 212, 259-60; Vol. 3, 345-46; Vol. 4, 120-21.

Sims, Naomi. "A Gift Truly Liberating." *Encore* 4 (June 23/July 4, 1975): 56-58.

Washington, John E. *They Knew Lincoln*. New York: Dutton, 1942. 53-55, 85, 205-41. Includes photographs.

Washington Star, 11 November 1935; 15 November 1935.

Wefer, Marion. "Another Assassination, Another Widow, Another Embattled Book." *American Heritage* 18 (August 1967): 79-88. Includes photographs.

Woodson, Carter G. "Communications." *Journal of Negro History* 21 (January 1936); 56-57.

Collections

The National Archives, the Library of Congress, and the Moorland-Spingarn Research Center at Howard University have papers relating to Elizabeth Keckley. Her work is noted in the First Ladies Collection of the Smithsonian Institution, the Black Fashion Museum, and the Costume Institute of the Metropolitan Museum of Art.

Marie Garrett

Leontine Kelly

(1920-)

Religious leader

Leontine Turpeau Current Kelly, a minister, church official, and the first black American woman elected bishop of a major religious denomination, was born March 5, 1920, in the parsonage of Mount Zion Methodist Episcopal Church in Washington, D.C. She was the seventh of eight children (four girls and four boys) born to the Reverend David De Witt Turpeau, Sr., and Ila (Marshall) Turpeau.

David Turpeau received two years of college education

Leontine Kelly

and two years of Biblical and theological study. He was ordained a Methodist Episcopal minister in 1900. At various times, he served as a pastor in Baltimore, Maryland; Washington, D.C.; Pittsburgh, Pennsylvania; and Cincinnati, Ohio. He also worked as an administrator, serving as the superintendent of the Colored Department of the Anti-Saloon League from 1912 to 1915 and as district superintendent in the Washington Conference of the Methodist Episcopal Church for five years in the 1920s. A district superintendent is the second highest office in the Methodist Church, one rank below bishop. Ila Marshall Turpeau was known as a staunch advocate of equality for blacks, an active supporter of the NAACP, and a cofounder of the Urban League in Cincinnati in September 1948 and the first black person to serve on the Cincinnati Camp Fire Girls Committee. Ila Turpeau was named one of the outstanding women of the year by the *Cincinnati Enquirer* newspaper in 1970.

When the David Turpeau family left Washington, D.C., they lived for two years in Pittsburgh before they settled in Cincinnati by the late 1920s, where Leontine Turpeau Kelly grew up. Kelly received her basic education in the public schools of Cincinnati. Her principal at the Harriet Beecher Stowe School, Jennie D. Porter, inspired Kelly to believe that sex or race should not be barriers to achievement. Porter was a pioneer: Cincinnati's first black principal and the first black person to earn a doctorate at the University of Cincinnati. Kelly later graduated from Woodward High School. Growing up in a parsonage, she learned how Methodist churches functioned and imbibed values from her parents about religion, race, gender, society, and the individual that would influence her life and later career.

When the Turpeau children discovered that the basement of their Cincinnati parsonage had been used as a station on the Underground Railroad, complete with a tunnel connecting it to the church, their father informed them that the aid given to fugitive slaves was a more important mission of the church than erecting unusually attractive buildings. David Turpeau practiced what he preached, making the churches he pastored centers for the cultural, political, and economic activities of their surrounding communities. He believed that social and political involvement was the duty of Christians, who should work actively in a variety of ways to improve society, and not merely pray for social change. He lived his religious philosophy by running for election to and serving in the Ohio State Legislature for four terms between 1939 and 1947. David Turpeau listed himself as politically independent in his *Who's Who in Colored America* entries (2nd through 6th editions), but he was elected to the Ohio legislature as a Republican.

During the years Leontine Turpeau Kelly was growing to adulthood, the Methodist church, like most Christian churches, maintained racial segregation in local churches and in its administrative structure. David Turpeau explained to his children that it was the duty of black Americans to be racial missionaries to the larger white church and change the attitudes of white Christians about racial issues and race relations as one step toward improving American society as a whole, racially and spiritually.

After graduating from high school, Kelly attended West Virginia State College (later West Virginia State University) between 1938 and 1941. After completing her junior year, she chose to leave college, get married, and start a family. She married Gloster Bryant Current, a fellow student at West Virginia who graduated in 1941. Current was a multitalented man who played in and directed his orchestra from 1930 to 1939, served as executive secretary of the Detroit branch of the NAACP from 1941 to 1946 and as director of branches for the National NAACP from 1946 to 1977. A deeply religious person, Current, without attending theology school, qualified to become assistant pastor of Saint Paul United Methodist Church from 1953 to 1978 and pastor of Westchester United Methodist Church from 1979 to 1983. Leontine Current became the mother of three children: Angella Patricia, Gloster Bryant, Jr., and John David.

By the mid-1950s Leontine and Gloster Current were divorced, posing a significant life challenge to Leontine, who felt devastated. Her children remained close to their father. She sensed a need for personal renewal, believing the faith system she developed while growing up was insufficient. So she disciplined herself "through prayer, meditation and Bible study," resulting in a deeper, more mature faith rooted in the spirituality of her ancestors (Reynolds, 126).

In 1956 she married James David Kelly, a Methodist minister who was then pastoring East Vine Avenue Methodist Church in Knoxville, Tennessee. In June 1958 the Kelly family moved when Reverend James Kelly was transferred to Leigh Street Church in Richmond, Virginia.

In this new location, Leontine Kelly took the steps that eventually led her to high achievement within the ordained ministry. Her husband encouraged her to complete her college degree and to develop her credentials within the Methodist church. She enrolled in Virginia Union University in Richmond, receiving a B.A. in 1960. Concurrently, she became a certified lay speaker in the Methodist church. She then worked as a social studies teacher from 1960 to 1966. She was enthusiastic about her teaching, seeing it an opportunity to help children develop their skills and use education as a means of pursuing equality in the future. Being a teacher fulfilled some of the social goals of her father's religious philosophy of personal involvement in enhancing the lives of others and improving society.

In 1966 James Kelly was transferred to pastor the Galilee United Methodist Church in Edwardsville, Virginia, where he remained until his death in 1969. Subsequently, Leontine Kelly adopted his great-granddaughter, Pamela Lynne Kelly. In the 1960s, Leontine Kelly had been active in church affairs and became a popular speaker whose style was described as "preaching" rather than speaking. Yet, up to 1969, Leontine Kelly had no plans to become an ordained minister in spite of her closeness to several ministers: her father, her brother (David D. Turpeau, Jr.), her first husband, who became a minister in the 1950s, and her second husband.

The death of James Kelly led the congregation of Galilee Church to ask Leontine Kelly to succeed her husband. She accepted, serving as a layperson in charge of the church. Less than a year after her husband's death, Leontine Kelly felt herself called by God to become an ordained minister. She began theological studies, first through the Conference Course of Study, then through summer school at Wesley Theological Seminary, Washington, D.C., in 1970 and 1971, and finally through enrolling in Union Theological Seminary in Richmond, receiving the master of divinity degree in 1976.

Leontine Kelly's status within the Methodist church began to advance as she received her first ordination as a minister, becoming a deacon in 1972. After completing her theological studies and satisfying all other requirements, she was ordained an elder in 1977. In 1975 she left the Galilee church to begin a two-year service as a staff member of the Virginia Conference Council of Ministries, directing social ministries. She was then appointed as pastor of Asbury-Church Hill United Methodist Church in Richmond, serving from 1977 to 1983. Kelly was also director of a cooperative urban ministry and outreach program that had its headquarters at Asbury. Due to her efforts, church membership doubled to four hundred. Kelly also served a four-year term on the Richmond School Board. She then became a member of the national staff of the United Methodist church, filling the position of evangelism executive, Board of Discipleship, from 1983 to 1984, giving her the prominence needed to be considered a candidate for bishop.

The Methodist church officially approved the full acceptance or ordination of women as ministers in 1956 and by 1984 approximately 1,400 women had entered the Methodist ministry (*New York Times,* 29 July 1984). By the 1970s clergywomen had organized and pressed the church leadership for increased opportunities for women in all aspects of the ministry. Leontine Kelly became active with the clergywomen's movement.

One result was that the United Methodist church became the first major religious denomination to elect women to their top ministerial office—bishop. In 1980 Marjorie Swank Matthews was elected bishop at the age of sixty-four, becoming one of the forty-six bishops of the church. Bishops are assigned to preside over an area for four years. Because church policy requires bishops who reach age sixty-six to retire at the end of their four-year term, Bishop Matthews retired in 1984 at the age of sixty-eight.

Methodists Elects First Black Woman Bishop

Faced with the retirement of the only woman bishop in the church, Methodist clergywomen were seeking candidates to put forward for the position. Traditionally, most men who became bishops did so after achieving prominence and experience either as president of a theological seminary or a Methodist college, district superintendent of an annual conference, director of a national Methodist board, or as editor of a widely-read Methodist publication. Though some women were becoming district superintendents, almost none had achieved any of the other three positions. In 1984, the *Washington Post* reported that only three women had ever served as heads of theological seminaries in the United States (29 September 1984, 36). Thus, hardly any women could qualify through the traditional routes. With nineteen new bishops to be elected in 1984, Methodist clergywomen sought competent female candidates who not only had experience as pastors and administrators but also had achieved enough prominence to gain broad-based support among male and female clergy and laypersons.

Leontine Kelly's personal maturity, her long-term involvement in the clergywomen's movement, and her administrative experience as a staff member in the Virginia Conference and on the National Board of Discipleship made her a viable candidate for bishop. As early as 1982, the national caucus of clergywomen had identified Kelly as the primary candidate to replace Bishop Matthews. In 1984 the clergywomen asked if they could place her name in nomination and Kelly consented. In order to maximize the chances of electing her, clergywomen arranged to nominate Kelly in four of the five Methodist jurisdictions that were meeting simultaneously to elect bishops. Usually, persons are elected bishops in the geographical jurisdiction they currently serve and clergywomen first sought enough support to elect Kelly in the Southeast Jurisdiction, where she was a member. When support seemed insufficient in the more conservative Southeast Jurisdiction, clergywomen switched tactics to concentrate on the Western Jurisdiction, notifying Kelly by telephone on Wednesday evening to take a plane to Boise, Idaho, to be present for the voting on Thursday, July 19, 1984. Election required a positive vote of sixty percent of those voting. By the thirteenth ballot, Kelly was clearly one of the frontrunners, and she was elected on the seventeenth ballot. She and the other new bishops were consecrated on Friday, July 20, 1984. Kelly became one of two or three persons ever to be elected bishop by one jurisdiction while serving as a member of a different jurisdiction.

Kelly thus became the second woman to be chosen bishop in the United Methodist church and the first black woman bishop in any major United States denomination. She remained the only one until the Episcopal church elected Barbara C. Harris a suffragan bishop in 1989. Black men had been elected as bishops in the Methodist church since the first two were chosen in 1920, the number increasing to seven by the mid-1970s. In 1984 Kelly and four black men were elected, bringing the total number of black bishops to eleven.

In September 1984 at the age of sixty-four, Kelly assumed her duties as bishop of the San Francisco area. She supervised the California and Nevada conferences of the United Methodist church, which included one hundred thousand members in 386 churches in Northern California and Nevada. As the spiritual leader and chief executive official for this area, Kelly was aided by seven district superintendents who advised her and were members of her cabinet. It was Kelly's responsibility, with the advice of her cabinet, to make appointments of four hundred ministers, to make numerous other appointments, to preside over conferences and meetings, to ordain ministers as deacons and elders, and subsequently to supervise their status.

The California and Nevada conferences have a diverse population of whites, blacks, Asians, Hispanics, and native Americans. Kelly "crusaded for women as well as all ethnics in the church" (Lanker, 112). She also worked to increase the church's involvement in the social and economic development of communities, especially black communities.

Kelly was widely respected by other bishops, as witnessed by her selection to the executive committee of the Council of Bishops, composed of all forty-six United Methodist bishops, and her service as president of the six-member Western Jurisdictional College of Bishops. She also was a member of the General Board of Church and Society while in office. Previously, she had been a member of the Health and Welfare Ministries Division of the General Board of Global Ministries.

As bishop, Kelly developed her own distinctive style of leadership based on her personal interpretation of the Bible. "As a black person, what I look for in the Bible is a sense of my own freedom and acceptance by God and the sense of liberation," she said. The Bible also gave her "the strength and . . . patience to wait for freedom" while actively seeking it, and the insight to share power in such a way as to encourage others to develop their full potential while she retained her ultimate responsibility for decisions and consequences (Lanker, 112).

In growing up, Kelly considered Ila Turpeau, her mother, and Mary McLeod Bethune, the college president, leader of black clubwomen, and government agency administrator under Franklin D. Roosevelt's presidency, to be her role models (*U.S.A. Today*, 127). In general, the first phase of Kelly's life followed the pattern of her mother and the second phase followed that of Mary McLeod Bethune's public career. In the first phase, Kelly filled the role of wife, mother, and family stabilizer while pursuing church and community projects as a volunteer. In the second phase, Kelly developed her own professional credentials, sought positions of power and authority in order to use them to educate and improve society and, unexpectedly, obtained a position and status as a pioneer previously unachieved by a black woman. In both phases, service to others and "uplift of the race" were paramount goals.

Significant Successes Mark Career

Kelly was reared to believe that blacks as a race could not afford a single failure. Thus, her career has been marked with significant successes. She is considered a dynamic preacher whose intellectually cogent messages are powerfully delivered. Her "soul-stirring sermons" surprise those who expect a small, grandmotherly Methodist to be less than forceful (Marshall, 166; *U.S.A. Today*, 125). Her leadership prompted fellow bishop Melvin G. Talbert to say that she "has proven herself a very competent leader at various levels of the church" (Marshall, 166). Through her career, Kelly has striven for high quality in all her activities, knowing that others would see her as a role model and as an "example." The strong sense of self-confidence, nurtured in her childhood and sustained throughout her continually deepening religious faith, is balanced by a sense of humor about life in general and humility about her personal achievements.

Honors and recognitions have come to Kelly during the 1980s, partly because of her unique status as the only black woman prelate and partly because of the effectiveness of her work. While still a local church pastor, she received the Grass Roots Leadership Award from the Virginia unit of the Southern Christian Leadership Conference (SCLC) in 1981. Garrett Evangelical Theological Seminary awarded her an honorary doctorate and the widely-read *Ebony* magazine capsulized her rise to become the "First Black Woman Bishop," in 1984. An April 5, 1985, an interview with Kelly in *U.S.A. Today* was reprinted in a book entitled *And Still We Rise: Interviews with 50 Black Role Models in 1988*. The national organization, SCLC, extended its highest award—The Drum Major for Peace award—to Kelly in 1987. In 1988 the *Ladies Home Journal* chose her as one of the most important women in America, and the Corcoran Gallery, Washington, D.C., chose her to be included in a nationwide touring exhibit of the nation's outstanding black women. In 1989, the exhibit photographs and accompanying biographies were published in book form, *I Dream a World: Portraits of Black Women Who Changed America*.

When the Fifteenth World Methodist Conference met in Nairobi, Kenya, July 22-29, 1986, Bishop Leontine Kelly spoke at the conference service of worship on Sunday, July

27. Commenting on her stellar performance the next morning, Bishop Desmond Tutu said:

> I would like to give you one very good theological reason why women ought not to be ordained, least of all made bishops. It is—Bishop Kelly. She was superb. . . . She really made men understand why women say that when God created man she was experimenting! (160).

On August 31, 1988, at the age of sixty-eight, Kelly relinquished her position in charge of the San Francisco area and retired as bishop. She became a part-time teacher, serving as visiting professor of Evangelism and Witness at the Pacific School of Religion in Berkeley, California. In addition, she became president of the newly-organized AIDS National Interfaith Network, which had plans to coordinate activities designed to minister to victims of AIDS, including training pastors and caretakers of AIDS sufferers. Kelly also has worked with "Chose Peace," an organization headed by Bishop C. Dale White. She continued to speak out, this time on how politics and the church can come together to bring about effective change. She said:

> How can you transform system and political structures if you stand outside? We shouldn't be afraid to be political, in our church or in our world. Nothing is more political than Moses being sent to tell Pharaoh to let the Hebrew people go! (*Jet* 75, 40).

References

"Biographical Directory of United Methodist Bishops, Spouses and Widows." Compiled by the Office of Secretary, Council of Bishops, United Methodist Church, November 1988. Located in church headquarters.

"Bishop Kelly to Head New National Network on AIDS." *Holston United Methodist Church Reporter* (19 August 1988).

Cincinnati's Black Peoples: A Chronology and Bibliography, 1787-1982. Cincinnati: Prepared for the Cincinnati Arts Consortium through the Center for Neighborhood and Community Studies, University of Cincinnati, June 1986.

Dykes, Sr., De Witt S., and Viola Logan Dykes. Interviews with the author, August 1989 and August 1990.

"Ex-Cincinnatian Becomes First Black Female Bishop." *Cincinnati Enquirer,* 8 August 1984.

Tutu, Desmond M. B. "God's Kingdom of Righteousness." *Proceedings of the Fifteenth World Conference.* Nairobi, Kenya, July 23-29, 1986. Published by the World Methodist Council, [1987]. 160-69.

Lanker, Brian. *I Dream a World.* New York: Stewart, Tabori and Chang, 1989. 112-13. Photograph, p. 113.

"Leontine Kelly to be 1st Woman to Preach on National Radio Pulpit." *Afro-American* (National Edition) (10 March 1984): 11.

Jet 75 (16 January 1989): 40.

Lincoln, C. Eric, and Lawrence H. Mamiya. *The Black Church in the African-American Experience.* Durham, North Carolina: Duke University Press, 1990.

"L. Kelly and Woodie White Become United Methodist Bishops." *Michigan Chronicle*, 11 August 1984. B-6.

Macklin, Beth. "Colorful Bishops." Tulsa *World* (5 August 1984).

Marshall, Marilyn. "First Black Woman Bishop." *Ebony* 40 (November 1984): 164-66, 168-70. Photograph, p. 165.

"Methodist Bishop, Leontine Kelly, Records Album of Stories." *Los Angeles Sentinel*, 23 August 1984. C-9.

"Methodist Bishop Records 'New Testament Stories' Album." *Afro-American*, 18 August 1984. 12.

"Methodists Elect 1st Black Woman." *Los Angeles Sentinel Times*, 2 August 1984. C-10.

"Methodists Elect 19 to Leadership." *New York Times,* 29 July 1984. 19.

"Methodists Vote for Bishops." *Washington Post,* 20 July 1984. B-3.

"New Bishop." *Washington Post,* 28 July 1984. B-6. Photograph and caption only.

Official Journal, Seventy-Ninth Session of East Tennessee Annual Conference, the Methodist Church, 1958, Bristol, Va., June 18-22, 1958.

Reed. W. A. "Methodist Women Pastors Receive Promise of Equality." *Tennessean,* 25 July 1984.

Reynolds, Barbara. *And Still We Rise: Interviews with 50 Black Role Models.* New York: USA Today Books, 1988. Photograph, p. 125.

Richardson, Harry V. *Dark Salvation: The Story of Methodism As It Developed among Blacks in America.* New York: Doubleday, 1976.

"Seminary's New Dean." *The Washington Post*, 29 September 1984. B-6.

"United Methodist Church Names Bishops." *Afro-American,* 28 July 1984. 15.

Weston, Rubin F. *Blacks in Ohio History.* Columbus, Oh.: Ohio Historical Society, 1976.

Who's Who Among Black Americans. 2nd ed. Lake Forest, Ill.: Educational Communications, 1977; 3rd ed. 1980; 4th ed., 1985; 5th ed., 1988. 6th ed. Detroit: Gale Research, 1990.

Who's Who in America. 46th ed. Wilmette, Ill.: Marquis, 1990.

Who's Who in Colored America. 1st ed. New York: Who's Who in Colored America Corp., 1927. 2nd ed., 1929. 3rd ed., 1930. 4th ed., 1933-1937. 5th ed., 1938-1940. 6th ed. Brooklyn: Thomas Yenser, 1941-1944. 7th ed. Yonkers: Christian E. Burckel, 1950.

Who's Who in the West. 22nd ed. Wilmette, Ill.: Marquis, 1990.

De Witt C. Dykes, Jr.

Florynce "Flo" Kennedy

(1916-)

Civil and women's rights activist, lawyer

> Her name is Florynce Rae Kennedy—Flo to friend and enemy alike—and she is the biggest, loudest and, indisputably, the rudest mouth on the battleground where feminist-activists and radical politics join in mostly common cause (Burstein, 54).

Florynce Rae Kennedy, born February 11, 1916, in Kansas City, Missouri, was the second of five daughters. Her formative years were spent primarily in Missouri and California. From 1942 to 1972, she called New York City her home; in 1972 she moved to San Francisco, California, where she still resides. At age seventy-four, Kennedy is still a very distinctive part of today's society, wearing the many hats of lawyer, activist, feminist, humanist, and spokesperson for civil rights issues. She has been cited in local and national publications, including the *Almanac of Famous People* (1989), *Who's Who Among Black Americans* (1990), and *Black Enterprise* (1977).

Kennedy has been described as intelligent, outrageous, outspoken, energetic, aggressive, dynamic, profane, prophetic, and/or shocking. She simply says of herself:

> I'm just a loud-mouthed middle-aged colored lady with a fused spine and three feet of intestines missing and a lot of people think I'm crazy. Maybe you do too, but I never stop to wonder why I'm not like other people. The mystery to me is why more people aren't like me (Kennedy, 79).

In her autobiography, *Color Me Flo: My Hard Life and Good Times* (1976), Kennedy describes her family as part of the "pooristocrats" of the black community. Her father, Wiley Kennedy, at various times worked as a Pullman porter, waiter, and ran his own taxi business. Her mother, Zella, was "awfully smart" and educated in the normal schools at a time when very few black people went to school. For the most part, Zella stayed at home and raised the children, but she went to work as a domestic during the Great Depression.

"Our parents had us so convinced we were precious that by the time I found out I was nothing, it was already too late—I knew I was something" (Kennedy, 76). Neither parent used excessive discipline, says Kennedy; "both parents taught each of us [Lynn, Grayce, Florynce, Joy, and Faye] never to take any s— from anyone" (27). She attributes this style of discipline as the major factor for her outspoken, aggressive nature:

> The whole concept of authority is what I think Women's Lib and Black liberation is about. The reason I have a pathological attitude toward authority, is because my parents did not establish their own authority, and did not require us to see the government, our teachers, or any of these people as unquestionable authority (Acton, LeMond, and Hodges, 113).

Education for Kennedy included the public schools of Missouri and California. "I must have been almost ready for high school when I decided to become a lawyer. My theory has always been that whatever the people who have all the money don't want you to do, that's what you ought to do" (Kennedy, 33). She graduated from Lincoln High School in Kansas City at the top of her class and went to work at various jobs—from selling hats to operating an elevator. Kennedy moved to New York City in 1942 to live with her sister Grayce. In 1944, at the age of 28, she entered Columbia University and four years later graduated with a bachelor's degree in pre-law with an "A" average. She then applied for admission to Columbia Law School. The institution initially rejected her. When Kennedy alleged that her denial was because of her race and threatened to fight it, the university changed its decision and admitted her. She obtained her law degree in 1951. Passing the New York Bar in 1952, she clerked for about three years with a New York law firm. By 1954, she had established her own private practice.

Though not a staunch supporter of the institution of marriage, Kennedy married Charles "Charlie" Dudley Dye in 1957 when she was 31 and he 41. She describes Dye as a "Welsh science-fiction writer and a drunk." The marriage dissolved after a short period of time. Later Dye died an alcoholic. Kennedy never remarried and there were no children born to this marriage.

Racism in Justice System Cited

For a brief period, Don Wilkes joined Kennedy as a law partner. The partnership was short-lived. One of the cases jointly handled by Kennedy and Wilkes was that of Eleanora McKay (Billie Holiday). Holiday's agent, Associate Booking Corporation, neglected to advise her of a federal statute that required persons convicted on charges of narcotics to register each time they left the country. Holiday had failed to do so and as a result, the United States attorney threatened to indict her when she returned from a European tour. A long, grueling legal battle ensued between the United States government and Holiday. Wilkes was able to persuade the United States attorney not to indict Billie Holiday, but she died just a few days after she won this major victory.

Kennedy continued to represent the Holiday estate and later took on the estate of Charlie Parker. According to Kennedy, both persons were fighting to recoup monies in royalties and sales denied them by their record companies and agents because they were black. Many black artists have died broke while money was due their estates. The struggle to recoup such royalties continues today.

In addition to representing the estates of Billie Holiday and Charlie Parker, Kennedy also represented the activist H. Rap Brown. In an interview with *Reconstruction* magazine, Kennedy states:

> I represented him a few times, but I wouldn't call myself his lawyer. Theoretically, I don't do criminal law. The only way I get into a case is if it's so important politically that no other lawyer will touch it, then sometimes I'll do something on it. But the courts are so racist and so bigoted. As a lawyer, you're looking for justice for people, but if you know there's no justice, what are you going to go looking there for? There's absolutely no justice for anybody I'd want to defend (Exerpted from "A Message for White Radicals" and printed in *Reconstruction*, as cited in *Color Me Flo,* 58).

These kinds of battles forced Kennedy to reevaluate her profession. The reevaluation process led to her eventual change in careers—a change that has spanned almost three decades. According to Kennedy:

> Handling the Holiday and Parker estates taught me more than I was really ready for about government and business delinquency and the hostility and helplessness of the courts in rectifying the imbalance between the talented performers and the millionaire parasites who suck their blood. These experiences, together with Wilkes' takeoff, marked the beginning of a serious disenchantment, if indeed I ever was enchanted with the practice of law. By this time I had learned a good deal about the justice system, and had begun to doubt my ability to work within it to accomplish social changes. Not only was I not earning a decent living, there began to be a serious question in my mind whether practicing law could ever be an effective means of changing society, or even of simple resistance to oppression (Kennedy, 52).

Kennedy has identified four types of oppression: personal, private, public, and political. "Her fight for equality does not end with either the civil rights movement or the feminist movement, but it entails all aspects of our oppressive society" (Excerpts from "Flo, Speak Out," reprinted in *Color Me Flo,* 132). It is not surprising that during the active but turbulent 1960s and 1970s, she stood on the forefront of a myriad of civil liberty causes and served as spokesperson for diverse groups, including homosexuals, prostitutes, minorities, women, and the poor—at a time long before it was in vogue to do so. Kennedy, a mover and shaker by anyone's definition, put before the public eye relevant and oftentimes unspoken issues that affected the lives of many.

In 1966 Kennedy founded the Media Workshop that she says was designed to "deal with racism in media and advertising." She was an original member of the National Organization for Women but broke away when "NOW got to be so boring and scared" (Kennedy, 62). Early on she spoke out on black women joining the women's liberation movement:

> It is obvious that black women are not prepared to work with white in liberation because of the divide and conquer techniques always employed by an exploitative society. However, in many towns there are movements where black and white woman are working one to one [in the movement]. It's the same wherever you are. Whether you're fighting for women's lib or just black lib, you're fighting the same enemies (King, 75).

Kennedy formed the Feminist Party whose first order of business was to support Shirley Chisholm as a presidential candidate. Still remaining friends even after the party split, Gloria Steinem says of Kennedy:

> For those who had been in the black movement when it was still known as the civil rights movement or in the consumers movement that predated Ralph Nader, or in the women's movement when it was still supposed to be a few malcontents in sneakers, or in the peace movement when there was more worry about nuclear fallout than about Vietnam, Flo was a political touchstone—a catalyst (Burstein, 54).

By the mid-seventies, Kennedy had lectured at more than two hundred colleges and universities and at rallies dealing with as many issues. She recalls in particular one incident that involved Bobby Seale. In 1967, while speaking at an anti-war convention in Montreal, she:

> became upset because Bobby Seale was not going to be allowed to speak. Seale was considered to be too radical for the group and the issues at hand. His purpose was to discuss racism

> where the group wanted to limit their discussion to the war (Vietnam). When they tried to stop him, I went berserk. I took the platform and started yelling and hollering. As a result, I was invited out to Washington to speak for a fee of $250 plus expenses, and that was the beginning of my speaking career (Kennedy, 61).

To Kennedy, racism is the most blatant form of oppression in the country and is something that everyone must combat on all fronts at all times. As such, she closely followed the activities of the black power conferences.

> I attended all four Black Power Conferences, including the planning stage of the First National Conference on Black Power. . . . The first Conference on Black Power was held in Newark in 1967, the second in Philadelphia in 1968, the third—an international conference—in Bermuda in 1969, and the fourth in Atlanta in 1970. There were also Black political caucuses in 1968 and 1972, both in Gary, Indiana, and I didn't miss them either, but I was disappointed in both of them, in 1968 because they failed to support Dick Gregory, and in 1972 when they failed to support Shirley Chisholm (Kennedy, 61-62).

Feminist Party Files Suit Against the Catholic Church

Kennedy moved her residence from New York to California in 1972. During that same year, she filed a complaint against the Catholic Church (Archdiocese of New York, Terence Cardinal Cooke, Birthright, and Knights of Columbus) with the Internal Revenue Service. She alleged that the Catholic Church violated the tax-exempt requirements in that it spent money to influence political decisions, particularly those that dealt with the abortion issue. The complaint, filed on behalf of the Feminist Party, basically stated that:

> the high level of organization is available to these tax-exempt groups largely because of their funding and because their pressure is so much the more difficult to resist because of their coming on as the "Church" with closer connection to God and "His" will. The church is organized as a strict hierarchy, with the Pope at the top. The Pope has been unbending in his stand on both contraception and abortion (*New York Times*, November 17, 1970: Exhibit 11). Individual legislators have been subjected to pressures in their individual parishes. All this, of course, is in blatant and flagrant violation of the First Amendment's proscription against the "establishment of religion." In recent times, separation of church and state has never been more clearly breached in this country (Kennedy, 152).

The central issue was that of abortion, or at least a woman's right to deal with this issue on her own terms without the dictates of the government or religion. The complaint alleged that the church's activities were unconstitutional in that they violated the basic principles of the First Amendment regarding the separation of church and state; fostered the establishment of a particular religious viewpoint; lobbied against women's rights at the taxpayer's expense; and denied the same type of equal protection under the law by denying tax-exempt status to groups who did less lobbying (Kennedy, 152). Nothing more is known about the outcome of the lawsuit.

One of the first books on abortion, *Abortion Rap*, was coauthored by Kennedy and Diane Schulter. The book describes the class action suit filed to test New York's abortion laws. Kennedy, as a part of the legal team that challenged the constitutionality of the New York law, collaborated on briefs and cross-examined witnesses in pretrial hearings (Burstein, 55).

In 1985 Flo Kennedy was roasted by friends and colleagues at an affair held at Playboy's Empire Club in New York City. The celebration marked her seventieth birthday. Among the guests were comic-activist Dick Gregory, civil rights lawyer William Kunstler, and television talk show host Phil Donahue. Kennedy was recognized as a civil rights activist, attorney, writer, television producer, national director of Voters, Artists, Anti-Nuclear Activists and Consumers for Political Action and Communication Coalition (VAC-PAC), and of the Ladies Aid and Trade Crusade. Kennedy described the latter two organizations as "tongue-in-cheek organizations" designed to make people aware of the fact that their dollars are more important than their votes because they use them everyday. "The Commandments of the organizations include Thou Shalt Not Use Our Dollars to Finance Racism and Sexism on Network television ("Activist, Attorney Flo Kennedy Roasted on 70th Birthday," 6).

A fitting tribute to Kennedy—a woman of many words and deeds—is the poem "She is Everywhere," written by Leonard Cohen, civil court judge, and published in *Color Me Flo*. Kennedy is still on the speaking circuit and can be found wherever there is a cause she believes needs to be championed and brought before the public consciousness.

References

"Activist, Attorney Flo Kennedy Roasted on 70th Birthday." *Jet* 70 (31 March 1986): 6.

Acton, Jay, Alan LeMond and Parker Hodges. *MUG Shots: Who's Who in the New Earth*. New York: World Pub. Co., 1972.

Burstein, Patricia. "Lawyer Flo Kennedy Enjoys Her Reputation As Radicalism's Rudest Mouth." *People Weekly* 3 (14 April 1974): 54.

"Flo Speaks Out." *The Megaphone*. Southwestern University, 9 October 1975.

Kennedy, Flo. *Color Me Flo: My Hard Life and Good Times*. Englewood Cliffs, N.J.: Prentice-Hall, 1976.

King, Helen H. "The Black Woman and Women's Lib." *Ebony* (March 1971): 68-70, 75-76.

Who's Who Among Black Americans, 1990/91. 6th ed. Detroit: Gale Research, 1990.

Marva Rudolph

Mae Taylor Street Kidd

(? -)

Politician, public relations consultant

Mae Taylor Street Kidd, an esteemed Kentucky legislator and public relations consultant, was born in Millersburg, Bourbon County, Kentucky. The daughter of James William Taylor and Anna Belle (Leer) Taylor, she graduated from Lincoln Institute, continued her education at Springfield Institute from 1948 to 1950, and later undertook further studies at American University from 1966 to 1967.

Before becoming involved in politics, Kidd had a distinguished career as a public relations consultant. In her nearly thirty-year association with the Mammoth Life and Accident Insurance Company, she served in diverse capacities: as supervisor of policy issues (1935-43), public relations counselor (1946-56), and sales representative. In the latter function she earned recognition as the outstanding producer in ordinary sales for three consecutive years (1961-64). Concurrent with her affiliation with that company, she assisted other business and professional organizations that sought her expertise as a consultant. She was director of programming and public relations for the United Seaman's Service in Portland, Maine (1945-46), special representative in the division of sales and personnel for Fuller Projects Company in Chicago (1947-50), and marketing consultant for William L. Higgins Property Management Company and for Continental National Bank of Kentucky. Since 1964 Kidd has been a consultant for the Supreme Life Insurance Company of America, from which she earned a gold plaque in 1966 for accumulating a sales total qualifying her as a member of the Half Million Dollar Club.

Availing herself of the experience gained in her professional pursuits, Kidd converted her talent in public relations and marketing into a successful sixteen-year political career. From 1968 to 1984, she served as a member of the Kentucky General Assembly, where she was a state representative for the Democratic Party and represented the Forty-first legislative district (Jefferson County-Louisville). Her political assignments and legislative committees include banking and insurance, cities and rules, elections and Constitutional amendment (vice-chairperson), Democratic caucus (secretary), and Democratic National Party Conference (delegate).

Kidd Sponsors Low-Income Housing Bill

Kidd is particularly noted for sponsoring a major piece of legislation, Kentucky House Bill 27, which called for establishing an agency to promote and finance low-income housing in the state. It was passed and signed into law in 1972.

Kidd's valuable professional and political accomplishments are complemented by her extensive contribution to community service. She has served on the board of directors of the Louisville Urban League and worked with the Plymouth House, a local branch of the YWCA, and has been instrumental in helping to raise funds for these as well as other organizations, such as the Girl Scouts. Her numerous memberships in and contributions to other organizations include the National Insurance Association (for which she served as treasurer, then as chairperson of the public relations committee), Iota Phi Lambda (charter member), Kentucky Business and Professional Women's Club (charter member), and the American Red Cross, where she was assistant director of the European Theatre from 1943 to 1945. Her devoted service has earned her countless awards, outstanding among which are the Unsung Heroine Award, bestowed by the National NAACP Women's Conference; the Top Ten Outstanding Kentuckians Award, Honor Award from the Louisville Urban League, Humanitarian Service Award from the United Cerebral Palsy Association, and Outstanding Service and Dedication Award from the Portland Area Council.

References

Editors of Ebony. *Ebony Success Library*. Vol. I. *1,000 Successful Blacks*. Chicago: Johnson Pub. Co., 1973. Photograph, p. 191.

Who's Who Among Black Americans. 2d ed. Vol. 1. Chicago: Who's Who Among Black Americans Corp., 1978.

Who's Who of American Women. 10th ed. Chicago: Marquis, 1978.

Carolyn R. Hodges

Jamaica Kincaid

(1949-)

Writer

The author of four books and dozens of short stories and essays, Jamaica Kincaid is one of the most innovative and provocative Caribbean-American writers of the late twentieth century.

Kincaid (Elaine Potter Richardson) was born on May 25, 1949, in Saint John's, the capital of the beautiful West Indies island, Antigua. For the first nine years of her life, she was the only child of an aging carpenter and his young wife, Annie Richards. Kincaid's grandmother, a tall, dark, Carib Indian who practiced *obeah,* significantly influenced Kincaid's formative years.

Kincaid's autobiographical novel, *Annie John* (1985), portrays her early years as almost idyllic: she was happily in love with her beautiful mother, who included her in everything and loved her best in the world. Kincaid describes Annie John—a representative of her childhood self—blissfully watching her mother going through the daily rituals of housekeeping, shopping, and cooking—rituals that seem magical. The older Annie constantly talks to Annie John, asking her opinion about everything and telling her wonderful stories about the times before and after she was born. "No small part of my life was so unimportant that she hadn't made a note of it, and now she would tell it to me over and over again," Annie John recalls. She delights in helping her mother. When her mother sends her to gather thyme or basil in their garden, Annie remembers that "sometimes when I gave her the herbs, she might stoop down and kiss me on my lips and then on my neck. It was in such a paradise that I lived."

However, dangerous poisons pervade this mother-daughter paradise. Kincaid hints at a source of poison in her earliest and most frequently anthologized short story, "Girl." In this story, which stars the young protagonist who is at the center of all of Kincaid's stories, the daughter is enchanted by her mother's ritual performance of daily activities and detailed advice about how to conduct herself in the world. However, the mother intersperses her beautiful, rhythmic discourse with variations of the theme: "try to walk like a lady and not the slut you are so bent on becoming" (*At the Bottom of the River,* 3).

The protagonist, Annie John loves and pities her elderly carpenter-father, but Kincaid never portrays him as a major force in her life. In fact, Kincaid learned that the man she had always called "father" was actually her stepfather. As an adult she has seen her biological father occasionally, but, she says, "I can't get myself to call him 'father.' He's sort of typical of West Indian men: I mean, they have children, but they never seem to connect themselves with these children" (Cudjoe, 219).

In a rare essay on her stepfather, Jamaica Kincaid describes "a snobby, critical, dignified man, who usually said very little about anything" (*New Yorker,* 7 July 1976, 23). However, he loved to tell stories about "how funny and great and attractive and smart Americans in general were . . . always the Americans were funnier, greater, smarter, and more attractive than anybody else, including himself." Satirically, Kincaid concludes that "I am very grateful to my father, who told me in his special way that, no matter what, I should always go with the cool people." Overall, Kincaid pays little attention to fathers—or to men in general. Rather, she sustains passionate interest in relations between women, especially mothers and daughters.

In 1988 Kincaid published *A Small Place,* an angry political analysis of the European-American exploitation of Antigua and a defense of the struggle of Antiguans to be "just human beings." This powerful book was highly praised by an international audience.

Recurring Theme Seen in Novels and Short Stories

In her most recent novel, *Lucy* (1990), Kincaid returns to the theme that concerns her the most: relations between women. *Lucy,* previously published as a series of short stories in *The New Yorker,* is "a sequel of sorts" to *Annie John* (Klepp 59). Lucy delightfully and defiantly explores her sexuality in various liaisons with men, but her emotional energy continues to be consumed by her simultaneous longing for and rejection of her mother. The fourth chapter of the novel, "Cold Heart," greatly illuminates the sense of loss that permeates *Annie John.* Lucy (an older version of Annie John) has lived in New York for several years, but she constantly hears her mother's voice, which she tries desperately to silence for fear that "I would die from longing for her." Finally, the narrator reveals what "I had never told anyone." Although Kincaid had always portrayed her central protagonist as an only child, Lucy surprisingly admits that "I was not an only child. . . . I was an only child until I was nine years old, and then in the space of five years my mother had three male children." Like her protagonist, Kincaid herself has three brothers: Joseph, Dalma, and Devon Drew. The protagonist is devastated by the fact that her mother, "Mrs. Judas," has greater plans and hopes for her sons than for her daughter. Kincaid ends "Cold Heart" with an observation that illuminates all of her previous work: "for ten of my nineteen years I had been mourning the end of a love affair, perhaps the only true love in my whole life I would ever know."

Approaching her twentieth year at the end of *Annie John,* Annie decides to leave her mother and go to England to become a nurse. But the nineteen-year-old heroine of *Lucy* leaves Antigua to become a writer in the United States. In

June 1965, at the age of sixteen, Jamaica Kincaid left Antigua, not to return for nineteen years. Like her heroine, Lucy, Kincaid worked in New York for some time as a live-in baby sitter. She studied at a variety of colleges and began to pursue a writing career. In 1973 she changed her name from Elaine Potter Richardson to Jamaica Kincaid. For three years (1974-1976) Kincaid contributed witty commentary on African-American and Caribbean culture to *The New Yorker*. She took George Trow, a regular contributor to "Talk of the Town" (a *New Yorker* column) to events such as roller-skate dances and Caribbean festivals, and eventually he suggested that Kincaid write her own stories for *The New Yorker*.

Kincaid has been a staff writer for *The New Yorker* since 1976. Her stories and essays have been published in many other magazines as well, including *Harper's, Rolling Stone,* and *The Paris Review*.

In 1983 Kincaid published her first book, a collection of short stories, dreams, and reflections entitled *At the Bottom of the River*. Although noting that parts of it were "almost insultingly obscure," critics generally praised the book as an innovative prose poem (Tyler, 32). Anne Tyler also noted that the collection was dominated by two themes: "the wonderful, terrible strength of a loving mother" and "the mysteriousness of ordinary life." David Leavitt observed that "in Kincaid's fiction, the relationship of a mother and daughter can recapitulate the genesis of mankind." In 1983 *At the Bottom of the River* won the Morton Dauwen Zabel Award from the American Academy and Institute of Arts and Letters.

In 1974 Kincaid was described in *The New Yorker* as a young woman who combined "Striking Black Looks with the syntax of Eve Arden" ("With Jamaica," 31). In 1990 she was described as a powerful, outspoken, fearless woman with a musical voice, "dreadlocks down to her shoulders," and a flair for drama (Garis, 70). A naturalized United States citizen who also holds Antiguan citizenship, the tall, dark Kincaid currently lives in Bennington, Vermont, with her husband, Allen Shawn. Shawn, a composer who teaches at Bennington College, is the son of "the former editor of *The New Yorker* . . . a man who is legendary for nurturing fragile writers" (Garis, 42, 80). Kincaid and Shawn have two children: Annie, born in 1985, and Harold, born in 1988.

References

Black Writers. Detroit: Gale Research, 1989.

Contemporary Literary Criticism. Vol. 43. Detroit: Gale Research, 1987.

Cudjoe, Selwyn R. "Jamaica Kincaid and the Modernist Project: An Interview." *Caribbean Women Writers*. Ed. S. R. Cudjoe. Wellesley, Mass.: Calaloux, 1990.

Garis, Leslie. "Through West Indian Eyes." *New York Times Magazine*, 7 October 1990: 42-91. Includes photograph.

Kincaid, Jamaica. *Annie John*. New York: Farrar, 1985.

———. *At the Bottom of the River*. New York: Farrar, 1983. Republished as an Aventura edition by Random House, 1985.

———. *Lucy*. New York: Farrar, 1990.

———. *The New Yorker* 50 (30 September 1974): 30-32.

———. *The New Yorker* 52 (14 July 1976): 23.

———. *A Small Place*. New York: Farrar, 1988.

Klepp, L. S. Review of *Lucy*, by Jamaica Kincaid. *Entertainment Weekly* 1 (2 November 1990): 59-60. Photograph, p. 60.

Leavitt, David. Review of *At the Bottom of the River*, by Jamaica Kincaid. *Village Voice* (17 January 1984): 41.

Tyler, Anne. "Mothers and Mysteries." *New Republic* (31 December 1983): 32-33.

"With Jamaica." *The New Yorker* 50 (25 February 1974): 31-33.

Kari Winter

Coretta Scott King

(1927-)

Civil rights activist

Coretta Scott King was born at Marion, Alabama, on April 27, 1927, one of three children of Obadiah Scott and Bernice (McMurry) Scott. Upon her graduation from the Marion Lincoln High School, King traveled to Yellow Springs, Ohio, to attend Antioch College, where in 1951 she earned a bachelor's degree in music and elementary education. Her sister, Edythe, was the first black student to attend Antioch College.

Antioch College opened many doors for Coretta King. In her words, "Antioch was a place which offered many opportunities for development" (King, 45). She recalled that, even as a student there, she had the opportunity to appear on a program with the world-famous baritone singer, Paul Robeson. After listening to and praising King's beautiful voice, Robeson urged her to continue advanced voice studies.

With the additional encouragement of two professors from Antioch College—Jessie Treichler and Walter Anderson,

Coretta Scott King

who was the only black faculty member—King finally decided to pursue advanced training at a conservatory of music. "Part of my dream had always been to study and graduate from a conservatory of music" she later wrote (King, 46-47). She has been able to utilize her voice training in varied ways. During trips abroad, she disclosed that while Dr. King made speeches, she sang on the same program.

Today, Coretta King has a very positive impression of her years at Antioch College. In her opinion, the college did a great deal for her, apart from the fine education she received. First and foremost, it taught her how to live in a white community. Since the authorities expected every student to alternate periods of work and study, she had to take a job every other semester and write evaluations of job experiences as part of the curriculum. King served as a waitress in a dining room and as a counselor at Karamu Camp, which belonged to a settlement house that specialized in the arts and music. For five months, she worked at the Friendly Inn Settlement House in one of the worst areas in Cleveland, Ohio. King also went home on some of her vacations to help her father, who was popularly called Obie, in the general store that he had opened in 1946. There she set up for him a system of bookkeeping, ordered the store's supplies, and waited on customers, jobs for which Antioch College gave her academic credit.

Faced with a difficult choice between the Juilliard School in New York and the New England Conservatory of Music in Boston, Coretta King was relieved when she received word that the New England Conservatory had accepted her as a student, and she promptly agreed to attend. Initially, King was worried about the fees, but she received a grant of $650 for her studies from the Jessie Smith Noyes Foundation. In her reaction to the grant, she wrote in her 1969 autobiography: "My prayers had been answered" (King, 48).

Mary Powell, an Atlantan residing in Boston, introduced Coretta Scott to the young Reverend Martin Luther King, Jr. King, who was affectionately called "ML" by his friends and classmates, was a doctoral student at Boston University. Reportedly, he had told Mary Powell, "Mary, I wish I knew a few girls from down home to go out with. I tell you, these Boston girls are something else. The ones I've been seeing are so reserved" (Lewis, 40-41).

Coretta Scott's and King's relationship blossomed. In November 1952 the Reverend Martin Luther King, Sr., and his wife, Alberta (Williams) King, visited Boston and met their future daughter-in-law, Coretta Scott. The meeting almost turned sour when the senior King, who was affectionately called Daddy King, insinuated that he wanted his son to marry a girl from Atlanta. Daddy King told Coretta Scott:

> You know, I don't understand this young man [his son, Martin]. He's gone out with some of the finest girls—beautiful girls, intelligent, from fine families. We love people and we want to be nice to everyone, but we don't know how to act. He gets us involved, and then he just seems to lose interest. Those girls have a lot to offer (King, 68).

Coretta King stated in her autobiography that by this time she was becoming irritated with Daddy King. She told her future father-in-law: "I have something to offer too" (King, 68). On June 18, 1953, Coretta Scott and Martin Luther King, Jr., were married in the garden of Scott's Alabama home in Marion. Daddy King officiated at the wedding and the Reverend A. D. King, his younger son, was the best man.

Coretta King wrote about the aftermath of her marriage in the following words:

> In September, 1953, after our marriage, Martin and I went back to Boston, he to finish the residence requirements and write the thesis for his doctorate and I to finish my musical education at the conservatory. We rented an apartment in a very old house right around the corner from the one Martin had when we were courting. It had four rooms—kitchen, bedroom, den and living room. Martin worked on his research in the den and I studied in the bedroom, though in order not to bother Martin or the neighbors, I never practiced my singing at home but used the practice rooms at the conservatory (King, 89).

In June 1954 Coretta King earned the Mus.B. degree in voice from the New England Conservatory of Music. By that time, her husband had completed his residency requirements at Boston University and was free to accept a job outside Boston while writing his dissertation. He completed his doctoral comprehensive examinations in August.

King had decided to return to the South to pastor a church, and he had been interviewed for the position of the pastor of Dexter Avenue Baptist Church in Montgomery, Alabama. Among those who received him warmly during his first visit to Montgomery was the Reverend Ralph David Abernathy, who was at the time the pastor of First Baptist Church in the city and had met him before in Atlanta. King was impressed with the officials of the Montgomery church, and he and Coretta King moved to Montgomery. It was on April 14, 1954, that he formally accepted the Dexter position, and he started his pastoral work there in September of that year.

Civil Rights Protests Begin

When Coretta King and her husband arrived in Montgomery, the officials of Dexter Avenue Baptist Church were still working feverishly to refurbish its parsonage at 309 South Jackson Street. Therefore, the couple had to stay with a church member. Their first child, Yolanda Denise King, born on November 17, 1955, was barely three weeks old when the Reverend King was chosen to lead the historic Montgomery bus boycott. The Kings were deeply involved in the incident in sympathy with Rosa Parks, the originator of the event. From that time on, Coretta King stood behind her husband in every civil rights protest meeting and demonstration from Montgomery to Memphis. Subsequently, three other children were born to them: Martin, III (October 23, 1957), Dexter (January 30, 1961), and Bernice (March 28, 1963).

Coretta King accompanied Martin Luther King, Jr., on his international travels as well. For example, in March 1957, the couple made their maiden overseas journey, which was a trip to Ghana to attend the country's independence celebrations, at which the British handed over the colony to the indigenous government headed by the late President Kwame Nkrumah. On their return to the United States, the Kings visited Nigeria, another British colony that would achieve its independence (in 1960). Accompanied by Professor Lawrence D. Reddick, an eminent black historian, the Kings visited India in 1959. In December 1964, Coretta King, other family members, and friends traveled with Martin Luther King, Jr., to Oslo, Norway, where he accepted the Nobel Peace Prize. At age thirty-nine, he was the youngest recipient of the prize.

Before going to Norway, King and his entourage of forty Americans visited London where he fulfilled several speaking engagements, including the preaching of a sermon at the famous St. Paul's Cathedral. In her memoirs, *My Life With Martin Luther King, Jr.* Coretta Scott King captured the essence of the Nobel ceremony:

> The next day, December 10, 1964, Martin received the Nobel Prize. We had quite a time getting him ready. He had to wear formal dress, striped trousers and a gray tailcoat. While several of us were working on the ascot, Martin kept fussing and making funny comments about having to wear such a ridiculous thing. Finally he said, "I vow never to wear one of these things again" (King, 11).

Dr. and Mrs. King had been received by King Olav of Norway on December 9, 1964, a day before the ceremony. It was the next day that they shared one of the high points of the American civil rights movement. Describing her personal impression of the prize as well as her contributions to the life of Martin Luther King, Jr., Coretta King wrote in 1969:

> We were all very emotional, and each of us felt we must say something, and in a very real sense this tribute from his friends meant as much to Martin as the formal [Nobel] ceremony which had preceded it. When my turn came, I talked about what my role had been—simply giving support to Martin over the years. I explained what a great privilege it had been, what a blessing, to live at the side of a man whose life would have so profound an impact on the world. It was the most important thing I could have done, and I had wanted to do it. I said, "This great experience has given me renewed faith. I will continue to give what support I can to my husband, and to the struggle" (King, 13-14).

Coretta King Pursues Civil Rights Interests

In the quest for civil rights for all minorities in America, Coretta King's support of her husband was unlimited. Through their indefatigable efforts, on August 6, 1965, President Lyndon B. Johnson signed the Voting Rights Bill. In Coretta King's assessment, the bill and the 1964 Civil Rights Act comprised a major step in the legal protection of the rights of black Americans. On several occasions, she traveled to civil rights events on her own, often as a representative of Martin Luther King, Jr. In 1967 she visited Chicago several times to participate in the Reverend Jesse Jackson's "Operation Breadbasket" program.

> I attended one of Rev. Jesse Jackson's meetings in Chicago in October, 1967, and I heard him give his regular message. It was terribly meaningful to me. I came home and said to Martin, 'I think that Jesse Jackson and Operation Breadbasket have something that is needed in every community across the nation.' (King, 289-90)

On April 4, 1968, Martin Luther King, Jr., was shot to death by an assassin at the Lorraine Motel in Memphis, Tennessee. King had gone to the city to take part in a demonstration to support striking garbage workers. After King's death, Coretta King did not retire from the civil rights movement. Instead, on Monday, April 8, 1969—barely four days after her husband's assassination—she and her children, accompanied by civil rights leaders, led a mammoth demonstration in Memphis, where she called for a "peaceful society" (Lukas, *New York Times*). In June of the same year, Coretta King and several civil rights leaders went to Washington, D.C., to take part in the so-called "Poor-Man's March or Campaign." She was the keynote speaker at the

Lincoln Memorial program of more than 50,000 people (Caldwell, *New York Times*).

To protect and expand the legacy of her late husband, Coretta King founded the Martin Luther King, Jr., Center for Nonviolent Social Change in Atlanta, Georgia. As founding president and chief executive officer of the center, she states that its purpose is to serve as a living memorial to King, to preserve his legacy, and carry forward his unfinished work.

Through the planning and lobbying efforts of Coretta King, the twenty-three-acre neighborhood surrounding King's birthplace in Atlanta was, in 1980, declared a National Historic Site by the National Park Service. The King center is situated in the area on historic Auburn Avenue. Coretta King led the twentieth-anniversary March on Washington in 1983, bringing together more than five hundred thousand people and eight hundred human rights organizations to form a "New Coalition of Conscience." In 1984, Coretta King was elected the chairperson of the Martin Luther King Holiday Commission, which was established by an Act of Congress to formalize plans for the 1986 first legal celebration of the holiday honoring King. Since then, she has coordinated the public observance of her late husband's holiday at home and abroad.

Coretta King has received numerous local and international honors. She was the first woman to deliver the Class Day address at Harvard University and the first woman to preach at a regular service at St. Paul's Cathedral in London, England, in 1969.

For her indefatigable efforts, Coretta King has been the recipient of several prestigious honors, including more than one hundred honorary doctoral degrees. President Jimmy Carter appointed her the alternate delegate of the United States delegation to the United Nations. In July 1977, Coretta King, accompanied by Daddy King and other family members, traveled to Washington, D.C., to receive the Presidential Medal of Freedom, awarded posthumously to her husband.

Coretta King has shown staunch support for the anti-apartheid movement. In addition to making public statements and writing a syndicated weekly newspaper column advocating social, economic, and political causes, she travels extensively. In April 1990, for example, she paid a visit to the so-called frontline nations of southern Africa, where she met with leaders of Namibia, Zimbabwe, Zambia, and the recently released African National Congress (ANC) leader, Nelson Mandela. In Zimbabwe, Coretta King participated in the observance of the country's ten years of independence. Her presence amply confirmed her abhorrence of colonialism and all forms of domination.

Today, Coretta King serves in various capacities. Apart from functioning actively as the chief executive officer of the King Center, she is also the co-chairperson of the Full Employment Action Council, and an active member of both the Black Leadership Forum and the Black Leadership Roundtable, speaking in support of human rights campaigns and social justice.

References

Assensoh, A. B. *Rev. Dr. Martin Luther King, Jr., and America's Quest for Racial Integration.* Devon, England: Arthur H. Stockwell, 1987.

Caldwell, Earl. "50,000 March in Capital to Support Demand by Poor for Sharing of Affluence." *New York Times,* 20 June 1968.

"Dr. King is Honored." *New York Times,* 12 July 1977.

"Dr. King's Widow in London." *New York Times,* 17 March 1969.

Garrow, David J. *Bearing the Cross: Martin Luther King, Jr., and the Southern Christian Leadership Conference.* New York: Morrow, 1986.

King, Coretta Scott. Biographical Sketch. Atlanta: The King Center, 1989. Official biography.

King, Coretta Scott. *My Life with Martin Luther King, Jr.* New York: Holt, 1969.

Lanker, Brian. *I Dream A World.* New York: Stewart, Tabori and Chang, 1989. 80-81. Photograph, p. 80.

Lewis, David Levering. *King: A Critical Biography.* New York: Praeger, 1970.

Lukas, J. Anthony. "Mrs. King Asks Peaceful Society." *New York Times,* 9 April 1968.

Who's Who Among Black Americans, 1990/91. Detroit: Gale Research, 1990. 737.

Collections

Photographs, correspondence, biographical materials, and other items on Coretta Scott King and the King family are in the files of the Center for Nonviolent Social Change in Atlanta.

A. B. Assensoh

Eartha Kitt

(1928-)

Actress, singer

Eartha Mae Kitt has acted on stage, screen, and television, earned critical acclaim as a singer and as a dancer, and has written two books. She was born January 26, 1928, in North, South Carolina, to William and Anna Mae (Riley) Kitt. She married William McDonald on June 9, 1960; they have one daughter, Kitt. They were divorced in 1965.

Eartha Kitt's parents were poverty-stricken blacks who worked as sharecroppers. Kitt was the older of two children; the other was a sister, Anna Pearl. Kitt's father disappeared when she was a very small child, and the mother left the girls to go off with a man who had eight children. The mother died, according to Kitt in *Thursday's Child*, her first autobiography, as a result of voodoo. *Thursday's Child*, a chronicle of racial conflict, abuse from other children who resented her light complexion, and dire poverty, is poignant and detailed. When Kitt was eight years old, her aunt, Mamie Lue Riley, a domestic in New York City, sent for the two little girls to live with her. They went to New York by train with catfish sandwiches for food. Kitt wore all the several sets of clothes the aunt sent her on her body.

Young Kitt was frequently alone in New York in a Puerto Rican-Italian section and so she developed a facility for language. Additionally, she created her own world of singing and dancing. She won prizes in dramatics at the New York School of the Performing Arts. Here she also learned that stark silence emerged when she spoke and that she could command an audience with her unusual voice.

A sports enthusiast, Kitt played baseball and became a champion pole vaulter. She left school at fourteen and worked in a Brooklyn factory sewing army uniforms. Some of the money she saved for piano lessons. When she was sixteen, a friend arranged for Eartha Kitt to meet Katherine Dunham. The meeting proved fortunate for Kitt, since through it she earned a dance training scholarship.

Kitt Launches Her Career

Katherine Dunham, then arguably the most renowned black dancer in the world, selected Kitt for the troupe that toured the United States, Mexico, and South America. Kitt soon emerged as a soloist. In 1947, she danced in the Hollywood film a sequence in *Casbah*. In 1948, she appeared with the Dunham troupe at the Prince of Wales Theatre in London before an audience that included members of the Royal Family. The tour also included Paris where Kitt earned more solo parts.

When the group returned to the United States, Kitt opted to stay in Paris. *Cue* mentioned how she found a room in a small hotel along the Seine and a singing job at Carroll's, one of the smart nightclubs, where she was an overnight success (27 November 1954). The French called her "the rage of Paris." Turkey, Egypt, Greece, New York City, Hollywood, Las Vegas, and Stockholm greeted her with equal acclaim. At the Kervansaray in Istanbul, "her dazzling gowns and the multilingual virtuosity of her singing" impressed her nightclub audiences.

In 1951, her Aunt Mamie died and Kitt flew home to the funeral. On her return to Paris, Orson Welles asked her to play Helen of Troy in *Faust*. But he chastised her speech, "It's too clear. You don't sound as though you came from anywhere. Everyone sounds as though he's from somewhere, but you—? No" (*Thursday's Child*, 185). With only two days to learn her part in *Faust*, she drew high praise from the critics. Ted Poston, the distinguished black journalist from the *New York Post*, wrote on January 30, 1955, quoting Kitt: "I learned so much from Orson Welles—just by keeping my mouth shut and listening. He gave me my first chance at a legitimate stage role."

Producer Leonard Sillman saw her at Max Gordon's Village Vanguard in 1952 singing "C'est Si Bon" and asked her to take a part in his revue, *New Faces*. Brooks Atkinson, probably the most revered critic in America at the time, wrote that her "combustible singing" of the song "Monotonous," described "the boredom of a worldly lady surfeited with luxury" (*New York Times*, 25 May 1952). For virtually the entire run of *New Faces*, Kitt sang at the after-dinner show at the Blue Angel nightclub, where she broke the all-time attendance record.

RCA Victor made the *Eartha Kitt Album* that popularized the Turkish folk song "Uska Dara." "C'est Si Bon," "I Want to Be Evil" and "Santa Baby" were also favorites. Her songs were sometimes considered racy; for example, "Santa Baby" was called "a catchy combination of sex and Santa Claus" (*Negro History Bulletin* 10). Twentieth Century Fox Film Corporation produced *New Faces* in Cinemascope with Kitt as the star.

After a tour of *New Faces*, the actress began to prepare for the leading role in the play *Mrs. Patterson* produced by Leonard Sillman. She appeared on a number of television shows including "The Colgate Comedy Hour", "Your Show of Shows", and "Toast of the Town." Edward R. Murrow's "Person to Person" program showed Kitt at home in her Riverside Drive penthouse on September 11, 1954. *Mrs. Patterson* closely resembled her life. Written by Charles Sebree and Greer Johnson, the play caused Walter F. Kerr to call Kitt in the *New York Herald Tribune*, "an enchanting gamin" in her portrayal of Teddy Hicks, the fifteen-year-old daughter of a Kentucky laundress who built a dream life around the white people whom she envied. James R. Howard said in the *Negro History Bulletin* that ". . . she has a fascinatingly alive face which can range from a savage look to one of tenderness. She prowls round the stage with a feline grace." After 101 performances, the show closed on February 26, 1955. Kitt appeared in two other Broadway Shows during the 1950s: *Shinbone Alley* (1957) and *Jolly's Progress* (1959). She was Mehitabel and Jolly, respectively. Also during the 1950s Kitt wrote *Thursday's Child* (1956), appeared in the film *St. Louis Blues* (1958), played the title role in the film *Anna Lucasta* (1958), and made a number of television shows.

The turbulence of the 1960s had an impact on Kitt's career. In her second autobiography, *Alone With Me* (1976), she writes of the unfortunate occurrence of the Johnson administration: "My country, which hasn't allowed me to work here but which takes a more than healthy chunk of my income because I refuse to be intimidated and leave it.'' A series of events generated this feeling. At the invitation of First Lady Mrs. Lyndon Johnson, Kitt attended a luncheon in January 1968 at the White House. The question under for discussion was, ''Why is there so much juvenile delinquency in the streets of America?'' Believing then (as she did as recently as December 3, 1989, on CBS's ''Sixty Minutes'') that her own poverty had colored her actions in every phase of her life, Kitt chose to respond to the question. Her feeling was that the war in Vietnam was a direct cause of the street crime in several ways. *Newsweek* (January 29, 1968), quoted her remarks to Mrs. Johnson as follows: ''I think we have missed the main point at this luncheon. We have forgotten the main reason we have juvenile delinquency. . . . No wonder the kids rebel and take pot. . . . '' Informing Mrs. Johnson that pot was marijuana, Kitt suddenly found her options for employment severely curtailed, and she became the subject of a lurid CIA investigation and other surveillance. Kitt says in *Alone With Me*, ''With God as my witness, I had no intention of launching a diatribe against the war in Vietnam.''

Kitt did not return to Broadway until the late 1970s when she appeared as Sahleem-La-Lume in Geoffrey Holder's reworking of *Kismet*, *Timbuktu* (1978). She returned to the White House in February 1978 with her sixteen-year-old daughter, Kitt McDonald. Kitt, five feet two inches and 105 pounds whose weekly earnings have ranged from $350 tp $10,000 during her career, says, ''Overall, I've had a very good life, a life of cotton and caviar. . . .''

References

Afro-American, 17 June, 1976: 1.

Bogle, Donald. *Toms, Coons, Mulattoes, Mammies and Bucks: An Interpretive History of Blacks in American Films*. New York: Viking Press, 1973.

Chicago Defender Accent, 18 November, 1978: 12.

Collier's, (June 11, 1954): 33-39

Cue, (27 November 1954).

Current Biography, New York: H.W. Wilson, 1955. 327-29.

Detroit Free Press, 17 September 1978.

Ebony, (December 1957): cover; 83-92.

Essence, (June 1978): 68-71.

Jet, (8 February 1968): 18-25.

Kitt, Eartha. *Alone With Me*. Chicago: Regnery, 1976.

———. *Thursday's Child*. New York: Duell, Sloan and Pierce, 1956.

Landay, Eileen. *Black Film Stars*. New York: Drake, 1973.

Negro History Bulletin, 19 (October 1955): 10.

NOW, (March 1978).

People, 18 July 1977.

Pittsburgh Courier, 18 February 1978.

Rollins, Charlemae H. *Famous Negro Entertainers of Stage, Screen, and TV*. New York: Dodd, Mead, 1967.

Shockley, Ann A. *Living Black American Authors*. New York: Bowker, 1973.

Time, (26 January 1968).

Washington Post, 19 January 1978.

Glenda E. Gill

Flemmie Kittrell

(1904-1980)

Educator, nutritionist

Flemmie Pansy Kittrell devoted her career to the improvement of family welfare around the world. She was successful in drawing attention to the important role of women to make a difference in a changing world and in providing assistance through home economics and nutrition education to governments at home and abroad.

Kittrell was born December 25, 1904, in Henderson, North Carolina, and died unexpectedly of cardiac arrest on October 3, 1980, in Washington, D.C. She was the seventh of nine children and the youngest daughter of James Lee Kittrell and Alice (Mills) Kittrell, both descendants of Cherokee Indian and African-American parents. Kittrell's parents encouraged family love and unity in the home and made learning a central activity. She shared many of her childhood secrets with her mother, whom she considered her best friend. Her father often entertained his family by reading stories and reciting poetry. He would heap praise on his children for their creative attempts and accomplishments. Kittrell's happy home life influenced her to formulate goals, initiate action, and persevere until her goals were met.

Kittrell's early education took place in the public schools of Vance County, North Carolina. After graduating from high school, she attended Hampton Institute (later University) in Virginia, where she received her bachelor of science degree (1928). Her professors at Hampton recognized her quick wit and keen abilities and continually urged her to enroll in graduate studies. Few black women in the 1920s attended graduate school, and she, too, was reluctant; nevertheless, she enrolled in Cornell University and received her M.A. (1930) and Ph.D. (1938) with honors. In addition, during several summers she took courses in guidance and women's education at Columbia University. Her positive educational experiences prompted her to become an advocate of higher education and training for other women.

Kittrell began her professional career as an instructor of home economics in 1928 at Bennett College in Greensboro, North Carolina. After obtaining her Ph.D. from Cornell, she returned to Bennett to continue teaching until accepting a position to serve as dean of women and director of the home economics division at Hampton Institute from 1940 to 1944. In September 1944, Kittrell assumed the position of head of the Department of Home Economics at Howard University in Washington, D.C., at the personal invitation of president Mordecai Johnson. This position gave her an opportunity to build a curriculum that transcended the traditional home economics model. Moreover, it reflected her own philosophy of home economics as a research-oriented discipline. Kittrell's program at Howard offered exciting new ideas and drew its content from the natural and social sciences as well as from the humanities. Her program also gave attention to the important task of women, both nationally and internationally, to make significant contributions in a constantly changing world.

Nutrition and Home Life Advanced in Developing Nations

Kittrell applied her research techniques and first gained international attention in 1947 when she conducted a nutritional survey of Liberia, under the auspices of the United States Department of State. The purpose of the study was to examine the nutritional value of food consumed by Liberians and to observe their general living conditions.

Kittrell's study's findings, published in the booklet *Preliminary Food and Nutrition Survey of Liberia* (1947), showed that ninety percent of the Liberian people experienced "hidden hunger" from subsisting largely on diets of rice and cassava dishes. To remedy malnutrition in Liberia, she made several long and short-range recommendations that included the refinement of agricultural production, development of the fishing industry, and enlargement of staff personnel within the agricultural bureau. In recognition of her expertise and services to its citizens and country, the Liberian government presented Kittrell with an award during the country's centennial-year celebration.

In 1950 Kittrell extended her international service in India. Under a Fulbright exchange program she assisted India's Baroda University to organize its college of Home Economics and to develop its food and nutritional research program. She returned to India in 1953 under the auspices of the Agency for International Development, and she conducted seminars on food and nutrition, taught courses in meal planning and child feeding, and gave home economics demonstrations. Baroda University students and faculty, as well as the government of India, credit Kittrell for advancement in home life skills in that country.

In 1957, as a leader of a team sponsored by the Department of State, Kittrell ventured to Japan and Hawaii to study home economics extension methods. In addition, she led three cultural tours to Africa for the Department of State: in 1957 to West Africa, in 1959 to West and Central Africa, and in 1961 to Guinea. In 1952 her worldwide efforts to improve the home life conditions of developing nations, primarily through education and demonstration, led Kittrell to Zaire to help organize the Congo Polytechnic Institute's School of Home Economics in 1952. Through diplomacy and persistence, Kittrell undertook the difficult task of convincing the Congolese men that higher education for women would enhance their home life.

The successful expansion of Kittrell's work abroad provided additional impetus for continuing her mission at home. In one corner of Howard University's quadrangle stands the School of Human Ecology, a brick and mortar testament to Kittrell's drive and determination. For fifteen years she almost single-handedly sought and finally obtained university approval for the construction of the building, which was dedicated in 1963. The four-story building offers innovative and functional classrooms, study center, and laboratory arrangements. It also houses a state-of-the-art nursery for the college's preschool program, a premier program that attracted national attention and provided a laboratory and proving ground for the nation's emerging Head Start program.

The emphasis of child development research within the framework of a home economics curriculum exemplified not only Kittrell's love of children but also her conviction of the importance of the environment in enhancing childrens' growth and development. In 1968 Cornell University acknowledged her unique accomplishments with an award for achievement in the study of human development and quality environment.

After a remarkable career that spanned more than four decades, Kittrell retired in 1972 from Howard University, achieving emeritus status. However, her active teaching life and her practice of nurturing and inspiring others continued. She was a Cornell Visiting Senior Fellow from 1974 to 1976, a Moton Center Senior Research Fellow in 1977, and a Fulbright lecturer in India in 1978.

Kittrell's humane and visionary contributions to the development of home economics and the improvement of family life were widely acknowledged over the years with awards from universities and professional organizations. Hampton University selected her as the outstanding alumna for 1955; the National Council of Negro Women presented her with the Scroll of Honor for special services in 1961; the University of North Carolina at Greensboro conferred on her an honorary degree in 1974; and the American Home Economics Association established an international student scholarship in her honor.

Kittrell attributed much of her success to her sustaining

faith, her family and friends, and the educational institutions she attended. Others attribute much of Kittrell's success to her unhesitating kind words, pats on the back, and endearing smile—in summary, her loving presence.

References

Brown, Herman. Interviewed, 6 April 1990.

Graves, Patsy. Interviewed, 10 May 1990.

Kittrell, Flemmie. "Liberians Do Not Eat Enough of Right Foods." *Service* (September 1948): 15-16. Photograph, p. 15.

Lee, Elinor. "She's Off to the Congo to Organize a College." *Washington Post,* 30 July 1962: B-6. Includes photograph.

McQueen, Adele. Interviewed, 10 May 1990.

Norfolk *Journal and Guide,* 8 October 1980. Obituary.

Ottley, Ester. "Flemmie Pansy Kittrell." *Profiles* 2 (December 1980): 1-22. Photographs pp. 1-19.

Rogers, Lydia. Interviewed, 9 May 1990.

Tynes, Jacqueline. Interviewed, 30 April 1990 and 2 May 1990.

Washington Afro-American, 11 October 1980. Obituary.

Washington Post, 5 October 1980. Obituary.

Who's Who in America. Vol. 1. Chicago: Marquis, 1981. 1853.

Who's Who of American Women. 12th ed. Chicago: Marquis, 1982. 415.

Collections

Information on Flemmie Pansy Kittrell is housed in the archives of Hampton University and in files at the Moorland-Spingarn Research Center, Howard University. A tape-recorded interview held on 11 April 1980 is available in the office of the dean of Howard University's Graduate School of Arts and Sciences. Numerous documents, awards, and articles spanning Kittrell's life accomplishments are in the possession of her niece, Jacqueline Tynes, of New York. Interviews noted above were held with her niece, friends, colleagues, and associates.

Virginia J. Newsome

Elizabeth Duncan Koontz

(1919-1989)

Educator, organization official

When she was president of the National Education Association (NEA) in 1968-1969—the first black elected to that position—Elizabeth Duncan Koontz urged members to organize, agitate, and, if the situation warranted, strike in order to bring about needed change in the public schools. After resigning her position with the NEA, she went on to head the United States Labor Department's Women's Bureau, where she spoke out in support of black women's rights. She served the education needs of her home state, North Carolina, as a teacher, as a leader in both the national and local teachers' associations, and as assistant state school superintendent.

Elizabeth Duncan Koontz was born June 3, 1919, in Salisbury, North Carolina, a college town about forty miles northeast of Charlotte. She was the youngest child of Lena Bell (Jordan) Duncan and Samuel E. Duncan's seven children. Both parents were educators. Samuel Duncan taught at Livingstone College and was principal of Dunbar High

Elizabeth Duncan Koontz

School in East Spencer. He was a man of logic and reason and often used mathematics to help his children solve problems. Lena Duncan was a teacher in Dunbar Elementary School and held the family together with a firm hand after the death of Samuel Duncan when Koontz was nine. Lena Duncan died in 1967.

Koontz entered elementary school at the age of four, already able to read and write. While still in elementary school, she would help check the lessons of illiterate adults whom her mother was teaching to read. She graduated from Salisbury's segregated Price High School as class salutatorian and began her college education at Livingstone College, where she graduated with honors in 1938 with a degree in English and elementary education. She earned a master's degree from Atlanta University in 1941 and did graduate work at Columbia University, Indiana University, and North Carolina College (now North Carolina Central University).

Elizabeth Duncan Koontz began her elementary school teaching career at Harnett County Training School in Dunn, North Carolina. She was fired from her first job in 1940 when she discovered the school principal was overcharging staff members at a school-owned boarding house and organized the teachers into a revolt against the system. She taught at Aggrey Memorial School in Landis, North Carolina, for the 1941-1942 year, then moved to the Fourteenth Street School in Winston-Salem for three years. Beginning in 1945 she taught high school and finally began specializing in special education classes at Price High School in Salisbury.

She continued her professional activities through the ranks of the National Education Association (NEA), its Council for Exceptional Children, the National Association for Retarded Children, and the President's Advisory Council on the Education of Disadvantaged Children.

Koontz became active in the NEA in 1952 when the black teachers' group to which she belonged, the North Carolina Negro Teachers Association (later "Negro" was dropped), was admitted to the North Carolina chapter of the National Education Association. By 1965, she had moved into office at the national level, and she was president of the NEA's Department of Classroom Teachers. Before becoming the first black president of the NEA Department of Classroom Teachers in 1965-1966, she had served two terms as secretary, one as vice-president, and one as president-elect.

As an educator, some of Koontz's major national concerns were teaching conditions, teacher training, the loss of teachers, and the challenge to pay better wages. Koontz believed that there were already opportunities on hand for teachers to take more responsibility for themselves and their students. Teachers needed to develop greater self-determination to help make the teacher an effective professional, improve the quality of education, study problems in recruiting and retaining competent teachers, and stimulate teachers to participate in politics at all levels. The time had come for teachers to take responsibility for their own destiny.

She also felt that teachers must be creative and fight for inclusion of materials that were missing from the curriculum. Along these lines, she developed a filmstrip, *The Negro American Citizen,* for the National School and Industrial Supply Corporation to help answer questions caused by the educational lag of segregation. The film contains the facts about black Americans and their contributions omitted from regular history textbooks.

National Education Association Elects First Black President

Koontz was installed as president at the National Education Association annual meeting in Dallas, Texas, on July 6, 1968. Speaking of her nomination, Koontz said, "The nomination moved me tremendously. It makes one humble to have such an honor thrust on her. Change is sweeping the American educational system. The concept of four immovable walls surrounding forty stationary children is a thing of the past" ("Educator's Leader," *Philadelphia Inquirer* 6 July 1967). In her inauguration speech, "A Time For Educational Statesmanship," she charted the course she wanted the NEA to follow. She noted that statesmanship must be the hallmark of the teaching profession. She saw the school as the way in which many Americans convert their dreams into reality, and those Americans who had no dream could build one (NEA, *Address and Proceedings,* Vol. 106, 43).

During her years as an educator, Koontz had a firsthand view of many contemporary issues in the area of vocational education. She felt that students needed a college education, but that there was also a need for students with twentieth-century skills—electronics, computer programming, appliance repair, drafting, and other talents. She noted that the first priority was to remove old stereotypes and free teachers and students from rigid habits. New paths should be made by taking the best from the old ways and developing more appropriate new ones. She called for schools to establish a background that would support such training. Public school preparation should include first-rate vocational education and establish with local industry cooperative vocational training programs. She advised that vocational education programs should call for high scholarship as well and should be just as demanding as college preparatory subjects.

As a teacher of special education classes for mentally retarded children, Koontz was extremely concerned about how these students were treated. She felt that slow learners needed more and better education geared to their individual capabilities. "Can we afford to say that there will be a beginning age of five when we know that there are children who need a kind of training before they are two?" (Koontz, "Education in Changing Times," 11-12). Koontz recognized a need for local communities to help set the direction that education of its citizens should take. In the same article, Koontz said, "we have a responsibility to let that community know that after it sets its goal, we as professional educators, have the right to determine the means by which we can produce it" (11).

Koontz saw a gap between the kind of education people

envision and the kind they are willing to support, noting that the gap should be closed. ''Too many taxpayers want the best teachers and programs . . . but they think it can be done with the same financial arrangements as fifteen years ago'' (Howell).

As one of the participants in a symposium on ''What's Right In American Education,'' Koontz commented that citizens fight to keep taxes down, yet, realizing that taxes are the means of support for the educational programs that they want, they are torn between a higher tax structure and meeting the aspirations and expectations of their schools (''A Symposium,'' 144). Koontz further stated:

> Though much is right about education, there is room for improvement. Until all institutions which bear responsibility for the education of our people accept professional responsibility for the entire spectrum of education that transcends structural lines and attainment levels, there will be gaps and chasms that prohibit or impede programs. Development of a more effective system for educating a population for changing times in which a college education may not necessarily be required for social or economic success must be a goal shared by the educational community and the public (145).
>
> The public must provide funds to furnish modern equipment and materials for the schools. The educator must readjust his/her approach to teaching and to learning. Is it reasonable—is it in the interest of society—to expect students to learn when outmoded equipment and methods of teaching are used in the schools? (Koontz, ''The Profession,'' 17).

Koontz brought to the NEA a change from traditionally conservative ideas to liberal activism. She spoke out in favor of teachers' strikes, saying that teachers should organize, agitate, and, if necessary, use their final weapon—the strike. ''Teachers who walk off the job after they have exhausted every other method of bringing needed improvement show dedication and commitment,'' she said (''NEW Views,'' 437). In July 1968, the Representative Assembly of the NEA adopted the following policy on strikes: ''The NEA recognizes the deplorable conditions in education in some school systems have brought about emergency situations which have forced educators to take drastic measures. . . . The Association denounces that practice of staffing schools with any personnel when in an effort to provide high quality education, educators withdraw their services'' (436).

Koontz endorsed militant teachers, and foresaw a time when, of necessity, they would become even more militant. On this issue she said:

> I am not sure that teachers are yet as militant as they must become, for many of today's barriers to the education of children will be removed only when teachers realize that teaching harder and longer will not achieve the goals unless some fundamental, basic conditions are provided by which teaching and learning may take place. Teachers have realized that as long as the old system of paternalism exists, their own professional competence, training, continued education, and love of teaching will avail them very little, for the decisions that can bring about change will be left to others (Koontz, ''Why Teachers Are Militant,'' 14).

Elizabeth Duncan Koontz felt strongly about teacher commitment and responsibility. In her final statements as president of the Classroom Teachers Department, Koontz pointed out some of the opportunities for responsibility that remained untapped—opportunities that the teaching profession must utilize if it is to achieve its full stature in American life. She also suggested directions for the future. Koontz said:

> The Department must have expanded programs, staff and budget. More staff members providing full service, including specialists who deal with issues of all teachers whether urban, suburban or rural. They need expanded communication programs to inform teachers at the grass roots level of its program. Teachers must avail themselves of the national professional organization (NEA, Department of Classroom Teachers, 5-9).

Her vision for the future included a profession that was strong, united, and proud of its achievements; a corps of classroom teachers who were confident of their abilities and secure in their rights, who were creative and innovative, who ever sought to improve their competence, and who would shoulder their full responsibility for providing leadership for their profession; and a nation that was aware of the contributions that education has made to its greatness and determined to protect that priceless heritage.

Koontz condemned ''moldering educational bureaucracies'' (*Current Biography,* 245) and had felt all along that boards of education must share decision-making with their teachers. She found untenable the practice of bureaucrats establishing policies that affect teachers and at the same time disregarding teacher attitudes, contributions, and potential effectiveness as those who must carry out the policies.

In a speech at the Arkansas Teachers Association in 1968, Elizabeth Duncan Koontz condemned the second-class citizen's role of teachers as professionals. She called for the freedom of teachers to practice the democracy that they teach in the classroom and called for teachers to fight to become professionally autonomous. ''We must accept our responsibility to work for adequate financing to do the job,'' she said (''NEA President Speaks at ATA'').

At the Office of Economic Opportunity Local Leaders Conference in 1968, Koontz spoke on actions that should be taken to decrease oppression in the educational system. ''It is our duty as educators to insist upon changes and conditions in which education can be relevant, can be personal, can be effective,'' she said. While the working teachers dedicated to this cause can make a difference, ''all of us as individuals, working together with awareness and sensitivity, can lick this business'' (Koontz, ''Can We Lick the Giants,'' 19).

School decentralization, then a hot issue in educational arenas, was of concern to Koontz: ''The best answer to the problem of overcentralization of public education is to return to the individual schools and to the separate publics they serve their rightful share of authority and responsibility for operation of schools'' (''President Koontz on Decentralization'').

Elizabeth Duncan Koontz spoke to many organizations before, during, and after her NEA presidency. Even as she went on to other duties, she was still extremely concerned about the educational system, the children, and the teachers. Delivering a speech to a group of retired teachers, she told them that ''even though they are retired, they still have a contribution to make to the school children of today because of their vast experience and wisdom'' (''Once A Teacher,'' 28).

At the twenty-first annual meeting of the American Association of Colleges for Teacher Education, held in Chicago, February 26, 1969, Elizabeth Duncan Koontz was the tenth Charles W. Hunt Lecturer. Her speech, ''A Consumer's Hopes and Dreams For Teacher Education,'' discussed her hopes and dreams for teacher education: Teacher education should become a joint endeavor between the practitioners in the field and the college and university personnel; it should become an educational continuum keeping abreast of new techniques in teaching; it should be individualized; and a systematic orientation and induction of prospective teachers into the actual world of teaching should be provided.

Koontz Heads Women's Bureau

In addition to her work in education, Koontz was also active in women's rights. In January 1969, President Richard Nixon appointed her director of the United States Department of Labor Women's Bureau—the first black director—and subsequently she became deputy assistant secretary for Labor Employment Standards. While in that position, she became the United States delegate to the United Nations' Commission on the Status of Women, which was responsible for the resolution on the International Women's Year Observance in 1975.

Upon assuming her new position, Koontz said:

> Women in America are not realizing their full potentials as workers, women do not have equal access to positions in all fields and many are in lower-paying jobs. They have not broken into that area so nebulously called, ''men's work.''
>
> When there was heavy work to be done, women were not capable of doing it, but in the push-button technology of today, when brains count more than brawn, there is no reason for women to be limited in their choice of jobs (''Black Women: Double Discrimination,'' 18).

The new Women's Bureau director also spoke out constantly for improving the working conditions of one of the lowest-paid menial occupations that has traditionally been the lot of minority women—domestic work.

Whether pointing out the unnecessary prejudices against women who work or proclaiming the rights of minority people to a decent life, Elizabeth Duncan Koontz continually expressed the deep-rooted belief that the most important factor involved in gaining meaningful employment is getting an adequate education. She believed education was the foundation of job training and preparation for all people in this country.

In March 1972 Koontz was designated as a special counselor on women's programs under the secretary of labor. Her duties were to coordinate women's programs with other federal agencies through the Interdepartmental Committee on the Status of Women. She also maintained public contact with groups, individuals, and organizations outside the federal government to strengthen the role of women in the work force. In March 1973 Elizabeth Duncan Koontz resigned as director of the Women's Bureau.

Koontz was a member of many professional and civic organizations, including the National Education Association (life member), the North Carolina Association of Educators, Phi Beta Kappa, Phi Delta Kappa Sorority, the National Academy of Public Administration, the National Black Child Development Institute, the Women's Equity Action League, the National Commission on Working Women, and the National Organization of Women.

Her participation in civic, religious, and educational organizations has long been rewarding and followed a family tradition of public service. She has been recognized for her work by honorary memberships in such groups as the American Home Economics Association, the Zeta Phi Beta Sorority, and the Altrusa Club, and holds honorary degrees from approximately three dozen colleges and universities throughout the country.

Elizabeth Duncan Koontz has received numerous other awards and honors. In May 1967 her alma mater, Livingstone College, awarded her an honorary doctor of humane letters. At the fifty-third annual meeting of the Association for the Study of Negro Life and History in 1968, she received the Distinguished Service Award, the highest honor bestowed by the association. The award is given to persons making outstanding contributions to Afro-American life and is given in honor of Carter G. Woodson, the association's founder. While she was director of the Women's Bureau, her hometown of Salisbury, North Carolina, honored her on ''Libby Koontz Day.''

On June 30, 1969, Koontz was the recipient of the H. Council Trenholm Memorial Award at the NEA Human

Rights Awards Dinner in Philadelphia. She was one of the women honored in 1970 by *Ladies Home Journal* as America's Seventy-five Most Important Women. The selection was made on the basis of those who have made the greatest impact on our civilization within the last five years.

In 1973 Koontz was honored by the National Education Association for four years of outstanding service to the advancement of women's rights in America. She was lauded for having federal contract compliance guidelines extended in 1970 to eliminate discrimination against women.

From 1973 to 1975 Koontz was coordinator of nutrition programs in the North Carolina Department of Human Resources. In 1975 she was assistant state superintendent for teacher education in the North Carolina Department of Public Instruction.

In 1975 President Gerald Ford presented awards to five women honored by the American Newspapers Women's Club for distinguished service in international affairs. Elizabeth Duncan Koontz was one of the recipients. And on October 26, 1976, she was recipient of the College Board Medal for Distinguished Service to Education at the 1976 College Entrance Examination Board National Forum.

From February to June 1977, Koontz was chair of the North Carolina International Women's Year Coordinating Committee and State Meeting. In July 1977 she chaired the National Commission on Working Women. In September 1977 she was a delegate to the National Women's Conference in Houston, Texas. From July 1977 to June 1979, she was a member of the North Carolina Council on the Status of Women. In October 1977 she was appointed as an advisory board member of the Institute for Education and Research on Women and Work, Cornell University, New York. In September 1977 she served as a national advisory committee member for Leadership Training for Women in the Public Service. From October 20 to November 10, 1977, Koontz participated in the American/Polish Education Scholars' Exchange sponsored by the United States Office of Education for three weeks in Poland. On November 28, 1977, she was the recipient of the North Carolina Medallion Award for Public Service for 1977.

In March, April, and May 1978, she participated in the second Government Executives Institute at the School of Business Administration of the University of North Carolina at Chapel Hill. On June 21, 1978, she coordinated a Proposal Writing Workshop sponsored by Far West Laboratory, contractor for the Women's Educational Equity program. In June 1978 Koontz was appointed by President Jimmy Carter to the National Advisory Committee for Women. In July 1978 she became a member of the Selection Committee for the Rockefeller Public Service Awards. In September 1978 she became a member of the Gallaudet College Board of Fellows in Washington. She was appointed in 1979 as vice-chairman of the Commission on North Carolina Year 2000 by Governor James B. Hunt, Jr. Koontz traveled extensively, both as a representative of the government and various organizations, as well as on a personal tour around the world.

Elizabeth Duncan Koontz's humanitarian interest in people of all ages, races, and socio-economic conditions has been widely recognized by private and public groups. Her personal commitment to service combined with skill and training have warranted the many honors, citations, and distinguished service awards she received during her lifetime.

Elizabeth Duncan Koontz retired in April 1982. She and her husband, Harry L. Koontz, whom she married on November 26, 1947, later athletic director and instructor at Dunbar High School in Spencer, North Carolina, made their home in Salisbury, where she continued to pursue her interests in education and the status of women, along with her many civic concerns. They were childless.

Soft-spoken, popular, charming, and highly effective Elizabeth Duncan Koontz has been referred to as one with "easy competence," and "serene self-confidence," who was unpretentious, tough, tactful, and fiercely committed to the young. She liked to hunt, fish, play tennis, bridge, and basketball, work crossword puzzles, and read. Koontz died on January 6, 1989, after a heart attack at her home in Salisbury, North Carolina.

References

Banas, Casey. "Urge Teachers Help in Forming Policies." *Chicago Tribune*, 7 July 1967.

"Black Women: Double Discrimination." *Sepia* 18 (September 1969): 18.

Current Biography Yearbook. New York: H. W. Wilson, 1969. 244-46. Photograph, p. 245.

"Educator's Leader." *Philadelphia Inquirer* 6 July 1967.

Edwards, Arlene. "The Nation Will Know About Libby's Concern." *Winston Salem (N.C.) Journal* (14 January 1968).

Howell, Deborah. "NEA Urged to Fight Tax, Quality Gap." *Minneapolis Star*, 6 July 1967.

Koontz, Elizabeth Duncan. "Education in Changing Times." *Wisconsin Education Association* (January 1968): 11-12.

———. "New Priorities and Old Prejudices." *Educational Digest* 36 (May 1971): 32-33.

———. "Why Teachers are Militant." *Education Digest* 33 (January 1968): 12-14.

———. "The Profession and the Media." *Today's Education* 58 (February 1969): 17.

———. "We Can Lick the Giants." *Ohio Schools* (October 1968).

National Education Association. Department of Classroom Teachers. *Official Report.* Miami Beach, Fla.: 1965-1966.

"NEA President Speaks at ATA." *NEA Today*, (8 November 1968).

"NEA Views on Teacher Strikes." *Childhood Education* 45 (April 1969): 435-37.

Obituary. *Current Biography Yearbook.* New York: H. W. Wilson, 1989. 665.

Obituary. *New York Times*, 8 January 1989. 26.

"Once A Teacher, Always A Teacher." *NTRA Journal* (November/December 1968): 28.

"President Koontz on Decentralization." *NEA Today* (24 September 1968).

"A Symposium: 'What's Right in American Education." *Educational Horizons* 54 (Spring 1976): 144-45.

Weil, Martin. "Elizabeth Koontz, Former Head of Women's Bureau, Dies." *Washington Post*, 7 January 1989. 36.

Janet Sims-Wood

L

Jewel Stradford Lafontant

(1928-)

Lawyer, ambassador

Ambassador Jewel Stradford Lafontant, a former Chicago attorney, is an ambassador-at-large and United States coordinator for refugee affairs. Lafontant, who reports directly to President Bush, was appointed to this position in August 1989. Lafontant was born in Chicago on April 22, 1928, the younger child of Francis Stradford and Aida Arbella (Carter) Stradford. Her mother, an artist, was born in Camden, South Carolina, on November 14, 1895, and died April 29, 1972. Francis Stradford, a lawyer, was born in Lawrenceburg, Kentucky, on September 3, 1892, and died April 29, 1963. Jewel Stradford was married to Ernest Lafontant, an attorney who was born on March 1, 1924, and died October 1976. She has one son, John W. Rogers, Jr., from this marriage. Nurtured by an environment of excellence and achievement, Lafontant's son, a Princeton graduate in economics, is president and chief executive of Ariel Capital Management. Jewel Stradford Lafontant is now married to Naguib S. Mankarious, an international business consultant.

Lafontant, who received a bachelor of arts degree from Oberlin College and a doctor of laws degree from the University of Chicago, was a trial attorney with the Legal Aid Bureau from 1947 to 1954. From 1955 to 1958 she was an assistant United States District Attorney in Chicago. An article in the Washington *Star News* (4 April 1974) notes that "Mrs. Lafontant is very conscientious in following her father's footsteps to the Supreme Court." The article further notes that it was because of her father that she attended Oberlin. As a young practicing attorney, Lafontant worked with her father. Francis Stradford's credits include the Hansberry case he won before the Supreme Court in the mid-1940s, which allowed blacks to live in previously segregated sections of Chicago. The case was that of Carl and Nannie Hansberry, the couple who moved their family to an all-white neighborhood on Chicago's South Side. The Hansberry family and the Stradfords were very close. Jewel Lafontant recalled sitting in the Hansberry's living room as bricks came through their windows. Lafontant believes that social changes can and should be made through the law. She also remembers going to Chicago restaurants during the 1940s and being turned away because they did not welcome blacks.

Legal History Embraces Lafontant

Lafontant's distinguished career as an attorney includes a senior partnership in the firm of Vedder, Price, Kaufman and Kammholz and executive vice president and director of the Ariel Capital Management Company. These connections were suspended when she became the first female deputy solicitor general of the United States during the Nixon administration. In this capacity, she argued cases before the United States Supreme Court and also served as United States representative to the United Nations. Lafontant's achievements and accomplishments have been numerous, including directorship of the following companies: Equitable Life, Revlon, Mobil Oil, Midway Airlines, the Hanes Corporation, Trans World Airlines, Pantry Pride, and TBG Broadcasting.

Lafontant, who was a fellow of the International Academy of Trial Lawyers and the American Bar Association, has served on numerous boards and civic interest groups as chairperson of the Illinois Advisory Committee to the United States Civil Rights Commission, commissioner of the Blue Ribbon Commission on the Administration of Justice in Cook County, commissioner of the Martin Luther King, Jr., Federal Holiday Commission, and commissioner of the Chicago Tourism Council. She has been a member of the Labor Relations Committee of the United States Chamber of Commerce, the President's Commission on Executive Exchange, the visiting committee of the University of Chicago Law School, the board of overseers for the Hoover Institution, director of the Capital Development Board of the State of Illinois, director of Project HOPE, director of the Council on Foreign Relations, director of the Illinois Humane Society—Serving Vulnerable Children, a trustee of Howard University, a member of the Chicago Committee, the Citizen's Committee on the Juvenile Court and the national advisory board of the Salvation Army, and an honorary member of Rotary International.

A guiding force in the recruitment of black entrepreneurs, Lafontant encourages blacks to build skills and pursue independence. In an interview in *Dollars and Sense*, December 1982, Lafontant articulated her position that black entrepreneurs should encourage blacks to be producers as well as consumers. Because of her prowess, acumen, and experience, Lafontant is respected by the corporate world as well as by members of the black community for her candor and influence. In the *Dollars and Sense* interview, she stated:

> They say that blacks don't measure up. Then you ask them where are they recruiting and they begin reciting all the black schools. I don't want to be treading on anyone's toes but I am partial to Oberlin College because I finished Oberlin and my father and his father, since it was the first college to admit blacks. . . . Some of the companies exclude schools like Oberlin and recruit from the all-black colleges in the deep South, where they have both good and bad schools. You also have some very poor ones that are barely accredited. So if you recruit at those you might have a legitimate reason for not hiring. . . . I asked them not to exclude black colleges, but include schools such as Oberlin. I hate those self-fulfilling prophecies, those "I gave you a chance and you couldn't make [it] kind of generalizations." So I see recruitment efforts as part of my role and I am not doing nearly enough (9).

Addressing the difficulty of overcoming certain misconceptions and biases blacks encounter in the corporate world and a racist attitude that is pervasive at the middle-management level, Lafontant believes that individuals must be educated so that they do not place people in stereotypical roles, recognizing that even though people may look different, they can achieve as well as other groups. "Incompetence is not distinguishable by color" (*Dollars and Sense*).

References

"Attorney Jewel Lafontant Joins 114 Lawyer Firm." *Jet* (3 October 1983): 33.

Contributions of Black Women to America. Volume 1. Ed. Marianna W. Davis. Columbia, S.C.: Kenday Press, 1982.

Editors of Ebony. *Ebony Success Library*. Volume 1. *1,000 Successful Blacks*. Chicago: Johnson Pub. Co. 1973.

Encyclopedia of Black America. Eds. W. Augustus Low and Virgil A. Clift. New York: McGraw Hill, 1981.

"Executive Changes." *New York Times*, 16 March 1972.

"Former Business and Professional Honoree to Chair Salute to Women." *Dollars and Sense* 14 (April/May 1988): 9.

Hine, Darlene Clark and Patrick Kay Bidelman. *Black Women in the Middle West Project: A Comprehensive Resource Guide*. Indiana: Indiana Historical Society and Purdue University, 1986.

"An Interview with Jewel S. Lafontant." *Dollars and Sense* 8 (December 1982/January 1983): 18-22.

"Jewel Lafontant Named to High Post by Nixon." *Jet* 43 (4 January 1973): 10.

"Jewel Lafontant to Chair Salute to 100 Women." *Dollars and Sense* 14 (February/March 1988): 9.

"Lafontant Oversees Refugee Affairs in New State Post." *Jet* 76 (7 August 1989): 9.

"The Lawyer is Truly a Lady: J. Lafontant, U. S. Deputy Solicitor General." *Ebony* 28 (April 1973): 146-152.

"Nixon Plan for Black Woman for Appeals Court Set Back." *Washington Post* 2 February 1974.

"Praising a Woman Lawyer." *Washington Post*, 18 April 1973.

Washington Star News, 4 April 1974.

Who's Who Among Black Americans, 1990/91. Detroit: Gale Research, 1990.

Simmona E. Simmons

Daisy Lampkin

(1888-1965)

Political activist, suffragist, civil rights reformer, organization official

Daisy Elizabeth Adams Lampkin was an activist for political rights, women's rights, and civil rights and particularly championed the rights of black Americans. Lampkin was a prominent black citizen of Pittsburgh, Pennsylvania, for more than half of the twentieth century. She served as a field secretary for the NAACP from 1927 to 1947. In 1935 Lampkin inherited the position of national field secretary from William Pickens. Due to recurring health problems with arthritis and sciatica, Lampkin was forced to step down from her position as field secretary in 1947. That year, Lampkin joined the board of directors of the NAACP and served on the board until her death in 1965. While working for the NAACP, Lampkin served on a variety of committees, including the Budget Committee, the Life Membership Committee, the 1964 National Nominating Committee, the Public Relations Committee, and the Committee on Branches.

Lampkin was born August 9, 1888, in Reading, Pennsylvania. She died on March 10, 1965, at her home in Pittsburgh, Pennsylvania, five months after suffering a stroke while conducting a membership drive campaign for the NAACP in Camden, New Jersey, on October 6, 1964. The telegram from Roy Wilkins, Executive director of the NAACP, announcing Lampkin's death praised her work as having "made a lasting contribution to the cause of civil rights."

Wilkins was a close friend of the Lampkins, and he commented in the same telegram:

> People throughout the nation offer their deepest sympathy upon the death of our distinguished Board member and dear friend Daisy Lampkin. [To] you and to those who knew her personally her death is especially grievous. To the civil rights movement her passing means the loss of a stalwart supporter and a courageous champion.

Lampkin was the only child of George S. Adams and Rosa Ann (Proctor) Adams. Lampkin moved to Pittsburgh in 1909. In 1912 she married William L. Lampkin, a restaurant operator. Daisy Lampkin was active in several organizations. These organizations included the *Pittsburgh Courier* Publishing Company, for which she served as vice-president from 1929 until 1965; and the Lucy Stone Civic League, of which Lampkin was president for more than forty years (the league awarded scholarships to local students and had awarded more than six thousand dollars to them by 1943); the Links; the National Association of Colored Women (NACW), which Lampkin served as the national organizer, as vice-president, and as chairperson of the executive board; the National Council of Negro Women, which she helped establish and of which she was a life member; the National Republican Convention (in 1933 Lampkin was the first black woman ever elected to serve as an alternate delegate-at-large); Delta Sigma Theta Sorority, for which she led the headquarter's fund-raising effort in 1952; and the NAACP. Lampkin was often in the forefront of these organizations as an outstanding worker and officer. Her fund-raising abilities were employed by several of the organizations to which she belonged.

Although Lampkin was an asset to any group she was associated with, her work with the NAACP appears to be among her best. During her tenure with the NAACP, Lampkin formed close personal and working friendships with NAACP notables and other prominent black leaders of the time, such as Walter White, Roy Wilkins, Nannie Helen Burroughs, and one of her assistant field secretaries, Ella Baker, who came to the NAACP in the 1940s and later became well-known in her own right as a prominent civil rights worker and activist. Lampkin is also credited with bringing Justice Thurgood Marshall to the NAACP to join its Legal Defense Committee.

When Lampkin had to resign as field secretary, her active pace did not lessen. Her work agenda remained quite active in the branch campaign drives and she continued to lend her fund-raising expertise while overseeing many of the membership activities of that division. During her longstanding career with the NAACP, Lampkin instituted a unique membership-drive technique—team method of fund-raising—that facilitated the arduous task of these drives. Cities were divided into four areas, each assigned a director. The directors held meetings twice a week and relied on churches throughout the cities to host the campaign efforts. This approach was highly successful. Lampkin's success in fund-

Daisy Lampkin

raising is clearly evidenced by her two campaigns in 1962 and 1963 in Pittsburgh, Pennsylvania, and Camden, New Jersey. Due to Lampkin's activities, the Pittsburgh chapter increased its membership by 4,647 members between 1962 and 1963. In 1963 that chapter boasted a membership of ten thousand. Similarly in Camden, membership in the chapter increased from 2,705 in 1962 to 4,078 in 1963.

During the Camden campaign, Lampkin was able to raise close to eleven thousand dollars. Her successful campaign drive in Camden in 1963 could have probably been repeated had she not fallen ill while conducting a similar campaign there in 1964. Lampkin is also credited with incorporating youth divisions among her campaign drives. She believed young people were the nation's and the race's future, and she likely realized that young people possessed the energy and verve needed to sustain these often tiresome endeavors. Lampkin's hopes for black youth were voiced in a speech she delivered in 1958, in which she attested to the necessity of black youth to know their history "so that they may be proud of their heritage" (Lampkin, "Integration Seen as Challenge to Negroes and Whites Alike").

In addition to working for the NAACP in a seemingly tireless capacity and holding membership in several organizations, Lampkin was also an active member of her church in Pittsburgh, Grace Memorial Presbyterian Church. In 1947 Lampkin was inducted into the Delta Sigma Theta Sorority as an honorary member. Delta Sigma Theta is a predominantly black sorority that emphasizes social service and community involvement. Lampkin was the first woman to be so honored by the sorority since 1935, when it admitted the outstanding black woman educator, activist, and presidential appointee, Mary McLeod Bethune. She was sworn into the Alpha

Epsilon Chapter of the sorority in Pittsburgh. In 1952 the national officers of Delta, including its president, Dorothy I. Height (a renowned activist in her own right), appointed Lampkin to head the fund-raising drive to purchase a national headquarters for the sorority in Washington, D.C. Writer Paula Giddings remarked that the sorority leaders needed someone who could run a "well-thought-out, systematic campaign . . . " and decided "to employ a seasoned specialist in such matters to lead it: Daisy Lampkin" (Giddings, *In Search of Sisterhood,* 227).

Black Women's Work Held Major Responsibility

Lampkin viewed the work done by black women for the rights of blacks and the rights of women as special responsibilities of herself and others like her. In a letter to her good friend, the prominent educator and activist Nannie Helen Burroughs of Washington, D.C., Lampkin stated that Burroughs was a prime example of "Negro womanhood" and that Burroughs's "every act must be the act of every Negro woman in America. It is a terrible responsibility, but it is yours" (Daisy E. Lampkin to Nannie Helen Burroughs, 20 May 1928, Nannie Burroughs Papers).

In other matters, Lampkin was equally adamant and vocal as well. In 1935 she and other prominent black women, such as Charlotte Hawkins Brown, Lugenia Burns Hope, and Mary McLeod Bethune, attended a meeting of the Association of Southern Women for the Prevention of Lynching (ASWPL), a white organization formed by activist Jessie Daniel Ames, to tell their white counterparts that the evils of lynching had far-reaching ramifications beyond the unjustifiable murder of often innocent black men and boys. Lampkin and other black women felt that the white women's position against lynching was not as hard as it should have been. At the time of the meeting in Atlanta, Georgia, the Costigan-Wagner Bill had been introduced in Congress. This act would have required federal intervention in cases of lynching when local authorities did not respond to the crime. The ASWPL did not endorse this measure and Lampkin warned these women that the act's opponents would use the white women's silence as a concession and they would also "use it to their advantage when they . . . say that . . . southern white women did not endorse the Costigan-Wagner Bill" (Quoted in Giddings, *When and Where I Enter,* 209).

Lampkin was also outspoken on the subject of integration. In a speech to the New Rochelle Branch of the NAACP, Lampkin outlined the importance of integration for black Americans. She declared, "No man is ready to meet the challenge of integration unless he is certain that he and his people have earned their place in an integrated society . . . and the Negro has earned his place. Living in an integrated society is his right; it is not a privilege extended to him by others" ("Integration Seen as Challenge to Negroes and Whites Alike").

It is apparent that Lampkin was a woman dedicated to the cause of civil rights for all, particularly black Americans. This is evidenced by her unselfish commitment to her race. Lampkin fell ill while conducting business for the NAACP. Her life's work and her commitment to civil rights and social justice is a testimony to all of those black women who worked so tirelessly before her and to those she helped to train and mold them into women of whom anyone could be proud. It is not surprising that a number of organizations honored Lampkin during her lifetime.

Shortly before her death, the North Jersey Chapter of the Links, a prominent black women's community and social society, planned to honor Lampkin. Unfortunately, Lampkin did not live to see this honor bestowed upon her. But Daisy Lampkin's work and life, her contributions to the NAACP, the black American community, and to all Americans will honor her memory. One of her former *Courier* employees and current biographer, Edna McKenzie, asserts that without Lampkin, "the NAACP would not have become a power." Lampkin was posthumously honored by the Pennsylvania Historical Commission in 1983 when her house was recognized as a historical landmark. The marker was placed at Lampkin's home largely through the tremendous efforts of McKenzie. This was a particularly significant occasion since Lampkin was the first black woman in the state of Pennsylvania to have been so honored.

References

"Biographical Sketch of Mrs. Daisy E. Lampkin." 9 February 1940, 24 November 1964, NAACP Papers.

Childs, Romaine. Interview with author, 12 November 1990.

Crisis NAACP 80th Anniversary Issue (January 1989): 85-98.

Current, Gloster B. Memo to Mr. [Henry Lee] Moon, 18 December 1963. Board of Directors Files, III, A, 24, NAACP Papers.

Forsythe, Frances T. To Roy Wilkins, 7 March 1965. NAACP Papers.

Giddings, Paula. *When and Where I Enter.* New York: Bantam Books, 1985.

———. *In Search of Sisterhood: Delta Sigma Theta and the Challenge of the Black Sorority Movement.* New York: William Morrow, 1988.

Howard, Elizabeth Fitzgerald. "Daisy Elizabeth Adams Lamkin." *Notable American Women: The Modern Period.* Cambridge: Harvard University Press, 1980.

Lampkin, Daisy E. "Integration Seen as Challenge to Negroes and Whites Alike," Press release of an address to the New Rochelle NAACP Branch, 24 October 1958. NAACP Papers.

Lampkin, Daisy E. To Nannie Helen Burroughs, 20 May 1928. Nannie Helen Burroughs Papers.

Lerner, Gerda, ed. *Black Women in White America*. New York: Pantheon Books, 1973.

McKenzie, Edna. Interview with author, 4 January 1991.

McKenzie, Edna. "Daisy Lampkin: A Life of Love and Service." *Pennsylvania Heritage* 9 (Summer 1983): 11.

"Mrs. Daisy Lampkin, NAACP Official." Special to the *Herald Tribune*, Pittsburgh, Pennsylvania, 11 March 1965.

"Mrs. Daisy Lampkin to Be Delta Honorary Soror: NAACP Executive is the First Honorary Member in Twenty Years." *Pittsburgh Courier*, 3 February 1947.

"Mrs. Lampkin Directs Over the Top Drive." NAACP Press Release, 20 December 1963. NAACP Papers.

Rouse, Jacqueline Anne. *Lugenia Burns Hope: Black Southern Reformer*. Athens, Georgia: University of Georgia Press, 1989.

Salem, Dorothy. *To Better Our World: Black Women in Organized Reform, 1890-1920*. Brooklyn: Carlson Publishing, 1990.

Wilkins, Roy. Telegram to William Lampkin, 11 March 1965.

Collections

Primary sources on Daisy Elizabeth Lampkin are in the Board of Directors Files, 1956-1960, NAACP, and in the Branch Files, 1940-1955, Library of Congress, Manuscript Division, Madison Building, Washington, D.C. Documents are also in the Nannie Helen Burroughs Papers, Library of Congress, Manuscript Division. The most complete collection of Lampkin's written work, interviews with Lampkin's friends, and Lampkin's personal papers are in the possession of Edna McKenzie, Roanoke, Pennsylvania.

Lisa Beth Hill

Pinkie Gordon Lane

(1923-)

Poet, writer

Pinkie Gordon Lane, the first black American to be appointed Louisiana State Poet Laureate—named by Governor Buddy Roemer in July 1989—was born in Philadelphia, Pennsylvania, on January 13, 1923, the daughter of a longshoreman, William Alexander Gordon, and a domestic worker, Inez Addie (West) Gordon. She was the youngest of four children and the only one to live past infancy. In her youth she was active in the Methodist church and graduated from the Philadelphia School for Girls in 1940, the same year that her father died. After she had worked in a sewing factory for five years, her mother also died, and Pinkie Gordon was persuaded by a friend to seek financial assistance for higher education. She applied to Spelman College in Atlanta, where her mother had attended secondary school. Winning a four-year scholarship to the college, she received her bachelor's degree in English with a minor in art, graduating magna cum laude and class valedictorian in 1949.

During her senior year at Spelman, she met and married Ulysses Simpson Lane, a teacher, and worked as an English teacher in the public schools of Florida and Georgia between 1949 and 1955. Returning to Atlanta, she received a master's degree in English in 1956 from Atlanta University; her thesis was "The Old and the New Philosophy in the Poetry of John Dryden." Later that year she moved with her husband to Baton Rouge, Louisiana, where he joined the faculty of the Education Division at Southern University, and she joined the English Department, first at Leland College in Baker, Louisiana (1957-1959), and then at Southern University (1959-1968). Her only child, Gordon (now a jazz musician who lives in Los Angeles), was born in 1963, and she soon began to pursue her Ph.D. in English at Louisiana State University, at the time still a segregated university on the undergraduate level. In 1967 she became the first black American woman to receive her Ph.D. at LSU; her area of specialization was Renaissance English literature, and her dissertation was on the subject of Sir Thomas Browne.

Sadly, after several years of regular trips to New Orleans hospitals, her husband died of liver and kidney disease in 1971, when her son was seven years old. She wrote about his sickness and death in several of her poems, particularly the four-part poem "Dying: Poems for Ulysses Simpson Lane."

Lane first started writing poetry in 1962 (before that she had written mainly fiction). In Lane's words, "In that same year a student of mine asked me had I ever heard of Gwendolyn Brooks. I said no. I found her book and was amazed because I had never read a book of poetry by a black woman. She became my role model" (Interview with Pinkie Gordon Lane, 28 July 1986). Since that time Lane has published poems in numerous journals, including *The Black Scholar, Callaloo, Ms. Magazine, Black American Literature Forum, The New Orleans Review, Nimrod, Obsidian: Black Literature in Review, The Southern Review*, and *Essence*. She has also published three volumes of poetry—*Wind Thoughts* (South and West, 1972), *The Mystic Female* (South and West, 1978), which was nominated by the publisher for the 1979 Pulitzer Prize for Poetry, and *I Never Scream* (Lotus, 1985); a fourth volume of poetry, *The Girl at the Window* (Baton Rouge: Louisiana State University Press), was scheduled for publication in the fall of 1991. She has also read her poetry throughout the nation and in four African countries—Ghana, Cameroon, Zambia, and South Africa—and has won numerous honors and awards. From 1974 to 1980 she directed the annual Melvin A. Butler Poetry Festival, sponsored by the Southern University Department of

English, bringing noted poets to the campus from all over the country. From 1974 to her retirement in 1986, she served as chair of the English department.

Lane's poems are largely autobiographical/confessional and have come to be called "quiet poems." Having begun her writing career in the 1960s and being extremely conscious of the themes and styles of acknowledged leaders of the Black Aesthetic movement in poetry, such as Imamu Amiri Baraka, Sonia Sanchez, and Nikki Giovanni, she felt compelled to recognize the existence of social violence and war, but she held on tenaciously to her right to compose personal, contemplative lyric poetry about nature, personal life, family, career, the city and its occupations.

Poetry Reflects Louisiana Landscape

Although Lane sometimes writes about her early childhood experiences in her poems, most often she refers to the Louisiana landscape, particularly Baton Rouge, and her experiences there. The words that recur most frequently in Lane's poems are *silence* and *stillness*. "I use the word *silence* in two ways," notes Lane. "In one way it can be a form of terror because of lack of communication. In another form, it is a way of getting into yourself—a kind of existential cutting yourself loose and getting back into the perimeters of your own confines. Existentially, we're alone and there is no way I can totally communicate with you, even while we're talking" (Interview with Pinkie Gordon Lane, 28 July 1986). It is obvious throughout the body of Lane's poetry that the evocation of place, even the attention to details of events in the "real" world, such as the condition of people on welfare, the war in Bangladesh, the murder of a newborn baby on board a plane—all of these things point decidedly inward toward the conflicts within the poet/speaker.

Lane believes that poetry should be made available to as many persons as possible, and she reads her works widely in public and at seminars and workshops. She has continued to promote the ideas of the annual Melvin A. Butler Poetry Festival in other similar activities. In 1985-1986 she developed "Louisiana Poetry"—a series of poetry readings by Lane, Tom Dent, Sue Owen, Roger Kamenetz, Charles de Gravelles, Daniel Fogel, and Glenn Swetman, on Louisiana Public Broadcasting—which was broadcast randomly during the day over several months. In September 1988 she and composer Dinos Constanides organized a program of poetry and music at the Louisiana State University School of Music. She has also participated in workshops with other noted black American scholar-writers, such as the workshop "A Con Fusion of Light," held at Radford University (Radford, Virginia) in September 1989; the other participants included Maya Angelou, Vertamae Grosvenor, Daryl Cumber Dance, Woodie King, Jr., and Houston A. Baker.

For her poetry, service as editor (poetry editor, *Black American Literature Forum;* contributing and advisory editor, *The Black Scholar* and *Callaloo)*, and community work in the promotion of poetry and literacy, Pinkie Gordon Lane has received numerous awards and honors, including the Louisiana State Poet Laureate; Image Award, NAACP; the Middle Atlantic Writers Association (MAWA) Creative Achievement Award; the Delta Pearl Award of the Baton Rouge Alumnae Chapter of Delta Sigma Theta Sorority; Arts Ambassador Award of the Arts Council of Greater Baton Rouge; National Award for Achievement in Poetry, College Language Association; the Black Caucus of the National Council of Teachers of English Award of Recognition for Artistic Achievement; Women of Achievement Award, Baton Rouge Area YWCA; and National Award for Outstanding Achievement in the Arts and Humanities, Washington, D.C., Chapter of the National Alumnae Association of Spelman College. In her poetry, reading, teaching, and dissemination of poetry, she works with the ideal that poetry is "restorative" and:

> that uttering truth is not the way to become popular, but it *is* the way to become whole; that beauty, after all, is what matters, and that it lifts us into the hemisphere of the spirit—our ultimate survival, our final and most profound union with our fellowman (Lane, "About the Author," *I Never Scream,* n.p.).

References

Bryan, Violet Harrington. "Evocations of Place and Culture in the Works of Four Contemporary Black Louisiana Writers: Brenda Marie Osbey, Sybil Kein, Elizabeth Brown-Guillory, and Pinkie Gordon Lane." *Louisiana Literature* 4 (Fall 1987): 49-60.

Craig, Marilyn B. "Pinkie Gordon Lane." *Dictionary of Literary Biography*. Vol. 41, *Afro-American Poets Since 1955*. Edited by Trudier Harris and Thadious Davis. Detroit: Gale Research, 1985. 212-16.

Goldsmith, Sarah Sue. "Pinkie Gordon Lane: A Poet in Search of New Mountains to Climb." *Sunday Advocate* (Baton Rouge), 31 August 1986. Includes photographs.

Henderson, Stephen. *Understanding the New Black Poetry, Black Speech, and Black Music as Poetic References.* New York: William Morrow, 1973.

Hullings, Jan. "Pinkie Gordon Lane." *States Times* (Baton Rouge), 27 February 1984.

Lane, Pinkie Gordon. *I Never Scream*. Detroit: Lotus Press, 1985.

Lane, Pinkie Gordon. Interview with the author, 28 July 1986.

———. *The Mystic Female*. Fort Smith, Ark.: South and West, 1978.

———. *Wind Thoughts*. Fort Smith, Ark.: South and West, 1972.

Newman, Dorothy W. "Lane's Mystic Female." *Callaloo* 2 (February 1979): 153-55.

Rowland, Lillian D. Review of Pinkie Gordon Lane's *I Never Scream: New and Selected Poems. Black American Literature Forum* 20 (Fall 1986): 294-98.

Salaam, Kalumu ya, ed. *Word Up: Black Poetry of the 80s from the Deep South.* Atlanta: Beans and Brown Rice Publishers, 1990.

Sexton, Anne. "For My Lover, Returning to His Wife." In *The Complete Poems.* Boston: Houghton Mifflin, 1981.

Tillman, Henry. "Not Just Another Poet." *Greater Baton Rouge METRO* (January 1986).

Ward, Jerry W. Introduction. "Poet in Lyric Space." Pinkie Gordon Lane. *The Mystic Female.* Fort Smith, Ark.: South and West, 1978.

Collections

Some of Pinkie Gordon Lane's papers are included in the James Weldon Johnson Collection of Negro Arts and Letters, the Beinecke Rare Book and Manuscript Library, Yale University.

Violet Harrington Bryan

Lucy Laney

(1854-1933)

School founder, educator

Educational reformer Lucy Craft Laney was born on April 11, 1854, in Macon, Georgia, one of ten children of David and Louisa Laney. Her father had been born a slave in South Carolina and later became a carpenter and a notable Presbyterian minister in Macon. Her mother was a slave of the prominent Campbell family of Macon. After her parents married, David Laney purchased his wife's freedom, assuring the freedom of their children.

Laney, who devoted her entire life to assuring black people—particularly women—the freedom to be educated and to educate others, was taught to read and write at age four by her mother, who realized the importance of education. Although Louisa Laney was married, she continued to work for the Campbells as a domestic. Her duties included dusting their library, in which the young Laney would snuggle in a big chair, and read fairy stories and other books. Laney's precociousness was noticed by the Campbell's daughter, who selected books for her education. Laney received her preparatory education at Lewis High School, later known as Ballard-Hudson High School. The Campbells saw to it that she entered Atlanta University at the age of fifteen.

Lucy Laney

Atlanta University had been founded by New Englanders of the American Missionary Association (AMA) and was headed by a Yale University man, Edmund Asa Ware. The school was deeply entrenched in the classical liberal arts tradition. Laney proved herself a brilliant student and graduated in Atlanta University's first class (1873) of its Higher Normal Department. She pursued graduate work at the University of Chicago during the summers.

Also after graduation Laney taught for two years in the public schools of Savannah, Georgia. When her health began to fail, she went to Augusta, Georgia, seeking a milder climate. Once she regained her strength, she briefly returned to Savannah. She taught for short periods of time in Macon and Milledgeville, Georgia, as well.

School Founded for Black Youth

After her second stint in Savannah, Laney returned to Augusta. She had promised the Reverend William J. White of the Harmony Baptist Church that she would open a school for Augusta's black youth. An Atlanta University trustee, White was very interested in education and figured prominently in the inauguration of the Augusta Baptist Seminary (which was later moved to Atlanta and became the acclaimed Morehouse College).

In 1883, virtually penniless, Laney opened her school. She used the lecture room of Christ Presbyterian Church at the corner of Tenth and Telfair streets, where she taught her five students. Laney was particularly interested in the education of females, although males were not excluded from her school, for she looked primarily to women as the regenerative force to uplift her race. By the end of the second year, the enrollment had grown to 234 pupils. In 1886, the school was chartered under Georgia law as a normal and industrial school.

The white women of the neighborhood objected to the noise at the swiftly growing school, so Laney relocated in rented quarters in the 800 block of Gwinnett Street. The school continued its successful development and conditions became crowded. A mortician named Platt allowed Laney the use of a two-story frame structure on lower Calhoun Street while the Gwinnett site was enlarged to handle the increased enrollment.

Fire, flood, and financial difficulties plagued the burgeoning school. In 1887 Laney traveled to the Minneapolis meeting of the Presbyterian Board of Missions seeking support for her cause. The board was impressed with her work but offered only moral support. She later met people who would help her, including Francine E. H. Haines, who was corresponding secretary of the Women's Executive Committee of Home Missions of the Presbyterian Church. Haines was so thoroughly impressed with Laney and her work that she encouraged her friends to assist the school. Laney was duly impressed with Haines's zeal and named the school in her honor—Haines Normal and Industrial Institute. The Presbyterian Board of Missions began to offer financial support for teachers' subsistence and maintenance. By 1914 Haines Normal had grown to more than nine hundred students and more than thirty teachers. This was an anomaly in the state of Georgia, where there were few public high schools. (Atlanta would not boast a public high school until 1924.) Laney's mission to prepare her students to enter good colleges and become qualified teachers had started. This was a bold step for Laney to take—developing a liberal arts curriculum when Booker T. Washington's industrial education model was the vogue for blacks. Nonetheless, Haines gained a reputation as the best school of its kind for black Georgians, with its graduates comparing favorably with white students in training and capability.

Kindergarten and Nursing Opportunities Begin

In the early 1890s Haines established Augusta's first kindergarten and nurse education department. The city of Augusta let Laney have an old pesthouse as a hospital (some sources indicate that it was an old dance hall). A Canadian-trained graduate nurse was put in charge to train young women. The program evolved into the school of nursing at Augusta's University Hospital. A U.S. Government report in 1917 said of Haines Institute: "The management is effective. The administration of the principal has won for the school the confidence of both white and Colored people. The teachers are well prepared and doing thorough work." By the 1930s, elementary education was dropped from Haines's offering, leaving a four-year high school program and an additional year of college-level offerings. However, as the Great Depression deepened, the church withdrew its support and the school declined. After more than sixty years of sterling service to colored youth of the South, Haines Normal and Industrial School closed its doors in 1949 and its buildings were razed. A modern public school structure, Lucy C. Laney High School, was built on the site.

Laney died of nephritis and hypertension on October 23, 1933 in Augusta. Her death was noted in the national press. The *New York Age*, 11 November 1933, stated: "Lucy Craft Laney was buried October 26th from McGregory Hall Chapel. A simple ritual of burial was performed, attended by dignitaries, educators and leading representatives from every walk of life who came to pay their tribute of respect to one of the greatest Negro women of the twentieth century." The *Augusta Chronicle* wrote: "Lucy Laney was great because she loved people. She believed that all God's children had wings, though some of the wings are weak, and have never been tried. She could see in the most backward that divine personality which she endeavored to coax into flame." More than five thousand mourners are said to have passed her bier.

William Howard Taft, shortly before his inauguration as President of the United States, visited Haines, and in referring to Laney, said, "That a colored woman could have constructed this great institution of learning and brought it to its present state of usefulness speaks volumes for her capacity. Therefore, I shall go out of this meeting, despite the distinguished presence here, carrying in my memory only the figure of that woman who has been able to create all of this" (Hartshorne, 207). Similarly, W. E. B. Du Bois described Laney as "the dark vestal virgin who kept the fires of Negro education fiercely flaming in the rich but mean-spirited city of Augusta, Georgia" and considered her the leading woman educator among Negroes of the South, if not the nation. Francis J. Grimké, Presbyterian minister and scholar, simply stated that Laney "was a woman who stood for the best and noblest things in life."

Laney was very dark-skinned and stocky with closely cropped hair. She never cared to be in the public eye and was usually simply dressed, eschewing ostentation. Laney had a sense of social need and emphasized scholarship and character. Many of her competitors in the area of education were envious of her eloquence, fearing that this gift would win friends they were also seeking. Because she was a woman, many thought she was ahead of her time, and she did lead the way for future women educators: Mary McLeod Bethune at Bethune-Cookman College, Nannie Helen Burroughs of the National Training School, and Charlotte Hawkins Brown at Palmer Memorial Institute. Professional men looked askance at her position as principal of a school, as it was considered unseemly. Yet in 1904 she was honored with an A.M. from Lincoln University, a men's Presbyterian-related college in Pennsylvania, becoming the first woman so honored. Laney was also awarded honorary degrees from Atlanta University (1898) and South Carolina State College (1925).

Although Laney may have held her tongue on occasions, she never pretended to acquiesce in what she believed to be wrong. In 1916 Joel Spingarn, an NAACP leader, felt the need to call a conference of influential blacks to create a common front to fight insidious racism in America. Laney was among the fifty people invited to Amenia, New York, for the conference. The whole array of black leadership was present, from the conservative Tuskegee machine to the radicals like Du Bois and William Monroe Trotter.

In a paper delivered at the Hampton Negro Conference Number III, July 1899, Laney read a paper on "The Burden of the Educated Colored Woman" in which she said:

> If the educated colored woman has a burden—and we believe she has—what is that burden? How can it be lightened, how may it be lifted? What it is can be readily seen perhaps better than told, for it constantly annoys to irritation; it bulges out as the load of Bunyan's Christian—ignorance—with its inseparable companions, shame and prejudice. . . . The educated Negro woman, the woman of character and culture, is needed in the school room not only in the kindergarten, and in the primary and the secondary schools; but she is needed in high school, the academy, and the college. Only those of character and culture can do successful lifting, for she who would mould character must herself possess it. Not alone in the schoolroom can the intelligent woman lend a lifting hand, but as a public lecturer she may give advice, helpful suggestions, and important knowledge that will change a whole community and start its people on the upward way.

References

Bacote, Clarence A. *The Story of Atlanta University*. Princeton: Princeton University Press, 1969.

Brawley, Benjamin G. *Negro Builders and Heroes*. Chapel Hill, University of North Carolina Press, 1937.

Coleman, Kenneth and Charles S. Gurr, eds. *Dictionary of Georgia Biography*. Athens: University of Georgia Press, 1985.

Daniel, Sadie Iola. *Women Builders*. Washington, D.C.: Associated Publishers, 1931.

Dannett, Sylvia G. L. *Profiles of Negro Womanhood*. Vol. I. Negro Heritage Library. Educational Heritage, 1964,

Hartshorne, William Newton, ed. *An Era of Progress and Promise*. Boston: Princilla Pub. Co., 1910.

Jet 46 (5 September 1974): 22.

Lerner, Gerda, ed. *Black Women in White America*. New York: Pantheon Books, Random House, 1972.

Loewenberg, Bert James, and Ruth Bogin, eds. *Black Women in Nineteenth-Century American Life*. Pennsylvania State University Press, 1976.

Logan, Rayford W. "Lucy Craft Laney." In *Dictionary of American Negro Biography*, edited by Rayford W. Logan and Michael R. Winston. New York: Norton, 1982.

Low, W. Augustus, and Virgil A. Clift, eds. *Encyclopedia of Black America*. New York: McGraw-Hill, 1981.

Ovington, Mary White. *Portraits in Color*. New York: Viking, 1927.

"Remembrance of Things Past." *Encore* 4 (December 22, 1975): 3.

Richardson, Clement, ed. *National Cyclopedia of the Colored Race*. Chicago: n.p., 1919.

Sepia 8 (May 1960): 75.

St. Clair, Sadie Daniel. "Lucy Craft Laney." In *Notable American Women*, edited by Edward T. James. Cambridge: Harvard University Press, 1971.

Who's Who in Colored America, 1928-1929. New York: Who's Who in Colored America Corp., 1929.

Photographs

A painting of Laney is located in the Georgia Capitol building. A mature Laney photograph is published in *Who's Who in Colored America, 1918-19*, p. 227. A striking younger Laney photograph and views of campus buildings are in Hartshorne's *An Era of Progress and Promise*, p. 207, and *National Cyclopedia of the Colored Race*, p. 502. A photograph circa 1902 is in G. F. Richings, *Evidences of Progress Among Colored People*, 9th ed., Ferguson, 1902.

Casper LeRoy Jordan

Nella Larsen

(1891-1964)

Writer, librarian, nurse

Nella Larsen, novelist, short story writer, children's librarian, and nurse, was born in Chicago on April 13, 1891, and died on March 30, 1964. Her mother was Danish and her father West Indian. Larsen disclosed few details of her personal life, especially of her childhood. All she revealed of her early years was that her biological father died when she was two years old, that her mother remarried a white man of Danish ancestry, that her mother gave birth to a daughter during her second marriage, and that she and her sister attended a private elementary school in Chicago, where they lived in a neighborhood populated largely by people of Scandinavian and German origin. As an adult, Larsen was apparently not close to her family—rarely seeing her mother and half-sister. Larsen seems to have consciously removed

Nella Larsen

herself from their sphere so that they would not be embarrassed by her blackness (Davis, 182-83).

After attending high school in Chicago, Larsen enrolled in Fisk University's high school division in 1909-1910; this experience was her first in an all-black context. Apparently, some of the early experiences of her protagonist Helga in *Quicksand* are modeled on Larsen's experiences in this setting. Her sojourns after her year at Fisk include a stay in Denmark from 1910 to 1912, during which she enrolled in classes at the University of Copenhagen; a stay in New York City from 1912 to 1915, during which she was a nursing student at Lincoln University; and a one-year stay at Tuskegee Institute from 1915 to 1916, during which she served as an assistant superintendent of nurses. After 1916, Larsen spent most of her remaining years in or near New York City. Upon her return to New York City in 1916, Larsen worked in two primary capacities—as a nurse and a children's librarian. She was a nurse from 1916 to 1918 at Lincoln Hospital and a nurse from 1918 to 1921 for the New York City Health Department. It was during this period that she wed Elmer S. Imes, a Ph.D. recipient from the University of Michigan who was chairman of the physics department at Fisk. They married on May 3, 1919.

In 1920 Larsen appeared for the first time in print. "Three Scandinavian Games" by Nella Larsen Imes was published in the "Playtime" section of the June 1920 issue of *The Brownies' Book,* a monthly children's magazine edited by Jessie Fauset and W. E. B. Du Bois from January 1920 through December 1921. In her preface to "Three Scandinavian Games," Larsen indicates that she learned the games from little Danish children long ago in Denmark. In the July 1920 issue, Larsen was again the "Playtime" contributor, writing "Danish Fun," in which she recalls three games that evoke "pleasant memories" of her "childish days in Denmark," a reference to the period she was in Copenhagen as a young adult.

In 1923 Larsen exhibited continuing interest in children's literature when she completed training that culminated in her receiving a certificate from the New York Public Library School. By 1924 she was employed as a children's librarian at the 135th Street Branch of the New York Public Library, the location at which the Schomburg Collection began. Larsen remained at the library until 1926. The timing as well as the location and the nature of her employment positioned Larsen well for literary success. As the wife of Elmer Imes, she had access to Harlem's social circles, in which she was able to cultivate relationships with influential men such as Walter White—a guiding force of the NAACP, and according to David Levering Lewis, the "best nursemaid of the Renaissance" (139)—and Carl Van Vechten—white writer of *Nigger Heaven,* who embraced Harlem during the 1920s. Both men encouraged her to write—White even persuading his secretary to type Larsen's manuscript of her first novel and Van Vechten finding a publisher for her works.

Career as Novelist Launched

Larsen abandoned her profession as a children's librarian so that she could launch her career as a full-time novelist. Lewis claims that she was in poor health during this period and that she began to write novels during her convalescence (231). In 1926 she began her first novel, *Quicksand.* Completed in a little over six months, the novel was accepted for publication by Alfred A. Knopf, who was so favorably impressed that he requested two other manuscripts from Larsen. The first copies of the novel appeared on March 20, 1928. Larsen dedicated *Quicksand* to her husband.

A novel that presents its central character's phases of development, *Quicksand* has as its protagonist Helga Crane, who, like Larsen, was of mixed parentage. The daughter of a Danish mother and a West Indian father, Helga is trapped as the novel begins at Naxos, a Southern school where she teaches. Complicated and restless, throughout the novel Helga tries to alter her inner condition by changing her geographic context. Never satisfied, she moves from place to place in pursuit of happiness. With each setting the protagonist moves to another stage of her quest for self-definition.

As the novel begins, Helga abandons Naxos, a school modeled no doubt on Fisk and Tuskegee. Larsen's negative view of black colleges and of black intellectuals who perceive themselves as racial spokespersons is suggested by the name she assigns to the institution. Naxos is an anagram for Saxon. The implication of the name is that Naxos, "a showplace in the Black Belt, exemplification of the white man's magnanimity, refutation of the black man's inefficiency," is a setting in which blacks imitate whites and hence that the school is just as sterile and deadening as larger white society. Feeling out-of-step at the school, Helga yearns to belong but is unable to interact with her peers in ways that would make her part of their group. Feeling hemmed in by the hypocrisy and class consciousness at Naxos, she decides to leave. Fleeing the school means she must break her engagement to fellow teacher Jim Vayle, scion of a prominent black family, who in many ways personifies much of what she abhors about Naxos. Helga almost reverses her decision to flee after she talks with the school principal, Robert Anderson, to whom she is drawn physically. Finally, though, she holds firm to her decision and departs from the confining South, thus beginning an odyssey that has as its goal the discovery of her self and the winning of her happiness.

Helga journeys initially to Chicago, where she seeks out a white uncle, whose new wife rejects her. After great difficulty, Helga finds a job that requires her to travel with her employer, Mrs. Hayes-Rore, a racial-uplift orator, to New York. Though limited to the black metropolis that is Harlem, she is happy for a time working for a black insurance company and residing with Anne Gray, a cosmopolitan black widow who, like many other black middle-class Harlemites "stood for the immediate advancement of all things Negroid" but who hypocritically preferred Pavlova to Florence Mills and Walter Hampden to Paul Robeson. Just as Helga becomes unhappy in Harlem, a deus ex machina in the form of a check from her white uncle arrives, and she suddenly has the means to travel again. This time she journeys to Copenhagen—as did Larsen at one point in her life—to visit her mother's family.

In Denmark, Helga is free of one strain of racism but is subject to another. In Copenhagen she is seen as an exotic, primitive creature; she is sought after because she is different. Feeling demeaned by the Danes' view of her and homesick for her fellow blacks, she returns to Harlem. When she returns, she offers herself to Anderson, now married to Anne Grey. When he rebuffs her, she is shattered. Distraught, she falls prey to a poor Southern preacher, the ironically named Reverend Pleasant Green, who marries her and returns her to the Southern prison from which she escaped at the novel's beginning. As the cyclical novel ends, Helga, whose sole happiness in her marriage to Reverend Green is the sexual fulfillment she finds, has had four children in four years, is pregnant with a fifth child, and is trapped in a marriage from which the only escape is death, which the novel suggests is imminent.

The end of the novel is in stark contrast with its beginning. At Naxos Helga surrounded herself with beautiful objects and availed herself of many creature comforts. In the Alabama community in which *Quicksand* concludes, she resides in "cleanly scrubbed ugliness." While both settings are constricting, the latter is more confining, for at the end of the novel, Helga is trapped biologically and cannot escape from becoming a mother over and over again. She cannot continue her elusive pursuit of selfhood by changing her context because she has children. Linking her lifelong unhappiness to the absence of her parents, she cannot wreak similar misery on her own progeny. Instead she must remain in quicksand of her own creating; she is doomed to end her days in "the bog into which she had strayed."

According to Thadious Davis, the ending of *Quicksand* is "graphic realism which may seem too drastic a shift of fortune for the search for self Helga Crane undertakes" (185). However, the critic contends that the resolution "is thematically and symbolically in keeping with her downward spiral into self-induced despair and destruction" (185). As Davis states, Helga is always a divided character who desires a life marked by achievement and fullness but who is paradoxically unable to keep to any specific path. Her inability to follow a single course (which resembles Larsen's similar inability throughout her life) stems from her not knowing what she wants to achieve and her not knowing when she excels.

Hortense E. Thornton sees Helga's picaresque wanderings, which culminate in the tragedy of her life with Reverend Green, as rooted primarily in sexism rather than in racism. Thornton believes that, as a woman living in a male-dominated society, Helga repressed her sexuality and thus made herself vulnerable to her "tragic degeneration" (188-89). Helga's repression of her sexual desires are attributable in large measure to the constrictions society in her literary world imposed upon black American women.

Their circumscribed existences are mirror reflections of the limitations imposed in actuality upon this group of women during the 1920s. In her December 1925 *Crisis* prize-winning essay "On Being Young—A Woman—and Colored," Marita Bonner—writing from Washington, D.C., where she was a high school teacher—railed against the restrictions that American women of all colors faced during this era:

> For you know that—being a woman—you cannot twice a month or twice a year, for that matter, break away to see or hear anything in a city that is supposed to see and hear too much.
>
> That's being a woman. A woman of any color.
>
> You decide that something is wrong with a world that stifles and chokes; that cuts off and stunts; hedging in, pressing down on eyes, ears and throat. Somehow all wrong (64).

While, on one hand, black American women's lives were affected by the same restraints that other women's lives were, black women's lives were complicated even more because they were seen, as Helga Crane was in Copenhagen, as sensual, primitive creatures. To this myth of the sexually-charged black woman, fictional Helga's reaction is flight from Denmark. To this myth, the real-life Bonner's response is disgust: "Why do they see a colored woman only as a gross collection of desires, all uncontrolled, reaching out for their Apollos and the Quasimodos with avid indiscrimination?" (64). In the fictional world of *Quicksand,* many of Helga's problems emanate from her inability to come to grips with her sexual desires in a world in which middle-class mores prohibit the expression of these yearnings outside of marriage, while at the same time the white world paints African-American women as carnality personified.

Although *Quicksand* was out of print from the 1930s to the 1970s, it did not fall from critical attention. Mainly, critics who assessed the work commend it. Robert Bone sees it as "tightly written, subtle, psychologically sound," and powerful in its development of its main dramatic tension (102). Invoking revealingly patriarchal critical dicta, Hiroko Sato praises Larsen for her "almost masculine detachment and her ability to expand a small, particular situation to a larger, universal one" (88). David Levering Lewis ranks *Quicksand* among the three best novels of the Harlem Renaissance, terming it an allegory that is so exemplary that he is unable to detect a single misplaced word or unnecessary sentence (231).

In Larsen's second published novel, *Passing*, a female character of mixed racial descent figures prominently again and, as in *Quicksand*, links Larsen's fiction and her life. Dedicated to Van Vechten and his actress wife, Fania Marinoff, *Passing*, published on April 26, 1929, focuses on two women who have known one another since childhood—Irene Redfield and Clare Kendry. Hailing from a prominent black family, Irene is married to a young black physician whose profession and earnings assure for her elevated status in Harlem's social circles. An unreliable narrator, Irene is the character from whose perspective most of the action unfolds. Clare Kendry is the mixed-race daughter of an alcoholic custodian. Raised by her white great-aunts, Clare marries a white man who believes she too is white. She weds him to escape the drudgery of her life with her white relatives.

Irene and Clare are so different that they appear to be literary doubles. Irene is associated throughout the novel with the need for security and the inability to take risks. She is so repressed and so concerned about appearances that she does not cry because weeping does not "become her"; she even goes so far as to bar her husband from discussing lynchings at the dinner table because such talk is, to her, inappropriate—because it disturbs the superficial tranquility of her family's lives. Although her husband, Brian, is unhappy with life in the United States and yearns to migrate to Brazil, where he hopes to elude racism, Irene will not even consider leaving her "safe" Harlem world for an unknown world. Clare, on the other hand, is constantly associated with risk-taking. First, she passes for white and marries a well-to-do white man. She even risks having a child, who might have been dark. Further, she risks all by resuming her acquaintanceship with Irene and by frequenting Harlem—because like Helga in *Quicksand*, she craves the companionship of blacks.

Throughout the novel Irene sees Clare as a threat to her safety and security. Near the end of the novel, Irene fears that Clare will take her physician husband away. Also, Irene fears Clare's ability to feel deeply and intensely. This ascendancy of feeling over reason spells danger to Clare herself and to others in her midst, Irene believes. As Clare has demonstrated time and again, she is likely, while in the throes of emotion, to cast aside caution—Irene fears—and to disrupt others' lives.

In one of the novel's final scenes, Clare's white husband appears suddenly in Harlem and finds her at a party with Irene and Brian Redfield and other blacks. During the chaos and confusion caused by his arrival and his discovery of Clare's blackness, she falls melodramatically from a window to her death.

The denouement suggests that, imagining that Clare is a threat to all that Irene cherishes, Irene may have pushed Clare to her death. While Addison Gayle has little difficulty seeing Irene as capable of a murder to save her marriage and thus prestige and position in Harlem (11), the possibility of such an act on Irene's part seems inconsistent with her characterization. Irene seems neurotic and insanely jealous, but nothing suggests that she has the capacity to take another person's life. Of course, if the novel were seen as a work presenting literary doubles, one implication of a possible murder of Clare by Irene is that Irene would, by killing Clare, permanently destroy within herself all remaining capacity for full self-expression.

Other possible conjectures about the denouement are that once discovered by her husband to be black, Clare leaped to her death; that her husband pushed her; or that she fell accidentally to her death. While the ending might cause the reader to wonder about what actually happened, the resolution—regardless of how Clare died—provides no valuable insights into human existence; aesthetically, it is not satisfying. Its "whodunit" quality lessens the work's literary value.

While Addison Gayle finds *Passing* superior to *Quicksand* (111), he is in the minority, for most critics believe that *Quicksand* is the more meritorious novel. Bone laments the "false and shoddy denouement" of *Passing*, which prevents the novel from "rising above mediocrity" (102). Sato acknowledges that *Passing* is "cleverly written and the psychology of the two women is coherently expressed" but believes that, compared to *Quicksand*, it is a "slight book" that "fails to present the deeper meaning of the question" of passing (89).

Close scrutiny of *Quicksand* and *Passing* reveals several striking similarities. Both novels treat middle-class black African-American women who could pass for white. The major characters in the novels are physically attractive, well-educated residents of the urban North—of Chicago and New York, where Larsen lived at different points of her life. Both Helga in *Quicksand* and Clare in *Passing* want to experience their existences to the fullest but are restricted by gender and race. Both Helga and Clare have white and black blood, but they desire to be in the company of blacks and come to prefer black life to white life in spite of the limitations of black American life. While her characters belong to the middle class, Larsen's novels do not celebrate black middle-class life in the manner of the Genteel School to which writer

Jessie Fauset belonged. Larsen's novels suggest that blacks who come to terms with the black and white world have a chance to lead happy lives, but she does not hesitate to assail blacks who ape white ways. Her descriptions of Naxos and Harlem middle-class life in *Quicksand* are examples of her willingness to attack such blacks; her description of Harlem middle-class life in *Passing* is another instance of her ability to expose Babbittry in African-American middle-class life and to judge its followers harshly.

Larsen's Writings Bring Recognition

During the latter 1920s, Larsen enjoyed the acclaim of her contemporaries. She was nominated in 1928 and 1929 for the Harlem Award for Distinguished Achievement Among Negroes in the literature section. Among her supporters for the awards were James Weldon Johnson—anthologist, literary historian, writer, and NAACP leader; W. E. B. Du Bois—*Crisis* editor, literary and social critic, scholar, and racial spokesperson; and Van Vechten—patron of black American artists and a writer himself. In 1928 Larsen won the Harmon Foundation's bronze medal for literature, placing second to Claude McKay, who won the gold medal for *Home to Harlem*. In 1930, she was the first black woman to win a prestigious Guggenheim Fellowship in creative writing, winning on the basis of her past novels, and the fourth black ever to win such an honor. Walter White won one in 1927; Countee Cullen and Eric Waldrond, in 1928.

Although Larsen's ability as a writer was recognized by people of prominence such as James Weldon Johnson, Walter White, and Van Vechten, and although she knew many Harlem Renaissance writers, she was removed from other black American writers of the period. She did not publish her work in *Opportunity* or *Crisis* as they did and was thus outside the literary circle that included writers such as Zora Neale Hurston, Langston Hughes, and Claude McKay. One reason she may not have published in these periodicals is her ambivalence about the black race, which she was alternately proud of and amused by. Racially marginal, she was socially unconventional and seemed odd to people. She wore short dresses, smoked cigarettes, defied rules that most women of her background and class adhered to, and eschewed religion—practices that set her apart. Additionally, Larsen was a reserved person who seemed aloof to others; this perception of her surely must have discouraged friendships. Finally, her age worked against her. Thirty-six years old when *Quicksand* was published, she was older than the younger generation of the New Negro writers and younger than the older generation of African-American writers publishing during the 1920s.

In 1930 Larsen's career as a writer, came for all practical purposes, to a close. That year she was charged with plagiarizing her short story "Sanctuary," which appeared in the January 1930 issue of *The Forum*, a mainstream periodical that included among its contributors that year luminaries such as Carl Jung and William Faulkner. In the story, Annie Poole, a tiny, withered black woman, hides Jim Hammer, a big black man who comes to her when he is in trouble for shooting a man. Though she appears physically frail, Annie possesses inner strength that she must summon when she discovers that the man Jim shot is not white, as he believes, but is instead her son, Obadiah, known in the community for his goodness. She shields Jim because "white folks is white folks," and she believes that blacks must band together against them. Because he is a fellow black, she protects Jim, who has "allus been triflin,' . . . no 'count trash." In her final words to Jim, she tells him that he should "nevah stop thankin' yo' Jesus he done gib you dat black face."

A reader of *The Forum* pointed out parallels between Larsen's story, which was ironically the only short story she ever had published, and a story titled "Mrs. Adis" written by Sheila Kaye-Smith that appeared in *Century* magazine in 1922. In her response to the accusation of plagiarism, Larsen denied that she was guilty of this offense, claiming that she had fictionalized a folk tale told to her by a black patient in a black hospital. Although the editors of *The Forum* supported her, Larsen was deeply affected by this incident. A fragile and vulnerable person whose confidence was undermined by the scandal, she never published again, although she wrote during her Guggenheim Fellowship year in Europe. Additionally, Mary Dearborn suggests that Larsen may have abandoned authorship because the writer was never thoroughly comfortable with the writing process and found writing bothersome and irritating (57).

After her return to the United States, Larsen moved to Nashville, Tennessee, where she joined her husband at Fisk. Although as early as 1929, Imes had allegedly fallen in love with a younger woman, Larsen remained married to him, largely because his position at Fisk carried with it a need for respectability. In 1933, she and her husband divorced. The divorce was the subject that year of sensational newspaper coverage by the *Baltimore Afro-American*, which printed rumors that the "other woman" in the case was white, that Larsen's frequent absences from her husband's side had precipitated the breakup, and that Larsen had tried to commit suicide at Fisk by jumping out of a window (Washington, 162). The year of the divorce, Larsen returned to New York City, residing on the lower East Side for a number of years. In 1941 she resumed her nursing career after her former husband died and she lost the alimony he had been paying her. For twenty years thereafter, she worked as a nurse at various Manhattan hospitals.

When Larsen died in 1964, she had fallen into self-decreed literary oblivion, from which she has been rescued only since the late 1960s and early 1970s. Since then, her novel *Quicksand* has been reprinted by Negro Universities Press (1969) and by Arno Press (Afro-American Culture Series) (1969), and *Passing* has been reprinted by Arno Press (Afro-American Culture Series) (1969). Also, both novels have been reprinted as part of Rutgers University's American Women Writers Series (1986). Since Larsen's rediscovery, her works have been the subject of critical scrutiny, especially by African-American women critics who see her fiction as seminal to the achievement of more recent African-American women writers. One of the first black women novelists to grapple with female sexuality and sexual politics and to treat black American women characters in urban landscapes, Larsen is a literary foremother to African-American fiction writers such as Ann Petry and Toni Morrison. Larsen and her works loom large in the annals of African-American women's fiction.

References

Bone, Robert A. *The Negro Novel in America.* New Haven: Yale University Press, 1958.

Bonner, Marita O. "On Being Young—a Woman—and Colored." *Crisis* 31 (December 1925): 63-65.

Carby, Hazel. *Reconstructing Womanhood: The Emergence of the Afro-American Woman Novelist.* New York: Oxford University Press, 1987.

Christian, Barbara. *Black Women Novelists: The Development of a Tradition, 1892-1976.* Westport, Conn.: Greenwood Press, 1980.

Davis, Thadious M. "Nella Larsen." In *Afro-American Writers from the Harlem Renaissance to 1940.* Vol. 51 of *Dictionary of Literary Biography.* Detroit: Gale Research, 1987.

Dearborn, Mary V. *Pocahantos's Daughters: Gender and Ethnicity in American Cultures.* New York: Oxford University Press, 1986.

Gayle, Addison. *The Way of the New World: The Black Novel in America.* Garden City, N.Y.: Doubleday, 1975.

Lewis, David Levering. *When Harlem Was in Vogue.* New York: Knopf, 1981.

Pryse, Marjorie, and Hortense J. Spillers, eds. *Conjuring: Black Women, Fiction, and Literary Tradition.* Bloomington: Indiana University Press, 1985.

Thornton, Hortense E. "Sexism as Quagmire: Nella Larsen's *Quicksand.*" *CLA Journal* 16.3 (1973): 285-301.

Sato, Hiroko. "Under the Harlem Shadow: A Study of Jessie Fauset and Nella Larsen." In *The Harlem Renaissance Remembered.* Ed. Arna Bontemps. New York: Dodd, Mead, 1972.

Washington, Mary Helen. "The Mulatta Trap: Nella Larsen's Women of the 1920's." In *Invented Lives: Narratives of Black Women, 1860-1960.* Garden City, N.Y.: Doubleday, 1987.

T. J. Bryan

Catherine A. Latimer

(1895?-1948)

Librarian

Catherine Allen Latimer was the first black professional librarian appointed by the New York Public Library. She was born in Nashville, Tennessee, the daughter of H. W. Allen and Minta (Bosley) Trotman. Latimer was educated in the public schools of Brooklyn, New York. Her college and library training were at Howard University. She later did graduate work at Columbia University. She worked one year at Tuskegee Institute as assistant librarian before going to the New York Public Library.

Educated during her early life in France and Germany, Catherine Latimer had a reading knowledge of German and spoke French fluently. She was appointed in 1920 to the 135th Street Branch Library in Harlem and later appointed reference librarian in charge of Negro literature and history, a field in which she specialized for a quarter of a century. Latimer was in charge of the collection until Arthur A. Schomburg, the man after whom it was later named, was appointed curator. Following Schomburg's death in 1938, Latimer again assumed full charge of that precious collection until Lawrence D. Reddick took over in 1939.

The Division of Negro Literature Branch and History at the 135th Street Branch, established in 1925, is considered the best collection of African works and black Americana. Schomburg's collection was purchased in 1926 with funds donated from the Carnegie Corporation. Latimer published in the *Crisis* magazine, June 1934, a description of some seven thousand books and pamphlets by and about blacks, approximately five hundred prints and rare portrait engravings "of eminent historical and literary characters, and about eight hundred manuscripts, letters, poems, plays, and sermons of writers and prominent citizens." She wrote:

> The purpose for which this Division was established is gradually being aroused and inspired. Through the preservation of these historical records there is in this wealth of material a virgin field along research lines and it is hoped in the future that the treasures may be more widely used and appreciated by all races.

Latimer's collection of clippings on items relating to black history and current events was hailed as one of the most comprehensive and useful resources for the study of blacks. That file was continued until 1985 and since then has been marketed under the title of the *Ernest D. Kaiser Index to Black Resources*. Kaiser was Latimer's protégé.

Latimer's influence was widely felt. She lectured to students of Wellesley, Columbia, Vassar, Smith, Hunter, and Pratt Institute, and many artists and writers gained inspiration through programs and exhibits that she sponsored.

In 1946 Latimer retired due to impaired eyesight and ill health. Prior to her retirement her coworkers had marveled at her ability to find information. Having worked with her books so many years, they had become part of her and she was content that all of the books were in place.

Latimer died in 1948 and was survived by her husband, Benton R. Latimer, son Bosley (then twelve), her mother Minta R. Trotman, and brother Henry B. Allen. The date of her birth is not established but her obituary in the *New York Age*, September 21, 1948, said that she was about fifty years old.

References

Kellner, Bruce, ed. *The Harlem Renaissance: A Historical Dictionary of the Era.* New York: Methuen, 1987. 215.

Latimer, Catherine A. "Where Can I Get Material on the Negro." *Crisis* 41 (June 1934): 164-65.

New York Age, 21 September 1948. Obituary.

Jean Blackwell Hutson

Margaret Morgan Lawrence

(1914-)

Psychiatrist, educator

In her journey in medicine, Margaret Cornelia Morgan Lawrence broke down many barriers for women and blacks. Now a prominent figure in American psychiatry, she is a living example of strength and perserverence.

Lawrence was born August 19, 1914, in New York City. She is the daughter of Sandy Alonzo Morgan, an Episcopal minister, and Mary Elizabeth (Smith) Morgan, a schoolteacher, both of whom were born near Richmond, Virginia. Lawrence was an only child, her parents having lost their firstborn, a son, to an undiagnosed congenital illness less than a year before Margaret Lawrence was born. This event motivated Lawrence to become a physician. She hoped that somehow she could spare other families the tragedy of losing a child. Because the Morgans did not wish to risk another childbirth in segregated southern hospitals, Margaret Morgan Lawrence was born at Sloan's Hospital for Women in New York. Her maternal grandmother and aunts resided in New York City at the time.

Lawrence was raised primarily in segregated Mississippi. For a brief time her parents lived in Widewater, Virginia, and then Mound Bayou, Mississippi, small communities where her father had ministerial calls. Her mother found existence in these rural areas difficult and "took to her bed" in sadness. Despite the difficulties of another move to the city, life in Vicksburg, Mississippi, proved to be more complete for Mary Morgan. Lawrence's father's ministry thrived, nurtured by the black parishioners, but also by white philanthropists in Mississippi. Her mother became a respected teacher and social figure. Despite the fact that Margaret Lawrence was a black child in the South, she grew up feeling "privileged." She understood the advantages of having educated parents who were respected by others. Although she felt the sting of being told by her white neighbor in Vicksburg that they could no longer play together since Lawrence was a Negro, she came to understand the segregated system early in life. Lawrence's world was filled with nurturing people. She and her mother made visits to New York City every other summer to visit Margaret's maternal grandmother, her aunts and uncle, and to experience urban life.

When Lawrence was fourteen, she decided to attend high school in New York in pursuit of her dream to become a physician. With her parents' blessing, she moved to the city where she lived with her maternal aunts. There she completed high school at Wadleigh High, one of two classical high schools for girls in New York. She excelled in her school work. She also established important relationships with blacks and whites who would support her in her endeavor to become a doctor. With the help of the teachers, all of whom were white, and Dean Anna Pearl MacVay at Wadleigh, Lawrence was accepted at three schools: Hunter College, Smith College, and Cornell University.

Lawrence attended Cornell University in Ithaca, New York, on scholarship from 1932 to 1936. When she was first admitted she was the only black undergraduate. She supported herself by working as a housekeeper and then as a laboratory assistant. For the first time she was removed from a nurturing environment and the company of black women who sustained her. She excelled at Cornell, but was not admitted to their medical college because another black, a man, admitted before had "not worked out."

Lawrence was the third black admitted to Columbia Medical School in 1936. After her rejection from Cornell, she was encouraged to apply to Columbia by Madeline Ramee, an administrator of the National Council of the Episcopal Church, a group that awarded her an undergraduate scholarship. Lawrence was one of ten women in her class of 104 who graduated in 1940. She was rejected for pediatric residency at Babies Hospital in New York because there were no accommodations for a black female intern. She was rejected at Grasslands Hospital in Westchester, New York, because she was married. (She married in 1938.) So, she began a pediatric internship at Harlem Hospital in 1940. During her two years there she learned firsthand about the problems of urban poverty. She completed a master of science in public health from the Columbia School of Public Health in 1943. There Lawrence had the opportunity to work with Benjamin Spock, who helped her focus her interests on children and their emotional concerns.

From 1943 to 1947 Lawrence taught pediatrics and public health at Meharry Medical College, beginning as an instructor and finishing as an associate professor of pediatrics. She returned to New York to fulfill her National Council Research Fellowship at Babies Hospital (1947-48). From 1948 to 1950, she pursued psychiatric training at the New York Psychiatric Institute. She also began psychoanalytic training at the Columbia Psychoanalytic Center in 1948; she was the first black admitted to the institute. From 1949 to 1951, Lawrence completed her fellowship in child psychiatry and pediatric consultation with the Council of Child Development Centers. She received her Certificate in Psychoanalytic Training from the Columbia Psychoanalytic Center in 1951.

Lawrence Contributes to Mental Health Field

After graduating from psychiatric training, Lawrence made many contributions to the field of mental health through her teaching, research, and clinical work. She spent many years at Harlem Hospital directing a therapeutic developmental nursery. She was one of the founders of the Rockland County Center for Mental Health and was the first child psychiatrist in Rockland County. Lawrence served on the New York State Planning Council for Mental Health in the 1970s and early 1980s. She retired from Columbia as an associate clinical professor of psychiatry in 1984. Although she was trained in classical psychoanalysis, Lawrence considers herself "a psychoanalytically oriented community psychiatrist" (Chapin, 116). She has presented many papers and is particularly interested in adaptation to trauma and ego strength. She has written two books, *The Mental Health Team in the Schools* (1971) and *Young Inner City Families* (1975). These works focus on her interdisciplinary, developmental, and generational approaches to treating children. Lawrence's daughter, Sarah Lawrence Lightfoot, has written a thorough and moving biography of her mother in *Balm in Gilead: Journey of a Healer*. A 1989 interview with Lawrence appears in the *Association for Psychoanalytic Medicine Bulletin*.

Currently, Lawrence is in private practice in Pomona, New York. She serves on several boards in the New York region, including Fountain House for seriously mentally ill adults and the Children's Stonefront School, a private school for inner city Harlem Children. She remains active with the Episcopal Peace Fellowship and serves on its national executive council. She maintains membership in many other peace fellowships in the New York area. She has been a member of the Susan Smith McKinney Stewart Society in Harlem for more than twenty years. This society of black women (of all ages) in medicine supports various organizations in New York while the members themselves are strengthened by the bonds within the society. Lawrence is working on her third book, *Out of Chaos: Living Stones*, which looks at black children identified as "strong" by their teachers in schools in Georgia and Mississippi and in East and West Africa. This book will study strengths as well as the pathologies and troubles of children. Some of the research for this study, she gathered with her husband, Charles Lawrence, during their sabbatical trip to Africa in 1973. Presently, Margaret Lawrence is working with others to found a Harlem psychoanalytic institute to train psychoanalysts and serve Harlem in a culturally sensitive environment.

Besides her family and the many important women in New York who are identified in *Balm in Gilead*, Lawrence feels her association with Benjamin Spock was also influential in her life. She cites Charles Pickett of the American Friends Service Committee for giving her the idea to become a psychiatrist for introducing her to Viola Bernard, who encouraged her to enter the Columbia Psychoanalytic Institute and served as her mentor.

Margaret Morgan met Charles Radford Lawrence II in Vicksburg, Mississippi, during her first summer home from Cornell in 1933. He was then a Morehouse College student with a strong social conscience. They were married in St. Mary's Episcopal Church in Vicksburg, Mississippi, on June 5, 1938. He was an eminent sociologist at Brooklyn College during much of his career. He was president of the House of Deputies of the General Convention of the Episcopal Church in the United States. His career interests influenced hers, and vice versa. Charles Lawrence died in 1988. The couple had three children: Charles Lawrence, who is now a professor of law at Stanford University; Sarah Lawrence Lightfoot, a sociologist at Harvard's School of Education; and Paula Lawrence Wehmiller, principal of the Wilmington Friends Lower School in Delaware.

Lawrence is petite, vivacious, and attractive. Her ability to understand and nurture others is immediately apparent. She has deep concern for all mankind and has remained committed to her goal to serve children and their families and to seek peace and equality for all people.

References

Chapin, Joanna. "Interview with Dr. Margaret Morgan Lawrence." *Association for Psychoanalytic Medicine Bulletin* 28 (March 1989): 116-22. Includes photographs.

Lawrence, Margaret Morgan. Interviewed, 14 March 1990.

Lawrence, Margaret Morgan and Charles R. Lawrence. Interviewed, 1979.

Lawrence, Margaret Morgan. *The Mental Health Team in the Schools*. New York: Behaviorial Publications, 1971.

Lightfoot, Sarah Lawrence. *Balm in Gilead: Journey of a*

Healer. Reading, Mass.: Addison-Wesley, 1988. Includes photographs.

Susan Brown Wallace

Marjorie McKenzie Lawson

(1912-)

Judge, civic activist, journalist

Marjorie McKenzie Lawson, the first black woman appointed to a judgeship by a president of the United States, has in her long, multifaceted professional life successfully combined the careers of jurist, civic activist, and newspaper columnist.

Lawson spent her early years in Pittsburgh, Pennsylvania, where she was born on March 2, 1912. After the death of her father, when she was only five years of age, Lawson was reared by her mother, who was from Bradford, Pennsylvania. Lawson attended the public schools in Pittsburgh, where she was the only black in her grammar and high school classes. Continuing her education at the University of Michigan, Lawson graduated in 1933 with a bachelor's degree in sociology. She remained at the University of Michigan to earn a certificate in social work in 1934.

In addition to her social work training, Lawson decided to obtain a law degree. After moving to Washington, D.C., she earned a degree from Terrell Law School, which offered an evening program. She was awarded her law degree and passed the District of Columbia bar in 1939.

Also in 1939, Marjorie McKenzie married Belford V. Lawson, Jr., a 1924 graduate of the University of Michigan, where he was the university's first black varsity football player. After earning his law degree at Howard University, Belford Lawson became a member of the District of Columbia bar in 1933. The Lawsons had one son, Belford V. Lawson III, an attorney.

For the Lawsons, marriage became a merger of their private and professional lives. After 1939 Marjorie Lawson primarily practiced law with her husband. However, from 1943 to 1946 she served as assistant director and later director of the Division of Review and Analysis of the President's Commission on Fair Employment Practices. After unsuccessfully competing for another federal position, which was won by a white Ivy League law school graduate, Lawson decided to enhance her professional credentials. As a result, she earned a J.D. from Columbia University in 1950. (Notwithstanding the fact that she was already a member of the District of Columbia bar, Columbia University required that she take the entire three-year legal course of study again.)

Lawson's partnership with her husband was not unusual for successful black women attorneys at that time. Examples of other black women who were part of husband-and-wife teams were Margaret Bush Wilson of Saint Louis, Jewel Stradford Lafontant of Chicago, and Sadie Tanner Alexander of Philadelphia. According to the August 1947 issue of *Ebony*, many of these women felt that their sex was a far greater barrier to their advancement than their color (''Lady Lawyers,'' 18-21).

Marjorie Lawson specialized in administrative law, while Belford Lawson concentrated on civil rights cases. He was the principal attorney in the 1937 landmark Supreme Court case of the *New Negro Alliance v. Sanitary Grocery*, which upheld the principle of the secondary boycott based on the slogan, ''Buy where you can work.'' In 1950 Belford Lawson, with the assistance of his wife, successfully argued the Supreme Court case *Henderson v. United States*, which abolished segregation in railroad dining cars.

Before going to Washington, D.C., Marjorie Lawson lived in Pittsburgh and Ann Arbor, Michigan, northern cities that were not rigidly segregated. Her move to Washington and her marriage to Belford Lawson, a native of Roanoke, Virginia, made her acutely aware of the discrimination against blacks in education, housing, and employment. Even though she was a professional, Marjorie Lawson found her life constrained by the boundaries of the black community in a segregated Washington, D.C. This abrupt contrast with her early life, as well as her training in social work and law, caused her to make a lifelong commitment to improving conditions in the black community. A considerable portion of Lawson's legal career and civic involvement centered on the development of low- and moderate-income housing for blacks.

Lawson's concern for social problems led her to join the National Council of Negro Women, where she served as vice-president from 1952 to 1954, and later as general counsel. Working with the council she assisted in the planning and building of Bethune House in 1957. Her interest in housing spurred her to join Walter Fauntroy, the first District of Columbia delegate to Congress, in founding the Model Inner City Community Organization in 1966. Through MICCO she encouraged citizen participation in rebuilding communities in the Shaw area of Washington during the turbulent 1960s.

During the 1950s and 1960s, Lawson simultaneously pursued a career as an attorney and a journalist. At the urging of Mrs. Robert Vann, wife of the publisher of the *Pittsburgh Courier* and a close friend from childhood, Lawson wrote a weekly public affairs column titled ''Pursuit of Democracy.'' For approximately fourteen years, Lawson wrote her column on perspectives in federal policies that affected blacks.

Lawson Appointed Juvenile Court Judge

The high point in Lawson's career came when President John F. Kennedy appointed her an associate judge in the District of Columbia Juvenile Court. Prior to this accomplishment she had been actively involved in Democratic party politics and John Kennedy's campaign for the United States Senate and presidency.

Through her husband, who attended the 1956 Democratic Convention, Lawson met John Kennedy, who made his initial bid for the United States presidency at that convention. Kennedy was considered a potential vice-presidential candidate on the ticket that was headed by Adlai Stevenson. However, Kennedy's Catholicism came to the fore as one of several potential drawbacks. Kennedy lost the nomination to Senator Estes Kefauver of Tennessee, who had been a leading opponent of Adlai Stevenson. At this time Belford Lawson became an early supporter of the Catholic senator, who was at that time unknown in the black community.

Between 1956 and 1960 the Lawsons became friends and informal advisors to John Kennedy. During this period the Lawsons were instrumental in introducing influential blacks such as George Weaver of the AFL-CIO, columnist Carl Rowan, publisher John Johnson, and Cincinnati councilman Theodore Berry to the future president. These contacts simultaneously helped Kennedy to gain an understanding of the black community and gave him visibility among politically active blacks.

In August 1960 presidential candidate Kennedy announced that Marjorie Lawson would head a newly created section of the Democratic campaign organization. Then general counsel to the National Council of Negro Women, Lawson was to direct research and advise Kennedy on civil rights and campaign issues. Among those working with her were Louis Martin, then vice-president of Defender Publications; Professor Harris Wofford, who was on leave from the Notre Dame Law School to serve as an assistant to Kennedy; Sargent Shriver, Kennedy's brother-in-law; and Christine Davis, staff director of the House Committee on Government Operations. Adam Yamolinsky joined this group as a coordinator of research on civil rights.

After President Kennedy's election, Marjorie Lawson played a prominent role on the inaugural committee. Shortly after Kennedy took office, Lawson's name surfaced as a possible nominee for a judgeship in Washington, D.C. Kennedy increased the possibilities of the appointment of a black judge when he signed a bill to create three juvenile courts for the District of Columbia. Since 1957 community leaders had fought for additional judges. The long-awaited new court was hailed as a community victory adding two judges to a previously one-person court where more than twenty-six hundred cases were pending. It was widely assumed that President Kennedy would appoint one black and one white to the new seats. Marjorie Lawson's name soon circulated as a likely nominee for one of the new ten-year appointments.

Lawson had reservations about accepting this appointment because she did not wish to serve under the sole and senior judge, Orem Ketchum, a Republican appointee. In holding out, Lawson asked that either she be appointed chief judge or be assured that the new chief judge share her views on handling court cases. This caused a delay in the announcement of the appointments. Kennedy resolved the matter by appointing attorney Morris Miller, a former chairman of the Juvenile Court Advisory Committee, as the chief judge. Since this compromise met with Lawson's approval, she accepted the appointment to the juvenile court.

Although this was a prestigious appointment for a black woman, Lawson remained on the bench only until 1965, when she submitted her resignation to President Lyndon B. Johnson. At this time President Johnson appointed attorney Aubrey Robinson to the vacant seat on the juvenile court. Not willing to let Lawson retire from national politics, Johnson appointed her United States representative to the Social Commission of the United Nations Economic and Social Council. She was a member of the delegation headed by then Ambassador Arthur J. Goldberg, who as secretary of labor had worked with Lawson when she was on President Kennedy's Commission on Equal Employment.

As a community activist, Lawson served as a member of the Washington Urban League board, vice-chairperson of the District of Columbia Crime Commission in 1966, the President's Task Force on Urban Renewal in 1969, the Committee on the Organization of the District of Columbia Government in 1970, the Mayor's Committee on Economic Development in 1971, and the board of the National Bank of Washington and the Madison National Bank in 1971.

After Lyndon Johnson's presidency, Lawson devoted her time to local politics. She credits much of her successful career to her husband, who supported and encouraged her involvement in national politics. A widow since 1985, the former judge, who is about five-feet four-inches tall, of light complexion with blond hair, and wearing glasses, continues to practice law.

The essence of Lawson's career in national politics is captured in the following quotation by a Democratic national committeewoman:

> There are two ways that you can get into politics—one is to go to a campaign office and stuff envelopes or knock on doors, or get in at the top as Marjorie Lawson did (Marjorie McKenzie Lawson).

References

Ebony 9 (January 1954): 70; 16 (March 1961): 88.

"Lady Lawyers." *Ebony* 2 (August 1947): 18-21).

Lawson, Marjorie McKenzie. Interviewed, 23 May 1990.

Lerner, Gerda, ed. *Black Women in White America.* New York: Pantheon Books, 1972.

Negro History Bulletin 39 (May 1976): 589.

Negro History Week Pamphlet, 1964. 2.

Pierce, Ponchitta. ''Problems of the Negro Intellecltual.'' *Ebony* 21 (August 1966): 146.

Ploski, Harry A., and James Williams, ed. *Negro Almanac.* Detroit: Gale Research, 1989. 1386.

Who's Who in America. Vol. 35. Chicago: Marquis, 1967. 244; Vol. 35, 1228; Vol. 36, 1324; Vol. 37, 1842; Vol. 38, 1824.

Toni-Michelle C. Travis

Jarena Lee

(1783- ?)

Religious leader, author

Jarena Lee was a nineteenth-century evangelist and itinerant preacher who published two autobiographies: *The Life and Religious Experience of Jarena Lee* (1836) and *Religious Experiences and Journal of Jarena Lee* (1849). Lee began her work as the leader of a predominantly female praying and singing band, eventually gaining prominence as an evangelist and published writer. A feminist, she wrote that ''the Savior died for the woman as well as for the man,'' and she overcame opposition from the male-dominated, independent black church to preach the doctrines of conversion, sanctification, and holiness through direct, individual contact with God. She relied on her religious visions, dreams, and experience as sources of power, wisdom, and authority.

Except for occasional references to Lee in histories of the AME church or in the biographies of AME church leaders, her autobiographies are the primary sources of information on the life of a woman who called herself ''the first female preacher of the First African Methodist Episcopal Church.'' She begins the 1836 account of her life:

> I was born on February 11th, 1783, at Cape May, state of New Jersey. At the age of seven years I was parted from my parents, and went to live as a servant maid, with a Mr. Sharp, at the distance of about sixty miles from the place of my birth (*Life* in Andrews, 27).

But she omits from both autobiographies important details of her personal life, including her family name, as well as the first names and occupations of her parents. In 1801, at age twenty-one, she was converted to Christianity at a religious meeting, but she suffered poor health and spiritual doubts for four years, considering suicide on three occasions before finding peace through sanctification. Several years later Lee decided to preach, but when she expressed this desire to Richard Allen, founder of Bethel African Methodist Episcopal Church in Philadelphia, the minister replied that the Methodist church ''did not call for women preachers.'' Lee reflected in her autobiography:

> And why should it be thought impossible, heterodox, or improper, for a woman to preach? seeing the Savior died for the woman as well as the man (*Life,* 36).

In 1811 Jarena Lee married Joseph Lee, the pastor of a black church in Snow Hill, about six miles outside of Philadelphia. In that rural community she experienced loneliness and isolation. Within a few years she lost six family members, including her husband, and was left to care for her two small children, a baby of six months and a two-year-old toddler. In 1818 Lee returned to Philadelphia, where she petitioned Richard Allen, now a bishop of the African Methodist Episcopal church, to permit her to hold prayer meetings in her home, and Allen granted her request. She began to think seriously about breaking up her home, leaving her sickly child (the only one mentioned from this point forward) in the care of friends, and forsaking all to preach the Gospel. In her mid-thirties, Lee began her career as an itinerant preacher, traveling throughout the northeast, where, according to her autobiographies, she preached to whites, blacks, and Indians in churches, schoolhouses, bush arbors, markets, private homes, and camp meetings. On one of her journeys she returned to her home in Cape May, New Jersey, where, after an absence of fourteen years, she was reunited with her mother and uncle. Her work as an itinerant preacher was exhausting. She wrote, ''I have travelled, in four years, sixteen hundred miles and of that I walked two hundred and eleven miles . . . '' (*Journal,* 36). Frequently ill, she often had to spend weeks in bed:

> My health was much destroyed by speaking so often and laboring so very hard, having a heavy fever preying upon my system (*Journal,* 58).

In 1823 Lee traveled from Philadelphia to New York with Bishop Allen to attend the annual conference of the AME church, and on her return, the bishop gave her a position at Bethel, but the church congregation opposed her appointment. Later, Bishop Allen assisted with the education of Lee's son, making provisions for him to attend school and learn a trade. After the bishop's death, Lee placed her son with a French cabinetmaker to continue his training. The young man later married and had children, including a son who died at an early age.

Like most nineteenth-century female evangelists, Lee had very little formal education, as she notes at the end of her 1849 autobiography:

Please to pardon errors, and excuse all imperfections, as I have been deprived of the advantages of education . . . as I am measurably a self-taught person (*Journal*, 97).

In 1833, when she was fifty years old, Lee rewrote her religious journal with the help of an editor, and three years later printed one thousand copies of her *Life* at a cost of thirty-eight dollars. In 1839 she reprinted an additional one thousand copies of *Life*, and in 1849, after the AME church's book committee refused to publish an expanded edition of her autobiography, she financed the printing of her *Religious Experience and Journal*. Derived from a two-hundred-page religious journal that she kept during her travels, the autobiographies have a tripartite structure, which parallels stages in Lee's spiritual development. She quotes extensively from hymns, poetry, and the Bible, while writing in the "plain language of the Quakers" (*Life*, 47).

Little is known about the life of Lee after the publication of her second autobiography in 1849.

References

Andrew, William L., ed. *Sisters of the Spirit: Three Black Women's Autobiographies of the Nineteenth Century*. Bloomington: Indiana University Press, 1986. 1-48.

Dodson, Jualynne. "Nineteenth-Century A.M.E. Preaching Women." In Hilah F. Thomas and Rosemary Skinner Keller, *Women in New Worlds*. Nashville: Abingdon, 1981. 287.

Lee, Jarena. *The Life and Religious Experiences of Jarena Lee*. Philadelphia: The Author, 1836.

———. *Religious Experience and Journal of Mrs. Jarena Lee*. Philadelphia: The Author, 1849.

Payne, Daniel A. *History of the African Methodist Episcopal Church*. Nashville: AME Sunday-School Union, 1891. 190, 237, 273.

Walker, Clarence E. *A Rock in a Weary Land: The African Methodist Episcopal Church During the Civil War and Reconstruction*. Baton Rouge: Louisiana State University Press, 1982. 25.

Wesley, Charles H. *Richard Allen*. Washington, D.C.: Associated Publishers, 1935. 197-98.

Wills, David M. "Womanhood and Domesticity in the A.M.E. Tradition: The Influence of Daniel Alexander Payne." In David W. Wills and Richard Newman, *Black Apostles at Home and Abroad*. Boston: G. K. Hall, 1982. 137-40.

Miriam DeCosta-Willis

Edmonia Lewis "Wildfire"

(1845?-?)

Sculptor

The dual heritage and accomplished marble sculpture of Edmonia Lewis distinguished her as the first major sculptor of black American and Native American heritage. Accounts of her early life are sketchy at best. Although Lewis claimed 1854 as her birthdate, it is more likely that she was born in 1843 or 1845. Various sources, including the artist herself, have noted Greenhigh, Ohio, and Greenbush, New York, as well as the vicinity of Albany, New York, as her birthplace, but none of these locales can be verified.

Lewis's father was a black American employed as a gentleman's servant and her mother was a Chippewa Indian, who may have been born near Albany, New York. It was she who presumably named her daughter "Wildfire." Lewis appears to have spent little if any time with her father, and instead lived with her mother's tribe. Orphaned before she was five, Lewis remained with the Chippewas until she was about twelve years old. As "Wildfire," she learned to fish, swim, make baskets, and embroider moccasins. Typically,

Edmonia Lewis

she sold her crafts as the tribe followed its nomadic life-style throughout New York state.

During the 1850s Lewis left the Chippewas because her brother "Sunrise," a California gold miner, had arranged for her schooling near Albany, New York. Adapting to her new circumstances proved difficult, but her brother persisted in efforts to educate her. In 1859, with his financial assistance, Lewis entered Oberlin College in Oberlin, Ohio. This event triggered her name change, and the school's records indicate that she assumed the name Mary Edmonia Lewis. Throughout her career, however, she seldom used her adopted first name, as reflected in her correspondence as well as the signatures on her sculptures.

Lewis was a moderately successful student, completing the Preparatory Department's high school courses and pursuing the College Department's liberal arts program. Her only extant drawing, "The Muse Urania," still in the Oberlin College Archives, was done in 1862 as a wedding present for her classmate Clara Steele Norton. Lewis may have been inspired by optional drawing courses offered by the Young Ladies' Preparatory Department. Later in life she recalled that "I had always wanted to make the form of things; and while at school I tried to make drawings of people and things" (Child, "Broken Fetter," 25).

Although Oberlin College and its namesake village actively promoted racial harmony, Lewis became the focus of a racially-motivated controversy in 1862, when two white female students accused her of poisoning them; Lewis was subsequently beaten by vigilantes. John Mercer Langston, a prominent lawyer also of African and Native American heritage, came to her defense and she was exonerated because of insufficient evidence. A year later she was accused of stealing art supplies. Despite her second acquittal, the college refused to allow her to graduate.

Shortly thereafter, Lewis moved to Boston, in part because her brother believed that the city's resources could support her interest in becoming a sculptor. Upon her arrival, she was greatly inspired by seeing Richard Greenough's life-size statue of Benjamin Franklin at City Hall. Using letters of introduction from Oberlin College, Lewis met William Lloyd Garrison, the abolitionist writer, who introduced her to Edward Brackett, a well-known portrait sculptor at that time. Brackett lent Lewis fragments of sculptures to copy in clay and critiqued her early efforts, then a customary alternative to academic training. Equipped only with this limited preparation, Lewis began to establish herself as a sculptor in Boston, and was listed as such in the city's directories in 1864 and 1865. According to these same directories, she worked in the Studio Building, where the black American painter Edward Mitchell Bannister and other artists maintained studios during the 1860s. To date, however, the extent of her interaction with this artistic community, specifically with Bannister, has not been established.

Exposure to Edward Brackett's sculpture and the impact of the Civil War combined to determine Lewis's first sculptures—medallion portraits of white antislavery leaders and Civil War heroes, which she modeled in plaster and clay. She also attempted her first portrait bust during this period. Its subject was Colonel Robert Gould Shaw, the young Boston Brahmin who was killed as he led his all-black battalion in battle against Confederate forces. The city's liberal white community subsequently lionized Shaw. Lewis's bust of Shaw as well as most of her early efforts are still unlocated, despite the fact that she made numerous plaster copies to help finance her move to Europe in 1865.

Lewis initially considered living in England because of its active abolitionist community. Following visits to London, Paris, and Florence, however, she established her studio in Rome during the winter of 1865-66. She was twenty-two years old at the time. Her interest in Italy and decision to settle in Rome were not unique. Since the 1820s, American sculptors, led by the example of Horatio Greenough, had been attracted by Italy's venerable artistic traditions, abundant marble supply, and cheap artisan labor. Moreover, women artists and writers considered Rome particularly congenial because it disregarded the sexist restrictions of their Ango-American world.

Settled into a large studio near the Piazza Barberini, Lewis quickly began learning to carve in marble and experimenting with the greater challenge of creating full-length figures. To increase her skills, she followed the common practice of copying classical sculptures in public collections. Proving adept in this direction, Lewis made copies of classical statuary, which she regularly sold to Americans who visited artists' studios in Italy as part of their grand European tours.

Lewis, however, shunned other customs of the art community, for she avoided instruction or criticism from her peers and also refused to hire native artisans to enlarge her small clay and plaster models and to carve the final marbles. Fierce pride in her heritage and the desire to achieve legitimacy as a sculptor led her to believe that her sculptures would not be considered original if she did not execute them herself (Anne Whitney Papers). Unwittingly, this attitude limited her production to the forty-six different compositions that have been identified to date though most of the actual works are still unlocated.

Commissions for small portrait busts in terra cotta and marble became Lewis's most reliable means of support. Patrons in Boston, especially prominent white men who were abolitionists and social reformers, were her regular clients. She also recognized the American market for "conceits" or "fancy pieces"—sculptures that used mythological children to convey human, often sentimental, themes. "Poor Cupid" (or "Love Ensnared") of 1876 is probably her best-known effort in this vein. (The sculpture is now in the National Museum of American Art, Washington, D.C.)

Sculptures Focus on Slavery and Racial Oppression

Financial security, however, was not Lewis's principal concern. Slavery and racial oppression were the central issues of her sculptures, a focus greatly facilitated by her distance from America. This focus also distinguished Lewis from her fellow sculptors in Italy, who derived their ideas and images from classical literature, history, and art. Between 1866 and 1883, Lewis created at least six major figurative groups featuring either black Americans or Native Americans. "The Freed Woman and Her Child" of 1866 (location unknown) and "Forever Free" of 1867 (Howard University collection, Washington, D.C.), for example, both capture the powerful emotion of emancipation. The latter's title is an adapted phrase from Abraham Lincoln's Emancipation Proclamation.

Lewis's exploration of the black figure reached as far as the African continent, when in 1868 she sculpted "Hagar," a marble also known as "Hagar in the Wilderness" (National Museum of American Art collection). Egyptians such as Hagar, the biblical maidservant to Abraham, were considered black by the nineteenth-century Western world, and in this sculpture, Lewis included the issues of gender and women's rights in her interpretation of oppression.

Lewis also reacted against the period's negative stereotypes of Native Americans as murderous savages or a dying, primitive race. Unlike the direct social commentary and ethnographic accuracy of her black figures, however, Lewis took a more literary, sentimental approach when carving her small-scale Indian groups such as "Old Arrow Maker" of 1872, also known as "The Old Arrow Maker and His Daughter" (National Museum of American Art collection). Lewis was greatly influenced by the narrative poem, "The Song of Hiawatha" (1855) by Henry Wadsworth Longfellow, whose portrait bust she began carving in Rome in 1869 and finished in 1871 (Harvard University Portrait Collection, Cambridge, Massachusetts).

Lewis's career in Rome coincided with the careers of other American women artists and writers who gathered around the neoclassical sculptor Harriet Hosmer and actress Charlotte Cushman. Both women welcomed Lewis to Rome, and it is widely believed that their influential circle greatly benefited her. However, social reformer Lydia Marie Child, one of Lewis's longtime patrons in Boston, wondered if American artists abroad would free themselves of "American prejudice" to help Lewis when she was deeply in debt and it became evident that Cushman and others had not come to her aid (Robie-Sewell Papers; James Thomas Fields Collection).

During the height of her popularity in the late 1860s and 1870s, Lewis's studio was a frequent stop for those who visited American artists abroad. She was also well-received during her several return visits to the United States between 1870 and 1876, when she exhibited works in Chicago, California, Boston, and Philadelphia. Perhaps the high point of her American career came in 1876 when her ambitious sculpture, "The Death of Cleopatra" (Forest Park Historical Society collection, Forest Park, Illinois), was exhibited and awarded a medal at the Centennial Exposition in Philadelphia.

From the outset, however, Lewis was considered "an interesting novelty . . . in a city [Rome] where all our surroundings are the olden Time" (Wreford, "A Negro Sculptress," 2001). Dressed in her rakish red cap and mannish costumes, Lewis captivated both Europeans and Americans, who often described her as childlike and charming. In 1863 she had already recognized the pitfalls of her triply disadvantaged heritage as a black Indian woman when she asked that her sculpture not be praised solely because of her background. Unfortunately, Lewis represented a tempting opportunity to those in Boston and Rome eager to demonstrate their support of human rights, and the encouragement she subsequently received ranged from sincere belief in her talents to well-meant but misguided indulgence.

Equally diverse, if not confused, are the descriptions of Lewis's appearance. Some described her hair as being black and straight like an Indian's and associated her complexion and willfully proud character with her mother's ancestry, while others believed that her facial features and hair reflected her father's background. Lewis herself was amused by a Bostonian's observation that "as her father had been a 'man of color' it would have seemed as though she ought to have been a painter, had it not been that her mother was a 'Chipp-e-way' Indian, and that made it natural for her to be a sculptor" (Wyman, 38).

In 1883 Lewis received her last major commission, "Adoration of the Magi," (location unknown) for a church in Baltimore, no doubt a reflection of her conversion to Catholism in Rome in 1868. After 1883 demand for her work declined, as it did for neoclassical sculpture in general. Her presence in Rome was reported in 1911, but the activities of her final decades are barely documented and the date and place of her death are unknown even today.

Following a visit to Lewis's studio, an anonymous American writer wondered in 1867 if "the youthful Indian girl" would create a "distinctive if not original style in sculpture" (Tuckerman, 604). Lewis indeed represented a fresh approach to the neoclassical sculpture tradition, injecting timely yet universal human rights issues and developing a more emotional, naturalistic style than her contemporaries.

References

Blodgett, Geoffrey. "John Mercer Langston and the Case of Edmonia Lewis: Oberlin, 1862." *Journal of Negro History* 53 (July 1968): 201-218.

Child, Lydia Maria. "Edmonia Lewis." *Broken Fetter* (3 March 1865): 25.

———. "Letter from L. Maria Child." *National Anti-Slavery Standard* 27 February 1864.

Ciovsky, Nicola, Jr., and William H. Gerdts. *The White, Marmorean Flock: Nineteenth-Century American Women Neocassical Sculptors.* Poughkeepsie, N.Y.: Vassar College Art Gallery, 1972. n.p.

Gerdts, William H. *American Neo-Classic Sculpture: The*

Marble Resurrection. New York: Viking, 1973. 48-49, 80-81, 132-33, 136-37.

Goldberg, Marcia. "A Drawing by Edmonia Lewis." *American Art Journal* 9 (November 1977): 104.

Hartigan, Lynda Roscoe. "Edmonia Lewis." In *Sharing Traditions: Five Black Artists in Nineteenth-Century America*. Washington, D.C.: Smithsonian Institution, 1985. 85-98. Includes photograph and illustrations.

James, Henry. *William Wetmore Story and His Friends*. Boston: Houghton, Mifflin, 1903. 357.

Leach, Joseph. *Bright Particular Star: The Life and Times of Charlotte Cushman*. New Haven: Yale University Press, 1970. 335.

Lewis, Edmonia. *The Revolution* (20 April 1871): n.p.

Locke, Alain. *The New Negro in Art*. Washington, D.C.: Associates in Negro Folk Education, 1940. 133.

Porter, James A. "Edmonia Lewis." *Notable American Women: 1607-1950*. Vol. 2. Cambridge: Harvard University Press, 1971. 397-99.

Sterling, Dorothy, ed. *We Are Your Sisters: Black Women in the Nineteenth Century*. New York: Norton, 1984. 202, 205-208, 459. Photograph, p. 207.

Tuckerman, Henry T. *Book of the Artists: American Artist Life, Comprising the Biographical and Critical Sketches of American Artists*. New York: Putnam, 1867.

Waterston, Anna Quincy. "Edmonia Lewis [the young colored woman who has successfully modeled the bust of Col. Shaw]." *National Anti-Slavery Standard* (24 December 1864). n.p.

Wreford, Henry. "Lady Artists in Rome." *Art-Journal* (March 1866): 177.

———. "A Negro Sculptress." *The Atheneum* (3 March 1866): 2001.

Wyman, Lillie Buffam Chase, and Arthur Crawford Wyman. *Elizabeth Buffum 1806-1899*. Boston: W. B. Clarke, 1914. 38.

Collections

Primary sources on Edmonia Lewis are in the James Thomas Fields Collection, F1650, Huntington Library, San Marino, California; Oberlin College Archives, Oberlin, Ohio; Robie-Sewall Papers, Massachusetts Historical Society, Boston; and the Anne Whitney Papers, Wellesley College Archives, Margaret Clapp Library, Wellesley, Massachusetts. Extensive primary and secondary research files on Lewis are available in the curatorial department and library of the National Museum of American Art, Washington, D.C. Two photographs of Edmonia Lewis in Chicago, by Henry Rocher, circa 1870, are in the Boston Atheneum, Boston, Massachusetts.

Lydia Maria Child and Annie Adams Fields correspondence is in the James Thomas Fields Collection, F1650, Huntington Library, San Marino, California.

Lydia Maria Child and Harriet Winslow Sewall correspondence is in the Robie-Sewall Papers, Massachusetts Historical Society, Boston, Massachusetts.

Lynda Roscoe Hartigan

Elma Lewis

(1921-)

Arts administrator, educator

Elma Lewis worked as a dancer, actress, dance teacher, director and choreographer, and speech therapist, put herself through college and post-graduate school, and then found her true niche when she opened the Elma Lewis school of Fine Arts in Roxbury. Her determined fund-raising and belief in the importance of her work led to the founding of the National Center of Afro-American Artists. According to the *New York Times*, Lewis "has almost single-handedly forged what is probably the nearest thing there is to a national center for Black culture and art in the United States today."

Elma Ina Lewis was born in Boston, Massachusetts, the only child of Edwardine (Jordan) Corbin Lewis and Clairmont Richard McDonald Lewis, who had both emigrated from Barbados. She had two older brothers born of her mother's first marriage; their father had died when the boys were still infants. One of her brothers helped Lewis to learn to read by the age of three. At that same age, at a meeting of Marcus Garvey's Universal Negro Improvement Association she recited a poem about the beauty of black women taught to her by her father. Her parents were ardent followers of Garvey and regular attendees at the Sunday meetings in Boston. Her mother was a Black Cross nurse, and her father was a member of the African Legion. She herself belonged to the Girl Guides and her brothers were newsboys for the Garvey newspaper. She said, "I really believe that being in the Garvey Movement gave me a sense of self" (*Washington Post*, 9).

Lewis attended Boston public schools, graduating from high school in 1939. As a child she studied dance, voice, and piano, and also received elocution lessons for one dollar a week. By the age of eleven she was earning as much as fifty dollars a week and could support herself through her dancing and dramatic performances. She also taught dance from 1935 to 1941 at the Doris W. Jones School of Dance in Boston and was a speech therapist at Roxbury Memorial High School for

Girls in Boston from 1942 to 1943. In addition, she worked as a student speech therapist for the Massachusetts Mental Health Habit Clinic in Boston. With income from performances and other jobs Lewis was able to pay her own way through Emerson College, where she graduated with the bachelors in Literature Interpretation degree in 1943. She played the role of Julie in Ferenc Molnar's *Liliom* in 1945 at the Copley Theatre in Boston. She wanted to become an actress, but realized there were very few opportunities for blacks and that such roles as were available were likely to be for menials. Being practical, she attended the Boston University School of Education, specializing in the education of exceptional children and receiving a master's degree in 1944.

In 1945 Lewis taught in the Boston public schools, then became a speech therapist again at the Massachusetts Mental Health Habit Clinic and from 1945 to 1949 was a fine-arts worker at the Harriet Tubman House, a social-work agency in Boston's South End. From 1946 to 1968 she worked with the Robert Gould Shaw House, also a social service agency, as director and choreographer for twenty-one operas and operettas presented by the Robert Gould Shaw House Chorus.

In 1950 Lewis founded the Elma Lewis School of Fine Arts in a six-room apartment in a racially mixed area in Roxbury, Massachusetts, to "offer quality education in the arts to children in the neighborhood" (Quinn, 14). With three hundred dollars from her father, some folding chairs and tables, and a rented second-hand piano, she began her school with four teachers and twenty-five students, teaching them dance and drama. The school led a nomadic existence until 1968, when she purchased for a token one dollar a former Hebrew synagogue and school valued at more than one million dollars, with the intention of using these facilities for her increasing activities. The population in the area had undergone a change with the influx of the black middle-class into a primarily Jewish community. Previously, the school had survived with the support of the black community through tuition, bake sales, and some gifts, but a permanent home was needed. Now having obtained property, Lewis began fund-raising in earnest for rehabilitating the buildings and for an endowment. After renovations, the doors of the Elma Lewis School of Fine Arts opened in January 1969 with 250 students.

Lewis stayed in Roxbury, her own community, working with friends and neighbors. Usually operating with very little money in hand, the staff often went unpaid for long periods of time. Although there was a constant need to ask for monetary and other contributions, Lewis developed an institution that the larger community began to notice and to consider worthy of support. The *Boston Globe*, Eastern Gas and Fuel, New England Telephone, the Permanent Charities of Boston, and other local agencies have given financial support over the years. The Rockefeller Foundation gave a grant in 1969 "to foster young talent in theatre and dance" (*New York Times*, 16 December 1969, 54) and in 1973 gave a $350,000 grant to the dance company. The Kresge Foundation and the National Endowment for the Arts have also been supporters. In 1969 the Ford Foundation gave a four-year grant of $400,000 that "had to be matched dollar to dollar the last three years (a feat accomplished within the first year)" (*Boston Globe*), The Ford Foundation in 1974 offered a $650,000 challenge grant toward endowment if Lewis could raise $1.3 million by August 1977.

On the occasion of the twenty-fifth anniversary of the school in 1975, Lewis sent out a call for more than six thousand alumni to come and celebrate. In introducing her at the anniversary dinner, Judge Harry Elam called her "an indomitable spirit who told her students over and over when something went wrong, that all they had to do was to pick themselves up, brush themselves off, and start all over again" (*Boston Globe*). The school has a long waiting list of students who wish to attend. As the school again planned renovations of its buildings in 1990, there were more than 350 students at scattered sites taking classes in dance (ballet and primitive), drama (from Shakespeare to Langston Hughes), African drumming, music (jazz and classical), and art. In addition to their studies, students at the school participate in many social events that would ordinarily be unavailable to them. They have been junior hostesses for an opening party of Ossie Davis's *Purlie Victorious*, they have heard presidential candidate Shirley Chisholm, they have met many international visitors, and designed a gown for singer Odetta. The school has done very little advertising; word-of-mouth has been the main vehicle of promotion. The tuition is minimal and flexible so as to enable all who wish to attend to do so. Most of the students come after school to take classes, but there are also evening programs for adults. Lewis has said, "I believe in Black artists rather Black art" (*Vogue*, 173). The Parent's Organization has been a strong support for the school, especially helping those young people who go to New York to further their development. Many thousands have seen *Black Nativity*, a Christmas pageant, in 1990 in its twenty-first year.

For many years the school has offered programs at the Massachusetts Correctional Institution at Norfolk. Inmates are taught African drumming and also have courses in dance, drama, music, writing, and art. The Technical Theatre Training Program was begun in 1970 to prepare the inmates for jobs in the theater as stage managers, sound men, electricians. Out of the program have come several very successful (as reviewed in the Boston papers) stage productions written and performed by inmates for other inmates. In 1972 Little, Brown published *Who Took the Weight*, a book of poetry, short stories, essays, and plays written by M.C.I. Norfolk inmates and a former inmate who at the time was a student at Rutgers University. Lewis contributed the foreword to the book.

National Center of Afro-American Artists Founded

In 1968 Lewis became founder/director of the National Center of Afro-American Artists, of which the Elma Lewis School is now a subsidiary. She hopes that the center will evolve into a national repository for the study and dissemination of black culture. The center at various times has included an experimental theater, both jazz and classical orchestras, and "Playhouse in the Park," summer theater in Franklin Park presenting both professional artists and the dance company of the National Center. From 1969 to 1980 Lewis was producer, and at times choreographer, for many of the programs and events offered. An internationally known entity of the center is the museum, under the direction of Barry Gaither. It is both an archive and an exhibitor of art of the African diaspora.

An article in the *New York Times* once said that Lewis "could be Black America's version of Sol Hurok, Tyrone Guthrie and P. T. Barnum—all fused into one generous package." In 1975 the artist John Wilson said of the Elma Lewis School:

> It's a landmark. In terms of developing tangible Black art, exposing a community to the arts, and stimulating involvement, I can't think of any other institution like this. The school has grown from nothing. I have seen it happen as she [Lewis] has been instrumental in getting it off the ground (*Boston Globe,* 31 January 1975, 13).

Lewis has been consultant to the Office of Program Development for the Boston public schools, to the National Educational Association, and to the National Endowment for the Arts. She has been involved in numerous civic organizations, boards, councils, and commissions, and has received numerous honors and awards, which can be described only briefly. She has been an overseer of the Museum of Fine Arts, Boston, and a member of the visiting committee of the Museum School; council member for the Massachusetts Council on the Arts and Humanities; a trustee of the Massachusetts College of Art and the Boston Zoological Society; a fellow of the Black Academy of Arts and Letters; an honorary member of the Alpha Kappa Alpha Sorority; and member of the American Academy of Arts and Sciences. She was on the board for the second World Festival of Black Art in Nigeria in 1977.

Lewis has received more than one hundred citations and awards, including a citation from Lambda Kappa Mu for outstanding cultural contribution in areas of dance (1965); from Omega Psi Phi for enriching the cultural life of the children of Boston (1967); the Mayor's Citation from the City of Boston (1970 and on several later occasions); the Henry O. Tanner Award from the Black Arts Council of California (1971); a resolution passed in both houses of the Massachusetts Legislature congratulating Lewis for twenty-five years of contributions to the black community, the world, and Afro-American culture (1975); an arts award from the Boston Chamber of Commerce (1978); an award in the area of arts from the NAACP, Boston Branch (1981); a Presidential Citation and medal from the President's Committee on the Arts and Humanities (1983); an Alumni Award for Distinguished Public Service to the Community from the Boston University Alumni Association (1984); the Ebony Award from the black seniors of Emerson College, recognizing Lewis as a role model for black youth (1984); and Black History Achiever Award from Northeastern University (1988).

Other institutions and organizations giving honors and awards to Lewis include the African Heritage Studies Association; Black Big Brother Association; Black Educators Alliance of Massachusetts; Boston State College; Children's Hospital, Boston; Governor's Committee on the Status of Women; Massachusetts Federation of Business and Professional Women's Club; Museum of Afro-American History, Boston; National Association of Dance, Health, and Recreation Workers; National Council of Teachers of English; New England Theatre Conference; Roxbury (Massachusetts) Community College; United States Department of Health, Education, and Welfare; University of Massachusetts Alumni Association; and Zeta Phi Beta Sorority.

In 1981 Lewis was among the first to receive a MacArthur Foundation Fellowship. Her five-year grant of $280,000 enabled her to have necessary surgery on her eyes, to travel, and to develop a curriculum on black culture. When interviewed at the end of the five-year grant period, she said that she wanted the National Center of Afro-American Artists to become "worthy to be called a world institute." She described herself as "a conceptualizer, a prophet, not a priest" (*New York Times,* 10 July 1986).

Lewis has received twenty-six honorary degrees, including degrees from Bates College, Brown University, Colby College, Emerson College, Harvard University, New England Conservatory of Music, Northeastern University, and the University of Massachusetts.

Although it was not Lewis's intention to train professional artists, many of her students have become professionals in the fields of dance, drama, and singing. "Our goal is to develop good human beings, human beings who can hold their heads up high and be proud of being black; if in the process we develop good artists, that's all right too" (Merchant, 29-30). In a story in *Essence*, Lewis said, "It is not in the realm of *luxury* but of *necessity* that the creative energies of the nation's Black population will be nurtured and preserved for prosperity" (Bailey, 40-41).

The meaning of the National Center of Afro-American Artists perhaps can best be described in Lewis's own words: "We expose the students to all of the art disciplines, and if they want to specialize they can do this and become professionals. But I like to think that the Center, most importantly, is a process during which the child, that most marvelous of human beings, not only learns cultural pride, but learns too, how to deal with the world" (*Boston Globe*, 31 January 1975).

References

Bailey, Peter. "Black Art's Amazing Fund-Raiser." *Ebony* 25 (June 1970): 70-78.

Bailey, Susan. "The Undeferred Dream of Elma Lewis." *Essence* 4 (July 1973): 40-41.

Boston Globe, 30 January, 22 September 1971; 26 February, 21 June 1974; 1 January, 31 January, 3 February, 1975.

Boston Herald Traveler, 27 April 12 June, 8 November 1971.

Editors of Ebony. *Ebony Success Library*. Vol. 1. *1,000 Successful Blacks*. Chicago: Johnson Pub. Co., 1973.

Garfinkel, Perry. "Big Boom in Black Arts and Culture." *Sepia* 25 (September 1976): 66-72.

Guralnick, Estelle Bond. "The Private Elma Lewis. *Boston Sunday Globe*, 23 January 1977.

Korzenik, Diana. "A Blend of Marcus Garvey and the 92nd Street Y: An Interview with Elma Lewis." *Art Education* 35 (March 1982): 24-26.

Lewis, Elma. "Celebrating Little People." *Boston Review of the Arts* 2 (September 1972): 89-92.

Merchant, Zarine. "Elma Lewis School of Fine Arts: The Fountainhead of Black Culture in Boston Started As a School and is Now a Mini-Empire." *Black Enterprise* 6 (August 1975): 29-31.

New York Times, 17 November 1968; 19 April 1968; 19 November 1968; 16 December 1969; 20 September 1970; 24 June 1974; 19 May, 25 May 1981; 10 July 1986.

Quinn, Susan. "Elma Lewis: Keeping African Culture Alive in Boston." *Ms.* 5 (May 1977): 14-15.

Record American (Boston) 25 May 1971.

Southern, Eileen. *Biographical Dictionary of Afro-American and African Musicians*. Westport, Conn.: Greenwood Press, 1982.

Spradling, Mary Mace. *In Black and White*. 3rd ed. Vol. 1. Detroit: Gale Research, 1980.

———. *In Black and White* Supplement. Detroit: Gale Research, 1985.

Vogue 153 (May 1969): 173.

Washington Post, 10 September 1975.

Who's Who Among Black Americans, 1990/91. 6th ed. Detroit: Gale Research, 1990.

Who's Who in American Art, 1989-90. 18th ed. New York: Bowker, 1989.

Who's Who of American Women, 1975-76. 9th ed. Chicago: Marquis, 1976.

Collections

Elma Ina Lewis's resume is in the Schlesinger Library, Radcliffe College, Cambridge, Massachusetts.

Ruth Edmonds Hill

Ida Elizabeth Lewis

(1935-)

Journalist, editor, publisher

There are few people who make childhood dreams a reality—and fewer still who enrich lives in the realization of their goals. Ida Lewis is one of those few special people. Her words are not just rhetoric about the fulfillment of potential for black American women; her words are articulations of her own rich example. Still involved in a lifelong career in journalism, the founder of two magazines, and the recipient of numerous awards, Ida Lewis is and has always been a strong advocate for black unity and the power of the black press as a force for shaping black America.

Ida Lewis is the second of six children born to Sam and Grace Lewis in Malvern, Pennsylvania. She appreciated the vitality and comraderie of a large family and feels it "was a joy growing up with a houseful of brothers and sisters. . . . We established a sort of Lewis Defense League—bother one, you bother them all sort of thing. A feeling which still exists" (*Essence*, 30). Her elementary school experience at the all-black Phillis Wheatley grammar school was positive, and she recalls, "We had loving teachers who cared, the school was part of the community" (Satterwhite, 33). Her high school days, however, were far less pleasant. All but one of the Lewis children attended the predominantly white Swarthmore High School. Of the experience she said that "many of my teachers were attentive to me because I was bright and they knew my parents stood behind me, but generally, their attitude was one of indifference," (Satterwhite, 33).

Lewis was an intelligent and inquisitive child. Years later in 1975, when she was the first black female journalist to appear as a panelist on "Meet the Press," she recalled how "as an adolescent, maybe about 13, she and her father would sit together engrossed in NBC's fledgling 'Meet the Press'" (Satterwhite, 33). Sam Lewis was a housepainter and laborer who loved to keep abreast of world news and who conveyed to his daughter his delight in seeing "history being made with the top journalists of the country" (Satterwhite, 33). Ida Lewis's mother ran an employment agency. Among the many gifts that Grace Lewis passed on to her daughter was a very practical business sense that Ida called upon much later in life.

As a child, Ida Lewis read a great deal and her imagination was always lively, her aspirations high. She already embodied some characteristics of a good journalist, conceiving a world larger than her immediate surroundings and reveling in the excitement of adventure:

> In our backyard, there was a big tree that I'd climb, a couple of books in hand, and I'd perch myself on the forked limbs and escape to far-away places like the South Seas or Siberia or to Africa or South America. My favorite hero was Matthew Henson, the black explorer who discovered the North Pole. In my tree we went on many adventures together (*Essence*, 31-32).

Besides a desire to expand her world, Ida Lewis's decision to become a journalist was rooted in several factors. First, she credits her mother with instilling in her a belief in herself and in her unlimited possibilities. Second, she recounts a senior year high school incident that she calls "humiliating" and "degrading":

> One of the requirements for graduation was a final paper for an English course. . . . I spent weeks gathering material in the Swarthmore College Library for the piece. I was the first to hand in the paper and the first to have it returned. The English teacher handed it back to me with a remark that she could not believe I had written such a high quality paper alone . . . [and] she gave me a C. I decided then and there that I would write for a living (*Essence*, 31).

Having determined her profession, Lewis chose to study at Boston University, receiving in 1956 a B.S. from the College of Communications. She also studied economics, and was honored for high academic achievement in the Scarlet Key Society. She immediately left for New York to pursue what was to become an auspicious career.

Lewis began her journalism career as a financial columnist for the *Amsterdam News* because the paper had no such column and she convinced the editor that young blacks needed to know more about financial and economic aspects of life. She held this position from 1956 to 1959. To augment the meager salary, Lewis found additional jobs, including opening a small coffeehouse on the East Side, a business venture that was unsuccessful. In 1959 she enjoyed a year as financial editor of the *New York Age* newspaper.

Soon she ventured into freelance writing: "At this time, in the early '60's, there was a lot of interest in the emerging African countries. I spent a lot of time at the UN, sent article ideas to magazines here and abroad" (Satterwhite, 33). In 1961 she made her first trip to Africa. This West African experience was added impetus for her book of essays, *The Deep Ditch and the Narrow Pit*, in 1964. The Pavilion Press commentary on the release of the book calls it an "absorbing volume in three sections: Poverty, Labor, and Africanization, which, also, serves as a subtitle. Its central design is so conceived as to present a black Africa in relationship to all black men and to impress the indispensable value of self-realization and self-government" (Press Release, 1). It also adds that throughout the remarkable series of essays, "one feels the unfailing presence of Ida Lewis: her own peculiar wit, humor, sympathy, and wisdom, vacillating between moments of overbearing realism and sparks of acute insight of human nature" (Press Release, 2).

Her second trip to Africa in 1964 was for coverage of John Okello, who successfully led the Zanzibar revolt. This article, a *Life* magazine piece, created much controversy among black Americans caught in the heightened black consciousness movement so prevalent in 1965. Lewis responded to the accusation of "selling out" by citing a journalistic "dilemma—how can you do investigative reporting as a black reporter and not tell the truth? I printed what he told me. He said he wanted black Americans to know about him" (Satterwhite, 33).

Journalistic integrity is a subject on which Lewis holds very definite ideas. She believes strongly in the power of the black press and its role in shaping the perspective and future of blacks in America. "Black journalists have a great responsibility. . . . Although they are earning their bread by giving the white point of view in a black way, they must be able to transcend that somehow and give a black perspective" (Charles, 31). This responsibility is tied to the distinction Lewis draws between being a reporter and being a journalist. "A reporter will just tell the relative truth, which happens to deal with the vehicle that he is employed by, but the journalist has a greater responsibility" (Charles, 31). The journalist for Lewis is a witness, dealing with the essential if delicate task of conveying the truth. Conveying such information involves more than objective observation: it involves intelligent interpretation.

Her journalistic career continued during her life abroad; living in Paris from 1963 to 1969, she wrote various pieces for a number of European newspapers and magazines. She covered the attitude of American blacks during the 1968 Nixon presidential campaign for *L'Express*, went to Biafra to write about the Nigerian Civil War for the Paris office of the *Washington Post*, interviewed Paris visitors for the British Broadcasting Corporation's African Service, and worked closely with and for the French international news weekly, *Jeune Afrique*. The Paris experience helped Lewis to solidify her career and her goals.

Journalist Becomes Editor and Publisher

Lewis returned to New York to become editor of *Essence*, a black women's magazine debuting in May 1970. Circulation grew, and *Essence* went from a circulation of zero in 1970 to 171,000 for its second anniversary issue.

After one year, however, Lewis left to realize her dream of someday publishing "a magazine like *Jeune Afrique*" (Satterwhite, 33). *Encore* was born in the spring of 1972—with forty thousand dollars from Lewis's personal savings, financial and emotional support from her friends, and dedication from an initially unsalaried staff. With a bank loan, credit, and continued dedication and support, it survived. With expertise, fine writers, and a novel concept, it flourished. As editor-publisher, Lewis fashioned her quarterly to realize her aims. In the premier edition, she stated the intention of this first black-owned-and-operated news magazine: "The chief value of *Encore* is informational. It proposes to stimulate and to be solution-oriented. *Encore* will provide a vehicle for Black adults to come face to face with the people and events that affect them" (2). In September of 1972, *Encore* began monthly publication. The magazine, similar in format to the already established *Time* and *Newsweek* but with an interpretation geared to the nonwhite world, branched into new areas of coverage:

> Among the unconventional contents: a debate between Black Poet Nikki Giovanni and Soviet Poet Yevgeny Yevtushenko over possible racist resonances in the term "Black Power"; an interview with Chinese Author-Physician Han Suyin on Women's Lib in Mao's Cultural Revolution; and an "*Encore* document" (now a regular feature), entitled "America: Neither Black Nor White," which included essays by George McGovern and black, Puerto Rican, Chicano, and American Indian spokesmen (*Time,* 85).

As founder, president, editor-in-chief, and publisher, Lewis remained with *Encore* from 1971 to 1982.

During those years, she was also involved in other journalistic activities. From 1978 to 1982 she was founder and board chairperson of the *Eagle and Swan,* a magazine for blacks in the military. She was a media consultant for several political candidates: Herman Danny Farrell for mayor in 1985 and Galen Kirkland for state senator in 1986 and subsequent campaigns. From 1978 to the present, she has been president of the Port Royal Communications Network, a communications and marketing company.

After she left *Encore* Lewis became, in 1984, editor and publisher of *Five Fifteen,* a newspaper with the subtitle "The First Black Women's Newspaper." A rich, full production, the paper is thick with coverage of diverse topics appealing to black women. In the premier May 1984 edition, Lewis pledges that *Five Fifteen* will:

> address issues relating to economics, politics, civil rights, crime and punishment. In addition, it will cover such areas as Black family life, personal care, health, travel, business and employment opportunities, the arts, literature, education and entertainment. Over and above serving the changing interests of the Black Woman, *Five Fifteen* will faithfully record her view of the world (3).

That Lewis has concentrated her efforts on a publication for intelligent black American women is appropriate. She has always championed the spirit of her sisters:

> Perseverance is the word that best describes the Black woman. It is a clue to what either always was or later became her basic nature. In every circumstance she displayed a spirit of survival, and the practicalities of that appear to have become an integral part of the very person and personality of the Black woman herself. . . . Even during periods of bleakest despair, racked by the image of grinning oppressors sitting on the bones of her children, the Black woman journeyed through the hells of America spirited and determined that one day, she, with her people, would embrace the moment of freedom (Lewis, *Five Fifteen,* 3).

Her feelings of admiration for her black American sisters come through not merely in Lewis's words; they shine in her decision to apply her considerable journalistic skills and business acumen to the expansion of the black woman's world.

Lewis is equally vocal on her views of racism in America, feeling that its eradication is impossible. "The fear of the black man's great potential combined with the white man's will to maintain power will always dictate the domestic policy of this country. We must fully understand that the aim of the Establishment will always be to subjugate each 'new Negro' who emerges at a given time" (*Essence,* 33). She feels that blacks must channel that great sense of survival that has served them throughout so much oppression into a great sense of will to realize full potential. "Our greatest weapon against oppression is black unity. . . . The only way we can measure black pride is by our degree of unity—not good looks, not money, not even professional competence, but unity" (*Essence,* 33).

Throughout the years, Lewis has received many awards: Journalism Award, Tougaloo College, 1973; Award of Achievement, the Association for the Study of Afro-American Life and History, 1974; Citizen of the Year, Omega Psi Phi Fraternity, 1974; Journalism Recognition Award, NAACP, 1976; Business Achievement Award, Harlem Commonwealth Council, 1979; First Annual Melnea A. Cass Citizenship Award, Boston University, 1980; National Alumni Council Award, Boston University, 1980; Partners in Education Award, New York City Public Schools, 1980; and Distinguished Alumni Award, Boston University College of Communication, 1982.

Her professional affiliations are numerous. Long interested in education, Lewis served as a trustee of Tougaloo College from 1976 to 1980 and as a professor of journalism at City University of New York from 1986 to 1987. Other affiliations mirror her myriad interests: board of directors, American Committee on Africa; National Council of Negro Women; National Association of Media Women; Alpha Kappa Alpha Sorority; commissioner, Commission of Inquiry into High School Journalism; and the National Alumni Council, Boston University.

Lewis considers herself a private person, a "loner" who guards the specialness of her personal life: "I don't really enjoy talking about myself, and it's not that I don't think it's important; it's just that it belongs to me and to people very close to me. I think one's private self is the only thing one has—it's the most sacred" (Charles, 45).

Never having been married, Lewis long ago chose the path wondrously imagined by a little girl in a backyard tree:

> I wanted to go around the world and taste strange foods and feel the heat of Africa and the chill of Paris in the fall. I wanted to see and feel people. So I just couldn't see getting married then (directly after college graduation). I don't like to think I was running away from anything, but I had dreamed so long, so long (*Essence*, 33).

Ida Lewis currently lives and works in New York City, residing in an apartment with bookshelves "dominated by (her) collection of black memorabilia and African sculpture picked up on trips to 23 countries" (Satterwhite, 33).

References

"Black Perspective." *Time* (30 October 1972): 85.

Charles, Pepsi. "Interview: Ida Lewis." *Black Collegian* (January/February 1972): 30-31.

"Conversation: Nikki Giovanni, Ida Lewis." *Essence* 1 (May 1971): 30-33.

Lewis, Ida. "In Focus." *Encore* (Spring 1972): 2.

———. *The Deep Ditch and the Narrow Pit*. New York: Pavilion Press, 1964.

———. "Our Time is Now." *Five Fifteen* (May 1984): 3.

Press Release for *The Deep Ditch and the Narrow Pit*. New York: Pavilion Press.

Satterwhite, Sandra. "The Black Executive, Article II: Ida Lewis, Publisher." *New York Post* 18 March 1975.

Terrell, Angela. "Black Publication, Third World Accent." *Washington Post* 30 April 1972.

Who's Who Among Black Americans, 1990/91. Detroit: Gale Research, 1990.

Collection

Biographical material on Ida Lewis is in her possession.

Margaret Duckworth

Samella Sanders Lewis

(1924-)

Art historian, artist, author, art curator, editor, educator, filmmaker

Lauded as one of the most prominent African-American art historians, Samella Sanders Lewis is a woman who skillfully fuses theory with practice in both her professional and political lives. She writes about art, but also makes it. She cares and stores for paintings and sculptures, but also makes them come alive for the public. She documents cultures in print and film, but also promotes them by merging the visual and performing arts in vivid presentations. She speaks about racial oppression, but also founds and directs institutions for immediate change. A medium-sized woman with an amiable, rounded countenance, she is an energetic source of fascinating information and activity.

Samella Sanders Lewis was born on February 27, 1924, to Samuel Sanders and Rachel (Taylor) Sanders in New Orleans, Louisiana. An honor student in high school, she received a Delta Sigma Theta Scholarship for college and studied at Dillard University in New Orleans for two years, 1941-1943. She then won a Hampton Institute Art Scholarship and completed her undergraduate education with a bachelor of science degree in art at Hampton in 1945. The following year she returned to her alma mater as an instructor in the art department. In 1947 Sanders left this position to pursue her education on an American University Scholarship at Ohio State University; she received her M.A. in art in 1948. On December 22 of that same year, she married Paul Gad Lewis. He would later receive his master's degree in mathematics from Ohio State University and teach computer programming at Freemont High School when the two moved to Los Angeles.

During the 1950s Lewis received her doctorate, raised her two children—Alan Stephen and Claude Anthony—and taught at three different universities. While teaching as an associate professor for two years at Morgan State College (1950-1952), Lewis wrote her dissertation and received her Ph.D. in art history in 1951 from Ohio State University. She was then appointed to the chair of the department of art at Florida Agricultural and Mechanical University and taught there from 1953 to 1958.

Lewis single-handedly built up the art department at Florida A.& M. When she arrived, there was virtually no material or equipment for art students. Lewis made a deal with the school's president that she would paint his portrait if he would spend more money on the art department. Although she began with just fifteen students, within five years Lewis's department had grown into one of the largest among black institutions. When her pupils won national prizes, several white students from Florida State flocked to the school trying to get into her classes.

While living in the Southeast, Lewis also became active with the local NAACP. She designed a Christmas greeting card for the group that read "Peace on Earth—Good Will to *All* Men." Because she underlined the word "all," the state of Florida accused her of communist sympathies and spent one hundred thousand dollars investigating her background. Lewis was not the only black American artist so charged—Elizabeth Catlett was also hounded by insinuations during the McCarthy era. The state subpoenaed and questioned Lewis and other members of the NAACP, but they were never officially cleared. Lewis's home became a target for racists—not only was the family barraged by obscene telephone calls and threats, but the Ku Klux Klan shot out the rear windows of their house. The police did nothing, however, claiming that they could take no action unless someone was killed.

Victor Lowenfeld, Lewis's mentor, was teaching at Hampton Institute at the time. Upon hearing of her difficulties, he found a position for her at the University of the State of New York in Plattsburg. There Lewis would teach art history and humanities for a decade (1958-1968).

At first the Lewises were pleased with their new neighborhood of Lake Placid and Plattsburg, but soon they discovered racial prejudice in the North, as well. Farmers imported black, migrant workers from the South and forced them to work long hours with very little pay. Additionally, black air personnel could not buy or rent decent housing. Alarmed at these conditions, the Lewises established the Plattsburg chapter of the NAACP. They attracted about ninety black and several white members and achieved some positive changes.

As her political and cultural consciousness grew, Lewis became more aware of non-European civilizations. During the 1960s she became fascinated with Asian culture and explored the subject in depth. In 1962 she was awarded a Fulbright Fellowship to study at the First Institute of Chinese Civilization and T'ung Hai University in Taiwan, and to travel to other capitals in Asia for the research of art history, language, and civilization. In 1964 and 1965 she was a National Defense Education Act post-doctoral fellow at the University of Southern California for the study of the Chinese language and Asian civilization. Lewis then received a New York State Ford Foundation Grant in 1965 to participate in seminars at New York University, the Metropolitan Museum of Art, the Boston Museum of Fine Arts, the Freer Gallery of Asian Art, and Harvard University for the study of Asian civilization and Chinese.

Lewis shared the fruits of her extensive investigations both in the public and academic sectors. She was the education coordinator at the Los Angeles County Museum of Art from 1968 to 1969, and in 1969 she was appointed professor of art history and humanities at Scripps College, one of the Claremont Colleges. The latter was a position she would hold until her retirement in 1984.

While at the Los Angeles County Museum of Art, Lewis noted that the few works of African art there were either poorly displayed on the top floor or hidden in the basement. Although she pointed this out to administrators, they never looked into the matter. Lewis then brought in black teachers to set up workshops for black students. Despite the fact that Lewis had three degrees in art and had been awarded numerous fellowships, the museum promptly hired a black investigator who tried to discredit Lewis by saying that she was not qualified to do museum work. The scholar's attorney handled the matter smoothly and Lewis received a handwritten apology from the museum.

Rather than continue to wage such battles, however, Lewis left the museum and resolved to establish an art gallery that would actively promote black culture. Together with the artist Bernie Casey, she spent four thousand dollars of their own money renovating an old building a few blocks from her home. In the early 1970s the Contemporary Crafts Gallery developed into a thriving hub of activity. At the suggestion of Howard Smith, an African-American artist living in Finland, the gallery supported the production of prints that could be sold inexpensively to the community, and it took only a small percentage if an artist sold work. While offering a wide variety of programs, Contemporary Crafts served primarily as a showcase for young black artists. Later, it would simply become known as The Gallery; Lewis would facilitate its activities until 1979.

In addition to managing Contemporary Crafts and teaching college, Lewis began to make films on African-American artists in the late 1960s. Her purpose was threefold: to document the achievements of past and living artists, to depict artists at work in their studios and allow them to have their say about their work, and to provide the public with educational as well as entertaining material. Her first film, *The Black Artists* (Afrographics, 1966), gives a brief history of African-American art. Each succeeding film is a short documentary (each twenty-one minutes long) on a single male artist; *John Outterbridge: Black Artist, Bernie Casey: Black Artist, To Follow a Star: The Sculpture of Richmond Barthé,* and *Feathers of Wood: The Art of Charles Hutchinson.* These films continue to be shown in museums and schools throughout the country.

Further realizing her goal of public education, Lewis joined forces with Elizabeth Waddy in publishing an illustrated guide to contemporary African-American artists. The two women amassed such a large collection of artists' statements and illustrations of their art that the work was published in two volumes. *Black Artists on Art* was produced by Contemporary Crafts and distributed by Hancraft Studios in 1969. In the preface to volume two, Lewis states her definition of the role of art in Africa and America. "Art has served man in a broad functional way throughout history,'' she said, and most works created ''expressed the deeds and aspirations of special interest groups. . . . The belief that art results from and serves man as an aesthetic non-essential, is a concept of the twentieth century'' (ix). Among traditional African art works, Lewis found art objects that were used in everyday life. Once a work was destroyed or lost, a new one was made to replace it. ''This attitude keeps the art alive instead of prolonging the life of an object'' (ix). She found that social art was used early in the United States as an instrument of communication or edification. People who are involved in a revolution and struggle for life, for example, will need to communicate socially and politically. Artists should produce what is needed. ''It all depends on the PLACE, TIME and THE PEOPLE'' (xi).

For a long time Lewis had recognized the need for a solid, well-researched textbook on the history of African-American art. Throughout the early 1970s she labored over a manuscript that would become a standard textbook in universities throughout the United States. In 1978 Harcourt, Brace, Jovanovich published her *Art: African American.* Lewis's aims were clear, to educate the public about a rich segment of American history and to challenge African-American artists ''to find ways to both use the spiritual and material powers of art in such a way that the visual arts become a vehicle of understanding for the people'' (5). In her preface, she issued additional, specific directives:

> Black artists today can do much to strengthen their role in society. In their search for direction, they must be mindful of the unique situations and purposes that confront them as artists. They must also be cognizant of their obligations and responsibilities to their communities. Since a lack of adequate knowledge of the past is frequently an obstacle to the present, a primary obligation is to understand the power of art and the use of that power to inform and educate.
>
> The Black artist should also establish a direct relationship with Black people at all socioeconomic and educational levels. In this role the artist is an interpreter, a voice that makes intelligible the deepest, most meaningful aspirations of the people. The artist is a channel through which their resentments, hopes, fears, ambitions, and all the other unconscious drives that condition behavior are expressed and become explicit. In this role the artist is a community resource, valued and supported because he or she forsakes the ''ivory tower'' and gets to the heart of community life (preface, p. 4).

Still used as an important textbook, Lewis's *Art: African American Revised* was published in 1990 by Hancraft Studios.

Art Works Widely Exhibited

The preface to *Art: African American* was both a call to all African-American artists and a personal statement for Lewis. She took her own advice to heart in both her academic and artistic lives. Not an ''ivory tower'' scholar, Lewis is an accomplished artist in painting, sculpture, and graphics; her own oil painting, *Royal Sacrifice* (1969), adorns the cover of *Art: African American.* She seems to have been most prolific in the visual arts in the 1940s before marriage and in the late 1960s after she raised her children. However, her work has continued to merit attention, and the bulk of her solo exhibitions have occurred in the last two decades. Lewis's works are primarily figurative and deal with the heritage of her people. She often depicts ordinary laborers, both in the city (*Garbage Man,* oil painting, 1969; *City,* oil, 1969) and in the country (*Canefield,* serigraph, 1969; *Migrants,* linoleum cut, 1967; *Sharecroppers,* 1949).

Lewis's art has won recognition in the form of one-woman shows, including those at Clark Museum (Claremont, California), 1979, and the University Union Gallery, 1980. Her work has also been included in the following group shows: Atlanta University National Negro Annual, 1943 and 1944; Virginia Museum of Fine Arts, 1943 and 1945; City Museum of Evansville, 1946; Central Library in Brooklyn, 1946; College of the Sacred Heart, 1946; Joseph Hirshhorn Collection at the Palm Springs Museum, 1969, ''Dimensions of Black'' at the La Jolla Museum of Art, 1970; ''Two Generations of Black Artists'' at California State University, Los Angeles, 1970; James A. Porter Gallery, 1970; State Armory, Wilmington, Delaware, 1971; Whitney Museum of American Art, New York, 1971; Rainbow Sign Gallery, Berkeley, 1972; The University Union Gallery, California State Polytechnic, 1980; Smithsonian Institution Traveling Print Exhibition in the United States and Canada, 1980-1983; The University of California, San Diego, 1981; Pasadena City College, 1981; the Print Club Invitational in Philadelphia, 1983; ''African American Art in Atlanta Public and Corporate Collections,'' High Museum of Art, Atlanta, 1984; The Museum of African American Art, Delta Art Center, Winston-Salem, 1989; and Hampton University Art Museum, 1990.

Lewis not only creates and writes about art, she also collects it. Her areas of specialty are rare African works (including Bakuba pieces from the 1890s), and paintings and sculptures by African-American and Caribbean artists.

The late 1970s saw Lewis serving on many important boards and panels throughout the world. From 1976 until 1979 she was a review panelist for the Expansion Arts segment of the National Endowment for the Arts. From 1976 until 1984 she directed and curated the Clark Humanities Museum of the Claremont Colleges, winning a State Arts Council of California Award for the institution in 1980-1981. In 1977 she worked in Nigeria for the United States Zone, Second World Black and African Festival of African Peoples. The same year and the following, Lewis was on the Advisory Panel of the Education Commission for the States. Beginning in 1977, Lewis contributed to the Far Eastern Studies Awards Panel of the Fulbright Fellowship Awards for three years. And in 1979 she aided the New World Festival of the African Diaspora, Haiti.

Lewis is perhaps best known, however, for her role in the development of two institutions—a journal and a museum beginning in 1976. Then she became editor-in-chief of the quarterly publication dedicated to artists of the African diaspora, *The International Review of African American Art* (formerly known as *Black Art Quarterly).* It was largely due to her efforts that the magazine achieved an award from the State Arts Council of California in 1980-1981. It was also in 1976 that Lewis founded the Museum of African American Art in Los Angeles. There she served as senior curator until 1986, supervising not only numerous exhibitions, but also the acquisition of the collections of artists Palmer Hayden and Richmond Barthé.

Lewis's philosophy regarding certain museum practices is articulated in an article she published in 1982, "Beyond Traditional Boundaries: Collecting for Black Art Museums." She calls for the acknowledgment of two factors in determining acquisitions—the art of tradition and the art of inspiration. In the first category she includes the art of Africa, the Caribbean, South America, and African-Americans and states that these cultures must be adequately documented in black art museums. Lewis terms "the art of inspiration" as that "which comes from the extension of an experience and is developed into extended possibilities . . . [and] makes possible visualization of nonvisual experiences" (43). With these two considerations in mind, the author argues for the acquisition not only of excellent works by early masters such as Robert S. Duncanson and Henry O. Tanner (scarce though they are), but also art in categories not always well-acknowledged by museums with Western European traditions. By this she means photographs, works made by self-taught artists, and forms that have been regarded as crafts, such as ceramics and textiles. This art has long held a position of significance in black cultures and should be esteemed as such. In order to make such works accessible to the public, Lewis holds that "black art museums [must] become institutions which *give* to people" (46-47). She believes in attracting support by offering programs that integrate the performing arts with the visual arts.

Lewis's vision of black art museums was heralded by others. As her prestige in the art community grew, so did the demand for her expertise in consulting, planning exhibitions, and writing catalogues. In 1981 she received two significant awards: an honorary doctorate in humanities from Chapman College, California, and a Ford Foundation Research Grant for the 1981-1982 year. In 1982, with aid from the National Endowment for the Humanities, she supervised a Black American Art Exhibits Exchange Program between African-American artists and artists from Fiji. The following year Lewis acted as Museum Program Review panelist for the National Endowment for the Humanities. In 1984 she was honored with the Women's Building Vesta Award.

During the early 1980s Lewis arranged numerous collections and exhibitions, including "Media, Style and Tradition: The California Artists," 1981; "Wildlife Sculpture: A Bayou Heritage," 1982; "California Museum of Afro-American History and Culture: Artist-teachers" at the University of Southern California, Santa Monica, 1983; and "African Images in the New World," Los Angeles, 1983. Also in 1983 Lewis was project director of an exhibition featuring the works of artists from Brazil, Columbia, Nigeria, Surinam, and the United States; in this she was sponsored by the Art Division of Los Angeles County Fair.

Lewis's curatorships served to double her efforts to make the public aware of the rich heritage of African-American art. In 1980 she founded and directed the Asanti Gallery in Pomona, California, for the promotion of artists. Next, recognizing the urgent need for scholarly monographs on African-American masters, she published a well-illustrated volume on her lifelong friend in 1984: *The Art of Elizabeth Catlett.* Throughout her life Lewis has persisted in highlighting the achievements of individual African-American artists such as Jacob Lawrence, Palmer Hayden, Richmond Barthé, John Outterbridge, Charles Hutchinson, and Bernie Casey with solo exhibitions, catalogues, and films. Among her publications in this vein are the following articles in *International Review of African American Art:* "A Portfolio of Surinamese Art," Vol. 5 (1985); "Jacob Lawrence," Vol. 5 (1985); "Richard Hunt," Vol. 7 (1987); "George Smith," Vol. 7 (1987); and "Best Village: The Legacy and the Odyssey," with Joyce Wong Sang, Vol. 8 (1988).

In addition to being an active curator, Lewis has many professional affiliations to her credit. Her memberships throughout the years have included those in the Association of Asian Studies, the College Art Association of America, the National Conference of Artists (she was cochair from 1970 to 1973), the Southern California History Association, and the Women's Caucus for Art.

For Lewis, the word retirement meant only being released from the administrative details of university life; she never considered slowing her remarkable activity and scholarly projects. In 1984 she received three special honors; she was given a Faculty Recognition Award and was named both Professor of the Year and Professor Emerita of Scripps College.

Just months after her nominal retirement in 1984, Lewis embarked on a series of curatorships that would extend through the decade. Her aim was to provide overviews of both historical and contemporary African, African-American, and Caribbean art and give special recognition to established African-American artists with solo shows. In 1985 she directed an exhibition and symposium on "Artists of the 1930s and 1940s" at the Museum of African American Art sponsored by the National Endowment for the Arts. The same year she supervised a major exhibition and symposium on Middle States African American Artists, also with the aid of the NEA. Lewis then oversaw solo exhibitions on three masters during the next two years—"Richmond Hunt: Sculptures and Drawings," Arts America, 1987 (NEA sponsorship); "Jacob Lawrence: Prints and Drawings," Arts

America, 1988; and "Echoes of Our Past: The Narrative Artistry of Palmer C. Hayden," Los Angeles, 1988 (the latter was curated by Allan Gordon; however, Lewis served as panel member and senior curator of the Museum of African American Art).

Lewis also delivered lectures throughout America, primarily focusing on celebrated artists; presentations included "The Life and Art of Elizabeth Catlett," 1985; "The Art of Richmond Barthé and the Harlem Renaissance," Bowdoin College, 1987; "The Art of Jacob Lawrence," The Brooklyn Museum, The Seattle Museum of Art, and the Crocker Museum of Art (Sacramento), 1987; "African American Women Artists," Delta Art Center in Winston-Salem, 1989; and "Social Art and the Art of Jacob Lawrence," The Museum of Contemporary Art in Caracas, Venezuela, 1989.

The art historian most recently curated "African Presence in the Art of the Caribbean" at the Museum of Art History in San Juan, Puerto Rico, in 1989 and "Celebrations/Sights and Sounds of Being," at the Fisher Gallery of the University of Southern California in 1990.

Throughout the 1970s and 1980s Lewis also persevered in aiding other institutions. She directed the Scripps College Mellon Foundation Internship Program of The Claremont Colleges (1978-1985) and served on the advisory board of the Women's Building in Los Angeles (1983-1987) as well as the National Board of the National Conference of Artists (1975-1987). Additionally, she was a panel member of the Hurd Museum in Phoenix and the San Antonio Texas Arts Commission in 1987. There she offered her insights on "The Importance of Developing Institutions and Methods of Building Collections." And in 1989 she became president of OXUM International, the institution that publishes *The International Review of African American Art.*

The second half of the 1980s ushered in yet more well-deserved prestigious awards and positions for Lewis. In 1985 she received the Women For, Los Angeles, Achievement Award. In 1988 Lewis served on the Arts Criticism Advisory Board of National Public Radio and won the National Conference of Artists Achievement Award. In 1989 she was a board member of the College Art Association of America and was given an Honor Award for Outstanding Achievement in the Visual Arts, Women's Caucus for Art. And in 1990 Hampton University, Lewis's alma mater, conferred upon her the Doctorate of Humane Letters.

Lewis continues to be extremely active in the world as a writer, lecturer, curator, consultant, and editor. During the summer of 1990 she traveled to Belo Horizonte, Brasilia, Recife, Rio de Janerio, Salvador, and Sao Paulo on a tour of conferences and lectures concerning African-American artists and their Brazilian counterparts. Her current research focuses on African retentions in the New World. Lewis and her husband now divide their time between their homes in Miami, Florida, and Los Angeles, California.

References

Igoe, Lynn M. *Two-Hundred-and-Fifty Years of Afro-American Art: An Annotated Bibliography.* New York: Bowker, 1981.

Lewis, Samella. *Art: African American.* New York: Harcourt Brace Jovanovich, 1976.

———. *Art: African American Revised.* Los Angeles: Hancraft Studios, 1990.

———. *The Art of Elizabeth Catlett.* Los Angeles: Museum of African American Art and Hancraft Studios, 1984.

———. "Beyond Traditional Boundaries: Collecting for Black Art Museums." *Museum News* 60 (January/February, 1982: 41-47.

Lewis, Samella, and Elizabeth Waddy. *Black Artists on Art.* 2 vols. Los Angeles: Contemporary Crafts, 1969. Revised 1976. Photograph of Samella Lewis inside jacket flap, Vol. 1.

Madeja, Stanley S. *Arts and Esthetics: An Agenda for the Future.* Aspen, Colo.: Cemrel, 1976. Lewis is a contributor to this publication, which is based on a conference held at Aspen, Colorado, in June 1976, cosponsored by Cemrel and the Educational Program of the Aspen Institute for Humanistic Studies.

Who's Who in America. Chicago: Marquis, 1983; 1989.

Who's Who in American Art. 18th ed. New York: Bowker, 1973, 1975, 1976, 1978, 1980, 1989-1990.

Who's Who Among Black Americans, 1990/1991. 6th ed. Detroit: Gale Research, 1990.

Wise, Leonard. "Portrait of Samella." *Essence* 3 (February 1973): 46-47, 80. This brief biography of Lewis provides extensive quotes from the artist as well as photographs of her and her painting, *Garbage Man.*

Collections

Art by Samella Lewis is in the following collections: Clark-Atlanta University Collection (Atlanta, Georgia); Baltimore Museum of Art (Baltimore, Maryland); Boys College (Aman, Jordan); Denison University (Granville, Ohio); Hampton University Collection (Hampton, Virginia); High Museum (Atlanta, Georgia); Oakland Museum of Art (Oakland, California); Ohio State University (Columbus, Ohio); Palm Springs Museum (Palm Springs, Florida); Pennsylvania State University (University Park, Pennsylvania); and Virginia Museum of Art (Richmond, Virginia).

Theresa Leininger

Abbey Lincoln

(1930-)

Singer, composer, actress, poet

Singer, composer, actress, poet Abbey Lincoln, whose true name is Anna Marie Woolridge Roach and who is also known as Gaby Lee and Aminata Moseka, was born August 6, 1930. Although born in Chicago the ninth of twelve children, she was raised in the country in Michigan because her mother thought that the country atmosphere would be better for the children. Abbey Lincoln attended a small country school in Michigan and graduated from Kalamazoo Central High School in Kalamazoo, Michigan.

Like many black women of her day, Lincoln worked as a maid for a short time after finishing high school, but her desire to perform and to sing led her, at the age of twenty, to begin her professional singing career in Jackson, Michigan, in 1950. In 1951 she moved to California and was performing in local clubs under her real name, Anna Marie Woolridge. After moving to Hollywood, she studied music for several years under prominent vocal and dramatic coaches. From 1952 to 1954, Lincoln performed in various clubs in Hawaii, using the name Gaby Lee. In 1956, she conceded to her manager's suggestion to change her name to Abbey Lincoln with the label "The Colored Bombshell." "I frankly didn't mind the name change," Lincoln said, "since Anna Marie was such a sweet name and I think people take on the character of the name they have. I liked Abbey because there's more protection in it. It seemed flexible and it swung." It was her agent's idea to name her Lincoln after the sixteenth president of the United States. "The Lincoln was kind of tongue in cheek, but no one from the beginning ever got the connection," says Abbey ("Abbey Lincoln Teams Up," 54). Once again she performed in the Hollywood clubs as a club vocalist from 1954 to 1957. Lincoln also recorded songs for Liberty Records in 1956.

Lincoln's club performances have won her rave reviews from numerous critics. In an article that appeared in *Time* magazine, one critic said that Lincoln "has a captivating, come-hither way with a song and the sinuous good looks that make audiences pay attention from ring side clear back to the chromium bar stools. . . . Abbey depends on an occasional shimmy of her spangled hips or a body shaping gesture of her hands to prime her audience for her blues-tinted ballads. Her timing and enunciation are precise. Usually she plays the elegant if slightly shopworn lady, but sometimes she drops that role to launch into a gusty celebration of the simple trials of being a woman" (45).

Another critic writing for *Essence* on the jazz grand divas said of her:

> On stage Abbey was electric with the music. Her lyrics flamed with messages of freedom. Her songs included cries and screams. Out of her mouth came pure instrumental sounds. She brought to her jazz performances cultural truth. She was a sultry diva resonant with pain. Delicate but defiant. Her vocal style was as savage as it was purposeful . . . Still evolving as a singer-composer. Dramatist, Poet. Critically acclaimed as one of jazz's most versatile performers. A truly gifted, creative woman with a new name. An African one, Aminata Moseka added to Abbey Lincoln. Still defiantly singing her own innovative personal style of jazz she fiercely called 'Moseka music" (De Veaux, 56).

Jazz critic Nat Hentoff said that Lincoln's singing comes from a self-liberation, a renewed and urgent pride in herself as a black woman. He ranks her among the great jazz singers of our time. "Abbey has been hailed by many of the outstanding black jazz performers of our era, including Coleman Hawkins, Benny Carter and Charlie Mingus, as a singer to be classed with the likes of Billie Holiday" (Ploski, 1976, 884).

Lincoln and Max Roach Become Jazz Team

When Lincoln began her professional career in the fifties, she was a provocative supperclub singer who was taught to think white. Lincoln says of herself, "I was told not to sound like a Negro. They put me into a Marilyn Monroe-type dress and I sang the more titillating standards and phony folk tunes" (Blackwell, 295). But as the country's political climate changed, so did Lincoln. She cut her hair into an Afro and married Max Roach, a master jazz drummer. Roach and Lincoln were the hottest couple of jazz during the sixties. Their decade-long relationship was also as tempestuous as the times. Roach and Lincoln enjoyed an international reputation and their collaborations became classics. Along with an all-star jazz group, Lincoln and Roach made numerous recordings for Riverside Records and many nightclub appearances, including the Astor Club in London.

Roach introduced Lincoln to New York's jazz scene as well as to some of the most inventive greats, such as Sonny Rollins, Thelonious Monk, John Coltrane, and Eric Dolphy. But Roach also had another affect on Lincoln—he encouraged her to look into herself and to "say something intelligent" (Blackwell, 295). He was also instrumental in her release from the "sepia siren" phase. Lincoln continued to go through her own transformation from a "glamor-struck novice to a self-aware and proud black artist" ("Abbey Lincoln Teams Up," 54). She believed that "there was something terrible happening to women in this country. They're all trying to be something they're not. . . . We've got to get past all the superficial things and look at the soul of a woman" (Ploski, 1976, 884).

Performing as a vocalist was not Lincoln's sole professional interest. She was also in several motion pictures. Lincoln recalled her first motion picture in 1957, *The Girl Can't Help It*, in which she appeared with Jane Mansfield. In one scene Lincoln wore the same famous purple gown once worn by Marilyn Monroe in *Gentlemen Prefer Blonds*. "I got to the preview, and then I saw a black girl singing. For a few seconds I wondered who that woman was. Then it hit, this was me! I didn't like that at all!" says Lincoln ("Abbey Lincoln Teams Up," 54). The billing line: "The Colored Bombshell" had come home to haunt her.

In 1974, Lincoln appeared in a second film. She gave a sensitive portrayal of Josie in *Nothing But a Man*, a low-budget film with a big message. Then in 1968, Lincoln costarred in the film *For The Love of Ivy* with Sidney Poiter. She portrayed Ivy. It is somewhat ironic that Lincoln should play Ivy, a domestic worker who wants to leave her job as a maid to take up another career, which is what Lincoln had done years before. Lincoln appeared in a fourth film, *A Short Walk to Daylight*, in 1972. There were also guest appearances on several television shows, such as "Marcus Welby, M.D." and "The Name of the Game."

As versatile as Abbey Lincoln is, it comes as no surprise that she has also performed in the theater. In 1959 she toured in the leading role with a Jamaican road company in *Wine in the Wilderness*. She has also written two plays, *A Pig in a Poke* and *A Steak O' Lean*.

References

"Abbey Lincoln Teams Up with Poiter in Romantic Comedy Film." *Ebony*, 23 (October 1968): 52-54. Includes photographs.

Blackwell, Earl, ed. *Celebrity Register*. 3rd ed. New York: Simon and Schuster, 1973.

De Veaux Alexis. "Do be do wow!" *Essence*, 17 (October 1986): 56.

Mapp, Edward. *Directory of Blacks in the Performing Arts*. Metuchen, N.J.: Scarecrow Press, 1978.

Ploski, Harry A., and Warren Marr, II, W. eds. *The Negro Almanac*. 3rd ed. New York: Bellwether Publishing Co., 1976.

Ploski, Harry A., and J. Williams, eds. *The Negro Almanac*. 4th ed. New York: Wiley, 1983.

"Topic A." *Time*, 71 (May 26, 1958): 45.

Who's Who of American Women. Vol. 2. Chicago: Marquis, 1975.

Nina T. Elliott

Inabel Burns Lindsay

(1900-1983)

Social worker, educator

Inabel Burns Lindsay, a social work educator who achieved national recognition for her work, was born in St. Joseph, Missouri, on February 13, 1900, the youngest of six children of Margaret (Hartshorn) Burns and Joseph Smith Burns. The mother was reared by her grandparents, former slaves who had purchased their freedom. The Hartshorn family had migrated from Virginia to Missouri during Reconstruction. Lindsay had three brothers and two sisters. She was eight years younger than her next sister. At one time the Hartshorn great-grandmother lived with the family and was Lindsay's babysitter.

Lindsay's father was a farmer. Her mother had only an eighth-grade education, but she stressed the importance of education and wanted her children to have more than she. Margaret Burns persuaded her husband to move the family into town, where he got a job. The parents separated when Lindsay was three years old. At that time, an older brother, Weyman, who was planning to enter Howard University's medical school in Washington, D.C., came home to look after the family. He and another brother, Ocie, who became a father-like figure took very good care of Lindsay. She had vision problems from about age three to age seven and consequently was taught at home, with a regular schedule, by her siblings. With improved eyesight, Lindsay finally entered school at age eight and was placed in the fourth grade. She graduated from high school when she was fifteen.

Lindsay enrolled at Howard University when she was only sixteen years old. Although there were institutions closer to home, the family was looking for a place in which a black girl could live in a dormitory, in a protected environment, because of her health and vision problems. She received a bachelor of arts degree in education in 1920 with a major in mathematics.

Lindsay participated in several student strikes against the university and also led one, which lasted about one month, when the price of board was raised with notification to parents but not to students. During the strike, she persuaded neighborhood housewives to feed the students. The university then moved against female students living in the dormitory with a ruling that they could not eat outside the dormitory. As graduation grew near, Lindsay did not feel optimistic about teaching; she preferred working one-on-one. While at Howard, she met Edward C. Williams, the chief librarian, who encouraged her to think about social work as a career, and sent for information about an Urban League Fellowship.

During her junior year at Howard, Inabel Burns met Arnett Grant Lindsay, who was a senior. He graduated in 1919 but stayed to study black history under Carter G. Woodson. After graduating from Howard, the couple moved to New York City.

First Position As Social Worker Offered

Inabel Burns Lindsay received a scholarship to the New York School of Social Work and stayed for one year (1920-21) of a two-year certificate program as an Urban League Fellow. There were only two other black students enrolled at the time. They were second-year students—E. Franklin Frazier and Frances Williams—who were both very helpful to Lindsay. Her first practice work was in the large tenements of Harlem. Again she found that she preferred a smaller situation, so she was moved to an agency in Brooklyn at midyear.

At the same time, Arnett Lindsay was attending the New York University School of Business Administration. He worked in New York for a year or two, but then moved to St. Louis where he worked as business manager of the black YMCA. He later became manager of the St. Louis Finance Company.

Inabel Burns Lindsay went to work at the Cleveland Urban League for the summer of 1921. Margaret Burns, who was unhappy about her daughter living in New York and about her being a social worker, had become ill. Inabel Lindsay's sister and brother had become teachers and their mother wanted Lindsay to do the same. She was offered jobs at the YWCA in Brooklyn and in Columbus, Ohio, but turned those down due to her mother's illness.

Lindsay's older sister took Lindsay's credentials to the St. Joseph, Missouri, school board and applied for a teaching position on her sister's behalf. Lindsay was given a job teaching a fifth-grade class of students who were selected by the principal.

One year later Lindsay took a position at the Attucks Elementary School in Kansas City. It was close to home and she received more pay. (Her mother, still protective, found an apartment nearby, and moved into it.) Lindsay did so well with her combination fourth- and fifth-grade class of children with behavioral problems that the principal of Lincoln High School invited her to teach there. She accepted the invitation, staying there for two years until her marriage to Arnett Lindsay in 1925. At the time it was generally expected that a married woman did not work and her husband did not wish her to work. She gave up teaching but the couple agreed that they would reconsider the situation after one year.

The National Urban League then asked Inabel Lindsay to repay her fellowship by being a research assistant for a survey in Springfield, Illinois. Since the position was for only six weeks, her husband agreed. The director of the study was the noted sociologist, Charles S. Johnson. It was hoped that recommendations resulting from the study would help ease racial tensions in the community. From this position Lindsay also wrote for *Opportunity* magazine.

Lindsay returned to St. Louis, where several social work agencies were interested in her. She accepted a position as a caseworker at the Provident Association, which was concerned with child and family welfare. She received promotions and soon became a senior worker. Because of her background in mathematics, she was chosen to compile the statistical reports for the agency. In 1929 the agency selected Lindsay as its representative at a one-month institute in New York City offered by the Family Welfare Association. She continued to receive promotions until she was next below the superintendent of the agency. About one year later she was made acting superintendent. Lindsay had a tendency to speak out when she saw something wrong, so at times she had difficulty with other people in the agency. At one of her evaluations, Lindsay told the overall agency supervisor that she had received insufficient supervision as a beginner and tried to explain the difficulties a new person faces. Although her own supervisor was extremely upset, the overall supervisor suggested that she would like to propose Lindsay for a position in another district, this one all-white, as opposed to the all-black district in which she was working. Lindsay stayed with the agency until about 1932, when she became ill and had to leave. When she returned to work in 1933, she was sent to another office.

When the Federal Emergency Relief Program was instituted in 1934, it supplemented the budgets of the private agencies. The Provident Association expanded the number of districts to sixteen, and Lindsay became a district superintendent. The private agencies eventually became public welfare agencies.

In 1936 Lindsay decided to go back to school, since she had completed only one year of the program at the New York School of Social Work. While working in St. Louis, she had taken a summer term at the University of Chicago and chose to go there. Her husband went to work with Carter G. Woodson while she was in Chicago and in late 1937 began to teach at Clark and Morris Brown colleges in Atlanta, Georgia. In 1937 Lindsay received her Master of Arts degree from the University of Chicago School of Social Service Administration.

Lindsay Becomes Social Work Educator and Administrator

E. Franklin Frazier, one of Lindsay's friends from the New York School of Social Work and head of the sociology department, was looking for a social worker to come to Howard University. The graduate program in social work had been started in 1935 but had become too much for Frazier to handle along with his other duties. Lindsay became director of the program and developed new courses that offered a certificate at the end of two years.

In 1938 Lindsay's husband became ill in Atlanta and went to Washington, D.C., for medical care. As they both felt that he should stay in Washington, he resigned from his positions in Atlanta and moved to the district. In the 1940s Arnett Lindsay became manager of a development and later opened his own real estate office.

About 1940 Howard University's social work program became a division within the graduate school. In 1944 the program became an autonomous unit, and Inabel Lindsay was named acting dean of the School of Social Work. The university continued to look for a man to take over the deanship. However, when the Association of Schools of Social Work would not accredit a school with only an acting dean, Howard University named Lindsay dean. Her goal was to make the school the best possible, open to students of all ethnic backgrounds. She introduced cultural content in the courses, prepared social workers to enter urban situations, and brought foreign students into the program.

When she was appointed dean, Lindsay decided to study for her doctoral degree. Although she had continued her study for an advanced degree at the University of Chicago during the summers of 1938 and 1940, she selected the University of Pittsburgh for completion of her study. She used her sabbatical and in 1952 received the doctorate of social work. Her doctoral dissertation was entitled: "The Participation of Negroes in the Establishment of Welfare Services, 1865-1900: with Special Reference to the District of Columbia, Maryland, and Virginia."

In 1958 the Department of State selected Lindsay to receive an award that enabled her to travel to Scandinavian countries to study their social welfare programs for the aged and children. On sabbatical in 1960-61, she traveled to the Caribbean as a visiting professor: One of her responsibilities was to help study the feasibility of establishing a school of social work at the University of the West Indies. Throughout her career, Lindsay participated in many institutes and seminars, both nationally and internationally.

After retirement in 1967 Lindsay served for more than two years as a consultant to the Department of Health, Education, and Welfare. In 1969 she was a visiting lecturer in the School of Social Work at the University of Maryland. In 1970 she was a special consultant to the Senate Special Committee on Aging, and wrote a pamphlet, "Multiple Hazards of Age and Race," a working paper (Washington, D.C.: U.S. Government Printing Office, 1971). She was on the board of the National Council on Aging and served in various capacities in the National Association of Social Workers, the National Social Welfare Assembly, and the Council on Social Work Education. She served on many committees during her tenure at Howard University. Other interests included the American Foundation for the Blind, the Edwin Gould Foundation for Children, the League of Women Voters, and the National Urban League. She was very active in the Episcopal church and served on the social relations board of the diocese of Washington, D.C., on the National Committee on Institutions for Children and Youth, and on the National Council of Bishops.

Lindsay published many articles in social work journals and served on the editorial advisory board of *Casework*. She participated in the 1950 White House Conference on Children and Youth and served as a leader for the 1960 conference. She was a delegate to the 1966 White House Conference on Civil Rights. Among her honors are alumnae awards from each of the educational institutions that she attended and an honorary doctorate from Howard University in 1982.

The Lindsays had no children but helped to raise and support children of relatives and friends.

Among Inabel Lindsay's friends and colleagues were sociologist E. Franklin Frazier, historians Charles H. Wesley and Rayford W. Logan, and Howard University president Mordecai Johnson. Lindsay, who became ill from diabetes, died September 10, 1983.

References

Black Women Oral History Project Interview with Inabel Burns Lindsay. Cambridge: Schlesinger Library, Radcliffe College, 1980.

Washington Post, 15 September 1983.

Collections

The tapes and transcript of an interview for the Black Women Oral History Project, as well as mimeographed material supplied by Inabel Burns Lindsay, are available at the Schlesinger Library, Radcliffe College, Cambridge. Other material is available at the Moorland-Spingarn Research Center, Howard University.

Ruth Edmonds Hill

Adella Hunt Logan

(1863-1915)

Educator, women's rights activist, clubwoman

Adella Hunt Logan, a forceful advocate for women's suffrage and education for blacks, was born in Sparta, Georgia, in February 1863. Her mother, Mariah Hunt, a free woman of color, was descended from blacks, whites, and Cherokee Indians. Her father, Henry Hunt, a white farmer and tanner, served in the Confederate army during Logan's early childhood. In deference to local opposition to overt interracial relationships, Mariah Hunt lived apart from her husband, with her eight children in a home on Hunt Hill, the Sparta neighborhood where the more comfortably situated black population resided. Their church was the Ebenezer Colored Methodist Episcopal.

The three older children in the Hunt family received only minimal education, but they helped to send the five younger ones through school and college. Logan, the fourth child, attended Sparta's Bass Academy and became a certified teacher at the age of sixteen. That same year, 1879, with the recommendation of her teacher and the county's state representative, she was granted a scholarship to attend Atlanta University and became the first black from Hancock County, Georgia, to acquire a college degree. Atlanta University later awarded her an honorary master of arts degree for her work in education.

For two years following the completion of her studies, Logan taught in an American Missionary School in Albany, Georgia. In 1883 she turned down an opportunity to take a "comfortable" teaching position at her alma mater, choosing instead to go to Tuskegee Institute at the urging of Booker T. Washington. During the early years at Tuskegee, Logan filled many positions on the small faculty and briefly worked at Alabama State Teachers' College. She taught English and social sciences, served as Tuskegee's first librarian, and for a short time became principal.

She also met Warren Logan, a Hampton schoolmate of Washington's, who had gone to Tuskegee Institute in 1882. He was Washington's oldest and most trusted friend on the faculty. In addition to teaching, he directed the traveling men's singing ensemble, served as treasurer, and was a member of the institute's board of trustees. These two dedicated teachers married in December 1888. Because Adella Logan's position was considered less critical to the institute, her work at the school was subordinated to her husband's. In 1890 she gave birth to the first of nine children—six of whom survived to adulthood. She had borne the last in 1909 when she was forty-six, and after she had come close to death when she lost a kidney.

Following her marriage, Logan taught only intermittently between difficult pregnancies, limited by the demands of her large household and official responsibilities as the wife of Tuskegee's second-ranking official. Nonetheless, she often called teaching her greatest passion. She became the guiding force behind the creation of the model school and teacher's training facilities at Tuskegee and participated in similar educational endeavors throughout the South.

Logan became immersed in the activities of the Tuskegee Woman's Club, a charter affiliate of the National Association of Colored Women's Clubs. The Tuskegee Woman's Club functioned in many arenas. Although Logan worked with reading seminars and theatrical productions, her most important club involvement centered around two subjects. First, she worked with local farm women in Macon County and attempted to improve standards of health, hygiene, and nutrition for them and for their children. She strongly advocated the importance of annual physical checkups for all children and championed the cause of full-time education for young people throughout the county.

Women's Suffrage Promoted

Logan's second major involvement with the Tuskegee Woman's Club was her work on behalf of women's suffrage. At a time when most white Alabamians either ignored or adamantly opposed the very idea of votes for women, at Tuskegee Logan led monthly discussions about the importance of suffrage. These endeavors also extended beyond the local club activities. She encouraged her students to hold demonstrations in participatory democracy as part of their course work. She lectured at regional and national conferences of the National Association of Colored Women's Clubs, and served briefly as that group's director of the divisions of Rural Affairs and of Suffrage. She amassed a large library of reading materials about suffrage that she shared with students and colleagues, and she wrote about the importance of suffrage for women—particularly for women of color—in the *Colored American* and the *Crisis*.

Logan was a small woman with piercing eyes, long dark hair, and great personal intensity who, to any uninformed observer, looked white. Because the cause of women's suffrage concerned her so greatly, she surreptitiously attended segregated meetings of the predominantly white National American Women's Suffrage Association in the South, without identifying herself as a "colored woman." Subsequently, she would bring back the information she gathered at these forums to share with her associates in the black community. For many years Logan was the only life member of the National American Women's Suffrage Association from the state of Alabama. She also contributed articles to that organization's newspaper about the activities of the National Association of Colored Women's Clubs.

Logan maneuvered along a tortuous path in the often-discussed ideological feud between Booker T. Washington and W. E. B. Du Bois over the appropriate direction for education in the black community. She maintained a philosophical adherence to Du Bois's philosophies while remaining a close personal friend, professional associate, and next-door neighbor to Washington. In addition, she encouraged scientist George Washington Carver in his work, particularly in his lesser-known endeavors as a painter.

In the fall of 1915, Logan suffered a severe emotional collapse, possibly triggered by a defeat for the women's suffrage movement in Alabama and undoubtedly aggravated by poor physical health, tensions in her marriage, and concerns about her children. She went to Michigan's famous Battle Creek Sanitarium for treatment. A few weeks later, however, she was summarily recalled to Tuskegee by news of Washington's impending death. After Washington died in November of that year, Logan's emotional health never returned. On December 12, as philanthropists, politicians, and other dignitaries gathered at Tuskegee to attend a memorial service for Washington, Logan jumped to her death from the top floor of one of the school's buildings.

References

Alexander, Adele Logan. "Ambiguous Lives: Free Women of Color in Rural Georgia.'' Master's thesis, Howard University, 1987.

Atlanta University Publications. No. 2. Social and Physical Condition of Negroes in Cities. Atlanta: May 1897.

Colored American 9 (September 1905): 487-89.

Culp. D.W., ed. *Twentieth-Century Negro Literature*. Napierville, Ill.: J. L. Nichols, 1902. Reprinted. Miami: Mnemosne Publishing, 1969.

Logan, Adella Hunt. ''Colored Women as Voters.'' *Crisis* 4 (September 1912): 242-43.

The Negro Farmer 14 (April 1914).

Washington, M. Booker T., comp. *Work for the Colored Woman of the South*. [Tuskagee, Ala.: Tuskagee Institute], 1894.

The Woman's Journal, January 26, 1901; January 17, 1903.

Collections

Letters of Adella Hunt Logan are in the Booker T. Washington Papers, Manuscript Division, Library of Congress, and in the Emily Howland Collection, Cornell University. Logan is mentioned in many of historian Rosalyn Terborg-Penn's writings about blacks in suffrage and the women's club movement.

Adele Logan Alexander

Audre Lorde

(1934-)

Poet, essayist, librarian

It is impossible to categorize the poet Audre Lorde, for the layers of complexity in her works and Lorde's courage in touching the center of her personal pain make it difficult. ''I cannot be categorized,'' Lorde has declared. Critics ''have always wanted to cast me in a particular light,'' she explains, to narrow her so that she can fulfill their expectations (Evans, 263).

If we cannot categorize Lorde, we can name her as she names herself. She is, in the world of art, the black unicorn she describes in one of her most popular poems—a rare individual. Like the unicorn, she is ''greedy,'' ''impatient.'' She was ''mistaken / for a shadow / or symbol. . . . / It is not on her lap where the horn rests / but deep in her moonpit / growing.'' She is ''restless.'' She is ''unrelenting'' and, like the black unicorn, she ''is not / free'' (*The Black Unicorn*, 7).

Lorde's avenue toward freedom is her writing. She began writing as a young woman because ''there was no one saying what I wanted and needed to hear'' (Evans, 263), and to work through very personal pain which continues to inform her poetry. She is the woman outsider: ''Child-woman seeking still a mother's love. Black mother agonizing the fated issue of her womb. Black lesbian feminist poet'' (Martin, 277).

Lorde's personal/private pain is a transforming experience for her readers. It transcends her childhood in Brooklyn and her reality as a lesbian. It educates, heals, and takes us to that space in the spiritual universe where there is no escaping truth or moral responsibility.

She invokes the spirit of ancestral women in her poetry. She travels to Africa, where there are mothers/women whose faces are her own. She celebrates the courage of defiant women, like Harriet and Assata, who give testimony to the strength of black women as survivors in such poems as the powerful ''A Litany of Survivors.''

Lorde is not a message-poet, but ''the question of social protest and art is inseparable'' for her. ''Art for art's sake doesn't exist for me'' (Evans, 264). When she airs her pain, which is not hers alone, ''That's the beginning of social protest'' (Evans, 264). As a black woman she protests racial oppression and sexual oppression. As a socialist she protests class oppression. As a lesbian she protests them all, bringing into focus the sharp edges of homophobia. More powerfully than any other writer, living or dead, Lorde broke the silence on lesbian love. In her autobiography *Zami: A New Spelling of My Name* she writes vividly of her love-making with several women, most especially Afrekete, ''whose print remains'' upon Lorde's life ''with the resonance and power of an emotional taboo'' (252-53).

> Afrekete Afrekete ride me to the crossroads where we shall sleep, coated in the woman's power. The sound of our bodies meeting is the prayer of all strangers and sisters, that the discarded evils, abandoned at all crossroads, will not follow us upon our journeys (*Zambi*, 252).

It is not only the passion/joy of her personal relationships Lorde celebrates in her writings, it is also ''the erotic urge, the place that is uniquely female'' (Evans, 265). ''Within a woman's capacity for feeling, our ability to love, to touch the erotic,'' Lorde writes, ''lies so much of our power, our ability to posit, to vision'' (Evans, 265).

Poetry Reflects Triumphs and Pain

For a woman who feels ''a duty to speak the truth as I see it and to share not just my triumphs, not just the things that felt good, but the pain, the intense often unmitigating pain,'' sharing the pain of her battling cancer and surviving is another example of her courage and her commitment to truth. *The Cancer Journals* (1980) is, therefore, another gift from

Lorde to those who would understand that only by walking through pain, and touching its inside, can we name ourselves, claim ourselves, and make a difference in the world. The *Journals* consist of prose entries which are really poems without the typography of a poem: "I want to write of the pain I am feeling right now, of the lukewarm tears that will not stop coming into my eyes."

Lorde was born in New York City on February 18, 1934, the daughter of Frederic Byron Lorde and Linda Belmar Lorde. She is the former wife of Edward A. Rollins, whom she married in 1962, and has two children, Elizabeth and Jonathan. Lorde studied for a year, 1954, at the National University of Mexico, received a B.A. from Hunter College in 1959, and an M.L.S. from Columbia University in 1961. By training a librarian, Lorde worked at Mount Vernon Public Library, 1960-62; Saint Clare's School of Nursing, 1965-66; the Towne School, 1966-68; City College of the City University of New York, 1968-69; Lehman College, 1969-70; John Jay College of Criminal Justice, 1970-80; and, since, 1980, at Hunter College.

Lorde's honors and awards include a National Endowment for the Arts grant, 1968; Creative Artists Public Service Award, 1972, 1976; Honorary Commission, governor of Louisiana, 1973; Woman of the Year Award, Staten Island Community College, 1975; Broadside Press Poet's Award, 1975; and Creative Artists Public Service Book Award for Poetry, 1974, for *From a Land Where Other People Live.*

Her writings include the books of poetry *The First Cities, Cables to Rage, From a Land Where Other People Live, New York Head Shop and Museum, Between Our Selves, Coal, Passion: New Poems, 1977-1980, Chosen Poems Old and New,* and *Our Dead Behind Us.* Among her other works are *Uses of the Erotic: The Erotic as Power, Sister Outsider,* and *Burst of Light.*

References

Black Writers. Detroit: Gale Research, 1989.

Evans, Mari. *Black Women Writers: A Critical Evaluation.* New York: Doubleday, 1984.

Lorde, Audre. *The Black Unicorn.* New York: Norton, 1978.

Who's Who in America. 43rd ed. Chicago, Marquis, 1984.

Who's Who of American Women. 8th ed. Chicago: Marquis, 1973.

Who's Who Among Black Americans, 1990/91. 6th ed. Detroit: Gale Research, 1991.

Gloria Wade-Gayles

Josephine Harreld Love

(1914-)

Pianist, arts administrator, musicologist

Josephine Harreld Love was born on December 11, 1914, in Atlanta, Georgia. She is of mixed parentage, her father being black and her mother white and American Indian. Her fascination with fine arts was apparent at an early age. Josephine Love says, "My father was my first and probably my most important teacher" (Parker, 3). Her grandfather, William Jefferson White, was one of the founders of Morehouse College, and her mother, Claudia Turner (White) Harreld, was a poet. Her father, Kemper Harreld, a concert violinist, was the first director of the Morehouse College Glee Club. For forty-five years he was head of the music departments of Morehouse and Spelman colleges. He encouraged and actively promoted his daughter's inclination toward music and fine arts.

At the age of three, Love began the study of music under the guidance and instruction of her father. By age ten she had decided to devote herself to the study of the piano, and by age twelve she was giving piano recitals. An announcement of one recital reads:

The Business and Industrial Assembly
presents
JOSEPHINE HARRELD
Child Pianist

TUESDAY EVENING, JUNE 12th.
8:15 o'clock
BLUE TRIANGLE Y.W.C.A.
Mary Hairston, President (Program, 1926).

Love began a process of self-discovery and development of her potentialities while she was a young student at Spelman. In addition to pursuing a major in English, she continued her study of piano under her father's tutelage and played the violin and viola in the college orchestra. She explored other interests as well. She was a member of the Spelman College Glee Club, the Spelman-Morehouse Chorus—a choreographic group that developed pantomimic interpretations of Negro spirituals—and the University Players, the dramatic organization of Spelman, Morehouse, and Atlanta University.

In 1932, in recognition of her creativity, she received the William Travers Jerome Award for arrangement of the Negro spiritual "You May Bury Me in the East," and in 1933 she won recognition for her musical setting for the Greek tragedy *Antigone*.

Love's artistic activities did not cease at the close of the academic year, for during the summer following her junior year in college she assisted the director of a children's theater, organized and developed by Atlanta University as an experiment in creative expression. Some of the girls in the group showed unusual ability in creating original airs, and fifteen melodies for nursery rhymes were produced and transcribed into musical notation by Josephine Love. Her unusual interest in children and her ability to work with them were evident even before her graduation from college.

It is a pleasure to hear Josephine Harreld Love relate some of her experiences with the little bands of blacks who, with her father, carried the torch of high culture during the dark years of passage of blacks in America. This group of cultural stalwarts included her father, Kemper Harreld, Clarence Cameron White, Paul Laurence Dunbar, Nathaniel Dett, Harry Burleigh, brothers James Weldon and J. Rosamond Johnson, William Grant Still, and Langston Hughes, who were stars in a firmament of high culture in America despite the color of their skin. This black elite seemed determined to prove that blacks could rise despite race to the highest levels of accepted culture whether in music, poetry, manners, literature, or other fields.

Love's educational background is impressive: a B.A. in English from Spelman College, 1933; diploma in piano from Juilliard School of Music, 1935; and an M.A. in musicology, Radcliffe College, 1936. While at Juilliard she attended sculpture classes. She studied with artist Hale Woodruff for two years. She also studied piano at Mozarteum Academy, Salzburg, Austria, 1935; and piano and musicology, University of Michigan, 1960-1965. She studied composition with Walter Piston at Harvard University and piano with Hazel Harrison in Chicago. Her professional experience includes positions at Bennett College, Greensboro, North Carolina, 1936-1937; Oakland University, Rochester, Michigan, 1970-1972; and the University of Michigan, Ann Arbor, 1987 to the present.

Black Heritage Cultural Center Founded

In 1939 Josephine Harreld Love made her concert debut as a piano soloist in San Diego, California. She was accompanist for Anne Wiggins Brown, who had been chosen by George Gershwin to play Bess in the original production of *Porgy and Bess*. She toured widely for several years and in 1942 she settled in Detroit, where she established a music studio. She is cofounder with Gwendolyn Hogue of Your Heritage House in the Detroit Cultural Center, an art museum and art school for children that includes an archive of materials from and about noted black Americans in the arts. She speaks of the importance of nurturing a child's interest in the arts and the necessity for having a supportive environment. Her childhood has been infused with art.

Josephine Love's special area of interest and expertise is the role of black colleges in the development of African-American music. On the founding of Heritage House, she said it was:

> the summation of dreams and experiences which I'd held fast to for most of my life. We called it by that name to emphasize that an individual's heritage is not simply their own immediate past but a legacy of their society's past (Parker, 3).

For her work in the arts, Josephine Harreld Love has received numerous awards and honors. These include an Award in Recognition from the Detroit Chapter of Jack and Jill of America, 1971; Great Contributions to Black America Award, Wayne County Community College, 1975; Children's Service Award, National Black Child Development Institute, 1978; Virginia Kiah Honor Certificate of Service Award, National Conference of Artists, 1980; Spirit of Detroit Award, 1982; Outstanding Leadership Award and Barbara Rose Collins Community Service Award, 1983; Creative Projects Award, Alpha Kappa Alpha Sorority, 1983; Focus and Impact Award, Oakland University, 1984; Arts Foundation of Michigan Patron Award, 1987; and Institution Builders Award, National Black Arts Festival, 1988. She serves on a number of boards and review panels, lectures widely on the arts, and has published a number of articles, including biographical sketches of Hazel Harrison and Azalia Hackley.

On June 18, 1941, Josephine Harreld married William Thomas Love, whom she met during a recital at Detroit's Second Baptist Church. He was assistant Wayne County Medical Examiner. The Love's have two children, Claudia Victoria Hopkins, a homemaker and civic volunteer in Washington, D.C., and William Thomas Love, Jr., a psychiatrist in Chicago, Illinois.

References

Parker, Barbara. "Your Heritage House Founded With, by Love." *Promenade*, 1978. 3. Includes photograph.

Southern, Eileen. *Biographical Dictionary of Afro-American and African Musicians*. Westport, Conn.: Greenwood Press, 1982.

Who's Who of American Women. 1st ed. Chicago: Marquis, 1964.

Photographs of Josephine Harreld Love appear in *Black Personalities of Detroit*, Detroit Public Library Calendar, 1970, and in *Black Photographers 1840-1940*, ed. Deborah Willis-Ryan, 1985.

Roy L. Hill

Ruth B. Love

(1935-)

Educator, school administrator, entrepreneur

Ruth Burnett Love (Holloway) is an American educational leader. She was born on April 22, 1935, in Lawton, Oklahoma, into a family with a long-term commitment to education. Love's grandfather was a faculty member at Langston University, her father founded the first school for blacks in Lawton, and she reported that her favorite game while growing up was playing school.

Love grew up in Bakersfield, California. She received her B.A. in elementary education from San Jose State University, her M.A. in guidance and counseling from San Francisco State University, and her Ph.D. in human behavior from United States International University in San Diego.

As seen in her photographs, Love is an attractive, self-possessed woman who carries herself with great confidence and flair. She married early in her career and used the name Ruth Love Holloway, but by the late 1970s she was divorced and had returned to the use of her maiden name, Love, in her published articles.

In the first decade of Love's career, she quickly gained experience in a variety of roles, moving between teaching in Oakland, California, and England, counseling in the Oakland schools, and beginning her role as an administrator in Africa and in the California state educational system. Love began her years as a teacher in the Oakland Unified School District from 1954 to 1959 and from 1961 to 1963. During 1958 she was also the project coordinator for the Girls' Correctional Institution. In 1960 Love was a Fulbright Exchange Teacher in Cheshire, England. From 1960 to 1962 she was a counselor for the Oakland school system and during the summer of 1962 she served as project director for Operation Crossroads in Ghana. Next she served as consultant to the Bureau of Pupil Personnel Services in the California State Department of Education from 1963 to 1965.

In the second decade of her career, Love moved into major administrative roles. From 1965 through 1971 she served as director of the Bureau of Compensatory Education in the California Department of Education. In 1971 Love became director of the Right to Read Program in the United States Department of Education. Her goals for the program and the approaches she used for tackling her role as director characterized her style in the positions she held for the next decade and a half: "The eradication of illiteracy [by 1980] is the goal of Right to Read." The program focused on "adults who are without the skills needed to read and on children who are potential illiterates." In the Right to Read Program, Love focused on identifying a goal, the eradication of illiteracy, and a collective mobilization strategy of all those involved, including teachers, teacher trainers, reading specialists, library aides, tutors, and student teachers. She encouraged them to use a variety of reading and learning methods, emphasized staff development processes, program planning, and stimulation processes to constantly engage all those involved.

Love also approached the problem of illiteracy conceptually. "She found black and poor children and adults 'failures' at reading because the schools were 'traditionally geared to the middle class and not really able to teach reading to children who varied from this limited norm.' She constructed the program based on Kenneth Clark's notion that children learn if their self-image is positively reinforced by the teacher and curricular materials. She also observed that teachers failed at teaching reading because they were only rarely trained in the subject. Eighteen states required only one course while sixteen required no reading courses for teacher certification at the elementary level. Love sought to change the public's expectations about reading ability, to encourage states to incorporate into their teacher education programs and to integrate the curricular materials used in the Right to Read program" (Pinderhughes, 305).

In 1975 Love was named superintendent of the Oakland Unified School District of California as a replacement for the system's first black superintendent, Marcus Foster, who had been assassinated by the Symbionese Liberation Army. The district had 97 schools and an enrollment of 59,000 students, of which 66 percent were black, 18 percent white, and the remainder other minorities. While Love was superintendent, the achievement scores of the students rose significantly; she reported they were "very near the national norm." She developed new programs to stimulate and motivate students and teachers. Programs to train administrators, especially principals, in program development and planning were implemented. The system also increased its spending on school construction contracts with minority contractors from 25 percent to 38 percent, at $73 million.

While she was being considered as a candidate for superintendent by the Chicago School Board, the local Chicago media summarized her relations with the Oakland environment as very strong and positive. She led the reorganization of the curriculum by having encouraged family, teacher, student, and parental involvement in the schools. Love also had good relations with business groups in Oakland and with the political community. She had also developed and maintained strong support from black grass-roots organizations.

Love Heads Chicago School System

In late 1980 Love was named superintendent of the Chicago school system and began service in March 1981. She was the first black and the first woman general superintendent of the Chicago public school system. The Chicago system was approximately ten times the size of the Oakland system: more than 550 schools, 450,000 students, a staff of 45,000 including 17,000 teachers, and an annual budget of $1.3 billion. Love arrived at a very critical time in the system. There was a budget crisis; the system was immersed in negotiations with the United States Department of Justice and the courts over the development and implementation of a desegregation plan, and the city was only one year into the turbulent administration of Jane Byrne, its first reform mayor. The schools were administered by the superintendent and by the school board, but the latter was appointed by the mayor. The city's racial and ethnic groups were engaged in a titanic struggle for control of the schools, the party, and the city government. Byrne had run for office on a reform platform but had just appointed two new white board members to replace two outgoing black school board members shortly before Love's arrival to assume the position.

On the day of Love's first school board meeting, for example, the schools had to deal with the desegregation plan, as they had been operating under a United States Justice Department consent decree and negotiating with the courts. The board asked for a third delay, but the courts refused and required the schools to implement a desegregation plan, which produced conflict and criticism from both the white and black communities. The NAACP also requested but was rejected in its effort to become a party to the suit. The Oakland schools had a large minority student population, but Love had not managed a district that had to draw up a desegregation plan. The city of Chicago was and remains divided along racial, ethnic, and partisan lines.

Some of Love's major programs in Chicago included the speeding up of the development and implementation of a citywide discipline code for the schools. Love transferred some of the programs she had developed in the Oakland schools into the Chicago system. "Principals of 387 schools are now given an opportunity, money, and detailed planning guidelines based on research on school effectiveness for deciding how to use this money to design programs to meet the special needs of their school." (Arnez, 316). She also developed the Adopt-A-School program in which "businessmen contribute money, equipment and other support to improve education" (*Crisis*. 23).

Earlier reference was made to Love's approaches in controlling her positions. Nancy Arnez noted in the *Journal of Negro Education* that Love had experienced problems of ageism and sexism when she first moved into the administrative position of counseling in the California state department of education. Although Arnez notes these problems subsided as Love dealt with the conflicts positively, in subsequent positions she faced increasing difficulties. In the Right to Read program and the Chicago superintendency, Love had attempted to enhance her ability to deal with such problems by strengthening the structural and budgetary resources at her disposal. Although Right to Read had "received little or no funding previously," Love "accepted the R2R post only after the U. S. Commissioner of Education, Sidney Marland, agreed to a $20 million budget, a 30-person staff and a $30,000 annual salary." After Love was in place she faced budget cuts and other problems and decided to resign shortly after she took office. "HEW Secretary under President Nixon, Elliot Richardson, coaxed her back into the program by responding to her complaints" (Pinderhughes, 306).

Love used a similar bargaining strategy before she agreed to accept the Chicago superintendency. She requested the right to hire with board approval a chief deputy superintendent, an assistant to the superintendent, a business advisor to serve as liaison with the chief financial officer for the school system who reported directly to the board, as well as securing an agreement that desegregation consultants would report to the superintendent rather than to the board.

Ruth Love, however, was unable to counter the difficulties she faced in Chicago. Their complexity was such that it is unlikely that any superintendent would have been able to. In previous positions, she had functioned primarily in her own area of expertise—teaching, counseling, reading—and within the geographic area in which she had grown up and become professionally active. She noted shortly after having been appointed Chicago superintendent that she had already known most of the Oakland school system's professionals when she became superintendent. She rose to the top of the Oakland system after experience within it as a teacher, counselor, and administrator and after experience as a consultant and bureau chief within the California state system.

When Love was named Chicago superintendent, she became one of the highest-paid officials within the state, but she was completely new to the state. Love arrived at a time when the city also had its first woman mayor, Jane Byrne, who was also a reformer. Chicago was divided by racial, ethnic, socioeconomic, and partisan desegregation conflicts as the old machine order had eroded and become disorganized in the year after Richard J. Daley's death.

The black community was also divided along machine and reform/grass roots lines, and it had its own black candidate for superintendent, Manfred Byrd, whom it favored over any outside candidate, black or white. There was significant support for Byrd and against earlier candidates for the superintendency even before Love was named the board's choice. She was the third individual asked to serve. Few of the superintendents before or after Love (including Byrd) lasted longer than her three-year tenure in office. Love faced a situation that was qualitatively different from Oakland's. The Chicago system itself was five times the size of Oakland's, but whereas Oakland had 97 schools for 59,000 students, Chicago had nearly nine times as many students in only five times as many schools. The basic school unit in Chicago was thus more than one third larger, making its management problems quite different.

Love served from 1981 until the summer of 1984, after which she became a commentator for WLS, one of Chicago's television stations. At present she resides in the San Francisco Bay Area, where she is director of Ruth Love Enterprises—an educational consulting firm that offers a number of services. The firm provides educational evaluation, trains teachers and administrators, produces videos, offers hands-on training, and conducts superintendent searches for cities and states. Love is also copublisher with Carleton Goodlett of *The Sun Reporter*, a series of metropolitan black American weekly newspapers in the Bay Area. Love publishes one of seven metropolitan weekly newspapers in Stockton, Vallejo, and elsewhere in the Bay Area. The *California Voice*, which Love publishes, is seventy-one years old and targeted at Oakland, Berkeley, and Richmond. The combined circulation for the papers is 159,000.

Love's publications include: "How Relevant is Equality?" *CTA Journal*, 65 (October 1969): 3-5; "Beyond the Ringing Phrase," *The Reading Teacher*, 25 (November 1971): 118-28; "Right to Read—A Chance to Change: Report from Washington," *The Reading Teacher*, 27 (October 1973): 33-36; "Let's Reward for Success; Not failure," *The Reading Teacher*, 30 (October 1976): 4-6; and with John Coons, "Would a Statewide Voucher System Work?" *Instructor*, 88 (May 1979): 28.

References

Arnez, Nancy L. "Selected Black Female Superintendents of Public School Systems." *Journal of Negro Education*, 51 (Summer 1982): 309-17.

Chicago Defender, 8 January 1981; 17 January 1981; 21 February 1981.

Chicago Sun Times, 21 March 1982.

Chicago Tribune, 5 January 1981, 9 January 1981, 14 January 1981, 16 April 1981.

Collins, Lisa. "Dr. Ruth Love: Bringing Excellence to Oakland Schools." *Sepia*, 28 (October 1979): 76-82.

"Love and Chicago Schools." *Crisis*, 89 (March 1982): 23.

Love, Ruth. Telephone interview with author. 2 July 1990.

Pinderhughes, Dianne M. "Black Women and National Educational Policy." *Journal of Negro Education*, 51 (Summer 1982): 301-308.

"Right to Read." *American Libraries*, 6 (March 1975): 143.

Who's Who Among Black Americans, 1990/91. 6th ed. Detroit: Gale Research, 1991. 1157.

Dianne M. Pinderhughes

M

Jackie "Moms" Mabley

(1894-1975)

Dancer, singer, comedienne

The black stand-up comedienne, Jackie "Moms" Mabley, who played the part of a cantankerous, spicy, raucous old lady with shabby wardrobe and broad, toothless smile in black nightclubs and vaudeville for half a century, gained in popularity through her recordings and televisions appearances during the mid-1960s. Her sudden popularity surprised the nation, and this cultural heroine was called "the funniest women in the world" (Bogle, 159). She had also appeared in films as early as the 1920s. Though she filled her act with insults toward old men, she felt enough generosity and compassion for all of her fellow performers that she earned the sobriquet "Moms." In the late 1980s Moms Mabley was revived in an off-Broadway act by Clarice Taylor and also in a play by Alice Childress designed to honor the talent of the comedienne and to give respect to her influence on humor.

Jackie "Moms" Mabley was born Loretta Mary Aiken in Brevard, North Carolina, in 1894. Accounts of her younger years are sketchy and often contradictory. However, a hazy portrait emerges. Loretta Aiken was one of twelve children. Jim Aiken, her father, owned several different businesses, including the local grocery store. He was also a volunteer fireman, and he died when the truck in which he was riding exploded. Harriet Smith, Loretta Aiken's great-grandmother, who had been a slave, was her religious inspiration. She told Aiken, "Put God in front and go ahead" (*Washington Post,* 4 October 1974, B-1).

By the time Loretta Aiken was eleven years old, she was raped by an older black man. Two years later she was raped again by the white town sheriff. Both rapes resulted in children. With two children to support and a stepfather she could not abide, she prayed to God for a job and a way to get away from her stepfather. It was because of him that she left Brevard, North Carolina. She left her children in the care of two women, and she moved to Cleveland at the age of fourteen, where she lived with a minister and his family. Since the boardinghouse next door was filled with people in show business, she was soon exposed to the art. There Aiken met a performer named Bonnie Belle Drew who thought that because she was beautiful, she should be in show business. (Aiken later named her fifth child after Bonnie.)

Loretta Aiken felt her prayers had been answered when Bonnie Drew invited her to accompany her to Pittsburgh the next day. Later that night, Aiken threw her clothes over the fence and went to Pittsburgh with Bonnie Drew and some other entertainers. Loretta Aiken did her first show that night dancing, singing, and doing some comedy. She met Jack Mabley, also an entertainer, and they became close friends. Loretta Aiken said in an interview for *New York* (14 October 1974) that, "He took a lot off me, the least I could do was take his name." Thus was born Jackie Mabley. Misfortune struck again when the two women who were taking care of her two children disappeared with her toddlers. Jackie Mabley never saw her children again until they were adults. Soon thereafter Mabley's mother was hit by a truck and killed on her way home from church on Christmas day.

Mabley Rises in the Chitlin' Circuit

Jackie Mabley started traveling throughout the country to the places catering to black artists, a round known as the chitlin' circuit. She started at twelve dollars a week. The routine was very difficult, especially in the South, where she did two performances a night—one for blacks and one for whites. In the *Washington Post* interview, Mabley said:

> All those white men had black mistresses, you know what I mean. But in the public they made like they didn't know. And one time, I can't forget this, we were going in a Jim Crow-car and we were travelling from Dallas to San Antone. And the train stops in Paris, Texas, and I look out and see this man tied to a stake. They were gonna burn him. So I pulled down that shade. Ignorance. Just ignorance, I say (B-1).

Jackie Mabley became pregnant again, and although it is unclear as to whether or not she was legally married, she gave birth to her third child. Mabley did not lose a beat, however, and she came right back to show business.

During the 1920s Jackie Mabley continued to develop her act. She was already dancing and singing. However, she became a comedienne and developed the character of the dirty old lady with a penchant for younger men. She would appear on stage dressed in baggy dresses, oversized shoes, a hat, and droopy stockings. Her trademarks became her bulging eyes, rubbery face, gravelly voice, and later, her toothless grin. She started calling her audience children. She described her character as a good woman with an eye for shady dealings. She envisioned her character as her granny—the most beautiful woman she ever knew.

On the black vaudeville circuit, Jackie Mabley appeared on bills with such talent as Pigmeat Markham, Cootie Williams, Tim "Kingfish" Moore, Bill "Bojangles" Robinson, Dusty "Open The Door, Richard" Fletcher, Peg Leg Bates, and John "Spider Bruce" Mason. It was Jackie Mabley who discovered the comic talent in Pearl Bailey. In the *Washington Post* interview, Jackie Mabley said, "I taught Pearl Bailey everything she knows. She was a blues singer. And I said, 'Girl, you're funny. You should be a comedienne'"(4 October 1974, B-1).

In the mid-1920s Jackie Mabley was discovered by the dance team of Butterbeans and Suzie. They later brought Mabley to New York, and she made her debut at Connie's Inn. From there her career really took off, and she often played the Cotton Club in Harlem and Club Harlem in Atlantic City. She appeared on the bill with Louis Armstrong, Cab Calloway, Duke Ellington, and Count Basie at those clubs.

Jackie Mabley's first motion picture roles were bit parts in movies, such as *Boarding House Blues* (RKO, 1929), also known as *Jazz Heaven*, and *The Emperor Jones* (United Artists, 1933), where she played Paul Robeson's landlady.

Moms Rules the Apollo

In 1939 Jackie Mabley became a regular at the Apollo Theatre in Harlem. She played fifteen weeks at a time. She was constantly changing her act. Many of the white comedians would venture up to the Apollo with their notebooks to see her show. Mabley appeared at the Apollo Theatre more than any other act in the history of the Apollo. Mabley said that, with the exception of Jack Benny and Redd Foxx, every comedian stole her material. But she was not disturbed because she felt that God always gave her more to draw from. She met and played with many other entertainers at the Apollo, such as Charles "Honi" Coles and Slappy White. She loved to play cards and always cheated, according to some of her colleagues. Louis Armstrong, Duke Ellington, and Sophie Tucker found that Mabley had a compassion for her coworkers and helped them in times of need, so they gave her the name of Moms, and it stuck.

Mabley played Broadway in such shows as *Fast and Furious, Swinging the Dream,* and *Blackbirds*. She was also a regular on the radio show "Swingtime at the Savoy." In the sixties the white audience discovered her. She began recording for Chess Records. Her first album was *Moms Mabley—The Funniest Woman in the World*. Then she went to Mercury Records in 1966, where she recorded *Now Hear This*. Her other LP's include *Moms Mabley At the UN*, and *Moms Mabley At the General Conferences*. Mabley then appeared on television and made her debut in "A Time For Laughter," which was an all-black comedy special produced by Harry Belafonte for the ABC network on April 6, 1967. After that Moms could be seen often on television, on shows hosted by Merv Griffin, the Smothers Brothers, Mike Douglas, Bill Cosby, and Flip Wilson. She turned down a repeat appearance on the Ed Sullivan show, because he would not give her four minutes.

"The only difference I found when I started doing TV," Moms said, "was that instead of looking at the audience as my children I looked at the world as my children" (*Current Biography,* 263). Mabley soared through television exposure, and the demand for her talent grew at such top white venues as the Copacabana in New York City, the Kennedy Center in Washington, D.C., and Carnegie Hall in New York City. In her early seventies, Moms got her first starring role in the movie *Amazing Grace*. During the filming she had a heart attack, and a pacemaker was implanted. She recovered and returned to filming.

After more than sixty years in the business, Mabley died of natural causes at 7:15 in the evening on May 23, 1975, in White Plains Hospital. She was presumed to be eighty-one. The funeral was held at Harlem's Abyssinian Baptist Church. At the time of her death Mabley was survived by her three daughters—Bonnie, with whom she lived in later years, Christine, and Yvonne—and a son, Charles, five grandchildren, two sisters, and three brothers, and Eddie Parto, with whom she wrote some of her material.

Mabley for many years was this country's only black comedienne, as well as the first to become widely recognized. She was a member of the NAACP and also a guest at the White House Conference on Civil Rights in 1966. A devout Baptist, she attended church regularly.

Alice Childress honored Moms Mabley in 1986, when she wrote "Moms: A Praise for a Black Comedienne." The play is based on Mabley's life, with music and lyrics by Childress and her husband, Nathan Woodard. It was first produced by Green Plays at Art Awareness, 1986, then off-Broadway at Hudson Guild Theatre on February 4, 1987 (*Black Writers,* 101). In 1987 Clarice Taylor, Bill Cosby's mom on "The Cosby Show," also brought Mabley back to life through an enactment of the late sharp-tongued comedienne on stage.

References

Black Writers. Detroit: Gale Research, 1989.

Bogle, Donald. *Brown Sugar*. New York: Harmony Books, 1980. 158-60. Photograph, p. 159.

Current Biography Yearbook. New York: H. W. Wilson, 1975. 261-64. Photograph of Mabley in a stage act, p. 262.

Focus (Summer 1983): 9.

"Moms Mabley Revisited." *Ebony* 46 (February 1988): 124, 126, 128, 130. Includes photographs.

"Moms Mabley: She Finally Makes the Movies." *Ebony* 29 (April 1974): 86-88, 90, 92. Includes photographs.

New York Times, 23 May 1975; 25 May 1975.

Newsday, 6 April 1967. A-3. Includes photograph. 13 May 1973, Sect. 2: 4. Includes photograph.

Obituary. *Black Perspective in Music* 3 (Fall 1975): 344-45.

Washington Post, 21 August 1972.

Washington Post, 4 October 1974. B-1. Includes photograph; 21 August 1972.

Southern, Eileen. *Biographical Dictionary of Afro-American and African Musicians*. Westport, Conn.: Greenwood Press, 1982.

Richelle B. Curl

Jane Ellen McAllister

(1899-)

Educator

During Jane Ellen McAllister's long career as an educator, she devoted herself to the uplift of black Americans through improved educational opportunities in a variety of practical and far-sighted ways.

McAllister was born October 24, 1899, in Vicksburg, Mississippi, and now resides in the family home on Main Street. She was the oldest of three children of Richard Nelson McAllister and Flora (McClellan) McAllister. Her brother, Richard, was born in 1901 and died in 1981, and her sister, Dorothy, was born in 1904 and died in 1974.

An autobiographical description of McAllister's childhood paints a vivid picture of a young girl growing up in a warm, loving, and close-knit family and experiencing a lifestyle that was unusual for the blacks and many of the whites of Vicksburg. Both her mother and father attended Natchez Seminary, which later became Jackson College. Her mother was the protégée of Charles Ayers, the president of the college, and his wife, and spent summers at their home on Martha's Vineyard in Massachusetts. There she learned to appreciate good books, good music, and excellent manners. During her childhood, Jane Ellen McAllister was surrounded by uncles, aunts, and cousins who were successful teachers, clergymen, seamstresses, skilled workmen, and governmental officials.

In recounting the story of her early years, Mcallister said:

> As I look back home now, my whole family were remarkably successful in that time just after slavery. From my earliest years, I can never remember them renting anything. And in their wills, they left all of the cousins a home. I live now in the home that they left me (McAllister, "Childhood" 25).

At the time of McAllister's birth, her mother was twenty-five and had taught school in Madison County for seven years; she later taught forty years in the Vicksburg public schools. McAllister's father was also a teacher for a brief period; later he worked in a Louisiana sugar refinery, and he spent the last forty years before his retirement as a mail carrier. The early influences of her family were a guiding force in McAllister's life and served her well throughout her productive career as an educator.

McAllister attended the Catholic Elementary School and completed her secondary education at Cherry Street High School. Her undergraduate studies were completed at Talladega College, where she received the A.B. degree in liberal arts in 1919. She received the M.A. degree in history and English in 1921 from the University of Michigan and was a member of the first class to be awarded masters' degrees by the institution. In 1929 she received the Ph.D. degree in education from Columbia University and was later selected one among two hundred most outstanding alumni to return to Columbia University, where she spent one-and-one-half years in post-doctoral study (Interview with Kara Vaughn Jackson).

McAllister's teaching experiences include Southern University, 1919-1920 and 1921-1922 and intermittently to 1927; principal, the Training School, Virginia State College, Norfolk, 1922-1924; director, teacher training, Southern University, Baton Rouge, Louisiana, 1924-1928; professor of education, Fisk University, 1929-30; professor of education and head of the department of education, Miner Teachers College, Washington, D. C., 1930-1951; professor of education, Jackson State College, Jackson, Mississippi, 1950-1967; director, Institute of Disadvantaged Youth, summers of 1965, 1966, 1967; professor of education (emeritus) Jackson State College, since 1967.

During McAllister's tenure at Miner Teachers College, she spent a year, 1937, revising the teacher-training program at Grambling State, and in 1941 she served as a consultant for curriculum revision at Jackson State. Returning to Jackson State in 1951, after her resignation from Miner Teachers College, McAllister stated that:

> For me, this is a return engagement; and for a teacher, as for an actor, there is nothing more flattering than a return engagement. Coming back to Jackson College means the privilege and stimulation of a decade of teacher education for, I was there, at the beginning of Jackson College as a state institution for teachers (*Mississippi Educational Journal*, 91).

Educational Uplift of Blacks Promoted

McAllister made great strides in the educational uplift of

blacks. During the approximately five decades of her career she was involved in the opening of the first extension class for black teachers in Louisiana in 1925; the initiation at Fisk University of a pilot program with the Nashville public schools that not only benefited both students and the community, but was also an important factor in the recognition of Fisk as a "Class A" institution by the Southern Association of Colleges and Secondary Schools. In 1937 she developed a teacher education program at Grambling State that featured a field services unit and was implemented at eight off-campus sites. It provided educational experiences for students and spread "the gospel of better food, housing and clothing, to rural people who were tenant farmers and wage earners on large plantations" (Burns 353). She was involved in the reorganization of the course sequence at Miner Teachers College and the institution of a program to allow inservice teachers with two-year certificates to earn degrees and update their skills; the development of a teacher education curriculum at Jackson State that was approved in 1942 and offered a degree program in elementary education, and she coordinated a telelecture course in 1963 called "Great Ideas In Antiquity." Sponsored by the Ford Foundation for the Advancement of Education with Moses Hadas as lecturer, the project included Jackson State, Grambling College, Southern University, and Tougaloo Southern Christian College. At Jackson State, McAllister instituted innovative programs such as the Student Sponsored Forum, the College Enrichment Program, "Town Meeting on the Air," National Defense Education Act (NDEA) institutes for teachers of disadvantaged youth, and from 1963-67 a college readiness program. She held memberships in many educational organizations and served on their committees. Penn School, located on an island off the coast of South Carolina, appointed McAllister to its board of trustees. From 1933 to 1968, she also served on the board of trustees of Talladega College in Alabama.

Of McAllister's notable contributions in education, a Columbia University professor stated that:

> The real history of the study of American Negro education on the advanced level in Teachers College began with the pioneer achievement of Doctor Jane Ellen McAllister in 1929. Miss McAllister, with the completion of her thesis on *The Training of the Negro Teacher in Louisiana* became not only the first colored candidate ever to receive the doctor's degree from this institution, but also the first colored woman throughout the world. This record and distinction Doctor McAllister has more than maintained through the high calibre of her work as Professor of Education at Miner Teacher College, Washington, D. C., and as Consultant in Rural Teacher Education for the General Education Board and the Rosenwald Fund at Grambling, Louisiana, and at Jackson State College, Jackson, Mississippi (Carney, 41-42).

McAllister's loyalty and dedication to the teaching profession were demonstrated in innumerable ways. She published articles in professional journals such as the *Journal of Secondary Education, Educational Administration and Supervision, Teachers College Record, Integrated Education*, and *Journal of Negro Education.* For sixteen years, her loyalty was demonstrated also in her daily round-trips by bus from her home in Vicksburg, Mississippi, to the campus of Jackson State College; she was never late. In 1971 the Jane Ellen McAllister Lecture Series was established in her honor by the School of Education and the Student National Education Association. She was again honorhd by the university October 19, 1989, during the celebration of the 112th Founder's Day with the dedication of the new dormitory for women in honor of McAllister and Mary G. Whiteside.

The friends and contemporaries of McAllister were Kara Vaughn Jackson of Grambling State, Florence O. Alexander of the Mississippi State Department of Education, Mary G. Whiteside of Coahoma Junior College, Mabel Carney of Columbia University's Teachers College, Naiomi Rushing of Howard University and Miner Teachers College, and Marjorie Holloman Parker of the board of trustees of the University of the District of Columbia.

In an April 1974 letter to George sewell, a friend and former colleage, Alleane Currie, described McAllister:

> A petite woman in stature, gifted with a brilliant mind, highly sensitive to others' needs, possessing a quiet charm, gentle and warm hearted, firm, serious and confident in her work, at times humorus and playful, poised, cooperative, modest, interesting to listen to.

References

Carney, Mabel. "Doctoral Dissertations and Projects Relating to the Education of Negroes." *The Advanced School Digest* 7 (February 1942): 41-42.

Currie, Alleane. Interview, 13 March 1990.

Currie, Aleane. Letter to George A. Sewell, 2 April 1974.

"Dr. Jane E. McAllister." *Mississippi Education Journal* 36 (February 1951): 91.

Jackson, Kara Vaughn. Interviewed by Winona Williams-Burns, 17 October 1981. "Jane Ellen McAllister: Pioneer for Excellence in Teacher Education." *Journal of Negro History* 51 (Summer 1982): 53.

McAllister, Jane Ellen. Curriculum Vitae. n.d.

McAllister, Jane Ellen. "Childhood As I Remember It." *Integrated Education* 51 (July 1973): 25.

Sewell, George Alexander and Margaret L. Dwight. "Jane Ellen McAllister: Pioneer in Black Education." *Mississippi Black History Makers*. Rev. and enl. ed. Jackson: University Press of Mississippi, 1977. 163-64.

Williams-Burns, Winona. "Jane Ellen McAllister: Pioneer for Excellence in Teacher Education.'' *Journal of Negro Education* 101 (1982): 342-57.

Collections

The personal papers of Jane Ellen McAllister are in her possession. The archives of the Henry T. Sampson Library, Jackson State University, contain course outlines, copies of proposals, photographs, and other materials. A tape recording of her response in absentia to the dedication of the building in her honor on October 19, 1989, is also available in the archives.

Cozetta W. Buckley

Gertrude P. McBrown

(1898?-1989)

Poet, playwright, educator, actress, stage director

Gertrude Parthenia McBrown dedicated her life to the dramatic arts and the presentation and communication of creative thought and the rich history of black America.

McBrown was born in Charleston, South Carolina, in 1898, the daughter of a Methodist minister. Little is known about McBrown's family and her early years in the South. As a child, McBrown had the opportunity to hear a reading by the great actor, Richard B. Harrison. This event inspired her to become an orator and actress.

Before entering college, McBrown attended Curry School of Expression in Boston, Massachusetts, where she studied under Florence H. Slack. Shortly thereafter, she attended Emerson College of Oratory (later Emerson College) in Boston from October 5, 1918, through May 1922. According to Emerson's records, McBrown was twenty years old at the time of admission.

As a drama student, McBrown prepared herself for a career as a writer, educator, and performer. She excelled academically at Emerson, where she was a member of the Children's Theatre and the debating team. Her dramatic ability won her places in the junior and senior recitals and the class play. She was chosen to direct the commencement play as well. After graduating from Emerson with a B.L.I. (Bachelor of Literary Interpretation), McBrown was hired as an instructor of English and dramatic art at Virginia State College. She returned to Boston a year later and continued her education at Boston University, where she received a M.Ed. in 1926. At Boston University, McBrown was assistant coach of the Dramatic Club. Following graduation, she taught in the public schools of Boston, at which time she engaged in experimental works in original children's poetry. During this period McBrown also submitted several children's poems to the *Saturday Evening Quill*, a short-lived black American magazine printed in Boston, and to the *Crisis* magazine. McBrown also became very active in the Boston dramatic and church community, where she was not only in charge of the choral group at the Ebenezer Baptist Church but also director of productions there.

During the late 1920s McBrown migrated south to head the drama department at Palmer Memorial Institute in Sedalia, North Carolina, under the direction of Charlotte Hawkins Brown. During her brief tenure at Palmer, McBrown staged a variety of productions, her most famous being George Hobart's *Experience*. The production received an excellent review in the August 1929 *Crisis*. From Palmer Memorial Institute she was hired to teach dramatic arts at North Carolina Agricultural and Technical College, Greensboro, where she succeeded her idol, Richard B. Harrison, who left to take the lead role in the Broadway production of *The Green Pastures*.

During the 1930s McBrown moved to Washington, D.C., where she was well known in dramatic and literary circles. During her years in Washington she became involved in numerous activities. McBrown was the director of the Southeast Children's Theatre, the Bronze Masque of Freedmen's Training School, and the Dramatic Club of the Lamda Rho Society of the Asbury Methodist Episcopal Church. She also taught speech at the Washington Conservatory of Music and taught English at the Frelinghuysen University, of which scholar Anna Julia Cooper was president and founder. In addition to all of these achievements, McBrown opened her own studio of expression.

Interest in Children's Poetry and Theater Escalates

While in Washington, McBrown's interest in children's poetry and theater escalated; she became more and more concerned with developing positive role models for black children and encouraging them to become more creative. In 1935 Associated Publishers issued McBrown's first book of poetry, *The Picture-Poetry Book,* with illustrations by renowned artist Lois Mailou Jones. Each poem in the small volume is accompanied by an appropriate sketch. In her preface, McBrown states that ''poetry is the language of childhood.'' She used illustrations because she believed that:

> The appreciation of pictures motivates reading. The picture stirs in the child certain emotions, creating for him impressions that serve as an incentive for expression. In many cases the pictures will stimulate children to create and illustrate their own poems (preface, *The Picture-Poetry Book*).

As McBrown's popularity as a children's poet increased, so also did her publications. Her poetry appeared in numerous journals and magazines, including *Opportunity, Popular Educator, Black Opals, Negro Women's World,* and *International Poetry Magazine.* She became managing editor of children's literature for the *Parent-Teacher Magazine* and a feature writer on drama for the Associated Negro Press.

McBrown became a board member of the *Negro History Bulletin,* headed by Carter G. Woodson, and maintained a long association with the publication. Through the *Negro History Bulletin* she published her first plays, *Bought With Cookies* (1949) and *Birthday Surprise* (1953). A one-act play, *Bought With Cookies* focuses on the life of young Frederick Douglass. The play examines Douglass's desire for knowledge and the sacrifices he made to obtain it. *The Birthday Surprise* highlights the poetry and career of the great poet Paul Laurence Dunbar.

McBrown gained popularity throughout the country for her one-woman dramatic recitals and impersonations of famous black American heroines. Gorgeously costumed in African attire, she also delighted children with stories from Africa.

McBrown moved to New York during the 1950s, where she taught speech and directed drama groups at the Carnegie Hall Studio. She initiated the founding of the Carter G. Woodson Memorial Research Collection in the Queens Public Library, Jamaica. She also wrote a weekly column, "Proud Heritage," for her local newspaper in the Jamaica section of New York, *Community Chatter*.

McBrown was a true scholar and world traveler. Throughout her life she constantly studied and shared her knowledge of African and black American culture. She pursued studies at such institutions as the Conservatoire Nationale de Musique et d'Art and took dramatics and advanced literature at the Institut Britannique in Paris. She also conducted research in African culture and folklore at the Royal Empire Society and the Royal Academy of Dramatic Art in London. McBrown traveled extensively in Africa, where she also performed her stories to enthusiastic audiences.

During her latter years, McBrown's struggle with crippling arthritis curtailed her numerous activities. She died in 1989.

McBrown's published dramatic works include *Bought with Cookies* and *The Birthday Surprise*. Selected poetry in published sources are: "Fairies and Brownies," *Crisis* 12 (1927); "Bubbles," "Fairies," "The Paint Pot Fairy," and "The Wise Owl," *Saturday Evening Quill* 6 (1928); and *The Picture-Poetry Book,* illustrated by Lois Mailou Jones.

References

Arata, Esther and Nicholas Rotoli. *Black American Playwrights, 1800 to the Present*. Metuchen, N.J.: Scarecrow Press, 1976. 136.

Cromwell, Otelia, Lorenzo Dow Turner, and Eva B. Dykes. *Readings from Negro Authors*. New York: Harcourt, Brace, 1931. 53-54.

Hatch, James and Abdullah Omanii. *Black Playwrights, 1823-1977: An Annotated Bibliography of Plays*. New York: Bowker, 1977. 151.

McBrown, Gertrude P. *The Picture-Poetry Book*. New York: Associated Publishers, 1935.

Profiles in Black: Biographical Sketches of 100 Living Black Unsung Heroes. Edited by Innis, Doris Funnye and Juliana Wu. New York: CORE Publications, 1976. 28-29.

Randolph, Ruth Elizabeth and Lorraine Elena Roses. *The Harlem Renaissance and Beyond: Literary Biographies of 100 Black Women Writers*. Boston: G. K. Hall, 1989. 229-31.

Who's Who Among Black Americans. 1980-81. 3d ed. Chicago: Who's Who Among Black Americans Corp., 1981. 530.

Collections

Vertical file materials on Gertrude Parthenia McBrown are in the Moorland-Spingarn Research Center, Howard University, Washington, D.C. Materials on Brown are also in the archives of Emerson College in Boston.

Kathy A. Perkins

Jewell Jackson McCabe

(1945-)

Entrepreneur, organization official

A fighter for the uplift of black women, Jewell Jackson McCabe believes that black women need an advocacy group to assist them in gaining the political and economic power that they need to effect social change. She believes that black women must transcend the barriers to their success and expose their myriad developments for the world to see. Convinced that these goals can be met, in 1981 she founded and became president of the National Coalition of 100 Black Women as the forum for addressing the concerns of black women.

Jewell Jackson Ward McCabe was born August 2, 1945, in Washington, D.C., the daughter of Harold "Hal" B. Jackson, a black broadcasting pioneer, and Julia O. (Hawkins) Jackson. She admits that she "grew up in a black upper-middle-class family." In addition to her father's status, her aunt was "the first black to graduate from the Boston Conservatory of Music." Their house was always "the biggest on the block'' (Lanker, 83). She graduated from the High School of Performing Arts at Bard College.

At age nineteen she married Frederick Ward, an advertising copywriter, and she later married Eugene McCabe, president of North General Hospital in New York City. Twice divorced, she has no children.

McCabe has served as consultant to the Commonwealth Fund on issues related to women, children, and family with a special focus on youth unemployment. She directed public affairs for the New York Urban Coalition, and later she became director of public information, Office of the Governor, Women's Division. As director of the Government and Community Affairs Department of WNET, Channel Thirteen, the public broadcasting station in New York City, McCabe designed and coordinated efforts to secure and maintain ten million dollars in federal and state financial assistance to support a significant portion of Channel Thirteen's annual operating budget.

In 1981 McCabe founded and organized the National Coalition of 100 Black Women—an outgrowth of the New York Coalition of 100 Black Women founded in 1970. McCabe is now chair of the coalition. The National Coalition of 100 Black Women was patterned after its counterpart, 100 Black Men, an influential group in New York and in other areas of the country. The organization is ''a coalition of high achievers combined with highly energetic women,'' said McCabe (Noel, 50). A volunteer group from the coalition serves as role models for the young, who are taught to leverage resources and how to survive. With more than five thousand members, the coalition is a leadership forum that engages professional black women to join together to meet their professional and personal needs and the needs of their communities, and to facilitate their access to mainstream America. Each year, the coalition presents the Candace (pronounced Can-day-say) Award to ten black women, honoring them in the arts, science, technology, and business. The name of the award is an Ethopian term for ''queen.''

McCabe Establishes Advisory Company

McCabe is also president of Jewell Jackson McCabe Associates. The firm serves as advisor to private and public sectors on government relations, marketing to minorities, and special issues and events. ''I want to establish a common ground between the public and private sectors,'' said McCabe (*Fortune*, 93). Her client list includes Panasonic, American Express, the NAACP Legal Defense and Education Fund, the Federation of Protestant Welfare Agencies, and the Associated Black Charities.

McCabe's professional career has led to several gubernatorial appointments. Her local and national affiliations include: member of the Education Committee, New York City Partnership, and chair of the State of New York Job Training Council; board member, New York State Council on Fiscal and Economic Priorities, and on the Tax Reform Committee; member of the New York State Council on Families, where she was assigned to the committee on Teen Pregnancy Prevention. Other affiliations include membership on the executive committee, Association for a Better New York; board of trustees, Economic Club of New York; board of directors, National Alliance of Business; board of directors, Overseas Education Fund; member, Government Relations Committee, United Way of America; board of directors, Coro Foundation; board of trustees, Phelps-Stokes Fund; member Committee for Economic Development; and board member, Schomburg Center for Research in Black Culture.

Jewell Jackson McCabe has received a number of honors. She has an honorary doctorate from Iona College, New Rochelle, New York, and one from Tougaloo College, Jackson, Mississippi. She was elected to participate in the Aspen Institute Executive Seminar. The *New York Daily News* selected her as one of ten women to watch in the eighties, and she is the recipient of the Women's Equity Action League Annual Award.

Published works by or under the direction of Jewell Jackson McCabe are *Commemorative Book: Motown Returns to the Apollo* (Fiftieth Anniversary); *Women in New York,* newsletter published by New York State, with a circulation of 100,000; and *Give a Damn,* newsletter published by the New York Urban Coalition, with a circulation of 20,000.

The influential, forthright McCabe, who works practically nonstop, has made a positive impression on the business world. John E. Jacob, former president of the National Urban League, called her ''one of the most articulate, provocative women I've met in years.'' David Rockefeller described McCabe as ''exceptionally energetic, creative, and sensitive,'' and James D. Robinson, formerly of American Express, noted that ''her contribution to the advancement of women and minorities is impressive and much to be admired'' (Noel, 50).

References

Fortune (17 August 1987): 93.

Lanker, Brian. *I Dream a World.* New York: Stewart, Tabori and Chang, 1989. 82-83. Photograph, p. 83.

New York Times, 3 June 1979. 56. Includes photograph.

Noel, Pamela. ''New Battler for Black Women.'' *Ebony* 39 (February 1984): 43-44, 48, 50. Includes photographs.

Weiss, Carol Zappelli. Interview with the author, 11 April 1991.

Jessie Carney Smith

Rosalie "Rose" McClendon

(1884-1936)

Actress

Rosalie Virginia Scott McClendon's itinerary from Greenville, North Carolina, to Broadway stardom can only be sketched in outline. Named Rosalie Virginia at her birth on August 27, 1884, to Sandy Scott and Tena (Jenkins) Scott, she was about forty-six years old when she first made a vivid impression on New York critics in a sustaining role in *Deep River*. Her earliest known contact with the world of professional theater began about ten years earlier. Nonetheless, from her appearance in *Deep River* in 1926 until her untimely death just short of ten years later on July 2, 1936, she was a highly respected actress on the stage, as well as a champion of black theater, actors, and playwrights.

Details about McClendon's early years are scanty. McClendon had an older brother and an older sister. The family moved from Greenville to New York City about 1890. Her father worked as a coachman and her mother as a housekeeper for a wealthy family. McClendon attended school at Public School Number Forty on East Twenty-eighth Street. At some point the family moved to West Fifty-third Street, and McClendon was active at Saint Mark's Methodist Episcopal Church, then located in that area of the city. On October 27, 1904, Rose Scott married Henry Pruden McClendon. Though he was a licensed chiropractor, he worked most of the time as a Pullman porter for the Pennsylvania Railroad. Both St. Mark's Church and the McClendons joined the black migration north to Harlem, where the McClendons lived on West 138th Street. The marriage was happy, but there were no children. She lived quietly as a housewife except for her active involvement in the social work of her church. As a child she had taken part in Sunday school plays, and as an adult performed in and directed plays and cantatas for St. Mark's. By 1927, the church had constructed an elaborate building with a gymnasium, a swimming pool, and several club rooms. Bruce Kellner states: "Saint Mark's Methodist Episcopal Church held elaborate services, with more ceremony than sermon, apparently, including a liturgy strongly influenced by Roman Catholicism, elegant robes on all participants, and Handel oratorios rather than familiar hymns from the choir" (313).

Rosalie "Rose" McClendon

In 1927, *Crisis* magazine printed one paragraph of a letter written in response to a query for personal information about Rose McClendon. In it McClendon claims she did not have a burning desire to be an actress during her early years. She states that her motive in accepting a scholarship around 1916 at the American Academy of Dramatic Art, housed in Carnegie Hall, was to teach the children in church to be better actors: "I have seen so many things badly done in churches that I wanted always to teach children what to do and when to do it." One may also speculate that the grand opening of the Anita Bush Players, the direct ancestors of the Lafayette Players, at the Lincoln Theatre in Harlem on November 15, 1915, played a role in awakening McClendon's interest in the theater. She studied at the academy with Franklin Sargent for three years and found herself in the 1919-1920 season doing a leading role—one of two for black actors, the other being taken by Frank Wilson—in the Bramhall Players' production of Butler Davenport's *Justice* at the playhouse on East Twenty-seventh Street.

In early 1924 McClendon worked in a production by the Lafayette Players in Harlem, starring in a revival of *Roseanne,* a play by the white author Nan Bagby Stevens. Previously the play had run forty-two performances at the Greenwich Village Theater with white actors in blackface, opening in December 1923. *Roseanne* told the story of the seduction of a young girl by a preacher entrusted with her education. Playing the girl's mother, McClendon had first urged the congregation to lynch the preacher, but then, after a change of heart, urged the congregation to spare his life leaving him to God's justice and mercy. The play opened with Charles Gilpin in the leading male role. He received bad notices while McClendon received excellent ones. During the run Gilpin was replaced by Paul Robeson, who was seeking more stage experience before undertaking *All God's Chillun Got Wings* for the Provincetown Players. The revival ran one week in Harlem and another week at the Dunbar

Theater in Philadelphia to enthusiastic, though small audiences.

McClendon Plays on Broadway

On October 4, 1926, McClendon appeared on Broadway in a supporting role that made her a legend. The production was a "native opera," *Deep River*, with book and lyrics by Laurence Stallings and music by Frank Harling. Appealing to neither devotees of musicals nor those of opera, the work managed only thirty-two performances. It presented the rivalry among two Kentuckians and a Creole over the selection of a mistress from the "débutantes" at the quadroon ball, ending in the death of all three men. McClendon played an aging mulatto, the hostess of the ball. In the third act, there was a moment when the stage was empty while the chorus sang softly offstage. McClendon appeared on an elevated veranda, walked down the outside stairs, and paused before exiting. McClendon managed to project an unforgettable moment of tragic pride and dignity in this short scene. The critics were caught, as was the audience, by this magical moment. Critic Alexander Woolcott told the classic anecdote about Ethel Barrymore, the reigning queen of Broadway, who caught part of the performance during tryouts in Philadelphia:

> "Stay till the last act if you can," Arthur Hopkins whispered to her, "and watch Rose McClendon come down those stairs. She can teach some of our most hoity-toity actresses distinction."

It was Miss Barrymore who hunted him up after the performance to say, "She can teach them all distinction" *(Crisis*, 55).

On December 30, 1926, McClendon opened in a starring role in Paul Green's play, *In Abraham's Bosom*. Her costar was Julius Bledsoe, a versatile actor and singer: in *Deep River* he had sung an heroic baritone role. But Bledsoe failed to appear at one performance and was replaced by Frank Wilson, who garnered praise for his performance. Paul Green, a farmer's son and war veteran who was then a teacher at the University of North Carolina, wrote a play about the dream of Abraham, a black worker in eastern North Carolina, to establish a school. The only two white characters in the play are Abraham's father and half-brother. The center of the drama is the Oedipal conflict between fathers and sons, made keener by racial barriers. Abraham is whipped by his own father in the first scene because Abraham has dared to attack his half-brother, who carries the white family's degeneration already evident in the father. The father acts from anger and the fear of Abraham being lynched. Pursued by a lynch mob Abraham kills his half-brother and is himself shot. Although male antagonism is the center of the play, it offered McClendon a chance to portray a woman who moves from being a tender and consoling wife in the first scene to a mother who survives her first two sons and finally witnesses the struggle between her husband and last son, seeing her husband shot.

Critics approved the play, but it did not attract the public in large numbers. When it received the Pulitzer Prize, the audience grew and the play ran for a total of 116 performances, first at the Provincetown Theatre in Greenwich Village, then at the Garrick, and after a hiatus, once again at the Provincetown. (In this era, one hundred performances constituted a success—two hundred, a hit.) For her performance in *In Abraham's Bosom*, McClendon received an acting award from the *Morning Telegraph*, as did Ethel Barrymore, Alice Brady, Jane Cowl, and Lynn Fontaine.

McClendon's next role was that of Serena in *Porgy*, which opened on October 10, 1927, and ran for 217 performances in New York and a return run of fourteen performances after several weeks in Boston. A decided hit, the play toured successfully for another season in the United States and abroad. The play is based on Du Bose Heyward's novel *Catfish Row* and served as a basis for George Gershwin's opera *Porgy and Bess*. Heyward's wife, Dorothy (Hartzell Kuhns) Heyward, an accomplished playwright in her own right, was the co-author. At the time, some black critics objected to the use of heavy black dialect and what they perceived as an excessively negative picture of black life written by a white South Carolina aristocrat. Later the problem of Heyward's treatment of black life was compounded by the question of authenticity and the appropriateness of George Gershwin's music in the 1935 opera *Porgy and Bess*. Nonetheless, the spectacle of a very large cast of black actors presenting a nonmusical hit-play about black life was a major breakthrough in 1927. As for the opera based on the material, its continuing popularity has given large numbers of black singers valuable stage experience, as well as serving as a launching pad for major careers. In another art medium, Richmond Barthé did a full-figure study of McClendon in her role as Serena.

In 1931 another play by Paul Green, *The House of Connelly*, opened September 28, and again offered McClendon a role on Broadway, this time through a supporting role. The play continues Green's preoccupation with the decline of a white family. This time, the symbolically impotent son of a domineering father, is pursued and won by the drivingly ambitious daughter of a tenant farmer, a woman who forces the young man's sisters to abandon the house and their brother. McClendon played "Big Sue" to Fanny De Knight's "Big Sis." They are the family retainers, but retainers with a difference. Pushing as near the line as they dare, the characters express contempt for white folk. Sardonic, disrespectful, and sassy, Big Sis and Big Sue mock their "betters" to their faces. It is clear that the white sisters' submission is forced: it is the victorious Patsy's threat with a poker in her hand that makes the two sisters grudgingly accept the new order at the end of the play. The play ran ninety-one performances.

McClendon Lauded as Leading Actress

Never No More opened at the Hudson Theatre January 7, 1932, and ran for only twelve performances, closing before Sterling A. Brown's eloquent appeal on its behalf in the February 1932 issue of *Opportunity* could save it. James Knox Millen, owner of an unremunerative plantation near

Memphis, Tennessee, based the play on a lynching he observed. McClendon played the matriarch of the family, Mammy. Brown's account makes clear the power of the play. The center of the play is the burning to death of Mammy's son Solomon, who in a panic killed a white girl. In the second act he is burned and tied to a stump in the family clearing; the family arms to defend itself against the mob, which turns its attention to them. The mob is not deterred until Mammy takes up the dynamite used for illegal fishing by one of her sons, and threatens to blow up everyone, attackers and defenders alike. "The curtain falls as the brothers go out to get the charred remains of Solomon, while Mammy slowly lays out his dressy Sunday suit for his burial" (55). If this act reached the intensity that Brown ascribes it, it is hard to imagine an effective third act to follow this one, although he maintains there was no letdown. In addition to his plea on behalf of the play, Brown also singles out McClendon for lavish praise as one of America's leading actresses.

McClendon appeared in Annie Nathan Myer's *Black Souls* with Juano Hernandez on March 30, 1932, at the Provincetown Playhouse. The play dealt with the lust of a white senator for the wife of the president of a black college. Condemned as poorly written, the play ran only thirteen performances. McClendon had a lead part in the radio program, "John Henry, Black River Giant" in 1933. Paul Green brought a new play, *Roll Sweet Chariot,* to Broadway on October 2, 1934. The stars were McClendon and Frank Wilson. Still treating the decline of the South, Green was trying new techniques in stagecraft in what he called a "Symphonic Poem of the Negro People." This play's run was brief. In November 1934 McClendon appeared in John Charles Bronelle's *Brainsweat,* which also managed only a brief run. She also appeared as a member of the crowd in John Houseman's production of *Panic,* a spectacle produced for a special three-day run.

In 1935 a new major project was being developed to showcase McClendon's talents. John Houseman had just launched his career with the remarkable success of Virgil Thompson's opera *Four Saints in Three Acts,* which was presented, as the composer stipulated, with an all-black cast of singers. At the suggestion of James Light and with the aid of Countee Cullen, both friends of McClendon, Houseman worked on a production of Euripedes' *Medea* to star her. Medea's two children would be mulattoes, and the chorus would be made up of black women while Jason and the rest of the actors would be white. With his school knowledge of Greek, cribs, and various printed versions of *Medea*, Houseman helped Cullen prepare the text. The verse choruses were set to music by Virgil Thompson, and Chick Austin designed the sets and costumes for a production in the winter of 1935-36. Unfortunately, the project fell through due to McClendon's illness and Austin's financial problems. Countee Cullen's *Medea* and Virgil Thompson's *Seven Choruses From the Medea of Euripides for Women's Voices and Percussion* are the published remains of the project. Carl Van Vechten took a photograph of McClendon as Medea in an improvised costume a month before her death.

It is important to note that these plays in which McClendon appeared were by white Americans writing about black life, produced by whites, and largely patronized on Broadway by white audiences. It was a step forward on Broadway that the plays were no longer being exclusively played by whites in blackface. Even after McClendon and other blacks had come to Broadway, Ethel Barrymore still put on blackface makeup to play in *Scarlet Sister Mary.* (McClendon kept a scrapbook of Barrymore's many hostile reviews.) Conversely, the stock of plays of black theater groups like the Lafayette Players was made up of plays from the Broadway repertoire with a sprinkling of holdovers from the nineteenth century. The Lafayette Players presented only a handful of plays about black life and even fewer by black playwrights. McClendon was well aware of the need to develop black talent in all facets of the theater and she used her influence to further this aim. Downtown she served on the board of the Theatre Union, which ran the Civic Repertory Theatre on West Fourteenth Street. Uptown, she directed plays for the Harlem Experimental Theatre, and with Dick Campbell, she organized the Negro People's Theatre, which merged into the Works Progress Administration's (WPA) Negro Theatre Project towards the end of 1935. During the course of 1935, the Negro People's Theatre produced a black version of Clifford Odets's *Waiting For Lefty.*

The last play in Rose McClendon appeared on Broadway was Langston Hughes's *Mulatto,* which was the first full-length play by a black author to be produced on Broadway. McClendon played the part of a mother whose son has been sent to the North to be educated. Rejected by his father upon his return, the son finally murders him. The play opened October 24, 1935, at the Vanderbilt Theatre and ran for 270 performances, although McClendon was forced to withdraw from the production due to illness. Arnold Rampersad's *The Life of Langston Hughes* traces some of the circumstances surrounding McClendon's performance. In the fall of 1930, Hughes and McClendon were together in Rose Valley near Media, Pennsylvania, home of the Hedgerow Players. Jasper Deeter, the director of the players, had proposed to do an entire season of black plays, with Hughes as resident black playwright and McClendon as one of the troupe of black actors. The project fell through because of money problems, but Hughes and McClendon were able to discuss the first draft of the play, then called *Cross.* In the period during which the production of the play got underway, Langston Hughes was not in New York: he had been in Russia and then on the West Coast trying to get a movie produced. He was so desperate for a theatrical success that would bring in money that he allowed the production to start without his presence, and he even consented to having rewrites done in his absence, assigning a quarter of the royalties to his collaborator, who turned out to be the producer, Martin Jones. Jones was a newcomer to the theater. He had just made a great deal of money with the sensational play *White Cargo* and hoped to duplicate the success with *Mulatto.* When Hughes arrived in

New York to discover that opening day was at hand, the major satisfaction he had in the short time before the opening was the presence in the cast of McClendon, whom he had envisioned in the role of Cora. Jones, who was adding scenes of sex and violence to the play with the aim of having a commercial hit that was far-removed from the original, treated the author very badly. Jones, who had been surprised to discover Hughes's ethnic identity, behaved no better after the opening. Not only did he avoid paying the royalties due the author, but Hughes asserted that "he had objected to paying Rose McClendon her full salary because he thought it too much for a Negro" (318).

Negro Theatre Project Promoted

The last service McClendon undertook for black theater was to become co-head of the Negro Theatre Project of the WPA. The Federal Theatre of the WPA came into being in late 1935 to address the pressing plight of unemployed theatrical personnel. The situation of black artists and actors, living even more precariously than their white counterparts, was desperate. It was quickly decided to set up black branches of the project in major cities. According to John Houseman, there were three factions involved in selecting the project head in New York. The first comprised the Lafayette Players, who had successfully run a Harlem repertory company until the competition from movies and radio became too great. They felt the project director should be black and one of their number. The second was the Harlem intelligentsia, who tended to look down on performers. Given the social and political climate, they felt the director should be a well-known white with national reputation and connections. Naturally, such a person would need black advisors, roles for which they felt themselves well qualified. The black performers who made their way into the downtown professional theater were the third group. They were torn between black pride, which called for a black director, and their perception of the realities of the social structure, which they shared with the intelligentsia. In this situation, all groups were willing to fall into agreement when Rose McClendon's name was proposed. She in turn accepted, but with the proviso that since she felt she was primarily a performer, a white codirector with equal authority be appointed. When her position was accepted, she nominated Houseman, who became co-head of the project. But she was already so ill that the collaboration became a matter of Housman's visiting her on her sick bed and trying to give her a sense of participation until her illness became so grave that she resigned.

McClendon withdrew from *Mulatto* officially because of pleurisy; she died six months later on July 2, 1936. Her death certificate lists the cause of death as pneumonia. But Houseman states that the disease that ravaged her was cancer. Given the reluctance to mention the disease at this time and Houseman's close contact with McClendon, cancer was likely the cause.

McClendon's professional life can be traced quite clearly, but at present her personal life is much less clear. Robert Lewis gives one of the few glimpses of her at home: "Rose McClendon is a perfect culinary artist in her home. Her house in Harlem is meeting place for the most prominent as well as the most promising artists of the day" (200). Reviews give a glimpse of her acting. For example, Brooks Atkinson says of her performance in *Never No More,* "She is both majestic and humble. She acts from the inside out" (*New York Times*). Her physical appearance is documented in photographs. She was strikingly beautiful. Small and thin, almost to the point of appearing frail, she was loved by the camera. It is no wonder that Carl Van Vechten took many pictures of her nor that he named the collection of one hundred photographs of black writers and artists, which he donated to Howard University, the Rose McClendon Collection. As a tribute to her work for black theater, her collaborator in the Negro People's Theatre, Dick Campbell, named the group he founded in 1937 to carry forward her vision of training the community in all aspects of the theater, The Rose McClendon Players.

References

Atkinson, Brooks. Review of *Never No More. New York Times,* 8 January 1932.

Brown, Sterling A. Review of *Never No More. Opportunity* 10 (February 1932): 56-57. A photograph of McClendon in the role of Mammy precedes the article.

Green, Paul. *The House of Connelly.* Condensed version in Burns Mantle, *The Best Plays of 1931-32.* New York: Dodd, Mead, 1932. 145-78.

———. *In Abraham's Bosom.* Condensed version in Burns Mantle, *The Best Plays of 1926-27.* New York: Dodd, Mead, 1927. 325-52.

Houseman, John. *Run-Through.* New York: Simon and Schuster, 1972. 129, 178-79.

Hughes, Langston and Milton Meltzer. *Black Magic.* Englewood Cliffs, N.J.: Prentice-Hall, 1967. Photographs pp. 108, 109.

Kellner, Bruce, ed. *The Harlem Renaissance: A Historical Dictionary for the Era.* New York: Methuen, 1984.

Lewis, Robert. "Rose McClendon." In *Negro: An Anthology.* Edited by Nancy Cunard. Edited and abridged by Hugh Ford. New York: Frederick Ungar, 1970. 199-200.

Locke, Alain. *Negro Art: Past and Present.* Washington, D.C.: Associates in Negro Folk Education, 1936. 79.

Mantle, Burns. *The Best Plays of . . . 1926-27*, "Deep River," 392-93. *1931-32*, "Never No More," 460-61. *1935-36*, "Mulatto," 424-25. New York: Dodd, Mead, 1927- .

Rampersad, Arnold. *The Life of Langston Hughes.* Vol. 1, *I, Too, Sing America.* New York: Oxford University Press, 1986. 191, 312-13, 318.

Voorhees, Lillian W. "Rose McClendon." In *Notable American Women 1607-1950*. Edited by Edward T. James amd others. Cambridge: Harvard University Press, 1971. 449-50.

Collections

There is a scrapbook of Rose McClendon in the Schomburg Collection on Black Culture. Letters and photographs of McClendon are in the James Weldon Johnson Memorial Collection, Yale University.

Robert L. Johns

Mary Eleanora McCoy

(1846-1923)

Philanthropist, clubwoman

A woman with meager formal education, Mary Eleanora McCoy became one of the most effective self-educated women of her time. Her concern for racial uplift was demonstrated in many ways, especially through her club work in Michigan in the McCoy Home for Colored Children, of which she was a major supporter, and in the Phillis Wheatley Home for the Aged, which she helped to organize. She was a powerful influence in the life of her husband, Elijah McCoy, internationally-known inventor whose devices revolutionized the railroad industry and the maintenance of machinery.

Mary Eleanora Delaney Brownlow McCoy was born in a stopping place on the Underground Railroad at Lawrenceburg, Indiana, on January 7, 1846. She was the daughter of Jacob C. Delaney and Eliza Ann (Montgomery) Delaney. Nothing more is known about her parents. The little formal instruction that she had came through mission schools conducted in homes in Indiana and at the Freedman's School in Saint Louis, Missouri, in 1869.

Elijah McCoy was born in Colchester, Ontario, Canada, on March 27, 1843, to George McCoy and Mildred (Goins) McCoy, slaves in Kentucky who escaped on the Underground Railroad to Canada in the fall of 1837. George McCoy served in the Canadian Army and upon his discharge was given a 160-acre farm in Colchester. Elijah McCoy worked on his father's farm while attending school, and when he was fifteen, his father sent him to Edinburgh, Scotland, to study mechanical engineering. Five years later, he returned to Canada as a master mechanic and engineer, and after a year he sought employment in the United States. Despite his training, the best job he was offered was that of railroad fireman with the Michigan Central Railroad. The manual method of lubricating the steam engine inspired him to find a better way to lubricate machines. By 1870 he was living in Ypsilanti, Michigan, and experimented with lubricators for steam engines. On June 23, 1872, he received his first patent but assigned his rights to obtain enough money to continue his inventions. Between 1872 and 1876 he obtained six patents for lubricators and one for an ironing table. Apparently discontinuing his inventions for a while, he went on to receive forty-four patents between 1882 and 1926. By 1920 he had organized the Elijah McCoy Manufacturing Company. He pioneered in devising a means for "steadily supplying oil to machinery in intermittent drops from a cup," making manual oiling unnecessary and eliminating the need to stop the machinery for oiling (*Dictionary of American Biography*, 617). The popular phrase "the real McCoy" applies to his oiling devices.

After his first wife, Ann Elizabeth Stewart, died, Elijah McCoy married Mary Eleanora Delaney Brownlow on February 25, 1873. Mary McCoy had had a previous marriage in 1869 to Henry Brownlow of Saint Louis. By 1882, Elijah and Mary McCoy moved to Detroit, where they purchased a house at 5730 Lincoln, later moving to 180 Rowens Street. The McCoys had one child. While they were said to have lived a quiet, private life, both were active in community affairs.

Women of color in Michigan in the mid-1890s began to organize clubs to address the needs of the black community. Mary Eleanora McCoy was instrumental in founding the earliest black women's club established in Michigan and several other organizations as well. This first organization, founded in Detroit in 1895, was called the In As Much Circle of King's Daughters and Sons Club. In 1895 Mary McCoy, along with Lucy Thurman, Frances Preston, Fannie Richards, and other prominent black women of the state, formed the Michigan State Association of Colored Women. McCoy was state organizer and vice-president of the Federated Colored Women's Clubs of Michigan. In 1898 the association joined the National Association of Colored Women (NACW). In 1914, when the eighth biennial session was held in Wilberforce, Ohio, McCoy presented to national president Margaret Murray Washington a gavel made from a cherry tree on the grounds of John Brown's home.

McCoy Called "Mother of Clubs"

Mary Eleanora McCoy was often called the "Mother of Clubs" due to her work in helping to organize the clubs as well as her involvement in numerous organizations. She was an organizer and in 1915 vice-president of the Phillis Wheatley Home for Aged Colored Women. She was vice-president of the Lydian Association of Detroit and the Willing Workers, the latter affiliated with the Bethel African Methodist Episcopal Church of Detroit, where she held membership. She also belonged to the Order of the Eastern Star. McCoy was the only black charter member of the Twentieth Century Club, which was organized in 1894 and included some of the best-known women of Michigan's metropolis. One of her primary interests was the McCoy Home for Colored Children, which she maintained as a major supporter. In addition to her club work, McCoy was active in the Women's Suffrage Movement, the NAACP, and the Democratic party. For her work with the Democratic party, she became flag bearer from Michigan in the Washington, D.C., parade of 1913 preceding the inauguration of President Woodrow Wilson.

Governor Woodbridge N. Ferris of Michigan appointed Mary McCoy to the highly-acclaimed Michigan Commission for the Half-Century Exposition of Freedmen's Progress. Several states came together for the exposition, held in Chicago, to recognize the progress of black Americans since the Emancipation Proclamation. The exposition was recorded in *Michigan Manual of Freedmen's Progress.*

The lynchings of black Americans during the first quarter of this century, particularly surrounding World War I, distressed McCoy. She wrote "An Appeal" in which she expressed her concern and called for relief:

> To All Lovers of Humanity, Everywhere!
>
> JUSTICE, where art thou? Thou Church of the Living God, why slumberest thou? Awake! Awake! and hear Ethiopia's cry for her people! Pray tell us, is there any premium on manhood? Is the Negro to educate himself and his children for citizenship only to be denied his rights?. . . . How long can a Civilized Nation stand by a human fellow being hung by a tree 'til dead, or burned at the stake and have his fingers and various other portions of his body cut off and mutilated, and used as souvenirs!. . . .
>
> We beg of you, as followers of Christ and citizens of this, our great America, "the Land of the free, and the home of the brave!" to lend us your aid in eradicating this evil, and by so doing you will help forward this movement towards solving the great Negro Problem which is now attracting the attention of all great minds (Marshall, 23).

Mary McCoy died in 1923 and her husband, Elijah, in 1929.

References

Dannett, Sylvia G. L. *Profiles of Negro Womanhood.* Vol. 1. Chicago: Educational Heritage, 1964. Line drawing, p. 284.

Dictionary of American Biography. Vol. VI. New York: Charles Scribner's Sons, 1933.

Ebony 22 (December 1966): 157. Line drawing of Elijah J. McCoy.

Hayden, Robert C. "Elijah McCoy." In *Eight Black American Inventors.* Reading, Mass.: Addison-Wesley, 1972.

Marshall, Albert P. *The "Real McCoy" of Ypsilanti.* Ypsilanti, Mich.: Marland Publishers, 1989.

Michigan Freedmen's Progress Commission. *Michigan Manual of Freedmen's Progress.* Compiled by Frances H. Warren. Lansing: 1915. Reprint. Detroit: John M. Green, 1985.

Peebles, Robin S. "Detroit's Black Women's Clubs." *Michigan History* 70 (January/February 1986): 48. Includes photograph.

Sammons, Vivian Ovelton. *Blacks in Science and Medicine.* New York: Hemisphere Publishing Corp., 1990.

Wesley, Charles Harris. *The History of the National Association of Colored Women's Clubs,* Washington, D.C.: NACW, 1984.

Who Was Who in America. Vol. IV. Chicago: Marquis, 1968. Rev. ed., 1967.

Who's Who of the Colored Race. Vol. 1. Ed. Frank Lincoln Mather. Chicago: 1915. Reprinted. Detroit: Gale Research Co., 1976.

De Witt S. Dykes, Jr.

Viola McCoy

(c. 1900-c. 1956)

Entertainer, singer

Viola McCoy, also known as Amanda Brown, Daisy Cliff, Fannie Johnson, Gladys Johnson, Violet McCoy, Clara White, Bessie Williams, and Susan Williams, an entertainer and blues singer, was born circa 1900 in Memphis, Tennessee, and died circa 1956 in Albany, New York.

McCoy went to New York and worked in cabarets in the early 1920s. She also appeared in four shows at the Lafayette Theater that included *Frolickers Revue* (1923), *Who Stole the Money?* (1924), *Hidden Treasure* (1924), and *Setting the Pace Revue* (1927). She owned, operated, and performed in Jack's Cabaret in 1927. In 1928 she was in a *New York Revue* at the Lincoln Theater. Following this were appearances in twenty-one shows at New York's Alhambra Theater—*Flying High Revue* (1928), *Joyland Revue* (1928), *Happiness Revue* (1928), *Brownskin Brevities Revue* (1928), *Laughing Through Revue* (1928), *Southbound Revue* (1928), *The Surprise Party Revue* (1929), *Ready Money Revue*

(1929), *Egg Nog Revue* (1929), *Hop Off Revue* (1929), *Sweethearts on Parade Revue* (1929), *Pearls of India Revue* (1929), *The Conjure Man Revue* (1929), *The Crazy Hotel* (1929), *At the Barbecue Revue* (1930), *By the Moonlight Revue* (1930), *Snake Hips Revue* (1930), *Fashion Plate Frolics Revue* (1930), *In the Swim Revue* (1930), *Edith Wilson Revue* (1930), and *Troy ''Bear'' Brown, Baby's Birthday Revue* (1930).

McCoy recorded in 1923 with the Gennett, Columbia, and Ajax labels in New York. She recorded during 1923 and 1926 with the Vocalion label, also in New York. In the three years that she was recording most prolifically, she rarely made a bad record. Her masterpiece was considered ''If Your Good Man Quits You, Don't Wear No Black,'' a fast blues accompanied by Fletcher Henderson's orchestral members. The opposite side of this recording was almost as impressive—''I Ain't Gonna Marry, Ain't Gonna Settle Down.''

During 1930 McCoy opened her own nightclub in Saratoga. She also returned to the Lafayette for three shows—*Scramblin' Roun' Revue* (1930), *Sweet Papa Garbage Revue* (1931), and *Plenty of It Revue* (1932). In 1932 she also appeared with Fletcher Henderson's Orchestra in *Harlem High Steppers Revue* at the Public Theater in New York City. The following year she performed at the Harlem Opera House. In 1934 McCoy appeared in two revues—one with Gladys Bentley's Urbangi Club at the Lafayette Theater and the other with Tiny Bradshaw's Orchestra, Walking On Air, at the Apollo Theater. She then performed with Leroy Smith's band at the Harlem Opera House in 1935. After a year of frequent club and theater engagements in Philadelphia, McCoy retired to Albany, New York, in about 1938. She is believed to have died there in 1956.

McCoy was a fine singer who had a very active career for more than a decade, appearing in theatrical revues and musical comedies. She was a grand performer with a lovely contralto voice that she projected with fine diction. Although she was from the vaudeville tradition, she performed using strong jazz stylistic characteristics.

References

Harris, Sheldon. *Blues Who's Who: A Biographical Dictionary of Blues Singers.* New Rochelle, N.Y.: Arlington House Publishers, 1979. 356-57. Viola McCoy is shown in a smiling bust pose, p. 356.

Stewart-Baxter, Derrick. *Ma Rainey and the Classic Blues Singers.* New York: Stein and Day, 1970. 94-95. Photograph, p. 94.

Marva Griffin Carter

M. A. McCurdy

(1852- ?)

Editor, educator, temperance leader

After overcoming adversities in her own life, M. A. McCurdy turned her energies toward independent learning and humanitarian efforts. She taught for a brief period, then became active in temperance and as editor of the *Southern Recorder* and *The Woman's World.* She used these papers as an outlet for her fight for temperance causes, women's suffrage, and morality and became widely-known and respected for her work. Deeply religious, she also served the community through church missions and helped to feed, clothe, and attend to the needs of the sick.

Born in the village of Carthage, Indiana, on August 10, 1852, to Alexander and Martha Harris, M. A. McCurdy attended racially-mixed schools in Rush County, Indiana. After her father died, she was unable to continue her formal education, but she read widely to prepare herself to become a teacher. Before she was nineteen, she secured a teaching position in a county school near her home. After teaching for awhile, she married J. A. Mason and had four children. Within eight years her husband and children had died. Her desire to work for the uplift of humanity led her to join the temperance movement in Richmond, Indiana. In 1884 she

M. A. McCurdy

was named secretary and editor of Richmond's temperance paper. Through her columns in the paper she gained fame as a staunch advocate of temperance.

McCurdy decided to move to the South, where she felt she could do the greatest good for black American people. On January 26, 1886, she arrived in Atlanta, Georgia, where she lived in the home of Bishop H. M. Turner and his wife and continued her temperance work. She became editor and secretary of the *Southern Recorder* when it was first issued on September 25, 1886; Turner was owner of the paper. Other papers commented on the *Recorder* and its information and wise sayings, often attributing the work to Turner, when in fact it was McCurdy, the secretary, who was responsible. Her work appeared in papers in the South as well as the West. She remained in Atlanta for four years and built up a respectable mission in Saint James Methodist Episcopal Church. She was Sunday school superintendent for three years. She visited the chain gang in the interest of temperance, acted as secretary of the city and county Woman's Christian Temperance Union (WCTU), and engaged in other church mission work.

McCurdy took a second husband on July 16, 1890, when she married C. McCurdy, a minister from Rome, Georgia. After moving to Rome, she continued her involvement in a variety of activities. She visited people in their homes for the purpose of instilling in them morality and religious beliefs. Through her daily visits she was known to comfort, feed, clothe, and help to heal the poor who lived in squalor and destitution in the damp and dark cellars of the city. Writing about her life in Rome, A. B. Allen said: "No home is too humble for her to enter, no person too base for her to labor to save" (Allen, 140).

M. A. McCurdy was active in industrial work among black American women. Through the Needlework Guild of America, Rome Branch, organized in 1894, three hundred three garments were made in two years and distributed throughout Rome and vicinity and to orphanages in Atlanta.

In Rome she continued her work as corresponding secretary of the state of Georgia's Women's Christian Temperance Union. She was superintendent of presswork for the state WCTU Number Two. She edited the temperance column in the *National Presbyterian*. With her sharp tongue and persuasive style, she is said to have made quite an impression on the reading public. "One has only to read her articles to become a total abstainer." She was known also as "a cogent writer" who was "always forceful and impressive whether writing or speaking" (Allen, 140).

Extremely loyal to her church, she was superintendent of the juvenile work of Knox Presbytery of the Presbyterian church. She was also president of missionary work and Sunday school teacher.

McCurdy Edits Paper

Although we do not know the date, McCurdy became editor of *The Woman's World*, a paper that focused on the intellectual, moral, and spiritual progress of people. The paper met with marked success; it was also wisely and ably managed. An ardent and firm advocate of women's suffrage, she made her views on women's rights known through the paper as well. In her article "Duty of the State to the Negro," she insisted that the state meet its obligation to black males and at the same time address the cause of thousands of women who called for equal franchise. She continued:

> [These are] women who are worthy of much consideration; women who would prove most valuable to the State on account of their executive ability, their culture, learning and wisdom, the four great somethings that assist mightily in bringing to pass those things that make for the good of all concerned. Then, there are women who can expound the law of the State in a precise manner and are therefore fully equipped for service in that capacity. . . . Emancipate the Anglo-Saxon and the Afro-American woman who are wearing a yoke of oppression, the equal of that which did hold the slave in bondage for more than two hundred years (M'Curdy [sic], 144-45.

If women were enfranchised, McCurdy believed that they would banish the alcohol traffic from the land permanently. Both through the WCTU and the *Woman's World* she became widely known throughout the state and in the major cities. She began many major reforms in society, especially in the area of temperance. Through her influence, the barrooms and other drinking places were closed during Christmas season.

McCurdy spoke in the cause of freedom for the race. She noted that the enslaved black American was "robbed of all privileges allotted to mankind to compete morally, intellectually and politically with other races," thus being rendered subservient (M'Curdy, 143). Once freed, blacks found themselves in need of moral, intellectual, and financial improvement, and schools and colleges were established to aid in this cause. There were also thousands of people imprisoned in poverty-stricken homes, correctional institutions, insane asylums, and in the few reformatory schools that existed. She believed that neither the schools nor the churches could correct the political wrongs that affected the black race, and that the state had a duty to "the Negro" to correct these political ills. Politicians in power "failed to do their duty toward the Negro," she said (144).

Nothing more is known about M. A. McCurdy. She bears further inquiry, particularly for her writing, her work as editor, and her efforts in the area of women's suffrage.

References

Allen, A. B. "[Mrs. M. A. McCurdy]. Sketch of Her Life and Labor in Rome, Ga." *Afro-American Encyclopaedia*. Comp. James T. Haley. Nashville: Haley and Florida, 1896. 139-42.

Gibson, J. W., and W. H. Crogman. *The Colored American from Slavery to Honorable Citizenship.* Atlanta: J. L. Nichols, 1901. 568-69.

Haley, James T., comp. *Afro-American Encyclopaedia.* Nashville: Haley and Florida, 1896. 137-39. Photograph, p. 138.

M'Curdy [sic], Mrs. M. A. "Duty of the State to the Negro." *Afro-American Encyclopaedia.* Nashville: Haley and Florida, 1896. 142-45.

Jessie Carney Smith

Hattie McDaniel "Hi-Hat Hattie"

(1895-1952)

Singer, actress

Show business is hard work, and Hattie McDaniel worked hard in show business all her life. She began as a singer and songwriter in vaudeville and worked her way into movies and radio. She made hundreds of films and became the star of a radio show that moved to television. In a business that could see her only as a mammy or a maid, McDaniel triumphed by taking the roles she was allotted and transcending them.

Hattie McDaniel

Born June 10, 1895, in Wichita, Kansas, Hattie McDaniel was the thirteenth child of the Reverend Henry McDaniel and Susan (Holbert) McDaniel. Reverend McDaniel pastored a local Baptist church and Susan McDaniel sang in the choir. Soon after Hattie McDaniel was born the family moved to Denver, Colorado. Reared in Denver, McDaniel attended East Denver High School. In 1910 at the age of fifteen, she was awarded a gold medal by the Women's Christian Temperance Union for excellence in "the dramatic art" for her recital of "Convict Joe." She moved many of the ladies to tears.

Possibly influenced by her mother's singing, coupled with her own experience in the church choir, McDaniel began her career as a singer. Joining her older brother Otis, who owned his own acting company, she wrote songs and performed them in small-town tent shows.

A prolific composer of more than a dozen songs, McDaniel recorded many of them with the Richard Jones Jazz Wizards at the Merritt Company in Kansas City and on the Okeh and Paramount labels in Chicago. However, most remain as sheet music. Reputed to be the first black American woman to sing on radio, she made her debut in 1915 singing with Professor George Morrison's Negro Orchestra in Denver.

Performing minstrel shows and working the vaudeville circuits, McDaniel continued her show business career, and by 1925 she had worked her way into a traveling production of *Show Boat.* By the late 1920s McDaniel found herself in Milwaukee and out of work. Accepting a job as a maid at Sam Pick's Suburban Inn, she worked until she was able to audition for a part in the Suburban Inn's show. In the audition she sang "St. Louis Blues." Winning a starring part in the show, she remained in Milwaukee for two years.

McDaniel moved to Hollywood in 1931 and made her movie debut in 1932 in the movie *The Golden West.* Her sisters Etta and Orlena and brother Sam had moved to California several years earlier; therefore she had family to depend on until she was able to establish her career. Over the next two decades she appeared in more than three hundred films but did not receive screen credit for them. Among the ones she is credited for are: *Hypnotized, Washington Masquerade, Blonde Venus* (1932); *I'm No Angel, Story of Temple Drake* (1933); *Judge Priest, Lost in the Stratosphere, Little Men, Operator 13, Babbit* (1934); *Another Face, Alice Adams, China Seas, Traveling Saleslady, Our Gang, Music is Magic* (1935); *The Prisoner of Shark Island, Showboat, The First Baby, Hearts Divided, High Tension, Star for a Night, Postal Inspector, The Bride Walks Out, Valiant is the Word for Carrie, Can This Be Dixie, Gentle Julia, Next Time We Love, Libeled Lady, The Singing Kid, Reunion* (1936); *Racing Lady, Don't Tell the Wife, The Crime Nobody Saw, True Confession, Over the Goal, Forty-five, Nothing Sacred, Saratoga, The Wildcatter* (1937); *Battle Broadway, The Shining Angel, Everybody's Baby* (1938); *Zenobia,*

Gone With the Wind (1939); *Maryland* (1940); *Affectionately Yours, The Great Lie, They Died With Their Boots On* (1941); *The Male Animal, George Washington Slept Here, In This Our Life* (1942); *Johnny Come Lately, Thank Your Lucky Stars* (1943); *Since You Went Away, There is a Family, Janie, Hi Beautiful* (1944); *Margie, Never Say Goodbye, Janie Gets Married, Song of the South* (1946); *The Flame* (1947); *Mickey,* and *Family Honeymoon* (1948).

Despite the number of films in which she appeared, McDaniel was never able to depend entirely upon her acting career for financial support. Forced to supplement her movie roles with other work, she often was heard on radio broadcasts. In Los Angeles she was broadcast on radio station KNX as Hi-Hat Hattie on "The Optimistic Donuts Show" (1931-32). She appeared on WGAR in Cleveland, Ohio (1940); the "Rudy Vallee Show" with Eddie Cantor on NBC (1941); later she broadcast on "Blueberry Hill," CBS (1943); the "Billie Burke Show," CBS (1944); on "Amos 'n Andy," NBC (1945); "The Beulah Show," CBS (1947), and the "Bing Crosby's Philco Radio Time."

Movie Career Brings Fame and Controversy

Limited by the stereotyped parts available to black actors, McDaniel's career was built on the image of "Mammy," a meek servant placating the whims of the white masters. However, McDaniel, a large woman with an expressive face and distinctive voice, transformed the image into a witty, sly, and perceptive observer of those she worked for. Although a servant, her performance often made clear her superior moral character and her wisdom regarding human nature.

A pragmatist, she never idealized the parts she played. She simply refused to allow the limitations of the roles to stop her from doing what she excelled in: acting. Often criticized and sometimes maligned by fellow blacks for playing the "mammy" roles, she replied with a verbal flippancy often characteristic of her acting: "It's better to get seven thousand dollars a week for playing a servant than seven dollars a week for being one" *(Notable American Women,* 445). In another, perhaps more thoughtful response, she said, "I portray the type of Negro woman who has worked honestly and proudly to give our nation the Marian Andersons, Roland Hayeses and Ralph Bunches" (Traylor, 415).

In 1939 McDaniel won an Academy Award for her portrayal of Mammy in *Gone With the Wind,* Named best supporting actress for her performance, she was the first black American to win the award. She donated her Oscar to Howard University.

McDaniel married four times. Of her first husband, George Langford, little is known except that he came from a prominent black Denver family and died young. They were married in 1922 and he died shortly afterward. McDaniel was married to Howard Hickman during the late 1930s. She was divorced from him in 1938. She and her third husband, James Lloyd Crawford, were married on March 21, 1941, in Tucson, Arizona, by the Reverend B. Cornelius at Union Baptist Church. Crawford was a Los Angeles real estate agent. McDaniel later divorced Crawford, and in 1949 she married Larry C. Williams, a successful Hollywood interior decorator. They were married in Yumma, Arizona, on June 11. This marriage also ended in divorce, lasting only four months.

McDaniel had no children but wanted desperately to become a mother. In May 1944, while still married to Crawford, McDaniel announced that she was pregnant. All of Hollywood celebrated with her. Clark Gable, Claudette Colbert, and Vivien Leigh showered her with gifts for the baby. But the baby never arrived. She had a false pregnancy threw her into a state of depression from which some people thought she never fully recovered.

During the 1940s, McDaniel chaired the black section of the Hollywood Victory Committee that organized entertainment for black troops serving in World War II. She was also an activist for black youth, working to raise funds for educational scholarships. Despite the roles she played on screen, off screen she was no accommodationist. McDaniel fought and won an antidiscrimination suit involving the purchase of her California home.

McDaniel Assumes "Beulah" Role

On October 31, 1947, McDaniel signed her first contract for the radio show "Beulah." She earned one thousand dollars a week starting salary, which rose to two thousand dollars weekly over a seven-year period. In her contract she insisted that she would not use dialect and demanded the right to alter any script that did not meet her approval. Both demands were met. Neither the NAACP nor the Urban League had complaints about McDaniel, who was so closely associated with the character that she often received mail addressed to Beulah McDaniel.

In 1950 when "Beulah" came to television, Ethel Waters was cast in the part. There was a public outcry for McDaniel to play the television part as well. Thus, when in 1951 Waters quit the role in order to do theater work in the East, McDaniel was given the assignment. During the summer of 1951, McDaniel filmed six episodes of the television show. On August 18 she became ill and was afterwards diagnosed as having suffered a heart attack. Her friend, Louise Beavers, was cast in the part. From August until early October McDaniel remained in Temple Hospital in Los Angeles. When she finally was allowed to go home near the end of October, she appeared to be on the road to recovery. But then in January 1952 she suffered a stroke. Returning to the hospital, she stayed only briefly and looked as though she would soon recover. In fact in the spring of 1952 she taped the first fifteen weekly episodes for the radio show "Beulah." Several years earlier, a boil or lump had appeared under McDaniel's left arm. She ignored it, and it appeared to go away. During the summer of 1952 it reappeared and was discovered to be breast cancer. Suffering from cancer, McDaniel died on October 26, 1952, at the Motion Picture Country House in San Fernando Valley, California. She was survived by one brother, Sam Deacon McDaniel, himself a film actor who died in 1963, a niece, Etta Emanuel, and a nephew, Elzei Emanuel, also an actor. Today the surviving members of the talented McDaniel family consist of Elzei Emanuel, Orlean McDaniel's grandson, and Edgar Goff, Etta Emanuel's grandson. Both reside in Los Angeles.

McDaniel's funeral took place on November 1, 1952, at People's Independent Church of Christ. Reverend Clayton D. Russell officiated. At one o'clock in the afternoon the church was crowded with one thousand people, all that it could seat. Four thousand more people stood outside. Lines of fans had been forming twelve hours prior to the funeral. There were 125 limousines in a lavish farewell. Buried in Rosedale Cemetery, McDaniel continued to make "firsts" for her race. She was the first black person to be buried at Rosedale, causing protests from some in Los Angeles.

References

Andreeva, Tamara. "Hattie Is Hep." *Denver Post,* 11 April 1948.

Aylesworth, Thomas G. and John Stewart Bowman. "Hattie McDaniel." *World Almanac Book of Who's Who in Film.* New York: World Almanac, 1987. 220.

Biography Index Vols. 2, 3, 6.19, 12. New York: H. W. Wilson, 1949.

Bogle, Donald. *Toms, Coons, Mullattoes, Mammies and Bucks.* New York: Viking Press, 1973. 23.

———. *Brown, Sugar: Eighty Years of American's Black Female Superstars.* New York: Harmony Books, 1980.

Crosby, John. "Radio in Review: Beulah." New York *Herald Tribune,* 14 March 1947.

Current Biography. New York: H. W. Wilson, 1940. 536-37.

Hooper, Hedda. "Hattie Hates Nobody." *Chicago Sunday Tribune,* 14 December 1947.

Horne, Lena. *Lena.* New York: Doubleday, 1965. 73-74.

Jackson, Carlton. *Hattie: The Life of Hattie McDaniel.* New York: Madison Books, 1990.

Kinkaid, Jamaica. "If Mammies Ruled the World." *Village Voice,* 5 May 1975.

Levette, Harry. "I Knew Hattie McDaniel." *American Negro Press,* 5 November 1952.

Mitchell, Lisa. "Hattie McDaniel, More Than A Mammy." *Hollywood Studio Magazine* (April 1977): 19-20.

———. "Mammy McDaniel As the Definitive Matriarch." *Los Angeles Times,* 7 November 1976.

Myrick, Susan. "40 years of Such Interesting People." *Atlanta Journal and Constitution Magazine,* 8 September 1974.

———. "Pardon My Un-Southern Accent." *Collier's* 118 (December 1939): 20-21, 32.

Nobel, Peter. *The Negro in Films: Literature of the Cinema* (1948). Reprinted. New York: Arno Press, 1970.

Nugent, Frank. "Gone With, Etc., Or The Making Of A Movie." *New York Times Magazine,* 10 December 1939.

O'Leary, Dorothy. "Regarding Miss Hattie McDaniel. *New York Times,* 7 March 1948.

Parsons, Louella. "Mammy's Gold Oscar: Most Popular Award." Syndicated column. *International News Service,* 9 March 1940.

Ploski, Harry A., and Warren Marr. eds. *Negro Almanac.* New York: Bellwether, 1976. 721.

Rea, E. B. "Natural Talent Made Her A Star." *Washington Afro-American,* 18 November 1952.

Skerrett, Joseph. "Hattie McDaniel." *Notable American Women: The Modern Period.* Cambridge: Harvard University Press, 1980. 445-46.

Sparks, Nancy. "Viewpoint." Wichita *Beacon,* 31 October 1967.

Time, 18 November 1946; 25 December 1939; 10 June 1940; 1 December 1947; 5 May 1961.

Traylor, Eleanor. "Hattie McDaniel." *Dictionary of American Negro Biography.* New York: Norton, 1982. 414-15.

Weaver, William R. Review of *Gone With the Wind. Motion Picture Herald,* 16 December 1939.

Zeigler, Ronny. "Hattie McDaniel (I'd) . . . Rather Play a Maid." *Amsterdam News,* 28 April 1979.

Collections

The vertical files at the Schomburg Center for Research in Black Culture and the Lincoln Center Library and Museum of Performing Arts of the New York Public Library contain valuable information as well as photographs of Hattie McDaniel. Photographs of McDaniel and members of her family are also held in the Margaret Herrick Library, Academy of Motion Picture Arts and Sciences, Beverly Hills, California.

Obituaries appear in the *Amsterdam News* 1 November 1952, *Our World Magazine* 2 February 1953, and the *New York Times* 27 October 1952. Most printed sources list McDaniel's birth date as June 10, 1898; however, her brother Samuel McDaniel listed it on her death certificate as 1895.

Nagueyalti Warren

Alice Woodby McKane

(1865-1948)

Physician, author, suffragist

Alice Woodby McKane, noted physician-author, was born in 1865 in Bridgewater, Pennsylvania. A practicing physician, poet, educator, and suffragette, McKane and her husband founded the first training school for nurses in southeast Georgia, which doubled as a dispensary for destitute people. McKane belonged to a number of organizations that promoted the health and welfare of black Americans and women's rights.

She was the daughter of Charles Woodby and Elizabeth B. (Frazier) Woodby. Both parents died before McKane was seven years old. She suffered the loss of her sight and remained blind for three years. She married Cornelius McKane, a practicing physician in Savannah, Georgia, on February 2, 1893. Cornelius McKane, born in Demarara, British Guiana, the grandson of a Liberian king, became a great scholar, linguist, orator, teacher, clergyman, author, editor, and race champion. Children born of this union included Cornelius, Jr., born May 14, 1897; Alice Fanny, born August 23, 1898; and William Francis, born May 14, 1902.

McKane was educated in the public schools of Bridgewater, Hampton Institute (1883-1886), and the Institute for Colored Youth in Pennsylvania (1886-1889). Her medical education was gained at the Women's Medical College of Pennsylvania (1889-1892), where in May 1892 she received the M.D. degree.

Nursing School and Hospital Established in Georgia

McKane was licensed as a physician in 1892. Two months after receiving her medical degree, she moved to Augusta, Georgia, as a practicing physician and began to train a class of young women to care for the sick. She also taught chemistry and physiology at Lucy Laney's Haines School. She said that "the training of women of my race as nurses was still of the greatest interest to me for many reasons, so I begged my husband to assist me to start such work in this city. He consented, and together we started work in our office. Few understood that our motives were to try to do good . . . " (*Southern Workman,* 1897). The team in 1893 established the first Training School for Nurses in southeast Georgia. A public dispensary was also started in conjunction with this work. Cornelius McKane took an active role in the operation of the school, and the first graduates finished in 1895. Many destitute people were treated free of charge in the small dispensary that the McKanes operated, while an average of ten people each week were turned away for lack of space and means to care for them. Local black churches provided some of the support needed to maintain the dispensary and training facility, but the funds were meager.

Some time during their stay in Savannah, the husband-wife team went to Monrovia, Liberia, where they were instrumental in organizing health facilities, and Alice McKane served as the Assistant United States Pension Medical Examiner for Civil War veterans residing in Liberia. Alice McKane was the co-organizer and in charge of the Department of Diseases of Women at the Private Hospital, Monrovia's first hospital.

McKane contracted an African fever that made it necessary to return to Savannah. She regained her health in 1896. In Savannah the husband and wife team established the McKane Hospital for Women and Children and Training School for Nurses, a state-chartered institution.

In April 1989, Alice Woodby McKane noted that:

> Our own people, the colored people, do not do very much for it [the hospital], and after careful observation and study I find the chief reasons to be ignorance and poverty. During the last year I have seen women give their last five cents for the cause, and then get trusted five cents for a loaf of bread the next morning, or do without. I have also seen them give one week's work to the cause, and found them objects of charity in the hospital the next. The beds are still all free, and the majority of the patients are women who live in service, and have no comfortable home nor anyone to care for them when they are sick (*Southern Workman,* August 1898).

Several of the local white physicians developed an interest in the facility and aided the McKanes with donations and by treating the sick.

The McKane's severed their connection with the Savannah project after several years and moved to Boston in order to provide a better education for their sons. They also had purchased a home in Boston. Two weeks after their arrival, the McKanes passed the State Medical Board and established medical practice. McKane restricted herself to office work, primarily in the treatment of women's diseases. She also lectured weekly to nurses in training at the Plymouth Hospital.

McKane was active in a number of organizations that included the office of Supreme Worthy Councillor of the Courts of Calanthe, Knights of Pythias of the Eastern and Western Hemispheres, St. Mary's Chapel Order of Eastern Stars, Scottish Rite Masons (Boston, Massachusetts), and joined St. Augustine's Mission. She was a member of the Robert A. Bell Women's Relief Corps No. 67, Grand Army of the Republic and the Ladies Auxiliary to Company L., Sixth Massachusetts National Guard. In the areas of health care she was a member of the St. Martin's Day Nursery Association in Boston and the Boston Okolona Hospital Club, for the Okolona (Mississippi) Institute. She was an active member of the Boston branch of the NAACP and a member of the National Equal Rights League. A poet, she was a member of the League of Colored Poets of the World.

McKane was a prominent and active Republican and was a member of the Business and Professional Women's Republican Club of Boston and the Republican Women's Council of Massachusetts. An activist in the women's suffrage movement, she was twice a delegate to the Republican Massachusetts State Convention and ward committeewoman and ward representative to the Eleventh Congressional District Convention.

McKane was an associate of Lucy Laney, founder of the Haines Institute, who appointed her teacher of natural science, resident physician, and instructor of nurses at Haines Institute, Augusta, Georgia, when she moved to the area in 1892. She was also associated with William Heard, African Methodist Episcopal (AME) church bishop and the United States Minister to Liberia. In her youth, McKane was private secretary of Fannie Jackson Coppin, principal of the Cheyney Institute for Youth and African missionary as wife of AME church bishop Levi Coppin.

McKane was a contributor to a number of religious magazines and journals. She authored *The Fraternal Society Sick Book,* 1913, which dealt with the art of healing. She also wrote *Clover Leaves,* a book of poems published in Boston in 1914. She died on March 6, 1948, of arteriosclerosis.

References

Boston Guardian, 9 March 1912.

Davis, Marianna W., ed. *Contributions of Black Women to America.* Vol. II. Columbia, S.C.: Kenday Press, 1982. 366.

Low, W. Augustus, and Virgil A. Clift, eds. *Encyclopedia of Black America.* New York: McGraw-Hill Book Co., 1981. 551.

Southern Workman 26 (August 1927): 151-52; 27 (August 1898): 157-58; 40 (March 1911): 191.

Who's Who in Colored America. Vol. 1. New York: Who's Who in Colored America Corp., 1927. 132.

Collections

Papers on Alice Woodby McKane are in the Black Women Physicians Project, Archives and Special Collections on Women, the Medical College of Pennsylvania. The archives of Hampton University also have materials on McKane.

Casper LeRoy

Nina Mae McKinney

(1912-1967)

Actress, dancer, singer

Nina Mae McKinney established a place for the sensuous black woman on screen, but her talents as a singer, dancer, and actress were largely overlooked in the Hollywood system of stereotyping black performers.

Born in Lancaster, South Carolina, on June 12, 1912, McKinney was a self-taught dancer who fled the South for the opportunity to sing and dance in New York City. She grew up on an estate owned by Colonel LeRoy Sanders in South Carolina, where her family had worked and lived for several generations. She was reared by her grandmother until she was twelve years old. Her parents, who lived in New York City, sent for her to live with them and attend school. McKinney attended Public School Number 126.

Discovered in the chorus line of Lew Leslie's *Blackbirds,* McKinney was cast in the starring role of Chick in King Vidor's film *Hallelujah* in 1928, replacing "Honey" Brown, who had been Vidor's first choice. On the eve of her departure for Hollywood, McKinney's father, a twenty-seven-year post office employee, died.

As Chick in *Hallelujah,* McKinney became the first recognized black woman actor in a Hollywood film. Unfortunately the role, while not the mammy type, was stereotypic. She introduced the first black temptress, a dubious distinction. Of her, Donald Bogle writes:

> In McKinney's hands and hips, Chick represented the black woman as an exotic sex object, half woman, half child. She was the black woman out of control of her emotions, split in two by her loyalties and her own vulnerabilities (*Toms*, 31).

McKinney's role in *Hallelujah* is important, for it establishes a sensual role for black women actors. *Hallelujah* was the first all-black musical and McKinney the first leading lady whose dance of seduction, Swanee Shuffle, created a tradition later expressed in the styles of Lena Horne and Dorothy Dandridge.

Richard Watts, Jr., of the *New York Post,* called McKinney one of the most beautiful women of that time. A mulatto, McKinney exemplified the standard for the women who would follow her in featured roles. McKinney's physical appearance, coupled with her performance in *Hallelujah,* prompted MGM to enthusiastically sign her to a five-year contract. McKinney was only seventeen years old. But ultimately Hollywood had no place for a beautiful, sexy black woman. Instead of *Hallelujah* catapulting her to other roles for leading ladies, she was disappointed with minor roles in obscure films.

Ignored by the American film public, McKinney went abroad with her pianist, Garland Wilson, in December 1929. In Europe she was billed as the black Garbo. Singing in cellars and cafes, she spent a month at Chez Florence in Paris and appeared at the Trocadero and the Cira clubs in London. McKinney also appeared in Dublin and Budapest. She encountered a European audience that appreciated her talents. While in England she met Paul Robeson and starred with him in *Congo Road* (1930) and *Sanders of the River* (1935). In 1930 McKinney returned to New York City for the Broadway premiere of *Congo Road.* Still unable to find employment as a Hollywood leading lady, McKinney appeared in a number of non-Hollywood films. She returned to Europe in 1932.

In 1940 McKinney returned to the United States and married Jimmy Monroe, a jazz artist. During the early 1940s she sang and toured the United States with her own band. Details of her later years are sketchy. She died in New York City on May 3, 1967, at the age of fifty-four.

McKinney's film credits include *Congo Road* (1930), *Safe in Hell, Swan Boat* (1931), *Pie, Pie Blackbird* (1932), *Reckless* (1935), *The Devil's Daughter* (1937), *Gang Smasher* (1938), *St. Louis Gal* (1938), *Pocomania* (1939), *Straight to Heaven* (1939), *Together Again* (1944), *Dark Waters* (1947), *Danger Street* (1947), *Night Train to Memphis* (1946), *Manhattan Messes Up* (1946), *Pinky* (1949), and *Rain* (1951).

In 1978 Nina Mae McKinney was inducted into the Black Filmmakers Hall of Fame.

References

Bogle, Donald. *Toms, Coons, Mulattoes, Mammies and Bucks.* New York: Viking, 1973. 31-34.

———. *Blacks in American Films and Television.* New York: Garland, 1988. 102, 418-20.

Chilton, John. *Who's Who of Jazz.* London: Macmillan, 1985. 241.

Claghorn, Charles. *Biographical Dictionary of Jazz.* Englewood Cliffs, N.J.: Prentice-Hall, 1982. 238.

Long, Richard A. *The Black Tradition in American Dance.* New York: Rizzoli, 1989. 44.

Mapp, Edward. *Directory of Blacks in the Performing Arts.* Metuchen, N.J.: Scarecrow Press, 1978. 328.

Sampson, Henry T. *Blacks in Black and White.* Metuchen, N.J.: Scarecrow Press, 1977. 232-34.

Nagueyalti Warren

Enolia Pettigen McMillan

(1904-)

Organization executive, educator, administrator

Enolia Pettigen McMillan, national president of the NAACP (1985-89), educator, and administrator, was born in Willow Grove, Pennsylvania, on October 20, 1904, the daughter of John Pettigen, born a slave in Virginia, and Elizabeth (Fortune) Pettigen, a domestic worker. McMillan graduated from Howard University in 1926 and went on to earn a master's degree in educational administration from Columbia University in 1933. On December 26, 1935, she married Betha D. McMillan. From this union came one son, Betha D., Jr., who currently resides in Baltimore, Maryland.

Enolia McMillan spent her early childhood years on the eastern shore of Maryland. In 1912, when McMillan was eight years old, her family moved to Baltimore. She grew up in a poor but relatively close-knit, stable family with her parents, two brothers, and one sister. Her family were longstanding members of Calvary Baptist Church in Baltimore, and McMillan, her mother, and her sister became active participants in the church's community-based programs. McMillan gained much of her experience as an organizer for the NAACP from her involvement with the church.

McMillan's parents and her school principal played prominent roles in her decision to pursue higher education. Impressed with McMillan's academic performance and enthusiasm for learning, her principal strongly encouraged her to attend college. Thus, after she graduated from high school in 1922, she began a daily commute by train to Washington, D.C., to attend Howard University. Seven years later, she earned her master's degree from Columbia University.

McMillan's earliest ambition was to become a doctor, but the racial discrimination of the 1920s often forced black American women to choose either teaching or domestic work. She chose teaching, beginning her career in Maryland at Pomonkey High School, where she served as principal from 1928 to 1935. She taught junior high school in Baltimore from 1935 to 1956, served as vice-principal at Clifton Park and Cherry Hill Junior High schools from 1956 to 1969 and as vice-principal at Paul Lawrence Dunbar Senior High School from 1963 to 1966. As a teacher and administrator, she voiced complaints about the inferior status of black American schools, and while president of the Maryland State Colored Teachers' Association she fought successfully against a law allowing "colored" teachers to be paid less than white teachers. Her earliest participation in the NAACP, which worked to change such laws, began during this period.

McMillan joined the NAACP in 1935, when the inactive Baltimore chapter was being revived, thus beginning her five decades of struggle for civil and human rights. She became president of the Baltimore chapter in 1969 at the age of sixty-five. Upon her election, she vowed to recruit younger members because she believed that the organization, with its cadre of older members, needed young people in order to grow. Under her presidency the previously declining membership increased to seven thousand members, both young and old, and fund-raising activities increased as well. In 1976, when the national organization had to pay $125 million in damages incurred from a boycott of white merchants in Mississippi, the Baltimore chapter raised $158,000—the largest local contribution—to help defray the expense.

By the early seventies the Baltimore chapter, through "negotiation, legislation, and litigation," had helped to effect considerable social change. One of the greatest areas of impact was employment—a greater variety of jobs had opened to black Americans. Still, because of continued racial discrimination, too few black Americans secured these jobs. As a result, McMillan helped to involve the chapter in every major job discrimination case and learned to redirect chapter goals as the needs of black Americans changed. Under her seventeen-year leadership, the Baltimore chapter distinguished itself as the "vibrant, effective vanguard" of the civil rights movement.

First Woman Heads the NAACP

In 1985, after having served on the national board, McMillan ran unsolicited and unopposed for the presidency of the national association and became the first woman to hold the unsalaried position. She was reelected each year until her retirement in December 1989. One of her major accomplishments was helping designate Baltimore as the new home for the NAACP national headquarters. When members of the national board agreed to relocate the headquarters, they considered Baltimore, among other cities, as a possible location because the Baltimore branch had made a thirty-three-thousand-dollar contribution to the national building fund. However, it was McMillan who took the initiative to invite the search committee to view the property in Baltimore, and her invitation led to the decision to purchase that property. She also worked actively on the campaign to secure funds to purchase the new headquarters building, which opened in 1986.

As president of the NAACP, McMillan emphasized the importance of the economic well-being of individuals as well as the organization. She believes that the future economic progress of black Americans will be based on educational achievement and economic empowerment. Because of her dedication to education, the Baltimore members established a scholarship fund in her name, providing financing for students from low-income families who attend college in Maryland.

McMillan has been committed to the work of the NAACP. She has never allowed personal ambitions and achievements to interfere with her work for black Americans as a people. She believes that many black Americans who have attained their personal goals no longer feel the need to continue fighting. She cites this lack of enthusiasm for civil rights and for the NAACP as a major source of frustration.

Small in stature, McMillan is described by colleagues as a giant in the struggle for civil rights and equal opportunity. She is a devout Christian who has always been unwilling to compromise her principles, and, therefore, has not wavered in her firm and righteous stand on critical issues. McMillan is humble, mild-mannered, yet clearly unshakable.

McMillan's strong sense of service to the community, her acute understanding of social injustice, and her extraordinary ability to mobilize forces have thrust her into positions of leadership throughout her long career. She was the first black American to serve as trustee to the executive committee of the Public School Teachers Association; the only woman elected president of the Maryland State Colored Teachers' Association; a member of the Governor's Commission on the Structure and Governance of Education in Maryland; the first secretary of the Maryland Federation of Colored Parent-Teachers' Association; chairperson of the Joint Committee to Equalize Teachers' Salaries in Maryland; and the first woman to chair the Morgan State College Trustee Board. Now, at age eighty-six, McMillan maintains that the greatest obstacle to progress was segregation but vows that she will continue her efforts to battle existing racism and discrimination.

References

Baltimore Afro-American, June 1984.

Baltimore *News American,* 8 May 1984.

Baltimore *Sun,* 16 January 1984.

Bunting, George. Interview with author. 8 February 1990.

McMillan, Enolia Pettigren. Interview with author. 26 May 1987 and 12 April 1990.

USA Today, 12 January 1984.

Who's Who Among Black Americans, 1990/91. Chicago, Detroit: Gale Research, 1990. 869.

Williams, James. Interview with author. 21 February 1990.

Collections

Articles on Enolia Pettigen McMillan are housed in the Maryland Room of Baltimore's Enoch Pratt Central Library. Papers and other literary effects from her presidency of the Baltimore chapter of the NAACP and those of her presidency of the national association can be secured through the NAACP's National Archives in Baltimore. Photographs of McMillan are on file at the Baltimore branch of the NAACP.

Deborah Tulani Salahu-Din

Thelma "Butterfly" McQueen

(1911-)

Actress

Actress Thelma Lincoln "Butterfly" McQueen, an only child, was born in Tampa, Florida, on January 8, 1911. (The only reference to the name "Lincoln" is found in *Our World*, 49). Known to many only for her role as Prissy in *Gone With the Wind*, McQueen was an accomplished dancer and stage actress as well as a screen actress. She also rebelled against the Hollywood system of racial typecasting, at great cost to her own career.

Her father was a stevedore on the Tampa docks and her mother worked as a domestic. Her mother was born in the 1880s in Augusta, Georgia, in a neighborhood her daughter described as a place where "whites and blacks lived side by side" (*Atlanta Constitution*, 19 February 1980). In 1916 McQueen's father left the family. A court decision awarded custody of Thelma McQueen to her mother. To provide financial support for herself and her daughter, Mrs. McQueen sought work in numerous locations from Florida to New Jersey, finally settling in Harlem. In the meantime, McQueen had begun to attend school in a Tampa church, but she was soon sent to Augusta, Georgia, while her mother looked for employment elsewhere. In Augusta, McQueen lived at St. Benedict's Convent and attended school there as well. Later she moved in with an aunt and went to school at Walker Baptist Church. Mrs. McQueen sent for her daughter after she had secured a steady job in Harlem as a cook. When Thelma McQueen arrived in New York, she was enrolled in what was then Public School Number 9 on West Eighty-third Street. In 1924 her restless mother decided to move again, this time to Babylon, New York, on Long Island. McQueen and her mother remained in Babylon long enough for the daughter to finish high school.

After graduation, McQueen entered nursing school at the Lincoln Training School in the Bronx, completing her training several years later at Georgia Medical College in Augusta. In 1946 McQueen began taking liberal arts courses in various subjects, including political science, Spanish, drama, dance, and music. She attended City College of Los Angeles, the University of California at Los Angeles, Southern Illinois University, Queen's College, and New York University. In 1975 she earned a bachelor of arts in political science from City University of New York.

McQueen's introduction to the theater began shortly after she had finished high school when she became a dancer in Venezuela Jones' Negro Youth Group. Membership in a dramatic club and a Works Progress Administration (WPA) youth theater project provided McQueen with her first acting opportunities. She began to study dramatic dancing, music, and ballet. Her dance instructors included Janet Collins, Katherine Dunham, Geoffrey Holder, and Venezuela Jones. She studied ballet with Mabel Hunt and voice with Adelaide Hall. In 1935 she made her stage debut as part of the Butterfly Ballet in Jones's adaptation of *A Midsummer Night's Dream* performed at New York City College. "Butterfly" became her stage name during this production and remained with her thereafter.

McQueen made her broadway debut on December 2, 1937, at the Biltmore Theatre in New York in the George Abbott production *Brown Sugar*. The play was a murder melodrama set among the blacks of Harlem and acted by an all-black cast. McQueen played the part of Lucille, the first of her many maid roles. It was a minor part—she had only one spoken line. Nonetheless, her talents did not go unnoticed. Brooks Atkinson wrote of:

> the extraordinary artistry of a high-stepping little dusky creature with a piping voice who describes herself as Butterfly McQueen . . . in 'Brown Sugar' she is an over-genteel parlor maid in an apartment of iniquitous leanings. All she does is flutter at the door, announce the black thugs with a gesture of grandeur and say, 'Step forward, please,' as though she were joyfully admitting them through the pearly gates. But she does it like a whole encyclopedia of etiquette. Butterfly has something on the ball (*New York Times*, 3 December 1937).

Another review condemned the play's portrayal of blacks as "condescending and vulgar exploitation" (*New York Evening Journal*, 3 December 1937). The show closed after only four performances.

McQueen's favorable review for her role in *Brown Sugar* prompted Abbott to cast her in future productions. As a result, she was added to the cast of *Brother Rat* in 1938. In contrast to the quick demise of *Brown Sugar*, *Brother Rat* ran for 577 performances. Later that same year she accepted a role in the Abbott production *What A Life*.

McQueen's role as Mary in *What A Life* was again a small one with only a few speaking lines. With her piping voice, she was credited with skillfully providing comic relief during the more solemn moments of the production. By now she had become a regular in the informal Abbott Acting Company and part of what was critically described as an "impeccable" cast (Leiter, 890-891). When Abbott decided to take *What A Life* on the road, McQueen was chosen to be a member of the touring company.

McQueen Stars in *Gone With the Wind*

In the late 1930s, while still working for Abbott, McQueen auditioned for the part of Prissy in the film *Gone With the*

Wind. At first, she was told that she was too fat, too dignified, and too old to play the part of a slave girl half her age. Later, producer David O. Selznick had other casting ideas. He preferred seasoned actors, choosing Hattie McDaniel to play Scarlett O'Hara's Mammy and McQueen, by now a veteran of Broadway revues, to play Prissy. McQueen had succeeded in winning the one role that author Margaret Mitchell wished she herself could have played (Haver, 34).

Susan Myrick, representing Mitchell on the set of *Gone With the Wind* and serving as technical advisor, noted in her journal her satisfaction with the choice of McQueen for the role of Prissy. Myrick's image of Prissy was that of purveyor of subtle comic relief, and in her eyes, McQueen's Prissy remained loyal to the novel. She reported back to Mitchell that McQueen was "really good in the role though not so young nor pipe-stem-legged as I could wish" (Letter to Mitchell, 12 February 1939). In her Macon, Georgia, newspaper column "Straight From Hollywood" Myrick wrote:

> I can hardly wait for the picture *[Gone With the Wind]* to be shown so you can laugh at the scenes where Prissy does her stuff. Butterfly McQueen is a good actress . . . Everytime Prissy worked in a scene we have a grand time. I know you'll get laughs when you see her (Myrick, 202).

McQueen's brand of comic relief was not of the old, vulgar sort. Instead, her controlled fright integrated beautifully with the flow of the film. She was at once delicate, pathetic, and humorous.

It was not until McQueen had arrived in Hollywood that she took time to reflect upon the role she was about to play. She had serious misgivings about the way Mitchell portrayed blacks in her novel. In particular, McQueen expressed a strong distaste for Mitchell's presentation of Prissy as inane and dull-witted. McQueen was stubbornly resistant to stereotyping, yet she played Prissy with remarkable conviction. Still, she was outspoken about certain aspects of her role: She refused to be filmed eating watermelon and spitting seeds, and she disapproved of the scene in which Scarlett slaps Prissy's face. In another scene, McQueen objected when the script called for Rhett Butler to refer to Prissy as a "simple-minded darkie" when Mitchell's words were "simple-minded wench" (Myrick, 88). A debate flared between Myrick and McQueen over the head attire to be worn by the female black servants. McQueen preferred her "pictorial" colorful bows while Myrick insisted on the more stereotyped "wrapped" heads. With Mitchell's approval, Myrick won out in the end (Susan Myrick to Margaret Mitchell, 15 January 1939; Margaret Mitchell to Susan Myrick, 19 January 1939).

Off the set, McQueen asserted her own brand of individualism as well, joining a delegation of blacks who threatened protest if restroom segregation wasn't abolished. She spoke out when all the black actors in the cast were packed into one car, while the white stars were provided with limousines.

Preparation for filming *Gone With the Wind* required numerous rehearsals and coaching sessions to perfect the southern accents of the novel's characters. McDaniel and McQueen both spent hours learning Mitchell's black dialect. Years later Myrick reminisced that "the most paradoxical dialect problem was presented by Butterfly McQueen who found the Uncle Remus-style dialect required by the film all but impossible" (*Atlanta Journal,* 25 March 1976). McQueen later explained that she "was not allowed to speak [in] dialect as a child" (*New York Times,* 12 July 1978).

Filming of *Gone With the Wind* began in January 1939 under the direction of George Cukor. Almost immediately, Selznick's disapproval of Cukor's script interpolations became apparent—a disagreement that eventually led to Cukor's resignation. Even so, much of what Cukor filmed remained uncut in the final version of the movie, including the famous birthing scene in which Prissy squeals, "Lawsy, Miss Scarlett, Ah don' know nuthin' 'bout birthin' babies!" For her frightened and ill-timed confession, the screenplay called for Prissy to be rebuked by a slap in the face from Scarlett. During the first take, Leigh slapped too hard, causing McQueen to step out of character, crying, "I can't do it, she's hurting me. . . . I'm no stunt man, I'm an actress" (Cripps, 144). She insisted that Leigh apologize before shooting could continue. Cukor was a stickler for detail and wanted Prissy to scream loudly when she was reprimanded by the irate Scarlett. McQueen later recalled, "I told them, if you really slap me, I won't scream, but if you pretend to slap me, I'll make the best scream you ever heard" (*Columbus [Ga.] Ledger Inquirer,* 5 November 1989). Cukor acquiesced and in the second shooting of the scene Leigh did not actually slap McQueen. Instead, a sound man clapped his hands off the set when Leigh swung her hand toward McQueen's face.

Myrick described Cukor's relationship with McQueen during the filming of *Gone With the Wind* in amicable terms. In her journal Myrick wrote that Cukor became "so tickled at her [McQueen] sometimes he could scarcely direct, and when Butterfly sees George is amused she breaks down and laughs" (Myrick, 83). Cukor enjoyed exchanging lighthearted quips with McQueen, though they were sometimes laced with racial overtones. At one point he told her that he "had a Prissy before her and he killed the last one" (Letter to Mitchell, 12 February 1939). Other times he quoted from the novel, threatening to " 'sell Butterfly down the river' if she didn't get the action just right" (Myrick, 83), or threatening to "use the Simon Legree whip on Prissy" (Letter to Mitchell, 12 February 1939). In another scene Cukor admonished, "Prissy, you better be careful how you try my patience. We had one Prissy here before you came, and I really did sell her South" (Myrick, 84).

Film Star Gains Popularity

In spite of the controversy and the love-hate relationship McQueen had with *Gone With the Wind,* she considered her part in the movie to be her best work. The role brought her instant international notoriety and financial security, albeit temporary. She recalled later that the role of Prissy paid well.

"I went through a full semester at UCLA on one day's pay" she said (Vance, 121-122).

Three weeks into production of *Gone With the Wind*, Cukor's resignation brought filming operations to a temporary standstill while a replacement was sought. Cukor immediately resurrected another project, the film *The Women*. McQueen was assigned the part of Lolla, a maid. She played opposite Joan Crawford and Virginia Grey, appearing in only one scene. Her recollection of working for Cukor in this project was anything but pleasant. She recalled that:

> His sole purpose in giving me the small part in *The Women* was to have the opportunity to vent his frustrations on me. The hurt I felt in having Mr.Cukor scream at me for some mistake I made, I remember vividly and will take with me to my grave. In the employ of David Selznick, he could not have done such a thing" (Summers, 7).

After the filming of *Gone With the Wind* was completed, McQueen returned to New York and to the stage. She appeared as Puck in the 1939 production *Swingin' the Dream*, a reinterpretation of *A Midsummer Night's Dream*. The show premiered on November 29 at the Center Theatre and lasted only thirteen performances. McQueen was singled out by one critic for her "piping-voiced Puck whose travesty is genuinely comic, her clowning as 'ladylike,' representing her peculiar artistry in finest fettle" (*New York Times*, 30 November 1939).

During the early 1940s, McQueen appeared in several more films, though never to the acclaim associated with *Gone With the Wind*. In 1941 she was again a maid, this time in *Affectionately Yours*. Playing Butterfly opposite Hattie McDaniel, she uttered the infamous line, "Who dat say who dat when you say dat." She later recalled, "I never thought I would have to say a line like that. I had imagined that since I am an intelligent woman, I could play any kind of role" (Bogle, *Toms, Coons*, 93). Ironically, her performance was considered by some critics to be the best of the film. As Bosley Crowther described it, "the only glints of brightness in the film are contributed by a hair-spring brownie called Butterfly McQueen, as a maid. Her frequent dissolves into tears upon the slightest provocation are ludicrous—and strangely prophetic" (*New York Times*, 24 May 1941).

Her next movie, *Cabin In The Sky*, released in 1943, was a monumental showcase for black musical talent. The all-star and entirely black cast included Duke Ellington's Orchestra, Louis Armstrong, John "Bubbles" Sublett, Ethel Waters, Mantan Moreland, Willie Best, Ruby Dandridge, Oscar Polk, and the Hall Johnson Choir. With a light plot, the film was carried along by the sheer wit and energy of the performers who transcended their stereotyped roles brilliantly.

The filming of *Cabin In The Sky* was not a happy time for McQueen. Owing to her thin-skinned nature, she was frequently at odds with various personalities in the cast. In particular, she recalled that Eddie "Rochester" Anderson teased her unmercifully, Lena Horne regarded her with contempt, and Vincente Minnelli was critical of her behind her back. Hattie McDaniel advised McQueen to be more tolerant and patient: "You complain too much, you'll never come back to Hollywood" (*Columbus [Ga.] Ledger Enquirer*, 5 November 1989).

Nonetheless, McQueen accepted another Minnelli role, that of Annette in the 1943 production, *I Dood It*. The film was a vehicle for the pianistic wizardry of Hazel Scott and the comedy antics of Red Skelton. Lavish music productions featured Scott and Lena Horne with a group of black singers whose performances of spirituals reflected white audiences' expectations of black religious fanaticism (Leab, 121).

During the next few years McQueen appeared in more minor film roles. In *Since You Went Away* (1944), a Selznick production, her role as a WAC sargeant was left on the cutting room floor. Working opposite Joan Crawford in *Mildred Pierce* (1945) as the servant Lottie, McQueen's character commanded more respect than her previous maid roles. In *Flame of Barbary Coast* (1945) starring John Wayne, she was Beulah, a maid. Selznick offered her another part in 1947, this time in *Duel in the Sun*. He cast her as the mysterious Vashti, an ethereal character who wandered in and out of the plot.

McQueen Refuses Stereotyped Roles

By this time, McQueen had tired of being typecast as a "handkerchief head" servant and she refused to accept any more maid roles. It was a stand that would cost her dearly. Except for a part in *Killer Diller* (1948) as a manager's secretary, she would not act again in a movie for twenty years.

The 1950s and 1960s were lean years for McQueen. Film producers weren't offering very many non-servant roles to black actors, so she returned to the stage. In 1951, she produced her own one-woman show in Carnegie Recital Hall. She played the part of Queen Elizabeth Victoria in the 1956 all-black production *The World's My Oyster*. It was not a critical success; one reviewer called the plot "dreary," the musical numbers "bumbling," adding, "even . . . potentially funny and charming players such as Butterfly McQueen . . . are victimized by their material" (*New York Times*, 10 August 1956).

The critics were not much more enthusiastic about a 1957 comedy, *School For Wives*, in which McQueen played Georgette. An adaptation of a Molière play, the work fell short of sustaining the "quicksilver shimmer" of its original version and succumbed to slapstick. A reviewer wrote:

> Admittedly, the idea was an intriguing one, if just for the trick of putting Butterfly McQueen in the role of the addlepated Georgette. But McQueen, for all her fluttery personal charm, heaving bosom and silver fingernails, is a fish out of water (*New York Times*, 20 June 1957).

In the 1964 production *The Athenian Touch,* McQueen was Ora, a maid and cook. The play was reviewed as "an exercise in tedium," in which " . . . Butterfly McQueen tries hard to make merry" but was trapped by the material (*New York Times,* 15 January 1964).

In her next few theater appearances, McQueen fared somewhat better. The character Hattie was added to the off-Broadway musical *Curley McDimple*—a role written especially for McQueen. She premiered the part on May 9, 1968. Her own musical revue, *Butterfly McQueen and Friends* appeared off-Broadway, premiering August 4, 1969. That same year she worked again with George Abbott, this time in *Three Men on a Horse.* She played the part of Dora Lee, an elevator operator, to favorable reviews. One critic wrote that he enjoyed "the itsy-little voice, fading over the far horizon of comprehension, that Butterfly McQueen contributed . . . with elevation and style" (*New York Times,* 17 October 1969).

The 1970s were sparse as well, but the decade was marked by McQueen's return to film. She appeared in a cameo role in the critical flop *The Phynx* in 1970. In 1974 she was Clarine in *Amazing Grace,* a vehicle for the aging Jackie "Moms" Mabley. Wrote one reviewer:

> the people around her [Mabley] never came up to her instep. . . . Two black performers associated with an earlier movie age—Stepin Fetchit and Butterfly McQueen—turn up in cameo roles that are unrewarding, both to us and to them (*New York Times,* 2 November 1974).

McQueen continued to find work in musical theater as well during the 1970s. She secured a part in a pre-Broadway production of *The Wiz* in 1975 and in 1976 she presented another one-woman show, *Prissy in Person.* In 1980, McQueen was a member of the touring company of the musical *Showboat.*

McQueen returned to the limelight in the later 1980s as a guest of honor at celebrations commemorating the fiftieth anniversary of the publication of the novel *Gone With the Wind,* and the production and premiere of the film. She appeared at numerous showings of the movie, signing autographs and quoting Prissy's "birthin' babies" line, much to the delight of her admirers.

In 1986, McQueen was offered another movie role, this time as Ma Kennywick, a villager in *Mosquito Coast.* Again, her part was a small one. In 1989, she appeared in the movie *Polly,* and had a cameo role in the Sam Irwin film *Stiff.*

Throughout the years, McQueen made numerous television appearances. She was a guest on several talk shows, including the "Mike Wallace Show," the "Virginia Graham Show," the "Mike Douglas Show," and the "Today Show." Her dramatic television roles have included a part in the 1957 Hallmark Hall of Fame production of "The Green Pastures," a 1979 children's special entitled "The Seven Wishes of Joanna Peabody," and a role in "Our World" (1987). She also had parts in several radio shows, including the "Dinah Shore Show," the "Jack Benny Show," and the "Danny Kaye Show."

Even though her movie roles were temporarily lucrative, McQueen found it necessary to support herself with various odd jobs. She taught at Southern Illinois University, sold toys at Macy's, dispatched taxi cabs in the Bronx, operated a restaurant, and managed a theater group. Much of her savings from her early movie roles was spent in financing her one-woman shows and paying fees in two unrelated legal suits. In 1968, McQueen won a court decision awarding her damages for unauthorized use of her photographs for promotional purposes by Stone Mountain Park in Georgia (*Jet,* 28 March 1968). Twelve years later, in 1980, McQueen filed a three-hundred-thousand-dollar suit against Greyhound Bus Lines and International Security of Virginia for injuries and damages sustained in a scuffle that erupted after a security guard at a Washington, D. C., bus station accused McQueen of pickpocketing. During the altercation, McQueen was thrown against a metal bench, injuring her ribs. A court settlement in 1984 awarded McQueen sixty thousand dollars.

Throughout McQueen's career, community service also occupied much of her time: "Community work comes first. I don't like people to call me a star. I'm not a star. I'm a community worker" (*Macon [Ga.] Telegraph and News,* 2 April 1984). Currently she enjoys teaching at neighborhood recreational centers, working with both the young and the elderly. A tireless supporter of animal rights, McQueen became a life member of the Anti-Vivisection Society in the 1940s. She is also active in urban cleanup and beautification projects and environmental protection.

McQueen, the actress, is best remembered for her high-pitched voice, ready smile, and large expressive eyes. Myrick once described her voice as "higher than soprano . . . about as high as the top note on Kreisler's violin." Author Donald Bogle characterized her as a "surreal creature . . . with a perplexed stare . . . and a quivering tremor of a voice . . . almost otherworldly." She never married, preferring the company of the residents of her Harlem neighborhood and her cats. A selfless individual, she chose to work for the betterment of her race rather than taking advantage of fame or seeking wealth. She once described her lifestyle as "square and straight-laced" (*Atlanta Constitution,* 19 February 1980). Her philosophy is refreshingly simple: "Each of us is born 'perfect'; we acquire habits of hate" (Summers, 7).

The many honors bestowed upon McQueen include the Rosemary Award in 1973, the Black Filmmakers Hall of Fame Award in 1975, and an Emmy Award for her role in *The Seven Wishes of Joanna Peabody* in 1979. In admiration of her acting ability, the author Edward Mapp dedicated his book *Blacks in American Films* to McQueen (iv-v). Editors Nash and Ross dedicated volume six of their *Motion Picture Guide* to "Butterfly McQueen . . . and all the great character people."

McQueen maintains residences in Augusta and Harlem.

References

Anderson, John. Review of *Brown Sugar*. *New York Evening Journal,* 3 December 1937.

Atkinson, Brooks. "Dark Town Melodrama." *New York Times,* 3 December 1937.

———. "Swinging Shakespeare's 'Dream' with Benny Goodman, Louise Armstrong and Maxine Sullivan." *New York Times,* 30 November 1939.

Barnes, Clive. "All-star Cast Excels in Betting Tale." *New York Times,* 17 October 1969.

Black, Doris. "Butterfly McQueen." *Sepia* 26 (February 1977): 80.

Bogle, Donald. "Butterfly McQueen." *Blacks in American Films and Television*. New York: Garland Publishing, 1988. 420-422.

———. *Toms, Coons, Mulattoes, Mammies, and Bucks*. Expanded ed. New York: Continuum Publishing Co., 1989. 93.

Bronner, Edwin. *The Encyclopedia of the American Theatre 1900-1975*. New York: A. S. Barnes, 1980. 69, 474, 514.

"Butterfly McQueen." *Our World* 2 (September 1947): 49.

"Butterfly McQueen Tells NYU to Mail Her Degree." *Jet* 48 (26 June 1975): 17.

"Butterfly McQueen Wins GA High Court Plea." *Jet* 33 (28 March 1968: 55.

Canby, Vincent. Review of *Amazing Grace*. *New York Times,* 2 November 1974.

Cripps, Thomas. *Slow Fade to Black*. New York: Oxford University Press, 1977. 143-44.

Crowther, Bosley. "Offer Rejected." *New York Times,* 24 May 1941.

Funke, Lewis. Review of *The Athenian Touch*. *New York Times,* 15 January 1964.

Gelb, Arthur. "*World's My Oyster* is Staged Downtown." *New York Times,* 10 August 1956.

———. Review of *School for Wives*. *New York Times,* 20 June 1957.

Haver, Ronald. *David O. Selznick's "Gone With the Wind."* New York: Bonanza Books, 1986. 34.

Howard, Sidney. *"G W T W:" The Screenplay*. Ed. Richard B. Harwell. New York: Macmillan, 1980. 196 and *passim*.

Lamparski, Richard. "Butterfly McQueen." In *Whatever Became of. . . ?* 2nd series. New York: Crown Publishers, 1968. 96-97.

Leab, Daniel J. *From Sambo to Superspade*. Boston: Houghton Mifflin, 1975. 121.

Leiter, Samuel L. *The Encyclopedia of the New York Stage, 1930-1940*. Westport, Conn.: Greenwood Press, 1989.

Mapp, Edward. "Butterfly McQueen." *Directory of Blacks in the Performing Arts*. Metuchen, N.J.: Scarecrow Press, 1972. iv-v, 239-40.

Mitchell, Margaret. To Susan Myrick, 19 January 1939. The Margaret Mitchell Marsh Collection, Rare Books and Special Collections, University of Georgia Library.

McCarter, Chris. "Actress Had a Strong Love-Hate Relationship with 'Prissy' Role." *Columbus [GA] Ledger-Enquirer,* 5 November 1989.

Myrick, Susan. *White Columns in Hollywood: Reports from the "Gone With the Wind" Sets.* Edited by Richard Harwell. Macon, Ga: Mercer University Press, 1982. 77, 83-84, 88, 202.

Nash, Jay Robert and Stanley Ralph Ross, eds. "The Phynx." In *The Motion Picture Guide*. Chicago: Cinebooks 1986. 6:2391.

Our World 2 (September 1947): 49.

Sampson, Henry T. "Thelma (Butterfly) McQueen." *Blacks in Black and White*. Metuchen, N.J.: Scarecrow Press, 1977. 234-235.

Smith, Helen C. "Butterfly: Still Flitting at 69." *Atlanta Constitution,* 19 February 1980.

Smith, Terri K. "She Sounds Like Prissy and She Looks Like Prissy, but Butterfly McQueen isn't 'Stupid and Backward.'" *Macon [GA] Telegraph and News,* 2 April 1984.

Summers, Murray. "Butterfly McQueen was one of *The Women*, Too (Let's Chat with Her About It)." *Filmograph* 3 (4 November 1973). 7-8.

Taylor, Ron. "Movie Memories Not Gone with Wind." *Atlanta Journal,* 25 March 1976.

Tomlinson, Doug. "Butterfly McQueen." *The International Dictionary of Films and Filmmakers*. Vol. 3, *Actors and Actresses*. Ed. James Vinson. Chicago: St. James Press, 1986. 427-428.

Vance, Malcolm. *Tara Revisited*. New York: Award Books, 1976. 121-22.

Wilson, John S. "Butterfly McQueen Squeaks Along. *New York Times,* 12 July 1978.

Wren, Dahlia. "Role in Epic Movie Cost Actress Career." *Augusta [GA] Chronicle,* 25 March 1984.

Collections

The largest selection of photographs of Thelma "Butterfly" McQueen is in the hands of Metro-Goldwyn-Mayer, Inc. One appears in *Black Film Stars* by Eileen Landay (New York: Drake Publishers, 1973), p. 79. Landay gives credit for the photograph to Culver Pictures. Another collection of rare publicity photographs is in the possession of Herb Bridges, Box 92, Sharpsburg, GA 30277, author of *The Filming of Gone With the Wind* (Macon, Ga.: Mercer University Press, 1984).

Juanita Karpf

Carmen McRae

(1922-)

Singer, pianist

Carmen McRae, well-known jazz singer who has been compared to Billie Holiday and Sarah Vaugh and is considered one of the great ones, was born in Brooklyn, New York, on April 8, 1922. The only child of Jamaican parents, Evadne and Oscar McRae, Carmen McRae studied piano privately from an early age and considered a career as a concert pianist. Formal music training is clearly evident in her later accomplishments as an arranger and pianist.

McRae began her musical career in 1944 as a singer with Benny Carter's big band after a brief stint as a government clerical worker in Washington, D.C. She also sang with various other bands in the forties, including Count Basie's and Mercer Ellington's, in a style strongly influenced by Billie Holliday.

McRae made her recording debut in 1946 as Carmen Clarke at a time when she was married to drummer Kenny Clarke. Clarke and McRae divorced in 1947. She really began to attract the attention of other musicians during the 1950s with her recordings for the Stardust and Venus labels. In 1954 she won *Down Beat* magazine's new singer award and signed a recording contract with Decca, which issued her superb renditions of "Yardbird Suite," "You Take Advantage of Me," and "Suppertime" in 1955. Her recordings since then have demonstrated her creativity and skill in arranging as well as a dynamic vocal and pianistic presence influenced by the be-bop players. McRae has also turned increasingly to mainstream popular music for raw material to use in club performances and recordings.

Carmen McRae worked hard to achieve her ultimate success, continuing to do clerical work on the side during the forties and fifties. She has polished her nightclub act, starting regularly as intermission pianist and singer at Minton's Playhouse in Harlem in the forties. From the fifties and sixties onward her career developed, and she continued to keep a very active solo and trio club performance schedule interspersed with frequent concert and recording dates.

McRae is personally very gregarious and public-minded and has never been secretive about her private life. She was married a second time to Ike Isaacs, from whom she was also divorced. She has no children. In addition to being a favorite on Marion McPartland's public radio program, she has appeared on television shows and in films, including *The Subterraneans* (1960), *Hotel* (1967), and *Monterey Jazz* (1968). Her scat singing and up-tempo playing border on virtuosity, while her ballad singing mixes dark musical colors with crisply pronounced lyrics, reflecting strong influences from both Billie Holiday and Sarah Vaughan.

McRae's approach to a song is in the tradition of a gifted jazz instrumentalist. She forcefully intones the melody, taking it in new directions, bending, massaging, emphasizing twists and turns, and making it her own. But the melody is always securely present, and her interpretations are more in the vein of a Billie Holiday, looking toward a blue shade. Her voice has its own quality; it is a biting, rich contralto, somewhat dry and raspy at times, and very pointed. Her lyrics are always crystal clear, with poignant accents to suit her textual readings.

Of her interpretations of a set of Billie Holiday's songs on her album *Carmen McRae Sings 'Lover Man' and other Billie Holiday Songs,* noted jazz critic Ralph Gleason wrote that she makes each song into "a bitter-sweet slice of life which she tells you about with finality because it is true." He goes on to compliment her "instant creativity, breathing raw salty life into every lyric," and "bringing just the right touch of wry and sometimes salty humor, of cynical inference and of sardonic, laughin' just to keep from cryin' feeling" (Gleason, album liner notes). The *Penguin Encyclopedia of Popular Music* credits her interpretations with "an intelligent female sensibility" (751).

Critic Phyl Garland, in describing McRae's singing on her duet album *Carmen McRae and Billie Carter,* reports that she "reaches out assertively and grabs a song with her rich contralto, immediately imposing her imprint on lyrics and melody alike" and that the album is able to capture something of the spontaneity and relaxed interplay of a performance before a live and appreciative audience (Garland, 136). In listening to her music one must be aware that as an artist she communicates best in such settings. She seems to be an artist who is always trying to reach out with her voice and share her thoughts and feelings directly with her listeners.

McRae's only fault may be a tendency to overreach herself and select current popular material that does not suit her style. All great jazz musicians have an experimental side and hers has surfaced in selecting and arranging well-known tunes rather than in composition or instrumental solos. The successes have been profound and a model for others who aspire both to create and to entertain.

References

Bemis, Ed. "Carmen McRae. *The New Grove Dictionary of American Music*. Eds. Wiley Hitchcock and Stanley Sadie. New York: Macmillan, 1986. 157-158.

"Carmen McRae: New Singer Challenges Ella for Jazz Supremacy." *Ebony* 11 (February 1956): 67-69.

Clarke, Donald, ed. *Penguin Encyclopedia of Popular Music*. New York: Viking, 1989. 750-751.

Dahl, Linda. *Stormy Weather: The Music and Lives of a Century of Jazzwomen*. New York: Pantheon Books, 1984. 142-143.

Feather, Leonard. *The New Edition of the Encyclopedia of Jazz*. New York: Bonanza Books, 1955. 329.

Garland, Phyl. "Carmen McRae and Betty Carter: The Carmen McRae-Betty Carter Duets." (Great American Music Hall 2706-1 and 2706-2). *Stereo Review* 53 (December 1988): 135-136.

———. "Sounds." *Ebony* 32 (December 1976): 27.

Gleason, Ralph J. *Carmen McRae Sings 'Lover Man' and other Billie Holiday Classics*. Columbia Jazz Odyssey Series. PC 37002. Liner notes.

Kernfeld, Barry, ed. *The New Grove Dictionary of Jazz*. Vol. 2. New York: Macmillan, 1988. 72.

Shaw, Arnold. *Black Popular Music in America; From the Spirituals, Minstrels, and Ragtime to Soul, Disco, and Hip-hop*. New York: Schirmer Books, 1986. 139-140, 330.

Southern, Eileen. *Biographical Dictionary of Afro-American and African Musicians*. Westport, Conn.: Greenwood Press, 1982. 262.

Donald Thieme

Naomi Long Madgett

(1923-)

Poet, publisher

Born July 5, 1923, in Norfolk, Virginia, poet and publisher Naomi Cornelia Long Madgett was the youngest of three children and the only daughter of Clarence Marcellus Long, a minister at Bank Street Baptist Church, and Maude (Hilton) Long, a schoolteacher. Before Madgett was two years old her family moved to East Orange, New Jersey, where she graduated from Ashland Grammar School. While growing up, Madgett was greatly influenced by her parents, who stressed the value of education. She was nurtured in her father's library, where at an early age she discovered the poetry of Alfred Lord Tennyson, whose poem "The Brook" she committed to memory, and Langston Hughes, whom she was privileged to meet when she was fourteen. Madgett believes her poetry reflects the variety of interests and style Hughes and Tennyson represent.

In December 1937, Madgett's parents moved the family to St. Louis, Missouri. This event has been described by Madgett as a turning point in her life. At age fourteen she entered the all-black Charles Sumner High School. Here her knowledge of black American achievement was enhanced and her own efforts to write encouraged. Following her high school graduation in June 1941, she published her first volume of poetry, *Songs to a Phantom Nightingale*. That same year she entered college, deciding to attend her mother's alma mater, Virginia State.

At Virginia State Madgett pledged the Alpha Kappa Alpha Sorority. Majoring in English, she graduated with a bachelor of arts degree with honors in 1945. Following graduation, Madgett began graduate school at New York University. After only one semester she withdrew to marry Julian F. Witherspoon, on March 31, 1946. The couple moved to Detroit where Madgett worked as a reporter and copyreader for the *Michigan Chronicle*, an African-American weekly, until the birth of her only child, Jill, in 1947. During this period her poems began to appear in anthologies under her married name. In 1948 she joined the Michigan Bell Telephone Company in Detroit as a service representative and remained there for six years. On April 27, 1949, Madgett divorced Witherspoon and ceased using his name.

Madgett Establishes Afro-American Literature Classes

On July 29, 1954, the poet married William Harold Madgett. Although this marriage ended in divorce in December 1960, she continues to use the name Madgett. In 1955 she began teaching at Burroughs Junior High school, then at Northern High School, and ended up teaching at Northwestern High School for twelve years. She introduced the first structured Afro-American literature course in the Detroit Public Schools, thus carrying the banner for black studies. Her first formal Afro-American literature class began as a specially funded course in the summer of 1965. Poet Melvin B. Tolson visited this class and talked to her students.

While working as a teacher in the Detroit public school system, Madgett completed a master's in English education at Wayne State University in the mid-1950s. In 1961 and 1962 she took postgraduate courses at the University of Detroit. The first recipient of the Mott Fellowship in English, Madgett used the $10,000 award and additional expense money provided to work as a resource associate at Oakland University in Rochester, Michigan, during the academic year

1965-66, where she wrote an Afro-American literature textbook. Madgett resigned from the Detroit public schools in 1968 to accept a position as associate professor of English at Eastern Michigan University in Ypsilanti.

On March 31, 1972, Madgett married Leonard Patton Andrews, an elementary school principal. The following year she was promoted to the rank of full professor of English at Eastern Michigan University. In 1980 she earned a Ph.D. in English from the International Institute for Advanced Studies. She retired as professor emeritus from Eastern Michigan University in 1984.

The Lotus Press Established

Retirement allowed Madgett to devote her full attention to the growth and development of Lotus Press, which she had taken over in 1974. In 1980, Madgett, along with her husband, Andrews, and daughter, Jill W. Boyer, incorporated the press as a non-profit, tax-exempt corporation. While this status offered some financial relief, despite her retirement the work load gradually increased. The number of unsolicited manuscripts grew as the name Lotus Press gained recognition. Madgett, who reads and responds to these manuscripts personally, says "the work load has become such that the press has postponed indefinitely the consideration of new manuscripts."

Despite these problems, Lotus Press has published seventy-four titles, sixty-seven of which are still in print. Madgett is devoted to the press, describing it as "one of only a few companies in the country dedicated to keeping black poetry alive." While the press must depend on donations and grants for its existence, she continues to struggle for the survival of the press because "it needs to be done."

Early Poetry Reflectes Artistic Choices

When Madgett began publishing her poetry in 1941, life for black American women was anything but conducive to literary careers. Although several well-known men had succeeded as poets (Hughes, Sterling Brown, Countee Cullen), few women had. Madgett did read the works of women poets, and Georgia Douglas Johnson was one of her favorites, but she did not enjoy the benefit of the number of role models a man would have. Published when she was seventeen, the age of Phillis Wheatley when her first poem was published, Madgett's first volume of poetry preceded Margaret Walker's first book by one year and Gwendolyn Brooks's by four. Thus Madgett's career has been a long one of setting precedents and breaking down barriers. She states that she cannot recall any time in her life when she "was not involved with poetry" (Foreword, *Phantom Nightingale*).

Having been born in 1923, Madgett experienced the Harlem Renaissance with its promotion of positive self-images, the Great Depression with its poignant and sometimes bitter images evoked by poverty and racism in America, and the World War II years, which produced a political climate rife with glaring inconsistencies between articulated war aims and actual domestic policy. Madgett witnessed the birth of the civil rights struggle and could see that black Americans had perhaps come midway. Surrounded by, if not affected by, the anger and militancy of the black power movement, the feminism of the seventies, and even the very apolitical nature that characterizes the eighties, Madgett has faced some difficult artistic choices. The poem "Ivory Tower" speaks to the poet's dilemma: As early as the 1940s, when this poem was written, Madgett questions the relevance of her lyric poems, saying they are "pretty, useless things" and wonders about social issues affecting "the hungry, beaten throng, / The hopeless, the defeated ones." Madgett states that black poets are caught in a dilemma: "out of one mouth you're told to be universal, and out of the other mouth you're told you're not black enough." She points out that during the 1960s "if a black poet was not ranting and raging about black themes, editors weren't interested" (*Detroit Free Press*, 1982).

However, Madgett chose to maintain the subtle lyric style she began to develop in *Songs to a Phantom Nightingale* (1941). Many of these early poems are nature poems. Madgett seems most heavily influenced during this early period by English romantic poetry. This is not unusual, as the Harlem Renaissance writers, Cullen in particular, were much affected by the romantics poets. Cullen happened to be a favorite of Madgett's. She was greatly influenced by him when as a college student she visited his home and was encouraged by him to perfect her poetic craft. Robert Sedlack observes that like Cullen, Madgett probably wanted to be recognized as a poet only, not as a "Negro" poet (*Dictionary of Literary Biography*, 105). Of her early poetry, Madgett writes: "I unwittingly imitated individual poets—Edgar A. Guest, Longfellow, Hughes, Georgia Douglas Johnson, Keats and Robert Browning" (Foreword, *Phantom Nightingale*).

Much of Madgett's early poetry is dominated by the use of Latin phrases and mythological and classical allusions, for example in "Threnody," "Pianissimo," and "Sonnetto." Madgett does not pay particular attention to elements of the black experience in her 1941 collection; instead she omits her colloquial poems. However, in *Phantom Nightingale: Juvenilia*, Madgett includes several poems that speak to the diversity of black American life. "On Democracy" calls to question American justice and "Market Street" celebrates the language and style of black people, as does "Refugee," which was selected by Langston Hughes and Arna Bontemps for their ground-breaking anthology, *The Poetry of the Negro, 1746-1949*.

Madgett Influenced by the Harlem Renaissance and Civil Rights Movement

Madgett says that she has been most deeply influenced by the Harlem Renaissance and civil rights movement. Her poem, "Nocturne," which states, "See how tenderly God pulls His blanket of blackness over the earth. / You think I am not beautiful? / You lie!" is reflective of the renaissance rather than the "Black Is Beautiful" motif found in the black art movement of the late sixties and early seventies. "The Race Question," found in *Star by Star*, expresses the ideas of the civil rights movement and echoes the integrationist impetus of the era. "The Race Question" speaks to the person or persons whose claim to fame rests upon the existence of a "race problem."

"Midway," perhaps Madgett's most popular poem, epitomizes the civil rights movement. In 1980 it was set to music by Gerald Savage and published by Lotus Press. *Pink Ladies in the Afternoon: New Poems, 1965-1971* has been described as a reflection of Madgett's "ever-deepening awareness of her heritage and identity" (*Dictionary of Literary Biography*, 108). But it seems Madgett's awareness of her heritage and identity was quite "deep" long before the 1972 publication of *Pink Ladies*. Reviewing *Pink Ladies* for *Black World*, Dudley Randall praised Madgett's ability to evoke crystal images in the reader's mind. *Pink Ladies* is poignantly reminiscent of times past; "Offspring" and "The Mother" muse over the effect of children growing up. "Late," which begins, "I sip Pink Ladies in the afternoon, / Peruse old yearbooks, wonder where / My old companions . . . / Went," captures the mood of this volume.

Madgett's mature pieces contained in *Exits and Entrances* (1978) have been favorably reviewed by Melba Boyd in *Black Scholar* and by Ray Fleming in *Black American Literature Forum*. Fleming, while impressed by Madgett's warm and vibrant lyrics, is somewhat unsure of the motivating forces behind such poems as "Mufflejaw" and "Fantasia." But of this collection, perhaps "City Nights" most appropriately represents Madgett's mature vision. It certainly captures the Zeitgeist of the urban 1970s. The poem begins: "My windows and doors are barred against the intrusion of thieves / The neighbor's dogs howl in pain / at the screech of sirens. / There is nothing you can tell me / about the city / I do not know."

Sedlack mistakenly compares Madgett's poem "In Search of Aunt Jemima (Alias Big Mama)" to Haki Madhubuti's earlier poem entitled "Big Momma," saying that Madgett associates herself with Madhubuti. However, Madgett denies any connection at all with Madhubuti's poem that uses the same term, saying she "was not in any way influenced by his poem" (Letter from Madgett to Warren). To compare Madgett with the so-called militant poets of the sixties is to do both a disservice. Black American poetry from Lucy Terry Prince onward reflects the uniquely personal aspects of the poet's life and mirrors the universals as well, commenting on nature, love, fear, and death. While protest appears to remain a constant in black American poetry, there were important variables during the sixties. Madgett represents one of the variables. Her poetry, while not shrill or angry, reflects the best of the black experience, abounds with the spirit of the ancestors, and flows with the rhythms of our times.

The most recent collection of poetry by Madgett, *Octavia and Other Poems* (1988), represents a lifetime of commitment to the craft of writing poetry. In this volume she quietly perfects what she begins in the 1941 publication. The title poem "Octavia" is inspired by Octavia Cornelia Long, Madgett's great-aunt, who died of tuberculosis at the age of thirty-four in Charlottesville, Virginia, three years before Madgett was born. As a child Madgett bore an uncanny resemblance to this aunt. She also carries her middle name. Thus from childhood Madgett was enchanted by the life and death of her grandparents' first child. The poetry of this volume, then, is an heirloom that contains the heritage of a black American family, depicting their sojourn in Texas, Oklahoma, Virginia, and northward. Carefully and lyrically rendering the experience of one family, Madgett speaks of the condition of many. She renders the universal emotions of love, hope, and fear, simultaneously depicting the black condition in America and elegizing the heroic struggles of black men and women during the early decades of this century.

Madgett's poetry is collected in seven volumes: *Songs to a Phantom Nightingale* (New York: Fortuny's, 1941); *One and the Many* (New York: Exposition Press, 1956); *Star by Star* (Detroit: Harlo, 1965; revised edition, Detroit: Evenill, 1970; reprinted in 1972 by Lotus Press); *Pink Ladies in the Afternoon: New Poems, 1965-1971* (Detroit: Lotus Press, 1972); *Exits and Entrances: New Poems* (Detroit: Lotus Press, 1978); *Phantom Nightingale: Juvenilia* (Detroit: Lotus Press, 1981); and *Octavia and Other Poems* (Chicago: Third World Press, 1988).

Translated into more than half a dozen languages, Madgett's poetry is anthologized in over one hundred collections. Her poems appear in: *The Poetry of the Negro, 1746-1949*, edited by Langston Hughes and Arna Bontemps (Doubleday, 1949); *American Literature by Negro Authors*, edited by Herman Dreer (Macmillan, 1950); *Beyond the Blues*, edited by Rosey E. Pool (Hand and Flower, 1962); *Afro-Amerikaanse Poesie*, edited by Rosie E. Pool and Paul Berman (Wesse-Luis, 1964); *Ik Ben de Nievwe*, edited by Rosie E. Pool and Bert Bakker, 1965; *Kaleidoscope*, edited by Robert Hayden (Harcourt, 1967); *Soulscript*, edited by June Jordan (Doubleday, 1970); *Mirror of Men's Minds II*, edited by Arnfield et.al. (Brown, 1967); *Literature for Listening*, edited by Eugene Bahn and L. LaMont Key (Allyn and Bacon, 1968); *Ten*, edited by Ellen Boyd (South and West, 1968); *Black Voices*, edited by Abraham Chapman (New American Library, 1968); *L'Idea degli Antenati*, edited by Roberto Giammanco Lerici, 1968; *Michigan Signatures*, edited by Albert Drake (Quixote, 1969); *Oral Interpretation*, edited by Charlotte I. Lee (Houghton Mifflin, 1971); *Black American Literature*, edited by Darwin Turner (Merrill, 1970); *Tomorrow Won't Wait*, edited by James Olsen and Laurence Swineburne (Noble and Noble, 1970); *Poems to Enjoy*, edited by Dorothy Pettit (Macmillan, 1970); *Right On!*, edited by Bradford Chambers (New American Library, 1970); *Britain America*, edited by L. Marandet and G. Merle (Delgrave, 1970); *The Black Poets*, edited by Dudley Randall (Bantam, 1971); *Black Insights*, edited by Nick Aaron Ford (1971); *Cavalcade*, edited by Arthur P. Davis and J. Saunders Redding (Houghton Mifflin, 1971); *A Broadside Treasury*, edited by Gwendolyn Brooks (Broadside, 1971); *Modern and Contemporary Afro-American Poetry*, edited by Bernard Bell (Allyn and Bacon, 1971); *Up Against the Wall, Mother . . .*, edited by Elsie Adams and Mary Louise Briscoe (Glenco, 1971); *New Black Voices*, edited by Abraham Chapman (1972); *Without You, Without You*, edited by Betsy Ryan (Scholastic Book Service, 1973); *On Freedom Side*, edited by Aaron Kramer (Macmillan, 1972); *The Comp Box*, edited by Ray Kytle (Aspen, 1972); *Afro-American Writing*, edited by Richard A. Long and Eugenia W. Collier (New York University, 1972); *On Our Way*, edited by Lee Bennett Hopkins (Knopf, 1974); *The Poetry of Black America*, edited by Arnold Adoff (Harper and Row, 1973); *Echoes From the Moon*, edited by Judith Goren, et. al. (Hot Apples Press, 1976); *I Hear My Sisters Saying*, edited by Carol Koner and Dorothy Walters (Crowell, 1976); *Lat Vaerlden bli en Svart Dikt*, edited by Bo Anderson and Gunilla Jensen, Forum (Stockholm, 1978); *Svarte Amerikanske Dikt*, edited by Ved Ivor Teigum (Det Norske Samlaget (Oslo), 1979); and *The Third Woman*, edited by Dexter Fischer (Houghton Mifflin, 1980).

Madgett's poetry appears in the following periodicals: *American Pen, Black World, Blue River Poetry Magazine, Detroit News, English Journal, Free Lance, Freedomways, Negro Digest, Negro History Bulletin, Michigan Challenge, Michigan Chronicle, Missouri School Journal, The Norwester, Phylon, Poetry Digest, Poetry Newsletter, The Virginia Stateman Journal of Black Poetry, Ebony, Great Lakes Review, Essence, Obsidian, Michigan Quarterly Review, Detroit Free Fress*, and *Callaloo*.

Madgett's scholarly books include: *Success in Language and Literature-B* with Ethel Tincher and Henry B. Maloney (Follett, 1967) and *A Student's Guide to Creative Writing* (Detroit, Penway Books, 1980). She also edited an anthology, *A Milestone Sampler: 15th Anniversary Anthology* (Detroit: Lotus Press, 1988).

Madgett is a member of the following organizations: College Language Association, National Council of Teachers of English, Modern Language Association, American Association of University Professors, Detroit Women Writers, National Writers Club, Alpha Kappa Alpha Sorority, Delta Kappa Gamma Society (International), NAACP, past member of Michigan Council for the Humanities, past member of Literature Panel, Michigan Council for the Arts, Poetry Society of Michigan, Metropolitan Detroit Alliance of Black School Educators, Alpha Rho Omega, and Cosmep (Committee of Small Magazine Editors and Publishers).

Madgett lists among her many honors and awards the Esther Beer Poetry Award for her poem "Native," presented by the National Writer's Club; the Distinguished English Teacher of the Year Award, given by the Metropolitan Detroit English Club in 1967; one of two Soror of the Year Awards by Alpha Kappa Alpha Sorority in 1969; the Josephine Nevins Keal Development Fund Award in 1979; the Distinguished Service Award presented by the Chesapeake/Virginia Beach Links in 1981. She has received citations from the Museum of African American History of Detroit (1983); National Coalition of 100 Black Women (1984); Black Caucus, National Council of Teachers of English (1984); and Alpha Kappa Alpha Sorority, Alpha Rho Omega Chapter (1969, 1984). Madgett was commissioned by the wife of the governor of Michigan to write the inaugural poem, which she read at the inaugural ceremonies at the State Capitol January 1, 1975. She was honored also by testamonial resolutions by the Detroit City Council (1982, 1985) and the Michigan State Legislature (1982-1984); inducted as an honorary member of the reactivated Stylus Society of Howard University (along with Alice Walker, Sterling Brown, and Dennis Brutus) (1984); received the Robert Hayden Runagate Award (Your Heritage House Writer Series) (1985); the Arts Achievement Award from Wayne State University (1985); the Creative Achievement Award for *Octavia and Other Poems* from the College Language Association (1988); and "In Her Lifetime" tribute by the African Poetry Theatre of Jamaica, New York (1989). The recognition for which she is most proud is the 1988 selection of her book, *Octavia and Other Poems*, as required reading for all eleventh grade students in Detroit public high schools. In 1986 she received a Creative Artist Award from the Michigan Council for the Arts to complete her seventh book of poetry. Highly acclaimed for her poetry, she has read in schools, colleges, and universities throughout the country. In 1978 she recorded her poems at the National Archives at the Library of Congress, Washington, D.C.

References

"Black Literature: Outstanding Writers Have Roots in Virginia." *Richmond News Leader*, 7 September, 1988: 15.

Dictionary of Literary Biography, Volume 76: Afro-American Writers, 1940-1955. Detroit: Gale Research, 1988.

"Ex-Detroit Teacher Carried Banner for Black Literature." *Detroit Free Press*, 1982.

Long, Richard A., and Eugenia Collier, eds. *Afro-American Writing*. New York: New York University Press, 1972.

Madgett, Naomi Long. Interview with Nagueyalti Warren, 26 December 1989.

———. Letter to Nagueyalti Warren, 29 December 1989.

Collections

Madgett's papers are being collected in the Special Collections of Fisk University Library in Nashville, Tennessee. Photographs of Naomi Long Madgett are available through Perry's Studio, Detroit, Michigan.

Nagueyalti Warren

Mary Mahoney

(1845-1926)

Nurse, civil rights activist, suffragist

Mary Eliza Mahoney was the first black professional nurse in America. Her career made her an example for nurses of all races; she gave more than forty years of expert nursing service in addition to making contributions to local and national organizations. She worked for the acceptance of black women in the nursing profession and for the improvement of the status of the black professional nurse.

Mahoney was born in Dorchester, a part of Boston, Massachusetts, on May 7, 1845, to Charles Mahoney and Mary Jane (Steward) Mahoney. There were three children in the family; Mahoney was the oldest and she had a younger sister and brother. She grew up in Roxbury, and at the age of eighteen began to show an interest in nursing as a career. Between the ages of eighteen and thirty-three, Mahoney worked at the New England Hospital for Women and Children, where she was employed to cook, wash, and scrub. However, in 1878, at the age of thirty-three, she was accepted as a student nurse.

Demands for performance at the school were high. Of the forty-two students who entered in 1878, only four students graduated. Mahoney was one of these, and she graduated on August 1, 1879.

The New England Hospital for Women and Children was progressive in its philosophy and took pride in the racially mixed patient population. This philosophy flowed to the School of Nursing, and by 1899 there were five other black graduates of the hospital's school of nursing. After graduation, Mahoney registered with the Nurses Directory at the Massachusetts Medical Library in Boston for work as a private-duty nurse. This directory—organized in 1873 and the first directory of its kind in the United States—provided a nurse's name and reference upon request for a private-duty nurse.

Mahoney's references specified that she was "colored." Families who had employed Mahoney were eager to employ her again. Her well-known calm and quiet efficiency instilled confidence and trust, which in some instances overcame the racial barrier. Her reputation spread, and she was called to nurse patients in New Jersey, Washington, D.C., and North Carolina.

Mahoney viewed herself as a professional and objected to the domestic work also assigned to the nurse. Although she performed these domestic tasks, she performed them with dignity. However, rather than eat in the kitchen with the household help, she chose to eat in the kitchen alone.

Through her alumnae association, Mahoney became a member of the Nurses Associated Alumnae of the United States and Canada, organized in 1896, which later became the American Nurses Association (ANA). She was one of the few early black members of the ANA.

Rights of Black Nurses Emphasized

By 1908 Mahoney had become convinced that if black nurses were to have the same privileges that white nurses were granted, they would have to organize. She enthusiastically welcomed and supported the organization of the National Association of Colored Graduate Nurses (NACGN), founded by Martha Franklin in 1908. At the first annual convention of the NACGN in Boston in August 1909, Mahoney delivered the welcoming address. Through this national endeavor, Mahoney developed a professional bond and friendship with Franklin and Adah Thoms.

In 1911 Mahoney was awarded life membership in the NACGN and was elected the national chaplain. She was responsible for the opening prayers and the induction of new officers, instructing them in their new duties and responsibilities. She rarely missed a national nursing meeting and her local and national involvements were extensive. She was a strong force in convincing other nurses to join the NACGN.

Mahoney attended the People's Baptist Church, a historic black church in Roxbury. She was a religious woman and attended church regularly. She loved to cook, was very good at it, and often cooked for her patients as well as her family. Mahoney had dark brown skin and stood less than five feet tall and weighed less than one hundred pounds. She never married. "She enjoyed being alone at times, valued her privacy, and enjoyed her own company," her great-nephew Frederick Saunders explained. Yet she knew many people and had ties with Boston's black medical circle through her good friends, prominent physician John B. Hall and his wife.

In 1911 Mahoney relocated to New York to take charge of the Howard Orphan Asylum for Black Children in Kings Park, Long Island. She held this position for more than a year, retiring in 1912.

Mahoney was concerned about the progress of women as citizens and worked diligently for their equality. She was a strong supporter of the women's suffrage movement. In 1921 when Mahoney was seventy-six years old, she was among the first women in her city to register to vote.

Mahoney became ill in 1923, suffering from metastatic cancer of the breast. She died on January 4, 1926, at the age of eighty-one, and was buried in Woodlawn Cemetery in Everett, Massachusetts. Since then her grave has been made into a shrine by Chi Eta Phi, a nursing sorority, and the American Nurses Association, and national pilgrimages are made to her grave.

Among many honors, several local affiliates of the NACGN

were named in honor of Mahoney. In 1936 the NACGN established an award in her name to honor her active participation in nursing organizations and her efforts to raise the status of black nurses in the profession. When the NACGN dissolved in 1951, the award was continued by the American Nurses Association. The Dimock Community Health Center, previously the New England Hospital for Women and Children, houses the Mary Mahoney Health Care Clinic, which is a comprehensive health care center.

References

Carnegie, M. E. *The Path We Tread.* Philadelphia: Lippincott, 1986.

Davis, Althea T. "Architects for Integration and Equality: Early Black American Leaders in Nursing." Ph. D. dissertation. Teachers College, Columbia University, 1987.

Saunders, Frederick. Interview with Althea T. Davis, 16 January 1987.

Althea T. Davis

Gerri Major
(1894-1984)
Journalist

In 1833, Geraldyn Hodges Major's great-grandfather left North Carolina with his family, driving a team of oxen, and arrived in Indiana with hope and determination to make a better life for his family. This move not only improved conditions for him and his loved ones, but for his great-granddaughter, Geraldyn Hodges Major, who was born sixty-one years later. Major was provided an opportunity to become one of the early black American journalists.

Major, a stately, attractive, and active woman, was born in Chicago, Illinois, on July 29, 1894, in a residence located in the 3200 block of Chicago's Wentworth Avenue. Major's mother died when she was born, and her mother's sister, Maude Powell Lawrence, raised her. However, Austin Curtis, a popular young society matron and close friend of the mother, nursed Geraldyn. She grew up on Wabash Avenue in Chicago and attended Douglas School, where she was one of two black students.

As a child, Major was accustomed to having nice possessions. Her aunt and uncle, Maude and David Lawrence, were both professionals. Major received many advantages that few black or white children had at that time. She dined out frequently in restaurants and hotels. She attended dancing school and parties given at the Appomattox Club located on Thirty-fifth Street and Wabash Avenue.

At the age of eighteen, Major attended Wendell Phillips High School. Although she applied to Howard University, Fisk University, and Spelman College—all considered the choice schools for contacts in the black community—she entered the University of Chicago. This decision was based on a work-study scholarship she was offered by the university. While attending classes at the University of Chicago, Major became a charter member of the Beta chapter of Alpha Kappa Alpha. The Beta chapter was the second chapter in the first sorority for black college women founded in 1913.

During her professional career, Major joined thirty different organizations. By attending summer school at the university, she completed a four-year program in three years, graduating in 1915, with a Ph.B. degree.

Her first professional position was a teaching appointment at Lincoln Institute, a black college founded by black soldiers who fought in the Civil War, located in Jefferson City, Missouri. While she was not trained to teach, she was determined to meet this challenge boldly and directly. A young, inexperienced woman with a tremendous task ahead of her, Major never thought about failing. Since she was unhappy at Lincoln Institute, she decided not to return to work at the institution for the fall 1916 school year. Instead, she would return to school to pursue a teacher's certificate from Chicago Normal College, where she completed the course in 1917.

While attending the University of Chicago Major had met a young man named Binga Dismond, who was on the track team. The two dated and were married on December 15, 1917, in Houston, Texas. Dismond went off to fight in World War I, and his bride attended Hampton Institute, Hampton, Virginia, during the summer. Later, she accepted a teaching position at Douglas School, her childhood alma mater in Chicago.

Major Becomes Journalist

Major's journalism career began in New York in 1925, with the publication of "Through the Lorgnette," which appeared in the *Pittsburgh Courier*. With the publication of a second article, "In New York Town," which appeared in the *Chicago Bee*, she was off and running. She was excited and enjoyed the challenge of the profession, and she organized the Geraldyn Dismond Bureau of Specialized Publicity in 1928. From 1928 to 1931, she became managing editor of the *Interstate Tatter*, where articles covered society news, entertainment, sports, politics, and gossip. In 1928 she began to write the column "New York Social Whirl" for the *Baltimore Afro-American*.

After Major divorced Dismond in 1933, she worked for the *Daily Citizen*, a newspaper edited during her six-month tenure by G. James Fleming. When this newspaper folded, she wrote for the New York Bureau of Public Health.

Major married Gilbert Holland during the Depression, but the marriage lasted only a short time. Her third and last marriage was to a mortician, John Major. The couple moved to Atlantic City. When John Major died, Gerri Major moved back to New York City. She worked for the *Amsterdam News* and was responsible for the women's pages.

Career with Johnson Publications Begins

In March 1953 Major began working for Johnson Publishing Company in Chicago and wrote articles for *Ebony* and *Jet* magazines. She submitted columns every week, continuing to write to age ninety, 1984. During her many years with Johnson Publishing Company, she traveled extensively. She covered the coronation of Queen Elizabeth II in England. Major lived in Paris because she was assigned the responsibility of the Paris bureau by John H. Johnson, president and chief executive officer of Johnson Publications. She traveled to Egypt, Brazil, Greece, and numerous other countries for work and enjoyment.

During her illustrious career, Major received citations from both New York City mayor Edward Koch and former New York governor Hugh L. Carey. She received a proclamation from borough president Andrew J. Stein of Manhattan declaring July 29, 1979, "Gerri Major Day." On this occasion she was presented with a telegram expressing best wishes from President and Mrs. Jimmy Carter.

Geraldyn Major, author of *Black Society,* died in New York Hospital on Friday, August 17, 1984, at age ninety, after suffering a stroke in her home.

References

"Backstage." *Ebony* 22 (June 1967): 24; Vol. 29 (October 1974): 34; Vol. 34 (October 1979): 24.

"Birthday Bash." *Jet* 47 (3 October 1974): 45.

Davis, Marianna W., ed. *Contributions of Back Women to America*. Vol. 1. Columbia, S.C.: Kenday Press, 1982.

Editors of Ebony. *Ebony Success Library*. Vol. 1. Chicago: Johnson Pub. Co., 1973. 214. Includes photograph.

"Jet Society Editor Gerri Major Feted on 85th Birthday." *Jet* 55 (23 August 1979): 17. Includes photograph.

Major, Gerri, with Doris E. Saunders. *Black Society*. Chicago: Johnson Publishing Company Inc., 1976. 325. Photographs, pp. 122, 193, 214, 318-20.

New York Times, 21 August 1984. II-6.

"Society Editor Gerri Major Dies of Stroke at Age 90." *Jet* 65 (3 September 1984): 55.

"Society Editors." *Ebony* 5 (March 1950): 50.

Vonita White Dandridge

Arenia C. Mallory

(1904-1977)

College president, clubwoman, religious leader

Arenia Conelia Mallory was a formidable woman in three areas: She served as president of a junior college for more than fifty years, during which time she inaugurated an astonishing number of "firsts"; she was a powerful member of the national network of black women's clubs; and she was an uncommon woman lay person in the Church of God in Christ. These women's conventions and missionary groups formed a power bloc in their structures around which even the most authoritarian church leaders learned to step gingerly. These organizations have been among the most independent national organizations of black American women, and their political role and influence have not been adequately examined. Several of these women, such as Mary McLeod Bethune and Nannie Helen Burroughs, who were staunch Baptists, and Arenia C. Mallory of the Church of God of Christ, were active on the national political scene as well as in the women's convention of their denominations. They all enjoyed national prominence.

Mallory was born in Jacksonville, Illinois, on December 28, 1904, to James Edward Mallory and Mazy (Brooks) Mallory. Edward Mallory was the son of one of the first African-American families to migrate from Missouri to Illinois in a mule-drawn wagon in the latter part of the nineteenth century. Edward and his brother, Frank, caught "show business fever" early. Eventually the two brothers and Edward's first wife, Grace, joined the circus and toured America and Europe as musicians. They moved from the circus to comedy routines and became nationally known as the Mallory Brothers. For a number of years they toured with the renowned Bert Williams.

After his first marriage ended in divorce, Edward Mallory met Mazy Brooks, a beautiful light-skinned woman whose father was said to be Italian. Brooks is reputed to have been the first black American to master the Italian concert harp and the first of her race to become a member of the Illinois State Federation of Musicians. She was an accomplished musician and actress. Edward and Mazy were married and the popular Mallory Brothers' duo became a popular trio. The group settled down in Jacksonville and operated a successful business and continued to perform locally.

Edward Mallory died during Arenia's high school senior year. She was a beautiful and talented young lady, and her mother, a seamstress after the death of her husband, kept her daughter beautifully dressed. Her mother had aspirations for her daughter to become a concert pianist and she was enrolled in the Whipple Academy of Music (1918-1922). Mallory's ensuing education included a B.S. degree from Simmons College, 1927, and an M.A. from the University of Illinois, 1950.

Still in her teens, Mallory had a religious experience while attending a revival meeting at a Pentecostal church. She lived with a Pentecostal missionary family and traveled with them as they conducted revivals in different cities. Among the seven historic African-American denominations, the black Pentecostals have a singular historical origin. Unlike black Methodists and Baptists, they trace their origins not to white churches but to a movement inaugurated and led by a black preacher. Also, unlike black Baptists and Methodists, these black Pentecostals began not as a separatist movement, but as part of a distinctly interracial movement from which whites subsequently withdrew. The modern Pentecostal movement in the United States dates from Los Angeles and the Azusa Street Revivals held from 1906 to 1909 by William J. Seymour, a black Holiness preacher. The Church of God in Christ (COGIC) was among the numerous denominations formed at the turn of the century in the wake of the Pentecostal movement. The founder, Charles Harrison Mason (1866-1961), was a former Baptist minister who had been dismissed from his church because of his belief in sanctification. In 1897, Elder Mason held religious meetings in Lexington, Mississippi, which were very successful, and he erected in 1906 Saint Paul Church of God in Christ, the first church of the fledgling denomination—the mother church.

Saints Academy Names Woman President

The COGIC maintained a junior college, Saints Academy, in Lexington, Mississippi, while All Saints University of Memphis, Tennessee, remains in the planning stages. Mallory served as the president of the junior college for more than fifty years, and in many respects her accomplishments have been equivalent to her more famous counterpart, Mary McLeod Bethune. In her early twenties Mallory answered the call to become a music teacher at Saints Academy, and in 1926 she departed from Chicago to take up her life's work in Lexington, Mississippi. After the death of the person who had been in charge of the school, Mallory was assigned the responsibility of the school and the entire focus of the school changed. Mallory modernized the physical plant, improved the curriculum, and it became Saints Academy and Junior College. She established the first high school for blacks in Holmes County, the first school band in the county, the first bus transportation for blacks, and the county's first integrated faculty.

During the 1940s Mallory's work spread. She became a life member of the National Council of Negro Women (NCNW), and she was a charter member of the group. Mallory was a regional director for eight years, during which period she organized southern regional meetings. She was first vice-president of NCNW for four years, and in 1954 she represented the council at the Convention of Women in Helsinki, Finland. She became a vice-president of the National Council of Women of the United States in 1956 and she was active in the International Council of Women. She played an active role in serving with the Women's Army for National Defense (WAND). The purpose of the organization was to take on the challenge anew for service in connection with the war. With a zealous interest in Africa, Mallory organized the Friends of Liberian Youth. The United States government called her to Washington in 1963 as an expert manpower development specialist in the Special Programs Division on the United States Department of Labor's Office of Manpower and Training.

Many honors came to Mallory over time. She was selected twice, in 1940 and 1945, by the National Council of Negro Women as one of the outstanding women of America. In 1956 the Utility Club of New York City lauded her as an educator and leader of women, designating her as "Woman of the Year"; she shared honors with Adam Clayton Powell, Jr., as "Man of the Year." In 1960 she was among the first Americans to visit the newly-independent African nation of Ghana, and in 1961 she was invited to return to Ghana as a member of the Conference for African Women and Women of African Descent. The National Negro Business and Professional Women's Clubs in 1963 gave her their Sojourner Truth Award for Meritorious Service in the Development and Advancement of the Status of Women. In 1965 Mallory received the National Council of Negro Women's tribute award and the Scroll of Honor for being a symbol of the accomplishment of Negro women in advancing education in the rural areas. The Delta Sigma Theta Sorority honored Mallory in 1966 as one of the top twelve women in government. In 1968 Mallory was cited by the Church Civic League of Cleveland, Ohio, as a woman of achievement; and she was the first person of color and the first woman to be elected to the Holmes County Board of Education in Mississippi. In 1969 she was commended by the NAACP and the Church of God in Christ International for outstanding work.

Mallory has received honorary degrees including an LL.D. from Bethune-Cookman College, 1951, and an M.A. from Jackson State College, 1936. The Holmes County Board of Supervisors in 1974 named a street in her honor in Lexington, Mississippi: Arenia C. Mallory Road.

Mallory maintained memberships in the Academy of Political Science, American Teachers Association, National Education Association, Administrators of Rural Education, Southern Conference on Human Relations, the Women's Organization of Higher Education, and the National Society for the Prevention of Juvenile Delinquency (which she served as vice-president). In 1952 she was elected as the only woman delegate of the Church of God in Christ to the World Pentecostal Convention in London, England. Her participation in many state, national, and international conferences included the White House Conference on Children and Youth and the White House Conference on the Aging.

Mallory married A. C. Clemmons on June 4, 1927. This was a mistake according to the COGIC standards, as Clemmons was not a member of the church. Many men of the church already resented her, since she headed the church's only institution of learning, and she paid a high price for marrying outside of the ranks of her church. She took a two-year leave of absence and was finally readmitted to the fellowship of her church. One daughter, Andrea Mazy E. Clemmons, was born of the union.

Mallory retired from the presidency of Saints Academy and Junior College in June 1976. In the following month the school was closed; it was reopened and remained in operation until May 1983.

Just after midnight on May 8, 1977, Mallory died at her home in Lexington. Memorial services were held on May 11, 1977, from 8:00 P.M. to midnight and citizens and friends came in great numbers to pay their last respects. The final service was held Thursday, May 12, at noon in the O. M. Kelly Chapel on the campus of Saints College. Her remains were flown to her birthplace, Jacksonville, Illinois, to be interred in her family plot. She was survived by her daughter.

References

Lincoln, C. Eric, and Lawrence H. Mamiya. *The Black Church in the African American Experience*. Durham: Duke University Press, 1990.

Personalities of the South. Raleigh: News Publishing Co., 1967.

Simmons, David Marie, and Olivia L. Martin. *Down Behind the Sun: The Story of Arenia Conelia Mallory*. Memphis: Riverside Press, 1983. Numerous photographs.

Who's Who in the South and Southwest. 10th ed. Chicago: Marquis, 1967.

Casper LeRoy Jordan

Annie Turnbo Malone

(1869-1957)

Entrepreneur

Annie Turnbo Malone

Annie Minerva Turnbo Pope Malone, a pioneer in black beauty culture, was acclaimed as the nation's first black millionairess. In the 1920s at the peak of her career, she was said to be worth fourteen million dollars; at her death her wealth had dwindled to a mere one hundred thousand dollars. Her birth in 1869 and death in 1957 marked the beginning and ending of key historic periods, which had a major impact on the economic, social, and political development of the African-American community. The significance of Malone as an entrepreneur, philanthropist, and founder of the first center for the study and teaching of beauty culture specifically related to African-Americans, is unknown to this generation of Americans and rarely mentioned in general black American histories.

Malone was born on a farm in Metropolis, Illinois, on August 9, 1869, the tenth of eleven children of Robert Turnbo and Isabella (Cook) Turnbo. Orphaned at a very young age, she was reared primarily by an older sister in Peoria, Illinois. It was in that setting, while still a very young girl, that Malone became aware of the different textures of hair, particularly as related to black and white women.

Concerned about the styling of her coarse hair, she rejected the hair-straightening techniques of Peoria women, who like many late-nineteenth-century black women, used soap, goose fat, and other heavy oils to straighten their hair. In the late 1890s she began to experiment with chemicals to develop a product that would straighten kinky hair without damaging the hair and scalp. A number of early hair straighteners used by black and white women damaged hair follicles and burned the scalp and skin. By 1900 Malone had developed successful straighteners, hair growers, tetter reliefs, and special hair oils.

Acknowledged by some sources as the first to develop and patent the pressing iron and comb in 1900, while residing in Lovejoy, Illinois, Annie Malone manufactured and sold Wonderful Hair Grower. In 1902 she moved her business to Saint Louis, Missouri, where she and three trained assistants sold her products door-to-door, providing free hair and scalp treatments to attract clients. In that same year, during the World's Fair, Malone opened her first business location. Within a year her products were being widely distributed to black women throughout the Midwest. During this period

Malone developed marketing strategies aimed at the national black consumer. Advertisements were placed in key black newspapers, press conferences were held, and women were recruited as agents to sell her products. Malone toured the South in an effort to expand her business to the nation's primarily black market. Also at this time, in 1903, she married a Mr. Pope; they soon divorced after he attempted to interfere with her business activities.

Coinciding with Annie Malone's expansion effort was the rise of Madame C. J. Walker. A former washerwoman, and one of Malone's first students, by 1905 Walker was employed as an agent for Poro products (Malone's business). Not content to sell Poro products and to work for Annie Malone, in 1905 Madame Walker began to perfect a hair formula similar to that of Malone's, to develop a complexion cream, and to market the hot iron as the primary straightener of black hair. In 1906 Walker moved to Denver, Colorado, where she organized her first office. In 1908 she organized a second office in Pittsburgh, Pennsylvania, and in 1910 she consolidated the two offices in Indianapolis, Indiana, where she built a plant to manufacture her products. At her death in 1919, Walker was an acknowledged millionaire.

Madame C. J. Walker is cited in numerous historical sources as the first successful major manufacturer of black beauty products. However, many sources indicate that Malone's business predated the Walker Company. Claude Barnett, founder of the Associated Negro Press and advertising advisor to Poro College for many years, asserted that Walker was a Poro trainee. Assailing what she termed "fraudulent imitations," in 1906 Malone copyrighted the trade name "Poro" for her products and merchandising systems. (Poro is a West African word for an organization dedicated to disciplining and enhancing the body physically and spiritually.) By 1910 there were numerous companies selling hair straighteners, pomades, and complexion creams. Poro products appear to have enjoyed a large part of the market because of Malone's system of exclusive franchised agent-operators, a system also utilized by Madame Walker.

Poro College Aids the Black Community

In 1902 the Poro business was located in Saint Louis at 2223 Market Street. In 1910 it was moved to larger quarters at 3100 Pine Street. Annie Malone was an entrepreneur; however, her special focus was the development of Poro College. In 1917 she built the Poro College complex at Poro Corner in Saint Louis. Poro College Building, Poro Annex Building, and Poro Garage Building comprised the Poro plant, with equipment and furnishings valued at more than one million dollars.

Poro College was a center for education and employment and was the social hub of the Saint Louis black community. Its facilities were used by diverse local and national organizations for special functions and as office space. In 1927 during the Saint Louis tornado disaster, Poro College served as one of the principal relief facilities of the Red Cross. Storm victims were sheltered, clothed, and fed at Poro College. The main building and its annex contained classrooms, barbershops, laboratories, an auditorium, a dining room, a cafeteria, an ice cream parlor, a bakery, a theater, and a roof garden. Malone taught her students how to use her products and how to present themselves.

In the early twentieth century, black leaders stressed the need for race improvement and the presentation of a positive self-image. Malone, imbued with the values of the black middle class, felt that one's deportment was just as important as education. Poro students were taught how to walk, talk, and eat properly. The college trained women as agents for the Poro System and provided jobs for workers and high school students. By 1926 Poro claimed to have 75,000 agents located throughout the United States, the Caribbean, and other parts of the world. The Poro College employed 175 people. In 1930 the business and college were moved to Chicago. Located at 44th Street on South Parkway, the area was called the Poro Block.

Annie Malone's tendency to rely upon managers to handle routine business affairs and her failure to hire capable and honest managers to aid her in the operation of Poro's vast hair preparation empire was a factor in Poro's demise. Historically, many black businesses have been beset by problems involving the level of capitalization, marketing, and distribution of products, and, generally speaking, a spate of difficulties related primarily to management techniques. Many of the early entrepreneurs had little training or experience in business and acquired most of their knowledge on the job.

Because of race needs for identifying and projecting black Americans who were successful, particularly those who had amassed some wealth, persons like Malone became major symbols of race success. Unlike white entrepreneurs, they were unable to live obscure existences. A part of their responsibility was to be available to the black community. Thus, a great amount of time was spent appearing and speaking at churches, conferences, conventions, and numerous social gatherings. This is possible if one has a good management team and a structure that operates efficiently without constant monitoring.

Management was weak at Poro, particularly during the crucial period following major expansion in the 1920s. Many businesses fail during times of major expansion. Moreover, Malone was engaged in a power struggle with her husband, Aaron Malone, who was the chief manager and president of Poro until 1927. For almost six years prior to their much-publicized divorce in 1927, they maintained a facade of happiness. Their relationship affected the operation of business.

Prior to suing Annie Malone for divorce, Aaron Malone actively courted Poro supporters, national black leaders, and key community sources for personal support that would be an effective weapon in wresting control of Poro from his wife. In the divorce suit, Aaron Malone asserted that Poro enterprises had succeeded because of his business acumen and ability to market the company through this extensive network of contacts developed prior to their marriage. He demanded one-half of the business assets. The black leadership was divided in their support for Annie and Aaron Malone. However, Annie Malone had the backing of powerful black clubwomen like Mary McLeod Bethune, who in 1927 was the national president of the National Association of Colored Women (NACW). Since Poro products were marketed primarily to women and Malone's philanthropic efforts affected many of these elements, she gained the edge. Annie Malone kept the business from going into receivership, negotiated a settlement of two hundred thousand dollars with Aaron Malone, and got a divorce. On the surface, she appeared victorious; however, Malone's self-image and the business had suffered. Following the divorce, she was sued for one hundred thousand dollars by Edgar Brown, editor of a local paper and former tennis champion. Although the case was dismissed for insufficient evidence, it increased her problems. She was dealt another blow in 1937 with the settlement of a long-standing lawsuit brought against her by a former employee who claimed credit for her success. These expenses forced the sale of her Saint Louis property.

An additional reason for the decline of Poro enterprises and an extension of Malone's management problems was her reluctance to pay the twenty percent excise tax, which the Federal government required for all luxuries and cosmetics in the 1920s. In 1943 she owed the government almost one hundred thousand dollars. In 1951 she owed forty-eight thousand dollars. Paying taxes never became a part of her business operation. Between 1943 and 1951 Malone was the constant object of government suits. By 1951 the government had taken control of Poro. Malone's failure to pay real estate taxes led to the sale of most of the Poro property.

Malone Called Nation's First Major Black Philanthropist

Annie Malone was the nation's first major black philanthropist. Because of her extensive philanthropy, she became known as a "freak giver." Malone supported nearly every known charity, giving phenomenal amounts. At one time she reportedly was supporting two full-time students in every black land-grant college in the United States. Numerous black orphanages received five thousand dollars or more annually. She purchased homes for her brothers and sisters and educated many of her nephews and nieces. During the 1920s, Howard University's Medical School Endowment received more than twenty-five thousand dollars from Malone. No other black American in history had made that kind of gift to any black college at that date. Between 1910 and 1918, Tuskegee Institute received numerous contributions, usually between one and two thousand dollars. In 1916 the Malones were said to have established a "world record among colored people" by giving five thousand dollars to the Saint Louis building campaign of the colored YWCA. In 1924 Annie Malone donated twenty-five thousand dollars to the Saint Louis Colored YWCA. When Poro College opened in 1918, it was said that the Malones had contributed more to charity and Christian associations than any hundred "colored Americans" in the United States.

Malone's philanthropy extended to employees. Her concern for their welfare was demonstrated in lavish gifts. At annual Poro Christmas banquets she gave diamond rings to five-year employees, gold awards to real estate investors, and prizes for punctuality and attendance. As noteworthy as Malone's philanthropy was, it too created a financial management problem that plagued Malone from beginning to end.

Throughout her life Malone was intensely concerned about the material and cultural uplift of her race. She held memberships and served as an officer in a number of organizations. She served as chairman of the board of directors of the Saint Louis Colored Orphans Home, an institution later named after her; president of the Colored Women's Federated Clubs in Saint Louis; a member of the executive committee of the National Negro Business League and the Commission on Interracial Cooperation; an honorary member of Zeta Phi Beta Sorority; a member of the African Methodist Episcopal church, and a lifelong Republican.

Annie Turnbo Malone died of a stroke on May 10, 1957, in Chicago's Provident Hospital. She had no children.

References

Bowles, Eva. "Opportunities for the Educated Colored Woman." *Opportunity* 1 (March 1923).

Embree, Edwin R. *Brown Americans: The Story of a Tenth of the Nation.* New York: Viking, 1946. 161, 163.

Frazier, E. Franklin. *The Negro in the United States.* New York: Macmillan, 1968.

"Missouri Women in History: Annie Turnbo Malone." *Missouri Historical Review* (July 1973). Includes photograph.

Mongold, Jeanne Conway. "Annie Minerva Turnbo-Malone." *Notable American Women: The Modern Period.* Cambridge: Harvard University Press, 1980. 700-702.

Kleitzing, Henry F., and William Crogman. *Progress of a Race.* Napierville, Ill.: J. L. Nichols, 1898.

Official Manual—State of Missouri, 1971-1972.

Porter, Gladys L. *Three Negro Pioneers in Beauty Culture.* New York: Vantage Press, 1966.

Who's Who in Colored America. 3rd ed. Brooklyn: Thomas Yenser, 1933. 292-93. Photograph, p. 292.

Woodson, Carter G. *The Negro in Our History.* 4th ed. Washington, D.C.: Associated Publishers, 1927. 461.

Collection

Information on Annie Turnbo Malone is in the Claude A. Barnett Papers, Chicago Historical Society. Photographs are included. Jean Conway Mongold also locates materials on

Poro College in the Western Historical Society, University of Missouri at Saint Louis.

Bettye Collier-Thomas

Vivian Malone

(1942-)

Civil rights activist

Vivian Malone, born in 1942, was a trailblazer during the civil rights era in the 1960s. She was one of two students who upstaged Alabama's Governor George Wallace as he stood in the doorway at the University of Alabama in June 1963, playing out his act of defiance in refusing to admit black students to the university. He stepped aside, however, when the federalized National Guard troops escorted Malone and the other black student, James Hood, through the halls of the University of Alabama to register.

Malone was the first black woman to attend and graduate from the University of Alabama. She spent her first two years of college at Alabama Agricultural and Mechanical College at Normal, Alabama, near Huntsville. Taking those first few steps inside the University of Alabama building with the cordon of guardsmen was a frightening experience for Malone. Nine months earlier a riot had erupted on the Ole Miss campus, and Malone says that she could not keep from thinking about what had happened in Mississippi and also thinking that something similar could happen at Alabama.

As it turned out, Malone's first day on campus was the worst time during her two-year stay at the university. Although Hood soon dropped out of school, leaving Malone the sole black student on campus, the attractive and poised Malone stabilized herself and was determined to complete her education. With the help of her classmates, Malone put aside her fears and the frightening experience of her first day and continued her effort toward achieving her goal. In 1965, two years after her admittance to the university, Malone received her baccalaureate degree.

Hood's departure from the university intensified Malone's sense of aloneness. In an interview with *Newsweek* in 1965, she recalled some of her most painful moments. Once, she said, while attending a football game, she was showered with a cupful of ice. There were times when the arranged seating charts for her classes left her surrounded by empty seats. As for her social life, she had occasional dates with black men from Tuscaloosa's Stillman College; (she later married Mack Jones, a physician she met at Stillman). She did not attend the university dances, however. Even though no attempt was made to prevent her from attending the dances, Malone chose not to attend because she did not want to go and stand around watching everyone else dance.

Not all of Malone's experiences were painful; there were times when she was treated just like everyone else and "not as a symbol but as a student" (*Newsweek*, 38). To her very pleasant surprise, Malone was often accepted just as she was:

> On my very first day of class when I went to my dorm that day some girls were sitting on the floor of the lounge to greet me. They asked me about playing bridge with them. That night, we went down and looked at TV together. Some girls even came by the room and said they were glad I could come there—that they thought they would profit by it personally (*Newsweek*, 38).

There were times when Malone experienced open hostility from others, but there were surprising rewards also. Not all of the white students shared the resentment at having blacks on their campus. Once when she was eating in the university cafeteria, a white girl walked away abruptly when Malone sat down with a group of friends. "It made the rest of the girls kind of mad, you know. They watched this girl going away and said, 'Well, what's wrong with her? I wonder what her trouble is?' And almost immediately, another girl came over and took the seat beside me" (*Newsweek*, 38). Soon the bodyguard of U. S. marshals who escorted her during the first few days on campus disappeared. Malone soon was able to make friends, distinguishing between those who merely made a gesture of friendship and those who became her real friends.

Malone scored a tremendous victory over George Wallace through both her personal and academic achievements. She graduated with better than a "B" average in a field, personnel management, that once was beyond the hopes of blacks. Malone had many job offers when she graduated, even one from her alma mater. However, some of the job offers were not of the magnitude of those offered to white male graduates. A few of the job offers to Malone were secretarial jobs, suggesting to her that she could work her way up. Yet a very important accomplishment for Malone was crossing the line between desegregating the University of Alabama and integrating it.

After becoming the University of Alabama's first acknowledged black graduate in 1965, Malone made a smooth transition from college to the workplace. She used her refined qualities of inner strength, patience, and determination to become involved in civil rights work. Malone's college experience heightened her awareness of the treatment of black people in America. It also inspired her to become involved in the civil rights movement and to make it an integral part of her life. She tried to obtain positions that would allow her to make a difference in the lives of black people. It is evident from the positions Malone has held that she has continued to be involved in work to improve the life of black people. She has worked for the Justice Department, the Veteran's Administration Hospital in Atlanta, and the Environmental Protection Agency as director of Civil Rights and Urban Affairs. Malone has also worked as executive director of the Voter Education Project.

In an interview with *Ebony* in December 1978, Vivian Malone commented on the civil rights movement:

> The civil rights movement is not dead, but it has gone into a deep sleep. It will be revived. We can't allow the masses of Black people to remain in the position they are in now. One way we can revive the movement is through the political process, but that is not the only answer or the only cure for the ills of this country. The economic development is tied to the political process. In the years since I finished college, some progress has been made in civil rights, but not nearly as much as should be. We have merely scratched the surface. And now that we are getting our hands on some power, we are being hit with reverse discrimination, and this takes some of the concentration away from the positive aspects of affirmative action. This has heightened our realization as Blacks as to where we are so far as civil right are concerned. We aren't as far as many thought we were (70).

References

"Learning the Hard Way." *Newsweek* 86 (October 6, 1975): 14.

"She Came Through." *Newsweek* 65 (June 14, 1965): 37-38.

"Whatever Happened to Vivian Malone?" *Ebony* 34 (December 1978): 65, 70, 78.

Nina T. Elliott

Paule Burke Marshall

(1929-)

Writer

Fiction writer Paule Burke Marshall was born April 9, 1929, in Brooklyn, New York, to Samuel and Ada Burke. Her parents immigrated to New York from Barbados in the early twenties, and Marshall was reared in a close-knit "Bajan" (West Indian-American) community in Brooklyn, where she attended grammar school and graduated from high school in 1949. In the fall of 1949 she entered Brooklyn College (now a branch of the City University of New York), where she studied sociology in preparation for a career in social work. However, an illness caused her to withdraw from college. During the interim a friend suggested that she write. She did, and she liked it. When she returned to college, Marshall changed her major to English literature. Receiving her bachelor of arts degree cum laude in 1953, she was inducted into Phi Beta Kappa.

Following graduation, Marshall was hired by John P. Davis, editor and publisher of *Our World* magazine. Initially hired to conduct research for other writers, she eventually was promoted to write copy for the fashion and food sections. Being the only woman on the magazine staff, she functioned in a precarious position. She recalls feeling as though "the men were waiting for me to fall" (*Dictionary of Literary Biography*, 163).

In 1955, Marshall became a graduate student at Hunter College (City University of New York), where she studied and continued to write for *Our World*. She often traveled to Brazil and the Caribbean on assignments for the magazine, but in 1956 she resigned from her position. As a student at Hunter College, she began writing her autobiographical first novel, *Brown Girl, Brownstones*. However, at this time, she had no intention of becoming a novelist. In 1957 she married Kenneth E. Marshall. They traveled to Barbados, where she completed the novel. The publication of *Brown Girl, Brownstones* was a turning point in Marshall's life, an event which led her to pursue a career as a writer.

Marshall says that while growing up she lacked role models in terms of black women writers. As a child she began writing poetry, inspired by a trip with her family to Barbados when she was ten years old. But in school she read Nancy Drew and later Jane Austen, and in college she read Joseph Conrad and Thomas Mann. She says that Mann's *Death in Venice* was a seminal book in her development. Upon discovering Richard Wright and other black American men writers, she was pleased but very much aware that her "particular experience as a young urban black American woman was not really being dealt with in that literature" (Brock, 194). Not until she discovered *Maude Martha* did she have a valid example of what was missing from black American literature; until Gwendolyn Brooks spoke, Marshall had not heard the black woman's voice.

Brown Girl, Brownstones was her effort to fill the void that existed in black American literature. What Marshall sensed in so much of the literature was:

> . . . that the reference was constantly the larger oppressive racist society, and that defined almost totally the hero or the heroine. I had a sense that even though that was valid . . . that a whole dimension was missing, that in the face of racism, in the face of oppression, there was a black community, that blacks had been able to elaborate, to make, to fashion a life in a community that was a means of sustaining them. And that our lives were not solely defined by racism, that

> we did most of the time love our children, our husbands and our wives and we had a family life and these were things that have to be celebrated because by celebrating we said that in the face of an oppressive society we were still able to maintain a sense of humanity (Brock, 195).

Brown Girl, Brownstones achieves much of what Marshall sets out to accomplish. She does indeed demonstrate that beyond white racist society a black world exists, does indeed sustain itself through love and trust and self-affirmation; young black girls do grow up and embrace their culture as Selina does. Silla, who buys wholeheartedly the corrupt American dream, symbolized by the brownstone, can be understood not as America has characterized her—castrating matriarch—but as a vulnerable dreamer, persistent in her dream, unaware of its nightmarish quality. *Brown Girl, Brownstones* is a rara avis, making, as it does, the ordinary special.

Despite the fact that the novel received excellent reviews, it was not a commercial success. Carol Field of the *New York Herald Tribune Book Review* heralded the novel, saying, "Rarely has a first novel come to hand which has the poignant appeal and the fresh, fierce emotion of *Brown Girl, Brownstones*." Marshall, however, was forced to recognize that writing a good book is not enough to create a commercial success.

Marshall believes that her failure to be self-promoting contributed to the disappointing sales of her first novel. She was naive and not inclined to appear in public or on the lecture circuit. Citing the success of other black writers and referring to Gwendolyn Brooks and Lorraine Hansberry in particular as women who were quite popular, Marshall blames neither racism nor sexism for the fate of her novel. She nevertheless does concede that the politics of the American literary establishment usually limit black exposures to one token spot on the horizon (Christian, *Dictionary of Literary Biography*, 168). Perhaps most importantly, Marshall is not concerned with commercial success; she would rather concentrate, as she has, on the craft and truth of her fiction.

Marshall Writes Second Novel

In 1960 Marshall won a Guggenheim Fellowship and used it to complete her second work, *Soul Clap Hands and Sing* (1961). This collection of novellas was completed after the birth of Marshall's only child, Eran-Keith, the son to whom she dedicates the book. In a revealing statement that points to the unique predicament of women writers, Marshall explained to DeVeaux how, despite her husband's objections, she hired someone to sit with her son so that she could go to a friend's apartment every day to complete her new book.

Soul Clap Hands and Sing was a test of Marshall's determination to be a writer. The title of this collection was taken from William Butler Yeats's "Sailing to Byzantium": "An aged man is but a paltry thing / A tattered coat upon a stick unless / Soul clap its hands and sing." The collection is focused on aged men who have fallen into the trap of materialism and have come close to losing their souls. Vernon Hall, Jr., described the work as "something of a renaissance in authentic feeling for real men, women and life" (*New York Herald Tribune*, 6). In this work Marshall broadens the sphere of the black community she is concerned with. The titles of each novella, "Barbados," "Brooklyn," "British Guiana," and "Brazil" embrace the African diaspora and speak of values that go beyond geographical boundaries. Marshall says that *Soul Clap Hands and Sing* is different from her first work because here she is consciously perusing a political theme. In *Soul* she stresses the politics of "Umoja"—unity with black people, community, and self.

Eight years elapsed before Marshall published her second novel, *The Chosen Place, the Timeless People* (1969). The intervening years found her working for *New World*, a Caribbean magazine, and as a librarian in the New York Public Library. Marshall also divorced her husband in 1963. While working on the novel she published three short stories: "Reena" (1962), "To Da-duh, In Memoria" (1967), and "Some Get Wasted" (1968).

Barbara Christian describes "Reena" as "one of the first pieces of Afro-American literature to delve into complex choices confronting the contemporary, educated black women" (*Dictionary of Literary Biography*, 165). Reena is a middle-aged woman who narrates her story during a wake for an aunt who has died and whose life is examined juxtaposed against Reena's dreams for herself and her children. "Reena" is quite contemporary in its articulation of black American women's problems in finding a suitable mate and portrays the educated black man's predilection for white women. These and other problems emerge in the story and Reena resolves to take her children to the source for an original black man. She believes Africa is where she will find black men living with pride in their heritage.

The Chosen Place, the Timeless People in manuscript form was entitled "Ceremonies of the Guest House." Robert Bone proclaimed it "the best novel to be written by an American black woman, one of the two important black novels of the 1960's (the other being William Demby's *The Catacombs*), and one of the four or five most impressive novels ever written by a black American " (*New York Times Book Review*, 31 November 1969). The novel embraces the collective self, focusing not on individual persons but on people. Bourne Island is a symbolic place located between Africa and the New World. Working with the past and manipulating history as deftly as Toni Morrison in *Beloved*, Marshall, eighteen years earlier, brings black history alive thorough her use of myth and ritual. The novel indeed is pan-African in scope with its meaning hinging on the ritualistic reenactment of carnival where the Bournehills people declare: "'If we had lived selfish, we couldn't have lived at all.' They half-spoke, half-sang the words. They had trusted one another, had set aside their differences and stood as one against their enemies. *They had been a people!*" (Marshall, *The Chosen Place*, 287).

In spite of Bone's declaration, *The Chosen Place, the Timeless People* received mixed reviews. Henrietta Buckmaster of *The Christian Science Monitor* wrote: "Paule Marshall is, I think, one of the best novelist writing in the United States. She has form, style and immense mastery of words." But Janet Burroway (*New Statesman*, 2 October 1970) wrote, "This is an impressive fat book with a superb thin book inside trying to get out." The novel's reception is not surprising, and Bell Chevigny's assessment shows why the novel might be hard to take:

> A novel that harbors an intelligent revolutionary politics and a compassionate, penetrating humanism is an event in any time. If the time is now, if the revolution is black, if the compassion transcends race, it is a freak or a miracle, depending on whether or not you trust it. I trust *The Chosen Place, the Timeless People*: I think it is an important and moving book. And Paule Marshall seems to me as wise as she is bold, for in compromising neither her politics nor her understanding of people, she makes better sense of both (*Village Voice*, 8 October 1970).

Marshall Confronts Past and Present

Praisesong for the Widow (1983), Marshall's latest novel, reflects perfectly the two themes most central to her work: "the importance of truly confronting the past, both in personal and historical terms, and the necessity of revising the present order" (Marshall, *New Letters*, 111). In *Praise Song*, Marshall examines the life of Avey Johnson, a black middle-aged widow very much submerged in American materialism and middle-class pretensions. On a luxury cruise to the West Indian island of Carriacou, Avey begins a journey to self-discovery. Marshall's use of dramatic irony permits the reader to know what Avey's problem is long before she discovers it. She leaves the cruise ship, finds herself alone on a small island, and becomes deathly ill before finally comprehending the meaning of her pilgrimage. Darryl Pinckney asserts that the construction of the novel is awkward and observes that the narration "wanders from the inside of Avey Johnson's dreams to speculations more proper to an omniscient voice." The flashbacks, Pinckney also complains, make for a "cumbersome reliance on the past perfect to keep chronology straight" (*Contemporary Literary Criticism*, 315.).

Anne Tyler's *New York Times Book Review* critique of *Praisesong* is a far more perceptive analysis of Marshall's novel than Pinckney's, which attempts to categorize Marshall's writing as a "one-dimension approach [that] comes from current strains in black feminism." He also charges, along with Lloyd Brown, that Marshall's views of the past and her concept of culture are romantic. But Marshall herself sets the record straight when she writes in *New letters*, "Anyone who had read my last novel [could not] accuse me of picturing the island as a tropical Eden [Pinckney does]. I am only too aware—painfully so—of the social and economic problems of the area where I have lived off and on for the past twenty years, but even more so of the psychological damage brought on by their history" (*New Letters*, 110). Marshall illuminates the significance of the islands to her work when she says:

> I am both Black American and West Indian and, by ancestry, African. The West Indies is so very important to me because it is part of a history that as a girl I tried to deny (Deveaux Interview, *Essence*, 123).

Marshall's writing deals with the past because she believes that African-Americans have not "really engaged our past. Part of the reason for this," she says, "is that we have been brainwashed into believing it's shameful—who wants to talk about slavery, for God's sake. But I think that until you do, you really can't begin creating your own proper image and proper self. Our history is not delimited by our presence in this part of the world" (DeVeaux Interview, *Essence*, 128).

Marshall first visited Africa in 1977 when she attended FESTAC in Lagos, Nigeria. In 1980, she visited Kenya and Uganda. These visits make Africa, the spiritual homeland to which she so often refers, "a concrete destination." Marshall believes that "a spiritual return to Africa is absolutely necessary for the reintegration of that which was lost in our collective historical past and the many national pasts which comprise it" (Williams, 53).

Reena and Other Stories was published in 1983. A collection of Marshall's short fiction that focuses on her female characters, this book includes "Barbados" and "Brooklyn," stories from *Soul Clap Hands and Sing*. "Reena," the title story, first appeared in *American Negro Short Stories* edited by John H. Clark in 1966.

In 1970 Marshall married her second husband, Nourry Menard, a Haitian businessman. He lives in Haiti, and she divides her time between New York and the island. This marriage, Marshall reveals, is "open and innovative" allowing her the time and freedom to create (Christian, *Dictionary of Literary Biography*, 168).

Marshall is recipient of the following awards: Guggenheim Fellowship (1960), Rosenthal Award from the National Institute of Arts and Letters (1962), Ford Foundation Grant (1964-65), National Endowment for the Arts Grant (1967-68), and the Before Columbus American Book Award for *Praisesong for the Widow* (1984).

Marshall is a member of the Harlem Writers Guild and during the 1960s was quite active in the Association of Artists for Freedom. She has worked as a free-lance writer and as lecturer on black literature at colleges and universities, among them Columbia, Michigan State, Cornell, and Oxford universities and Lake Forest College. She attempts to maintain a low public profile and reveals that she does not especially enjoy teaching, preferring to do what she does best: write. Nevertheless, she is currently on the graduate faculty at Virginia Commonwealth University in Richmond, Virginia.

References

Bone, Robert A. "A Review of *The Chosen Place, the Timeless People.*" *New York Times Book Review* 31 (November 1969): 4, 54.

Brock, Sabine. "Talk as a Form of Action: An Interview with Paule Marshall." *History and Tradition in Afro-American Culture*. Frankfurt: Campus Verlag, 1984.

———. "Transcending the Loophole of Retreat: Paule Marshall's Placing of Female Generations." *Callaloo* 10 (Winter 1987): 79-90.

Buckmaster, Henrietta. "I'm Somebody Now. Recognize Me." *Christian Science Monitor* (22 January 1970): 9.

Burroway, Janet. "Golden Pulp." *New Statesman* (2 October 1970): 426.

Chevigny, Bell. "A Review of *The Chosen Place, the Timeless People.*" *Village Voice* (8 October 1970).

Christian, Barbara. "Paule Marshall." In *Dictionary of Literary Biography*. Vol. 33, edited by Thadious M. Davis and Trudier Harris. Detroit: Gale Research, 1984.

———. "Ritualistic Process and the Structure of *Praisesong for the Widow.*" *Callaloo* 18 (Spring-Summer 1983): 74-84.

———. "Sculpture and Space: The Interdependency of Chaucer and Culture in the Novels of Paule Marshall." In *Black Women Novelists*. Westport, Conn.: Greenwood Press, 1980: 80-136.

Collier, Eugenia. "The Closing of the Circle: Movement from Division to Wholeness in Paule Marshall's Fiction." In *Black Women Writers, 1950-1980*, edited by Mari Evans. New York: Doubleday, 1984.

Contemporary Authors. Vols. 77-80. Detroit: Gale Research, 1979.

Contemporary Literary Criticism. Vol. 27. Detroit: Gale Research, 1984.

Davies, Carole Boyce. "Black Woman's Journey into Self: A Womanist Reading of Paule Marshall's *Praisesong for the Widow.*" *MATAU* 1 (1987): 19-34.

De Veaux, Alexis. "Paule Marshall: In Celebration of Our Triumphs." *Essence* 1 (May 1979): 96, 98, 123-34.

Marshall, Paule. "Characterizations of Black Women in the American Novel." In *The Memory of the Spirit of Frances, Zora and Lorraine: Essays and Interviews on Black Women and Writing*, edited by Juliette Bowles. Washington, D.C.: Howard University Press, 1979.

———. *The Chosen Place, The Timeless People*. New York: Harcourt, 1969.

———. "The Negro Woman in American Literature." *Freedomways* 6 (Winter 1966): 21-25.

———. "Shaping the World of My Art." *New Letters* 40 (October 1973): 97-112.

McCluskey, John Jr. "And Called Every Generation Blessed: Theme, Setting and Ritual in the Works of Paule Marshall." In *Black Women Writers, 1950-1980*, edited by Mari Evans. New York: Doubleday, 1984.

Michaelson, Judy. "Black Before Her Time." *New York Post* 6 (December 1969).

Tyler, Anne. "A Widow's Tale." *New York Times Book Review* 20 February 1983: 7, 34.

Williams, John. "Return of a Native Daughter: An Interview with Paule Marshall and Maryse Conde." *Sage* 3 (Fall 1986): 52-53.

Nagueyalti Warren

Sara Martin
(1884-1955)
Singer

Blues singer Sara (Sarah) Dunn Martin, also known as Margaret Johnson and Sally Roberts, was born June 18, 1884, in Louisville, Kentucky. Sara was born to William Dunn and Katie (Pope) Dunn and began solo vaudeville acts as a teenager in her hometown. Around 1915 she moved north and formed a singing act in a vaudeville circuit out of Chicago. By the early 1920s she was singing in the cabarets and clubs of New York City, and Clarence Williams collaborated with her on several blues songs during her tenure with Okeh Records from 1922 to 1928, the earliest being "Uncle Sam Blues" and "A Green Gal Can't Catch On." She also recorded on the Columbia label with her own Brown Skin Syncopators in 1922 and with Fats Waller, Eva Taylor, and Shelton Brooks on the Okeh label in 1923.

Martin's singing engagements expanded to include theatrical houses. She performed at the Princess Theater in Harrisburg, Pennsylvania, in 1922. The next year she worked at the Bijou Theater in Nashville, the Lyric Theater in New Orleans, the Regent Theater in Baltimore, the New Star Casino in New York, the Monogram Theater in Chicago, and the Paradise Cabaret in Atlantic City. Martin was popular on the Theatre Owners Booking Association (TOBA) show circuits and toured extensively with Fats Waller from 1922 to 1923 and with the W. C. Handy Band in 1923. During the next three years she had many engagements throughout the United States, including the Dunbar Theater in Columbus,

Ohio, the Howard Theater in Washington, D.C., and the Grand and Coliseum theaters in Chicago.

Sara Martin was known for her dramatic stage presence as well as her lavish gowns, which were changed two or three times during a performance. Her song repertoire reflected versatility ranging from the traditional twelve- and sixteen-bar blues to vaudeville comedy songs. She also sang fox-trots that reflected Sophie Tucker's singing style and was billed as "The Colored Sophie Tucker." Her singing encompassed the moaning style as well as the country ballad style. During the 1920s Martin created a family act with her three-year-old son and her husband, William Myers, on the banjo that heightened her popularity.

Throughout her career Martin appeared in many reviews, theatrical shows, and musicals, including the *Jump Steady Revue* at the Lafayette Theater in New York in 1922 and the *Up and Down* show, which toured the east coast in 1922. Four years later she was featured in Leigh Whipper's *Golden Brown Reasons*. In 1927 she worked with the Doc Straine Company at the Lincoln Theater in New York. She also appeared with Eva Taylor in the musical comedy *Bottomland* at the Savoy Theater in Atlantic City and at the Princess Theater in New York in 1927. Her tours with William Benbow's *Get Happy Follies Revue* (1928) took her to theaters in Cuba, Jamaica, and Puerto Rico, among others. In 1929 she appeared with Mamie Smith in the musical comedy *Sun-Tan Frolics* at the Lincoln Theater. During the next year Martin toured the theaters of the East Coast and the clubs of Cleveland, Ohio.

Martin's audiences also extended to radio; she appeared on WFAA in Dallas (1924) and with the Clarence Williams Trio on WHN in New York (1927). She has been credited with having appeared in one film, *Hello Bill* (1927).

In the latter part of her career she shifted from blues singing to gospel and began working with Thomas A. Dorsey, who had made the same transition. They toured together in local churches in the Chicago area in 1932. Martin was never noted for singing gospel, however, as she had been for singing the blues.

More than a decade before her death, Martin made another career change, this time outside the field of music. She owned and operated a private nursing home in Louisville, Kentucky. On May 24, 1955, she died of a stroke at the Louisville General Hospital and was buried at the Louisville Cemetery.

Sara Martin was one of four outstanding female blues singers produced in Louisville—the others being Edith Wilson, Helen Humes, and Edmonia Henderson. As a contemporary of Ma Rainey and Bessie Smith, Martin had a lengthy career as a vaudeville blues queen and was instrumental in popularizing the blues through recorded and stage performances during the 1920s.

Martin's recorded songs include "Cage of Apes," "Can't Find Nobody to Do Like My Daddy Do," "Daddy Ease This Pain of Mine," "Death Sting Me Blues," "Don't You Quit Me Daddy," "Down at the Razor Ball," "Every Woman Needs a Man," "Gonna Be a Lovin' Old Soul," "Good Bye Blues," "Got to Leave My Home Blues," "Green Gal Can't Catch On," "Guitar Blues," "Guitar Rag," "I Can Always Tell When (My/A) Man is Treatin' Me Cool," "I Won't Be Back If I Don't Find My Brown At All," "I'll Forget Your Blues," "I'm Gonna Hoodoo You," "I'm Sorry Blues," "I've Got to (Go and) Leave My Daddy Behind," "It's Too Late Now to Get Your Baby Back," "Longing for Daddy Blues," "Mama's Got the Blues," "Mistreating Man Blues," "Papa Papa Blues," "Roamin' Blues," "Sad and Sorry Blues," "Squabbling Blues," "Strange Lovin' Blues," "Sweet Man's the Cause of It All," "Troubled Blues," "Uncle Sam Blues," "What More Can a Monkey Woman Do?," "You Don't Wan Me Honey," and "Your Going Ain't Giving Me the Blues."

References

Harris, Sheldon. *Blues Who's Who: A Biographical Dictionary of Blues Singers*. New Rochelle, N.Y.: Arlington House Publishers, 1979.

Harrison, Daphne Duval. *Black Pearls: Blues Queens of the 1920s*. New Brunswick, N.J.: Rutgers University Press, 1988.

Kellner, Bruce, ed. *The Harlem Renaissance: A Historical Dictionary for the Era*. New York: Methuen, 1987.

"Sara in New York." *Chicago Defender*, 23 April 1927.

Collections

Materials on Sara Martin are in the James Weldon Johnson Memorial Collection, Beinecke Rare Book and Manuscript Library at Yale University. Materials on Martin dating around 1924 are in the Music Division, vertical files, New York Public Library, Lincoln Center.

Marva Griffin Carter

Biddy Mason

(1818-1891)

Entrepreneur, midwife, nurse, philanthropist, humanitarian

Born into slavery on August 15, 1818, and named Bridget, this former slave turned entrepreneur quickly came to be known as Biddy and retained that name the remaining years of her life. The exact place of her birth is unknown. Researchers have given both Georgia and Logtown, Mississip-

Biddy Mason

pi, as her place of birth. Her obituary in the *Los Angeles Times*, 16 January 1891, gives Hancock County, Georgia, as her birthplace. Biddy Mason was the slave of Robert Marion Smith and Rebecca (Crosby) Smith, who owed a plantation in Mississippi.

Mason had three children. Her first child, Ellen, was born on October 15, 1838, when Mason was twenty years old. Ann was born six years later and Harriet was born four years afterward. It is possible that Mason's children were fathered by her owner, Robert Smith.

Smith became a Mormon convert in 1847 and decided to migrate to the Utah Territory in order to make his contribution to building the Kingdom of the Saints in Salt Lake City. On March 10, 1848, Mason began her strenuous cross-country journey with the Smith family and others, including another slave of Smith's named Hannah, who had several daughters. Mason exhibited great endurance and an impressive variety of skills in fulfilling her responsibilities as organizer of a camp of fifty-six whites and thirty-four slaves. She herded the two yoke of oxen, seven milk cows, and eight mules that belonged to the party. She also prepared the meals, cared for her own children, and acted as midwife for several births during the long and arduous two-thousand-mile trek.

The Smith clan and their slaves, including Mason, remained in the Mormon environs for only a few years, from 1848 to 1851. During this brief period, however, Mason witnessed and was subjected to the indignities of the Mormons' firm and often outspoken belief in the inferiority of blacks. Robert Smith learned of a newly established Mormon community in San Bernardino, California, and decided to leave the Salt Lake Valley and move to this new community in September 1851, taking his slaves with him.

Smith obviously did not know of the legislation that had passed in California. The California state constitution, as drafted in 1849, forbade slavery. The debates between the pro- and antislavery forces continued until September 1850, when California was admitted to the Union as a free state. Despite being a free state, the status of people of color who entered the state as slaves both before and after the admission of California was ambiguous. Mason's owner became alarmed over the confused status of slaves and began making preparations to move his family and slaves to Texas, a slave state.

Mason told two free black men of Los Angeles her fear of being forced to leave California and remaining hopelessly entrapped in the merciless status of a slave. The two men, Charles Owens and Manuel Pepper, were determined to keep Smith from separating them from Biddy's and Hannah's young daughters, with whom they had romantic relationships. Owens's father, Bob Owens, was an influential and well known black businessman in Los Angeles. These gentlemen decided that Smith's plot to keep his slaves in bondage, particularly Mason, Hannah, and their daughters, had to be thwarted. They, along with sheriffs and others, disrupted Smith's plan by invading his hideout encampment in the Santa Monica Mountains of Los Angeles. There, Smith was served with a writ of habeas corpus by Mason and her family.

To appreciate the boldness and courage of Mason's challenge, it must be seen within the context of her previous existence in the tortuous reality of Mississippi plantation life. Mason was compelled to remain silent during the court proceedings to rule on her petition for freedom because of an 1850 California law that disallowed the testimony of blacks, mulattoes, and Indians against white people in both criminal and civil cases of law. When Smith failed to appear in court on January 21, 1856, Mason's petition for manumission was approved. Not only did Mason gain her own freedom, but Judge Benjamin Hayes, who presided over the two-day hearing, also freed all members of her family when he rendered the final decision against Smith.

Upon her entry into the life of a free person of color, Mason was invited by Robert Owens, to remain in Los Angeles. Mason accepted his invitation for her and her daughters to live with him, his wife, Winnie, and their children—Charles, Sarah Jane, and Martha. The strong bond between these two families culminated in the marriage of Charles Owens and Ellen Mason. They had two sons, Robert Curry Owens and Henry L. Owens.

Nurse and Midwife Becomes an Entrepreneur

Mason's reputation as a skilled nurse and midwife was quickly established and respected among newly arrived Anglo immigrants, American Indians, and the wealthy. Mason's finely-honed midwifery and nursing skills were probably learned on the Southern plantations from older slaves and knowledgeable practitioners of successful treatments through the use of herbs, roots, exercise, and diet. Her consistently high standards in the successful practice of her midwifery skills among all social classes allowed her to attain economic independence.

Through her work and her thrift, Mason achieved her dream of owning a home for her family only ten years after gaining her freedom. She bought a site on Spring Street, now a bustling commercial center in the heart of downtown Los Angeles. The purchase price was $250 and she was one of the first black women to own land in Los Angeles. From the time of purchase, she referred to the lot as "the Homestead" and sternly instructed her children that it was never to be abandoned. Mason actually rented a small dwelling for eighteen years after the purchase of her land. Although she was not a speculator, she was saving money to build a revenue-producing structure on part of her land.

By 1884, at the age of sixty-six, Mason moved onto her own land. She also sold a parcel for $1,500 and built a commercial building with rental spaces in this rapidly developing urban center of Los Angeles. Mason had made wise and prudent decisions regarding her business and real estate transactions, establishing a secure and financially independent future for herself and her family. Through her astute observations of the struggles of ethnically diverse groups of Chinese-Americans, Japanese-Americans, Mexican-Americans, and American Indians, it became clear to her that those who were beginning to prosper in nineteenth-century Los Angeles possessed skills that enabled them to acquire land and to educate their children. These observations of success among nonwhite newcomers to Los Angeles helped to inspire Mason's goal of possessing a homestead in perpetuity for her family. Mason's acquisitions of land provided her heirs with wealth and status in the Los Angeles community. Her grandson, Robert, was described at the turn of the century as the "richest Negro in Los Angeles." He was a real estate developer and politician.

Mason's homestead was more than a secure place for her family. She used it as a base for her generous charitable and philanthropic work with the poor, often providing a refuge for needy people of all races. Mason was well-known for her frequent visits to the jails, and those who were incarcerated often found that they were neither abandoned nor forgotten. People seeking her assistance often formed lines at 331 South Spring Street.

In addition to being a philanthropist, she was a deeply religious woman. She, along with Charles Owens, her son-in-law, invited a group of people to her home to found in 1872 the Los Angeles branch of the First African Methodist Episcopal church. Mason's legacy of legal precedents, social philanthropy, civic participation, familial nurturing, and the spiritual enrichment of the Los Angeles community has been appropriately acknowledged in a recent series of community celebrations of her life.

Although many mourned Mason's passing when she died on January 15, 1891, she was interned in an unmarked grave at Evergreen cemetery in the Boyle Heights area of Los Angeles. The grave remained unmarked for nearly one hundred years. On Palm Sunday, March 27, 1988, Mayor Tom Bradley and about three thousand members of the First African Methodist Episcopal church, founded by Mason, paid homage to her by unveiling an impressive tombstone to mark her grave.

Thursday, November 16, 1989, was declared Biddy Mason Day and a ceremony at a new mixed-use building called the Broadway Spring Center unveiled a memorial depicting the highlights of her lifetime achievements in nineteenth-century Los Angeles. It is in the form of an eight-by-eighty-one-foot timeline wall. Both ceremonies were attended by Gladys Owens Smith, Biddy Mason's ninety-five-year-old great-granddaughter, and her great-granddaughter, Linda Cox.

References

Beasley, Delilah L. *The Negro Trailblazers in California*. Los Angeles: Times Mirror Printing and Binding House, 1919.

Bunch, Lonnie G. *Black Angelenos: The Afro-American in Los Angeles, 1850-1950*. Exhibit catalog. Los Angeles: California Afro-American Museum, 1988.

Crouch, Gregory. "Early Black Heroine of L.A. Finally Receives Her Due." *Los Angeles Times*, 28 March 1988.

Hayden, Dolores. "Biddy Mason's Los Angeles, 1856-1891." *California History*, 68 (Fall 1989): 86-99. Hayden's article is the definitive account of Biddy Mason's life and work.

Jackson, Bobi. "Biddy Mason: Pioneer 1818-1891." Unpublished essay. University of California, Los Angeles Center for the Study of Women, 1985.

Oliver, Myrna. "A Lot of History." *Los Angeles Times*, 17 November 1989.

Oscar L. Sims

Lena Doolin Mason

(1864-?)

Religious leader, poet, lecturer

Lena Doolin Mason, known primarily for her work as a Methodist minister and evangelist, also wrote poetry, and painted. Described by Daniel W. Culp as "powerful in argument and picture making,'' Mason ''possesse[d] considerable ability as a poet and ha[d] written several poems and songs that do not suffer by comparison with poems by the best poets'' (*Twentieth Century Negro Literature*, 444). Given her artistic talents and her gifts as a minister, it is indeed surprising that so little is known about this energetic, multitalented woman.

Mason was born on May 8, 1864, in Quincy, Illinois. Apparently her parents, Reba and Vaughn Doolin, were free and devout Christians. Mason attended Douglass High School in Hannibal, Missouri, and Professor Knott's School in Chicago. On March 9, 1883, she married George Mason. The couple had six children—four boys and two girls. Only one child, a daughter Bertha Mae, survived to adulthood. A photograph in *Twentieth Century Negro Literature* shows Mason to have been a handsome woman. Her hair is parted in the middle and cut short or pulled back. Dressed simply in a button-down jacket, a necklace around her neck, and a pin with a star and a moon in her lapel, Lena Mason has a pensive, determined look of serenity.

Christianity played an important role in Mason's development, and at the age of twenty-three, she entered the ministry. She began her ministerial career, which eventually took her to almost every state in the United States, by preaching for three years to all-white congregations. She later preached to racially mixed congregations and was affiliated with the Colored Conference of the Methodist church. At some point in her career she spent five months in Minneapolis working in black and white churches.

Numerous Religious Conversions Spurred

Clearly an enormously powerful preacher, during the course of her ministry Mason, sources say, spurred 1,617 people to convert. A fellow minister, C. L. Leonard, pastor of the Central German Methodist Episcopal church, said of Mason:

> I desire to express my highest appreciation of Mrs. Mason's church and effective evangelical work in my church and in many others. Mrs. Mason is now making a tour of the South; and by her lectures and sermons is doing a work among the colored people that will bear good fruit in the future. One only needs to hear Mrs. Mason to understand how it is that one never tires listening to her (444).

And Culp writes: ''Few preachers can excel her in preaching.'' The critic also cites Mason's excellent work in Minneapolis. ''Her five months work in colored and white churches,'' he says, ''will never be forgotten'' (444).

Two of Mason's poems are included in *Twentieth Century Negro Literature* and at the present are the only known examples of her poetry. These two works,''The Negro and Education'' and ''A Negro in It,'' reveal Mason's commitment to the black liberation movement of that period. She writes the two poems in the sort of verse form and rhyme that characterize much of the poetry written in the late-nineteenth and early-twentieth centuries. But her subject matter, her bold and direct style, her flair for irony, and most importantly, the skillful way she weaves her argument for racial equality into her poetry, set her apart from other poets whom some might dismiss as too ''conventional.''

In ''A Negro in It,'' Mason focuses on the role black Americans have played in American history. The poem argues against history's marginalization of blacks and the discrimination and violence that continue in spite of emancipation. Mason devotes the first ten stanzas of the poem to describing the crucial role black soldiers played in the battle of San Juan Hill and to noting how J. B. Parker, a black man, courageously captured President McKinley's assassin. The evidence she offers clearly disputes the logic behind bigoted efforts to keep blacks from attaining social equality. Having presented her case for her race's historical significance, she advances her argument for racial equality in religious terms:

> White man, stop lynching and burning
> This black race trying to thin it,
> For if you go to heaven or hell
> You will find some Negroes in it.

Like so many other black Americans, Mason identified education as the means by which blacks will overcome the legacy of slavery. ''The Negro and Education'' deals with a theme that Robert B. Stepto, in his book, *From Behind the Veil: A Study of Afro-American Narrative*, and others have identified as the most crucial one in black American literature, namely ''the quest for freedom and literacy.'' In this poem Mason boldly and convincingly unites her faith in God with her pride in her race. The poem chronicles the progress black Americans have made as they emerge from what Mason calls ''the dismal cave of slavery'' and the oppressive illiteracy that kept so many blacks within ''the darkness of its walls near three long centuries.'' Each stanza ends with a variation of the oft-quoted observation made by slaveholders, ''If you educate a Negro you will unfit him for a slave.''

Two stanzas allude, directly and indirectly, to Frederick Douglass's autobiography, *The Narrative of Frederick Douglass, an American Slave*. In this work Douglass recounts his master's efforts to keep him illiterate. This master's observations to his wife, Mrs. Auld, who had begun teaching Douglass to read, about the so-called ill effects of literacy on slaves are echoed in the following lines: ''No knowledge shall they have, / For if you educate a Negro / You unfit him for a slave.''

The poem continues in a religious tone as Mason relates the progress blacks have made, with God's help, overcoming both illiteracy and slavery. In the last three stanzas the poet proclaims her belief that the cave of slavery will never again hold her people captive. Once ''the yoke of bondage'' had been removed, the Negro ''caught the wheels of progress, / Gave them another roll.''

Mason thus enables herself to complete her argument for

the importance of education and the equality of blacks. Education may have rendered the Negro "unfit to be a slave," but it has now made him more than fit for a variety of other roles. In the final stanza, she effectively catalogues the varied accomplishments of black Americans. "We have lawyers and we've doctors, / Teachers and preachers brave." These two poems suggest that Mason was an optimist. And perhaps it was her optimism that inspired so many people who heard her preach to convert to Christianity.

Throughout the poem "The Negro and Education," Mason uses the third person singular masculine pronoun to prefer to the entire black race, a common rhetorical convention at the time she was writing. Nevertheless, she includes in the final stanza a reference to "a host of noble women / who have safely crossed the wave." This line strongly suggests she was indeed aware of the unique hardships women faced. Though few biographical facts are known, one can speculate that she knew something about these women's struggles, having accomplished more than most people, male and female, do in a lifetime. Like the heroic J. B. Parker and the black soldiers who saved the day for the Rough Riders at San Juan Hill, she has already taken her place in American history. Perhaps in the future more will be known about the role this remarkable woman played in it. For surely Mason—evangelist, minister, lecturer, poet, painter, as well as wife and mother—should be counted among the "host of noble women" she praises in her poem, women whose works have only recently begun to be discovered.

References

Culp, Daniel W. *Twentieth Century Negro Literature*. Atlanta: J. L. Nichols Co., 1902. Reprinted. Miami: Mnemosyne Pub. Co., 1969.

Dannett, Sylvia G. L. *Profiles of Negro Womanhood*. Vol. 1, 1619-1900. Philadelphia: M. W. Lads, 1964.

Douglass, Frederick. *The Narrative of Frederick Douglass: an American Slave*. 1846. Reprinted. Cambridge: Harvard University Press, 1960.

Richardson, Marilyn. *Black Women and Religion: A Bibliography*. Boston: G. K. Hall, 1980.

Stepto, Robert B. *From Behind the Veil: A Study of Afro-American Narrative*. Urbana: University of Illinois Press, 1979.

Candis LaPrade

Victoria Earle Matthews

(1861-1907)

Author, journalist, clubwoman, social worker

Victoria Earle Matthews was among an impressive number of black women writers near the turn of the century—during what poet, abolitionist France E. W. Harper saw as "a woman's era." Matthews was born one month after the Civil War began in Fort Valley, Georgia, about ninety miles south of Atlanta. She was one of nine children of a slave mother, Caroline Smith. Her mother escaped from her master during the war and upon her return after emancipation, she found only four of her children. After a legal struggle, Caroline Smith gained custody of her two fair-complexioned daughters, Anna and Victoria Smith, who were being reared in her former master's home. According to oral family history, both Matthews and her older sister were the offspring of their mother's slave owner. Matthews, with her mother, arrived in New York around 1873 after living in Richmond and Norfolk, Virginia, for nearly four years.

Matthews attended Grammar School 48 in New York City until she was compelled to leave due to the illness of a family

Victoria Earle Matthews

member. She began working as a domestic, which was the only work available to her. Matthews was a great reader and very intelligent despite her disadvantaged background. She read, "whatever she could lay her hands on" (Brown, 209). She was largely self-taught, acquiring knowledge by reading the books from the library of one of her employers and through lectures, special studies, and contact with educated persons. She took advantage of every opportunity to improve herself, intellectually and culturally. In 1876, at the age of 18, she married William Matthews, a carriage driver and native of Petersburg, Virginia. During the early years of her marriage, she wrote stories about her childhood that were published in *Waverly* magazine, *New York Weekly*, the *Family Story Paper*, and other journals.

In 1893, under the pen name "Victoria Earle," she published a slim volume, *Aunt Lindy*, a tale of a former slave in postwar Georgia who resisted temptation and murdered her former master. Matthews did free-lance writing for the *New York Times*, the *New York Herald*, the *Brooklyn Eagle*, and wrote articles for the leading black newspapers: the Boston *Advocate*, *Washington Bee*, *Richmond Planet*, *Cleveland Gazette*, and the *New York Globe*. She became a journalist for the *New York Age* and with encouragement from its editor, T. Thomas Fortune, she selected and edited *Black Belt Diamonds: Gems from the Speeches, Addresses, and Talks of Booker T. Washington* (1898).

As a sympathetic journalist, Matthews was the prime organizer of a testimonial for the antilynching crusader, Ida B. Wells, held October 5, 1892, in New York City's Lyric Hall. The cosponsor of the event was Maritcha Remond Lyons, a Brooklyn school teacher. Two hundred and fifty women were present to honor Wells, including Josephine St. Pierre Ruffin of Boston, Sarah S. T. Garnet, the widow of abolitionist Henry Highland Garnet and a New York City grammar-school principal, and her sister, Susan McKinney Steward, a physician from Brooklyn. At this gathering a "generous purse" of $700 was collected to support the protest efforts and writings of Ida B. Wells. Immediately after the mass meeting of black women, Matthews, McKinney Steward, and Ruffin announced plans to form women's clubs in New York City, Brooklyn (then a separate city), and Boston. Between 1892 and 1894 black women's clubs emerged across the country, of which the most prominent were the Women's Era Club of Boston, the Woman's League of Washington, D.C., the Woman's Loyal Union of New York (Manhattan) and Brooklyn, and the Ida B. Wells Club of Chicago.

Matthews was the founder and first president of the Woman's Loyal Union of New York City and Brooklyn. More than seventy women, among whom were school teachers, literary women, journalists, businesswomen, artists, homemakers, and housekeepers, joined the Loyal Union club after it was organized December 5, 1892. The group emphasized social and political improvement, especially better schools and employment.

As a delegate of the Women's Loyal Union, Matthews attended the first national conference of black women on July 29-31, 1895. Along with other prominent women—Josephine Ruffin, Florida Ruffin Ridley, and Margaret Washington—Matthews assumed a leadership role at the meeting and was appointed to the platform committee. On the second day of the conference, she addressed the body of club women on "The Value of Race Literature." Matthews emphasized the importance of collecting the writings of black men and women, including histories, biographies, sermons, speeches, essays, and articles, in order to preserve the culture and contributions of people of African descent.

The outgrowth of the first national women's conference was the founding of the National Federation of Afro-American Women (NFAAW). Among the officers elected were Margaret Washington as president and Victoria Matthews as chair of the executive board. The *Women's Era* was named the official newspaper of the NFAAW and Matthews was one of its correspondents.

In her powerful position on the executive board of the National Federation of Afro-American Women, Matthews played a primary role in planning its 1896 convention in Washington, D.C. She was an astute politician; her suggestions in the general meetings, service on committees, and resourcefulness were invaluable in the formation of a new black women's organization. Plans were announced for the meeting of two separate national organizations of black women in July 1896: the National Colored Women's League of Washington and the Federation of Afro-American Women. Matthews, presiding over the first session, informed the body of clubwomen that the NFAAW "began its work in 1895 with approximately twenty-eight clubs in the United States . . . but one year later, in 1896, there are sixty-seven clubs represented at this second annual meeting." Matthews was appointed to a joint committee of seven women from each body, the Colored Women's League and the Federation of Afro-American Women, to consider a program of unity. The consensus of the committee stipulated that the two women's organizations consolidate under the name National Association of Colored Women (NACW). In the interest of their club work for the moral and social uplift of black people, they chose the motto "Lifting As We Climb." With Mary Church Terrell as president of the NACW, Matthews served as the first national organizer from 1897 to 1899.

Victoria Matthews, tall, slender, with straight brown hair and large soulful eyes, was a woman of rare intelligence, courage, and persistence. She attended the Congress of Colored Women of the United States meeting at the Cotton States and International Exposition held in Atlanta, December 1895. Matthews was actively involved in the committees and other decision-making groups. Immediately after the congress, Matthews began a tour of the South. Although she was impressed with the self-help efforts of blacks in Alabama, she was disappointed by the red-light districts in New Orleans and other southern cities. Following her investigations, Matthews returned to New York to continue her uplift and improvement work there.

White Rose Mission Attracts Widespread Attention

Matthews's concern for social welfare work in the black community increased after the death of her son and only child, Larmartine Matthews, at the age of sixteen:

> And immediately my heart went out to other people's boys and girls . . . . I found that this was my field so I began to visit families. I selected the ones I thought needed me most and tried to be a real friend to the mothers . . . . Then I began to hold mothers' meetings at the various homes where I visited; and you may not believe this, but one day at one of these meetings we prayed especially for a permanent home where we might train boys and girls and make a social center for them where the only influence would be good and true and pure. Almost immediately Winthrop Phelps, who owns an apartment house, offered us one of its flats, rent free for three months to make our experiment. We opened here on February 11, 1897 (Brown, 211-12).

The mission was founded by Victoria Matthews with the purpose of "establishing and maintaining a Christian, nonsectarian Home for Colored Girls and Women, where they may be trained in the principles of practical self-help and right living" (Meier, 134). It offered a social center for community women and children as well as shelter and protection to young women coming from the South in search of employment. Matthews organized a group of women from different religious denominations to assist in the operation of her program. Thus, "many a young girl learned something of the art of doing things before she ventured out in [domestic] service" (Brown, 212). The children, both males and females, were three to fifteen years old. The boys engaged in vocational and handicraft courses while sewing, cooking, and housekeeping courses were offered to the girls. A kindergarten class was taught by Alice Ruth Moore, who married the poet Paul Laurence Dunbar. Matthews, a frail woman in a black hooded coat, was frequently seen outside, lovingly surrounded by the children of the mission.

Possessing the desire to do practical, useful work, Matthews, at the same time, expanded her efforts in cultural pursuits for black people. A gifted lecturer with a talent for dramatic, forceful speeches, she often spoke before black audiences on the political and social responsibilities of black Americans in self-improvement. She encouraged respect for black women, their work, and accomplishments. In 1897 she delivered a lecture on "The Awakening of the Afro-American Woman."

News of the Matthews's mission spread, and she gained a national reputation for her charitable work. Matthews and her helpers began to meet the boats at the Old Dominion pier and assist the inexperienced young women from the rural South. Matthews was a pioneer in travelers' aid work. A series of services, like a perfect chain of white roses, was established from Norfolk to New York. The founder decided that her mission should be known as the White Rose Mission, "and I shall always feel that the girls will think of the meaning—purity, goodness and virtue—and strive to live up to our beautiful name" (Brown, 214). In 1905 the White Rose Travelers' Aid Society was established. White Rose agents, including Matthews's sister, Anna Rich, watched the docks to prevent the black women from becoming victims of a "white slave" traffic that existed from New Orleans to New York. Later, the White Rose Home, the National League for the Protection of Colored Women, and the YWCA supported each other in sponsoring travelers' aid services.

The White Rose Mission received contributions and advice from black and white patrons in the White Rose Industrial Association. Persuaded by T. Thomas Fortune, Booker T. Washington visited the White Rose Mission and spoke at a fund-raising dinner that enabled the settlement house to move to larger quarters on Eighty-sixth Street. The home contained a library that was described as "one of the most unique special libraries in New York" (Brown, 215). Many of the books, written by and about black people, were used in a class that Matthews taught on Race History.

Matthews's work was her life, and she approached it with dedication and intensity. A New York newspaper reporter once described her as "a Salvation Army field officer, a College Settlement worker, a missionary, a teacher, a preacher, a Sister of Mercy, all in one, and without being in the least conscious of it" (Brown, 215). Matthews was ahead of her time; a woman of great foresight, assertive, impatient, and sometimes misunderstood by others around her. Perhaps she realized that the tasks of "race work" that she set for herself had to be accomplished quickly. As her health gradually failed, her duties as superintendent of the White Rose Home were assumed by her able assistants.

Matthews, residing at Thirty-three Poplar Street in Brooklyn Heights and a member of Brooklyn's Saint Philips Episcopal Church, died on March 10, 1907, of tuberculosis at the age of forty-five. She was buried in the Maple Grove Cemetery, Kew Gardens, Long Island City. The White Rose Home and Industrial Association for Working Girls and Women, as it was called, remained on 95th Street for several years before moving, in 1918, to 136th Street in Harlem. A plaque outside the brownstone distinguished "The White Rose Home," and a large photograph of Victoria Matthews that dominated the entry hall are memorials to her dedicated service and inspiration to others.

References

Brown, Hallie Q. *Homespun Heroine and Other Women of Distinction*. Xenia, Ohio: Aldine Pub. Co., 1926. Reprinted. New York: Oxford University Press, 1988. 208-16.

Best, Lasalle. "History of the White Rose Mission and Industrial Association." WPA Research Paper, n. d., Schomburg Center for Research and Black Culture, New York Public Library.

Daniels, Mattie K., member White Rose Home Association, NACW Club, Empire State Federation of Women's Clubs. Interview with author.

Davis, Elizabeth, Lindsay, comp. *Lifting As They Climb.* [Washington, D.C.]: National Association of Colored Women, 1933. 232-34.

Hutson, Jean Blackwell. "Victoria Earle Matthews." *Notable American Women, 1607-1950.* Vol. 3. Cambridge: Harvard University Press, 1971. 510-11.

Lewis, Mary L. "The White Rose Industrial Association: The Friend of the Strange Girl in New York." *Messinger*, 7 (April 1925): 158.

Logan, Rayford. "Victoria Earle Matthews." *Dictionary of American Negro Biography.* Eds. Rayford Logan and Michael R. Winston. New York: Norton, 1982. 428-29.

Osofsky, Gilbert. *Harlem: The Making of a Ghetto, Negro New York, 1890-1930.* New York: Harper, 1971. 9-12, 13-15.

Richings, G. F. *Evidence of Progress Among Colored People.* Philadelphia: George S. Ferguson, 1897. 414-15.

Scruggs, Larson A. *Women of Distinction.* Raleigh: The Author, 1893. 30-32.

Obituary. *New York Age*, 14 March 1907.

A photograph of Victoria Earle Matthews is in the Print and Photo Collection, Schomburg Center for Research and Black Culture, New York Public Library.

Floris Barnett Cash

Dorothy Maynor

(1910-)

Opera singer, choral director, school founder

Dorothy Maynor, singer and founder of the Harlem School for the Arts, first came to prominence in the musical world when she auditioned for conductor Serge Koussevitzky at the Berkshire Musical Festival in Tanglewood, Massachusetts, in 1939. Impressed by Maynor's singing, Koussevitzky exclaimed, "An American Flagstad!" (Taubman, 11). He invited her to sing the next day at a picnic for members of his orchestra, guests, and music critics. Maynor sang the aria "O Sleep, Why Dost Thou Leave Me" from Handel's *Semele*, Pamina's aria "Ach Ich Fuehl's" from Mozart's *The Magic Flute*, and Charpentier's "Depuis Le Jour" from *Louise*, and immediately established herself to this highly critical audience "as one of the most gifted vocalists of the younger generation" ("Dorothy Maynor Wins Prize," 8).

Reviewing the performance that day, the *New York Times* music critic Noel Strauss commended her artistry: "Miss Maynor sang with a poise worthy of a veteran of the concert stage. . . . The feeling for phrase, for melodic outline, for a just interpretation of text and music, was that of the mature and fully equipped artist of prime rank. . . . In all numbers, Miss Maynor made known a grasp of style, a control of tone and unusual gifts as interpreter" (14). An unknown without professional experience as a concert singer, Maynor scored as one of the greatest operatic triumphs of the year. Later that year on a broadcast recap of the highlights of 1939, she was introduced as "the musical discovery of the year" (Taubman, 11).

Dorothy Leigh Maynor (born Mainor—she changed her name professionally) was born in Norfolk, Virginia, on September 3, 1910. One of three children, including a sister and brother, Maynor's childhood was happy in a close-knit family. Her parents, John J. Mainor, the pastor of a small Norfolk Methodist church, and Alice (Jefferies) Mainor, shared a strong interest in their children's musical development: "The family atmosphere was one of piety and affection; there were evenings of music and singing" (*Current Biography*, 419). Endowed with an excellent voice, Dorothy sang in the church choir, accompanied by her sister, Helen.

At age fourteen, Maynor enrolled in the preparatory school at Hampton Institute in Hampton, Virginia. After graduating in 1929, she entered the college program as a four-year scholarship student, majoring in home economics with a specialty in dress designing. Maynor's goal was to become a public school teacher. In addition to numerous extra-curricular activities, Maynor played flute in the school orchestra and sang in the Hampton choir under the direction of R. Nathaniel Dett, distinguished conductor, teacher, and composer. She toured Europe with the choir in the summer of 1929. With Dett's encouragement, Maynor studied for a music career in the public schools. Taking voice training as well as piano and orchestral instruments, she soon turned her full attention towards a professional music career. Maynor was awarded a bachelor's degree from Hampton in May 1933. In that same year she received a scholarship from the Westminster Choir College in Princeton, New Jersey, where she studied conducting and choral works with John Finley Williamson. Receiving a bachelor of music degree in 1935, Maynor returned to Hampton to teach at the Phoenix School. While there, Harriet S. Curtis, dean of women at Hampton, became her major patron and encouraged Maynor to prepare for a concert career. In the fall of 1935, Maynor went to New York to study under Wilfried Klamroth and later in 1937 was a student of John Alan Houghton. By 1939 she was preparing for her New York debut in November of that year.

Maynor Launches Concert Career

Her triumphant debut at Town Hall on November 19, 1939, with accompanist Arpad Sandor, before an enthusiastic, capacity house audience established Maynor ''as one of the most remarkable soprano voices of this rising generation'' (*Current Biography*, 420). By the end of the season she had performed in the leading concert halls in the United States.

In succeeding seasons, Maynor sang such diverse works as Strauss's ''Ruhe Meine Seele,'' Brahms's ''Meine Liebe ist gruen,'' Handel's ''Atalanta,'' and Debussy's ''Air de Lia,'' not only with the New York Philharmonic Orchestra, but also with the Boston Symphony, the Philadelphia Orchestra, and the Chicago Symphony. In the 1950s she rapidly forged an international reputation with performances in Central and South America, Australia, and Europe.

On November 19, 1950, Maynor celebrated the twentieth anniversary of her historic New York debut with a Town Hall recital. Hailed by one critic as ''one of the supreme communicative artists of our time,'' he continued, ''the commemorative program Miss Maynor offered her admirers displayed her great gifts as interpreter of songs of diverse style to the full. . . . No vocal instrument could be lovelier in timbre than Miss Maynor's was in the recital. . . . She is today . . . a great singer with a vision who not only has much to give but gives it unstintedly, straight from the heart'' (*Musical America*, 24).

After a successful twenty-five years as a concert artist, Maynor decided to retire and fulfill a lifelong dream. ''During her years of travels and tours, Dorothy Maynor never missed an opportunity to help groups devoted to increasing opportunities for Negro youth,'' reported Soria J. Dorle (''Artist Life,'' 3). As the wife of Shelby Rooks, pastor of Saint James Presbyterian Church (whom she married on June 24, 1942), she developed a music education program at the church for neighborhood children. Now she wanted to provide music instruction for underprivileged community children. In 1964 Maynor founded the Harlem School for the Arts to provide instruction in the performing arts—piano, painting, string orchestra, dance—classical and modern—and voice, with master classes for advanced singers. With a professional faculty comprised of graduates from Juilliard and the Mannes School of Music, the Harlem School for the Arts provided a comprehensive cultural education for five hundred inner-city youths. Maynor served as its director from 1964 to 1979. Acutely aware of her social responsibility, Maynor told one interviewer:

> I decided the need was for cultural education rather than play. Many groups are trying to help juvenile delinquents, but our goal was to prevent children from becoming delinquents. Children who are kept busy under supervision are not apt to get into trouble. It is the unsupervised child with nothing special to do who falls into evil ways (Fisher, 38).

Maynor's honors include the Town Hall Endowment Service Award (1940-1941); Hampton Alumni Association Award (1941) for distinguished service; honorary doctorates from Bennett College (1945), Howard University (1960), Duquesne University (1970), Oberlin College (1971), and Carnegie Mellon University (1972); and appointment to the Metropolitan Opera Board of Directors (1975).

References

Current Biography. New York: H. W. Wilson, 1951.

Dorle, Soria J. ''Artist Life.'' *High Fidelity*, August 1967.

''Dorothy Maynor Wins Prize.'' *New York Times*, 25 February 1940.

Fisher, Marjorie M. ''Community Concerts to Community Services.'' *Music Journal* 24 (November 1966): 38.

Musical America 79 (December 15, 1959): 24.

Reyus, Sylvia G. ''American Songbird.'' *Liberty* 17 (30 November 1940): 46.

Southern, Eileen. *The Music of Black Americans*. 2nd ed. New York: Norton, 1983.

Straus, Noel. ''Dorothy Maynor Berkshire Soloist.'' *New York Times*, 10 August 1939.

Story, Rosalyn M. *And So I Sing*. New York: Warner Books, 1990.

Taubman, Howard. ''Million-Dollar Voice.'' *Collier's* 105 (2 March 1940): 11.

Turner, Patricia. *Dictionary of Afro-American Performers*. New York: Garland Press, 1990. Photograph, discography, p. 265.

Collections

Patricia Turner locates collections on Dorothy Maynor in the following repositories: Hampton University archives; James Weldon Johnson Collection, Beinecke Library, Yale University; Schomburg Center for Research on Black Culture; Oral History Collection, Columbia University, and the Black Oral History Collection, Fisk University Library.

Jacquelyn L. Jackson

Adah Isaacs Menken "The Naked Lady"

(1835-1868)

Actress, poet

In Adah Isaacs Menken's short, intensely vivid life she rose to fame as one of the most alluring and celebrated actresses of her time and was considered to be a talented poet by many literary figures of the era.

Menken was born in 1835 in Chartrain (now Milneburg), Louisiana, near New Orleans. Although her life is documented in no less than four biographies and featured in dozens of articles and in the personal letters and diaries of the many famous people with whom she came into contact, there exist several conflicting accounts of her origins and early background. Her own equivocal statements in a diary and her autobiographical fragment, *Notes of My Life,* combined with incomplete records, disclose a background shrouded in the mysterious aura which became the trademark of her enigmatic personality. She died in Paris on August 10, 1868, reportedly of a malignant abscess under her left side, now presumed more likely to have been a combination of ailments, possibly including tuberculosis and cancer.

Often referred to as "The Naked Lady," "Queen of the Plaza," or "La Belle Menken," sobriquets associated with her stage career, and at times known as Dolores Adios Fuertes and Adeline McCord, two of the names with which she whimsically signed herself, Menken is most commonly identified as Adah Bertha Theodore or by her name from her first marriage, Adah Isaacs Menken, and designated of Creole heritage. Her father was Auguste Theodore, a storekeeper of mixed-blood origin, who belonged to a broad and varied ethnic group referred to at that time as *hommes de couleur libres* or "free men of color" (Bontemps and Conroy, 123). Her mother, Marie Theodore, was a native of Bordeaux. Several months after Adah Theodore's birth, Auguste Theodore died, and Marie Theodore married Campbell Josephs, who taught Latin and Greek at a private boys' academy in New Orleans. To this marriage was born Adah's sister, Annie. Most of Menken's formal education was acquired during her first twelve years, during which, under the tutelage of her stepfather, she became proficient in French, Spanish, Greek, and Latin and became an accomplished horsewoman.

Menken never lost her thirst for learning, particularly her passion for poetry, from which evolved a volume of poems, *Infelicia,* dedicated to Charles Dickens and published two months after her death. An ardent admirer, mentor, and confidante of Walt Whitman, who praised her intellect, she styled her own work after his. At various times throughout her life she published essays and poems in local newspapers, and she was admired and encouraged by an illustrious following of friends, including, along with Dickens and Whitman, Bret Harte, Dante Gabriel Rossetti, George Sand, and Theophile Gautier, and lovers, including Algernon Swinborne and Alexander Dumas *père.* While her verse remained largely unfamiliar to the general public, literary historians have nonetheless praised Menken's genuine, if uneven, talent, and she has been included in numerous biographical dictionaries of literature. Menken's love of the written word was matched by her love of the theater, to which she was drawn at an early age. Although many have judged her acting ability as limited, the stage was nevertheless the foremost arena of her success and notoriety.

"Lo! This is she that was the world's delight." These words, inscribed by Swinburne on the flyleaf of a copy of Menken's volume of poetry, reflect the effect that the provocative, enigmatic, and, above all, irresistibly charming Menken was to have on audiences in cities across the United States, in London, and in Paris. Often acclaimed for her remarkable beauty and petite, well-shaped physique, she combined her vivaciousness and intellect with a flamboyance and daring that defied the Victorian principles of her time. Menken is perhaps best described in her own words, as leading a "double life," being "possessed of *two souls*, one that lives on the surface of life, pleasing and pleased; the other as deep and as unfathomable as the ocean; a mystery to me and all who know me" (quoted in Lesser, 255-56). The surface soul was her guiding spirit on the stage and in her personal relationships that, every bit as sensational as her stage roles, included four husbands and a host of admirers and lovers.

Menken's early fascination with the stage and flair for the dramatic took a firm hold in 1853 when, at the age of eighteen, she traveled to Havana as mistress of Baron Friedrich von Eberstadt, an Austrian nobleman whose daughter she had tutored. Although Menken never performed on stage during her two years there and, in fact, turned to prostitution after the baron abandoned her, she repeatedly referred to her successful stage career in Havana, where she claimed to have been known as "Queen of the Plaza." Her actual stage debut did not take place until 1857, two years after her return to the United States from Havana and one year after her marriage in Livingston, Texas, to Alexander Isaac Menken (she added the "s" to Isaac for use in her own), a Jewish would-be violinist who worked in the family drygoods business in Cincinnati. In order to please his family, she converted to Judaism and went so far as to learn Hebrew; Adah Menken continued to avow Judaism throughout her life. It was in April 1857 that she was introduced to theatergoers in Shreveport, Louisiana as Pauline in *The Lady of Lyons.* After a successful run in Shreveport, the play was moved to New Orleans, where Menken was again well-received. She then took the role of Bianca in *Fazio* and, throughout the next year, she was steadily employed.

The "Naked Lady" Gains Popularity on Stage

Isaac Menken encouraged his wife's writing and helped launch her acting career, but her rapidly increasing popularity and love of the adulation heaped upon her by her followers drove the two apart. In New York in the spring of 1859 she and her husband separated, after which she landed a small role in *The Soldier's Daughter,* then a more demanding part in *The French Spy*. She divorced him one year later, but not before secretly marrying the boxer John Carmel Heenan, billed as "Benicia Boy." This marriage, too, ended abruptly in 1861, after the estranged Heenan, having left her pregnant and without money, went off to pursue his boxing career. After suffering a miscarriage, she returned to the stage, this time in the role that was to earn her the sobriquet "Naked Lady." She opened in June 1861 at Albany's Green Street Theater in *Mazeppa,* an adaptation of Byron's poem, in which she appeared in the title role of the noble Tartar youth captured by Poles. In the climactic scene that made her famous, she appeared to be naked—actually clad neck to ankles in flesh-colored tights—and was strapped to the back of a charging horse that carried her up a narrow runway. Audiences were at once shocked and delighted and reviewers raved about her sensational performance. Throughout the next year she starred in repeated performances of the play, which had successful runs at the Broadway Theater in New York, then in Baltimore and Philadelphia.

Menken married again in 1862, this time to Robert Henry Newell, a New York journalist famous for his satirical sketches that he signed as Orpheus C. Kerr. A staunch supporter of her literary endeavors, Newell did much to encourage her, as well as assisting in managing her theatrical pursuits. She toured the West and Midwest. Audiences flocked to see her in *Mazeppa*; she also performed in *The French Spy, Three Fast Women, Dick Turpin, Jack Sheppard,* and *Lola Montez*. Menken's success continued to grow as she traveled to London to appear in *Mazeppa* at Astley's Theatre in 1864, when she commanded the highest salary (five hundred dollars per performance) any actress had ever received. She later opened in that same theater in *The Child of the Sun,* but it was soon replaced, by popular demand, with *Mazeppa*.

While traveling in Austria, she met Johann Strauss and Emperor Franz Josef of the Austro-Hungarian Empire. Seeking revenge against von Ebersadt, who had abandoned her many years earlier, she appeared before the emperor in a tight-fitting, flesh-colored costume similar to the one designed for her role in *Mazeppa*. Although the incident earned her banishment from the empire, she felt much vindicated in the lifelong disgrace it caused the baron. Menken then returned to France with high hopes for continuing her career.

Menken's third marriage, too, had suffered from the strains of her flamboyant life, and she divorced Newell in 1865. The following year marked her final American tour as well as her fourth marriage, in New York, to Paul Barkley, a professional gambler. The marriage lasted but three days, after which the pregnant Menken returned to Europe. Her son, whose godmother was Menken's close friend and protectress, writer George Sand, was born four months later and christened Louis Dudevan Victor Emmanuel Barkley. Nothing is known about his life; it is presumed that after Menken's death, his adoptive family provided him with a new identity.

Late in 1866 Menken returned to the stage, this time appearing in *The Pirates of the Savannah* in Paris. She enjoyed a brief comeback on the stage and another amorous fling when she was romantically linked with Alexander Dumas *père,* but her newfound glory was short-lived. The aging Dumas *père* was sharply criticized for his affair with Menken, and although she received the highest salary ever paid to an actress in Paris up to that time, overwork and poor health soon took their toll. Her last performance was on May 30, 1868, in London in *The Pirates of the Savannah* at the Sadler Wells Theatre. Shortly thereafter, while rehearsing in Paris for a new production of that same play, she collapsed and was unable to continue. Initially buried in the Jewish section of Père Lachaise cemetery in Paris, her remains were later moved to Montparnasse, where her tomb carries the inscription "Thou Knowest," from Swinburne's "Ilicet." These words seal a permanent veil of mystery over the enigmatic image that Menken ardently worked to create. In the final chapter of his biography of Menken, *Enchanting Rebel,* Lesser poses the question, "Who was Adah Isaacs Menken?" He proposes that:

> It was perhaps the beautiful Menken's ironic jest, that the world which had cheered the spectacle of her bared body might never know the secret of her soul. Somewhere she must be laughing (251).

References

American Authors. New York: H. W. Wilson, 1938. 527. Includes photograph.

Bontemps, Arna, and Jack Conroy. *They Seek a City*. 1945. Reprinted as *Anyplace but Here*. New York: Hill and Wang, 1966.

Falk, Bernard. *The Naked Lady or Storm Over Adah*. London: Hutchinson, 1934.

Famous Actors and Actresses on the Stage. Vol. 2. New York: Bowker, 1975. 780-83.

Jenkins, William. "We Were Both in the Photographs." *The Baker Street Journal* 36 (1986): 1-15. Photographs, pp. 7, 9, 11, 14.

Lesser, Allen. *Enchanting Rebel: The Secret of Adah Isaacs Menken*. Philadelphia: Ruttle, Shaw, and Wetherill, 1947. Photograph, p. 128.

Lewis, Paul. *Queen of the Plaza*. New York: Funk and Wagnalls, 1964.

Monfried, Walter. "The Negro Beauty Who Bewitched Two Continents." *Negro Digest* 14 (1965): 86-90. Photographs, pp. 86-87.

The Oxford Companion to American Literature. 5th ed. New York: Oxford University Press, 1983. 487-88.

Palmer, Pamela. "Adah Isaacs Menken: From Texas to Paris." In *Legendary Ladies of Texas*. Ed. Frances Edward Abernethy. Dallas: E-Heart Press, 1981. 85-93.

Wilkins, Thurman. *Notable American Women: 1607-1950*. Vol. 2. Cambridge: Harvard University Press, 1971. 526-29.

Collections

Menken's diary, autobiographical fragment, and other personal papers are located in the Adah Isaacs Menken Collection in the Harvard University Library. Copies of these documents can also be found in the private collection of Henry Ewing Hibbard, New York City.

Carolyn R. Hodges

Louise Meriwether

(1923-)

Writer, social activist

With the publication of her first novel, *Daddy Was a Number Runner* (1970), Louise Meriwether was hailed by critics as a writer of considerable power. Receiving favorable and enthusiastic reviews, the novel was selected by the *New York Times* and *Library Journal* as one of the major books of 1970. Critic James Baldwin, who wrote the Foreword to the novel, sees the significance of the work in relation to the social climate of the times. The success of the novel lies as much in its powerful statement of what it means to be black in America as in the exploration of a menacing, oppressive world from the perspective of a young black girl: "Because she has so truthfully conveyed what the world looks like from a black girl's point of view, she has told everyone who can read or feel what it means to be a black man or woman in this country. She has achieved an assessment, in a deliberately minor key, of a major tragedy. It is a considerable tragedy" (Foreword, 7).

Publishers Weekly wrote that the novel "breaches reality and heartbreak. A tough, tender, bitter novel of a black girl struggling toward womanhood and survival" (78). Other critics praised Meriwether's technical skills; in *Saturday Review* Ruth Bauerle observes, "Miss Meriwether's skill as a writer makes it vivid to the reader. It is this considerable talent that produces a hopeful book" (62). Paule Marshall, of the *New York Times Book Review*, significantly links Meriwether to the African-American tradition:

> The novel's greatest achievement lies in the strong sense of black life that it conveys; the vitality and force behind the despair. It celebrates the positive values of the black experience: the tenderness and love that often underlie the abrasive surface of relationships . . . the humor that has long been an important part of the black survival kit, and the heroism of ordinary folk. . . . It is the exposition of these qualities as well as the book's language, which draws its beat and poetry directly from Harlem's speech, that lend such power and authenticity to Louise Meriwether's story. Honestly told and carefully crafted, it is a most important novel (28 June 1970).

The third of five children—four boys and one girl—Louise Jenkins Meriwether was born in Haverstraw, New York, on May 8, 1923, to Marion Lloyd Jenkins, a bricklayer and house painter, and Julia Jenkins, a domestic worker. During the depression years, the family moved to Brooklyn and later to Harlem where the father, unable to find work, became a number runner in order to support his family. Meriwether attended Public School Eighty-one in Harlem and graduated from Central Commercial High School in downtown Manhattan. Working briefly as a secretary, she eventually enrolled in New York University, where she received a B.A. degree in English. She married Angelo Meriwether, a teacher. Shortly thereafter they moved to the Midwest, where he secured a teaching position; later they moved to Los Angeles. After her marriage to Meriwether ended in divorce—though she continues to use the name—she later married Earle Howe, whom she subsequently divorced.

From childhood, Meriwether was firmly committed to a career as a writer. In Los Angeles, she began graduate study at UCLA, interspersing her studies with jobs as a legal secretary, a real estate salesperson, a reporter for the *Los Angeles Sentinel*, and as story analyst at Universal Studios, the first black to be hired in that position. In her writings of this period, Meriwether was already concerned with important themes—racial oppression, the effects of racism and poverty on the black family, the victimization of black Americans—that would appear in her later works: "One of her graduate theses, rewritten and published in the October 1965 issue of *Negro Digest* as "The Negro: Half a Man in a White World," is a militant rendering of the mistreatment of blacks in America and documents her early preoccupation with this subject" (Danderidge, 183). She received a master's degree in journalism from the University of California at Los Angeles in 1965. In an interview, she said of her journalism career, "I worked as a journalist first and then went back to school for a higher degree" (*Ebony*, 98).

From the mid to late 1960s, Meriwether had published

book reviews for the *Los Angeles Times* and *Los Angeles Sentinel* and numerous articles for black journals, including "James Baldwin: The Fiery Voice of the Negro Revolt," (*Negro Digest,* August 1963), "No Race Pride," (*Bronze America,* June 1964), "The Negro: Half a Man in a White World," (*Negro Digest* 14, October 1965), "The New Face of Negro History" (1965), and "The Tick End Is for Whipping" (1968). Crucial to her work at this time was the need to expose institutionalized racism and its effect on black Americans as well as to present heroic models of strong black survivors: "Admitting that she 'always had a budding romance with history,' Meriwether generally wrote articles about blacks who overcame great odds to achieve success: Matthew Henson, Leontyne Price, Grace Bumbry, and attorney Audrey Boswell" (Danderidge, 183).

A social activist, Louise Meriwether worked in Bogalusa, Louisiana, in the summer of 1965 with the Congress of Racial Equality (CORE) "as a gun toter" for a radical group, the Deacons, who were protecting blacks from harassment by the Ku Klux Klan" (McKay, 232-33). In the late 1960s she joined the Watts Writers Workshop as a staff member of the project. In 1967 when *Antioch Review* invited the group to submit its work, her fiction began appearing in that journal. "She viewed the opportunity to publish in the *Antioch Review* as a means of getting doors opened to book publishers who searched literary quarterlies for prospective novelists," says Danderidge (183). By the fall of 1967 Meriwether had published a short story, "Daddy Was a Number Runner," in *Antioch Review;* and in the spring issue of that journal a second short story, "A Happening in Barbados" appeared. The latter story drew the attention of Bill Gross, an editor with Prentice-Hall, who "admired its veracity and boldness and requested chapters from the novel in progress" (Danderidge, 183).

In between the time that the idea for the novel *Daddy Was a Number Runner* began to germinate in her mind and its actual completion, Meriwether subordinated her career as a writer for nine months to political activism. Offended by the historical inaccuracies and the distorted portrait of Nat Turner, Meriwether was motivated "to do battle with Hollywood director Norman Jewison and Twentieth Century-Fox producer David L. Wolper, the latter of whom bought the film rights of William Styron's *The Confessions of Nat Turner* (1967) for $600,000" (Danderidge, 183). With the assistance of Vantile Whitfield, founder of the Performing Arts Society of Los Angeles, she cofounded the Black Anti-Defamation Association in order to oppose the use of Styron's book as the basis of the proposed motion picture. Receiving assistance from other political activists, writers, and organizations, such as Ossie Davis, Imamu Baraka, the Los Angeles NAACP, the Urban League, Karenga's US, the Black Panther Party, the black student unions, churches, and support from historian John Henrik Clarke, who edited and published a collection of essays from black writers, in response to Styron's novel, entitled *William Styron's Nat Turner: Ten Black Writers Respond* (1968), the Black Anti-Defamation Association's battle was successful, for the movie was not produced.

Novel Reflects Racial Oppression

Written over a five-year period, *Daddy Was a Number Runner* was the first novel published from the Watts Writers Workshop. The novel explores the bitter and painful effects of racial oppression on a twelve-year-old black girl, as she struggles to survive amid the tough and bleak environment of the Harlem ghetto. An initiation story, the novel's focus is on Francie's maturation—her consciousness and the formation of her character. But the story is also a social indictment, a powerful social document of racial oppression and poverty in America and the devastating effects of racism on the lives of black families and the black community as they struggle against insurmountable odds. *Daddy Was a Number Runner* is a story of defeat and survival of the black community: While it is a "growing up" story, it:

> also belongs to all of the people who make up Francie's world—all of the men and women and children who live and hate each other, who quarrel and fight among themselves, but who are also capable of expressing concern and tenderness for each other at moments when we least expect them to do so. These are people who feel deeply about everything, because for each one, life is a constant struggle against a barrage of circumstance that threatens to destroy all of their humanity" (McKay, 210).

After the publication of the novel Meriwether was awarded two grants to continue her writing—a National Foundation of the Arts grant and a Creative Arts Service program grant.

Louise Meriwether moved back to New York in the 1970s and turned her attention to writing biographies for adolescents. Generally disappointed with the lack of black heroes in nonfiction for elementary school children, she realized that "the deliberate omission of blacks from American history has been damaging to children of both races. It reinforces in one a feeling of inferiority and in the other a myth of superiority" (Washington, 63). Meriwether has written three biographies of famous African-Americans. *The Freedom Ship of Robert Smalls* (1971) is an inspiring portrait of Robert Smalls, a slave in Beaufort, South Carolina, who escaped by hijacking a Confederate gunboat; he reached the Union fleet in safety. In later years, he returned to Beaufort, where as a prominent politician he served five consecutive terms as a representative to Congress. Meriwether's next two children's books were *The Heart Man* (1972), a story of the life and struggles of Daniel Hale Williams, a nineteenth century black physician, surgeon, and pioneer who performed the first successful heart surgery in 1893 and opened the first hospital in Chicago in 1891 for training black nurses and treating patients of all races. In *Don't Ride the Bus on Monday: The Rosa Parks Story* (1973), Meriwether traces the life and courageous heroism of Rosa Parks, whose refusal to give up her seat on a segregated bus in Montgomery,

Alabama, spurred the famous Alabama bus boycott that precipitated the civil rights movement of the late 1950s and 1960s.

Meriwether has remained strongly active socially and politically. She is an organizer and member of Black Concern, an anti-Apartheid group, seeking to influence black Americans against breaking the Organization of African Unity (OAU) boycott against the Republic of South Africa. Along with coorganizer John Henrik Clarke, she has helped publish a pamphlet, *Black Americans Stay Out of South Africa,* and spoken on radio and at the United Nations in an effort to gain support of others against apartheid.

Louise Meriwether has taught fiction workshops at the Frederick Douglass Creative Arts Center in New York for several years and writing courses at Sarah Lawrence College. She has produced one short story, "That Girl from Creektown," (*Black Review,* 1972), based on her CORE experiences in Louisiana. The story focuses on the explosive racial tensions in Creektown, Mississippi, and on the social issues that a young black woman faces in this racially-charged environment. In recent years she has written an unpublished novel and completed the research for a historical novel about the Civil War and Reconstruction.

References

Baldwin, James. Foreword. In Louise Meriwether. *Daddy Was a Number Runner*. Englewood Cliffs, N.J.: Prentice-Hall, 1970.

Bauerle, Ruth. Review of *Daddy Was a Number Runner. Saturday Review* 33 (23 May 1970): 51-62.

Danderidge, Rita B. "Louise Meriwether." In *Dictionary of Literary Biography*. Vol. 33, *Afro-American Fiction Writers after 1955*. Eds. Thadious M. Davis and Trudier Harris. Detroit: Gale Research, 1984. 182-86.

Ebony 25 (July 1970): 98-103.

Marshall, Paule. Review of *Daddy Was a Number Runner. New York Times Book Review*, 28 June 1970.

McKay, Nellie. "Afterword." Louise Meriwether. *Daddy Was a Number Runner*. New York: Englewood Cliffs, N.J.: Prentice-Hall, 1970.

Meriwether, Louise. "A Happening in Barbados." In *Black-Eyed Susans*. Ed. Mary Helen Washington. New York: Anchor Press, 1975.

———. *Daddy Was a Number Runner*. Englewood Cliffs, N.J.: Prentice-Hall, 1970.

Publishers Weekly 192 (19 January 1970): 78.

Jacquelyn Jackson

Lyda Moore Merrick

(1890-1987)

Journal founder, editor

Education, compassion, and success were integral parts of Lyda Moore Merrick's illustrious birthright. Later in her life she said, "My father passed a torch to me which I have never let go out. We are blessed to serve" (Wilson, 70). The depth of this belief and the breadth of its vision is shown in the successful works of her life.

Merrick was born the older daughter of Aaron McDuffie Moore and Sarah McCotta (Dancy) Moore in Durham, North Carolina. Aaron Moore, originally from Columbus County, North Carolina, had studied medicine at the Leonard Medical School, then a part of Shaw University in Raleigh, North Carolina. In 1888, after his graduation, he became the first black physician in Durham. "Cottie" Dancy Moore, the daughter of a well-known political leader, was born and grew up in Tarboro, North Carolina. She attended Saint Augustine's College and became a teacher. While teaching in Charlotte, she met Aaron Moore when he attended a medical conference there. They were later married and made their home in Durham. In 1898, Aaron Moore, John Merrick—Lyda's future father-in-law—and others founded the North Carolina Mutual Life Insurance Company in Durham. This is the largest business owned by blacks in the United States. Aaron Moore, John Merrick, and Charles C. Spaulding, a nephew of Moore's, operated and controlled the business. Under their leadership the insurance company prospered, as did the black community. The city of Durham became well-known for its black enterprise. In 1901, with both moral and financial support from businessman Washington Duke, Aaron Moore founded Lincoln Hospital with the intent that black doctors could practice there and black nurses could be trained. It was a two-story wooden structure built on Proctor Street. In 1910, with the wheels of progress steadily turning, North Carolina Central University was founded as the the first state-supported black liberal arts college in the South. The college was under the leadership of James Shepard, also one of the founders of North Carolina Mutual Life Insurance Company.

Being an educated man, Moore was greatly concerned that blacks could not use the public library facilities. His words, as recalled by Lyda Merrick years later, were: "If only my people had something to read!" (Wilson, 72). With this incentive, he started a small library in the basement of the White Rock Baptist Church, which he and his family attended. The library project soon demanded more space, and he, businessman Stanford Warren, and others secured larger properties for housing the library. Upon moving into new quarters, the small church library became the Durham Colored Library, a first of its kind. One corner of the library was designated for the blind; sighted persons read to them there. From its small beginnings in the church basement, this facility has continued to grow, and today it is known as the Stanford Warren branch of the Durham County Library system. Upon her father's death, Lyda Moore Merrick became the chairperson of the library board. It was here, in the corner for the blind, that Merrick's deaf and sightless friend, John Carter Washington, first pointed out to her the need for a Braille news publication geared to a black audience. Being reared in this atmosphere of love, success, enlightened warmth, and educated awareness was surely the major influence in Merrick's destiny, and perhaps the foundation upon which she formed the creed of her life:

> "When you see a need, fill it to the best of your ability" (leaflet, *Negro Braille Magazine*, n.d.).

Merrick grew up and was educated through the ninth grade in Durham. She and her sister, Mattie Louise, were then sent to Scotia Seminary in Concord, North Carolina, to finish high school. After graduation, both girls attended Fisk University in Nashville, Tennessee, graduating magna cum laude in 1911, with Merrick earning a degree in music. They were encouraged by their father to continue their educations at Columbia University. After further study at Columbia, Merrick returned home and began teaching private piano students. Her talent as a portrait artist was also greatly appreciated by her family and friends. She continued painting until shortly before her death.

On November 20, 1916, Lyda Vivian Moore married Edward Richard Merrick of Durham. Edward Merrick was treasurer of the North Carolina Mutual Life Insurance Company. They had two daughters, Vivian Merrick Sansom, who resides in Raleigh, and Constance Merrick Watts, who resides in Durham. As well as being a wife, mother, and homemaker, Lyda Merrick was very active in school, church, and community activities, and was always an avid member of the North Carolina Federation of Negro Women's Clubs. Edward and Lyda Merrick not only provided a wonderful home for themselves and their daughters, but they also willingly shared it with other family members and friends who needed a place to stay while either visiting or attending college in the area.

Braille Magazine for Blacks Founded

In 1951, with John Washington's words ringing within her, Merrick, being true to her creed of filling a need, began investigating the possibilities for publishing a Braille magazine geared to the black audience. Her queries led her to the American Printing House for the Blind of Louisville, Kentucky. With the help of these editors, she collected material for the first issue and mailed it to Louisville. There it was set in Braille and mailed to blind readers. The first issue of the *Negro Braille Magazine* was published in June 1952. Today, the magazine is published by the National Braille Press in Boston, Massachusetts. The original purpose of the magazine was "to give the Negro blind a bridge between themselves and the sighted world" (leaflet, *NBM*, n.d.). Though this philosophy remains the same, today the magazine is available to all blind readers, regardless of color. In filling this need, Lyda Merrick became the founder and first editor of the *Negro Braille Magazine*, following in her family's footsteps with yet another "first of its kind." Merrick said of the magazine:

> I was destined to do it. It was in my heart and in my lap, and I did the best I could do day by day (Wilson, 72).

Merrick served as unpaid editor of the magazine for eighteen years. She financed it from contributions, solicitations, support from her husband, and from her own personal resources. In 1969, she resigned as editor and Charlotte Hackett assumed the position. The magazine continued to make great progress, and a management and editorial board was formed. Hackett resigned in 1975 and was succeeded by Margret Whisenton. The present editor is Ila Blue of Durham. Approximately ten years ago (circa 1980) the name of the magazine was changed to the *Merrick-Washington Magazine for the Blind* in honor of Lyda Merrick and John C. Washington.

The magazine, printed in grade two Braille, has seventy-six pages and carries no advertising. Its mailing list includes readers from all parts of the United States and many foreign countries. The contents consist of articles excerpted from nationally known periodicals, listed under various subject headings such as National and International News, History, Editorials, Entertainment, People, and others. There is also an editor's column and an "Our Reader's Write" section, edited by the associate editor, plus announcements of special interest to readers. The magazine is free to blind readers upon request. Institutions and organizations serving the visually impaired are also eligible for this service (leaflet, *NBM*, n.d.). The primary source of funding for the magazine comes from donations of the Durham Colored Library Board, even though the library is now merged into the county system. The next largest single financial contributor is the North Carolina Federation of Negro Women's Clubs. Merrick was a key figure in both of these organizations and remained an influential participant until her death. Civic organizations and interested individuals also provide financial support to the magazine.

Lyda Moore Merrick's impressive list of awards and honors include the Artra Achievement Award "for outstanding and unselfish efforts for the nation's blind," 1969; the Daughter's of Dorcas Plaque; the Negro Braille Magazine Plaque for founding and fostering the magazine, 1952-1977; Links, Inc., of Durham for "dedication to bringing light to many in darkness," 1969; recognition by Walter Cronkite, CBS News, 1969; the Twenty-fifth Anniversary Celebration of the Negro Braille Magazine dedicated to her honor, June, 1977; honorary membership in the North Carolina Library Association, 1977; and honorary membership in the Delta Sigma Theta Sorority 1979.

After Edward Merrick's death on February 12, 1967, Lyda Moore Merrick continued to carry on the many projects they had begun. In 1977 she moved to the home of her daughter, Constance M. Watts, in Durham. She remained there until her death on February 14, 1987. She was ninety-seven years old. Constance Merrick Watts characterizes her mother as being a person "who loved her family, and who was always interested and involved in church and community projects" (Interview with Constance Merrick Watts, October 1990). Viewing her many accomplishments, an afterword might be: How deep was her love; how bright and far reaching was her torch!

References

Negro Braille Magazine. Leaflet. n.d.

Watts, Mrs. Constance Merrick. Interview with author, October 1990.

Wilson, Emily Herring. *Hope and Dignity.* Philadelphia: Temple University Press, 1983.

Collections

Records of the beginning of *Negro Braille Magazine* as well as current editions are being collected in the Moorland-Spingarn Research Center, Howard University, Washington, D.C. Inquiries concerning the magazine should be addressed to: *The Merrick-Washington Magazine for the Blind,* 319 Wayne Circle, Durham, NC 27707.

Information on Lydia Moore Merrick can be found in the Biography File, Fisk University Library, Nashville, Tennessee.

Phyllis Wood

Emma F. G. Merritt

(1860-1933)

Singer, educator, lecturer, social worker

Emma Frances Grayson Merritt was an educator of educators, a lecturer, social worker, and community volunteer. She was just three years old when her parents, John Merritt and Sophia (Cook) Merritt, brought her to Washington, D.C., from Dumfries (Cherry Hill), Prince William County, Virginia. The third girl in a family of four daughters and three sons, she was born January 11, 1860, two years before Abraham Lincoln began to advocate publicly the emancipation of the slaves. By the time the Merritt family arrived in Washington, D.C., the Civil War was nearing an end. Slaves in the District of Columbia had been emancipated in April 1862, and in "1864 Congress passed legislation to provide funds for a free public school for the great influx of newly freed slaves" (Caulton, B-4). In the public schools of Washington, Emma Merritt fostered a love for learning that would propel her into one of the District of Columbia's most outstanding educators.

Merritt's family can still be traced to the District of Columbia area today. Her erudite nature has had profound influence on her family, many of whom have become educators. Her scholarly influence is particularly evinced in two sisters who are great-nieces, Estelle Wormley Taylor, director of graduate expository writing at Howard University in Washington, D.C., and Emma Merritt Wormley Thomas, associate professor of English at Montgomery College in Montgomery County, Maryland. In the tradition of their great-aunt, both sisters were educated in the segregated public schools of the District of Columbia. After high school, they attended Miner's Teachers College, an academy that was originally established for black girls in 1851 by Myrtilla Miner, a white woman from New York. Presently, the school is a part of the University of the District of Columbia. Both educators earned master's degrees from Howard University, and Taylor went on to receive her doctorate from Catholic University in Washington, D.C.

Thomas, goddaughter and namesake of Emma Frances Grayson Merritt, has fond but sketchy memories of the history of the Merritt family. In a telephone conversation with the writer (n.d.) she recalls that "Aunt Nen," as she was fondly called by her great-nieces, described her mother, Sophia Cook Merritt, as a Cherokee Indian and her father, John Merritt, as "very dignified in his bearing with jet-black skin and a silky white beard." Her sisters were Georgianna C. Merritt Jordan, Gertrude Merritt Payne, and Matt or Matilda Merritt. Robert Merritt, John Merritt, Jr., and Washington Merritt were her brothers. Thomas also has fond memories of a steamer trunk of books given to the sisters by their great-aunt, which became a "treasure trove" to them. She humorously recalls her great-aunt being referred to as an old maid because in those days female teachers were not expected to marry. Although she had gentlemen callers, she never made a matrimonial commitment to any of them, preferring instead to live out her existence as a dedicated career woman.

The African-American church in the days following the Civil War was a many-sided institution. It fed the spirits of the newly-freed slaves but also metamorphosed itself into a makeshift classroom to educate the minds of those freed slaves. Some of the monies that Congress allocated for public education found their way to the Ebenezer African Methodist Episcopal (AME) Church (Ebenezer United Methodist today) at 420 D Street Southeast, the first school attended by Merritt. In 1875 she graduated from "the Old M Street High School, later Dunbar High" (Taylor, 434), or possibly from the Washington High School. The years 1883-1887 were spent in collegiate normal preparation at Howard University under professors James M. Gregory and Wiley Lane. During 1887-1890 she studied at Columbian University (George

Washington University today), in Washington, D.C. but *Who's Who in Colored America* records 1898 as the date of attendance. The years 1889-1892 were spent pursuing a specialization in mathematics at Howard University. From 1895 to 1898 she studied psychology, child study, and sociology under professor Craven at the Columbian University.

During 1898-1901 she studied mathematics at the Cook County Normal School in Chicago, Illinois, as well as psychology, child study, and primary methods. In 1901 she graduated from the Phoebe Hearst (Kindergarten) Training School in Washington, D.C. In 1913-1914 she studied at the Berlitz School of Languages, Paris, France, and Washington, D.C., where she obtained credit for extension courses, and she also received credit for courses taken at Columbia University in New York City. As a salute to her intellectual pursuits and achievements and her community service, the board of trustees of Howard University conferred upon her an honorary degree of master of arts in June 1925.

Merritt was fifteen years old in 1875 when she began her career as educator in the public schools of Washington, D.C. The next fifty-five years would be a gradual progression of promotions and achievements. Her first assignment was first grade teacher at the Stevens School at Twenty-first and K streets Northwest, where she volunteered her services to begin the first summer school. In 1887, after a brief span of eleven years, she assumed the principalship of the Banneker Elementary School on Third Street Northwest. In 1896 at the Garnet School on U Street, she established the first kindergarten for African-American students, equipped and maintained it, and raised the teachers' salary to assure its success.

System Supervisor Revolutionizes Teaching Methods

Merritt was promoted to primary instructor and director of grades one through four in 1898 and retained this position until 1925. The zenith of her career came in 1926 when she was appointed supervising principal of the colored school system of the District of Columbia, divisions ten and eleven, or possibly the eleven schools that comprised divisions ten through thirteen (divisions one to nine were for whites only).

Carter G. Woodson, known to many as the father of African-American history, credits Merritt with bringing teaching methodology in the District of Columbia into the twentieth century. She developed a primary department for black American students and modernized instruction in that department; organized demonstration and observation schools to improve teachers and teaching methods; grouped students homogeneously for teaching purposes; innovated observational study, excursions, visits to interesting points and places in and about the city (that is, she is the innovator of field trips); and introduced silent reading in the schools before any provision had been made for it in the curricula. Moreover, she corresponded with former students who had secured teaching positions in the rural South and provided them with new ideas in education.

Between the years 1898 and 1932 Merritt was a demonstrator in modern educational work and lectured as an institute speaker at the State College in Delaware, Howard University, Cheyney Institute in Pennsylvania, Manassas Industrial School and Hampton Institute in Virginia, the Normal School in Baltimore (Coppin State College today), West Virginia State College, and Dallas Institute in Texas.

The superintendent of schools in the District of Columbia at that time, F. W. Ballou, commented, "Miss Merritt is demonstrating the last word in education. Go and see it" (Woodson, 245). On another occasion, he remarked that "Miss Merritt has blazed a new trail in modern education." Because he perceived her acute sensitivity in the cultivation of young minds, "he asked the Board of Education to establish two laboratory or demonstration schools in which her modern methods could be used and observed" (Taylor, 435).

Merritt's civic contributions complemented her numerous achievements in public education. In 1898 she organized and presided over the Teachers' Benefit and Annuity Association of Washington, D.C., which had capital of approximately $35,000 in 1932, and she organized and presided over the Prudence Crandal Association for needy children. From 1905 to 1933 she was financial chairperson of the Phillis Wheatley YWCA. During the years 1910-1925 she served as director of the executive board of the Southwest Social Settlement House. From 1929 to 1933 she was director of the Mother-Child Center. From 1930 to 1933 she was president of the District of Columbia branch of the NAACP and a member of its executive committee. From 1931 to 1933 she was treasurer of the Banneker Boys Club, and she was treasurer of the Lend-a-Hand Club, which helped unwed mothers. In addition, she was a supporter of the Association for the Study of Negro Life and History and was associated with the Ionia R. Whipper Home for Unwed Mothers.

Merritt was chosen as a delegate from the Colored Women's league to attend a joint assembly of the League and the Federation of Afro-American Women. The two organizations merged, and she became a founding member in the National Association of Colored Women's Clubs (NACW), which was dedicated to the improvement of the moral, intellectual, and social growth of colored women. The NACW held its first convention in Nashville, Tennessee, on September 15-17, 1887.

Merritt's travels were not limited to visits to institutions to demonstrate modern teaching methods; she traveled for pleasure as well, visiting many United States cities, northern Mexico, the southern provinces of Canada, the British Isles, France, Switzerland, and Belgium.

The fact that she was a political independent sheds light on her as being autonomous, a free thinker, and a self-made woman. Religiously, she preferred to worship as a Congregationalist.

Merritt resided at two addresses in the District of Columbia during her lifetime, 1913 Nineteenth Street Northwest and 1960 Tenth Street Northwest, which has been demolished to make room for the playground of the current Shaw Junior High School. In 1930 she retired from the formal vocation of education; she lived three years after her retirement. She was under the care of physician Ionia R. Whipper at 5ll Florida Avenue Northwest from March 12, 1933, until she expired at her Tenth Street address on June 8, 1933, at the age of seventy-three. Death occurred at 10:20 P.M.; the cause of death was a malignant stomach tumor and an aneurysm of the thoracic aorta. A liver tumor was a contributing cause of death. She was survived by a sister (Gertrude Paynel), a niece, nephew, and two great-nieces.

The Board of Education of the District of Columbia did not forget Merritt's tireless dedication to a progressive school system. In the community of Deanwood, "a triangle of about three square miles on Washington's northwest border with Maryland" (Caulton, B-4), where Merritt's great-nieces grew up, an elementary school was posthumously dedicated in her memory on November 10, 1944. This honor was most prestigious, and one that would have pleased her. That school was demolished in 1976 to make room for the new one that replaced it. The new school sits on the old playground of the original Merritt Elementary. Construction of the new school began in 1974, and students and faculty moved into the new building in February 1976. The new Emma Frances Merritt Elementary School is located at Fiftieth and Hayes Streets Northeast, and its current principal is Nancy Shannon. A photograph of Merritt that ironically seems to maintain an Argus-eyed watch over the students and faculty hangs in the entrance of the Merritt Elementary School.

Carter G. Woodson wrote in his essay in *Opportunity*, "There is no doubt that the District of Columbia has never had a teacher whose influence has been more widely exerted for the enlightenment of the Negroes at large . . . and though her active influence . . . ends, her silent influence will go on forever" (245).

References

Afro-American Encyclopedia. Vol. 6. North Miami, Fla.: Educational Book Publishers, 1974.

Blackburn, Helen M. "Emma F[rances] G[rayson] Merritt." *Dictionary of American Negro Biography*. Edited by Rayford W. Logan and Michael R. Winston. New York: Norton, 1982.

Caulton, Jane R. "Innovative D.C. Teacher Started Family Tradition." *Washington Times* (8 February 1990): B-1, 4.

Colored Y.W.C.A. Annual Reports, 1907-09.

Contributions of Black Women to America. Vol. 2. Edited by Marianna W. Davis. Columbia, S.C.: Kenday Press, 1982.

Dannett, Sylvia G. L. *Profiles of Negro Womanhood*. Vol. 1: *1600-1900*. Yonkers, N.Y.: Educational Heritage, 1964.

Du Bois, W. E. B., ed. "Along the Color Line." *Crisis* 37 (September 1930). Reprinted. New York: Arno Press, 1969.

"Educators of the First Half Century of Public Schools of the District of Columbia." *Journal of Negro History* 17 (April 1932): 131.

Franklin, John Hope. *From Slavery to Freedom*. 3rd ed. New York: Vintage Books, 1969.

Low, W. Augustus, and Virgil A. Clift, eds. *Encyclopedia of Black America*. New York: McGraw-Hill, 1981.

Ploski, Harry A., and Warren Marr II, eds. *The Negro Almanac*. New York: Bellwether, 1976.

Quarles, Benjamin. *The Negro in the Making of America*. Rev. Ed. London: Macmillan, 1969.

Robinson, Omelia. "Contributions of Black American Academic Women to American Higher Education." Ph.D. dissertation. Wayne State University, 1978.

Taylor, Estelle. "Emma Frances Grayson Merritt: Pioneer in Negro Education." *Negro History Bulletin* 38 (August-September 1975): 434-35.

Thomas, Emma Merritt Wormley. Interview with Gerri Bates.

Wesley, Charles Harris. *The History of the National Association of Colored Women's Clubs*. Washington, D.C.: NACW, 1984.

Who's Who in Colored America. 3rd ed. Brooklyn: Who's Who in Colored America, 1932.

Woodson, Carter G. "Emma Frances Grayson Merritt." *Opportunity* 18 (August 1930): 244-45. Photograph, p. 244.

Gerri Bates

May Miller

(1899-)

Playwright, educator, poet

May Miller, one of the most celebrated women playwrights of the Harlem Renaissance, turned to poetry after a full career as a teacher and playwright and achieved equal acclaim as a poet. In her writing, Miller deals with humanism and social and political issues, and she questions the morality and humanity of the society in which we all live.

May Miller was born January 26, 1899, in Washington, D.C. One of five children born to Kelly Miller and the former

Annie Mae Butler of Baltimore, Miller grew up in the old John M. Langston house on Howard University's campus, where her father was a prominent professor and dean. The first black to attend John Hopkins University, Kelly Miller's position as a nationally-recognized sociologist, essayist, and educator put him in close social and political contact with such eminent black Americans as W. E. B. Du Bois, Mary Church Terrell, Paul Laurence Dunbar, Booker T. Washington, Lucy Diggs Slowe, Jessie Fauset, Carter G. Woodson, William Stanley Braithwaite, and Charles S. Johnson. A strong advocate of preserving African and African-American culture and history, Kelly Miller, along with a committee that included Benjamin Brawley, Dorothy B. Porter (Wesley), and Charles Wesley, established the Moorland Spingarn Collection at Howard during the 1930s.

In addition to these accomplishments, Kelly Miller was a published poet and orator who could recite many poems. His creativity and oratorical skills influenced young May Miller. Her life was also impacted by her attendance at the noted M Street School (later Paul Laurence Dunbar High School), where she studied under playwrights Mary P. Burrill and Angelina Grimké, two of the earliest black American female dramatists of the twentieth century. Under Burrill's tutelage, May Miller was encouraged to write her first play, *Pandora's Box,* which was submitted and published in the *School Progress* magazine in 1914.

Miller graduated from Dunbar High School in 1916 and entered Howard University that same year. She received further encouragement to continue her dramatic writing through the Howard Drama Club (later the Howard Players) under the direction of professors Alain Locke and Montgomery T. Gregory. Her years at Howard also included writing essays. For the one-hundredth-anniversary commemoration of Frederick Douglass, she wrote and delivered an essay that was sponsored by Howard's History Club. Academically at the helm of her class, she earned a bachelor of arts degree in 1920. In recognition of her abilities as a playwright, Howard awarded Miller a prize for her one-act play, *Within the Shadows*. The honor was significant, because Miller was the first student at Howard to win such an outstanding award.

The 1920s and 1930s were Miller's most prolific and productive years. After graduating from Howard, she taught drama, speech, and dance at the Frederick Douglass High School in Baltimore. Although she wrote the bulk of her plays and various essays while at Douglass, it was in Baltimore that Miller joined the Krigwa Players. Originated by Du Bois during the mid-1920s, the Krigwa Players was an early "Little Negro Theatre" group dedicated to "acting out plays that were written by Negroes." Krigwa groups were located in such cities as New York, Washington, D.C., and Denver. As a member of the group, Miller not only directed but acted as well; she performed in poet/playwright Georgia Douglas Johnson's *Blue Blood* and Willis Richardson's *The Broken Banjo*. Her classmates included Frank Horne, Sam Popel, Randolph Edmonds, Leander Hill, and Ruth Cornell.

Miller's creative impulses were further stimulated by the vitality of Georgia Douglas Johnson's "S Street Salon," which was a gathering place at Johnson's Washington home for writers to share their works. Miller commuted on weekends to S Street, where she cultivated an array of friendships among such writers as Jean Toomer, Langston Hughes, Alice Dunbar Nelson, Countee Cullen, Alain Locke, Mary P. Burrill, Jessie Redmon Fauset, Carter G. Woodson, Marita Bonner, Willis Richardson, and Zora Neale Hurston. Through the activity of the salon, Miller and Johnson formed a strong bond of friendship. Miller was at Johnson's deathbed in 1966. Also, during this period, Miller met Zora Neale Hurston and encouraged her to transfer from Morgan State University to Howard University, thus marking the beginning of another personal and literary friendship.

During the summer months, Miller studied playwriting at Columbia University under the eminent theater scholar Frederick Koch. Koch, who was also the teacher of playwrights Paul Green and Elizabeth Lay, recognized Miller's talents and encouraged her to stress the "Negro folk idiom." He was very pleased when Miller's play, *Scratches* (1929), was published in the University of North Carolina's *Caroline Magazine*.

In 1925 her play *The Bog Guide* placed third in the Urban League's *Opportunity* contest, an important vehicle for aspiring young Negro writers of the 1920s. *Opportunity* also awarded her an honorable mention the next year for *The Cuss'd Thing*.

During the 1930s Miller wrote history plays in order to educate her students at Douglass. She, along with many of the black writers of the time, saw drama as a vehicle for effecting social change and for educating the young about African-American history. In 1934 Carter G. Woodson encouraged Miller and the noted playwright Willis Richardson to collaborate on an anthology dramatizing the lives of black heroes and heroines. As a result of this encouragement, in 1935 *Negro History in Thirteen Plays* was published. Miller contributed the plays *Harriet Tubman, Sojourner Truth, Christophe's Daughters,* and *Samory* to the anthology and thereby garnered national recognition for herself.

Plays Focus on Social and Political Issues

Like many of the black women writers of the 1920s and 1930s, Miller focused on social and political issues. Yet at the same time, her work stands out from those of other black women writers because she dared to venture from the home; and in several plays she incorporated white characters in major roles. While most of her contemporaries utilized an all-black cast, with the action occurring primarily in the home and in the United States, the action of Miller's plays occurred as far away as Africa and Haiti, as in *The Bog Guide* and *Christophe's Daughters*. Miller included white characters in many of her works as an effective method of dealing with racial issues of the time; for example, *Stragglers in the Dust* (1930) explores the issue of blacks in World War I and *Nails and Thorns* (1933) focuses on the topic of lynching.

Along with Georgia Douglas Johnson and Eulalie Spence,

Miller was recognized as one of the most outstanding black playwrights during the Harlem Renaissance. She was also the most widely-published black female playwright of her era. Of her fifteen plays, nine were published; many of them were staged at numerous colleges and little-theater groups throughout the country. Miller wrote her last play, *Freedom's Children on the March,* in 1943. A dramatic folk ballad with music, this play was performed at the Frederick Douglass commencement. The same year, Miller retired from the Baltimore Public School System. Feeling that she no longer had a platform to perform her plays, Miller began to focus on poetry. She moved to Washington, D.C., with her husband, John Sullivan, whom she had married in 1940. John Sullivan was a high school principal in Alexandria, Virginia, when the two met, and he later became an accountant for the United States Postal Service. He was always supportive of Miller's aspirations as an author and would often attend various literary engagements.

Miller's career as a poet is just as outstanding and expansive as her life as a playwright. Upon returning to Washington, D.C., in 1943, she joined a poetry workshop conducted by Inez Boulton, who came to Washington after an affiliation in Chicago with *Poetry Magazine*. Miller says, "This workshop which was located at New Hampshire and S allowed me the opportunity to meet the great creative space with other poets and artists" (Interview with May Miller Sullivan, 1 August 1986). Those who frequented the workshop included Ester Popel Shaw, Elsie Austin Dorothy Weaver, Paul Lawson, founder of Charioteer Press, and Owen Dodson. In her reminiscences, Miller refers to this period as the golden years.

Miller's poetry speaks of humanist issues. Like her plays, her poetry also poses important moral questions for a society that continues to embrace non-humanist values. Her poems have been published in many periodicals, anthologies, and journals; she has conducted readings throughout the Washington, D.C., area at many notable institutions, including the Smithsonian, the Library of Congress, and the Folger Library.

While Miller has given up playwriting, the 1980s and 1990s have seen a resurgence in the production and publication of her plays, many of which appear in recent anthologies—some for the first time. Written in 1930 and recently published, *Stragglers in the Dust* premiered in 1991 at the University of Illinois at Urbana-Champaign. May Miller's career is distinguished with many honors. In 1986 she was presented the Mister Brown Award (Mr. William Brown was manager of the African Company in New York from 1816 to 1823) for Excellence in Drama and Poetry by the National Conference of African-American Theatre at Morgan State University in Baltimore.

Miller resides in Washington, D.C., and continues to write poetry in her home.

Miller's published plays are *The Bog Guide* (1925), in *Plays and Pageants; Christophe's Daughters* (1935) in *Negro History in Thirteen Plays* and *Black Female Playwrights; The Cussed Things* (1926); *Freedom's Children on the March* (1943); *Graven Images* (1929) in *Plays and Pageants,* and *Black Theatre U.S.A.*; *Harriet Tubman* (1935), in *Negro History in Thirteen Plays* and *Black Female Playwrights; Moving Caravans* (193?); *Nails and Thorns* (1933), in *The Roots of African-American Theatre; Pandora's Box* (1914) in *School's Progress; Riding the Goat* (1925), in *Plays and Pageants, Black Female Playwrights,* and *Wines in the Wilderness; Samory* (1935), in *Negro History in Thirteen Plays; Scratches* (1929), in *Carolina* 49 (April 1929); *Sojourner Truth* (1935), in *Negro History in Thirteen Plays* and *Black Female Playwrights; Stragglers in the Dust* (1930), in *Black Female Playwrights;* and *Within the Shadow* (1920). Her poetry includes *Collected Poetry* (Detroit: Lotus Press, 1989); *The Clearing and Beyond* (Washington, D.C.: Charioteer Press, 1974); *Dust of Uncertain Joy* (Lotus Press, 1975); *Halfway to the Sun* (Washington, D.C.: Washington Writer's Publishing House, 1981); *Into the Clearing* (Charioteer Press, 1959); and *The Ransomed Wait* (Lotus Press, 1983).

References

Brown-Guillory, Elizabeth, ed. *Wines in the Wilderness.* Westport, Conn.: Greenwood Press, 1990.

Hatch, James V., and Leo Hamalian, eds. *The Roots of African-American Theatre.* Detroit: Wayne State University Press, 1991.

Hatch, James V., and Ted Shines, ed. *Black Theatre U.S.A.: Forty-five Plays by Black Americans, 1847-1974.* New York: Free Press, 1974.

Miller, May, and Willis Richardson, eds. *Negro History in Thirteen Plays.* Washington, D.C.: Associated Publishers, 1935.

Perkins, Kathy Ann, ed. *Black Female Playwrights: An Anthology of Plays Before 1950.* Bloomington: Indiana University Press, 1989.

Randolph, Ruth Elizabeth, and Lorraine Eleana Roses, ed. *Harlem Renaissance and Beyond: Literary Biographies of 100 Black Women Writers, 1900-1945.* Boston: G. . Hall, 1989.

Richardson, Willis, ed. *Plays and Pageants from the Life of the Negro.* Washington, D.C.: Associated Publishers, 1930.

Sullivan, May Miller. Interview, 1 August 1986.

Kathy A. Perkins

Florence Mills

(1896-1927)

Entertainer

Florence Mills, the leading black American musical comedy singer and dancer of the Jazz Age and the Harlem Renaissance, was born January 25, 1896, in Washington, D.C., to John Winfree and Nellie (Simons) Winfree. She died from paralytic ileus and peritonitis in New York City on November 1, 1927.

Born in slavery in Amherst County, Virginia, the Winfrees migrated to Washington from Lynchburg because of economic depression in the tobacco industry where both were employed. They settled first in a middle-class neighborhood on K Street, where Florence was born, but were soon forced to move to Goat Alley, one of the capital's most poverty-stricken, unhealthy, and crime-ridden black slums. John Winfree worked sporadically as a day laborer and Nellie Winfree took in laundry to keep their family together. Both were illiterate, and even in a city with unusual opportunities for people of color, their prospects and futures were limited.

"Baby Florence," however, demonstrated early her extraordinary gifts for singing and dancing, and as young as age three appeared at local theater amateur hours, where she won prizes. She was even invited to entertain the British ambassador, Lord Poncefote, and his guests. The child received public recognition that no doubt contributed to her developing sense of self-worth, and she became an important source of her family's income, which imbued her with a profound sense of responsibility for those around her.

Florence Mills

The high point of Mills's childhood occurred in 1903 when she appeared as an extra attraction in the road company production of Bert Williams and George Walker's *Sons of Ham,* where she sang "Miss Hannah from Savannah." She was taught the song by Aida Overton Walker, the great cakewalk dancer and ragtime singer who had sung it in the original show. Walker was a beautiful, sophisticated, and highly talented star who took time with a ghetto child, thereby becoming Mills's mentor and role model. Walker demonstrated that blacks with ability and determination could find a successful vocation in entertainment.

As a result of her abilities, Mills was hired at about age eight by the traveling white vaudeville team of Bonita and Hearn, entertainers who used her as a singing and dancing "pickaninny" in their routine. Mills may well have felt both gratitude for the opportunity to work on the stage and support her family as well as resentment at the crude exploitation.

At age fourteen, Mills and her sisters Maude and Olivia organized their own traveling song-and-dance act as the Mills Sisters. They played the East Coast colored vaudeville houses and received good notices in the black press for their lively performances. Sometimes dressed in male attire, Florence Mills specialized in traditional ballads and the popular tunes of the day. In 1912 she contracted a brief marriage with James Randolph.

Just before World War I, Mills found herself in Chicago weary of long hours, low pay, and the difficult traveling conditions all blacks faced. She decided to move from vaudeville to cabaret and through Ada "Bricktop" Smith obtained a job at the notorious Panama Cafe on State Street. In the heart of the South Side's honky-tonk and red-light district, the Panama was a black and tan club well known for sexual liaisons across the color line.

With Bricktop, Cora Green, and occasionally others, Mills formed the Panama Trio, a singing group with the legendary Tony Jackson on piano. This was an exciting time in Chicago: the city was the center of black migration from the rural South, and the white gangsters who controlled the cabarets in the black community fostered the new jazz music and an open social environment. Respectable people, both black and white, however, perceived the Panama as a center of vice, and it was finally closed down.

Mills returned to vaudeville and joined the Tennessee Ten, a traveling black show then on the Keith circuit. A member of the troupe was Ulysses "Slow Kid" Thompson, an acrobatic, tap, and "rubber legs" dancer of considerable skill. Born in Arkansas in 1888, Thompson had spent his life in various circuses, carnivals, medicine, and minstrel shows. He and

Mills became romantically involved, were married, and established a devoted relationship that lasted until her death.

The connection with Thompson and the success of the Tennessee Ten brought Mills closer to the center of show business than she had been in cabaret and vaudeville. She was singing at Barron's Club in Harlem when she received an offer that moved her into public notice and the front rank of black entertainers. It was the opportunity to replace Gertrude Sanders as the lead in *Shuffle Along*.

Shuffle Along opened off-Broadway in New York in the spring of 1921. Music and lyrics were by Noble Sissle and Eubie Blake and the book by Flournoy E. Miller and Aubrey Lyles. It was an instantaneous and total hit. Actually, there was nothing new about *Shuffle Along;* similar shows had existed in the black entertainment world for years. What was new was the discovery by white America of the zesty abandon of jazzy music and fast, high-stepping black dancing. Langston Hughes believed *Shuffle Along* even initiated the Harlem Renaissance and inaugurated the decade when "the Negro was in vogue."

Mills Presented to National Audience as Singer and Dancer

Besides reintroducting blacks into mainstream musical theater and setting the rhythmic beat for the Roaring Twenties, *Shuffle Along* presented Mills to a national audience. Now twenty-six years old, she was a dainty woman, five-feet-four, never weighing much more than one hundred pounds, bronze colored with beautiful skin texture. She moved deftly and in her strange high voice sang "I'm Simply Full of Jazz" and "I'm Craving for That Kind of Love."

The critics could never quite describe Mills's voice with its curious breaks, soft accents, sudden molten notes, and haunting undertones. Bird-like and flute-like were among the reviewers' frequently-used adjectives. It was Mills's dancing, however, and the dancing in all the black shows spawned by *Shuffle Along* during the 1920s that completely stunned audiences. The jazz rhythms, accelerated pace, skilled precision, intricate steps, and uninhibited movement brought dance rooted in African-American folk culture to white audiences eager to break loose from restrained and respectable convention.

Mills's performances were memorable, too, for her charismatic effectiveness in presentation. Demure and modest personally and in her private life, on stage she was assured, vivacious, and as capable of intimate mutual interaction with her audiences as a black preacher. With her fey and fragile appearance she could be intense as well as melancholy, impudent as well as communicating pathos, risqué without being vulgar. Mills's popularity, however, did not mean race and racism were no longer realities; Irving Berlin said if he could find a white woman who could put over a song like Mills, he would be inspired to write a hit a week.

Anticipating the fad for black entertainment and entertainers, Lew Leslie, a white promoter, hired Mills and Kid Thompson to appear nightly after *Shuffle Along* at the Plantation Club, a remodeled night spot over the Winter Garden Theatre. The Plantation's decor included an imitation log cabin, a chandelier in the form of a watermelon slice, and a black mammy cooking waffles. Featuring Mills, the revue itself was a constellation of black talent: Will Vodery's orchestra, Johnny Dunn's cornet, Edith Wilson's double-entendre songs, and visiting performers like Paul Robeson.

The Plantation, as Thompson pointed out, was "the first highclass colored cabaret on Broadway" (Thompson, 320). It drew fashionable white clientele and helped create an accepting atmosphere for things Negro, though old stereotypical images died hard. Florence Mills left *Shuffle Along* to work full-time for Leslie, a mutually beneficial relationship that lasted throughout her career. Also, the Plantation established the format for Mills's and Leslie's future shows: unconnected singing and dancing and musical acts in the vaudeville style with a touch of minstrelsy, and with all black performers.

Leslie soon realized his nightclub production could be turned into a Broadway show. The *Plantation Review* opened at the Forty-eighth Street Theatre on July 22, 1922. Sheldon Brooks presided as master of ceremonies and did a comedy routine; otherwise the bill was the same as the club's. Audiences and reviewers were impressed with the cast's genuineness and enthusiasm and the show's bouyant spontaniety, especially the breathtaking dancing. It was all "strutting and stepping and syncopating," said the *Tribune* on July 18.

The *Plantation Review* was important for Mills, for it was here she was first seen by the New York critics. They liked her energy and vitality, her sinuous dancing, her lack of self-consciousness. She sang Irving Berlin's "Some Sunny Day" and led the Six Dixie Vamps in a "Hawaiian Night in Dixie Land" dance number. There was some criticism of her song "I've Got What It Takes But It Breaks My Heart to Give It Away," not quite the sweet, crooning number that was her specialty. But there was real appreciation for the authenticity of black song and dance, and the realization that Negro portrayals by blackface performers like Al Jolson and Eddie Cantor were only imitations of the real thing.

With *Shuffle Along* and the *Plantation Revue* behind her, Mills emerged as a preeminent black female performer with the potential of breaking into the racially restricted preserves of establishment show business. America was not ready for such a bold move, but the British impresario Sir Charles B. Cochran was looking for ready-made attractions for the London stage. He made arrangements to take the Plantation company to the Pavilion in the spring of 1923. There were immediate problems. British entertainers strenuously objected, citing the competition for jobs but reinforcing that fear with color prejudice. "Nigger Problem Brought to London" ran the headline of one of Hannen Swaffer's articles in the *Daily Graphic*.

The show Cochran devised was a hybrid called *Dover Street to Dixie*. A mild comedy with an all-English cast,

"Dover Street" constituted the first half and was totally unrelated to "Dixie," the second half, which was Mills and the Plantation cast in a variation of their standard routines. Prejudice against the visiting black Americans had escalated and demonstrations were expected in the theater on opening night. Tension intensified because "Dover Street" was a disaster and the audience was restless and bored.

"Dixie" began with a fast number by Vodery's orchestra, a troupe of frantic dancers, and Edith Wilson belting out a song. Then Mills quietly made her entrance and in a small plaintive voice sang "The Sleeping Hills of Tennessee." She electrified the audience. Any threat of opposition vanished, and for the rest of that night and the remainder of the show's run, she received a fervent ovation *before* every song she sang. This was a tribute, Cochran said, he had never known London to give to any other performer.

Perhaps the most significant consequence of *Dover Street to Dixie* was the serious attention it was paid by British intellectuals. The essence of their response was that Mills's performance and that of her fellow black Americans was art, even high art, and not mere entertainment. One reviewer made the astonishing statement that Mills was "by far the most artistic person London has ever had the good fortune to see"(Johnson, 198). Constant Lambert, musical director of Sadler's Wells Ballet, was deeply inspired by Mills and "Dixie" and began adapting jazz rhythms and techniques to his work, narrowing the separation between popular and "serious" music and infusing the latter with new vitality.

Upon her return to New York, Mills received an unusual invitation—to appear as an added attraction in the *Greenwich Village Follies* annual production opening that autumn at the Winter Garden. With Bert Williams's death the previous year there were now no blacks in mainstream shows. This was the first time a black woman was offered a part in a major white production. The *Follies* cast responded by threatening to walk out. Even after management smoothed their feelings, the white cast continued to resent Mills's participation.

All-Black Musical Comedy Opens

Mills's talent and popularity brought an even more extraordinary opportunity. Florenz Ziegfeld offered her a contract to join the *Ziegfeld Follies,* the country's leading musical revue and the apex of show business success. But Mills turned Ziegfeld down. She decided to stay with Lew Leslie and create a rival show—but with an all-black cast. Bert Williams had broken the color barrier as an individual, she said, but she could best serve the race not by merely following him herself but by providing a venue for an entire company.

Mills wanted to break through Broadway's racial restrictions *and* to create an opportunity for black American entertainers to demonstrate the uniqueness of their culture. Her decision, and what she meant by it, was not lost on the black community. The *Amsterdam News* said:

> Loyalty of Florence Mills to the race as against temptation to become a renowned star of an Anglo-Saxon musical extravaganza has saved for the stage and the race what promises to be one of the most distinctive forms of American entertainment ever created—an All-Colored revue (Undated news clipping).

The first step toward Mills's goal was *From Dixie to Broadway,* which opened at the Broadhurst Theatre in October 1924. A black musical comedy in the heart of Broadway had been the dream of black entertainers since the turn of the century, and it was now realized. The price for this acceptance was a certain modification of the show's black elements by the whites who controlled the production, but the cast's superactive energy and expressive power broke through and the show was a critical and popular hit.

The cooperative effort between blacks and whites set a pattern for "crossovers" from the black entertainment milieu to the larger, more lucrative, and more influential white world. This resulted in a minimum of traditional "darky" stage imagery. This was an absence some critics missed, but the reviewers could only applaud the vital black American style and exuberant tempo now more free from racist stereotypes.

In *From Dixie to Broadway* Mills sang "Dixie Dreams," "Mandy, Make Up Your Mind," and the song that became her theme and trademark, "I'm a Little Blackbird Looking for a Bluebird"; behind the song's sentimentality Mills saw a subliminal message: "the struggle of a race" seeking satisfaction. Most critics thought the show's high point was its satirical jazz treatment of Balieffe's "March of the Wooden Soldiers," in which Mills led the male dancers.

Mills clearly dominated *From Dixie to Broadway* and the reviewers lauded her as "a slender streak of genius" and "an artist in jazz." Writing in the *New York Telegram and Evening Mail* on October 30, 1924, Gilbert W. Gabriel gives a fuller picture of the Florence Mills who captured Broadway, as well as revealing his inability to comprehend the distinctive black American elements in her art:

> This sensational little personality, slim, jaunty, strung on fine and tremulous wires, continues to tease the public's sense of the beautiful and odd. There is an impudent fragility about her, a grace of grotesqueness, a humor of wrists, ankles, pitching hips and perky shoulders that are not to be resisted. Her voice continues to be sometimes sweet and sometimes further from the pitch than Dixie is from Broadway. She is an exotic done in brass.

After the show's road tour, Mills broke another racial barrier. On June 27, 1924, she was the first black woman to headline at "The Taj Mahal of Vaudeville," the Palace Theatre. On Broadway at Forty-seventh Street, the Palace was the country's premier variety theatre, and it was every entertainer's dream to play there. Other blacks had been in

Palace programs, but as a headliner Mills received money, billing, the best dressing room, and courtesy from management—real and symbolic achievements for a black American woman.

Mills achieved her great goal of creating a major all-black revue, but she was destined never to return to Broadway. The new show was *Blackbirds* and it opened at the Alhambra Theatre in Harlem after having been constructed at Plantation Club performances. After successful runs in Harlem and Paris, *Blackbirds of 1926* moved to London's Pavilion Theatre, opening September 26 and lasting for an impressive 276 performances, after which it toured the British provinces.

Blackbirds was an extraordinary hit. Mills sang "Silver Rose" and repeated "I'm a Little Blackbird." She was so popular she became to London what Josephine Baker was to Paris. The Prince of Wales saw *Blackbirds* more than twenty times and Mills played to him when he was in the theater. She and the cast were taken up by England's ultra-sophisticated "Bright Young People" and joined their outrageous parties in London, Oxford, and Cambridge.

Mills is mentioned in all the diaries of the period and even turns up as a character in Evelyn Waugh's *Brideshead Revisited.* It is likely she had an affair with the King's youngest son, the handsome, wild, and charming Prince George, who later became Duke of Kent. It was not only royalty and decadent aristocrats who were impressed, however; artists and intellectuals caught the infectious freedom and style of the black performers and the energizing tempo of their music and dance. "For the first time," exclaimed critic Arnold Haskell, "I was *seeing* true jazz."

Perhaps because she felt more secure in a less racially-prejudiced country or perhaps because the British public and press treated her more seriously than the American public and press did, Mills expressed her race consciousness more strongly in England than at home. At an exclusive dinner party where she was lauded by Sir Charles Cochran as a great artist, she ignored his personal tributes in her response and instead made a moving plea for black freedom. "I am coal black and proud of it," she announced at a fashionable soiree where there was some question about black and white seating *arrangements (Variety,* undated clipping).

Mills saw her work as a crusade on behalf of racial justice and understanding. She literally believed that every white person pleased by her performance was a friend won for the race. Her passion led her to drive herself without respite, and it broke her health. She left *Blackbirds* and after an unsuccessful attempt at a rest cure in Germany, sailed for New York. Her condition did not improve, however, and she entered the Hospital for Joint Diseases, where she died following an operation. She was thirty-one years old.

Mills was one of the most popular people in Harlem during the 1920s. Blacks understood that she had never forgotten her roots, that she never put on airs, that she affirmed over and over again the heritage—and the struggle—they shared together. In appreciation for everything she meant to them, the people of Harlem gave her the grandest funeral within their considerable power, an outpouring of affection and recognition, music and flowers, tears and drama.

On a cold November day in 1927 a congregation of five thousand, a choir of six hundred, and an orchestra of two hundred jammed Mother African Methodist Episcopal Church on 137th Street. More than 150,000 people crowded the Harlem streets to glimpse the famous mourners and participate in a bit of history, but mostly to pay their own silent tributes and say good-bye to a sister they knew was their own. It is reported that a flock of blackbirds flew over the funeral cortege as it slowly made its way up Seventh Avenue toward Woodlawn Cemetery in the Bronx.

The public tributes were lavish. In an unprecedented editorial, *The New York Times* praised "the slim dancer who blazed the way" for others to follow (4 November 1927). George Jean Nathan called her "America's foremost feminine player" (*New York Telegram,* 16 April 1927). Theophilus Lewis said Mills "always regarded herself as our envoy to the world at large and she was probably the best one we ever had" ("Florence Mills, An Appreciation"). One London newspaper commented that if Mills had been a white woman she would have been acknowledged as one of the greatest artists of her time.

Except among the cognoscenti and in black folk legend, Mills did not achieve permanent fame. Plans for a memorial fizzled in disputes over money. There were no films or recordings to perpetuate her memory. The Great Depression of 1929 abruptly rang down the curtain on the vim and verve of the Jazz Age. Lew Leslie tried to continue the *Blackbirds* series, which was her dream for celebrating authentic black American performing art, but the effort faded without Mills's vibrant and vivacious presence.

Mills made her mark in several ways. *Shuffle Along* introduced jazz song and dance to Broadway musical theater. In *From Dixie to Broadway* she starred in a black revue built around female singing and dancing rather than traditional male blackface comedy. In *Blackbirds* she created a major show composed of vital black American music and movement. She helped minimize the "darky" element in show business while bringing special black qualities to her crossover numbers. Through it all Florence Mills was first and foremost a "race woman" proud of her heritage, uncompromising in her identity, and always using her artistry to build bridges to the white world in the hope of securing greater justice for her people.

References

Amsterdam News. Undated clipping.

"Florence Mills, An Appreciation." *Inter-State Tattler*, 27 November 1927.

Johnson, James Weldon. *Black Manhattan*. New York:

Knopf, 1930. 188-89, 196-201, 209-210, 217, 224. Photographs, pp. 198 and 199.

Logan, Rayford W. "Florence Mills." *Dictionary of American Negro Biography*. Edited by Rayford W. Logan and Michael R. Winston. New York: Norton, 1982. 440.

New York Telegram and Evening Mail, 30 October 1924, 16 April 1927.

New York Times, 4 November 1927.

New York *Tribune*.

Variety. Undated clipping.

Reid, Anne Cooke. "Florence Mills." *Notable American Women, 1607-1950*. Vol. 3. Cambridge: Harvard University Press, 1971. 545-46.

Thompson, U. S. "Florence Mills." *Negro: Anthology by Nancy Cunard, 1931-1933*. London: Nancy Cunard and Wishard and Co., 1934. 320.

Collections

Reviews, programs, clippings, photographs, and other materials on Florence Mills are in the libraries of Columbia University, the Hatch-Billops Collection, Harvard University, Howard University, Yale University, the Museum of the City of New York, and the New York Public Library, including the Theatre Collection and the Performing Arts Research Center at the Schomburg Center for Research in Black Culture.

Richard Newman

Abbie Mitchell

(1884-1960)

Singer, actress

Abbie Mitchell an internationally-known singer and stage actress in both musical comedy and serious drama, was born on September 25, 1884, in New York City, to a Jewish father and black mother, Luella (Holiday) Mitchell. An only child, Abbie Mitchell was reared by a maternal aunt, Alice Payne, in Baltimore, Maryland, where she enrolled in a convent.

Displaying a talent for singing at a very early age, Abbie Mitchell studied voice under the tutelage of Harry T. Burleigh and Emilia Serrano. In 1898 at the age of thirteen, she won the lead role in the play *Clorindy: The Origin of the Cakewalk*, a comedy with lyrics by Paul Laurence Dunbar and music by Will Marion Cook, whom she would later marry. James Weldon Johnson considered this play to be "the first demonstration of the possibilities of syncopated Negro music" (Johnson, 103). The choruses and finales in *Clorindy* were described as breathtaking, and the play was so popular that it ran the entire summer season at the Casino Roof Garden.

In 1900 and 1903 a daughter, Marion Abigail, and a son, Will Mercer, were born to Abbie Mitchell and Will Cook. Just as Mitchell herself was raised by a maternal aunt, so also was Marion Abigail cared for by relatives. Only scant information about Marion appears in biographical sketches of her mother, and she is not mentioned at all in her mother's obituary that appeared in the *New York Times*, 20 March 1960. But Mitchell's son, Mercer, was written about quite often, perhaps because he traveled from infancy with his mother, making trips abroad as well. Will Mercer became a professor of romance languages at Howard University and United States Ambassador to Niger and to Senegal.

Mitchell appeared in numerous revues as well as many of her husband's productions, including *Jes Lak White Folks* (1899) and *The Southerners* (1904). In 1903 the production of *In Dahomey*, produced by the well-known team of Walker and Williams, appeared in London. Mitchell achieved international acclaim when she sang the lead in this musical, the music for which was composed by her husband. While in London she gave a command performance for King Edward VIII at Buckingham Place. *In Dahomey* made theatrical history by opening at the New York Theatre in Times Square, and in London the play made the cakewalk dance a fad.

Mitchell later appeared in *Bandana Land* (1908) by Cook and *The Red Moon* (1908) by Bob Cole and J. Rosamond Johnson. She took part in a command performance of *The Red Moon* before Czar Nicholas II of Russia. Although her marriage to Cook was failing during this time and would eventually end in divorce, it was a testimony to her professionalism that her musical association with Cook did not also terminate.

Singer Also Becomes Actress

Until this time, Mitchell had achieved note as a singer; however, she went on to gain equal attention as a dramatic actress. In 1915 she joined the all-black stock company of the Lafayette Players in Harlem, where she was soon counted among a group of favorite actors. Such notables included Anita Bush, Ida Anderson, Inez Clough, Lottie Grady, Laura Bowman, Susie Sutton, Cleo Desmond, Edna Thomas, Charles Gilpin, Frank Wilson, Sidney Kirkpatrick, Walter Thompson, Charles Olden, and Andrew Bishop. In 1920 she accompanied Cook's Southern (American) Syncopated Orchestra. During the ensuing years she continued to sing and to develop her skills as an actress as well.

Mitchell was well-received in the many European countries in which she performed. Her repertoire included operatic arias and songs by Will Marion Cook, Harry T. Burleigh, and Margaret Bonds, who was a close friend. A noted perfectionist, Mitchell's quest for excellence led her to Paris to study with Jean de Reszke. Throughout her long career,

Mitchell was associated with many great performers, including J. Rosamond Johnson, Bert Williams, and Bob Cole, as well as the poet Paul Laurence Dunbar. Mitchell also sang on National Broadcast Company radio shows, and from 1931 to 1934 she taught voice at Tuskegee Institute in Alabama. She also served as executive secretary of the Negro Actors Guild of America.

Mitchell's career as a dramatic actress is noteworthy. In 1926 she starred with Julius Bledsoe and Rose McClendon in the play *In Abraham's Bosom*, which won a Pulitzer Prize for its use of the stage as an educational tool. James Weldon Johnson wrote: "[*In Abraham's Bosom*] was closer and truer to actual Negro life and probed deeper into it than any drama of the kind that had yet been produced." In 1927 Mitchell appeared with Helen Hayes in *Coquette;* in 1937 she starred in Langston Hughes's *Mulatto*, a play banned in Philadelphia for its supposedly inflammatory theme. She is also fondly remembered for her parts as Clara in *Porgy and Bess* and Addie in *The Little Foxes*.

Mitchell gave recitals in Paris, Berlin, and Vienna and in many cities in the United States. The mellifluousness and purity of her voice, as well as her elegant bearing, were widely praised. Eugene Stinson of the Chicago *Daily News* said:

> I have never before heard singing of such consistently sage and beautiful workmanship, or such pure and elaborated vocal effect to the disclosure of style, turned with such dignity of purpose and such satisfying effect to the disclosure of how fine a musical instrument the human voice can make. In this respect Miss Mitchell stands quite alone among all the singers of the present day. A rare intelligence has also had its part in her attainment of vocal pre-eminence (*Chicago Daily News*, 22 October 1930).

The critic for the *New York Sun* wrote on April 22, 1927, "Her voice is one of the most beautiful heard this season. And her stage presence bespeaks the singer to the manner born." Noted not only for her astounding voice, Mitchell was a woman of equally rare physical beauty.

Mitchell associated with prominent opera singers and was awarded equal acclaim with them, but her dream to sing opera remained unrealized. "Refused admittance into opera's inner circles" (Robinson, 229), she exhausted her voice by the heavy demands of singing in vaudeville and musical comedies. Mitchell's long and successful dual career as an actress and singer is marked by outstanding accomplishments in both fields. As a result of her numerous precedent-setting performances, she opened the door for many who would follow. Her standards could well be emulated by all who strive for excellence. In 1960, succumbing to a lengthy and protracted illness, Abbie Mitchell died.

References

"Abbie Mitchell, Actress, Is Dead; Singer Was Widow of Composer." *New York Times,* 20 March 1960.

"Abbie Mitchell Sets Standards in Recital Here." *Chicago Daily News,* 22 October 1930.

Isaacs, Edith. *The Negro in the American Theatre.* College Park, Md.: McGraw, 1947. 36.

Johnson, James Weldon. *Black Manhattan.* 1930. Reprint. New York: Arno Press and *The New York Times,* 1968. 103, 207.

Robinson, Wilhelmina S. "Historical Negro Biographies." In *International Library of Negro Life and History.* New York: Publishers Company, 1967. 229-30.

Ryder, Georgia. "Abbie Mitchell." *Notable American Women: The Modern Period.* Cambridge: Harvard University Press, 1980. 483-84.

Collections

The Schomburg Center for Research in Black Culture, New York Public Library, has a file of newspaper clippings about Abbie Mitchell.

Rita D. Disroe

Juanita Mitchell

(1913-)

Lawyer, community activist, civil rights leader

While Juanita Mitchell has her own story, it is complete only when one discusses her in the context of her family. Her family can be documented as far back as 1801 when William Bowen, her great-great grandfather, was born free in Montgomery County, Maryland. "The Bowens believed in bricks and mortar," Mitchell is fond of saying, meaning they were builders. They built churches and businesses near the Quaker settlement of Sandy Spring. On the other side of the family, her grandmother married a man who claimed descent from Charles Carroll of Carrollton, a signer of the Declaration of Independence. Thus, statesmanship is in the family line, too.

Born in Hot Springs, Arkansas, Mitchell was the second of four children—three daughters and a son—born to Keiffer Jackson and Lillie May (Carroll) Jackson. The Jackson family traveled extensively because of the father's early occupation of showing movies. At that time, the only way for many blacks to see a movie was in the basement of their church. So, while their father changed reels, Mitchell recited poetry and her sisters Virginia and Marion sang and played the piano. Those who knew Mitchell then describe her as a pretty, rosy-cheeked little girl. Eventually the family came back to Maryland and settled in Baltimore.

Mitchell graduated from Frederick Douglass High School in 1927 with honors and then, having been denied admission to the University of Maryland because of her race, attended Morgan State College for two years. Transferring to the University of Pennsylvania, she earned a bachelor's degree in education in 1931 and, following a brief teaching stint, earned a master's degree in sociology in 1935. During the summers, she traveled throughout the southern and western parts of the United States with the National Council of Methodist Youth and in September 1935 joined the NAACP national staff. Her picture graces the cover of that issue of the *Crisis* magazine.

Mitchell's mother did not take kindly to the University of Maryland's denying admission to her daughter in 1927. She was further angered by a refusal of service in a downtown Baltimore department store. In 1931 Lillie Jackson formed an advisory council to address racial problems, the counterpart of which was the City-Wide Young People's Forum founded by Juanita Mitchell. The meetings provided education, information, discussion, and opportunities for social action. They attracted large numbers of youth. Under the banner, "Buy Where You Can Work," the two groups launched a campaign to break down economic discrimination. Eventually, the groups merged with the Baltimore Branch of the NAACP under Lillie Carroll Jackson's leadership, making the branch the largest in the national civil rights organization.

Meanwhile, in 1933 a young reporter for the black American newspapers went to Princess Anne, Maryland, to cover the activities of a mob set on lynching a black man. When Clarence M. Mitchell, Jr., arrived, the man had been hanged. The mob then set fire to his body and took parts of the charred remains as souvenirs. Returning to Baltimore the next day, Clarence Mitchell turned in his story, then went home. At the dinner table before his horrified family, he became sickened by the activities he had witnessed. At that time, he and his younger brother, Parren, became determined to dedicate their lives to the advancement of blacks. At a Young People's Forum meeting, Clarence Mitchell met Juanita Jackson. The two were married at Sharp Street Memorial United Methodist Church on September 7, 1938, by the same pastor who had united Juanita Mitchell's parents at that church twenty-eight years earlier. This union brought together two people committed to the battle for civil rights.

Citizen's Rights Issues Promoted

In April 1942, Juanita Mitchell directed a citizens' march of two thousand people on Maryland's capitol in Annapolis. This resulted in the appointment of the Governor's Interracial Commission, the appointment of black police officers, and an investigation into charges of police brutality. In that same year, she directed a voter campaign that placed eleven thousand new voters on the books.

Remembering that Mitchell had been denied admission to the University of Maryland, the Baltimore branch of the NAACP, under the leadership of Lillie Jackson, began filing cases through their attorneys, challenging the school's racial barriers. When the battle ended, the university agreed to admit black Americans to the School of Law. Graduating in 1950, Mitchell received the first law degree that institution had ever awarded to a black woman and became the first black woman to practice law in Maryland. She was admitted to practice before the Court of Appeals of Maryland, the United States District Court for Maryland, the United States Court of Appeals for the Fourth Circuit, and the United States Supreme Court.

Mitchell was later to say, "I've done a lot of living and a lot of fighting. I've found that the best ways to fight are with the ballot, through educating public opinion and through the courts" *Baltimore Sun*, 16 May 1972). And fight she did, winning major desegregation suits in the nation's highest court against Maryland's practices in recreation areas, schools, and restaurants. She entered her first case in 1950 aimed at eliminating racial segregation at municipal and state beaches and swimming pools. She won this case before the United States Supreme Court in 1955. She then served as counsel in suits that desegregated schools, making Baltimore the first southern city to desegregate following the United States Supreme Court's 1954 decision that declared segregated schools unconstitutional. She faced the high court again in 1965 and won a case that led to the desegregation of Maryland restaurants.

After several heinous crimes committed by two local blacks, the police department conducted, without warrants, mass searches of the private homes of blacks. Mitchell represented black homeowners in proceedings to enjoin the commissioner of police of Baltimore from any further searches. She won an appeal before the United States District Court and before the United States Court of Appeals in 1966. Following this victory, the Fourth Legislative District elected her to serve in the Constitutional Convention of Maryland in 1967. Mitchell said:

> We believe in the Constitution. There's nothing wrong with the American system. The trouble is with the people who run it. To get the [changes we want], we just have to get the right people to run it. This is the genius and vitality of democracy. We just want democracy to be real and to work. (*Baltimore Sun*, 16 May 1972).

Her husband, Clarence, who was chief of the NAACP's Washington Bureau from 1950 to 1979, was said to carry a copy of the Constitution with him.

Clarence and Juanita Mitchell purchased their first and only home, on Druid Hill Avenue in 1942. As a result of residential desegregation, many blacks with the means to do so eventually moved out of the inner city, but the Mitchells remained. In the heart of the black community, they continued their work, recruiting members for the NAACP, conducting voter registration drives, and leading social change. Their home served as a staging ground for civil rights strategies for forty years.

> Some people don't want to live in an integrated society,'' she once said, ''but they don't understand the irreparable damage that happens to people who live separately. The development of the human personality to the fullest depends on the degree to which we learn to live with people of all backgrounds (*Baltimore Sun*, 16 May 1972).

One of Mitchell's sons, Michael, went into the legal profession, forming, with his parents, the firm of Mitchell, Mitchell and Mitchell. Keiffer is a physician and did some integrating of his own in the medical community. Clarence III is a politician, and George manages the family property. The Mitchell family, never known for money or high social standing, achieved great fame for their work in civil rights, and two sons easily won election to local political offices. The eldest, Clarence III, won election to the Maryland legislature at age twenty-two. In 1975 Michael won a seat on the Baltimore City Council. However, around the time their Uncle Parren became the first black congressman from Maryland in the Mitchell's began referring to themselves as ''the black Kennedys.'' This continued into the early 1980s, when the sons faced legal difficulties.

To pay her sons' legal fees, Juanita Mitchell, a widow since 1984, borrowed against everything she owned, including the house in which she lives. In June 1989, when she could not repay the loans, the bank foreclosed on the family property, including her home. But those who worked with her through the years and had met many times at her Druid Hill Avenue home were determined that she would not lose it. Within a matter of weeks, local black leaders raised more than ninety-three-thousand dollars, with contributions ranging from twenty-five cents to five thousand dollars. This was enough to save the Mitchell residence, with a small amount earmarked to convert the home to a museum after her death. The bank that held the mortgage forgave a large part of the interest fees as a contribution to the Mitchell house, which had opened its doors to Eleanor Roosevelt, President and Mrs. Lyndon Johnson, and many other dignitaries.

During the stress of this ordeal, Mitchell's health began to decline. Yet, always one to give credit to others, she wrote an article for the *Baltimore Sun*, 20 June 1989, paying tribute to Owen Lattimore, whom she called a teacher and statesman. It says in part that in 1947 the Baltimore branch of the NAACP began a picket line in front of Ford's Theater. ''We picketed Ford's for seven long years without missing a performance. Owen Lattimore, arriving with a party of his friends, refused to cross the picket line. He took up a sign and walked with us.''

On the eve of the 1983 march on Washington for jobs, Juanita Mitchell said:

> Look what has happened in this State. The integrated schools, the barriers that have fallen in voting rights. When we started out, we had no laws, no legal precedents. And I think we've been so busy tearing down the walls that have separated our society that our children have come into this world of new opportunities and freedoms with no sense of what we went through to get here (*Baltimore Sun* Magazine).

Presidents Franklin D. Roosevelt, John F. Kennedy, and Lyndon B. Johnson appointed Mitchell to White House commissions during their terms in office. She is a member of many bar associations and of Alpha Kappa Alpha Sorority. Honors and awards for her work have been bestowed by many groups, including the National Association of Negro Business and Professional Women's Clubs, the National Council for Negro Women, and the Black American Law Students Association of the University of Maryland School of Law. She received the Loyola College Andrew White Award for Distinguished Public Service in 1971, the Baltimore's Best Award in 1985, and was elected to the Maryland Women's Hall of Fame.

References

Baltimore Sun, 22 June 1989.

Baltimore Sun Magazine (21 August 1983): 12.

''Black Community Acts to Save Mitchell House.'' *Baltimore Sun*, 22 June 1989.

Hathaway, Phillis. ''Lillie May Jackson.'' *Notable Maryland Women*. Cambridge, Md.: Tidewater Publishers, 1977. 187-91.

Jacobs, Bradford. ''Mitchells of the Middle.'' *Baltimore Evening Sun*, 28 September 1965. A20.

Jonnes, Jill. ''Defiant Dynasty: Matriarch of the 'Black Kennedys,' Juanita Mitchell Fights to Perpetuate the Legacy of a Family under Fire.'' *Baltimore Magazine*, October 1986: 99.

''Juanita E. Jackson to Join NAACP National Staff.'' *Crisis* 42 (September 1935): 272. Illustration of Jackson on cover.

''Juanita Mitchell Hospitalized after Spinal Injury, Stroke.'' *Baltimore Sun* 3 January 1990.

Mitchell, Juanita. ''Courage to Light a Candle.'' *Baltimore Evening Sun* 20 June 1989. A13.

Mitchell, Juanita. Interview, 1984.

Nast, Lenora H., Laurence K. Krause, and R. C. Monk, eds. *Baltimore: A Living Renaissance*, Baltimore: Historic Baltimore Society, 1982. 287-88.

"Outpouring of Love Aids Mrs. Mitchell." *Baltimore Afro-American,* 24 June 1989. A1.

Pagan, Margaret D. "The Bowens of Montgomery County, Maryland." *Flower of the Forest Black Genealogical Journal.* 1 (1984). 88-89.

Pollack, Randi M. "Mrs. Mitchell Prime Force in Civil Rights Battle." *Baltimore Sun,* 16 May 1972. B1.

"Sale Set for Mitchell Buildings." *Baltimore Daily Record,* 17 January 1990. 1.

Tucker, Sam. "Clarence M. Mitchell, Jr.: 'Senator' for the Poor and Dispossessed." *Metropolitan Baltimore/Washington Magazine* (February/March, 1979): 42-45.

Washington Post, 1 February 1976.

Who's Who in Colored America. 5th ed. Brooklyn, N.Y.: Thomas Yenser, 1940. 276.

Margaret D. Pagan

Mollie Moon

(1912-1990)

Pharmacist, civic worker, organization founder, public relations executive, activist

For nearly fifty years, Mollie Moon was president of the National Urban League Guild, New York City, which she founded in 1942. She worked tirelessly for equal rights and was honored accordingly throughout her life. Her commitment to racial uplift and the National Urban League was unwavering.

Mollie V. Lewis Moon was born July 21, 1912, in Hattisburg, Mississippi, the daughter of Telious Lewis and Beulah (Rodgers) Lewis. She graduated from Meharry Medical College, Nashville, Tennessee, in 1929 with the Phr.C. She undertook further study at Teachers College, Columbia University, and the New School of Social Research in New York City, where she studied housing and public relations. For two years she was a student at the University of Berlin, where she studied biology and education and became fluent in German. In 1933 Mollie Moon was a pharmacist in Douglas Pharmacy, New Orleans, Louisiana. She moved to Gary, Indiana, and in 1934 she became a pharmacist for Shultz's Pharmacy. In 1937 she was a pharmacist with La Morrell's Drug Store in New York City. She left that profession and from 1938 to 1972 she was a social worker with the Department of Social Services in New York.

Already established in social circles and by then a prominent New Yorker, Mollie Moon was in a convenient position to help the league overcome the financial woes it faced in the early 1940s. Lester B. Granger, then the executive director of the league, asked Moon to call together a group of volunteers to help the league become financially stable. "She accepted Granger's challenge with the fervor and ecumenical spirit that became her hallmark" ("In Memoriam," National Urban League, n.d.). She crossed racial and class lines in her fund-raising plan, and she became a pioneer in race relations, thus establishing in the public's mind her early concern for community unity.

Early in 1942 Mollie Lewis Moon and a group of friends sponsored a benefit Victory Cocktail Party as a fund-raiser for the league. The affair was so successful that she established what was to become a New York tradition—a black-tie Beaux-Arts Ball held each February. The popular ball attracts entertainers, movie stars, business people, and a broad spectrum of interested persons. In 1948 she went to Canton, Ohio, to help launch the first guild outside New York City. Through her efforts also, the Council of Urban League Guilds was formed and over the years raised more than $3.4 million to help support the league's programs and initiatives. From the time of the founding of the league until Mollie Moon's death on June 24, 1990, she was its only president.

Mollie Moon was active in various community organizations, committees, and projects and held numerous appointments. From 1972 to 1976 she was a member of the national advisory board, Food and Drug Committee, Department of Health, Education and Welfare in Washington, D.C. She became a member of the board of directors for the Ladies of Charity, Arthur Mitchell's Dance Theater of Harlem, the Coalition of 100 Black Women, National Committee Against Discrimination in Housing, and the Sickle Cell Foundation of New York. From 1955 to 1962 she was secretary of the board of directors of the National Urban League.

She was a member of the distinguished group of Americans who were invited by the government of Iran to participate in a ten-day symposium on "Iran—Past, Present and Future" held in Persepolis, Iran, in September 1975. In the early eighties she represented the National Urban League as an observer at sessions of the United Nations.

Mollie Moon's contributions to community affairs resulted in a number of recognitions and awards. She received the Medallion of Honor as a Woman of Achievement from the Women's International Institute (1960); Humanitarian Award, Committee for United Negro Relief (1962); Citation, Empire State Federation of Women's Clubs for New York and Westchester regions (1963); tribute, Morningside Community Center, New York City (1964); Scroll of Honor, National Association of Negro Business and Professional Women's Clubs (1975); the Hoey Award, Catholic Interracial Council (1981); Robert Kitchen Award for outstanding work in the community, American Cancer Society (1983); the Ruth Standish Baldwin-Eugene Kinckle Jones Volunteer Service

Award given by the league in recognition of forty-five years of outstanding volunteer service (1985); and the Whitney M. Young, Jr., Award, Whitney M. Young Training Center, National Urban League (1987). In 1989 she received the league's highest honor—the Equal Opportunity Award. In that year also the league created a volunteer award named in her honor to be awarded annually to a guild member with outstanding service to the league. Its first recipient, Helen E. Harden, was Mollie Moon's cherished friend and colleague. A special Mollie Moon Distinguished Service Award was established in her name by the Whitney M. Young Training Center in 1989. Also in her honor, the Southwestern Fairfield County Urban League Guild established the Mollie Moon Award to be presented annually to a person who has contributed substantially to the advancement of black people.

Civil Rights Library Founded

An ardent supporter of the National Urban League, Mollie Moon's interest in its success never wavered. She chaired a committee to raise funds to maintain the Henry Lee Moon Civil Rights Library in Baltimore, Maryland, at the NAACP headquarters. The library was named in honor of her husband, Henry Lee Moon, a longtime director of public relations for the NAACP and editor of *Crisis* magazine.

Perhaps the last honor that Mollie Moon received was the President's Volunteer Action Award from President George Bush, presented to her in 1990 by Mayor David N. Dinkins of New York City. After apparently suffering a heart attack, Mollie Moon died in her Long Island residence on June 24, 1990, and was survived by a daughter, Mollie Moon Elliot, and five grandchildren. On her death, National Urban League president and chief executive officer John E. Jacob recognized "her landmark efforts in race relations for helping pave the way for such historic accomplishments as the election of New York's first Black major, the Honorable David N. Dinkins. We have lost a true promoter of equal opportunity" (*Jet*, 17).

Those who knew Mollie Moon well knew the extent of her commitment to racial uplift, as evidenced by the way it was expressed in her work. On this matter she wrote:

> At an early age I became aware of my obligation to participate in organized efforts to level the onerous barriers which locked me and my people in a ghastly cultural, political, and economic ghetto. Neither I nor my family had sufficient income to make significant financial contribution to this cause. We did, however, have commitment, energy and time to contribute (Questionnaire, Fisk University Library, 27 May 1982).

She consciously made voluntary contributions to various organizations and causes, but her "principal effort has been . . . volunteer work on behalf of the National Urban League through the National Urban League Guild" (Questionnaire). On this matter she wrote:

> I chose the National Urban League because I believe in the soundness of its program, dedicated as it is to the enlargement of social, political and economic opportunities for Black folk; because I am committed to interracial cooperation which the National Urban League advocates and practices; and because I have profound faith in the integrity and ability of its leadership now personified by John E. Jacob, the League's . . . energetic and outspoken Executive Director (Questionnaire).

References

Biographical information, National Urban League. Includes photograph.

Birmingham, Stephen. *Certain People*. Boston: Little, Brown, 1977. Photographs, including scene from the Beaux Arts Ball, inserted between pp. 144-45.

"In Memorian." National Urban League, n.d.

"National Urban League Guild President Mollie Moon Dies." *Jet* 78 (16 July 1990): 17. Includes photograph.

Questionnaire, Fisk University Library, 27 May 1982.

Jessie Carney Smith

Melba Moore

(1945-)

Actress, singer, comedienne

Since she first attracted the attention and affection of Broadway theatergoers between 1968 and 1971, Melba Moore rapidly established herself as a leading actress, singer, and comedienne. Her singing virtuosity and strong dramatic and comedic skills have captivated audiences and elevated her to stardom.

According to the *New York Times*'s John Rockwell, "Her musical diversity and her theatrical background are also reflected in the variegated nature of her audience" (8 December 1976). A jazz pianist by training, Moore brings to her craft ample vocal artistry: a four-octave range, powerful delivery and stage presence, and stylistic flexibility that showcases her gospel-blues-classical roots. Hubert Saal describes her voice as having "a variety of registers, a range of colors, and a mixture of styles—gospel, blues, rock, pop—shaping every song to suit her extraordinary versatility" (*Newsweek*). "Miss Moore is marvelous," a reviewer wrote for *Life* Magazine's "TV Review," "shifting from sleepy sex to high jive to gospel low-down as though her voice box were a bicycle with six gears. She assumes the shape of the song she sings, fire into water into champagne . . ." (Cyclops). Impressively, she has continued to garner pioneering roles in Broadway musicals, movies, television specials and sitcoms, and nightclub and concert performances and has received critical acclaim for her numerous recordings.

Moore was born in New York City on October 29, 1945, to singer Melba (Bonnie) Smith and jazz saxophonist Teddy Hill. Her mother later married pianist Clem Moorman, and this marriage produced three step-siblings, Clementine, Dennis, and Elliot, and a half brother Girard. Born into a musical family, Moore says, "My brothers, and my sister and I were all musically inclined and we enjoyed taking lessons . . . " (Garland, 31).

As a child living in Harlem for nine years and later in Newark, New Jersey, during the 1950s and 1960s, Moore gained an acute sense of pain from the isolation, violence, and corruption that surrounded her. Harlem, her love, according to Saal, made her. And scarred her ("Peach Melba," 94). She admitted to him, "Personally, I was protected. But I was surrounded by violence, by uncles in and out of jail, people cutting each other up. It was a world of the streets, of too many kids, a whole different code of living. . . . I had never learned to talk to people. In Harlem they taught me not only not to be heard but not to be seen." A shy "gloomy child, always feeling lonesome . . . " (*Essence*), Moore was, nevertheless, able to transcend her environment and alienation by focusing on school and on her music. She attended Waverly Avenue Elementary School and later Cleveland Junior High School in Newark. "I went to Catholic school and even that I liked," she explained to Alan Ebert. "It was cold and mechanical—exactly what I knew and felt comfortable with . . . . The only way I communicated was through music" (*Essence*, July 1973, 56).

During Moore's high school years at the Arts High School in Newark, she majored in music. Moore enrolled at Montclair State Teachers College after her high school graduation and also chose a major in music education with the intention of being a public school teacher. Following her graduation from college, she spent the next year as a music teacher at Pershine Avenue Elementary School, a job that she hated because of the poor facilities and curriculum, particularly for black students, and because of her greater love for show business: "I taught in a black school and I enjoyed imparting my love for performing and music to the kids, but the more I performed, the less I liked teaching," she recalled (Garland, 31).

Moore began her professional music career while performing part-time with a group called "Voices", composed of other " . . . practical-minded school teachers with an eye for the entertainment world" (Garland, 31). Over the next few years, she worked as a stand-up singer on the resort circuit in the Catskill Mountains area and in a succession of performances as a background singer for such superstars as Aretha Franklin and Frank Sinatra. Moore supported herself during these early years by performing in television commercials. Her apprenticeship paid off; Moore recalled, "By the time I left the mountains, I was pretty well respected and they knew who Melba Moore was" (Garland, 32). In early 1968 she was doing a background session for Gualt and MacDermott, composers for the off-Broadway hit rock musical *Hair*. Impressed by her performance, MacDermott asked Moore to audition for the new production of the show, which she did successfully.

Actress Gains Fame

Making her Broadway debut in the long-running musical *Hair*, Moore attracted widespread attention "as the first Black lead of any of the Broadway rock musical *Hair* companies around the world" (*Jet*, 5 October 1972, 57). Melba Moore recollected her first big-time Broadway experience: "I cringed throughout the tryout. The fear was unrelenting . . . for me it was terror, except when I was singing" (*Essence*, July 1973, 58). Phyl Garland reports that her experience was a growing one. "Melba Moore, who had no experience or training whatsoever as an actress, cropped the part and did most of her learning on stage each night" (*Ebony*, July 1970, 32). Under Tom O'Horgan's direction, *Hair*, confirmed Ebert, taught Moore improvisational acting and gave her the stage training she needed (*Essence*, July 1973, 58). The *Newsweek* critic Saal went on to say that "*Hair* was her emancipation. Just as its counterculture attitudes opened the eyes of an older generation, it liberated Melba." Melba Moore also recognized the therapeutic value of the experience: "I had been a misfit, a rule breaker. . . . But the *Hair* experience informed and reformed my deepest feelings. . . . What *Hair* taught me was to take a chance, to try. . . ." (*Newsweek*).

After eighteen months, Moore left the cast of *Hair* to star in the award-winning Broadway musical *Purlie*, based on the stage play *Purlie Victorious*, written and produced by Ossie Davis in 1961. As the delightful country bumpkin Lutiebelle, playing opposite Cleavon Little, Moore was an instant hit. Herschel Johnson exclaimed, "In *Purlie*, Melba's dynamic voice, with its four-octave range, drew audiences and critics alike into the fold, as she established herself as a powerhouse of an entertainer" (*Essence*, September 1984, 94). Other critics, including David Ewen, were deeply impressed by Moore's performance in *Purlie* and predicted stardom for the young actress: "Miss Moore . . . proved herself to be a luminous star, about whom much undoubtedly will be heard in the years to come . . . " (*American Musical Theater Awards*, 441). Typical of the critical consensus on her performance, Richard Watts wrote, "She walked off with the evening. You emphatically didn't forget her" (*American Musical Theater Awards*, 441). Moore has since appeared in two other Broadway musicals, as Mansinah in *Timbuktu* (March 1, 1978) and in the starring role in the comedy *Inacent Black* (May 6, 1981).

Moore made her film debut in *Cotton Comes to Harlem* (1970), followed by *Pigeons* (aka *The Sidelong Glance of A*

Pigeon Kicker) (1970), the musical drama *Lost in the Stars* (a musical adaptation of Alan Paton's *Cry The Beloved Country* (1974), *Hair* (1979), and *Flamingo Road* (1980).

Called one of the fastest-rising young black female stars of stage and cabaret (M. Cordell Thompson, *Jet*, October 5, 1972, 56), Moore continues to broaden her repertoire. For her, musical diversity is the key to continued growth and mass appeal: "I use a lot of different voices and styles," said Moore, "Why not? I'm a lot of different people inside. Aren't we all? I'm a child sometimes, and a woman, and angry or sad, and black and human" (*Newsweek*, 28 June 1971, 94). Touring widely in the United States and Europe as an entertainer, she has appeared in nightclubs in Lake Geneva, Cannes, Lake Tahoe, and Las Vegas, at New York's Philharmonic Hall, in the Empire Room of the Palmer House in Chicago and on television shows, including the "Tonight Show" and "Hotel." In 1972, along with costar Clifton Davis, Moore cohosted the CBS television summer musical and variety series "The Melba Moore-Clifton Davis Show." In addition, she shared star billing with Ben Vereen, Richard Burton, Faye Dunaway, and Ann Jillian in the CBS miniseries *Ellis Island* (1984). Having the distinction of being the first black actress to have her own network sitcom named after her, she had the lead role in the short-lived "Melba," which premiered on January 28, 1986. Her return to television to portray Harriet Tubman in the television special "The American Woman: Portrayals of Courage" won critical acclaim. Moore also filmed three appearances for the dramatic series of the nighttime soap "Falcon Crest," portraying an attorney for the show's star, Maggie (1987).

Moore has won the approval of a wider audience with her extensive recordings. According to *People Weekly*, "She was on the crest again with two disco smashes, *You Stepped Into My Life* and *Pick Me Up I'll Dance*" and received rave reviews for her albums—*Melba Moore, Peach Melba, This Is It, A Portrait of Melba, The Other Side of The Mountain Never Say Never, Read My Lips*, and *A Lot of Love*. In 1990, she climbed to the top of the music charts in a collaborative hit record with Dionne Warwick, Anita Baker, and others, "Lift Every Voice and Sing."

Winning her first awards for her stellar performance in *Purlie* (1970), Moore captured the Tony Award, New York Drama Critics' Award, and the Drama Desk Award. She also won the Outer Circle Award and Entertainer-of-the Year Award. In 1985 Moore was nominated for two Grammy Awards for her albums, *This Is It* and *Read My Lips*.

The petite Moore is five-feet four-inches tall and weighs approximately one hundred pounds. She has been described as a "winsome stick of dynamite" (*Jet*, 27 January 1972, 57). Hubert Saal says of her dynamic voice, "Suddenly out of that child came this mountain of a voice, big and strong, green valleys below and bleak snowcaps above, where winds howled" (*Newsweek*). In Moore's interview with Saal, he found her "comfortable to talk with, given to straight and thoughtful answers, unsuspicious and responsive."

Early in her career, Moore committed herself to being a role model for young blacks and the black community: "I want to be careful not to alienate anybody because I'm proud to be black but I also want to give black people something to look up to, an image they can be proud of and kids can emulate. . . . I want the white community to *dig* me, but I'm really more concerned about the black community . . . " (Garland, 34). Moore has used her talents to keep this commitment. In the 1970s, she made appearances at the Cook County Jail in Chicago and the Manhattan House of Detention in New York. Inspiring young black entertainers to succeed, she coached Freddie Jackson, her protégé to success: "She hired him as a backup singer and composer, introduced him to her management firm, and later took him to Capitol Records, where she records and requested they give him a recording contract. . . . She also took him with her on a sizzling 70-city U. S. tour and introduced him to the public" (*Jet*). Moore believes that "Black entertainers must help each other. . . . It increases your own treasures" (*Jet*), She continues to work with young promising artists; her other protégés are Lillo Thomas and Paul Laurence.

Moore is married to Charles Huggins, and they are the proud parents of a daughter, Charli. Moore's career is still primed for takeoff; She continues to emerge. Superstar, pioneer, international actress, singer, comedienne, Moore still sees her role as helping to make America a better place:

> The veils we wear have changed but underneath the situation is pretty much the same economically and racially. . . . There is a melting pot, and eventually we're going to be more like one another, but there still are differences. . . . The important thing is to be kind to each other. . . . The rest will take care of itself" ("Melba Moore Still Has Hope for the Melting Pot," *New York Times*, 6 July 1981).

References

American Musical Theater Awards. Ed. David Ewen. New York: Holt, Rinehart, 1970. 440-41.

Current Biography. 34 New York: H. W. Wilson, 1973. 305-307.

Cyclops. "Toast to Melba, A Summer Peach." "Life TV Review." *Life* 43 (July-August 1972). 17.

Essence 4 (July 1973): 28-29.

Garland, Phyl. "The Prize Winners." *Ebony* 25 (July 1970): 28-37

Jet 41 (January 27, 1972): 56-59.

Jet 69 (November 4, 1985): 22-24.

Johnson, Herschel. "MELBA MOORE." *Essence* 15 (September 1984): 101.

"Melba Moore Still Has Hope for the Melting Pot." *New York Times* 6 July 1981.

"Melbamoors." *People Weekly*. 11 (April 30, 1979): 80.

New York Times, 8 December 1976.

Saal, Hubert. "Peach Melba." *Newsweek* 77 (June 28, 1971): 94.

Jacquelyn L. Jackson

Queen Mother Audley Moore

(1898-)

Pan-African, community organizer

A tireless crusader for civil rights, women's rights, and Pan African nationalism, Andley Moore was involved in almost every important political group, organization, and movement that worked toward these aims, as well as acting as the driving force behind a great many economic and political efforts for the improvement of African-Americans' lives.

Audley Moore was born in New Iberia, Louisiana. Moore was the oldest of three daughters born to Henry and St. Cyr Moore. Her father, a onetime sheriff's deputy in Iberia Parish, had married three times and fathered eight children. Her mother, the granddaughter of an African woman raped by her white owner, died when Audley Moore was only five, leaving Moore and her sisters, Eloise and Lorita, to live with their maternal grandmother in New Iberia while their father moved to New Orleans. Moore recalls that her mother's father had been lynched and she witnessed the lynching of her grandmother's husband. A few years later the sisters were reunited with their father in New Orleans; he died when Moore was in the fourth grade. She then dropped out of school to take care of her sisters, selling some of her father's mules to rent a house and lying about her age in order to become a hairdresser to support the family.

Queen Mother Audley Moore

Moving to New Orleans around the turn of the century would prove to be a bittersweet experience for Moore and her sisters. It was here that they would experience the brunt of racial violence and segregation but also the awakening of racial pride. She vividly recalls the violence and segregation of their early years in Louisiana:

> I remember when I was a kid in Louisiana, the Catholic convents took black girls but no black boys for the priesthood. . . . Then I remember police rounding up our men just because they were standing on the corner . . . talking to one another, hauling them in for vagrancy . . . rounding them up at fish fries. They would take all the men and put them in a van, then go back and rape the women" (*Black Scholar*, 49).

She and her sisters traveled to Anniston, Alabama, during World War I, where they were appalled at the separate and unequal treatment of black soldiers. The sisters canvassed the black community for food and other supplies for the soldiers. Moore credits her sister, Eloise, with organizing the first USO in an abandoned church building and becoming the first unofficial member of the Women's Army Corps (WAC). While in Alabama, Moore supported her family primarily through hairdressing and sewing. They eventually returned to New Orleans, where Moore married and opened a small store with her husband.

It was the repressive climate of racial violence and segregation that led many outraged blacks in New Orleans to flock to a local meeting hall in 1914 to hear a little-known Jamaican. Calling for the establishment of an independent black nation, Marcus Garvey embarked on a five-month lecture tour across the United States before settling in Harlem in 1916. On the lecture circuit in 1919, Garvey's appearance in New Orleans provoked a local disturbance but had a profound affect on the nineteen-year-old Moore. At first the police prohibited Garvey from speaking to the incensed crowd. The following night, when Garvey returned to the hall, the crowd came fully prepared to hear him—most armed with guns. Moore carried two—"one in my bosom and one in my pocketbook." When the police attempted to silence Garvey this time, they met armed resistance. The crowd stood on benches, waved their guns, and exhorted Garvey to speak. Moore recalls the police "turned red as crawfish and filed out like wounded puppy dogs'' (Lanker, 103). Garvey's impact on Moore was immediate and lasting; it set her on a lifelong quest for black consciousness and nationhood. She became a life member of Garvey's United Negro Improvement Association (UNIA), buying stock in the ill-fated Black Star Shipping Line. She says Garvey ''raised in me a certain knowledge of the history of the wealth of Africa'' *Black Women Oral History Interview*, transcript, 7).

Moore, her husband, and sisters joined thousands of other blacks fleeing the South in search of freedom and employment in the West and the North. After traveling to California and Chicago, they eventually settled in Harlem in 1922, only to discover the same appalling conditions they were trying to escape in the South. From 1900 to 1930, the black population of New York City grew dramatically by 250 percent, from 91,709 in 1910 to 327,706 in 1930. Although most of these migrants came from the South, a large influx also came from the West Indies, creating a dynamic fusion of Afro-American cultures. As the geographic and cultural boundaries of Harlem took shape, ''Black Manhattan'' emerged as the mecca of black life. But beneath the glamour and appeal of Harlem lay a gloomy underside consisting of congested housing conditions, widespread unemployment and job discrimination, and poor health conditions.

Moore was particularly disturbed by the plight and exploitation of black working women in Harlem, most of whom were domestic workers in white homes. She compares labor conditions in Harlem to slavery in the South. White women would meet African-American women on the street corners in the Bronx, examine their knees for crust (a sign of a hard worker), and hire them for as little as fifteen cents a day. She set out to organize these women by founding the Harriet Tubman Association, one of the many organizations she would found and head in her lifetime.

Community Uplift Activities Organized

By 1930 her organizing efforts in Harlem led to a twenty-year affiliation with the Communist party, which recruited strongly in the African-American community in the 1920s and 1930s. Moore initially joined the International Labor Defense, thinking it was the Communist party because of its large number of Communist members. She officially joined the party in 1933, encouraged by its involvement with the Scottsboro Case (1931-1933) and its advocacy of voters' rights and civil rights. The party helped her to hone her organizational skills among working-class people and gave her an in-depth understanding of capitalism. While active in the party, she fought racial segregation on a number of fronts, helping to integrate major league baseball and the Coast Guard, fighting evictions, and organizing early rent strikes in Harlem.

> I had the first rent strike in New York City. Getting the landlord not only to raise rents, but to roll back rents from where he had them. [I] went from apartment to apartment and rolled back the people's rent (*Black Women Oral History Interview*, transcript, 69).

She served as the campaign manager to Benjamin E. Davis, Jr., an African-American Communist leader in New York, who served two successive terms on the New York City Council in the 1940s. In 1950 she resigned from the party, denouncing it as ''racist to the core,'' and became an advocate of poor people in the South, returning to her home state of Louisiana to lead a successful campaign to restore twenty-three thousand black and white families to the welfare rolls after they were cut off by state authorities. Through her organization, the University Association of Ethiopian Women, she also sought to overturn the death sentences of African-American prisoners.

Moore's affiliations with the Garvey movement, the Communist party, and other grass roots organizations did not prevent her from associating with or joining more mainline groups such as Mary McLeod Bethune's National Council of Negro Women (NCNW), organized in 1935 in Washington, D.C., as an umbrella organization for black women's organizations. Personally acquainted with the renowned educator and reformer, Moore was present at the organizational meeting of the NCNW. She credits both Bethune and historian Lawrence Reddick with helping her to develop confidence in public speaking by providing speaking opportunities for her in Washington; both were impressed with Moore's persuasive oratory and clear analysis. Her associations with prominent black male leaders from 1930 to 1950 were less than favorable because of their blatant sexism and class consciousness. She claims that African-American women were wrongly excluded from the first two Pan-African Congresses (1919, 1921), organized principally by W. E. B. Du Bois. It was not until the founding of the Organization of African Unity that Moore says she got an opportunity to participate in the Pan-African Movement and to travel to Africa. She claims that Elijah Muhammad, the head of the Nation of Islam, was unreceptive to developing any cultural or political ties with Africa. In fact, she claims it was she and her sister, Eloise Moore, who introduced Malcom X to African history and Pan-Africanism.

Moore Calls for Reparations

Beginning in the 1950s, Moore's Pan-African nationalism broadened to include such issues as economic reparations, cultural identity, and education. Although she was hardly the first African American to issue a call for reparations, she was instrumental in making it a central issue prior to the inauguration of the civil rights and the black power movements. She launched her campaign for reparations in 1955 while in New Orleans, after reading in ''an old Methodist encyclopedia'' that ''a captive people have one hundred years to state their judicial claims against their captors or international law will consider you satisfied with your condition.'' With the one-hundredth anniversary of the Emancipation Proclamation just five years away, Moore launched a national crusade to rally support for reparations, even going to the White House in 1962 to meet with President John F.

Kennedy. She organized and directed the Reparations Committee of the Descendants of United States Slaves, which filed a claim in California in late 1962. Though her cries fell on deaf ears—the Civil Rights Act of 1964 and the Civil Rights Bill of 1965 fell far short of her demands for five-hundred million dollars—she had persisted in her efforts.

> They owe us more than they could ever pay. They stole our language, they stole our culture. They stole our mothers and fathers and took our names away from us . . . It's past due. The United State will never be able to pay us all they owe us (Lanker, 103).

For Moore the issue of reparations was more than a question of assuaging any guilt white Americans harbored for the enslavement and dehumanization of African-Americans. Reparations were a constructive step in the rebuilding of African-American cultural identity—the first step in Black Nationalist ideology. She founded and headed a number of organizations to achieve her goal of teaching racial pride and cultural identity in African-Americans. With Harlem as her base, she organized the African-American Cultural Foundation, which led the fight against the names "Negro" and "black." She contends that both terms are pejorative labels used by white oppressors to brainwash African-Americans; she advocates the use of "African" as a more appropriate term.

Moore also founded the World Federation of African People and was a founding member of the Ethiopian Orthodox Church of North and South America, the Congress of African Peoples (1970), and the Republic of New Africa, which were in part inspired by her trips to Africa, the West Indies, and Europe. On her first trip to Africa in 1966, she attended the funeral of Kwame Nkrumah. The trip was a memorable experience for Moore:

> When the plane landed such a thrill came over me, I became hysterical. For some reason, I couldn't keep it in any longer. All the years, all I had suffered, all of the separation, all of the whips on our black, all the rapes . . . came before me. I cried and cried (*Black Scholar*, 50).

She would return to Africa many times, visiting the heads of states of Uganda, Nigeria, Guinea, Tanzania, and Zimbabwe, and participating in such conferences as the All-African Women's Conference (1972) and the Sixth Pan-African Conference (1974)—both in Tanzania. While in Ghana, she was initiated as "Queen Mother" of the Ashanti people in recognition of her lifetime service to the African people.

One of Moore's most tangible contributions to people of African descent has been the Eloise Moore College of African Studies, founded on a two-hundred-acre plot of land in Mount Addis Ababa, New York. Named in honor of her sister, the fledgling school is designed to "embrace the cultural, education, and industrial needs" of African-Americans.

> We wanted to buy a school to teach our children, who are being severed from public schools—so called drop-outs. . . . We wanted to give our children skills that automation could not eradicate like soil conservation, skills like pruning trees, like landscaping, like poultry rearing. . . . Africa needs those skills. So if we could teach our children to be teachers—to go to Africa to teach the young ones their skills, we could have a flow of interests and collective work reaching across the seas (*Black Scholar*, 51).

Although the school burned down in 1961, Moore's vision of a school promoting African identity and vocational training has not diminished.

More recently Moore has been campaigning to establish a national monument in memory of the millions of Africans who died during the trans-Atlantic slave period. She has also been active in the Ethiopian Orthodox church of North and South America, which she cofounded with her sister, Lorita Moore. Although raised as Catholics, the two sisters became disenchanted with the Roman Catholic church in 1935 when the Pope blessed Italy's ammunition used to invade Ethiopia. The Moore sisters joined with a number of other African-American groups in organizing for Ethiopia's defense. In 1969 Moore was baptized by Abuna Tehopholis, head of the Ethiopian Orthodox Church, and became an abbess and later an archabbess.

Despite her more than eighty years as an activist and organizer, Moore remains virtually unknown. No full-length biography has been written of her life, but several good primary sources are available for such an endeavor. In addition to Cheryl Townsend Gilkes's extensive interview in the Black Women Oral History Collection at Radcliffe College, Brian Lanker's *I Dream a World: Portraits of Black Women Who Changed America* presents brief excepts from an interview, a short biographical sketch, and a recent photo of Moore. *Black Scholar* also published a wide-ranging interview with Moore in 1973.

References

Black Scholar (Interview) 4 (March-April, 1973): 47-55.

Black Women Oral History Interview with Queen Mother Audley Moore. Cambridge: Schleslinger Library, Radcliffe College, 1980.

Lanker, Brian. *I Dream A World*. New York: Stewart, Tabori and Chang, 1989. 102-103.

Women of Courage. An Exhibition of Photographs by Judith Sedwick. Based on the Black Women Oral History Project, Schlesinger Library, Cambridge: Radcliffe College, 1984. 59. Photograph, p. 59.

Collections

The most extensive biographical materials of Queen Mother Audley Moore are an undated vita published by the World

Federation of African People, Inc., at Mount Addis Ababa, New York, located in files at the Fisk University Library, and the Black Women Oral History Collection at Radcliffe College. A transcript of the interview is also in the Fisk collection. The 1983 interview, conducted by Cheryl Towsend Gilkes, traces the developments of Moore's life. The oral history sources, however, must be utilized with care since the interviews were conducted when Moore was older, and could not recall some significant dates and events.

Raymond R. Sommerville

Undine Smith Moore

(1904-1989)

Composer, arranger, educator

Undine Smith Moore belongs to a special group of black American composers who have not only achieved significant recognition through the performance of their musical compositions but also enjoyed long and successful teaching careers. Moore felt that while "it is a great thing to be a musician . . . the only thing that matches it is perhaps the opportunity to be a teacher" (*Black Creative Artists*). In addition to the love and respect of generations of students, she received many awards for her contributions to education. There is no doubt that her music has earned her a prominent place among black composers, especially in the field of choral music.

Moore was born on August 25, 1905, in Jarret, Virginia. She was the youngest of three children of James William Smith and Hattie (Turnbull) Smith. Her father worked as a brakeman for the railroad. When she was four, the family moved to Petersburg, Virginia, but returned to Jarret each summer to visit the family. Moore felt that those formative years in Jarret, among the rich musical culture endemic to "Southside" Virginia, inspired many of her later compositions. Her family was extremely affectionate and supportive and instilled in the children the value of education. Even with limited financial resources, they provided their daughter a Steinway piano. Although many people thought she would become a concert pianist, upon graduation from college she chose to begin her teaching career.

Moore graduated at the top of her class with a B.A. and B.Mus. (piano and theory) from Fisk University and went on to receive the M.A. professional diploma from Columbia University Teachers College. She also attended Juilliard as Fisk's first scholarship recipient and later studied theory and composition at Manhattan School of Music and Eastman School of Music. She taught high school music for one year before her long and celebrated forty-five-year (1927-1972) tenure at Virginia State College. Her students included many illustrious contributors to the music world, such as jazz pianist Billy Taylor, opera singer Camilla Williams, conductor Leon Thompson, gospel singer Robert Fryson, music educators Michael V. W. Gordon and James Mumford, and composer Phil Medley.

A principal achievement was her cofounding with Altona Trent Johns of the Black Music Center. In the interview for *Black Creative Artists* in 1980, she expressed their shared concern "that each generation appeared to know less and less about Black achievement." Determined to address this concern, they secured a grant from the National Endowment for the Humanities to bring a series of seminars on black music, art, dance, and drama to the campus. The philosophic basis for this project was to focus not only upon classical music, but on what Moore felt was the "true creative genius of the black people in the ditches and in the sawmills."

Upon her retirement from Virginia State University she was awarded an honorary doctorate of music for her exceptional work as a teacher. The degree was presented at New York City's Town Hall as part of a celebration in her honor orchestrated by former students. It included performances of her works as well as the presentation of a certificate of appreciation by Mayor John Lindsay; the certificate read: "To one who knows the true meaning of Service, Dedication, Beauty, and Love."

Retirement might also be characterized as commencement, as she continued to teach part-time at Virginia Union University and other colleges. During this period she was in great demand as a lecturer on the music of black composers; and as a result she traveled extensively, lecturing and conducting workshops at Howard University, Fisk University, and Indiana University, among others. In 1976 she received an honorary doctoral degree from Indiana University, where she also served as senior advisor to the Afro-American Arts Institute for many years.

Moore was a composer who worked in a variety of forms, including choral works, works for solo instruments and solo voice, chamber ensembles, and orchestra; her music is heard frequently at concerts, conventions, festivals, on college campuses, and in churches, such as the Peoples Congregational in Washington, D.C.. Her numerous commissioned works have been performed at Fisk University's Fine Arts Festival and Jubilee Day celebration, among others. Her many honors in the field of music include the proclamation of Undine Moore Day in Petersburg, Virginia, a 1980 Black Music Caucus Achievement Award, and the title Music Laureate bestowed in 1977 by the Commonwealth of Virginia. Her cantata, *Scenes From the Life of a Martyr: To the Memory of Martin Luther King,* which premiered in 1982, was nominated for a Pulitzer Prize.

Moore's work has been the focus of many musical events, including a series of concerts sponsored by the Midwest conference of American Women Composers and Kennedy-King College in honor of Black History Month, the Seventh

Annual Afro-American Music Workshop at Atlanta University Center in January 1978, and the New York Philharmonic's "Celebration of Black Composers Week" at Lincoln Center in August 1977, the first sizable tribute to black artists to be sponsored by a major symphony. Other composers and artists honored at the concert were pianists Leon Bates and Natalie Hinderas, violinists Sanford Allen and Aaron Rosand, and composers Howard Swanson and Olly Wilson.

Carl Harris, professor of music and director of choral activities at Virginia State University, has had a long association with Undine Smith Moore. He described her work in an article that appeared in *The Choral Journal* in April 1974, entitled "Three Schools of Black Choral Composers and Arrangers 1900-1970." Here he describes the work of Moore as belonging to a group designated as "Black Innovators," which includes Ulysses Kay and Hale Smith, composers who "have made dramatic and effective use of old compositional techniques coupled with many contemporary ideas" (16).

Harris described Moore's work in greater detail in his January 1976 article in the same journal, entitled "The Unique World of Undine Smith Moore." Here he describes the style of her choral works as "free, through composed style with frequent usage of recitative for expressive effects [where] contrasting moods are set by shifting of melodic and rhythmic patterns, functional harmonies with sporadic uses for mild dissonances and for dynamic contrasts, the expansion of basic four-part writing from five to eight parts" (7). In describing Moore's choral works in the black idiom, Harris points to a tendency in modern-day arrangements of Negro spirituals to get away from the original style of the songs. He continues, "the original melodies and characteristic rhythmic vitality found in Mrs. Moore's arrangements, however, assure us that much of their real import is still present and that fairly authentic performances can be realized" (7).

Negro Spirituals Influence Work

Harris speaks of the influence of Negro spirituals on Undine Smith Moore's work. It was not until her years at Columbia University that she realized the profound impact the songs sung by her deeply religious parents had upon her. She realized that many of these spirituals from Southside Virginia were not commonly heard and decided to document them for future use. She thought the songs so beautiful that she "wanted to have them experienced in a variety of ways—by concert choirs, soloists and by instrumental groups. To attempt to do this has given me much musical pleasure and strengthened the memories of the people who loved me and gave direction to my life" (Harris, "The Unique World," 6-7). Other influences on her style include ragtime, blues, jazz, and gospel music, as well as the Harlem Renaissance of the 1920s, as seen in the use of poems of Langston Hughes.

Undine Smith Moore's best-known published choral works include *Mother to Son* and *Tambourines to Glory*, based on the poetry of Langston Hughes; *Striving after God*, based on a text by Michelangelo Buonarotti; *Let Us Make Man in Our Own Image*, based upon text from John Milton's *Paradise Lost; The Lamb*, from a poem by William Blake, and *Lord We Give Thanks to Thee*, with text from Leviticus, commissioned in 1971 for the Centennial Celebration (1871-1971) of the Fisk Jubilee Singers. Choral works in the black idiom include *Fare You Well, Long Fare You Well, Daniel, Daniel, Servant of the Lord, Bound for Canaan's Land, Hail, Warrior, I Just Came From the Fountain,* and *Sinner You Can't Walk From My Path.* In *Black American Music Past and Present,* Hildred Roach describes *Glory to God* and *I Would Be True,* two more recent pieces, as follows:

> The opening of "Glory to God" depicts the rhythmic influence of Africa as well as the gospelized response to the Black church as the intricacy of movements among voices glorifies the God of mankind. "I Would Be True" reveals a portion of her piano style as it syncopates against the voices in parallel chord frames within a polymetric scheme (14).

The influences of spirituals can also be heard in *Afro-American Suite* for flute, cello and piano (commissioned by Trio Pro Viva). This piece, in addition to *Three Pieces for Flute and Piano,* are a departure from previous works in the use of dissonance employed by block chords of clusters and twelve-tone assimilations.

Moore was married to James Arthur Moore, who was chairman of health and physical education at Virginia State University. They had one daughter, Mary Hardie Moore Easter, a professional dancer and dance instructor at Carlton College. Undine Smith Moore died on February 6, 1989, at the age of eighty-three.

References

Abdul, Raoul. "Reading the Score. Honoring Undine Smith Moore." *Amsterdam News* (11 February 1978): B-10.

Black Creative Artists: Close-up. Video interview in three parts produced by Indiana University Instructional Television and the Afro-American Institute, 1980.

Gann, Kyle. "Concerts Honor Black Women Composers." *Chicago Sun-Times* (6 February 1987): 9.

Harris, Carl. "Three Schools of Black Choral Composers and Arrangers, 1900-1970." *Choral Journal* 14 (April 1974): 11-18.

———. "The Unique World of Undine Smith Moore." *Choral Journal* 16 (January 1976): 6-7.

Moore, Undine Smith. Biography File, Fisk University Library.

"Philharmonic Honors Black Composers." *New York Times*, 11 July 1977.

Roach, Hildred. *Black American Music Past and Present.* Boston: Crescendo Pub. Co., 1973. Includes photograph.

———. *Black American Music Past and Present.* Vol. 2. Malabar, Fla.: Krieger Pub. Co., 1985. Includes score excerpts.

Southern, Eileen. *The Music of Black Americans.* 2nd ed. New York: Norton, 1983.

Collections

Papers of Undine Smith Moore are at Indiana University.

Robert W. Stephens

Rose Morgan

(19?-)

Entrepreneur

Chaptle Morgan, a sharecropper, left Shelby, Mississippi, with a family of thirteen when Rose Meta Morgan was six years old, and settled in Chicago, Illinois. It was Chaptle Morgan, with demonstrated perseverance, who encouraged and instilled in his daughter Rose the desire to strive for the best life has to offer. Rose Morgan was determined to do just that. When she was fourteen years of age, she started a small beauty business in her neighborhood. She was the only beautician for many of her friends, which allowed her to earn her spending money.

After completing high school in Chicago, Rose Morgan attended Morris School of Beauty. Due to her special ability in styling, cutting, and grooming hair, attending beauty school simply enhanced her talents. Morgan began her first professional job when she leased a booth in a beauty salon in her neighborhood and established full-time clients. Her customers were pleased and her list of clients grew. Her big break occurred when she styled Ethel Waters's hair for a performance in Chicago in 1938. Ethel Waters was impressed with the style Morgan gave her and extended an invitation to Morgan to go with her to New York City. After being in the city for less than a year, Morgan had developed a growing business with a friend, Olivia Clark. They purchased a ten-year lease on a building that was soon to be called Rose Meta House of Beauty.

In the 1940s, Rose Meta House of Beauty was the largest black-owned beauty shop in the United States. However, Morgan did not become complacent with what seemingly was an overnight success. Instead, she worked hard to build her business and to maintain a reputation that would attract and appeal to her customers. She was determined to keep up with the times; therefore, she began developing and marketing Rose Meta cosmetics, producing fashion shows, and continuing to build her beauty salon. She traveled to Paris, France, to demonstrate her techniques on women of color in that city, and she was a smash in Europe.

Elaborate House of Beauty Opened

The grand opening for her second beauty salon, the House of Beauty, was in February 1955. Harlem was packed with women who came to see the elaborate and flamboyant new salon. Rose Meta Morgan was indeed a distinguished businesswoman—an entrepreneur by the standards of any nation.

Morgan was less successful in matrimony. However, out of her three marriages, the most widely publicized marriage was her second, to heavyweight boxer Joe Louis. The couple was married December 25, 1955, in New York. They were also involved in a business venture together. Rose and Joe Louis developed and promoted cologne for men. It was called "My Man," and Joe Louis was the man. The venture, a business idea implemented too soon for the times, did not survive.

The couple separated the summer of 1957, and the marriage was annulled in 1958. Morgan's third and final marriage was to Louis Saunders, an attorney. She pursued another business venture with her new husband. The couple cofounded a savings and loan association in New Jersey. After two years of marriage,the couple decided to separate. A divorce was never sought and soon after, Louis Saunders died.

After returning to New York, Morgan joined a group forming the Freedom National Bank in Harlem. In 1972 Morgan began franchising a new business, Trim-Away Figure Contouring (*Ebony* Editors, 228). As of this writing, Morgan is still living in New York City.

References

Davis, Marianna W., ed. *Contributions of Black Women to America.* Vol. 1. Columbia, S.C.: Kenday Press, 1982.

Editors of Ebony. *Ebony Success Library.* Vol. 1. Chicago: Johnson Pub. Co., 1973. 228.

"House of Beauty." *Ebony* 1 (May 1946): 25-29.

Moore, Mike. "Rose Morgan: Success in Grand Style." *Essence* 12 (June 1981): 34-44.

"Single Standard for Training Emphasized in Nation's Leading Profession for Women." *Ebony* 21 (August 1966): 142.

Vonita White Dandridge

Toni Morrison

(1931-)

Educator, editor, writer

Toni Morrison, a writer who has published five works of long fiction, is one of the country's most significant novelists of the twentieth century. She is praised for her mastery of language, especially her achievements in voice and movement in narrative and dialogue, and her control of verbal nuance, metaphor, image, and point of view. Modernist critics often compare her fiction to that of William Faulkner and James Joyce. But, in spite of formal literary training, she perceives her creativity as emanating from central forces in black American culture and not from the Eurocentric traditions implicit in the works of most authors to whom she is likened. Specifically, she believes that her novels have their foundations in the qualities of black culture that, so far, only black musicians have been able to express and that still reside in some undefinable culture-gen that survives in isolation because the black community manages to hold on to it. She explains that writing novels gives her a sense of encompassing that ineffable "something" (McKay, 426).

In form and content, Morrison believes that the best art is political and insists on the highest standard—the "irrevocably beautiful"—in her own craft of writing (Morrison, 5). One function of her novels, she points out, is to tell those stories of black people—stories that though articulated and memorized long before they appeared in print, have not been heard outside of the black community, nor by younger black people who are distant from the community. Another important quality of her stories comes from her conscious effort to transpose the orality of black language into the written text. In finely crafted "meandering" dialogue that needs no adverbs to communicate tones and moods, her fiction accommodates silent reading and oral presentation equally effectively. Readers hear her words as vividly as they see them on a page.

Toni Morrison

Her work upholds the integrity of black American cultural aesthetic traditions in the translation of those art forms into a print medium. That medium becomes a critical voice, upholding the functionality, improvisational nature, and relationship to audience performance that is central to the black tradition. Morrison has tried her hand at playwriting, and one drama of hers had one discrete public performance, but this work has not yet been released to the general public. Still, more than one critic notes dramatic qualities in several of her novels. One of the most notable characteristics of her writing is that while she carefully avoids the pitfalls of feminist rhetoric and dogma, she presents powerful images of the psychic realities of black women's experiences in her art.

Morrison, the second of the four children of George and Ramah Wofford, was born in Lorraine, Ohio, shortly after the onset of the Great Depression. She claims southern roots on both sides of her family. On her mother's side, the journey north was from Greenville and Birmingham, Alabama, by way of Kentucky, early in the century, in a flight from poverty, sexism, and racism. In Kentucky her grandfather, a farmer and carpenter, worked in the coal mines for a while; then, in search of better educational opportunities for the children, moved his family to Ohio.

Morrison's father hailed from Georgia, where racial violence precipitated his early departure from that region, even as it made such an indelible impact on him that throughout his entire life he found it impossible to trust or believe in the humanity of white people. A shipyard welder, he was a man of such enormous self-pride and self-respect that he welded his name into the sides of the ships on which he worked whenever he achieved a perfect seam. Frightened by the possibilities of unemployment, for seventeen years, during the early lives of his children, he held three jobs simultaneously. His most important legacy to his famous daughter is the strong sense of self-worth that she possesses.

Although Morrison grew up in an integrated community of blacks and ethnically diverse Europeans in which everyone was poor and blacks were not social outcasts, from her family's background she could not avoid a knowledge of the history of race in America. At home, with the maternal grandparents and her parents, she grew up amidst four separate, conflicting philosophical positions on the future of blacks in America. Her grandfather, John Solomon Willis, who after Emancipation lost the eighty-eight acres of his

Indian mother's land to unscrupulous whites, was convinced that there was no hope for black people in America. His wife, Ardelia, disagreed, and she placed her trust in her religious faith and the effort of will. While Morrison's grandparents argued about how and if black people could improve themselves, and who would help or hinder them, her parents disputed the possibility of white people's improvement. Morrison's father felt that was impossible and did his best to keep them out of his life; her mother was open-minded and approached each new encounter with whites with patience and reason. Only on the virtues of black culture did these four people agree.

Morrison's most vivid memories of childhood include learning about the richness of black folklore, music, myths, and the cultural rituals of her family and community. Her mother sang in the church choir; her grandfather, an artist, once supported his family by means of his violin performances; her grandmother decoded dreams from a book of symbols and played the numbers based on her translations; and there were signs, visitations, and ways of knowing well beyond traditional wisdom. Storytelling, in which Morrison is an expert, was also a major form of family entertainment during her young life. She recalls that the men and women in the family participated in this activity. Even now, the magic and the inexhaustible source of nonconventional wisdom embedded in folk life are so real to Morrison that she continues to find her dream life as interesting and absorbing to her as the more concrete aspects of her existence.

Not surprisingly, Morrison learned to read at an early age and was the only child in her first-grade class to enter with reading skills. Later, as a teenager, she read widely, from Jane Austen to the great French and Russian novelists to the literature of the supernatural. The specificity with which European writers presented their cultures in writing fascinated her. In this, she imagined that they spoke to her and everyone outside of their cultures. Morrison, like Langston Hughes before her, was so impressed by this aspect of literary achievement that she, like Hughes, works hard to capture a similar quality of specificity in black culture in her writing—to present as cogently as she can what black people do, and the meanings of the actions of black people. This specificity includes helping readers recognize the roles of magical elements in black cosmology. For example, in the world of Morrison's novels one needs to be attentive, learn to recognize, and understand the outrage and hurt that trees are capable of, and the meaning of the absence or presence of birds or animals in a narrative.

Morrison attended Loraine High School where, for four years, among other subjects, she studied Latin. She graduated with honors. Her mother was a high school graduate, her father was not, and only one relative of hers, an uncle, attended college. After high school, the family expected her to find work, get married, and settle down. Instead, Morrison went to Howard University, where she majored in English, minored in the classics, and changed her given name to Toni. In general, the social aspects of college life disappointed her, especially the emphasis on trivial elements such as clothes and parties. To counteract the superficiality that surrounded her, she joined the Howard University Players and traveled with the student repertory troupe in the summers, performing in plays across the South. These trips were the first contacts she had with that region and they brought her face to face with experiences she had heard about in childhood from the adults in her family.

Following graduation from Howard in 1953, Morrison entered Cornell University, where in 1955 she earned a master's degree in English. Her thesis was on the theme of suicide in the works of William Faulkner and Virginia Woolf. For the next two years Morrison taught at Texas Southern University, and in 1957 she accepted an appointment at Howard University and married a Jamaican architect named Harold Morrison. Among her most well-known students in the late 1950s and early 1960s were Claude Brown, author of the acclaimed *Manchild in the Promised Land* and *Children of Ham,* and Stokley Carmichael, famous for his civil rights activities in the 1960s. Morrison's marriage lasted for only a few years. By 1964 she was a divorced mother of two young sons, Harold Ford and Slade Kevin.

Morrison Accepts Editorial Position

In 1965 Morrison accepted a job as textbook editor for a subsidiary of Random House Publishing in Syracuse, New York. In 1968 she moved to New York City as senior editor in the trade department of Random House, a position she held until 1983. During her years as senior editor, she had particular concerns for young black writers and used her influence to bring several of their works to publication. Among those who gained from her interest in them were Toni Cade Bambara, Angela Davis, Henry Dumas, Leon Forrest, and Gayl Jones. The demands of editorship and single parenthood did not halt Morrison's teaching career in Afro-American literature and creative writing. From 1969 to 1970 she was an instructor at the State University of New York at Purchase; from 1975 to 1977, Distinguished Visiting Professor at Yale University; and from 1979 to 1980, Distinguished Visiting Lecturer at Bard College. Meanwhile, her first novel appeared in 1970. In 1984 Morrison left the world of publishing to accept the Albert Schweitzer Chair of the Humanities at the State University of New York at Albany, a position she held until 1989 when she moved to Princeton University as the Robert F. Goheen Professor of the Council of the Humanities. There she teaches in the Afro-American studies and the creative writing programs. The Princeton position makes Morrison the first black woman writer in America to hold a named chair in an Ivy League university. In addition to her fiction, her publications include a 1965 textbook on college reading skills and several essays and articles in popular and scholarly journals and newspapers on American literature, black American writing, life, and culture, and the worlds of black women.

Novel Wins Pulitzer Prize

Morrison's writing has enjoyed wide recognition in the academy at large, the general literary establishment, and the world that takes an interest in the humanities and culture. In addition to Faulkner and Joyce, her books are favorably compared with works by, among others, Vladimir Nabokov, Gunter Grass, and Gabriel Garcia Marquez. She has more than fifteen honorary degrees from American colleges and universities, including Harvard, Yale, Columbia, Georgetown, and Dartmouth. Likewise, she is the recipient of numerous honors and awards. In addition to the Pulitzer Prize for *Beloved*, her fifth novel, she holds the Chianti Ruffino Antico Fattore International Literary Prize (1990), the Modern Language Association of America's Commonwealth Award in Literature (1989), the Melcher Book Award (1988), the Elmer Holmes Bobst Award for Fiction (1988), City College of New York's Langston Hughes Festival Award (1986), the Distinguished Writer of 1978 Award from the American Academy and Institute of Arts and Letters, and the National Book Critics Circle Award (1978). She is cochairperson of the Schomburg Library's Commission for the Preservation of Black Culture and a member of the American Academy of Arts and Sciences, the American Academy and Institute of Arts and Letters, the board of trustees of the New York Public Library, the national advisory board for the Center for the Study of Southern Culture, the advisory board of Queens College, New York, and the Helsinki Watch Committee. A show in the PBS series, "Writers in America," features her life.

From their earliest fiction, autobiographies, and nonfiction prose in the nineteenth century, in general, black women writers in America focused on the experiences of black women. Throughout this long period, social marginalization based on race and sex almost entirely excluded them from literary history. Although most people were unaware of the black American literary tradition until the 1960s, the writings of men, even then, took precedence over those of women, and this state of affairs continued for almost another two decades. Interestingly, although Morrison did not read the works of earlier black women writers until after she published her first two books, her literary career followed in the tradition of the women who preceded her.

Morrison first turned to writing in the late 1950s when she joined a group of ten black writers in Washington, D.C. They met monthly and each participant brought something to read. Once she took a hurriedly-written story about a young black girl who wanted blue eyes. The idea originated from a conversation she had as a child with another black girl who rejected the existence of God after she had prayed unsuccessfully for two years for blue eyes. Even then, Morrison did not pursue the idea or think seriously of becoming a writer. Later, living alone with her sons in Syracuse, she turned to writing as a means of coping with loneliness. She developed more fully the idea of the effects of pain and yearning for a certain kind of physical beauty by women for whom that standard was unattainable. *The Bluest Eye* appeared in 1970.

Although reviewed in such well-known magazines and newspapers as *The New York Times Book Review, Newsweek*, the *New Yorker, The Times Literary Supplement, The New Republic*, and the *Chicago Tribune*, *The Bluest Eye* was not an instant success. Nor was *Sula*, Morrison's second novel. In fact, by 1974, when *Sula* appeared, the earlier book was out of print. While the handful of predominantly white critics who reviewed *The Bluest Eye* were unanimous in praise of Morrison's stylistic articulation of her vision of black life and the power of her poetic prose, their reactions to the plot were guarded, ambivalent, and sometimes negative. Only two black women, writing for *Black World* and *Freedomways*, openly admired *The Bluest Eye*. *Sula*, with more notice from black reviewers, fared better than its predecessor. Among other things, it was an alternate selection of the Book-of-the-Month Club and appeared in excerpts in *Redbook*. Most reviewers called this novel "thought-provoking" and a bold attempt to address the black female situation within the black community. The *New York Times* Sunday book reviewer, however, while praising Morrison's artistic talents and skills, implored her to break out of the provinciality of confining her writings to the lives of black girls and women. By 1977, when *Song of Solomon* was published, both early works were out of print.

If *The Bluest Eye* and *Sula* did not catch hold of the imagination of the book-buying public, their emergence nevertheless changed the life of their author. By 1970 Morrison's opinions were widely sought by the print media for comments on black life and black books in particular. Between 1971 and 1972 she reviewed twenty-eight books for the *New York Times* and wrote an essay on the women's liberation movement that appeared in its pages. She had gained national recognition.

Set in the Midwest, *The Bluest Eye*, told from the viewpoint of a nine-year-old narrator's experiences, is the story of Claudia McTeer, her ten-year-old sister, Frieda, and their friend, Pecola Breedlove. The narrative revolves around Pecola's physical and psychological destruction, a result of her impoverished sense of self. Feeling unloved by her family and the black community, Pecola surmises that a problem in herself keeps others from loving her and concludes her flaw is the ugliness of her blackness. Thus convinced, she transforms her need for love into an obsession for the symbol of beauty: blue eyes. She yearns to be like Shirley Temple, whom everyone, even the adults in the black community, adores.

Conversely, Claudia and Frieda live with their parents in a poor but emotionally secure home and resist such a self-destructive value system. They spend their time engaged with school activities, with play, and in watching how grown-ups respond to them. They learn to love themselves and have no sense of inherent unworthiness. In telling the story of Pecola Breedlove, the woman Claudia comes to better understand herself, the community, and why she and Frieda survived and Pecola did not.

Also set in the Midwest, and embodying the lives of several other memorable women characters, *Sula* focuses on the lives and friendship of two black girls in the 1920s and 1930s, Nel Wright and Sula Peace. The novel follows them from childhood to womanhood to the end of the friendship that precedes Sula's early death, and to a time many years later, when Nel experiences an epiphany about the meaning of her early relationship with Sula. In their extraordinary friendship, Sula is the social rebel, the town's scandal and embarrassment who, in Morrison's words, lives an experimental life; and Nel is the conformist who uncritically accepts the bondage of the stereotypes of woman's social function as her life.

Morrison has spoken of the character Sula as the best idea she ever had but admits to having had difficulty making her up. One problem was that Morrison never knew a woman exactly like Sula but wanted to describe her as a prototype of a classic evil force without making her repulsive or wholly unattractive to readers. However difficult the depiction might have been to execute, critics agree that Morrison succeeded. In the juxtaposition of Nel and Sula, Morrison explodes old ideas of good and evil by showing them to be intricate parts of each other.

The Bluest Eye and *Sula,* along with the works of such women as Paule Marshall, Alice Walker, Gayl Jones, and Toni Cade Bambara, made it clear that although previously neglected, black women writers of the 1970s claimed literary territory by their insistence on women's consciousness separate from men's. Joined with black men in the struggle against racial oppression, they also highlighted other equally significant considerations affecting the lives and welfare of black Americans. Like Gwendolyn Brooks's *Maude Martha* (1953), which was almost entirely overlooked in literary commentary when it was published, *The Bluest Eye* focused on ordinary black girls, giving them voice and agency, and called attention to much-neglected aspects of the lives of the majority of black women in this country. *Sula* moves beyond Morrison's first novel to engage with the lives of the black girls who survive childhood—to examine the importance of black women's friendships and the meanings of the decisions they make for themselves. Black feminist critics especially understand Nel and Sula as projections of different aspects of a single self—as representations of the connected differences within the self in process. With these ideas, Toni Morrison became one of the clear new voices of black women writing in the 1970s.

New Era of Writing Seen

Song of Solomon (1977) ushered in a new era for Morrison as a writer. Until the publication of *Beloved* (1987), this was her most widely acclaimed work. With this book, she was no longer the aspiring writer; she had become a giant in the field. In a short time, *Song of Solomon,* featured on the front page of the *New York Times Book Review,* received considerably more notice than *The Blues Eye* and *Sula* combined. It was also a Book-of-the-Month Club selection. In the wake of the novel's success, Morrison received the National Book Critics Circle Award and an appointment to the American Academy and Institute of Arts and Letters. A year following its publication, when *Song of Solomon* was a paperback best-seller with 570,000 copies in print, President Jimmy Carter appointed Morrison to the National Council of the Arts, and she was elected a member of the American Academy and Institute of Arts and Letters.

Song of Solomon differs from the earlier stories largely because of Morrison's choice of a central character. For the first time in her writings, a male took center stage. White critics and admirers in particular had other reasons to praise it more heartily than *The Bluest Eye* and *Sula* with their deeply disturbing themes of rape, incest, and black women attempting to define themselves in a social milieu that refused to accommodate deviance. *Song of Solomon* embodied the more familiar western themes of flight, journey, family quarrels, physical and psychological male violence, and the world of the black community, known for its well-defined social codes, superstitions, fables, myths, and songs.

Literary audiences responded to *Tar Baby* (1981), Morrison's next novel, in much the same way they did to *Song of Solomon.* Obviously enjoying the fame that was now hers, in an interview with *Newsweek* shortly after the novel appeared, Morrison quipped to the attendant photographer: "Are you really going to put a middle-aged, gray-haired, colored lady on the cover of this magazine?" (Strouse, 52). The smiling, successful writer made history when she became the first black American woman to appear on the cover of *Newsweek* (30 March 1981). A month after its publication, *Tar Baby* was on the *New York Times* best-seller list and remained there for nearly four months.

Tar Baby is different from Morrison's previous books in setting and structure. A fusion of fantasy and realism, the story has roots in the black American folktale of the white farmer who uses a tarbaby to trap the rabbit that has been foraging in his fields, but who is himself outwitted by the clever animal. Equally as important as Morrison's use of black folklore to provide the foundations of her plot was her decision to move the action beyond the borders of America and to separate her characters from their familiar social contexts. Most of the novel occurs on the exotic Isle des Chevaliers, an Edenic Caribbean locale, invaded by wealthy white Americans. But there is more. The sophistication of Paris, the excitement of New York City, the certainty of Philadelphia, and the search for black origins in Eloe, Florida, make up the landscape of *Tar Baby.* In the broadest sense, this novel suggests the scope of the black experience in confrontation with white America and the search for an identity.

The Pulitzer Prize-winning *Beloved* (1987) is a meditation on the legacy of slavery, a work that Morrison describes as an effort to rescue the "sixty million and more" to whom she dedicates it from the oblivion to which they had been consigned by history. The idea for the novel grew from a newspaper clipping about a slave woman, Margaret Garner, who in 1851, with her four children, escaped from Kentucky to a small neighborhood outside of Cincinnati, Ohio. Facing capture and a return to slavery, Garner killed one of the children and attempted to do the same to two others, whom she only succeeded in hurting. Morrison was especially struck by the reports in subsequent interviews of a calm, quiet, and self-possessed Garner while she was in prison. She expressed no remorse for her actions, explaining only that she did not want her children to live under the system from which she tried to rescue them.

Morrison's interest in the incident focuses largely on the nature of mother love. Garner had loved her children so much that she displaced herself, making them her best part, and putting on them the value of her own life. In so doing, she preferred to see them dead than to have them sullied or hurt by slavery. One question the author raises is the nature of excess, even of virtue. But the book is also a memorial that focuses readers on a recollection of slave and slavery. From Morrison's point of view, no suitable memorial wreath or plaque or building or tower exists—not even a tree—to remind us of those who endured the terrible experience. *Beloved* is such a monument.

Set outside Cincinnati, in a house called "124," with flashbacks to a slave plantation in Kentucky named Sweet Home, the key players in Morrison's novel are Beloved, the ghost/person of the murdered child; Sethe, the mother; Paul D., a former slave who knew Sethe when they were together at Sweet Home; and Denver, one of Seth's three other children who were not killed. Discovered by slave trackers a month after her escape from Sweet Home, Sethe kills her older daughter as a first step in attempting to save herself and her family from a return to slavery. The act both saves and destroys Sethe, for although she and the living children go free, she is more feared than loved by those around her, and the memory of the dead child remains with her.

Beloved is a novel about a community confronting its collective past of slavery, suffering, endurance, and strength, and a woman forced into remembering her past. Healing and self-acceptance come through confrontation that moves toward reconciliation, acceptance, and rebirth. The novel embraces an abundance of psychological subtlety and is filled with Morrison's most consoling as well as her most horrific images. Through Sethe's search for love and healing, Morrison seems to indicate that these goals are unattained in the absence of community. Only when Sethe's ties with the community are reestablished does she undergo healing. In the most intimate form of community, Paul D. and Sethe come together at the conclusion of the novel, and their stories, placed next to each other, create the promise of a future together.

To date, Morrison has published five novels and won many awards for them. She is a superb storyteller and an excellent stylist who creates unforgettable, haunting images to portray human experiences. Critics are unanimous in their praise of her illuminating metaphors, her skill with dialogue, and her graceful syntax. She admits that writing affords her an opportunity to find coherence in the world, that the discipline it requires helps her to sort out the past—her own as well as the collective past of black people in America. From the point of view of her own enjoyment, at least in the early years, it was work she did for and by herself. She likens her pleasure in the process of writing to that of a dancer's on stage in relation to gravity, time, and space. In writing, she finds energy, balance, repose, and the constant possibilities of growth. One of her great desires is that her writing continues to develop an element she admires in black music, especially in jazz—the absence of a final chord that keeps listeners on the edge, always wanting something more. Morrison's novels offer many avenues for explorations of American culture. They are crucial instruments in the refiguring of the black American and American literary traditions as the world approaches the end of the twentieth century.

Morrison's novels have been the subjects of three book-length studies: Karla F. C. Holloway and Stephanie A. Demetrakopoulos, *New Dimensions of Spirituality: A Biracial and Bicultural Reading of the Novels of Toni Morrison* (1987); Bessie W. Jones and Audrey L. Vinson, *The World of Toni Morrison: Explorations in Literary Criticism* (1985); Terry Otten, *The Crime of Innocence in the Fiction of Toni Morrison* (1989); and one anthology, Nellie Y. McKay's *Critical Essays on Toni Morrison* (1987). Dozens of critical essays on Morrison include Jane S. Bakerman, "Failures of Love: Female Imitation in the Novels of Toni Morrison," *American Literature* (1981); Barbara Christian, "Community and Nature: The Novels of Toni Morrison," *Black Feminist Criticism* (1985); Cynthia A. Davis. "Self, Society, and Myth in Toni Morrison's Fiction," *Contemporary Literature* (1982); Melvin Dixon, "Like an Eagle in the Air: Toni Morrison," *Ride Out the Wilderness: Geography and Identity in Afro-American Literature* (1987); Valerie Smith, "Toni Morrison's Narratives of Community," *Self-Discovery and Authority in Afro-American Narrative* (1987); Michael Awkward, "The Evil of Fulfillment: Scapegoating and Narration in *The Bluest Eye*," *Inspiring Influences: Tradition, Revision, and Afro-American Women's Novels* (1989); Robert J. Butler, "Open Movement and Selfhood in Toni Morrison's *Song of Solomon*," *Centennial Review* (1985); Theodore O. Mason, Jr., "The Novelist as Conservator: Stories and Comprehension in Toni Morrison's *Song of Solomon*," *Contemporary Literature* (1988); Ruth Rosenberg, "And the Children May Know Their Names: Toni Morrison's *Song of Solomon*," *Literary Onomastics Studies* (1981); Lawrence W. Hogue, "The Song of Morrison's *Sula*: History, Mythical Thought, and the Production of the Afro-American Text," *Discourse and the Other: The Production of the Afro-American Text* (1986); Victoria Middleton, "*Sula*: An Experimental Life," *CLA Journal* (1984); Maureen T. Reddy, "The Tripled Plot and Center of *Sula*," *Black American Literature Forum* (1988); Peter B. Erickson, "Images of Nurturance in Toni Morrison's *Tar Baby*," *CLA Journal* (1984); Lauren Lepow, "Paradise Lost and Found: Dualism and Edenic Myth in Toni Morrison's *Tar Baby*, *Contemporary Literature* (1987); and Marilyn E. Mobley, "Narrative Dilemma: Jadine as Cultural Orphan in Toni Morrison's *Tar Baby*," *The Southern Review* (1987). For additional listings of sources, see David L. Middleton, *Toni Morrison, An Annotated Bibliography* (1987), and Craig Werner, "Toni Morrison," *Black American Women Novelists* (1989).

References

Dictionary of Literary Biography. Vol. 33. *Afro-American Fiction Writers After 1955*. Ed. Thadious M. Davis. Detroit: Gale Research, 1984. 194.

McKay, Nellie. "An Interview with Toni Morrison." *Contemporary Literature* 24 (Winter 1983): 413-39.

Morrison, Toni. "Rootedness: The Ancestor as Foundation." *Black Women Writers*. Ed. Mari Evans. New York: Anchor Books, 1983. 339-45.

Stepto, Robert B. "'Intimate Things in Place': A Conversation with Toni Morrison." *Chant of Saints*. Eds. Michael S. Harper and Robert B. Stepto. Urbana: University of Illinois Press, 1979. 213-29.

Ruas, Charles. "Toni Morrison." *Conversations with American Writers*. New York: Knopf, 1985. 215-43.

Strouse, Jean. "Toni Morrison's Black Magic." *Newsweek* 97 (30 March 1981): 52-57.

Nellie Y. McKay

Gertrude Bustill Mossell

(1855-1948)

Educator, journalist, feminist

Gertrude Bustill Mossell

Gertrude E. M. Bustill Mossell, educator, journalist, and feminist, was born in Philadelphia, Pennsylvania, on July 3, 1855. Mossell died on January 21, 1948 at the age of ninety-two in Philadelphia, the city where she spent most of her life and did most of her campaigning for equal rights and women's rights. She had been ill for about three months before she died in Frederick Douglass Memorial Hospital, an institution she and her husband founded.

Mossell's parents, Charles H. Bustill and Emily (Robinson) Bustill, were among the free black elite of Philadelphia. The prominent Bustill family included generations of achievers, including Gertrude's great-grandfather, former slave Cyrus Bustill (1732-1806), who earned his freedom and served on George Washington's staff as a baker during the War for Independence. He owned his own bakeshop and was a schoolmaster during the late eighteenth century and a member of the Free African Society, a Philadelphia benevolent society. One of Bustill's daughters, Grace Bustill Douglass (1782-1842), was an abolitionist and a member and officer of the Philadelphia Female Anti-Slavery Society, as was her daughter, Sarah Mapps Douglass Douglass (1806-1882). Sarah Douglass was not only an abolitionist but a feminist and noted educator. Perhaps the most illustrious member of the Bustill family was Gertrude Bustill's cousin, actor and political activist Paul Bustill Robeson (1898-1976), who became a Rhodes Scholar after graduating from Rutgers University.

Mossell and her elder sister, who later became Mrs. William D. Robertson, were raised as Quakers, as were many of the Bustills. Both women later followed the lead of several family members and joined the Presbyterian denomination. They were educated in Philadelphia's "colored" schools, but while they were still children, their mother died. The girls were boarded with family friends until reaching adolescence, when they were returned to their father's house.

After completing her education the Roberts Vaux Grammar School, Mossell taught school for a period of seven years at various places, including Camden, New Jersey, and Frankford, Delaware. Marriage to physician Nathan F. Mossell of Lockport, Pennsylvania, probably in the early 1880s, ended her formal teaching career as married women were not allowed to teach. She returned to live in Philadelphia, where she raised two daughters, Mazie and Florence. Nathan Mossell's paternal grandmother was the sister to Paul Robeson's mother, Louise Bustill Robeson, revealing intermarriage patterns among Philadelphia's black elite. Hence Nathan Mossell and Gertrude Mossell were distantly related. A few years after her marriage, Gertrude Mossell resumed her writing and developed a career as a journalist, educating the public about women's rights and social reform movements.

Her career goal is not surprising because Mossell's early

life was characterized by her exceptional ability as a writer, and she came from a family of political activists and feminists. The Reverend Benjamin Tucker Tanner discovered Mossell's writing potential, probably in the late 1860s, as a guest at the closing exercises of the Roberts Vaux Grammar School, where he heard Bustill read her essay, "Influence." He invited her to submit it for publication to the periodical he edited, *The Christian Recorder*. As a result of this first literary success, Mossell began an outstanding literary career, writing essays and columns for numerous newspapers and periodicals and eventually writing two books: *The Work of the Afro-American Woman* (1894) and *Little Dansie's One Day at Sabbath School* (1902).

National Reputation as Journalist Developed

Mossell developed a national reputation as a journalist writing for African-American newspapers. Her articles and columns appeared in the *A.M.E. Church Review*, the *New York Freeman*, the *Indianapolis Freeman*, the *Richmond Rankin Institute*, *Our Women and Children*, and the *Indianapolis World*. In Philadelphia she wrote for leading papers with syndicated columns in the *Echo*, the *Philadelphia Times*, the *Independent*, and the *Press Republican*. In addition, Mossell assisted in editing the *Lincoln Alumni Magazine*, the journal of her husband's alma mater. During the late nineteenth and early twentieth century, Lincoln University in Pennsylvania became a prestigious institution that educated black American men.

Through her articles and columns Mossell wrote about her political and social ideology, reflecting the views of a feminist and social reformer. There were few black American women journalists during the 1880s when Mossell wrote the column, "Our Woman's Department," in the first issue of T. Thomas Fortune's *New York Freeman*, December 1885. Mossell introduced her column, entitling the first one "Woman's Suffrage." She said that her column would "be devoted to the interest of women" and that she would "promote true womanhood especially that of the African race" (*New York Freeman*, 26 December 1885).

After soliciting suggestions from her readers, Mossell discussed the politics of the women's suffrage movement. She expressed gratitude to Senator Blair of Massachusetts, who introduced a women's suffrage amendment in the United States Senate. Mossell encouraged readers who did not know about the issues of women's suffrage to read books and periodicals to educate themselves. Her hope was that those who thought unfavorably about votes for women would be convinced through awareness to change their opinions. Married women, Mossell argued, supported women's suffrage. Her words indicated a significant political awareness and sophistication that she shared with only a few outspoken black women suffragists in the 1880s.

Mossell's column appeared every other week throughout 1886: In it she promoted career development in business and the professions for women of her race. She called for training of women in skills that would prepare them for businesses such as the restaurant industry. She encouraged women to go into professions such as medicine, journalism, and training school education. Views such as these would not be seriously considered by representative black Americans for at least another generation. As for literary and journalism careers, Mossell introduced her readers to role models such as poets Frances Ellen Watkins Harper, Josephine Turpin Washington, and Charlotte Ray, essayist and journalist Mary Ann Shadd Cary, and journalists such as Ida B. Wells, Clarissa Thompson, and Mattie Horton. Throughout her column Mossell promoted women and encouraged them to seek their rights.

As to black American women seeking careers and also being wives and mothers, Mossell encouraged the women of her race to follow in her own footsteps, which many of them did. As a result, Mossell, like Ida B. Wells and other black women leaders of the late nineteenth and early twentieth century, combined roles as activists with those of wife and mother.

In Mossell's opinion, all types of black American women needed to ally to help themselves and one another. At the time, women such as Mossell called this process "racial uplift." Mossell looked beyond lines of status when she called for "domestic women, the intellectual, the temperance reformer, the White Cross worker, the suffragist, the missionary worker and the mother to come together to work for the race" (*New York Freeman*, 9 January 1886; 25 December 1886).

As a feminist, Mossell criticized male efforts to discriminate against women and white women's attempts to discriminate against black women. In an article she wrote for *The Afro-American Encyclopedia* (1895), "The Power of the Press," Mossell concluded that women journalists functioned as "satellites revolving round the sun of masculine journalism." Although women were respected as reporters in the black industry, she argued that they were not in "the thick of the battle" (169). Mossell diplomatically called for an end to male prejudice against women and encouraged women to assert themselves in industry.

Mossell was less diplomatic in her response to white feminists who attempted to ostracize black feminists from the movement. When a white woman from the Women's National Press Association wrote asking if Mossell wanted this white woman's organization to assist black women journalists in organizing, Mossell refused the help. Her priority was to encourage women of her race to work harder to be recognized by black men. Black women, she argued, could advance themselves more by joining their state press associations and the "National Association already established" (*New York Freeman*, 25 December 1886). Her views were consistent with other black women activists of the time who felt the rebuff of white feminists. Women like Mary Church Terrell and Ida B. Wells also admonished white women for giving into the racism by attempting to segregate black women into separate women's rights organizations.

Continuing to note the prejudices of white women in her writings, at the end of the nineteenth century Mossell noted that when books about American women's accomplishments were written, black American women were consistently left out. These omissions were part of her motivation for writing her first book, *The Work of The Afro-American Woman*, published for the first time in 1894. Dividing the manuscript into several sections, the book was more than a collection of biographical sketches like the two published in 1893: *Noted Negro Women*, by Monroe A. Majors, and *Afro-American Women of Distinction*, by Lawson A. Scruggs. Mossell's goal was to analyze the roles of women of her race within the context of the social movements of the day and to look at the professional development of these women. She noted that the women's suffrage movement "had passed the era of ridicule" as women began to look at suffrage issues more critically. She also commented on the Women's Christian Temperance Union and how it became a strong reform factor in women's work nationwide (*The Work of the Afro-American Woman*, 9).

Perhaps the largest profession for educated black American women at the end of the nineteenth century was the field of education. Mossell listed every woman of her race who had founded a school or developed an educational institution, from Fanny Jackson Coppin at the Institute for Colored Youth at Philadelphia during the antebellum period to Lucy Moten, who was principal of the Normal School of Washington, D.C., in the 1890s.

Mossell went on to cite black American women literary figures, journalists, lawyers, physicians, and others. Her nearly fifty-page list noted hundreds of names of black women and their professions. She ended her book with the following words:

> We close this tribute to Afro-American womanhood with a heart warmed cheered feeling that we have proven our case. Hath not the bondwoman and her scarce emancipated daughters done what they could? (9).

In the later half of Mossell's long life she became more actively involved in several race-oriented, social welfare activities, as did many of the women who worked to uplift the race. She organized the Philadelphia branch of the National Afro-American Council, a precursor to the NAACP. She was the major force behind fund-raising for the Frederick Douglass Memorial Hospital, a black institution founded by her husband because most hospitals in Philadelphia denied admission to blacks. Through Gertrude Mossell's leadership, black American women of Philadelphia raised the funds necessary—some thirty thousand dollars—to erect a three-story building in 1895. Not surprisingly, the hospital included the Training School for Nurses, an example of a program Mossell had long encouraged women of her race to seek. Much of her community efforts during the more than fifty years of the Douglass hospital's existence went toward fund-raising for the institution. She was the president of its Social Service Auxiliary. After considerable turmoil with its rival black medical facility, Mercy Hospital, founded in 1907, the Douglass hospital merged with it in 1948, the year of Mossell's death. The new institution became the Mercy-Douglass Hospital. By that time, the two major benefactors of the old Douglass hospital had died—Nathan and Gertrude Mossell.

Mossell, who was one year older than her husband, shared his life of activism, supporting human rights causes and equal justice for black Americans, especially in Philadelphia. He died in the fall of 1946 at the age of ninety. She survived him by fifteen months. They were survived by their two daughters, Mazie Griffin and Florence Holmes, four grandchildren, and several other relatives.

References

Alexander, Raymond Pace. "Nathan Francis Mossell." *Dictionary of American Negro Biography*. Eds. Rayford W. Logan and Michael R. Winston. New York: Norton, 1982. 457-58.

Brown, Claudette. "Gertrude E. M. Bustill Mossell." *Dictionary of American Negro Biography*. Eds. Rayford W. Logan and Michael R. Winston. New York; Norton, 1982. 457.

Majors, Monroe A. *Noted Negro Women*. Chicago: Dononue and Henneberry, 1893. 129-33.

Mossell, Gertrude E. B. Bustill. *The Work of the Afro-American Women*. Philadelphia: George S. Ferguson Co., 1908. A photograph of Gertrude Bustill Mossell with her young daughters is in the 1908 edition of this work (frontispiece).

Mossell, Mrs. N. F. "Our Woman's Department." *The (New York) Freeman*, 9 January 1886; 25 December 1886.

———. "The Power of the Press." *The Afro-American Encyclopedia*. Nashville, Tenn.: Haley and Florida, 1895. 167-67.

Penn, Irvine Garland. *The Afro-American Press and Its Editors*. Springfield, Mass.: Wiley, 1891. 405-407. Photograph p. 489.

Rosalyn Terborg-Penn

Lucy Ellen Moten

(1851-1933)

Educator

Lucy Ellen Moten's strong influence as an educator of black school teachers changed Washington, D.C.'s entire educational system. She held in highest regard ample education for future teachers as well as refinement of culture and moral character. She herself fully embraced these ideals, thus serving as an esteemed role model for her students.

Moten's own extensive education started early. She was born in 1851 to Benjamin Moten and Julia (Withers) Moten, free blacks who soon recognized their daughter's intellectual promise. In order to accommodate this, they moved from Moten's birthplace in Fauquier County, Virginia, to Washington, D.C., so that she could receive a substantial elementary education. Moten started in Washington's tuition schools for free blacks and then switched to the black public schools when they were established in 1862. Upon graduating, she began her secondary education in Howard University's normal and preparatory departments, where she studied for two years. Then she began teaching and thereafter spent most of her life both as an educator and as a student, often filling the two positions simultaneously.

Moten's first teaching employment began in 1870 in the primary classes at Washington's O Street School, a public grammar school. She continued this post until 1873, when she resumed her education at the State Normal School in Salem, Massachusetts. After graduating in 1875, she returned to teaching. Later she attended Spencerian Business College, graduating in 1883. In that same year, she undertook what was to become a lifelong endeavor, the position of principal for the Miner Normal School, a training school for black American elementary teachers. It was this post in which she was the most influential and for which she became the most well-known. Ironically, she was initially turned down for the position, not because of deficient credentials, but because of her striking appearance. Miner School board member Frederick Douglass had recommended her, and although the trustees accorded that her educational qualifications were highly satisfactory, they feared that her character was not moral or strong enough to assume the responsibility of such a position. Douglass explained this situation to Moten and asked her if she would relinquish certain recreations, such as theater, card playing, and dancing. When she assented, he recommended her a second time, and "upon the statement that he, himself, would stand surety for her promise, the board approved her appointment to the position" (Carrothers, 103). She remained at Miner until 1920, demonstrating through the many changes she instituted that the school, now part of the University of the District of Columbia, would have been radically different without her.

Moten Heads Miner Normal School

In educating her students, Moten stressed cleanliness, health, and physiology as well as strong technical education. While she was principal, she began studying medicine "so that she might better deal with students' health problems and to assist her in establishing a hygiene course in the school's curriculum" (West, 459). In 1893 she began attending Howard University Medical School, and received her M.D. degree in 1897. She expanded Miner's curriculum to include health and hygiene, first giving lectures herself and later bringing in another physician to lecture on children's diseases and health care. Beginning in 1903, she ensured that her students were in good health by bringing in a doctor to conduct regular checkups.

Moten firmly believed that educators should be highly educated, and she influenced the entire college population of Miner School and Washington in this regard. Under her principalship, Miner extended the school's program to two years and added student-teaching to the curriculum. In this way, students benefited from supervision as they practiced teaching. Her graduates were said to have been "sought by state superintendents throughout the country because of the efficient service they rendered whenever they were employed" (Wormley, 127). Moten also initiated a special one-year teacher training course for college graduates. Upon completing this course, the graduates were eligible for employment in Washington's elementary schools.

While at Miner, Moten was constantly expanding her own education and experience. She instructed aspiring teachers in several vocation schools in the South, and as a result of this experience, took graduate courses in education at New York University. She also spent several summers in Europe.

Moten's educational accomplishments earned her the post of vice-president of an annual educational conference. The *Colored American*, regarding this honor, said of Moten, "It is conceded by those best posted on educational affairs that the explanation of the art of teaching by Miss Moten is equal to any of either race in this country" (Majors, 319).

Moten left Miner in 1920 and about four years later moved to New York City. In 1933, she was struck by a taxicab in Times Square and died from her injuries on August 24 of that same year. She is buried in Harmony Memorial Park Cemetery outside Washington, D.C.

There exist two testaments to Moten's educational accomplishments and strength of character. In her will, she left more than fifty-one thousand dollars to her alma mater, Howard University, which recognizes her for that donation. Also, a Washington elementary school has held her name since 1954.

References

Contributions of Black Women to America. Vol. 2. Ed. Marianna W. Davis. Columbia, S.C.: Kenday Press, 1982. 295-96.

Corrothers, Thomasine. "Lucy Ellen Moten." *Journal of Negro History* 19 (January 1934): 102-106.

Majors, M.A. *Noted Negro Women: Their Triumphs and Activities.* Chicago: Donohue and Henneberry, 1893. Reprinted. Salem, N.H.: Ayer Co., Publishing, 1986. 318-319.

Peterson, Gladys Tignor. "Lucy Ella [sic] Moten." *Nota-*

ble American Women: A Biographical Dictionary. Vol. 2. Cambridge: Harvard University Press, 1971. 591-92.

West, Earle H. "Lucy Ellen Moten." *Dictionary of American Negro Biography*. Eds. Rayford W. Logan and Michael R. Winston. New York: Norton, 1982. 458-59.

Wormley, G. Smith. "Lucy Ellen Moten." *Journal of Negro History* 17 (January 1932): 124-40.

Evonne Lack with Adrienne Lash Jones

Constance Baker Motley

(1921-)

Lawyer, politician, judge

Constance Baker Motley served as an associate counsel for the NAACP Legal Defense Fund over a period of twenty years, becoming part of a civil rights movement that was involved in spectacular legal victories against segregation. She is presently a senior district judge for the Southern District of New York, which covers Manhattan, the Bronx, and six counties north of New York City.

Constance Baker Motley

Constance Baker Motley was born on September 14, 1921, in New Haven, Connecticut. Her parents, Willoughby Alva Baker and Rachel (Huggins) Baker, migrated to the United States from the Caribbean island of Nevis. Although blacks composed only about two percent of the total population of New Haven at the time, Motley, fortunately, was exposed to black history and culture through her religious affiliation. She attended Sunday school at an Episcopal church, where the minister offered lectures on black history. The minister and his wife, who was from the South, served as mentors to her.

Motley attended elementary and high schools in New Haven. When she entered New Haven High School at the age of fifteen, she was well-prepared for the rigors of academic life, but she encountered her first experiences with racial discrimination. The first incident occurred when she and a group of friends went to Bridgeport, Connecticut, for a picnic. The group of youths were refused admission when they tried to enter the roller-skating rink. On another occasion in Milford, Connecticut, Motley and several black and white youths were prohibited from swimming at a local beach because the group was interracial. These incidents raised her consciousness on racial discrimination and helped influence her decision later to join the civil rights movement. Since she was tall and by the age of fifteen could easily pass for twenty-one, Motley participated in local community affairs, becoming president of the New Haven Youth Council and secretary of the New Haven Adult Community Council. Both organizations were established to promote civil rights.

Motley graduated from high school with honors in 1939. As one of nine children during the depression era, however, college seemed a remote possibility. A year and a half later, Clarence Blakeslee, a contractor and successful businessman, offered to pay her college expenses. Blakeslee, who contributed to many black causes, offered financial assistance after hearing Motley speak at a New Haven community center that he had built. The facility was not used by the black population, and Motley offered the explanation that "blacks were not involved because they were not on the Board of Directors and therefore they were not really concerned" (Motley, "Some Recollections of My Career," 36). Blakeslee was impressed with Motley's intelligence and outspoken demeanor. When he asked her why she was not in college, she told him she did not have the money to go to college, but she wanted to be a lawyer. Blakeslee admitted that "he didn't know much about women and law," but he was willing to provide the means for her to pursue her goals (36). Motley's parents didn't really believe her when she told them the story, but they did not discourage her. "They thought I should be a hairdresser. I even thought I should be an interior decorator when I was in the eighth grade." Thus, Motley's opportunity to continue her education due to the kindness of a benefactor allowed her to exceed the expectations that she or her parents held.

Motley attended Fisk University in Nashville, Tennessee, from February 1941 to June 1942, transferring during the war to New York University and graduating from its Washington Square College in October 1943 with a major in economics. Motley was admitted to Columbia Law School and began her studies in February 1944. There were very few women there, but they survived and graduated. "When I graduated in 1946, you would not have been able to find a single person willing to bet twenty-five cents that I would be successful in the legal profession," recalled Motley (Motley, "Civil Rights: Our Legacy and Our Responsibility," 1; "Some Recollections," 37).

Motley, like her sisters from the nineteenth century—Mary Church Terrell, Mary Ann Shadd Cary, Charlotte Ray, Harriet Tubman, and Sojourner Truth—dreamed of helping black people. The dream became reality in Motley's last year of law school when she was selected as a law clerk for Thurgood Marshall, the chief counsel of the NAACP Legal Defense and Education Fund, future Solicitor General of the United States and Supreme Court Justice.

A tall, gracious, stately woman, Motley successfully combined career and marriage. She and Joel Wilson Motley, a real estate and insurance broker, were married on August 18, 1946, in New Haven. Their son, Joel, Jr., born on May 13, 1952, later graduated from Harvard Law School. For Motley, the quality of time spent with her family was very important. Early in her career, she traveled a lot and devoted much of her time to her legal work. However, she maintained close contact with her husband and son through their weekend visits.

Motley observed gender and racial prejudice as she traveled throughout the United States. "During the course of my work with the NAACP Legal Defense and Educational Fund, I traveled around the country trying school and other kinds of desegregation cases. One of the early cases in which I appeared as a trial lawyer was a case in Mississippi [*Bates* v. *Batte*], involving the equalization of black teachers' salaries in 1949" (Motley, "Some Recollections," 37). The local newspapers had a big story on the day the trial began because there were two black lawyers from New York who were going to try the case and one was a woman. The courthouse was packed; not only because this was the first case in this century in which blacks in Mississippi sought to attack the establishment and try to end segregation, but because, as the local newspaper stated, "there was a black woman lawyer from New York" (37).

Motley notes a distinct connection between the black struggle for equality and justice and the increasing momentum for civil rights following World War II. Even before the war, the strategy of the NAACP Legal Defense Fund was "to change the laws back to make them conform to what we believed was the intent of the Civil War Amendments. There was no prior precedent, therefore, it was the task of the Legal Defense lawyers to create new legal theory" (Blount, 30; Motley, "Civil Rights," 129-30). These legal cases were interrupted by World War II, when the country turned its attention to helping in the war effort while soft pedaling the business of discrimination. "World War II created a type of psychological stress whereby segregation in the armed forces became a national embarrassment," Motley believes (Blount, 30). The returning servicemen brought a new sense of pride in their American citizenship and this gave them the strength to unite in the struggle against discrimination and oppression. According to Motley, "They enrolled in the NAACP in unprecedented numbers" (Blount, 31).

School Segregation Laws Attacked in Court

After the war, Motley helped write the briefs filed in the United States Supreme Court in the school desegregation cases, *Brown* v. *Board of Education* (1954). After winning the historic case, in a series of cases the Supreme Court declared segregation unconstitutional in other areas where restrictive state statutes and polices were based exclusively on race. "The Brown decision was the catalyst which changed our society from a closed society to an open society and created the momentum for other minority groups to establish public interest law firms to secure their rights," states Motley ("Civil Rights," 132). In addition, she reminds us that it provided the impetus for the women's rights movement, the poor people's movement, and other public interest concerns, including prisoners' rights, consumer rights, and environmental law.

Motley was always well-prepared during her years as a trial lawyer. Setting a record of personal achievement unequaled by most lawyers, she argued ten civil rights cases in the Supreme Court, winning nine. Among others, Motley represented James Meredith in his long fight to enter the University of Mississippi (*Meredith v. Fair*), Charlayne Hunter and Hamilton Holmes (*Holmes v. Danner*) in their fight to enter the University of Georgia, James Hood and Vivian Malone, the University of Alabama, and similar college and professional school-level cases. Motley played a key role in gaining Meredith's entrance into the university on September 30, 1962. He was admitted after sixteen months of constant legal work, almost fifteen court hearings, and an expense to the Legal Defense Fund of an estimated thirty thousand dollars. As a result of Meredith's case, the last segregated university gave up peacefully. Harvey Gantt was admitted to Clemson College, the state college in South Carolina, the year after the first court order.

In court, Motley was a keen and perceptive lawyer, always firm and forceful in her legal presentations. During her years as associate counsel of the NAACP Legal Defense Fund, she appeared before state and federal courts in eleven southern states and the District of Columbia in numerous cases involving public school desegregation, public and publicly-aided housing, transportation, recreation, and public accommodations (the sit-in cases). Jack Greenberg, who succeeded Thurgood Marshall in 1962 as NAACP Legal Defense Fund director-counsel, regarded Motley as "anchor woman of his team" ("Mme. Borough President," 225). She and other attorneys of the NAACP Legal Defense Fund represented the "sit-inners" in the early sixties— Martin Luther King, Ralph Abernathy, Fred Shuttlesworth, and other demonstrators in the civl rights protest movement— and succeeded in having various injunctions against them lifted. In the civil rights movement, blacks demonstrated that they could do something with their law degrees—could make a significant contribution. "Black lawyers became respectable in the legal profession because they had accomplished something on their own," said Motley (Interview with Constance Baker Motley).

As a result of Motley's work in civil rights during the 1950s and early 1960s, her legal career broadened and future appointments opened to her. In February 1964, she was elected to the New York State Senate, setting a precedent as the first black woman to hold the office. During her first seven weeks in the state legislature, she began a campaign for the extension of civil rights legislation in employment, education, and housing. However, Motley's tenure in Albany was brief. In a special election in February 1965, called by the New York City Council, she was elected to fill a one-year vacancy as president of the Borough of Manhattan. Motley was reelected in the city-wide elections of November 1965 to a full four-year term. As the first woman and the third black to hold the office of borough president, Motley made tremendous accomplishments despite both race and gender. While in office, she drew up a plan to revitalize Harlem and other underprivileged areas of the city.

Motley Appointed Federal Judge

In 1966, Motley received national acclaim for her achievements in civil rights. That year President Lyndon B. Johnson appointed her to the United States District Court for the Southern District of New York. There was tremendous opposition to her appointment, not only from southern senators but from other federal judges as well, but "she finally made it through the senate" and was confirmed in August 1966 (Motley, "Some Recollections," 39). She became the chief judge of her court on June 1, 1982, and served as such until October 1, 1986, when she took senior status.

Motley's appointment to the federal judiciary marked the climax of a distinguished career in politics and civic affairs. Throughout the years she had exerted honest, determined, and frank leadership in the legal field. She is personally pleased with the historically significant changes that have been made and the progress that has taken place over the last twenty years. She believes, however, that "there is still a lot to be done." On civil rights, Judge Motley firmly states, "If we have to litigate the basic issues of racial discrimination into the next century, then that's what we must do" (Blount, 31).

Motley receives support and encouragement from her husband, Joel Motley, and from her son, Joel Motley, Jr., a graduate of Harvard, a lawyer, and an investment banker. Joel Motley, whose career has not been adversely affected by his wife's prominence, maintains his own identity by "being considerate and understanding of his wife's career" (Berry, 158). The Motleys are members of the Riverside Church. For relaxation, they enjoy the theater, entertaining friends, and occasional weekends at their country home in Chester, Connecticut. In addition, they spend a few weeks each year in the Caribbean.

Motley is optimistic about the future of the legal profession, especially the increasing demand for black lawyers. She predicts a bright future for intelligent, young, dedicated men and women in the legal profession. Motley believes the problems that black Americans face today do not include strictly legal barriers to full participation in the American community. The formal legal barriers have been removed by civil rights litigation. "Most of the problems blacks now face require political solutions. The most pressing need among blacks is the need for greater political power," she concludes. The momentum will come from a new breed of lawyers. "Lawyers are natural leaders and activists in the black community. More and more blacks will become involved in policy making agencies, in government, in politics, in business and diplomacy—in areas where blacks have not been before and where decisions and changes are going to be made," Motley asserted (Interview with Constance Baker Motley).

Motley has received many honors and achievements from some of the most prestigious institutions in the country, including honorary degrees from the following institutions: Tulane University and the University of Connecticut, 1990; Georgetown University School of Law and Princeton University, 1989; Yale University and Colgate University, 1987; New York University, 1985; University of Bridgeport Law School, 1984; New York Law School, 1982; Spelman College, John Jay Institute of Criminal Justice, Trinity College, Connecticut, 1979; Atlanta University, University of Hartford, 1973; Brown University, 1971; Fordham University, 1970; Howard University, Morgan State University, and Virginia State University, 1966; and Smith College, 1965. She has also received the Elizabeth Blackwell Award, Hobart and William Smith College, 1965; Columbia Law School Medal for Excellence, 1987; and the New York State Bar Association Gold Medal Award, 1988.

In addition to her work in law, Judge Motley has written extensively in legal and professional journals. The following articles are just a few of her publications: "Prisoners' Rights," *Brooklyn Law Review,* 62 (Spring 1976): 887-94; "From Brown to Bakke: The Long Road to Equality" *Harvard Civil Rights-Liberties Law Review,* 14 (Spring 1979): 315-527; "Race Discrimination Cases: The Legacy of Justice Lewis F. Powell," *Suffolk University Law Review*, 21 (Winter 1987): 971-87; "Desegregation and Education," *Mississippi Law Journal*, 58 (Fall 1988): 241-46; "Civil Rights: Our Legacy and Our Responsibility," *North Dakota Law Review*, 64 (1988): 121-33; "Massive Resistance: America's Second Civil War," *Arkansas Law Review*, 41 (1988): 123-40; "Some Recollections of My Career," *Law and Inequality: A Journal of Theory and Practice*, 6 (May 1988): 35-40; "Standing On His Shoulders: Thurgood Marshall's Early Career, *The Harvard Blackletter Journal*, Harvard Law School, (Spring 1989): 9-17; and "The Legal Aspects of the Amistad Case," *Journal of the New Haven Colony Historical Society*, 36 (Spring 1990): 23-31.

References

Berry, Bill. "Husbands of Well Known Women." *Ebony* 33 (April 1987): 154, 156-58.

"Constance Baker Motley Biography." December 1990. Typewritten document.

Dannett, Sylvia G. *Profiles of Negro Womanhood*. Vol. 2. Yonkers, New York: Educational Heritage, 1964. 320-27.

Duckett, Alfred A. *Changing of the Guard: The New Breed of Black Politicians*. New York: Coward McCann and Geoghegan, 1972. 108-12.

Lamson, Peggy. *Few Are Chosen; American Women in Political Life*. Boston: Houghton Mifflin, 1968. 127-61.

Lerner, Gerda. Ed. *Black Women in White America: A Documentary History*. New York: Vintage Books, 1973. 323.

Low, Augustus W. *Encyclopedia of Black Americans*. New York: McGraw-Hill, 1981. 582.

"Mme. Borough President: Constance Baker Motley." *Crisis* 72 (April 1965): 224-25.

Motley, Constance Baker. Interview with author. 21 July 1990.

Motley, Constance Baker. "James Meredith in Perspective." *Crisis* 70 (January 1963): 5-11.

Ploski, Harry A., and James Williams, comps. and eds. *The Negro Almanac: A Reference Work on the African American*. New York: Gale Research 1989. 38, 345-46. Photograph with President Lyndon Johnson, p. 345.

Reasons, George and Sam Patrick. *They Had A Dream*. New York: New American Library, 1971. 42.

Robinson, Wilhelmena S. *Historical Afro-American Biographies*. Cornwells Heights, Pa.: Publishers Agency, 1978. 230-31.

Spiegler, Charles, ed. *They Were First*. New York: C. E. Merrill, 1968. 85-89.

Smythe, Mable M., ed. *The Black American Reference Book*. Englewood Cliffs, N.J.: Prentice-Hall, 1976. 95-121.

Who's Who Among Black Americans. Detroit: Gale Research, 1990-1991. 929.

Floris Barnett Cash

Joan Murray

(1941-)

Broadcast journalist, entrepreneur

Joan Murray, who worked her way up the ladder go become the first black woman to report the news on television, later opened her own ad agency and was equally successful in her second career. She was born on November 6, 1941, in Ithaca, New York. Murray, who is an identical twin, attended Ithaca College for one year and then moved to New York City with her sister, June, and attended Hunter College and the New School for Social Research. Besides attending schools in New York, Murray studied at the French Institute and Harvard University. Her father, Isaiah, was a Fulbright scholar, and her mother is the former Amanda Pearl Yates of Kentucky. She also has a younger sister ("Joan Murray: TV News Broadcaster," 4, Biography file).

When Joan Murray and her twin sister, June, moved to New York to attend school and break into commercial television, little did Murray know that she would be carving a place in history as the first black American news correspondent appearing on television in the United States.

Like many early television journalists, Murray worked her way up the ladder, starting as a court reporter and then moving to the CBS-TV press department as secretary. While working in that position, Murray was known "as one of the best secretaries in the building" (*Sepia*, 29). Murray left the CBS-TV press department in 1959 to work as a secretary for Allen Funt, the man who created "Candid Camera." She worked in that position for six months while also working as a model and appearing in television and other productions. In fact, "Joan and her twin sister, June, were hired to appear in the first series of TV commercials ever produced for the Black consumer market" ("Joan Murray: TV News Broadcaster," 3, Biography file).

Murray received her first real break in television in 1963 when she landed a job with NBC on Kitty Carlisle's daytime show entitled "Women on the Move." There, Murray started writing for television and appearing on the air "presenting light news stories and women's features" (*Ebony*, 50).

While the NBC show was a good break for Murray, she wanted to be in television news. In 1965 Carlisle's show was killed by NBC, which caused Murray to set some new goals for herself. Murray said:

> I always looked forward to the time when the job would be opened for a Negro woman. However,

> as time went on, I realized I would have to make my own opening (*Sepia*, 29).

Murray wrote a letter to CBS-TV "outlining her experience and ability. That move landed her an audition, and she was hired the following week" (*Ebony*, 50), thus joining CBS as the first black American woman to appear on a major television show. The time was right and Murray was there making history.

> The job was virtually created for Joan because CBS realized that the climate was right and the time appropriate for putting a Negro woman on the air. The other two networks already had Negro reporters on the air—Mel Goode at ABC and Bob Teague at NBC (*Sepia*, 30).

While it was fashionable in the 1960s to put a minority person on the air because of the racial climate at that time, CBS realized "that they had found the right woman, and they were not mistaken" (*Sepia*, 30). Murray was more than just a token journalist who was going to be used as a symbol or window dressing.

Joan Murray left a legacy; she was more than just a pretty face. She was known as an intelligent, hard-working journalist whose primary goal and motivation was centered around the perfection of her craft. Murray worked as a correspondent on the 6:00 and 11:00 P.M. newscasts and was a contributor to various other television specials, news, and public affairs programming. Murray was described as a television reporter who reports the news "with cocksure crispness without the slightest sign of nervousness and with tonal quality which would do justice to an old hand in the business" (*Sepia*, 28).

Murray Forms Advertising Agency

Despite her success, Murray left the television news business in 1969 to form Zebra Associates, a successful and lucrative advertising agency serving several national clients, including General Foods, Gillette, Gulf Oil, and Miller Brewing, to name a few.

During her tenure in the news and advertising business, Murray was the recipient of more than seventy-six honors and awards (*Who's Who in America*, 2375). Some of her honors include the Mademoiselle Award for Outstanding Achievement, John Russwurm Award, Urban League's Certificate of Merit, Media Woman of the Year, Matrix Award from the New York chapter of Women in Communication, Links Distinguished Service Award, and the Mary McLeod Bethune Achievement Award. Murray was also the first black American woman to enter the Powder Puff Derby, where she flew solo in a small plane. She is also the author of *A Week with the News*, an autobiography published by McGraw-Hill in 1968.

References

Ebony 21 (October 1966): 50.

"Joan Murray: CBS Girl on the Go." *Sepia* 7 (February 1966): 28-33.

"Joan Murray: TV News Broadcaster—Businesswoman—Author—Lecturer—Pilot." Typewritten document. Biography File, Fisk University Library.

Mapp, Edward. *Directory of Blacks in the Performing Arts*. 2nd ed. Metuchen, N.J.: Scarecrow Press, 1990.

Ploski, Harry A. and Ernest Kaiser, eds. *The Negro Alamanac*. 2d ed. New York: Bellwether, 1971.

Who's Who in America. 46th ed. Chicago: Marquis, 1990.

Dhyana Ziegler

Pauli Murray

(1910-1985)

Lawyer, poet, scholar, author, educator, administrator, religious leader, civil rights and women's movement activist

Pauli Murray's career and interests transcended categories. In the course of achieving noteworthy stature in the fields of literature, law, and religion, she became a distin-

Pauli Murray

guished educator and an ardent leader in the civil rights and women's movements. She illustrated in her writings, legal arguments, lectures, sermons, and personal activities that knowledge must be committed to the search for freedom and justice if it is to contribute fully to society.

Born in Baltimore, Maryland, on November 20, 1910, Pauli Murray was the fourth of six children. Her father, William Henry Murray, was a graduate of Howard University and a teacher and principal in the Baltimore public schools. Her mother, Agnes (Fitzgerald) Murray, was a graduate of the Hampton Training School for Nurses. Christened Anna Pauline Murray, she was the namesake of her father's mother, Annie Price Murray, and her mother's sister, Pauline Fitzgerald Dame. When her mother died of a cerebral hemorrhage in 1914, Pauli Murray went to live with her Aunt Pauline and her maternal grandparents, Robert George Fitzgerald and Cornelia (Smith) Fitzgerald, in Durham, North Carolina. Her father, who suffered from long-term effects of typhoid fever, was too ill to cope with his six children and was committed to Crownsville State Hospital. The other five Murray children were raised in Baltimore by their father's sister and unmarried brother. Pauli Murray's ambition as a young girl was to have her father released and to restore her family when she reached the age of majority, but her father was allegedly killed by a hospital attendant in 1923. It was through others that Pauli Murray learned of her mother's beauty, her dark flashing eyes, her high spirits, her quick temper, and her forgiving spirit. Stories about her mother and father conveyed both love and sadness to her and had a strong influence on her development. "From a realm beyond my senses," she said, "they both inspired and gave me my first stern lessons in the meaning of adversity" (Murray, *Song in a Weary Throat*, 1).

In the segregated South, Murray learned to live with intricate racial codes while learning from her grandparents the pride, strength, and spirit of the blend of races and cultures in her ancestry—black, white, and Cherokee Indian; slave, free black, and white aristocrat. Years later Murray described herself as having been "biologically and psychologically integrated in a world where the separation of the races was upheld by the Supreme Court of the United States" (Leland, *The Chapel Hill Newspaper*).

Perhaps the strongest influence on Murray was the legacy of her mother's family, a story she made famous in her family memoir, *Proud Shoes*. Her grandmother, Cornelia, was the daughter of a young white attorney, Sidney Smith, and his sister's beautiful slave, Harriet Day, who was part Cherokee Indian. Smith raped Harriet, and she gave birth to his daughter, Cornelia, who was raised in the Smith household by the spinster sister, Mary Ruffin Smith. Sidney Smith was proud of his daughter and spent hours in her company, practicing his eloquent courtroom arguments on his audience of one. Mary Ruffin Smith supervised Cornelia's religious training at the Chapel of the Cross Episcopal Church in Chapel Hill, North Carolina. Grandmother Cornelia instilled in her granddaughter, Pauli Murray, her sense of pride in this heritage.

Murray's grandfather, Robert Fitzgerald, was a native of Delaware and the son of a half-Irish free black and a white farm girl. He was educated at the Ashmun Institute (now Lincoln University) in Pennsylvania and served in the Union forces in the Civil War. He met and married Cornelia Smith when he went to North Carolina to teach the freed slaves after the war. He imparted to Murray his self-reliance, his pride in his military service, and his fervor for learning, teaching her to read the newspaper to him when he became blind and she was not yet of school age.

Murray's aunt, Pauline Fitzgerald, was a forty-three-year-old school teacher when she took Pauli Murray to live with her. She kept Pauli with her in her classroom, where the young child unobtrusively learned along with the third-graders until she was old enough to enroll in school. Murray was confirmed in the Episcopal Church when she was nine years old, and was adopted by her Aunt Pauline that same year. In 1926, when she was fifteen years old, she graduated at the head her class of forty at Hillside High School in Durham.

Determined to attend college, Murray went with her Aunt Pauline to New York to see if she could be admitted to Columbia University, but learned that Columbia did not admit women. She then talked with the admissions officer at Hunter College, and when she discovered that she did not have a sufficient number of high school courses for admission, she met the difficulty with her "competitive spirit" (Murray, *Song*, 67), deciding to study in a New York high school and gain the credentials to qualify for admission. In 1927, Murray was one of twenty-five to graduate with honors in a class of more than two hundred at Richmond Hill High School. She returned to Durham and worked for a year before entering the freshman class at Hunter College in the fall of 1928. She had to leave school her sophomore year after the stock market crashed and she lost her jobs. When Murray was twenty years old she secretly married a man whom she later identified as "Billy" (Murray, *Song*, 77), but they separated after several months of living in poverty and later had the marriage annulled.

In the spring of 1931, Murray drove to California with a friend to look for work, but returned to the East Coast almost immediately in response to a letter from her Aunt Pauline, who was ill. With no money for train fare, she traveled as a hobo aboard cattle, fruit, and express trains. Being five feet tall and slender, with short hair, she dressed as a teenage boy and traveled unharmed. After her aunt improved, Murray returned to New York to work and to resume her studies. She graduated from Hunter College in January 1933, with a major in English and a minor in history. She was one of only four black students in her class of 247 women.

Talent for Writing Developed Early

Although Murray constantly pushed aside her career in literature for service in other professions, it was always first in her heart. When she was fifteen, she wrote a novel, *The Angel of the Desert*, which she described as being stereotypic and lurid, with a blond, blue-eyed heroine and a wicked, dark-haired sister. The novel was published in serial form in the *Carolina Times*, the black-owned newspaper in Durham. During her years at Hunter College she began to focus on her "long-simmering ambition to become a writer" (Murray, *Song*, 86). As part of her studies there, she wrote an essay on her Grandfather Fitzgerald, which was the origin of *Proud Shoes*, published twenty-eight years later. While driving to California in the spring of 1931, she wrote the first poem that she published, "Song of the Highway," which appeared in the anthology *Color* in 1934. She published her first article, "A Working Student," in the December 1932 issue of *Echo*, the Hunter College magazine.

In the 1930s, Murray worked for the Works Progress Administration (WPA) as a teacher in the Remedial Reading Project in the New York City public schools, and then in the WPA Workers' Education Project, and kept alive her desire to be a writer. She developed a friendship with the Pulitzer Prize-winning poet Stephen Vincent Benét, who guided and encouraged her in her poetry writing and urged her to write a novel about her family. She also associated with Harlem Renaissance writers such as Countee Cullen and Langston Hughes. Through the years she continued to write poems and articles that were published in various magazines.

Innovation in Civil Rights Movement Begins

Always ahead of her time, Murray was an innovator in the movements to gain racial and sexual equality in the United States. Beginning in the late 1930s, her activism in the civil rights movement was so influential that it could be considered a career in itself, but for her it was a logical involvement that grew out of her everyday struggle to overcome social injustice. Her first protest against the Jim Crow practices in the South occurred when as a young girl she would walk miles in Durham rather than ride the segregated city buses. Her first overt stand against racial segregation came when she refused to consider attending a segregated college after she graduated from high school.

In the fall of 1938, Murray took an even more unorthodox step in attacking racial discrimination in regard to her own education, a step unthinkable for a black person to take at the time: she applied for admission to the graduate school at the University of North Carolina. On December 14, 1938, she received a letter from the dean of the UNC graduate school rejecting her application on the grounds that "members of your race are not admitted to the University" (Murray, *Song*, 115). Her personal quest for admission to the university suddenly became public news because the United States Supreme Court had ruled on December 12, in the *Gaines v. Canada* case, that it was the duty of a state to furnish graduate and professional training to all the residents of the state based on an equality of right. The decision affected sixteen southern states, including North Carolina, which barred black students from attending the state universities.

Only the second black person ever to apply to the university, Murray became the topic of articles in the national black-owned newspapers, debates in the UNC student newspaper, and finally articles in white-owned newspapers all over the country. Her case was the first of its kind to receive wide publicity, and resulted in black students' filing applications almost immediately at other southern universities. With the admission of several black students to the University of North Carolina law school in 1951, Murray began to see the importance of her role as a pioneer in this struggle for equality of opportunity in higher education. When other southern state universities were facing the issue of racial integration for the first time more than twenty years later, her example took on even greater significance.

The greatest ironies of the case were not acknowledged in the editorial comments—that the Smith family, of which Murray's grandmother, Cornelia Smith Fitzgerald, was a member, had created a permanent trust fund for the education of students at the university; that her grandmother Cornelia's grandfather, James S. Smith, had been a member of the board of trustees of the university; and that the family inheritance that her grandmother should have received had been directed to the university instead. As Murray recounts in her autobiography, the final irony in her battle for admission to the university came forty years later in 1978, when the university decided to award her an honorary degree. To her it was more than an academic honor. She recalled, "It was a symbol of acceptance stretching back to my Grandmother Cornelia and her relationship to the Chapel Hill Smiths, whose position as benefactors of the university from which I was excluded had intensified my feeling of being disinherited" (Murray, *Song*, 128). Although she initially accepted the invitation, Murray unhappily declined later because of the university system's refusal to produce and implement a more adequate desegregation plan for its sixteen campuses, which it had been directed to do by the United States Department of Health, Education, and Welfare.

Civil Rights Violation Spurs Interest in Law

Murray's serious interest in a career in law was sparked when she was arrested in Virginia in March 1940. While on a trip to Durham, she and her friend, Adelene McBean, were arrested on a Greyhound bus in Petersburg, Virginia, charged with disorderly conduct and creating a public disturbance. Although they had observed the Jim Crow laws on the bus, they had refused to move further back to a broken seat where the driver had directed them. They were jailed for three days, and despite efforts of the NAACP attorneys, they were found guilty and had to pay a fine. Through this experience, Murray began to realize how Mahatma Gandhi's method of nonviolent protest could be used to fight racial discrimination in this country. To the Gandhian techniques, she added her own "American techniques of showmanship" (Murray, *Song*, 201).

While in jail, Murray and her friend drafted a "Statement of Facts" about the case, which their attorneys praised for its form and accuracy. Murray found herself able to follow and anticipate the legal arguments that the attorneys made, and to envision her case as part of a large effort to overthrow all segregation laws. Vindication for her came in 1946 when, in the *Morgan v. Virginia* case, the United States Supreme Court held the Virginia Jim Crow statute invalid.

Murray's job as field secretary for the Workers Defense League took her from coast to coast during the next two years to raise funds for the defense of Odell Waller, a black Virginia sharecropper who had been sentenced to death for killing a white landowner, Oscar Davis, in a dispute over Waller's crops. Convinced of Waller's innocence, Murray believed the jury to have been prejudiced and worked with an all-consuming passion to prove the crucial issue that nonpayers of poll tax were barred from jury service by the discriminatory administration of jury law. This human tragedy so affected her that it changed the course of her life.

In the fall of 1941, Murray enrolled at the Howard University law school with the intent of becoming a civil rights lawyer. She continued to work on Waller's behalf, publishing, with Murray Kempton, "All for Mr. Davis: The Story of Sharecropper Odell Waller," to acquaint the nation with the facts of the case. All appeals failed and Waller was executed in 1942. Murray's legal argument was finally won twenty-four years later when the United States Supreme Court struck down the Virginia poll tax.

Murray's interest in fighting racial discrimination remained steady as she worked with the NAACP and joined the Congress of Racial Equality (CORE), a pacifist organization experimenting with Gandhian techniques, led by Bayard Rustin and James Farmer. Murray also developed a close friendship with Eleanor Roosevelt, with whom she had corresponded since 1938 and had met for the first time in 1940. For more than twenty years she and Eleanor Roosevelt visited frequently and had ongoing discussions about the problems of racial discrimination in this country. While still a law student, Murray organized and led sit-in demonstrations aimed at desegregating restaurants in Washington, D.C.

During this time, Murray's journalistic writing began to gain attention. Her article, "Negroes Are Fed Up," appeared in *Common Sense* magazine, and her article about the Harlem race riot in 1943 was published in the Socialist *Call*. In 1943 she also finished "Dark Testament," her most famous poem, in which she related the history of black and white Americans and expressed the ideas that blacks must accept the challenge of their existence, and that whites must work to restore America's professed ideals and to promote universal brotherhood. It was published two years later in *South Today* magazine, which paid her one hundred dollars, the first money that she earned for writing poetry.

During her senior year Murray was elected president of her class and chief justice of the Court of Peers at Howard University. Her senior law thesis, in which she examined the Supreme Court's civil rights decisions in the late nineteenth century, was significant because of her argument that the "separate but equal" doctrine did violence to the personality of the minority individual. The lawyers for Oliver Brown, et al. used her argument successfully ten years later to help win the *Brown v. Board of Education of Topeka* case, in which the United States Supreme Court ruled that the doctrine of "separate but equal" had no place in American public education. In May 1944 Murray graduated cum laude from the Howard University law school, and won a Rosenwald Fellowship for graduate study in law at Harvard University. After the public announcement, however, she was rejected by Harvard law school on the basis of gender. When she noticed that her male colleagues at Howard found her rejection from Harvard to be amusing rather than outrageous, she began to feel more keenly and militantly the injustice of gender discrimination.

That fall Murray entered the Boalt Hall of Law at the University of California, Berkeley. In 1945, she received an LLM degree in law and passed the California bar examination. Her master's thesis, "The Right to Equal Opportunity in Employment," was the first definitive published law review article on this issue. In January 1946 she became the first black deputy attorney general of California, but she had to leave the job shortly thereafter because of a personal illness and the illness of her Aunt Pauline.

After several years, in which Murray worked as a law clerk, gained admission to the New York bar, and moved her aging aunts, Pauline and Sallie, to live with her in Brooklyn, she opened a law office in New York City. In 1949 she ran for a New York City Council seat from Brooklyn's tenth senatorial district as candidate for the Liberal Party. She made a remarkable showing, coming in second to the Democratic candidate.

In 1951 Murray published her first book, *States' Laws on Race and Color*, which added to her eminence as a legal scholar. Thurgood Marshall later affirmed the importance of this book, saying that it was the Bible for the civil rights lawyers who were fighting segregation laws. In the early 1950s, Murray and James Baldwin were residents at the famous McDowell Colony for artists in Peterborough, New Hampshire, the first black writers admitted to the colony.

In 1956 Murray published *Proud Shoes: The Story of an American Family*, a biography of her grandparents, Robert and Cornelia Fitzgerald, and also the story of courageous black Americans coping with racial conflict. With *Proud Shoes*, she established a new genre in American literature, the Afro-American family history, which preceded by twenty years Alex Haley's *Roots*, the book that attracted public attention to the genre. With the revival of interest in this subject and literary genre, *Proud Shoes* was reprinted in 1978.

In 1956 Murray was hired as an associate attorney in the nationally prestigious law firm of Paul, Weiss, Rifkind, Wharton and Garrison in New York City, where she worked until 1960. The only female attorney in the firm, she again experienced the discrimination practiced against women in many areas of professional life.

Murray was deeply affected by the lynching of Mack

Parker in Poplarville, Mississippi, in 1959, and felt that she had to get away from the United States. In February 1960, she left New York for an eighteen-month sojourn in Ghana to teach constitutional and administrative law as a senior lecturer at the Ghana School of Law, and to explore her African cultural roots. In 1961 she and Leslie Rubin published an original textbook, *The Constitution and Government of Ghana*. Murray returned to the United States and began graduate study at Yale law school in the fall of 1961.

In 1962 Murray, whose stature as a legal scholar and educator and as an activist in a number of civil rights groups had become well-known, was selected as a member of the Committee on Civil and Political Rights, one of seven study committees set up by the President's Commission on the Status of Women. She wrote "A Proposal to Reexamine the Applicability of the Fourteenth Amendment to State Laws and Practices Which Discriminate on the Basis of Sex *Per Se*," a memorandum that developed a new approach to the issue and was used by the committee as the substance of its final report.

Murray Helps Found National Organization for Women

In 1965, Murray received the degree of Doctor of Juridical Science from Yale law school, the first black person awarded this degree by the law school. She met Betty Friedan that fall and told Friedan about her idea for an independent national civil rights organization, like the NAACP, for women. In October of 1966, Murray was one of the thirty-two women who met in Washington and founded the National Organization for Women (NOW).

About this time, Murray began to lean more and more toward service in the Episcopal church, but with no specific goal other than lay Christian service. In 1966, she left the church for a year because of its refusal to include women in active roles in worship services. The following year, cancer struck her friend Renee Barlow and made Murray think more deeply about the questions of human destiny, but she left the immediate questioning behind as she began a one-year residence as vice-president of Benedict College in Columbia, South Carolina.

Murray's work as a consultant at the Fourth Assembly of the World Council of Churches in Uppsala, Sweden, called in 1968 to contribute to the elimination of white racism, fired her with enthusiasm to proclaim through her life and work the universal sisterhood and brotherhood (Murray, *Song*, 385). Once again, however, she attended to other business, beginning a five-year tenure as a professor of American Studies at Brandeis University.

Murray's only collection of poetry, *Dark Testament and Other Poems*, was published in 1970. In addition to the title poem, this volume includes forty-seven poems that deal with such topics as historical events and personages, love, death, friendship, and the universal difficulties of life.

In 1972 Murray was named Louis Stulberg Professor of Law and Politics at Brandeis. The following year, her friend Renee Barlow died in New York. With no priest available, Murray ministered to Barlow when she died, as she had with her Aunt Pauline in 1955. After this experience, Murray felt the call of total commitment to service in the church. She applied for admission to holy orders and entered the General Theological Seminary in September 1973, the only black woman and the oldest student enrolled.

Episcopal Church Ordains First Black Woman

The last decade of her life, a time usually reserved for retirement, saw the full flowering of Murray's talents and gifts—ongoing study, the writing of her autobiography, ordination in the ministry of the Episcopal church, and speaking engagements across the country. In 1976 she received the Master of Divinity degree, cum laude, from the General Theological Seminary and was ordained to the Holy Order of the Deacons of the Episcopal Church, USA.

On January 8, 1977, Murray was ordained an Episcopal priest at the National Cathedral in Washington, D.C. She was the first black woman ordained a priest in the two-hundred-year history of the Protestant Episcopal Church. On February 13, 1977, Murray celebrated her first Holy Eucharist in Chapel Hill, North Carolina, at the Chapel of the Cross Episcopal Church, whose archives recorded that her grandmother, Cornelia, a "servant child," had been baptized there on December 20, 1854. The event was recorded on national television by Charles Kuralt of CBS in his "On the Road" program.

Along a course of dedicated and innovative leadership in the ministry, Murray served as priest of the Episcopal Church of the Atonement in Washington, D.C., as priest of a "floating parish" for the hospitalized and homebound in Alexandria, Virginia, and as priest of the Church of the Holy Nativity in Baltimore, Maryland. In January 1984, she retired and moved to Pittsburgh, Pennsylvania.

On July 1, 1985, Pauli Murray died of cancer at her home in Pittsburgh. Funeral rites were held on July 5 in Washington, D.C., at the National Cathedral, where she had been ordained.

Murray's last literary contribution was her autobiography, *Song in a Weary Throat: An American Pilgrimage*, which was published posthumously in 1987 and which documents her career and her search for personal identity. In 1988 this work received both the Robert F. Kennedy Book Award and the Christopher Award. In 1989 it was reprinted as *Pauli Murray: The Autobiography of a Black Activist, Feminist, Lawyer, Priest, and Poet*.

During her lifetime, Murray received wide acclaim for her service to society, from recognition in 1946 as "Woman of the Year" by the National Council of Negro Women, to the Eleanor Roosevelt Award from the Professional Women's Caucus in 1971, to honorary degrees from Dartmouth, Radcliffe, and Yale, among other colleges and universities. In 1990, the University of North Carolina added one more voice, a significant voice in view of its historical encounters with Pauli Murray, to those throughout the nation that have affirmed the ideals and aspirations that she personified. The Pauli Murray Scholarship was established by the university to be awarded annually to an undergraduate student with documented financial need who has made significant contributions to the improvement of race relations on the campus of the University of North Carolina at Chapel Hill.

Murray's entire life was one of broadening interests, multiplying talents, and response to new challenges. In an age of the deliberate oppression of America's black citizens, she contributed to the reordering of the national agenda, insisted on rational discourse, and fostered conciliation among all people. Her observation that she had "lived to see [her] lost causes found" (McNeil, "Interview with Pauli Murray," 77), stands as a convincing testament to her contributions to the betterment of American society.

References

Contemporary Authors. Detroit: Gale Research, 1989. 352-354.

Diamonstein, Barbaralee. *Open Secrets: Ninety-four Women in Touch With Our Time*. New York: Viking, 1972. 289-294.

Leland, Elizabeth. "Pauli Murray Returns to Fulfill A Prophesy." *The Chapel Hill Newspaper*, 14 February 1977.

McKay, Nellie. "Pauli Murray." *Dictionary of Literary Biography*. Vol. 41, *Afro-American Poets Since 1955*. Detroit: Gale Research, 1985. 248-251.

McNeil, Genna Rae. "Interview with Pauli Murray, February 12, 1976, Alexandria, Virginia." Southern Historical Collection and Manuscripts, Wilson Library, University of North Carolina, Chapel Hill, N.C.

Murray, Pauli. *Dark Testament and Other Poems*. Norwalk, Conn.: Silvermine Publishers, 1970.

———. *Proud Shoes: The Story of an American Family*. New York: Harper and Row, 1956. Reprinted, 1978.

———. *Song in a Weary Throat: An American Pilgrimage*. New York: Harper, 1987.

———. *States' Laws on Race and Color*. Cincinnati, Oh.: Women's Division of Christian Service, Methodist Church, 1951.

Murray, Pauli and Murray Kempton. "All for Mr. Davis: The Story of Sharecropper Odell Waller." New York: Workers Defense League, c.1942.

Murray, Pauli and Leslie Rubin. *The Constitution and Government of Ghana*. London: Sweet and Maxwell, 1961.

Thomas, Gwendolyn. "Pauli Murray." *American Women Writers*. Vol. 125. New York: Frederick Ungar, 1981. 241-243.

Collections

The Pauli Murray Papers, 1941-1973, are in the Schlesinger Library, Radcliffe College, Cambridge, Massashusetts. The library also houses the Marie T. Monahan Collection of Pauli Murray Papers, 1971-1972, and the Lillian H. Nelson Collection of Pauli Murray Papers, 1977-1981. Correspondence between Pauli Murray and the Roosevelts, 1939-1962 may be found in the Franklin D. Roosevelt Library, Hyde Park, New York. Photographs of Murray are in the Schomburg Center for Research in Black Culture, Prints and Photo Collection, New York City.

Marsha C. Vick

N

Ethel Ray Nance

(1899-)

Secretary, museum assistant, historian, writer

During the Harlem Renaissance of the 1920s, Ethel Ray Nance encouraged young black intellectuals to go to New York and participate in the great cultural awakening that was taking place. So that the young members of the renaissance would not be lost, she kept a file of their dossiers. She also kept a diary of their achievements and other occurrences within the literary and cultural movement of that time. The apartment that she shared with playwright and librarian Regina Anderson (Andrews) and Louella Tucker, known as "580," was a "Renaissance USO" (Lewis, 127) for the emerging and aspiring black artists and writers, where they could find food, shelter, a receptive ear, and a meaningful introduction to society. Working closely with Charles S. Johnson on *Opportunity,* the journal of the National Urban League, she was involved in the literary contests and social events that gave these young men and women their start up the literary and artistic ladder. She was an important figure in the Harlem Renaissance. To Nance, however, her work as assistant to W. E. B. Du Bois when he was consultant to the United Nations at its founding in San Francisco in 1945 was the most important part of her career.

Ethel Ray Nance was born April 13, 1899, in Duluth, Minnesota, one of four children of Inga (Nordquist) Ray and William H. Ray. Her mother, who was white, was born on a farm in Sweden. She moved to live with her brother in Minneapolis and there she met and married William Ray. Nance's father was born near Raleigh, North Carolina, orphaned at an early age, and raised by an uncle on a farm in North Carolina. When William H. Ray was about nine or ten, he moved to Iowa where he lived with a German family and completed elementary and high school. He respected his German teachers for their thoroughness. Nance never saw her grandparents nor were they discussed much in the family.

The Ray family was among the two hundred blacks in a population of one hundred thousand in Duluth. Nance recalls seeing passenger ships in Duluth, with students from Howard and Fisk universities aboard, and the impressionable young girl dreamed of sailing away to a different place. After graduating from high school Nance worked in Duluth from 1918 to 1919 as a stenographer, then became secretary to the director of relief work for the Minnesota State Relief Commission in connection with the Red Cross in Moose Lake, where she remained for four years (1919-1922). In an effort to broaden her perspective and knowledge of black people, Nance's father took her on a long trip to Chicago (where she saw the black YMCA, YWCA, and the Urban League), Toledo, Detroit, Rochester, Boston, (where she saw the Crispus Attucks monument and visited the Old North Church), and on to New York. There she was to meet W. E. B. Du Bois, but in his absence she met A. Philip Randolph and visited his *Messenger* office, George Schuyler, and a few other prominent blacks. The father and daughter went on to Washington, D.C. (where she visited Howard University), and to Raleigh, North Carolina. There Nance met many of her relatives and important businesspeople such as Charles C. Spaulding of the North Carolina Mutual Life Insurance Company. The final stop was Atlanta, Georgia, where she met other businesspeople. Her father's carefully planned itinerary provided for the business contacts. On each meeting Nance asked, "Is there an opening for a stenographer, hoping someone would say there might be" (Ann Allen Shockley interview with Ethel Ray Nance, 18 November 1970).

After returning to Minnesota, Nance secured a position in the Minnesota House of Representatives as a stenographer for one year (1923). She was then offered a position with the Urban League in Kansas City. Nance held the position from 1924 to 1925. There she saw totally segregated living—a condition to which she was unaccustomed. Then twenty-two years old, she was placed in charge of employment. In 1924 the National Urban League and the National Conference of Social Work both met in Kansas City. "The world came to Kansas City," she said (Interview, 18 November 1970). Nance met many prominent blacks. She renewed her acquaintance with Charles C. Spaulding and met Eric Waldrond, Charles S. Johnson, and others. This was a time when the National Urban League was looking for secretaries to work in its various branches.

The contact with Charles S. Johnson led to an offer to come to New York City to work with the National Urban League and to assist with his research on blacks in cities in the United States. The Harlem Renaissance was already in full bloom. The young, inexperienced Nance was not easily persuaded and Johnson wrote to her approximately three times before she accepted. She was won over by his letters as he told her about the movement for young black writers. In his most persuasive letter Johnson said:

> Everything centers in New York. You have your selection of contacts. Eventually if you grow you will come here anyway. There are half dozen schools, all the magazines, and practically all the colored writers of any standing. I suspect the loadstone for them is some degree of contact with the white writers. This is undoubtedly helpful. You could have been of enormous assistance to me this past week when I was arranging for the debut of a younger Negro writer. It was a most unusual affair—a dinner meeting at the Civic Club [held to honor Jessie Redmond Fauset and her new book *There is Confusion*] at which all of the younger Negro writers met and chatted with the passing generation. It would have given you firsthand introduction to the last worders in literature. But principally it served to stimulate a market for the new stuff which these younger writers are turning out. A big plug was bitten off. Now it's a question of their living up to the reputation (Charles S. Johnson to Ethel Ray, cited in interview, 18 November 1970).

Nance moved to New York in 1925, telling her parents that she had been "promoted" to the Urban League office there. Their reluctance was tempered by the fact that A. Philip Randolph would be her guardian. Nance's father would have chosen his friend, W. E. B. Du Bois, but he knew that Du Bois was often away. Beginning in 1925 Nance was assistant to Johnson on *Opportunity* magazine and was to plan for the first Opportunity Awards celebration to be held in May 1926.

"Dream Haven" Nourishes the Harlem Renaissance

Nance assured her father that Harlem was much more than a social center. Searching for housing, she soon met Regina Anderson, a librarian at the 125th Street Branch of the New York Public Library. With Anderson's friend from Ohio, Louella Tucker, the young women shared an apartment that they called "Dream Haven." Located at 580 Saint Nicholas Avenue, it was popularly known as "580" and the mere mention of 580 to a taxi driver was all that was needed to reach the apartment. Their neighbor across the hall was singer, actress Ethel Waters. Harlem was still being discovered. Publishers and white writers were coming there. Magazines were publishing articles by black writers such as Countee Cullen and Langston Hughes, and Eric Waldrond was very much on the scene. Regina Anderson also had met many young writers and publishers who came to the library to do research. Five Eighty became the place to be in Harlem. There was Anderson with her group of young scholars, and there was Nance with the backing of influential Charles S. Johnson and *Opportunity* magazine, a catalyst between a young scholar's obscurity and popularity.

Five Eighty attracted many scholars and writers, such as Jean Toomer, Walter White, Paul Robeson, Countee Cullen, Langston Hughes, Zora Neale Hurston, Arna Bontemps, Eric Waldrond, Aaron Douglas, Jessie Faucet, Gwendolyn Bennett, Carl Van Vechten, and countless others. Five Eighty meant different things to different people.

> It was a casual billet only by appearances. For Toomer and Hughes, it was an evening furlough from the literary battlefront. For Eric Waldrond, making his rounds with fascinated whites, it was a genteel waystop, a relaxed forum for contact between Uptown and Downtown New York. In reality, it functioned as a combination probation office and intelligence outpost for the Urban League (Lewis, 128).

According to Nance, Countee Cullen came often to 580. A student at nearby City College, the charming, unassuming young man used the young women as audience for his new poetry. He seemed to apologize for his new product. Nance learned the personalities of Harlem's black literati: Gwendolyn Bennett had a sense of humor but was unpredictable. She came to parties at 580, but they never knew when she was coming. "I think she lived pretty much the life that she planned for herself," said Nance (Interview, 18 November 1970). Jessie Fauset, one of the younger writers, held Sunday afternoon teas always with a certain decorum. Astonished to see her smoking in a pubic place, Nance later was to hear her say, "Men don't give me candy, they give me cigarettes" (Interview, 18 November 1970). Eric Waldrond made friends easily and fit different situations well. He was perhaps the only member of the groups who had a relationship with Marcus Garvey and worked with him on *New World*. The other groups did not recognize Garvey at all, nor was he interested in them. Nance knew Weinold Reiss, the German-American painter who influenced Aaron Douglas, and who was in Harlem when he painted Harold Jackman, Cullen, Elise Johnson McDougald, C. C. Spaulding, and other blacks for the March 1925 special edition of *Survey Graphic*, "Harlem: Mecca of the New Negro." Nance witnessed the actual painting of some of his portraits. She had already known Douglas when they were in Kansas City while she was with the Urban League there and he taught at Lincoln High School. For quite some time Weinold Reiss had tried to persuade Douglas to come to New York but had no success. Nance wrote to him, saying, "It would be better to be a dishwasher in New York than a teacher in Kansas" (Ann Allen Shockley interview, 6 September 1981). He was persuaded. She met Nella Larsen once. Zora Neale Hurston was "hard to keep in bounds" (Ann Allen Shockley interview, 23 December 1970). Charles S. Johnson helped her by getting her a scholarship to Columbia and introducing her to Fannie Hurst. "Don't accept the idea that Carl Van Vechten was the only one who did things for black people" during the Harlem Renaissance, she said (Interview, 23 December 1970).

Ethel Ray Nance and Regina Anderson played important roles in the Harlem Renaissance. Anderson, an intelligent woman with a retentive memory, was a "delicate, little person with long hair" that she combed high on her head, giving her a Spanish look (Interview, 18 November 1970). She loved to be surrounded by people. She met freely the writers, publishers, and students who came to the library. At night she brought home stacks of books that she had to review for the next day, and together the women enjoyed reading the new works. "I suppose we complemented each other," Nance said. "Regina was little and I suppose I was above average" (Interview, 18 November 1970). Anderson's role in this matter was to persuade librarian Ernestine Rose, her employer, "that the community had a new talent whose works cried out for the audition at the 135th Street Library" (Lewis, 129). Nance kept a diary of the 580 guests, the occurrences at the National Urban League, and later the awards banquet. She also sought out new manuscripts for *Opportunity* magazine and the literary contests and gave the works their first reading when they came into the office. Her assignment also was to deliver the manuscripts to the various judges, who were always influential people. This was her introduction to black intellectual James Weldon Johnson, one of the judges.

Nance's influential employer, Johnson, had a powerful grip on Harlem's cultural activities. He brought artists and writers to Harlem and to public attention. In time, he probably touched the lives of every young artist or writer who came to Harlem. It was generally known that the way to success was through the public notice that Johnson could give, and Nance was the way to Johnson. But, as noted earlier, she carried her own weight in her role as talent scout and manuscript reviewer in the *Opportunity* office. The 580 women knew W. E. Du Bois well and called on him to help Harlem's newcomers find employment. They also relied on him when their meager salaries ran out toward the end of the month.

By 1927, Nance had returned to Minnesota, having already reestablished connections there beginning in 1926 as associate head resident of the Phillis Wheatley Settlement House—a position that she held until 1928. On August 2, 1929, she married Clarence A. Nance. Apparently some of her work with Johnson continued after she returned to Minnesota. Through her father's work with the NAACP in the late 1920s, Nance had another connection with Du Bois. The relationship was to continue later. From 1928 to 1931 Ethel Ray Nance was a police officer in the Women's Bureau of the Minneapolis Police Department. Between 1932 and 1934 the Nances had two sons: Thatcher Popel Nance (named for teacher and poet Esther Popel Shaw, who worked for Carter G. Woodson on the *Negro History Bulletin*) and Glenn Ray Nance. During this time also she cataloged two private libraries and was a public stenographer. From 1935 to 1936 Nance conducted a housing survey of displaced residents of the north side of Minneapolis for the board of directors of the Phillis Wheatley Settlement House in Minneapolis.

Ethel Ray Nance continued to work in various positions. She was secretary to the administrative assistant of the commissioner of education, State Department of Education in Saint Paul (1937-40); secretary to the dean of instruction, Hampton Institute, Hampton, Virginia (1940-43); secretary to the Port of Embarkation in Seattle, Washington, for the War Department Army Transportation (May-September 1943); deputy clerk, United States District Court, Seattle (September 1943-August 1944); office manager, USO Club, Seattle (August-October 1944); and from October 1944 to May 1945 she was secretary to the race relations advisor, Regional Office, Federal Public Housing Authority in Seattle. By then she reestablished her relationship with W. E. B. Du Bois, and from May to June 1945, when he was consultant to the American delegation for the founding of the United Nations in San Francisco, she was his secretary. She continued work with Du Bois as his research assistant in the NAACP's national office in New York from June to July 1945 and was a special administrative assistant to the West Coast Regional Office of the NAACP in San Francisco from 1945 to 1955.

Relationship with Charles S. Johnson Reestablished

Overlapping these years, from 1953 to 1954 Nance reestablished her working relationship with Charles S. Johnson, now president of Fisk University, Nashville, Tennessee, when she became his administrative assistant. Johnson's work took him away from the campus much of the time. The United Sates Supreme Court was preparing for its cases on segregation in the public schools, and Johnson and his staff were involved in research and pulling information from files for the courts. Nance said that Johnson was "probably a difficult person to know." She had known him for many years then and they understood each other and worked together well. But he "could be very short" (Interview, 23 December 1970). He was a very busy person with many irons in the fire. He worked on many activities that would benefit Fisk but were generally unknown to the public or to his faculty and staff. "At times he could be quite ruthless," she said. For example, sometimes faculty members expected to be rehired, but if Johnson found a better, more qualified person the new person was hired. He sought and hired the best. (Interview, 23 December 1970).

When asked to compare Charles S. Johnson and W. E. B. Du Bois, Nance said that both were scholars but had totally different personalities. Du Bois was easier to work with. He kept his own calendar and knew precisely what he would be doing every day in the year. He would not be disturbed in his work, which probably allowed him to accomplish so much. He knew exactly what he wanted, thus facilitating the staff's library research for him. He expected his staff to complete their work in the office and not take it home with them. On the other hand, Johnson had little concern for the length of the workday and knew full well that his staff took work home. He was less organized, gave vague instructions, and expected his staff to follow through. As noted above, some people found him difficult.

Nance left Fisk and became secretary in the Loan Service and Claim Section, Loan Guaranty Division, Veterans Administration Regional Office in San Francisco, where she remained from September 1954 to June 1956. Then she became secretary to the director of instructional materials, San Francisco Unified School District, district headquarters in San Francisco, 1956 to 1964. The next five years (1964-1969) she was secretary in the Real Estate Division, Regional Office, United States Post Office in San Francisco. From January through December 1969 she supervised the clerical staff in the Twin Cities Opportunity Industrialization Center (TCOIC) in Minneapolis. For two months in 1971 she conducted research for a handbook, "Chronology of African-Americans in New York, 1621-1966," edited by Regina T. Anderson (Andrews). Her last employment before retirement began in 1970 and ended in 1977, when she was administrative assistant in the San Francisco African-American Historical and Cultural Society. The next year, at age seventy-nine, she received a B.A. degree in public service from the University of California.

Nance was active in preserving and promoting black history and culture in Minnesota and San Francisco. In 1975 she gathered family history materials and presented them to the Minnesota Historical Society for inclusion in the publication *Blacks in Minnesota—A Preliminary Guide to Historical Sources* (1976). She was featured at a public forum in May 1979 on "Black Women in Minnesota, 1920-40," sponsored by the Minnesota Black Women's Historical Project and the local YWCA. She also volunteered for projects in the San Francisco Public Library.

Throughout the years Ethel Ray Nance and Regina Anderson (Andrews) maintained contacted with each other. Nance mentioned her travel to New York to visit Anderson (Andrews) in her 1981 interview.

Ethel Ray Nance has been honored for some of her work; however, the significance of her contribution to the internal structure of the Harlem Renaissance is yet to be appropriately acknowledged. David Levering makes a fine start in *When Harlem Was in Vogue,* which brought some prominence to her. Her honors, awards, prizes, and special achievements include certificate of recognition, San Francisco Public Schools, 1964; certificate of merit, Negro Historical Society, San Francisco, 1965; honoree, first annual achievement luncheon, African American Historical and Cultural Society, 1978; and Sojourner Truth Award, National Association of Negro Business and Professional Women's Clubs, San Francisco, 1981.

From her earliest years of employment through the early 1980s Nance held membership in numerous organizations. Some of these are the Oral History Association (national); Friends of the San Francisco Public Library; board member, Sickle Cell Anemia Disease Research Federation; board, San Francisco Historical and Cultural Society; advisory board, San Francisco Neighborhood Legal Assistance; Association for the United Nations; National Council on Negro Women; auxiliary president, Phillis Wheatley Settlement House in Minneapolis; American Federation of Teachers; International Association of Police Women; National Conference of Social Work; Minnesota State Conference and Institute of Social Work; and the NAACP.

Her writings include: "Along Came Ben," *Opportunity* (January 1924); "More About Phyllis Wheatley House," Women's Christian Association, Minneapolis, 1927; "Women at San Francisco," *North West Herald* (Seattle, Washington); editor, newsletter for the Council for Minority Rights, Seattle; and "New York Renaissance, 1924-26," *Negro History Bulletin* (1968). She prepared an unpublished essay titled "Remembrances of Dr. W. E. B. Du Bois," as well as "Recollections of Amos White (musician)," and she taped an interview with S. Edward Hall for the Historical Society, Saint Paul, Minnesota.

In retrospect, were Ethel Ray Nance and Regina Anderson (Andrews) socialites of the Harlem Renaissance, as some have suggested? Nance replied:

> We never regarded ourselves in that light. We were all struggling. Three of us girls had an apartment. The salaries were not very high but the rent was high. We couldn't do any lavish entertaining. . . . With the younger people who were starting to write and draw it [the apartment] was a place where they could drop in and they could meet others, and it was a place where . . . anyone [who] had . . . any kind of success would get together and . . . rejoice. I don't recall . . . any instances of jealousy because one person was successful in getting in print and someone else had not been accepted. I think that was the thing that held us together. We were sort of a little family (Interview, 23 December 1970).

The little family of Ethel Ray Nance and Regina Anderson (Andrews) were the scholars who produced the poetry, novels, essays, and works of art of that time that we know as products of the Harlem Renaissance era.

Ethel Ray Nance, now ninety-one, lives in a retirement home in the San Francisco area.

References

Lewis, David Levering. *When Harlem Was in Vogue.* New York: Knopf, 1981.

Nance, Ethel Ray. Interview with Ann Allen Shockley, 18 November 1970; 23 December 1970; 6 September 1981.

Who's Who of American Women. 10th ed. Chicago, Marquis, 1977.

Collections

Information on Ethel Ray Nance is included in the oral history collection of the National Council of Negro Women, Washington, D.C., and the Black Oral History Collection at Fisk University, Nashville, Tennessee.

Jessie Carney Smith

Nettie Langston Napier

(1861-1938)

Clubwoman, activist

In the latter part of the nineteenth century and into the twentieth century, poor black working women often left their children at home unattended. In the early 1900s, Nettie DeElla Langston Napier recognized the need to care for these children, help them enrich their young years, and aid their mothers, who were unable to provide for their welfare. Napier established a new concept in Nashville, Tennessee, known as the Day Home Club to provide immediate assistance to Nashville's needy children and their mothers. While the home was short-lived, the trend was set for other organizations to serve this purpose, as seen subsequently in the work of local YWCAs and Phillis Wheatley homes.

Nettie DeElla Langston Napier was born June 17, 1861, in Oberlin, Ohio, the daughter of John Mercer Langston and Caroline M. (Wall) Langston. Her parents, both educated at Oberlin College, married on October 25, 1854, and had five children. The eldest daughter was born in Oberlin, died and was buried there before the family moved to Washington, D.C. Napier was the second daughter. (There is confusion about Napier's middle name. Records of the academy or preparatory department of Oberlin College, where she attended school, and Davis, *Lifting As They Climb,* p. 222, give her middle name as DeElla and De. Ella, respectively. John Mercer Langston's book, *From the Virginia Plantation to the National Capitol,* p. 526, gives the name Matilda. Napier used DeElla on her records.) The Langstons also had three sons—Arthur D., Ralph E., and Frank Mercer. Napier's mother was born in North Carolina and grew up in Harveyburg, Ohio. Her father was born on a plantation near Louisa Court House, in Louisa County, Virginia, on December 14, 1829, the son of Ralph Quarles, a white plantation owner, and Lucy Langston, his mistress of the "great house," who was of Indian and Negro extraction. When Napier was nine years old, the family moved to Washington, D.C. There John Langston rose to become a prominent lawyer and founder in October 1868 and then head of the law school at Howard University, Washington, D.C. He later moved on to the halls of the United States Congress.

Nettie Langston Napier

Napier attended public schools and later Howard University in Washington, D.C., and after one year there she returned to Oberlin to complete her education in music. From 1876 to 1878 she was enrolled in Oberlin's academy or preparatory department. In 1878, she married James Carroll Napier, a native of Nashville and one of four children of William Carroll Napier and Jane Elizabeth (Watkins) Napier, both free blacks. After studying at Wilberforce College in Ohio and later at Oberlin College, James Napier returned to Nashville. While at Oberlin he met John Langston. It is said that John Langston came to Nashville and convinced Napier's parents to send him to law school. Napier studied at Howard University and lived with the Langstons. On his return to Nashville he was admitted to the bar and employed in the Internal Revenue Service. After Grover Cleveland was elected president in 1885 and removed the Republicans from office, Napier left the IRS.

Nettie Langston and James Napier were married in 1878. The Napiers appear to have lived in Nashville, Tennessee, until they returned to Washington, D.C., in 1910. While in Washington they lived in historic "Hillside Cottage," the Langston home located at Fourth and Bryant Streets N.W., in the vicinity of Howard University. Sometime later they adopted a daughter and named her Carrie Langston Napier. John Langston died in his home of apoplexy on November 15, 1897, and was buried in Woodlawn Cemetery, Washington, D.C. His widow continued to live in the home with her daughter and son-in-law.

James Napier was Tennessee's ranking black Republican until the early part of the twentieth century, and he represented his party at the National Republican Convention several times. He also had a respectable law practice and was engaged in local politics. James Napier became an investor in 1903 in the One Cent Savings Bank in Nashville and served as the nonsalaried cashier almost continuously until his death in 1940 at the age of ninety-five. In 1911 he was named by

President Robert Taft to the high office of Register of the Treasury.

James Napier belonged to the elite social and economic class in Nashville and in Washington. The Napiers, therefore, moved in Washington's prominent social circles and entertained lavishly in Hillside Cottage. Nettie Napier, who stood about five-feet four-inches tall and was a fair-skinned, attractive woman, was often labeled "queenly" because of her elaborate dress and proud and stately manner. Booker T. Washington and the Napiers were close friends, and when Washington visited the nation's capital, he made Hillside Cottage his local headquarters as he had when John Langston was alive. The Napiers also maintained a permanent residence in Nashville and a summer home, "Ogedankee," outside of Nashville.

Day Home Club Founded

The Napiers returned to Nashville after Napier's two-year stint in the treasury and after his resignation to protest President Woodrow Wilson's policies on segregation. He continued his work with the One Cent Savings Bank, which later became Citizen's Savings Bank. Aside from the social circles in which the Napiers moved, Nettie Napier had her own areas of interest in Nashville. She was very concerned for Nashville's poor black children who were left at home unattended while their mothers worked. It was Nettie Napier's belief that the children needed food, training, and health care; therefore, she was compelled to found the Day Home Club, one of Nashville's several black women's organizations that addressed the needs of the black community, such as the Phillis Wheatley Club, one of the most active local organizations associated with the City Federation of Colored Women's Clubs.

Napier founded the new program in a house located at 618 Fourth Avenue South in early January 1907. Later the home became known as Porter Homestead. As president, she called a meeting on January 14, 1907, of women who were interested in supporting activities to address the needs of poor black women and their children. The club wrote a constitution, elected officers, and appointed Josie E. Wells, a medical doctor who specialized in diseases of women and children, physician-in-charge. The group aimed to appoint a superintendent for the home and several vice-presidents for the city's wards. The next month Napier convened a mass meeting of black women to review the concept of the home and to hear reports on activities undertaken. Minnie Lou Crosthwaite reported on educational activities, and another report on temperance was heard. Both reports drew heated reaction. Josie Wells noted the public opposition to women becoming physicians but encouraged young women to pursue training in nursing and medicine. Following general discussion and reports, Napier took the floor and presented her views on neglected children in the area.

The local black press gave attention to the home, its activities and problems, and called the object of the day home praiseworthy and needy. For example, the press reported on a "very important meeting" of the Day Home Club held on Wednesday, October 31, 1908—the first meeting held after the summer's vacation:

> There was a full attendance and an interesting and spirited discussion as to the advisability of again opening the home. . . . We attempted to fill what we considered a long felt need and for a year and a half we have successfully carried on a Home, where ten and twelve children have been kept by the week: bathed, combed, dressed (often in the clothes that have been contributed or that the women of the club have made), and those who were old enough were taught to read, write and sew.

The report continues to identify the conditions that affected the school's operations and concluded:

> We are not discouraged and we will continue to use our means, live [sic] and effort to allay suffering humanity and will be grateful for contributions that will assist us in our work ("Meeting of Day Home Club," *Nashville Globe*, 30 October 1908).

Though the need for the home was great, the session generated minimal interest. After eighteen months of operation, the home's problems began to mount. Few women were active in the club's activities, the facilities were inadequate, furnishing, clothing, and fuel were needed, and the operational funds had been depleted. Initially, the home was to open during the day, but the irregular working hours of the mothers meant that some provisions were needed to care for children at various times during the day and night. From ten to twelve children were kept as boarders during the week; however, the extended hours required building security and expenses that could be met only through additional funding.

Fees were one dollar and ninety-five cents a week per child with an adjusted fee for two or more children from the same household. Expenses included fifteen dollars monthly for the matron, twenty dollars for rent, eight to ten dollars monthly for the cook, thirty-five to forty dollars monthly for food, and an additional amount for fuel. Napier announced that the home was unable to sustain itself and more funds were needed to ensure its continuance. The date on which Porter Homestead closed has not been determined. Neverton-Morton notes the combination of efforts in black communities that could finance social service programs such as Porter Homestead and suggests that its failure was due to other causes.

Beginning in 1901 at the Buffalo meeting, Napier worked with leaders in the women's club movement from other states through the National Association of Colored Women's Clubs (NACW). She appeared on the program in Buffalo and spoke on a subject with which she had considerable familiarity and interest—"Woman's Domain." After the meeting she commented: "I put woman in the home and let her stay there" (Davis, 224). From 1916 through 1933 she is known to have held various positions with the national body. She was auditor of the association and national treasurer and later "custodian" of the NACW's project to restore and maintain the Douglass home in the Anacostia section of Washington, D.C. When the sixteenth biennial session of the NACW was held in the District of Columbia in 1928, she reported on the home improvement and maintenance of the home. By the 1930 meeting she had been named head of the Committee on the Frederick Douglass Home and reported that their purpose at this time was "to wipe out the indebtness on the home of the late Frederick Douglass and to restore it to its former beauty, that we may make of this historic place a hallowed spot where our boys and girls may gather during the years to come and receive hope, inspiration, and encouragement to go forth like Douglass delighted to win." The association needed fifteen thousand dollars to reach this objective.

Locally, Napier was a member of the executive committee of the New Idea Club and the City Federation. She chaired a committee of black women for Red Cross activities. Napier was known to contribute financially to the work of women's clubs, philanthropies, the church, education, and the preservation of historic places. With her "accomplished musical education," and "deep, rich contralto voice of great power," she participated freely in "musical entertainments. . .of public and general interest" (Davis, 223). On the occasion of James C. Napier's eighty-seventh birthday celebration held in the reception rooms of the AME Sunday School Union on June 9, 1932, people came from far and near to pay tribute to Napier and his "queenly wife," including Mary McLeod Bethune, Josie E. Wells, and Minnie Lou Crosthwaite.

Nettie Napier was hailed as a philanthropist. Although she was a member of Howard Congregational Church, in October 1930 she and J. C. Napier donated to St. Andrews Presbyterian Church a parcel of land adjoining the site of St. Andrews. It was given "in memory of our deceased mothers, Jane E. Napier and Caroline Langston and our dear little daughter, Carrie Langston Napier, and in recognition and appreciation of the many blessings which have been bestowed upon us in the more than fifty-two years of marital happiness" ("Honorable and Mrs. J. C. Napier," 1). When no one else would do so, even though the family had already made a generous donation, Napier gave fifty dollars to support the maternity ward at the new Hubbard Hospital (Wells, 1-2).

Napier's views on the "duty of a wife to her husband" appeared to have no boundaries. She has been praised consistently for being a model wife and homemaker. Wells notes Napier's attention to her ailing husband after his comforts had been addressed, medicine given, diet provided for, and nothing remained for his wife to do. "In a most distressing voice you will hear something like this. 'Ugh! Oh, dear.' 'What is it, Sug?' 'Come here and listen to me grunt.' And believe me. . . she sits by the bed and listens" (Wells, 3).

Napier died of congestive heart failure at her residence, 120 Fifteenth Avenue North, on September 27, 1938, at 10:25 P.M. without any surviving children. She was sixty-seven years old. Her funeral was held at Howard Congregational Church on Friday, September 30, at 2:00 P.M. "God Be With You Till We Meet Again," Napier's favorite hymn, was sung. It was written by Jeremiah Rankin, who officiated at the marriage of the Napiers. She was buried in Nashville's Greenwood Cemetery under the care of the W. H. McGavock Funeral Home.

Not only did local and national groups recognize Napier's talent and interests, but her father, John Langston, wrote of her earlier in his book *From the Virginia Plantation to the National Capitol* (526-28). Though obviously biased in his views, he gave accurate accounts of her private life and interest in education, religion, and community affairs. Her devotion to her parents and her husband was deep and permanent.

References

Bethune, Mary McLeod. Untitled speech delivered by Mrs. W. T. Francis at the Ira Bryant sponsored celebration of J. C. Napier's Eighty-Seventh Birthday, Nashville, Tennessee, 9 June 1932.

Crosthwaite, Mrs. S. W. [Minnie Lou]. "The Model Woman: A Toast." Paper delivered at the Ira Bryant sponsored celebration of J. C. Napier's Eighty-Seventh Birthday, Nashville, Tennessee, 9 June 1932.

Davis, Elizabeth Lindsay. *Lifting As They Climb.* Washington, D.C.: National Association of Colored Women, 1933. 222-24.

"Emancipation Anniversary." Nashville *Globe,* 11 January 1907; 18 January 1907.

"Honorable and Mrs. J. C. Napier Benefactors of Saint Andrews' Presbyterian Church." "The Saint Andrew's News" 13 (February 1931): 1.

Langston, John Mercer. *From the Virginia Plantation to the National Capitol.* Hartford, Conn.: American Pub. Co., 1898. Portrait between pp. 526 and 527. The chapter on "Hillside Cottage and His Family," pp. 521-34.

"Meeting of Day Home Club." *Nashville Globe,* 30 October 1908.

Neverdon-Morton, Cynthia. *Afro-American Women of the South and the Advancement of the Race, 1895-1925.* Knoxville: University of Tennessee Press, 1989. 171-72.

Oberlin College Archives. Alumni file for Nora DeElla Langston.

Washington, Margaret Murray. "The Beginnings of the National Club Movement: Club Work Among Negro Women." In Gerda Lerner, ed. *Black Women in White America.* New York: Random House, 1972. 443-47.

Wells, Josie E. "As a Philanthropist: A Toast." Paper delivered at the Ira Bryant sponsored celebration of J. C.

Napier's eighty-seventh birthday, Nashville, Tennessee, 9 June 1932.

Wesley, Charles Harris. *The History of the National Association of Colored Women's Clubs: A Legacy of Service*. Washington: NACW, 1984. 36, 72, 84-85, 87, 89, 104-105, 111.

"Women's Meeting Held in the Interest of 'Day Home' Project." *Nashville Globe*, 22 February 1907.

Collections

The Oberlin College Archives contains information on Nella DeElla Langston Napier and James Carroll Napier. Photographs and other information on Nettie Napier are in the James C. Napier Papers and the Nettie Napier file, Special Collections, Fisk University Library. A death certificate was obtained from the Tennessee State Library and Archives. Her funeral program was also obtained.

Jessie Carney Smith

Diane Nash

(1938-)

Civil rights activist, educator

Diane Judith Nash was born in 1938 and grew up in Chicago in a middle-class Catholic family. At one time she planned to become a nun, but was discouraged. Her formal education was in progress during the years of the *Brown* v. *Board of Education* decision handed down by the Federal courts. This decision affected her life as it did that of all Americans, especially black Americans. Diane Nash was enrolled at Howard University, Washington, D.C., in the late 1950s. She later transferred to Fisk University in Nashville, Tennessee, where she became an English major. Fair-skinned and attractive, runner-up in Chicago's Miss America trials (*Jet*, 49), she might have easily become involved in the social aspects of campus life. However, by the time she arrived at Fisk she had already developed an interest in the problems of discrimination that all black Americans faced and the possible solution through social change. Nashville's segregated restaurants, theaters, water fountains, and other facilities disturbed her tremendously. She became a key figure in the sit-in movement of the 1960s that led to radical reform in the racially segregated American communities.

In fall 1959, several dozen students from Tennessee State University, American Baptist Theological Seminary, Meharry Medical College, and Fisk University, all in Nashville, Tennessee, and a group of adults from the community came together for the purpose of organizing to address the critical need for social change—initially to begin a movement to desegregate downtown Nashville. They became involved in workshops on nonviolence led by James Lawson, a black American student studying at Vanderbilt University's Divinity School. Lawson had learned Mahatma Gandhi's technique while studying in India. The workshops met weekly from September through November, enacted the potential experience of a sit-in, trained in nonviolent self-protection and protection of each other, and were given demonstrations in various nonviolent techniques. Diane Nash heard about the workshops through Paul LaPrad, a white student at Fisk, and she became a workshop participant. By the end of November those trained became the initial sit-in group. Diane Nash became the first unofficial leader of these organizing students, who, along with Lawson, included James Bevel, Bernard Lafayette, and John Lewis, and who within a few years would become "the backbone of the younger, more assertive wing of the civil rights movement" (Powledge, 204).

In 1959 Nashville was still a tightly segregated city. This troubled Diane Nash, who had known about segregation but was just then witnessing it and wounded by it. Reflecting on that period, she said to Fred Powledge in a December 7, 1988, interview:

> My stepfather was a waiter on the railroads and he had to make trips to the South. He would tell about the segregated facilities down there. I believed him and listened to the stories, but I think that it was an intellectual understanding. But when I actually got down there and saw signs, it really hit me that I wasn't, quote-unquote, "supposed" to go in this rest room or use a particular facility, then I understood it emotionally as well (Powledge, 207).

James Lawson saw segregated Nashville as an excellent place for an initial test for social change by use of a nonviolent sit-in. The sit-in technique was not new: lunch counters and restaurants in Chicago were tested by members of the Congress of Racial Equality (CORE) in 1943; those in Washington, D.C., in the 1940s; and those in Saint Louis and Baltimore in 1949 and 1953. There were rumblings in some sixteen southern and border states in the late 1950s as blacks grew impatient with the segregated accommodations in libraries, theaters, hotels, restaurants, schools, and elsewhere. In December 1959, two months before sit-ins were staged in Greensboro, North Carolina, a test sit-in was launched at two Nashville department stores. The official Nashville sit-in began on February 7, 1960, a Saturday, and the busiest shopping day for Nashville department stores. This was not to be a one-day effort. The sit-ins continued throughout February 1960. The Nashville police began making arrests, and eighty-two students were charged with disorderly conduct and taken to jail.

At first Diane Nash had been skeptical of James Lawson's teachings. The nonviolent techniques worked and she was impressed with their effectiveness. She learned about herself for the first time and found unknown courage. "I found beautiful things in people who would care enough about other people to put their bodies between another person and danger," she said. "A lot of things started making sense to me through the learning of nonviolence as well as the practice of it. And I developed it as a way of life" (Powledge, 208). Her early work in the movement was not without fear. The local press published her photograph, thus introducing her to a wide audience, including staunch racists. While checking on demonstrators at a local store she encountered a large number of whites and heard one of a group of teenagers say, "That's Diane Nash. She was in the paper. She's the one to get" (Powledge, 208-209). From then on she replaced fear with function in the movement.

Diane Nash, the unofficial leader, now became the unofficial spokesperson for the group, and her statements were often quoted in the Nashville newspapers. When the students decided to serve their jail terms rather than pay the fifty-dollar fine or let someone else pay the fine for them or bail them out, Nash, an articulate speaker, said to the judge at the trials on Monday, February 29: "We feel that if we pay these fines we would be contributing to and supporting the injustice and immoral practices that have been performed in the arrest and conviction of the defendants" (Branch, 279). Sixteen students, including Nash and John Lewis of the American Baptist Theological Seminary, were jailed. James Bevel, another student from the seminary, led the second wave of protesters to jail and the movement was well on its way.

In an effort to halt the demonstrations, Nashville Mayor Ben West offered to release the students and establish a biracial committee to make recommendations about the segregated downtown stores. In the meantime, no further sit-ins at downtown stores were to occur. Nash, Bevel, and the jailed students emerged victorious, for they had forced a segregated southern city to address its laws and practices on segregation and discrimination. In March the Nashville sit-ins were suspended, and a truce was declared when a group of black clergymen announced the formation of a local biracial citizens' committee to study the matter. Subsequently Nash, James Bevel, and Rodney Powell, a Meharry Medical College student, became members of the committee. While the committee planned, Diane Nash led a group to the segregated Greyhound bus terminal's lunch counter—a site not originally approached or included in the mayor's agreement. The students were served without incident. Early in the movement, the sit-in pattern had been established: "constant surprises, all-night meetings, serial victories, and setbacks, with the elders of both races often on the defensive against their young" (Branch, 280).

Two serious incidents impacted significantly on the students' determination and on public sentiment. First, the board of trustees summarily expelled James Lawson from Vanderbilt Divinity School for his involvement in the movement. After faculty threats of mass resignation and national condemnation of the university's board and its action, he was reinstated. Second, on April 19 the home of Z. Alexander Looby and his wife was bombed, and damage was shared by nearby homes and Meharry Medical College. Looby, a prominent, outspoken black attorney and politician, had represented the students when they were jailed and had been plagued constantly by threatening telephone calls. After the bombing, a massive crowd of black and white protesters marched on city hall and Mayor West, who pledged to catch the bombers and claimed that the desegregation of the lunch counters was a matter beyond his power. When he asked the group to pray together, Diane Nash pushed to the front of the crowd and asked: "How about eating together?" When she asked, "Then, Mayor, do you recommend that the lunch counters be desegregated?" the response was "Yes," to which the crowd cheered (Branch, 295). She had another victory. In retrospect, Nash commented:

> I have a lot of respect for the way he responded. He didn't have to respond the way he did. He said that he felt it was wrong for citizens of Nashville to be discriminated against at the lunch counters solely on the basis of the color of their skin. That was the turning point. The Nashville newspaper reported this statement in the headlines the next day, and it was one step toward desegregating the lunch counters. That day was very important (Hampton, 66).

From the lunch counters, protesters moved to theaters, churches, and other public gathering places to effect desegregation. One cannot overlook the impact of economic withdrawal as a key weapon in the desegregation efforts. Many adults, black and white alike, felt that they could not endure the abuses that the students suffered, but they could refuse to shop at establishments that discriminated against blacks. While it has been said that economic withdrawal originated in Nashville, it spread rapidly to other cities where sit-ins were in place and helped to accelerate the actions that the student protesters envisioned.

The Nashville movement brought about other changes aimed to effect better race relations. In March a major conference on community relations was held in Christ Episcopal Church to examine ways to improve human relations in the city. More than four hundred persons attended. Included on the panel was Kelly Miller Smith, pastor of the black First Baptist Church—the control site for the sit-in movement. He had worked closely with Nash, Bevel, Lewis, and the other leaders and supporters of the movement.

Sit-In Movement Changes Course of History

The sit-ins marked a turning point in the black American community locally and nationwide as attention was focused on a condition that had existed for more than three hundred years—that of racial discrimination. Diane Nash emerged as a leader of that protest. By June 1960 lunch counters in seven Tennessee cities had been opened to black American patrons.

Thus, two historic sit-ins were launched from an entirely different perspective. While the Greensboro movement was spontaneous and involved four students from one college—North Carolina Agricultural and Technical State University—the Nashville movement had been planned over several months, drawing on the wisdom of students in several colleges as well as adults from the community. From the Greensboro movement, sit-ins flared in nearby Durham and Winston-Salem, then in South Carolina, Virginia, and Florida. While both movements were necessary and influential in removing barriers to equality, the Nashville activity became the most successful primarily because it was well organized, it led to negotiated settlements with the white power structure, and it became a model for the national student movement that followed.

Training for student leaders continued. In April 1960 students who had staged sit-down protests against lunch counter segregation in Tennessee, Georgia, and South Carolina held a workshop on "The New Generation Fights for Equality" at Highlander Folk School, Monteagle, Tennessee, to map the future course of action. About fifty students, both black and white, analyzed their successes and failures and then broke into smaller groups to review the detailed aspects of their actions and the course that their work would take in the future. They discussed methods of protest, problems of communication, relation of community and schools, and philosophy of the movement. Without announcing the specific targets of their plan, the students advocated stepping up the campaign for racial integration, proposed picketing and boycotts, and advocated better-planned demonstrations. Such workshops were held periodically and helped keep the movement on target, as well as ensured that the leaders remained well prepared for their work.

Nash Extends Activism to the Deep South

Diane Nash had become highly charged during the sit-ins, and as a nonviolent activist she had to continue her work. Her total dedication to the movement had been publicly recognized. By mid-April, some fifty thousand black and white students and sympathizers had been involved in the movement. Student protesters felt a need to establish their own civil rights organization that would operate beyond the methods and perspectives seen in established civil rights groups. The Student Nonviolent Coordinating Committee (SNCC) was formed on the weekend of April 15-17, 1960, on the campus of Shaw University in Raleigh, North Carolina. Black women already had been leaders in the sit-ins and continued to distinguish themselves as activists. Nash was invited to attend the conference as a leader of a sit-in movement and secretary of the Nashville SCLC. Nash was not only in attendance but played a major role in assisting Ella Baker, then executive secretary of the Southern Christian Leadership Conference (SCLC) and an associate of Martin Luther King, Jr. Baker, a seasoned civil rights activist, had been one of the few women in a leadership role in the SCLC. Her experience in organizing NAACP chapters throughout the South was invaluable.

SNCC advocated the "jail, no bail" strategy to avoid the continuing dependency on families, friends, and groups for bail or fines seen during the first year of the sit-in movement. The new tactic would be tried in Rock Hill, South Carolina, with students from CORE and the NAACP. Demonstrators who attended a CORE meeting were arrested, and they refused bail. Then CORE asked SNCC to continue the strategy in Rock Hill, and Diane Nash of Fisk, Ruby Doris Smith of Spelman College in Atlanta, Charles Sherrod of Virginia Union University, and Charles Jones of Johnson C. Smith University in Charlotte, volunteered. They were arrested also and served thirty-seven days in jail, where they were put to hard labor and exposed to racial insults. They came to be known as "The Rock Hill Four." The "jail, no bail" strategy proved a problem for authorities as jails overflowed. As well, it brought public attention to the cities or towns involved, dramatized the issues, and forged a closer relationship between the students. Nash and Smith left college and worked for SNCC full-time—Nash as a salaried field staff member and Smith later as executive secretary. The plan had worked well throughout the period of the movement. "Initiated by CORE, used and developed by SNCC, and utilized most effectively by Martin Luther King, Jr., the 'jail, no bail' stratagem revolutionized the southern movement" (Giddings, 279).

Nash Becomes Active in Freedom Rides

Nash, Smith, and other students, including several women who survived the sit-ins, went on to a baptism of fire in the freedom rides, which James Farmer, head and founder of CORE, conceived. The riders were to leave Washington, D.C., gather passengers in Virginia, North Carolina, South Carolina, Georgia, and Alabama, and finally stop in New Orleans. Assuming responsibility for the freedom rides gave SNCC a sense of identity and the ability for direct action.

The freedom rides began on May 4, 1961, with little fanfare, but outside Anniston, Alabama, on May 14—Mother's Day—a mob of whites attacked blacks, and white protesters bombed and burned the bus on which they were riding. The bus company refused to honor the tickets of the freedom riders. Nash, the direct action leader, quickly organized the militant Nashville students. Meanwhile, she talked with James Farmer, the head of CORE, and suggested the Nashville contingent might go to Birmingham to replace the original riders. He consented. John Seigenthaler, special assistant to United States Attorney General Robert Kennedy, who was dispatched to Birmingham to meet with the governor, knew the grim realities of Birmingham and advised the group to turn around when he reached Nash by telephone. But Nash pushed to keep the plan in place, and chairman James Bevel selected the ten students who would go. Those selected were John Lewis (for leadership), six male and two female students who were black, and one white male and one white female student. They became the "nonviolent standing army" (Branch, 431). Nash was not selected because she was too valuable on the homefront. This group intended to go to New Orleans by way of Birmingham and Montgomery, Alabama, then through Jackson, Mississippi. They were joined by some members of the first group, including James Farmer and Henry Thomas.

Of the student plan, Nash said:

> I strongly felt that the future of the movement was going to be cut short if the Freedom Ride had been stopped as result of violence. . . .
>
> The students who were going to pick up the Freedom Ride selected me coordinator. As coordinator, part of my responsibility was to stay in touch with the Justice Department. Our whole way of operating was that we took ultimate responsibility for what we were going to do. But it was felt that they should be advised, in Washington, of what our plans were. . . .
>
> I was also to keep the press informed, and communities that were participating, such as Birmingham, Montgomery, Jackson, and Nashville. And I coordinated the training and recruitment of more people to take up the Freedom Ride (Hampton, 82).

The riders traveled by bus, initially without the knowledge of the Birmingham police, who later learned of the plan. The bus was intercepted in Alabama and all students ticketed to New Orleans were considered freedom riders. They were removed from the bus and left stranded just over the Tennessee state line. Learning of their fate from a telephone call that John Lewis placed, informing her in coded message that "all seven packages were ready to return to Birmingham," Nash sent Leo Lillard to drive them. They continued to Birmingham.

By August 1961, Diane Nash suffered obvious disillusionment with the support many students were receiving from their colleges. She questioned black faculty in the black colleges who failed to support the expelled students and refused to associate with the movement. "Why are the faculty members and administrators of southern Negro colleges not on the picket lines and sitting at the lunch counters? I think the answer lies within the answer of what Jim Crow does to the Negro," she concluded ("Inside the Sit-ins," 47). SNCC at that time also had internal controversy: one faction favored direct action as a primary approach and another favored voter registration as an additional approach. After a debate at a Highlander Folk School seminar on August 11, 1961, Ella Baker suggested a compromise that was accepted: "SNCC would have two wings, one for direct action and one for voter registration" (Carson, 42). Diane Nash headed direct action—the protest wing, while Jones headed voter registration.

The students' efforts helped to effect essential legislation, and on September 22, 1961, the Interstate Commerce Commission banned racial discrimination in public interstate travel and facilities. Clayborn Carson states quite trenchantly the importance of the freedom rides:

> The significance of the freedom rides was not merely that they led to desegregation of southern transportation facilities. The rides also contributed to the development of a self-consciously radical southern student movement prepared to direct its militancy toward others concerned (37).

Neither the work of SNCC nor Diane Nash was finished. SNCC moved the struggle into the deep South, and churches, women's organizations, colleges, and other groups and organizations joined forces with them to test the ICC ruling and to fight other racial injustices, particularly the denial of the right to vote. Nash and other leaders of SNCC came to feel that voter registration was now the pivotal purpose for the committee and its work in the deep South. They emphasized the need for black Americans to become involved in the political process. Charles Jones, who headed voter registration, would not lead the political awareness focus of SNCC and there would no longer be two separate wings. Shortly after the Albany, Georgia, movement was formed, the SCLC hired James Bevel from SNCC. Diane Nash also went to work for the SCLC. Bevel says he was hired to smooth out the conflict that developed between SNCC and the SCLC. SNCC grew militant while the SCLC remained moderate. By this time also, the NAACP was at odds with both of the organizations and opposed mass protest. In May 1962, Diane Nash Bevel, then four months pregnant, was jailed in Jackson, Mississippi, for teaching the techniques of nonviolence to black children. She insisted on sitting in jail rather than putting up bail. She condemned the court system and vowed not to cooperate with its evil and corrupt acts. Sentenced to two years in prison, she was released after a short stay.

Nash's work brought her in close contact with other prominent leaders in the movement: Martin Luther King, Jr., Fred Shuttlesworth, Ella Bates, and James Farmer. In fact, Nash's planning strategies were often studied and adopted in part or in entirety in various struggles. The SCLC's Selma, Alabama, voting rights campaign of 1965 grew out of ideas she had shared with King.

At the March on Washington rally held in August 1963, Diane Nash Bevel was introduced by the chairman, A. Philip Randolph, as one of the outstanding women of the civil rights struggle. She had earned this recognition and more. Ironically, she and the other wives of male leaders were not permitted to participate in the main procession. In fact, a week before the march was to occur, no woman was listed as speaker. Anna Arnold Hedgeman, member of the administrative committee for the march, wrote to A. Philip Randolph in protest. She said:

> In light of the role of Negro women in the struggle for freedom and especially in light of the extra burden they have carried . . . it is incredible that no woman should appear as a speaker at the historic March on Washington Meeting at the Lincoln Memorial. . . . I would like to suggest . . . [t]hat a Negro woman make a brief statement and present the Heroines just as you have suggested that the Chairman might do (179).

Although Rosa Parks, Daisy Bates, and Gloria Richardson shared the recognition given to Diane Nash Bevel, and Parks was allowed to make a brief statement, there were no women speakers scheduled during the three-hour program.

When Sixteenth Street Baptist Church in Birmingham was bombed on September 15, 1963, and four little black girls were killed while attending Sunday school, Nash and James Bevel were deeply shaken. They felt the young girls who were killed were their own—an understandable reaction, since the entire movement had brought about a close relationship between the leaders and the ones they were to lead. The Bevels decided that they would devote whatever time needed to see that Alabama blacks exercised their right to vote—a right denied by laws of segregation. The day of the bombing they drew up an initial strategy draft for a plan to get the right to vote.

By 1963 SNCC had become a militant organization. Once an organization of nonviolent activists who aimed to appeal to the nation's conscience, it became a cadre of organizers who sought to coerce the federal government into enforcing civil rights goals. Some SNCC members believed that economic and political change would not occur through nonviolent protests alone. At a retreat at Kingston Springs, near Nashville, Stokeley Carmichael became head of SNCC. He advocated black power both by slogan and by leading SNCC organizers to establish black power bases in the black community. Relations between SNCC and the SCLC became even more strained. SNCC's relations with the NAACP and the SCLC also were damaged when it sought to become the dominant group within the civil rights movement. From here on Nash appears to have had no connection with either group.

The struggle continued, and by 1965 two major goals of the movement had been realized. Civil Rights Acts and the Voting Rights Act were passed, yet the ills of society were not healed by the legislation. Diane Nash and the other leaders and supporters had taken monumental steps in their attack on racial oppression in the structurally-flawed American society.

Diane Nash Bevel continued her concern for the oppression of the underclass and the need for social change. Her involvement in the issues affecting the Vietnam War brought her an invitation to visit Hanoi. Nash brought the same fervor and involvement to the antiwar protest that she had exhibited in the civil rights struggle. She has constantly been a signal voice to those groups who needed leadership for change. Now divorced and teaching in Chicago, during the 1980s she lectured nationally on issues pertaining to women's rights and frequently on a retrospective of the civil rights movement. Her December 7, 1988, interview with Fred Powledge, published in *Free at Last,* is the most comprehensive source known on her involvement in the civil rights movement and her reflections on that involvement. Though highly successful in the cause for social change in the South, Diane Nash is an uncelebrated figure in this important period in history.

References

Branch, Taylor. *Parting the Waters: America in the King Years 1954-63.* New York: Simon and Schuster, 1988.

Brisbane, Robert H. *Black Activism.* Valley Forge, Pa.: Judson Press, 1974.

Carson, Clayborne. *In Struggle: SNCC and the Black Awakening of the 1960s.* Cambridge: Harvard University Press, 1981.

Garrow, David J., ed. *Martin Luther King,Jr., and the Civil Rights Movement.* New York: Carlson Pub. Co., 1990.

Giddings, Paula. *When and Where I Enter.* New York: Bantam Books, 1984.

Hampton, Henry, and Steve Fayer. *Voices of Freedom: An Oral History of the Civil Rights Movement from the 1950s Through the 1980s.* New York: Bantam Books, 1990.

Hedgeman, Anna Arnold. *The Trumpet Sounds.* New York: Holt, Rinehart and Winston, 1964.

Jet 20 (29 June 1961): 49.

King, Mary. *Freedom Songs.* New York: Morrow, 1988.

Morris, Aldon D. *The Origins of the Civil Rights Movement.* New York: Free Press, 1984.

Nash, Diane. ''Inside the Sit-ins and Freedom Rides: Testimony of a Southern Student. In Mathew H. Ahmann, ed. *The New Negro.* New York: Biblio and Tannen, 1969.

Nashville *Banner* 4 April 1960.

Nashville *Tennessean* 28 February 1960; 17 March 1960; 3 April 1960.

Powledge, Fred. *Free At Last? The Civil Rights Movement and the People Who Made It.* Boston: Little, Brown, 1991. Photograph with Kelly Miller Smith, I-2.

Warren, Robert Penn. *Who Speaks for the Negro?* New York: Random House, 1965.

Zinn, Howard. *SNCC: The New Abolitionists.* Boston: Beacon Press, 1964.

Collections

The sit-ins and the civil rights movement are documented in the SNCC Freedom Center Collection, University of Illinois, Chicago Circle and in the Braden Papers, Civil Rights Collection, State Historical Society of Wisconsin, Madison. Newsclippings, photographs, and other materials on Diane Nash and the civil rights movement in Nashville are in the Special Collections, Fisk University Library. A photograph of Nash in a protest march and another with her daughter, Sherrilynn, and James Bevel are published in *Ebony* 18 (September 1963), p. 43.

Reavis Mitchell and Jessie Carney Smith

Annie Greene Nelson

(1902-)

Writer, nurse, educator

Annie Greene Nelson is South Carolina's first known black woman novelist of the twentieth century. Despite having published three novels and many other literary works, Nelson is virtually unrecognized by the general public except in her hometown of Carterville, South Carolina, and Columbia, South Carolina, where she has made her home for more than half her life; however, many are gradually recognizing the importance of her works, which were reprinted in the middle seventies.

During the 1940s and 1950s when many writers loathed the minstrel tradition and were faced with the dilemma of writing on "universal" topics or protest literature, Nelson wrote fictitious stories about blacks and whites interacting harmoniously against an imaginary backdrop of tightly-knit communities of teachers, preachers, and elders. Like Victorian heroines, the female characters are vulnerable and committed to their families and friends. They look to the community for identity, affirmation, and recognition.

After the Storm (1942), for example, is an inspirational tale of an innocent Christian girl who loses her social position by becoming pregnant out of wedlock and then regains her social standing by marrying a physician and living a life of service. Nelson's second published novel, *The Dawn Appears* (1944)—divided into two sections, one evaluating the moral character of an unwed mother and one exploring the religious and patriotic fervor of a struggling couple during the Second World War—follows a similar strand of assessing morality, chastity, democracy, social acceptance and rejection, and race relations. Although the first two novels were published by a local black publisher, Hampton Printing Company, Nelson published and distributed her third novel, *Don't Walk On My Dreams* (1961). In her unpublished autobiography, *Letters to Paw,* which included a series of letters written to her father, Nelson details her family history and openly discusses lynchings, murder, and the civil rights movement.

Annie Greene was born on December 1, 1902, the first of thirteen children born to Sylvester Greene and Nancy (Muldrow) Greene. She grew up on Parrott's Plantation in Darlington County, South Carolina, where her father worked as a sharecropper and a music teacher.

Her talent as a writer was recognized in her early youth. Out of affection for her class sweetheart, Nelson wrote "Sugar is sweet, lard is greasy, if you love me honey, don't be uneasy." She later continued the rhapsody, "As the grass grows in the pine, you're my darling all the time." (Maryemma Graham interview with Annie Greene Nelson, June 1986).

Nelson graduated from Voorhees College in Denmark, South Carolina, in 1923, receiving her degree in education and nursing. She served as a schoolteacher, librarian, and textbook binder during the Works Progress Administration (WPA) period. Her employer, Catherine Wheeler, then head librarian at Columbia's black library, commented that Nelson spent more time reading than working at the library (Maryemma Graham interview with Catherine Wheeler, June 1987). Additionally, Nelson admits she was the founder and teacher of the first kindergarten for black children in Columbia, South Carolina. Her career as a nurse lasted twenty years, and at age eighty, Nelson went back to college to study the performing arts to improve her acting. She used this training in her one-woman show, *Happenings on the Parrot Plantation*.

Nelson devoted some of her time to community organizations and activities. She was a volunteer in the community during the Great Depression and again during World War II. For two years she was a member of the YWCA board. She was also president of the C. A. Johnson High School Parent-Teachers Association, and treasurer of the Drew Park Mothers Organization.

Nelson suggests that the reason she is largely unknown outside of South Carolina is her devotion to her six children and her husband, which she considered a high priority. "I had a chance to do better with my books, but I wouldn't have left my husband or children to push [the books] for anything," said Nelson. "The happiest moments of my life have been my children" (Maryemma Graham interview with Annie Greene Nelson, June 1986). A widow when she married Edward Nelson in 1935, Annie Greene Nelson is now a great-great-grandmother.

Nelson's unpublished works include a song, "I Wish You Were Here Tonight"; the play, *Parrott's Plantation;* and a musical drama, *The Weary Fireside Blues,* which may have been patterned after the well-known collection by Langston Hughes. Nelson is in great demand as a speaker at many high schools and colleges and has received many awards, including a Budweiser of Columbia Community Drama Award (1980-1981) and the Arts Award for Excellence in the Arts from the Columbia Urban League (1982). She was also honored in 1987 by Benedict College with a testimonial and special exhibition of her works and by the South Carolina Humanities Council.

After having contributed to black American and mainstream literature, Annie Greene Nelson is currently writing about the experience of growing old. The book's proposed title is *80, So What?*

References

Biography File, Fisk University Library.

Graham, Maryemma. Afro-American Novel Project interview with Annie Greene Nelson, Columbia, South Carolina, June 1986; North Myrtle Beach, South Carolina, June 1987.

Nelson, Annie Greene. *After the Story*. Spartanburg, S.C.: The Author [1974].

———. *The Dawn Appears*. Spartanburg, S.C.: Reprint Company [1944].

———. *Don't Walk on My Dreams: A Novel*. Spartanburg, S.C.: Reprint Company, 1976.

———. *Letters to Paw*. unpublished manuscript.

Norman, Cassandra M. "Annie Greene Nelson: A Brief Biography." [Columbia, S.C.: Benedict College, n.d.] Includes photograph.

Kelley Norman

Effie Lee Newsome

(1885-1979)

Poet, author, illustrator, librarian

Mary Effie Lee Newsome, a poet, prose writer, illustrator, and librarian, was a prolific writer for both children and adults who sought to foster a sense of racial pride in her young readers and an understanding of the realities of race relations in her adult readers. One of five children (four daughters and one son) born to Benjamin Franklin Lee and Mary Elizabeth Lee. Effie Lee Newsome was born January 19, 1885. Newsome's father attended Wilberforce University, where he became an instructor of homiletics and related subjects; in 1873 he rose to the presidency of the university, succeeding Bishop Daniel A. Payne, Wilberforce's first president. Later Benjamin Franklin Lee edited *The Christian Record*, the African Methodist Episcopal (AME) church's official organ, published in Philadelphia—the city in which Newsome was born—and was elected to the AME bishopric, his dioceses including first Louisiana, Texas, Washington, and Oregon; second, Ohio and other states; and later, the Pacific Coast.

During the Lee family's years in Philadelphia, the children's leisure time was consumed by reading—especially the Bible, poetry, fairy tales, and children's magazines. Books about nature appealed especially to Newsome and her younger sister Consuelo. It was during these years in Philadelphia that Newsome began writing at the age of five. Also, it was then that she developed a love of the visual arts, as she and Consuelo "plied the brushes joyously," as Newsome states in "Pigments," a June 1929 prose sketch in *Crisis*, the organ of the NAACP. Newsome's interest in painting and drawing later manifested itself in the illustrations she created to accompany her poems and prose sketches in *The Brownies' Book* and in "The Little Page" in *Crisis*.

In 1896 the Lee family moved from Philadelphia to Wilberforce, Ohio, which was to become the family's permanent home. Like her father, Newsome attended Wilberforce University. After her 1904 graduation, she attended Oberlin College's Academy in 1904-1905, the Academy of Fine Arts in 1907-1908, and the University of Pennsylvania from 1911 to 1914. In 1920, when she was thirty-five years old, Newsome married a minister, the Reverend Henry Newsome. At that time she decided to change her pen name from Mary Effie Lee to Effie Lee Newsome because, in her words, "four names in a row would be like the long row of houses on our street in Philadelphia" (Rollins, 58).

Newsome and her husband resided the rest of their lives in Wilberforce, Ohio, where she was a librarian first at Central State College and later at Wilberforce University. During those years she developed ties with local librarians and with local churches; through these relationships she promoted the reading of good books. In 1963 Newsome retired from her position as librarian in the College of Education at Wilberforce University.

Works of Prose Written for Children

During virtually all of her life, Newsome was a prolific poet and prose writer whose works were generally created for an audience of children. Containing relatively simple language and metrics, her poems for children treat nature and the universal aspects of childhood. A tireless bird-watcher and observer of nature's marvels, Newsome attempted in her poems to connect with her readers by recalling her own childhood—largely spent attuning herself to nature's beauties. Through her poems, Newsome tries to help children see the miraculous and the beautiful in the familiar. In the tradition of Walt Whitman and Emily Dickinson, Newsome's poems for children are optimistic, exuberant works that rely heavily upon visual images to convey their wonder. In her poems for adults, Newsome also celebrates nature, but it is her wont in these works to wax nostalgic. In "Memory" and "Ohio," the adult speakers yearn for nature's beauty. In "Capriccio," the adult speaker yearns for summer and "the petals of a rose."

Most of Newsome's works for children appear primarily in *The Brownies' Book* and in "The Little Page" in *Crisis*. A frequent contributor to *The Brownies' Book*, a short-lived magazine for black children published by W. E. B. Du Bois and Augustus Dill in 1920 and 1921, Newsome saw eleven of her poems, one prose sketch, and one letter appear in the magazine's twenty-four issues. Her association with the periodical began with the April 1920 issue when her nature sketch "The Birds at My Door" appeared. In the following month's issue, two of her nature poems, both titled "May Basket," were published. Throughout the remainder of

1920, she contributed at least one poem to almost every issue. The last work of hers to appear in *The Brownies' Book* was the nature poem "When Comes the Wavering Spring," published in April 1921.

Four years after *The Brownies' Book* ceased publication, Newsome began writing "The Little Page" for *Crisis*. A one-to-two-page feature that appeared most months in the magazine from March 1925 to June 1929, "The Little Page" was a miniature *Brownies' Book* of sorts—including within its limited space poems, prose, and pen-and-ink illustrations by Newsome.

In 1944, thirteen years after the last appearance of "The Little Page," Newsome's only book of poems was published. Titled *Gladiola Garden: Poems of Outdoors and Indoors for Second Grade Readers*, the collection was released by Associated Publishers, the publishing arm of the Association for the Study of Negro Life and History formed by Carter G. Woodson so that authentic books on black culture might be published. Many of the poems in *Gladiola Garden* appeared initially in either *The Brownies' Book* or in "The Little Page." In theme and form, the poems written for *Gladiola Garden* mirror Newsome's previously published poems. Short, clearly expressed poems on nature and on generic childhood experiences are the rule.

While *Gladiola Garden* contains poems exclusively and while Newsome's *Brownies' Book* contributions are primarily poems, approximately half of her "The Little Page" consists of prose, much of which was written for "Calendar Chat." Each "Chat" in "The Little Page" described some feature, usually of nature, that was unique to a specific month. Like Newsome's poems, the "Chat" was designed to bring joy and happiness to child readers, but unlike the poems, in which the primary mission was usually to amuse or please, the "Chat" seems to have been equally committed to instruction.

In addition to "Calendar Chat," Newsome wrote other prose sketches for "The Little Page." What distinguishes these sketches from those in "Chat" is that several of them treat race—a topic that appears rarely in Newsome's canon for children. Perhaps she generally avoided race in her works for children and opted instead to treat the commonplace because she knew that children's lives encompassed the ordinary far more often than they revolved around race relations. In her poems for adults, Newsome was much more willing, however, to treat racial themes. Newsome's "Morning Light the Dew Drier" and "Father and Son" present bleak racial visions. But their perspectives are balanced by "The Bronze Legacy (To a Brown Boy)," "Negro Serenade (In the South)," and "Gourds"—all of which brim with racial pride.

Patently political, Newsome's racial sketches are designed to teach the history of Africans and their descendants in the diaspora and create, therefore, feelings of racial pride in black American readers. As such, these sketches are directly tied to *The Brownies' Book*, wherein biographies of black achievers were included to inspire black American children and to build self-esteem in these readers.

In an editorial in the October 1926 issue of *Crisis*, W. E. B. Du Bois wrote:

> Few magazines have tried to do more for the children than *The Crisis*. The space we have given them is indeed much too small and of this they have frequently complained; but at any rate, we have given them space every year and during the last years, with the help of Effie Lee Newsome, almost each month. This is as it should be, for the development of sound children and the youth among us is the astonishing thing of our history (283).

Newsome devoted herself to this "astonishing thing" throughout her long life.

When Effie Lee Newsome died on May 12, 1979, she left an extensive canon. Although she was a respected writer during the 1920s, 1930s, and 1940s, she has since been largely forgotten as indeed have many of the women writers who were her contemporaries. No doubt she and her oeuvre now wear a cloak of invisibility because the majority of her works were written for children and because her only published collection consists of poems for this audience.

As a writer and illustrator, Newsome merits a place in black American literary history. A pioneering writer of works for children, she created resonant poems and prose sketches whose chief virtues are her mastery of visual imagery and her deftness at treating themes as far-ranging as nature, the timeless world of childhood, and racial pride.

Effie Lee Newsome's works appear in the following collections or anthologies: Robert T. Kerlin, *Negro Poets and Their Poems* (Washington, D.C.: Associated Press, 1923); Countee Cullen, ed., *Caroling Dusk: An Anthology of Verse by Negro Poets* (New York: Harper, 1927); Arna Bontemps, comp., *Golden Slippers: An Anthology of Negro Poetry for Young Readers* (New York: Harper, 1941); Effie Lee Newsome, *Gladiola Garden: Poems of Outdoors and Indoors for Second Grade Readers* (Washington, D.C.: Associated Press, 1944); Arthur P. Davis and Michael W. Peplow, eds., *The New Negro Renaissance: An Anthology* (New York: Holt, Rinehart, Winston, 1975); and Maureen Honey, ed., *Shadowed Dreams: Women's Poetry of the Harlem Renaissance* (New Brunswick: Rutgers University Press, 1989).

References

Du Bois, W. E. B. "Opinion." *Crisis* 32 (October 1926): 283.

Greene, J. Lee. *Time's Unfading Garden: Anne Spencer's Life and Poetry*. Baton Rouge: Louisiana State University Press, 1977. 86.

Hull, Gloria T. "Afro-American Women Poets: A Bio-

Critical Survey.'' In *Shakespeare's Sisters: Feminist Essays on Women Poets*. Ed., introd. Sandra W. Gilbert and Susan Gubar. Bloomington: Indiana University Press, 1979. 173.

———. *Color, Sex, and Poetry: Three Women Writers of the Harlem Renaissance*. Bloomington: Indiana University Press, 1987. 13.

Johnson, Abby Arthur, and Ronald Maberry Johnson. *Propaganda and Aesthetics: The Literary Politics of Afro-American Magazines in the Twentieth Century*. Amherst: University of Massachusetts Press, 1979. 40, 154.

MacCann, Donnarae. ''Effie Lee Newsome: African-American Poet of the 1920s.'' *Children's Literature Association Quarterly* 13 (1988): 60-65.

Newsome, Effie Lee. ''The Bronze Legacy (To a Brown Boy).'' *Crisis* 24 (October 1922): 265.

———. ''Capriccio.'' *Crisis* 32 (September 1926): 247.

———. ''Father and Son.'' *Crisis* 48 (September 1941): 295.

———. ''Gourds.'' *Crisis* 39 (November 1932): 349.

———. ''A Great Prelate: Bishop Lee at Home.'' *Crisis* 32 (June 1926): 69-71.

———. ''Memory.'' *Crisis* 38 (January 1931): 15.

———. Morning Light the Dew Drier.'' *Crisis* 17 (November 1918): 17.

———. ''Negro Serenade (In the South).'' *Crisis* 32 (July 1926): 136.

———. ''Ohio.'' *Crisis* 38 (September 1931): 306.

———. ''Pigments.'' *Crisis* 36 (June 1929): 194, 209.

Redmond, Eugene B. *Drumvoices: The Mission of Afro-American Poetry: A Critical History*. Garden City, N.Y.: Doubleday, 1976. 215.

Rollins, Charlemae. ''Effie Lee Newsome.'' In *Famous American Negro Poets*. New York: Dodd, Mead, 1965. 56-60.

Shockley, Ann Allen, ed. *Afro-American Women Writers: 1746-1933: An Anthology and Critical Guide*. Boston: G. K. Hall, 1988. 403, 409.

T. J. Bryan

Camille Nickerson ''The Louisiana Lady''

(1888-1982)

Collector, arranger, composer, musician, educator

Camille Lucie Nickerson's life exemplified discipline, hard work, and a desire to validate and immortalize the artful melodies of her Creole ancestors. She recalled:

> A composer once was heard to say:—''Artists like Bach and Beethoven erected Churches and Temples on the Heights.'' I wanted . . . to build simple dwellings for men, in which they might feel at home and happy (The Camille Nickerson Papers).

Nickerson, ''The Louisiana Lady,'' was born March 30, 1888, in the French Quarter of New Orleans; she died of pneumonia at Howard University Hospital on April 27, 1982, at age ninety-six. She never married or had children. Nickerson's contribution to the performance, preservation, and appreciation of music was her lagacy to the world.

Nickerson grew up in an environment of musicians. A child prodigy, at age nine she was pianist for the Nickerson Ladies' Orchestra conducted by her father, William Joseph Nickerson. In addition to being a conductor, her father was a violinist and music teacher. Her brother Henry became a violinist and jazz bandleader, and her brother Philip played in a local dance orchestra. Her mother, Julia Ellen, played violin and cello, was a music teacher, and founded and conducted a ladies' orchestra. As a teenager Camille Nickerson tutored many of the local Crescent City youth in her father's famous studio. Nurtured under his watchful eyes, she developed an early love of music.

Realizing that his daughter needed formal training in music theory, Nickerson arranged for her to seek more structured training at Oberlin Conservatory. Here, Nickerson obtained a bachelor of music degree, thus fortifying her skills in piano, organ, voice, theory, history, and composition. Already an accomplished musician upon her arrival, she quickly won the confidence of her instructors, who placed her in charge of various choral groups. Her natural propensity for music earned her membership in Pi Kappa Lambda, the national honor society in music.

In addition to her ability to conduct music, while at

Oberlin Nickerson discovered her skill at composing and publishing Creole music. She recalls one of several stories concerning the publication of her songs:

> On one of my vacation periods, while a student at Oberlin, I visited Chicago, and while there was introduced to a music publisher. When I showed him a song I had written, as an assignment in theory, he was quite pleased and offered to publish it. And so, "When Love Is Done" was my first publication (The Camille Nickerson Papers).

This was to become the first of many publications for Nickerson. During the span of her career as composer, she published the following Creole songs: "Go to Sleep, Dear," "I Love You So," "Mister Banjo," "Mam'selle Zi Zi," "Susanne, Bel Femme," "Suzanne," "Christmas Everywhere," and "The Women of the U.S.A." She also published one interracial hymn entitled "A Precious Lullaby" and, in addition to her first published song, "When Love Is Done," the song "Lizette" joins her list of credits.

As a child, Nickerson was fascinated by the "simple, appealing, even 'comforting'" lyrics of Creole songs. Herself of Creole extraction, she developed profound satisfaction in collecting and publicizing folk songs from fellow native New Orleanians. Possessing the same determination to preserve her native culture as noted folklorist Zora Neale Hurston did, Nickerson turned a great deal of energy while she was in an academic environment where research support was available for compiling existing lyrics and melodies as well as composing her own Creole arrangements. As she collected, she took great care to abide by her father's wish that she not "destroy the Primitive and basic image of these melodies by the use of settings foreign to their Native Simplicity" (The Camille Nickerson Papers).

"The Louisiana Lady" Emerges

Upon her graduation from Oberlin, Nickerson returned to New Orleans to teach with her father in the Nickerson School of Music. While there she made her debut as a concert artist and later played such cities as Atlanta, Birmingham, and Nashville. During this time Nickerson adopted the stage name "The Louisiana Lady," adding a mysterious aura to her performances. In addition, she dressed in Creole costume for authenticity. Audiences—especially those in France where she toured in 1954 under the sponsorship of the United States Information Agency—raved about her performances. Also, while based in New Orleans, Nickerson's consciousness of native Creole music was reawakened. In an interview conducted during the 1973-74 academic year while she was a member of the department of music faculty at Howard University, she seemed deeply disturbed about her people's apathy toward Creole music. She told Howard University musiciologist Doris E. McGinty:

> We didn't think that the Creole song was important, just as I suppose people sang spirituals in churches for years and years, and nobody thought that they were important until somebody came along to arrange them to show how important they were. But I was always delighted with the sound of the song and always very happy when hearing it. So after I finished high school and normal school and had finished Oberlin and had gone back to New Orleans to teach, I began to think about the songs (McGinty, 82).

Not until Nickerson was deceived by a fellow New Orleanian and fellow admirer of Creole songs named Edna Thomas, did she seriously acknowledge her own competence at collecting, arranging, and publishing the music. Under the pretense of adding to a depleted supply of songs to be performed on various local programs, Thomas convinced the unassuming Nickerson to assist her by seeking a fresh repertoire. With the help of an equally unsuspecting father, some cousins, and a few friends, Nickerson not only collected five new songs, but, after yet another request from Thomas, she arranged all five and presented them to her. Nickerson noted in hindsight that this episode of extreme naivete ironically gave her the on-the-job training that she needed to put her talent to work for herself.

After several successful seasons on the concert circuit, Nickerson shocked both friends and associates with her decision to give up a blossoming career as a performing musician to become part of Howard University's music faculty. Nickerson confessed in a personal note that Howard made a total of three offers while she remained in New Orleans at the Nickerson School of Music. When the third offer came, her father's nod of approval facilitated her decision between "entertaining the many and preparing a few to take their place in the profession" (The Camille Nickerson Papers).

Nickerson's career took a decidedly different turn at Howard University, where she tutored numerous aspiring musicians during her thirty-six-year stay there—from 1926 to 1962—retiring with the title professor emerita. When several of Nickerson's former students who attended the junior preparatory department were queried on their impressions of her, they were unanimous in using accolades like "no-nonsense," "iron fist and velvet glove," "exacting," and "extremely demanding." Nickerson is fondly remembered by several alumna for her emphasis upon decorum, manners, appearance, and behavior.

After several years of exemplary teaching in the school of music's junior preparatory department, Nickerson was granted leave made possible by a Rosenwald Fellowship, during which she sought to collect and transcribe Creole music in Louisiana as the basis of her graduate study. This project evolved into her master's thesis, "Afro-Creole Music of Louisiana." Nickerson's graduate research uncovered an abundance of Creole folk music, but it also revealed impressive accomplishments made by black American musicians that have gone largely unnoticed. She notes:

> The Black composer has made a definite and significant contribution to Music Literature, and can take his place among composers of the other groups without apology. When we consider the handicaps—lack of encouragement, very little opportunity of being heard—one marvels at what has come from his pen notwithstanding (The Camille Nickerson Papers).

Nickerson returned to Howard after her graduate studies, and she was eventually promoted to head of the school of music's junior preparatory department and remained there until her retirement.

During her stay at Howard University, Nickerson was a member of many social and professional organizations both on and off campus. She was a past president of the National Association of Negro Musicians, the Faculty Women's Club of Howard University, and the Round Table Club. Nickerson was also a member of the American Association of University Women, Kennedy Center, the Washington Performing Arts Society, the advisory board of the National Folk Festival Association, and the Friday Morning Music Club.

References

Anderson, Ruth E. *Contemporary American Composers: A Biographical Dictionary*. Boston: G. K. Hall, 1976.

Handy, D. Antoinette. *Black Women in American Bands and Orchestras*. Metuchen, N.J.: Scarecrow Press, 1981.

McGinty, Doris E. "Conversation with Camille Nickerson, The Louisiana Lady." *The Black Perspective in Music* 7 (Spring 1979).

Southern, Eileen. *Biographical Dictionary of Afro-American and African Musicians*. Westport, Conn.: Greenwood Press, 1982.

Washington Post, 1 May 1982.

Collections

The Camille Nickerson papers are in the Moorland-Spingarn Research Center, Howard University. They were donated to the university by her long-time friend and associate, R. Louise Burge. Photographs are included.

Sandra G. Shannon

Jessye Norman

(1945-)

Singer

As a young girl growing up in Augusta, Georgia, Jessye Norman remembers hearing the great black contralto, Marian Anderson, sing Brahms's *Alto Rhapsody* and being swept away by the richness and beauty of her voice. Norman played and replayed a recording of Leontyne Price singing *Aida* and thought it the most heavenly sound she had ever heard. The impact of these early inspirations, as well as an abiding appreciation of the role these black singers played in paving the way for others to follow are still with Norman today as she pursues one of the most illustrious singing careers of our time. From her earliest performances, Norman has received resounding praise from the critics. Paul Hume of the *Washington Post* had this to say about her 1968 Washington, D.C., performance of the soprano solos in Handel's *Messiah:* "So great is the future promise in Jessye Norman that her singing, which is today immensely moving and exciting, can only be heard as the prelude to something quite extraordinary." This future promise became a reality in concert halls and opera houses the world over as Norman established herself at the top of her profession. Her voice has been described as "a marvel of expressive power and control (*Life*), an "instrument unmatched in its combined sumptuousness, range, force, and expressivity" (*Connoisseur*).

Norman was born on September 15, 1945, in Augusta, Georgia, one of five children of Silas Norman and Janie (King) Norman. Jessye Norman comes from a happy and financially secure environment. As she told Matthew Gurewitsch in an interview with *Connoisseur* magazine, "My parents were happy to have us, happy to have us around, to support and encourage us." She feels this encouragement inspired her greatly as a child. Both parents worked: her father as an insurance salesman, her mother as a secretary for the Democratic party and an auditor for a local church. Both parents had an avid interest in music, which was a natural and integral part of family life. Her mother was an amateur pianist and her father a singer in the church choir. All of the Norman children studied piano from an early age. Although Jessye Norman loved to sing, she did not begin serious vocal instruction until her college years. She has often mentioned in interviews that she is grateful she did not begin studying voice at an early age. As she told Matthew Gurewitsch:

> Singing isn't like playing the violin. We don't start having lessons at age three. The very best thing that could happen to a voice, if it shows any promise at all, is when it is very young to leave it

> alone, and to let it develop quite naturally, and to let the person go on for as long as possible with the sheer joy of singing—rather than being concerned with what comes later: the necessary concern over vocal technique (98).

However, she recalls, that she was always encouraged to perform by family and friends.

At age seven, Norman entered her first vocal competition, taking third prize at the Mount Calvary Baptist Church in Augusta with her rendition of "God Will Take Care of You." Having discovered and instantly fallen in love with opera through the Metropolitan Opera radio broadcasts, she eventually sang arias for Girl Scout and PTA meetings in Georgia and South Carolina. Singing in local choirs was also an important element of Norman's musical development. In high school, her choral director provided special instruction in voice and took her to compete in the Marian Anderson Music Scholarship Competition in Philadelphia when Norman was sixteen years old. Although she did not place in the competition, Norman's teacher arranged for her an audition with Carolyn Grant, a voice teacher at Howard University in Washington, D.C. Based on the audition, Grant recommended Norman for a full scholarship at Howard, where Norman later studied voice, piano, and music education, earning a bachelor of music degree with honors in 1967. During her years at Howard, she sang with the university chorus and local choirs. Upon graduation, she went on to study with Alice Duschak at the prestigious Peabody Conservatory of Music in Baltimore, Maryland, continuing with Pierre Bernac and Elizabeth Mannion at the University of Michigan at Ann Arbor, where Norman earned her master's degree in 1968.

In her early twenties, Norman successfully competed in several important vocal competitions, receiving in 1965 first prize from the National Society of Arts and Letters in Washington, D.C. In 1968 she was selected to participate in a State Department People-to-People tour of South America. That same year, a scholarship from the Institute of International Education would take her to Europe to compete in the International Music Competition sponsored by Munich Radio. Norman won first prize in that competition, which led to the first of many debuts in European cities. Settling in West Berlin in late 1969, she signed a three-year contract (1970-1973) with the Deutsche Oper Berlin requiring her to appear in principal soprano roles two-and-one-half months each year. In December 1969 her operatic debut there as Elisabeth in Wagner's *Tannhäuser* drew praise from the local critics for her musicianship and sensuous voice. At the end of her contract, Norman took a calculated risk and decided not to renew, but to expand her repertoire in the concert halls, opera houses, and music festivals across Europe.

Throughout the 1970s Norman continued her European debuts—in Florence at the Teatro Comunale in Handel's oratorio *Deborah;* at the Festival of Two Worlds in Spoleto, Italy, in renditions of Mahler's songs; in Rome as Idamante in a concert version of Mozart's *Idomeneo* with the Radiotelevisione Italiana Orchestra; in London performing Wagner's *Wesendonck Lieder* at the Last Night of the Proms and as Cassandra in Berlioz's operatic masterpiece, *Les Troyens,* at the Royal Opera House, Covent Garden. Although she performed in America as well during this period, it was with European audiences that Norman first became an established presence. In this phase of her career, she also made the first of many recordings for Philips as the countess in *The Marriage of Figaro*, Colin Davis conducting. That recording further expanded her audience at home and abroad. She also appeared in numerous concerts and festivals in Germany, Spain, Holland, France, Austria, Argentina, Mexico, and Israel. In these performances her roles included Marguerite in Berlioz's four-part dramatic legend, *The Damnation of Faust;* the title role of Verdi's *Aida,* directed by Claudio Abbada; and Selika, the captured African queen in Giacomo Meyerbeer's tragic opera, *L'Africaine.*

Performance in *Aida* Marks American Debut

Norman's professional American debut is generally considered the 1972 performance of *Aida* at the Hollywood Bowl in Los Angeles, with James Levine conducting. She returned in 1973 as Donna Elvira in *Don Giovanni,* the second of Mozart's comic operas, also conducted by Levine. Her East Coast debut came in 1973 at Lincoln Center in New York City. This performance of songs by Brahms, Wolf, Strauss, Mahler, Wagner, and Satie was extremely well-received and "stamped her a singer of extraordinary intelligence, taste and emotional depth" (Henahan, *New York Times*). Other United States appearances during this period include the National Symphony at Wolf Trap Farm Park for the Performing Arts in Vienna, Virginia; an appearance in an all-Wagner program at the Berkshire Music Festival in Lenox, Massachusetts, with Colin Davis conducting; under the direction of Julius Rudel at the Caramoor Festival in Katonah, New York; at the Kennedy Center for the Performing Arts in Washington, D.C.; at Carnegie Hall in New York City; with the Los Angeles Philharmonic, Zubin Mehta conducting; and with the Chicago Orchestra and Daniel Barenboim at the Ravinia Festival.

In late 1983, Norman followed in the footsteps of her heroines, Marian Anderson and Leontyne Price, when she appeared on the stage of the Metropolitan Opera. Norman's debut at the one hundredth-anniversary production of *Les Troyens*, in which she sang both female leads, the prophetess Cassandra and Queen Dido of Carthage, firmly established Norman's popularity with American audiences as an extraordinary vocalist and a gifted actress. The performance was broadcast nationally over public television. Norman continues to appear at the Met most seasons. She recently appeared in a history-making production of Arnold Schonberg's *Erwartung,* a one-character opera composed in the post-Romantic atonal style, and in Wagner's *Die Walümkure* as Sieglinde. Of the latter role, Donal Henahan said in his *New York Times* review that "Miss Norman, assuming her role for the first time at the Metropolitan, sang both richly and sensitively and entered into the character with the ease and skill of a veteran Wagnerian." Subsequent roles at the Met have included Jocasta in Stravinsky's *Oedipus Rex,* Strauss's

Ariadne auf Naxos, Madame Lidoine in Poulenc's *Dialogues of the Carmélites,* and Elisabeth in Wagner's *Tannhäuser*.

In addition to her Metropolitan Opera performances, Norman continues to perform with major orchestras the world over, including Berlin, Vienna, New York, Boston, London, Dresden, Leipzig, Toronto, Tokyo, Taipei, and Hong Kong. Her September 1989 performance at the 148th opening of the New York Philharmonic was broadcast live from Lincoln Center. Norman received rave reviews from the New York opera critics for her performances of the "Liebestod," a mainstay of her repertoire and one of the highlights of Wagner's greatest opera, *Tristan und Isolde,* and for Mahler's five *Ruckert* songs. In addition to the Metropolitan and Lincoln Center broadcasts, a 1987 special entitled "Christmastide," was also televised.

She especially enjoys recitals, which offer the opportunity to perform art songs, spirituals, and popular music, for which she has gained an ardent following. In 1989, she gave recitals at San Francisco's War Memorial Opera house and Pasadena's Ambassador Auditorium as well as in Europe. In 1990, she appeared for the first time in south Florida in a recital of Spanish, French, and German songs, and Purcell arias. The *Miami Herald* describes Norman as "more than just an opulent soprano that can soar through a wide range of music with superb accuracy and effortless ease. She has an etcher's skill in carving the phrases of German lieder." The *Atlanta Journal* describes a recital at the Atlanta Symphony's Great Performers Series that "spanned four languages and three centuries. . . . Time and again she found just the right inflection or color to illuminate the text. . . . Her trademark, 'He's Got the Whole World in His Hands,' [was] sung with such spellbinding intensity that even the stoniest misanthrope might be forgiven for shedding a few tears."

Norman was invited to sing the French National Anthem, "La Marseillaise," at the bicentennial celebration of the French Revolution held in Paris on July 14, 1989, a distinct honor for someone who is not a French citizen. Norman is a special favorite in France and has received the country's highest cultural honors, including, in 1984, the title "Commandeur de l'Ordre des Arts et des Lettres," and the Legion of Honor from President Mitterand in 1989. Norman has also received many honors at home, including honorary doctoral degrees from Howard University, the University of Michigan, Boston Conservatory, University of the South, Brandeis University, and Harvard University. Cambridge University and the American University of Paris have similarly honored her.

Since the 1970s, Norman has recorded prolifically. Her discography includes more than fifty recordings, most with Philips and others with EMI, CBS, Erato, Deutsche Grammophon, Orfeo, Eurodisc, and Decca. The recordings include lieder by Mahler, Schubert, Schumann, Poulenc, Wagner, Brahms, and Strauss; art songs by Ravel, Satie, Duparc, Gounod, and Franck; Mozart's *Die Gartnerin Aus Liebe,* and Mahler's *Das Lied Von Der Erde;* solos in Mahler's Second and Third Symphonies, Beethoven's Ninth Symphony, and Bruckner's *Te Deum;* Wagnerian arias including the "Liebestod" from *Tristan Und Isolde;* and Berlioz's *La Mort de Cléopatre*. Operas include Mozart's *Le Nozze di Figaro,* Wagner's *Die Walküre,* Haydn's *Armida,* Gluck's *Alceste,* and Offenbach's *La Belle Hélène*. Norman has also recorded an album of popular music entitled *With a Song in My Heart,* containing songs of Cole Porter, Harold Arlen, and George Gershwin. Her recordings have won numerous prestigious awards, including the Paris Grand Prix National du Disque, the Gramophone Award (London), the Edison Prize (Amsterdam), and in the United States, a Grammy Award as Best Classical Vocalist.

Although Norman is usually described as a soprano, her repertoire spans soprano, mezzo-soprano, and true contralto parts. In a 1989 interview with *Stereo Review,* she said "When I began singing, I had three separate voices. My work over my professional life has been to connect them. I feel that I've made some progress in that respect, and it's now more comfortable to use all parts of my voice." Her working range has been reported to run from high C-sharp to low G. She has, however, always resisted pigeonholing and likes to do what she is able to do, rather than what seems most comfortable. Then, too, technical prowess is only one aspect of what makes a successful opera singer. The performance must be credible, and to be credible it must be understood by the performer. Perhaps the key to Norman's ability to portray a variety of enslaved, abandoned, and condemned heroines from centuries past is made up in equal parts of catharsis, imagination, and literal understanding of the words. She has said she must "feel absorbed by the character," visualizing each scene down to the most minute detail to use as a reference point. The fact that she is often singing the words of queens and princesses caught up in the struggles that myths are made of does not affect her ability to relate to the characters as human beings. As Norman told William Livingstone in a 1989 interview with *Stereo Review:*

> I can't explain why, coming from Georgia, I'm so interested in Greek heroines, but I am whether it's Phèdre in an opera by Rameau or Dido in *Les Troyens* of Berlioz. In Purcell's *Dido* or in *Les Troyens,* when duty calls and Aeneas decides to leave, I can feel that the world is coming to an end because Dido is abandoned. On the other hand, when Aida and Radames don't get together, I just think: Oh, well, it'll be all right. Aida will find somebody else (104).

Norman's agility with languages (she sings in English, German, French, Italian, Spanish, Hebrew, and Latin) is also an essential component of her acting ability. She has said that she does not memorize sounds but understands every word she sings. This ability is also responsible for her huge popularity in other countries, especially France, where there is a great deal of pride in the national language. As she also told William Livingstone in *Stereo Review:*

> Yes, I've been singing French in France, and they've loved it because it shows that I've made

> a terrific effort since I wasn't born singing this language. To enjoy the marvelous songs of Poulenc and Satie the audience must be able to follow the text, and I know if I pronounce the words correctly, the text will be understood. I love watching the faces of the people who are listening as I sing these songs and know that they understand. I think that's what every performer wants: to communicate, to be understood in many ways and on many levels (103).

Norman's appearance was beautifully described in a 1982 article that appeared in *Newsweek*:

> Everything about Jessye Norman is larger than life—her size, her voice and her vibrant personality. . . . On an opera stage, her eyes flash, her head arches high and she moves with the inexorable surge of a ship at sea. Her creamy, richly colored voice extends from the mezzo-soprano range to such dramatic soprano parts as Aida and Isolde. It soars thrillingly up the scale from the dark, chocolate-thick tone of her lower voice to ringing high notes that fill an opera house.

The same article describes her offstage persona:

> Offstage Norman can seem, at first, as intimidating as she looks. Her speaking voice is rich and resonant, her accent tony British; she has lived in London's fashionable Belgravia section since 1975. . . . But for all her European cultivation, there is a girlish openness and warmth about her. Her laugh ripples up and down the scale. And, yes, she goes home to her native Georgia two or three times a year (128).

Norman makes her home in Westchester County, New York, also maintaining a London residence. When she is not performing, she likes her privacy and enjoys close relationships with family and friends and has strong ties to the Augusta community where she grew up. Norman loves to garden, is an avid reader, and has many civic interests, including black educational institutions, Girl Scouts of America, and Save the Children.

References

Abdul, Raoul. *Blacks in Classical Music.* New York: Dodd, Mead, 1977.

Cunningham, Carl. "Soprano Jessye Norman Turns In Sterling Performance at Recital." *Houston Post,* 5 March 1990.

Current Biography Yearbook. New York: H. W. Wilson, 1976. 292-295. Includes photograph.

Ewen, David. *Musicians Since 1900: Performers in Concert and Opera.* New York: H. W. Wilson, 1978.

Garland, Phyl. "Jessye Norman: Diva." *Ebony* 43 (March 1988): 52-56.

Gurewitsch, Matthew. "The Norman Conquests." *Connoisseur* 217 (January 1987): 96-101. Includes photograph.

Henahan, Donal. "A Benefit of Wagner Begins a Season." *New York Times,* 22 September 1989.

——. "First Walkure of Met Season." *New York Times,* 26 March 1989.

Henry, Derrick. "Norman Has Whole Audience in Her Hands at Symphony Hall." *Atlanta Journal,* 11 March 1989.

Kretschmer, Johan Thomson. "Mehta Leads Glorious Philharmonic Opener." *New York Post,* 22 September 1989.

Livingstone, William. "Jessye Norman. 'I want to communicate, to be understood in many ways and on many levels.'" *Stereo Review* 54 (October 1989): 102-105. Includes photograph.

Page, Tim. "Call It the Philharmonic's Home Opener for Fall." New York *Newsday,* 22 September 1989.

Rockwell, John. "Muti and the Philadelphia Offer Two American Works." *New York Times,* 27 April 1989.

Roos, James. "A Beautiful Evening with Jessye Norman." *Miami Herald,* 16 April 1990.

Sanburn, J. C. *Life* 8 (March 1985): 99-102. Includes photograph.

Shaw Concert program. New York, February 1990.

Swan, Annalyn. "A Modern Norman Conquest." *Newsweek* 100 (6 December 1982): 128. Includes photograph.

Washington Post, 30 December 1968.

Who's Who in America. 44th Ed. Vol. 2. Marquis Who's Who, 1987.

Robert W. Stephens

Eleanor Holmes Norton

(1938-)

Lawyer, government official, politician, educator

Eleanor Holmes Norton has always been a forerunner in politics, law, and human rights. Championship of equality and the rights of poor and working people has been the overriding theme of her life and career as a constitutional, civil rights, and labor lawyer, as Human Rights commissioner of New York City, and as chair of the Equal Employment Opportunity Commission from 1977 to 1983 during President Jimmy Carter's administration, and in every other phase of her career.

Norton, the oldest of three girls, was born April 8, 1938, in Washington, D.C. Her father, Coleman Holmes, was a civil servant in the housing department of the District of Columbia; her mother, Vela Holmes, was a schoolteacher. Both parents were college graduates and instilled in their children the importance of hard work and a good education. Her father returned to school to earn his law degree while Norton was still a child. She said that her father always wanted a boy but was not disappointed that he has all girls. "He was proud of us and just assumed that girls could do whatever boys did. My mother and grandmother felt the same way, and my sisters and I had a sense that little girls can grow up to be somebody" (*Current Biography*, 295).

Norton was raised not only by her parents, but by a neighborhood and community that was shaped by solid working and aspiring people. She was raised by people who fought to transform a segregated city into a metropolitan center that takes pride in its pluralism today.

Norton attended Monroe Elementary School (now Bruce-Monroe), Banneker Junior High School, and Dunbar High School in Washington, D.C. In 1955, after graduating from high school, she enrolled in Antioch College in Yellow Springs, Ohio. Norton went on to Yale University, where she earned both a master's degree in American studies in 1963 and her doctor of jurisprudence degree in 1964.

In 1964 Norton moved to Philadelphia, where she worked for a year as a clerk for a federal judge. There she met her husband, Edward Norton, whom she married on October 9, 1965. "He liked the fact that I was a highly educated woman," she told Greta Walker in an interview for the *Women Today*. "Nobody would have married me who didn't want a woman with a career. By the time my husband met me, a career was totally built into my being. I would never have attracted a man who wanted a wife to stay home." Later that year the Nortons moved to New York City, where she took a job as the assistant legal director of the American Civil Liberties Union (ACLU).

During her career with the ACLU Norton represented alleged criminals, Vietnam War protesters, civil rights activists, Ku Klux Klansmen, politicians, and feminists. In one case she won promotions for sixty women employees who accused *Newsweek* magazine of job discrimination based on sex.

Norton specialized in cases involving freedom of speech. She was a member of the team of lawyers that drew up a brief in defense of Julian Bond, then a Georgia state representative, when the Georgia House of Representatives voted to deny the young black legislator his seat for his outspoken opposition to the Vietnam War. When Governor George C. Wallace, the American Independent party's candidate for the presidency, was denied a permit to hold a rally at Shea Stadium during the 1968 election campaign, Norton asked to represent the governor in his lawsuit against the city. "If people like George Wallace are denied free expression, then the same thing can happen to black people," she explained to the interviewer. "Black people understand this. No black person ever said to me, 'Sister, how come you're representing George Wallace?' They knew how come" (*Current Biography*, 296). Wallace's ACLU lawyers won their case, but when New York City appealed the decision, Wallace moved the rally to Madison Square Garden to save the time and expense of litigation.

In October 1968 Norton argued and won her first case before the Supreme Court as the legal representative of the National States Rights Party, a white supremist group that had been denied permission for a rally in Maryland two years earlier because local authorities thought that the group's vocal denunciation of Jews, blacks, and others might provoke angry responses from nonparty members. During these years, in addition to practicing law, Norton taught courses in black history at the Pratt Institute in Brooklyn, New York.

Norton Heads New York City's Human Rights Commission

In April 1970 Mayor John V. Lindsay appointed Norton chairman of the New York City Commission on Human Rights. Norton decided to accept the position mainly because the Human Rights Commission, by law, acts as the representative of and advocate for the complainants. Shortly after the appointment she told newsmen at a press conference:

> As commissioner, I will attempt to see that no man is judged by the irrational criteria of race, religion, or national origin. And I assure you that I use the word "man" in the generic sense, for I mean to see that the principle of nondiscrimination becomes a reality for women as well (*Current Biography*, 297).

Because many working women do not see themselves as objects of discrimination, Norton observed, women are more exploited by business than any other group. "Most people think civil rights today is about 'whether or not I'm turning down somebody at the door because he is black or female,'" Norton explained to one interviewer. "It doesn't happen that way anymore. It is more subtle. It happens when women are asked at a job interview, 'Do you intend to get pregnant within the next two years?' And it happens to women much more than it happens to blacks, because blacks have spent more than 300 years trying to educate the country about how perverse it all is" (*Current Biography*, 297).

Norton is the first woman to head New York City's most powerful anti-discrimination agency. As head of the Human Rights Commission, she became known for her ability to obtain federal grants to assist her in her all-out efforts to end all forms of discrimination. "There are certain substantive principles that I believe in strongly," she once said. "One is racial equality. The other is free speech. As it turns out, if I want to implement the principle of equality, I do it through participation in the civil rights movement. To implement my belief in free speech, I represent anyone whose free speech has been infringed" (*Current Biography*, 295).

In support of working women's individual complaints, she obtained liberal maternity benefits, including maternity leave for single women, from an airline company, a major bank, and a blue-collar employer; convinced another company to allow a pregnant secretary to remain on the job past her seventh month of pregnancy; won for a woman sports reporter the right to sit in the press box at hockey games; forced the chic Twenty-one Club to serve women on an equal basis with men; and ordered the Biltmore Hotel to change the name of its Men's Bar and open it up to women. Working closely with national and local women's groups, Norton promoted the revision of outdated federal and state laws regulating workmen's compensation and minimum wages, the liberalization of abortion laws, and the establishment of adequate day care centers.

To address the particular problems of black women who have had to contend with both racial and sexual discrimination, Norton helped to found the National Black Feminist Organization in August 1973.

In an effort to combat job discrimination against blacks, Hispanics, Vietnam veterans, ex-offenders, and older employees, Norton urged businessmen to give these people access to "higher-level, skilled, and better-paid jobs in every industry" (*Current Biography*, 297). In a speech to the Association of Personnel Agencies of New York meeting at the Pierre Hotel in New York City on April 2, 1971, Norton noted that while most companies had made an effort to recruit minority group members for entry-level positions, few offered these employees any real chance for advancement.

Getting the nation's strictest law prohibiting discriminatory real estate practices through the New York State legislature was made possible with the aid of Norton. She convened public hearings on the New York City Schools Board of Education's employment practices in January 1971. Citing a 1959 Board of Education survey that showed that minority groups comprised fifty-five percent of the students, nine percent of the teachers, and four percent of the principals, she ordered Human Rights Commission investigators to look into recruitment, appointment, and promotion procedures and to outline constructive proposals for improvement. Norton conducted a census of city employees to check for racial or sexual discrimination, set up affirmative action programs, and broadened maternity leave policies.

Norton was reappointed to the Human Rights Commission of New York City for a second term in 1974. Her reappointment was supported by 100 Black Men, the NAACP, the National Urban League, feminists, leading city politicians, and both of New York City's black newspapers.

In 1988 Norton was designated by the Reverend Jesse Jackson to handle platform discussions during his presidential campaign. Her appointment was greeted with some relief by the campaign of Governor Michael S. Dukakis of Massachusetts, the probable Democratic nominee, and by Democratic party leaders. According to the *New York Times*, her appointment seemed to be symbolic of Jackson's desire to make peace with the party and help it win the 1988 election.

Civil Rights Record Leads to Federal Appointment

Norton was among the members of a distinguished panel appointed by President Gerald Ford to investigate the American welfare state. Among the ideas endorsed by this panel was a "limit on the length of time that those who can work are entitled to welfare benefits." Welfare mothers who bumped up against the time limit would be offered a public-sector job and told by the government to choose "between the job we offer and making it on your own." Prominent black figures such as Eleanor Norton endorsed kicking mothers off welfare if they would not work ("Gaining Ground," 11).

Norton was also among the one hundred scholars and experts who produced the study "A Common Destiny: Blacks and American Society," released by the National Research Council in 1989. "Americans face an unfinished agenda," states the report, regarded as the most substantial study of black life in America since World War II. "Many black Americans remain separated from the mainstream of national life under conditions of great inequality." Congress could use the report to hold hearings on its own, comments Eleanor Holmes Norton. "The important function of this report is that it is not options; it's basically data that seems to me to be irrefutable" (Watts, 26).

Norton contends that affirmative action has been effective in the advancement of blacks:

> Affirmative action is the most important modern anti-discrimination technique ever instituted in the United States. It is the one tool that has had a demonstrable effect on discrimination. No one who knows anything about the subject would say it hasn't worked. It has certainly done something, or else it wouldn't have provoked so much opposition. In just one decade—the 1970s—the number of sales, technical and professional jobs Blacks hold increased by 50 percent. Affirmative action, by all statistical measures, has been the central ingredient to the creation of the Black middle class (Villarosa, 66).

Although the Democratic primary campaign was badly shaken by the fact that she and her husband, a lawyer who once headed the city's Board of Elections and Ethics, had failed to file local income tax returns for eight years, in October 1990 Norton won the nomination to replace Walter Fauntroy as Congressional delegate representing the District of Columbia. Norton said that she did not know that her husband never mailed the 1982 through 1989 tax returns she signed. She boldly confronted the crisis at a tearful press conference attended by her two children and Edward, her attorney husband of twenty-five years, who explained that he handles family finances and was personally responsible for the oversight. She lost votes because of the flap but handily won the election (Haywood, 106). As she ran for public office, Norton gave up her tenured position as professor in the Georgetown University Law Center and her seat on several corporate and philanthropic boards. She became one of the three black women to join Cardiss Collins (Democrat, Illinois) in the United States Congress. The others are Maxine Walters (Democrat, California) and Barbara-Rose Collins (Democrat, Michigan).

Among her many other accomplishments, Norton was recognized by *Washington Magazine* as "One of the Most Powerful Women in Washington," and *Ladies Home Journal* counted her among the magazine's "One Hundred Most Important Women" in America. Norton has been awarded nearly fifty honorary degrees, including honorary doctorates from Howard University, Gallaudet College, the University of the District of Columbia, and Georgetown University.

Norton's service locally and nationally has been usually diverse, including the board of governors of the District of Columbia Bar and the board of such organizations as the Community Foundation of Greater Washington, the Martin Luther King, Jr., Center for Social Change, the Southern Christian Leadership Conference, and the National Women's Political Caucus Advisory Board.

Norton, eloquent, tall, striking, with short-cropped hair, is devoted to her family. She relaxes by jogging and spends much of her leisure time with her husband and her two children—John and Katherine. Because Katherine has Down's syndrome, Norton spends a significant amount of time working with her. "Katherine is an extraordinary human being," she says, "and it's a pleasure to bring out the best in her" (Haywood, 106).

References

Afro-American Encyclopedia. Vol. 3. North Miami, Fla.: Educational Book Publishers, 1974.

Ayres, Drummond B. "Women Nominated for Capital Mayor." *New York Times* 12 September 1990.

"Candidate Owing Back Taxes Won't Quit Race." *New York Times* 10 September 1990.

Current Biography. New York: H. W. Wilson, 1976.

Dionne, E. J. "Two Party Insiders to Lead Jackson's Convention Drive." *New York Times* 14 May 1988.

Dreifus, Claudia. "'I Hope I'm Not a Token.'" *McCall's* 99 (October 1971): 51.

"Gaining Ground." *New Republic* 200 (5 June 1989): 10, 11.

Haywood, Richetta. "Eleanor Holmes Norton Takes D. C. Seat." *Ebony* 46 (January 1991): 105-106. Photographs, pp. 104-106.

Ploski, Harry. *The Negro Almanac*. New York: Bellwether Pub. Co., 1976.

Pyatt, Richard I. "Eleanor Holmes Norton: From Human Rights to Equal Opportunity." *Encore* 6 (20 June 1977): 47, 48.

Villarosa, Linda. "What Have They Done For Us Lately." *Essence* 21 (May 1990): 66-68. Photograph, p. 66.

Walker, Greta. "Eleanor Holmes Norton." *Women Today* (1975): 29.

Watts, Daud. "The American Dilemma Has Not Been Solved." *Black Enterprise* 19 (October 1989): 26. Includes photograph.

Who's Who among Black Americans, 1990/91. 6th ed. Detroit: Gale Research, 1991.

Jo Ann Lahmon

O

Oblate Sisters of Providence

Religious leaders, educators

On July 2, 1829, four black women—Mary Rosine Boegues and Mary Frances Balas of San Domingo, Haiti, Mary Theresa Duchemin of Baltimore, and Elizabeth Lange of Santiago, Cuba—made their final vows as nuns in Baltimore, Maryland, founding the oldest congregation of black American nuns in the United States. Sister Mary Elizabeth Lange became superior, a position she held until her death at the age of ninety-five in 1882. The new order received papal approval on October 2, 1831.

The names of the sisters are given as in the *Catholic Encyclopedia* of 1911. The *New Catholic Encyclopedia* of 1967 lists the names as Elizabeth Lange, Marie Magdalen Balas, Rosine Boegue (without an *s*), and Almaide Duchemin. The discrepancy seems due to a confusion of secular and religious names; for example, Elizabeth Lange took the name Mary Elizabeth when she made her vows.

The order of Oblate Sisters of Providence has its roots in nineteenth-century Haiti. The convulsions of the struggle for liberty in that country sent a number of free mulattoes and blacks as refugees to Baltimore around 1800. The conditions these refugees faced reduced them to poverty and made it extremely difficult for them to provide education for their children. The group of French-speaking blacks posed a challenge and an opportunity for the church. Furthermore, their children were growing up English-speaking and largely illiterate. The young women who were the first members of the Oblate Sisters of Providence felt both a call to the religious life and a desire to offer schooling to their fellow blacks. Their goals were fulfilled after Jaques Hector Nicholas Joubert de la Muraille, a Supplician priest, was assigned pastoral responsibility for the blacks of Saint Mary's chapel.

Joubert was born September 6, 1777, in France. After attending artillery school, he became a tax collector and was sent to San Domingo, Haiti in 1800. In 1803 his family in San Domingo was massacred. With an uncle and nephew who had taken refuge earlier in Cuba, Joubert went to Baltimore. In 1805 he began to study for the priesthood and was ordained in 1810. In 1827 he was assigned to address the religious needs of the black Catholics in Baltimore. (A somewhat fuller account of his early life can be found in the biographical sketch in Bede, 112). The conjunction of the women's vocation and Joubert's pastoral concerns led them to act together to establish the Oblate sisters, of whom he became the spiritual director. The sisters began their educational work by opening a school with twenty-four girls.

The obstacles the Oblate sisters faced were formidable. To the disabilities of race, color, and gender must be added the effects of virulent anti-Catholic prejudice in the nineteenth century that led to incidents like the attack on the convent by a white mob in 1837. Within the church, there was the tension between a strong and genuinely shared religious commitment and the difficulty of establishing a real community among members of different ethnic groups. For example, before the establishment of the motherhouse as a place for them to worship, black Catholics were segregated on the rear benches of the churches and took communion last. Among Protestant denominations the problem of community was usually solved by the withdrawal of blacks and the establishment of a separate church organization, an option not open to Catholics who wished to remain faithful to the teachings of their church.

A particularly difficult period for the order appears to have occurred at the death of Joubert on November 5, 1843, when it was still suffering from the aftereffects of the panic of 1837. According to Brother Bede, "The work had declined; the attendance had fallen off in the school; and the institution seemed moribund" (46). Tentatively, one may assign to this period the alleged statement of an archbishop. He is said to have had "little regard for the Oblate sisters and no faith in their abilities as nuns" and wished to see the order dissolved (*Ebony*, 144). The situation was corrected with the 1847 appointment of Thaddeus Anwander, a Redemptorist priest, as director. With his guidance and the effort of the sisters, the situation was redressed, and by 1857 the Oblate sisters began to expand their efforts outside of Baltimore.

The segregation prevalent within the church had a direct impact on the teaching mission of the sisters; for many years no Catholic college would accept black students, making it very difficult for the sisters to prepare themselves properly for their teaching mission. Two fellow orders of white nuns did much to assist them. The School Sisters of Notre Dame, who began to work in Baltimore in 1847, offered valuable assistance and opened the doors of Notre Dame College, founded in 1895, to blacks at an early date. In addition, the Sisters of the Blessed Sacrament, founded in 1889 to work with blacks, did much to help; this order established Xavier College in 1915. Praising them for the efforts, Brother Bede says, "Many of the administrative officers of the Society of Oblates of Providence are products of schools conducted by the Sisters of the Blessed Sacrament" (77).

In face of these difficulties, the Oblate sisters, along with the other congregation of black nuns founded in the nineteenth century—the Sisters of the Holy Family—persevered. (The third order of black nuns, the Franciscan Handmaids of Mary, was founded in the early twentieth century. Among them, the three orders comprised in 1982 between seventy and eighty percent of the approximately seven hundred black nuns, who in turn comprise about .5 percent of nuns in the United States (calculation based on numbers in Rector, 240). In that year, there were 191 Oblate sisters.

Oblate Sisters Establish Schools and Orphanage

Until 1857, the sisters confined their efforts to Baltimore where they had a flourishing girls school—30 boarders and 105 day students in 1853—a recently established boys' day school, and an orphanage. According to the *Catholic Encyclopedia*, around 1910 the 130 sisters of the order ran schools in Baltimore; Washington, D.C.; Leavenworth, Kansas; Saint Louis; and Normandy, Missouri; and had four houses in Cuba. (The Cuban operations ceased in 1961, during the early days of the Castro regime.)

The Oblate sisters have continued to face problems in the twentieth century as society and the church continue to change. Since the 1950s there has been a decline in the number of vocations, a problem faced by all religious orders. Marked changes also occurred in the patterns of Catholic education: As the migration of Catholics to the suburbs caused a decline in the number of schools, the number of lay teachers rose to more than three times that of teaching sisters, and the schools faced modest rises in the number of black students and declines in the number of Catholic students.

The Oblate Sisters of Providence have responded with unimpaired faith and with flexibility to the challenges of a changing society. Rector offers a table detailing the scope of their activities in 1982, when they operated twenty-four institutions in the United States and three in Costa Rica. The three largest schools were Holy Comforter, Washington, D.C. (365 students); Buffalo Educational Center, Buffalo, New York (523 students); and Holy Name of Mary School, Chicago (300 students).

At the time of the order's 150th anniversary in 1976, reflecting on the mission of the community and the struggle to construct the new motherhouse, Our Lady of Mount Providence Convent, completed in 1960, Sister Marie Infanta said:

> This is still a struggling community. But we were able to build the Mother House ourselves; no one gave us any money for this. Some of our old projects will have to die as new ones are born and we will continue to grow. We will always continue in service to God and address ourselves to the needs of the times (*Ebony*, 146).

References

Bede, Brother (Michael Francis Rouse). *A Study of the Development of Negro Education Under Catholic Auspices in Maryland and the District of Columbia*. Baltimore: The Johns Hopkins Press, 1935.

Chineworth, M. A. "Oblate Sisters of Providence." In *New Catholic Encyclopedia*. Vol. 10. New York: McGraw-Hill, 1967.

Gratin, Magdalen. "Oblate Sisters of Providence." In *The Catholic Encyclopedia*. Vol. 11. Ed. Charles G. Herbermann, et al. New York: Robert Appleton, 1911.

Norment, Lynn. "The Miracle of Providence." *Ebony* 34 (September 1979): 142-44, 146.

Rector, Theresa A. "Black Nuns as Educators." *Journal of Negro Education* 51 (Summer 1982): 238-53.

Collections

The archives of the order are housed in Our Lady of Mount Providence Convent, Baltimore, Maryland.

Robert L. Johns

Odetta

(1930-)

Singer

Odetta Holmes Felious Gordon Shead Minter, eclectic folksinger and guitarist recognized simply by her first name, hopes to be for her audience "a mirror, in front of each individual, where they look into it and see some part of their own reflection that they like" (Yelin, 17).

Odetta was born December 31, 1930, New Year's Eve, in Birmingham, Jefferson County, Alabama. She was the only child of Reuben Holmes and Flora Sanders Holmes. When she was six years old, her family moved to Los Angeles, California, where she grew up. In 1937 she took the surname of her stepfather, Zadock Felious. She was married to Don Gordon in 1959, to Gary Shead in the late sixties, and to Iversen "Louisiana Red" Minter in 1977. Although she currently lives in New York, it was in Los Angeles that she began her career as a folk artist.

Odetta's education, like that of many folk artists, is a

composite of formal and informal training. In Los Angeles, she attended Belmont High School, graduating in 1947. She attended night courses at Los Angeles City College. Today she continues her study by researching much of her material at the Library of Congress in Washington, D.C.

Odetta's study of music began as a child when she took lessons and practiced on her grandmother's piano. As a member of the glee club during her junior high school years, she took voice lessons. As a teenager, she continued taking music lessons, with an emphasis on classical music. At Los Angeles City College, she majored in music and obtained a degree in classical music and musical comedy.

Odetta's career began early. In 1945, while she was still in high school and only fourteen years old, she worked as an amateur at Hollywood's Turnabout Theater. In 1949, when she was nineteen, she made her initial professional stage appearance, performing as a member of the chorus in a local production of *Finian's Rainbow* in San Francisco. Until this point, she had no interest in folk music, but as a result of the tour, she became interested in folk song. She was, according to Robert Yelin, "deeply affected by the new experience and by the atmosphere of social reform in which she discovered it" (914). As a result of this association with folksingers and folklorists, Odetta began teaching herself to play the guitar.

She began her career as a professional folksinger with an impromptu performance in 1952 at San Francisco's hungry i club. She went on to appear at local parties and in nightclubs in Los Angeles and San Francisco. She spent 1953 in residence performing at another such club, the Tin Angel. While there, she was booked to perform a two-week engagement at New York City's Blue Angel; its manager, Herb Jacobi, took an interest in her upon reading a review in the *San Francisco Chronicle*. Later in the fifties, Odetta performed in clubs in New York's Greenwich Village, one of the folk revival's most active centers.

Odetta's concert appearances are too numerous to name. She has performed around the world from folk festivals to Carnegie Hall, where she played in 1960 and in 1968.

In 1957 Odetta performed with Bill Broonzy at a benefit concert in Chicago, in 1959 with the Count Basie Orchestra at Hunter College in New York City, in 1960 with Pete Seeger at Yale University, and in 1968 with Harry Belafonte in a concert for children in New York. She appeared frequently at the Newport Folk Festival, and performed at the New Orleans Jazz Festival in 1977. She appeared at London's Hyde Park in 1970, and, four years later, toured the Soviet Union and Eastern Europe. At the 1980 Toronto Festival, she appeared on stage with Salome Bey and Elizabeth "Libba" Cotten. In September 1989, she was still performing, appearing in New York City's Merkin Concert Hall series, Voices of Change. From Nashville's Grand Ole Opry to Africa and Asia, Odetta has lent her talent to the folk art genre.

Artist Performs in Several Music Genres

Odetta's folk repertoire encompasses several musical genres, including blues, gospel, and European-based folk song, her guitar providing her major accompaniment. With her discovery of folk music, Odetta was impressed by the works and styles of Bessie Smith and Leadbelly. As well, some of Odetta's arrangements reveal the influence of folk sounds collected in fieldwork done by the Lomaxes and perhaps researched at the Library of Congress.

If Odetta's choice of material is somewhat complex for its mixture, the choice has been often defended. Langston Hughes placed her in the company of Josh White, Leon Bibb, and others who, for example, "made use of spirituals in nightclub appearances" (131). Indeed, Odetta's repertoire extends from her renditions of Bob Dylan to prison work songs of the chain gang and social protest songs of the labor struggle.

Odetta's early influence by Leadbelly is recounted by Pete Seeger who, with Harry Belafonte, took a strong role in promoting Odetta's early career:

> In 1952, at a party at Bob DeWitt's, Topanga Canyon, California, I first heard Odetta sing. Someone told me that there was a young woman who really knew how to sing Leadbelly's songs. We had to hunt to find her, very shy, sitting in the farthest corner. But when she was persuaded to sing—Power, power, intensity and power! I told her she was the first person since Leadbelly had died to do justice to the song "Take this Hammer" (313).

Janis Joplin is said to have begun with "an imitation of Odetta's huge 'Take this Hammer' voice" (Pavletich, 55). Also, according to Seeger, Odetta's revival of Leadbelly's "Old Cotton Fields at Home," which she taught to Harry Belafonte, made the Hit Parade: "When I was a little bitty baby / My mother would rock me in the cradle / In the old, old cotton fields at home" (313). Thus, she was impressed with Leadbelly's music and, interpreting it in her own right, influenced other folk performers with it.

Odetta's performance of spirituals and gospel music provides for her repertoire a wealth of folk material while displaying the range of her voice and her mastery of tone. Her arrangement of "Joshua," for example, is said to display a "power and intensity that could well have tumbled the walls of Jericho" (Gitter). At the other end of the spectrum is the soft sadness of "Sometimes I Feel Like a Motherless Child" and the solemn tone of "Glory, Glory." When backed by the choir of the Church of the Master, under the direction of Theodore Stent, "she offers what appears to be unadulterated Gospel music, as in her versions of the spirituals 'Hold On' and 'Ain't No Grave Can Hold Me Down'" (Mellers, 69). Her a cappella arrangement of "God's a-goin' to Cut You Down" demonstrates her use of handclapping, a prevalent factor in her performance.

Just as it includes blues and gospel, Odetta's repertoire takes in many more music forms. Her interpretation of "All the Pretty Little Horses" is heartrending for its evocation of the injustice of plantation life, wherein a mother must attend the child of her mistress to the neglect of her own child, who is left in the field, open to the elements, its cries unheeded. She can inspirit such well-known tunes as "900 Miles," "Shenandoah," and "Blowing in the Wind," a song often associated with Bob Dylan. On the same program, she can perform a prison song such as "Been in the Pen."

Odetta's eclecticism and her performance style won her success as a professional folk artist and sustained for her a high level of popularity through and beyond the fifties and sixties, a period of high profile for the folk song movement of which she was a vital part. In a review of Merkin Concert Hall's 1989 Voices of Change series, which was "devoted to political songs" on a program that "looked back to the 19th century," Jon Peeples describes Odetta's performance as "a virtually free-form set of songs that seemed unconnected to the series' theme—their protests were existential rather than political or topical" (79). According to Peeples:

> She strung together blues and spirituals, many of them familiar. Over the steady rhythm of her guitar and her tapping foot, she sent her voice to its clear heights and its nasal depths, bringing out the field holler roots of her music (79).

Although the traditional significance of the field holler content may have grown distant with time, Odetta's voice range, her guitar, and her use of hand claps and foot taps typify the appeal of her audience-oriented performance as a folk artist. She explains that her perception of her audience tends to direct her choice of material as she goes; thus she prefers to perform solo to have the freedom to sing what she feels like singing. This approach reveals her attitude toward the range of material comprising the repertoire of her performance programs.

Odetta refuses to yield to the dogmas of folk purists, either with her guitar technique or with her personal background. When asked about her limitations as a self-taught guitarist, for example, she responds:

> If a song is important enough for me to sing, I'll find a way to accompany myself on guitar. I would make up chords to fit the singing—I'm not a purist in any way, shape, or form. If I felt I needed to sing a song so badly, and I couldn't play accompaniment for it, I would sing it a cappella (Yelin, 17).

When questioned about the strict dogmas of folk audiences that demand a folk artist perform out of the personal background and experience of penury, she responds: "We're trained in stereotypes. I know there have been an awful lot of people who have been disappointed with me because I didn't have runover heels and my slip hanging down in front of my dress. . . . I figure that's their problem" (Pavletich, 55). Odetta's formal training is perhaps what enables her to achieve a level of objectivity that assumes her audience appreciates the inspiration of the direction her program takes.

Odetta Known as Accomplished Guitarist

Odetta's use of the guitar is well-known. She began by teaching herself, using a guitar belonging to an associate who showed her "C, G, and an easy F chord" (Yelin, 14). When she was employed at the Tin Angel, she used her rent money to purchase from a pawn shop a wood-bodied National guitar that she named "Baby" and on which she did all of her arrangements for years. She is known for making up chords, a process that she describes:

> I'll usually take the first-position open chords that I know, like E, Al, or B7, and slide them up the neck. By playing them that way, I am harmonizing fretted strings with open strings. That is how I create my new chords and harmonies. I have been told that my playing chords that way has made my guitar sound like a 12-string guitar. I also adore playing in open D tuning [D-A-D-F#-A-D] (Yelin, 17).

Placing her interest in singing above her technical proficiency with the guitar, Odetta also describes her guitar style as "self-defense," explaining her effort to achieve fuller sound from her self-acquired knowledge of the guitar:

> I'll play the same few chords, but by varying my strumming, by harmonizing notes within a chord and picking some other notes—that way I'll achieve the sounds of fullness. I love the opposite forces I can create by singing a smooth melody line and hearing my rhythm playing churning away beneath it. I love those dramatics in music (Yelin, 14).

Aside from its role in her song, Odetta's guitar is for her a private means of getting in touch with herself. The vibrations have a healing effect on her. Her guitar is, in a less personal sense, a tool making up part of her stage presence, for her art is, in Mellers's terms, "an actress' projection" (71), a comment that brings to mind her career in drama. Her guitar combines with an expansive contralto voice, an introspective mood, and a modest attitude to give to this imposing figure a stage presence in remarkable contrast to the quiet delicacy of her off-stage personality.

Odetta has appeared frequently as a dramatic performer on stage and in film. From her early years on the local stage, she ascended to perform on countless occasions. When she left New York City's Blue Angel club, she returned to California to appear in the 1954 film *The Last Time I Saw Paris* and to sing "Santy Anno" in the 1955 film *Cinerama Holiday*. For the next two years she performed at Los Angeles's Turnabout Theater. In 1959 she appeared with Langston Hughes on CBS-TV's "Lamp unto My Feet" and was featured on CBS-TV's "Tonight with Belafonte." In 1960 she took a role in the motion picture *Sanctuary*; in 1961 she appeared in CBS-TV's *Have Gun Will Travel*, in the episode, "The Hanging of Aaron Gibbs." Two years later she appeared in the television special "Dinner with the President," sponsored by the B'nai B'rith Anti-Defamation League. In 1974 she appeared in the popular CBS movie, *The Autobiography of Miss Jane Pittman*, starring Cicely Tyson and in 1976 sang and acted in Gian Carlo Menotti's opera, *The Medium*. She has also made television appearances with hosts Joey Bishop, Mike Douglas, David Frost, Virginia Graham, Della Reese, Pierre Salinger, and Woody Guthrie.

Besides performing on film, at festivals, and in concert halls, Odetta is a prolific recording artist. In 1956 she recorded her first album, *Odetta Sings Ballads and Blues* (Tradition TLP 1010), and in 1957 she recorded live *Odetta at the Gate of Horn*, while engaged there, with Albert Grossman, the club's owner, as her manager. Between 1956 and 1981, she recorded more than fifteen albums with seven record companies. Among her releases were the blues album *Sometimes I Feel Like Crying*, her first album with RCA Victor (LPM/LSP 2573); *Odetta Sings Dylan*; *Odetta at Carnegie Hall*; and *Odetta Sings Christmas Spirituals*. Among the recording companies she worked with were Tradition, Vanguard, RCA Victor, Everest, Riverside, and Verve-Forecast. Although she primarily performs solo, bassists Bill Lee, Leslie Grinage, and Victor Sproles accompany her on various albums, with Bruce Langhorne on second guitar. She has also recorded on album anthologies, including *The Sound of Folk Music and Folk Festival at Newport*, Volume 2.

Odetta's talent has been publicly recognized. In addition to her awards from the music industry, in 1959 she won the Sylvania Award for Excellence for her appearance in "Tonight with Belafonte." In 1965 she was presented with the Key to the City of Birmingham, Alabama. Odetta was recipient of Yale University's Duke Ellington Fellowship Award. She currently lives in New York where she continues her career as a folk artist.

References

Baggelaar, Kristin and Donald Milton. *Folk Music: More than a Song*. New York: Crowell, 1976.

Barnes, Adam. Record notes for *Odetta Sings Folk Songs*. RCA Victor, LPM/LSP, 1963.

Budds, Michael J. "Odetta." *The New Grove Dictionary of American Music*. Edited by H. Wiley Hitchcock and Stanley Sadie. New York: Macmillan, 1986.

"Commentary." *Black Perspectives in Music* 2 (1974): 228.

De Lerma, Dominique-René. *Reflections on Afro-American Music*. Kent, Ohio: Kent State University Press, 1973.

Gitter, Dean. Record notes for *Odetta Sings Ballads and Blues*. Tradition, TLP, 1956.

Harris, Sheldon. *Blues Who's Who: A Biographical Dictionary of Blues Singers*. New York: Da Capo Press, 1979.

Hughes, Langston and Milton Meltzer. *Black Magic: A Pictorial History of Black Entertainers in America*. New York: Bonanza Books, 1967.

Mellers, Wilfred. *Angels of the Night: Popular Female Singers of Our Time*. New York: Basil Blackwell, 1986.

Pavletich, Aida. *Rock-A-Bye, Baby*. New York: Doubleday, 1980.

Peeples, Jon. "19th Century Songfest." Review of Voices of Change, Merkin Concert Hall, New York. *New York Times*, 17 September 1989.

Seeger, Pete. *The Incompleat Folksinger*. New York: Simon and Schuster, 1972.

Southern, Eileen. *Biographical Dictionary of Afro-American and African Musicians*. Westport, Connecticut: Greenwood Press, 1982.

Terkel, Studs. Record notes for *Folk Festival at Newport*, Vol. 2. Vanguard, 1959.

Vassal, Jacques. *Electric Children: Roots and Branches of Modern Folkrock*. Translated by Paul Barnett. New York: Paplinger Pub. Co., 1976.

Yelin, Robert. "Odetta: Folk Music's Majestic Leading Lady." *Frets Magazine* (April 1981): 14-17.

Laura C. Jarmon

P

Nell Irvin Painter

(1942-)

Historian, educator, author

History professor and author Nell Irvin Painter describes herself as "a historian of the United States South in the 19th and 20th centuries" (Moseley, 12); however, she is also known as one whose teaching, lectures, and writing are concerned with social history, labor history, African-American history, and women's history.

Nell Irvin Painter was born on August 2, 1942, in Houston, Texas, to Frank Edward Irvin, Sr., and Dona Lolita (McGruder) Irvin. Painter's fraternal grandfather, Ed Irvin, was a pioneer skilled black mechanic on the Missouri Pacific Railroad. He was one of the first black Americans to service the steam engines that came into the system's maintenance yards in Houston. Her maternal grandfather, Charles Hosewell McGruder, Sr., a teacher at Straight University in New Orleans, Louisiana (now incorporated into Dillard University), married Nellie Eugenie Donato, who had been his student. After she graduated they settled in Victoria, Texas, where he became principal of the Victoria Colored High School. When Dona, their youngest child, was seven, the family of mother, father, and five children moved to Houston, Texas. Until his death in 1935, McGruder worked in Houston as local, state, and national official of the black fraternal and benevolent order, United Brothers of Friendship and Sisters of the Mysterious Ten, familiarly referred to as the UBF and SMT.

In the mid 1930s Painter's parents met when they were students at Houston College for Negroes (now Texas Southern University). With the mass migration of black Americans during World War II, the Irvins came to Oakland, California, in October 1942, when Painter was ten weeks old. For more than thirty years Frank Irvin, Sr., was the non-official father figure and mentor for black students and employees—American, African, and Caribbean—at the University of California at Berkeley, where he worked as an administrator in the college of chemistry. After age fifty, Dona Irvin developed a career in the teacher education department of University of California, Berkeley, and the personnel office of Oakland Public Schools.

Painter's memory of her junior and senior high school years when she attended Downs Memorial United Methodist Church in Oakland and took part in its youth activities is primarily related to being in the company of some of her peers whose thoughts and ambitions were in tune with her own. Downs gave her the further opportunity to observe the model set by the pastor, Bishop Roy C. Nichols, and other congregants in their highly visible participation in the political and social action of the community. Painter knew that her parents' encouragement for her to associate with a church was intended to aid in the development of a moral philosophy for her adult life.

Growing up as an only child, Painter enjoyed the companionship of friends outside of her home. One of her favorite preschool playmates, Robin Fox, showed the same early evidence of an inquiring mind as Painter did. The two girls engaged in typical child's play, and they shared the accomplishment of having taught themselves to read long before entering kindergarten. Painter built upon this advantage with the added experiences of travel to places near and far away from her home, trips to the ballet, opera, and theater to augment the popular entertainment of the day, and exposure to museums to explore cultures unlike her own, with emphasis upon the African.

From the upper elementary grades through Oakland Technical High School and the first four years at the University of California, Berkeley, Painter questioned the quality of the education she had received. She was a serious student who felt that few of her teachers had demanded that she use her mental abilities to the fullest extent, and she is convinced that the meaningful part of her education did not start until the mid-1960s, when she went to West Africa with her parents.

Painter spent the summer of 1962 in Kano, in northern Nigeria, with Project Crossroads Africa. She was part of a group of American college students who joined their counterparts in selected African countries to undertake projects that would contribute to raising the living conditions of the indigenous people. Near Kano, Nigerian and American students constructed a school building for the children of a middle-sized village. This first visit to Nigeria set the stage for Painter's subsequent return to Africa.

In college well before the invention of African-American studies, Painter chose anthropology as an undergraduate major so that she could pursue her interest in people of African descent in the United States and elsewhere, past as well as present. She avoided classes in American history because of what she saw as their failure to address the actualities of life in the United States as she knew it, notably segregation and racial discrimination. Her interest in history was initially sparked in the University of California's Education Abroad Program in Bordeaux, France, where, as a third-year student she enrolled in courses in French medieval history and visited some of the sites of major historical events. The real commitment to history came later when she discovered the satisfaction of delving into the past of West Africa by studying its history at the University of Ghana's Institute of African Studies.

After graduation from the University of California, in June 1964 with a bachelor of arts degree, Painter returned to West Africa for a second stay, this time in Ghana. As a post-baccalaureate student in the University of Ghana's Institute of African Studies in Accra, she encountered a different approach to history that included knowledge about the Third World, imperialism, the class aspect of human history, and the economic dimension of political issues—aspects of history that she believes are fundamental.

When Painter came back to the United States she earned a master's degree in history from the University of California, Los Angeles, in 1967. Then she realized that she wanted freedom to read extensively for additional knowledge in her chosen field, and that this, and significant career advancement, would depend upon study beyond the master's level. A Ph.D. would enable her to write history as she wanted to, and interpret it according to her own vision. With this motivation she left California, began graduate study at Harvard, and received a doctorate in 1974. Being a black woman in graduate school at the time of the birth of Afro-American Studies programs taught Painter to focus upon "more than one variable at a time—class, race and gender all at once" (Moseley, 12), and thus to consider each one in the interpretation of historical events.

Painter gives credit to two distinguished historians for their influence upon the direction that her career has taken. The guidance of Frank Fridel, her dissertation adviser at Harvard, showed her the workings of the craft of the professional historian, and she has passed this knowledge on to her students. She has often sought and received the advice of John Hope Franklin, a prominent black historian with great intellectual integrity, one who identifies himself very clearly as a black person concerned with black people. Painter has relied upon the examples of the quality of his work and the generosity of his spirit.

Professional Life Addresses Various Aspects of History

Painter's approach to southern history sees all its people as actors, no matter what their race, class, or gender. In her view, the South has long been a region so rent by conflicts that it is difficult to generalize about "the South." Her focus on conflict carried over into her third book, *Standing at Armageddon: The United States, 1877-1919* (Norton, 1987). This book's main thesis holds that Americans differed over the meaning and distribution of the fruits of industrialization. The content of *Standing at Armageddon* is, in Painter's words, "the way I do history. It's political history, but from the bottom up. I take the working class seriously; I'm interested in their religion, their music, their entertainments" (Moseley, 12).

Exodusters, Black Migration to Kansas after Reconstruction (Knopf, 1976), Painter's first book, initially appeared as a dissertation for the doctorate at Harvard. It later became a major publication. *Exodusters* is a study of black southern social history immediately after emancipation and shows that many black people feared they would be reenslaved at the end of Reconstruction. As a result, large numbers were willing to leave the South and settle in other parts of the country.

The Narrative of Hosea Hudson, His Life as a Negro Communist in the South (Harvard University Press, 1979), Painter's second book, recounts the experiences of a black man who was born in the rural South in 1898 and died in 1988. In the preface Painter describes *The Narrative of Hosea Hudson* as "a collaborative oral autobiography, produced by a young historian and an old radical." It tells the story of Hudson's life as a working man and a member of the Alabama Communist party until he moved to New York City in 1954, where he continued to be politically active.

Painter's commitment to women's rights is reflected in her involvement in professional associations and editorial boards of women's groups, and the scope of her published articles and other writing in this area. Of the three major works in progress, one is a study of sexuality in the South in the nineteenth and twentieth centuries, the second is a biography of the abolitionist and woman's suffrage advocate Sojourner Truth, and the third is a history of the South since 1865. Through her written work Painter's aim is to provide a critical, balanced, feminist analysis of southern society.

As a professor of history Painter is taking a great deal of satisfaction from training a new generation of southern and African-American historians. She enjoys lecturing and guiding young people through the kind of preparation they need as historians; but she loves writing even more. Given her choice in the use of time, she would write more prolifically on a broad assortment of subjects. Had she time, she would write two biographies beyond that of Sojourner Truth. One would be of Martin Delany, a free-born black man known as the father of black nationalism for having spoken out in the 1840s and 1850s for black solidarity and for having advocated the immigration of African-Americans to West Africa. The other would be of William Randolph Hearst, the newspaper publisher who wielded widespread influence through the print media in the first half of the twentieth century. Painter also wishes she could document the origin and status of the steel bands of the West Indies as the music of the African diaspora and investigate them as a symbol for a new music for a new people, from the West Indies to New York to London. She would take pleasure in writing about the Irish in Great Britain and in the United States.

Painter's political orientation faces two ways. Her parents

and her early environment turned her toward liberalism and a humanistic approach with a sensitivity to the needs of people whose advantages are less than hers, and an accompanying willingness to support measures that will bring beneficial changes in their lives. This puts her on the left side of the political spectrum, a position reinforced by her awakening to the importance of economics and the class aspect of history that came from her study in West Africa. Her second orientation, somewhat in contradiction to her liberalism, is a deeply-ingrained race feeling, stemming from having grown up in a pan-African household.

Two instances of political action provide an indication of her views. In 1961, as an undergraduate student at Berkeley, she was part of the Monroe Defense Committee for the defense of Robert Williams, president of the NAACP chapter of Monroe, North Carolina, who had been indicted in the aftermath of a Ku Klux Klan assault upon Native Americans and black people in Monroe. At a different time and in different circumstances, in 1987, she was nominated and backed by the Harvard Radcliffe Alumni/Alumnae Association Against Apartheid as a candidate for the Harvard Board of Overseers and has remained a member of the association's executive committee.

Physically, Painter is a strikingly attractive, tall, slender, dark-skinned woman whose face gives a clear indication of intelligence. She wears her hair cut short, in the unprocessed, untinted, natural "Afro" style that emerged with the black awareness period of the 1960s. Painter takes regular morning jogs for fitness, but would welcome more frequent opportunities to indulge in her favorite exercise, swimming laps in the university pool. For relaxation and to pass the hours of travel or airport waits she knits sweaters for herself, family, and friends.

Since 1976 Painter has maintained a steady correspondence with Nellie McKay, professor of Afro-American Studies and English at University of Wisconsin, Madison. McKay and Painter met in 1969, when both were beginning graduate students at Harvard—McKay in English and Painter in history. Their correspondence has continued without interruption.

During the two years that Painter lived in Ghana she met Colin Painter, a teacher in the linguistics department at the University of Ghana; she was married to him from 1965 to 1966. They had no children. In 1989 she married Glenn R. Shafer, a professor in the business school of the University of Kansas. Shafer has two children from a former marriage, Richard and Dennis.

In addition to teaching in the Ghana Institute of Languages, 1964-1965, Painter has taught at Harvard University, the University of Pennsylvania, the University of North Carolina, Hunter College of the City University of New York (where she was Russell Sage Visiting Professor), and Princeton University (where in 1990-91 she headed the Afro-American Studies Department).

Painter is a member of the Mortar Board, and is an American Council of Learned Societies Fellow, Guggenheim Fellow, and Center for Advanced Study in the Behavioral Sciences Fellow. She received the Candace Award, National Coalition of One Hundred Black Women.

Painter's numerous articles, reviews, and review essays on a variety of aspects of black history and current black life include these two recent articles: "The Journal of Ella Gertrude Clanton Thomas: An Educated White Woman in the Eras of Slavery, War, and Reconstruction," introduction to Virginia Burr, ed., *The Secret Eye: The Journal of Ella Gertrude Clanton Thomas, 1848-1889*, Chapel Hill, 1990, and "Sojourner Truth in Life and Memory: Writing the Biography of an American Exotic," *Gender and History* 2 (Spring 1990).

References

Moseley, Caroline. "Painter Presents History of the Souths." *Princeton Today* 4 (Summer 1990): 12. Includes photograph.

Collections

Nell Painter's personal papers have not been collected in an archive. Tapes and documents relating to the publication of *The Narrative of Hosea Hudson* are housed in the Southern Oral History Collection of the Southern Historical Collection at the University of North Carolina at Chapel Hill.

Dona L. Irvin

Rosa Parks

(1913-)

Civil rights activist

Rosa Louise McCauley Parks, a long-time advocate of civil rights, is best known for her December 1, 1955, refusal to surrender her seat to a white passenger in a crowded Montgomery, Alabama, bus. Parks's landmark act is described as having "breathed life" into the civil rights movement (Hymowitz).

Parks was born February 4, 1913, in Tuskegee, Alabama, one of two children of Leona (Edwards) McCauley and James McCauley. Her father was a carpenter and her mother taught in rural schools. Her parents separated in 1915 soon after Parks's brother, Sylvester James, was born. After her father went north to live, she had very little contact with him. Her mother returned with her children to Pine Level, Alabama, to live with her parents, Rosa and Sylvester Edwards. Parks also knew her great grandparents, Mary Jane Nobles,

Rosa Parks

of African descent, and James Percival, of Scotch-Irish descent, who both died when Parks was young.

Parks helped with the household chores, not only because her mother was teaching much of the time, but also because her mother and both grandparents were not in good health. Parks often had to take care of everyone. But she especially liked making quilts and cooking. Her mother taught in rural one-room schools and other buildings where classes could be held, and for about three years was Parks's teacher. When she was eleven years old, Parks was sent to a private school, the Montgomery Industrial School for Girls, living with her mother's sister, Fanny Williamson. In addition to chores in her aunt's home, Parks often went with her aunt to help with her domestic work because Fanny Williamson too was in ill health.

The Montgomery Industrial School for Girls was run by Miss White, and the teachers were liberal women from the North. In exchange for tuition, Parks cleaned two classrooms. With her duties at school and at home, there was little time for Parks to enjoy childhood. At school she had academic studies in addition to domestic arts, and she enjoyed reading. She entered Booker T. Washington High School but dropped out when her mother became seriously ill. Parks learned about the hardships of slavery and about emancipation from stories told by her maternal grandparents. From her family's teaching, from her own observations as a child, and from her experiences at Miss White's school, Parks realized that segregation and discrimination were wrong.

Hoping that her daughter would become a teacher, Leona McCauley helped Parks financially so she could attend Alabama State Teachers College. But perhaps because she had cared for the sick people in her family, Parks thought more about nursing as a possible career. She had learned sewing at home and at Miss White's school but did not consider it a way to make a living. She did, however, sew for family and friends.

The family attended the African Methodist Episcopal Church where Parks enjoyed singing and praying. She has been a member throughout her life. As a young person, she belonged to the Allen Christian Endeavor League.

In December 1932, Rosa McCauley was married in Pine Level, Alabama, to Raymond Parks, who was originally from Randolph County, Alabama. He had very little formal education, as there was no "colored" school near him. Later he attended Tuskegee Institute when he was about twenty-one years old. When the couple met, he was a barber at the Atlas Barber Shop in Montgomery. Raymond Parks often talked to Rosa Parks of the poverty and cruelty of his childhood. He was very interested in the case of the Scottsboro boys, who were charged with raping two white girls, and he often brought food to the young men while they were in jail awaiting trial. Raymond Parks was a member of the National Committee to Save the Scottsboro boys.

Raymond Parks and Rosa Parks shared a common interest in the problems of inequality and segregation in the South. After the marriage, Rosa Parks held a variety of jobs in order to supplement her husband's income from barbering. She sewed at home, worked as a domestic, as an insurance salesperson, and as an office clerk.

In 1943 Parks became a member of the Montgomery Chapter of the NAACP, one of the first women to do so. She served as the organization's secretary from 1943 to 1956, and for several years as youth advisor. She also ran the office for Edgar Daniel Nixon, the state NAACP president and regional officer of the Brotherhood of Sleeping Car Porters. She joined the Montgomery Voters League and encouraged blacks to register to vote. In the summer of 1955 Parks attended workshops at the integrated Highlander Folk School in Monteagle, Tennessee, which had been engaged in the civil rights struggle since the 1930s. Whenever she could, Parks avoided the segregated drinking fountains, the "Colored Only" elevators, and other reminders of the low status imposed on blacks in the South. She often walked home from work.

Parks Sparks the Famous Montgomery Bus Boycott

On Thursday, December 1, 1955, Rosa Parks was riding home on the Cleveland Avenue bus from her job at Montgomery Fair, a downtown Montgomery department store where she worked as an assistant tailor. The first ten seats on the city buses, which were always reserved for whites, soon filled up. She sat down next to a man in the front of the section designated for blacks. A white male got on and looked for a seat. In such situations, the black section was made smaller. The driver, who was white, requested that the four blacks move. The others complied, but Rosa Parks refused to surrender her seat. The driver called the police.

(From his point of view, he was only doing his duty.) Parks had been evicted from a bus twelve years earlier by the same driver, but this time it was different. In an interview she said, "I didn't consider myself breaking any segregation laws . . . because he was extending what we considered our section of the bus" (*Black Women Oral History Project Interview*, 10). At another time she said, "I felt just resigned to give what I could to protest against the way I was being treated" (*Black Women*, 10). Three-quarters of the bus ridership were from the black community. There had already been fruitless meetings with the bus company about the rudeness of the drivers and other issues, including trying to get the bus line extended farther into the black community. In the previous year three black women, two of them teenagers, had been arrested for defying the seating laws on the Montgomery buses. The community had talked many times about a citywide demonstration such as boycotting the bus line, but it never developed. The Women's Political Council already had a network of volunteers in place and had preprinted fliers; they needed only a time and place for a meeting.

About six o'clock in the evening, Parks was arrested and sent to jail. She was released on a one-hundred-dollar bond to Edgar Daniel Nixon, Clifford Durr, a liberal white lawyer, and his wife, Virginia. Trial was scheduled for December 5, 1955. On Friday, December 2, the Women's Political Council distributed more than fifty-two thousand fliers throughout Montgomery calling for a one-day bus boycott on the day of Parks's trial. On December 5, four days after her arrest, there was a mass meeting of more than seven thousand blacks at the Holt Street Baptist Church. The Montgomery Improvement Association was formed by the black community, and Martin Luther King, Jr., was elected president. At Nixon's urging, Parks had agreed to allow her case to become the focus for a struggle against the system of segregation. The success of the bus boycott on December 5 led to its continuation. In the second month it was almost one hundred percent effective, involving thirty thousand black riders. When Parks was tried, she was found guilty and fined ten dollars and court costs of four dollars. She refused to pay and appealed the case to the Montgomery Circuit Court. Following her release from jail, Parks went back to work but later lost her job, as did her husband. At home, the couple had to deal with threatening telephone calls. Rosa Parks devoted her time to arranging rides in support of the boycott. Blacks were harassed and intimidated by the authorities in Montgomery, and there was an attempt to break up the carpools. Parks served for a time on the board of directors of the Montgomery Improvement Association, and often was invited elsewhere to speak about the boycott.

On February 1, 1956, in a case designed to have the Alabama segregation laws declared unconstitutional, the Montgomery Improvement Association filed a suit in the United States District Court in the names of four women and on behalf of all who had suffered indignities on the buses. On June 2 the lower court declared segregated seating on the buses unconstitutional. The Supreme Court upheld the lower court order that Montgomery buses must be integrated, and on December 20, 1956, the order was served on Montgomery officials. After 381 days of boycotting, resulting in extreme financial loss to the bus company, segregation and other discriminatory practices were outlawed on the city buses. Parks's refusal to give up her seat on a bus was the beginning of the civil rights movement of the 1950s and 1960s. Parks's action marked the beginning of a time of struggle by black Americans, supported by their sympathizers both northerners and southerners, as they sought to become an integral part of America.

With the notoriety surrounding her name, Parks was unable to find employment in Montgomery. Her husband became ill and could not work. So Parks, her husband, and mother moved to Detroit in 1957 to join Parks's brother, Sylvester McCauley. Since Raymond Park did not have a Michigan barber's license, he worked in a training school for barbers. In 1958 Rosa Parks accepted a position at Hampton Institute in Virginia for one year, after which she returned to Detroit and worked as a seamstress. She continued her efforts to improve life for the black community, working with the Southern Christian Leadership Conference in Detroit.

In 1965 Parks became a staff assistant in the Detroit office of United States Representative John Conyers; she retired in 1988. Raymond Parks died in 1977 and Parks's mother died in 1980. Parks has been a member of the AME church throughout her life, and served as a deaconess in St. Matthew AME Church in Detroit.

Rosa Parks has been called "the first lady of civil rights" (*Sunday News Magazine*, New York, 24 May 1961) and "the mother of the freedom movement" (Flier from the National Committee for the Rosa L. Parks Shrine). The *New York Times* (15 January 1980) reported that Coretta Scott King and former diplomat Andrew Young assured Parks that "as the 'mother of the civil rights movement,' she had a permanent place in history." She is the recipient of many awards, including the NAACP's Spingarn Medal (1979). In 1980 Parks was the ninth person, and the first woman, to receive the Martin Luther King, Jr., Nonviolent Peace Prize, accepting it from Coretta Scott King, Martin Luther King's widow. She holds ten honorary degrees, including one from Shaw College in Detroit. The citation for an honorary degree from Mount Holyoke College in 1981 read in part, "When you led, you had no way of knowing if anyone would follow" (*Boston Globe*, 25 May 1981). In 1984 Parks was the recipient of a special award, the Eleanor Roosevelt Women of Courage Award, from the Wonder Woman Foundation. In 1986 as part of the celebration for the Statue of Liberty's one-hundredth birthday, Parks was one of eighty people to receive a medal of honor for their contributions to American ethnic diversity.

Parks continues to make speeches across the country to raise money for the NAACP, and speaks to young people about the civil rights movement. She is still active in the Southern Christian Leadership Conference, which since 1963 has sponsored the annual Rosa Parks Freedom Award. Her many honors in Detroit have included the naming of Rosa

Parks Boulevard, which runs through the black community, and the Rosa Parks Art Center. In 1987 she established the Rosa and Raymond Parks Institute for Self-Development, incorporated as a nonprofit organization in Detroit, to work with young people between the ages of eleven and fifteen. In January 1988 the Museum of African-American History in Detroit unveiled a portrait of Parks on her seventy-fifth birthday. On June 30, 1989, the twenty-fifth anniversary of the Civil Rights Act, she attended ceremonies at the White House. The National Committee for the Rosa Parks Shrine is soliciting money for a home on Rosa Parks Boulevard for Parks after her retirement. It will also serve as a library for her personal papers. In 1990, her seventy-seventh birthday was celebrated at the Kennedy Center in Washington, D.C., with three thousand black leaders, government dignitaries, entertainers, and social leaders on stage and in attendance. In her own remarks, Rosa Parks took the occasion to speak again on behalf of freedom and equality. She said, "Pray and work for the freedom of Nelson Mandela and all of our sisters and brothers in South Africa" (*Washington Post*, 6 February 1990).

References

Bennett, Lerone, Jr. *Wade in the Water*. Chicago: Johnson Publishing Co., 1979.

Black Women Oral History Project Interview with Rosa Parks. Cambridge: Schlesinger Library, Radcliffe College, 1984.

Boston Globe, 25 May 1981.

Current Biography Yearbook. New York: H. W. Wilson, 1989.

Giddings, Paula. *When and Where I Enter*. New York: Morrow, 1984.

Hymowitz, Carol and Michaele Weissman. *A History of Women in America*. New York: Bantam Books, 1978.

Metcalf, George R. *Black Profiles*. New York: McGraw-Hill, 1988.

Miller, Judi. *Women Who Changed America*. New York: Manor Books, 1976.

National Committee for the Rosa L. Parks Shrine. Flier.

New York Times, 15 January 1980.

People's Almanac 2. New York: Morrow, 1978.

Raines, Howell. *My Soul Is Rested*. New York: Penguin Books, 1983.

Robinson, Jo Ann. *The Montgomery Bus Boycott and the Women Who Started It*. Knoxville: University of Tennessee Press, 1987.

Sunday News Magazine, New York, 24 May 1981.

USA Today, 1 February 1988.

Washington Post, 6 February 1990.

Collections

The tapes and transcript of the Black Women Oral History Project interview, as well as photographs and clippings, are available at the Schlesinger Library, Radcliffe College, Cambridge.

Ruth Edmonds Hill

Mary Parrish (Grace Ermine)

(c. 1863-?)

Journalist, educator, church worker

The life of Mary Virginia Cook Parrish risks being overlooked in the shadows cast by her mentor, William J. Simmons, and her husband, Charles Henry Parrish, both very important Baptist leaders. Fortunately, enough remains in the account of her early life to draw the portrait of an intelligent and dedicated woman who accomplished much in her own right. After her marriage to the eminent minister, her activities were subordinated to his, as they had been in a long relationships as minister and laywoman and employer and employee. With her commitment to religion and her intense involvement in a socially conservative denomination, she may have had no prolonged doubt about the choices she made in her life. Unlike many women in her situation and of her era, Parrish left enough of a record that we can judge her on specific accomplishments rather than the vague generalities that are often used to describe the wives of distinguished men.

Parrish was the daughter of Ellen Buckner; nothing is known of her father. A "gentle and mild" woman (Penn, 368), Buckner gave birth to Mary Virginia Cook in Bowling Green, Kentucky, during the Civil War, at a time when the daughter's status as "slave" or "free" hung in the balance. Parrish's mother was well-positioned to hear the news and rumors of war, since Bowling Green is on the Louisville and Nashville Railroad, a vital link for the Union armies. When Parrish was old enough to seek schooling, she made do with the scanty resources available. She won a reputation as the best student in town. and she won a silver cup for spelling in a competition between three schools. She won another prize for oral reading at a teacher's institute on September 30, 1881, after she had turned to teaching herself at the invitation of her pastor, C. C. Stumm, who had started an academy. For Parrish, the most important event during this period was almost certainly her conversion in 1876: For the rest of her life she associated with people who shared her beliefs and her commitment to Christianity.

The word "exploited" with all its modern connotations would not have been part of Parrish's vocabulary, but even though she was as "gentle and mild" as her mother, Parrish was near tears after a dispute with Stumm about her share of the monthly earnings of the school (she taught the largest number of students). On October 15, 1881, she received a scholarship to State University (later Simmons University) in Louisville, Kentucky. State University had recently been founded by the Baptists, and it was entirely black-controlled, with black teachers and board of trustees. The president of the university, William J. Simmons, had identified Parrish as a potential student the preceding year when he had visited Bowling Green in search of students. Simmons, one of the most outstanding Baptist leaders of the nineteenth century, was a mentor of both Parrish and her future husband, Charles Henry Parrish. The sketch of Simmons's extraordinary life by Henry M. Turner is the prefix to Simmons's book *Men of Mark* and deserves to be read. That book also includes a biography of Parrish who was then twenty-eight years old.

Parrish entered State University as a member of the third normal class on November 28, 1881. She became dining-room matron and was a student teacher. During the year she finished the normal course, she taught five hours a day, maintained a ninety-five percent mark, was valedictorian of her class, and served as president of the Athenaeum and the Young Men and Women's Christian Association. Simmons wrote of her:

> As a student, she was prompt to obey and always ready to recite. She has a good intellect and well developed moral faculties, and is very refined, sensitive, benevolent and sympathetic in her nature, and well adapted to the work of a Christian missionary (Penn, 370).

Parrish graduated from the normal course on May 17, 1883, and was immediately made principal of the normal department and professor of Latin and mathematics. In addition to her teaching duties, the board of trustees allowed her to continue in the college department, and she received her B.A. four years later in May 1887. This "bright-faced, intelligent little woman" who had just recently come to weigh one hundred pounds for the first time, was "deep in many subjects," "especially fond of Latin, biography, and mental and moral philosophy," much respected, and very charitable (Penn, 37). She continued to teach at State University until May 1890.

Work as Journalist Begins

In 1886 Parrish began writing for the *American Baptist*. This denominational newspaper advertised in 1888 that it was the "Oldest Religious and Family Journal in the South among colored people. It is bright, newsy, and ably edited" (*Diamond Jubilee*, 66). The fact that early black women journalists such as Lucy Wilmot Smith, Lucretia Newman Coleman, and Mrs. C. C. Stumm are among the contributors to this newspaper suggests its importance in studying the history of black American women. In publishing, Parrish disguised her name but not her sex under the pseudonym Grace Ermine. Penn states that "in 1887 [Parrish] edited a column of *The South Carolina Tribune*. At the same time she controlled a column in *The American Baptist*" (373). About 1889 Parrish is credited with editing the educational department of *Our Women and Children*, another Louisville publication frequently associated with women writers. While Parrish's exact writing and editing activities remain somewhat indefinite, the samples provided by I. Garland Penn show Parrish was a very competent writer not afraid of expressing her opinion. Commenting on the current state of relations between blacks and whites, Parrish wrote:

> White faces seem to think it their heaven-born right to practice civil war on negroes, to the extent of blood-shed and death. They look upon the life of their brother in black as a bubble to be blown away at their pleasure. The same spirit that existed in the South twenty-four years ago is still recognized in its posterity. The negro is still clothed in swarthy skin, and he is still robbed of his rights as a citizen, made dear and fairly won to him by the death of those who fell in the late Rebellion. This outrage cannot endure. God still lives, and that which has been sown shall be reaped (Penn, 373-74).

Parrish's strictures were addressed to whites as well as blacks, and she expressed freely her opinion on the difficulties within the black community:

> As a people we are not easily led, and we often slaughter the one who attempts it. There is always fault to be found, which thing should be left to our enemies, while we, like faithful Aarons, should uphold the arms of those who have dared to strike for us. There is a natural antipathy against our leaders. If they act as gentlemen, dress decently, and have ability, we call them stuck-up and big-headed; and often a majority will join hands with the Irish, or some other nationality, to get them defeated (Penn, 374).

Parrish also traveled and spoke extensively. In 1887 she attended the National Convention of Baptists in Mobile, where she spoke on "Woman's Work in the Denomination." She addressed the Kentucky State Teacher's Association with a paper on "Women, a Potent Factor in Public Reform," and spoke to the National Press convention on the subject "Is Juvenile Literature Demanded on the Part of Colored Children?" As a corresponding secretary of the Baptist Women's Educational Convention, an organization in which she held various offices from 1884 to 1887, she delivered in 1889 the convention history in a manner that drew high praise from the *American Baptist*, which commented, "Miss Cook is never more in earnest than when saying a word for the women's work'' (Penn, 372). In the same year she talked on ''Female Education'' before the Nashville meeting of the Baptist Home Mission Society. It was also in 1889 that State University awarded her and Charles H. Parrish honorary M.A.s. She did not share the honors in 1896 when Parrish received an honorary D.D. from State University. An indication of the social milieu in which she lived can be seen in the honorary degrees awarded by the university in its first ten years: Of the forty-seven honorary degrees only four went to women, all M.A.s . While one man did have to be satisfied with a B.S., the thirty-three doctorates all went to men.

After this promising beginning in Parrish's life story, current sources reduce her to the status of an appendage of her husband's eminent career. Charles Henry Parrish was born near Lexington, Kentucky, on April 18, 1859. His early struggles to support himself and his family and to gain an education have an epic quality well-depicted in William J. Simmons's *Men of Mark*. When Simmons, Charles Parrish's pastor in Lexington, was named president of the year-old State University, Simmons took the young Parrish with him. By extraordinary exertion, Parrish managed to graduate as valedictorian of the first class to complete the academic course in 1886, earning a B.A. He was immediately named professor of Greek and secretary-treasurer of the university. Parrish was ordained on January 2, 1886, and on September 27 became the pastor of Calvary Baptist Church in Louisville. He began his very successful career as a minister by more than doubling the church's membership in eighteen months. Parrish remained at Calvary until his death. But he also filled such eminent positions as moderator of the General Association of Colored Baptists in Kentucky from 1915 to 1917 and president of Simmons University (formerly State University) from 1918 to 1931. Since he was a member of the class just before Mary Parrish's at a small school, he knew her for some time before she became his teaching colleague.

In the spring of 1890 William J. Simmons left State to found Eckstein-Norton Institute in Cane Spring, Kentucky, a small town about thirty miles from Louisville, halfway between Shepherdsville and Bardstown on a branch of the Louisville and Nashville railroad. This move is characteristic of Simmons's career, during which he periodically sought to refresh himself and find new fields for his endeavors. Charles Parrish and Mary Parrish (then Cook) followed Simmons to Eckstein-Norton. Simmons died in August, leaving Charles Parrish to assume the presidency of the institute, a position he held until 1912 when it merged with Lincoln Institute in Jefferson City, Missouri (now Lincoln University). While not certain, it is probable that Mary Cook remained there until her marriage to Parrish.

In the two-page summary of the highlights of Charles Henry Parrish's life in the *Diamond Jubilee of the General Association of Colored Baptists in Kentucky* (40-41), the marriage rates only two lines: ''January 26, 1898, married to Miss Mary V. Cook, of Bowling Green, Kentucky, to which happy union one child, Charles H. Parrish was born.'' Mary V. Cook was eclipsed by Mrs. Charles H. Parrish. Still her work continued and the *Golden Jubilee* lists some of her activities, most of which involve, as is natural, church activities, such as missionary secretary, Calvary Baptist Church; state vice-president for the Women's Auxiliary to the National Baptist Convention; and member of the board of managers of the Baptist Women's Educational Convention. She also filled the posts of chairperson of the board of trustees of the National Training School for Women and Girls in Washington, D.C., statistician of the National Association of Colored Women, and president of the Parent-Teacher Association of Central High School in Louisville. The American Baptist Press published, in pamphlet form, one of her statistical reports for NACW in 1914.

The post Mary Parrish held longest was that of corresponding secretary of the State Baptist Women's Missionary Convention, one that she held continuously from its founding in 1903 until at least 1943 at the time of the diamond jubilee celebration, some years after her husband's death on April 7, 1931. The women of the missionary convention were not idle. Paraphrasing Mary Parrish's report of 1915 (*Golden Jubilee*, 157), the women attended prayer meetings, distributed Bibles and tracts, made religious visits, induced children and non-church goers to attend church, gave religious talks, visited the sick, aided the poor and suffering, distributed clothing, read Bible chapters, and raised money. And finally, although women were barred from the pulpit and lacked the authority to baptize, in an actively proselytizing denomination, Parrish would have taken great satisfaction in the 4,431 ''sinners brought to Christ'' by the association between 1903 and 1915. Some of these were surely among the fifteen hundred persons her husband baptized between 1886 and 1915.

References

Diamond Jubilee of the General Association of Colored Baptists in Kentucky. Louisville: American Baptist, 1943. Photograph, p. 78.

Dunnigan, Alice E. ''Early History of Negro Women in Journalism.'' *Negro History Bulletin* 28 (May 1965): 178-79, 193.

Parrish, C. H., ed. *Golden Jubilee of the General Association of Colored Baptists in Kentucky*. Louisville: Mays Printing Co., 1915. Photograph, p. 23.

Penn, I. Garland. *The Afro-American Press and Its Editors*. Springfield, Mass.: Willey and Co., 1891. Portrait p. 369.

Simmons, William J. *Men of Mark: Eminent, Progressive and Rising*. Cleveland: George M. Rewell and Co., 1887.

Robert L. Johns

Mary Jane Patterson
(1840-1894)
Educator, educational administrator

Mary Jane Patterson, a woman who took great strides in the advancement of black education in the nineteenth century, was born in 1840 to Henry Irving Patterson (b. 1805) and Emmeline Eliza (Taylor) Patterson, in Raleigh, North Carolina. There, Henry Patterson's mother, Chancy, and her family lived for some time near the home of the family of Andrew Johnson. Johnson, Henry's brother John, and Henry were boyhood friends. Henry Patterson was a bricklayer and a plasterer who, after obtaining his freedom, moved his family to Ohio, probably leaving North Carolina in 1852 and arriving in Oberlin, Ohio, around March of 1856. In Oberlin, he worked as a skilled mason.

On the second of March, 1856, Mary Jane and John E. Patterson (probably Mary Patterson's brother, who was born August 13, 1848) were entered into the records of the First Congregational Church in Oberlin. Besides John, Mary Patterson had at least eight brothers and sisters, of whom it is thought she was the oldest. Brother Henry (b. 1844) enlisted in 1863 and fought in the Fifty-fourth Massachusetts Volunteer Infantry in the Civil War until 1865.

Mary Jane Patterson

In 1857, Mary Patterson entered the preparatory course at Oberlin College. She studied in that program for one year, and then entered the "gentleman's" or classical course, at a time when most women studied in the "ladies'" or literary course. Emma Brown and Fanny Jackson (Coppin), who were educators, and Edmonia Lewis, a sculptor, were among the other black students at Oberlin College at that time. Although Oberlin was progressive in the education it offered to black students, Emma Brown wrote of Oberlin on May 22, 1860, "There is considerable prejudice here which I did not at first perceive" (Sterling, 199). She also wrote on May 27, 1860:

> There are 200 lady students. Quite a number. . . . There are very few colored students—that is comparatively speaking. . . . There is one colored girl [presumably Mary Jane Patterson] taking a Classical Course. I have been told that she is a pretty good scholar (Sterling, 200).

Patterson graduated with a B.A. with highest honors from Oberlin College in 1862. At her graduation she read her own address, which was entitled "The Hero of Italy" (referring to Garibaldi). The *Oberlin Evangelist* reported that "in the College Graduating Class of 28 [students], including six young ladies, the colored race has had one representative of each sex. Both appeared well on the stage, their pieces not below the average of the class." While Patterson is thought by many to have been the first black woman to receive a B.A., another black woman, Grace A. Mapps, reportedly graduated from New York Central College at McGrawville in the 1850s. Patterson's brother John graduated from Oberlin in 1867, and two sisters—Emma (b. 1853) and Chanie Ann (b. 1848)—graduated from Oberlin's "ladies' course" and became teachers.

In 1863, Mary Patterson was listed in the *Triennial Catalogue of Oberlin College*, as teaching in Chillocothe, Ohio. However, she apparently did not stay there long, and on September 21, 1864, she wrote a letter addressed from Oberlin to W. H. Woodbury in Norfolk, Virginia, to apply for a teaching position in the school for black children there. On October 7 of that year, E. H. Fairchild, principal of Oberlin College's preparatory department from 1853 to 1869, wrote to recommend Patterson for an "appointment from the American Missionary Association as a . . . teacher among freedmen" (AMA Manuscripts).

In this letter, Fairchild described Patterson as "a light quadroon, a graduate of this college [Oberlin], a superior scholar, a good singer, a faithful Christian, and a genteel lady." He "asked her if she had a heart for . . . sinners. She replied that this was what interested her most. She had experience and success in teaching [presumably in Chillicothe] and is worthy of the highest . . . you pay to ladies" (AMA Manuscripts).

Patterson moved to Philadelphia in the 1860s. There she began teaching (probably in 1865) as an assistant to Fanny

Jackson (Coppin) at the Institute for Colored Youth. The members of the administration at the institute:

> were impressed by the ability of Miss Jackson and her assistant, Mary Jane Patterson . . . to give "thoroughness and perfect understanding" to every portion of the student recitations. The ladies' experience in public speaking and elocution at Oberlin were reflected in their teaching (Perkins, 25).

Patterson moved to Washington, D.C., in 1869, where she lived at 1532 Fifteenth Street Northwest, with her two sisters, Emma and Chanie, and her brother John. In the 1880s the children also took in their parents who they were having financial difficulties.

First Black High School Principal in the Nation's Capital Appointed

From 1869 to 1871, Patterson taught school in Washington; then she was appointed as principal of the one-year Preparatory High School for Colored Youth (later Dunbar High School). She was the Preparatory High School's first black principal, and is recorded as the first black principal of a high school in Washington, D.C. After filling this position for one year, Patterson was replaced by Richard T. Green, the first black graduate of Harvard University. Patterson served under Green as assistant principal. When he left the school after only one year, Patterson was reappointed as principal.

Patterson continued in that position until 1884, when the school had grown from fewer than fifty to 172 pupils. Her reasons for stepping down are unclear—whether due to failing health or because it was decided that the growth of the student body made it "advisable to place a male in charge" (*Evening Star*). The latter explanation is perhaps more likely, since after Patterson was replaced by F. L. Cardozo, Sr., she reportedly continued to teach at the Preparatory High School until her death in 1894. However, according to a letter she wrote in January 1885, Patterson was unemployed and experienced financial difficulties for some time after she lost her job to Cardozo.

Patterson was an effective teacher and administrator. When writing of Patterson during her time as principal of the Preparatory High School, Mary Church Terrell, another Oberlin graduate, described Patterson and her accomplishments in the following manner:

> She was a woman with a strong, forceful personality, and showed tremendous power for good in establishing high intellectual standards in the public schools. Thoroughness was one of Miss Patterson's most striking characteristics as a teacher. She was a quick, alert, vivacious and indefatigable worker. During Miss Patterson's administration, which lasted altogether twelve years, three important events occurred: the name "Preparatory High School" was dropped; in 1877, the first high school commencement was held; and the normal department was added with the principal of the high school as its head (Terrell, 256).

Hallie Q. Brown described Patterson similarly, writing:

> Miss Patterson had in the school-room a vivacity of manner and a sympathetic interest that gave her a strong influence over the youth with whom she came in contact and many successful men and women of to-day remember with gratitude her influence on their lives (Brown, 145).

While living in Washington, D.C., Patterson was very active outside her work at the high school. She is reported by the *Evening Star* in her obituary as having "co-operated heartily in sustaining the Home for the Aged and Inform Colored People in this city, and other Kindred organizations," and having "devoted much of her means and time to forming and sustaining an [unknown] industrial school for girls of her race."

Patterson died on September 24, 1894, at her home in Washington, D.C.

References

American Missionary Association. Manuscripts. LS [Microfilm]. Ohio Roll No. 13.

Amsterdam News, June 19, 1954.

Bigglestone, William E. *They Stopped in Oberlin: Black Residents and Visitors of the Nineteenth Century*. Scottsdale, Ariz.: Innovation Group, 1981.

Brown, Hallie Quinn. *Homespun Heroines and Other Women of Distinction*. Xenia, Ohio: Aldine Pub. Co., 1926.

Evening Star, 25 September 1894.

First Congregational Church Records, 1839-1856. D. Archives, Oberlin College Library, Oberlin, Ohio.

Fletcher, Robert S. *History of Oberlin College, From Its Foundation Through the Civil War*. 2 vols. Chicago: R. R. Donnelley, 1943.

Lawson, Ellen N. and Marlene D. Merrill. *The Three Sarahs: Documents of Antebellum Black College Women*. Studies in Women and Religion 13. New York: Edwin Mellen Press, 1984.

———. "The Antebellum 'Talented Thousandth': Black College Students at Oberlin Before the Civil War." *Journal of Negro Education* 52 (Spring 1983): 142-55.

Noble, Jeanne L. *The Negro Woman's College Education*. New York: American Book, Stradford Press, 1956.

Patterson, Allan, ed. *Oberlin Community History*. Oberlin School District, Board of Education: 1981.

Oberlin Evangelist. Archives. Oberlin College Library, Oberlin, Ohio.

Oberlin College Necrology for the Year 1894-95. Oberlin, [1895].

Perkins, Linda M. "Quaker Beneficence and Black Control: The Institute for Colored Youth, 1852-1903." In *New Perspectives on Black Educational History*. Edited by V. P. Franklin and J. D. Anderson. Boston: G. K. Hall, 1978.

Sterling, Dorothy, ed. *We Are Your Sisters: Black Women in the Nineteenth Century*. New York: Norton, 1984.

Tapley, Melvin. "Our People: Pages from History." New York *Amsterdam News,* 19 June 1954.

Terrell, Mary Church. "History of the High School for Negroes in Washington." *Journal of Negro History* 2 (July 1917): 252-66.

Triennial Catalogue of Oberlin College. Oberlin, [1863].

Wormley, G. Smith. "Educators of the First Half Century of Public Schools of the District of Columbia." *Journal of Negro History* 17 (July 1932): 124-40.

Collections

Information on Mary Jane Patterson, a negative of a photograph of her, as well as newspaper photographs are in the Oberlin College Archives, Oberlin, Ohio.

Maureen A. McCarthy with Adrienne Lash Jones

Georgia E. L. Patton

(1864-1900)

Physician, religious worker

Georgia Esther Lee Patton Washington was the first black woman to graduate from Meharry Medical College and the first Meharry graduate to serve as a missionary to Africa. She was also the first black woman to be licensed as a physician and surgeon in Tennessee, and was the first to practice medicine in Memphis. Patton was born a slave on April 16, 1864, in Grundy County, an area of small farms and mountain ranges in southeast Tennessee. In 1886, at the age of twenty-two, she went to Nashville where she entered Central Tennessee College and after completing the senior normal course in 1890 she enrolled in the Meharry Medical Department of Central Tennessee College, which was later renamed Meharry Medical College.

The dean of Meharry, George W. Hubbard, wrote in the

Georgia E. L. Patton

January 1901 issue of *The Christian Education* that Patton was a gifted student whose "percentage marks of class-standing were above the average." She completed her medical studies in only two-and-one-half years, graduating in February 1893. Her name and photograph appear on two documents housed in the Meharry Medical College Archives: a list of the thirty-six graduates of 1893 and a composite photograph of the Meharry Medical Department faculty and graduates.

Two months after graduation from medical school, Patton left the United States to become a medical missionary in Africa. When she set sail on April 5, 1893, her cabinmate was a young journalist and antilynching lecturer, Ida B. Wells, who wrote in her travel diary, excerpted in *Crusader for Justice*:

> *Third Day* [April 7, 1893] Seasick. So is Dr. Georgia E. L. Patton. We have a stateroom to ourselves and lie in two berths looking at each other. Ugh.

According to Wells, they landed in Liverpool, England, on April 13 and shared a room at the Shaftsbury Hotel until the following Saturday, when Patton sailed for Africa. Wells wrote the following short biographical sketch of Patton:

> Miss Patton was a graduate of Meharry Medical College, one of its first woman graduates, if not the first. She was early imbued with the desire to go to Africa as a medical missionary. . . .
>
> Georgia Patton stayed in Liberia a number of years practicing medicine, until her health broke down and she returned to the United States. She

settled in Memphis, my old home, and built up a practice there. She afterward married David Washington, one of the most highly respected letter carriers there and one of the few substantial citizens who did not leave Memphis when the rest of us did. Georgia Patton Washington had one child, which died, and later she herself passed away before she had reached the noonday of life (Wells, 88-89).

Physician Visits Africa as Self-Supporting Missionary

Unable to get the financial backing of her church's missionary society, Patton went to Monrovia, Liberia, as a self-supporting missionary who labored to gain the confidence of her patients, as she explained to Meharry's dean, George Hubbard:

> For the first few days after my arrival the surroundings looked very discouraging for my professional work. On examining my first case, remarks made by the natives were: "Patients in his conditions never get well; we always expect them to die." After careful treatment and watching for two months he was able to leave his bed, and finally went to his work. The next two cases were also considered to be hopeless, yet both recovered (Hubbard, 5).

Later she reported to the dean, "I have treated over one hundred cases, and have lost four" (Hubbard, 5). Hubbard printed a photograph of Patton at work in Africa, and the inscription reads: "Mrs. Washington [though Patton was single at the time] in Africa Removing Ulcers From the Leg of a Native Boy; The Other Lady Physician is Bishop Taylor's Niece" (Hubbard, 6). The thirty-year-old doctor, neatly attired in a cotton dress and long white apron, is working in a frame shelter. The photograph reveals the crude conditions under which Patton worked with inadequate equipment, medical supplies, and operating facilities. Eventually, her health began to fail, and after two years in Liberia, Patton had to return to the United States.

In 1895 Patton opened a medical practice in downtown Memphis, where, according to Hubbard, she "soon secured a large and lucrative practice" but also "found many difficulties to contend with" (Hubbard, 5). Her name first appears in the *City Directory of 1897*: "Patton Georgia E.L. c[olored], physician 282 2nd, res[idence] 250 Washington." That same year her photograph was printed in James T. Haley's *Sparkling Gems of Race Pride*, where she is depicted as a lovely young woman, small and fair-skinned, with dark hair pulled back from an oval face. Her looks and intelligence must have appealed to David W. Washington because on December 29, 1897, he and Georgia E. L. Patton were married. Twelve years older than his wife, David Washington was a distinguished looking gentleman with piercing black eyes, chiseled features, a thick mustache, and close-cropped hair. Born a slave in 1852 at La Grange, Tennessee, he was the first black hired as a letter carrier in Memphis, and he became one of the city's most successful businessmen and property owners.

The Washingtons were active church members; he belonged to Avery Chapel AME Church, while she attended Centenary Methodist Episcopal Church. Patton shared her husband's interest in philanthropy; "constantly ministering to others," according to George Hubbard, "she literally forgot herself . . . " (Hubbard, 5). Officials of the Freedmen's Aid Society called her the "Gold Lady" because she donated ten dollars a month to the society. She was also a feminist who chastised a society clerk in a letter dated May 24, 1900, for failing to address her properly:

> Dear Brother Mason:
>
> Some weeks ago I sent you a letter with a little money inclosed. In reply you said, "Dear Brother." I am not a brother. Do you not remember Georgia Patton? Well, it is she, with a little more attached. I send ten dollars more, and hope to be able to keep sending until I have given $100, asked by you of the alumni of the schools; and even more if possible.
>
> Yours, with best wishes for the Society.
>
> G. E. L. Patton Washington
>
> P.S. Say "Sister" next time (Hubbard, 6).

Patton sent money to the Freedmen's Aid Society at a time when she was not working because of a serious illness—tuberculosis—which became manifest in Africa. A year before, on February 14, 1899, she had given birth to her first child, Willie Patton Washington, who died the same day. When she wrote to Brother Mason, she was pregnant with her second child, David W. Washington, who was born on July 11, 1900. But she had been in poor health for several years and apparently had to give up the practice of medicine, for her name does not appear in the *City Directory* of 1899. On Thursday, November 8, 1900, Patton died in her Washington home. Her funeral was held at Centenary Methodist Episcopal Church on South Street at two in the afternoon on Saturday, November 10. Thirteen days later, her baby died. The thirty-six-year-old doctor and her two sons are buried under a magnolia tree in Zion Cemetery, Memphis's oldest black cemetery.

References

City Directory of Memphis, Tennessee, 1897.

The Commercial Appeal, 9 November 1900; 10 November 1900.

Haley, James T. *Sparkling Gems of Race Pride Worth Reading*. Nashville: J. T. Haley, 1897.

Hubbard, G. W. "Dr. Georgia E. L. Patton Washington." *The Christian Education*, January 1901.

Summerville, James. *Educating Black Doctors, A History of Meharry Medical College*. Alabama: University of Alabama Press, 1983.

Wells, Ida B. *Crusader for Justice*. Edited by Alfreda M. Duster. Chicago: University of Chicago Press, 1970.

Collections

Records of Georgia Patton, a list of the 1893 graduates, and photograph of the faculty and graduates of Meharry Medical College are in the Meharry archives.

Miriam DeCosta-Willis

Ethel Payne
(1911-1991)
Journalist

As a journalist Ethel Lois Payne crusaded against injustice, exposed problems in the black community, and offered possible solutions to problems of education, health, and welfare. Of her journalistic battle, Payne said: "There is a zest for waging battles within me that lends exuberance to the struggle" (Afro-American).

Ethel Payne

Payne was born on August 14, 1911, in Chicago, Illinois. She was the daughter of William Payne, who was a Pullman porter, and Bessie (Austin) Payne, who was a high school Latin teacher. Ethel Payne attended school at Crane Junior College, the Garrett Institute, and the Medill School of Journalism at Northwestern University in Evanston, Illinois.

Payne grew up in a poor but stable and supportive household. She came from a family of six children—three older sisters, an older brother, and a younger sister. Early in life Payne learned a sense of responsibility to others and felt that the strong had an obligation to protect the weak. She had many nieces and nephews, all of whom have excelled in their studies. Her oldest two nephews are doctors in San Diego, California, and a younger nephew has completed his senior year in the School of Engineering at Northwestern University, on a full scholarship. In an interview on April 6, 1990, Payne was also proud to mention a young niece who attends Sidwell Friends School, Washington, D.C., and who has won a merit scholarship.

The walls of Payne's apartment were covered from one end to the other by awards, honors, and accolades that she received for her writing talent. Interspersed with these plaques were memorabilia, pictures, paintings, and souvenirs from her travels around the world.

Meeting Payne was like greeting and conversing with an old friend. Her voice was soft and her speech well-articulated, commanding undivided attention. Approaching her eightieth birthday at the time of the interview, she was a handsome woman. Payne said that she had recently completed an eight-hour oral history for the Washington Press Club and Women's Organization, which has been transcribed and edited and will be housed at Columbia University in the Women's Archives. Hers was the first such oral history to be recorded. As Payne wrote her memoirs, this oral history, which took two years to complete, served as her guide.

During the interview Payne expressed concern about the current plight of black journalists. She had recently attended a dinner recognizing black journalists for outstanding contributions to the field of journalism and she observed that, of those honored, a total of fifteen had received the Pulitzer Prize for outstanding journalism. She was a staunch believer and advocate of the power and impact of the black press. She said it is a *voice* that must continue to speak out and be heard, opposing the injustices and indignaties so blatantly created and perpetuated by racism.

Payne Launches Career in Journalism

In 1949 Payne held a position as director of an army club in Tokyo, Japan. Two black correspondents from the Chicago *Daily Defender* visited her in Tokyo and asked her to send her observations on discrimination to the *Defender*. She did so and also kept a diary of her impressions of Asia: specifically, the combat and social atrocities of the Korean War. Payne recorded her admiration for the Japanese male-female social contact. These articles caused quite a national furor and Payne was ordered to Allied Headquarters and called down by General Douglas McArthur's aide for allegedly disrupting the morale of the troops.

Shortly after returning to Chicago and graduating from the Medill School of Journalism Payne began as a staff member for the *Chicago Defender*. Within the year she was transferred to the Washington bureau, where she replaced Venice Tipton Spraggs. Spraggs had run the office since 1943 and Payne found her "a formidable person to follow" (*Contributions of Black Women to America,* 278). The duties of Payne's position were demanding and required a thorough indoctrination in the ways of Washington. But she persevered, establishing "one of the most exciting and demanding reportorial roles of all, where the endless round of press conferences and cocktail parties leading to establishment of news and background sources for stories, were all essential to the job" (*Contributions,* 278).

Payne's concern for the future of mankind prevented her from slowing her journalistic activities. From her self-described "box seat on history, she . . . chronicled and monitored the social and political policies of seven presidents. Her unique grasp of complex social and political issues [was] a result of her extensive travel and broad journalistic experience"(*Distinguished Black Women, 1981-1986,* 41).

While the majority of the American press ignored or avoided race issues, Payne sought to raise the public's awareness. Her first major attempt to publicize southern racial problems was a series of articles, "The South at the Crossroads," published in 1953. She quickly established herself as a tough and talented journalist.

Payne noted:

> I applied for White House credentials and was welcomed to the corps by Jim Hagerty, press secretary to President Eisenhower. He was famed for his Irish temper and a pet ulcer. I later activated both of them ("Loneliness in the Capital," 155).

President Eisenhower held regularly scheduled formal press conferences and, according to Payne, was known to give a "fairly equitable spread" among media giants, the wire services, television and radio networks, and the "little fellas" with small circulations. Shortly after she was accredited as a correspondent, Payne attended a press conference and asked a question that brought her regular recognition at the press conferences. She asked why the Howard University choir had been turned away from a Republican Lincoln Day celebration, when it was to have performed alongside choirs from Emory and Duke universities. Payne said that President Eisenhower "expressed surprise at the news and said that if, as I implied, there was any racial snub involved he would be the first to apologize."

This was a major story covered by all the media. While this matter brought her much attention, it also caused problems between Payne and the black press:

> It was painfully upsetting for me when I was attacked by some of my fellow black journalists who accused me of showboating to get my name in the *New York Times* transcripts. I felt that it was unfair since those blacks who were accredited along with me had the same right to try and ask questions as I. The fact that they kept silent was self-exclusion to me.
>
> Secondly, every question that I put to the President was carefully thought out in advance and it dealt with an issue of vital concern to minorities. I thought that I was acting as a conduit through which presidential thinking would flow to a segment of people whose interests were not normally recognized. Clarence Mitchell, the forthright director of the Washington Bureau of the NAACP, often called to express his appreciation for the questions I asked. In turn, I sought his advice on occasions when I needed background expertise ("Loneliness," 156).

In the press as well as in press conferences, Payne was relentless in her attack on segregation and the treatment of minorities. After the Interstate Commerce Commission handed down an opinion calling for an end to segregated practices in interstate travel, she asked Eisenhower his intentions concerning such travel and caused a furor that had far-reaching effects.

> Ike took this as a personal affront. Drawing upon his five-star general authority, he proceeded to chew me out as he would one of his top sergeants, "What makes you think," he demanded icily, "that I should do any special favors for any special interest group? I will do what I believe is in the best interest of the country" ("Loneliness," 156).

In addition to reports of the incident in the Washington *Evening Star* and other newspapers, the White House put Payne into "deep freeze" and banned her from the White House press conferences.

While Payne recognized the shortcomings of the black media at that time, she resented the second-class status that they received. Thus, she continued to fight for equality and to work as a supporter of the historically adversarial role upon which the black press was founded.

In addition to her White House assignments, Payne covered "Capitol Hill, the Labor Department, Housing and Urban Development Department, the State Department, and such independent agencies as the Equal Employment Opportunity Commission and the United States Information Agency. All create or enforce policies that directly bear on black people. She also kept in close contact with the African embassies, whose news was of increasing interest to observers of the struggle to end white domination here and in the black ancestral homeland" (*Contributions,* 160).

During her career Payne served as staff writer of the AFL-CIO Committee on Political Education; writer-in-residence, George Washington University, Washington, D.C.; Ford Foundation fellow in educational journalism; regular columnist for the *Afro-American, Miami Times,* San Francisco *Sun-Reporter, Miami Herald, St. Louis Sentinel,* Sengstack Newspaper Chain, Chicago *Defender, Michigan Chronicle,* and Pittsburgh *Courier.* From 1953 to 1973 she was White House correspondent. In 1967 Payne was the first black female war correspondent in the Vietnam War. She went to the front and became "one of the most seasoned of national or foreign correspondents Black or white, male or female" (*Contributions,* 278). Payne was commentator for "Matters of Opinion," WBBM, CBS, Chicago, 1978-82, and she was one of six commentators for "Spectrum," the CBS opinion program, 1981. She was writer-in-residence, Jackson State College, Jackson, Mississippi, in 1983. From 1982 to the time of her death, she was a free-lance writer. In 1982-83 she was given a distinguished honor: The *Washington Afro-American* reported that Fisk University had named Payne the "first recipient of the Ida B. Wells Distinguished Journalism Chair." Named for a courageous black newspaper editor who wrote about lynching in the South and discrimination in the North and who helped found the NAACP, the Ida B. Wells chair became black America's "first fully funded chair organized by black journalists." The establishment of the chair aimed to build a repository for works by and about America's black journalists. It would "provide an outlet for research, writing and publishing." In support of this effort, a Fisk-Payne Fund was established (May 13, 1982).

In November 1989 Payne and an entourage from the press visited Namibia to cover the Independence Celebration and Inaugural.

Payne Expresses Views

Payne believed that black newspapers lack vision and that they need high-quality writers and articles that attract advertisements in order to support the paper. Payne also believed there must also be a willingness to pay the best workers top dollar for their work. An article entitled "Ethel Payne," written by Grayson Mitchell in the March 1974 issue of *Essence,* states that "the world, as seen through [Ethel Payne's] eyes, is a battleground where the powerless are unmercifully pitted against the powerful and it is her self-appointed mission to even the odds."

Payne's views on the role of black women in the military were included in the *Delta Journal.* She cited the work of Harriet Tubman, whom she called a "general" and a "first":

> The legendary Harriet Tubman not only led more than 300 slaves to freedom, but she served in the Union Army as nurse, cook, scout and spy. At the outbreak of the Civil War, she presented herself to Gen. David Hunter at Hilton Head, South Carolina, handing him a letter from Gov. John Andrew of Massachusetts recommending her for service to the unit. In the spring and summer of 1865, she worked at Freedmens Hospital in Monroe, Virginia.
>
> Yet it took 30 years for the federal government to finally recognize her services. She was rewarded with a pension of $20 a month. Hers is the first recorded history of Black women in the military. It was not until 1942 and the advent of the United States entry into World War II that women were officially admitted into the services. There was an immediate necessity for backup support to the war effort. On May 15, 1942, President Franklin Delano Roosevelt signed the bill establishing the Women's Auxiliary Army Corps (WAAC). Scores of women volunteered for the national defense. ("Black Women in the Military," 15).

After the Civil War into the twentieth century, Payne found that blacks were still adjusting to two societies—one black and one white, and this was demonstrated nowhere more clearly than in the armed services. Separatism had become a fact of life and, with few exceptions, blacks learned to live with the dual system.

> Women entering the service faced the reality of segregation and discrimination. They were buffeted between racism and sexism. Still, the challenge for a different kind of career drew them to enter the military. Like their male counterparts, it offered job security at a time when other channels of employment were slim for Blacks. In many ways, pride and patriotism superseded the harshness of racism (*Delta Journal*).

Payne received numerous awards and achievements. Among these were the first prize from the Illinois Press Association for "Issues on Adoption," 1952; third annual World Understanding Award, Chicago Council on Foreign Relations, 1956; and Outstanding Reporting Award, Windy City Press Club, 1957. She was twice the recipient of the Newsman's Award, Capital Press Club Award for Vietnam Report, Washington, D.C., 1967; president, Capital Press Club, 1970-1973; honorary member of the Delta Sigma Theta Sorority, 1973; and first recipient of Fisk University's Ida B. Wells Distinguished Journalism Chair, 1973. Payne was named "Woman of Action" for outstanding achievements in journalism, given by the National Association of Negro Business and Professional Women's Club, 1980; recipient of the Gertrude Johnson-Williams Award, given in memory of the mother of John H. Johnson of Johnson Publishing Company. A tribute dinner was given in Payne's honor on June 12, 1982, and a thirty-minute documentary film entitled *Portrait of A Queen: Legacy of Ethel Lois Payne* was prepared for showing at the dinner. She was named board member of Africare, Washington, D.C., 1983; received the Candace Award of the Coalition of 100 Women, 1988; and elected to the Washington, D.C., Women's Hall of Fame, 1988. She is included in the Gallery of Greats: "Black Journalists—Then and Now," a collection of oil portraits commissioned by the Miller Brewing Co., 1988; and on March 27, 1990, she was the recipient of an award from Kappa Tau Alpha at Hampton University in Hampton, Virginia. The organization is a member of the National Journalism Scholarship Society.

A few of Payne's colleagues and associates were former Congresswoman Shirley Chisholm, former *Michigan Chronicle* editor and publisher Louis Martin, Washington, D.C., bureau chief for Johnson Publications Simeon Booker, and Alice Dunnigan, the first black woman accredited as a member of the White House press corps (*Washington Afro-American*).

Before she was found dead on May 28, 1991, of an apparent heart attack, Payne was a free-lance writer, and made personal television appearances and conducted radio interviews. She was once the owner of a very expensive and unique doll collection from around the world. Payne donated this collection to the Washington, D.C., public school system for exhibition to the children of the District of Columbia who may share and delight in the dolls' beauty.

Payne authored *A Profile on Black Colleges; Roots, Rewards, Renewal* (Chicago, published under the auspices of Delta Sigma Theta Sorority and George Johnson, 1980). She also published a report on women refugees in Somalia, Sudan, Zambia, and Zimbawe sponsored by Africare and the Board of Global Ministries, United Methodist Church, 1982.

Two video productions on Payne's life are *Portrait of a Queen: Legacy of Ethel Lois Payne*, a thirty-minute documentary that chronicles her more than thirty years as a distinguished journalist (WHMM-TV, Channel 32, Howard University, Washington, D.C., 1982), and *Personal Diary* (PD No. 10, Black Entertainment Television, December 1989).

References

Contributions of Black Women to America. Vol. 1. Ed. Marianna W. Davis. Columbia, S.C.: Kenday Press, 1982.

Distinguished Black Women, 1981-1986. Washington, D.C.: Black Women and Sisterhood for Action, 1986.

Mitchell, Grayson. "Ethel Payne." *Essence* 4 (March 1974): 66, 96.

Payne, Ethel L. "Behind the Scenes." *Washington Afro-American,* 3 November 1985; 12 November 1985; 23 November 1985; 14 December 1985; 14 January 1986; 8 February 1986; 8 March 1986; 18 March 1986.

——. "Black Women in the Military." *Delta Journal* (Winter 1986/87): 8-10, 15-16.

——. "Black Youth and the Ballot: An Alternate to Frustration." *Negro History Bulletin* 35 (May 1972): 115-17.

——. "Loneliness in the Capital: The Black National Correspondent." Chapter 13 of *Perspectives in the Black Press.* Kennebunkport, Me.: Mercer House Press, 1974.

Payne, Ethel Lois. Interview with author, April 6, 1990.

Washington Afro-American, 13 March 1982; 3 October 1985.

Washington *Star,* 20 October 1970; 12 May 1972.

Who's Who Among Black Americans, 1990-1991. Detroit: Gale Research, 1990.

Collections

Ethel Payne's personal papers are in the Moorland-Spingarn Research Center at Howard University in Washington, D.C., and the Schomburg Center for Research in Black Culture in New York City.

Dorothea W. Slocum

Carolyn Robertson Payton

(1925-)

Psychologist, educator, government official

Carolyn Robertson Payton, the first black female director of the Peace Corp, was born in Norfolk, Virginia, on May 13, 1925, to LeRoy and Bertha Robertson. After receiving her early education in Norfolk, she went on to receive a bachelor of science degree in home economics at Bennett College (1945) in Greensboro, North Carolina, a master of science in psychology (1948) from the University of Wisconsin at Madison, and a doctorate in counseling (1962) from the Columbia University Teachers College in New York.

Her first position after graduating with her master's was with Livingston College in Livingston, Alabama, as instructor in psychology education. While there she also created a freshman orientation program. In 1953 she moved on to Elizabeth City State Teachers College in North Carolina to become dean of women. Leaving North Carolina in 1956, she accepted a position as associate professor of psychology at Virginia State College. In 1959 she moved still farther north to accept an assistant professorship in psychology at Howard University in Washington, D.C. In 1964 Payton resigned her position at Howard to serve as chief field selection officer for the Peace Corps.

Peace Corps Names First Female Director

The Peace Corps was formed in 1961 under mandate of President John F. Kennedy. Charged with the sharing of technical skills with requesting countries, trained volunteers spent two years in host countries working primarily in the areas of agriculture, rural development, health, and education. At its inception the Peace Corps sent volunteers to Latin America, Africa, and the Middle East. By 1990, with the Cold War ending, Eastern Bloc countries were also requesting volunteers.

By 1966 Payton had been promoted to the position of deputy director of the Peace Corps's Eastern Caribbean section, where she served until 1971. She then returned to Howard University to become the dean of counseling and career services. In 1977 the Peace Corps again called her into service, when President Jimmy Carter named Payton director of the organization. When she took the oath of office in 1978, she became the first woman and the first black to head the Peace Corps.

The Peace Corps had undergone some changes since her earlier stint with the organization. First, under the Nixon administration, "the focus of recruitment shifted away from new [college] graduates with liberal arts backgrounds to experienced, highly skilled persons who could fill the specialized needs of developing countries in Africa, Asia, and Latin America" (Coughlin, 8). Payton recognized that the use of highly specialized volunteers had its own problems, such as "teaching down to the people they are sent to help" rather than developing respectful teacher-student relationships (Coughlin, 8). To remedy this, she planned a paraprofessional training program to train volunteers to be better teachers. The change to specialists had also caused the volunteer populace to be mainly white and male. Payton hoped to recruit substantially more blacks and women for the program.

The second change was that the Peace Corps was no longer an autonomous organization. Instead, it was now administered by ACTION, an umbrella organization for the United States domestic and foreign volunteer programs. ACTION agency head Samuel Brown did not see the Peace Corps in the same light as did Carolyn Payton. His plan to have a small but better-trained field force was in direct opposition to her plan to have a larger corps of better teachers rather than a minimal number of specialists. The battle grew to a war, forcing Payton to resign after only one year in office. "Mrs. Payton's departure concluded several weeks of wrangling with Brown over the direction of her agency" ("First Black Peace Corps Head," 6). Payton would later reflect that her 1978 resignation had the positive effect of forcing the president to realize that the Peace Corps operated better as an autonomous organization and to separate it from ACTION in 1979. In 1981 the agency was given its formal independence by the International Security and Development Act.

After her tenure with the Peace Corps, Carolyn Payton returned to Howard University as director of counseling services. Her other involvements include fellowship in the American Psychological Association, membership on the editorial board of the *Journal of College Student Personnel* (1979-1982), and a seat on the District of Columbia Board of Psychologists Examiners (1980-1983), and she is a member of the Delta Sigma Theta Sorority. In 1978 the Capitol Press Club honored Payton for her humanitarian efforts by naming her "Woman of the Year."

Her only marriage was to Raymond Rudolph Payton. The couple divorced in 1951.

References

Academic American Encyclopedia. Vol. 1. Danbury, Conn.: Grolier, 1982.

Coughlin, E. K. "Changing the Peace Corps." *Chronicle of Higher Education* 15 (11 October 1977): 8.

"First Black Peace Corps Head Forced to Resign Her Post." *Jet* 55 (14 December 1978): 6.

Redmond, Coates. *Come As You Are—The Peace Corps Story.* San Diego: Harcourt Brace Jovanovich, 1986.

Soviet Union and East European Political Dictionary. Oxford: ABC Clio Information Services, 1984.

"Sweat in Payton, Lewis. . . ." *Jet* 53 (3 November 1977): 7.

United States Government Manual 1990/1991. Washington, D.C.: U.S. Government Printing Office, 1990.

Who's Who Among Black Americans, 1990/1991. 6th ed. Detroit: Gale Research, 1990.

Who's Who in America. 45th ed. Vol. 2. Wilmette, Ill: Macmillan Directory Division, 1988.

Sarah Elizabeth Crest

Mary S. Peake

(1823-1862)

Educator

Mary Smith Kelsey Peake, a teacher during slavery and the Civil War, "was not satisfied with the ordinary routine of the weekday schoolroom, but felt that the teacher of a mission school should aim to educate the children for eternity as well as for time" (Lockwood, 31-32).

Peake was born in Norfolk, Virginia, in 1823. She was the daughter of a free mulatto woman and a prominent Englishman. When Peake was six years old, her mother sent her to Alexandria, Virginia, to attend a private school for free blacks. Peake lived with her aunt and uncle, Mary and John Paine, while learning mathematics and English. She also learned the trades of needlework and dressmaking.

Several years later, Peake's education was terminated after a law was passed closing all "colored" schools in Virginia. Peake moved back to Norfolk, where she established herself as a seamstress. Influenced by her mother and aunt, Peake became a devoted Christian. She was an active member of the First Baptist Church in Norfolk.

In 1847 Peake's mother married Thompson Walker and the family moved to Hampton, Virginia. It was Peake's deep concern for the plight of her people that led her to begin teaching children and adults, slave and free, in her home in Hampton. In addition, she founded the Daughters of Zion to assist the poor and the sick. In 1851 Mary married Thomas D. Peake, who was a free man. Five years later her daughter, Hattie, nicknamed Daisy, was born.

Shortly after the Civil War began, Confederate forces under the command of General John Magruder were ordered to burn Hampton because of the overwhelming support of black villagers for the Union cause and to discourage this black alliance with the Union army. Many of the beautiful and stately homes of black families who resided in Hampton were destroyed, including the home of Mary Peake.

The Peake family, along with other black families from Hampton, sought refuge at Fortress Monroe. Reverend Lewis C. Lockwood, who was commissioned at Fortress Monroe by the American Missionary Association, enlisted Mary Peake to teach the children at the fortress. In September 1861 Peake started a school teaching approximately six students, but this number grew to more than fifty in just a few days. It was one of the first schools of its kind, and Peake was the first teacher in the American Missionary Association schools. An old house known as Brown Cottage near the Hampton River, was the site of school. The Peakes lived on the second floor and the schoolroom was on the first. In addition to teaching her students how to read and write, she taught them to pray and sing hymns. Peake also began an evening school for adults.

Peake was a truly dedicated teacher. Her health began to fail shortly after she was married and it steadily declined during the years that followed. She continued to teach her students—even when she was too sick and weak to leave her bed. Peake died of tuberculosis on February 22, 1862.

References

Dannett, Sylvia G. L. *Profiles of Negro Womanhood*. Vol. 1, *1619-1900*. Yonkers, New York: Educational Heritage, 1964.

Lockwood, Lewis C. *Mary S. Peake, The Colored Teacher at Fortress Monroe*. Boston: American Tract Society, 1863.

Logan, Rayford W. "Mary S. Peake." *Dictionary of American Negro Biography*. Edited by Rayford W. Logan and Michael R. Winston. New York: Norton, 1982.

Sandra M. Lawson and Ibrahim Kargbo

Anna Belle Rhodes Penn

(1865-?)

Writer, poet, educator

In *Noted Negro Women: Their Triumphs and Activities*, M.A. Majors praises Anna Belle Rhodes Penn—essayist, poet, and educator—for being a member of "[t]hat younger class of women in our national life who are slowly, but surely, making themselves an enviable place in the literary future" (75). During the early years of her life she developed a reputation in her Lynchburg, Virginia, community for being an excellent elocutionist, though she apparently did not accept invitations to travel to other places for speaking engagements.

This talented woman about whom we have very little information was born in Paris, Kentucky, on June 18, 1865, to William and Sophia Rhodes. The family moved to Lynchburg, Virginia, when Penn was still very young. Clearly intellectually gifted, Penn first attended a private school in Lynchburg taught by Mrs. C. C. Ellis. In the year she turned thirteen, 1878, Penn began her studies at Shaw University. According to Majors, her parents asked the president of Shaw University, the Reverend H. M. Tupper, and his wife to take care of their precocious young daughter, who more than lived up to the potential her parents saw in her. Majors says that "[a]s a student she enjoys the record of having been a brilliant one, of having always pursued her studies with diligence and profit" (76).

As a result of her intelligence and her diligence, Penn received a bachelor's degree in 1880 from Shaw's Classical Department. The May 1880 issue of the Shaw University Bulletin also lists her as a student in the AM course (master's degree). Penn began her teaching career at Shaw, where she taught for two years in the normal department before returning to Virginia to teach first in Chatham and then in the primary department of a school in Lynchburg. In 1886, she attended at least one summer institute held at the Virginia Normal and Collegiate Institute in Petersburg, Virginia, now known as Virginia State University. Lucius Edwards, librarian at Virginia State University, says that at this point in Virginia's history the state required that its teachers attend anywhere from one to three of these summer institutes depending on their previous training. Virginia Normal and Collegiate held its first summer institute in 1884, so Penn was among the first black women to participate in this program.

On December 26, 1889 or 1890 (Majors says 1890 but *The National Cyclopedia of the Colored Race* lists 1889), Anna Belle Rhodes married Irvine Garland Penn, also an educator. At the time of their marriage, both were working in the Lynchburg, Virginia, public schools, she as a teacher and he as a principal. Majors states that "she ranks among the first-class primary teachers in Virginia and is one of the three best-salaried lady teachers in a group of eighteen or twenty belonging to the corps" (77). The most recent source of information about the Penns, *The National Cyclopedia of the Colored Race*, published in 1919, says the couple had seven children: Mrs. Wilhemina Franklin, of Cincinatti; Reverend I. Garland Penn, Jr., Maysville, Kentucky; Mrs. Georgia S. Williams, Little Rock; and Elizabeth, Louise, Marie, and Anna B. Penn; and three grandchildren. I. Garland Penn is best known for having written *The Afro-American Press and Its Editors*. Anna Belle Rhodes Penn "was of very much service to her husband in the preparation of his great work," Majors observes. He also notes that "the reading Afro-American must not be surprised if the Madame gives a book to the world of letters in the near future" (82). Curiously, Penn does not include his wife in the book's acknowledgments.

Majors reprints two of Anna Belle Rhodes Penn's poems, "A Grief Unknown" and ten of the fifteen stanzas of "Light Out of Darkness." At the present these are the only available examples of Penn's literary contributions. She read "Light Out of Darkness" at the December 1, 1890, Quarto Centennial Celebration of Shaw University. Among those present at this event were Shaw's president, H. M. Tupper, The Honorable Elijah J. Shaw, and the Reverend Dr. McVicar. The poem celebrates Shaw's role in alleviating the illiteracy slavery inflicted on black Americans and consists of eight-line stanzas that roughly follow an *ababcdcd* rhyme scheme. The dominant images in this work are light and dark, thus giving the poem a Biblical as well as a political tone. The poet describes Shaw as one of God's "restitutions" to the wronged black Americans held in slavery and praises God and New England benefactors for making Shaw and other institutions of its kind possible. Penn expresses her own gratitude as well as that of her race for her alma mater when she writes:

> Year after year she [Shaw] has labor'd
> To rescue the youth of this age,
> From Ignorance's thralling savor,
> Which has darken'd History's page.
> Some are in the rural districts,
> Where the light has recently gone,
> Where the neat and comely rustics
> Are eager, anxious for the morn (Majors, 79).

Shaw, Penn says, faced much opposition when she "[t]hrew her college doors open wide / To Africa's sons and daughters" (79).

Though Penn clearly wrote effectively about large issues affecting the entire black race—and indeed the whole of the American public—namely, slavery and education, she also used her poetic skills to explore feelings of a more personal nature. "The Grief Unknown" explores an age-old poetic theme, a young girl's lost love, once again using the same eight-stanza form she employs in "Light Out of Darkness." The poem opens with the following stanza:

> Who can tell the bitter anguish
> Of a true and noble heart?
> Who can quote in simple language
> Words which bid its grief depart?
> When its dearest earthly treasure,
> When its life, its love, its all,
> He who ever sought its pleasure
> From earth to heaven is called (Majors, 80).

"The Grief Unknown" gives voice to the feelings that those who find themselves "confined / Within sorrow's dungeon cell" cannot express. The sensitivity with which she approaches this subject conveys deep empathy for others and also suggests that she may have written other poems of this nature for the benefit of people whom she knew to be suffering.

Majors mentions another of Penn's poems, "No Footsteps Backwards," which she read at her graduation from Shaw. According to him, many people regard this first poem as her best effort, but unfortunately he does not include it in his article. He also refers to an essay titled "All That Glitters Is Not Gold." She read this essay at the closing exercises of the Virginia Normal and Collegiate Institute's summer normal school program. According to Edwards, each teacher who completed the summer program read an essay at the closing exercises. Unfortunately, the text of this essay is not available. But Majors does describe the praise Penn's efforts received from John Mercer Langston, the university's president—and the uncle for whom the famous poet of the Harlem Renaissance, Langston Hughes, was named. Paraphrasing Langston, Majors writes that this famous nineteenth-century black American "commenting on the essay, its delivery, etc., said that for chasteness of language, beauty of diction and composition it was one of the best he had ever heard. He was very elaborate in his complimentary comment, showing that under its mellifluous flow he had grown rapturously dizzy" (77). Although Majors mentions this essay as one of the many Anna Belle Rhodes Penn read in public, he does not offer any other examples.

Anna Belle Rhodes Penn is but one of the many long-overlooked black American women whose lives are a rich source of information about the experiences of black women born in the period immediately following the Emancipation. The information available about Penn gives us insight into the educational and vocational opportunities available to nineteenth-century black women living in the southern

United States. Though one reason for her obscurity may be that she chose to devote herself to her husband and her children, the possibility still exists that someone will stumble upon the book M. A. Majors predicted she would write. This gifted woman may have left poems and essays that at this moment lie waiting to be rediscovered, for she started down a literary path at a very young age.

References

Edwards, Lucius. Telephone interview with author, 18 December 1990.

Elliot, Patrick. Telephone interview with author, 21 June 1990.

Majors, M. A. "Anna Belle Rhodes Penn." *Noted Negro Women: Their Triumphs and Acivities*. Chicago: Donohue and Henneberry, Printers, 1983.

The National Cyclopedia of The Colored Race. Vol. 1. Ed. Clement Richardson. Montgomery, Ala.: National Pub. Co., 1919.

Candis LaPrade

Carrie Saxon Perry

Carrie Saxon Perry

(1931-)

Politician, community activist, social worker

Women in general and in Hartford, Connecticut, in particular, congratulated a black history-maker when Carrie Saxon Perry became the first black woman mayor of the city. This extraordinary woman's name is now added to the list of those great black Americans to whom we pay tribute.

On August 10, 1931, in Hartford, Connecticut, Carrie Saxon Perry, an only child, was born to Mabel Lee Saxon. The mother and daughter found themselves in a circle of poverty, as did many black families during the depression of the thirties. Perry considers her mother her greatest asset throughout her life. In order to provide comfort, warmth, and protection for her, her mother used ingenuity and hard work. In spite of the poverty around them, they found beauty in their family relationships. Perry says that her grandmother and aunt served as role models and gave her continuous encouragement in her life's goals. Reared in Hartford, she graduated from the Hartford public schools. Upon completion of high school, she attended Howard University in Washington, D.C., as an undergraduate political science major in the liberal arts college in 1949. She studied two years at Howard's School of Law. She returned to Hartford, married James Perry, Sr., and they had one son—James Perry, Jr. They later divorced.

After her return to Hartford, Perry became a social worker for the state of Connecticut, an administrator for the Community Renewal Team of Greater Hartford, and executive director of Amistad House.

As a social worker in a northeastern urban center, she became more conscious of the conditions that have an impact on lower economic families and their rearing of children. Poverty affects the attitudes, self-esteem, values, code of conduct, job training opportunities, and family activities of poor people. In an interview she stated:

> Years ago I lived in a housing project in Hartford. Now I am mayor of the city of Hartford, Connecticut. We've made real progress. You and I have opportunities that our parents and grandparents did not have. To be sure, morally intolerable disparities exist between white and black Americans. And, many live in neighborhoods with high crime, drug abuse, few jobs and little hope. Since I have benefitted from the gains that blacks have made, I owe an obligation to those left behind (Richardson).

From her experiences as a social worker Perry feels that the black family must develop a sense of pride, competence, and confidence, perpetuate memories of black leaders and heroes, and disseminate information on black history to the child. If blacks are to overcome the negative effects of teenage pregnancy, they must instruct the child in sex education and advise against early sexual activity. Moreover, parents should emphasize to their children their role in the lives of their children as nurturer, caretaker, protector, and provider, says the mayor.

"As a novice in politics, I had a problem insofar as support and networking were concerned because of the gender bias and color prejudice imposed on us by society," she said. "That's all breaking down today, but there's still some residue."

In 1976 Perry decided to run for the General Assembly of the Connecticut State Legislature. She, with the help of her son, jumped in the race and almost won over the machine, although she was not endorsed by anyone. She said:

> I was not endorsed by a single soul. I won on the machine. We were partying, just dancing and everything, and then they came in with the absentee ballots and said, "You lost." It was kind of crushing (Lanker, 61).

During the campaign Perry's opponent talked about his experience versus her inexperience. Perry said:

> I have a right to go up there and make a fool of myself. I'll never know until I get up there. If you're going to always judge people—women, blacks, Indians, whatever—against a white person who has had more advantages, more opportunities, and a quicker starting time, then we should never participate in anything (Lanker, 61).

When Perry ran successfully in 1980, no one endorsed her again. She was reelected state representative to the Connecticut State Legislature three additional times.

Ernest N. Abate, speaker of the House, appointed Perry assistant majority leader of the House in her freshman year. A member of the Education Committee and the Finance, Revenue, and Bonding Committee throughout her tenure at the capitol, Perry chaired the House Subcommittee on Bonding. As chair, she used her persuasive powers to obtain funds for the Riverfront Recapture, the Artists' Collective, and the Old State House Restoration. Furthermore, she was able to assist in the allocation of funds for minority contractors in the state. Concerned with human rights in the United States as well as abroad, she convinced the state legislature to divest state funds linked to the apartheid-supporting government of South Africa. Continuing her sensitivity for the disadvantaged in the community, Perry supported programs and legislation for quality education for Hartford's schools, job training programs to reduce high school dropout rates, and programs to prevent teenage pregnancies and the high rate of infant mortality. She also fought for the right of the homeless to have the right to vote.

A member of the Democratic party, Perry served as alternate delegate from Connecticut to the Democratic National Convention in San Francisco in 1984, while in 1988 she served as state vice-chair for the Connecticut delegation at the Democratic National Convention in Atlanta, Georgia. In Atlanta she spoke in the nationally-televised platform debate on funding for social programs and limited funding for the military.

Carrie Saxon Perry, the sixtieth mayor of Hartford, was elected on November 3, 1987, and inaugurated on December 1 of that year. Her election followed that of Mayor Thurman Milner, who was New England's first black mayor. Becoming the first black female mayor of a northeastern city, she won the election by defeating her white male Republican opponent by a vote of 10,304 to 7,613.

While Perry sees racist attitudes continuing in Hartford, she finds that as more and more people judge individuals less by color, gender and class, there is a greater chance for all the people to participate in the political process:

> The idea of community embraces a diversity of individuals, groups, experiences, interests and viewpoints. Believing that diversity strengthens the community I strongly support efforts to make the political process more representative and responsive to all constituencies of the community (Marshall, 60).

Mayor Attacks City's Problems

Perry's constituents see her as an answer to their problems. Her weekly telephone logs reveal complaints about homelessness, mental health problems, abandoned cars, discrimination, landlord and tenant problems, crime, police behavior, housing, and parking tickets. She said, "It also shows that people look at the mayor's office as the hub of the city" (Richardson).

A description of Hartford in 1990 gives a picture of the problems that Perry faced. Hartford, the capitol city of Connecticut and the insurance capitol of the world, housed a population of 136,000. More than a third of the citizens were black, while twenty-two percent were Hispanic. She and both groups have worked diligently to achieve political power. In 1990 the city council had three blacks and two Hispanic members out of nine. In 1989 the public schools of Hartford were approximately ninety percent black and Puerto Rican, while outside the city limits the schools were decidedly white.

Although the state of Connecticut had the highest per capita income in the United States, twenty-two percent of the residents of Hartford existed below the poverty line in 1989. On the one hand, the corporate world with its insurance companies and banks boomed with growth and prosperity. On the other hand, the inner-city neighborhoods were in decline. Perry is extremely sensitive to this issue. Hartford had the fourth-highest crime rate in the United States. Crime, a major problem, was sustained by drug trafficking and gang growth. Teenage crime has overwhelmed the authorities since cocaine took root.

Urban poverty is contrasted with New England affluence,

the world of the rich with the poor. According to the 1980 census, Perry is mayor of the nation's fourth-poorest city among those with populations of more than one hundred thousand. In the poorest sections of the city, unemployment is at least thirty percent, while in neighboring towns the rate is under four percent and in several, under two percent.

Conscious of poverty, racism, and sexism, Perry knows that changes must take place in society in order for a birth of new ideas and directions to take place. She stated:

> I believe that you have to force change. It doesn't always have to be by violence. You rebel, you organize, you force issues, you threaten the status quo, you show numbers, you promise upheaval: there are numbers of things you have to do. You have to be committed to long distance and accept the fact that it doesn't happen overnight, and that you're doing it probably for another generation (Lanker, 61).

Perry is as interested in the cultural and business life of the city as she is in its social problems. At a conference on American Cities in Crisis held at Bryn Mawr College in Pennsylvania in 1989, Perry said that "the state of our cities is more of a threat to our national security than the Warsaw Pact." Because of her concern, she has allocated funds for after-school and weekend recreation programs to provide wholesome outlets for underprivileged youth. Disturbed by the value system that is developing among some inner-city school children, she felt the need to form Operation Bridge, which targets potential dropouts and those with negative behavior patterns. (There has been a rash of murders by young people over gold chains, tennis shoes, and Gucci and Louis Vitton apparel). In this program, young middle-class Hartford residents work with the dropouts by encouraging them to stay in school. Although the program is expensive, evaluators claim it to be highly successful.

Perry initiated another program about which she stated:

> Operation Break trains people living in housing projects for good jobs that will give them a livable wage. The program offers support services such as drug rehabilitation, remedial education, instruction in English as a second language and day care (Fahy, M-3).

Sensitive to the plight of the deprived, Perry constantly uses innovative programs to uplift these persons to a level where they can compete with the middle class in Hartford. Since her election as mayor, she walks in unannounced at community meetings and listens to her constituents. She attended a community meeting in Clay Hall, a North End neighborhood known for drug dealers and drug addicts. She was there to let the people know that she cares and is on their side. She made no speeches nor promises.

Her caring attitude extends to the men behind bars. On February 14, 1990, she traveled to the state's maximum security prison to deliver a message during the prison's observation of Black History Month. She said that Hispanics and blacks make up eleven percent of the country's population, but sixty-seven percent of the prison residents. Appalled by these statistics, she exhorted the inmates to return to family values. In addition, she made the point that black women need black men at home. Too much waste and potential go down the drain every time another black person fills up another bed in the penitentiary.

> Everyone is breaking walls down all over the world—people crying, fighting, dying for freedom, and we're wasting it. This is unacceptable (Moser, "Inmates Cheer Hartford Mayor").

Women as Political Leaders Advocated

According to Perry, women have established themselves in greater numbers in the American political scene, but a very few have made it to the upper levels. Female politicians encounter what has been called the "glass ceiling" syndrome. They were free to lick stamps and stuff envelopes but were seldom elected to the senior positions in the political arena. Historically, women have been undervalued as serious political contenders. She urged women to become aware of the change for women in politics. At a conference on "Gender, Authority and Leadership: Perspectives from the Political World," held at Smith College, she stated:

> It is very lonely being a woman in politics. We have to become much more comfortable with these positions. Women, African-American women in particular, have to consider public office as a position that is most honorable (Speech at Smith College, 20 February 1990, 4).

Many problems facing the 1990s could use the woman's perspective. She continued:

> The 1960s, plagued by racial inequality, had such leaders as Martin Luther King and Malcolm X. The leaders of the 90s, faced with the tyranny of infant mortality, drugs, AIDS and homelessness, will be women. There will be opportunities for women as the heads of colleges and universities, not to be clones of men, but rather to bring special perspectives to leadership (Speech at Smith College, 20 February 1990, 8).

To succeed as political leaders, women have to change their attitudes toward men, power, and politics. Perry feels that women in too many cases still acquiesce to men when they sit in the same room. For fear of appearing aggressive, traditionally a masculine characteristic, women frequently fail to assert themselves in politics. When men and women are together in decision-making attitudes, the women become automatically reticent.

Although she is proud of her visibility around Hartford, Perry could do more if the office of the mayor had more power. Perry feels that the Hartford city charter should be revised. Since the city charter provides most of the power to the city council and the city manager, the mayor's office represents influence rather than power. If reelected, she said, she would push to have a vote on the council, add another member to maintain an uneven number of council votes, lengthen the mayor's term to four years, and stagger four-year terms for council members.

Responding to the question of why she ran for mayor, she said:

> I thought about it. And the fact that Mount Everest is there, why not climb it? It was a challenge, an opportunity.
>
> I feel strongly that government should be representative of the community. I'm the 60th mayor, and 57 of them have been white men. One has been a white woman and one a black man (Keveney and Pazniokas).

Perry is moving cautiously with the city council as she develops her position in the political system of the city. She attends most committee meetings of the council since these committees settle most issues that come before the city. In addition, she participates in the Democratic caucuses. Mary Phil Guinan, the Democratic town chairwoman, said:

> I think Carrie has really done an impressive job so far. She has developed a leadership role within the Democratic caucus and at city hall (Keveney and Pazniokas, ''Mellow Style'').

The mayor presides over council meetings, reviews the municipal budget, and is designated in the charter as the city's policy leader.

Perry's colleagues and constituents find her friendly and congenial. They exhort her to be outspoken and forceful since the city is in decline and needs strong leadership. At this point she has not faced any issues with the council that have caused confrontations. Instead of fighting the city council, Perry works harmoniously with the council to a degree that has not been seen in recent years.

Perry, known also for the hats she wears, claims that she is not trying to make a fashion statement. She simply has such a busy schedule that ''she does not have time to comb her hair'' (Marshall, 64). Nevertheless, her hats have become her trademark. In her office, she placed an antique brass hat rack for her broad brimmed trademarks.

As a social worker, member of the House of Representatives for the State of Connecticut, and mayor of Hartford, she has risen to the challenge with vision and intelligence. In these positions she has had the chance to interact with the poor and disadvantaged, the middle class, and prominent, political, educational, civic and business leaders of the state. She has shared her thoughts and opinions and discussed answers to today's tough problems.

Just as a quilt ties a multiplicity of pieces together into one whole, Carrie Saxon Perry hopes to bring together a diversity of people, programs, and resources in order to improve the lives of her community.

References

Condon, Tom. ''Mayor Merits a Little Heart in Hartford.'' *Hartford Courant*, 8 February 1990.

Fahy, Anne. ''Mayor Urges Rescue Efforts for Cities.'' *Philadelphia Inquirer* 3 December 1989.

Graham, George. ''Hartford Mayor Foresees Opportunities for Women.'' *Union News*, 21 February 1990.

Hartford Courant, 20 May 1989.

Johnson, Kirk. ''In Hartford, Drug Violence May Draw Region's Concern.'' *New York Times*, 11 November 1989.

Keveney, Bill and Mary Pazniokas. ''Mellow Style Suits Perry.'' *Hartford Courant*, 31 May 1988.

Lanker, Brian. *I Dream a World.* New York: Stewart, Tabori, and Chang, 1989. Photograph, p. 60.

Marshall, Marilyn. ''Carrie Saxon Perry: More Than a Pretty Hat.'' *Ebony* 43 (April 1988): 60.

Moser, Matthew. ''Inmates Cheer Hartford Mayor.'' *Hartford Courant*, 15 February 1990.

Perry, Carrie Saxon.''Gender, Authority and Leadership.'' Speech delivered at Smith College, 20 February 1990.

———. Inaugural Address: Hartford, Connecticut, 5 December 1989.

Richardson, Lisa. ''Choice for Mayor of Hartford.'' Editorial. *Hartford Courant*, 29 October 1987.

''Speaking Out: What Must be Done. (Four Black Leaders' Opinions on Government's Anti-drug Efforts) (War! The Drug Crisis: Programs and Solutions.)'' *Ebony* 44 (August 1989): 156.

''What Did Rainbow Tuesday Mean? (Race as a Factor in American Politics).'' *Ebony* 45 (February 1990): 32.

Who's Who Among Black Americans. 5th ed. Lake Forest Illinois: Educational Communications, 1988.

Who's Who in America. 45th ed. Vol. 2. Chicago: Marquis, 1988.

Who's Who in American Politics. 12th ed. New York: Bowker, 1989-90.

Who's Who of American Women. 16th ed. Chicago: Marquis, 1989-90.

Joan Curl Elliott

Julia Perry
(1924-1979)
Composer, musician, educator

Julia Amanda Perry's career as a composer perhaps mirrored those of many creative persons of her generation: excellent preparation, including study abroad, recognition through awards and grants, major performances, accolades in the press. But there were also rejections, insufficient opportunities for public hearings, and unanswered correspondence. A serious illness impeded her work and made it difficult for her to write and copy music, but it did not still her creativity.

Perry was born in Lexington, Kentucky, on March 25, 1924, and died in Akron, Ohio, on April 24, 1979. Her family moved to Akron in 1934. Perry had two older sisters, both of whom studied violin; she studied piano as a child.

Following her public school education in Lexington and Akron, Perry attended Akron University and the Westminster Choir College, where she received the B. A. in music in 1947 and the M. A. in music in 1948. Talented in piano, she was also a gifted singer and became interested in composition. Following advanced study in 1950 at the Juilliard School of Music, she attended the Berkshire Music Center at Tanglewood, Massachusetts, in the summer of 1951. There she met several influential persons, among them Leonard Bernstein, Howard Shanet, and Luigi Dallapiccola. Perry also met many aspiring young artists, including conductor Lorin Maazel and contralto Betty Allen, who would both achieve success on the concert stage.

In composition classes at Tanglewood under Dallapiccola, Perry became greatly inspired by his genius for combining the lyrical line with uncompromisingly contemporary harmonic and contrapuntal elements. In addition, the breadth of knowledge of music of all ages—Mozart, Palestrina, Berg, Bartok, Bach, and Monteverdi—that Dallapicolla revealed in his composition classes enabled students to view their efforts in a wide context.

Following study at Tanglewood, Perry spent several years abroad, returning to the United States for performances and to make grant applications. While abroad, she studied composition with Dallapiccola in Florence and Nadia Boulanger in Paris, and gave a series of lectures on American music for the United States Information Service (U.S.I.S.). She also studied conducting with Emanuel Balaban and Alceo Galliera and conducted a number of European orchestras, presenting performances of her works for orchestra and chamber music ensembles. Her studies abroad included two summers (1956 and 1957) spent at the Academia Chigiana in Siena, Italy. Awards enabling her European studies included two Guggenheim fellowships (1954 and 1956), a Boulanger Grand Prix, and the U.S.I.S. sponsorship.

Perry Becomes Active Composer

Returning to the United States, Perry was active as a composer and teacher. She received the National Institute of Arts and Letters Award in 1965, and taught at Florida A. & M. University, 1967-68, and Atlanta University, 1968-69, as well as at Bronx Community College and New York University. Her works have been performed by numerous American orchestras and chamber music ensembles, including the New York Philharmonic Orchestra (*Study for Orchestra*, 1965) and Clarion Concerts (*Stabat Mater*, Carnegie Hall, 1958). Her opera, *The Cask of Amontillado*, was performed at Columbia University in 1954. Her work for percussion ensemble, *Homunculus C. F.*, was recorded by Composers Recordings in 1960 (CRSD 252).

In her compositions, Perry exhibits a continuity and cohesiveness of style, featuring uncompromisingly modern sounds contrasted with lyrical, flowing melodies. Her Prelude (*Lament*) for piano of 1946, for example, exhibits block-chord harmonies and a diverse modern tonal palette, supporting an expressive melodic contour. Thirty years later, some of these same compositional traits can be found in her 1977 *Bicentennial Reflections* for tenor soloist and six instruments. The latter work also reveals her subtle sense of satire, irony, and humor. The three percussionists in the ensemble are to be dressed in red, white, and blue, and the score calls for them to be black, Chinese, and Jewish or "Aryan." In the poetic text by Perry, the tenor soloist poses and answers Rumpelstiltskin-like riddles concerning freedom in America. Sadly, the work also shows how severely her writing had deteriorated. It is difficult to read, although well worth the effort. Like a Beethoven manuscript, it is almost illegible—one has the impression of a creative genie imprisoned in a bottle and struggling to burst free.

A trained and talented singer, Perry's writing for the voice shows much care and sensitivity. As an example, her acclaimed *Stabat Mater* was first performed at Tanglewood in 1951 and later recorded by the Japan Philharmonic with Betty Allen as soloist. Ross Parmenter of the *New York Times*, reviewing a performance in 1958, commented that "the intensity of her feeling frequently conveyed through vividly expressive string colorations makes the work impressive." He added that she knows "how to write effective declamation for the voice," and that the composition was "brilliantly sung and it had a marked success with the audience."

Perry's willingness to experiment with new forms is shown in her *Homunculus, C. F.* for percussion ensemble. Making use of autogenetic contrapuntal technique but preserving tonal cohesion, Perry constructs a thematic "Homunculus" and brings it to life in a process of complex development, featuring novel sound combinations, dynamic variations, and expressive colorations. She writes expertly for percussion and enjoyed composing this work. Her inspiration for the piece, as the title alludes, is in Goethe's *Faust*, where Wagner, Faust's apprentice, brings to life his artificial creation, "Homunculus."

The problem of opera also interested Perry. She responded well to the dramatic element, being a poet as well as a singer, pianist, and composer. One answer to the challenge of achieving a performance within practical limits of personnel and resources seemed to be available in chamber opera. One of her works in this medium, *The Cask of Amontillado*, fits well within these limits. It was performed in 1954 at Columbia University, with Howard Shanet conducting. There are two major roles, limited scenery, and the work lasts about half an hour. It is an affective work, and the audience gave the performance a favorable response despite the somber nature of Poe's tale, as told with empathy by Perry. Reviews, however, were mixed.

Taken as a group, Perry's works reveal her ability to express sacred themes, (as in the *Stabat Mater* and her several shorter choral works), as well as her love of the voice, (as shown in her opera and chamber music settings). She was an excellent writer for orchestra, with probably twelve symphonies to her credit (a letter of October 1978 refers to the twelfth, with its second movement completed and a third, "Rondo," nearly completed). Other symphonic works include her *Suite Symphony* (1976), *Slums*, and *Global Warfare*. Her choral training found expression in numerous choral works, in which she shows a good sense of balance, range, and text declamation. Her chamber music shows an appreciation for the possibilities of small ensemble cohesion and contrast. She also wrote several works for the piano and solo songs. In summary, her muse found expression through many musical forms that she used with considerable professional skill.

References

Abdul, Raoul. *Blacks in Classical Music*. New York, Dodd, Mead, 1977.

Black Perspective in Music (Fall 1974): 153.

Ebony (August 1966) 66.

Green, Mildred D. A. *Study of the Lives and Works of Five Black Women Composers in America*. Ph.D. dissertation, University of Oklahoma, 1975.

Musical America (December 1, 1954): 32.

The Negro Almanac. Letter from Julia Perry to Ed. Harry A. Ploski. New York: Wiley, 1983.

New York Times, 19 December 1958.

Southern, Eileen, ed. *Biographical Dictionary of Afro-American and African Musicians*. Westport, Conn., Greenwood Press, 1982.

———. *The Music of Black Americans*. 2d ed. New York, Norton, 1983.

Collections

The Fisk University Library, Special Collections, includes personal letters and five manuscripts of Julia Perry's works: *Bicentennial Reflections* (1977) for tenor and six instruments, *Module for orchestra* (1969) piano transcription, *Prelude* for piano (1946, rev. 1962), *Triptych* for Bass Baritone and five instruments (1976), and *Hymn to Pan* (facsimile, 1963) for chorus (SATB) and organ.

Darius Thieme

Dorothy Peterson

(c. 1900-?)

Patron of the arts, theater founder, educator, manuscripts collector

Committed to the support and advancement of the Harlem intellectuals of the 1920s and 1930s, Dorothy Randolph Peterson transformed her family's Brooklyn home and later her East Side apartment into gathering places where many aspiring artists and writers came to socialize and form alliances. In 1929, she and Regina Andrews founded the Negro Experimental Theatre, a small theater group that was also commonly referred to as the Harlem Experimental Theatre. Almost a decade later, she devoted much of her time and artistic energies to the Harlem Suitcase Theatre, which Langston Hughes formed with the help of Louise Thompson. After 1940, Peterson concentrated largely on her teaching and the collecting of many documents and manuscripts of the black literati of her day. Through her efforts, Carl Van Vechten greatly enlarged the James Weldon Johnson Memorial Collection of Negro Arts and Letters at Yale University.

Dorothy Peterson was born around the turn of the century. Her father, Jerome Bowers Peterson (born September 12, 1859), was a risk-taking, industrious young man whose career interest ultimately gravitated to journalism. In 1873, at the age of fourteen, he discontinued his schooling in Brooklyn to work as a messenger for Freedman's Savings and Trust Company. Realizing the importance of education, however, he attended night school, and after his graduation cofounded a weekly publication that eventually became the *New York Age*. There he worked as a contributing editor with T. Thomas Fortune, a fellow black journalist known for his militancy. In 1904, Jerome Peterson accepted the appointment of United States Consul to Puerto Cabello, Venezuela, for two years. Once his appointment ended, he served as

Deputy Collector of the Internal Revenue first in San Juan, Puerto Rico and later in New York City.

Dorothy Peterson's mother, Cornelia S. White, married James Peterson in 1895. The daughter of Philip A. White, the first black member of the Board of Education of Brooklyn, Cornelia Peterson served as a board member of the Brooklyn Home for Aged Colored People, chairperson of the Relief Circle, president of a section of the Needlework Guild, and a member of the Circle for Peace and Foreign Relations. She died following an operation for appendicitis on July 30, 1926. Dorothy Peterson's brother, Jerome Sidney Peterson, studied medicine and, at the completion of his training, took positions at Seaview Hospital on Staten Island and in New York City's Department of Health.

Dorothy Peterson finished her secondary education locally, graduated from Puerto Rico University, and took post-graduate courses at some of the leading universities in the United States. Like many black women, she secured employment as a teacher in the public school system. In later years, she taught at Wadleigh High School for Girls in Harlem. She also worked at the Harlem branch of the New York Public Library.

During the 1920s, the Petersons's Brooklyn home at 380 Monroe Street served as a literary salon that encouraged racially mixed gatherings. Carl Van Vechten, in his controversial novel *Nigger Heaven* (1926), used the Peterson residence as the model for the home of his character Aaron Summers. He attempted to capture the ambiance of the location and the literary meetings that took place there. Van Vechten also modeled the heroine of the novel, Mary Love—a prim, beautiful librarian concerned with her racial heritage—after Dorothy Peterson.

Once Peterson and her brother obtained an apartment on the East Side, they established a literary salon for artists comparable to the one Regina Andrews and Ethel Ray Nance had formed on Harlem's West Side. Many distinguished writers became their guests, and Peterson's involvement and support extended beyond their visits. Taking an interest in their literary endeavors, she, for example, became one of the first nine patrons of *Fire* (1926), a publication that novelist and dramatist Wallace Thurman launched with the help of Langston Hughes, Zora Neale Hurston, John P. Davis, Richard Bruce Nugent, Gwendolyn Bennett, and the painter Aaron Douglas.

In the mid-1920s, Peterson became interested in the teaching of George Ivanovich Gurdjieff, the Russian who espoused Oriental thought and disciplines, and she became smitten with one of his most distinguished disciples, Jean Toomer. After the publication of *Cane* in 1923 and a visit to Gurdjieff's Institute for the Harmonious Development of Man in Fontainebleau, France, in 1924, Toomer came to Harlem preaching Gurdjieff's doctrine and seeking converts. Some of those he proselytized included Aaron Douglas, Wallace Thurman, Nella Larsen, and two individuals who conducted literary salons, Muriel Draper and Dorothy Peterson. Toomer quickly had an enormous impact on Peterson and under his influence she finished a manuscript. In October 1931, Toomer married a white woman but there still remained "the one Afro-American woman Toomer was once thought to care about: a sad-eyed, beautiful teacher of Spanish and aspiring actress named Dorothy Peterson, whose love for Jean Toomer was legend among their Harlem friends" (Berry, 214).

Negro Experimental Theatre Founded

In February of 1929, Peterson and Regina Andrews spearheaded The Negro Experimental Theatre. They and one or two more young Harlemites met at the 135th Street Branch of the New York Public Library to discuss recreating a small theater similar to the type W. E. B. Du Bois had established with the Krigwa Players. The playwrights, Inez Wilson and Andrew Brown, had been successful with a serious drama entitled *Retribution* at the Lincoln Theatre, one of the first theaters in Harlem; therefore, the group felt encouraged that a theater devoted to serious dramatic presentations would thrive. Four months later the group, with the help of Jessie Redmond Fauset, Harold Jackman, Theophilus Lewis, Ira De Augustine Reid, and the Lincoln actors, gave what the *Inter-State Tattle* of July 5, 1929, called "an unusually brilliant" performance of Georgia Douglas Johnson's one-act play *Plumes*, which Jackman directed. The theater moved in February of 1931 to Saint Philip's Episcopal Church on West 134th Street, which served as the group's "creative production center for the playwright, the actor, the costume and stage designer, and the director" (Mitchell, 76). Serafin Alvarez and Joaquin Alvarez Quintero's play, *A Sunny Morning*, which Peterson directed, Ridgely Torrence's *Rider of Dreams*, Andrew Burris's *You Must Be Born Again*, Ted Martin's *Eviction*, George Calderon's *Little Stone House*, and Regina Anderson's *Climbing Jacob's Ladder*, a story about lynching that she wrote under the pseudonym Ursala Trelling, were a few of the dramas staged by the Negro Experimental Theatre during its existence.

One evening in 1930, Richard B. Harrison, the star of Marc Connelly's Broadway hit, *The Green Pastures*, attended one of the Negro Experimental Theatre's productions. He selected Peterson, who was then the theater's executive director, and Inez Wilson to perform in an all-black production of Connelly's play. Peterson took a leave of absence from her teaching, and Regina Andrews assumed her duties at the theater during Peterson's appearance as Cain's girlfriend at the Mansfield Theatre on West Forty-seventy Street as Cain's girlfriend. Lucien H. White, a reporter for the *New York Age*, touted the three-hour production as the "biggest sensation New York has had in ages" (Walton, *New York Age*, 8 March 1930, 7).

When the Harlem Suitcase Theatre came into being on the second floor of the International Workers Order's Community Center at 317 West 125th Street in 1937, Peterson was quick to offer her assistance. She served as technical director for the theater, which had approximately forty-seven official members. And at one point she rehearsed for the role of the mother in *Don't You Want To Be Free?*, the one-act play written by the theater's founder, Langston Hughes. Undoubtedly Hughes thought very highly of Peterson throughout their friendship, as evidenced by his dedication to her of *Laughing to Keep from Crying* (1952), a collection of short stories.

The life span of the Harlem Suitcase Theatre, like that of the Negro Experimental Theatre, was only a few years. Limited finances and scenery and a lack of new dramatic material that was anticapitalistic in nature inevitably led to its demise. Peterson, as technical director, at one point sharply asserted: "We can't go on forever doing sceneryless plays" (Rampersad, 364). Various members of the group felt the theater's death could be traced to Hughes's move to California and "personality problems" among its officers. Some accused Louise Thompson, who had located the space and was a communist sponsor for the theater, of being "too domineering" and Peterson of being "too cosmopolitan" (Rampersad, 369).

In the following decade, Peterson committed herself to another task: the preservation of black arts and letters. Carl Van Vechten, with whom she had a long-standing friendship, founded the James Weldon Johnson Memorial Collection of Negro Arts and Letters at Yale University. Van Vechten credited Peterson with securing "many interesting volumes by Puerto Rican Negroes . . . the second volume of *Opportunity* not on my own shelves" and successfully soliciting "many gifts from others" (Kellner, *"Keep A-Inchin' Along"*, 131). Van Vechten repeatedly acknowledged her and others who helped him assemble the collection:

> As I have intimated, in the work behind me I have received able assistance from a great number of persons, but I would be ungrateful if I did not mention the fact that Dorothy Peterson, Harold Jackman, Walter White, and Langston Hughes seemed to be at one with me in their willingness to make the forming of the collection a lifework. Hardly a day passes in which I do not hear from several of them, now with letters or information, and again with packages bulging with valuable material. (239)

Peterson reciprocated Van Vechten's kindness. Harlem's Wadleigh High School dedicated its 1944 yearbook, *The Owl*, to him. Peterson had arranged the honor.

In February of 1949, Peterson, with Van Vechten's help, formed the Jerome Bowers Peterson Memorial Collection of Photographs of Celebrated Negroes at Wadleigh High School. Peterson's father had died of a stroke in February 1943. Van Vechten supplied the photographs that comprise the collection.

Dorothy Peterson's continued work as a teacher allowed her to expand the minds of a future generation. Her involvement in the preservation of the manuscripts and letters of the black literati of the Harlem Renaissance and of post-renaissance writers has helped shape our memories of the past.

References

Berry, Faith. *Langston Hughes, Before and Beyond Harlem*. Westport, Conn.: Lawrence Hill, 1983.

Bontemps, Arna. *The Harlem Renaissance Remembered*. New York: Dodd, Mead, 1972.

Interstate Tatler, 5 July 1929: 12.

Kellner, Bruce. "Dorothy [Randolph] Peterson." *The Harlem Renaissance, A Historical Dictionary for the Era*. Westport, Conn.: Greenwood Press, 1984.

———. "Jerome Bowers Peterson," *The Harlem Renaissance, A Historical Dictionary for the Era*. Westport, Conn.: Greenwood Press, 1984.

———. *"Keep A-Inchin' Along."* Westport, Conn.: Greenwood Press, 1979.

Lewis, David Levering. *When Harlem Was in Vogue*. New York: Knopf, 1981.

Mitchell, Loften. *Voices of the Black Theatre*. Clifton, New Jersey: White, 1975.

"Mrs. Jerome B. Peterson Dies After Operation." *New York Age*, 7 August 1926.

Rampersad, Arnold. *The Life of Langston Hughes Volume I: 1902-1941*. New York: Oxford University Press, 1986. Photographs pps. 278-279.

Walton, Lester A. "Negro Players Star in New Success, 'Green Pastures' Furnishes Great Vehicle for Stage Veterans." *New York Age*, 15 March 1930.

White, Lucien H. "'The Green Pastures,' Given by An All-Negro Cast of 100, is Biggest Sensation New York Has Had in Age." *New York Age*, 8 March 1930.

La Vinia Delois Jennings

Ann Petry

(1911-)

Writer

Ann Lane Petry, the "first black female author to address problems black women face" (*Black Writers*, 455) and the writer of important books for young readers, including

Harriet Tubman: Conductor on the Underground Railroad, said of her work:

> I hope that I have created characters who are real, believable, alive. For I am of the opinion that most Americans regard Negroes as types—not quite human—who fit into a special category and I wanted to show them as people with the same capacity for love and hate, for tears and laughter, and the same instincts for survival possessed by all men (Ivy, 49).

Petry was born on October 12, 1911, "in the morning (upstairs over [her] father's drugstore in Old Saybrook, Connecticut)" (*Third Book of Junior Authors*, 223). Her parents were Peter C. Lane and Bertha (James) Lane. Petry came from a New England family that owned pharmacies in Old Saybrook and Old Lyme. The Lane family was part of a very small minority in these towns: in 1910 the census counted 367 black Americans in all Middlesex County, 0.8 percent of the population. Petry's grandfather had been a pharmaceutical chemist, and her father, uncle, and aunt were all pharmacists. Petry attended the local schools and high school. She read widely from childhood because, as she expressed it, "I was born and reared in a small town, and in a small town, you know, there is really nothing much to do except read" (Ivy, 49). When she was fourteen years old she decided that she wanted to be a writer. In high school she wrote poetry and one-act plays. Upon graduation from high school in 1929, she followed the family tradition and expectations and entered the Connecticut College of Pharmacy (now part of the University of Connecticut), where she completed the program in 1931. She then worked in Pharmacist James' Pharmacy in Old Saybrook, as well as in Old Lyme, until 1938 when she married George David Petry on February 22 and the couple moved to New York.

In New York, Ann Petry worked in the advertising department of the *Amsterdam News* between 1938 and 1941. She then edited the woman's page and did general reporting for the rival news weekly, *People's Voice* from 1941 to 1944. For nine months she worked in an experimental program in Harlem schools designed to explore and combat the effects of segregation. She also took classes at Columbia University (1943-1944), taught a class in business for the YWCA, and was, at least briefly, a member of the American Negro Theatre. Meanwhile she also worked on her writing, as she had since childhood, although until 1943 she garnered only rejection slips.

Petry's first published story, "On Saturday the Siren Sounds at Noon," appeared in the December 1943 issue of *Crisis*. The magazine could not accept her second submission "In Darkness and Confusion," which treated the Harlem riot of August 1943, because of its length. However, "Olaf and His Girl Friend" did appear in *Crisis* in May 1945, as well as "Like A Winding Sheet" in November of that year. The latter was named best American short story of 1946. The first of these stories had a direct impact on the writing of Petry's first novel, *The Street*. "On Saturday the Siren Sounds at Noon" was read by an editor at Houghton Mifflin, who asked her if she was working on a novel. The following year Petry submitted the first five chapters and an outline of the remainder. Houghton Mifflin awarded her the Houghton Mifflin Literary Fellowship of $2,400 for 1945. This fellowship was intended to allow promising young writers to work uninterruptedly on their literary project, and it allowed Petry to devote ten months to the completion of *The Street*, which was published in January 1946.

Petry's experience as a reporter in Harlem gave her the background for her story of Lutie Johnson, and in an interview with James W. Ivy in *Crisis*, Petry expressed her purpose in writing the novel:

> In *The Street* my aim is to show how simply and easily the environment can change the course of a person's life. For this purpose I have made Lindy [*sic*] Johnson an intelligent, ambitious, attractive woman with a fair degree of education. She lives in the squalor of 116th Street, but she retains her self-respect and fights to bring up her little son decently . . . There are no statistics in the book though they are present in the background . . . in terms of what life is like for people who live in over-crowded tenements. . . . (Ivy, 49).

In the novel, Lutie Johnson shares the dream she sees embodied in the Italian grocers, the Pizzinis, who help Lutie by having their daughter write her a recommendation for a maid's job. Nearly illiterate, the Pizzini's have nonetheless worked their way out of poverty, have been able to buy a beautiful home in the suburbs, and have given their daughter a good education. Although Lutie shares with them the values of hard work, honesty, and a strict sense of sexual morality, she is ultimately defeated by her surroundings. *Black Writers* states that "Ann Petry became the first black female author to address the problems black women face as they struggle to cope with life in the slums" (455). Over the years *The Street* has sold more than one million copies.

Because of *The Street's* subject matter, reviewers placed Petry in the school of Richard Wright, but this judgement was soon revealed to be wrong. Petry's subsequent novels were quite different, and there are critics who feel that her best work is in the later novels, despite the success of her first. Petry published *Country Place* in 1947. The imaginative germ of the novel was the effects of a devastating hurricane on a small town in Connecticut. *Country Place* represents a marked change of location and cast of characters from those in *The Street*. Not only do she move from Harlem to a New England town, all of the main characters are white. In *Country Place*, Petry deals with the effects of the war on the women who stayed home and the breakdown of conventional codes of morality. The character Johnnie Roane comes home from WW II and discovers, under very dramatic circumstances, the infidelity of his wife, Glory.

Thelma J. Shinn sees the novel as continuing an exploration of values begun in *The Street*: "[Petry] not only demonstrates the collapse of tradition but also shows what society has become; Lil and Glory are vehicles of their society as Lutie is of hers, without, however, her underlying integrity" (115). Petry's choice of subject matter in this novel is, of course, controversial. Jeanne Nobel, for example, expresses a succinct negative opinion: "for blacks at least, it has little meaning . . . it scarcely added to the need for a strong literature on the black experience" (177).

Petry herself reacts against attempts to categorize her as a certain type of writer: "I always want to do something different from what I have done before; I don't want to repeat myself. If I belong to a certain tradition, I don't want to belong, because my writing would be very boring if I always wrote in a particular style" (O'Brien, 160). Of her relationship to other black writers, she says:

> [W]e're all black. As I said, we do have a common theme. We write about relationships between whites and blacks because it's in the very air we breathe. We can't escape it. But we write about it in a thousand different ways and from a thousand different points of view (O'Brien, 157).

It is not certain exactly when Petry and her family moved back to Old Saybrook, but she states that she wrote *The Drugstore Cat*, the first of her juvenile books, published in 1949, while she was still living in New York. She is characteristically reticent about her private life, but it is known she has at least one daughter, Elizabeth Ann. John O'Brien tells us that "Petry lives in a house that was built in 1800 and has been preserved in its original state" (154). In 1972, she shared her home with "a slow-moving, majestic black cat" named Tobermory, called Mr. Toby (*Third Book*, 223-24). Petry loves mornings and says that when she writes she works from about eight o'clock to noon, saving the afternoons for any needed revising. She is nontemperamental about her writing, saying, "I doubt if my family or anyone else can tell when I'm thinking about writing" (O'Brien, 160). Her hobbies are painting and playing the piano, and she also enjoys gardening, sewing, cooking, and writing poetry. That her taste may not be entirely for modern mass culture is indicated by her identification of it with "pro-football, beer, TV serials, and cars" (O'Brien, 158). (It is, however, a loaded question that provoked this response.)

The setting of Petry's third novel, *The Narrows* (1953), is again a small New England town. It deals with the love affair of a young black man of considerable integrity, Link Williams, and a blonde, rich, and bored wife, Camilo. Neither blacks nor whites approve of the affair when it becomes public. Again in this novel social pressure and the demands of the individual collide, resulting in Link's murder. But there is an increased emphasis on the way the pressures of the past shape the lives of people. Thelma J. Shinn has chosen a passage that aptly illustrates this point; an older woman is talking of her life:

> I see my father . . . and he's saying, "Frank, you know you've got a man's mind." Anywhere I go here in Monmouth, I can always see myself—too tall, too thin, too bony. Even at twelve. And too bright, able, and unable and unwilling to conceal the fact that I had brains. When I finished high school I went to college, to Wellesley, where I was a kind of Eighth Wonder of the World, because I was colored. I hadn't been there very long when the dean sent for me and asked me if I was happy there. I looked straight at her and I said, "My father didn't send me here to be happy, he sent me here to learn." . . . . A college graduate. All hung over with honors and awards and prizes. And I knew I'd never get married, never have any children. So I was going to be a doctor. . . . My father was alone here and I couldn't bear to leave him, and there was the business he had built up so slowly and so carefully. So I became an undertaker too (119).

Although some reviewers, such as Arna Bontemps, mostly approved of *The Narrows*, the *New Yorker* capsule is more typical of the mixed reactions of others: It is "an anguished book, written with an enormous amount of emotion and some thought, that does not succeed because there is far too much of it. It seems to choke on itself, with so many people trying to tell everything about themselves all at once" (29 August 1953, 78). But writing some twelve years later, David Littlejohn finds in Petry's writing "more intelligence in her novels, paragraph for paragraph, than in those of any other writer I have mentioned . . . a prose that is rich and crisp . . . and . . . characters of shape and dimension, people made out of love, with whole histories evoked in a page" (155).

Following these novels came three works destined for young readers. Petry wrote *Harriet Tubman: Conductor on the Underground Railroad* (1955) out of her dissatisfaction with the way slavery had been presented in her schoolbooks. Petry also found herself fascinated by a young black woman caught up the Salem witch trials, and wrote *Tituba of Salem Village* published in 1964. Petry is torn between her interest in history and the limits that the necessity for research and accuracy put on the imagination, and so she abandoned two projects for further juvenile works. One was the story of Daniel Drayton and Edward Syres, two ship captains who tried to help slaves escape from the District of Columbia; the other dealt with Jacintha de Siqueira, an African woman in Brazilian history. In 1970 appeared *Legends of the Saints*, which retells the stories of ten saints, from Christopher to Martin de Porres.

Miss Muriel and Other Stories, a collection of Petry's short stories from the first that appeared in print, was published in 1971 and underlines the individuality of Petry's writing voice. Alfred Kazin reviewed the collection together with a number of other books by black American writers published at the same time, including two by Imamu Amiri Baraka. Kazin notes that in comparison "Ann Petry seems old-fashioned, so surprisingly 'slow' in her narrative rhythm.'' He adds: ''Her stories are very far from contemporary black nationalist writing, and by no means necessarily more interesting. But they are certainly different'' (34-35).

Petry has remained true to her individual vision regardless of current fashion, and she dislikes discussing the meaning of her work as a writer. She says, ''My feeling is that once I've written something I don't have anything more to say about it. That's it. Talking about it isn't going to change what I did or didn't do'' (O'Brien, 155). She writes for herself, first of all. She says, ''If I permitted myself to think in terms of the reader, I would become so inhibited I wouldn't write—at least for publication'' (O'Brien, 158). Bernard W. Bell makes this claim for Petry's importance:

> Petry's vision of black personality is not only different from that of Himes and Wright, it is also more faithful to the complexities and varieties of black women. . . . Ann Petry thus moves beyond the naturalistic vision of Himes and Wright to a demythologizing of American culture and Afro-American character. This is her most valuable achievement in the tradition of the Afro-American novel (183).

In recent years, Petry was professor of English at the University of Hawaii from 1974 to 1975. She received honorary degrees from Suffolk University, the University of Connecticut, and Mount Holyoke College. She has been a member of several professional writers' organizations, including PEN, the Authors Guild, and the Authors League, of which she was secretary in 1960. Her work continues to engage the attention of readers, critics, and scholars.

References

Bell, Bernard W. *The Afro-American Novel and Its Tradition*. Amherst, Mass.: University of Massachusetts Press, 1987.

De Montreville, Doris and Donna Hill, eds. *Third Book of Junior Authors*. New York: H. W. Wilson, 1972. Photograph, p. 223.

Ivy, James W. ''Ann Petry Talks About First Novel.'' *The Crisis* 53 (February 1946): 48-49. Photograph, p. 48.

Kazin, Alfred. ''Brothers Crying Out of More Access to Life.'' *Saturday Review* 54 (2 October 1971): 33-35.

Littlejohn, David. *Black on White*. New York: Grossman, 1966.

Metzger, Linda, ed. *Black Writers*. Detroit: Gale Research, 1989. 454-56.

The *New Yorker* 29 (29 August 1953): 78.

Noble, Jeanne. *Beautiful, Also, Are the Souls of My Black Sisters*. Englewood Cliffs, N. J.: Prentice-Hall, 1978.

O'Brien, John, ed. *Interviews with Black Writers*. New York: Liveright, 1973. Photograph, p. 153.

Poirier, Suzanne. ''Ann Petry: From Pharmacist to Novelist.'' *Pharmacy in History* 28 (No. 1 1986): 26-33.

Robinson, Wilhelmena S. *Historical Negro Biographies*. New York: Publishers Company, 1968. Sketch of Petry, p. 235.

Rothe, Anna, ed. *Current Biography* 1946. New York: H. W. Wilson, 1947. Photograph, p. 476.

Shockley, Ann Allen and Sue P. Chandler. *Living Black American Authors*. New York: Bowker, 1973.

Shinn, Thelma J. ''Women in the Novels of Ann Petry.'' *Critique* 16 (No.1 1974-75): 110-120.

Who's Who Among Black Americans. 6th ed. Detroit: Gale Research, 1990.

Who's Who of American Women. 8th ed. Chicago: Marquis, 1974.

Collections

The letters and papers of Ann Petry are housed at Boston University.

Robert L. Johns

L. Eudora Pettigrew

(1928-)

Educator

L. Eudora Williams Pettigrew, educator and administrator, was born in Hopkinsville, Kentucky, on March 1, 1928, the daughter of Warren Cicero Williams and Corrye Lee (Newell) Williams. Now divorced, Pettigrew is the mother of two children, Peter W. Woodard and Jonathan R. Pettigrew.

In 1950, Pettigrew earned a bachelor of music degree from West Virginia State College. She received her master of arts degree from Southern Illinois University in 1964 and her Ph.D. in educational psychology in 1966.

Pettigrew began her professional career as a music and English instructor at Swift Memorial Junior College in Rogersville, Tennessee, in 1950. For the academic year 1951-52, she was an instructor of music and librarian at Western Kentucky Vocational School in Paducah. Continuing her work in higher education, Pettigrew again worked as a music and English instructor, this time at Voorhees College in Denmark, South Carolina, in 1954-55.

Leaving the field of higher education and returning home, Pettigrew became the director of music and recreation therapy at the Western Kentucky State Psychiatric Hospital in Hopkinsville, Kentucky, from 1956 to 1961. From 1961 to 1963, she was a research fellow at the Rehabilitation Institute at Southern Illinois University, Carbondale.

Eudora Pettigrew returned to the field of higher education in 1963. She was both instructor of educational psychology and coordinator of the undergraduate educational psychology program at Southern Illinois from 1963 to 1966. At the same time, she served as acting chairman of the Educational Psychology Teacher Corps.

In 1966, Pettigrew became an assistant professor of psychology at the University of Bridgeport in Connecticut. She was promoted to associate professor in 1970. Leaving the University of Bridgeport, Pettigrew went to Michigan State University as associate professor of psychology at the Center of Urban Affairs and College of Education. In 1973 she was promoted to professor.

During her years in higher education, Pettigrew held several concurrent positions. She was a consultant for Hall Neighborhood House Day Care Project for the State of Connecticut, 1966-68; consultant for the Bridgeport Public Schools, 1967-68; and a consultant for research and evaluation for the United States Eastern Regional Laboratory Education Development Center, Newton, Massachusetts, 1967-1969. In 1971 she worked as a consultant for the Lansing Model Cities Agency Day Care Program in Lansing, Michigan. Pettigrew also found the time to serve as program development specialist for the Lansing public school's Teacher Corps program from 1971 to 1973. From 1973 to 1977 she served as consultant for the universities of Pittsburgh, Michigan, and Wayne State, as well as the Wayne County Public Health Nurses Association and the Illinois State Board of Education.

Pettigrew was professor and chairperson of the Department of Urban and Metropolitan Studies in the College of Urban Development at Michigan State University in East Lansing from 1974 to 1981. From Michigan State, she went to the University of Delaware in Newark as associate provost in 1981.

Pettigrew has made guest appearances on radio and television, discussing issues of black women, equality, career, and integration in schools.

Pettigrew has been named Outstanding Black Educator, and Outstanding Woman Educator, and has received the Diana Award from the Lansing YWCA, among many other awards.

Pettigrew has coauthored several publications, among them: *Cheating Behavior of Fifth Grade Youngsters: A Concern of the Elementary Counselor* in 1966 and *The Effects of Study Questions on College Students' Test Performances* in 1967. She is the author of other publications, one of which is "Reverse Discrimination—Fact or Fantasy?" published in the *Journal of Integrated Education*, 1976. In this article Pettigrew concludes that "even though Federal legislation designed to equalize employment opportunities for all U. S. citizens has been enacted, the only group to enhance its employment status over the past ten years has been that of white males" (3).

Another article written by Pettigrew is "Competency Based Teacher Education: Teacher Training for Multi-Cultural Education," published by the U.S. Department of Health, Education and Welfare, National Institute of Education, 1973. In this article she defines "competency based teacher education and discusses relevant competencies, some problems and issues, and some assessment strategies."

Pettigrew continues to research, publish, teach and work in administration. Currently she is the president of SUNY College of Old Westbury in New York.

References

American Men and Women of Science. Vol. 2. New York: Bowker, 1973.

Pettigrew, L. Eudora. "Reverse Discrimination—Fact or Fantasy?" *Journal of Integrated Education*, 14 (November-December 1976): 3-4.

Who's Who in America. 44th ed. Vol. 2 Wilmette, Ill.: Marquis, 1986-87.

Nina T. Elliott

Vel R. Phillips

(1924-)

Politician

"It just happened," is how Vel Rogers Phillips refers to all of the firsts she has accomplished in her life. She further explains that she feels guilty to some extent, because many times she did not even know she was making history. If such a person could be imagined, she might be depicted as a political dynamo or a power-hungry person. But Phillips is a direct contradiction to the stereotypical politician. She is petite, soft-spoken, bubbly, talkative, and a pleasant and warm individual.

Phillips was the first black woman to graduate from Wisconsin Law School in 1951; part of the first husband-and-wife team to practice before the federal bar; the first woman and first black woman elected to Milwaukee Common Council in 1956; the first black in the United States ever elected to serve on the National Committee of either major party (1958); the first black woman judge in Wisconsin (1972); and the first black elected to the position of secretary of state in Wisconsin (1978).

Vel Phillips attributes her accomplishments to her parents and her husband, Dale Phillips, who were always "helpful and supportive emotionally and financially." Throughout Phillips's career she states that her husband was always there for her and was very accepting of her being in the forefront. It was Dale Phillips who first pushed her into the political arena.

Born Velvalea Rogers on February 18, 1924, in Milwaukee, Wisconsin, she later had her name legally changed to Vel because it was easier to pronounce. She has been a career blazer since the early age of seventeen when she entered a nationwide oratorical contest sponsored by the Elks and won a four-year scholarship to Howard University. She graduated with a B.S. degree in 1946.

While working on a master's degree, Vel Phillips met her husband. She states it was "love at first sight" and "we were perfectly matched"; they married in 1948. Dale Phillips was still in law school when they went on their honeymoon. Vel Phillips told her husband that she had always wanted to go to law school. In an effort to please his wife, he took a year off to save money, and the next year both Phillipses enrolled in Wisconsin School of Law. Dale Phillips graduated in 1950, a year ahead of Vel Phillips.

Phillips remembers law school being very difficult, and her instructors telling law students to look to the left and then to the right for those who would not graduate. It was also difficult financially: the Phillipses lived in a trailer to cut expenses. When she reflects on those years, Vel Phillips recalls the sexism exhibited by her fellow classmates. They would often say to her husband that he was lucky because with his wife in law school, he had a built-in secretary. Her response was, "If I wanted to be a secretary, why would I go to law school?"

Vel Phillips explains that a friend would have been the first black woman to graduate from Wisconsin School of Law, but circumstances forestalled that woman's graduation, opening the door for Phillips to become the first black woman to graduate. Years later she would serve on the board of trustees and the board of visitors at Wisconsin School of Law.

In 1951 Vel and Dale Phillips opened the law firm of Phillips and Phillips. It was Dale Phillips who suggested that they apply to practice before the federal bar. Once admitted to the bar, they discovered they were the first husband and wife attorney team to practice before Milwaukee's federal bar.

Vel Phillips started her political career shortly after graduating from law school. At the age of twenty-nine in 1953, she ran for a school board post in Milwaukee. This resulted in one of the few losses Phillips would encounter in her lengthy political career. Phillips believes that it was her hard work as a member of the League of Women Voters that helped create Milwaukee's second ward in 1955. When she realized that the second ward did not have an incumbent alderman, she asked her husband to run for the position. He agreed to run but later changed his mind. When she announced her own candidacy in October 1955, she discovered that no other woman, black or white, had ever served on the city council. She was told by her detractors that she was too delicate and fragile for the position and that she should stay home and bake bread.

Once it was decided that Vel Phillips would run for office, the next question was where she would get money to finance her campaign. She had saved more than three thousand dollars to buy a mink coat but decided instead to sink the money into her campaign. She started a campaign drive entitled "Get Out and Vote," having volunteers cover the entire one hundred sixty blocks that comprised the second ward. Due to her affiliation with the League of Women Voters, she became aware of the crowded living conditions, disease, and other problems affecting the second ward. These problems became the issues she spoke about throughout her campaign. In addition, she asked for advice and reviewed books and newspapers to discover techniques that had worked for other candidates.

In the March primary Phillips had the backing of the Democratic party but was in a four-way race with LeRoy J. Simmons, also black, and two write-in candidates, Frank J. Kanavz and Julian A. Nagel for the April election.

After the primary, Phillips discovered she was pregnant and considered dropping out of the race. However, her husband and friends convinced her to stay. She won the election by 1,713 votes. Phillips conceded that winning was not the most important thing, but "alerting people to the responsibility of exercising their voting privilege was in itself worthwhile to the community" (Clayton, 135).

When Phillips was sworn in she was wearing maternity clothes. After the birth of her first son, she stated that having a child gave her the ability to see her ward not only through the eyes of a woman but through those of a mother. Since she was the first woman to sit on the city council in its 115-year history, the seventeen other aldermen were presented with the question of how to address Phillips. After they reviewed several etiquette books, she was informed the council would address her as "Madame Alderman."

While she was working on the city council, Phillips continued working at the law firm. Due to her busy schedule, a full-time housekeeper was employed who did the cleaning and cooking. Phillips worked at home most of the time, attended council meetings on Tuesdays, took only interesting law cases, and gave speeches in the evening after her two children were sleeping. This routine allowed Phillips to be a wife, mother, lawyer and politician.

After sitting two years on the city council, Philips was

waging a battle for the seat of national committeewoman of the Democratic party a party elective office that allows one to cast a vote for the presidential nominee. She was running against Marguerite Benson, state vice-chairman, who in twenty-eight years had held various positions in the Democratic party. Phillips thought that Benson was getting too powerful. Phillips was sponsored by labor elements and Frank Wallick, Milwaukee editor of the *Wisconsin CIO News*. The campaign caused a bitter factional battle between blacks and whites. Phillips won, but only by 120 votes, and voices of dissent were still in the air after the election.

This position made Phillips the first black in the United States elected to serve on the National Democratic Convention Commission, and she held the position until 1964. Phillips was so respected that on May 24, 1960, she was named cochairman of the Committee on Rules and Order of Business.

Phillips had an easier election year in 1960 when she ran for reelection to her city council position. She beat her opponent, Edwin W. Froemming, by almost one thousand votes, and when she ran against Eleanora Wickstrom for national committee member, Phillips was reelected, and there were no voices of dissent this time.

While serving on the city council, Phillips viewed housing as her first priority and worked constantly to bring public housing and urban renewal programs to Milwaukee. She worked very hard to pass a bill outlawing housing bias; however, the council in 1961 would not pass such a bill. Phillips did not let this discourage her and, along with supporters, staged a sit-in campaign at the state capitol in Madison, Wisconsin. In 1962 Phillips proposed an ordinance that would end discrimination in the sale and rental of housing in Milwaukee, but again the council would not pass the ordinance. In fact, this proposed ordinance did not even get out of committee. But due to Phillip's persistance, Milwaukee passed a fair housing ordinance in 1968. Phillips continued her fight for laws outlawing discrimination, along with being an advocate for civil rights, women's equality, the conservation of energy, and full employment until she left office in 1972. While serving on the city council for sixteen years, Phillips served on the following committees: Board of Estimates, Special Recreation Committee, Finance Committee, and Special Radio and Television Program Committee.

An important milestone occurred in Phillips's career in 1971 when Governor Patrick J. Lucey appointed her a county judge of children's court to fill an unexpired term. She was the first black woman and one of a few women to become a judge in Wisconsin. In the same year, she was a graduate of the Summer College for Juvenile Court Judges. However, Phillips was defeated in 1974 when she ran for reelection.

Wisconsin's First Black Secretary of State Seated

After a four-year hiatus, Phillips achieved the highest pinnacle in her political career by becoming secretary of state in Wisconsin. She again would hold the distinction of being the first, this time the first black to hold this position in that state. Her husband, whom she describes as her greatest fan and severest critic, did not think she would win based on the polls. To his surprise and to that of others, not only did she win the election, but she received more votes than the Republican governor and lieutenant governor. While she held this position, many people thought she was the secretary of state's wife. This position allowed her to be acting governor at times, and there was talk the she might run for governor. She believes that is the reason there was a vigorous campaign against her when she ran for reelection. Phillips recalls wanting four more years as secretary of state, but she was defeated in 1982.

From 1982 through 1988, Phillips was Mrs. Dale Phillips, but she found the position boring, and it is not surprising that in 1988 she threw her hat back in the political arena by deciding to run for Congress. But her plan fell through due to her husband's illness; and on April 14, 1988, Dale Phillips died of a heart attack. She still misses him very much but continues to keep busy by giving speeches, participating in civic work, and practicing law. Phillips's life is also filled by grandchildren. "Whenever I am feeling down I call 442-1620," she says. This is the number of the YWCA named after her in Milwaukee.

During Phillips's illustrious career she has been involved in various organizations. She established the Vel Phillips Federated Girls Club under the auspices of the Wisconsin State Association of Colored Women's Clubs. She has been a member of the following: American Association of University Women; Women's International League for Peace and Freedom; board of the NAACP Day Care and Child Development Council, John F. Kennedy School; advisory board of Department of Local Affairs; Wisconsin Citizens for Fair Housing; United Church Women's Committee of One-Hundred; Milwaukee County Human Relations Television Council; National Citizens Committee for Community Relations; Links; board of Wisconsin Alliance for Children; board of Community Brain Storming Conference; Delta Sigma Theta; and board of Women's Court and Civil Conference. Phillips was also the cochair of the National Democratic Convention Committee on Rules and Order of Business.

The honors Phillips has received include the following: Howard University Alumni Achievement Award, 1960; Milwaukee Star Award for Service to Milwaukee Youths, 1967; "Woman of the Year" by Milwaukee Marquette University Chapter of Theta Sigma Phi Sorority, 1968; Junior Achievement Award; Junior Chamber of Commerce Award; and Hadassah Award. She was voted one of the Doers of the Decade by Theta Sigma Phi Sorority. She represented President Kennedy at Independence Day Ceremonies for the Upper Volta in 1961; visited Germany on a goodwill information trip in 1964; and was selected by the State Department to appear in a Voice of America film illustrating achievements of American blacks.

References

"Busiest Woman." *Crisis* 65 (October 1958): 506.

Clayton, Edward T. *The Negro Politician: His Success and Failure*. Chicago: Johnson Pub. Co., 1964.

Editors of Ebony. *The Ebony Success Library*. Vol. 1. *1,000 Successful Blacks*. Chicago: Johnson Pub. Co., 1973.

"Husband and Wife Teams." *Ebony* (January 1954): 68.

Jet (26 May 1966): 11; (16 September 1971): 10.

"Milwaukee." *Black Enterprise* (July 1972): 42.

"Milwaukee's First Lady Councilman." *Ebony* (June 1958): 40-45.

"The Negro Woman in Politics." *Ebony* (August 1966): 96-100.

Ploski, Harry A. and Warren Marr, II. *Negro Almanac*. New York: Bellwether.

"Pride in Achievement: Delta Woman." *Delta* 54 (May 1968): 30-38.

Scott, Gilbert. "In the News." *Black Enterprise* (January 1979): 10. Includes photograph.

"Two States Choose Black Women As Secretaries." *Ebony* (October 1979): 74-80. Photographs, pp. 74, 76, 80.

Who's Who Among Black Americans, 1990/91. 6th ed. Detroit: Gale Research, 1990.

"Women in Politics." *Ebony* (August 1956): 81-84. Photograph, p. 84.

Valerie S. Hartman

Annette L. Phinazee

(1920-1983)

Librarian, educator

Alethia Annette Lewis Hoage Phinazee, called a trailblazer for her work as a librarian and educator, was born on July 23, 1920, in Orangeburg, South Carolina. She had one brother and no sisters. Her parents, William Charles Lewis and Alethia Minnie Lewis, were educators who cherished the ideals of service, excellence, and active involvement in church and civic life. Annette Phinazee died in Durham, North Carolina, on September 17, 1983, after a long bout with cancer.

Annette Lewis married George Lafayette Hoage on April 22, 1944, and was widowed on August 22, 1945. The union was blessed with one child, a daughter, Ramona, who now directs the National Urban Coalition in Silver Spring, Maryland. Hoage's second marriage to Joseph Phinazee took place on July 14, 1962.

Phinazee attended the public schools of Orangeburg and graduated with a bachelor of arts degree in modern foreign languages from Fisk University in 1939. She received the bachelor of library science degree in 1941 and the master of library science degree in 1948 from the University of Illinois. In 1961 she was the first woman and the first black American woman to earn the doctorate in library science from Columbia University; and her dissertation, "The Library of Congress Classification in the United States," is a seminal and authoritative library science classic.

Phinazee launched her teaching career in North Carolina at the Caswell County Training School from 1939 to 1940 as a teacher-librarian. She was a cataloger in the library at Talladega College in Alabama from 1941 to 1942. From 1942 until 1944 she held the position of journalism librarian at Missouri's Lincoln University. She taught cataloging and classification courses at the Atlanta University School of Library Service (1946-57) and would become renowned as teacher and counselor to generations of black American librarians. Phinazee served for a period of time as a cataloger at Southern Illinois University (1957-62). She returned to Atlanta University as head of special services, which included the administration of the Trevor Arnett Library's Negro Collection—a world-renowned depository of American Africana (1962-67)—and returned to a professorship at the School of Library Service (1963-69). In 1969 Phinazee shouldered the assistant directorship of the Cooperative College Library Center in Atlanta. This was a library-centered service adjunct of the United Board for College Development whose mission was to develop college libraries in the historically black college and university sector of American academia.

Phinazee Chosen Dean

In 1970 Phinazee was chosen dean of the School of Library Science at North Carolina Central University in Durham. She held this position until her death in 1983. She provided innovative leadership as dean, and the school's program, founded in 1939, was accredited by the American Library Association for the first time in 1975. The Early Childhood Learning Center established under her leadership at North Carolina Central is unique among library information science offerings in the nation.

Phinazee was an active, respected, and concerned member of the American Library Association (ALA)—attending her first conference in 1948. She was concerned and disturbed about the racist attitudes and style of the association, and at the 1961 annual conference of the ALA meeting in Cleveland, Ohio, she expressed her displeasure at the fashion in which blacks were treated. The ALA soon passed stringent resolutions concerning freedom of access to libraries and curtailed the recognition of separate professional organizations in the segregated south. She was a member and chair of the Classification Committee of the ALA (1962-67) and was cochairperson of the Institute on the Use of the Library of Congress Classification in 1966—one of the benchmark meetings in the history of library classification in the United States. Phinazee chaired the Ad Hoc Committee on Cataloging Juvenile Literature in 1967. She held memberships in various ALA subdivisions: the Library Education Division, the ALA Council, the Intellectual Freedom Committee, Resources and Technical Services Division, the Association of College and Research Libraries Internship Committee, and the Advisory Committee to the Office of Personnel Resources. She was the first chairperson of the ALA's Standing Committee on Library Education and was elected the first black president of the North Carolina Library Association (NCLA). Additionally, she was a member of the Citizens Advisory Committee to the Governor's Conference on Library and Information Services and a delegate to the conference, later heading the North Carolina delegation to the White House Conference on Library and Information Sciences which was held in the nation's capital in the early 1980s. At its 1989 conference in Charlotte, North Carolina, NCLA awarded Phinazee a posthumous award as a "Trail Blazer" in North Carolina librarianship. She received distinguished service awards from the Black Caucus of the American Library Association and the Durham (North Carolina) Library Association. She served as a member of the executive committee of Beta Phi Mu Library Science Honorary Fraternity and was a charter member of Xi Chapter at Atlanta University.

Phinazee had a longtime interest in the bibliographical control of black library resources. While in Atlanta University, she spearheaded several national conferences on the bibliographical treatment of black library resources and goaded the Library of Congress to rethink its continued use of "Negro/Negroes" associations as descriptors in its subject cataloging. When the Institute on Materials By and About Negroes was held at Atlanta in 1965, Phinazee served as institute moderator, and later edited the proceedings. She was a consultant for a Ford Foundation project to improve library services in black colleges, codirected with Casper L. Jordan the feasibility study for the Cooperative College Library Center, and served on the United Negro College Fund Library Development Committee.

Bibliographical Control of African-American Materials Promoted

After taking the deanship in North Carolina, Phinazee continued to exhibit her interest and expertise in black American librarianship. She headed a three-year (1971-74), federally-funded project dealing with black library resources in six southeastern states: the African-American Materials Project. This was a cooperative venture initiated by selected historically black colleges and universities in Virginia, North Carolina, South Carolina, Georgia, Tennessee, and Alabama. During the life of the project a census of holdings in black Americana was made in these libraries. Several finding lists were published. AAMP, as the project was known, was the protype for a national project, but it was never funded. Phinazee played a stellar role in conducting, summarizing, and reporting most conferences covering black materials. She summarized an Institute for Training Librarians for Special Black Collections and Archives meeting held in Montgomery, Alabama, in 1973, and she served on the advisory board that planned the conference on Bibliographical Control of Afro-American Literature held in Chicago in 1976. She served on the board of directors of the Southeastern Black Press Institute of the University of North Carolina at Chapel Hill, which was transferred under her direction to North Carolina Central University in 1979.

A lifelong member of the United Presbyterian Church, Phinazee functioned as a ruling elder in Atlanta and Durham, superintendent of the Church School in Carbondale, Illinois, and as a member of the Board of Christian Education. She was the second vice-president of the Atlanta-Fulton County League of Women Voters. In Durham, she chaired the Citizen's Advisory Committee of the City Council and was a member of a New Horizons Fair Housing Task Force committee. She was designated a member of the North Carolina Assembly on Women and the Economy and was often called to testify before state and federal legislative hearings on matters concerning higher education. Two governors of North Carolina appointed Phinazee to serve on the North Carolina Public Librarian Certification Commission, the State Library Committee, and the State Advisory Council on Libraries.

Phinazee was a member of the Delta Sigma Theta sorority, Order of Eastern Star, Golden Circle, and Daughters of Isis.

Phinazees' first article, "Survey of Journalism Libraries," was published in *Special Libraries* in 1943. Her master's thesis, "Resignations in Two University Libraries," was the first turnover study of librarians, and her doctoral study on library classification, "The Library of Congress Classification in the United States" was a germinal study. She edited *The Black Librarian in the Southeast* (1980), a compilation of the proceedings of a 1976 colloquium on the historic place of black librarians in the southeast.

Phinazee was a tall, statuesque woman of medium brown complexion and, regardless of the dictates of style, she wore rimless glasses. A possessor of a dry sense of humor, she gave guidance and love to many of her former students. She was highly cerebral and disdained pedantry and superficiality. Her associates were many in educational, civic, and religious circles.

Speaking to black American librarians at the institute at Montgomery in April of 1973, she said:

> In the past, black librarians have made great personal sacrifices to identify, collect and preserve our heritage. We must continue to feel an obligation and do this. We cannot survive if we regress rather than progress—even standing still constitutes a loss. If our children in the streets can say "ain't nobody goin' to turn me around," librarians can too. We are better prepared to

defend ourselves than they are. The entire profession of librarianship is in the precarious position that it is because we have been selfish, intellectually snobbish, and short sighted. Black librarians cannot afford to use this model. We learned how to share our home. We have had to be shrewd, resourceful, and plan ahead in order to survive. We are learning (I hope) that it is foolish to be snobbish and prejudiced. We have made less progress in getting organized, but I hope that we now realize that this is a "must" and that we will "get with it" as quickly as possible. We have the ability—all we need is the desire and determination. I am optimistic about our future *if* we are willing to give what it takes. I warn you that it will not be easy, but I can tell you from experience it's a wonderful feeling when you have "given your all" to a worthy cause (*Lift Ev'ry Voice and Sing*, 105).

References

ALA Yearbook of Library & Information Science. Chicago: American Library Association, 1985. Obituary and photograph, p. 27.

Black Caucus of Librarians, eds. *Lift Ev'ry Voice and Sing*. Proceedings of the Institute for Training Librarians for Special Black Collections and Archives. Montgomery: Alabama State University, 1974.

Dean's Report to the Alumni. North Carolina Central University. School of Library Science. Durham: 1983.

Phinazee, Annette L., ed. *The Black Librarian in the Southeast; Reminiscences, Activities, Challenges*. Papers presented for a colloquium . . . October 8-9, 1975. Durham: North Carolina Central University, 1980.

Who's Who Among Black Americans. 2d ed., 1977-78. Chicago: Who's Who Among Black Americans, Inc., 1978.

Who's Who in Library and Information Services. Chicago: American Library Association, 1981.

Collections

Personal papers of Annette L. Phinazee are in the Woodruff Library of the Atlanta University Center and at North Carolina Central University.

Casper LeRoy Jordan

Ann Plato

(c. 1820-?)

Poet, educator

As is the case of many African-Americans born in the early decades of the nineteenth century, the facts of poet Ann Plato's birth are obscure. Several sources, however, list her birth date as 1820 or thereabouts. Born in Hartford, Connecticut, where she escaped the plague of chattel slavery, Ann Plato became a teacher. She taught very young children, being only fifteen or so herself. "The Infant Class" is a poem that describes her teaching experience.

Information regarding Ann Plato's family is nonexistent. We do know, however, that she grew up and resided in Hartford, Connecticut, where a small African-American community existed and where Congregationalism was the prevailing religion. Undoubtedly, Ann Plato benefited from both. A devout Congregationalist, she joined the church when she was thirteen years old. She reveals this information in one of her poems titled "Advice to Young Ladies." From her poetry we can also surmise that her paternal ancestors were native American. In "The Natives of America" she bemoans the oppression they felt and the land that they lost. "I Have No Brother" is the only other poem that gives any information about Plato's family. Apparently, she had a brother named Henry. He died when she was quite young.

Ann Plato's single volume of essays and poetry published in 1841 is introduced by the famous abolitionist, W. C. Pennington, pastor of the Colored Congregational Church in Hartford (Shockley, 26). In the introduction to Plato's book, *Essays; Including Biographies and Miscellaneous Pieces in Prose and Poetry*, Pennington writes:

> I am not in the habit of introducing myself or others to notice by the adjective "colored," &c., but it seems proper that I should just say here, that my authoress is a colored lady, a member of my church, of pleasing piety and modest worth (Plato, 1).

Pennington stresses Plato's youth. At the publication of her book, she would have been around twenty years old. However, many of the pieces were composed some years earlier. Pennington's "To the Reader" states the significance of Plato's work. He says: "The book contains her own thoughts, expressed in her own way" (Plato, 1). He also warns the reader not to be hypercritical of her style. "The best way to do justice to young writers," he advises, "is to weigh their thoughts without so strict a regard to their style as we should pay in the case of elder writers" (1).

Plato's book contains sixteen essays that range in topic from religion and education to the changing seasons and death. Commenting on her work, Joan Sherman states that Plato's writings are "the pious, moralistic effusions of a Puritan girl" (33). Shockley also places Plato's essays in the Puritan tradition, noting that her subjects are "Education," "Religion," "Benevolence," and "Employment" (27). These essays, judged harshly or otherwise ignored, nonetheless represent the *only* book by a black American between 1840 and 1865 "avowedly issued as a collection of essays" (Shockley, 26). The book is also only the second published by a black American woman.

William Robinson, commenting on Plato's essays, says that they are "self-righteous, routine essays . . . which, mercifully brief, have most value as species of essay compositions of the times" (13). His statement ignores that Plato is a woman, and an African-American, writing during a period in American history when neither was acknowledged as a full citizen and where the latter was thought subhuman and ineducable.

An interesting aspect of Plato's little book is the inclusion of four biographies. Plato eulogizes Louisa Sebury, Julia Ann Pell, Eliza Loomis Sherman, and Elizabeth Low in these brief biographies. Each young woman suffered ill health and died before age thirty. Seabury and Low both died in 1838, within months of each other. Pell and Sherman both died in 1839. Although not articulated in her biographies, these events must have traumatized young Ann Plato. Her essay, "Reflections Upon the Close of Life," voices some of her emotions:

> When we contemplate the close of life, the termination of man's designs and hopes; the silence that now reigns among those who, a little while ago, were so busy or so gay; who can avoid being touched with sensations at once awful and tender? (Plato, 72)

Plato's biographies provide a glimpse of what life must have been like for young, middle-class black women of New England. Even though these women appear to live sheltered and even charmed lives when compared to their enslaved southern sisters, slavery actually cast its malevolent shadow everywhere. Eliza Sherman endured pulmonary consumption. Plato reveals that the climate in Georgia would have suited Sherman better but "the laws" (slavery) prevented her going there (85).

Verse Typifies Early Works

Ann Plato's verse, consisting of twenty poems, typifies early nineteenth-century works. Her verse form is iambic tetrameter. Plato rarely departs from this form, and when she does, she does so unsuccessfully. The Puritan themes that dominate her essays also pervade the poetry. Considering the rate at which her young companions died, it is no wonder she is obsessed with the subject of death. Of the twenty poems, eleven have death as their themes.

Although her poetry is harshly criticized for lack of originality and political protest, perhaps Plato's most appealing poem is the romantic "Forget Me Not." Containing seven stanzas, the first one is representative of all:

> When in morning's misty hour,
> When the sun beems [sic] gently o'er each flower;
> When thou dost cease to smile benign,
> And think each heart responds with thine,
> When seeking rest among divine,
> Forget me not (106).

The sole poem concerning slavery is "To The First of August," which celebrates the abolition of slavery in the West Indies in 1838.

We know not when or how Ann Plato died. We know only that she sought to express herself in writing during a time when literacy for most black Americans was illegal. Thus, her efforts alone are noteworthy and for them she is remembered.

References

Plato, Ann. *Essays; Including Biographies and Miscellaneous Pieces, in Prose and Poetry*. Hartford: Printed for the Author, 1841. Reprinted. New York: Oxford University Press, 1988.

Robinson, William H., Jr. *Early Black American Poets*. Dubuque, Iowa: William C. Brown, 1969.

Sherman, Joan. *Invisible Poets*. Urbana: University of Illinois Press, 1974.

Shockley, Ann Allen. *Afro-American Women Writers 1746-1933*. Boston: G. K. Hall, 1988.

Nagueyalti Warren

Willa B. Player

(1909-)

Educator, government official, consultant

Willa Beatrice Player, a woman with many careers who moved to the top of her profession as an academician and college president, has only to point to her own life and work as an example to women who struggle to make strides in their own careers.

The daughter of Clarence E. and Beatrice D. Player, Willa Player was born in Jackson, Mississippi, the last of three children. The family moved to Akron, Ohio, in 1916, where

Willa B. Player

she attended elementary and high school. Her parents, who were identified with Methodism, insisted from her early childhood that she become involved with Sunday school, the youth choir, and other church organizations. Influenced by the Methodist church, Player attended a Methodist college, Ohio Wesleyan University, in Delaware, Ohio.

After graduating from college with a B.A. degree in 1929, Player began a teaching career in Latin and French at Bennett College, Greensboro, North Carolina. Bennett College had been cofounded in 1926 as a college for women by the Board of Education of the Methodist Episcopal Church and the Woman's Home Missionary Society. Obtaining her master's degree from Oberlin College, Oberlin, Ohio, in 1930, Player continued her studies in French at the University of Grenoble, France, and received the Certificat d'Edutes in 1935. Continuing her graduate studies at the University of Chicago and the University of Wisconsin in Madison, she eventually received a doctorate of education at Columbia University in New York City in 1948. Beginning her professional experience as an instructor in French and Latin at Bennett College, she was later promoted to the director of admissions, coordinator of instruction, and vice-president of Bennett College. On October 22, 1955, she became the first black woman president of Bennett College, a four-year women's college, and held this position until February 28, 1966.

In spite of the fact that Player had worked at Bennett College since 1930, many outsiders were shocked that the board of trustees had selected her as president of the college. According to many, the decision dealt men a shattering blow by breaking precedent. However, she had done such a remarkable job at the college that the move did not seem as startling on campus as it did off campus. She was questioned constantly about how it felt to be the center of all the attention—the first black woman employed as president of a four-year women's college. "All I was thinking about was that I had a job to do," she stated (Guy-Sheftall, 17). Most importantly, Player's breakthrough freed scores of other women to aim for the pinnacle of their profession. However, after she retired, a man became the next president of Bennett College. (In 1987, Bennett's second woman president, Gloria Scott, was elected.) Bennett College, to which Player devoted twenty-six years of her life, designated her as president emerita and endowed a chair in the humanities at the college in her honor in 1988.

As a former president of Bennett College, Player responded frequently to questions about the goals, purposes, and objectives of the college. According to her:

> Bennett College wants to be widely-known as a place where important questions are asked about life and human purpose, where students are taught to consider such topics with vitality, sensitivity, and concern. The college wants to be known as a place which prepares young women to face this complex world as they make their way through life (Telephone interview with Willa B. Player, 21 January 1991).

During her tenure as president of Bennett College, Player was repeatedly questioned about the relevance of a women's college in the twentieth century. Admittedly, since the sixties the number of women entering colleges and different careers attest to the steady progress women have made. Women are assuming leadership positions in all areas of employment. Yet a subtle prejudice still exists. Women still need to find out who they are before they enter into competition with males. Women's colleges provide such a stimulus and commitment to women. Player stated:

> I think the special mission of women's colleges is to ensure that all opportunities where women are able to combine all their talents are open to them. I believe that women have two outstanding talents that are not always present in males. One is the sense of commitment to serving others, coupled with their compassion for other people, and their ability to empathize with others. I think that a women's college can bring this out better than coed colleges. At a women's college, women have the opportunity to hold all the positions where their talents may be exercised without feeling that they have to complete with men (Guy-Sheftall, 16).

Feminism stresses the idea that neither of the two sexes should be directed by gender into a particular field. Each person has the right to pursue his or her hopes, dreams, or ambitions without regard to stereotypical thinking. A man or woman should be allowed to do what he or she wants or does not want to do, or can or cannot do, according to Player (Telephone interview with Player).

As an educator, Player is constantly questioned about the value of a liberal arts education in modern technological America:

> A liberal arts education furnishes a basic background which helps students to maintain a structure and discipline in their decision-making. Basic truths come out of liberal arts study; these truths serve as a guide as persons analyze and evaluate the needs of society today. In spite of the fact we are moving toward a technologically-oriented society, the critical thinking skills of a liberal educated person are still necessary (Telephone interview with Player).

Player feels that a danger exists in moving too rapidly from the liberal arts component of education as we respond to a technological society. The liberal arts have a real place in our culture as we try to understand values and develop a personal philosophy of life.

As a student, Player's interests are in the humanities, especially French and Latin. However, as a college president and curriculum specialist, she had an equal interest in the sciences for her students:

> The science education is important because of its critical importance in developing students' natural curiosity into the more abstract concepts and processes of science. Furthermore, our world has become more scientific-oriented and our students need to understand the underlying principles (Telephone interview with Willa B. Player).

Although the number of women enrolling in colleges and universities has remained constant, career goals have changed dramatically. No longer is a woman limited to home economics, foreign languages, education, and library science. In the past, women chose majors due to cultural indoctrination, but now we see more and more women moving into full-time careers in engineering, medicine, law, and computer science. This would have been rare in the fifties. Player stated:

> In large measure, we live in a male-oriented society and women have not been considered for certain roles. Women have been brought up by mothers and grandmothers to feel as if men should play the major roles in our society. There is a temerity there which is disappearing in the younger generation of women who are more aggressive. Secondly, whenever men and women have been in competition, women have tended to accept more responsibility, and this has been a danger signal for men that they dare not let this woman get too far, for she might surpass the mold and become the dominant person in controlling what happens in our world (Guy-Sheftall, 17).

Most professional positions today are filled through search committees that are designed, literally, to screen out prejudice on the basis of sex, race, age, or physical appearance. In spite of these committees, the picture is still not rosy. Black women still face color as well as gender bias. Player explains:

> While black women have chalked up a number of successes throughout history, they still face obstacles that leave them in a peculiar position today. Despite the odds a black woman is a woman for all seasons (Lumpkins, C-1).

In spite of her own achievement, Player is conscious of the stumbling blocks that women face in order to move up the ladder. Women still do the work, while most men do the directing. An ingrained prejudice that exists in society is detrimental to the potential of most women. If a woman is successful in management or higher education, then she stands out as highly unusual.

Player was able to assume the presidency of Bennett College because of her experiences in academe. No major in a given field prepared her for the responsibilities of the president of a college. She had taught, interpreted, and evaluated the curriculum throughout the years on all levels at the college. From a gradual accumulation of knowledge on the workings of a university, she developed the necessary experience to make meaningful decisions. In fact, her liberal arts background gave her the analytical, interpretative, and evaluative skills needed to think critically. With this background, she tackled problems and made decisions:

> I'm not sure that you can really train for the presidency. . . . I think you get to that role by simply combining your knowledge and your experience in such a way that you take the initiative in as many situations as you can in whatever work situation you find yourself. . . . You see the way you learn how to be an administrator is to be chair of the committee, is to lead a particular activity or even to plan a particular activity. And in this sense, I think women are preparing themselves for these kinds of roles without even realizing it. They are frequently unchallenged when they take the initiative because the men will permit the women to do all the work (Guy-Sheftall, 17).

For Player a person does not need a role model as much as critical thinking skills. When a person has confidence, self-esteem, plus acumen, she can manage to bring a situation to a logical conclusion. However, she does admire other people in academe and sees value in their positions. Player explains:

> I suppose if I were going to indicate who the one person was who had the greatest influence on me (and there were many people at Bennett who helped), it was Constance Warren, the president of Sarah Lawrence College. She had more of a vision of what women could become than all the rest of those people put together, but what we

> had to do with the rest of those people was to take their philosophies and remold them in terms of what our students needed. So, it wasn't just one role model. It was a whole lot of people who became involved in building a total college (Guy-Sheftall, 17).

Women Students Supported in Sit-Ins

Player was president of Bennett College at the outbreak of the civil rights movement in the sixties. The sit-ins at lunch counters, which began in Greensboro, North Carolina, affected the civil rights of black America and precipitated the dismantling of segregation in public accommodations in the United States. Although four male students at North Carolina Agricultural and Technical College, as it was known then, began these sit-ins, Player's students at Bennett College participated in these historic protests. She recalls:

> I was extremely proud of the Bennett girls as they questioned segregated Greensboro of the sixties. The college had always encouraged students' questioning and had equipped students with the tools to make responsible choices. Therefore, when the students questioned the validity of the continuation of segregation and wanted to participate in the sit-ins, I viewed that as dissent of a most reasonable kind (Telephone interview with Willa B. Player, 21 January 1991).

Player advised the women students to understand and evaluate their role and purpose in the civil rights struggle and then commit themselves to their goal. Her most recent award, "the Stepping Stone to Freedom Award," was presented to her for significant contributions to the civil rights movement of the sixties. She recalled that at the height of the sit-ins (1960-1964), Martin Luther King, Jr., could only speak at Bennett College when the Student Leadership Conference held a conference or institute in Greensboro.

Since the civil rights movement of the sixties, with its cry of elitism and racism, foreign-language departments have come under attack. The protesters consider the study of foreign languages as elitist. According to Player, this is not necessarily true:

> The value of the foreign language study is as valid today as in the past. The study of languages helps you to understand another culture, to contrast your own culture with another, and to appreciate your own even more. As a cosmopolitan person you identify with literature, art, music, and architecture on a much broader basis. The study of languages and literature does not have to exclude the languages, heritage, and culture of Africa and other non-European countries (Telephone interview with Willa B. Player, 21 January 1991).

Multiculturalism has become a goal for curriculum committees of the nineties. Increasing demands from ethnic groups have caused curriculum committees to encourage a need for cultural diversity in the curriculum. One reality of our times, according to Player, is that we have to deal with cultural diversity. The study of foreign languages can be helpful in this endeavor. A person can compare and contrast similarities and differences in other cultures and this, in turn, creates more understanding among people.

> Multiculturalism's day has arrived. Administrators must realize that the USA is not a melting pot, but represents many representatives of different cultures who wish to remain part of their cultural identity.
>
> The college or university should urge administrators to develop a multicultural curricula, demonstrate an institution-wide commitment to diversity and equality, and train faculty and staff in cross-cultural understanding (Telephone interview with Willa B. Player, 21 January 1991).

Praised as a visionary educator and an enlightened leader, Player received several honorary doctorates from colleges and universities across the United States. In constant demand as a consultant in higher education, she served the academic community diligently and well. A member of the board of trustees for the Charles Stuart Mott Foundation, she is a member of its Advisement Committee for Black Higher Education. Due to her expertise and knowledge as president of an historically black college, she served on the board of directors of the United Negro College Fund.

Federal Appointment Helps Strengthen Black Colleges

Upon her retirement from Bennett College, Player became the director, Division of Institutional Development, Bureau of Postsecondary Education, Washington, D.C., where she remained from February 1966 to April 1977. As director of the Division of College Support in the United States Office of Education, historically black colleges increased their federal support under Title III considerably. Under her direction, colleges and universities benefiting from the Strengthening Developing Institutions programs grew from 158 in 1966 to 555 in 1972.

A recipient of many awards, Player received the Superior Service Award in 1970 and the Distinguished Service Award from the United States Department of Health, Education and Welfare in 1972. As an outstanding alumna, she received a distinguished achievement citation from Ohio Wesleyan University in 1980. On September 15, 1984, the selection committee for the Ohio Women's Hall of Fame in Columbus chose Willa Player of Akron, Ohio, as an inductee for this honor, since she was the first black woman in America to become president of a four-year women's college.

Because of her affiliation with the United Methodist church, since 1984 she has served as a member of the University Senate of the United Methodist Church in Nashville, Tennessee. The United Methodist church supports several historically black colleges. After Willa Player was elected president of Bennett College, she continued her participation in the meetings of the Home Missionary Society both on campus and in the local church. However, because the college was supported on the national level by the church, she began to support more activities of the church nationally. Receiving invitations from Methodist women from all jurisdictions, she spoke at annual meetings, conducted seminars, and taught in mission schools for youth and adults. She held training sessions at Scarritt College in Nashville in preparation for schools of mission on issues related to the mission. For the first time for the church, she hosted an integrated national seminar for Methodist women at Bennett College on the theme "The Family in a World of Radical Social Change." In addition, she assisted United Methodist Women in an interpretation of the Charter for Racial Policy. She attended the Quadrennial Assemblies of the Women's Division, devoted to education and the conduct of world Christian missions. From 1962 to 1963 she was elected president of the National Association of Schools and Colleges of the Methodist Church. She has been deeply involved in the leadership among United Methodist Women as a representative of one of these outstanding institutions. Her life illustrates how a woman can be involved in the highest academic professional world and yet remain involved in mission work through the church.

Due to Willa Player's experience as president of a black college, she was a member of the Commission on Funding Black Colleges in Nashville from 1976 to 1984. The Ford Foundation made an extensive study on black colleges and again named her as a member of this committee. In addition, she served as a member of the board of trustees of Clark College in Atlanta, Georgia, until 1985 and as a member of the board of trustees of the Methodist Theological School in Ohio. She was a member of the board of trustees of Mount Union College in Alliance, Ohio, for one year. During her academic career and in retirement, she has been a consultant in higher education from 1977 to the present.

After retirement from government service in 1977, she has continued to provide her wisdom on many issues for the younger generations:

> One never really retires. My retirement has been wonderful. The younger people tend to value your experiences and you have time to respond to questions which they raise. You are constantly bringing forth your experiences to fortify the resolutions of their problems. The younger generation needs support for their decision and seems to appreciate helpful exchanges. They do not necessarily throw experience out of the window, and the retiree enjoys that (Interview with Willa B. Player, 21 January 1991).

Throughout the twentieth century Willa B. Player established a reputation as one of the century's most outstanding academicians.

References

"Educator Honored." *Atlanta Daily World*, 1 May 1984.

Guy-Sheftall, Beverly. "A Conversation with Willa B. Player." *Sage: A Scholarly Journal on Black Women* 1 (Spring 1984): 16-19. Photograph, p. 16.

Lumpkins, Barbara. "Black Women: Special Challenges, Rewards." *Akron Beacon Journal*, 4 February 1985. C-1.

Player, Willa B. Interview with author, 21 January 1991.

Who's Who Among Black Americans, 1990/91. Detroit: Gale Research, 1990. 1015.

Collections

Information on Willa B. Player can be found in the Bennett College Archives. Interviews with Player are in the Black Oral History Collection, Fisk University Library, and The Civil Rights Movement Project, Greensboro Public Library.

Joan Curl Elliott

Mary Ellen Pleasant "Mammy Pleasant"

(c. 1814-1904)

Civil rights activist, entrepreneur

Depending on the source, Mary Ellen "Mammy" Williams Smith Pleasant was either San Francisco's most venturesome civil rights pioneer or its most notorious procuress/madame/extortionist. Corroborative evidence tends to support both portraits, due to Pleasant's involvement in a number of California's most infamous court cases. As a civil rights pioneer, she did, in fact, help bring an end to racial discrimination on California's street cars in the case *Pleasants v. the North Beach and Mission Railroad Company*, appellant, brought before the California State Supreme Court in 1868. Other data, primarily newspaper and biographical sketches, credit Pleasant with helping to free blacks who were illegally held as slaves in California in the 1850s and she is credited with helping to secure the rights of blacks to have their testimonies accepted in California courts. Perhaps the most widely-reported account (and the most difficult to substantiate) has Pleasant providing financial support to John Brown for his raid on Harper's Ferry.

But yellow journalism and a healthy (or unhealthy) curiosity for pruriency aside, the preponderance of evidence,

Mary Ellen Pleasant

based on most newspaper and other written accounts, records Pleasant as a crafty survivor, whose sustenance and/or subsistence were the wealthy and powerful white male "clients" and the emotionally vulnerable "ingenues" whom she brought together as "partners" during the 1850s and 1860s in San Francisco.

Part of the imbalance in the historical portrait of Pleasant is due, perhaps, to the few corroborative details about her life. In the year of her eightieth birthday, Pleasant granted an interview to the *San Francisco Examiner* (13 October 1895). And she provided some sketchy details to an interviewer, Samuel Post Davis, for a *Pandex of the Press* article that appeared in January 1902, also in San Francisco. Helen Holdredge's partially fictionalized biography, *Mammy Pleasant*, 1953, lacks documentation. Apparently, Pleasant made few, if any, individuals privy to details about her private life. Perhaps her silence was linked to her fierce protection of the secrets, incriminating or otherwise, of her many business clients. Simply stated, no one is likely to know the full story of the life of one of California's most colorful individuals.

A *San Francisco Chronicle* article (9 July 1899) claims that Pleasant was reared on the Helmcken estate in Virginia. Other accounts list Georgia as her place of birth (*The Oakland Tribune*, 3 September 1916). In *Pandex of the Press*, Pleasant stated that her birth took place 19 August 1814 at 9 Barley Street, Philadelphia, Pennsylvania. To add to the confusion, Pleasant also claimed that she was born, not a slave, but a free black to a black Louisiana mother and a Kanaka or Hawaiian father, named Louis Alexander Williams, who was an importer of silks. Meanwhile, other speculation has it that Pleasant was the slave-born daughter of a black—possibly mulatto mother—and a white plantation owner father. The *Oakland Tribune* (3 September 1916) reported that, as a young girl, Pleasant so impressed a visitor to the Georgia plantation where she was a slave that he told her owner that Pleasant was too smart to be a slave and the visitor purchased Pleasant's freedom for six hundred dollars. But, at the age of six Pleasant worked as a store clerk for the family of Phoebe Hussey, who were Quakers in Nantucket, Massachusets, and she did not receive the Boston education that the visitor promised.

Later moving to Boston, Pleasant first married a wealthy black Cuban tobacco planter named Alexander Smith, who moved in abolitionist circles with the likes of William Lloyd Garrison and Wendell Phillips. Upon Smith's death, he reportedly left Pleasant a forty-five-thousand-dollar legacy, mostly bonds, and made her promise to use the money for the abolition of slavery (*Oakland Tribune*). After Smith's death in 1848, Mary Ellen Smith married John J. or James Pleasant (or Plaissance, depending on the source). J. Pleasant had been an overseer for Alexander Smith. Though the Pleasants moved west to California in 1849, during the California gold rush, James Pleasant dropped out of accounts of Mary Ellen Pleasant's life in California.

Shortly after Mary Ellen Pleasant's arrival in San Francisco in 1850, wealthy merchants and miners participated in an auction for her services as a five-hundred-dollar-a-month cook. In a lengthy account of Pleasant's arrival and of the subsequent bidding war for her culinary services, the *San Francisco Call* (7 May 1899) uncovered the aura and the smart business sense associated with Pleasant, which were to become her trademarks. A crowd of wealthy white merchants and miners rushed to the waterfront where a ship had just come in from around Cape Horn, bearing a number of pioneers and one rather well-known black woman, hailed as "one of the great Southern cooks," reported the *Call*. The demand for her services as a cook were so high that Pleasant instructed the group to conduct a bidding and offered to work for the highest bidder. The bidding stopped at five hundred dollars per month for cooking services that excluded dishwashing or washing of any other kind. But as the *Call* reported, "when the lucky bidder offered at once to escort her with becoming pomp to his bachelor's quarters and install her as goddess of the cook stove, Mammy suddenly folded her arms and calmly announced that she had changed her mind." She demanded time to think the offer over.

The *San Francisco Call* account depicts dejected men of means, many of them bachelors, anxiously awaiting a decision to work from the only reputable cook in the scarcely-settled mining district. Many of the miners and merchants likely had southern roots and were more than a little familiar with the southern, Louisiana-style cuisine of a former slave woman. But Pleasant declined the offer, choosing instead to open up a boardinghouse where all the bidders could enjoy her cooking skills.

Pleasant lent, at 10 percent interest, portions of the Smith legacy to miners and other businessmen. She told the *San*

Francisco Examiner that she came to San Francisco with fifteen thousand dollars in gold coins, which she lent to several businessmen. "My custom was to deposit silver and draw out gold, by which means I was able to turn my money over rapidly," she said. For the next ten years, until 1858, Pleasant's Washington Street boardinghouse grew and prospered, housing some of the most important and influential businessmen in California. During this time, Pleasant gained the reputation of procuress, reportedly matching wealthy, often married, men with attractive young women, primarily as mistresses, though some were brief affairs, and some of the liaisons among singles resulted in marriage. Charles C. Dobie, who wrote of having seen Pleasant when he was a child, described the climate of the mining community in which Pleasant lived and worked:

> San Francisco, in 1848, did not offer much in the matter of diversions to men of taste. The dancing-halls, the gambling-halls, the houses of joy were crass and bawdy. Mammy Pleasant's boarding-houses provided similar entertainment leavened with quality, with finesse: After the table was cleared there were cards and drinks and even female companionship (*San Francisco: A Pageant*, 318).

According to the *San Francisco Chronicle* (9 July 1899), Pleasant guarded the private indiscretions of her clients until her death, a practice that doubtless earned her even more clients and led to profitable business ventures. The *Chronicle* reported that although she was offered numerous bribes, Pleasant fiercely protected the secrets or "family skeletons" that involved her clients. Once offered fifty thousand dollars to divulge potentially damaging information about a prominent San Francisco man, Pleasant declined, saying that she "never needed money badly enough to betray a friend."

Civil Rights of Blacks Promoted

In the 1850s and 1860s, Pleasant reportedly secured a reputation as a helpmate to blacks in California who were illegally held as slaves. The Compromise of 1850 resulted in California being brought into the Union as a free state. W. Sherman Savage writes that Pleasant rescued blacks from owners who had recently come to California, bringing their slaves with them. The *San Francisco Call* (7 May 1899) reported, without attribution, that Pleasant had come to California with "a price on her head in the South" due to her involvement with the Underground Railroad that moved slaves from the South to the North and Canada. Planters whose slaves Pleasant had allegedly helped to escape sought her capture.

Details are scarce about Pleasant's exact role in securing freedom for California blacks in illegal captivity. But court records do prove Pleasant's involvement in helping establish civil rights and legal redress for blacks in and around San Francisco. For example, she is credited with winning the right of blacks to have their testimonies accepted in California courts in 1863. And in 1868, Pleasant successfully sued two San Francisco railway companies for refusing to permit blacks to ride on the city's streetcars. (Pleasant had been refused admittance by a conductor on a city streetcar, prompting a lawsuit.)

In January 1868 the California State Supreme Court, in *Pleasants v. North Beach and Mission Railroad*, upheld the ruling of a lower court that had returned a damage action against a railway company for refusing to allow Pleasant passage. The District Court of the Twelfth Judicial District of San Francisco had awarded Pleasant five hundred dollars in damages against the North Beach and Mission Railroad Company, which then appealed the case to the State Supreme Court. Records from the January 1868 session of the California State Supreme Court give the following account:

> Measure of Damages For Refusing to Receive Passenger on Street Car.—Plaintiff, Mary E. Pleasants, who is a person of color, being desirous to take passage on defendant's street railroad car in San Francisco, hailed the Conductor, requesting him to take on board, which he failed to do. The Conductor stated immediately after, in reply to a request of a passenger to take plaintiff up, as requested, that "We don't take colored people in the cars." There was at the time ample room in the car to accommodate plaintiff, who was ready and willing to pay the fare. There was no proof of any special damage. Plaintiffs had a verdict and judgment for five hundred dollars (*Reports of Cases Determined in The Supreme Court of the State of California*, 586).

Interestingly, the railroad company based its appeal not on its right to refuse passage to blacks but on the assumption that there was no evidence of malice or ill will in the conductor's refusal to admit Pleasant, and that the damages awarded were, at most, excessive, and at the least, unwarranted. To fully appreciate Pleasant's valiance and ultimate contribution in bringing forth the lawsuit, it is important to note that neither the California State Supreme Court nor the lower San Francisco Twelfth Judicial District Court held any precedent in the form of legal statutes for cases involving individual and racial discrimination prior to the Pleasant case in 1868, and a similar case, *Turner v. North Beach and Mission Railroad*, in 1866. In view of the railroad's failure to base its defense on a right to deny admission to persons of color and in the subsequent rulings of both the district court and the state supreme court, one can conclude, perhaps, that all parties recognized the common-law duty of a railway company to allow admittance and passage to the public without regard to race or color. It was in 1893, in fact, that the California legislature enacted a statute prohibiting racial discrimination in places of public accommodation.

In an analysis of the Pleasant case, the *Hastings Law Journal* concludes that the decision of the California courts was based on "concern for monopoly status of a common carrier that would refuse service to someone for no antagonistic reason'' rather than on a desire to remedy racial discrimination. ''Historically there was early common law doctrine that . . . common carriers had a duty to extend their facilities to all members of the public in the absence of some reasonable justification for not doing so'' (276).

But the most persistent (and thus far unproven) account of Pleasant's support of abolitionism is her alleged financial support of John Brown in his raid on Harper's Ferry. Details about this alleged deed appear in Delilah Beasley's *The Negro Trail Blazers*, Dobie's *San Francisco; A Pageant*, and numerous newspaper accounts, such as the *Oakland Tribune* (3 September 1916). The *San Francisco Chronicle* writes that in 1858, Pleasant returned East, met and befriended John Brown at Chatham, Canada, and gave him thirty thousand dollars to finance the raid on Harper's Ferry. Pleasant was supposed to aid Brown by inciting slaves to revolt. She was said to have blamed the failure of the raid on Brown's premature attack, started before large forces could be organized. Upon capture, Brown supposedly carried a note signed ''W. E. P.'' which Pleasant claimed were her initials, the ''W'' being mistaken for what was really the letter ''M.'' W. Sherman Savage writes that although Pleasant evidently traveled East and bought property in Chatham, Massachusetts in September 1858, there is insufficient evidence that she met John Brown or provided him with money, especially since he had left Canada in May of that year. Furthermore, John Brown's biographer, Oswald Garrison Villard, who was the grandson of William Lloyd Garrison, gives no credence to the story.

Questionable Businesses Practices Developed

Returning to California after the alleged involvement in John Brown's activities, Pleasant began building favor among California's wealthiest miners. In 1869, she opened an establishment, Geneva's Cottage, on San Jose Road. There she entertained ''proteges'' until business slowed, and she turned to ranching and raising produce. Pleasant was seen often driving a team to the old Washington Market where she, dressed in blue jeans, a woolen shirt, and wearing a slouch hat, would trade produce. But the innocent country woman of simple pleasures is a far cry from the swarthy, mysterious woman observers say later moved into the home of Thomas Bell, a wealthy white businessman, and his new wife, the former Teresa Clingan, and entered into a strange, triangular business relationship with the couple.

This portrait of Pleasant, according to the *San Francisco Examiner*, is that of a ''tall, spare, and erect'' woman who ''always affected a black dress and hat, with white apron and neckerchief, and a green and black tartan shawl thrown over her shoulders.'' The image evoked was that of a marketer and household manager, a far cry from the image of a shrewd financier. Charles C. Dobie describes Pleasant as ''ashen black'' and having high cheek bones, a well-formed nose, thin ''scornful'' lips and ''one blue eye.'' According to Dobie, Bell was a wealthy Scotch banker whom Pleasant had met in her boardinghouse operator days. Pleasant reportedly had brought the couple together before moving with them into a three-story San Francisco mansion, dubbed ''The House of Mystery.''

Transcripts resulting from a lawsuit that developed between Pleasant and the Bell family, after the death of Thomas Bell, reveal that she held an unusual amount of power and influence over the couple and their finances. Bell had died after a mysterious fall from an upper-floor window at his home. But suspicion surrounding Pleasant's possible role in his death dissolved when Bell's will revealed that he left no money or property to her. Trial records reveal that Pleasant's name appeared on the deeds to numerous properties apparently owned by Bell. The ''House of Mystery'' itself was reportedly planned and designed by Pleasant, though purchased with the Bells's money (Dobie, 320). The *San Francisco Chronicle* reports the following story: In a scheme to get money from Thomas Bell, Pleasant sent Mrs. Bell to San Leandro but told Thomas that his wife was vacationing in New York and in need of twenty-five thousand dollars. After Bell sent the money, Pleasant went to him, claiming that his wife had been robbed of the money. Bell sent another twenty-five thousand dollars, and his wife returned home.

In another scam, Pleasant reportedly charged the Bell estate with stall fees of twenty-five dollars a month for carriages that, in actuality, she had sold to Slocum and Company years earlier. Yet another story tells of William Tomlinson, a blind butler to the Bell family, who received one hundred thirty dollars from relatives in his native Scotland. Pleasant offered to keep the money for Tomlinson and to pay him higher interest than the banks. He never saw the money again. Such was Pleasant's apparent ability to manage, freely, the financial and business affairs of Thomas Bell that her name was found on the deed to the Bell homestead. The legal entanglements resulting from Pleasant's financial involvement with the Bells were so complicated that litigation continued well past Pleasant's death, with a showing of far less than a million dollars remaining in the estate (*Chronicle*).

In yet another case involving the mysterious deeds of Pleasant, a young woman named Sarah Althea Hill sued a United States senator from Nevada, William Sharon, for breach of a marriage contract. Allegedly, Hill had been Sharon's mistress. When he broke off the relationship, Hill sued and was backed by five thousand dollars from Pleasant to cover legal fees Speculation is that Pleasant spent money from the Thomas Bell estate to finance the Hill case. Hill argued that William Sharon had signed a contract of marriage with her. Pleasant, who talked extensively about the famous case in the *Examiner*, claimed that she befriended Sarah Hill just prior to the broken engagement and counseled her to sue Sharon for financial damages. Pleasant blamed Sharon for trying to discard an unwanted mistress. Sharon blamed Pleasant (and Hill) for forging a marriage contract. Although Hill won her case in a state court, a federal judge later overturned the decision, declaring the marriage contract a forgery. The judge also pronounced Pleasant a ''scheming, trafficking, crafty old woman'' for her role in the case (Savage, 76).

Pleasant is said to have spent part of the fortune she wrested from the Bell estate on numerous "proteges and retainers," many of them apparently black. For example, one account has Pleasant securing a monopoly on domestic jobs for black women in California (*Schomburg Clipping File*). Another account claims that Pleasant "gained a reputation of generosity" by giving charitable support to black families and to churches "out of bounty extracted from her employer" (*San Francisco Examiner,* 1 January 1904). Pleasant herself told the *Examiner* that she frequently loaded her carriage with food and took it to churches and hospitals. But other accounts suggest that the true beneficiary of Pleasant's philanthropy was Pleasant herself. Numerous black families who had made Pleasant executrix of their estates ended up penniless. According to the *San Francisco Examiner*, "little or no benefit resulted to the heirs from [her] administration of their properties," and she proved elusive to the courts that sought to punish her.

After a quarrel with Teresa Bell, following the death of Thomas Bell, Pleasant was evicted from the House of Mystery on Octavia and at Bush Streets in San Francisco. In June 1899, Pleasant went to bankruptcy court and was declared financially insolvent, though she was actually worth from thirty-five thousand dollars to 150 thousand dollars (*Oakland Tribune*). Reportedly, Pleasant made a few well-publicized trips to various individuals, asking for bread and other essentials. A few years later, an acquaintance, Mrs. Lyman Sherwood, visited Pleasant at her 2107 1/2 Webster Street home and found her without food. Mentally acute to the end, though in frail health physically, Pleasant moved in with Mr. and Mrs. Sherwood, November 19, 1903, and reportedly gave them power of attorney over what remained of her estate. But in Peasant's will she designated another friend, Samuel Post Davis, to continue the many lawsuits she brought against the Bell estate after her death. Additionally Pleasant had transferred all of her property to Davis before her death, saying that he aided her during her insolvency (*Oakland Tribune*).

Pleasant died of old age at 10:55 on the morning of Monday, January 11, 1904, at the home of Lyman M. Sherwood (described in the *San Francisco Examiner* as a pension attorney) at 2751 Filbert Street in San Francisco, California. She was buried in the Sherwood burial lot at Napa on the following Wednesday.

References

"Angel or Arch Fiend in the House of Mystery?" *The San Francisco Call*, 7 May 1899.

Beasley, Delilah. *The Negro Trail Blazers of California*. Los Angeles: 1919. Reprinted. San Francisco: R and E. Associates, 1968.

Davis, Samuel Post. *Pandex of the Press*. San Francisco: January 1902.

Dobie, Charles C. *San Francisco; A Pageant*. New York: Appleton-Century Co., 1939.

The Hastings Law Journal 17 (1965-66). University of California. Hastings College of the Law. San Francisco, California.

Holdredge, Helen. *Mammy Pleasant*. New York: Putnam, 1953.

Index to the Schomburg Clipping File. New York Public Library. Alexandria, Va.: Chadwyck-Healey, 1986.

"Life Story of Mammy Pleasant." *The San Francisco Examiner,* 13 October 1895.

"Mammy Pleasant is Dead at Age of Ninety." *San Francisco Chronicle,* 12 January 1904.

"Mammy Pleasant Will Work Weird Spells No More." *San Francisco Examiner,* 11 January 1904.

Oakland Tribune, 3 September 1916.

"Remarkable Career of Mammy Pleasant and Her Wonderful Influence Over Men and Women." *San Francisco Chronicle,* 9 July 1899.

Reports of Cases determined in The Supreme Court of the State of California, at the October Term, 1867, and January Term, 1868. Vol. 34. San Francisco: Bancroft-Whitney Company, 1887.

San Francisco Chronicle, 9 July 1899.

San Francisco Examiner, 13 October 1895; 1 January 1904.

Savage, W. Sherman and Rayford W. Logan. "Mary Pleasant." *Notable American Women: 1607-1950*. Vol. 3. Cambridge, Mass: Harvard University Press, 1971.

"The True Story of Mammy Pleasant." *The Oakland Tribune*, 3 September 1916. Reprinted from *The San Francisco News-Letter*.

Collections

Photographs of Mary Ellen "Mammy" Pleasant are available at the Bancroft Library, University of California at Berkeley. The Schomburg Clipping File of the Schomburg Center for Research on Black Culture, also contains materials on Pleasant.

Helena Woodard

Dorothy Porter

(1905-)

Library curator, librarian

Dorothy Porter has played a pivotal role in setting standards for collecting African-Americana. This exemplary role began with collecting the invaluable manuscripts and archives that laid a foundation for building at Howard University in Washington, D.C., the largest repository for the study of African-American history in an academic institution. Her work helped bring recognition to the value of African-American research resources and the importance of their collection, preservation, and dissemination and served as a model for structuring similar collections, particularly in black libraries.

Dorothy Louise Burnett Porter was born in Warrenton, Virginia, to Hayes Joseph Burnett and Bertha (Ball) Burnett, on May 25, 1905. Her father was a physician and her mother an expert tennis player. She was the oldest of the four offspring—Hayes Joseph Burnett, Jr., Leonie Withers, and Alice Earnestine. Dorothy Burnett attended elementary, junior, and senior high schools in the middle-class suburban neighborhood of Montclair, New Jersey. She came to Washington, D.C., in 1923 and by 1925 she had attained a diploma from the Miner Normal School in the city. She continued her formal education at Howard University, Washington, D.C., and by 1928 earned a B.A. degree.

Dorothy Porter received her B.S. in 1931 and the M.S. in 1932, both library science degrees from Columbia University in New York. This was accomplished despite the fact that she was told that she would be unable to achieve her goal. She became the first black American to graduate from Columbia's library school.

In 1930 she married James Amos Porter, an artist and member of the fine arts department and later department head at Howard University. They had one child, Constance Burnett, born in 1939. Constance Burnett married Milan Uzelac, and they live in Marina Del Rey, California. James Porter died in 1970, and on November 30, 1979, Dorothy Porter married historian Charles Harris Wesley, who died on August 16, 1987. Her religious affiliation has been Episcopalian, and her sorority is Delta Sigma Theta.

Dorothy Porter began her professional career in 1925 as librarian of the Miner Teachers College, where she substituted for one year for the librarian who was on leave. She was cataloger at the Carnegie Library of Howard University from 1928 to 1930, being appointed to build a collection on blacks. She met this responsibility with complete dedication. Soon the collection that she developed was named the Moorland Foundation, the Negro Collection, the Library of Negro Life and History. Her assignment became her life's avocation and resulted in an outstanding collection that flourishes today to the benefit of thousands of researchers. It is currently known as the Moorland-Spingarn Research Center.

By the time black studies became recognized as an academic discipline after the clamor for civil rights in the 1960s, Dorothy Porter was a deft professional—one who had cultivated the skills, collected the resources, and mastered the craft, and hence was an ardent and enthusiastic guide to those who were trying to teach themselves black history so they could be effective pacesetter instructors—those who suddenly found themselves teaching neglected black American history to the history-hungry youth of the post-Martin Luther King, Jr., era.

Dorothy Porter in 1930 began her charge of building the Moorland Collection by literally walking the stacks of Howard's library. She isolated and organized into a cohesive collection all of the approximately three thousand items on African-Americans that were to form the nucleus of a collection that evolved from the original gift by Jesse E. Moorland of his private library in 1914. An earlier gift in 1873 of Lewis Tappan's antislavery material was incorporated into this Negro collection, which grew phenomenally before Dorothy Porter retired in 1973. Along with books, pamphlets, serials, and periodicals, these materials include an original collection of pioneering black newspapers, vertical file items, microfilm, prints and photographs, manuscript and oral history materials, and three-dimensional memorabilia and artifacts that now constitute the pride of the center's museum collection. By the time of her retirement, the collection had reached a phenomenal size, having grown to 180,000 cataloged items from its humble 3,000 item core collection.

It is through the acumen and perspicacity of curator Dorothy Porter that the richness and diversity of the collection is cataloged in an effective and precise manner. She found the traditional system inappropriate for the collection and insufficient to incorporate the multiplicity and diversity of materials on African-American history and culture. Porter developed a pragmatic arrangement that is extremely effective and functional.

The success of Dorothy Porter's mission was not to be hampered by bureaucratic limitations, inadequate budgets, insufficient staff size, and inadequate support services. Her dedication, persistence, and perseverance, coupled with her ingenuity, caused her to triumph in spite of all odds against success. The knowledge she acquired from the collections that she acquired and processed became her richest resource. Armed with this intelligence, Dorothy Porter actively pursued every lead, no matter how remote, to acquire another deserving item for the collection. She routinely contacted book dealers and collections through correspondence and personal visits to accomplish her goals. This noble pursuit remained central during her travels and vacations and continues to motivate her. Her quest then, as now, is to document the richness of experience of African people without limits of language, geography, or chronology.

Dorothy Porter has been a productive scholar who practiced what her efforts silently preached. She has compiled several bibliographies and finding aids for study and research on African-American themes. A prolific writer, she has made major contributions through the following works: *Early Negro Writing, 1760-1837* (Boston: Beacon Press, 1971); *North American Negro Poets* (Hattiesburg, Miss.: The Book Farm, 1945); *Negro Protest Pamphlets* (New York: Arno Press, 1969); *The Negro in the United States: A Selected Bibliography* (Washington, D.C.: The Library of Congress, 1970); and *Afro-Braziliana, A Working Bibliography* (Boston: G. K. Hall, 1978). Her other publications, too numerous to identify here, appeared in serials such as the *Journal of Negro History, Howard University Bulletin, Phylon, Journal of Negro Education, Bulletin of Negro History, Opportunity,* and *African Studies Bulletin.* Included in these works are a number of articles on building black collections and documenting the black experience in library collections.

Dorothy Porter's list of honors and awards is impressive. Many of these came in recognition of her contributions to the study of African-American history. She was Ford Foundation consultant to the National Library, Lagos, Nigeria, from 1962 to 1964. She received the distinguished service award from students of Howard University's College of Liberal Arts in 1971. The University of Susquehanna, Pennsylvania, in 1971 awarded her the doctor of letters, and in 1989 Syracuse University awarded her the doctor of humane letters. Her most recent honorary degree—doctor of humane letters—was awarded in February 1990 from Radcliffe College. Upon her retirement, Founder's Library at Howard University dedicated the Dorothy B. Porter Room in her honor on June 8, 1973. For the 1988-1989 year she was visiting senior scholar at the W. E. B. Du Bois Institute for Afro-American Research at Harvard University. On October 27, 1989, the University of Utah honored her with the Oladah Equino award of "excellence for pioneering achievements." She is a member of Phi Beta Kappa and holds membership in numerous professional organizations.

An informal survey in 1990 of scholars around the country on Dorothy Porter's professional contributions brought recognition of her scholarship and documents further her position in American and African-American history. John Hope Franklin expressed deep appreciation for her work; Louis Harlan recognizes the "remarkable example" she set with her "legendary knowledge"; Henry S. Robinson called her a "walking encyclopedia"; and James H. Billington sees her as "a librarian extraordinaire." Darlene Clark-Hine recognizes her as a "beacon light" and Adelaide Cromwell said that her "desire to help goes beyond the walls of the library." Donald Stewart says Dorothy Porter is a "librarian's librarian and a scholar's scholar"; she "knows more about black history than anyone else in the country," said Dorothy Sterling, and Benjamin Quarles concludes that she is "destined to live in history" (Bhan, "Profile of a Collector").

Dorothy Porter Wesley currently resides in Washington, D.C.

References

Bhan, Esme. "Dorothy Porter: Profile of a Collector." Paper read at the Seventy-Fifth Annual Conference of the Association for the Study of African-American Life and History, Chicago, October 26, 1990.

Wesley, Dorothy Porter. Interviews with the author, June 1990-January 1991.

Who's Who Among Black Americans, 1990/1991. Detroit: Gale Research, 1990. 1022.

Collections

The personal papers of Dorothy Porter Wesley are in her possession. The vertical file of the Moorland-Spingarn Research Center, Howard University, also contains photographs and information on her.

Esme E. Bhan

Ersa Hines Poston

(1921-)

Government official

Ersa Hines Poston, apart from a career in public service as a government official in a number of capacities, has been a member of many professional organizations, and worked for many civic causes, foundations, seminars, and clubs. Her life has been dedicated to improving the economic opportunities of women, particularly black women. It was her efficient, intelligent, and caring approach to problem solving that prompted New York governor Nelson A. Rockefeller to call her "an able administrator and a creative planner of programs to expand opportunities and horizons" (*Ebony Success Library,* Vol. 2, 200).

Ersa Hines Poston was born in Paducah, Kentucky, May 3, 1921, to Vivian (Johnson) Hines and Sherman Hines. Her mother, a Cherokee Indian, died of tuberculosis when Poston was four, and she was brought up by her paternal grandmother. She later said that "in our family education was an obsession. Accomplishment was something that was driven into me every moment of my life" (*Ebony Success Library,* Vol. 2, 198). She eventually graduated from Kentucky State College with a bachelor of arts in 1942 and from Atlanta

University with a master of social work in 1946. She thought of medicine and then aimed for social work. Later she said that she "became interested in social work during the depression when so many people around us were going hungry" (199). She did not marry until 1957. Then she wed Theodore "Ted" Poston, a well-known journalist with the *New York Post*. They had no children and Poston has been a widow for many years. She now resides in Maryland.

After finishing her master of social work degree at Atlanta University, her first job was in Hartford, Connecticut, with the Tuberculosis and Health Association. Her interest in both medicine and social work and in this first job was probably inspired by the circumstances of her mother's death.

Once she began her career, her rise was very rapid. Soon she moved to the state of New York, where she stayed for two years. Her rise in government ranks could be seen as spectacular. Ersa Hines Poston herself would see it quite differently. She said that "what might have appeared to others as significant accomplishments may have been the result of being *in place* at the *right time*. In order to be 'in place' meant years of training and experience to be prepared to assume such responsibilities and positions which brought some degree of recognition" (Poston, 4).

Government Positions Held

When she moved to New York, it was first to New York City government and eventually to New York State government. First, Poston was the director of the Clinton Community Center on the West Side of Manhattan, from 1950 to 1953. Next, she became field secretary for the New York City Welfare and Health Council and then, from 1955 to 1957, she was assistant director, Office of the Mayor, New York City Youth Board. She then went to the state government as the area director, New York State Youth Commission, from 1957 to 1962, and Youth Work Progress director, New York State Division of Youth. From 1962 to 1964 she was confidential assistant to Governor Nelson A. Rockefeller in Albany, and from 1965 to 1967 she was director of the New York State Office of Economic Opportunity. She seemed well on her way to fulfilling her own statement of a goal—"to be one day in a top leadership position in the Federal Government where, hopefully, one might have the opportunity to influence the social and public policies that shape the life and destinies of many people" (Poston, 4). Her next position was as president and member of the New York State Civil Service Commission. In this job she was responsible for ensuring that people were rewarded for merit and for no other reason; her task was to make the New York Civil Service fair to all its workers, and to prevent capricious or even spiteful punishments. That she did so very well is indicated by her next position as vice-chair, Merit Systems Protection Board, Washington, D.C., which she assumed in 1977. "Explaining the Special Council (of that Board) she said that it 'would have the power to propose disciplinary action. . . .' For example, you—having 'blown the whistle' on your boss—might find yourself suddenly reassigned to Lower Slobovia. Is this a reprisal? The Special Council could stop that reassignment or similar action while investigating, could cancel the move, and bring charges against your boss" (Keathley, 25).

As a member of that board she has stated that she believes "both conceptually and philosophically that a representative work force is good, sound, public policy. In order to achieve this, one does not have to compromise the merit principles nor lower the quality of the public work force" (Poston, 4). Indeed, while in New York, she developed a career development plan that over a number of years trained and employed thousands of people that others seemed to have given up on. "Our retention figure is 70 percent. We've just gone into the ghettos and found candidates. We have to have social commitments if we are going to meet our manpower needs. . . . The program is designed to start workers on a career ladder and then help them move up" (*Ebony Success Library*, Vol. 2, 200).

She has won many awards, undoubtedly as a result of her businesslike approach to problems, her attempts to use her position to be of help to as many as possible, and her fairness to all. She was awarded the Distinguished Alumni Award from Kentucky State University, 1965; a Kentucky Colonel Commission from the Commonwealth of Kentucky in 1965; Populus Dei Award, Mercy College, 1967; Voice of Democracy Award, from the Veterans of Foreign Wars, 1967; Award for Achievement in Government, from the 369th Veterans Association; Woman of Achievement Award, New York Chapter, The Northeasterners, 1969; Benjamin Potoker Brotherhood Award, New York State Employees Brotherhood Committee, 1970; Distinguished Alumni Citation, Atlanta University, 1971; Distinguished Service Award, Caucus of Black Legislators of the State of New York, 1971; Achievement Award, New York Council, United Negro College Fund, 1972; Equal Opportunity Day Award, National Urban League, 1976; Distinguished Public Servant Award, Capital Press Club, 1977; National Black Personnel Association's First Award for Outstanding Achievements in Public Personnel, 1978; and the Governor of New York's Citation and Induction into New York State Woman's Hall of Fame, 1980.

References

Editors of Ebony. *Ebony Success Library*. Chicago: Johnson Publishing Co., 1973. Vols. 1 and 2.

Encyclopedia of Black American Women. New York: McGraw-Hill, 1981.

Keathley, Virginia. "Federal Systems, No People, Cited in Reform." *Tennessean*, 22 March 1978.

Negro Almanac. 5th ed. Detroit: Gale Research, 1989.

Poston, Ersa Hines. "Personal Statement." Biography File, Fisk University Library.

Who's Who Among Black Americans. 4th ed. Lake Forest, Ill.: Wolk Krouse Publishing, 1985. 6th ed. Detroit: Gale Research, 1991.

Who's Who in Government. 2nd ed. Chicago: Marquis, 1976.

Who's Who of American Women. 5th ed. Chicago: Marquis, 1988.

Women in Public Office. 2nd ed. Metuchen, N.J.: Scarecrow Press, 1978.

James Duckworth

Renee Francine Poussaint

(1944-)

Broadcast journalist

Renee Francine Pouissaint, a poised and well-respected journalist and social activist, is an excellent role-model for black Americans and others who aspire to become journalists.

Poussaint was born on August 12, 1944, in New York, New York. She graduated from Sarah Lawrence College with a bachelor of arts degree in comparative literature in 1966 and received a master of arts degree in African studies from the University of California. She has continued to advance her education through non-degree studies at Yale Law School, Columbia University Journalism School, Indiana University, and the Sorbonne in Paris, France. She is married to Henry Richardson, who is a law professor.

Poussaint's early career was not as a news reporter, but she worked in a variety of other areas of the mass media and entertainment. In 1967, she was a dancer for the Jean Leon Destine Haitian Dance Company. From 1967 to 1969, Poussaint was a program director of the Association Internationale des Etudiants et Commerciales (AIESEC) in New York. She also worked as a translator for the University of California Press in 1970 and was an editor for the *African Arts* magazine in Los Angeles from 1969 to 1973. Although her early career was not in the field of journalism, her career choices and skills complemented her academic studies in literature and African studies.

Poussaint's television news experience can be traced to WBBM-TV in Chicago where she worked from 1973 to 1977. She was on the air in a variety of positions including news reporter, news anchor, and show host. Poussaint's career as a television news reporter continued to flourish, and she advanced in her journalistic career, becoming a CBS network correspondent for the Midwest and Washington bureaus from 1977 to 1978. Her credibility and reputation as a journalist continued to blossom. In 1978 she became an anchor/reporter for WJLA-TV "News 7," a newscast airing in Washington, D.C., at 5:30 p.m. and 11:00 p.m.

Poussaint has a commanding presence on the air. She is poised, articulate, and serious, making a clear statement that she is in control of the message she is delivering to the public.

But she is not only a working journalist, she also works in the community helping solve problems. She tutors children, has testified before Congress on the problems of illiteracy, and writes for *The Washington Post* and *Ms.* magazine. Poussaint also serves as a national advisor to UNICEF on issues involving children and is a member of the board of directors of the Capital Area Community Food Bank and of the Robert F. Kennedy Journalism Awards for reporting on the disadvantaged.

Poussaint's work reaches beyond the Washington, D.C., area and addresses global issues around the world. Besides covering presidential campaigns in the United States, Poussaint's stories have focused on a variety of topics, including apartheid in South Africa, peace struggles in the Middle East, AIDS and its impact on women, as well as the plight of migrant workers. She has done several news specials and documentaries on societal issues affecting the community.

Her work in journalism has earned Poussaint numerous honors. She has received several local and national awards, including six Washington Emmys. She has been honored by several organizations, including the National Association of Media Women, Illinois Mental Health Association, the YWCA in Chicago, American Firefighters Association, American Association of University Women, and the United States Department of Labor. She has also been awarded two honorary doctorates of humane letters, one of those from Georgetown University.

Poussaint is a member of Women in Communications, the Society of Professional Journalists (Sigma Delta Chi), and a lifetime member of the NAACP.

References

"Change of Heart." *VARIETY,* 30 November 1988.

"Renee Poussaint Biography." WJLA-TV "News 7," 1990.

Scheurer, Steven H., ed. *Who's Who in Television and Cable.* New York: Facts on File, 1983.

"The Stress Factor." *VARIETY,* 30 November 1988.

Who's Who Among Black Americans, 1990-1991. Detroit: Gale Research, 1990.

Dhyana Ziegler

Georgia Powers

(1933-)

Politician, entrepreneur

By age fifty-five most people are well settled in their careers and would never consider leaving their job to start a new career. But this is just what Georgia Powers decided to do in 1967 when she chose to run for a seat in the Kentucky State Senate. This decision was courageous not just because she was choosing a new career but also because no other black or woman had ever held a seat in the Kentucky Senate. Powers is an extraordinary person who has faced challenges and controversies with a sense of enthusiasm and courage that enabled her to succeed where women and people of color were not welcome.

Born Georgia Montgomery on October 29, 1923, in Springfield, Kentucky, to Frances (Walker) Montgomery and Ben Montgomery, Powers was the second of nine children. In a telephone interview on September 20, 1990, Powers stated that being the product of interracial parents did not present her with any special problems. Her biggest problem was her parents believing her eight brothers could do everything, but since she was a girl she should stay at home. She never allowed this double standard to stop her.

In 1925 the Montgomery family moved from Springfield to Louisville, where Georgia Powers has resided most of her life. She attended Mary B. Talbert Elementary School from 1928 to 1929, Virginia Avenue Elementary School from 1929 to 1934, Madison Junior High School from 1934 to 1937, Central High School from 1937 to 1940, and Louisville Municipal College from 1940 to 1942. She received certificates from Central Business School and the United States Government IBM Supervisory School.

In 1943 Georgia Montgomery married Norman F. Davis and this union produced one child. They divorced in 1968. In 1973 she married her present husband, James F. Powers.

Georgia Powers's political career started when someone in her church asked her to work for Wilson Wyatt, who was campaigning for the United States Senate in 1962. With no previous experience, she was put in charge of training volunteers for his campaign. This position proved to be so challenging that she continued to work as chairperson of election campaigns for candidates for the United States Senate, governor of Kentucky, United States President, mayor of Louisville, and United States Congress from 1962 to 1967. In 1964 Powers was elected to the Jefferson County Democratic Executive Committee for a four-year term. She felt that the position was an "unresponsive political structure"; therefore, after two years she resigned. Powers, along with a black man, were the first two black people to serve on the committee. She also attended three Democratic National Conventions—1968 in Chicago, where she spoke on behalf of Hubert H. Humphrey's platform; 1984 in San Francisco; and 1988 in Atlanta.

During the 1960s Georgia Powers immersed herself in civil rights issues. In 1964 she was one of the organizers of Allied Organizations for Civil Rights, which pushed for the passage of state-wide public accommodations and fair employment laws. This group sponsored the March on Frankfort with more than 25,000 participants. The main speaker was Martin Luther King, Jr. Due to the success of the march, the Kentucky General Assembly passed the bill in 1965. Also in 1965, she was an organizer of the Kentucky Christian Leadership Conference, an affiliate of the Southern Christian Leadership Conference (SCLC), and participated in the Selma march that supported the National Voting Rights Act. She marched daily for open housing in Louisville, led marches in Saint Petersburg, Florida, for more than two hundred sanitation workers who had been fired, joined Martin Luther King, Jr., in a march in Memphis, and was a local organizer for the Poor People's Campaign in Washington, D.C., in 1968. She also participated in many voter registration campaigns throughout the 1960s.

After several years of running other campaigns, Powers finally caught the "political bug" and realized that "a political office is where the power is, and where you could bring about changes." So she went from "protest to politics."

At the time Powers decided to run for office she was a supervisor for the United States Census Bureau, and she took a leave of absence but never returned. During her first campaign she ran against a white opponent "in a district that was 60 percent white and that same district today is 85 percent black." The Democratic party did not endorse Powers or her opponent in the primary, but during the general election she had endorsements from the Kentucky and Louisville education associations, Kentucky Medical Association, the AFL-CIO, and Louisville Chamber of Commerce. These endorsements proved to be very effective and Powers went on to win the general election by a four-thousand-vote majority, making her the first black and first woman ever elected to the Kentucky State Senate. The years of running other campaigns proved to be very beneficial.

Legislator Addresses Civil Rights, Housing, Gender and Sex Bias Issues

Once in office Powers continued her fight for civil rights issues. The first bill she introduced was for statewide fair housing. The bill was later passed by the senate. During her twenty-one years in office she sponsored legislation for civil rights, against sex discrimination, job discrimination, and age discrimination, and for pay increases for the police and firefighters, improved insurance regulation, and improved education for the physically and mentally handicapped.

Reflecting on her five terms in the senate, during which time she remained the only women and the only black in the senate, Powers realized that she was the only senator who introduced bills related to civil rights.

Powers introduced the first open housing law in the South. The Kentucky House of Representatives gave the bill the title "The Georgia M. Davis, Mae Street Kidd, Hughes E. McGill Civil Rights Act of 1968"—so titled to smooth bruised feelings that resulted from competition over sponsorship and legislation for open housing. The bill was later passed. She also introduced low-cost housing bills, a bill to eliminate "race" from Kentucky motor vehicle operators' licenses; an amendment of the Kentucky Civil Rights Act (1966) to eliminate discrimination based on race, sex, and age; a displaced homemaker's law; the Equal Rights Amendment Resolution; and a bill to increase the minimum wage in Kentucky.

While holding office, Powers was chairperson of the Health and Welfare Committee (1970-1976), the Rules Committee (1976-1978), and the Labor and Industry Committee (1978-1988); secretary of the Democratic Caucus for twenty-one years; and a member of the Cities' Committee and the Elections and Constitutional Amendments Committee.

Powers explains that she was able to push for legislation for women, black Americans, and the poor in a district that was sixty percent white because it was a working-class-to-poor district, and her constituents did not vote in large numbers. "I did not have to worry about getting voted out," she said. She concentrated in the black areas and when the complexion of her district gradually changed to a black majority it was unnecessary for her to change her views on important issues.

In 1981 Powers fought to maintain historically black Kentucky State University as a four-year institution. In 1982 and 1983 she was successful in helping defeat a referendum to merge Louisville and Jefferson into one county. On a national level, Powers was Kentucky chairperson for Jesse L. Jackson's candidacy for the democratic presidential nomination in 1984 and 1988.

Powers did not let her business training go to waste. In 1969, while she was in the senate she opened a fast-food restaurant called "Senators" and a dry-cleaning business. However, by 1974 "it was too much, so I sold both enterprises."

In January 1988 Powers, at the age of sixty-five, decided not to run for senate, to the disappointment of many. "It was time for someone else to run, a younger person with fresh ideas, and I need more free time," she said. Powers was hesitant about leaving office earlier because "I did not want to leave office until someone was able to promulgate my wishes and carry out the things I wanted to accomplish. I am pleased that Gerald Neale is the person who has my seat. I work closely with him and am consulted on various bills." Neale is the same man who ran against Powers in 1979 and at that time she explained to him, "it wasn't his time, he could not win, it was a waste of his money and time." Powers's assessment proved correct but now there is no animosity between the former combatants.

The present controversy that surrounds Powers concerns what Ralph Abernathy wrote in his book, *And the Walls Came Tumbling Down* (1990). Abernathy wrote that Martin Luther King, Jr., had a close relationship with a black woman who was a member of the Kentucky legislature. However, Powers did not find his book upsetting:

> He had a right to write a book and I am surprised it took someone close to Martin so long to write about that time. It was a good book and I do not understand why people are so upset about a few pages. He stated that we were close and we were; he did not say we were having a love affair.

Even though Powers worked closely with King, she did not see him as a great man during the 1960s. "He was an ordinary man with extraordinary abilities and a great orator. I realized he was great after his death."

Powers has one son, three stepchildren, and three grandsons. She is not disappointed that none are interested in politics. Three of her brothers are dead but she is close to her five remaining brothers. They meet monthly with their spouses and take turns informing each other about their immediate family.

Presently Powers is completing her autobiography, *Pride, Passion, and Politics,* and she thinks some people will be upset but says, "it will not bother me; I am only dealing with facts." She also has many speaking engagements and is active in the Covenant Memorial Presbyterian Church. Powers states that she wants to be remembered as one who "really cared about people and their situation."

Powers's various organizations and affiliations include chairwoman, Senate Committee on Wages and Hours; board of directors, Louisville Red Cross, Fund of Women, and the Kentucky Indiana Planning and Development Agency; former member Board of Overseers, University of Louisville; member, International Afro-Musical and Cultural Foundation, SCLC, Jefferson County Democratic Executive Committee (1964-66), YMCA, NAACP, Urban League, Subcommittee on Narcotics, and Cities and Labor Committee. She was appointed by the governor to serve on the Desegregation of Higher Education Implementation Committee.

Powers has received numerous awards, including: King/Kennedy Award, Kentucky Young Democrats (1968); University of Louisville Board of Appreciation Award; "Woman of the Year Award," Women's Coalition; Kentucky Chapter, NAACP Award of Recognition; Kentucky State University Distinguished Service Award; and the Kentucky State University Alumni Association Award. Other organizations presenting awards include the Mount Zion Baptist Church, American Red Cross, Fraternal Order of Police, Morehead University, Kentucky Circuit Judges Association,

Park DuValle Health Center, YMCA, YWCA, Alpha Kappa Mu, Alpha Phi Alpha Fraternity, Sigma Gamma Rho Sorority, and Black Women's Political Action. On May 7, 1989, the doctor of laws degree was conferred upon Powers by the University of Kentucky, and on May 21, 1989, the University of Louisville conferred on Powers the doctor of humane letters.

References

Alpha Kappa Alpha Sorority. Heritage Series # 2. *Women in Politics.* Chicago: AKA, July 1969. Includes photograph.

Ebony Editors. *1000 Successful Blacks.* Vol. 1, *The Ebony Success Library.* Chicago: Johnson Pub. Co., 1973. Includes photograph.

Kaukas, Dick. "Georgia On Their Minds." *Courier-Journal Magazine*, 11 March 1990. Photograph, pp. 5-6.

Lanker, Brian. *I Dream A World.* New York: Stewart, Tabori and Chang, 1989. Photograph, p. 70.

"Louisville, A Slow Track for Blacks in Derbytown." *Black Enterprise* 2 (February 1972): 42-46. Photograph, p. 45.

Low, W. Augustus, and Virgil A. Clift, eds. *Encyclopedia of Black America.* New York: McGraw-Hill, 1981.

Ploski, Harry A. and James Williams, eds. *The Negro Almanac.* Detroit: Gale Research, 1989.

Powers, Georgia Montgomery Davis. Interview with author, 20 September 1990.

Who's Who Among Black Americans, 1990/91. 6th ed. Detroit: Gale Research, 1990.

Valerie S. Hartman

Evelyn Preer

(1896-1932)

Actress

Evelyn Preer Thompson, an independent-minded actress during Hollywood's early days, blazed the trail for black women in motion pictures.

Preer was born July 26, 1896, in Vicksburg, Mississippi. No sources indicate whether she had siblings. At the age of two, she moved with her parents to Chicago, where she attended grammar school and Wendell Phillips High School. Preer made her acting debut in high school when she appeared on stage in *Lady American Minstrels*. After graduating from high school, she toured the Orpheum Circuit as a leading lady with Charley Johnson's vaudeville troupe.

Preer later moved to New York City and joined the Lafayette Players at the Avenue Theatre. During her two years with the company, she appeared in such productions as *Why Wives Go Wrong*, *The Good Li'l Bad Girl*, and on Broadway in *Lulu Bell*, *Rang Tang*, and *Porgy*. In 1923, she was part of a triple bill presented by the Ethiopian Art players, in which she played the title role in *Salome*. The bill also included *The Chipwoman's Fortune* and *A Comedy of Errors*. It was Preer's performance in *A Comedy of Errors* that garnered her a favorable review from a *New York Times* theater critic who wrote that the actress displayed "excellent comedy talent" (8 May 1923).

In 1924, Preer met and married fellow actor Edward Thompson when the two appeared together in *The Warning*. The couple had one child.

At the same time Preer was performing in stage productions, she was also embarking on her career in feature films. She was the pioneer black woman in the cinema world. In 1918, she appeared in *The Homesteader* and during the next decade starred in a number of Oscar Micheaux films, including *Deceit; Within Our Gates* and *The Brute* in 1920; *The Gunsaulus Mystery* in 1921; *Birthright* in 1924; *The Devil's Disciple* (which she considered her best work) and *The Conjure Woman* in 1926; *Melancholy Dame* in 1929; and *Georgia Rose* in 1930. Her last feature film was *Blonde Venus* with Marlene Dietrich in 1932.

Very little seems to have been written about Preer's personal life. Most material about her contains information relating to her films. She reflected on her experiences in movies in a series of articles for the Pittsburgh *Courier* in 1927, in which she talked of the realism in her acting that resulted many times in physical pain.

In the June 11 article in the *Pittsburgh* Courier, Preer discussed her first picture, *The Homesteader*, and her 1922 film *Birthright*. She described *The Homesteader* as a dramatic tragedy in which she played the leading role of a mistreated daughter who stabs her father and then herself. Preer commented that the only thing she remembered about the picture was "the terribly long time it took the cameraman to film the scene of my spirit coming back to haunt the people who had mistreated me."

In the same article, Preer discussed her 1922 film *Birthright*, which was filmed in Roanoke, Virginia. Real bloodhounds were supposed to chase her across a hill and through a swamp. Instead of chasing her, however, they liked her, and the only way the film crew could get the dogs to chase Preer was to have her hold out a piece of meat and call them. Preer also stated that she still had scars on her ankle from one scene that required her to roll down a long hill: to get to the hill, she had to wade through a pond of water that was much deeper than she thought and she nearly drowned. "My back being to the camera,'' said Preer, ''I expressed my feeling freely to Micheaux as I waded out.''

In the second *Courier* article, which ran on June 18, Preer recounted her roles in *Within Our Gates* and *The Brute*. *Within Our Gates* was filmed in Chicago, and Preer contended that the best scene she ever played was in that movie. The story was set in Mississippi, and Preer's character and her family were being run away from their home by angry whites. During the night, Preer's character slipped back to the house to get some clothes and, without her knowledge, was followed by a member of the would-be lynching party. When she entered the house, the man also entered and locked the door. The ''grand fight,'' as she describes it, began, in which tables, chairs, and other furniture were overturned. The actress grabbed a vase, but just before she crowned the villain, her lover leaped on the villain's back and the two of them began ''one of the most realistic fights [she] witnessed since being in the movies.'' However, all of the excitement did not occur on the screen. The premiere of *Within Our Gates*, which Preer attended, was held at the Vendome Theatre in Chicago. One of the actress's fans became so overzealous that he had to be guarded by the ushers during the performance. During the scene where Preer raised the vase to hit the villain, she said this man ''leaped up and yelled 'kill him!' and uttering words that I will leave to your imagination.''

But the real thrills, according to Preer, came with *The Brute*. She played opposite actor A. B. Comanthiere, who was to knock her to the floor, blackening her eye in the process. Ever the realist, Preer said she begged Comanthiere to hit her. He did, and the actress had a black eye for several days. Comanthiere actually dragged Preer around the room by her hair at her suggestion. ''Since that scene,'' said Preer, ''I have worn bobbed hair and I haven't made a picture with Comanthiere, thank God!''

In the *Courier* article on June 25, Preer described yet another first—her first fight with a woman, on or off the screen. Set in Chicago, the film was *Deceit*, and Cleo Despond played Preer's mean sister, who forced her to leave her husband. In the scene, Preer said she really hit Despond and the actress in turn retaliated. ''For two days,'' commented Preer, ''I saw my teeth prints on her fingers. I can't call that my thrill—it belongs to Despond. But I don't mind—I'm awfully nice like that.''

Preer returned to Broadway in 1927 where she appeared in a brief run of *Rang Tang*. The actress died in 1932. She was survived by her husband, Edward, and their child. In 1933, actor Clarence Muse originated an annual radio program in her memory on station KRKD in Los Angeles.

References

Kellner, Bruce, ed. *The Harlem Renaissance: A Historical Dictionary for the Era*. New York: Methuen, 1987.

Mapp, Edward. *Directory of Blacks in the Performing Arts*. Metuchen, N.J.: Scarecrow Press, 1978.

New York Times, 8 May 1923.

Sampson, Henry T. *Blacks in Black and White: A Source Book on Black Films*. Metuchen, N.J.: Scarecrow Press, 1977.

Woll, Allen. *Dictionary of the Black Theatre: Broadway, Off-Broadway, and Selected Harlem Theatre*. Westport, Conn.: Greenwood Press, 1983.

Delores Hudson

Frances E. L. Preston

(c. 1840-1929)

Elocutionist, entrepreneur, school founder, temperance lecturer, organist

Frances E. L. Preston rose from a slave background to become a highly-respected elocutionist, temperance lecturer, and clubwoman, and along the way founded a school for black girls. She achieved greatness and exemplifies the efforts of countless African-American women in history.

Frances E. L. Preston was born in Richmond, Virginia, possibly in 1840, although 1845 is also suggested, the only daughter of a free father and a slave mother. Since children at that time acquired their mother's status, Preston was born a slave. She received some education while living in Richmond, and when the family moved to Detroit, Michigan, during her early years, she enrolled in one of the black schools. The talented Preston learned to play the organ and the piano, taught music early, and for a number of years was organist for the Second Baptist Church in Detroit. Expanding her early education, in 1880 at the age of about forty, she enrolled in the Detroit Training School of Elocution, where for two-and-a-half years she studied English literature and graduated on May 19, 1882. Academically, she ranked second among a large number of graduates, most of whom were women who had come with a much better education that she had.

At that time, Frances E. L. Preston was a widow with one child. To support her family, she had a large hairdressing business in Detroit. After graduating, she traveled for one year with the Donivan Famous Tennesseans concert group on a recital tour. She returned to Detroit and taught in her alma mater, the Detroit Training School. It is probable that she also did postgraduate work at the school at this time. Her training and experiences led to her appointment later on as lecturer and organizer for the National Women's Christian Temperance Union.

She lectured throughout eastern Virginia in 1884 and gave public programs. According to Sylvia G. L. Dannett, she taught in Baptist academies in Jacksonville, Florida, and Louisville, Kentucky, and was engaged in educational activities in Alabama, Georgia, Oklahoma, and Texas (305). With her daughter, Lillie, she moved to Augusta, Georgia, in 1884 and opened a Baptist school for girls. The school had only one teacher. To support the school, Preston traveled and gave recitals but her mother's illness ended the activities.

In July 1890 Frances E. L. Preston was appointed agent to a Dr. Derrick of New York City to assist in fund-raising for the Baptist foreign missionary board. In April 1891 she became a member of the Women's Christian Temperance Union's lecture bureau. This position facilitated her speaking engagements and recitations before lecture associations, clubs, churches, lyceums, and other groups, and she went on to receive high praise for her performance. The *Detroit Free Press* wrote of her early work:

> The debut of Mrs. Frances Preston, at Abstract Hall, possessed peculiar interest, from the fact that she is the first colored lady in this city to essay public readings. She is to be congratulated on winning a very emphatic success. She has a melodious voice of excellent range and flexibility, enunciates with agreeable clearness, and manifests feeling and appreciation in selections, grave and gay (Major, 97).

The press often reminded the public of Preston's slave background and educational achievements, and also called her a "fine reader" with "elocutionary talent of no small order." The charm of her readings was in her "naturalness and grace of manner" (Major, 98). One of her most inspiring pieces appears to have been "The Black Regiment." A Newport News, Virginia, appearance in the First Baptist Church, held as a fund-raiser for the church, drew a large audience that was so moved by her performance that no one wanted to leave at the end of the program. The local newspaper, *The Caret,* said:

> Mrs. Preston has a rich contralto voice, over which she has perfect control. She has a fine stage presence, and whatever the character of her selection—pathetic, sentimental or humorous—she portrays each with equal skill, and is one of the most finished readers before the public (Major, 98).

Powhatan Beatty, who was associated with theaters in Cincinnati, said:

> Miss Preston is a pleasant reader, and thoroughly understands the principles of elocution. Her gestures are graceful and full of expression. . . . Her modulation is excellent, and in the lower and middle register of her voice she has not an equal. . . . I have heard all of the great readers, and so far as my judgment goes I would place her in the front ranks. She has a voice full of pathos, and at times her audiences are melted to tears, and at other times are convulsed with laughter (Major, 99).

Preston's daughter accompanied her on some occasions, apparently as a singer, and was known for her "remarkably sweet voice" that was developing well.

Elocutionist Demonstrates Talent as Civic Organizer and Leader

Frances E. L. Preston was also an active civic organizer and leader, and for four years (1909-1913) she was president of the Michigan Federation of Colored Women's Clubs. She was also active in the National Federation of Colored Women's Clubs. At the second convention of the national group held in Atlanta in December 1895, under the presidency of Josephine B. Bruce, she was a member of the Committee on Courtesies, along with such well-known leaders as Fannie Barrier Williams, Frances E. W. Harper, and Nettie Langston Napier. In 1910 Preston attended the sixth biennial session held at Louisville, Kentucky, under the leadership of Elizabeth C. Carter. She was one of several outstanding women who delivered addresses and papers. The others included Ida Wells Barnett, Nannie Helen Burroughs, Janie Porter Barrett, and Elizabeth Ross (later Haynes).

Frances E. L. Preston worked with other black women in the Women's Christian Temperance Union (WCTU), which "offered black women an organized vehicle through which they would improve family life, health, and morality" (Salem, 36). The black elite of the mid-nineteenth century had been active in the temperance movement, and after the Civil War, when considerably more stress was placed on black families, the WCTU increased its activities and expanded them globally. Black women became more involved, and Rosetta Douglass Sprague (daughter of Frederick Douglass), Frances Joseph, Amanda Berry Smith, and Lucy Thurman were organizers at the national level. Under Thurman's presidency, the NACW added temperance as a major focus.

References

Dannett, Sylvia G. L. *Profiles of Negro Womanhood.* Vol. 1, 1619-1900. Yonkers: Educational Heritage, 1964. Drawing of Frances E. L. Preston, p. 204.

Major, M. A. *Noted Negro Women.* Chicago: Donohue and Henneberry, 1893. Line engraving, p. 96.

Salem, Dorothy. "National Movements and Issues: Women, Race, and the National Association of Colored Women, 1890-1910." In *To Better Our World: Black Women in Organized Reform, 1890-1920.* Brooklyn: Carlson Publishing, 1990.

Wesley, Charles Harris. *The History of the National Association of Colored Women's Clubs.* Washington, D.C.: NACW, 1984.

Jessie Carney Smith

Florence Price

(1888-1953)

Composer, musician

Florence Price published a musical composition at the age of eleven, went on to study serious music, and became a composer who made a name for herself among her contemporaries. She is perhaps best known for her art songs and piano teaching pieces, and she sought to infuse her work with the rich fund of African-American musical idioms in order to create a truly American form of music.

Florence Beatrice Smith Price was born April 9, 1888, in Little Rock, Arkansas, and died June 3, 1953, in Chicago of a stroke. Born Florence Smith into a solidly middle-class family where her father, James H. Smith, was a dentist and her mother, Florence Irene (Gulliver) Smith, was a schoolteacher, she had the advantage of a sound general and musical education. She and her brother, Charles, and sister, Gertrude, began their musical education under the tutelage of their mother, who was well known as a singer and pianist and who had taught music as part of her duties as a public school teacher in her native Indianapolis. The mother presented the daughter in public performance at age four.

James Smith was born in Camden, Delaware, of free parents and grew up in New Jersey, where he was eventually a private secretary to the wealthy Mrs. J. Bastrop, who was instrumental in arranging for him to study dentistry in the Philadelphia office of Kennard, Longfellow, and Flagg. Although not a college graduate, Smith's studies prepared him for a lucrative practice in the Chicago Loop, where he had an office until the Chicago fire of 1871, during which his practice was destroyed. Dr. Smith moved to Arkansas and became a public school teacher. In 1876 he married Florence Gulliver and opened his Little Rock practice in 1878. It is quite likely that Gulliver had family ties to Arkansas, since the family is known to have owned land there.

This background allowed Price to grow up in an environment where education and the arts were valued. Her father was an amateur painter, her mother a musician, and the family associated with other blacks who were similarly situated. They were friends with the family of city judge Mifflin Gibbs, whose daughter, Harriet, was the first black female graduate of the famed Oberlin Conservatory, where so many of the earliest black classical musicians trained. They were also acquainted with Thomas Shepperson the stepfather of William Grant Still, a well-known black American composer who had come in infancy in 1895 to live with his widowed mother in Little Rock, where she met and married Shepperson.

Price and Still both attended elementary school under Charlotte Stephens, who had studied music at Oberlin but was prevented from completing her studies for lack of financial support. Without doubt, Stephens recognized the talents of Price and Still and encouraged them. It is not clear that she taught them music, however. Price also attended elementary school in Chicago but completed high school in Little Rock.

Conflicting dates of Price's graduation from high school are given. Green reports the year as 1902 while Jackson reports the date as 1903. Price was valedictorian of her class and enrolled in the New England Conservatory of Music shortly after graduation from high school.

At New England, Price majored in piano and organ, but more importantly, she studied music theory and composition with the renowned George Chadwick, who used African-American musical idioms in his works and no doubt encouraged his several black students to do so. Florence Smith also studied with other musical leaders of the day such as Benjamin Cutter and Frederick Converse. She had already exhibited talent for composition before entering New England, having published a composition as early as age eleven. At New England she wrote a string quartet and a symphony and also performed as an organist and pianist and held a church position in Nantucket. In 1906—Green gives the date as 1907—she graduated and returned to Little Rock and shortly thereafter began a teaching career at Arkadelphia Academy in Cotton Plant, Arkansas. Her talents came to the attention of Neumon Leighton, a white musician, who encouraged her by lecturing about her works and teaching her art songs to his students at Memphis State University.

From 1906 to 1910, Price was employed as a music teacher at Shorter College in North Little Rock. She also taught privately, giving violin, piano, and organ lessons. For two years, 1910-1912, she taught at Clark College in Atlanta. Her career as a college teacher ended when she married Thomas Price, a young Little Rock attorney. At this point, Price limited her teaching to private lessons as she attempted to rear her children, Tommy, Florence Louise, and Edith. Tommy died in infancy, and her song, "To My Little Son," was written as a tribute to his memory.

Racial unrest characterized by lynchings and discrimination led the Prices to move to Chicago in 1927. Chicago offered Price rich opportunities for further musical education and for association with other talented musicians. She resumed her general and musical studies by matriculating at Chicago Musical College, the American Conservatory, the University of Chicago, Chicago Teachers College, Central YMCA College, and Lewis Institute. She was able to study with outstanding music figures such as Arthur Olaf Anderson, Carl Busch, and Leo Sowerby and earned fees by writing radio commercials. In Chicago she was able to associate with Langston Hughes, Will Marion Cook, Abbie Mitchell, William Dawson (who later won fame as an arranger of spirituals and as a choral director at Tuskegee Institute—now University), and other black artists and intellectuals. Here she also became the mentor of another black woman, Margaret Bonds, who would later make a mark in the musical world. Bonds studied piano and composition with Price and later performed Price's works. A notable instance was in 1934 when Bonds appeared as the pianist with the Women's Symphony of Chicago playing Price's Concerto in F Minor at the Chicago World's Fair. Little is known about Price as a conductor, but a photograph of her conducting pianist Margaret Bonds and the Women's Symphony of Chicago is given in Southern's second edition of *Black American Music*. As her career progressed, Price came to know and correspond with artists such as Roland Hayes, Harry T. Burleigh, and John Alden Carpenter. Carpenter sponsored her membership in the American Society of Composers, Authors, and Publishers in 1940.

Composer's Career Flourishes in Chicago

Perhaps Chicago was most important in Price's career because it was here that she began to find publishers and audiences for her works. By 1928 G. Schirmer had published the piano piece *At the Cotton Gin* and McKinley Publishing Company became interested in her short teaching pieces. By the 1940s publishers were soliciting works from Price after Marian Anderson had used her setting of a Langston Hughes poem, "Songs to a Dark Virgin," while still in manuscript on her second American tour. G. Schirmer published the work in 1941. Other artists including Carol Brice, Leontyne Price, Roland Hayes, Blanche Thebom, Etta Moten, Camilla Williams, Grace Bumbry, Todd Duncan, William Warfield, and Ellabelle Davis included Price's songs on their programs. Gamble Hinged Music Company, Edwards B. Marks Corporation, Clayton Summy, Theodore Presser, Carl Fischer, and Handy Brothers Music Company were among publishers who carried compositions by Price in their catalogs.

Although known best for her art songs ("Songs to a Dark Virgin," "Moon Bridge," "Out of the South Blew a Wind," "April Day," and "Night") and for her short piano teaching pieces such as *Three Little Negro Dances,* Price also wrote in the more extended forms. Her Symphony in A Minor and a piano sonata won Wanamaker Awards in 1930. The symphony had its first public performance with the Chicago Symphony Orchestra under the baton of Frederick Stock at the Chicago World's Fair in 1933. Price won prizes in other competitions such as the Holstein (1925, 1927) and the G. Schirmer (1928). The Concerto in D Minor was played by Price at Chicago Musical College in 1934. Symphony No. 3 in C Minor was given its premier performance in 1940 by the Detroit WPA Orchestra. She also wrote chamber works that were performed by several groups. Perhaps the crowning glory came for Price when she was asked by Sir John Barbirolli to write a suite for strings based on spirituals. The work was premiered in Manchester England.

Price has been characterized by Eileen Southern as a neoromanticist and black nationalist (Southern, *The Music of Black Americans,* 418). Nationalistic tendencies are present in many of her works that draw upon black folk material—for example, *Suite of Negro Dances, Three Little Negro Dances,* Symphony No. 3 in C Minor, Symphony in E Minor, Concert Overture No. 1, Concert Overture No. 2, and Sonata in E Minor. Jackson reports that Price wrote of her third symphony, "It is intended to be Negroid in character and expression. In it no attempt, however, has been made to project Negro music solely in the purely traditional manner. None of the themes are adaptations or derivations of folk songs" (Jackson, 38). Thus, she subscribed to the aesthetic creed held by major black composers of the period that black idioms were rich resources for the creation of a body of uniquely American concert music.

A partial list of Price's works includes: "Adoration," for organ (Lorenz); "Anticipation," for piano (McKinley Music Co.); "An April Day," for voice (Handy Brothers); "Bright Eyes," voice (Theodore Presser); "The Butterfly," for piano (in *Pieces We Like to Play,* Carl Fischer); "Cabin Song," for piano (Theodore Pressler); Concert Overture No. 1 (unpublished); Concert Overture No. 2 (unpublished); Concerto for Piano and Orchestra (unpublished); "Dances in the Canebrakes," for piano (Affiliated Musicians); "Dances in the Canebrakes," orchestral suite (Mills); "Doll Waltz," "The Engine," "The Waltzing Fairy," "The Waterfall," from *Five Easy Compositions for Piano* (McKinley Music Company); "Heav'n Bound Soldier," for women's voices (Handy Brothers); "Here and There," for piano (McKinley Music Company); "Hoe Cake," "Rabbit Foot," and "Ticklin' Toes" from *Three Little Negro Dances* (Theodore Presser); "I am Bound for the Kingdom" and "I'm Workin' on My Building" from *Two Traditional Negro Spirituals* (Handy Brothers); "In a Quiet Mood," for organ (Summy); Sonata in E Minor (unpublished); "Songs to a Dark Virgin" (G. Schirmer); Suite No. 1, for organ (unpublished); Symphony in C Minor (unpublished); Symphony in D Minor (unpublished); Symphony in E Minor (unpublished, and Symphony in G Minor (unpublished). A more complete listing of Price's works is included in Samuel Floyd's *Black Music in the Harlem Renaissance*, pp. 205-208.

Unfortunately, there is not an extensive list of recordings of Price's music. The eminent pianist Natalie Hinderas did not include any works by Price or any other black female composer in her historic album, *Natalie Hinderas, Pianist, Plays Music by Black Composers* (Desto 7102-3); nor is Price or any black woman composer represented in the monumental multivolume recording, the CBS *Black Composers Series* (P919424). "My Soul's Been Anchored in de Lord," has been recorded by Ellabelle Davis on London LPS 182 and Victor 1799. A very fine disc (C 1027), *Althea Waites Performs the Music of Florence Price,* has been released by Cambria Records of Lomita, California. Works include: Sonata in E Minor, "The Old Boatman," "Cotton Dance," "Dances in the Canebrakes," "Nimble Feet," "Tropical Noon," and "Silk Hat and Walking Cane."

References

Abdul, Raoul. *Blacks in Classical Music.* New York: Dodd, Mead, 1977. Photograph inserted between pp. 96-97.

Anderson, E. Ruth. *Contemporary American Composers: A Biographical Dictionary*. 2nd ed. Boston: G. K. Hall, 1982.

Butcher, Margaret Just. *The Negro in American Culture*. New York: Knopf, 1957.

Contributions of Black Women to America. Vol. 1. Ed. Marianna W. Davis. Columbia, S.C.: Kenday Press, 1981.

Cuney-Hare, Maud. *Negro Musicians and Their Music*. Washington, D.C.: Associated Publishers, 1936. Reprinted. New York: Da Capo Press, 1974.

de Lerma, Dominique-René. *Black Music in Our Culture*. Kent, Ohio: Kent State University Press, 1970.

———. *Reflections on Afro-American Music*. Kent, Ohio: Kent State University Press, 1973.

Floyd, Samuel A., Jr., ed. *Black Music in the Harlem Renaissance*. Westport, Conn.: Greenwood Press, 1990.

Graham, Shirley. "Spirituals to Symphonies." *Etude* 54 (November 1936): 691.

Green, Mildred Denby. *Black Women Composers: A Genesis*. Boston: G. K. Hall, 1983. Photograph, p. 31.

Jackson, Barbara Garvey. "Florence Beatrice Price." *Notable American Women: The Modern Period*. Cambridge: Harvard University Press, 1980.

———. "Florence Price, Composer." *Black Perspective in Music*. 5 (Spring 1977): 30-43. Photograph, p. 30.

Locke, Alain. *The Negro and His Music*. Washington, D.C.: Associates in Negro Folk Education, 1936. Reprinted. New York: Arno Press and the New York Times, 1969.

Roach, Hildred. *Black American Music: Past and Present*. Boston: Crescendo Pub. Co., 1973.

Southern, Eileen. *Biographical Dictionary of Afro-American and African Musicians*. Westport, Conn.: Greenwood Press, 1982.

———. *The Music of Black Americans*. 2nd ed. New York: Norton, 1977. Photograph of Price conducting Women's Symphony Orchestra in one of her works, p. 417.

Wilson, Olly. "The Black-American Composer and the Orchestra in the Twentieth Century." *Black Perspective in Music* 14 (Winter 1986): 26-34.

Williams, Ora. *American Black Women in the Arts and Sciences*. Metuchen, N.J.: Scarecrow Press, 1978.

Collections

Unpublished manuscripts of some of Price's works may be found in the Special Collections of the library of the University of Arkansas at Fayetteville. There are more than eighty published and unpublished scores, several letters, photographs, notebooks, and clippings. Biographical material is in the Julius Rosenwald Collection at Fisk University.

Ben E. Bailey

Leontyne Price
(1927-)
Singer

Mary Violet Leontyne Price (originally Leontine), the first black lyric soprano (*lirico spinto*) to achieve international diva status in our time, emerged in the 1950s as a major artist. Hers became a preeminent career that ushered in a new era that opened the international operatic stages to younger black singers. From the beginning of her student performances at Juilliard School of Music, she was recognized as an extraordinary talent. When Frederick Cohen, director of Juilliard's opera department, first heard her sing "Lament" from *Dido and Aeneas* in his Introduction to Opera course, he proclaimed: "We have the voice of the century" (Lyon, 57). Internationally acclaimed by music critics and fans, Leontyne Price has been crowned Diva, "*A Prima Donna Assoluta*" of the international world of music, "the Stradivarius of singers" (Schonberg), and "the prototypical . . . black singer, to

Leontyne Price

whose pinnacle all who have followed aspire'' (Jacobson, 19).

Price was born in Laurel, Mississippi, February 10, 1927. Her brother George was born two years later. They grew up during the depression and were reared by hardworking, proud, self-reliant, and deeply religious parents. Their father, James Anthony Price, born in the 1880s, left his hometown of Enterprise, Mississippi, shortly before the turn of the century in search of a secure livelihood. He settled in Laurel, where he found employment as a carpenter with a local lumber company. Katherine (Kate) Baker, a native of Hernando, Mississippi, moved to Holly Springs, Mississippi, where she attended Rust College in hopes of becoming a nurse. Her education disrupted by financial difficulties, Kate Baker moved to Laurel in 1915 to live with her sister and brother-in-law. There she met and married James Price. Both children of Methodist ministers, they centered their lives around the church, where James Price played the tuba in the church band and Kate Price sang in the choir. During these years, Kate Price worked as a midwife to supplement her husband's meager earnings.

Leontyne Price's parents were powerful influences on the lives of their two children. Her father, a quiet, hardworking, inspiring man, ''was my first hero. I always looked up to him. As a child, I would see my father coming across the road from his job, heading toward the house, and I knew everything was alright,'' she told Phyl Garland of *Ebony* magazine. Price's mother, a determined, insightful woman, recognized her daughter's promising musical talents early and enrolled her at the age of three in Hattie V. J. McInnis's private piano classes. Both parents instilled positive values in their children. During the middle of the Depression, Leontyne Price and George Price received such strong spiritual and material support that they never felt deprived. These strong roots, according to Leontyne Price, became the foundation for their future successes: ''We were raised with love, discipline, respect for hard work, and faith in ourselves. We both worked our way through college and through our advanced training, with *great* sacrifices from our parents, but we never felt poor. We were rich in other ways'' (Garland, 35). George Price, now her manager, retired as a brigadier general after twenty-eight years of distinguished services in the United States Army.

Leontyne Price was a popular, outgoing, and excellent student throughout her years at Sandy Gavin Elementary School. Her teachers—whom she credits for their strong sense of encouragement and inspiration—recognized and supported her talents. Not only did she excel in music but she was also the star performer in the annual dance and acrobatic programs. By this time, Price was firmly committed to a career in music. Nothing distracted her from her love of singing and playing the piano, and in her dedication to music she was totally supported by her mother who took her talents very seriously. Kate Price intuitively believed that her daughter was destined for greatness and thus made sure that nothing interfered with her music.

Marian Anderson Influences Price

An added stimulus for Leontyne Price's ambitions occurred at the age of nine when she accompanied her mother to hear Marian Anderson at a concert in Jackson, Mississippi: ''It accomplished exactly what she wanted it to accomplish,'' Price recalls. ''I woke up! I was excited! I was thrilled with this woman's manner, her carriage, her pride, her voice. This was something else again'' (*Ebony*). As Leontyne Price listened to Anderson, her ambition became focused: ''When I first heard Marian Anderson, it was a vision of elegance and nobility. It was one of the most enthralling, marvelous experiences I've ever had. I can't tell you how inspired I was to do something even similar to what she was doing. That was what you might call the original kick-off'' (*Current Biography*, 329).

This strong guidance in Price's early life paid off, for at the age of eleven, she was an accomplished pianist, playing for both the Sunday school and regular church services. She gained local recognition; singing and playing at community affairs—small soirees in private homes, weddings, and funerals—made her a local celebrity and, at the same time, allowed her to make extra money. Even at this young age, her performances revealed the sensitivity and expressiveness that would later make her an international diva.

Price entered the sixth grade at Oak Park Vocational High School in the fall of 1937, firmly committed to a career in music. Oak Park, one of the best high schools in Mississippi, had a very effective music program. Under the tutelage of Hattie McInnis, Price's longtime piano instructor, Price's music abilities were showcased. She sang first soprano with the prestigious Oak Park Choral Group and was selected to play for all school concerts. On December 17, 1943, she presented her first recital. Meanwhile, Price also found time for majorette practice and for competing for the title of Miss Oak Park, which she won in her senior year. In addition to traveling with both the choral group and football team, she dated and went to parties and movies with friends.

Leontyne Price, graduating cum laude from Oak Park Vocational High School, was awarded a full four-year scholarship at Wilberforce College (now divided into Wilberforce and Central State universities) in Wilberforce, Ohio. Initially, she sang alto, unaware of the full potential of her vocal range. Majoring in music, Price hoped to obtain a degree in public school music and return to Laurel to teach. However, during her freshman year, she progressed rapidly in her classes, mastering fundamental techniques.

As her visibility increased, Price's professors realized that there was something special about her abilities and advised her to change her major to voice: Catherine Van Buren, Price's first voice teacher at Wilberforce, instructed her to seek expert voice training. Also, during her audition for the Wilberforce Choir, a visiting pianist informed her that she was not a mezzo-soprano. Encouraging Price to sing a song written for a lyric soprano, the pianist lifted the range of Price's voice. For the first time in her life, she realized that she had a vocal instrument for a professional career. Charles Wesley, president of Wilberforce, also advised Price to change her major to voice. And, recognizing her spectacular talent, he asked Price to represent the school at special functions. She became a campus celebrity.

Interspersing her studies with extracurricular activities, Price accompanied the college choir, performed with the local church choir, and with the Wilberforce Singers—a select group of the best vocal talent at the college. As their featured soloist, Price traveled throughout Ohio and neighboring states to perform concerts and raise money from the school's alumni.

Enrolling at Juilliard in the fall of 1948, Price's classmates included an impressive group of promising talent: Andrew Frierson, Martha Flowers, Billie Lynn Daniels, Gloria Davy, and Mary Robbs, many of whom remained Price's lifelong friends. Although her parents contributed, they did not have enough money to cover Price's living expenses. Elizabeth Chisholm, a close and longtime family friend from Laurel, provided much-needed financial assistance. During her years at Juilliard, Price helped support herself by working as a receptionist at International House. Here she found an enriching experience that brought her into close contact with other serious and talented students from all over the world.

Even more important to Price was the opportunity to study vocal technique with Florence Page Kimball, a former concert singer, who was her teacher for four years and her lifetime adviser, coach, and friend. Kimball not only coached Price in voice, diction, and lieder, but also gave her personal advice as well as valuable criticism of her singing. Initially, Kimball was not impressed by Price's voice but was encouraged by her seriousness, determination, and charm. Price worked very hard and steadily improved. After the first year, Kimball's confidence in the young soprano was manifest not only in presenting her students in a small concert, but also in inviting noted film composer Max Steiner to hear the production. His recognition of Price's superb vocal power was immediate. Steiner, looking for someone to cast in the role of Bess in his revival of Gershwin's *Porgy and Bess*, promptly invited Price to star in the role of Bess.

Price Makes Operatic Debut

While a student at Juilliard, the excitement that Price experienced when she attended her first operatic performances, Puccini's *Turandot* at the City Center in New York City and Strauss's *Salome* at the Metropolitan, thoroughly convinced her to become an opera singer, in spite of the limited roles for blacks in the standard repertoire. During her sophomore year, she auditioned for Juilliard's Opera Workshop, a very difficult task because of the exceptional talent and stiff competition. Frederick Cohen immediately recognized Price's extraordinary, powerful talent. She gained experience by singing in as many roles in student productions as she could. Her first role, that of Aunt Nella in Puccini's *Gianni Schicchi,* was followed by an appearance as Mistress Ford in Verdi's *Falstaff.* After hearing her, composer and critic Virgil Thompson cast her as Saint Cecilia in a revival of his *Four Saints in Three Acts*, a production that ran in New York and Paris in the spring of 1952. That same year she made her triumphant international debut as Bess in Gershwin's *Porgy and Bess.*

Between 1952 and 1954, she and baritone William Warfield (then her husband) made international headlines. John Rosenfield of the *Saturday Review* declared: "The voice, a bright and focused soprano, has great impact, but even this is only half of it. She brought a lively theatrical imagination to the role . . . and . . . such vivid detail that the first night audience lost its composure when she took her final curtain call." David Hume of the *Washington Post* observed: "Leontyne Price sings the most exciting and thrilling Bess we have heard. . . . Price will no doubt spend a long time in the role of Bess. But when she is available for other music, she will have a dramatic career. And her acting is as fiery as her singing." European critics hailed her as well.

The role of Bess marked an acceleration in the career of Price. She attracted recognition from notable musicians and composers such as Stravinsky, Lou Harrison, Henri Sauget, William Killmayer, and John LaMontaine. Her producers arranged her schedule to allow her to expand her repertoire and she accepted invitations to perform at the Museum of Modern Art, the Metropolitan Museum of Art, and Constitution Hall. On November 14, 1954, Price, accompanied by Samuel Barber, gave a demonstration of her steadily maturing abilities in a Town Hall recital. Her performance, however, was received with mixed reviews. Despite the criticism of her "consistent tremolo" and "unevenness of tone," Jay Harrison of the *New York Herald Tribune* praised her elegance and charm and "a personality that literally spills charm over the footlights."

In 1955, Price's appearance in the role of Flora Tosca on a nationally televised production by NBC-TV Opera Workshop was historic—the first black to appear in opera on television—and won for her a succession of leading roles in subsequent NBC productions, such as Mozart's *The Magic Flute* in 1956 and *Don Giovanni* in 1960. Price made her American operatic debut on September 20, 1957, with the San Francisco Opera as Madame Liodine in *Dialogues of the Carmelites*, making her a major talent. In subsequent seasons she starred in such diverse operas as Verdi's *Aida* and *Il Trovatore*, Orff's *The Wise Maiden*, Mozart's *Don Giovanni*, and Massenet's *Thaïs*, performing in major opera houses throughout the United States. Her European reputation was established when conductor Herbert von Karajan cast her as Aida with the Vienna State Opera in 1958, after which Price appeared in a succession of roles at the Vienna Arena, the Salzburg Festival, and London's Covent Garden. When she sang *Aida* at La Scala in 1960, Price emerged as *the* Verdi soprano. One Italian critic exclaimed: "our great Verdi would have found her the ideal Aida" (Walsh, 67).

Price Sings at the Met

Price was well prepared when she made her historic debut

as Leonora in Verdi's *Il Trovatore* at New York's Metropolitan Opera on January 27, 1961. As the fifth black artist to sing a major role at the Met since Marian Anderson made the breakthrough in 1955, Price was triumphant: "Miss Price overcame . . . technical hurdles with the utmost ease . . . giving the part a special dramatic eloquence, which arose partly from the rich, vibrant quality of her voice and partly from the authoritative artistry with which she used it. Her interpretation was virtually without flaws" (Sargeant, the *New Yorker*). At the conclusion of the performance, Price received "an unprecedented forty-two minute ovation" (Garland, 35). The season was an extraordinary one—five starring roles in one season. In addition to Leonora in *Il Trovatore*, she sang the title role in *Aida*, Doña Anna in *Don Giovanni*, Cio-Cio-San in *Madame Butterfly*, and Liu in *Turandot*. Critics raved about Price's perfect Verdi and Mozart voice, admired her musical style, and noted her regal appearance on stage.

Alfred Frankenstein in the San Francisco *Chronicle* described Price voice and musical style: "Miss Price's voice is a little lighter in texture than those we are accustomed to hearing in this role. It has all the power the music demands, but it floats with a special quality that is new so far as *Aida* is concerned, and is profoundly moving. But no singer, no matter how beautiful and individual the timbre of her voice could have accomplished what Miss Price accomplished on her vocal quality alone. . . . Her ear is impeccable and so is her command of phrasing and nuance; over and above everything is her warm, vital, youthful and immensely appealing stage personality . . . " (Lyon, 80). Price's grace and regal appearance have also drawn considerable attention. She is five-feet, six-inches tall with full lips and broad nose making her "a strikingly attractive woman. . . . Her best features are her almost translucent brown skin, high cheekbones and expressive eyes set in charcoal shadows" (Lyon, 145). In the role of Aida, critics acclaimed her as a statuesque Aida, the most impressive they had seen in years. According to Ross Parmenter of the *New York Times*, "The glory of her performance was its singing, but its excellence in other respects should not go unnoticed. . . . She was Aida of such physical attractiveness that, for once, it was thoroughly understandable that Radames should prefer her to the high-born princess" (Lyon, 101).

Although she had a "couple of terrible crises in her career" (Sargeant, 148)—most notably that of the role of Minnie in Puccini's *Fanciulla del West* and as Cleopatra in *Anthony and Cleopatra*—Price continued broadening her repertoire and achieving triumphant successes. Her greatest roles include Aida, Amelia in *Un Ballo in Maschera*, Leonora in *Il Trovatore* and in *La Forza del Destino*, and as Doña Elvira in *Ernani*. Price was chosen as the star to open the new Met in Lincoln Center with the world premiere of Barber's *Anthony and Cleopatra* on September 16, 1966. Although the premiere was technically flawed, starring in the role was an honor for Price. She said "It was a beautiful score and I have tremendous respect for Barber as a composer. . . . I don't think you can find music more beautiful than some of it" (Lyon, 118).

Although a veteran of 118 Metropolitan performances between 1961 and 1969, Price reduced her appearances at the Met considerably during the 1970s. She stated:

> "I feel that you rest the voice and avoid pressure for considerable periods. You have to reflect too. I've been singing less and less everywhere. . . . I think a career, if it is good, should be handled like something really beautiful. . . . I have a very personal reason for not singing so much. It's just Leontyne trying to find out about Leontyne. I'm beginning to forget what I started out with—the completely natural joy of singing. It's almost coming back, and I'm trying not to lose it" (Sargeant, *Divas*, 160).

Price was more selective in her repertoire during the 1970s: "Price annexed several new operatic roles to her repertory. . . . A phalanx of disappointed critics regretted as 'deserving her own interest' her choice of Puccini's *Manon Lescait*, which she sang at the Metropolitan Opera House on February 7, 1975" (*Current Biography*, 331). However, her debut as Ariadne in Strauss's *Ariadne auf Naxos* at the San Francisco Opera on October 19, 1977, was, according to Arthur Bloomfield, "one of her greatest achievements" (*San Francisco Examiner*).

Price Returns to Recitals

From the late 1970s to her retirement in 1985, Price concentrated on her "first love," recitals, which allowed her to " . . . indulge a long standing prediliction both for spirituals and for songs by such contemporary composers as Samuel Barber, John LaMontaine, Ned Rorem, Margaret Bonds, and Dominick Argento" (Walsh, 67).

Price bade farewell to the opera stage on January 3, 1985, singing *Aida* to a tumultuous ovation. Robert Jacobson sums up her distinguished reign: "Perhaps *the* opera event of 1985 was the stage farewell of Leontyne Price who bid adieu with *Aida* . . . on the stage of the Metropolitan Opera—a fitting platform for the Mississippi born soprano, who over the decades had become *the* American prima donna personified. No natural born singer of her era has been so honored as Leontyne Price, and few singers of any nationality have captured the hearts of their public as she has over the years. . . ." (*Opera News*, 19). Price is quick to remind that she is departing from the opera stage but not from the platform, favoring more concerts and recitals and teaching master classes.

Among Price's many awards are the Presidential Medal of Freedom and an American Academy of Arts and Sciences' Fellow. She was awarded honorary doctorates from Dartmouth College, Howard University, Fordham University, Central State University, and Rust College. Besides being a trustee and member of the Board of Directors of International House and a member of the Advisory Board of the National

Cultural Center, Washington, D.C., Price also has served as honorary vice-chairperson of the U.S. National Committee of UNESCO. She received the Spirit of Achievement Award from Albert Einstein College of Medicine and the NAACP's Spingarn Medal, as well as the Order of Merit from the Republic of Italy. During her career she was presented twenty Grammy awards from the National Academy of Recording Arts and Sciences.

Since 1958, Price has recorded almost exclusively for RCA Victor. Her records include Negro spirituals, pop tunes, Christmas carols, hymns, American, French, and German art songs, and complete operas.

Price lives in a spacious federal-era townhouse in New York's Greenwich Village. Relishing her privacy, she enjoys working with her neighborhood block association and gardening. Price continues, however, to accept new challenges; in addition to her recitals, she is working on her autobiography and is actively involved with civic organizations. Of interest to both young readers and adults is the book *Aida*, told by Leontyne Price and illustrated by Leo and Diane Dillon (New York: Harcourt Brace Jovanovich, 1990), which captures the thrill of the opera as told by a diva.

Price is especially proud of the part she has played in opening the world's stages to younger black singers. She insists, "to the end of time . . . I will be the vehicle for major exposure for young black artists—sopranos, baritones, the whole thing" (*Opera News*).

References

Bloomfield, Arthur. *San Francisco Examiner*, 20 October 1977. Quoted in *Current Biography*, 1978.

Current Biography. New York: H. W. Wilson Co., 1978.

Eaton, Quaintance. *The Miracle of the Met*. New York: Meredith Press, 1968.

Frankenstein, Alfred. *San Francisco Chronicle*. Quoted in Hugh Lee Lyon. *Leontyne Price: Highlights of a Prima Donna*. New York: Vantage Press, 1973.

Garland, Phyl. "Leontyne Price: Getting Out At the Top." *Ebony* (June 1985): 31-36.

Harrison, Jay. *New York Herald Tribune*, 18 November 1954. Quoted in *Current Biography*, 1978. 330.

Hume, David. *Washington Post* August 1952. Quoted in Lyon, 66.

"I'm Just a Girl from Laurel Mississippi." *Ebony* 30 (February 1975): 40-41. Includes photograph.

Jacobson, Robert. "Collard Greens and Caviar." *Opera News* 50 (July 1985): 18-23.

Lanker, Brian. *I Dream a World*. New York: Stewart, Tabori and Chang, 1989. Photograph p. 45.

Lyon, Hugh Lee. *Leontyne Price: Highlights of a Prima Donna*. New York: Vantage Press, 1973.

Parmenter, Ross. *New York Times*. Quoted in Lyons, 101.

Rosenfield, John. "A New Porgy in Dallas." *Saturday Review*, 28 June 1952: 44.

Sargeant, Winthrop. *Divas*. New York: Coward, McCann & Geoghean, 1973.

———. "Musical Events. A Great Night." The *New Yorker* 4 February 1961: 102.

Schonberg, Harold. "A New and Handsome Aida Opens at Met." *New York Times*, 4 February, 1961.

Southern, Eileen. *Biographical Dictionary of Afro-American and African Musicians*. Westport, Conn.: Greenwood Press, 1982.

Story, Rosalyn M. *And So I Sing: Afro-American Divas of Opera and Concert*. New York: Warner Books, 1990.

Walsh, Maurice. "What Price Glory, Leontyne!" *Time* 14 January 1985.

Jacquelyn Jackson

Amelia Perry Pride

(1858-1932)

Educator, institution founder

Amelia Perry Pride was recognized as a distinguished teacher and civic leader in Lynchburg, Virginia. She was born in 1858 to William Perry and Ellen (George) Perry. She grew up in Lynchburg and later attended Hampton Institute, where she prepared herself for her life's work among the poor in her hometown. She graduated in 1876.

A teacher in the public schools for thirty-three years, Pride went on to become principal of Polk Street School for twenty years. Not content simply to reach the children who came to school, she organized and taught night school for adults and children who were unable to attend classes during the day. By the time the city established night schools, Pride's work with adults and children was already legendary.

Pride firmly believed that education was the salvation of her race and that education included more than the basic skills of reading, writing, and arithmetic. She opened a sewing school and a cooking school for girls who wanted to learn a vocation. So strong was her devotion to education for life that she joined the Red Cross and worked teaching conservation (home economics) to adults who needed to know how to make the most of meager funds.

Describing challenges she faced, Pride wrote about her philosophy and work in letters to Hampton Institute's alumni office. Of her concern for the destitute and her efforts to help them, she wrote:

> The salvation of our boys and girls is to be effected through industrial training. That they need it as individuals and as a whole has long been decided. How and in what form to give it when all are needy and means are wanting is a serious problem. In my work among the destitute I have been forced time and again to ask myself the question, am I really helping, when those who are aided do not know how to husband what is given them, is there economy in giving, when what has been given is destroyed or not utilized? (Amelia Perry Pride to the Alumni Office, Hampton Institute, n.d.).

Pride also wrote of her concern for self-help, a philosophy that Booker T. Washington, also a Hampton graduate, espoused:

> I believe in training the head, heart, and hands. It is impossible to have good boys and girls unless they are industrious (Amelia Perry Pride to the Alumni Office, Hampton Institute, n.d.).

Her contributions were cited in an article in the *Daily Advance*, February 1918, in which the writer noted that Pride worked in the campaign in the interest of food conservation among "colored people" in Lynchburg. Her channels of contact came through churches, clubs, and homes of black families. Her experience as a domestic science teacher in "colored" schools was credited with aiding her greatly in her instruction about food substitutes.

Home for the Elderly Destitute Founded

As a member of the Eighth Street Baptist Church, Pride spread her message of the importance of education, values, and concern to older residents of the community. A staunch fund-raiser, she secured enough support from women in the neighborhood to open Dorchester Home for elderly women in Lynchburg. To provide the services and goods needed by the older women who were taken into the home, Amelia Pride organized one hundred women into working committees. The leadership required to manage this task was enormous. Nevertheless, she continued her work as an elementary school teacher, church worker, and general counselor in the community.

Continuing to solicit additional funds for the home for the elderly, Pride attracted the attention of residents of Dorchester, Massachusetts. They contributed funds to purchase a building and provide food, fuel, clothing, and other supplies. She named the Dorchester Home in honor of these contributors.

While working in schools and community, Pride maintained a strong family life. She was married on December 27, 1881, to Claiborne G. Pride, a barber from Lynchburg. They had three sons and two granddaughters. Amelia Pride's health was impaired as a result of two automobile accidents. She died on June 4, 1932.

The esteem in which Amelia Perry Pride was held is reflected in the honor given her name in 1950. The following exerpt of a letter to her niece, Marian Pride Kyle, from Paul M. Munro, then Superintendent of Schools in Lynchburg, Virginia, describes the naming of a school in her honor.

> This is to officially advise you that in the Fall of 1949, upon the completion of a lovely building to house the Vocational Home Economics classes of the Dunbar High School, on my recommendation, the house was named by the Lynchburg School Board, Amelia Pride House, in honor of your late grandmother, who I understand was largely responsible many years ago for the introduction of Home Economics into the course of study in the Negro upper schools of Lynchburg. You will be interested to know that across the entrance to this lovely building are the words in black letters against a light background, Amelia Pride House (3 September 1950).

References

Daily Advance, Lynchburg, Virginia, February 1918.

Munro, Paul M. to Marian Pride Kyle. 3 September 1950.

Neverdon-Morton, Cynthia. *Afro-American Women of the South and the Advancement of the Race, 1895-1925.* Knoxville: University of Tennessee Press, 1987.

Pride, Amelia Perry. Letters to the Alumni Office, Hampton Institute, Lynchburg, Virginia, n.d.

Collections

Materials on Amelia Perry Pride are in the University Archives, Hampton University.

Elaine P. Witty

Pearl Primus

(1919-)

Dancer

Pearl Primus has been a pioneer in the development of black dance as an art rather than as simple entertainment. For her, not only has dance played a crucial role in her own personal and artistic growth, it also has a vital role to play in black liberation.

Primus, the only daughter of Edward Primus and Emily (Jackson) Primus, was born in Trinidad on November 29, 1919. The family moved to New York when she was two. She attended Hunter High School and graduated from Hunter College in 1940 with a major in biology. One of the school's finest athletes, she was a sprinter who set school records in the broad and high jumps. She had no intention of becoming a dancer, but there were no laboratory jobs open to blacks at that time and the lingering depression continued to make jobs of any sort scarce.

Initiating a pattern that would recur over the years, Primus combined taking further classes with her other activities. She continued her education in night school at New York University (NYU), taking health education courses in her first year and psychology courses in the second. The National Youth Administration could find no daytime job for her in her field and placed her as an understudy in one of the dance groups it sponsored. This was her first experience in dance and her progress was rapid. About July 1941 she tried for and won a scholarship from the New Dance Group, becoming the first black student at the school—at one stage of her connection with this organization, she cleaned the studio in exchange for lessons. When the NYA's dance program was closed down in the summer of 1941, she held a series of unrelated jobs to support herself, ranging from welder-burner to switchboard operator.

At the same time, Primus continued to work and perform with the New Dance Group's performing company, and by the middle of 1942 she had made a decision to pursue a career as a dancer. Her debut appearance at the New York Young Men's Hebrew (YMHA) Association on February 14, 1943, was successful, and she accepted the subsequent offer of Cafe Society Downtown to appear there as an entertainer. She worked there for ten months beginning in April. In April 1944 she presented a solo performance, again at the YMHA, and worked after this at Cafe Society Uptown. Backed by her own troupe, which included four male dancers, seven musicians, two singers, a narrator, and the folksinger Josh White, Primus appeared in a ten-day run on Broadway at the Belasco Theater in October 1944; she also had a month's engagement at the Roxy Theater in New York before the end of that year. Between January 1 and November 2, 1946, she appeared as a featured dancer in a revival of *Show Boat,* and she also appeared as a witch doctor in a two-performance production of *The Emperor Jones* at the Chicago Civic Opera in October of that year. From November 1946 to February 1947, Primus toured with her own company, principally in the South.

Primus's appearance at the University of the Dance in Jacob's Pillow, Massachusetts, in August 1947 gave the *Time* reviewer occasion to describe her dancing:

> Her forte is force. Says she: "My body is built for heavy stomping, powerful dignity." She usually dances to an accompaniment of pulsing drums. In one of her new works, *Santo,* a psychological study of the clash of Voodooism and Christianity in Cuba, fascinated students watched an exhibition of primitive panther-like power and grace. In *The Shouters of Sobo,* a work based on the traditions of African stonecutters, students got a lesson in gripping, concentrated intensity. With muscled shoulders hunched over bended knees, her powerful arms pounding, her whole body dynamically dramatic, everything about her was directed downward with terrible force ("Little Primitive," 42-43).

In 1948 Pearl Primus was awarded the last fellowship given by the Rosenwald Foundation; her original idea had been to build a work around a poem from James Weldon Johnson's *God's Trombones,* but she finally proposed going to Liberia to study African dance. Her interest in Africa was already well-developed; many of her own dance creations were built on African elements, and she had written an article on African Dance that appeared in *Dance Magazine* in July 1946. Compared to her predecessor in seeking inspiration in African tradition, Katherine Dunham, Primus was to remain closer to the original dances in her recreations, conceding less to the demands of her American audiences. Thus, her dances appeared less sexy and flamboyant than Dunham's but were more authentic. Her experiences in Liberia—where President William V. S. Tubman awarded her the Order of the Star of Africa medal—were expanded by time in Ghana, Angola, Cameroon, Senegal, and Zaire. For many years during this period she was pursuing a doctorate in anthropology at Columbia University in addition to performing and teaching dance.

During a period of folklore research in Trinidad in 1953, Primus met Percival Borde. Impressed by his potential as a dancer, she invited him to New York to her school. Borde was able to make his professional debut in late 1958 to rave reviews, and in early 1959 her dance group became Pearl Primus, Percival Borde, and Company. The school also became a joint operation. The two had married in 1954 and they have one son, Onwin, born about 1955, who is now a dancer, musician, and stage manager for his mother's programs. Primus and Borde shared their professional lives, and they have traveled in Africa together, spending a two-year period as guests of the Liberian government and making another trip in 1962 under the sponsorship of the Rebekah Harkness Foundation and the State Department.

In 1966 Primus's continuing interests in Africa, dance, and education were reflected in "A Pilot Study in the Integration of Visual Form and Anthropological Content for Use in Teaching Children Ages Six to Eleven about Cultures and Peoples of the World," with funding from the United States Office of Education and the Unitarian Universalist Service Committee. This study brought dance into several schools and had a research component, which was designed to serve as part of the requirements for the completion of her doctorate at the New York University School of Education.

Primus said in 1968, "The dance has been my teacher, ever so patiently revealing to me the dignity, beauty, and strength in the cultural heritage of my people as a vital part of the great heritage of *all* mankind" (Estrada, 56). She adds:

> Why do I dance? Dance is my medicine. It's the scream which eases for a while the terrible frustration common to all human beings who, because of race, creed or color, are "invisible." Dance is the fist with which I fight the sickening ignorance of prejudice. It is the veiled contempt I feel for those who patronize with false smiles, handouts, empty promises, insincere compliments. . . . Instead of growing twisted like a gnarled tree inside myself, I am able to dance out my anger and frustrations (Estrada, 58).

A day later in an afterthought to the interview, Primus added, "Because through dance I have experienced the wordless joy of freedom, I seek it more fully now for my people and for people everywhere" (60).

Judith Jamison and the Alvin Ailey Dance Company recognize their debts to pioneering African-American dancers and choreographers like Primus. Her work, *Impinyuza* (1952) was featured in their 1990-1991 season. Primus is currently far from being only a precursor. She actively presents a series of dances and lectures using African dances and music. She also serves as professor of ethnic studies at the Five Colleges, an educational consortium made up of Amherst, Smith, Hampshire, and Mount Holyoke colleges and the University of Massachusetts.

References

Estrada, Ric. "Three Leading Negro Artists, and How They Feel about Dance in the Community." *Dance* 42 (November 1968): 45-60. Includes photographs.

Hentoff, Nat. "An Inheritance Comes to P.S. 83." *American Education* 2 (February 1966): 29-32. Includes photographs.

"Little Primitive." *Time* 50 (25 August 1947): 42-43. Includes photographs.

Patterson, Lindsay, ed. *Anthology of the American Negro in the Theatre*. New York: Publishers Company, 1970.

"Pearl Primus." *Current Biography*. New York: H. W. Wilson, 1945.

"Pearl Primus." *Ebony* 6 (January 1951): 54-58.

"Pearl's Prodigy." *Ebony* 14 (March 1959): 46-53.

Primus, Pearl. Publicity leaflet. Lordly and Dame, 51 Church Street, Boston, MA 02116.

Who's Who Among Black Americans. 3rd ed. Northbrook, Ill.: Who's Who Among Black Americans, 1981.

Who's Who of American Women. 8th ed. Chicago: Marquis, 1975.

Collections

The Julius Rosenwald Fund Archives, Fisk University Library, includes biographical material and photographs of Pearl Primus.

Robert L. Johns

Lucy Terry Prince

(c. 1730-1821)

Poet, orator

The mother of six children, wife to an aging man, and former slave, Lucy Terry Prince is a remarkable example of the black woman's legacy of achievement. She is noted for her eloquent oration and one printed poem. The text of her poem appears in anthologies including *The Poetry of the Negro*, *Introduction to Black Literature in America*, *The Black Poets*, and *Afro-American Women Writers*.

Born somewhere in West Africa circa 1730, Lucy Terry (slave name) was kidnapped and brought to Rhode Island as an infant. From infancy to the age of five there is no record of her life.

In 1735 Terry was sold to Ensign Ebenezer Wells. She toiled as a slave in the Wells's household in Deerfield, Massachusetts. On June 15, 1735, at the age of five, young Lucy was baptized. The Great Awakening in New England and the missionary impetus to christianize Africans no doubt prompted Terry's mistress to have the small slave girl baptized. Terry joined the church in 1744, when she was fourteen years old.

Two years later on August 25, 1746, the sixteen-year-old Terry was witness to an Indian ambush. This event gave rise to her poem, the only example of her poetry known to exist, "Bars Fight":

> August, 'twas the twenty-fifth,
> Seventeen hundred forty-six
> The Indians did in ambush lay,
> Some very valient men to slay,
> The names of whom I'll not leave out
> Samuel Allen like a hero fout,
> And though he was so brace and bold,
> His face no more shall we behold.
>
> Eleazer Hawks was killed outright,
> Before he had time to fight,—
> Before he did the Indians see,
> Was shot and killed immediately.

Oliver Amsden he was slain,
Which caused his friends much grief and pain.
Simeon Amsden they found dead
Not many rods distant from his head.

Adonijah Gillett we do hear,
Did lose his life which was so dear.
John Sadler fled across the water
And thus escaped the dreadful slaughter.

Eunice Allen see the Indians coming
And hopes to save herself by running;
And had not her petticoats stopped her,
The awful creatures had not catched her,
Nor tommy hawked her on the head
And left her on the ground for dead.
Young Samuel Allen, Oh, lack-a-day,
Was taken and carried to Canada.

Terry's poem was first printed in 1855 by Josiah Gilbert Holland, who included it in his *History of Western Massachusetts*.

Although there is but one surviving poem, Terry's life is testimony to her remarkable talent and abilities. Described as "a twenty-eight-line vivid doggered description," the simple ballad is possibly equal to any of the early verse of colonial America, including Anne Bradstreet's.

On May 16, 1756, Terry married Bijah Prince before the local justice of the peace, Major Wells. Bijah Prince was a former slave who was set free and given land by the terms of his master's will. Prince purchased his wife's freedom, and they moved from Deerfield, Massachusetts, to Guilford, Vermont, where Prince was given a "hundred-acre lot by Deacon Samuel Feild" (Wright). Terry and her husband also owned land in Sunderland, Vermont, a lot not far from the home of Ethan Allen.

Prince Argues for Justice

Terry gave birth to six children. Each child was baptized and their names duly recorded: Caesar, born January 14, 1757; Durexa, born June 1, 1758; Drucella, August 7, 1770; Festus, December 12, 1763; Tatnai, September 2, 1765, and Abijah, June 12, 1769. The children were educated in the local Guilford schools, but when Ceasar was ready to attend college, he was barred from admission because of his race. Terry spent several hours before the Board of Trustees of Williams College (Massachusetts) trying to persuade them to change their racist policy. She was unsuccessful, but she was perhaps the first African-American woman to fight publicly against discrimination, reportedly arguing for three hours, quoting Gospel and law verbatim.

The Prince home was a center for political and literary discussions. One of the Prince daughters, Durexa, reportedly was a poet, and Terry was "noted for her rhyme and stories" and also for "her wit and wisdom" (Wright, 159).

Terry was a gifted orator as well as a poet. "Her gift for oratory gained national prominence when she brought a suit against Colonel Eli Bronson, a neighbor in Sunderland" (Shockley, 14). Colonel Bronson attempted to claim some of the Prince land for his own. Terry retained Isaac Ticknor, who would later become governor of Vermont, as her attorney. However, when the case reached the Vermont Supreme Court, she became dissatisfied with Ticknor's arguments and pleaded her own case. Justice Samuel Chase presided and is reported to have said that "Lucy made a better argument than he had heard from any lawyer at the Vermont Bar" (Katz, 184).

Prince, who was twenty-four years his wife's senior, died in 1794, and Terry moved to Sunderland, where she lived the remainder of her life. In 1812, she lost her oldest daughter, Durexa. The cause of death is unknown. For years Terry made an annual pilgrimage on horseback from Sunderland over the Green Mountains to Guilford in order to visit her husband's grave.

Terry lived to be ninety-one. She died in Sunderland, Vermont, in 1821. She was survived by her oldest son, Ceasar, who fought in the Revolutionary War, settled in Sunderland, and died in 1836. She was also survived by four other children: Drucella; Festus, who married a white woman and settled in Sunderland; Tatnai, who married a Quaker shopkeeper and moved to Salem, New York; and Abijah.

References

Green, Lorenzo J. *The Negro in Colonial New England.* New York: Columbia University Press, 1942.

Katz, Bernard. "A Second Version of Lucy Terry's Early Ballad." *Negro History Bulletin* 29 (1966): 183-84.

Sheldon, George. *A History of Deerfield, Massachusetts.* Vol. 1. Greenfield, Mass.: E. M. Hall, 1895.

Stetson, Erlene. *Black Sister: Poetry of Black American Women, 1746-1980.* Bloomington: Indiana University Press, 1981.

Wright, Martha R, "Bijah's Luce of Guilford." *Negro History Bulletin* 27 (1965): 152-53, 159.

Nagueyalti Warren

Nancy Gardner Prince

(1799- ?)

Servant, seamstress, religious worker, writer

In *A Narrative of the Life and Travels of Mrs. Nancy Prince,* Nancy Gardner Prince recorded her travels and published her observations of life as a freeborn nineteenth-century domestic servant from Massachusetts, whose marriage led her to the Russian Courts of Alexander I and Nicholas I, and whose humanitarian interests later led her to serve among the recently emancipated slaves of Jamaica.

Prince was born on September 15, 1799, in the commercial seaport of Newburyport, Massachusetts. She was the second of her mother's eight children by the second of her mother's four husbands. Prince's father, Thomas Gardner, was born of African descent in Nantucket and died when Prince was three months old; her mother was born in Gloucester, she recalls in her autobiography (5). (The name is spelled "Gardener" in the narrative's first edition [1850], "Gardner" in the second and third editions [1853, 1856]. Prince's mother's name is not provided in the narrative, but her maiden name was, presumably, Wornton.)

Prince provided more detail about her maternal grandparents and stepfather. Her grandfather, Tobias Wornton (also called "Backus"), a slave who had been abducted from Africa in his youth, was "in the Revolutionary army, and at the battle of Bunker Hill"; her grandmother, an "Indian of this country" who became "a captive of the English, or their descendants," served "as a domestic in the Parsons family" (5). Stepfather Money Vose, whom Prince repeatedly refers to as having been abusive to herself and her older sister, came to America as an African slave; he jumped ship at an unspecified free-state port, was employed as a seaman, was pressed into British maritime service during the War of 1812, suffered "dropsy," and "died oppressed, in the English dominions" (7).

Although Prince had little if any formal education, she "had enjoyed the happy privilege of religious instruction," thanks to her maternal grandfather, a devout member of the Congregational Church (11). Prince states that she "was very limited in education" (44); she may have had some schooling, however, for she makes an otherwise curious statement that her grandfather "thought it was wrong for us to go to school where the teacher was not devoted to God" (11). In addition, she learned a trade (presumably that of seamstress) prior to her marriage and move to Saint Petersburg, Russia, and within six months after that move, had learned enough of the languages spoken at court "to be able to attend to" the business that she started there (38).

With the death of Prince's stepfather, her mother and six younger siblings were left unprovided for. Not yet fifteen years of age, Prince helped by picking and selling berries, and was later compelled to leave Gloucester to work for wages as a domestic; first in Essex, then in Salem, where she attended upon a "sanctimonious" family of seven for three months—until "hard labor and unkindness" had deteriorated Prince's health to the extent that she was sent back to her mother (11-12).

Prince labored tirelessly and often unsuccessfully on behalf of her family. During the winter of 1815-1816, Prince walked to Boston from Salem to rescue her "deluded" older sister Silvia from a house of "harlots" (12, 14). Working in Boston in 1817, Prince anticipated that the combined wages of herself and eldest siblings might finally provide her family "comfort and respectability"; however, her mother then married a man who expected the older children to support him, and for Prince this was "like death to us all" (18). Baptized in 1817 by Reverend Thomas Paul, Prince's religious faith sustained her during this "seven years of anxiety and toil" in which she labored to assist her mother and find homes and employment for her siblings (20).

In 1822 Prince left her position in Boston to learn a trade and made up her mind to leave her country. The following year, her future husband, identified only as Mr. Prince, arrived from an earlier voyage to Russia; on February 15, 1824, the twenty-three-year-old married Mr. Prince, departing with him for St. Petersburg two months later. Mr. Prince was born in "Marlborough" (probably Marlboro, Massachusetts), lived with families there during his youth, and went to Gloucester in 1810, sailing for Russia with Captain Theodore Stanwood. Prince's description of her husband is vague and ambiguous; it is likely that Mr. Prince was freeborn to a poor family or was possibly orphaned and placed in homes during his youth, as were Prince and her siblings. On his second voyage to Saint Petersburg (1812), Mr. Prince stayed behind to serve a noblewoman of the royal court and, later, to replace one of twenty "colored men" serving as hall sentries at the palace of the Czar (23). Prince may have met or known about Mr. Prince previously; she mentions that he visited her mother during a period of time subsequent to his first voyage; Prince could have been at that time about twelve years old.

Prince Establishes Orphanage

Arriving in Saint Petersburg on June 21, 1824, the Princes were later presented to Emperor Alexander I and Empress Elizabeth. Prince weaves into her description of this event a subtle reference to the racism she had left behind: "There was no prejudice against color; there were there all castes, and the people of all nations, each in their place" (23). The enterprising Prince began boarding children and started her own business making baby linens and children's garments "handsomely wrought in the French and English styles," which were purchased by the "present Empress" (that is, in 1850) "and by other nobility" (39). Her business was apparently successful enough to warrant employing a journeywoman and apprentices. She attended Protestant services, was active in a ladies' society, helped establish an asylum for orphans in Saint Petersburg, and passed out Bibles at the royal palace.

Nearly ten years after her arrival, Prince left Saint Petersburg in 1833 for reasons of health. Mr. Prince felt it best that he remain for a time in Saint Petersburg to accumulate property—also, as Prince suggests, "It is difficult for any one in the Emperor's employment to leave when they please" (40). Mr. Prince died, however, before he could return, leaving his thirty-four-year-old wife on her own.

Returning to Boston, Prince devoted herself to humanitarian service. Empathizing with the plight of the orphans in the city, Prince organized an institution for homeless children who "on account of color" were "shut out from all the asylums for poor children" (41). She worked on this project for three months, but the orphan asylum closed for lack of adequate funding. She began attending meetings of the antislavery societies, and eventually met a Reverend Ingraham who lectured on the conditions of emancipated slaves in Jamaica and sought to enlist help for his mission in Kingston. Seeing a "field of usefulness" spread out before her, Prince Prince volunteered, justifying her decision with these words: "I hoped that I might aid, in some small degree, to raise up and encourage the emancipated inhabitants, and teach the young children to read and work, to fear God, and put their trust in the Saviour" (43, 45). (Slaves under British domination in the West Indies had been emancipated in 1833.)

Prince eventually made two voyages to Jamaica. In December 1840 she arrived at Saint Ann Harbor, planning to continue on to Kingston and help Mr. Ingraham; convinced by a Mr. Abbott to help with the mission in Saint Ann, however, Prince stayed there. Repeatedly witnessing what she felt was inappropriate conduct on the part of teachers and leaders there, Prince complained to the minister, who threatened her with dismissal if she could not obey established policies. Before her dismissal became necessary, Prince became ill and gave up her position with the Saint Ann school. Unaware that Reverend Ingraham had lost his position in Kingston, Prince traveled there in April 1841 and established a society whose goal was to provide a Free Labor School "for the poor girls that were destitute" (55). Prince returned to America in July 1841, raising funds for her school throughout Boston, New York, and Philadelphia.

Prince arrived in Kingston for the second time in May 1842, in the aftermath of a bloody insurrection. She called upon the American Consul to request assistance in leaving Kingston, but was persuaded by her Kingston colleagues to manage her Free Labor School for a three-month trial period. Realizing afterwards that these colleagues were merely trying to swindle her, she departed Jamaica in August as soon as passage was available. Her voyage was fraught with danger. The ship's captain tried to induce Prince into disembarking at Key West, where free "colored" persons could be legally taken into "custody"; a storm threatened food and water supplies; and many of Prince's personal belongings were stolen.

In New York City, with the help of Lewis Tappan and others, Prince was able to retrieve some of her goods from the ship and finally made her way to Boston in August 1843. Despite frequent infirmities, she labored with success to support herself during her first twenty months there, but was later "broken up in business" on three occasions, embarrassing her and obliging her to move (85). During the period 1848-1849, friends came to her relief, and in the following year she published the first edition of her narrative in the hopes that by doing so, she could "obtain the means to help supply my necessities" (preface). Sometime between the publication of her narrative's second and third editions (1853-1856), Prince's health deteriorated seriously; to the preface of her third and last edition, she added that she had lost the power of her arms. Circumstances of her life beyond 1856 remain unrevealed.

Among the notable contemporaries whom Prince met or associated with during the first half of the nineteenth century were the Russian Czar Alexander I, the wives of Alexander I and Nicholas I, and the American philanthropists and abolitionists Lewis Tappan and Lucretia Mott.

Prince's narrative includes a travelogue of Copenhagen, Saint Petersburg, and the West Indies. She incorporates details about the royal court at Saint Petersburg, Russian religious and educational practices, geography, holidays, languages, the flood of 1824 (during which she nearly lost her own life), the cholera epidemic of 1831, the deaths of Emperor Alexander I and Empress Elizabeth, the succession of Nicholas I, the Decembrist revolt of 1826, and more. She incorporated into her narrative her fifteen-page pamphlet, *The West Indies: Being a Description of the Islands, Progress of Christianity, Education, and Liberty among the Colored Population Generally,* with a general history of slavery and British domination in the West Indies, and an account of the Sierra Leone resettlement experiment—all of which is permeated with Prince's repeated denunciation of poverty, inhumanity, and the greed and corruption she observed among teachers and clergymen of many ethnic backgrounds serving in Jamaica during her two visits.

References

Foster, Frances Smith. "Adding Color and Contour to Early American Self-Portraitures: Autobiographical Writings of Afro-American Women." In *Conjuring: Black Women, Fiction, and Literary Tradition.* Edited by Marjorie Pryse and Hortense J. Spillers. Bloomington: Indiana University Press, 1985.

Loewenberg, Bert James, and Ruth Bogin. *Black Women in Nineteenth-Century American Life.* University Park: Pennsylvania State University Press, 1976.

Prince, Nancy. *A Narrative of the Life and Travels of Mrs. Nancy Prince.* 2nd ed. Boston: Privately printed, 1853. 3rd ed. 1856.

———. *The West Indies: Being a Description of the Islands, Progress of Christianity, Education, and Liberty among the Colored Population Generally.* Boston: Dow and Jackson, 1841.

Shockley, Ann Allen, ed. "Nancy Gardener Prince." *Afro-American Women Writers, 1756-1933.* Boston: G. K. Hall, 1988.

Jo Dawn McEwan

Ernesta G. Procope

(19?-)

Entrepreneur

Ernesta Gertrude Foster Bowman Procope is the founder and president of the nation's largest black-owned insurance brokerage agency, E.G. Bowman Company, with an estimated thirty million dollars in annual premium sales and a client list that includes more than fifty Fortune 500 corporations. She is married to John Procope, publisher and editor of the *Amsterdam News*, the nation's largest weekly newspaper for blacks, who also serves as chief executive officer of E. G. Bowman Company. She has no children.

Procope was born in Brooklyn, New York, the only daughter among the four children born of West Indian immigrants, Clarence and Elvira Lord Foster, who entered the Bedford-Stuyvesant section of Brooklyn in the 1910s. She studied music at an early age, performing in concert with eight other students at Carnegie Hall. She graduated from the New York High School of Music and Art, attended Brooklyn College for a short time, and entered Pohs Institute of Insurance and Real Estate. In 1950 she gained her real estate license.

Procope began her career in insurance as a result of the encouragement she received from her first husband, Albin Bowman, a real estate developer whom she married in the late 1940s. Many neighborhoods in which he owned property, including his own office building in the Bedford-Stuyvesant neighborhood, were poor, and because insurance for these buildings was difficult to obtain, he had the idea of insuring them himself. Bowman encouraged his wife to enter the Pohs Institute in 1950 and at the time of Bowman's death in 1952, Procope was handling all their insurance needs. She formed the E. G. Bowman Company in 1953. At the time, hers was one of only a handful of companies providing insurance to black families for new and existing homes.

Ernesta G. Procope

During the late 1960s, most of Procope's business centered around Bedford-Stuyvesant, and insurance companies, fearful of the urban rioting going on elsewhere and threatening in that area, canceled some 80 percent of her clients' insurance. She then became actively involved in the Bedford-Stuyvesant Restoration Corporation, a community-based economic development program founded in 1967 to stem the rapid deterioration of the area, and by 1968 Procope was handling all the property-casualty insurance of the program. She kept her office in this section of Brooklyn until 1979.

In 1970, Procope began courting the commercial insurance market accounts, expanding her client list to include corporate enterprises. She also successfully bid for the entire employee benefits package of the Community Development Agency (CDA), an umbrella organization for the city's antipoverty agencies. She established a subdivision, Bowman-Procope Associates, to oversee those benefit programs, that now cover seventeen thousand employees.

Innovative programs begun by Procope included a data-processing system to solve the problems of reporting and documentation at the CDA, employee education programs about health and safety, and an approach to corporate accounts that included a scripted cassette called "We Can't Let George Do It Anymore," pointing out the need for managers to be more cautious and responsible for safety and programming. "These demonstrated not only her commitment to providing clients with adequate insurance coverage, but her concern with keeping costs within the client cost at a minimum by preventing loss" (Schwab 121).

Using affirmative-action program techniques and innovative employment policies and applying these principles to the acquisition of corporate accounts resulted in a client list that now includes such giants as Control Data, Pepsi-Co, IBM, General Motors, and Gulf Oil.

During the early 1970s, Procope was instrumental in the passage of the New York State Fair Plan, which guaranteed homeowner's insurance in poor neighborhoods. Keeping her ties to the old Bedford-Stuyvesant neighborhood, Procope continues to insure churches, organizations, and schools such as Howard University, although these clients and personal-property and casualty insurance make up only five percent of her current business. In 1972, she was named "Woman of the Year" by the black newspaper supplement

Tuesday at Home. By 1973, Avon Products had become a client, and in 1974 she joined its board of directors, now serving as chair of its audit committee. Procope was honored to serve as the United States representative to Gambia's tenth anniversary celebration in 1975. In 1979, she moved her company to new offices at 97 Wall Street, a move she felt would bring her company into the mainstream of commercial insurance brokerage. Her continuing aim is to stress cost reduction, emphasize risk analysis, and encourage clients to improve on-the-job-safety techniques. She is also on the board of directors of many other corporations and organizations including the Salvation Army, Chubb Corporation, and the Urban National Corporation, which invests in minority businesses nationwide.

Procope is a diminutive woman who nonetheless radiates stature and warmth, tenderness, and depth. Her genteel elegance complements a powerful, astute mind and has aided her rise to prominence and tremendous success among client companies, large and small. Her youthful physical appearance is evidence of her belief in the importance of good health. She enjoys relaxing in the pool and sauna installed in the Queens home she shares with her husband and credits this relaxation technique with elevating her creative energy level. Procope prefers not to reveal her age, projecting a youthfulness and energetic spirit that makes age irrelevant.

Insurance Company Reflects Business Philosophy

From the very start of her career, Procope's business philosophy has reflected her concern for the need to provide insurance to all client companies, regardless of size. Although she founded her company primarily to handle the needs of her first husband's investment properties, as word of her abilities spread, she soon branched out into the areas of homeowner's and business insurance sales.

From the beginning, Procope's primary business goal has been to build a professional insurance company that would be accepted and respected by the mainstream American business establishment. This goal, she knew, was a lofty one for a small, black-owned agency operating in a ghetto and run by a woman, but Procope persevered, never forgetting the commitment she made in the early years to serve the needs of her traditional clients. Even with that commitment, she knew the firm would have to grow and expand if it was going to be financially successful.

Developing the necessary skills to make her company a success, Procope says, was a combination of her formal education at the Pohs Institute and what she refers to as on-the-job-training:

> In order to develop an insurance-brokerage agency, the skill one must have is the ability to sell. When I first became interested in insurance, I didn't really equate it with sales—that came later. But, if you have a product to offer, you have to sell it (Gayle, 22).

Continuing skills development remains Procope's major concern, both for herself and her staff, who regularly attend seminars and keep abreast of changes in the industry by reading periodicals and professional journals. "It's a dynamic field—it changes almost daily," Procope says (Gayle, 22). The challenge of staying ahead of these changes and incorporating new ideas into the company's way of doing business has helped to create a firm to be reckoned with. She attributes her success to a willingness to work hard and show tenacity in the face of seemingly insurmountable odds, characteristics she believes are not necessarily associated with her sex.

> I don't think the fact that I'm a woman has hindered me, but I do believe that being black has been somewhat of a deterrent in moving ahead. To build the company, I needed to get large commercial accounts. I could get in the door because I'm black and a woman and they were curious to see what I'm all about. That doesn't necessarily mean I would be able to sell the account. I think it was harder to sell commercial accounts because my company was small and black-owned rather than because of the fact that it was owned by a woman (Gayle, 22).

Procope believes in building a strong organization in support of existing management, a cue she took from large corporations, and in encouraging other women to enter the insurance field. Regular employee seminars and a predominantly female staff are the legacy of these efforts.

"I think it's important to create a dialogue among employees—it makes them feel involved with the company," Procope says. "It's constructive communication: we get their input about how they feel about the company and where they want to go within it, and they keep up-to-date on what the company is doing" (Gayle, 22).

Procope believes her exposure to the inner workings of large corporations has provided her an opportunity to benefit from their success, particularly in the area of structural organization. This exposure, she adds, "has been a great experience for me—just in that area if nothing else. I believe in perpetuity. I want to build an organization that is not here just while I'm here. That is why I've always attempted to build people behind me. I want this organization to prosper, and I want it to become a meaningful entity in this country" (Gayle, 22).

While she is modest about her own accomplishments and the role she has played in the phenomenal growth of her company, Procope is vocal about her pride in serving on the boards of directors of numerous organizations and corporations, especially the Urban National Corporation, which was set up to make equity investments in minority businesses.

"Being on boards of directors is a very important role," Procope explains. "The board oversees what management does, setting up committees such as compensation, which examines salaries, pension plans and benefits. It's very much how the government works" (Mourges-Rudolph, 31). She feels uniquely qualified to advise other board members about possible improvements and innovations in insurance needs because she understands both what the insurance carriers and the employees require concerning coverage. It is this balanced perspective and her goal to provide consistent improvement that have enabled Procope to gain a voice in the process of creating quality insurance coverage as well as gaining her the respect and admiration of her peers and business associates.

Ambitious, energetic, and unwilling to settle for the success her firm has earned to date, Procope keeps a firm hand on the present and an ever-watchful eye on the future. Having made great strides in developing a solid customer base nationwide, she says the next step is to expand the company beyond the boundaries of the fifty states, particularly to Puerto Rico and Canada. She admits that while her goals may seem lofty, they are attainable:

> It falls to us to convince major corporations that we can handle their needs—effectively and competently . . . the key word is exposure. We know our own capabilities and when to stop. All we ask is an opportunity, because one day we might be in a position to be world-wide ourselves (Mourges-Rudolph, 31).

With persistence, driven by the desire to help both clients and employees benefit, Procope has created a strong and growing company.

References

''A View From the Top.'' *Black Enterprise* 5 (June 1975): 79.

Gayle, Rosalie. ''Procope: Premium Power Broker.'' *Working Woman* 4 (December 1978): 21, 22.

Iverem, Esther. ''Wall Street Success Story: How One Woman Guided Her Insurance Company to the Top.'' *Essence* 19 (October 1988): 130.

McLeod, Douglas. ''Small Fish Swims in Exclusive Pond of Corporate Clients.'' *Crains New York Business*, 25 July 1988.

Mourges-Rudolph, Denise. ''Ernesta Procope: No. 1 in Insurance.'' *Sepia* 27 (May 1978): 27, 31.

Prufer, Diana. ''A Premium Life: Ernesta Procope Battled Scandal and Racism to Build a Twenty-five Million Dollar Insurance Brokerage.'' *Savvy* 9 (October 1988): 40.

Schwab, Priscilla. ''A Little Tokenism Can Help.'' *Nation's Business* 67 (December 1979): 121.

Wansley, Joy. ''Opening Doors, Especially on Wall Street, is no Easy Task, but Ernesta Procope Managed It.'' *People Weekly* (December 1978): 203.

Who's Who among Black Americans, 1990/91. Detroit: Gale Research, 1990.

Thura R. Mack

Barbara Gardner Proctor

(1933-)

Entrepreneur, writer

Barbara Gardner Proctor's career as an advertising entrepreneur is marked by her courage to maintain high standards, and unwavering belief in her abilities and talents, and her willingness to assume risks. Through determination, she has been able to overcome discriminatory barriers, becoming a highly respected business leader.

Proctor was born November 30, 1933, in Black Mountain, North Carolina, the only child of a single mother. She was raised by her grandmother and an uncle, Morgan. Proctor's early academic achievements led to a scholarship at Talladega College in Alabama, which she attended in the 1950s, earning a B.A. in English education and a B.A. in psycholo-

Barbara Gardner Proctor

gy and social science. There she was a recipient of the Armstrong Creative Writing Award in 1954.

Proctor's transition from college to the multimillion-dollar career she is presently involved in was a gradual one. Her resume includes: jazz music critic and contributing editor, *Downbeat* magazine, beginning in 1958; Vee-Jay Records International, Chicago, 1961-64, where she began by writing descriptive comments for jazz record album covers and became international director; Post-Keys-Gardner Advertising, Chicago, 1965-68; Gene Taylor Associates, Chicago, 1968-69; and North Advertising Agency, Chicago, where she was copy supervisor, from 1969 to 1970. Proctor has a strong belief in "the need for quality and equality in advertising" (Brown, 307). Armed with her degrees, her professional experience, and the will to succeed, she formed her own firm in 1971. Now chief executive officer, founder-president, and creative director of Proctor & Gardner Advertising, Proctor has demonstrated successful performances with impressive blue-chip clients, boards of directors, and varied industries.

Proctor's credibility, vivacious personality, and leadership skills put her in constant demand in the business arena; a demand evidenced by her service on the boards of directors of Illinois Bell Telephone Company, Northwestern Hospital, the 1988 Illinois Olympic Committee, the council of the Chicago Better Business Bureau, the *Louisville Courier-Journal*, the Girl Scouts of Chicago, and the Economic Club. In 1983 and 1984, Proctor served, by special appointment from the governor of Illinois, as cochairperson of the Gannon-Proctor Commission; she is also a governing council member of the Illinois State Bar Association's Institute for Public Affairs. Her contributions to the American marketplace have earned numerous awards, citations, and honors. Professional and community affiliations are: board of directors, Bingham Companies, Louisville, Kentucky; board of directors, Dusable Museum of Black History; honorary board of directors, Handicapped Organized Women, Charlotte, North Carolina; delegate and task force member, White House Conference on Small Business; founding member, Committee of 200; life member, NAACP; president, League of Black Women (1978-1982); Prominent Women in Advertising Award, 1983; American National Business Hall of Fame Museum, Western Illinois University, 1983; council member, American Advertising Federation; 100 Most Successful Black Women in America, *Dollars and Sense* magazine, 1985; committee member, Chicago Council of Fine Arts (Business Advisory Committee); committee member, Chicago Historical Society; committee member, Business Advisory Council of the University of Illinois; mayor's appointee, Financial Planning Council; appointee, Build Illinois; associate council member, Northwestern University; Lincoln Academy Trustee, Office of the Governor.

Proctor's rich background as a writer combined with and her business savvy have led to the status she enjoys in the business community. Her career reveals the resilience, forthrightness, individualism, and style that have become her trademarks in the advertising business. Her honors include: "Hero of the 80s" in 1987, named by President Ronald Reagan; honorary doctoral degrees from Lake Forest College and Summons College, 1986; Chicago Advertising "Woman of the Year", 1974-1975; Frederick Douglass Humanitarian Award, 1975; Black Media, Inc., Leadership Award, 1975; Small Business Woman of the Year, 1978; Headline Award, 1978; Charles A. Stevens International Organization of Women Executive Achievers Award, 1978; ADDY awards, (two Gold and one Silver,) 1978; Small Business of the Year Award, 1978; Black Media Award for Outstanding Professional, 1980. She is also a recipient of more than twenty advertising industry awards for excellence, including Clio Awards from the American Television Commercial Festival.

Advertising Firm Developed Early

Proctor's willingness to take on tough challenges has allowed her to realize her dream: a timely entrance into the entrepreneurial sphere of the 1970s made for a dynamic beginning for her advertising firm. According to *Contemporary Newsmakers*,

> the climate was right for a minority agency; commercial awareness of the black consumer marker was gradually mounting. Thus, Proctor & Gardner was able to tap into a virtually untouched market, totaling millions of dollars annually, and at the same time had the opportunity to improve the public's perception of blacks by creatively casting them in a positive and constructive manner.

Proctor's career has been marked by clear direction, while her refusal to play it safe is an example of her leadership ability, her intense desire to succeed, and her willingness to reach beyond barriers.

Proctor has a youthful, expressive face and immaculately coiffed hair. Critics describe her as a lithe and fashionable woman who maintains a chic appearance and businesslike, though relaxed, demeanor. Proctor is at home in a twenty-two-room condominium that includes exercise facilities (though she confesses that working—often as much as fifteen hours a day—is her truest form of relaxation).

Proctor is energetic and has impeccable instincts. And at her agency, she has been successful in creating a relaxed atmosphere for staff and clients. She thrives on countering problems through timely innovations and strategic planning. A prime example of her clever planning is her choice of a name for the firm, Proctor and Gardner. "I found the advertising world wasn't ready for a female (in charge of the firm)," she says, "so I called my agency Proctor and Gardner. I'm both of them, but men assumed there was a Mr. Gardner back running the company" (Ball, 7).

Undaunted by early setbacks, Proctor obtained her first account after being in business for six months. Having created her agency through the assistance of a loan from the Small Business Administration (SBA) and finding herself in need of additional working capital at the end of four years,

Proctor again approached the SBA. Following her request, she says, "they sent an accountant to review my books, and he said I'd been out of business in three years. I didn't know it. I just kept going to work" (Ball, 7).

"In advertising, the only thing worse than being a woman was being an old woman," says Proctor. "I was over 30, female and black. I had so many things wrong with me that it would have taken all day to figure out which one to blame for my rejections. So I decided not to spend any time worrying about it" (Ball, 7).

True to her belief in the power of positive thinking, Proctor falls back on earlier successes as her ace in the hole for handling setbacks and conflicts. She says, "In every case where something would have been an obstacle, I've found a way to turn it to an advantage . . . I cannot buy the concept that anyone outside is responsible" (Ball, 7).

Rather than being a hindrance to her success, Proctor believes being black and female helped her to get that first SBA loan. "I think blacks have a different acceptance of reality than white people," she says. "We're more realistic. There is less fear. Being poor was good for me. Once you've been poor and black and you survive, there's nothing left to be afraid of. Most people are afraid of taking risks" (Francke, 19).

Women Urged to Enter Business World

As a business leader, Proctor encourages women to seek viable opportunities and make good use of them. "Risk is one trademark in business," she points out, adding that women have often been afraid to fail and are too quick to blame others for their own lack of success in the business world.

> One of the things women fear is risk. They don't want to risk anything; they want guarantees. If you are able to risk, able to lose, then you will gain. When women get to the point where they take the risk, fail and try again, without any loss of self-esteem, they will be free (Francke, 19).

Proctor holds that women have assets, talents, and skills they often overlook or do not emphasize.

> I think women are more multi-talented and have less self-esteem (than men), so they don't worry about being above doing things that need to be done. I brought my baby with me everywhere. I did my work in bed. I did what I had to do. I think women have this sort of flexibility (Ball, 7).

Exercising this flexibility and learning to use teamwork, which she says is often not a part of women's early training, can lead to dynamic performance. "Women learn very early to count on individual effort, but we continue to draw on our differences from other women rather than on our similarities with other executives" (Ball, 7). Once women have overcome barriers in their own thinking, she believes, no door will be closed to them and there is no limit to the amount of success women can achieve.

Proctor points out that while women have made significant gains in the workplace over the past twenty years, many have not reached the pinnacle of success because they have been taught that power is unfeminine. She urges women to abandon the attitudes of self-effacement and self-sacrifice that have sabotaged them. In part, this effort requires inspiring others to succeed, just as she was inspired through the early influence of the grandmother who raised her:

> My grandmother always thought I would do something. She taught me what is important isn't on the outside, but inside. She said it was important to put something inside you, some courage, knowledge, and a skill, things that no one can take from you (Francke, 19).

With these thoughts to sustain and bolster her confidence from an early age, Proctor has yet to find a door she cannot open and has maintained a sense of pride.

But one use to which she will not lend her talents is what she refers to as "ethically dubious advertising pitches" aimed at women and minorities. She is unrepentant in her criticism of advertising by drug, tobacco, and alcohol companies that target women and minorities, believing these companies have been responsible for the increased use of psychoactive drugs, sleep-inducing medications, and tobacco among the target groups. Her firm refuses liquor and cigarette accounts, choosing to handle accounts that reflect family values and lend themselves to quality promotional ideas. This policy cost Proctor her first job in the advertising business in 1970. According to Proctor, the agency came up with the concept of a television commercial that parodied the civil rights marches and sit-ins, "a mass demonstration of housewives running down the street waving a can demanding that their hairdressers foam their hair" (Stravro, 124). She found the commercial's concept tasteless and offensive, particularly to blacks, and was fired for her refusal to work on the project. Again, timing was an important force behind the success of her agency: The 1970s reflected an increasing awareness of the black consumer market. Proctor has insisted on maintaining accounts that reflect her own high standards. "Advertising is the single most important way of reaching everyone in America, and I feel a deep sense of responsibility for my work," she says, adding that she has no fear of turning away business that she believes provides reinforcement of negative stereotypes of women and blacks (Francke, 19).

References

"Advertising Exec. Barbara Proctor Discusses Her Career." *New Orleans Times-Picayune*, 30 April 1984.

Ball, Millie. "Ad Whiz was on Her Way with Her First SBA Loan." *New Orleans Times-Picayune*, 30 April 1984.

Bergen, Michele. "They are Owners, Bosses Workers." *Ebony* 32 (August 1977): 122.

Brown, Michelle. "Barbara Gardner Proctor." *Contemporary Newmakers*, 1985 Cumulation. Detroit: Gale Research, 1986.

Dudley, Percy. "Entrepreneur Urges Women to Take Control of Their Lives." *Atlanta Constitution*, 24 September 1987.

Francke, Richie L. "Proctor Takes a Gamble and Hits the Jackpot." *Working Woman* 4 (August 1979): 19.

Gottschalk, Earl C., Jr. "More Women Start up Their Own Business with Major Successes." *Wall Street Journal*, 17 May 1983.

Klose, Kevin. "In the Spirit of Enterprise: Barbara Proctor and her Presidential Mention." *Washington Post*, 27 January 1984.

McFadden, Robert D. "President's 5 Heroes for the 80's Seek to Share Their Spotlight." *New York Times*, 27 January 1984.

Morton, Carol A. "Black Women in Corporate America." *Ebony* 32 (November 1975): 107.

"Profile of Chicagoan Barbara Proctor, Head of Advertising Agency, who President Reagan praised in his State of the Union Address." *Chicago Tribune*, 26 January 1984.

Runde, Robert. "The Ad Agency Chief." *Money* 10 (September 1981): 50.

Stravro, Barry. "The Best Collateral (Barbara Gardner Proctor)." *Forbes* 132 (21 November 1983): 124.

Winako, Bess. "Success Wasn't So Elusive for These Black Women." *Chicago Tribune*, 5 September 1971.

Who's Who Among Black Americans, 1990/91. Detroit: Gale Research, 1990.

Who's Who in America. 39th-45th ed. Chicago: Marquis, 1975-88.

Who's Who in Finance and Industry. 20th-22nd ed. Chicago: Marquis, 1977-81.

Who's Who in the Midwest. 14th-15th ed. Chicago: Marquis, 1974-77.

Who's Who of American Women. 11th-16th ed. Chicago: Marquis, 1979-88.

Thura R. Mack

Elizabeth Prophet

(1890-1960)

Sculptor, educator

A strong individualist with high ideals, Nancy Elizabeth Prophet was an artist whose portrait busts and figurative sculptures earned her international acclaim in the 1920s and 1930s. Along with Edmonia Lewis (who worked in Rome) and Meta Vaux Warrick Fuller (who studied in France), she was one of the first black American sculptors to launch her career by studying abroad. She lived in Paris for twelve years, often on the brink of starvation, but exhibited her work at prestigious salons both in France and in the United States. At the requests of W. E. B. Du Bois and John Hope, president of Atlanta University, Prophet accepted a teaching position at Spelman College in 1934. There she built up Atlanta University's art department for ten years and continued to exhibit her work. The last two decades of her life, however, were marked by poverty and obscurity.

Prophet was born on March 19, 1890, the second child of Rosa E. (Walker) Prophet and William H. Prophet in Warwick, Rhode Island. A brother and a sister would join the family during the next four years. Prophet's paternal grandmother was Narranganset-Pequod; she bought her husband out of slavery. Prophet's father worked for the Providence

Elizabeth Prophet

Parks Department. Her mother, who had an African-American heritage, was a homemaker. Prophet's parents did not encourage her in the visual arts. In fact, she was compelled to hide when painting or drawing; such things were considered frivolous, and therefore were forbidden. Nevertheless, Prophet maintained that both of her parents were "of extraordinary energy, wisdom, and activity" (Harmon Foundation Questionnaire, 14 July 1938).

Little is known about Prophet's early life. It is likely, however, that she helped finance her education by working as a housekeeper for a private family on the well-to-do East Side in Providence. In 1914 she entered the Rhode Island School of Design. Reserved and self-conscious, Prophet worked diligently but kept to herself. The following year, on January 30, she married Francis Ford in an Episcopal ceremony. He was thirty-four years old, she twenty-four. Although Ford's family came from Maryland, he graduated from Hope High School in Providence in 1900; there he was the only black student to complete the classical course of study, and he also founded the Athletic Association. In 1900 Ford entered Brown University as a freshman, and did the same again in 1904-1905, but never graduated from college. Prophet apparently felt ambiguous about her relationship with him; few people knew about their marriage and it would later dissolve in France.

Although she had studied sculpture at the Rhode Island School of Design, Prophet graduated with a degree in painting and freehand drawing with a specific interest in portraiture in 1918. For four years she tried to earn a living by making portraits, to no avail. When she submitted an example of her work to a local exhibition, it was accepted with the proviso that she not attend the opening. Prophet withdrew her entry in protest. Later, a wealthy American asked her to submit designs and prices for a fountain group. Wanting to save money, the patron suggested that Prophet use less-costly materials. The artist responded that if she were able to commission a work of art, gold would not be too precious a medium for casting. Prophet did not accept the offer. Frustrated with the lack of opportunities in Providence and perhaps already unhappy with her marriage, she fled to Paris, leaving her husband behind.

Prophet arrived in Paris on August 11, 1922, with just $380. She quickly obtained a studio at 36 Avenue du Chatillon in Montparnasse, the most active artistic neighborhood, but stayed in bed for the first two months from nervous exhaustion. In her diary she recalled that in a moment of weakness, she wrote to her husband asking him to join her; this was a decision she would later regret. She then began work on her first piece of sculpture abroad "with a calm assurance and a savage pleasure of revenge" (Diary, 11 August 1922). The physical activity gave her strength and confidence:

> I remember how sure I was that it [the sculpture] was going to be a living thing, a master stroke, how my arms felt as I swung them up to put on a piece of clay. I was conscious of a great rhythm as they swung through the air, they seemed so long and powerful (Diary of Nancy Elizabeth Prophet, dated 11 August 1922 but written circa fall 1925).

For weeks Prophet labored on the sculpture in the morning, then all day during the following month. Two weeks before the piece was completed, however, she ran out of money. Desperate for sustenance, she stole a piece of meat and a potato from a dog's food bowl. Although starving, Prophet found the incident "humourous" and wrote of her starvation, "It was then interesting to feel how I felt each day, my mind was very clear, I could think with a great ease, though my belt was always dropping down around my feet" (Diary, circa 1925).

The twin struggles of escaping poverty and creating art would mark the rest of Prophet's life. Constantly seeking inexpensive housing, she lived with the artist Ellen Barrows in Versailles for three months in early 1923 and would move four times in the next two years. Despite her peripatetic lifestyle, Prophet maintained a rigorous work schedule and studied with the noted sculptor Victor Joseph Segoffin at L'Ecole Nationale des Beaux Arts. She completed at least two busts in 1923. One of these, a wooden piece, was included in the Salon d'Automne the following year.

In 1924 Prophet earned her living by making and selling batik. One woman sympathized with the sculptor's plight and gave her two thousand francs for materials. Prophet then began her first life-size statue, *Volonté* (will or wish). At the end of April 1926, in desperation with her perceived lack of progress, she would smash this work, vowing to improve herself.

Despite one benefactor's aid, Prophet continued to have monetary difficulties. She tried to sustain herself by growing vegetables near her self-described "filthy shack" outside of Paris but finally had to be admitted to the American Hospital for malnutrition in the summer of 1925. Upon noting her emaciated condition, medical practitioners there accused her of drug addiction and cautioned her not to exert herself for a year lest a relapse occur. Within three weeks, however, the artist was back at work.

In the middle of 1925, Prophet sublet a studio on the Rue Vercingétorix in Montparnasse, but was determined to have her own atelier. By November she found someone who promised to build a studio for her for the sum of four thousand francs, a year's rent in advance. Prophet borrowed the money and waited impatiently. During this time she was plagued by periods of loneliness and self-doubt and filled her diary with melancholic outpourings in her large, distinctive handwriting. She wrote that she was "so hungry to work that it seems I must go completely insane. My head is full of ideas, a fever to execute" (4 June 1924).

Prophet was further disturbed by the unexpected appearance of her drunken husband. Ford came in December bearing an enormous bouquet of roses and then passed out on her couch. By April 1926, she determined to leave him. It was not until April 1929, however, that he left his itinerant job as a waiter in France and went back to the United States. Prophet paid his fare by selling a piece of sculpture. By way of acknowledging the death of the relationship, she listed herself as a widow on the Harmon nomination form the same year. She made the separation official in June 1932 by obtaining an affidavit to change her name legally from Ford back to Prophet.

At the end of June 1926 Prophet moved into her cramped quarters at 147 rue Broca, where she would live for the next seven years. Her atelier was at the end of a narrow passage-way strewn with the broken rejects of other sculptors in the neighborhood. Prophet partitioned off a corner of her studio in which to sleep and brightened the walls with books and a coat of cool gray-green paint. Although she was finally settled in Paris, she continued to have financial difficulties. The first work Prophet made in her new atelier she christened *Poverty*. In her diary she recorded her constant battle against destitution, as well as her new-found independence:

> How swiftly the happy days slip by, it's only the unhappy ones that linger and drag. Almost a month has fled, a month of battles fought and won with all the glory that comes with success. Days of spiritual freedom, days of harmony in body and soul, days when the body was healthy and heard [sic], days of passion and desire, days of sadness and of joy. Days of laughter and days of tears. Nights of sweet sleep and pleasant awakening. Days of plenty, and then days of want. Poverty, detestable poverty, how you trail behind me ever screeching out your presence. Think you to ever make me a subject of your kingdom? Never! Though I die of hunger I shall never bend the knee to your majesty for I am not of your race. And yet what new phases of poverty are there for me to learn. Going without eating is common, to regain my health and strength only to lose it through fasting, it comes as a periodical occurence so frequent that it neither interests or frightens me. Poverty, weary not yourself in trying to humiliate me. Sometimes the face of life becomes but a mocking leer. Poverty, your grace, I accept your challenge (19 September 1926).

Mabel Gardner, an American sculptor in Paris, noted Prophet's condition and wrote to the actress Louise Brooks on her behalf. Through Brooks's influence, the Students Fund of Boston supplied Prophet with thirty dollars a month for two years, beginning in July 1927.

Often hungry and without sleep, Prophet persevered in sculpting, asking people she met in cafes to model without pay. Haunted by the threat of mediocrity, she hid her works from her own eyes with black cloths. Her persistence, however, paid off; her sculptures were included in the Salon d'Automne of 1925, 1926, and 1927 (the latter exhibited her *Tete de jeune fille)*. She also continued to send her work to the United States; it appeared in the Rhode Island School of Design Museum exhibition and the Boston Independent Exposition in 1928.

These pieces reflected the predominant sensibility of French sculpture in the 1920s. Like the work of Antoine Bourdelle, student of Auguste Rodin, her figures and busts had an androgynous quality with their close-cropped or covered hair, heavy-lidded eyes, enigmatic smiles, and small breasts. A series of her masks in plaster and clay from this period also recalls ancient Etruscan statues with their broad, calm fore-heads and archaic smiles. By depicting few details and concentrating on human busts, Prophet imbued her works with strong spiritual and humanistic qualities.

Real Life Reflected in Sculptures

The artist preferred to create sculptures from life, and modeled pieces after an Argentinian friend (*Poise*, for exam-ple), men she met in cafes, a woman named Povisipkine, and possibly performers (one work, *Reptile Woman*, bears the title of a common circus figure, a *femme serpent)*. More often, however, she sculpted from imagination for lack of money to pay sitters.

Prophet worked primarily in marble and wood (cherry, sycamore, ebony, and pear), but also in bronze, alabaster, granite, terra-cotta, plaster, and clay. She also lightly painted some of her bas-relief carvings, occasionally adding gold highlights. Prophet made a conscious effort to docu-ment all of her work and diligently transported each piece to the next arrondissement to be photographed in black and white. Unfortunately, those images seem to be all that remain of most of her sculpture.

Despite her exhibition success, Prophet made very little money and lived alone quite frugally. The titles of some of her works, *Discontent*, *Bitter Laughter*, and *Prayer* (also called *Poverty*) reflect her physical and emotional discom-fort. Prophet preferred to keep her woes to herself; she believed mute endurance would give her strength. *Silence*, a woman's head in marble, held special significance for the artist. She sculpted the bust after months of solitary living and wrote verses about it, one of which concludes, "Si-lence—the unifying quality of the body, mind and soul" (quoted in "Nancy Prophet Wins Success as Sculptress"). Du Bois stored the bronze version for Prophet in his office after the 56th Galleries in New York (where the work had been on exhibit in 1931) closed for the summer and often commented on it in his correspondence to her. At the beginning of 1932, Prophet wrote that he could keep it. By the end of 1935, however, she requested that Du Bois sign a certificate stating that the work belonged to her.

Despite her silence, friends in Paris were not unaware of Prophet's harsh life. Discovering that she was nearly on the point of starvation in 1928, Henry Ossawa Tanner wrote a strong letter of recommendation on her behalf to the Harmon Foundation. He praised her potential, disregarding her racial background: "Of the many, many students over here either white or black I know of none with such promise as Mrs.

Prophet. On the Harmon application, Prophet listed her high school as "the College of serious thought & bitter experience, situated on the Campus of Poverty & Ambition." She was disqualified for technical reasons but won the $250 Otto Kahn Prize for sculpture the next year; *Head of a Negro* was exhibited in New York at the International House in 1929.

Although Prophet generally maintained a self-imposed isolation in Paris, she took great interest in current events in the United States and received the *Crisis* magazine on a regular basis. She was particularly interested in black American achievements and kept up devoted correspondence with W. E. B. Du Bois. Du Bois's son-in-law, the writer Countee Cullen, met Prophet in Tanner's studio in 1929 and published an article on her the following year in *Opportunity* magazine. Du Bois encouraged Prophet to advise another black American sculptor who came to study in Paris, Augusta Savage. The two met in September 1929, and Savage later worked in Prophet's first atelier on the Avenue Chatillon.

Shortly after her meeting with Savage, Prophet returned to the United States in October 1929 for an eleven-month visit to promote her art. She was boosted by the exhibition of her marble *Buste d'homme* at the Société des Artistes Français the previous April. Prophet was immediately lionized in social circles, attending a Christmas party given by Roland Hayes, visiting in New York and sketching at the Metropolitan Musem of Art, residing with the Du Bois family for several months, and staying with various friends in Providence through the summer of 1930. Prophet would also socialize with such notables as Owen Dodson, Harold Jackman, and Emily Post. Despite the warm reception, however, Prophet yearned to be back in France and by herself. She wrote to Countee Cullen, "What is dear Paris doing these days? I long to be there in the solitude of my own studio, I do not like being famous, Cullen" (16 January 1930, Amistad Research Center).

While in the United States, Prophet made several artistic coups. Her work was exhibited at the Salons of America, American-Anderson Galleries, and the Boston Society of Independent Artists; she was also elected a member of the latter group. Through the 56th Galleries in New York, Prophet sold *Discontent* to Ellen D. Sharpe and Eleanor Green for one thousand dollars. These wealthy white women then donated the work to the Museum of Art at Prophet's alma mater. However, the galleries' commission was a third of the sale and Prophet still needed funding to continue living in France. Du Bois labored to secure further monetary aid on her behalf by writing to the banker Otto Kahn and the Harmon Foundation. He had little success, and Prophet sailed back to France with just five hundred dollars.

Prophet was apparently frustrated not only with Du Bois's futile efforts to obtain financial backing for her work but also with what she perceived as a lack of recognition of her achievements by black Americans. Du Bois tried to soothe the artist by writing to her:

> Do not blame me and do not blame the colored people of the United States. We are still curiously helpless. When eventually you triumph, as I am sure you will, it will not be altogether wrong to give people of colored blood here a part of the glory. They are a kindred-hearted and sympathetic folk but they are ignorant and inexperienced (18 May 1931, Du Bois Papers).

Prophet did not comment on these remarks, but recognized that her country was still in severe straits from the Great Depression, and both black and white people had difficulty in supporting the arts. She was grateful for Du Bois's continued moral support and sent him several books and many letters from Paris.

In the early 1930s, Prophet's luck turned, and she found devoted French patrons in Edouard and Julia Champion. Edouard Champion was a well known author of more than twenty books, including a multivolume anthology of French comedy. He and his wife supported Prophet by paying for her rent and frequently offering her dinner. Bolstered by their interest in her, Prophet produced more sculptures and succeeded in exhibiting them in the Société des Artistes Français—a marble bust was shown in 1931 and two works, *Violence* and *Buste ébène,* were displayed in 1932. French critics praised Prophet's work; in 1931 Jean Patézon wrote in *Le Rayonnement Intellectuel:*

> Elizabeth Prophet has a broad and grand vision, which is a guarantee of the quality of her work. Her vision follows her thought which is original and with no outward influences and this is what makes her work so strong and expressive ("Along the Color Line," 308).

In May 1932 Prophet returned to the United States once more to promote her art there, staying this time for ten months. Her sculpture was exhibited at the Robert C. Vose, Jr., Galleries in Boston and at the Boston Society of Independent Artists. In June she was elected as a member of the Art Association of Newport just in time for her works to be displayed in the Twenty-first Annual Exhibition by that group; on view were *Discontent, Silence, Poise, Peace,* and *Congolaise.* The first work won the Richard B. Greenough grand prize of seventy-five dollars and the last was later purchased by the Whitney Museum of American Art. *Congolaise* (circa 1930), the artist's best known piece, is a cherry wood head of an African figure with a Masai warrior's headdress. Newspapers in Rhode Island duly noted both Prophet's artistic and social success during her second visit to the United States. Her work was admired not only by Gertrude Payne Whitney, but also by Mrs. William Vanderbilt, Mrs. William Randolph Hearst, Mrs. Vincent Astor, and the Countess Cocini.

Sculptor Shares Talent Through Teaching

Inspired by her growing fame and wanting to share her knowledge with others, Prophet approached the Harmon Foundation with the idea of being sponsored for one semester to teach at a black university. She offered to give instruction in modeling, batik, and art history. Enthusiastic about the idea, the president of the institution contacted Florence Read, president of Spelman College, who immediately agreed. Prophet, however, had a sudden change of heart and went back to Paris in February 1933.

Unfortunately, the year was a grim one for the sculptor. She did not receive the anticipated Guggenheim Fellowship and she exhibited no works. Because her funds were dwindling, Prophet was forced to borrow money from her concierge to pay heat and grocery bills. Next, the police hounded her for avoiding import taxes. After she appealed to the Minister of Fine Arts, the Minister of Finance granted her three hundred dollars to cover expenses. By mid-1934, however, she was ten thousand francs in debt, had nearly wrecked her relationship with the Champions, and was living on a diet of tea and marmalade. Despite this, Prophet worked frantically from six o'clock A.M. to midnight renovating her studio in the spring. She hoped to reserve the ground floor for her studio work and rent the upstairs studio for living quarters. Shocked at Prophet's emaciation, Julia Champion loaned her the money to pay for the rent in July.

Fortunately, although they had been rebuffed once, administrators at Spelman College were still interested in hiring Prophet. Finally, with the encouragement of Du Bois, who called her "our greatest Negro sculptor" (Kirschenbaum, 51), and at the request of John Hope, president of Atlanta University, Prophet began teaching at Spelman College in the fall of 1934. Her salary of two thousand dollars was sponsored by the Harmon Foundation.

Together with painter Hale Woodruff, who had been recruited by John Hope in 1932, Prophet expanded the arts department of the Atlanta University Center. She taught courses in clay modeling and the history of art and architecture. Prophet also continued to exhibit her work and participated in the Whitney Sculpture Biennials of 1935 and 1937 and the Philadelphia Museum of Art's Sculpture International of 1940.

Early in 1940 Prophet outlined her philosophy on the interaction of art and life in an article published in *Phylon* magazine; this was to be her only publication. The sculptor firmly believed that the mark of civilized people was the degree to which they embraced the arts:

> If the purpose of art is to give aesthetic pleasure, that objective has not been fulfilled until some higher aesthetic quality has been reflected in the lives, habits, and manners of the people. The artist has always had a strong educational influence, and the obligation of the modern artist is no less today than it was in the Golden Age of Greece or the Renaissance of Italy. Intelligent America and her educators are well aware of this and are attempting to give some cultural education to the people, for this can no longer be neglected if America is to take her place in the civilized world (Prophet, 325).

Convinced of her own obligation to society, Prophet devoted herself to teaching while she was at Spelman, at the expense of her own art. She believed that artists should act as role models by embodying the principles of art:

> The principles of the arts which are form, rhythm, harmony; and the abstract qualities, some of which are poise and courage, are factors which no civilized man who aspires to be educated can live successfully without attaining (324).

Prophet always strove to attain those "abstract qualities" of poise and courage; the titles of some of her works reflect this ambition—*Confidence, Peace, Le Pélerin* (the pilgrim), *La Volonté* (will or wish), and *Poise*. The latter work is the bust of a man, executed in marble. With a calm brow, tensed throat muscles, and squared chin, it embodies the "inner intensity and outer calm" that Prophet said necessarily compounded the quality of poise. She maintained that every one of her works embodied "an experience, something I have lived—or its result" ("Nancy Prophet Wins Success as Sculptress," n.p.).

Initially, the relationship between Prophet and Spelman was warm and mutually beneficial. She was frequently invited to attend faculty functions, and she participated in academic events on campus, socializing primarily with Du Bois and William Stanley Brathwaite. Du Bois even invited her to speak to his sociology class about the French attitude towards Jews, Negroes, Asiatics, and Americans. Prophet grew disappointed, however, with the cynical attitude of some of her students, and frustrated with the lack of proper teaching equipment, such as lantern slides of art historical masterpieces and tables for modeling. She was most unhappy with the new demands on her time and the fact that she had no studio in which to work. She continued to maintain her atelier in Paris at the rate of five thousand francs a year and longed to go back there. Prophet did return briefly in the summer of 1936 but only to collect the remainder of her art materials, books, and furnishings.

Despondent with the limitations of a small, Southern community, Prophet gradually withdrew from social life. While still appearing elegantly attired for dinner (often in a dramatic black cape and felt hat), she became increasingly eccentric and was said to speak in whispers, carry around a live rooster, and cover her sculptures with damp cloths so that no one could see them. She despairingly called her makeshift studio in the power plant a grave and longed to have private space in which to work. Sympathizing with Prophet, Frederick Keppel of the Harmon Foundation arranged to have a studio for her in 1939. That year she was also included in *Who's Who Among American Women*.

Encouraged by this recognition, Prophet applied again for a Guggenheim Fellowship and asked the Harmon Foundation for yet more money. There were a number of works she wanted to have cast or made in marble, and she also wanted to attend the Women's Congress in New York. Her savings were again minimal; she claimed she had used part of her salary to help her students, having taken particular interest in the blossoming sculptor, Edward Scott. She was rejected by the Guggenheim Foundation, but in 1941 the Grant-in-Aid committee of the Carnegie Foundation awarded Prophet one thousand dollars for the purchase of marble and a potter's wheel. By the spring of 1944, however, Prophet felt that she had fulfilled her duty to society with ten years of teaching. In June she went back home to Providence, Rhode Island, and stayed with friends.

Little is known about the last two decades of Prophet's life, except that she did various housekeeping jobs, sometimes as a live-in domestic servant. Her artistic activity, unfortunately, diminished greatly. She had one small exhibition at the Providence Public Library in 1945, the year after she returned to that city, but never exhibited her sculpture again.

Prophet worked for a ceramics factory in Rhode Island for some time making busts for a commercial market. A photograph of three pieces from this period survives. The works recall turn-of-the-century symbolist content and style. If the artist continued to sculpt for herself, she let few people know. The postal carrier who managed the ceramics shop later acquired Prophet's sculpting tools. He recalled seeing one of her mahogany pieces in storage; it depicted a Madonna and child with the Devil lurking in the background. Prophet may have created the work after her conversion to Catholicism; she joined the church in 1951, apparently believing that it was the last hope for sculpture. In Paris she had been enthusiastically encouraged by a Catholic abbé who marvelled at her sculpture, saying, "You have works here that will live for two thousand years, think what your life can mean to generations to come" (Prophet to W. E. B. Du Bois, 20 August 1931, Du Bois Papers). This priest was R. P. Félix Anizan, who wrote philosophical and theological essays for *Le Rayonnement Intellectuel.*

Prophet received a small pension and public assistance, but still had pecuniary difficulties. Concerned about making ends meet, she continued to write the Harmon and Carnegie Foundations to request funding. She also made a notary statement in 1946 disinheriting Francis Ford, claiming that he had been a moral and financial handicap to her and that her father had supported them at the beginning of their marriage. It is unclear whether she ever divorced Ford.

Throughout her life Prophet was ambivalent about her racially mixed heritage. At times she embraced her African-American background, and at times she fiercely denied it. She was a slender, copper-colored woman with high cheekbones and straight black hair she often wore tightly pulled back in a bun. Journalists made much of her striking appearance and commented on her dual lineage. For instance, Cullen recalled first meeting her when she swept into Henry O. Tanner's studio "revealing her Indian ancestry in her straight, unbending gait; unleashing her Negro blood in a warm smile." Likewise, critics were quick racially to categorize the artist. Headlines read "Negress Wins the First Prize at Newport" (*Art Digest,* 14) and "First Prize for Indian Woman" (*Newport Herald*). Americans were not alone in focusing on Prophet's heritage; French critics did the same. One writer from *L'Art Contemporain* stated "Elizabeth Prophet is a sculptor of race: one feels it in everything, in her work, in the firmness of her will, in her independence." Although the French were more tolerant than Americans as a whole, they were also fascinated by black culture in the early twentieth century. Prophet's success came right after that of Josephine Baker, who added to the rising enthusiasm for black art first prompted by cubism over a decade earlier.

Prophet never firmly identified herself as belonging to any race, preferring to be known first as an artist, yet she sought the attention of her people. As noted above, she complained to Du Bois about not being recognized by African-Americans to her satisfaction. She did not cross him, however, when he wrote to her that he had told John Hope that "a person who is doing artistic work, and particularly a colored person, needs the freedom and inspiration of Paris" (8 February 1934, Du Bois Papers). In her article, "Art and Life," Prophet criticizes what she sees as a lack of cultural awareness among black people, but then includes herself in that group, and praises the artistic achievements of Americans in general:

> Many of the indignities inflicted by whites on Negroes are due to the former's lack of the finer sensibilities. They resent the limitations of the Negro, and pay it back in crude brutality. It would be regrettable if, as a group, we should insist upon clinging to the early ignorance of the pioneer Americans in regard to art and the artists, for there is no country at present making a more eager effort to develop its artistic expression than here in America (325).

On the other hand, Prophet was pleased that *Crisis* stated that "she was not an amateur or a 'colored artist' but an artist" ("Can I Become a Sculptor?," 315).

Nonetheless, art historians discerned distinctive racial characteristics in Prophet's work. James Porter wrote:

> Without exception her subjects have been Negroes, and usually they reflect the super-personal trait of the individual. The pride of race that this sculptor feels resolves itself into an intimation of noble conflict marking the features of each carved head (*Modern Negro Art,* 139).

Additionally, Cedric Dover asked for permission to include photographs of *Congolaise* and *Discontent* in his forthcoming book, *American Negro Art.* Prophet begged him not to discuss her work in this context, stating unequivocally that as an anthropologist, he "must certainly know" that "I am not a negro" (Dover, 56).

Despite her protestations about being identified as black, Prophet was proud of her African history. She eagerly wrote to Du Bois about the African sculptures that were on view at the Colonial Exposition in Paris in 1931:

> . . . heads that are such a mental development that are rarely seen among Europeans. Heads of thought and reflection, types of great beauty and dignity of carriage. I believe it is the first time that this type of African has been brought to the attention of the world of modern times. Am I right? People are seeing the aristocracy of Africa (20 August 1931, Du Bois Papers).

Thus, while Prophet sometimes suffered from her racially mixed heritage, she also took pride in it. Determined not to let others categorize her, she took pains to create her own identity. "I am a fighter," she wrote in her diary, "determined and non-retreating. I only stop when I drop" (2 June 1927).

Without the support of family and friends, several months before her death, Prophet wrote once more to her former patron, Julia Champion. She had lost communication with her over the years, discovering that the government had restricted communications during World War II. Prophet wanted to inform her old friend of her depressed condition and thank her for the many gifts she had received in Paris. She never mailed the letter, however, and passed away from a heart attack in December 1960. A man for whom Prophet had worked as a housekeeper for six months, Edward J. Carley, hastily raised funds to keep her from a pauper's funeral.

Because Prophet died without a will, the whereabouts of her effects is unknown. In the late 1970s a sketchbook of pastel compositions, newspaper clippings, and photographs of the artist and her work surfaced and were donated to Rhode Island College. Less than ten of Prophet's sculptures are in ascertained collections; the rest (less than two dozen) seem to have disappeared and their existence is known only from archival photographs or publications. Admittedly, Prophet herself destroyed works when she was not satisfied with them, and some she could not afford to transport from France. Other rotted outdoors for lack of storage. However, several of her sculptures, as well as watercolors and oil paintings, must be in private collections throughout the United States.

Prophet was a talented sculptor with exceptional vision. Her representative works and writings reveal the complex psychology of a highly imaginative and intelligent artist. Never wholly a part of one community, she will be remembered both as a fiercely independent woman and someone who worked to make a lasting contribution to civilization. She believed, "Someday people will realize that this is my medium of expression, that it is still possible to say something through sculpture, that a sculptor may yet live again (Diary, 7 June 1927).

References

"Along the Color Line." *Crisis* 38 (September 1931): 308.

"Art: Woman Artist." *Crisis* 39 (August 1932): 259.

"Beth Prophit [sic] is Hailed in Paris as Real Artist." *African American* (Baltimore), 3 August 1929.

"Can I Become a Sculptor? The Story of Elizabeth Prophet." *Crisis* 39 (October 1932): 315.

Cullen, Countee. "Elizabeth Prophet: Sculptress." *Opportunity* 8 (July 1930): 204-205. With photographs of the artist and *Bust of Roland Hayes, Silence,* and *Discontent.*

Dover, Cedric. *American Negro Art.* Greenwich, Conn.: New York Graphic Society, 1960.

"Elizabeth Prophet Named among Famous Women in America." Atlanta University *Bulletin* (December 1939): 11.

"Elizabeth Prophet, Sculptor." *Crisis* 36 (December 1929): 407, 427.

"Elizabeth Prophet, Sculpture Prize Winner." *Providence Evening Bulletin*, February 1930.

"First Prize for Indian Woman." *Newport Herald*, 9 July 1932.

Four From Providence: Bannister, Prophet, Alston, Jennings. Providence: Rhode Island Black Heritage Society and Rhode Island College, 1978.

Kirschenbaum, Blossom S. "Nancy Elizabeth Prophet, Sculptor." *SAGE* 4 (Spring 1987): 45-52. With illustrations of Prophet and *Congolaisy*, *Silence*, and *Head of a Negro*. One of the most comprehensive articles ever written on the artist.

"Nancy Prophet Wins Success As Sculptress." *Providence Evening Bulletin,* 8 July 1932. Includes photographs of the artist and her marble bust, *Poise*.

"Negress Wins the First Prize at Newport." *Art Digest* (1 August 1932): 14.

Patézon, Jean. "Elizabeth Prophet, artiste américaine." *Le Rayonnement Intellectuel,* ca. 1931.

Porter, James. *Modern Negro Art.* New York: Arno Press, 1943.

Prophet, Nancy Elizabeth. "Art and Life," *Phylon* 1 (Third Quarter 1940): 322-26.

———. Diary, John Hay Collection, Brown University.

———. Harmon Foundation Questionnaire, 14 July 1938, Harmon Foundation Papers.

Reynolds, Gary A., and Beryl J. Wright. *Against the Odds: African-American Artists and the Harmon Foundation.* Newark, N.J.: The Newark Museum, 1989. Photographs of Prophet at work and reproductions of *Silence* and *Discontent*.

Saint-Hilaire, Jules de and Raymond Sélig. "Elisabeth [sic] Prophet." In "Les Salons des Artistes Français, de la

Nationale et des Indépendants.'' *Revue du Vrai et du Beau* 8 (10 August 1929): 7.

Tanner, Henry Ossawa. Letter to George Haynes, 22 October 1928, Harmon Foundation files.

Who's Who in American Art. New York: Bowker, 1941.

Who's Who of American Women. Chicago: Marquis, 1939.

Collections

Art by Nancy Elizabeth Prophet is in the following collections: Rhode Island Black Heritage Society; Rhode Island College, Adams Library; Rhode Island School of Design; Rhode Island Urban League; Schomburg Center for Research in Black Culture, New York Public Library; and Whitney Museum of American Art in New York City.

Photographs of Prophet and her work as well as newspaper clippings are in the Carl Russell Gross Papers (1888-1971), Special Collections, Adams Library of Rhode Island College. The original diary kept by Prophet when she was in Paris from 1922-1934 is in the John Hay Collection at Brown University. Correspondence with and grant and exhibition applications to the Harmon Foundation are in the Library of Congress. Correspondence with W. E. B. Du Bois is in his papers at the University of Massachusetts at Amherst and on microfilm at the Library of Congress.

Theresa Leininger

Mary Ann Prout ''Aunt Mary Prout''

(1801-1884)

School founder, educator, church worker, humanitarian, social activist

Though there is some confusion about the circumstances into which she was born, Mary Ann Prout, also known as ''Aunt Mary Prout,'' is believed to have been born in Baltimore, of free, mixed-African parentage, on February 14, 1801 (one account cites 1800). However, Sylvia Dannett, in *Profiles of Negro Womanhood*, states that Prout was born a slave in South River, Maryland, on February 14, 1801, and that during her childhood her parents moved to Baltimore. Nevertheless, according to the Daniel Murray Papers, Mary and her two older brothers, William A. (b. 1790) and Jacob W. (b. 1797), were born free in Baltimore. And considering that the Prout family was actively involved in the American Colonization Society of Maryland and that William and Jacob later immigrated to Liberia, a colony in West Africa for free blacks, it is probable that the Prout siblings were free.

Records indicate that the Prout family was intelligent and actively involved with religions, civic, and social matters. There is no record of where and how the members of the family received their educations. Like Mary Prout, William A. and Jacob M. Prout were noted teachers as well as lecturers. Jacob Prout often lectured on behalf of the American Colonization Society. The *National Intelligencer* of May 4, 1831, recounts Jacob Prout's lecture in Washington, D.C., at the Israel Methodist Church. William A. Prout became governor of Liberia for a brief time in 1854. And Jacob Prout's son, Samuel J. Prout, was postmaster general in Liberia for many years.

While her brothers and nephew, as well as other members of the family, were making their marks in the United States and Liberia, Prout remained in Baltimore, Maryland, to aid people there. All biographical accounts agree that Prout was ''converted'' and became devoted to religion as a member of Bethel African Methodist Episcopal Church on Saratoga Street, which was near her home at eleven Saratoga Street. From the time Mary Prout became a communicant of Bethel at the age of twelve, she devoted her entire life to religious activities. For years she was a member of the church association known as the Daughters of Conference at Bethel AME in Baltimore. Spradling mentions that Prout was a soprano and since there is no record of her performing in concerts, it is assumed she was a member of Bethel's choir.

According to Bishop James Anderson Handy, ''During the early days of Bethel, when it was poor and in debt, Prout was constantly devising ways and means of relieving it. She lived to a great old age and was never married'' (Dannett, 141). At Bethel, Prout was assistant to Annie Dickerson, one of the pillars of the church, who took under her care the new female converts, indoctrinating them into their duties to God and the church. Prout would read the Bible on Sunday, and Dickerson would explain the scriptures to her. Prout was a pious and devoted christian.

Day School and Benevolent Organization Founded

Prout founded a day school in 1830, where she taught until 1867. (Again, there is some confusion: The Daniel Murray Papers give 1820-1821 as the founding dates for Prout's day school.) Whatever the founding date, many men and women of color in Baltimore received their educations from this eminent teacher.

Not only was she a faithful church member and a dedicated teacher, Prout was a also humanitarian. She was one of the two black trustees of the Gregory Aged Women's Home, which officially opened July 21, 1867, in Baltimore. Prout was also the president of the association in charge of the home. Leroy Graham's *Baltimore: The Nineteenth Century Black Capital* makes no mention of the association, but it is believed to be the National Reform Educational Association. Graham reports that the Gregory Aged Women's Home was named after General Edward M. Gregory, head of the Maryland Freedmen's Bureau.

The year 1867, in which the day school is said to have closed, was the same year that Prout founded a secret order from which evolved the Independent Order of St. Luke. (Graham dates the order's founding year as 1856.) Early in her life, Prout recognized the need for a black organization that would supply financial aid to the sick and funds for the burial of the dead.

The *Baltimore Afro-American Ledger* (31 October 1903) states that "there was a split in the Order, and the part which split off from the parent body took up its headquarters in the city of Richmond." Maggie Lena Walker, who was president of the Richmond organization, never failed to pay homage to Prout as founder of the order. In the May 4, 1907, issue of the *Ledger* the following account was given:

> The meeting that was held on last Monday evening in the main auditorium of Bethel A.M.E. Church under the auspices of the Baltimore Bethel Council Independent Order of St. Luke was attended by a large and appreciative audience. . . . The speaker of the evening was Mrs. Maggie L. Walker . . . of Richmond Virginia [who] delivered a very interesting as well as instructive address on the order of St. Luke. She also said that she was proud of the opportunity to speak to the members of the Order in Baltimore, as this is the place where the founder of the Noble Order lived and founded this work, Miss Mary Prout, [who] was a member of this church and whose memory still lives in the minds of many today and if every St. Luke in this city would unite under one head, it would not be too long before they could see the results of her [Mary Ann Prout's] labor.

Under Maggie L. Walker's leadership, the Independent Order of St. Luke branched out into several institutions that benefited blacks. These included the *St. Luke Herald* (1902)—a newspaper that reported the order's financial affairs, the St. Luke's Penny Saving Bank (1903), and the short-lived St. Luke Emporium, a department store founded in Richmond. In twenty-five years the order grew from fifty-seven local chapters to fifteen hundred chapters, from thirty-four hundred members to more than fifty thousand members, and from an indebtedness of four hundred dollars to assets of nearly four hundred thousand dollars.

An organization founded to provide insurance for the sick and financial aid to help with the burial of the dead became one of the most important assets for blacks in the early part of the twentieth century. The order was still in existence in the late 1920s and perhaps into the 1930s, but the changed economic and social conditions, notably the stock market crash of 1929 and the Great Depression reduced, if not eliminated, fraternal insurance cooperatives.

The work started in Baltimore by a relatively unknown lady to help poor blacks spread across the United States. Prout's social and religious activities exemplify the motto: "Charity begins at home and then spreads abroad." For her efforts and the good work that evolved, Prout should be acclaimed not only as a prominent member of Bethel A.M.E. Church and as one of its shining lights but as eminent teacher and social activist. Prout died in Baltimore in 1884.

References

Baltimore Afro-American Ledger, 24 August 1901; 31 October 1903; 4 May 1907. The August 24, 1901 issue contains a photograph of Mary Ann Prout.

Bragg, George F., Jr. *Men of Maryland*. Baltimore: Church Advocate Press, 1925.

Dannett, Sylvia G. L. *Profiles of Negro Womanhood*. Vol. 1, 1619-1900. Yonkers, N.Y.: Educational Heritage, 1964.

Graham, Leroy. *Baltimore: The Nineteenth Century Black Capital*. Washington, D.C.: University Press of America, 1982.

Majors, Monroe. *Noted Negro Women: Their Triumphs and Activities*. Chicago: Donohue and Henneberry, 1893.

National Intelligencer, 4 May 1931.

St. Clair, Sadie Daniel. "Maggie Lena Walker." *Notable American Women*, 1607-1950. Vol. III. Cambridge: Harvard University Press, 1971.

Spradling, Mary Mace, ed. *In Black and White*. 3rd ed. Supplement. Detroit: Gale Research, 1980.

Collections

The Daniel Murray Papers contain information on Mary Ann Prout. They are housed in the Beulah Davis Special Collections, Soper Library, Morgan State University, Baltimore.

Margaret Ann Reid

Harriet Forten Purvis

(1810-1909)

Activist

A member of one of the most prominent and respected black abolitionist families in the country, and famous in her own right as an abolitionist, Harriet Davy Forten Purvis was the second child of the wealthy freeborn businessman James

Harriet Forten Purvis

Forten (1766-1842) and his wife, Charlotte (Vandine) Forten (1785-1884).* She was born in Philadelphia in 1810 and was named for the daughter of Forten's benefactor, Robert Bridges. It was Bridges who had taught Forten the craft of sail-making, assisted him in purchasing real estate, and eventually sold his business to him. Bridges's young daughter, Harriet, had apparently been a great favorite of Forten's. She married John Broome Davy, a Philadelphia merchant, and died at the age of twenty-four in 1809, just a few months before the birth of Harriet Forten. Forten may have named two of his other daughters, Sarah and Mary, for members of the Bridges family. His second son was named for Robert Bridges. Two other sons were named for white merchants who had assisted him—Thomas Willing and William Deas.

Like her brothers and sisters, Harriet Forten enjoyed the benefits of a private education. Her father was unable to get his children admitted to Philadelphia's exclusive academies and was unwilling to send them to the schools set aside for black children because he believed they could receive only an inferior education in such schools. Drawing on his financial resources and cooperating with other wealthy black parents, Forten established a school of his own where black children could study the same subjects at the same level as white children. He also arranged for his daughters to be tutored at home in music and languages. Many visitors to the Forten home commented on the refinement of James Forten's daughters. One, the abolitionist poet John Greenleaf Whittier, was moved to express his admiration in some verses for Harriet Forten's album (*Journals of Charlotte Forten Grimké*, 15 April 1858).

Sisters!—the proud and vain may pass ye by
With the rude taunt and cold malicious eye;
Point the pale hand deridingly and slow,
In scorn's vile gesture at the darker brow;
Curl the pressed lip with sneers which might befit
Some smocking spirit from the nether pit;
Yet, from a heart whence Truth and Love have borne
The last remains of Prejudice and Scorn,
From a warm heart, which, thanks to God, hath felt
Pride's charm to loosen and its iron melt,
Fervent and pure let this frail tribute bear
A Brother's blessing and a Brother's prayer.

And what, my sisters, though upon your brows
The deeper coloring of your kindred glows
Shall I less love the workmanship of Him
Before whose wisdom all our own is dim?
Shall my heart learn to graduate its thrill?
Beat for the White, and for the Black be still?
Let the thought perish, while the heart can feel
The blessed memory of your grateful zeal.
While it can prize the excellence of mind
The chaste demeanor and the state refined.
Still are ye all my sisters, meet to share
A Brother's blessing and a Brother's prayer.

Forten eventually married Robert Purvis, a young migrant from the South. Purvis had been born in Charleston, South Carolina, on August 4, 1810, and was several months Harriet's junior. His father, William Purvis, was an English immigrant to South Carolina who had prospered as a cotton merchant. His mother, Harriet Judah (1784/85-1869), was a free woman of German-Jewish and North African descent. Robert Purvis was the second of their three sons. William Purvis had moved his family to Philadelphia when Robert was ten years old. Six years later, at the age of sixty-four, he died of typhus. Although he never married the woman he referred to as his "beloved friend," Purvis acknowledged that he was the father of her children. Under the terms of his will, she received bank stock to the value of $10,000 and the rest of his estate, valued in excess of $230,000, was divided among their sons, William, Jr., Robert, and Joseph. In the spring of 1828 Robert Purvis's elder brother, William, died of consumption at the age of twenty-one. He was unmarried and his share of his father's estate was divided between Robert and Joseph (Philadelphia County Wills, 1828, Book 9, p. 189).

It was not long before Robert and Joseph Purvis were drawn into the Forten family circle. The Fortens and the two young Purvis brothers shared wealth, education, and a strong commitment to social reform, particularly abolitionism. A warm relationship based on mutual respect soon developed between James Forten and Robert Purvis. In many ways, James Forten replaced the father the young man had lost, while Forten admired the fact that Purvis took pride in his African heritage, instead of attempting to deny it. Robert Purvis was light-skinned enough to "pass," had he chosen to do so. He told abolitionist Samuel J. May that he "had travelled much in stage-coaches, and stopped days and weeks at Saratoga and other fashionable summer resorts, and mingled, without question, among the beaux and belles" (May, 288). However, in the choice of a wife Purvis made it clear where his sense of racial identity, as well as his affections, lay. He proposed to Harriet Forten and was accepted.

Robert Purvis and Harriet Forten were married in a ceremony at her father's home on September 13, 1831. Bishop Onderdonk, a white Episcopalian, officiated. The marriage evidently gave rise to much uninformed gossip. As one observer of the social scene recalled, Forten "had a family, and of course strove for a respectable platform for its members; and to this end it was said of him that he coveted to wed his daughter to a whiter species at some sacrifice of his fortune. This was an *on dit* of the day" (Ritter, 46-47). In fact, if there was any "sacrifice of fortune," it was on the part of Robert Purvis, rather than James Forten, and the "whiter species" Forten had secured for his daughter was an ardent abolitionist unwilling to make a secret of his family background.

By all accounts, Harriet and Robert Purvis were very happy in their marriage. Abolitionist William Lloyd Garrison, who often visited them, thought them ideally suited in temperament and outlook. Their strong mutual affection was coupled with a determination to advance the social agenda they had both espoused since childhood.

During the first few months of their married life, Harriet Purvis and her husband probably lived with her parents. Then, in June 1832 Robert Purvis paid more than three thousand dollars for a two-story brick house on Lombard Street, near Ninth. It was in that house that their first child, William, was born in the late fall of 1832.

By the time of his marriage, Purvis had already embarked on a career as an abolitionist lecturer. Harriet Purvis supported him in every way possible and when, in 1834, he announced his intention of undertaking a tour of Britain to spread the antislavery message, she made no objection to staying behind to care for their infant son.

Philadelphia Female Anti-Slavery Society Supported

If childcare responsibilities kept Harriet Purvis in Philadelphia, they certainly did not prevent her from participating in the struggle for abolition. Like her mother, Charlotte, two of her sisters, Margaretta and Sarah, and many of her closest friends from Philadelphia's black upper class, Harriet Purvis was a member of the interracial Philadelphia Female Anti-Slavery Society. Over the years she served the organization in many capacities. She was frequently chosen to serve on the committee that planned the society's annual Christmas fair. In some respects, the Philadelphia Female Anti-Slavery Society was a Forten family enterprise. Not only were Charlotte Forten and her daughters officers and members, but the men in the family, including Robert Forten, James Forten, Jr., and Robert Purvis, were often invited to address the society. Family friends also appeared at meetings of the society. For instance, Joseph R. Daily attended one meeting to answer questions regarding conditions in Liberia, where he had spent six years. He was an old friend of the Purvises and it was Harriet Purvis who had kept him supplied with small luxuries from home during his years in Africa.

In addition to their membership in the Philadelphia Female Anti-Slavery Society, Harriet Purvis and her sisters participated in the antislavery struggle at the national level. Despite the fact that she was expecting her second child, Harriet Purvis traveled to New York with Sarah and Margaretta in 1837 to be present at the first Women's Anti-Slavery Convention. A delegate at the second convention in Philadelphia's newly-built Pennsylvania Hall in 1838, she inadvertently helped to cause a riot. Her husband accompanied her and was seen helping her from their carriage. Hostile onlookers concluded that they were an interracial couple and that the hall was indeed a meeting place for "amalgamationists." Undaunted by the mob scenes that accompanied the destruction of Pennsylvania Hall, Harriet Purvis was present the following year when the third and last female antislavery convention was held in Philadelphia.

At the state level, both Harriet and Robert Purvis were active in the Pennsylvania Anti-Slavery Society. Robert Purvis was the president of the organization from 1845-50. Their support of abolition often took the Purvises away from home. The demands of her children kept Harriet Purvis from traveling quite as extensively as Robert, but she still managed to attend meetings in Pennsylvania and further afield. In May 1840, for example, she and Robert were in Harrisburg for the convention of the Pennsylvania Anti-Slavery Society; Harriet Purvis was a delegate from the Philadelphia Female Anti-Slavery Society and Robert a delegate from the Philadelphia City Anti-Slavery Society. Shortly afterwards, they made their way to New York for a meeting of the American Anti-Slavery Society. Harriet Purvis also traveled without her husband. In the summer of 1854, for instance, she and her younger brother, Robert Bridges Forten, were in Boston when the fugitive Anthony Burns was tried and ordered returned to the South. The case left a lasting impression on both brother and sister.

Again and again, Harriet Purvis balanced the demands of her large family with her commitment to abolition. Always the support of her husband was crucial. Their marriage was truly an abolitionist partnership. That partnership was seen in action many times. In 1848, for example, Harriet Purvis took part in a huge antislavery revival in Philadelphia. Together with other women from the black elite, including Eliza Bias and Harriet Smith, the wife of businessman Stephen Smith, she was elected to the business committee that organized a massive abolitionist convention. Again, Robert Purvis played a significant role in the proceedings.

Educational Uplift Promoted

Abolition was not the only cause Harriet and Robert Purvis championed. Both were active in promoting education.

When Daniel Alexander Payne, the future AME bishop, arrived in Philadelphia as a young emigre from Charleston, the couple befriended him and agreed to act as referees for the school he was trying to establish in the city. Harriet Purvis's brother, Robert Bridges Forten, a gifted amateur scientist, was recruited to teach astronomy.

In many respects, raising a family seemed to deepen Harriet Purvis's commitment to abolition and the eradication of racial prejudice as she reflected on the nature of the society into which her children were being born. Harriet and Robert Purvis had eight children—William (b. 1832), Joseph Parrish (b. 1837), Harriet (b. 1839), Charles Burleigh (b. 1840/41), Henry (b. 1843/4), Robert (b. 1844/45), Granville Sharp (b. 1845/46), and Georgianna (b. 1848/49). In seeking a good education for her children, Harriet Purvis encountered many of the same problems that had faced her own parents decades before. Her husband's wealth could not spare them from the effects of prejudice. In 1853, angry that his children were excluded from the better public schools and relegated to a vastly inferior black school in the neighborhood, Robert Purvis refused to pay his school tax. He observed that his assessment was one of the highest in the neighborhood, and yet his children were denied the right to attend the schools he helped to finance.

Other means had to be found of educating the Purvis children. Fortunately, there were a few interracial, abolitionist-oriented schools in existence by the 1840s. Joseph and Robert Purvis were sent off to New York Central College, in McGrawville, Courtland County, New York. (Their cousin, James Forten, was also enrolled in the school.) Hattie Purvis was sent to Eagleswood, a school in Fort Lee, New Jersey, run by close friends of the Forten and Purvis families—Angelina and Theodore Weld and Angelina's sister, Sarah Grimké. When Hattie Purvis left school, she helped to teach her younger siblings. As she wrote to her old school friend, Ellen Wright, the niece of Lucretia Mott, "I have been teaching my little brothers and sisters this winter, for there is no school here for them to go to, except a *Public School*, and there they are made [to] sit by their selves, because their faces are not as white as the rest of the scholars" (Hattie Purvis to Ellen Wright, 16 January 1856). In 1858 Harriet Purvis arranged for her niece, Charlotte, to teach her younger children. (Charlotte was the daughter of Harriet's younger brother, Robert Bridges Forten, and Harriet had long taken an interest in her—ever since the death of Charlotte's mother in 1840. With Charlotte's father's business difficulties and his second marriage, Byberry, Harriet and Robert Purvis's farm, became a second home to Charlotte.)

Her early education had instilled in Harriet Purvis a great love of literature. She read whatever came her way—antislavery works, religious literature, contemporary novels, and works of literary criticism. According to her niece, Harriet was very familiar with the writings of Charlotte Bronte. Like other members of the family, she had a clear speaking voice and a talent for reading aloud. She could also sustain her part in an argument. For instance, discussing the authorship of Shakespeare's plays with her niece, Charlotte, she insisted on siding with the Baconians—although Charlotte believed she only did so to be perverse. Her love of music, art, and fine literature led her to seek out others who shared those tastes. In 1841 she and her husband were among the founding members of the Gilbert Lyceum, a cultural and literary society that differed from most in Philadelphia's free black community in that membership was open to both men and women.

In addition to being a gifted antislavery lecturer, Robert Purvis was a shrewd businessman. The fortune his father had left him was prudently invested in real estate in Philadelphia, in nearby Bucks County, and in Burlington County, New Jersey. Sometimes Purvis would buy up houses and vacant lots, sometimes he would acquire ground-rents. Seldom did he sell without reaping a handsome profit. Occasionally he teamed up with Joseph Cassey, an immigrant from the French West Indies who had prospered as a barber and wigmaker. If a potentially profitable investment materialized, the two men could raise the purchase price between them. Harriet Purvis was necessarily involved in her husband's business activities. Under Pennsylvania law, no sale of land by a married man was legal unless his wife gave her informed consent to it. In order to ensure, insofar as was possible, that a wife's consent was freely given, the law required that she appear before an alderman or justice of the peace without her husband. As the wife of a man regularly involved in real estate deals, Harriet Purvis was frequently required to testify that she was aware of the transactions he was involved in, that she understood them, and that they were being made with her full agreement.

The wealth of the Purvises steadily increased. In the fall of 1843 Robert Purvis paid $13,000 for a "Mansion" and one hundred and four acres of land in Byberry township in Philadelphia County. He did not farm all the land himself: much of it was sold off when a good price was offered. The farm and its equipment represented only a fraction of Robert Purvis's wealth. He kept livestock, and cultivated various grain and root crops. However, Purvis was basically a gentleman farmer. His show horses were famous in the neighborhood, and he won many prizes with them. Harriet Purvis shared her husband's interest in fine horses. In fact, her niece, Charlotte Forten, was surprised at the extent of her knowledge of horses.

In writing of the Byberry household, Charlotte Forten praised its "elegance and order" (*Journals of Charlotte Forten Grimké*, 6 July 1858). Harriet Purvis had been a gracious hostess at her home in Philadelphia. Now, established at Byberry, she had far greater scope. Abolitionists from all over the United States and from Europe were sure of a warm welcome at the Purvis home when they visited the Philadelphia area. Garrison, Sarah Parker Remond, Daniel Alexander Payne, Susan B. Anthony, and many others were guests of the Purvises over the years. In 1852 a British abolitionist, Sallie Holley, visited Byberry. She described the home as "elegant" and praised the Purvises for their hospitality: their "style of living is quite uncommonly rich and elegant. . . . The house and grounds are in tasteful

English style.'' As for Harriet Purvis, she was ''very ladylike in manners and conversation [with] something of the ease and blandness of a Southern lady'' (Holley, 101-103).

Fugitive Slaves Find Shelter

There were often other guests at Byberry whose presence the Purvises were careful not to reveal. For many years Harriet and Robert Purvis knowingly broke the law and sheltered fugitive slaves. Runaways were hidden in their Philadelphia house in the 1830s. Before they moved their children to Byberry, the Purvises decided to have some renovations done to their new house. Those renovations consisted of the construction of a secret room. Robert Purvis kept meticulous records regarding all those he and his wife had aided, until, according to Wilbur Siebert, ''the trepidation of his family after the passage of the Fugitive Slave Bill in 1850 forced him to destroy it.''

According to Frederick Douglass, one of those the Purvises sheltered in their Philadelphia home was Madison Washington. He had fled from slavery in Virginia and made his way to Canada. However, he was tormented by the knowledge that he had left his wife behind and he was determined to return for her. On his way back to Virginia the Purvises sheltered him. Robert Purvis begged him not to attempt the rescue: he would almost certainly be recaptured and that would not help his wife. Madison rejected the warning, returned to Virginia and, as Purvis had predicted, was soon taken. However, Harriet and Robert Purvis could not have foreseen the sequel. Madison Washington was sold to a slave-dealer and put on a vessel, the *Creole*, en route to New Orleans. When they were a few nights out from Richmond, he led his fellow slaves in a mutiny, seized the ship, and forced the crew to take it to a Bahamian port. There the slaves secured their freedom.

The Purvises also assisted Joseph Cinque and the other captives from the *Amistad*. Robert Purvis commissioned a portrait of Cinque and presented it to the Philadelphia Academy. It was returned to him with a note explaining that the picture was too controversial to be exhibited.

Time and again Harriet and Robert Purvis opened their homes to fugitives, gave them food, clothing, and money, and arranged for their journey north to Canada. In April 1859 Robert Purvis and others mobilized when a man by the name of Daniel Webster was seized in Philadelphia as a fugitive. He was released, ostensibly because the evidence of identification was not considered strong enough, although Charlotte Forten believed that officials had been swayed by public sentiment. It was Robert and Harriet Purvis who took Webster into their home and arranged for his passage to Canada.

Unlike so many of their white coworkers, Harriet and Robert Purvis did not believe that the abolitionist struggle had ended with the passage of the Thirteenth Amendment. In September 1866, as a member of the Philadelphia Female Anti-Slavery Society, Harriet Purvis attended a lecture on the state of affairs in the South. She did not hesitate to point out that there were battles to be won in the North as well as the South. In the City of Brotherly Love, the city where she had been born and where her family had lived since the days of William Penn, she was barred from riding in the streetcars. Abolition only made men and women like Harriet and Robert Purvis more keenly aware of the barriers that still had to be removed. Throughout the 1860s and into the 1870s both were active in the American Equal Rights Association and the Pennsylvania Equal Rights League.

Happy though the Purvises were in many ways, one tragedy after another struck over the years, uniting family members in grief. Harriet and Robert Purvis lost three of their sons to tuberculosis. Joseph Parrish Purvis died at Central College on May 8, 1851, at the age of fourteen. William, their eldest child, died on August 28, 1857. Robert, Jr., who had already embarked on a promising career as a merchant in Philadelphia, also fell victim to consumption. He died on March 19, 1862, when he was in his twenty-eighth year. Georgianna survived her mother by barely two years.

Harriet Purvis died of tuberculosis on June 11, 1875, at the age of sixty-five. She was buried at the Friends Fair Hill Burial Ground in Germantown, Philadelphia. Robert Purvis outlived her by almost twenty-three years. He was survived by his second wife, Tacy Townsend Purvis, and four of his children by Harriet—Hattie, Granville Sharp, Charles, and William. Of those four, three continued the activist tradition of Harriet and Robert Purvis. Charles Burleigh Purvis studied law before turning to medicine. He graduated from the Medical College of the Western Reserve in 1865. Moving to Washington, D.C., he worked at the Freedmen's Hospital and taught at Howard University as professor of medical jurisprudence. Henry W. Purvis went to South Carolina during Reconstruction and entered politics. He served as a state representative and then as the adjutant-general of the state militia. After the overthrow of the state's Reconstruction government he returned to Pennsylvania. As for Hattie Purvis, with the disbanding of the Philadelphia Female Anti-Slavery Society, in which she had been an active member for many years, she turned her attention to the fight for women's political rights.

References

Anti-Slavery Advocate June 1859.

Blassingame, John W., ed. *Frederick Douglass Papers*. Series 1, *Speeches, Debates and Interviews*, Vol. 2. New Haven: Yale University Press, 1983. 154-55.

Colored American 3 April 1841.

Dannett, Sylvia G. L. *Profiles of Negro Womanhood*. Vol. 1. Yonkers, N.Y: Educational Heritage, 1964. 84.

Garrison, William Lloyd. Letter to Robert Purvis, 10 December 1832. Anti-slavery Manuscripts, Boston Public Library.

''Harriet Bridges Davy.'' *Poulson's American Daily Advertiser* 10 May 1804, 18 May 1809.

History of Pennsylvania Hall, Which Was Destroyed by a

Mob on the 17th of May, 1838. Philadelphia: Merrihew and Gunn, 1838.

Holley, Sallie. *A Life for Liberty: Anti-Slavery and Other Letters of Sallie Holley*. Ed. John White Chapwick. New York: Putnam's, 1899. 101-103. Cited in Sumler-Lewis, "The Fortens," 104.

Liberator 16 December 1853.

May, Samuel J. *Recollections of Our Antislavery Conflict*. Boston: Fields, Osgood, 1869. Reprint. New York: Arno Press, 1968. 288.

National Anti-Slavery Standard 25 April 1844, 20 December 1849.

Pennsylvania Freeman 7 April 1841.

Philadelphia Board of Health Records, 1803-60. City Hall Annex, Philadelphia, Pennsylvania.

Philadelphia County Agricultural Census, 1850, Byberry Township.

Philadelphia County Deeds, A. M., Book 26, p. 469. R. L. L., Book 8, p. 351. City Hall Annex, Philadelphia, Pennsylvania.

Philadelphia County Wills, 1826, #150, Book 9, p. 5.; 1828, #72, Book 9, p. 189; 1898, #661, Book 200, p. 291. City Hall, Philadelphia, Pennsylvania.

Philadelphia Death Registers, 1875. City Hall Annex, Philadelphia.

Population Census, 1860. Philadelphia, Twenty-third Ward.

Poulson's American Daily Advertiser 10 May 1804, 18 May 1809, 3 September 1831.

Purvis, Hattie. Letter to Ellen Wright, 16 January 1856. Sophia Smith Garrison Papers, Smith College, in *Black Abolitionist Papers Microfilm*. New York: Microfilming Corporation of America, 1981-83.

Records of Friends Fair Hill Burial Ground. Collections of the Genealogical Society of Pennsylvania. Historical Society of Pennsylvania.

Ritter, Abram. *Philadelphia and Her Merchants, As Constituted Fifty and Seventy Years Ago*. Philadelphia: The Author, 1860. 46-47.

St. Peter's P. E. Church, Philadelphia, Pa.—Marriages, Burials, Confirmations, Communicants, 1828-1884. Records of the Genealogical Society of Pennsylvania, I. Historical Society of Pennsylvania.

Siebert, Wilbur H. *The Underground Railroad from Slavery to Freedom*. New York: Macmillan, 1898. Reprinted. New York: Arno Press, 1968. 10.

Sterling, Dorothy, ed. *We Are Your Sisters: Black Women in the Nineteenth Century*. New York: Norton, 1984. 187-88. The education of Hattie Purvis is discussed.

Stevenson, Brenda. ed. *The Journals of Charlotte Forten Grimké*. New York: Oxford University Press, 1988. 1 June and 5 June, 1854, pp. 64-65, 67; 12 April 1858, p. 300; 28 April 1858, p. 305; 17 June 1858, p. 317; 6 July 1858, p. 322; 4-9 April 1859, pp. 356-58.

Sumler-Lewis, Janice. "The Fortens of Philadelphia: An Afro-American Family and Nineteenth-Century Reform." Ph.D. dissertation Georgetown University, 1978. 106, 206.

Julie Winch

(The family background is given in more detail in the entries for Charlotte Forten Grimké and for Margaretta Forten.)

Sarah Forten Purvis

(c. 1811-1898?)

Poet, activist

Sarah Louisa Forten Purvis, noted poet and abolitionist, was born in Philadelphia in 1811 or 1812 to the wealthy freeborn businessman James Forten and his second wife, Charlotte Vandine Forten. She was the third of their eight children.*

If her poem "Hours of Childhood" is, to any great degree, autobiographical, it suggests that Sarah Forten grew up in a warm and supportive atmosphere. She writes of "dear cherished hours" of childhood, of beloved family members and friends, and "of schoolday mirth" (*Liberator,* 18 January 1834). Like her brothers and sisters, Sarah Forten Purvis had the benefits of a private education. The decision to cooperate with other wealthy free black parents to establish a separate school was one forced on James Forten. He would not enroll his children in the only schools that would admit them because of what he considered the inferior quality of the education available in those schools, and the private academies were closed to them on account of their race.

The formal education Sarah Forten Purvis and her siblings received at school was supplemented by tutoring at home. James Forten hired teachers to train them in music and languages. The Forten daughters were described by many who visited their home as refined and accomplished young women, well able to take their place in genteel society. Like several of her brothers, Sarah Forten Purvis had a fine singing voice, and took great pleasure in music. Throughout her life she evidently read extensively, devouring whatever works of literature she could find—from Hannah More's

Strictures on the Modern System of Education to Washington Irving's *Tales of the Alhambra*.

Her father's wealth, the social status of her family, and the fact that she was freeborn did not blind Sarah Forten Purvis to the evils of racial prejudice nor alienate her from the slaves. In 1837, in a revealing letter to the white abolitionist Angelina Grimké, she described the impact of racism on herself and her family. "[I]t has often embittered my feelings . . . I must also own that *it* has often engendered feelings of discontent and mortification in my breast when I saw that many were preferred before me, who by education, birth, or worldly circumstances were no better than myself." She was fully sensible of the fact that her father's wealth insulated her from the worst effects of racial injustice, but, even so, racism confronted her once she stepped outside her comfortable home. "For our own family—we have to thank a kind Providence for placing us in a situation that has hitherto prevented us from falling under the weight of this evil. We feel it but in a slight degree compared with many others. . . . We are not disturbed in our social relations—we never travel far from home and seldom go to public places unless quite sure that admission is free to all—therefore, we meet with none of the mortifications which might otherwise ensue (Sarah Forten to Angelina Grimké, 15 April 1837).

From her earliest years Purvis had been raised to oppose slavery, to work for its eradication, and to reject the notion that her freeborn status somehow divorced her from those held in bondage in the South. Although, writing to Angelina Grimké, she credited Garrisonian abolitionism with awakening her "from apathy and indifference, [and] shedding light into a Mind which has been too long wrapped in selfish darkness," it is hardly likely that she needed to be won over to the antislavery ranks by abolitionist journalist William Lloyd Garrison or any other white activist (*Weld-Grimké Letters*, 380).

Forten Writes Antislavery Verse

What the antislavery ferment of the 1830s did offer Purvis was a chance to make her voice heard. Under the penname "Ada," she began writing antislavery verse for Garrison's abolitionist journal the *Liberator* in 1831, when she was nineteen or twenty years old. After two of her poems had been published, James Forten revealed the true identity of "Ada" to Garrison.

Purvis's first poem was entitled "The Grave of the Slave" and it was published in the third number of the *Liberator* on 22 January 1831. Her theme was a conventional one—that in death the slave would find rest from his labors. However, she took the opportunity to remind slaveowners that all were equal in death and that no earthly master could rouse the slave "with voice of command." She ended:

> Poor slave! shall we sorrow that death was thy friend, The last, and the kindest, that heaven could send? The grave to the weary is welcomed and blest;
> And death, to the captive, is freedom and rest
> (*Liberator* 22 January 1831).

The subject of "Past Joys" received similar treatment. The theme was again conventional enough—sadness at leaving home and friends. What "Ada" explored was the far deeper sorrow that afflicted the slave:

> Poor Afric's son—ah! he must feel
> How hard it is to part
> From all he lov'd—from all that life
> Had twined around his heart.
>
> His is a sorrow deeper far,
> Than all that we can show;
> His is a lasting grief, o'er which
> No healing balm can flow.
> The mother, wife, or child he loved,
> He ne'er shall see again;
> To him they're lost—ay, dead indeed:
> What for him doth remain?
> (*Liberator*, 19 March 1831).

Other poems followed. In "The Slave Girl's Address to Her Mother" and "Prayer" she spoke of religion as affording consolation to the slave, but she was no apologist for slavery.

> Oh! ye who boast of Freedom's sacred claims,
> Do ye not blush to see our galling chains;
> To hear that sounding word—'that all are free'
> When thousands groan in hopeless *slavery*?
>
> Upon your land it is a cruel stain —
> Freedom, what are thou?—nothing but a name.
> No more, no more! Oh God, this cannot be;
> Thou to thy children's aid wilt surely flee:
> In thine own time deliverance thou wilt give,
> And bid us rise from slavery, and live
> (*Liberator*, 29 January 1831).

A recurring theme in her poetry was America's abandonment of its revolutionary principles. Purvis was the daughter of a man who had fought for the independence of his country and suffered imprisonment in the defense of liberty. The bitter irony that so many of her fellow citizens could espouse liberty while sanctioning slavery aroused her anger. In "The Slave" she wrote:

> Our sires who once in freedom's cause,
> Their boasted freedom sought and won,
> For deeds of glory gained applause,
> When patriot feelings led them on.
> And can their sons now speak with pride,
> Of rights for which they bled and died,—
> Or while the captive is oppressed,
> Think of the wrongs they once redress'd?

She could only conclude:

> On, surely they have quite forgot,
> That bondage once had been their lot;
> The sweets of freedom now they know,

They care not for the captive's wo[e]
(*Liberator*, 16 April 1831).

Oh! speak not of heathenish darkness again,
Nor tell me of lands in error's dread chain!
Where—where is the nation so erring as we,
Who claim the proud name of the 'HOME OF THE FREE'? . . .
Speak not of 'my country,' unless she shall be,
In truth, the bright home of the 'brave and the free.'
Till the dark stain of slavery is washed from her hand,
A tribute of homage she cannot command
(*Liberator*, 4 January 1834).

Her message was equally forceful when she forsook poetry for prose. In the spring of 1831, in a letter signed "Magawisca," she addressed the theme of "The Abuse of Liberty." She pointed out that the enjoyment of life, liberty, and property was confined to white men. "I say every white man, because those who cannot shew [sic] a fair exterior, no matter what be the noble qualities of their mind, may be robbed of the rights [with] which they were endowed by an all-wise and merciful Creator, who, in his great wisdom, cast a sable hue over some of the 'lords of creation.'" She expressed pity for the slaveholder, even as she condemned him for his injustice and prayed that he might see the error of his ways. "[T]here is no state of life so anxious as his . . . he is in constant dread lest they, who he unjustly condemns to bondage, will burst their fetters and become oppressors in their turn." She ended with a warning about the inevitability of divine retribution. "[C]an you think . . . He, who made the sun to shine on the black man as well as the white, will always allow you to rest tranquil on your downy couches? No,—He is just, and his anger will not always slumber. He will wipe the tears from Ethiopia's eye; He will shake the tree of liberty, and its blossoms shall spread over the earth" (*Liberator*, 26 March 1831).

Like her older sister, Margaretta, she was moved to put into verse her sentiments on the formation of the American Anti-Slavery Society. Some of those who had traveled to Philadelphia in December 1833 to establish the organization had dined at the Forten home. A few were already valued friends; others she met for the first time that winter. As they left the city to return to their homes she experienced conflicting emotions:

We joy that duties call them forth,
Clad in an armor bright;
With shield of faith, their surest guard,
And sword of truth and light. . . .

And yet, we sorrow most of all.
And from the heart deplore,
That we perchance on earth again
May see these friends no more
("The Separation," *Liberator*, 21 December 1833).

Purvis shared the fervent admiration for William Lloyd Garrison so often expressed by her father and other members of her family. When Garrison left the United States in 1833 to take his antislavery message to Britain, she wrote a poem to the *Hibernia*, the "gallant bark" that carried:

. . . to old Britain's shores,
The Champion of the slave. . . .
. . . He goes to raise the standard high,
And freedom's flag unfurl,
And to proclaim the rallying cry
Of freedom to the world
(*Liberator*, 21 December 1833).

Occasionally she penned sentimental verses that contained no mention of the plight of the slave. "Hours of Childhood" is one such piece and "The Farewell," written in 1832, is another. In "The Farewell," the writer addresses a young man who, she fears, will soon forget her and transfer his affections to another when they are no longer together:

Another's lips will charm thee then,
Another's voice will praise;
Thou wilt forget we e'er have met
In past and happy days. . . .

Farewell—farewell!—'t were better far
That we had never met,
Than meeting one brief moment here,
To part—and then forget
(*Liberator*, 30 June 1832).

In a third poem, "A Mother's Grief," she describes the sufferings of a widowed mother who has just lost her one remaining child (*Liberator*, 7 July 1832). However, these three compositions are exceptions to her main theme—the iniquities of slavery and prejudice.

What is probably her best-known poem, "An Appeal to Woman," was published in the *Liberator* on February 1, 1834. It had already appeared in the Lowell *Observer*. In that poem she called upon white women to "nobly dare to act a Christian's part":

Dare to be good, as thou canst dare be great,
Despise the taunts of envy, scorn and hate;
Our 'skins may differ,' but from thee we claim
A sister's privilege, in a sister's name.

As in some of her earlier works, she reminded her white readers that all would be equal in death:

Oh, woman!—though upon thy fairer brow
The hues of roses and of lilies glow-
These soon must wither in their kindred earth,
From when the fair and dark have equal birth.
Let a bright halo o'er thy virtues shed
A lustre, that shall live when thou art dead
(*Liberator*, February 1834).

More than three years after the poem's first publication, the delegates to the first women's antislavery convention reprinted the second verse on the title page of their *Appeal to the Women of the Nominally Free States*.

Female Anti-Slavery Society Founded

Purvis did not confine her antislavery activism to writing poetry and prose. With her older sisters, Harriet and Margaretta, she signed the charter incorporating the Philadelphia Female Anti-Slavery Society in December 1833. She served several terms on the society's board of managers in the 1830s and took part in campaigns to petition for the abolition of slavery in the District of Columbia, and for an end to schemes to annex Texas for the benefit of Southern slaveholders. In November 1836 Sarah Forten and her mother, together with a close family friend, Grace Douglass, were appointed to the committee that issued a statement praising the work of Angelina Grimké as she embarked on her first antislavery speaking tour. Sarah Forten also played a role in the efforts of the society to finance the building of the ill-fated Pennsylvania Hall. She was active in the work of the Philadelphia Female Anti-Slavery Society until her marriage and her departure from the city.

During her Philadelphia years abolition was central to almost all of her activities. She attended antislavery meetings, she helped her parents to entertain visiting abolitionists, and she found most of her friends, black and white, among those active in the abolitionist movement. One of her correspondents was Elizabeth Whittier, the sister of the poet John Greenleaf Whittier. In the spring of 1835 she sent Elizabeth Whittier an enthusiastic description of the visit of the British abolitionist George Thompson to Philadelphia (Sarah Forten to Elizabeth Whittier, 23 March 1835. She refers in her letter to another white abolitionist with whom she corresponded—a Mrs. Fuller of Boston). A second letter, a lively account of the Christmas Fair organized by the Philadelphia Female Anti-Slavery Society, also conveys a sense of the extent to which abolitionist activities and abolitionist contacts dominated her life.

In 1837 Purvis and her sisters, Margaretta and Harriet, joined with other female abolitionists and attended the Female Anti-Slavery Convention in New York. While in the city, they stayed with Reverend Peter Williams, the minister of St. Philip's Episcopal Church and the father of a family friend, Amy Matilda Cassey. In 1838 and 1839 the women's antislavery conventions met in their own city. Harriet and Margaretta evidently attended those conventions, but Sarah Forten left Philadelphia early in 1838 and may not have been present on either occasion.

On January 7, 1838, Sarah Forten married Joseph Purvis, the younger brother of her sister's husband, in a civil ceremony in Burlington County, New Jersey. Joseph Purvis was the youngest son of William Purvis (1762-1826), an English immigrant who had amassed great wealth as a cotton merchant in South Carolina. Purvis had taken as his mistress Harriet Judah, a native of Charleston, many years his junior. Harriet Judah, a freeborn woman of German-Jewish and North African descent, bore Purvis three sons—William, Jr. (1807-1828), Robert (1810-1898), and Joseph (1812-1857). William Purvis, Sr., acknowledged the children and, after making generous provision for their mother, he left his estate to be divided among them. (Harriet Judah subsequently married Reverend William Miller, a future AME bishop.) The death of William Purvis, Jr., unmarried and without children, meant that his share of his father's estate was shared by his two surviving brothers.

When Sarah Forten married him, Joseph Purvis was a man of means. While his older brother made substantial investments in urban properties, Joseph Purvis had used his share of his inheritance to establish himself as a farmer. Two-and-a-half years before his marriage he had purchased a two hundred-acre farm in Bensalem, Bucks County, for more than $13,500. In 1838 he moved his bride there to a life markedly different from that she had known in the city. Raising a family and helping to manage a farm left Sarah Purvis little time for writing antislavery verse. (Poems by a writer who signed herself "Ada" continued to appear in antislavery periodicals. However, Sarah Forten Purvis was almost certainly not their author: the writer refers to growing up in New England and also favors the Quaker style of dating her work.) In twelve years Sarah Forten had eight children, Joseph (b. 1838/39), James (b. 1839/40), William (b. 1841/42), Sarah (b. 1842/43), Emily (b. 1844), Alfred (b. 1845/46), Harriet (also known as Annie, b. 1847/48) and Alexander (b. 1850).

Joseph Purvis was wealthy enough to hire domestic servants. According to the federal census of 1850, he employed two female servants to assist his wife with the household chores and four farm laborers to work with him in the fields. There was no reason for Sarah Purvis to be apprehensive that her standard of living would deteriorate. The main farm in Bensalem produced a good income for the family in the 1840s and early 1850s. Purvis invested substantial amounts in farm machinery and livestock. He concentrated on grain and meat production, dairy farming, and beekeeping. He also continued to buy up real estate. Some months after his marriage, he acquired a second farm, in Bristol township, which he eventually sold. In 1839 he bought another farm, once the property of his brother. However, unlike his brother, he kept his investments in Philadelphia property small. Presumably he was gambling on a steady rise in the value of agricultural land—especially land at no great distance from a large urban industrial center where thousands of people needed to be supplied with food.

Joseph Purvis may have been too rash with some of his investments. He was in the midst of a series of complicated land deals when he died suddenly on January 17, 1857. He died intestate and with all of his eight children still minors. The Bucks County Orphans' Court stepped in. It was soon apparent that his reserves of cash were "not Sufficient for the payment of his debts," and with Sarah Purvis's consent (she waived her right to act as administrator), portions of his property were ordered to be sold off. The property holdings were considerable: the bulk of Joseph Purvis's real estate was in Bucks County, but there were Philadelphia interests and a vacant lot in Richmond, Virginia, to be disposed of. Purvis's administrator did his best, but in 1857 the nation was gripped by a financial panic. People were being cautious; selling real estate and securing a good price was not easy. There were also Purvis's promissory notes. Purvis had apparently loaned money to other farmers in the neighborhood. The administrator was able to call in two of the notes Purvis had given, but it is probable that there were other creditors who could not pay their debts.

Sarah Purvis and her children were not immediately faced with ruin. Her niece, Charlotte Forten, on a visit some months after the death of Joseph Purvis, observed that the farm, "Fairview," "is very pleasant, and with the elegant cultivation which distinguishes Aunt H[arriet]'s would be far more beautiful" (*Journals of Charlotte Forten Grimké*, 233, entry for 26 June 1857). On a subsequent visit she was less favorably impressed. "Went to Aunt S.'s this morning. As usual a scene of confusion and disorder greeted me. What a contrast to Byberry [the home of Harriet and Robert Purvis]. Every thing, every body is so very, very different. It grieves me to think of it."(*Journals of Charlotte Forten Grimké*, 322-23, entry for 6 July 1858). The descent into genteel poverty might be slow, but it was inevitable. The census of 1860 reveals that the servants and farmhands had gone: Sarah Purvis had no real estate of her own (the property was held in trust for her children), and her personal property amounted to just over six hundred dollars. The family's finances received some much-needed help when Sarah Purvis's mother-in-law, Harriet Judah Miller, died in 1869. A woman of means, she left her estate to be divided between the families of her two sons, Robert and Joseph Purvis. This windfall might have enabled Sarah Purvis to settle some of her debts, but it could not save her family's fortunes. By 1871 Joseph Purvis's once considerable estate had dwindled to three small properties comprising forty acres and two houses. It was by no means a negligible holding, but it did not go far when it had to be divided among his surviving children and his widow. Sarah Purvis was eventually obliged to declare bankruptcy in 1875 and have her few remaining possessions auctioned off.

In addition to her financial woes, Sarah Purvis also endured the loss of three of her children in less than a decade. Alfred Purvis died on April 27, 1865, at the age of nineteen. James Forten Purvis died in February 1870 at the age of twenty-nine. Emily Purvis, who had married and gone to live with her husband in Albany, New York, died in the early 1870s. Two more of Sarah Purvis's children left Pennsylvania to join the exodus of black settlers to Kansas. Sarah Purvis's eldest daughter, Sarah, had married William Boseman, probably a younger brother of Benjamin Boseman, a New York native, who became an important figure in the political life of Charleston, South Carolina, during Reconstruction, When the Bosemans decided to try their luck in Kansas, they were joined by Sarah Purvis's youngest brother, Alexander. By 1873 they had settled in Neosha Falls, Woodson County, Kansas.

Sarah Purvis returned, a poor widow, with two of her children, Annie and William, to the childhood home she had left almost four decades earlier to marry Joseph Purvis. (Her eldest son, Joseph, stayed on in Bensalem and tried to make a living from farming.) Under the terms of a property transfer made by her father shortly before his death, she had a one-eighth interest in the Lombard Street house. For many years her unmarried elder sister, Margaretta, had kept house for her mother and her two bachelor brothers, Thomas and William Forten. Margaretta Forten died of pneumonia in January 1875 and Sarah Purvis took over the day-to-day running of the household. The census of 1880 lists Sarah, Annie, and William Purvis living at 336 Lombard Street. (After the consolidation of Philadelphia, the houses were renumbered. By 1860, the house that had been 92 Lombard Street was 336 Lombard.)

A search of the Philadelphia death records has so far failed to reveal the exact date of Sarah Forten Purvis's death. She is listed in the census for 1880 and in the city directory for that year. She had presumably died by 1898 when the daughter of abolitionist William Still observed that William Deas Forten was the last surviving member of the family. Sarah Forten Purvis was buried in a lot owned by William Forten in the cemetery of the Episcopal church of St. James the Less of Philadelphia. Her grave is unmarked.

References

Agricultural Census, 18509, Bensalem Township, Bucks County, Pennsylvania.

An Appeal to the Women of the Nominally Free States, Issued by an Anti-Slavery Convention of American Women, Held by Adjournments from the 9th to the 12th of May, 1837. 2d ed. Boston: Isaac Knapp, 1838.

Bucks County Administrations, File #10075, Adm. 8, no. 49. Bucks County Courthouse, Doylestown, Pennsylvania.

Bucks County Deeds. Book 60, p. 111; Book 64, p. 130. For the various property settlements made for Emily (Purvis) Allen, Sarah (Purvis) Boseman, and Alexander Purvis see Bucks County Deeds, Book 158, 462; Book 160, 406; Book 178,397. On the bankruptcy of Sarah Purvis and two of her children, William and Annie, see Bucks County, Misc., Book 18, 436, Bucks County Courthouse, Doylestown, Pennsylvania.

Bucks County Mortgages, Book 17, p. 312.

Federal Census, 1850, 1860, 1880. The exact year of Sarah Forten's birth cannot be determined. In the census of 1850 her age is given as 36, indicating that she was born in 1813 or 1814. In the census of 1860 her age is recorded as 48, meaning that she was born in 1811 or 1812. In the census of 1880 her age is given as 70. If that is accurate, it would mean that she and her sister, Harriet, were twins. For further information on James and Charlotte Forten, see the entry on *Margaretta Forten*.

Forten, James. Letter to William Lloyd Garrison, 23

February 1831. Anti-Slavery Manuscripts, Boston Public Library.

Purvis, Sarah Forten. Letter to Angelina Grimké, 15 April 1837. *Letters of Theodore Dwight Weld, Angelina Grimké Weld, and Sarah Grimké, 1822-1844*. Eds. Gilbert H. Barnes and Dwight L. Dumond. New York: D. Appleton-Century, 1934. 379-82.

———. Letter to Elizabeth Whittier, 23 March 1835. Whittier Papers, Central Michigan University, in *Black Abolitionist Papers Microfilm*. New York: Microfilming Corporation of America, 1981-83.

———. Letter to Elizabeth Whittier, 25 December 1836. Whittier Papers, Central Michigan University, in *Black Abolitionist Papers Microfilm*. New York: Microfilming Corporation of America, 1981-83.

———. "Magawisca." "The Abuse of Liberty." *Liberator* 26 March 1831.

———, Under penname "Ada." Various Poems in *Liberator* 22 January 1831; 29 January 1831; 19 March 1831; 26 March 1831; 16 April 1831; 7 July 1832; 21 December 1833; 4 January 1834; 18 January 1834; 27 June 1835; *Philanthropist* 11 March 1835.

———, Under penname "Sarah Louisa." *Liberator* 30 June 1832; 25 May 1833; 18 January 1834; 1 February 1834; "The Slave Girl's Farewell" 27 June 1835; "The Slave" 11 March 1837; 29 March 1839. The "Grave of the Slave" was reprinted in the *Philanthropist* 11 March 1836.

Pennsylvania *Freeman* 19 November 1836.

Philadelphia County Deeds, G.S., Book 35, p. 621; R.L.I., Book 19, p. 241 and Book 48, p. 267. City Hall Annex, Philadelphia.

Philadelphia County Wills, 1869, #639, Book 66, 109. City Hall, Philadelphia.

Philadelphia *Public Ledger* 12 January 1838.

Population Census, 1850, Bensalem Township, Bucks County, Pennsylvania.

St. James the Less Episcopal Church, Philadelphia, Pennsylvania—Cemetery Records. Handwritten volume, Genealogical Society of Pennsylvania, Historical Society of Pennsylvania.

Stevenson, Brenda, ed. *The Journals of Charlotte Forten Grimké*. New York: Oxford University Press, 1988. 233, entry for 28 June 1857; p. 322-23, entry for 6 July 1858.

Collections

No photographs of Sarah Forten Purvis have so far been located. Although there is apparently no collection of her personal papers, examples of her prose and poetry are to be found in a number of antislavery journals.

Julie Winch

**(See the entries for Charlotte Forten Grimké and Margaretta Forten for a more detailed account of the family background.)*

Q

Norma Quarles

(1936-)

Broadcast journalist, disk jockey

Television journalist Norma R. Quarles was born on November 11, 1936, in New York. Quarles is an alumna of Hunter College in New York and the City College of New York. She is divorced with two children—a daughter, Susan, and a son, Lawrence.

Quarles did not begin her career in the field of journalism or television news. She first worked as buyer at a specialty shop in New York. She then moved to Chicago, and from 1957 to 1965 she worked as a licensed real estate broker for Katherine King Associates. It was not until 1965 that she made the transition to a broadcasting career and landed her first job in radio where she performed as a disc jockey, news reporter, and public service director for WSDM Radio in Chicago. She worked at the WSDM radio station for one year.

The civil rights movement of the sixties began to apply pressure on the news media to involve more minorities in its efforts to provide balanced news coverage to the public. As a result of this criticism, doors begun to open up in the broadcasting news industry for women and minorities, and training programs targeted for the purpose of attracting more women and minorities to the news business were established. In 1966 Quarles was selected to attend a one-year news training program sponsored by NBC in New York.

The 1960s were challenging times for women and minorities interested in entering the news media because these pioneers would go down in history as the ones responsible for paving the way and opening future doors for women and minorities. Quarles did exactly that. After attending the NBC training program, Quarles moved to Cleveland to work as a news reporter and anchor for WKYC-TV. She stayed in that position for three years. She was then transferred back to WNBC-TV in New York, where her career began to skyrocket in her first year. While working as a reporter for WNBC-TV, Quarles substituted as a hostess of a women's show and as a result of that three-week performance, Quarles was selected as the first woman in the city to coanchor a 6 P.M. news program.

According to an *Ebony* article on television newswomen, Quarles did not have an easy time climbing up the ladder and was criticized "by some blacks for not being militant enough when she first began television work." However, Quarles did not quit because of the criticism she received from members of her own race. Her attitude was, "You have to be willing to constantly learn and grow. Most of all, if a person wants to be in this business, she has to love it" (*Ebony*, 170).

Quarles's family obligations, however, had a major impact on the direction of her early career. A divorced mother of two, Quarles discussed how her family obligations limited her career aspirations:

> I have never really pitched for a network assignment job because it involves traveling all over the country, all over the world. And as a mother with the responsibility of children, I really can't do that. Yet it would be an upgrade both financially and professionally (Gelfman, 133).

At the time, Quarles's son was seventeen years old and her daughter was thirteen. It was very important for her to balance her two careers as a mother and a journalist.

Quarles worked with the NBC network and its affiliates for twenty-one years. During her tenure at NBC, Quarles covered major stories for NBC's Midwest bureau and was an award-winning reporter and anchor for WNBC-TV, where she won a Sigma Delta Chi Deadline Club Award as well as a Front Page Award for news stories reported on the film story "The Stripper." In addition to those awards, she won an Emmy for reporting for her "Urban Journal" series while working with WMAQ-TV, NBC's Chicago station. While working as an NBC New York correspondent, Quarles also covered the highly-publicized Bernhard Goetz shooting and the Baby M case. In 1984, she was selected to serve as a panelist on the League of Women Voters Vice-Presidential Debate. She also anchored the NBC News "Evening Digest."

In 1988, Quarles left NBC after working there for twenty-one years and joined the Cable News Network's (CNN) New York bureau. She is currently coanchoring CNN's weekday news programs "Daybreak" and "Daywatch."

Being the first woman to coanchor a 6 P.M. newscast has definitely earned Quarles a place in history. She is not only a skilled and dedicated journalist but a very personable and witty individual. It is evident that her success has not altered her personality.

Norma Quarles is a member of the National Academy of Televison Arts and Sciences, Sigma Delta Chi, and a board member of the Governor's National Academy of Television Arts and Sciences.

References

Gelfman, Judith S. *Women in Television News.* New York: Columbia University Press, 1976. 133.

"Norma Quarles Biography." Cable News Network (CNN), 1990.

Polski, Harry A., and James Williams, comps. and eds. *The Negro Almanac: A Reference Work on the Afro-American.* 5th ed. Detroit: Gale Research, 1990. 1284. Includes photograph.

Scheurer, Steven H., ed. *Who's Who in Television and Cable.* New York: Facts on File, 1983. 389.

"Upsurge in TV News Girls." *Ebony* 26 (June 1971): 169-70.

Who's Who Among Black Americans, 1990-1991. 6th ed. Detroit: Gale Research, 1990. 1040-41.

Dhyana Ziegler

R

Muriel Rahn

(1911-1961)

Singer, actress

Muriel Ellen Rahn—gifted concert soprano, opera star, and stage personality—was born in Boston in 1911, the only child of Willie and Bessie Rahn. When Willie Rahn died, Muriel Rahn continued to live for a while in Boston with her father's sister, Mamie Davenport. Later, Muriel was taken to New York, where her mother had found employment. It was in New York, also, that Bessie Rahn met and married Cornelius Battey, who became director of the photography division at Tuskegee Institute, Alabama. She worked as a bookkeeper in the office of R. R. Moton, Tuskegee University's second president.

Rahn finished high school at Tuskegee Institute, as it was called then, attended Atlanta University for two years, and completed a degree at the Music Conservatory of the University of Nebraska at Lincoln. In addition, she pursued special course work at Teachers' College, Columbia University, and subsequently taught public school music for two years in Winston-Salem, North Carolina. Upon her return to New York, she studied voice at the Juilliard School of Music.

Rahn began exploring and developing her natural talent for singing during her Tuskegee and Atlanta University days. She sang so frequently that her parents became concerned about her academic progress at Atlanta and gently chastised her, "A college course to you seems to be a singing vacation" ("Broadway Finds Muriel Rahn," *Chicago Defender*, 12 May 1945). Muriel Rahn demonstrated, however, that she was serious and continued to sing whenever asked. With music training and experience behind her, she launched a professional career in 1929 with Eva Jessye's Jubilee Singers. This group provided background music in the Players' Club revival of *Uncle Tom's Cabin* staged at the Capitol Theater in New York. Also in 1929 she joined the casts of at least two Broadway musicals, Lew Leslie's *Blackbirds of 1929* and Connie Inn's *Hot Chocolates* (1929-30). These groups included many other leading vocalists—Cab Calloway, Edith Wilson, the Five Crackerjacks, Billy Higgins, Roland Holden, and Dick Campbell, Muriel Rahn's future husband and producer/manager. Between Broadway shows, she sang in numerous music halls, speakeasies, and supper clubs in New York.

About 1932, Rahn married Charles Rountree, a young Boston student. When they separated shortly thereafter, she returned to New York; then in 1933 she moved on to Paris where she sang at the fashionable Chez La DuBarry. Both the French critics and the public applauded her. By 1934, she had married Dick Campbell and was again on Broadway appearing with Judith Anderson in the Broadway production of Clemence Dane's *Come of Age*. Early in her career Muriel Rahn established an alternating schedule of successful singing and acting, becoming known as one of those rare individuals who combined outstanding vocal and dramatic talents.

Though her reputation rests primarily on concert appearances, Rahn was an accomplished artist in grand opera and on Broadway. On May 12, 1945, in "Broadway Finds Muriel Rahn Jack of All Theatre Trade," the *Chicago Defender* summarized her outstanding career and quoted one of her directors, Alfred Lunt, on her versatility: "Many people can act and a goodly number can sing but only a handful have achieved fame in both fields-and MURIEL RAHN is one of them." She herself assigned "about fifty-fifty" to acting and singing in their importance for her.

By the 1940s Muriel Rahn was active in the opera division of New York City's National Orchestral Association, a perfect outlet for further developing her dual talents. Already an anomaly as the only black member of the association, she distinguished herself even more by auditioning and being chosen over more than 250 white vocalists to perform in Mozart's *Abduction from the Seraglio*, presented by the association in January 1942. In this role Muriel Rahn became the first black to appear in opera at Carnegie Hall with an all-white opera company. Other National Orchestral Association productions in which she performed include Puccini's *Suor Angelica* and *Gianni Schicchi*. And in 1948 when the Salmaggi Opera presented Verdi's *Aida*, it was Muriel Rahn who sang the title role. She repeated this performance twice in 1949—with the San Carlo Opera and with Mary Cardwell Dawson's National Negro Opera Company. In 1954, performing still another demanding operatic lead, Muriel Rahn opened in Newark, New Jersey, in *Salome*, Richard Strauss's modern opera on the New Testament story. She studied with former assistant Metropolitan Opera conductor Herman Weigert and with choreographer Charles Weidman in preparing the role of Salome, a grueling part requiring acting, singing, and dancing. According to an account in the January 1955 *Ebony*, she was equal to the challenge: "The audience cheered Miss Rahn for a versatile exhibition of first-rate singing of a difficult score, believable acting of a complex role and a spirited interpretation of a bizarre dance.'' Moreover, described as ''a coffee-with-cream complexioned songbird, with big brown eyes and that come-hither look,'' she was persuasive as the impassioned temptress Salome.

Rahn also created roles in two American operas—Harry Freeman's *The Martyr*, presented at Carnegie Hall in 1947, and the Langston Hughes-Jan Meyerowitz production, *The Barrier*, which premiered at Columbia University on January 18, 1950. Based on Hughes's play *The Mulatto*, *The Barrier* featured Rahn in the lead role of Cora Lewis, mother of the mulatto boy. Howard Taubman, music critic for *The New York Times*, wrote a glowing tribute: ''Muriel Rahn . . . gives a stunning performance. She brings a personal dignity and sincerity to the part, and her singing is not only accurate and full-bodied, but charged with dramatic cogency. Miss Rahn's Cora is the core of the piece—its fire and artistic conscience.'' After a brief run of five performances in Washington, D. C., *The Barrier* opened on Broadway in November 1950 at the Broadhurst Theater, starring Lawrence Tibbett, Wilton Clary, and Muriel Rahn in what was to be her last Broadway appearance.

Rahn Performs in Broadway musicals

Earlier, however, Rahn had starred in numerous musical dramas on Broadway. She won a featured dramatic role in *The Pirate*, an Alfred Lunt-Lynn Fontaine production staged at the Martin Beck Theater in September 1942. Indeed, it was on Broadway that she portrayed Carmen, the character for whom she became best known. Alternating with Muriel Smith in the title role, Rahn sang in Billy Rose's *Carmen Jones*, which enjoyed a run of 231 performances at the Broadway Theater during 1943-44. Clearly a consummate performer, she won rave reviews for her work in every form—in opera, in musical drama, in the supper club, and on the concert stage.

Yet her professional life was not without trouble. She sometimes experienced problems that were common for black American artists during the 1930s, 1940s, and early 1950s. In September 1950, protesting segregated seating at the Ford Theatre in Baltimore, Maryland, where *The Barrier* was to be presented, Rahn promised to honor her contract by performing but to picket the theater while not on stage. The theater owner canceled the production, however, thereby avoiding difficulties with both opponents and proponents of Jim Crow. Aside from laws and customs that prohibited or limited access to public accommodations, there was also the perennial problem of the exploitation of black artists. In *Voices of the Black Theatre*, Dick Campbell recounts an incident of the early thirties in which a Mr. Slatko offered him and Rahn seventy-five dollars of a promised fee of one hundred fifty dollars. Following Rahn's angry response, ''The whole world should know how this man treats black performers,'' Campbell created a disturbance involving policeman, firemen, and interested bystanders who heard the robbery charges levied against Slatko. Perhaps a combination of moral pressure, embarrassment, and fear convinced him to pay the Rahn-Campbell team the entire one hundred fifty dollars. On a larger scale, Billy Rose failed to keep his promise of an increase in Rahn's salary based on the escalating success of *Carmen Jones*. Again, Rahn resisted exploitation and exposed the would-be exploiter. *The Chicago Defender* of December 25, 1943, carries the article, ''Rahn Quits Carmen in Tilt with Billy Rose,'' denouncing the ''millionaire producer.''

After *Carmen Jones*, Rahn embarked upon an extensive concert tour of three different trips—from New York to Texas, through the Midwest to the Pacific coast, and through the New England states—totaling approximately forty-five appearances. Her program included works by black American writers and composers Langston Hughes, William Grant Still, and William Dawson. Continuing to combine concert and theater, she performed in 1955 with Diana Barrymore in an off-Broadway production of *The Ivory Branch* and worked during 1959-60 as musical director of *Bells Are Ringing*, produced by the German State Theatre at Frankfurt.

About his fellow performer, friend, and wife of twenty-seven years, Dick Campbell fondly recalls:

> She was a beautiful, light brownskin woman about five feet two, slim with large eyes and always a lovely smile. She was also one of the most intelligent women I have ever known—a gifted speaker, on most any subject or occasion and a fantastic personality.
>
> Langston Hughes was one of her greatest admirers and he brought all of his work to her to read before publishing, including the lyrics to songs that she often sang in her own concerts at Town Hall in New York . . . Other friends were Harold Jackman, Countee Cullen, a young Marian Anderson, Paul Robeson, Canada Lee, Todd Duncan and many more (Campbell, 7 March 1990).

On August 8, 1961, Muriel Rahn, ''sensational songbird'' and serious artist, died of cancer at Sydenham Hospital in New York City.

References

Abdul, Raoul. *Blacks in Classical Music*. New York: Dodd, Mead 1977. 104-105, 150.

'''Aida' at Armory Saturday.'' *Washington Post* 24 April 1949.

The Black Perspective in Music 3 (Fall 1975): 310.

''Break No. 3 Comes to Soprano Star, Muriel Rahn.'' *Journal and Guide* 15 August 1942.

''Broadway Finds Muriel Rahn Jack of All Theatre Trade.'' *Chicago Defender* 12 May 1945.

Calvin, Dolores. ''Muriel Rahn Excited Over Concert

Tour; Gives Interview of Future Plans.'' *Journal and Guide* 28 August 1944.

———. ''Rahn Quits Carmen in Tilt With Billy Rose.'' *Chicago Defender* 25 December 1943.

Campbell, Dick. ''Muriel Rahn's Life and Career.'' In Letter to author 7 March 1990.

Campbell, Dick. Telephone interview with author, 9 February 1990.

''Carmen Jones.'' *Playbill* 2 April 1944.

Hughes, Langston. *Fight for Freedom. The Story of the NAACP*. New York: Norton, 1962. 178-79.

Guzman, Jessie P., ed. *Negro Yearbook*. New York: William H. Wise, 1952. 56-57.

Hughes, Langston and Milton Meltzer. *Black Magic: A Pictorial History of the Negro in American Entertainment*. Englewood Cliffs, N. J.: Prentice Hall, 1967. 135, 160-61, 163, 214, 238.

Jessy, Eva. Telephone interview with author, 16 February 1990.

Mapp, Edward. *Directory of Blacks in the Performing Arts*. Metuchen, N. J.: Scarecrow Press, 1978. 301.

Mitchell. Loften. *Voices of the Black Theatre*. Clifton, New Jersey: James T. White and Company, 1975. 91-92.

''Muriel Rahn Has Wide Range Tour.'' *Afro-American* 19 August 1944.

''Muriel Rahn, Negro Singer in Opera and Concert, Dies.'' New York *Herald Tribune* 9 August 1961.

''Muriel Rahn's Dance of Seven Veils.'' *Ebony* 10 (January 1955): 64-73.

''Muriel Rahn, Soprano Is Dead; Had 'Carmen Jones' Title Role.'' *New York Times* 9 August 1961.

''Muriel Rahn To Sing in Columbia University Opera Drama.'' *Journal and Guide* 24 December 1949.

''The Pirate.'' *Playbill* 6 December 1942.

Rampersad, Arnold. *The Life of Langston Hughes. Vol. II: 1941-1967: I Dream A World*. New York: Oxford University Press, 1988. 71, 176, 183-84, 307.

Sampson, Henry T. *Black in Blackface: A Sourcebook on Early Black Musical Shows*. Metuchen, N. J.: Scarecrow Press, 1980. 414-15.

Southern Eileen, ed. *Biographical Dictionary of Afro-American and African Musicians*. Westport, Conn.: Greenwood Press, 1982. 316.

———. *The Music of Black Americans: A History*. 2nd ed. New York: Norton, 1983. 413-14.

Collections

Photographs and other materials on Muriel Rahn are in Dick Campbell's collection.

Patsy Perry

Ma Rainey (Gertrude Pridgett)

(1886-1939)

Singer

Ma Rainey, ''Mother of the Blues,'' was born Gertrude Malissa Nix Pridgett on April 26, 1886, in Columbus, Georgia, to Thomas Pridgett and Ella (Allen) Pridgett, both Alabamians. She was the second of five children, including two brothers, Thomas, Jr., and Essie, a younger sister, Malissa, and another child whose name is unknown.

Very little is known about the singer's early and formative years. The gleanings from available biographical sources report that Gertrude Pridgett was baptized in the First African Baptist Church and that her grandmother may have performed on stage after Emancipation. These sources have

Ma Rainey (Gertrude Pridgett)

even less to say about the dispositions, activities, and livelihoods of Rainey's parents, though it has been determined that her mother was employed by Central Railway of Georgia after the death of Thomas Pridgett in 1896. Rainey's biography essentially begins with her first public appearance at the age of fourteen in a local talent revue, *Bunch of Black Berries*, at the Springer Opera House around 1900. Shortly after this stage debut, she began to perform in tent shows and is reported to have started singing the blues as early as 1902.

On February 23, 1904, when she was in her eighteenth year, Gertrude Pridgett married Will Rainey, a comedy singer who was purportedly performing with one of the minstrel shows that passed through Columbus when he and Gertrude Pridgett met and fell in love. Traveling with the Rabbit Foot Minstrels, husband and wife for many years did a song-and-dance routine as "Ma" and "Pa" Rainey, "Assassinators of the Blues." Together they continued to work tent shows, circuses, minstrel shows, and black variety circuits. Though notable events in Ma Rainey's marital life remain undated, the sequence of events has been established. Gertrude and Will Rainey adopted a son, Little Danny Rainey, who performed as a dancer with the troupe and was billed as "the world's greatest juvenile stepper." He was one of several children for whom Ma Rainey was a foster mother. Some years later, Gertrude and Will Rainey separated. Will, who was older than Gertrude, died; she later married a younger man not involved with show business.

During the early teens, as Ma and Pa Rainey continued to tour in the South with such companies as the Rabbit Foot Minstrels, the George Smart Set, the Florida Cotton Blossoms, and Shufflin' Sam from Alabam', her popularity grew to such an extent that she eventually got separate billing as "Madame Gertrude Rainey." The program of the troupes with which she traveled included singers, novelty acts, jungle scenes, comedians, jugglers, vaudeville, and minstrels. Rainey did comedy, dancing, novelties, ballads, and topical songs. Reputed to be one of the first singers to add blues to her selections in minstrel shows, Rainey's fame grew simultaneously with the spread of the blues that soon became her specialty. She was usually accompanied by a small jug band, a pianist, or a small jazz band.

Influence of Minstrelsy and Vaudeville Demonstrated

Ma Rainey sang what is called classic blues, which, according to Sandra Lieb in *Mother of the Blues: A Study of Ma Rainey*, "emerged partly from black minstrelsy and vaudeville and partly from the work of anonymous male folk blues singers whose songs appeared most prolifically in the East Texas and Mississippi Delta regions after 1890". Rainey sang what came to be known as the classic blues in a decidedly down-home style—a raw, gritty singing rooted in the living and the feeling and the folk. And the black rural southern people loved jazz and respected this woman who, in the words of the great composer and gospel singer Thomas Dorsey, "was a natural-born artist [who] didn't need no school, didn't go to no school; didn't take no music, didn't need no music" (Harrison, 36). In a voice that, according to Daphne Duval Harrison, "retained those characteristics most admired by Africans and Afro-Americans—buzzing sounds, huskiness, satirical inflections, ability to translate everyday experiences unto living sound" (39), Rainey deeply moved her audiences as she sang songs about everyday life, about "the drudgery, pain, and joys of her folk," and songs more specifically about "mistreatment, desertion, infidelity, revenge, sex, alienation" (Harrison, 39), songs about being, living, having the blues. According to Lieb, who has written the most in-depth study of Rainey to date, the blues singer spoke to the "poverty, suffering, heartbreak, and pain, as well as humor, fortitude, strength, and endurance" characteristic of the black experience (82). "Her great theme is the intense sexual love between men and women, and her secondary themes concern the sensual, earthy, and often rough side of life: music and dancing, drunkenness and superstition, lesbianism and homosexuality, women in prison, jealousy and murder" (Lieb, 82).

Compassionate, tender, willing to help others, Rainey has been variously described as heavy, round, short, dark, squat, and homely. Daphne Dural Harrison writes in *Black Pearls: Blues Queens of the 1920s* that Rainey was "a flashy dresser who loved jewelry, the more glitter the better. Announcements for shows often included pictures of her in a lamé headband, necklace and earrings fashioned from gold-eagle dollars, and a heavily beaded dress draped over her stocky torso (37). Another account pictures a woman who was "volcanic and spoke her mind, though underneath her apparent sternness she was soft-hearted and generous; but she was a tigress when roused. A picture . . . emerge[s] of a woman fond of flashy jewelry and flashy clothes. A warm-hearted, generous human being, wrapped up in the world of the theatre, the vaudeville stage with its songs, and the blues of her race were very much part of her. All the toughness of her life and character is there in her singing" (Stewart-Baxter, 42).

And when Ma Rainey sang, she required, whether seriously or comically, that her audience, in the words of "Those Dogs of Mine," "look, listen, and believe" because she was telling the truth. Singing, Ma Rainey put her finger on the special places of her audience's being. Again it is Dorsey whose panegyric probably best expresses how an audience usually experienced a performance by the Mother of the Blues when he declares that "Ma had the real thing she just issued out there. It had everything in it needed, just like somebody issued a plate of food out say everything's on the plate. And that's the way Ma handed it to 'em—take it or leave it" (Harrison, 39).

The audience took it, as Rainey inspired, confirmed, affirmed, and simply stirred profound feelings in those, white and black, who gave themselves up to the power of her voice. Rainey's songs bodied forth much of the disorientation, flux, and change that Americans felt in the wake of World War I. Lieb suggests that the white members of Rainey's audiences were appreciative of what they perceived to be the exoticness of the black blues singer. Ma Rainey's gift to the black members of her audience who suffered race prejudice, lynchings, and the Ku Klux Klan is found at a deeper level of consciousness. For though Rainey's songs, like many recorded blues, do not address but rather tend to "omit" and "ignore," as Lieb points out, "national affairs, politics, and racial protest" (82), her blues singing communicated the mixed feelings of fear and frustration that was the portion of those who experienced Jim Crow law and lynchings and the feelings of hope and deracination that attended black migration to the North and Midwest. In any event, her songs were a connection to the past and to roots as Lieb indicates:

> Ma Rainey's itinerant life and the development of her career in many ways paralleled the growth of an important segment of black consciousness, from roughly 1900 to 1930—from rural folk culture to modern urban metropolis; from privation in the South to opportunity and cultural chaos in the North. . . . . For her audience, Ma Rainey was a folk figure who reached her greatest popularity at the same time that black writers like Jean Toomer, Zora Neale Hurston, Langston Hughes, and Sterling Brown were all celebrating the Southern folk experience in novels, poems, essays, and plays (Lieb, 168-69).

Herself a part of the Southern folk experience, Ma Rainey was also celebrated. Poet Sterling Brown wrote, for instance, a poem about the great singer who worked with such managers as Al Gaines, Silas Green, and C. W. Parks and such renowned musicians as Lovie Austin, Louis Armstrong, Thomas Dorsey, Fletcher Henderson, King Joe Oliver, Pops Foster, Sidney Bichet, Don Redmond, Buster Bailey, and Tom Ladnier.

Rainey and Bessie Smith Share Blues Circuit

Another important figure to whom Rainey was no doubt an inspiration was Bessie Smith, whose career would eventually receive even greater acclaim than Ma Rainey's. The two women met sometime between 1912 and 1916 when, it has been determined, the two worked together "in at least two traveling shows." Several unconfirmed stories lace the biographical accounts of the relations of these two blues singers. Ma Rainey, for instance, is said to have kidnapped the young and talented Bessie Smith and trained her as a blues singer while the two traveled with the minstrel show. Another story suggests that Ma Rainey and Bessie Smith, who were both undoubtedly "interested in women," at some point had a homosexual relationship. Even the status of their professional relations is not particularly clear-cut. Though some aficionados and critics circulate the idea that Smith was an apprentice of Rainey, others, like Derrick Stewart-Baxter find it "inconceivable" that Rainey "would train a girl so talented, and far more likely that she would look upon her [Bessie] as a potential rival" (47). All that can finally be said is that Rainey, the "Mother of the Blues," influenced the young woman from Chattanooga, Tennessee, who would soon become "Empress of the Blues."

Ma Rainey extended her audience with her recordings at Paramount Record Company. The thirty-seven-year-old Rainey had already been singing and developing her talents for about twenty-five years before she made her first eight recordings in Chicago in December 1923. Rainey, who had been performing before Southern audiences, black and white, as a Paramount recording star now reached a Northern audience which, unexposed to the performances of blacks in the tent shows of the rural South, had not cultivated to the same extent as their Southern counterparts their ear for Rainey's down-home or countrified style.

Ma Rainey recorded exclusively with Paramount in Chicago, though she made two trips to New York. Music critics bemoan this fact because the poor acoustical quality of the recordings has given later generations neither the clearest nor the truest nor the best sense of Rainey's artistry and voice; these recordings, some believe, are a factor in her relative obscurity. Another factor, according to Lieb, which may have contributed to Rainey's obscurity is that Rainey, based in Chicago as she was, never got the attention of the New York-based Carl Van Vechten, the writer and critic and "self-styled interpreter of black culture, who idolized Bessie Smith" (25). Lieb writes that "this lack of a Northern white audience and significant promotion by a white critic no doubt contributed to Ma Rainey's relative obscurity to this day" (25).

Though Mother of the Blues, Ma Rainey was not the first black woman to record. This distinction belongs to Mamie Smith, who on February 14, 1920, recorded "That Thing Called Love" and "You Can't Keep a Good Man Down." Because these recordings by Smith were such a great success, other blues singers were able to follow suit. From 1923 to 1928, Ma Rainey, who composed some of her own original songs but used a lot of traditional material too, made ninety-two recordings representative of, as Lieb reminds, "only part of her work" (54). Her first eight recordings were "Bad Luck Blues," "Bo-Weevil Blues," "Barrel House Blues," "Those All Night Long Blues," "Moonshine Blues," "Last Minute Blues," "Southern Blues," and "Walking Blues." Other titles include such selections as "Honey Where You Been So Long," "Ya-Da-Do," "Those Dogs of Mine," "Lawd Send Me a Man Blues," "See, See Rider Blues," "Jelly Bean Blues," "Goodbye Daddy Blues," "Memphis Bound Blues," "Down In the Basement," "Sissy Blues," "Blame It on the Blues," and "Big Feeling Blues."

While these recordings extended Rainey's audiences, her bookings around 1924 through the Theatre Owners Booking Association (TOBA) circuit also expanded her audience and marked her move up into the world of entertainment. The association, organized, according to Harrison in 1909 in Memphis by one Anselmo Barrasso, targeted Southern and Midwestern audiences and scheduled the performances of great numbers of black entertainers in sixty-seven theaters in these regions. Though the white-controlled TOBA had a mixed reputation among black performers (some, for example, renamed it "Tough on Black Actors or Asses"), it was, as Eileen Southern in *The Music of Black Americans: A*

History has pointed out, a "showcase for black talent," a showcase that had featured such important entertainers as Butterbeans and Susie, the Whitemore Sisters, Ma Rainey, Bessie Smith, and Ethel Waters. To be on the TOBA circuit was to have the opportunity to ride to such big-time circuits, as the Pantages, Orpheum, Columbia, and Keith Albee.

TOBA collapsed around the time of the depression in 1931. Only three years earlier on December 28, 1928, Rainey had made her last recording with Paramount. The climate of the entertainment industry was changing in ways that proved unfavorable for TOBA and some blues singers. Harrison, writing about the decline of TOBA, sheds some light on the end of Ma Rainey's career:

> TOBA was instrumental in the development and expansion of the black entertainment industry from 1907 until its destruction by the economic forces of the Depression. It could not compete with the competition from "talkie" movies, radio programs and dance music as opposed to vaudeville and minstrel acts. . . . Fortunately for some of the blues women, there were opportunities in brief roles in the movies; for others the radio weekly shows kept them singing for a while; and those who could adjust their style and repertoire were able to continue as cabaret or revue performers. . . . But none of these activities brought them the fame and fortune that were theirs in the heyday of the 1920s. Like the TOBA, the blues women lost in a market that disappeared (40-41).

Apparently Ma Rainey was one of the women who suffered in the wake of a disappearing market. Stewart-Baxter reports that a Paramount official declared in 1928 that "Ma's down-home material had gone out of fashion" (44).

When her sister, Malissa, died in 1935, Ma Rainey went back to the family home she had built with her earnings. Months later that same year, the blues singer's mother died. No longer performing by this time, Ma Rainey operated two theaters that she owned—the Lyric in Columbus and the Airdome in Rome, Georgia. She later joined the Friendship Baptist Church where her brother, Thomas Pridgett, Jr., was a deacon.

Ma Rainey, "the earliest professional blues singer," died December 22, 1939, at the age of fifty-three of heart disease and was buried in the family plot at Porterdale Cemetery in Columbus, Georgia.

References

Brown, Sterling. "Ma Rainey." In *The Collected Poems of Sterling A. Brown*. Selected by Michael S. Harper. New York: Harper, 1983. 62-63.

Harrison, Daphne Duval. *Black Pearls: Blues Queens of the 1920s*. New Brunswick: Rutgers University Press, 1988. 34-41.

Kellner, Bruce, ed. *The Harlem Renaissance: A Historical Dictionary for the Era*. New York: Methuen, 1987. 293-94.

Lieb, Sandra R. *Mother of the Blues: A Study of Ma Rainey*. Amherst: University of Massachusetts Press, 1981. Photographs, pp. 6, 9, 29, and 34.

Southern, Eileen. *The Music of Black America*. 2nd ed. New York: Norton, 1983. 293-94, 330, 368-69, 452.

Stewart-Baxter, Derrick. *Ma Rainey and the Classic Blues Singers*. New York: Stein and Day, 1970. 35-47. Photographs, pp. 39 and 41.

Vanessa D. Dickerson

Amanda Randolph

(c. 1902-1967)

Actress, singer

Even to those scholars whose main objective is the careful historical cataloging of Hollywood film, the name Amanda Randolph may not immediately conjure up memories of an outstanding portrayal in an important or otherwise noteworthy Hollywood production. Indeed, those who do remember Amanda Randolph oftentimes confuse her with her sister, Lillian Randolph, whose acting credits include not only the role of Birdie in the radio, film, and television versions of *The Great Gildersleeve* but also a respectable performance as the family housekeeper in the Christmas staple, *It's a Wonderful Life*.

Confusion notwithstanding, Amanda Randolph was a talented and versatile actress and singer in her own right. And while her name may not necessarily top the list as one of black America's most cherished Hollywood stars, her long and illustrious career was a remarkable one—spanning almost fifty years and including stints on the legitimate stage, on television, radio, and in film.

Amanda Randolph was born in 1902 of 1905 in Louisville, Kentucky, some ten years before her sister, Lillian. She was a musician and hearty singer with a strong voice and began performing at an early age, appearing in Cleveland nightclubs and musical comedies. During the 1930s she toured Europe with the Scott and Whaley show and the Glenn and Jenkins Review, in addition to appearing in several hit musical revues, including *Chili Peppers*, *In the Alley*, *Joy Cruise*, *Dusty Lane*, and *Fall Frolics*. In 1932 she teamed with Catherine Handy (the daughter of composer W. C. Handy); they were billed as the Dixie Nightingales.

A few years later, Randolph made the transition to film in a career that included at least a dozen film roles, a career that was no doubt stunted by the overt racism that was characteristic of the Hollywood studio system. More often than not, black American actresses with Randolph's looks—brown-skinned and full-figured—were relegated to film roles as maid, servants, or housekeepers. Randolph was afforded little opportunity to display her true talent as singer or actress.

Randolph's film debut appears to have been in 1936 in the musical short, *The Black Network,* a race movie also featuring Nina Mae McKinney and the Nicholas Brothers. Race movies were a particular genre of films that featured mostly black American characters and a plot line especially written for a black audience. Randolph also appeared in a number of features written and produced by Oscar Micheaux, a black American independent film producer. These include *Swing* (1938), *Lying Lips* (1939), and *The Notorious Elinor Lee*, a movie about boxing that opened in 1940 at the RKO Regent, billed as the movie made as a tribute to "the important part played by the Colored fighter" (Cripps, 344). These movies, written, produced, directed, and distributed by Micheaux, were, unfortunately, often technically inferior. However, they at least offered a glimpse of black life that contrasted with Hollywood's often unfavorable images of black people. In addition to the above titles, Randolph appeared in the film *Comes Midnight* (1940), which was produced by the Sepia Arts Company.

In the 1950s Randolph appeared in a number of Hollywood productions. Even an ideologically-charged world war and a host of important antidiscrimination legislation had not effected much real change in the way black American women were portrayed on the screen. Yet postwar American film of this period offered several thoughtful portrayals of black American men, portrayed as soldiers fighting alongside their comrades, as college students, professionals, and otherwise literate and contributing members of society. However, except for a few uncommon portrayals, black American women were still assigned to the same stereotypic roles as decades past. Randolph's screen credits include *She's Working Her Way Through College*, produced by Warner Brothers in 1952 and featuring Ronald Reagan, in which she plays a maid to Virginia Mayo; *Mr. Scoutmaster* (1953); and the role of Gladys in the film noir classic, *No Way Out* (1950), which featured Sidney Poitier and Richard Widmark.

Since they represented less of a threat to the existing status quo, female black American servant characters were often allowed "smartly witty lines" in their portrayals as "sassy maids" or loyal confidantes. Still, their importance to the film was usually carefully muted, often to the point where their scenes could be left out altogether to avoid offending the Southern box office. Though Randolph's parts were in general very small, it is evident that she possessed talent beyond the ability to play a maid or servant. Sadly, little of her true ability was highlighted during her career as a Hollywood actress.

Randolph Featured in "Amos 'n Andy" Programs

Amanda Randolph was a featured performer in the immensely popular and long-running radio show, "Amos 'n Andy." Partly because of the adverse publicity suffered by this program during its television run, many have forgotten the tremendous popularity of the radio version of the show. The "Amos 'n Andy" show began on March 19, 1928, on WMAQ radio, Chicago. It went on to become the longest-running radio program in broadcast history. Its cast of characters included, among others: Andy, the not-so-bright president of the Fresh Air Cab Company; Amos, his level-headed business associate; and "Kingfish" Stevens, a conniving smoothie. During the 1940s Randolph and her sister, Lillian, had featured roles in the popular program, with Amanda Randolph playing the role of "Madame Queen," Andy's romantic interest.

Amanda Randolph was one of the only two performers in the radio cast of "Amos 'n Andy" to be featured in the television version. However, this was not her television debut. Earlier, she had appeared in the cast of the short-lived domestic comedy, "The Laytons" which appeared from August to October of 1948. For black Americans, the popularity of the television medium heralded a period of hopeful excitement. Derogatory images of black American people had been communicated in popular culture for several decades. Television had the capacity to change and to nullify these images. A 1950 article in *Ebony* magazine endorsed television's liberal exploitation of black talent as a sure sign that the medium was "free of racial barriers" ("Negroes Get Better Roles in TV," June 1950).

"Amos 'n Andy," which featured Amanda Randolph as Mama, the outspoken mother of the Sapphire Stevens character, lasted some two years before the program was canceled in the midst of an ideological hurricane in 1955. The program's portrayal of black life and culture was deemed an insulting return to the days of blackface and minstrelsy. The controversy surrounding this program probably equalled that of the popularity of the radio version and the reasons why are much too numerous to discuss here. However, "Amos 'n Andy's" significance to television history cannot be overlooked, as it was the first television series with an all-black cast, the only one for another eighteen years.

In 1953 Amanda Randolph was cast as Louise, the family housekeeper, in the popular television show "Make Room for Daddy," which starred Danny Thomas. "Make Room for Daddy," later retitled "The Danny Thomas Show," was one of the few television programs to last more than a decade. It received accolades as best situation comedy and also best new program.

On August 24, 1967, at the age of about sixty-five, Randolph died of complications following a stroke. The *New York Times* said of her upon her death, "She played the cantankerous, meddling mother-in-law in the Amos 'n Andy show on radio and TV" (Obituary, 25 August 1967, 35). The obituary was only partially correct, as it was Lillian who had played the part for radio. Still, Amanda Randolph should be remembered not so much for a long-forgotten role on a short-lived but controversial television program. It is easy to overlook the contributions of the many gifted black American women whose careers as Hollywood performers were limited to minor roles as domestic servants. Today, these roles may appear even more menial and insulting and they are often carefully edited out of television screenings. However, their importance to film history is immeasurable. Amanda Randolph made a successful transition from the stage to radio, television, and film. Her appearance on the "Danny Thomas Show," which ran for more than ten years, rendered her one of the few black women to appear consistently on television. And though she was hardly given the opportunity to display her gifts as a singer and musician, she managed to carve out a respectable film career that spanned almost twenty years. Randolph must be remembered not just for one particular role but for her significant contributions to American film and American popular culture.

References

Bogle, Donald. *Blacks in American Film and Television*. New York: Garland Press, 1988. 155.

Cripps, Thomas. *Slow Fade to Black: The Negro in American Film, 1900-1940*. New York: Oxford University Press, 1977. 344-45.

Brooks, Tim and Earl Marsh. *The Complete Directory to Prime Time Network TV Shows, 1946 - Present*. 3rd ed. New York: Ballentine Books, 1985. 39-40, 199-200, 472.

"Negroes Get Better Roles in TV Than in Any Other Entertainment." *Ebony* 5 (June 1950): 22-25.

Klotman, Phyllis Rauch. *Frame by Frame: A Black Filmography*. Bloomington: Indiana University Press, 1979. 67, 116, 327, 382-83, 385, 464, 508.

New York Times 24 August, 1967. 35.

Sampson, Henry T. *Blacks in Black and White: A Source Book on Black Films*. Metuchen, N.J.: Scarecrow Press, 1977. 255-56 for brief biographical information, and 275, 287, 291, 297 for information on specific films.

Terrance, Vincent. *Radio's Golden Years: The Encyclopedia of Radio Programs, 1930-1960*. New York: Barnes, 1981. 16.

Pamala S. Deane

Virginia Randolph

(1870-1958)

Educator, social worker

Virginia Estelle Randolph, the first Jeanes teacher, was one of the most influential educators of her day. Born in Richmond, Virginia, on June 6, 1870, of slave parents Nelson Randolph and Sarah Elizabeth Randolph, she lived to see many schools following curriculums patterned after her ideas and a school named in her honor. Virginia Randolph is responsible for designing the format of the Jeanes teachers' program. She developed an approach to education for rural black children that focused on community involvement, industrial training along with academic training, and clean, healthy, and attractive school environments. The Jeanes teacher program was modeled after her successful experiences at the Mountain Road School in Henrico County, Virginia. Through the Jeanes teacher movement that spanned 1908 to 1968, Virginia Randolph was instrumental in bringing about improvements in the lives of thousands of teachers, children, and community residents.

Virginia Randolph's early years were difficult. Her father died when she was quite young, leaving her mother to raise four young children. Using skills learned while a slave of professors at Richmond College, now the University of

Virginia Randolph

Richmond, Virginia's mother worked night and day sewing, cooking, washing, and keeping house for white families. Virginia began working on her first job when she was eight years old. Her mother taught her how to knit, sew, and crochet—skills that later served her well when she initiated her instructional methods in schools.

Virginia Randolph received her early education at the Bacon School and the City Normal School in Richmond. At the young age of sixteen, she was appointed to a teaching job in Goochland County. Three years later she took a teaching job at a one-room schoolhouse in Henrico County—the Mountain Road School.

Randolph started her career at Mountain Road School with fourteen students. Her first effort was to improve the physical appearance and condition of the school and its surroundings. Like other segregated schools for blacks at that time, there was nothing inviting about the building or equipment. She planted grass on the red clay and had gravel placed where hard surface areas were needed. To support her efforts, she organized a Willing Workers Club to raise funds.

One of the memorable events of the early years of her career was the initiation of the first Arbor Day celebration in Henrico County. Following the governor's lead in announcing the Arbor Day proclamation, Randolph asked twelve school patrons each to bring a tree to the school. The trees were planted and given the names of the twelve Apostles. Ten of the trees remain standing as living monuments. The two trees that died from disease were replaced in November 1977 by the Henrico County Bicentennial Commission in honor of Robert Bracey, the first curator of the Virginia Randolph Museum.

During her twelve years as a teacher at the Mountain Road School, Virginia Randolph organized a Patrons' Improvement League, beautified the schoolyard with flowers, shrubbery, and trees, and made a gravel pathway to the building to provide easy access from the high road. She whitewashed the building frequently and always kept it clean and inviting.

Firmly convinced that children needed something more than the regular school curriculum, Randolph organized a Sunday school. She was able to secure Bibles, books, and an organ from Joseph Bryan, father of the chairman of the school board at that time. Randolph also taught Sunday school nearly every Sunday for five years.

She visited the children's homes and initiated "Patrons' Day" to get the parents to come to the school. To launch her "Better Homes" campaign, Randolph taught the children how to make things from scraps. She invited the parents to extend the idea of making things to improve their homes. She was able to persuade some of the parents to work cooperatively to improve the home of a sick woman in the neighborhood. Her emphasis on cleanliness and use of odds and ends to brighten the school and home sparked the attention of families.

Randolph placed just as much emphasis on the school curriculum and on teaching the academic basics as she did on the school environment and community. She believed in "learning by doing" and in honest work as the best of all character builders. She taught the children to sew and weave and gradually included industrial education in the curriculum. Her school program reflected her belief that education is the all-around development of the child.

To assure herself that she was providing the best programs possible, Randolph visited what she identified as a progressive school for white children to ask the teachers for help and suggestions. The teachers shared some of their materials with her. She was convinced that her approach to education was the right one. She began to ask the public for funds to support the school's work. Many of the school patrons responded and the Mountain Road School became the "center of life in the community" (Jones, 33).

Virginia Randolph, small and slender in stature, though sometimes appearing too unassuming, was firm yet kind, humble yet independent. She was patient, tactful, good-humored, faithful, and possessed a quiet tenacity of purpose. Her personal and professional qualities as well as her success with students and parents of the Mountain Road School were noticed by the superintendent of schools for Henrico County, Jackson Davis. He believed that what she was doing ought to be spread to other places. Her emphasis on vocational skills and her approach to education was in sharp contrast to the academic orientation of other schools at that time. Davis arranged for her to visit other rural schools on one or two days a week to share her ideas with other teachers. Convincing other teachers to follow her program was often difficult, but the possibilities of using this method to improve many of the other schools was attractive to Davis.

Virginia Randolph Becomes First Jeanes Teacher

The superintendent's interest in placing Virginia Randolph in a position to help other black teachers implement her ideas was assisted by Anna T. Jeanes. A Philadelphia Quaker who wanted to help improve education for black youth in rural schools in the South, Jeanes donated one million dollars that was used to establish a fund for supporting teachers who supervised other teachers. This was called the Jeanes fund. Jeanes set aside a fund consisting of income-bearing securities to be used to foster improvements in small black rural schools. Completing her plans just before her death on September 24, 1907, Anna T. Jeanes presented the securities to Hollis S. Frissell, Booker T. Washington, and George Foster Peabody, three of the men she designated to serve on the board of trustees.

Upon receiving Randolph's word that she would leave Mountain Road School and devote full-time to supervision, Jackson Davis wrote the following letter to James H. Dillard, chairman of the board of the Jeanes Fund:

October 26, 1908

Dear Dr. Dillard:

> I have secured Miss Virginia E. Randolph (colored), 813 Moore Street, Richmond, as the industrial teacher for the Negro schools in the county and her work in this field began today. I think we are fortunate in securing her, as she has had twelve years' experience in the public schools, and in her own school she has accomplished many of the results in industrial work that we now hope for in all the schools. She possesses common sense and tact in an unusual degree and has the confidence of all who know her, both among white people and those of her own race. We are a little late in starting, but I could not get her released from the school that she was teaching until this time. I called a meeting of the Negro teachers on the 23rd for the purpose of discussing the industrial work that we felt it would be practicable to undertake, and the outcome of the discussion was gratifying. I feel that they are all interested and will work faithfully to accomplish results. Our aim is to organize Improvement Leagues at each school and have the Negroes provide the equipment themselves. Several schools have already begun this. I am sure that will be most valuable on the principle of selfhelp, making use of whatever material may be at hand.
>
> Her salary is forty dollars a month (four weeks), and I would like to ask how you wish to pay her, whether by direct check to her or through our School Board. I should also be glad if you would like to have reports as to her work and how often, etc.
>
> Very truly yours,
>
> Jackson Davis (Williams, 25-26)

In October 1908, Virginia Randolph became the first Jeanes teacher, and in time she worked as a supervisor in Virginia, North Carolina, and Georgia. Her success led to the introduction of Jeanes teachers, supervising industrial teachers in rural schools all over the South. Most of them were experienced and, like Randolph, had already achieved outstanding status in the public schools. About half of them had been educated at Hampton or Tuskegee Institute or at other normal and industrial schools. Others had no industrial training but, considering the various needs and activities of the schools, their talents enabled them to perform well.

The work of Jeanes teachers went beyond supervision of industrial instruction for the rural children. While concentrating heavily on improving physical facilities for one-room, one-teacher rural schools, the Jeanes teachers also worked to build community support for schools. They raised money for school projects and buildings. They organized programs for commencement, county-wide field days, and other activities designed to bring students, parents, teachers, and patrons together. Gradually, the Jeanes teachers' focus broadened from physical improvement and industrial instruction to supervision of classroom instruction in regular academic curriculums.

By 1913-14, 118 Jeanes teachers were employed by 119 counties in Southern States. The money provided by Anna T. Jeanes for the original Jeanes Fund was merged with other funds to expand the programs and services provided. After April 22, 1907, the Anna T. Jeanes Foundation became known at the Negro Rural School Fund. It was later merged with the Virginia Randolph Fund, which was established as a tribute to Randolph on December 17, 1936. The George Foster Peabody Fund, established on February 7, 1867, by New England financier George Peabody, began to provide for the intellectual, moral, and industrial education in the destitute portions of the southern and southwestern states. On April 25, 1882, John Fox Slater, a Connecticut manufacturer, established the John F. Slater Fund to uplift and emancipate the population of the southern states. On July 1, 1937, the Peabody, Slater, Jeanes, and Virginia Randolph funds merged to establish the Southern Education Foundation (SEF) in Atlanta, Georgia. SEF works with private and public school officials and others to improve education and living conditions, with special emphasis on the needs of black Americans. For sixty years, however, from 1908 to 1968, the Jeanes supervision was an impressive movement in American education.

The success of the Jeanes teachers eventually led to the end of the movement. Having worked effectively to improve educational environments and programs for rural black children and teachers, Jeanes teachers were perceived as influential and powerful persons in the community and in the school system. With the initiation of desegregation, the question of power became very important. Federally-funded programs for schools supplied money for new staff positions, such as director of federal and special programs, reading consultants, and instructional assistants. Confusion over the role of the Jeanes teachers in the expanding lineup of educational specialists produced many difficulties. New titles and positions eventually replaced Jeanes teachers.

While the position of Jeanes teacher or Jeanes supervisor is no longer found in schools of the South, the work that the Jeanes teacher performed is remembered well.

After more than fifty-seven years in education, Virginia Randolph retired from her position as supervisor of black education for Henrico County in 1948.

Community Problems Addressed

Virginia Randolph's activities reached into areas other than education. She was deeply interested in the problems of juveniles and worked with the Richmond Juvenile and Domestic Court in aiding such youth with their problems. She opened her home to needy children and at one time she had seventeen of them living with her.

Randolph was a member of the Moore Street Baptist Church and the Queen Esther Elks Temple. Many honors were bestowed upon her. The Virginia Randolph School at Glen Allen, Virginia, was named in her honor. She was appointed by Governor Peery to the Board of Directors for Virginia's Industrial School for Negroes. In 1926 she received the Harmon Award for her social service contributions. In 1949 she was honored with an Appreciation Service that was attended by black and white educators who acknowledged her service. A bust of Randolph was unveiled in 1954 in the Virginia Randolph School.

In 1970 the Virginia Randolph Museum was dedicated in her honor, and in 1976 the United States Department of Interior, National Park Service, named the museum a National Historic Landmark. It was also designated as a State Historic Landmark by the Virginia Historic Landmarks Commission. The original sycamore trees planted by Randolph were named the first National Historic Trees in Virginia. The museum is probably the only one of its kind in the South. The decision to name the Virginia E. Randolph Museum a national shrine created considerable interest in her hometown of Richmond, Virginia. A lengthy newspaper article described the procedures of investigation that were conducted prior to the decision. The writer noted that the investigator toured the facility (then the Creighton Cardwell Cottage at the Virginia Randolph Educational Center) and reviewed the documents, personal letters, and artifacts connected with Randolph's work. The recommendation to name the museum a national shrine was presented to two national historic committees and to the Secretary of the Interior, who was Rogers B. Morton. Morton made the final decision.

One of the most interesting descriptions of Randolph's contributions to education was written by Lance G. E. Jones, a lecturer and tutor in the Oxford University department of education. In identifying the qualities that characterized Randolph, he said:

> What, we may ask, are the qualities which have enabled this small, slender, unassuming Negro woman, to win through? Some of them have already been noticed, others are revealed by the incidents we have recorded—patience and faith, tact, kindliness, good humor, a humility that shows itself in her willingness to learn from others, and a quiet tenacity of purpose that overcomes all difficulties. But though humble she is independent, and though patient and tenacious, she has not been lacking in enthusiasm and vigor (Jones, 36).

Virginia Randolph died on March 16, 1958, at age eighty-eight, at her home at 817 West Marshall Street, Richmond, Virginia. She was survived by an adopted daughter, Carrie Brown Sample, and a niece, Aretha R. Davis. When writing about her death, a newspaper reporter for the Richmond *Times Dispatch*, 17 March 1958, noted her international reputation. Calling her a pioneer educator, the writer said, "Her reputation spread. Schools here and abroad adopted her methods of teaching manual skills, and her vocational programs were used by Great Britain in its African Colonies."

Noting her unusual contributions to education, a Henrico school official called Randolph a "liberal investor." He said that "she invested her life and means in the lives and characters of those for whom she has labored" (*Richmond Times Dispatch*, 8 November 1970).

Virginia Estelle Randolph's philosophy of education guided her tremendous influence on the lives of many children. She generously used her private funds to purchase items for schools. She opened her home to youth who needed a place to stay. She believed, as she stated in her first report as a Jeanes teacher, *A Brief Report of the Manual Training Work Done in the Colored Schools of Henrico County, Virginia, for Session, 1908-1909*, "The destiny of our race depends, largely, upon the training the children receive in the schoolroom."

References

Crisis 65 (May 1958): 296, 298-99. Includes full-length photograph.

Dannett, Sylvia G. L. *Profiles of Negro Womanhood*. Vol. 1. Yonkers, N.Y.: Educational Heritage, 1964. 306-307.

Davis, Marianna W., ed. *Contributions of Black Women to America*. Vol. 2. Columbia, S.C.: Kenday Press, 1982. 307-309.

The Jeanes Story: A Chapter in the History of American Education 1908-1968. Prepared by the National Association of Supervisors and Consultants Interim History Writing Committee. Atlanta: Southern Education Foundation, 1979. A photograph of Virginia Estelle Randolph appears in the back of this volume. A larger portrait of Randolph hangs in the Southern Education Foundation's facilities.

Jenness, Mary. *Twelve Negro Americans*. New York: Friendship Press, 1936. 24-27.

Jones, Lance G. E. *The Jeanes Teacher in the United States 1908-1933: An Account of Twenty-Five Years' Experience in the Supervision of Negro Rural Schools*. Chapel Hill: University of North Carolina Press, 1937.

Mather, Frank Lincoln, ed. *Who's Who of the Colored Race: A General Biographical Dictionary of Men and Women of African Descent*. Vol. 1. Chicago: n.p., 1915.

"Miss Randolph Dies; Was Pioneer Educator." Richmond *Times Dispatch* 17 March 1974.

"Randolph Museum in Henrico: Site Eyed as National Shrine." Richmond *News Leader* 28 June 1974.

Who's Who in Colored America: 4th ed. 1933-37. New York: Who's Who in Colored America Corporation, 1937. 429-30.

Elaine P. Witty

Charlotte E. Ray
(1850-1911)
Lawyer

In the 1870's, when the social and political climate in the U.S. was at best tenuous for blacks, Charlotte E. Ray (Fraim) moved with quiet determination to overcome prejudices toward blacks—and women—to become the first black American woman lawyer in the United States and the third woman admitted to the practice of law in this country.

Born in New York City January 13, 1850, Ray was one of seven children of Charles Bennett Ray and Charlotte Augusta (Burroughs) Ray. Her father was a minister and a well-known abolitionist descended from early New England Negro, Indian, and white ancestry, while her mother was a native of Savannah, Georgia.

As a journalist, Congregational minister, antislavery activist, and conductor of the Underground Railroad, it is natural that her father, Charles Ray, knew the value of a good education. Accordingly, it was he who saw to it that his children, including Charlotte, had the benefit of formal study. As a child, she attended the Institution for the Education of Colored Youth in Washington, D.C., founded by Myrtilla Miner. Ray demonstrated scholarly excellence that she would later replicate in law school. Once Ray completed the prescribed program of study for students in 1869, she became a teacher in the Normal and Preparatory Department at Howard University.

Ray's father used ingenuity combined with dedication and hard work as a conductor of the Underground Railroad. As to whether Ray's propensity for ingenuity was derived from her father, one cannot say with absolute certainty. One can say, however, that it was her ingenuity that helped her gain admission to Howard's law school. When applying, she submitted her name as "C. E. Ray," since she was aware that there was a reluctance to admit women to the study of law. Ray's awareness of this opposition to women in the legal profession was confirmed by the Illinois Supreme Court in 1872, when it refused to grant Myra Bradwell a license to practice law in the courts of that state. The Illinois Court declared:

> It is sufficient to say that, in our opinion, the other implied limitations upon our power . . . must operate to prevent our admitting women to the office of attorney-at-law. If we were to admit them, we would be exercising the authority conferred upon us in a manner which, we are fully satisfied, was never contemplated by the legislature.

Ray did not permit the stereotyping of roles for women by the Supreme Court in Illinois and traditional mores of society to deter her from pursuing a career in the legal profession.

With quiet determination, Ray impressed her classmates in law school and later was inducted into Phi Beta Kappa. Several references were made to Ray's intellectual ability and achievement as well as her presence as a female law student. General O. O. Howard, the founder and first president of Howard University, stated in his third annual report dated July 1870, that a trustee of the law school was amazed to find "a colored woman who read us a thesis on corporations, not copied from the books but from her brain, a clear incisive analysis of one of the most delicate legal questions."

James C. Napier, an 1869 classmate of Ray's, presented one of the few written descriptions of her as well as a comment on her intellectual ability. Napier described Ray as "a Negro girl about the complexion of Frederick Douglass, with long straight hair. There was never the least doubt that she was what we term a Negro. She was an apt scholar."

While a student at Howard, Ray matriculated with several black American men who went on to have distinguished careers. An examination of the class rosters found in the *Catalog of Howard University for the Years 1870-1871* (located in the Moorland-Spingarn Collection) elicits the following names: John C. Napier, C. H. Gardner, and John H. Smyth. Napier served as a member of Howard's board of trustees and as registrar of the United States Treasury; Gardner was a well-known abolitionist leader and speaker for several abolitionist groups; and Smyth was one of several prominent black Americans who served as Minister to Liberia. Perusal of the class rosters for the period 1869-1872 reads almost like a *Who's Who in Black America*. By any reasonable academic measure, Ray's intellect and industry as a student equipped her for comparable achievements and work.

Howard's law department admissions policy stated that a certain degree of mental discipline was indispensable to enable the student to master principles of law, and any person of suitable age and good moral character could be admitted to the classes and exercises of the department. The graduation requirement for the students more pointedly indicated that women were not expected to undertake the rigors of legal studies. Accordingly, "graduation of each depended upon the regularity of his attendance, the diligence of his application, his proficiency in the studies pursued, and his success in passing the final examination and in presenting and delivering a legal dissertation acceptable to the faculty at the close of the course."

The course of study in the law department at Howard was intensive. Even so, Ray had begun to specialize in commercial law before the conclusion of her studies in 1872. She presented a paper on "Chancery," which was well received. As a legal academician, she was regarded as one of the best lawyers on corporation law in this country. Ray graduated in February 1872, and took the bar examination for the District of Columbia and passed it. She was admitted to the practice of law on April 23, 1872. Fortunately for Ray and other women who would follow, the District of Columbia's legal code had been revised to omit the word "male" in connection with admission to the bar. It appears that Ray's application caused no great furor at the time.

Sexual Bias Denies Ray Legal Practice

It was Ray's anticipation that she would have a future in law. Her contemporaries in academia and the legal profession regarded her potential and academic achievements as noteworthy. An article in the *Woman's Journal* in May 1872 noted Ray's unique achievement:

> In the city of Washington, where a few years ago colored women were bought and sold under sanction of law, a woman of African descent has been admitted to practice at the bar of the Supreme Court of the District of Columbia. Miss Charlotte E. Ray, who has the honor of being the first lady lawyer in Washington, is a graduate of the Law College of Howard University, and is said to be a dusky mulatto, possessing quite an intelligent countenance. She doubtless has a fine mind and deserves success (161).

Others who made observations that further illuminate the life and times of Ray include Kate Kane Rossi and M. A. Majors. Kate Rossi has identified herself as a friend of Ray's. A criminal lawyer by profession, she was very much impressed with Ray's breadth of knowledge about the legal profession. She indicated in an interview with a reporter from the *Chicago Legal Times* that Ray, "although a lawyer of decided ability, on account of prejudice, was not able to obtain sufficient legal business and has to give up active practice" (23 October 1887). M. A. Majors, who wrote *Noted Negro Women*—one of the early works on black American women (1893)—discussed Ray's achievements: "Her special endowments make her one of the best lawyers on corporations in this country; her eloquence is commendable for her sex in the court-room, and her advice is authoritative" (184). As Rossi stated, in spite of outstanding achievement and recognition as a legal authority on corporation law, Ray was unable to maintain a law practice because of a lack of business. This lack of legal business forced Ray to close her law office in Washington, and she later returned to New York.

Ray attended the annual convention of the National Women's Suffrage Association in New York. Also, she was an active member in the National Association of Colored Women after 1895. Ray's activities after leaving the District of Columbia, however, are less clear. By 1879, she had returned to her native New York City to live. Once there, she became employed in the Brooklyn public school system, where her two younger sisters also worked. Sometime after 1886, she married a man with the surname Fraim, of whom very little is known, and by 1897 she was living in Woodside, Long Island. Ray died on January 4, 1911, of acute bronchitis at the age of 60. She was buried in the family plot in Cypress Hills Cemetery in Brooklyn.

In spite of the notable success of Ray's career, there is little doubt that being a woman prevented her from even greater achievements and perhaps a more "glamorous" career, such as those enjoyed by two of her fellow classmates, James C. Napier and John Smyth. Most certainly, the Greater Washington Area Chapter, Women Lawyers Division of the National Bar Association (GWAC) recognized Ray's contributions when it dedicated its annual award presentation in honor of Ray. The GWAC is a group of black women lawyers in the District of Columbia metropolitan area whose major effort has been devoted to establishing and endowing a program for law students. the GWAC has established a legal intern program for law students, and affiliated members study a wide array of subjects, including copyright laws, federal procurement policy, domestic violence, tax law changes, legislative issues affecting attorneys, women and children, and numerous other issues. Additionally, GWAC is an active participant with many governmental, legal, and community groups throughout the District of Columbia's metropolitan area, such as the District of Columbia Commission on Women, the National Committee on Pay Equity, and the Women's Legal Defense Fund. In addition to intensive research under way on the life and times of Ray, the GWAC Charlotte W. Ray Annual Award is a glowing tribute to the contributions of a truly outstanding black American woman.

References

Alexander, Sadie T. M. "Women as Practitioners of the Law in the U.S." *National Bar Journal* 1 (July 1941): 60.

"Brief Biographical Sketch of Charlotte Ray." Washington, D.C.: Howard University, 22 February 1983. Moorland-Spingarn Research Center.

Catalogue of Howard University for the Years 1869-1870. Washington, D.C.: Judd and Detweiler, 1870, 1870-71.

"Charlotte E. Ray." Interview with Kathryn A. Ellis, Greater Washington Area Chapter, Women Lawyers Division, National Bar Association, 12 July 1990.

Chicago Legal News, 23 October 1897.

Contributions of Black Women to America. Vol. 1. Ed. Marianna W. Davis. Columbia, S.C.: Kenday Press, 1982.

"Charlotte E. Ray Award Program," Greater Washington Area Chapter, Woman Lawyer's Division, National Bar Association. February 28, 1990.

Howard, O. O. Third Annual Report, Howard University, Washington, D.C., July 1870.

Logan, Rayford W. *Howard University: The First Hun-*

dred Years, 1867-1967. New York: New York University Press, 1969.

Low, W. Augustus and Virgil A. Clift, eds. *Encyclopedia of Black America*. New York: McGraw-Hill, 1981.

Majors, Monroe A. *Noted Negro Women: Their Triumphs and Activities*. Chicago: Donohue and Henneberry, 1893. Reprinted. Freeport, New York: Books for Libraries, 1971.

Morello, Karen Berger. *The Invisible Bar: The Woman Lawyer in America, 1638 to the Present*. New York: Random House, 1986.

Negro Yearbook: An Annual Encyclopedia of the Negro, 1925-1926. Nashville: Sunday School Union Print, 1925. 301.

New National Era 23 February 1872. 2.

Ray, F. T. *Sketch of the Life of Rev. Charles B. Ray*. New York: Press of J. J. Little, 1887.

Stanton, Elizabeth C., et. al., eds. *History of Woman Suffrage*. Vol. 3. New York: Fowler and Wells, 1886.

Thomas, Dorothy. "Charlotte E. Ray." *Notable American Women: 1607-1950*. Vol. 3. Cambridge: Harvard University Press, 1971.

Wesley, Charles. *In Freedom's Footsteps—From the African Background to the Civil War*. Washington, D.C.: Association for the Study of Afro-American Life and History, 1978.

The Woman's Journal 111 (25 May 1872): 161.

Larry L. Martin

H. Cordelia Ray

(c. 1849-1916)

Poet, educator

Poet and scholar Cordelia Ray achieved recognition and some acclaim for her poetry during her lifetime, but she also earned criticism for her refusal to politicize her work. Cordelia, as she was called, was the second daughter born to Charles Bennett Ray and Charlotte (Burrough) Ray.

Henrietta Cordelia Ray's birth date appears in various sources as 1849 (Brown), 1850 (Shockley), and 1852 (Kerlin). Although born in New York City, her family reputedly derived from "the first Negroes of New England, aboriginal Indian, and English stock of Massachusetts" (Brown, 171).

Charles B. Ray, a Congregational minister, fathered an illustrious family. He married Charlotte Augusta Burrough of Savannah, Georgia, his second wife, and together they created a home where "birth, breeding and culture were regarded as important assets" (Brown, 172). He edited the *Colored American*, an abolitionist newspaper, and insured that his children were well educated, including his daughters. The family consisted of seven children—two boys and five girls. Two girls died in their youth. The surviving children were all college graduates.

Cordelia Ray graduated from the University of the City of New York in 1891 with a master of pedagogy degree. She also attended Sauveneur School of Languages, where she perfected her fluency in French, Greek, Latin, and German. Florence, the older sister closest to Cordelia, became a teacher. Charlotte E., a younger sister, became the first black American woman in the United States to attend and graduate from the Howard University School of Law. Admitted to the bar in Washington, D.C., she became the first black American woman attorney to practice in the nation's capital.

Impressed by her sister Florence's position as a teacher, Ray also applied for a teaching position. She taught in the girls' department of the Colored Grammar School Number One. However, she soon found teaching boring. Arrangements were thus made to enable her to pursue, unhampered, her literary work, a comparatively rare advantage for a black American woman.

Cordelia Ray lived in Woodside, Long Island. She never married, devoting herself instead to the care of her sister Florence, who became an invalid. Ray often taught pupils individually or in small groups. She conducted lessons in music, mathematics, and foreign languages. Once she offered a course in English literature for teachers. She also worked as corresponding editor to *New Era* a publication of the National Colored Democratic League, Washington, D.C. Together Cordelia and Florence Ray wrote and published a short biography of their father. *Sketches of the Life of Rev. Charles E. Ray* (1887) is a seventy-nine-page document describing their father's work as an editor and as an advocate for the abolition of slavery.

Cordelia Ray's poetry received special recognition when William E. Matthews read her eighty-line ode entitled "Lincoln," for the unveiling of the Freedman's Monument. The event took place on April 14, 1876, in Washington, D.C. Frederick Douglass's keynote address and Ray's poem were the highlights of the occasion. In 1893 Ray published a collection of her poetry entitled *Sonnets*. A second volume titled *Poems* appeared in 1910.

Poetry Equals Best Writing of the Period

Many of Ray's poems appeared in the *AME Review*, a publication of the African Methodist Episcopal church. She wrote prolifically around the turn of the century. Her major poetic concerns included nature, Christian idealism, morality, love (Platonic), and literature. Often criticized for lacking passion, emotion, and vitality, her poetry, nonetheless, is characteristic of the best writing of her time. For example, "Verses to My Heart's-Sister," perhaps her most well-known poem, is as emotional a poem as any Victorian poet was likely to write. The following first stanza is not unlike the sentimental poetry found in Rufus W. Griswold's *Female Poets of America*, all of whom were white:

> We've traveled long together,
> O sister of my heart,
> Since first as little children
> All bouyant, we did start
> Upon Life's checkered pathway,
> Nor dreamed of aught save joy;
> But ah! To-day can tell us
> Naught is without alloy (Shockley, 330).

The entire poem is a revealing confession of her emotional response to the loss of her closest sister, Florence, and other members of her family. Sentimentality was the dominating mode, so in this sense Ray's poetry is typical.

Despite the criticism of her poetry for lacking a racial consciousness and being void of a political agenda, Ray's technical skills are excellent. Joan Sherman comments on Ray's skillful use of stanza forms and the rhythmic nature of her poems. Ray often invents her own forms, freeing herself from conventional versification. Ray's verse is compared to Mary Weston Fordham's poetry, which never considers racial issues, in spite of the Introduction to her *Magnolia Leaves* (1878) by Booker T. Washington.

Ray's poetry falls into three categories. The philosophical poems are serious, idealistic, and "deeply pious" (Sherman, xxx). In "Broken Heart" the poet utters real pain, which she ultimately surrenders to Jesus. Ray is accused of seeing the world, particularly her world—fresh from slavery, steeped in the recoil from Reconstruction, and suffused by the horrors of Ku Klux Klan terror—through rose-colored glasses. Despite the fact that her life must have been quite sheltered from southern horrors and grueling poverty, her father's militant crusade as an operator of the Underground Railroad and the fact that their New York home was a station causes one to look for some remnant of protest in her poetry. There is none.

More damaging to her poetry than a lack of social consciousness is Ray's fondness for "antique diction and syntax, for personification, mythological allusions, and copious adjectives." These elements, Sherman claims, "further stiffens the wax flower, stuffed birds, and canvas sunsets in her verse museums" (xxx).

"Chansons D'Amour" constitutes the second category into which Ray's poems fall. These poems express disappointment in love. Several are warm and candid. For instance, "Love's Vista" reveals true emotion: "Love oped a vista rare with stars," the poem begins. The final stanza, "Yet sweet, sweet dove, when life is drear, / Come chant again that dreamy lay, / O tender Love, send shining stars / To light her soul, once more, some day" (Sherman, 136), reveals her lost love but few regrets.

The third section of Ray's poems are eulogies to freedom fighters like her own father, William Lloyd Garrison, Abraham Lincoln, Frederick Douglass, Toussaint L'Ouverture, and others. This section also contains poems celebrating other writers, among them Paul Laurence Dunbar and Harriet Beecher Stowe. These poems are as close as Ray comes to speaking to the issues of her time. Ray versified only socially-acceptable sentiments, not unlike her contemporaries, both African-American and white (Sherman, xxx).

Her poetry received a mixed response. There were times when Ray must have felt herself a failure. The poem "Failure" poignantly summarizes what it must have been like to be a black American woman poet in the early years of this century. She writes:

> What is failure? When the poet
> Hears his verse harshly scorned,
> Can he yet forget the rapture,
> That upon his spirit dawned (Sherman, 59).

In 1988 the Schomburg Center for Research in Black Culture joined with Henry Louis Gates to produce a series of books and publications that constitute the Schomburg Library of Nineteenth-Century Black Women Writers. H. Cordelia Ray is included in *Collected Black Women's Poetry,* volume 3, edited by Joan R. Sherman. Years after her death in 1916, Ray's inclusion in this prestigious series solidifies her place in what is being acknowledged in literary history as "The Black Woman's Era," 1890 to 1910.

References

Brown, Hallie Q. *Homespun Heroines and Other Women of Distinction.* Xenia, Ohio: Aldine Pub. Co., 1926.

Kerlin, Robert T. *Negro Poets and Their Poems.* Washington, D.C.: Associated Publishers, 1947.

Ray, H. Cordelia. "Poems." *Collected Black Women's Poetry.* Ed. Joan R. Sherman. New York: Oxford University Press, 1988. Separately paginated.

Sampson, Henry T. *Blacks in Black and White.* Metuchen, N.J.: Scarecrow Press, 1977.

Shockley, Ann Allen. *Afro-American Women Writers 1746-1933.* Boston: G. K. Hall, 1988.

Nagueyalti Warren

Bernice J. Reagon

(1942-)

Museum curator, writer, historian, musician, civil rights activist

Inspired by the civil rights movement of the 1960s, Bernice Johnson Reagon had woven her skills as a singer, writer, and historian into a life's work to make the field of black studies "credible." On October 4, 1942, the Reverend Jessie Johnson and Beatrice (Wise) Johnson welcomed the third of their eight children, Bernice. In the little cluster of homes near Albany, Georgia, where they lived, the Johnson family were black pioneers. From a modern perspective, the struggles of black pioneers often look small: fighting for a bus to take children to school, risking lives to cast a ballot. Yet, blacks fought for every American right we have, and children like Bernice Johnson Reagon looked on, grew up, and continued the struggle.

Reagon began to distinguish herself as a singer at age five in her father's church and credits him, a singer also, for her style. But for her, the church meant more than singing. Her heart heard the collective voice of people united in struggle.

Entering Albany State College, Albany, Georgia, in 1959 as a music major, she studied German leider and Italian arias.

Bernice J. Reagon

But soon the rising voices of the civil rights struggle caught her attention. Her political activities led her to hold the office of secretary of the local NAACP Youth Chapter.

Later, when the Student Nonviolent Coordinating Committee (SNCC) moved into Albany to help organize the community, Reagon found she preferred their confrontational style to the legal battle that the NAACP waged. In December 1961 during her junior year, she participated in a SNCC-coordinated march protesting the arrest of two fellow students. Commenting on the protest, Reagon said:

> The SNCC workers told us we were not supposed to hit back if we were hit. It didn't make sense to me. I had nothing in my brain to absorb the word nonviolence. But the SNCC people gave a long speech on marching with dignity and there was a discussion among them as to whether we would sing. It was decided we would be quiet, marching in pairs around the city jail. I was not moved by nonviolence as a way of life. What I was moved by was the hundreds and thousands of people in the streets. I was moved by hearing songs, and after hearing them all my life, for the first time, I understood what they meant. They were saying what I was feeling. Somehow, it felt like all those words that Black people had been praying and saying was a language for us, a language we could not understand unless we were involved in practical, everyday struggle. I remember feeling incomplete and humble, yet really powerful. It was the most powerful thing that happened to me (DeVeaux, 145).

For her part in these activities, Reagon was suspended from school, and on the third day of the Albany march she was arrested. What held her together in jail, she says, was music—unaccompanied vocal music sung by the forty to fifty incarcerated women. Before leaving Albany State College, where she was the school's highest-ranking student, she had changed her major. When she resumed her studies at Spelman College in Atlanta in 1962, she returned to her music, though majoring in nonwestern history.

That same year, Reagon left school to join the Freedom Singers of SNCC. This group of young people sang at mass meetings and in jails, traveled around the country raising money for the movement, and often drew attention to voter registration drives. In 1963 she sang with a group during the March on Washington and later directed the Harambee Singers.

Reagon joined the Harambee Singers at a time when she felt herself growing away from the integrationist posture of the civil rights movement and into a separatist posture. She looks back on this as a time when she wrote her most militant songs.

During this period she married Cordell Reagon, a SNCC field worker and Freedom Singer from Nashville, Tennessee, whom she met at Albany State. Before their painful separation, they had a daughter, Toshi, who is now a singer also, and a son, Kwan, who recently graduated from the Baltimore International Culinary College. Bernice and Cordell Reagon were divorced in 1967.

Sweet Honey in the Rock Singers Organized

Folkway Records released Reagon's first solo album of traditional songs, *Songs of the South,* in 1966 and Kintel Records her second, *Sound of Thunder,* in 1967. Following these successes, Reagon began to integrate her music and education. At Spelman, she completed her degree in 1970, then moved to Washington, D.C. As vocal director at the District of Columbia Black Repertory Theater, she organized the folk-music group Sweet Honey in the Rock and began her career with the Smithsonian Institution with the program in Black American Culture. By 1975 she had earned a Ph.D. from Howard University with a dissertation about songs of the civil rights movement.

Despite their name, which comes from a gospel song, Sweet Honey in the Rock's message is more often political than religious. "I think everything is political," said Reagon, "We are about being accountable" (*People*).

The *Washington Post* stated on October 11, 1978:

> This rare composite of a cappella virtuosos, directed by American music historian Bernice Reagon, has just released an important new album of original songs entitled "Believe I'll Run On, See What the End's Gonna Be." In this new album as well as on their earlier disc, the vitality of these ladies' natural singing voices squarely competes with more popularized and exploited music forms (B-9).

The group has turned down offers from many record labels who wanted to commercialize Sweet Honey's sound.

High Fidelity magazine described the group's singular and uncommercial sound as "breathtaking excursions into harmony singing" (Camacho, 82). *Downbeat* magazine called it "neck-hair raising" (Palmer, 74).

With eight albums to their credit, Sweet Honey opened to a sold-out performance at Carnegie Hall in May 1989. The group is presently composed of Reagon, Ysaye Maria Barnwell, Carol Lynn Maillard, Nitanju Bolade-Casel, Aisha Kahlil, and Shirley Childress Johnson, who signs the group's songs for the hearing impaired. (Since 1979 the group has made sign-language interpretation for the deaf an integral part of their concern.) Over the years, others have joined and left the group for various reasons. One former member, Evelyn Harris, penned several of their songs, though Reagon, too, is a songwriter. Many of her songs are showcased on *Believe I'll Run On, See What the End's Gonna Be.*

Sweet Honey has performed at churches, concerts, and festivals in Washington, D.C., New York City, and Ann Arbor, Michigan. By their fifth anniversary, Sweet Honey's fans filled Washington's All Souls Church. A performance at "Sisterfire" in Washington in 1987, a multicultural outdoor women's arts festival, drew a large following, as did New York's Caribbean Cultural Center's "Tribute to Women of Color." Reagon's humourous storytelling on stage is a part of Sweet Honey's attraction. The group also contributed to an album produced to benefit the environmental and peace movements.

On the international scene, they performed at the New Song Festivals in Ecuador and Mexico; toured Germany, Japan, England, Canada, Australia, and the Caribbean; and served as coordinators of the closing cultural festivities at the United Nations Decade for Women Conference in Nairobi, Kenya, in 1985. In 1990 Sweet Honey in the Rock toured Africa, performing in Uganda, Zimbabwe, Mozambique, Swaziland, and Namibia. They also performed in several events in the United States celebrating the release of Nelson Mandela, South African freedom fighter. "Sweet Honey's song stylizing is to black music what Alex Haley's *Roots* was to black written history. They both offer a much needed legacy of black culture" (*Mind Is,* 40).

Even as the fame of Sweet Honey grew, Reagon continued to establish her role as a solo artist on such albums as *Joan Little*, and *Give Your Hands to the Struggle*.

Reagon's career as a scholar has kept pace with her musical career. The *Washington Post* reported, "The Smithsonian Institution has recently come out with a three-record collection called 'Voices of the Civil Rights Movement: Black American Freedom Songs 1960-66.' One of those voices is both on the record and behind it: Dr. Bernice Reagon." The illustrated booklet in the Smithsonian Collection that accompanies the record collection is, itself, a music history journal.

In a 1978 interview, Reagon asserted, "I'm a performer, teacher, researcher and historian with a strong social, political, and economic consciousness" (Morris, 40). She has lived up to it all, earning her doctoral degree in 1975. While working as cultural historian for the Smithsonian Institution's Division of Performing Arts/African Diaspora Project, she did extensive research on the black American artistic expression and its relationship to similar Caribbean and African experiences. The result was her article, "African Diaspora Women: The Making of Cultural Workers." Here she traces the cultural growth of black women from West Africa, Brazil, and America. As a result of the African diaspora, she says:

> There is the struggle to contend with a new space where . . . people and children are defined in new ways. . . . [The Diaspora] disrupted and threw in severe trauma cultural practices that had been nursed in African societies. Mothering therefore required a kind of nurturing that would both provide food and stamina for survival within a cruel slave society and the passing on of

> nurturing that would allow for the development of a community that was not of but beyond the slave society. . . . Nurturing was not only reconciling what was passed to them with the day-to-day reality, but also sifting and transforming this experience to feed this child, unborn, this new Black community, in preparation for what it would face (87).

Despite our other roles in society, Reagon urges us to continue to nurture and transform "a new space for a new people in a new time" (89).

A future book is planned on Ruby Doris Robinson, a strong supporter of civil rights workers in Mississippi during the movement. It also is not surprising that when filmmakers decided to explore life-changing experiences of people caught up in social change, they called on Reagon to narrate her experiences during the civil rights movement in Albany, Georgia. Reviewers described her presentation as forceful, yet unpretentious (Wood, 1117). Further showing the range of respect for her talent, Reagon wrote the program notes for "A Program of Spirituals," given by Kathleen Battle and Jessye Norman at Carnegie Hall in March 1990.

Among Reagon's most recent awards is the John D. and Catherine T. MacArthur Foundation Fellowship in the amount of $285,000. She was notified of her selection while doing research in Georgia in 1989 on worship communities and traditions in black churches.

Reagon Appointed Curator of National Museum

Until her recent promotion to curator of the National Museum of American History, Reagon served as director of the Smithsonian's program in black American culture. She is credited with bringing black studies into the mainstream. "Her work is of such high scholastic quality that the legitimacy of the field has come to be unquestioned." Speaking of the folks like those she grew up with in the backwoods of Georgia, Reagon said, "If these people have a sense that the National Museum of American History knows they exist, then I know I'm doing my job" (*Evening Sun,* M-3).

Washingtonian magazine in December 1984 described Bernice Johnson Reagon as lush-looking. Despite the fact that she is a petite five feet one inch tall, *Essence* magazine called her voluptuous. The Baltimore Evening *Sun* said that "on stage, Dr. Reagon appears majestic, a matriarchal figure rooted in black American tradition and steeped in African lore. In her curator's role . . . she looks younger and less formidable, but still light-years from drab. Her black hair is twirled into short dreadlocks" (G-1).

A fine photograph of Reagon singing appeared in the *Washington Post* on November 16, 1980. *High Fidelity* magazine pictured Sweet Honey in the Rock in its May 1989 issue. Interviews with Reagon reveal her warmth and easiness with people, her concern for accurate comments about her life and work, and, above all, give her the opportunity to convey her message to black people—that they have a cultural history worth knowing. She resides in Washington, D.C.

References

Camacho, Mildred. "The Other Side." *High Fidelity* (April 1986): 82.

"Coda." *Ms.* 13 (May 1985): 53.

DeVeaux, Alexis. "Bernice Reagon." *Essence* 11 (June 1980: 92-93, 142, 145, 148, 150.

"Inspired by Gospel and African Rhythms, Sweet Honey in the Rock Delivers Political Punch A Capella." *People* 33 (28 May 1990): 108.

"Limelight." *Washington Post* 16 November 1980. M-3.

McHenry, Susan. "Stepping across the Line: Voter Registration Then and Now." *Ms.* 13 (November 1984): 86.

Morris, Rachel. "Essence Women." *Essence* 8 (February 1978): 40.

Palmer, Don. "Sweet Honey in the Rock: Live at Carnegie Hall." *Downbeat* (May 1989): 74.

"Performer, Researcher, Curator: Her Life Is a Commitment to African-American Culture." Baltimore *Evening Sun* (30 July 1989). G-1.

Reagon, Bernice J. "African Diaspora Women: The Making of Cultural Workers." *Black Women's History*. Vol. 2. Edited by Darlene Clark-Hine. Brooklyn: Carlson Pub. Co.

———. Interviews with Margaret D. Pagan, January 1991.

"Reagon Makes Sweet Music." *A Mind Is a Terrible Thing to Waste* 1 (Winter 1991): 24-25, 40.

"Sweet Honey Runs on with a Strong New Album." *Washington Post*, 11 October 1978.

Wood, Peter H. "You Got to Move." Movie review. *Journal of American History* 74 (December 1987): 1117.

Young, Ivy. "Sweet Honey in the Rock." *Essence* 18 (May 1987): 92.

Margaret D. Pagan

Sarah P. Remond

(1826-1894)

Activist, physician

During the late 1850s and early Civil War years, Sarah Parker Remond devoted herself to keeping the moral issue of American slavery before the public in Great Britain. With the example and support of her older brother, Charles Lenox Remond, she also became an antislavery lecturer. As a Garrisonian abolitionist, Remond was interested in women's rights as well as antislavery and antiracist education. She was also a member of the platform group at the National Women's Rights Convention in New York City in May 1858.

Remond was born on June 6, 1826, in Salem, Massachusetts, into a prominent and prosperous black family, many of whom became antislavery activists. Her family was a vital influence in shaping Remond's public career as an antislavery lecturer and an advocate of women's rights. Remond's early home life emphasized the importance of skilled work, education, and politics for the girls as well as the boys. Her mother, Nancy Lenox Remond (1788-1867), was the daughter of Cornelius Lenox, a veteran of the Revolutionary War who settled in Newton, Massachusetts. Nancy Lenox was a cakemaker by trade at the time of her marriage to John Remond. Four of the six girls in the Remond family worked in their parents' trades as adults, including one who followed in Nancy Lenox Remond's footsteps. Cecelia, Maritcha, and Caroline Remond operated a wig factory and sold a medicated hair tonic. Susan Remond had a bakery at home, and her kitchen is remembered by a visitor as a place "where gathered radicals, free thinkers, abolitionists, female suffragists, fugitives" (Sterling, 96-97). Nancy Remond was also actively involved in the antislavery movement as a member of the Salem Female Anti-Slavery Society founded by a group of black women in 1832. Nancy Remond's involvement in the movement was as hostess to visiting abolitionist luminaries, including William Lloyd Garrison, Wendell Phillips, and William Wells Brown. Caroline Remond Putnam was both a member and an officer in the Salem Female Anti-Slavery Society.

Sarah P. Remond

Remond's father, John, was an immigrant from Curaçao, who wemt to Salem in 1798 and took up hairdressing, wigmaking, catering, and trading in wines, spices, and food. He became a United States citizen on May 2, 1811, and a life member of the Massachusetts Anti-Slavery Society in the 1830s.

According to Dorothy Porter's research, Sarah Remond and her sisters "encountered much racial prejudice" in the public schools of Salem *(Dictionary of American Negro Biography,* 522). When Remond was ready for high school in 1835, she was refused admission on the grounds of color. This was just a year after the Salem school committee instituted a separate school for "African" children, in an apparent response to community pressure against integration in the girls' high school (Bogin, 138). The separate school for blacks lasted only ten years and was boycotted by parents who could afford private instruction. The Remond family promptly moved to Newport, Rhode Island, and enrolled their daughters in a private school for black American children there.

When the family returned to Salem in 1841, Remond continued her informal education through reading and attendance at political and cultural events. By the time she was launched on her lecturing career, she was impressively "well read . . . in English literature and the English poets," according to one British observer (Bogin, 123). Yet she felt inadequately educated when she came to undertake her public career, and when the opportunity arose, she pursued formal education again.

Remond's brother, Charles, sixteen years older than she, began to lecture as an agent for the Massachusetts Anti-Slavery Society when she was just entering her teen years, in 1838. When she was fourteen he served as a delegate to the World Anti-Slavery Convention in London (1840) and, with William Lloyd Garrison, sat in the visitors' galleries with the American women delegates, who had not been seated. Charles Remond spent a full year lecturing in England and Ireland on the antislavery cause at this time, before returning to New England. Sarah Remond's first experience of public lecturing with her brother took place in July 1842 in Groton,

Massachusetts, when she was only sixteen (Porter, *DANB*, 522).

Remond's personal involvement in antiracist politics intensified in the 1850s. One incident was reported in detail in the antislavery press. In May 1853, Remond and two friends refused to sit in the segregated gallery of the Howard Athenaeum in Boston for a performance of a Mozart opera. Roughly handled by the policeman who ejected her, she fell down the stairs. Asserting her equal rights in a Salem police court, she won a significant moral and legal victory. She was awarded five hundred dollars in damages in a civil suit, and the principle of desegregated seating in the hall was upheld. (Dorothy Porter first retold this incident in the *Journal of Negro History*, citing the American and Foreign Anti-Slavery Society's *Thirteenth Annual Report*, 1853, 288).

Remond was living in the Dean Street household of her brother, Charles, and his wife, Amy Matilda Remond, at least as early as 1854. James Forten, the prominent sailmaker and abolitionist of Philadelphia, sent his young daughter Charlotte to the Remond household in order to give her an opportunity to attend the now-integrated Salem schools. Her journal for 1854-1858 provides interesting glimpses of the exciting political atmosphere in which Sarah Remond lived at this time.

Remond Appointed Antislavery Agent

Remond's first official appointment as an antislavery agent came in 1856 when she was thirty years old. She toured New York state as part of a team of lecturers hired by the American Anti-Slavery Society, including Charles Remond, Wendell Phillips, Abby Kelley and her husband, Stephen Foster, and Susan B. Anthony. William Lloyd Garrison wrote approvingly in the *Liberator* about Remond's "calm, dignified manner, her winning personal appearance, and her earnest appeals to the conscience and the heart" (Bogin, 129-30). One of the other lecturers, Aaron M. Powell, recorded in his memoirs that because of anticipated "heartless and vulgar prejudice" at hotels and boardinghouses, arrangements had to be made with other antislavery friends for private overnight accommodations for the two black abolitionists on this tour (Bogin, 130).

Once well-launched on a career as a public speaker, Remond wrote a letter to Abby Kelley Foster suggesting how strongly she felt her own deficiencies of education at this time:

> We have attended some interesting meetings in this state, and my only regret is that I did not sooner begin to do what I might, in this particular field of labour. I feel almost sure I never should have made the attempt but for the words of encouragement I received from you. Although my heart was in the work, I felt that I was in need of a good English education. Every hour since I met you I have endeavoured as far as possible to make up this loss. And when I consider that the only reason why I did not obtain what I so much desired was because I was the possessor of an unpopular complexion, it adds to my discomfort (Sterling, 176).

As she wrote this letter, Remond was preparing to sail for England, where with support from American abolitionist friends Parker Pillsbury and Samuel J. May, she had arranged for an extensive lecture tour. She arrived in Liverpool in January 1859. A British paper, *The Anti-Slavery Advocate*, provided extensive coverage of her lectures in Scotland, England, and Ireland during the next two years, and praised her reasoned style of lecture as "well-adapted to English audiences" (Porter, *JNH*, 291). As a black woman lecturer, Remond was at first a novelty and frequently drew unusually large crowds.

In Warrington, near Liverpool, Remond's lectures stimulated the mayor to propose the formation of a "ladies' committee," and in a subsequent Music Hall lecture she spoke to a primarily female audience. As Harriet Jacobs later did in *Incidents in the Life of a Slave Girl* (1861), Remond spoke about the special sexual oppression experienced by the slave woman and the laws that made "immorality" economically profitable to the slaveholder. On this occasion she was presented with a watch inscribed "Presented to S. P. Remond by Englishwomen, her sisters, in Warrington, February 2d, 1859," and she was reported as deeply moved by the event (Bogin, 132).

In Ireland, Remond spoke about the Irish immigrants to the United States who had too quickly forgotten their own oppression and joined the ranks of slaveholders and their sympathizers. She reminded her audience of the continuing illegal importation of African slaves in the United States and urged that Great Britain and Ireland use their great influence and prestige to undermine the institution of slavery in the United States. In London, she visited famous runaway ex-slaves William and Ellen Craft, participated in meetings that led to the formation of the London Emancipation Committee, and spoke in rebuttal of the proslavery lecture by dancer Lola Montez. In November 1859 she was involved in a highly-publicized episode of discrimination, when the American legation in London refused her request for a visa to visit France, asserting that her color was a barrier to United States citizenship (*Notable American Women*, 135-37).

During her second year abroad, Remond alternated antislavery speaking with liberal arts studies at the Bedford College for Ladies in London. The founder of this college, Elisabeth Jesser Reid, was an active supporter of American abolitionists. During holidays, Remond lectured in Yorkshire for the Leeds Young Men's Anti-Slavery Society and in September 1860 she spoke in Edinburgh at the behest of the Ladies' Emancipation Society. She stayed in Great Britain throughout the Civil War, and as a member of the London Emancipation Society and the Freedman's Aid Association, worked to influence British public opinion to support the Union blockade of the Confederacy and to raise money for the newly enfranchised slaves. (See her letter to Garrison, dated October 22, 1864, included in Sterling, 179-80. A speech she made before the International Congress of Charities, Correction and Philanthropy, in London, in 1862, appears under the title, "The Negroes in the United States of America," in the *Journal of Negro History* 27.)

Remond spent only about a year in the United States after the close of the Civil War. With Charles Remond and Frederick Douglass and others in the American Equal Rights Association, she worked for universal suffrage—specifically on the unsuccessful campaign to have the New York Constitutional Convention of 1867 eliminate the words "white" and "male" from the Constitution. But by 1867 she was back in England. Bogin notes that she was one of those who "helped to honor William Lloyd Garrison on his visit to London" (148). Soon thereafter she moved to Italy, where she apparently remained for the rest of her life. It seems likely that she, like other black American expatriates before and after her time, sought in Europe a haven from the kind of color prejudice she had spent much of her life fighting.

Remond's later life in Italy is sparsely documented. She is said to have studied medicine at the Santa Maria Nuova Hospital in Florence from 1866 to 1868. According to Bogin, one former antislavery associate, Parker Pillsbury, in *Anti-Slavery Apostles*, said that Remond "studied medicine in London, went to Italy, married, and settled in large medical practice in Florence." Porter notes that "no official record has been found of her enrollment or the completion of her medical work, but Remond is said to have pursued a regular course of study together with hospital practice and to have received a diploma certifying her for 'Professional Medical Practice'" (*NAW*, 137).

Remond married Lazzaro Pinto, an Italian man, on April 25, 1877. A letter from Frederick Douglass, dated Rome, February 11, 1887, refers to a visit to his "old friends the Remonds," probably including Sarah and her two sisters, Maritcha Remond and Caroline Remond Putnam, who joined her in 1885 (Sterling, 180). Sarah Remond died on December 13, 1894, and is buried in the Protestant Cemetery in Rome (Porter, *DANB*, 523).

References

Anti-Slavery Advocate (London), 1858-1860. April, May, July, September, October 1859; February, November 1860.

Billington, Ray Allen, ed. *The Journal of Charlotte L. Forten*. (London: Collier, 1961). Original manuscript diary in the Moorland-Spingarn Research Center at Howard University.

Bogin, Ruth. "Sarah Parker Remond: Black Abolitionist from Salem." Essex Institute Historical Collection, C (April 1974). Reprinted in *Black Women in American History from Colonial Times Through the Nineteenth Century*. Vol. I. Ed. Darlene Clark Hine. Brooklyn, N.Y.: Carlson, 1990.

Liberator, 6 March 1857; 11 March 1859; 22 October 1864; 11 November 1864.

Liverpool Mercury, January 1859.

Nelson, Larry E. "Black Leaders and the Presidential Election of 1864." *Journal of Negro History* 63 (January 1978): 42-58.

Porter, Dorothy B. "Sarah Parker Remond." *Dictionary of American Negro Biography*. Eds. Rayford W. Logan and Michael R. Winston. New York: Norton, 1982.

———. "Sarah Parker Remond." *Notable American Women 1607-1950*. Vol. III. Cambridge: Harvard University Press, 1971.

———. "Sarah Parker Remond, Abolitionist and Physician." *Journal of Negro History* 20 (July 1935): 287-93.

Remond, Sarah P. "Colonization." *Freed-man* 1 February 1866.

———. *The Negroes & Anglo-Africans as Freedmen and Soldiers*. Ladies' London Emancipation Society Tract Number 7, 1864.

———. "The Negroes in the United States of America." *Journal of Negro History* 27 (April 1942): 216-18.

Stanton, Elizabeth Cady, and others, eds. *History of Woman Suffrage*. Vol. 1. New York: Fowler and Wells, 1881.

Sterling, Dorothy, ed. *We Are Your Sisters: Black Women in the Nineteenth Century*. New York: Norton, 1984.

Warrington Guardian, March 1859.

Warrington Times, February, 1859.

Wyman, Lillie B. C., and Arthur Crawford Wyman. *Elizabeth Buffum Chace, 1806-1899, Her Life and Environment*. Vol. II. Boston: W. B. Clark, 1914. The Quaker abolitionist Elizabeth Buffum Chace visited Remond in Florence in 1873.

Collections

Information relating to Sarah Parker Remond is in the Abigail Kelley-Foster Papers, American Antiquarian Society, Worchester, Massachusetts, and the Post Family Papers, Department of Rare Books and Special Collections, University of Rochester. Several of Sarah Remond's letters are in the William Lloyd Garrison Collection, Rare Books and Manuscripts, Boston Public Library. a photograph portrait is housed in the Essex Institute, Salem, Massachusetts.

Jean McMahon Humez

Beah Richards

(1926-)

Actress

On stage, in television productions, and in movies, Beah Richards has usually been a woman of quiet and restrained dignity. Her *personal* expression, however, reveals a woman with a strong sense of self, definite convictions, and distinctive racial pride. "In my family the word *black* was always a beautiful word. . . . When everybody was saying 'Negro' and 'colored,' my family would use the term *black*" (Lanker, 59).

Richards was born in Vicksburg, Mississippi, on July 12, 1926, to Beulah and Wesley Richardson, a minister. She recalled, "Everybody in Vicksburg told me I was going to be an actor. We didn't even have a theater, and if they had one, I couldn't go to it." She attended college at Dillard University in New Orleans and then moved to San Diego, where she studied dance with Serge Oukrainsky and drama with Craig Noel at the Old Globe Theatre. She also appeared in numerous productions, including *The Little Foxes* and *Another Part of the Forest*.

After three years Richards moved to New York City in 1950. Throughout that decade and early 1960s, her parts were scattered. She added continuity to her life by becoming a teacher in a charm school. "Curiously enough, later in some of her important roles she often had the air of a well-brought up and mannerly woman, determined to remain polite and ladylike no matter what the situation" (Bogle, *Blacks in American Films and Television*, 453).

Beah Richards

Richrds's initial roles were in productions of *Take a Giant Step* (off-Broadway, 1954), *The Miracle Worker* (1959), and *Purlie Victorious* (1961) and as understudy for Claudia NcNeil in *A Raisin in the Sun*, before assuming the role of Lena Younger in a national tour. Along with Godfrey Cambridge and eighteen other actors, she initiated the Harlem Community Theatre in 1958. It was her striking performance in James Baldwin's *The Amen Corner* that contributed most to her national reputation.

The Amen Corner was written in 1953-1954 and first produced at Howard University a year later. Frank Silvera presented the play in Los Angeles, where it attracted the attention of Nat King Cole and others. In 1965 Cole's widow, Maria Cole, acting as producer, brought it to New York City with Silvera as actor and director. "This sensitive, moving play had Beah Richards prominently co-starred with Mr. Silvera, and both poured into the work their complete artistry" (Mitchell, 204). The critical response to the play was not totally favorable, but Richards's performance received rave reviews. In the words of one critic, "to see Beah Richards in the role of the lady minister (Sister Margaret Alexander) of a storefront church who has to learn about false piety was to witness a performance that gave the play special stature" (Abramson, 274).

The reaction of Walter Kerr, a white reviewer for the *Herald Tribune*, to the moment in third act moment when Richards, as Sister Alexander, recognizes the meaning of her existence, is significant:

> I do not normally care much for actresses who actually cry on stage and I was offering the moment some resistance because Miss Richards was actually crying. But that is when she fooled me, on the double. Suddenly, as though a meat-axe had cut straight through all of the inhibitions binding her, she turned her tears into a whoop of laughter, slapped the table hard with an open palm, and let her left leg slide into an abandoned 18-year-old limpness. She was that girl, after all, released by a bolt of lightning. The moment is a remarkable one, swiftly intelligible in spite of all that has gone to contradict it beforehand.

Josie Dotson, a black actress in the play, was also deeply affected:

> In that scene where Beah broke into laughter, one of the most marvelous laughs in the world, in that scene, I understood how we, a people, could be the kinda people who could take it. I knew that Beah knew that black people had got something. We don't get wiped out. We don't. Par-

> ticular individuals get wiped out, but the people do not. No! No! What is that something that keeps us doing it?
>
> In that moment of Beah Richards' laughter, I knew what it was. She showed me that, forever. It was one of the greatest moments the theater has ever seen. I knew that Beah knew what she was talking about and she wasn't just living the lines, she was really talking about it (Hatch, 515).

The play only ran for twelve weeks, but Richards was given the New York Drama Critics Circle Award and the *Theatre World* Award and she topped *Variety*'s Drama Critics Poll. The All-American Press Association Award was to follow in 1968.

The context of the movie *Hurry Sundown* (1967) provides some of the most meaningful evaluation of Richards's acting skills. Donald Bogle offers this analysis:

> Beah Richards, as Mammy Rose, came off better than any other black actor . . . presenting to the audience a middle-class mammy in revolt. . . . There had never been anyone quite like her before. . . . For one thing, she was very dark and had "Negroid" features. . . . For another thing, she looked hard and "evil," as if she would bite back in a minute if anyone dared step on her toes. In her dying moments Mammy Rose told her son, "I was wrong . . . I was a white folks' nigger . . . I truly grieve for the sorry thing that has been my life" (*Toms, Coons*, 211-12).

Although the film was in some ways a shaky melodrama, with Jane Fonda and Michael Caine as unconvincing Southerners, it did link the modern era to the experiences of slavery and Reconstruction.

Richards Nominated for Academy Award

Interestingly, another film in 1967, containing less candor, drew a great deal more attention and an Academy Award nomination for best supporting actress for Beah Richards: Stanley Kramer's *Guess Who's Coming to Dinner*. In the film, Sidney Poitier plays an obviously over-qualified black Albert Schweitzer seeking parental acceptance for the hand of an empty-headed white San Francisco socialite. As Isabell Sanford, who played the maid in the movie, comments: "Civil Rights is one thing, but this here is another" (Bogle, *Toms, Coons*, 217). Bogle's evaluation of the charade as "innocuous" and "pure 1949 clap trap" seems appropriate. But again Richards manages to salvage her personal dignity. "Every word is measured and each line is delivered with a fascinating precision. . . . Intuitively, we feel she has too much sense to stand by so idly—and silently—in this hopelessly fake movie. But the script does not allow her an explosion" (Bogle, *Blacks in American Films and Television*, 453-54).

The actress has also made her voice heard in the selection of roles. She has rejected many offered to her: "There are a lot of movies out there that I would hate to be paid to do, some real demeaning, real woman-denigrating stuff. It is up to women to change their roles. They are going to have to write the stuff and do it. And they will" (Lanker, 59). In 1973 she participated in a Boston University conference on "Black Images in Film: Stereotyping, and Self-Perception as Viewed by Black Actresses." She advocated an even more activist response:

> You don't dig those naked movies and all that crap, don't go to them. Don't. All of them should be picketed. That's where the attack ought to be. If they continue to make movies like that, don't just say that black people don't do it. If the whites continue to do it, don't support them. That's where I think the attack should be. I think it will be like Rosa Parks. Rosa Parks was not a militant. Rosa Parks didn't see herself as a great leader of anything. But one day she sat down and all of Alabama sat down and all of Alabama got up and walked. And I think it's going to be simple as that. One day some actor is going to say no, and he's going to say it so loud, and in such a definite way, that all the actors are going to say no (Sims-Wood, 246).

Richards added her special qualities to the unique television series "Frank's Place," set in New Orleans. *New York Post* critic David N. Rosenthal identified part of the uniqueness of the short-lived series, which was canceled in 1988: "It builds slowly, drawing its humor from its rich characters instead of cheap one-liners. It's a gentle show that grows on you with a lilting rhythm seldom seen on television." Richards received an Emmy Award for Outstanding Guest Appearance in a Comedy Series for an episode called "The Bridge."

Richards's other television appearances have been so numerous and varied that an exhaustive listing is almost impossible. Among those listed on her professional resume include the movies of the week and miniseries "Roots II: The Next Generation," "Sophisticated Gents," "Y.E.S., Inc.," and "And the Children Shall Lead." Her episodic works include "Brewster Place," "Equal Justice," "Beauty and the Beast," "Hill Street Blues," "227," "Sanford and Son," and "Room 222." Her film appearances include: *Take a Giant Step* (1960), *The Miracle Worker* (1962), *Gone Are the Days* (1963), *Guess Who's Coming to Dinner* (1967), *In the Heat of the Night* (1967), *Hurry Sundown* (1967), *The Great White Hope* (1970), *The Biscuit Eater* (1972), *Mahogany* (1975), *Inside Out* (1987), *Big Shots* (1987), and *Drugstore Cowboy* (1989).

Richards was selected to the Black Filmmakers Hall of Fame in 1974. She is a member of the Screen Actor's Guild and The Actor's Equity Association. In addition to her performances in vehicles authored by others she has directed plays and television shows and taught courses at the University of Southern California. She directed *Stoop* in 1983 in productions in both San Francisco and San Antonio.

Recently Richards elaborated on the impact of the late actor-director Frank Silvera on her. He told her in 1962:

> ''Don't act, just be.'' That's when I became an actor. I ran into this philosophy of being. I was a liberated person after that. I think before I was a reactor. Now I am an actor, I can take the initiative (Lanker, 59).

Bogle refers to the actress's special quality, even offstage, of seeming to ''be up in the clouds, operating in some enlightened but unfathomable, highly personal state of Grace'' (*Blacks in American Films & Television*, 453).

Richards has written three plays. One was called *All's Well That Ends*, dealing with segregation. The second was *One Is a Crowd*, written in 1951 and produced in 1971 in Los Angeles. Margaret B. Wilkerson writes in *9 Plays by Black Women:* ''Ms. Richards stunned the Los Angeles theatre community as both writer and actress in her first full-length play, 'One Is a Crowd.' Playing the lead role, she made the soliloquy form from her one-woman shows the centerpiece of a compelling drama about a black singer's lifelong pursuit of revenge against a white man whose casual lust had destroyed her family'' (28).

Insight Into Actress Reflected in Poetry

More insight into the mind of the actress is offered in her 1974 collection of fourteen poems, *A Black Woman Speaks*. The book was dedicated to Richards's parents and includes two related poems, ''My Father Made Souls'' and ''Mother, Please Go to Bed.'' Her purpose is indicated in the preface: ''I have found life to be incredibly theatrical and theatre to be profoundly lifeless . . . let us set aside our theatrically conditioned view and see how it is that blacks and whites agree so little culturally'' (v).

In Part One Richards expresses her views on ''The Law of Love,'' starting with ''My Gods Are Not of Virgin Birth.'' The impact of a segregated society is suggested in ''It's Time for Love'':

> I have never been a lady.
> I have always been a woman.
> They come in colors, you know —
> the woman Black —
> the lady white (4).

In ''Love Is Cause It Has to Be'' she celebrates the beauty of black romantic expression.

In Part Three, ''Stranger in a Strange Land,'' she challenges ''The Liberal'' and denounces words of pity:

> Pity implies superior situation
> but, reflecting upon things in their proper
> relations,
> victim though I am,
> I am not disgraced (23).

Richards adds that the real pathology is in the impact on white society.

''A Black Woman Speaks,'' a pungent eight-page poem, first written in 1950 and performed before the Women for Peace group in Chicago, was to remain a part of her repertoire more than twenty years later. It was published as a part of Richards's book of poetry in 1974, and her one-woman dramatization on television was later to result in an Emmy Award (1975). She has also performed it at colleges, libraries, and book fairs.

Richards's message is to white women. She implores them to ''remember'' history. She identifies both black and white women as victims of the white supremacists:

> White womanhood too is enslaved;
> the difference is degree. . . .
>
> If they counted my teeth,
> they did appraise your thigh.
> Sold to the highest bidder the same as I. . . .
>
> Oh God, how great is a woman's fear
> who for a stone, a cold, cold stone
> would not defend honor,
> love nor dignity.

White women were ''exiled to vanity'' while black women fought a battle for all women. Richards concludes with an appeal for unity and common purpose:

> Remember, you have never known me.
> You've been seeing me as white supremacy
> would have me be.
> But I will be myself —
> FREE!
>
> JUSTICE!
> PEACE!
> PLENTY!
> for every MAN
> WOMAN
> CHILD
> who walks the earth!
> This is my fight.
> If you will fight with me, then take my hand,
> that our land may come at last to be a place of
> peace
> and human dignity.

References

Abramson, Doris E. *Negro Playwrights in The American Theatre, 1925-1959*. New York: Columbia University Press, 1969.

''Beah Richards, Max Roach, William Marshall to Teach.'' *Jet* 42 (21 September 1972): 56.

Bogle, Donald. *Black Arts Annual 1987/88*. New York: Garland Publishing, 1989.

———. *Blacks in American Films and Television.* New York: Garland Publishing, 1988.

———. *Toms, Coons, Mulattoes, Mammies, & Bucks.* New York: Viking Press, 1973.

Hatch, James V., editor. *Black Theater, U.S.A., Forty-five Plays by Black Americans, 1847-1974.* New York: Macmillan, 1974.

"How to Survive in Hollywood between Gigs." *Ebony* 33 (October 1978): 33-40.

Lanker, Brian. *I Dream A World.* New York: Stewart, Tabori and Chang, 1989. Photograph, p. 58.

Marill, Alvin H. *The Films of Sidney Poitier.* Secaucus, N.J.: Citadel Press, 1978.

Mitchell, Loften. *Black Drama.* San Francisco: Leswing Press, 1967.

Poitier, Sidney. *This Life.* New York: Knopf, 1980.

Peterson, Bernard L., Jr. *Contemporary Black American Playwrights and Their Plays.* Westport Conn.: Greenwood Press, 1988.

Richards, Beah. *A Black Woman Speaks.* Los Angeles: Inner City Press, 1974.

Rush, Theressa G., ed. *Black American Writers.* Vol. 2. Westport, Conn.: Greenwood, 1983.

Sims-Wood, Janet. "The Black Female: Mammy, Jemima, Sapphire, and Other Images." In *Images of Blacks in American Culture.* Edited by Jessie Carney Smith. Westport, Conn.: Greenwood Press, 1988.

Who's Who among Black America, 1990/91. 6th ed. Detroit: Gale Research, 1990.

Wilkerson, Margaret B., ed. *9 Plays by Black Women.* New York: New American Library, 1986.

Keith A. Winsell

Fannie M. Richards

(1840-1922)

Educator, school founder, social reformer, civil rights activist

In December 1970 students from Jones Annex Elementary School in Detroit, Michigan, attended a tea in honor of Fannie Moore Richards. The tea resulted from Pearlye J. Rudolph's search to answer her students' question, "Who was Detroit's first professional black teacher?"

Fannie Moore Richards was born October 1, 1840, in Fredericksburg, Virginia. Some biographies give the year as 1841 and one family history lists the date as 1842. Her father, Adolph Richards, born in Guadaloupe, had come to Virginia seeking a more favorable climate because of his poor health. "He was a Latin of some Negro blood, had noble ancestry, and had led an honorable career." When he came to Fredericksburg he chose not to emphasize his nobility or his London education but to open: "a shop for wood-turning, painting and glazing" (Hartgrove, 24).

Fannie Richards's mother, Maria Louise (Moore) Richards, a native of Fredericksburg, was the daughter of Edwin Moore, a Scotchman of Edinburgh, and his wife, who was a free black woman from Toronto. Having been born in a time and a place where the teaching of blacks was allowed, Maria Richards also had been well educated. She actively sought to provide a strong education for each of her fourteen—or five (see Jackson's article)—children. "All of them were well grounded in the rudiments of education and given a taste for higher things" (Hartgrove, 23-24).

By the time the Richards children were school age, Virginia laws had made the task of educating black children a difficult one. Some of the Richards secretly received their education in the homes of free blacks. In some homes, courageous teachers reclined on couches while presenting their lessons to avoid the penalty of a law that forbade anyone to sit or to stand to teach a black. Often the teachers kept wood splinters close by so that they could pretend to be teaching the children how to make matches. One of the Richards boys risked being exiled from his home state by attending school in Washington.

Despite such hardships, many members of the Richards household grew to become contributing members of their own communities. Maria Moore Richards "lived to see . . . the distinguished services they rendered and the desirable connections that they made after the Civil War." John D. Richards actively participated in Republican party politics in Detroit. Evalina Richards married Joseph Ferguson, who studied medicine and became a Detroit physician. Julia Richards's husband, Thomas F. Carey, owned a business in Detroit. The Carey's daughter married David Augustus Straker, a lawyer, Louisiana administrator, and then Michigan's first black judge. Fannie Richards, along with her friend Booker T. Washington, believed that education provided a key to a better life and chose to devote her own life to teaching.

A part of Fannie Richards's commitment may have come not only from her parents' concern for education but also from watching and hearing about the challenges that her older brothers and sisters faced in their efforts to obtain an education. One source states that her own education probably began in a clandestine school in the home of Richard De Baptiste. Another article gives Toronto, Canada, as the site of her first schooling. However, a June 20, 1915, *Detroit News Tribune* interview with Richards states that her early education took place in the Detroit school system. The family moved to Detroit after Adolph Richards's death in 1851.

Some accounts record that the Richards family moved first to Toronto and then to Detroit when Fannie Richards was a teenager. Whether she was in Toronto as a young child or not, Fannie Richards did attend normal school in Toronto, studying English, history, drawing and needlework. No mention of further education appears in the *News Tribune* article or in other biographies. A family history, however, states that following normal school, Richards studied in Germany, where she was introduced to the concept of kindergarten.

Richards Begins Teaching Career

The exact nature of her own education is not as important as what she did with it. Fannie Richards returned to Detroit and in 1863 opened a private school for black children. By 1868 she was teaching in the public school system, a task to which she devoted herself for more than forty years. Other blacks before her had taught in the schools of Detroit, but Fannie Richards was the first black to become a full-time professional teacher in the city.

W. B. Hartgrove's story in the *Journal of Negro History* tells of how her public school career began and illustrates Fannie Richards' resourcefulness and her determination to pursue what was best for those whom she taught:

> Going to her private school one morning, she saw a carpenter repairing a building. Upon inquiry she learned that it was to be opened as Colored School Number 2. She went immediately to William D. Wilkins, a member of the board of education, who, impressed with the personality of the young woman, escorted her to the office of superintendent of schools, Duane Dotty. After some discussion of the matter Miss Richards filed an application, assured that she would be notified to take the next examination. At the appointed time she presented herself along with several other applicants who hoped to obtain the position. Miss Richards ranked highest and was notified to report for duty the following September. Early one morning she proceeded to her private school in time to inform her forty pupils of the desirable change and conducted them in a body to their new home (Hartgrove, 31).

Concern for her students later led Richards to campaign actively against the school board in favor of desegregation. At that time, whites received twelve years of schooling, blacks only six. Richards felt that blacks deserved equal rights to the benefits provided by public education. She and her family, especially her brother John, took part in the struggle to obtain those rights. John Bagley, who later became the governor of Michigan, led the campaign that was carried to the supreme court in Lansing. Understanding Richards's concern about the court decision, Bagley waved a white handkerchief, a prearranged symbol of victory, from the train window as he returned to Detroit. "Fannie Richards and her pupils cheered. They formed a circle, held hands, and danced around the room" ("First Black Teacher," 9).

Members of the school board must have recognized Richards's ability to teach. They retained her as one of three black teachers in the school system. For the rest of her career, she faithfully and enthusiastically fulfilled her role as teacher in Detroit's Everett Elementary School. During part of that time she served as the city's first kindergarten teacher. When she retired, she was able to tell a newspaper reporter, "There was never a day when I wasn't glad to go to the children—when I did not really enjoy what I had to do" ("Colored Teacher Loved Children").

The school board's confidence in Richards was well-founded. She worked hard at the task that she enjoyed so much. As she sought to provide a quality education for her students, she continued to educate herself. W. B. Hartgrove comments that even in her early days of teaching in the school that she started Richards was "doing a higher grade of work than that then undertaken in the public schools" (Hartgrove, 30). Five years before her retirement, an article in a Detroit newspaper praised her because "she had kept her interest in modern pedagogic methods, [and] maintained a high standard of scholarship in her school" (Hartgrove, 32). Fannie Richards herself stated:

> The methods have changed a good deal since the time that I started in and it would be easy to lag behind, but I try not to. It means continual reading and study to keep up with the modern way of doing things, but I manage to do it, and when the time comes that I cannot do my work in a satisfactory manner I want the Board of Education to discharge me and get some one else (Hartgrove, 31-32).

Richards's love for her students knew no barriers of class or of color. She taught students, rich and poor, of many nationalities and rejoiced in the particular strengths that she observed among them. Her love also extended beyond the walls of her classroom. Many children "were accustomed to surrounding and clinging to her as she walked to and from school. She visited the homes of her pupils and invited them to her home" (Hayden, 525). For more than fifty years she taught Sunday school at Detroit's Second Baptist Church, the oldest black congregation in the city.

Phillis Wheatley Home Founded

Richards's active concern for others included older people as well as younger ones. Seeing the plight of elderly black women who had no one to support them, she determined to provide help. With savings from her salary and with the assistance of other people, she founded Phillis Wheatley Home, an organization that cared for the needs of aging black women from 1898 to 1967. She served as its first president, and after its incorporation in 1901, as chairman of the board of trustees. Some writers estimate that Richards donated to this society almost half of her salary, which ranged from $450 in her early days of teaching to $700 at the time of her retirement. The choice of the name Phillis Wheatley, "the first African American, the first slave, and only the second woman to publish poetry in the United States," typifies Fannie Richards's belief in the abilities of blacks.

Faith in black Americans comprised an integral part of Richards's personality, and that faith undoubtedly played a significant role in motivating her students of all races to achieve. She exhibited in her own life her belief in what blacks, or any other people, could accomplish if they desired to do so. She took special delight in the advancements that she witnessed in Detroit's black community. She said:

> No race has advanced more rapidly than ours, and it has not shown all that it can do yet. Just since I have been in the schools here in Detroit there have been great changes for our people and all due to educational advantages. We have Negroes who are actually wealthy, who have seen the opportunities in real estate and have taken advantage of them; we have fine doctors and excellent lawyers, but over and above all this they have gained culture, refinement and can take their place equally with any race ("Colored Teacher Loved Children").

Richards did take her place equally among Detroit educators. She recognized the existence of prejudice, but her dedication, expertise, and pleasing, sweet personality merited and received respect. At the close of her career she was able to state:

> I was accepted always for what I could do and there was no discrimination made against me because of my color. If there was something to be decided by the teachers in our school, my word carried as much weight as another's, and if there were plans made for picnics or excursions I was always consulted too. . . . I accompanied the teachers on their annual trips to Washington, not so much for the educational advantages of the trip, but just to lend "color" to the excursions, I always told them ("Colored Teacher Loved Children").

Such optimism and humor must have contributed to Richards's success not only in working with other teachers but also in working with her students and with the school administration. Her selection as honorary vice-president of the Freedman's Progress Commission, created by the Michigan legislature on April 21, 1915, stood as an appropriate recognition of her success and of her contribution to the state.

On June 6, 1915, Fannie Richards retired from teaching and was granted a pension by the school board. A newspaper reporter described her as "a tall, stately white-haired Negro woman" who "has the same kindly manner and the same enthusiasm today that she had for her work away back in 1871, when as a young girl she entered the Everett School." In talking with the reporter, she emphasized the invaluable contribution that others had made to her own life rather than the service that she had rendered: "I know my children loved me; I have enjoyed every minute of my life ("Colored Teacher Loved Children").

Fannie Moore Richards died on February 13, 1922, at the home that she shared with her nieces, Mrs. W. H. Bailey and Mrs. C. P. Covington, and was buried in a family plot at Elmwood Cemetery. The newspapers of the times seldom carried stories about black deaths, but editorial writers in Detroit and throughout Michigan paid fulsome tribute to this "woman of impeccable reputation" ("First Black Teacher"). The Detroit Association of Colored Women's Clubs held a memorial service in her honor.

In the half-century following her death, Richards has been honored on a number of occasions. For American Education Week, October 25-31, 1970, the Detroit Public Library and the public school system prepared an exhibit about her work. On December 21, 1970, artist Carl Owens presented his portrait of Fannie Richards to the Detroit Historical Commission. The unveiling took place at the Detroit Historical Museum during a tea sponsored by the museum, the public schools, and the public library. Ten students from Jones Annex Elementary School paid their tribute to her alongside adults who told Richards's story and reminisced about her life. Eugene Thomas created an edible cake-portrait of the honoree for the occasion. Richards's niece, Frances Covington, was also included in the honors that day.

Detroit's mayor declared October 1, 1975, as Fannie Richards' Day in the city. Second Baptist Church hosted a Marker Dedication Program. The Detroit Historical Museum invited citizens to visit its continuing exhibit of the life and works of Fannie Richards in its Urban History Hall.

As recently as 1987, Richards and other family members were featured at a symposium on Blacks in Our Sesquicentennial as a part of the African World Festival in Detroit. In February of that year, the *Detroit Free Press* carried an article about her, mentioning the marker that stands at Richards's homesite and reviewing the major events in her life.

In the interview following Richards's retirement, she told the reporter, "It is through education that blacks are going to make their mark, and that mark has not yet been reached" ("Colored Teacher Loved Children"). In his article written less than a year later, W. B. Hartgrove assessed the influence of this one black teacher:

> Miss Richards estimates that in the years of school work, she has had in her room an average of fifty pupils a term, although sometimes the attendance overflowed to a much greater number. With eighty-eight terms of teaching to her credit, the number of pupils who owe part of their education to "this gentle and cultured woman" amounts well up into the tens of thou-

sands, enough to populate a fair-sized city (Hartgrove, 32).

More than fifty years later, the *Detroit Historical Society Bulletin* paid tribute to Fannie Moore Richards, a woman who "left an indelible mark on education in Detroit" ("Tea at Museum").

References

Black Historic Sites Committee. *BHS: Black Historical Sites in Detroit*. Detroit: Detroit Historical Department, 1989. Includes photograph of Richards.

"City Honors 1st Black Teacher." *Detroit News* 30 September 1975.

"Colored Teacher Loved Children and Enjoyed 44 Years in Service." Interview. *Detroit News Tribune* 20 June 1915.

"Family Portrait. . . . Fanny Richards" *Ferguson/Webb News* July/August 1987. Includes photograph.

"First Black Teacher to be Honored." *Detroit Schools* 20 October 1970. 9-10. Includes photograph.

Hartgrove, W. B. "The Story of Maria Louise Moore and Fannie M. Richards." *Journal of Negro History* 1 (January 1916): 23-33.

Hayden, J. Carleton. "Fannie Moore Richards." Eds. Rayford W. Logan and Michael R. Winston. *Dictionary of American Negro Biography*. New York: Norton, 1982. 524-25.

Jackson, Harvey C. "Pioneers and Builders in Michigan." *Negro History Bulietin* 5 (May 1942): 177. Includes photograph.

Lawrence, Beverly Hall. "This Teacher Was a Pioneer." Detroit *Free Press* February 1987. Includes photograph.

"Negress, Teacher, Honored in Death." *Detroit Times* 21 March 1922.

"Oldest Negro Teacher in Detroit Dies at 80." *Detroit News* 16 February 1922.

Robinson, Wilhelmena S. *Historical Negro Biographies*. Cornwell Heights, Pa.: Association for the Study of Afro-American Life and History, 1978. 116-17.

"Tea at Museum Honors First Negro Teacher." *Detroit Historical Society Bulletin*, (January 1971): 14-15. Includes portrait of Richards.

"Tea to Honor Fannie M. Richards, First Black Career Teacher in Detroit." *Detroit Schools* 18 December 1970.

Collections

The Burton Historical Collection of the Detroit Public Library contains miscellaneous records and publications on Fannie Moore Richards.

Marie Garrett

Gloria Richardson

(1922-)

Civil rights activist

Gloria St. Clair Hayes Richardson led the Second Ward of Cambridge, Maryland, during the turbulent sixties in efforts to desegregate the city. Richardson was born May 6, 1922, in Baltimore, Maryland, the only child of John Edwards Hayes and Madel Pauline (St. Clair) Hayes. She lived in Baltimore six years before moving to Cambridge, Maryland. Her family was one of the free black families in Maryland. Her grandfather, H. Maynadier St. Clair, was a city council member in Cambridge from 1912 to 1946. Gloria St. Clair Hayes Richardson attended Frederick Douglass High School (now Maces Lane High School), and in 1942 graduated from Howard University.

In June 1962, Richardson became cochair of Cambridge Non-violent Action Committee (CNAC), and with that she became the virtual leader of the black community in Cambridge. Richardson saw fundamental problems facing blacks in Cambridge as a lack of adequate housing, discrimination in the educational process, lack of equal job opportunity, and poor health. After a survey of the total black community, fifteen demands were made in the areas of employment, housing, and health care. The attack was on the entire system of segregation with demands for equal treatment on all scores, including employment, police protection, and schools. Then, in addition to segregation itself, the economic and social systems that segregation defended were attacked—housing, employment, working conditions, and education.

During spring 1963, Richardson and the CNAC appealed to the City Council to hear its demands and organized outside support for possible demonstrations. On March 25, 1963, Richardson and cochair Inez Grubb appeared at a meeting of the city council to inform Mayor Calvin Mowbray that blacks wanted integration immediately. Several days later Richardson and her followers began picketing and sit-ins. The next seven weeks saw demonstrations at City Hall, the County Courthouse, and the jail. In all, Richardson and eighty protesters were arrested.

In May 1963, the much publicized "Penny Trials" were held. A mass trial of the eighty activists resulted in each being fined a penny and given a suspended sentence (CNAC,

47). On May 14, 1963, Richardson, her daughter Donna, and her mother, Mabel St. Clair Booth, were arrested. Richardson and her mother were arrested at the Dizzyland Restaurant. By night's end, sixty-two persons had been arrested and state police and K-9 dogs arrived to assist local police (*Daily Banner*, 15 May 1963).

A tenuous peace followed, with a committee appointed by Judge W. Laird Henry agreeing that five demands should be met: complete desegregation of public places; complete desegregation of public schools, with Negro students assigned to schools nearest them; creation of equal employment opportunities in industries and stores, beginning with an initial minimum goal of ten percent hiring of Negroes in each place; building of a public housing project for Negroes and a study of sewer and sidewalk needs; and an end to all forms of public brutality and appointment of a Negro deputy sheriff (*Washington Post*, 19 May 1963).

This peace was shattered on May 25, 1963, when twelve juveniles were arrested for creating a disturbance while picketing the Board of Education office. They were released in the custody of their parents and expelled from school. Picketing, as well as a general economic boycott, continued in Cambridge. On May 31, 1963, Richardson appealed to Attorney General Robert F. Kennedy for a federal investigation of violations of constitutional rights in Cambridge. Compounding the restlessness in Cambridge was action on the state level by segregationist groups to block the June 2, 1963, application of the Public Accommodation Law by securing petitions to put the statute to a referendum vote in 1964. Further, the sentencing on June 10, 1963, of two juveniles, Dinez White and Dwight Cromwell, to indeterminate terms in correction schools, precipitated immediate, all-out demonstrations. Violence broke out. Fires started and incendiary bombs were found. Richardson again appealed to Robert Kennedy for federal aid.

On June 13, 1963, state troopers blocked all approaches to the black district. The next day, Governor Tawes of Maryland met with Richardson and other leaders in Annapolis and announced that he was sending in the National Guard to create a climate for a peaceful settlement (*New York Times*, 15 June 1963). Martial law was imposed on Cambridge. On June 15, 1963, about 500 Maryland National Guard troops—the entire Eastern Shore Battalion—and about 235 troopers of the Maryland State Police force were either on patrol or on call in the bivouacs in the Cambridge Armory, the American Legion Hall, and in nearby motels.

The National Guard remained in Cambridge until July 8, 1963. The day the National Guard left Cambridge, students tried to enter Dizzyland Restaurant, resulting in a much-publicized confrontation. The next day, racial violence flared again. On July 10, 1963, Richardson met with Maceo Hubbard, a seventeen-year veteran of the Justice Department and civil rights lawyer sent to calm Cambridge. Violence continued, becoming most pronounced on July 11, 1963. The National Guard returned on that evening and imposed new, more restrictive bans on the citizens.

Demonstrators were halted by a brief moratorium to allow a biracial commission to demonstrate good faith. In the meantime, Robert Kennedy, in a speech on July 17, criticized Richardson for the violence in Cambridge. She immediately sent a letter of protest. During this period, Richardson warned that President Kennedy might have to visit Cambridge to avert a civil war.

On July 22, at the invitation of Assistant Attorney General Burke Marshall, Civil Rights Division, a conference was convened in Washington. The session included Attorney General Kennedy and Robert Weaver, head of the Housing and Home Finance Agency. On June 23, 1963, the five-point Treaty of Cambridge was signed by blacks and Cambridge city officials in Attorney General Kennedy's office.

The points of the agreement called for complete and immediate desegregation of the public schools (with integrated busing) and hospitals in the county; construction of two hundred units of low-rent public housing for Negroes; employment of a Negro in the Cambridge office of the Maryland Department of Employment Security and in the post office; appointment of a human relations commission; and adoption of a charter amendment that provided for desegregation of places of public accommodation.

If twenty percent of the voters filed a petition for a referendum, the desired implementation would not occur. In spite of the hopes of those who signed the "treaty," more than twenty-five percent of the voters signed petitions, forcing a referendum.

Richardson and the local NAACP divided on support of the public accommodation amendment. Richardson's view was that, as a moral issue, blacks already had these constitutional rights and they should not be subjected to a vote: "Public Accommodations are a right that cannot be given or taken away by a vote" (Kempton, 15-17). The defeat of the referendum was laid at Gloria Richardson's feet.

Activist's Efforts Desegregate Cambridge, Maryland

The following occurred in the aftermath of the concords: The day immediately following the signing, county-wide desegregation of the school system was ordered; bus transportation was desegregated with students discharged at the closest school; a black woman was placed in the local Maryland employment office within a week to ensure all job listings were available; steps were put in motion for hiring black postal carriers in the post office; urban renewal was brought into Cambridge; the hospital and library were desegregated; and a black policeman was promoted.

In September 1963, Richardson's quest for civil and economic justice continued to be realized when twenty-eight black children entered previously all-white schools. A second success was the decision of the Maryland Court of Appeals on October 8, 1963, reversing the sentences of Dinez White and Dwight Cromwell. Additionally, in January 1964, the United States Civil Rights Commission released a forty-nine page report that underscored the findings of the CNAC in Cambridge—criticizing the governor, private industry, economic conditions, and the state personnel commissioner for contributing to the problems of blacks in Cambridge. In March 1964 distribution of federal surplus food parcels began.

In June, Secretary of Labor Willard Wirtz and Attorney General Kennedy announced an on-the-job-training program for two hundred employed blacks in Cambridge. Designed by the Urban League under the Manpower Development Act, the program would be administered by Morgan State College. This was a long-sought goal of Richardson, who presaged the War on Poverty view that economic oppression was just as violent as civil injustice.

Yet new obstacles were created. Perhaps the most disheartening episode occurred when Alabama Governor George Wallace spoke on May 2, 1964, at the Fireman's Arena (the skating rink that had been the focus of many desegregation efforts). His presence sparked spontaneous reactions all over the country. Many civil rights leaders and students attended a rally at the Elks Club the same evening. Following the Elks Club rally the marchers, led by Richardson, were dispersed by tear gas. Richardson and thirteen others were arrested. In July 1964, the same month the National Guard officially withdrew from Cambridge, President Lyndon B. Johnson signed into law the Civil Rights Act. In August, Gloria Richardson left Cambridge to move to New York. She married her second husband, Frank Dandridge, whom she met during the Cambridge movement. He was a free-lance photographer on assignment there. Richardson believed that the Johnson Administration's War on Poverty and the Civil Rights Act would make a substantial difference in the lives of blacks.

Criticized by many, including Kennedy, Martin Luther King, the NAACP, columnists, and television commentators, Richardson held true to her faith in a moral cause, her belief in how to achieve results, and her compassion for the alienated. Her direct action had been a powerful weapon in the civil rights movement. She created a climate for change in Cambridge. Richardson said, "This was a first plateau. Since then other steps [were] made. Blacks philosophically [believed] they [could] challenge the status quo" (Gloria Richardson memorandum to Brock, December 1989).

Throughout the Cambridge Movement, Richardson established working contacts with many of the prominent civil rights proponents; Malcolm X, Stokely Carmichael, Adam Clayton Powell, Lena Storne, Dick Gregory, and John Lewis are a few. She worked with William Hansen and Reginald Robinson, field secretaries of the Student Non-Violent Coordinating Committee (SNCC), Clarence Logan of the Civic Interest Group (Cambridge), and others.

Commenting on persons who influenced her life, Richardson said:

> One of my inspirations, and I had a lot of them, was Rayford Logan who taught me history at Howard, and Highland Lewis (Ja Jahannes interview with Gloria Richardson, 1988).

Richardson is currently program officer in the Department for the Aging, New York City.

References

Carson, Clayborne. In *Struggle: SNCC and the Black Awakening of the 1960's*. Cambridge: Harvard University Press, 1981.

CNAC Summer Staff. "The Negro World of Cambridge, Maryland: A Study in Social Change." Cambridge, Maryland, 1963.

Daily Banner 15 May 1963.

Giddings, Paula. *When and Where I Enter*. New York: Morrow, 1984.

Kempton, Murray. "Gloria, Gloria." *New Republic* (16 November 1963): 15-17.

Kent, George Robert. "The Negro in Politics in Dorchester County, Maryland, 1920-1960." Master's Thesis, University of Maryland, 1961.

New York Times, 15 June 1963.

New York Times, July 1963.

Richardson, Gloria. Interview with Gil Noble, 26 February 1981.

Richardson, Gloria. Interview with Ja Jahannes, 1988.

Washington Post, 19 May 1963.

Wilmington News, 13 June 1963.

Wolk, Allan. *The Presidency and Civil Rights: Eisenhower to Nixon*. Cranbury, N.J.: Associated University Presses, 1971.

Zinn, Howard. *SNCC: The New Abolitionists*. Boston: Beacon Press, 1964.

Collections

The Ja Jahannes interview and the Gil Noble interviews with Gloria Richardson are located in the dean's office, School of Humanities and Social Sciences, Savannah State College, Savannah, GA 31404. Some personal papers may be in Richardson's possession but many files of SNCC and CNAC were lost as a result of fire in the Cambridge headquarters. Very little scholarship is devoted to Richardson outside of current newspapers and magazines. Photographs of Richardson can be secured from UPI/Bettmann Newsphotos.

Annette K. Brock

Florida Ruffin Ridley

(1861-1943)

Clubwoman, writer, educator, social worker

Florida Yates Ruffin Ridley, clubwoman, writer, educator, and social worker, was born in Boston, Massachusetts, the second of five children and only daughter of Josephine (St. Pierre) Ruffin and George Lewis Ruffin. Like her mother, with whom Ridley often worked closely, Ridley was one of the exceptional women who provided leadership for the black community at the turn of the century. They began the women's club movement with the aim of social reform and their extaordinary work produced outstanding accomplishments.

Ridley's mother, a prominent clubwoman and civic activist, was a charter member of the Women's Era Club, the National Federation of Afro-American Women, the National Association of Colored Women, and the Northeastern Federation of Women's Clubs. Her father was one of the first blacks admitted to practice law in Boston, was a graduate of Harvard law school and a municipal court judge for the Charleston district.

Florida Ruffin Ridley, whose maternal grandparents were of English, French, African, and Indian ancestry, resembled her mother, having the same light brown complexion and soft curly hair, which she wore long and twisted on top of her head. An eloquent speaker and charming woman, she was educated at Boston Teachers College and Boston University. Ridley taught in the Boston public schools. She and her husband, Ulysses A. Ridley, were the parents of two children, Ulysses A. Ridley, Jr., and Constance J. Ridley. Versatile and active in community affairs, Ridley was one of the founders of the Society for the Collection of Negro Folklore in Boston in March 1890. The society, which met at the Revere Street Church, was one of the earliest groups of black folklorists.

In February 1893 Florida Ridley assisted her mother, Josephine Ruffin, and Maria Baldwin, principal of the Agassiz High School in Cambridge, in organizing the Woman's Era Club. Josephine Ruffin was president of the Woman's Era Club for many years. Florida Ridley read a report at the first meeting indicating that the club was open to all women regardless of race, but black women provided the leadership. She spoke of a leaflet published by the club to protest lynching. The Woman's Era Club supported work outside of Boston, namely, a kindergarten conducted by the Georgia Educational League. The club contributed twenty dollars a month for the support of the kindergarten. Florida Ridley spent three years in Atlanta, Georgia, working with this project.

Ridley joined her mother in promoting a national organization of black clubwomen. She served as corresponding secretary of the Committee on Arrangements, which organized the first national conference of black women in Boston at Berkeley Hall in July 1895. Circulars, with the program, dates, and other information, were mailed to black women throughout the United States. Letters of response from women who were engaged in missionary and charitable work, sewing circles, reading clubs, literary societies, mothers' meetings, and community service organizations were sent to the Woman's Era Club, in Ruffin's home, at 103 Charles Street. The conference convened under the leadership of Josephine Ruffin, who delivered the keynote address challenging the women to recognize and accept the need for advancement and reform. Delegates from sixteen states and the District of Columbia attended the opening session. The convention discussed issues that were critical to the black community, including temperance, education, political equality, lynching, and the convict lease system. Ridley was appointed to the committee concerned with the Georgia convict lease system, Florida state school law, and lynching.

Ridley Becomes Officer of National Women's Federation

The outcome of the national conference was the organization of the National Federation of Afro-American Women (NFAAW) and the selection of the *Woman's Era* as its official organ. The primary objective of the NFAAW was the establishment of a sisterhood of Afro-American women and the encouragement of joint efforts in uplifting the race. Margaret Murray Washington, the wife of Booker T. Washington, was elected president of the NFAAW, and Florida Ridley became the recording secretary.

The following year, 1896, two national women's organizations held their conferences in Washington, D.C. The Colored Women's League, under the presidency of Helen A. Cook, met on July 14-15. The National Federation of Afro-American Women held its meeting on July 20-22. The two organizations merged into a permanent organization, the National Association of Colored Women. Florida Ridley assisted in editing the *Woman's Era* until 1900.

Efforts were made to strengthen the new national association through its department that served the interests of its members—Sarah Garnet, Mary Church Terrell, Florida Ruffin Ridley, Josephine St. Pierre Ruffin, and others—who were involved in the suffrage movement. Ridley was active in the Brookline Equal Suffrage Association between 1894 and 1898.

During World War I, Florida Ridley and other clubwomen were encouraged to join the war effort. She took a special secretarial course at Boston University in 1916 and upon completing it devoted her time to war activities. Ridley worked at the YWCA Hostess House at Camp Upton, Long Island, New York, and was executive secretary of the

Soldiers Comfort Unit from 1917 to 1919. This organization, the Solider's Comfort Unit, later became the League of Women for Community Service and retained Ridley as its executive secretary until 1925. Ridley broadened the scope of her political involvement during the presidential campaign of 1924 by campaigning for the Democratic nominee, John W. Davis. She toured several cities on the east coast, speaking in Atlantic City and Trenton, New Jersey, and Wilmington, Delaware.

Ridley had a keen sense of social consciousness and dedication to community service. Active in social welfare work, she was a member of the board of directors of the Robert Gould Shaw Settlement House from 1919 to 1925. A cooperative committee centralized the social service group, including the Robert Shaw Settlement House, the Harriet Tubman House, and the Boston Urban League. Ridley was the first editor of the *Social Service News*, the journal of the Co-operative Committee of Social Agencies, and she was affiliated with the Urban League.

In 1929 Ridley was elected secretary of the Lewis Hayden Memorial Association. She remained at her home in Boston until the latter part of her life, when she moved to Toledo, Ohio, to live with her daughter, Jessie Heslip. A pioneer in the founding and development of black women's clubs and a leader in Boston civic and social life, Florida Ruffin Ridley died in March 1943 at the age of eighty-two. Funeral services were held in Toledo and in Boston at the St. Bartholomew Episcopal Church.

References

Amsterdam News 27 March 1943.

Brown, Hallie Q. *Homespun Heroines and Other Women of Distinction*. 1926. Reprinted. New York: Oxford University Press, 1988. 152-53.

A History of the Club Movement Among the Colored Women of the United States of America. Washington, D.C.: National Association of Colored Women's Clubs, 1902. A photograph of Florida Ruffin Ridley appears opposite p. 5.

Ridley, Florida Ruffin. "Memorial to Josephine St. Pierre Ruffin." *National Notes* Septemer/October 1928.

———. "The Negro in Boston." *Our Boston* 2 (January 1927): 15-20.

The Woman's Era 24 March 1894.

Who's Who in Colored America. New York: Who's Who in Colored America Corp., 1941-44. 309-310.

Collections

Birth and death records of Florida Ridley Ruffin are in the Massachusetts Bureau of Vital Statistics. Incomplete files of *The Woman's Era* are in the Moorland-Spingarn Research Center, Howard University, and in the Boston Public Library. Copies of the NACW *National Notes* are in the Moorland-Spingarn Collection.

Floris Barnett Cash

Eslanda Goode Robeson

(1896-1965)

Chemist, business manager, Pan-Africanist, anthropologist, activist, writer

Although biographical and critical material abounds on the career of Paul Robeson, a full-length biography of his wife, Eslanda Goode Robeson, who is astonishing in her own right, has not yet been attempted. In addition to her role as Robeson's loving partner and a tireless promoter of his career, she distinguished herself equally through her own endeavors in anthropology and political activism.

Eslanda Cardoza Goode Robeson was born into the black middle-class community of Washington, D.C. Her father, John Goode, had risen above his slave origins and held a position as a clerk in the War Department. Her mother, Eslanda (Cardoza) Goode, was a product of South Carolina's

Eslanda Goode Robeson

free black community and was descended from the union of Isaac Nuñez Cardozo, a Spanish Jew of considerable wealth, and an octoroon slave woman. His son, Essie Robeson's grandfather, Francis Louis Cardozo, was one of six children from this union. He graduated from the University of Glasgow and became a pastor of a Congregational church in New Haven, Connecticut. Henry Ward Beecher proudly referred to him as "the most highly educated Negro in America" (Duberman, 35).

Cardozo, through the American Missionary Association, received a grant of ten thousand dollars to found the Avery Institute, the first black secondary school in Charleston, South Carolina. After the Civil War, Cardozo became a prominent racial spokesman and held the office of state treasurer during Reconstruction.

When Robeson, or Essie, as she was known to all her intimates, was six, her father died from the effects of alcoholism and her mother took her and her two brothers to live in New York City, where they would not have to attend segregated schools. The elder Eslanda set an example for her daughter by plunging into the study of osteopathy and beauty culture. Within a short period of time, she opened her own practice, charged high fees, and promptly became a success. Eslanda Goode's clientele included such wealthy society figures as Mrs. Joseph Pulitzer and Mrs. George Gould.

Robeson had arrived in Harlem at a propitious time. Thus, she was fortunate to see and experience the glorious beginnings of the Harlem Renaissance. She first attended the State University of Illinois but went on to complete her education at Teachers College of Columbia University. She also completed one year at Columbia University Medical School.

Historian Barbara Ransby says that it was during these years that Robeson first became politically active (22). The Bolshevik Revolution stimulated radical thinking among young intellectuals in New York, and Robeson's natural interest in racial equality propelled her into this realm. She became close friends with John Reed and other activists and developed both left-wing political views and a deepened commitment to social change. While her future husband, Paul Robeson, became known for his social and political views, he came to them gradually through his experience singing and performing in different parts of the world. Eslanda Robeson preceded him in his thinking and probably deserves some credit for impressing upon him the importance of such commitment. The fact that Robeson literally sacrificed his fortunes and career to the cause of equality dramatically illustrates how much he came to share in his wife's beliefs and goals.

When Eslanda Goode first saw Paul Bustill Robeson at Devann's Restaurant in Harlem during the autumn of 1920, Robeson was already a well-known figure. He had graduated Phi Beta Kappa from Rutgers, where he had also been an outstanding athlete on both the football and basketball teams. In 1919 he had moved to Harlem and was pursuing a law degree at Columbia. Although the huge, jovial, handsome young man naturally captured Essie Goode's eye, she did not meet him until several weeks later, when he was brought to Columbia's Presbyterian Hospital, where she worked, after an accident on the football field.

Although Paul Robeson was besieged by pretty girls, Essie Goode set her cap for Robeson and went after him in a calculated and systematic way that characterized much of her later life. In spite of this, their courtship was not all clear sailing. Paul Robeson still held intense feelings for Geraldine Maimie Neale, a young woman he had courted in his undergraduate days. Duberman suggests that although Essie Goode interested him, Robeson actually proposed to Neale first, only to be rebuffed. After a somewhat impulsive proposal to Goode in August 1921, the pair were married on the seventeenth of the month in Portchester, New York (Duberman, 38-41).

A wedding photograph readily explains the almost immediate attraction each felt for the other. Few men could match Robeson's masculine good looks when he was in his prime. In those days he stood six feet four inches tall and easily carried 205 pounds on his muscular frame. With the charm of his smile, he made friends wherever he went. Eslanda Robeson, small of stature, could not have been more different in her physical and emotional makeup. The photograph reveals that she had a fair complexion, regular features, and rich, full dark hair. Like her husband, she, too, had a charming and winning smile.

Essie Robeson graduated from Columbia with a bachelor of science degree in chemistry. She immediately made history by becoming the first black person to obtain employment as an analytical chemist and technician in the surgery and pathology department at Columbia Presbyterian Medical Center, where she was in charge of the laboratory. She was engaged in several research projects while in the laboratory.

Robeson himself graduated from Columbia Law School with the same distinction that characterized his undergraduate education and was hired by a prestigious white law firm. In spite of this, he found the work he was assigned to be without challenge. He realized that there would be few real opportunities for a black lawyer, even one with his gifts, and the realization was a depressing one.

Paul Robeson Changes Career

According to Graham, Paul and Essie Robeson had become friends with some of the show people who were putting on the many musical extravaganzas that were so much a part of the Harlem scene in the 1920s, and Paul had once accompanied some of them in some impromptu songs at a party. Essie had seen what an impression Paul's powerful baritone voice had made on the audience, and she got the idea of channeling her husband into show business. She convinced him to take the lead in a YMCA production of *Simon the Cyrenian*, one of *Three Plays for a Negro Theatre* written by Ridgely Torrence, a white lyric poet.

Against his better judgement, Paul Robeson took the lead

role of Simon, a black African who carries Christ's cross to Calvary. Robeson played to a packed house that was mesmerized by his performance. Later, this play would be considered a turning point in the depiction of blacks in American theater, because it was the first time that they were depicted as real people of human depth rather than as comical stereotypes (Hamilton, 19).

Members of the prestigious Provincetown Playhouse were in the audience, and they enthusiastically offered Robeson the lead in Eugene O'Neill's *The Emperor Jones*. Robeson, always a man of principle, refused the role on the grounds that he found the depiction of blacks as savages to be repugnant.

Robeson had made an impact, however, and in 1922 he was offered the lead in Mary Hoyt Wyborg's play *Taboo*. Essie Robeson encouraged him in this pursuit and hid from her husband the fact that she was seriously ill and required immediate surgery for adhesions from an old appendectomy. With characteristic precision, she gaily saw Paul off at the dock and wrote and postdated twenty-one letters that she gave to friends to mail to Europe for her, sent him a cheery cable at sea, then promptly checked herself into the hospital. Although the operation was successful, she suffered a variety of postoperative complications that kept her hospitalized for weeks. All of this she kept from Robeson for much of the duration of his tour (Duberman, 47-49).

Success on the stage had made Paul Robeson restless and dissatisfied with the law, and his return to his studies was marked with mediocrity. At graduation, two-thirds of his course grades were C's.

Louis William Stotesbury, a successful white alumnus of Rutgers and a trustee of the school, offered what seemed a golden opportunity to Paul Robeson. He became the first black man in the firm's offices. He gave Robeson the job of preparing an important brief for trial and, for a while, Robeson was diligent. However, the specter of racism in the office made him uncomfortable and, recognizing the hardships the younger man would face, Stotesbury told him frankly that his prospects in the law were probably limited. Unwilling to face such restrictions on his future, Paul Robeson left the firm and gave up law, something that caused him little anguish, considering the new direction his life seemed to be taking.

Success in London was followed by another offer in the fall of 1923 to play the leads in Eugene O'Neill's *All God's Chillun Got Wings* and a revival of *The Emperor Jones*. Eslanda Robeson resigned her position at Columbia Presbyterian Medical Center in fall 1925 and accompanied her husband to London. Soon Robeson was the toast of two continents and was regularly performing in both the United States and Europe. By 1926 they were making a European concert tour and Essie had left her career as a chemist to become Paul's full-time manager, booking him into concerts, shows, and motion picture roles.

The great irony was that although Paul Robeson was performing in white theaters and concert halls, he and Essie Robeson found that they could still be refused service at a coffee shop across the street. The adulation Paul Robeson received from white intellectuals did nothing to counteract the effects of this prejudice. Hamilton notes that "no single situation of their daily lives served to radicalize Paul and Essie more than these endless, petty incidents of racial discrimination and prejudice" (38). Essie Robeson began staying home more, partly in order to avoid these humiliations, but also because they were expecting a child. In 1927 their son, Paul, afterwards known as Pauli, was born.

In April 1928 the pair went to London, where Paul Robeson was starring in *Show Boat*. There they found themselves lionized by the British aristocracy, but they found other reasons to like Britain, too. In November 1928 the British Labor Party held a luncheon at the House of Commons for the Robesons. While there, each realized that there were other people besides American blacks for whom life was less than equal. They also realized that they were intensely sympathetic to Labor's views on social equality. They decided to settle in London in 1928 and maintained a residence there.

In the years that followed, Paul Robeson starred in *Othello*, a role he could never have played in the United States. Essie Robeson also began to come into her own, writing a compelling and at times revealing biography about Paul that came out in 1930. The biography was considered somewhat shocking because she discussed the possibility of Paul's infidelities with other women and lampooned whites who came to tour Harlem. Although the *New Republic* condemned the book, it was nonetheless tremendously successful and made for her a reputation as a writer.

The early thirties were turbulent times in Europe, as in the rest of the world. The Great Depression had affected most of the world, and political unrest in Germany saw the emigration of many German Jews into Great Britain. Times were no less turbulent for the Robesons, who separated for a couple of years. According to Duberman, Paul's entanglements with a number of white women in Great Britain strained, but did not sever the bonds between them (139-64).

At the end of 1934 the Robesons traveled to the Soviet Union. This was a particularly moving experience for both of them, because they were impressed with the ethnic tolerance they found everywhere they went. When they left to return to England a year later, it was with the wish that they could spend a part of every year there. It was a wish that was not to be fulfilled.

In spite of all this traveling and meeting the demands of Paul Robeson's career, Eslanda Robeson had undertaken a new direction in her own life—a growing interest in Africa and the study of anthropology. From 1935 to 1937 she studied anthropology at London University and in 1938 she studied at the London School of Economics. Here she began to understand that racism was being fostered by what she termed "interpreting" the Negro mind and character by white students and teachers. She later derided this thinking in her book *African Journey:*

> After more than a year of very wide reading and intensive study I began to get my intellectual feet wet. I am afraid that I began to be obstreperous. I soon became fed up with white students and teachers "interpreting" the Negro mind and character to me. Especially when I felt, as I did very often, that their interpretation was wrong.
>
> It went something like this: Me, I am a Negro, I know what we think, how we feel. I know this means that, and that means so-and-so.
>
> "Ah, no my dear, you're wrong. You see, you are a European. You can't possibly know how the primitive mind works until you study it, as we have done."
>
> "What do you mean I'm European? I am a Negro. I'm African myself. I'm what you call primitive. I have studied my mind, our minds. How dare you call me European!"
>
> "No, you're not primitive, my dear," they told me patiently, tolerantly, "you're educated and cultured, like us."
>
> "I'm educated because I went to school, because I was taught. You're educated because you went to school, were taught. I'm cultured because my people had the education and the means to achieve a good standard of living; that's the reason you're cultured. . . . Going to school and having money doesn't make me European. Having no schools and no money doesn't make the African primitive," I protested furiously.
>
> "No, no," they explained, "the primitive mind cannot grasp the kind of ideas we can; they have schools, but their schools have only simple subjects and crafts; it's all very different. . . . You've never been out there, you've never seen them and talked with them on their own home ground; you can't possibly know" (Robeson, *Negro Digest,* 87).

This kind of condescension to a woman of Eslanda Robeson's stripe was like adding a spark to fuel. In 1936 she decided to go to Africa to do the field work for her degree and, along with her she took her eight-year-old son, Pauli. She later explained this momentous decision:

> We have been profoundly disturbed by the realization that he (Paul, Jr.) had been living in an entirely white world since we had brought him and my mother to live with us in England . . . we must do something about that, we had said . . . a trip to the heart of Africa itself will be a revelation. He will see millions of other brown and black people, he will see a black world, he will see a black continent. So it was decided that Paul would go with me to Africa ("What Do the People of Africa Want," quoted in Ransby, 23).

This trip would prove to be a revelation to Essie Robeson as she explored the political, economic, and social realities of this black world. She quickly found that the suffering of the peasant population of this huge continent touched her more deeply than anything else she saw. Ransby tells us that she became a Pan-Africanist in the sense that she recognized the importance of racial pride and unity for the defeat of racism as an ideology. She also saw the need for African people to overcome tribalism and other divisions in order to combat successfully colonialism and imperialism. At the same time, Ransby asserts, she was not a black separatist and never hesitated to link the cause of African peoples with the cause of oppressed minorities the world over (23).

After her return to London, she and Paul Robeson traveled to Barcelona, where Paul entertained members of the International Brigade. What they saw there deeply impressed both of them, so much so that when Republican Spain fell in 1939, Paul Robeson discovered the strength of his own commitment to freedom and openly declared himself against oppression of any kind.

The Robesons returned to America in September 1939 and, after living on Edgecombe Avenue in Harlem for a couple of years, purchased a rural retreat in Enfield, Connecticut, which they named "The Beeches." Essie Robeson enrolled at Hartford Seminary and began work on a Ph.D. in anthropology.

Pan-Africanist Condemns Western Imperialism

She was not content merely to engage in academic life during this period. In 1941 she joined with her husband and other influential black people to found the Council on African Affairs. It was the task of this council to inform American public opinion on the current events in Africa with a view to rallying the Negro and progressive-minded public circles of the United States to the support of the African peoples in their struggle for independence. Eslanda Robeson became one of the most outspoken and articulate members of this organization and was often blunt in her criticism of western colonial powers, which would subjugate Africans and other non-white peoples for political and economic reasons. In 1944 she wrote:

> Until this war, the only people who were even vaguely aware of Africans as human beings were missionaries. Tourists, businessmen, government officials, and politicians—with few exceptions—considered the Africans (if they considered them at all) as savages, labor fodder, and pawns.
>
> This war has changed all that. The people of the world, in fighting for their own freedom, have come at long last to sense that no man can be free until all men are free. . . . I believe there will

never be peace in the world until people achieve what they fought and died for.

Africans are people ("African Journey," *Freedomways*, 346).

The middle forties were to bring more accolades and fame to both of the Robesons and, with the end of war, hope for the future. In 1945 Eslanda Robeson's book *African Journey* was published and Paul Robeson was awarded the Spingarn Medal. Paul Robeson was off again to Europe to entertain victorious Allied troops, and Essie Robeson was sent by the Council on African Affairs as a delegate to the San Francisco Conference, which would create the United Nations. In 1946 Essie Robeson returned to Africa and traveled on foot, on horseback, and by car, airplane, and boat throughout the Congo, Ruanda-Urundi, and French Equatorial Africa. She later used the knowledge she gained on this trip to argue and discuss the problems of the region before the United Nations Trusteeship Council. Rayford Logan has mentioned that the support of the Soviet Union to these emerging self-governing and independent nations reinforced Essie Robeson's already strong sympathies for the Soviet Union (528).

Unfortunately, dark forces were afoot in the United States that would try to subvert the meaning of the Allied victories in Europe and Asia and rekindle the racist-inspired fear and hatred that had characterized race relations in the United States for many years. Inevitably, as the Robesons spoke out against these tyrannical forces, they would come to pay the price for their outspokenness.

Paul Robeson, particularly, invited this wrath when he spoke out against racism and pointed to the apparent success of the Soviet Union in producing a system rooted in equality of all peoples. Remarks he made at the Paris World Congress of Partisans of Peace in April 1949 were distorted in the American press, and he was made to seem a subversive voice favoring communism. Members of the American Legion and other anti-communist elements swarmed over the grounds of an outdoor concert where Paul Robeson was to sing in Peekskill, New York. In the violence that followed much of the outdoor concert hall was destroyed, many people were hurt, and others were terrorized. The Robesons themselves were prevented from being there, thanks to a timely warning. As Hamilton succinctly put it in her book, "the year 1949 marked the end of America's enthrallment with Paul Robeson" (134).

Paul Robeson was called before the House Un-American Activities Committee, where he was questioned by hostile congressmen about his political sympathies and possible membership in the Communist Party of the United States. Armed only with the force of his personality and intellect and a controlled anger, Robeson fought the committee to a standstill. It was forced to dismiss him without having proven anything against him.

Later Essie Robeson was called before the committee. When questioned regarding her political activities, she, in turn, questioned members of the committee on the lack of civil rights for blacks in the United States. Finally, Senator Joseph McCarthy dismissed her from the stand, saying that only her sex had prevented her from being held in contempt. She got in the last lick, however, writing in *Freedomways* that "before any committee starts yelling for first class loyalty and cooperation from me, they'd better get busy and put me and my Negro people in the first class department by making US first class citizens" (Quoted in Ransby, 25).

Unable to prove anything against the Robesons, the State Department nonetheless revoked their passports, effectively destroying any opportunity for Paul Robeson to continue his career as a concert singer. Almost overnight their income dropped from more than one hundred thousand dollars a year to about two thousand. They were forced to sell The Beeches in order to live.

Even this did not stop them from speaking out against injustice to others. Eslanda Robeson often wielded her pen like a sword, as she did in January 1952 after the Christmas slaying of Harry T. and Harriet Moore by racists in Florida:

> Every loyal American citizen, especially every Negro citizen, and more especially every Negro soldier, should stop right here and now and take time out to consider the blasting to death of Harry T. Moore and his wife Harriet, not on Heartbreak Ridge on the distant battlefield of Korea, but on Heartbreak Ridge here in Mims, Florida, U.S.A., on Christmas night. *Christmas night!* . . . .
>
> While these UnAmericans rave and rant and pant about the glory of Freedom and Democracy, and the need for defending them by fighting Communism in Europe and Asia and particularly in Korea, they are very busy fighting American Constitutional Democracy here in the United States; they fight Civil Rights legislation; and they fight—politically, economically, socially and physically, often with force and violence to the death—these loyal American citizens who refuse to agree with or obey them ("Re the Assassination of Harry T. Moore and His Wife," 350).

Not satisfied simply to criticize wrongdoing at home, Eslanda Robeson again took up her pen to criticize American foreign policy in an open letter to President Dwight D. Eisenhower in the March 19, 1953, issue of the *Daily Worker*. Here she attacked the foreign policy that urged friendship with former enemies (Germany and Japan), yet openly supported opposition to Russia and China (Logan, 528).

The persecution of the Robesons did not go unnoticed by their friends overseas. Government and private groups on both sides of the Iron Curtain openly deplored Washington's refusal to reissue their passports. But the State Department wilfully ignored this plea.

By the end of the fifties, things finally began to turn around. In 1958 Paul Robeson was invited to give his first concert in nearly ten years at Carnegie Hall. That same year they also finally got back their passports, leaving them free to go first to Great Britain and then to the Soviet Union, where they temporarily settled among people for whom they felt a great gratitude and kinship.

The years and their troubles had taken their toll on both Robesons, however, and in 1959 they were hospitalized for fatigue and other complaints. Still tired and ill, they returned to the United States in 1963, after stopping in East Germany, where Essie Robeson spoke to a crowd of more than twenty thousand and was awarded both the Peace Medal and the Clara Zetkin Medal, an award made by the East German government to women who have been distinguished by their fight for world peace.

Back in the United States, Essie Robeson's health continued to decline, although she remained outspoken in her criticism of both imperialist and colonialist foreign policy and inequality at home and abroad. She died of cancer on December 13, 1965, at Beth Israel Hospital in New York City. Paul Robeson died in 1976.

Eslanda Robeson's career can be considered as nothing less than astounding. Although she had no problem with being identified as the wife of Paul Robeson, she was not swallowed up by this role. Her pride of self and of race enabled her to go places and do things from which others would shrink. At the same time, her relationship to Robeson was a deep and close one. Robeson, for all his greatness, was subject to the same frailties as a lesser man, something that placed a strain on, yet did not destroy their marriage. Her support of his career and of him as her husband was unfaltering in spite of the stresses that inevitably come with a relationship with a man of such towering ego.

R. L. Prattis has noted of Eslanda Goode Robeson that "although a talented woman in her own right, she forgot self in love of her husband. . . . If Paul is great, so was Essie for indeed they were one and the same person" (338).

References

Duberman, Martin Bauml. *Paul Robeson: A Biography.* New York: Knopf, 1988.

Golden, Lillie. "Remembrances of Eslanda." *Freedomways* (Fourth Quarter 1966): 330-32.

Graham, Shirley. *Paul Robeson: Citizen of the World.* New York: Messner, 1946.

Hamilton, Virginia. *Paul Robeson: The Life and Times of a Free Black Man.* New York: Harper, 1974.

Logan, Rayford W. "Eslanda Cardoza Goode Robeson." *Dictionary of American Negro Biography.* Eds. Rayford W. Logan and Michael R. Winston. New York: Norton, 1982. 527-28.

Prattis, R. L. "Remembrances of Eslanda." *Freedomways* (Fourth Quarter 1966): 337-38.

Ransby, Barbara. "Eslanda Goode Robeson, Pan-Africanist." *Sage* 3 (Fall 1986): 22-26.

Robeson, Eslanda Goode. "African Journey." *Freedomways* (Fourth Quarter 1966): 346-47.

———. "African Journey" [condensation]. *Negro Digest* 3 (October 1945): 86-93.

———. *Paul Robeson, Negro.* New York: Harper and Brothers, 1930.

———. "Re the Assassination of Harry T. Moore and His Wife at Mims, Florida, Christmas, 1951." *Freedomways* (Fourth Quarter 1966): 350-53.

———. "What Do the People of Africa Want?" Quoted in Barbara Ransby, "Eslanda Goode Robeson, Pan-Africanist." *Sage* 3 (Fall 1986): 22.

Sullivan, Patricia. "Eslanda Cardoza Goode Robeson." *Notable Black American Women: The Modern Period.* Cambridge: Harvard University Press, 1980. 583-84.

Who's Who in Colored America. Vol. 1. New York: Who's Who in Colored America, 1927. 171.

Collections

The Eslanda Goode Robeson papers in the Moorland-Spingarn Research Center, Howard University, contain correspondence, speeches, the original manuscripts of her three books, unpublished manuscripts, a number of short stories, two plays, and one novel. There are detailed notebooks on her trips to the Soviet Union, Africa, Spain, Central America, and China. Of particular importance are the detailed and vivid diaries, which she kept fairly continuously from 1924 through 1928. The Paul Robeson Collection as well as the research files for Martin Duberman's biography of Robeson, also in Moorland-Spingarn, contain additional information on Eslanda Robeson.

Robert E. Skinner

Rubye Doris Robinson

(1942-1967)

Civil rights activist

Rubye Doris Smith Robinson typifies the army of women whose labors energized, organized, and maintained the civil rights revolution in the United States. Long before the young activists of the Student Non-Violent Coordinating Committee (SNCC) took to the field and before any national leaders stepped to the front of local demonstrations, the civil rights movement's female volunteers had been working long days and nights preparing the campaign and maintaining its momentum—and Robinson was among the hardest working of those women.

Rubye Smith Robinson was born on April 25, 1942, in Atlanta to Georgians Alice (Banks) Smith and John Thomas Smith. Her father was a self-employed mover (he later became a minister) and her mother was a beautician who ran the family store. The Smith family had seven children, Rubye being the second child and second daughter. In later years Robinson told an interviewer that her mother had been a powerful and primary influence on her life:

> She has so much social conscience for one thing. I remember when I was little our house was on the escape route for Negro men on the prison chain gangs. . . . Well my mother always kept a suit of men's clothes in the house and a package of things—a little silver money, matches, names and telephones maybe of certain preachers around the South who would help. . . .
>
> She took a big risk. Didn't matter what he did or who he was—he was a Negro man off the chain gang and if they caught him, they'd beat him to death. So she helped him escape (Carson, 253-54).

Her family's commitment to what would become the black liberation movement gave her a sense of direction, but it was by watching the television coverage of the Montgomery bus boycott when she was thirteen that she found her dedication to activism. Ironically, given the important symbolic role of young people's sacrifices to the later movement, it was the old people's walking, day after day, that inspired the young Rubye Smith.

In line with her family's emphasis on education, Robinson entered Spelman College in 1959, eventually graduating with a degree in English. It was there as a sophomore that she found her life's work after being inspired by the Greensboro, North Carolina, lunchcounter sit-ins. Along with her older sister and other students from the Atlanta University Center, Robinson joined in the first Atlanta sit-ins. In April 1960 she became a founder of SNCC and a disciple of Ella Baker's call for a wider vision of liberation than the right to eat hamburgers at a lunch counter. From then on, Robinson would be front and center at most of the turning points of the civil rights movement.

The next great watershed came in February 1961 when students honoring the anniversary of the Greensboro sit-in were arrested in Rock Hill, South Carolina, and chose jail over paying their fines. This "jail no bail" tactic could solve the movement's growing problem of scarce bail money and would represent a quantum leap in commitment if only it could be reinforced. Robinson joined the SNCC contingent of four volunteers who traveled to Rock Hill to give the needed support by willingly following the original protesters to jail. For the first time, the national SNCC organization was blending into a local movement, a principle of grass roots organization that would influence later SNCC ideology.

When the original Congress of Racial Equality (CORE) sponsored Freedom Rides of 1961 to end state-mandated segregation on interstate travel were in danger of being stopped by white violence in Birmingham, Alabama, Robinson, fresh out of jail, took up the challenge by personally telephoning SNCC affiliates across the nation for reinforcements. Then she joined the SNCC freedom riders who put their bodies on the line. The new riders were violently attacked and beaten in Montgomery and later arrested in Jackson, Mississippi, for the crime of "inflammatory" traveling. In accord with the "jail no bail" policy, Robinson accepted a two-month prison term served out in both county jail and the dreaded Parchman Penitentiary. Through this extension of the Freedom Rides the students had won national attention and shown that mob violence would not easily stop the freedom movement.

Robinson then joined the SNCC summer voter-registration project in violent McComb, Mississippi, and shortly thereafter, sensing the need for blacks to be able to strike back against violence, she became one of a growing number of activists who thought of nonviolence as a tactic rather than a way of life. During this period she also took part in the abortive Albany, Georgia, demonstrations and in SNCC's Cairo, Illinois, project of 1962.

Commitment to Civil Rights Struggle Sealed

In 1963 Robinson became a full-time revolutionary, taking the post of administrative assistant to SNCC's executive secretary, James Forman. He described her during this period as "of medium height with plain features," "brilliant," "extremely talented," and "one of the few genuine revolutionaries in the black liberation movement." While others typically dropped in and out of the struggle, their commitment limited to one summer or one local action, Rubye Robinson had become a professional activist. For the next four years she was the nuts-and-bolts operative of SNCC. She described herself to an interviewer as the coordinator of the Coordinating Committee: "I'm a sort of coordinator of finances. I decide what we can spend for what and usually I have to tell them that we can't afford it no matter what it is" (Carson, 253). In every organization there must be someone strong enough to accept the job of saying no. In SNCC, it was Rubye Robinson.

In 1964, however, she said yes to Clifford Robinson, marrying the veteran who, she said, was "the only fellow I met. . . . stronger than me." Their son, Kenneth Touré, was named for the president of Guinea, who dropped in on a SNCC team visiting Africa. Rubye Robinson had been a part of that team. President Touré reminded them that the black struggle must also be a part of a wider struggle against economic exploitation. In taking up this idea as critical to the movement, she again found herself moving ahead of the mainstream.

In May of 1966 Rubye Smith Robinson was elected executive secretary of SNCC as the organization's leadership changed from the southern nonviolence of John Lewis to the militant black nationalism of northerner Stokely Carmichael. Soon thereafter, when SNCC field secretary Willis Ricks created the "Black Power" slogan to give a rallying cry to the masses, Rubye Robinson stood behind him, in part because the new slogan mirrored her own internal conflict and anger over white women's dominance of American standards of beauty and behavior. "I spent three years hating white women so much it nearly made me crazy," she later said of this period.

As the leadership of SNCC was changing, Robinson had to endure more and more of what James Forman later called "vicious attacks" from male chauvinists in the movement who resented her lectures to them about dedication to organizational responsibility and self-discipline. Yet despite some nascent feminism, she generally rejected the growing women's movement (as she did antiwar activism) as a distracting diversion from the main cause. This same sense of party dedication showed up when she tried to silence SNCC chairman Stokely Carmichael for six months because his radical public statements had not been cleared by the organization and brought too much heat onto SNCC's organizers in the field. She believed in quiet organization for the armed struggle, not in announcing it openly beforehand to friend and foe alike. Robinson left her position as executive secretary in the spring of 1967.

Only months later, on October 7, 1967, she would die from leukemia, struck down while still in her prime. Near the end she reflected on the meaning of the movement to which she had given her life; she found irony in the thought that in victory the civil rights revolution might destroy the very thing for which she had been fighting:

> So, in a way I'm working for the extinction of the African type in America because I want black people to have their own businesses and hold high political offices, but I know that when they do, they are going to become more and more a part of the American character. And the black soul is going to die in the middle of the white soul (Carson, 256).

It is impossible to know how Robinson would assess civil rights progress in the 1990s, of how her own views and predictions might have changed along the way. To the end, she was ahead of her peers. Rubye Doris Smith Robinson had been the iron in SNCC. It was Robinson and women like her who had done much of the grunt work for liberation, while men, in a kind of shadow play, usually received the honors. Robinson had dreams for her own son, and when she placed him with her mother so that she could work full-time to make his life better, she gladly took up an old burden shared by her people and by women and parents everywhere. In this, as in so much else, her life remained at once revolutionary and traditional.

References

Carson, Josephine. *Silent Voices*. New York: Delacorte Press, 1969. Rubye Robinson is discussed as "Sarah" on pages 253-56.

Farmer, James. *The Making of Black Revolutionaries*. New York: Macmillan, 1972.

King, Mary. *Freedom Song*. New York: Morrow, 1987.

Reagon, Bernice Johnson. "Rubye Doris Smith Robinson." *Notable American Women: The Modern Period*. Cambridge: The Harvard University Press, 1980.

Zinn, Howard. *The New Abolitionists*. Boston: Beacon Press, 1964.

Collections

Robinson's papers are in the possession of her family.

William D. Piersen

Charlemae Hill Rollins

(1897-1979)

Librarian, storyteller, author

A lasting tribute was made to Charlemae Hill Rollins on October 21, 1989, when the Chicago Public Library honored her memory with a special ceremony. Included in the program was an official proclamation from the Office of the Mayor of the City of Chicago. Highlighting her career as a librarian, humanitarian, speaker, author, and authority on black literature, it also indicated the ultimate objective for this singular event:

> I, Richard M. Daley, Mayor of the City of Chicago, do hereby duly honor and recognize that the children's area of the George Cleveland Hall Branch Library be called "The Charlemae Hill Rollins Children's Room (Daley, Proclamation, 12 October 1989).

This is truly a living memorial to an individual whose life *is* and *was* a life of celebration.

A native of Yazoo City, a small farming community in Mississippi, Charlemae Hill Rollins was born June 20, 1897,

Charlemae Hill Rollins

the daughter and oldest child of Allen G. Hill, a farmer, and Birdie (Tucker) Hill, a teacher. When her father was forced to leave Mississippi, he took his family and fled to the Indian territory that is now Oklahoma. Rollins had fond memories of her childhood years. Although there was a lack of money, this was no deterrent for happiness: "We were very rich in family life—parents, brothers, and sisters and lots of cousins, aunts and uncles . . . " (Hopkins, 300).

In retrospect, she paid tribute to her grandmother, a former slave:

> Grandma told wonderful stories of her life as a slave. I've always loved books because of her. She gave us all the books that belonged to her master who was the father of her children, one of whom was my father. We enjoyed the books in his library, even though most of them were medical books. But I would read anything and everything (Hopkins, 300).

Denied equal educational opportunities in their new location, the town of Beggs, the children attended a school for black youngsters that was founded by the Hill family. Rollins's mother, Birdie Hill, was "one of the first black teachers in this Indian territory" (Hopkins, 300). Completing her elementary education when she was thirteen, she enrolled in the black secondary schools in St. Louis, Missouri, and Holly Springs, Mississippi. The year 1916 marked her graduation from high school at Western University, a segregated boarding school in Quindoro, Kansas. For a brief period Rollins taught in Beggs, Oklahoma, after she passed the required teaching examination.

Her desire for further education led her to Howard University in Washington, D.C. However, she remained only for one year before she returned to Oklahoma. In that locale on April 8, 1918, she married Joseph Walter Rollins, who became a devoted friend, loving husband, caring father, and lifelong companion. During her husband's service in the United States Army in World War I in France, Charlemae Rollins remained in Oklahoma; then, in 1919 with his return, the young couple moved to Chicago, which was to be their permanent home. The birth of their son, Joseph Walter Rollins, Jr., in 1920, occurred on a return trip to Oklahoma.

It was Rollins's fondness for reading, acquired at an early age, coupled with her teaching experience, that propelled her into the library profession. She said that it was "the best thing I ever did." Entering into the employment of the Chicago Public Library in 1927 as a children's librarian, she was assigned to the Harding Square Branch Library. This branch served a multicultural, multiethnic population, but there was an absence of black patrons.

Librarian Rollins Heads Children's Department

Recognizing her need for a proper educational preparation, Charlemae Rollins secured funds from the library system to receive training in library schools at Columbia University in the summer of 1932 and the graduate library school at the University of Chicago, 1934-36. When the George Cleveland Hall Branch Library opened in 1923, she was appointed head of the children's department, a position that she held until her retirement in 1963.

Named after a distinguished black surgeon and civic leader who also served on the library's board of directors, this branch agency became a cultural, educational, and recreational center for the black community. Built on land that was donated by philanthropist Julius C. Rosenwald, the library served a diverse population. Entering through its doors were patrons who resided in tri-level brownstones, elegant old mansions, or in the Rosenwald apartment complex. Every socioeconomic level of society was represented and all were welcomed into this edifice. It was the first branch built in a black neighborhood.

Working closely with Vivian Harsh, the library's first director, Rollins demonstrated her abilities as an imaginative librarian and a dedicated humanitarian. In response to her warmth and interest, the children found a friend and a confidante from whom they were able to receive inspiration and meaningful guidance to the world of books. Among those who were fortunate to benefit from her selfless giving was Gwendolyn Brooks, eminent Pulitzer Prize-winning poet.

Dorothy Evans recalls with warmth the storytelling sessions that Charlemae Rollins held in the branch library:

> As a child growing up at 45th and Indiana, Hall Branch was my second home. To be able to go to the Library to take books out and to see the librarians check books in and out with their

> pencil stamps was fascinating. The biggest thrill, however, was listening to Mrs. Rollins tell stories, At the time I did not know what a treasure was before me. I just know the stories transported me to another time and to being another person . . . (Questionnaire, Hall Branch Library).

Developing a comprehensive scope of services and programs in a new branch library provided a wide range of opportunities for Rollins to be creative. With her skills in reference work, she met the informational and research needs of children, parents, and educators. She encouraged class visits to the library and visited neighborhood schools with her outreach programs. Capitalizing upon the inducements to encourage library use, she organized book fairs, reading and dramatic clubs, a Negro History Club, and a series of Appreciation Hours at the library. A major purpose in both of these latter programs was to highlight the contributions of black people.

Her work with adults enabled her to involve families with a program of Reading Guidance Clinic for Parents and to establish strong relationships with many parent-teacher association groups. During the depression years, Rollins met Langston Hughes, who visited the branch library many times. Referring to these encounters, she said:

> Ours was one of the branches that sponsored a WPA Writers Project. Langston spoke to our various groups and read and discussed his poetry. We all fell in love with him. He visited my home often. He enjoyed Southern cooking which is one of my hobbies (Hopkins, 302).

The storytelling sessions were an important aspect of the library's services and programs. For Rollins these were more than a "key" to guide eager listeners to lands of enchantment:

> Storytelling is a wonderful way of breaking down barriers, or getting acquainted with new people, and drawing groups and individuals together. Hearing a wonderful story well-told, can bring escape from hunger, from drab surroundings, from hate and rejection, and escape from injustices of all kinds (Rollins, "The Art of Storytelling," 22).

Viewing her audiences of children during these sessions with a sensitive perception, Charlemae Hill Rollins underscored her conclusions regarding their potential and their uniqueness:

> Should you stand at the edge of a South Side playground in Chicago and listen to the children at their games, you would hear their palms clapping, their voices lifted in a singsong chant, and see their hips and arms and bodies swaying in rhythms unlike those of any other American children. It is not one song, but a dozen, with patterns of words unheard elsewhere, about corn bread and stepping out to the dance, and Saturday nights, and all the delights that are not wholly denied them.
>
> Of this great mass of dark-skinned children it has been said that they are culturally deprived, yet here is a culture as spontaneous as it is unrecognized. It tells us again that the spirit of man can still endure under whatever misery and deprivation, on crowded streets and in back alleys where the garbage cans overflow, that here there is even laughter and dance and song (Rollins, "Foreword," n.p.).

With a feverent desire to nourish the potential and the uniqueness of her young adventures, Rollins focused her attention upon the areas of book selection and the library collection. From her diligent searching, she realized that the children's book collection was lacking materials in the sphere of the black experience. An opportunity to fill this void was provided to Rollins during her period of study at the University of Chicago. In an evening class taught by Agatha L. Shea, director of work with children at the Chicago Public Library, Rollins submitted a research paper relating to this problem. This became a forerunner of her pamphlet that was later published as *The Negro in Children's Books*. In recognition of her competency as an evaluator, coupled with her objective insights into literature by and about blacks, Rollins became a valued member of the library's advisory committee to work with Shea in formulating principles and policies related to book selection.

Racial Stereotypes in Children's Books Opposed

The year 1941 heralded a significant landmark for authors, illustrators, and publishers of children's books and for librarians and educators who selected these materials. Crusading against the stereotypical images of blacks in children's literature, Rollins prepared her first edition of the excellent work, *We Build Together, a Reader's Guide to Negro Life and Literature for Elementary and High School Use*, published by the National Council of Teachers of English. Replete with an introductory essay and recommended criteria to evaluate literature concerned with the black experience, the publication contained an annotated bibliography of recommended books, arranged by subject. There was an immediate enthusiastic response to this publication that resulted in the issuing of revised editions in 1948 and 1967.

Considered an authority in this specialized area of literature, Rollins's career was given an added dimension as she gained national prominence. Major publishers sent her manuscripts to review, authors requested her advice and suggestions. Invitations to lecture, to write, and to teach were received in unprecedented numbers. Traveling beyond the immediate environs of the George Hall Branch Library during her nonscheduled work days, she spoke at conferences and engaged in workshops and summer school sessions. Rollins was welcomed on the campuses of Fisk

University, Morgan State College, the University of Mississippi, Rosary College, San Francisco State College, and the University of Chicago. In 1946 she began to teach the course, "Children's Literature," at Roosevelt University in Chicago. Considered a success, it was a required subject for education majors by 1955.

Committed to the principle that involvement in professional organizations was vital to one's career, Rollins assumed an active role in state and national library associations. In 1954-55 she was chair of the Children's Section, the Illinois Library Association, and in 1953-54, chair of the Elementary Section of the Illinois unit of the Catholic Library Association. Her affiliation with the American Library Association (ALA) spanned many years. During the 1950s she was a member of the council for four years and also served as treasurer for the Children's Library Association from 1954 to 1956. Elected vice president and president-elect of the Children's Services Division in 1956, she served as chair of the Newbery/Caldecott Awards Committee. When she assumed the position of president in 1957, she was the first black librarian to attain this office.

Additional responsibilities beyond her duties as children's librarian enabled her to serve as a member of the editorial advisory board of *World Book Encyclopedia* and *The American Educator*. Her involvement as a member of the advisory committee for the *Bulletin of the Center for Children's Books*, published by the University of Chicago, extended from 1941 to 1977. She also chaired the Jane Addams Book Award Committee for the Women's International League for Peace and Justice from 1964 to 1965. Another highlight in her distinguished career was her trip to Oslo, Norway, to present the Jane Addams Book Award to Aimee Sommerfelt, author of *The Road to Agra*.

Rollins Becomes A Creative Writer

Completing thirty-six years of service as a children's librarian in the Chicago Public Library system, Rollins retired on August 29, 1963; however, her driving zeal to pursue other interests directed her efforts toward the field of creative writing:

> I got hooked on books and children while working at the library. I was also hooked on writers and listened to all the authors (Richard Wright, Langston Hughes, Arna Bontemps and others) who visited the library. I attended lots of lectures on writing by many famous authors. I just had to try to do a book on my own (Hopkins, 300-301).

What resulted from her literary efforts were several publications. She enhanced the biographical genre with important works: *They Showed the Way* (Crowell, 1964), *Famous American Negro Poets for Children* (Dodd, 1965), *Famous Negro Entertainers of Stage and Screen* (Dodd, 1967, affectionately dedicated to her mother, "Mrs. Birdie Tucker Hill, aged 95, who listens with pride and enjoyment to all the young Negro entertainers"), and *Black Troubadour, Langston Hughes* (Rand McNally, 1971).

Charlemae Rollins made an invaluable, lasting contribution to the field of literature with her superb publication, *Christmas Gif', an Anthology of Christmas Poems, Songs and Stories Written by and about Negroes* (Follett, 1963). She dedicated this volume to "my husband—my perennial Christmas Gif'—and my understanding family—all of whom have helped me remember rich Christmas Gif's from the past." What was the catalyst that motivated her to compile this notable work?

> The custom of "Christmas Gif'" has been a part of the holiday celebration in my family for as long as I can remember.
>
> As a child I spent much time with my grandmother, who had been a slave. From her I learned that "Christmas Gif'" was a surprise game played by the slaves on Christmas Day. Two people meeting for the first time that day, would compete to be the first to call out, "Christmas Gif'!" The loser happily paid a forfeit of a simple present—maybe a Christmas tea cake or a handful of nuts. Truly, there was more pleasure in being "caught," and having to give a present—the giving, though comically protested, was heartwarming to a people who had so little they could with dignity share with others.
>
> The practice of "Christmas Gif'" spread from the slave cabins to the "Big House," and soon became a traditional part of the celebration of Christmas, a joyful time felt and shared even by an enslaved people (Rollins, *Christmas Gif'*, "Foreword," n.p.).

As an extension of her distinguished career as a librarian, a dedicated humanitarian, and a mentor to thousands of children, young adults, and adults, Charlemae Hill Rollins became a recipient of many honors and awards. These included the American Brotherhood Award from the National Conference of Christians and Jews (1952), Library Letter Award, the American Library Association (1953), and from the same association, the Grolier Foundation Award (1955), that read in part:

> because she has led thousands of children to read good books . . . and inspired many authors to write better books for children (Obituary, *Chicago Sun Times*, 7 February 1979).

Further acknowledgements of her achievements include the "Woman of the Year" Award, given by Zeta Phi Beta (1956), honorary member, Phi Delta Kappa (teacher's sorority) (1959), Good American Award of the Chicago Committee of One Hundred (1962), three Negro Centennial Awards (1963), Children's Reading Round Table Award (1963), Woman's National Book Association's Constance Lindsay Skinner Award (1970), New Jersey Library and Media Association, Coretta Scott King Award (1971, for her book, *Black Troubador Langston Hughes*), the Torch Bearers Award of the Alpha Kappa Alpha Sorority (1972).

On June 30, 1972, Rollins was elected to honorary life membership, American Library Association, by the ALA Council. Once again, she had the distinction of being the first black librarian to be accorded this prestigious award.

In 1974 Columbia College in Chicago awarded Rollins a doctorate of humane letters. Three years later, November 19, 1977, the Chicago Public Library dedicated a room to this renowned scholar at the Carter G. Woodson Regional Library.

The memorable career of a most remarkable individual came to an end on February 3, 1979, when Rollins died at the age of eighty-one. One of the most endearing tributes rendered to her was the poem by Gwendolyn Brooks, who had been one of the many children befriended and inspired by their library companion:

> Her gift is long delayed,
> And even now is paid
> In insufficient measure,
> Rhymful reverence,
> For such excellence,
> Is microscopic treasure,
> Nothing is enough
> For one who gave us clarity—
> Who gave us sentience—
> Who gave us definition—
> Who gave us her vision (Wirth, 279).

Although she is no longer with us, the influence of Charlemae Hill Rollins is still cherished and perpetuated. One is the biennial "Charlemae Hill Rollins Colloquium" that is presented by the School of Library and Information Science, North Carolina Central University in Durham. The second occasion is the presentation of the Charlemae Rollins President's Program by the American Library Association for Library Service to Children, a division of the American Library Association. Begun in Los Angeles, California, in June 1983, this major activity is presented during the association's annual summer conference.

References

American Library Association. *Top of the News* 29 (November 1972): 11-12.

Commire, Anne. *Something About the Author: Facts and Pictures About Contemporary Authors of Books for Young People*. Detroit: Gale Research, 1972.

Daley, Richard M. *Proclamation*. Office of the Mayor of the City of Chicago, 12 October 1989.

Evans, Dorothy. Response to a questionnaire from the George Cleveland Hall Library, 15 September 1989.

Hopkins, Lee Bennett. "Charlemae Rollins." In *More Books by More People; Interviews with Sixty-five Authors of Books for Children*. New York: Citation Press, 1974.

Nichols, Charles H., ed. *Arna Bontemps-Langston Hughes Letters, 1925 - 1967*. New York, Dodd, Mead, 1980.

Obituary. "Charlemae Rollins Dies; Librarian." *Chicago Sun Times* 7 February 1979.

Randle, Wilma. "Kids Are Still the Story at Hall Library." *Chicago Tribune* 16 March 1990.

Rollins, Charlemae. "The Art of Storytelling." *Illinois Libraries* 51 (January 1969): 22-26.

———. *Christmas Gif', an Anthology of Christmas Poems, Songs, and Stories Written by and about Negroes*. Chicago: Follett Pub. Co., 1963.

———. "Foreword." In Arnold Adoff, ed. *I Am the Darker Brother; an Anthology of Modern Poems by Negro Americans*. New York: Macmillan, 1968.

———. "Library Work with Negroes." *Illinois Libraries* 25 (February 1945): 92-94.

———. *We Build Together; a Reader's Guide to Negro Life and Literature for Elementary and High School Use*. Urbana, Ill.: National Council of Teachers of English, 1967.

Shaw, Spencer G. "Charlemae Hill Rollins, 1897-1979: In Tribute." *Public Libraries* 21 (Fall 1982): 102-104.

Wirth, Otto. "Roosevelt University Honors and 'Is Honored.'" American Library Association. *Top of the News* (May 20, 1964): 279.

Collections

The books, including those autographed by black authors, are in the Vivian G. Harsh Collection of Afro-American History and Literature, Carter G. Woodson Regional Library in Chicago and have been designated the Charlemae Hill Rollins Collection of Children's Literature.

Spencer G. Shaw

Diana Ross

(1944-)

Singer, actress

"She wants to be somebody and she wants that for her audience as well as for herself. And she's going to *be* somebody because she works at it. I know she's going to be a *great*, great star because there is nobody who works at it as

Diana Ross

hard as Diane Ross does . . . and there's nobody better than her at it,'' predicted Berry Gordy, Jr., Motown mogul and founder in 1965 about his protégée (Taraborrelli, 67). Diana Ross's meteoric rise to international fame is ''so familiar to us that it has taken on a mythic quality'' (Cleage, 72). It is one of the most fascinating rags-to-riches legends in pop music history. ''She's earned stardom the old fashioned way: through hard work and determination,'' says Susan L. Taylor in *Essence* magazine (50).

Starting in obscurity as a teenage singer from the Brewster-Douglass housing project in Detroit, Michigan, Diana Ross has become a multitalented megastar, acclaimed popular vocalist, Academy Award-nominated actress, one of the most glamorous stars in show business, fashion designer, and successful businesswoman who heads her own multimillion-dollar corporation, Diana Ross Enterprises. Hers is the American Dream success story. Geoff Brown commented in his book *Diana Ross*, ''If an individual's rise from rags to riches, from relative poverty to a position of power, is still at the heart of the American Dream, then the career of Diana Ross is as good an example of that perhaps mythical Dream at work as one could wish to see'' (6).

Diane Ross (she changed her professional name to Diana when she joined Motown) was born in Detroit, Michigan, on March 26, 1944, to Fred Ross, a factory worker, and Ernestine Ross. The second of six children, Ross has two sisters, Barbara and Marguarita, and three brothers, Fred, Jr., Arthur, and William Alex. Growing up in inner-city Detroit, she remembers her childhood as comfortable and ''fun, fun, fun'' (*Ladies Home Journal*, 44). ''Kids in the ghetto,'' she said,''at least when I was growing up, were very lucky to have a lot of little things to get involved in, instead of just hanging around the streets'' (Taraborrelli, 24). The Brewster Center was the focal point of all the social and recreational activities in the projects: ''There was roller skating in the streets,'' Ross explained. '' There was swimming, baseball, basketball. . . . It was really an incredible center to be that close to. A lot of creative people, musical people came from the Detroit area'' (*Ladies Home Journal*, 44).

Music has always been Diana Ross's love. Both of her parents sang in the choir at Detroit's Olivet Baptist Church, where Ross and her siblings also sang in the junior choir. Influenced from her early years by her parents' love of music, young Diana Ross enjoyed singing with them: she loved the quiet times when her mother would stop working and take a rest. She would put some Billie Holiday records on the record player and sing along with them. By the age of six, Ross had decided that she would be a singer. ''When company came, Diana's parents would often ask her to sing for them. Diana loved the attention . . . . She was only about six years old when she learned that her singing could get her things that she wanted'' (Haskins, 7). Another strong musical influence in her childhood were her neighborhood peers. Street-corner singing and dancing to the latest records of the day was a favorite pastime for many youngsters in the Brewster Projects: ''Some serious-minded budding talents in the projects would proudly form vocal groups and improvise their own arrangements of songs by their favorite artists. . . . To form a vocal group had become a very prestigious thing to do and most young Brewsterites were preoccupied with the idea'' (Taraborrelli, 39). Numerous future R & B singers and musicians lived in the neighborhood, including Smokey Robinson, Mary Wilson, Paul Williams, Florence Ballard, and Eddie Kendricks. ''Aside from church choir singing, the natural tendency was for kids to form vocal groups, imitating their elders and idols whom they heard on the radio, singing on street corners or down subways where the echo enhanced their vocals,'' says Geoff Brown (24).

At Balch Elementary School, Ross sang and danced in numerous school performances. One of her teachers, Mrs. Julia Page, remembered her impressive leadership skills and competitive spirit:

> Throughout all six years she was at Balch, Diane participated in the activities we had in the auditorium that involved her class group. Diane would always be the one to set up and inspire the class program . . . . She had an uncanny ability to organize . . . . She was just a leader . . . The other kids would just follow Diane's lead and she would take charge and get it all done (Taraborrelli, 20-21).

Because of her high grade point average while at Dwyer Junior High School, Diana Ross was accepted at the prestigious Cass Technical High School, one of the best high schools in the city. There, she was intent upon pursuing a career as a fashion designer or model, taking courses in dress design, sewing, costume illustration, and cosmetology. Not only was she friendly and outgoing but was also determined and serious about becoming a singer. In addition to her studies, Ross participated in extracurricular activities—the girls swimming team, the letter girl club, and charm school—but her love of singing continued. Between classes and work after school at Hudson's department store, she sang with friends on weekends at social functions. Ross graduated from Cass in 1962 and was voted Best Dressed Girl in her senior class.

Her big break came while in high school when Diana Ross was asked to join a neighborhood vocal group composed of Mary Wilson, Florence Ballard, and Betty Anderson (later replaced by Barbara Martin). This foursome called themselves the Primettes, the female counterpart to their brother group the Primes (Eddie Kendricks, Melvin Franklin, Paul Williams, and Cal Osborne—soon to become the Temptations). Singing locally at parties and record hops, the Primettes made their first appeal for an audition and recording contract with Berry Gordy, president of Hitsville, who advised them to complete high school before embarking on a music career. Disappointed but undaunted by his rejection, the Primettes continued to sing, gaining confidence, showmanship, and local fame by performing at churches, block dances, sock hops, talent shows, and clubs. Shortly afterward, they landed a contract with the Detroit-based Lu Pine label and recorded two singles, *Tears of Sorrow* and *Pretty Baby*.

Ross Launches Career with the Supremes

After graduation from high school, the fourth Primette, Barbara Martin, departed from the group, and the trio was signed with Hitsville as backup vocalists for other Motown acts such as Marvin Gaye, Mary Wells, and Martha Reeves and the Vandellas. In 1962, after renaming them the Supremes, Gordy carefully planned their debut: "Gordy sent them to . . . the Motown finishing school . . . . This was Gordy's own dream factory. Here he shaped mere singers into charming, poised entertainers, by giving them months of dancing, modeling and acting lessons . . . and upon 'graduation' [they] were given a special reward . . . . ("Real Dreamgirls").

The Supremes cut their debut album *Meet The Supremes* (1963) with two of the singles, "I Want A Guy" and "Buttered Popcorn" unimpressively reaching the top one hundred on the charts. The next six singles, "Your Heart Belongs to Me," "Let Me Go the Right Way," "My Heart Can't Take It No More," "A Breathtaking . . . Guy," "When The Lovelight Starts Shining Through His Eyes," and "Run, Run, Run" met with modest success. It was not until late 1963 that the group was assigned new producers, Holland-Dozier-Holland (H-D-H). From that day on for Motown and the Supremes "international fame was just a hit away" (*The Illustrated Encyclopedia of Black Music*, 101). This combination, stated *Ebony*, "From the outset . . . was a match made in heaven. The H-D-H team gave the girls a strong new beat, highlighted Diana's tender vocals against a background of resounding pianos, and the resulting mix was 'Where Did Our Love Go?' (Mid 1964), the first of the Supremes' million-plus sellers" ("Real Dreamgirls," 46). "Where Did Our Love Go?" was released while the Supremes were on their first national tour and became a number one hit, a million seller that remained on the charts for more than three months. By the end of the tour, the Supremes "were topping the bill and the record was topping the charts—all over the world" (*The Illustrated Encyclopedia of Black Music*, 101). Geoff Brown recounted the appeal and popularity of their next two hits:

> "Where Did Our Love Go?" and "Baby Love" had displayed most of the facets of Diana's voice which made it perfect for pop music. There was a coy, sexual quality, a certain natural grace, a definite nasal tone occasionally . . . and a sense of versatility in that this voice could be able to adapt to most pop settings in which it was placed (38).

These two were the first in a breathtaking number of hits for the Supremes under the guidance of H-D-H. "The greatest of Motown's female groups had twelve number one singles, sold over fifty million records, and were more famous than any other black performing group in American history" (Bogle, 169).

"From the first, hers was the dominant voice, supple, breathily sexy, and it bore the group to major stardom and wealth," reported *Life* magazine (42). Diana Ross had the commercial voice. Randy J.Taraborrelli says in his book *Diana* that " Diana had one of those flexible voices that easily adapted to show tunes as well as to rock and roll. She *looked* the part" (2). "No one else should have been the Supremes' 'lead singer,'" recalled songwriter Eddie Holland; "She had a unique sound—once you hear her you know it's her. . . . She doesn't sound like any other singer. . . . Her ability is to have her own sound and she has a very sensuous sound. . . . And that's the key to her (Nelson, 85-86).

With Ross as the leader, the Supremes were Motown's trailblazers, according to James Haskins in *Diana Ross—Star Supreme* (32), winning a vast crossover audience. By 1965, they were international celebrities—one of the most successful R & B groups in America with an endless list of accomplishments; they "helped to shape sixties' pop music sensibility"(Brown, 69). Pioneering the Motown Sound, they played the big supper clubs, the Copa in New York and Las Vegas; between 1965 and 1966, the Supremes had appeared in more than twenty national television shows, including "The Ed Sullivan Show," "Hullabaloo," "Shindig," "The Mike Douglas Show," "The Hollywood Palace," "Sammy Davis Special," and the "Orange Bowl Parade." They had toured in Europe, recorded theme songs to motion pictures, entertained President Johnson, and made an appearance at Philharmonic Hall in New York. With five number one records in a row, the Supremes were one of only three groups—the other two being the Beach Boys and the Four

Seasons—confidently able to challenge the dominance of the Beatles on the pop charts.

In the midst of this spectacular success, Diana Ross had bigger dreams; she would not settle for group success—she wanted to be a star. As Gordy's favorite protégeé, Ross worked hard in expanding her artistry; and he, impressed by her determination and perserverance, recognized her remarkable talents and fashioned her into a superstar. She seized every opportunity that she could to learn everything she could, Ross contends:

> I have never felt I was a great talent. I have to work hard on everything. I really do. When I record, I stay in the studio a long time. I know I'm the total of all the intense work and of all of my experiences. Nothing I've learned in my life is wasted (Taraborrelli, 2).

Attending John Powers School for Social Grace, theatrical performing classes, and studying techniques and demo tapes made by other female artists, Ross "was a perfectionist always anxious to be the best at her craft" (Taraborrelli, 89).

On the first Supremes recordings, Ross and Florence Ballard alternated lead vocals, but during this two-year period of extra grooming (1965-1967), Ross made steady growth as a vocalist and as a performer. In 1967 Gordy renamed the group Diana Ross and the Supremes (along with changing the company name to Motown) to showcase Ross's talents. "True she had come to be accepted by Motown as the most distinctive voice in the group," says Brown,

> and therefore the lead singer and because of that the most attention was fixed on her. . . . Her emergence as the focal point of the group was timely, for she had exactly the type of figure which the models of the sixties . . . would popularize. . . . She had a universal appeal to be more than a singer in one of his groups, using a lightly sexy, breathing style of delivery. . . . What is unarguable is that Diana's singing with the Supremes helped define the label's particular sound and become a blueprint to which other artists adapted their work. Not every singer was as vocally pliable as Ross (33).

Ross's ascendancy to solo stardom began long before the group's name change. Her electrifying presence and drive enhanced the group's showmanship but drew attention to her. Reporters wanted to interview her alone; television producers booked her as a guest on their television shows. She was also booked alone on specials, appeared in skits, and finally appeared by herself on the cover of *Look* magazine on August 23, 1969. Even at this time Ross was interested in diversifying her career. She discovered the Jackson Five and brought them to the attention of Gordy, who was so impressed that he signed them to a longtime contract with Motown. As their mentor Ross advised them and offered assistance. Their first debut album, *Diana Presents The Jackson 5*, launched their career.

On January 14, 1970, Diana Ross and the Supremes gave their farewell performance at the Frontier Hotel in Las Vegas, riding on the crest of yet another successful recording, "Someday We'll Be Together." Ross's replacement was Jean Terrell. Joseph N. Bell states:

> Diana had a ten-year run with the Supremes—always as the lead singer, pushed farther front-and-center each year. The departure of Florence Ballard, the changing music scene, the steady growth in Diana's performing stature all contributed to her leaving the group in 1970 to take her sequined gowns and multiple wigs and electric arrangements into a solo act, backed and carefully synchronized by Berry Gordy and Motown (92).

Leaving to form an even more successful solo career, Diana Ross utilized the talents of successful Motown song-writers Nick Ashford and Valerie Simpson and released her first solo single "Reach Out and Touch Somebody's Hand" in 1970. Between 1970 and 1984, she recorded more than fifty singles and thirty-one albums in addition to teaming with such superstars as Marvin Gaye, Stevie Wonder, Michael Jackson, Lionel Richie, and Julio Iglesias.

Singer Embarks on Acting Career

In 1971 Ross married businessman Robert Silberstein, and three daughters—Rhonda Suzanne, Tracee Joy, and Chudney Lane—were born to this union. Although she refocused most of her energy and time to raising her daughters and making a home for her family, Ross continued to find the time to accelerate her professional growth. She embarked on a movie career and began working on her first film acting role in a portrayal of Billie Holiday in the critically-acclaimed *Lady Sings The Blues* (1972), for which she received an Academy Award nomination. After her impressive film debut, Ross was much in demand for other movie roles. They were *Mahogany* (1975), a financial disaster but a smash for her performance of the title song, "Do You Know Where You're Going To," which reached number one on the pop charts in 1976; and *The Wiz* (1978). Though neither film was a critical success, each one was important to Ross's professional growth: "for the first time in my life," said Ross, "I'm on my own—and that is *something*. I'm finding it very important for *me* to rely on me" (Bell, 173).

Artistic growth has always been significant for Diana Ross. Since 1978 she had wanted to be independent—to handle her own business affairs. Although 1980 was a blockbuster year for her at Motown with the album *Diana*—one of her biggest sellers since going solo—both gold and platinum records during the year for the single "Upside Down," and the album *20 Golden Great*, television specials, and other guest appearances, she still had the need to control her own life: "She had been glamorous Diana Ross of Motown for so long that she had lost track of Diana Ross, person. . . . She decided to look for that Diana Ross" (Haskins, 53).

Diana Ross took her career in hand. By 1981 she left Gordy and Motown to sign a contract with RCA Records. After nearly twenty years with Motown, she knew that the move would be extremely difficult but vitally necessary—a part of growing up: "Look," she says, "I had to grow. . . . You've got to leave home. It's a natural part of life" (Hirshey, 164). In a December 1985 interview with Susan L. Taylor of *Essence*, Diana Ross elaborated on her need to be independent: "I think I know what's right for me. There isn't anything anyone can tell me about my career that I haven't already considered somehow. I have given my career a lot of thought, and if I haven't done something, it's because it was not the way I wanted to do it or because I made another choice. . . . I go with what I believe, that's all" (54).

Out on her own, Ross has had periods of diminished commercial and critical success. Still touring and making recordings, she has, according to *Essence*, sometimes succeeded—as in *Why Do Fools Fall In Love?*—and sometimes failed—her album *Red Hot Rhythm & Blues* was an artistic and commercial disappointment. But she views all her post-Motown experiences as chances to learn and grow: "When I left the company it was a real important pivotal point in my life. It was important for me to stand on my two feet and make decisions for myself. I had opportunities on my own that I never would have had at Motown" (Cleage, 128).

Divorced in 1977, Ross moved from the West Coast to New York and set up Diana Enterprises, a record production company. In recent years, she has diversified her corporation. Meanwhile, her projects divert her time and attention increasingly away from recording and touring. She founded RTC Management Company, not only to oversee and produce her career but also the careers of other performers; her own production company, Anaid Films; JFF (Just For Fun) Enterprises to handle all independent projects outside of her career—proposed cosmetics, fashions, and merchandizing lines; Chondee, Inc., and Rossville and Rosstown publishing companies; Rosco, an advertising company; and the Diana Ross Foundation, designed for charity projects.

Ross is the recipient of numerous awards. In 1970 she was named Female Entertainer of the Year by the NAACP; she won a Grammy Award in that same year; became the honorary chairwoman of the Image Awards Presentation (1971) and at that gala won the Best TV Special of the Year Award for her "Diana" show; won the Cue award as Entertainer of the Year (1972), the Golden Apple Award (1972), the Gold Medal Award Photoplay (1972), an Academy Award nomination for Best Actress of the Year (1973), a Golden Globe Award (1972), an Antoinette Perry Award (1977); she was named to the Rock & Roll Hall of Fame and received awards from Billboard, Cash Box, and Record World, such as World's Outstanding Singer; she was awarded a star on Hollywood Walk of Fame; and received citations from Vice-President Humphrey for efforts on behalf of President Johnson's Youth Opportunity Program and from Coretta Scott King and Reverend Ralph Abernathy for her contributions to the SCLC cause.

Described by one writer as:

> Probably weighing in at not much more than one hundred and twenty pounds, she has a strength of presence in the room that has nothing to do with physical size and everything to do with concentrated energy. She is one of those people who charges the air . . . simply by moving through it. She easily looks a decade younger than her 45 years (Cleage, 72).

To stay fit, Ross bicycles, swims, walks, and runs.

The singer married Norwegian shipping magnate and mountaineer Arne Naess in 1985. Along with their children from previous marriages, Ross and Naess have two sons, Ross and Evan. Spending her time between her New York-based corporation and Norway, Ross says, "I'm happier now than I have ever been. . . . I'm much wiser now. Much more forgiving and loving. The more I live, the more I know what things are not worth wasting energy on" (*Essence*, 72).

Ross's drive and energy have not abated. Assessing her career, Pearl Cleage says in *Essense*, "She seems to be curious and excited about what 'the next phase' will bring. 'I'm learning so much,' Diana responded. . . . 'I love thinking about new things. I am excited by the possibilities I see'" (128). In addition to being a devoted mother and wife, she is involved in numerous projects: looking at scripts for other film projects, cutting albums, performing at concerts and clubs, and investigating the possibilities of managing other artists. But Ross has not forgotten her roots. "Instead of always looking at the past, I put myself 20 years ahead and try to look backward through my mind's eye. I don't think life is horizontal. I don't think you move through it like that at all. It's more like. . . . It's like I believe magic" (*Essence*, 133).

In some ways, her life has come full circle—she returned to her musical home, her roots, and Motown. Her new album *Working Overtime* (1989) was released on the Motown label and on that album she has incorporated the new street rhythms from her hometown into her music with the hope that "her interpretation of the music will be a positive force in the lives of her audience" (*Essence*, 128). More significantly, Ross is giving back to the home that nurtured her. In 1989 she accepted an offer to return to Motown as an artist, an equity partner, and director of the company. Diana Ross, superstar, "The Boss," is doing what she likes best: helping younger black artists succeed. "I really thought it was a terrific opportunity. I will be working with some new artists, probably in a management role, trying to pass on to them some of what I've learned about the music business. That part will sort of be an extension of what I'm doing now, and of course I'll continue with my own music" (*Essence*, 130).

References

Bell, Joseph N. "Diana Ross Grows Up." *Good Housekeeping* 176 (April 1973): 92, 172, 174, 184.

———. "I Love Being Diana Ross." *McCalls* 106 (October 1978): 122, 172-73.

Bogle, Donald. *Brown Sugar*. New York: Harmony Books, 1980.

Brown, Geoff. *Diana Ross*. London: Sidquick and Jackson, 1981.

Cleage, Pearl. "DIANA." *Essence* 20 (October 1989: 70-72.

"Diana Ross." *Ladies Home Journal* 95 (November 1978): 36, 42-44, 213-14.

Haskins, James. *Diana Ross—Star Supreme*. New York: Viking 1985.

Hirshey, Gerri. "Did the Dream (Girls) Come True?" *Esquire* 101 (May 1984): 163-67.

The Illustrated Encyclopedia of Black Music. New York: Harmony Books, 1983.

Nelson, George. *Where Did Our Love Go*? New York: St. Martins Press, 1985.

"New Day For Diana." *Life* 73 (8 December 1972): 42-45.

"Real Dreamgirls." *Ebony* 41 (October 1986): 44-46, 48, 50.

Taraborrelli, J. Randy. *Diana*. New York: Doubleday, 1985.

Taylor, Susan L. "Diana!" *Essence* 16 (December 1985): 50-52.

Jacquelyn Jackson

Wilma Rudolph

(1940-)

Athlete

Wilma Goldean Rudolph was born on June 23, 1940, the fifth of eight children born to Ed and Blanche Rudolph in Bethlehem, Tennessee. Given the achievements that she was to make later in life, the physical problems that surrounded her from birth until she was eight years old give cause to wonder how she survived and excelled. Rudolph, who was born with polio, weighed only four-and-a-half pounds at birth. She suffered from double pneumonia twice and scarlet fever by the time she was four years old, and was left with the use of only her right leg from the crippling effect of polio. The nurturing of her mother, the optimism of her doctor, the support of her track coach, and her own will to overcome her adversity led her to become one of the world's most noted track stars.

Wilma Rudolph

Since Rudolph's father had eleven children by a previous marriage, there were nineteen children in the family. Shortly after Wilma Rudolph's birth, the family moved to a house on Kellogg Street in Clarksville, Tennessee, some forty-five miles west of Nashville. Wilma Rudolph's father worked as a railroad porter and also did odd jobs around Clarksville; her mother was a maid in the homes of prominent Clarksville white families. Wilma Rudolph realized early that race made a difference in her little town of Clarksville, that blacks were expected to accept an inferior status in their dealings with whites. But what was especially curious to her was the belief of her parents' generation that they were protecting their children by not allowing them to challenge the assumption of their inferior status. Wilma Rudolph's mother was a strict and staunch Baptist, her father a little less so, but firm nonetheless. He was a disciplinarian. He took pride in the fact that none of his large family of children had been arrested for a crime, picked up by the police for anything, or jailed. In his view, these were crucial matters.

When doctors at Meharry Medical College in Nashville advised the Rudolphs that Wilma might regain the use of her leg through daily therapeutic massages, for two years the mother and daughter made weekly visits to Meharry for heat and water therapy treatment. On all other days the mother, with the assistance of three of her older children, massaged Wilma Rudolph's crippled leg at least four times each day. The hospital and home treatment was to prove immensely beneficial to Rudolph. It was her many rides from Clarksville to Nashville's Meharry Medical College for therapy that left on Rudolph the deepest, most enduring impressions of the place of her race in southern society. The trip was always taken on the segregated Greyhound bus; the same route was followed each time and blacks were the ones who sat in the back. The bus station had a separate ticket window, waiting area, and toilet for blacks. Blacks were expected to give up their seats, even those in the back of the bus, and stand in the aisle if the front of the bus became overcrowded with whites. The bus driver enforced the seating arrangement.

At age five, Wilma Rudolph was fitted for a steel brace to correct her polio condition, and for the next six years she wore that brace from arising in the morning until she went to bed at night. Psychologically the brace was devastating, since it served as a constant reminder that "something was wrong" with her. She also endured other illnesses and surgeries for the first decade of her life. She rebelled against her sickness and developed a competitive spirit that would contribute to her success in sports later on. At age nine, she rook off her brace after forcing herself to walk normally by "faking a no-limp walk." Losing her brace liberated Rudolph:

> From that day on, people were going to start separating me from that brace, start thinking about me differently, start saying that Wilma is a healthy kid, just like the rest of them (Rudolph, *Wilma*, 32).

Wilma Rudolph entered Cobb Elementary School in Clarksville in 1947 at the age of seven, and although she had missed kindergarten and the first grade because of her physical problems, she was allowed to enter at the second grade level. The school building included all grades from elementary through twelfth. Typical of many black schools of its time in the South, the curriculum, materials, and facilities were inferior to those of white schools. But her teachers stressed the basics—reading, writing, and arithmetic—which, though not a well-rounded program, provided skills that were beneficial then and later. Rudolph's first year of school changed her life. "I went from being a sickly kid the other kids teased to a normal person accepted by my peer group, and that was the most important thing that could have happened to me at that point in my life. I needed to belong, and I finally did," said Rudolph (*Wilma*, 22).

Rudolph's first teacher was a Mrs. Allison, who became Rudolph's role model. By her acts of kindness and generosity she helped to increase young Wilma's self-esteem and self-acceptance. On the other hand, her fourth-grade teacher, a Mrs. Hoskins, was the "meanest, toughest teacher in the whole school" (Rudolph, 22). She gave Rudolph her first spanking in school. But Rudolph grew to love Hoskins, who "had no pets in class, no favorites, and treated everybody equally" (22). Hoskins instilled in Rudolph positive thinking. "Do it," she said to Rudolph, "don't daydream about it. Wilma, I want you to do it." This advice was to have a lasting impact on Wilma Rudolph and was a strong force that shaped her thinking later as she emerged as a track star.

Rudolph's education at Cobb did little to prepare her for black life at the time nor for the black experience in the United States. The black history course that was taught at the school was geared toward "providing us with black heroes, not telling us the facts of life. The object of it all was to give us black kids somebody to be proud of, not to tell us we were still oppressed" (Rudolph, 27).

Rudolph Introduced to Organized Sports

The seventh grade proved to be the pivotal year of Wilma Rudolph's life. The new high school that was constructed for blacks in Clarksville "gave all of the kids something to look forward to each day" (Rudolph, 40). All social activities in the black community revolved around Burt High School, and it was at Burt Wilma Rudolph was introduced to organized sports, specifically, basketball. During her basketball career she first encountered the distorted views that many people had toward women participating in sports. Some believed that a woman "couldn't be a lady and a good athlete at the same time" (43). Rudolph never allowed such attitudes to affect her participation in sports. "When I played," she later wrote "I went all out" (44).

When she was in the eighth grade, Rudolph's seventh grade basketball coach, Clinton Gray, decided to resurrect the track team that had been started the previous year. He invited girls on the school's basketball team to join the track program. Because this would occupy her time after school and she wanted to keep busy, Rudolph signed up. Since she still preferred basketball, Rudolph continued to play and improve her game well into the ninth grade.

Rudolph ran in five different events in high school—the 50 meter, 75 meter, 100 meter, 200 meter, and the relay. She was thirteen years old and ran twenty different races that season. She won every one.

In her sophomore year she scored 803 points to set a new record for high school girls' basketball. Her team won the Middle East Tennessee Conference title. Rudolph was a starter on this team that won eleven conference games while losing four nonconference contests. In winning the conference title, Burt High School earned a spot on the Tennessee High School Girls' Championship, played at Pearl High School in Nashville. They lost the second game and they were eliminated from the tournament. It was at this tournament that Rudolph remembered one of the referees who worked many of the girls' basketball games. He was a track coach at Tennessee State University, Edward Temple. Temple took an interest in Rudolph because he saw her as a good prospect for his women's track team at Tennessee State University.

It was in her sophomore year at Clarksville's Burt High School that Wilma Rudolph entered her first serious track meet, held at Tuskegee Institute in Alabama. The meet attracted girls from all over the South. Rudolph lost every race. This was the first time she had suffered defeat in track; it had a devastating effect on her morale. But this was a sobering experience that made her realize that she could not "always win on natural ability alone, and that there was more to track than just running fast" (Rudolph, 64). The Tuskegee meet also had a tremendous psychological impact upon her. If it shattered her confidence, it also made her determined "to go back the following year and wipe them out" (64). It taught her, too, that champions come back after crushing defeats. The May following the Tuskegee meet, Coach Temple came from Nashville to see if Rudolph's parents would allow her to spend the summer at Tennessee State University. He wanted to teach her the techniques of running. At this summer camp, Coach Temple ran his girls "about twenty miles a day, five days a week, cross country to build up endurance" (69). At the end of the summer Temple took his team to the National Amateur Athletic Union (AAU) contest in Philadelphia. Rudolph won all nine races that she entered, and the women from Tennessee State swept the whole junior division of the National AAU. She also demonstrated her potential for the 1956 Olympic Games in Melbourne, Australia. It was at this meet that Rudolph was photographed with two baseball greats—Jackie Robinson and Don Newcomb of the Brooklyn Dodgers. Robinson became her first black hero.

Rudolph attended the Olympic trials in Seattle as a high school junior and qualified for the United States Olympic Team. Her confidence as a runner reached an all-time high. As the youngest member of the United States Olympic Team, Rudolph took her first trip to Los Angeles and her first airplane flight in 1956. At the trials, she was looked after by Bill Russell, captain of the United States men's basketball team. In Melbourne, Rudolph felt a psychological letdown because Coach Temple was not there, "a feeling shared by all of the other girls from Tennessee as well" (Rudolph, 95). Wilma Rudolph was eliminated from the 200 meter, but she ran the third leg of the relay, and the team placed third for a United States Bronze Medal. In Melbourne she decided that someday she would return to the Olympics "and win more medals, gold ones" (99).

The team scored three outstanding firsts in the history of Olympic competition: It was the first time that any school or club had six members qualify for Olympic competition in any sport; it was the first time all four members of the women's relay team came from the same team; and it was the first time that three teams broke the world's record in the same event (Lewis and Thomas, 128).

In September 1958, Rudolph entered Tennessee State University as a freshman, majoring in elementary education and psychology. Although an athlete and soon to become a member of the track team, she did not attend college on an athletic scholarship. Except when running track, Rudolph was not known to hurry and was usually late for classes.

"Tigerbelle" Becomes Three-Gold-Medal Winner

Rudolph and other members of the famed "Tigerbelles" helped support their education through the work assistance program (work-aid). Each athlete worked two hours a day, five days a week, at various jobs all over the campus to stay in school. In Rudolph's sophomore year, the first stop on the way to the 1960 Olympics was Corpus Christi, Texas, where the National AAU meet was held. The best women athletes were invited to the Olympic trials two weeks later at Texas Christian University. Rudolph set a world record in the 200 meter that was to stand for eight years, and she qualified for the Olympic team in three events—the 100 meter, 200 meter, and relay. In Rome she became the first American woman to win three gold medals. Of her Rome performance a reporter wrote:

> Running for gold medal glory, Miss Rudolph regularly got away to good starts with her arms pumping in classic style, then smoothly shifted gears to a flowing stride that made the rest of the pack seem to be churning on a treadmill (*Time*, 19 September 1960).

Afterward, she and the whole American team were invited to the Vatican to meet Pope John XXIII.

From Rome, Coach Temple took his winning team to the British Empire Games in London. Rudolph won all of the events she entered. From London the team went to Stuttgart, West Germany, and on to Holland and throughout Europe. Wherever Rudolph went, crowds of admirers came to see her. Journalists in Europe admired her running technique and scissoring stride. "The French called her 'La Gazelle,' 'La Chattanooga Choo Choo,' and 'La Perle Noire'; to the Italians she became known as 'La Gazzélla Nera.'" Rudolph duplicated her previous successes in all of these meets. When she returned to the United States, she and her teammates were honored with a parade in her hometown, Clarksville. More than forty thousand people attended the parade. The parade had a social significance beyond the celebration of Rudolph's achievements—it was the first integrated event in Clarksville's segregated history. From Clarksville Rudolph went to Chicago, where she received the key to the city from Mayor Richard Daley, then on to Detroit, Atlanta, Philadelphia, and Washington, D.C., where she met Vice President Lyndon B. Johnson and President John F. Kennedy. She was called on to attend numerous banquets, give television appearances, sign autographs, and make countless speeches. Always poised, she met the challenges well.

In 1961, after returning from Rome, Rudolph received the Sullivan Award—given to the top amateur athlete in the United States—and the Female Athlete of the Year Award. She was the first woman to be invited to run in such meets as the New York Athletic Club Meet, the Melrose Games, the Los Angeles Times Games, the Penn Relays, and the Drake Relays. She later ran track against the Russians and made two goodwill trips—one to French West Africa and another with the evangelist Billy Graham and the Baptist Christian Athletes, who went to Japan.

Next to coaches Ed Temple and Clinton Gray, May Faggs

was an important influence on Rudolph's athletic career. Faggs held several records in United States Women's Track, and she won medals in the Olympic competitions before Rudolph completed high school. She encouraged Rudolph to "perform as an individual" and not to be concerned with the loss of the friendship of her teammates if she should defeat them (Rudolph, 85).

Rudolph was born with red, sandy hair, a light complexion, and she was skinny. Later the attractive, gracious, and congenial athlete reached five feet eleven inches tall and weighed about one hundred and thirty pounds. Her friends called her "Skeeter" because of her size and her continuous movement, contending that she moved like a mosquito. Her first track coach, Clinton Gray, is credited with giving her the nickname—short for mosquito—since she was always "buzzing around." It was possible to mistake her for a white person, and beside some of her very dark brothers and sisters, she later wrote, "I felt like an albino" (11). The treatment of her race and the role and status attached to color had a deep psychological effect upon Rudolph, making her believe at the time that "all white people were mean and evil" (11). Her bitterness, however, was tempered by religion. She made a commitment to Christ at the age of fifteen. Religion and faith would carry her through many challenges in her career.

After graduating from Tennessee State University on May 27, 1963, Rudolph was offered the job as girls' track coach and teacher of the second grade at the elementary school she attended as a child. She married her high school sweetheart, Robert Eldridge, and later moved to Evansville, Indiana, where she became a director of a community center. From Evansville she moved to Boston, where she became involved in the Job Corps program in Poland Springs, Maine.

In 1967 Vice President Hubert Humphrey invited her to work with him in Operation Champion. The aim of the program was to take star athletes into sixteen of the largest city ghettoes of the United States to give young people training in sports. Ralph Boston, another Tennessee State track star and a graduate of the school, and Rudolph were the track specialists. After this project ended, the Job Corps transferred Rudolph to St. Louis, which allowed her to be closer to her home state. From St. Louis she went to Detroit and took a teaching position at Palham Junior High School. Later, at the advice of Bill Russell, she went to California, where she worked with the Watts Community Action Committee. She returned to Clarksville, Tennessee, in 1977 before her final return to Detroit, where she and her family reside today. She is president of the Indianapolis-based Wilma Rudolph Foundation. Wilma Rudolph and her husband, Robert Eldridge, have two daughters—Yolanda and Djuana—and two sons—Robert, Jr., and Xurry. Wilma Rudolph is active in her community as a member of Delta Sigma Theta Sorority, which she joined as a sophomore in college.

A major autobiographical work, *Wilma: The Story of Wilma Rudolph*, published in 1977 and produced as an NBC television movie by the same name, starring Cicely Tyson, told Wilma Rudolph's story to the world. The book and movie also provided encouragement to handicapped youth who otherwise might never work to achieve their goals despite their physical problems.

References

Biracree, Tom. *Wilma Rudolph*. New York: Chelsea House, 1988. Contains photographs.

Current Biography. New York: H. W. Wilson, 1961. 399-401.

Jacobs, Linda. *Wilma Rudolph: Run for Glory*. St. Paul, Minn.: Eric Corp., 1975.

Lanker, Brian. *I Dream a World*. New York: Stewart, Tabori and Chang, 1989. 140-41. Photograph, p. 141.

Lewis, Dwight, and Susan Thomas. *A Will to Win*. Mt. Juliet, Tenn.: Cumberland Press, 1983. Includes photographs.

Rudolph, Wilma. *Wilma: The Story of Wilma Rudolph*. New York: New American Library, 1977. Includes eight pages of photographs of Rudolph and scenes from the parade in her honor in Nashville following the 1960 Olympics in Rome.

Time 19 September 1960.

Collections

The Special Collections Department in the Tennessee State University Library contains news clippings from throughout the nation documenting Rudolph's life and activities, reviews of the NBC production *Wilma*, photographs, and Tigerbelle trophies.

James E. Haney

Josephine St. Pierre Ruffin

(1842-1924)

Clubwoman, civic leader, civil and women's rights activist

Josephine St. Pierre Ruffin, clubwoman, civic leader, and reformer, was born in Boston, Massachusetts, the fifth daughter and youngest of six children of John and Elizabeth Matilda (Menhenick) St. Pierre. Ruffin was a charter member of the Women's Era Club, the National Federation of

Josephine St. Pierre Ruffin

Afro-American women, the National Association of Colored Women, and the Northeastern Federation of Women's Clubs.

Her mother was born in Cornwall, England. Her father's background stemmed from African, French, and Indian heritage. He was the son of Jean Jacques St. Pierre, a French immigrant from Martinique, who married Betsey Hill, the descendant of an African prince who settled among Indians near Tauton, Massachusetts, after he apparently escaped from a slave ship. John St. Pierre was a clothes dealer who, like black shop owners on Battle and Union streets, sold new and used clothing. He was also the founder of the Zion Church in Boston. Ruffin's appearance was a mirror of her diverse ethnic heritage. She was a small woman with distinguished features, light brown complexion, and soft wavy hair. In her later years she projected a proud, matronly image.

Ruffin was sent to public schools in Charleston and Salem and, later, to a private school in New York to escape the segregated schools in Boston. She returned to Boston in 1855 and attended the Bowdoin School after the racial barriers were broken. In 1858, at the age of sixteen, she married George Lewis Ruffin, who was twenty-one at the time. George Ruffin was the oldest of the eight children of George W. and Nancy (Lewis) Ruffin, who were free blacks in Richmond, Virginia. Seeking better opportunities for her family, Nancy Ruffin migrated to Boston in 1853. George Ruffin attended the Chapman Hall School. Immediately after his marriage to Josephine St. Pierre, the couple sailed for Liverpool, England, to escape discrimination and social injustice in the North. They returned after six months, however, and George Ruffin began working as a barber in one of the well-patronized black establishments scattered throughout the city. In 1869 he graduated from the Harvard law school, and thereafter developed a thriving law practice, won a seat in the state legislature, was elected to the city council, and in 1883 became Boston's first black municipal judge. He was appointed resident consul in Boston for the Dominican Republic the same year.

Josephine St. Pierre Ruffin was actively involved in community and national reforms. She and her husband joined the freedom struggle prior to the Civil War. Although George Ruffin was unable to enlist because he was nearsighted, they recruited soldiers for the Fifty-fourth and Fifty-fifth Colored Regiments of Massachusetts. They were members of the Home Guard and worked for the United States Sanitary Commission. Following the war, Josephine Ruffin organized the Kansas Relief Association and through it collected money and clothing to provide relief for southern blacks in the exodus to Kansas. Ruffin expanded her career after her husband's death in 1886. During her marriage she acquired prestige and self-identity, but she was left with little material wealth, since her husband had contributed generously to charities and racial uplift. The Ruffins had five children: Hubert St. Pierre, who became a lawyer; Florida Yates, a clubwoman and teacher in the Boston public schools; Stanley, an inventor and manufacturer; George Lewis, a church organist and concert baritone; and a fourth son, Robert, who died in infancy. Despite family responsibilities, Ruffin became a well-known journalist, organizer, and clubwoman. Her keen interest in charity led her to write a letter in 1889 to the Educational League of Georgia informing the members that black women in the North were willing to assist them in undertaking the moral and industrial training of black children in Georgia. "It is the first time, we believe, in the history of the South where a body of representative Southern white women have shown interest in the welfare of the children of their former slaves as to be willing to undertake to make them more worthy [of] the duties and responsibilities of citizenship." Ruffin suggested also that "helpful inspiring lessons in morals and good conduct" could be conducted on Sabbath afternoons "without [the] contribution of a dollar from any pocket, Northern or Southern" (Dunbar Nelson, 173-76).

With increasing awareness of the crucial issues of the times, Ruffin conscientiously extended herself beyond the black community. She served on the executive board of the Massachusetts Moral Education Association and for eleven years was a volunteer visitor for Associated Charities. She was acquainted with Julia Ward Howe, Lucy Stone, Edna Cheney, and other reformers. Ruffin was active in many influential women's organizations in Massachusetts, including the Massachusetts School Suffrage and the New England Women's Club. In 1893 while working as an editor of a black newspaper, the weekly *Boston Courant*, she joined the New England Women's Press Association and retained her membership for several years.

Woman's Era Club Founded

In February 1893 Josephine Ruffin organized the Woman's Era Club, in association with her daughter, Florida Ridley, and Maria Baldwin, principal of the Agassiz High School in Cambridge. This local woman's club, with Ruffin as president, was founded to promote the interests of blacks in general and women in particular. Membership was open to all women, regardless of race. The first meeting was attended by several prominent white activists, including Lucy Stone Blackwell and Edna Dow Cheney. The Woman's Era Club adopted the motto, "Make the World Better," which were the last words of Lucy Stone Blackwell, an abolitionist and feminist who died on October 18, 1893. Yet, it is clear that Ruffin was especially interested in the progress and advancement of blacks. The Woman's Era Club, a self-help organization, encouraged unity among black clubwomen primarily:

> Our aim has been for practical work and we have tried in every particular to live up to the object of our club. How far we have succeeded is demonstrated in the interest which has been taken in all things pertaining to the uplifting of the race (*A History of the Club Movement*, 116).

A special project of the club was the presentation of scholarships to achieving students. The Woman's Era Club was the most representative organization of black people in New England. It initiated many reforms and movements that had a profound impact on racial uplift and advancement. By 1895 there were more than 133 members of the club, which met twice a month and collected an annual fee of one dollar from each member. A Sewing Circle affiliated with the club provided aid to St. Monica's Home, a hospital for black women. The Women's Era Club not only supported work in Boston but outside the area as well. The club contributed twenty dollars monthly toward the support of a kindergarten conducted under the auspices of the Educational League of Georgia.

Ruffin and her daughter, Florida Ridley, worked closely in club work and, together, they founded the *Woman's Era*, a monthly illustrated magazine available to the club members. The first issue was published in March 1894; the subscription rate was fifty cents a year for persons who subscribed prior to November 1 and afterwards, seventy-five cents to members and one dollar for nonmembers. The *Woman's Era* published articles that deal not only with women's issues but also with political and economic matters. It was the first newspaper in the United States to be owned, managed, and published by black women.

The Woman's Era Club of Boston, the Woman's Loyal Union of Brooklyn and Manhattan, and the Colored Women's League of Washington, D.C., were among the oldest black women's clubs. Ruffin's interest in the women's club movement led to national prominence. A woman of extraordinary skill in planning and organizing. she provided the inspirational power of the movement for a national organization of black women. The first national conference of colored women convened in Boston at Berkeley Hall under Ruffin's leadership. A committee on arrangements, composed of members of the Woman's Era Club, was formed with Ruffin as president and Ridley as corresponding secretary. The announcement of the national conference read:

> We, the women of the Woman's Era Club of Boston, send forth as call to our sisters all over the country, members of all clubs, societies, associations, or circles, to meet with us in conference in this city of Boston, July 29, 30, and 31, 1895 (Davis, 14).

Various black women's organizations responded to Ruffin's call, sending their letters to her home at 103 Charles Street. Ruffin informed the women that although the need for a national convention had been expressed for some time, the meeting was precipitated by a letter to England written by a Missouri editor, John W. Jacks, which denounced the moral character of all black women. Ruffin refused to publish the letter in the *Woman's Era*, but she sent a copy to all the women's organizations throughout the country emphasizing the pressing need for unity—for their own protection. In her opening address to the conference Josephine Ruffin challenged the women to seize every opportunity to do their part as black women and as American women:

> These women's clubs, which have sprung up all over the country, built and run upon broad and strong lines, have all been a preparation, small conferences in themselves, and their spontaneous birth and enthusiastic support have been . . . inspirational on the part of our women and a general preparation for a large union such as it is hoped this conference will lead to. . . . It is a good showing. It shows that we are truly American women, with all the adaptability, readiness to seize and possess our opportunities, willingness to do our part for good as other American women (Davis, 17).

Ruffin further stated that it was the right and duty of black women to declare their principles and "to teach an ignorant and suspicious world that our aims and interests are identical with those of all good aspiring women" (Davis, 18). She maintained that black women had been silent too long and silence under unjust charges only helped to protect the accuser. She urged black women to protest against the stereotyped images of black women. "It is to break this silence, not by noisy protests of what we are not, but by a dignified showing of what we are and hope to become that we are impelled to take this step, to make of this gathering an object lesson to the world," she proclaimed (Davis, 19). Ruffin insisted upon black women assuming the leadership in a club movement that would sympathize with the black race and with white activist women. She said, "Our movement is a woman's movement in that it is led and directed by women for the good of women and men, for the benefit of all humanity" (Davis, 19). Exclusion was not a factor in the formation of a black women's organization. "We are not drawing the color line," Ruffin asserted, " . . . we are not alienating or withdrawing, we are only coming to the front, willing to join any others in the same work and cordially inviting and welcoming any others to join us.'' The opening session in Berkeley Hall and several of the following meetings were held at the Charles Street African Methodist Episcopal Church.

National Unity Sought Among Women's Clubs

The outcome of the first national conference of black women was the founding of the National Federation of Afro-American Women (NFAAW). Josephine Ruffin was adamant in her goal to achieve a broad sisterhood of black women, and therefore encouraged the selection of Margaret Murray Washington, the wife of prominent educator Booker T. Washington, as president of the NFAAW. Florida Ridley was chosen recording secretary and Elizabeth Carter of Massachusetts was selected corresponding secretary. The *Woman's Era*, with Ruffin as editor, became the official journal of the NFAAW.

Meanwhile, a similar movement toward national unity was taking place in Washington, D.C., under the leadership of the Colored Women's League, which had affiliate clubs in other parts of the country. In July 1896 both national women's organizations held nearly simultaneous conventions in Washington. The Colored Women's League, led by Helen C. Cook, held its convention at the Fifteenth Street Presbyterian Church on July 14-15. The Federation of Afro-American Women met at the Nineteenth Street Church on July 20-22. Several progressive black women leaders—Margaret Murray Washington, Victoria Earle Matthews, Josephine St. Pierre Ruffin, and Mary Church Terrell—were present at the conference. A proposed merger of the two national bodies of black women stirred a great deal of emotion in both organizations. However, the clubwomen realized that a strong national organization was needed to achieve their objectives of improvement and reform. Thus, in 1896 the National Association of Colored Women (NACW) was founded and Mary Church Terrell of Washington, D.C. was chosen as president. Josephine St. Pierre Ruffin, Fanny Jackson Coppin, and Lucy Thurman were among the seven vice-presidents. The NACW motto, ''Lifting As We Climb,'' reflected the views of Josephine Ruffin, who had been involved in racial uplift more than three decades before the founding of a permanent national association of black women. News for the association was printed in the *Woman's Era*, which was edited by Ruffin and Florida Ridley until 1900. Other associates with the magazine were Victoria Matthews in New York, Fannie Barrier Williams in Chicago, Josephine Yates in Kansas City, Alice Ruth Moore in New Orleans, and Mary Church Terrell in Washington. The *Woman's Era*, which published the news of the work and activities of women's clubs across the nation, did more to promote the idea of a national association than any other source. The NACW worked through its leading departments of suffrage, patriotism, education, music, literature and art, mothers' meetings and night schools, child welfare, and public speaking, which combined the activities and work of the Woman's Era Club and other local clubs within the national association.

After national unity was achieved, the local clubs began to broaden their program through a system of federation. Josephine Ruffin organized, in 1896, the oldest regional federation in the NACW, the Northeastern Federation of Women's Clubs. The first meeting was held in Ruffin's home and Mary Dickerson of Newport, Rhode Island, was elected president. Ruffin was the vice-president and Elizabeth Carter was chosen secretary.

Josephine St. Pierre Ruffin's strong leadership ability, experience, and knowledge of women's clubs was derived, in part, from her long years of association with several prestigious white organizations. The New England Woman's Club, of which Ruffin was the first black member, was organized in 1868. The dominant figure in the club was Julia Ward Howe. She was joined by other reform-minded members concerned with abolition, the United States Sanitation Commission, temperance, and education. The Woman's Era Club became affiliated with the Massachusetts State Federation of Women's Clubs and Ruffin was a member of the executive board from 1899 to 1902. Delegations from the Woman's Era Club were cordially received when attending federation meetings, receptions, and conventions.

''The Ruffin Incident'' Stirs Controversy

It was not until the turn of the century that Josephine St. Pierre Ruffin experienced racism within the club movement. The incident stemmed from the General Federation of Women's Clubs' (GFWC) efforts to exclude black women from that organization. The GFWC, founded in 1890 just six years prior to the National Association of Colored Women, was the most substantial organization supporting reform. However, racism within the club movement surfaced as the number of clubwomen increased and as the scope of the GFWC broadened. In May 1900, after the GFWC invited the Woman's Era Club to join the organization and issued a certificate of membership, Ruffin decided to attend its biennial convention in Milwaukee, Wisconsin, as a delegate from the Woman's Era Club and the New England Women's Press Association. The officers of the GFWC became concerned when they realized that they had admitted a club with a black membership. The president, Rebecca Lowe, a southerner from Atlanta, Georgia, decided to return the dues the Woman's Era Club had paid and request the club to return its certificate of membership. Upon arriving at Milwaukee, Ruffin was told that she could not enter the convention representing a black club but would be accepted as a delegate from either of the other organizations she represented. To enforce the ruling, an attempt was made to snatch the membership badge from her chest. Ruffin refused to enter the convention under the conditions offered her. The ''Ruffin incident'' received publicity across the country; however, newspapers generally supported the strong stand Ruffin took for equal rights for black women. Despite considerable protests from some state delegations and the withdrawal of several Massachusetts clubs from the General Federation of Women's Clubs, the organization maintained its discriminatory admission policy for several decades. Although Ruffin was outspoken and aggressive in her demands for equality, she was not seeking interracial women's clubs. Instead, she sought equality of opportunity based on individual worth. The impact of the "Ruffin incident" on black women's clubs was tremendous, providing the incentive for them to develop their goals and improve their own communities through self-help organizations.

Ruffin, a founder of white and black civic organizations in Boston, was active in community and charitable work throughout her life. She was the founder of the Association for the Promotion of Child Training in the South and among the fifty-six charter members of the NAACP. The Boston NAACP, organized in 1910, was the first branch of the national association. Ruffin was a founder and later chairperson of the League of Women for Community Service. The league and the Women's Service Club opened homes on Massachusetts Avenue from which black women could direct social service work. This motivated old organizations and encouraged new ones with social service objectives. The city social service groups cooperated in attempting to solve the problems of housing, recreation, and employment opportunities. Ruffin's interest in improving conditions in Africa led to membership in the American Mount Coffee School Association. As vice-president of the association, which she helped organize, she assisted in fund-raising to expand Mrs. Jennie (Davis) Sharpe's school at Mount Coffee, Liberia. In later years, Ruffin was active in the Calhoun Club and was elected to the board of management of the Sedalia Club of Boston.

Josephine St. Pierre Ruffin was optimistic about the future of black women. She was a leader in the club movement among black women and active in both the struggle for racial equality and the movement for women's rights. Ruffin was a spirited worker who refused to leave any tasks unfinished. She labored incessantly for the cause in which she believed—racial uplift and women's rights. Florida Ridley wrote intimately of her mother, recalling that in her eightieth year she attended Women's Day at the Copley Plaza Hotel on November 16, 1921, and headed a receiving line of distinguished Massachusetts women. She was active in the Massachusetts Founders Day celebration on February 10, 1924, and on the twenty-eighth of the same month she attended the annual meeting of the League of Women for Community Service. The following month, on March 13, 1924, Josephine St. Pierre Ruffin died of nephritis at her home on St. Botolph Street. Visitation was held at the house of the League of Women for Community Service, of which Florida Ruffin Ridley was secretary. Prominent Bostonians, white and black, attended the funeral services at her church, the Trinity Episcopal Church of Boston, where her son George had been a soloist with the choir for thirty years. Josephine Ruffin was buried at Mt. Auburn cemetery in Cambridge, Massachusetts. Flowers and telegrams were sent by many organizations and individuals, including the National Association of Colored Women's Clubs, Northeastern Federation, Women's Era Club, Massachusetts State Union, Sedalia Club, and League of Women for Community Service.

References

Brown, Hallie Q. *Homespun Heroines and Other Women of Distinction*. Xenia, Ohio: Aldine Pub. Co., 1926. Reprint-ed. New York: Oxford University Press, 1988. 151-53. A photograph of Josephine St. Pierre Ruffin is published opposite p. 146.

Countee, Clarence G. "Josephine St. Pierre Ruffin." *Dictionary of American Negro Biography*. Eds. Rayford Logan and Michael R. Winston. New York: Norton, 1982.

Dannett, Sylvia G. L. *Profiles of Negro Womanhood*. Vol. 1. Yonkers, N.Y.: Educational Heritage, 1964.

Davis, Elizabeth Lindsay, ed. *Lifting As They Climb:* [Washington, D.C.]: National Association of Colored Women, 1933.

Dunbar Nelson, Alice, ed. *Masterpieces of Negro Eloquences*. New York: Johnson Reprint, 1974.

Hill, Adelaide C. "Josephine St. Pierre Ruffin." *Notable American Women, 1607-1950*. Vol. 3. Cambridge: Harvard University Press, 1971.

A History of the Club Movement Among the Colored Women of the United States of America. Washington, D.C.: NACW, 1902.

Hopkins, Pauline. "Josephine St. Pierre Ruffin at Milwaukee, 1900." *Colored American Magazine* 5 (July 1902): 210-13.

Kolmer, Elizabeth. "Nineteenth Century Woman's Rights Movement: Black and White." *Journal of Negro History* 59 (April 1974): 178-80.

Lerner, Gerda, ed. *Black Women in White America: A Documentary History*. New York: Vintage Books, 1972.

———. "Early Community Work of Black Club Movement." *Journal of Negro History* 59 (April 1974): 158-67.

Lord, Myra B. *History of the New England Woman's Press Association*. Newton, Mass.: Graphic Press, 1932.

Richings, G. F. *Evidence of Progress Among Colored People*. Philadelphia: George S. Ferguson Co., 1897.

Scruggs, Larson A. *Women of Distinction*. Raleigh, N.C.: The Author, 1893.

Washington, Booker T., ed. *New Negro for a New Century*. Chicago: American Publishing House, 1900. Photograph p. 391.

The Woman's Era (September 1895): 14.

Wood, Mary I. *History of the General Federation of Women's Clubs*. New York: Norwood Press, 1912.

Work, Monroe N., ed. "Josephine St. Pierre Ruffin." *Negro Yearbook* 1925/26. 422.

Collections

The Moorland-Spingarn Research Center, Howard University, Washington, D.C., contains the papers of George Ruffin which includes a photograph of Josephine St. Pierre Ruffin. Incomplete files of the *Woman's Era* are also in the center and in the Boston Public Library.

Floris Barnett Cash

S

Betye Saar

(1926-)

Artist, educator

Artist Betye I. Saar has been an inveterate collector of family memorabilia, photographs, printed ephemera, buttons, shells, feathers, beads, and other odds and ends since childhood. When she was small she often visited her grandmother, who lived in the shadows of Simon Rodia's Watts Towers. Rodia piled shards of broken tile, china, pottery, glass, old bottletops, and other "junk" onto steel skeletons to build what is probably the most monumental work of folk art in United States history. Saar has described these fantastic towering spirals as a fundamental influence on her own work, which is indeed based on collage. The technique appears as a natural outgrowth of her faith in the power of art to recover meaning from old fragments.

A native of Los Angeles, Saar was born on July 30, 1926, to Jefferson and Beatrice Brown. She received her B.A. in design from the University of California at Los Angeles in 1949 and pursued graduate studies at California State University at Long Beach (1958-1962), the University of Southern California (1962), California State University at Northridge (1966), the Pasadena School of Fine Arts Filmmaking (1970), and the American Film Institute (1972). She has taught at UCLA and at the Parsons-Otis Institute in Los Angeles.

At first Saar was basically a printmaker, focusing especially on mysticism and the occult, as in her *Mystique Scene* (1965) and *The House of Tarot* (1966). These works often combined drawing with intaglio or etching. Other works were silverpoint drawings, such as *Bone Conjuring Sirens* (1967). Toward the end of the 1960s, however, she began to place her prints within already-existing windowframes or specially made boxes, such as in *Black Girl's Window*. The use of boxes has been said to reflect the influence of Joseph Cornell. Gradually Saar introduced more and more elements of three-dimensional collage into essentially two-dimensional works until her constructions became predominantly three dimensional, as in her 1971 creation *Eshu [The Trickster]*, although still wall-hung. Eventually she replaced her own prints as parts of her assemblages with already-existing collected items or photo-mechanical reproductions of such images, including color xerographs. For her 1973 piece *Shrine: Mti*, she piled boxes on boxes to form a kind of altar, representing an evolution toward freestanding sculpture.

In 1974 Saar received a grant from the National Endowment for the Arts to build a series of floor standing pieces intended to evoke her mysterious, magical, and ritualistic feelings. She traveled to Haiti, Mexico, and Nigeria to collect some of the materials for the series. She became inspired by a then-recent article by Arnold Rubin, "Accumulation: Power and Display in African Sculpture," in which the author distinguishes between European and African concepts of art. European connoisseurship promotes the concept of an artwork as the product of a singular creator and seeks the restoration of any particular work to its original state at the time of creation. In traditional African society, a single artwork can be the product of any number of makers over an indefinite period of time. "The evolution of such objects," said Rubin, "may be thus said to begin rather than end when the basic forms have been defined" (47). Anything possible could be added to the work to enhance its impact as display, so as to yield greater detail, ornamentation, or variety of color. Its power also could be increased by adding materials symbolic of high status, family, ancestry, wealth, or spiritual force. As a result, many works of traditional African art are assemblages of already-existing natural or manufactured objects or fragments not originally intended as art materials. This, of course, could also describe Saar's work. She seized upon this Afrocentric definition of art as her own and used it to direct her production of the NEA-sponsored series of altars. A popular category of free-standing works (for example, *Indigo Mercy*, 1975), the ritual altars of the 1970s and 1980s have appreciated more greatly in value over the years than perhaps any other category of her work.

"To recapture the past, in both an autobiographical and more general sense," said New York art critic Deborah C. Phillips, "has been the primary motivation behind all of Saar's work" (Knowlton, 231). The artist herself has called this her cumulative consciousness: "That's the part of my accumulative memory from way back to the beginning of time. It includes all the things that have touched my existence even before my birth" ("Interview with Betye Saar," quoted in Conwill, 14). Among references that are autobiographical in the narrow sense, pieces of family memorabilia often have figured in the collected items that find their way into Saar's art. A good example is *Record: For Hattie* (1975), a mixed media assemblage that brings together objects associated with the artist's great aunt Hattie, then recently deceased. A poignant mood of reminiscences arises from the juxtaposition of Hattie's jewelry, a mirror, pressed dried flowers, a baby photograph, and cosmetics along with multicultural symbols of the life of the spirit. Autobiography also becomes African ancestral memory in such works as *Gris Gris Box* (1972), essentially a collage, *The Protector: The Earth* (1977), an altar, and *Spirit Catcher* (1976-77), a freestanding work in natural fibers.

Ethnic Imagery Seen in Works

After the death of Martin Luther King, Jr., a theme of personal protest surfaced in Saar's works through irony or satire. The exemplar of this trend is her "Aunt Jemima" series. Saar added to her palette of collective imagery certain popular American depictions of black people. Exposing the racism underlying the images, she created droll assemblages that transformed pejorative stereotypes into hard-hitting political statements. *The Liberation of Aunt Jemima* (1972), now held by the Art Museum of the University of California at Berkeley, uses repeating smiling faces of nurturant black womanhood from commercial pancake mix labels as background to a big black mammy doll carrying a broom in her left hand but toting a big black rifle in her right. This aunt is bent on freedom by any means necessary. Similar works are *I've Got Rhythm (We Shall Overcome)* (1972) and *Mammy's Little Coal Black Rose (We Shall Overcome)* (1973). Art historian Samella Lewis has characterized such works as "attacks on traditional Western attitudes" (174). Saar acknowledges this orientation: "At first, my work was overtly political. I used stereotypic and derogatory images of blacks—Black Sambo, Aunt Jemima, Uncle Remus—as images of power" (Lilly Wei interview with Betye Saar, quoted in "The Peripatetic Artist," 135).

However, the artist, a Unitarian, rarely limits her material to African-American or African imagery. She usually combines in the same work items collected from Latin America, the Pacific, and Asia with things from the United States, the Caribbean, and Africa. The same work sometimes combines such disparate spiritual symbols as crescent and star, cross, star of David, and tarot card. As early as 1977 she asserted that "there is no difference in kinds of religions or kinds of people." She regarded her art as "just about folks" (Conwill, 13).

Although Saar's work has been featured in many women's exhibitions and some all-black exhibitions, by the end of the 1980s she had become bored with that kind of segregation: "I want the art to be considered for itself. Midway through 1989 I made a decision . . . not to become involved with shows that had 'woman' or 'black' in the title" (Brown, 23). At first she tended to use images of women as objects associated with them more than she used traditionally male subjects. "But now," she says, "the politics are more submerged, subversive, softer, as my work becomes more about a universal feeling" (Lilly Wei interview with Betye Saar, 135). Her hope for the 1990s is "that we will move away from separatist issues and begin to address how we are going to survive the next 100 years, what's going to happen to the planet" (Brown, 23).

The scope of Saar's vision has widened. In moving from assemblages to installations, she also has become interested in extending the African artistic characteristics of display and power: "I began to create an area around the sculpture/assemblage which expanded the 'power' and 'display' to include the viewer in the space, in the art environment itself" (Saar, 44). For some of her room-size installations she has invited the public to participate by contributing objects to the "altar" in imitation of the accumulation in traditional African artworks. Some of the trash and treasures thus accumulated the artist has permanently added to the works for future exhibition. Other contributions by viewers have taken the form of dances danced, music played, songs sung, and poetry read within the space of the installation. Other installations incorporate more autobiographical, personal statements with the addition of quotations, other text, and silhouettes of the artist herself. All of these things she regards as having enhanced the displays and increased their power. As her installations have evolved so has her repertoire of images expanded: "I have seen that with installation art, at least, there is an energy that bypasses national and cultural limitations. It's as if cultural boundaries are erased. Perhaps it is because this kind of work is so new and there is no tradition other than an international one" (Lilly Wei interview with Betye Saar, 135).

Exhibitions of Saar's work have ranged widely in venue and genre. In addition to showing three-dimensional assemblages and site installations, California and New York Galleries have exhibited lesser-known two-dimensional works of the 1980s, including paper collages and collages on women's handkerchiefs. In 1983 she showed her assemblages on books along with others by her daughters Lezley and Alison. (She also has a third daughter, Tracye.) In 1990 Betye and Alison Saar had a well-received joint show of their assemblages and installations along with *House of Gris Gris,* a collaborative installation. Since 1972 Betye Saar has had over forty solo shows, including ones at California State University at Los Angeles (1973), the Whitney Museum of American Art (1975), the Studio Museum of Harlem (1980), Carnbena School of Art, Australia (1984), and the Museum of Contemporary Art, Los Angeles (1984). Among major group shows in which her work has appeared are *Painting and Sculpture in California: The Modern Era,* National Gallery of Art (1967), *The Object as Poet,* the Museum of Contemporary Crafts, New York (1977), and *Ritual and Myth,* the Studio Museum in Harlem (1982). Pieces by Saar are in the permanent collections of the High Museum in Atlanta, the Hirshorn Collection in Naples, Florida, the Oakland Museum, the San Francisco Museum of Modern Art, the State Museum of New Jersey, the University of California at Berkeley, and the University of Massachusetts at Amherst.

In 1974 she was the subject of "Spirit Catcher: The Art of Betye Saar," a half-hour documentary in the *Women in the Arts* series on WNET-TV in New York City. In 1984 she received a second grant from the National Endowment for the Arts.

References

Brown, Betty Ann. "On Compiling Relics: The Magic of Works by Alison and Betye Saar Transcends Postmodernism." *Artweek* 21 (1 February 1990): 1, 20.

Burke, Carolyn. "Images from Dream and Memory." *Artweek* 15 (14 January 1984): 4.

Cornwill, Houston. "Interview with Betye Saar." *Black Art* 3 (1978): 4-15.

Exhibition catalogs, California State University at Los Angeles, 1973; Museum of Contemporary Art, Los Angeles, 1984; Studio Museum in Harlem, 1980; and Whitney Museum of American Art, 1975.

Hammond, Pamela, "Betye and Alison Saar, Wight Art Gallery, UCLA." *Art News* 89 (April 1990): 176.

Hollie, Pamela. "Betye Saar: Eminently Collectible." *Black Enterprise* 2 (December 1980): 40.

Hollis, Sara. "Afro-American Artists: A Handbook." Ph.D. dissertation, Atlanta University, 1985.

Hugo, Joan. "Sophisticated Ladies." *Artweek* 14 (8 January 1983): 16.

Knowlton, Monique. "Betye Saar." *Art News* 80 (September 1981): 231.

Lewis, Samella. *Art: African American.* New York: Harcourt Brace Jovanovich, 1978.

Rubin, Arnold. "Accumulation: Power and Display in African Sculpture." *Artforum* 13 (May 1975): 35-47.

Saar, Betye. "Installation as Sculpture: Site Works." *International Review of African American Art* 6 (1984): 44.

Wei, Lilly. "The Peripatic Artist: 14 Statements." *Art in America* 77 (July 1989): 135.

Who's Who Among Black Americans, 1990/91. 6th ed. Detroit: Gale Research, 1990.

Lester Sullivan

Edith S. Sampson

(1901-1979)

Lawyer, judge

Edith S. Sampson accomplished a long list of firsts: first woman to be awarded a master of laws degree from Loyola University; among the earliest of black women admitted to practice before the Supreme Court; first black woman elected judge in the United States; and first black person appointed as delegate to the United Nations.

Edith Spurlock Sampson was born on October 13, 1901, in Pittsburgh, Pennsylvania. She grew up in a large family of seven brothers and sisters under the direction of their frugal parents, Louis Spurlock and Elizabeth (McGruder) Spurlock. By all reports, including her own, the family was quite poor; her father "managed a cleaning and dying establishment," and her mother made buckram hat-frames and switches of false hair and earned enough money to buy the family a home. They avoided even the smallest waste: "Clothing went from child to child, but it was always fitted to the new owner, and was always neat and clean" (Sampson, "I Like America," 6).

The family was so poor that Sampson interrupted her schooling in order to work even in grade school. "My first job was in a fish market after school, scaling and boning fish when I was fourteen" (Sampson, "I Like America," 6). She returned to school and eventually graduated from Peabody High School in Pittsburgh. Her Sunday school teacher helped Sampson obtain a job with Associated Charities, which later helped her gain admission to the New York School of Social Work. She frequently discussed her experiences there in a course in criminology in which she earned the highest grade. The teacher, George W. Kirchwey of the Columbia University School of Law, commented: "You are in the wrong field. You have the earmarks of a lawyer." When she had moved to Chicago and had begun working as a social worker at the Illinois Children's Home and Aid Society, she encountered Kirchwey again when he gave a speech in the city. With his encouragement and support, she enrolled in the John Marshall Law School at night. She "placed dependent children in new homes and found adoptive homes for the neglected" during the day (Sampson, "I Like America," 7), and as the highest ranking student among ninety-five in the course on jurisprudence, she received special commendation from Dean Edward T. Lee.

Sampson failed the bar, an event that she attributed to overconfidence, and she commented, "that was the best thing that could have happened to me" (*New York Times*). She then enrolled in a master of laws program at the graduate law school of Loyola University. She was awarded the LL.M. in 1927 from Loyola, the first woman to have received the degree from the university. She was also admitted to the Illinois bar in the same year.

Sampson effectively maintained dual careers in social work and law for much of her life. She worked at the Young Women's Christian Association and the Illinois Children's Home and Aid Society while she was in law school. By 1925 she became a probation officer and eventually a referee for the Juvenile Court of Cook County, Illinois, for eighteen years, where, she reported, she "learned the practical side of law." She also began a law practice, specializing in criminal law and domestic relations, in 1924 and continued it until 1942. During those years she was admitted to practice before the Supreme Court of the United States (1934), among the earliest of black women to have been so honored. In 1934 she married attorney Joseph E. Clayton, who joined her in her practice in Chicago. Edith Spurlock Clayton became Edith S. Sampson after her marriage to Rufus Sampson, a field agent for Tuskegee Institute in Alabama. Although she later divorced him, she continued to use that name in her public life. Her law office on South State Street, in the heart of the Chicago black belt, became a kind of clinic for thousands of poor people who would have had difficulty getting legal advice elsewhere. A friend describes her in court as "a kind of free-wheeler with a completely unorthodox approach to law." Sampson said of her court manner: "I talk from my heart and let the law take care of itself" (Ratcliff, "Thorn in Russia's Side," 6). In 1947 Sampson was appointed Assistant State's Attorney of Cook County.

In the late 1940s Sampson began a third, international phase to her career that intersected with post-World War II

Edith S. Sampson

cold war politics. This role first became apparent when Sampson participated in a seventy-two day around-the-world featuring the "America's Town Meeting of the Air" radio program. During the trip, representatives of various types of American interest groups broadcast discussions of current problems in twelve countries. The National Council of Negro Women (NACW) selected Sampson as its representative. She was chairwoman of the executive committee of the NACW. Sampson reported that a lot of misinformation about the status of blacks in American was clarified on the trip:

> Wherever we went we found that people had been misled into believing that fifteen million American Negroes lived behind barbed wire. They were amazed that I had a law degree, attended a white church, and had never been to a segregated school (Ratcliff, "Thorn in Russia's Side," 6).

Supreme Court Justice William O. Douglas said that:

> [a] speech in New Delhi, 16 August 1949 by Edith Sampson . . . created such a profound impression. She made it clear that while she would fight for the rights of her people at home, she would stand for no criticism of America abroad by reason of the color issue. That speech created more good will and understanding in India that any other act by any American ("A Tribute to the Hon. Edith S. Sampson," n.p.).

At the conclusion of the trip the delegates organized the World Town Hall Seminar and elected Sampson president of the group. She and her husband were practicing criminal law at the time, but Sampson reported:

> My decision to make the Town Hall trip proved to be the turning point of my life. After visiting and talking with the peoples of other countries, I knew that I could never make my law practice the primary business of my life; I would have to devote myself to the course of world brotherhood and world peace.
>
> That is why I was so delighted when the President of the United Sates appointed me as a member of the U. S. Delegation to the United Nations (Sampson, "I Like America," 8).

Sampson Appointed Delegate to the United Nations

Sampson was appointed by President Truman in August 1950 to serve as an alternate United States delegate (substituting for Eleanor Roosevelt) to the fifth regular session of the General Assembly. "When her appointment was announced, she was canning peaches in the kitchen of her Chicago home. She received reporters, went on with the canning" (Ratcliff, "Thorn in Russia's Side," 6).

At the United Nations, Sampson served on the Social, Humanitarian and Cultural Committee, Committee Three, which was responsible for a number of areas, including land reform, reparation of prisoners, the repatriation of Greek children, a general resolution on the work of the Commission on Human Rights, and radio jamming. The committee also monitored and secured the release of German and Japanese prisoners of war held captive by the Russians in the early 1950s. The Soviets were very slow about repatriating their prisoners of war. Sampson was reappointed alternate delegate in 1952 and later member-at-large of the U.S. Commission for UNESCO early in the Eisenhower administration.

During her years with the United Nations, Sampson was called upon the travel abroad and address the status of the black population in America. In 1951, for example, she traveled in Europe and visited Austria. *Ebony* magazine reported on her trip:

> When the Austro-American Institute of Education recently found itself backed to the wall by questions about the status of Negroes in America, they put in a quick SOS to Washington. Secretary of State Dean Acheson responded immediately with one of the country's most potent weapons against Communist distortion of the Negro's status in the U.S. He sent dynamic and brilliant Chicago lawyer, alternate U.S. delegate to the United Nations General Assembly, on a special assignment to tour Austria and answer questions about the Negro. . . .
>
> She was given carte blanche to tell the truth and when she returned to the United States, President Harry S. Truman personally congratulated her on the job she had done (''Edith Sampson Goes to Austria,'' 80-81).

Sampson herself said of the trip and of her discussion of racism in the United States:

> There were times when I had to bow my head in shame when talking about how some Negroes have been treated in the United States. . . . But I could truthfully point out that these cases, bad as they are, are the exceptions—the Negro got justice for every one where justice was denied. I could tell them that Negroes have a greater opportunity in America to work out their salvation than anywhere else in the world (''Edith Sampson Goes to Austria,'' 80-81).

At least one article by William Worthy, published in the *Crisis*, offered some criticism of Sampson's comments about the status of blacks in the United States in a speech and in questions and answers given during a trip to Copenhagen in 1952. Marguerite Cartwright also discussed the controversial question of Sampson's characterization of the status of blacks in the United States in her travels abroad.

Sampson readily assumed this role of speaking up against communism on behalf of the place of and achievements of blacks in the United States on a number of occasions. *Ebony* quoted her comment, ''I would rather be a Negro in America than a citizen in any other land,'' with great approval. In fact the magazine used Sampson and her expression of opinion to describe ''Where *Ebony* Stands Today'' in an editorial on its fifth anniversary:

> The very career of Mrs. Sampson [whose picture was on the opposite page] in itself is a symbol of the greatness of American democracy with its story of a girl born in the slums, and unable to finish grade school working her way through law school and becoming a member of the U. S. delegation to the world tribunal.
>
> Ebony insists that is precisely because America is great that Negroes will continue to uphold, protect and fight for their native land as unceasingly as they battle to correct the flaws in the democracy they cherish (94).

Sampson also recognized the significance racial conflict within the United States had for the rest of the world. In 1951 she concluded an address to the American Home Economics Association:

> You may not realize that these peoples [in the Eastern part of the world] represent two-thirds of the population of the world, and they are dark people. We need their help and co-operation. They are questioning our sincerity. They are of the opinion that the same discriminatory practices affecting Negroes in this country would affect them because of their color if they joined with America (Sampson, ''World Security Begins at Home,'' 517).

In 1961 and 1962 she was appointed by the vice president to serve on the United States Citizens Commission on the North Atlantic Treaty Organization. In 1964 and 1965 she was a member of the Advisory Committee on Private Enterprise in Foreign Aid.

Chicago Elects Sampson to Judgeship

In 1962 Sampson was elected associate judge of the Municipal Court of Chicago, the first black woman so elected in the United States. In 1964 *Harper's Magazine* reported on her work in Branch Forty-one of the Municipal Court of Chicago, which dealt with domestic relations. She managed a reconciliation between a man and his estranged and unwilling wife. Sampson addressed the wife:

> I know what you're thinking. ''When we leave here it will begin all over again. Nothing has been changed.'' But there you're wrong. Your husband isn't the same man anymore. He's changed, and you've changed, too. Something has been added to both your lives—me (Schiller, 147).

By the late 1960s she was judge of a branch of the Circuit Court of Cook County, handling landlord-tenant cases. She was consistently opposed to evicting tenants, to the distress of the landlords.

Sampson's election to the court reflected her close and cordial relations with the Chicago machine run by Mayor Richard Daley. Daley considered her a friend and supported Sampson as a candidate for the court when William Dawson, leader of the black South Side, opposed her. On another, earlier occasion, Harold Washington reported that she visited him as an emissary of the mayor. She came to encourage Washington to get along with the staff in the prosecutor's office, as Daley wanted to support her career. Washington was unable to handle the opposition he faced at the time and eventually left his position in the city's prosecuting division.

Sampson's strong personality impressed all who met her. In 1955, when she was fifty-four, she was described as follows: ''She works like a dynamo; talks like a pneumatic drill; and her warmth penetrates any room she enters'' (*Chicago Defender*, 11 October 1979, 21). On issues of race and racial identity Sampson said, ''Color never bothered me very much. I know what I am, and a blonde I am not'' (Ratcliff, ''Justice—Edith Sampson Style,'' 169).

Edith Sampson was awarded an honorary degree of doctor of laws from the John Marshall Law School. She led a very full life. Although Sampson had no children, three of her seven siblings had children, and she was very much involved in the lives of some of her nieces and nephews. She enjoyed interior decorating, canasta, canning preserves, and making jelly. She had a powerful impact on her entire family, and two of her nephews not only followed her into the legal profession, but are judges: Oliver Spurlock in Chicago and Charles T. Spurlock in Boston. Sampson's career has not yet been the subject of a historical biography, but it is one that cries out for the attention of a serious scholar.

References

Bennett, Lerone Jr. *Before The Mayflower History of Black America.* Chicago: Johnson Publishing Company, 1987.

Cartwright, Marguerite. ''The United Nations and the U.S. Negro.'' *The Negro History Bulletin* 18 (March 1955): 148, 133-35.

Chicago Defender 11 October 1979. 4, 21.

Chicago Sun-Times 14 February 1990.

Chicago Tribune 10 October 1979. Section 6, 11.

Christmas, Walter, ed. *Negroes in Public Affairs and Government.* Yonkers N.Y.: Educational Heritage, 1966.

Contributions of Black Women To America. Vol. 1. Ed. Marianna W. Davis. Columbia, S.C.: Kenday Press, 1982.

''Edith Sampson Goes to Austria.'' *Ebony* 6 (October 1951): 80-82.

''Edith S. Sampson.'' *Current Biography.* New York: H. W. Wilson, 1975.

Hymer, Esther W. ''On The Team For The Assembly.'' *Independent Woman* 29 (December 1950): 365, 380.

Jones, Claybin. Interview with author, 2 July 1990.

Jones, Douglas. Interview with author, 2 July 1990.

Jones, Joyce, Interview with author, 7 July 1990.

Kramer, Dale. ''America's Newest Diplomat.'' *New Republic* 124 (22 January 1951): 15-16.

''In Memoriam, Judge Edith S. Sampson.'' Funeral Program, October 11, 1979.

New York Times, October 1979.

''Pioneers of American Law and Government.'' General Motors Corp., n.d.

Ratcliff, J. D. ''Edith Sampson, Thorn in Russia's Side.'' *United National World* 5 (March 1951): 24-25.

———. ''Thorn in Russia's Side.'' *Negro Digest* 9 (September 1951): 6.

———. ''Justice—Edith Sampson Style.'' *Reader's Digest* (November 1968): 167-74.

Robinson, Wilhelmena S. *Historical Negro Biographies.* New York: Publishers Company, 1969.

Sampson, Edith S. ''I Like America.'' *Negro Digest* 9 (December 1950): 3-8.

———. ''Impartial Commission To Investigate The Prisoners of War Question.'' *Department of State Bulletin* 24 (8 January 1951): 68-74.

———. ''World Security Begins At Home.'' *Journal of Home Economics* 43 (September 1951): 516-17.

———. ''Citation for Person Killed in Service of the U.N.'' *Department of State Bulletin* 27 (22 December 1952): 997.

———. ''Statement Made on 20 November, 1952, in the Ad Hoc Committee on Repatriation of Greek Children.'' *Department of State Bulletin* 29 (31 August 1953): 296-297.

———. ''Equal Opportunity—Equal Responsibility, These Are Two Sides of the Same Single Coin.'' *Vital Speeches of the Day* 23 (15 June 1957): 519-21.

———. ''Show the East How the Freedom Revolution Works, Industrial Civilizations Are Built From the Bottom Up.'' *Vital Speeches of The Day* 17 (15 February 1951): 272-75.

———. ''Choose One of Five, It's Your Life.'' *Vital Speeches of The Day* 31 (15 August 1956): 661-63.

Schiller, Andrew. "Two Views of Chicago, II. People in Trouble." *Harper's Magazine* 228 (April 1964): 145-48.

Spurlock, Charles Thomas. Telephone interview with author, 11 July 1990.

Spurlock, Oliver. Telephone interview with author, 7 July 1990.

Travis, Dempsey. *An Autobiography of Black Politics.* Chicago: Urban Research Press, 1987.

"A Tribute to the Hon. Edith S. Sampson, 1901-1979." Commemorative flyer. The John Marshall Law School, 1979.

"Where Ebony Stands Today." *Ebony* 6 (November 1950): 94.

"Who's New At the U. N." *Senior Scholastic* 57 (27 September 1950): 16.

Worthy, William. "In Cloud-Cuckoo Land." *Crisis* 59 (April 1952): 226-30.

Collections

Edith S. Sampson's papers which include numerous speeches and photographs are in Special Collections, Arthur and Elizabeth Schlesinger Library on the History of Women in America, Radcliffe College.

Dianne M. Pinderhughes

Deborah Sampson (Robert Shurtleff)

(1760-1827)

Soldier, educator

Deborah Sampson's legacy is one of heroism and adventure as a Revolutionary soldier. Her decision to serve in the Continental Army simply represented an intense patriotism; she was injured three times and finally became too ill to serve. Sampson was no doubt the first woman ever to draw a soldier's pension, which Paul Revere helped her secure.

Deborah Sampson was born December 17, 1760, and died April 29, 1827. The daughter of Jonathan Sampson and Deborah (Bradford) Sampson, she was born in Plymouth, Massachusetts. One of six children, she could trace her ancestry back to old Pilgrim stock. Her mother's lineage was traced to Governor William Bradford, and Miles Standish and John Alden were among her father's ancestors. Despite their illustrious background, the Sampsons were not wealthy people. As a means to provide a better life for his family, Jonathan Sampson decided to become a sailor. Most likely as a result of a storm or shipwreck at sea, he disappeared and was never seen or heard from again. With the sole responsibility for her children, Mrs. Sampson found herself unable to find work that would allow her to take care of them. After experiencing continued chronic financial difficulties, and desiring to see to it that her children would receive adequate food and clothing, she dispersed them to different families with the hope that they would have a chance to improve their lot.

Dispatched from home at about age five, Sampson went to live initially with a cousin. Upon the death of her cousin when Sampson was about eight, she went to live with a pastor's wife, where she remained for approximately two years. She was then bound out as a servant in the home of Benjamin Thomas of Middleborough, where she remained until the age of eighteen. During the time she was with the Thomas family, she carried on her chores in an exemplary manner. She was able to acquire skills in many of the domestic arts associated with female work expectations, and she became generally adept as a cook and a seamstress. She became accustomed to long and grueling hours of work while with the Thomases. In addition to gaining expertise in the domestics arts, Sampson—owing in large part to her tall and well-proportioned physical stature—plowed the fields, fed the farm animals, and engaged in several other "manly" chores, including carpentry.

While her stay at the Thomas home was characterized by long and hard hours of work, it also allowed her to develop her interest in learning and to acquire some education. Sampson had the advantage of part-time attendance at the Middleborough public school. In 1770, few females were able to go to school, and Sampson used every opportunity to read and become more educated. Her part-time attendance at school was supplemented by instruction from the Thomas children. As her education progressed, she became an avid reader of newspapers and other printed materials. In time, much of her reading centered on the major issues of her day: the quarrel between Britain and the colonies, the vexing concern about Britain's financial problems, and the hateful regard for the taxes imposed on the colonies by Britain. Eventually, her interest in reading about the events of the day would prompt her to enter the Continental Army as a soldier in the war against Britain.

Sampson's interest in education and learning was developed enough that after her term of service to the Thomas family ended, and with some limited instruction at the local Middleborough school, she was able to teach for six months at the same school. She took a very definite interest in the teaching profession and would likely have remained a teacher except that she did have some difficulty with the local establishment. Deborah Sampson had been accused of dressing in male clothing and of conduct unbecoming a respectable lady. This difficulty seems to have been quite pronounced not only with the school officials but also with the local church with which she was affiliated at the time. Records of the First Baptist Church of Middleborough, which she joined in November 1780, show that she was excommunicated. Concerned about her sudden disappearance and her conduct prior to her reappearance, church officials "concluded it was the Church's duty to withdraw fellowship until she returned and [made] Christian satisfaction" (Mann, xxviii).

It was the venturesome Sampson who continually busied herself with not only female undertakings but the "concerns of men" relative to her avid interest in colonial and British politics. She was less than thirteen years of age at the time of the Boston Tea Party. In 1775, she read the latest news about developments between Britain and the Colonists; the American Revolution had begun as the British soldiers and the colonists had engaged in battle at Lexington and Concord. Although only fourteen at the time, Sampson continued to follow the events of the war. Seven years later, when she was twenty-one and the war was still being fought, she began to entertain the idea of active involvement in the colonial army. Each day her reading and interest in the issues brought her closer and closer to the decision to involve herself in the colonial war effort.

Sampson's move to action is perhaps reflected in the following lines attributed to her in this regard by Mann:

> For several years I looked on the scenes of havoc, rapacity and devastation, as one looks on a drowning man, on the conflagration of a city—where are not only centered his coffers of gold, but with them his choicest hopes, friends, companions, his all—without being able to extend the rescuing hand to either (Gannett, *An Address With Applause, At the Federal Street Theatre,* 17).

Speaking of Sampson's motivation for participation, Elizabeth F. Ellet wrote:

> There is no reason to believe that any consideration foreign to the purest patriotism, impelled her to the resolution of assuming male attire, and enlisting in the army. She could have been actuated by no desire of gaining applause; for the private manner in which she quitted her home and associates, entrusting no one with her design, subjected her to surmises of a painful nature; and the careful preservation of her secret during the period of her military service, exonerates her from the least suspicion of having been urged to the step by an imprudent attachment (369).

Having completed her period of indenture to the Thomas family, and alone, without the attachment of a spouse or other immediate family, Sampson was unrestrained in her patriotic dream to serve her country.

Sampson Serves in Continental Army

Her actual preparation for participation began in early 1782. From her work in the local school district, Sampson had accrued a sum of twelve dollars, which she used for purchasing materials for a man's suit. It appears that she selected times when she could work in private, and, using a skill perfected while with the Benjamin Thomas family, she sewed her suit to her liking. She then made her way on foot to Billingham, Massachusetts, where she presented herself for enlistment for the duration of the war. Disguised in men's clothing and using the alias Robert Shurtleff (Shirtliff or Shirtlieff), Deborah Sampson enlisted as a volunteer in the Continental forces on May 20, 1782. She was mustered into the service by Captain Eliphalet Thorp at Worcester, May 23, 1782, and served in Captain George Webb's company, Colonel Shepard's (later Colonel Jackson's) Fourth Massachusetts Regiment until discharged by General Knox at West Point on October 23, 1783 (*Massachusetts Soldiers and Sailors,* 164).

Sampson's height was above average for a female, and her "strong features, her stamina, and her remarkable adaptability enabled her to conceal her identity and perform her military duties well" (Cometti, 228). As a soldier in the Fourth Regiment, Sampson's robust strength and stamina served her well during her months of dangerous and hard fighting at White Plains, Tarrytown, and Yorktown. It was in the battle at Tarrytown that she received a sword-cut on the head and two musket balls went into one of her legs. She was seriously wounded but afraid to go to a hospital lest her sex be discovered. Her fellow soldiers recognized that she was seriously injured and took her to the nearest hospital, which was six miles away. There Sampson received treatment for her head injury, but she was able to disguise her leg injury from the doctor. Once alone, she used metal probes to remove one of the musket balls from her leg; the other was too deep and it remained in her leg. Sampson's wounds were now healing and although she had not completely recovered, she returned to active duty.

Four months later, Sampson was shot through the shoulder. "Her first emotion was described as a sickening terror at the probability that her sex would be discovered" (Ellet, 373). Again, it was her robust health that was her ally temporarily in coping with her shoulder injury. However, on the march north after the battle of Yorktown, Sampson's good fortune eluded her. The winter had been extremely cold, and the soldiers in the regiment were without proper clothing for warmth and comfort. During the extreme cold temperature, she succumbed to brain fever and was once again taken to a hospital by fellow soldiers. She was unconscious when she arrived at the hospital of Barnabas Binney, a physician in Philadelphia. Her ailment was considered hopeless, and consequently it appears that very little attention was devoted to her. After several days of hospitalization, however, Binney inquired of her state. Upon being informed that she was dead, Binney examined her for a pulse and learned that she was still alive. During this examination, he discovered that she was female. Even so, Binney did not divulge

Sampson's secret. He treated her until she could be safely taken to his house, where she remained until she recovered and was thereafter discharged from the army.

Sampson returned to her native New England in November 1783, where she resided with an uncle in Sharon, Massachusetts. She resumed female attire and seems to have settled comfortably into the Sharon community life. It was there that she met a farmer by the name of Benjamin Gannett, who lived on a nearby farm. Deborah Sampson and Benjamin Gannett were married on April 7, 1784. From the union three children were born: Earl Bradford, Mary, and Patience; they adopted a fourth, Susannah Shepherd, whose mother had died in childbirth.

Sampson's experience as Robert Shurtleff in the Continental Army began to attract attention. In the late 1790s Sampson met Herman Mann. Mann published what many regard as a much-romanticized biography of Sampson under the title *The Female Review* (Dedham, 1797; new ed., Boston 1866). Mann also wrote a lecture on her adventures, and here again his propensity to romanticize her experiences was evident.

Beginning with her appearance at the Federal Street Theatre in Boston on March 22, 1802, Sampson adapted the lecture written for her by Mann to her own liking and toured several New England towns, where she told of her Revolutionary War experience. It appears that Deborah and Benjamin Gannett were not doing well at farming, and in addition to personal satisfaction gained as a result of telling her story, Sampson used the speaking engagements as a means of earning money.

Soldier's Heroism Recognized

Sampson's story awed the listener and helped to spread the word about her phenomenal and daring adventure as a soldier. She met many outstanding Revolutionary War participants, became an acquaintance of Paul Revere, and visited General John Paterson, one of her former commanding officers; several social affairs were held in her honor to recognize her heroism.

Sampson was awarded pensions from the state of Massachusetts and from the federal government for her services to the nation. She received her first pension in 1792 from Massachusetts. In 1804 Paul Revere wrote to a member of Congress on behalf of Sampson, who was then in poor health and experiencing financial difficulties. Revere's appeal included the following comments:

> This extraordinary woman is now in her 62d year of her age; she possesses a clear understanding, and a general knowledge of passing events; fluent in speech, and delivers her sentiment in correct language, with deliberate and measured accent; easy in deportment, affable in manners, robust and masculine in her appearance.
>
> There are many living witnesses in this county, who recognized her on her appearance at the court, and were ready to attest to her services (Niles, 417).

On March 11, 1805, Sampson was listed among those receiving pension payments from the United States government.

Circumstances of Deborah Sampson Gannett's life after the turn of the century until her death in April 1827 are sketchy. It is known that in 1820 she renewed her claims for a pension for services rendered as a soldier in the Revolutionary War. After her death, her husband petitioned the federal government for claims as her widower in December 1837. He presented himself as worthy of her pension for his having cared for her during her long and protracted illnesses resulting from participation in the war. Her illnesses had also caused him to accumulate several medical bills, and he found himself in indigent circumstances. Congress responded favorably in July 1837, and Benjamin Gannett was granted eighty dollars per annum for the remainder of his life.

Deborah Sampson Gannett is buried in Rockridge Cemetery in Sharon, Massachusetts. The back of her tombstone reads, "Deborah Sampson Gannett, Robert Shurtleff, The Female Soldier: 1781-1783."

References

Cometti, Elizabeth. "Deborah Sampson." *Notable American Women: 1607-1950.* Vol 3. Cambridge: Harvard University Press, 1971.

Ellet, Elizabeth F. *The Eminent and Heroic Women of America.* New York: McMenamy, Hess, 1873. Reprinted. New York: Arno Press, 1974.

Forbes, Esther. *Paul Revere and the World He Lived In.* Cambridge: Riverside Press, 1942.

Gannett, Deborah. *An Address Delivered With Applause, At the Federal Street Theatre, Boston. . . .* Dedham, Mass., 1802. Reprinted. Publications of the Sharon Historical Society of Sharon Massachusetts. No. 1. Boston: Press of H. M. Hight, 76 Summer Street, 1904.

Gannett, Michael R. *Gannett Descendants of Matthew and Hannah Gannett.* Chevy Chase, Md.: The Author, 1976.

Hart, James D. *The Oxford Dictionary of American Literature.* Chevy Chase, Maryland, 1976.

Niles, Hezekiah. *Principles and Acts of the Revolution in America.* Baltimore: Printed and Published for the Editor by William Ogden Niles, 1822.

Mann, Herman. *The Female Review: Life of Deborah Sampson.* Introduction and Notes by John Vinton. Boston: J. K. Wiggin and William Parsons Lunt, 1866.

Massachusetts Soldiers and Sailors of the Revolutionary War: A Compilation from the Archives Prepared and Published by the Secretary of the Commonwealth. Vol. 14. Boston: Wright and Potter Printing Co., 1896.

Stickley, Julia Ward. "The Records of Deborah Sampson Gannett, Woman Soldier of the American Revolution." *Prologue: The Journal of the National Archives* 4 (Winter 1972): 233-241.

The National Cyclopedia of American Biography. Vol. 8. NewYork: James T. White and Co., 1983.

Larry Martin

Sonia Sanchez

(1934-)

Poet, playwright, activist, lecturer

Sonia Sanchez, poet, playwright, activist, editor, and national and international lecturer, is recognized as a political activist for black culture, racial justice, women's liberation, and peace and as one of the most prolific and influential living black American writers. She was born Wilsonia Benita Driver in Birmingham, Alabama, September 9, 1934, to Lena (Jones) Driver and Wilson L. Driver. She has one brother and one sister. She is the former wife of poet Etheridge Knight and the mother of three children. For several years she was a member of the Nation of Islam (Black Muslims in USA).

Sanchez began her writing career during the black arts movement of the sixties. Along with Don L. Lee, Nikki Giovanni, and Etheridge Knight, she formed the "Broadside Quartet" of provocative young poets, introduced and promoted by Dudley Randall. A major voice in this quartet, Sanchez, daring and revolutionary in her poetry, made the struggle for liberation as "palpable in [her] writings as it was in the streets" (Fuller, 7). She used the language of the people rather than the polished language of the academy, mixing images of the ghetto, lower-case letters, dashes, slashes, hyphenated lines, abbreviations, unorthodox spelling, and other experiments with language and form to redefine what a poem is, what it does, and for whom it is written.

In order to write, which is "to tell the truth," Sanchez explains, "I had to wash my ego in the needs/aspiration of my people" (Evans, 415). In the sixties, this creative washing produced compelling and passionate poetry that screamed out in a rage against racial/economic oppression and exhorted black people, who are "baddDDD," to deprogram themselves for the revolution.

By the early seventies, Sanchez was no longer a poet in the Broadside Quartet. Without question, she became/is a *solo* poet: distinctive, poignant, and gifted. She is not a one-theme, one-style, one-decade poet. She is not a "movement" poet. There is nothing tired or so very familiar about her writing that we feel we have read it before in a different volume. Every volume of Sanchez's poetry is a new experience in which she opens her artistic lens to new insights, images, feelings, details, truths; new experiments with language and form. She writes ballads, poetic letters, and haikus. Indeed, black American literary history will celebrate Sanchez as the preeminent writer of haikus. Intense, profound, complex, image-rich, and masterfully crafted, her haikus, interspersed in volumes that contain lengthy poems, are gifts to the reader. Even in haikus, traditionally known for "happy" scenes, Sanchez "washes" in the pain of her people.

Sanchez works with different poetic forms as an artist works with different colors and textures, matching form with subject matter and feeling and always producing poems that are detailed and original. She chants, sings, dances with her words. She sings the blues and the gospels. She writes long poems and short poems. She writes poems with revolutionary language and poems with traditional language. She is personal and political. She writes about war and pain; she writes about love and passion. She is in a state of rage; she is connected to peace.

Black American literary history will also record Sanchez as the artist who immortalized leaders and ordinary people in poetry that breaches the pulse of their lives. Indeed, there is a gallery in Sanchez's poetry: among them, her father, papa Joe Jones, domestic workers in the African diaspora, johnbrown, Margaret Walker, Jesse Jackson, and Malcolm X.

Poet Pioneers as Black Woman Writer

From the very beginning of her writing career, even when the focus was not on women, Sanchez was a black *woman* writer. In *Homegirls and Handgrenades*, *A Blue Book for Blue Black Magical Women*, *I've Been a Woman*, and *Sister Sonji*, as the titles indicate, Sanchez reaches into her woman's viscera.

There is no mistaking the signature of Sanchez: palpitating passion; provocative questions and disturbing answers; fresh and dazzling images; rhythms that you can dance to, run to, think to, rage to; details, the smallest of details, that are sprinkled like glitter in every line; power and force, message and craft, that are the hand grenades of her truth.

Sanchez received a B.A. at Hunter College in 1955 and did further study at New York University in 1958. She has taught and lectured at universities across the nation: instructor at San Francisco State College, 1966-67; instructor at the University of Pittsburgh, 1968-69; assistant professor at Rutgers University, 1969-70; assistant professor of black literature and creative writing at Manhattan Community College, 1971-73; teacher of writing at City College of the City University of New York, 1972; associate professor at Amherst College, 1972-73; poet-in-residence at Spelman College, 1988-89; poet-in-residence and professor of English at Temple University, (present).

In 1972, Sanchez won the P.E.N. Writing Award and the American Academy of Art and Letters' $1,000 award to continue writing. She was awarded an honorary Ph.D. in fine arts by Wilberforce University in 1973 and received a National Education Association Award in 1977-78. She was named Honorary Citizen of Atlanta in 1982 and, that same year, received the Tribute to Black Womanhood Award by the black students of Smith College. Other honors are: the Patricia Lucretia Mott Award from Women's Way and NEA in 1984; the Outstanding Arts Award from the Pennsylvania Coalition of 100 Black Women, and the Community Service Award from the National Black Caucus of State Legislatures. She is a 1985 winner of the American Book Award for her work *Homegirls and Handgrenades*. She serves on the literature panel of the Pennsylvania Council on the Arts and is a sponsor of the Women's International League for Peace and Freedom.

In addition to writing poetry, plays, and children's books, Sanchez is an Egyptologist whose study of Egyptian queens appeared in the highly touted *Black Women of Antiquity* edited by Ivan Van Sertima (Transaction Books, 1988). Sanchez is a contributing editor to *Black Scholar* and *Journal of African Studies*, editor of two anthologies, and author of more than twelve books. Her works are: *Homecoming: Poems* (Detroit: Broadside Press, 1969); *We a BaddDDD People*, play (produced at Theatre Blac'd, New York City, October 3, 1970; Broadside Press, 1970); *Liberation Poems* (Broadside Press, 1970); *It's a New Day: Poems for Young Brothas and Sistuhs* (Broadside Press, 1971); *Ima Talking about the Nation of Islam* (Truth Del, 1972); *A Blues Book for Blue Black Magical Women* (Broadside Press, 1973); *The Adventures of Fathead, Smallhead and Squarehead* (Third Press, 1973); *Love Poems* (Third Press, 1973); *A Sound Investment*, poems (Third World, 1980); *I've Been a Woman: New and Selected Poems* (Black Scholar Press, 1981); *Crisis in Culture: Two Speeches by Sonia Sanchez* (Black Liberation, 1981); *Homegirls and Handgrenades*, poems (Third World, 1985); and *Under a Soprano Sky*, poems (Africa World Press, 1987). Scheduled for publication in 1991 are *Shake Down Memory* and *Continuous Fire* (Africa World Press, 1991).

Her published plays are: *The Bronx is Next* (*Tulane Drama Review*, 1968); *Sister Sonji* (*New Plays from Black Theatre*, 1970); *Malcolm/Man Don't Live Here No Mo'* (*Black Theatre*, 1972); *Uh, Huh; But How Do it Free us?*; *I'm Black When I'm Singing, I'm Blue When I Ain't* (OIC Theatre, 1982); and *Dirty Hearts* (*Scripts* I, 1971).

Sanchez's recordings are: *Sonia Sanchez* (Pacifica Tape Library, 1968); *We a BaddDDD People* (Broadside, 1969); *Homecoming* (Broadside, 1969); *A Sun Lady for All Seasons Reads Her Poetry* (Folkways, 1971); *Sonia Sanchez and Robert Bly* (Blackbox, 1971); *Sonia Sanchez: Selected Poems, 1974* (Watershed Intermedia, 1975); and *IDKT: Capturing Facts about the Heritage of Black Americans* (Ujima, 1982).

References

Basel, Marilyn K. "Sonia Sanchez." *Black Writers*. Detroit: Gale Research, 1989.

Contemporary Literary Criticism. Vol. 5. Detroit, Gale Research, 1976.

Davis, Marianna W., ed. *Contributions of Black Woman to America*. Vol. 1. Columbia, S.C.: Kenday Press, 1982.

Evans, Mari. *Black Women Writers: A Critical Evaluation*. New York: Doubleday, 1984.

Shockley, Ann A. and Sue P. Chandler, eds. *Living Black American Authors*. New York: Bowker, 1973.

Tate, Claudia, ed. *Black Women Writers at Work*. New York: Continuum, 1983.

Gloria Wade-Gayles

Doris Saunders

(1921-)

Publishing executive, journalist, librarian, educator

When Doris Evans Saunders was a sophomore in high school, she met Joseph Rollins, Jr., at a Christmas party. He asked her out, but since she could not date, they went to the library. When he introduced Doris Saunders to his mother, the children's librarian at Hall Branch Library, his mother looked her over and later told Doris, "I wondered where my son had found this little hussy" (Saunders's mother was studying beauty culture at the time and had made Saunders's hair henna-colored). Charlemae Hill Rollins asked Doris Saunders about the books she had read and shortly discovered that, although she read widely, she had read no black American writers except Booker T. Washington and Paul Laurence Dunbar. Charlemae Rollins introduced Saunders to this wide field of knowledge and to many writers and editors who were her friends. Saunders soon determined that she would be a librarian when she grew up. She was under Charlemae Hill Rollins's influence completely and attended American Library Association (ALA) conventions and Children's Reading roundtable meetings long before she became a librarian in the Chicago Public Library.

While Joseph Rollins, Jr., found other girlfriends, and Saunders found other boyfriends, Charlemae Rollins became, in essence, Saunders's other mother. Saunders was born in Chicago on August 8, 1921 to Alvesta Stewart Evans and Thelma (Rice) Evans. Her father died the year before she met Charlemae Rollins, and her mother had gone to work. The family had to live with the maternal grandparents; therefore, Charlemae Rollins filled a significant void in the life of Doris Saunders in a very constructive way.

Saunders attended Chicago's Englewood High School. She entered Northwestern University in 1938 and remained until 1940, and later pursued studies at Central YMCA College in 1940-41. Also in 1941, she entered the Chicago Public Library Training Class and completed the course of study and practice. Nine months later, in May 1942, she became a junior library assistant and shortly thereafter, she passed the Civil Service examination for senior library assistant. She was first assigned to the book selection department, later to the Hall Branch Library, and then the George M. Pullman Branch Library. While at Pullman, she was the only black among nine persons who passed the principal reference librarians' examination. She was appointed to work in the social science and business division of the main library as the first black reference librarian. She was still fairly young, although by 1947, when she went to the social science and business division of the library, she was already divorced from Sydney S. Smith, childless, and had returned to Roosevelt University part-time to complete the bachelor of arts degree in philosophy. Saunders earned her degree in June 1951.

On a cold and dreary Saturday afternoon in January 1949, one of Saunders's white coworkers, a little tipsy on her luncheon martini, made the mistake of speaking about "those people" in her hearing. Saunders realized the coworker was referring to her. She left the library, took the bus directly to Charlemae Rollins's and informed her that she was quitting her job. Rollins listened to her story, sympathized, and suggested that before quitting her present position she should seek employment elsewhere. She suggested that Saunders write a letter to John H. Johnson, who had just bought a building that he was renovating for *Ebony* magazine offices. Using Rollins's paper, typewriter, envelope, and stamp, she wrote and mailed the letter to John H. Johnson, and suggested that he establish a special library for his editorial and advertising staff and clients. The following week his secretary called Saunders to come for an interview, and on February 1, 1949, she became the librarian at Johnson Publishing Company. She never really looked back, nor did she ever have to ask for a raise. John H. Johnson was completely supportive of the library, and today it is an outstanding special reference library on the contemporary black in the twentieth century.

On October 28, 1950, Doris Evans married Vincent E. Saunders, Jr., a Chicago health educator, and they had two children, Ann Camille and Vincent III. They were divorced in August 1963. He has remarried; Doris Saunders has not.

Saunders Influences the Publishing of Black Books

In 1960 John H. Johnson responded to Doris Saunders's request to publish hardcover books that would fill the gap in information about black people, and Saunders became director of the book division. The requests for information from schools, colleges, and readers had tripled and the movement for more and better information on black history, which had really started with the *Brown* vs. *Board of Education* decision, was reaching a groundswell. This was an unparalled opportunity not only for a black woman but for any woman to make a mark in the publishing business. The first nonfiction book was Lerone Bennett, Jr.'s *Before the Mayflower*. It has become a classic.

In 1966, following a policy disagreement, Saunders left Johnson Publishing Company and established her own public relations firm, the Plus Factor and Information. During the six years that she was away from Johnson Publishing Company, she did promotions for clients as varied as Ravinia Festival's production of *Ceremonies in Dark Old Men*, and the changing of the guard at a community bank as the white president was forced out and a black president replaced him. For the *Chicago Daily Defender* she wrote columns, one titled "Confetti," two social columns a week, and one for the food pages on Thursdays. She had a local radio show on WBEE, "The Doris Saunders Show," where she interviewed guests at lunchtime at Lake Meadows Restaurant and Lounge, a popular dining place in Chicago's black community. She later wrote and served as associate producer for "Our People" on WTTW-TV, a magazine-format television program that ran from 1968 to 1970.

In 1968 Saunders became the director of community relations for Chicago State University and later added the duties of acting director of institutional development. In 1970-72, she was staff associate in the office of the chancellor at the University of Illinois, Chicago. This gave her a real taste for involvement with students, and when she left this job at John H. Johnson's request to return to her former position as director of the book division, Doris Saunders was determined to go back to school for a higher degree. At the urging of Lowell Martin, dean of the University of Chicago Library School, she did not go to library school for a master's degree in library science. Rather, when the opportunity presented itself after her own children had completed college, she went to Boston University and earned in one academic year the master of science in journalism from the School of Public Communication and the master of arts in Afro-American studies from the graduate school. These degrees were awarded in 1977. During the year 1983-84 she studied toward a Ph.D. in history at Vanderbilt University in Nashville, Tennessee. Meanwhile, Saunders had commuted to Chicago on weekends at John H. Johnson's expense to continue working on the books in progress. One was *Black Society*, which she wrote with Geraldyn ("Gerri") Major and published in 1976. Doris Saunders edited *The Day They March* (1963) and *The Kennedy Years and the Negro* (1964). She compiled the *Negro Handbook* (1966).

Saunders has been affiliated with the following organizations: board member, Black Academy of Arts and Letters; board member, Illinois Chapter, American Civil Liberties Union; member Chicago Leadership Resource Program, National Association of Media Women, Chicago Publicity

Club, Alpha Gamma Pi Sorority, and Black Advisory Commission for the 1980 census in Washington, D.C.

Saunders began working at Jackson State University, Jackson, Mississippi, in January 1978 for a one-semester writer-in-residence position. Johnson of Johnson Publishing Company grew tired of her continuing absence and requested that she make a decision. She did. Saunders accepted the position of professor and coordinator of print journalism at Jackson State University, where she has been in daily contact with students ever since. She officially began her employment with the institution on July 1, 1978.

She anticipates retiring in spring 1991. She will be seventy years old on August 8, 1991, and retirement at seventy is mandatory in Mississippi. What will she do? She has no idea, but Doris Saunders will probably stay involved with ancestor hunting, her personal history system that she sells by mailorder, and *Kith and kin*, her newsletter in genealogy and family history.

References

Crump, Paul. "Prisoner Becomes a Writer." *Ebony* 18 (November 1962): 94.

Ebony 28 (January 1973). 22. Includes photograph.

Editors of Ebony. *Ebony Success Library*. Vol. 1. Chicago: Johnson Pub. Co., 1973. Includes photograph.

"Jackson State University Educator Named to U. S. Census Advisory Board." *Jet* 56 (26 April 1979): 18. Includes photograph.

Saunders, Doris. Interview with author, 24 September 1990, 7 January 1991.

Saunders, Doris E. To Vonita W. Dandridge, 27 September, 4 October, 10 October, 15 October, 1990.

Who's Who Among Black Americans, 1990/91. Detroit: Gale Research, 1990.

Vonita White Dandridge

Augusta Savage

(1892-1962)

Sculptor, educator

Augusta Fells Savage faced the obstacles of racism, poverty, and tragedy as a talented sculptor, whose proclivity for creating and love for her work and art led her to become one of the nation's most distinguished black artists of the Harlem Renaissance and beyond. With her career in the balance, the sharp, demanding sculptor and educator generously shared her expertise by teaching and encouraging young, talented, and promising black youth and by fighting for the recognition of black artists. While she worked in several mediums, she is known for her high artistic work as a sculptor of portraits in bronze, plaster, and wood. Unable to cast many of her works in bronze, Savage could not ensure the permanency of her sculpture; hence, many of her pieces did not survive. The daring quality of her genius, however, is immediately evident in the works that are known.

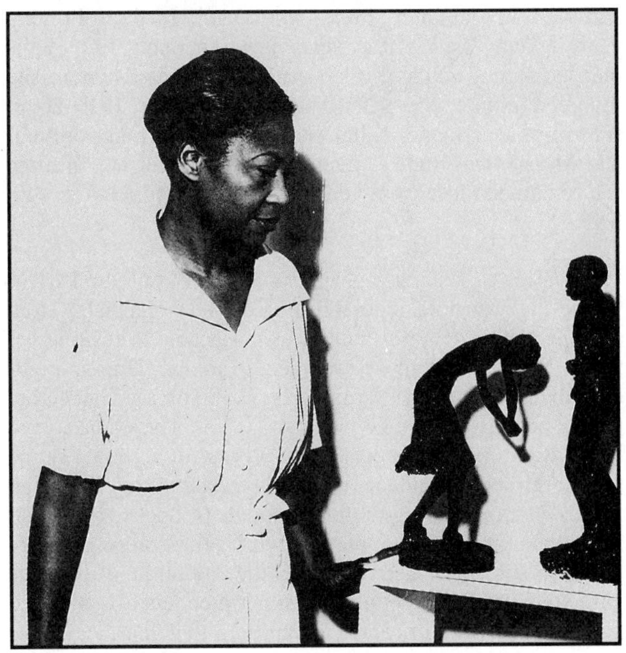

Augusta Savage

The red clay of Green Cove Springs in northern Florida, where Augusta Christine Fells Savage was born on February 29, 1892, fascinated her early, became her primary play object, and was the seed of her later fame as a sculptor. From the red clay she shaped art forms and taught the technique to her playmates and siblings. "At the mud pie age, I began to make 'things' instead of mud pies," she said ("Augusta Savage: An Autobiography," 269). She often missed the local public school in which she was enrolled in order to visit the clay pit of the town's brick yard, making ducks from clay. Augusta Fells, the daughter of Edward Fells and Cornelia (Murphy) Fells, was the seventh child in a family of fourteen, nine of whom lived to maturity. Her father loved good books but was unable to afford them on his housepainter's income. A minister who was deeply religious and strict, Edward Fells was disturbed over the "graven images" that the young sculptor made. "My father licked me five or six times a week and almost whipped all the art out of me," she said (Bearden and Henderson, 78). She learned to keep her work from his sight.

Augusta Fells and John T. Moore were married in 1907

and had one daughter, Irene, who was born the following year. Moore died a few years later. Around 1915 Fells married James Savage, a laborer and carpenter, whom she divorced in the early 1920s. She spent one year, 1919-20, at state normal school in Tallahassee, now Florida Agricultural and Mechanical State University. Throughout her lifetime she remained close to her daughter and shared a home with her.

By 1915 Augusta Savage had moved to West Palm Beach, where clay was not a natural resource. She begged clay from a small factory, Chase Pottery, and was able to resume her work. Her creation of several pieces, among them an eighteen-inch statue of the Virgin Mary, so impressed her father that he began to accept her work and talent. The statue stirred local excitement and opened new vistas for Savage. While still a high school student, she taught a class in clay modeling for six months. Along with her models of ducks, chickens, and other animals, her pieces, which then were of more difficult subjects, also came to the attention of George Graham Currie, the county fair superintendent. He allowed her to exhibit her work at the fair and saw to it that she receive a special prize of twenty-five dollars for her sculptures. Local support raised her earnings to $175—enough to finance her stay in Jacksonville, where she had gone to sculpt busts for of well-to-do black residents to earn money for formal instruction. Ultimately she was unsuccessful in her attempt because the "rich folks refused to be 'done'" ("Augusta Savage: An Autobiography," 269), she moved to New York City in 1920, where she arrived with four dollars and sixty cents, a letter of introduction from George Currie to Solon Borglum, prominent New York sculptor, and "a burning desire to become an artist in six months" (Poston, "Augusta Savage," 66).

In New York, Savage supported herself as an apartment caretaker and went to see Borglum, who arranged for her to study sculpture at Cooper Union, a tuition-free school, instead of studying with him, for he charged enormous fees for his teaching. From 1921 to 1924 she was enrolled in the school and for the most part, studied with sculptor George Brewster. Three months after enrolling, she lost her job as apartment caretaker. However Cooper Union's director offered her a scholarship in 1921-22 to cover her living expenses. She took a cheap room in Upper Harlem to reduce her expenses. Meanwhile, news of both her talent and her plight spread. She had become known at the 135th Street branch of the New York Public Library, where she read about African art. Librarian Sadie Peterson (Delaney) persuaded the friends of the library to commission Savage to do a portrait of W. E. B. Du Bois. Elton Fax said of Savage's Du Bois sculpture: "Her handling of the planes of Du Bois's finely formed head clearly expressed the resolute militancy and intelligence of the scholar" (Fax, 543). Other patrons of the arts followed the library's lead, and she received commissions for portraits of other prominent black leaders. Notable among them was Marcus Garvey, who had promoted pride in African heritage and gained fame as leader of the United Negro Improvement Association. He sat for her on Sunday mornings in his Harlem apartment. Elton Fax said that the Garvey sculpture "became her response to the hero-image of the black nationalist" (543). The commissions brought Savage wide recognition in the black community, provided financial support, and gained her wide acceptance among the Harlem Renaissance figures. Meanwhile, Savage completed the four-year course at Cooper Union in three years.

Racial Incident Stirs Controversy

When the French government announced that one hundred American women students would be admitted to study in a summer art school at the Palace of Fontainebleau outside Paris, in 1923 Augusta Savage applied for and was granted a five-hundred-dollar scholarship. Learning that she was black, the scholarship committee withdrew its offer. This flagrant incident of racial discrimination angered her and led her to see that the matter receive widespread attention in the New York press. "I don't care much for myself because I will get along all right here, but other and better colored students might wish to apply sometime. . . . I am the first colored girl to apply. I don't like to see them establish a precedent," she said (Bearden and Henderson, 86). Front-page coverage of the account was seen daily, while *Nation* magazine and leading newspapers joined the protest. The scholarship committee was publicly embarrassed and hid in silence, although one member, Hermon MacNeil, came forward to admit his shame. MacNeil, who once shared a Paris studio with Henry Ossawa Tanner and was known for his American Indian sculptures, offered Savage an opportunity to work with him in his studio at College Point. She accepted his offer. Meanwhile, Savage became known as a talented troublemaker to be avoided. It has been suggested that the prominent white critics, museum heads, artists, and dealers saw to it that she was excluded from exhibits and galleries (Bearden and Henderson, 88).

Undaunted by her experience with racial intolerance, Savage received occasional commissions and modeled small figures and portraits of ordinary people, including a bust of Theodore Upshure, a handicapped black youth from Greenwich Village. Her exhibits in 1926 at the 135th Street branch library kept her work visible locally, while she sent some pieces to the Frederick Douglass High School in Baltimore, Maryland, and to Philadelphia for its sesquicentennial exhibition. Her statue "The New Negro" was inspired by Alain Locke's anthology by the same title—further evidence of the influence of black culture on Savage's work.

A series of events occurred in the middle 1920s that impacted significantly on Savage's personal life, yet did not deter her. Savage married again in October 1923, this time to journalist Robert L. Poston, a Marcus Garvey associate. He died in March 1924. Through the efforts of W. E. B. Du Bois, in 1925 Countess Irene Di Robilant, of the Italian-American Society, gave Savage a scholarship to study at the Royal Academy of Fine Arts in Rome, Italy. Savage worked in a laundry to earn enough money to support her European travel, but had to use the funds for family matters. Unable to pay the required travel expenses or to secure contributions from friends and philanthropists, she refused the fellowship. Discouraged, she wondered if she would ever study in Rome.

The third major sculpture for which Augusta Savage is known—her most popular statue—is a piece through which Elton Fax says "the young artist brought her earliest experiences to full flower" (Fax, 543). Savage approached the model, an attractive black youth whom she saw on a Harlem street, and persuaded him to sit for a portrait. She fashioned a head in clay that "caught the vitality, the humanity, the tenderness, and the wisdom of a boy child who has lived in the streets" (Bearden and Henderson, 90). She etched into its base the title "Gamin."

The work attracted immediate attention and rewards for the sculptor. *Opportunity* magazine pictured the work on its front cover for June 1929. "The jaunty angle of his cap, the knowing twinkle in his eye, the scornful twist of his mouth, are eternal qualities" of the "mischievous urchin revealed in this bust" (Poston, "Augusta Savage," 67). Perhaps this is what attracted Eugene Kinckle Jones, executive secretary of the National Urban League, in 1929 to ask the Julius Rosenwald Fund to award Augusta Savage a fellowship for study in Paris. Certainly "Gamin" had influenced the granting of the award. Savage won her second Rosenwald Fellowship in 1931. Her application letter for the first grant noted that she had studied with Onorio Ruotolo of New York, Italian sculptor Antonio Salemme, and Hermon MacNeil. In addition to locating her works at the 135th Street branch library and an important piece, "Green Apples" in the personal collection of Harlem realtor John E. Nail, Savage had "done some work with children on soap sculpture for the Proctor and Gamble Co." (Augusta Savage to George R. Arthur, 19 April, 1929). She had influential contacts; her grant application was also endorsed by Frederick P. Keppel of the Carnegie Corporation and sculptor Victor Salvatore, who had Savage under his tutelage so that she would be "better equipped to begin her work abroad" (Eugene Kinckle Jones to George R. Arthur).

Charles R. Richards, director of the Industrial Art Division of the General Education Board, also wrote to the Rosenwald Fund in support of Augusta Savage and noted that her recently executed works "show exceptional ability and a fine feeling for sculpturesque form" and were of professional quality. He praised the work she was doing "with colored children at her home," where she taught them the techniques of sculpture. Her tutor, Victor Salvatore, recommended to Richards that Savage "consider her future work largely in relation to her own people" (Charles R. Richards to Edwin R. Embree).

In Paris, Savage studied sculpture and woodcarving privately for one year with Félix Beauneteaux and Mademoiselle Hadjii at the Académie de la Chaumière and later with Charles Despiau, one of the foremost modern portrait sculptors. Savage's works were shown in several European salons and brought citations from the Salon d'Automne and the Salon du Printemps Grand-Palais in Paris. Savage won an additional grant from the Carnegie Corporation to travel through France, Belgium, and Germany, where she studied sculpture in the cathedrals.

Embree and Arthur, both Rosenwald officials, were delighted with the photographs of Savage's work sent to document her activities in Paris in 1930. Like Charles R. Richards earlier, George Arthur hoped that Savage would continue to work primarily with "Negro" models. He wanted her to do original work born out of a deep spirituality that she, as a black woman, must have felt. He cautioned her:

> [Avoid becoming] too much imbued with European standards of technique, if they are going to kill the other something which in my opinion some Negro will eventually give to American art, maybe in sculpture, maybe in music, painting or literature. . . . Know the culture and technique of other races, but do not simply be a copy of them at the expense of originality of your own. . . . There is just one field in which the Negro has an equal chance with the white man in American life and that field is art. If he follows standards or even the white Americans, which in turn have copied them from Europe, then the Negro can at best be but a copy of the copy (George R. Arthur to Augusta Savage, 28 May 1930).

Savage was already following the trend among young black realists of the time, who found their materials in the life of their people. She assured Arthur that she appreciated his "brotherly advice" and was glad they shared the same views. While she was working in a different style then, she was "timid about it" because she unsure how it would be received. She said:

> I have lately been trying to develop an original technique . . . but I find that the masters here are not in sympathy as they all have their own definite ideas and usually wish their pupils to follow their particular method, so I have been working alone for the past three or four months only calling in a critic for suggestions which I have found better for me if I am to develop along the line that I have decided on for my self (Augusta Savage to George R. Arthur, 15 June 1930).

Savage felt that the Chicago World's Fair, scheduled for 1933, should display a major work by a competent black sculptor, in this case a monument to Jean Baptiste Pointe de Sable, the first settler of Chicago, as the black American's contribution to the exhibition. She wrote to George R. Arthur to inquire about the possibility of Rosenwald support for the project, but apparently received no encouragement.

Savage continued sculpting after her return to New York in 1931. Her work, already seen in the prestigious Harmon Foundation exhibit of 1928, was seen again in the foundation's exhibit of 1930-31. Frederick P. Keppel of the Carnegie Corporation had offered her, through the Boykin

Art School, the position of teacher of sculpture. She created busts of poet James Weldon Johnson, surgeon Walter Gray Crump, abolitionist Frederick Douglass, Eugene Kinckle Jones, composer W. C. Handy, and others. During the 1930s Savage showed the daring quality of her imagination in the woodcarving "Envy," and two other strong sculptures—"A Woman of Martinique," a head carved in black Belgian marble, and "After the Glory," a bronze model on granite erected on the triangular park bounded by 155th Street, Seventh, and Eighth avenues in New York City, in commemoration of the World War service of the Fifteenth Regiment, New York National Guard. She founded the Savage Studio of Arts and Crafts. At first she sustained herself by teaching a small class in her studio on West 143rd Street and a second class sponsored by the adult education department of the University of the State of New York. Later she obtained a $1,500 grant from the Carnegie Foundation to teach children in her larger quarters at 239 West 135th Street. As the Great Depression worsened, Savage became a leader in enrolling black artists in the Works Progress Administration's Federal Art Project (FAP) and became one of the most effective spokespersons on behalf of the artists.

During the 1930s and 1940s Savage's exhibitions of works by her students, other black artists, and her own works reached larger audiences and were widely received. Her popularity and influence soared, and in 1934 she was the first black elected to the National Association of Women Painters and Sculptors. In 1935 she recognized the "native talent in Harlem" and said she wanted to "teach [the students] the essentials without making them bound down with academic tradition which will spoil the freshness of their work" ("Negro Students Hold Their Own Art Exhibition," n.p.). Savage presented the work of her pupils at a local YWCA. The students were drawn from all strata of Harlem life and included Norman Lewis, the most talented of the group who, in time, Savage felt, would eclipse Henry Ossawa Tanner as the premier black painter. Another promising student, Robert Jones, was discovered wandering the streets and sleeping in subways. Students who came from better circumstances were also instructed at the Savage studio. Subsequently Savage became an assistant supervisor of the Federal Art Project for New York City.

In 1936 the Rosenwald Fund asked its grant recipients of the past seven years to report on the benefits of the fellowship. Savage wrote in praise of her first-hand encounter with great artists. She described her visits to the galleries where the world famous works of art were shown as highlights. She had also welcomed the opportunity to study woodcarving and sculpture in the free manner in which Europeans taught, in contrast to the formal, conventional training that she had in the United States. And when the fellowship had ended and she set up classes for young black students, she was able to pass on to them what she had learned during her European study (Questionnaire, Julius Rosenwald Fund, 18 March 1936).

Savage was appointed the first director of the Harlem Community Art Center in 1937, where she organized programs in recreation, education, and art. One of the principal organizers of the Harlem Artists Guild, Savage continued her efforts to recognize and promote black artists. Harlem Renaissance painter and muralist Aaron Douglas was the guild's first president and Savage became the second. She also established the Vanguard Club to keep alive the political and social issues affecting Harlem's black artists. When Communists infiltrated the group, she withdrew.

Sculptor Commissioned for World's Fair

Savage received her last major commission in the late 1930s, when she was asked to create a sculpture for the New York World's Fair of 1939-40. One of four women and the only black woman so honored, she created the famous work, "Lift Every Voice and Sing," inspired by the song known as the "Negro National Anthem," with lyrics by her friend, James Weldon Johnson, and music by his brother, J. Rosamond Johnson. Savage's sculpture is a sixteen-foot harp composed of blacks of various sizes and ages, who lift their voices to sing and form strings, tapered from each head to the base. A mammoth forearm and hand with fingers curved upward, representing the Creator, form the base. In front, the kneeling figure with outstretched arms offers the gift of black music to the world. While the sculpture, cast in plaster and finished in black basalt (bronze was too costly), was destroyed, replicas that were cast in pot metal as souvenirs of the fair are extant, and photographs of the sculpture are published in numerous works. "Lift Every Voice and Sing" became Savage's best known and most widely recognized work.

Savage's position at the Harlem Art Center was filled during her leave-of-absence to create the sculpture for the World's Fair. In 1939 Savage headed a corporation that opened the Salon of Contemporary Negro Art, devoted to the exhibition and sale of works by black artists. A useful enterprise, the salon closed after a few years due to lack of funds.

Savage's productivity subsequently declined. She became weary, possibly discouraged, and she abandoned her friends and her work as art educator, promoter of black art and artists, and sculptor in New York City. She moved to a farm located near an art colony in Saugerties, New York, in the Catskill Mountains, where she continued her art work. She is said to have raised and sold chickens and eggs, created portrait sculptures for tourists, and taught children in local camps. She made infrequent trips to New York City to make minor repairs on the plaster sculptures of her close friends. When her health began to fail, she returned to New York City to live with her daughter, Irene Allen. Overcome by cancer, Savage died in virtual obscurity in Abraham Jacobi Hospital on March 26, 1962.

Savage has been called "the true artist, in love with Art," who positioned art above everything. "Real art is created solely for art's sake," she said. Her motto was, "Life is fleeting, Art is eternal" (Poston, "Augusta Savage," 51, 67). Certainly Savage made art the focus of her life. Her aim to create something "really beautiful, really lasting" was realized through her legacy to black American culture.

References

Arthur, George R. To Augusta Savage, 28 May 1930; 24 October 1931. Augusta Savage Folder, Rosenwald Fund Archives.

"Augusta Savage: An Autobiography." *Crisis* 36 (August 1929): 269. Includes photograph.

Bearden, Romare, and Harry Henderson. "Augusta Savage." *Six Black Masters of American Art*. New York: Doubleday, 1972. 76-98. Includes photographs of Savage and her work.

Bontemps, Arna Alexander, and Jacqueline Fonvielle-Bontemps. *Forever Free: Art by African-American Women 1862-1980*. Alexandria, Va.: Stephenson, 1980. 124-25, 203-204. Photographs, pp. 124-25.

Cederholm, Theresa Dickason, comp. and ed. *Afro-American Artists*. Boston: Boston Public Library, 1973. 247-48.

Current Biography. New York: H. W. Wilson, 1941. 752-54.

Dykes, De Witt S., Jr. "Augusta Savage." *Notable American Women: The Modern Period*. Cambridge: Harvard University Press, 1980. 627-29.

Fax, Elton C. "Augusta Savage." *Dictionary of American Negro Biography*. Eds. Rayford W. Logan and Michael R. Winston. New York: Norton, 1982. 542-43.

Jones, Eugene Kinckle. To George R. Arthur, 19 April 1929. Augusta Savage Folder, Rosenwald Fund Archives.

Kellner, Bruce, ed. *The Harlem Renaissance*. Methuen, N.Y.: Routledge and Kegan Paul, 1984. 315-16.

Lewis, Samella. *Art: African American*. New York: Harcourt Brace Jovanovich, 1978. 84-86.

"Negro Students Hold Their Own Art Exhibition." *New York Herald Tribune* 15 February 1935.

Poston, T. R. "Augusta Savage." *The Metropolitan* (January 1935): 28-31, 51, 66-67.

———. "Harlem Will See Self as Others See It at Novel Show." *Amsterdam News* 9 February 1935.

Questionnaire, 18 March 1936. Julius Rosenwald Fund Archives.

Richards, Charles R. To Augusta Savage, 8 May 1929. Augusta Savage Folder, Rosenwald Fund Archives.

Savage, Augusta. George R. Arthur, 19 April 1929; 15 June 1930; 19 October 1931. Augusta Savage Folder, Rosenwald Fund Archives.

"Sculptress Commissioned to do Group." *Journal and Guide,* 18 December 1937.

Collections

Works of Augusta Savage are located in the Jacob Lawrence Collection (Seattle, Washington), Morgan State University (Baltimore, Maryland), National Archives (Washington, D.C.), the Schomburg Center for Research in Black Culture (New York City), and the Quinto O'Brien Studios (Jamaica, British West Indies). While her papers are uncollected, the Julius Rosenwald Fund Archives, Fisk University Library, contain a fellowship application, news clippings, correspondence, photographs, and other items on Augusta Savage.

Jessie Carney Smith

Philippa Schuyler

(1931 - 1967)

Musician

My old man died in a fine big house,
My ma died in a shack.
I wonder where I'm gonna die,

Philippa Schuyler

Being neither white nor black.
Langston Hughes

Philippa Duke Schuyler was born in Harlem in 1931 during the Great Depression, to George Schuyler, a well-known and controversial black journalist hailing from Syracuse, New York, whose family took pride in never having been slaves; and to Josephine Cogdell, a white artist and writer who spent much of her pampered childhood in west Texas being raised by the family's black servants in a baronial mansion on the meandering Brazos River. A troubled genius who was proficient in music, languages, and writing, Philippa Schuyler traveled the world for most of her adult life without ever finding her place in it. She was both celebrated and victimized as a result of her parents' grand experiment and, by extension, her own country's inability to accept her as one of their own.

George Schuyler and Josephine "Jody" Cogdell met in New York during the spring of 1927. She had gone there to pursue her career as a journalist and to meet George Schuyler, whose writings and ideas she had admired for years. In the back of her mind was also a plan that had been incubating for some time: that the progeny of an interracial marriage, through hybrid vigor, would be extraordinary. This, she believed, could prove to be the final solution to America's race problems.

The attraction between George Schuyler and Jody Cogdell was immediate and intense. After six months, she moved from her comfortable Greenwich Village apartment to Schuyler's spartan one in Harlem. "I have dropped completely out of sight," Jody Cogdell wrote in her ongoing journal shortly after marrying Schuyler (*Diaries of Josephine Cogdell*). "No one in the white world knows my whereabouts or will ever know."

Both George and Josephine Schuyler believed in the theory of hybrid vigor and they expected great things from their daughter (named after Philip of Macedonia and Philip Schuyler, a Revolutionary War hero). From the very beginning, the pressures on Philippa Schuyler were enormous. She, however, seemed to take everything in stride. At the age of two and a half she could read and write; by age four she was composing music and by age five performing Mozart. Her IQ, tested by New York University and others, was 185.

Philippa Schuyler grew tall and healthy on her mother's diet: orange juice, unpasteurized milk, a piece of slightly steamed fish, raw cauliflower, broccoli, carrots, avocados, and six teaspoons of cod liver oil was a typical breakfast. (Schuyler followed a strict diet her entire life. She ate no meat, sugar, or cooked foods, drank no sodas, and used no artificial ingredients. She neither smoked nor drank.) By adolescence she was a slim five feet six inches; her face—described by George Schuyler as "the color of lightly done toast with dark liquid eyes of a fawn, and eyelashes like the black glistening stems of maiden hair ferns, turned back to meet your eyebrows"—was delicate and finely drawn (Scrapbooks, 1931-1945, *The Schuyler Collection*). Later, Philippa Schuyler's beauty would take on a vulnerable and aloof quality, a beauty that Ishmael Reed described as "haunting."

Schuyler Becomes Child Prodigy

Josephine Schuyler became her daughter's impresario, business manager, confidante, and best friend. Philippa Schuyler never strayed far from her mother's eye. Nor did she have the opportunity, for much of her education was done at home with a tutor, except for a brief spate at the Convent School on the grounds of Manhattanville College, then in Harlem. But if she were isolated from children her own age, she was also effectively isolated from the ravages of the country's depression and America's racial problems. "I was born and grew up without any consciousness of America's race prejudices," Philippa Schuyler would later write ("My Black and White World," 13).

Initially, white America was fascinated by this interracial child prodigy; black America, proud. She was profiled in the *New York Herald Tribune*, *The New Yorker*, *Look Magazine*, *Time* magazine, *The Pittsburgh Courier* (the paper her father wrote for), and others. And, indeed, she had spectacular success as a child prodigy, winning innumerable prizes for compositions and performance; she was featured by the National Guild of Piano Teachers, the New York Philharmonic Concerts for Young People, Detroit's Grinnel Foundation (where they compared her compositional prowess to Mozart at the same age and called her "the brightest young composer in America"), and others. At not quite nine years old, she had a day named after her at the New York World's Fair; at ten, she became the youngest member of the National Association of American Composers and Conductors; and at fifteen made her debut in the unusual double role as composer and pianist with the Philharmonic Symphony Orchestra at Lewisohn Stadium in New York City before an audience of twelve thousand people.

Schuyler's visibility was due not only to Josephine Schuyler's relentless drive to prove that the child of a mixed marriage could succeed, but also to George Schuyler. His connections and reputation as a black journalist had enabled the Schuylers to interest the white newspaper world, very early on, in their extraordinary daughter. Without his long arm, *Time*, *Look*, the *New York Herald Tribune* and others would probably have turned a blind eye to a young mulatto protégée growing up in Harlem in the 1930s and 1940s.

It was George Schuyler, too, who was able to construct a "role model" of his daughter for the black American community, through his constant coverage of her in the *Pittsburgh Courier*. If Josephine Schuyler "created" her image, George Schuyler, through the black press, was able to perpetuate it, giving his daughter wide publicity. Hylan Lewis, with his typical sharp insights, once called Philippa Schuyler a "protegé puppet," adding somewhat wryly, "and she had two very good puppeteers" (Conversation with Hylan Lewis, June 1988).

But without Schuyler's own genius as a pianist and composer, the efforts of her parents would have turned to dust. As a young pianist, her reviews by both black and white critics were uniformly exceptional. Her compositions, although efforts of a young mind, were also judged to be exceptional. Composing seemed to come as naturally to Schuyler as seeing and hearing. She would visit a toy shop with her mother and then sit down to write *The Toy Maker's Ball* with the clacking of little mechanical figures beating steadily in the background. She would go to the shores of Lake Ontario and write a composition in which you can almost hear the wind and the lapping of the water on the shore.

Despite Philippa Schuyler's successes as a child prodigy in both fields of composition and performance, her appeal to white America faded as soon as she entered young adulthood. It was becoming more and more difficult for her mother (who had always been the family's business manager) to obtain concerts that were not backed by black organizations. And it was becoming more apparent to Josephine Schuyler—although not yet to Philippa—that her daughter's chances of succeeding in America were not improving. She was no longer an intriguing child prodigy; she was (to borrow Philippa Schuyler's description of herself many years later) a strange curiosity. "I became intellectually aware of race prejudice," she wrote, "when I grew up and entered the world of economic competition . . . Then I encountered vicious barriers of prejudice . . . because I was the offspring of what America calls a mixed marriage. It was a ruthless shock to me that, at first, made the walls of my self-confidence crumble. It horrified, humiliated me" ("My Black and White World," 13). In her mind was a new skepticism, a scrutiny that concluded that the world's promise of reciprocation on which she was raised was a sham. "But instead of breaking under the strain," she wrote, "I adjusted to it. I left" ("My Black and White World," 13).

Schuyler Seeks Identity in Travel

As a concert pianist, Philippa Schuyler traveled first to Latin America, where she discovered a tripartite color system—black, white, and mulatto—casting her own country's one-drop-of-black-blood theory in an even more disturbing light. And while momentarily gratified to find a category for herself, it was not the same as finding an identity. While traveling in Europe she encountered another perspective: here she was admired as "the exotic beauty with the jade complexion and the Dutch name." Much later in her travels, Philippa Schuyler would come closer to finding a sense of self: in Madagascar, her father's tap root, and in Portuguese Africa, the only country, she wrote, that was virtually free of racial prejudice. But these identities were always borrowed, and she ultimately discarded them as unsatisfactory.

Philippa Schuyler was more comfortable outside of America and could easily have settled overseas. Instead, she chose to be on the move, almost constantly. During her last ten years, she spent more than half her time abroad, performing in more than eighty countries, from Iceland to Malaysia, Argentina to Vietnam. In Haiti she played at the inauguration of three successive presidents. In Africa, she performed for such notables as Haile Selassie, Lumumba, and Kasavubu on Congo's Independence Day, President Nkrumah in celebration of Ghana's independence, the President of Madagascar, King George of Toro, King Kalonji of the Baluba tribe, and Albert Schweitzer in his isolated and far-flung leper colony in Lamberene. In Belgium, she performed for Queen Elizabeth; in Malaysia, for the prince and his wife. But she was never invited to play before a major American figure.

Rejected by her own county, she roamed the globe looking for a home. Constant travel and work became an anodyne, her palliative. "I am a woman of color," she wrote toward the end of her life, "with all its accompanying sadness and suffering. I was born in New York, but I never truly felt like other Americans. An invisible wall surrounded me, divided me from others" (Phillipa Schuyler, "Une metisse à la recherche de son ame"). Several years earlier, while in Rome, she had scribbled "Wounds and hurt. I'm a beauty but I'm half colored, so I'm not to be accepted anyplace. I'm always destined to be an outsider, never, never part of anything. I hate my country and no one wants me in any other. I am emotionally part of nothing . . . . And that will always be my destiny" (*The Schuyler Collection*, Letters).

To the end, her American audiences remained largely segregated; not many whites knew her as a musician. To a couple in North Carolina who were trying to secure her concerts with white audiences in the South, she wrote a year before her death: "You can't imagine how grateful I am for your kindness. For years I have deplored the way I have been effectively segregated. . . . So I have spent most of my time abroad where I could play as an individual for individuals" (Private Collection).

As a concert artist, Philippa Schuyler never attained the status of one of the musical greats, although those experts who followed her career uniformly ranked her exceptionally high. Too many barriers, both personal and musical, had stood in her way, and at times her wide spectrum of talents and interest distracted her from concentrating on a single career. Equally compelling, in later years, was the fact that she had become the main support of the Schuyler family because of her father's steadily declining income. The fact that there was racial as well as sexual discrimination in her field was obviously another hindrance.

In 1960, when money from performing alone became lean, Philippa Schuyler added a second profession: that of a journalist and writer. During the next seven years, she published more than one hundred newspaper and magazine articles and was syndicated by UPI and NANA, one of the very few black writers of her day to do so. Proficient in five languages, she also wrote for European journals—in French, Portuguese, and Italian.

Philippa Schuyler published four full-length books during her life: in 1960, a somewhat specious biography *Adventures in Black and White*; in 1962, *Who Killed the Congo?*, an idiosyncratic book about the aftermath of the Belgian Congo's independence; in 1963, *Jungle Saints*, an encomium to the missionaries of Africa; and in 1966, in collaboration with her mother, *Kingdom of Dreams*, a "scientific" investigation of the interpretation of dreams. Published posthumously was Schuyler's book about the Vietnam War entitled *Good Men Die*.

All her published books are nonfiction and if they are not Pulitzer Prize material, they are provocative and controversial. An intrepid traveler and a quick-sketch artist of landscapes and people, she reported on the political scenes of the day. In Saigon, she visited an overcrowded and undermanned city hospital where the bug-ridden wards stank in the sweltering heat and live patients might stay in the same bed with a corpse for a whole day or more. "This is the incarnation of a seventeenth century charnel house," she wrote in her notes. In Africa, she saw the rioting in Leopoldville. From her hotel window she watched as the severed heads of rival tribesmen were paraded through the street on spears of the victors. In Buenos Aires, caught in the midst of an uprising against the Peronistas, revolution raging in the streets, she heard machine gun and mortar fire, saw bombs exploding, and passed dead bodies in the gutters.

Philippa Schuyler also wrote fiction, none of which was ever published. An incomplete novel called *Sophie Daw*, set in the late eighteenth century, a mixture of Dickens and Fielding, with a dash of Marquis de Sade thrown in, addresses a fundamental concern of hers: the plight of women worldwide. As Schuyler witnessed firsthand the low regard for women in third-world countries, where even educated families were performing the barbaric ritual of female circumcision, as she struggled with her own dilemma of how to have a family and a career, as she found herself a helpless victim in the face of attempted rapes in Africa, her alarm over crimes of gender escalated. It is a cause that if she were alive today, would have consumed much of her time.

During her final trip to Vietnam, Schuyler began her last fiction, *Dau Tranh*. Even more autobiographic than an earlier novel, *Appassionata*, it held the promise of a personal catharsis. Jeanne, an American mulatto, is an erstwhile child prodigy and a musician, traveling and working in Vietnam as a foreign correspondent. For dramatic effect, the protagonist is illegitimate, but other than that, she is Philippa Schuyler herself:

> Jeanne was in a state of struggle. Dau Tranh that agonized cry of pain and defiance that typified all the movements for the liberation in Vietnam also expressed her own drama. She had inherited the handicaps of illegitimacy and a skin that was not white. The first burden could be concealed, but the second never could. Her skin was light enough for her to be accepted as a second-class white in Rhodesia, Kenya, or South Africa, and its color made no difference in Europe. But to Americans, it was the most important characteristic. It categorized one as a person to be insulted, to be treated as a pariah, to be deprived of respect in all deeper relationships (*Dau Tranh*, incomplete manuscript, *The Schuyler Collection*).

Philippa Schuyler's saga is a tragic and complex one. Her final decade is deeply lined with intrigues, anomalies, and contradictions. It was fragmented by her search for identity and her curious religiosity—a combination of Catholicism, fatalism, and mysticism: she was a daily thrower of tarot cards, a firm believer in the horoscope, and a frequent visitor to seers and clairvoyants, especially in the Far East. She also believed in reincarnation. "One must go forth, to meet one's fate," she wrote. "Often when I reach a place, I know that I have been there before, in some dream or in some former life" (Philippa Schuyler, *Adventures in Black and White*, 222). Her life was still further fragmented by her desire to marry and have children but never being able to reconcile a peripatetic career with home. Her relationship to her mother was particularly crippling, perpetuating her search for identity. Schuyler continued to exercise ferocious control over her daughter, even thousands of miles away. And despite Philippa Schuyler's seeming independence, she wrote her mother constantly when abroad, often daily, dutifully translating reviews, or consulting her on a man she might have met. These letters, while an incredible source for a biographer, speak equally to the codependent relationship that did not allow Philippa Schuyler to mature as a person, a woman, and finally, as an artist.

Her final decade also saw the ripening of a political ultraconservatism that tended to obviate lasting romances with many of the men she met; her increasingly difficult relationship with Africa—initially envisioned as a homecoming but which turned sour; and her own growing disaffection. Several days before she died, Philippa wrote her mother, "Remember, my bitterness requires mobility and relocation" (*The Schuyler Collection*, Letters).

Philippa Schuyler Becomes Felipa Monterro

At the end of 1962, Philippa Schuyler applied for a new United States passport, but not under her own name. Instead she chose Felipa Monterro y Schuyler, trying to reflect an Iberian-American heritage. She traveled on this passport until 1966 as Felipa Monterro, dropping the name Schuyler.

Philippa Schuyler's new persona was the final hope in her quest for identity. She ventured to synthesize a new human being—to graft another profile onto her own self-portrait. Monterro would preserve all of Schuyler's talents but drop the ballast of her former self. Monterro would be an independent writer without being identified as "the daughter of the Negro journalist, George Schuyler." Monterro would be a pianist and a composer but without critics comparing her to a child prodigy, wondering if she had, indeed, matured as an artist. Monterro's life would not be "ruined by carrying segregation against me wherever I went" (*The Schuyler Collection*, Letters).

Initially, Monterro was to be an Iberian-American. But by

the end of 1963, Schuyler had given Monterro a European provenance. Writing from Belgium to the American John Birch Society offering to join their lecture circuit on such topics as "The Red Menace in Africa," she described herself as a social worker, born and educated in Europe but working in Africa with the missionaries. Her disguise was apparently effective. They wrote back confirming their interest but expressing concern whether her English would be good enough for American audiences. Philippa Schuyler sent a voice-tape of Monterro: her English, they replied, was flawless. The Birchites took her into their camp, and Monterro earned a sizeable sum from several lecture tours.

But the crowning objective of the Monterro gambit was to break into white America as a classical pianist. Both Schuyler and her mother hoped that if Monterro could establish a solid reputation in Europe, she could re-enter the American concert scene as a white and be able to perform for an audience so far denied Philippa Schuyler. In April 1963, Felipa Monterro debuted in Switzerland. Her reviews, however, were mediocre, although the critics were all impressed with the technical prowess, and few concerts followed. They seemed to be confused by the sudden appearance from nowhere of such an accomplished pianist.

But the successes or failures of Monterro—while important to Schuyler—were less significant than the plan itself. For years, Schuyler had stumbled around in a landscape whose signposts all showed retreats rather than ways to selfhood. Philippa Schuyler's problem, like that of Nella Larsen's protagonist, Helga Crane, in *Quicksand* (1929), was deeper than lack of racial identity: at bottom was her inability to be a whole person, regardless of race, and her frantic movement from place to place was her attempt to "escape-into-wholeness" (McClendon, [86]).

Philippa Schuyler died on Tuesday, May 9, 1967, in a helicopter crash in Vietnam. She had gone there as correspondent for William Loeb's *Manchester Union Leader* to perform for the troops, and in her unofficial capacity as lay missionary—evacuating young children, nuns, and priests from Hué to Da Nang. She was on her last "mission of mercy" when the helicopter crashed yards from shore. Schuyler was thirty-five years old. Ironically, she had visited a clairvoyant several days before, asking his advice on a variety of matters. He had told her that on Tuesday, May 9, "her malefic period would be over and that she would emerge from the mouth of the Dragon." In her very last letter home to her mother, she had written: "God, I can't wait to emerge from the Dragon's mouth" (*The Schuyler Collection*, Letters).

Noted in America as a child prodigy but rebuffed as a young adult because of the color of her skin, Philippa Schuyler spent most of her life searching for an identity. Her journey included but transcended Du Bois's "double consciousness," for hers was a duality within a duality. Lavishly entertained in Latin America as a mulatto, she was a second-class citizen in her own country; performing in Europe, the Far East, and Africa for kings and queens as an American Negro, she chose—in order to further her concert career—to pass as white in apartheid South Africa and Rhodesia, playing for all-white audiences. Unsuccessful in her own country as a "Negro" musician, she was nonetheless syndicated by UPI and others as an "American" journalist. Unable to prevail as herself, wrestling with two professions, two "skins," and two souls, she adopted an alternate identity in hopes of obtaining the recognition she so richly deserved. Behind her life of awards and medals, of travels and applause, lies the tragedy of promise denied.

References

In compiling this biography the author interviewed numerous individuals, including Olive Abbot, the Codgell family, Eschila Cosi, Leonard de Paur, Gerd Gamborg, Kathleen Houston, Hylan Lewis in June 1988, Carolyn Mitchell, Joseph and Mary Myers, Tohanan Ramati, Robert Speller, and Theo and Linede Snijders van Eyk.

McLendon, Jacquelyn Y. "The Myth of the Mulatto Psyche: A Study of the Works of Jessie Fauset and Nella Larsen." Ph.D. dissertation. Case Western Reserve University, 1986.

The Schuyler Collection. Dau Tranh, incomplete manuscript, 1966-67; *Diaries of Josephine Cogdell*; letters; Philippa Schuyler, "Une metisse a la recherche de son ame." Scrapbooks, 1931-1945.

Schuyler, Josephine. *Philippa: The Beautiful American*. New York: The Philippa Schuyler Memorial Foundation, 1969.

Schuyler, Philippa. *Adventures in Black and White*. New York: Robert Speller & Sons, 1960.

———. *Good Men Die*. New York: Twin Circle Publishers, 1969.

———. *Jungle Saints*. Rome: Herder, 1963.

———. "My Black and White World." *Sepia* (June 1962): 10-15.

———. *Who Killed the Congo*? New York: Devin Adair Company, 1962.

Schuyler, Philippa and Josephine Schuyler. *Kingdom of Dreams*. New York: Robert Speller & Sons, 1966.

Collections

Music manuscripts, journals, letters, literary effects, personal papers, and photographs are located at the Schomburg Center, and the George Arents Research Library, Syracuse University, Syracuse, New York. Other American libraries have some, but very little primary materials on the Schuyler family.

Kathryn Talalay

Esther Mae Scott "Mother Scott"

(1893-1979)

Musician

Blues artist Esther Mae Scott, often addressed as Mother Scott, was born on March 25, 1893, in Bovina, Warren County, Mississippi, on Polk Plantation. She was the seventh child among fourteen born to Henry S. Erves and Mary Liza Erves.

Scott's parents were poor sharecroppers. Her mother's father, Monroe Cox Prentiss, was a blacksmith in Holland and was smuggled into America, where he was bought by Sergeant S. Prentiss and married Agnes Jane Garrett, who was half-white. Since the British Abolition Act eliminated slavery in 1833, Prentiss was probably sold before he could be freed. He was the blacksmith and caretaker on Polk Plantation and lived in the Polk household. He could read and write, and at a later date purchased five hundred acres of Polk Plantation, which he left to his son Jeff. He died in 1912, at the age of eighty-seven. Esther Scott's mother, Mary Liza Scott, did not inherit any of the property. She was born free in 1867 and died in 1947.

Because her family was poor and were farmers, Esther Scott's early childhood was difficult. They lived in a shotgun house, had no doctors, and were often hungry. In a 1976 interview with Theresa Danley, Mother Scott recalled: "I remember going to the briar patches with a stick—and we had some molasses at home—and I'm telling the snakes, 'You done been in the briar patches and got yours, now get out of the way and I'll get . . . (laughs)" (Black Women Oral History Interview, 31). Their food often consisted of berries gathered in the briar patches, and food gathered from their small garden or purchased from the commissary. Their only meat was sourbelly and picklepoke, which she explained was pickled horse meat for cooking vegetables.

Esther Mae Scott was delivered by a midwife and was the seventh child and born in the seventh month with a veil over her face. The midwife told her mother, "If you could raise her, then she'd be something special" (Goren, 13). She interpreted the auspices of her birth to mean she was psychic and illustrated her point with: "If there's something I want to do, I can meditate over it and think about it and the next day I pretty well do what I want. I'm psychic. I guess that's some of the special stuff the midwife was talking about" (Goren, 13).

By age five, Scott was an active member of the farm's workforce. She and her nine-year-old brother were water carriers for the men and boys ploughing in the fields. She was paid nothing at that age, but by age eight or nine, she received a quarter a day. By then she had long been helping to clean and open the ground, a job done by hand in order to farm the land for cotton, sugarcane, corn, and potatoes. According to Mother Scott, "in the country you wouldn't be a baby . . . we used to work from 'kin' to 'cain't'! That's from when you could see to when you couldn't see" (Goren, 13). It was her task to gather the cows, and in the winter she often suffered frostbite because she had no shoes or socks. She recalled that while she was gathering the cows, her heels split open, and her mother tended her with home remedies: "My mother would roast turnips and she would get them out, just like some people roast sweet potatoes, and put it open and stick it to my heels as hard as she could bear, and put socks on me. Sometime my grandfather would give us socks" (Black Women Oral History Interview, 31).

Scott's formal education consisted of a few short periods of school attendance structured around the farm activity, as the crops received greater attention than school. She first attended school at around the age of six or seven, a few years after her watercarrying responsibilities began, and she remembered a time when there were no schools in the area. She explained:

> Later on there was a school; Julius Rosenwald, a Jewish fellow, put some schools out there for Blacks. And we had one teacher, and the teacher would have the children who could say the alphabets or read and write, to help him with the children who would come to him. It was more than he could handle. That was the best we could do. And for my schooling, to go to school we had to pick. . . . And if on the man's place, if Christmas come and you wasn't through picking cotton, when New Year's come, you had to start. So that was one week from Christmas to New Year's. And from then, if we could go and finish the cotton, picking the cotton and getting the crops and things, I say long in February, they started turning over the land with ploughs and mules again. We had to get out there, and if I didn't carry water, I had to burn brush, or knock stalks—I cut down stalks with a hoe or something like that—and work. I had no time for school much. I imagine to go to school I was grade, say about second grade (Black Women Oral History Interview, 30).

The name of the school was Clover Valley Baptist School, and it was affiliated with a church of the same name. Scott went to school "about a month in this season before, and no time before Christmas." Because they were always late with the cotton, "you'd go to school after Christmas, I'd say two or three weeks" (Black Women Oral History Interview, 30).

Her early musical experience was informal. She stated that all her people "were singers because they were slaves"

(Silver, 7). She noted the connection between work and song: "I started to sing around five because I started to work around five" (Goren, 13). She explained that "the average Negro from Mississippi and other slave counties knew how to sing because singing is something to raise your ego up enough to help you solve the task you got to do. And singing looked like it'd make the day shorter for you" (Silver, 7). Indeed, Warren County, Mississippi, the area in which Esther Scott grew up, was in "a region that spawned a diverse range of blues musicians, from Charlie Patton to Son House to Muddy Waters" (Goren, 13). Her grandfather, Monroe Prentiss, played the violin, and from him she heard "such tunes as 'Turkey in the Straw' and ragtimes and jigs" (Black Women Oral History Interview, 23).

When Scott was about eight years old, she began learning the guitar. An eleven-year-old boy, Kiser Suder, who worked for her uncle and had the only guitar among the children in the area, taught her to play. Prior to the guitar, she and her cohorts used various homemade instruments:

> Well, you see, we'd been making music with jugs; and brooms, you draw across your hand, make bass; and sardine cans what you make violins; and we had all kinds of crazy things going. And tin pans and rhythms, and that's what we would do (Black Women Oral History Interview, 33).

Scott did not own a guitar in her early years but eventually played numerous instruments, "borrowing her friends' 'Stella' guitars and playing whatever else was around," including a mandolin, banjo, and piano: "It just come to me and I hit the notes" (Goren, 13). Thus, her early musical training was informal and derived from work, family, and community affiliations.

Entertainer Joins Minstrel Show

When Scott was about fourteen or fifteen years old, she put her age forward by two years and became a professional entertainer by joining W. S. Wolcott's Rabbit Foot Minstrels, with whom she worked in vaudeville for two years touring the South. She traveled the Delta area, singing, dancing, playing the guitar, and demonstrating hair pomade in such areas as New Orleans, Baton Rouge, Fort Gibson, Natchez, and Vicksburg. Her reason for joining Rabbit Foot and Wolcott was poverty: "I wanted a shiny dress. I wanted to wear pretty clothes. My mother wasn't able to get them for us, she had so many children" (Goren, 14). She asked the girls performing how she could get on the show as a dancer. According to Ward Silver in *Great Speckled Bird*, the show was called the *Dark Town Follies*, and at that point Scott was not interested in joining as a guitarist. She told the girls, "If I could just get me a shiny dress like you all got, I can sing and dance as good as you" (Goren, 14). Mother Scott received one dollar a day with the show and took her first paycheck to her mother, who was disappointed at her choice. Scott apologized to her and said, "I get so tired of seeing you eat the same thing" (Goren, 14).

With Wolcott's show, Scott was an all-around entertainer whose major responsibility was to promote the sale of Jack Rabbit and Bentone Liniment to make hair grow. As Scott put it, "I had to tell people how great this liniment was" (Silver, 7). In her act, she sang, danced, played guitar, told jokes, and demonstrated the pomade as effective on her own hair:

> I'd come out and say, "Yes, it'll make hair grow on your head. It'll make hair grow on lamp posts, lamplights, light bulbs," and things like that. And I knew I was lying. . . . But that's the way I had to make a living. And that's what I was doing for a living, I was getting a dollar a day to lie (Black Women Oral History Interview, 37).

The show, according to Scott, was run by whites but employed only blacks "masked up just like in the time of Al Jolson . . . [with] this white stuff on their lips, black around the eyes, and they looked real funny . . . bow ties and things under their shirts and long shoes and split-tail coats and them little derbies that sits on their head" (Silver, 7). The liniment was sold only to blacks, "and it got every nickel these people would make" (Black Women Oral History Interview, 37). The claim was that the liniment would straighten hair and make it grow; to illustrate, the viewers witnessed pictures of attractive people with beautiful hair, as well as the entertainers themselves, of whom Scott was one. While she used her own hair ostensibly as an example, she never used the product: "I knew better, 'cause it was red devil lye, what you scrub with, was in that stuff, what they put in that hair pomade" (Black Women Oral History Interview, 37). And she explained, "when they washed their hair, their hair came out. And nobody in Mississippi was gonna lay a suit on a white man. He knew that meant death so he better go bald headed or die" (Silver, 7).

In her work with Wolcott's Rabbit Foot Minstrels, Scott developed a sense of audience. In her shiny dress, she was "just like a proud peacock" (Black Women Oral History Interview, 37). She was "Old Miss, very beautiful," weighing 118 pounds and holding the stage name "Big Baby" (Black Women Oral History Interview, 38). She made up songs and used those of others, such as Leadbelly's "Hop around, jump around, pick a bale of cotton. Oh Lordy me and my gal gonna pick a bale of cotton" (Goren, 14). She explained: "When I would be saying that I would be telling the truth because me and my father, so many of us, were sharecroppers. . . . [We'd] go down the rows and come up with a bale of cotton" (Goren, 14). She sang spirituals as well as blues, which she defined as being "when you sorry for yourself" (Goren, 14). She worked seven days a week, never earning more than two dollars a day. She also sang and played on the guitar songs she learned with Kiser Suder, such as "Oh Babe, Babe, please don't let me fall / If you do, you won't have no baby at all / We gonna have a good time, a hot time / In the town tonight."

After two years, Scott left the show, ending her early career as a professional entertainer. She spent the next fifty years as a domestic and nanny. She worked for twenty-seven years as a domestic with a family of German Jewish caterers, Ed Klaus and Adele Klaus Gottheld of Vicksburg, Mississippi. With this family she was a maid and nurse and during their vacations traveled the East Coast between Martha's Vineyard and Biloxi, Florida. In 1938, still in the depression years, the family moved to a hotel, fired her without severance pay and offered her only a ticket to Cary Plantation in Mississippi. Instead of going there she went to Baltimore, Maryland, by way of a visit to her daughter, Ruth, in Washington, D.C. In Baltimore she became the maid and wet nurse for Merty Landau Shoemaker, the cousin of her former employer. Around 1958, she left Baltimore and moved to Washington, D.C., where she began a new career as a professional entertainer.

While in domestic service, however, she played the guitar only sporadically but kept up with the musical arena. As well, during her years with the Klaus family in Vicksburg, Mother Scott kept in touch with entertainers she had met in vaudeville and also met others. Two such acquaintances were Leadbelly and Bessie Smith.

Mother Scott's friendship with Leadbelly began when she met him on tour in New Orleans in 1910. This friendship continued through the years. Mother Scott said of Leadbelly:

> He was like a chunky, big black bull! The thing about Leadbelly . . . he wanted women and he loved women. He'd love to have them around and play around . . . a playboy. But his girlfriend—don't fool around with her! He was a jealous man and that's the part I didn't like him for. I just couldn't understand that. He wasn't my cup of tea, but he was a very dear friend of mine.
>
> Leadbelly was just so much greater than I was. He could make anything rhyme. He's just smart, let's put it like that. I wasn't quick like that. Leadbelly was just a performer, a real performer from the heart (Goren, 14).

While Mother Scott was employed with the Klaus's family, Leadbelly took her to meet Bessie Smith, whom she recalled seeing on two separate occasions. As to her introduction to Smith, however, Mother Scott remembered it variously. By one account, she met her at the Daisy Theater in Clarksdale, Mississippi. By the other account, she met her in Memphis, Tennessee.

In a 1978 interview with David Goren, and in a 1976 interview with Theresa Danley, Mother Scott described the experience of meeting Bessie Smith in Clarksdale. According to Scott, one Friday she asked her employers for and was granted permission to go to Clarksdale to see Bessie Smith perform. Because she was afraid they would change their minds, she hurriedly left with Leadbelly:

> We got in his car and off we went. And when we got to Clarksdale, we met Bessie. And I was telling Bessie how much I thought of her. She didn't believe me. Bessie was the kind of person, she drinked all the time. And she just believed everybody was after her boyfriend, which I was proud—there wasn't a thing I wanted but her voice. I just wanted to learn her songs and to hear how she sang and hear how she performed. And on and on, I made her know that I meant it and I was on the square with her. That was all I wanted, was her songs. And I idolized the "Gulf Coast Blues" (Black History Oral History Interview, 40).

Of this same meeting, Mother Scott informed Goren:

> She was auditioning and her boyfriend Clarence Williams was playing the piano. You know she was kind of shy. I been looking at her boyfriend and she was a jealous person. I caught her in the wrong mood . . . simply because she was drinking. She loved to drink. But she could do her best singing when she was just half high . . . drinking that wine. It never did appeal to me. All I wanted to do was to get her way of singing (14).

The other account of her introduction to Bessie Smith was recounted to Jerry Silver in 1975. When asked how she came into contact with Smith, Mother Scott replied:

> After this show (Around 1910). Bessie was gonna play in Memphis. And I was up there on a peach barrel with these white people I was working for and Leadbelly (who was a close friend) said, "How about we goin' to Memphis to hear Bessie?" and I said, you know I've idolized her all my life and if I could just get to see and talk to her. So we went and I heard her sing the "Gulfcoast Blues." I went crazy because I knew I wanted to sing like her.
>
> I had heard her on record, but I wasn't satisfied. I wanted to hear her (live) and when I met her I let her know who I was and what songs I wanted to hear, she really played them and she sang it for me (7).

Mother Scott further told Silver that her second time seeing Bessie was in New Orleans. On this occasion, Mother Scott played in a funeral procession with Louis Armstrong and his Knights of Pytheon, performing "When the Saints Go Marching In" (7).

When Silver interviewed Mother Scott, he noticed that on her living room wall were posters of Roy Buchanan and Leadbelly, and one of her accompanists present at the interview, Phillip Terry, informed Silver, "Mother Scott knew Charlie Patto [sic] rather well" (7).

Scott Reenters the Music World

Quite some years following these early experiences and after her career as a domestic, Mother Scott's career in professional music began anew in Washington, D.C., where she lived and performed until her death. Upon moving to Washington, Mother Scott became a member of St. Stephen and the Incarnation Episcopal Church and became active in its song programs as well as in civil rights and senior citizens' interests. According to Goren, "Through her church she began singing at weddings and funerals, and eventually she travelled widely to perform at night clubs, demonstrations, and festivals" (Goren, 14). Theresa Danley suggests that Mother Scott's reentry into the music world coincided with a period during the sixties when the church became "interested in folk music as part of the liturgical mass" (Black Women Oral History Interview, 44).

Mother Scott's late career in music was in several ways enhanced by her association with the church. At St. Stephen's, she was prompted to branch out by then rector, the Reverend William A. Wendt. As Mother Scott recalled:

> I had my first guitar, my own guitar, I could call my own, at St. Stephen and the Incarnation, and Father William A. Wendt told me, "Get out and go down to Pogoe's and get you a guitar. And you get out on your own because you got enough talent. You're wasting it. And get out and make you some money" (Black Women Oral History Interview, 44).

Indeed, in a letter to the author, the Reverend Wendt remembered Scott as an "important lady" who was "near and dear" to him (2 June 1990). In another letter to the author, one of Mother Scott's fellow parishioners, Edith C. H. Eder, currently the "oldest-in-terms-of-service parishioner working in the office" of Stephen and the Incarnation, states: "She often was asked to play at weddings, for people in no way connected to the church, and would reduce congregations to tears by singing "He's Got the Whole World in His Hands" and ending it "He's got [Bruce] (groom) and [Wendy] (bride) in His hands" (8 May 1990). Mother Scott also "worked with electric bands in churches long before it became socially accepted, performing with various groups of young people" (Black Women Oral History Interview, iii). Most of her church-related work she performed gratis.

Mother Scott also played blues at local Washington clubs, such as the Cellar Door, known for its blues and jazz entertainment. She was a member of the musician's union and earned union wages for her performances on radio and television. She performed at folk festivals, at colleges and universities, and for various groups from Boston to Miami. During the seventies, Mother Scott performed rather widely. Among her engagements were appearances at the bicentennial celebrations for the Smithsonian Folk Festival in southwest Washington, D.C. (1976), and in Columbia, Baltimore, and Westminster, Maryland (1976). As well, she responded to the Reverend Don Howard's request that she appear at the United Methodist Church Bicentennial Program. She also performed on the Mall at the Smithsonian Festival of American Folklife (1978); in a 1978 concert at Rutgers University, from which her granddaughter Ruette Madrice Watson graduated in 1977; at Washington National Cathedral; and in Louisville during the Episcopal Church General Convention, where, on Cabaret Night, she was on stage with the orchestra performing "When the Saints Go Marching In" to an audience of priests and bishops. She performed to an audience of 72,000 people in the Pocono Mountains.

At the Ford Theater in Washington, D.C., she attended *Bessie and I* and was invited onto the stage by Linda Hopkins:

> She made a mistake and asked me up on the stage with her. And I got up there and stole the show from her. I told her I knew Bessie Smith before she was born and I did. And I got up and sang the "Gulf Coast Blues" (Black Women Oral History Interview, 40).

Scott also played on stage with Elizabeth Cotten, another Washington area blues singer and guitarist. She has performed with Joan Baez, Kris Kristoffersen, Judy Collins, and Alice Cooper.

Mother Scott released only one album, *Moma Ain't Nobody's Fool*, on the Bomp label in 1971. This album was partly the result of her association with a young musician, Michael Butler, who died tragically. According to Danley, Butler's mother "was so impressed by Esther and her musical ability that she asked the pastor of St. Stephen's Church, Father Wendt, if she could financially assist Mother Scott in making a record" (Black Women Oral History Interview, iii). Thus, Mother Scott recorded her first and only album at the age of seventy-eight. The album contains performances by Vassar Clements and Emmy Lou Harris as well as Mother Scott's version of "Gulf Coast Blues." At the age of seventy-nine, Mother Scott was still composing and wrote "Keep a Goin'" for her eightieth birthday. It was, according to her, "a favorite for senior citizens" (Black Women Oral History Interview, 48). The song was transcribed by Danley:

> If you strike a thorny rose, Keep a goin'
> If it hails or if it rains, Keep on goin'
>
> Tain't no use to sit and whine, When the fish
> ain't on your line.
> Bait your hook and keep on trying, Keep a goin'
>
> If the weather kills your crops, Keep a goin'
> Though it's work, Keep a goin'
>
> Suppose you out of every dime, Getting broke
> ain't any crime
> Tell the world you're feeling fine, Keep a goin'
>
> When they said it all was up, Keep a goin'
> Drain the sweet milk from the cup, Keep a goin'
>
> See the wild birds on the wing, Listen to the bell
> sweetly ring
> If you feel like singing, sing, Keep a goin'

> If a task is once begun, Keep a goin'
> Never leave it until it's done, Keep a goin'
>
> Be the labor great or small, Do it well or not at all
> Answer your name when the roll is called, Keep a goin'
>
> It's all I'm saying, Keep a goin'
> (Black Women Oral History Interview, 48).

As an inspiration to senior citizens, Mother Scott espoused a proud approach to life and aging. As she stated several years after composing the song:

> My brain, this old house, is still 82 years old and age kill trees and I can't do with my body, darling, what I used to do. I can think, thanks be to Jesus I'm not senile. I can think and do things. But I don't want to be put in a home with old people—listen who's saying about old—I don't want to hear this gruntin' and achin' and complainin' cause I don't do that. If somethin' hurt me you wouldn't know it. I tells it in my prayer and I'll go to the cross with it (Silver, 7).

Although Mother Scott's late career spanned both blues and gospel performance, she saw no conflict between the two. At age eighty-six, just prior to her death, she explained:

> Age makes you want to speak to God [and] I sing more spirituals now. You put your heart into it. When I'm singing I look around the audience. I see people who I have really got to. You don't know what a happy person I am when I do that (Goren, 15).

Mother Scott, to a great extent, accepted music as a kind of ministry, and when hospitalized for eye surgery she entertained the other patients because, as she said, "I thought it was my duty" (Black Women Oral History Interview, 45).

Mother Scott's having been born with a veil over her face perhaps contributed in part to her unique composing style. Referring to her song "God Called Adam," she indicated that "many of her ideas came to her in dreams and visions" (Goren, 15). Of the song, she stated, "One night, two o'clock in the morning, I had a vision with the angels, the 4 and 40,000. And I began to hear them sing 'God Called Adam'" (Goren, 15).

Still, though, her works were a mixture of the sacred and the secular. The year before her death she changed the ending to her performance from "Goodnight ladies, I'm bound to leave you now" to a new one she had made up:

> An old lady sat under a tree,
> Sewing as long as her eyes could see
> She pulled her work and she smoothed it right
> And she said Dear work goodnight goodnight.
> A flock of black crows flew over her head
> Crying caw caw on her way to bed
> She said as she noticed the noisy flight
> Little black thing goodnight goodnight
> The horses neighed and the cattle lowed
> The lambs were bleatin' way down the road
> They all seemed to say with quiet delight
> All God's creatures, Goodnight, Goodnight.
> (Goren, 15).

Toward her performance of both blues and gospel music, Mother Scott held a practical attitude. She rationalized that it was difficult to live on an income of $146 a month from her social security allotment when her rent was $115 and her other expenses exceeded the balance. She stated:

> God helps him who helps himself. And I will not tell you I don't sing the blues. The average person retires at age 65 and I'm 82 and I'm still goin' and I'll go 82 more years rather than be at the mercy of people so I can live like any other person. I'm willing to work as long as God gives me the strength (Silver, 7).

As she grew older, she suffered from various problems, none of which kept her from being active. She was operated on for glaucoma and was almost without sight in one eye. She was diabetic, had high blood pressure, and had difficulty walking; she underwent physical therapy twice a month. Because she was so dearly loved, however, she had many friends who escorted her on errands.

She lived in a one-bedroom apartment in the Mount Pleasant area of northwest Washington, D.C., and on one occasion was mugged on Newton Street and assisted to nearby St. Stephen's by community citizens who were concerned for her safety. As her friend Edith Eder explained, "everybody knew her; she was in *loco matris* to the young girls and on winking and joking terms with the men." According to Eder, Mother Scott "loved to share whatever she had and would make scrumptious southern foods and give them to people in the office or whoever she was with at the moment. As a diabetic she often couldn't eat them herself."

When her older sister Clara was widowed in 1960, Mother Scott traveled to Mississippi and brought her to Washington, D.C., where they lived together until Clara's death in 1970. Reverend Wendt recalled Mother Scott's response to her sister's passing:

> I remember—the day we buried her sister's ashes in the church yard. When we placed them in the hole, she looked up to the heavens and said, "Well God, we sure cheated the worms."
>
> She cheated no one in life, and will be long remembered by folks like me (William A. Wendt to Laura C. Jarmon, 2 June 1990).

Mother Scott's music career was full and combined the outstanding poles of traditional black music. A guitarist, she could not read music, but, in her words, "I know when it's right and I know when it's wrong" (Goren, 13). She also taught herself to read guitar notes by getting a book. She was a trainer to the younger musicians with whom she worked. Of her voice, Danley suggested that she learned vibrato from Bessie Smith. Of her repertoire, Edith Eder states that it was huge. She is generally described as having been cheerful, and, indeed, Mother Scott herself said that from childhood she "always believed that one thing wouldn't last always" (Silver, 7).

In response to the author's inquiry about Mother Scott's album, *Moma Ain't Nobody's Fool*, Eder descriptively wrote:

> Too bad you can't see her singing it, with her loving, twinkling eyes beaming, pale, nimble fingers drawing music from her very special guitar, and her warm, expressive voice reaching out to everybody (Edith C. H. Eder to Laura C. Jarmon).

Mother Scott was, in her late years, a product of the folk revival, and she brought to the public a talent and style unique to the Mississippi delta region of America's first quarter century. She died of a stroke in Washington, D.C. on October 16, 1979, at the age of eighty-six.

References

Barlow, Bill. "Esther Mae 'Mother' Scott." *Living Blues Magazine* 44 (Autumn 1979): 57.

Barlow, William. *"Looking Up at Down:" The Emergence of Blues Culture*. Philadelphia: Temple University Press, 1989. 74.

Eder, Edith C. H. Interview with author, 8 May 1990.

Goren, David. "Remembering 'Mother' Scott: An Interview." *Sing Out* 27 (June 1979): 13-15. Includes photograph.

Scott, Esther Mae. Black Women Oral History Interview, 11 August 1976 and 3 November 1977. Schlesinger Library, Radcliff College, 1986.

Scott, Esther Mae. *Moma Ain't Nobody's Fool*. Bomp. RI3384. 1971.

Silver, Ward H. "Born Under a Good Sign." *Great Speckled Bird* 8 (20 February 1975): 7. Includes photograph.

Wendt, William A. Interview with author, 2 June 1990.

Women of Courage: An Exhibition of Photographs by Judith Sedwick. Based on the Black Women Oral History Project. Cambridge: Schlesinger Library, Radcliffe College, 1984.

Laura C. Jarmon

Gloria Scott

(1938-)

Educator, organization official

Gloria Dean Randle Scott, distinguished leader in higher education and an advocate of women's issues, is the second woman chief administrator of Bennett College, Greensboro, North Carolina. A zoologist by training, she rose rapidly in academia to hold professorial administrative posts outside the field of science. She is known also for her leadership in Girls Scouts, USA, for which she served as national president.

Born April 14, 1938, in Houston, Texas, Gloria Dean Randle Scott is the middle of five children born to Freeman Randle, a Houston cook, and Juanita (Bell) Randle, a domestic and part-time nurse. Gloria Randle Scott's first-grade teacher was a strong influence in her life. "She made learning interesting and let us know that, because we were black, we had to be doubly achievement-oriented," said Scott. "She had no children of her own, but she would have us to her house, tell us how to study, take us on outings. As a result, I found learning a challenge" (Demaret, 39). Scott graduated from Jack Yates High School in Houston in 1955, where she was salutatorian. She received three degrees from Indiana University: a B.A. in zoology with minors in botany

Gloria Scott

and French, 1959; M.A. in zoology with a minor in botany, 1960; and a Ph.D. with a major in higher education and minors in zoology and botany, 1965.

She taught at Marian College, Indianapolis, Indiana, from 1961 to 1965 and moved to Knoxville College, Knoxville, Tennessee, in 1965, where she joined the teaching faculty and was also dean of students and deputy director of the Upward Bound program until 1967. From 1967 to 1968 Scott was special assistant to the president at North Carolina Agricultural and Technical State University, Greensboro, where she developed a ten-year institutional long range plan for the university as part of the North Carolina State Plan for Higher Education and set up an Office of Institutional Research and Planning. From 1968 to 1972 she was director of institutional research and planning and at the same time taught on the faculty. On leave from 1973 to 1975, Scott was senior research associate and head of post-secondary education at the National Institute of Education, Washington, D.C., and returned to the university for one year, 1975-1976, as director of educational research and planning.

Moving to Houston, Scott was professor of higher education in 1976-1977 and assistant to the president for educational planning and evaluation, Texas Southern University, for the 1977-1978 year. She spent the next nine years at Clark College in Atlanta as vice-president. From 1978 to 1987 she taught at several colleges—Clark, Bryn Mawr, Atlanta University, and Grambling State University. In 1987 Scott was elected president of Bennett College, Greensboro, North Carolina, becoming the second woman president in the school's history. (Willa B. Player was the first woman president of Bennett from 1955 to 1966.) "Having a woman president earlier made it easier for the college to select another," Scott said "There are far more capable women who should be college presidents or who should be in other high level academic positions" (Interview with Gloria Randle Scott, 2 February 1991). She presides over the academic life of 660 young women in this historically black liberal arts college.

Role of the Black Women's College Viewed

Scott refers to herself as a "race woman." "Giving something back, influencing what happens to Black people has always been important. . . . I suppose I'm one of the vestiges of what you call 'race women'—people who really believe in African Americans" (Mercer, 14). Her presence at Bennett College allows her the opportunity to give back to women and to black people. Scott sees the black college as an institution with a mission to provide an education "that allows economic, social and intellectual mobility," but it is also potentially "a corporate citizen," particularly since black high schools have closed and the community must look elsewhere for advocates for black students (Mercer, 14). A black woman's college goes a step beyond the coeducational institution. Scott said in a recent interview: "If you attend a woman's college, you have the opportunity to be everything. . . . You don't have to deal with the competitive personal development issue of whether you challenge the males, or if you're a good student, the question of whether you tailor that so you won't appear to be too smart" (Mercer, 10).

When asked to identify any problems peculiar to a single-sex college, especially for black women, Scott said, "Black women still don't have money. The alumnae pool is small, but the level of giving at Bennett is high. Funding is a problem as well as a challenge. We must sell the college. High school counselors don't steer students to women's colleges or the black colleges in general" (Interview with Gloria Randle Scott, 2 February 1991).

Planning for the black women's college of the future is equally challenging. On this issue Scott said that as we look toward the end of this decade, we must look at those forces that affect black women. Black women themselves must continue to be a strong part of the family, community, and the professional structure. Scott said:

> I hope to educate Bennett women in the area of applied technology. This started to change our lives and will change it in the future. Women must harness that learning. . . . They must take on the role of being informed citizens and influence social and economic policy. They must be educated to become parents. Attention needs to be given to being a new kind of parent. We must educate women beyond a narrow band. A very good liberal arts base is critical . . . and the student must gain some depth in an interest area (Interview with Gloria Randle Scott, 2 February 1991).

She sees black women in a leadership role in the future and actively pursues means to help them get there. "Part of my leadership style is to help enable . . . younger women, especially, to develop leadership qualities. I've made a deliberate decision to try to bring some women along in the pipeline . . . to give them challenges and then be supportive," she said. While the women will make mistakes, they will then "try to correct those mistakes and understand what that means" (Jones, 30).

Scott is as much concerned with the black community and black students in the schools as she is with Bennett College and higher education. She is troubled over a national problem that seems to defy resolution—the countless numbers of black students who need good higher education but are unable to get it. She is distressed that black students lost a role model when the black teacher was displaced and the community suffered as well. "Black students need to see some validation about what they can do." Black teachers also make a tremendous impact on white youth, "who need to know that blacks are leaders too," she said (Interview with Gloria Randle Scott, 2 February 1991).

Black women's colleges will need to look toward other leaders in the future—when Johnnetta Cole at Spelman College and Gloria Randle Scott at Bennett move on to other arenas. Black women who aspire to become college presidents or hold other senior-level positions will need knowledge that a good liberal arts program can provide, said Scott. In addition to the general qualities required for effective management, "black or other ethnic women must carry with them their culture and history" (Jones, 32).

In the area of governance, Scott's experiences have come from academic institutions noted earlier as well as from affiliations with other institutions and agencies. She was a founding member and secretary of Persons Responsive to Educational Problems, 1966-1982. Since then she has served as board member, Southern Education Foundation, 1967-1977; and vice-chair, National Advisory Committee on Black Higher Education and Black Colleges and Universities (to the United States Department of Education and the office of Health, Education and Welfare), 1976-1983.

In 1975 she was on the Education Commissions of States Task Force on Equal Education Opportunity for Women. President Gerald Ford and later President Jimmy Carter appointed Scott to the National Commission on International Women's Year, from 1976 to 1978. She was chairperson of the education committee and member of the board of directors, National Urban League, 1976-1985. From 1978 to 1980 she held yet another presidential appointment from President Carter, this time to the National Commission on International Year of the Child.

She was also a member of: Defense Advisory Committee on Women in the Services, Department of Defense, 1979-81, and chair 1981; board of trustees, Wilson College, Chambersburg, Pennsylvania, 1979-1984; National Commission on Higher Education Issues, American Council on Education, 1982-83; Council of Chief Academic Officers, American Council on Education, 1982-1984; board of directors (and chairperson), SERO/National Scholarship for Negro Students, 1982-1985; board of directors, American Association of Higher Education, 1982-1985; board of directors, Association of American Colleges, 1982-1985; board of directors, InRoads Atlanta, 1986-1988; and board member of the Educational Corporation. She has served on other state and local advisory committees and commissions in North Carolina, Tennessee, Georgia, and Texas. During 1989-1990 she was a member of the Greensboro Area Chamber of Commerce and a member of the board of directors and cochairperson of the minority task force, National Association of Independent Colleges and Universities, 1989-1992.

Affiliations in professional associations continue. Scott is on the board of directors of the following associations and institutions: Africa University (and secretary of the board), 1988-1991; member of the University Senate, United Methodist Church, 1988-1991; North Carolina Governor's Internship Council, 1988-1990; First Home Federal Savings and Loan (Greensboro, N.C.); Loews Corporation; and President's Board of Advisors on Historically Black Colleges and Universities, 1990. Gloria Scott and the board of advisors for the Historically Black Colleges met in Washington, D.C., in 1991 when Education Assistant Secretary Michael Williams issued a public statement and held a press conference in which he reported that the Department of Education deemed unlawful the provision of minority-only scholarships for students in college. The board of advisors urged President George Bush to nullify the Education Department's interpretation of the law, which he did, called for a review of the Education Department's policy, and asked that educators have an opportunity to develop a strategy.

Professional organizations and regional agencies have benefited extensively from Scott's leadership ability. She has been active in extensive program development for the Southern Regional Education Board, the Council on Social Work Education, professional regional accreditation agencies, and miscellaneous education-related groups. Gloria Scott has participated in institutional accreditation evaluation in numerous institutions within the area accredited by the Southern Association of Colleges and Schools and has chaired numerous committees with responsibility for final reports to the Commission on Colleges. Of particular importance in the dismantling of dual systems of higher education, between 1973 and 1976 she has conducted program review and evaluation for the United States Office of Education in states where dual systems existed. In addition, she reviewed programs in other institutions to determine whether or not they complied with regulations of Title VI, Title VII, and Title IX. Currently she serves on the external review board for Stanford University's Minority Participation and Presence.

Scott Rises to Helm of Girl Scouts

Gloria Scott is well known for her work with the Girl Scouts, USA. Her interest in scouting was nurtured while she was growing up in Houston, and she saw it as both an opportunity for personal development and a means of enhancing the lives of poor and minority children. Her nature trips, which she took during her early teens as a Girl Scout, created an abiding interest in the outdoors. She has been a member of the board of directors of the Girl Scouts since 1969. From 1969 to 1972 she served as chair of the Program Committee and member of the Minority Task Force. From 1972 to 1975 she was first vice-president, and from 1975 to 1978 she was national president—the first black in the organization's history of more than sixty-five years. From February 28 through March 10, 1977, she conducted workshop training sessions for heads of national organizations for member countries in the Western Hemisphere of the World Association of Girl Guides and Girl Scouts in Rio de Janeiro. This involved conducting training sessions for volunteer and staff administrators of associations from Central America, South America, and the Caribbean.

Scott directed an unprecedented array of innovations early in her term as Girl Scout president. In Florida a statewide scout conference explored women's issues, land use, and justice for juveniles. Scouts in North Dakota who were interested in law, politics, and public administration became state legislative interns. Baltimore scouts organized a coalition to increase the participation of black youth and adults in the movement. Leadership training for black and Puerto

Rican teenagers was held in Hartford, Connecticut; therapeutic programs for mentally handicapped girls as well as those with psychiatric problems were held in Nashville, Tennessee; and scouts in Maine attended classes on venereal disease.

Volunteer and other civic activities have come to Scott's attention, and she has devoted tireless service to these groups. She served the Delta Sigma Theta Sorority as national second vice president, 1958-1960; national secretary, 1971-1975; and executive board member, 1958-1960 and 1971-1975. Among other areas of special interest for Gloria Scott are women's issues. She participated in the Women in Passage Conference in 1975 sponsored by *Goodhousekeeping*, and Phase II, Women in Passage—The Male Point of View, May 1977. In November of that year she was the official presiding chair for the opening of the National Women's Conference held in Houston, Texas. She was national cochairperson of the 1981 Black Women's Summit, Washington, D.C., July 1981. When Clark College held its Conference on American Black Women titled "Have We Come a Long Way, Baby?" (A Report on the Status of America's First Female Work Force) on May 3-5, 1985, she was conference convener and led a delegation to the International Women's Decade meeting in Nairobi, Kenya.

Honors and awards for Gloria Scott have been numerous. These include: the Indiana Governor's Award and being named Outstanding Negro Student in Indiana, 1964; the Student Government Award for Outstanding Service to the University, North Carolina Agricultural and Technical State University, 1970; "Woman of the Year" in humanitarian and community services, *Ladies' Home Journal,* May 1977; selection as a Legendary Woman, Birmingham Southern College, September 1977; Distinguished Service Citation, Southern Education Foundation, 1977; citation from the Texas House of Representatives for "Outstanding Leadership and Contribution through Services," January 1978; "Woman of the Year for Achievement" by *Post Standard* newspaper, Syracuse, New York, February 1978; "Woman of Achievement," YWCA, Houston, Texas, 1978; "Black Woman of the Year," Community Action Program, Evansville, Indiana, November 1978; Whitney M. Young, Jr., Service Award from the Boy Scouts of America, February 1979; induction into the Academy of Women Achievers, YWCA, Atlanta, Georgia, 1986; and selection as honoree of the Museum of African-American Life and Culture and inclusion in the Texas Sesquicentennial Celebration, "They Showed the Way," a traveling exhibition that will be housed in the museum at Dallas, 1986. In May 1977 Indiana University awarded Gloria Scott the doctor of laws degree, and in June 1978 Fairleigh Dickinson University awarded her the doctor of humane letters degree.

Editorial experiences span a number of years. Gloria Scott gave editorial service to the American College Personnel Association Monograph Commission on Student Personnel Monographs from 1966 to 1970. She was guest editor, *Journal of Black Higher Education,* September 1975, and member of the Editorial Committee from 1973 to 1978. From 1985 to the present she has been a member of the Editorial Advisory Committee, *Journal of the American Black Nurses Association,* and from 1986 to 1988 she was on the Liberal Education Editorial Advisory Board of the American Association of Colleges. From 1984 to 1987 Gloria Scott was host on "Community Journal," WGNX-TV in Atlanta. Currently she appears on "Education Update," the Black College Student Network broadcast weekly from Washington, D.C.

Her writings include "Can Black Institutions Organize to Survive?" (Institute for Services to Education, Conference Report); "Educational Needs of Black Women" (*Occupational and Educational Needs of Black Women,* National Institute of Education, 1977); and "The Economic Future: Institutional and Student Financial Aid for Blacks in Higher Education," in *Black Students in Higher Education: Conditions and Experiences,* edited by Gail E. Thomas (Westport, Conn.: Greenwood Press, 1980).

Gloria Dean Randle Scott is "an activist president" who manages by visiting other offices on campus for conferences. "In moving back and forth, I see things on campus, and get a better sense of what's going on," she said (Jones, 30). She is a carefully-spoken, dynamic leader with will and determination, quiet reserve, and a wry sense of humor. Rarely is she without pencil and notepad to record conversations and meeting highlights; she uses the information for planning, action, and evaluation. The five feet two inch president lights up her royal-blue and white, well-appointed office. On the wall in her outer office is a framed photograph of Septima Clark from the exhibit "I Dream a World," in which Scott's photograph is also included. An early riser, she walks three miles around the campus each day as much for exercise as to examine the campus and its condition. In 1959 Scott married Will Braxton Scott, currently a professor of sociology and social work at Bennett College. While they have no children, they were surrogate parents to more than three million Girl Scouts and hundreds of former students.

References

"Biography: Gloria R. Scott, Eleventh President of Bennett College." n.d.

"Bush's Black College Board Lauds Call for Review of Minority Scholarship Plan." *Jet* 79 (21 January 1991): 33. Includes photograph of the commission of black educators in which Gloria Scott is shown.

Contributions of Black Women to America. Vol. II. Ed. Marianna W. Davis. Columbia, S.C.: Kenday Press, 1982.

Demaret, Kent. "The Old Girl Scout Cookie Crumbling? No Way, It's Got a New Activist—And Its First Black—Prez: Gloria Scott." *People* (25 July 1977): 38-39. Includes photographs.

"Essence Women." *Essence* 8 (January 1978): 6. Includes photograph.

Jones, M. Colleen. "An Interview with Gloria Scott." Special Issue: "Black Women in Higher Education." *Jour-*

nal of the National Association of Women Deans, Administrators, and Counselors 53 (Spring 1999): 29-32.

Ladies' Home Journal (June 1977): 75-76. Includes photographs.

Lanker, Brian. *I Dream a World.* New York: Stewart, Tabori, and Chang, 1989. 118-19. Photograph, p. 119.

Mercer, Joye. "Difficult Winds Ahead: Five Women Chart the Course for HBCUs in the 1990s." *Black Issues in Higher Education* 7 (27 September 1990): 10-15. Includes photographs.

People (3 October 1977): 69. Includes photograph.

Scott, Gloria Dean Randle. Interview with author, 2 February 1991.

"Speaking of People." *Ebony* 32 (August 1977): 3. Includes photograph.

Who's Who Among Black Americans, 1990/91. 6th ed. Detroit: Gale Research, 1990.

Who's Who of American Women. 10th ed. Chicago: Marquis, 1978.

Collections

A historical collection of information about Gloria Dean Randle Scott is in the Special Collections of the Atlanta Public Library, while the archives of Bennett College house current materials on the president.

Jessie Carney Smith

Hazel Scott

(1920-1981)

Musician, singer, actress, social activist

A gifted musician, Hazel Scott had a long and varied career as a performer in nightclubs, on concert and Broadway stages, in radio, television, and film; she remained an outspoken critic of racial discrimination and helped pave the way for other black and women artists.

Hazel Dorothy Scott was the daughter of an educator and a musician (her father was a college professor and her mother was a pianist-saxophonist). Scott, a child prodigy at the piano, was born June 11, 1920, in Port-of-Spain, Trinidad. Her exceptional musical abilities became evident when she was about two-and-a-half years old. Her first teacher was her mother, Alma Long Scott. Hazel Scott made her debut in Port-of-Spain at the age of three, at which point, she later admitted, she was playing everything by ear. The next year the family moved to the United States and her mother realized that she needed formal training in playing the piano. A year later, at age five, she made her American debut at Town Hall in New York. Scott continued her studies and by the time she was eight she had received a six-year scholarship to attend the Juilliard School of Music. At that time, a student had to be sixteen years old to enroll in Juilliard.

After the death of Hazel Scott's father in 1931 or 1932, her mother joined the all-woman orchestra, the Harlem Harlicans, led by Lil (Mrs. Louis) Armstrong. Alma Long Scott eventually formed her own all-female orchestra, the American Creolians Orchestra. When Scott was about fourteen years old, she played piano and trumpet in her mother's orchestra.

In 1936, at age sixteen, Scott was featured on her own radio program on the Mutual Broadcasting System. Her performances included a mixture of the classics and jazz. She was known for her very showy style of playing. That same year, she also made her Broadway debut playing with the Count Basie Orchestra at the Roseland Dance Hall. (Although the Roseland is located on Fifty-second Street, it is a part of the area referred to as Broadway.)

Scott's career changed directions slightly when she appeared in the musical *Sing Out the News* on Broadway in 1938. In 1939 she made her recording debut with a sextet called the Rhythm Club of London—three blacks of West Indian descent and three British musicians. From 1939 to 1945 she was associated with Barney Josephson's Cafe Society Downtown and Uptown in New York and gained national recognition for her performances. Josephson had begun to feature performers who had participated in John Hammond's Spirituals to Swing concert dedicated to the memory of Bessie Smith. Ida Cox was included, but she became too ill to perform, so a "new performer" was substituted. A very young Hazel Scott replaced Cox and became so popular she was kept on for about six years as she gained national recognition.

Scott Established as Pianist-Singer

In 1942 Scott returned to Broadway to perform in the show *Priorities of 1942*. She toured throughout the United States and established herself as a leading pianist-singer. In 1943 she performed in four films: *Something to Shout About*, *I Dood It*, *Tropicana*, and *The Heat's On*. During the next two years she appeared in more films, including *Broadway Rhythm* (1944) and *Rhapsody in Blue* (1945), which portrayed the life of George Gershwin.

Scott had a busy year in 1945 with a Carnegie Hall recital and her marriage to the brilliant, handsome, powerful pastor of the Abyssinian Baptist Church in Harlem, Adam Clayton Powell, Jr. Powell had just been elected to Congress from Harlem in 1944. Their wedding was one of the social events of the year. To this union was born one son, Adam Clayton Powell III. After a period of separation, the marriage ended in divorce in October 1956.

As a nightclub performer, Scott developed her very individualistic talents. Generally unrestricted in this setting, she blended classics with a high jazz style. Her style included a very fresh wit along with a rather physically moving way of playing the piano. Her performances were always buoyant and vibrant, showing her natural technique at the keyboard and her jubilant personality. She had the distinction of being the first black woman to have a television show all to herself in the late forties and early fifties. It was the persecution of the McCarthy era that led to her show's cancellation in 1950.

Scott Fights for Equality

On more than one occasion Scott faced the unpleasantness that racial discrimination can bring. In 1945 she was involved in a racial incident in Washington, D.C. The downtown theaters would not admit blacks whether or not they sat in the balcony, as was usually the case in segregated theaters. When she attempted to see *Rhapsody in Blue*, in which she had a starring role, the manager told her that he was sorry but he could not admit her to the theater.

In 1950, Scott was accused of being a communist sympathizer. She released an anticommunist statement that was to be read when she appeared before the House Un-American Activities Committee. She defended her many performances before groups that were raising funds to fight for equality. Her outspokenness was well-known and she fought long for racial freedom and equality. She even insisted on including a clause in her contract that required forfeiture if the audience was segregated racially. She was also very proud and very conscious of her African roots. "My father was a Garveyite; he was very hung up on Marcus and the Black Nationalist Movement, so that I was exposed to it from when I was about four years old" (Taylor, 265).

In 1962 Scott went abroad for a five-year stay and lived mainly in France and Switzerland. She returned to the United States in 1967 and became active again as a performer. She appeared in several television shows on the West Coast, including "The Bold Ones," " The Doctors," Diahann Carroll's show, "Julia," and "CBS Playhouse 90." She also returned to performing in nightclubs on the East Coast, including Emerson, Ltd., in Washington, D.C., and Downbeat and Ali Baba East in New York.

In 1978 Scott was inducted into the Black Filmmakers Hall of Fame. Inductees were selected around the theme "The Black Musical Presence in Cinema." Scott continued to perform in clubs until 1981, when her health deteriorated. She died in the fall of that year, leaving a legacy for pianists, women performers, and blacks. Scott was "gifted, sophisticated, elegant, glamourous, outspoken and uncompromising" (Handy, 183). Her racial pride led her to speak out against discrimination and injustice.

References

Handy, D. Antoinette. *Black Women in American Bands and Orchestras*. Metuchen, New Jersey: Scarecrow Press, 1981.

Lewis, Claude. *Adam Clayton Powell*. Greenwich, Conn.: Fawcett Publications, 1963.

Placksin, Sally. *American Women in Jazz*. Wideview Books, 1982.

Powell, Adam Clayton, Jr. *Adam by Adam*. New York: Dial Press, 1971.

Shaw, Arnold. *Black Popular Music*. New York: Schirmer Books, 1986.

Southern, Eileen. *Biographical Dictionary of Afro-American and African Musicians*. Westport, Conn.: Greenwood Press, 1982.

Taylor, Arthur. *Notes and Tones*. New York: Coward, McCann, 1977.

Mildred Green

Mary Ann Shadd

(1823-1893)

Journalist, orator, educator, activist

A fiery and controversial exponent of abolition, equal rights, and women's suffrage, Mary Ann Shadd used her

Mary Ann Shadd

talents as a writer, editor, speaker, teacher, and lawyer to aid the people and causes she believed in and fought for so vigorously. Perhaps best known for her groundbreaking work as an editor and journalist, Shadd led the way for the women who followed and added color and drama to what was already a colorful and difficult period in American history.

Mary Ann Shadd was born October 9, 1823, in Wilmington, Delaware, the oldest of thirteen children of Abraham Doras Shadd and Harriet (Parnell) Shadd, who were well-to-do free blacks. (Variants in the spelling of her name are Anne and Schad or Shad; however, the family adopted the Anglicized spelling of the surname, Shadd.) Early in life Shadd was exposed to runaway slaves who often took shelter in her father's house. Abraham Shadd, a shoemaker, was an active abolitionist as early as 1830, and in 1830, 1831, and 1832 he represented Delaware at the National Convention for the Improvement of Free People of Color in Philadelphia. During his presidency at the 1833 convention he made public his views on education, condemned the American Colonization Society for supporting black expatriation to Liberia, and stressed the need for the society to assist blacks in becoming educated. His view was that education, thrift, and hard work would bring about racial parity for blacks.

Thus, early in her life Mary Ann Shadd saw the evils of slavery and was influenced by it as well as by her father's views on racial equality and education for blacks. Since Delaware was a slave state and education for blacks was forbidden, her parents took her at the age of ten to Price's Boarding School, founded by Quakers in 1830, in West Chester, Pennsylvania. She completed six years there and, having been affected by the denial of education in Delaware earlier, she returned to Wilmington and organized a private school for black children where she taught from 1839-1850. Some years later when public schools were opened and tuition was free, she moved to teaching positions in West Chester and Norristown, Pennsylvania, and in New York City.

Shadd Favors Black Emigration to Canada

The Fugitive Slave Act of 1850 produced mixed reactions among America's citizens and led eventually to a considerable migration to Canada. At first the act was condemned by liberty-loving citizens, and the fugitives felt that they would be able to protect themselves. In a short time, however, men and women were arrested or, if they resisted, were killed. For twenty years or more, some blacks had lived in freedom and had acquired considerable property, yet found themselves only marginally free. Whole families were grabbed in the middle of the night, beaten, and forced back into slavery. Black and white citizens met privately and publicly, sermons were preached from the pulpits, and many resolutions were debated. To preserve their freedom, thousands of black men, women, and children sought safety in Canada. Many had to depend on charity in the new land until they could find employment, for they had no money left after the escape. Shortly after the Fugitive Slave Act was passed, some three thousand blacks made their flight to Canada for safety. By the end of the 1850s, more than fifteen thousand had fled.

Shadd decided to give up teaching, and with her brother Isaac moved to Windsor, Canada West in 1851. She was determined to ascertain what Canada offered to make it appealing to the settlement of black emigrants from the American north and west, and she subsequently became one of the chief protagonists of the Canadian emigration. Henry Bibb, Samuel Ringgold Ward, Henry Highland Garnett, Alexander Crummell, Martin R. Delany, and other black luminaries supported the emigration movement and caused thousands of blacks to immigrate to Canada to seek freedom and equality.

Shadd had seen the effects of slavery knew it to be amoral and dehumanizing. She and her brother taught in a segregated school in Windsor, adjacent to Detroit, where a great number of fugitives initially went. The school was supported by the American Missionary Association (AMA) of New York and by the students themselves, who each paid thirty-seven cents a month to attend. Her assignment as the only black among the 263 AMA home missionaries was to promote better schools. In general, white teachers in AMA schools in Canada West did not fare well. Shadd tried to conceal her relationship with the AMA, and by 1853, when the association had overextended itself in the Canada Mission, the Windsor project was suspended.

The year following Shadd's departure, her father left West Chester for this section of Canada to examine living conditions in order to make decisions about relocating Shadd's mother and younger brothers and sisters, and advising other families from Pennsylvania who might wish to settle there. Confident that Canada West offered many opportunities to blacks, the Shadd family settled at Windsor and later moved to Chatham, the headquarters and terminal point of the Underground Railroad. Both Mary Shadd and her family were deeply sympathetic to the cause, and she immediately published a pamphlet that would aid in their vigorous and active campaign to help the fugitives. The descriptive forty-four page pamphlet, *A Plea for Emigration, or Notes on Canada West, in its Moral, Social and Political Aspect* (1852), provided fugitives information on what to expect in this British possession in such matters as climate and soil, the moral, social, and political atmosphere, and "suggestions respecting Mexico, the West Indies and Vancouver's Island." Written clearly, it was widely circulated in the United States.

Henry Bibb and Mary Shadd became bitter and persistent opponents over the issue of segregation in Canada. In his bimonthly newspaper, *Voice of the Fugitive*, he accused Shadd of race betrayal and said that those who accepted "the deluded sister['s]" views on integration were traitors (Silverman, 92). Bibb, born a slave in Kentucky in 1815, became an incorrigible and was sold to six different masters before escaping to Detroit and later joining fellow fugitives who crossed the Canadian border. He strongly supported separate and segregated communities and facilities for blacks, as expressed in the newspaper that he established, in the day school that he founded, the Methodist church that he helped to build, and in educational, temperance, and antislavery societies that he assisted in creating. On the contrary, Mary Shadd's aims were integrated schools and facilities.

Shadd Edits the *Provincial Freeman*

By this time her talent as a journalist was taking shape. Realizing that a newspaper was needed to address the interests of blacks, particularly the fugitive slaves, Shadd enlisted the timely help of a committee of local luminaries and black abolitionist and prominent fugitive slave Samuel Ringgold Ward. In March 1853 Shadd published the first edition of the *Provincial Freeman*. Its motto was prominently placed at the head: "Self Reliance Is the True Road to Independence." It was essentially an advertising tool. The first number of this attractive, outspoken, well-edited journal, issued from Windsor, listed Mary Ann Shadd as its publishing agent, and it was Canada West's first antislavery organ. The newspaper declared war on slavery, attacked the all-black settlements in Canada, and sought funds to help the fugitives. Originally Shadd had intended to head the paper until an editor from the United States could be designated, but she agreed to remain when no other editor arrived. By May 1854 the *Provincial Freeman* resumed publication from a headquarters in Toronto and was issued weekly. It is likely that the presence of several prosperous black businessmen and the concentration there of blacks who were interested in the paper influenced the selection of the headquarters' location. The site of publication changed again in the summer of 1855, when it was moved back to Chatham, where most fugitive settlements were established. Abraham Shadd and Samuel Ward brought their printing presses with them to Chatham and became the official printers to the Chatham Town Council. Ward was fully involved on the lecture circuit throughout the province and in Britain for the Anti-Slavery Society of Canada founded four years earlier.

Editorial responsibilities remained with Mary Shadd and for a brief period William P. Newman was the nominal editor. William Still, agent for the *Provincial Freeman* in Philadelphia, recognized her authority, and by spring of 1856, she, H. Ford Douglass, and Mary Shadd's brother Isaac became formal editors. In the second issue she justified the need for the paper, stating that black people in the United States had to be kept informed about actual conditions in Canada to help them decide "whether or not to leave Yankeedom with disenfranchisement and oppression" and settle "in a land of impartial laws and a Constitution having no distinctions of color." Accounts of blacks starving in Canada had to be dispelled, and Shadd also wanted to demonstrate to the white citizens the noble deeds and heroic acts of black Americans and to justify their claim for equal and exact justice. Sympathizers with slavery who lived in Windsor, St. Catherine's, and on the United States border made countless efforts to suppress the paper. Many people sent insulting letters to the editors and demanded that they stop mailing copies of the paper to them. Mary Shadd worked diligently and fearlessly for three years and endured the ravages of the sympathizers and at the same time became firmly entrenched in American and Canadian history as the first black woman editor and the first educated black woman lecturer.

The *Voice of the Fugitive*, Bibb's competing newspaper, was the target of Mary Shadd's criticism for encouraging fugitive blacks to believe that they were temporary residents in Canada West. This was the paper's primary mission and contrasted sharply with the mission of the *Provincial Freeman*, which urged blacks to make the most of their new home and conditions in the new land. Josiah Henson, Hiram Wilson, and Bibb were singled out in the attack. (It was Bibb who exposed the fact that earlier Mary Shadd accepted support from the AMA, even though subsequently she had made attacks on the organization.) In her view, conventions, caucuses, and resolutions supported by these men would bear watching, for Shadd believed their meetings to be solely to build their own egos. Neither John Scoble nor the British and Foreign Anti-Slavery Society were acceptable to her. Her devotion to her people never interfered with her criticism of them when she thought the cause would be beneficial. In an editorial published on Sunday, 31 January 1857, she lashed out at Canadian blacks who complained about various issues, stating that they lived in a land where equal laws and equal rights prevailed, but they were still dissatisfied. John Scoble's warning in a public lecture that people would lose their friends if publication of the *Provincial Freeman* continued, and his call for its discontinuation provoked a bitter response. Shadd replied in an editorial, "Such a barefaced attack was never made by any mortal enemy against any paper as this made by a PRETENDED friend of colored people. . . . Every device that a wicked heart would suggest, was used to prejudice the minds of the people" (Dannett I: 156). Scoble was unsuccessful in his efforts to close the paper. Even though Shadd broke off relations with Ward and the Anti-Slavery Society of Canada and weakened her position with moderate readers, her sentiments on fugitive slaves, the plight of the race, and black pride in general never wavered.

The depression of the late 1850s claimed as its victims by 1858 the *British Colonist*, the *Provincial Freeman*, and other papers. During the Civil War, Isaac Shadd appears to have revived it for a brief period before he moved to Mississippi where he became a prominent figure and held a seat in the Mississippi legislature for several terms.

Lectures Address Race Issues

To ensure the effectiveness of her work, Mary Shadd returned to the United States in 1855-1856 and lectured by invitation in Michigan, Ohio, Pennsylvania, and Illinois. Poet and reformer Frances Ellen Watkins and Mary Shadd became the black women trailblazers on the lecture circuit. Antislavery lecturers Abbey Kelley, Lucretia Mott, and Lucy Stone were also speaking on this subject and put their lives in danger whenever they spoke. The risk that Shadd took was much greater. She had already moved to Canada and spoke publicly to encourage fugitive slaves to go there, and she offered the means necessary to get them there. She attacked blacks and whites who compromised with slavery or who accepted the concept of second-class citizenship. She sought aid for runaway slaves. Having relinquished editorial responsibility for the journal, she worked to increase circulation and to speak publicly on matters of race. On November 19, 1855, Elizabeth Taylor Greenfield, the "Black Swan," held a benefit concert for Shadd. Greenfield paid the piano accompanist herself because of the heavy repertoire, which included a group of antislavery songs.

Mary Shadd spoke on a variety of themes relating to race as a self-appointed spokesperson for fugitives who had taken permanent residence in Canada. Several issues were disturbing to her, and she was disillusioned by the dissension among abolitionists and their supporters and by the tactics that some used. She saw disunity among free blacks in America and in the black Canadian communities as well. She deplored the tactics of ministers who sought to support their congregations by begging and soliciting funds. Self-segregated black settlements such as those found in Canada West were another target of her attack, and she called for fugitives to become active in the broad community. One of her chief interests and an area of her support was The True Band Society of Amherstburg (in Canada West), a militant group who opposed begging and favored settling the many internecine quarrels through arbitration boards of colored members rather than by airing the dissension among fugitive leaders in the public press.

The Refugee Home Society, legally based in Michigan and a self-segregated community led by white men and Henry Bibb, was a target for her attack. She accused all of its agents of malfeasance for granting the fugitives five acres of land on the condition that they purchase twenty more—a requirement that demanded a financial responsibility that most fugitives were unable to honor—and for keeping between twenty and twenty-five percent of solicited funds for administrative expenses. The formation of the experimental black communities in Canada had a positive motive—to prove to whites and blacks that blacks could be successful outside slavery. Mary Shadd's visit to Chicago in January 1856 was encouraging, for there she witnessed the growth since her last visit of a strong Free Soil sentiment that advocated the dismantling of slavery in the states and territories. The manner in which whites dealt with blacks showed a self-consciousness on their part: Whites treated their political inferior, "the colored man," with great consideration; they were fully aware of the great power that they had over them. Whites were "too proud-spirited to strike their prostrate victim, too conscious of their own strength to fear that he will ever be politically equal, and too American to recognize him as a part in a common brotherhood" (Dannett I, 155).

Mary Shadd's comments on terminology used to refer to her race make interesting study. She objected to the overuse of what she labeled an inaccurate and loose term, the word "Negro," and used it only in quotations. "Colored people" and "colored persons" were acceptable, as was "complexion" to describe people of color ("dark complexioned," "complexional differences," and so forth), although "complexional differences" troubled her, for she felt that one who emphasized such appearances ran the risk of establishing an artificial caste system that could ultimately impact negatively on "colored" people.

A popular lecturer, she received praise for her intellect, logic, literary cultivation, tenacious character, modest manner, and original ideas. Mary Shadd, a slender, attractive, person with an imperious manner, was also a witty and sharp-tongued speaker who could handle delicate and difficult situations that arose during the course of a lecture. Her persuasiveness led to the achievement of the task that she defined for herself. When early Negro conventions were held to discuss matters of suffrage, women were excluded until after 1848. The 1855 convention was held in Philadelphia, and Mary Shadd, the first black woman to be admitted as a corresponding member of the convention movement, was accepted only after she became a part of a spirited discussion. She was heralded "a conductor of the Freeman" when she addressed a large audience in Elkhorn, New York, on March 25, 1858. Anti-abolitionists often paid hecklers to disrupt her lecturers while other slavery sympathizers engaged in equally disrespectful acts. While on tour she continued to write letters to the *Provincial Freeman* to give important information on the status of blacks in the different sections of the country where she traveled. Her journey took her by rail and steamer, often in extreme weather conditions (once she was severely frostbitten), but she always fulfilled her obligations and met her schedule. Insults because of her color came also as she traveled; yet personal grievances and experiences were never published in her journal. Space was reserved for "matters of greater importance."

Amelia Freeman, a professor at the Avery College of Pittsburgh, Pennsylvania, came to Chatham in March 1856. In that year she married Isaac Shadd. She aimed to bring culture to her people, and by May 16 she had established a school in Stringer's Building. Writing an editorial on the school, Shadd called the institution a "School For All" where young people of both sexes would receive a thorough instruction in primary and secondary grades. There would be a modest charge for those who could pay and no cost to children of poor widows and respectable destitute people. They would be given courses in the arts—painting, drawing, music, and writing. According to the editorial, "no complexional distinctions" were to be made.

In the summer of 1856 Mary Ann Shadd married Thomas F. Cary of Toronto. They lived in Chatham and had a daughter, Sally. The added responsibilities of wife and mother in no way interfered with Shadd's editorial work on the *Provincial Freeman* with her brother and Henry Douglass or with her dedication to fugitives and matters of race.

Civil War Elicits Shadd's Union Help

On May 8, 1858, John Brown held a secret "convention" at Isaac Shadd's Chatham home where he and his companions adopted a "Provisional Constitution." He went there also to seek and to save those who were lost. He was successful in his project and found many who came to his assistance. Mary Shadd immediately became interested in Brown's movement. She compiled and published in 1861 the notes of Osborne P. Anderson, sole survivor of Brown's group that had raided Harper's Ferry, in a work entitled "Voice from Harper's Ferry."

By the time the Civil War began, Mary Shadd was teaching in Michigan and remained there for a brief period (1862). She returned to Chatham in 1863 to become a naturalized British subject. She made peace with the AMA and taught school for the missionary group in Chatham. When President Lincoln called for 500,000 men to strengthen the Union Army after the bloody battles at Gettysburg and Vicksburg, Mary Shadd responded, and in August 1863 she was appointed a recruiting officer to enlist black volunteers to the federal armies in Indiana. She accepted the commission from Levi P. Morton, governor of Indiana, and she helped recruit solders to serve at the front.

When the war ended, she obtained a certificate to teach in America and taught first in Detroit. The fiery abolitionist then moved to Washington, D.C., and taught school under the direction of Howard University. For seventeen years she was principal of three large public schools in the district. During this same time she wrote regularly for *The New National Era*, which Frederick Douglass edited, and for *The Advocate*, edited by John Cromwell. Then, in her forties, Shadd became the first woman to enroll in the law department of the newly-opened Howard University and in 1883 she received an LL.B. degree. She continued to write articles on sociopolitical issues, and noting the efforts of Reconstruction politics to separate and exploit the black community, she called for a boycott of white businesses.

Shadd Advocates Women's Suffrage

Long recognized for her views on racial equality, Shadd also became a staunch suffragette. She argued before the Judiciary Committee of the United States House of Representatives in Washington, D.C., that women had a right to vote. She argued that the Fourteenth and Fifteenth Amendments provided that right to good citizens and taxpayers. She tested her case and became a registered voter in the District, one of the few women to achieve the privilege that the law provided. When bitter antiblack arguments by white women began to soften in 1876, Mary Shadd wrote to the National Women's Suffrage Association (NWSA) to argue on behalf of ninety-four black women from Washington that they be enrolled in the centennial autograph book as supporters of the declaration of sentiment calling for immediate enfranchisement. She joined the National Women's Suffrage Association. Susan B. Anthony and Lucretia Mott recognized her importance to the movement, and in 1878 she was invited to address the association's convention. Later, she founded the short-lived Colored Women's Progressive Franchise Association in Washington, D. C. Through the association she made plans to publish a newspaper and to bring into being a joint stock company with women in official controlling power. Published dates marking the founding of the assocation and her initial membership in the NWSA are conflicting.

Shadd returned to Canada briefly and held a "Votes for Women" rally. Still at the center of controversy, she enraged opponents of suffrage for women, and as result she was threatened with physical violence. She fled across the border to Detroit but returned later to hold a second meeting. Both sessions were well attended. Most of her work from that time forward was devoted to the lecture circuit and to writing.

Views on the level of Shadd's success vary. The *Provincial Freeman* had a limited audience all along and at the time had little prospect of increasing circulation, since few of the emigrants could read, and many were unable to afford the few cents for a newspaper. Shadd's outspoken manner and the caustic views stated in the press and in public lectures were unpalatable for many, even among those who claimed to be abolitionists in the truest sense of the word. There are claims that, out of a compulsion to persuade free American blacks to relocate in Canada and to help slaves and fugitive slaves find freedom, she glossed over the problems of Canadian resettlement. She died in Washington, D.C., on June 5, 1893, having become enfeebled with rheumatism and presumably cancer, and was buried in Harmony Cemetery. Shadd left the legacy of a pioneer who built a foundation for other black women journalists who followed. During her tenure at the *Provincial Freeman*, she established herself unequivocally as one of the best editors in Canada.

Jason H. Silverman's biographical essay, "Mary Ann Shadd and the Search for Equality," summarizes quite succinctly Shadd's legacy:

> Her lifelong goal was to see equality achieved for all black men and women. To achieve this she was ready at various times during her life to endorse emigration and even separate institutions. Throughout her career . . . she always retained her basic belief that through education, thrift, and hard work blacks could achieve integration. . . . Shadd spoke for all oppressed men and women by her actions. She aired her views as early as 1849, when she was only twenty-six. She emigrated, and then facilitated the way for others by authoring her *Notes on Canada West*. She became the first black woman editor of a newspaper, writing scathing editorials on those she thought had betrayed the fugitives. She actively participated in the women's suffrage movement, agitating alongside white women for something in which she believed. She lectured, published, and rarely compromised, and in so doing Mary Ann Shadd assuredly made her voice heard and her ideas known" (100).

References

Bearden, Jim, and Linda Jean Butler. *Shadd: The Life and Times of Mary Shadd*. Toronto: N.C. Press, 1977. This work is designed for young readers.

Brown, Hallie Quinn. *Homespun Heroines and Other Women of Distinction*. Xenia, Ohio: The Aldine Publishing Co., 1926. Inaccurate in some details.

Dannett, Sylvia G. L. *Profiles of Negro Womanhood*. Vol. I, 1619-1900. Yonkers, N.Y.: Educational Heritage, Inc., 1964.

Davis, Marianna W. *Contributions of Black Women to America*. Columbia, S.C.: Kenday Press, 1982. Vol. I, *The Arts, Business & Commerce, Media, Law, Sports*. Vol. II, *Civil Rights, Politics and Government, Education Medicine, Sciences*. Shadd's married name in this set is spelled Carey as well as Cary.

Hancock, Harold B. "Mary Ann Shadd: Negro Editor, and Lawyer." *Delaware History* 15 (April 1973).

Lewis, Elsie M. "Mary Ann Shadd Cary." *Notable American Women 1607-1950*. Vol. I. Boston: Radcliffe College, 1971.

Murray, Alexander L. "The Provincial Freeman: A New Source for the History of the Negro in Canada and the United States." *Journal of Negro History* 44 (April 1959).

Quarles, Benjamin. *Black Abolitionists*. New York: Oxford University Press, 1969. This work contains brief but important material useful to place in perspective work of black men and women who were abolitionists.

Silverman, Jason H. "Mary Ann Shadd and the Search for Equality." *Black Leaders of the Nineteenth Century*. Eds. Leon Litwack and August Meyer. Urbana: University of Illinois Press, 1988. Contains excellent references to other sources.

Winks, Robin W. *The Blacks in Canada: A History*. New Haven: Yale University Press, 1971: 394-95, 207.

———. "Mary Ann Shadd Cary." *Dictionary of American Negro Biography*. Eds. Rayford W. Logan and Michael R. Winston. New York: Norton, 1982. The bibliography locates Shadd Cary's papers at the Moorland-Spingarn Research Center, Howard University, and identifies other important works.

Collections

The papers of Mary Ann Shadd (Cary) are in the Moorland-Spingarn Collection, Howard University.

Jessie Carney Smith

Ntosake Shange

(1948-)

Poet, playwright, performer, writer

Ntosake Shange, the brilliant poet, playwright, performer, and novelist who in the early 1970s changed her name to one that in Zulu means "She who comes with her own things/ she who walks with lions," was born October 18, 1948, in Trenton, New Jersey. The daughter of Paul T. Williams, an air force surgeon, and Eloise Owens Williams, a psychiatric social worker and educator, Shange was originally named Paulette Williams, after her father. The eldest of four children, she spent her childhood with her family in upstate New York and in Saint Louis, Missouri.

By all accounts—including her own in the autobiographical *Betsey Brown: A Novel* (St. Martin's, 1987)—Shange had an interesting, even extraordinary, childhood. Paul and Eloise Williams enjoyed and were able to provide for their children upper-middle-class comfort and social standing and access to their American and African-American cultural heritage. Their foreign travel to such destinations as Cuba, Haiti, Mexico, and Europe; Eloise Williams's wide reading, which encompassed the major works of the African-American canon and which she shared with her children; and Paul Williams's love of the rich and varied musical expression of Africa (Williams played the conga drums and at one time had his own band), all contributed to an intellectually and aurally stimulating childhood. There was "always different music in our house all the time," noted Shange in an early interview (Stella Dong, *Publishers Weekly* 3 May 1985, 75). The Williams children came into frequent contact with numerous visiting musicians, writers, and thinkers, a reflection of their parents' interests. Dizzy Gillespie, Chuck Berry, Miles Davis, and Chico Hamilton were among the well-known musical guests at the Williams's home. One evening, according to family lore, only the renowned scholar W. E. B. Du Bois could coax the reluctant young Shange into going to bed.

The day-by-day presence of musical expression, the constant reading and declamation of black poetry and prose, the family's attendance at concerts, dance performances, and the ballet, the impact of foreign travel, and the intellectual vibrancy of the Williams's household all had an early and profound effect on Shange's development as a writer. "I live in language / sound falls round me like rain on other folks," she wrote in *Nappy Edges* (St. Martin's, 1975, 19). The anger that infuses Shange's poems, novels, and plays stems in part from her awakening as a child to the racial cruelty that she unavoidably witnessed and endured at the newly-integrated school she attended in St. Louis, Missouri, following the 1954 Supreme Court desegregation decision. And the fierce and protective love for young, black American girls that also pervades her work can be explained by her other painful awakening to the concomitant oppression of women.

A writer all of her life, even as a child, Shange's most recent publication, *Ridin' the Moon in Texas* (St. Martin's, 1987), is a collection of poetry and prose inspired by the creations of fourteen, visual artists. Shange's full-length books of poetry include *Nappy Edges*; *A Daughter's Geography* (St. Martin's, 1983) and *From Okra to Greens: Poems* (Coffee House Press, 1984). Her novels to date are *Sassafrass, Cypress & Indigo* (St. Martin's, 1982) and *Betsey Brown*. Shange has written and directed many theater pieces, including: *A Photograph: A Study in Cruelty*, a poem-play that was first produced off-Broadway in 1977 and in a revised version in 1979 at the Equinox Theatre in Houston, Texas; *Boogie Woogie Landscapes*, a play first produced in workshop in New York in 1979 and then on Broadway and at the Kennedy Center in Washington, D.C.; and *Spell #7: A Geechee Quick Magic Trance Manual*, a play produced on Broadway in 1979 at Joseph Papp's New York Shakespeare Festival Public Theatre. In addition to directing and sometimes performing in her own theater pieces, Shange has directed those of others, among them Richard Wesley's *The Mighty Gents* in 1979 at the New York Shakespeare Festival and *Tribute to Sojourner Truth*, a work coauthored by poet June Jordan and scholar/performer, Bernice Reagon.

Prize-Winning Choreopoem Brings Fame

It was *for colored girls who have considered suicide / when the rainbow is enuf*, Shange's prize-winning, controversial and dramatic choreopoem, that catapulted her to fame. Nominated for Tony, Emmy, and Grammy Awards in 1977, *for colored girls* won the Outer Circle Critics Award, Obie awards for Shange, the producers (Joseph Papp and Woodie King, Jr.), and actress Tanzana Beverly. An unblenched feminist statement on behalf of black women, the production was a combination of music, dance, and poetry in the form of soliloquies, dialogue, stories, and chants performed by an ensemble of seven black actresses. It ran for two years on Broadway and traveled to major cities throughout the United States as well as abroad. *for colored girls* was first published as a book of twenty poems in 1975 and was adapted for an "American Playhouse" public television series in 1982.

In the foreword to the 1976 edition of *for colored girls*, Shange explains the genesis of the play. While living and working in northern California in the early 1970s, she began writing a series of poems about the reality of the lives of seven different kinds of women. The poems were first presented at Bacchanal, a women's bar near Berkeley and one of a number of bars and clubs in the area where poetry, dance, and music were being experimentally combined to form a dynamic women's theater. In fact, the vitality of the emergent women's movement during this period was a significant factor in helping to define Shange's feminist point of view. She writes in the foreword that her three-year association with the women's studies program at Sonoma State College was "inextricably bound" to the development of her sense of the world, herself, and women's language. Shange also credits as influential the poetry readings then being staged by small women's presses such as Shameless Hussy Press, The Oakland Women's Press, and Third World Communications. She had much in common with other women writers whose energies were being directed "toward clarifying our lives—& the lives of our mothers, daughters, & grandmothers—as women" (9-10).

Shange was involved at the same time in the theory and practice of African-American dance as student, teacher, and performer, another aspect of her California residence that contributed to her development as a performance artist and writer. She danced in Halifu Osumure's all-female dance troupe and taught theater and dance in San Francisco and Berkeley public schools. "Just as women's studies had rooted me to an articulated female heritage & imperative," she wrote, "so dance as explicated by Raymond Sawyer & Ed Mock insisted that everything African, everything halfway colloquial, a grimace, a strut, an arched back over a yawn, waz mine" (*for colored girls*, 10). Similar to the Afrocentric dance she learned, performed, and taught, Shange's own writing is infused with and ordered by African-American cultural elements—literary, musical, and folk.

The mother of a daughter, Shange writes also out of a trenchant sense of obligation to young, African-American women for whom she hopes to provide "information I did not have." Passionately, she proclaims: "When I die, I will not be guilty of having left a generation of girls behind thinking that anyone can tend to their emotional health other than themselves" (Claudia Tate, *Black Women Writers at Work*, 1983, 161-62). She says in the dedication to her novella *Sassafras* (1976) that she wrote the story, "to make her daughter's dreams as real as her menses." Still, in spite of her special concern for black women, Shange's work displays great empathy for other categories of the oppressed. Her extensive travel and sympathy with peoples of Latin America and the Caribbean are readily apparent in her poems.

The polemical force and impact of her creative efforts notwithstanding, Ntosake Shange's purpose and achievement is that of the true artist. At a national Afro-American writers conference held in 1977 at Howard University, she insisted:

> When I take my voice into a poem or a story / i am trying desperately to give you that. i am not trying to give you a history of my family / the struggle of black people all over the world or the fight goin on upstairs tween Susie and Matt. i am giving you a moment / like an alto solo in december in nashville in 1937. as we demand to be heard / we want you to hear us. we come to you the way leroi jenkins comes or cecil taylor / or b. b. king. we come to you alone / in the

theatre / in the story / & the poem. like with billie holiday or betty carter / we shd give you a moment that cannot be recreated / a specificity that cannot be confused. our language shd let you know who's talkin, what we're talking abt & how we cant stop saying this to you. some urgency accompanies the text. something important is going on. we are speaking. reaching for yr person / we cannot hold it / we dont wanna sell it / we give you ourselves / if you listen (*Nappy Edges*, 11).

Shange attended Barnard College in New York and graduated with honors in 1970; she received an M.A. in American Studies in 1973 from the University of Southern California, Los Angeles, and has pursued other graduate study at the University of Southern California.

Throughout her career as a writer, performer, and director, Shange has taught courses in women's studies, creative writing, drama, and related subjects at colleges and universities across the United States. In 1981, she received a Guggenheim Fellowship for writing and the Medal of Excellence from Columbia University. Among other awards, she has received the Pushcart Prize, the *Los Angeles Times* Book Prize for Poetry (1981) for *Three Pieces*, and an Obie for *Mother Courage and Her Children*, her adaptation of Bertolt Brecht's play.

Shange currently lives in Philadelphia, works as a performance artist and is artist-in-residence at Villanova University. She is writing a novel and adapting Harriet Beecher Stowe's *Uncle Tom's Cabin* for performance by the San Francisco Mime Troupes.

References

Betsko, Kathleen, and Rachel Koenig, eds. *Interviews with Contemporary Women Playwrights*. New York: Beech Tree Books, 1987.

Christ, Carol P. *Diving Deep and Surfacing: Women Writers on Spiritual Quest*. Boston: Beacon Press, 1980.

Contemporary Authors. New Revision Series. Vol. 27. Detroit: Gale Research, 1989.

Contemporary Literary Criticism. Vol. 8. 1978; Vol. 25, 1983; Vol. 38, 1986. Detroit: Gale Research.

Dictionary of Literary Biography. Vol. 38, *Afro-American Writers after 1955: Dramatists and Prose Writers*. Detroit: Gale Research, 1985.

Dong, Stella. "Ntosake Shange." *Publishers Weekly* (5 May 1985): 74-75.

Shange, Ntosake. *See No Evil: Prefaces, Essays and Accounts, 1976-1983*. San Francisco: Momo's Press, 1984.

———. *A Daughter's Geography*. New York: St. Martin's Press, 1983.

———. *for colored girls who have considered suicide / when the rainbow is enuf*. New York: St. Martin's Press, 1976.

———. *From Okra to Greens*. St. Paul: Coffee House Press, 1972.

———. *Nappy Edges*. New York: St. Martin's Press, 1972.

———. *Ridin' the Moon in Texas*. New York: St. Martin's Press, 1987.

———. *Sassafras*. Berkeley: Shameless Hussy Press, 1976.

———. *Sassafrass, Cypress & Indigo*. New York: St. Martin's Press, 1982.

Squier, Susan Merrill, ed. *Women Writers and the City: Essays in Feminist Literary Criticism*. Knoxville: University of Tennessee Press, 1984.

Tate, Claudia, ed. *Black Women Writers At Work*. New York: Continuum Publishing Company, 1983.

Carole McAlpine Watson

Ella Sheppard Moore

(1851-1914)

Pianist, choral director

In 1870 George L. White, treasurer of Fisk University in Nashville, Tennessee, organized a band of singers who had the best voices in Fisk's music classes to study the slave songs that at that time were heard primarily in black religious meetings. The original intention was not to sing the songs in public, since they represented slavery, the dark past, and deep sorrow songs of the black enslaved. But the voices blended so melodiously and the message was so moving that White decided to take the small band of singers on tour to raise money for the struggling school. On October 6, 1871, the original troupe of singers left on a tour of the northern states. The company of nine was comprised of Phoebe Anderson, I. P. Dickerson, Green Evans, Benjamin M. Holmes, Jennie Jackson, Maggie Porter, Thomas Rutling, Minnie Tate, Eliza Walker, and Ella Sheppard. Despite hardships and opposition from the outset, the singers raised twenty thousand dollars in the first year to be used to erect a building that would be named Jubilee Hall. The Fisk Jubilee Singers soon became an internationally-recognized group of some of the finest singers ever heard. The unwritten music that they popularized and gave to the world was the Negro

Ella Sheppard Moore

spiritual. Ella Sheppard's name is enshrined in the history of the Fisk Jubilee Singers as pianist and assistant trainer. Because she was so closely connected with the preservation of the spiritual and presentation of the spiritual to the world, John Wesley Work called her "a folk song of the American Negro" (97).

Ella Sheppard was born on February 4, 1851, in Nashville, Tennessee, of slave parents Simon Sheppard, a coachman, and Sarah Hannah Sheppard, head nurse and housekeeper. The Sheppards had married in the parlor of the slave master's mansion when Sarah Hannah was seventeen. Their first child died and Ella, the second, was born six years later. Simon Sheppard persuaded his master to allow him to hire himself out. He worked hard and earned $1,800 to buy his freedom. Simon had been promised the opportunity to buy Sarah from her mistress, but the slaveowner refused to honor the agreement. When Ella was three years old, Sarah Sheppard heard the master pleading with the mistress to keep her promise but she argued that Sarah would never belong to Simon and that Sarah would be hers until she died. Sarah declared, "If you will sell Ella to her father immediately I will remain your slave; if you do not you lose both of us. My baby shall never be a slave" (Moore, "Before Emancipation," 3). The distraught Sarah was determined that Ella would not grow up in slavery and threatened to "take Ella and jump in the river than see her a slave" (Howse, [2]). This is the course that some slave mothers had taken, while others took their lives in other ways (see Sheppard, "Negro Womanhood," 6). To avoid loss of her property in this manner, the mistress sold Ella Sheppard to Simon for $350. Sarah "was taken to Mississippi, the most dreaded of all the slave states," (3) while Ella and Simon remained in Nashville. Since Sarah was never to return, as Simon knew well, Simon married another slave woman and purchased her freedom for $1,300.

In 1856 a race riot in Nashville caused whites to tighten control on free blacks there, and white vigilantes were rampant in their repressive measures. The vigilantes forced Daniel Wadkins, a free black, to close his school for free black children where Ella Sheppard was a student. When he was unable to pay his bills during the 1857 depression and was threatened with having his family seized and his assets sold, Simon Sheppard and his family fled to Cincinnati. There Ella Sheppard studied music in a local black school and developed such a talent for music that her father bought her a piano.

Simon Sheppard died suddenly in 1866, leaving his bills paid but his family in extreme poverty. Ella Sheppard also had been an invalid for nearly two years. To earn a living for the family Ella Sheppard played the piano at local functions. Her musical training had become very important to her, and a local piano teacher of prominence agreed to help her continue her training. Since his school was segregated and Sheppard was his only black pupil, she secretly entered his school through the back door between nine and ten o'clock at night for lessons. Her earlier health problems left her frail, yet she worked diligently for the little monies that she received. In addition to the money earned while playing for functions, she said that she "took in washing and ironing, worked in a family, and had a few music pupils" who paid sporadically (Moore, "Historical Sketch of the Jubilee Singers," 4).

In her lifetime Sheppard was rewarded manyfold—perhaps chief among the rewards was her finding her mother and a sister who had been sent to Mississippi earlier, and bringing them to Nashville. Her family had known well the pain and suffering of slavery which had penetrated the sanctity of their home and family. "Slavery broke my mother's heart. She often says, 'My back was never struck, but my heart is like a checkerboard with its stripes of sorrow.' Slavery separated my father and mother, and I was taken from her when three years of age. I never saw her again until after freedom, when a girl of fifteen I found her. I did not even know her face" ("Negro Womanhood," 5-6). The stepmother, who until then had lived in Ohio, Sarah Sheppard, Ella, and Ella's sister lived together in a home on the Fisk campus, which was to be known as the Moore House (Ella's married name), probably until they died.

In 1868 Ella Sheppard returned to Tennessee and taught school in Gallatin, a small town near Nashville. Realizing her educational deficiencies and the difficulties she would have in earning a respectable living with limited training, in September of that year Sheppard enrolled in Fisk University. The few possessions that she had fit into a trunk with some space remaining but the trunk was so small that her schoolmates called it a "pie box." She also had six dollars in savings—barely enough to last barely more than three weeks in school. Opportunities for work at Fisk were limited, since most students attending the school at that time were needy and sought jobs to help support their education. While she decided to stay at Fisk only until her money was spent, she soon found three students who paid her four dollars each month for music lessons. She also waited tables in the campus dining room and washed dishes to supplement her income. During the summers she was assistant music teacher at Fisk. The school was also poor and struggling; food was scarce and the beef that was served to the students "was so tough that the boys called it 'old Ben,' and declared that everytime they met a cow they felt like apologizing" (Moore, 42). The students shivered in the cold winters, often without "an inch of flannel" on their bodies. But the "Fisk spirit" that was to become recognized as a part of the school's living history was set then, for they were jolly, determined, and enthusiastic. When they were not studying or working, the students often played with abandoned children in the area, and once a month when they were allowed to go to the city for church and for entertainment, they went to Baptist College (later Roger Williams University, which subsequently closed).

Fisk and its students were fully absorbed by poverty and the wind whistled fiercely through the hospital barracks that served as dormitories, sometimes causing the students to tremble in fear that "the sounds were the cries of lost spirits of the soldiers who had died in them" (Moore, 43). Something had to be done or the American Missionary Association that had founded the school would close it. They prayed fervently for food, shelter, clothing, and survival.

Fisk Jubilee Singers Begin Tour

George L. White collected his meager resources, all the money that he could borrow, all that the school's treasury could spare, and on October 7, 1871, set out "with his little band of singers to sing the money out of the hearts and pockets of the people" (Moore, "Historical Sketch," 46). The school had to be saved. The fifty thousand dollars raised in their first tour of churches in Ohio was donated to the Chicago Relief Fund to help the victims of the great Chicago fire. White was manager of the fund-raising venture and placed Ella Sheppard in charge of voice training and the general care of the singers. The talented Sheppard was well prepared for the job. She "had that discernment of tone which is called 'absolute pitch.'" In addition, "In intellect, in spirit, and in musical attainment she was one of the gifted women of the world" (Spence, 77).

Segregation was still rampant, ugly, and intolerable. The singing group was denied accommodations in hotels, ill-treated on railroads, and, despite their melodious voices, they were ridiculed when they sang. While en route to a large city to give a concert, a railroad accident compelled the Jubilee Singers to spend the day at a railroad station in the woods until the night train came. The presence of a black group with a white man, the singers' director, George L. White, aroused the attention of the whites gathered at election time, who opposed the "Yankee nigger school teacher" (Moore, "Historical Sketch," 43). Following the typical behavioral patterns of rural or small-town southern whites of that era, threats were shouted and uneasiness began. Reporting further on the strained situation, Sheppard stated:

> Mr. White, anxious and fearful for us, had us stroll to the railway platform, and sitting on a pile of shingles we prayed through song for deliverance and protection. Mr. White stood between us and the men, directing our singing. One by one the riotous crowd left off their jeering and swearing and slunk back, until only the leader stood near Mr. White, and he finally took off his hat. Our hearts were fearful and tender and darkness was falling. We were softly finishing the last verse of "Beyond the smiling and the weeping I shall be soon," when we saw the bull's eye of the coming engine and knew that we were saved. The leader begged us with tears falling to sing the hymn again, which we did. As the train passed slowly by I heard him repeating, "Love, rest and home, sweet, sweet home" (Moore, "Historical Sketch," 43).

This was one of many incidents in which the singers effected change with their jubilee songs.

The Fisk Jubilee Singers knew slave songs well. They sang them privately to their music instructor Adam K. Spence, willingly—that they might learn to feel the spirit known by their fathers, and often that they might appreciate the wonderful power and beauty of the songs. At first their public repertoire contained what they called "white man's music," or the usual choruses, duets, and solos learned at school, such as "Songs of Summer," "Hail America," "Old Folks at Home," "Comin' Through the Rye," and a temperance medley. The sorrow songs associated with slavery and the dark past that represented events and experiences best forgotten were at first difficult for them even in a private setting; they were sacred to their parents, "who used them in their religious worship and shouted over them" (Moore, "Historical Sketch," 43). In time, the slave or sorrow songs were to become a primary part of the singers' repertoire and were popularized by them.

When they first set out on tour the group was unnamed. While visiting Columbus, Ohio, they held a prayer meeting in the presence of the Fisk minister, H. S. Bennett. The next morning George L. White, who had prayed alone all night, announced: "Children, it [the name] shall be Jubilee Singers in memory of the Jewish year of Jubilee" (Moore, 47).

The singers traveled widely—to New York, New Jersey, New England, Washington, D.C., and elsewhere, and they met such notable personalities as Wendell Phillips, William Lloyd Garrison, and Henry Ward Beecher, who helped introduce them to the audiences. They gave private performances when requested, including one for "Parson" Brownlow, a senator from Tennessee whose illness prevented him from attending a public concert. "He wept like a child as he listened to the humble slave melodies," Ella Sheppard said (Richardson, 30). They electrified audiences and raised considerable funds for Fisk. They raised forty thousand dollars to pay off school debts and to purchase twenty-five acres of land for the new site of the school. The New England tour also brought them an invitation to sing at the White House for President Ulysses S. Grant.

On May 6, 1873, the Jubilee Singers traveled to Great Britain, where the Earl of Shaftsbury had invited them to give a concert. They drew favorable reviews in the local press. On the night of the concert they were invited to visit the Duke and Duchess of Argyle in their home, where Queen Victoria came to meet them and hear them sing. It was also during this tour (1873-74) that Queen Victoria commissioned her court painter, Edmund Havel, to paint a portrait of the celebrated singers. For three months they were busy filling engagements, often moving in Quaker circles since the Quakers had worldwide contacts and were known for their friendship for the oppressed. They received the attention of William Gladstone, the British politician, and visited him and his wife at home. In appreciation for their music and for the university, Gladstone later sent a valuable collection of books to the library at Fisk. The group journeyed through Scotland, Ireland and Wales, and their concerts, preceded by a letter from Lord Shaftsbury, were crowded and successful. They often sang at as many as six Sunday worship services. They also sang at breakfasts for thousands of the poor, to working people and outcasts, in hospitals and prisons, beside sickbeds, in the open air to thousands, and in private homes. They earned nearly fifty thousand dollars on their first campaign abroad and returned to Fisk on May 27, 1874. These funds, too, went to support Fisk University and, among other purposes, were used to build Jubilee Hall, a women's dormitory erected on the campus in 1875—"a structure sometimes lovingly called 'frozen music,' a memorial to the songs that were its building" (Collins, n.p.).

On May 15, 1875, the singers, whose numbers had increased to eleven, began a second campaign abroad, visiting England, Ireland, Switzerland, and Holland. They arrived in London on May 31, in time to sing before the Freedmen's Aid Society's annual meeting. Evangelist Dwight L. Moody invited them to sing before his service at Haymarket Opera House. The singers continued their work with Moody for more than a month, often appearing before crowds of from ten to twelve thousand. Their reward at the end was one autographed Bible for each singer (Moore, "Historical Sketch," 54).

Sheppard found the English "a stiff set" and "so stupid or ignorant" about Americans and blacks (Richardson, 36). The singers traveled in Great Britain until summer 1876 and the whirlwind tour began to take its toll on the group. Ella Sheppard was ill, prompting a physician to advise her to stop work in order to recover. Funds from this tour went toward the erection of Livingstone Hall, a dormitory and classroom building named in honor of David Livingstone. While in Rotterdam, Sheppard directed the singers in George White's absence, as noted in her diary entry on October 27, 1877. Appearing in a cathedral in Rotterdam on a rainy evening, Sheppard found "the Cathedral . . . well filled. The stage was too small" and the group was cramped. "It seemed that I should never get them to the stage" partly because of the limited space and partly because of confusion in the presence of so many of their friends and well-wishers. By 1877 the group entered Germany. Sheppard wrote of the singers' experiences in Berlin:

> Practiced as usual after worship. This morning we attended a private reception at Rev. Davis'—and sang for the first time before the Germans. Everyone seemed highly pleased & expressed warmest interest. Were many distinguished persons present. Dr. or Rev. Kögel, "Hofpredegan" or Court Preacher—the leading preacher of influence & in eloquence expressed—in German—the appreciation of interest not only of himself but of those present & said that we must consider his silence as keener appreciation than clapping—that the songs sank far too deeply into the heart to be expressed with the hands. How I wish I could remember all the good expressions which he used (Diary of Ella Sheppard, 31 October 1877).

The singers spent eight months in Germany. In Pottsdam they were received by the Crown Prince and Crown Princesses at the New Palace. Queen Victoria had already written to her daughter, the Crown Princess, giving her an enthusiastic account of the Jubilee Singers earlier performance at the Duke of Argyle's. Sheppard wrote of the group's meeting with the crown prince and princess:

> A day long to be remembered!. . . . I had glanced at the frescoed walls—a full length mirror between each fresco, in the beautiful polished floor—when the Crown Prince & Princess entered along and advancing quickly toward us greeted us with a hearty & cordial welcome—going from one to the other till each had been greeted & there chatted pleasantly with different ones. The prince picked out one & another—those whom he recognized as having seen in the photo in our history which Mr. C[ravath] had sent them. To Mr. L[oudin] he said "I remember you, you stand leaning on a book in the photograph." & to Rutling "and you I know from the mischievous expressions," & to Mag[gie] P[orter] "and you are one of the old members" and so on—showing how keenly he had studied the picture & the faces of the singers, particularly (Diary of Ella Sheppard, 4 November 1877).

While the Jubilee Singers were well received, their tour was somewhat less successful financially than the first tour, due in part to the economic depressions in Great Britain and Germany. The singers were ready to leave Germany and return home to school and family. By then also, some of the singers had left the group because of illness or other reasons. George White resigned, leaving Sheppard full responsibility for managing the group's music. The singers prepared to disband, leaving the Continent and arriving home in July 1878. According to Marsh, at the close of the second campaign "future prospects for successful concert work abroad seemed so uncertain that it was deemed best to disband the company. Some of the Singers remained on the Continent for study," while the others returned home (100). In seven years the singers had raised $150,000 in the U.S. and Europe, with Sheppard serving "as backbone and trainer for the group" (Howse, [2]).

In 1879 George L. White re-organized the troupe as an independent group and they toured again. Sheppard was a part of the reconstructed singers until 1882, when she married George W. Moore. The ceremony took place in White's home in Fredonia, New York. According to Doug Seroff, "the Jubilee Singers' tours of 1879 to 1882 are especially interesting, as they were quite politicized, speaking out in favor of the ill-fated Civil Rights Act of 1875, and forming alliances with such notable figures as President James Garfield, John Greenleaf Whittier, and Rev. Joseph Cook" (interview with Doug Seroff).

Sheppard lived with her husband in Washington, D.C., where he pastored Lincoln Memorial Church. For many years she joined with her husband in his work for the American Missionary Association, as he lectured throughout the South and organized jubilee choirs. After returning to Nashville in 1890, she trained a group of talented Fisk students, most of whom were members of the Mozart Society. They began a new fundraising tour of the North, the first as a university-sponsored Jubilee Singers group since 1878. On October 16, 1890, that company went on tour until May 1891. Since this venture was not ultimately as lucrative as the university officials hoped, the company disbanded. Since then, other university-sponsored companies toured at different times. For many years, Sheppard was in charge of the fine Jubilee Club at Fisk, and in early 1902 the group gave a command performance for Prince Henry of Prussia during his stop in Nashville (interview with Doug Seroff).

Views on the Black Slave Woman Expressed

While she had been known for her fine voice and skill as pianist and choir director, Sheppard was less known for her views on black womanhood. Writing on this theme, she said:

> From the cradle to the grave the Negro woman lived in constant dread; no matter how favorably situated with kind and intelligent owners, there was no assurance that on tomorrow she would not be torn from her children and loved ones and sold to the coarsest and most illiterate master, and subjected to that from which only death could release her ("Negro Womanhood,"5).

Sheppard noted that, even if laws had permitted the black slave woman and the master to marry, unless he freed her and their children, they still could be sold on the slave market. The slave woman was always subject to the whims of the master:

> The Negro woman's position and moral status were largely controlled by environment and the degree of morality possessed by the master. There were different degrees of degradation. If the master desired to share the wife of a slave, the husband was powerless to interfere or prevent, and sometimes had to behold two sets of children in the little cabin. Friends of mine have looked into the faces of colored children whose white father was also their grandfather. . . . Negro's life did not more fully illustrate the depth to which unbridled license could sink the human heart, than the experiences of Negro women in the stockades, on the breeding farms and in the chain gangs of American slavery (5-6).

Sheppard believed that if there had been a continuing bond between slave and mistress, particularly where her mother was concerned, life would have been better for the slave woman.

> If all the Negro women, slave and free, had been thus considered, our God had probably not bathed this beautiful land in human blood—requiring a drop of blood for every tear wrung, from the crushed hearts and bruised bodies of our mothers ("Negro Womanhood," 5).

Though she often considered serious topics in her writing, humor did not elude Ella Sheppard Moore. Writing on the black preacher, she noted that the text for the black minister's sermon often came from the white minister. In an effort to repeat "I am Alpha and Omega," a black minister said, "O Lord, I am an African Nigger" ("Before Emancipation," 6-7).

Sheppard died on June 9, 1914. Folklorist Thomas W. Talley, who had been a member of the short-lived Fisk Jubilee Singers company of 1890, said in his eulogy of Sheppard in the *Fisk University News:*

> As a leader of music, Mrs. Moore had few equals. Well do I remember, when, more than a score of years ago, she trained a Jubilee chorus in which I sang bass. We were young, life was all a dream, but she had had us only a few hours when we began to realize that "the Lord had laid His hands on" her. . . . Our music, inspired through her, made the hearts of others purer and better (12).

Descendants of Sheppard include a niece, three great-granddaughters, four great-grandsons, thirteen great-great-grandchildren, and four great-great-great-grandchildren. Beth Madison Howse, a great-granddaughter, is reference librarian in Special Collections, Fisk University Library.

References

Collins, Leslie M. "Jubilee Singers." Unpublished document. Special Collections, Fisk University Library, Fisk University, n.d.

Howse, Beth. "Ella Sheppard (Moore) 1851-1914." "Leaders of Afro-American Nashville." A publication of the 1987 Nashville Conference on Afro-American Culture and History. n.p.

———. "One Fisk Family." *Fisk* (July 1978): 16.

Marsh, J. B. T. *The Story of the Jubilee Singers with Their Songs*. Rev. ed. Boston: Houghton Mifflin, 1881. 103-105.

Moore, Ella Sheppard. "Before Emancipation." New York: American Missionary Association, n.d.

———. Diary, 19 October 1877-15 July 1878. Jubilee Singers Collection, Fisk University.

———. "Historical Sketch of the Jubilee Singers." Part I. Personal. *Fisk University News: The Jubilee Singers* 2 (October 1911). Photographs p. 41, and p. 45.

———. "Negro Womanhood: Its Past." New York: American Missionary Association, n.d.

Pike, Gustavus D. *The Jubilee Singers*. London: Hodder and Stoughton, 1873. 49-54. Engraving, p. 40.

Richardson, Joe. *A History of Fisk University, 1865-1945*. Tuscaloosa, Alabama: University of Alabama Press, 1980.

Seroff, Doug. Interview with the author, 8 March 1991.

Spence, Mary E. "The Jubilee of Jubilees." *The Southern Workman* 51 (January 1922): 73-80.

Talley, Thomas W. "Appreciation of Mrs. Ella Sheppard Moore by a Fellow Student." *Fisk University News*, November 1914.

Work, John Wesley. *Folk Song of the American Negro*. Nashville: Press of Fisk University, 1915. Photographs, p. 81.

Collections

The Jubilee Singers Collection is housed in Special Collections, Fisk University Library, and contains letters, diaries, scrapbooks, photographs, autographs, memorabilia, and other items relating to Sheppard and the other singers. The Ella Sheppard Moore diary is a part of the collection. The works by Marsh and Pike cited above are in Special Collections at Fisk. The history of the singers is told in other works also in the collection. The portrait of the Jubilee Singers by Edmund Havel hangs in Jubilee Hall, Fisk University. It is reproduced often in published works.

Jessie Carney Smith

Olivia Shipp (Olivia Porter)

(1880-1980)

Musician, organization founder

This intriguing pioneer left many mementos on the musical scene in this country. Known professionally primarily as a bass violinist, Olivia Shipp performed in many dance and jazz bands, chamber music ensembles, and orchestras in New York City and elsewhere, with a performing career extending from about 1900 into the post-World War II era. Her influence was perhaps larger, as she formed a very important performing group, the Negro Women's Orchestral and Civic Association, was very active during the Harlem Renaissance, and knew a great many of the country's outstanding musicians during her lifetime of one hundred years.

Olivia Sophie L'Ange Shipp was born in New Orleans May 17, 1880, and died in New York City June 18, 1980. She and her sister, May Kemp, developed some musical talents in the home, and Shipp subsequently learned to play a parlor organ and later helped with a local church choir. May Kemp was also an actress, and she soon left New Orleans to join the Black Patti Troubadour Company and then the Bob and Kemp vaudeville team, moving to New York City.

May Kemp soon invited Shipp to join her in New York around the turn of the century, and Shipp's career developed rapidly from that point. Adopting the performing name of Olivia Porter, she was active as a pianist, cellist, and finally as a bassist. She subsequently used her married name, Olivia Shipp, for most of her professional work as a musician.

From working in chamber music groups as a pianist, Shipp came to admire the sound of the cello. She took lessons from fellow musicians, including Wesley Johnson and Leonard Jeter (band leader, composer, and cellist in the Shuffle Along orchestra). Next, she became active with the Martin-Smith School of Music and studied bass violin with a Mr. Buldreni of the New York Philharmonic. She played bass with Marie Lucas's Lafayette Theatre Ladies' Orchestra and organized another orchestra with a title very reminiscent of the character and spirit of the emerging Harlem Renaissance: Olivia Shipp's Jazz-Mines.

Shipp's next major venture involved forming the Negro Women's Orchestra and Civic Association. In this undertaking she had assistance from Local 802 of the American Federation of Musicians and a then-emerging major New York political figure: United States Representative (and later, Mayor) Fiorello H. LaGuardia. This orchestra subsequently furnished musicians for an appearance by Lil Hardin Armstrong in Harlem's Apollo Theatre. Shipp's activities in music circles and civic affairs continued from that point on. She performed frequently as a free-lance musician in stage shows, for dances, and with various ensembles. As she confirmed in a personal interview with D. Antoinette Handy on February 22, 1979, at the age of ninety-eight: "I played the best of shows; I worked with the best of them" (Handy, 78).

References

Handy, D. Antoinette. *Black Women in American Bands and Orchestras*. Metuchen, N.J.: Scarecrow Press, 1981. Biographical coverage is based on personal interviews. Contains photographs of Shipp and her orchestra.

Kellner, Bruce. *The Harlem Renaissance; A Historical Dictionary for the Era*. New York: Methuen, 1984. Contains photographs of Shipp and her orchestra.

Southern, Eileen. *Biographical Dictionary of Afro-American and African Musicians*. Westport, Conn.: Greenwood Press, 1982.

Darius L. Thieme

Modjeska Simkins

(1899-)

Civil rights activist, educator

Mary Modjeska Monteith Simkins is medium-tall (five feet three inches), with straight hair, and fair-skin, being the offspring of mulattoes. She is strong-willed, direct, outspoken, bold, nurturing, and independent-minded. In her speech and writing, she is caustic, abrasive, and confrontational. As an orator, she is witty and humorous, preferring to use colloquial speech patterns. At times she seems a scolding matriarch in her mannerisms.

Simkins's affiliation with progressive and vanguard organizations and movements on state, regional, and national levels provided her an enlarged perspective that exceeded the bounds of provincialism in her native South Carolina. Her exposure to persons in the midst of the political ferment of reform and radical organizations led her to support groups as diverse in philosophy as the labor unions, the Communist party, and the NAACP. Her multifaceted activities also helped to preserve her independence and open-mindedness. While she functioned in the continuum of an ongoing tradition in the black community, she maintained an elevated position of service that few have been able to reach.

Modjeska Simkins

Mary Modjeska Monteith was born December 5, 1899, the eldest child of Henry Clarence Monteith and Rachel Evelyn (Hull) Monteith, who had eight children—five daughters and three sons. Simkins attended Benedict College, Columbia, South Carolina, from grade one through the completion of her bachelor's degree. She received an A.B. degree in 1921. Shortly after leaving Benedict, she took courses at Columbia University and at Morehouse College during summer sessions. In connection with her employment as director of Negro work for the South Carolina Tuberculosis Association, she completed graduate work in public health at the University of Michigan at Ann Arbor and, during the 1930s, at Michigan State Normal College (now Eastern Michigan University), Ypsilanti.

Being the oldest child of a large family placed Simkins in a responsible position: She was expected to set an example for the younger children. While her mother was recuperating from childbirth and her father was out of town as foreman of brick work with a construction company, Simkins was in charge of the family. She would go into town alone to take care of family business and she supervised the children at work on the family farm. She was the first child allowed to drive the family's horse and buggy.

These experiences of leadership and responsibility gave Simkins a practical and realistic perspective. She was taught that life was not easy or frivolous and the consequences of one's actions were reaped through punishment as well as rewards. While she enjoyed childhood, she also learned to be frugal, respect work, be independent, serve humanity, love knowledge, and have pride in self and race.

Simkins's career as a schoolteacher followed the path of

her mother and maternal aunts, beginning at the teacher-training division of Benedict College and continuing to teach at the Booker T. Washington School in Columbia. She remained an employee there until her marriage to Andrew Whitfield Simkins, a prosperous black businessman who owned real estate and operated a service station in Columbia. Because the public school system in Columbia did not allow married women to teach, Modjeska Monteith Simkins was forced to give up her job. But her marriage to Simkins, who embodied the business acumen that she admired, strengthened her business skills and fostered her leadership ability.

The next employment Simkins accepted prepared her for a career of activism and public service: In 1931 she began a tenure as director of Negro work for the South Carolina Tuberculosis Association where her role was to raise funds and assist in health education among blacks in South Carolina. Working in one of the poorest states in the nation during the Great Depression, Simkins was exposed to the dire poverty and utter deprivation that existed in the rural areas where the majority of the black population lived and worked. This was the awakening of Simkin's political consciousness.

Simkins established clinics for tuberculosis testing at churches, schools, mills (on company time), and sometimes in the fields of plantations where blacks were working. She worked with black teachers at summer schools and training institutes. In order to facilitate her work, she published a newsletter and organized a state conference of black leaders and held annual meetings. During her career with the State Tuberculosis Association, 1931-1942, Simkins made crucial contributions to the physical and political well-being of black South Carolinians. But the conservative, tradition-bound administrators at the South Carolina Tuberculosis Association, who regarded her political work as subversive, put pressure on Simkins to sever ties with the NAACP. Since she did not bow to the demands, Simkins was tactfully "fired." In 1942, released from full-time paid employment, Simkins came into her own as spokesperson and agitator for civil rights—a full-time public service career that she maintained until 1956, when she accepted a position as public relations director for the Victory Savings Bank in Columbia. Simkins had become skilled in methods of publicity and propaganda, public speaking, journalism, and letter-writing, and she had met and worked with black leadership on the state level.

In 1942, Simkins was elected to the voluntary office of state secretary of the South Carolina Conference of the NAACP. A member of the initial group of founders of the state conference in 1939, she had worked as corresponding secretary from the outset. In 1941 she was elected head of the publicity committee and member of the Speakers Bureau of the organization. In the late 1930s, she had worked with the Columbia branch of the NAACP as publicity director and as a member of the Executive Board.

From 1939 to 1957, the South Carolina Conference of the NAACP undertook lawsuits on behalf of black citizens, and Simkins was in the forefront of these activities. The organization's first lawsuit, a fight for equalization of teachers' salaries across the state, was won by black teachers of Charleston in 1944. In 1945, the Columbia teachers won a similar case. Simkins was active with the Columbia teachers who worked to establish a case on behalf of the black teachers. She penned letters, wrote articles for the black newspapers, and assisted in arranging meetings of black teachers to discuss the inequities of the salary scale and to take action against it. When the campaign for teachers' salaries was undertaken in 1943 by the state conference, she was the only woman of a committee of four who was appointed to raise funds to support the lawsuit. Once the Teachers' Defense Fund was established, she served as its secretary.

Because state employees were being threatened with the loss of their jobs if they donated to cases being prepared by the NAACP, the state conference formed a companion organization through which money could be routed to the NAACP. The new organization, the South Carolina Citizens Committee, had the same leaders as the state and local branches of NAACP. Simkins, elected reporter, was the only woman officer and she was asked to write the charter of the new organization.

After the teachers' salary cases were won, full attention was directed to dismantling South Carolina's white primary, a project that had been the rallying cry in the move to form the state conference. In the voting cases, Simkins was actively involved in planning in-court proceedings, and she attended the sessions at the courthouse. Thurgood Marshall, the attorney representing the national office of the NAACP, suggested that Simkins, who had been involved in the correspondence of the NAACP's case, pay special attention in court so that she could possibly advise the NAACP lawyers on points they might have missed. In addition to her financial support of George Elmore, the plaintiff in the first voting rights case, she also lent her moral and emotional support. While the *Elmore* v. *Rice* case was won in 1947, the South Carolina Democratic party formulated devices to circumvent the ruling. But the members of the NAACP developed a second case, *Brown* v. *Baskins,* in order to obtain full voting rights. The second case was won in July 1948.

Activist Fights State Public School Segregation

The most far-reaching South Carolina case was that which came out of Clarendon County in the 1950s. Beginning in 1947 as an attempt to secure bus transportation for black students, in 1949 the case became a demand for equal education opportunities. Finally, upon the joint decision of Walter White of the national office of the NAACP and federal judge J. Waties Waring of South Carolina, the case was changed to an attack on segregation in public schools. In her capacity as secretary, Simkins worked with NAACP leader Reverend J. A. Delaine, in writing the background of the case. The Clarendon County case became one of those argued before the Supreme Court in the famous *Brown* v.

Board of Education of Topeka case; the decision in 1954 invalidated racial segregation in the nation's public schools.

Great economic suffering attended the South Carolina blacks who petitioned the State's school boards to comply with the *Brown* decision. Again, Simkins was active in providing relief and support, this time to the victims of economic reprisal. Her assistance took the form of direct appeals for funds from persons and organizations outside the state as well as personal involvement in the distribution of food and clothing to needy victims. One such appeal Simkins made was at the Abyssinian Baptist Church in Harlem, New York, with the support of Reverend Adam Clayton Powell, Jr. Further, Simkins wrote and distributed eyewitness accounts of the distressing situation.

But in November 1957 Simkins was not reelected to her post as NAACP state secretary, most likely due to her affiliation with radical groups such as the Southern Negro Youth Congress and the Communist party. In the early 1940s, Simkins had begun a term as a member of the National Adult Advisory Board of the Southern Negro Youth Congress (SNYC). Organized in 1937 in Richmond, Virginia, the SNYC was a group that "focused on activism as distinct from the legal route of redress of grievances with specialized lawyers as the main staff" (Interview with James and Esther Jackson, 11 December 1977). In 1946, she coordinated a major conference of the SNYC in Columbia, bringing in delegates from across the country.

Simkins's affiliation with the Communist party came through her support of black and white leaders who were Communists and through financial donations to projects carried out by the party. She never joined, but she wholeheartedly supported prominent Communists such as William Patterson, Benjamin Davis, James and Esther Jackson, and Herbert Aptheker.

After 1957, when Simkins was not reelected to her post as state secretary of the NAACP, she concentrated on projects on the local and regional levels in Columbia and central South Carolina. But she had begun working with local projects long before: In the late 1930s she worked with the Civic Welfare League, a body that sought to improve municipal conditions for blacks in Columbia by working to get playgrounds and better housing for blacks, end police brutality against blacks, reduce crime and most importantly regain the ballot. Simkins was secretary of the organization. During the mid-forties, she had worked with the Columbia Town Hall Congress and the Columbia Women's Council as director of publicity and public relations. The Columbia Town Hall Congress, an interracial body, sought to provide intellectual stimulation and social outlets for the enlisted men at Fort Jackson in Columbia. Their meetings included a concert, an address, a discussion period, and a movie. The Columbia Women's Council, organized in 1947 by Mrs. Horatio Nelson and Simkins, was a local political-action group of black women who developed projects that increased the number of registered women voters.

Simkins Fights Segregation at the Local Level

Before 1957, Simkins had also worked with the Richland County Citizens Committee (RCCC, chartered in 1956), an offshoot of the South Carolina Citizens Committee, organized in 1944. After 1957 Simkins chose to use the committee as the vehicle for her multifaceted projects in Columbia. These included the integration of the University of South Carolina, the improvement of living conditions for black mental health patients at the state's institution, and the desegregation of the Columbia public school system. In 1963, through the efforts of Simkins and others in her family—including her sister, R. Rebecca Monteith— Henri D. Monteith, Rebecca's seventeen-year-old daughter, was admitted by court order as the first black student at the University of South Carolina since Reconstruction. South Carolina was the last state to admit blacks to its all-white public school system ("USC to Admit Negro," 11 July 1963). The Monteiths, sisters Rebecca and Modjeska in the forefront, worked together on other projects, including one to improve conditions for black patients in the state's mental health hospital. In Simkins's official capacity as public relations director for the RCCC in 1964, charges were leveled against the governing board of the State Mental Health Commission for having substandard conditions at the all-black mental health facility, the Palmetto State Hospital for Negroes. The RCCC managed to get wide publicity for its complaint. And in February 1965 the governor of South Carolina, Donald S. Russell, toured both state mental health facilities, the South Carolina Hospital for Whites and the Palmetto State Hospital for Negroes, to investigate the charges. Conditions were improved after the publicity.

Another RCCC project in 1964 was the desegregation of Columbia's public schools. With the assistance of the RCCC, parents of twenty-six black students applied for transfer to all-white public schools, and the Columbia School Board complied without the threat of a court-ordered plan. By 1965, black students were admitted to the white Columbia public schools without violence or disruption.

Simkins's local activities included working with branches of regional organizations, including the Commission on Interracial Cooperation (CIC), the Southern Regional Council (SRC), and the Southern Conference for Human Welfare (SCHW) and its offspring, the Southern Conference Educational Fund (1948). In her work with the South Carolina Committee of the CIC, Simkins participated in meetings and projects with fellow blacks and a middle- and upper-class whites to promote harmony between the races. This involvement led to her affiliation with the Durham Conference of black leaders who were part of the organizing body of the Southern Regional Council (SRC). Although Simkins was a charter member who supported the work of the SRC, their moderate approach to the problem of segregation caused disenchantment on her part. In her official capacity as vice-president of the Richland County division of the SRC, Simkins handled much of the written correspondence and the duplication of materials.

The regional organizations with which Simkins was most active were the Southern Conference for Human Welfare and its successor in 1948, the Southern Conference Educational Fund (SCEF). By the mid-1940s, Simkins, the group's liaison in South Carolina, was actively involved in projects of the SCHW, sending letters of protest to officials and placing advertisements in the papers. She attempted unsuccessfully in 1947 to establish a chapter of the organization in South Carolina. In 1952, Simkins chaired the local committee for a SCEF-sponsored conference in Columbia, and in December of the same year, she was elected vice-president of SCEF, being the first woman to hold such a high office in the organization (her election came after the resignation of Benjamin E. Mays from the position).

Simkins's activities with regional groups were supplemented by service to at least four national organizations, the Civil Rights Congress (CRC), the United Negro and Allied Veterans of America (UNAVA), the National Republican party, and the National Progressive party. After attending the Detroit founding meeting of the Civil Rights Congress in 1946, Simkins worked as a state liaison in supporting the projects of this organization. Her work in the late 1940s with the UNAVA, an organization that assisted black veterans in securing the benefits provided by the GI Bill of Rights, resulted in the organization's establishing a chapter in Columbia, South Carolina. Also, she was instrumental in planning a National Council Meeting of UNAVA in Columbia in 1948.

Simkins's political activities on the local level were tied the national Republican party for years, and for a brief span, a third party movement, the national Progressive party. Her participation and support in this area emanated from her desire to foster the development of real competition among political parties, and to create a solid base of support within South Carolina for the national Republicans. Simkins's work with the Republicans led to her being named in 1948 to the National Convention Committee on Permanent Organization from South Carolina. But during the same period, she became discontented with South Carolina's Republican party for their welcoming disgruntled Democrats who disapproved of President Harry Truman's support of civil rights. Later, this led to Simkins's complete withdrawal from the party, and shortly before that, to her support of the national Progressive party. In December 1947, Simkins was a member of a delegation of fifty-one black leaders who urged Henry Wallace to run for president on the Progressive party ticket. She supported Wallace's campaign through projects she carried out under the auspices of the Southern Conference for Human Welfare.

Simkins preferred to work as public relations director, secretary, or program chairperson for many of the diverse organizations with which she was affiliated. She ran for public office four times but she was never elected. These bids for public office included: candidate for the Columbia City Council in February 1966 (she placed third of six candidates—five white males and herself—for two seats); candidate for membership in the legislature, the South Carolina State House of Representatives (Richland County representative) in June 1966; candidate for the Columbia School Board; and another candidacy for the Columbia City Council in 1983.

Simkins was a prolific writer, although most of her work is not published, since it is in the form of speeches, radio scripts, and letters in her official capacities with numerous organizations. Her earliest writings take the form of letters of protest to newspaper editors and public officials. Some of these are: a protest against black women prisoners being forced to work on the Columbia street chain gangs; a protest against separate seating of the races in a Columbia concert featuring black vocalist Marian Anderson; a protest against the "work or go to jail" decree issued by the Mayor of Columbia; a letter in support of Paul Robeson's right of free speech; a letter suggesting that blacks arm themselves since the police were not providing adequate protection; a letter protesting public officials' and candidates for offices' use of the word "nigger" and race-baiting in South Carolina's elections; and a letter defending and explaining the contribution of the black race in the building of America. Letters to public officials requested support for specific legislation, such as the Anti-Lynching Bill.

Simkins was a correspondent for the Associated Negro Press and wrote an editorial column in the Norfolk *Journal and Guide*, "Palmetto State," for two years, from 1946-1948 (the other editorial writers were men). She also wrote articles regularly for two black newspapers in Columbia during the 1940s—the *Palmetto Leader* and *The Lighthouse and Informer*. During the 1950s, she worked as editor of *The Lighthouse and Informer*, when former editor John McCray was imprisoned. Occasionally Simkins wrote articles for other newspapers.

Simkins was a close friend and contemporary of several major figures in the interracial southern civil rights movement. Close friends of national prominence included leaders of the national NAACP such as Associate Supreme Court Justice Thurgood Marshall, Walter White, Roy Wilkins, Ella Baker, Gloster Current, and Ruby Hurley. Leaders with more radical political perspectives who were Simkins's friends and associates were James and Esther Jackson, Paul Robeson, W. E. B. Du Bois, William Patterson, and Herbert Aptheker. Prominent contemporaries in other civil rights organizations were Septima P. Clark of the Southern Christian Leadership Conference, Myles Horton (cofounder and director of Highlander Folk School), the Reverend Fred Shuttlesworth, Virginia Durr, Anne Braden, Judy Hand, and the Reverend Ben Chavis. In South Carolina, Simkins is considered the matriarch of the state's civil rights movement; she has worked with leadership there from the 1940s to the present.

References

Abyssinian Baptist Church, New York, N.Y. Young Women's Civic League. Press release, 12 December 1955.

"Columbia Schools Set Racial Policy." *The State*, 4 February 1965.

Hurley, Ruby. Interviewed, Atlanta, Georgia, 1 March 1977.

"Information from the Files of the Committee on Un-American Activities, United States House of Representatives: Subject—Modjeska Simkins (Mrs. Andrew Simkins)," 13 June 1965.

Jackson, James and Esther. Interviewed, Brooklyn, New York, 11 December 1977.

Johnson, Minnie. Interviewed, 26 January 1977.

Key, V. O., Jr. *Southern Politics in State and Nation.* New York: Knopf, 1950.

Macdougall, Curtis D. *Gideon's Army*. Vol. 3: *The Campaign and the Vote.* New York: Marzani and Munsell, 1965.

"Minutes of Meetings of the Board of Directors, 1941-44," meeting of 28 February 1943. South Carolina State Conference, NAACP. Modjeska Simkins Personal Collection.

"Minutes of the Board of Directors, 1939-1949." South Carolina Tuberculosis Association. South Carolina Tuberculosis Association Papers.

Montgomery, Eugene. Interviewed, Orangeburg, South Carolina, 3 October 1977.

"Negro Citizens Committee of South Carolina Organized." *Palmetto Leader* 1942(?) or 1944(?). Modjeska Simkins Personal Collection.

Newman, I. DeQuincey. Interviewed, Columbia, South Carolina, 26 January 1977.

Newsreel. Newsletter. Prepared by Modjeska Simkins for the South Carolina Tuberculosis Association. n.d.

"The Orangeburg-Ellorree Story." Leaflet. Modjeska Simkins Personal Files.

"Palmetto State Hospital Defense Given." *The State* 10 February 1965.

"Russell and Negroes Tour Asylums for Five Hours." *The Charlotte Observer,* 14 February 1965.

"Russell to Tour Negro Hospital." *The State,* 30 January 1965.

Simkins, Modjeska. Interviewed, 13 September 1975; 18 November 1975; 4 July 1977; 10 July 1977; 20 July 1977; 31 July 1977; 17 September 1977; 9 November 1977; 20 November 1977; 14 December 1977; 3 June 1978; 4 July 1978.

Simkins, Modjeska and Byrd., Levi. G. Interviewed Cheraw, South Carolina, 23 July 1977.

Simkins, Modjeska. Interviewed by Jacquelyn Hall, 15 November 1974; 28-31 July 1976. Southern Oral History Program, University of North Carolina, Chapel Hill.

Teachers' Defense Fund. Circular. Modjeska Simkins Personal Collection.

"Twenty-Fifth Annual Report, 1941-1942." South Carolina Tuberculosis Association. South Carolina Tuberculosis Association Papers.

"UNAVA News" [United Negro and Allied Veterans of America] 2 May 1946.

"USC to Admit Negro." *The State,* 11 July 1963.

Woods, Barbara A. "Modjeska Simkins and the South Carolina Carolina Conference of the NAACP, 1939-1957." In *Women in the Civil Rights Movement: Trailblazers and Torchbearers, 1941-1965.*" Brooklyn: Carlson Pub. Co., 1990.

Collections

Papers of Mary Modjeska Monteith Simkins are at Winthrop College, Rock Hill, South Carolina (limited collection); Benedict College, Columbia, South Carolina (limited collection); Caroliniana Special Collections Library, University of South Carolina, Columbia; and in the home of Modjeska Simkins, in Columbia.

Newspaper archives that include information on Simkins are *The State,* (Columbia Newspapers), Columbia; *The News and Courier,* Charleston, South Carolina. Photographs are in the Southern Women's Oral History Project, University of North Carolina-Chapel Hill; Columbia newspapers (several photos over a few decades); and Caroliniana Special Collections Library, University of South Carolina.

Oral history collections in which Simkins is included are the Southern Women's Oral History Project, University of North Carolina, Chapel Hill; University Library, Winthrop College, Rock Hill, S.C.; and "The Quest for Human Rights: the Oral Recollections of Black South Carolinians" (audiovisual tapes), Afro-American Studies Program, University of South Carolina. Many interviews with Simkins's coworkers are also in this collection. Extensive collection of taped interviews are at the South Carolina Educational Television Network, Columbia, South Carolina.

Barbara A. Woods

Althea T. L. Simmons

(1924-1990)

Lawyer, lobbyist, organization official

The segregated community of Monroe, Louisiana, where Althea T. L. Simmons grew up, provided a backdrop for the fierce and uncompromising desire that she had throughout her life to remove apartheid-like conditions wherever they existed. From her experiences as fieldworker for the NAACP, she rose in the ranks of the organization to head its Washington Bureau and became its chief lobbyist. She fought relentlessly for legislation to support civil rights. Her faithfulness to the cause also led to voting rights extensions, a strengthened Fair Housing Law, and a bill to establish the Martin Luther King Holiday, later made into law. A fierce fighter, uncompromising expert on civil rights issues, and faithful servant of the NAACP, Simmons wrestled with the organization's problems efficiently and effectively for more than twenty-eight years. Above all, she spent a lifetime fighting racism.

Simmons was born in Shreveport, Louisiana, on April 17, 1924, the daughter of M. M. Simmons, a high school principal, and Lillian (Littleton) Simmons, a high school teacher. Since kindergarten days she has used the initials "T. L." When asked to define the initials, she responded, "That's one secret I will keep" (Williams, A-26). She grew up in a family of an older brother and a younger sister. She received her bachelor of science degree with honors from the black, state-supported institution Southern University in New Orleans, Louisiana, 1945; a master's degree in marketing from the University of Illinois, Urbana, 1951; and a law degree from Howard University, Washington, D.C., 1956. She pursued further study in contract compliance at the University of California, Los Angeles, and took additional work at the American Society for Training Development, the American Management Association, the New School for Social Work in New York City, and the National Training Laboratory. This training was necessary for Simmons, who after graduation from law school, immediately set her sights on climbing unclimbable mountains and achieving the seemingly unachievable, with a particular interest in eliminating the color, gender, and economic barriers to racial unity.

Simmons was associated with the W. J. Durham law office from 1956 to 1961. A former college teacher and journalist, in 1961 Simmons began twenty-eight years of service to the NAACP. Before that she had been an NAACP volunteer as executive secretary of the Texas State Conference of NAACP branches and chairperson of the executive committee of the Dallas branch. From 1961 to 1964 she was field secretary and worked out of the NAACP subregional office in Los Angeles. When a management consultant firm submitted a reorganization plan to the NAACP Board of Directors in 1964, their report called for an office of secretary for training. Roy L. Wilkins, then executive director, appointed Althea T. L. Simmons to the newly-created position of secretary for training, a position that she held until 1974. Working under the supervision of Gloster B. Current, who directed branches and field administration, Simmons was responsible for compiling and distributing all training manuals and materials. She planned and implemented training and executive development programs for the NAACP's national office, in the field, and for the executive secretaries of branches. She set up training sessions for volunteers in numerous small cities, towns, villages and hamlets across the country.

In 1964 Simmons was also director of the NAACP's National Voter Registration Drive. Later, as NAACP national education director, 1974-1977, she developed handbooks, pamphlets, programs, and other instructional materials designed to uplift black youth. As associate director of branch and field services, 1977-1979, she supervised the NAACP's nationwide network of branches, field staff, and the membership and youth and college division.

Simmons worked in the "Boot Heel" of Missouri on an NAACP special Voter Registration Summer Project. When Medgar Evers was assassinated on June 11, 1963, the NAACP sent her to work with Evers's wife, Myrlie, and the Evers family and to relocate them to California. "Her quiet courage and demeanor was a source of strength to Myrlie and the children," said Benjamin L. Hooks ("Statement of Benjamin L. Hooks," 41).

Chief NAACP Lobbyist Named

In 1979 Simmons was appointed director of the Washington Bureau and chief lobbyist for the NAACP. She had already excelled in her various assignments with the organization and she said that her years of field service within the NAACP "taught her the value of grassroots mobilization" (Williams, A-28). It was in Washington that Simmons's work finally gained her the national respect and recognition that she had earned considerably earlier. But the shadow of her predecessor, legendary Clarence Mitchell, was inescapably there as her stewardship was often compared to his. There were those who disregarded her as a worthy successor to Mitchell and who opposed her on the basis of her gender, "convinced that being black and female would be a double liability in a predominantly white male world" (Williams, A-28). She was also reminded of her uncanny resemblance to then Congresswoman Barbara Jordan. None of this would deter Simmons, for she had a mission and her own agenda, and she knew that the larger problem dealt with the organization's civil rights agenda. Immediately she began her usual pattern of working tirelessly and incessantly, late in the evenings and on weekends, to get the job done. She never viewed her role as one of self-glorification. She was an expert on civil rights and had a comprehensive understanding of the civil rights agenda. Thus, the fierce, determined, and uncompromising Simmons buttonholed congressmen and senators and "cajoled them . . . into supporting Civil Rights legislation" ("Statement of Benjamin L. Hooks," 41). Her forceful determination also helped to bring about extensions of voting rights, passage of the Fair Housing Act, and a bill to establish a Martin Luther King, Jr., national holiday. Simmons played a pivotal role in causing Congress to deny Robert Bork's appointment to the United States Supreme Court. She was "one of the most effective, intelligent lobbyists on the Hill," said Senator Orrin G. Hatch, Republican of Utah (Williams, A-26). She facilitated the work of the Resolutions Committee at the NAACP conventions in planning summits, conferences, marches, and various protests and demonstrations.

Simmons's commitment to social action was manifest in other positions that she held outside of the NAACP. She was a member of the National Manpower Advisory Committee, United States Department of Labor, 1969-1974; Filer Commission on Private Philanthropy and Public Needs, 1973-1975; vice-president, American Society for Training and Development, 1973; vice-president NOW Legal Defense and Education Fund, 1974-1977; and National Advisory Council for Mental Health, 1973-1976. She served on the editorial board of *Integrated Education* and of the *Journal of Afro-American Issues*. Simmons was a member of the United States Census Advisory Committee on Black Populations, 1980 Census, from 1975 forward; board of trustees, Teachers College United Seamen's Service, 1976 forward; board of directors of the National Council on the Aging; and a member of the executive board of Delta Sigma Theta Sorority, 1988 until her death, where she cochaired the Commission on Social Action. She was consultant to the Office of Federal Contract Compliance; National Advisory Council; and member, Equality of Educational Opportunity.

During her distinguished career, Simmons received a number of awards and recognitions professionally and in community service. These included Washburn University's President's Award, 1975; Howard University's 1987 Alumni Award for Postgraduate Achievement in Law and Public Service and 1988 Leadership Award; and a 1987 Distinguished Alumni Award and 1988 Leadership Award from the National Association for Equal Opportunity in Education (NAFEO). Althea Simmons was named recipient of the National Bar Association's Gertrude E. Rush award for 1990.

Simmons has been featured in *Ms., Essence,* and *Savvy* magazines; *U.S.A. Today,* the *New York Times,* the *Washington Post,* and is profiled in *Beacham's Guide to Key Lobbyists* and the "I Dream a World" exhibition of black women who changed the world, 1989. A multitalented person, she was skilled as a writer, speaker, planner, organizer, motivator, and facilitator. These are the qualities that led the NAACP to promote her and made her widely-sought as a speaker before church, education, political, business, fraternal, and professional forums.

Simmons was a member of Asbury United Methodist Church, where she once chaired the administrative board; member of the General Board of Pensions of the United Methodist Church and its Committee on Corporate Fiduciary Responsibility, Committee on Appeals, and chaired the Committee on Legal Concerns.

Simmons had one daughter, a lawyer. Tall and stately, Simmons had the bearing of an African queen with the forcefulness and resolve that made her an awesome opponent and a fearless leader. She was straightforward and to the point in her transactions. She had a brisk walk, always appearing to be in a hurry. Though ill for a number of months, Althea Simmons set up office in her Howard University Hospital room to continue her work rather than take leave. "The job must go on. There is little time for rest," she said (Althea Simmons Runs Civil Rights Drive," 7). After a long illness, she died in her hospital room on September 13, 1990. She left a legacy in the civil rights struggle that may never be equalled.

References

"Althea Simmons Runs Civil Rights Drive from Hospital." *Jet* 78 (16 April 1990): 7.

"Biographical Sketch. Althea T. L. Simmons." Washington Bureau, NAACP, n.d.

Booker, Simeon. "Ticker Tape U.S.A." *Jet* 78 (10 April 1990): 10.

Guess, Jerry M. "Reflections on a Life." *Crisis* 97 (October 1990): 37-40, 51. Includes photographs.

Lanker, Brian. *I Dream a World.* New York: Stewart, Tabori and Chang, 1989. Includes photograph.

"Miss Simmons in New Post." *Crisis* 72 (March 1965): 166-67.

"Statement of Benjamin L. Hooks on the Death of Althea T. L. Simmons." *Crisis* 97 (October 1990): 41, 51-52.

Who's Who Among Black Americans, 1990/91. 6th ed. Detroit: Gale Research, 1990.

Williams, Lena. "Black and Female, and Now Deemed Effective." *New York Times,* 30 June 1987. Includes photograph.

Jessie Carney Smith

Judy Simmons

(1944-)

Poet, journalist, editor, singer, pianist

Judy Dothard Simmons is a great communicator. However, unlike many a politician, she does not need a teleprompter, nor is she restricted to a single medium. Whether in print, on the radio, or seated at a piano, she always leaves her audience cognizant of the beauty and the pain of being born a woman of vision and compassion in an inequitable social system.

Judy Simmons was born on August 29, 1944, in Westerly, Rhode Island. She is the only child of the union of Amanda Catherine Dothard of Choccolocco, Alabama, and Edward Everett Simmons of Newport, Rhode Island. Both of Simmons's parents are college educated; her mother had a career in education, and her father was in the United States Army and later in the civil service. Although Simmons was born in Rhode Island, her formative years were spent in various rural towns in Alabama. This bifurcated upbringing would provide the future artist with different perspectives on the same country. Simmons once commented that while she was "happy for the both experiences," the move was nevertheless a culture shock and an experience "from which I may never recover" ("Judy Simmons Has 'Decent Intentions,'" 3).

In 1960 Simmons graduated as class valedictorian from the Allen High School, a boarding school in Asheville, North Carolina. She went on to attend Talladega College in Talladega, Alabama, but after a year she transferred to her father's alma mater California State University at Sacramento, where, while working full and part-time, she earned her B.A. in psychology (1967). In 1967 Simmons returned east and soon made the New York metropolitan area her home. From 1968 to 1974 Simmons worked for AT&T Long Lines Department in managerial positions of divisions staff supervisor, public relations supervisor, and accounting operations supervisor.

In addition to taking various managerial courses at AT&T and several business courses at Iona College, in 1984 Simmons went on to further her formal education as a Revson Fellow at Columbia University's Graduate School for the Arts Writing Division, where she began work towards an MFA in poetry.

Simmons the poet came of age literarily during the black consciousness movement. Over the years her poetry has appeared in numerous periodicals, including *Conditions 5*, *Bopp*, *Elan*, *Essence*, *Persea 2*, and has been anthologized in *Black Review No. 2* (William Morrow, 1972), *Understanding the New Black Poetry* (William Morrow, 1973), *Giant Talk; An Anthology of Third World Writing* (Random House, 1975), *Drumvoices* (Doubleday, 1976), and *New Rain No. 1* (Blind Beggar Press, 1981, 1985). Simmons also has three volumes of poetry to her credit: *Judith's Blues* (Broadside Press, 1973), *A Light in the Dark* (Cambridge Adult Books, 1983), which was commissioned by Literacy Volunteers of America and is widely used in adult literacy programs, and *Decent Intentions* (Blind Beggar Press, 1984). The dynamism of Simmons's poetry attests to the fact that she is more than a wordsmith: she is a truthteller. As June Jordan said in her advance praise for *Decent Intentions*:

> She means it; the intention alternately sings and singes the nerve endings alert. Hers is a particular and complicated and faithfully lyrical spirit among us. Be gentle and wake yourself up to these poems (Bookjacket, *Decent Intentions*).

In the field of journalism Simmons has worked in both the print and broadcast media. She began broadcasting in 1978 at New York's WBAI-FM, a public station where she hosted the weekly talk show, "On The Real Side." In 1981 she joined the black-oriented news and information station WLIB-AM, where until 1984 she graced the air waves with "The Judy Simmons Show," produced by Fern Gillespie. The show, which aired four hours a day, five days a week, ran the gamut from tofu to South Africa in terms of discussion topics, providing a mixed bag of lifestyle and current events issues relevant to people of color regionally, nationally, and internationally. In terms of her outlook on herself as a radio personality, Simmons was once quoted as saying:

> I see what I do as a social responsibility. . . . Media needs to be used to improve the quality of human life on this planet. That means that what I do is more important than celebrity-hood (*Gannett Westchester Newspapers*, 12 October 1982).

Simmons's career in print journalism has included positions at *Essence* magazine as senior editor and business editor (1980 to 1981) and as editor-at-large and in various other editing and writing capacities (1985 to 1989); senior editor at *MS* magazine (1988 to present) and free-lance editor for *Emerge* magazine (1990 to present). As a print journalist, Simmons has written numerous articles on a broad range of topics including racism, sexism, abortion, parenting, relationships, business, and art. Her articles include: "Cartoons As Commerce" (*Black Enterprise*, May 1977), "Back to College at 34" (*Family Circle*, September 1979), "The Many Faces of Audre Lorde" (*Contacts II*, 1983), "Struggle for the Executive Suite" (*Black Enterprise*, September 1980), "Staying Power in Publishing" (*Essence*, May 1987), "Spirituality: An African View" (*Essence*, December 1987), and "Dangling Man," a profile of Bill Robinson (*Village Voice*, 5 September 1989). Two of Simmons's articles of particular note are "The Necessary Bitch," in which she deals with one of the most pervasive stereotypes about black women (*Essence*, September 1986), and "A Matter of Choice," on abortion (*Essence*, October 1987). The former has been anthologized in *Psychopathology of Everyday Ra-*

cism and Sexism (Hayworth Press, 1988); and the latter, for which Simmons received a Planned Parenthood Federation of America Maggie Award (1988), has been anthologized in *The Black Women's Health Book: Speaking for Ourselves* (Seal Press, 1990). One of the signature features of Simmons's writing is the use of her own experience as a point of departure and the frankness with which she shares scenes from her private life. Her writing is physical, dynamic, always promoting a response from the reader. It is impossible to read her work and not be affected emotionally, because her spirit and energy so radiate from the pages.

Simmons has also had this same effect on people through her work as a singer-pianist with a repertoire that includes jazz and Broadway show tunes. Her performance venues have included Manhattan's Silver Lining and various lounges on the east coast and in California.

Like other black artists of conscience and consciousness, Simmons has understood that special responsibility to give back and to educate. Clearly, Judy Simmons's work as a poet and print and broadcast journalist has been about the business of information and educating. But Simmons has also logged hours in the classroom. Her teaching posts include: professor of English and social studies at Rodman Job Corps Center (1967 to 1968), adjunct professor of English at Empire State College (1980), and instructor of creative writing for various workshops and seminars sponsored by the New York State Council on the Arts (1970 to present).

The multitalented Judy Simmons defies singular definition and pigeonholing. It might be better to let her speak for herself:

> I'm five feet eight inches tall, weigh 180 pounds and am black-haired, brown-eyed, ferociously intelligent, kinda wild and determined to run as much of my life and the world as I can get under my control ("The Necessary Bitch," 152).

The title of the article in no way describes the personhood of Judy Simmons. And based on her work as poet, journalist, and performer, one suspects that if she were to run more of the world, she would strive to make it a better place. As she wrote on the dedication page of *Decent Intentions*:

> If you become the thing you kill
> it exists still
> and you are
> what you wished to rid the world of.

Judy Simmons's notable friends include poets Audre Lorde and Amiri Baraka. Her professional affiliations include: PEN American Center; International Woman's Writing Guild; Women's Media Group. Her honors and awards include: Freedom's Journal Award (Committee for a Free Press); Outstanding Citizen of the Year (Omega Psi Phi Fraternity); Ophelia Devore Achievement Award; Radio Personality of the Year (Independent Order of Foresters); Community Service Award (The Black Experimental Theatre); and the Superior Achievement Award (National Council of Teachers of English).

References

Gannett Westchester Newspapers (12 October 1982).

Jordan, June. Statement on bookjacket. Judy Simmons. *Decent Intentions*. Bronx, N.Y.: Blind Beggar Press, 1984.

"Judy Simmons Has 'Decent Intentions.'" *The Black American* 23/24 (October 1984): 25-31.

Simmons, Judy. *Decent Intentions*. Bronx, N.Y.: Blind Beggar Press, 1984.

———. "The Necessary Bitch." *Essence* 17 (September 1986): 73-77, 149, 152, 155.

Tonya Bolden

Hilda Simms

(1920-)

Actress

Hilda Simms is a black actress who in 1944 achieved critical acclaim in the play *Anna Lucasta*, in which she played Anna, a prostitute whose plotting and grasping family brings her back from the streets of Brooklyn to manipulate her into marriage with an unsuspecting graduate of an agricultural school newly arrived from the South with eight hundred dollars in his pocket. Prior to this production, no black cast of performers had ever appeared in a play that did not address the issue of race. Under the direction of Abraham Hill, the play, which was first performed June 8, 1944, in the basement of the Harlem Public Library, soon moved to Broadway, where it was produced by John Wildberg and directed by Harry Wagstaff Gribble. Described as beautiful and intelligent, as a "vivacious, versatile 25 year old . . . a siren of sepia" who "personified every man's idea of a dream girl" (*Ebony*, 1 December 1945, p. 21), Hilda Simms turned the corner from amateur to professional with her first nineteen performances of the play, which showcased her talent and beauty.

Born April 15, 1920, in Minneapolis, Minnesota, to Lydia (Webber) Moses, who was by one account reared in a convent, and to Emil Moses, a musician (one biographical sketch identifies his occupation as engineer), Hilda Theresa was the eldest of thirteen children. Since the family was poor, Simms, at about the age of ten, started to do odd jobs after school and on weekends, "lighting fires on Saturday mornings for religious Jewish neighbors" and "taking care of children'' (*Ebony,* 1 December 1945, 21). In the meantime, her work at school paid off, for Simms won a scholarship to St. Margaret's Academy, becoming one of the first blacks to be admitted there. After graduating from the academy, Simms worked in her spare time and attended the University of Minnesota, first entering the General College, from which she would eventually transfer to the College of Education to prepare for a teaching career. After about a year and a half at the university, Simms, unable to afford school, left to make salads in a Minneapolis restaurant.

Though her earliest professional interest, one report goes, was in the field of social work, Simms in her part-time work and her spare time was often indirectly or directly drawn to the stage. While attending the University of Minnesota, Simms had worked as a maid in the Homewood Theater. At the age of eighteen, the light-skinned, dark-haired, beautiful young woman became one of the first black women to model for portrait and sculpture classes at the Minnesota Art Institute. From 1936 until she went East, she also worked as a girl's recreational assistant in the Phillis Wheatley Settlement House, where she taught the first classes ever held in modern dancing for blacks. Her first public appearance was at the age of fifteen in the Frank Buck *Bring 'Em Black Alive* show, then stopping in Minnesota, where Simms appeared as a Malayan girl. Her first appearance in the theater was in 1937 in St. Paul, Minnesota, as Maimie in Claire Booth's *Kiss the Boys Good-Bye*, where Simms appeared with the Edythe Bushe Players. College offered and Simms availed herself of some of the best opportunities to hone her acting skills. While attending the University of Minnesota, Simms joined its Little Theater group and played the part of Marion in Noel Coward's *Cavalcade* and the part of Irene in Eugene O'Neill's *The Dreaming Kid*.

On August 15, 1941, she married a graduate of Coe College whom she had met six years before, Williams Simms. A week after the marriage, Malcolm MacLean, the president of Hampton Institute (now University) in Virginia, who had founded the General College of the University of Minnesota and left that college to head the institute, offered Hilda Simms a teaching fellowship, the first of its kind ever granted by Hampton. The Simmses moved to Virginia, where William worked as director of public relations at Virginia State College and where Hilda simultaneously worked to get her B.S. degree and taught English, radio drama, and speech correction. While teaching and studying at Hampton, Hilda Simms also organized and directed a USO group called First Nighters. Made up of townsfolk from Newport News, the group toured black army camps throughout the South. In 1943 Simms completed her course at Hampton and moved to New York, where she eventually established herself as an actress.

By the time the twenty-three-year-old Hilda Simms arrived in New York she had experience on the stage. Shortly after her arrival she joined the American Negro Theater (ANT), founded in 1940 in Harlem by Frederick O'Neal, a young actor from Mississippi, with the help of Abraham Hill and six associates. As a member of ANT, Simms participated in a cooperative organization in which members gave their time and money. Simms is reported to have said that at different times she was ''actress, sound effects woman, property custodian, and publicity agent,'' depending on the needs of the theater group (*Current Biography*, 623). Members of the ANT were also required to give ''two percent of their outside acting income'' to the group treasury. Apparently Hilda Simms, like most of the other performers, had jobs outside the theater and donated her services to ANT. While living in New York and rehearsing and performing with ANT, Simms worked as a writer of broadcast scripts and as a publicity assistant with Artkino Pictures (later she became an assistant to the vice-president of this agency, which distributed Russian motion pictures in the United States). She also sang or had small parts in programs broadcast by WLIB, WNYC, WOR, and WEVD.

Simms Scores Hit in *Anna Lucasta*

Simms's first performance with the ANT was as Marion in *Three Is a Family*. Her most resounding performance was in the production of Phillip Yordan's *Anna Lucasta*, which has been called ''an important event in American theater'' and ''the most successful Negro hit in theatrical history'' (*Ebony* 1, December 1945, p. 17). Hilda Simms herself commented, ''The fact that a Negro cast is entertaining white audiences with a play that is not typically negroid is history-making. It's the first time it ever happened. To me, it's indicative of our growing democracy'' (18). In October Simms received the Achievement Award as the outstanding actress of the year offered by the Salute to Young Americans Committee.

One source indicates that Hilda Simms's husband, William, had difficulty with her role as Anna. ''He doesn't like the idea that everyone knows me as a prostitute,'' Simms is reported to have remarked with a smile. ''I asked him, 'Would you like me better as Juliet even if I were the world's biggest failure?' and he said, 'Yes!''' (21). Though Simms was amused by her husband's possessive response, the marriage ended, and on September 20, 1948, the actress married the Chicago actor Richard Angarola. Simms lived with her husband in Paris, where she attended the University of Paris from 1950 to 1952.

Throughout her acting career Simms attended various drama schools and studied with prominent theatrical figures. She was at the American Academy of Dramatic Art from 1948 to 1959. She studied at the Carnegie Hall Drama School from 1959 to 1960. Simms also studied acting with Abbe Mitchell, Ezra Stone, Betty Cashman, and Harry Wagstaff Gribble in New York City.

Some of the honors she received include the *Chicago Defender* Race Relations Honor Roll (1944), Allied Forces (Central Europe) Award (1951), Minneapolis Urban League Award (1953), New York City YMCA Award (1954), and the National Council of Negro Women Award (1956). Other organizations honored Simms—the Hampton Alumni Association (1955), Harlem Hospital School of Nursing (1956),

Vocational Guidance and Workshop Center (1956), and the Boy Scouts of America, Harlem (1957).

In the wake of her Broadway success, Hilda Simms, whose favorite roles are those of Saint Joan and Juliet, appeared in many plays at home and abroad. It was as Anna Lucasta that Simms made her debut in London at His Majesty's Theatre on October 29, 1947. She also appeared at the Rudolph Steiner Hall in Picasso's *Desire Caught by the Tail* (February 1950), at the Embassy as Stella Goodman in *The Gentle People* (April 1950), and at the Cambridge Theatre as Pervaneh in *Hassan* (May 1951). In New York, Simms performed the part of Miss Dewpoint in the play *The Cool World* at the Eugene O'Neill in February 1960, and at the Red Barn in Northport, New York, she starred in July 1961 in *The Captain's Paradise* and *Black Monday*. At the Little Theatre, Simms played Laura Wright Reed in *Tambourines to Glory* in November 1963, and at Sokol, New York, March 1970, she appeared as Therese in *The Madwoman of Chaillot*.

In 1953 Simms flew back from Paris to play the part of Joe Louis's wife in the film *The Joe Louis Story*, and she appeared in 1954 in the film *Black Widow*. From 1954 to 1957 she had her own radio program, "Ladies' Day with Hilda Simms"; she toured in a one-woman show, *Letters of Famous Courtesans*, which opened in 1961. Simms has figured in several television dramas and in the series "The Nurses," which aired in 1962. Simms, who is interested in writing a novel, became a feature writer for *Tuesday* magazine. She has worked in political campaigns and was, at the time of one of the more recent biographical accounts, director of the Theater Therapy Addiction Research and Treatment Center. Although Hilda Simms made history on the stage, her career has many other facets.

References

Current Biography. New York: H. W. Wilson, 1945. Photograph, p. 622.

"A Date with Anna: At Tale of a Two-City Triumph by a Love-Hungry Girl from Harlem." *Ebony* 1 (December 1945): 17-23. Cover photograph.

Ebony 3 (February 1975). Cover photograph.

DeKnight, Freda. "A Date With a Dish." *Ebony* 9 (January 1954): 56-59.

Mapp, Edward. *Directory of Blacks in the Performing Arts*. Metuchen, N.J.: Scarecrow Press, 1978.

Notable Names in the American Theater. Clifton, N.J.: J. T. White, 1976.

Poussaint, Alvin F. "The Problems of Light-skinned Blacks." *Ebony* 30 (February 1975): 85-91.

Who's Who in the Theatre 16th ed. Vol. 1. Detroit: Gale Research, 1977.

Vanessa D. Dickerson

Nina Simone "High Priestess of Soul"

(1933-)

Musician, singer

> For Nina Simone, the "high priestess of soul," music is not only an art, but an expression of life in all its verities. More than any other popular performer of the day, she has captured the essence of the black revolution and sings of it without biting her tongue. However, her stature as a versatile musician is considerable regardless of what she happens to be singing about, for this sorceress of song is an outstanding eclectic, a sort of one woman summation of musical confluence (*Ebony*, 1969 170).

Born Eunice Kathleen Waymon to a minister mother, Mary Kate (Irvin) Waymon, and a handyman father, John Divan Waymon, in Tyron, North Carolina, in 1933, she is the sixth of eight children—four boys and four girls. Nina Simone developed her musical talents at an early age. For example, at the age of three, she accompanied her minister mother as a musician to shouting revival meetings in nearby towns. She also played and sang with two sisters in a trio called The Waymon Sisters.

Simone's formal musical education began at the age of eight under the supervision of Mrs. Lawrence Mazzanovich, a local teacher. Subsequently, she earned the honor of being the "brightest little girl in the town" but did not feel comfortable with this title, especially when she was requested to perform recitals by her teacher. She was encouraged to pursue her intellectual and musical capabilities during her boarding school years in Asheville, North Carolina. She graduated valedictorian of her class. A piano prodigy with the financial support of her hometown, she first studied piano and theory with Carl Friedburg at the Juilliard School of Music in New York and later at the Curtis Institute in Philadelphia.

In 1954 the possibility of a concert career seemed hopeless, just as it had been for most blacks of that era. Simone obtained a position as a cocktail pianist in the resort area of Atlantic City. She was asked to sing as well as play, so she included in her repertoire songs from her church years.

The year 1959 is the beginning of her recording years. She recorded a soulful rendition of "I Loves You, Porgy," which was a Gershwin composition that was modified by Billie Holiday. According to Arnold Shaw's *Black Popular Music in America*, "I Loves You, Porgy" was "released on a small, independent label (Bethlehem) in 1959" and "became her sole million seller." It paved the way for a recording contract with Colpix, an affiliate of Mercury, and in the late 1960s with RCA. Simone also changed her name during this time. She said that as a Waymon it would be unacceptable for her to perform on the nightclub circuit and as a teacher she tried to remain free of deviant behavior that would be embarrassing to her religious parents. The name Nina means "little girl." She had been called "Nina" in her childhood. She selected Simone because she felt that it was compatible with Nina.

Simone called Political Diva

Donald Bogle views Nina Simone as a political diva. In this context, the songs "Four Women" and "Mississippi Goddam" describe directly and bitterly the racial situation in America. "Mississippi Goddam" was written in 1963 and seldom heard on the radio. The song protested the killings of Addie Mae Collins, Denise McNair, Carole Robertson, and Cynthia Wesley at the Sixteenth Street Baptist Church in Birmingham, Alabama, and that of Medgar Evers in front of his home in Jackson, Mississippi. These acts of violence outraged Simone, and she sang about "Mississippi Godamm": "I mean every word of it." In the song she expressed many of the grievances blacks endured at the time and sneered at those who wanted blacks to lessen their pace in the drive toward freedom and the elimination of intolerance and discrimination.

"Four Women," written and recorded during this same time (1966), examines the varying life styles and attitudes of four black women in the context of skin color. These four women include: the black woolly-headed Aunt Sarah; the high-yellow, straight-haired Safronia; the pretty, tan-hued Sweet Thing; and the unruly, loud-talking, streetwise Peaches. Phyl Garland asked Nina Simone in an interview in 1969 if she was the sort of person who believed that the artist should reflect the time in which he or she lives. She said:

> It has to be that way, my friend. I live that. There's no other purpose, so far as I'm concerned, for us except to reflect the times, the situations around us and the things that we're able to say through our art, the things that millions of people can't say. I think that's the function of an artist and, of course, those of us who are lucky leave a legacy so that when we're dead, we also live on. That's people like Billie Holiday and I hope that I will be that lucky, but meanwhile, the function, so far as I'm concerned, is to reflect the times, whatever that might be (183).

"I Wish That I Knew How It Would Feel to Be Free" was a song composed by jazz pianist and lecturer Billy Taylor and recorded by Simone. Its final lines reflected the times and Simone's own feelings:

> Say it clear, say it loud, I am black and I am proud!

Simone's first spouse was Donald Ross, and the marriage ended in a divorce. She married Benjamin Stroud in 1961. He became her manager and booking agent. They have one daughter, Lisa Celeste Stroud.

Nina Simone has had numerous best-selling albums. They include: *Wild in the Wind, High Priestess of Soul, Silk and Soul, Pastel Blue, I Put a Spell on You, Let it All Out,* and *Nina Simone Sings the Blues*. She has been the recipient of various awards. For example, the Radio DiscJockeys named her the Most Promising Singer of the Year in 1960. Being the first woman to receive the Jazz Cultural Award, she was honored as "Woman of the Year" by the Jazz at Home Club in New York City in 1966. In 1967 the National Association of Television and Radio Announcers designated her as Female Jazz Singer of the Year.

References

Donald Bogle. *Brown Sugar*. New York, 1980. Includes photograph.

Current Biography Yearbook. New York: H. W. Wilson, 1968. Includes photograph.

Feather, Leonard. *New Edition of the Encyclopedia of Jazz*. New York: Bonanza Books, 1960.

Garland, Phyl. "Nina Simone—High Priestess of Soul." *Ebony* 24 (August 1969): 156-59.

——. *Sound of Soul: The Music and Its Meaning*. Chicago: Regnery, 1969.

Shaw, Arnold. *Black Popular Music in America*. New York: Schirmer Bros, 1986.

Mary R. Holley

Carole Simpson

(1940-)

Broadcast journalist

Carole Simpson has made outstanding contributions to the field of journalism and, through her work, to society at large. Though not allowing herself to be pigeonholed as a reporter of "black" news—indeed, since 1988 she has been anchor of ABC's "World News Saturday"—she has brought sensitivity and perspective to her coverage of news and features concerning black America.

Carole Simpson Marshall was born on December 7, 1940, in Chicago, Illinois. Simpson graduated from the University of Michigan in 1962 with a bachelor of arts degree in journalism and did graduate study in journalism at the University of Iowa. Simpson is married to James Marshall and has two children, a daughter named Mallika and a son named Adam.

Simpson is a well-respected journalist and news anchor with more than twenty years of experience covering a wide array of topics, including Capitol Hill, health care, housing, education, the environment, and the release of Nelson Mandela. Early in her career, Simpson worked as a stringer correspondent for Voice of America. She then spent two years as a journalism instructor and director of the Information Bureau at Tuskegee Institute in Alabama.

From 1965 to 1968 she worked as a news reporter and anchor as well as a movie and book reviewer for WCFL Radio in Chicago. From 1968 to 1970, Simpson served as a special correspondent and weekend anchor at WBBM Radio in Chicago. While serving in that capacity, Simpson also performed as a commentator on "Our People," a minority affairs program on WTTW-TV, a public television station in Chicago. From there, Carole Simpson became Chicago's first black woman television reporter.

Simpson continued to make strides in her career. She became a television news correspondent for WMAQ-TV and worked at that station from 1970 to 1974. At the same time, she worked as a journalism instructor for Northwestern University's Medill School of Journalism from 1971 to 1974. While working at WMAQ-TV, Simpson had her priorities concerning the types of stories she covered. Although she enjoyed covering hard news stories, she preferred feature stories "that allow more creativity" (*Ebony*, 1971, 168). She also stated at that time the following regarding the coverage of black stories:

> I want to cover black stories because I feel I bring them sensitivity and a perspective that white reporters don't have. I wouldn't want to cover just black news though, because you often lose your credibility that way (*Ebony*, 1971, 170).

Carole Simpson continued to rise in the area of television news and earned her credibility through excellence in her work.

Moving on to Washington, D.C., Carole Simpson worked as a host of a women's public affairs program called "Her-Rah," which aired on WRC-TV, an NBC Washington affiliate television station. She then became a substitute anchor for "NBC Nightly News" and also anchored NBC's "Newsbreak" on the weekends. Simpson's news delivery style, camera presence, and finesse on the air evolved, and she was selected to cover Capitol Hill as a news correspondent; she performed in that position from 1978 to 1981. Simpson was then chosen to serve as a perimeter reporter during the Republican and Democratic conventions in 1980. The visibility she received on Capitol Hill as well as her coverage during the conventions earned Simpson respect and a national reputation. In 1982, Simpson joined ABC in Washington as a general assignment correspondent.

Simpson Receives Presidential Assignment

Simpson has been covering George Bush since 1980. She has accompanied him on domestic and foreign trips since his vice-presidency. In 1984 Simpson covered his vice-presidential reelection campaign and in 1988 his bid for the presidency. She also served as a perimeter reporter during the 1988 Republican Convention in New Orleans.

Simpson is articulate and has a rhythmic flow in her news delivery in addition to a manner that exhibits confidence. Her excellent skills, combined with her many years of experience in the news business, are apparent in her role as anchor of ABC's "World News Saturday." Simpson was named anchor in June 1988. In addition to her performance as news anchor, she contributed to reports concerning family issues for the "American Agenda" segment on "World News Tonight" with Peter Jennings. Some of her "American Agenda" segments include stories on children under stress, battered women, teen pregnancy, and a 1988 report on children with AIDS that earned her an Emmy nomination. Simpson can also be seen on "Nightline" and "20/20."

Carole Simpson is a versatile journalist. Besides anchoring half-hour news shows and doing news segments, Simpson has also anchored three hour-long ABC news specials: "The Changing American Family," "Public Schools in Conflict," and "Sex and Violence in the Media." Simpson reported the release of Nelson Mandela, who had been imprisoned in South Africa for twenty-seven years. While covering Mandela, Simpson also did a special report on South African women. However, Simpson was assaulted by a South African police officer during a disturbance in Johannesburg while she was covering a church service the day before the African National Congress leader was released. Simpson says she "will not return to the country until its apartheid policy ends" (*Jet*, 12).

Simpson is listed in *Who's Who in America* and *Who's Who Among Black Americans*. She served as president of the Radio and Television Correspondents Association from 1982 to 1983. She was named to the University of Iowa's School of Communications Hall of Fame, and in 1986 she was elected chairperson of the ABC News Women's Advisory Board. She is a member of the board of directors for the Washington chapter of the Society of Professional Journalists of the Fund for Investigative Journalism, and of the Distinguished Journalists Advisory Committee of the American University. In 1988 she was the recipient of the Milestone Award in Broadcast Journalism from the National Commission on Working Women and received the Silver Bell Award from the Ad Council in 1989.

References

"'ABC News' Carole Simpson Won't Return to South Africa." *Jet* 768 (30 April 1990): 12.

"Carole Simpson Biography." Capital Cities/ABC Inc. Television Network Group, 1980-1990. Washington, D.C.

"Upsurge in TV News." *Ebony* 26 (June 1971) 168, 170.

"Tops in TV Newscasters." *Ebony* 34 (January 1979): 111.

Who's Who Among Black Americans, 1990-1991. Detroit: Gale Research, 1990.

Who's Who in America. 40th ed. Chicago: Marquis, 1979.

Dhyana Ziegler

Naomi Sims
(1948-)
Model, entrepreneur, lecturer, author

Naomi Sims, haute couture model, author, lecturer, and business executive, was born March 30, 1948, in Oxford, Mississippi. She rose to become one of the nation's premier black woman entrepreneurs. The product of a broken home, Sims had only faint memories of her father, who divorced her mother when Sims was a baby. Her mother suffered a nervous breakdown when Sims was only eight. The subsequent separation from her mother and her other sisters, Betty and Doris, and shifts from one home to another, created a lonely childhood for young Naomi Sims. She therefore spent many nights longing for her natural mother and the security of the fairy tale that could always be found in the elementary readers. She was never returned to her natural mother; instead, she was placed with loving foster parents who raised her.

Young Sims continued to battle the usual adolescent insecurities that were magnified by a height that would one day propel her to the pinnacle of a modeling career. The insecurity remained for years, but her sense of self-reliance assisted her in transforming the gangling adolescent into a striking teenager. "At 13, Naomi Sims was already 5 feet 10 inches in height. She felt tall, dark, and different" (Summers, 41). At fourteen, Sims's proclivity for modeling and fashion was recognized by friends who suggested modeling as a career. It was a natural suggestion; by Sims's admission, she had "always been a clotheshorse" (Lurie, 144). After graduating from Westinghouse High School in Pittsburgh, Sims enrolled in New York's Fashion Institute of Technology. A shortage of money precipitated Sims's foray into modeling. She began posing for a fashion illustrator at $6 an hour. To further increase her earnings, Sims had to take drastic measures. At this time she did the unheard-of, and it ended up launching her modeling career. Without benefit of an agent or an introduction, she boldly telephoned prominent fashion photographer Gosta Peterson. Her purpose was served and the association led to a marked increase in her earnings. She went from six to sixty dollars an hour. Sims found the juggling of a growing modeling career and the study demands of school too taxing; consequently, she left school.

Notwithstanding the tenfold increase in her modeling fees, the road to success was still to be an uphill struggle. Sims went through weeks of unemployment, living on borrowed money from the modeling agency that was then representing her. Not surprisingly, Sims eagerly accepted the *New York Times* assignment that placed her on the cover of its *Fashion of the Times* supplement—the first for a black model. That cover photograph was to change the fashion industry and the national perception of beauty. Never before had a woman of such deep, rich color been used to exemplify beauty. Fashion designer Halston understood the significance of the exposure of Sims. He surmised that "she was the great ambassador for all black people. . . . She broke down all the social barriers" (Keveles, 14). While it was an optimistic overstatement to say that she broke down "all" of the social barriers, many did fall as she appeared in the AT&T commercial and became the first black model published on the covers and pages of such Anglo-American bastions of fashion as *Vogue, Ladies Home Journal, Life,* and *Cosmopolitan.*

Sims found the fashion world superficial, boring, and unnatural. In the 1968 interview for *Ladies Home Journal,* Sims said:

> I can't see myself modeling at 30—it's too competitive and often shallow. When you're young its great because you can make fantastic money. I like money. . . . But I think I can be happy just making enough to buy what I want. Once you've got success, it's empty. The fun is in reaching for it (Lurie, 145).

Sims Opens Manufacturing Business

At the age of twenty-four, Sims had experienced tremendous success in the modeling field and gave it up to reach for success in her own business. Her goal in her private enterprise was to manufacture quality wigs that were complimentary to women of color. Utilizing a synthetic fiber she invented and patented, Kanekalon Presselle, she attempted to place her wigs on the market. Many businesses were reluctant to carry her line. In her typical take-charge stance, Sims explained the procedure for opening the market: "I took a slide show to those in the industry who resisted and gave them an education. I told them if they would just leave me and Black women alone, it would be fine" (Summers, 102). In spite of the obvious risks in any new business, the Naomi Sims Collection was more than just "fine"; it was a financial success that assured Sims' status as an accomplished businesswoman. Naomi Sims Beauty Products was incorporated in 1985 with Sims serving as founder and chairperson of the board. The company expanded to include a complete line of beauty products for women of color that could be found in department and specialty stores in the United States and the Bahamas.

The company business was just one aspect of Sims's busy life. As wife to art dealer Michael Findlay and mother to their son, John Phillip, Sims felt that nurturing the family was important, and she sought to keep her private life sheltered. However, that did not hinder her public and civic participation as she attempted to give back to her community and her people. She used her fashion and beauty expertise to write several books. Her first, *All about Health and Beauty for the Black Woman*, published in 1975 by Doubleday, became the health and beauty reference book for black women. After multiple printings, Sims published a revised edition in 1986. She also wrote *How to Be a Top Model* (1979), *All about Hair Care for the Black Woman* (1982), and *All about Success for the Black Woman* (1983), all published by Doubleday. She contributed regularly to *Right On!*, a magazine with a nationwide black teenage audience. Her insightfulness and ability to speak cast her as lecturer and participant in numerous seminars, panel discussions, and gatherings on topics as diverse as drug abuse, sickle-cell anemia, and education, as well as health and beauty.

Over the years Sims compiled a lengthy list of awards and special recognitions. Among them are Model of the Year Award, 1969 and 1970; Modeling Hall of Fame International Mannequins, 1977; and International Best-Dressed List, 1971-1973, 1976, 1977. She was named one of the Women of Achievement, *Ladies Home Journal*, 1970; the governor of Illinois proclaimed September 20, 1973 Naomi Sims Day, and in 1971 she received the key to the city of Cleveland, Ohio. In 1970 she received the New York City Board of Education Award.

Sims has been a member of the board of directors of the Northside Center Child Development in Harlem, and a participant in the Sickle-Cell Anemia Drive and the New York State Drug Habilitation Program. In 1980 she was invited to be executive-in-residence for the School of Business Administration of Georgetown University in Washington, D.C. Her business acumen was recognized again in 1984 when she was selected as a participant in the President's Panel at the Twelfth Annual Career/Alumni Conference of the Harvard Business School.

Long absent from the modeling world, Sims has continued to be a model for humanity—a complementary ensemble of social conscience, community involvement, religious faith, and family love.

References

Kevels, Barbara. ''From Cover Girl to Cover Up: Naomi Sims Turns Wigs into Millions.'' *People* (22 August 1977): 14-19.

Lurie, Diane. ''Naomi.'' *Ladies Home Journal* (November 1968): 114.

Summers, Barbara. ''Naomi Sims.'' *Essence* 16 (January 1986): 41.

Bonnie Shipp

Barbara Sizemore

(1927-)

Educator

Barbara Ann Laffoon Sizemore, educator, educational consultant, school superintendent, and author, was born in Chicago, Illinois, on December 17, 1927. She was the only child of Sylvester Walter Laffoon and Delila (Alexander) Laffoon Stewart, who were both born in Terre Haute, Indiana. Her mother and stepfather, Aldwin E. Stewart, currently reside in Evanston, Illinois. Her father died in 1935.

Sizemore grew up in Terre Haute, Indiana, where she attended Booker T. Washington Elementary School and graduated from Wiley High School. She went on to obtain a bachelor of arts degree in classical languages in 1947 and a master of arts degree in elementary education in 1954 from Northwestern University. In 1979 she completed a Ph.D. program, majoring in educational administration at the University of Chicago.

Currently, Sizemore resides in Pittsburgh, Pennsylvania, with her husband, Jake Milliones, Jr., a native of Marietta, Georgia. They have four children: Beatena, DuBois, Momar, and Marimba. Although these are her stepchildren, she says, ''They are just like my own'' (Barbara Sizemore to Brenda J. Ingram, 22 March 1990). She also has two children from a previous marriage: Kymara Sizemore Chase Spikes and Furman G. Sizemore. She is the proud grandmother of two—Lansing and Kafi Chase. She revels in the accomplishments of her children and grandchildren and describes them as the ''bright light in her life'' (Telephone interview with Barbara Sizemore, May 1990). She is a member of the Macedonia Baptist Church and Delta Sigma Theta Sorority. In her spare time she enjoys reading, writing, photography, and listening to jazz.

Sizemore began her professional career in the Chicago public schools, where she taught for sixteen years (1947-1963). During this time she served as a substitute, teaching Latin at Wendell Phillips High School from 1947 to 1948. From 1950 to 1954, she taught sixth, seventh, and eighth grades at John Shoop Elementary School. During the next three years, she taught reading English and English for the Spanish-speaking at Frank Gillespie Elementary School. Until 1962 she taught grades two to five at Charles Richard Drew Elementary School.

During the next four years, Sizemore served as principal of Anton Dvořák Elementary School (nongraded kindergarten through fifth grade) and Forrestville High School in the Chicago public school system. Following this, she was appointed as director of the Woodlawn Experimental Schools Project from 1969 to 1971. This project was a collaboration between the Chicago public schools, the University of Chicago, and the Woodlawn Organization under the ESEA Title IV, a government-funded program in community control. During the same time (1965-1971), Sizemore was an instructor at the Center for Inner City Studies, Northeastern Illinois State University. Her last position in the Chicago area was as coordinator for government-funded programs associated with the Chicago public schools.

Sizemore Becomes Washington's Superintendent of Schools

Upon arriving in the greater Washington, D.C., area, Sizemore made her most noteworthy accomplishments. She served as the first woman and first black associate secretary for the American Association of School Administrators in Arlington, Virginia (1972-1973). She went on to be elected superintendent of schools for the District of Columbia Public School System from 1973 to 1975. During her tenure as school superintendent, Sizemore was committed to quality education. Her effort to permit more parental involvement led to some political ramifications that eventually led to her dismissal. In the next two years, she was self-employed as an educational consultant. In 1977 Sizemore ran for the office of city council member in the District of Columbia. After a defeat by Hilda Howland Mason, she relocated to Pittsburgh, Pennsylvania, and was employed as an associate professor in the Department of Black Community Education and Development at the University of Pittsburgh. In 1989 she was promoted to full professor.

Sizemore has made significant scholarly contributions to the field of education and its relevance to ethnic minorities and has a special interest in promoting multiculturalism. Between the years 1969 and 1990, Sizemore has published about twenty book chapters. She also has published twenty-two journal articles and six book reviews. Further, she has written three pamphlets, two educational reports for grant funded projects, and has authored or coauthored four books. As a consultant, Sizemore has served as a lecturer and expert advisor and witness on more than 375 occasions during the past nineteen years in thirty-five states and British Columbia. She has served as a consultant for numerous public school systems and has been the keynote speaker for many conferences and African-American history college programs.

Sizemore has been awarded many honors. These include listing in *Who's Who Among Black Americans*, 1990/1991 and *World's Who's Who of Women*, 1978; and the United Nations Association Human Rights Award, 1985. Between 1974 and 1975 Sizemore also was awarded three honorary doctorates—one each from Delaware State College, Central State University, in Wilberforce, Ohio, and Baltimore College of the Bible.

Upon reviewing her life, Sizemore views her mother as her greatest inspiration: "She has always been there, motivated me, and challenged me to be the best person I could be." She quickly adds, "All (my family and friends) have contributed to my development." Sizemore also gives special accolades to her husband, Jake Milliones, Jr.: "I am away from home a lot. He is very understanding, supportive and caring. He takes care of things while I am away" (Telephone Interview with Barbara Sizemore, May 1990). For these things and many more, Sizemore is appreciative of her husband. She is extremely modest and gives credit to the people around her for her success. Two very special people, Charshee Lawrence-McIntyre, president of the Africa Heritage Studies Association, and Nancy Arnez of Howard University were described as good supportive friends. Sizemore is a warm and friendly yet very humble person who is enthusiastically committed to the improvement of education for black American children.

She describes several important values for her life that include "striving to live a Christian life, helping the poor, and being available to people in trouble." Sizemore has made many notable contributions to the black American community and plans to continue to quench her thirst for knowledge by her scholarly efforts. Her long-range goals are to continue at the University of Pittsburgh until 1998 and then retire.

References

Barbara Sizemore to Brenda J. Ingram, 22 March 1990.

Telephone Interview with Barbara Sizemore, May 1990.

Who's Who Among Black Americans, 1977-78. 2nd ed. Northbrook, Ill.: Who's Who Among Black Americans Corp., 1978.

Who's Who Among Black Americans, 1990/1991. Detroit: Gale Research, 1991.

World Who's Who of Women, 1978. 4th ed. Vol. 1. Cambridge, England: International Biographical Centre, 1978.

Brenda J. Ingram

Norma Merrick Sklarek

(1928-)

Architect

Norma Merrick Sklarek has been guided by the wisdom of her parents who told her: "Things that are worthwhile and from which one receives great satisfaction are never easy but require perseverance and hard work." Sklarek is the first black woman to be licensed as an architect in New York (1954) and in California (1962). A highly respected architect, she has had a distinguished career in which she has overcome longstanding barriers to women and blacks.

Norma Merrick Sklarek was born on April 15, 1928, in New York City, to Walter Merrick and Amy (Willoughby) Merrick. Sklarek obtained her training in architecture at Barnard College of Columbia University, where she received the bachelor of architecture degree in 1950. About that experience, she notes:

> I had never seen a T-square or a triangle before I entered the School of Architecture at Columbia University. I found throughout my experiences that if something is tough initially, after I work at it, I not only catch up but move on ahead (Lanker, 40).

After passing the rigorous four-day licensing examination in New York on her first attempt in 1954, she became that state's first black woman licensed architect.

Sklarek soon began to move ahead and remained in lead positions. She was hired in 1955 to work for the prestigious New York City architectural firm of Skidmore, Owens, Merrill, where she remained for five years. With her experience there in handling complicated detail work on major projects and her design expertise, she was able to move to her next position in 1960 with Gruen and Associates in Los Angeles, where she was employed for twenty years. After six years there, she became the first woman to occupy the position of director of architecture, which called for her to manage twenty to fifty architects.

The uniqueness and magnitude of Sklarek's accomplishments early in her career are underscored by the fact that while she became a licensed architect in California in 1962, twenty more years were to pass before that achievement was to be repeated by another black woman. While working at Gruen, Sklarek achieved another first, in 1966: the first woman to be honored with a fellowship in the American Institute of Architects. Although she was the first woman in the long history of the Los Angeles chapter of that association to be so highly recognized, she was still not at the time a partner at Gruen. Sklarek later went on to become vice-president of the California chapter of the American Institute of Architects.

Largest Woman-Owned Architectural Firm Established

In 1980, after leaving Gruen, she became project director for Weldon, Becket, and Associates, in Santa Monica, California. Sklarek took on an even greater role as a leader in her field in 1985 when she formed her own architectural firm, Siegel, Sklarek, Diamond, which she proudly described as "the largest totally woman-owned architectural firm in the United States" (Lanker, 40). Since 1989 she has served as a principal in the Jerde Partnership in Venice, California.

Sklarek feels strongly that architecture should be appealing, functional, and most importantly, pleasing for the persons for whom it is designed, "not just in the image of the architect's ego" (Lanker, 40). Although she has been very successful, at times it has nevertheless been very frustrating when she has tried to realize those goals, not only because of the restrictions placed on her by her clients but also because of the difficulty of obtaining projects for which many established male firms also complete. She explains:

> Projects don't just come to us. Most of our projects are not in the public sector, government projects. Even though there is an affirmative-action policy with government work, we still have to do an enormous marketing job and spend an awful lot of money in order to get it, to prove that we're not just equal to, but better than any of the male firms (Lanker, 40).

The principal works credited to Sklarek include: The American Embassy, Tokyo; Pacific Design Center, Los Angeles; Courthouse Center, Columbus, Indiana; Fox Plaza, San Francisco; City Hall, San Bernardino, California; and Terminal One at Los Angeles International Airport.

Sklarek has served as a role model not only through her projects but also through her community service and work as an educator. She has taught at New York City College (1957-60) and at the University of California, Los Angeles (1972-78). She also served, since 1970, as commissioner on the California State Board of Architectural Examiners and from 1984-87 she was director of the University of Southern California Architects Guild. She has also served on the Design Grading Jury in California.

Sklarek has been married twice: first in 1967, to Rolf Sklarek, deceased in 1984; currently, since 1985, to Cornelius Welch, a physician. Her children are Gregory Ranson and David Fairweather from the first marriage, and Susan.

References

American Architects Directory. 3rd ed. New York: Bowker, 1970.

Lanker, Brian. *I Dream a World.* New York: Stewart, Tabori and Chang, 1989. Photograph, p. 41.

Lewis, S. D. "Professional Woman: Her Fields Have Widened." *Ebony* 32 (August 1977): 115. Includes photograph.

Questionnaire, Biography File, Fisk University Library.

Who's Who Among Black Americans, 1990/91. 6th ed. Detroit: Gale Research, 1991.

Who's Who in America, 1988-1989. 45th ed. Vol. 2. Wilmette, Illinois: Marquis, 1989.

Who's Who of American Women, 1989-1990. 16th ed. Wilmette, Illinois: Marquis, 1989.

Carolyn Hodges

Edith Barksdale Sloan

(1940-)

Politician, lawyer

Edith Sloan began her career in public service as a volunteer for the World Council Mission and for the Peace Corps. When she returned to the United States, she channeled her skills and energies into achieving human rights for people in her own country. Sloan has worked in government service from the Johnson through part of the Reagan administrations, championing civil rights, workers' rights, and consumer rights, among other causes.

Edith Barksdale Sloan was born on November 29, 1940, to Odell Barksdale, an electrician and postal worker, and to Elizabeth (Watts) Barksdale, a buyer and homemaker. Sloan was the youngest of four daughters; she has one younger brother. She grew up in the Bronx, New York.

Sloan's parents sought every opportunity to expose their five children to a variety of social, cultural, and political knowledge. "We may not have been economically well off but we were middle class in culture," Sloan remembers. She took weekly piano lessons from ages six to eleven and often acted in plays. She learned to cook, sew, and to acquire all the skills and tastes of a lady. In addition, the Barksdales also exposed the children to as many black leaders as found their way to New York, and eventually they all came to the Big Apple to give a talk or to participate in a cultural event or political demonstration. Sloan met Mary Church Terrell, Mary McLeod Bethune, and Ralph Bunche, among others. These leaders had a tremendous impact on Sloan's growing awareness of social and political change, not only in the black community, but in the world at large. Sloan also vividly remembers meeting Eleanor Roosevelt several times. In fact, young Edith and her mother had the distinct pleasure of personally escorting Eleanor Roosevelt to her cab after she spoke at Trinity Methodist Church.

Like so many young black girls growing up in the 1940s and 1950s, Sloan's idols were Dorothy Dandridge and Lena Horne. But becoming a world-renowned actress or singer seemed a bit too much like dreaming. Eleanor Roosevelt and Judge Edith Sampson of Chicago appeared to be more accessible role models that a black girl could not only admire from afar but also emulate. When she learned of the black Judge Sampson, Sloan remembers thinking rather self-assuredly, "I'm going to make it! I can be Edith Sampson."

By the age of nine, Sloan had already determined, "I want to make a mark on the world. I do not want to just grow up, get married, have children, be a housewife. I want to contribute [in other ways as well]." Her parents put a premium on education. She graduated from high school at the age of sixteen and from Hunter College at nineteen, in 1959. Sloan absolutely loved attending Hunter College. High school had been academically rewarding but still very difficult emotionally. She recalls observing racism at its harshest in the classroom as white teachers often mercilessly berated black students who, unlike Sloan, had not grown up in that predominantly white educational system. But at Hunter, Sloan blossomed academically and professionally into a strong, determined personality set on making her mark on the world.

Having always been a history buff with a strong desire to travel all over the world, Sloan studied international affairs at Hunter College. She had already done some European travel before completing her studies. Now she longed to see other parts of the world. In 1960 she had been selected for the first Peace Corps mission to Ghana but had to decline the offer because she had just accepted another offer from the World Council Mission to participate in a work camp program in Lebanon. "Lebanon was fascinating," Sloan remembers. "It was the first time I had been in a church where the women all sat in the back segregated according to sex." Sloan was outraged and "wanted to walk out," but also "knew we couldn't do that to our host." The volunteers worked in the fields helping the farmers to harvest their corn and to rebuild the fences around an agricultural college that some Moslems had blown up.

It was while Sloan was stationed in Lebanon that she had the opportunity to visit Egypt. "I felt totally at home; I was their sister." The memory of that trip made an indelible impression on her sense of belonging to a race of world leaders.

Sloan Accepts Peace Corps Assignment

When the Lebanon experience ended, Sloan returned to New York only briefly, working a two-month stint in Bloomingdale's. The Peace Corps contacted her concerning another mission. Sloan accepted the offer to work in the

Philippines, reluctantly, because she thought that it would be too Americanized.

Once she arrived in western Leytey, Sloan immediately discovered that the American influence was at best surface: At the island's heart was a combination of Malaysian and Polynesian culture. "I learned to appreciate their culture," she notes. And the Filipinos, in turn, learned to accept Sloan. She had taken some getting used to, though, because they had expected a blond, blue-eyed person. Sloan, along with the other volunteers, helped to establish a kindergarten where she taught English as a second language, a little mathematics, and science.

Often the volunteers became the doctors in their small towns, which were sometime miles and miles from any medical facilities. Besides, the "jitney" cab system did not run at night, leaving sick people to their own resources if emergencies occurred during off hours. Although it is difficult to effect massive change in such a short period of time, Sloan is perhaps most proud of the work that volunteers accomplished in locating and transporting all the children they could find who had any physical abnormalities to a hospital in Sagou. There they received free medical treatment, and the volunteers needed only return them to their families and supervise their care during recuperation: "We tried to find every one of these deformed children with fangs, etc., because the culture is very cruel if you have any kind of defect. It's no chance for a girl to get married that way."

At the age of twenty-three, while still living in Baybay in western Leytey, Sloan received two shocking pieces of news from the United States. President Kennedy had been shot and killed. And perhaps even more important for Sloan, she learned that a church had been bombed in Birmingham, Alabama, and four little black girls lay dead. "I don't think I've ever gotten over that. Every time I see that I cry," she remembers painfully. Already very much involved in the struggle to improve the human condition at home and abroad, the deaths became a major deciding factor in what this young Peace Corps volunteer would do with her life once she returned to the United States. After the bombing Sloan found herself thinking, "This [the Peace Corps] is great for you, but what are you doing for the people back home? . . . What are you doing now?" It was then that she knew that once she returned home she would participate in the fight for civil rights, to put her body on the frontline, so to speak.

Back home, Sloan almost immediately began pursuing her commitment to achieving human rights for all people in this country. She served for almost a year as a human relations intern at the Eleanor Roosevelt Memorial Foundation in New York. As an intern assigned to the New York Urban League, she worked with the housing director on code violations, and assisted in the League's voter registration and education campaign for the 1964 general election, among other things.

Sloan Enters Other Arenas of Government Service

By 1965, Sloan had moved to Washington, D.C., and had become public information specialist for the U. S. Commission on Civil Rights. In this position, she assisted national private organizations in developing programs utilizing commission materials to inform constituents of civil rights issues and progress in education, voting rights, administration of justice, housing, and public accommodations. She also served as assistant manager of the National Conference on Race and Education in 1967, in addition to arranging briefings for visitors and staff institutes. It was also in this position that Sloan had the opportunity to develop her public speaking skills more fully. She not only prepared White House messages on civil rights but spoke to national groups on behalf of the agency.

Four years later, Edith Barksdale Sloan (now married to attorney Ned Sloan) had become Executive Director of the National Committee on Household Employment. It was Dorothy Height, president of the National Council of Negro Women, who had known Sloan since she was a teenager and who by this time had become her mentor, who said "Edith, this has great possibilities and you can do a lot with this."

Sloan took the position to obtain fair wages and hours for domestic workers and to send a message that household workers wanted respect for the work they did. But she also had a hidden agenda to change the workers' ways of thinking about themselves, because herein would lie the power to make lasting change at both personal and political levels. During her first year at this post, Sloan hired a field worker, Josephine Huett, who had been a domestic herself and who was both extremely articulate and a motivator. The second year, Huett and Sloan, now pregnant, in law school, and working full time, began traveling across the country to churches, community action programs, and other community groups to organize the workers into local chapters.

While most of the workers were afraid of "unionizing," they were very interested in forming their own association. They were tired of the poor wages, poor hours, and lack of respect afforded them. Moreover, "they did not want to take home clothes and grapefruit rather than money." Forty-five local chapters were organized in twenty-one states with two to three million actual constituents.

On July 16, 1971, the first conference of National Household Workers convened at the Marriott Hotel in Washington, D. C. Six hundred women from across the United States arrived by bus for two unforgettable days of fellowship and organization. Sloan remembers that weekend with deepest gratitude, humility, and compassion. "It was as if the women all joined together in one chorus to let the world know 'This is mine. This is mine.'" That sense of ownership of an organization that truly belonged to them was absolutely electrifying as the women joined forces to make their voices heard in Congress.

In the opening plenary session, Sloan delivered the keynote address with these lines: "This must be one of those 'great days a coming' which hasad been promised to us for so long . . . . Let's make hay while our sun is shining." And in a cry for respect, she reminded the audience to demand the respect they deserved: "We refuse to be your mammies, nannies, aunties, uncles, girls, handmaidens any longer. What we will be are skilled, professional household technicians, child care specialists, caterers, cooks, and health aides with the same rights and benefits and the respect other workers receive throughout the nation."

The media provided excellent coverage of the conference. Sloan spoke of its significance on Phil Donahue's talk show, then stationed in Dayton, Ohio, and to numerous regional, state, and local newspapers. *Newsweek* also covered the story, and Bill Monroe of "NBC Today" conducted a ten-to-twelve-minute interview about the conference and its implications for household workers. The largest actual coverage of the conference itself came from Sloan's own hometown paper: *The New York Times*. The conference had created such a stir that it made the Sunday front page of *The New York Times*.

When the bill to obtain fair wages and hours for household workers was first presented to President Nixon in 1973, he vetoed it. But the veto did little to dampen the enthusiasm of the workers. Vista volunteers, churches, and other organizations joined the workers to lobby for the basic benefits they were fighting to obtain. Their staunchest opposition, however, was not Richard Nixon but George Meany. If Meany would hear their pleas for equality, justice, and respect, then convincing Congress and the president would be considerably easier. That's exactly what happened. Through the unfailing efforts of the Vista volunteers and the workers, the word finally reached Meany and by late 1973, Meany announced to Nixon and the Congress that there would not be a minimum wage act that year without including household workers. With Meany's go-ahead, all knew they had indeed persevered and won.

Because the household workers did not have another immediate rallying point, Sloan could clearly see "the heydey was ebbing." A little later that same year she received a call from Carole Foreman of the Consumer Federation of America, who announced that the office needed a new head. Sloan accepted the post of director of the District of Columbia's Office of Consumer Protection in 1976 and served a two-year term. Appointed by the mayor, she served as a member of his cabinet and formulated policies for the District and directed and implemented consumer protection programs and activities. In addition to extending hours, Sloan also coordinated an all-out effort to recall and clear the shelves of fireproof children's pajamas that had been discovered to contain carcinogens. Again drawing upon community involvement and working this time with CETA (Comprehensive Employment Training Act) workers, Sloan was able to have the pajamas removed from the shelves throughout the District.

Sloan Becomes a Commissioner for Consumer Protection

Shortly after that project was completed, Sloan received a call from President Jimmy Carter asking her to serve as one of five commissioners for the Consumer Product Safety Commission. She was nominated in the fall of 1977, and with her husband, Ned Sloan, by her side and her eight-year-old-son, Douglass Sloan, holding the Bible, Edith Barksdale Sloan was sworn in as a United States Commissioner for Consumer Protection Safety on March 20, 1978. That appointment made Sloan one of the highest-ranking female appointees in the Carter Administration.

The experience as commissioner also brought with it many rewards and professional gains. As a member of this collegial body, Sloan had a mandate to protect the public against "unreasonable risk of injury associated with consumer products." To that end, she participated in establishing mandatory safety standards for consumer products and in requiring the recall, repair, replacement, or refund of the purchase price of products deemed to present substantial hazard. She also participated in decisions to ban imminently hazardous products and sat as a member of the appellate panel for cases on appeal from the rulings of the administrative law judge. Again, Sloan's work carried her across the country as she served as a spokesperson for the agency on national, regional, and local levels. Since Sloan had a fixed term, she did not leave that office with the Carter Administration, but continued with the agency under the Reagan Administration until November 1983.

Since that time, Sloan has returned to the practice of law as an independent practitioner with the firm of Fortas, Porkop, and Hardman. While she continues to practice law, her career has now taken a different turn. In January of 1989, she officially matriculated as a full-time student at Wesley Theological Seminary. Upon successfully completing her program, she will receive a master of divinity degree and become officially ordained as a minister in Unity Church.

The Sloans have raised four sons. The youngest, Douglass Ned, was named for the great abolitionist, orator, and newspaper publisher Frederick Douglass. With Douglass now in college, Sloan turns her attention more fully to a new career that has, perhaps, always been quietly in the making, waiting for just the right time to ferment and grow. Through her work, her talents, and spiritual gifts, she continues to make a mark on the world.

References

Bill Monroe, interview with Edith Barksdale Sloan. "Today Show," July 18, 1971.

"The Donahue Show." Dayton, Oh., August 5, 1971.

Evening Star. Jacqueline Trescott. 16-17 July 1971.

"Farewell to Dinah." *Newsweek* 2 August 1971: 67.

Interview with Edith Barksdale Sloan, 9 March 1990. This essay is based upon that interview.

Sunday New York Times 18 July 1971.

Washington Post. Jeannette Smyth. 17 July 1971.

Collections

Speeches that Edith Barksdale Sloan delivered while United States Commissioner and photographs taken of her during her tenure can be found in the National Archives. Speeches given and photographs taken while Sloan was director of the National Committee on Household Employment, which is now housed under the aegis of the National Urban League, are located there. Other speeches, personal papers, and photographs are housed in Sloan's personal files. Coverage of the National Conference on Household Employment can be found in the files of NBC's "Today Show" (July 18, 1971), *Newsweek* (2 August 1871), *The New York Times* (18 July 1971), "The Phil Donahue Show" (August 5, 1971), *The Evening Star*, and other local papers. Copies of her plays are housed with Unity Church and Edith Sloan.

Shirley M. Jordan

Lucy Diggs Slowe

(1885-1937)

Educator

In 1922 Lucy Diggs Slowe was offered the position of Dean of Women at Howard University. In accepting this post, which she held until her death in 1937, Slowe became the first black woman dean of the university. It was in this position that Slowe grew in prominence and became the foremost spokesperson for black women's higher education and leadership training. She worked throughout her tenure at Howard to ensure that the position "Dean of Women" at that and other black institutions carried with it the same status and authority as other administrative posts held by men. She also sought to have this position elevated from the image of "matron" or "chaperone" who kept watch over the morals of women students to one that was perceived as being concerned with all aspects of women's education.

Lucy Diggs Slowe was born July 4, 1885, in Berryville, Virginia. She was the youngest of seven children born to Henry Slowe and Fannie (Porter) Slowe. Her father died when she was six months old and her mother died when she was six years old. After the death of Slowe's parents, she was raised by a paternal aunt, Martha Slowe Prince, in Lexington, Virginia. When Slowe was thirteen, her family moved to Baltimore, Maryland, where she attended the public schools. She graduated second in her class from the Colored High School in Baltimore in 1904 and enrolled in Howard University, Washington, D.C., with scholarship aid that same year. While a student at Howard, Slowe excelled scholastically and became involved in many student activities. In 1908 she was one of the founders and vice-presidents of Alpha Kappa Alpha Sorority, the first Greek-letter organization for black women. During her senior year at Howard, Slowe was selected to be a chaperone for other women students in the dormitory for shopping trips downtown.

After Slowe graduated from Howard University in 1908, she taught English at Baltimore Colored High School. In 1915 she earned an M.A. degree in English from Columbia University and taught in a Washington, D.C., high school until 1919. When Shaw, the first junior high school for blacks, was established in the District of Columbia in 1919, Slowe was appointed principal. While at Shaw, Slowe instituted an integrated inservice course for junior high school teachers, which was conducted by Columbia University. Slowe's next and final professiona position was Dean of Women at Howard.

Slowe was greatly influenced by the works of several white women in the growing field of student personnel services, such as Esther Lloyd-Jones, Harriet Hayes, and Sarah Sturtvant at Teachers College of Columbia University and Thyrsa Amos of the University of Pittsburgh. During a period when emphasis in American higher education was being placed on educating the "whole" student, Slowe was extremely concerned that black women students were not reaping the benefits of this new movement. This concept included career guidance, athletics, health services, food service, and cultural activities, as well as academic concerns.

Slowe was not a timid person and was usually quite direct in addressing her concerns to people. From the beginning of her tenure at Howard, Slowe sought to establish a presence of authority equivalent to those of the male administrators. In January 1923 she wrote J. Stanley Durkee, the white president of Howard, requesting that all matters concerning disciplinary problems with women students be referred to her and not to him. She stated that if Durkee did not agree with her opinion on this matter, she would "become a non-entity in the University." In May 1923 Slowe proposed that the university build more dormitories for women so that she could better coordinate and supervise women's activities. Slowe noted that the women who lived off-campus were not bound by the rules of the university as were the on-campus women. These women often went to the dancehalls and theaters in the community. Consequently, Slowe believed that the activities of the off-campus women reflected poorly on the reputation of Howard's women students (Lucy Diggs Slowe to J. Stanley Durkee, 22 January 1923; May 1923, *Slowe Papers).*

Slowe was actually more concerned with developing black women culturally and preparing them for leadership rather than imposing upon them stringent rules, which were common to black colleges. Slowe was quite outspoken concerning the archaic rules that were imposed on women students and said that they were degrading and insulting. Slowe commented that "when a college woman cannot be trusted to go shopping without a chaperone she is not likely to develop powers of leadership'' (Slowe, ''The Education of Negro Women and Girls,'' 14).

Slowe was often quite critical of the traditional black church. She believed that in many instances the black church impeded the growth of women. Slowe wrote:

> It is to be remembered, too, that much of the religious philosophy upon which Negro women have been nurtured has tended toward suppressing in them their own powers. Many of them have been brought up on the antiquated philosophy of Saint Paul in reference to woman's place in the scheme of things, and all too frequently have been influenced by the philosophy of patient waiting, rather than the philosophy of developing their talents to the fullest extent (''The Colored Girl Enters College,'' 276).

Like many educated middle-class blacks of her era, Slowe tended to be Eurocentric in her cultural and religious orientation. She instituted a Cultural Series in the late 1920s and sought to stress ''high'' culture to her women students. During this period of jazz, ragtime, and blues, Slowe sought to expose her students to the fine arts, which were devoid of the sexuality and emotionalism of much of the black arts of the 1920s. In a letter of protest to the YWCA in 1925, Slowe complained that some of the performances of a benefit revue sponsored by the Y had been ''coarse and suggestive.'' Slowe characterized a ragtime piece done by a child as ''reprehensible.'' In her opinion, the YWCA needed to uphold the ideals of ''modesty, decency, and culture'' (Lucy Diggs Slowe to Martha McAdoo, 13 January 1925, *Slowe Papers*).

In addition to the Cultural Series, Slowe organized teas for the women's dormitories and gave an annual garden party at her home for the students.

In September 1926, Mordecai W. Johnson, a Baptist minister, became the first black president at Howard. Although Slowe had to challenge many decisions of the Howard administration prior to Johnson's arrival, for the duration of her term at Howard, Slowe and Johnson constantly clashed.

The first major confrontation came a few months after Johnson's arrival. In January 1927 Slowe received a complaint from a Howard parent that a male professor had used ''improper and vulgar'' language in a class of women students. Slowe discussed this incident with the professor, who then sent Slowe a letter attacking her motives and her morals. When Slowe approached President Johnson concerning this matter, he supported the male professor. Only after Slowe threatened to resign did Johnson refer the matter to the Howard Board of Trustees. The accused professor was subsequently placed on leave-of-absence with half-salary. Although Slowe could not confirm it, it was her belief that Johnson never presented all of the facts of this event to the board. With her insistence in upholding dignity and respect of the black women students, her challenge of Johnson's decision in this matter resulted in a ''persecution of Dean Slowe [that] was continuous and heartless'' (Note attached to the letter from Clarence Harvey Mills to Lucy Diggs Slowe, 11 January 1927, *Slowe Papers*).

Activities in National Women's Organizations Increase

In 1923 Slowe became the first president of the National Association of College Women (NACW), an organization of black women college graduates of accredited liberal arts colleges and universities. In her inaugural statement Slowe stressed the uniqueness and purpose of this organization. She noted that the organization was formed to raise the standards in the colleges where black women were educated; to inspire conditions for black women faculty; and to encourage advanced scholarship among women. Slowe also envisioned this organization to be the ''center of guidance, encouragement and information'' to black girls (''Proceedings of the Conference Called by the College Alumnae Club of Washington, D.C., 1923,'' in *Slowe Papers*).

Committed to the purposes of the NACW, Slowe conducted a study on the status of women on black college campuses. The results of this study were published in an article in the *Journal of Negro Education* in 1933. Slowe wrote that black women received little in courses, activities, or role-models to prepare them for leadership. A priority of the NACW was to influence the presidents of black colleges to appoint well-trained deans of women (''The Higher Education of Negro Women,'' 355). As the number of women deans and advisors to women grew on black college campuses, Slowe organized in 1929 the National Association of Deans of Women and Advisors to Girls in Negro Schools as part of the NACW. In 1935 this group became an organization independent from the NACW.

In addition to the National Association of College Women and the National Association of Deans of Women and Advisors to Girls in Negro Schools, Slowe was active in an array of women's and civic organizations. She helped found the National Council of Negro Women with Mary McLeod Bethune and served as the organization's first executive secretary. She was an active member of the YWCA and served on the advisory board of the National Youth Administration and a member of the predominantly white National Association of Deans of Women. Slowe was also extremely interested in the peace movement and attempted to encourage more black women to join this cause. She was an active member of the Women's International League for Peace and Freedom.

Slowe was a prize-winning tennis player, winning seventeen cups in an era when few blacks competed with whites in that sport. She sang contralto in Saint Francis Catholic Church and in her own Madison Street Presbyterian Church in Baltimore. Slowe's companion and housemate during the last fifteen years of her life was Mary Burrill, a well-known Washington, D.C., public school teacher and playwright.

Slowe died of kidney disease in October 1937 in her home.

She is buried in Lincoln Cemetery in Washington, D.C. There is a stained-glass window in Howard University's chapel and a dormitory named in her memory. Throughout her professional career, Slowe fought to elevate black women to a position of equality with whites and black men. She believed that black women should be prepared for the world and not just for their own communities.

References

Logan, Rayford W. "Lucy Diggs Slowe." *Dictionary of American Negro Biography*. Eds. Rayford W. Logan and Michael R. Winston. New York: Norton, 1982.

Lucy Diggs Slowe to J. Stanley Durkee, 22 January 1923; May 1923. *Slowe Papers*.

Lucy Diggs Slowe to Martha McAdoo, 13 January 1925, *Slowe Papers*.

Mills, Clarence Harvey. Letter to Lucy Diggs Slowe. Note attached to letter, 11 January 1927. *Slowe Papers*.

"Proceedings of the Conference Called by the College Alumnae Club of Washington, D.C., 1923." *Slowe Papers*.

Slowe, Lucy Diggs. "The Colored Girl Enters College." *Opportunity* 15 (September 1937): 276-79.

———. "The Education of Negro Women and Girls." Address delivered at Teachers College, Columbia University, 11 March 1931. *Slowe Papers*.

———. "The Higher Education of Negro Women." *Journal of Negro Education* 2 (July 1933): 352-58.

Wright, Marion Thompson. "Lucy Diggs Slowe." *Notable American Women*. Vol. 3. Cambridge: Harvard University Press, 1971.

Collections

Information concerning the National Association of College Women and the National Association of Deans of Women and Advisors to Girls in Negro Schools is found in the Slowe Papers, Moorland-Spingarn Research Center, Howard University. The papers also contain photographs of Slowe. An excellent account of Slowe's career is given in "Brickbats and Roses: The Career of Lucy Diggs Slowe," unpublished paper of Karen Anderson (in possession of the author).

Linda M. Perkins

Ada Smith "Bricktop"

(1894-1984)

Singer, entertainer, nightclub hostess

Ada Beatrice Queen Victoria Louise Virginia "Bricktop" Smith, an entertainer and nightclub owner in New York, Paris, Rome, and Mexico City, who rubbed shoulders with the wealthy and artistic elite on two continents, was born in Alderson, West Virginia, on August 14, 1894. T. S. Eliot commented about the event thirty years later: "And on that day Bricktop was born, and to her thorn, she gave a rose" (Neimark, 70). Choosing a name for their daughter proved to be a difficult task for Ada Smith's parents. Not only didn't they want to offend anyone, but they wanted to please certain significant individuals as well. The only solution was to select several names, thereby placating as many people as possible. Beatrice was their pharmacist's choice; Ada and Queen Victoria were probably her mother's idea; the other names were chosen to appease the neighbors (Bricktop and Haskins, 3-4).

Ada Smith was the third daughter and the youngest of the five children of Thomas Smith, a barber, and Hattie E. (Thompson) Smith. Hattie Smith, who was of Irish descent and seven-eighths white, was born into slavery about 1861. Ada Smith's maternal grandmother had white skin, blue-gray eyes, and blond hair. Her maternal grandfather was probably her mother's master. Little is known of Thomas Smith's family. He died in his mid-forties after a series of strokes when his youngest child was four years old.

One of Ada Smith's four siblings died in infancy. There were two sisters, Etta "Blonzetta" Smith Belfant, born about 1883, and Ethel Smith, born about 1889. Ethel Smith was shot to death in 1920 by her husband's girlfriend. A brother, Robert Smith, was born in about 1891 and died in 1913 at age twenty-two of tuberculosis.

Shortly after the death of her father, Smith's mother decided to move her family to Chicago. Hattie Smith's first job was as a housekeeper, but she soon began to run rooming houses. Ada Smith attended public school in Chicago but dropped out at age sixteen to pursue a full-time stage career (Bricktop and Haskins, 7-23).

Ada Smith's stage debut came long before she had begun school. Shortly after the family arrived in Chicago, a company rehearsing a production of *Uncle Tom's Cabin* announced that the part of a small child remained unfilled. Someone in the company had seen Smith and asked for her mother's permission to allow her to play the part. Hattie Smith reluctantly consented.

Singing and dancing became an increasingly important activity for Smith. She accepted parts in many plays and shows at school. Her childhood dream was to be an acrobatic dancer. On one memorable occasion, Smith's mother took her to the local jail to sing and dance for the inmates. She envied her sister Ethel, who was invited to sing at a local saloon. Nonetheless, it was the nearby Pekin Theatre that fascinated Smith the most.

The Pekin Theatre was the first theater of any consequence in Chicago to be devoted to black drama. Owned and operated by Bob Motts and his nephews, the Pekin opened in 1902. It boasted its own resident stock company, the Pekin Players. Attending productions at the Pekin was a special thrill for the Smith children. Ever present in the back of Smith's mind was a desire to be on the stage rather than in the audience. Her opportunity came when she was about fifteen. She auditioned for a place in the chorus of the Pekin Players and won a part. Her career was short-lived however, as her mother insisted that she return to school.

When Smith was sixteen, she left school permanently and began her entertainment career. Bob Motts was preparing to take the vaudeville comedy team of Flournoy Miller and Aubrey Lyles on tour and he needed young singers for the chorus. Ada Smith was chosen to be a member of the touring company, but lack of funding forced the show to cancel after only a few performances.

Ada Smith was still too young to sing in saloons, so she continued to look for theater work. She accepted a job as a chorus member with the Georgia Troubadours, which featured comedian Bill McCabe in stock minstrel numbers. The lyrics of the songs, such as those of the notorious minstrel tune "Rufus Rastus Johnson Brown" were degrading, but Smith remained unperturbed. She later remarked that "it didn't bother me to sing that kind of song. That's what you did in a minstrel show. It's what the audience wanted, and if you wanted to be on stage, you gave the audiences what they came for" (Bricktop and Haskins, 26).

Ada Smith left the Georgia Troubadours after several months to return to Chicago and look for a better paying job. She was asked by Oma Crosby to join the Oma Crosby Trio as a replacement member for their upcoming tour. While on tour the hours were grueling, but the salary was slightly higher than what Smith had earned in the past. What's more, she was grateful for the opportunity to perform in distant cities, including Cincinnati, New York, and Philadelphia.

During her stay in New York with the Crosby Trio, Smith met saloon owner Barron Wilkins. She was not yet eighteen years old but had managed to gain admission to Wilkins's well-known cafe on Seventh Avenue and 134th Street. Wilkins was so taken with Smith's red hair that he decided to call her "Bricktop"—and the name remained with her thereafer.

Entertainer Performs at Nightlubs and Saloons

Smith longed to become a saloon performer, and her first opportunity came just shy of her eighteenth birthday as a replacement for Rose Brown, an entertainer at Roy Jones's saloon in Chicago. Ada Smith was immediately popular with the customers, and when Brown recovered, Jones kept Smith on. While working at Jones's, Smith met boxing champion Jack Johnson, who invited her to perform at his saloon, the Cabaret de Champion. Johnson's cafe was the first such establishment in Chicago to be racially integrated. Smith remained at the Cabaret de Champion until it closed in 1912.

Numerous saloon engagements followed for Smith, including performances with Florence Mills at the Panama Club. Along with Cora Green, the three young women became known as the Panama Trio. Their act flourished and they might have continued at the Panama indefinitely if a scandal involving a shooting incident at the bar had not forced the cafe to close.

In 1917, Smith left the Panama Trio and set out for Los Angeles, where she accepted a job entertaining at the Watts Country Club. She began to keep company with Walter Delaney, a friend of the club's owner. Eventually they rented a bungalow together, but their relationship soon became stormy. Delaney had a history of involvement with drugs, gambling, and prostitution, and his efforts to curtail his illicit activities frequently met with failure. When the Los Angeles police began a vice eradication campaign, he and Smith were forced to flee to San Francisco. Eventually Delaney left Smith and moved to Seattle, preferring to live without her rather than continue to drag her down with him in his mire of hopeless drug addiction. They were never together again. Smith recalled years later:

> If I ever loved anyone in my life, it was Walter. How can you help but love a man who tries to lift himself up because he loves you? He was bitter with himself because he failed to do what he wanted to do. But he did try. What else can you ask of a man but that he try? (Bricktop and Haskins, 69).

In 1922, Smith returned to New York and worked again at Barron's cafe. Barron's now catered to a rich, famous, and mostly white clientele. Smith made the acquaintance of many notables while there, including Joan Crawford, John Barrymore, playwright Charles MacArthur, and gangster Jack "Legs" Diamond. Occasionally Smith took time off from Barron's to travel to Washington, D.C., to perform at the Oriental Gardens Cafe. The music for Smith's act was provided by the Washingtonians, whose pianist was Duke Ellington.

In 1924, while still employed by Barron, Smith accepted an invitation to travel to Paris to perform. At that time, there were fewer than a dozen black entertainers in all of Paris. Smith was hired by Sammy Richardson to replace Florence Jones at the Cafe Le Grand Duc. She traveled on the luxury oceanliner *America* and arrived in Le Havre on May 11, 1924, after an eleven-day voyage.

Le Grand Duc was located in Montmartre at Fifty-two Rue Pigalle. The diminutive size and cramped quarters of the Montmartre cafes were a disappointment to Smith, who was accustomed to a dance floor large enough to accommodate several musicians and dancers. Nonetheless she enjoyed her work and made new friends. One of her first acquaintances at Le Grand Duc was a busboy, the young and fledgling author Langston Hughes. Members of the Parisian artistic and wealthy crowd who discovered Smith and Le Grand Duc included Zelda and F. Scott Fitzgerald, Fred Astaire, Ernest Hemingway, Man Ray, Pablo Picasso, John Steinbeck, Josephine Baker, Elsa Maxwell, and Cole and Linda Porter. Smith was earning one hundred dollars a week—a respectable salary in those days.

In 1925 Cole Porter began to give "Charleston" parties at his house—two or three a week. He invited Smith to attend and teach his guests how to dance the Charleston. Porter's friends represented the best-known of Parisian society, most of whom were eager to learn the latest American dance crazes. The Charleston had not yet reached Europe, and Porter wanted to be at least partially responsible for its introduction in Paris. Smith's friendship with the Porters' grew, and in 1926 she was invited to spend the summer with them at their palazzo in Venice. She wasn't missed at Le Grand Duc, as most of the Montmartre night life ceased during the hot Parisian summers. At the Porters there were frequent and lavish parties, with Smith teaching the Charleston and overseeing the other entertainment. In her later years, Smith gratefully acknowledged Porter's assistance in helping establish her career as a cafe entertainer. He purchased expensive clothing for her and introduced her to the Parisian elite. At no time, however, did she feel patronized by Porter: Their genuine friendship never took on the air of a sponsor-protégée relationship.

Shortly after returning to Paris in the fall of 1926, Smith followed the advice of a friend and decided to open up her own saloon. It was called the Music Box and was located just down the street from Le Grand Duc. Before opening to the public, the Prince of Wales hosted a party at Smith's cafe. He brought with him his royal entourage and an enthusiasm for the latest in American dances—the Charleston and the more recent black bottom. Smith applied for and was granted a *provisoire*—a temporary operating license—and the public flocked to the Music Box. With Porter's following and the continued patronage of various members of the British royalty, Smith's cafe was a smash success, but the provisional license expired and Smith was unable to obtain a permanent permit. Regrettably, the Music Box closed its doors.

Bricktop Opens Cafe in Paris

Smith returned to Le Grand Duc only to find that its owners, George Jamerson and his wife, were eager to retire from the nightclub business. They requested that she take over the cafe—an offer she accepted only after consultation with Cole Porter. Within the year, however, Smith wanted a more chic establishment. She settled on a location across the street from Le Grand Duc. Again she sought Porter's advice, this time on choosing a name for her newly-acquired cafe. His response was succinct and telling: "Bricktop's," he said. "That's the only thing you should call it. It's your place, it's you. You're the reason why people come" (Bricktop and Haskins, 119). Within a year Bricktop's became widely known as one of the most elegant clubs in Paris.

In 1927 Smith met saxophonist Peter Ducongé. He grew up in New Orleans and had come to Paris with Leon Abbey's band. Like many black musicians in Paris in the late 1920s, he gravitated to Bricktop's. Ducongé was easygoing, likeable, and a stylish dresser. He and Smith developed an immediate rapport, and for her birthday in 1928, Ducongé gave Smith a nine-carat diamond ring.

In spite of the depression, the cafe business continued to be profitable for Smith. She moved to a larger apartment, one with three bedrooms, a living room, a kitchen, and two bathrooms—spacious by Parisian standards. Ducongé moved in with her and on December 19, 1929, they were married. The reception was held at Bricktop's. In 1930 the Ducongés purchased an estate in Bougival, outside Paris. Smith took up gardening as a hobby and Ducongé started a chicken farm.

In 1931 Smith opened a bigger cafe—three times the size of the original Bricktop's. She hired the well-known George Hoyningen-Huené to design the lighting and Neil Martin as interior decorator. The new Bricktop's opened in November 1931. Ducongé wasn't interested in becoming a partner in the cafe business, so Smith took on Mabel Mercer as her assistant. It was at Bricktop's that Mercer tried her wings. She later recalled, "If I know anything about taking care of people, I got it from Bricktop" (Bricktop and Haskins, 161).

As was the custom for all Montmartre cafes, Bricktop's closed for the hot month of August. At the suggestion of friends, Smith filled the void by opening another cafe in Biarritz, a resort where the rich and famous spent the hottest five or six weeks of the year. Opening night was a huge success, attended by the Prince of Wales and other notables. At the end of the brief Biarritz season, the Ducongés and Mercer returned to Paris to reopen the original Bricktop's.

Shortly after the 1932 fall season was underway, Cole Porter arrived at Bricktop's with a new song he had just written. Based on the Frankie and Johnnie legend, it was called "Miss Otis Regrets She's Unable to Lunch Today." The song became popular with Smith's customers, so much so that she recalled singing it several times an evening on more than one occasion. It was dedicated to their mutual friend Elsa Maxwell, but Smith laid false claim to the song and even announced to her audiences and clientele that Porter had actually written it for her.

Smith's relationship with Ducongé began to falter sometime in 1933. At Smith's insistence, he moved out of their country estate, but it was agreed that he could continue to perform at Bricktop's until other employment was found. He left Paris several months later when Louis Armstrong summoned him to London. In spite of their separation, Smith and Ducongé remained friends and frequently sought each other's assistance. Years later Smith loaned Ducongé a substantial sum of money to help finance his cafe in Harlem. When he became seriously ill in the 1960s, Smith again offered assistance. They did not have any children and were never divorced.

The year 1934 was a difficult time in Paris. The depression gradually impinged upon the cafe business until Smith was forced to give up her country villa and move Bricktop's to a smaller, more affordable location. It was a time when esprit de corps in Montmartre reached new levels as the artistic and rich banded together to help each other out. Smith borrowed money from her mother, who was visiting from the United States at the time, and from Ducongé, who was still performing in London.

By the fall of 1936 Smith could no longer gather up enough cash to reopen Bricktop's for another season. To make ends meet, she and her constant companion and friend, Mabel Mercer, entertained at various nightspots both in Paris and in Cannes. Smith's mother returned to the United States, and Mercer followed shortly thereafter in October 1938. About a month later a cablegram arrived from Blonzetta Smith Belfant in Chicago with the news that Smith's mother had died. She was buried in the family plot in Alderson, West Virginia. Smith was unable to make the trip back to the United States to attend her mother's funeral.

When Hitler marched into Poland in August 1939, the reality and suffering of war hit Paris. The American consulate insisted that all Americans leave France. To stay meant risking internment under German rule. Fearful of her future in a country she had left behind sixteen years earlier, Smith was reluctant to leave. Paris had become her home. But there was no alternative and with the financial assistance of her friends, the Duchess of Windsor and Lady Elsie de Wolfe Mendl, Smith was booked in a private cabin on the *Washington* for her return voyage. She set sail on October 26, 1939, and was among the last American entertainers to leave France.

Smith almost immediately found life in New York to be vastly different than what she had grown accustomed to in Paris. Racial segregation was just beginning to break down, but out of habit Smith headed straight for Harlem: "I had just taken it for granted that I would have to go to Harlem," she later recalled (Bricktop and Haskins, 208). Most nightclubs were still segregated and black entertainers scrounged for work. Smith first sought employment in the white nightclubs and met only moderate success. She remarked, "Across the pond things are different. Negroes were as welcome in my place as any of the ritziest white people. I made no distinction. In America it's far different and one finds himself at wit's end to keep clear of ugly or embarrassing situations" (Burley, 8). To some, she had gotten "too big for her britches during those years in Paris" (Bricktop and Haskins, 211). Even her Jewish acquaintances seemed resentful at times. Speaking to a Jewish friend, she summed up her assessment of the situation: "I always thought Negroes and Jews needed each other. Maybe you haven't seen what's happening to your people in Europe, but I have" (Bricktop and Haskins, 211).

Nonetheless, Smith entertained at a number of cafes and attracted the Paris crowd that had settled in New York. But when her Bricktop's following headed for warmer climates in the dead of winter, she found herself without a steady clientele. Undaunted, she made the acquaintance of several important nightclub operators and was a partner in the financing and management of a new cafe, the Brittwood, which opened June 12, 1940, on 140th Street. The media linked her romantically with Harry Robinson, the club's master of ceremonies, and claimed that they were engaged. The marriage never took place (*New York Amsterdam News*, 22 June 1940, 21).

At first the Brittwood was a successful venture, attracting New York celebrities and such well-known entertainers as Earl Hines, Anna Jones, Willie Grant, Minnie Hilton, and Robert Taylor. But a friend of Smith's who told her, "America isn't ready for you, Bricktop," was correct. Without people she knew from Paris she was lost. And even when they were in town, they were displaced persons—it was impossible to recapture the ambience of Montmartre. She decided to try her luck in Mexico City, but before departing, she made one more major change in her life. In 1943 she converted to Catholicism.

Mexico City was home for Smith for the next six years. She was part-owner of two well-known clubs, the Minuit and Chavez's. In time she grew to love Mexico and its people. Her new-found religious zeal helped make the difficult times bearable. She left Mexico reluctantly in July 1949, eager to start anew in Paris.

The Paris Smith returned to was vastly different from the pre-war days. Parisians had begun to reflect some of the distinctly American attitudes towards blacks—an attitude Smith believes was imported and perpetuated by white American soldiers.

Starting a new business in post-war Paris was a process impeded every inch of the way by bureaucratic snarls, but Smith persevered. The new Bricktop's opened in May 1950 to a grateful clientele. Janet Flanner wrote in *The New Yorker*: "With pleasure, this correspondent can announce that Bricktop, still unspoiled in 1950, is back again in Paris, in a new red, gold, and white damask club of her own, on the Rue Fontaine. Her recent opening night was an extraordinary, chic jam of people who were in Bricktop's circle twenty-five years ago" (Genét [Janet Flanner], 60-61).

The magic of old Montmartre proved to be capricious and fleeting, with few nights as glorious as opening night. By Christmas 1950 business was bleak, forcing Smith to close the club. She traveled to Rome and opened the first Rome Bricktop's on Via Veneto in early 1951. The clientele of opening night read like a *Who's Who* of Italian high society and royalty.

While in Italy, Smith became involved in Catholic charity work. In various fund-raising projects, she was able to take advantage of her comfortable position as an internationally-known hostess and entertainer. She raised money for institutions housing children orphaned during the war. Her dedication drew the attention of many church leaders, including Bishop Fulton J. Sheen, with whom she became close friends. A favorite possession of Smith's was a book by Sheen autographed "To my child in Christ, Bricktop, who proves every walk of life can be spiritualized—from Bishop Sheen" (Bricktop and Haskins, 253-261).

On March 6, 1964, Smith announced that she was retiring from the nightclub business: "I'm tired, honey. Tired of staying up until dawn every day" (Bricktop and Haskins, 279-80). She had begun to feel the discomfort of arthritis and was recently diagnosed as having a heart condition. She returned to Chicago in 1965 to be with her ailing sister Blonzetta, who died two years later.

With no one to keep her in Chicago any longer, she traveled to various places, including Los Angeles and London, finally settling in New York. She made her only recording in 1970—a rendition of "So Long, Baby"—with the assistance of Cy Coleman. In 1973 she shared the stage with an aging Josephine Baker, who was attempting a comeback, and that same year she made a film documentary entitled *Honeybaby, honeybaby!* (Bogle, 193). Columbia College in Chicago awarded Smith an honorary doctor of arts degree in 1975. She made few public appearances after 1979 owing to her frail health. On her last birthday, in 1983, New York City Mayor Edward Koch presented Smith with a seal of the city and a certificate of appreciation for "extraordinary talent and indomitable spirit" (Slonimsky, 2152). Her autobiography, entitled *Bricktop*, written with the assistance of author James Haskins, was published in 1983.

Smith died in her sleep on January 31, 1984. A mass was celebrated in her honor at St. Malachy's Church in New York with more than three-hundred people in attendance. Participants in the mass included Ruth Ellington, sister of Duke Ellington, James Haskins, and columnist Jack O'Brian. Smith was buried in Woodlawn Cemetery in the Bronx (*New York Times* 5 February 1984; Levy, 12-14).

References

Bogle, Donald. *Brown Sugar: Eighty Years of America's Black Female Superstars*. New York: Harmony Books, 1980.

"Bricktop." *Our World* 2 (September 1947): 46-47.

Bricktop [Ada Smith Ducongé], and James Haskins. *Bricktop*. New York: Athenaeum, 1983.

"Bricktop's $$ [*sic*] Backs Nitery." *New York Amsterdam News* (22 June 1940): 21.

———. "Bricktop: The Name On a Thousand Lips." *New York Amsterdam News* (25 November 1939): 8.

Genét [Janet Flanner]. "Letter from Paris." *The New Yorker* 26 (27 May 1950): 60-61.

Grafton, David. *Red, Hot and Rich*. New York: Stein and Day, 1987.

Hughes, Langston. "Bricktop." In *The Big Sea*. New York: Hill and Wang, 1963. Reprinted. New York: Thunder's Mouth Press, 1986.

Krebs, Albin. "Bricktop, Cabaret Queen in Paris and Rome, Dead." *The New York Times* (1 February 1984): B-10.

Levy, Margot, ed. "Bricktop." In *The Annual Obituary: 1984*. Chicago: St. James Press, 1984.

Neimark, Paul. "Queen of Saloon Keepers." *Sepia* 24 (August 1975): 69-77.

New York Amsterdam News (22 June 1940): 21.

Slonimsky, Nicolas. *Baker's Biographical Dictionary of Musicians*. 7th ed. New York: Schirmer Books, 1984.

"Smith, Ada Beatrice Queen Victoria Louise Virginia (Bricktop), 1894-1984." *Contemporary Authors*. Vol. 3. Detroit: Gale Research, 1984.

Southern, Eileen. "Smith, Ada Beatrice ('Bricktop')." *Biographical Dictionary of Afro-American and African Musicians*. Westport, Conn.: Greenwood Press, 1982.

"300 Attend Service for the Singer Bricktop." *New York Times* (5 February 1984): 32.

Collections

Smith bequeathed all her personal papers to author James Haskins, who in turn donated them to the Schomburg Center for Research in Black Culture of the New York Public Library.

Juanita Karpf

Amanda Berry Smith

(1837-1915)

Missionary, religious leader

Amanda Berry Smith, a remarkable missionary-evangelist who worked on four continents and whose life was a testament to indefatigable service to humanity, was born a

Amanda Berry Smith

slave on January 23, 1837, in Long Green, Maryland, about twenty miles from Baltimore. Her father, Samuel Berry, and her mother, Mariam (Matthews) Berry, were slaves on the adjoining farms of Shadrach Green and Darby Insor. She was one of thirteen children, five of them born in slavery. Samuel Berry was a favorite of his young mistress, daughter of his owner, who, on her deathbed, exacted from her parents the promise that he would be allowed to purchase his freedom and, subsequently, that of his wife and children. He was a man of great physical stamina, determination, and intelligence, and he was able to move his freed family to a farm in York County, Pennsylvania, a number of years before the Civil War. The Berry home soon became a station on the Underground Railroad. Smith heard many stories of the work of helping slaves to escape northward, and she began to dream of securing an education for herself and working in the freedom movement.

Both parents could read and strongly desired education for their children. They taught Smith what they could at home, but she was able to obtain very little formal education, the whole of it amounting to only a few months. However, she began at a very early age to grasp every opportunity to learn. She had already decided on her life's work, and she was never to be turned back.

Spiritual Conversion Compels Smith

Family life grew more difficult for the Berrys as the number of children continued to increase. Smith became a domestic worker and in September of 1854, at age 17, she married Calvin Devine of Columbia, Pennsylvania. It was not a happy marriage, but she drew considerable strength from her conversion, which took place in Columbia in 1856. Several of the women for whom she worked at one time or another as a domestic encouraged her to attend some of the camp meetings and tent revivals that were so popular at that time, not always because of their religious import. For a time she attended the Tuesday night meetings that Phoebe Palmer held in New Utrecht, New York, when she was living there. But her life was truly transformed on a Sunday in November 1870, in Brooklyn. Smith later wrote in her *Autobiography*:

> Sister Scott, my band sister and myself went to the Fleet Street A. M. E. Church. It was Communion Sunday. . . . Brother . . . took his text. I was sitting with my eyes closed in silent prayer to God, and after he had been preaching about ten minutes, as I opened my eyes, just over his head I seemed to see a beautiful star, and as I looked at it, it seemed to form into the shape of a large white tulip; and I said, "Lord, is that what you want me to see? If so, what else?" And then I leaned back and closed my eyes. Just then I saw a large letter G, and I said, "Lord, do you want me to read in Genesis or in Galatians? Lord, what does this mean?" Just then I saw the letter O. I said, "Why, that means Go." And I said, "What else?" And a voice distinctly said to me, "Go preach."

It was for Amanda Smith an unmistakable call to the Christian ministry, a call that she answered with immediate, total commitment and enthusiasm.

Her first husband having been killed in the Civil War, Amanda Smith had met and married James Smith in Philadelphia. Smith was an ordained deacon in that city's Bethel Church, the founding congregation of the African Methodist Episcopal (AME) Church. After the marriage he decided, much to Amanda Smith's disappointment, to leave the deaconry, and he died not long after she received her call. Although she had given birth to several children during her two marriages, by 1870 only her daughter Mazie survived. Amanda Smith decided to devote herself diligently to her evangelistic work. She began her work in Salem, New Jersey. It soon became evident that this woman possessed a most compelling spiritual presence, which she was able to communicate to others in a most remarkable way. Her sermons were further enhanced by her rich singing voice, and she often burst into song as she preached and testified and ministered to those who came around her.

Sexism Encountered in the Pulpit

Through her husband, Amanda Smith had come into contact with and under the influence of the AME Church, which was spreading throughout America, the Caribbean countries, and Africa. But as she became more involved in the church, she met considerable resistance from many of the men who pastored these congregations and were opposed to the admission of women to the pulpit. Nevertheless, there were always those whom she was quickly able to win over to her support. She was to recall in her book:

> In May, '70 or '71 (actually '72), the General Conference of the A. M. E. Church was held at Nashville, Tennessee. . . .
>
> The election of delegates to the General Conference the next year was a very prominent feature of the Conference; of course every minister wanted, or hoped to be elected as delegate. As I listened, my heart throbbed. This was the first time in all these years that this religious body of black men, with a black church from beginning to end, was to be assembled south of Mason and Dixon's line. . . . I ventured to ask one of the brethren, who had been elected delegate to tell me how much it would cost to go to Nashville. I would like to go if it did not cost too much.
>
> He looked at me in surprise, mingled with half disgust; the very idea of one looking like me to want to go to the General Conference; they cut their eye at my big poke bonnet, with not a flower, not a feather. He said "I tell you, Sister, it will cost money to go down there; and if you ain't got plenty of it, it's no use to go," and turned away and smiled; and another said:
>
> "What does she want to go for?"
>
> "Woman preacher; they want to be ordained," was the reply.
>
> "I mean to fight this thing," said the other.
>
> "Yes, indeed, so will I," said another.
>
> Then a slight look to see if I took it in. I did; but in spite of it all I believed God would have me go. He knew that the thought of ordination came from Him, Who said, "Ye have not chosen Me, but I have chosen you, and ordained you, that you might go and bring forth fruit, and that your fruit might remain". . . .

Amanda Smith persisted. Moreover, her testimony and religious experiences were interdenominational in spirit, and she cultivated relationships with religious groups of varying orientation.

Smith Spreads Evangelism Abroad

During the AME general conference of 1872 Amanda Smith heard that the church was sending missionaries to Africa. She resolved to prepare her daughter, Mazie, for such a ministry, thinking herself academically and intellectually incapable of such work. She devoted her best efforts over the ensuing six years to this endeavor. The daughter, upon reaching maturity, decided against going to Africa, married, and remained in the United States. Smith resolved that she herself would go to Africa as soon as she could. In 1876 she went to conduct services in England, where her fame spread. She toured several European countries, notably France and Italy, before being persuaded by a friend to move her evangelistic activities to India. Accordingly, after having made provisions for her daughter's comfort in America, she sailed from Suez, bound for Bombay, on October 26, 1879.

Her sojourn in India was a great success, exceeding even her most expansive expectations. Attendance at her service remained consistently high, even when her associates were unable to sustain the interest of large numbers of people. Most people initially came out of a pleasure-seeking kind of curiosity, but they returned because of the religious fervor and magnetism of the evangelist.

Inevitably, Amanda Berry Smith's activities generated much controversy concerning the appropriateness of women as preachers and evangelists. But her abilities as speaker and singer made of her a most commanding communicator who was able to overcome much of the prejudice that had existed before her coming. During her time in India she regained the strength she had earlier lost, and found herself refreshed and ready for more years to be spent in Christian service.

Amanda Smith returned to America for a period of about six months. Then in 1881 she set out for Africa for a period of service that was to last for eight years. She had long had a concern for the spiritual and economic development of that continent, especially its westernmost areas. It was a concern engendered in her by her parents, and one to which she had hoped to be able to respond. During her years in Africa she worked with several Methodist missionaries, the most prominent of whom was William Taylor, Methodist Episcopal Bishop of Africa. Bishop Taylor became one of her most vocal admirers, and he maintained that she was phenomenal in her influence upon the lives of all with whom she came in contact. Amanda Berry Smith, said the bishop, had done more for the cause of missions in Africa than all of her predecessors combined. She also worked with people from other denominations that were active in the countries of West Africa at the time, mainly Liberia and Sierra Leone. She organized numerous temperance societies.

Her gift of communication remained strong, as did her joy in her work. It was indeed amazing how she could establish almost instant sympathy with her listeners and coworkers, even among people who spoke no English, just as she did not speak their language. But her appeal cut across all lines of race, class, and age. One individual writing from India after he had worked with this extraordinary woman declared, "India has had many visitors of rank and wealth, but we are sure that very few of them have contributed as much to her real advantage as this obscure colored woman, poor in this world's riches and unschooled in earthly learning, but very rich toward God and well instructed in the school of Christ. How earnestly this land and every other, cries out for much such." The same statement might have been offered in any of the locations to which Smith turned her attention, both earlier and later.

Surely it must have been very difficult for Smith to observe many of the indignities and cruelties and un-Christian practices to which the native African women were subjected, but though she identified with these women on an ethnic basis, she was convinced that the culture of America, tempered by the presence of Christian belief, was superior to the habits and requirements of the people to whom she ministered. Part of the conversion that she strove to bring about was concerned with the transfer of these cultural values to their own daily lives.

While Smith was in Africa she adopted a native boy and girl, with the intention of educating them and returning them to Africa where they would continue her work. When, in 1890, she planned several months of evangelizing in Great Britain prior to her return to the United States that year, she brought these two young people with her and arranged to place them in English schools. However, on the eve of her departure for America, the girl, who had difficulty in adjusting to the climate of the country, fell ill and was soon returned to Africa under Smith's continuing responsibility. The boy remained in England and returned home to work as a missionary after having finished his educational course.

Orphans Receive Attention

It had been fourteen years since Smith had left for Europe and Africa. For a time after her return she preached in various locations along the eastern seaboard before relocating to Chicago. Her life to this point had been very eventful. She wanted now to pause and reflect on many rich experiences, write an account of her life, and continue her work in the temperance movement, but at a more subdued level. She published her *Autobiography* in 1893. By her own account, it was in 1894, while attending the convention of the Women's Christian Temperance Union, that she considered the question, "What have you done to help your own people in a permanent way that will live after you are gone?" The idea of establishing a home for orphans occurred to her, and she set about acquiring land in Harvey, Illinois, the site of a temperance community that had commanded her attention. She supported this new endeavor with her savings, the proceeds from the sale of her book, and the profits from her newspaper, *The Helper*. In spite of the support she also received from several large donors, it was necessary for her to return to her singing and preaching in the churches in order to obtain sufficient funds to advance her project. She was able to purchase a twelve-room house in Harvey, for which she paid six thousand dollars, and in 1899 the Amanda Smith Industrial Home opened its doors.

A wealthy Florida real estate dealer, George Sebring, who had become interested in Smith's life and work, had repeatedly offered her a house in Sebring, Florida, for her use as a retirement home. In October of 1912 she accepted his offer and moved to Florida. A very comfortable and attractive cottage was outfitted for her use, and she was lovingly attended and cared for in this setting. Here Smith would be able to achieve the rest and repose that she had so richly earned.

Upon her decision to move to Florida, the orphanage that she had directed since its inception applied for and received a state charter. But the school had been mired in financial difficulties since its opening and had remained open only under the most difficult of circumstances. It was not surprising that, given the school's financial status, Smith had experienced great problems in retaining a staff of adequate size and training. It was only by the force of her personality that she had been able to keep it in operation as long as she had, for the school had been threatened with closure on numerous occasions. Besides, it had been the only Protestant-run home in the state that offered care to black children. The home continued in operation for several years after Smith's departure, albeit at a substandard level, until the building was destroyed by fire in 1918.

It was in the cottage at Sebring that Amanda Berry Smith lived out the remaining years of her life. There was so much of her work on which she could reflect—the years of preaching and evangelizing, her work in the temperance movement worldwide, her impact upon scores, even hundreds, of other religious workers, her service to children on four continents—Europe, Africa, Asia, and North America—and her advocacy for women's rights. She maintained her interest in missionary activities both in America and abroad, and her memory remained fresh among those fortunate people who had the privilege of knowing and working with her.

In 1915, in Sebring, Amanda Berry Smith succumbed to a paralytic stroke. Her seventy-eight years had been as productive as any individual might hope a life to be. Her body was returned to Chicago, where a heavily-attended celebration of her life was held at Quinn Chapel African Methodist Episcopal Church. The leading local and national figures of that denomination's hierarchy paid her tribute, along with the many leaders of the Women's Christian Temperance Union and the Methodist Episcopal Church. She was buried in Harvey, Illinois.

References

"Amanda Berry Smith." *Afro-American Women Writers 1746-1933: An Anthology and Critical Guide*. Ann Allen Shockley, ed. Boston: G. K. Hall, 1988.

Bracey, John H., Jr. "Amanda Berry Smith." *Notable American Women*. Vol. III, P-Z. Edward T. James, ed. Cambridge: The Belknap Press of Harvard University Press, 1971.

Brown, Hallie Q., ed. *Homespun Heroines*. Xenia, Ohio: Aldine Publishing Co., 1926.

Cadbury, M. H. *The Life of Amanda Smith*. Birmingham, England: 1916.

Loewenberg, Bert James, and Keith Bogin, eds. *Black Women in Nineteenth Century American Life*. University Park, Pa.: Pennsylvania State University Press, 1976.

Miller, Basil. *Ten Slaves Who Became Famous*. Grand Rapids, Mich.: Zondervan Publishing House, 1951.

Smith, Amanda. *An Autobiography: The Story of the*

Lord's Dealings with Amanda Smith, the Colored Evangelist. Chicago: 1893.

Spear, Allan. *Black Chicago: The Making of a Negro Elite 1890-1920*. Chicago: University of Chicago Press, 1967.

Collections

The Julius Rosenwald Papers at the Regenstein Library, the University of Chicago, contain information on the management of the orphanage. A full-lenth biography of Amanda Berry Smith is in progress.

Lois L. Dunn

Bessie Smith "Empress of the Blues"

(1894-1937)

Singer

Bessie Smith is one of the most important women in the history of American music: She was the first to change a folk expression into an indigenous art form by successfully blending African and Western modes of music. The blues-jazz she sang is a significant base of one of America's chief contributions to world culture. She was a master performer with a commanding stage presence and a rich contralto that could project the deepest emotions. She set a new standard of excellence. People who saw her perform described her as Junoesque, mesmerizing, hypnotic, and majestic, earning her the name, Empress of the Blues.

Bessie Smith

Louis Armstrong, another American jazz genius, who was the trumpeter on nine of Smith's records, admired the way she expressed her deep feeling and spoke about how thrilling he found the way she phrased her blues notes. Another view of Smith comes from Gunther Schuller's *Early Jazz*, the book he wrote when he was the president of the New England Conservatory of Music:

> [M]ore than any other singer, she set the blues tradition in terms of style and quality. She not only gave a special musical aura to this tradition but her own singing and the accompaniments of the many great jazz artists who assisted her in her recordings placed it firmly in the broader jazz tradition (227).

Bessie Smith was born in Chattanooga, Tennessee, on April 15, 1894, and died on September 26, 1937, in Clarksdale, Mississippi. Contrary to popular belief, she was unrelated to Mamie, Clara, and Trixie Smith. Her given name was Bessie, not Elizabeth, as some sources suggest. She was one of six children in a poor family. Her father, William Smith, a part-time preacher, died shortly after her birth and her mother, Laura, who did laundry to support the family, died when Bessie was nine years old. Her oldest sister, Viola, also did laundry while trying to raise her sisters and brothers as well as her own baby.

Heroic figures are always surrounded by myths and legends, making it difficult to separate the fact from the fiction. The fictions about Smith are often taken as gospel truth and are repeated. Part of the legend about young Bessie is that she cared very little for school except for performing in school plays, but we know that she learned to read and write. Additionally, Smith had to be extremely bright to organize and produce shows, write more than twenty-five songs, and forge a synthesis of various musics. As a child she performed for pennies on the streets of Chattanooga, singing and dancing to the guitar accompaniment of her brother Andrew.

Smith's brother Clarence had joined the Moses Stokes Show, and when they played in Chattanooga, he arranged an audition for his younger sister. The most believable story about the episode is that Bessie Smith joined the troupe as a dancer in the chorus, and later became a singer and comedienne. At the time, she may have been as young as fourteen years old, passing for sixteen since she was tall and full-bosomed. As an orphan from an impoverished home, and with a brother in the show, it is easy to see how the lure of the tents would have loomed large to the young Bessie Smith.

Gertrude (Pridgett) Rainey and her husband, Will, were among the dozen members of the troupe. They were billed as Ma and Pa Rainey. A stage-struck child would certainly have been impressed by a successful performer like Ma Rainey, who sported gold teeth and a necklace of twenty-dollar gold pieces and who wore diamond-studded tiaras, rings, bracelets, bangles, silks, satins, feathers, and furbelows.

Another version of Smith's start in the traveling shows is that she began with the Rabbit Foot Minstrels, a company Ma Rainey worked with many times. Yet another story has it that Smith and Ma Rainey met in Tolliver's Circus and Musical Extravaganza. In any case, they met early in Smith's career and worked together on two occasions as Smith was starting out. They remained good friends during their lives. Rainey was about ten years Smith's senior. Smith used some of the songs Ma Rainey wrote in her own repertoire and recorded some, including "Boll Weevil Blues" and "Moonshine Blues." They wrote a couple of songs together later in their lives: "Don't Fish in My Sea" and "Weepin' Woman Blues," which Ma Rainey recorded in 1928.

Ma Rainey's influence on Smith's musical style is clearly identifiable in Smith's earliest recordings of 1923 and 1924. But Smith's charisma is clearly her own, and as she became more successful and worldly, especially after feeling at home in New York City, her singing reflected the changes and became more urban and sophisticated, less country-sounding.

Smith invented herself. She developed the technique to execute her fertile imagination of how the music should sound, like no one else before her. As far as music was concerned, she became sure of herself early, performing as she wanted.

Not long after Smith joined the road shows, when she was in her mid-teens, she wound up in a working residence at the 81 Theater in Atlanta. It was one of the theaters on the Theatre Owners Booking Association (TOBA) circuit. She worked in various venues on the circuit and barnstormed the rural areas, performing in cabarets, dance halls, and levee camps. For a while Smith traveled with F. S. Wolcott's Rabbit Foot Minstrels. She joined Pete Werley's Minstel Show for a time, then Silas Green's, then the Florida Cotton Pickers, where she worked with Clarence Williams, who later became the piano player on many of her records. She continued to return to the theater at 81 Decatur Street in Atlanta, using it as a base.

By about 1920, Smith was producing her own shows for the 81 Theater, then taking them on the road. One, called *Liberty Belles*, had been written because her chorus line was so hot and hard-driving: They were not the usual "sepia lovelies," instead, they were plump and dark. Some theater owners gave Smith a hard time about the chorus line but she was obstinate, and if they didn't work she wouldn't either. She used the same kind of chorus line fourteen years later at the Apollo in New York City and was politely asked by Frank Schiffman, the owner, to permit him to supply her with another line. Again, she was immovable and got her way.

Smith left the South in 1921 to work alone with a band at the Standard Theater in Philadelphia, but in 1922 she was in a show again at the Paradise Gardens in Atlantic City. She bought a house in Philadelphia and brought her family up from Chattanooga. She fulfilled one of her secret wishes, to garden, when she bought a farmhouse in New Jersey. In Philadelphia she joined a show called *How Come* with Sidney Bechet at the Dunbar Theater. It was a big success, particularly their duet on "St. Louis Blues," pairing her voice with his offstage clarinet. As Bechet describes it in his autobiography, "Most of the time before we was even through, people would be calling and yelling. They'd just never heard anything like that before; there was nothing better of that kind that could be given to them" (135). Smith and Bechet toured with the show—Cleveland, Cincinnati, Chicago—but when it was about to hit New York, the promoters felt it should be "fancied up" and hired Alberta Hunter to replace Smith. That was before Smith made records, and Alberta Hunter had already recorded a dozen for Black Swan and Paramount.

Blues Queen Excels as Recording Star

Smith wanted to record too. Since Mamie Smith's "Crazy Blues" had become a revolutionary hit—she was the first black person to sing the blues on a record—Bessie Smith knew she could be successful, too. But it took many tries, about five of them, before she signed a contract with Columbia. In 1921 she reportedly made tests with Emerson Records, Columbia, and Black Swan, which advertised itself as the only "genuine colored" record label. But all of them rejected her for sounding "too rough." Black Swan did take Alberta Hunter and Ethel Waters. Thomas Edison turned Smith's voice down too, and so did Fred Hager of the Okeh Record Company.

In April 1923 Smith finally signed a contract with Frank Walker, who took over the race records for Columbia. Her first record issued, "Downhearted Blues," backed by "Gulf Coast Blues," sold the unheard-of amount of three quarters of a million records in the first months. In the summer of that year Smith married Jack Gee, a poor nightwatchman whom she allowed to be her manager and with whom she lived and fought, off and on, for six years.

With the records, Smith's star truly began to shine, and during the next ten years while she was with Columbia, she played the best theaters for the best money. The first stop on her southern tour, where she opened after recording nine songs, was her old home base, the 81 Theater on Decatur Street in Atlanta. Every performance was a sellout. One of the local white radio stations broadcast her show live—an unprecedented event in those days.

Smith continued to record and perform. Full-page advertisements appeared in the black press announcing her new record releases. After hearing her on record, fans wanted to see her perform live. It was common for lines two blocks long to form with people waiting for her shows. She was the biggest name and the biggest draw in the realm of the TOBA and the records.

Smith became an urban blues singer and did not limit herself to a twelve-bar format. She recorded a wide variety of songs, including Tin Pan Alley tunes, which were always informed by the blues when she sang them. For example, one of the great standards in the history of American song was written as a popular tune in 1918, "After You've Gone." The way Smith sang it is an exquisite example of her genius, of the way she interpreted the music. She sang the word "gone" in ten different ways. Her sense of rhythm was superb and she could place her phrases on, off, before, or after the beat; even on top of or below it. And she could bend a note or stop in the middle of it to create the tension she wanted. This subtle timing and phrasing was carefully planned in spite of her innate musicianship and flawless technique (she practiced frequently, with and without her musicians). What sounds like improvising is the result of hard work and an understanding of the infinite possibilities of invention.

Smith used her voice as an instrument. Her moans, groans, slurs, swoops, scoops, slides (sometimes down a whole octave), and stretches were as carefully employed as each stroke on a master's canvas. Her perfect pitch and control of her rich vibrato and intonation gave a freshness to everything she sang. These are qualities that arguably made her the first jazz singer. Some writers have claimed that title for Louis Armstrong, but Smith had been working professionally for a longer period of time than Armstrong and she was about five years older. When they recorded together for the first time in January 1925, Bessie Smith was already a big success due to her records and vaudeville tours. She was being billed as "the Greatest and Highest Salaried Race Star in the World."

Billie Holiday acknowledged learning her technique from listening to Smith. Holiday, too, kept the blues in her heart and used those intonations when she sang pop. In this way, these women transcended some of the ordinary songs they sang, turning them into art. Mahalia Jackson also claimed Smith as a mentor, as did Mildred Bailey, Connie Boswell, Jimmy Rushing, Dinah Washington, Big Mama Thornton, and others.

Many people wrongly assume the songs that Bessie Smith performed are autobiographical. One mistake made was identifying her with "Me and My Gin," by songwriter Harry Burke. Several old friends of Smith's say that she preferred scotch. The hit "Nobody Knows You When You're Down and Out") (by Jimmie Cox) which Smith recorded in May 1929 in New York City, where she was living very comfortably in a luxurious apartment, is another of the songs people mistakenly presume is autobiographical. Perhaps such assumptions can be attributed to Smith's persuasive performances.

Smith bought an eighty-foot Pullman railroad car in 1925 to make traveling easier and to spare herself and her troupe the indignities they suffered due to a lack of hotels that accommodated blacks.

In 1926 she adopted a child and kept a housekeeper to attend to him. Smith supported a huge number of relatives in a style to which they easily became accustomed. She set her sister Viola up in the restaurant business in Philadelphia and bought her a house, too.

One of Smith's masterpieces, among the legacy of 160 recorded songs she left us, was her rendering of "Backwater Blues" in February 1927. She was accompanied—rather, complemented—by James P. Johnson's piano; they had a magnificent rapport while recording. Floods in the South brought terrible destruction to poor people living in rickety houses on river banks, including the Mississippi River. In "Backwater Blues" she transmuted the tragic into the anecdotal, personalizing it for her listeners. When she sings the closing line she is at her most dramatic and intense: "There ain't no place for a poor old girl to go."

When many blues singers were finding it hard to get work because of the Great Depression and the advent of "talking pictures" and radio, which caused the demise of the TOBA, Smith was still traveling and earning "good money," even into 1931. She continued to work until the day she died.

When her fans saw her, Smith always fulfilled their expectations. As she walked onto the stage, all the rowdiness in the theater stopped, and one could hear a pin drop. She was a splendid figure of a woman with an assured presence and statuesque carriage—five feet nine with two hundred pounds of firm flesh—with dark-chocolate skin and animated black eyes. Her distinctive honey contralto could have filled the demands of opera. Microphones did not exist in the early years, and by using a vocal chord technique colloqually called "throwing it from the velvet," Smith could be heard in the last seat of any theater or tent, and even across the street.

People in the small towns in the South could not wait to get her new release through mail order and willingly went down to the railroad station to pay the pullman porters as much as five dollars for a 75-cent record. Her importance as a folk hero in the black community was best expressed by Ralph Ellison in his book of essays, *Shadow and Act*:

> Bessie Smith might have been a "blues queen" to the society at large, but within the tighter Negro community where the blues were part of a total way of life, and a major expression of an attitude toward life, she was a priestess, a celebrant who affirmed the values of the group and man's ability to deal with chaos (257).

During the ten years that Miss Bessie, as she preferred to be called, recorded, starting in 1923 with "Downhearted Blues" to "Do Your Duty" in 1933, she gave us a body of work that is one of the landmarks of twentieth century music.

Smith's dignity, grandeur, and authority can clearly be

heard on her records and seen in her photographs. Too much has been made of her roughness, her drinking, and her love affairs. She was a multifaceted and complex person: independent and in control of her own life, she was also generous and caring. Cooking was one of her pleasures and while traveling in her long yellow railroad car, at the height of her popularity, she was known to move the chef out of the kitchen to cook up a mess of collard greens for the troupe.

In 1929 Smith starred in the only movie she made, a seventeen-minute two-reeler filmed in Astoria, Long Island. In spite of being racist, sexist, and full of clichés and stereotypes, it is the only example we have of her on film. It is also the closest we can come to seeing her ''live'' and hearing her sing the title song, ''St. Louis Blues,'' with the marvelous piano music of James P. Johnson and the Fletcher Henderson Band and the Hall Johnson Choir as backup. Rather than being cast as the empress she was, she was cast as an unlucky prostitute whose pimp preferred a light-skinned woman. The cabaret setting, however, is authentic.

In 1929 Smith and Jack Gee separated and in the next year she made a permanent association with Richard Morgan (Lionel Hampton's uncle). She had known him and liked him for many years. He was sophisticated and rich—entirely opposite from Jack Gee. Morgan left bootlegging in Chicago to join Smith and become her manager.

In spite of the Great Depression—when Smith, too felt the slump because the TOBA had closed, the record companies were hardly recording, and the theaters that remained open were paying modest salaries—she continued to work, even if the pace was slower. Her relationship with Morgan was solid and although the blues were out of date in New York, they were still popular in the South. She traveled more there and took less money. Her style changed with the times; she abandoned the 1920s look for the simpler, more elegant bias-cut style for her gowns in the 1930s, and she was singing more of the popular songs of the day with the new sound of swing as backup.

In New York Smith worked at the Harlem Opera House, The Apollo, and Connie's Inn in midtown, then had a long stint as the star of a nightclub show in Philadelphia. Recording prospects were in the offing and in the fall of 1937 she was working in a traveling show in the South called ''Broadway Rastus.'' On her way from Memphis to Darling, Mississippi, on Route 61 in the early morning of September 16, 1937, with Richard Morgan driving the Packard, she was fatally wounded in a car accident. The official death certificate states that Smith died in the black hospital in Clarksdale on September 26, 1937, at 11:30 A.M. Her arm was almost severed at the elbow and her death resulted from shock, loss of blood, and internal injuries.

One month later John Hammond wrote an article based on hearsay for *Downbeat* magazine, stating that Smith's death was the result of her bleeding to death in the foyer of a white hospital in Memphis where they allegedly would not treat her because she was black. This untrue and irresponsible story was compounded by Edward Albee in a play he wrote called *The Death of Bessie Smith*, which was produced in New York in 1961.

The Empress of the Blues was buried in an unmarked grave in Mount Lawn Cemetery in Philadelphia. Thirty-three years later, in August 1970, a gravestone was erected and dedicated. It was paid for by Juanita Green, president of the North Philadelphia NAACP, who as a child had washed Bessie Smith's floors, and Janis Joplin, both joined by officials from Columbia Records.

There have been many queens of the blues, but Bessie Smith was the only empress and remains unchallenged. In 1984 she was inducted into the National Women's Hall of Fame along with Mary Harris ''Mother'' Jones, the crusading labor organizer. Miss Bessie took her place along with other outstanding American women who created a significant change in American culture, including Emily Dickinson, Eleanor Roosevelt, and Helen Keller. Since 1980 a campaign has been underway to have Smith's image published on a United State postage stamp, in the Performing Arts series, to commemorate her contribution to American music.

References

Albertson, Chris. *Bessie*. New York: Stein and Day, 1972.

Bechet, Sidney. *Treat It Gentle: An Autobiography*. New York: Hill and Wang, 1960. Reprinted. New York: Da Capo Press, 1978.

Bradford, Perry. *Born with the Blues*. New York: Oak Publications, 1965.

Ellison, Ralph. *Shadow and Act*. New York: Random House, 1964. 257.

Gara, Larry. ''Bessie Smith.'' *Notable American Women*. Vol. 3. Cambridge: Harvard University Press, 1971. 306-307.

Harris, Sheldon. *Blues Who's Who*. New Rochelle, N.Y.: Arlington House, 1979. 462-65.

Lieb, Sandra. *Mother of the Blues: A Study of Ma Rainey*. Amherst: University of Massachusetts Press, 1981.

Oliver, Paul. *Bessie Smith*. New York: A. S. Barnes, 1961.

Pleasants, Henry. *The Great American Popular Singers*. New York: Simon and Schuster, 1974. 63-79.

Schuller, Gunther. *Early Jazz: Its Roots and Musical Development*. New York: Oxford University Press, 1968.

Shapiro, Nat, and Nat Hentoff, eds. *Hear Me Talkin' to Ya*. New York: Dover Publications, 1955.

Southern, Eileen. *Biographical Dictionary of Afro-*

American and African Musicians. Westport, Conn.: Greenwood Press, 1982. 343.

Stewart-Baxter, Derrick. *Ma Rainey and the Classic Blues Singers.* New York: Stein and Day, 1970.

Rosetta Reitz

Clara Smith "Queen of the Moaners"

(1894-1935)

Singer, musician

Clara Smith began her career in vaudeville, where she developed a reputation as a blues performer, singer, and pianist. She is believed to have started her career around 1910, when she was about sixteen and began working the theater circuit. She is particularly associated with the Theatre Owners Booking Association (TOBA), with which she was a star by 1918. Although she toured throughout her career, in 1923 she settled in Harlem, New York, where she performed in clubs, managed revues, and recorded, and made her mark as one of the great blues singers of the era.

Smith was born in 1894 in Spartanburg, South Carolina. She married former baseball manager Charles Wesley in 1926. At the age of forty she entered Parkside Hospital in Detroit, Michigan, and died of a heart attack on February 21, 1935. She is buried in Lincoln Cemetery in Macomb County, Michigan. Little else is known of her personal life.

Smith's vaudeville career was extensive. During her time with the TOBA she performed throughout the South, appearing at the Lyric Theater in New Orleans, Louisiana, and at the Bijou Theater in Nashville, Tennessee, among many other places. She toured with Al Well's *Smart Set* tent show in 1920, worked in Columbus, Georgia, at the Dream Theater, and performed in Saint Louis, Missouri, at the Booker T. Washington Theater (*Blues Who's Who,* 466).

In New York, Smith's career included various activities, not the least of which was managing her own revues. In 1924 she opened her own club, the Clara Smith Theatrical Club. In 1927 she appeared in two shows of her own, the *Black Bottom Revue* and the *Clara Smith Revue*. Between 1927 and 1935 Clara Smith appeared in revues, including the *Swanee Club Revue*, the *Ophelia Show From Baltimo Revue*, *Dream Girls Revue*, *Candied Sweets Revue*, and a number of others in New York City. She performed many of these shows in the Alhambra Theater, also playing at the Lafayette, the Lincoln, the Ambassador, Harlem Fifth Avenue Theater, Harlem Opera House, and the Apollo (in Atlantic City, New Jersey). During this time Smith also toured to the Standard Theater in Philadelphia, Pennsylvania, and Orchestra Gardens in Detroit, Michigan, performing quite a number of dates in other places such as Cleveland, Ohio, and as far west as California. In addition to these performances, Smith performed on radio radio in New York City, in the "Swanee Club Revue" (1928). She also performed in *Trouble on the Ranch,* an all-black musical western (1931).

Another important aspect of Smith's career includes her performance as a recording artist. She recorded for Columbia, Paramount, and Okeh, releasing as many as 125 recorded selections. According to Sally Placksin, Smith "began recording for Paramount in 1923, and her first song was 'Every Woman's Blues'" (39). It was also in 1923 that Smith "was put under contract by Columbia" and according to Harris, "she remained with the company for more than a decade except for one release on Okeh in October 1930 under the pseudonym Violet Green" (240).

Smith's professional associates include well-known blues and jazz performers. Her recording accompanists included Fletcher Henderson, Louis Armstrong, Don Redman, James P. Johnson, Coleman Hawkins, Charlie Green, and Joe Smith, among others. In the extravagant *Club Alabam' Revue* she worked with comedian Doc Straine. In the early thirties she paired up with Paul Barbarin in New York. Just as important, however, is her professional relationship with Bessie Smith, with whom she recorded for Columbia. Clara Smith was Columbia's second most prolific female blues recording artist, yielding only to Bessie (the two were not related). They shared the same accompanists. While Columbia promoted Bessie as the Queen of the Blues, it promoted Clara as the Queen of the Moaners.

Clara Smith's performance and blues style appealed to a large audience. With broad experience in vaudeville and musical revues, Smith's performance style was highly dramatic and often somewhat comedic. Her delivery was emotional, insinuating, and witty. Harris writes, for example, that Smith "took advantage of each opportunity for dramatizing her lyrics by shedding tears, emitting mournful wails, and clutching her stole or the stage curtains around her body in obvious anguish" (241). Harris further quotes Coy Herndon's description of Smith:

> Her voice is a typical blues singer type, combined with a wonderful personality, but she is a comedienne . . . of the highest order. Her blues gained numerous encores and her facial expressions, combined with a distinct personality, caused the audience to ache from laughter (243).

Singer Called "Queen of the Moaners"

Smith's blues style prompted her description as the Queen of the Moaners. The melodrama and pathos referred to by

Harris provided Smith a distinct avenue of appeal to her audience. She has been labeled a classic blues performer by some and an urban blues performer by others. Referring to female blues singers whose lyrics included sexual innuendo, William Barlow includes Smith and her "Whip It to a Jelly" among the likes of Martha Copeland, Cleo Gibson, and Lil Johnson, all of whom he identifies as performers of "classic blues that reflects the influence of commercialism compris[ing] vaudeville-based songs featuring graphic metaphors for sexual activity, which were often linked to culinary delights" (142). Barlow indicates that "It's Tight Like That" exemplifies the type, and although it was composed by Thomas Dorsey and Tampa Red, it was first recorded by Smith. According to Harris, furthermore, "Clara Smith sang straight country blues as well as Ma Rainey did, or the city blues like Sippie Wallace. . . . Clara Smith cannot be labeled a vaudeville or ballad singer who sometimes performed the blues; her voice and style are categorically city blues with a touch of country soul" (242).

Smith appealed to an audience that appreciated not only her emotive delivery but also her humor. Placksin reveals that she "drew a tough, raucous crowd . . . the more 'evil' her routines and singing got, the more her audiences loved it" (40). She frequently included her audience through a technique in which she engaged them in dialogue related to a song's content. Her more emotive tunes are exemplified by "Awful Moaning Blues," which combines song text and tonality as devices that justify her dramatic presentation and her audience's empathetic appreciation. The song concerns a woman left alone without friends. The tonality derives from prefatory moans that continue throughout the song and are accompanied by voice tremors and quavers. In Harris's opinion, "Smith's voice conveys a down-in-the-mouth mood, alternating between a hard, dry sound and a tremulous, tragic whine" (240).

Clara Smith's recording career included several duets with the famous Bessie Smith, also recording on the Columbia label. Edward Brooks notes that they recorded together three times, each with Bessie Smith as the dominant figure: "Far Away Blues," accompanied by Fletcher Henderson, "I'm Going Back to My Used to Be," and "My Man Blues," a Bessie Smith composition (93). This latter song, "My Man Blues," is a playful argument with each singer laying claim to one "Charlie Grey." Chris Albertson states that although Clara and Bessie never performed together live, they got along well together until their friendship ended during a disagreement at a party in New York in 1925 (105).

Clara Smith was, according to Al Wynn, "very attractive, and a nice person" (Oliver, 136). She is also described as having been "one of the 'dressiest' women on stage" (Placksin, 39). Harris describes her: "Clara Smith was a handsome woman with a broad face and a big smile. Her large wide-set eyes and broad nose gave her a resemblance to Bessie" (239). Although Clara Smith was relatively small in physical stature, she was a great figure in the development and legacy of blues sound.

References

Albertson, Chris. *Bessie.* New York: Stein and Day, 1972.

Barlow, William. *"Looking Up at Down": The Emergence of Blues Culture.* Philadelphia: Temple University Press, 1989.

Brooks, Edward. *The Bessie Smith Companion.* New York: Da Capo Press, 1982.

Harris, Daphne Duval. *Black Pearls: Blues Queens of the 1920's.* New Brunswick, N.J.: Rutgers University Press, 1988.

Harris, Sheldon, ed. *Blues Who's Who: A Biographical Dictionary of Blues Singers.* New York: Da Capo Press, 1979. Photograph, p. 466.

Oliver, Paul. *Conversation With the Blues.* New York: Horizon Press, 1965.

Placksin, Sally. *American Women in Jazz: 1900 to the Present.* New York: Seaview Books, 1982.

Rye, Howard. *The New Grove Dictionary of Jazz.* Ed. Barry Kernfeld. New York: Macmillan, 1988.

Southern, Eileen. *Biographical Dictionary of Afro-American and African Musicians.* Westport, Conn.: Greenwood Press, 1982.

Laura C. Jarmon

Lucie Wilmot Smith

(1861-1888)

Journalist, editor

African-American history has its heroes and great names, but like other history, it has in large measure been written upon the achievements of dedicated people for whom meaningful work was its own reward. Lucie Wilmot Smith, nineteenth-century journalist and editor, was one such person.

As is true of many people of color who emerged from slavery in 1865, little is known about Lucie Smith. She was born in Lexington, Kentucky, on November 16, 1861, to Margaret Smith. Since Kentucky was a border state and her birth came after the start of the Civil War, it is equally possible that she could have been born slave or free. The fact that her father is unknown lends some credence to the suggestion that Smith was born to an enslaved mother and that therefore in her own early years she likely lived as a slave.

Since freedom from slavery did not mean freedom from want for most post-bellum black Americans, Lucie Smith was forced to begin teaching at the age of sixteen to help support herself and her mother. Somehow she also managed to graduate from the normal school at the State University in Louisville in 1887. Considering the paucity of her resources, the possibility exists that she attended school while she was teaching, a factor that may explain the number of years between the beginning of her teaching career and the actual date of her graduation.

It is probable that during these years she studied at State University, she first came to the attention of William J. Simmons, a circumstance that was to prove beneficial to her in more ways than one. At this time Simmons was president of the university and already a man of some note. He was president of the National Press Convention, secretary of the American Baptist Home Mission Society, and editor of the society's organ, *The American Baptist.* By 1887 he had published *Men of Mark,* a book that remains an important reference to those interested in the progress of black Americans during the latter part of the nineteenth century.

Early in Smith's association with Simmons she became his secretary. Although it is not known precisely when this association began, it still may be surmised that she assisted him in the writing of *Men of Mark.* Certainly he was to influence her greatly, since I. Garland Penn has observed in *The Afro-American Press and Its Editors* that through Simmons "she was introduced to the world of thinkers and writers in newspaper life" (373).

It is unfortunate that the newspapers to which she contributed have not survived, since few of her words are otherwise available for study. However, some things are known about her publishing career. Under Simmons's guidance Smith became the editor of the children's column in *The American Baptist.* Simultaneously or sometime after that, she also worked on the staff of *The Baptist Journal,* which was published in Saint Louis by the Reverend R. H. Coles. Little is known about the Reverend Coles and his paper, of which no known copies have survived.

By the late 1880s and early 1890s, Smith was also contributing articles to *The Journalist,* a black newspaper published in New York City. Penn notes that she contributed sketches of black female newspaper writers to this paper and that these articles were reproduced in *The Boston Advocate* and *The Freeman,* published in Indianapolis, and several others (378).

Smith seems to have reached the pinnacle of her career by the early 1890s. Mrs. N. F. Mossell (Gertrude E. M. Bustill Mossell), a successful black Philadelphia journalist, described Smith's writing as particularly crisp and complimented her on her descriptive powers (Quoted in Penn, 380). Penn praises Smith for her work on *Our Women and Children,* a magazine that began publication in 1888 in Louisville. Here she edited the "Women and Women's Work" department and used it to campaign strongly for women's equality and suffrage (380).

In an article about black women journalists, Smith wrote sketches of ten such women, including N. F. Mossell, Lucretia Mott, Newton Coleman, Ida B. Wells, Victoria Earle Matthews, Mary V. Cook, and Amelia F. Johnson. Originally published in *The Journal,* she begins the article with the following introduction:

> The Negro woman's history is marvelously strange and pathetic. From the womb of the future must come that poet or author to glorify her womanhood by idealizing the various phases of her character. . . . Born and bred under the hindrance of slavery and the limitations of her sex, the mothers of the race have kept pace with the fathers. . . . The educated Negro woman occupies vantage ground over the Caucasian woman of America, in that the former has had to contest with her brother every inch of the ground for recognition; the negro man, having had his sister by his side on plantations and in rice swamps, keeps her there, now that he moves in other spheres. As she wins laurels, he accords her the royal crown. This is especially true of journalism. Doors are opened before we knock, and as well-equipped young women emerge from the class-room, the brotherhood of the race, men whose energies have been repressed and distorted by the interposition of circumstances, give them opportunities to prove themselves; and right well are they doing this, by voice and pen (Reprinted in Dann, 61).

She also held a faculty position at State University in Louisville and was active in religious societies and other national bodies, before which she often expounded upon her philosophies.

A contemporary steel engraving in Penn's book of Smith at the age of about thirty depicts her as a handsome woman with an oval face and a chiseled aquiline nose. The set of her jaw suggests the determination she often expressed in her writings about the elevation of the woman's place in society and the encouragement of woman's suffrage.

Regretfully, after 1891 nothing about Lucie Wilmot Smith's life or career is known, although her date of death was December 1, 1888. It is probable that she continued her career into the twentieth century and was one of the many unsung black women who, through their example, urged others on to educate themselves and become, themselves, examples to younger generations.

References

Penn, I. Garland. *The Afro-American Press and Its Editors.* Springfield, Mass.: Willey and Co., 1891. Engraving, p. 379.

Smith, Lucy Wilmot. "Women as Journalists." Reprinted in *The Black Press 1827-1890*. Ed. Martin E. Dann. New York: Putnams, 1971. Originally published in *The Journal*, n.d., and reprinted in *The Freeman*, 23 February 1889.

Robert E. Skinner

Mamie Smith

(1883-1946)

Singer

Hundreds of blues singers owe Mamie Smith a debt: She was the first black woman to record the blues. She was unrelated to the other "blues" Smiths—Bessie, Clara, Laura, and Trixie—of similar but sometimes confused musical fame. Physically impressive, Mamie Smith inspired others and is brilliantly described in Daphne Duval Harrison's *Black Pearls* (Rutgers, 1988), which is dedicated to the memory of Sippie Wallace and Edith Wilson. But Smith's life deserves at least a full treatment that locates her within the special vanguard to which she belongs.

Mamie Robinson Smith was born May 26, 1883, in Cincinnati, Ohio. If her birth date is correct, Mamie Smith left home when she was about ten years old (in 1893) with a white touring company, the Four Dancing Mitchells, as a dancer. By 1912 she had performed with Salem Tutt Whitney's Smart Set. By the time she was thirty, New York had become her home and she was established as an important cabaret singer. She performed at the Goldgraben's, Barron Wilkins's Leroy's, Percy Brown's, and Edmund's—names that certified her as a serious entertainer, especially in vaudeville. She starred in Perry Bradford's *Maid in Harlem* at the Lincoln Theatre in Harlem in 1918.

As early as 1895, George W. Johnson had recorded "Laughing Son," and the brilliant comedian Bert Williams was on a disc with the Dinwiddle Colored Quartet in 1902. Also, the Fisk Jubilee Singers' "sorrow songs" as well as the "coon" songs by a few black minstrel men existed on wax. Smith's stellar accomplishment—being the first black woman to record the blues—is due to several factors: Major white entertainers were seeking new materials for their acts; soldiers returning from World War I brought with them a race consciousness and a wider world view than was possible at the beginning of the decade; the historical moment was right; Smith had experience and talent; and Perry Bradford helped promote Smith. He was a genuine talent broker, street smart and tenacious. He was also a composer, bandleader, singer, and mentor to Smith.

W. C. Handy, the "Memphis Father of the Blues," had a good relationship with Bradford; both had composed and published sheet music for piano rolls and were known to several of the "A & R" men—Artist and repertoire or recording managers of some of the major companies—especially at Victor and Columbia. Said Bradford:

> It was my humble belief that the people were craving for something to lift them up so they could forget about the war and to those same mothers and sweethearts, war songs weren't any relief. . . our folks had a story to tell and it could be told only in vocal—not instrumental—recordings (Bradford, 114).

But Columbia Records, then recording numerous jazz bands, "wouldn't think of recording a colored girl at [that] time [1912-16]" (Bradford, 115). So Bradford contacted Columbia's chief competition, Victor Records, about the star of the musical revue *Maid in Harlem*. Smith made a test record, "That Thing Called Love," but Victor didn't release it. However, dealers bootlegged the Smith record and the public response was so tremendous—something Bradford used as leverage. Fred W. Hogen was the manager of General Phonograph Corporation's recording department, and he gave a receptive ear to Bradford and Smith. On February 14, 1920, Mamie Smith's contralto voice shouted:

> That thing called love—money cannot buy—
> That thing called love—will make you weep and cry,
> Something you're sad—romantic and glad;
> The most wonderful thrill—you ever had.

The flip side of "That Thing Called Love" was "You Can't Keep a Good Man Down," also written by Bradford, and OKeh Records (of General Phonograph Corporation) became the first company to record a solo black artist singing the blues.

Within six months, Smith was back at OKeh singing two more of Bradford's "dressed up blues": "The Crazy Blues" (originally titled "Harlem Blues") and "It's Right Here For You." The first month, seventy-five thousand copies at one dollar each, were sold, and Smith's popularity soared. Together with her band, the Jazz Hounds, Smith commanded fees from twenty-five hundred to three thousand dollars per performance.

Smith made twenty-three more records in 1921-1922 for OKeh. Beside touring extensively, between 1923 and 1931 she appeared in nine musical revues at either the Lafayette or Lincoln theaters in Harlem. She recorded for Ajax in 1924, for Victor in 1926, and for OKeh in 1929 and 1931. In 1932-1934, Mamie Smith toured in *Yelping Hounds* with Fats Pichon's orchestra. Besides the short *Jailhouse Blues* in 1929, she appeared in the following Hollywood films: *Paradise in Harlem* (1939), *Mystery in Swing* (1940), *Murder on*

Lennox Avenue (1941), *Sunday Sinners* (1941), and *Because I Love You* (1943). About 1936 she made a European tour. She was married to William "Smitty" Smith, a singer (1912); Sam Gardner, a comedian (1920s); and a man named Goldberg (1929).

In 1946, Smith died at Harlem Hospital in New York after a lengthy illness and was buried at Frederick Douglass Memorial Park Cemetery on Staten Island. But it was only through the efforts of German jazz buffs that we now know where her body rests. From *Records Research: The Magazine of Record Information and Statistics*, we learn that:

> One December 30 [Smith's] gravestone arrived free of freight in New Orleans aboard the Hamburg-American line M/S Iserlohn from Iserlohn, West Germany, under the personal care of the Captain of the vessel. It was there in Iserlohn that Gunter and Lore Boas with the cooperative members of their Hot Club sponsored the construction of the [head] stone by running a benefit concert on November 30, with no less than 6 jazz bands. . . There aboard the ship, three musicians . . . gave Mamie Smith a final blues send off. The stone was in plain view . . . and the carved inscription was to "Mamie Smith 1883-1946 FIRST LADY OF THE BLUES Dedicated from the Hot Club and the city of Iserlohn" (October 1964).

Blueswoman Victoria Spivey and others were present when, on Monday, January 27, 1964, there was a memorial concert to cover expenses for Smith's reinterment. It was appropriate for Spivey to be involved; years earlier, in *Record Research*, Spivey had noted:

> Wow! Miss Smith walked out on that stage and I could not breathe for a minute. She threw those big sparkling eyes on us with that lovely smile showing those pearly white teeth with a diamond the size of one of her teeth. Then I looked at her dress. Nothing but sequins and rhinestones plus a velvet cape with white fur on it . . . and when she sung she tore the house down.

Of herself, perhaps modestly, Smith had this to say:

> Thousands of people who come to hear me . . . expect much, and I do not intend that they shall be disappointed. They have heard my phonograph records and they want to hear me sing these songs the same as I do in my studio in New York. . . . Another thing I believe my audiences want to see me becomingly gowned, and I have spared no expense or pains . . . for I feel that the best is none too good for the public that pays to hear a singer.

References

Arthur, Desmond. "Mamie Smith." *The Harlem Renaissance: A Historical Dictionary for the Era*. Ed. Bruce Kellner. New York: Methuen, 1984.

Bradford, Perry. *Born With The Blues: Perry Bradford's Own Story*. New York: Oak Publishers, 1965.

Downbeat Magazine. Numerous editions, 1940, 1941, 1946.

Harris, Sheldon. *Blues Who's Who*. New Rochelle, N.Y.: Arlington House, 1979.

Harrison, Daphne Duval. *Black Pearls: Blues Queens of the 1920's*. New Brunswick, N.J.: Rutgers University Press, 1988.

Kinkle, Roger D. *The Complete Encyclopedia of Popular Music and Jazz 1900-1950*. New Rochelle, N.Y.: Arlington House, 1974.

The Paramount "Book of the Blues." Port Washington, Wis.: New York Recording Laboratories, [1927?].

Record Research: The Magazine of Record Statistic and Information. Vol. 65 (October 1964).

Southern, Eileen. *Biographical Dictionary of Afro-American and African Musicians*. Westport, Conn.: Greenwood Press, 1982.

Stewart-Baxter, Derrick. *Ma Rainey and the Classic Blues Singers*. New York: Stein and Day, 1970.

Roseann P. Bell

Willie Mae Ford Smith "Mother Smith"

(1904-)

Singer, religious leader

Willie Mae Ford Smith, a groundbreaking evangelist and gospel singer who stirred up both congregations and church leaders and who is frequently addressed as Mother Smith, was born June 23, 1904, in Rolling Fort, Mississippi; her year of birth frequently appears as 1906. She was the seventh of fourteen children, and her parents were Mary (Williams) Ford and Clarence Ford. When she was a child, her family moved to Memphis, Tennessee, and when she was twelve, around 1917, they moved to Saint Louis, Missouri, which became Mother Smith's lifelong home and her base of operations during her extensive career as an evangelist and gospel performer.

Smith's parents were hard-working and active church members. Her father was a railway brakeman, and it is perhaps due to his job that the family relocated to Memphis. In Saint Louis, her mother opened a restaurant, where Smith worked for a time. The family were strict Baptists, and her father was a deacon. Smith's maternal grandmother was a slave and later babysat the Ford children. The family was poor during its early years, and often the children slept four in a bed, using their coats for cover.

Smith's early education was more informal than formal. In her eighth-grade year of school, she quit in order to help in her mother's restaurant. Her musical training was informal; however, it began early and continued for many years. She recalled her maternal grandmother "singing, clapping, and doing the 'Rock Daniel,' her name for the holy dance" (Broughten, 50). Her father and mother sang duets in churches around their area, and in 1922, her father formed a family quartet, The Ford Sisters, comprised of Mary, Emma, Geneva, and Willie Mae as lead singer. In the twenties, as the sisters gradually married, the quartet broke up, but the other sisters encouraged Smith toward solo performance by sponsoring her as the group's representative. At this point, Smith chose music as a career and intended to study classical music.

In 1924, Willie Mae Ford married James Peter Smith, a man nearly twenty years her senior. By then a resident of Saint Louis, James Smith was from New Orleans, Louisiana. He was a small businessman with a general hauling business. They had two children—Willie James Smith, who attended Tennessee Agricultural and Industrial State University in Nashville, Tennessee, and Jacquelyn Smith Jackson. Although Mother Smith had music interests during the twenties, during the thirties she traveled widely, and the children often were attended to by their father and aunts. Mother Smith's husband died in 1950.

Mother Smith's early music career, which was highlighted by her roles in the Ford Sisters quartet and the National Baptist Convention, was varied. The Ford Sisters performed at the National Baptist Convention in 1924 and received a lukewarm reception. They sang their own arrangements of "Ezekiel Saw the Wheel" and "I'm in His Care" (Heilbut, 226). Their style was too lively and dramatic for the audience of the time, which "hadn't really accepted gospel" (Dargan, 251). Despite this early reaction, Mother Smith maintained a lifelong active affiliation with the National Baptist Convention.

Although her early range of musical interest was broad, in 1921 she decided to commit her talent to gospel song. She made her commitment after hearing Detroit's Madame Artelia Hutchins: "My God, how she sang 'Careless Soul, Why Do You Linger?' Now she wasn't too emotional, I was the one. When I knew anything, I was gone like a light, and she'd keep on anyhow. I knew then I had to be a gospel singer" (Heilbut, 226). From this choice, Mother Smith advanced into a career as gospel soloist, and through the thirties, she was a favored solo performer at the conventions: "If I wasn't the first to sing free, as the spirit told me, I don't know who was. I didn't hear anybody sing with a beat before me, either, not gospel solo" (Heilbut, 226). Thus, Mother Smith was in the vanguard of black gospel music's development, particularly in the area of solo performance.

Mother Smith's role in the development of gospel music performance connects with the roles of gospel pioneers Thomas A. Dorsey and Sallie Martin. Dorsey, former pianist for blueswoman Ma Rainey, first heard Mother Smith when she was with the Ford Sisters and performing in Louisville, at which time he was performing blues. In 1932 he and Sallie Martin were performing gospel tours in black churches and met Mother Smith, upon which she joined their pioneer gospel movement. She accepted the task of organizing Saint Louis for Dorsey, and in 1936 formed and became director of the Soloists Bureau of Dorsey's National Convention of Gospel Choirs and Choruses, part of the National Baptist Convention. In this capacity, for many years she trained up-and-coming young gospel music performers, imprinting upon them her style and lending them use of her arrangements. In 1937, with her composition and rendition of "If You Just Keep Still," she "set the standard for solo singing" (Boyer, 252).

In 1939, Mother Smith's career shifted from gospel solo performance to evangelism, as she left the Baptist church and became a member of the Church of God Apostolic, which baptizes, as she states, "in the name of Jesus, period, not the Trinity" (Heilbut, 227). She remembered the occasion:

> When the Lord filled me with the Holy Ghost . . . I was in Ohio singing, and Mrs. [Artelia] Hutchins was [there] singing "Let it breathe on me, Let the Holy Ghost breathe on me." When the Holy Ghost hit me, I hit the floor. On the train coming back to St. Louis, I kept everybody up all night long, trying to talk, speaking in tongues. . . . Honey, this child got soused good. The Lord had to fix me up, because you see I was a wild person, just like a wild buck. I made fun of holiness people. I laughed at 'em and tried to do the holy dance. I would just cut up (Dargan, 251).

According to Dargan, "also in the late 1930s and 1940s Smith acknowledged a calling to the ministry and was ordained by the African Methodist Episcopal Zion Church" (251). As well, he reveals that "during the mid-1950s, Mother Smith joined and was ordained a minister in the Lively Stone Apostolic Church in Saint Louis, an affiliate of the Pentecostal Assemblies of the World, the largest of several Pentecostal-Apostolic denominations" (253).

As both soloist and evangelist, Mother Smith traveled and performed widely. During the late thirties and the forties, she was on the road three out of four weeks a month. She did concert appearances and recitals, conducted revivals, and "performed frequently at churches in places like Buffalo, Detroit, Cleveland, and Chicago, and small towns around the midwest" (Dargan, 252). Aside from the appearances during these more active years, she made appearances later in life, working at the Newport Jazz Festival and at Radio City Music Hall in New York City.

Influence on Black Gospel Music Extensive

Mother Smith's influence on the development of black gospel music is extensive, and the names of her trainees and associates are impressive. She is considered among the top five gospel pioneers, alongside Thomas Dorsey, Sallie Martin, Roberta Martin, and Mahalia Jackson, all of whom she knew and worked with. For years, Roberta Martin was her accompanist at the Soloists Bureau. In the thirties, Mother Smith and her husband adopted Bertha Smith, who was her accompanist into the early fifties. Her better-known protégés were Myrtle Scott, who at one time sang with the Roberta Martin Singers; Martha Bass, who worked with the Ward Singers and is mother of soul singer Fontella Bass; the O'Neal Twins; Edna Gallman Cooke, "The Sweetheart of the Potomac"; and Brother Joe May, "The Thunderbolt of the Middle West." Her favorite performers were Queen C. Anderson, Edna Cooke, the Ward Singers, the Sallie Martin Singers, Marion Williams, and Delores Campbell (Heilbut, 230). Many of these singers visited her home in Saint Louis, along with others, including The Simons-Akers Singers, The Caravans, Inez Andrews, and the Reverend Clarence Cobb (Dargan, 250).

Mahalia Jackson, the most commercially successful of Mother Smith's contemporaries, was a beautician when Mother Smith was already performing. Mother Smith recalled Mahalia Jackson's admiring words, "Willie Mae, I'm gonna leave this beauty shop. I wanna be like you" (Broughten, 53). Mother Smith invited Jackson and Dorsey to her church in 1940. As Jackson's career took hold and became financially fruitful, Mother Smith continued evangelizing. In the late forties, "Mother Smith and Mahalia Jackson sang for an Easter Sunrise Service at the Hollywood Bowl in California, where a company arranged to record several selections and offered each a contract" (Dargan, 252). According to Mother Smith's son:

> This man heard both her and Mahalia and wanted to sign 'em up [But] Mother never did anything without the advice of my father and my grandfather. . . . They said, "Naw, don't sign up with this. . . . " They thought it was something slick. They didn't even want to be associated with anything that was supposed to be slick. So she didn't sign up (Dargan, 252).

Mother Smith did not record during her early years. However, many of her protégées did so, and some of them made almost verbatim recordings of her arrangements. Edna Cooke recorded for Nashboro Records, Martha Bass recorded "I'm So Grateful" on the Checker label, and Mahalia Jackson sang "If You Just Keep Still." Roberta Martin used Mother Smith's arrangement of "What a Friend We Have in Jesus," "making it her best-known solo. She published the new arrangement, adding in small letters 'as sung by Willie Mae Ford Smith of St Louis,' but Willie Mae didn't see a cent in royalties" (Heilbut, 227). Brother Joe May's "Search Me Lord," "Old Ship of Zion," and "He'll Understand" "were also note-for-note copies of Willie Mae's arrangements," and may be taken as "documentation of her style" (Heilbut, 230). Mother Smith's income, however, depended upon the collection plate.

Mother Smith's performance style was highly dramatic and led to her designation as the forerunner in the tradition of using introductory sermonettes and song text explication. The sermonette and song form is one "whereby the singer delivers a five-or-ten minute sermon before, during, or after the performance of a song" (Boyer, 252). She viewed her evangelical performances as means of saving souls. She embellished a song, interspersing song and talk: "Before each song, Willie Mae would 'talk it up,' setting the pace for all the sermonettes gospel singers now employ. Between her explications of the text and the demands of the spirit, Willie Mae could easily get a two-hour concert out of ten songs" (Heilbut, 228). This song and explication form blended with a highly dramatic performance style. Mother Smith explains her approach: "I always did have emotional gestures. You just move with the feeling. You sway with the feelings. I'll sing with my hands, with my feet—when I got saved, my feet got saved too—I believe we should use everything we got" (Heilbut, 224).

In a 1989 interview, Mother Smith's daughter, Jackie Jackson, gives an instructively detailed description of Smith's sermonette style as she performed her popular arrangement of "Give Me Wings." Jackson reports the many dramatic gestures with which Mother Smith illustrated the words of the song. In Jackson's words, "She was a dramatic singer, and her gestures were always on time with what she was singing. . . . It was like she was talking to an audience as one would stand before a podium and say, 'let me tell you something.' She would have her hands in front of her, shall I say, soloist style" (Dargan, 255). Jackson describes and interprets the various expressions and movements of the eyes, head, arms, and torso as Mother Smith sang "Give Me Wings."

Although Mother Smith's revival performances were referred to as programs, they were worship services, "a revival in song" (Dargan, 255). Mother Smith began her programs with "Lest I Forget" and closed them with the benedictory "God Be With You Till We Meet Again" (Dargan, 255). She conducted her own offertory collection and prayer, asking for a set number of coins more. She performed half of her songs before the collection and the other half afterwards, and after her, guests sang. She responded to requests, frequently conducted an altar call, and "sometimes they would stop and actually open the doors of the church" (Dargan, 255). Mother Smith's audiences loved her and awaited her appearance; although she made a habit of arriving late, "nobody would leave, . . . they'd just sit and wait" (Dargan,

254). Zella Jackson Price, who was for a while Mother Smith's road manager, recalled: "She was a singer. I've seen her walk out singing . . . on the way to her next appearance . . . and folks is just shoutin' everywhere, hats flyin' and carryin' on, just something terrible. She'd come in and just wreck all them buildings. That was Mother Smith, and she loved it" (Dargan, 254).

Song and Ministry Stir Controversy

Mother Smith's song and her ministry provoked controversy among church conservatives. Her song performance often alarmed church officials who felt it too closely resembled blues, and, indeed, until her commitment to the ministry, she was interested in blues. In Memphis, during her childhood, she heard blues at a club behind their home, and the men "would throw money down out of the window for [her] to sing the 'Boll Weevil'" (Dargan, 250). She sang "everything [she] could sing, blues, reels, you name it, when [her] Moma wasn't around" (Heilbut, 225). As she put it: "You know I used to love to party, to dance and to sing. Count Basie, Bessie Smith, Cab Calloway. Before I got saved. I used to have a ball. I imagine I'd have gone into blues myself. It's just when I got saved, nothing interested me but serving God" (Heilbut, 227). According to Mother Smith, Dorsey told her that she "had the vocal power to surpass Bessie Smith" (Broughten, 50). Mother Smith further commented, "The gospel song is the Christian blues. I'm like the blues singer, when something's rubbing me wrong, I sing out of my soul to settle me down" (Heilbut, 216). Her song, like Dorsey's arrangements, blended the blues and sanctified music.

The conservative reaction to her music indicates her experience as a gospel pioneer who "got into [gospel] before churches accepted it" (Kael, 124). Mother Smith recalled the early attitude:

> They said I was bringing the blues into the church. "You might as well be Mamie Smith, Bessie Smith, one of those Smith Sisters, you make me sick with that stuff." Well, I said, that's all the stuff I know. When I first started out singing gospel, they said "We don't want that Coonshine stuff in here," but that didn't stop me. I kept going because that's what the Lord wanted (Broughten, 51).

Her voice was said to be "distinctive for her powerful, blues-like contralto . . . and her free use of roars and crooning" (Southern, 350). Drawing a similarity between Mother Smith and Sister Rosetta Tharpe, Heilbut suggests that both would have made great blues singers. Smith's "Give Me Wings" is often referred to for its resemblance to blues. Wilfred Mellers calls attention to "her breathy, wide-vibrato-ed, explosive vocal production [which] resembles that of 'heavy' blueswomen such as Ma Rainey and Bessie Smith" (8). According to Dargan:

> Sometimes called "gospel blues" (because of its use of phrasing and harmonic patterns similar to twelve-bar blues), the sixteen-bar structure of "Give Me Wings" identifies the performance both with the congregational singing tradition in black holiness churches and with the works of Dorsey, W. Herbert Brewster, Alex Bradford, and other gospel song composers (262).

As well, according to Heilbut, "in 1937, she tore up the Baptist Convention with her own composition of "If You Just Keep Still," a triumph of the gospel idiom" (227). He describes the song as a sixteen-bar blues:

> Sometimes I want to be in company
> Then again Lord I want to be alone
> When enemies press me hard,
> And confusion's all in my home.
> Sometimes I stand with folded arms
> And the tears Lord come running down.
> Lord you said you'd fight my battles
> If I just keep still (227).

He refers to this song as reflecting Mother Smith's resemblance to Bessie Smith in "background and musical taste" (227).

Mother Smith carried this style beyond her solo performance and into her training and evangelical performances. As well as being a composer in her own right, she "performed anybody's tunes among them her pianist Sam Windom's 'Canaan'" (Heilbut, 229). In her role as director of the Soloists Bureau of the National Convention of Gospel Choirs and Choruses, she taught her style to younger singers "to demonstrate that slurs and note-bending fit any tunes. . . . She performed many standard hymns, revised, rephrased, reconceived into whole new numbers," telling her pupils, "it isn't in the music or the words, it's the way you demonstrate it" (Heilbut, 226). Heilbut describes her as "evangelist, Sunday School teacher, 'cultured' neo-concert singer, and gutsy blues shouter, rolled up in one" (225).

Dargan presents a detailed technical analysis of Mother Smith's "Give Me Wings" and "The Lifeboat Is Coming." He writes that "the scale structures most frequently heard in Smith recordings vary from the five-note pentatonic scale to the seven-note major scale, with the lowered third and seventh degrees idiomatic to black vocal style. These 'blue notes' are most often heard in major tonalities, with minor keys being used more sparingly" (259). He also explains that her tempo and rhythmic structure "fall into two broad categories: metered and non-metered songs," and adds:

> Several important characteristics of Smith's performances emerge from this study: First, vocal lines constantly alternate between avoidance of and coincidence with the downbeat formed by meter, text, and/or harmony, thus generating a floating, unhindered, dance-like quality. Second, upbeat phrases are frequently prolonged or extended, especially at points of cadence. Third, cadences are continuously interrupted or overlapped by new material, preventing any sense of

> resolution until the end of the piece. These characteristics, which help to generate the tremendous intensity of the performances, result from the interaction of vocal lines with text, harmony, meter, phrasing, and accompaniment (259).

Along with his instructive analysis, Dargan provides textual and musical transcriptions of the two songs. He credits her with effecting "the transfer of worried notes, bends, scoops, growls, and melismas from the blues and spirituals to the gospel idiom" (264).

Just as Mother Smith's gospel style engendered conservative resistance, so did her evangelism. Performing in churches, she was rarely invited into the pulpit, despite having been ordained. By her report, preachers told her, "'You can sit down there, you don't need to come up here. Don't get in my program. You a woman, didn't you realize?' No respect at all. Well it don't make no difference to me. So I turn around in my pew and sing to that audience. Next thing I know, 'Come on up here, get up and let them all see you'" (*National Geographic*, 211).

Along with her influence on the development of gospel music, Mother Smith had other achievements. She served seventeen years as director of the National Baptist Convention's Education Department. In 1982, she was a featured subject in the gospel film documentary, *Say Amen Somebody*. As well, in 1988 she received from the National Endowment for the Arts a Heritage Award in recognition of her outstanding performance as an American folk artist.

Although she did not record until her late years, there are available recordings of her sound. Some examples are "I Believe I'll Run On" and "Going On With the Spirit," both produced on the Nashboro Label, as well as "I Am Bound For Canaan Land" (Savoy SL 14739).

References

Boyer, Horace Clarence. "Willie Mae Ford Smith." *The New Grove Dictionary of American Music*. Eds. H. Wiley Hitchcock and Stanley Sadie. New York: Macmillan, 1986.

Broughten, Viv. *Black Gospel: An Illustration of the Gospel Sound*. Dorset, England: Blanford Press, 1985. Photograph of Willie Mae Ford Smith, p. 50.

Dargan, William Thomas, and Kathy White Bullock. "Willie Mae Ford Smith of St. Louis: A Shaping Influence Upon Black Gospel Singing Style." *Black Music Research Journal* 9 (Fall 1989): 249-270.

Goreau, Laurraine. *Just Mahalia Baby: The Mahalia Jackson Story*. Louisiana: Pelican Pub. Co., 1975.

Heilbut, Anthony. *The Gospel Sound: Good News and Bad Times*. New York: Simon and Schuster, 1971.

Kael, Pauline. Review of *Say Amen, Somebody*. *New Yorker* 59 (4 April 1983): 124-8.

Lanker, Brian. *I Dream a World*. New York: Steward, Tabori, and Chang, 1989. Photograph of Smith, p. 79.

———. "I Dream a World." *National Geographic* 176 (August 1989): 211.

Mellers, Wilfred. *Angels of the Night: Popular Female Singers of Our Time*. New York: Basil Blackwell, 1986.

"Righting Wrongs: Sexual Equality Counts Too." *Life Magazine* 11 (Special Issue, Spring 1988): 60. Includes photograph of Smith.

Schickel, Richard. Review of *Say Amen, Somebody*. *Time* 121 (2 May 1983): 76. Includes photograph of Smith.

Southern, Eileen. *Biographical Dictionary of Afro-American and African Musicians*. Westport, Conn.: Greenwood Press, 1982.

Laura C. Jarmon

Mabel Murphy Smythe-Haithe

(1918-)

Educator, government official

Mabel Smythe-Haithe has been a major force in international education, development, and relations. As an educator, a consultant, and an ambassador, she has continuously been committed to global understanding among nations.

Born on April 3, 1918, in Montgomery, Alabama, Mabel Murphy Smythe-Haithe was the daughter of Harry Saunders Murphy and Josephine (Dibble) Murphy. She was the third child and the third girl out of four children. Her brother was born when she was nine years old. At the time of Mable Murphy's birth, her father was on the faculty at Alabama State Normal College.

As a child Smythe-Haithe grew up in a middle-class family with parents who cared about her sisters, her brother, and herself. As a united family, they cared about accomplishing personal goals and giving back to the community. Her parents were interested in social issues and encouraged blacks to register and become voters. As a teenager, Smythe-Haithe would accompany her mother and father as they went into the community to explain the process of registration and voting. Her parents, as a part of the NAACP and voter registration drives, took people to the polls. The children of the Murphy family were taught to seek solutions for social issues.

Smythe-Haithe's father, a creative writer, constantly wrote articles for newspapers, including the *Atlanta Daily World*. At age seven, Smythe-Haithe enjoyed writing and received awards in school for being the best speller. Having a lot of self-esteem, she felt that she could do anything. Though modest and shy and not necessarily a leader, she was oriented toward action. During her childhood, she was a bookworm and read everything available. In her household the question never arose whether she, her sisters, and brother would attend college or not. Smythe-Haithe attended private school on the campus of Alabama State Normal College and high school at Atlanta University Laboratory School. Her mother and father both were college graduates; hence, she had a strong academic background. She attended Spelman College from 1933 to 1936, but since her father had studied in Boston, he wanted her to study in New England. She received a scholarship from Mount Holyoke College in South Hampton, Massachusetts, in 1937 and earned her N.S. degree from the college in that year. From 1937 to 1939 she began her teaching career at Fort Valley Normal and Industrial Institute in Fort Valley, Georgia.

In 1938 she met Hugh H. Smythe at the University of Wisconsin and married him on July 26, 1939. From this union a daughter, Karen Pamela, was born. She received her master's and doctorate in economics with a minor in law from the University of Wisconsin. After her husband finished his studies at Wisconsin, he entered the army. While he was in the army, she taught at Lincoln University in Jefferson City, Missouri, a historically black college. She still sees a need for black colleges today:

> Black colleges fulfill a need that white colleges fail to provide for black students. The black colleges receive the black students wholeheartedly and work with them until they reach acceptable levels. Today, the black college continues to believe in the black student, for they know that students will succeed if motivated. Again, they provide black role models when blacks were seldom acknowledged in the public media. Then and now, black colleges provide an artistic and cultural life in the black community. At such colleges, students do not face prejudice against their blackness and their cultural background (Interview with Mabel Murphy Smythe-Haithe, November 1990).

From 1945 to 1946, Smythe-Haithe was professor of economics at Tennessee Agricultural and Industrial College (now Tennessee State University). Afterwards, in 1946-1947, she taught economics in Brooklyn. Her daughter, Karen, was born in 1947.

Although Smythe-Haithe studied accounting and economics as an undergraduate, she wanted to work with people. She and her husband decided to work overseas in the foreign service. At that time the NAACP encouraged the United States Department of State to employ blacks and encouraged the Smythes to apply. Both accepted appointments to teach in Japan at two different universities. She taught at Shiga University from 1951 to 1953 while Hugh Smythe taught at the University of Janaikechi. From 1951 to 1953 she taught English as a second language to the Japanese and eventually wrote a book, *Intensive English Conversation*. The experiences in Japan made her conscious of the world at large, and her interest in international education developed. She said:

> I began to see value in other cultures, other values, and other philosophies of life. My new learning enabled me to enjoy and relate more wholly to different races. Experience made me realize that there were many minorities in the United States besides black Americans. At the same time I felt the need for multilinguistic skills (Interview with Mable Murphy Smythe-Haithe, November 1990).

Upon her return to the United States from Japan on June 30, 1953, she began working for the NAACP Legal Defense and Education Fund. As deputy director for nonlegal research for school desegregation cases in 1953, she gathered information on the upcoming desegregation court case, *Brown v. Topeka Board of Education*. Familiar with the arguments before the Supreme Court, she sent reports to newspapers and was a reporter for the *Amsterdam News*.

> I felt that I was taking part in history during the development of the information for this famous case. Thurgood Marshall and the staff realized that this case would have a greater effect on black people than any case since the *Plessey v. Ferguson* decision in 1898 (Interview with Mabel Murphy Smythe-Haithe, November 1990).

From 1954 to 1959 she was an instructor at New Lincoln School in New York City and served as coordinating principal from 1959 to 1969. She was adjunct professor at the Baruch School in 1959-1960 at Queens College as well as adjunct professor in 1962 at City University of New York. She supplied articles for the Encyclopedia Brittanica Educational Corporation from 1969 to 1973. Serving as director of research and publications for the Phelps-Stokes Fund, serving from 1970 to 1972, she was promoted later to vice-president of the Phelps-Stokes Fund from 1972 to 1977. She extended her interest in Africa in this position:

> After participation in the United States foreign service in Japan, my interest in Africa began to grow. While in Japan in 1953, James Robinson, founder of Crossroads Africa, visited me and my husband in our home. I began to assist him in working on a project on taking students to Africa and bringing Africans to the United States. During this period, I took my trips to Europe and Africa. On board ship I would organize the newsletter and language classes. Working with

> American University admission officers, I organized the African Scholarship Program for Nigerian students for Harvard and other American universities. Twenty-six students from Nigeria studied for the first time in the United States. On board I interpreted the British and American culture, the educational system, and American life to these international students. After I became vice-president for research for the Phelps-Stokes Fund, my interest in Africa became full bloom (Interview with Mabel Murphy Smythe-Haithe, November 1990).

Scholar Twice Appointed Ambassador

As a scholar in residence for the United States Commission on Civil Rights, she served from 1973 to 1974. Designated by President Jimmy Carter, she was the United States Ambassador to the United Republic of Cameroon in Yaounde from 1977 to 1980 and United States Ambassador to the Republic of Equatorial Guinea in 1979-1980. In addition, she was a part of the United States delegation to the South African Development Coordination Conference in Maputo, Mozambique, in 1980. She accompanied Ambassador Donald McHenry to Zimbabwe and to Liberia to consult with their presidents in 1980. From 1980 to 1981 she was the deputy assistant secretary for African Affairs for the United States Department of State in Washington, D.C. As part of the United States delegation, she participated in the International Conference for Assistance to Refugees in Africa in 1981, in the Refugee Policy Group in 1983, and accompanied United States officials to the funeral of Sir Seretse Khama, the president of Botswana.

From 1981 to 1983 she was Melville J. Herskovits Professor of African Studies at Northwestern University in Evanston, Illinois, and the associate director of African studies from 1983 to 1985. By 1986 she became a member of the board of the Ralph Bunche Institute on the United Nations at the City University of New York, a Julius Rosenwald Fellow, and a Harriet-Remington Laird Fellow.

In 1985 she served as co-leader for a group of faculty members from black institutions for a West African seminar sponsored by the National Association of Equal Opportunity in Higher Education. Supported by a grant from the United States Information Agency, this group visited Senegal and three additional African countries:

> In this group the black faculty members experienced cultural diversity on one hand and multiculturalism on the other in West African nations. Through human contact, communication among participants and host countrymen was able to find points of commonality, yet survive points of differences (Interview with Mabel Murphy Smythe-Haithe, November 1990).

Smythe-Haithe was a member of the United States Advisory Committee on Educational Exchange, 1961-1962, on International Educational and Cultural Affairs, 1962-1965, a delegate to the UNESCO General Conference in Paris, 1964, member of the United States National Commission for UNESCO in 1965-1970, member of the Advisory Council for African Affairs for the United States State Department 1962-1969, and a member of the advisory committee for Operation Crossroads Africa, 1958-1965. Furthermore, she was a member of the Public Affairs Committee for the national YWCA from 1959 to 1965 and a member of the National Resources Committee from 1963 to 1965. Other memberships include the Women's African Committee from 1959 to 1964, the Committee for Second Progress in Education from 1964 to 1969, and a panel for Board of Examiners for the New York State Civil Service Commission from 1960 to 1965. In addition, she became a member of the Committee on Research Development for the International Institute from 1965 to 1967 and the International Cooperation Year Committee in 1965. Along with these memberships she was on the advisory committee of the National Assessment of Educational Progress from 1969 to 1976, and a member of the executive committee of LAWS, a division of the Atlantic Foundation, from 1968 to 1977. Mabel Smythe-Haithe comments on her involvement with diverse groups:

> Since I am basically a people's person, I participate in many groups which serve people who struggle for global understanding, global communication, and at the same time, respect cultural diversity. Memberships on boards and organizations reflect my interest in these issues (Interview with Mable Murphy Smythe-Haithe, November 1990).

She served on the board of directors for the African-American Institution from 1964 to 1965. Continuing her civic duties, she was on the board of directors of the New York Center, International Visitors, International School Services from 1964 to 1971, and the National Cooperation of Housing Partnerships. She showed her continued interest in education by serving as a trustee at Cottonwood Foundation from 1964 to 1965 and from 1969 to 1977, Connecticut College from 1964 to 1965 and 1968 to 1977, Hampshire College from 1971 to 1977, Mount Holyoke College from 1971 to 1976, and Spelman College from 1980.She is a member of the Council on Foreign Relations, the Congressional Black Caucus, the American Economic Association, the Smithsonian Institution, Museum of the American Indian, Cosmopolitan Club, Council of American Ambassadors, and Association of Black American Ambassadors. She is also a fellow of the African Studies Association.

She is listed in the *Dictionary of International Biography*, *Who's Who in America*, *Who's Who in the World*, *Who's Who of American Women*, *Contemporary Authors*, the *Writer's Directory*, *Who's Who in the Social Sciences in Africa*, the *International Scholars Directory*, and *Living Black American Authors*. She received the Top Hat Award from the *Pittsburgh Courier* in 1979. In Africa she was decorated Gran Dama D'Inore, Order Royal Crown in Malta, and grand officer, Order of Valor in Cameroon in 1980. In 1981 she received the Mary McLeod Bethune Women of Achievement Award; in 1982, the Ellen S. Grasso Award from Mount Holyoke College, and the Decade of Service Award from the Phelps-Stokes Fund. In 1983 she was the guest scholar at the Woodrow Wilson International Center for Scholars and was named Alumna of the Year at Northwestern University. In 1984 she received the National Coalition of One Hundred Black Women Award, while in 1985 she received an award from the Association of Black Ambassadors for its study mission to Japan. In 1986 she was awarded the United States Information Service Award. Smythe-Haithe received the Distinguished Service Award from the New York Chapter of the Links. She received a Doctorate of Humane Letters from Mount Holyoke College in 1977 and an honorary law degree in 1980 from Spelman College.

After the death of her husband, Hugh H. Smythe, the former United States Ambassador to Syria and Malta, she married Robert Haithe and now resides in Washington, D.C. Mable Smythe-Haithe is author of *Intensive English Conversation,* with Alan B. Howes (Japan: Kai Ryudo, 1953); *The New Nigerian Elite,* with H. H. Smythe (Stanford, Calif.: Stanford University Press, 1960); *Curriculum for Understanding*, with Edgar S. Bley (Union Free School District Thirteen, 1965); and *Introduction to a Slaver's Log Book* (Evanston, Ill., 1976). She is editor of *The Black American Reference Book* (Englewood Cliffs, N.J.: Prentice-Hall, 1976), and *American Negro Reference Book* (Prentice-Hall, 1974).

References

Contemporary Authors. Vol. 37-40. Detroit: Gale Research 1973.

Leavitt, Judith A., ed. *American Women Managers and Administrators*. Westport, Conn.: Greenwood Press, 1985.

Smythe-Haithe, Mabel Murphy. Interview with author. November 1990.

Stineman, Esther, ed. *American Political Woman*. Littleton, Colo.: Libraries Unlimited, 1980.

Who's Who Among Black Americans. 5th ed. Lake Forest, Ill.: Who's Who Among Black America, 1988.

Who's Who of American Women. 14th ed. Wilmette, Ill.: Marquis, 1985-86.

Joan Curl Elliott

Valaida Snow

(c. 1900-1956)

Musician, singer, dancer

Summarizing a tribute by Rudolf Hopf (''Valaida Snow, Queen of [the] Trumpet,'' *Jazz Podium,* October 1972, 8-9), Handy writes:

> Snow's trumpet playing was inventive, effortless, highly stylized and exceptionally improvisational. He acknowledged a strong Louis Armstrong influence . . . but asked, who of that period (1930s) was not influenced (and judged) by Armstrong? Her treatment of lyrical themes was suggestive of Billie Holiday—highly personal and reflective (132).

The life of Valaida Snow is imperfectly known. She was born by most accounts in Chattanooga, Tennessee, on June 2. The year is variously given as 1900, 1903, and 1909. The last date is highly improbable since that would mean that she was working in a New York speakeasy at the age of thirteen, but either of the earlier ones is possible. John Chilton proposes either Chattanooga or Washington, D.C., as the birthplace (348). D. Antoinette Handy says that her mother was trained at Howard University and that both parents were performers (131). There were three sisters, Lavaida, Alvaida, and possibly Hattie. It is not clear whether the claims that the parents were in show business are well-founded or merely an inference, but it does appear that the children were trained in music by their mother, and Lavaida, Alvaida, and Valaida were all in show business. Handy identifies Snow's instruments as ''cello, guitar, accordion, harp, saxophone, clarinet, bass violin, banjo, mandolin, and trumpet'' (131). Given the prejudices against women instrumentalists in all-male bands, it was to be as a singer, dancer, and trumpeter that she made her career.

Valaida Snow began appearing in East Coast clubs around 1920 and toured with Will Mastin's shows in the early twenties. Her first appearance at a widely-known venue was in 1922 at the Exclusive Club, a Harlem cabaret run by Barron Wilkins. She appeared in several different shows in 1923, and in 1924 she appeared in Sissle and Noble's *Chocolate Dandies* alongside Josephine Baker, who was very shortly afterwards to make her sensational Paris debut. Continuing to work throughout the United States, Snow went to Shanghai in August 1926 with Jack Carter's band. According to Lotz, her sister Lavaida later married Carter's brother, Herman (477). On her return, Snow toured, principally out of Chicago, and in 1929 toured in Europe, Russia, and the Middle East. She performed in Flornoy Miller and Aubrey

Lyle's attempt to revive *Shuffle Along* at a moment when the appeal of black shows to white audiences had declined, and in 1931 she costarred in *Rhapsody in Black* with Ethel Waters. Among the songs she sang were "Saint James Infirmary" and "Till the Real Thing Comes Along," and she conducted a vocal arrangement of Gershwin's "Rhapsody in Blue." She appeared with Earl Hines in Chicago in 1933 and joined his band on a tour for a year. This also the first year she cut a record.

In 1934 she married dancer Ananias Berry, who left the Berry brothers' act. There was some problem in connection with the marriage, since she was tried and acquitted on a charge of bigamy. *Blackbirds of 1934,* unlike its predecessors, did not make it to Broadway; in New York it played in a Harlem theater. However, it did have a fairly successful run in London with Valaida Snow conducting the show's band. Then for a while she worked on the West Coast with her husband in a double act. She made appearances in two films, *Take It From Me* and *Irresistible You,* while she was there. Snow then made another tour of the Far East before returning to Harlem to appear at the Apollo Theatre. Sometime during this period, her marriage apparently broke up, since Ananias Berry returned to the brothers' act after an absence of a year or so.

An energetic woman who realized the importance of putting on a good show, it was while she was operating out of Chicago that she impressed the young Bobby Short. For him she was the "fabled Valaida Show, who traveled in an orchid-colored Mercedes-Benz, dressed in an orchid suit, her pet monkey rigged out in an orchid jacket and cap, with a chauffeur in orchid as well" (99). Many felt that as a trumpet player she was second only to Louis Armstrong. Mary Lou Williams said: "I have always liked her trumpet playing. She was hitting those high C's just like Louis Armstrong. She would have been a great trumpet player if she had dropped the singing and concentrated on the trumpet" (Dahl, 81).

Favorable European Reputation Developed

After playing the Apollo Theatre again in 1936, Valaida Snow returned to Europe for a stay that was to last until about 1942. She built up a brilliant European reputation and appeared in two French films, *L'Alibi* (1936) and *Pièges* (1939). Will Friedwald, who remains cool to much of her music, pays tribute to her achievements in Europe by stating:

> By performing like Armstrong reincarnated in the body and voice of Adelaide Hall (according to Rosetta Reitz, they called Valaida "Little Louis" in Europe), Valaida broke down traditional notions of what male instrumentalists and female canaries are supposed to do over the course of several dozen very exciting records made with the cream of English and Scandinavian musicians (352).

It was in Scandinavia during the early forties that her most celebrated misadventure happened. She was arrested in Denmark or Sweden for theft and drug possession and deported to Germany, spent two years (or more) in a German concentration camp and was released in a prisoner of war exchange. Or she was arrested in Sweden and deported to the United States. Other variants also exist. For the moment the truth is uncertain: What is sure is that she returned to the United States in 1941 or 1942, and she was in very poor physical shape. Earl Edwards, a producer, nursed her back to health; he also became her husband. In 1943 she was able to front a band at the Apollo Theatre again and take up her career as a performer. She was to remain an active performer until her death, although some feel that the level of her music never again reached that of her prewar efforts. Still, she was a working musician and recorded regularly. Melba Liston remembered being in a show with Snow about 1945:

> There was something about her, the way she acted that saddened me and that I never forgot. . . . I said, "Boy when I get her age I'm not going to let that happen to me"—whatever it was. She was so talented, so beautiful and so sweet. But she was so unhappy. She was like hurt all the time. In my youth I didn't understand. But I felt the pain from her all the time. . . . There was that confusion that I couldn't understand in my youth (Dahl, 257).

Valaida Snow's last engagement was at the Palace Theatre in New York City. Shortly afterwards she suffered a massive cerebral hemorrhage while she was at home and died on May 30, 1956, in King's County Hospital.

Reissued recordings include: *Hot Snow: Queen of the Trumpet Sings and Swings* (Foremothers Series, Vol 2), Rosetta RR-1305; *Jazzwomen: A Feminist Retrospective,* Stash ST-109; and *High Hat Trumpet and Rhythm,* World Records SH-309.

References

Chilton, John. *Who's Who of Jazz.* Philadelphia: Chilton, 1972.

Dahl, Linda. *Stormy Weather: The Music and Lives of a Century of Jazzwomen.* New York: Pantheon, 1984. Photograph, p. 83.

Friedwald, Will. *Jazz Singing.* New York: Charles Scribner's, 1990.

Handy, D. Antoinette. *Black Women in American Bands and Orchestras.* Metuchen, N.J.: Scarecrow Press, 1981. Photograph in unnumbered section following p. 170.

Lotz, Rainer E. "Valaida Snow." *The New Grove Dictionary of Jazz.* Vol. 2. Ed. Barry Kernfeld. London: Macmillan, 1988.

Mapp, Edward. *Directory of Blacks in the Performing Arts.* 2nd ed. Metuchen, N.J.: Scarecrow Press, 1990.

Oppenheimer, Priscilla. "Valaida Snow." In *The Harlem*

Renaissance: A Historical Dictionary for the Era. Ed. Bruce Kellner. New York: Methuen, 1984.

Short, Bobby. *Black and White Baby*. New York: Dodd, Mead, 1971.

Stearns, Marshall, and Jean Stearns. *Jazz Dance*. New York: Macmillan, 1968.

Taylor, Frank C., with Gerald Cook. *Alberta Hunter*. New York: McGraw-Hill, 1987.

Robert L. Johns

Eileen Southern

(1920-)

Pianist, musicologist, educator, writer

Eileen Stanza Jackson Southern, a multifaceted artist and renowned scholar, has been a concert pianist, music educator, and music historian whose most important achievement, and the one of which she is proudest, has been her contribution to the preservation and documentation of black American music and the reintroduction of countless black American musicians to a world that had forgotten their achievements.

Eileen Jackson Southern, born in Minneapolis, Minnesota, February 19, 1920, to Lilla (Gibson) Jackson and Walter Wade Jackson, rarely speaks of her younger years. She spent her childhood in Chicago, Minneapolis, and Sioux Falls, South Dakota, with one or the other of her parents, who were divorced. She was the oldest of three sisters, the other two being Elizabeth "Libby" and Estella "Stella." Her father was a graduate of Lincoln University in Pennsylvania (1911) and Brown University, Providence, Rhode Island (1912). During the years he lived in the North, he could find work only in steel foundries or on the railroad. From 1913 to 1925 he taught at Jackson State College, Jackson, Mississippi; Johnson C. Smith University, Charlotte, North Carolina; West Virginia State College in Institute, West Virginia; and Morris Brown College, Atlanta, Georgia.

When Southern was eight, her parents separated permanently, and the three children spent the first four years after the divorce with their father in Minneapolis and Sioux Falls, then rejoined their mother in Chicago.

Southern studied piano wherever she was. She played her first concert when she was seven, in Chicago. "Wherever I was, with my father or mother, they made sure that we had music lessons." She played often as a child and spent nearly every evening during the years she lived with her father at the piano. "He was a violinist, and every night he would play, and I would play and my two sisters, Libby and Stella, would sing. It seemed natural at the time; I thought everybody lived that way" (Interview with Eileen Southern, 1990. Unless otherwise noted, all subsequent quotes in this essay are from various interviews with Southern in 1990).

Often traveling musicians would stay at her father's house, particularly in Sioux Falls, where there were few black people and no hotel would accommodate them. "I remember Louis Armstrong staying there one night when he had come to town to play. Of course he wasn't so famous then."

Her mother was insightful. Hours after Southern's birth, she chose her middle name with great care—Stanza. She knew that Eileen would be a concert pianist and that her music would bring joy and happiness to lonely souls. Southern had some feelings for jazz, but her iron-willed mother kept her in classical music. In those days, she said, "My favorite radio program was 'Red Hot and Low Down.' I presume the equivalent now would be rhythm and blues, but she insisted I stick to classical."

After finishing public schools in Chicago, Eileen Southern enrolled in the music department at the University of Chicago, where she earned the B.A. degree in 1940 and the M.A. degree in 1941. When Southern graduated from the University of Chicago, black scholars were generally unable to obtain teaching positions in northern institutions, so she sought positions in southern black colleges. For the next ten years she combined college teaching with concertizing. When Lilla Jackson did missionary work in Port-au-Prince, Haiti, in 1951, she had her daughter Eileen presented in concerts there.

In 1941 Southern accepted employment at Prairie View Agricultural and Mechanical College in Texas, where she met Joseph Southern, who was employed in the business office at the college. They were married the following year, and the two taught at several schools in the South during the next eight or nine years. It was during this time that her daughter, April Myra, was born (1946). In 1955 the Southerns adopted Edward Joseph Southern (b.1952).

At the end of this period, and after additional study at Chicago Musical College, Boston University, and Juilliard School of Music, Eileen Southern took a brief vacation as a homemaker in Kentucky. Her husband was teaching at Kentucky State College in Frankfort.

Eileen Southern appeared in concert at the following: YMCA, Buffalo, New York; Bishop College and Wiley College, Marshall, Texas (Bishop was located in Wiley at that time); B Sharp Club, New Orleans, Louisiana; Johnson C. Smith University, Charlotte, North Carolina; Edward Waters College, Jacksonville, Florida; Bethune-Cookman College, Daytona Beach, Florida; Florida Agricultural and Mechanical University, Tallahassee, Florida; Claflin College and South Carolina State College, Orangeburg, South Carolina; Alcorn State University, Lorman, Mississippi; Prairie View State College, Prairie View, Texas; Southern University, Baton Rouge, Louisiana; Carnegie Hall, New

York; and at Orchestra Hall and Lincoln Center, both in Chicago, Illinois. In 1951 she appeared as guest soloist with the Louisville Symphony Orchestra, Louisville, Kentucky, playing the Grieg Concerto, and in 1955 she appeared in concert at the Harlem YMCA in the YMCA Annual New Year's Day Concert.

In 1951 Eileen Southern came to New York to study for her doctorate at New York University, where she wrote her dissertation on Renaissance music. The following year her husband and her daughter joined her. In 1958 she went to Brooklyn College and later became a full, tenured professor of music at York College, which was the newest senior college in the City University system at the time. She would have been department chairperson if York had had chairmen, or departments, she recalls. "We completely reorganized things. With a brand new school you could get away with breaking a lot of rules in the first few years."

In the spring of 1968, black students at Brooklyn College, another campus of the City University of New York system, demanded, among other things, a program of black studies. The university's music faculty, meeting to discuss a program in the music school, heard one faculty member say, "Black music? Besides jazz, what is there?" Eileen Southern, the only black member of the department, told him, and has since told the rest of us, in *The Music of Black Americans, A History* (New York: Norton, 1971; rev. ed. 1983).

In this volume Southern outlines the course of black music, from the arrival in 1619 of the first slaves, who brought the West African's traditional love of music with them, to rhythm and blues. She actually devotes only about a fifth of the book to what is usually thought of as "black music"—jazz and the blues—and spends the remaining four hundred or more pages on the choral works, symphonies, folk music, spirituals, and popular music produced by black Americans during the last 450 years. She makes it clear that blacks have been fully involved in all types of music since long before Emancipation, and she tells who and where and mentions the social and political contexts of these contributions.

Notable Works on Black Music and Musicians Published

Although Eileen Southern has been a concert pianist as well as an educator and has published a number of journal articles and books on both Renaissance and black American music history, the publication of *The Music of Black Americans* is her favorite achievement. She says:

> It has given me a real feeling of accomplishment. I always had the feeling that I was not really making a contribution to the history of my people. Now I feel that I have done something worthwhile. It's really the one thing I have ever done that I have not felt frustrated about.

She has published another book on the same subject called *Source Readings in Black American Music* (New York: Norton, 1971, 1983).

In 1976 she went to Harvard. She came to the university when the Afro-American studies department and the music department offered her a joint professorship. She chaired the Afro-American Studies Department and taught a variety of courses in both departments, including Renaissance Notation, a seminar in the performance of Renaissance music; Black Musical Theatre; History of Afro-American Music; the Black Church and its Music; and Oral Traditions in Afro-American Culture.

Although she is the foremost authority on black American music, she has found it "difficult at times" to be a "double minority" on the Harvard faculty. Eileen Southern is aware of the similarities between her feelings and those of other faculty women, "but they can't understand what it means to be a double minority," she says. In Southern's case it was not only sexism, but racism, which delayed her being acknowledged as a scholar.

> I didn't figure it out until I was a graduate student at New York University. Finally it occurs to you: I received the same honors as the others. I have published in the same journals. What makes me inferior? Then you realize it's your color, and you can't do anything that will ever make any difference.

In 1973 Eileen Southern and her able husband established *The Black Perspective in Music*, the first musicological journal on the study of black music. After publishing numerous articles in journals and encyclopedias, she made her fourth major contribution to the study of Afro-American music, the *Biographical Dictionary of Afro-American and African Musicians* (Greenwood Press, 1982).

Eileen Southern has received many outstanding awards and honors. These include the Founders Day Award, New York University, 1961; Sojourner Truth Award, National Association of Negro Business and Professional Women's Clubs, 1969; Alumni Achievement Award, University of Chicago, 1970; Outstanding Contributor to Music, National Association of Negro Musicians, 1971; Deems Taylor Award, ASCAP, 1973; Outstanding Educator in the Field of Music, Phi Delta Kappa, 1973; honorary M.A., Harvard University, 1976; and Distinguished Achievement Award, National Black Music Caucus, 1986. From 1979 to 1983 she was recipient of a National Endowment of the Humanities grant. She became an honorary member of Phi Beta Kappa, Harvard-Radcliffe Chapter, in 1982, and in 1990 she became a Sterling Patron of the Mu Phi Epsilon Music Fraternity. She is a member of the Alpha Kappa Alpha Sorority.

In recognition of her outstanding achievements as a scholar and editor, in 1985 she received an honorary degree of Doctor of Arts from Columbia College of Chicago.

References

Morgan, Paula. "Eileen Southern." *New Grove Dictionary of American Music*. Vol. 4. Eds. H. Wiley Hitchcock and Stanley Sadie. New York: Macmillan, 1986. 277.

Southern, Eileen Jackson. Interviews with the author, 1990.

Who's Who Among Black Americans, 1990/1991. 6th ed. Detroit: Gale Research, 1990. 1185.

Who's Who in America. 41st ed. Vol. 2. Chicago: Marquis, 1980. 3118.

Who's Who of American Women. 12th ed. Chicago: Marquis, 1981. 704.

Roy L. Hill

Eulalie Spence

(1894-1981)

Playwright, educator, theater critic

A prolific playwright, dedicated teacher, and drama critic, Eulalie Spence believed that theater could portray black life in America without having to drive home a "message," and she achieved a fair amount of success as a playwright.

Eulalie Spence was born June 11, 1894, on the island of Nevis, British West Indies. The daughter of a sugar planter, she was the eldest of seven girls. At the turn of the century, her father's sugar crop was destroyed during a hurricane. Devastated by the event, the family left the island for the United States. Spence migrated with her parents and four of her five sisters through Ellis Island to New York City in 1902; a seventh sister would be born in the United States. The family first settled in Harlem and later moved to Brooklyn.

In an unpublished 1973 audio interview located in the Hatch-Billops Collection in New York City, Spence speaks of the difficulty her family had in this country because they were West Indian and possessed a certain level of education. Spence's mother, who was well-educated, was employed as a seamstress with a company that manufactured girls' school uniforms. Since her mother was allowed to have the previous year's uniform, the Spence girls were always well-dressed. It was not until later in life that Eulalie Spence realized she had grown up poor. Her mother had instilled in her daughters the idea that they were very important people, no matter how little they possessed.

In the same 1973 interview, Spence tells how she was inspired by her mother, who often read stories of adventure to the girls. These tales inspired Spence to become a writer. She also speaks of her father as being a very quiet man who left all of the decisions concerning the girls up to his wife. Spence indicated that perhaps the female characters in her plays are such strong personalities compared to the male figures because of her upbringing. Thus, she did not consciously intend for the female characters to appear strong nor for the males to appear weak. In speaking about her father, Spence believed that he died at an early age from a broken heart because he never secured the type of work he deserved in America, and also because of his desire to return to Nevis.

Very fair-complexioned, of medium height, and thin, Eulalie Spence was prim and ultracorrect in her speech and dress. She was also very loving, generous, and the backbone of the family of seven girls. Spence graduated from New York City's Wadleigh High School and the New York Training School for Teachers. She later continued her education at New York University, receiving a B.A. in 1937 and an M.A. in speech from Teachers College, Columbia University, in 1939. At Columbia, Spence had the opportunity to study playwriting with such noted professors as Hughes Hatcher and Estelle H. Davis. She also performed with the drama club at Columbia.

In 1918 Spence joined the New York public school system, and in 1927 she was assigned to Eastern District High School, Brooklyn, where she taught elocution, English, and dramatics, as well as heading the drama group until her retirement in 1958. According to former students such as Joseph Papp and Bina Mozell, Spence was a very dedicated and inspiring teacher.

Spence Becomes Prolific Playwright

During the 1920s, Spence became one of the most prolific and experienced black female playwrights, writing more than a dozen plays. Of her fourteen known plays, at least eight have been published and seven produced. With the exception of *Her* and *Undertow*, Spence wrote only comedies on Harlem life. *Her*, a ghost play, centers around a foreigner who attempts to find happiness in a strange country. Spence is perhaps speaking of her own family. The play is also interesting because *Her* illustrates Spence's use of the strong female character and the weak male. While the main character, Martha, is a dominating woman, she is also very loyal to her invalid husband. *Undertow* explores infidelity and a troubled marriage in a Harlem tenement building. Spence's themes were universal, but her characters were undeniably black.

While many of the early black women dramatists wrote propaganda plays—plays written to effect social change—Spence insisted on writing folk plays that entertained. She adamantly believed that a play could not depend on propaganda for success. Spence also emphasized that her rationale for avoiding propaganda issues was that she knew nothing about lynchings, rapes, nor the blatant injustices experienced by blacks in this country. As a West Indian, she claimed these issues were not part of her background. In her role as drama critic for *Opportunity* magazine, Spence often criticized propaganda plays and any play of poor quality written by blacks. In one of her critiques she requested "a little more laughter and fewer spirituals" (Spence, 180). Spence was constantly at odds with W. E. B. Du Bois because he insisted that she utilize her talents to write propaganda works. While these two very strong personalities had their differences, Du Bois and Spence managed to work together for several years.

Foreign Mail—possibly Spence's first play—placed second in the NAACP's *Crisis* magazine competition for playwriting in 1926. (Unfortunately, the script has been lost.) The next year proved to be Spence's most exciting year; she won the Urban League's *Opportunity* second place award for *The Hunch* and one half of third place for *The Starter*, in which a young woman attempts to persuade her boyfriend to marry her. That same year, W. E. B. Du Bois entered the comedies *Foreign Mail* and *Fool's Errand* in the David Belasco Little Theatre Tournament. *Fool's Errand*, which explores a group of female busybodies in a church who are convinced that a young woman is pregnant, won the Samuel French two-hundred-dollar prize, and both plays had the distinction of being published by French. Two of Spence's sisters, Doralyne and Olga, performed in her plays. Spence also coached Doralyne when she took over Rose McClendon's role in *In Abraham's Bosom*. In 1927, Du Bois and his group, The Krigwa Players, presented *Her* as part of their second season at the 135th Street New York Public Library.

Spence's only full-length play, *The Whipping*, a three-act comedy based on a novel by Ray Flanagan, was the only play that ever made money for her. It was to have opened in Bridgeport, Connecticut, during the 1933 season but was canceled at the last minute. The play was later optioned and sold to Paramount Pictures but never produced.

Spence, who never married, devoted most of her life to her students at Eastern District. Because of her commitment to the school, it is speculated that she had little time to meet the many writers of the Harlem Renaissance. She did correspond with Alain Locke at Howard University a great deal, and it is possible that she and Zora Neale Hurston crossed paths, since both were active with the Krigwa Players. Spence died March 7, 1981, in Pennsylvania.

Spence's plays include: *Being Forty*, *Brothers and Sisters of the Church Council* (1920), *Foreign Mail* (1926) (New York: Samuel French, 1927); *Fool's Errand* (1927) (New York: Samuel French, 1927). Also found in *Black Female Playwrights and Black Theatre U.S.A.* (New York: Free Press, 1974); *The Hunch* (1926) (*Carolina* 4: May 1927); *The Starter* (1926), *Plays of Negro Life* (New York: Harper, 1927); *Hot Stuff* (1927?), (unpublished, Howard University Moorland-Spingarn Research Center); *Episode* (1928), (*The Archive* 40: April 1928, Duke University and Trinity College Publication); *Her* (1927), *Black Female Playwrights* (Bloomington: Indiana University Press, 1989); *Wife Errant* (1928), *La Divinia Pastora* (1929), (unpublished, Spence Estate); *Undertow* (1929), (*Carolina*, No. 49: April 1929); *The Whipping* (1932), (unpublished, Spence Estate).

References

Hatch, James V., and Ted Shine, eds. *Black Theatre U.S.A.: Forty-Five Plays by Black Americans, 1847-1974.* New York: the Free Press, 1974.

Locke, Alain, and Montgomery T. Gregory, eds. *Plays of Negro Life: A Sourcebook of Native American Drama*. New York: Harper, 1927.

Oral History Interview with Eulalie Spence in the Hatch-Billops Collection, New York, N.Y.

Perkins, Kathy Anne, ed. *Black Female Playwrights: An Anthology of Plays Before 1950*. Bloomington: Indiana University Press, 1989.

Randolph, Ruth Elizabeth, and Lorraine Elena Roses, eds. *Harlem Renaissance and Beyond: Literary Biographies of 100 Black Women Writers, 1900-1945*. Boston: G. K. Hall, 1989.

Spence, Eulalie. "A Criticism of the Negro Drama." *Opportunity* (June 28, 1928): 180.

Kathy A. Perkins

Anne Spencer

(1882-1975)

Poet, librarian

Among its many accomplishments, the civil rights movement of the 1960s inaugurated a resurgence of interest in Harlem's literary renaissance of the 1920s. This reawakening among scholars and non-scholars alike again spotlighted such male writers as Langston Hughes, Countee Cullen, Claude McKay, Jean Toomer, and James Weldon Johnson. The works of women writers of the renaissance remained essentially in the background, though Nella Larsen was mentioned occasionally and Zora Neale Hurston was cited frequently for the works she produced at the end of the 1920s literary movement. It would be the mid-1970s before women writers of the Harlem Renaissance would share the foreground with their male counterparts. One of these women writers was Anne Spencer, a poet whose works were published primarily in the 1920s and a woman who was a close friend and confidante of many Harlem Renaissance luminaries. This black female—and feminist—voice was brought to light again with the publication of J. Lee Greene's *Time's Unfading Garden: Anne Spencer's Life and Poetry* (1977).

Anne Spencer

This study was one of the first post-1960s biographies of Harlem Renaissance writers, and Greene's bio-critical examination of Spencer's life and art remains the standard on which subsequent studies about her are based.

Born in Henry County, Virginia, on February 6, 1882, Annie Bethel Bannister was the only child of Joel Cephus Bannister and Sarah Louise (Scales) Bannister. Her parents were as much alike as they were different, both with unyielding personalities that inevitably clashed and caused their permanent separation. According to Spencer, "Fate let them escape chattel slavery by a hair. Good thing, too, for the slaveowner!" (Greene, 3). When the marriage ended, the couple was living in Martinsville, Virginia, where Joel Bannister remained and operated a saloon. Sarah and Annie Bannister left Martinsville, eventually settling in Bramwell, West Virginia.

After arriving in Bramwell, Sarah Bannister soon learned that, for her, employment and motherhood were incompatible. Thus, she secured her daughter a place in the home of William T. Dixie, a barber and a respected member of the black community. Better educated than Sarah Scales (who had resumed her maiden name), the Dixies were better equipped to nurture Spencer's native intelligence, which already had begun to bear fruit. Reading the dime novels and newspapers that William Dixie would bring home from the shop and under his wife's tutelage, Spencer learned the rudiments of reading and writing. Sarah Scales, though barely literate, took a great interest in her daughter's education, refusing to let her attend the black "free schools," where most of the students were the children of miners. The resourceful mother saw in the Virginia Seminary (previously the Lynchburg Baptist Seminary) an opportunity to acquaint her daughter with affluent blacks.

Commencing in 1893, her education at the seminary marked a crucial point in Spencer's young life. She exhibited a fervent desire to learn, and her precociousness sparked the first instance of her intellectual "rebelliousness"; she once recalled, "I disagreed with the religion being taught at the Seminary, and I wrote about going to hell" (Greene, 31). Her inquisitiveness resulted in what she remembered as her first poem, a sonnet entitled "The Skeptic." The fervor of her independent thought and her intellectual aggressiveness, rather than her academic performance, resulted in her selection to do the 1899 valedictory in place of the actual valedictorian, who was a brilliant but bland classmate. Spencer's tenure at the seminary proved to be a turning point in her personal life as well, for it is here that she first met Edward Spencer, who graduated with her in 1899.

Spencer and Her Garden Attract the Black Intelligentsia

Edward Spencer and Annie Bethel Scales married on May 15, 1901, and soon established a lifelong residency at 1313 Pierce Street in Lynchburg. The couple had three children (two girls and a boy). The Spencer home soon became a major stopping point for blacks traveling to the South, particularly artists and educators, as well as persons from the middle and upper classes of black society. Indeed, the Spencer household was the black equivalent of Gertrude Stein's famous salon in Paris during the 1920s, as the list of those "passing through" reads like a *Who's Who* of the black intelligentsia: Sterling Brown, George Washington Carver, W. E. B. Du Bois, Langston Hughes, Georgia Douglas Johnson, Claude McKay, Adam Clayton Powell, and Paul Robeson are among the memorable visitors before the mid-1960s. As one might expect, this august body of visitors left Spencer with myriad memories: She warmly remembers Hughes's friendship, while she had a more "warring friendship" with Du Bois, with whom she sparred verbally (Greene, 72). And even after her death in the 1970s, her home has attracted visitors as diverse as Lady Bird Johnson and Virginia ex-governor Charles Robb from the political world; poets Gwendolyn Brooks and Maya Angelou; actors Thalmus Rasulala and Carl Anderson; and a host of other public and many private citizens, all in recognition of the prominent place Anne Spencer and her garden occupied in the cultural life of east-coast America.

Although for more than half a century Spencer and her garden attracted the famous and the affluent, the poet felt a great responsibility to black people from the ordinary walks of life. Her biographer notes that just prior to 1920, she embarked on a campaign to rid black Jackson High School (Lynchburg, Virginia), of white teachers, mainly because black teachers could not work in white schools and were left unemployed; she was willing to teach at the seminary for free in times of financial exigency. In her position as librarian at Dunbar High School in Lynchburg from 1923 to 1945, she exposed black students to books otherwise unavailable to them; and in the late 1950s she opposed school integration on the grounds that it merely perpetuated "tokenism." She challenged racism in personal ways, often refusing to ride segregated public transportation or to submit to pernicious Jim Crow laws. Spencer was active in more public ways as well, serving on a human relations committee that was instrumental in organizing a Lynchburg chapter of the NAACP in 1918. The national organization agreed to send James Weldon Johnson to help lay the necessary groundwork, and his visit marked a crucial point in terms of Spencer's career as a poet.

While the notion of "discovering" an artist can be somewhat prickly, the term accurately describes Johnson's role in Spencer's literary life: The author of *The Autobiography of an Ex-Coloured Man* even selected her pen name, Anne Spencer. Johnson introduced her work to H. L. Mencken, who played a seminal role in launching the careers of black writers—one reminiscent of William Dean Howells's influence on the careers of Charles Waddell Chesnutt and Paul Laurence Dunbar. Apparently, Mencken was responsible for the publication of "Before the Feast at Shushan," the first of her poems to appear in print. Unlike her male counterparts, however, Spencer subsequently declined his patronage. True to her forthright nature, she resented Mencken's criticism of her work on the grounds that his non-poet status prevented him from understanding her art.

Apex of Spencer's Career Reached

The 1920s was the apex of Spencer's career, as the majority of her poems were published during this period. Editors and readers quickly recognized her talents, and her work (with biographical headnotes) appeared in some of the decade's most prominent anthologies: James Weldon Johnson's *The Book of American Negro Poetry* (1922); Robert T. Kerlin's *Negro Poets and Their Poems* (1923); Louis Untermeyer's *American Poetry Since 1900* (1923), that included one other black poet, Claude McKay; Alain Locke's groundbreaking *The New Negro* (1925); and finally Countee Cullen's *Caroling Dusk* (1927), a collection of black poets' work which included ten of Spencer's poems. While many editors solicited her work, Spencer seldom obliged, and thus fewer than thirty of her poems appeared in print during her lifetime.

Spencer went against the grain vis-á-vis her black literary counterparts, many of whom protested against racism much more stridently. The author herself retorted, "I react to life more as a human being than as a Negro being. . . . The Tom-Tom *forced* into poetry seems a sad state to me" (Green, 139); author's emphasis). Many of her poems—"At the Carnival," "Subjugation," "Questing," and "Change," for example—represent an almost existential concern with a decaying modern world and man's inexorable search for values and beauty in it. The persona of "At the Carnival" passes through a sideshow of hideous, deformed figures, and the "Girl-of-the-Diving-Tank" signifies the presence of beauty in the midst of degeneracy:

> Gleaming Girl, how intimately pure and free
> The gaze you send the crowd,
> As though you know the dearth of beauty
> In its sordid life (Greene, 177).

At other times Spencer expresses awe at the wonders of God's natural world, as evident in "Life-Long, Poor Browning" and "Change," poetic expressions that derive from the spiritual and aesthetic stimulation of the garden she cultivated for several decades. In a short, untitled poem, Spencer decries man's violation of God's divine, natural world:

> God never planted a garden
> But He placed a keeper there;
> And the keeper ever razed the ground
> And built a city where
> God cannot walk at the eve of day
> Nor take the morning air (Greene, 182).

In espousing the sanctity of the garden, Spencer adumbrates a motif evident in other black women writers of this century, most notably in the works of Zora Neale Hurston and Alice Walker—two vibrant voices in black feminist literature.

While her work primarily addresses the themes of man's quest for beauty in a squalid world and the search for immortality, Spencer did not write in a vacuum. "White Things" (1923) is the quintessential "protest" poem; Maureen Honey in her introduction to *Shadowed Dreams: Women's Poetry of the Harlem Renaissance* (1989) cogently notes that "the connection between male domination, white supremacy, and the destruction of nature is evident in Anne Spencer's 'White Things'" (8). While the preponderance of her works deals with more universal themes, clearly a stentorian voice emerges from time to time; incidentally, in her later life Spencer expressed an admiration for the work of poet-dramatist Amiri Baraka, father of the nationalistic Black Arts Movement of the 1960s.

After Johnson, her cherished friend, died in 1938, Spencer gradually retired from public life, becoming a virtual recluse following her husband's death in 1964. By 1973 failing eyesight, coupled with general physical deterioration, forced Spencer to abandon the reading and writing she practiced for three-quarters of a century. The last two years of her life consisted of intermittent stays in the hospital and a nursing home, taking her away from her beloved home on Pierce Street. The debilitating illness even prevented her from attending a ceremony at the Virginia Seminary and College, where her alma mater bestowed an honorary degree upon her in May 1975. Having outlived her literary contemporaries (Hughes was the last to die in 1967), as well as her beloved Edward, Anne Spencer died on July 27, 1975, at the age of ninety-three. Regrettably, many of her writings were lost, largely due to her idiosyncratic method of writing: "On paper bags, in the margins and fly leaves of books, on envelopes, in tablets, on the telephone bill, on the back of a check, a new line to a poem, a revision of a line, an entire poem, data about her life, or just 'thoughts' would appear" (Green, 164).

This iconoclastic woman once proclaimed that "My life is an open crook," and indeed she remains one of the most engaging artists to emerge from the Harlem Renaissance. An appendix to Green's study includes forty-two of her poems, and her poems now appear in several anthologies of Harlem Renaissance and twentieth-century black women writers.

References

The Anne Spencer Memorial Foundation. *Echoes from the Garden: The Anne Spencer Story*. Documentary Film. Washington, D.C.: Byron Studios, 1980.

Greene, J. Lee. *Time's Unfading Garden: Anne Spencer's Life and Poetry*. Baton Rouge: Louisiana State University Press, 1977. Includes photographs of Anne Spencer.

———. "Anne Spencer of Lynchburg." *Virginia Calvacade* 27 (Spring 1978): 178-85. Illustrated.

Honey, Maureen, ed. *Shadowed Dreams: Women's Poetry of the Harlem Renaissance*. New Brunswick, N.J.: Rutgers University Press, 1989.

Hull, Gloria T. "Afro-American Women Poets: A Bio-Critical Survey." In *Shakespeare Sisters*. Eds. Sandra Gilbert and Susan Gubar. Bloomington: Indiana University Press, 1979.

Stetson, Erlene. "Anne Spencer." *CLA Journal* 21 (March 1978): 400-409.

———. *Black Sister: Poetry by Black American Women 1746-1980*. Bloomington: Indiana University Press, 1981.

Collections

Many of Anne Spencer's letters to James Weldon Johnson and others are housed in the James Weldon Johnson Memorial Collection of Negro Arts and Letters, Collection of American Literature, Beinecke Rare Book and Manuscript Library at Yale University. Her personal literary effects are contained in the Spencer Family Papers in the Anne Spencer House and Garden Historic Landmark, Lynchburg, Virginia.

Keith Clark

Isabele Taliaferro Spiller

(1888-1974)

School cofounder, educator, performer

Isabele Spiller, a musician and performer for many years whose students and friends included some of the hottest musicians of her day, cofounded the Spiller Music School in Harlem and taught there in New York public schools, and for the Federal Music Project in New York City. She was a supporter of the move to teach instrumental music as a regular class subject in the public schools.

Isabele Taliaferro Spiller was born March 18, 1888, in Abingdon, Virginia, in Washington County. Her parents, Granville L. P. Taliaferro (1860-1916) and Josephine (Outlaw) Taliaferro (1865-1910) were both college educated. Spiller was the oldest of two daughters; her sister, Bessie, was born in 1889.

Spiller was born Cary Isabele Tallifero [sic] and according to her birth certificate, her father reported that she was white rather than black. According to Bessie Taliaferro, their father was a mulatto, the first generation offspring of a white father and black slave mother. While Isabele apparently had a very fair complexion and could sometimes pass for white, she was black.

Isabele Taliaferro received her public school education in Philadelphia, Pennsylvania, at the U. S. Grant Elementary School (1899-1903) and the Girls Commercial High School. In 1901 she earned a music certificate in public school music at the New England Conservatory of Music in Boston.

In 1912 Isabele Taliaferro joined the Musical Spillers, a black vaudeville group and, as a result, met and eventually married the founder and director of the group, William Newmeyer Spiller (1876-1944). From 1912 to 1925 she toured the United States, Canada, Mexico, and South America.

Isabele Spiller developed a large circle of friends as a result of her tenure with the Musical Spillers. Several musicians working in the 1920s had their first professional experience with the Musical Spillers, including Sam Patterson, ragtime pianist and vaudeville entertainer; Rex William Stewart, who was best known as the solo trumpeter with Duke Ellington; and Walter Bennett, who later played with Fletcher Henderson.

During her association with the Musical Spillers, Isabele Taliaferro Spiller became an accomplished performer. In 1925 a reporter from the *Chicago Defender* characterized her work: "Mrs. Spiller tickles a mean set of ivories and toots a mean moaning saxophone, too" (*Chicago Defender*, 18 July 1925).

From 1926 to 1930 Spiller studied music education at Teachers College, Columbia University. For a number of years she also studied with Melville Charlton, reputed to be one of the first blacks to gain admission to the American Guild of Organists.

In 1920 William and Isabele Spiller purchased a home on Striver's Row, the residential section of Harlem where the black elite lived and socialized. The location of their home in Harlem allowed Isabele Spiller to meet other black professionals, including W. C. Handy, Leigh Whipper, Bill

''Bojangles'' Robinson, and Noble Sissle, who also lived on Striver's Row. Luckeyeth Roberts, J. Rosamond Johnson, Leontyne Price, and Will Marion Cook were among those who regularly met at Spiller's house to study theory with Charlton.

William and Isabele Spiller founded the Spiller Music School in 1925 in response to the needs of black musicians in Harlem who could not attend the white schools and who could play with extraordinary skill but could not read music. At least six other music schools were established in Harlem by black professional musicians during the early part of the twentieth century, including David I. Martin, Carl Diton, Eva Jessye, Felix Fowler Weir, Alfred Jack Thomas, and Harry and Laura Prampin.

Around 1928 William Spiller returned to his performing career, but Isabele Spiller remained in New York City and focused her energies on her music school. William contracted an unidentified disease during his last concert tour and, after a five-year illness, he died on September 3, 1944, in New York City (''William Spiller, Vet Showman is Dead,'' *New York Amsterdam News,* 9 September 1944).

Spiller's work in her private music school was probably one of her greatest contributions as a music teacher. From 1925 to 1940 she touched the lives of hundreds of black adults and children, thus providing a valuable service, which the black community recognized.

During the early part of the twentieth century some public schools offered class instrumental music education for the first time. Spiller contributed to the development of instrumental music in Harlem because, aside from theory classes, her school was devoted exclusively to teaching students to play instruments. Her programs demonstrated the process and result of class instrumental music.

Spiller also taught at the segregated Young Women's Christian Association in Brooklyn from 1928 to 1930 and the Moorland Young Men's Christian Association in Plainfield, New Jersey, from 1938 to 1940. In 1942, at age fifty-four, Isabele Spiller began teaching in the New York public schools. For ten years she worked as an orchestral conductor and music teacher at Wadleigh High School, where she directed instrumental music classes.

According to several former members of the Wadleigh High School Orchestra, Spiller was an excellent teacher and orchestra conductor. June Carter Bentham spoke of Spiller as:

> A marvelous teacher. She was not only a music teacher but she knew classics, jazz, popular music, and ragtime. She knew history, current events, and she would keep her students up-to-date in black cultural events (Telephone interview with June Carter Bentham, 8 January 1988).

Etta Person Norris offered the perspective of the student who observed Spiller in assembly programs:

> I can remember assembly days. I can still picture her with the baton in her hand and she would be on the podium. To see her conduct that band was a marvelous sight to behold. It was really a treat. We ran to the auditorium on assembly days mostly to hear the band (Telephone interview with Etta Person Norris, 5 January 1988).

As a former member of Spiller's orchestra, Bentham offered a firsthand account of what it was like to play under Spiller:

> I can see her now standing before me; every time she led the orchestra, she always used to pivot around on her toes and she would look directly at you though those round glasses. She was always at a rise on her toes. . . . I remember her with that baton in her hand and she would swing into one of those grand Sousa marches. And then you would play your heart out because she was standing in front of you (Telephone with June Carter Bentham, 5 January 1988).

Spiller held three appointments as a music supervisor. From 1929 to 1933 she supervised the music department at the Columbus Hill Community Center. For a brief time in 1936 and 1937 Spiller served as music consultant at the Breeze Hill Civilian Conservation Corps Camp. In 1952, while still working at Wadleigh High School, Spiller accepted a position at Harlem Evening School, her last professional appointment in music education.

Spiller Excels in Federal Music Project

Spiller's most significant contribution was made as a supervisor of instrumental music in the music education division of New York City's Federal Music Project. From 1933 to 1941 she directed the activities of eight music centers, which included music classes. For two years, as a part of her employment with the Federal Music Project, Spiller also worked as music supervisor with the 1939 World's Fair in New York City.

Spiller distinguished herself as one of a few blacks who worked as a music supervisor with the Federal Music Project in New York City. She coordinated the efforts of two black teachers—one man and one woman—and six white men. Ruth Hannas, director of the music education of the project, evaluated Spiller's work as a music supervisor and expressed her delight in having Spiller as a female supervisor:

> Mrs. Isabele Taliaferro Spiller is considered by us as one of the most valuable supervisors functioning on the Federal Music Project. Her pedagogical equipment is unusually fine and temperamentally fitted for the work. Her ability to handle difficult people and difficult situations is outstanding. It is unusual to find a woman so well equipped in charge of the Woodwind, Brass,

and Percussion program (Ruth Hannas, letter to whom it may concern, n.d.).

Between 1927 and 1938 Spiller wrote nineteen articles relating to music education. Her writings included letters to parents and other teachers, editorials, and complete articles that ranged in length from several paragraphs to several pages. Most of her articles concentrate on methodology, with particular advice for the studio teacher.

Spiller applauded the efforts of the public schools to offer instrumental music in classes on the same basis as other subjects. She learned to be an instrumentalist under the conservatory approach, as had other teachers. Spiller's endorsement of the class method of instrumental instruction was based on her belief that the class method was actually a better way to teach music and to allow more children to study music. In one of her articles she explained:

> Instruction in the schools, where every child may have the privilege of playing an instrument, means not only large opportunities for the children, but also [a] far wider scope for the private teachers, because all talented children are advised by the music teachers in school to take private instruction ("Public School Orchestras," 550).

Spiller's work in New York City was recognized through her publications. Clarence Byrne, public school editor of *Jacob's Orchestra Monthly*, published Spiller's articles. In a brief introduction to one of the articles, Byrn wrote:

> Mrs. Spiller is qualified for this discussion by a very broad and thorough training in vocal and instrumental music; her methods of instruction embrace the best of long-established traditions combined with the latest developments in modern musical pedagogy (10).

Her publications included "Drum Instruction in Public Schools and How to Begin; Practical Suggestions and Instructions for Rhythmical Development Through Class Work," *Metronome*, November 1, 1927; "Free Instruction," *Amsterdam News*, November 1928; "Mrs. Spiller on Music," *New York Age*, 23 November 1929; "Music is a Preventive," *Amsterdam News*, 10 October 1936; "Products and Results of Instrumental Music Classes," *Jacobs' Orchestra Monthly*, March 1927; "Selecting an Instrument for the School Child," *Metronome*, August 1928; "Testing Musical Intelligence," *The Etude*, April 1932; and "Violin Class Instruction," *School Music*, November-December 1928.

Spiller's activities within the black community of New York City were quite varied. She was active in the United States Citizens Defense Corps, the Boys Club of America, the Harlem Riverside Community Council, and the West Harlem Riverside Neighborhood Defense Council. As a member of the Harlem Music Week Committee, she was acquainted with more than forty black musicians, including Hall Johnson, W. C. Handy, J. Rosamond Johnson, Cleveland G. Allen, Felix Fowler Weir, Carl Rossini Diton, Jules Bledsoe, and Clarence Williams.

From the mid-1920s until her death in 1974, events in Spiller's personal and professional life were chronicled in the *New York Age* and New York *Amsterdam News*. Cleveland G. Allen, music journalist for the *New York Age, Chicago Defender*, and *The Freeman*, reviewed Spiller's concerts.

In 1958 at the age of seventy, Spiller retired from her work as a public school orchestra conductor after sixteen years of service with the New York public schools. She conducted the orchestra for the last time at the Harlem High commencement program on June 30, 1958. Spiller's retirement was announced in *The Juilliard Review* in the fall of 1958 (24).

During her last years, Isabele Spiller was plagued by attacks of acute indigestion, the eventual cause of her death. At age eighty-six, Isabele Taliaferro Spiller died on May 14, 1974, at ten o'clock A.M. in Harlem Hospital. Her funeral, sponsored by the Negro Actors Guild, was held in Trumbo's Funeral Chapel. She was buried at Fairlawn Cemetery in Fairlawn, New Jersey, and her obituary was published in *The Black Perspective in Music*.

References

Berry, Lemuel. *Biographical Dictionary of Black Musicians and Educators*. Guthrie, Okla.: Educational Book Publishers, 1978.

Byrne, Clarence. "Products and Results of Instrumental Music Classes." *Jacob's Band Monthly* (March 1927): 10.

Chicago Defender, (18 July 1925).

Handy, D. Antoinette. *Black Women in American Bands and Orchestras*. Metuchen, N.J.: Scarecrow Press, 1981.

Interview with Bessie Taliaferro, 28 July 1987, 29 July 1987, 24 September 1987, 25 September 1987; Audrey Toppin, 22 September 1987, 25 September 1987; and Chester J. Trumbo, 25 September 1987.

"Isabele Taliaferro Spiller." Alumni Notes. *Juilliard Review* (Fall 1958): 24.

Kellner, Bruce, ed. *The Harlem Renaissance: A Historical Dictionary for the Era*. Westport, Conn.: Greenwood Press, 1984.

Layne, Maude Wanzer. *The Negro's Contribution to Music*. Philadelphia: Theodore Presser, 1942.

Obituary. *Black Perspective in Music* 2 (Spring 1974): 227.

Ruth Hannas, letter to whom it may concern., n.d.

Southern, Eileen. *Biographical Dictionary of Afro-American and African Musicians*. Westport, Conn.: Greenwood Press, 1982.

Spiller, Isabele Taliaferro. "Public School Orchestras." *The Etude* (July 1928): 550.

Spradling, Mary Mace, ed. *In Black and White.* 3rd ed. Vol. 2. Detroit: Gale Research, 1980.

Telephone interview with June Carter Bentham, 5 January 1988; Pearl Case, 24 September 1987; Eddie Coastes, 7 October 1988; Marion Cumbo, 14 January 1988; Ouida Blackman Edwards, 5 January 1988; Lawrence Hudson, 12 November 1987, 5 January 1988; Etta Person Norris, 5 January 1988; Bessie Taliaferro, 1 November 1987; Audrey Toppin, 13 January 1988; and Florence Von Kuren, 13 October 1987.

Who's Who in Colored America. Yonkers-on-Hudson, N.Y.: Christian E. Burckel, 1950.

"William Spiller, Vet Showman is Dead." *Amsterdam News* (9 September 1944).

Collections

Research on Spiller has been facilitated by the two collections of primary source material that Spiller prepared and donated between 1952 and 1960. The collections include correspondence, newspaper clippings, photographs, publicity circulars, programs, and family biographies. One collection is housed in the Moorland-Spingarn Research Center in Washington, D.C., and the other at the New York Public Library's Schomburg Center for Research in Black Culture. The Isabele Taliaferro Spiller Collection at Moorland-Spingarn is divided into five series: Isabele Taliaferro Spiller; William N. Spiller; The Musical Spillers; The Spiller School of Music; Photographs. The William N. and Isabele T. Spiller Papers at the Schomburg Center consist of four series: Personal Papers; The Musical Spillers; The Spiller School of Music; and Isabele Taliaferro Spiller. Aside from the Schomburg and Moorland-Spingarn collections, an extremely valuable source was the interviews held with Bessie Taliaferro, Spiller's sister and only known surviving relative. These interviews were particularly important since Spiller had no children and Taliaferro lived with Spiller most of her life. Taliaferro was an excellent source of Spiller memorabilia.

Phyllis W. Anderson

Hortense Spillers

(1942-)

Educator, author

A strikingly tall, dark, slender woman of regal beauty with close-cropped hair, Hortense Jeanette Spillers, literary scholar and writer of fiction, draws from several disciplines to explore her theories of race, gender, and nationality and to explain the genesis of the African-American as a people who have been culturally displaced. The last of four children of Curtis and Evelyn (Taylor) Spillers, was born on April 24, 1942, in Memphis, Tennessee, still the family hometown. She grew up "in the church," an institution whose influence would be decisive in her later life, particularly as the sermon became a focus of much of her scholarly work.

Hortense Spillers's formal education, punctuated with honors and awards, began in 1948 at Melrose High School in Memphis, where she received primary, elementary, and secondary training, completed with her graduation in 1960. College studies followed. She studied at Bennett College, Greensboro, North Carolina (1960-1961) and at Memphis State University (1961-1966), where she received a bachelor of arts degree in English literature and United States history (1964) and a master of arts degree in English and American literature (1966). Her master's thesis was titled "A Study of the Symbolism of William Blake's *Vala, or the Four Zoas.*" While she was at Memphis State, in 1965 she was elected to Phi Alpha Theta National Historical Society. After two years of teaching (September 1966-June 1968) at Kentucky State College (now University) with a summer of study in the humanities in between at Wesleyan University (Connecticut), in fall 1968 Hortense Spillers began scholarship-supported graduate study in the department of English and American literature of Brandeis University. She continued her teaching throughout the period of graduate study: in programs for young people in Memphis, the University of Massachusetts Boston, and Brandeis University; in the Verde Valley School (Sedona, Arizona), and Millersville State College (Millersville, Pennsylvania); in the African-American Studies program at Brandeis (1972-1973), and as a lecturer in American and African-American literature at Wellesley College in Massachusetts. On May 17, 1974, she was officially recognized for the completion of her graduate studies and dissertation, "Fabrics of History: Essays on the Black Sermon," and awarded the doctor of philosophy degree.

Full-time devotion to a career of teaching, scholarship, and creative writing followed immediately with a joint appointment in English and black studies at Wellesley College, which she held for five years (1974-1979), during which time (June 1974) she also studied at the Afro-American Institute of Culture at the University of Iowa, directed by Darwin T. Turner. Her career has continued through appointments at the University of Nebraska (1979-1981); Haverford College in Haverford, Pennsylvania (1981-1988); Cornell University (1988-1990); and Emory University (1990-). Along the way she has received numerous awards and honors, among them the National Magazine Award for Excellence in Fiction and Belle Letters (1976), nomination for the Pushcart Award in Fiction, and post-doctoral fellowships from the National Endowment for the Humanities and the School of Criticism and Theory at the University of California in Irvine (1976), the Rockefeller Foundation

(1980-1981), and the Ford Foundation through the National Research Council (1985-1986). She was appointed Senior Fellow, Society for the Humanities, Cornell University (Spring semester, 1988) and seminar leader and lecturer, School of Criticism and Theory, Dartmouth College (summer 1990).

Perspectives from Variety of Disciplines Explored

Hortense Spillers has emerged from her journey from Memphis to Atlanta as a premier scholar of literary criticism and theory, and of African-American literature in particular. Her peers, world-wide, include such persons as Henry Louis Gates, Jr. (Duke University), Houston Baker (University of Pennsylvania), Valerie Smith (University of California at Los Angeles), Nellie MacKay (University of Wisconsin), and Kimberly Benston (Haverford College). In the words of Benston:

> Hortense . . . is among the most advanced theoreticians and interpreters of American literature, women's studies, and African-American culture today. Her work combines perspectives from a wide variety of disciplines—anthropology, semiotics, cultural studies, feminist theory—to provide . . . the most sophisticated and provocative analysis of black women's literature and expressive culture we have today (Kimberly Benston to Lucius Outlaw, 20 May 1990).

Benston's assessment is, in part, both based on and confirmed by a record of scholarship that is more than impressive. In Spillers's own words: "I have managed to publish everything I've ever written in my life . . . " (Hortense Spillers to Lucius Outlaw, 20 March 1990). The list of her publications includes: two edited collections (*Conjuring: Black Women, Fiction, and Literary Tradition*, eds. Hortense Spillers and Marjorie Pryse (Bloomington: Indiana University Press, 1985); *American Identities: Race, Sex, and Nationality in the Modern Text: Selected Papers from the English Institute*, ed. with an introduction by Hortense Spillers (New York: Routledge, Hall, 1990); twenty-seven essays and reviews; and three short stories. A major work centering on the expressive culture of black women, *In the Flesh: A Situation for Feminist Inquiry*, is well under way.

A major focus of Spillers's work is what she has insightfully construed as "The American Grammar Book" ("Mama's Baby, Papa's Maybe: An American Grammar Book," 65-81). This "book," however, is not simply a collection of inscribed pages, whether her own or those of others. Rather, it is the coming-to-be of the African-American, in and through enslavement and domination, as what Spillers terms "the hyphenated proper noun" constituted through "the black person's relationship to and apprenticeship in American culture" ("Moving on Down the Line," 86). Words, Spillers tells us in this essay, are articulations of inscription on the flesh under domination. African life in America is thus a "book"; for her, it is one to be "read" and "rewritten."

What makes the book distinctively American for Spillers is its "grammar": the symbolic order manifest in discursive practices and social relations that generates and configures the meanings constitutive of African-Americans, and of European-Americans, and their interrelations ("Notes on an alternative model-neither/nor," 165-66). It is the outcome of African-American life under the pressure of events that began with the "rupture and radically different kind of cultural continuation" by way of "massive demographic shifts, the violent formation of a modern African consciousness" effected by the trade in African slaves, which "interrupted hundreds of years of black African culture" ("Mama's Baby, Papa's Maybe," 68). Finally, it is a symbolic order shaped by strategies of terministic violence dedicated to defacing and dehumanization (the denial and attempted destruction of African humanity), and to displacement, "deferment of place": Africans in America are neither fully "here" (America) nor "there" (Africa). A closer look at several pieces of Spillers's work will reveal her reading and re-writing of chapters in the American Grammar Book.

African-American Sermons Analyzed

Tapping her early immersion in Baptist church-centered community life in Memphis, one of Spillers's earliest and most sustained scholarly efforts involves her studies of African-American sermons. These studies include, for example: "Martin Luther King and the Style of the Black Sermon," *The Black Scholar*, 3 (September 1971), 14-27; reprinted in *The Black Experience in Religion*, C. Eric Lincoln, ed. (New York: Anchor Books, 1974); her doctoral dissertation, "Fabrics of History: Essays on the Black Sermon," Brandeis University, 1974; "Moving on Down the Line: On African-American Sermons": and a major, ongoing research project involving the analysis of more than three hundred sermons. It is work that demonstrates the creative insights of a critical literary theorist whose interpretive reconstructions are guided by an ear tuned to "hearing and reading" the sermons as crucial "texts." For a sense of the grounding of her approach, it is best to have Spillers speak for herself:

> If African-Americans have been "taught" anything under the regimes of New-World domination, it adheres in the very close analogy between dominant behavior and the shape of information in which it is conveyed. . . . If "I am" captive and under dominance, there can be no doubt of this "reading" in the woundings and rendings of "my" flesh. As African-Americans read their own history in the United States, the wounded, divided flesh opens itself to a metaphorical rendering both for the principle of self-determination and as a figurative economy for its peculiar national encounter. In other words, one seeks an adequate expression of equivalence, in "reading" the culture, between the situation of captivity and its violent markings. The imprint of words articulates with "inscriptions" made on the material body, so that an actual "reading" of captivity brings us to consider those changes in

> the tissue-life of the organism; to consider those differences of nuance inflicted on individual and collective identities, which help create the American regime of difference that only the Gospel, from a certain perspective, can reconcile or satisfy ("Moving on Down the Line," 102-103).

As the African-American is the hyphenated proper noun in the deferred place of neither "here" nor "there," for Spillers the black person's relationship to, and apprenticeship in, American culture are thereby inherently structured by ambivalence. African-American sermons are paradigmatic carriers of this decisive constitutive element of African-American being and consciousness, and thus are primary material for a "reading" in support of an examination of the nature of that relationship. In "Moving on Down the Line" Spillers pursues what she terms a "fundamental assumption": namely, "the religious sentiment and the documents of homiletics that inscribe it bring into play the pre-eminent mode of discourse by which African-Americans envisioned a transcendent human possibility under captive conditions" (84). The sermon is "the primary instrument of moral and political change within the community" that catalyzes, embodies, is the movement for change. It is a symbolic form that not only helps to shape verbal fortunes, but plays a major role in shaping the psyche of the African-American community (86).

Drawing out the narrative implications of these sermons requires a major shift in the project of literary theorizing: the requirements of "literacy" must be redirected "as the ear takes on the functions of 'reading'" ("Moving on Down the Line," 84-86). Furthermore:

> Because the oral/spoken sermon is granted, at the moment, privileged status in African-American life and thought . . . we must seek a place for the written/spoken documents. An American community that reads itself primarily as "oral" and "musical" and remains, in its critical/theoretical disposition, divided between "folklore"/ "vernacular" on the one hand, the "literary"/ "theory" on the other, is presently called upon to rethink itself. We have yet to examine fully the dramatic encounters of New-World Africans as texts and the impact of the latter on the culture development of strangers in a strange land (87).

We should cease, Spillers tells us, regarding the African-American situation as "basically text-deprived"; written sermons provide "another line of inquiry . . . another dimension of discursive possibility" (87). Further still, study of African-American sermons sheds historical light on an element of self-consciousness effected through a form too often thought of as simply "spontaneous": "The written sermon suggests that no sermon is without contrivance, or a considerable degree of forethought. . . . Not that a written sermon might not sustain an important element of the extemporaneous, but that the sermon itself, written down, or 'remembered' from other sermonic practice, inscribes the self-conscious pursuit of form" (88). And in the making of the African-American, sermons play a critical role by providing "a strategy of identity for persons forced to operate under a foreign code of culture" (89). Consequently, the hearer/'reader' of the sermon, "in participatory readership, is given a history at the same time that s/he seeks to fabricate one" (90).

Another chapter in the American Grammar Book read and rewritten by Spillers is that constituted by the re-formation of African women in America: the "grammar" ordering the meanings constitutive of the lives of black females in America effects their ungendering. Since gender, says Spillers, is "a category of social production . . . not yet assimilated to women of color," black women become "the very negation of femaleness" ("Notes on an alternative model-neither/ nor," 166, 170). Spillers provides us profound insight into the social construction of the African-American woman in life and literature, in part through an examination of the mulatto/a figure in literature ("Mama's Baby, Papa's Maybe") with whom the African-American female shares much common ground: a proximity between real and imagined properties; both constitute radical "alterities" to "the Dominant One," i.e. white males. An interracial figure, the mulatto/a, Spillers argues, is stranded in cultural ambiguity, a neither/nor proposition without historic locus or materiality that has been violently appropriated by dominating genocidal forces. So, too, the African-American female. Consequently, the mulatto/a figure, and the African-American woman conceal, and thus, through a proper reading, are revelatory of the "strategy of terministic violence and displacement" that makes possible what Spillers calls the problematics of alterity that African-Americans in the United States present. By coming to see how both the mulatto/a and the African-American female are socially constructed, we come to understand "the extent to which modes of substitution can be adopted as strategies of containment." In other words:

> If African-American women's community can be silenced in its historic movement, then it will happen because the narratives concerning them have managed successfully to captivate the historic subject in time's vacuum. By denying the presence of the African-American female, or assimilating her historic identity, more precisely, to a false body, ventriloquized through a factitious public discourse concerning the 'blood' and 'breeding,' the dominant mode succeeds in transposing the real into the mythical/magical ("Notes on an alternative model-neither/nor," 177-78).

The African-American female, with an identity and being constructed under the conditions of slavery and domination, was "robbed of the benefits of the 'reproduction of mothering'" and became, as noted, "the very negation of femaleness that accrues as the peculiar cultural property of Anglo-American women, in the national instance, and more generally, of the female of not-color ("Notes on an alternative model-neither/nor,'' 170). As an instance of ''alterity,'' black women share what Spillers calls the ''cultural unmaking'' of Africans that was effected during the Middle Passage from Africa to the New World that left the enslaved ones nowhere, ''literally suspended in the 'oceanic''' destined for they knew not where, without recognizable names. We know little or nothing of what this was like for women and children, of ''the fate of the pregnant female captive and the unborn'' (''Mama's Baby, Papa's Maybe,'' 72). Further: ''What confuses and enriches the picture is precisely the sameness of anonymous portrayal that adheres tenaciously across the division of gender. . . . If in no other way, the destruction of the African name, of kin, of linguistic, and ritual connections is so obvious in the vital stats sheet [of slave ships] that we tend to overlook it (''Mama's Baby, Papa's Maybe,'' 73).

> The loss of the indigenous name/land provides a metaphor of displacement for other human and cultural features and relations, including the displacement of the genitalia, the female's and the male's desire that engenders future. The fact that the enslaved person's access to the issue of his/her own body is not entirely clear in this historic period throws in crisis all aspects of the blood relations, as captors apparently felt no obligation to acknowledge them. Actually trying to understand how the confusions of consanguinity worked becomes the project, because the outcome goes far to explain the rule of gender and its application to the African female in captivity (''Mama's Baby, Papa's Maybe,'' 73).

This ''relative silence of the record'' is for Spillers ''the nickname of distortion, of the unknown human factor''; it is a ''disquieting lacunae'' that bequeaths a particular task for a critical literary theory and feminist investigation: to fill the lacunae, that is, to contribute to a revised public discourse that would both ''undo and reveal the distorting silence . . . '' and ''search out the metaphorical implications of naming as one of the key sources of a bitter Americanizing for African persons'' (''Mama's Baby, Papa's Maybe,'' 73).

It is to this principled speaking out against the distorting silencing of African-American people, through a ''reading'' and ''rewriting'' of the American Grammar Book that Hortense Jeanette Spillers has devoted her life, now, especially, with regard to the situation of African-American females. Of her present book, *In the Flesh*, she says:

> I am trying to work out a theoretical position from which African-American women might speak to a number of discursive postures that surround them, including feminist inquiry and its various staked-out positions. I am arguing that gender, at least as far as the socio-political instance of the United States goes, defines nothing more than an instrument of racial solidarity in the Anglo-American rise to power. For that reason, some women in America ''have'' gender, others don't, so that ''gender'' becomes itself as problematic a category of analysis as ''race'' and ''class'' (Hortense Spillers to Lucius Outlaw, 20 March 1990).

Given her commitments, her record to date, and her desire and sustained effort to be, in her words, ''not just a good . . . but a great'' writer of scholarship and fiction, there is every reason to believe that Spillers will achieve her goal and, in doing so, will continue to reward us with some of the most challenging theoretical, critical, and creative writing of this historical period. Already, Hortense Jeanette Spillers is well on her way.

References

Hortense Spillers to Lucius Outlaw, 20 March 1990.

Kimberly Benston to Lucius Outlaw, 20 May 1990.

Spillers, Hortense. ''Mama's Baby, Papa's Maybe: An American Grammar Book.'' *Diacritics* 17 (Summer 1987): 65-81.

———. ''Moving On Down the Line: On African-American Sermons.'' *The American Quarterly* 40 (March 1988): 83-109.

———. ''Notes on an alternative model-neither/nor.'' In *The Difference Within: Feminism and Critical Theory*. Eds. Elizabeth Meese and Alice Parker. Philadelphia: John Benjamins Pub. Co., 1988.

Lucius Outlaw

Victoria Spivey ''Queen Victoria''

(1906-1976)

Singer, entertainer, entrepreneur

Victoria Regina Spivey, ''Queen Victoria Spivey,'' was born on October 19, 1906, in Houston, Texas, and died of a liver ailment in New York on October 3, 1976. Spivey, who established herself as a classic blues singer, pianist, and composer in the 1920s, was born into a musical family. Her mother, Addie, a nurse, sang semiclassical and religious songs, and her father, Grant, and her brothers played in a family string band. Thus, it is not surprising that Victoria Spivey began to play piano early in her childhood. Later, she and her sister Addie and her brother Elton toured the vaudeville circuit and performed in barrelhouses and theaters throughout Texas, Michigan, and Missouri. Spivey went on to perform and record until her retirement in 1952; in the late

1950s, she made a comeback when the blues were "discovered" by white audiences.

The parents of Grant and Addie had been slaves. After freedom came, Grant's father amassed land holdings in Texas and Louisiana but was unable to retain them. After moving to Houston, where they sought a more economically stable life, Grant was accidentally killed while at work, leaving Addie with a family to rear. Apparently, Spivey's musical talents were drawn upon to help support the family, for her mother reluctantly allowed her to play piano at various places of questionable character in Houston. As a preteen, Spivey also played for the Lincoln Theater in Houston. When it was discovered that she could not read music, she was fired from the job. She and her brother Willie began to play for black entertainments and in whorehouses around Houston.

Spivey very early came under the influence of early blues women such as Ida Cox, Ma Rainey, Mamie Smith, and others through hearing them perform in clubs and theaters and on recordings. She was also influenced by bluesmen such as Daddy Fillmore, with whom she played, and Robert and John Calvin. Perhaps one of the most important influences upon Spivey's musical development and style came from her association with Blind Lemon Jefferson as they performed together at picnics and house parties. Eventually, Ida Cox heard Spivey perform at such a house party and encouraged Spivey to join her show; however, nothing came of this because Cox, for some unexplained reason, left without Spivey. Spivey later went to Saint Louis with the intention of recording.

Spivey aggressively appealed to Jesse Johnson, the owner of a Saint Louis record store and scout for Okeh Records, and in 1926 her "Black Snake Blues" was issued on the Okeh Record label. When Blind Lemon Jefferson's recording of "Black Snake Blues" proved to be more popular than Spivey's, Spivey accused Jefferson of stealing her song. The dispute was settled amicably and Jefferson and Spivey remained friends. In rapid succession Spivey released a string of hits such as "Dirty Woman Blues," "Spider Web Blues," and "Arkansas Blues," the latter with Lonnie Johnson on the guitar. By 1928 she had written and recorded at least thirty-eight titles for Okeh.

Perhaps the best known of all of Spivey's songs was "TB Blues," which was written while she was employed as a songwriter by the Saint Louis Music Company. It was recorded in 1927 (Okeh 8494). Blues singers tended to write and sing about contemporary events and conditions, and Spivey's "TB Blues" was just one of many such songs that grew out of black people's concern about the devastating disease, tuberculosis, which was spreading rampantly throughout the country and to which black people, more so than any other group, were falling prey. A popular notion was that tuberculosis was God's punishment for "loose living." Another Spivey version known as "Dirty TB Blues" was recorded with Luis Russell's Orchestra in 1929.

Spivey's vocal style was characterized by angularity, nasality, and a type of moan, which she called "tiger moan," reminiscent of a style of black church singing. She used slightly inflected tones that Leonard Kunstadt is reported to have described as "off-tones" (Placksin, 351). She also altered the familiar twelve-bar blues structure by adding another four bars, resulting in a sixteen-bar form. Her songs were filled with sexual overtones, double entendres, and outright pornography. The lyrics dealt with contemporary subjects and problems including drugs, the penal system, capital punishment, and lesbianism, all of which were of concern in the daily lives of her listeners.

Spivey Appears in the Musicals and Films

It has been suggested that Spivey was an assertive personality. This, coupled with an innate business acumen and ambition, led her into areas other than merely singing blues. Spivey went on the musical stage in 1927 in *Hits and Bits from Africana,* a production that also featured Jackie Mabley, who was later to win fame as the shameless comedienne, "Moms" Mabley. In 1929 Spivey entered the film world in the minor role of Missy Rose in King Vidor's musical, *Hallelujah.* She later toured Oklahoma and Texas in the starring role in *Tan Town Topics 1933*. She and her husband, dancer Bill Adams, were featured in the revue *Hellzapoppin* on the Glaser booking circuit. These activities brought occasional performances with stars such as Louis Armstrong and Bessie Smith.

From 1934 to 1951 she managed her husband's career as a dancer. She had in 1930 settled in Chicago, where she worked with or knew other blues musicians such as "Tampa Red," "Georgia Tom" (Thomas Dorsey of gospel music fame), "Memphis Minnie," "Washboard Sam," Lil Green, Sonny Boy Williamson, Big Bill Broonzy, and "Memphis Slim." She also recorded for Vocalion and Decca in Chicago, occasionally under the name Jane Lucas. She toured the country as the featured singer with her own band, The Hunter Serenaders, which included Ben Webster on tenor saxophone, Reuben Floyd on trumpet, and Joe Jones on drums. Her driving energy, business sense, and passion for perfection enabled her to continue to pursue her career long after many other blues artists had been forgotten.

After she and Adams ended their marriage and after a brief stint with the Balaban and Katz shows, Spivey left the entertainment world in 1952 to become a church organist in Brooklyn, although she continued to perform in clubs occasionally.

The discovery and acceptance of blues by white America in the late 1950s brought recognition once more to many of the early blues performers. Spivey was among the most visible of these "discoveries." Spurred by the enthusiastic support of white blues lover Leonard Kunstadt, Spivey began to appear frequently in New York clubs and was engaged by promoters of blues festivals, which had by this time become popular. Ever the businesswoman, Spivey set up her own record company, Spivey Records, and reissued many of her old works and recorded such early performers as Lucille Hegamin, Lonnie Johnson, Little Brother Montgomery, Memphis Slim, Big Joe Williams, and younger musicians such as John Hammond, Bill Dicey, and Bob Dylan. A notable issue of Spivey Records was *Spivey's Blues Cavalcade* which featured "Bunka" White and Bob Dylan among other performers.

In 1963 Spivey participated in the American Blues Festival in Europe and sang her famous "TB Blues." In 1965 she and an old friend, Sippi Wallace, appeared together at festivals. Spivey was generous in helping other show business personalities. She made her last stage appearance in 1963 in a benefit to help the ailing Mamie Smith. She continued to write blues until her death in 1976.

A partial discography of Victoria Spivey's recordings includes: *Woman Blues* (Bluesville, 1054); *The Blues is Life* (Folkways, FS 3541); *Basket of Blues* (Spivey, 1001); *Victoria and Her Blues* (Spivey, 1002); *Three Kings and the Queen* (Spivey, 1004); *The Queen and Her Knights* (Spivey, 1006); *Three Kings and the Queen, Vol. 3* (Spivey, 1014); and *Victoria Spivey's Recorded Legacy of the Blues, 1927-'37* (Spivey, 2001).

References

Barlow, William. *Looking Up at Down: The Emergence of Blues Culture*. Philadelphia: Temple University Press, 1989.

Groom, Bob. *The Blues Revival*. London: Studio Vista, 1971. Photograph, p. 70.

Harris, Sheldon. *Blues Who's Who: A Biographical Dictionary of Blues Singers*. New Rochelle, N.Y.: Arlington House Publishers, 1979. Photograph, p. 480.

Harrison, Daphne Duvall. *Blues Queens of the 1920's: Black Pearls*. New Brunswick, N.J.: Rutgers University Press, 1988.

The New Grove Dictionary of American Music. Vol. 4. Eds. E. Wiley Hitchcock and Stanley Sadie. New York: Macmillan, 1986.

Oakley, Giles. *The Devil's Music: A History of the Blues*. New York: Harcourt Brace Jovanovich, 1976. Photograph, p. 119.

Oliver, Paul. *The Meaning of the Blues*. New York: Collier Books, 1963.

Oliver, Paul, and others. *The New Grove: Gospel, Blues and Jazz*. New York: Norton, 1986.

Placksin, Sally. *American Women in Jazz: 1900 to Present*. New York: Seaview Books, 1982.

Southern, Eileen. *Biographical Dictionary of Afro-American and African Musicians*. Westport, Conn.: Greenwood Press, 1982.

———. *The Music of Black Americans: A History*. 2nd ed. New York: Norton, 1983.

Stewart-Baxter, Derrick. *Ma Rainey and the Classical Blues Singers*. New York: Stein and Day, 1976. Photograph, pp. 61, 63.

Ben E. Bailey

Jeanne Spurlock

(1921-)

Psychiatrist, educator, administrator

Physician, educator, and writer Jeanne Spurlock has devoted her career to improving the practice and attitudes of medicine toward women, blacks, and other minority groups. She was born July 21, 1921, in Sandusky, Ohio, to Godene (Anthony) Spurlock and Frank Spurlock. She was the oldest of the couple's seven children. Frank Spurlock was born in Pittsburgh; Godene Anthony Spurlock was born in the upper peninsula of Michigan. When Jeanne Spurlock was six months old her family moved to Detroit; she lived there through high school. She considered herself as growing up in an economically poor family that was rich in dreams of upward mobility. Her earliest sense that she might go into medicine occurred when she suffered a severe leg fracture when she was nine years old. She felt she was mishandled in the Detroit hospital that treated her and thought about becoming a better kind of doctor. She felt that she would not have enough money to pursue a medical education, however. She had always loved history and felt perhaps one day she would teach history.

After graduation from high school in 1940, Spurlock entered Spelman College on a tuition scholarship. She had to work almost fulltime to meet her other expenses for room, board, and supplies while she attended classes fulltime. She attended Spelman from 1940 until 1942, when it became too expensive for her. She then entered Roosevelt University in Chicago. She attended until March of 1943, when she entered medical school at Howard University on a special accelerated program. She never completed a bachelor's degree.

Jeanne Spurlock studied at Howard from 1943 until her graduation with an M.D. in 1947. Psychiatry residencies were very difficult for minorities to obtain at that time, and she had considered obstetrics/gynecology as an alternative to psychiatry when she was in medical school. She returned to Chicago to do an internship at Provident Hospital from 1947 to 1948. She then completed a residency program in general psychiatry at Cook County Hospital in Chicago, 1948-1950. From 1950 to 1951 she studied child psychiatry in the fellowship program at the Institute for Juvenile Research in Chicago. In her work with adult patients, Spurlock had often listened to their accounts of trouble during childhood and felt that intervention at that stage might be more effective. She continued as a staff psychiatrist at the Institute for Juvenile Research (1951-1953) and also served as a staff psychiatrist at the Mental Hygiene Clinic at Women's and Children's Hospital in Chicago during this period (1951-1953). She also consulted at the Illinois School for the Deaf in Jackson, Illinois, from 1951 to 1952.

In 1953 she began her adult and child psychoanalytic training at the Chicago Institute for Psychoanalysis. She did her training part-time and also worked until completion of the program in 1962. During this time she served as director of the Children's Psychosomatic Unit, Neuropsychiatric Institute (Chicago) from 1953 to 1959. She was an assistant professor of psychiatry at the University of Illinois College of Medicine during that period (1953-1959). From 1960 to 1968 she was an attending psychiatrist and chief of the Child Psychiatry Clinic at Michael Reese Hospital in Chicago while serving as clinical assistant professor of psychiatry at the Illinois College of Medicine. She maintained a private practice in psychiatry in Chicago from 1951 to 1968.

Significant Contributions Made in Mental Health Field

In 1968 Jeanne Spurlock left Chicago to be chairperson of the Department of Psychiatry at Meharry Medical College. She served in that position until 1973. Spurlock left Meharry Medical College to go to Washington, D.C., in 1973. She was a visiting scientist at the National Institute of Mental Health, Division of Special Mental Health Programs, from 1973 to 1974. In 1974, she became deputy medical director of the American Psychiatric Association, a position she holds at this time. Since that time, her work has been largely administrative, although she maintains a small private practice. She also holds clinical professorships at George Washington University College of Medicine and Howard University College of Medicine. She finds herself serving as a lobbyist to policymakers to ensure funding for medical education and post-medical education, particularly for minorities. She is often called upon to speak and remembers a presentation she made at Psychiatry Grand Rounds at UCLA, the first year they recognized Black History Month.

As deputy medical director of the American Psychiatric Association, much of Spurlock's work focuses on issues of minority and powerless people. She fights for populations subject to discrimination, including children, minorities, and women. Recently, her work has included gay populations and graduates of foreign medical schools who practice in the United States. These physicians, many of whom are American, face discrimination when they attempt to practice medicine in the United States. She is a codirector of recruitment and training efforts of minorities in research. She also directs a fellowship program for minority psychiatry residents sponsored by the American Psychiatric Association.

When asked during a 1990 interview what challenges remain in medicine and psychiatry, Spurlock noted several. First, the high cost of medical care prohibits many from seeking adequate access to care. Public health issues, such as teenage pregnancy, drugs, and smoking, also remain. Targeting vulnerable populations, such as minorities and women of childbearing age, to refrain from smoking and drinking is of concern. There are changes in families and communities that must be addressed. Parents and communities must support our schools. Parents and teachers have become alienated from each other and this has caused problems. The press continues to focus upon the negatives of black people, rather than reporting how groups such as churches and fraternities in the community have made a difference for many people, and how many have been successful despite serious odds.

Spurlock has written numerous works. She was coeditor with A. F. Coner-Edwards of *Black Families in Crises: The Middle Class*. Her own personal chapters in the 1988 book included ones on "Stresses in Parenting" and "Male-Female Relationships: The Woman's Perspective." She has written several works on such subjects as the effects of racism on children, self-concept in Afro-American children, and culturally sensitive assessment and therapeutic intervention for minorities. She has also written about sexism in medicine and psychiatry, minority issues in training physicians in child and adolescent psychiatry, and about issues affecting black Americans, especially black children. She is presently coauthoring another book on the treatment of minority group children.

Spurlock has served on the editorial boards of several professional journals, including *Journal of the American Academy of Child Psychiatry* (1969-1974), *Journal of Medical Aspects of Human Sexuality* (1972-1987), *Integrated Education* (1974-1980), and *The Pharos* (1976-1988), and continues to serve on the boards of *The Journal of Psychiatric Education* (since 1975), *Women in Context: Development and Stresses* (since 1974), and *Psychiatric Annuals* (since 1971). She has served on the board of directors of the National Urban League (1970-1978, 1979), Carnegie Corporation (1973-1980), Hillcrest Children's Center, Washington, D.C. (1977-1979), and the Green Door in Washington, D.C. (1978-1984), a halfway house program for individuals who have been psychiatrically hospitalized. The Green Door was identified during the Carter Administration as a successful example of such programs.

Spurlock is listed in *Who's Who Among Black Americans*, 1990/1991. Oral histories of Dr. Spurlock are housed at Fisk University and the Medical College of Pennsylvania. The oral history at the Medical College of Pennsylvania includes a transcript of an interview conducted by Joyce Antler on June 2, 1978, as part of the school's oral history project on women in medicine.

Jeanne Spurlock comes from a family that has supported

her throughout her career. She feels that they have contributed greatly to her success. Once, while a student, Spurlock had the opportunity to meet Mary McLeod Bethune, who was president of the National Council of Negro Women. Bethune awarded her a promissory note when she ran out of money. Spurlock was touched by her concern and financial help. Viola Bernard, a New York psychoanalyst served as her mentor, teacher, and friend. Charles Pinderhughes, a Boston psychiatrist, has been an important supportive colleague. Spurlock also sought guidance, training, and therapeutic experience from her analysts Charlotte Babcock and Fritz Mollenhoff. She feels that there are too many others who have supported her in her work to mention individually.

Jeanne Spurlock never married. She has many nieces, nephews, and former students and friends. She has served as a special mentor to many who will spread the word about cultural sensitivity in psychiatry and medicine, as she has so earnestly and successfully taught it.

References

Interview wih Jeanne Spurlock, 12 March 1990.

Spurlock, Jeanne. "Development of Self-Concept in Afro-American Children." *Hospital and Community Psychiatry* 37 (January 1986): 66-70.

———. "Survival Guilt and the Afro-American of Achievement." *Journal of the National Medical Association* 77 (1985): 29-32.

Who's Who Among Black Americans, 1990/1991. Detroit: Gale Research, 1990.

Collections

An oral interview of Jeanne Spurlock is in the Black Oral History Collection, Fisk University Library.

Susan Brown Wallace

Mabel Keaton Staupers

(1890-1989)

Nurse, organization executive

Mabel Keaton Staupers

Mabel Doyle Keaton Staupers led the decades-long struggle of black nurses to win full integration into the mainstream of the American nursing profession. During the Great Depression, Staupers assumed the leadership of the almost moribund National Association of Colored Graduate Nurses (NACGN). Possessed of superb organizing skills and a remarkable talent for political maneuvering, Staupers served as the executive secretary of the NACGN from 1934 to 1949, when she became its president. Staupers is perhaps best known for the major role she played in the desegregation of the Armed Forces Nurse Corps during World War II. She published an illuminating account of this and other battles of black nurses in *No Time for Prejudice: A Story of the Integration of Negroes in the United States* (1961). It is impossible to grasp the full significance of the history of black women in the nursing profession without devoting considerable attention to her life and work.

Staupers was born in Barbados, West Indies, on February 27, 1890. In April 1903 she and her parents, Thomas and Pauline Doyle, migrated to the United States, settling into the Harlem community in New York City. She completed primary and secondary school in the city and in 1914 matriculated at Freedmen's Hospital School of Nursing (now Howard University College of Nursing) in Washington, D.C. Three years later, Staupers graduated with class honors from the nursing program and was married to James Max Keaton of Asheville, North Carolina. The marriage, however, ended in divorce. A second marriage in 1931 to Fritz C. Staupers of New York City proved more resilient, ending only with his death in 1949. When Mabel Staupers died on November 29, 1989, she was survived by a sister, Dorothy Harrison, of Washington, D.C.

Black women encountered virtually insurmountable obstacles in their pursuit of nursing training. Although the first three schools of nursing opened in America in 1873, few welcomed black students. Mary Eliza Mahoney (1845-1926) became in 1879 the first black professional nurse after completing requirements at the New England Hospital for Women and Children. Most institutions either excluded black women altogether, as was the case in the South, or, as was seen in the North, regulated quotas for admission along racial and ethnic lines. Black communities in both the North and South, often with financial contributions from white philanthropists, assumed the major responsibility of establishing a network of hospitals, clinics, and nursing schools in order to provide black women a means to enter the nursing profession and to provide facilities for black physicians to attend their patients. By 1927 the nation's 1,797 nursing schools had trained 18,623 graduate nurses. In 1925 the number of black graduate nurses stood at 2,784. There were thirty-six schools of nursing available to them.

By the 1920s graduate nurses practiced their profession in one of three settings: private duty nurses in the homes of patients; hospital staff nurses; and as visiting nurses affiliated with municipal health departments, various public health agencies, or settlement houses. Like the vast majority of both black and white graduate nurses, Staupers began her professional career by accepting private-duty cases. Her private-duty work, however, was short-lived. In 1920, in cooperation with black physicians Louis T. Wright and James Wilson, Staupers helped to organize the Booker T. Washington Sanitarium in 1922 and became the first executive secretary of the Harlem tuberculosis committee of the New York Tuberculosis and Health Association. The Washington Sanatarium was the first inpatient center in Harlem for black patients with tuberculosis and was one of a few city facilities that permitted black physicians to treat their patients.

Staupers's work with black health care facilities and organizations enlarged her awareness of the discrimination and segregation that blacks encountered in their search for adequate treatment. A 1921 working fellowship at the Henry Phipps Institute for Tuberculosis in Philadelphia enabled her to leave New York. While in Philadelphia, Staupers accepted an assignment at the Jefferson Hospital Medical College. First-hand observations of the ill-treatment and lack of respect for blacks by college administrators and physicians left an indelible impression on the young nurse.

In 1922 the New York Tuberculosis and Health Association invited Staupers to conduct a survey of the health needs of the Harlem community, and she readily accepted. She assessed and found wanting the city's efforts to meet the health needs of the Harlem community. With consummate thoroughness, Staupers evaluated the services offered for the care of minorities in tuberculosis institutions in the city and state. Her subsequent report led to the establishment of the Harlem Committee of the New York Tuberculosis and Health Association. For twelve years Staupers served as the organization's executive secretary. She worked assiduously to channel aid and resources to minority groups afflicted with tuberculosis. Staupers's work with the Tuberculosis and Health Association left her well-prepared to assume the leadership of the NACGN.

In 1908 a group of fifty-two black nurses under the urging of Adah Belle Thoms (1870-1943) of New York and Martha Franklin (1870-1968) of Connecticut met to form the NACGN. Franklin served two terms as the NACGN's first president. The objectives of the new organization focused on securing for the black nurse integration into the mainstream of the profession. The integration sought included full membership in the key professional bodies, in particular the American Nurses' Association (ANA), and unfettered access to all schools, hospitals, and advanced study programs, along with equal salaries and fair opportunities for advancement to administrative positions. The organization would promote higher nursing standards and raise the requirements for admission into the black schools of nursing. That there existed a need for such an organization was undeniable. Both the ANA and the National League of Nursing Education had refused to accept individual membership from black nurses residing in seventeen states. Every southern state association barred black women, thereby making the majority of black nurses professional outcasts in a large section of the country. The NACGN pledged to advance the status of black nurses on many fronts. Thoms, who served as acting director of the Lincoln Hospital Nursing School from 1906 through 1923, also served as president of the NACGN from 1916 to 1923. The exclusion of black nurses from the Armed Forces Nurse Corps during World War I had been one of the most trying episodes of Thoms's presidency.

The NACGN achieved mixed results during its early years. The lack of a salaried official seriously hindered its effectiveness. In the mid-thirties the organization's fate improved as grants from the General Education Board of the Rockefeller Foundation and the Julius Rosenwald Fund enabled the NACGN both to employ Staupers and to move into permanent headquarters at Rockefeller Center, where all the major national nursing organizations had offices. Fortuitously, Staupers took the post of executive secretary just as Estelle Masse Riddle (1903-1981), the superintendent of nurses at the Homer G. Phillips Hospital in Saint Louis, Missouri, assumed the presidency of the NACGN. In 1933 Riddle had become the first black nurse to earn a master of arts degree in nursing education. Together Staupers and Riddle fought to win integration and acceptance of black nurses into the mainstream of American nursing.

The fight for integration involved a series of strategies. Staupers decided the first requirement was a stronger, more resilient NACGN replete with programs that addressed the immediate needs of black nurses. Accordingly, she spent the first few years in her new position collecting data, organizing state and local nursing associations, advising and counseling black nurses, and representing them in the larger community. She worked closely with the NACGN's biracial national advisory council that she organized in 1928 in order to develop greater public interest in, and support for, the association's programs.

Efforts Lead to Desegregation of Armed Forces Nurse Corps

The struggle to win professional recognition and integration of black nurses into American nursing acquired new momentum and urgency with the outbreak of World War II. Staupers adroitly seized the opportunity created by the war emergency and the increased demand for nurses to project the plight of the black nurse into the national limelight. By the time of the Japanese attack on Pearl Harbor in December 1941, Staupers had developed a sharp sense of political timing. When the army set a quota of fifty-six black nurses and the navy refused even to consider admitting black nurses into the nurse corps, Staupers swung the NACGN into action. She publicized the quotas. She joined with other black leaders to meet directly with the army generals and high-ranking government officials to protest the imposition of quotas. The pressure did result in some success, although not as much as desired.

In 1943 Staupers received notice that the navy had decided to place the induction of black nurses under consideration. The army raised its quotas of black nurses to 160. In an effort to draw even more attention to the unfairness of quotas, Staupers requested a meeting with Eleanor Roosevelt. In November 1944, the First Lady and Staupers met, at which time Staupers described in detail the black nurses' troubled relationship with the armed forces. Eleanor Roosevelt, apparently moved by the discussion, applied her own subtle pressure on Norman T. Kirk, the surgeon general of the United States Army, Secretary of War Henry Stimson, and Navy Rear Admiral W. J. C. Agnew.

Actually, a well-publicized confrontation between Staupers and Kirk best demonstrated Staupers's indomitable courage and political adroitness. In January 1945 Kirk announced the possibility of a draft to remedy a nursing shortage within the armed forces. Staupers immediately challenged him: "If nurses are needed so desperately, why isn't the Army using colored nurses?" (Hine, *Black Women in White*, 179). Her question exposed the hypocrisy of the call for a draft. Afterwards she encouraged nursing groups, black and white, to write letters and send telegrams protesting the discrimination against black nurses in the Army and Navy Nurse corps. This groundswell of public support for the removal of quotas that so severely restricted the enrollment of capable and willing black women proved effective.

Buried beneath the avalanche of telegrams and seared by the heat of an inflamed public, Kirk, Agnew, and the War Department declared an end to quotas and exclusion. On January 20, 1945, Kirk stated that nurses would be accepted into the Army Nurse Corps without regard to race. Five days later Admiral Agnew announced that the Navy Nurse Corps was now open to black women, and within a few weeks Phyllis Daley became the first black woman to break the color barrier and receive induction into the corps. The end of discriminatory practices by a key American institution helped to erode entrenched beliefs about the alleged inferiority of black health care professionals and paved the way for the integration of the American Nurses' Association.

The battle to integrate blacks into the Army and Navy Nurse Corps exhausted Staupers. In 1946 she relinquished her position as executive secretary to take a much-needed and well-deserved rest. It was to be of short duration, however, for Staupers considered her work incomplete. She had not accomplished her major objective, the integration of black women into the American Nurses' Association. Beginning in 1934, Staupers and Riddle had appeared before the House of Delegates at the biennial meeting of the ANA. After the 1944 meeting Staupers expressed optimism that integration would soon be accomplished. Indeed, so convinced was she of this possibility that she advised the black nurses attending the four NACGN regional conferences in 1944 to recommend to the board of directors that it be "ready and willing to vote for complete integration, if and when the American Nurses' Association House of Delegates accept us to full membership" (Hine, *Black Women in White*, 183).

General integration into the ANA did not come until four years later. In 1948 the ANA's House of Delegates opened the gates to black membership, appointed a black nurse as assistant executive secretary in its national headquarters, and witnessed the election of Estelle Riddle to the board of directors. The decision to grant individual membership to black nurses barred from state associations in Georgia, Louisiana, South Carolina, Texas, Virginia, Arkansas, Alabama, and the District of Columbia was followed by the adoption of a resolution to establish biracial committees in districts and state associations to implement educational programs and promote development of harmonious intergroup relations.

With the removal of the overtly discriminatory barriers to membership in the ANA, Staupers and the leadership of the NACGN persuaded the members that the organization was now obsolete. The ANA agreed to take over the functions of the NACGN. Furthermore, it agreed to continue to award the Mary Mahoney Medal to the individual contributing the most to intergroup relations within a given period, regardless of race. Thus, during the NACGN's 1949 convention, the members voted the organization out of existence. The following year Staupers, then president of the NACGN, presided over its formal dissolution.

Staupers Wins Spingarn Medal

Staupers received many accolades for her leadership. The crowning acknowledgement of her role in and contribution to the quest of black nurses for civil rights and human dignity came from an unexpected source. The Spingarn Committee of the NAACP chose her to receive the Spingarn Medal for 1951. Channing H. Tobias, director of the Phelps-Stokes Fund, confided to Staupers, "I know the committee was especially appreciative of the fact that you were willing to sacrifice organization to ideals when you advocated and succeeded in realizing the full integration of Negro nurses into the organized ranks of the nursing profession in this country'' (Hine, *Black Women in White*, 186).

Staupers well deserved the praise, awards, and recognition heaped upon her in the aftermath of the dissolution of the NACGN. For more than fifteen years she and Estelle Masse Riddle had labored to develop cooperative relations with leading white women and black male heads of organizations. More significantly, they had cultivated and sustained mutually beneficial ties with the leaders of the NAACP, the National Medical Association, the National Urban League, and the National Council of Negro Women. Staupers, furthermore, manipulated the press extremely well by releasing statements at the most strategic moments. Her public remarks unfailingly emphasized the cause for which she was fighting. In so doing, she constantly reminded the country of the plight of black nurses, of the racism and sexism that robbed them of the opportunities to develop their full human potential. Small of frame, energetic, and fast-talking, Staupers knew when to accept a half-loaf of advancement and when to press on for total victory. It is unlikely that the eventually complete integration of black women into American nursing on all levels could have been accomplished without Mabel Keaton Staupers at the helm of the NACGN.

References

Cobbs, W. M. ''Mabel Keaton Staupers, RN (1890-).'' *Journal of the National Medical Association* 61 (March 1969): 198-99.

Hine, Darlene Clark. *Black Women in White: Racial Conflict and Cooperation in the Nursing Profession, 1890-1950*. Bloomington: Indiana University Press, 1989.

———. ''Mabel K. Staupers and the Integration of Black Nurses into the Armed Forces.'' In *Black Leaders of the Twentieth Century*. Eds. John Hope Franklin and August Meier. Urbana: University of Illinois Press, 1981. Photograph of Mabel Keaton Staupers facing p. 241.

''Mabel Staupers, 99, Who Led Black Nurses.'' Obituary. *New York Times* (6 October 1989).

Collections

The Mabel Keaton Staupers papers are located in the Moorland-Spingarn Research Center, Howard University, and the Amistad Research Center, Tulane University. A list of unpublished sources on Staupers, black nurses, and the work of the National Association of Colored Graduate Nurses is given on p. 247 of *Black Leaders of the Twentieth Century*.

Darlene Clark Hine

Susan McKinney Steward

(1847-1918)

Physician, hospital founder, women's rights activist

Susan Maria Smith McKinney Steward devoted forty-eight years to an outstanding career in medicine. Her name and memory live in at least two public tributes: the renaming of Brooklyn's Junior High School Number 265 as the Dr. Susan Smith McKinney Junior High School and the naming of the society of the black female physicians of the New York-New Jersey-Connecticut area in honor of Susan McKinney Steward.

Susan Maria Smith McKinney Steward was born in 1847 in Brooklyn, New York, as Susan Maria Smith. She was the seventh of ten children of Sylvanus Smith and Anne (Springsteel) Smith. Her father was a successful and prosperous farmer especially noted for his raising of pigs in then rural Brooklyn. Her mother was the daughter of a Shinnecock Indian woman married to a French colonel. Her paternal great-great-grandmother, Libby Larkins, was a Montauk

Susan McKinney Steward

Indian. Susan Smith's great-grandfather, Solomon Hubbs, was an African who escaped from a slave ship.

Growing up in Brooklyn, Steward became in her teens a serious student of the organ, taking lessons from two well-known teachers: John Zundel of the Plymouth Church and Henry Eyre Browne of the Brooklyn Tabernacle. She evidently gained great proficiency in playing and in her musical knowledge because she taught music in the public school system of the District of Columbia for two years. Later, while practicing medicine, she was the choir director and organist at the Bridge Street African Methodist Episcopal Church in Brooklyn for twenty-eight years. Her tenure ended in March 1893, when, in advance of her dismissal by the board of trustees of the church, she resigned over some uproar between the choir and the trustees.

In 1867 she was admitted to the New York Medical College for Women, four years after its founder, Clemence Sophia Lozier, a wealthy physician of abolitionist background, opened it on November 1, 1863. Lozier was not only Steward's mentor but also was a close friend until the former's death in 1888. Steward wrote of her friend, "Dr. Clemence Lozier was a most remarkable type of noble, energetic, womanhood. She was firm though generous; kind though judicious; she attracted very closely to her those fortunate enough to receive training under supervision" (Seraile, 29).

The school taught homeopathic medicine chiefly in the clinical years, and included, as in the more traditional medical education programs, anatomy, physiology, chemistry, and materia medica as the preclinical medical sciences.

Students had to pay tuition and Steward managed to pay her own and according to some reports took considerable pride in the fact. Her three years in medical school were evidently marked with hard work and high intelligence, for she was graduated with the M.D. degree on March 23, 1870, as valedictorian of her class. There is no known record of her valedictory. One newspaper that covered the graduation described Steward as being "3/4 white, [with] good features, charming black eyes, and soft, black, wavy ringlets." In describing her attire, the paper noted "her black silk dress and that her chignon was bound with narrow red ribbons" (Seraile, 31). Thus, Steward became the first black woman to receive a medical degree from a medical college in New York and the third in the United States to receive the M.D. degree. The other two were Rebecca Lee in 1864 from New England Female Medical College, Boston, and Rebecca Cole in 1867 from Women's Medical College in Philadelphia.

Steward was the only one among her siblings to become a health professional, but four of her sisters were successful in other fields of endeavor. Her oldest sister, Minsarah Tompkins, was principal of Grammar School Number Four in 1864 and continued to be a principal at Public School Eighty-Eight in Manhattan until her retirement in 1901. Like Steward, she married twice, and like Steward, her first husband was an Episcopal minister. After his death, Minsarah Tompkins married Henry Highland Garnet, a famous antislavery orator and minister to Liberia. Another sister, Mary, was a hairdresser, a lucrative business in those days. Emma Smith Thomas, a third sister, was a schoolteacher; a fourth, Clara Smith Brown, was a piano teacher. There were three brothers, two of whom were killed in the Civil War and one who was stillborn.

Lucrative Medical Practice Develops

Steward began her practice of medicine in Brooklyn in 1870, five years after the end of the Civil War. Her office in Brooklyn was located at 205 DeKalb Avenue. "Business grew slowly but steadily. . . . Certain endowments of temper and temperament helped to abridge the probationary period, and in a few years she became a popular [and] prosperous family physician" (Brown 162). She opened another office in Manhattan, thus maintaining offices in two widely separated sections of the city. She practiced medicine in Brooklyn from 1870 to 1895. The practice included black and white patients of all walks of life. One biographer quotes a reference to her as "the most successful practitioner of medicine of her sex or race in the United States. Her practice is . . . among . . . the high, the low, the rich and the poor" (Seraile, 31).

Four years after opening her practice, she married the Reverend William G. McKinney, an Episcopal minister from Charleston, South Carolina. Having taken his name in marriage, the doctor used it in her practice as Dr. Susan McKinney until his death. There were two children from this marriage: Anna McKinney (later Holly-Carty), a schoolteacher in Brooklyn for many years, and William Sylvanus McKinney, who followed in his father's footsteps by becoming a Protestant Episcopal priest. He served at St. Stephen's Episcopal Church in Jamaica, Long Island.

In 1881, Steward participated in the organizing and founding of the Brooklyn Woman's Homeopathic Hospital and Dispensary, located at Myrtle and Grand avenues. It was later renamed Memorial Hospital for Women and Children and relocated at 800 Prospect Place. Steward remained a member of the staff until 1895 and was a member of the governing board from 1892 to 1895. She also served as a member of the medical staff of the New York Medical College and Hospital for Women in 1882. She was a member for just that year. It is interesting to note that she was engaged in postgraduate study—the only woman in the class—at Long Island Medical College from 1887 to 1888, and that she evinced interest in organized medicine through her memberships in the Kings County Homeopathic Medical Society and the Homeopathic Medical Society of the State of New York. As an active member of the latter society, she presented two papers and was appointed as a delegate to the New Jersey Homeopathic Society's semiannual meeting in Jersey City on October 1, 1889. Steward was also official physician to the Brooklyn Home for Aged Colored People.

Issues on Women in Medicine, Suffrage, and Temperance Advanced

Even with her busy practice, Steward found the energy and time to advance the cause of women in medicine and was one of the founders of the Women's Loyal Union of New York and Brooklyn. In 1890 her husband became seriously disabled after a cerebral hemorrhage and was able to perform only limited preaching activities and pamphlet writing. He died on November 24, 1895. Steward, now forty-eight years old, continued her practice of medicine and family responsibilities, which included the care of her mother and providing lodging and food for several other relatives. She made public speeches about women in medicine, was later active in the women's suffrage and temperance movements, and was one of the founders of the first black women's club in New York. In 1911 she addressed the Interracial Conference in London, England, on ''Women in Medicine in the United States'' and on ''Colored Women in America.''

On November 4, 1896, Ann Eliza Smith, Steward's eighty-one-year-old mother, died unexpectedly at the family home at 205 DeKalb Avenue. This was also the scheduled wedding date of Annie McKinney and M. Louis Holly, a son of the famed Bishop Theodore Holly of Haiti. The wedding could not be postponed, since Holly and his wife were scheduled to leave for Haiti three days later. A few weeks later, on November 26, the widowed Susan McKinney married the Reverend Theophilus Gould Steward, who was then serving as chaplain of the Twenty-fifth United States Colored Infantry, and according to one report, had been her minister at an earlier time.

Now once again Steward changed her professional name to include that of her second husband, and with him moved to Fort Missoula in Montana where she became licensed and practiced medicine. From 1898 to 1902 Chaplain Steward was stationed in Cuba and the Philippines. During that time Susan Steward was employed as college physician at Wilberforce University in Ohio. She rejoined her husband at Fort Niobrara in Nebraska when he returned to the States. Here she was also licensed and practiced medicine in the small town of Valentine and among the soldiers at the fort. In addition, she participated in the Women's Christian Temperance Union. In 1906 she went with Chaplain Steward to Fort McIntosh in Texas. Not long thereafter she returned with her husband to Wilberforce, where he joined the faculty as a professor in history. With him she made frequent trips away from Ohio, both in the United States and abroad. One of her more remarkable trips was made alone in 1897 to Haiti to deliver her first grandson, Louis Holly.

She died at Wilberforce University on March 7, 1918, and was interred on March 10 at Greenwood Cemetery in Brooklyn following funeral services at the home of her daughter, Annie Holly.

References

Alexander, Leslie L. ''Susan Smith McKinney, M.D., 1847-1918.'' *Journal of the National Medical Association* 67 (March 1975): 173-75.

Brown, Hallie Q. *Homespun Heroines and Other Women of Distinction*. Xenia, Ohio: Aldine Publishing Co., 1926.

Seraile, William. ''Susan McKinney Steward: New York State's First African-American Woman Physician.'' *Afro-Americans in N.Y. Life & History* 9 (July 1985). This is a source of detailed information about Susan McKinney Steward.

Ralph J. Cazort

Ella P. Stewart

(1893-1987)

Pharmacist, entrepreneur, clubwoman, editor

When Ella Nora Phillips Myers Stewart was interviewed in 1980 at the age of eighty-seven for the biographical sketch later published in *Contributions of Black Women to America* (397-401), she was the oldest living black woman pharmacist in the United States. As a black woman, she pioneered in her field and used her talent as an organizer, editor, and community worker to support various causes dedicated to

Ella P. Stewart

uplifting black women and black people. Chief among these causes were her activities with the Ohio Association of Colored Women's Clubs, which she served as president and for six years as chaplain. She spread her talent beyond the local community to the National Association of Colored Women's Clubs which she headed from 1948 to 1952. She received national acclaim for her editorial work on *National Notes*, the official organ of NACW; for writing an edition of *Lifting As They Climb*, a history of the association; and for her goodwill tour around the world for the Education Exchange Service, United States Department of State. For more than fifty years she lived her life as a notable black American woman.

Ella Nora Phillips was born on March 6, 1893, in Stringtown, a small village near Berryville, Clark County, Virginia, the first child of Henry H. Philips and Eliza T. (Carr) Phillips, who were sharecroppers. Her paternal grandmother was an Indian—a mixture of Massassoit and Cherokee—and her paternal grandfather was white. Four children were born to the Phillips marriage but the parents had wanted a boy when Ella was born: until she was five years old, Ella was dressed in overalls and was often unrecognizable as a girl. The family was highly respected and associated freely with blacks and whites in Berryville and the surrounding area. Since Jim Crow was unknown to Stewart for a while, her ability to deal with racial injustice as well as her role as a crusader for justice later in life may well have been the result of her early upbringing. At age six she was sent to Berryville to live with her grandmother Phillips and attend school. An outstanding student in grade school, Stewart graduated at the head of her class and won four major scholarships to Storer College in Harper's Ferry, West Virginia, which she entered at the age of twelve. After Stewart graduated in 1910, she married Charles Myers, a classmate, and they moved to Pittsburgh, Pennsylvania. The couple divorced three years later, after their only child, Virginia, died at age three.

In Pittsburgh, Stewart worked as a bookkeeper and cashier for the Lincoln Drug Company. A local physician encouraged her to become a pharmacist, but her friends discouraged her on the ground that pharmacy schools would not accept black women students. Stewart applied to the University of Pittsburgh School of Pharmacy and was accepted. She entered in the fall of 1914, graduating in 1916 with a Ph.C. to become the first black woman graduate of the College of Pharmacy. While a student, she was one of the founders of Pitt Lyceum and throughout her studies she was its first vice-president. In 1917 she did postgraduate work at the University of Pittsburgh, and later she studied at the University of Toledo. Stewart became assistant pharmacist for the Mendelsson Drug Company, owned by two of her Jewish classmates. From there she became manager of Howard's Drugstore in Braddock, Pennsylvania, the first black to be employed in that capacity. Having become interested in owning her own drugstore, she purchased the firm and operated it until 1918. Moving to Pittsburgh, Stewart bought the stock of Sellers Pharmacy, combined it with that of Howard's Pharmacy, and formed Myers Pharmacy, which she operated from 1918 to 1920. She sold the store when labor was scarce as a result of World War I.

Ella Myers married William Wyatt "Doc" Stewart, a prominent druggist from Pittsburgh, on May 1, 1920. They lived in Youngstown, Ohio, where she was pharmacist and purchasing agent in Youngstown City Hospital. In summer 1922 the Stewarts bought a building at the corner of Indiana and City Park avenues in Toledo and in July opened Stewart's Pharmacy, which they operated until 1945, when they sold the business. Theirs was the first drugstore in the area and many doubted that it would succeed. Initially the Stewarts's clients were predominantly white and in time the business boomed; lines often formed before the store opened. Situated in the vicinity of the Indiana Avenue YMCA, where black social activities were often held, the drugstore became a popular gathering place and the center of activities in the black community. On Sundays young people would meet there after church services, partly, but not entirely, because there was no place else to go. The pattern of using drugstores for social gatherings was set in many black communities. Stewart's Pharmacy had long hours and accommodated many people who brought their problems that the Stewart's might offer a solution. The store also became a training ground for blacks interested in pharmacy and an unofficial recruitment center for blacks in the profession.

Spacious quarters consisting of eight rooms above the pharmacy served as the Stewarts's residence. In the absence of hotel accommodations for blacks in Toledo from the 1920s to the 1940s, the Stewarts did what many blacks who lived in segregated areas felt obligated to do—they opened their residence to visitors and passersby. Many of the great black entertainers and other noted blacks were their guests. Among the luminaries who visited their quarters, some on several occasions, were singer Marian Anderson, educator Mary McLeod Bethune, cartoonist E. Simms Campbell, activist and early NAACP leader W. E. B. Du Bois, historian Carter G. Woodson, ranking black United States Army General Benjamin O. Davis, singer Paul Robeson, and educator Rayford Logan. Perhaps through Mary McLeod Bethune's relationship with President Franklin Roosevelt and his wife, Eleanor, as adviser on Negro affairs, Ella Stewart became an unofficial member of Eleanor Roosevelt's black cabinet.

The drugstore arrangement had far-reaching effects. It permitted Art Tatum, the blind pianist who played almost from infancy, to enter the show business arena. The Tatums were customers in the pharmacy. While Adelaide Hall of vaudeville note stayed with the Stewarts, Art Tatum played for her at All Saints Episcopal Church and was hired on the spot.

Stewart took an active role in local and national service organizations. Prior to becoming president of the National Association of Colored Women (NACW), she was national treasurer for twelve years and editor-in-chief of *National Notes*. She was also national chairperson of the Department of Negro Women in Industry. Stewart's love for human rights is expressed in her review of the association's developments during her administration from 1948 to 1952:

> I have tried to be fairminded, tolerant, and have consistently fought for human and civil rights with love in rendering a service to all people, regardless of race, color, or creed, locally, nationally, and internationally (Wesley, 123).

The urge for equal opportunity for blacks was a driving force behind Stewart and her husband.

Business Skills Applied to National Organization

Ella Stewart had a keen sense of business, perhaps derived in part from her experiences as owner and manager of drugstores and in part from years of service as national treasurer of NACW. As treasurer, for example, in 1941 she called for an audit before the convention, a voucher system for expenditures, a budget for officers and chairpersons, and other measures that reflected good business practice. By the time of her presidency in 1948, Stewart still maintained that the organization needed to operate more efficiently. During the first two years of her administration she worked to set the organization on a businesslike course. In addition to internal matters in headquarters, she began a national life-membership drive. During her travels to state meetings, she visited homes and collected local archives for deposit in the headquarters files, thereby preserving the historical records of NACW. By 1950 the association was in its fifty-fourth year when Stewart presided over the Atlantic City convention as fourteenth president. In her address before the national body she recalled the "clear vision" and "serene confidence" of the association's pioneer leaders and the growth that was witnessed. Projects of the association included restoration of the Frederick Douglass home as a shrine, the establishment of the Hallie Quinn Brown Scholarship Fund for educating young men and women, the establishment and maintenance of the national headquarters building in Washington, D.C., and the organization of the National Association of Colored Girls—the youth organization—to provide leadership training for young women and girls. National trends by 1950 presented new conditions, opportunities, and responsibilities that required the association's attention if its original purpose of service was to be maintained. Stewart saw "the bodies of hatred and prejudice . . . erected in law and custom between races and creeds in the United States" slowly eroding. Blacks were being allowed to vote, barriers to education were being dismantled, and discrimination in housing gradually was losing enforceable covenants. In Stewart's view, the mandate for the association was clear:

> [to] develop a program of service and action, based upon an intelligent, common sense view of public affairs of our day. The larger experiences of our day and time will require deeper insights, greater emotional maturity, more specific education and sound spiritual convictions (Wesley, 124).

During Stewart's administration she updated the history of the NACW, which was published as *Lifting As They Climb*.

Stewart was active in numerous other arenas; for example, she was vice-chairperson of the American Committee, Pacific and Southeast Asian Women's Association. The United States Department of State sponsored a study of social conditions in Asia and in October 1954 named Stewart and Helen M. Fowler of New York City as goodwill ambassadors for the Education Exchange Service. They studied conditions in the principal cities of West Pakistan, India, Ceylon, Indonesia, and the Philippines and also traveled deep into the rural recesses as the United States government aimed to raise the literacy standards of the Asian masses. They gave formal and informal lectures to women's groups. Perhaps the strongest impression of the tour was that "men, women and children are not much different wherever they live."

In 1957 the state of Virginia was to honor Stewart and Clilan B. Powell, a black physician living in New York City, by naming each as one of the state's distinguished citizens. The 350th Anniversary Committee for the Commonwealth of Virginia had made the selection, and a dinner was to be held on May 17 for the distinguished Virginians. On learning that they were black, the offer to attend was rescinded and the two were asked to return the invitations. Powell's reaction to the awkward request is unknown; however, Stewart refused to return the invitation or, of course, to actually attend the affair. In recognition of Stewart's contributions as a gifted leader, local supporters held an interracial testimonial dinner for her on May 17.

Commitments to Community and Governmental Service Demonstrated

Many other honors, awards, and recognitions came to Stewart for her work. Appointments to federal and international committees on which she served came from both Democratic and Republican administrations. The United States Department of Labor in 1951 named her to the Women's Advisory Committee on Defense Manpower. In 1952 the NACW selected her as delegate to the International Council of Women of the World in Athens, Greece, and in 1963 Secretary of State Dean Rusk appointed her to the executive board, United States Commission of UNESCO. Among her honors and awards are the Community Service Award from the Council of Churches (1952); Chamber of Commerce recognition (1955); Toledo "Woman of the Year" (1955); Distinguished Citizenship Award from *The Toledo Blade*; Golden Brotherhood Award, Temple B'nai Israel (1967); induction into Ohio Women's Hall of Fame; Stella Maris Award from Mary Manse College, Toledo, in recognition of her community work and for exemplifying the ideals of the college (1970); Doctor of Humane Letters, University of Toledo (1974); NACW's Silver Platter Award; one of ten Outstanding Senior Citizens of the Toledo-Lucas County areas; and the Ohio Senior Citizens Hall of Fame Plaque, Ohio Commission on Aging. The Toledo Board of Education honored Stewart when it named a three million-dollar elementary school after her. A museum was added to the school in 1974 to house the numerous plaques and awards that Stewart received, as well as art, carvings, and other items that she gathered on her international tours.

Stewart loved humanity but especially children. She visited regularly the school named in her honor—a practice that she continued into her nineties—and each spring, for as long as she was able, she feted the graduating classes with a dinner that she prepared. She encouraged the children to learn about the past and to know their own history. "I never had any children," she said to a fifth grade class. "I want you to remember that you're all my boys and girls." She could not bear to tell them of her own child's death at the age of three.

Stewart was a member of the board of directors of the Toledo Council of World Affairs, Community Relations, and the Toledo Community Chest, and she was on the advisory board for the Douglass Community Center. Memberships in addition to the NACW included NAACP, YWCA, American Academy of Political Science, Toledo Municipal League, Preschool Council of Toledo, League of Women Voters, Toledo Art Museum, Toledo Council of Churches, Department of Christian Social Relations of the Dioceses of Ohio, and Intercircle of Toledo. Stewart was a life member of the Frederick Douglass Historical Association, National Council of Negro Women, Delta Sigma Theta Sorority, and Iota Phi Lambda Sorority. She was honorary member of Phi Delta Kappa. She was editor of the Ohio Association of Colored Women's *Queens' Gardens*. Her church affiliation was Episcopalian, and she was "a lifelong Republican" but a "quiet one" (Lee, 3). When she joined the League of City Mothers, she said:

> Although I had no children of my own I joined the League of City Mothers because I felt I really had a great many children. I was the first Negro "Mother." There were no complications. I understand that an organization of women's clubs in Toledo threatened to drop the league from its rolls if the league accepted my membership. The league just sat tight and nothing ever happened (Rothman, 24).

Later Ella Phillips Stewart was named treasurer of the league.

William Wyatt Stewart died in 1976 at the age of 83. Still, Ella Stewart continued her community activities and was called on frequently to assist groups at the local, national, and international levels that sought advice on educational, social, and community issues. A stately figure throughout her lifetime, Stewart's grace, poise, and strength are seen clearly in later years. Photographs of her are published in *The History of the National Association of Colored Women's Clubs,* where she is pictured in 1980 or 1981 with four living past presidents, presenting plaques to Mary Church Terrell and Mary McLeod Bethune, and placing a wreath on the grave of Mary Church Terrell.

Ella Phillips Stewart died after critical surgery in Toledo on Friday, November 27, 1987, at the age of ninety-four. An editorial in *The Toledo Blade,* 30 November 1984, paid tribute to the humanitarian and civic leader, noting that "although she suffered from racial discrimination that many of her fellow black Americans did throughout the years, she overcame prejudice by refusing to reciprocate it or show bitterness over it. In her own friendships here and in other parts of the world she simply declined to judge people by color or racial differences." A black American woman of distinction, she exemplified high ideals as a pharmacist and community leader. Doubtless her thoroughness, orderliness, business acumen, interest in the uplift of her race, and concern for wholesome race relations made local and national leaders take notice and caused groups at both levels to draw upon her skills when needed. And Ella Phillips Stewart responded with dignity and completeness.

References

"Black Women Achievements Against the Odds." Traveling Exhibition from the Smithsonian Institute [sic], Washington, D.C., and "A Salute to . . . Ella P. Stewart." Program. Held at Phillips Temple CME Church, February 18, 1984.

Cole, Edrene B. "Blacks in Toledo: A Resource Unit for Elementary Teachers." Master's thesis, University of Toledo, 1972.

Davis, Elizabeth Lindsay. *Lifting As They Climb.* [Washington, D.C.]: National Association of Colored Women's Clubs, 1932.

Davis, Marianna W., ed. *Contributions of Black Women to America.* Vol. 2. Columbia, S.C.: Kenday Press, 1982. Photograph, p. 398.

"Ella P. Stewart." Editorial. *The Toledo Blade*, 30 November 1987.

Grigsby, John. "Black History Program Honors Ella P. Stewart." *The Toledo Blade*, 19 February 1984.

Lane, Tahreen. "Ella P. Stewart and Her School." *The Toledo Blade*, 12 November 1985.

Lawrence, Lord. "A Toledoan's View of the Far East." *The Toledo Blade*, 13 March 1955.

Lee, Stan. "What a Difference a Lifetimes Makes." Toledo *Blade* 28 February 1988. Includes photographs.

"Mrs. Stewart Won't Attend Virginia Meeting." *The Toledo Blade*, 13 March 1955.

Pan-Pacific and South East Asia Women's Association. Toledo Chapter. Fiftieth Anniversary, Fourteenth Conference. Program. n.d. Includes photograph.

Rothman, Seymour. "The 'First' Lady." *The Toledo Blade*, 13 March 1955. Includes photograph.

"Toledo Board Will Protest to Virginians." *The Toledo Blade*, 1 May 1957.

"Toledo Woman Attains Leadership of 50,000." *The Toledo Blade*, 20 August 1948.

Wesley, Charles Harris. *The History of the National Association of Colored Women's Clubs.* Washington: The Association, 1984. Photographs, pp. viii, 121, 122.

Who's Who in Colored America. 7th ed. Yonkers-on-Hudson, N.Y.: Christian E. Burckel, 1950. Includes photograph.

Collections

Awards, plaques, scrapbooks, costumes, furniture, and memorabilia of Stewart are in the museum of the school named in her honor in Toledo. Papers from her administration with the state and national NACW are in the local and national offices. Some of her papers are in the Bowling Green State University Center for Archival Collections, Bowling Green, Ohio, and include an oral history interview with Stewart. An Ella Phillips Stewart file is maintained in the Toledo-Lucas County Public Library, which also contains a taped interview with Stewart.

Jessie Carney Smith

Maria W. Stewart

(1803-1879)

Women's rights activist, journalist, educator

In 1832 Frances Maria Miller W. Stewart was the first American-born woman to speak publicly on political themes to a mixed audience of both men and women. She was also likely the first African-American woman to lecture in defense of women's rights. Although her public speaking lasted less than two years, she made a profound impact and stands at the forefront of the black female activist and literary tradition. A reader, writer, and student of texts, she spoke and wrote on the importance of education, the need for black unity and collective action toward liberation, and the special responsibilities and rights of women. These themes were carried out in her own activism throughout her life. Although rooted in the abolitionist movement, she was not just an opponent of slavery but of political and economic exploitation, and racism and sexism as well. Stewart's unqualified militancy and willingness to accept armed struggle if necessary set her apart from most abolitionists and showed her true dedication and political pragmatism. According to biographer Marilyn Richardson, "Her calling was not merely reformist, it was subversive" (26).

Stewart was born in 1803 in Hartford, Connecticut. Nothing is known about her family except that they were free. She had no known siblings. Left an orphan at the age of five, she was bound to the family of a clergyman until the age of fifteen. She learned to read, apparently in "Sabbath schools," and had access to books in the family library, which she states gave her a thirst for knowledge. The religious and theoretical texts she encountered in the family, as well as her contact with the art of public address, were to have a great impact upon her later life. Between the ages of fifteen and twenty she furthered her religious education and literacy in Sabbath schools while working as a domestic servant. At some point she moved to Boston, but it is not certain if this occurred before or after she lived with the clergyman's family.

On August 10, 1826, at the age of twenty-three, she was married in Boston, Massachusetts, to James W. Stewart. He was about forty-four years old and worked as an independent shipping agent outfitting whaling and fishing vessels. He had served as a seaman in the War of 1812 and was captured and held as a prisoner of war in England. At the time of the marriage he had one or two illegitimate daughters. He and Maria were married by the Reverend Thomas Paul, the founding minister of Boston's African Baptist Church, located in the African Meeting House on Beacon Hill. The church was a focal point of Boston's black community and was known for its support of social and political causes. Their choice of this church for their wedding suggests that the couple had some interests along these lines.

At her husband's suggestion, Maria Stewart added his middle initial to her name. They settled as members of Boston's small black middle class. The entire black population of Boston made up three percent of the city's total population in 1830. The couple enjoyed approximately three years of marriage until on December 17, 1829, James Stewart died of a "severe illness." They had no children. After his death the executors of the estate, a group of white businessmen, through what was described as "shameless legal maneuvers" in two years of litigation, defrauded Maria Stewart of a substantial inheritance.

In 1830, anguish over her husband's death as well as the death of David Walker, an important black activist in the antislavery movement, led Stewart to reassess the place of religion in her life and experience a religious conversion. She had previously been affiliated with the First African Baptist Church, but the "born again" experience deepened her religious commitment and caused her to see religion as more personal and central to her daily life. She wrote that her new commitment made her a "warrior" and potential martyr for "the cause of oppressed Africa," and a "strong advocate for the cause of God and for the cause of freedom"(Richardson, 8). It is important to understand her religious vision, as it is intrinsically connected to her political agenda. She wrote:

> From the moment I experienced the change I felt a strong desire . . . to devote the remainder of my days to piety and virtue and now possess that spirit of independence that, were I called upon, I

> would willingly sacrifice my life for the cause of God and my brethren. All the nations of the earth are crying out for liberty and equality. Away, away with tyranny and oppression! (Richardson, 9).

Her religious beliefs were her own and not based upon the doctrines of any one church. At various times she was affiliated with Methodist, Baptist, and Episcopal congregations.

Abolitionist William Lloyd Garrison Recruits Stewart

In the fall of 1831, Maria Stewart learned that the editors of the *Liberator* wanted to recruit black women to write for them. Founded by William Lloyd Garrison and Isaac Knapp, the *Liberator* was a weekly paper based in Boston that became a major voice of the abolitionist movement. The news "fired" Stewart "with holy zeal," and she brought a completed manuscript to the editors. *Religion and the Pure Principles of Morality, the Sure Foundation On Which We Must Build* was published by Garrison and Knapp as a twelve-page pamphlet in 1831 (with Stewart's name misspelled as Steward). Published two months after Nat Turner's famous slave revolt in Virginia, the militant essay urged the black community to "sue for your rights and privileges" and warned whites that "our souls are fired with the . . . love of liberty and independence" (Loewenberg, 189-91).

The publication of this essay began an important friendship and professional affiliation between Stewart and Garrison. Over the next two years, Garrison published three texts of Stewart's speeches in the *Liberator*; in line with the conventions of the day they appeared in the paper's "Ladies' Department." As well, an essay entitled "Cause for Encouragement" appeared in the July 14, 1832, issue and a poem, "The Negro's Complaint," was also published.

Stewart's public speaking career, which was to last slightly less than two years, began in the spring of 1832 when she addressed the Afric-American Female Intelligence Society of America. This address was published in the *Liberator* on April 28, 1932. Her second public lecture was on September 21, 1832, at Franklin Hall, the site of meetings of the New England Anti-Slavery Society. It was the first public lecture by an American born woman before an audience of both men and women. The Grimké sisters are often cited as the first American women to speak in public, but Stewart preceded them by five years. Frances Wright, a British-born woman, had earlier shocked audiences with a public speech in 1828.

The third lecture was delivered at the African Masonic Hall on February 27, 1833. Both the second and third lectures were published in the *Liberator*. "Mrs. Stewart's Farewell Address To Her Friends in the City of Boston" occurred on September 21, 1833, and was her last public speaking appearance. In *Contributions of Black Women to America*, it is stated that Maria Stewart was "employed as a full-time activist for the Maine Anti-Slavery Association" and that she "became a well known public speaker, delivering four speeches in a day during a time when women were forbidden to speak publicly" (422). No other available information on Stewart suggests that she was ever paid for her activist efforts or that she ever delivered more than four public lectures spaced over about eighteen months.

Maria Stewart's farewell address showed an uncharacteristic serenity that would seem to imply that she had made a decision to end her public career. She cited disfavor on the part of the black community with her religious exhortations and her audacity as a woman. She noted that there was a "hissing and a reproach among the people." In the speech she said:

> Having God for my friend and portion, what have I to fear? As long as it is the will of God, I rejoice that I am as I am; for man, in his best estate, is altogether vanity. Men of eminence have mostly risen from obscurity; nor will I, although a female of darker hue, and far more obscure than they, bend my head or hang my harp upon the willows (Loewenberg, 200).

With that she departed and moved to New York City in 1833.

In 1835 Garrison published *Productions of Mrs. Maria W. Stewart*, which consisted of texts of her four public speeches, some biographical facts, and several essays and poems, including a reprint of *Religion and the Pure Principles of Morality*. Stewart arranged for this publication from New York.

New York may have been more appealing, as it had a larger black population than Boston. There, Stewart kept a low public profile, but she did find a circle of black intellectuals and became a member of one of the city's two black female literary societies. These literary organizations were the foundations of the later black women's club movement. Stewart joined at first to further her own education but soon became an active member. She continued her political activism in New York, working for the North Star Association and attending the American Women's Anti-Slavery convention in 1837. It appears that she did no public speaking after leaving Boston, although advertisements for her book, published in 1879, profess that she lectured at some time in New York.

During the 1830s Stewart became a teacher in the public schools, first in Manhattan, then in Brooklyn, two separate cities at that time. In Brooklyn she taught at the Willamsburg School and in 1847 was appointed assistant to the principal, Hezekiah Green. In 1852 she lost her post for unknown reasons, and in 1853 she moved to Baltimore, Maryland, where she taught privately to individual pupils.

Sometime between 1861 and 1863 Stewart moved to Washington, D.C., where she was to spend the remainder of her life. She taught in the public school system during the Civil War and became friends with Elizabeth Keckley, the seamstress and modiste to Mary Todd Lincoln, the president's wife.

Stewart also worked at the Freedmen's Hospital, affiliated

with Howard University, and in the early 1870s was appointed matron, or head of housekeeping services. This position was held earlier by abolitionist and women's rights activist Sojourner Truth. Stewart lived and worked in the hospital for about nine years, her job being to "promote order, cleanliness, industry and virtue among the patients" (Richardson, 84). She continued to teach school while working at the hospital.

Freedmen's Hospital, located on the square between Fifth, Seventh, Boundary, and Pomeroy streets, had room for three hundred patients and was noted for its excellent medical facilities. At the end of the Civil War it was virtually a refugee camp for former slaves, who received food, clothing, and medicine in return for working on the hospital grounds or making clothes for the patients. By 1877 all classes of patients were received without distinction of sex or color.

In 1871 Stewart opened a Sunday school for poor and destitute children in the neighborhood as well as those who could pay. She raised two hundred dollars to buy a building for the school. It was located near Howard University, whose students occasionally assisted in the teaching.

In the late 1870s, Stewart learned of the passage of a pension law covering veterans of the War of 1812. This entitled her to a claim as the widow of a Navy veteran. She traveled to Boston to collect evidence of her marriage. With the help of a friend, Louise C. Hatton, she searched for individuals and official records to document her claim. In March 1879 Stewart received from Congress a pension of eight dollars a month, retroactive to the date of the law's passage. She used this money to finance the publication of *Meditations From the Pen of Mrs. Maria W. Stewart*, printed in Washington, D.C., in 1879. It consisted of a reprint of her earlier book with additional sections titled "Letters and Commendations," "Sufferings During the War," and "Biographical Sketch."

To understand the context of Stewart's activism, one must look at the abolition movement centered in the North in the 1820s. Progressing from a conciliatory, moralistic approach in the first two decades of the century, a new spirit of militancy and political action emerged. In 1831 the *Liberator* was started, calling for immediate emancipation, the New England Anti-Slavery Society was formed by Garrison, and the Nat Turner insurrection occurred in Virginia. During this time the condition of Northern free blacks was little better than that of slaves. Even the first interracial abolitionist societies were not immune to this, as the question of mass black participation was hotly debated. Paula Giddings writes that for whites, "abolitionist activism was primarily a means of releasing their suppressed political energies—energies which they directed toward the goal not of Black liberation, but of their own" (Giddings, 55). Through their participation in abolition struggles, northern white women became aware of their own oppression and began to form autonomous women's rights organizations.

Black Protest Impacts Stewart's Abolitionist Efforts

While closely tied with the interracial abolitionist movement, Stewart's arguments grew out of a black protest and abolitionist tradition that was independent of the later white and integrated groups. Probably the most influential figure for Stewart was David Walker (1785-1830), a member of the Massachusetts General Colored Association during the late 1820s. In 1829 he published *Walker's Appeal*, denouncing slavery and argued for the overthrow of white supremacy by violent means if necessary. Walker's influence on Stewart can be seen in many ways: her willingness to be a martyr to her cause, resistance to physical and political oppression, trust in the strength and potential of the black community, and the promotion of its cultural as well as physical survival. Like Walker, her words were addressed to black audiences and her ideas were uncompromising even though they might have been alienating to some.

Her contact with the abolitionist movement and her early years in the home of a clergyman gave Stewart's speeches a religious, sermon-like quality. She had a command of sophisticated rhetorical techniques and set paths for other black public speakers such as Sojourner Truth, Frances E. W. Harper, and Frederick Douglass. She spoke "as a writer under siege," challenging and pushing her audiences to action.

Religion was interspersed throughout Stewart's rhetoric. Much of the language and themes she used came from the Old Testament, where she found the Book of Revelations to be a favorite. She warned whites of the judgement to come for the sin of slavery, and some might consider her use of Biblical images as justification for inciting to rebellion. Religion, however, did not stand alone in Stewart's analysis; it was interconnected with social justice and a politically pragmatic world view. Her activism combined a sense of duty and urgency—"resistance to oppression was the highest form of obedience to God."

Stewart had a wide and varied political agenda and spoke of abolition issues in an international context. She noted the European national uprisings of the 1830s, but also berated those in the United States who only sent aid to liberation struggles outside their own country. She urged blacks to strengthen the black community and institutions within it and to plan wisely for the future. She denounced the colonization movement to send blacks to Africa, stating: "And now that we have enriched their soil and filled their coffers. . .they would drive us to a strange land. But before I go, the bayonet shall pierce me through." Along with this, however, Stewart talked about pride in accomplishments of the historical past of blacks in Africa: "Though we are looked upon as things, we sprang from a scientific people" (Loewenberg).

Stewart was critical of her black audiences as well as white oppressors, finding fault especially with free blacks in the North for doing less than they could to fight oppression. She often goaded her audiences toward activism: "If you are men, convince them [white people] that you possess the spirit of men,'' and spoke out against those who would today be labeled ''armchair activists.'' Some blacks, she said, were ''abundantly capable'' but ''talk, without effort, is nothing . . . and this gross neglect, on your part, causes my blood to boil within me!'' (O'Connor, 146).

At times Stewart was vulnerable to racist ideologies of the day, believing that if whites saw evidence of black worthiness and refinement they might acknowledge their inherent equality, and asking blacks to aspire to white standards. However, she also wrote of challenging and transcending the standards, and overall believed that the racism and exploitative actions of the larger white society were the primary cause of black oppression.

Her eloquent words and the fact that her four public speeches were published have made Stewart a most popular and widely quoted figure in discussions of black women and feminism. At the time she lived it was considered extremely inappropriate for women to give speeches or to be in any way involved in public political activism. Their place was in the home, and when they were allowed to participate in political organizations they were delegated to auxiliaries that had a moralistic focus. Stewart claimed the women were entitled and indeed obligated to speak and act in the struggle against oppression and exploitation.

Addressing the Afric-American Female Intelligence Society in 1832, Stewart put forth the unique responsibilities of women in the black community:

> O woman, woman! Upon you I call; for upon your exertions almost entirely depends whether the rising generation shall be any thing more than we have been or not. O woman, woman! Your example is powerful, your influence great; it extends over your husbands and over your children, and throughout the circle of your acquaintance (Richardson, 55).

The importance of education is central to the black woman's responsibility. Stewart felt she should develop her intellectual capacities in order to participate in all aspects of their communities: religion, education, politics, business. She hoped that through education, notions of female subservience would be dispelled. Stewart's is the earliest recorded call to black women to become teachers; she also charges mothers with instilling a ''thirst for knowledge'' in their children (Loewenberg, 188).

Stewart directly addressed her message to black women:

> It is of no use for us to sit with our hands folded, hanging our heads like bulrushes, lamenting our wretched condition; but let us make a mighty effort, and arise. Let every female heart become united, and let us raise a fund ourselves; and at the end of one year and a half, we might be able to lay the corner-stone for the building of a High School, that the higher branches of knowledge might be enjoyed by us.
>
> Do you ask, what can we do? Unite and build a store of your own. . . . We have never had the opportunity of displaying our talents; therefore the world thinks we know nothing (Loewenberg, 189).

Notions of feminine weaknesses were used to bar women from public activism, but it was not seen as a contradiction to this that many black and working-class white women worked as domestic servants. Stewart did call upon black women to be good housewives and mothers but did not see domesticity and political action as diametrically opposed. Rather, she condemned the fact that black women often had to work as domestic servants:

> Few white persons of either sex are willing to spend their lives and bury their talents in performing mean, servile labor. And such is the horrible idea that I entertain respecting a life of servitude, that if I conceived of there being no possibility of my rising above the condition of servant, I would gladly hail death as a welcome messenger. . . . Most of our color have dragged out a miserable existence of servitude from the cradle to the grave. And what literary acquirements can be made, or useful knowledge derived, from either maps, books, or charts, by those who continually drudge from Monday morning until Sunday noon? (Sterling, 154-55).

At one point, Stewart addressed white women regarding their privilege:

> O, ye fairer sisters, whose hands are never soiled, whose nerves and muscles are never strained, go learn by experience. . .! Had it been our lot to have been nursed in the lap of affluence and ease . . . should we not have naturally supposed that we were never made to toil? And why are not our forms as delicate and our constitutions as slender as yours? Is not the workmanship as curious and complete? (Sterling, 155).

Stewart's ideas encompassed both the Victorian ethic and notion of ''true womanhood'' as well as criticism of it. She believed that women could exercise moral influence but opposed the idea that morality was inherent to any particular class or race. She felt that the ''true womanhood'' idealized by the dominant culture was determined by external circumstances and privilege rather than natural law. Her opposition to the idea that women are responsible for their own degradation is radical even today.

In her farewell address in Boston in 1833, Stewart placed herself in the historical tradition of women activists, asserting the right of women to aspire to positions of responsibilities and authority:

> What if I am a woman? Is not the God of ancient times the God of these modern days? Did he not raise up Deborah to be a mother and a judge in

> Israel?. . . St. Paul declared it was a shame for a woman to speak in public, yet our Great High Priest and Advocate did not condemn women for a more notorious offense than this; neither will he condemn this worthless worm (O'Connor, 142).

She mentions many women throughout history: Queen Esther, Mary Magdalene, the Greek oracles, Jewish and Egyptian prophetesses, a woman professor of law in the thirteenth century, and many more. All this fortifies the theme of women's ability and activism found throughout her work. She urges her contemporaries to take note of the achievements of women throughout history and accept and encourage public activism in the present:

> God at this eventful period should raise up your females to strive . . . both in public and private, to assist those who are endeavoring to stop the strong current of prejudice that flows so profusely against us at present.
>
> No longer ridicule their [women's] efforts. It will be counted as sin (Loewenberg, 199).

"Daughters of Africa, awake! arise! distinguish yourselves." These words of Maria Stewart stand in a long tradition of black women struggling against oppression. Notable not only in the fact that she was the first to speak publicly but in what she said and in her militancy and dedication, hers is a life combining theory and practice, inspiration and activism. Maria W. Stewart died on December 17, 1879, at Freedman's Hospital in Washington D.C. at the age of seventy-six.

References

Black Women in Nineteenth Century American Life. Eds. Bert James Loewenberg and Ruth Bogin. University Park: Pennsylvania State University Press, 1977.

Giddings, Paula. *When and Where I Enter*. New York: William Morrow, 1984.

Contributions of Black Women to America. Vol. 1. Ed. Marianna W. Davis. Columbia, S.C.: Kenday Press, 1982.

O'Connor, Lillian. *Pioneer Women Orators*. New York: Columbia University Press, 1954.

Quarles, Benjamin. *Black Abolitionists*. New York: Oxford University Press, 1969.

Richardson, Marilyn. *Maria Stewart: America's First Black Woman Political Writer*. Bloomington: Indiana University Press, 1987. The most thorough and complete source on Stewart, and the main source used for this essay.

Sterling, Dorothy, ed. *We Are Your Sisters*. New York: Norton, 1984.

Stewart, Maria W. *Meditations From the Pen of Mrs. Maria W. Stewart*. The Author, 1879. Reprinted in Marilyn Richardson. *Maria Stewart*.

——. *Productions of Mrs. Maria W. Stewart*. Boston: Garrison and Knapp, 1835. Reprinted in Marilyn Richardson. *Maria Sewart*.

Flexner, Eleanor. "Maria W. Stewart." *Notable American Women*. Vol. 3. Cambridge: Harvard University Press, 1971.

Lisa Studier with Adrienne Lash Jones

Juanita Kidd Stout

(1919-)

Judge

Juanita Kidd Stout, retired Justice of the Supreme Court of Pennsylvania, is the first black woman to serve on the highest appellate court of any state. She was appointed to that position in January 1988 by Pennsylvania governor Robert P. Casey. Upon her election in 1959 to the Municipal—the name was later changed to County—Court of Philadelphia, she became the first black woman to be elected to a court of record in the United States. She held that position until 1968. After serving a ten-year term on the Municipal (County) Court she was elected to two ten-year terms on the Court of Common Pleas. She then served the court of general trial jurisdiction and then was appointed to the Supreme Court of Pennsylvania. Upon reaching the mandatory retirement age of seventy, Stout retired from the Supreme Court of Pennsylvania and returned to the Court of Common Pleas as a senior judge in the homicide division.

Stout was born on March 7, 1919, in Wewoka, Oklahoma, the only child of Henry M. and Mary Chandler Kidd. From her parents, who were schoolteachers, she learned to be obedient, studious and, above all, "useful," her mother's favorite word. Her parents taught her to read by the time she was three and, when she was six, she started school in the third grade. She graduated at the head of her class in grade school and high school but had to leave Oklahoma at age sixteen to attend an accredited college. For two years, beginning in 1935, she studied at Lincoln University in Jefferson City, Missouri, then transferred to the University of Iowa in Iowa City to study music. Stout had studied piano diligently since she was five and she received a bachelor of arts degree in music in 1939. For two summers she did graduate study in piano at the University of Colorado in Boulder, Colorado, and at the University of Minnesota in Minneapolis.

At the age of twenty, Stout began her career as a teacher in Seminole, Oklahoma, where she taught grade school and high school music for two years at the Booker T. Washington High School. She also taught one year at Sand Springs, near Tulsa, Oklahoma. It was there she met her future husband, Charles Otis Stout, who taught history and Spanish and also assisted as boys' counselor. Although a few of Stout's students were older than she, and most of them were larger—she weighed only eighty-eight pounds—she believed that the first prerequisite for learning was order in the classroom and "order I was determined to have." Discipline, however, was the one shortcoming of her principal, "a wonderful, kindly man," who had built an excellent school with an enthusiastic faculty. Because of her future husband's commanding physical presence, she formed the habit of sending "the large boys who were troublesome" to him, and her discipline problems "began to fade away" (Telephone interview with Juanita Kidd Stout, May 1990).

The relationship between the two teachers grew closer than either realized at that time. They spent much of their spare time together playing the piano and singing and playing bridge. After a year of teaching together, World War II broke out and they went their separate ways: he to the army and she to Washington, D.C., with another teacher from Sand Springs, Eula Mae Smith, and found employment as a secretary.

The two young ladies, in their early twenties, found Washington more exciting then Sand Springs, and decided to remain there. For a very brief period, Stout took a job with the National Housing Authority. After passing the examination for a job as junior professional assistant, which was the only qualification for the job, Stout observed that others were being given these jobs while she was not. After a heated and futile discussion with the personnel manager, Stout decided to quit rather than to stay in a job paying only eighteen hundred dollars a year. Good fortune, however, awaited her. That evening Smith told her that she had learned that the prominent law firm of Houston, Houston, and Hastie was seeking an additional secretary. Because Stout was excellent in typing and shorthand and also because she loved the law, she was hired. She worked directly with Charles Hamilton Houston, who inspired her and whom she still describes as "the best lawyer I have ever met" (Telephone interview with Juanita Kidd Stout, May 1990).

When Stout left Sand Springs there were no plans for marriage. Before his first leave, however, her future husband located her through their former school principal. On his first leave, he went to Washington to renew his relationship with her. She says, "He never asked me to marry him. He just walked in and said 'We're getting married.' He never gave me a chance to say 'No.' " (Telephone interview with Juanita Kidd Stout, May 1990). On June 23, 1942, they were married.

From the time she was three years old, Stout knew she wanted to be a lawyer. She had "never even seen a woman lawyer, never mind a black woman lawyer," she says. "I can't explain it even today. It was my dream" (Telephone interview with Juanita Kidd Stout, May 1990).

Stout's legal training was started at Howard University, but she transferred to Indiana University in Bloomington, Indiana, where her husband was completing his doctoral studies. This arrangement proved to be her golden opportunity to accomplish her dream of becoming a lawyer. She earned two law degrees: a doctor of jurisprudence in 1948 and a master of law, specializing in legislation, in 1954.

Stout Begins Law Career

Stout passed the grueling Pennsylvania Bar examination in 1954 and went into private practice with Mabel G. Turner, who later became assistant U.S. attorney. In April 1956 Stout joined the Philadelphia district attorney's office. Three-and-one half years later she was promoted to chief of the Appeals, Pardons, and Parole Division. During her tenure in this office she still maintained a private practice, limited to civil cases. Stout became the first black woman to sit on the bench in Philadelphia. Her appointment as judge of the municipal court was made by Governor David L. Lawrence in September 1959. In November of that year she ran in a citywide election and won a ten-year term—beating her opponent by a two-to-one margin—and thus became the nation's first elected black woman judge.

During the mid-1960s, while serving a brief period in the juvenile division of the court, Stout attracted national attention because of her handling of youth gang problems, which turned some neighborhoods into battlegrounds. *Life* magazine featured her in an article titled "Her Honor Bops the Hoodlums," which paid a special tribute to Philadelphia for having a "tough" but fair judge on the bench. However, she was criticized by the American Civil Liberties Union, which felt she paid insufficient attention to the "constitutional niceties" in meting out her "swift justice" (*Time*, 42). Despite this criticism, which Stout "[doesn't] understand," she has earned a reputation for her intellectual prowess (Telephone interview with Juanita Kidd Stout, May 1990). Many of her colleagues say that her special talent "is that she knows when to take the long-term view" (*Ebony*, 44).

Stout is known among her peers for the clarity of her legal writing and opinions. She has published several articles, including "The Separate but Equal Theory," published in John Franks's *Cases on Constitutional Law in 1950*; "Executive Clemency in Pennsylvania," in the May 1959 issue of *The Shingle*, the official publication of the Philadelphia Bar Association; "The Suitable Home—One Proposal for Preventing Juvenile Delinquency," in the Winter 1960 issue of *Temple Law Quarterly*, and "Troubled Children and Reading Achievement" in *Catholic Library World* in 1965.

Stout has been active in many professional and civic organizations. These include the American Judicature Society, Philadelphia Bar Association, Pennsylvania Bar Association, American Bar Association, National Association of Women Lawyers, and the American Judges Association. She has held board memberships with Rockford College, Saint

Augustine's College, the National Conference of Christians and Jews, and the Women's Medical College of Pennsylvania.

Her unique ability has been recognized by eleven universities, which have awarded her honorary degrees, and by Rockford College, Rockford, Illinois, which awarded her the prestigious Jane Adams Medal in August 1965. Her alma mater, the University of Iowa, named her a distinguished alumnus in June 1974.

Stout has received over two hundred awards from professional and civic organizations. She has been awarded the Charles Hamilton Houston Medallion of Merit by the Washington Bar Association and was named the outstanding woman lawyer of the year by the National Association of Women Lawyers in 1965. She was named the justice of the year by the National Association of Women Judges in 1988. In 1989 she was awarded the Gimbel Award for Humanitarian Services by the Medical College of Pennsylvania and was named a distinguished daughter of Pennsylvania by Governor Robert P. Casey. Stout's special ability also gained the attention of Presidents John F. Kennedy and Lyndon B. Johnson, each of whom named her to missions to Africa. On November 16, 1981, a very special event occurred: Her home state of Oklahoma—which had not admitted her to any of its accredited colleges or to its law school—inducted her into its Hall of Fame. She was inducted into the Oklahoma Women's Hall of Fame on November 18, 1983.

Stout is a warm and attractive woman with beautiful eyes and a winning smile. Her dress is elegant and impeccable. She enjoys bridge and swimming when she has the time. She also loves to travel, but says "cruises are a little too slow for me" (Telephone interview with Juanita Kidd Stout, May 1990).

Stout is cognizant that her accomplishments are unprecedented but attributes them to the many people who have helped her along the way, especially her parents, who taught her the value of education and moral living, and to the unswerving support of her husband, Charles Otis Stout, who died August 15, 1988. They had no children.

Stout continues to find pleasure in forming new legal theories and in applying the law in a manner "that will serve people, make for the overall good, and be useful to American society" (Telephone interview with Juanita Kidd Stout, May 1990).

References

"A Career of Firsts." *Ebony* 44 (February 1989): 76, 78, 80.

Dannett, Sylvia G. L. *Profiles of Negro Womanhood.* Vol. 2. Yonkers, N.Y.: Educational Heritage, 1966.

"Her Honor Bops the Hoodlums." *Life* 59 (9 July, 1965): 74.

Philadelphia Inquirer (7 March 1988) F-1; (30 October 1989) F-6.

Stout, Juanita Kidd. Resume.

——. Telephone interviews with Emery Wimbish, Jr., May 1990, July 1990.

"Unfrightened Crusader." *Time* 85 (16 April 1965): 47.

Collections

Photographs of Juanita Kidd Stout are in the John Mosley Photograph Collection of the Charles L. Blockson Afro-American Collection, Temple University Libraries.

Emery Wimbish, Jr.

Niara Sudarkasa

(1938-)

Educator, anthropologist

On September 29, 1986, the Board of Trustees at Lincoln University announced that from a field of 103 candidates, Niara Sudarkasa had been unanimously chosen as president of that historic black academic institution. Lincoln, founded in 1854, is the oldest of America's black colleges established

Niara Sudarkasa

and maintained on the original site to develop into a baccalaureate degree-granting institution. In the history of this famed institution, Sudarkasa is the first woman to be appointed president. Her inauguration was held on October 1, 1987. At the ceremony one of the committee members said, "When we looked around to find the best man we could for this position, we discovered that he was a woman" (Washington , 108).

Sudarkasa's devotion to higher education for people of African descent is only one of her many qualifications; she is a guiding light for black scholars whose future has been jeopardized by political decisions and racism. She values higher learning but places the importance of peace above that of education: "As concerned as we are about education, our paramount concern is for peace" (Oberlin College Master File). As her Swahili name indicates, she is a woman of high purpose.

On August 14, 1938, in Fort Lauderdale, Florida, Gloria Albertha Marshall was born to George and Rowena Marshall. She has three brothers. Her mother was a silkfinisher and presser in New York City, and her father was in the United States Army. They later separated and then divorced. Her stepfather, Alex Charlton, owned a cocktail lounge in Fort Lauderdale. Growing up in Florida, Sudarkasa was often called a "Nassau" because her grandparents were from the Bahamas. Sudarkasa's grandparents reared her in their large Caribbean family: her grandmother was one of twenty children, and her grandfather, Alpheus Evans, worked as a foreman at Port Everglades.

While living in Florida, Sudarkasa attended Dillard High School from 1948 to 1952, where she was an honor student. At age fourteen she won a Ford Foundation Early Entrant Scholarship to Fisk University in Nashville, Tennessee. In her junior year at Fisk she went to Oberlin College as a semester exchange student, where she subsequently decided to apply for admission to the college of arts and science, and Oberlin accepted her as a transfer student. She became active with WOBC (Oberlin's radio station), the Interracial Committee, and the Young Democrats. On her admission application she listed as special interests the clarinet, ping-pong, and tennis. In 1955-56 she lived in the dormitory designated for graduate students—Mallory House. The second year, 1956-57, she lived in Baldwin Cottage—a women's dormitory.

At Oberlin College Sudarkasa became interested in studying about Africa. She had taken a course on Caribbean culture and came across the word "esusu / esu"—a word that she heard frequently among her family. "Esusu or esu . . . are savings associations in Haiti and Jamaica and almost every part of the Caribbean. An article by a student of the Yoruba in Nigeria described esu as a Yoruba credit association. I believe that was the beginning of my determination to study Africa," she said (Lanker, 139). This was the first time that Sudarkasa fully realized black people's cultural ties to Africa; consequently, she decided to go to Africa and learn its history.

At the age of eighteen in 1957, Sudarkasa graduated from Oberlin College with a bachelor of arts degree in sociology, ranking in the top ten percent of her class. She went to Columbia University in New York, where she earned a master's degree in anthropology in 1959. In 1959-60 she was awarded the John Hay Whitney Opportunity Fellowship to pursue a Ph.D. degree. In 1960-63 Sudarkasa received a Ford Foundation Foreign Area Training Fellowship to study the Yoruba language and the role of Yoruba women in the markets, first at the University of London School of Oriental and African Studies, then in Nigeria. In 1963-64 she became a fellow with the Carnegie Foundation Study of New Nations at the University of Chicago, where she served on the Committee for the Comparative Study of New Nations. Sudarkasa received her Ph.D. in anthropology from Columbia University in 1964.

Sudarkasa Promoted in Academia

Niara Sudarkasa taught at Columbia University as a visiting faculty member and then at New York University in 1964. In 1967 she moved to the University of Michigan in Ann Arbor, where she served for twenty years. While at Michigan she served first as assistant professor from 1967 to 1970, then associate professor from 1970 to 1976, and finally in 1976 she became the first black woman to be promoted to full professor in the division of arts and sciences. She was also the first tenured black woman professor. She directed the Center for Afro-American and African Studies in 1981-84 and also was research scientist at the Center for Research in Economic Development.

Sudarkasa's academic activities at the University of Michigan were matched by her political activism. Describing her role, she stated:

> At the University of Michigan, I was part of the establishment. But I was very politicized about Africa so I was a vocal spokesperson for all the things that the students were advocating in those days, the early seventies: black studies, more black and minority students in the university. At Michigan I became the activist I had not been in the sixties, and most people knew me there as an activist-scholar (Lanker, 139).

In 1984 Sudarkasa was appointed associate vice-president for academic affairs. She was responsible for academic policy, special academic projects, and minority student affairs. In addition, she was in charge of initiating, evaluating, and monitoring the university's efforts to recruit and retain minority students.

Sudarkasa Internationally Acclaimed Anthropologist

Sudarkasa's academic research has made her an internationally acclaimed anthropologist. She has more than thirty scholarly publications to her credit. Further, she has conducted research in Nigeria, Ghana, and the Republic of Benin. She is a recognized authority in the fields of African women, especially Yoruba women traders; West African migration;

and the African-American and African family. She has also studied higher education policies for black Americans and other minorities, and she is an advocate for minority access to education at the university level.

Sudarkasa has applied her study of West African culture to that of the African-American family structure, with emphasis on the role of black women within the family and society. She has protested the imposition of Eurocentric models of white middle-class family norms onto the study of black community life. Her work has shown that the African family, whether polygamous or monogamous, is consanguineal or has a blood kinship pattern. Each family member works in favor of the group or clan rather than for a select part of the group. Since slave owners disrupted this pattern by deliberately separating blood kin, they also unintentionally forced slaves to alter their definitions of family to include those whose children, parents, spouse, or other family members were sold or killed. That pattern is seen in the contemporary black community. Black conjugal units may have an elderly relative, an unmarried male or female relative, an unmarried female relative with children. Sudarkasa concludes that traditional African and African-American families do not encourage members to leave the group. Instead, the group or clan enlarges to make any necessary accommodations.

Like the black family, black women have been severely criticized and blamed because of their roles in the family and society. Sudarkasa's research shows that African-American women's active participation has roots in pre-colonial Africa. Before the imposition of European norms in Africa, women's roles were different from men's while still complementary.

> Given the interdependence and relative parity of male and female economic roles in most precolonial African societies, if one were to apply the "beast of burden" stereotypes to women, one should also apply it to men. The disparities that are evident in the economic roles of men and women in contemporary Africa are for the most part resultant from socioeconomic changes that have taken place in the twentieth century (Sudarkasa, "Sex Roles, Education, and Development in Africa," 280).

Unlike their European counterparts, African women traditionally have been more active in economic and social activities outside the home, and they participate equally in family responsibilities. For her example, Sudarkasa used Yoruba women who work in the markets. These women maintain their own economic independence, while at the same time keeping family duties intact by working together to supply a child-care network for one another.

Sudarkasa notes also that the sexism that is prevalent in Africa today is a result of Western disruption of traditional economic systems. Introduction of Western technology eliminated many traditional jobs; thus, women have been denied access to the necessary education to qualify for the new types of employment. With distribution of jobs on the basis of sex, those jobs that women dominate are classified as low status and are poorly financed. Sudarkasa stresses that Africa cannot expect to advance if the importance of women's contribution is denied and women are deprived of their rights in the social and economic sphere.

Black Colleges Called Essential

Sudarkasa also stresses that in order for black Americans to achieve in the United States, black students must have access to quality higher education. She has devoted her life to ensuring that educational opportunities are available to blacks and other minority students. She strongly believes in the necessity of black institutions of higher learning because they are unique in their ability to teach students of African descent to survive in a racist society.

In her inaugural speech at Lincoln, Sudarkasa noted that "mainstream academia is pulling in the welcome mats it recently laid out to minorities. . . . Equality of access to higher education is a long way off. . . . Recent gains by blacks . . . are now being lost" (Oberlin College Master File). She added that despite this setback, major steps forward have been taken in this century, and accomplishment is not wholly dependent on a person's social and economic status.

She stressed the importance of black colleges because they provide for black students in ways that white colleges cannot. Although a large percentage of black students attend predominantly white universities, black colleges have historically produced leaders. Black college graduates contribute more to society and they are seven times more likely to pursue Ph.D.'s than their counterparts in white colleges. Her commitment to the continuity of black colleges coincides with their struggles as many face financial constraints and loss of black students.

A reporter asked Sudarkasa why, if she is such an advocate of black colleges, her son attended a predominantly white undergraduate and professional school. She responded:

> I believe that black students are entitled to a choice. They must have the right to enroll in those institutions if they choose. My son has never forgotten the struggles that put him in those institutions, and he has always sought out opportunities for service on behalf of the Black community (Reynolds, 36).

Michael Eric Mabogunje Sudarkasa, born on August 5, 1964, is a graduate of the University of Michigan and Harvard Law School, and is with the African Development Bank in the Ivory Coast.

In addition to her son, since 1977 Sudarkasa has shared her life with her husband, John L. Clark, an inventor, sculptor, and contractor. Of her husband she says: "Everybody has told me that he is the anchor I needed" (Washington, 108). They have opposite personalities: While she is active and intellectual, he is reserved and intuitive. John Clark is not disturbed by his wife's public fame because they each concentrate on their own activities; and they seek to promote peace in their house, which is decorated with African arts and antiques.

Sudarkasa and Clark are both willing to compromise for the other when necessary. Before Niara Sudarkasa was asked to accept the presidency at Lincoln, John Clark wanted to relocate to the Republic of Benin to start a construction company and to work on his inventions. They agreed that whoever got the opportunity first would accept it and the other would follow. Her offer from Lincoln came first, so they moved to Lincoln University, Pennsylvania.

Sudarkasa Assumes University Presidency

As president of Lincoln University, Sudarkasa intends to carry its long tradition of educational excellence into the twenty-first century. She promotes the university's strong science reputation and its international studies program. She makes herself accessible to the students, who fondly refer to her as Madame President. She is delighted that students think nothing of giving her a hug and kiss.

Sudarkasa's mission is to prepare Lincoln graduates to walk in the shoes of alumni like Thurgood Marshall and Nnamdi Azikiwe: "These men graduated with a sense of mission. . . . They wanted to make a contribution to African people—to better our condition." She would like to convey this same sense of urgency to today's students. "Unless a sense of service and duty is instilled . . . our upward mobility will only be measured by cars and styling." Ideally, she hopes her graduating students will "have a zeal to be somebody with a purpose larger than material acquisition"—learned adults with Afrocentric views (Washington, 108). Sudarkasa also plans to preserve the institution's ties to the African continent. Currently, the university has a large collection of African paintings, sculpture, textiles, jewelry, and other art objects in addition to Sudarkasa's collection. Current plans include opening an African museum on the college campus.

The cultural ties with Africa that she discovered at Oberlin College led Sudarkasa to affirm her association with the African continent. She feels that the continent is the home she does not have in America: "I feel that it [America] was my country but not my land. But when I went to West Africa, I had the deep sense not only of belonging, but of possession. This was ours! The whole continent was ours!" (Lanker, 139). She adopted an African name, in addition to Gloria Marshall Clark, to symbolize her ties to the continent. "The word 'nia' in Swahili means purpose. So Niara was an adaptation and the name was given to me to mean a woman of high purpose" (Lanker, 139). The name 'Sudarkasa' came by marriage.

President Sudarkasa's inaugural gown also symbolized her ties to Africa. It is royal-blue appliqued and trimmed with blue and gold kente, with matching cap. The kente cloth was given to her mother, who is now deceased, when she visited Ghana in 1968. Sudarkasa used some of that kente cloth for her inaugural robe in 1987:

> Something told me to use the kente in the robe. I saw it as a way of having my mother always with me. I also reflected on the connections of the kente with Ghana and Kwame Nkrumah, that country's first president and one of Lincoln's greatest sons. Having the kente on my robe was a magnificent coming together of many things (Washington, 108).

Sudarkasa was described in the May 1988 commencement exercises program as a:

> renowned anthropological explorer of African heritages and linkages among persons in many lands, tireless leader in the struggle for justice, equality, and excellence in the education of black Americans, women, and persons of Third World background (Oberlin College Master File).

Fellowships and study grants sudarkasa received include the Social Science Research Council Fellowship in 1973-74, the Senior Fulbright Research Scholarship in 1982-83 for research in the Republic of Benin, a Ford Foundation grant in 1983-84, a National Endowment for the Humanities grant in 1983-84, Ford Foundation Middle East and Africa research fellow in 1973-74, and Social Science Research Council African Studies fellow 1973-74.

Sudarkasa has long been active with a number of organizations. She served as a member of the African Studies Association, 1959-1969; fellow of the American Anthropological Association, 1964 to date; member of the American Anthropological Association executive board, 1972-1975; chairperson of the State of Michigan Committee on Minorities, Women, and Handicapped in Higher Education, 1984; member of the board of directors of Ann Arbor Community Center, 1983; member of the Association of Black Anthropologists; chairperson of the Special Advisory Committee on Minority Enrollment, 1985-86; member of the American Association for Higher Education, 1986; member of the American Ethnological Society; and a member of the African Studies Association.

Sudarkasa is a member of the advisory board for the Ford Foundation Project on New Immigrants; American Council on Educational Study of Undergraduate International Programs; American Council for Educational Study of Graduate Opportunities for Minority Students and board of directors of the Pennsylvania Economic Development Partnership, appointed by Governor Robert P. Casey in 1987.

Sudarkasa has been honored for outstanding accomplishments by organizations such as Zeta Phi Beta Sorority in 1971, Alpha Kappa Alpha Sorority in 1976, the city of Fort Lauderdale (which celebrated Dr. Niara Sudarkasa Day) in 1976, the Michigan Senate in 1986, the Michigan State House of Representatives in 1986, the Borough of Manhattan in 1987, and the Association of Black Anthropologists, the Links, Inc., and the Elks.

References

Lanker, Brian. *I Dream a World.* New York: Stewart, Tabori and Chang, 1989. Photograph of Niara Sudarkasa in academic regalia, p. 138.

McKinney, Rhoda E. "'Sister' Presidents." *Ebony* 43 (February 1988): 82-88.

Reynolds, Rhoda E. "Inquiry: Black Colleges." *USA Today* 12 October 1987.

Sudarkasa, Niara. "An Exposition on the Value Premises Underlying Black Family Studies." *Journal of the National Medical Association* 67 (May 1975).

———. "Female Employment and Family Organization in West Africa." In *The Black Woman Cross-Culturally.* Edited by Filomina Steady. Cambridge: Schenkman Publishing, 1981.

———. "Sex Roles, Education and Development in Africa." *Anthropology and Education Quarterly* 13 (Fall 1982): 278-88.

Washington, Elsie B. "Niara Sudarkasa: Educator for the 1990's." *Essence* 20 (May 1989): 106-108.

Who's Who among Black Americans. 5th ed. Lake Forest, Ill.: Educational Communications, 1988.

Who's Who in America, 45th ed. Vol. 2. Wilmette, Ill.: Marquis, 1988.

Collections

Information on Niara Sudarkasa, Oberlin College Class of 1957, is located in Oberlin College Master File, Alumni Office, file No. 1774301. Photographs are included.

Deborah Stewart with Adrienne Lash Jones

Madame Sul-Te-Wan

(1873-1959)

Actress

Madame Sul-Te-Wan is known almost exclusively by her professional name. Edward Mapp supplies a real name, Nellie Conley, and an exact birth date, September 12, 1873. The name Conley may be that of her first husband, since a photograph in a 1954 *Our World* identifies an Onest Conley, aged forty-seven, as the only surviving son of her first marriage. The most reliable details of her early life come from Delilah L. Beasley's *The Negro Trail Blazers of California* (1919). The account appears to be based on direct contact with Madame Sul-Te-Wan.

Sul-Te-Wan was the daughter of a Louisville, Kentucky, washerwoman who worked for actresses, among others. According to *Our World*, by 1954 Sul-Te-Wan's washerwoman mother became a burlesque dancer and her father was a Hindu minister who gave his daughter his father's name. Sul-Te-Wan had the job of delivering the laundry at the stage door and was sometimes permitted to watch shows from backstage. Stage-struck, she rehearsed the acts she had seen and boasted to her schoolmates that she would someday be a performer. Sul-Te-Wan mentioned two famous performers, Mary Anderson and Fanny Davenport, as giving encouragement to her ambitions. They are supposed to have intervened with the owner of the Buckingham Theater, James Whalen, who was also mayor of Louisville at the time, urging him to give the young girl a chance. After giving her a tryout, Whalen engaged twenty-five black girls to sing and dance as a novelty act. He also staged a buck-and-wing contest. Sul-Te-Wan won the prize, a dishpan and a spoon. Following this, her mother allowed Sul-Te-Wan to continue to accept theatrical work in Louisville, and they eventually moved to Cincinnati, which offered greater possibilities in this line of work.

In Cincinnati, Sul-Te-Wan secured long engagements at the Dime Museum on Vine Street and also appeared in family theaters in a section of the city known as Over the Rhine. Eventually she joined a company called The Three Black Cloaks, using the name Creole Nell. She also had a small part in one of Fanny Davenport's touring plays during the play's Cincinnati run. Overall, Sul-Te-Wan was successful enough in show business that she began organizing her own companies to tour. Her first company, consisting of sixteen performers and fourteen musicians, was The Black Four Hundred. The next year she organized The Rair Back Minstrels. Her success with both companies brought her numerous offers of marriage, and she did marry, possibly around 1906 (if Onest Conley, born around 1907, is the first son of that marriage).

After her marriage Sul-Te-Wan moved to Arcadia, California, sometime about 1912, where after two years her husband abandoned her with her three sons, the youngest three weeks old. (In the *Our World* article the number of sons is listed as eight.) Thrown to the resources of charity, she moved to Los Angeles, where a lodging was rented for her. She was in dire straits in the search for work because she had been performing since she was a child and she knew nothing about housework—the most readily available work for a black woman of her generation—and she met with very little encouragement from white booking agencies. Although she did manage to secure a short engagement at the Pier Theater in Venice, her money was running very short when she turned to D. W. Griffith.

Actress Appears in Infamous Stereotypical Film

Griffith was at the time filming *The Clansman*, as Madame Sul-Te-Wan consistently refers to it in the account she gave Beasley: the film is of course *The Birth of a Nation*. Although many of the blacks in the film were played by whites in blackface, she found a job at three dollars a day, raised to five after the first day's work. She was filmed in a sequence "as a rich colored lady, finely gowned and owner of a Negro colony of educated colored citizens, who not only owned their own land, but she drove her own coach and four-in-hand. This scene was to show the advancement of the Negro from ante-bellum days to this period" (Beasley, 240). According to this rather implausible account, the scene, along with others favorable to blacks was cut by the "censor." In the film as we have it Sul-Te-Wan has been identified as the woman who spits on the old colonel. After the completion of *Birth of a Nation,* Sul-Te-Wan sought Griffith out to ask for money to replace a keepsake fan of hers, which had been destroyed during the filming. Griffith gave her twenty-five dollars to replace the fan and put her on the payroll at five dollars a day whether she was working or not. This would make her the first black American to be hired by a major movie producer on a continuing basis.

After *Birth of a Nation* opened in Los Angeles, Sul-Te-Wan was fired on the basis of accusations that she had helped organize black protest against the film and that she had stolen a Christian Science book from another actress. She sought the aid of prominent black lawyer Edward Burton Ceruti, who wrote on her behalf and secured her reinstatement. This may be the basis for later statements that she sued to enforce a contract and won. She was featured in *The Marriage Market, Intolerance, Happy Valley's Oldest Boy,* and *Up From the Depths* for Griffith's studio, for which she worked at least until April 1917.

Sul-Te-Wan went on to have a career in the motion pictures as a featured player. This career is more remarkable for its duration than the number of films: Klotman identifies eleven films spaced fairly evenly at one or two year intervals from *Birth of a Nation* (1915) to *Maryland* (Twentieth Century Fox, 1940). There are undoubtedly other fleeting appearances as an extra without credit; for example, the *Our World* article adds *Drums of Love, Tarzan of the Apes,* and *Mighty Joe Young* to Klotman's list (81). There is a still from *Rhapsody in Blue* (1945), with Sul-Te-Wan as the middle card player, in the book *Black Hollywood* (143). A slim and elegant woman who won first prize in a cakewalk contest held at the Hollywood Bowl when she was sixty-eight, Sul-Te-Wan had an acerbic comment on one of her difficulties in getting roles among the narrow range of those available to blacks at this time, especially playing maids: Referring to her more successful younger contemporaries, Hattie McDaniel and Louise Brooks, she said, "For many roles I'm dark enough, not fat enough" (81). In addition, when she reached seventy, studios were very reluctant to consider her because of insurance requirements.

Sul-Te-Wan married twice in later life, both times to white husbands. The second was "a German, Count William Holt who died shortly after their marriage" (*Our World,* 81). She married Anton Ebenthur, an interior decorator, about 1943, when he would have been about forty-eight and she about seventy. They were still apparently happily married some ten years later. Sul-Te-Wan died February 1, 1959.

References

Beasley, Delilah L. *The Negro Trail Blazers of California*. Los Angeles: The Author, 1919. Photograph, p. 237.

Goode, Kenneth G. *California's Black Pioneers.* Santa Barbara: McNally and Laftin, 1974. Photograph between pp. 80-81.

Klotman, Phyllis Raunch. *Frame By Frame: A Black Filmography*. Bloomington: Indiana University Press, 1979.

Null, Gary. *Black Hollywood: The Negro in Motion Pictures.* Secaucus, N.J.: The Citadel Press, 1975.

"The Case Against Mixed Marriage." *Ebony* 6 (November 1950): 50-57. Photograph, p. 56.

"Madame Sul-Te-Wan." *Our World* 9 (February 1954): 80-82. Includes photographs.

Mapp, Edward. *Directory of Blacks in the Performing Arts.* 2nd ed. Metuchen, N.J.: Scarecrow Press, 1990.

Robert L. Johns

T

Mary Morris Talbert

(1866-1923)

Educator, civil rights activist

Mary Morris Burnett Talbert, educator and civil rights activist, was born on September 17, 1866, in Oberlin, Ohio. She was the youngest of eight surviving children born to Cornelius J. Burnett and Caroline Nichols Burnett. Her father was born of free parents in Fayetteville, North Carolina, on June 29, 1813; her paternal grandfather was a veteran of the American Revolutionary War. Caroline Nichols was born in Raleigh, North Carolina, about 1830 and reputedly was the great-granddaughter of Richard Nicholls, who captured New Amsterdam in 1644 and renamed it New York. A barber by trade, Cornelius Burnett in 1860 purchased land in the commercial district of Oberlin, where he hoped to relocate his family so that his children could take advantage of the superior educational opportunities the town offered. After the outbreak of the Civil War, Burnett decided to postpone the move until peace returned to the nation and in 1865 the Burnetts relocated to Ohio.

Cornelius Burnett ran a successful barber shop and was elected delegate to several Republican state conventions while Caroline Burnett operated a boarding house and restaurant that catered to the Oberlin College community. The Burnetts, devout Episcopalians, joined the Christ Episcopal Church in Oberlin, but they later affiliated with the Second Congregational Church. While history does not record why the Burnetts changed their religious affiliation, the Congregational church is known for its pursuit of a social gospel that included a number of reform measures aimed at alleviating black suffering.

In this nourishing, rich environment Talbert grew into womanhood. Like her parents, she attended the Congregational church; she also was pianist for the Methodist church. The politics of the post-Reconstruction era and her father's involvement in Ohio Republican politics, as well as her parents' successful business enterprises, had a profound effect upon her. They taught her that she could carve out her own niche in spite of race and gender.

Talbert attended the public schools in Oberlin and was graduated from high school at age sixteen. Through the aid of former college president James Fairbanks, she enrolled in the literary program at Oberlin College in 1883 and completed her course of study three years later. Oberlin College awarded her the S.P. degree in 1886 and the B.A. degree in 1894.

Talbert was in an excellent position to take advantage of the new opportunities available to blacks and to help engineer the subsequent direction that black struggles for liberation would take in the twentieth century. Her liberal arts training at Oberlin College introduced her to some of the most eminent intellectuals in the United States, while it also brought her into contact with other young, progressive black women, like Mary Church Terrell and Anna Julia Cooper, who later became renowned for their struggles against racism, gender-bias and colonial domination. These three women later would provide enlightened leadership for the National Association of Colored Women's Clubs (NACW) for nearly half a century, and this organization would become the major forum for the articulation of black women's concerns.

Talbert launched a teaching career in the segregated school system of Little Rock, Arkansas, after she completed her studies at Oberlin College. While Oberlin, in many ways, provided an harmonious environment for blacks, Talbert was well aware of the social constrictions it placed upon them. On the other hand, Little Rock provided her with first-hand experience of the atrocities perpetrated against blacks—the inequities in the education system and a denial of economic opportunities, which resulted in deprivation for a disproportionate number of blacks.

Talbert Gains Fame as Educator

The Little Rock experience first catapulted Talbert into national limelight. She taught algebra, geometry, Latin, and history, and educators across the nation praised her teaching ability. In 1887 she became assistant principal of Bethel University, the first woman in the state to hold the position. The following year she resigned to become principal of Union High School. The respect accorded teachers in the black community allowed Talbert ample opportunity to participate in public events and gained her recognition. Building such bases of support across the country greatly enhanced her ascent through the hierarchy of the NACW later. She remained in Little Rock until 1891 when she married William Talbert, a wealthy Buffalo city clerk and realtor, whose family had resided in the Buffalo region for nearly a century. Their marriage was a partnership that allowed them the opportunity to pursue their separate goals. Politics played an important role in the Talbert household.

For years William Talbert was president of the Buffalo Colored Republican Club, and he also was an organizer of the Niagara Movement of 1905.

During the first year of her marriage Talbert experienced a difficult pregnancy and returned to her family in Oberlin where she gave birth to her only child, a daughter, Sarah May, who later was graduated from the New England Conservatory of Music and became an accomplished pianist and composer. She remained in Oberlin for several months afterwards and upon her return to Buffalo devoted her time to taking care of her baby and managing the extended Talbert household. There is no evidence that she was involved actively in the public sector until the twentieth century, although she was a charter member of the Phyllis Wheatley Club, founded in 1899 and one of the most effective catalysts for change in the Buffalo black community.

At the turn of the century black women organized professional clubs that responded in new ways to both the conservative racial climate and gender restrictions. Many of their clubs were affiliated with the National Association of Colored Women founded in Washington, D.C., in 1896. It was in this context that Talbert would carve out her political niche and rise to national prominence as she crusaded for black freedom and women's rights.

Nineteenth-century forces also shaped Talbert's values and philosophy. Talbert held deep religious convictions and had internalized Christianity's commitment to agape or mutual support. But she also was imbued with the contemporary black ideology of self-help and racial solidarity as expounded by Booker T. Washington, a frequent guest in her Buffalo home. She interacted with W. E. B. Du Bois at the 1905 organizational meeting of the Niagara Movement that met at her home and at the sessions arranged to establish a Buffalo chapter of the NAACP. A few years later she and Du Bois served as directors of the NAACP during the same period. Yet she, like her sisters in the struggle, succeeded in perfecting a delicate balancing act which allowed her to be independent of these apparently divergent camps.

Mary Morris Talbert

Women's Place in the Modern World Identified

Talbert was a womanist who believed that black women had a unique role to play in the shaping of the modern world and it was incumbent upon them to lead in this era of hope for blacks. She argued that black women were at the dawn of a better day and maintained that a woman's sphere is not limited and woman should enter any sphere where she can do the most good. Talbert further contended, "Clear and insistent is the call to the woman of my race today—the call to self-development and to unselfish service. We cannot turn a deaf ear to the cries of the neglected little children, the untrained youth, the aged and the poor." (Mary Church Terrell Papers, reel 17, frame 257, Library of Congress). Black women needed the suffrage amendment to guarantee their freedom and Talbert participated in such forums as "Votes for Women: A Symposium by Leading Thinkers of Colored Women," held in Washington, D.C., in 1915. She also attended the NAACP Amenia Conference that met in upstate New York in 1916 to discuss practical ways of redressing racism. When Talbert addressed the Baltimore NACW conference in 1916, she told delegates:

> No negro woman can afford to be a drone in the social and club bee-hive in our country. No negro woman can afford to be an indifferent spectator of the social, moral, religious, economic, and uplift problems that are agitated around us. No negro woman can afford to be idle but must take an active personal interest in everything that concerns the welfare of her home, her church, her community, her state . . . her religion . . . for once [women] have struck out in this great work [they] are doing the work of God . . . and when God is with us who can be against us? (*National Notes*, 17, October 1916, p. 3).

Talbert adhered to a kind of liberation theology. She enjoyed telling audiences about the lessons that could be drawn from the Old Testament Book of Esther. Even at the risk of her own death Esther never waivered in her efforts to create a world in which Jews would no longer be persecuted. The implications for African-American women were clear. But just as the responsibilities for black women were great, Talbert saw the twentieth century as one that offered great opportunities for them as well. She explained:

> Never in the history of our race have our women had so great a privilege as is granted to us, the privilege to be and to do what we will, to develop our highest powers . . . to satisfy our deepest

longings for educational advantages (*National Notes*, 17, November-December 1914, p. 2).

Talbert embraced the view that black women had to address a "simultaneity of oppression" that included race, class, and gender discrimination. She also contended that the oppression of people of color around the globe was connected and that their struggle for self-determination was black Americans' struggle too. Consequently, her reform activities emphasized the need to aid the liberation movements of colonized Africans who sought freedom from their European oppressors, as well as Caribbean nations, like Haiti, whose government was toppled by the United States's desire to protect its business community's interests. On such occasions she joined forces with black men to redress their mutual grievances. But women around the world formed a critical link in this social movement. These beliefs governed Talbert's life and politics.

In Buffalo Talbert had attracted attention by using the local media to address issues and social concerns that affected her community. The Michigan Avenue Baptist Church, founded by the Talberts in 1832 and foremost in black protest movements, also provided a base of operation for Talbert. There in 1901 she founded the Christian Culture Congress, a literary society and forum to address the critical problems that blacks faced. Talbert invited nationally prominent spokespersons, such as Nannie Helen Burroughs and Du Bois, to address the Buffalo community. She had also gained a reputation as a teacher in Buffalo. Under the auspices of her church she trained over three hundred Sunday school teachers to assure that they were knowledgeable and used sound pedagogical techniques to educate African-Americans.

Talbert from the outset became an important force in the Buffalo Phillis Wheatley Club. In a public forum sponsored by the Phillis Wheatley Club and held at the Michigan Avenue Baptist Church, Talbert addressed an integrated audience on the reasons "Why the American Negro Should Be at the 1901 Pan American Exhibition." Arguing from a pragmatic view, she noted that such exhibits had attracted thousands of visitors at previous world fairs and observed that the Buffalo exhibition was the only one in recent history where an African-American was not appointed commissioner. Talbert argued that displays on black history and culture had focused upon the progress blacks had made since slavery and had helped to win support for improvements in race relations. She is credited with the club's successful bid to host the second biennial conference of the NACW in 1901. This was an astute move for Talbert because her home was the headquarters for the conference and once more she was reunited with her fellow Oberlin College alumnae Anna J. Cooper and Mary Church Terrell, who introduced her to other influential NACW members. NACW members earlier had learned of Talbert's protest against the exclusionary policies of the Pan-American Exhibition's board of directors through the NACW publication *National Notes*. This was also an astute move for the NACW, for the press gave widespread coverage to its sessions and helped to catapult the activities of black women's clubs into the national limelight.

The NACW affiliates were important in Talbert's rise to national prominence. Talbert was elected second president of the Phillis Wheatley Club. During her administration the club invited the NAACP to organize in Buffalo. The Buffalo chapter was established in 1910 following a meeting with local black representatives and Du Bois and Fanny Garrison Villard of the national office. Talbert served on the local board of directors and in 1918 became a director and later a vice-president of the national organization, a position she held until her death. Under NAACP auspices she travelled throughout the South and established a number of branches in Texas and Louisiana, including Galveston, Austin, Texarkana, and Alexandria.

Talbert Becomes Noted for NACW Leadership

Shortly after the biennial meeting in Buffalo, Talbert assumed several administrative positions in the NACW and its affiliates. NACW clubs in New York formed a federation in 1909 and elected Talbert its second president in 1911, a position she held until 1916. From 1910 to 1912 she was NACW parliamentarian and chair of the executive committee during 1912 through 1914; delegates elected her vice-president-at-large in 1914. At the Baltimore Biennial meeting in 1916, delegates elected her president of the national organization, and she served two terms that ended in 1920.

Little is known about the political struggles that resulted in Talbert's rise to power within the NACW or the NAACP. Yet it is evident that she was able to consolidate her power locally and then draw upon the national networks which she had established during her student days at Oberlin, while teaching in Arkansas, and during her presidency of the Empire State Federation. Her NAACP contacts which included Terrell and Maggie Lena Walker, among others, also proved useful. A past Worthy Matron of the Order of the Eastern Stars, Talbert could rely upon the support of this national benevolent organization too. Talbert, known for her oratorical skills, was a popular lecturer and was always in demand; the black press gave widespread coverage to her speeches. She also could depend upon the Talbert family resources should the occasion warrant.

Talbert envisioned a world in which racial harmony and justice would prevail. She devised a multifaceted program to address the social ills which threatened her dreams. The promotion of black history and culture was a key element in her plans, and she pursued a number of projects at the local as well as national level. The elimination of mob violence and Jim Crow and the colonial domination of Africa were other issues which Talbert addressed. She believed strongly that clubwomen should address the plight of black women and children. Talbert noted, "The average clubwoman is in the work because she loves her sister. . . . It needed love to awaken sympathy in woman to help woman" (*National Notes*, 19, October 1916, p. 3). The NACW provided a nationwide network of women and their supporters to help implement plans to address these considerations.

Talbert, like other black Americans, perceived education as a tool for liberation from economic exploitation. In keeping with its mandate to uplift "fallen" women and to protect children, the Phyllis Wheatley Club, under Talbert's leadership, initiated educational programs which stressed practical job training. The club established a settlement house in the heart of the black community and offered courses in sewing, cooking, music, health care, and other special programs for mothers; it also sponsored kindergarten classes. The local community supported such efforts by donations.

As president of the NACW Talbert spearheaded a number of projects designed to provide education for black children and to protect them from the racist judiciary system. During her travels throughout the South, Talbert observed that children, sometimes under five years of age, had been incarcerated for stealing food or a toy. Since most southern jurisdictions did not provide reformatories for black children, they were placed in prisons with hardcore criminals and deprived of the opportunity to advance themselves intellectually or spiritually. Talbert noted the connection between the incarceration of young blacks and the municipalities' needs for a pool of cheap labor to build roads, bridges, and other such projects; she deplored such exploitation.

To counteract the negative impact of such abuse, Talbert urged NACW affiliates to establish their own reformatories where black youngsters would be placed in a wholesome environment where they could be educated. At the biennial meeting of the association in Denver in 1920, she announced its successes in getting children released from prison and in securing lighter sentences for them. Under Talbert's leadership the NACW established homes for delinquent children throughout the South and helped to bring about penal reform in that area of the country.

Talbert was interested in the total well-being of children. Her concern led her to address their legal status. Arguing that the status of illegitimacy jeopardized the lives of innocent children, Talbert urged clubwomen, regardless of race, to lobby their state representatives to enact legislation to protect the welfare of these children. The first black elected delegate, she took her crusade for the children to the International Council of Women's conference that met in Christiania, Norway, in 1920. After Talbert addressed the delegates, they unanimously adopted her resolution which provided the right for illegitimate children to receive financial support from their father and the right to bear their father's name. After delegates returned to the United States, those in Minnesota and Wisconsin immediately lobbied their legislators in an effort to get them to ratify the Talbert resolution.

Black history and culture were significant in Talbert's scheme for the liberation of black people. She seemed to internalize the adage that people are condemned to repeat their history, if they do not know it. In her writings Talbert frequently focused upon the deeds of black female historical and contemporary figures "so that our youth may receive inspiration from [their] work and life" (*National Notes*, 24, January-March, 1922, p. 5).

The most extensive historical project which Talbert spearheaded involved the purchase and restoration of the Frederick Douglass home in Anacostia, D.C., as a monument to Douglass and black achievement. It would also serve as the national headquarters of the National Association of Colored Women. This was the NACW's first major fundraising project and it was successful. Talbert wrote:

> Our purpose [is] to wipe out the indebtedness of the home of the late Frederick Douglass and to restore it to its former beauty, that we may make of this a historic place, a hallowed spot where our boys and girls may gather during the years to come, and receive hope and inspiration and encouragement to go forth like Douglass and fight to win (*National Notes*, 19 January, 1917, p. 5).

She noted that "we rely upon race loyalty and pride as [our] energizing power" to complete this project. In Denver in 1920 Talbert announced that the NACW had succeeded in acquiring the Douglass home. Its restoration, however, would remain to be completed as a memorial to Talbert.

Talbert devoted her entire life to the eradication of Jim Crow and human rights violations wherever they manifested themselves. Both the NAACP and the NACW and its affiliates provided forums for her to campaign against these atrocities. As NAACP vice-president Talbert conducted a national crusade in support of the Dyer Anti-Lynching Bill which had been introduced into Congress in 1921. The crusade also hoped to elicit international support in its efforts to raise one million dollars to fight the lynching of black men and women in the United States, as well as other crimes perpetrated against them. Talbert helped to raise over twelve thousand dollars during a nationwide lecture tour. Her NACW network contributed to this success. Congress, however, failed to ratify the anti-lynching bill, and in response Talbert urged clubwomen to exercise their newly won right to vote and withhold their support from candidates who voted against the bill. On September 28, 1921, she also joined the delegation of thirty prominent African-Americans who went to the White House to urge President Warren G. Harding to grant clemency to the Twenty-fourth United States Colored Infantry, convicted of inciting the Houston, Texas, riots in 1917.

Just as she fought to overturn racism in the United States, Talbert joined other progressive black women to expose human rights violations around the world. On one occasion she wrote King Albert of Belgium and urged him to grant democracy and humane treatment to his colonized Africans. At the International Council of Women's conference, she asked the 660 delegates "to appeal to your strong men to justify their claim as leaders of mankind by . . . upholding law and order with righteousness [and] with a firm hand, till no individual or race shall feel the hoof of oppression upon them." She continued in the same vein, arguing that "the greatness of nations is shown by their strict regard for human rights, rigid enforcement of the law without bias, and a just administration of the affairs of life'' (*National Notes*, 23, October-December 1920, p. 13). Fluent in several languages, she traveled to eleven European nations and lectured on the conditions of black Americans. She was the guest of Queen Wilhelmina of the Netherlands and Lady Aberdeen of Scotland.

Talbert also protested the conditions of Haitian women and children following the invasion of the country by the United States in 1921. Reports indicated that U.S. marines had slaughtered innocent women and children and had raped black women. There is some evidence that she influenced the NAACP's decision to send James Weldon Johnson, acting secretary, to investigate and he verified that the United States had committed grave human rights violations. As a member of the Education Committee of the International Council of Women of the Darker Races, established in Washington, D.C., in 1922, Talbert continued to apprise her constituents of the conditions of women and children of color around the world.

World War I provided black American women an opportunity to show their patriotism by once again aiding the United States's war and reconstruction efforts. Talbert, a member of the Women's Committee on National Defense, traveled for the government to gain black support for the Third Liberty Bond Drive; black women contributed five million dollars to this fund. For four months in 1919 Talbert served as YMCA Secretary and Red Cross nurse in Romagne, France. Upon President Warren Harding's invitation, Talbert traveled across the country to lecture black clubwomen regarding the government's food conservation program. She was appointed to the League of Nations' Women's Committee on International Relations in 1920.

Talbert's involvement in all of these reform movements set her apart from the rest of her community. Yet Talbert was not unique; she was one of many dedicated women bent upon serving their race. She was a charismatic leader, an acclaimed orator, and a brilliant strategist, characteristics which accounted for her preeminence in the NACW. Hallie Q. Brown described her personality as ''most pleasing and her smile an object of beauty'' (*Homespun Heroines*, 217). Talbert's rise to prominence and the world-wide visibility it brought her only fueled her commitment to bring about social change and to improve the status of black Americans. She once noted, ''we are a group of women representing fifty thousand women in this labor of love, yet responsible for the ten million of our race'' (*National Notes*, 19, October 1916, p. 3). Talbert's feminist ideology also embodied the traditions and customs of blacks. Talbert had ''caught the vision'' of what the possibilities were for black people in her world.

Her vision included the promotion of their rich African-American heritage as a safeguard for black freedom. Her vision also included the protection of black youth through education, penal reform, and other protective legislation. She further envisioned a world in which human rights violations would be exposed and eliminated. To realize her dream, Talbert believed that black women should cooperate with white women when it was mutually beneficial. She believed also that black men were an important component in the creation of the world that she wished for her granddaughter and subsequent generations. She frequently took her campaign for support for NACW projects to such groups as the National Negro Business League. Talbert's beliefs and actions embraced a multifaceted approach to the liberation of her people.

Talbert's impact upon the National Association of Colored Women is notable. During her presidency the organization became national in scope, for she maintained close ties to the branches and frequently visited them. She also standardized procedures. During Talbert's administration the NACW was recognized as a full-fledge member of the International Council of Women. For the first time, too, the NACW embarked upon a national project, the purchase of the Frederick Douglass home, and clubwomen rallied to the support of their president. Talbert served as president and trustee for life of the Douglass Memorial and Historical Association. The Douglass home today stands as a tribute, not only to the great achievements of Douglass, but also as a monument to the tireless efforts of these women to preserve it. NACW members began discussions about the establishment of a national headquarters to allow them greater visibility and efficiency; Talbert suggested that the NACW could use the Douglass home for this purpose. The NACW established the ten-thousand-dollar Mary B. Talbert Memorial Fund to honor her memory; monies collected would be used to maintain the Douglass home.

Talbert's contributions to the NAACP were equally notable. The establishment of branches in the South was especially important as the NAACP also wished to expand its influence. The anti-lynching drive that she headed raised crucial funds with which the NAACP could advertize the atrocities of lynching and win white support for its elimination. The NAACP awarded Talbert the Spingarn medal in 1922 in recognition of her efforts to preserve the Douglass home and the contributions she made to advancing human rights. She was the first woman to receive this coveted honor.

Talbert's essay, ''Did the American Negro Make, in the Nineteenth Century, Achievements Along the Lines of Wealth, Morality, Education, Etc., Commensurate With Opportunities? If So, What Achievements Did He Make?'' was published in D. W. Culp's 1901 volume *Twentieth Century Negro Literature*. Talbert was a frequent contributor to the *Crisis* and served on the editorial boards of *Woman's Voice* and the *Champion*.

Talbert died of coronary thrombosis in Buffalo, New York, on October 15, 1923, after nearly a year's illness.

References

Brown, Hallie Q. *Homespun Heroines and Other Women of Distinction*. Xenia, Ohio: Aldine Publishing, 1926.

Contributions of Black Women to America. Vol. 2. Edited by Marianna W. Davis. Columbia, S.C.: Kenday Press, 1982.

Dannett, Sylvia G. *Profiles of Negro Womanhood*. Vol. 1. Yonkers, N.Y.: Educational Heritage, 1964.

Hill, John Lewis. *When Black Meets White*. Cleveland: Argyle Publishing Company, 1924.

Logan, Rayford. "Mary Burnett Talbert." *Dictionary of American Negro Biography*. Edited by Rayford W. Logan and Michael R. Winston. New York: Norton, 1984.

Mather, Frank Lincoln. *Who's Who of the Colored Race*. Vol. 1. 1915. Reprinted. Detroit: Gale Research, 1976.

National Notes. National Association of Colored Women, 17 (November-December 1914): 2; 19 (October 1916): 3; 19 (January 1917): 5; 23 (October-December 1920): 13; 24 (January-March, 1922): 5.

Robinson, Wilhelmina S. *Historical Negro Biographies*. New York: Publishers Co., 1967.

Rywell, Martin. *Afro-American Encyclopedia*. Vol. 9. North Miami, Fla.: Educational Book Publishers, 1974.

Terrell, Mary Church. Papers. Reel 17, Frame 257. Library of Congress.

Williams, Lillian S. "Mary Morris Burnett Talbert." *The Encyclopedia of World Biography*. Edited by David Eggenberger. Vol. 15. Palatine, Ill: McGraw Hill/Jack Heraty, 1988.

Collections

There is no extant body of Talbert papers. The Mary Church Terrell collection at the Library of Congress contains the most comprehensive body of Terrell's letters concerning NACW matters. *National Notes*, the NACW publication contains some of her reports and speeches. For information on her NAACP activities, see Talbert's special correspondence files in the NAACP papers at the Library of Congress.

An oil on canvas portrait of Talbert and several photographs of her are housed in collections at the Buffalo and Erie County Historical Society in Buffalo, N.Y.

Lillian S. Williams

Ann Tanneyhill

(1906-)

Organization administrator

Ann (Anna) Elizabeth Tanneyhill is a black American woman who has dedicated her entire adult life to serving others. Tanneyhill's professional career is rather unique, since all of her adult work was done within the National Urban League structure. Tanneyhill's career with the league began in 1928 when she worked for the Springfield, Massachusetts, league affiliate office as secretary to the executive director. Between 1947 and 1961, Tanneyhill undertook the directorship of vocational services for the league's national office in New York.

Tanneyhill was born in Norwood, Massachusetts, on January 19, 1906. She is the daughter of Alfred Weems Tanneyhill and Adelaide (Grandison) Tanneyhill. In 1928 Tanneyhill earned a bachelor of science degree from Simmons College in Boston. Ten years later she received a master of arts degree in vocational guidance and personnel administration from Teachers College of Columbia University in New York City. In addition to the above degrees, Tanneyhill was awarded a certificate from the Radio Workshop of New York University. Tanneyhill never married.

As director of vocational studies for two decades, Tanneyhill organized the Vocational Opportunity Campaigns at the predominantly black high schools and at historically black institutions (HBI's) throughout the South. These campaigns were devised to provide vocational guidance and counseling to black youth.

Tanneyhill's career within the league was particularly full. After she left the league's affiliate office in Springfield in 1930, she moved to New York City, where she continued working for the league at its national headquarters. Between 1930 and 1940, Tanneyhill was secretary to the director of industrial relations. For the following year she was the assistant in charge of guidance and personnel. From 1941 through 1981, the year she retired, Tanneyhill had served in a number of professional posts at the league, including secretary, Bureau of Guidance and Placement (1941-1945); executive assistant (1946); director of vocational services (1947-1961); assistant director of public relations (1961-1963), associate director of public relations (1964-1968), and director of conferences (1969-70). In 1970 she served as consultant to the executive director of the league (1971-1979); and director of the George Edmund Haynes Fellowship Program (1979-1981). Tanneyhill officially ended her long years of stalwart service to the National Urban League in 1981. In addition to holding several key positions within the league, between the years 1940 and 1961, Tanneyhill's service was spread among the several organizations, and she served on the boards of many associations as well. Some of these organizations include, but are not limited to, the Advisory Committee on Young Workers of the Bureau of Standards, United States Department of Labor, the National Vocational Guidance Association, the Advisory Commission of the New York Vocational High School in New York City, and the New York Citizens Committee for Nursing Education.

Career Conferences in Black Colleges Held

Tanneyhill is also a charter member of the Urban League's Quarter Century Club, which is composed of those who have been in service to the league for twenty-five years or longer. Her commitment to black youth in particular is extraordinary. Tanneyhill once wrote that the most serious problems facing the nation included the "high rate of unemployment among black and other minority youth." She continued, "There is great need to place more attention on basic education, and on the guidance, counseling and preparation of youth for jobs and careers" ("A Biographical Sketch, [after 1963]"). She emphasized the need for a "massive upgrading" of the current inner-city schools to better prepare the students for post secondary education and employment. Tanneyhill also voiced her concerns for voter registration among black Americans and other ethnic minorities. "The need for a massive 'voter education' program . . . is essential," she said. She is also extremely concerned that minority youth understand the "privilege of the ballot box" (Questionnaire, 28 September 1977, 4).

The career conferences on HBI's in the 1950s were the brainchild of Tanneyhill. Between 1950 and 1955, these conferences were invaluable, because they established the industry recruitment efforts on the black college campuses, thereby exposing black students to the professional work world and providing access to potential employers and companies, which often had systematically denied them employment due to racist and discriminatory practices. Another of Tanneyhill's creative endeavors took the form of the Tomorrow's Scientists and Technicians Project (TST), which was a national effort to encourage competent black youth to explore their vocational talents and interests in science and technology.

As should be expected of someone of Tanneyhill's talents and dedication, she was the recipient of several awards and honors. In 1963 Tanneyhill was presented with two awards, the Merit Award of the New York Personnel and Guidance Association and the National Vocational Guidance Association Award. It can be argued that her most special award was the Ann Tanneyhill Award, named in her honor from the National Urban League in 1970. The award is presented annually to a league staff member "for excellence and extraordinary commitment to the Urban League Movement" (Questionnaire, Supplemental Information Sheet for Section 12, 28 September 1977, 4; "Tanneyhill Award," n.p.). In 1971 Tanneyhill was honored by her alma mater, Simmons College, with its Alumnae Achievement Award.

Although Tanneyhill was quite busy in her career alone, she wrote several published articles, vocational guidance aids, radio programs, and a number of other publications, including *From School to Job: Guidance for Minority Youth*, Public Affairs Pamphlet Number 200 (1953); *Program Aids for the Vocational Opportunity Campaign* (many editions), and *Whitney M. Young, Jr.: 'The Voice of the Voiceless'* (1977). Tanneyhill used a variety of resources to promote her work among minority youth, including radio. In the 1940s Tanneyhill arranged two radio programs for CBS. In 1941 she supervised the radio program, "The Negro and National Defense." In 1943 she also promoted the "Heroines in Bronze" radio program, "which was an appeal for the inclusion of black women in the war effort" (Questionnaire, Supplemental Information Sheet for Section 19, n.p.). In 1960 Tanneyhill was the primary consultant to the television documentary film, *'A Morning for Jimmy,* which was sponsored by the National Urban League.

Tanneyhill's work was also the subject of a number of publications. Her career was featured in *Charm* magazine in 1957. During this interview, Tanneyhill discussed her work for the league and her commitment to minority vocational training and employment. When Tanneyhill received the Merit Award from the New York Personnel and Guidance Association in 1963 for her outstanding work in education and vocational guidance, she was the subject of an article in the *Journal and Guide* publication. The article proclaimed that Tanneyhill's "dedication to the League program . . . has endured as incentive to thousands of Negro youth" ("Urban League Staffer Honored with Merit Award," n.p.)

The contributions Tanneyhill made to the league are many. Tanneyhill is affectionately called "Miss 'T'" by Urban League staff members who worked with her at some point in her long and meaningful career there. The life and work of Ann Tanneyhill are living testimonies of her dedication to the black community and her unswerving devotion to promoting the talents of minority youth in America. The importance of her contributions to the black American community and to American society at large cannot be overlooked.

References

"Ann Tanneyhill Award." Press Release. National Urban League, 1971.

"Biographical Sketch of Ann Tanneyhill." Department of Public Relations. National Urban League, National Office, New York, N.Y., April 1963.

"Biographical Sketch of Ann Tanneyhill (After 1963)." Department of Public Relations. National Urban League, National Office, New York, N.Y.

Donnelly, Susan. "Young Ghetto Negroes Urged to 'Reach for Stars.'" *Oregonian* 22 August 1967. 23.

Fisk University, Biography File. Questionnaire, 28 September 1977.

Fisk University, Biography File. Questionnaire, 15 December 1980.

Giddings, Paula. *When and Where I Enter*. New York: Bantam Books, 1985.

Kaufman, Vie. Telephone interview with author, 17 December 1990.

"News from National Urban League Conference." Press Release. National Urban League Press, National Office, New York, N.Y., 22 July 1970.

Parkinson, Margaret B. "How Did She Get There? Ann Tanneyhill, Vocational Counselor, Who Has Opened the Job Door for Thousands." *Charm* (May 1957): 210-30).

Parris, Guichard and Lester Brooks. *Blacks in the City: A History of the National Urban League*. Boston: Little, Brown, 1971.

"Urban League Staffer Honored with Merit Award." Women in the News. *Journal and Guide* 30 November 1963.

Weiss, Nancy. *The National Urban League, 1910-1940*. New York: Oxford University Press, 1974.

Collections

An interview with Ann E. Tanneyhill dated 11 August 1978 is in the Black Women Oral History Collection, Radcliffe College.

Lisa Beth Hill

Ellen Tarry

(1906-)

Author, journalist

"I . . . thank God for endowing me with a simple, trusting nature . . . [a] quality which was responsible for the happy childhood that allowed me to achieve a degree of maturity before I was scarred by racial prejudice," Ellen Tarry Patton opens her autobiography, *The Third Door*. "I was born a Southern Negro" (vii). She was born a Baptist but converted to Catholicism. These two factors, race and religion, inform her life and work. A journalist and the author of numerous books, Tarry's writing reflects her faith in humanity and seeks to portray black cultures and people in a meaningful and truthful way.

Tarry was born September 26, 1906, in Birmingham, Alabama, the first child of Eula (Meadows) Tarry, a seamstress for some of the wealthy white women of Birmingham, where she settled after leaving a very small community near the Alabama border. She married John Barber Tarry, who was born in Athens, Alabama, around 1886 and moved to Birmingham, where he became a barber of the wealthy gentry. Tarry's childhood was a happy one with the exception of having to lose some of the limelight with the birth of her sisters, especially the second one, Ida Mae, in 1911; she had to "share the joy of being 'Bob Tarry's little girl' " (Tarry, 7). At age seven, she entered Slater Elementary School. Here, she was taunted for her appearance—reddish hair, gray eyes, fair complexion—and height—she was taller than most of her classmates. However, it was also here that she became aware of her writing ability. A teacher, after receiving "a descriptive composition on a camping trip outside Eutaw, Alabama," asserted to the class that someday Tarry would be a writer (Tarry, 21). This idea grew. On completion of Slater and after the death of her father, she entered St. Francis de Sales Institute in Rock Castle, Virginia, a Catholic boarding school for blacks. By 1923 she had converted to Catholicism.

After graduation, Tarry enrolled in Alabama State Normal at Montgomery (now Alabama State College). Following her work there, she became a substitute teacher in the Birmingham school system in spite of the fact that she had been told that they would not hire a Catholic. In addition, she became a teacher at the Knights of Columbus Evening School for Adults. It was about this time that she was faced with her first real lesson in racial segregation and discrimination and came to understand her situation. She saw a blatant case of police brutality that went unpunished. She finally became a fourth-grade teacher and later a fifth-grade teacher at her alma mater. Even though teaching, she was still trying to find a way to fulfill her proclivity for writing. Her writing skill and her concern for the race, especially the young, manifested itself in her research and presentation to her students. She sought to provide them with sketches of people from Alabama who had left the state and excelled. These were written up for the class. Based upon these sketches, the editor of *The Birmingham Truth* (organ for the Knights of Pythias and the Court of Calanthes), Guillermo Talliferro, hired her. Tarry saw this as a stepping-stone to her real work of writing books and continued to seek ways to go to New York and enter Columbia University's School of Journalism. She became a combination reporter-columnist-editorial writer. Her column was called "Negroes of Note." Based on one of her editorials, Theodore Bilbo, the notorious Mississippi politician, suggested she "should be burned" (Dannett, 249). She was quite successful, but believed she could be more so with more training.

Finally, in 1929, Tarry moved to New York. Here she worked as a waitress, a governess, an elevator operator, and a nightclub attendant. Frequently these jobs were terminated once her race was discovered; however, she was not trying to pass; she just did not volunteer the information. She was able to get an apartment in a "swanky building" and wear "enough clothes" to be "dub[bed] the Mae West of Sugar Hill" (Dannett, 250). Tarry became a writer-researcher on the Federal Writers' Project and later studied under Lucy Sprague Mitchell in the Writers' Laboratory at Bank Street College in New York City. She became acquainted with the poet-novelist Claude McKay (with whom she formed a lasting friendship), the sculptor Augusta Savage, the writer and Howard professor Sterling Brown, and the writer James Weldon Johnson. These artists, especially McKay and Johnson, were quite influential in her development. She later studied at Fordham University's School of Communication Arts in public relations (Dannett, 251).

Tarry served as the codirector for Friendship House on the South Side of Chicago, and during the war she served as a USO worker in several cities. In 1944 she became the regional director of the New York National Catholic County Services (NCSS) Club, which was housed in the Harlem Serviceman's Center. In 1951 she was appointed director of community relations for the Saint Charles (Borremeo) School and Community Center Fund. This was during a campaign launched by Catholic, Protestant, and Jewish leaders—both black and white—to build a new Saint Charles.

For two years Tarry served as director of the Public School Number Sixty-eight Community Center. "In 1958, [she] joined the Housing and Home Finance Agency (HHFA) as a relocation advisor. Two years later she was appointed Intergroup Relations Specialist for HHFA'S Region One, which included New York and six New England states" (Dannett, 254). Tarry became the assistant to the Regional Administrator for Equal Opportunity, Department of Housing and Urban Development.

Tarry Emerges as Journalist and Author

Through all of her varied experiences, Tarry continued her writing. She was a reporter for the *Amsterdam News* and contributed to *The Catholic World* and *Commonweal*. In 1940 her first book was published. *Janie Belle*, illustrated by Myrtle Sheldon and published by Garden City Publishers (1940) was the story of a foundling and her adoption; it was significant for its positive portrayal of a black individual as a main character. Other books were to follow that did not present negative images, which reflected her love and faith in the human race, and which grew out of her experiences and the world around her. For example, two of her books, *Hezekiah Horton* and *The Runaway Elephant*, both illustrated by Oliver Harrington, the black creator of the cartoon "Bootsie," have "Mr. Ed" as a character. He is based on Edward Doherty, a journalist who was to become the husband of Baroness Catherine de Hueck, who was in charge of Friendship House. In an attempt to gain a valid picture of Harlem, he sought and received the help of Tarry. Because of his gratitude for her help, he threw a party for the children of Friendship House. A part of this celebration was to transport the children in his car to the party. Tarry says, "The instant I saw tall, blond Eddie standing alongside a shiny red convertible full of wiggling, giggling brown urchins my story was started" (*The Third Door*, 174). The early concern for her elementary students and the untold history of the black man is evident in her juvenile literature. This includes biographies such as *Young Jim: The Early Years of James Weldon Johnson* and *The Other Toussaint: A Modern Biography of Pierre Toussaint, a Post-Revolutionary Black*. Other works by Tarry are *Katherine Drexel: Friend of the Neglected* (illustrated by Donald Bolognese) and *Martin de Porres: Saint of the New World* (illustrated by James Fox).

Tarry details her maturation and the events that surrounded it in *The Third Door: The Autobiography of An American Negro Woman*. In the foreword, she says, "This . . . is a part of the story of a young, growing America . . . told so that future generations may avoid the mistakes of our time; so that they may know the price we have paid for tomorrow" (viii). The foreword ends on a note that reflects her optimistic and trusting nature: "It is the hope of the author that this book will sow happiness in place of discord, hope in place of despair, and faith in our American future" (viii).

References

Black Writers: A Selection of Sketches from Contemporary Authors. Detroit: Gale Research, 1989.

Dannett, Sylvia G. L. *Profiles of Negro Womanhood*. Vol. 2. Yokers, N.Y.: Educational Heriage, 1966. Photograph, p. 244.

Something about the Author. Vol. 16. Detroit: Gale Research, 1979. Photograph, p. 251.

Tarry, Ellen. *The Third Door: The Autobiography of an American Negro Woman*. New York: McKay, 1955. Reprinted. New York: Negro Universities Press, 1971.

Helen Houston

Anna Diggs Taylor

(1932-)

Judge

After an active career as a lawyer in private practice, government service, and the civil rights movement, Anna Diggs Taylor became the first black woman federal judge in Michigan, appointed to a life term by President Jimmy Carter. An advocate of civil rights, women's rights, and equal justice for all, Judge Taylor handles both praise and criticism squarely.

Born on December 9, 1932, in Washington, D.C., Anna Johnston Diggs Taylor is the daughter of Virginius Douglass

Johnston and Hazel (Bramlette) Johnston, both of whom were educators. Growing up in a city in which systematic racial segregation was practiced, Taylor attended the public schools of Washington, D.C., through the ninth grade. Since her parents valued education for personal development and as a means to secure a solid position in a changing society, they wanted Taylor to attend a more intellectually challenging school. In 1947 she enrolled in Northfield School for girls in East Northfield, Massachusetts, graduating in 1950. She has described her years there as "a very difficult experience" because she rarely saw her family ("Women in the Law," 491). But she believes Northfield acquainted her with a much larger world than she otherwise would have experienced. It also gave her a sound academic preparation for college. She was admitted to Barnard College, Columbia University, and earned a degree in economics in 1954.

Taylor was uncertain about her choice of graduate study, whether it should be business or law, so she applied to both graduate and law schools. She chose law when Yale's law school admitted her and offered her a scholarship, making additional education easier to afford. Enrolling to test the curriculum, she said she "discovered I really loved the Law. By then history was as important as economics to me, especially American history. The law is obviously at the root of everything, so I really loved it and did pretty well" (*Michigan Bar Journal*, 491). Graduation with a degree of LL.B. came in 1957.

Upon graduation, Taylor interviewed with law firms in New York and Washington, D.C., none of which offered her a job. Finally, she obtained a job in the Solicitor's Office of the United States Department of Labor through the efforts of J. Ernest Wilkins, the assistant secretary of labor. Wilkins was a political appointee and the first black person to be employed in a subcabinet position. "I'd be unemployed today if it hadn't been for that man," Taylor said in a 1984 interview (*Michigan Bar Journal*, 491). Admitted to practice law in the District of Columbia in 1957, she remained an assistant solicitor in the Department of Labor until 1960.

Anna Johnston married Charles C. Diggs, Jr., in 1960. A divorced father of three children, Diggs was a mortician by profession, a former Michigan state senator and, since 1955, a United States congressman elected from the city of Detroit. Taylor moved to Detroit, was admitted to practice law in Michigan in 1961, and worked as assistant Wayne County prosecutor from 1961 to 1962. Her first child, Douglass Johnston Diggs, was born in 1964. Five months later, as the major civil rights organizations were coordinating a comprehensive program of voter registration, educational tutoring in "Freedom Schools" and antisegregation demonstrations for the entire state of Mississippi, Taylor volunteered to spend the summer in Jackson, Mississippi, working for the National Lawyers Guild. The guild coordinated a team of seventy lawyers handling all types of civil rights cases arising from the activities of the 1964 "Freedom Summer," with Taylor and Claudia Shropshire being the only women attorneys donating their services.

Taylor resumed her career by working as an assistant United States attorney, Eastern District of Michigan, in 1966. Her second child, Carla Cecile Diggs, was born in 1967. Subsequently, she worked as a legislative assistant and as Detroit office manager for her husband, Congressman Charles Diggs, from 1967 to 1970 (*Almanac of the Federal Judiciary*, Vol. 1, 13). In 1972 Anna and Charles Diggs divorced. In May 1976, she married attorney S. Martin Taylor, who was then director of the Michigan Employment Security Commission (1971-1983) and later became director of the State of Michigan Department of Labor (1983-1984), executive vice-president and president of New Detroit (1984-1989), and vice-president for community and governmental affairs for the Detroit Edison Company (1989-).

In 1970 Taylor entered the private practice of law by becoming a partner in the firm of Zwerdling, Maurer, Diggs and Papp. Specializing in labor law, she also taught as an adjunct professor in labor law, first for the Wayne State University School of Labor and Industrial Relations from 1972 to 1975 and then for the Wayne State University Law School in 1976. Service on a panel of arbitrators for the American Arbitration Association occurred during these years. During her employment in the United States Department of Labor, she came to realize the considerable opportunities in government and the court system to increase racial equality and to improve society. She decided to become politically active, supporting causes and candidates who shared her vision.

In the process, her own career eventually benefited, as she was afforded greater opportunities to demonstrate her skills and ability. When Taylor moved to Michigan, her political involvement increased. She worked on her first husband's campaigns for Congress and even ran, unsuccessfully, as a candidate for a judgeship in the 1960s. She also served as chairperson of Lawyers for Humphrey and Lawyers for McGovern. In 1973 she was active in the campaign of Coleman A. Young to become Detroit's first black mayor. His election brought into office an administration that wanted to increase the number of qualified blacks employed in the city. Thus, in 1975 Taylor left her law firm and became the supervising assistant corporation counsel in the Law Department for the City of Detroit until 1979.

Eastern District Judge Appointed to Office

In 1976 Anna Diggs Taylor was active in the campaign to elect Jimmy Carter President of the United States. During his term of office, the number of federal judgeships was expanded, and Carter personally requested that special efforts be made to find competent and experienced women and minority candidates for these positions. Anna Diggs Taylor was recommended and appointed to a life term as judge, United States District Court, Eastern District of Michigan, beginning on November 15, 1979. She became the first black American woman federal judge in Michigan.

As a judge, she handled a wide range of cases, including conflicts over attempted takeovers of billion-dollar companies, air pollution and environmental issues, the civil rights of Cuban nationals detained in federal prisons, racial violence as a civil rights issue, the fairness of political party processes, and the constitutionality of Christmas nativity scenes on government property. A widely-publicized case was her 1984 sentencing of a white man, Ronald Ebens, to twenty-five years in prison for hitting Vincent Chin, a Chinese-American, with a baseball bat, which led to his death. When tried in a state court, the state judge had sentenced Ebens only to three years probation and a fine. The federal trial, however, convicted Ebens of violating Chin's civil rights and drew a stiffer sentence from Judge Taylor, whose decision was overturned on appeal.

Judge Taylor has not let judicial reticence keep her from commenting on important social and racial issues as long as there is no related court case before her. For example, she reprimanded the chief judge of her own court for remarks reported in a newspaper interview. In an August 26, 1984, *Detroit Free Press* story, John Feikens, chief judge of the United States Court, Eastern District of Michigan, criticized Mayor Coleman Young's administration of the Detroit Water and Sewerage Department. Some decisions of that department resulted in the department head and one of Mayor Young's alleged associates, along with four others, being convicted of crimes and sentenced to jail.

Judge Feikens was quoted as saying these events were evidence "that we have to give back people the time to learn . . . how to run city governments, to run projects like the water and sewer plant. . . . As the black people come into political power in all the big cities of the United States, they will have to learn how to climb hills. Some won't. Some will not understand how to run government. Some will not understand leadership." Within a few days, Judge Taylor had written a letter to Judge Feikens and distributed it to other judges. She wrote that "it is an extraordinary insult to all black professionals and/or administrators, and indicates a total failure to value human individuals on their individual merit: the essence of bigotry." Taylor concluded that Feikens's statements "can only be described as racist" and cast "a cloud upon the quality of justice to be expected from the Eastern District of Michigan" (*Detroit Free Press,* 26 August 1984, 29 August 1984; *The National Law Journal,* 3, 11).

Most lawyers who practice in Judge Taylor's courtroom have a positive impression of her work as a judge, though she has a few detractors. Most lawyers think she is fair to all, "usually has knowledge of current legal developments and a good understanding of the issues in ordinary cases, accommodates emergency requests, and usually rules on motions promptly and knowledgeably." In addition, some lawyers think Taylor "tends to rule for the plaintiff in civil rights cases and tends to favor the defendant in criminal cases." She is described as taking an active role in the courtroom, placing strict controls on "a lawyer's questioning of and general behavior toward witnesses." Detractors say that she "sometimes does not have a good understanding of the issues in complex cases," and she "sometimes produces very good, sophisticated opinions; sometimes doesn't" (*Almanac of the Federal Judiciary,* 14).

Taylor believes that women attorneys must "work extremely hard all the time" to develop "superior" credentials. Though she has personally followed this path, she also feels that her good fortune has been greatly aided by luck. On the differences in career development between men and women, Taylor believes that women are more cautious, try harder to attain perfection, to avoid making mistakes and appearing foolish. On the contrary, men are more willing to take risks that might result in their appearing foolish, to concentrate more on making impressions on people and fostering relationships that can aid advancement, while women concentrate on perfecting their "work product." Still, Taylor is optimistic about the future of women attorneys, since the large numbers and high caliber of young women entering the field of law will command their recognition.

Anna Diggs Taylor is active with numerous bar associations, such as the Women Judges Association, Women Lawyers of Michigan, State Bar Committee on the United States Courts, Federal Bar Association, and the Michigan Bar Association. She is active in community activities, serving, for example, on the board of directors or trustee board of Sinai Hospital, Detroit Science Center, Planned Parenthood League of Detroit, Detroit Receiving Hospital, and the Detroit Symphony Orchestra. She is also a member of the Women's National Democratic Club, United Community Services, Women's Economic Club, Detroit Commission on Community Relations (Women's Committee), and Metropolitan Detroit YWCA Public Affairs.

Among her awards are the National Bar Association Women Lawyers' Division Award, 1981; Michigan SCLC Millender Award, 1984; Alpha Phi Alpha Award, Epsilon Chapter, 1984; Sojourner Truth Award, National Negro Business and Professional Women, 1986; and Absalom Jones Award of Michigan Black Episcopalians, 1986.

References

Almanac of the Federal Judiciary. Vol. 2. Sixth Circuit. Englewood Cliffs, N.J.: Prentice Hall Law and Business, 1990.

The American Bench: Judges of the Nation. 5th ed. Sacramento: Forster-Long, 1990.

Biographical Directory of the United States Congress 1774-1989. Bicentennial Edition. Washington, D.C.: U.S. Government Printing Office, 1989.

Curriculum Vitae.

"Feikens Assesses Mayor Young, VISTA, Sewage Cleanup." *Detroit Free Press,* 26 August 1984.

"Feikens's Comments Are Racist, Judge Says." *Detroit Free Press,* 29 August 1984.

Higgins, Chester. "Lady Legal Eagles Learn of 'Mississippi Way of Life.'" *Jet* 26 (9 July 1964): 16-19.

"U. S. Judge Focus of Racial Dispute." *National Law Journal* (September 17, 1984): 3, 11.

Who's Who Among Black Americans, 1990/1991. 6th ed. Detroit: Gale Research, 1990. 1225.

Who's Who in American Law. 3rd ed. Chicago: Marquis, 1983. 692. 6th ed. Wilmette, Ill.: Marquis, 1990. 869.

Who's Who in American Politics. 9th ed. New York: Bowker, 1984. 691.

Who's Who of American Women. 14th ed. Chicago: Marquis, 1986. 790.

"Women in the Law—Comments from Some Women Judges." *Michigan Bar Journal* 63 (June 1984): 490-95.

De Witt S. Dykes, Jr.

Eva Taylor

(1895-1977)

Singer, dancer, radio show hostess

Irene Gibbons Williams, popularly known as Eva Taylor, contributed significantly as a vocalist in the theater, radio, and recording industries of the Harlem Renaissance (1920s and 1930s). She was born January 22, 1895, in Saint Louis, Missouri, one of twelve children of Frank Gibbons and Julia (Evans) Gibbons, and was educated at Sumner High School in Saint Louis. Having performed internationally with a vaudeville show in her youth, she married Clarence Williams (pianist, vocalist, arranger, composer, bandleader) on October 8, 1921, settled in New York City, and pursued an active singing career. During her singing career she also raised her three children—Clarence, Jr. (b. March 18, 1923); Spencer Patrick (b. March 17, 1926); and Irene (b. April 18, 1928). She remained married to Clarence Williams until his death in 1965. Taylor died of cancer in Mineola, New York, on October 31, 1977.

Taylor began her career as a toddler in vaudeville, singing and dancing with Josephine Gassman and Her Pickaninnies at the Orpheum Theater in Saint Louis (1898). Prior to World War I, she toured with this troupe nationally and internationally (Hawaii, Australia, New Zealand, England, Germany, France, the Netherlands). Taylor appeared with Al Jolson in New York City as a chorus girl in *Vera Violetta* (1911), returned with the Gassman troupe to tour Australia, Tasmania, and New Zealand (1914-1915), and remained with the troupe as a ballad singer and dancer touring American cities after 1915.

In 1921 she married Clarence Williams and settled in New York City, where she frequently sang blues and ballads in local clubs and theaters with her husband's group, the Clarence Williams Trio. In 1922, she performed with Florence Mills in the musical comedy *Shuffle Along* (Sixty-third Street Theater), in *Queen O'Hearts* (George M. Cohan Theater), and with the Miller and Lyles variety show *Step On It* (in theaters along the East Coast).

From 1923 until 1930 Taylor performed frequently in New York City—at Madison Square Garden, the Lincoln, The New Douglas, and Lafayette theaters, the Renaissance and Savoy ballrooms, the Harlem Casino—and served as understudy to Florence Mills in the highly acclaimed musical revue *Dixie to Broadway*, which opened in 1924 at the Broadhurst Theater. According to John Hope Franklin, "Negro revues had previously starred two black-face comedians"—the "domination of the show by Florence Mills" was therefore a significant "break with long-established traditions" (370). Taylor performed with her husband at the Sesquicentennial International Exposition in Philadelphia, in New York City at Carnegie Hall, and in the *Clarence Williams Revue* at Lincoln Theater. In 1927 she appeared in the Broadway musical comedy *Bottomland,* and in 1929 appeared in Miller and Lyles musical show *Keep Shufflin'*.

Career in Radio Flourishes

Taylor's involvement in music during this time coincided with the rise of the American radio industry. Her career in radio began when she appeared with the Clarence Williams Trio in 1922 on Vaughn De Leath's "Musical Program" (NBC-affiliate WEAF-radio, New York City) and led to two specific honors: Taylor became the first black American female soloist to be broadcast nationally and internationally (1929); and she also hosted her own radio program, "Eva Taylor, Crooner Show" (WEAF/WJZ-radio, 1932-1933). Primarily affiliated with WEAF/WJZ, Taylor made appearances on several other New York City stations during the 1920s, with Piron's New Orleans Orchestra, Clarence Todd, and her husband's groups (the Clarence Williams Radio Trio, Blue Three, Blue Five Orchestra) on WJZ, WGBS, WHN, and WPAP/WPCH. She performed on the "Florence Mills Memorial Hour" and "Below the Mason-Dixon Line" shows, and sang on the "Clarence Williams and Pals Show" (WABC, 1928; WOV, 1929).

During the 1930s Taylor's involvement in New York City radio expanded further. At WEAF/WJZ she worked as staff soloist, frequently sang with the Knickerbockers Orchestra, and appeared on the following radio shows (1929-1935): "Major Bowes Capitol Family Show"; "Morning Glories"; "The Rise of the Goldbergs"; "Harlem" (with the Cab Calloway Orchestra); "Rye Crisp"; "The Eveready Hour" (with Nat Shilkret); "Atwater Kent Hour"; a black adaptation of "Samson and Delilah" on "Alpha and Omega Opera Company Deluxe"; "Blue Streaks Orchestra"; "General

Eva Taylor

Motors'' (with Erno Rapee); ''Careless Love''; Hugo Mariana's ''Marionettes Orchestra''; ''Harlem Fantasy''; ''Club Valspar''; ''Slow River Show'' (with Lil Armstrong and Clarence Williams Trio); ''Kraft Music Hall Show'' (with Paul Whiteman Orchestra); and ''Soft Lights and Sweet Music.''

In addition to her WEAF/WJZ performances during the 1930s, Taylor appeared on ''Sixty Minutes of Broadway Entertainment'' on WGY (1930, Schenectady, New York). She performed with the ''Clarence Williams Trio,'' the ''Dixie Nightingales,'' ''The Lowland Singers/Trio,'' and ''The Sheep and Goat Club'' shows on WOR-radio (1930-1940). She also performed on the ''Grandmother's Trunk Show,'' the ''Clarence Williams Quartet,'' ''Folks From Dixie,'' ''Drowsy Rhythm,'' and ''Youth on Parade'' shows on WMCA, NBC, WENR, and a local station (1931-1939, New York City and Chicago, Illinois). During this period she appeared in the musical revue *Melodies of 1933* (Harlem Opera House), headlined at the Harlem Opera House (1934), sang at the Apollo Theatre (1936), appeared in *Mr. Jiggins of Jigginstown* (Labor Stage Theater, 1936), and performed again with her husband at Carnegie Hall (1939).

Taylor and Clarence Williams were actively engaged in recording their music. Taylor recorded free-lance and with her husband and others throughout the 1920s and 1930s under the Black Swan, Okeh, Columbia, Edison, Victor, Velvetone, Vocalion, Bluebird, and ARC labels. She recorded under several names (including Irene Gibbons, Catherine Henderson, the Charleston Chasers, and the Riffers), and frequently recorded with her husband's groups.

Taylor retired from public performance to entertain for the Hospital Reserve Corps in New York City hospitals during the World War II era. She performed at the Bessie Smith Memorial Concert in 1948 (Town Hall, New York City), though she became increasingly inactive in music through the 1950s and 1960s. In 1967, she appeared with the Anglo-American Alliance Jazz Groups on BBC-radio in London, recorded with the Anglo-American Boy Friends in Burnham, England, and appeared on the ''Joe Franklin Show'' (WOR-TV, New York City). During a hiatus from retirement during the mid-1970s, she worked at the Overseas Press Club (Biltmore Hotel, New York City), performed in concert with the Sweet Peruna Jazz Band and Maggie's Blue Five group (Copenhagen, Denmark and Lund, Sweden), performed at the Stampen Club (Stockholm, Sweden), and appeared on national television in Sweden.

Often with her husband, Taylor worked with a number of notable contemporary singers, musicians, and stage and radio performers, such as Bessie Smith, Ethel Waters, King Oliver, Al Jolson, Florence Mills, Miss Vaughn de Leath (''The Original Radio Girl''), Armand J. Piron, Sarah Martin, Lawrence Lomax, Clarence Todd, and Cab Calloway.

Taylor is recognized as the author of ''May We Meet Again, Florence Mills,'' and is credited with the following recordings: (under Irene Gibbons) ''That Da Da Strain,'' ''My Pillow and Me,'' ''Longing/Let Me Forget''; (under Eva Taylor) ''My Pillow and Me/I'm Going Away Just to Wear You Off My Mind,'' ''From Now On Blues/Church Street Sobbin' Blues,'' ''Original Charleston Strut/If You Don't, I Know Who Will,'' ''Terrible Blues/Arkansas Blues,'' ''Shake That Thing/Get It Fixed,'' ''Scatter Your Smiles/Candy Lips,'' ''Back in Your Own Backyard/Chlo-e,'' ''Happy Days and Lonely Nights/If You Want the Rainbow,'' ''Senorita Mine/Charleston Hound,'' ''Have You Ever Felt That Way?/West End Blues,'' ''And Her Anglo-American Boy Friends''; (under Charleston Chasers) ''Ain't Misbehaving/Moanin' Low,'' ''Turn On the Heat/What Wouldn't I Do for That Man?,'' ''You're Lucky to Me/Loving You the Way I Do''; (under Clarence Williams) ''Of All the Wrongs You've Done to Me/Everybody Loves My Baby,'' ''Coal Cart Blues/Santa Claus Blues,'' ''Mandy, Make Up Your Mind/I'm a Little Blackbird Looking for a Bluebird,'' ''Zonky/You've Got to Be Modernistic,'' ''Papa De-Da-Da/Baby,'' ''Won't You Please Come Home?,'' ''Shout Sister Shout,'' ''Top of the Town/More Than That,'' ''Wanted,'' and ''Thriller Blues/Uncle Sammy, Here I Am.''

It has been noted that Taylor's singing style was influenced by Katherine Henderson and Sippie Wallace. Brian Rust has suggested that although Taylor was ''not possessed of a big voice like Bessie Smith or Sara Martin, her rich and thrilling contralto is nevertheless ideally suited to all kinds of songs, flexible, warm and human as its owner'' (Parlophone album).

References

Chilton, John. *Who's Who of Jazz: Storyville to Swing Street*. Philadelphia: Chilton, 1972.

Franklin, John Hope. *From Slavery to Freedom*. 5th ed. New York: Knopf, 1980.

Harris, Sheldon. *Blues Who's Who*. New Rochelle, N.Y.: Arlington House, 1979.

Kinkle, Roger D. *The Complete Encyclopedia of Popular Music and Jazz: 1900-1950*. Vol. 3. New Rochelle, N.Y.: Arlington House, 1974.

Who's Who in Colored America. 5th ed. Yonkers, N.Y.: Christian E. Burckel, 1938.

Jo Dawn McEwan

Susie King Taylor

(1848-1912)

Nurse, activist, author

Among the legacies of the nineteenth century, the names of only a few women of color are found in American history books. Harriet Tubman, the fugitive slave, Underground Railroad conductor, Civil War spy and nurse, and women's activist, is usually considered to be the most prominent woman of her era. Similarly, when discussing black American women and the nursing profession, thoughts generally focus on Mary Mahoney, the first professionally trained nurse. In neither context is the name of Susan Baker King Taylor mentioned. Although her writings alone should warrant some distinction, Susie King Taylor is usually not found on any list. Instead, this former slave, Civil War nurse, teacher, and author has become one of the many unsung heroes of the late nineteenth century.

Susie King Taylor

Like many of her counterparts, Taylor was born a slave and died a free woman. Here is where such similarities end. Unlike most of her contemporaries, she was raised in an intact household that was able to maintain the family structure. Baker knew her family as well as its history, which extended back to a great-great-grandmother. This young woman grew up a member of a proud family, and she displayed abilities normally denied to the slave community. Susie Taylor was able to leave the plantation to visit and eventually live with her grandmother, and she could read, write, and sew before she was nine. From this very strong base, she spent her life trying to improve the lives of others.

In the first chapter of her autobiographical work, Taylor a brief sketch of her ancestors. Her remarkable origins began with her great-great-grandmother. This woman of mixed African and Indian ancestry lived for roughly one hundred twenty years. Of her seven children, five participated in the American Revolution. Susanna, Taylor's great-grandmother, also lived to be over a hundred. A midwife by profession, she gave birth to twenty-four children—twenty-three daughters and one son. In 1820 Taylor's maternal grandmother, Dolly, was born. She married Fortune Lambert Reed some thirteen years later and gave birth to two children: James, who died when he was twelve, and Hagar Ann, Taylor's mother.

Born in 1834, Hagar Ann married Raymond Baker in 1847. They had nine children and six survived. While it is not clear whether Raymond Baker was a slave, his wife and children were held in bondage. Susie, born on August 5, 1848, was their first child. Apparently she lived with her mother on the Grest farm on the Isle of Wight in Liberty County, Georgia, some thirty-five miles from the city of Savannah.

Both Dolly Reed and Hagar Baker developed important relationships with their masters that were crucial to Taylor's development. Dolly Reed was hired out and allowed to live in Savannah under the supervision of a guardian. Similarly, Hagar Ann Baker was a well-liked house servant and privy to special considerations. Thus, both Taylor's mother and grandmother lived lives that were distinct from the majority of other slaves. Although they were enslaved, their minds were free. They were able to retain levels of dignity and pride that they passed onto their children.

Obviously, this tremendous pride and inner strength influenced Taylor. Even in a world filled with blatant racial and sexual prejudices, she was able to maintain a positive outlook. Her attitude was shaped by her strong religious convictions, as well as by the surrounding environment.

The Grest family took an active interest in the Baker children. Taylor became one of Mrs. Grest's favorites. When Mr. Grest went away on business, Mrs. Grest was quite maternal. She would place Taylor and her brother on the foot of her bed to sleep and keep her company. However, there were fine lines drawn between the slaves, mistresses, and master. For example, if Mr. Grest arrived home unexpectedly, she would put them on the floor.

In contrast to Mrs. Grest, Dolly Reed never hid her true feelings. It was clear that she was especially proud of her family. Taylor remained in close contact with her throughout her life. Taylor reported that her grandmother visited her mother every three months. As the trip was a lengthy ordeal, Dolly Reed mixed business with pleasure. For each visit, she hired a wagon to carry foodstuffs that she would trade with the neighboring residents. In return, she would take other foodstuffs back to Savannah to sell in local markets. From this and other ventures, Dolly Reed earned a decent living.

Young Slave Taught to Read and Write

When Taylor was seven, Mr. Grest allowed Dolly Reed to take her and a younger sister and her brother and raise them in Savannah. Although it was against the law, their grandmother sent Taylor and her brother to a free woman's home to learn how to read and write. The two children walked nearly a half mile to the home of a Mrs. Woodhouse where they were taught with more than twenty other children. Marching in one by one, they carried their books wrapped in paper to disguise their actions. Two years later, when Taylor had learned all that she could from Mrs. Woodhouse and her daughter, Mary Jane, she continued her education under Mary Beasley. Such schooling continued until she outgrew all of her teachers.

After leaving Beasley in May 1860, Taylor began her informal education. As she did not know of any other black teachers, she utilized the services of neighboring white children. The first of these illegal tutors was Katie O'Connor. O'Connor volunteered to teach Taylor if she promised not to tell her father. After securing this promise, the two young women met every evening over a four-month period. Their sessions came to an end when O'Connor entered a convent.

James Blouis, the son of Dolly Reed's landlord, served as the second tutor. Reed secretly recruited this high school student to give Taylor a few lessons. However, they too would be interrupted. Blouis, a soldier of the Confederate army, was sent to the battlefront in the middle of 1861. Like O'Connor, he would also never return to Savannah.

While the Civil War effectively ended the official education of Susie Baker Taylor, her life experiences were only beginning. The significance of President Lincoln's war to save the Union was not lost on this bright teenager. Whether through the conversations she overheard in the street or based upon what her grandmother had told her, Taylor hoped that a Union victory would spell emancipation for the millions of African-Americans held in perpetual bondage.

As Dolly Reed took an active role in the affairs of Savannah's black community, so did her granddaughter. From the outbreak of the conflict, Reed went to meetings and discussed current events with other knowledgeable citizens. On several occasions, Taylor accompanied her grandmother and developed her own opinions. Almost immediately, Taylor was pressed into action. She used her skills by writing passes for slaves and freemen alike, allowing them to expand the limits of their mobility.

Unfortunately, such contributions came to an abrupt end. Following a police raid on a suburban church meeting, Dolly Reed was arrested and handed over to her guardian. As a result of her participation in this clandestine freedom meeting, he imposed tighter restrictions to limit her bold and independent spirit. It was clear that she would no longer be allowed to influence her grandchildren. Around April 1, 1862, Taylor was sent back to her mother on the Grest farm.

As the war raged around Savannah and several area forts, the fear of the Yankees increased. When Fort Pulaski fell to the Union troops, Taylor, an uncle, and several members of his family escaped to St. Catherine Island. They were placed under the protection of the Union fleet and remained on the island for roughly two weeks. With thirty other African-Americans, Taylor and her family were transported to St. Simon's Island.

As white Southerners had continually stressed to their slaves that Northerners were quite different from Southerners, Taylor longed to see the "dreaded Yankees." While she was living in Savannah, it was believed that blacks sang hymns with hidden meanings. One such hymn contained the lines: "Yes, we all shall be free, When the Lord shall appear." Paranoid members of the white community believed that the slaves sang "the Lord" in place of "the Yankee." Dolly Reed was singing that particular hymn on the evening she was caught in the police raid at the suburban church. Therefore, the "Yankees" were very important to Taylor. They represented freedom and much more.

During the voyage to St. Simon's Island, Taylor finally had her first conversation with a Yankee. The Yankee was Captain Whitmore, the commander of the boat. He asked the fourteen-year-old Taylor where she was from and if she could read or write or sew. To prove all of her affirmative replies, she had to demonstrate each skill. When convinced, the captain replied, "You seem to be so different from the other colored people who came from the same place you did." Taylor responded, "No! The only difference is, they were reared in the country and I in the city." After her statement, she recalled that Whitmore seemed satisfied with her comment, and there was no further conversation on that subject (Taylor, 9).

As Captain Whitmore recognized Taylor's abilities, her

services were instantly utilized. Just three days after arriving on St. Simon's Island, a Commodore Goldsborough approached her to operate a small school on the island. Upon receiving the necessary supplies, she started a school at Gaston Bluff. Her earliest groups consisted of two sessions. She taught forty children during the day and a handful of eager adults at night. The school operated for most of 1862.

Slaves Prepared for Emancipation

Unknown to Taylor and the other African-American refugees on the Sea Islands, they were part of an experiment in freedom. Although they were not officially informed that they were free, they were granted rights beyond those of slaves. While President Lincoln maintained a strict policy of retaining slavery to preserve the Union, these officers clearly disregarded the orders. With the assistance of northern missionaries, the soldiers distributed some of the confiscated lands and convinced blacks to resume cotton production. In her role as a teacher, Taylor made an important contribution by preparing members of her race for their eventual emancipation.

As the war waged on along the Georgia coast, it became obvious to the Union officers that the outpost on St. Simon's Island was not secure. In the late fall of 1862, a decision was made to evacuate the black residents, and Taylor was relocated to Camp Saxton in Beauford, South Carolina. The school came to an end, and Taylor was recruited to serve as a laundress. She was assigned to Company E, an all-black unit led by white officers.

Company E, the first South Carolina Volunteers, was the first black regiment formed in the South. In reality, it was an outgrowth of the experiments waged by Lincoln's pro-abolition generals. Supported by General David Hunter, General Rufus Saxton formed the regiment from free blacks and fugitive slaves who wanted to fight for the freedom of their race. Captain, later Colonel, C. T. Trowbridge was responsible for the enlistment of many of the recruits, and in 1863, Harvard-educated Thomas Wentworth Higginson took command of the regiment.

From the outbreak of the war well into 1862, Lincoln was against the use of slaves in the conflict. While he knew of the formation of Company E and similar regiments in Kansas and Louisiana, he refused to sanction them. His rejection of regiments composed of northern free blacks was based on the same principles. Although this policy annoyed many northern white and black leaders, the president stood his ground. However, following the response to the reading of the Emancipation Proclamation in 1863, President Lincoln agreed to the involvement of blacks in the conflict. He then authorized the formation of the United States Colored Troops (USCT). The USCT became the all-black regiments under the control of the Union army. They would be led by northern white officers, including colonels Robert Gould Shaw and Thomas Wentworth Higginson, Bostonians of great social prominence. Company E became the Thirty-third Regiment of the USCT.

While morale in these regiments was extremely high, conditions were poor. Taylor reported that despite the support of their commanding officers, the black troops were ill-clad, were not paid for eighteen months, and then were given a lower salary than white troops. She proudly related that although General Saxton provided services to some of the needier soldiers from his own funds, the men refused their wages until they received equal compensation.

Colonel Higginson spoke well of his men in his own work, *Army Life in a Black Regiment*. He also was an active participant in the fight of the black soldiers to receive equal pay. Higginson wrote several letters to the editors of the *New York Tribune* and the *New York Times* and a petition to Congress complaining about the injustice done to his troops. He praised his men as "dedicated, brave, and loyal."

Company E became very important to Taylor. She remained with the regiment throughout the course of the war and dedicated all of her time and energies to those who fought for freedom. The company also gained a personal importance. Members of her family, including several uncles and cousins, joined the regiment. However, in her eyes, the most important member of the regiment was Sergeant Edward King. Also from Georgia, Edward King had lived in the city. After escaping from his master, he joined the First South Carolina Volunteers. Although Taylor had known Sergeant King before arriving in Beaufort, the two became very close during the war. Her care and concern for him grew, and they eventually married. (Taylor never wrote when she married Edward King; however, it is clear that they married sometime during the war, either in 1862 or 1863. It seems more probable that they married in 1862).

Susie Baker King Becomes Camp Nurse for Black Regiment

Although a married woman, the young bride could not stop to celebrate. In fact, her life continued as it had before the marriage. Taylor, now fifteen, was gaining responsibilities beyond her original charge. She was taught how to use and care for a rifle, and during her spare time she cooked meals for the wounded and taught eager soldiers how to read and write. As the war pressed on these duties multiplied. Due to an increasing number of casualties, Taylor began a new occupation as a camp nurse.

Historically, nursing had always been a trade assigned to slave women. Throughout the antebellum period, black nurses breast-fed and cared for babies of both races. In addition, on most southern plantations they played a role in caring for the sick, from the families of the master down to the slaves. The racial tendencies of the nineteenth century dictated the separation of the races on the battlefield and in the field hospitals, and as a result, the majority of black women were restricted to care for those of their own race.

At mid-century, nursing was still developing as a profession. Only whites, mainly women, were able to gain academic training. However, the majority of America's nurses during the Civil War were untrained white male volunteers.

Although there is a tendency to think of Clara Barton as America's first nurse and that the majority of Civil War nurses were women, these views are somewhat inaccurate. While Barton was one of the first, others, including Elizabeth Blackwell and Dorothea Dix, had greater prestige. Following the First Battle of Bull Run in 1861, Barton quit her job at the United States Patent Office to organize field nurses and stretcher bearers. At roughly the same time, Dorothea Dix was appointed government superintendent of nurses. Dix set the directives for female nurses; the minimum age was thirty, and they had to wear clothing of a somber color, without hoops, and unadorned with bows or lace. And less than a year later, Blackwell was put in charge of a professional training program for nurses. Yet, no more than twenty percent of the army nurses during the war were women, and it is believed that this number was even lower in the South. Most were concerned participants who donated their time and energies taking orders from more skilled physicians.

Taylor's role as a nurse was no different. It was an indirect result of her participation as a laundress. While caring for the uniforms, bandages, and other supplies, she began to assist the military surgeons. Her voluntary duties included the soothing of the sick and other tasks assigned by the doctors. Later, when the need for competent persons increased, she donated the majority of her time to this task.

Taylor proved to be an excellent practitioner. The soldiers were constantly thanking her for taking care of them. They felt that she always went out of her way to provide that extra touch. Regardless of their company, she treated all of the men the same. When her kindness was noted, Taylor replied, "You are all doing the same duty, and I will do just the same for you" (Taylor, 30).

Perhaps one of her greatest memories of the war was meeting Clara Barton, the founder of the American Red Cross. The two met during Barton's stay at the hospital in Beaufort in the summer of 1863. In the course of Taylor's hospital visits, the two women conversed. Taylor enjoyed these encounters and wrote: "Miss Barton was always very cordial toward me, and I honored her for her devotion and care of those men" (Taylor, 30).

There were other meetings that also became fond memories. Although they were only in the same camp for a short period, she would later describe Colonel Robert Gould Shaw as one of her heroes. One of the camps visited by the Thirty-third Regiment during the campaigns of 1863 was named in his honor. Later that year, the young commander of the Fifty-fourth Massachusetts Regiment would die with his troops during the assault on Fort Wagner.

Yet of all the important people she met during the war, Taylor's relationship with Colonel Higginson became a lifelong association. While she spoke highly of other officers in the regiment, it was clear that the dashing abolitionist-minister turned soldier was her favorite. Taylor was distressed when he left the regiment after suffering injuries in May 1864. She wrote:

> All the men were sorry to lose him. They did not want to see him go, they loved him so. He was kind and devoted to his men, thoughtful for their comfort, and we missed his genial presence from the camp (Taylor, 32).

In October, still infirm, the colonel felt compelled to resign his commission. With the exception of Taylor and Cyrus Wiggins, he never again saw any person associated with his beloved regiment.

Thomas Higginson also spoke highly of Taylor, who had married sometime after she moved to Boston, and wrote the introduction to *Reminiscences of My Life in Camp*. When the colonel died in May 1911, his honor guard was composed of young black soldiers. Taylor was also there to pay tribute to her friend for the last time.

Following Higginson's resignation, C. T. Trowbridge reassumed command. Taylor also had a good relationship with Trowbridge. She said, "There was no other like him, for he was a 'man' among the soldiers" (Taylor, 45). He too, was fond of the young nurse. He often told her about the North and introduced her to any Northerners who visited the camp. Trowbridge guided the Thirty-third until they were mustered out of the service. In a farewell speech given on February 9, 1866, he praised the men and thanked them for their service. Taylor was so touched by the speech and the significance of the day that she kept the copy of the address.

With the war finally over and a new life beginning, Taylor felt a sense of relief and joy. The war had provided many happy and hectic moments. She vividly remembered playing with "Piggie," the camp's pet pig, anxiously waiting to hear from Edward King when the Thirty-third went to Edisto, W. H. Brisbane's reading of the Emancipation Proclamation and the subsequent celebration on the evening of January 1, 1863, and the time that she nearly died when her transport ship had overturned, leaving her in the cold Atlantic Ocean for hours before she was rescued. Yet these thoughts were overshadowed by the more gruesome aspects of the war. The images of death and the devastation of the human spirit remained with her.

Freedom had been achieved, and she was among those who had contributed to making that goal a reality. However, despite her efforts during the war, she received no pay or certificate of service. And since she was not officially credited as a Union nurse, she was also denied a post-war pension.

For the first time, the Kings could start their life together. They returned to Savannah and settled on South Broad Street (Oglethorpe Avenue). Taylor settled in as a housewife; due to racial prejudice, Edward, a boss carpenter by trade, took a job as a longshoreman.

Taylor's inactivity was short-lived. Since there was no school for black Americans within the community, she established one in her home. She had twenty day pupils and several night students, charging each a dollar per month.

Unexpectedly, on September 16, 1866, Taylor's world was shattered. Edward King was killed in an accident unloading vessels at the pier. Not yet twenty, Taylor was a widow and an expectant mother. In December her condition and the arrival of the Beach Institute, a free school, forced her to stop teaching. Shortly after the birth of her son, she resumed her work, briefly operating a country school in Liberty County (the name of her son was never mentioned in any documents). However, within a year she grew tired and relinquished control of the school to a Susie Carter.

Once back in Savannah, her enthusiasm returned. With the assistance of her brother-in-law, Taylor ran a night school for adults. Within the following year this school was also forced to close. Once again there was competition; the Beach Institute started a free evening program.

Facing mounting financial difficulties, Taylor sought assistance. She placed her son with her mother, who would practically raise him, and applied for Edward King's army pension of one hundred dollars. Upon receiving the money, she heeded Dolly Reed's suggestion and placed some of this money in the Freedmen's Bank. Both Taylor and her grandmother lost their savings when the bank collapsed.

While waiting for her claim, she gained employment as a laundress for Mrs. Charles Green. In 1873 the Greens relocated to Rye Beach for the summer and they took Taylor as their cook. It was her first time in the North, a place that she had only heard about from the white officers. To Taylor, Boston was a magical city, and she was captivated by its charm and lack of prejudice. This first exposure to northern living left a lasting impression. Besides, it was extremely profitable. While there, Taylor entered and won a prize for excellence in cooking at a church fair.

In 1874 she returned to Boston, this time in the employ of the James Barnards. Although she would make several trips back to the South, Boston became her home. During the subsequent five-year period she worked for the Barnards, a Thomas Smith, and later for a Mrs. Gorham Gray. In 1879 she met and married Russell L. Taylor.

As late as 1886, Susie Taylor was still influenced by the Civil War. In that year her undying patriotic fever led to the organization of Corps Sixty-seven, Women's Relief Corps, auxiliary to the Grand Army of the Republic. Taylor was very loyal to the organization she helped to found, serving as a guard, secretary, treasurer (for three years), and in 1893 as president. A red, white, and blue quilt that she made for a future occasion won praises and was awarded to the next president.

Three years later, in 1896, she was involved in another war-related venture. Taylor compiled a list of war veterans living in Massachusetts. She found both black and white soldiers who had been forgotten by their peers. Her work was respected and within the veteran's association she was highly admired.

Tragedy struck again in 1898. Taylor had lost her father in 1867, her grandmother in 1889, and now she had received news that her son was seriously ill in Louisiana. Her son, who was an actor traveling with Nickens and Company, had been performing in *The Lion's Bride*. He had taken ill in January and was bedridden in Shreveport. As he could not travel to Boston, Taylor went south to take care of him. Although she had grown up in the South, she had never been to Louisiana. The railroad trip and the reactions of the people she encountered stirred up a great hatred of southern culture.

Although she met influential people of both races, the impact of segregation was devastating. Because of her color she had to ride in segregated cars, and in the deep South she was relegated to the smoking car. As a result she had to endure several indignities. She learned that most Southerners accepted the situation as it was rather than effecting change. Even many of the black veterans suffered because they proudly wore their military buttons. To make matters even worse, on the ride home she witnessed a lynching. It appalled her that the citizens of Clarksdale, the scene of this crime, were not disturbed by this heinous act.

Her son was suffering from a hemorrhage and could not be moved. However, even if she wanted to, her race made it impossible to secure a sleeping car to transport him to Cincinnati. From there they could have traveled in comfort. Instead, Susie Taylor was forced to care for her son in the South. With tremendous regrets, his mother buried him in the South and returned to Boston.

Autobiographical Work Relates Racial Progress

Although she probably had the idea at a much earlier date, in 1901 Taylor finished a manuscript about her life. The book, *Reminiscences of My Life in Camp*, was more than an autobiography; rather it was a personal account of the struggles and achievements of Americans, but particularly black Americans, from the Civil War to the turn of the century. Although she highlighted some of the accomplishments of blacks since the war, the legacy of racism and discrimination was a theme in the second half of the work. Many of her comments were influenced by her travels, especially the trip to Shreveport. Taylor believed that racism was a national problem. However, she felt it was much more pronounced in the South.

Taylor's views were well developed in the last two chapters. In chapter thirteen, Taylor offered her thoughts on present conditions. On the subject of racism and progress she wrote:

> I wonder if our white fellow men realize the true sense or meaning of brotherhood? For two hundred years we had toiled for them; the war of 1861 came and was ended, and we thought our race was forever free from bondage, and that the two races could live in unity with each other, but when we read almost every day of what is done to my race by some whites in the South, I sometimes ask, "Was the war in vain? Has it

> brought freedom, in the full sense of the word, or has it not made our condition more hopeless?''
>
> In this ''land of the free'' we are burned, tortured, and denied a fair trial, murdered for any imaginary wrong conceived in the brain of the negro-hating white man. There is no redress for us from a government which promised to protect all under its flag. . . . No, we cannot sing, ''My country 'tis of thee, Sweet land of Liberty!'' It is hollow mockery (Taylor, 61-62).

It was her desire that the book would awaken a social consciousness within the nation. This woman who had seen the horrors of war desperately wanted to see the harmonious unification of the races and the nation.

Taylor published the manuscript in 1902. Although there were no reviewers of the work or records of its sales, it could be assumed they were very modest. Most of the purchases were probably by her fellow clubwomen and their families.

Following the publication of *Reminiscences*, there is virtually nothing known about the activities of Taylor. In all probability, she continued to work as a domestic and spent her free time involved with the war organizations. Sometime before the publication of the book, Russell Taylor died, and it is apparent that she lived alone. (As the only detailed source of her life, *Reminiscences* leaves many questions unanswered.) Taylor did not write very much about her mother after she escaped from the Grest farm. Outside of her owning a grocery store in post-war Savannah, nothing is said of her activities. Even less is mentioned about her only son. Taylor wrote that she left him with her mother, and it appears that he was raised by Hagar Ann Baker. Other sources have challenged this notion and believe that Dolly Reed raised Taylor's son. Despite the controversy, it seems clear that he did not live with her in Boston. The nature of the relationship between mother and son is unknown. Similarly, outside of his name, Taylor did not write anything about her second husband. Therefore, all of the important facts about Russell Taylor also remain unknown. Simeon Baker, in his work on Susie Taylor, indicates that Russell Taylor died before Susie Taylor. He believes that she was buried next to him. Most likely, Susie Taylor moved into a rooming house. By 1908 Taylor was sixty years old, but based on the longevity of her great-great grandmother and great-grandmother, she was probably still quite active.

On the morning of October 6, 1912, the landlady was making her rounds at the rooming house. She knocked at Taylor's door but received no answer. When she opened the door, she found Taylor slumped by her bed. A doctor was summoned, and he pronounced her dead.

Taylor was buried in Boston's Mount Hope Cemetery with an unmarked headstone. The local papers did not carry an obituary or a funeral notice. She had outlived her only son, two husbands, and all of her close relatives and friends. In essence, she died alone and unknown.

Although Taylor's life seemed to be of little significance, her deeds certainly touched all who knew her. She was a dreamer, a woman of peace, love, and brotherhood. Her quest was to bring about a better world, and in her roles as a teacher, nurse, author, and organizer, she did her best to make that dream a reality.

References

Black Women in Nineteenth-Century American Life: Their Words, Their Thoughts, Their Feelings. Eds. Bert James Loewenberg and Ruth Bogin. University Park: Pennsylvania State University Press, 1976. 898-94.

Booker, Simeon. *Susie King Taylor: Civil War Nurse*. New York: McGraw-Hill, 1969.

Burchard, Peter. *One Gallant Rush: Robert Gould Shaw and His Brave Black Regiment*. New York: St. Martin's Press, 1965.

Carnegie, Mary Elizabeth. *The Path We Tread: Blacks in Nursing 1854-1984*. Philadelphia: Lippincott, 1986. Includes photograph.

Dannett, Sylvia G. L. *Profiles of Negro Womanhood*. Vol. 1. Yonkers, N.Y.: Educational Heritage, 1964.

Driver, Paul J. *Black Giants in Science*. New York: Vantage Presss, 1978.

Gaines, Edith M. *Terrible Tuesday*. Cleveland: New Day Press, 1972. Includes illustrations.

Higginson, Thomas Wentworth. *Army Life in a Black Regiment*. Reprinted. New York: Norton, 1984.

Lerner, Gerda, ed. *Black Women in White America*. New York: Pantheon Books, 1972.

Merriam, Eve. *Growing Up Female in America: Ten Lives*. Garden City, N.Y.: Doubleday, 1917.

Risjord, Normal K. *America: A History of the United States*. Englewood Cliffs, N.J.: Prentice-Hall, 1985.

Taylor, Susie King. *Reminiscences of My Life in Camp*. Boston: Privately printed, 1902. Reprinted. New York: Arno Press, 1968.

''Teen-age Civil War Nurse: Susie King Taylor.'' *Ebony* 24 (February 1970): 96-102.

Leslie Wilson

Susan L. Taylor

(1946-)

Editor, television show host

> Something so delicious is happening in Black America. We're only 120 years up from slavery. We are doing incredibly well if we look at the fact that the people we're comparing ourselves with have been in this [rat] race for 400 years with all of the assets, all of the support. We've been running that same race with shackles on our ankles trying to hold us back (Susan L. Taylor, *Excel,* 13).

Few American women of any race have the style and finesse of Susan L. Taylor. As editor-in-chief of *Essence* magazine, she exudes a glowing personal energy from the inside out that enhances her strikingly beautiful appearance. This magnetism, coupled with old fashioned intelligence and foresight, has gotten Susan Taylor where she is today. Along with editing *Essence*, she is also vice president of Essence Communications and past host and producer of the Essence television show. The magazine has a readership of fifty thousand, with revenues of more than twenty million. The television show was the first nationally-syndicated black-oriented magazine show. It ran for four seasons in more than sixty countries.

This is a far cry from Susan Taylor's early days. Born on January 23, 1946 in Harlem, the daughter of a shopkeeper and a homemaker, she became a licensed cosmetologist and dabbled in acting with the Negro Ensemble Company before joining *Essence* as a free-lance beauty writer in 1970. A year later she was named the magazine's beauty editor, and the following year her position was expanded to include both fashion and beauty.

Much of Susan Taylor's life exemplifies the kinds of triumphant struggles *Essence* readers know intimately. The determination to advance personally and professionally and the desire to promote positive images and take pride in one's accomplishments are values Taylor shares with her readers. These are reflected in her editorial column "In the Spirit" and in the kinds of topics regularly covered by *Essence.*

Susan Taylor notes the magazine was among the first to deal editorially with incest, cocaine, heroin, and rape. Recent issues have run the gamut from an interview with Winnie Mandela, wife of South African National Congress Vice President Nelson Mandela, to romantic meals for two, male/female relationships, hair styling tips, spa and European vacations, and even facial bleaching.

She sees the two Essences—magazine and television show—as having two different missions: "The magazine is a hands-on, how-to vehicle for helping black women move their lives forward," she said, while "the television show [was] aimed at everyone to project a positive image of black Americans. People tend to have negative views of what black people are all about" (*Detroit News,* 30 October 1986).

Susan Taylor, who has been a strong source of inspiration at many college seminars, shares her secret of inner strength:

> My day starts with quiet time about 6 a.m. I meditate. It's not any formal kind of meditation. It's just getting centered. I try to tap into that spiritual side of me. Cause when I go out without that intact, I get crazy, befuddled, and depressed. I read some psalms or the Lord's Prayer just to affirm some things for myself; that I am gonna move through this day from the highest perspective—that I'm going to be a problem solver and not fall victim to the things I see. That's what I have to tell myself (*Excel,* 15).

Lifestyle Magazine for Black Women Emerges

When asked what *Essence* means to her personally, Susan Taylor often has pointed to society's negligence: "Imagine yourself as a white woman, wanting to buy a magazine and seeing black faces on every cover," she once told the white press. "Wouldn't you feel isolated and ignored?" (*Detroit News,* 30 October 1986).

Evoking this uncomfortable picture in reverse clearly tells all of Susan Taylor's frustration before spring 1970, when *Essence* became the first lifestyle magazine devoted to black women. She said:

> I was so happy I didn't know whether to read it or hug it. Let's be real. We live in a racist society, and that makes it difficult to keep our faith high. . . . [T]here is little to remind us daily of how powerful and capable we are, so we must do that for ourselves and for each other. . . . [W]e can make a difference in our lives and in the world. We black folks have to believe this is true. It's time to dream big dreams and make them real (*Los Angeles Times,* 13 April 1986).

Susan Taylor likes to talk with people about taking charge of their lives and moving forward so they start to believe they can. Explaining her feelings and what life was like when she became a single mother she said:

> I've come from a place where I didn't believe in myself. I had no money, no man, My car was broken. I was making $500 a month working at *Essence* and paying $368 a month for rent. I could not see tomorrow (*Los Angeles Times,* 13 April 1986).

What turned it around for her, she said, was a conversation

with a minister who implored her to believes in herself. "Nobody had ever said that to me," she said.

Susan Taylor personifies the *Essence* woman in much the same way Helen Gurley Brown personifies *Cosmopolitan*. But she still remains close to home in her heart. "There's still that little girl in me that jumped double-dutch on 116th Street. I want to keep her alive" (*Excel,* 15).

Taylor is a member of the National Association of Black Journalists, the Society of Professional Journalists, the American Society of Magazine Editors, the Alliance Directors Resource Council for the National Women's Economic Alliance Foundation, and Women in Communications. She is a board member of the Edwin Gould Services for Children, an adoption and foster-care agency. She has received the Women in Communications Matrix Award, and an honorary Doctorate of Humane Letters from Lincoln University in 1988, among many other awards.

Susan Taylor's personal commitment is to empower the poor, to work with women in prison, and to work with teenage mothers to help them realize their strengths and take charge of their lives.

Susan Taylor earned a B.A. degree in social science and economics from Fordham University in 1990 in New York City. Recently married to Kephera Burns, she has one daughter, Shana, age 21.

References

Detroit News (30 October 1986).

Excel 2 (Fall 1986): 13-15. Full-page photograph, p. 14.

Los Angeles Times (13 April 1986).

Dianne Marshall

Mary Church Terrell

(1863-1954)

Writer, lecturer, educator, clubwoman

During Mary Church Terrell's long and notable life, it seemed that there was very little she *didn't* attempt in order to improve the social, economic, and political conditions of black Americans. Her excellent education and her travels abroad helped equip her for a career that began with teaching and continued with leadership positions in the Colored Women's League and later the National Association of Colored Women. Terrell worked vigorously for women's suffrage and women's rights, particularly black women's rights. She was an internationally-known speaker and lecturer, a widely-published writer, a member of numerous boards and associations, a founding member of a church in Washington, D.C., and an active member of the Republican party, and a charter member of the NAACP. Terrell led and won the fight to desegregate Washington, D.C., a struggle that was finally resolved in 1953, just a year before her death.

Mary Church Terrell

Mary Eliza Church Terrell, born in Memphis, Tennessee, on September 23, 1863, was the eldest child of Louisa (Ayers) Church and Robert Reed Church, both former slaves. Her father was the son of his master, Charles B. Church, who treated him decently but never gave him his freedom. After Robert Church's mother died, his father gave him work on his riverboat as a dishwasher, but the young man's diligence eventually earned him the position of procurement steward for the vessel. After emancipation, Robert Church opened a saloon that proved to be a reasonably successful operation. During the Memphis race riots of 1866 when Mollie Church, as the young Mary was commonly known, was about three years old, Robert Church was shot in the head and left for dead. However, he survived the attack and was able to open another establishment.

Although Church was a shrewd businessman, it was Louisa Church's hair salon—patronized by many of the well-to-do white women of Memphis—that enabled the young family to buy their first fashionable home. Life between Terrell's parents was not peaceful, however, and they were divorced while she was very young. Custody of Terrell and her brother, Thomas, was awarded to Louisa Church, but Robert Church continued generous support to his children throughout their lives.

During the yellow fever epidemic in Memphis in 1878-79, many people fled the city and were willing to sell their property at almost give-away prices. By that time Robert Church's business was prosperous and he was willing to buy as much abandoned real estate as he could afford. Observers felt that Church was foolish to believe that the city of Memphis would recover after the epidemic, but they were wrong, and Robert became an extremely wealthy real estate holder who was able to support his daughter in a manner to which few blacks of the period were accustomed.

Terrell's early schooling was in Memphis but schools for black children there were so inadequate that her parents decided to send her to the Antioch College Model School in Yellow Springs, Ohio, when she was about six years old, where she was often the only black child among her classmates. She boarded with a kind black family, the Hunsters, and when she was older, divided her summers between her parents' homes. While she was away at school, her mother and younger brother moved to New York City, so she would often travel by train up and down the eastern seaboard to visit her parents. Terrell's mother sent her boxes of clothes and gifts at various times during the school year but visits were a rarity.

Even as a young child, Terrell seemed conscious of the special opportunities that were afforded her and did not complain about the separation from her loved ones. She had a well-balanced and gregarious disposition that caused her to adapt easily to new situations. Although Terrell was so light-skinned that she was sometimes mistaken for white, she was subject at various times to racial indignities. While Terrell was yet in elementary school, one incident between her and either prejudiced or uncaring white classmates who condemned her race helped Terrell decide that she would show everyone that a black student could be academically superior. She thoroughly enjoyed school, rarely had problems with fellow students, and consistently demonstrated an excellent grasp of her assignments, often winning the distinction of being first in her class. After two years at the Model School, Mary attended public school in Yellow Springs, then began eighth grade at the public high school in Oberlin, Ohio, graduating in 1879.

Terrell was one of several black students at Oberlin, a college operated by abolitionists. One of the few integrated institutions of higher learning in the United States, it had first opened its doors to blacks in 1835. Most women at Oberlin chose the two-year ladies curriculum, but Terrell decided to pursue the "gentleman's course"—four years of classical studies. She performed well in classes and was active in many campus activities including Bible studies, the church choir, literary societies, and various recreational activities such as dancing. Many years after her 1884 graduation, Terrell wrote in her autobiography, *A Colored Woman in a White World* (1940), that she felt the sting of racial discrimination only a few times during her years at Oberlin. Terrell probably protected herself to a degree by refusing to thrust herself into white student social circles or date white male students. Nevertheless, she found to her surprise that she was popular with her fellow students and respected by her teachers and was often invited to participate in their school and outside social activities. In 1929 she was named among the one hundred most successful students to graduate from Oberlin.

After her graduation in 1884, Terrell's father wanted her to return to Memphis to live the life of a lady of education and refinement. College women who decided to work professionally were generally frowned upon during the nineteenth century, and Church had no desire for his daughter to be counted among that group. Terrell was one of the few black women in the United States who had ever received a bachelor's degree. By the time that Terrell returned home, Church was so wealthy that he was considered to be both a millionaire and the wealthiest black man in the South. Both at school and at home with her father, Terrell had the opportunity to meet many nationally prominent black Americans, such as Frederick Douglass, Senator Blanche Kelso Bruce and his wife, Josephine, Booker T. Washington, and Paul Laurence Dunbar. Terrell especially admired Douglass and commenced a friendship with him while she was at Oberlin that lasted until he died in 1895.

Terrell agreed for a time to be her father's hostess, but her heart's desire was to be a professional woman. She was soon impatient with her inactivity, especially after her father married an old family friend, Anna Wright, who naturally assumed the role of mistress of the home. Terrell secretly began sending inquiries about teaching positions with the hope that she would be able to share the knowledge she had gained during her years in the educational arena with eager students.

Teaching Career Launched

When she accepted a job in Ohio at Wilberforce College in 1885, her father was livid and refused to speak to her for almost a year. Although pained by the estrangement, Terrell nevertheless pursued her goal, teaching five different courses and acting as the college secretary. After her first school year at Wilberforce, Terrell went to visit her mother in New York and then decided that she would go to Memphis to try to achieve reconciliation with her father. On the way to Tennessee, she wired him informing him of the time of her arrival. She was relieved to find him waiting for her at the station and willing to forget their differences. From then on, he relinquished all efforts to keep her from a professional career.

Terrell returned to Wilberforce for another year but then accepted a position in the Latin department of the Colored High School in Washington, D.C. There she worked under the direction of Robert Heberton Terrell, a very light mulatto born in Orange, Virginia, in 1857, who had graduated with honors from Harvard College in 1884. While she was working in the District of Columbia she completed the requirements for a master of arts degree from Oberlin, which she received in 1888. She enjoyed working with Terrell but would not allow him or the job to keep her from accepting her father's offer to send her on a European tour. She spent two years—from 1888 to 1890—traveling and studying in France, Germany, Switzerland, Italy, and England. During her time there, on separate occasions, her mother and brother and her father and his new family visited and traveled with her. She relished the cultural opportunities that were open to her in Europe because of the freedom from racial tensions. She attended plays and concerts frequently and regularly practiced her language skills with nationals. She kept diaries in French and German detailing her activities and describing her friends and acquaintances. She resisted several opportunities to marry European men, feeling that such a marriage would cause her to relinquish her Afro-American identity.

After she returned to the United States, she was soon convinced that she should marry Terrell, who had finished his law degree at Howard University while she was gone. She was momentarily tempted to postpone the planning for the wedding because she received an offer to work as the registrar at Oberlin College, a position of responsibility that she believed no other black person had ever held at any predominantly white institution of higher education. However, romance won, and she decided to marry Terrell as scheduled in October 1891. Her father gave her an elaborate ceremony in Memphis that received favorable coverage in both white and black-owned newspapers.

Her new husband, Robert Terrell, taught at M Street High School in Washington, D.C., from 1884 to 1889 and served as principal of the school ten years later from 1899 to 1901. He was admitted to the bar in 1883 and opened a law firm with John Roy Lynch, a black man who had served in the United States House of Representatives during the Reconstruction period. In 1889 he was appointed chief of division, Office of the Fourth Auditor of the Treasury Department. From 1911 until 1925, Terecrell was an instructor in law at Howard University. His most outstanding accomplishment, however, was his appointment in 1902 as judge of the District of Columbia Municipal Court (called Justice of the Peace Courts until 1901), a position to which he was appointed consecutively by four presidents—Democrat and Republican—until his death in 1925.

Because married women were legally barred from working as teachers, Terrell decided to dedicate herself to managing her household. During the early years of her marriage, she was depressed by three miscarriages that she attributed to poor medical facilities for blacks and finally traveled to New York to be with her mother when she gave birth to a healthy baby girl, Phyllis (named after Phillis Wheatley, the black poetess), in 1898. Later, in 1905, the Terrells adopted her brother Thomas's daughter, who had been named after her aunt, Terrell Church.

The primary event that drove Terrell back into the political and professional arena was the 1892 lynching of her lifelong friend from Memphis, Tom Moss, who was murdered by whites jealous of the success of his grocery store. Never had such blatant injustice struck Terrell so personally. She and Frederick Douglass were able to make an appointment with President Benjamin Harrison to urge him to speak out forcibly about such racial violence. Although the president gave them a sympathetic hearing, he made no public statement.

Leader of Women's Club Becomes Orator

In the same year, 1892, Terrell assumed the leadership of a new group formed in the District of Columbia, the Colored Women's League. Three years later black women in Boston under the leadership of Josephine St. Pierre Ruffin formed the Federation of Afro-American Women. Margaret Murray Washington, the wife of Booker T. Washington, was elected president of the Boston organization. In 1896 the two groups, along with other black women's organizations, merged to become the National Association of Colored Women and elected Terrell as the first president. Thus began one of the endeavors for which Terrell would become most well-known—the fight for equal rights for women in general and black women in particular. She was later elected to a second and a third term and then named honorary president for life. One of the women's early endeavors was to establish kindergartens and day nurseries for black working mothers. They also were concerned with equal rights for blacks, work opportunities for black women, female suffrage, and the criminal justice system. During her many years of work with the association, Terrell came into contact with most of the black women leaders, such as Mary McLeod Bethune and Nannie Helen Burroughs.

Because of her leadership in the association, Terrell was given many opportunities for service, including meeting with and speaking before white women's suffrage groups. In 1898 she delivered a speech before the National American Women's Suffrage Association entitled "The Progress of Colored Women" and in 1900 gave a thirty-minute presentation before the same group entitled "Justice of Women Suffrage." Perhaps Terrell's most celebrated speaking engagements were in 1904, 1919, and 1937. In 1904 she spoke at the Berlin International Congress of Women, at which she was the only representative of the darker races of the world. Terrell, determined to make a good impression for her race, noted the German women's impatience with the English-speaking women who made no attempt to speak to their audiences in German. She decided only several days before her presentation that she could deliver her speech in her hosts' tongue. After she translated her remarks, she engaged a German to check the grammar and sentence structure. Terrell created a sensation among the delegates by not only delivering her remarks in German but in French and English also. After this meeting, Terrell had the opportunity to travel to several countries in Europe to meet old friends and see places she had frequented during her first European tour.

Terrell had two additional opportunities to make presentations before international groups in Europe. In 1919 she addressed the delegates of the International League for Peace and Freedom, meeting in Zurich, and in 1937 she represented black American women at the World Fellowship of Faiths held in London. Meeting with women's groups both at home and abroad, Terrell had the opportunity to become acquainted with many of the leaders of suffrage organizations, including Susan B. Anthony, Alice Paul, Carrie Chapman Catt, and Jane Addams. In the years leading up to the passage of the Nineteenth Amendment, Terrell and her daughter marched with suffrage groups, picketed in front of the White House, and pointed out to some of their white counterparts the inconsistency of their lukewarm stance about suffrage for black women.

In addition to Terrell's ongoing work with both black and white women's organizations, she was recruited in the 1890s by the Slayton Lyceum Bureau (also called the Eastern Lyceum) to be a professional lecturer. Poise, graciousness, and gifted speaking ability led to a highly successful public speaking career for Terrell that lasted about thirty years. She composed a number of speeches on subjects such as black women's progress since Emancipation, racial injustice, lynching, female suffrage, economics, crime, and various aspects of black history and culture. Although she wrote her speeches, she memorized them, so that she would not have to use notes when she gave her presentations. While preparing and practicing her addresses Terrell became interested in publishing articles on a wide variety of social issues. Early in her career she wrote under the pen name Euphemia Kirk, but soon abandoned it and used her own name. She published in newspapers, magazines, and journals, both domestic and foreign. Copies of many of her publications are among the Mary Church Terrell papers in the Manuscript Division of the Library of Congress.

In 1895 Terrell was appointed to the District of Columbia School Board, served until 1901, was reappointed in 1906 and served five more years until 1911. One of the first black women in the country to serve in such a capacity, she was careful to work for equal treatment of black students and faculty members in Washington's segregated school system. Terrell and her husband were also pioneers in church work. They were among the founders of the Lincoln Temple Congregational Church in northeast Washington, D.C., a church attended by many members of Washington's black elite. She was also the first black woman to be elected to the presidency of the Bethel Literary and Historical Association in Washington, D.C., serving the 1892-93 term, and was one of the early members of the Association for the Study of Negro (later Afro-American) Life and History, which was organized in 1915. Terrell joined Delta Sigma Theta sorority and was the author of the Delta pledge, part of which seemed to summarize her life philosophy:

> I will not shrink from undertaking what seems wise and good because I labor under the double handicap of race and sex, but, striving to preserve a calm mind with a courageous and cheerful spirit, barring bitterness from my heart, I will struggle all the more earnestly to reach the goal (*The Delta*, 10, January 1941, 4a).

Terrell demonstrated this philosophy many times in her life. For example, when three companies of black soldiers were dismissed without honor and without a hearing in 1906 after a racial disturbance in Brownsville, Texas, during which one white man was killed and several others wounded, Terrell, at the urging of the leader of the Constitution League, a civil rights organization, went to see the Secretary of War, William H. Taft, to request that the action against the black troops be rescinded until they could be given a fair hearing. Her request was granted after Taft appealed to President Theodore Roosevelt and the Constitution League sent in lawyers to hear the soldiers' side of the story. The brief reprieve was to no avail, however, because none of the men would tell which of their number actually caused the disturbance, and in consequence, all were dismissed.

Terrell vacillated in her feelings toward the Booker T. Washington philosophy of accommodation and industrial education, but after visiting Tuskegee Institute decided that Washington was doing a great work and thereafter generally supported his strategies and programs. She was further influenced in Washington's favor because he was influential in helping her husband retain his judicial appointment. However, Terrell was shocked when Washington attempted to apologize for the severity of President Roosevelt's treatment of the soldiers in Brownsville. Thus, several years later, in 1901, when the NAACP was organized, Terrell was willing to become a charter member of the organization at the invitation of W. E. B. Du Bois, Washington's intellectual rival, and cooperate with Du Bois's more militant political tactics. As Terrell grew older she became bolder in her expressions of social and political dissent.

In 1911 Terrell became very involved in organizing a birthday centenary celebration in memory of abolitionist Harriet Beecher Stowe, author of *Uncle Tom's Cabin*. A few years later, after the United States entered World War I, Terrell worked at the War Risk Insurance Bureau, where she soon became involved in a protest about the treatment of black women. Soon after the armistice, Terrell worked for a short time with the War Camp Community Service as the director of work among black women and girls. In this capacity she traveled to various cities to discuss with community leaders the means of providing better community services to black females. In performing both of these jobs Terrell met with a great deal of resistance from whites who did not want to provide equal treatment for black people. In 1920 she was asked by the Republican National Committee to be the supervisor of the work among black women in the east. Her assignment was to talk with women's groups about exercising their newly-acquired right to vote by supporting the Republican party platform. Terrell continued to work with the Republican party, campaigning in 1929 for Ruth Hannah McCormick, who ran unsuccessfully for United States senator from Illinois. In 1932 Terrell served as an advisor to the Republican National Committee during the Hoover campaign. During the intervening years she was active with the party, helping in whatever way she could. She remained a Republican until 1952, when she decided to vote for Democratic presidential candidate Adlai Stevenson.

Famous Autobiographical Work Published

In 1940, the culmination of Terrell's writing career involved the publication of her autobiography, *A Colored Woman in a White World*, with a preface by H. G. Wells. In this work she traced her life from early childhood days, emphasizing her experiences growing up and living in white-dominated America. She dedicated much of the book to the discussion of the community activism in which she had been involved for much of her life. At seventy-seven years of age when the book was published, she was still not ready to leave the civil rights arena. After a long court battle to renew her membership with the Washington, D.C., branch of the American Association of University Women, Terrell was backed by the national organization, which insisted in 1949 that Terrell be reinstated as a member of the D.C. branch (she had been a member earlier but had allowed her membership to lapse). Most of the D.C. branch members refused to associate with her, resigned, and formed a new organization. In the same year, 1949, Terrell was elected chair of the Coordinating Committee for the Enforcement of District of Columbia Anti-Discrimination Laws. These laws, forbidding discrimination in the district's public accommodations, had been passed in 1872 and 1873 and never repealed. Segregated public facilities had become the norm in the nation's capital, and blacks who attempted to integrate were fined or jailed. The coordinating committee, under Terrell's direction, decided to test the laws both in practice and in court. Terrell joined a small demonstration in the city targeting Thompson's Restaurant, which refused to serve the group. The group sued and the case went all the way to the Supreme Court, where Terrell had the opportunity to testify in behalf of the cause of equal accommodations. The committee won the case in 1953, and the desegregation of the capital was set in motion.

One of Terrell's last major crusades was in behalf of Rosa Ingram, a black sharecropper from Georgia, who was sentenced to death along with her two sons for killing a white man who had assaulted them. Terrell agreed to head the National Committee to Free the Ingram Family. She led a delegation to the United Nations where she spoke in the Ingram's behalf and then traveled to Georgia in an unsuccessful attempt to win a pardon from the state governor. After a decade-long campaign, the Ingrams were finally freed in 1959, five years after Terrell's death.

Terrell died on July 24, 1954, a scant two months after the Supreme Court's *Brown* v. *Board of Education* decision sounded the death knell of segregation in the United States. Her funeral was held on Thursday, July 29, at one o'clock in the afternoon at the Lincoln Temple Congregational Church, where she had been a member for many years. She was buried in Lincoln Memorial Cemetery.

Terrell had been honored many times during her long life for her accomplishments and had received honorary doctorates from Howard University, Wilberforce and Oberlin colleges, and numerous citations and plaques from the organizations she had worked with or supported. A Washington, D.C., school was named in her honor, and many black women's clubs are named in her memory.

References

Current Biography New York: H. W. Wilson, 1942, 1954.

The Delta 10 (January 1941): 4.

Giddings, Paula. *When and Where I Enter; The Impact of Black Women on Race and Sex in America*. New York: Morrow, 1984.

Jones, Beverly Washington. *Quest for Equality: The Life and Writings of Mary Church Terrell*. Brooklyn, N.Y.: Carlson Publishers, 1990.

New York Times, 29 July 1954.

Shepperd, Gladys B. *Mary Church Terrell—Respectable Person*. Baltimore: Human Relations Press, 1959.

Sterling, Dorothy. *Black Foremothers*. Old Westbury, N.Y.: Feminist Press, 1979. Revised 1988. A children's book.

———. "Mary Church Terrell." *Notable American Women: The Modern Period*. Vol. 4. Cambridge: Harvard University Press, 1980.

Terrell, Mary Church. *A Colored Woman in a White World*. Washington, D.C.: Ransdell, 1940. Reprinted. New York: Arno Press, 1980.

Washington Post, 25 July 1954.

Washington Star, 25 July 1954.

Wesley, Charles H. *History of the National Association of Colored Women's Clubs, Inc., A Legacy of Service*. Washington, D.C.: National Association of Colored Women's Clubs, 1984.

Collections

The most informative sources for Mary Church Terrell are her autobiography and her papers at the Library of Congress Manuscript Division and the Moorland-Spingarn Research Center at Howard University. The papers at the Library of Congress include several drafts of her published autobiography, her correspondence, copies of her speeches and articles, newspaper clippings and testimonials about her life, and her extensive subject file. Correspondence between the members of the Terrell family are among Mary Church Terrell's papers. There are several photographs of Terrell in the Prints and Photographs Division of the Library of Congress.

Debra Newman Ham

Sister Rosetta Tharpe

(1915-1973)

Singer, guitarist

Sister Rosetta Tharpe's career as a gospel singer spanned fifty years. From her beginnings as a child performer in 1921 until her death in 1973 (Tharpe was to record at Savoy Records on the day before her death), she entertained audiences with her singing and guitar playing.

Rosetta Nubin was born March 20, 1915, in Cotton Plant, Arkansas, and died October 9, 1973, of a stroke, in Philadelphia, Pennsylvania. She was the only daughter of Katie (Bell) Nubin (1880-1969), a singing and mandolin-playing evangelist in the Holiness Church. The Nubins moved to Chicago around 1920, where Rosetta, known as "Little Sister," made her debut with her mother before an audience of 1,000, singing "I Looked Down the Line and I Wondered." Tharpe began touring as a professional when she was six years old with evangelist F. W. McGee on the tent-meeting circuit, sometimes singing to her mother's mandolin accompaniment but usually to her own guitar playing. The Nubins traveled widely between 1923 and 1934 as Rosetta Tharpe's reputation as a sanctified singer continued to grow in the Holiness church. Her singing and guitar styles were influenced by Arizona Dranes, a blind pianist who also traveled with Reverend F. W. McGee.

Tharpe's gospel singing career paralleled the rise of gospel music in the United States and falls into four periods: 1921-1937, 1938-1950, 1951-1960, and 1961-1973.

The years 1921-1937 represent the early years of gospel music. Tharpe sang the gospel hymns of Luci Campbell and W. H. Brewster and the blues-tinted gospels of Thomas Andrew Dorsey. Tharpe was influenced in her guitar playing by her mother and Arizona Dranes, a blind, foot-stomping, sanctified pianist. Three events in 1938-1939 propelled Tharpe into national prominence: she received a contract with Decca Records and her record of "Rock Me" with Lucky Millender became a hit; *Life* magazine featured Rosetta Tharpe in an article describing her gospel singing in church and in the Cotton Club revue, singing with Cab Calloway; and she performed in the historic "Spirituals to Swing" concert in Carnegie Hall on December 23, 1938.

The forties were her decade. Gospel became the most important black music since early jazz and Tharpe's three hits made the gospel sound become familiar to the country. She performed in the exclusive Cafe Society Downtown and in the Blue Angel Club, both in New York City.

Next came the decade of the fifties—mid-century and gospel's golden period. Tharpe, Willie Mae Ford Smith, Sallie Martin, Roberta Martin, and Mahalia Jackson were the prima donnas of gospel music. During the decade of the sixties Tharpe took her guitar and gospel singing to European audiences and jazz festivals.

Tharpe's song repertoire was wide and varied. During her early period she performed the tunes of the Holiness church, many of them older than the gospel songs of Dorsey and others. Many of the sanctified songs are anonymous, others are written by pioneers in the Holiness movement. Her recording hits in the forties included Thomas Dorsey's "Rock Me," "This Train," and "Precious Lord." In clubs she sang her arrangements of up-tempo spirituals, such as "Down By the Riverside." She recorded "Strange Things Happening Every Day" in 1944 with Sammy Price, the boogie-woogie pianist. She teamed with Marie Knight in 1946 and their duet, "Up Above My Head" made the Billboard race charts. Tharpe recorded several blues songs around 1952, including "Trouble In Mind" and "Lonesome Road." Her repertoire also included band arrangements of spirituals.

Singer Takes Gospel Music to Europe

Tharpe was the first gospel singer to travel extensively in Europe. Her first trip in the early 1950s lasted almost a year, followed in 1957 with a tour of England. She performed at the Antibes Festival in 1960 and again at the Paris Jazz Festival in 1968. One of her last European tours was with blues singer Muddy Waters.

Because of her many years as a gospel entertainer, Tharpe appeared with many outstanding performers. Among the nationally recognized performers were Cab Calloway, Bill Robinson, Andy Kirk, Roy Acuff, Mary Lou Williams, and Lucky Millender.

Among her achievements as a pioneer in gospel music, Tharpe attained several firsts: the first nationally known gospel singer; first gospel singer to record with a major recording company—Decca Records; first to go public with gospel by performing on the secular stage; and first to perform gospel in a theater—the Apollo Theater in New York City.

Tharpe's secularizing of gospel music brought her national recognition but in the words of Anthony Heilbut, "she became *persona non grata* in the Sanctified church." The breach was never healed, and in her later years she joined the Baptist church. As early as the thirties, Tharpe had adopted a more secular style of playing her guitar and singing than the other gospel singers. Describing her songstyle as the gospel blues, Heilbut said:

> She could pick blues guitar like a Memphis Minnie. Her song style was filled with blues inversion, and a resonating vibrato. She bent her notes like a horn player, and syncopated in swing band manner. And, starting in 1938, she scored as no gospel singer has done since (191-92).

Tharpe performed mainly gospel songs throughout her lifetime. She sang them in concerts, theaters, clubs, music halls, festivals, and on radio. She performed with gospel groups, such as the Caravans, James Cleveland singers, Golden Gate Quartet, the Dixie Hummingbirds, and the Rosettes.

The last five years of Tharpe's life were filled with tragedies. Her mother, Katie Bell Nubin, died in 1969. Rosetta Tharpe suffered her first stroke in 1970 while touring in Europe. Her leg had to be amputated when complications occurred; however, she managed a few tours in 1972 and early 1973. Mahalia Jackson, her friend and contemporary, died in 1972. On October 8 Rosetta Tharpe had a second stroke while planning for a recording session arranged by Anthony Heilbut.

Tharpe was married three times. In 1934 she became the wife of Pastor Thorpe, an elder in the Holiness church, in Pittsburgh, Pennsylvania. After the marriage ended, she kept his name but changed the spelling to Tharpe. During the forties she married Forrest Allen, a New York booking agent for spiritual music. Tharpe's third marriage to Russell Morrison, her manager and seven years her junior, was the most successful and also a spectacular event that took place in 1951 in Griffin Stadium, Washington, D.C.

Tharpe's flamboyant stage presence and colorful outfits contrasted sharply with those of most of her gospel contemporaries. (Clara Ward and the Ward Singers also wore exotic stagewear and performed in nightclubs.) Even during the late sixties she would appear in her red-orange wig, blue jeans, high heels, and an elaborate feather boa. She had her own followers, both in the United States and Europe, and her popularity continued into the early sixties. However, by 1965 a new generation of gospel singers and audiences were on the scene. Tharpe's reputation continued, but her following became smaller and smaller.

A discography of the singer's works includes *Sister Rosetta Tharpe, Gospel, Blues, Jazz* (Foremothers, Vol. 8, RR1317, Women's Heritage Series); *Brighten the Corner Where You Are: Black and White Urban Hymnody* (New World NW 224); *Gospel Train* (MCA 1317); *Soul Sister* (MCA 510 148, import, 1946-1949), and *Sister Rosetta Tharpe* (Savgos RI 5008).

References

Broughton, Viv. *Black Gospel: An Illustrated History of the Gospel Sound.* New York: Blandford Press, 1985.

"Gospel Singers." *Ebony* 6 (December 1950): 91-95. Includes photograph.

Heilbut, Anthony. *The Gospel Sound.* New York: LimeLight Editions: 1985. 270-72, 313-16. Includes photograph.

"Sincerely, Sister Rosetta Tharpe." Notes from Foremothers Album Jacket, Woman's Heritage Series, Vol. 8. Includes photograph.

"Sister Tharpe Swings Same Songs in Church and Night Club." *Life* 7 (28 August 1939): 37. Includes photograph.

Southern, Eileen. *Biographical Dictionary of Afro-American and African Musicians.* Westport, Conn.: Greenwood Press, 1982.

"20,000 Watch Wedding of Sister Rosetta Tharpe." *Ebony* 6 (October 1951): 27-30.

Ellistine P. Holly

Alma Thomas

(1891-1978)

Educator, artist

Believing that as an artist she had freedom to make independent statements using her unique art as visual communication, Alma Thomas spent her entire life of eighty-seven years observing the world, painting, and teaching others what she felt. Her vision of the world was tied to her career as art teacher for children as well as to her appreciation of flowers and to her grand and joyous abstract art. This diversity confirms the breadth of her creativity. Each of her paintings reveals the inspiration of her experience and is

Alma Thomas

shaped by her life's challenges. Since her art has a greatness of spirit, and because her delightful patterns and exuberant colors convey her joie de vivre, Thomas's paintings "testify to the integrity of the artist's commitment to the vision of art that sustained her all of her life" (Foresta, 34).

Born on September 22, 1891, in Columbus, Georgia, Alma Woodsey Thomas was the oldest of four daughters. She grew up in a Victorian house with a loving family. Her father, John Harris Thomas, was a businessman and her mother, Amelia (Cantey) Thomas, was a violinist and teacher. They were middle-class progressive parents, and Thomas was reared as a southern lady. This early educational influence led Alma Thomas to follow her aunts, mother, and sisters into teaching.

Better educational opportunities and anxiety over race riots led the family to move to Washington, D.C. In 1907, when Thomas was sixteen, they purchased a substantial brick house at 1520 Fifteenth Street, where she lived most of the rest of her life, more than seventy years, in a sophisticated world. While attending Armstrong Technical High School, she felt the art room was as "beautiful as heaven" (Foresta, 16). To prepare for her career, she took teachers' preparatory courses at Miner Teachers Normal School. After graduation, she taught for six years in Wilmington, Delaware, at the Thomas Garrett Settlement House. Projects for her students there included painting life-sized animals and designing costumes and stage sets for theatrical performances. Starting in 1921, Thomas continued her education at Howard University, where as a fine arts student, she received her bachelor of science in 1924. Her influential art instructors at Howard included Lois Mailou Jones and James V. Herring. Lois Jones and Alma Thomas both had paintings in an exhibition called "Black Matri-Images" in 1973 in Baltimore. Herring, who remained one of her closest friends, set an example of achievement and professionalism that Thomas followed all her life as an artist.

Adelyn D. Breeskin, Senior Curatorial Adviser at the National Museum of American Art in Washington D. C., writes that she went two or three times with museum director Joshua C. Taylor to visit Thomas and to select from her many paintings for the museum at Howard University. Breeskin stated that Thomas would stack against the walls of her living room those paintings that she especially wanted to become part of the museum's collection (Foresta, 8). The National Museum of American Art now has thirty works by Alma Thomas. Taylor often asked for her lovely little oil, *Wind and Crepe Myrtle Concerto,* to be displayed in his office. It was there at the time of his death in 1981, three years after Thomas died.

Thomas's "Earth Paintings" treated wind and flower subjects. They were inspired, she claimed, "by the display of azaleas at the Arboretum, the cherry blossoms, circular flower beds, the nurseries as seen from planes that are airborne, and by the foliage of trees in the fall" (Foresta, 23).

The holly tree that pressed against the window of Thomas's living room also inspired her paintings of the designs formed by the leaves framed against the windowpanes and the interrupted patterns of light and shade the tree cast on the floor and walls of her kitchen. By changing these patterns and heightening glimpses of color beyond them, light continually renewed her subject. Thomas had known the holly tree for almost sixty years, and her responses to it, as to all her immediate surroundings, were spontaneous and deeply felt.

In 1943 Herring joined with Alonzo Aden, a former curator at Howard University's Gallery of Art, to found the Barnett-Aden Gallery. Thomas's association with this gallery was pivotal to her own development as an artist. Breeskin writes, "Alma went around the room with me, letting me see how enthusiastic she was about this Gallery. I soon concluded that her taste in art was exceptionally broad, leading her to admire all styles of art. During the 1960's I often saw her there with Professor Herring" (Foresta, 7). Her longtime friend, David C. Driskell, remembers the significant learning experience he had with Thomas at the Barnett-Aden Gallery, as he watched her mingle with such luminaries as poets Langston Hughes and Georgia Douglas Johnson, poet and playwright May Miller Sullivan, opera star Lillian Evanti, and sociologist E. Franklin Frazier.

As long as James Herring and his successor, James Porter, were at Howard University, Thomas felt close to that institution. In later years she relied on artist Jacob Kainen and Taylor. She was to be seen year after year at almost every opening held by Washington art galleries. Always she was smartly dressed in colorful clothes, with hat and gloves, for above all Thomas loved color. "She struggled to fit herself to the mold of propriety pressed upon her, but under her satin bows and lace gowns lurked a true Bohemian spirit—impatient of convention, fiercely independent, iconoclastic, hungry for recognition, and fixed upon a high ideal of personal achievement," according to Adolphus Ealey, then director of the Barnett-Aden Gallery (Foresta, 9).

There was only one period in Thomas's life during which she was able to taste the heady brew of Bohemian life. This was in the early 1930s, while she was earning a master's degree in art education from Columbia University. Ealey states that she loved the festive Harlem she had known during its renaissance (Foresta, 11). According to Ealey, she was both fashionable and dramatic during her life in Harlem. He continues:

> Always possessed of a flair for the dramatic, she loved to make appearances on Lenox Avenue and 125th Street attired in clothes of the latest fashions, all beautifully handmade by her mother. She also spoke of Washington's Carter G. Woodson, the historian and pioneer in black studies, who enjoyed showing her off around the capital. "He used to call me his little Spanish doll" (Foresta, 11).

At an art exhibition at Howard University, Adolphus

Ealey was warned by Herring not to come within her range unless he was prepared to do battle over any conflicts of opinion. Somewhat daunted, Ealey contented himself by studying her from afar. He saw a petite woman clad in a billowing mink coat and hat, worn with careless assurance. She had positioned herself, as it were, on center stage and greeted her admirers. "Milady is receiving," he thought with amusement, then, "but how well she carries it off!" (Foresta, 10). Herring had often spoken of her determination and industriousness. "Alma is a tough little woman and a very hard, devoted worker. You either love Alma or hate her" (Foresta, 10).

Although Thomas was a small woman, barely five feet tall and arthritic, a sense of strength is common to all of her large paintings. Foresta describes Thomas's painting technique:

> Using her kitchen or small living room as a studio, she propped the huge canvases in her lap or balanced them on a sofa, bracing the sometimes considerable weight of the wooden stretcher with her leg and applying her acrylic paints like oils, with a firm stroke and definite attack. Working as she did without the benefit of seeing the painting from a distance, she often turned the canvas around to reach its unpainted areas. Although she made many watercolor studies in preparation for her paintings, each canvas represents a series of spontaneous decisions based on the problems and challenges of the moment (Foresta, 26).

Thomas's volatile temperament was generally revealed only to her intimates, who had to accept being alternately bullied and defended, castigated and humored. Whenever the occasion called for it, she summoned forth the charm and gracious manners of a southern gentlewoman, the gentility she had learned in childhood.

Thomas Dedicated to Teaching Art

One can imagine how broad the exposure to different media was for Thomas's many students. She, in many cases, directed their leisure time with many art ideas for life. Her ideas of putting on plays and designing costumes and puppet shows have always delighted the imagination of children everywhere.

From 1924 until her retirement in 1960, Thomas taught art at Shaw Junior High in Washington, D.C. Although encouraged by Herring to continue painting full-time, she maintained her independence by pursuing a teaching career that gave her both social and economic freedom. Self-reliance was a special virtue to her and she placed the demands of her art above the pleasure of having a family of her own. Her decision to postpone a career as a painter until her tenure as a school teacher was completed is in part explained by her focused sense of responsibility to her students and her personal standard of excellence, which allowed no room for distraction from her professional duties.

"During her years of teaching in public school, Thomas's creativity surfaced in the activities she organized for the students: classes in arts and crafts and clay modeling, marionette plays, and lectures about art" (Foresta, 17). Her students became aware of their own creativity. She saw power in education and believed that one is free who is able to express himself or herself accurately. As she taught, she enhanced her own ability to communicate through painting. David C. Driskell recalls that "she was a teacher who cared for young people who made known their commitment to art" ("Alma Thomas, A Personal Reflection," 3).

Thomas began graduate study in art education in 1930 at Columbia University and later earned a master of arts degree. She focused on marionette plays, which enabled her to combine her talents for sculpture, costume design, and theater. New York exposed her to large museums and modern art galleries. "The masters sharpened her eye; she knew every painting in the Corcoran Gallery of Art in Washington," and her knowledge of art history was wide-ranging and deep (Foresta, 18).

Adolphus Ealey gives us insight into Thomas's personality. He writes, "From the beginning, she told me, she was driven by an irresistible urge to accomplish, to make things—a compelling need that she felt her sisters had never understood. She said, 'I could not sit around and read, cook, and sew like them. I had to get out and create new things'" (Foresta, 11).

Thomas continues:

> I always wanted to succeed on my own terms, as a woman, an individual. Maybe I would have become an artist sooner if I'd grown up in Harlem instead of Washington. You know how reserved the black community here was in the old days, how it admired successful black people. Well, my family succeeded in Georgia, right in the heart of the South, and they did better than most after we came to Washington. I was proud of them and I still am. But for educated young black people there were so many expectations then, so many pressures to conform. I don't know why I never lost this need to create something original, something all my own (Foresta, 11).

After she retired in 1960, Thomas devoted endless hours to the study of painting. She had begun to study at American University in Washington, D.C., with Robert Gates, Jacob Kainen, and Ben Summerford. Foresta notes that as Thomas was nearing seventy, her work began to show color more gloriously than ever before. She was painting in earnest and in the early 1960s she demonstrated freshness and spontaneity in the many watercolors that she painted. Her first solo exhibition, which was also highly successful, was held in 1960 at the Du Pont Theatre Art Gallery in Washington, D.C.

Artist Recognized for Form and Color

At the end of the 1960s Thomas was deeply inspired by the space program. Her ''Space Paintings'' ''had deeper or hotter color, evocative of the energy required to leave earth's boundaries'' (Foresta, 26). Foresta continues:

> ''Snoopy—Early Sun Display on Earth'' is one of many paintings inspired by the circumlunar-module spacecraft, which anticipated the expedition of moon-walking astronauts. Made up of predominantly blue strokes of paint, the painting's circular form resembles a magnificent, fantastical sun rising upon the world and growing more radiant at the edges as the sphere dissolves through the spectrum toward orange and yellow (Foresta, 26).

Thomas learned a great deal about color and form from her aesthetic contemporaries Kenneth Noland, Gene Davis, and Morris Louis. An affiliation between Thomas and these artists began in the 1950s at the Barnett-Aden Gallery at Howard. Davis and Louis were leaders of the ''Washington Color School,'' as Noland called the new romanticism (Kutner, C-14). Noland painted horizontal colored bands, which were stunning, and circles of different colors like an archery target. Thomas learned about the power of geometric form and color from the veils of Morris Louis, the stripes of Gene Davis, and the targets of Kenneth Noland. According to Adolphus Ealey, ''although she was exposed to many styles and techniques, Miss Thomas always maintained her own personal style of flowing colors freely moving with dark lines appearing here and there to direct space and form'' (''Introduction,'' *Alma W. Thomas, Recent Paintings*).

Thomas's most popular painting, to many people, at the Studio in Harlem is called *The Eclipse*, a dark circle surrounded by hundreds of mosaic squares of many colors, which reminds one of a glorious quilt and of Noland's style.

Gene Davis's work shows hard-edged vertical stripes resembling wallpaper, which Thomas apparently liked. Hard-edged refers to the sharp edges of bright color and is typical of the Washington Color school artists. Davis and Louis are also well known for their huge canvasses. While Davis's largest painting is ten by twenty feet, Thomas's *Red Azaleas* is six feet by thirteen feet, or ''mural'' sized. Her *Light Blue Nursery* is influenced by Davis's stripes. Jacob Kainen writes that ''Miss Thomas certainly drew some of her basic ideas from Noland and Davis, but she also studied the work of Dorazio, Capogrossi, Nay and the French tachists'' (Foresta, 14). Thomas was eclectic, gathering ideas and interpreting them in her own way. Thomas's *Gray Night* has stripes and hatchmarks like a print dress material.

''She assembled shapes in a synthetic balance of form and color. This is not like her later works which are images from nature'' (Foresta, 22). ''Though her surfaces sometimes look tweedy or fabricky, Alma Thomas's ideas came straight from nature, which includes the hollyhocks that pressed against the window of her house, an eclipse of the sun, ice on a pond, the action of the wind on leaves. Yet she was tuned into twentieth century life and her titles for example, refer to the comic strip 'Peanuts,' astronauts and rock-and-roll music. There is, in fact, a rhythm and energy in this work not at all dissimilar to a slightly older form of music, jazz'' (Glueck, B-1).

Thomas's early works were modest still lifes, jugs of flowers and bowls of fruit. ''The classically inspired head, placed back in the empty space created by heavy folds of painted fabric, produces a feeling of isolation. Most of the pieces she produced for her classes were copied from classical or Renaissance models or recreated the standard models used to teach form and design'' (Foresta, 17). Next she moved to abstraction, producing much tighter versions of her expressionistic paintings. She painted ''narrow vertical and rectangular shapes joined like building blocks of color placed determinedly one on top of the other, and the dense, earth-toned color enforces their solidity'' (Foresta, 22).

Thomas modified and softened her style in the direction of a freer, more lyrical impulse. Her former mosaic-like style of color abstraction, with its very strict, often symmetrical patterns, is very little in evidence later.

Morris Louis also influenced Thomas with his background color showing through the top layer of details. His painting with successive colored waves produces a ''single continuous configuration while a single color is still visible'' (Kutner, B-1). Antares appears as shiny white flecks in the background and sumptuous square dabs of red paint. Thomas achieved counterpoint by textured application of her palette knife to lay down rough patches on painted backgrounds, with the two colors blending.

Bill Marvel of the *Dallas Times Herald* said, ''Certainly Alma Thomas would agree with famous artist Paul Klee as he said, 'Color and I are one.''' Piet Mondrian said, ''Things give us everything. Representation of things gives us nothing'' (Marvel, E-3). Thomas's abstract circles, stripes, and tiny squares would indicate she believes as Klee and Mondrian do. She was obviously influenced by Henri Matisse, one of the great colorists. Thomas painted abstract geometrics in her first period. Her second period often focused on the theme of flowers, many of which were immense. Almost hidden among tiny squares of contrasting colored backgrounds, such as green, were flowers completely made of mauve square-like petals. Colors that Louis and Thomas both enjoyed include shades of pink and moss green. A joyous work entitled *Wind and Crepe Myrtle Concerto* has flowered waves of sunset pinks and fuchsias on a green background.

In explaining the format of her paintings, Thomas said, ''You see, all the gardens are so formal. They're formalized by man.'' Her use of color and pattern reinterprets this control, and many of her paintings, such as *A Joyful Scene of Spring*, form geometric designs. *A Joyful Scene of Spring* recalls the large, circular gardens planted throughout the city of Washington. Committed to her palette of exuberant color, she used wedges of paint to suggest a variety of flowers, the reflections of pools, and the unplanted earth. She agreed with Johannes Itten, a Swiss artist, who said, "Color is life; for a world without color appears to us as dead" (Foresta, 24).

Thomas uses primitive patterns to enter the nature world. She often painted what she saw from the window of her kitchen. *Hydrangeas* looks as if hundreds of petals are falling in the wind. *Double Cherry Blossoms* is one of her most engaging pictures. Musical themes also run through Thomas's work. Her painting titled *Red Azaleas Singing and Dancing Rock and Roll Music* was done in 1976 when she was eighty-five. It has motion such as billowing waves with a mosaic of patterns and paint strokes of long curves with quilt-like squares and rectangles in vivid reds on a raw canvas, like a whirlwind of leaves, or "notes of jazz" (Moser, 142).

Although Thomas loved the idea of flying, until the early 1970s the images she formed of aerial views were only imaginary: "I began to think about what I would see if I were in an airplane. You look down on things. You streak through the clouds so fast you don't know whether the flower below is a violet or what. You see only streaks of color. And so, I began to paint as if I were in that plane," she said (Foresta, 36). To Thomas, "color is the sole architect of space" (Driskell, "A Personal Reflection," 6).

Creativity Spans Many Subjects

Thomas's vast creativity spanned many subjects in "a rapidly changing world of science, economics, religion, and society where through my impressions of nature and the space program, I hoped to impart beauty, joy, love and peace," Thomas said (Foresta, 24). Her watercolors reveal her adherence to the Washington color school through light and broad fields of color with wide bands of patchy squares or vertical stripes such as her teachers, Gene Davis and Kenneth Noland, had painted.

The year 1972 saw honors for Thomas at the retrospective exhibit held at the Corcoran Gallery that included forty of her paintings and nine works on paper. In the Corcoran exhibition catalog, David C. Driskell notes that Thomas remained "aware of the need to expand her painting beyond a colorist format even though color is mainly what her art is about. . . . Much of what one finds to be abstract in her art is often related to a pleasant experience that she enjoys sharing with friends" ("A Personal Response, *Alma W. Thomas, Retrospective Exhibition*). Also in 1972, when she was eighty-one, she became the first black woman to have a solo exhibition at the Whitney Museum of American Art in New York. In 1977 Thomas, age eighty-six, enjoyed her first Corcoran biennial exhibit of Contemporary American Painting, where her colorful mosaic-like paintings *Babbling Brook and Whistling Poplar Symphony* and *Red Azaleas Jubilee* looked graciously in place with the work of the younger abstract painters.

"Honey, you should have been there. I was a knockout," Thomas would say to friends, reporting gleefully on the honors accorded her during her last years, when she had exhibited her works in more than twenty galleries including the Studio Museum in Harlem and the Whitney in New York. According to Jacob Kainen, her one-woman show held in 1972 at the Whitney Museum "brought her to a national attention" ("Introduction," *Alma W. Thomas, Retrospective Exhibition*). Other galleries that honored her art include the Dupont Theatre Art Gallery, the Gallery of Art at Howard University, the Margaret Dickey Gallery of Art, and the Franz Bader Gallery, all in Washington, D.C.; the Carl Van Vechten Gallery in Nashville; the Martha Jackson Gallery in New York; the H. C. Taylor Art Gallery in Greensboro, North Carolina, at North Carolina Agricultural and Technical State University; the Philadelphia Afro-American History and Culture Museum; and the Museum of Fine Arts and the Liz Harris Gallery in Boston, Massachusetts.

Thomas was first invited to exhibit her paintings at the White House in 1969 and 1970, during the Nixon administration. Another thrill that she very much enjoyed was Alma Thomas Day on September 9, 1972 (Foresta, 40). She was again invited to the White House by President Jimmy Carter in 1977, only eight months before she died.

She died on February 25, 1978, after undergoing aortal surgery. In her seventies and eighties she was handicapped by chronic arthritis, but she still attended openings, on the arm of her nephew. She was a tiny person, but she stood out in a crowd because of her natural presence, her spontaneous enjoyment of festive occasions, and her charming personality.

> Alma Thomas was black, a woman, and an artist, each a circumstance presenting its own difficulties. But she was persistent and committed to overcoming these barriers and made the choices necessary to adapt her life to her vision. As if answering the criticism that she did not more militantly confront the issues of her race or sex and that she did not use her art more definitively to represent these problems, Thomas wrote: "Creative art is for all time and is therefore independent of time. It is of all ages, of every land, and if by this we mean the creative spirit in man which produces a picture of a statue is common to the whole civilized world, independent of age, race and nationality, the statement may stand unchallenged" (Foresta, 34).

References

Driskell, David C. "Alma Thomas: A Personal Reflection." Unpublished manuscript, n.d. David Driskell's personal collection.

———. "A Personal Response." *Alma W. Thomas, Retrospective Exhibition.* Catalogue. Corcoran Gallery of Art, Washington, D.C., September 8, October 15, 1972.

Ealey, Adolphus. "Introduction." *Alma W. Thomas, Recent Paintings.* Catalogue. Howard University Gallery of

Art, Washington, D.C., October 22-November 14, 1975. Includes photograph of Thomas.

Fonville-Bontemps, Jacqueline and Arna Alex Bontemps. *Forever Free: Art by African-American Women, 1862-1980.* Alexandria, Va.: Stephenson, 1980. Photograph, p. 132.

Foresta, Merry A. *A Life in Art—Alma Thomas.* Washington, D.C.: Smithsonian Institution Press, 1981.

Forgey, Benjamin. "The Nation: The Corcoran Biennial. A Generation Split." *Art News* 76 (May 1977): 106-114.

Glueck, Grace. "Art: Studio Museum Exhibits Alma Thomas." *New York Times*, 20 October 1973.

Kainen, Jacob." "Introduction." *Alma W. Thomas, Retrospective Exhibition.* Catalogue. Corcoran Gallery of Art, Washington, D.C., September 8-October 15, 1972.

Kutner, Janet. "Artist: Alma Thomas." *Dallas Morning News*, 13 February 1987.

Marvel, Bill. "Lesser Artist, More Spectacle." *Dallas Times Herald*, 26 April 1986.

Moser, Charlotte. "Alma Thomas." *Art News* 81 (May 1982): 142.

Virginia Wilson Wallace

Edna Thomas

(1886-1974)

Actress

Born in Lawrenceville, Virginia, in 1886, Edna Lewis Thomas came to the attention of filmmaker Orson Welles in 1936 because of her work in black theaters, vaudeville, and on Broadway. After having resisted earlier invitations to enter the professional theater, she made her debut in 1920 with the Quality Amusement Corporation, the contractual name of the Lafayette Players, a group that had branches on both coasts. Thomas performed in this distinguished group with Clarence Muse, Dooley Wilson, Jack Carter, and Evelyn Preer. Her first production was *Turn to the Right*, which appeared in 1920.

It was during the 1920s and the fervent Harlem Renaissance that Thomas received considerable recognition. A'Lelia Walker, daughter of the black woman millionaire Madame C. J. Walker, gave lavish parties to which artists, writers, musicians, actors, and others flocked. Thomas, one of the most popular figures of this era, was among the guests.

Thomas's work with the Lafayette Players led to a part in Shakespeare's *Comedy of Errors*. Staged in a circus tent on May 15, 1923, the play cast Thomas as Adriana's sister. Percy Hammond, distinguished critic of the Republican newspaper the *New York Herald Tribune*, labeled Thomas "an ingenue." So striking was her beauty, little did he know that she was thirty-seven years old. Three years later, Thomas played a small part in David Belasco's production of *Lulu Belle*, which attracted a wide circle of critics. Many condemned the play, with the *New York Times Theatre Review* referring to it as "the wages of sin in four acts." Thomas wrote Carl Van Vechten, Harlem Renaissance patron, that the play went over "big."

In 1927, following the 1921 success of *Shuffle Along*, black plays were in vogue; *Porgy*, produced by the famed Theatre Guild, played, and Thomas sang at the Palace. This is the only instance that appears to be recorded of her singing Negro spirituals and plantation melodies.

With the waning of the Harlem Renaissance and the onset of the Great Depression, black actors, who even in more affluent times had little work, met with unusually hard times. Thomas was not spared and was without work after her vaudeville stint for five years. She was married at the time to Lloyd Thomas and had a household guest, Olivia Wyndham, who, according to Thomas's letters to Carl Van Vechten, helped with expenses.

In 1932 Thomas played Maggie in *Ol' Man Satan* with a cast of one hundred twenty-five. A cast of this size would bankrupt a show in 1990, but large casts were not unusual in the 1930s. Neither was exploitation or abuse. The majority of performers worked with little, if any, legal protection. Most had no affiliations with unions. *Ol' Man Satan* was rehearsed for one year, a phenomenal period of time. If the show had closed, the actors would have received no pay. Actors Equity covered few actors of color then.

In 1933 the role of Sis Ella in Hall Johnson's famed *Run, Little Chillun* became available, and the producers sought Edna Thomas for the part. Sis Ella is the wife of the minister's son, Jim, who is lured away from the fold and his wife by the "animalistic adulteress," Sulamai, a member of the pagan cult across the river. Thomas played the forgiving wife who receives her penitent husband as he returns to the fold and God strikes Sulamai dead with lightning. Leonard de Paur, of the de Paur Infantry Chorus and Hall Johnson's protege, said: "Edna Thomas was one of the three great ladies of the theatre we had at that time. She, Rose McClendon and Laura Bowman could have played any type of theatre that was ever staged."

Following the success of *Run, Little Chillun*, Thomas opened April 18, 1934, in *Stevedore*, by Paul Peters and George Sklar, white playwrights. This vehicle on the unionizing of dock workers alarmed members of Congress, who labeled it a "Communistic lynch drama" (Moorland-Spingarn Collection). Thomas played Ruby Oxley.

Thomas Becomes Active in Federal Theater

On April 8, 1936, Roi Ottley reviewed the touted all-black voodoo *Macbeth*, which Orson Welles adapted for the stage of the Works Progress Administration's (WPA) Federal Theatre. Thomas played Lady Macbeth at Harlem's Lafayette Theatre. Ottley wrote on "Harlem's Lord and Lady Macbeth in Full Regalia" in the *New York Amsterdam News*: "In Edna Thomas' last scene as Lady Macbeth, she literally tore the heart of the audience with her sensitive and magnificent portrayal of the crazed Lady Macbeth."

Thomas was an exceptionally good-looking woman with straight hair and fair complexion. In many ways this was a hindrance, as she was too light-skinned for many black roles and yet not white. On the other hand, Josephine Baker initially lost a role in the chorus of *Shuffle Along* because she was too dark. Thomas could play Lady Macbeth and other white roles with such groups as the New York City unit of the WPA Federal Theatre or the Lafayette Players, but as years passed she found that Broadway would cast her only in roles for black women. Loften Mitchell, who saw her in *Macbeth*, said, "She was literate, expansive, sincere—unflinching — always in the forefront of the struggle for human rights."

In her struggle for roles, in November 1938 Thomas wrote to Carl Van Vechten, a major white supporter of black artists:

> When I first met you, and on mentioning my burning ambition to do something worthwhile in the theatre, I was told "How dare you—you've never slept on a bench in the park." That was before I knew how much you wished I might achieve my aim—park bench or no park bench.

In the same year, the WPA Federal Theatre asked Thomas to play the slave girl, Lavinia, in the George Bernard Shaw play *Androcles and the Lion*, sometimes referred to as "The Negro Version," because of its having substituted Negro spirituals for the music Shaw suggested. Thomas and the players reached an artistic high, according to critic Brooks Atkinson of the *New York Times* and an article in the *New York Amsterdam News*. Dooley Wilson played Androcles and Add Bates, a dancer, the lion.

Androcles and the Lion was the third in popularity among the audiences of the black units of the WPA Federal Theatre. There is the element of stage romance between the captain, played by P. Jay Sidney, and Thomas. There was the hilarious scene at the end of the play where Androcles dances with the lion who is expected to eat him. This brought the crowd to its feet and is reputed to have "turned out the theater." In spite of the success of *Androcles and the Lion* and the entire Federal Theatre Project, six months after the Shavian drama opened, Congress closed the Federal Theatre. Martin Dies and the House Un-American Activities Committee began their search for communists in the theater. Threatened Broadway producers such as Mike Todd also helped to destroy the government project and the opportunity for actors of color. The $46,000,000 grant was a great help to the 851 black actors, and the other 11,000 or more persons on the Federal Theatre Project.

Thomas, and other players as well, looked for greener pastures. In 1943 and 1944 Thomas went on Broadway in *Harriett*, a play about Harriett Beecher Stowe. Thomas played Sukey, a "helpless Negress" who escapes via the Underground Railroad, is captured and returned to slavery. Helen Hayes starred in the play. Thomas wrote to Fania and Carl Van Vechten:

> I can only say that God has been good to me, and I am fortunate to have, and indeed so deeply grateful for, this job.

In spite of the controversy surrounding *Harriett*—that it was dynamite and explosive—Federal Theatre actors, because of their visibility in the 1930s, were by now in Hollywood and on Broadway.

One Broadway drama with a racial theme—miscegenation—came Thomas's way in 1945—Lillian Smith's *Strange Fruit*. Produced and directed by José Ferrer, the production cost $100,000. Many critics considered the dramatization of Smith's novel a failure. Thomas's character, Mamie McIntosh, constantly urges her son, Henry, played by Robert Earl Jones (father of James Earl Jones), to remember his place. Abram Hill wrote an account of the play in the *New York Amsterdam News*:

> Of the thirteen scenes of the play, only two really broke through as vital theatre. The memorable scene of Mamie McIntosh, whipping young Henry and planting in his hide and head the fact that he is inferior to white people, is translated with earthly conviction to the stage by Edna Thomas and Ken Kenard.

Two years later, an aging Thomas got her last stage role—the Mexican woman in Tennessee Williams's *A Streetcar Named Desire*. She was also in the movie version with Marlon Brando.

Thomas spent her retirement years in New York City, where she died of a heart condition on July 22, 1974. She was eighty-two years old. Both the *New York Times* and *Variety* noted her death. Sister Francesca Thompson, who interviewed Thomas in 1972, made a comment that characterizes the noted actress: "She was a *grande dame* in every sense of the word."

References

de Paur, Leonard. Interview with Glenda E. Gill, 29 March 1982.

Gill, Glenda E. "Edna Thomas: The Grand Dame." In *White Grease Paint: A Study of the Federal Theatre, 1935-1939*. New York: Peter Lang, 1988. 67-90. Photographs of Thomas, p. 73 and p. 86. Includes an extensive bibliography.

Mitchell, Loften. Letter to Glenda E. Gill, 6 December 1979.

New York Amsterdam News, 8 April 1936; 1 December 1945.

New York Times Theatre Review, 10 February 1926.

Ottley, Roi. "Harlem's Lord and Lady Macbeth in Full Regalia." *New York Amsterdam News*, 8 April 1936.

Thomas, Edna. Interview with Richard Fraule, 1972.

Thompson, Sister Francesca. Letter to Glenda E. Gill, 6 September 1977.

Collections

Materials on Edna Lewis Thomas, including letters to Fania and Carl Van Vechten, are in the Beinicke Library, Yale University. The Moorland-Spingarn Research Center, Howard University, has a clipping file on Thomas.

Glenda E. Gill

Lillian Parker Thomas

(1857- ?)

Journalist, social reformer, women's rights activist

Lillian May Parker Thomas was a truly remarkable woman of her time. A champion of civil and women's rights, Thomas's political and editorial activities helped to enlighten and to shape the public consciousness concerning racial equality and changing gender roles. Her position with a black midwestern publication enabled her to disseminate information to the black female community of her region about the activities of its native and distant sisters.

Born in Chicago, Illinois, in 1857, Thomas was the oldest child of Reverend Byrd Parker and Jane Jeanetta Parker. Her father pastored Quinn Chapel, one of the city's Methodist churches. He later accepted pastorates at Saint Paul's, a church in Saint Louis, and at Bethel, an assembly in Indianapolis. Her mother, a graduate of Spiceland University—a Quaker institution in Indiana—was the first salaried teacher for black children in Indianapolis. She later held teaching positions in Saint Louis and a few other midwestern cities.

Just after Thomas turned nine months old, her parents moved to Oshkosh, Wisconsin. The formal education she received there in the School Lyceum was of an exceptional quality. She excelled in all of her subjects and demonstrated a particularly strong aptitude for grammar and composition. Her marriage at the end of her junior year ended her secondary education at Oshkosh High School, but it did not end her quest for knowledge nor her love of books.

Between 1880 and 1885, Thomas publicly displayed her skill as a writer and political activist. Known for her "luminous ideas," she became a "much solicited contributor to that great dissemination of public opinion, the weekly and daily press" (Scruggs, 237). One of her first solicited articles, "The Rights of Colored People, or A Plea for the Negro," appeared in two Wisconsin newspapers, *The Northwestern* of Oshkosh and *The Evening Wisconsin* of Milwaukee. Her column-and-a-half article attacked the United States Supreme Court's October 15, 1883, ruling that the first and second sections of the Civil Rights Act, passed March 1, 1875, were unconstitutional. Five civil rights cases had reached the high court involving whites' denial of lodging, entertainment, and transportation accommodations and privileges to people of color. The Supreme Court asserted that neither the Thirteenth nor the Fourteenth Amendment of the Constitution authorized the civil rights enactments. Moreover, the Court ruled that the Thirteenth Amendment related solely to slavery and involuntary servitude. Only one member of the bench, Justice John Marshall Harlan, dissented. Many readers of Thomas's rebuttal to the Court's decision praised her stunning logic and superior diction. Her political insight and literary prowess secured her a respectable position among both black and white contemporary women writers and journalists.

In 1885, Thomas moved to Indianapolis after "being thrown on her own responsibility for maintenance" (Scruggs, 239). Described as "being a lady of fine voice and attractive personality," she studied elocution under Mrs. Prunk and later with Lucia Julian Martin (239). Once settled in the city, she quickly associated herself with the literary circles of the area and became an active participant.

Thomas Joins *The Freeman* as Writer and Editor

In September 1891, Thomas accepted the positions of feature writer and correspondent with *The Freeman*, one of the nation's leading weekly illustrated black publications of the day. Features of the journal, "Church," "Stage," and "Race Gleanings" expanded in scope under her influence. "Women's World," a column devoted to "instructing and interesting items of news, gleaned from philosophers puns and press comments pertaining to women," appeared shortly after her staff appointment. The column covered the activities of noted white and black women, such as Ida B. Wells, Susan B. Anthony, and Frances Ellen Harper. It also announced new publications of interest to women, such as L. A. Scruggs' 1893 book devoted to the achievement of black American women, and imparted words of wisdom as well as health and beauty tips. Her presence at *The Freeman* afforded black women and men a constant source of racial uplift and inspiration, demonstrated black capability, and provided an excellent example of a nontraditional career option for black and white women.

Although she is credited with addressing primarily the turn-of-the-century black woman and serving as one of the most outstanding female role models of her race, Thomas's feminist politics resonate as strikingly modern and raceless:

> We believe that what should most interest women is woman; despite the glaring indication that her chief consideration, as well as chief glorification, is man. Woman's condition to-day, as compared with her condition in no far remote time, stands out in contra distinction in favor of the present. But even now she is environed with untoward odds which operate in many instances to stultify her aspiration or palsy her effort, and yet a number sufficient to wield telling influence have in the last few decades invaded . . . the ranks of the arts, sciences and industries. . . . The loom, spinning wheel and quilting frames have been exchanged for the desk, the ledger, the brush and palette, the caligraph and the camera. . . . [Y]et woman has not abandoned the duties incumbent upon her as wife and mother. . . . But in this, a day of great possibilities, the feminine heart yearns for broader paths wherein to work, an intellectual highway whereon all nations or sex may walk abreast (Majors, 206-07).

The record bears few details of Lillian Thomas's later life and death. Her earlier years, however, reveal the profile of a woman unafraid to speak out for her race and her gender.

References

Majors, M. A. "Lillian Parker Thomas." *Noted Negro Women*. Chicago: Donohue and Henneberry, 1893.

Scruggs. L. A. "Mrs Lillian May Thomas." *Women of Distinction*. Raleigh, N.C.: Scruggs, 1893.

La Vinia Delois Jennings

Eloise Bibb Thompson

(1878-1928)

Writer, journalist

Eloise Bibb Thompson, poet, short story writer, journalist, lecturer, and playwright, became prominent in social and religious circles of the late 1890s and early 1900s. A devout Catholic with a need for self-fulfillment, she devoted her life to the advancement of her race. According to one of her contemporaries, Delilah Beasley, in *The Negro Trail Blazers of California*, Thompson's solution for the plight of the more than seven million blacks living on the East and West Coasts in 1919 was simple—to "enter the bosom of the church" to find meaning and purpose in life (255). This proselytizing approach pervaded all of her work.

Born in New Orleans, Louisiana, on June 29, 1878, Eloise Alberta Veronica Bibb Thompson was the only child of middle-class parents, Charles H. Bibb and Catherine Adele Bibb. Her father was a United States customs inspector for roughly forty years. Following an early education in New Orleans, Thompson published her first volume of verse, *Poems* (Boston: Monthly Review Press, 1895), when she was seventeen. Though critics of this small volume failed to take into account her youth, one critic remarked that the verse was "neat and prim" (Loggins, 355). Another critic concluded that "over half the poems . . . are romantic narratives of star-crossed lovers and agonized heroes [and] . . . the poetic sentiments are those of a girl in love with love, the more tempestuous the better" (Sherman, 205). Despite this criticism, Eloise Bibb's poems reveal a range of interests—religion, history, personal tributes, and love—that is unusual in a girl so young. Her personal tribute to Alice Ruth Moore reveals a light-hearted imagination:

> I peer adown a shining group,
> Where sages grace the throng,
> And see the bard of Wheatley Club
> Proclaimed the Queen of Song.
>
> Fair Alice! shed thy radiance more
> And charm us with thy verse;
> So dulcet, so harmonious,
> So graceful, sweet, and terse.

Dedicated to Alice Ruth Moore, who later married Paul Lawrence Dunbar, "To the Sweet Bard of the Women's Club" suggests that Thompson perceived Moore as her mentor and as a source of inspiration. According to R. Baxter Miller, African-American scholar, Thompson's poetry reveals occasionally "brilliant originality of thought" that is "typical of the late nineteenth century" (Interview with R. Baxter Miller, 21 June 1990).

From 1899 to 1901, five years after the publication of her first volume of poetry, Thompson attended Oberlin College Preparatory Academy. At the end of her fifth term, she returned to New Orleans and taught in the public schools for two years. In the fall of 1902, she entered Teachers College of Howard University in Washington, D.C., and graduated in January 1908. Shortly afterwards, she became head of the Social Settlement at Howard from 1908 to 1911.

In Chicago on August 4, 1911, Eloise Bibb married Noah Thompson, a well-known black Catholic journalist who was prominent in black literary circles in Los Angeles, California. He was a thirty-three-year-old widower with a son, Noah Murphy. According to Mary Scally's *Negro Catholic Writers*, Eloise Bibb and Noah Murphy were "well matched because of their common interest in religion, literature, and the advancement of the Negro in the United States" (115).

While still newlyweds, the two moved to Los Angeles, where they became active immediately in church work and continued their careers as well. Besides the real estate business, Noah Thompson was on the editorial staff of the *Evening Express* and the *Morning Tribune*. Meanwhile, Eloise Bibb Thompson "made her mark as a rising star" as a special writer for the *Los Angeles Tribune* and the *Morning Sun* (Shockley, 234).

In addition to her career in journalism, Eloise Bibb Thompson contributed articles and poetry to the popular magazines *Out West* and *The Tidings*, an organ of the Diocese of Monterey and Los Angeles. The latter magazine published her article, "The Church and the Negro," which her contemporaries considered a significant contribution. When she addressed the Catholic Women's Clubs of Los Angeles in the Knights of Columbus Hall, Thompson made a lasting impression. The daily newspaper commented favorably on Thompson's appearance and speech delivery but made no mention of her race. Performances of this kind by black women, however, were indeed rare.

Journalist Becomes Playwright

Eloise Bibb Thompson turned to playwriting and short fiction around 1915. Because she spoke candidly to mixed audiences about racial issues, her first dramatic work, *A Reply to Clansmen*, was created in the midst of controversy. *Opportunity* reports that the play, "a scenario in form," was sold to Thomas H. Ince in 1915 for one hundred five dollars (63). However, the play was never produced by the Triangle Film Corporation, forcing Thompson to hire a lawyer to gain its return. Further complications ensued when D. W. Griffith expressed interest in producing "an exceptional story of great possibilities [and] material of remarkable caliber" (*Opportunity*, 63). He, too, faltered on the oral commitment. The underlying reason for the rejection of Thompson's play is that it was a response to Thomas Dixon's novel, *The Clansman*, an account glorifying the Ku Klux Klan. In 1915 D. W. Griffith bought the rights from Dixon and made *The Birth of a Nation*.

In the decade of the 1920s, Eloise Bibb Thompson produced three plays. The Playcrafters performed *Caught* (1920) at the Gamut Club. Frank Egan, owner of Egan Theatre, purchased *Africannus*, also referred to as *Africans* (1922). The plot centers on a group of Bantus who involve American interests in their liberation plans. Although one Los Angeles reviewer noted that the piece was episodic and melodramatic, she related that it was the "first time in Los Angeles theatre history that a drama about an African country, written by a black author and intended for a black audience had been realized by an all black cast" (Durham, 249). The performance featured Pauline Jones and Malcolm Patton, Jr. A more successful play for Eloise Bibb Thompson was *Cooped Up* (1924), a roominghouse drama of sexual passion written when she was a member of the National Ethiopian Art Theatre students. Cast members included Ardell Dabney, F. Eugene Corbie, Lillian Creamer, G. Alfred Woods, Joseph A. Steber, and Hemsley Winfield (Kellner, 261). Critics hailed the play as "amazingly realistic . . . [with] the possibility of romanticizing Negro life" (*Opportunity*, 64).

The racial issue permeated Eloise Bibb Thompson's short fiction as it had her playwriting. In both "Mademoiselle 'Tasie—A Story" and "Masks," the "passing" issue plagues blacks within and without the Creole subculture. In the first story, which Edward O'Brien of the *Boston Transcript* called one of the "best short stories of 1925," Thompson portrays 'Tasie, as the youngest daughter "of an exceptional Creole family," speaking only "patois French." A thirty-seven-year-old woman with "very crinkled red hair," she is forced to work for a former slave. The notion of color pervades all of 'Tasie's and her family's thinking. To them, the worst crime was to be seen on the street with an American Negro—"Negre aux grosse oreilles"—of dark complexion and with big ears. Realizing the disparity between her dreams and reality, 'Tasie meets dark-skinned Titus Johnson, a forty-year-old businessman. She learns a valuable lesson about life and love. By her own admission, 'Tasie becomes "entirely forgetful of his color" and marries ("Mademoiselle 'Tasie," 278).

In her second story, "Masks," Eloise Bibb Thompson addresses the question of passing and the color line for two mulattoes. Julie, a quadroon, and her husband, Paupet, an octoroon, live in the French Quarter of New Orleans. The plot focuses on the efforts of her grandfather, Aristile Blanchard, to defy nature by designing a mask of the white man's face, feeling that it would "open the barred and bolted doors of privilege for those who knocked thereon" (Masks: A Story, 302). He dies unsuccessful in his attempts to cease judging a person by skin color. Trying to come to grips with her grandfather's "half-crazed tirade" against the white oppressors, Julie takes the idea of passing one step further. She marries the "whitest octoroon that she had ever seen," hoping to insure her offspring can pass and never face racial discrimination. Eloise Bibb Thompson gives an ironic ending to the story; Julie gives birth to a black offspring. The inscription on her tombstone reads, "Because she saw with the eyes of her grandfather, she died at the sight of her babe's face."

Eloise Bibb Thompson's concern for the welfare of her people permeated her life and work. Unafraid to express faith in her race, she lent her voice to the movement toward equality of opportunity throughout the United States. Though much of her writing is scattered, she and her husband, Noah, worked hard to improve conditions for blacks. Her sudden and untimely death on January 8, 1928, extinguished a "magnificent spirit which lighted her approach to life" (Obituary, 37).

References

Abajian, James de T. *Blacks in Selected Newspapers, Censuses, and Other Sources*. Boston: G. K. Hall, 1977.

Arata, Esther Spring. *Black American Playwrights, 1800 to the Present: A Bibliography*. Metuchen, N.J.: Scarecrow Press, 1976. 191.

Beasley, Delilah L. *The Negro Trail Blazers of California.* Los Angeles: The Author, 1919. Reprinted. New York: Negro Universities Press, 1969. 130, 254-55.

Bibb, Eloise. *Poems.* 1895. In *Collected Black Women's Poetry.* Vol. 4. Ed. Joan Sherman. New York: Oxford University Press, 1988.

———. "Mademoiselle 'Tasie—A Story." *Opportunity* 3 (September 1925): 272-78.

———. "Masks: A Story." *Opportunity* 5 (October 1927): 300-302.

Durham, Weldon B., ed. *American Theatre Companies, 1888-1930.* New York: Greenwood Press, 1987.

Hatch, James V., and Omanni Abdullah, eds. *Black Playwrights, 1823-1977.* New York: Bowker, 1977.

Interview with R. Baxter Miller, 21 June 1990.

Kellner, Bruce, ed. *The Harlem Renaissance: A Historical Dictionary for the Era.* Westport, Conn.: Greenwood Press, 1984. 261.

Loggins, Vernon. *The Negro Author.* Port Washington, N.Y.: Kennikat Press, 1964. 355.

Miller, R. Baxter. Interview with authors, 21 June 1990.

Obituary. *Opportunity* 6 (February 1928): 37.

Rush, Theressa Bunnels, Carol Fairbanks Myers, and Esther Spring Arata, eds. *Black American Writers Past and Present.* Metuchen, N.J.: Scarecrow Press, 1975. 75.

Scally, Mary Anthony. *Negro Catholic Writers 1900-1943.* Grosse Pointe, Mich.: Walter Romig, 1945. 144-45.

Sherman, Joan R. *Invisible Poets: Afro-Americans of the Nineteenth Century.* Urbana: University of Illinois Press, 1989. 204-206.

Shockley, Ann Allen, ed. *Afro-American Women Writers 1746-1933.* Boston: G. K. Hall, 1988. 233-35.

Stetson, Erlene. "Black Women in and out of Print." *Women in Print: Opportunities for Women's Studies Research in Language and Literature.* Vol. 1. Eds. Joan R. Hartman and Ellen Messer-Davidow. New York: Modern Language Association, 1982. 99.

Sharynn Owens Etheridge

Era Bell Thompson

(1906-1986)

Journalist, author

Era Bell Thompson had a natural talent for writing, which manifested itself while she was in college. She progressed from preparing essays for class to writing for the school paper. From there she became a correspondent for the *Chicago Defender* and wrote an article for *Physical Culture* that netted her three dollars. With the newfound success in writing, Thompson notes that "I traded contortionism for journalism and hooked my wagon to a literary star." She went on to become editor of *Negro Digest* and *Ebony*, and eventually international editor of *Ebony* and a noted journalist.

Thompson was born August 10, 1906, in Des Moines, Iowa, and died on December 29, 1986, in Chicago, Illinois. She was buried in the family plot in Driscoll, North Dakota. She was the only girl in a family of six—her father and mother, Steward C. Thompson and Mary (Logan) Thompson, and three brothers. Her father was a waiter, cook, coal miner, operator of a secondhand store, and a farmer.

Thompson graduated from high school in Driscoll and enrolled at North Dakota State University in Grand Forks. Here she became a track star and played against major colleges. In her second year at North Dakota State she began to live in the home of the Reverend Edward O'Brian, and when he became president of Morningside College in Sioux City, Iowa, the next year, Thompson went along as a part of the family to finish her college training.

The writing skills of the budding journalist were honed in college. Her spelling skills, however, left much to be desired, yet the problems were never discouraging to Thompson. Addressing the matter in her autobiography, Thompson said:

> My interest in writing met with unexpected encouragement and a few setbacks. Mr. Lewis [her teacher] read my first theme, a short autobiography, to the class. When he finished, he said, "Well, Miss Thompson, there isn't much of yourself; there are many misspelled words; but the general impression is so good that I can't help it. 'A.'" My next theme was a little more daring, less conventional, for here in college they took the broad view, they let you out on your own. For a while my papers returned with neat praise for the writing and subtle hints about spelling and construction, but I paid small heed. It was

> during the height of the Darwin controversy, and I put everything I had into an article entitled "Evolution." The gist of it was that women were fine people but all men were monkeys—and I misspelled "monkeys" (Thompson, *American Daughter*, 176).

The talent for writing notwithstanding, Thompson's primary interest in her college years was acrobatics. She "couldn't resist the gymnasium long," she said. "I played basketball with all four teams and stayed after school to practice acrobatics, because right then my sole desire was to become a lady contortionist." Her white friends at school were as curious about her athletic skills as they were about her color. While showering in the dressing room, her friends watched her "undress, watched to see if the color went all the way up and if any washed off in the water, and . . . they were glad when it didn't because they knew then I wasn't a phony" (Thompson, *American Daughter*, 150).

That winter she found a new interest—the *Chicago Defender*. Thompson enlarged upon commonplace experiences that she knew and "created enough news to become a correspondent." Her first feature was an attack upon Marcus Garvey's "Back to Africa" movement, and it brought her first fan mail, including "a letter from one of his followers who even scorched the outside of the letter." She gave up social reform and began to write under the pseudonym "Dakota Dick." She wrote in the "Lights and Shadows" column as a "bad, bad cowboy from the wild and wooly West." The fan mail became friendly and came from black pen pals. After she received three dollars for an article in *Physical Culture* magazine, Thompson was persuaded that her career would be in journalism (Thompson, *American Daughter*, 150).

Thompson received a bachelor's degree from Morningside College in 1933 and studied at Medill School of Journalism at Northwestern University. She arrived in a depression-ridden Chicago in 1933 with her college diploma but without a job. For a short time she lived and worked at the Settlement House under the supervision of Mary McDowell. Eventually she was able to get positions with the Works Projects Administration (night shifts), the Chicago Department of Public Works, the Chicago Relief Administration, the Chicago Board of Trade, and finally the Illinois State Employment Services. Interspersed with these positions, which she held between 1933 and 1945, she was a waitress, domestic worker, writer, elevator operator, and housekeeper, and when all else failed, her real estate friend would give her part-time employment. Thompson received the Newbery Fellowship to write her autobiography in 1945, and it was published by the University of Chicago Press a year later under the title *American Daughter*.

Journalism Career Opens

In 1947 John H. Johnson, the young and enterprising publisher of two new national magazines—*Negro Digest* and *Ebony*, persuaded Era Bell Thompson to leave her position with the Illinois State Employment Service to become an editor of these two journals. From 1947 to 1951 she was managing editor of *Negro Digest*, later called *Black World*, and she was co-managing editor of *Ebony* from 1951 to 1964.

In 1964, Thompson became international editor and remained in that position until her death in 1986. As international editor she traveled extensively on six continents and was entertained in "thatch huts and palaces." On one occasion she visited India, where she had an appointment with the renowned guru Maharishi Babesh Yogi, who preached transcendental meditation as a solution to the world's problems. On her return to the United States, she wrote stories on the Maharishi and her other experiences in *Ebony* magazine.

Thompson received numerous honors and awards. These included a Bread Loaf Writer's Fellowship, 1949; National Press Club citation, Washington, D.C., 1961; Iota Phi Lambda Outstanding Woman of the Year, 1965; honorary degrees from Morningside College, 1965, and the University of North Dakota, 1969; Society of Midland Authors' Patrons Saints Award, 1968, for *American Daughter*; and in 1978 selection by Radcliffe College as one of fifty women of courage who are recorded and photographed for the Black Women Oral History Project. In that year also she was noted in the Iowa Hall of Fame, and the University of North Dakota Cultural Center was named for her. Her memberships included the board of directors of Hull House 1960-64; the North Central Manpower Advisory Commission from 1965 to 1967; Urban League; Chicago Council on Foreign Relations; and the Chicago Press Club.

In addition to her autobiography, Thompson wrote *Africa, Land of My Fathers*, in which she expressed her love for her African heritage:

> I am proud of the African blood in my veins and proud of my black heritage, for I have seen evidences of that ancient African civilization in the excavations of Ife, and I have talked with black kings who are the descendants of African conquerors, and I have walked in the streets of a black kingdom whose Christianity is among the oldest in the world.

She added, however, that America was her home. In 1963, Thompson coedited with Herbert Nipson *White on Black*. One of her most revealing stories, "I Was a Cancer Coward," printed in *Ebony*, tells of her fears when, as a consequence of cancer, she had to undergo a radical mastectomy. The article aimed to help relieve the fears of others who had the same need.

Thompson has been described as petite, and tough (she was four feet eight inches tall). Among her notable friends, companions, and contemporaries were John H. Johnson, Herbert Nipson, Linda H. Rice, Simeon Booker, Lerone Bennett, Jr., Gerri Majors, Phyl Garland, Alex Poinsett, and Joyce A. Smith. During her years with Johnson Publishing

Company she became known as one of the most prominent women journalists in the nation.

References

"Backstage." *Ebony* 23 (April 1968): 26.

Barton, Rebecca. *Witnesses for Freedom: Negro Americans in Autobiography*. New York: Harper, 1948.

Ebony 42 (March 1987): 25.

Ebony Success Library: 1,000 Successful Blacks. Chicago: Johnson Pub. Co., 1973.

Major, Gerri, with Doris Saunders. *Black Society*. Chicago: Johnson Publishing Co., 1976.

Shockley, Ann A., and Sue P. Chandler. *Living Black American Authors*. New York: Bowker, 1973.

Thompson, Era Bell. *Africa, Land of My Fathers*. New York: Doubleday, 1954.

———. *American Daughter*. Chicago: University of Chicago Press, 1946.

———. "I Was a Cancer Coward." *Ebony* 26 (September 1971): 64-71.

Collections

Papers and photographs of Era Bell Thompson are in the Carter G. Woodson Library in Chicago. Thompson is included in the Black Oral History Collection at Fisk University, and the Radcliffe College Black Women Oral History Project and accompanying catalog of photographs, *Women of Courage*. Photographs are also in the North Dakota Hall of Fame, *Ebony* (March 1987) with her obituary p. 25, and *Ebony: 1,000 Successful Blacks*, p. 303.

Lois C. McDougald

Louise Thompson

(1901-)

Educator, labor organizer, social reformer

Educator, labor organizer, and social reformer, Louise Thompson influenced the lives of many artists and writers of the Harlem Renaissance. Her circle of friends and acquaintances included Aaron Douglas, Langston Hughes, Zora Neale Hurston, and the novelist and playwright Wallace Thurman, who became her first husband. A particularly close bond developed between Thompson and Hughes, and at various stages throughout his literary career she served as his stenographer, advisor, and critic.

Born in Chicago on September 9, 1901, Thompson was reared and educated in the West. Her stepfather, a restless man who worked as a chef, moved his family from one small town to another throughout the western and midwestern states. Obtaining employment at each new location was not a difficult task for her mother, Louise, who worked as a domestic, but acquiring a sense of belonging and identity became increasingly difficult for both mother and daughter, who often found themselves the only black family in a small Idaho, Oregon, or California town. To cope with the recurring feelings of racial alienation and isolation that assailed them at each new location, the light-complexioned mother and daughter occasionally passed for white or Mexican, whichever affiliation suited their communal or economic needs of the moment.

In May of 1923, Thompson graduated from the University of California at Berkeley with a major in business administration and a minor in Spanish. Racial inequities at this juncture of her life continued to motivate her to alter her ethnic identity. She "briefly passed as a Mexican to work as a girl Friday in a San Francisco office, after finding all such employment opportunities closed to 'colored' applicants" (Berry, 100). Before leaving Berkeley, however, she attended a lecture of the great sociologist and historian, W. E. B. Du Bois, whose message of racial uplift greatly impressed her. He stirred her racial pride and sparked her desire to move East and to become a part of the black literary renaissance that he had helped to inspire.

A few years and two teaching appointments intervened before Thompson became a part of the New Negro Movement underway in Harlem. Her first teaching position took her to Pine Bluff, Arkansas. One source describes her employment there as simply a "teaching position at a black college" (Berry, 100), while another more descriptive account states that "her students were barely able to read, although she was expected to teach them Spanish among other subjects" and that it was there she discovered "racism in its violent manifestations" (Kellner, 353). Yet another source generalizes her experience by simply stating that she "spent a year teaching at a hopelessly reactionary black school in Pine Bluff, before coming to Hampton at the start of the school year" (Rampersad, 162). Thus, Thompson began the 1926 school term teaching business administration at Hampton Institute in Virginia.

The following year, Thompson's support of a student strike that erupted on Hampton's campus on October 8, coupled with her intolerance of refined racism, eventually drove her from her job. Dubbed "The Glorious Revolution," hundreds of Hampton's students opposed the subtly racist and repressive paternalistic policies and treatment that the school's predominantly white administration and faculty imposed upon them. Since the passage of the Massenburg Bill, a bill that required the separation of the races in public halls in Virginia, including Hampton, students charged that the white principal had become even less social to students, that he had placed known Klan members in some of the trade departments, and that members of the faculty from the North referred to students as "heathens." Furthermore, Thompson and other black faculty were denied social interaction with their students, while the administration discouraged socializing between black and white faculty. Because the predominantly white administration believed "that the students were of such low character that they would undertake sexual contact during a play, the school would not sponsor such activities unless the lights were on, even to the extent of destroying the effect of the moving picture or play" ("The Hampton Strike," 345-46). Moreover, social activities required one faculty chaperon present for every four students in attendance. A walk-out of students in silent protest against the administration's expectation that they sing a spiritual for the South African prime minister Jan Christiaan Smuts before a segregated audience precipitated the strike. The action of the students along with "Louise Thompson's letter to W. E. B. Du Bois recounting these antiquated attempts to insure gentility (published anonymously in *The Crisis* to protect her job), effected some minor changes at Hampton" (Kellner, 354).

The Thompson-Langston Hughes Friendship Begins

Before ending the academic year of unrest and her final semester at Hampton, Thompson met Langston Hughes. Rampersad notes the circumstances surrounding the meeting:

> On March 11, Hughes read his poems in Ogden Hall at Hampton Institute. . . . His host was a junior faculty member, Susie Elvie Bailey . . . who introduced him to another teacher, Louise Thompson, with whom Hughes would be very close in the years to come. . . . Both Louise Thompson and Sue Bailey were under a cloud. The independent-minded Bailey was suspected of having written an anonymous letter about conditions at Hampton to Du Bois at the *Crisis*. . . . [I]n fact, Louise Thompson had done so, intending only to give information to Du Bois, who had promptly published the entire text. Now the two young women, glumly expecting to be fired, were planning to leave for New York. Hughes tried to cheer them up with brave talk about their prospects in the city (Rampersad, 161-62).

Harlem immediately embraced the spirited, bright, and attractive Thompson upon her arrival in June of 1928. Aaron Douglas, the most outstanding painter of the Harlem Renaissance, and his wife, Alta, befriended her. Wallace Thurman, needing help with the novel on which he was working, hired her as his typist. Like Thompson, Thurman had grown up in the West and had been educated in California at the University of Southern California. By the end of August, they were married, but within six months, Thompson had gone to Reno, Nevada, with the intention of remaining long enough to establish residency in order to obtain a quick divorce. She asserted that their incompatibility stemmed from his homosexuality (Thurman had been arrested in a New York men's room). His chronic alcoholism, depression, and suicidal tendencies only compounded her need to be free of the marriage. "'I *never* understood Wallace,' she would later admit. 'He took nothing seriously. He laughed about everything. He would often threaten to commit suicide but you knew he would never try it. And he would never admit that he was homosexual. *Never, never*, not to me at any rate'" (Rampersad, 172). The notification that her mother had cancer cut short her Nevada trip and first attempt to divorce Thurman, and yet another attempt failed when he refused to finance a Mexican divorce. The termination of their marriage came finally with the death of Thurman on December 22, 1934. Though estranged since their initial separation in 1928, Louise Thompson visited him in the Staten Island Welfare home where he died. She also attended his funeral.

Just as she was completing study at the New York School of Social Work on an Urban League fellowship in 1929, Thompson, needing employment, accepted a secretarial job from Charlotte Louise Vandervere Quick Mason, an affluent and influential white philanthropist who resided at 399 Park Avenue. Alain Locke had recommended her for the position. Mason, who had established herself as the "Godmother" and publicly anonymous patron of struggling young black writers and artists such as Langston Hughes, Zora Neale Hurston, Aaron Douglas, Claude McKay, Alain Locke, Richmond Barthé, and Hall Johnson, expected Thompson to write her thank-you notes for what Thompson considered her pay for services rendered. She acquiesced to Mason's whimsical eccentricity, however, because the flexible hours and steady income enabled her to care for her ailing mother. Nonetheless, the Mason-Thompson liaison lasted less than a year because for Thompson, Mason's stifling patronage, strong bias as to what black art should be, and racist attitudes bore strong resemblances to the white, paternalistic control she had despised at Hampton. She resented Mason's stereotypical indulgences about blacks: "I might comment on the beauty of a flower arrangement in her apartment, and she would be greatly pleased. 'I knew you would like them, you *would* like red'" (Huggins, 130). Despite Mason's faults, Thompson acknowledged her generosity and graciousness. Still, she was shaken and hurt when, after almost a year in her employment, Mason summoned her and launched a bitter attack upon her and all black people. Mason's attack severed their relationship permanently. Although Thompson had occasionally suggested to Hughes that Mason's interest only in primitivism and not in social protest stifled his political independence, she was not responsible for Hughes's break with Mason. In fact, Mason's own scathing attack on Hughes in an attempt to manipulate him brought about the disintegration of their relationship several months later.

Thompson's initial attraction to Mason's employment stemmed from the opportunity to work as an assistant to Hughes, and she spent the term of her employment as his stenographer. Her first assignment was to help him with the revision of *Not Without Laughter*, which Knopf accepted for publication at the end of 1929. The relationship that developed between the two can be best described as one shared by "kindred spirits" (Berry, 100). Six months separated their births in western cities, and both in their childhoods had been shuttled from city to city. Similar circumstances had also dictated that their mothers work as domestics. Thompson and Hughes spent much recreational time with each other. They often shared an evening out with Aaron and Alta Douglas, attended football games, and danced at the Savoy Ballroom. On one occasion the *Inter-State Tattler*, a black gossip sheet, reported that they had been seen holding hands on Seventh Avenue (Rampersad, 174). Hughes often visited her apartment, which she shared with Sue Bailey, at 435 Convent Avenue near City College. Not only would Thompson and Hughes spend time together in Harlem, but their future paths would cross in Russia and Spain. In 1942, Hughes would dedicate "to Louise" *Shakespeare in Harlem*, a book of poems. Though they were close friends, a romantic intrigue never developed between them.

While in Mason's employment, Thompson, serving as the stenographer for Hughes and Zora Neale Hurston, who were collaborating on a play, found herself in the middle of a dispute that eventually led to the dissolution of friendship between the two writers. Hughes and Hurston worked incessantly in a Westfield, New Jersey, boarding house in March and April of 1930 on *Mule Bone*, a comedy about two hunters who quarrel over a turkey until one knocks the other unconscious with a mule's hock bone. With a draft completed but still many revisions needing to be done, Hurston took a copy of the script with the proposed plan of traveling South and working there. Hughes later discovered that Hurston had retitled the play *De Turkey and De Law* and had copyrighted it solely under her name. She had also given it to Carl Van Vechten to submit for performance with a theatre guild. When Hughes confronted her with her betrayal, Hurston responded that she objected to an earlier suggestion of his that Thompson share the royalties. She also accused Thompson of trying to pit Hughes against her. After a long, drawn out fracas between the two, which included Thompson being called to Cleveland where the play was in a rehearsal to verify the coauthorship and Hughes threatening to bring suit against Hurston, the theatre guild canceled the play's performance. Hurston vowed it would never be performed. Some critics speculate that Hurston, who was no stranger to charges of plagiarism, was attempting again to appropriate someone else's work (Lewis, 261). Others maintain that the bone of contention that grew between Hughes and Hurston stemmed from Hurston's jealousy of Thompson and her resentment of the attention Hughes paid to Thompson and not her.

Group Recruited for Film in Moscow

Seeking new employment, Thompson became the assistant to the director of the Congregational Education Society in the department of social relations. Her duties included conducting seminars on a Pullman Car that traveled throughout the South and editing the society's newsletter. Becoming more politically radical, Thompson also helped to form a Harlem branch of the Friends of the Soviet Union. Her work caught the attention of James W. Ford, the leading black American Communist of the day and future vice-presidential candidate for his party. Ford, who had just returned from the Soviet Union, had been asked to recruit a group of black performers and intellectuals who would come to Moscow to make a motion picture entitled *Black and White*. The plot, set in Birmingham, Alabama, was to depict the exploitation of the American Negro from slavery to the present. Ford recruited Thompson to serve as executive secretary and to spearhead the search for young artists able to afford the fare of ninety dollars to Moscow, where Meschrabpom Film Corporation of the Worker's International would reimburse them. Thompson had difficulty attracting seasoned actors because of the fare stipulation but finally managed to assemble twenty-one participants of diverse backgrounds and talents. Dorothy West, a New England poet and fiction writer; two *New York Amsterdam News* journalists, Henry Lee Moon and Ted Poston; Juanita Lewis, a singer; Allen Mackenzie, the only bona fide Communist party member, and two other communist sympathizers; two experienced performers, Sylvia Garner and Wayland Rudd; and eleven others who were neither political nor artistic arrived at the Brooklyn Pier on June 14, 1932, to board the German ship *Europa* en route to Russia. From the onset of the project, Thompson had contacted Hughes and asked him to be a part of the group and to help write the English dialogue for the screenplay. He assented. Thus Mackenzie, Hughes, Thompson, and two others, Loren Miller and Matt Crawford, were the only committed socialists in the group.

The *Black and White* project was ill-fated from its inception. The majority of the troupe brought over to act and sing could do neither. While waiting for the start of the filming, some grew restless and began to "behave as tempestuously as movie stars on a Hollywood set" despite Thompson's plea for them "to uphold the honor of our race" (Berry, 160). Two factions sprang up within the group. One was interested in Moscow purely as a pleasure jaunt, while the other was interested in finding out more about the socialist system and its people. The latter group became upset with the former group, whose scandalous behavior reflected poorly on the group as a whole. The original screenplay for the movie was also problematic. Written by a Russian who had never been to America, the plot was "so interwoven with major and minor impossibilities and improbabilities that it would have seemed like a burlesque on the screen" (Hughes, 76).

Ironically, the group learned of the film's cancellation from the newspaper. A front-page story in the European edition of the *New York Herald Tribune* on 12 August attributed the film's termination to the Soviets' fear of a negative American reaction. Four days later, Boris Babitsky, director of the Meschrabpom Film Corporation, met with the group to explain that an unsatisfactory scenario, unsuitable cast members, the lack of trained Negroid-looking extras for the mass scenes, and the lack of technical facilities had blocked the completion of the project. The media, however, carried the charges that the United States' granting diplomatic recognition to the Soviets killed the project. Hoping to set the record straight about the failure of the Moscow film project, Thompson wrote two articles: "The Soviet Film," which appeared in *Crisis* in February 1933, and another, "With Langston Hughes in the USSR," which appeared in *Freedomways* in 1968. She also provided first-hand affirmation of the warm reception and preferential treatment bestowed on the members of her group because of the color of their skin.

> I have had many occasions to wonder at the great generosity of the Soviet people. Realizing that foreigners who come to this country may have different standards of living, they make available to them many things not available to their own people. Yet I have never experienced any resentment on the part of the people about this preferential treatment. Wherever we went as a group, or in pairs,the Russians would push us to the front of the queue line for a bus ticket, or offer us eats in a crowded streetcar. For all of us who experienced discrimination based on color in our own land, it was strange to find our color a badge of honor, our key to the city, so to speak ("With Langston Hughes in the USSR," 155-56).

Apprising her mother in a letter of the "honored guests" status she and her companions received, Thompson wrote "It will really be difficult to scramble back into obscurity when we return to the old U.S.A." (Rampersad, 246).

Thompson's Radical Political Activities Continue

Thompson returned to the United States more politically radical than ever. She became involved in the Scottsboro case, in which nine black youths ranging in age from thirteen to nineteen were accused in Scottsboro, Alabama, of raping two white prostitutes in a railroad boxcar and then sentenced to death. She participated in the May 1933 march on Washington, D. C., which drew more than three thousand demonstrators to demand the release of the boys. Thompson, the secretary of the Scottsboro Action Committee, was among the group of twenty-five—which included James W. Ford and Ruby Bates, one of the white prostitutes who had admitted her perjury—with which President Franklin Roosevelt refused to meet.

In 1933, Thompson also began her fifteen years of service to the International Workers Order (IWO), the powerful, fraternal society affiliated with the Communist party. Thompson used her IWO connection to aid a broke Hughes who had recently returned from Madrid, Spain. Prior to his return in 1937, Thompson had traveled to Spain as a member of a relief delegation and visited him while there. Upon her return to the States she had forwarded his correspondence to newspapers and magazines. Through the IWO, she arranged a series of lectures for Hughes entitled "A Negro Poet Looks at a Troubled World." Since Hughes had strained his ties with Knopf, his old publisher, and since it was not uncommon for leftist unions to support social literature, she also persuaded the IWO to publish a pamphlet of radical poems by Hughes, which she entitled *A New Song*. Costing only fifteen cents, the thirty-one page booklet, of which the IWO ten thousand copies, was a huge success. Thompson felt Hughes was becoming the social protest writer that he had always showed promise of being. The poems stimulated her to suggest that he write a play based upon some of them. Her suggestion gave rise to the one-act play, *Don't You Want To Be Free? A Poetry Play: From Slavery Through The Blues To Now—and Then Some! With Singing, Music, and Dancing*.

Hughes struck upon the idea of starting a theater, and Thompson found the space and the sponsor for what would become the Harlem Suitcase Theatre. The IWO allowed them to use the second floor of its community center at 317 West 125th Street. Because the IWO supplied the location, the theatre was to produce and to perform works anticapitalistic in nature and theme. First, only IWO workers Edith Jones, her husband, Robert Earl Jones, Grace Johnson, Mary Savage, and Thompson staffed the theatre. Later, Dorothy Peterson, Hilary Phillips, and Toy Harper joined the ranks. *Don't You Want To Be Free?*, the one-act play Thompson had inspired, became the theatre's first production.

Thompson's marriage in 1940 to William Lorenzo Patterson, lawyer and executive secretary of the International Labor Defense, which defended the Scottsboro boys, took her to Chicago, where she continued to work in various fields devoted to the liberation of the masses and social justice. In 1943, she gave birth to the only child of their union, Mary Louise. She and her husband eventually returned to New York, and it is there that he died on March 5, 1980. Though many of her early years in New York afforded her a closeness with Hughes, she also had the opportunity to work with other literary figures, such as Arna Bontemps on his 1931 novel *God Sends Sunday*, and to exchange books with Ralph Ellison. Throughout her career, Louise Thompson remained true to her friends and true to her political ideals.

References

Berry, Faith. *Langston Hughes, Before and Beyond Harlem*. Westport, Conn.: Lawrence Hill, 1983.

"The Hampton Strike." *Crisis* 34 (December 1927): 345-56.

Huggins, Nathan Irvin. *Harlem Renaissance*. New York: Oxford University Press, 1971.

Hughes, Langston. *I Wonder as I Wander*. New York: Hill and Wang, 1956.

Kellner, Bruce. "Louise Thompson [Patterson]." *The Harlem Renaissance, A Historical Dictionary for the Era*. Westport, Conn.: Greenwood Press, 1984.

Lewis, David Levering. *When Harlem Was in Vogue*. New York: Knopf, 1981.

Rampersad, Arnold. *The Life of Langston Hughes, Volume I: 1902-1941*. New York: Oxford University Press, 1986.

Thompson, Louise. "The Soviet Film." *Crisis* 40 (February 1933): 37, 46.

———. "With Langston Hughes in the USSR." *Freedomways* 8 (Spring 1968): 152-58.

La Vinia Jennings

Adah Thoms

(1870?-1943)

Nurse, civil rights activist, feminist

Adah Belle Samuels Thoms (Smith) was a pioneer for equal opportunity for black women in nursing and was committed to improving race relations. As president of the National Association of Colored Graduate Nurses (NACGN), she campaigned for acceptance of black nurses in the American Red Cross and the United States Army Nurse Corps during World War I. She wrote the first book, *Pathfinders*, to record the experiences of black nurses.

Thoms was born on January 12, circa 1870, in Richmond, Virginia, to Harry and Melvina Samuels. Although little is recorded about her early years, Thoms had at least one sibling. Her early education was in the elementary public and normal school of Richmond before she choose nursing as a career. She was briefly married and carried the surname Thoms throughout her nursing career.

Thoms came to New York City in 1893 and established a residence in Harlem. During the 1890s she studied elocution and public speaking at the Cooper Union in New York. She entered the Woman's Infirmary and School of Therapeutic Massage in New York for a course in nursing, the only black student in a class of thirty, and graduated in 1900.

She spent the next three years working as a nurse in New York City and in North Carolina. Dissatisfied with her informal nursing course, in 1903 Thoms entered the school of nursing at the Lincoln Hospital and Home in New York City. She graduated in 1905 and was employed at the hospital as its operating room nurse and supervisor of the surgical division.

In 1906 Thoms was appointed the assistant superintendent of nurses, a position she held until her retirement eighteen years later. Until a director was selected, Thoms served as the acting director of the school of nursing from 1906 through 1923. Despite her longevity in this position and her competence, it was not the custom to promote a black woman to a major administrative position, even in an institution for black students.

In 1908 Thoms played a key role with Martha Franklin in organizing the National Association of Colored Graduate Nurses (NACGN). As president of the Lincoln nurses' alumnae, Thoms invited Franklin to have the first meeting of the NACGN in New York, under the sponsorship of the alumnae association. The meeting took place at St. Mark's Methodist Episcopal Church, of which Thoms was a member. A charter member of this new organization, Thoms was elected its first treasurer and thereafter she organized the New York chapter of the NACGN. Through this national endeavor Thoms developed a professional bond and personal friendship with Mary Mahoney, the first trained black nurse, and with Martha Franklin.

Thoms served as president of the NACGN from 1916 to 1923. During these seven years she set forth ideas and established policies that in later years were the foundation for advances in education, employment, and community alliances for black nurses. In 1916 she began working with the National Urban League and the NAACP in efforts to change the inadequate conditions of black hospitals and training schools for black nurses. As president, Thoms traveled and addressed state and local nurses' associations. Thoms was a charismatic leader who loved poetry and song, which she always included in her addresses.

Army Nurse Corps Integrated

When Congress declared war on Germany in April 1917, Thoms as president of the NACGN immediately alerted black nurses, urging them to enroll in the American Red Cross nursing service, the only avenue to the United States Army Nurse Corps. When black nurses applied to the American Red Cross, they were constantly rejected because of their race.

During the winter of 1917-1918, the supply of civilian registered nurses was critically depleted due to the war, and meanwhile a massive influenza epidemic was in progress, resulting in an even more critical shortage. This nurse shortage finally impelled the surgeon general to authorize the use of black nurses. Although the first black nurse enrolled in July 1918, it was not until December 1918, after the war was over, that eighteen qualified black nurses were appointed to the Army Nurse Corps with full rank and pay. Assigned to separate living quarters and recreational facilities, black nurses met the influenza epidemic with a zest that proved their worth beyond any doubt.

During the 1921 NACGN national convention in Washington, D.C., President and Mrs. Warren G. Harding received the association at the White House. As Thoms presented a large basket of roses to the president and first lady, Thoms requested that the NACGN be placed on record as an organized body of two thousand trained nurses, ready when needed for world service.

A firm believer in the professional identity of nursing, Thoms was outspoken against the NACGN merging with the National Medical Association, the black association for physicians. Thoms thought there could be an affiliation without a merger, allowing nurses to retain their identity as a group of nurses. Thoms swayed the majority and this position later facilitated the merger of the NACGN in 1951 into the American Nurses Association (ANA).

Thoms was a crusader for equal rights for women. When the Nineteenth Amendment was ratified in 1920, Thoms advised members of the NACGN to look upon the ballot as a practical power as much as they do the privilege to work. She organized a campaign to urge members of NACGN to make a careful study of suffrage, be nonpartisan, and vote for worthy candidates.

Thoms had an interest in furthering her own education. She took continuing education courses at Hunter College and the New School for Social Research, both in New York City. She encouraged black nurses to follow her example and continue their education.

By 1921 Thoms's leadership assumed an additional dimension. That year she was appointed by the assistant surgeon general of the Army to serve on the Women's Advisory Council on Venereal Diseases of the United States Public Health Service.

Throughout her career and after retirement, Thoms was an active member of many professional organizations. She retired from Lincoln School for Nurses in 1923. She subsequently married Henry Smith, who died within one year. In 1929 she wrote the first account of black nurses entitled *Pathfinders*. It is a classic historical source of the unique experience of black nurses. For this contribution to nursing and for her efforts in 1917 to have black nurses accepted in the Army Nurse Corps, Thoms became the first nurse to receive the NACGN's Mary Mahoney Award in 1936.

Thoms was a well-built, medium-brown-skinned woman. She resided in Harlem from the time she came to New York until her death. Thoms died from a stroke on February 21, 1943, and is buried in Woodlawn Cemetery, New York, under the surname of Smith.

Thoms's work, *Pathfinders*, originally published by Kay Printing House, New York, in 1919, was reprinted by Garland Publishers in New York in 1985. A photograph of Thoms is included. She also coauthored with C. E. Bullock the article ''Development of Facilities for Colored Nurse Education.''

References

Carnegie, E. M. *The Path We Tread*. Philadelphia: Lippincott, 1986. Photograph of Thoms, p. 97.

Davis, Althea T. ''Architects for Integration and Equality: Early Black American Leaders in Nursing.'' Ph.D. Dissertation. Teachers College, Columbia University, 1987. Photographs of Thoms, pp. 114, 138.

Althea T. Davis

Lucinda ''Lucy'' Thurman

(1849-1918)

Temperance leader, clubwoman

The temperance movement had as one of its chief advocates Lucinda ''Lucy'' Smith Thurman, an organizer and a woman dedicated to purpose. Her early interest in racial uplift was nourished and brought to full flower in her work with local club activities in Michigan and in the National Association of Colored Women (NACW), where under her leadership a temperance department was established and where her interests in addressing the racial issues of the time were compatible with those of NACW. The merging interests worked to the mutual benefit of NACW, Thurman, and the black American people.

Thurman was born on October 22, 1849, in Ottawa, Canada, the daughter of William and Katherine Smith. (Her father is also identified as Nehemiah Henry Smith and her mother as Catherine.) She attended the schools of Canada, and at the age of seventeen she had become concerned about the need to uplift the black race. Leaving her Canadian home in about 1866, she went to Rochester, New York, were she met black abolitionists Frederick Douglass, William Wells Brown, and other great leaders of the day. By then she had developed recognizable leadership and educational abilities. Through the assistance of Douglass and Brown, she obtained a teaching position in Maryland, which she held for three years. From there she moved to Jackson, Michigan. She first married in Cleveland, Ohio, and had two sons. She was married a second time to Frank Marion Thurman of Detroit in 1883 and had two additional children.

Thurman's first known work with the temperance movement was in 1873, when she was among the first of the band known as the Blue Ribboners. The women lectured on temperance, and she was among those who joined the Woman's Christian Temperance Union (WCTU) when it was formed. Thurman was one of its most popular, dedicated, and successful lecturers. Her work at that time was largely confined to Indiana, Illinois, and Michigan, and wholly among whites. Thurman is known as the first black American woman to attend a convention of the Temperance Union. The 1893 WCTU convention was held in conjunction with the 1893 World's Fair, where Thurman was elected Superintendent of Temperance Work Among Colored People. This association required her to travel to California and every southern state in performance of her duties. While in the South she concentrated on lectures in the schools. Her reputation and performance earned her a place as a delegate to the World WCTU convention held in England in 1896, where she was a guest in the home of Lady Henry Somerset. When Frances Willard, a white woman who headed the Women's Christian Temperance Union, died in 1898, Thurman served as one of the honor guards at the funeral.

Thurman had a keen interest in women's clubwork. In 1898 she organized the Michigan State Association of Colored Women and was elected its first president. She served the association in this capacity for several years—1898-1909. Her work took her to women's groups throughout the country to help organize groups for the improvement of family life and educational opportunities, for programs to advance women, and to improve the quality of life and care for the elderly. With the assistance of other interested women, a Phillis Wheatley Home was organized in Michigan.

Clubwork Reflects Thurman's View on Temperance

Thurman took an active role in the national club movement. When the NACW met in Chicago in 1898, she lectured on"The Relation of the WCTU to the Home." She was elected chairperson of the Ways and Means Committee for the period 1901-1904 and reelected to serve from 1904 to 1906. From 1906 to 1908 Thurman was the third national president of the National Association of Colored Women. Presiding at the sixth biennial session held in the Concord Baptist Church, Brooklyn, New York, August 24-29, 1908, she urged the convention to "strive for the White Ribbon Standard for all our homes. There must be bands of white ribbons throughout the National" (Wesley, 66). During the convention Thurman received a flag and "the occasion reached a climax when, upon receiving the flag, Mrs. Thurman waved it and the audience joined heartily in singing 'My Country 'Tis of Thee'" (Wesley, 67). By the end of the convention, which also marked the end of her term, she had been elected honorary president for life, along with Mary Church Terrell and Josephine Silone Yates. During her presidency the NACW's Department of Temperance became highly developed, and the association's work was enhanced in the areas of "suffrage, health, business education, railroad travel, anti-lynching, literature, art, and night school" ("Ain't I A Woman," 17). Thurman visited the Oregon Association of Colored Women, organized in 1899, and probably stressed the importance of temperance. The Oregon women established a temperance union and named it for her in 1911. Thurman in 1912 sent invitations to all black women of Portland to meet on January 1, 1912, to encourage them to join NACW. By June 14, they had done so.

Retiring from her career of service in 1910, Thurman continued to influence the community. In 1933 a branch of the Young Women's Christian Association was opened at 569 East Elizabeth at St. Antoine in Detroit and was named in her honor. Like other black branches, the Lucy Thurman YWCA provided housing for black women. Facilities included sixty-five residential rooms, a pool, gymnasium, cafeteria, and conference rooms. In recent years the Lucy Thurman Branch became an alcoholic treatment center and represents the interest in service to humankind that Thurman's activities and interests embraced.

On March 29, 1918, this dedicated clubwoman and temperance leader died. She is buried in Evergreen Cemetery in Jackson, Michigan. Her grave is identified with a marker on which are inscribed the words "Erected by the Michigan Association of Colored Womens' Clubs"—a fitting tribute to one who was committed to work with black women and black issues.

References

Ain't I A Woman. An exhibition catalog of the Museum of African American History. Detroit: Museum of African American History, 1989.

Brown, Hallie Q., *Homespun Heroines and Other Women of Distinction.* Xenia, Ohio: Aldine Pub. Co., 1926.

Salem, Dorothy. "Foundations for Organized Reform." In *To Better Our World: Black Women in Organized Reform, 1890-1920.* New York, Carlson, 1990.

Wesley, Charles Harris. *The History of the National Association of Colored Women's Clubs.* Washington: NACW, 1984.

Jessie Carney Smith

Sue Thurman

(1903-)

Editor, religious worker, lecturer, community worker

A tireless promoter of spirirual and social uplift for black Americans and for all peoples of the world, Sue Bailey Thurman's accomplishments, both as an individual and in tandem with her husband, Howard Thurman, are too numerous and varied to fit readily into a summary. Her most notable achievements, however, may be helping to establish the first integrated church in the United States and being the first black woman to discuss nonviolent resistance as a political weapon with Mahatma Gandhi.

Thurman was born in Pine Bluff, Arkansas, the youngest of ten children of Susie (Ford) Bailey and Isaac George Bailey. At the time, a sister, Dorcas, and a brother, Isaac, were the only survivors. Her maternal grandmother was Elvie Ford, who was the slave housekeeper/mistress of Thomas Ford, a plantation owner in Mississippi. Her paternal grandparents were Virginia and Perry Bailey. He was a former slave, and she a Cherokee Indian.

Thurman's parents were dedicated workers in the community. Her mother, who had found a way to get an education for herself, tried to set up schools in the country to teach former slaves. Her father, who was about ten years old at the time of Emancipation, later became a minister. He was in the Arkansas legislature for a time and noted the lack of schools for black children. Determined to organize one, he founded an academy in Dermott, Arkansas, for high school students, both male and female, to prepare them to go on to college. Thurman's, brother, Isaac was a graduate. Her father died when she was ten years old. When Mrs. Bailey died in 1948, Thurman was the only child still living.

After her father's death, her mother no longer had a close connection with the academy other than to help them whenever she could. She held adult education classes for women in her home. She decided that there was insufficient educational opportunity for her daughter and in 1914 sent her to Nannie Burroughs School for Girls in Washington, D.C. Isaac Bailey was in Washington studying medicine, and her mother felt that it would help Thurman to be near a member of the family.

At the age of thirteen, Thurman went to Spelman Seminary (now Spelman College) in Atlanta, Georgia. She finished in three years, in 1919. While there she met Howard Thurman; she was a senior at Spelman, and he a sophomore at Morehouse College. Both were involved in other close friendships at the time. She also was friends with Katie Kelly, who later became Howard Thurman's first wife. After finishing Spelman she applied for admission to Oberlin College, which had been suggested by a friend of her brother. The college required additional preparation in Latin and mathematics, which she took at Morehouse.

She enrolled at Oberlin, studying American culture and at the same time taking music education with piano in the conservatory. Although the college was considered liberal, open to women and minorities, only two black girls could live in the dormitory at one time. But because of the international nature of the student body, this was the first time in her life that Thurman had an opportunity to form friendships without regard to race or color.

Thurman graduated from Oberlin Conservatory in 1926, the first black student to receive the bachelor of science in music degree. After an additional summer session, she received her liberal arts degree from the college. While a student at Oberlin, Thurman was president of the International Club and cochair of the World Fellowship Committee of the YWCA. She served as the first president of the Negro Student Forum.

After her graduation from Oberlin, the composer R. Nathaniel Dett, who was director of the music department at Hampton Institute (now University) in Virginia, offered her a teaching position. Many of the teachers were white women from the North, and many had not finished college. She stayed two years, in the morning working on a music program for all the Virginia schools, and in the afternoon teaching music at the institute. She also worked as an advisor to the YWCA girls on campus. Thurman knew early that she would not stay in music, as she was being pulled in a spiritual direction. In her second year at Hampton, she could feel disturbance in the air. The students protested and struck over various issues. Although most of the teachers separated themselves from the situation, Thurman supported and helped the women students find places to stay when they were expelled and the school closed. It reopened in three weeks. In the summer of 1928, under the auspices of the World Christian Student Federation, she went to Europe with a YWCA group.

In 1930, at the age of twenty-six, Thurman took a position as a traveling secretary of the national staff of the YWCA, working out of New York City. She was invited because staff members felt that she had at least tried to do something for the striking students at Hampton. Her job was to work with women's student groups on the campuses of the black colleges. For two years one of her companions on these travels was Benjamin Mays, who later became president of Morehouse College. He was working in a similar capacity with the YMCA. Howard Thurman was often invited to be a speaker at the YWCA and YMCA state conferences. It was at a Spelman College dinner that he and Sue Thurman met again on a more personal level.

At one of the national conferences of YWCA and YMCA student volunteers in 1931 in Detroit, the hotel had promised integrated facilities. The hotel reneged on this promise, and Thurman decided to move into the Phillis Wheatley residence, the black YWCA. A few delegates went with her. Reinhold Niebuhr, later a professor of theology at Union Theological Seminary; Buell Gallagher, later in his life president of Talladega College; and others decided to take a stand on her behalf to force the YWCA and YMCA to think about their roles as Christian organizations.

Howard Thurman's first wife died in 1930 after a long illness. He was married to Sue Bailey on June 12, 1932, at King's Mountain, North Carolina. They were the parents of two daughters, Olive, born in 1927 from his first marriage, and Anne, born in 1933. Thurman's life has been very much intertwined with that of her husband. There seems to have been no separation of interests or goals; theirs was a true partnership.

Thurmans Learn Ideas of Nonviolent Resistance

Howard Thurman was professor of theology and dean of the chapel of Howard University from 1932 to 1944. The Howard University Faculty Wives group was organized under Sue Thurman's leadership to serve as hostesses to the many students and international visitors. Leaving the children in Geneva, Switzerland, with her sister-in-law, Madaline

Thurman, from October 1935 to April 1936, she and Howard Thurman and others, as guests of the Student Christian Federation, went on a "pilgrimage of friendship" to Burma, Ceylon, and India. They visited forty-five university centers. They met the poet Rabindranath Tagore, and Thurman took classes at his university, Santineeketan, in Bengal. She was the first black woman to have an audience with Gandhi and to discuss with him nonviolent resistance in the struggle for political freedom. He presented to the Thurmans a cloth that was to be brought back to the United States as a token of love for the students, and especially for the black people of America. At the end of the meeting, Thurman sang two Negro spirituals for Gandhi. After their return, she lectured in colleges and universities in the United States and Canada on "The Beauties of Indian Civilization." She used the proceeds for scholarships to enable young black women to study in India at Tagore's university. Both she and her husband lectured on the idea of nonviolent resistance.

The Thurmans returned also with a vision of a new kind of church. Dr. Alfred Fisk, a Presbyterian minister, had gathered together a small group of people of different ethnic backgrounds. Looking for a black co-pastor, he asked Howard Thurman for a recommendation. The Thurmans saw this as a possible realization of their idea of a church and decided to go themselves. She felt that what she had done at Howard University was in preparation for this work. Beginning in 1944 with only a one-year leave of absence granted by the university, the Thurmans spent ten years of their lives working with the Reverend Fisk to establish the Church for the Fellowship of All Peoples in San Francisco, the first completely integrated church in America. Sue Thurman served as the chairperson of the Intercultural Workshop. She also established the Adventures in Friendship department in the church, which sent a delegation to the Fourth Plenary session of UNESCO in Paris.

Thurman has been involved in the community wherever she lived. In 1940 she was the founder-editor of the *Aframerican Women's Journal*, a publication of the National Council of Negro Women in Washington, D.C. She also founded and was the first chairperson of the organization's library, archives, and museum department. While at Howard University, she made connections between academe and the black community through exhibits and writing and lecturing on African-American history. She has been on the board and served as chairperson of the YWCA's World Fellowship Committee in Boston, San Francisco, and Washington. She also participated in international student centers in Cambridge and San Francisco.

President Harold Case asked Howard Thurman to come to Boston University in 1953 as a professor of theology. He also offered him the opportunity to become dean of Marsh Chapel, the highest administrative position for a black in a large university. At Boston University from 1953 to 1964, Sue Thurman organized the Faculty Wives Hostess Committee for Service to International Students. She was the first chairperson, and editor of the organization's *International Cuisine* (Boston, Kairos Press, 1957). Sales of the cookbook enabled the group to establish a loan fund for international students at the university. She was chairperson of the World Refugee Arts and Crafts Program of the Women's Committee of Marsh Chapel and served on the board of the Boston University Women's Council.

It was through Thurman's efforts that the black poet Phillis Wheatley was honored on the 175th anniversary of her death. Tenor Roland Hayes, poet Georgia Douglas Johnson, and sculptor Meta Warrick Fuller were among the guests of honor. Later Harriet Tubman was honored at Marsh Chapel in a similar manner. As she had been at Howard University, Thurman was hostess to Boston University's numerous local, national, and international guests. In 1963 Thurman and her daughter Anne Thurman Chiarenza created a map, "Freedom Trails of Negro History in Boston." While living in Boston, she also was on the boards of the Harriet Tubman Community House and the South End Music Center and founded the Museum of Afro-American History. She is now an honorary president of the museum.

In 1957 Thurman commissioned the noted sculptor Meta Warrick Fuller to create dolls heads representing fourteen famous nineteenth- and twentieth-century black women. Bodies were attached, and the dolls were dressed in clothes of their period. This formed an exhibition that was shown all over the United States. The collection was presented to Spelman College for the International Rooms, which were renamed the Thurman International Rooms in her honor.

After Howard Thurman retired from Marsh Chapel in 1964, the couple traveled with some support from Boston University on a ministry-at-large to Africa and the Far East. They then returned to San Francisco and the Church for the Fellowship of All Peoples. In San Francisco Thurman was for a time director of the African American Historical and Cultural Society, serving for one dollar a year. When an executive director was hired, she then worked as a volunteer on the personnel committee and for the seniors program.

In order to promote international understanding and friendship, Thurman established international library-museum centers at several black colleges. The first three were at Arkansas State College in Pine Bluff, Spelman College, and Livingstone College. The International-Historical Bailey Memorial Room at Arkansas State College was established as a memorial to Sue Thurman's family.

Thurman has received a number of awards, among them a citation from the San Francisco chapter of Theta Sigma Phi, the national honorary journalism fraternity. The Women Graduates Club of Boston University chose her as an honorary member, and she received an honorary doctorate in 1967 from Livingstone College in Salisbury, North Carolina. She has established there the Poets and Dreamers Garden honoring literary and historical figures.

Thurman's writings include "Veena, Lady of India"

Pioneers of Negro Origin in California (San Francisco: ACME Publishing Co., 1949); and the April chapter in the anthology *Meditations for Women* (Nashville: Abingdon Press, 1944, pp. 97-127). Under the sponsorship of the National Council of Negro Women, she compiled and edited *The Historical Cookbook of the American Negro* (Washington, D.C.: NCNW, 1958). She also reported for the press from San Francisco during the organization of the United Nations in 1945.

Both Howard and Sue Thurman's friendships have been wide ranging. The door to their home was always open. She knew the mother of Martin Luther King, Jr., very well, as they had gone to high school together. The Thurmans taught King about nonviolent resistance. They were there for him, Andrew Young, Jesse Jackson, and others in the civil rights movement who turned to them for talk or spiritual sustenance. They knew Channing Tobias, a trustee of Howard University, who had been executive secretary for the YMCA's work with blacks; they knew James Farmer of the Congress of Racial Equality (CORE). They worked with young Byron Rushing, before he became a state representative in Massachusetts, and Henry Hampton, who later became a film producer, in developing the Museum of Afro-American History in Boston. The Thurmans were longtime friends of Edward Carroll and Phenola Carroll, who had accompanied them on the visit to India. Edward later became a bishop of the African Methodist Episcopal Church. The Harold Cases were friends of the Thurmans long before Case became president of Boston University.

After her husband's death in 1981, Thurman took over the care of the Howard Thurman Educational Trust, which he had started in 1964. Originally the idea was to offer grants enabling black students to go to college, but since that time seminars and workshops have been added, as well as the dissemination of Howard Thurman's books and tapes.

Thurman was not only spiritual guide and grounding for her husband, Howard Thurman, and their children, but also for the many thousands of students, friends, and acquaintances whom she has met throughout her life in Washington, Boston, San Francisco, and around the world.

References

Thurman, Sue Bailey. Interview collected for Black Women Oral History Project of Schlesinger Library, Radcliffe College. Photographs of Thurman are a part of the project's files.

Yates, Elizabeth. *Howard Thurman, Portrait of a Practical Dreamer*. New York: Day, 1964.

Ruth Edmonds Hill

Jackie Torrence "The Story Lady"

(1944-)

Storyteller

> There is a new breed of storyteller—the professional—who chooses to make a living travelling throughout the nation spinning tales to all who will listen (Torrence, 280).

This statement by Jackie Torrence introduces an individual who has been on the road as a teller of tales for the past seventeen years. What prompted her to use her creative talents as an outstanding exponent of the oral tradition is a story containing within itself some of the essential ingredients inherent in a folktale.

Born February 12, 1944, in Chicago, Illinois, Torrence spent much of her early childhood on Second Creek near Salisbury, North Carolina. Living in this farming settlement with her grandparents, she experienced both happiness and sadness. Through a warm family relationship with her older kin, she remembered being "surrounded by a family who told lovely old stories" (Smith, 46). With fondness she

Jackie Torrence

recalled her grandfather, Jim Carson, son of a slave. Known affectionately as "Mister Jim," he spun innumerable tales to her as they spent hours together. While her grandmother baked bread in an old wood cookstove, she responded with more tales to her ever curious, questioning granddaughter. From such a legacy Torrence can rightfully claim, "I know stories Uncle Remus never heard of" (Smith, 47).

Her departure from Second Creek occurred when she was ready to enter school in Salisbury. Living with her Aunt Mildred, who had never married, she was a lonely girl who was limited in any opportunities to make friends. In school she endured the taunts and ridicule of her classmates because of a speech impediment. Fortunately for Torrence, she found an outlet from these traumatic experiences through the sensitive intervention of two dedicated teachers. In a poignant reflective note, she recalls these bittersweet days:

> You see, I was a fat child, had no daddy, and felt unattractive. . . . In the fifth grade, I realized I didn't talk like everyone else. I had a speech impediment [and] . . . whenever I began to talk, it sounded as though I had rocks in my mouth, and the other kids laughed at me. I was shattered (Smith, 47).

Helping her to overcome this obstacle and to regain a sense of self-worth, her teacher, Pauline Pharr, encouraged her to write stories that she would read to the class as a substitute for Torrence. Together, these two shared her creative efforts with the other children, and, for once, Torrence became a figure in her own right.

Through an accident when she was struck in her mouth with a thrown bottle, it was discovered that Torrence had a dental abnormality. She had impacted teeth—an unusual occurrence of a complete set of extra teeth in her mouth that prevented her from speaking clearly. When this defect was corrected, her ability to express herself improved over the next four years in high school. This progress was made during and after school hours with the careful guidance and selfless support of her English teacher, Abna Aggrey Lancaster. In a personal tribute to this extraordinary individual, Torrence called her:

> one of the most incredible people I have ever met, says that in me she found an eagle among her chickens. She worked with me day and night and Saturdays to change my speech. She will tell you that she never taught school, she taught students. (Lanker, 125).

Torrence added:

> Mrs. Lancaster gave me the courage to stand in front of an audience and to say what I wanted to say and do what I wanted to do (Smith, 48).

The ability to perform before an audience was nurtured during her high school years when she read the Scriptures in the school assembly programs. Completing her secondary education, Torrence matriculated at Livingstone College. Finding sororities too expensive, she became a member of the Drama Club, where she starred in the play *A Raisin in the Sun*. Encouraged by her success in this venture, she cherished the afterglow of this event; however, her college days ended before she graduated. Marrying a ministerial student, Torrence was confronted with the rigors of a difficult existence as she and her husband went from one southern community to another, from one impoverished church to another.

For a period of eight years their church-related odyssey compelled them to travel throughout Georgia, Mississippi, Arkansas, Oklahoma, and Texas. It was in Little Rock, Arkansas, that Torrence assumed a new role during the absence of her husband. She fulfilled the pastoral duties, reading the Scriptures, praying, and usually relating a Bible story. She recalled:

> . . . when I told the congregation a Bible story, I thought I was teaching. I didn't know—didn't have no idea under the sun—that I was *storytelling* (Smith, 49).

Realizing with regret that her marriage was unsuccessful, Torrence returned to North Carolina, where she left her daughter, Lori, in the care of her mother in Granite Quarry. Seeking employment in High Point, North Carolina, she became an uncertified reference librarian in the public library until a chance event helped to chart for her a new and exciting future.

Storytelling Career Evolves

On a snowy day in 1972 the children's librarian was ill and the library director approached her. The scenario remains vivid in her memory:

> He said, "The storyteller's not here. There's nobody to tell and the children are yellin' and screamin'. Will you tell 'em a story?"
>
> I was a reference librarian. I had never told a story at the library before. "No, I have a stack of questions to answer and telephone calls to make."
>
> But he begged me. Then he bribed me, "I'll give you an extra hour off, any time you choose, if you'll just do it for me!" So, reluctantly, I went into the children's department. . . . I was terrified (Smith, 49-50).

What followed next had far-reaching repercussions for Torrence. The youngsters' reception of her stories from Richard Chase's, *The Grandfather Tales* was overwhelming. From this well-received storytime with three- and four-year-old children, a new career eventually evolved. In subsequent weeks Torrence charmed countless audiences in the library as she became the full-time storyteller, known affectionately as "The Story Lady." With a fast-growing reputation and repertoire of stories, Torrence lured large crowds into the library, eager to fall under the spell of her telling. Within a short time her skills as a raconteur brought her numerous requests to present programs in neighboring communities. Now she was faced with a dilemma. She had a choice of relinquishing her free-lance engagements and confining her storytelling activities to the library or of resigning. Faced with this decision and experiencing some trepidation, Torrence severed her relationship with the library.

In succeeding years Torrence has excelled as a storyteller, giving unstintingly of herself and adding luster to the revival of the old art of storytelling. Traveling throughout the United States, Canada, Hawaii, England, and Mexico, she has revealed hitherto unexplored worlds of wonder to eager listeners in storytelling festivals, at schools, colleges and universities, and through radio, television, and recordings. In an April 1980 article from the *Wall Street Journal* titled "Br'er Possum, Meet Br'er Snake, but You Better Be Careful" Torrence remarked:

> many people think storytelling and storytellers are weird. Somehow they think it's not a legitimate thing to do. It's like being a shepherd. What do you say to a shepherd? "Where's your flock?"

On the stage she notes: "I can't wait to tell the stories. . . ." When the performance ends, she says, "I feel like I'm waking up from a very beautiful night's sleep."

What does a storyteller of Torrence's stature relate? Her selections are broad and come from varied sources; however, she is well-known for her retelling of tall tales, ghost stories, African-American tales, and Appalachian lore. Recognizing the reluctance of many tellers to use the Uncle Remus stories as recorded in heavy dialect by Joel Chandler Harris, she feels that these tales are an indigenous part of American lore and the legacy of the African-American:

> As a teaching tool, the tales implied great morals when they told of the sly ways the slaves had outsmarted the master; they were warning devices and were used as signals to those who were hiding—needing information about people who could and would help.
>
> . . . why do we resent them now? The fact that the tales came from the evil days of slavery could be a major reason. We also seem to be uncomfortable with the imagery in the stories, and we seem to be uncomfortable with the dialect and with their overall ideals. Whatever the reason, we are making a grave mistake. These stories are important to the black as well as to the white heritage of America. . . . (Torrence, 282-83).

A distinguished raconteur, Torrence has insights on the merits and value of perpetuating the art of storytelling. Considering the use of language as a vehicle to transport listeners into distant times and places, she realizes that understanding will come when the heart is touched. In tribute to her heritage, she acknowledges:

> I am proud to know that my ancestry was from Africa. I'm proud that my great-grandparents were slaves and they made it through. They must have been strong, because I'm here. . . . If it had not been for storytelling, the black family would not have survived. . . . I wish you could see all my uncles and aunts when we get together and the stories come out. They are storytellers on a higher level than I will ever be (Lanker, 125).

An audience waits, their eyes focused upon Torrence, who sits comfortably; then, in a quiet moment, all are mesmerized as they hear her say, "Once upon a time. . . ."

References

"Br'er Possum, Meet Br'er Snake, but You Better Be Careful." *Wall Street Journal*, 4 April 1980.

Lanker, Brian. *I Dream a World.* New York: Stewart, Tabori and Chang, 1989.

National Directory of Storytelling, 1990. Jonesborough, Tenn.: National Association for the Preservation and Perpetuation of Storytelling, 1990.

Smith, Jimmy Neil, ed. *Homespun: Tales from America's Favorite Storytellers.* New York: Crown, 1988.

Storytelling, 1990, Catalog of Storytelling Resources. Jonesborough, Tenn.: National Association for the Preservation and Perpetuation on Storytelling, 1990. A photograph of Torrence appears on p. 6.

Torrence, Jackie. "Storytelling." *Horn Book* 69 (February 1983): 280-83.

Wellner, Cathy. "Paying Your Dues: An Interview with Jackie Torrence." *National Storytelling Journal* 2 (Summer 1985): 12-13 Includes a photograph of Torrence.

Spencer G. Shaw

Geraldine "Deenie" Pindell Trotter

(1872-1918)

Editor, entrepreneur, activist, civic worker

Dedicated to the cause of equal rights, Geraldine Pindell Trotter worked as copartner with her husband, William

Geraldine "Deenie" Pindell Trotter

Monroe Trotter. She was active also in areas of her own interests and was involved in much public-spirited work. An able newspaperwoman and public speaker, she moved in Boston's prominent, elite black militant circles as supporter and activist and reached thousands of people through her work as associate manager, coeditor, and society editor of the *Boston Guardian*, an organ for equal rights for black Americans. The *Guardian* was founded by her husband who, along with W. E. B. Du Bois and their adversary, Booker T. Washington, were considered three of America's most important spokespersons at the time. While Monroe Trotter has been labeled "the precursor of the Negro Protest Movement of the twentieth century" (book jacket), he was successful possibly only through the support of Geraldine Pindell Trotter—his vocal and active partner.

Geraldine Louise Pindell Trotter, known to her friends as "Deenie," was born on October 3, 1872, the daughter of Charles E. and Mary Pindell. She is known to have had at least one sister and a foster brother. The Pindell family had a tradition of racial militancy. Her uncle, William Pindell, led a successful fight to integrate Boston's schools in the 1850s. Trotter attended grammar school in Everett, Massachusetts, and continued her education in the Boston schools. For ten years she was bookkeeper and stenographer for Eli Cooley, a china decorator, until she married.

As a child, she had known William Monroe Trotter, who was only six months older than she. She had also dated W. E. B. Du Bois, who remained her good friend through her life. William Monroe Trotter (1872-1934) was the only son of James Monroe Trotter and Virginia (Isaac) Trotter. Two other Trotter children died in infancy. The affluent, race-conscious James Monroe Trotter was known for his political interests, his position as recorder of deeds for the United States government, and perhaps more popularly, as author of *Music and Some Highly Musical People*, published in 1878, which quickly sold more than seven thousand copies. James Trotter was a "demanding patriarch" and set high expectations for his children. They had associated with the Archibald Grimkés and other prominent black families of the Boston area. Monroe Trotter lived up to his father's expectations, entered Harvard in fall 1891, stood third in his freshman class of 376, and in his junior year was elected to Phi Beta Kappa—the first black at Harvard elected to this prestigious honor society—and graduated in 1894 magna cum laude.

Monroe Trotter, "one of the young luminaries in Boston's polite Negro society," was "prestigiously educated, talented, handsome, and heir to a small fortune" (Fox, 21). He was active in the exclusive black literary group, the Omar Khayyam Circle, that met at the Cambridge home of schoolteacher Maria L. Baldwin. About this time he became serious in his relationship with Geraldine Pindell. Trotter had seen Geraldine Pindell occasionally during his college days at Harvard. The petite, vivacious, blond, blue-eyed, fair-skinned, and fragile Geraldine Pindell nearly died of pneumonia in 1895. When William Trotter's class day was held at Harvard the following spring, she was still weak but attended the activity. Her relationship with William Trotter strengthened after he escorted her home from a party and kissed her goodnight. Trotter later wrote that he "found his love for once and for all time" (Fox, 22).

William Trotter and Geraldine Pindell were married on June 27, 1899, and moved to their new home at 97 Sawyer Avenue in Dorchester. The site has been described as "on top of a hill in a previously white neighborhood" (Fox, 23). Trotter later wrote: "From the sitting room window" they could see "over all the country as far as Blue Hill and from my bed-room window all the bay down to the red building on Deer Island" (in Fox, 23). From the start the marriage was a happy one, and the childless couple apparently had no serious conflicts in life together. "She was to become a major source of strength for him in the troubled days which lay ahead" (Puttkammer, 5).

Monroe Trotter's Harvard degree and Phi Beta Kappa key by no means provided an entrée into the Boston job market, for the racial barriers there would not be penetrated. An offer to teach at a segregated school in Washington, D.C., was unappealing to Trotter who preferred a business career in the Boston area. After a stint with a white real estate firm, in 1899 he opened his own insurance business and soon owned several pieces of property. Like his father, he and Geraldine Trotter lived and worked among white people as Monroe Trotter dabbled in politics while maintaining his elitist black militancy. The Trotters became active in a number of local groups. For example, in March 1901 Monroe Trotter helped to found the Boston Literary and Historical Association, which became a forum for militants. Among lecturers to the group were Du Bois, Charles Waddell Chesnutt, Kelly Miller, and Maria Baldwin. White sympathizers who attended included George Washington Cable, Oswald Garrison

Villard (of the New York *Evening Post*), and William Lloyd Garrison, Jr. Trotter also joined the Massachusetts Racial Protective Association.

On November 9, 1901, the first issue of the *Guardian*, Monroe Trotter's newspaper, was published. For a few years of their marriage, Geraldine Trotter enjoyed a comfortable, unencumbered life with the young, enterprising, rising young businessman. Monroe Trotter was aggressive and uncompromising in racial reform activities and capable of producing large quantities of work within the arenas of his interest, and the Trotters abandoned the pleasures normally found in the home to devote their full energies to agitation for equal rights. Geraldine Trotter "protested mildly" when he established the *Guardian*, particularly because it made more demands on his time and caused him to extend his hours away from home. She also opposed his abandoning his real estate business but later understood and appreciated the paper's cause (Puttkammer, 8, 12).

Beginning in about 1900, Trotter became a leading critic of Booker T. Washington as leader of the race. He saw Washington and his followers, the Bookerites, as subservient to Southern whites, while Washington viewed Trotter and his followers, the Trotterites, as radicals. They had vastly opposing views on education for blacks and on political issues as well, and they became extraordinarily bitter toward each other. On July 30, 1903, Trotter and several Trotterites were involved in a protest against Booker T. Washington called the "Boston Riot," in which Trotter interrupted a public meeting of the National Negro Business League held at the Columbus Avenue African Methodist Episcopal (AME) Church by reading from a list of questions to challenge Washington. Claims were made that Trotter aimed to prevent Washington from speaking. Trotter and his sister, Maude, were arrested, but soon bailed out by his mother. Later, he spent thirty days in jail for the so-called riot.

Influential Editor Manages Newspaper

Geraldine Trotter considered the circumstances surrounding Monroe Trotter's imprisonment crucial and started working for the *Guardian* as accountant. She also helped with the society columns. "Quite, almost invariably, she became his most important supporter and co-worker. By 1905 she could speak from her own experience, on the needs of making personal sacrifices in the greater interest of the race" (*Guardian,* 28 December 1914, 4, quoted in Fox, 80). By then her activism had become firmly entrenched. Geraldine Trotter and the Trotter friends kept the paper going.

By 1905, Du Bois and Trotter, still in harmony with each other, had been the power behind a group of twenty-nine black men in the founding of the Niagara Movement. In fact, Trotter's *Guardian*, according to Kelly Miller, was so influential that he almost single-handedly created the climate that made it possible. In 1906 Du Bois organized a "woman's auxiliary of the movement" (Fox, 103). Although Trotter supported women's suffrage, he opposed sexual parity and saw women as followers rather than leaders (*Guardian* 18 October 1902). He thus opposed the admission of women to this movement. In time, however, as he continued to depend more and more on Geraldine Trotter and recognized other talented black women in Boston, he compromised and agreed that Geraldine Trotter should join. She resigned in August due to internal strife in the group. By 1909 the Niagara Movement has lost momentum, and the next year it was totally ineffective and gave way to the newly-formed National Association for the Advancement of Colored People (NAACP).

For the next ten years, there were other rival factions that affected the *Guardian* and the Trotters. The *New York Age* was perhaps chief among these factions: It was a rival newspaper, and it attacked Trotter and the *Guardian*. Trotter continued the attacks on inequality and segregation; for a while he was active in the NAACP but soon kept his distance and was never known to be fully committed to it. During this period there also existed rapidly-growing ill-will between Trotter and Du Bois, possibly accounting for Trotter's lack of enthusiasm for the NAACP, which Du Bois helped to found.

By 1916 Trotter's health was impaired from a heavy work load. While he was hospitalized for two weeks and recuperated for several additional weeks at home, publication of the *Guardian* was not interrupted. Geraldine Trotter commented that, while Trotter did some work during his illness, "it does him no good" (Fox, 211). Her commitment to the *Guardian* and to correcting racial problems matched her husband's. Her work with the *Guardian* after the Boston Riot and Trotter's imprisonment helped her to see firsthand the harsh realities of racial agitation. In 1905, when Bostonians held several centennial celebrations to honor the birth of William Lloyd Garrison, she spoke on the need for self-sacrifice. She said: "That is the great lesson we Colored people should learn. . . . Those of us who have had the advantages of education, who have seen life in its broadest light, [should] be willing to sacrifice . . . to do for our own down-trodden people all in our power . . . to make their cause our cause, their suffering our suffering" ("The Celebration of the One Hundredth Anniversary . . . of William Lloyd Garrison," 14, cited in Fox, 212).

The *Guardian* and its persuasive power was possibly the Trotters' central focus in life. The newspaper was an obsession with them, perhaps the replacement they needed for the children they never had. Geraldine Trotter was a partner in the truest sense, spending her time as bookkeeper, subscriptions clerk, billing clerk, editor of the society columns, and attending to other matters of management while Monroe Trotter busied himself in his various activist groups in Boston and the business attendant to such work. Geraldine Trotter's versatility was seen in her activities beyond the *Guardian* as well. Her civic interests were important to her. She was fundraiser for the Saint Monica's Home for elderly black women. Geraldine Trotter was executive chairperson of the Boston Literary Association and arranged the loving cup presentation to Moorfield Storey in Faneuil Hall. Storey was a Trotter supporter and at one time president of the NAACP. She organized a women's antilynching committee and was a member of the National Equal Rights League, which Monroe Trotter helped to found. She addressed the needs of black soldiers at Camp Devens during World War I and was successful in her petition to release from prison William Hill, a veteran of James Monroe Trotter's Fifty-fifth Regiment, who served forty years of a life sentence. She secured pardons for several other black inmates at the state prison. She presented the national colors to the 519th Engineers at Fort Devens on behalf of the state. She organized the Godmother's Association to this, the only black unit that went overseas from Massachusetts, and was a member of the Soldier's Comfort Unit and Sunday hostess at its War Service Center. "Her last act was to send fruit to the colored soldiers at Camp Devens who were ill with influenza" ("Funeral of Mrs. G. L. Trotter," 1).

In fall 1918 Geraldine Trotter fell victim to the influenza epidemic that spread across Camp Devens and the nation. After seeming to rally, the petite and frail warrior died on October 8, 1818—just five days after her forty-sixth birthday—in the same house where she had married Monroe Trotter. Her obituary gives October 9 as the date of her death. A communicant of Saint Mary's Episcopal Church in Dorchester, her funeral was held from her home at 97 Sawyer Avenue in Dorchester. "Few members of her race were better known," said the *Boston Post* ("Funeral of Mrs. G. L. Trotter," 1).

On the death of Geraldine Trotter, her longtime friend W. E. B. Du Bois said:

> She never hesitated or wavered, and she yielded every little temptation of home and dress and company and leisure for the narrow office and late hours of public life; yet through it all she shone clear and fine, and died as one whom death cannot conquer (Quoted in Fox, 213).

Monroe Trotter, devastated over the death of his wife and coeditor of his newspaper, wrote:

> To my Fallen Comrade, Geraldine L. Trotter, my Loyal wife, who is no more. To honoring her memory, who helped me so loyally, faithfully, conscientiously, unselfishly, I shall devote my remaining days; and to perpetuating the Guardian and my Equal Rights cause and work for which she made such noble, and total sacrifice, I dedicate the best that is in me till I die" (*Crisis* 17, 75; *Guardian* 28 December 1918, 4; 15 February 1919).

The Guardian's editorial page published her photograph for many years afterward.

References

Fox, Stephen R. *The Guardian of Boston: William Monroe Trotter*. New York: Atheneum, 1970.

"Funeral of Mrs. G. L. Trotter." *Boston Post* 13 October 1918. Reprinted. *Washington Bee*, 19 October 1918. 1.

Guardian, 18 October 1902; 28 December 1918, 15 February 1919.

"Men of the Month." *Crisis* 17 (December 1918): 75. Includes photograph.

Puttkammer, Charles W., "William Monroe Trotter: An Evaluation of the Life of a Radical Negro Newspaper Editor, 1901-1934." Senior Thesis, Department of History, Princeton University, April 17, 1958. Microfilm.

Puttkammer, Charles W., and William Worthy. "William Monroe Trotter." *Journal of Negro History* 43 (October 1958): 298-316.

Jessie Carney Smith

Sojourner Truth

(1797-1883)

Abolitionist, women's rights activist, lecturer, religious leader

One of the most famous nineteenth-century black American women, Sojourner Truth, like Harriet Tubman, was an uneducated former slave known for active opposition to slavery. A tall, big, raw-boned black woman, Truth is

Sojourner Truth

admired for her ability to voice fearlessly and pungently the necessary truths that her fellow, self-censoring abolitionists and feminists probably dared not conceive and certainly could not utter. Over the years she has stood for the nexus connecting race and sex in liberal reform. As a symbol of the unintimidated, articulate black woman, Truth both reminds black Americans that black women have gender as well as racial self-interests and refuses to let white feminists forget that black women are women too. Even though she never learned to read or write and could not generate the books, letters, or other historical documents that usually guarantee historical longevity, she is one of a very small number of Americans whose reputations have endured more than a century after their deaths.

Having begun to gain recognition as a gifted preacher around New York City in the 1830s, Isabella Van Wagenen, or Sojourner Truth, is remembered today as a prophetic presence on the antislavery and women's rights lecture circuit in the 1840s and 1850s. Truth symbolized enslaved black women in predominantly white reform movements that portrayed "the slave" as male and "woman" as middle- or upper-class and white.

Truth was born a slave to James and Elizabeth (Mau-Mau Bett) Baumfree in 1797 in Ulster County, New York, the second youngest of ten or twelve children. As a child, Truth belonged to several owners before being sold in 1810 to her longtime master, John Dumont of New Paltz. At an unknown date, Truth married an older slave named Thomas, who also belonged to Dumont, with whom she had five children. Shortly after her emancipation by New York State law in 1827, Truth left her children with her husband on Dumont's place. Several years later Thomas died in a workhouse.

Truth had three pivotal experiences in 1826 and 1827. Her youngest child, Peter, was sold and transported illegally to Alabama. She secured the assistance of Ulster County Quakers, who helped her successfully bring suit to secure his return. This was the first instance in which Truth showed that she would not be one of slavery's passive victims. She was willing to take the initiative and go to extraordinary lengths to secure her rights, no matter how circumscribed.

In 1826 she also seized her own freedom by leaving John Dumont and spending a year in the employ of Maria and Isaac Van Wagenen. During this same period she underwent a conversion experience, in which she recognized Jesus as her "intercessor" to the more remote figure of God, of whose existence her mother had taught her. Following this third important episode, Truth joined a Methodist church in Kingston where she made the acquaintance of a Miss Grear, who took her to New York City in about 1828.

In New York, Truth attended the predominantly white John Street Methodist Church and the black African Methodist Episcopal Zion Church. She also began to forge a reputation as a gifted Methodist preacher and visionary at the camp meetings that were frequently held around New York City during the Second Great Awakening. Grear introduced Truth to James Latourette, who brought her to the Magdalene Asylum, a mission of middle-class New Yorkers to prostitutes on Bowery Hill. Truth spent only a short time with the Magdalene Asylum but continued her acquaintance with a coworker there, Elijah Pierson, with whom she stayed on as a household worker.

Through Pierson, Truth met Robert Matthews, an American of Scottish descent, who by then called himself Matthias. Matthews had been an itinerant preacher in and around Albany in the late 1820s. In 1830 he had declared himself a prophet and a Jew and had taken the name Matthias. Truth became one of his followers in 1832. With Pierson's support he established a "kingdom," a sort of religious commune, first in New York City, then in Sing Sing, of which Truth was the only black American member.

Truth occupied an anomalous position in Matthias's kingdom. She, like the white members, had contributed her material resources to the commune. Yet she did more than her share of domestic work. The white women in the commune did some housework, but the brunt of the hardest and dirtiest labor fell on Truth. Nonetheless, she was clearly a far more integral member of the commune than a mere domestic drudge. She had joined the kingdom out of religious conviction and stuck with it as a conscious decision. Without her being a leader—the leaders were male—her opinion mattered within the commune. The Matthias kingdom disintegrated in 1835, after spouse-swapping at Matthias's behest and Pierson's death in questionable circumstances. Truth was not involved in the sexual complications, but she was accused and acquitted of poisoning Pierson.

Isabella Becomes Sojourner Truth

Truth remained in New York, taking in washing and doing housework, as she had since her arrival in the city. In 1843, however, she was feeling fed up with urban life, particularly with her inability to save and with the money-grubbing that accompanied the depression following the panic of 1837. As the depression deepened, she was appalled by her own lack of charity toward the poor. Then God spoke to her, commanding her to leave the city and take a new name, Sojourner. She herself took the last name Truth. On June 1, 1843, she left New York and set out, as God instructed her, toward the East. She spoke at camp meetings on Long Island, then crossed over into Connecticut.

It is not an accident that Truth took to the roads to preach when she did. During the year 1843, Millerism—a mass movement in the Northeast that expected the second advent to occur between 1843 and 1844—was at its height. William Miller was a farmer from Vermont and northern New York whose chronology and inspirations closely paralleled, and perhaps stimulated, his neighbor, Robert Matthews. Inspired by a Charles Finney-type revival, Miller, like Matthews, had begun in about 1831 to preach the approaching end of the world. Thanks to the support of a gifted abolitionist organizer from Boston, Miller's message reached hundreds of thousands from Maine to Michigan via a series of widely-distributed periodicals and the words of scores of itinerant preachers who held forth at frequent and massive camp meetings.

Hence when she took the name Sojourner Truth, she did so at a moment when hundreds of Northerners heard God command them to go out and preach their message to others and when large numbers were particularly receptive toward wandering, unlettered, itinerant preachers of many sorts and both sexes. Truth was joining an established tradition of Quaker and Methodist itinerant women preachers, some of whom, like Zilpha Elaw and Jarena Lee, were black. Quite to the point, her new name translates as ''itinerant preacher,'' for Sojourner means temporary visitor and telling the truth, she said, was her mission.

Once she took to the roads, Truth was immediately able to reach large, ready-made audiences at Millerite camp meetings at which she was welcome to preach. Millerites were accustomed to charismatic itinerant preachers, including women, so Truth did not seem entirely strange. Her audiences were not necessarily all confirmed second adventists, for northern evangelical Protestants were generally agitated in 1843, whether or not they were expecting the literal end of the world.

Truth was not a Millerite, and in Connecticut she denounced second adventism as totally wrongheaded. Despite the tongue-lashing, Millerites thought her a gifted, inspired preacher and singer, and they continued to invite her to their homes and meetings. Through invitations that she received at second advent meetings at which she preached, Truth followed a Millerite network up the Connecticut River valley into western Massachusetts.

Millerites steered Truth to the utopian Northampton Association, which seems odd, for second adventists, expecting the world to end momentarily, were not motivated to improve it. But many of them had been active in moral reform, such as antislavery, and the connection between Millerite millennialism and utopianism was also close. When the world failed to end by 1844, disappointed second adventists flocked to utopian communities. The people in the Northampton Association were not millenarians. But they did aim to regenerate the world through reform of the political economy, which in the last several years had been wrenched by a serious panic and deep depression. The Northampton Association was starting on a small scale with the cooperative production of silk.

In the Northampton Association, Sojourner Truth lived with well-off, well-educated people whose main concerns were political. Although she later became disaffected with this version of communal life, at Northampton she encountered Garrisonian abolitionism for the first time. George Benson, the Northampton Association's leading figure, was William Lloyd Garrison's brother-in-law, and the association's residents were reform-minded. Abolitionists and supporters of women's rights, like Garrison and Frederick Douglass, were frequent visitors. Truth embraced abolitionism and women's rights and, when she was ready to leave the commune, found a new means of subsistence in reform-minded audiences. In the late 1840s, she joined the antislavery lecture circuit, speaking and selling personal mementos.

Truth fed and clothed herself and paid off the mortgage on her house in Massachusetts through the sale of *The Narrative of Sojourner Truth*, which an abolitionist, Olive Gilbert, had taken down and which Truth published herself in 1850. A friend in Battle Creek, Michigan, Frances Titus, added new material and published a second edition of the *Narrative* around 1875. For the rest of Truth's life, she supported herself through sales and charitable contributions, which she solicited through antislavery newspapers and collected from the reform-minded audiences who were her market. After she moved to Battle Creek, Michigan, in 1856, she was able to repay mortgages on two buildings through money earned from the Freedmen's Bureau and contributions.

Truth Joins the Abolitionist Circuit

Truth started out on the abolitionist circuit in the late 1840s, initially in company with the British antislavery member of Parliament, George Thompson. In 1850 she attended her first women's rights convention in Worcester, Massachusetts, where she and another former slave soon to gain great prominence, Frederick Douglass, were listed as representatives of the ''enslaved African race.''

In 1851 Truth spoke her first (and now most famous) lines at a women's rights conference in Akron, Ohio, which she had attended primarily to sell copies of her *Narrative*. The standard account of Truth's appearance in Akron (rendered in dialect) is by Frances Dana Gage, who chaired the meeting, and is reprinted in the second edition of Truth's *Narrative* and in the first volume of *History of Woman Suffrage* (1881).

Gage says that Truth sat on the steps of the pulpit—the rest of the audience was in the pews—and said nothing the first day. Several ministers in the audience had denied women's claim to equal rights on account of women's lack of intelligence, the fact that Jesus Christ was a man, not a woman, and the sex of Eve, who had tempted man into original sin. None of the white women in the convention was brave enough to respond to these charges publicly. On the second day, Sojourner Truth stood up and spoke. Her words are well-known, but what is not usually appreciated is the contrast between her self-confidence and the timidity of the white women who had organized the meeting. Whereas Gage herself was apprehensive about chairing a meeting for the first time, Truth had boldly taken a seat at the front of the room. Having won over audiences—welcoming and hostile—at many a camp meeting, Truth was not shy. An experienced preacher, she was well aware of the power of her persona and her words. The white women had failed to answer the ministers who trounced women's rights, but Truth, an uninvited speaker, defended all women in phrases that silenced the male opposition. She said:

> Wall, chilern, whar dar is so much racket dar

> must be somethin' out o' kilter. I tink dat 'twixt de niggers of the Souf and de womin at de Norf, all talkin' 'bout rights, de white men will be in a fix pretty soon. But what's all dis here talkin' 'bout?
>
> Dat man over dar say dat womin needs to be helped into carriages, and lifted over ditches, and to hab de best place everywhar. Nobody eber helps me into carriages, or ober mud-puddles, or gibs me any best place! And a'n't I a woman? Look at me! Look at my arm! (and she bared her right arm to the shoulder, showing her tremendous muscular power). I have ploughed, and planted, and gathered into barns, and no man could head me! And a'n't I a woman? I could work as much and eat as much as a man—when I could get it—and bear de lash as well! And a'n't I a woman? I have borne thirteen chilern, and seen 'em mos' all sold off to slavery, and when I cried out with my mother's grief, none but Jesus heard me! And a'n't I a woman?

Before her 1851 audience, Truth asserted her identity as a woman, even though she was working-class and black. She demanded the broadening of the category of "woman" to include not only those who were treated as ladies but those who, enslaved, could not protect their children. Interestingly enough, in this speech Truth appropriated her mother's tragic experience: Mau-Mau Bett had lost ten or twelve children who were sold away from her. But none of Truth's five children had been sold away from her permanently. This was not to be the only time that Truth heightened the drama of her life as a slave for rhetorical power. In the 1870s she routinely claimed that she had been a slave for forty years—instead of thirty—and that she had suckled white infants, which was more common practice on southern plantations than in Ulster County, New York. As early as 1851, Truth was making herself into the emblematic slave woman.

In Indiana in the fall of 1858 Truth made another memorable gesture before an audience of both sexes, again related to gender. According to a report published in the abolitionist newspaper, the *Boston Liberator*, and republished in the second edition of Truth's *Narrative*, after a hostile minister claimed that she was a man:

> Sojourner told them that her breasts had suckled many a white babe, to the exclusion of her own offspring; that some of those white babies had grown to man's estate; that, although they had sucked her colored breasts, they were, in her estimation, far more manly than they (her persecutors) appeared to be; and she quietly asked them, as she disrobed her bosom, if they, too, wished to suck! In vindication of her truthfulness, she told them that she would show her breast to the whole congregation; that it was not to her shame that she uncovered her breast before them, but to their shame.

Again, the demand was to be seen as a woman, despite her strength.

In the late twentieth century, Truth's remarks and gestures regarding gender, race, and class are her signature. But during the nineteenth century her most famous remark was religious. Today the rhetorical question through which she would not let Frederick Douglass forget God's ultimate goodness is no longer so well-appreciated. It appears in an essay that made Truth widely known in her own lifetime. Harriet Beecher Stowe's "The Libyan Sibyl," was published in the April 1863 issue of the *Atlantic Monthly*.

According to Stowe's report and Douglass's remembrances in his *Life and Times of Frederick Douglass*, Douglass was a speaker at a meeting in Boston. Following the passage of the Fugitive Slave Act of 1850, Douglass had been influenced by the reasoning of his friend, John Brown, who subsequently attempted to instigate a slave revolt in Virginia in 1859. Douglass began to exhort southern slaves to seize their own freedom by force of arms. His advocacy of violent action and his despair shocked Truth, whose faith in God's power was boundless. From the front row of the audience, she asked a rhetorical question that carried all over Faneuil Hall: "Frederick, is God Dead?"

The definition of the historically symbolic figure of Sojourner Truth is completed with her remarks on women's suffrage. During the debates over black and women's suffrage that surrounded the drafting and ratification of the Fourteenth Amendment to the United States Constitution, Truth was one of a minority of black American abolitionists who favored the inclusion of women in the provisions for widened citizenship. While most male and black abolitionists agreed with Frederick Douglass that Reconstruction was the "Negro's hour" and that women should not imperil black suffrage by insisting on women's suffrage immediately, Truth sided with white feminists who advocated the deletion of the word "male" from the Fourteenth Amendment. At an 1867 equal rights convention she noted that in debates over enfranchising black men, no one had thought about black women. Truth held that if black men but not women were enfranchised, "colored men will be masters over the women, and it will be just as bad as it was before" (Stanton, Vol. 2, 193).

Truth lived many more years and was active in public life as an advocate of the cause of ex-slave refugees, but this part of her history has not entered the realm of black American or feminine history. In 1864 she recovered from a bout of ill-health and went to Washington, D.C., where she met President Abraham Lincoln. Truth remained in the Washington area for several years, working alongside former abolitionist colleagues like Josephine Griffing. Ministering to the needs of the freed refugees in the District, Truth worked with the Freedmen's Bureau of the federal government and the private, New York-based National Freedmen's Relief Association in the Freedmen's Village at Arlington Heights, Virginia, and at Freedmen's Hospital.

By the late 1860s she became discouraged about the future of unemployed and impoverished freedpeople in the District of Columbia. Together with friends and colleagues in Battle Creek, Michigan (such as Quaker Henry Willis), and Rochester, New York (such as Isaac and Amy Post), Truth helped several freedpeople relocate and find employment.

Distressed that this piecemeal approach could never solve the overwhelming social and economic problems of the black poor in the Washington area, Truth conceived of a plan by which freedpeople would be allocated government lands in the West. She had a petition drafted to submit to Congress and solicited signatures, beginning in Providence, Rhode Island, in 1870. In the following year she accepted an invitation from a supportive Kansan and visited the state that eight years later would become the goal of migrants from the deep South fearing reenslavement after the end of Reconstruction. She was never able to persuade Congress to take action on her petition.

By the time of the exodus to Kansas in 1879, however, Truth's health had deteriorated badly. Her grandson, Sammy Banks, who had accompanied her over the years and written her letters, had died in Battle Creek in 1875. After several years' painful suffering, Truth died in Battle Creek in 1883 of ulcerated sores on her legs, perhaps from diabetes or gangrene. She is buried in Battle Creek, Michigan.

References

Douglass, Frederick. *Life and Times of Frederick Douglass.* 1892. Reprinted. New York: Bonanza Books, 1962.

Stanton, Elizabeth Cady, et al., eds. *History of Woman Suffrage.* 2 vols. New York: Fowler and Wells, 1881-82.

Stowe, Harriet Beecher. "The Libyan Sibyl." *Atlantic Monthly* 11 (April 1863): 473-81.

Truth, Sojourner, and Olive Gilbert. *The Narrative of Sojourner Truth.* By Olive Gilbert. Privately printed, 1850. 1875/78 ed. Edited by Frances Titus. Battle Creek: Privately printed, 1875/78.

Photographs of Sojourner Truth are to be found in the Sophia Smith Collection, Women's History Archive, at Smith College, the Bentley Library, Michigan Historical Collection of the University of Michigan, and at the Schomburg Center for Research in Black Culture.

Nell Irvin Painter

Harriet Tubman "Moses"

(c. 1820-1913)

Underground railroad conductor, Union scout and spy, nurse, feminist

"I had crossed the line of which I had so long been dreaming. I was free; but there was no one to welcome me to the land of freedom," Harriet Tubman spoke of her accomplishment and the intense loneliness that led to her resolve to free her family and other slaves (Bradford, 31). Although she escaped from slavery, her heart was "down in the old cabin quarters, with the old folks and my brothers and sisters" (Bradford, 32). With this resolve she began her work as a conductor on the Underground Railway, a venture that would last for ten years and make her famous. Tubman made at least fifteen trips from the North into southern slave states, leading over two hundred slaves into free northern states. On her first trip into slave territory, she led her sister, Mary Ann Bowley, and two children to freedom in the North, eventually freeing all her brothers and sisters as well as her parents. Although Harriet Tubman achieved historical importance primarily in this role, she was also a spy, nurse, feminist, and social reformer, if indeed these terms can adequately describe her

Harriet Tubman

various activities during a period of profound racial, social, and economic upheaval in the United States in the nineteenth century.

The term conductor was, of course, a euphemism for guide or leader, as the Underground Railroad was for illegal transportation. These terms have a romantic ring today, but Tubman's work was far from romantic; it was extremely dangerous and demanded great strength and endurance, both physically and mentally. Tubman's physical appearance was decidedly not that of a leader, as she was not an imposing figure like Sojourner Truth, a slave who became a famous orator and feminist. She was of slight build and only five feet tall. Even more curious for a person whose leadership depended upon physical action, Tubman suffered from seizures of sudden and deep sleep because of a head injury received as a young girl. Nevertheless, Tubman possessed leadership qualities that were quickly recognized by the slaves she led to freedom and the abolitionists with whom she worked. Thomas Wentworth Higginson, the author and reformer, called her "the greatest heroine of the age," in an 1859 letter to his mother. "Her tales of adventure are beyond anything in fiction and her ingenuity and generalship are extraordinary. I have known her for some time—the slaves call her Moses" (Conrad, 107).

Tubman made up for her small size through the expedient of carrying a long rifle—a weapon she would use to encourage any slaves who became fainthearted during their journey north as well as to discourage pro-slavers—and her innate leadership abilities. She was not taught to read or write but relied upon her memory, knowledge of nature—the only resource she had at times when guiding slaves under cover of darkness—and natural shrewdness. When some whites expressed unusual curiosity while observing Tubman and some slaves in a small southern town, she bought railway tickets for a train going south. What slave attempting to escape from a southern state would travel south? The ploy was one of a number Tubman would use to elude escape from authorities. Tubman was well versed in the Bible, music, and folklore of her time and place in the South, and her repertoire of biblical verse and song was important in communicating. Harriet Tubman used her strong singing voice to communicate her presence to slaves in the South and to communicate danger or safety to slaves that were hidden while she was scouting their surroundings.

Tubman's unwavering resolve and courage, like that of other great leaders, is more difficult to account for. Scholars and historians can only examine the particular environment and events that produce leaders in particular places at particular times and speculate at the synergy of people, environment, and events. Of her environment, Tubman said, "I grew up like a neglected weed—ignorant of liberty, having no experience of it," when she was interviewed by Benjamin Drew, an educator and part-time journalist, in St. Catherines, Ontario, in the summer of 1855 (Conrad, 73). Although she was ignorant of liberty as a slave, Tubman was nurtured and cared for in a large family. Born in 1820 in Dorchester County near Cambridge, Maryland, one of eleven children of Benjamin and Harriet (Green) Ross, Tubman was called Araminta as a child but later adopted the name of her mother. Tubman had stability of place while growing up, unlike some slaves who were sold to landowners in the deep South, although that stability was constantly under threat. Tubman was hired out for housework for families living near her owner at various times as a young child but was always returned to her family between jobs. While she and her family were subject to the orders of their owner and hired out to neighboring farmers, they were a family unit in which care and support was given and received and in which religion and folklore were shared.

Tubman Examines the Institution of Slavery

Tubman was returned to the care of her family after a severe head injury, an injury that caused recurring seizures of sleep for the rest of her life. The injury had a profound influence on her emotionally as well as physically. When she was about thirteen years of age and working in the field one autumn, one of her fellow slaves left his field work early and went to the general store. The overseer caught up with the man in the store and attempted to bind him for a whipping. As the slave ran out the door, Tubman attempted to shield the man and was knocked unconscious by a two-pound weight the angry overseer had thrown at the running slave. She recovered from the blow, but her convalescence was slow because the injury to her head was serious. While her body was healing, Tubman, raised in a deeply religious family, began praying. While seeking a solution to her condition as a slave, she began to examine that condition and, as well, the institution of slavery in general from a philosophical and practical perspective.

Speaking of this recovery period in her youth to her friend and biographer, Sarah Elizabeth Bradford, Tubman said "And so, as I lay so sick on my bed, from Christmas till March, I was always praying for poor old master. Oh, dear Lord, change that man's heart, and make him a Christian" (Bradford, 23-24). Tubman's prayers changed when she heard that she and her brothers were to be sent in a chain gang to the far South. She prayed, "Lord, if you ain't never going to change that man's heart, kill him, Lord, and take him out of the way, so he won't do no more mischief" (Bradford, 24). When her owner died shortly afterwards, Tubman again changed her prayers. She began praying in different ways and at different times for the Lord to "cleanse her heart of sin," beginning the process of taking control, so much as she could, of her life rather than passively accepting things as they were.

During this period of illness, prayer, and rumors of slave-selling, Tubman began to formulate a personal philosophy that transcended the laws of men. She trusted herself, God, and Divine Providence, in that order. Although she did not formulate this philosophy in a stroke of flashing illumination, it is probable that Tubman's character and intelligence, combined with the experience of her illness, prayer, and changing circumstances, produced an individual who, paradoxically, through both desire and necessity, developed self-reliant courage and strength of purpose. It was Tubman's courage and purpose that led her to become an important figure to both blacks and whites.

Tubman had a calm respite after she slowly healed from her injury. It was during this period that two events took place that are important: she married a free black man, and she discovered that her mother legally should have been freed years earlier upon the death of her former owner. Shortly after her recovery, her father became a valuable laborer for a neighboring timber operator, and Tubman began working for the man, slowly regaining her strength and becoming a valuable laborer also. In 1844, she married John Tubman, a free black in the Cambridge area. Little is known about Tubman's relationship with her husband; there are reports that he was not an ambitious man, and that he thought his wife worried too much about her condition as a slave. While Tubman was reticent about her relationship with John Tubman, she apparently cared for him. About a year after marrying, while she was still a slave, Tubman's curiosity about legal matters affecting the status of blacks led her to pay a lawyer to search for legal documents relating to her mother's owners to trace her mother's history in slavery. She discovered that her mother, Harriet Green Ross, had been legally free at one time because of the untimely death of one of her owners, a young woman named Mary Patterson who died young and unmarried, leaving no provisions for Harriet Green Ross. It was the lawyer's opinion that Tubman's mother was emancipated at that time. No one informed Harriet Ross of her rights, and she remained a slave. Although Tubman was illiterate, she examined the workings of literacy in a social order in which she had not power. Tubman realized that literacy had been denied her, but she began to understand the social order enslaved her. In 1849 Tubman escaped to freedom in Pennsylvania alone and unaided.

The self-reliance of Tubman was twofold: she began supporting herself economically, and within a year of her escape, she began the task of freeing her relatives. Tubman's first stop was Baltimore, Maryland, for her sister and two children. Tubman embarked on her career as a conductor alone and unaided by the simple expedient of working as a cook and domestic in Philadelphia until she had saved enough money to provide for her needs. She provided for herself in between her trips to the South before the Civil War and also between her political interventions after the war.

By 1857 she had freed her entire family, including her aging parents. John Bell Robinson, a pro-slavery advocate, criticized Tubman's work in his book *Pictures of Slavery and Freedom*, stating, "The most noted point in this act of horror was the bringing away from ease and comfortable homes two old slaves over seventy years of age" (Conrad, 99). Pro-slavery writing criticizing Tubman was indicative not only of the economic damage she was responsible for in the South but also intended as a corrective to the increasing agitation in the North to abolish slavery. Tubman did not remember a life of ease and comfort as a slave. While Tubman began the work of leading her family and others from slavery to freedom in the North single-handedly after her own escape, she soon worked in concert with other abolitionists in the North, both black and white. The end of slavery was a personal issue for Harriet Tubman.

Tubman's self-appointed purpose led her to be closely involved with progressive social leaders in the North, first abolitionists, then feminists, and political and military leaders as she became well known as an abolitionist and a black leader. Her primary goal was to work for the freedom of slaves. Tubman's career led her to associate with people who shared her goal of the emancipation of blacks, regardless of the boundaries of gender, color, and socioeconomic status. She became closely associated with John Brown before his raid on the federal arsenal at Harper's Ferry and admired him enormously all of her life. Other white leaders she personally knew were Thomas Garrett and William H. Seward, as well as Susan B. Anthony, Ralph Waldo Emerson, and the Alcotts. The settlement and growth of the western states led to increased agitation over the institution of slavery, and white progressive leaders supported Tubman's work financially and welcomed her into their homes when she needed shelter, generally in conjunction with her trips to the South or when she was attending an antislavery feminist meeting. As the controversy over slavery intensified, Tubman became an effective and acknowledged leader in the abolitionist movement, which had a strong and effective organization in Philadelphia.

Tubman and William Still Join Forces

As Boston was the center of progressive thought in New England, so Philadelphia was the center of progressive social thought and action further south on the Atlantic seaboard. It was in Philadelphia that Tubman became acquainted with William Still and other well-known and well-organized abolitionists. The first organized society against slavery was established in Philadelphia in 1775, the Pennsylvania Society for Promoting the Abolition of Slavery, the Relief of Free Negroes Unlawfully Held in Bondage, and for Improving the Condition of the African Race, indicating the long-held sympathetic views of the inhabitants. Tubman became closely associated with William Still, the energetic and active executive director of the General Vigilance Committee. Still was the most important black man that Tubman was closely associated with. The Underground Railroad was effectively organized into networks for the safe transport of slaves, and communication between leaders and workers in the system was necessary for safety and efficiency. On the other hand, written records were dangerous to keep, as abolitionists became aware after John Brown's papers were seized after the Harper's Ferry raid. Although many written records and letters were destroyed, Still kept a chronicle that has survived. Of Harriet Tubman he later wrote, "She was a woman of no pretensions; indeed, a more ordinary specimen of humanity could hardly be found among the most unfortunate-looking farm hands of the South. Yet in point of courage, shrewdness, and disinterested exertions to rescue her fellow-man, she was without equal" (Conrad, 54).

William Still and the other members of the General

Vigilance Committee worked closely with Harriet Tubman; through their organization she met Thomas Garrett, a prominent white Quaker abolitionist in Wilmington, Delaware. Thomas Garrett thought highly of Tubman and her work and provided her with shelter, money, or whatever else she needed for her trips on the Underground Railway, especially when Tubman was leading groups of slaves into Canada. He corresponded with friends united in the abolitionist movement as far away as Scotland, describing the activities of antislavers in the United States as well as Tubman's activities and raising money for her needs. His help was especially important as she freed members of her family from Delaware and began taking slaves to St. Catherines in western Canada for complete safety "under the lion's paw" of England. Passage of the Fugitive Slave Law in 1850 made freedom precarious for blacks in the North.

After living intermittently in St. Catherines, Ontario, from 1851 until 1857, Tubman moved to Auburn, New York, eventually settling there with her parents after the Civil War. Auburn was the center of progressive thought in New York. Abolition and women's suffrage thrived in Auburn. As well, it was the home of one of Harriet Tubman's strongest supporters, William H. Seward, governor of New York, and a publishing center for abolitionist literature. William H. Seward sold Tubman a home in Auburn on generous terms, for which she paid through unsolicited donations from white supporters. At the annual meeting of the Massachusetts Anti-Slavery Society in 1859, the president, Thomas Wentworth Higginson, asked for a collection to assist her in buying the house so "her father and mother could support themselves, and enable her to resume the practice of her profession!" There was much "laughter and applause" after Higginson's announcement (Conrad, 109).

Tubman's profession changed but little during the Civil War. She was sent to Beaufort after the fall of Port Royal, South Carolina, in 1862 for Reconstruction work by Governor Andrew of Massachusetts. Her position with the War Department was one of irregular attachment yet solicited by officials. Tubman nursed the sick and wounded soldiers and taught newly-freed blacks strategies for self-sufficiency. She was sent to Florida for a time to nurse soldiers who were ill with fever. After her return to South Carolina, she resumed her nursing duties there. When the young schoolteacher, Charlotte L. Forten, visited Beaufort, she enthusiastically wrote the following entry in her diary on 31 January 1863: "We spent all our time at Harriet Tubman's. She is a wonderful woman—a real heroine" (Quarles, 49). Harriet Tubman also organized a group of eight black men to scout the inland waterway area of South Carolina for Union raids under the direction of Colonel James Montgomery. She personally assisted Colonel Montgomery when he led a raid in the Combahee area, coming under fire herself from Confederate troops in the battle.

Returning to Auburn after the Civil War, Tubman devoted herself to caring for her parents, raising funds for schools for former slaves, collecting clothes for destitute children, and helping the poor and disabled. Tubman worked closely with black churches that had provided overnight shelter for runaway slaves on the Underground Railroad and raised money for Tubman's work as a conductor. She was active in the growth of the AME Zion church in central and western New York and raised funds for the Thompson Memorial African Methodist Episcopal Zion Church in Auburn. Always concerned with the most vulnerable—children and the elderly—Tubman was the agent of her church in collecting clothes for destitute children and was concerned with homes for the elderly. With her characteristic penchant for action, Tubman purchased twenty-five acres of land adjoining her house in 1896. The land was to be sold at auction, and Tubman hid in a corner of the crowd, bidding on the property until all others dropped out. It was not until she won the bidding that she identified herself as the buyer. The astonished crowd wondered where she would obtain the money for her purchase, but Harriet Tubman went to the bank and secured funds by mortgage. The Harriet Tubman Home for Aged and Indigent Colored People was incorporated in 1903 with the assistance of the AMEZ church, and formally opened in 1908.

Tubman resumed her affiliation with women's groups because she viewed racial liberation and women's liberation as being strongly linked. Tubman had a long-lasting and cordial relationship with the suffragist pioneer and leader, Susan B. Anthony, both being active in the New England Anti-Slavery Society. Tubman strongly believed in racial equality and thought that the greatest benefit could be reaped when blacks and whites worked together. She was also a delegate to the first annual convention of the National Federation of Afro-American Women in 1896 and when she was asked to give a talk at this first meeting, her theme was "More Homes for Our Aged." Victoria Earle Matthews, chairperson of the evening session, introduced Mother Harriet, as she was called, and commented on the great services that she had rendered to the race. Tubman's initial appearance before the delegates as speaker was a momentous occasion:

> Mrs. Tubman stood alone on the front of the rostrum, the audience, which not only filled every seat, but also much of the standing room in the aisles, rose as one person and greeted her with the waving of handerchiefs and clapping of hands. This was kept up for at least one minute, and Mrs. Tubman was much affected by the hearty reception given her (*A History of The Club Movement*, 41).

The National Association of Colored Women would later pay for Tubman's funeral and for the marble headstone over her grave. In April 1897 the New England Women's Suffrage Association held a reception in her honor. When asked later in life whether she believed that women should have the right to vote, Tubman replied, "I have suffered enough to believe it" (Conrad, 217).

While Tubman was active in Reconstruction work, women's rights organizations, and in caring for her parents in her home, she also remarried. Her first husband, John Tubman, did not join her after her dash for freedom, and he died in 1867. In 1869 Tubman married a Union soldier, Nelson Davis, a black man twenty-two years younger than she. Little is known of Davis except that he was a former slave who served in the Union Army. The facts that have survived him are a result of documentation of his war service, documentation that enabled Harriet Tubman to draw a pension after his death as the widow of a Civil War veteran. For two decades white supporters attempted unsuccessfully to secure a government pension for Tubman based upon her three years of service during the Civil War. The only other facts about the marriage of Tubman to Nelson Davis come from a description of the wedding ceremony that appeared in an unidentified Auburn newspaper. Earl Conrad, in his book, *Harriet Tubman*, states, "It has been said that her husband, Nelson Davis, in spite of being a large man was not a healthy man, that he suffered with tuberculosis, and she married him to take care of him" (145). This information was based upon an oral statement of a friend. The fact that Nelson Davis lived for twenty years after his marriage to Tubman appears to invalidate this claim and to reflect Victorian patriarchal sentiments. Other writers assert that Tubman cared deeply for her first husband because she kept his name. Tubman probably did care for her first husband, but again, retaining the Tubman surname was probably a practical matter for Tubman because of her age and fame, rather than a mythic and romantic matter. Tubman's second marriage, a marriage to a much younger man, has consistently been marginalized even by scholars and writers today. Readers of biographies and articles on Tubman's life are required to pay close attention to dates of births and deaths to discover that Harriet Tubman was a vital woman in middle age—not just a very good nurse.

Tubman died of pneumonia on March 10, 1913, after a two-year residence in the Harriet Tubman Home for Aged and Indigent Colored People. A memorial service was held a year later by the citizens of Auburn, at which time a tablet erected in her honor was unveiled. Booker T. Washington was the featured speaker at the evening service. Although biographies of Tubman contain elements of myth as well as fact, her fame has endured, most recently because of new interest in the role of women in history and in literature. A liberty ship was christened the *Harriet Tubman* during World War II, and in 1978 the United States Postal Service issued a Harriet Tubman commemorative stamp, the first in a Black Heritage USA Series. Poets, artists, and musicians have written, portrayed, and sung their admiration of this nineteenth-century black woman. Harriet Tubman personified strength and the quest for freedom, and her fame is enduring.

References

Bradford, Sarah. *Harriet Tubman: The Moses of Her People*. 1886. Reprinted. New York: Corinth, 1961.

Conrad, Carl. *Harriet Tubman*. New York: Erickson, 1943.

Contributions of Black Women to America. Vol. 2. Edited by Marianna W. Davis. Columbia, S.C.: Kenday Press.

A History of the Club Movement among the Colored Women of the United States of America as Contained in the Minutes of the Conventions, Held in Boston, July 29, 30, 31, 1895, and of the National Federation of Afro-American Women, Held in Washington, D.C., July 209, 21, 22, 1896. Washington, 1902.

McPherson, James M., et. al. *Blacks in America: Bibliographic Essays*. Garden City, N.Y.: Doubleday, 1971.

Quarles, Benjamin. "Harriet Tubman's Unlikely Leadership." *Black Leaders of the Nineteenth Century*. Edited by Leon Litwack and August Meier. Urbana: University of Illinois Press, 1988.

Williams, Lorraine A. "Harriet Tubman." *Dictionary of American Negro Biography*. Edited by Rayford W. Logan and Michael R. Winston. New York: Norton, 1982.

Collections

A famous portrait of Harriet Tubman appears opposite the title page of the first edition of Sarah Bradford's *Scenes in the Life of Harriet Tubman*. A well-known picture of Harriet Tubman formally posed standing by a chair is often reproduced; *Ebony* magazine's archives apparently has this picture.

Nancy A. Davidson

C. DeLores Tucker

(1927-)

Civic leader, politician

Cynthia DeLores (C. DeLores) Nottage Tucker, civic leader and public official, was born on October 4, 1927, in Philadelphia, Pennsylvania. Her parents, the Reverend Whitfield Nottage and Captilda (Gardiner) Nottage, inspired her to work hard and believe in Christian teachings. The details of her early life appear in an interview in *Biography News* (July/ August, 1975). Tucker said:

> My parents were strict fundamental, Puritan Christians. We couldn't smoke, play cards, drink, dance, or listen to popular music. No male company until I was 21. My father was a minister, from a family of ministers. He never took a salary, always believing God would provide, even though he had 11 children. But my mother realized she had to feed us, so she opened up an

> employment agency, then a grocery store, then she rented houses. We weren't taught to value material things, But we were taught that we were spiritual aristocracy, that we were special, were children of the King, and were taught to place all our values in relationships—to heal the sick, to love everybody, to feed the poor, not to care about anything worldly.

One of Tucker's earliest memories was of her family living on a farm in Montgomery County. In the ninth grade she was the only black. She was called "Black Beauty," which was not taken as a compliment since that was the name of a horse. She says, "All the doors were open, all the children's heads were peepin' out, all the teachers' heads were above, and they were watching one little black girl come into that school. I just don't know how I survived."

Tucker's early ambition was to become a doctor and during the summer months she worked in hospitals. For her graduation from Girls' High in Philadelphia, her father took her on a trip to the Bahamas and they were told that because they were black, they had to sleep in a different compartment. She refused these accommodations and instead stayed up on deck, spending the night outside in the damp air. When she got back home, a spot was found on her lung. She was ill for a year, needing complete rest. That prevented her from going to college and into medicine and ultimately altered the direction of her life.

Not all of Tucker's early experiences were bleak. One of the more personal consequences of her change in plans was her meeting with William J. Tucker, a Philadelphia real estate executive. Two years later, in July 1951, they were married, and now they often work together on business ventures. Although they have no children of their own, the Tuckers have served as surrogate parents to many children. Tucker attended Temple University, Pennsylvania State University, and the University of Pennsylvania. She holds honorary doctor of laws degrees from Villa Maria College in Erie, Pennsylvania, and Morris College in Sumter, South Carolina.

Involvement in Polities Begins

The first black and the first woman member of the Philadelphia Zoning Board, Tucker has had many years of involvement in the civil rights movement. In 1965, she participated in Martin Luther King, Jr.'s White House Conference on Civil Rights. She was a founding member of the National Women's Caucus and cofounder of the national Black Women's Political Caucus. Tucker has also been an active force in national, state, and local NAACP organizations, serving as vice-president of the Pennsylvania NAACP and in 1982 on the national board of this body's Special Contribution Fund.

Tucker has been described as a tall, striking woman with a spellbinding voice, which was trained by her father, the Reverend Whitfield Nottage. She has been named by *Ebony* magazine as one of the best-dressed women of the year and has been active in politics since she worked as a teenager in the 1950 mayoral campaign of Joseph Clark. Beginning in 1972, her name has often been listed in *Ebony* magazine's "100 Most Influential Black Americans." Forceful and articulate, she once offered the following advice to a group of black women regarding the need to get involved in politics:

> Many of you are in the position to bring influence to bear if you have the courage of Esther, who could say, "I'll go in unto the King, which is not according to the law, and if I perish, I perish" (Book of Esther).

As secretary of state of the Commonwealth during Governor Milton J. Shapp's administration, she was the highest ranking black woman in state government in the country. In this capacity, Tucker worked aggressively to regulate the business of corporations and individuals affecting the lives of almost everyone in Pennsylvania. Her dismissal from this position in 1977 was sparked by a controversy that alleged that she used state employees and state property to help prepare speeches for which she accepted thousands of dollars in speaking fees.

An effective leader and organizer, Tucker was nominated by the *Ladies Home Journal* in 1975 and 1976 for "Woman of the Year," and *Redbook* magazine named her as the woman best qualified to be Ambassador to the United Nations on a slate of twenty-two women who could save America. In the 1987 primary election in Pennsylvania, she achieved another significant milestone. Tucker was drafted by 150 organizational leaders as the first black candidate to run for the office of lieutenant governor, and she finished third in a field of fourteen candidates.

A longtime friend and associate of the Reverend Jesse Jackson, Tucker was an active supporter in his presidential campaign in 1984. She is president of the Philadelphia chapter of the Martin Luther King, Jr., Association and has served as coordinator of the annual Martin Luther King, Jr., luncheon. She played a key role in the founding of the Philadelphia chapter of this organization after working closely with Coretta Scott King, widow of the slain civil rights leader, and other prominent Atlanta community leaders.

By her oratory and her example, Tucker continues to inspire others to achieve greater levels of service to their communities. In spite of her busy schedule, she maintains a family home in Philadelphia and finds enough time to relax and to enjoy reading, traveling, and good music.

References

Biography News, July/August 1975.

Ebony 27 (July 1972): 60-62.

Philadelphia Inquirer, 22 September 1977.

Philadelphia Evening Bulletin, 19 March 1975.

Philadelphia Tribune, 17 December 1985. 3-A.

Tucker, C. DeLores. Resume.

Photographs of C. Delores Tucker are in the John Mosley Photograph Collection of the Charles L. Blockson Afro-American Collection, Temple University Libraries.

Emery Wimbish, Jr.

Tina Turner

(1939-)

Singer, actress

Tina Turner, after a long career as an entertainer and singer, remains one of the hottest properties in the music business. Now in her fifties, Turner still electrifies audiences all over the world. A survivor of a difficult, nomadic childhood and an abusive marriage, Turner has been able to find a home for herself on stage and has taken her place in music and show biz history.

Tina Turner began life as Anna Mae Bullock on November 26, 1939, in Brownsville, Tennessee, in Haywood Memorial Hospital. Her early life was spent with her mother, Zelma, "a black Indian of high spirits" (Turner, 12), and her father, Floyd Richard Bullock, a Baptist deacon, on the Poindexter farm, for which he was the resident overseer. Located in Nut Bush (sometimes spelled Nutbush), the Poindexter farm was home for Anna Mae and her older sister, Alline, as well as their half sister, Evelyn Currie, who lived with the girls' maternal grandparents in a small home just across Forked Deer Road. Josephus and Georgianna Currie were both three-quarter Indian and had been sharecroppers for the Poindexters for some time. The paternal grandparents, Alex and Roxanna Bullock, lived just up the highway. "Mama Roxanna was a big, fine, church-centered woman of sober demeanor and harsh, starchy virtues" (13) while, in sharp contrast, her husband was an inebriate.

Turner felt unwanted by her parents. Born into a union already full of disagreements and lacking in marital affection, the last child was yet another detracting force in the tenuous relationship between her parents. Though the marriage was full of "wall banger" arguments and anger, her parents were able to find time for Alline but not Turner, leaving her feeling left out and on her own. Turner would later reflect, "My mother wasn't mean to me, but she wasn't warm, she wasn't close, the way she was with Alline. She just didn't want me. But she was my mother and I loved her" (17).

When the United States entered World War II in 1941, Zelma and Floyd Bullock left Nut Bush to look for nonagrarian work in the defense industries in Knoxville. The two daughters were left behind—Alline in the warm family comfort of the Curries and Turner with the stiff, acrid Mama Roxanna. During the two years the Bullocks worked in the city, the girls were allowed one short visit and then returned to their grandparents in Nut Bush. It was during this visit that Turner first sang for money. When her mother took the girls shopping, Turner sang for the salesladies and was often rewarded with quarters. It was also here she got her first taste of worship in the Sanctified Church. For the first time Turner witnessed the full out style of worship so different from the rather constrained worship at Mama Roxanna's Baptist church. Observing and later participating in the "Holy Dance," Turner was able, for the first time, to experience totally uninhibited self-expression. (Black evangelicals feel the Holy Dance is the physical manifestation of the Holy Spirit. The Sanctified Church is known for its freewill style of worship that includes the Holy Dance, usually to the accompaniment of gospel music. Drums and other musical instruments are often included in the worship but are not requisite.)

When the defense factories closed, the Bullocks collected Turner and Alline and moved to Flagg Grove and later to Spring Hill. Turner began singing in the Spring Hill Baptist Church Choir. Though she was the youngest member of the choir, she took the lead on all of the upbeat songs.

The Bullocks's marriage, which was always rocky, began to reach the breaking point. In 1950 Zelma Bullock left her daughters and her husband and moved to Saint Louis to live with one of her aunts. Floyd Bullock quickly remarried and was just as quickly divorced. When Turner was thirteen, her father moved to Detroit, leaving the girls in the care of a cousin, Ella Vera. Neither parent kept close contact with the girls, though their father did send money for their care. Eventually the money stopped coming, and the girls had to go to live with Mama Roxanna. Finding that home unbearable after Alline graduated high school and moved to Detroit to live with her father, Turner moved in with Mama Georgie Currie. In 1956 Mama Georgie died. When Zelma Bullock came down to her mother's funeral, she took her daughter back to Saint Louis to live. Alline had only spent a short time in Detroit and was now also living with her mother in Saint Louis.

Saint Louis spelled an awakening for Turner. She was once again united with the sister she idolized. Under Alline's tutelage she learned about life in the city. Though she was only sixteen, she began to wear makeup and go to East Saint Louis nightclubs with Alline and her girlfriends. At the Club Manhattan all the women were buzzing about the band they were to see. The Kings of Rhythm were the hottest band on the chitlin' circuit. The group drew large crowds of mostly women. Ike Turner, the diminutive, charismatic lead musician, commanded the greatest share of the attention.

Ike Turner was born as Izear Turner on November 15, 1931, in Clarksdale, Mississippi. He was raised primarily by his mother, a seamstress, after his father, a Baptist minister, was murdered by the boyfriend of a woman with whom the minister was committing adultery. Ike Turner learned to play the guitar from the wife of a blind man for whom he served as a guide. He grew up on the music of the Grand Ole Opry and the blues as performed in clubs in Clarksdale's black entertainment district. As early as age eight, Turner was spending time at the local radio station, filling in for the disc jockey during his coffee breaks and finally securing his own program.

After playing in another local band, Ike Turner and several other band members broke with the group and formed the Kings of Rhythm. The band was a local success. During one road swing the group had an opportune meeting with B. B. King, who, after hearing them, recommended the group to his record producer. Upon hearing the group, the producer felt that Ike Turner was an excellent musician but lacking as a lead vocalist. With Jackie Brenston as lead singer, the group cut its first record, ''Rocket 88,'' and it was a number one hit on rhythm and blues charts in June 1951. Though the record was a chart success, it did not spell financial success for the group. The Kings of Rhythm disbanded over a monetary dispute and reorganized with part of the band forming the road group for the former lead singer, Jackie Brenston, now a solo act, and the others, with Ike Turner, forming a new Kings of Rhythm.

In 1954 Ike Turner, in search of new opportunities, took his second wife and moved to Saint Louis. The Kings of Rhythm, who had now been rejoined by several members of the original band, began to play in the hot clubs of East Saint Louis. By 1956 the group was again a local success and one of the main attractions at East Saint Louis's Manhattan Club.

Singer Makes Stage Debut

Young Anna Mae Bullock struck up friendships with several of the bandmembers while Alline dated Gene Washington, the group's drummer. Listening and singing along as she watched the band, Turner developed a real desire to perform on stage. After weeks of yearning, an opportunity finally presented itself. During a break between sets, Ike Turner played the organ on stage while Washington tried to coax a reluctant Alline to sing into a microphone. Turner, seated at the table with her sister, realized that she knew the B. B. King song being played, took the microphone, and began singing. Ike Turner was so impressed that he immediately wanted to include her in the act and was finally able to do so after some negotiation with her mother. She first performed under the name of Little Ann.

During her first year of performance Turner became close to Raymond Hill, the band's saxophone player, and gave birth to his son, Raymond Craig, in 1958. For some time the relationship between Ike Turner and Anna Bullock remained platonic, with Ike Turner exhibiting a protective, mentoring attitude toward his newest singer. A short while after high school graduation, Anna moved into Ike's house and some time later became his lover. Although she was disturbed by his violent reputation, she fell in love with him and in 1960 gave birth to his son, Ronald Renelle. The couple later entered into a questionable marriage in Tijuana, Mexico. Ike Turner would later admit that he had not divorced his previous wife until 1974.

Their debut song, ''A Fool in Love,'' was released in summer 1960. The lead vocal was written for Art Lassiter, who never recorded the song due to a dispute with Ike Turner. After hearing the demonstration piece with the lead sung by Anna Mae Bullock, Henry ''Juggy'' Murray of Sue Records contracted with Ike Turner to press and sell the record and advised Turner not to seek a male lead. Murray further advised Ike Turner to build the group around Tina Turner. The record was released under the names Ike and Tina Turner. Although Turner felt apprehensive about being named for a woman from one of Ike's jungle fantasies, she wanted to support him in his quest for success. The song reached number two on the rhythm and blues charts, creating a demand for personal appearances.

The Ike and Tina Turner Revue debuted on a bill with Jackie Wilson. With Tina Turner's ''soul-drenched quaking, pleading and shaking'' (*Current Biography Yearbook,* 411), the energetic backup of the Ikettes, and Ike's musical skills and direction, the revue became one of the hottest acts of its time. Though laden with monetary disputes with the band, singers, and record producers, the revue was able to record several songs that reached the charts, including ''It's Going to Work Out Fine,'' ''I Pity the Fool,'' ''I Idolize You,'' ''Poor Fool,'' and ''Tra La La La La.''

Throughout the sixties and early seventies the band toured the United States and Europe performing their special style, considered a mix of blues, rock, and gospel. The miniskirted Tina Turner and the Ikettes proved to be a provocative combination. In 1965 noted record producer Phil Spector took notice of Tina Turner's voice during a club date at the Galaxy on Sunset Boulevard in Los Angeles. He recruited the revue for The Big TNT Show, which featured such other performers as the Byrds, Ray Charles, and Petula Clark. In 1966 Spector decided to have Tina Turner record the song he had just cowritten with Jeff Barry and Ellie Greenwich. The deal was such that only Tina Turner would be involved in the sessions and Ike Turner would not be permitted to accompany her to the studio. ''River Deep, Mountain High'' was a huge success in Britain, remaining on the Top Fifty charts for thirteen weeks. In the United States it was a failure, going only to eighty-eight on the pop charts and then falling down. Tina Turner surmised ''that record never found a home. It was too black for the pop stations and too pop for the black stations'' (Turner, 110).

''River Deep, Mountain High'' proved to be the group's pass to Europe. Just as the song had been such a hit in Great Britain, so was the group. As the opening act for the Rolling Stones 1966 European tour, the revue gathered a large following. Purveying the band's trademark of hard-driving rhythm and blues with Tina Turner's unforgettable voice and mien, a new level of crossover was achieved. By 1971 their successful combination of pop/rock and rhythm and blues produced a Grammy Award for ''Proud Mary.'' Tina Turner's provocative introduction to that song—''We never,

ever, do nothin' nice and easy. So we're gonna do it nice and rough''—became a key phrase in the history of the Ike and Tina Turner Revue and indeed of the popular music of that era.

Back in the United States the group finally began to reach the middle American audience Ike Turner so coveted. Appearances on shows hosted by such big-name entertainers as Pearl Bailey, Ed Sullivan, and Andy Williams sealed their position as true crossover artists.

The group's public success did not spell private success for Ike and Tina Turner's relationship. Tina had begun to glean information about both the business and performance aspects of their venture but felt that Ike left her no creative outlet. As her maturing self-image began to surface, she felt stymied and considered leaving the group. At the same time Ike became increasingly physically abusive, often causing Tina to sing through badly swollen lips. The combination of Tina's emerging self and Ike's abuse proved to be a powerful catalyst. On a 1976 tour that would place the revue in Dallas, Texas, for the Fourth of July, Ike, in a drug-induced violent binge, began to beat Tina, and she fought back for the first time. Tina Turner would never make it to that Fourth of July performance. Deciding that this would be the last beating she would ever take, she left the group in Dallas on July 1.

On her own, Tina Turner began to rebuild her career. Drawing strength from chanting in the practice of Buddhism, she took a year off to settle her personal affairs, including divorcing Ike. Slowly, she began to create a show. At first her performances were on the cabaret circuit. By 1978 she had recorded an album, *Rough,* which received little commercial success or critical acclaim. She was still able to draw on her European success and performed there frequently. The Rolling Stones also recalled her success and asked her to join their 1981 United States tour. Recognition from that tour rekindled interest and independent bookings followed. She also made artistic changes in her show, returning to her blues roots for some of her selections and incorporating some of the new reggae influenced music for others.

Her career once again on track, Tina Turner performed on a record-breaking 1983-1984 European tour and achieved special-guest billing on Lionel Richie's 1984 United States tour. That same year also marked her return to the recording studio. The album *Private Dancer* went gold (selling more than a half million copies) immediately and sold more than eleven million copies worldwide. *Private Dancer* also received four Grammy Awards for her, including Record of the Year for ''What's Love Got to Do with It?''

The next year Tina Turner returned to the big screen. Her first role had been the Acid Queen in the 1975 movie *Tommy.* She won a role as Aunty Entity in the Mel Gibson film *Mad Max: Beyond the Thunderdome.* The film also produced a hit song, ''We Don't Need Another Hero,'' for Tina Turner.

Tina Turner's 1986 album *Break Every Rule* went multiplatinum, firmly establishing her as ''rock n' roll's queen diva'' Her 1987-1988 world tour included one performance in Brazil that drew a crowd of 182,000 fans, making it one of the largest on record.

Although she has declared that each of last three tours would be the last, Tina Turner's most recent tour (the Foreign Affair) has taken her to every continent. Her ''raw, gritty voice'' (*Jet,* 57) and overwhelming stage presence have enabled her to sell out every concert on the tour. Though fifty years old when the tour began in April 1990, audiences would agree she has not lost a provocative step prancing about in her trademark high heels and mini skirts. Tina Turner has firmly stated, ''This is definitely my last tour and I mean it!'' (*Jet,* 60). In the near future she wishes to secure more acting roles in either movies or a television series. On January 11, 1991, Tina Turner was inducted into the Rock and Roll Hall of Fame.

References

Current Biography Yearbook. New York: H. W. Wilson, 1984. 410-13.

Hardy, Phil, and Dave Laing. *Encyclopedia of Rock.* New York: Schirmer Books, 1988.

Helander, Brock. *Rock Who's Who.* New York: Schirmer Books, 1982. 595-96.

Hitchcock, Wiley H., and Stanley Sadie, eds. *New Grove Dictionary of American Music.* Vol. 4. New York: Macmillan, 1986.

Lippy, Charles H., and Peter H. Williams, eds. *Encyclopedia of the American Religious Experience.* Vol. 1. New York: Scribner's Sons, 1988.

Norment, Lynn. ''Rich, Free and in Control—the Foreign Affairs of Tina Turner.'' *Ebony* 45 (November 1989): 166-68, 172.

Pareles, Jon, and Patricia Romanowski, eds. *Rolling Stone Encyclopedia of Rock.* New York: Rolling Stone Press, 1983.

Southern, Eileen. *Biographical Dictionary of Afro-American and African Music.* Westport, Conn.: Greenwood Press, 1982.

Tennessean 30 November 1991.

''Tina Turner Still Sexy and Going Strong.'' *Jet* 78 (9 July 1990): 56-58, 60.

Turner, Tina, with Kurt Loder. *I, Tina.* New York: William Morrow, 1986. Includes photographs.

Sarah Crest

Cicely Tyson

(1942-)

Actress

Lights! Camera! Action! These three words heard frequently by actors and actresses translate automatically into Talent! Drive! Determination! when it comes to describing award-winning actress Cicely Tyson. Early in her career she came face to face with an inner drive that caused her one day to stop typing abruptly:

> I know God did not put me on the face of this earth to bang on a typewriter for the rest of my life. I don't know what it is or where it is, but I am certainly going to find it (Klemesrud, 35).

And she found it. Tyson has become not only a successful star of stage, screen, and television, but an actress committed to the honest and dignified portrayal of black Americans.

At the age of eighteen, while working as a secretary for the American Red Cross, Tyson was determined to rise above her present status in life. When her hairdresser, Walter Johnson, asked her to model one of his hairstyles in a style show, she agreed. The decision to comply with her hairdresser's wishes turned out to be one of the most dramatic decisions Tyson would make during her early career. After the style show she received many compliments. Some friends even encouraged her to study modeling, and she did that. Although she continued to work for the Red Cross, she enrolled in the Barbara Watson Modeling School and used her lunch hour and weekends to fulfill her modeling engagements.

Cicely Tyson

Modeling Career Progresses

As her modeling career progressed, Tyson soon became one of the top ten black models in the United States, earning as much as sixty-five dollars an hour in the mid-1950s. "Blessed with poise and natural grace, Cicely's modeling career led her to new heights. In 1956, she appeared on the cover of *Harper's Bazaar* and *Vogue,* two of America's foremost fashion magazines" (*Negro Almanac,* 1118). The motivation from her friends to pursue a career in modeling proved to be beneficial.

The youngest of three children, Tyson was born December 19, 1942, in the east Harlem section of New York City. She has an older sister, Emily, and "an older brother who since childhood was known only by his last name, and whose first name to this day Cicely will not reveal" (Robinson, 34). Her parents, William and Theodosia (or Frederika) Tyson, were immigrants from Nevis, the smallest of the Leeward Islands in the West Indies.

Before entering Barbara Watson's School of Modeling, Tyson received her high school diploma from Charles Evans High School in Manhattan. Educated in the public schools of New York City, she attended Public School 121 and Margaret Knox Junior High School.

Both of Tyson's parents worked hard to provide for their children. Although her father was a carpenter and a painter, sometimes it was necessary for him to sell fruits and vegetables from a fruit stand. To supplement the family's income, Tyson sold shopping bags in nearby neighborhoods at the early age of nine.

While her family experienced poverty, Cicely Tyson even as a child "refused to accept the poverty of the Harlem ghetto as the totality of existence" (Klemesrud, 35). She told Arthur Unger of the *Christian Science Monitor* that she always wandered on the bus and subway reaffirming her belief that there was "a world outside. . .and she always looked toward tomorrow." Like most black children who grow up in a ghetto area, Cicely Tyson wanted to find a way out. She knew there had to be something else outside of 102nd Street. "My choice was to go a different way" (Klemesrud, 35).

In addition to living with the consequences of finding and creating choices, Tyson was also considered her father's favorite. She tells of the incident of her mother's leaving their father:

> My mother was strict. . . . Mother watched me like a hawk. Mother, who left my father when I

> was ten years old, said I was Daddy's baby. She seemed to resent that and I adored him so much and that I had been his favorite. . . . I suppose I understand why. She knew if anything happened to me, I mean, if I "went wrong," my father would never forgive her . . . so my mother watched me like a hawk (Robinson, 35).

Theodosia Tyson dedicated her life to her children, especially after the father died in 1962. Religion was a dominant force in Tyson's childhood and she spent a lot of her time at Saint John's Episcopal Church. Having a devout, religious mother, her activities as well as those of her sister and brother were restricted to the church because the mother felt that the church was the safest place for them to be. Tyson sang in the choir and played the piano and the organ. Her talent and ability to sing and play the piano earned her the nickname "Come Thou Almighty King" from her grade school friends (Robinson, 34). The long hours she spent practicing the piano paid off, for she became a pianist of concert standard, giving recitals at many of New York's concert halls. Tyson made another choice during those years, which she later saw as youthful rebellion: "When I can dictate my own life, I will never touch another piano." (Angelou, 40).

As a child Tyson was not permitted to attend movies with her girlfriends, but she was exposed to them in Sunday school. Her friends would tell her about the movies that they had seen, but they did not interest her. Nor was she enthusiastic about being terrified by Dracula. Despite the restrictions placed on Tyson by her mother while she was growing up, she is "grateful to her when I think of the many kids we grew up with who are either dead from drugs or in prison" (35). Whether or not she was impressed by the stories behind the movies her girlfriends told her, Tyson was in store for the surprise career of her life. Little did she know that one day critic Rex Reed would write in the *New York Daily News*: "Cicely Tyson is not a great black actress. She is a great actress, who quite incidentally, just happens also to be black." In this review of Tyson's Emmy Award-winning portrayal of an ex-slave in the title role of the 1974 television special, "The Autobiography of Miss Jane Pittman." Reed goes on to say of her performance:

> I would need twice this space again to describe the fully detailed nuances of her voice, body and movement, but suffice it to say it is one of the most brilliant performances I have ever seen by a woman of any color, any age, any season.

Where did all this talent come from? Once Tyson described herself as a "puzzlement" (Angelou, 41). She used this term because at times she finds herself in a lifelong search and is sure of what she is searching for, and at other times, this search is not only unknown, but hard to understand. One such search culminated in an illustrious career in acting. It all began accidentally while she was on an interview for a modeling job and an actress who had a role in a film spotted her. Encouraged by the fashion editor to read a script for the producer, who was looking for an ingenue to play the lead, Tyson complied reluctantly. Several months went by before the producer called to tell her that she had been selected.

Tyson is grateful to the late Freda DeKnight, a fashion editor for *Ebony* magazine during the mid-1970s, and to Evelyn Davis, a character actress. These talented young women thought she would be the perfect person for a part in *The Spectrum,* an independent black film that was being shot by Warren Coleman in New York. In addition to starring Tyson in his film, he became her friend. He believed in her and the black film even then, ten years before both she and it made it big.

This experience caused Tyson to follow the advice of her friends and study acting. "I went to every acting school in New York City, including the Actor's Workshop and Paul Mann's workshop," she told Lloyd Shearer in an interview for *Parade* magazine (3 December 1972). As a student at New York University, she took classes at the Actors' Studio, where she studied with Lloyd Richards and Vinnette Carroll, among others. Carroll made the observation that Tyson possesses all the qualities for a successful actress: strong determination, a strong desire to achieve, an enormous capacity for work and self-motivation. Hard work and self-determination, coupled with a strong desire to achieve, would not let her settle for anything less than the best. Carroll also observed: "There was never any doubt in my mind that Miss Cicely (that's my pet name for her) was going to make it" (Webster, 24).

Career in Acting Begins

Tyson's first role in a motion picture was in the movie *Twelve Angry Men*, produced by United Artists in 1957, starring Henry Fonda. In 1959, she played in *Odds Against Tomorrow*, a United Artists production.

Beginning in 1959 with her first theatrical role as Barbara Allen in Carroll's off-Broadway revival of the musical *The Dark of the Moon*, Tyson has had a brilliant career as an actress. This performance was followed by six additional appearances during that same year. She won a role in the short-lived play, "The Spectrum." During that same year, she played a young African woman in "Between Yesterday and Today" for "Camera Three," a CBS cultural series that aired on Sunday mornings, "with what is believed to be the first African natural hair style on television" (Norment, 127). Later that year she was featured in the production of another television special, "Americans: A Portrait in Verse." In addition to appearing in these feature television productions, she participated in John Effrat's variety show, "Talent '59," at the Broadhurst Theatre on Broadway. On December 5, 1959, she appeared in New York at the Longacre in the Theatre Guild's production of *Jolly's Progress,* in which she also understudied Eartha Kitt in the role of Jolly Rivers.

It was in the amateur production of *The Dark of the Moon,* directed by Carroll, that Tyson's mother saw her perform for the first time. The mother's reaction to the daughter's performance as a prostitute in the role of Virtue, for which

Tyson received the Vernon Rice Award, was to come backstage and cover Tyson with her coat.

Eventually, television work in series, soap operas, and dramatic specials came along. In February 1960, Cicely Tyson played the part of Girl in Eugene O'Neill's play, *The Cool World.* During that same year, she appeared in a television adaptation of *Brown Girl, Brownstones* by Paule Marshall. In 1969 she was one of the original cast members of the off-Broadway production of Jean Genet's drama, *The Blacks*, where she played the part of Stephanie Virtue Diop. It opened at the Saint Mark's Playhouse on May 4, 1961, and ran for more than two years.

Impressed by Tyson's appearance in *The Blacks*, George C. Scott recruited her for a leading part in "East Side/West Side," a 1963 CBS-TV series about social workers, in which Tyson was cast as Scott's assistant, becoming the first black actress ever to have a continuing role in a dramatic television series. Over the years she had appeared in many other television programs, including "Naked City," "The Nurses," "Slattery's People," "To Tell the Truth," "I Spy," "Frontiers of Faith," and "The Bill Cosby Show."

From 1962 to 1969 Tyson was featured in many different acting roles. She performed in such productions as *Moon on a Rainbow,* produced by Errol John, at the East Eleventh Street Theatre in January 1962. For her outstanding performance in this off-Broadway production she won another Rice Award. In the winter of 1962-1963, she played Celeste Chipley in the Broadway production of *Tiger, Tiger, Burning Bright* at the Booth Theatre. She appeared with Alvin Ailey, Claudia McNeil, and Diana Sands. Her next performance on stage was in April 1963 at the Masque, where she played the part of Joan in *The Blue Boy in Black*, with Billy Dee Williams. Reverend Marion Alexander was the role she played in Vinnette Carroll's musical, *Trumpets of the Lord*, at the Astor Place Playhouse in December 1963.

During the fall of 1966, Cicely Tyson participated in a revue produced by the Longacre Theatre. Entitled *A Hand is on the Gates*, it included black poetry and folk music. In February 1968 she played Myrna Jessup in *Carry Me Back to Morningside Heights* at the John Golden Theatre. During January 1969 she participated in a program of dramatic readings from Robert Nemiroff's collage of assorted writings of the late Lorraine Hansberry, including letters to him, her former husband. Later that year Tyson found herself in a repeat performance of *Trumpets of the Lord*. This production was produced by the Cherry Lane Theatre.

The 1970s turned out to be banner years for Cicely Tyson, beginning with the 1970-1971 Playhouse in the Park series in Cincinnati, Ohio, where she performed in *The Blacks* to flattering recognition from Harvard University. "In 1974 she was the first actor, of any race or sex, to be honored with a day by the Harvard University Faculty Club" (*Negro Almanac*, 1118).

Since 1957, when Tyson received her first featured role in the motion picture *Twelve Angry Men*, she has starred in at least ten other films, including *The Comedians* (MGM, 1967); *A Man Called Adam,* costarring Sammy Davis, Jr., (Embassy, 1966), a film about a jazz musician; and *The Heart Is a Lonely Hunter* (Warner-Seven Arts, 1968).

Four years went by before Tyson accepted another movie role. She played the part of Rebecca Morgan in *Sounder*. Early in her career, she decided what kind of roles she would accept. She refused to accept roles in blaxploitation films, saying: "Every race has them (con men and whores and those kinds of characters). Don't have the world believing this is all we are capable of being or doing or that this is all we are. That's not only unfair, it's criminal" (Bright, 18).

Released by Twentieth Century Fox in 1972, *Sounder* is based on a novel by William H. Armstrong that won the Newbery Medal Award in 1970. Tyson feels "Sounder really is significant for the black woman. She has always been the strength of our race, and she has always had to carry the ball . . . like Rebecca . . . a positive image of her . . . with warmth, beauty, love and understanding. We do have that. It does exist. I grew up in that kind of setting here in New York where the only thing that kept the family together was the parents' love for each other" (Klemesrud, 13).

In the role of Rebecca, Cicely Tyson portrays a strong, dignified, loving wife of a sharecropper, played by Paul Winfield, in the South during the depression years. For her superb performance in this movie, she received many accolades from top movie critics whose columns appear regularly in newspapers and magazines like the *New York Sunday News*, the *New York* magazine, and the *New York Times*. Tyson feels "Rebecca is the first positive portrayal of a black woman on the screen. . . . The time has come for blacks to look back at our history and be proud of it, and not ashamed" (*New York Sunday News*).

In his assessment of Tyson's performance in *Sounder*, film director Martin Ritt said, "I rank her with the best actresses I ever worked with" ("Black Actors Don't Make Any Money," 62). In 1972, "Cicely got a bit of practice in winning awards at the Atlanta Film Festival where, before an audience that was seventy-five percent white, the National Society of Film Critics named her best actress for her performance in *Sounder*. For her role as Rebecca Morgan, a sharecropper's wife, in this film, she received a five-minute standing ovation. 'My knees went to water,' she confides. . . . 'I just stood there, so astonished. Finally, I turned around and hugged Marty (Martin Ritt, the film's director)' " (Klemesrud, 13).

After her magnificent performance in *Sounder*, she went on to star in *The Blue Bird* (1976), *The River Niger* (1976), *A Hero Ain't Nothing but a Sandwich* (1978), *The Concorde Airport 79* (1979), and, "Just an Old Sweet Song" (1976), a television special.

Tyson Wins Emmy

Television audiences around the nation watched, with utter amazement, Tyson's performance in the television drama "The Autobiography of Miss Jane Pittman." In the title role as Jane Pittman, she was required to play the life of the character from the age of 19 to her death at 110. Directed by John Korty and adapted for the screen by Tracy Keenan Wynn, the story was based on a prize-winning novel by Ernest J. Gaines. Aired by CBS in January 1974, the action is centered around "the life of an ex-slave from the post-Civil War years to the civil rights movement of the 1960s" (*Jet*). "The plot . . . presents without any compromise the black experience in the deep South" (Bright, 18).

Critics heaped well-deserved praise on her for her magnificent performance in "The Autobiography of Miss Jane Pittman." "Movie critic Judith Crist called Miss Tyson's virtuoso performance as Jane Pittman 'sheer perfection,' and Pauline Kael wrote in the *New Yorker* (January 28, 1974): 'She's an actress, all right, and as tough-minded and honorable in her methods as any we've got. . . . I'm comparing Tyson to the highest, because that's the comparison she invites and has earned'" (*Current Biography,* 425).

Tuesday, May 28, 1974, is a day Tyson shall never forget, for it was on this date that she stood before family, friends, and fans to receive the coveted Emmy Award as actress of the year for television. "Those who heard Cicely's acceptance speech when she won the 'Emmy' awards for Pittman were not aware of the meaning of her words when she stared right into the camera and said, 'You see, Mom, it really wasn't all a den of iniquity after all.' She said that with a smile, and she was referring to Mrs. Tyson's long-standing opposition to what she called Cicely's 'foolishness work'—her decision to be an actress" (Sanders, 30). Tyson also said of her mother:

> Mother thought that anything having to do with the theater, with entertainment period, was pure sin. . . . She would tell me "It's all a den of iniquity" (Sanders, 30).

Ivan Webster outlines his own theory about Cicely Tyson's stardom: "Since Miss Jane Pittman, television is where Tyson has shone, and where she has perhaps staked out the territory in which she will make her deepest claims on all of us" (Webster, 25). Between 1976 and 1978 she appeared in four television specials. On December 11 and 12, 1976, she appeared on NBC-TV as Harriet Tubman, the Maryland slave who led three hundred other slaves to freedom on the Underground Railroad, in "A Woman Called Moses." It was adapted for television from Marcy Heidish's novel of the same name. In the television adaptation of Alex Haley's powerful saga "Roots" (1977), she played Kunta Kinte's mother. In "King" (1978), she played the part of Coretta Scott King, wife of the slain civil rights leader, Martin Luther King, Jr., and appeared as the mother of Olympic track star Wilma Rudolph in "Wilma."

On November 26, 1981, Thanksgiving Day, Tyson married jazz trumpeter Miles Davis in Amherst, Massachusetts. After her marriage she appeared in "The Marva Collins Story" (1981), portraying the schoolteacher Marva Collins; "Benny's Place" (1982); "Cry Freedom" (1987), the first movie on apartheid; and "The Women of Brewster Place" (1989).

How does Tyson spend her time when she has an hour or so a day to do whatever she wants to do? She told Lynn Norment, "I do just that—whatever I want to do that is going to give me one of those rare moments. I might just take off in the morning and go from one movie house to another. Or I might decide to cook. I do love to cook, but I seldom eat what I prepare. My gratification is watching other people enjoy it" (Norment, 130). As an avid reader, she reads everything she can find. "I spent a lot of time in the library as a child. I think that has to do with the fact that the library is a quiet, peaceful place. I always seek quiet, peaceful places. That's probably why I love early mornings. And I love to walk. When I'm in New York, I walk all over" (Norment, 130-32).

Tyson never had second thoughts about her profession:

> When I decided to become an actress I never had any doubt that I would be successful. Once I began to study, I was in it totally. My mother had always instilled into us that whatever you try to do, do it as best you possibly can and if you are good at what you're doing, then success will come to you. I was never preoccupied with whether or not I was going to be successful, I was preoccupied with doing whatever I was doing the best possible way. If I iron a handkerchief, it's going to be done the best I can possibly do it. I am a perfectionist (Salaam, 90).

That same character trait of being a perfectionist is evident throughout her acting career. For instance, as she was preparing for the role of the aged Jane Pittman, Tyson spent several days with elderly women in a nursing home. This experience helped her "tremendously in playing Jane Pittman, not because I copied them," she said, "but because they shared with me the perspective and quiet dignity that comes with old age. If I learned one thing from this role, it was a deep respect for people who have been down the road and can look back on where they've been" (Bright, 18).

Looking back on where she has been conjures up mixed emotions for Tyson. Receiving recognition and awards from many places she dreamed of as a child growing up in Harlem, she has graciously accepted these honors, including an honorary Doctor of Fine Arts degree from Marymount College in 1979. She holds similar honorary doctorate degrees from Atlanta, Fisk, Loyola, and Lincoln universities.

Recipient of the Vernon Rice Award two times in 1962, Cicely Tyson has received numerous distinguished citations. Among them are awards from the NAACP; the National Council of Negro Women; Urban Gateways, a Chicago social service agency; and the Capitol Press Award.

As cofounder of the Dance Theatre of Harlem, Tyson is responsible for discovering and nurturing new talent. One such discovery was made while filming *The Blue Bird* in Russia. There she met a talented young Russian girl and arranged for her to study at the Dance Theatre of Harlem. In addition to this commitment to the dance theatre, Tyson serves as a trustee for the Human Family Institute and the American Film Institute. She is a member of the board of directors of Urban Gateways.

When Lynn Norment of *Ebony* magazine asked Tyson how she feels about fame and success, she responded:

> I performed . . . for two presidents at the same time. President Shehu Shagari from Nigeria was honored at a state dinner given by President Carter, who invited me to be the guest performer. I was the only performer. When I received the call, I couldn't believe it!! When I came from under the shock of it all, I said, "Well, Cicely, I guess you've arrived." It's one of the highest compliments that I've received (Norment, 132).

Determined to control her destiny, Tyson began making significant choices early in her life. She continues to practice an age-old maxim: "Destiny is not a matter of chance; it is a matter of choice." When Tyson hears: Lights! Camera! Action!, these words take on a different meaning for her because of the choices she made.

References

Angelou, Maya. "Cicely Tyson: Reflections on a Lone Black Rose." *Ladies Home Journal* 94 (February 1977): 40-41.

"Black Actors Don't Make Any Money: Cicely Tyson." *Jet* 44 (17 May 1973): 62.

Bright, Daniel. "Emmy Award for Cicely." *Sepia* 23 (April 1974): 16-20.

"Cicely, Miles Wed on Thanksgiving Day." *Jet* 61 (17 December 1981): 59.

"Cicely Tyson Scores in TV's Jane Pittman Autobiography." *Jet* 45 (21 February 1974): 62.

Crist, Judith. "Sounder." *New York* 5 (2 October 1972): 70-71.

Current Biography Yearbook. New York: H. W. Wilson, 1975.

Ebert, Albert. "Inside Cicely." *Essence* 3 (February 1973): 40-41.

Ebony Success Library. Vol. I. *1,000 Successful Blacks*. Chicago: Johnson Pub. Co., 1973.

Feather, Leonard. "Miles Davis' Miraculous Recovery from Stroke." *Ebony* 38 (December 1982): 60.

Grant, Liz. "Beauty Talk with the Stars." Interview. *Essence* 4 (January 1974): 38-39.

Klemesrud, Judy. "Cicely, the Looker from 'Sounder,'" *New York Times*, 1 October 1972.

Norment, Lynn. "Cicely Tyson: Hollywood's Advocate of Positive Black Images Talks about the 'Bo Derek look' Rip-Off, Her New Movie. . . ." Interview. *Ebony* 36 (February 1981): 124-126.

Peterson, M. "Black Imagery on the Silver Screen." *Essence* 3 (December 1972): 34.

Ploski, Harry A., ed. *The Negro Almanac*. 5th ed. Detroit: Gale Research 1989.

Robinson, Louie. "Cicely Tyson: A Very Unlikely Movie Star." *Ebony* 29 (May 1974): 33-43.

Salaam, Kalamu ya [Val Ferdinand]. "Cicely Tyson: A Communicator of Pride." *Black Collegian* 9 (November/December 1978): 52-54, 86-91.

Sanders, Charles L. "Cicely Tyson: She Can Smile Again after a Three-Year Ordeal." *Ebony* 34 (January 1979): 27-36.

Spradling, Mary Mace, ed. *In Black and White*. 3rd ed. Detroit: Gale Research, 1980.

Webster, Ivan. "Woman Called Tyson." *Encore* 7 (November 1978): 24-27.

Who's Who among Black Americans, 6th ed. Detroit: Gale Research, 1990.

Who's Who in America. Wilmette, Ill: Marquis, 1988-1989.

Who's Who in the Theatre. 17th ed. Detroit: Gale Research, 1981.

Felicia H. (Felder) Hoehne and Barbara Lynne Ivey Yarn

V

Susan Paul Vashon

(1838-1912)

Civil War relief organizer

Civil War relief organizer, educator, and clubwoman Susan Paul Smith Vashon was born in Boston in 1838 to one of the city's leading black families. Her mother, Bostonian Anne Paul Smith, was the eldest daughter of Thomas Paul, a Baptist clergyman and arguably the most influential black man in the city. The Reverend Paul was pastor of Boston's foremost black congregation that met in the three story African Baptist Church, the first church in the city constructed entirely by black laborers. Paul also sponsored the African school, which met in the church's basement, to educate black youngsters denied schooling in Boston's public schools. In addition, Paul was socially active as a Mason and chaplain for the well-known home lodge of black masonry—African Grand Lodge No. 459. The Reverend Paul's work in uplifting former slaves soon involved him in the growing abolitionist movement, and his interest in the nationalist emigration plans of the era resulted in his leading the first Baptist mission to Haiti in 1823, where he was warmly received by President Jean Pierre Boyer. Later Paul became a general agent with his friend, David C. Walker, for the abolitionist *Freedom's Journal* when it was first published by John Russwurm and Samuel Cornish.

Susan Paul Vashon

While Susan Smith's mother, Anne Paul Smith, died when Susan was still very young, the activities of the Paul family remained formative because Susan was taken in by her material grandmother, Katherine Paul. In the Paul household the young Susan doubtless fell under the influence of her aunt Susan Paul for whom she had been named. Susan Paul was a teacher and abolitionist who was an officer in the Boston Female Anti-Slavery Society and served as one of the vice presidents of the Second Annual Anti-Slavery Convention of American Women. In addition to her abolition work, Susan Paul was secretary to Boston's all-black temperance organization and a speaker for women's rights. She worked as a music teacher at Boston Primary School Number 6 and often performed as a vocalist during concerts at the African Baptist Church.

Less is known about Susan Paul Smith's father, Elijah W. Smith. He probably met his wife-to-be at one of the fashionable concerts held at her father's church, for the Boston headwaiter was noted for his skills as a poet, cornetist, and composer. Later his music would take him to London where in 1850 he played in concert at Windsor Castle at the command of Queen Victoria.

At about the same period as his European tour, his daughter Susan entered Miss O'Mears Seminary in Somerville, Massachusetts (three miles northwest of Boston). When she graduated from the school in 1854 she was both valedictorian and the only black pupil in her class. The choice to send her to a private school was probably the result of increasing black resistance to the segregation of public education in Boston which had reached a fever pitch in 1849. Influenced by complaints and boycotts, but too late for Susan Paul Smith, Boston eventually became the first large American city to integrate its schools—requiring racial integration in public education in 1855.

After graduation from Miss O'Mears, Smith moved to Pittsburgh, Pennsylvania, where her father had relocated. She took a teaching post in the segregated local school system under principal George Boyer Vashon, a man fourteen years her senior, whom she married in 1857.

Her new husband had a family and personal history very much like her own. Vashon had been born into an active abolitionist family that resided in Pittsburgh, Pennsylvania, during his youth. At sixteen Vashon went west to Oberlin College and became its first black graduate in 1844. He began a career in education by teaching school in Chillicothe, Ohio, during college, and after graduation he studied law in Pittsburgh. In 1848, after taking the bar examination in New York, Vashon became the first black lawyer to practice in the state; he had originally intended to take the bar examination in Pennsylvania but had been denied the privilege because of his African ancestry.

Frustrated and angry with American racial discrimination, Vashon left for Haiti that same year. It is interesting to speculate that he may have been motivated by his father's interest in an emigration plan popular in Philadelphia during 1824, the year of his birth. Haiti's president Jean Pierre Boyer (the same leader who had welcomed the missionary Thomas Paul the year before) had sent agents to Pennsylvania to recruit free blacks to emigrate to Haiti where their skills would help develop the island and where they could be free of the virulent racism common in the United States. Whatever his motives, Vashon spent the years 1848-1850 in Haiti teaching in Port-au-Prince. He then returned to practice law in Syracuse, New York, (where he wrote his great epic poem, "Vincent Ogé" about the Haitian revolution in 1853) and became professor of belle-lettres and mathematics at New York Central College. In 1857 Vashon moved back to Pittsburgh to take a position as principal and teacher in the city's "colored" public schools.

Clearly Susan Paul Vashon and her husband, George Boyer Vashon, were a well-matched couple. Each had a family active in fostering black education and the abolition movement, and both families were connected to the black republic of Haiti. Susan and George Vashon had both struggled for their educations in schools where black students were a rarity, and both had succeeded with high honors. That both also became teachers is reflective of the professional opportunities available in that era. In the course of their marriage the well-matched Vashons had seven children.

Soldiers and Refugees Receive Care

It is highly probable that prior to the war the newly-married Vashons were active participants in the underground railroad aiding runaway slaves, since both George and his father, John Bethune Vashon, were known to have been conductors in Pittsburgh. Susan Vashon carried on the same tradition during the Civil War. She cared not only for the sick and wounded soldiers, but she also raised funds to house black refugees with a series of sanitary relief bazaars in 1864-65 which netted thousands of dollars to relocate displaced freedmen in Pittsburgh. Such charitable activities, although on a smaller scale, had long marked the black elite of Philadelphia and Boston; in her nursing and work with former slaves in Pittsburgh, Susan Vashon was carrying on well-established traditions.

In 1867 the Vashons moved to Washington, D.C. where George Boyer Vashon became the first black instructor at Howard University (1867-1868) teaching in the evening school; he then took a position as a solicitor for the Freedmen's Bureau. Susan Vashon began teaching in the "colored" public schools of Washington in 1872 and remained active for the next eight years before becoming the principal of the Thaddeus Stevens School. Then in 1874 George Boyer Vashon returned to college teaching by taking a teaching position at the new Alcorn University in Rodney, Mississippi, just three years after its founding. George Boyer Vashon died there in 1878.

The widow Susan Vashon moved with her four surviving children to Saint Louis in 1882 where she remained true to both the Paul and Vashon family traditions of community uplift—working for the All Saints Episcopal Church, the Book Lover's Club, the Mother's Club (guiding young women) and the Women's Federation—until her death in 1912.

Her work to foster the women's club movement in Missouri is especially noteworthy. She helped organize the Missouri Association of Colored Women's Clubs in 1900 and in 1902 she served as president of the Missouri State Federation of Colored Women's Clubs of the National Association of Colored Women's Clubs (NACW), working to unify the efforts of the state's first black women's association. She was instrumental in forming the Saint Louis Association of Colored Women's Clubs and was persuasive enough to bring the national convention of the NACW to Saint Louis during the great World's Fair in 1904.

Vashon lived in Saint Louis with her son John B. Vashon who, like his parents, was a highly respected educator. The three other children who moved to Saint Louis also became part of the city's black elite. George Boyer Vashon worked as a clerk in Saint Louis City Hall, Emma Vashon Gossin was a teacher at Sumner High School, and Frank C. Vashon took up service as a postal worker.

Vashon High School in Saint Louis was named in honor of the Vashon family's many achievements. Susan Paul Vashon, herself, is buried in Bellfontaine Cemetery in Saint Louis.

References

Brown, Hallie Q. *Homespun Heroines and Other Women of Distinction*. Xenia, Ohio: Aldine Publishing Co., 1926.

Dannett, Sylvia G. *Profiles of Negro Womanhood*. Vol. 1. Chicago: Negro Heritage Library, 1964.

Manning, Erma. *Herstory Silhouettes, Profiles of Black Womanhood*. Saint Louis Public Schools Publication, 1980.

Collections

Biographical information on Susan Paul Vashon is located in the Missouri Historical Society, Newspaper Morgue Files.

William D. Piersen

Sarah Vaughan

(1924-1990)

Singer

Critics called Sarah Vaughan "The Divine." Some of her friends called her by the nickname "Sassy." The former name was first used by Dave Garroway, the latter by accompanist John Malachi. She was well known as "a musician's singer," particularly because it was a very rare occasion when a performance did not meet with their praise.

Sarah Vaughan was born on March 27, 1924, in Newark, New Jersey, to Ada and Asbury Vaughan. She went to Arts High School and sang at Mount Zion Baptist Church in Newark. Appropriately, a student from Arts High School, Kwan Nelson, sang "Precious Lord" at her funeral, held on April 9, 1990, at Mount Zion Church, where more than a thousand people came to pay their respects.

Vaughan was married four times: to George Treadwell in 1956, George Atkins in 1959, Marshall Fisher in 1971, and Waymon Reed in 1978. The first three marriages ended in divorce. George Treadwell, a trumpeter and subsequently her manager, had a strong effect on her early career development, as did trumpeter and manager Waymon Reed in her later career. She had an adopted daughter, Deborah, and she lived with her mother and husband on Vaughan's estate in Hidden Hills, California, until her death in April 1990.

Sarah Vaughan

Vaughan's musical training began early. Her father was an amateur guitarist and pianist, and her mother sang in the choir at Mount Zion. She joined her mother in the choir and began piano and organ lessons at the age of eight. She was an organist at Mount Zion at the age of twelve. Her interest in music theory began from her days playing piano in the band at Arts High School, teaching herself to analyze the music and discovering new and different ways to sing melodies.

It was during her school days also that Vaughan's interest in jazz performance began. She reported later that she learned from other musicians, particularly horn players. She used to sneak into a bar in her neighborhood and listen to trumpet player Jabbo Smith. Charlie Parker and Dizzy Gillespie were other early mentors. She met them in 1943, during her first year in show business.

Vaughan's career started fortuitously in 1942. On a friend's dare, she entered a jazz contest at Harlem's Apollo Theatre and won first prize with her performance of "Body and Soul": ten dollars and a week's engagement at the Apollo. Billy Eckstein, the great vocalist, heard her there and recommended her to his bandleader, Earl "Fatha" Hines. She was hired as vocalist and pianist, playing with him at the Apollo and traveling with the band for a year. Eckstein then formed his own bop-oriented big band and hired her as vocalist. Subsequent engagements followed with John Kirby and the J. C. Heard sextet. Another leading influence in her early career was trumpeter George Treadwell, who became her manager and then her husband in 1947.

Early champions of Vaughan's career included critic and pianist Leonard Feather, who arranged her first solo recording session with Continental Records. Dave Garroway heard her and featured her on radio and television shows. Successful appearances and recordings followed that led to her winning *Downbeat* magazine's best female singer award (1947 through 1952) and similar awards from *Metronome* magazine (1948 through 1953).

Concerning her typical tour experiences, Vaughan's accompanist at that time, John Malachi, reports:

> You'd play a few key cities—New York, Washington, Philadelphia, Pittsburgh, Chicago—and then you'd go on tour and play tobacco warehouses and barns all through the South. We'd be on the road for three to eight months of the year. I can remember the times when Sarah was cussin' every minute. She had this beautiful voice and they weren't paying her any attention. They wanted to hear Billy Eckstein. Billy had the hit records as far as the black circuit was concerned. Being a black girl, you know, had definite limitations in those days (*Current Biography,* 408).

Early in her career Vaughan was often seen as a vocalist, accompanied by a stage band or studio orchestra. She was usually featured in soulful ballads, where her sultry voice with beautiful nuances of vibrato could be heard and enjoyed. Her range, precision, and musical ability were important trademarks, along with personalized interpretations. She also appeared with small ensembles and jazz groups, tending to favor this setting more in later years. As a jazz singer, her reputation was first solidified with her recording of "Lover Man" in 1945 with Charlie Parker and Dizzy Gillespie, followed by "Body and Soul" in 1946.

Various attempts have been made to classify her art. Vaughan was above all else a jazz singer in the deepest essential meaning of the term. The dimensions of jazz were always broad enough for her to find the expressive quality she sought for a particular song, and the pages of countless reviews are full of exclamations of praise for the particular insights and nuances she brought to her music. What does one expect of a jazz singer: improvisation? interpretation? vocal technique used for expressive purposes? word-painting? a studied grasp of the art of variation? She had these, and more.

Perhaps versatility, beyond the hackneyed present-day use of the word "crossover," might be a point of departure to use in drawing a musical sketch of Vaughan's art form. She could take a pop song like "I Left my Heart in San Francisco" and paint it a new and different hue. Her 1950s "Mean to Me" shows her early skill in improvising a new second melody to fit the prescribed changes. Can "Tenderly" be colored blue? Listen to hers. Her "Misty" and "Foggy Day" touch your skin with the impressionistic texture she conveys to their moist and thoughtful moods. Her "April in Paris" is a jazz tour de force. Do you want up-tempo? Try her "Sweet Georgia Brown." Slow? Try one of her mournful blues renditions. Bossa? Try her "If You Went Away."

For Vaughan, boundaries seemingly didn't exist for jazz. She wasn't "crossing" to reach for the audience; they came to her. Of her rendition of the Broadway show tune, "Dancing in the Dark," critic Martin Williams commented that it was "a gloriously dramatic version, in which every note seems to be bursting out of the confines of that song" (*Saturday Review,* August 26, 1967, 81).

Vaughan's career may be seen as moving along several tracks with some shifts and turns in the process. She performed in virtually all available settings from solo appearances to small combos to concerts accompanied by a full symphony orchestra. She performed in small clubs, theaters, concert halls, and large stadiums; at jazz festivals, for presidents, and on college campuses; from New York's Cafe Society Downtown to Copenhagen's Tivoli Gardens to the Hollywood Bowl to New York's Avery Fisher Hall to the Copacabana to Mister Kelly's in Chicago.

As a recording artist, Vaughan began with recordings for Continental and Musicraft Records *Lover Man*, 1945, and moved to contracts with Columbia, Mercury, Mainstream, Roulette and Pablo Records. Some of her most famous albums include *The Divine One* (Roulette), *Live in Japan* (Mainstream), *Lullaby of Birdland* (EmArcy), *Sassy* (EmArcy), *Broken Hearted Melody*(Mercury), *Sassy Swings Again* (Mercury), and her more recent *I Love Brazil*(Pablo), *The Duke Ellington Songbook*(Pablo) and *Brazilian Romance* (Columbia).

Her accompanying groups have ranged from combos featuring jazz artists the caliber of Ray Brown, Oscar Peterson, Joe Pass, and Louis Bellson, to orchestras including the Los Angeles Philharmonic, National Symphony Orchestra, and Duke Ellington's Orchestra. Her first European tour was in 1953, and subsequent European and international tours included an extensive tour in the 1960s with the Count Basie Orchestra, and tours to South America, Japan, Africa, Australia, and England. As a result, her acclaim was extended widely abroad and won her the Downbeat International Jazz Critics award for world's best female singer during the years 1973 and 1975 to 1979, and she headed the 1990 list of inductees into the Jazz Hall of Fame.

Following Vaughan's first television performance with Dave Garroway, she has been featured on a broad variety of shows, with hosts including Ed Sullivan, Johnny Carson, Jackie Gleason, Merv Griffin, and Sammy Davis, Jr. Jazz festivals in which she has performed include a variety of international festivals and the Monterey and Newport Jazz Festivals in the United States.

In describing Vaughan's vocal abilities, one should begin with Ella Fitzgerald's affirmative statement: "The greatest singing talent in the world today is Sarah Vaughan" (*Current Biography,* 407). Gifted with a wide-ranging voice centered primarily in the contralto register, Vaughan made excellent use of all of her vocal strengths. Her control was strong throughout her range. There was a sultry, soulful nature to the lower voice, great strength in the mid-range, and a more pointed, clear, and bell-like quality to the upper register.

Improvisation Called Vaughan's Greatest Gift

An early discovery of the potentials of vibrato led to her use of this technique to color her lower range with dark, whispery caresses, or bright dynamic colorations in her higher ranges, and to use these nuances for a beautifully embroidered painting of notes, ideas, and moods. Precise musicianship enabled her to complete slides and embellishments with pinpoint accuracy. The art of improvisation was one of her greatest gifts.

She could move easily throughout her range, adding, subtracting, and using a full palette of dynamics from a subtle pianissimo to a proud fortissimo. Several musicians commented that she sang using the fullest vocal possibilities, thought as a musician, and was also somewhat instrumental in her approach. She herself said that beginning in her early career she admired instruments, particularly horns: "When I was singing with the (Hines) band, I always wanted to imitate the horns. Parker and Gillespie, they were my teachers" (*Current Biography,* 408).

Perhaps Martin Williams best summarizes her technical prowess:

> Her voice has range, body, volume. More important, her control of her voice is phenomenal. Her pitch is just about impeccable, and she can jump the most difficult intervals and land true. No other singer has such an effortless command of dynamics. I know of no one who can move from a whisper to full volume in the course of a few notes and make the move sound less affected than Sarah Vaughan (*Saturday Review,* 50, August 26, 1967, 81).

He also wrote that:

> Sarah Vaughan has one of the biggest and most powerful voices—in range, in volume, in body, in variety of texture, in flexibility—that our "popular music" has ever seen. Indeed, listen to a performance like her astonishing "Dancing in the Dark" and you may come away convinced that hers is a voice, and a control and use of a voice, that is quite beyond category or style (*Smithsonian Collection of Classical Jazz,* album notes, 35).

Whitney Balliett (*New Yorker,* October 1, 1990, 89) adds the following critique:

> She was a wonderful embellisher and improviser, who never sang a song the same way twice. . . . At her most unfettered, she became a horn singer. Yet her melodic lines were of such complexity and daring that no horn player could have played them. Ultimately, she became a kind of abstract singer, whose materials were inadequate for what she did but were all that she had.

Bill Cosby recounts a humorous event that shows another, lighter dimension of this versatile personality. At a performance on Vaughan's birthday, she apparently had celebrated a bit too much, but nevertheless went ahead with a high-speed virtuoso rendition of "Sweet Georgia Brown." She forgot the words, but improvised all kinds of impossible words and sounds to fit the notes, always homing in on "Sweet Georgia Brown," to the point where Camille Cosby fell on the floor, overcome with laughter. Cosby comments that, "My wife, though she's married to a comedian, never laughed so hard in all her life" (*Jazziz*, vol 7, no. 7, June/July 1990, p. 67-68).

Finally, we might close with another very apt Cosby anecdote. Vaughan's husband, Wayman Reed, was talking to Cosby on the night she died, and said: "No, you have to listen to me. I have your singing album." Cosby said, "What?" He said, "Yeah, I have your singing album." Cosby said, "Oh, man. Well, don't play it." He said, "No man, I won't play it because you can't sing worth a beep-t-beep, you know." Cosby said, "Yeah, but after Sarah dies you can play it again, because there'll be nothing to measure great singing with" (*Jazziz,* June/July 1990, 68).

References

Aldred, Michael, "The Divine Sarah Vaughan—The Columbia Years, 1949-1955." *Audio* 73 (October 1989): 172.

Balliett, Whitney. "Jazz Giants." *The New Yorker* 66 (October 1990): 89-90.

Cosby, Bill, "Sarah Vaughan." *Jazziz* 7 (June/July 1990): 67-68.

Current Biography. New York: H. W. Wilson, 1980.

Driggs, Frank. "Everything I Have is Yours—The MGM Years." *Audio* 71 (October 1987): 41.

Feather, Leonard. *Pleasures of Jazz.* New York: Horizon, 1976.

Gelly, Dave. *The Giants of Jazz.* New York: Schirmer, 1986.

Jones, Max. *Talking Jazz.* New York: Norton, 1988.

Kernfeld, Barry. "Sarah Vaughan." *The New Grove Dictionary of American Music.* London: Macmillan, 1986.

———. "Sarah Vaughan." *The New Grove Dictionary of Jazz.* New York: Macmillan, 1988.

Leydi, Roberto. *Sarah Vaughan.* Milan: G. Ricordi, 1961.

Liska, James. "Sarah Vaughan: I'm Not a Jazz Singer." *Down Beat* 49 (May 1982): 19-21.

Lyons, Leonard and Don Perlo. *Jazz Portraits.* New York: Morrow, 1989.

McDonough, J. "50th Annual Down Beat Readers Poll." *Down Beat* 52 (December 1985): 22-24.

Morgenstern, Dan. *Jazz People.* Englewood Cliffs, N.J.: Prentice-Hall, 1976.

Morrison, Allan. "Sarah Vaughan Adopts a Baby." *Ebony* 16 (September 1961): 88-94.

Quinn, B. "Sassy '67." *Down Beat* 34 (1967): 20.

Reisner, Robert. *Jazz Titans.* New York: DaCapo Press, 1977.

Robinson, Louie. "The Divine Sarah." *Ebony* 30 (April 1975): 94-102.

"Sarah Vaughan." *Variety* 330 (20 April 1988): 140. (Concert review, Sydney, Australia, Opera House).

"Sarah Vaughan Inducted Into Jazz Hall of Fame." *Jet* 78 (8 October 1990): 56.

Shaw, Arnold. *Black Popular Music in America.* New York, Schirmer, 1986.

Simon, George T. *Best of the Music Makers.* New York: Doubleday, 1979.

"Singer Sarah Vaughan Dies." The *Tennessean*, 5 April 1990.

Southern, Eileen, ed. *Biographical Dictionary of African and Afro-American Musicians.* Westport, Conn.: Greenwood Press, 1982.

Watrous, Peter. "Sarah Vaughan is Eulogized in Church Where She Sang as a Child." *New York Times*, 10 April 1990.

Williams, Martin. "Words for Sarah Vaughan." *Saturday Review* 50 (26 August 1967): 81.

Williams, Martin, ed. *Smithsonian Collection of Classic Jazz.* Washington, D.C.: Smithsonian Institution and Norton, 1973.

Woodward, Richard B. "The Jazz Singer." *Connoiseur* 219 (March 1989): 146-49.

Darius L. Thieme

W

Reverend Mother Charleszetta Waddles (Mother Waddles)

(1912-)

Religious leader and visionary, humanitarian

In Detroit, a city plagued with problems of every magnitude, the Reverend Mother Charleszetta Waddles has devoted her life to uplifting the human spirit and bettering the human condition in a ministry to others that has earned her the name "Mother Waddles." An ordained Pentecostal minister and a visionary, Mother Waddles believes that God reveals His grace through the good works of people: "It's not me that's doing the good, it's God" (Interview with Helen Cooks, 12 November, 1990. Unless otherwise indicated, all quotations are from that interview).

Seeing the need to help humankind, she has guided the Mother Waddles's Perpetual Help Mission for more than three decades. Since the mission opened, it has grown from a collection place for food items for hungry people in the basement of her home to a total of ten urban missions, including two in Africa, answering the needs of more than one hundred thousand people a year, with assistance ranging from job training and placement to health care and counseling to providing food, utility payments, or other solutions to emergency situations (Nagy, 6). Her nonprofit mission has its headquarters at 12479 Grand River, on Detroit's commercial west side. Although there are specific hours of operation, Mother Waddles is on call around the clock, regularly putting in a twelve-hour day for the needy.

Mother Waddles befriends people submerged in poverty and personal tragedy. But it is not just her love that she gives away; she teaches people how to hope. She believes that all unresolved human conflicts and problems result from myopia—incorrect vision or thinking. Her optimistic attitude, faith, and vision keep her from being overwhelmed by the privations of the many hungry and needy people who come to her for help.

Charleszetta Lena Campbell was born on October 7, 1912, in Saint Louis, Missouri. She was the oldest of Henry Campbell and Ella (Brown) Campbell's seven children, only three of whom survived to adulthood. Her parents' third child lives in California; her youngest sister, born three months after her father's death, and Mother Waddles both reside in Detroit.

Helping was not a lesson Waddles learned through any particular experience, but came naturally to her from her earliest years. From the early days of her childhood, she remembers numerous incidents of people stopping her mother along the street to comment about the unusual nature and the promise they saw in the child. Mother Waddles recalls her mother saying that when she was four or five years old, spiritual readers and other mediums would say, "Oh, that child you have is going to do this and is going to do that," but, she regrets that her mother never grasped the full magnitude of their message.

> I remember when I was eleven or twelve years old, my mother used to say, "I wish I had a heart like you." I guess up until the time I did get the calling, all through my younger years and the times I married and remarried, and went through the changes that young people go through, I considered myself freehearted. Then I found out that there's no such animal. There are no freehearted persons, that all good is God, whether you recognize it or not. God was working through me; I just didn't understand it (Interview with Mother Waddles, 12 November 1990, 5 March 1991).

Despite the hardship of her father's death, which forced her to leave school at twelve, Mother Waddles has become self-educated through her wide-ranging and productive experience and diligent Bible study. Even though life seemed to have dealt her a heavy blow at an early age, Charleszetta Waddles says that having to leave school to go to work to help support her family because of her mother's heart condition was no burden: "It just didn't bother me. I had started doing little chores in the neighborhood and washing windows for people when I was nine years old and I would take food to the fair."

Mother Waddles believes that death is not the worst experience that can happen to someone. Her father's rejection by church members after his earnings declined and his resultant feelings of dejection had a greater impact on her than his death and helped prepare her for her life's work:

> I had the experience of watching my dad go from affluence to dejection. He had a person who came in [to the barber shop] and he had impetigo. My dad was not a learned barber. He did not go to school to learn about impetigo, so he lost his trade, by not being aware. I saw him go from that business to working in a black shop where there was no money to be made. And I watched the people in our church, go from saying "Come here, darling," to"Not now, I'm in a hurry." And, boy, I felt that. I saw my dad go stand on corners, for hours at a time. And, so many, many times, I saw my mother cry. When my father died, there weren't hardly any of those people from the church at his funeral. . . . I think that was the foundation for what I am today (Interview with Mother Waddles, 12 November 1990, 5 March 1991).

Her faith has seen her through what others might believe to be impossible odds. Married and a mother by the age of fourteen, she was treated as a "little toy" by her first husband, Clifford Walker, who was nineteen at that time—a man whom she says loved her, but who was a man of the streets and was "not what he said he was." Mother Waddles faced the harsh reality of widowhood at the age of nineteen. By the time she was twenty-one, she was married again, this time to a man twice her age. Like her father, this husband experienced financial setbacks. Expecting to get a good job, he decided to leave Saint Louis, with twenty-four-year-old Charleszetta, and her child, for Detroit, where he landed a job in a restaurant, making eleven dollars a week. Believing her second husband to be unchallenged and uninspired to strive for a better life, Mother Waddles left with her seven children and returned to Saint Louis to help care for her ailing mother. After ending that marriage, she had a short common-law relationship, with which alcohol interfered.

After the death of her mother, she returned to Detroit. Eventually, Mother Waddles found satisfaction in a marriage to Payton Waddles, whom she believes God sent to her and her nine children at a time when they were living on welfare and having trouble making ends meet.

Because thirteen years had passed since the births of her first two children, she thought she was destined to have only two. She says of her third child and the surprise of her unexpected pregnancy, "Oh boy, I thought he was a tumor, a cancer." After the third, though, they came more quickly, even two in one year. By the time she was seventy-nine, she was the mother of ten children, grandmother of thirty-seven, and great-grandmother of twenty-three.

Activities Guided by Early Vision

From her early years, Waddles took risks to help those in need. This behavior came to be her way of life. Years later, despite her limited resources as a mother alone with her nine children after several bad experiences with marriage, living on Aid to Dependent Children, Charleszetta Waddles once again stepped forward to answer a need. One of her friends,

Reverend Mother Charleszetta Waddles

the mother of two children, was about to lose her home. "I said to her, 'I'm going to give up my house,'" she related, "'and I'm going to move into your house so you won't lose it.' I didn't want her to lose that house, so I moved into her unfinished basement." It was in the basement of this house that Mother Waddles at the age of thirty-six had her first vision directing her to "create a church that had a social conscience, that would feed the hungry, clothe the naked, and take folks in from outdoors." A woman with drive, creativity, and spirit, Mother Waddles undertook the responsibility to raise money for a church function. She was selling barbecue at the church when a man on his way to gamble stopped to buy something to eat. Mother Waddles recalls, "I'd never seen that man before in my life. But, I married that man. He not only got the barbecue, he got me and my nine children . . . and today, I draw his social security; he passed away in 1980. I've never been back on welfare, and I'm still living off the love that he gave me."

Mother Waddles believes that God made it possible for her to submit to His will. He had sent her a man to help her carry out the work. She began to have prayer meetings at her house. She would tell the small group of ladies gathered that they were never too poor to give to the less fortunate, that they could take a can of food from the shelf and give it to someone in need. She says, "You can create a thing, and it can be a step. I wanted a black, religious, charitable church . . . one that tended to the earthly things as well as the heavenly things."

Love for humanity led Mother Waddles to open in 1950 a "thirty-five-cent restaurant," where all meals cost just thirty-five cents. Mother Waddles did the cooking, the laundry, and almost everything that had to be done for the restaurant. The menu offered a wide variety, and patrons from all walks of life were welcome. Some who could afford it gave as much as three dollars for a cup of coffee. All patrons of the restaurant were offered the same food choices and the same service—a napkin, a glass, silverware, a flower on the table, a menu, and a waitress. The needy could eat with dignity. The affluent could humble themselves. And what astounded everyone was that no one took advantage of the situation or the generosity before them.

Church and Charitable Mission Opened

In the mid-fifties, while reading the newspaper, Mother Waddles found an advertisement that read "Store for Rent, two months rent free." In responding, however, she learned that the occupant would have to pay two months rent up front before receiving the two months free. Mother Waddles told the owner, "I have nothing but an idea, and I just happened to see the two months free rent." Convinced by her determination, the owner let her have the space. And thus began her black religious charitable church, the Perpetual Help Mission.

Mother Waddles is a living testament to her conviction of the importance of love and service for others. Many people have assisted her in carrying out her mission. Mother Waddles reflects, "That's how I keep my business going. Some give food, some give clothes, some give shoes." Being creative and resourceful, Mother Waddles has also written a philosophy book, a book on self-awareness and self-esteem, and two cookbooks. She has sold more than 85,000 copies of her cookbooks over the past thirty years; the proceeds go to help continue her work.

Sustained by her faith in God, Mother Waddles remembers one of God's divine blessings in this way:

> I fell and broke my pelvic bone and they said, "Well she won't walk." The newspapers were rolling it off the press; TV folks were coming. After two weeks, I was sitting up on the side of the bed. In the middle of night, I heard, "The earth is without form or order." That is all I heard, and I said, "Oh, that's just like a poor woman's kitchen, without food or water." Sometimes you got the meat and you ain't got the bread. Sometimes you got the bread and you ain't got the potatoes. I wrote a poem:
>
> Creating a meal is a poem, I'm saying.
> All you have to do is have imagination
> And a gospel song to sing. Then when it
> Comes time to eat,
> You sit down to a meal you can't beat.
> Say, 'God's amazing grace done it again,
> Amen.' (Interview with Mother Waddles, 12
> November 1990, 5 March 1991).

Mother Waddles seeks to bring hope to desperate, destitute, and dispossessed persons caught in the web of poverty and deprivation, the thousands of men, women, and youths who find themselves entrapped in the vicious whirlwind of drugs and associated crimes. Mother Waddles explains that many black Americans and poor people have been brainwashed into thinking that those who have to struggle and work hard are people devoid of dignity. Thus, in the past, parents overprotected their children, hoping that they might avoid the hardships they themselves have had to face. Consequently, this generation of young adults is unable to cope with the realities of life. It is her belief that many of today's poor could have bought a home with half of the money they have spent for overpriced or non-nutritious food if only they had learned to economize and to develop vision and priorities. She claims, "Most of their money has gone to drugs, gone to the bathroom." She insists that many of life's tragedies could be circumvented if people would develop positive attitudes towards living and learn to help themselves. About many situations, she says, "We've got to help them to help themselves."

Mother Waddles also knows the value of education and strongly encourages young people to stay in school to acquire the skills they will need to realize their potential. She expresses a desire to get on a speaking circuit to talk to young people. She believes they need to know the importance of family, relationships, and marriage. She recognizes the obstacles many men face in this society, especially those who live in large urban areas experiencing economic woes, such as Detroit. With threats to the automobile industry all around, she has been inspired to open a school to retrain people who have lost their jobs through plant closings and permanent layoffs. She is keenly aware of the technological advances made in this society and the shift to industrial production with highly technical skill requirements. While she is taking steps to move the mission into the future, she has not abandoned her founding purpose. The school will offer classes in adult basic education, as well.

Mother Waddles was the featured subject of a 1989 PBS documentary on her endless devotion to serve the needy. The thirty-minute *Ya Done Good,* described her endeavors and commitment to those who need help and to those who have "fallen through the cracks" of other social service systems. The program's producer and director, Daphne Boyd Kilgore, said in an article appearing in the *Detroit Free Press* that "there's strong interest in Hollywood for a miniseries docudrama" (Chargot, B-1, B-5).

Mother Waddles has accomplished much in the eight decades since her mission began. Municipalities, civic, service, and social organizations have recognized her leadership and contributions, presenting her with more than three hundred awards, plaques and honoraria. Many of her weekly sermons have been published and are available to the public, as are her cookbooks and book of philosophy. She uses the proceeds from her writings to continue the work of her mission.

Mother Waddles says she is a simple person, doing the Lord's work because it is her calling to serve the needs of others. She says, "I think that's why He picked me. Because

I was simple. I didn't have all that technical knowledge, and He didn't let me get it. I had to get down to the nitty-gritty. . . . So, I've kept my feet on the ground and stayed with the people. I'm the one God gave [the calling] to. If I don't keep doing it until the day I die, then I have lived beneath my privilege." She laments, "I guess I'm just a nobody trying to tell somebody I'm somebody who loves everybody." Asked what she would be if she were not a missionary, she leaned back in her chair, and with characteristic smile, confidence, determination, and humor, she replied, "I'd be a revolutionary."

References

Briscoe, Stephen. "Mother Waddles: City's Poor 'Worse than Ever.'" *Michigan Chronicle* 3-9 October 1990. Includes line drawing.

Chargot, Patricia. "Mother Waddles, City's Helper of Poor, Stars in Documentary." *Detroit Free Press* 16 February 1990). Includes photograph.

"Mother Waddles: One Woman's War on Poverty." Essence 21 (October 1990): 48. Includes photograph.

Nagy, Mike. "Mother Waddles Speaks at the University of Detroit about Charity and Self-Esteem." University of Detroit *Student Illustrated* 10 February 1988.

Waddles, Reverend Mother Charleszetta. Interview with author. 12 November 1990, 5 March 1991.

Collections

An earlier oral history interview with Mother Waddles is in the Black Women Oral History Project collection, Schlesinger Library, Radcliffe College.

Helen C. Cooks

A(i)da Walker

(1870-1914)

Entertainer

Aida (or Ada) Walker (scholars differ on the spelling) was a pioneer black stage performer who could do it all: sing, dance and act. Throughout her short but notable career she was given high praise for all three.

As with many early performers, little is known for certain about Walker's early life. She was born in Richmond, Virginia, in 1870. The date is unknown, as is much about her family. A few years after her birth, Walker came with her mother to live in New York City, which was to be her chief

A(i)da Overton Walker

place of residence until her death on October 11, 1914. No hard data is available as to the cause of her death, but many show-business people succumbed to the rigors of the profession: high stress and little sleep culminating in exhaustion often complicated by pneumonia. Her husband, George Walker, died years before her of advanced venereal disease, and that certainly could have contributed to the decline of Aida's health. What is known is that during her performing years she was a lithe and attractive woman of about five feet three inches. She was as quiet and reserved offstage as she was uninhibited on stage.

About her formal education still less is known. One might easily deduce the presence of a mentor in the performing arts, as by 1886 at age sixteen she "began to attract attention as a soubrette with the Black Patti Company and later with the Oriental American Company in 1888" (Sampson, 438). Both companies provided training grounds for Walker's prodigious talents. The extravaganzas they would produce for the burlesque house circuits served to hone the entire company's skills for later appearances on Broadway. Slowly but surely Walker worked her way up to featured performer.

When manager John W. Isham was looking for cast for his minstrel-tradition Negro show in 1895, "The Octoroons," he recruited Billy Johnson, Tom Brown, Tom McIntosh, the Hyer Sisters, Mattie Wilkes, Walter Smart, George Williams, and Walker. The women all had prominent roles, and the closing number, "Cakewalk Jubilee," featured the dancing talents of the brash Walker. She was a natural for Isham's next venture, a complete departure from the burlesque and minstrel traditions: the first production with a Negro cast to open on Broadway. Another all-star cast was assembled that included Sidney Woodward, J. Rosamond Johnson, William

C. Elkins, Maggie Scott, and Inez Clough. The production de-emphasized dancing and featured solos and choruses from Carmen, Martha, Faust, Il Trovatore, and other operas. But Walker had proven her versatility and that would propel her to superstardom on the stage from then on.

By 1899 another major element had been added to black theater: black ownership and management with Bob Cole and his associates Bill Johnson, Sam Lucas, Jesse Shipp, and others. His first effort, *A Trip to Coontown*, was the first black musical comedy, a show with a continuous storyline from beginning to end. It was a tremendous success, running for three seasons between 1898 and 1900. Walker stood out in her chorus role.

This success inspired giant leaps in black theatrical efforts, and Walker was literally right in the middle of them. At various times she worked with great co-stars: Bert Williams and George Walker, Will Vodery, Sissieretta Jones, Ernest Hogan, and Alex Rogers; and she used material from writers Will Marion Cook, Paul Laurence Dunbar and many more.

Stage Performer Featured with Williams and Walker Team

Before the close of *A Trip to Coontown*, an 1899 show, *Senegambian Carnival*, brought George Walker and Aida Walker together. On June 22, 1899, they were married. Next came *The Policy Players* in which George Walker was featured in the musical number, "The Broadway Coon." Very shortly thereafter Bert Williams and George Walker's biggest success to date was mounted, *The Sons of Ham* in 1900. Not coincidentally Aida Walker had a featured role, that of a citizen of the town the characters played by Williams and Walker were trying to hoodwink.

The Cannibal King in 1901 was a flop, but it was followed by the hugely successful *In Dahomey* in 1902, the first black show to open on Times Square. It played the Grand Opera House in August and then went on a forty-week tour of the country. Aida Walker played the role of Rosetta Lightfoot, "a troublesome young thing" and was featured in the Act II musical number, "Actor Lady." Later the show went to London's Shaftesbury Theater, and there was a command performance at Buckingham Palace. Walker was the toast of royalty and gentry as she introduced the cakewalk dance to Britain and France.

In 1906 the most lavish of the Williams and Walker productions, *In Abyssinia*, with a large cast, elaborate scenery, and live animals, including camels, continued their winning ways. Aida Walker was cast as an Abyssinian, "Miriam, a market girl," and arranged, sang, and danced in three elaborate production numbers. The production's run at the Majestic Theater on Columbus Circle and Fifty-eighth Street was sufficiently long to make a handsome profit. At this point the salaries of all the featured performers lifted them above all but the captains of industry.

Aida Walker was by then a full-fledged member of New York's high society, as she was one of the luminaries of Marshall's, the "in-spot" for first black, and then white show business giants. But her life was not all glitz: Jimmie Marshall's hotel was a place to trade stories and discuss race problems. Author, civil rights leader, James Weldon Johnson remembers: "Our room, particularly of nights, was the scene of many discussions; the main question talked about and wrangled over being always the status of the Negro as a writer, composer and performer in the New York theater and world of music" (Osofsky, 15). Aida Walker had overcome other obtacles of the period. On this issue Mary White Ovington, National Association for the Advancement of Colored People co-founders, commented: "Lightness of color seems a requisite for a stage position, unless a dark skin is offset by very great ability, as in the case of Aida Walker, one of the most graceful and charming women in musical comedy" (157).

By the time *Bandanna Land* opened in 1908, Walker's husband George was so ill that he retired from show business after only a few performances. Walker sang not only her own numbers like "It's Hard to Love Somebody When Somebody Don't Love You," but in male attire all of George's, including his signature "Bon Bon Buddy, The Chocolate Drop." She was considered nothing less than a marvel. After receiving the best of care in various sanitariums, George Walker died in 1911.

It was pretty much downhill for Aida Walker after that as well. She was contracted by the *Smart Set* company for the 1909-1910 season and performed in several less-successful productions, though well-regarded as a fabulous dancer of great talent. For the 1911-12 season she appeared in vaudeville and toured in both the East and West. "For the next two years, Walker devoted more of her time to producing acts than to appearing on the stage and was financially interested in the Porto Rico Girls and the Happy Girls" (Sampson, 439). She was also instrumental in the careers of Lottie Gee and Anita Bush. The last entertainment under her management was given at the Manhattan Casino on August 16, 1914. She died shortly afterwards on October 11, 1914.

James Weldon Johnson called Aida Walker "beyond comparison the brightest star among women on the Negro stage of this period, and it is a question whether or not she had since been surpassed. She was an attraction in the company not many degrees less than the two principals (Williams and Walker)" (Johnson, 107). It was quite an accomplishment even to hold one's own in the company of the stars with whom she shared the stage. Still, she did quite well:

> Ada Walker was a singer who did ragtime songs and ballads equally well. As a dancer she could do almost anything, and no matter whether it was a "buck-and-wing," "cake walk" or some form of grotesque dancing, she lent the performance a neat gracefulness of movement which was unsurpassed by anyone. Those of us who can actually remember her, are pretty well agreed that she was a Florence Mills and Josephine Baker rolled into one. The late Florence Mills

herself admitted that Ada Overton Walker was her idol, and that she had tried to follow in Ada's footsteps. Ada in fact taught Florence Mills the song, "Miss Hannah From Savannah" which started the immortal little "Blackbird" to fame and stardom (Fletcher, 181-82).

References

Charters, Ann. *Nobody: The Story of Bert Williams.* London: Macmillan, 1970. Includes photographs of Ada Overton Walker.

Fletcher, Tom. *One-Hundred Years of the Negro in Show Business.* New York: Da Capo Press, 1984.

Johnson, James Weldon. *Black Manhattan.* New York: Knopf, 1940. Reprinted. New York: Arno Press, 1968.

Osofsky, Gilbert. *Harlem: The Making of a Ghetto: Negro New York, 1890-1930.* 2nd ed. New York: Harper Torchbooks, 1971.

Ovington, Mary White. *Half A Man: The Status of the Negro in New York.* New York: Longmans, Green, 1911.

Sampson, Henry T. *Blacks in Blackface: A Sourcebook on Early Black Musical Shows.* Metuchen, N.J.: Scarecrow Press, 1980. Photographs of Ada Overton Walker, p. 439.

Shaw, Arnold. *Black Popular Music in America: From the Spirituals, Minstrels, and Ragtime to Soul, Disco, and Hip-Hop.* New York: Schirmer Books, 1986.

Stearns, Marshall and Jean. "Williams and Walker and the Beginnings of Vernacular Dance on Broadway." *Keystone Folklore Quarterly* 11 (Spring 1966): 3-12.

Denis Mercier

A'Lelia Walker

(1885-1931)

Arts patron, entrepreneur

Entrepreneur and Harlem Renaissance patron A'Lelia Walker was born in Vicksburg, Mississippi, in 1885, to Sarah (Breedlove) McWilliams and Moses McWilliams. She became famous as the fabulous A'Lelia Walker of Harlem, New York. Originally she was named Lelia; as an adult she changed her name to the more breathless A'Lelia. According to rumor, her father was killed by a lynch mob when she was two years old. Her mother and the two-year-old Lelia moved from Vicksburg to Saint Louis, Missouri, where her mother had relatives, found work as a cook and a laundress, and

A'Lelia Walker

supported her daughter with her meager earnings. In spite of their poverty, Lelia attended the public schools in Saint Louis and eventually graduated from a private biack college, Knoxville College, in Knoxville, Tennessee.

Since her mother was illiterate at that time, Lelia Walker became the chief asset in her mother's beauty-care business. Working side by side with her mother, she assisted in the manufacturing of products, helped with business decisions, and traveled around the country selling the products. In 1906 Madame Walker placed her daughter in charge of the mail order operation in Pittsburgh while she continued to introduce the products in different parts of the South and East. Finally Madame moved to Pittsburgh, Pennsylvania, and joined her daughter, who was now a young married woman. Together they resolved problems in the business and established their system of beauty culture.

By 1908 mother and daughter set up a beauty school, Lelia College, in Pittsburgh in order to train beauty culturists in the Walker method. Lelia was left to take care of Lelia College and local business, and Madame traveled to take care of business on a national level. In addition, Lelia set up a special correspondence course that cost twenty-five dollars. Diplomas and contracts were provided from the Lelia College with the signatures of Madame C. J. Walker, president, and Lelia Robinson, secretary. In 1910 Madame Walker moved her headquarters to Indianapolis, Indiana. By 1913, Lelia moved part of the business operations and set up another Lelia College in New York. Whether dealing with speaking engagements, business decisions, or sales tips, mother and daughter were in accord. Their experiences bound them together professionally and personally.

After her mother's death, A'Lelia Walker, became the president of the company; she threw herself into the business of running the company and put her mark on it. She had the Walker Building at 617 Indiana Avenue in Indianapolis erected in 1928. The building contained the Walker Manufacturing Company, the Walker College of Beauty Culture, a beauty salon, barbershop, pharmacy, grocery store, professional offices, and the Majestic Walker Theater. The Walker Building was the first black owned and operated building of its kind in the country. It became a haven for black professionals, entrepreneurs, and patrons of the arts since segregation disallowed the use of white office buildings during this period. The building was renovated in 1988 and has again become a focal point of black life in Indianapolis. It has been placed on the state and national registers of historic places.

The "Joy Goddess" of Harlem Blossoms

It was in New York that Madame Walker built her palatial villa in the village of Irvington, New York, facing the Palisades on the Hudson River. Lelia, by now known as A'Lelia, was a patron of the arts and was referred to by Langston Hughes as the "joy goddess" of Harlem's 1920s when the Harlem Renaissance was in full flower. A'Lelia Walker remodeled her own town house on 136th Street and christened it "The Dark Tower". As party hostess, A'Lelia Walker served as a stimulus to careers of many talented blacks and helped to promote interest in the young, black avant-garde poets, artists, and writers. A'Lelia Walker entertained everybody, the famous and the not so famous, the intellects and the not too intellectual. No matter who they were, they all had a good time.

Although Walker's apartment could hold only a hundred people, she nevertheless, invited hundreds of people to each party. The guests would have to arrive early if they planned to get in the door. Langston Hughes tells of the arrival of "some royal personage"—a Scandinavian prince—who was unable to penetrate the crowded entrance hall and enter the party area. Hughes added:

> Word was sent in to A'Lelia Walker that His Highness, the Prince, was waiting without. A'Lelia sent word back that she saw no way of getting His Highness in, either, nor could she herself get out through the crowd to greet him. But she offered to send refreshments downstairs to the Prince's car (Hughes, 244-45).

In spite of the enormous crowd, people enjoyed milling around in the hallway or standing wherever they could find space. Walker not only entertained in her town house and her apartment in New York City, but she held parties at her country mansion Villa Lewaro, at Irvington-on-the-Hudson where she awakened overnight guests with pipe organ programs each morning.

It was A'Lelia Walker who asked the singer Caruso to name her mother's villa. The name comes from the first two syllables of Lelia Walker's name:

> Lelia Walker Robinson
> Le Wa Ro

When Madame Walker died, she left her daughter the bulk of her estate and the mansion, Villa Lewaro, was bequeathed at the end of A'Lelia Walker's life to the NAACP. In spite of her emotional grief over the loss of her mother, she ran the business wholeheartedly and added her own touch to the business.

With a physically commanding presence, A'Lelia Walker was almost six feet tall and had bold African features with a chocolate brown coloring. She wore jeweled turbans on her cropped hair. Madame Walker provided her daughter with wealth and she lived lavishly. At the time of Madame Walker's death in 1919, A'Lelia Walker and her adopted daughter, Mae, were in Panama. Upon her return home she buried her mother with extreme personal grief. Three days after her mother's death she became the wife of Wiley Wilson, however this marriage did not last. Then she resurrected her relationship with James Arthur Kennedy and married him. They also obtained a divorce shortly afterwards. All in all she married four times.

A'Lelia Walker died unexpectedly at the home of friends in Long Branch, New Jersey, in August 1931. The Reverend Adam Clayton Powell, Sr., eulogized her in an exclusive funeral parlor in Harlem on Seventh Avenue. The funeral was by invitation only. Langston Hughes described the occasion, the playing of soft music for the solemn ceremony, and the amazement of the crowd:

> We were startled to find De Lawd standing over A'Lelia's casket. It was a truly amazing illusion. At that time *The Green Pastures* was at the height of its fame and there stood De Lawd in the person of Rev. E. Clayton Powell, a Harlem minister, who looked exactly like Richard B. Harrison in the famous role in the play. . . .
>
> A night club quartette that had often performed at A'Lelia's parties arose and sang for her. They sang Noel Coward's "I'll See You Again," and they swung it slightly, as she might have liked it. It was a grand funeral and very much like a party. Mrs. Mary McLeod Bethune spoke in that great deep voice of hers, as only she can speak. She recalled the poor mother of A'Lelia Walker in old clothes, who had labored to bring the gift of beauty to Negro womanhood, and had taught them the care of their skin and their hair, and had built up a great business and a great fortune to the pride and glory of the Negro race—and then had given it all to her daughter, A'Lelia.
>
> Then a poem of mine was read . . . "To A'Lelia." And after that the girls from the various Walker beauty shops throughout America brought their flowers and laid them on the bier (Hughes, 246-47).

References

Bundles, A'Lelia. Interview with author, 4 November 1988.

Bundles, A'Lelia. "Madame C. J. Walker To Her Daughter A'Lelia Walker—The Last Letter." *Sage* 1 (Fall 1984): 34-35.

Fisher, Walter. "Sarah Breedlove Walker." *Notable American Women 1607-1950*. Vol. III. Cambridge: Harvard University Press, 1971.

"Henry Bundles and the Madame C. J. Walker Co." *Shoptalk*, Spring Journal, 1989: 108.

Higgins, Will. "On the Verge of Big Growth? 76 year old Madame Walker firm considers leaving Indianapolis." *Indianapolis Business Journal* 29 June 29 1987: 9-11.

Hughes, Langston. *The Big Sea: An Autobiography*. New York: Thunder's Mouth Press, 1940.

Lewis, David Levering. *When Harlem Was in Vogue*. New York: Knopf, 1981.

Logan, Rayford W. "Madame C. J. Walker [Sarah Breedlove]." *Dictionary of American Negro Biography*. Eds. Rayford W. Logan and Michael R. Winston. New York: Norton, 1982.

Lyons, Douglas C. "History Children: Descendants of Legendary Figures Continue The Tradition." *Ebony* (February 1988): 33-37.

The Madame C. J. Walker Beauty Manual. Indianapolis: Mme. C. J. Walker Manufacturing Company, 1925.

Nelson, Jill. "The Fortune That Madame Built." *Essence* (June 1983): 84-89.

Ploski, Harry A. and Roscoe C. Brown, Jr., eds. *The Negro Almanac*. New York: Bellwether Pub. Co., 1967.

The Story of a Remarkable Woman. Indianapolis: Mme. C. J. Walker Manufacturing Co., 1970.

Trescott, Jacqueline. "The Hair Way to Success: The Business Dynasty of Madame Walker." *Washington Post* 25 May 1973.

Collections

Papers, photographs, and memorabilia of A'Lelia Walker (Robinson) are in the possession of Madame Walker's granddaughter, A'Lelia Bundles of Washington, D.C., the Walker Urban Life Center, and the Indiana Historical Society in Indianapolis. Photographs are in numerous publications, including Lewis's *When Harlem was in Vogue*.

Joan Curl Elliott

Alice Walker

(1944-)

Writer, poet, lecturer

Alice Malsenior Walker, award-winning poet, novelist, essayist, biographer, short story writer, and lecturer, was born on February 8, 1944, in Eatonton, Georgia. Her parents, Willie Lee Walker and Minnie Tallulah (Grant) Walker, were sharecroppers and dairy farmers who supported their eight children—of whom Alice was the youngest—on three hundred dollars a year and on the mother's small salary earned as a part-time maid. In 1952, at the age of eight, Alice Walker suffered temporary disfigurement and permanent blindness in her right eye when one of her brothers shot her with a B.B. gun. Although the injury was traumatic for Walker, causing her to become shy and introspective, it nevertheless marked the emergence of the creative spirit lying dormant in the young girl. Having been nurtured on the folk stories told by her parents, grandparents, and neighbors, at this time Walker began to record their tales and to write original poetry. Her physical vision had been impaired; however, Walker later stated the paradoxical, salutary effects of the accident:

> I believe, though, that it was from this period—
> from my solitary, lonely position of an outcast—

Alice Walker

> that I began really to see people and things, really to notice relationships and to learn to be patient enough to care about how they turned out. I no longer felt like the little girl I was. I felt old, and because I felt I was unpleasant to look at, filled with shame. I retreated into solitude, and read stories, and began to write poems (*In Search of Our Mother's Gardens,* 244-45).

Much of Walker's literary talent is devoted to expressing this "inner" vision. In her works, especially in her poetry, Walker illustrates her sensitivity to, and insistence upon, the worth of the individual and of human relationships. Since her teenage years, Walker has read widely in the literature of all cultures from Greek classics to Russian writers to other American Southern writers like William Faulkner and Flannery O'Conner. However, she prefers to focus on presenting and interpreting the tradition of African-Americans, especially African-American women. According to one critic, who quotes Walker, "To her, to lose those traditions is not only to lose 'our literary and cultural heritage, but, more insidiously, to lose ourselves'" (Mainiero, 314).

Although Alice Walker's parents could not provide their daughter with an abundance of physical comforts, they did provide her with a way of viewing and interpreting the world around her. In addition to their vivid memories of the rural South, the Walkers gave their daughter sources for potential characters and ways to develop them for her later fiction. In her essay "Father," included in *Living by the Word* (1988), Walker recalls that her father seemed like two different fathers to his two sets of children—healthy and vibrant to the first four children and weak and sickly to the second set of four, which included Alice. By the time Alice Walker was born in 1944, her father, the first black man to vote in Eatonton, Georgia, was old and sickly. Although Walker resembled her father in physical features, emotionally they were worlds apart. Walker says that, "I am positive my father never understood why I wrote" (9). In fact. she states that her father tended to be "like some of my worst characters the older he got" (11). It was not until after her father's death, when she went to the cemetery and lay on his grave and meditated, that Walker was able to achieve a "wonderful reconciliation" with her parent (Bradley, 32).

In contrast, Walker expresses a closer bond with her mother, who quietly encouraged Walker to pursue her literary career. This encouragement was symbolized by three gifts: a sewing machine when Walker was fifteen or sixteen, which, in Walker's mind, gave the young girl courage to be independent; a suitcase for Walker's graduation from high school, which, recalls Walker, "gave me permission to travel"; and a typewriter when Walker was in high school, a gift that symbolized to Walker her mother's message—"Go write your ass off" (Washington, 38). Walker especially remembers these gifts because at the time, her mother was earning less than twenty dollars a week.

To her daughter, Tallulah Walker was "a large, soft, loving-eyed woman who was rarely impatient in our home. Her quick, violent temper was on view only a few times a year, when she battled with the white landlord who had the misfortune to suggest that her children did not need to go to school" (*In Search,* 238). Walker views her mother as a forerunner of the women's movement:

> I grew up believing that there was nothing, literally nothing, my mother couldn't do once she set her mind to it . . . so in a way when . . . the women's movement happened, I was really delighted because I felt they were trying to go where my mother was and where I always assumed I would go (*Current Biography,* 430-31).

After graduating from high school as valedictorian and senior class queen, Alice Walker enrolled as a freshman at Spelman College in Atlanta, Georgia, having been awarded a scholarship for handicapped students. Her neighbors collected her seventy-five-dollar bus fare to Spelman. Walker did not feel comfortable at the elite black woman's college because of its "puritanical atmosphere" (Bradley, 28). While there, however, Walker met the historians Staughton Lynd and Howard Zinn and became active in Atlanta's civil rights movement. Leaving Spelman in 1963 after completing her sophomore year, she enrolled in the more liberal Sarah Lawrence College in Bronxville, New York.

After completing her junior year at Sarah Lawrence, Alice Walker spent the summer in Africa, an experience that, ironically, provided her with some of the material for her first collection of poetry, *Once.* Written when Walker, having returned from Africa, was alone and pregnant in her dormitory room experiencing one of the darkest periods in her life and contemplating suicide, the volume contains poetry that reflects her most influential experiences up to and following that critical moment when she decided to have an abortion. As she searched for a meaning to her life, Walker wrote the poems in the following order: first those about Africa, then the poems on suicide, then those on love, and finally the poems on the civil rights movement. She wrote most of the poems during the week after the abortion and secretly placed them as fast as they were written under the door of her teacher, Muriel Rukeyser, a noted poet. Rukeyser, appreciating the poems of love, suicide, civil rights, and Africa shared them with Hiram Hayden, an editor at Harcourt Brace Jovanovich, who eventually had the volume published in 1968 (*In Search,* 248-49).

Walker's poems show influences of Zen epigrams and Japanese haiku—"simple brief and mysterious poems about love, pain, struggle, and the joy of being alive and whole" (Mainiero, 314). *Current Biography* quotes Lisel Mueller's praise of the poems in *Once:* "Feeling is channeled into a style that is direct and sharp, honest speech pared down to essentials. Her poems are like pencil sketches which are all graven outline: no shaded areas, no embellishments. Wit and tenderness combine into humanity" (431). This collection of poems has a special significance for Walker herself, who stated in an interview, when explaining the genesis of the poems in *Once:*

> I have gone into this memory because I think it might be important for other women to share. I don't enjoy contemplating it; I wish it had never happened. But if it had not, I firmly believe I would never have survived to be a writer. I know I would not have survived at all (*In Search,* 249).

Walker received her B.A. from Sarah Lawrence College in 1965. While working in Liberty County, Georgia, canvassing voters, and for New York City's Welfare Department, Walker spent her free time writing. In 1966 she won a writing fellowship. Although eager to move to Senegal, West Africa, she remained in the states, in Mississippi "to be in the heart of the civil rights movement, to help blacks who had dared to register to vote" (*Current Biography,* 431). It was there that she met Melvyn Rosenman Leventhal, a Jewish civil rights attorney, whom she married on March 17, 1967, in New York City. A daughter, Rebecca Grant, was born November 17, 1969. In 1984 Walker stated that her interracial marriage had a negative effect on her career: "My own work was often dismissed by black reviewers because of my lifestyle: a euphemism for my interracial marriage" (*People Weekly,* 86). She and her husband were divorced amicably in 1977.

In 1967 while still in New York, Walker had two short works published: her essay "The Civil Rights Movement: What Good Was It?" won first prize in *American Scholar*'s annual essay contest and appeared in that journal in August 1967. In the same year her first short story, "To Hell with Dying," was published. In September 1967 Walker and her husband returned to Jackson, Mississippi, where they lived seven years as the first legally married interracial couple in the state (*Current Biography,* 431). While Leventhal fought for desegregation of schools, Walker was for a while a black history consultant to Friends of the Children of Mississippi Head Start program and writer-in-residence at Jackson State College (1968-1969). She also was writer-in-residence at Tougaloo College in 1970-1971 and served on the board of trustees at Sarah Lawrence from 1971 to 1973.

Walker Publishes First Novel

During the next few years, the prolific Walker established herself on the literary scene with several important works. In 1967 Walker wrote her first novel, *The Third Life of Grange Copeland,* while on a fellowship at the MacDowell Colony in New Hampshire. This realistic novel, published in 1970, received reviews ranging from enthusiastic to noncommittal. According to Walker, *The Third Life of Grange Copeland* is "a grave book in which the characters see the world as almost entirely menacing" (Tate, 314). Some critics, however, feel that the characters lack the depth of analysis seen in Walker's later works (*Current Biography,* 432). The main objection concerns the depiction of Brownfield, Grange Copeland's son, whose meanness, some critics think, is exaggerated. In response to this criticism, Walker, in an interview with Claudia Tate, defends her characterization of Brownfield:

> I had a lot of criticism about Brownfield, and my response is that I know many Brownfields, and it's a shame that I know so many. I will not ignore people like Brownfield. I want you to know I know they exist. I want to tell you about them, and there is no way you are going to avoid them. I wish people would do that rather than tell me this is not the right image (*Black Women Writers at Work,* 177).

In 1972-1973 Walker moved to Massachusetts, while her husband remained in Mississippi. In 1973 two more of her works were published, *In Love and Trouble,* a collection of thirteen short stories, and *Revolutionary Petunias and Other Poems.* The collection of short stories, written between 1967 and 1973, had been previously published in magazines such as *Harper's* and *Ms.,* as well as in periodicals directed to black readers. In the collection, Walker draws on her admiration of Zora Neale Hurston and Jean Toomer, depicting, according to critic Lillie P. Howard, "the oppressions, the insanities, the loyalties, and the triumphs of black women," the only people she respects "collectively and with no reservations" (*American Women Writers,* 314). In 1974, *In Love and Trouble* won the American Academy and Institute of Arts and Letters Rosenthal Award.

Revolutionary Petunias, however, is largely autobiographical and is written "in honor of incorrect people like Sammy Lou, the heroine of the title poem who struggled against oppression and won" (*American Women Writers,* 314). The poems focus on revolution and love, which to Walker is essential to a true revolution. Divided into five parts, "with a flower as the symbol of revolution," the poems, according to Barbara Christian, show "that beauty, love, and revolution exist in a necessary relationship" (Evans, 473). Praising the book for its "plain, unaffected diction and its revelations of human behavior and emotion" critic Darwin Turner also observed that "some phrases bordered on the banal" (*Current Biography,* 432). Walker herself has admitted, in an interview, that at least one of the poems included in the volume, "Nothing is Right," is "trite" (*In Search,* 271). Nevertheless, *Revolutionary Petunias* was nominated for the National Book Award and won the Lillian Smith Award of the Southern Regional Council in 1974.

After having two more works published in 1974, *The Life of Thomas Hodge* and *Langston Hughes, American Poet,* a biography for children, Walker saw the publication of her second novel, *Meridian,* in 1976. Abandoning the realism seen in *The Third Life,* Walker, in *Meridian,* attempted a more evocative rendering of the life of the protagonist, Meridian, a civil rights worker. In her interview with Claudia Tate, Walker explains the reason for the nonlinear structure of her second novel:

> All I was thinking of when I wrote *Meridian,* in terms of structure, was that I wanted one that would continue to be interesting to me. The chronological sequence in *The Third Life of Grange Copeland* was interesting as a one-time

> shot, since I had never before written a novel. So when I wrote *Meridian*, I realized that the chronological sequence is not one that permits me the kind of freedom I need in order to create. And I wanted to do something like a crazy quilt, or like *Cane* [by Jean Toomer]—if you want to be literary—something that works on the mind in different patterns. As for the metaphors and symbols, I suppose, like most writers, I really didn't think of them; they just sort of happened (176).

Meridian has been praised "as one of the finest novels to come out of the civil-rights movement" (*Current Biography*, 432). Walker explains her use of the term "crazy quilt."

> You know, there's a lot of difference between a crazy quilt and a patchwork quilt. A patchwork quilt is exactly what the name implies—a quilt made of patches. A crazy quilt, on the other hand, only *looks* crazy. It is not "patched," it is planned. A patchwork quilt would perhaps be a good metaphor for capitalism; a crazy quilt is perhaps a metaphor for socialism. A crazy quilt story is one that can jump back and forth in time, work on many different levels, and one that can include myth. It is generally much more evocative of metaphor and symbolism than in a novel that is chronological in structure, or one devoted, more or less, to rigorous realism, as in *The Third Life of Grange Copeland* (Tate, 176).

Between 1979 and 1982, when Walker's third novel, *The Color Purple*, was published, Harcourt published another volume of Walker's poetry, *Goodnight, Willie Lee, I'll See You in the Morning* (1979), her Zora Neale Hurston Reader, *I Love Myself When I am Laughing in and Then Again When I am Looking Mean and Impressive* (1979), and her second collection of short stories, *You Can't Keep a Good Woman Down* (1981). The title poem of the volume of poetry, "Good Night, Willie Lee, I'll See You in the Morning," comes from Walker's mother's final words to her husband.

Author Wins Pulitzer Prize

It was *The Color Purple* that established Walker as a major American writer, remaining twenty-five weeks on *The New York Times* best seller list and claiming the American Book Award as well as the prestigious Pulitzer Prize for Fiction in 1983. An epistolary novel that recounts the life of the main character, Celie, a young, sexually abused black woman living in the rural South, *The Color Purple* opens with Celie's plaintive expostulation: "Dear God, I am fourteen years old. I have always been a good girl. Maybe you can give me a sign letting me know what is happening to me" (11). The novel includes Celie's letters to God, her later letters to her sister, Nettie, and Nettie's letters to Celie. In an essay included in *Black Women Writers*, Walker recounts the initial difficulty that she had in writing *The Color Purple*. Although Walker conceived of the novel while living in New York, she states that her characters objected to being conceived in New York, that they "spoke" to her these words, rejecting the tall buildings of the city: "'What is this tall shit, anyway?' they would say." Listening to her characters, Walker packed her bags and moved to San Francisco in 1978. It took a while, however, before Walker found the right spot in California for her characters to be "born" (453-55).

According to Walker, Celie is the voice of her step-grandmother, Rachel: "I tried very hard to record her voice for America because America doesn't really hear Rachel's voice" (*People Weekly*, 87). Warner Brothers paid Walker $350,000 for movie rights to *The Color Purple* (*People Weekly*, 87). *The Color Purple* illustrates the writer's feminist allegiance as well as the black woman's tenuous place in American society. Celie's emergence as a strong woman despite her early incestuous rape and marriage of convenience to a man who tortures her mentally and physically, gives testimony to the tenacity of black women in a male-dominated society. The critical acclaim of *The Color Purple* prompted Walker to remark, "I think to many people I could not be a name brand until I was certified by the Pulitzer people. I understand it and I'm not angry at all" (*People Weekly*, 85).

In 1989, Walker's fourth novel, *The Temple of My Familiar*, was published. The critical reception of this novel ranged from very positive to lukewarm. Although it was hailed as a "great" by the *New York Times*, James Wolcott in *New Republic* called it "the nuttiest novel I've ever read" (28). Wolcott is not alone in his objection to what he views as the overly "political" focus of *Temple*. Wolcott acknowledges the merit of "the geographical center [of the novel] being . . . Mother Africa, its moral and spiritual center the black African woman" (30). However, Wolcott obviously bristles at what he sees as Walker's "tedious" effort to emasculate the black male. Many readers will agree that with the many characters and shifting scenes, reading the novel requires patience. However, Walker might advise such readers as she advised readers of *Meridian:* Read the novel twice—to fully appreciate the intent and meaning.

Since the publication of *The Color Purple*, Walker has published another volume of poetry, *Horses Make a Landscape Look More Beautiful*, and two non-fiction works, *Living by the Word* (1988) and *In Search of Our Mother's Gardens* (1983), a collection of essays, articles, reviews, and statements written between 1966 and 1982. The subtitle of the second collection, "Womanist Prose," clarifies Walker's position as a "black feminist." Walker prefers the term "womanist" to "feminist," defining her use of the designation:

> I just like to have words that describe things *correctly*. Now, to me, "black feminist" does not do that. I need a word that is organic, that really comes out of the culture, that really expresses the spirit that we see in black women. And it's just that . . . *womanist* (Bradley, 30).

The term "womanist," which Walker employs to describe her prose, can also describe her poetry, fiction, and Walker herself. From a shy, self-conscious, albeit precocious, child living in the rural South, Walker has become at times a powerful spokesperson for black American women. Walker attributes some of her stories, as well as the "urgency" to record them, to her mother's storehouse of tales and to the urgency with which her mother narrated them. In a sense, Walker's voice is her mother's voice telling of the struggles of her ancestors (*In Search,* 240). Moreover, in a sense, Walker herself can be compared to one of Walker's favorite characters, Zora Neale Hurston's Janie Crawford, the protagonist in *Their Eyes Were Watching God:* self-reliant, adventuresome, willing to take risks. In her volume *Good Night, Willie, I'll See You in the Morning,* Walker pays tribute to Janie, who refused to be either a "mule" or a "queen," who refused to submit to male domination and who refused to accept male depictions of womanhood.

If asked why she writes what she writes, Walker may refer the questioner to Toni Morrison's reply to that same question, "Because they are the kind of books I want to read" (*In Search,* 7). In her own words, Walker says:

> I'm really paying homage to the people I love, the people who are thought to be dumb and backward but who taught me to see beauty (*Current Biography,* 433).

There are many reasons that the works of this gifted writer will endure, but one of the most important reasons is that she has captured the essence of African-American life and of an African-American woman's life as she has heard it and lived it. In an interview, Walker stated:

> One thing I try to have in my life and my fiction is an awareness of and openness to mystery, which, to me, is deeper than any politics, race, or geographical location (*In Search,* 252).

Walker's poetry, refreshingly direct, sometimes antithetical, always honest, reveals this openness and awareness to mystery as felt by a woman who has loved and lost and gained in the process, as a black American living in a troubled society, and as a human being struggling to maintain her dignity and integrity in an increasingly impersonal world. One has only to read one of Walkers poems, such as "These Days," to appreciate Walker's apprehension of the beautiful complexity of life and her rendering of that apprehension into art.

Walker's stature as a writer of fiction has been compared to that of William Faulkner, who stated, when he received the Nobel Prize for Literature in 1950, that the modern novelist had "forgotten the problems of the human heart in conflict with itself, which alone can make good writing because only that is worth writing about, worth the agony and the sweat" (O'Connor, 147). Whether or not Walker cares to be compared to Faulkner, her works reveal similar concern. Alice Walker has been both criticized and lauded for her depiction of African-American life in the early twentieth century. However, her commitment to her craft has never been questioned. In an interview on October 11, 1990, Alice Walker discussed her work with frankness, warmth, and enthusiasm; she is not egotistical, but a writer willing and able to talk about her craft. Although Walker has been offered many academic awards and honorary degrees, she has generally refused to accept such recognition, valuing instead the satisfaction she derives from exploring and writing about the African-American experience.

References

Bradley, David. "Telling the Black Woman's Story." *New York Times*, 8 January 1984. 24-37.

Christian, Barbara. "Alice Walker: The Black Woman Artist as Wayward." In *Black Women Writers (1950-1980): A Critical Evaluation*. Ed. Mari Evans. New York: Anchor, 1984. 457-77.

Current Biography. New York: H. W. Wilson, 1984. Includes photograph.

Mainiero, Linda, ed. *American Women Writers*. Vol. 4. Vois, N.Y.: Frederick Ungar, 1982.

O'Connor, William Van. *The Tangled Fire of William Faulkner*. Minneapolis: University of Minnesota Press, 1954.

Tate, Claudia, ed. *Black Women Writers at Work: Conversations*. New York: Continuum, 1983. 175-87.

Walker, Alice. *The Color Purple*. New York: Washington Square Press, 1982.

———. *Good Night, Willie Lee, I'll See You in the Morning*. New York: Harcourt, 1979.

———. *In Search of Our Mothers' Gardens: Womanist Prose*. New York: Harvest, 1983.

———. "Letters to God are Postmarked with a Pulitzer." *People Weekly* 20 (2 January 1984): 85-86.

———. *Living by the Word*. New York: Harcourt, 1988.

Walker, Alice. Telephone interview with the author. 11 October 1990.

———. "Writing the Color Purple." *Black Women Writers (1950-1980): A Critical Evaluation*. Ed. Mari Evans. New York: Anchor, 1984.

Washington, Mary Helen. "Her Mother's Gifts." *Ms*. 10 (June 1982): 38. Includes photograph.

Who's Who Among Black Americans, 1990/1991. 6th ed. Detroit: Gale Research, 1990.

Wolcott, James. "Party of Animals." *New Republic* 200 (29 May 1989): 28-30.

Grace E. Collins

Lelia Walker

(1886-1954)

Philanthropist, civic worker, humanitarian

Lelia O'Neal Walker, philanthropist, church and community worker, and humanitarian, was the daughter of a well-to-do family. Her father, Ireland O'Neal, (who died when Walker was six years old), was from Shannon, Ireland, and her mother, Tennie Fannie O'Neal, was of African descent. Born May 2, 1886 in Tchula, Mississippi, Walker began school near Jackson, Mississippi, and later attended school at Knoxville College in Tennessee, probably in the preparatory department. From there she entered Tougaloo College, Tougaloo, Mississippi. On October 26, 1906, the "belle and sweetheart of Sunflower County," as she was called, married Joseph Edison Walker. Born March 31, 1880, in Claiborne County, Mississippi, to a mother affectionately known as Aunt Patsy Walker, Joseph Walker grew up in meager circumstances within a Christian home. He graduated from Alcorn Agricultural and Mechanical College, Lorman, Mississippi, in 1903 and received the M.D. degree from Meharry Medical College, Nashville, Tennessee, in 1906. From medical school he went to Indianola, Mississippi, where he met and married Lelia O'Neal. They had two children—Johnetta and A. Maceo.

The young couple moved swiftly into an established place in the black community. Indianola, the county seat of Sunflower County, had a black woman postmistress whom President Theodore Roosevelt had appointed over the objections of local whites. Joseph Walker was to establish medical practice there, giving the community two highly visible and influential black leaders. The black community took notice: "Dese white folks just now getting over having 'er nigger postmaster and now here comes 'er nigger doctor—Dis Ros'velt send 'm 'ere too?" (Sewell, *Clarion-Ledger*, 27 July 1975, F-7).

The penniless Walkers achieved considerable stature in Indianola; in addition to his medical practice, Joseph Walker helped to found and became president of the Delta Penny Savings Bank and then became president of Mississippi Life Insurance Company. In 1920 the insurance company moved to Memphis but was barely supported by the Beale Street leaders. Walker was displaced from his position. In 1923 he planned, organized, and established a new financial institution—Universal Life Insurance Company. The insurance company's assets grew, and six months after discussing the idea with his family members, Joseph Walker and his son founded the Tri-State Bank in Memphis. Contrary to some accounts, Lelia Walker was not a partner in the founding and removed herself from the family's business matters. The financial giant, Joseph Walker, was a recognized business leader and was president of the National Negro Insurance Association and the National Negro Business League. He guided the political awakening and expression of blacks in Memphis and the mid-South. He died in his office on July 28, 1958.

After the move to Memphis, Lelia Walker continued to provide the moral support needed for a successful bank and insurance company leader, and her son, A. Maceo, took an active part in the business. Lelia Walker, however, devoted her time to a variety of other interests and essential community activities. She was loyal to each of her causes. Her religious interests were seen in the church; in 1921 she and Roxie Crawford raised the first one thousand dollars needed for their new church on Mississippi Boulevard. The Walker family gave the church a piano and an organ. During the 1940s and 1950s, as a member of the Star Supporters, an affiliate of the Missionary Convention (now the Missionary Convocation), Lelia Walker helped to raise money to educate young ministers. She and her husband also founded the Walker Memorial Christian Church and the Riverview Christian Church.

Lelia Walker was sympathetic to the needs of the poor, both in the church and within the community. She provided food, clothing, and encouragement to countless needy families. Many young blacks were able to attend LeMoyne College in Memphis because Lelia Walker paid their tuition. She also was active in the black women's club movement. As a member of the Hiawatha Club, she gave liberally of her time, services, and financial resources. She purchased a five-room home and provided the furnishings for the clubhouse that served the City Federation of Colored Women's Clubs and enabled the women to move the meetings from their homes, where they originally met, to the clubhouse. The meeting house was named in her honor and, as required by Walker, members of the Hiawatha Club would forever be members of its board of directors. The City Federation in Memphis was at that time the only chapter with its own clubhouse. Now more than forty years old, the clubhouse is still being used. Subsequently, another women's club was established and named in honor of Lelia Walker.

Johnetta Walker Kelso, the Walkers's daughter, described her mother as "a lover of beauty, an accomplished dressmaker and designer," and always impeccably dressed (Johnetta Walker Kelso to Marion Roberts, 21 November 1989). She was a devoted wife and mother who was dedicated to community and humanitarian causes.

Lelia Walker died in Memphis Tennessee, on September 30, 1954, of complications from a brain tumor. Her funeral was held in Mississippi Boulevard Christian Church—the institution that she helped develop into a spacious complex on Raines Road and aided as it served the spiritual life of the Memphis community. She is buried in Elmwood Cemetery.

References

Handbook of City Federation of Colored Women's Clubs. Memphis, Tenn: September 1967.

Johnson, T. J. *From the Driftwood of Bayou Pierre.* Louisville: Dunne Press, 1949. Photograph inserted between pages 52-53.

Kelso, Johnetta Walker. To Marion Roberts, 21 November 1989.

Kelso, Johnetta Walker. Interview with author, 16 January 1991.

"Mrs. Lelia Walker." Flier. Mississippi Boulevard Christian Church, n.d.

Memphis Negro Chamber of Commerce Directory. Memphis: 1941.

Sewell, George. "Dr. J. E. Walker—Physician, Banker, Insurance Executive." *Clarion-Ledger*, 27 July 1975.

The Ulico, Thirty Fifth Anniversary Edition, 7 (Fall 1958): 6. Official organ of the Universal Life Insurance Company.

Walker, A. Maceo. Interview with author, 17 January 1991.

Ward, Zana, To Johnetta Walker Kelso, n.d.

Collections

Information on Lelia O'Neal Walker and the Walker family is in the family's possession, the Memphis Public Library and Information Center, and the Mississippi Valley Collection, John Willard Brister Library, Memphis State University. News articles are in the office of the *Tri-State Defender*, located in Memphis. The Walker's church records are in the files of the Mississippi Boulevard Christian Church. Information on the Universal Life Insurance Company is in the files of the office.

Jessie Carney Smith

Madame C. J. Walker

(1867-1919)

Entrepreneur, philanthropist

Among the early entrepreneurs of the twentieth century, no one is more intriguing than the black beauty culture genius Madame C. J. Walker—not only because of her development of the "hot" comb but also because of her remarkable business acumen. A black woman with one dollar and fifty-cents in her pocket in 1904, Walker was the first woman in the United States to become a millionaire through her own efforts. Walker burst on the scene in 1904 and changed the way business people marketed their products. She also revolutionized the methods for treating black hair. Walker, an original, dreamed of a world in which all things were possible. As one reads about her life, one senses that Walker was a brilliant woman, capable of remarkable insights with the capacity to carry them out.

Madame C. J. Walker

Sarah Breedlove Leaves the Plantation

Sarah Breedlove McWilliams Walker, later known as Madame C. J. Walker, was born in 1867 in Louisiana and died on May 12, 1919, in New York. Born to Owen and Minerva Breedlove, indigent former slaves, Walker lived in a dilapidated shack with her parents on the Burney family plantation in Delta, Louisiana, on the Mississippi River. Her parents worked as sharecroppers on the plantation until their deaths. As a child and an adult, Walker toiled in the cotton fields with other black laborers. Cotton, still ranked as the main souce of income for southern farmers, was produced by hand and mule labor and required a warm to hot climate. Working conditions were unbearable for laborers. Hardened, sharp cotton bolls pricked and cut their fingers as they picked cotton in the hot sun. With no child labor laws, Walker, a mere child, worked from sunrise to sunset.

During the Reconstruction era, 1865-1898, Walker could not have lived in a more hostile environment. Although blacks had changed their name of slave to sharecropper, nothing on a plantation had changed. Walker experienced extreme poverty which was manifested in all aspects of her daily life. The windowless shack in which she lived had one door, no water, no toilet, and a dirt floor. She and other family members slept on the ground. As a child, she received the coarse materials for one dress a year that was handed out by the plantation owner. She suffered all the humiliations and indignities that a black suffered at that time.

After her parents died in her childhood, Walker moved to Mississippi with her married sister Louvenia and Louvenia's husband at which time she experienced domestic violence and abuse. Insensitive and tyrannical, the brother-in-law showered only cruelty on seven-year-old Sarah. She eventually responded to the abusive situation by moving away and marrying Moses McWilliams at the age of fourteen. Four years later in 1885, she had a daughter, Lelia. Two years later when Sarah McWilliams was twenty years old, it is said that her husband was killed by a lynch mob.

Her difficulties continued to mount as she became a single parent with a two-year-old child to rear. Vicksburg, Mississippi, was not an ideal place for blacks. Blacks had the best chance for employment and education in urban areas, so Walker moved to Saint Louis, Missouri, where she had relatives, found work as a cook and a laundress, and supported her daughter with her meager earnings. Although she was unable to read and write at the time, she sent her daughter, Lelia Walker, not only to school but to Knoxville College, a private black college located in Knoxville, Tennessee. As an uneducated black, Walker was proud of this accomplishment.

Sarah Walker Finds Her System

Poverty continued to haunt Walker. At the same time she began to experience baldness due to the stressful wrap and twist method which was used to straighten the hair of blacks. This method caused only pain. Growing out of intimate knowledge of hair loss, agony, and the inconvenience of black hair care, she addressed the hair problems of the black woman. Walker, using patent medicines of the day and her own secret ingredients (supposedly sulfur), stopped her own hair loss. She was amazed how quickly her hair grew back. Her friends, using the products, were intrigued with her efforts and became enthusiastic customers. She said her formula came to her in a dream after she had prayed to God to save her hair:

> He answered my prayer, for one night I had a dream, and in that dream a big black man appeared to me and told me what to mix up for my hair. Some of the remedy was grown in Africa, but I sent for it, mixed it, put it on my scalp, and in a few weeks my hair was coming in faster than it had ever fallen out. I tried it on my friends; it helped them. I made up my mind to begin to sell it (Bundles, *Ms. Magazine*, 92).

Black people needed methods for handling hair since no running water, supplies, and equipment existed for them. Bringing water from outdoors and placing the body in awkward positions to shampoo it, Walker and other black women found taking care of their hair was one more arduous task to deal with. By responding to a need, she developed the hot comb and her Wonderful Hair Grower. She eventually prepared five hair-care. Faced with the prospect of domestic and laundry work for life, Walker took her chance with destiny and became a successful businesswoman.

Walker Establishes a Hair Preparations Company

After the death of her brother, Walker moved to Denver, Colorado, to reside with her sister-in-law and her four nieces. With one dollar and fifty cents, she began a hair preparations company. She gradually moved away from working as a domestic to manufacturing hair products. Encouraged by the success of her formula on the hair of other black women, she, her daughter, her sister-in-law and her nieces began to fill jars with the hair preparations in the attic of their home. Six months after her arrival in Denver, she married C. J. Walker, a newspaper man who had knowledge of advertising and mail order procedures, which she used successfully.

Although the business gradually became successful, she experienced incompatible differences with her husband. He failed to share the dream for the company that she envisioned. Walker began to have confidence in herself and hope in the future. At the same time she felt a feeling of stagnation in her marriage:

> When I started in business . . . with my husband, I had business disagreements with him, for when he began to make ten dollars a day, he thought that amount was enough and that I should be satisfied. . . . But I was convinced that my hair preparations would fill a long-felt want, and when we found it impossible to agree, due to his narrowness of vision, I embarked in business for myself (Bundles, *Ms. Magazine*, 92).

She continued to use the initials of his name after the dissolution of the marriage. At the time whites called all black women by their first names no matter who they were, so black women frequently kept their first names a secret, if possible. Hence, she is referred to as Madame C. J. Walker rather than Sarah Breedlove Walker.

Like most inventors, no one is totally original, for the inventor responds to a situation, improves upon it, and draws from the environment around him or her. Walker was not the first to organize a hair preparations company, since Annie N. Turnbo Malone with her Poro Company and "Wonderful Hair Grower" proceeded her in 1900. Some sources suggest that Walker was first an agent for Malone and later her rival in the beauty empire business. Walker was also not the first to heat a comb to straighten hair since the French Jews pressed hair in the early eighteenth century. Nor was she the first to send products through the mail, for many white companies had used this strategy with much success. In fact, her husband, Charles Walker, recommended the idea from his experiences with the newspaper business and advertisements. However, she was the first woman to organize supplies for black hair preparations, develop a steel comb with teeth spaced to comb the strands of blacks, place the comb on a hot stove, send the products through the mail, organize door-to-door agents, and develop her own beauty school. From a combination of these ideas she nursed her company and it grew.

In spite of her early struggles as a single parent, her daughter, Lelia Walker, became her chief asset in the business. Working side by side with her mother, she assisted in the product manufacturing, helped with business decisions, trained the students in the Walker method, and traveled around the country to sell the products. In 1906, Walker placed her daughter in charge of the mail-order operation while she continued to introduce the products in different parts of the South and East. By 1908 mother and daughter moved to Pittsburgh, Pennsylvania and set up a beauty school, Lelia College, in order to train cosmetologists in the Walker method. Lelia Walker handled the manufacture of the hair products as well as the beauty school, while Madame Walker continued to sell the products personally to black women around the country. Through her personal endeavors and travels she contacted thousands of women who became Walker agents. During one of her stops in 1910 she decided that Indianapolis, centrally located in mid-America, would be an ideal location for the company's headquarters. This became a sound business decision. In the meantime Lelia Walker moved part of the business operations to New York in 1913 and set up another Lelia College.

Walker Becomes a Millionaire

Although she began her company with door-to-door selling techniques, Walker knew that she would have to sell on a national level in order to make a fortune. She established a chain of beauty parlors throughout the United States, the Caribbean, and South America. She built her own factories and laboratories with the most modern equipment available. By 1910 Walker had five thousand black agents selling her products on a commission basis. These agents averaged over one thousand dollars a day, seven days a week. In addition, they removed themselves from the tyranny of domestic work. Walker not only provided jobs for blacks, but others obtained jobs as a result of the improvement of their appearance.

Since part of her mode of operations was to make contacts personally with the Walker agents in the marketplace, Walker employed Freeman B. Ransom to run her operations in Indianapolis after his graduation from law school. While traveling, she had met him when he was a train porter, and felt intuitively that he would be a strong link in the chain of command at her headquarters.

Walker's career as an entrepreneur continued as an odyssey of personal discovery. She continued to expand her distribution by recruiting and retaining her sales force of black women. They used, demonstrated, and sold products. Her agents taught other women to set up beauty shops in their homes and to learn techniques of bookkeeping. By 1919, 25,000 women called themselves Walker agents.

Often racism stifles the ingenuity and creativity of blacks. However, in this instance, it worked in Walker's favor. Although whites controlled the economy, they left two types of businesses in the hands of blacks: the funeral and the hair preparations businesses.

Many in the black community accused Walker of trying to make black women in the image of white women. The conservatives spoke against this artificially, straightened hair. They accused her of trying to remake black women into an imitation white Europeans.

Even the church became an opposing force. Walker believed that she could make contact with large groups of black women if she approached churches. The churches, in many instances, rejected her. Black clergymen claimed if God meant for blacks to have straight hair, he would have endowed them with it. Notwithstanding, black women took to these products. Since blacks still had negative feelings about themselves, they subsciously took up straightened hair to eliminate the stigma assigned to the hair of the lower socioeconomic caste.

Illiteracy was another negative force which Walker overcame. As an uneducated child of former slaves, she was unable to read and write. Nevertheless, she surrounded herself with educators and lawyers to assist in her business transactions. Indeed, for a while she wrote her name in an illegible script on checks and bank documents. As she gradually became financially able, she employed tutors to teach her to read and write. In fact her handwriting became so legible that the bank called her to ascertain if her present handwriting was really hers. She eventually learned to read and enjoy American literature and history. Moving from illiteracy to literacy was a long, arduous struggle Walker overcame.

After she became wealthy, Walker built a palatial mansion on the Hudson River in Irvington, New York. She named the mansion Villa Lewaro, after her daughter Lelia Walker Robinson, now married, using the first syllables from the first, middle, and last names. Madame Walker and A'Lelia Walker Robinson (Lelia added an A' to her name) invited leaders of the black community to socials, soirees, and dinners at the mansion. She claimed she was not necessarily interested in this palatial mansion for herself, but she wanted blacks to feel proud of it. Nevertheless, she did not deny herself, in addition to this thirty-four-room architecturally designed mansion, an electric car, and exquisitely decorated brownstones. She bequeathed the mansion to her daughter, A'Lelia, at her death with the idea that the NAACP would inherit from A'Lelia. Due to the depression the NAACP could not support the mansion; it was sold and the NAACP received the proceeds.

Walker Becomes Benefactor

Even at the height of her success, Walker was unable to

forget the black experience that had produced her. She contributed to philanthropic causes and black educational institutions. She donated five thousand dollars to Mary McLeod Bethune's school in Florida, Daytona Normal and Industrial Institute for Negro Girls; she left five thousand dollars to Lucy Laney's Haines Institute in Augusta, Georgia; and she sponsored a teacher at Charlotte Hawkins Brown's Palmer Memorial Institute, a black preparatory school in Sedalia, North Carolina. She gave five hundred dollars to redeem Frederick Douglass's home, Cedar Hill, in southeastern Washington, D.C. The Douglas home restoration was a project of the National Association of Colored Women's Clubs.

Although Walker placed emphasis on education, which was almost a religion to her, she also promoted the idea of black economic self-help. If women could develop a business, they could manage their lives:

> The girls and women of our race must not be afraid to take hold of business endeavors. I started in business eight years ago with one dollar and fifty cents. [Now I am] giving employment to more than a thousand women. . . . I have made it possible for many colored women to abandon the washtub for a more pleasant and profitable occupation (Bundles, *Ms. Magazine*, 91).

She was proud of the fact that she could offer black women a challenge and could relieve the pressure for employment placed on poor black people. By developing the beauty schools in cities in the United States, she could help poor black women with jobs and skills. She felt as if these schools were an emancipatory project for black women.

Walker became a source of inspiration, and all black women who were designated as Walker agents were proud of her and themselves. She gave hope for employment to many persons and provided dignity to persons concerned about their appearance. She strengthened the skills of these women and provided a stimulus for their performance. Partly as a result of her business acumen and experience, Walker opened the way for black women to think of other careers besides domestic work.

Walker, faced with prejudice throughout her life, remembered her roots, became a social activist, and supported causes which fought the policies of racism. She provided funds for Monroe Trotter's National Equal Rights League. She gave support to the NAACP's anti-lynching drive. In 1917 she accompanied other black leaders from Harlem to the White House to attempt to confront President Woodrow Wilson concerning federal anti-lynching legislation. The president pretended he was too busy to see the black coalition. At the Walker agents' convention in 1917, the women sent a telegram encouraging President Wilson to give support to the federal anti-lynching legislation. These women also voiced their concern over the killing of black people in a riot in East St. Louis, Illinois. Notwithstanding the lack of a vote, she insisted that women should express their thoughts and ideas.

Gender bias in the workplace was a force Walker experienced all of her life. Limited to working as a laundress and maid, she dared to take a chance and developed her company. Even after she became a success she still faced the male chauvinism of black men. At the National Negro Business League in 1912, Booker T. Washington and other men at the convention did not intend to let her speak. As Washington praised a black male banker for his bank's operations, Walker proceeded to the podium and stated emphatically:

> I am a woman who came from the cotton fields of the South. I was promoted from there to the washtub. Then I was promoted to the cook kitchen, and from there I PROMOTED MYSELF into the business of manufacturing hair goods and preparations. . . . I have built my own factory on my own ground (Walker Collection, A'Lelia Bundles).

At the 1913 convention Walker was a presenter on the program.

Walker had a decided influence on people—an effect that made many people feel that their lives had been changed, deepened, and enriched. A letter from a Walker agent stated:

> You have opened up a trade for hundreds of colored women to make an honest and profitable living where they make as much in one week as a month's salary would bring from any other position that a colored woman can secure (Walker Collection, A'Lelia Bundles).

Her company was not just her expression of her own possibilities, but became an ethnic statement giving credence to the ingenuity of black people. As a result of an individual's determination, she proved to the world that a black could overcome lack of white business support and lack of capital with a creative idea. Her dramatic commercial success was intriguing to her people. News articles invariably stressed her wealth and material acquisitions, as they have always done when discussing a folk-derived entrepreneur who has made it big. Admittedly, Walker's earnings and investments were enough to attract anyone's notice. By 1914 her gross from company earnings were over a million dollars.

Walker died on May 25, 1919. Funeral services were conducted in the Villa Lewaro by the pastor of her church, the Mother Zion African Methodist Episcopal Zion Church of New York, and she was buried in Woodlawn Cemetery in the Bronx.

Madame C. J. Walker, strong and admirable, had everything against her, but she won. Powerful and determined, she overcame overwhelming odds. Her success, accepted with pride by black communities across the land, was mind-boggling for the average person. Indeed, once one understands what was involved in the management of a company by a black woman in 1904, one has the highest respect for her. She attained her strong reputation in American business accomplishments by meeting a need prudently and imaginatively. In spite of her fame, she was down-to-earth and remained mindful of her roots. She knew that she arose from a poor, black heritage and she would not let herself forget it.

References

Bundles, A'Lelia. "America's First Self-Made Woman Millionaire." *Radcliffe Quarterly* (December 1987): 11-12.

———. "Black Foremothers: Our Trail Blazers." *Spelman Messenger*: 18-19.

———. Interview with author, 4 November 1988.

———. "Madame C. J. Walker—Cosmetics Tycoon." *Ms*. July 1983: 91-94.

———. "Madame C. J. Walker To Her Daughter A'Lelia Walker—The Last Letter." *Sage* 1 (Fall 1984): 34-35.

Doyle, Kathleen. "Madame C. J. Walker: First Black Woman Millionaire." *Illustrated* March 1989: 24-26.

Fisher, Walter. "Sarah Breedlove Walker." *Notable American Women*. Vol. 3. Cambridge: Harvard University Press, 1971.

"Henry Bundles and the Madame C. J. Walker Co." *Shoptalk* Spring Journal, 1989: 108.

Higgins, Will. "On the Verge of Big Growth? 76 year old Madame Walker firm considers leaving Indianapolis." *Indianapolis Business Journal* 29 June 1987: 9-11.

Hughes, Langston. *The Big Sea: An Autobiography*. New York Thunder's Mouth Press, 1940.

Lewis, David Levering. *When Harlem Was in Vogue*. New York: Knopf, 1981.

Logan, Rayford W. "Madame C. J. Walker [Sarah Breedlove]." *Dictionary of American Negro Biography*." Eds. Rayford W. Logan and Michael R. Winston. New York: Norton, 1982.

Lyons, Douglas C. "History Children: Descendants of Legendary Figures Continue The Tradition." *Ebony* (February 1988): 33-37.

The Madame C. J. Walker Beauty Manual. Indianapolis: Mme. C. J. Walker Manufacturing Co. 1925.

"Madame Walker and Urban Life Center." Indianapolis: Mme. C. J. Walker Manufacturing Co., n.d.

"Mme. C. J. Walker Honored: The Rebirth of the Walker Theatre." *Jet* (October 1988): 54.

Nelson, Jill. "The Fortune That Madame Built." *Essence* (June 1983): (June 1983): 84-89.

Ploski, Harry A. and Roscoe C. Brown, Jr., eds. *The Negro Almanac*.

The Story of a Remarkable Woman. Indianapolis: Mme. C. J. Walker Manufacturing Co., 1970.

Trescott, Jacqueline. "The Hair Way to Success: The Business Dynasty of Madame Walker." *Washington Post* 25 May 1973.

Wells, Ida B. *Crusade for Justice*. Chicago: University of Chicago Press, 1970.

Collections

Papers, photographs, and memorabilia of Madame C. J. Walker (Sarah Breedlove) are in the possession of Madame Walker's granddaughter, A'Lelia Bundles of Washington, D.C., the Walker Urban Life Center, and the Indiana Historical Society in Indianapolis. Photographs are in numerous publications, including Lewis's *When Harlem was in Vogue*.

Joan Curl Elliott

Maggie L. Walker

(1867-1934)

Entrepreneur, feminist, civil rights activist, newspaper founder, lecturer

On December 18, 1934, the *Richmond News Leader* ran a lengthy obituary for Maggie Lena Walker. Its praise was noteworthy:

> Mrs. Maggie Walker was the greatest of all Negro leaders of Richmond. She probably was the most distinguished Negress ever born in Richmond and, in solid achievement, one of three or four ablest women her race ever produced in America.

Three days before, on Saturday, December 15, this legendary woman had died. At sixty-eight—after a lifetime of personal tragedy and public triumph—she had died peacefully at 8:30 p.m. in the family home that she so dearly loved and that has come to be recognized as a monument to her remarkable life.

Maggie Lena Walker was born black in a society governed by prejudice, female in a society dominated by male achievement, and poor in a community in which poverty was accepted. Against these overwhelming circumstances, or perhaps because of them, Walker became the country's first woman bank president and used her economic and social

Maggie L. Walker

position to fight for greater educational opportunities, for black pride, and for feminine rights. Her beginnings were humble. In a speech given to a group of young people in 1907, this wealthy, prominent woman alluded to her childhood: "I was not born with a silver spoon in mouth: but instead, with a clothes basket almost upon my head" ("Stumbling Blocks" 1907 in *Addresses 1909*).

Elizabeth Draper Mitchell, an ex-slave, was a cook's helper in the Van Lew mansion on Church Hill in Richmond, Virginia. Her mistress, Miss Van Lew, was both an eccentric spinster and an ardent abolitionist. Maggie Walker was born to Elizabeth, affectionately known as Lizzie, on July 15, 1867. The child spent her early years at the elegant home in free-spirited happiness. "The household afforded its servants not only an exceptionally good education, but unusual encouragements to enterprise as well" (Bird, 167). William Mitchell, Elizabeth's husband, who was a butler in the mansion, decided that opportunities were greater in downtown Richmond. The family then moved to one of two small clapboard houses located in an alley running from Broad to Marshall streets. It was here, at the place later to be called "Maggie Mitchell's Alley" in recognition of her mother's constant calling to her, that Maggie Lena Walker was reared with her younger brother, Johnnie. Her childhood friend, Wendell Dabney, claims that "she was spoiled by all but one. The mother ruled with a rod of iron"(26).

Maggie learned well her mother's lessons of industry and became an extremely conscientious child. Her sense of responsibility was tested in the first of her life's several tragedies. William Mitchell, who worked as a head waiter at the Saint Charles Hotel, mysteriously disappeared. Five days later, he was found floating in the James River, apparently the victim of robbery and murder. As support for her family, Elizabeth Mitchell increased her laundry business; to her young daughter fell the responsibility of caring for a rambunctious Johnnie and of carrying laundry back and forth to her mother's white clients. There is little doubt that Elizabeth's exemplary drive and frugality greatly shaped the daughter's sense of industry and thrift.

Walker's adolescence was filled with school, work, church, and her involvement with the Order of Saint Luke. All of these activities created the woman who was within the girl. Her attitudes and beliefs were firmly rooted in these formative, busy years.

Educated in the segregated Richmond public school system, Walker led her class at Armstrong Normal and High School. Her senior class protest was a foreshadowing of the aggressive stand for racial equality that she would later espouse. The 1883 black graduating class objected strongly to receiving diplomas in a church and wanted to join their white counterparts who would march in a theater. Told by their principal that they could do so only if separate seating were accorded white and black audience members, the students decided to graduate from their school auditorium. Wendell Dabney, who also participated in this protest, claims that "this event stands recorded as the first school strike of Negroes in America" (33). Walker and her classmates were evincing a new spirit of racial defiance that would later manifest itself in her passionate articulation of race solidarity and activism:

> God will not and does not one whit more for the Negro than He does for the Italian, the Sweede [sic] or the Jew. God has promised but one thing—"I will help," He says and that help is something that comes only when we are doing, striving and making the best effort of which our brains and hands are capable. We can do; we will do; we are going to do now ("Race Unity," *Addresses 1909*).

Walker believed ardently that blacks must aggressively seize that which the racist society has denied. She fervently called her people to be the best each could be; to constantly strive for the betterment of every individual was the way to improve the black community. She carried forth this belief in education by teaching for three years at the Lancaster School after graduation. She also took classes in accounting and business management.

Walker never left school during her childhood, but she did devote much time and energy to helping her mother support her family. She shopped, carried baskets of laundry, did washing and ironing. Side by side with her beloved mother, she learned the rewards of drive and endeavor. She grew up as one of two women who supported a family, and all her life she realized the virtues of her black sisters. In 1909 she spoke of this appreciation:

> And the great all absorbing interest, this thing which has driven sleep from my eyes and fatigue

> from my body, is the love I bear women, our Negro women, hemmed, circumscribed with every imaginable obstacle in our way, blocked and held down by the fears and prejudices of the whites, ridiculed and sneered at by the intelligent blacks ("Nothing But Leaves," *Addresses 1909*).

Black Feminism Advocated

Maggie Lena Walker's passionate plea to young women was that they should work diligently and find in themselves the source of feminine power she so admired: "I wish to God that I could imbue you with the spirit of push and energy that would awaken your dormant powers" ("Women in the Business World," *Addresses 1909*). For Walker, the industry of women was mandatory if racial progress was to be made. Perhaps it was the absence of William Mitchell during her formative years; perhaps it was the carefree indolence of her brother; perhaps it was the frustration and pain she saw in the community's menfolk who were so severely beaten by the racist system—whatever the factors, Walker repeatedly urged women to better themselves educationally and economically. She saw this industry as necessary not only for personal improvement but also for racial progress:

> The timidity and retiring disposition of women unfit them for the strife, competition and worry of business life. But, we must do something. We are up and doing, working and suffering because our needs and necessities and our ambitions force us to enter the world and contend for a living. . . .
>
> If our men are so slothful and indifferent as to sleep upon their opportunities, I am here to-day to ask the women of North Carolina to awake, gird their armor and go to work for race uplift and betterment ("Women," *Addresses 1909*).

Walker was an ardent feminist but she was careful to explain that she was not "an advocate for what is called 'New Woman and the Bachelor Girl'" ("Traps," *Addresses 1909*). She enjoyed men and loved her family dearly. What she called for was the fulfillment of women as individuals in a time when they were often merely appendages to their husbands.

As a child Walker joined the Old First Baptist Church and became very active in the Thursday night Sunday school meetings. It was at one of these meetings that she met a young contractor, Armstead Walker, who would become her husband. Maggie was active in the church and soon took charge of a Sunday school class. Religion proved to be an important and lifelong force in her life. For Walker, belief in God was not posture and was not superficial; she held a deep abiding faith that carried her through many difficulties. In her May 8, 1931, diary entry, she evidences this sustaining faith. After describing the trials of a particularly trying day in business and the discomfort of not feeling well, she concludes, "A quiet meditation brought me back to myself and I remembered that *God* is our helper." She relied on the constancy and prevalence of her faith and felt that her success, her very practical daily endeavors, were all rooted in a divine force. Written while she was on an extended vacation in Florida, a journal notation illustrates how integrated were God and her routine activities:

> Up and dressed at 12 n.
>
> Day spent reading, and thinking of God and His goodness—How He has led me by the side of still waters, through pastures green, and restoreth my soul.—I thank Him for this Divine leadership.—He still leads and guides.—All will be well, home, loved ones; work and workers, citizens and community interests will all work together for good, because *I* love and fear the Lord.
>
> An official check of $35.00 received (1931 *Diary*).

Walker spoke often at churches, and she remained a forceful presence in the religious community of Jackson Ward.

At fourteen, Maggie joined the Independent Order of Saint Luke (IOSL). In 1886, when she and Armstead Walker were married, she stopped teaching to devote herself to her new family. An ever active woman, she filled the void of not teaching by increasing her activities in the order. Basically an insurance company started by Mary Prout in 1867 in Baltimore, the IOSL was created for blacks to help the sick and bury the dead during the post-Civil War period. It also encouraged self-help and racial solidarity—two goals that appealed to Maggie Lena Walker. The order proved a natural outlet for her unbridled energy; from the time of her joining, she moved through the ranks from secretary of the Good Idea Council, Number Sixteen, to appointment as delegate to the annual convention in Petersburg, and to Grand Sentinel. In 1890 the Magdelena Council, Number 125 was named in her honor. Eventually, she became Right Worthy Grand Secretary, succeeding William T. Forrester in 1899. When she accepted the post at a reduced salary of eight dollars per month, the treasury contained $31.61 against a stack of unpaid bills. There were only 1,080 members. Through increased memberships, through the formation of a department store and a bank, and through the charismatic competency of its secretary treasurer, the order expanded tremendously. A *Richmond Times Dispatch* news article of August 23, 1924, reports that "the $31 that was placed in her hands has grown until the order has collected $3,480,540.19." But the black beneficent society was more than just economic; "the Order demonstrated a special commitment to expanding the economic opportunities within the community in the face of racism and sexism" (Brown, 1587). The organization also operated in a religious spirit. "Though it offered a hundred-dollar policy without a doctor's examination, it refused to insure anyone who did not confess his or her faith in the Supreme Being" (Bird, 169). The Independent Order of Saint Luke, then, proved an ideal organization in which

Walker could channel her energies; it bought her beliefs about education, religion, race, and sexism under the umbrella of economic enterprise.

The young woman who emerged at the turn of the century was a confident, articulate champion of her strong beliefs. Walker, however, was much more than a mere spokesperson. She realized her convictions with concrete action and delicately balanced her public and private lives. As she was becoming active socially and economically in the community, indeed in the nation, she was also becoming a young wife and mother who needed to meet the emotional demands of an ever-growing family.

In the community she became a visible force. Through the Order of Saint Luke, she established *The St. Luke Herald* on March 29, 1902. She saw the need for a newspaper to provide increased communication between the community and the order and to illuminate black concerns. "The first issue espoused lofty ideals and came out foresquare against injustice, mob law, Jim Crow laws, the curtailment of public school privileges and the enactment and enforcement of laws that constricted the roles of blacks in Virginia politics" (Jordan, 32, 34). As a forum for community and national issues, the paper squarely faced controversy. A reader would expect no less; for three decades, Walker served as editor of the weekly journal. "She also devoted a special section . . . to children. 'The Childrens' [sic] Page' contained bits of wisdom from the Right Worthy Grand Matron (Maggie Walker), as well as letters to 'The St. Luke Grandmother' from tykes all across the country" (Chandler, i).

Walker Founds Savings Bank

In 1903 Maggie Walker determined the order needed a bank. In its Historical Overview, the currently named Consolidated Bank and Trust Company—built diagonally across the street from the original Saint Luke's Penny Thrift Savings Bank—relates Walker's purpose in founding the institution: she "persuaded the Richmond-based organization (I.O.S.L.) to establish a bank to monitor and house funds accruing from its expanding operations in states along the Atlantic seaboard" (1). She also sought a bank to help black people turn pennies and nickels into dollars and to finance black home ownership. Walker was proud of this mortgaging success and observed that "by 1920 there were 645 black homes 'entirely paid for through our bank's help'" (Field, 15). This enterprise had a marked effect on the quality of black life in Richmond and "was a magnificent achievement in a time when blacks, segregated from the white mainstream of society, rallied behind the banner of self-help and racial solidarity" (Field, 15). Walker served as president of the bank until poor health dictated her retirement in 1932, at which time she became chairman of the board. She had seen the bank through a name change to the Saint Luke Bank and Trust Company after the Virginia Banking Division forced the separation of secret orders and their banks, and through a second name change after two mergers. When she died, she left an institution strong enough to weather the Great Depression and exist today. For Walker, this bank—black-owned and run—was another way to help her race. The bank's slogan reflects this intention of keeping black people's money in black people's pockets: "Bring It All Back Home."

Children always held a special place in Walker's heart and she used the bank and the IOSL to help them. She encouraged a sense of thrift in the children of Jackson Ward by providing small cardboard boxes in which they were encouraged to save pennies; when the pennies had reached a dollar, the children were praised for opening bank accounts. Walker proudly reported their progress: "Numbers of children have bank accounts from one hundred to four hundred dollars. They sell papers, cut grass, do chores, run errands, and work in stores on Saturdays" (Daniel, 9). Walker also used the juvenile division of the order to instill values of industry, thrift, and generosity. In 1895 she had founded this division for youngsters to encourage "children to study the *Bible*, save, keep clean, and work" (Bird, 169). The youngsters were encouraged not only to save but also to help those in need. "On 'Sunshine Day,' held on Thanksgiving each year, they were told to send out a 'ray of sunshine' by visiting or giving a gift to someone" (Field, 15). "Miss Maggie," as she was called, enjoyed the children and they idolized her. She would often visit their meetings, speaking to them of the possibilities that might be theirs. Pearle Mankins, a child in the IOSL, remembers with deep affection the woman whom the youngsters adored: "'Miss Maggie Walker' was always said in deference to everything else, with a great deal of respect; she was very warm and loved by the children" (Interview with Pearle Mankins, 18 October 1990). Walker tried to inculcate values in the juvenile members and often created little lessons for them to learn. Because she wanted the children to have successful futures, she also established an educational loan fund for those who wished to attend college.

Walker's vast community contributions extended far beyond the confines of the Saint Luke order. Her many varied activities and honors reflected the concerns she held closest: racial improvement and education. She was instrumental in establishing and maintaining a Community House in Richmond, in securing and keeping a visiting nurse for blacks, and in supporting and advising the Piedmont Tuberculosis Sanitorium for Negroes in Burkeville. She was active in many organizations to promote black interests: founder and president of the Council of Colored Women, cofounder of the Richmond branch of the NAACP, vice-president of the Negro Organization Society of Virginia, and board member of several organizations, including the national NAACP, Colored Women's Clubs, National Urban League, and the Virginia Interracial Committee. She served in various groups, including the State Federation of Colored Women, the International Council of Women of the Darker Races, and the National Association of Wage Earners. She also channeled her considerable energies into organizations of an educational nature: she was a trustee of both Virginia Union University (1931) and the National Training School in Washington, D.C. "Several governors of the state in turn appointed Mrs. Walker as the Negro member of the board of the Virginia

Industrial School for Girls and the Virginia Manual Labor School in Hanover County'' (''Negro Leaders' Rites Arranged,'' 2).

It would have been difficult for such a community activist to refrain from the political arena. She ''and other of the St. Luke women were instrumental in political activities of the black community including the struggle for women's suffrage, voter registration campaigns after the passage of the Nineteenth Amendment, and the formation of the Virginia Lily-Black Republican Party'' (Brown, 1587). The Lily-Blacks were a splinter faction of the Virginia Republican party. They not only created their own platform but also nominated their own candidates. Walker ran unsuccessfully for state superintendent of public instruction. She also was active in the National League of Republican Colored Women and handled that organization's funds.

Domestically, Walker's life was both rich and tragic. While she married on September 14, 1886, her views on marriage were rather advanced for the turn of the century:

> And since marriage is an equal partnership, I believe that the woman and the man are equal in power and should by consultation and agreement, mutually decide as to the conduct of the home and the government of the children (''Stumbling Blocks,'' *Addresses 1909*).

Three sons were born: Russell Ecles Talmage (1890), one who died in infancy, and Melvin DeWitt (1897). In 1905 the family moved into the lovely two-story brick row house at 110 1/2 East Leigh Street. Eventually, Walker expanded the house to accommodate her extended family—all of whom lived with her: her sons, their wives and children; her mother; her companion/housekeeper/friend, Polly, and Polly's husband. The house grew quite large with twenty-two rooms, including eight bedrooms, two parlors, sitting and dining rooms, and a playroom. She took pride in the huge rooms and mirrors, carefully decorated with her fine taste. Today the house has been designated a National Historic Landmark.

Walker enjoyed being surrounded by her extended family, but tragedies did mar her happiness. In 1915 Armstead died in an accident. Russell mistook his father for a prowler on the porch and shot him. During his ensuing trials, his mother remained a steadfast support. Russell was acquitted of the murder charge but never quite recovered from the ordeal. He died in 1923, leaving his wife and child to live with Maggie. Her beloved mother, Elizabeth, also passed away. A diary entry reads, ''My darling mother left us February 12, 1922 - *Rest for her*'' (1921 *Diary*). Tragedy also touched Maggie Walker physically. In 1907 she fell on the front steps of her home and injured her knees, damaging several nerves and tendons. She subsequently suffered severe pain and, during her last ten years, spent much time in an upstairs suite and on a window-enclosed porch from which she would greet neighbors. ''To the people who passed her house . . . , she was a revered friend and neighbor with whom to pass the time of day and discuss the news of the city and nation'' (Pettiger, A-7). In 1928 she was confined to a caned wheelchair and made two major accommodations to the inconvenience: a hand-operated elevator at the back of her home and a 1929 eight-passenger Packard modified to accept her chair.

Respected and renowned, Walker was hostess to many important people. She loved to entertain, choosing personally her china and menus. ''The house was then (1922) a hub of black business, civic and social leadership in Richmond, and Maggie Walker was in her prime'' (White, 20). Famous visitors graced this lovely home, including W. E. B. Du Bois, Langston Hughes, and Mary McLeod Bethune. Her granddaughter recalls the activity: ''There were always guests seated at the large dining room table'' (White, 20). She also describes her grandmother as ''always full of fun. . . . She loved people and flowers, bright lights and music'' (White, 20).

Maggie Walker's brilliance shone in so many lives that awards in later life were profuse. Among them were a 1924 ''testimonial of life'' celebration for her at City Auditorium given by the people of Richmond and the IOSL, an honorary master of science degree from Virginia Union, and, posthumously, a high school bearing her name. An October 4, 1934, *Richmond News Leader* article discusses the creation of ''Maggie Walker Month'' by black organizations across the country:

> The celebration of the month (October) has been proposed . . . in recognition of her outstanding achievements as Christian mother, fraternalist, banker, philanthropist, and minister of interracial good will.

Two months later, Walker died, her death certificate citing ''diabetes gangrene'' as the cause of death. The service at First American Baptist Church was one of the largest in Richmond history. She was buried on Wednesday, December 19, in the family section of Evergreen cemetery.

Maggie Lena Walker had moved from being the daughter of an ex-slave washerwoman to being one of America's wealthiest, most influential black women during the early twentieth century. It would have been easy for one whose life was filled with so much success to have been insensitive to others; however, Pearle Mankins recalls that ''As a child, I never heard a negative word about her'' (Interview with Pearle Mankins, 18 October 1990). That comment fifty-six years later would have pleased Maggie Walker; one of her small journal notations echoes that very wish for her life:

> . . . hoping that no act of mine, no word spoken has given any person heartache—I feel at peace with the whole world (1921 *Diary*).

References

Bird, Caroline. ''The Innovators: Maggie Walker, Kate Gleason.'' *Enterprising Women*. New York: Norton, 1976.

"A Brief History of Consolidated Bank and Trust Company in Richmond, Virginia." Historical Overview. n.d.

Brown, Elsa Barkley. "Maggie Lena Walker." *Encyclopedia of Southern Culture.* Edited by Charles Wilson and William Ferris. Chapel Hill: University of North Carolina Press, 1989.

Chandler, Sally. *Maggie Walker: An Abstract of Her Life and Activities.* Bound Study. 28 April 1975.

Dabney, Wendell. *Maggie L. Walker and the I.O. of St. Luke.* Cincinnati: Dabney, 1927. Photographs included.

Daniel, Sadie Iola. *Women Builders.* Washington, D.C.: The Associated Publishers, 1931.

Field, Sue and Stephanie Halloran. "Maggie Walker—Lifting as We Climb." Richmond, Virginia, January 1976. Maggie Walker Papers, Maggie Walker National Historic Site.

Jordan, Daniel. "Indomitable Maggie Walker." *Commonwealth* 48 (March 1981): 32-4.

"'Maggie Walker Month Set Apart." *Richmond News Leader*, 4 October 1934.

Mankins, Pearle. Interview with author, 18 October 1990.

"Negro Leader's Rites Arranged." *Richmond News Leader*, 17 December 1934.

Pettiger, Betty. "Maggie Walker House: Park Service to Rescue." *Richmond Times Dispatch* 28 July 1981.

Richmond News Leader, 18 December 1934. Obituary.

Richmond Times Dispatch, 23 August 1924.

Walker, Maggie. *Addresses—Maggie Walker.* 1909, 1921, 1931. Maggie Walker National Historic Site, Richmond, Va.

———. *Diaries of Maggie Walker.* 1921, 1931. Maggie Walker National Historic Site, Richmond, Va.

White, Pam. "Famous Grandma Walker was 'Full of Fun.'" *Richmond News Leader*, 16 July 1979.

Collections

The papers of Maggie Lena Mitchell Walker, including addresses, diaries, and photographs, are in the Maggie Walker National Historic Site, Richmond, Virginia, in the care of the United States Park Service. The Valentine Museum in Richmond also has an extensive collection of photographs.

Margaret Duckworth

Margaret Walker

(1915-)

Author, poet, educator

Margaret Abigail Walker, renowned author, poet, and educator, was born July 7, 1915, in Birmingham, Alabama. She was born to Sigismund C. Walker (a Methodist minister) and Marion (Dozier) Walker, a music teacher. The family moved frequently because of the father's occupation. Yet, her family which included of parents, three sisters, a brother, and a maternal grandmother, was supportive and instilled in Margaret Walker a pride in her race, a fact of which she is ever mindful.

In *This is My Century: New Collected Poems by Margaret Walker* (University of Georgia Press, 1989), she writes of her influences:

> My father was . . . my first teacher of poetics. He said I must remember to include three elements in every poem: pictures or images; music or rhyme; and meaning. I think my parents were also my first sources of poetic inspiration. My mother's music, vocal and instrumental, gave me my only sense of rhythm. Whenever the music was classical—Bach, Beethoven and

Margaret Walker

> Brahms—church hymns or anthems, folk songs such as spirituals, work songs, blues, or ragtime and popular ballads and jazz, I heard music, my mother's music, as my earliest memory. My images have always come from the southern landscape of my childhood and adolescence. The meaning or philosophy came from my father, from his books and from his sermons. Most of all, it came from reading the Bible'' (xi-xii).

In response to those who attempt to pinpoint the sources of her poetry, Walker says they are the result of ''a lifetime of reading the Bible and wisdom literature of the East—*Mahabharata, Bhagavad-Gita, Gilgamesh, Sundiata,* and the *Book of the Dead*'' (xvi).

Walker began writing at an early age; her first poems were written between the ages of eleven and fourteen while she was in Gilbert Academy in New Orleans. At age sixteen she met Langston Hughes who read her poetry, said she had talent, and encouraged her parents and her teacher, Miss Fluke, to '''Get [her] out of the South so she . . . [could] develop into a writer''' (*This is My Century*, xii). Upon graduation Walker entered Northwestern University and earned a bachelor's degree in 1935. Here she was influenced by editor, scholar, author W. E. B. Du Bois, who published her poetry in *Crisis* magazine, and Edward Buell Hungerford, her creative writing teacher who had her admitted to the Northwestern chapter of the Poetry Society of America. Walker earned both her M.A. and her Ph.D. from the University of Iowa and for both degrees she presented original works.

Chicago Renaissance Poet Emerges

Following graduation from Northwestern Walker spent four years in Chicago. Part of this time was spent working with the Works Progress Administration. She was also a member of the South Side Writers' Group, initiated by novelist Richard Wright. Both the WPA and the South Side Writers' Group represented two important avenues for advancing Walker's talents. It was here that she mixed with a group of talented artists, writers and other scholars who formed a ''Chicago Renaissance'' movement. Walker developed a friendship with Wright and worked on various projects with him. For a time after he moved to New York, they corresponded. However realizing the need for job security which writing would not always provide, Walker decided to seek a master's degree in order to enter college teaching. She completed the degree with her collection *For My People* (Yale University Press, 1942; reprinted, Ayer Co., 1969). The title poem is her best known and most anthologized work. It was at this point that she began her teaching career, never losing sight of her writing.

Walker taught at Livingstone College, Salisbury, North Carolina; West Virginia College in Institute, West Virginia; and Jackson State College (later University) in Jackson, Mississippi, from which she retired. At Jackson State College she served in many capacities including the director of the Institute for the Study of the History, Life, and Culture of Black People. She details the plight of the teacher in ''Black Women in Academic,'' an essay in *Why I Wrote Jubilee,* edited by Maryemma Graham (Feminist Press, 1990). In this essay Walker says, ''My teaching career has been fraught with conflict, insults, humiliation, and disappointments. In every case where I have attempted to make a creative contribution and succeeded, I have immediately been replaced by a man'' (Graham, 24). Additionally, she has served as a lecturer, National Concert and Artists Corporation Lecture Bureau; Visiting Professor in Writing, Northwestern University; staff member of the Cape Cod Writers Conference; and participant, Library of Congress Conference on the Teaching of Creative Writing.

Since the early years of her life, Walker has pursued her writing career. In fifty two years, Walker has published ten books, including her first collection of essays. An untold number of poems, short stories, essays, reviews, letters and speeches remain to be collected. She laments the fact that in her seventh decade she does not write as she did in her adolescence when she wrote every day.

Maryemma Graham says, ''Walker's remarkable achievement has met with mixed response and somewhat scanty critical attention over the years despite the appearance of her early and best known volume *For My People,* winner of the Yale Series of Younger Poets Award in 1942'' (viii). With this collection of twenty-six poems, Richard Barksdale in *Black American Poets Between Worlds, 1940-1960* says, ''she became one of the youngest Black writers ever to have published a volume of poetry in this century'' and ''the first Black woman in American literary history to be so honored in a prestigious national competition'' (575). This collection, like her later work, affirms the heritage of the black American folk and presents strong positive images in accessible language. Three of the poems from this collection appeared in early issues of *Poetry:* ''For My People'' which took fifteen minutes to write, ''We Have Been Believers,'' and ''The Struggle Staggers Us,'' a sonnet.

Other published collections of poetry followed. *Ballad of the Free* was published by Broadside Press in 1966. *Prophets for a New Day* (Broadside Press, 1970), poems reflective of her faith, are her civil rights poems which were influenced by the turbulence of the sixties. She was emotionally involved in the movement on several levels. Medgar Evers was her neighbor and was assassinated on the street where she lived, one of the girls killed at Sixteenth Street Baptist Church in Birmingham was the granddaughter of a former neighbor, her cousins were members of that church which she had also attended in her youth. Three years later she published *October Journey* (Broadside Press, 1973). She says the title poem has multiple meanings in her life:

> In 1943 after a few weeks at Yaddo, where I wrote the ballad ''Harriet Tubman,'' I was actually making the journey South in October, and ''October Journey'' expresses my emotions at that time. I met my husband in October, and after

thirty-seven years of marriage he died in October (*This is My Century*, xv).

Subjects of poems include poets Paul Laurence Dunbar and Phillis Wheatley, educator Mary McLeod Bethune, and poet/dramatist Owen Dodson. This work was followed by *This is My Century* which contains five volumes of poetry. Walker said: "All of these poems have come out of my living. They express my ideas and emotions about being a woman and a black person in these United States—Land of the *Free* and Home of the Brave?" (*This is My Century*, xvi).

Throughout, she has combined her pursuit of education, her occupation, and literary work with her roles as wife and mother. In 1943 Walker married Firnist James Alexander (now deceased). To this union were born four children: Marion Elizabeth (1944), Firnist James, Jr., (1946), Sigismund Walker (1949) and Margaret Elvira (1954).

Historical Novel *Jubilee* Enhances Reputation

In 1966 Walker's historical novel *Jubilee* was published (Houghton Mifflin, 1965; Bantam, 1981). It has been quite popular and was adapted into an opera. She incorporates actual and historical events into the fictionalized life of her maternal great-grandmother, Margaret Duggins, from slavery to Reconstruction. Walker details the writing of this novel, which began when she was nineteen, in *How I Wrote Jubilee* (Third World Press, 1972). In this she says, "Long before Jubilee had a name I was living with it and imagining its reality. Most of my life I have been involved with writing this study about my great-grandmother" (11). It spans the period before and after the Civil War. She is currently working on a sequel to the novel.

In 1974, *A Poetic Equation: Conversations Between Nikki Giovanni and Margaret Walker* (Howard University Press; reprinted with new postscript, 1983) appeared; it presented a dialogue between these two poets representing different generations and different ideologies. She has recently completed the definitive biography of Richard Wright, *The Daemonic Genius of Richard Wright: A Portrait of the Man, a Critical Look at His Works* (Dodd, 1987). This grew out of her thirties association with the writer. The biography is based on the premise that his creative genius was driven through his career by the demons of anger, ambivalence, alienation, and aberrations resulted from his Mississippi childhood.

Even though Walker has not received the acclaim a poet of her stature and contribution should, she has received honors and awards and has not allowed the lack of recognition to stifle her creativity. In addition to the Yale Series of Young Poets Award, she received a Rosenwald Fellowship (1944), a Ford Fellowship for study at Yale University (1954), a Houghton Mifflin Literary Fellowship (1966), a Fulbright Fellowship to Norway (1971), and a Senior Fellowship from the National Endowment for the Humanities (1972). She has received honorary degrees from Northwestern University, Rust College, Dennison University, and Morgan State University. Additionally, she received the White House Award for Distinguished Senior Citizen, participated in the inaugural activities of William F. Winter, governor of Mississippi from 1980 to 1984, and July 12, 1980 was proclaimed Margaret Walker Day in Jackson, Mississippi. Walker is presently working on another novel and her autobiography.

References

The Archival Collection of Margaret Walker. Harry T. Sampson Library. Prepared by Lelia G. Rhodes. Jackson State University, 1980.

Basel, Marilyn K. "Margaret Abigail Walker, 1915- ." *Black Writers, A Selection of Sketches from Contemporary Authors.* Detroit: Gale Research, 1989.

Gilken, Ronda. *Black American Women in Literature: A Bibliography, 1976 Through 1987.* Jefferson, N.C.: McFarland, 1989.

Tate, Claudia, ed. *Black Women Writers at Work.* New York: Contiuum, 1983.

Walker, Margaret. *Richard Wright, Daemonic Genius.* New York: Warner Books, 1988.

——. *How I Wrote "Jubilee" and Other Essays on Life and Literature.* Ed. Maryemma Graham. New York: Feminist Press, 1990.

——. *This is My Century: New and Collected Poems.* Athens: University of Georgia Press, 1989.

Collections

The archival holdings at Jackson State University include essays, speeches, awards, tapes, and photographs relative to the career of Margaret Walker as both literary figure and educator.

Helen Houston

Joan Scott Wallace

(1930-)

Social scientist, educator, governmental official

Joan Scott Wallace is a distinguished social scientist, educator, government administrator, and diplomat. She was born in Chicago, Illinois, on November 8, 1930, and is the only child of the late William Edouard Scott and Esther Fulks Scott. Her father was a portrait and mural painter of the "Chicago Renaissance" era (1930-1950) who had studied under the famous black artist, Henry O. Tanner. Her mother was a social worker who was actively involved in the profession until her death at age seventy-four. From her parents Wallace developed a strong commitment to racial equality, an appreciation for hard work, and an understanding of the importance of a good education. Wallace is married to Maurice A. Dawkins, a government relations consultant. She is the mother of three sons by a previous marriage.

Wallace's academic and educational achievements began in high school where she was the school's first black salutatorian and winner of the Robert S. Abbott Award for leadership and academic excellence. Following graduation, she enrolled in Bradley University as a premedical student and later changed her major to sociology. She was inducted as a member of Pi Gamma Mu (national social science honor society) at the end of her sophomore year. In 1952 she earned an A.B. degree in sociology with honors. She received a fellowship in social work and continued her studies at Columbia University where her M.S.W. was completed in 1954. Northwestern University conferred her Ph.D. in social psychology in 1973.

Her academic and professional training led to a variety of positions in education and administration. From 1967 to 1973, Wallace was assistant and associate professor in the department of psychology, at the Jane Addams School of Social Work, University of Illinois at Chicago. She has also held the position of dean of the School of Social Work at Western Michigan University and vice president for programs at the National Urban League. From 1973 to 1976, Wallace was associate dean and professor, School of Social Work, Howard University; and from 1976 to 1977 she held the position of vice president for administration at Morgan State University.

Department of Agriculture Has First Black Woman Leader

Given her significant administrative experience, it was not surprising that Wallace would continue the pattern of achievement that was developed earlier in life. In June 1978 she was offered the job of assistant secretary for administration at the United States Department of Agriculture (USDA). A few months later she became the first black and the third woman to serve in this position since 1862. Her appointment to this position during the Carter administration was significant in that it marked a change in the pattern of black appointments to high-level federal positions. Many blacks were placed in top positions across the entire range of government, outside the cluster of federal agencies primarily concerned with minority, poverty-related, or civil rights issues.

As assistant secretary for administration, Wallace was responsible for departmental leadership in administrative management. Moreover, she was in charge of an eighty-million dollar budget and two thousand employees. Her office provided administrative direction to those departments under her jurisdiction: Operations and Finance, Safety and Health Management, Personnel, Equal Opportunity, Small and Disadvantaged Business Utilization, and the quasi-judicial activities of Administrative Law Judges and the Board of Contract Appeals.

During her tenure at USDA, Wallace's accomplishments were extensive. Her leadership resulted in improved productivity of managers, professionals, and white-collar workers. In 1979 she was presented the Udall/Derwinsky Award for leadership in implementing the Civil Service Reform Act in USDA. The Presidential Rank of Meritorious Executive is an award given to members of the Senior Executive Service (SES) within the Federal government. In 1980 this award was presented to Wallace "for sustained superior performance in management of programs of the United States government, and for noteworthy achievement of quality and efficiency in public service." She also created an Equal Employment Opportunity evaluation and planning system to document employment practices and provide statistics on minority employment, and a mechanism to draw up realistic affirmative action plans.

In addition to implementing significant administrative changes within USDA's equal employment opportunity area, Wallace engaged in major efforts to publicize programs and opportunities for blacks and to include affirmative action procedures as a part of the budget review process. She initiated career seminars addressing the scarcity of black agriculturalists. Black farmers complained that their needs were not addressed through existing USDA programs. Wallace responded to the complaints by instituting a series of national forums to inform black farmers of available programs. She was also actively involved in efforts to recruit blacks to USDA. She spoke to numerous youth groups and organizations such as the NAACP. In an interview with *Essence* magazine, she spoke of her recruiting efforts: "Agriculture isn't just farming. It encompasses forestry, consumer affairs, foreign agriculture, science, and education" (56). In 1978 the federal government awarded a grant of sixteen million dollars to black colleges and universities in an attempt to bring minorities back into the area of agriculture. The grant was awarded under the Food and Agriculture Act of 1977, as a way for USDA to help black institutions develop research facilities in the area of agriculture. In an address at the 1978 Research Symposium of the Historically Black Land-Grant Colleges and State Universities, she expressed the hope that the farm act would "stimulate college presidents to encourage people into the field of agriculture" (*St. Louis American*, 16 November 1978).

In July 1981 Wallace was appointed administrator of the Office of International Cooperation and Development (USDA). She assumed responsibility for the coordination and implementation of international policies and programs. She remained in this position until 1989, when she was appointed representative to the Inter-American Institute for Cooperative Agriculture (IICA), Tacarigua, Trinidad and Tobago. This most recent appointment is another in a long list of accomplishments for the "Joan of Agriculture," as she is known in Trinidad. While her list of awards and honors is extensive, only a few are listed here: Delta Sigma Theta

Meritorious Award (1979); Doctor of Humanities, University of Maryland (1979); Doctor of Humane Letters, Bowie State College (1981), and Doctor of Laws, Alabama Agricultural and Mechanical University (1990).

Wallace has represented the United States Department of Agriculture in bilateral and multilateral conferences and consultants in more than thirty countries in Africa, Asia, Australia, Europe, and Latin America. She has also represented USDA to various International Food and Agriculture Organizations including the United States/Indo Subcommittee, World Food Council, United States/Saudi Joint Commission, and others.

In addition to her many achievements at home and in the international arena, Wallace has found time to write a variety of publications. She has contributed articles to the *Howard Law Review*, *Diversity*, *Focus*, *Atlantic Economic Journal*, and the *Journal of Sociology and Social Work*.

References

"Essence Women." *Essence* 9 (November 1978): 56.

Poole, Isaiah. "New Yield At Agriculture." *Black Enterprise* 10 (November 1979): 49-50.

Smith, Carol Hobson. "Black Female Achievers in Academe." *Journal of Negro Education* 51 (Summer 1982) 318-35.

Walker, Daphne. "Government Tries to Lure Blacks Back to Agriculture Thru Grants." St. Louis *American* (16 November 1978).

Collections

Biographical data, newspaper articles and clippings, USDA documents and other materials on Joan Scott Wallace are in the Inter-American Institute for Cooperation on Agriculture office, Trinidad and Tobago, and in the Office of International Cooperation and Development, United States Department of Agriculture, Washington, D.C.

Lena Boyd-Brown

Phyllis Ann Wallace

(c. 1920s-)

Economist, educator, scholar, activist

Described by her peers as a "scholar-activist," Phyllis Ann Wallace is an economist who earned her doctorate at a time when few black women pursued such studies. Her professional career has included stints in government and academia and on private sector boards. Wallace has made unique contributions to labor economics with her research on affirmative action, the status of black women, and the career path of people in business. She is a leader in her profession, serving as president of the Industrial Relations Research Association, the first woman as well as the first black to hold that post.

Baltimore native Wallace is the daughter of John Wallace, a craftsman, and Stevella Wallace, a housewife. The oldest of seven children, she graduated in 1939 from the segregated Frederick Douglas High school, one of the foremost high schools in the state. Although she ranked first in her class, state law prevented her from attending the all-white University of Maryland. Yet Maryland state law also paid out-of-state educational expenses for those black students whose chosen major was not offered at all-black Morgan State College. Wallace majored in economics at New York University, graduating magna cum laude and Phi Beta Kappa in 1943.

Wallace initially planned to teach in Baltimore's high schools after her graduation. But encouraged by one of her economics professors, she applied to and was accepted by Yale University, where she received a master's degree in 1944 and a doctorate in 1948. One of few women in Yale's economics department, Wallace experienced both subtle and blatant discrimination. For example, department regulations prevented her from holding traditional graduate student employment as a teaching assistant. However, a research assistantship and fellowship support from the Julius Rosenwald Foundation and Yale's Sterling Fund made it possible for her to complete her course of study.

A research stint with a defense-related federal agency convinced Wallace to focus on international economics. She wrote her dissertation on commodity trade relationships, focusing on international sugar agreements. After receiving the doctorate from Yale, Wallace lived in New York City, where she taught at City College of New York and did research at the National Bureau of Economic Research, focusing on international trade and productivity issues.

In 1953 Wallace joined the economics faculty at Atlanta University, a position she held for four years. Some of the pivotal friendships of her lifetime, including those with M. Carl Holman, Whitney and Margaret Young, Sam Westerfield, Hylan Lewis, and Nese and Ves Harper were made at this time. She left Atlanta to continue research in international economics, working for the federal government as an economic analyst in intelligence until 1965. She published articles about Soviet economic growth and development during this period.

Wallace says the atmosphere of social change that infused the mid-1960s made her consider a shift in her research focus. The Equal Employment Opportunity Commission (EEOC) set up operations in July 1965; Wallace began working as its chief of technical studies a few months later. She was a pioneer in research on the economics of discrimination and also distinguished herself by stretching scarce resources to provide government data to academicians for analysis. Lester Thurow, Orley Ashenfelter, James Heckman, Ray Marshall, and Robert McKersie were among the economists who worked closely with Wallace on early EEOC data sets.

Wallace's other key contribution to the economics of discrimination research was her effort to build interdisciplinary teams to address issues of discrimination. She worked with legal scholars like Rutgers University's Al Blumrosen in the Griggs *v.* Duke Power case. She assembled a team of industrial psychologists to write the first guidelines about testing for EEOC in 1966. She convened hearings to raise questions about discrimination issues in a number of industries. Her involvement of scholars from a range of disciplines in issues of discrimination set the tone for research for the next generation.

Black Women in the Labor Market Examined

After three years at EEOC, Wallace moved to the Metropolitan Applied Research Center to study on urban youth in labor markets. Her 1974 book *Pathways To Work: Unemployment among Black Teenage Females* emphasizes the labor market experiences and aspirations of young black women, an area that had been unexplored until that time. In 1972 she joined the faculty of the Massachusetts Institute of Technology (MIT) and three years later became the first tenured black woman on the faculty. During her early years at MIT, Wallace combined her knowledge of the public and nonprofit sector with her research ability to produce conferences, workshops, and a series of publications on minorities and women in the work force. During this period she wrote *Equal Opportunity and the AT&T Case*, *Women, Minorities and Employment Discrimination*, *Black Women in the Labor Force*, and *Women in the Workplace*.

Wallace's years in the nonprofit and academic sectors have been distinguished by service on a series of advisory groups, panels, and boards. She has served on the boards of the Brookings Institution, the Museum of Fine Arts (in Boston, as MIT's representative), and the Wellesley College Center for Research on Women (1983-86). Her other commitments include service on the President's Pay Advisory Committee (1979-1980), the Minimum Wage Study Commission (1978-82), the Economic Advisory Panel of *Black Enterprise* magazine (1982-85), the visiting committee of Harvard's Graduate School of Business Administration (1977-1982), the advisory committee to the National Academy of Sciences on the Status of Black Americans (1985-89). Wallace has also been one of few black women to serve on corporate boards, including that of the State Street Bank and Trust Company (beginning in 1975), the Stop and Shop Corporation (1981-88), and the Teacher's Insurance and Annuity Corporation (beginning in 1980).

A theme of all of this service as well as her professional work has been, according to her colleague Alice Rivlin, the application of "the skills of a well-trained scholar/activist to some of the most important and intractable problems of our time, especially the problems of alleviating poverty and the damage of racial and sexual discrimination" (19-22). Yet only in retrospect has Wallace seen barriers to her full professional participation. "I felt, go in and do your work and that's it," she noted, indicating that she cleared hurdles without even realizing they were there.

Wallace retired from active teaching at MIT in 1986, choosing to continue research, board service, and writing. In 1988 she served as president of the Industrial Relations Research Association, developing a research and conference program for the organization. As she concluded her term of office and addressed the membership, Wallace exhorted them to expand their view of industrial relations research, encouraging labor economists, trade unionists, and corporate human resource specialists to dismantle the barriers to advancement of minorities and women in internal labor markets. In 1989 she published *MBAs on the Fast Track*, the results of surveys on career progress that she had administered while at MIT.

Wallace has received honorary degrees from Valparaiso University (1977), Mount Holyoke College (1983), Brown University (1986), and Northeastern University (1987). She has also received awards from Yale University (1980), the National Economics Association (1981), and the Graduate School of Business at Harvard University. In the years since her retirement, she has also received commendations from universities, research organizations, and black woman's groups, both for her research on the labor market and for her committed and distinguished service to her profession. In her leisure time Wallace performs historical research on her family, who were free blacks in Maryland prior to the Civil War, and pursues her interest in the arts by such activities as serving since 1989 on the board of trustees of the Society of Arts and Crafts. She has also been an active mentor to young black women and men and to others in economics, academia, the corporate sector, and the arts.

References

Rivlin, Alice. "Phyllis A. Wallace: Scholar/Activist." *Sloan Magazine* (Winter 1987): 19-22.

Wallace, Phyllis A. Interview with Julianne Malveaux, 8 June 1990.

———. "Presidential Address." Industrial Relations Association, December 1988.

Julianne Malveaux

Sippie Wallace
(1898-1976)
Singer

Eminent blues artist Beulah Belle Wallace was born to George and Fanny Thomas on November 1, 1898, in Houston, Texas. Houston had been a frontier town with a burgeoning black population at the turn of the century. Those blacks who worked in towns and cities were laborers or domestics, and among these were the Thomases, who had thirteen children. Beulah was the fourth child of the religious, hard-working couple who neither approved of nor indulged in the Saturday night house parties which spawned such blues notables as "Ragtime" Henry Thomas and Blind Lemon Jefferson. Though the Thomases did not live to see it, two of their sons, George, Jr., and Hersal, and one of their daughters, Beulah, rose to stardom on the vaudeville circuit as a result of their musical talents.

Beulah, nicknamed Sippie by her siblings, spent her preteen years singing and playing at the family church, Shiloh Baptist. It was there she earned a "certificate for singing" from a teacher in Sunday school. Although she had very little formal education beyond elementary school, she was given encouragement for her musical career by her older brother and sister, George and Lillie. Under George's tutelage she began to learn the popular music which her mother disdained. Wallace described how she also began writing her own lyrics, with his coaching.

> You see my brother wrote music, you know, and I use to always hang around him all the time. And my brother never did have no words and I use to hear the words, get the words from different women, you know, girls come around singing. I get the words, I put them down on a piece of paper and I carry them. And then by listening then I learn how to put them together (Interview with Sippie Wallace, 24 January 1975).

By the time she was in her teens, Sippie succumbed to the catchy rhythms of her brother's piano playing and joined him in his creative efforts. When George, Jr., went to New Orleans to pursue his musical career in 1912, fifteen-year-old Sippie soon followed him there. In New Orleans she met and married Frank Seals. She later said this was a mistake, caused by her youth and her inexperience with men.

> I've been the biggest fool in the world. I believe everything everybody said was true, you know. Just like if you'd say I love you. Well, I got a little enough sense to believe that you love. I ain't got no better sense than that. And mostly—and then when I first, you know when I first married, I thought that you get a husband wasn't nobody going to have him but you. But that's the wrongest thing and it's the wrongest way to teach a child, cause can't no woman have a man by herself. Girl, if you going to have help. I don't care how good you are, you going to have help. Then you couldn't have no husband by yourself, nohow.
>
> So, my brother, me and him wrote "Adam and Eve had the Blues". I got all mine [ideas], got it from the Bible . . . . this is true facts. . . .
>
> And Eve is the true cause of all of us having the blues, child. Even little dogs have the blues, even little birds have the blues, even little bees, even everything has it. Everything been having trouble . . . (Interview with Sippie Wallace, 24 January 1975).

The broken marriage was obviously not Wallace's first unhappy experience, but it affected her profoundly enough for her to recount her mother's advice about men. She later paid tribute to her mother's admonitions about "keeping company" in the first blues she wrote, "Caledonia."

Both parents had died when Wallace returned home around 1918 to live with her siblings. However, the stage-struck young woman could not forget her experiences in New Orleans's Storyville district where brother George's friends included King Oliver and the soon-to-be famous Louis Armstrong. Disappointment in love was overshadowed by the burning desire to dance and sing in one of the tent shows which visited Houston on the Theater Owner's Booking Association (TOBA) circuit. The teeming crowds gathered to watch the parade and hear the lively orchestras play the latest ragtime and marching tunes. She figured that with her talent, she might get a chance to play or sing for one of the show people, so she and other budding musicians waited around all day hoping to be noticed. Sippie Wallace began her road show career as a maid and stage assistant to a Madam Dante, a snakedancer with Phillip's Reptile Show. When she described one of these experiences she could barely contain the laughter that bubbled inside.

> So when Madame was all loosed up she'd motion for me to bring the cane basket with the snake, you know. And I was just as scared as I can be and I had that thing just like this here when one time out of the middle of the stage the old snake come sticking his head up and I let it fall. [She laughed heartily.] It was jumping all out that thing. Child, I let that thing go and I flew. I never will forget that (Interview with Sippie Wallace, 24 January 1975).

By mentioning her lack of dancing talent and her willingness to work as a maid, Wallace underscored two things: jobs on stage were scarce but much sought after, and domestic labor was a mainstay for black women, even in show business. There was no bitterness in that compromise for Wallace because it brought her closer to her goal as a performer. As Madame Dante's maid she began her travels around Texas, from Houston to Dallas, Galveston, Waco, and all the little towns in between.

Wallace soon gained a reputation as the "Texas Nightingale" as she sang with small bands for picnics, dances and holiday celebrations. From these she went with tent shows around Texas a singer, not a maid.

Wallace's first recordings demonstrated a mature seasoned performer who had learned her craft well. She owed much to her brother, George, who was a respected composer and music publisher when he sent for her to come to Chicago. He was on the recording staff of the W. W. Kimball Company's music roll division and director of his own orchestra when Sippie, Hociel, her niece who was also an aspiring blues singer, and Hersal, her baby brother arrived. George's influence played a significant part in getting the trio going. Sippie and George renewed their song-writing partnership to produce the popular "Shorty George" and "Underworld Blues."

Hersal Thomas, was a superb pianist who often accompanied his sister when she performed, although he was only thirteen or fourteen years old. His musical gifts also included composition and his name was listed in the credits on George's sheet music and on recordings. The musically talented Thomases—George, Sippie, and Hersal—quikly became famous in the recording field. George's "Muscle Shoals Blues" was a best-seller in 1922 but it did not match the popularity of Sippie Wallace's first recordings on the Okeh label, "Shorty George" and "Up the Country Blues." With these titles, Wallace and pianist Eddie Heywood hit the blues recording market with a force like the blustering winds from Lake Michigan. The Windy City had a new star who would challenge any blues singer on the scene. Her first recording purportedly sold one hundred thousand copies—quite a feat for a newcomer in a young field. In just a few months, Wallace's portrait was featured in the advertisements for her recordings hailing the "Texas Nightingale" as one of General Phonograph Corporation's new race stars. The dignified portrait was often accompanied by "exceptionally high-type dialect, especially prepared to appeal to the colored race," according to a trade magazine for the phonograph industry (*Talking Machine World*, 116).

Wallace's blues style is a mix of Southwestern rolling honky-tonk and Chicago shouting moan, a seductive brew that fit, her personality. She had a strong, smooth voice and good articulation that pushed the words straight forward. Her ability to shift moods within a song adds a dimension that is missing in singers such as Victoria Spivey and Mamie Smith. Her unorthodox sense of timing and accentuation of words gives her lyrics punch and tension.

"Shorty George" remains a Wallace classic after more than sixty years because of her distinctive phrasing, punctuated by mournful slides and shifting moods. In "Special Delivery Blues," with Louis Armstrong on cornet and Hersal on piano, Wallace portrays the scorned woman who is unwilling to accept the finality of rejection by her lover.

Many of the ideas for her blues came as Sippie Wallace mulled over her personal concerns. She repeatedly said that she would just be "thinking it over in my mind, child, and it would just come to me to make a song about what was troubling me." For example, the joy and satisfaction which grew out of the creative interaction she shared with her brothers is reflected in her exuberant renditions of "Shorty George" and "Up the Country Blues." But there were other occasions and relationships which inspired her to write in a different mood. Among them were "Can Anybody Take Sweet Mama's Place?" and "He's the Cause of the Me Being Blue" with Clarence Williams.

A very attractive buxom young woman, Sippie had already remarried by the time she joined her brother in Chicago. Her second husband was Matthew Wallace, a dapper Houstonian whom she adored. For a while Matthew played a major role in the further development of his wife's career, serving as her manager and, on occasion, as emcee. Unfortunately, Matt's penchant for gambling interfered with his effectiveness and eventually led to financial problems for the couple. Sippie Wallace's recording about gambling was "Jack O' Diamond Blues" which was issued in March 1926 along with "Special Delivery Blues." "Jack O' Diamonds" was written by Wallace and featured Armstrong and Hersal Thomas.

Wallace was promoted as a recording artist in 1923 and 1924 enhancing her stage career as well. Soon she was a regular headliner on the TOBA circuit. Her life was busy with travel. Always a lover of beautiful, fancy stage costumes, Wallace would wear feathers and sequined gowns, low-cut to emphasize her full-bosomed figure. Her pecan-brown round face was accented by full lips and big soft brown eyes, which were most expressive as she sang. In between shows she could be found in Okeh's studios in New York or Chicago. Meanwhile, Detroit had replaced Chicago as home base for her, Matt, Hociel and Hersal. Both Hersal and Hociel had cut their own recordings by 1925, so the Thomases were a musical family of quite some note. They settled into an area on Detroit's eastside, which was densely populated by blacks, Russian Jews and Italians, and Matt worked as a laborer when he could find work.

Wallace counted among her close friends blues singer Sara Martin and the comedy team, Butter Beans and Susie, all of whom were on the Okeh label at one time, and who served time on the TOBA. Wallace entertained these and other show business friends with fine dinners and was the guest of many other friends as she travelled.

The deaths of the three siblings who had been instrumental in the development of her career came unexpectedly during her peak years on stage. In 1925, she was summoned to the bedside of her dying older sister, Lillie, who had taught her how to sing as a child. Then, in June, 1926, her beloved Hersal succumbed at sixteen to a case of food poisoning. In 1928, George Thomas's song writing and publishing career ended suddenly when he was run down by a streetcar in Chicago, bringing an end to the brilliant trio's collaborations.

In their years together, the talented brothers and sister produced some solid winners in the blues field. During this recording period, Wallace's initiative and hard push for her career on stage was derived not only from her desire to make it big but also from the fact that singing and playing were the only tools she had for making a living other than as a domestic. She exercised the option so she could better her existence while expressing herself creatively. Her vivid, matter-of-fact style was an outgrowth of life on the rugged road from poverty to prosperity. Still, Sippie Wallace's early religious experiences tempered her behavior and served her well as she struggled with career, family, and marital strife.

When asked if the rough conditions of stage life may have caused many of the performers to drink heavily, Wallace gave a forthright answer that revealed the vestiges of her early upbringing.

> People just get besides theirselves, you know. They get an inch and take a foot. Because they made some heroes some people can make a "pure D ass" out of themselves, you know, hurt their own self. . . . I drank beer but I didn't act like a fool, I was not a party girl. I was a theatrical woman and loved it, but I knew how to act, you know (Interview with Sippie Wallace, 1976).

"Knowing how to carry yourself" was important to the Texas warbler who believed that proper manners gained respect from others. She and most of her peers valued their personal integrity and did not sell themselves short in order to achieve their goals.

In an interview with Wallace about the attitudes of the men with whom she performed towards the women singers and pianists, she admitted that she was not readily accepted as a leader of a group, but the deciding factor was getting a job and being able to pay the players. Wallace could play the piano as well as sing so she was hired by local musicians for socials and club dates, a practice she continued in Detroit long after her blues recording career had ended in 1929.

An unexplained recording hiatus of two years was ended when she was put under contract in 1929 by Victor Records. There, she made four sides but only two were issued, the popular, "I'm a Mighty Tight Woman" and "You Gonna Need My Help." The 1926 Okeh recording had Cicero Thomas on cornet and Hersal on piano. Wallace accompanied herself on piano backed by Natty Dominique on the Victor reissues. "Mighty Tight Woman" (RCA Victor, February 1929), one of the few erotic blues recorded by Wallace, demonstrated her superb vocal phrasing and her pianistic abilities. Although it was one of the last records Sippie Wallace cut in the 1920s, "Mighty Tight Woman" has not only remained a favorite of old-timers but has also become a hit with the present generation of blues lovers.

Wallace produced some noteworthy sides during her Okeh years. Her subject matter ranged from jealousy, vengeance, and skin color, to mistreatment and natural disaster; all treated with equal verve and vigor.

Her career suffered the same decline as that of her peers when the record industry declined with the Depression. She had not developed the versatility of style and repertoire of an Edith Wilson or Alberta Hunter, so she could not gain employment as a comedienne or sultry chanteuse. Wallace had a raw country-style talent well-suited to belting the blues but not to sweet, mellow ballads. And Detroit was a blues city not a Cotton Club Revue town. She lacked the training and experience to change, and she sorely missed the guidance of her brother, George, at this critical point in her career. Without him, she had no strong writing partner to inspire her and to put her musical ideas on paper.

Wallace's stage bookings dwindled and finally petered out. By 1932 she had slipped into obscurity along with many of her other singing sisters. Her husband, family, and church became the focal point of her life. In the 1940s she became the guardian of Hociel's three orphaned daughters. Her installation as a nurse in her church brought her joy and satisfaction, as did her work with the choir.

She turned her song-writing and piano-playing abilities to church music for the next three decades. Conversations about "her"church and "her" choir sparkled with an ardor that flowed out with each statement.

During an interview in 1974, Wallace played and sang several religious songs she had written for her choir, interlacing the songs with comments. She explained her feelings about the church and her music, the spirituals and blues, in the following manner:

> I shout sometime, it feels so good. Because I mostly do blues for jobs. But for my heart it's at church. That's why I make it to church all the time. Everytime I go I always ask can I sing the spirituals.

Sippie Wallace, the blues singer, might have remained obscure for the rest of her life, except for an occasional club date in Detroit, were it not for the issuance of two recordings. In 1945, Mercury Records issued her great "Bedroom Blues." Backed by Albert Ammons, piano, and his Rhythm Kings—Artie Starks, clarinet, Lonnie Johnson, guitar, and John Lindsay, bass—she proved, without a doubt, that her voice and style had not diminished during her absence. Although the recording was excellent, the blues audience had already shifted its attention to the Chicago and Memphis sound of male singers. Bebop, swing, rhythm and blues were all struggling for the attention of the listening public, so the record did not sell and she slipped back into obscurity.

The next recording on Detroit's Fine Arts Label, in 1959,

suffered the same anonymity, but it must have convinced her friend, Victoria Spivey, to keep urging her to come out of "retirement" and try the folk-blues festival circuit that was sweeping the country. As a result, Wallace went to Europe in 1966 and captivated a new, younger generation of blues enthusiasts. The Storyville recording of her Copenhagen performance demonstrated that the second coming of Sippie Wallace was long overdue. With Roosevelt Sykes and Little Brother Montgomery sharing the piano, she presented new renditions of her old classics, "Trouble Everywhere I Roam," "Shorty George Blues," "Special Delivery" and "I'm a Mighty Tight Woman," and introduced "Women Be Wise, Don't Advertise Your Man," the blues which inspired Bonnie Raitt, a young white singer. One reviewer wrote: "Visiting Europe in 1966, Sippie Wallace astonished by the breadth of her singing and a delivery recalling Bessie Smith." He commented that the remakes with Montgomery and Sykes in Denmark were of "exceptional merit" (Kunstadt, 3).

Raitt was instrumental in the revival of interest in and enthusiasm for artists such as Wallace, Sykes, and Montgomery in the early 1970s. That exposure to audiences all across the United States created a new demand for Wallace's style of blues singing—the shouting wail.

Bathed by the spotlight of Lincoln Center's Avery Fisher Hall, Sippie Thomas Wallace, at eighty, could still evoke some of the deepest emotions as she sang the blues in 1977.

In numerous ways, Wallace was the archetypal women blues singer—gusty, yet tender; bereft, but not downtrodden; disappointed, yet hopeful; long on talent, short on funds; legendary, but not widely acclaimed; exploited but not resentful; independent, yet vulnerable. Her life story is not resplendent with dramatic events that capture the imagination, a bronze Cinderella whom Prince Charming rescued from drudgery and cruelty. Instead it might be considered quite pedestrian except for her musical talent; it did not save her from toil, drudgery, and grief, but it did enable her to communicate her feelings about life's triumphs and disasters.

The ravages of old age and crippling arthritis did not stop Wallace from singing the blues whenever and wherever she was called. So in the Spring of 1986, six months before her death, Wallace sang to an audience in Germany, "Women Be Wise, Don't Advertise Yo' Man."

References

Chicago *Defender* 12 June 1926; 12 August 1929.

Harrison, Daphne Duval. "'Up Country . . . ' and Still Singing the Blues: Sippie Wallace." In Daphne DuVal Harrison. *Black Pearls: Blues Queens of the 1920s*. New Brunswick, N.J.: Rutgers University Press, 1988. 112-45. Photographs of Sippie Wallace appear on pp. 112, 124.

Kunstadt, Len. "The Comeback of Sippie Wallace." *Record Research* 88 (January 1968): 3.

"Mighty Tight Woman," RCA Victor BVE 48870-2. February 1929. Reissued. RCA Victor LPO 534. 1966.

Polk's Detroit Dictionary, 1923-24 ed. 35.

Price, Sammy. Interview with author, April 1977.

Talking Machine World 21 (May 15, 1925): 116.

Wallace, Sippie. Interview with author, 24 January 1975, 1976.

Daphne Duval Harrison

Clara Mae Ward

(1924-1973)

Singer

Gospel singer Clara Mae Ward was born on April 21, 1924, in Philadelphia, Pennsylvania, the second daughter of Gertrude Mae Murphy and George Ward. The couple's first child, Willa, was born in 1922, at about the time the Wards moved to Philadelphia from South Carolina. The harsh economic conditions the family was attempting to escape in the South were similar to the ones they found in the North. The onslaught of the Great Depression forced Gertrude Ward

Clara Mae Ward

to provide for her family by serving as a domestic worker for wealthy white families in Philadelphia.

In 1931 Gertrude Ward embarked on a career as a gospel singer, the result of a revelation she received in a dream. For the next several years, she performed at various churches in Philadelphia, and in 1934 she included daughters Willa and Clara in her first solo concert. The Ward Trio was born. The preparation for this occasion had begun many years before. Clara Ward started singing at age five and began piano lessons a few years later. Her extraordinary musical talents were apparent at an early age. Stories of her childhood renditions of "When the Saints Go Marching In" are frequent reminiscences of old-timers at Ebenezer Baptist Church, where Ward attended in her youth. Much like her protégé, Aretha Franklin, Ward developed solid keyboard abilities that never received proper recognition or exposure. Except for an early period when Ward and jazz great Dinah Washington served as accompanists for Gertrude Ward and Sallie Martin performances, Ward's singing always was the talent highlighted. For the next nine years, the Ward Singers, as they came to be know, sang wherever and whenever there was an opportunity. They often visited several churches on a Sunday morning to announce their performance that evening. Fees were small and frequently didn't exist at all. Money had not become an issue and engagements were never turned down because the sponsors couldn't pay.

In 1943 nineteen-year-old Ward was introduced to the national gospel circuit, performing with the Ward Singers at the National Baptist Convention in Philadelphia. Hers was a sensational reception, but while she was aware of her gift for singing and its effect on others, she remained grounded in humility. Gertrude, however, a consummate promoter, took full advantage of the convention triumph. She skillfully rode the wave of this success for the next twenty years. After the Philadelphia Convention, calls came in from all over the United Sates, particularly from the eastern and southeastern states. The Ward Singers began to tour extensively, and even though their popularity was growing, they continued to perform for very little money. However, in 1947 a record review and the addition of two singers, Marion Ward and Henrietta Waddy, positioned the Ward Singers for greater success. By 1949 the group had begun what was to become a long and fruitful relationship with preacher and songwriter W. Herbert Brewster. Gertrude Ward's dream predicting a successful career in gospel music had become a reality, and Ward was to take her own career to even greater heights than her mother.

Although a petite woman—only five-feet three-inches tall and weighing 103 pounds—Ward was a powerhouse of energy and charisma. As time passed, she began to take more control over the artistic direction of the group from her mother and introduced striking gowns and new hair-styles. For many years, the women in the group wore their hair in trademark ponytails. The departure from the usual concert attire gave Ward new fashion freedom. Attention to detail was essential, and mink-trimmed shoes were occasionally the final touch to complete an outfit. The Ward Singers were undoubtedly the most successful female gospel group of the 1950s, and they looked the part. With dazzling gowns, sling-back shoes, and elaborate wigs, they ushered gospel music into the arena of big business.

Trends Set in Gospel Music

The Ward Singers were trendsetters in gospel music. They had laid the foundation for its development in the east by introducing in 1935 the music of Sallie Martin and Thomas A. Dorsey, composer of "Precious Lord," to Philadelphia churches. "Surely God Is Able," a Brewster composition, was the first gospel song to use rhythmic triplets and was a huge success for the Ward Singers. Also, the group employed switch-leads for solo parts in their songs. In the early 1950s, a life-long relationship developed between the Ward Singers and the Reverend C. L. Franklin, father of Aretha Franklin. The group frequently toured with him, and several of its members became close family friends. The Reverend Franklin once described Ward's singing as having created a "whole new dimension of expression for gospel singers." Franklin and Ward had great respect and admiration for each other's abilities, and they toured the Holy Land together in the late 1950s.

Of all the singers who were inspired and influenced by her, Ward's impact on the singing style of Aretha Franklin is best known. Franklin idolized Ward and readily credits her as the inspiration behind her climb to singing superstardom. When Franklin was twelve years old, Ward sang at the funeral of Franklin's aunt. It was this witnessing of Ward's spirited solo that made Franklin decide, on the spot, to become a singer.

"Queen of Moaners" Attracts Crowds

An emotional singer with the power of a seasoned preacher, Ward had a long list of best-selling records. "Surely, God Is Able" sold more than one million copies. Other successes included "How I Got Over," "Come in the Room," and"The Day Is Past and Gone." Her power and conviction were eminently clear on her records, and she constantly filled auditoriums and churches to capacity and broke attendance records for gospel concerts. Over thirteen thousand people attended her concerts at Convention Hall in Philadelphia and twenty-five thousand at Washington's Griffith Stadium. Known best for her delivery of hymns, Ward, at her peak, had an exceptionally beautiful and clear alto voice. Although she developed the theatrical vocal effects associated with her later years, Ward is still affectionately remembered as the "Queen of the Moaners." A master of vocal phrasing and a brilliant and innovative arranger, she and James Cleveland were the top gospel arrangers in the mid-1950s.

Ward's penchant for introducing new music, both her own and that of other composers, led to the establishment of a publishing company. Ward's House of Music was a big success and eventually operated out of the basement of her fourteen-room Philadelphia home. At the height of operation, the company grossed over fifty thousand dollars annually. Its publications included souvenir booklets, song collections, and many of the more than five hundred songs that Ward composed during her lifetime.

Between 1943 and 1957 the Ward Singers wore out fifteen cars and logged a million miles of travel. The "Big Gospel Cavalcade of 1957" is a good example of the kind of scheduling they experienced. During the run of the "Cavalcade," the Ward Singers appeared in a different city every night of the week except Saturdays. A 1955 appearance at the Apollo Theater in Harlem was considered a major breakthrough, but even more amazing opportunities were to come. As a result of an appearance at Carnegie Hall with Mahalia Jackson, the Ward Singers were invited to sing on an all-gospel matinee program at the 1957 Newport Jazz Festival.

Clara Ward Singers Emerge

The Ward Singers rose from performing free concerts for anyone who would listen to receiving five thousand dollars for single performances. Growth and change were inevitable. The year 1958 was one of much unrest within the group, caused primarily by personnel changes and a shift in artistic direction. However, with "Mother" Gertrude Ward at the helm, the singers regrouped and continued their upward climb. In 1959 they went on an immensely successful Scandinavian tour. In 1961, because of Clara Ward's decision to perform at the Village Vanguard in New York City, the singing group was propelled into a totally different environment from that of the churches and religious services to which they had become accustomed. Ward's audiences were absolutely captivated by what they saw and heard at the Vanguard. Engagements at other clubs—such as the Elegant, Birdland, and the Blue Angel—followed. The most publicized and profitable of these performances was a two-week engagement in 1961 at the New Frontier Hotel in Las Vegas. This engagement was extended to forty weeks and was repeated the following year. At the time, it was the longest consecutive booking for any performer in Las Vegas history.

Eventually, the name of the group was changed from the Ward Singers to the Clara Ward Specials and then, finally, to the Clara Ward Singers. In 1962, the Clara Ward Singers first appeared in Disneyland. After that performance, the group was engaged so often at Disneyland that they became regulars. Having already visited more than twenty countries, Ward and her singers continued a rigorous travel schedule, returning to Vietnam and the Far East for a second tour in 1968. They performed for President Lyndon B. Johnson, appeared at Radio City Music Hall, made the film *It's Your Thing*, and appeared on shows with Jack Benny at the Ziegfeld Theater in New York City. A winner of the Courier Theatrical Poll, Clara Ward was extremely popular and also appeared frequently on television. Ed Sullivan, Mike Douglas, Danny Thomas, Steve Allen, Ernie Ford, and the "Today" show all vied for her group's time.

As the act continued to change, so did the repertoire and the appeal of their recordings. Ward recorded an album with the Isley Brothers and for MGM/Verve she recorded *Born Free* and *America the Beautiful*. Clara's showmanship and flexibility carried her to the Broadway stage, where she was musical director and costar of Langston Hughes's "God's Trombones," with Lou Gossett, Jr.

Ward's transition from traditional gospel to pop-gospel had taken nearly twenty years. Much had been gained in the switch, but indeed much had been lost. The physical strain had taken its toll, and a stroke while performing at a Florida hotel left her temporarily unable to sing. Undaunted by her illness, Ward continued to perform, expanding her role as accompanist for the group, she thus provided her mother with yet another promotional angle, as Clara, God's Miracle Girl. Many will say that Ward sacrificed her artistic principles for fame and fortune, but her spiritual integrity remained intact. About gospel music she once said, "It's from the heart. It gets you so much all over, you just can't be still." Despite her musical transition from "Precious Lord" to "Zippety-Dooh-Dah," she never lost her spiritual center. Ward was genuinely concerned that her early supporters would not understand what she was trying to do and spent much of her time explaining her motives. Despite the fact that no alcohol was served while she performed, her appearances in nightclubs was a great point of contention between her and her good friend of many years, Mahalia Jackson.

Ward brought a broader audience to gospel music than ever before. In 1967, the Clara Ward Singers were the first gospel group to appear at the Philadelphia Academy of Music. Her influences are far-reaching, from the singing of Franklin and Ray Charles to gospel-oriented theatrical productions. Gospel music became and remains big business, largely because of the efforts of Clara and Gertrude Ward. It is accepted in the mainstream market and can be heard from rural churches to Carnegie Hall.

After lapsing into a coma following her second stroke in five weeks, Ward died in Los Angeles on January 16, 1973. Before she reached her final resting place in the Freedom Mausoleum at Forest Lawn in Glendale, California, Mother Ward organized two elaborate funerals. A "service of triumph" was held in Philadelphia on January 23, 1973, at the old Metropolitan Opera House. Included on the program were Kitty Parham, Rosie Wallace, and Franklin, who sang Clara Ward's greatest hymn, "The Day Is Past and Gone." A second memorial service was held at the Shrine Auditorium in Los Angeles. Former Ward Singers member Marion Williams thrilled the crowd of over four thousand mourners with "Surely, God Is Able," and Gertrude Ward sang "When the Storms of Life Are Raging." For forty years Ward sang gospel music and she left a rich legacy of musical innovations and personal triumphs. The world of gospel music is much different from the one she was introduced to at the National Baptist Convention in 1943, and we are all benefactors of the musical and social effects of her work.

References

"Benny Finds Gospel Songs through Clara Ward." Chicago *Defender*, Bishop, Louise Williams. Interview with Maurice B. Wheeler, (8 April 1990.)

Broughton, Viv. *Black Gospel: An Illustrated History of the Gospel Sound*. Dorset, England: Blandford Press, 1985.

Cummings, Tony. *The Sound of Philadelphia*. London, England: Methuen, 1975.

"Glamour Girl of Gospel Singer." *Ebony*, January 1957.

"Gospel Singer Clara Ward Dies at 48: Grew Up Here." Philadelphia *Inquirer*, 22 April 1973.

Heath, Linwood. Interview with Maurice B. Wheeler, 18 April 1990.

Heilbut, Tony. *The Gospel Sound*. New York: Limelight Editions, 1985.

"Jazz Fans Went Wild over the Clara Ward Singers." *Melody Maker*, 4 April 1959.

Oliver, Paul. *New Grove Gospel, Blues, and Jazz*. New York: Norton, 1986.

"On the Beat." *Billboard*, 9 March 1959.

"One of the Last Great Hymn Singers." *Washington Post*, 21 January 1973.

Southern, Eileen. *Biographical Dictionary of Afro-American and African Musicians*. Westport, Conn.: Greenwood Press, 1982.

Maurice B. Wheeler

Laura Wheeler Waring

(1887-1948)

Artist, educator

Laura Wheeler Waring was born in Hartford, Connecticut, in 1887, a year when the giants of French painting—Gaugin, Renoir, Degas, and Cézanne—were creating some of their finest works. Waring, who would become one of America's outstanding women artists and whose masterpieces would hang in some of this country's most prestigious galleries, was born into a progressive family which was already prominent in the community.

Waring's father was Robert Foster Wheeler, a graduate of Howard University's theological school and longtime minister of the Talcott Street Congregational Church. Her mother, Mary Freeman Wheeler, was from Brooklyn, New York. Laura was the second daughter of six children. All the Waring children were educated in Hartford, at the Arsenal Grade School and the Hartford High School. Achievement came early to Waring: out of a graduating class of 149 students, she was chosen as one of eight to appear on the program.

Laura Wheeler Waring

After high school, Waring, who had shown unusual talent in art early on, went to Philadelphia, where she enrolled in the beginner's class of the Pennsylvania Academy of Fine Arts in September 1906. She studied there for six years under such masters as Henry McCarter, William Chase, and Thomas Anshutz. Because of her originality and mastery of technique, in 1914 she was awarded the coveted Cresson Travel Scholarship. This award enabled her to travel to most of the countries of western Europe, where she had the opportunity to study the old masters as well as the newer ones.

This first trip abroad was an important milestone in Waring's life. Many of the scenes that she saw in London, Dublin, Paris, and Rome are reflected in her earlier works. Her studies were interrupted by the First World War, and before the year was over Waring returned to Philadelphia and the studios of the academy to complete her studies.

On completion of her studies, Waring was invited to direct the art and music departments at Cheyney State Teachers' College near Philadelphia. For three decades she would teach there and inspire hundreds of students. While at Cheyney Waring produced some of her finest portraits—of president emeritus Leslie Pickney Hill, several trustees, and a faculty member—as well as excellent landscapes of Chester and Delaware County, Pennsylvania, which are among her most original and creative works. Her paintings are outstanding because of the unique manner in which she combined impressionism and academicism, masterfully executed, for example, in her portrait of Evangeline R. Hall, presented to the college on Cheyney Day.

In 1924, while still teaching at Cheyney, Waring traveled abroad for a second time accompanied by her friend, the novelist Jessie Redmond Fauset. On her arrival in Paris Waring enrolled in the Académie de la Grande Chaumière. Here she came under the influence of the French masters Boutet de Monvel and Eugène Delécluse. While on this trip she also traveled in Italy and North Africa.

Wheeler's Art Gains Recognition

On her return to the United States, Waring's reputation grew rapidly and her work received increasing recognition. In 1926 she served as an official in charge of the Negro Art section at the Sesquicentennial Exposition in Philadelphia. The following year she served in a similar capacity at the Texas Centennial Exposition. Also in 1927 she won a gold medal in the annual Harmon Foundation Salon. Increasingly, Waring's works were exhibited in such notable galleries as the Pennsylvania Academy of Fine Arts, the Philadelphia Museum of Art, the Carlen Galleries, the National Collection of Arts, the Corcoran Gallery, the Art Institute of Chicago, the Brooklyn Museum, and Howard University. She exhibited also at the Harmon Foundation, the American Negro Exhibition in Chicago, the Texas Centennial, and the Tanner Art Gallery-Negro Exhibition in Chicago. In her third and last trip abroad, the artist, now Mrs. Walter E. Waring, exhibited at a one-woman show in Paris at the famed Galerie du Luxembourg.

Primarily a portrait painter, Waring made a significant contribution to American and world art. She preserved in her paintings the personalities of many distinguished blacks who have done much to accelerate the liberation struggle in America. A master painter, Waring possessed a highly developed imagination, a skilled hand in drawing, and a fertile appreciation of color, all requirements for creating great art.

In 1946 Waring began a series of religious paintings depicting her concept of the Negro spiritual. Her works in this series include *Jacob's Ladder, The Coming of the Lord,* and *Heaven, Heaven,* a small canvas depicting Saint Peter listening and looking at a tired black woman as she passes through Heaven's door where nine serene angels welcome her.

On February 3, 1948, Waring died after a long and painful illness. Though her mortal presence was gone, Waring lives on in such works as *Mother and Daughter,* a poetic canvas depicting a mulatto mother and her quadroon daughter that clearly shows the harmonious blending of the races, and *Sunday Best,* illustrating the technique and subject matter she addressed in her final and highly impressionistic period. Waring also lives in her penetrating portraits of great personalities such as James Weldon Johnson, W. E. B. DuBois, John Haynes Holmes, and Mary White Ovington. Other influential and outstanding blacks whose portraits have been left as a legacy include Sadie T. M. Alexander, Raymond Pace Alexander, Marian Anderson, Harry T. Burleigh, Jessie Redmond Fauset, and George E. Haynes.

Examples of Waring's work are reproduced in the *Negro Almanac,* Cedric Dover's *American Negro Art,* Alain Locke's *The Negro in Art,* Benjamin Brawley's *Art of the American Negro,* Margaret Just Butcher's *The Negro Genius,* Carroll Greene, Jr.'s *Afro-American Artists: 1800-1968,* and *African-American Artists: 1880-1987.*

References

Cederholm, Theresa Dickason. *Afro-American Artists.* Boston: Boston Public Library, 1973.

Chase, Judith Wragg. *Afro-American Art and Craft.* New Yor: Van Nostrand-Reinhold, 1971.

Driskell, David C. *Two Centuries of Black American Art.* New York: Los Angeles Museum of Art/Knopf, 1976.

Fonvielle-Bontemps, Jacqueline. *Forever Free: Art by African-American Women, 1862-1980.* Alexandria, Va.: Stephenson, 1981.

James, Milton M. ''Laura Wheeler Waring.'' *Negro History Bulletin* 19 (March 1956): 126-28. Includes photograph.

Lewis, Samella. *Art: African-American.* New York: Harcourt Brace Jovanovich, 1978.

Collections

Laura Wheeler Waring's works are in the possession of the Smithsonian Institution, National Portrait Gallery, Barnett-Aden Collection, and Cheney State University. Private collectors who hold her works are Marian Anderson, Charles M. Day, the G. James Flemings, Eleanor Forrester, the Martin Jenkinses, Marie Johnson, Lois Pierre Noel, Robert C. McNeill, Robert H. McNeill, and Madeline Wheeler Murphy.

Margaret Burroughs

Dionne Warwick

(1940-)
Singer

Known throughout the world as Dionne Warwick(e), Marie Dionne Warrick, Grammy Award winning singer of numerous hit songs, including "Do You Know the Way to San Jose," "Promises, Promises," and "I'll Never Fall in Love Again," was born December 12, 1940, the eldest child of Mancel (or Marcel, depending on the source) and Lee Warrick. Her name change resulted from an error on a recording contract. But this transformation is slight compared to those Dionne Warwick has helped bring about in the world of popular music. One source credits "the distinctive, versatile voice of Dionne Warwick" with having "demolished the barriers that used to separate blues, jazz, and gospel singing" (*Current Biography*, 442).

For Warwick, music has always been a family matter. She and her two siblings, sister Dee Dee and brother Mancel, Jr., were raised in a racially mixed neighborhood by devoutly religious parents, both of whom worked in the music business. Her mother, Lee Warrick, managed the Drinkard Singers, the first gospel music group to sing at the Newport Jazz Festival and to be recorded by RCA Victor. Mancel Warrick served as a gospel music promotion director for Chess Records. Recognizing their daughter's talent, Warwick's parents saw to it that she received vocal training. Not surprisingly, gospel music played a significant role in her musical development. As a teenager she sometimes performed with the Drinkard Singers as a pianist or substitute vocalist and sang in the choir of the New Hope Baptist Church in Newark, New Jersey. Her mother once said: "You just know she's had gospel training. She's got that deep soul feeling" (*Current Biography*, 442). Well-known poet and playwright Le Roi Jones (Imiri Baraka) also notes the uniquely African-American quality of Warwick's music. In spite of her success within the white-dominated popular music establishment, Warwick's gospel music beginnings are evident, Jones maintains. "The strings and softness of her arrangements, and of many of her songs, are like white torch singers' delight but her beat (she used to be a gospel singer in New Jersey) and sound take her most times into a warmth undreamed of by the whites" (*Black Music*, 202).

In 1954, at the age of fourteen, Warwick took part in another family music venture, joining her sister Dee Dee and a cousin—Cissy Houston, mother of the popular singer Whitney Houston—in a group called the Gospelaires. The Gospelaires performed together for seven years and enjoyed some success as backup singers. Warwick clearly set her sights on a musical career early on, but apparently she did not envision the glamorous life as a world famous singer that awaited her. Instead, in 1959, she started her way down a more traditional vocational path and entered the Hartt College of Music at the University of Hartford, where she took classes in piano, theory, and voice. The Gospelaires continued to perform as backup singers for groups such as the Drifters and Sam "The Man" Taylor at Harlem's Apollo Theatre and other traditionally black theaters during summers and school vacations.

But it was Warwick, the group's leader, who drew the attention of composer Burt Bacharach during a recording session. He was conducting the Drifters, backed up by none-other-than the Gospelaires, in a version of his tune "Mexican Divorce." *Ebony Magazine* quotes Bacharach as having said of his first encounter with the woman whose talents would lead to international recognition of his own: "She was singing louder than anybody else, so I couldn't help noticing her. Not only was she clearly audible, but Dionne had something. Just the way she carries herself, the way she works, her flow and feeling for the music—it was there when I first met her. She had, and still has, a kind of elegance, a grace that few other people have" (quoted in *Current Biography*, 443). Thus began the highly successful partnership between Bachrach, his lyricist Hal David, and Warwick, though creative and business disagreements in the 1970s caused the three musicians to part on rather strained terms. Fortunately, Bacharach and Warwick resolved their difficulties in 1986.

From the beginning it was evident that Warwick was one of the few singers who could do justice to Bacharach's unusual, rhythmically challenging, and difficult compositions. Stephen Holden notes that Bacharach and David:

> devised a sophisticated, effervescent style for Warwick, which minimized her gospel mannerisms while preserving the direct emotionalism of soul music. Bacharach's ingenious melodies, with their open-ended structures, unconventional time signatures, and rapid modulations, combined with David's lyrics to create a narrative urgency that perfectly suited Warwick's dark husky alto, staccato diction, and slurred phrasing. But it was Warwick's fervent yet colloquial style that gave what were essentially pop songs an individual and convincing soul feeling (480-81).

By 1962, Warwick was well on her way to musical success when she, Bacharach, and David signed a contract with Scepter Records and recorded the top-ten pop-chart hit "Don't Make Me Over." Warwick gave up her studies at Hartt College in 1963 and with the encouragement of her manager, Paul Cantor, as well as Bacharach, began a strenuous but rewarding concert tour. France received her especially well; Parisians nicknamed her "Paris' black Pearl" (Stambler, 726).

Throughout the 1960s, the Warwick, Bacharach, and

David combination continuously made the charts with hit singles and albums. Popular music fans whose memories reach back to the mid-1960s will definitely recognize the titles of the following Dionne Warwick hit singles: "Walk on By," "Anybody Who Had a Heart," "You'll Never Get to Heaven," "Are You There," "I Just Don't Know What to Do with Myself," "Trains and Boats and Planes," "Message to Michael," "Alfie," and the gold record hit "I Say a Little Prayer for You." Her highly successful albums from this period include *Presenting Dionne Warwick, Anyone Who Has a Heart, Make Way for Dionne Warwick, The Sensitive Sound of Dionne Warwick, Dionne Warwick in Paris,* and *Dionne Warwick on Stage and in the Movies.* Warwick recorded all of these hits on the Scepter Records label.

In 1968 and 1969, Warwick produced the hit singles "Do You Know the Way to San Jose" (this city consequently made her an honorary citizen), "Valley of the Dolls," "There's Always Something There to Remind Me," and "You've Lost That Lovin' Feeling," all on the Scepter label. She cut four albums for Scepter in 1968, *Dionne in the Valley of the Dolls, Windows of the World, Dionne Warwick's Golden Hits, Part l,* and *Promises, Promises.* And she made her screen debut in the 1969 movie *The Slaves.*

The 1970s mark a period of personal and professional change for Warwick. Irwin Stambler in the *Encyclopedia of Pop, Rock, and Soul* calls the mid 1970s a "low period" for Warwick, though she certainly remained productive throughout this decade (Stambler, 727). Her marriage to drummer-turned-actor Bill Elliot in September 1967 ended in divorce in 1975. Their union produced one son, born in January 1969. As previously mentioned, she cut her ties with Bacharach and David during this period, a rift that involved legal disputes. Nevertheless, she continued to perform in concert halls and clubs as well as to make appearances on television variety and talk shows and to make movie soundtracks. Her hit singles from the early part of this decade include "Let Me Go to Him," "The Green Grass Starts to Grow," and "Make It Easy on Yourself," a song from the musical score of *Promises, Promises.* She made the album charts in 1970 with *Golden Hits Volume 2, Soulful,* and *I'll Never Fall in Love Again.* Her 1971 efforts—*Very Dionne,* the movie soundtrack to *Love Machine,* and *The Dionne Warwick Story,* which went gold—also made the album charts.

But in 1971 she switched from Scepter Records to Warner Brothers. This arrangement produced fewer successful records than she had enjoyed while under contract to Scepter. Among her hits on the Warner label were the 1973 singles "If We Only Have Love" and "Just Being Myself." Her albums for Warner Brothers include *Then Came You* and *Track of the Cat* (1975) and *Loved at First Sight* (1977). She also released her best-selling hit single "Then Came You" during this time. This single, the result of her five-week summer concert tour with the Spinners, was the number one Billboard single during the week of October 26, 1974. Warner Brothers gave permission for this song to be recorded by Atlantic, part of their corporation.

Warwick Produces Platinum Album

By 1979, Warwick began to recover lost ground. First, she switched from Warner Brothers to Arista Records and produced the platinum album *Dionne,* which includes the gold record top-five single "I'll Never Love This Way Again." Her other successful ventures with Arista include the albums *No Night So Long* (1980), *Hot Live and Otherwise* (1981), *Heartbreaker* (1982), *How Many Times Can We Say Goodbye* (1983), and the gold *Friends* (1985). This album contains the Grammy Award-winning single for Best Pop Performance by a Duo or Group with Vocal and Song of the Year "That's What Friends Are For," written by Burt Bacharach and Carole Bayer Sager. Gladys Knight, Stevie Wonder, and Elton John can also be heard on this single, attributed to "Dionne and Friends". These stars united to benefit AIDS research. Also among the honors Warwick received in the 1980s is first prize at the Ninth Annual Tokyo Music Festival in 1980.

In mid-1985, Warwick began to take on new sorts of projects. She was one of the forty-five performers who united their talents on the internationally successful "We Are the World" single, sponsored by USA for Africa. Profits were donated to African hunger relief efforts. In 1986 Warwick began promoting a perfume named "Dionne," and she and Johnny Mathis embarked on tour. Among her 1987 accomplishments were a part in the movie *Rent-a-Cop,* a new album on the Arista label, *Reservations for Two,* and a reunion tour with Burt Bacharach. In a review of an appearance the two made at Radio City Music Hall on this tour, *Variety* bestows the following praise on Warwick:

> Her performance, relaxed and confident as ever, was something of a revelation in this decade of female vocalists who approach singing as an athletic exercise. Climbing into falsetto range, changing keys, or holding notes for dramatic effect, Warwick made it all look effortless. She brought the crowd to its feet with "Make It Easy on Yourself," and one of her non-Bacharach hits, "I'll Never Love This Way Again" (216).

Clearly her early hits have not lost their appeal. But Warwick is not content to rest on her past laurels. Instead, with her most recent album, *Dionne Warwick Sings Cole Porter* (1990), she charts a new musical course for herself and combines her artistic maturity with the talent that has brought her worldwide recognition since the 1960s. Her voice, though it changes as she grows older, is still enormously compelling. A *New York Times* reviewer writes that on two of this album's cuts, "What Is This Thing Called Love" and "So in Love," Warwick "spreads the wings of an alto that has grown so deep that at moments it sounds almost forbidding" (H-34).

And surely the accolades will continue to pour in as Warwick's career enters its fourth decade. In one sense this remarkably gifted woman with the captivating, unique voice has achieved her original goal of becoming a music teacher.

For she has clearly inspired other musicians and has generously used her talent to benefit others. Robert J. McNatt mused in the November 1981 issue of *Essence*: "If music is a woman, one of her names must be Dionne Warwick" (18). It is truly a name that will long be heard, remembered, and enjoyed.

References

Current Biography Yearbook. New York: H. W. Wilson, 1969.

"Dionne Warwick and Burt Bacharach. Concert Review." *Variety* (14 October 1987): 216.

"Dionne Warwick Sings Cole Porter." *New York Times* 19 August 1990.

"Dionne Warwick." *Who's Who of American Women*. 15th ed. Chicago: Marquis, 1988.

Holden, Stephen. "Dionne Warwick(e). *The New Grove Dictionary of American Music*. Eds. H. Wiley Hichcock and Stanley Sadie. New York: Macmillan, 1986.

Jones, Le Roi. *Black Music*. New York: William Morrow, 1969.

McNatt, Robert J. "Main Events." *Essence* 12 (November 1981): 18.

Stambler, Irwin. "Dionne Warwick." *The Encyclopedia of Pop, Rock, and Soul*. Rev. ed. New York: St. Martin's Press, 1989.

Who's Who Among Black Americans, 1990/91. 6th ed. Detroit: Gale Research, 1990.

Candis LaPrade

Dinah Washington

(1924-1963)

Singer

One of the greatest blues and popular singers of her time, Dinah Washington seemed to know everyone, go everywhere, do everything—and she could sing anything. Her life was cut tragically short, but even that seems to fit the life of a women who created herself in the image of a shooting star.

Dinah Washington was born Ruth Lee Jones on August 29, 1924, in Tuscaloosa, Alabama, to Alice Williams and Ollie Jones; she and her family moved to Chicago's South Side when she was four years old. She had a brother and two sisters and attended Chicago's public schools, including Wendell Phillips High School, which numbers among its graduates Nat Cole, Ray Nance, and Milt Hinton. She was married seven times, to John Young, Robert Grayson, George Jenkins, Walter Buchanan, Eddie Chamblee, Rafael Campos, and Richard "Night Train" Lane, and had two sons, Robert Grayson, Jr., and George Jenkins, Jr. Two additional marriages (to Rusty Maillard and Larry Wrice) were announced but did not take place. She moved to New York about midway into her career, and then finally to Detroit, following her marriage to Dick Lane. She died at home in Detroit on December 14, 1963, of an accidental overdose of diet pills and prescription drugs.

Singing and performing began for her at an early age. Her mother was a pianist at Saint Luke's Baptist Church and taught her daughter piano. Soon she was playing the piano and singing gospel at the church. Her mother realized that her daughter had potential as a gospel singer and coached her. She became a favorite as a gospel soloist at Saint Luke's and was hired by Sallie Martin as an accompanist, also singing with her at numerous churches in the Chicago area. It was through Sallie Martin that she met Mahalia Jackson, the evangelist preacher, singer C. L. Franklin, and Roberta Martin (her favorite gospel singer). She also became a member of the Sallie Martin Colored Ladies' Quartet, the first all-woman gospel group founded by Sallie Martin.

From her peers, Dinah Washington developed a liking for popular song, and her first love as a popular singer was Billie Holiday. She began to sing regularly and entered an amateur contest at the Regal Theater when she was fifteen years of age. She won, singing "I Can't Face the Music." After this, she began to sing at various local clubs without her mother's permission, performing in churches often enough to please her mother, while bringing money home. At a certain point, she realized that she had greater earning power singing in clubs than in churches, and she left the Martin Singers. However, her love of gospel singers remained strong throughout her life, and she was a lifetime member of the Gospel Singers' Convention. Nevertheless, her mother was a very religious person, and the shift in Dinah Washington's career probably caused some permanent friction.

Her first husband, John Young, was also her manager. At this point, she was still in her teens, but eager to leave home and follow her singing career. Marriage also gave her the opportunity to gain a measure of personal freedom and leave the poverty of her South Side home. She appeared at many local clubs and began to develop a reputation both as a pianist and singer. In this respect, John Young helped considerably. Her marriage, however, soured, lasting barely three months.

Dinah Washington's career continued. A friend took her to hear Billie Holiday at the Garrick Stage Lounge, and Dinah Washington was determined to get a job singing there. She auditioned for the owner, Joe Sherman, and was hired to sing at the upstairs room while Billie Holiday sang downstairs. After singing upstairs, she rushed downstairs to hear Billie Holiday perform. She remained at the Garrick Stage

Lounge after Holiday's engagement was over, and the owner helped greatly to further her career. He is credited with suggesting her name change to Dinah Washington. He also arranged for the agent Joe Glaser to hear her in 1943 and, through him, Lionel Hampton. Hampton hired her, and this began an important association with his band, taking her to stage engagements at major cities and on tour. Glaser subsequently became her agent.

Following engagements with Hampton at New York's Apollo Theatre in 1943, pianist and composer Leonard Feather asked her to record with him as pianist, and she cut several of his blues songs for a new company, Keynote Records. The records did very well, and this caused a bit of a stir with Hampton's company, Decca, which had not given permission. The recording group had been billed as the Lionel Hampton Sextet, and this had to be deleted. Decca was only interested in recording Hampton in instrumental numbers, and this caused a problem for Dinah Washington. She continued with Hampton, however, and in 1945 she was finally able to have her own contractually legal recording session with Decca Records, at which she introduced another Feather Song, "Blowtop Blues." Soon thereafter she broke with Hampton, arguing over more opportunities to sing and performance rights to "Blowtop Blues," some say at gunpoint (Haskins, 36).

Fame As Blues Singer Launched

From this point on, her career as an independent artist was launched, as well as her fame as an exponent of the blues. She branched out ever more into the role of a traveling superstar, and soon earned her moniker of "Queen of the Blues." She toured widely, visiting all sections of urban and near-urban America with her talents. Utilizing a format of a basic small group, she favored primarily youthful artists in her ensemble, usually men in their twenties and early thirties: Jimmy Cobb, Wynton Kelly, Keter Betts, Jack Wilson, and Eddie Chamblee. When she added musicians according to the needs of the occasion, she literally sampled from the very best of talent available.

Her regular ensemble often included musicians whose talents she personally discovered, and for recording sessions she regularly brought in others. In fact, one can readily count Dinah Washington as having made a lasting contribution to American music through her discovery and promotion of new talent. To mention only a few names in addition to those cited above, one can list Patti Austin, Paul Quinichette, Quincy Jones, and Lola Folana.

Alongside her personal appearances, a burgeoning recording career was fast developing. Following her initial successes, she had numerous sessions, including those in 1945 for Apollo, ABC, Grand Award, and Parrot, that led to twelve sides, mostly of blues songs, and all recorded in Los Angeles. Very soon thereafter, she was approached by agent Ben Bart with a contractual deal with Mercury Records. Dinah Washington signed with Mercury and stayed with the company for some fifteen years, also taking on Bart as her new agent and leaving Joe Glaser (she resumed working with Glaser in 1954). She recorded her first sides for Mercury in Chicago, also in 1945. An excellent list of her recordings may be found in Jim Haskins's *Lady Sings the Blues*, pp. 203-230.

Her records were doing quite well, and were helped initially by her substantial popularity in the "race records" market, as well as her ability to charm a variety of audiences in person, thereby creating yet further demands for her recordings. An important development in the record market then ensued, with the commercial coinage of a new term: "Rhythm & Blues" (replacing the term "Race Records"), first used in the *Billboard* magazine record charts on June 25, 1949. The new term was tailor-made for Dinah Washington. She had long issued records and sung popular songs of all varieties and types, not limiting herself to "blues" in the strictly formal sense, but songs often imbued with her particular soulful interpretations of lyrics and capturing the rhythmic essence of the blues as well. From the institution of this new term, Dinah Washington's songs were regularly among the leaders on the *Billboard* R&B charts.

With a keen eye for the market, Mercury Records fed her public with a goodly supply of blues songs, as well as giving Dinah Washington the opportunity to record standard popular songs targeted to her followers. Thus, she could be called on in 1949 to issue such standards as "How Deep Is the Ocean" and "Harbor Lights," as well as blues songs like "Fast Movin' Mama" and "Shuckin' and Jivin'." Frequently, Dinah Washington would be their "cover" singer, recording for the black market a song originally introduced by a white singer (Haskins, 54). For the most part, however, her albums and singles included songs designed to suit her market and the R&B charts, where she retained a leadership position for many years.

That she was an excellent musician with an outstanding sense of pitch is attested to by the musical quality of her records. The vocal presence she assumed always suited the lyrics. At times there was a biting quality to the voice, at times a velvety smoothness, but always very clear diction. Her vocal quality had a somewhat instrumental timbre, according to Haskins (64), now like that of a clarinet, now like a tenor saxophone.

She prided herself on excellent enunciation, prompting Ernestine McClendon's husband to remark, "You listen at her. Her and Ella. You can. It's not mumble jumble. You can hear every word they say." Dick Lane commented on her ability to reach people: "I didn't realize how many hundreds of thousands of people were sitting behind closed doors, with whatever their problems were, with Dinah, how she could take a song and sing it to all those people and really make them feel that they shouldn't be lonely because they had her" (Haskins, 64). Said baritone sax player Charles Davis, "I never experienced anything with a vocalist that could make a whole band cry. That happened quite frequently" (Haskins, 127).

Dinah Washington said of her interpretative style, "I like to get inside of a song. When you honest-to-goodness get inside of a song there's a feeling, a strong feeling, that comes out. That's what should always happen. When anyone sings they ought to let the soul come out of them. You just step back and let that soul come out—just let it flow out. That's what I try to do" (Sanders, 151).

Perhaps the most poignant and personal example of this is her rendition of "I Don't Hurt Anymore," recorded in 1954 after her relationship with Jimmy Cobb had ended. She also "lets the soul come out" with all of the textual nuances in "What a Difference a Day Makes," which finally and firmly established her qualifications as a mainstream artist in 1959. Or, reflect on how she tells you just how salty a salty papa is, in her "Salty Papa Blues." Or, be thrilled as she sings her "Dentist's Song" ("You Thrill Me When You Drill Me").

Clearly, her life informed her singing. She lived life to its fullest. She loved parties and special occasions, especially birthdays and Christmas. She empathized with others' problems, frequently helping those in need with car payments, rent, loans, hospital bills, and the like. She fired her assistants one day, and gave them lavish presents the next. As a demanding musician, she had a somewhat stormy career, leaving the bandstand when conditions were not right and feuding with her musicians; she was hit with a trombone stand and even threw Eddie Chamblee's saxophone against a wall after an argument. In addition to her seven husbands, there were always men in her life. Her travels took her everywhere; she experienced deep South "Jim Crow" at its worst, poor working conditions, and the press of the one-night stand circuit.

She was a devoted family person, and shared all of her family's problems. She remained close to her father and mother, even after her father remarried. She bought her mother a house and set her father up in an apartment house she owned. Her two sons stayed with her mother at first, and after her mother remarried to James Kimbrough in 1953, there were ten children at home with her mother and stepfather. She took on the added financial responsibility and delighted in cooking when she was at home, particularly at Christmas.

She set up another home in New York to accommodate her career. Here she had an apartment with enough room for LaRue Manns, her longtime personal manager, and to have guests, friends, and parties. Ironically, it was at Christmastime that she died, in her new house in Detroit, with her two sons home for the holidays from boarding school, apparently very happy with her new husband, Dick Lane.

She retained her familial closeness wherever her career took her. Consequently, there was always a need to earn more money, make more records, take more one-night stands. This soon began to wear on her physically. In addition, she worried constantly over her physical appearance, and this occasioned the diet pills and medication. Also, she took great pains to dress well and look good on stage, which called for special dresses and constant attention to her hair (she freely admitted that she changed her hair as often as she changed her men). Consequently, she had a constant need for hairdressers and seamstresses, and she had a large entourage, including LaRue Manns, Ruth Bowen, her business manager, her hairdresser, seamstress, her man, her band, her chauffeur, and various others.

All of the foregoing can readily be distilled into a life full of fun, pathos, deep caring, a soulful feeling for others, and responses to the feelings and needs of others. Add to this her frequent shifts of mood and temper, the anecdotal references to her brushes with the law, her throwing a glass and injuring a woman in a bar, her threatening people with a gun, her receiving a gift parcel of candy laced with glass slivers, her receiving a gift parcel of very stale and fragrant chitlins from a fellow musician with whom she was feuding, and one certainly has an image of her "life to its fullest." It is, then, certainly no wonder that her songs are full of empathy and poignancy.

The following quotation aptly sums up her contribution to music history:

> The tragedy of Dinah Washington was the tragedy of all powerful black females who often cannot find a place of honor and respect—be it in show business or in society. Yet there is still glory to be found amid the tragedy, and the glory of Dinah Washington lies in the simple power and triumph of her music and the personal statement of power she made as a woman—an image untouched by time and a music seldom surpassed (De Ramus and Gourse, 78).

References

Bogle, Donald. *Brown Sugar; Eighty Years of America's Black Female Superstars*. New York: Harmony Books, 1980. 111, 139, 172.

"Darling of the Hi-Fi Set." *Ebony* 12 (November 1956): 37-42.

DeMille, Darcy. "What a Difference a Day Makes." *Sepia* 13 (February 1964): 78-79.

De Ramus, Betty, and Leslie Gourse. "Remembering Dinah." *Essence* 14 (May 1983): 76-78, 134, 137.

"Dinah Washington." *Ebony* 5 (June 1950): 59-62.

Harris, Sheldon. *Blues Who's Who: A Biographical Dictionary of Blues Singers*. New Rochelle, N.Y.: Arlington House, 1979. 536-538.

Haskins, Jim. *Queen of the Blues*. New York: William Morrow, 1987.

Kernfeld, Barry. "Dinah Washington." *New Grove Dictionary of American Music*. Vol. 4. Eds. H. Wiley Hitchcock and Stanley Sadie. New York: Macmillan, 1986. 489.

Noble, Jeanne. *Beautiful, Also, Are the Souls of My Black Sisters.* Englewood Cliffs, N.J.: Prentice-Hall, 1978. 228-229.

Sanders, Charles L. "Requiem for Queen Dinah." *Ebony* 19 (March 1964): 146-154.

Shaw, Arnold. *Black Popular Music in America.* New York: Schirmer Books, 1986. 181-182, 189, 279, 284, 306, 344-345.

Darius L. Thieme

Fredi Washington

(1903-)

Dancer, actress, organization founder

Fredricka "Fredi" Carolyn Washington exemplified the cultural dilemma of mulattoes who were physically white and socially black. "To pass," she said, "for economic or other advantages would mean that I swallowed, whole hog, the idea of black inferiority. I am a black woman, and I am proud of it. I will fight injustices until the day I die or until there is nothing to fight against" (Darden, 105). These lines reveal much about Washington: a sense of inner beauty and pride in her race. They also reveal her willingness to fight injustice wherever it surfaced. Best known for a stage and screen career in the 1930s and 1940s, there was another side to Washington few people knew existed. She founded the Negro Actors Guild and served as its first executive secretary. She was editor of *The People's Voice* and contributed theater reviews to area newspapers. She also worked actively with the NAACP to secure better hotel accommodations for black actors and actresses.

Fredi, a nickname given to her by her mother, was born December 23, 1903, in Savannah, Georgia. As the oldest girl, she ran the household and cared for her other brothers and sisters: Isabell, Bubba, Alonzo, and Rosebud. After the death of her mother when Washington was eleven years old and after her father's remarriage, Fredi Washington, along with Isabell, entered Saint Elizabeth's Convent in Cornwell Heights, Pennsylvania, run by the Reverend Mother Katherine Biddle. Both sisters left the cloistered life of the convent; however, only Washington moved to New York to live with her grandmother and an aunt. Washington's education was later interrupted temporarily at sixteen, but she graduated from Julia Richmond High School. Further studies, completed at two professional schools, Egri School of Dramatic Writing and the Christophe School of Languages, marked the end of Washington's formal education. But this background, combined with some informal training, would enhance her acting ability on the stage and the silver screen.

A series of jobs followed, such as stockroom clerk in a dress company, but the one at the W. C. Handy Black Swan Record Company yielded the best result for Washington. Working there as a bookkeeper, she heard about a dance audition for the black musical, *Shuffle Along*. One critic believes that this 1921 musical "initiated the return of black shows to Broadway on a regular basis" (Sampson, *Blacks in Black Face*, 20). The play, written, directed, produced, and staged by Eubie Blake, Noble Sissle, Flournoy E. Miller, and Aubrey Lyles, featured the black chorus line in the style of the white *Follies* or *Vanities* on the Broadway stage. With the help of the black choreographer, Elida Webb, Fredi Washington landed a spot in the chorus and earned thirty-five dollars a week despite the fact that she lacked professional training as a dancer.

The decade of the twenties gave Washington exposure to directors, producers, and movie-company moguls who cast her in plays and films. After *Shuffle Along*, Washington appeared as a dancer at New York's Club Alabam' and came to the attention of Lee Shubert. He insisted that she audition for *Black Boy* (1926), a story based on the life of Jack Johnson, starring Paul Robeson as the prizefighter. The play opened on Broadway at the Comedy Theatre to mixed reviews. One review criticized Robeson but praised Washington as the "colored girl who . . . passes for white, but finally declares she is coloured and goes home to live with Black Boy" (Johnson, 206). Another critic hailed Washington as one of the "most talked about ingenues" and some theatergoers went to see if she was as white as reputed by the media (Bogle, *Brown Sugar,* 76). The play established a dangerous precedent in that Washington became typecast as the tragic mulatto: a fair-skinned black woman who decides to pass for white. Ironically, just as it had been Washington's fair appearance that brought her to prominence, it was her fair appearance that drove her ultimately from both stage and screen.

At the end of the decade, Washington toured Europe and returned to the United States to star in a series of films such as *Hot Chocolates* (1929) and *Great Day* (1929). However, the musical film, *Black and Tan Fantasy* (1929), reminiscent of her *Shuffle Along* days, established Washington's career as a dancer. According to one film critic, "this picture was produced primarily to showcase Duke Ellington and his Orchestra" (Sampson, *Blacks in Black and White,* 134). Washington plays a sick dancer who dances to the music composed by her sweetheart and succumbs to death. Also, Washington appeared in *Sweet Chariot* (1930), a musical play based on Marcus Garvey's Universal Negro Improvement Association. In 1931 Washington, along with her sister Isabell, starred in *Singin' the Blues,* a melodrama of night life in Harlem. Two years later Washington starred in *Run, Little Chillun,* a Hall Johnson folk drama contrasting the strength of religion as pitted against savagery.

In the 1930s Washington emerged as one of America's

great black dramatic actresses. She had strong roles in movies like *The Emperor Jones* (1933), playing a Harlem prostitute in a drama in which the protagonist rises from a Pullman car porter to emperor of an island of blacks. But there is an underside to the filming of this movie in that the Will Hays Office, the movie industry's censoring agency, "insisted on seeing the rushes. . . . Hays insisted that it be reshot, lest the light-skinned Miss Washington come across as a white woman" to the film's audience making love to a black man (Duberman, 168). Hence, dark make-up was applied to Washington each day. The recurring issue of Washington's appearance baffled movie producers and directors in the years to come. Other movie roles like *The Old Man of the Mountain* (1933) and *Mills Blue Rhythm Band* (1933) gave Washington an avenue to showcase her talent. However, the movie *Imitation of Life* (1934), a Universal film production of the same name, was Washington's greatest success and her greatest failure. Again typecast as the tragic mulatto in the role of Peola, Washington became the center of controversy.

The story proper centers on two mothers, one white (Bea Pullman, portrayed by Claudette Colbert) and one black (Delilah Johnson, portrayed by Louise Beavers) who supported their daughters on a meager income. The subplot focuses on the conflict between Delilah and her daughter, Peola. However, the crux of the problem lies in Peola experiencing an identity crisis when she compares herself to Jessie, Bea's daughter. Unable to accept her blackness, Peola passes for white, dates white men, and ultimately marries a white, blond engineer. The two leave the United States for the jungles of Bolivia. In the movie version Delilah, disappointed with her daughter's actions, asserts "Black wimmin who pass, pass into damnation" (Short, 115). With a broken heart and ill health, Delilah gives detailed arrangements for her own funeral to her white employer, readies herself to meet Jesus, and dies. As her mother's white horse-drawn coffin moves slowly down the street, Peola runs toward it screaming, "I've killed my own mother" (Short, 116).

After the initial previewing of the movie, Sterling Brown, then of Howard University and film critic for the magazine *Opportunity*, and Fannie Hurst, the author of the book, were greatly divided in their critique of the film's artistic impact. Despite mixed reviews, the movie was a box-office success. It appears that *Imitation of Life*, more than any other film, not only typecast Washington as the tragic mulatto but served to deepen society's ambivalence toward her as a person and as an actress. The motion picture industry mirrored similar ambivalence in that numerous roles awaited Washington as the tragic mulatto but few roles as a serious dramatic actress.

In 1935 Washington returned to the silver screen in *Drums of the Jungle*, playing a half-breed, and two years later she starred as Flora Jackson in *One Mile From Heaven*, a Twentieth Century-Fox film, which one critic describes as a "hodgepodge of Class C celluloid" (*New York Times*, 19 August 1937). In this drama, Jackson befriends a white foundling named Sunny, whose father is killed in a gangland war. She rears the child as her own until Sunny's mother discovers her whereabouts. The ending surprises the audience because Sunny reunites with her mother and millionaire stepfather. Jackson joins Sunny and becomes her governess and maid. Others who appeared in this cast are Claire Trevor as Lucy (Tex) Warren and Bill Robinson as Officer Joe.

According to one film critic, the late 1930s was a period of "optimism in Negro Theatrical circles [and] Ethel Waters, Willie Bryan, Georgette Harvey, Fredi Washington, Anne Wiggins Brown, [and] Jose Ferrer . . . brought dynamic performances to *Mamba's Daughters*" (Mitchell, 108). This production provided Washington a chance to return to her first love, the Broadway stage. As the character Lissa, she played opposite Ethel Waters. The stage, Washington felt, offered some relief from the typecasting she had experienced in Hollywood.

Negro Actors Guild Founded

Washington, sensing that typecast roles had been her undoing, became more politically oriented and founded the Negro Actors Guild of America and served as its first executive secretary (1937-1938). The aim of the guild was to create "a number of important moves toward the bettering of roles for coloured actors and the elimination of sequences in plays and shows which were considered racially out of date" (Noble, 223). Also, Washington, maintaining a scaled-down career in stage and screen, served as theater editor and columnist for *The People's Voice*, a weekly newspaper published by Adam Clayton Powell, Jr. With the guild and the newspaper as support, Washington wielded more credibility in the political arena when she fought to secure good hotel accommodations and worked for black performers with the NAACP for more black participation in the arts. Other involvement included work in the Joint Actors Equity Theatre League Committee on Hotel Accommodations for blacks throughout the United States and as a registrar for the Henry da Silver School of Acting.

Washington worked at various jobs in the late 1940s and early 1950s such as casting consultant for *Carmen Jones* (1943), *Porgy and Bess* (1943), and *Cry the Beloved Country* (1952). Her theater roles include: *Lysistrata* (1946), *A Long Way From Home* (1948), in which she portrayed a character named Celine, and *How Long Til Summer* (1949). Radio and television roles consisted of specials for the National Urban League, the CBS network, and "The Goldbergs," a weekly family drama.

Fredricka Carolyn Washington was born too soon to be in the true sense a Broadway stage actress and silver screen star, because whites of her generation perceived blacks narrowly. Only the stereotypical roles of mammies, Jemimas, and tragic mulattoes seemed appropriate for the white-controlled movie industry. However, Washington had all the talent, beauty, and stage presence that any actress needed or wanted. Hollywood was not ready to accept a black leading lady with poise, intelligence, and professionalism. The tragic side of Washington's dilemma was the fact that no studio offered her a chance to show her creativity and range of talent. *Imitation of Life* was both a blessing and a curse in that Washington brought sympathy and feeling to the role of Peola and transformed, in the minds of critics, a subplot on the issue of passing for white into a main plot. Moreover, audiences remained ambivalent about her personally and professionally for years to come. The movie ostensibly gave Washington the exposure needed to secure future roles, yet her fair complexion frustrated her ambitions. As with *The Emperor Jones,* her face had to be darkened in *Imitation of Life* so that audiences would not confuse her with the leading lady. Though bitter momentarily, Washington knew that the Peola myth remained intact and that the big roles had eluded her.

As a casting consultant, founder of the Negro Actors Guild, and theater editor of *The People's Choice,* Washington became a "bridge for others" and dedicated her life to improving the quality of the profession for fellow black performers (Darden, 109). Today, Washington is a civil rights activist. She resides with her second husband, a prominent black dentist, in Stamford, Connecticut.

References

Bogle, David. *Blacks in American Films and Television.* New York: Garland, 1988. Photograph, p. 61.

——. *Brown Sugar: Eighty Years of America's Black Female Superstars.* New York: Harmony, 1980. Photographs, pp, 81-82.

——. *Toms, Coons, Mulattoes, Mammies, and Bucks: An Interpretive History of Blacks in American Films.* New York: Viking, 1973. Photograph, p. 478.

Brown, Sterling A. "The End of a Controversy." *Opportunity* 13 (August 1935): 231.

——. "Imitation of Life: Once a Pancake." *Opportunity* 13 (1935): 87-88.

" 'Confession' at the Strand, 'Roaring Timber' at the Rialto, 'One Mile From Heaven' at the Palace." *New York Times,* 19 August 1937.

Contributions of Black Women to America. Vol. 1. Ed. Marianna W. Davis. Columbia, S.C.: Kenday Press, 1982.

Cripps, Thomas. *Slow Fade to Black: The Negro in American Film, 1900-1942.* New York: Oxford University Press, 1977.

Darden, Norma Jean. "O Sister! Fredi and Isabel Washington Relive 1930s Razzmatazz." *Essence* 9 (September 1978): 98-111. Photographs, pp. 98-99.

Duberman, Martin Bauml. *Paul Robeson.* New York: Knopf, 1989.

"Fredi Washington as Lissa in 'Mamba's Daughters.' " *New York Dispatch,* 4 February 1939.

Hurst, Fannie. "Editorial." *Opportunity* 13 (April 1935): 121-22.

Isaacs, Edith J. R. *The Negro in the American Theatre.* College Park, Md.: McGrath, 1947.

Johnson, James Weldon. *Black Manhattan.* New York: Knopf, 1930. Reprinted. New York: Arno Press, 1968.

Kellner, Bruce, ed. *The Harlem Renaissance: A Historical Dictionary.* Westport, Conn.: Greenwood Press, 1984.

Leab, Daniel J. *From Sambo to Superspade: The Black Experience in Motion Pictures.* Boston: Houghton Mifflin, 1976.

Mapp, Edward. *Dictionary of Blacks in the Performing Arts.* Metuchen, N.J.: Scarecrow, 1978.

Mitchell, Loften. *Black Drama: The Story of the American Negro in the Theatre.* New York: Hawthorn Books, 1967.

Noble, Peter. "The Coming of the Sound Film." *Anthology of the Afro American in the Theatre.* Ed. Lindsay Patterson. Cornwell Heights, N.Y.: Publishers Agency, 1967.

——. *The Negro in Films.* Port Washington: Kennikat Press, 1969.

Oshana, Maryann. *Women of Color: A Filmography of Minority and Third World Women.* New York: Garland, 1985.

Sampson, Henry T. *Blacks in Black and White.* Metuchen, N.J.: Scarecrow Press, 1977.

——. *Blacks in Black Face.* Metuchen, N.J.: Scarecrow Press, 1980.

Sennwald, Andre. "The Screen Version of Fannie Hurst's 'Imitation of Life,' at the Roxy—'College Rhythm.' " *New York Times,* 24 November 1934.

Short, Bobby. *Black and White Baby.* New York: Dodd, Mead, 1971.

Smythe, Mabel M., ed. *The Black American Reference Book.* Englewood Cliffs, N.J.: Prentice-Hall, 1976.

Sharynn Etheridge

Josephine Washington

(1861-1949)

Writer, educator

Author and educator, Josephine Turpin Washington. was a significant historical figure whose life and works escaed popular recognition. She was born in Goochland County, Virginia, on July 31, 1861, the daughter of Augustus A. and Maria V. Turpin. As a young child Washington was taught to read by an employee who worked for the family. The family later moved to Richmond, where she graduated from normal and high schools and the Richmond Institute, which became the Richmond Theological Seminary. Washington entered Howard University and completed her study there in 1886. During summer vacations she served as a copyist in the office of Frederick Douglass, Recorder of the District.

She soon married Samuel H. H. Washington, a physician practicing in Birmingham, Alabama, and moved there in 1888, after her marriage. Although the date of her entry into the literary world is unclear, Washington gained her literary reputation before she was married. Her first literary piece was published in 1877 in the *Virginia Star*, Virginia's only black newspaper at that time. The focus of the article, "A Talk about Church Fairs," was to protest the selling of wine at social functions given by church members for the benefit of the church.

Washington addressed a variety of themes in her writings, including racial problems and women's issues. In her essay, "Higher Education for Women" appearing in the *People's Advocate*, she emphasizes that through education women could increase earning power, become better mothers, expand their job opportunities beyond the limits of domestic service, and develop communication skills which would improve their ability to relate to men. Her feminist views are apparent in her introductory essay to Lawson A. Scruggs's *Women of Distinction* as well:

> Woman is not undeveloped man but diverse . . . the true woman takes her place by the side of man as his companion, his co-worker, his helpmate, his equal, but she never forgets she is a woman and not a man. Whether in the home as a wife or mother, struggling in the ranks of business or professional life, she retains her womanly dignity and sweetness, which is at once her strength and her shield. . . . Because many noble and lovable women have been content to abide beneath the shadow of the home-roof, and never have sought to extend their influence beyond the domestic circle, they deny the fitness of any woman's doing so, regardless of the difference in the nature of the circumstances of different individuals and even of the fact that many women have no roof-tree under which to abide. The "progressive woman" is caricatured and held up as a horror and a warning to that portion of the feminine world who might be tempted into like forbidden paths. She is out of her sphere, she ought to be in her home, she is trying to be a man, she is losing the tender consideration and the reverence once accorded to womanhood. . . . The woman is a human being as well as a woman. It is within the range of possibility that sometimes she may be endowed with great gifts which it is fortunate for all minds if she can find opportunity to exercise. . . . The contact with the outer world, a little rubbing of minds, an occasional directing of the energies into new channels, refreshes and invigorates the tired wife and mother and enables her to give the best to the dear ones at home (xii).

Washington's essay on "Impressions of a Southern Federation," which appeared in *Colored American Magazine*, combines problems of race and gender. When the sixth annual meeting of the State Federation of Colored Women's Clubs was held in Mobile, Alabama, in 1904, Washington wrote a vivid account of the topics addressed and the ambience of the city. Twenty clubs were represented with thirty-five representatives of women's organizations from all areas of the state. Washington gives a glimpse of the dress of the attendants and describes activities some clubs sponsored, such as the yearly birthday celebration of Frederick Douglass and efforts to foster racial pride by giving an annual prize for the best essay on "a race subject." She also reported on the delegates' emphasis on black womanhood, motherhood, character and standards of morality, and the establishment of a reformatory for youth convicted of minor offenses.

Mobile, the host city for the convention, had a progressive black community comprised of merchants, including owners of grocery stores, drug stores, and livery stables. There were also doctors, lawyers, and other professionals. The city was still steeped in racial prejudice—a condition that Washington describes in the introduction to her essay "Impressions":

> Mobile, city of the sea, true to her name—Mobile—changing, responsive, susceptible, like the waters of her shimmering gulf; tender, dreamy, beautiful, and smiling, she lies under the semitropic skies. . . .
>
> But even in this inviting spot the petty prejudices of our little life obtrude. Yonder swings are not for the dusky children of the sun. Some heart moved to sympathy with the childhood's joys, when that childhood is Anglo-Saxon of race, made possible this pleasant pastime. Dark-hued little men and maids look on longingly, but dare not touch the sacred structure. Even in the lovely

city of the dead something of the baneful influence follows. Will this ever-present discrimination have effect "when the general roll is called" and we all, according to promise, are "there?"

Views on Race and Gender Expressed in Poetry

Scruggs, in *Women of Distinction,* confirms that Washington's writings were both prose and poetry. He highlighted the poem "Thoughts for Decoration Day":

Throughout our country's broad domain,
In North and East and South and West,
In city street and village lane,
The nation pauses and takes rest.

Yet honor we the men who gave
Their lives and all that makes life dear,
To save our land and free the slave
From cruel fate than death more drear.

For women who, like Spartans brave,
Had tied the sash round soldiers gay,
And sent them forth a land to save,
And cheered them as they marched away.

We are not one; an alien race,
Distinct, the negro dwells apart;
The crime of color his disgrace,
What matters, brain, brawn, or heart?

Through ages dark in bondage held,
And freed by accident of state,
Deemed strangers where our fathers dwelled,
The strife of party feud and hate.

Arouse, awake, bend to your oars!
Much work remains yet to be done;
Til opened, wide all closed doors,
Rest not, nor think the battle won.

Unite to build the race in wealth,
For money is a magic key;
Seek power frankly, not by stealth,
And use it wisely as may be.

With all thy getting, wisdom get:
Acquaint thyself with minds that soared;
Tis knowledge makes the distance set
'Twixt cultured men and savage horde.

No cloud of doubt disturbs my mind,
This nation's destined to be one,
And futures ages sure must find
The night dispelled by risen sun.

Hence, let us pass with hope renewed,
Fresh courage for daily care;
Forget past wrongs, avoid all feud,
And only what is noble dare.

The brave men we have honored here
Knew how to die like heroes true:
Who questions we will be their peer,
If we like heroes learn to do!

Washington also had an interest in the education of ministers and teachers and has been credited with playing a significant part in the development of Selma University in Alabama. Founded in 1878 to provide training to ministers and teachers, later the school began to offer degrees in liberal arts and general curricula. Selma University still operates today with an enrollment of less than five hundred and offers preparation in business and theology.

Washington's salient contributions have been underemphasized. Her prose and poetry contributions indicate that she was not reticent; she was persuaded by her religious convictions, felt women were equal to men, and was eager to rid the country of the "monster of prejudice whose voracious appetite is appeased only when individuals are reduced to abject servitude and are content to remain hewers of wood and drawers of water" (Scruggs, xix).

Selected writings of Washington include "The Benefits of Trouble, *Richmond Virginia Star*, 11 November 1882; "Good Old Times," *People's Advocate*, 8 September and 15 September, 1883; "Higher Education for Women," *People's Advocate*, 12 April 1884; "Wendell Phillips," *People's Advocate*, 8 March 1884; and "Impressions of a Southern Federation," *The Colored American*, November.

The facts of Washington's later life and the circumstances of her death are yet unknown. Of her life, however, Scruggs said that she was "a student from whom one could always catch new inspiration . . . a real genius in the class-room, yet gentle, never arrogant, always wearing a pleasant smile, occasionally interrupted by a blush passing over her face" (91).

References

Brown, Hallie Q. *Homespun Heroines and Other Women of Distinction*. Xenia, Ohio: Aldine Publishing Co., 1926.

Dannett, Sylvia G. *Profiles of Negro Womanhood*. Vol. 1. Yonkers, N.Y.: Educational Heritage, 1964.

Davis, Marianna W., ed. *Contributions of Black Women to America*. Vol. 1. Columbia, S.C.: Kenday Press, 1982.

Majors, Monroe A. *Noted Negro Women: Their Triumphs and Activities*. Chicago: Donohue and Henneberry, 1893. Reprinted. New York: Books for Libraries, 1971.

Penn, I. Garland. *Afro-American Press*. 1891. Reprinted. New York: Arno Press, 1969.

Scruggs, Lawson A. *Women of Distinction*. Raleigh, N.C.: privately printed, 1893.

Twenty 19th Century Black Women. Washington, D.C.: National Council of Negro Women, 1979.

Washington, Josephine. "Impressions of a Southern Federation.'' *Colored American Magazine* 7 (November 1904): 676-680. Includes photograph.

Wesley, Charles Harris. *The History of the National Association of Colored Women's Clubs: A Legacy of Service*. Washington, D.C.: NACW, 1984.

Simmona E. Simmons

Margaret Murray Washington

(c. 1861-1925)

Educator, clubwoman

From the frequency with which her name appears in print, there would seem to be no doubt that educator and clubwoman Margaret Murray Washington was a major figure in her time. This makes the fact that she has received little attention in recent studies all the more surprising. For example, there is no listing of her in the index to Darlene Clark Hines's sixteen-volume series of reprints, *Black Women in United States History* (Brooklyn: Carlson, 1990). With few exceptions, printed sources are panegyrics or brief mentions. Even if it is felt by some that her role was no more than that of a well-oiled cog in Booker T. Washington's Tuskegee machine, she did survive him by nearly a decade and continued to make an impression on the women's club movement and on Tuskegee. While there is nothing to suggest that she did not heartily support her husband's policies and programs, the scattered letters printed in the *Booker T. Washington Papers* do support the proposition that she is of considerable interest and importance in her own right.

Margaret Murray Washington

Despite the date of March 9, 1865, inscribed on her gravestone, Margaret James Murray Washington was probably born in 1861. Louis R. Harlan, who presents the data succinctly as an editor of the *Booker T. Washington Papers*, speculates that she may have decreased her age when she entered Fisk Preparatory School in 1881. The census of 1870 lists Laura, aged ten, Margaret, nine, Willis, seven, and Thomas, four, as living in Macon, Mississippi, with their mother, Lucy Murray, whose occupation is given as that of washerwoman. The first three children were labeled mulatto and the last black. There seems to be no documentary trace of Margaret Murray's white father, characterized as an Irish immigrant, beyond the statement, in an article she must have seen before publication, that he died when she was seven. In the 1880 census Margaret Murray was still listed as living with her mother, who was now married to an African-American named Henry Brown. According to the 1880 census, Margaret Murray was still living at home; her sister, ''Laury,'' aged twenty-two, was working as a cook and still living at home, and the two younger brothers have now become sisters, seventeen and thirteen.

Now married to educator and statesman Booker T. Washington and living in Alabama Margaret Murray Washington stated in 1898 that she had nine siblings who lived long enough to have children but that only the youngest girl, aged twenty-seven, actually had any—two. This sister would have been born about 1871. In 1904, after their parents' deaths, a nephew and a niece came to Tuskegee to live with the Washingtons. The older, Thomas J. Murray, already nearly full-grown, was soon working at the Tuskegee Institute Savings Bank. The younger was not yet of school age. Taken into the family, she took the name Laura Murray Washington and called her aunt ''Mama.'' She received several houses in Tuskegee and elsewhere as a bequest at Margaret Murray Washington's death.

An article that gives further information about Margaret Murray's Washington's early life is by Booker T. Washington's private secretary, Emmett J. Scott, ''Mrs. Booker T. Washington's Part in Her Husband's work'' (*Ladies Home Journal* 24 (May 1907), 42. According to this article, Margaret James Murray was taken in by a Quaker brother and sister on her father's death when she was seven; when she was fourteen her protectors suggested she become a teacher, which she did. Harlan is unable to identify positively her protectors.

To further whatever education she had acquired, Margaret Washington entered Fisk University's preparatory school in 1881, working to pay part of her expenses. A model student, she completed the preparatory and college class in eight years, in the process forming a lifelong friendship with W. E. B. Du Bois, her contemporary at the school. In her final years at Fisk she was an associate editor of the student newspaper and president of one of the campus literary societies. After completion of her degree in 1889, she went to Tuskegee to teach. She was highly recommended by Fisk president Erastus Milo Cravath and by the principal of women, Anna Thankful Ballantine; the latter wrote that she was "of good mind, of conscientious religious convictions, of unusual power in gaining influence over those younger than herself, and of ability to direct them" (*BTW Papers,* Vol. 3, 3). The following academic year Margaret Murray Washington became lady principal at a salary of five hundred dollars a year and board.

Booker T. Washington first met Margaret Murray at a dinner with the seniors just prior to the June 1889 Fisk commencement, about a month after the death of his second wife, Olivia Davidson Washington, on May 9, 1889. He must have been impressed by her teaching and executive abilities when he named her lady principal a year later, but the course of the affection that sprang up between them is not easy to discern from the surviving documents. However, by late 1891 he had proposed.

The proposal seems to have brought her doubts to the fore. She is concerned with her own bad temper: "I am awful when my temper gets the best of me. I hear you say Amen" (*BTW Papers,* Vol. 3, 175). She did not get on well with the family: she quarrelled with James Washington, Booker's favorite brother and could not bear James's wife. She questioned her own sympathy for and ability to deal with Washington's three children, even though she felt definitely that she was more capable than Mrs. James Washington, who, she said, knew "as much as a cat about caring for children" (*BTW Papers,* Vol. 3, 251). Nonetheless, she got on well with the two young boys, and her major concern was the relation with Portia, the oldest of the three, whose dislike of her prospective stepmother was reciprocated. On October or November 1, 1891, she writes:

> My Dear Booker. . . . I wish very much that I might be of some help to you in your hard duty but *I never can be*. . . . Mr. Washington, you have no idea how I feel because I can not feel toward Portia as I should. And I somehow dread bring thrown with her for a life time. I sometimes make up my mind that I will not let any talk to me of the child and then I forget. She kinder understands it too and I hate it. I wonder Mr. Washington if it is a wise and Christian thing for me to love you feeling as I do? Still I shall be absolutely honest with you and if you feel that you prefer giving me up I should find no fault with you. Don't be angry or annoyed (*BTW Papers,* Vol. 3, 178).

The doubts were resolved, although it was some time before Portia Washington's hostility abated, and by July 1892 Margaret Murray was pressing for marriage: "I do not wish to be away from you longer and if we find it necessary to wait longer I shall break the engagement because I do not feel that we have any right to be to each other what we are and still remain from each other. And then too, the longer we wait, the harder it will be for the friends on both sides" (*BTW Papers,* Vol. 3, 246). Booker T. Washington and Margaret Murray were married on October 12, 1892, in Tuskegee.

The quality of the marriage over the years is difficult to evaluate; there are surprisingly few published letters between the two. Although Booker T. Washington had yet to know the full flowering of his power and celebrity that followed his speech at the Atlanta Exposition in September 1895, at the time of his marriage he was already established in a pattern of work that left little time for family life. Typically, he was away from Tuskegee for six months every year, speaking and raising money. Margaret Murray Washington usually joined him at whatever place in the North that he had chosen as his summer headquarters and in 1899 accompanied him on a European trip.

After the publication of the *Booker T. Washington Papers* and Harlan's biography of Booker T. Washington, a representative judgement on the marriage is Lawrence J. Friedman's statement: "His third marriage to Margaret Murray represents a practical, bourgeoisie marriage of convenience. Margaret Murray gave him a stable home life and cared for his children, but neither husband or wife was emotionally involved with the other" ("Life 'In the Lion's Mouth,'" *Journal of Negro History,* 349). The paucity of evidence about the marriage suggests caution on this point; what is clear, however, is that Margaret Murray Washington was working nearly as hard as her husband in support of their common goals, and there was never any visible disunity between the two. She could be an effective aide in fundraising. For example, her husband relied on Andrew Carnegie's admiration for her and the fact that she was a Fisk graduate to persuade the financier philanthropist to drop the condition that a gift of $25,000 he made to Fisk be matched (Harlan, *Booker T. Washington,* Vol. 1, 181-82). Harlan states that Booker T. Washington habitually went over his speeches with Margaret, at least in the earlier years (*Booker T. Washington,* Vol. 1, 213); he further speculates that she may have influenced Booker T. Washington's extremely uncharacteristic attack on the black clergy at the 1890 Fisk commencement, when uttered such inflammatory statements as "out of four hundred Colored Baptist churches in Alabama only about fifteen intelligent pastors could be found" (*Booker T. Washington,* Vol. 1, 194-96). Margaret Murray Washington was at Booker T. Washington's side as the fatally ill man was brought south to die at Tuskegee, and she in turn would lie beside him in the grave on Tuskegee's campus, as does his second wife, Olivia Davidson Washington.

As she had wished before the marriage, Margaret continued to work at Tuskegee. This possibility was of some concern to her, for she did not wish to be dependent on her husband for all the money at her disposal—she put it tactfully, "I love to work in the class room, and I want to make some money too because I shall need many things for the house and the children that you will not know of. I like a pretty home" (*BTW Papers,* Vol. 3, 214). In 1900, for example, she is director of the department of domestic sciences—"laundering, cooking, dressmaking, plain sewing, millinery and mattress making" (Booker T. Washington, *The Story of My Life and Work,* in *BTW Papers,* Vol. 1, 175). She was very involved in the construction of Dorothy Hall, which housed the girls' industries and later served as a guest house. It is perhaps useful to add here that Tuskegee was not training servants, and the institute was severely embarrassed when persons who supposed the contrary wrote seeking to hire domestics. Margaret Murray Washington also served on the fifteen-person executive committee, which ran Tuskegee while Booker T. Washington was absent. (Her official correspondence with him begins with Mr. Washington and is signed Mrs. Washington.) Eventually she became dean of women and continued her service to the institution after his death. Her marriage also meant that she was responsible for the tasks traditionally assigned to a president's wife, most notably the reception and entertainment of the constant stream of distinguished visitors drawn by the favorable publicity the institution received. Still in conjunction with the campus, she worked with the school's woman's club, which met twice a month. This group was extremely active, placing great emphasis on temperance work.

Work with Mother's Groups Initiated

Tuskegee also maintained a tradition of reaching out to local black American farmers. Around the turn of the century Margaret Murray Washington was, for example, doing plantation work in a settlement eight miles away. In addition, Saturdays were devoted to the mothers' meeting she ran in Tuskegee in two rented rooms above a local black grocery store. Students went into the streets to invite women to attend when they came with their families on the weekly expedition into town. The children were entertained in one of the rooms, while the mothers had coffee and cake and an uplifting talk in the other. Margaret Murray Washington comments on the place of these meetings in her life and the women's lives:

> With all of my school work, I often grow tired and feel that I must give up these meetings, these outside interests, but when I look into the faces of these children and women, I just pick up the threads and go on. I have not had any one meeting this fall less than fifty or sixty, until yesterday when it had been raining a week and there were even then two women who came in from seven miles around. It is the one bright spot in their lives. I am thinking of putting in a bathing apparatus where we carry on the sewing classes for the girls. They seldom get a real bath (*BTW Papers,* Vol. 6, 11).

By 1904 the mothers' meetings were attracting nearly three hundred women (Hunter, 86).

Margaret Murray Washington did not limit her speeches to the confines of club work in Macon County, Alabama. Often she would speak on the same program as her husband. The pattern was that Booker T. Washington addressed a group of ministers and civic leaders in the morning and a mass community meeting in the evening, while Margaret Murray Washington addressed the women in the afternoon. A typical specimen of her oratory is the "plain, earnest talk" she delivered in Charleston, South Carolina, in September 1898 (*BTW Papers,* Vol. 4, 462-68). She sounded the appeal to self-improvement:

> We need, as a race, a good, strong public sentiment in favor of a sounder, healthier body and a cleaner and higher-toned morality. . . . No nation or race has ever come up by entirely overlooking its members who are less fortunate, less ambitious, less sound in body and hence in soul, and we cannot do it. We must not do it. There are too many of us down. The condition of race, brought about by slavery, the ignorance, poverty, intemperance, ought to make us women know that in half a century we cannot afford to lose sight of the large majority of the race who have not, as yet, thrown off the badge of the evils which I have just mentioned (463).

Specifically, she was concerned to address "the awful death rate and the alarming increasingly illegitimate birth rate among our women and girls" (464), and the actions she recommends to the women are personal hygiene—"bathe at least twice a week" (467); a better diet—"get fresh fruit, fresh eggs, good meat, etc." (467); and keeping regular hours—"do not stay in church till 12 and 1 o'clock at night" (467). On the moral front she urges the use of home influence—"teach the boys to come home at night . . . [and] the sin of ruining some man's daughter" (468)—combined with the influence of ministers and teachers. Her concluding words reinforce the commitment she seeks from the women: "Above all let us who have had an opportunity, who have educational advantages, modify our caste line—stoop down now and then and lift up others" (468).

"Lifting as We Climb" is the motto of the National Association of Colored Women's Clubs (NACW). Given Margaret Murray Washington's position and commitment to improvement, it is natural that she devoted a considerable part of her energies to the women's club movement. She answered the call by Josephine St. Pierre Ruffin to attend the meeting in Boston at the end of July 1895 that resulted in the formation of the National Federation of Afro-American Women, of which she became vice-president. Margaret Murray Washington was president of the federation at the meeting in Washington, D.C., in July 1896, by which time the number of affiliated clubs had grown from twenty-eight to sixty-seven. A delegation from the federation met with a delegation from the Colored Women's League, which had held its convention just before, and the fusion of the two groups created the National Association of Colored Women, with a call for its first convention to be held in Nashville in

September 1897. At that meeting Margaret Murray Washington was elected secretary of the executive board.

Official Publication of National Clubwomen Inaugurated

In 1901 the biennial convention was held in Buffalo, New York. Margaret Murray Washington was a candidate for president, along with Josephine B. Bruce. Both ruined their chances by declining an invitation to an event held by the local Phillis Wheatley Club, alleging a prior commitment to one held by a white women's club. In the event, Josephine Silone Yates was elected, and Washington was not to be president of NACW until 1914, although she held several offices in the organization and inaugurated at Tuskegee the series of *Notes* that eventually became the *National Notes,* the official publication of the organization. The entire movement needs study in depth; the problems in the organization and tensions between leaders are known only in a very vague way. For example, in 1924 before the NACW convention in Chicago, Hallie Q. Brown held a meeting of selected women, excluding Washington. Washington in turn solicited the support of Nannie H. Burroughs in preventing factionalism from disrupting the organization; the election of Mary McLeod Bethune to the presidency at the convention did much to calm the storm (Neverdon-Morton, 196).

In Alabama, Margaret Murray Washington was president of the Alabama Association of Women's Clubs from 1919 until her death in 1925. During her tenure, the Rescue Home for Girls (later known as the Girls Home) in Mt. Meigs was planned and completed. She was also influential in the tentative and very cautious approach of black clubwomen to the Commission on Inter-racial Cooperation (CIC), a basically white organization founded in December 1918. Lugenia Hope, Jennie Moton, and Washington were involved in the attempt to bring black and white clubwomen together for a common program of action in 1920. There was some degree of cooperation developed, although most white southern clubwomen were not attracted to the CIC. By the time of Washington's death, black clubwomen and the CIC had had a certain amount of success in improving educational opportunities for blacks.

In 1920 also, a group of black women, all active in club work, formed the International Council of Women of the Darker Races, an organization designed for "the dissemination of knowledge of peoples of color the world over, in order that there may be a larger appreciation of their history and accomplishment and so that they themselves may have a greater degree of race pride for their own achievements and touch a greater themselves" (Margaret Murray Washington letter printed in Hoytt, 54). The first public meeting was held in Chicago in the summer of 1924. Margaret Murray Washington was a prime mover in the formation of this organization and its first president. The women involved recognized the importance of building links to women of color throughout the world, but this organization was short-lived due to the fact that the members were already very busy in other activities and the fact that Washington died before the council was firmly established. Margaret Murray Washington died on June 4, 1925.

References

Bethune, Mary McLeod. "Margaret Murray Washington—A Tribute." *The Tuskegee Messenger* 1 (1 August 1925): 3.

Friedman, Lawrence J. "Life 'In the Lion's Mouth'" Another Look at Booker T. Washington." *Journal of Negro History* 49 (October 1974): 337-51.

Harlan, Louis R. *Booker T. Washington.* Vol. 1, *The Making of a Black Leader 1856-1901.* New York: Oxford University Press, 1972. Photograph.

———. *Booker T. Washington.* Vol. 2, *The Wizard of Tuskegee, 1901-1915.* New York: Oxford University Press,

Harlan, Louis R., and others, eds. *The Booker T. Washington Papers.* 13 Vols. Urbana: University of Illinois Press, 1972, 1984.

Haynes, Elizabeth Ross. "Margaret Murray Washington." *Opportunity* 3 (July 1925): 207-109. Photograph.

Hoytt, Eleanor Hinton. "International Council of Women of the Darker Races: Historical Notes." *Sage* 3 (Fall 1896): 54-55.

Hunter, Wilma King. "Three Women at Tuskegee: 1885-1922: The Wives of Booker T. Washington." *Journal of Ethnic Studies* 3 (September 1976): 76-89.

Lerner, Gerda. "Early Community Work of Black Club Women." *Journal of Negro History* 49 (April 1974): 158-67.

Moton, Jennie B. "Margaret M. Washington." In Hallie W. Brown. *Homespun Heroines and Other Women of Distinction.* Xenia, Ohio: Aldine Pub. Co., 1926. Photograph.

Neverdon-Morton, Cynthia. *Afro-American Women of the South and the Advancement of the Race, 1895-1925.* Knoxville: University of Tennessee Press, 1989.

"Short Sketch of the Life of Mrs. Margaret Murray Washington." In *Lifting As They Climb.* Ed. Elizabeth Lindsay Davis. [Washington, D.C.] National Association of Colored Women, 1933.

"The Three Wives of Booker T. Washington." *Ebony* 37 (September 1972): 29-30, 32, 34. Reprinted. *Ebony* 46 (February 1991): 36, 38, 40, 42.

The Tuskegee Messenger. 1 (27 June 1927). Memorial edition. Photograph of Margaret Murray Washington on cover.

Wesley, Charles Harris. *The History of the National Association of Colored Women's Clubs.* Washington, D.C.: NACW, 1984. Photograph.

Collections

The papers of Margaret James Murray Washington are in the Tuskegee University Archives. Additional information may be found in the Luther Hilton Foster Papers at Tuskegee, the Booker T. Washington Papers at the Library of Congress, and the National Association of Colored Women Clipping File at Hampton University.

Robert L. Johns

Olivia Davidson Washington

(1854-1889)

Educator, school founder

Olivia America Davidson Washington, founder of Tuskegee Institute with her husband Booker T. Washington, was born free on June 11, 1854, in Mercer County, Virginia. Her father, Elias, listed as a slave in 1846 in the will of his owner, Joseph Davidson, was recorded as a free laborer in the 1850 census. Her mother, Eliza Webb, who had ten children, is thought to be the daughter of a "free colored" woman.

Olivia Davidson Washington

The Davidson's were forced to leave Virginia when pressures against free blacks in the state grew too intense. They joined the migration into southern Ohio and settled in Ironton. The older Davidson children attended school in Ironton, and there is no reason not to believe that Washington, who turned six in 1860, started her schooling here. Washington was living with her sister Mary and her sister's doctor husband, Noah Elliott, in Gallipolis, Ohio, where it is assumed she attended high school.

Washington's sister Mary operated dressmaking and millinery establishments in several Ohio cities as she and her husband moved, seeking greater opportunities. They eventually settled in Columbus, the state capital. Another sister, Margaret, was a teacher, and Washington followed her south to teach among the freedmen. Her eventual relocation to Memphis was thought to have occurred to allow her to be closer to Margaret and her brother Joseph, who was living with her. Margaret's death shortly afterwards, followed by the Ku Klux Klan's killing of Joseph, devastated Washington.

Concerns for Stronger Race Stressed

Washington began teaching school in Ohio when she was barely sixteen. It is not known if economic need, the strong sense of mission, or a combination of both, was the motivating factor, but after going south, Washington taught during summer vacations, in Mississippi and Arkansas. There are two pieces of evidence that shed some light on her experiences in these plantation and country schools. Booker T. Washington's autobiography, *Up from Slavery*, tells of her closing her school to nurse one of her students stricken with smallpox, because every one else was too frightened to do so. In 1886 Washington addressed the members of the Alabama State Teachers' Association on "How Shall We Make the Women of Our Race Stronger?" After discussing the evils of alcohol, tobacco, and drugs, and the need for good personal hygiene, proper food, and cleanliness in the home, she focused her concern on reaching the girls because she felt they were the "hope of the race." She cautioned the teachers that black school teachers could not be "mere school teachers in the narrowest use of the term, but had to do much work outside the classroom. She described the "two years' earnest, patient work" of a teacher with positive results, which was most likely her work at Spencer, Mississippi (Harlan, *Booker T. Washington Papers,* Vol. 1,281). In 1874 she left the rural area and took a position as a sixth-grade teacher in a new school in Memphis, Tennessee.

The opening of this school, Clay Street School, was front-front-page news because it was one of the first brick school buildings in Memphis. Here Washington was caught up in a controversy over integrated staffs at black schools. (Clay Street School had a white principal and four black and four white teachers.) Blacks were demanding that their schools be staffed only with black teachers and principals. Despite this, as well as the continuing problem of inadequate funding, Washington was in a positive learning situation, for the superintendent, Aaron Pickett, introduced new teaching methods and curriculum changes. By 1878, worn out by the constant work and saddened over the death of her sister and brother, Washington returned to Ohio to rest for the summer. It was during this time that a yellow fever epidemic occurred in Memphis. She offered to return as a nurse, but because of the danger was advised, instead, to use the time to study at Hampton Institute.

In fall 1878 Washington enrolled in the senior class at Hampton Institute with her scholarship paid for by the wife of President Rutherford B. Hayes. The senior year program included the study of reading, English literature, algebra, bookkeeping, history, political economy, elements of agriculture, civil government, grammar, chemistry, and the Bible. The culminating experience was a three-week institute "as special preparation for teaching." She delivered one of ten essays during the graduation program on May 22, 1879, "Decision of Character." Her future partner in institution building, Booker T. Washington, as the postgraduate speaker, described "The Force That Wins."

While at Hampton Institute, Washington's old desire for a college course returned and she planned "to enter a school of higher grade." This desire was evidently transmitted to one of Hampton's instructors, who brought Washington to the attention of his aunt, Mrs. Mary (Augustus) Hemenway, a philanthropist and supporter of Hampton Institute. Hemenway, impressed with Washington, supported two years of study for her at the Framingham, Massachusetts, State Normal School. Washington enrolled on September 3, 1879, and graduated on June 29, 1881.

Washington, twenty-five years old on admission to Framingham, was older than most students and had nearly six years' teaching experience in Tennessee, Ohio, and Mississippi. Like other students, she spent time observing and teaching at an ungraded model school in the area. This Framingham experience, added to that of Hampton Institute and the nearly six years' teaching experience, prepared her well for her role as cofounder of Tuskegee Institute. For not only did Washington learn sophisticated pedagogical techniques, but she established important contacts which proved invaluable during fundraising for the future Tuskegee Institute.

Washington Helps Establish Tuskegee Institute

Washington excelled at Framingham and was one of six honor students in a graduating class of twenty-five. Her essay presented during the graduation exercises on June 29, 1881, was titled, "Work among the Freedmen." Following graduation, Washington fell ill and returned to Hampton Institute to rest and to teach the Indians during the summer. Booker T. Washington, who arrived in Tuskegee on June 14, and opened the school on July 4, wrote to her urging her to join him immediately in the building of Tuskegee. When word reached him of her poor physical condition, he suggested she rest until September and then come. She arrived on August 25, and in a letter less than two months later, Washington wrote that "Miss Washington's services are inestimable," a phrase repeated on several occasions (*BTW Papers,* Vol. 2, 150).

The illness twenty-seven year old Washington experienced as she left Framingham is the first known reference to serious health problems. She had worked tirelessly since sixteen years of age and had undoubtedly been exposed to several diseases in the rural areas where she worked, to yellow fever in Memphis, and to diphtheria in Framingham. Nevertheless, she continued inestimable efforts at Tuskegee. Washington, in *Up From Slavery,* commented that she threw her whole self into the work and that "she was never very strong, but never seemed happy unless she was giving all of her strength to the cause she loved" (*BTW Papers, Vol. 1 The Autobiographical Writings*, 290).

In less than three years, late in 1883, Booker T. Washington, who was fundraising in the North, had to return home because Washington's condition worsened. Her ensuing convalescence was long, for she was resting in Montgomery in February 1884 and in September was still resting but now in the mountains of Jackson, New Hampshire. She was unsure of the state of her health, and she wrote of having completely broken down. Booker T. Washington's first wife, Fannie N. Smith, had died on May 4, 1884. Some two years later, on August 11, 1886, he married his Tuskagee Institute cofounder. Washington returned to her sister Mary's home in Athens, Ohio, for the wedding ceremony. Booker, Jr., was born May 29, 1887, and although there was concern over her health for a number of months, she became pregnant again in about a year. It was reported in *The Southern Letter*, the Tuskegee paper, that in October, 1888, Washington began to have throat trouble that "grew from month to month." Early in the next year, on February 6, a son, Ernest Davidson was born. Two days later, because of a defective flue, Washington's house burned down at 5:00 a.m. Davidson was taken out into the early morning chill and never recovered from the exposure. She was taken first to Montgomery and then to Boston for medical treatment. She died of tuberculosis of the larynx on May 9, 1889, at Massachusetts General Hospital.

There was literally nothing at Tuskegee when Washington first arrived. After complaining a bit in a letter to one of her former Framingham classmates, Mary Berry, her strong sense of mission surfaced and she wrote, "I shall try to be grateful that I have so soon found work to do in such great abundance" (*BTW Papers,* Vol. 2, 147). She put her full energies into this work from the day she arrived until her early death eight years later. She truly, "in every way . . . played an equal part with Washington in founding and operating the school," and he acknowledged it. He stated, "The success of the school, especially during the first half dozen years of its existence, was due more to Miss Davidson than any one else" (*BTW Papers*, Vol. 1, 32).

It is impossible to identify any area in which Washington did not play a role. It is also difficult to give priorities among her public roles of teacher, curriculum specialist, lady principal, fundraiser, and builder and the private roles of confidant, wife, and mother.

Since the state provided very little financial support and that only for instructors' salaries, fundraising was vital to the survival of the school. Land had to be purchased, structures built, salaries paid, and very poor students helped in various ways. Washington helped to organize local fundraising efforts and went North to raise funds when necessary, utilizing contacts made when she was a student at Framingham. During these trips she drew heavily on her limited physical strength as she followed a strenuous fund-raising schedule. She no doubt found the work both trying and on occasion embarrassing, but she experienced success, chiefly due to the favorable impression she made on donors.

There are similarities between the educational backgrounds and training of Booker T. Washington and Olivia Davidson Washington, but she brought more experience as a practicing teacher and more content and theory as a result of the Framingham experience. Her husband stated in *Up from Slavery* that she came to Tuskegee with "many valuable and fresh ideas as to the best methods of teaching," and these found their way quickly into the curriculum and classrooms (*BTW Papers*, Vol. 1, 282). In the role of lady principal, she had general oversight of the female students in all aspects of their on-campus lives—dormitory living, industrial work, and class work. Louis R. Harlan wrote that Washington's "special forte was in persuading the girl students, fresh from the tenant shacks of the Black Belt, to emulate her genteel sensibility, New England self-restraint and feminine modesty" (*Booker T. Washington*, 149). Her influence and work were felt everywhere, both on and off campus.

When people work as closely together as these two founders did, it is difficult to separate the private areas from the public. She was the first staff person to join Washington, and one can only imagine the hours these two spent together talking and planning for Tuskegee Institute. She was in every way an equal partner. Her husband said that when the last effort seemed exhausted, Washington discovered a way out. Their relationship appears to have been a warm and loving one and despite her consistently poor health, she worried about him and paid for a physical education summer training course at Harvard for him. Washington's knowledge of literature, history, and poetry were soon reflected in her husband's speeches in the form of classical and literary allusions. In return, he lost some of his "brusque, full-of-business air," undoubtedly picked up from General Samuel Armstrong at Hampton Institute, and was an affectionate husband and father (Harlan, *Booker T. Washington*, 153-55, 185).

Not only did Washington have two sons, she became stepmother to her husband's daughter, Portia, who grew to love her and call her "mama." Her friends eventually made it possible for Portia to attend the practice school at Framingham.

Washington's uniqueness is reflected in all that is written about her. Phrases such as "christian martyr," "good and lovely woman," "inspiring faith." "refinement," "essential truthfulness of her character," and "strength of mind" appear throughout. Her admirers speak of her "earnest desire to work for her people" and of her refusal to pass for white when she enrolled at Framingham. She was "greatly revered" and "appreciated by others." Washington said she was a "rare moral character" and that her life was one of unselfishnes, which had seldom been equalled (Marshall, *Christian Register*, 6 June 1889). Her early death was truly a great loss not only to Washington and her children and Tuskegee but to all of black education.

References

"Albany Site of Famed Romance." *Athens Messinger*, 16 February 1925.

Ambler, Charles Henry. *West Virginia: The Mountain State*. Englewood Cliffs, N.J.: Prentice-Hall, 1940.

"Anniversary Exercises at Hampton Institute." *Southern Workman* 8 (June 1879): 71.

"A Crown of Life." *Southern Workman* 18 (July 1889): 84.

Davidson, Joseph. Last Will and Testament of Joseph Davidson, 30 May 1846. West Virginia Historic Records Survey, Box 87. West Virginia University.

Davidson, Olivia A. "Dear Friend" *Southern Workman* 8 (March 1879): 29.

"The Death of Mrs. B. T. Washington." *Southern Letter* 5 (May 1889): 1.

Dorsey, Carolyn A. "Despite Poor Health: Olivia Davidson

———. "The Pre-Hampton Years of Olivia A. Davidson." The Hampton Review 2 (Fall 1985): 69-72.

Framingham Gazette, 3 October 1879; 28 November 1879; 1 July 1881.

Harlan, Louis R. *Booker T. Washington: The Making of a Black Leader, 1856-1901*. New York: Oxford University Press, 1972.

———. ed. *The Booker T. Washington Papers*. 3 vols. Urbana: University of Illinois Press, 1972-74.

Hilliard, David Moss. *The Development of Public Education in Memphis, Tennessee, 1884-1945*. Chicago: University of Chicago Press, 1946.

Majors, Monroe A. "Mrs. Olivia Davidson Washington: Educator, Financier and Christian Martyr." *Noted Negro Women: Their Triumphs and Activities*. Chicago: Donohue and Henneberry, 1893.

Marshall, James Fowle Baldwin. Obituary, Olivia A. Davidson. *Christian Register*, 6 June 1889.

"Mrs. Olivia Davidson Washington and the Training of the Colored Girls." *Southern Letter*, August 1890.

"Our Colored Children: The Grand Demonstration Yesterday on the Opening of the New Public School Building." *Memphis Daily Appeal*, 14 March 1874.

Phillips, Sarah, A. Letter to Carolyn A. Dorsey, 3 July 1980.

———. Letter to Connie Perdreau, 26 September 1977.

Tribe, Ivan M. "Rise and Decline of Private Academies in Albany, Ohio." *Ohio History* 78 (Summer 1969): 188-201.

U.S. Bureau of the Census, Seventh Census: 1850; Eighth Census, 1860; Ninth Census, 1870; Tenth Census, 1880.

Collections

Selected letters of Olivia A. Davidson Washington appear in Louis R. Harlan, ed., *The Booker T. Washington Papers, 1860-1889*. Vol. 2. (Urbana: University of Illinois Press, 1972). Others are in the Booker T. Washington Papers housed at the Manuscript Division of the Library of Congress. A reproduction of her photograph is available in the Hampton University Archives and *Ebony*, 37 (September 1982), 29.

Carolyn A. Dorsey

Sarah (Sara) Spencer Washington

(1889-?)

Entrepreneur, philanthropist

Cosmetics mogul and philanthropist Sarah (Sara) Spencer Washington was born June 6, 1889, in Berkley, Virginia, the daughter of Joshua and Ellen Douglass Phillips. She was educated in the public schools of Berkley, the Lincoln Preparatory School in Philadelphia, Pennsylvania, and the Norfolk Mission College in Norfolk, Virginia. She studied beauty culture in York, Pennsylvania, and later did advanced work in chemistry at Columbia University.

Washington was a dressmaker from 1905 until 1913. Overriding the objections of her family, who wanted her to become a schoolteacher, Washington embarked upon a career in the then comparatively new field of beauty culture. In 1913, in Atlantic City, New Jersey, she founded a small hairdressing establishment where she worked as an operator and taught her system to others. She spent her evenings taking her products from house to house. In 1919 she became the founder, sole owner, and president of Apex Hair and News Company. She conducted Apex colleges and supply stations in New York and New Jersey. This was to be her principal interest for the rest of her life.

From 1937 to 1939, in Atlantic City, Washington built her own laboratories, where she manufactured seventy-five different kinds of beauty preparations. Apex Beauty Colleges boasted 215 regular employees. At one time, there were more than thirty-five thousand Apex agents throughout the United States.

In 1939, because of her great achievements, Washington was awarded a medallion at the New York World's Fair, representing her attainment of international stature in the business world.

Washington Supports Worthy Causes

Washington's philanthropies were pronounced. She endowed a home for girls devoted to the educational features of the National Youth Administration program and she donated twenty acres of farmland as a campsite for black youth. She gave annual scholarships to ambitious students throughout the country and contributed large sums of money to worthy institutions.

That Washington became a millionaire is second in importance to the fact that she stood as a source of inspiration to black women throughout the country. She moved along a path that had been emblazoned by Madame C. J. Walker (Sarah Breedlove Walker) and Madame Annie N. Turnbo Malone, founder of the Poro Method of beauty culture. Better educated than either of her predecessors, Washington led scores of black women to financial independence as entrepreneurs and placed professional personal grooming within the reach of tens of thousands of women in America.

Another of Washington's contributions was seen in the employment she was able to provide for large numbers of men and women throughout the Apex System. Her dedication in this regard is evidenced in the story of how she chose to forego the increased production possible with machinery and thus retain hundreds of workers during the Great Depression to perform tasks manually. She created the slogan "Now is the time to plan your future by learning a depression-proof business."

Washington, one of the golden triumvirate who pioneered what was to become a lucrative field for black women and, later, men, left both a legacy and a self-erected monument in the far flung Apex System.

References

Contributions of Black Women to America. Vol. 1. Edited by Marianna E. Davis. Columbia, S.C.: Kenday Press, 1982.

Distaff to History. Scott Paper Co., n.d. A drawing of Washington appears on page 27.

Porter, Gladys L. *Three Pioneers in Beauty Culture*. New York: Vantage Press, 1966.

Who's Who in Colored America, 1928-29. New York: Who's Who in Colored America Corporation, 1929. Page 381 features a photograph of Washington.

Casper LeRoy Jordan

Ethel Waters

(1896-1977)

Singer, dancer, actress

As an exemplar of true artistry in her long and successful career as a singer, dancer, and actress, Ethel Waters pursued and exercised her great gifts of musical creativity and dramatic expression, and in doing so achieved prominence and critical acclaim in a white-dominated profession. She brilliantly distinguished herself in nightclubs, motion pictures, and the theater, and for more than half a century was recognized and held in affectionate esteem throughout America.

Waters was born in Chester, Pennsylvania, on October 31, 1896, the daughter of Louise Anderson, a black woman, and John Waters a white man. Louise, who was twelve years old when Ethel was born, had been the victim of rape at knife point, a scheme perpetrated by her sister, Viola, and John Waters. Anderson married another man soon after Ethel's birth and left her daughter in the care of her mother, Sally Anderson. John Waters, a popular pianist, died when Ethel was three years old.

Ethel Waters

Shunned by her mother and her well-to-do paternal grandmother, Lydia Waters, Waters always loved Sally Anderson as her mother, and called her "Mom." Because her maternal grandmother was a live-in domestic, Waters raised herself, living in makeshift homes with her aunts who constantly moved to be close to where her grandmother was working in the three neighboring cities of Philadelphia, Chester, and Camden. Though she worked hard, Anderson was unable to provide a good home or enough food for her family, and because she was home only one day a week she could not provide enough supervision for Waters's well-being. Forced to live in neighborhoods plagued by alcohol, drugs, violence, and prostitution, Ethel Waters as a child watched the effects of these substances and activities on friends and members of her own family. Possessing a "great inner strength and a will power" (Waters, *His Eye Is on the Sparrow*, 36), she refused throughout her life any association with these vices.

Billed as "Baby Star," Waters made her first public appearance as an entertainer when she was five years old. As a singer in a children's program in a Philadelphia church, she was a great success, with calls for a number of encores. When she was eight years old, Waters saw her first vaudeville stage shows, whose performers she liked to imitate at home. During this time her mother, whom she called "Momweeze," periodically took her to live with her and Waters's half sister, Genevieve, so that she could hire Waters out to work. It was not until she was nine years old and her grandmother enrolled her in a Catholic school that Waters began to "walk for a little while in a clean and brightly shining world" (Waters, *Sparrow*, 33). Though the ill treatment she received from her alcoholic aunts remained unchanged, she was accepted and treated kindly by the nuns in the school. Waters was in this school only two years before moving again, but she found there the beginnings of a refuge in religion that remained throughout her life.

When she was twelve years old, Waters experienced a spiritual awakening at a children's revival at a black protestant church in Chester. Even though she had been attending the Catholic church with her grandmother, she felt uneasy about her relationship to God. It was at this revival meeting, she recalled in her autobiography *His Eye Is on the Sparrow*, that she "came truly to know and to reverence Christ, the Redeemer" (52) Subsequently, her fear of being a hypocrite by going to church while harboring anger toward a young girl who had wronged her caused her to leave the organized church, but after her conversion she always prayed and called on God to guide her daily life.

Against her wishes, Waters married Merritt "Buddy"

Purnsley in April 1910, when she was thirteen years old. After her mother gave Purnsley permission to marry her, Waters acquiesced to please her family and tried to preserve the marriage for a year before leaving her husband. With only a sixth-grade education and the grief of losing her beloved grandmother that same year, Waters began supporting herself by working as a cleaning woman in Philadelphia. Always a fast and conscientious worker, she would finish her work ahead of schedule and imitate the vaudeville actresses and singers in front of the mirrors in the apartments she cleaned. At fifteen, she worked as a waitress in Wildwood, New Jersey, where she entertained the hotel workers by singing and dancing in the saloon. While Waters was working there, her grandmother, Lydia Waters, tried to reconcile with this granddaughter who resembled so much her late son, but Ethel Waters could not overcome the hurtful effects of her grandmother's lifelong rejection. Years later, Waters speculated on the inheritance that she had received from each grandmother—her "fighting heart" from Anderson and her "poise, dignity, and whatever intelligence" from Waters (Waters, *Sparrow*, 70).

Career as Blues Singer in Vaudeville Begins

On October 31, 1917, Waters was coaxed into her singing debut in a neighborhood Philadelphia saloon. Braxton and Nugent, small-time vaudeville agents who were in attendance that night, consequently hired her for a job on the stage in Baltimore. During that two-week engagement she became the first woman to sing professionally "St. Louis Blues," one of America's greatest blues tunes. Waters's blues singing, characterized by sophistication and dignity, was the first of its kind to be accepted by black audiences who then were accustomed to the full-voiced, unrestrained style of Bessie Smith and Ma Rainey. Performing song-and-dance routines as "Sweet Mama Stringbean," a stage name given to her because she was tall and thin, Waters was unconvinced of her talent even after the audiences showered the stage with money following her performances.

When she learned that she was being paid only a fraction of the money that Braxton and Nugent were making from her act, Waters quit the show and went on a tour of the South as the featured singer in Maggie and Jo Hill's vaudeville act. After working for a while with a carnival, she began working regularly on the black vaudeville circuit with such stars as Smith, Rainey, and the Whitman sisters. She experienced cruel and painful Jim Crow treatment in the South, however, nearly losing a leg after she was in an automobile accident and was denied proper treatment in a hospital in Anniston, Alabama. Unable to walk for more than a month afterwards, Waters was still in demand by bookers and fans who wanted to hear her blues. After a year on the road, Waters returned in triumph to perform in Philadelphia. When this engagement was concluded, she moved in with her mother, half sister, and aunt and took a job busing dishes while trying also to rest and take care of her injured leg. She subsequently took a job in Barney Gordon's saloon, where her blues drew large crowds. She then began her lifelong practice of supporting her whole family, including her half sister's child, Waters, whom she adored.

Waters Introduces Jazz Style in Popular Songs

In 1919 Waters accepted an engagement at the Lincoln Theatre in Harlem. She got a good reception there, attracting a number of entertainers who had seen her perform in Philadelphia. She then regularly appeared at Edmond Johnson's Cellar, a nightclub in Harlem, where she began to characterize and act out the popular ballads of the day and to attract a sophisticated clientele. She portrayed difficult and tragic experiences in song, but also was a masterful comedienne. With her refined voice, polished diction, innovative rhythm and phrasing, sense of intimacy, and flair for dramatizing each song, she created a new style of singing popular music. Rather than relying solely on the words of a song to convey its story, she instinctively used these vocal styles to express her conception of the song, thus establishing a jazz style that influenced later popular singers such as Billie Holiday, Ella Fitzgerald, and Sarah Vaughn. Modern critic Leonard Feather described her uniqueness as a singer: "Her clear, rich, vibrant sound with its touch of huskiness, and the vibrato that was so distinctive . . . gave her a character she shared with no other singer, blues or pop, black or white" (Passion, 65). Her performances attracted such stars as Bill "Bojangles" Robinson, Florence Mills, and Sophie Tucker, the latter of whom paid Waters to sing privately so that she could study her style. Waters later characterized these years at Edmond's Cellar as among the happiest in her life.

Waters performed at the Lafayette Theatre in Harlem and became popular with Harlem's well-to-do patrons, but she was developing an ambition to perform in a stage show, an ambition she realized in *Hello, 1919!*, a black-face comedy in which she had to perform in burnt cork. After the show closed in Ohio, Waters returned to New York and resumed her work at Edmond's Cellar.

In March 1921 Waters made her first record for the Cardinal Company, with "New York Glide" on one side and "At the New Jump Steady Ball" on the other. She was the first prominent black recording artist who was not primarily a blues singer. Shortly afterwards she recorded "Down Home Blues" and "Oh, Daddy" for Black Swan. During the next two years she recorded a total of twenty-six titles for the Black Swan label. While at Edmond's Cellar, she turned down a lucrative contract with an agent for the white vaudeville circuit and traveled and performed, instead, with Fletcher Henderson's Black Swan Troubadours. Though Waters could not read music, she guided Henderson to play the piano the way she felt the music and he developed a jazz style with the distinctive trills and bass technique for which he became well-known. While touring the South they became the first black entertainers to perform on radio.

The show in which Waters first appeared as a name performer was *Oh Joy!*, which opened in Boston in 1922. She was acclaimed for her singing of "Georgia Blues" in this revue. In the early 1920s she worked for the black

Theater Owners Booking Association, traveling and performing in the Midwest, East, and South with her talented accompanist, Pearl Wright. Her fame on Black Swan records obscured her talent as a dancer, which her public began to appreciate and request in these theaters. Having been "the world's champion shimmy shaker in Chester, Pennsylvania" (Waters, *Sparrow*, 207), she still loved to dance. As a headliner who stopped the show, Waters enticed the black audiences from the balconies in the competing white theaters. She also attracted white patrons, who were allowed to sit in the rear of the black theaters. While playing in Atlanta, she narrowly escaped being lynched by a tough, white theater owner who resented her insistence that the piano be tuned properly. She credited God with arranging her miraculous escape.

In 1924 Waters starred in the *Plantation Revue* in Chicago. Ashton Stevens, the influential Chicago newspaper critic, proclaimed that "Ethel Waters is the greatest artist of her race and generation," a statement that was reprinted in newspapers all over the country (Waters, *Sparrow*, 182). In 1925 she performed at the Plantation Club on Broadway, where she introduced "Dinah." Her recording of this song made it the first international hit to come out of an American nightclub and also brought her enthusiastic and wide recognition.

Earl Dancer, owner of the Golden Gate Inn in New York, recognized Waters's genius and persuaded her to audition on the white Keith vaudeville circuit in 1925. Her tryout was at Chicago's Kedzie Theatre, the first big-time vaudeville theater in which she worked. Although she had been reluctant to work before the more subdued white audiences, Waters was an immediate success. She performed with Dancer on the white Orpheum circuit and made her first trip to the west coast. Soon becoming headliners, Waters and Dancer worked in vaudeville with Jack Benny and other famous performers.

Waters Performs in Musicials on Broadway and in Films

Waters's first Broadway appearance was in *Africana*, a black musical produced by Dancer in 1927. After starring in the long run on Broadway, Waters went on the road with the show. When it closed in Saint Louis, she returned to New York and worked as a single act in nightclubs and all-star shows. She developed a friendship during this time with Carl Van Vechten, the writer, photographer, and recorder of black cultural life during the Harlem Renaissance. Van Vechten, she said, was the only person who understood the shyness deep inside her. In the late 1920s, Waters married Clyde Edward "Eddie" Matthews and continued her work on the Orpheum circuit. During these years she was recording on the Paramount, Vocalion, and Columbia labels, with forty-eight titles to her credit on Columbia alone. In 1929 she made her first movie, *On with the Show*, in which she sang the popular "Am I Blue?" which she later recorded.

In 1930 Waters was having trouble with her throat and sailed for Europe with her husband and her goddaughter, Algretta Holmes, who was eighteen months old. They spent several months in France, after which Waters performed at England's most famous music hall, the Palladium in London. An English physician, Dr. Cyril Horsford, discovered that Waters's throat trouble was being caused by a nodule on her left vocal cord and would require a dangerous operation to remove it. Putting the situation in the hands of God, Waters agreed to the operation, and Dr. Horsford successfully removed the nodule.

Upon her return to the United States, Waters immediately set up vaudeville dates and began making new records on the Columbia label. She starred in *Blackbirds of 1930*, a revue produced by Lew Leslie in New York, and in *Rhapsody in Black*, a revue that opened at the Belasco Theatre in Washington in 1931. While on the road with this show, she worked with the legendary Al Jolson in Chicago.

In the early 1930s, Waters became the highest paid star ever to perform at the Cotton Club in Harlem. While appearing there in 1933 with Duke Ellington's orchestra, she introduced "Stormy Weather," which she considered to be the theme song of her life at that time and which became the first dramatic song hit to come out of a night club. At the time Waters and "Stormy Weather" became the talk of New York. Irving Berlin heard her at the Cotton Club and signed her for his musical, *As Thousands Cheer*, which was an overwhelming success on Broadway in 1934. With this engagement, Waters became the first black person to perform in an all-white cast on Broadway. She sang three of Berlin's songs in the show, "Heat Wave," "Harlem on my Mind," and "Supper Time," the latter being a dirge that told the story of a black woman whose husband had been lynched. Stopping the show with this song, which she described as "a type of song never heard before in a revue," Waters became the highest paid female performer on Broadway (Waters, *Sparrow*, 221). She claimed another first when *As Thousands Cheer* went on the road and she became the first black person to costar with white players below the Mason-Dixon line. She was with the show for two years, traveling to the west coast and back to Rochester. During this time she separated from her husband.

Waters received excellent reviews when she costarred with Beatrice Lillie in the Broadway revue *At Home Abroad* in 1935 and 1936. Although lucrative movie-house engagements were waiting for her after the show closed, Waters chose to go into vaudeville with Eddie Mallory, a trumpet player whom she had worked with and admired. She toured the South with Mallory's band, whose pianist was her half brother, Johnny Waters.

Waters Emerges as Dramatic Actress

In 1939 Waters became the first black woman to perform the leading role in a dramatic play on Broadway. As Hagar in *Mamba's Daughters*, she alone received seventeen curtain calls on opening night, and she later remembered that experience as the most important of her life as a performer. Waters "became" Hagar, as she interpreted the character from the torment, loneliness, and uncomplaining courage of her own mother's life. After wide critical acclaim and a long run on Broadway, Waters and the company took *Mamba's Daughters* on tour before returning to New York for a second engagement. Her triumph in the role of Hagar assured her status as a ranking actress.

Waters's talents as a singer and actress were extraordinarily combined in her role as Petunia Jackson in the Broadway musical *Cabin in the Sky*, which opened in 1940. After a five-month run in New York, she went with the show to Los Angeles and San Francisco. While performing her individual act at the Orpheum Theatre in Los Angeles, Waters was offered and accepted a part in an episodic film *Tales of Manhattan*.

In 1942 Waters bought a house in Los Angeles. She appeared in the film *Cairo* with Jeanette MacDonald and in the screen version of *Cabin in the Sky* in 1943 with Lena Horne, Louis Armstrong, and Eddie "Rochester" Anderson. During the next several years she continued to perform in night clubs, but parts for her in plays and movies were nonexistent because of the absence of substantive roles for blacks and because of the lack of production funds. Discouraged, she moved back to New York and lived in mid-Manhattan white hotels. She wanted to be with members of her own race, so she began spending more time in Harlem and living with various friends there, causing the public to believe that she was down and out. She performed at the Club Zanzibar in New York in late 1947 and at Madison Square Garden early in 1948, but was unemployed until mid-summer in 1948. After she was robbed of money and clothes in Harlem, she moved in with another friend and became a recluse. Waters, who had commanded exceptionally high salaries during most of her career, had been financially generous with others, remembering what it was like to be poor, and also spent a great deal of money on fine clothes, jewelry, and cars, which she thought her public expected. Now, unable to figure out how to pay her mother's expenses, her own living expenses, the expenses of her house in California, income taxes, and still donate to charity, Waters decided to go back to California to get a new perspective on her career. She was not able to leave New York right away, however, because of various obligations, and accepted several night club jobs and benefits on the road. While traveling she lost the chance to play in the Broadway production of *Medea* because the correspondence reached her too late. Waters later recalled her feelings about this period in her life: "It was as though the entire theatrical world had forgotten there ever had been an Ethel Waters" (Waters, *Sparrow*, 267).

Although Waters hit bottom professionally in the winter of 1948-49, she finally was fulfilled emotionally when her mother sensed that she was down and for the first time told her that she loved her and was proud of her. Until that time, Waters had never been accepted by her mother, who was ashamed of the circumstances of her daughter's birth. Waters began working in clubs again, but many of the clubs had added bars and television sets and she found that the quiet atmosphere necessary for her intimate performing was often missing. Nevertheless, she was still wowing the audiences, even those who were not familiar with her previous work and reputation. In February 1949 Twentieth Century-Fox studios asked Waters to audition for a part in the film *Pinky*. She was cast in the part of Granny, for which she later received an Oscar nomination. "All I had to do to play Granny well," she said, "was remember my own grandmother, Sally Anderson" (Waters, *Sparrow*, 272). In her later years Waters attributed her success as an actress to the fact that she acted instinctively, "reliving" her life and the lives of the relatives who were close to her.

When first asked to star as Berenice Sadie Brown in Carson McCullers's play *The Member of the Wedding*, Waters refused the part because the character lacked faith in God and therefore did not seem authentic. McCullers later permitted Waters to give the role her own interpretation, so she signed the contract. Waters substituted a Russian lullaby for "His Eye Is on the Sparrow," a song that she had learned in church as a child, which would become her trademark. The play, which also starred Julie Harris and Brandon DeWilde, opened in New York at the Empire Theatre on January 5, 1950. Critics proclaimed that Waters, at fifty-four years old, had her finest artistic success in this role.

While performing in *The Member of the Wedding*, which ran for 501 performances on Broadway, Waters wrote, with Charles Samuels, her first autobiography, *His Eye Is on the Sparrow*. The book was published in 1951 and was praised for its frank self-revelations and its disclosures about racial discrimination and the entertainment business in America. In 1952 Waters was nominated for an Academy Award for her role in the film version of *The Member of the Wedding*. The following year she starred in the weekly television series "Beulah." During the next few years she was extremely successful with her one-woman show, *An Evening with Ethel Waters*, but was gaining weight rapidly for the first time in her life. Weighing 350 pounds, she found it difficult to adjust to her large body, and she became deeply troubled. Her comfort at the time was to sing "His Eye Is on the Sparrow," which she included in every performance, and which she later called "the marrow in my bones" (Waters, *To Me It's Wonderful*, 11).

New Career Begins as Singer for Jesus Christ

In May 1957, living alone in a hotel room in New York, Waters pondered her successful career and her personal unhappiness. "I had fame, but I was empty," she stated (DeKorte, 74). Desolation was overwhelming her when she went to Madison Square Garden to hear Evangelist Billy Graham preach at his New York Crusade. Graham clarified her spiritual dilemmas for her as she went night after night to hear him preach. She unobtrusively joined the choir, but was soon asked by Cliff Barrows to sing "His Eye Is on the Sparrow" for several television broadcasts of the crusade. After the New York Crusade ended, Waters returned to her home in Los Angeles, where she was forced to cancel her west coast engagements because of heart problems related to her weight. She received the medical help that she had needed for a long time, remaining in intensive care for twenty-three days, and ultimately losing more than two hundred pounds over several years. Thereafter, she crowned her diverse and prolific career by devoting her energy and talents to singing for Jesus Christ at the Billy Graham Crusades. Graham commented on the force of her presence: "When she walks out on the platform, I've seen 75,000 people all rise at once. Ethel Waters is one of the most beloved, remarkable, and *electric* women of the century" (Rankin, 82).

Waters's last films, *The Sound and the Fury* and *The Heart Is a Rebel*, were made in the late 1950s. She performed her one-woman show in the early sixties, and in 1964 performed in successful revivals of *The Member of the Wedding* in Pasadena, LaJolla, and Santa Barbara. In 1970 she again played in a six-week run of this play in Chicago. Most of her time, however, was spent singing for the Billy Graham Crusades and giving sacred concerts in churches, Youth for Christ meetings, and religious conventions.

Although she was at peace spiritually in her last years, Waters suffered from heart disease, diabetes, deteriorating eyesight, and hypertension. Her supreme courage and faith in God made it possible for her to bear these physical burdens and to keep singing. In 1971 she sang at the Sunday Worship Service at the White House, a service in which she broke the familiar barriers of stiffness and protocol with her warmth, laughter, and deeply inspired singing. She returned to the White House later that year as a guest at Tricia Nixon's wedding. In 1972 she wrote a second autobiography, *To Me It's Wonderful*, which chronicles her life after she rededicated her life to Jesus Christ in 1957.

On October 6, 1972, after fifteen years of singing in the Billy Graham Crusades, Waters was honored by Graham with a testimonial dinner in California. Tributes regarding her place of distinction in American theater, music, vaudeville, film, television, radio, and religious life were presented by such celebrities as Tricia Nixon Cox, Bob Hope, Hugh Downs, Julie Harris, and Graham.

Waters sang for the last time at Billy Graham's San Diego Crusade in August 1976. Referring to herself as "damaged goods" (Knaack, 137), she was diagnosed that same month as having cancer. Her health gradually declined over the next year, and she died at the home of Julianne and Paul DeKorte in Chatsworth, California, on September 1, 1977.

From her earliest days of singing and dancing in vaudeville as "Sweet Mama Stringbean" to her recording of numerous hit songs, to her achievements in acting on the stage and screen to her later career as a singer of religious music, Waters boldly presented through her art the message of her life and her race and her Savior. She is remembered as "The Mother of Modern Popular Singing," a distinction that signifies her formidable contributions in providing a jazz interpretation of popular music that was a major influence on American popular singing. As a dramatic actress, Waters expressed for the first time in this white-dominated artistic medium the soul and heritage of black Americans, and is recognized as one of the American theater's greatest performers. Above all, she was one of this country's native geniuses, whose extraordinary artistic imagination and sense of theater set the standard for the work of future generations.

References

DeKorte, Juliann. *Ethel Waters: Finally Home*. Old Tappan, N.J.: Fleming H. Revell Company, 1978.

Feather, Leonard. *The Passion for Jazz*. New York: Horizon Press, 1980.

Giddins, Gary. *Riding on a Blue Note: Jazz and American Pop*. New York: Oxford University Press, 1981.

Knaack, Twila. *Ethel Waters: I Touched a Sparrow*. Waco, Texas: Word Books, 1978.

Placksin, Sally. *American Women in Jazz, 1900 to the Present*. New York: Seaview Books, 1982.

Rankin, Allen. "The Three Lives of Ethel Waters." *Reader's Digest* (December 1972): 81-85.

Waters, Ethel. *His Eye Iis on the Sparrow*. Garden City, N.Y.: Doubleday, 1951. Reprinted. New York: Jove Publications, 1978.

———. *To Me It's Wonderful*. New York: Harper, 1972.

Collections

George Finola of New Orleans, Louisiana, has compiled the only known complete discography of Ethel Waters's recordings. The list includes 259 recordings. Sizable collections of Waters's recordings are available in the Historical Sound Recordings Collection in the Yale University Library, New Haven, Connecticut; in the Motion Picture, Broadcasting, and Recorded Sound Division of the Library of Congress, Washington, D.C.; and in the Rogers and Hammerstein Archive of Recorded Sound in the New York Public Library's General Library and Museum of the Performing Arts at Lincoln Center, New York City.

The Beinecke Rare Book Library at Yale University has, in its Carl Van Vechten Collection, a bust of Waters sculpted by Antonio Salemme and photographs of her by Van Vechten. There are also photographs of Waters in the Schomburg Center for Research in Black Culture, Prints and Photo Collection, New York City. The Music Division, Special Collections, of the Library of Congress has ninety-three of Waters's personal letters.

Marsha C. Vick

Faye Wattleton

(1943-)

Organization executive, reproductive rights activist

Faye Wattleton has been one of the most influential black American women in the area of reproductive rights. She transformed a declining service-oriented organization into a high-profile and aggressive proponent of women's reproductive rights.

The only child of George Edward Wattleton and Ozie (Garrett) Wattleton, Alyce Faye Wattleton was born on July 8, 1943, in Saint Louis, Missouri. George Wattleton, who died in 1970, was a factory worker. Ozie Wattleton—one of Faye Wattleton's role models, along with Martin Luther King, Jr., and John F. Kennedy—was a seamstress and minister of the Church of God. Living one's politics was important in the Wattleton family. Her father, for example, refused to buy gas from a service station that failed to provide bathroom facilities for "coloreds." "It was [her] parents' way of protesting the system economically" (Lanker, 97).

Faye Wattleton's family was very poor but stressed the importance of helping those who were less fortunate. She "was expected to become a missionary helping 'the poor and maimed' of Africa" (Epstein, 46). At the age of sixteen she entered Ohio State University Nursing School, and in 1964 was the first person in her family to receive a college degree. Her first postgraduate job was as a maternity nursing instructor for the Miami Valley Hospital School of Nursing in Dayton, Ohio. It was during her two years there that she was first exposed "to the medical and emotional complications of women who had life-threatening illegal abortions" (Green, 42). In 1966 Wattleton moved to New York to study at Columbia University on a government stipend; a year later she received an M.S. in maternal and infant health care, with certification as a nurse-midwife. While a student at Columbia, she was an intern at Harlem Hospital, where the importance of access to safe abortion became clear to her. As she recalls: "One of the cases I remember in Harlem was a really beautiful 17-year-old girl. She and her mother had decided to induce an abortion by inserting a Lysol douche into her uterus. It killed her" (Epstein, 48).

Wattleton Heads Planned Parenthood Association

In 1967 Wattleton moved to Dayton, Ohio, to work as consultant and assistant director of Public Health Nursing Services in the City of Dayton Public Health Department. She was asked to join the local Planned Parenthood board and a year and a half later, at the age of twenty-seven, was asked to serve as its executive director. Under her leadership, the number of clients tripled and the budget increased from less than four hundred thousand dollars to just under one million dollars. In 1973 she married Franklin Gordon, a social worker raised in Roxbury, Massachusetts. Two years later she not only became a mother but also the chairwoman of the national executive director's Council of Planned Parenthood Federation of America (PPFA). In fact, Wattleton was in labor with her daughter, Felicia, when she won the election to the position. Three years later she was appointed president of PPFA.

As the first black person, first woman, and youngest individual to head the organization, it is no surprise that many people were shocked at Wattleton's appointment. According to one local director, "Nobody believed our board would settle on 'a little nurse from Dayton' with no national experience for the highest-paid job [seventy thousand dollars a year] in the largest voluntary health agency in the country" (Epstein, 48). How, then, did the board decide to appoint a woman, particularly a black woman, as president? In Wattleton's opinion, there were at least three factors involved: her demonstrated compassion for human suffering, the organization's realization that its primary reason for existence was women's issues, and her competence.

Even Wattleton, however, could not have imagined just how tough her job would be. The Hyde Amendment, passed in 1977 and "aimed to prohibit the use of any federal funding for abortion, unless the life of the mother was endangered," was one of the early indicators that Right to Life groups were having a significant influence on the political process. During that same year, Planned Parenthood of Miami Valley came under attack from the local Baptist group and Right to Life chapter and also received a federal inquiry into its use of federal financing. In addition, Planned Parenthood clinics in Minnesota, Virginia, Nebraska, Vermont, and Ohio, were burned or bombed. Thus the antichoice stage had been set. One of the ongoing efforts of the Reagan administration was an attempt to repeal the United States family planning program, Title I of the Public Health Service Act. As family planning services and their funding were being threatened, Wattleton worked to bring PPFA into public view. She appeared on radio and television talk shows, including "Donahue," to rally support around her cause. In fact, Phil Donahue called Wattleton "a talk show host's dream guest" because she got to the point and was always well-informed (Rubin, 107).

President Reagan also attempted to enact a "squeal rule," which would have required federally-funded clinics to receive parental consent before distributing diaphragms, intra-uterine devices, or birth control pills to minors. Wattleton, however, argued that the notification of parents requirements would merely lead to an increase in teen pregnancies. A "gag rule," which would prevent abortion counseling by federally-funded family-planning agencies was also proposed.

Because PPFA served men and women in the developing

countries of Africa, Asia, and Latin America, the Reagan administration's "Mexico City" policy also disturbed Wattleton. In essence, the policy was an attempt to restrict United States family-planning aid to foreign organizations that refered, performed, or advocated abortion. However, according to Wattleton and the majority of Americans who participated in the 1988 Harris poll, the United States should provide family-planning funds to developing nations—even those nations where abortion was a legal option.

"By engaging in political activism, Ms. Wattleton has brought Planned Parenthood full circle" (Rubin, 107). When Margaret Sanger, also a public health nurse, opened the nation's first birth control clinic in 1916, she was jailed and contraceptives were confiscated. The early 1900s was a time when "contraceptives were classified as 'obscene materials;' when Kotex was not yet on the market and when most women were 'prisoners of their own fecundity'"(Epstein, 54). Because of early efforts such as those of Sanger and her associates, the distribution of and information about birth control became widely accepted by the medical establishment.

Almost seventy years later, Wattleton would have to struggle to keep family planning on the national agenda. By this time, Planned Parenthood had lost much of its attraction among middle and upperclass women. Most of the clients were poor or of the working class and thus were particularly vulnerable to reductions in federal funding, such as Medicaid. The Hyde Amendment, for example, cut off Medicaid abortion funding, which meant that hundreds of thousands of poor women could no longer have their abortions paid for by Medicaid. Wattleton argued that poor people, like the rich, should have access to the full range of health care services.

> The women who came to my hospitals under less than dignified circumstances were not affluent. That girl in Harlem who died was not affluent. . . . *That's* when I became aware of the political significance of these people. If they really cared about equity and fairness in life they would say that as long as abortion is legal in this country, poor people should have the same access as the rich (Epstein, 45).

Equal access was not the only issue raised concerning reproductive choice and freedom. Wattleton attempted to locate the reproductive issue in a wider context of federal neglect. In her view, the Reagan/Bush administration tried to dismantle programs designed to confront not only the issue of inadequate health care but also homelessness and poor education. Thus, one had to look at the circumstances under which so many women chose to end their pregnancies—many of which were unintended.

Public Advocacy Drive Initiated

Planned Parenthood is dedicated to working for a society where unintended pregnancies would be reduced. Sex education and information about contraceptives are very important elements of this commitment. Under Wattleton's leadership the agency "expanded its public advocacy drive through newspaper and television advertisements geared toward educating teens, parents and public officials on the financial and human costs of runaway teen pregnancy" (Green, 42). Wattleton also coauthored a book entitled *How to Talk to Your Child About Sex*, which sold more than thirty thousand copies. It angered her, however, that by 1989 "no major network [would] accept contraceptive advertising [and] only 17 states and the District of Columbia require[d[] sex education in their school systems" (Gillespie, 52). In her view, children needed to be taught about sexuality before they became adolescents. Wattleton attributes the increase of teen pregnancies to children's contradictory exposure to sex: children are bombarded with sexual messages and exploitation by a society that is, for the most part, sexually illiterate.

Wattleton's demanding role as president of PPFA unfortunately took its toll on her personal life. Although she commuted from New York to Dayton on weekends to be with her husband and daughter, her marriage to Franklin Gordon crumbled in 1981. In retrospect, Wattleton said that her demanding schedule "probably accelerated" the demise of an already shaky marriage (Rubin, 83). In spite of her personal problems, however, her calm and rational outward demeanor were not shaken. In fact, cool composure and articulation have become her trademarks. These qualities have allowed her to disarm enemies and inspire supporters. John Willke, a medical doctor and president of the National Right to Life Committee, called Wattleton "an attractive and articulate spokesman for her cause" (Rubin, 107). Journalists have also commented on her physical appearance. One source referred to "the immaculately tailored, carefully maintained surface" and went on to describe in detail her impeccable dress: "Wattleton wears a pale mauve leather suit with a deep purple silk tank top. Her fingernail polish matches her suit" (Szegedy-Maszak, 18).

Wattleton, a slender woman of five-feet-eleven inches, enjoys playing tennis as well as collecting antiques. She and her former husband also bred Afghan hounds. Her life currently centers around her job and her daughter. Wattleton's only complaint about her very demanding schedule is that it allows little time for Felicia. Wattleton spends a great deal of time on the road, lecturing and appearing on television and radio talk shows, and usually works at least twelve hours a day. However, she reserves weekends for herself and her daughter.

Wattleton's awards and accomplishments are impressive. In 1980 *Savvy* magazine named her one of the country's outstanding not-for-profit executives. In 1984 she was named to the Young Presidents' Organization. She received the 1986 American Humanist Award, the World Institute of Black Communication's 1986 Excellence in Black Communications Award, the 1986 Women's Honors in Public Service from the American Nursing Association, and in that same year was appointed to the board of directors of the United States Commission for the United Nations Children's Education Fund. She received the Independent Sector's 1987 John Gardner Award, the 1989 Congressional Black Caucus Humanitarian Award, the Better World Society's 1989 Better

World Population Medal, and the American Public Health Association's 1989 Award of Excellence. She has been featured in a national exhibit, "I Dream a World: Portraits of Black Women Who Changed America." Wattleton is included in *And Still We Rise*, a book containing interviews with fifty black role models. She has appeared on "Good Morning America," "World News Tonight," "CBS Evening News," "This Week with David Brinkley," "Sixty Minutes." "McNeil/Lehrer Report," "Today Show," "Donahue," "Nightline," "NBC Nightly News," and "20/20." In addition, *Ms.* magazine selected her as one of the "80 Women to Watch in the 80s."

Wattleton is also a member of numerous organizations: the National Academy of the Sciences' Institute of Medicine's Study Committee on the Role of State and Local Public Health Departments, the advisory committee of the Women's Leadership Conference on National Security, and the President's Advisory Council on the Peace Corps. She is also a board member of the Ohio State University Alumni Association and the National Urban Coalition.

PPFA is currently served by twenty-one thousand volunteers and staff nationwide. This three-hundred-million-dollar organization (according to its 1988 budget) "provides medical and educational services to nearly four million Americans through 178 affiliates in 47 states and the District of Columbia . . . [and] serves an additional four million men and women in the developing world through its international division, Family Planning International Assistance" (Faye Wattleton, news release, 1989). PPFA has also become the largest pro-choice organization in a pro-choice coalition that includes the National Organization for Women, the National Abortion Rights Action League, the Fund for the Feminist Majority, and the American Civil Liberties Union.

One of the major setbacks for PPFA as well as other advocates of reproductive choice was the Supreme Court's ruling in the *Webster v. Reproductive Health Services*. The case challenged certain aspects of *Roe v. Wade*, the 1973 Supreme Court decision that legalized abortion. On July 3, 1989, the Supreme Court gave states the right to limit access to abortion. Although this event may have signaled defeat to even the most resolute leader, Wattleton confidently asserted after hearing the decision, "my commitment and my determination is in no way diminished. I am furious as can be" (Szegedy-Maszak, 62).

When interviewed in mid-November 1988 by *Savvy Woman* magazine, Faye Wattleton revealed that she was not sure how long she was going to continue the very demanding schedule she had set for herself at PPFA and added that "whoever is providing leadership needs to be as fresh and thoughtful and reflective as possible to make the very best fight" (Rubin, 108).

References

Dionne, E. J., Jr. "On Both Sides, Advocates Predict a 50-State Battle." *New York Times*, 4 July 1989.

Epstein, Helen. "Abortion: An Issue That Won't Go Away." *New York Times Magazine*, 20 March 1980.

Gillespie, Marcia Ann. "Repro Woman." *Ms.* 18 (October 1989): 50-53.

Green, Constance M. "A View from the Top." *Black Enterprise* 17 (April 1987): 40-48.

Greenhouse, Linda. "Change in Course." *New York Times*, 4 July 1989.

Lanker, Brian. *I Dream A World.* New York: Stewart, Tabori and Chang, 1989. Photograph, p. 96.

Leavitt, Judith A. *American Women Managers and Administrators.* Westport, Conn.: Greenwood Press, 1985.

Lewis, Shawn D. "Family Planning's Top Advocate." *Ebony* 33 (September 1978): 85-86.

Reynolds, Barbara. *And Still We Rise: Interviews with 50 Black Role Models.* Washington, D.C.: USA Today Books, Gannett Co., 1988.

Rubin, Nancy. "The Politics of Parenthood." *Savvy Woman* (April 1989): 81-83.

Szegedy-Maszak, Marianne. "Calm, Cool and Beleaguered." *New York Times Magazine*, 6 August 1989. 16-19.

Wattleton, Faye. Planned Parenthood Federation of America. News Release. December 1989.

Carolyn Cunningham with Adrienne Lash Jones

Ida B. Wells Barnett

(1862-1930)

Journalist, lecturer, social activist, clubwoman, feminist, antilynching crusader

Characterized throughout the print media as courageous, determined, forceful, fearless, fiery, and militant, the life and career of Ida Bell Wells Barnett covers several epochs of the black American saga. Born in slavery six months prior to the signing of the Emancipation Proclamation and reared during Reconstruction, she came of age during the post-Reconstruction period and spent her adult life fighting to redress the inequities brought about by Jim Crow.

Wells Barnett was born a slave on July 16, 1862, in Holly Springs, Mississippi, to James Wells and Elizabeth "Lizzie" (Bell) Wells. Her mother was the child of a slave mother and an Indian father who had moved to Holly Springs. James

Ida B. Wells Barnett

Wells was apprenticed by his master, who was his acknowledged father, to learn the carpentry trade. The oldest in a family of four boys and four girls, Ida Wells Barnett attended Rust College, a freedmen's high school and industrial school. Formerly called Shaw University, Rust College was established in 1866 by northern Methodist missionaries in Holly Springs and provided instruction at all levels and grades, including the basic elementary subjects. Wells Barnett's parents impressed upon her the importance of receiving an education and, with the guidance and instruction of the teachers at Rust, she was an excellent student.

The yellow fever epidemic of 1878, which ravaged Memphis, Tennessee, and northern Mississippi, claimed the lives of Ida Wells Barnett's parents and that of her youngest brother. Following their deaths, at the age of sixteen Wells Barnett assumed responsibility for her siblings. After passing the teachers' examination, she taught for a short time in the rural district of Holly Springs, earning twenty-five dollars a month.

In the 1880s, Wells Barnett engaged her brothers and sisters in apprenticeships and with her two younger sisters moved to Memphis to be close to her father's sister, Fannie Butler, and to obtain a better-paying teaching position. While preparing for the teachers' examination for the black public schools of Memphis, Wells Barnett taught at a rural school in Woodstock, outside Memphis.

Legal Suit Filed Against Railroad

A train ride from Memphis to Woodstock was the beginning of Wells Barnett's lifelong public campaign against the inequities and injustices faced by blacks throughout the South. In May 1884 she purchased a first-class ticket on a local Memphis-to-Woodstock line operated by the Chesapeake, Ohio, and Southwestern Railroad Company. Taking a seat in the ladies' coach, she was asked by the conductor to move to the forward car, which was a smoker. Wells Barnett refused, got off the train, returned to Memphis, and subsequently filed suit against the railroad company for refusing to provide her the first-class accommodations for which she had paid.

In December 1884 the Memphis circuit court ruled in favor of Wells Barnett, levied the maximum fine of three hundred dollars against the railroad company, and awarded her personal damages of five hundred dollars. Headlines in the Christmas edition of the Memphis *Daily Appeal* (25 December 1894) read, "A Darky Damsel Obtains a Verdict for Damages Against the Chesapeake and Ohio Railroad—What It Cost to Put a Colored Teacher in a Smoking Car-Verdict for $500." Wells Barnett's success against the railroad company was short-lived. The railroad appealed the case to the Tennessee Supreme Court, which on April 5, 1887, reversed the lower court's decision on the grounds that the railroad had satisfied the statutory requirements to provide "like accommodations." Six days after the court's decision, Wells Barnett noted:

> I felt so disappointed because I had hoped such great things from my suit for my people generally. I [had] firmly believed all along that the law was on our side and would, when we appealed to it, give us justice. I feel shorn of that belief and utterly discouraged, and just now, if it were possible, I would gather my race in my arms and fly away with them. O God, is there no redress, no peace, no justice in this land for us? Thou hast always fought the battles of the weak and oppressed. Come to my aid this moment and teach me what to do, for I am sorely, bitterly, disappointed. Show us the way even as thou led the children of Israel out of bondage into the promise land (Duster, xvii).

Wells Barnett taught in the Memphis city schools from 1884 to 1891. During her tenure, she devoted herself to the education of black children and sharpened her own academic skills by attending summer sessions at Fisk University, in Nashville, Tennessee. On Friday afternoons, Wells Barnett met with other teachers at the Memphis Vance Street Christian Church to play music, give recitals, read essays, and engage in debates. These literary meetings closed with the reading of the *Evening Star*, an internal journal of current events, prepared and read by the editor. When the editor's position became vacant, Wells Barnett was elected to fill it. While serving in this capacity, she became known throughout the community and in 1887 was invited by Reverend R. N. Countee, pastor of the Tabernacle Missionary Baptist Church, to write for the *Living Way*, a religious weekly. Using the story of her suit against the Chesapeake, Ohio, and Southwestern Railroad and its outcome as her first article, Wells Barnett contributed to the weekly for two years under the pseudonym "Iola." After publishing an account of her experiences in the local black press, Wells Barnett began writing regularly for the black press throughout the country. At the 1889 meeting of the Colored Press Association, later called the Afro-American Press Association, held in Washington, D.C., she was elected secretary. During this same year, the "Princess of the Press," was invited to become editor of and partner in the *Free Speech and Headlight*, a militant journal owned by the Reverend Taylor Nightingale, pastor of the Beale Street Baptist Church, and J. L. Fleming.

Wells Barnett Called a Fearless Journalist

Wells Barnett gained a reputation for fearlessness because of the scathing and militant opinions she openly expressed in print. Her protest editorials were angry and to the point. In 1891 Wells Barnett openly sanctioned retaliatory violence by blacks in Georgetown, Kentucky, who avenged the lynching of a black man by setting fire to the town. "Not until the Negro rises in his might and takes a hand in resenting such cold-blooded murders, if he has to burn up whole towns, will a halt be called in wholesale lynching."

Because Wells Barnett wrote an editorial critical of the Memphis Board of Education and its unequal distribution of resources allocated to the segregated black schools, the board dismissed her from its employment in 1891. Wells Barnett's dismissal came as no surprise; as a matter of fact, she had anticipated the board's negative reaction. Disheartened, but not discouraged, Wells Barnett devoted all of her time and energy to the paper. She shortened its name to the *Free Speech* and worked diligently to expand its circulation. In less than a year, the circulation had increased by 38 percent.

In 1892 events in Memphis changed the course of Wells Barnett's life. Thomas Moss, Calvin McDowell, and William Stewart, all friends of hers, opened the People's Grocery Store on the curve of Walker Avenue and Mississippi Boulevard, in a black section of Memphis. The black entrepreneurs successfully competed with white merchant, W. H. Barrett, who operated a grocery store across the street. Barrett's loss of the market share to the People's Grocery aroused animosities that ultimately led to violence. After several episodes, the Shelby County grand jury indicted the owners of People's for maintaining a nuisance. Subsequently, on Saturday, March 5, after dark, when nine deputy sheriffs dressed in civilian attire converged upon the grocery store owners, the deputies were taken for a mob and fired upon by a group of blacks determined to protect the owners. Three deputies were wounded; McDowell, Stewart, Moss, and scores of other accused rioters were arrested.

Judge Dubose of the Shelby County criminal court illegally disarmed the Tennessee Rifles, a black state militia company that guarded the jail for three nights in an attempt to protect the prisoners. On Wednesday, March 9, 1892, nine white men abducted Moss, McDowell, and Stewart from the jail, carried them one mile north, and barbarously shot them to death. Wells Barnett wrote the following:

> The city of Memphis had demonstrated that neither character nor standing avails the Negro if he dares to protect himself against the white man or become his rival. There is nothing we can do now about the lynching, as we are out-numbered and without arms. The white mob could help itself to ammunition without pay, but the order was rigidly enforced against the selling of guns to Negroes. There is therefore only one thing left that we can do; save our money and leave a town which will neither protect our lives and property, nor give us a fair trial in the courts, but take us out and murder us in cold blood when accused by a white person (Duster, 52).

Outraged by this, the most heinous act of brutality perpetrated against blacks since the Memphis police riot of 1866, the black community retaliated by encouraging all who could to leave the Bluff City, and those who stayed to refrain from patronizing the City Railroad Company. Prodded by angry editorials in the *Free Speech* and the calls of "On to Oklahoma," two thousand blacks left Memphis and put the streetcar company in dire financial straits. Throughout the following weeks and into the spring, Wells Barnett's editorials "demanded that the murders of Moss, McDowell, and Stewart be brought to justice" (21 May 1892).

The Memphis daily journals which had played a pivotal role in igniting the smoldering embers of racial bigotry that emboldened, fostered, and incited the merciless lynching, now attempted to prevent this westward exodus by publishing tales of adversities experienced by those blacks who had already traveled west. On the advice of Isaac F. Norris, a former member of the Tennessee House of Representatives and an in-law of Wells Barnett, she went to Oklahoma to determine for herself the future of black migration. She conveyed her findings through the *Free Speech*, informed the readers of what she witnessed, and wrote of their chances of progress in this new territory.

The third week in May 1892, Wells Barnett left for Philadelphia to attend the African Methodist Episcopal church convention. However, before her departure, she left behind an editorial to be printed in the May 21 edition of the *Free Speech*. Provoked by the lynching of eight more Negroes, her fiery pen punctured the ego of white men of the South. Wells Barnett called into question the hackneyed excuses used by whites for executing blacks without due process of the law, by inferring that white women of the South were sexually attracted to black men. Undaunted by fear, she audaciously wrote, "Nobody in this section of the country believes the old thread-bare lies that Negro men rape white women. If Southern white men are not careful they will over-reach themselves and public sentiment will have a reaction; a conclusion will be reached which will be very damaging to the moral reputation of their women" (*Free Speech*).

Terrorizing statements poured forth from the local papers. The *Memphis Scimitar* credited the editorial to J.L. Fleming and responded that "unless the Negroes promptly applied the remedy it would be the duty of whites to tie the author to a stake, brand him on the forehead and perform a surgical operation on him with a pair of shears.'' The *Memphis Commercial* stated, ''There are some things the Southern white man will not tolerate, and the obscene intimations of the foregoing have brought the writer to outermost limit of public patience'' Later that evening, a group of leading white citizens convened a meeting at the Merchants Exchange and voted to send a committee to warn the proprietors of the *Free Speech* that never again were they to print such sentiments or they would ''suffer the consequences'' (*Nashville American*). Neither Wells Barnett nor Fleming were there to receive the delegation's warning. The *Free Speech* presses and offices were destroyed on May 27, 1892, and Wells Barnett was warned not to return to Memphis.

Fiery Journalist Exiled from the South

The ''lynching at the curve'' and her forceful pen denouncing the atrocity perpetrated by Memphis whites brought Wells Barnett national and international attention. Exiled from the South, she persevered in her struggle against racial injustice and the lynching of blacks as a columnist for the *New York Age*, a paper owned and edited by T. Thomas Fortune and Jerome B. Patterson. She exchanged the circulation list of the *Free Speech* for a one-fourth interest in the paper and wrote a series on lynching. On June 7, 1892, the *New York Age* published a full seven-column page giving a detailed analysis of lynching and refuting the myth that the white men in Memphis intended to shield white women against rape. Ten thousand copies were printed and distributed throughout the country. One thousand copies were sold in the streets of Memphis. This report became the foundation for two booklets: *Southern Horrors*, published in 1892, and *A Red Record: Tabulated Statistics and Alleged Causes of Lynching in the United States, 1892, 1893, and 1894*, published in 1895. *A Red Record* was more than a statistical tabulation of lynching in America. It gave the history of black and other lynchings since 1863. This work later appeared in London under the title, *United States Atrocities*.

Wells Barnett Begins the Lecture Circuit

Discontented with narrating the story in the black press, Wells Barnett, with the assistance of Fortune, began lecturing throughout the Northeast. This lecture circuit brought her international attention, and in 1893 she was invited by Catherine Impey, the British editor of the *Anti-Caste*, to speak in England. Wells Barnett departed the United States on April 5, 1893. Arriving nine days later, she lectured throughout England, Scotland, and Wales, with the tour ending in May 1893. Wells Barnett's lectures were praised as clear, enlightening, and powerful, and they provided the British an opportunity to learn of the black American's opposition to lynching. The *Manchester Guardian* said of Wells Barnett, ''Her quiet, refined manner, her intelligence and earnestness, her avoidance of all oratorical tricks, and her dependence upon the simple eloquence of facts makes her a powerful and convincing advocate.''

Founding of Black Women's Clubs Spurred

While abroad, Wells Barnett told the English about America's inhumanity to the black American and learned of the enterprising endeavors of the women of England through their civic groups. Upon her return home she strongly advised her sisters to become more involved in the matters of their communities, cities, and the nation, through organized civic groups. Wells Barnett's urgings were taken to heart. According to Gerder Lerner, on the eve of Wells Barnett's depature for England, she spoke at a fund-raising rally that a group of prominent New York women organized in her support. This meeting had a profound effect on the black women's club movement:

> This 1892 meeting, which brought together Mrs. Josephine St. Pierre Ruffin of Boston, Victoria Earle Matthews of New York and Dr. Susan McKinney of Brooklyn, inspired the formation of the first two black women's clubs. The New York and Brooklyn women formed the Women's Loyal Union and somewhat later, Mrs. St. Pierre Ruffin organized the Woman's Era Club of Boston (Lerner, 161).

Josephine Pierre Ruffin in 1895 had actively promoted a national organization, the First National Conference of Colored Women. In that same year, the National Federation of Afro-American Women was founded with Mary Margaret Washington as president. Thus, the local club movement as well as the national efforts promoted the views of Wells Barnett and her contemporaries who saw a need for women to become involved in local and national issues.

Wells Barnett's concern for black Americans was not limited to the lynching issue. In 1893 she focused her attention on the exclusion of blacks from the World's Columbian Exposition in Chicago. Working with the ''sage of Anacostia,'' Frederick Douglass, Ferdinand Lee Barnett of Chicago, and I. Garland Penn, Wells Barnett wrote an eighty-one page pamphlet entitled *The Reason Why the Colored American is Not in the World's Columbian Exposition—The Afro-American's Contribution to Columbian Literature*.

Wells Barnett moved to Chicago in 1893 and began working for the *Chicago Conservator*, the first black American paper in the city, founded by Barnett. She continued her interest in women's clubs and organized Chicago's first civic club for black women, which was later named in her honor.

In February 1894 Wells Barnett returned to England. During her six-month stay, a Chicago daily paper, the *Inter-Ocean*, edited by William Penn Nixon, published her articles in a column entitled ''Ida B. Wells Abroad.'' While there, she appeared before more than one hundred churches, clubs, and gatherings where she apprised her audiences of the increasing occurrences and savageness of lynchings in the South, of the remissness of regional authorities, and she demanded that due process of the law replace riotous crowd ferocity. Wells Barnett requested and obtained the pledge that the English would sanction the fundamental right to a fair trial for southern blacks accused of a crime.

Wells Barnett's lectures were well received by the press, and she granted special interviews to the *Daily Chronicle*, The *Christian World*, the Westminster *Gazette*, the London *Sun*, and the *Labor Leader*. She also was the impetus behind Britons' forming an antilynching committee for the purpose of investigating and publicizing the persecution of blacks in America's southland.

"Crusader for Justice" Continues the Struggle

The "crusader for justice" returned from her successful European tour in July 1894. Upon her return, Wells Barnett lectured throughout the northern and western states and organized antilynching committees, where possible, until spring 1895.

On June 27, 1895, Wells Barnett married Ferdinand L. Barnett, a black attorney and editor and founder of the *Chicago Conservator*. Barnett shared his wife's interests and together they championed the black cause for equal rights. They had four children: Charles Aked, born in 1896; Herman Kohlsaat, born in 1897; Ida B. Wells, born in 1901; and Alfreda M., born in 1904.

Domesticity did not detract Ida Wells Barnett from her crusade. She continued to write articles and took an interest in local and national affairs. In 1898 she was a member of a delegation that called on President William McKinley to seek redress in the case of a black postmaster lynched in South Carolina. She was also active in the Afro-American Council and served as secretary until 1902.

After the birth of her second child, Wells Barnett traveled less and concentrated her activities in Chicago. In 1893 she had organized a women's club in Chicago which adopted the name "Ida B. Wells Club." Later, as president of the club, she initiated the establishment of a kindergarten for the black community at the Bethel African Methodist Episcopal Church. In 1900, when Robert W. Patterson, editor of the *Chicago Tribune*, published a series of articles advocating a segregated school system in Chicago, Wells Barnett sought the assistance of her friend Jane Addams, the famous Chicago social worker. Addams agreed to help and called a meeting of the city's influential citizens. Wells Barnett successfully presented her case against segregated education, and those in attendance formed a seven-member committee chaired by Addams. After the committee met with Patterson and made known their sentiments, the articles ceased.

In 1909 Wells Barnett was one of two black women—Mary Church Terrell was the other—who signed the "Call" for a conference on the Negro, which came in response to the three days of racial violence in Springfield, Illinois, in August 1908. On May 31, 1909, the conference convened in New York City and led to the formation of the National Association for the Advancement of Colored People (NAACP). Wells Barnett was an active participant in the deliberations of the conference, delivering one of the principal speeches during the public sessions. At the close of the conference, Wells Barnett was placed on the NAACP's executive committee and was a strong advocate of the NAACP's having its own publication to express the views of the organization. Thus, *Crisis* was founded in 1910.

An ideological opponent of the accommodationist tenets espoused by Booker T. Washington and a proponent of the protest views expressed by W. E. B. Du Bois, Wells Barnett was a strong ally of the Du Bois faction. Yet, while her philosophical views on economic accumulation and self-help had much in common with Washington's ideology, there was a major difference: for Wells Barnett, economic power was a weapon to be used to force changes in white behavior. After the NAACP's formation, she distanced herself from the organization. She belittled the organization's handling of the lawsuit in Chicago to ban the movie, "Birth of a Nation," in 1915, and a number of times she disagreed with the NAACP's field representatives while investigating lynchings and mob violence in East Saint Louis, Illinois, and in Elaine and Helena, Arkansas, on which she reported.

Wells Barnett continued to fight injustice and discrimination in Chicago and throughout the United States. The Springfield riots had motivated her with students in her Sunday School class at Grace Presbyterian Church, to establish an organization called the Negro Fellowship League. Just before the NAACP was chartered in May 1910, the Negro Fellowship League established a settlement house in Chicago. Supported by contributions from Victor F. Lawson, owner and editor of the *Daily News*, the house provided low-cost lodging for men without homes, a reading room, a social center, and an employment service. When a branch of the Young Men's Christian Association for Negroes opened in 1913, Lawson ceased funding the Fellowship League. The same year Judge Harry Olson of the municipal court appointed Wells Barnett adult probation officer. She worked out of the Fellowship League's social center and contributed her monthly salary of $150 to the center's budget. Wells Barnett worked as a probation officer until 1916.

Wells Barnett believed in the power of the ballot box and encouraged black men to register and exercise their right to vote. She worked in the women's suffrage movement and on January 30, 1913, founded the Alpha Suffrage Club of Chicago, the first black suffrage organization. Wells Barnett marched in suffrage parades and led her club members in the parade of June 16, when suffragists marched to the Republication National Convention and demanded a plank to give women the right to vote.

In December 1920 Wells Barnett was hospitalized and underwent surgery. The settlement house and center of the Negro Fellowship League continued to experience difficulty and closed the same year. After her recovery, a year later, Wells Barnett again became active in the civic and political affairs of Chicago and was one of the founders of the Cook County League of Women's Clubs. When the National Association of Colored Women met in Chicago in 1924,

Wells Barnett ran for president of the organization. She was defeated by Mary McLeod Bethune. Although the black women's club movement was a direct outgrowth of her campaign, Wells Barnett was never elected to a major office in the national club organization.

Six years later, in 1930, Wells Barnett entered Chicago's political arena as an independent candidate for state senator. Running against Warren B. Douglas and Adelbert H. Roberts, she was defeated handily.

On March 21, 1931, Wells Barnett became ill and was rushed to Daily Hospital on Monday, March 23, suffering from uremic poisoning. Two days later, on March 25, at the age of sixty-nine, the ever-vocal "crusader for justice" died. She was buried in Chicago's Oakwood Cemetery.

As a black American leader of the nineteenth and twentieth century, the life of Wells Barnett has been memorialized. In 1941 the Chicago Housing Authority opened the Ida B. Wells Housing Project, and in 1950 the City of Chicago named her one of twenty-five outstanding women in the city's history. On July 16, 1987, the 125th anniversary year of her birth and ninety-five years since she had been forced from the "Bluff City," the Memphis Community Relations Commission, through the Tennessee Historical Commission, dedicated a historical marker at the former site of the *Free Speech* newspaper offices:

> Ida B. Wells crusaded against lynchings in Memphis and the South. In 1892 while editor of the Memphis Free Speech, located in this vicinity, she wrote of the lynching of three Black businessmen. As a result, her newspaper office was destroyed and her life threatened. After moving to New York, she began an international speaking tour where she influenced the establishment of the British Anti-Lynching Society. She co-founded the NAACP and organized the first Black women's political organization. A Chicago housing project is named in her honor.

For the 1990 Black History Month observance, the United States Postal Service issued a stamp honoring this civil rights activist. Also, in 1990, the first full-length biography of Wells Barnett, *Ida B. Wells Barnett*, by Mildred Thompson, was published in the sixteen-volume series entitled *Black Women in the United States History: From Colonial Times to the Present.*

References

Cartwright, Joseph H. *The Triumph of Jim Crow: Tennessee Race Relations in the 1880s.* Knoxville: University of Tennessee Press, 1976.

Church, Annette E. and Roberta Church. *The Robert R. Churches of Memphis.* Ann Arbor, Michigan: Edwards Brothers, 1974.

Church, Roberta and Ronald Walter. *Nineteenth Century Memphis Families of Color, 1850-1900.* Memphis: Murdock Printing Co., 1987.

Duster, Alfreda M., ed. *Crusader for Justice, the Autobiography of Ida B. Wells.* Chicago: University of Chicago Press, 1970.

Flexner, Eleanor. "Ida B. Wells-Barnett." *Notable American Women 1607-1950.* Vol. 3. Cambridge: Harvard University Press, 1971.

Free Speech, 21 May 1892.

Holt, Thomas C. "The Lonely Warrior: Ida B. Wells Barnett and the Struggle for Black Leadership." *Black Leaders of the Twentieth Century.* Edited by John Hope Franklin and August Meier. Urbana: University of Illinois Press, 1982. Photograph, p. 38.

Lerner, Gerda. "Early Community Work of Black Club Women." *Journal of Negro History* 59 (April 1954): 158-67.

Manchester Guardian, 8 May 1893.

Memphis Commercial, 25 May 1892.

Memphis Daily Appeal, 25 December 1884.

Memphis Scimitar, 25 May 1892.

Nashville American, 26 May 1892.

Neverdon-Morton, Cynthia. *Afro-American Women of the South and the Advancement of Race, 1895-1925.* Knoxville: University of Tennessee Press, 1989.

Pacyga, Dominic A. and Ellen Skerrett. *Chicago: City of Neighborhood Histories & Tours.* Chicago: Loyola University Press, 1986.

Sterling, Dorothy. *Black Foremothers: Three Lives.* Old Westbury, N.Y.: Feminist Press, 1979.

Thompson, Mildred. *Ida B. Wells-Barnett: An Exploratory Story of an American Black Woman, 1893-1930.* Vol.16 *Black Women in United States History.* Edited by Darlene Clark-Hine. Brooklyn: Carlson Publishing Co., 1990. The biography was originally written as a doctoral dissertation at George Washington University in 1979. Includes photographs.

Tucker, David M. *Black Pastors and Leaders: The Memphis Clergy 1819-1972.* Memphis: Memphis State University, 1975.

———. "Miss Ida B. Wells and Memphis Lynching." *Phylon* 32 (Summer 1971):

Wilson, Charles R. and William Ferris. *Encyclopedia of Southern Culture.* Chapel Hill: University of North Carolina Press, 1989.

Collections

Papers of Ida Bell Wells Barnett are housed in the Chicago Historical Society, the Regenstein Library of the University of Chicago, Moorland-Spingarn Research Center at Howard University in Washigton, D.C., Newberry Library, Schomburg Center for Research on Black Culture in New York City, and the Vivian G. Harsh Collection of the Carter G. Woodson Library in Chicago. Photographs of Wells Barnett are included in these collections.

Linda T. Wynn

Dorothy West

(1907-)

Writer, editor, journalist

Dorothy West is a novelist, short story writer, editor, and journalist who began her literary career in the 1920s during the Harlem Renaissance. She was born June 2, 1907, in Boston, Massachusetts, the only child of Rachel Pease Benson and Isaac Christopher West. Her mother had moved from her native home of Camden, South Carolina, to Massachusetts as a teenager. Years later she met and married the older Isaac West, a former slave from Virginia who lived first in Springfield, Massachusetts, where he opened an ice cream parlor and food store, then in Boston, where he owned a wholesale fruit company and became known as the "Black Banana King" of Boston (Ferguson, 187-88).

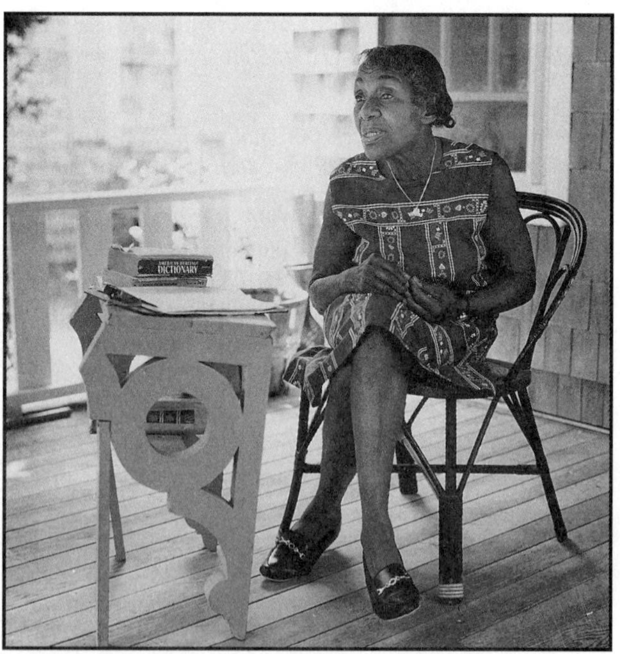

Dorothy West

West received her formal education in Boston. At the age of two she began lessons under the tutelage of Bessie Trotter, sister of *Boston Guardian* editor, Monroe Nathan Trotter, and then under Grace Turner. West entered the Farragut School in Boston when she was four, able to do second-grade-level work because of the excellent tutoring she had received. The rest of her elementary education was at the Martin School in the Mission Hill District of Boston. Upon graduating from Girl's Latin High School in 1923, West attended Boston University and later the Columbia University School of Journalism.

West began writing short stories at age seven. Her first short story, "Promise and Fulfillment," was published in *The Boston Post*. Subsequently she became a regular contributor to this paper which awarded her several literary prizes for her well-written stories. Just after high school graduation, not yet eighteen, West and her cousin, poet Helen Johnson, received invitations to attend *Opportunity* magazine's annual awards dinner in New York. The two young ladies attended the dinner and settled in at the Harlem YWCA. West later moved into the apartment that was vacated by Zora Neale Hurston.

During her stay in New York, West developed her writing skills and became one of the Harlem Renaissance writers and artists that included Langston Hughes, Zora Neale Hurston, Bruce Nugent, Wallace Thurman, and Aaron Douglas. Of her association with these now well-known figures, West said:

> I went to the Harlem Renaissance and never said a word. I was young and a girl so they never asked me to say anything. I didn't know I had anything to say. I was just a little girl from Boston, a place of dull people with funny accents (Washington, 150).

In 1926 West won a second-place short story prize from *Opportunity* magazine for her short story "The Typewriter." (West shared the award with Zora Neale Hurston.) In West's biographical statement in that issue, she stated, "To be conventional, my favorite author is Dostoevsky, my favorite pastime, the play" ("Our Authors," 189). "The Typewriter" is about a nonachieving, unfulfilled black man who lives out his dream to be someone important through a series of fantasy letters he dictates to his daughter who is practicing to increase her typing speed. Each evening he looks forward to this escape from his dull world, until the day he gets home from work and learns that his daughter has returned the rented typewriter because she has gotten a job as a stenographer and no longer needs it. His world is shattered, and he dies.

Other short stories written by West include "Hannah Byde" (*Messenger* 8, July 1926: 197-99), "An Unimportant Man" (*Saturday Evening Quill* 1, June 1928: 21-23), "Prologue to a Life" (*Saturday Evening Quill* 2, April 1929: 5-10), "The Black Dress" (*Opportunity* 12, May 1934: and "Mammy" (*Opportunity* 18, October 1940: 298-302). Dostoevskian elements are evident in some of these stories which, according to Margaret Perry, tend "to emphasize confinement, in moral, psychological, emotional, and physical aspects, [and] the idea of salvation through suffering" (Perry, 132). The characters in West's stories are unfulfilled, frustrated people who feel trapped by their environment, by racism, and by sexism.

Challenge and *New Challenge* Literary Magazines Founded

In 1927, West had a bit part in the original stage production of *Porgy* and went on a three-month tour of the play in London. During the 1930s, she traveled to the Soviet Union with a group of twenty-two black Americans to film *Black and White*, a project that was never completed. Despite the failure of this project, West remained in Russia for about a year. Upon returning to New York West founded *Challenge* magazine in 1934, and then *New Challenge* magazine in 1937. These two literary journals sought to provide an avenue for the publication of high-quality writing by some of the Harlem Renaissance writers as well as younger writers who were just beginning their careers. Although West had high hopes for her magazines, they were both short-lived because many of the entries were of poor quality and had to be rejected; the magazines had financial difficulties; and by the time the one and only issue of *New Challenge* was printed, West's editorial policy had shifted to reflect a proletarian ideology, with Richard Wright as one of the associate editors.

After the demise of the two magazines, West worked as a welfare investigator in Harlem for eighteen months, then joined the Federal Writers Project of the Works Progress Administration where she remained until the project ended in the 1940s. She continued to write and became a regular contributor of short stories to the *New York Daily News* from 1940 to 1960. In 1945, she left New York permanently and moved to Martha's Vineyard where she continues to reside.

In 1948 West's novel *The Living is Easy* was published. It is a semi-autobiographical novel in which the main characters, Cleo, Bart, and Judy Judson, are patterned after Rachel, Isaac, and Dorothy West, respectively. Like Rachel West, the beautiful, light-skinned Cleo Judson is a domineering woman who wishes her dark-skinned daughter, Judy, were more like her in both appearance and personality. Cleo gathers her sisters and their children in hers and Bart's large home, subsequently breaking up their marriage. She is also cold and scornful to her husband, Bart, who is the main financial support of the household. The novel satirizes the black Boston elites who were disdainful of "ordinary" black people. Racism, sexism, and class-consciousness are all evident themes in West's only published novel, which received mixed reviews when it first appeared. Since the reprint of the novel by Feminist Press in 1982, critics have tended to look at the novel in feminist terms, focusing on the role and importance of the mother in the household, the mother-daughter relationship, and the complexities of the character of Cleo. Robert Bone calls the work "a diamond in the rough . . . bitingly ironic," and of "a primarily Renaissance consciousness" (187, 190).

While she remains a resident of Martha's Vineyard, West continues to write, contributing a weekly column to the *Martha's Vineyard Gazette*, lecturing periodically, and granting interviews on occasion.

References

Bone, Robert. *The Negro Novel in America*. New Haven: Yale University Press, 1965.

Daniel, Walter C. "*Challenge* Magazine: An Experiment That Failed." *CLA* Journal 26 (June 1976): 494-503.

Ferguson, Sally Ann H. "Dorothy West." *Dictionary of Literary Biography: Afro-American Writers, 1940-1955*. Vol. 76. Ed. Trudier Harris. Detroit: Gale Research, 1988.

Johnson, Abby Arthur, and Ronald Maberry Johnson. *Propaganda and Aesthetics: The Literary Politics of Afro-American Magazines in the Twentieth Century*. Amherst: University of Massachusetts Press, 1979.

"Our Authors and What They Say Themselves." *Opportunity* 4 (July 1926): 189.

Perry, Margaret. *Silence to the Drums: A Survey of the Literature of the Harlem Renaissance*. Westport, Conn: Greenwood Press, 1976.

Rampersad, Arnold. *The Life of Langston Hughes*. Vol. 1. "I, Too, Sing America: 1902-1941." New York: Oxford University Press, 1986.

Schraufnagel, Noel. *From Apology to Protest: The Black American Novel*. Deland, Fla.: Everett/Edwards, 1973.

Washington, Mary Helen. "I Sign My Mother's Name: Alice Walker, Dorothy West, Paule Marshall." In *Mothering the Mind: Twelve Studies of Writers and Their Silent Partners*. Ed. Ruth Perry and Martine Watson Brownley. New York: Holmes and Meier, 1984.

———. *Invented Lives: Narratives of Black Women 1860-1960*. Garden City, N.Y.: Doubleday, 1987.

West, Dorothy. "Elephant's Dance: A Memoir of Wallace Thurman." *Black World* 20 (November 1970): 77-85.

———. *The Living is Easy*. Boston: Houghton Mifflin, 1948. Reprinted, New York: arno Press, 1969. Reprinted, Old Westbury, New York: Feminist Press, 1982.

———. "The Richer, the Poorer." In *The Best Short Stories by Negro Writers*. Ed. Langston Hughes. Boston: Little, Brown, 1967.

———. "The Typewriter," *Opportunity* 4 (July 1926): 220-222.

Collections

The papers of Dorothy West are housed in the Mugar Memorial Library, Boston University, and the James Weldon Johnson Memorial Collection at Yale University. Photographs of West are with her papers at Boston University Library, in Vol. 1 of Arnold Rampersad's *The Life of Langston Hughes*, in Sally Ann Ferguson's article on West in *Dictionary of Literary Biography*, and in Mary Helen Washington's article "I Sign My Mother's Name," *Mothering the Mind*.

Elwanda D. Ingram

Doris L. Wethers

(1927-)

Pediatrician

Doris L. Wethers, eminent pediatrician and leader in the fight to combat sickle-cell anemia, was born on December 14, 1927, in Passaic, New Jersey, to William Wethers and Vivian (Wilkerson) Wethers. Wethers is the youngest of two daughters. Her sister, Agnes Wethers Timpson, is married to Richard Timpson, a family physician. They have six children and reside in Connecticut. Her mother was born in Washington, D.C, and attended Miner's Normal School. Her father, who was born in Charleston, South Carolina, graduated from Howard University Medical School, and was the first physician in the family. After her parents' marriage and the birth of her sister, the family moved to Passaic, New Jersey. Her father practiced medicine there until his World War I reservist status made him eligible for recall in World War II. He was discharged with the rank of major and relocated to New York City, where he practiced medicine. He was one of the founding physicians of the HIP Upper Manhattan Group in Harlem, a member group in the Health Insurance Plan. He was a significantly motivating factor in Doris Wethers's decision to become a physician and subsequent decisions to accept appointments in the program.

Wethers attended public schools in New York City and in 1948 graduated from Queens College in Flushing, New York, magna cum laude. She was accepted to Yale University School of Medicine and graduated in 1952. After completing a rotating internship at General Hospital in Washington, D.C., in 1953, Wethers immediately began a straight internship in pediatrics at Bellevue Hospital in New York City, which she completed in 1954. Wethers took her residency in pediatrics at Kings County Hospital in Brooklyn, New York, from 1954 to 1955 and was appointed chief resident in pediatrics from 1955 to 1956. During that time she was also an assistant instructor in pediatrics at the College of Medicine, State University of New York.

After completing her residency in 1956, Wethers practiced pediatrics in an office adjacent to her father's for ten years. During those years she developed her interest in sickle-cell disease in children and expanded her involvement in children's health problems in general.

In 1961 Doris Wethers accepted the position of medical director for Speedwell Services for Children (Foster Care and Adoptions), a post she occupied until 1973. In 1965 while at Speedwell, she accepted the post of chief pediatrician for the Washington Heights Medical Group, where she remained until 1982.

In 1965 Wethers started a sickle-cell program at the Arthur B. Logan Memorial Hospital (formerly Knickerbocker Hospital) in New York City. She continued her sickle-cell work there and also began a similar program at Sydenham Hospital. She directed the departments of pediatrics at both hospitals. When both hospitals closed in 1974, Wethers became director of the department of pediatrics at Saint Luke's Hospital in New York City and continued the sickle-cell program there, where it has been a tremendous success.

Wethers Heads Sickle-Cell Program and Research

Wethers has been at Saint Luke's for approximately thirty-two years. She started as an assistant in the pediatrics clinic in 1958 and she became the first black American attending physician accepted by the hospital. She was director of pediatrics from 1974 to 1979, when Saint Luke's Hospital merged with Roosevelt Hospital. Wethers then resigned her directorship to devote more time to sickle-cell concerns and assume directorship of the Comprehensive Sickle-Cell Program at Saint Luke's Hospital and has retained that position until the present time. She also directs pediatrics at Manhattan HIP and continues to be actively involved in general pediatric care.

In 1979 Wethers received a grant for and has since been involved in a cooperative study of sickle-cell anemia focusing on the natural history and sickle-cell anemia disease in children and adolescents. She has been particularly interested in the functioning of the spleen, growth and development of the child, and infection in the blood and bones. The cooperative study as a whole basically looks at the incidence and spectrum of complications in sickle-cell diseases and the causes of death and disability.

In discussing her many responsibilities, Wethers perceives herself as "wearing two hats in my pediatric practice. First, focusing on sickle-cell care for ill patients but also preventive total care of infants and children, regular immunizations, watching their growth and development, being sure that they eat adequately, and guarding against various complications'' (Interview with Doris L. Wethers, 19 April 1990).

When asked whether she has seen many changes in sickle-cell disease and its treatment, Wethers indicated that:

> Sickle cell disease has changed very little in the past thirty years. The manifestations are about the same, for example, varying degrees of anemia, pain, infections and stroke. The treatment has varied little. We treat the potentially infected patient with broad spectrum antibiotics. Transfusions are indicated for severe anemia problems and gallstones. The types of antibiotics have changed with newer antibiotics. Some preventive aspects have changed. If children are given prophylactic penicillin shortly after birth, infectious complications are reduced—that's been introduced broadly over the last few years. Also there has been standardization in the use of transfusion for stroke patients. Newer forms of vaccines help prevent infections although they are not the total answer and they can only be used with certain aged children, and are not completely effective. There are some new medications but further study must be conducted to test their toxicity. Cures have been reported with bone marrow transplantation. This procedure has a thirty percent mortality, whereas the mortality statistics for the disease is nowhere near that. With good care the mortality rate for sickle-cell disease is quite low. However, if there are certain coexisting diseases, for example, leukemia, bone marrow transplantation may be appropriate. More positive findings should be reported in the near future (Interview with Doris L. Wethers, 19 April 1990).

Wethers works closely with groups of mothers of sickle-cell patients in conjunction with social workers at HIP and Saint Luke's/Roosevelt. The mothers of newborns in particular need the pediatrician's and the social worker's expertise in the disease and behavioral responses to the situation, respectively. There is also an adolescent support program that focuses on diet, pain control, and how to deal with feelings of being different.

Wethers finds it very rewarding and challenging working with students from high school through premedical courses to medical school. Each summer premedical students have participated in the sickle-cell program, and during the summer of 1990 she had several premedical students who represented various racial groups. Saint Luke's/Roosevelt is an affiliate of the Columbia University School of Medicine and in 1990, for the first time, she had medical students who chose a month in the summer sickle-cell program as a curriculum elective.

Wethers has authored or coauthored more than forty published articles and reports, as well as books related to the care and management and support of sickle-cell patients and their families. The articles relate to, for example, research and analyses of specific aspects of the disease. She has written an encyclopedia that provides information on the health of children for the lay public; she has published reports on symposia and position papers on sickle-cell disease, as well as those that take an advocacy position.

Wethers has served on numerous committees, organizations, and planning boards. Currently, she is a member of the New York State Governor's Advisory Committee for Black Affairs; the Committee on Minorities of the New York County Medical Society; the executive council of the New York City chapter of the American Academy of Pediatrics; board of the Children's Aid Society; editorial board of *Viewpoints* a publication of the National Association for Sickle-Cell Disease; and chairperson of the New York State Sickle Cell Advisory Committee. Wethers is also a member of the American Pediatric Society and a fellow of the American Academy of Pediatrics. She has been a consultant to the Premedical Research and Education Program, working with promising minority high school and college students who are aspiring physicians. Wethers is a founder of the Susan Smith McKinney-Steward Medical Society, comprised of black American women physicians who serve as role models for the very student population mentioned above.

Among her many honors, Wethers has received the Southern Christian Leadership Conference Award for Sickle-Cell Anemia (1972), Public Health Association of New York Award for Merit (1977), Council of Churches City of New York Distinguished Service Award (1978), and the Charles Drew Memorial Award, Charles Drew Premedical Society, Columbia University (1984).

Wethers shares her work between administration, research, and clinical practice. She describes her medical career as extremely satisfying: ''I am doing what I like best, clinical medicine in pediatrics, plus working with children, with just enough administration to add spice and enough research to add challenge and heighten intellectual interest'' (Interview with Doris L. Wethers, 19 April 1990).

Doris L. Wethers has been married to Garvell Booker, a dentist, since 1953. They have three sons—Garvell Booker IV, Clifford Wethers Booker, and David Boyd Booker.

References

Wethers, Doris L. Interview with author, 19 April 1990.

Juanita R. Howard

Laura Frances Wheatley

(18?-19?)

Educator, social and political activist, patron of the arts, writer, entrepreneur

Laura Frances Dickerson Wheatley was a multi-faceted community leader whose noted accomplishments include co-founding the Neighborhood Improvement League. Established in 1915, the league was comprised of black and white citizens who worked together to effect change in Baltimore neighborhoods.

Wheatley was born in Cincinnati, Ohio (no birth date available), the daughter of Henry Dickerson and Mary Spalding Dickerson. On June 21, 1906, she married Edward J. Wheatley, a physician who had a private practice in Baltimore, Maryland. Wheatley received her early education at Central High and Normal School in Louisville, Kentucky, the A.B. degree from Morgan College in 1917, and the M.A. from New York University in 1940. Her graduate study was done at Cook County Normal School in Chicago (dates unknown), the University of Maryland in 1928, and Howard University in 1939. Wheatley was a teacher in the Louisville public schools (1900-1905) and in Baltimore where she also served as chairperson of the department of English of Douglas High School.

Jean Fisher Turpin, an educator, organist, and civic and church worker, remembers Wheatley as a very active person who was devoted to civic responsibilities. Turpin recalls that Wheatley was a very principled person, very outspoken, but polite and thoughtful. She was most concerned about social problems in Baltimore. Wheatley was also involved in many cultural activities in the city: She was instrumental in presenting many lectures and concerts at Bethel African Methodist Episcopal Church on Druid Hill Avenue. The Wheatleys lived at 1230 Druid Hill Avenue which was very near Bethel, where they were faithful and devoted members, and near Edward Wheatley's office on Druid Hill.) *Who's Who in Colored America* (1950) corroborates Turpin's reminiscences. The biography describes Wheatley as "an impresario who presented numerous artists to Baltimore audiences and who sponsored art exhibits displaying Negro art works" (546).

Wheatley's community interest is evident in her involvement in several civic, political, and social organizations.

> She was a volunteer civic worker for better schools for Colored Children from 1928-50. She was directly responsible for getting the White Parent-Teachers Association and the Colored Parent Teachers Association to attend a Teachers Training School. In 1923, she was unanimously elected first president of the Baltimore Federation of Colored Parent Teacher Clubs, which is one of the largest organizations in Baltimore with a membership of over 10,000 (*Who's Who in Colored America*, 455).

Wheatley was also a member of the Women's Auxiliary to the Monumental Medical Association, the Alpha Wives, DuBois Circle, Provident Hospital Guild, YWCA, Home Friendly Society, and Fortnightly Whist Club.

Social and Economic Uplift of the Community Promoted

As a member of the NAACP, and at one time the executive secretary, Wheatley worked diligently in the Baltimore chapter. The October 1, 1920, issue of the *Afro-American Ledger* asserts:

> A huge mass meeting to be held at Trinity Baptist Church next Sunday afternoon at 4 o'clock under the auspices of the local branch of the National Association for the Advancement of Colored People will launch one of the biggest membership campaigns ever staged in the city. The Association plans to secure ten thousand new members. . . .
>
> Mrs. Wheatley, chairman at the local end, [has] been working night and day . . . to perfect their plans for the ten day campaign.

Another example of Wheatley's community involvement was cited in the March 17, 1915, issue of the *Afro-American Ledger*:

> Probably no institution in this city is doing more at the present time for civic betterment than the Neighborhood Improvement League of the 1200 block of Druid Hill Avenue and environs. The League was organized about a year ago by Mrs. E. J. Wheatley [Laura Frances] and Miss Edythe Cooper who have been active ever since. While the working membership is composed entirely of ladies, an Advisory Committee, composed of men, formed an important part of the activities of the League. The fact that the white residents take an active interest in the work of the League makes it unique among organizations of its kind. The officers of the League are Mrs. Laura Wheatley, president. . . . The officers of the Advisory Committee [include] . . . Dr. E. J. Wheatley.

This organization was not only unique because of its racially integrated membership but because of the various social improvements that the league effected. The same issue of the *Afro-American Ledger* lists the various subcommittees and the results of their efforts. There were the Committee on Sanitation and Public Improvement, which had Druid Hill Avenue paved and had frosted lamps placed in front of Bethel AME church and Trinity Baptist Church; the Aesthetic Committee, which urged residents to "use paint a little more freely and to repair broken shutters"; and the Committee on Social Order, "which had eight boys returned to school and which looked after their regular attendance." The Committee on Social Order also sought a desirable tenant in a building whose occupants were a menace to the neighborhood. The Committee on Business Interests in the Community reported five new businesses established "by young men of the race and . . . urged members to patronize them." The Committee on the Care of Children was most effective in that five motherless children were returned to school, "glasses procured for one child, hospital treatment for another child; infants' food was distributed to needy mothers, children were placed from a poorly conditioned nursery into a better one." The accomplishments of the neighborhood Improvement League were astounding.

Wheatley's social concerns did not stop in Baltimore. She was elected to give President Herbert Hoover an appraisal of the conditions that prevailed in Haiti; this appraisal resulted in actions being taken to improve the quality of life there.

In addition to Wheatley's political and social activities, she was also culturally active. She was known for her literary abilities and her talents were recognized in several forums. She won three national essay contests: The Timothy Todd Contest, the Boston Brown Book Contest in 1905, and the *Opportunity* Magazine Essay Contest in 1925. There is no mention of what prize she received in the Timothy Todd Contest; however, the Boston Brown Book Company awarded her a trip to Europe, but Wheatley opted for the cash equivalent. In July 1931, however, she did go on a study tour to England, Norway, Sweden, Denmark, Finland, Russia, Poland, Germany, Austria, Italy, Switzerland, France, and Belgium. The prize from *Opportunity* magazine was small. The June 1925 issue announced the "Third prize of $10.00 to THE NEGRO POET by Laura D. Wheatley of Baltimore, Md." (142). Unfortunately, neither this issue nor subsequent ones printed the essay "The Negro Poet" written by Wheatley. The first prize essay winner was E. Franklin Frazier, who became an eminent sociologist, and second prize went to Sterling Brown, who became a renowned poet and professor at Howard University. Wheatley was certainly in good literary company: Langston Hughes, Zora Neale Hurston, and Countee Cullen were winners in other categories.

Wheatley was also the author of the "Universal Obligatory Military Training and Service" written in 1917 for the National Defense League, and *Manila, Phillipine Islands* written in 1905. Since this is the same year that she won the Boston Brown Book Contest, it is guessed that the prize of a free trip to Europe was for this book.

In spite of her many activities, Wheatley still found time to be a realtor. She was also active in politics. While the 1930-32 edition of *Who's Who in Colored America* lists her as a Republican, the 1950 edition lists her as a Democrat.

Wheatley lived a full, well-rounded life and was very devoted to helping humanity. It is unfortunate that records documenting her life are scant, and that a fuller picture of this diligent civic worker is not unavailable.

References

Afro-American Ledger, 25 March 1915; 1 October 1920.

Neverdon-Marton, Cynthia. *Afro-American Women of the Soviet* and the Advancement of the Race, 1895-1925. Knoxville: University of Tennessee Press, 1989. 87-89, 207.

Opportunity 3 (June 1925): 186. Includes photograph.

Turpin, Jean Fisher. Interview with author, 6 February 1990.

Who's Who in Colored America. Yonkers-on-Hudson, N.Y.: Christian E. Burckel, 1930-32, 1938-40, 1950. Photograph, 1938-40 ed., p. 555.

Margaret Ann Reid

Phillis Wheatley

(c. 1753-1784)

Poet

Phillis Wheatley, who after her marriage usually signed her name Phillis Peters, was America's first black to publish a book, a collection of poems. After Anne Bradstreet, she was America's second woman to publish a book of poems, her 1773 *Poems on Various Subjects Religious and Moral*.

The commentary that surrounds Wheatley's life and work describes two Wheatleys: a *pseudo*-Wheatley, a person "petted" as a slave (according to Wheatley, an impossible condition for any human being) while as an artist called a derivative imitator of Alexander Pope; and a *real* Wheatley who consciously engaged in an unflagging struggle for freedom and who constructed a poetry that is recreative and original. At the present time, as has been the case for the past two hundred years, the psuedo-Wheatley dominates both biographical sketches and critical commentary. Attendant on these sketches are numerous assertions including that Pope was the major influence on her work, that she read only British poets, that she was honored on her trip to London by the lord mayor of that city, that her poetry reveals almost no presence either of her color or her enslaved state, that she was

Phillis Wheatley

not concerned for the freedom of her black brothers and sisters, that she gained her freedom only after both John Wheatley and Susanna Wheatley died, and even the truly impossible notion that Wheatley was a loyalist, not a patriot, during the American Revolution.

However, other evidence indicates Pope was only one of many poets Wheatley read, including the American poets Mather Byles, and Samuel Cooper. Reports also indicate that at the time Wheatley was in London, Brook Watson had not yet assumed the office of lord mayor, this distinction to come several years later. Additionally the recent recovery of her letters and poems reveals Wheatley's unmistakable concern for the problem of slavery, these works written *after* she achieved emancipation. Before she was freed, however, her poems and her 1773 volume amply reveal that she not only accepted her African origins, she was proud of them. Interpretation of her published work establishes that the central concern of her writing was the quest for freedom. The early September 1773 publication of *Poems* led to her manumission before mid-October of the same year, some four months before the death of her mistress Susanna and at least four years before John Wheatley's death. Finally Wheatley's own poems and letters offer irrefutable testimony that, from her first published poem, the 1767 "On Messrs. Hussey and Coffin," until the year of her death in 1784 when she published "Liberty and Peace," which celebrates the victory of the American Revolution, she remained a constant patriot.

Because in "Phillis's Reply" Wheatley herself identifies Gambia as the land of her birth and because her slender facial features (long forehead, thin lips, well-defined cheek bones, and small nose) remarkably resemble those of the present-day Fulani, a people who occupied the region of the Gambia River during the eighteenth century, it is plausible that Wheatley was born of the Gambian Fulani. Since at the time of her purchase in Boston, on or about July 11, 1761, she was losing her front baby teeth, it is suggested that the year of her birth was 1753. The ship that transported her from Africa was the *Phillis*, and so it is speculated that this name was foisted upon her. Such a name might have served as a life-long reminder of the horrid middle passage that was partial cost of her having been brought from Africa to America.

The only memory of her mother Wheatley cared to recall to her white captors was that of her mother pouring "*out water before the sun at his rising*" (Oddell, 12)? This self-same sun subsequently become the central image of her poetry. On the numerous occasions when the poet employs solar imagery, she infrequently articulates the commonly occurring eighteenth-century pun on sun-Son. Wheatley's sun is more often simply the life-giving sun of nature, echoing her mother's devotion. It is worth pointing out that her mother's practice of this daily ritual suggests hierophantic solar worship (usually practiced by the African aristocracy) and Islam, which had made, by the mid-eighteenth century, some headway in the Gambian region of West Africa. Wheatley's blending of solar imagery, Judaeo-Christian thought and figures, and images from ancient classicism reveal complex multicultural origins, not the least of which derives from her African heritage.

African Heritage Reflected in Elegies

Another manifestation of Wheatley's African heritage is her practice of the funeral elegy. Among the Akan peoples, a group neighboring the Fula, for example, tradition dictated that all girls sang and composed funeral elegies for the deceased. Given this heritage, Wheatley's memories of her African days very likely included performances of dirges sung by young women. As practiced in Africa, however, the oral elegy bears other parallels to Wheatley's. For example, in Africa the singer of the dirge is expected in *her* performance to point out numerous examples of the departed's wisdom; such references are typically drawn by young women lamenting that they have lost a wise counselor. In her elegies on Joseph Sewall and Samuel Cooper, Wheatley carries out these specifications. Of Joseph Sewall, who was for fifty-six years pastor of the famous Old South Church of Boston and whose services the poet attended until his death in 1769, Wheatley wrote: "I, too have cause this mighty loss to mourn, / For he my monitor will not return" (Wheatley, 21). From Sewall's youth, the poet continues, "He sought the paths of piety and truth." While Sewall apparently served as Wheatley's spiritual advisor during her adolescent days, Cooper, who baptized her on August 18, 1771, served as her counselor. In her early 1784 elegy on this latitudinarian minister of Boston's Brattle Street Meeting House, Wheatley, not quite a year before her own death, identifies Cooper as one "drawn by rhetoric's commanding laws," who "Encourag'd oft and oft approv'd [my] lays" (Wheatley, 153). The poet also celebrates Cooper's intellectual gifts in the arresting line, "The Sons of Learning on thy lessons hung."

Such personal acknowledgements as those appearing in Wheatley's elegies on Cooper and Sewall are uncharacteristic of American and English elegies of the time. Also uncharacteristic of the genre was Wheatley's penchant for the dramatic, which appears in many of her elegies. For example, in her elegy to Whitefield, Whitefield speaks five verse couplets. In another elegy, a deceased girl of five utters six lines of advice from her heavenly abode. Other elegies offer suggestions from the departed to the living describing how they may imitate the lives of those who have died and have been received into heaven. As African funeral elegies frequently focus on the living and adopt the form of dramatic testimony, perhaps Wheatley's own flare for the dramatic and concentration on the conduct of the living throughout her elegies are other manifestations of her heritage.

Wheatley's principal biographer, Margaretta Matilda Oddell, has recorded that Wheatley "was frequently seen," very shortly after her purchase by John and Susanna Wheatley, "endeavoring to make letters upon the wall with a piece of chalk or charcoal" (12). Such accounts attest to the young girl's verbal giftedness. And it was not long before Mary Wheatley, one of the Wheatley twins (Nathaniel was the other), began to instruct Phillis in reading the English Bible. Her master John wrote in a letter dated November 14, 1772, which comprises a portion of the prefatory material of Phillis Wheatley's 1773 *Poems* that "by only what she was taught in the Family, she, in sixteen Months Time from her Arrival, attained the English Language" (Wheatley, 6). He also noted that "She has a great Inclination to learn the Latin Tongue, and has made some Progress in it." Some progress indeed! Wheatley had, by the publication of her 1773 *Poems*, mastered Latin so well that she rendered into heroic couplets the Niobe episode from Ovid's *Metamorphoses* with such dexterity that she created one of the best English translations of this episode. Significantly, Wheatley did not stop with mere translation; she added so many elements to Ovid's original (such as invocation to the muse, long speeches by Niobe and a goddess, and machinery of the gods) that she effectively recast the Latin to create an epyllion, or short epic. Wheatley was no stranger to the manipulation of language and its poetic forms.

Wheatley's first noted composition was a letter to Samson Occom, the Mohegan Indian minister, described in the letter by her master as having been composed in the year 1765. Her first published poem was printed on December 21, 1767, in the *Newport Mercury*, a colonial newspaper of Newport, Rhode Island, where her black friend Obour Tanner resided. Some have speculated that Wheatley and Tanner came over together on the *Phillis*. In any event, Wheatley corresponded with Tanner with great tenacity. Recent evidence has suggested that these two visited with some frequency as well, with Wheatley traveling from Boston to Newport.

Wheatley's Linguistic Talent Recognized

Wheatley's linguistic talent soon brought her to "the attention of the literati of the day," so Oddell observes, "many of whom furnished her with books." Oddell further notes that Wheatley was to be "frequently visited by clergymen, and other individuals of high standing in society." One of those individuals was probably Mather Byles, sometime poet who became first Congregational minister of the Hollis Street Church. It has been argued that Wheatley designed her 1773 *Poems* after Byles's 1744 *Poems on Several Occasions* (Shields). It is plausible that Byles, as a practicing poet, gloried in flattery from emulators and welcomed the opportunity to work with a student of poetry who showed as much promise as Wheatley. It is also widely known that as a young man Byles carried on an active correspondence with Alexander Pope, the British poet he most highly esteemed. Pope sent Byles copies of his famous translations of the *Iliad* and *Odyssey*. It may have been through these very volumes that Wheatley was introduced to Pope's mighty couplets. Byles, a Harvard graduate and, of course, no stranger to Latin, may have served Wheatley as occasional tutor in the ancient language. His inheritance of the library of his uncle, Cotton Mather—this library being one of the most extensive in the colonies—would have equipped Byles to teach his enthusiastic student. Byles numbered among the volumes in his library plays by Terrence (the other African author Wheatley cites in "To Maecenas" which opens her 1773 *Poems*), several elementary Latin grammars, and virtually all the standard Latin texts used in the grammar schools before 1784 in America, including works by such authors as Horace, Virgil, Homer and Ovid—all of whose works Wheatley was thoroughly familiar.

As a young woman, Wheatley may have socialized with the other young women of Boston who joined the regular meetings of the singing schools conducted by William Billings, America's first full-time composer-choirmaster. Evidence that Wheatley and Billings did in fact know each other has surfaced from the publication of Wheatley's elegy on Samuel Cooper's death, for appended to a six-page version of the Cooper elegy is a two page anthem "set to Musick by Mr. Billings" to be sung at Cooper's funeral. In Billings' 1770 *The New England Psalm-Singer*, the first collection of original anthems published by an American, he included one piece entitled "Africa," a tribute to Wheatley's homeland. As early as October 2, 1769, Billings ran an advertisement in the *Boston Gazette* that read:

> John Barrey and William Billings Begs [sic] Leave to inform the Publick, that they propose to open a Singing School THIS NIGHT, near the Old South Meeting-House, where any Person inclining to learn to sing may be attended upon at said School with fidelity and Dispatch (quoted in McKay and Crawford, 36)

The Old South Boston Meeting House was Wheatley's church and the designation "any Person," not limiting sex or race, likely appealed to her.

Another repository of knowledge on which the young Wheatley may have drawn is the extensive and scholarly library of Thomas Prince. In 1718 this Harvard-trained minister, scholar, and bibliophile joined Joseph Sewall,

Wheatley's spiritual "monitor" at Old South Church, as assistant minister where he remained in this capacity until his death in 1758. Prince's defense of George Whitefield, the subject of Wheatley's her most famous elegy, along with his alignment with Sewall, would have recommended him to the young Wheatley. During his career, Prince acquired such a number of volumes that the size of his library was exceeded only by that of Byles and perhaps by the holdings of Governor Hutchinson. On his death Prince left this extensive library, to Old South Church.

With the colonies' best libraries and better minds available to Wheatley, this developing poet was enabled to pursue her scholarly interests, very likely at her own pace and with little hindrance. As well, she probably participated in the singing schools, thereby creating opportunities to meet the young women whose families later became the subjects of her elegies. As suggested earlier, however, Wheatley was not merely a student-scholar and social participant; she was also a politically active, as her many poems about political events attest. One possible motivation for her political position may well have been her close association with Old South Church. The church was the site of the town meeting held after the Boston Massacre, a meeting that resulted in the expulsion of the royal governor. Wheatley's non-extant poem "On the Affray in King-Street, on the Evening of the 5th of March," was most likely about the Boston Massacre and the martyrdom of Crispus Attucks, the black man who organized the "affray." This same Old South Church became the site of the Massacre's anniversary orations, one of which was delivered by John Hancock, who lent his signature, of course, to the Declaration of Independence, but also to Wheatley's letter of attestation. And here was held the organizational meeting of the Boston Tea Party.

Wheatley would not have required anyone to teach her the meaning of freedom. As a slave until mid-October of 1773, she chose the American quest for independence. Indeed American patriot rhetoric must have held an inexorable attraction for one who in her poetry struggled so determinedly for freedom. The fact that Wheatley was a communicant of the largely-patriot Old South Church, while John and Susanna Wheatley attended the more loyalist New South Church has gone relatively unnoticed. For example, as recently as 1982 J. Saunders Redding published a sketch of Wheatley in which he claimed she was, along with the entire Wheatley family, a faithful British loyalist.

However Wheatley wrote no poetry on behalf of the Torys' predicament. It is true that John and Susanna Wheatley were indeed loyalists, and it is also very likely that their son Nathaniel, who remained in England was a staunch loyalist. But Benjamin Franklin, remarks in a letter of July 7, 1773 that "I went to see the black Poetess and offer'd her any Services I could do her. Before I left the House, I understood her Master was there and had sent her to me but did not come into the Room himself, and I thought was not pleased with the Visit" (Franklin, 291-292). Nathaniel Wheatley was probably not pleased to receive a colonist whose political views he opposed. Phillis Wheatley's political stance must have been uncomfortable to maintain. Yet she did maintain a patriotic stance throughout her career, writing poems dedicated to George Washington, General David Wooster, and the declaration of peace in the 1783 Treaty of Paris, ("Liberty and Peace").

Such a political position, doubtless known by the citizens of Boston, may have contributed to Wheatley's failure to publish a volume of her poems in Boston in 1772. Whether or not the poet's politics played a role in the failure of "Proposals for Printing by Subscription" to find sufficient subscribers, racism did play a decisive role. As William H. Robinson has ably demonstrated, the Boston public would not support "anything of the kind" to be printed (*Black New England Letters*, 50-51). Wheatley, however, found a more sympathetic backer in England. Largely because of Wheatley's publication in 1770 of her most famous elegy, "On The Death of the Mr. George Whitefield," a poem widely printed in broadside on both sides of the Atlantic, the poet came to the attention of Selina Hastings, Countess of Huntingdon, a wealthy philanthropist whose personal chaplain Whitefield had been. When the Countess heard that Boston subscribers would not endorse Wheatley's volume, she agreed to finance it in London.

Almost a year and a half passed before the volume went to press. During that interval many titles of the 1772 "Proposals" were radically altered. Such titles as "On America," "On the Death of Master Seider [Snider], who was killed by Edenezer Richardson, 1770" (Snider was according to Wheatley, "the first martyr for the common good" [Wheatley, 136]), "On the Arrival of the Ships of War, and landing of the Troops," "On the Affray in King-Street, on the Evening of the 5th of March," and "To Samuel Quincy, Esq; a Panegyrick" were all eliminated and replaced by new titles such as "To Maecenas," "Thoughts on the Works of Providence," "Hymn to the Morning," "Hymn to the Evening," "Isaiah," "On Recollection," "On Imagination," "Hymn to Humanity," "To S.M.," and "Niobe in Distress."

The replacement of so many poems reveals that the earlier 1772 volume would, had it appeared, have taken on a character different from the later 1773 *Poems*. While the earlier volume would have had much more appeal to an American, patriot audience, the 1773 *Poems* had more of an aesthetic appeal to an audience that would have found pro-American poems inflammatory. The 1772 volume's subject was patriot American politics; if published, Wheatley could arguably have been the author of the first book of Revolutionary War poems, challenging Philip Freneau's claim to this distinction.

Poet Matures as Artist

Nevertheless, the year and a half between March 1772 and July 1773 was an unusually productive one that saw Wheatley's maturation as a poet. Not finding her freedom realizable as yet in this world, Wheatley turned inward to construct a poetics of liberation. In her poem, "On Imagination," she can, as poet with absolute power over the words of *her* poems, "with new worlds amaze th'unbounded soul" (Wheatley, 66). In the very next line of this piece, she begins immediately to construct a new world not bound by winter's iron bands but one populated by fragrant flowers and forests heavy with verdant leaves. This world into which she escapes is more redolent of her African Gambia than of a Christian paradise. But Wheatley realizes that no poet can indefinitely sustain a poetic world; hence she reluctantly leaves "the pleasing views" and returns to a winter whose most stark reality is the condition of slavery.

After the appearance of Wheatley's *Poems on Various Subjects, Religious and Moral*, however, she was not to endure slavery much longer. When *Poems* appeared in London in early September, the volume was reviewed at least nine times in British newspapers, many of which expressed indignation for the fact that Wheatley, obviously an extremely talented artist, remained a slave. These notices crossed the Atlantic along with the first copies of Wheatley's *Poems*. It is probable that these notices, which praised the poet but attacked her masters, played a role in bringing about Phillis Wheatley's manumission. Another fact that may have contributed to the poet's release from slavery was the famous Somerset judgment of 1772, which was widely interpreted to mean that any slave who set foot on the English shore was thereafter considered free. Thus, technically Wheatley received manumission when she arrived in London on June 17, 1773. Her masters were doubtless faced with something of a dilemma when their "slave" returned to Boston, according to British law no longer a slave. Surely the reviews expressing displeasure and surprise regarding this young woman's enslavement placed additional pressure on the Wheatley's to free her.

In any event, by the time the poet penned a letter on the eighteenth of October 1773 to David Wooster, in which she enumerates her activities in London during the past summer, she also announces: "Since my return to America my Master, has at the desire of my friends in England given me my freedom" (Wheatley, 170). It is important to note that Wheatley does not say John Wheatley freed her out of his own generosity but at the behest "of my friends in England". This same letter reveals that Wheatley made good use of her limited time in London where she met such dignitaries as Thomas Gibbons, Granville Sharp, Brook Watson, and the Earl of Dartmouth. Dartmouth gave Wheatley five guineas with which he encouraged her to use to purchase Alexander Pope's *Complete Works* "as the best he could recommend to my perusal." While it is certain that Wheatley was well acquainted with many of Pope's works before this time (*The Collected Works*, pp. 276-279), Dartmouth's recommendation that she examine Pope's complete opus suggests either that the Earl was unaware of Wheatley's knowledge of Pope or that the young black poet was not as thoroughly steeped in Pope's works as has heretofore been assumed.

Wheatley returned to Boston on July 26, 1773 to be at the side of her mistress whose health was in a state of rapid decline. While taking care of her mistress, Wheatley carried on active correspondence, writing to such figures as the Countess of Huntingdon, David Wooster who later became a general in the American revolutionary forces), John Thornton (British philanthropist and friend of the Countess), Samson Occom (the Mohegan Indian minister and graduate of what later became Dartmouth College), and the Reverend Samuel Hopkins, as well as Obour Tanner. In these letters, Wheatley seized every opportunity to promote her *Poems*. In her epistle to Occom, Wheatley presents her most eloquent and emphatic condemnation of slavery, when she declares: "In every human Breast, God has implanted a Principle, which we call Love of Freedom; it is impatient of Oppression, and pants for Deliverance" (Wheatley, 177). This magnificent indictment of slavery refutes the notion that she was unconcerned for the fate of her black brothers and sisters still suffering under the yoke of slavery. The letter had more than a dozen reprintings in New England newspapers before 1780.

Despite solicitous care, Susanna Wheatley died on March 3, 1774, at the age of sixty-five. It was about this time that Wheatley began to see John Peters, a free Black whom she married on April 1, 1778. Most sources give little time and no kindness to the figure of John Peters. Sidney Kaplan, however, paints a favorable portrait describing Peters as a multitalented, enterprising man whose vocations included grocer and advocate on behalf of blacks before Massachusetts tribunals. Kaplan said Peters seemed "to have been a black man of dignity, who valued himself, did not kowtow to patronizing whites, struggled to climb the educational and economic ladder and failed" (186). It is largely because of Peter's failure that Wheatley's own fortunes began to deteriorate. Another factor which undeniably contributed to the decline of the Peters family was the American Revolutionary War.

In October of 1775, Wheatley wrote a poem in honor of George Washington, which she mailed to the commander-in-chief of the Continental Army, receiving an enthusiastic reply and an invitation to visit him at his headquarters. Washington passed on Wheatley's tribute to a friend; subsequently the poem was printed several times as an instrument for the patriot cause. Wheatley was able to take Washington up on his invitation, visiting him at his Cambridge headquarters. It is guessed that Wheatley (she spent thirty to forty-five minutes with him in private) told Washington first-hand that Jefferson was grossly unjust in his assessment of blacks as having intelligence and aesthetic capacities inferior to those of whites.

Wheatley's final years, nevertheless, numbered disappointment after disappointment. In 1778, the year of her marriage to Peters, John Wheatley died, leaving her with greatly limited resources. The very next year, one senses a desperation behind her decision to publish a set of "Proposals" for a new volume of poems. Surely this attempt failed, not because of racist reasons alone but largely because a country in revolution has little time or money for poetry. Even so, this volume projects some three hundred pages of poetry, only a small portion of which has been reclaimed. Until that manuscript is recovered (many think John Peters took the manuscript south to Philadelphia after his wife's death), poems by Wheatley will probably continue to surface. During the last year of her life, Wheatley published what is perhaps her most moving funeral elegy (on the death of her mentor, Samuel Cooper), a poem celebrating the victory and peace of the American Revolution, and another elegy. The elegy on Cooper describes its subject as "A Friend sincere, whose mild indulgent rays / Encouraged oft, and oft approv'd her lays" (Wheatley, 225). The tribute to the Revolution boldly asserts "And new-born Rome shall give *Britannia* Law" (154).

While neither of these poems suggests a weakening of Wheatley's poetic ability, "An Elegy on Leaving ______" does imply that the poet's career may indeed be coming to an end, for she bids farewell to "friendly bow'rs" and streams, protesting that she leaves "with sorrow each sequester'd seat." (156). In these poems, she seems to know she will soon cease to visit in her imagination the plains and shepherds of the pastoral land of pure poetry. Yet even in this condition, "sweet Hope" may "Bring calm content to gild my gloomy seat" (157). On December 5, 1784, Phillis Wheatley Peters died in Boston, unattended, of complications arising from having given birth to her third child. This child died mercifully with her, two other children having preceded them.

References

Franklin, Benjamin. *The Papers of Benjamin Franklin*. Ed. William B. Willcox. New Haven: Yale University Press, 1976. 20.

Kaplan, Sidney, and Emma Nogrady Kaplan. *The Black Presence in the Era of the American Revolution*. Rev. ed. Amherst: University of Massachusetts Press, 1989.

McKay, David P., and Richard Crawford. *William Billings of Boston: Eighteenth-Century Composer*. Princeton: Princeton University Press, 1975.

Oddell, Margarita Matilda. *Memoir*. Boston, 1834.

Redding, J. Saunders. "Phillis Wheatley." *Dictionary of American Negro Biography*. Eds. Rayford W. Logan and Michael R. Winston. New York: Norton, 1982.

Robinson, William H. *Black New England Letters*. Boston: Boston Public Library, 1977.

———. *Phillis Wheatley and Her Writings*. New York: Garland Publishing, 1984.

Shields, John C. "Phillis Wheatley and Mather Byles: A Study in Literary Relationship." *College Language Association Journal* 23 (June 1980): 377-390.

Wheatley, Phillis. *The Collected Works of Phillis Wheatley*. Ed. John C. Shields. New York: Oxford University Press, 1988.

Collections

Wheatley's manuscripts are housed at Cambridge University (within the Countess of Huntingdon Papers), at the Massachusetts Historical Society (Phillis Wheatley Letters), at Dartmouth College (which has several elegies), and at Harvard University's Houghton Library (a version of the elegy on Charles Eliot). The largest collection of Wheatley materials may be found in the Schomburg Center for Research on Black Culture, New York City Public Library.

John C. Shields

Ionia Rollin Whipper

(1872-1953)

Physician, religious leader

Ionia Rollin Whipper was a Washington, D.C., physician who opened a much-needed and still-surviving home for unwed mothers. Born September 8, 1872, in Beaufort, South Carolina, she was the third of five children born to William J. Whipper and Frances A. Rollin Whipper. Her maternal grandfather, William Whipper (1804?-1876) was a conductor on the Underground Railroad, a moral reformer, and entrepreneur in the North. Her father Williams J. Whipper, a carpet-bagger lawyer, migrated to Charleston from Detroit in 1864. Active in Republican Party politics, he was a delegate to the 1868 South Carolina Constitutional Convention, a municipal judge, and a member of the 1868 state constitutional convention. Her mother, Frances Rollin, came from a well-to-do, well-educated family of mulattoes in Charleston. She wrote, under the pseudonym Frank Rollin, *The Life and Services of Martin R. Delaney* (1868). Along with her sisters Lottie Rollin, Louisa Rollin, and K. Rollin, Frances was active in feminist and political causes.

In the 1880s Whipper's mother, Frances, moved to Washington, D.C., where she attended Howard University School of Medicine and became one of the first black women physicians in the United States. Following the path of her mother, Ionia Whipper also pursued a career in medicine. Specializing in obstetrics, she graduated from Howard School of Medicine in 1903. Her mother died before Ionia Whipper completed her studies, compelling her to borrow money and teach before starting her own practice in 1911.

Like many other professional black women of her time, Whipper embraced moral reform, focusing her time and resources on the plight of unwed mothers in the nation's capital. Many of these women, whose babies she delivered at Freedmen's Hospital, were often homeless during and after their pregnancy. Consequently, Whipper opened her home to them, and in 1931 she organized the Lend-A-Hand Club to raise funds for a permanent shelter for unwed mothers. Within ten years the club had reached its goal: the Ionia R. Whipper Home for Unwed Mothers was opened in 1941, and "remained the only such institution for Negroes in Washington until similar facilities for whites were desegregated in the 1960s" (Penn, 642). Due to chronic funding and personnel shortages, Whipper had to assume many roles at the shelter—administrator, social worker, teacher, and physician. Financial support came primarily from the black community of Washington.

Whipper's medical practice and reform activities in Washington spanned more than forty years. She died after a long illness in Harlem Hospital, New York, on April 23, 1953. Her funeral was held at St. Martin's Protestant Episcopal Church with interment at Fresh Pond Crematorium. Single, she was survived by her brother, Leigh Whipper, a stage and screen actor, and a niece, Leighla Whipper Ford. Following Ionia whipper's death the shelter she established was temporarily closed, but reopened in 1955 at a new location under the name of the Ionia Whipper Rehabilitation Home for Unwed Mothers.

References

Majors, Gerri, and Doris Saunders. *Black Society*. Chicago: Johnson Publishing Co., 1876.

Obituary. *New York Times*, 25 April 1953; Washington *Evening Star*, 24 April 1953; and St. Luke's Episcopal Church in Washington, D. C.

Terborg-Penn Rosalyn. "Ionia Rollin Whipper." *Dictionary of American Negro Biography*. Eds. Rayford W. Logan and Michael R. Winston. New York: Norton, 1982.

Collections

Biographical source material on Whipper and her family may be found in the vertical file on the Whipper Home at the Martin Luther King Memorial Library in Washington, D.C., and in the Leigh R. Whipper Papers in the Moorland-Spingarn Research Center at Howard University in Washington, D.C.

Raymond R. Sommerville

Eartha White

(1876-1974)

Social worker, community leader, businesswoman, teacher

Eartha Mary Magdalene White, a dynamic woman who spent most of her ninety-four years in her native Jacksonville, Florida, made many important contributions to her community. She gained status as a business leader by buying small ventures, which she nurtured to success, and then sold for a profit. But White reinvested these profits in the community, establishing recreation and civic centers, most notably a home for the transient and homeless, the Clare White Mission, named for her adoptive mother.

White was born on November 8, 1876 in Jacksonville, Florida to the former slave, Molly Chapman, and a white man from a prominent family. Her father's name was never revealed. As an infant she was adopted by Lafayette White and Clara (English) White. Clara English was the daughter of freed slaves. She made a living by working as a domestic, cook, and stewardess on several steamship lines. Lafayette, a former slave, was a member of the thirty-fourth Regiment, Company D, United States Colored Troops, and was a soldier in the Civil War. White's adopted parents instilled in her a great appreciation for her black American heritage.

Beginning her education in Stanton School in Jacksonville, White often recalled the influence of one of her elementary teachers, Mary Still. Still's family had been abolitionists and supporters of the Underground Railroad in Pennsylvania. This teacher helped foster a deep sense of pride in White—for herself and her people.

In 1881 Lafayette White died. Eartha White and her mother remained in Jacksonville until 1888. Eartha White completed the eighth grade at the Stanton School. During an outbreak of yellow fever in 1888, Eartha and Clara White moved to New York City where Eartha attended school. In 1889 she entered Dr. Reason's School, later transferring to Madam Hall's School, where she studied hairdressing and manicuring. She also attended Madam Thurber's National Conservatory of Music, where she was given voice lessons by the highly acclaimed Harry T. Burleigh.

Invited to join one of the first Black opera companies in the United States in 1895, she began touring with the Oriental-American Company. During 1895-1896 she traveled throughout America, Europe, and Asia. While touring with the opera company, she met James Lloyd Jordan, a handsome black man from South Carolina. They fell in love and planned to marry. Tragically, a month before the wedding, Jordan died. Eartha White never married.

Giving up her singing career, White returned to Jacksonville. She attended Florida Baptist Academy from 1896 to 1898. Later she found a position teaching in Bayard (just outside Jacksonville) at the Stanton School. Ambitious and energetic, White also worked as a secretary for the Afro-American Life Insurance Company. In 1901 she saved the company's records from the great fire that destroyed Jacksonville.

Saving $150 from her teacher's salary, in 1904 White opened a department store that catered to black people. This venture was very successful and set her on the path of acquiring real estate. Between 1905 and 1930 White became an active entrepreneur. She owned a dry-goods store, a

Eartha White

general store, an employment agency, a janitorial service, a real-estate business, and a steam laundry. She would buy a small business, invest her time and energy until it was successful, then sell the business for a profit and start a new one. She eventually owned an investment portfolio worth more than one million dollars. She used the profits form her buying and selling to support her philanthropic activities. White became the first black social worker and census taker in Jacksonville.

Racial Uplift Programs Initiated

Philosophically and politically aligned with Booker T. Washington, in 1900 White joined him as a charter member of the National Negro Business League. "Like Washington, she believed that education, business success, and racial uplift could be effective instruments against prejudice." White seemed to think "cooperation" was the best means for achieving racial equality (Shafer, 727).

White's life is a paradigm of what she believed everyone is capable of attaining. Her highly developed social consciousness led her to operate for many years the only orphanage for black children in the entire state of Florida. In 1904 she established the Boy's Improvement Club and initiated a campaign to "Save 1,000 Boys from Juvenile Court." The campaign was to raise money for a recreational center. The project failed, but White convinced a friend to donate land for a park and used her own money to hire someone to run the recreational program. Finally, in 1916 the city council was persuaded to take over the project. For more than fifty years White conducted Sunday Bible classes at the county prison and worked untiringly to improve conditions for the inmates.

White's enthusiasm for public service was inspired by her adoptive mother, Clara White, who always made generous contributions to the ill and destitute members of Jacksonville's "Black Bottom." Clara White died in 1920. Eight years later Eartha White established a memorial to her beloved parent, calling it the Clara White Mission. Considered her most important contribution to Jacksonville, the mission on West Ashley Street rivaled Chicago's Hull House. White resided in the mission with the transient and homeless people. During the Great Depression more than twenty-five hundred persons received food from the mission in one month alone, February 1933.

During World War I, White directed the War Camp Community Services and coordinated recreational activities in Savannah, Georgia. She was the only woman to participate in the Southeast War Camp Community Service, held in Jacksonville and the only black woman to attend a White House meeting of the Council of National Defense.

Politically conservative, White became more radical during World War II. In 1941 she worked with A. Philip Randolph to organize a march on Washington to protest job discrimination and racism. Even though the march never materialized, the protest led to Executive Order 8802 issued by President Franklin D. Roosevelt, banning discrimination in employment in defense industries and in the Federal government. The order also established the Fair Employment Practices Committee.

White was most proud of the Eartha M. White Nursing Home completed in 1976. She initiated the project with her personal funds, later garnering support from federal grants. The 120-bed facility offered physical and occupational therapy, and recreational activities for county and state welfare patients.

A remarkable woman, White almost single-handedly established a long line of social service agencies including: a maternity home for unwed mothers, a child placement center, an orphanage, the Harriet Beecher Stowe Community Center, and a tuberculous rest home. Her motto was, "Service is the price we pay for the space we occupy on this planet" (Gibson, 123). Among White's many honors and awards are: Good Citizenship Award by local Jaycees, (1969), Lane Bryant Volunteer Award (1970), American Nursing Home Association Better Life Award (1971), and appointment to the President's National Center for Voluntary Action, for which she was honored at a White House reception (1971). In 1973 the National Negro Business League honored her as its official historian with the Booker T. Washington Symbol of Service Award.

Although confined to a wheelchair in her later years after she fell and broke her hip, White remained active until her death on January 18, 1974. She died from heart failure in Jacksonville, Florida, at age ninety-four.

References

Gray, Lawrence E. "Eartha M. White." *Biographical*

Dictionary of Social Welfare in American. Westport, Conn: Greenwood, 1986. 753-56.

Gibson, Harold. "My Most Unforgettable Character." *Reader's Digest* 105 (1974): 123-127.

Shafer, Daniel. "Mary Magdalene White." *Notable American Women: The Modern Period*. Cambridge: Harvard University Press, 1980.

Collections

The Eartha White Collection is held at the Library of the University of North Florida. The collection contains more than one thousand documents, letters, photographs, and other items. Rollins College Archives in Winter Park, Florida, also contains primary source materials on White.

The *Deed Books* in the Nassau County courthouse, Fernandiana Beech, Florida; the Duval County Courthouse in Jacksonville, and the National Archives, *Record Group 94*, all contain information on White's adoption. Interviews with White are published in the St. Petersburg *Times*, 1 August 1971, and the *New York Times* in 1970.

Nagueyalti Warren

Fannie B. Williams

(1855-1944)

Lecturer, civic leader, clubwoman, journalist

Fannie Barrier Williams, one of the founders of the National League of Colored Woman and its successor, the National Association of Colored Women, was active all her life in political and civic groups and women's clubs involved in the struggle to uplift the race. She and her husband were prominent and respected leaders in the battle for equal rights.

Williams was born in Brockport, New York, on February 12, 1855, the youngest of three children, two daughters and a son, of Anthony J. Barrier and Harriet (Prince) Barrier. Her parents and grandparents were freeborn and for many years her family was the only black family in town. Her mother was a native of Cherburne, New York. Her father, a native of Philadelphia, had lived in Brockport and became a modestly successful barber and sometime coal merchant; thus, he provided a comfortable and secure life for his family. Well-respected in the community, he was a homeowner and a leader in the local Baptist church.

The family of Anthony J. Barrier associated freely with whites. Williams attended local schools and in 1870 graduated from the academic and classical course of the State Normal School in Brockport. Like many educated Northern black women of the Reconstruction era, she taught school in the South and in Washington, D. C. Race relations in the South dealt a shattering blow to her ideals of what life was like, especially in view of her childhood years in an environment free from overt prejudice or discrimination. On her experiences with discrimination for the first time, she wrote, "I have never quite recovered from the shock and pain of my first bitter realization that to be a colored woman is to be discredited, mistrusted and often meanly hated" ("A Northern Negro's Biography," 91). She lamented that prejudice was everywhere, but not as vividly as it was in the South. Regardless of where she lived, Williams's knowledge of its ills was firm: ". . . I cannot be counted for my full value, be that much or little, I dare not cease to hope and aspire and believe in human love and justice, but progress is painful and my faith is often strained to the breaking point" ("A Northern Negro's Autobiography," 96). She returned to Boston to study in the New England Conservatory of Music and then in the School of Fine Arts in Washington, D. C.

Fannie B. Williams

While in Washington, Fannie Barrier met S. Laing Williams, a native of Georgia, who was a young, recent graduate of the University of Michigan and an honors graduate of the Columbia Law School in Washington (later the George Washington Law School). They married in Brockport in 1887 and moved to Chicago; he was admitted to the Illinois bar and Fannie Williams helped her husband establish a law practice. For a short time he shared a law office with Ferdinand Barnett, the husband of noted anti-lynching crusader and clubwoman Ida Wells Barnett, and immediately became a leader in Chicago's black society. They soon found a place in the small, closely-knit black community and became members of the All Souls Church (Unitarian) of the Reverend Jenkin Lloyd Jones. They had no children. S. Laing Williams in 1887 organized a literary society known as the Prudence Crandall Club. The society attracted membership from practically every socially prominent black Chicagoan.

Williams Becomes Renowned Lecturer

Public life for Fannie Williams began in 1893 and spanned more than thirty years. When the World's Columbian Exposition of 1893 was planned for Chicago, she worked diligently to secure recognition for blacks. The exposition coincided with the rising tide of Jim Crow legislation, increased incidences of lynching, and among other slanderous claims, allegations of rape by black men and sexual immorality of black women. Though she was relatively unknown until then, the exposition provided Williams a rostrum before the World's Congress of Representative Women held at that time. Her address in May of that year on the subject "The Intellectual Progress of the Colored Women of the United States since the Emancipation" was highly acclaimed. This also led to a second successful address during the exposition, this time before World's Parliament of Religions on "Religious Duty to the Negro." So impressive were both presentations that she soon won a local and a national reputation as an able and eloquent speaker.

The speeches reflected the traditional views of the black elite of the time. Williams favored union and organization among blacks as a vehicle to advance the race, and she reminded her white audiences that slavery provoked "every moral imperfection that mars the character of the colored American." The denial of equal opportunity to blacks meant that "the American people are but repeating the common folly of history in thus attempting to repress the yearnings of common humanity." In her speech on "Intellectual Progress of the Colored Women," she spoke in the name of humanity and dismissed the charges of sexual immorality that a diseased public opinion created. She lamented that "less is known of our women than of any other class of Americans." When freedom came, it was "one of the most wonderful things in human history how promptly and eagerly these suddenly liberated women tried to lay hold upon all that there is in human excellence. There is a touching pathos in the eagerness of these millions of new home-makers to taste the blessedness of intelligent womanhood."

She expressed a concern that was explored later in her work with black women's clubs that "the power of organized womanhood is one of the most interesting studies of modern sociology." Williams was outraged that "black women can find no employment in this free America." Her concern for the black family was evident, and she noted in her speech on "Religious Duty" that the "heart of every social evil and disorder among the colored people, especially in the rural South, is the lack of those inherent moral potencies of home and family," and that slavery had been savage and relentless in its "attempted destruction of the family instincts of the negro race in America." She found black history pathetic: When freedom came, blacks groped about in search of their scattered offspring with the hope of knitting broken ties of family kinship, but they had only instinct to guide them in the search ("The Intellectual Progress of the Colored Woman of the United States" which includes "Religious Duty to the Negro").

Through her work in Chicago's social welfare activities, Williams won a well-deserved reputation as an able organizer. In 1891 she assisted Daniel Hale Williams in the founding of Provident Hospital, with its biracial staff of doctors and its training school for nurses, and she remained an active supporter. Provident was one of the first black-controlled medical centers in the country. Her nomination in 1894 for membership in the Chicago Women's Club brought considerable public attention. After fourteen months of bitter wrangling, she won a victory for the social equality that she had supported in her speeches. She was admitted to membership in 1895 and for thirty years she remained the club's only black member.

For her performance before the exposition as well as the notoriety surrounding her election to the Chicago Women's Club, Williams was hailed by the press and by black leaders, and for the next decade the demands on her as lecturer and writer made her travel extensively. She addressed women's clubs and church groups and lectured on various black American themes. A talented musician, she sometimes combined her lecture with a concert. She was a journalist for several newspapers, including the *Chicago Record-Herald* and the *New York Age*. Her ability as a civic leader was soon recognized, and she also devoted her talent to developing an organizational and institutional life in black Chicago.

Women's Club Movement Aids Black Women

Williams helped to found the National League of Colored Women (NLCW) in 1893 and was one of its primary leaders. With women's rights reformer Mary Church Terrell, she helped to found its successor in 1896, the National Association of Colored Women (NACW).

The women's club movement fought the ills of mounting discrimination by providing various kinds of self-help. Three leading black women, Williams, Terrell, and Ida Wells Barnett, were in Chicago and they worked diligently to make it succeed. In doing so, they placed Chicago at the vanguard in the movement. Before the NACW was established, there had been Ida Wells clubs that had similar interests. By 1900, however, there were more than a half dozen such clubs and they came together to form the Colored Women's Conference of Chicago. The clubs operated kindergartens, mother's clubs, sewing schools, day nurseries, employment bureaus, parent-teacher associations, and a penny-savings bank. The clubs also sponsored several welfare organizations, the first of which was the Phillis Wheatley Home for Girls, which opened in 1896.

Along with many other prominent black women of this era, Williams saw the club movement among black women as a means of ameliorating the subsocial conditions of an entire race of people. For white women, the clubs already meant forward movement among the best women in the interest of what was best for womanhood. The movement worked for those already uplifted. For black women, the club represented the efforts of a few competent women who worked on behalf of many who were less competent, if not incompetent at the time. The club became only one of several means for social and racial uplift. In Williams's view, the masses of black women needed to advance and to emancipate the mind and spirit. Legislation alone could not do it and had not done it. Time, patience, suffering, and charity would be needed to complete the work that the club movement helped to advance. The movement brought about great unity and helped the women put new social values on themselves. Perhaps Williams's best view of the movement is given in the statement that "The club movement is well-purposed. . . . It is not a fad. . . . It is rather the force of a new intelligence against the old ignorance. The struggle of an enlightened conscience against the whole brood of social miseries, born out of the stress and pain of a hated past" ("Club Movement Among Colored Women of America").

Among her other affiliations, Williams was active in the Illinois Women's Alliance. In 1905 she became a director of the Frederick Douglass Center (a social settlement on Chicago's South Side), and she was corresponding secretary of the board of directors of the Phillis Wheatley Home for Girls. An active member of the Reverend Jenkin Lloyd Jones's All Souls Church (Unitarian), she worked with its social welfare adjunct, the Abraham Lincoln Center.

Fannie Barrier Williams was petite, light complexioned, and vivacious in conversation. Described by her contemporaries as charming, attractive, and witty, she was more familiar with the black elite but worked fervently for the uplift of the black masses. Doubtless her vivaciousness, mixed with her intelligence and perseverance, led to her involvement in the various activities already noted. Sometimes she used her skin coloring and knowledge of French to escape the laws of Jim Crowism. "Je suis française," she said to the conductor of a Southern train in order to retain her seat in the first-class (white) section. Writing on this issue later, she said: "I quieted my conscious by recalling that there was a strain of French blood in my ancestry, and too that their barbarous laws did not allow a lady to be both comfortable and honest" ("A Northern Negro's Autobiography," 95).

As attested to in her speech at the Chicago Exhibition, Williams took up the cause of black women, whom she said were the "least known and most ill-favored class of women in the country." Her comments on their unemployment also helped to stir a stream of letters from women asking for help in obtaining employment. With quiet success, she urged employers to hire qualified black women applicants for responsible positions. She pointed out that many were qualified for stenographic and clerical jobs but because of their color alone were not hired. She used her lectures and writings to plead the cause of black women. Her concerns, timely for that period, are still important, critical issues that face black woman today. Williams urged black women to organize as white women had done and to focus attention on the double bind of race and sex, particularly in such areas as employment, child welfare, the family, education, and religion. She emphasized the importance of the black women's club movement as "a new intelligence against an old ignorance," and she believed that the movement could be a vehicle for arousing black women from their "do-nothing, unsympathetic and discouraged condition."

Williams Tempers Her Views

In her early lectures and writings, Williams adhered to the militant protest ideology of leaders like Frederick Douglass. She argued for the eradication of segregation and discrimination as the means for solving America's racial problems. Her views were tempered by 1900, when she began to drift to the conciliatory and practical views of Booker T. Washington, the noted educator and founder of Tuskegee Institute (now University) in Alabama. Where employment was concerned, for example, she began to echo Washington's emphasis on practical training while holding on to the value of a broader education. She conceded that the narrow scope of "industrial education" could be broadened by embracing science and the arts to complement practical instruction. Blacks had to depend on the dominant race to fulfill the hope for advancement, she argued, and she disregarded problems of social discrimination.

Added to her views was a new position: Blacks needed to acquire property and cultivate their own strength against adversity. The devotion that she demonstrated for Washington continued in her support in his quarrel with the militant activist, educator, and social reformer W. E. B. Du Bois. Many other popular black leaders at the turn of the century also joined Washington's camp in the face of mounting social discrimination. It was in 1900 that Washington, black newspaper editor T. Thomas Fortune, and Washington's secretary Emmett J. Scott, founded the National Negro Business League. In that year also, Williams and Washington contributed to the book *A New Negro for a New Century*. When the Afro-American Council was held in Saint Paul in 1902, the supporters of Washington, Fortune, and Scott maintained control, and Williams was elected corresponding secretary, succeeding Ida B. Wells Barnett. By then, Wells Barnett and her husband, Ferdinand had joined the opposition. In 1902 also, Williams restated her views on the role of black women in her essay on the club movement: "The Negro woman's club of to-day represents the New Negro with new powers of self-help" (203).

Thus Fannie Barrier Williams, once a voice of the militant protest ideology of Frederick Douglass, drifted to the conciliatory approach of Booker T. Washington. While Williams changed her approach from militancy to conciliation, she apparently never lost faith in equal rights and equal opportunity. Her support of Washington and her most active work with Tuskegee came at the same time her husband was seeking a federal job, which he hoped to secure through the influential Washington and his extensive patronage connections. In fact, Laing Williams and Washington benefited each other: Williams had been Washington's primary Chicago contact and reportedly kept Washington informed about issues important to the progress and political activities of black people, including the important Niagara group in Chicago. He had delivered Tuskegee's commencement address in 1895 and later arranged for Washington's periodic visits to Chicago. The relationship led to his appointment in 1908 as Assistant U. S. District Attorney for Illinois and Eastern Wisconsin. A year later, however, he was discharged, but Washington assisted in having him reappointed. By 1912, Laing Williams had lost the position permanently. It has been said that Woodrow Wilson's election in that year led to Washington's loss of favor and power in the White House. President Wilson removed from office several prominent black leaders, including James C. Napier (Register of the Treasury) and S. Laing Williams. Despite his relationship with Washington, some of Laing Williams's contemporaries believed that through the new public views that she expressed on self-help and racial solidarity and her public support of Washington, Fannie Williams played a major role in her husband's federal appointment. Either she had a change in view on what was best for the race, or she leaned toward what was politically expedient for her husband's cause.

During 1912 the famous Washington-Du Bois controversy began to ebb, and the Williamses began to work with Du Bois and the newly-established National Association for the Advancement of Colored People (NAACP). As was seen earlier in the work of Mary Ann Shadd Cary, Fannie Williams became interested in the women's suffrage movement. This was manifest in her work and her lectures, and she urged black women to take a leading role in fighting for the rights of all women.

Laing Williams died in 1921, after which time Fannie Williams was less active. In 1924-1926, however, she served on the Library Board of Chicago and is credited as being the first black and the first woman to hold this appointment. She retired from the board at the end of her term in 1926 and moved to the family home in Brockport, where she lived her remaining years with her unmarried sister. Arteriosclerosis brought an end to her life on March 4, 1944, when she was eighty-nine years old. She was buried in the Barrier family plot located in the High Street Cemetery. Fannie Williams is preserved in history as a pioneer in the political and social development of black women.

References

Davis, Elizabeth Lindsay, ed. *Lifting as They Climb.* [Washington, D.C.] National Association of Colored Women, 1933.

Fishel, Leslie H., Jr. "Fannie Barrier Williams." *Notable American Women 1607-1950*. Vol. 3. Cambridge: Harvard University Press, 1971.

Loewenberg, Bert James and Ruth Bogin, eds. "Fannie Barrier Williams." *Black Women in Nineteenth Century American Life*. University Park, Pa.: Pennsylvania State University Press, 1976.

Logan, Rayford W. "Fannie Barrier Williams." *Dictionary of American Negro Biography*. Edited by Rayford W. Logan and Michael R. Winston. New York: Norton, 1982.

Mossell, Mrs. N. F. *Work of the Afro-American Woman*. 2nd ed. Philadelphia: Ferguson, 1908.

Spear, Allan H. *Black Chicago: The Making of a Negro Elite 1890-1920*. Chicago: University of Chicago Press, 1967.

———. "Fannie Barrier Williams." *Dictionary of American Biography*. Supplement Three, 1941-45. New York: Charles Scribner's Sons, 1973.

Williams, Fannie Barrier. "A Northern Woman's Autobiography." *Independent*, 14 July, 1904.

———. "The Club Movement Among Colored Women in America." Booker T. Washington. *A New Negro for a New Century*. Chicago: American Publishing House, 1900. 405.

Jessie Carney Smith

Lorraine A. Williams

(1923-)

Educator, clubwoman

(Evelyn) Lorraine Anderson Williams, who ended her illustrations career as an educator with an appontment by President Carter to the United States Circuit Judge Nominating Panel for the District of Columbia, was born on August 6, 1923, in Washington, D.C., in the Capitol Hill home of her parents, Allen and Alice Anderson. Williams had a heart defect that was considered so serious that the doctor warned Anderson's parents that she would probably not live to be twelve years old. The concerned parents invited Alice's mother, Mary Ann (Scott) Winston, a preacher's daughter who worked as a pastry cook, to live with them so that she could take care of the baby while they worked. Williams's grandmother gave the child loving, meticulous care and prepared special foods designed to improve her health.

As Williams grew she always felt and looked very healthy, but her parents were careful to keep her away from strenuous activities. She could play quiet games with her friends and especially enjoyed playing school. After she began to attend the Joshua Giddings Elementary School, she was delighted to find that the younger children would wait for her in the afternoon so that she could teach them what she had learned that day. Thus from the time that she was a small child, she decided that she wanted to be a teacher.

On many quiet evenings her grandmother carefully led Williams in interesting discussions that she called "lessons from life." Grandmother Winston, a graduate of the District of Columbia's segregated M Street High School, had a special love for history and often told her about the achievements of blacks in America. She regaled her grandchild with genealogical information about their family and carefully taught her stories from the Bible. Williams developed a special love for the Old Testament during these years that did not diminish as she grew older. Winston designed these evening talks to keep Williams interested in sedentary activities so that she would not miss the lack of play. Williams did sometime yearn for greater freedom, but she learned to enjoy books and good conversation.

Alice Anderson, Lorraine Williams's mother, was a choir director at Mount Jezreel Baptist Church. The child often went with her mother to rehearsals and concerts, where she learned to appreciate hymns, spirituals, and classical music. She liked to play a game of discerning the difference between the vocal parts and in so doing gained a genuine appreciation of music. Other than church activities, Williams's social life was very limited. By the time Anderson entered Jefferson Junior High School, her health still showed no signs of failing. She was an excellent student, an eloquent public speaker, and a good singer. Sometimes she felt overprotected—like the time that her grandmother wanted to go to the ninth-grade prom with her and her young date and was only dissuaded when Williams convinced her to wait for them at the home of a friend who lived near the school—but mostly she felt loved.

Williams excelled at the Dunbar Senior High School, where she finished sixth in her class of eighty-eight, a semester ahead of schedule. Realizing her lifelong dream of attending Howard University in 1940, she decided that she would major in history and minor in education so that she could teach history on the secondary level. Still cautious about her health, although it rarely gave her any problems, Williams was afraid of too much activity with younger school children.

During Williams's sophomore year she joined a sorority, Sigma Gamma Rho, that was new to Howard's campus, but quite strong in the Midwest where it was founded. The group, composed largely of teachers and other professional women, emphasized academic excellence. She was elected president of the undergraduate chapter in 1942 and would continue to hold leadership roles in that sorority—composed of more than twenty thousand black professional women—for much of her life.

In her senior year, 1944, the history department at Howard, chaired by Rayford W. Logan, awarded Williams a fellowship for the completion of her master's degree. She gratefully commenced her graduate work under the leadership of Merze Tate, a black female graduate of Oxford University, choosing as a thesis topic "Germany's Imperalist Policies in the Pacific." This gruelling topic required that she not only know German and Pacific Ocean history but also the German language.

In addition to her exacting studies, her graduate year was rendered even more intense because she had agreed to marry an upperclassman, Charles Edward Williams, who had returned to Howard from a two-year Army stint. The pressures of preparing for her wedding, which was to take place several days after the graduation ceremony in 1945, along with the completion of the thesis, drove Williams to the end of her patience. Nevertheless, both ceremonies were beautifully executed, and Lorraine Anderson Williams found herself a married woman and a beginning historian within the same week.

After staying at home as a housewife for a year, Lorraine Williams was delighted to be invited back to Howard to teach in the social science program, a two-course sequence required for all freshmen. The ranks of entering students had swelled because of the young men who were taking advantage of their veterans benefits. The teachers in the social science program were mostly women with master's degrees who taught five large classes each semester according to a prescribed syllabus. Most of these women did not receive promotions or stay on at the University because their course load was so heavy that they had no time to write articles or pursue their doctorates. Williams was determined that since she had the good fortune to work at Howard, she would get her doctorate and publish articles so that she could ultimately become a full professor.

Lorraine Williams commenced doctorate work in intellectual history at American University while her husband began to pursue his doctorate in law at Georgetown. In 1955 she and her husband finished their degrees within a month of each other. Williams, whose dissertation focused on Northern intellectual attitudes toward the Civil War, was one of the first two black women to receive a doctor of philosophy degree from American University. With her degree and subsequent publications, Lorraine Williams received a steady series of promotions at Howard.

While she was still working on her degree, Williams became president of the Washington, D.C., graduate chapter of Sigma Gamma Rho. She was subsequently chosen national vice president of the sorority, in 1959 she was made national president (Grand Basileus), and in 1967 she was honored by being elected to the leadership of the sorority again, serving until 1971. She worked concurrently with the National Council of Negro Woman as national historian from 1959 to 1960 and national vice president from 1961 to 1962.

After her first term as Sigma national president ended in 1962, Williams was appointed chairperson of the social science program at Howard, the first time that position was held by a woman. She worked hard to standardize the approach that the professors took toward their classes, enhance the holdings for students in the university library and encourage the students to use them, and improve the budget and facilities available for the social science students and faculty. Williams was also able to offer several different classes, including some community service programs for interested students. She served as chair of the social science program until 1969, except for a brief period from 1967 to 1968 when she acted as associate dean of liberal arts.

Professors in the social science program were not well-regarded academically by their colleagues because of the program's two-course limitation and because so few had doctorates. After more than twenty years, Lorraine Williams longed to leave the program to teach in the history department. She had occasionally taught history courses before 1970 and had published several historical articles in reputable journals, but she was not successful in switching departments until that year. She was elected chairperson of the history department soon after she joined the faculty.

The late 1960s and early 1970s were turbulent times at Howard as well as at other universities. Civil rights and student rights protests, as well as anti-Vietnam War demonstrations, swept American campuses. Sit-ins, freedom rides, and protest marches kept students in a constant state of turmoil. Many cities were torn by race riots, during which lives and property were lost, but no single occurrence loosed Howard students' anger and violence like the assassination of Martin Luther King, Jr., in the spring of 1968.

Williams's leadership at Howard and in the sorority was severely tested during this period. Howard students were demanding a reexamination of every aspect of the school's curriculum to determine its relevance to the needs of the black students. Members of the sorority wanted to know how they could provide meaningful help and leadership to the black community. Williams interacted with student and community leaders, trying to be as open as possible to new ideas, courses, and programs while remaining dedicated to academic excellence. During the period that Williams was chair of the history department, the curriculum was greatly modified for the purpose of developing more courses with an Afrocentric perspective—courses relating to black life and culture in various parts of the world.

While serving chair of the history department, Lorraine Williams was the editor of several publications, including the Howard University *Second Series of Historical Publications* (Washington, D.C.: Department of History, 1970-74); *Afro-American and Africans: Historical and Political Linkages* (Washington, D.C.: Adams Press, 1974); and *Africa and the Afro-American Experience* (Washington, D.C.; University Press, 1977).

Howard University Appoints Its First Woman Chief Academic Officer

In 1974 Lorraine Williams was appointed the editor of the *Journal of Negro History*, the first woman to hold the position since the publication was founded in 1916 by Carter G. Woodson. Later that same year, Howard president James Cheek offered her the position of vice president for academic affairs. In Howard's 107-year history, no woman had ever held a vice presidency. After some soul searching, she agreed to accept the position. Because of the pressures of the new office, she relinquished her editorship of the *Journal* in 1976 but continued to serve as a member of the executive council of the Association for the Study of Afro-American Life and History, the journal's parent organization.

As vice president, Lorraine Williams supervised twelve of Howard's seventeen schools and colleges, several research institutes, the university press, and the entire university library system. Because Williams had been at Howard as a student and faculty member for more than thirty years at the time of her appointment, she was familiar with many of the faculty, staff, and programs. Nevertheless, moving from departmental to university-wide administration, with only a brief period as a dean, Williams had a lot to learn. Many of the deans who worked under her leadership commented favorably on her administrative ability and her accessibility.

In 1978 President Jimmy Carter appointed Lorraine Williams to the United States Circuit Judge Nominating Panel for the District of Columbia and in 1980 she was appointed to the board of trustees of Johnson C. Smith University. In 1983 Lorraine Williams retired, although she maintains an active interest in the university and funds scholarships in the history department and the divinity school.

References

Aurora. Chicago: the Sigma Gamma Rho Sorority. Various issues since 1955.

Cherry, Gwendolyn. *Portraits in Color: The Lives of Colorful Negro Women*. New York: Pageant Press. 1962.

The Hilltop. Washington, D.C.: Howard University Student Newspaper. Various issues, especially 1970-83.

Miller, Carroll L. *Role Model Blacks: Known but Little Known Role Models of Successful Blacks*. Muncie, Ind.: Accelerated Development, Inc., 1982.

Winston, Michael R. *Howard University Department of History, 1913-1973*. Washington, D.C.: Department of History, 1973.

Photographs of Lorraine A. Williams may be obtained from the Moorland-Springarn Research Center at Howard University in Washington, D.C.

Debra Newman Ham

Madame Maria Selika Williams

(1849?-1937)

Singer

Madame Maria Selika was the stage name of Maria Smith of Natchez, Mississippi, who later became Mrs. Sampson Williams and finally took the name of Maria Selika Williams. The name "Selika," which was added to her stage identification, was taken directly from the heroine of Giacomo Meyerbeer's opera *L'Africaine*. The choice of the name Selika indicates the early affinity for opera by Madame Selika, as well as her identity with her heritage—for Selika, in the opera, is a slave girl. The concert stage was to become the vehicle for the distinguished career of Madame Selika in the last two decades of the 1800s.

Born in Natchez, Mississippi around 1849, Madame Selika was as an infant taken to Cincinnati, Ohio, where she began the study of music at an early age under the patronage of a wealthy family. In fact, Natchez produced two great black prima donnas—Elizabeth Taylor Greenfield (twenty years earlier) and Madame Selika. Few details about Madame Selika's early life have been found. It is known that she traveled in Mississippi, Ohio, Illinois, and California before settling in the East. Her debut as a concert singer was made in San Francisco in 1876 and shortly thereafter she moved to Boston to continue her studies. By this time her unusual musical talent was attracting attention in such cities as Boston and Philadelphia. This led her to continue further study in England. In 1883 she made an appearance before Queen Victoria of England and attracted the attention of music critics there.

This critical acclaim was not without a sound musical basis. Madame Selika was one of the first of her race to prepare rigorously for a concert and operatic career by studying with reputable teachers and by subjecting herself to the kind of systematic and meticulous training necessary to command respect on the concert stage or in the opera house. She studied languages while in Boston and became proficient in French, Italian, and German. She worked with knowledgeable coaches such as Signora G. Bianchi during her stay in San Francisco. She persevered in this pursuit of a career in singing despite the fact that the odds were distinctly against her. It was not until December 1, 1923, that tenor Roland Hayes became the first black singer to give a concert in Carnegie Hall, and it was not until January 7, 1955, that a black singer made an appearance at the famed Metropolitan Opera House in New York—contralto Marian Anderson made her debut in the role of Ulrica, a sorceress, in Guiseppe Verdi's *Un Ballo in Maschera*.

Madame Selika was married to Sampson Williams, who was himself a singer. He is variously identified as "the Hawaiian tenor" or "an inspiring baritone," which gives some indication of the scant attention he received in contrast to that given to Madame Selika. He, too, took a stage name: Viloski. Together they toured the United States, Europe, and the West Indies. It was in Philadelphia that Sampson Williams died. Various reports list the date as 1911 and 1921, again some indication of the attention paid to the husband of Madame Selika. Sources further indicate that Madame Selika's insistence that her husband be included in many of her appearances may have negatively affected her own career. It was generally conceded that her husband was less talented than she was, yet she continued to perform with him. Following his death, Madame Selika moved to New York City and taught at the Martin-Smith School of Music in Harlem until her death.

Madame Selika was known as a coloratura soprano. The coloratura range is characterized by a high, flexible, flute-like quality that has been possessed by only a few singers throughout the centuries. Henry Pleasants, in *The Great Singers: From the Dawn of Opera to Our Time*, writes that:

> . . . we tend to think of the coloratura soprano as a sweet-voiced girl with more or less secure high notes, and with agility and fluency enough to get through the arias of Zerbinetta and the Queen of the Night, but there have always been singers who could do more than that . . . who could ascend to the higher E or F without resorting to a detached, tricky head voice, and who, in lyrical and dramatic passages, could sing persuasively and beautifully.

Pleasants further traces the like of such singers during the time in which Madame Selika was active, but fails to mention her by name. He speaks of Henriette Sontag, Jenny Lind, Adelina Patti, and Marcella Sembrich—but no mention of Madame Selika, who was identified in other sources as "the greatest colored singer of the globe." In the book *Noted Negro Women: Their Triumphs and Activities* by M. A. Majors, M.D., the author writes: "Her rightful position as an accomplished singer is by the side of Jenny Lind, Parodi, Nilsson, Patti and Elizabeth Greenfield."

Critics Praise the Coloratura Soprano

According to reviews, Madame Selika astonished audiences with the strength of her voice as well as the execution of her trills—the stock and trade of coloratura singers. She was also cited for her style and her demeanor—poised, attractive, and of great presence. "Her 'Echo Song' cannot be surpassed—it is beyond criticism," wrote a critic in *Le Figaro* of Paris. The *Tageblatt* was to write, following her appearance in Berlin, that "the artist gave us genuine pleasure. She roused the audience to only say that she is endowed with a voice of surpassing sweetness and extraordinary compass.

With her pure tones, her trills and roulades, her correct rendering of the most difficult intervals, she not only gains the admiration of amateurs but also that of the professional musicians and critics. It is almost impossible to describe the effect of her voice. One must hear it to appreciate its thrilling beauty.'' British impresario James Mapleson, upon hearing her in concert in Philadelphia, was to write: ''She [Madame Selika] sang the 'Shadow Song' from *Dinorah* delightfully, and in reply to a general encore, gave the Valse from the *Romeo and Juliet* of Gounod. In fact, no better singing have I heard.''

Following an appearance in Washington, D.C., *The Colored American* was to carry this account of her concert: ''Despite the awful inclemency of the weather, hundreds came to hear the greatest colored singer of the globe last Wednesday night. . . . The talent and programme were the finest, combining in one the magnificent soprano, Madame Selika; the peerless little Lotta, the renowned tenor and instrumentalist, Prof. Laurance, and the famous baritone Prof. Velosko [sic].''

The choice of Selika as a stage name is an interesting aside. *L'Africaine*, or *The Slave Maid*, along with *Les Huguenots* and *Le Prophète*, are the best-known works of the composer Giacomo Meyerbeer. It is said that the creation of *L'Africaine*, which was twenty years in the making, might have cost the composer his life. He died in the midst of preparing for the opening performance of this opera on Monday, May 2, 1864—the day after the final copy of the opera was completed. It was probably the story that appealed to Madame Selika, for it entails the sacrifice of Selika for explorer Vasco da Gama, in an act of love. Selika eventually kills herself by breathing the perfume of a mancanilla tree, whose perfume is deadly to anyone who inhales its odors, but not before she has been returned to her homeland and there welcomed back as queen and given the sacred oath. The appellation ''Madame,'' along with the acquired name of ''Selika,'' bespeak a quality of grandness that was associated with Madame Selika. According to some sources, her beauty, coupled with her talent, made her especially appealing. Her skin was fair and her hair was long and straight.

The Color Line Denies Selika Recognition

Madame Selika was a prima donna of the late nineteenth century who, because of her color, did not receive the recognition and credit that she deserved. A pioneer in a field that hitherto had been closed to persons of African descent, she was forced to accept concert engagements and solo performances whenever they became available. Not permitted to sing on the famous opera stages of the world, she spent most of her career giving concerts in the United States and abroad. Her career ended as she attempted to pass on to young singers what she had learned in the course of her career. Her last years demonstrated that she harbored no bitterness over the fact that her own career had been severely limited by her color, but that despite such obstacles, young singers must be trained in the operatic and concert traditions. This goal she pursued in the waning years of her life.

Madame Selika was the best-known of black singers in the 1880s and the 1890s. Her fame was international and her career was exceptional. She sang before the Queen of England, the Czar of Russia and, by special invitation, before President Hayes of the United States.

Persons who figured prominently in her development were: Frances Bailey Baskin of San Francisco, who persuaded her to pursue a career in the East; Signora G. Bianchi of San Francisco, under whom she studied voice; Carlotta Patti and Percy Blandford, with whom she appeared in concerts; and her husband, Signor Viloski (Sampson Williams), with whom she appeared in a number of duet performances. Madame Selika died in New York City in 1937 at the age of eighty-seven.

In the volume *Noted Negro Women*, published in 1893, this statement appears: ''The world has heard Madame Selika and has been delighted with her singing. The press everywhere has spoken in very high praise of the wonderful range of her sweet voice, the masters in music have found new beauties in their songs when sung by her, and in no compromising terms, have placed her where she rightly belongs, second to none of her time.''

References

Afro-American Encyclopedia, Vol. 10. North Miami, Fl.: Educational Book Publishers, 1974.

Brawley, Benjamin, *The Negro Genius*. New York: Dodd, Mead and Co., 1971.

Dannett, Sylvia G. L., ed. *Profiles of Negro Womanhood*. Vol I. Yonkers, N. Y.: 1964.

Dictionary of Black Culture. Edited by Wade Baskin and Richard N. Runes. New York: Philosophical Library, 1973.

Johnson, James Weldon. *Black Manhattan*. New York: Knopf, 1930.

Pleasants, Henry. *The Great Singers: From the Dawn of Opera to Our Time*. New York: Simon and Schuster, 1966.

Smythe, Mabel M., ed. *Black American Reference Book*. Englewood Cliffs, N.J.: Prentice-Hall, 1976.

Southern, Eileen. *The Music of Black Americans*. 2nd ed. New York: Norton, 1982.

Story, Rosalyn M. *And So I Sing: African-American Divas of Opera and Concert*. New York: Warner Books, 1990.

Huel D. Perkins

Mamie Williams

(1872-1951)

Civic leader

Mamie Williams served the black community of Savannah, Georgia, her hometown, as one of its most notable civic leaders, as its representative to the National Republican convention in 1924, and as Republican National Committeewoman for Georgia from 1928 to 1932.

Named Mary Miller at her birth to Reverend and Mrs. James A. Miller in April 1872 in Savannah, by 1880 she, her widowed mother, and two brothers resided with a maternal uncle and his family. She completed her basic education at the Beach Institute, a missionary school sponsored by the Congregational Church. Widowed by 1900, the then Mamie Lambert married George S. Williams on June 17, 1902.

During World War I Mamie Williams organized and worked tirelessly in the Toussaint L'Ouverture branch of the American Red Cross. She received a service pin from the organization in recognition of the more than 2,400 hours she volunteered. During that same time she was active in Liberty Loan Drives and the War Camp Community Service.

After the war, Mamie George Williams, as she was known in Savannah, organized a black Girl Scout troop in Savannah that is still named the Mamie George Council. During the 1920s and the 1930s she was in turn Grand Worthy Inspectrix of Courts of Calanthe of Georgia, president of the Georgia Federation of Women's Clubs, member of the Interracial Commission of Georgia, director of the Georgia State Savings and Realty Corporation, president of the Chatham County Colored Citizen Council, and matron-in-charge of the Chatham County Protective Home for Girls. In 1935 she was awarded the Waldorf Club silver loving cup for having rendered the most outstanding civic service. During the 1940s Williams led the movement that resulted in securing the Colored Recreation Center and Swimming Pool at Savannah. She was also a member of the committee that secured a federal grant to establish the State Home for Colored Girls at Macon, Georgia. In recognition of her efforts on behalf of black women in Savannah, she was elected an honorary member of the Iota Phi Lambda Sorority.

While her tireless efforts on behalf of the black community in Savannah and in the state of Georgia are noteworthy, Williams also made an important contribution to the political history of the United States. When women were first appointed as members of the National Republican Committee in the early 1920s, she was the first black woman named to such a position. Later, following the adoption of the "fifty-fifty Resolution" designed to give equal representation to black and white members of the Republican party, Williams was the first black woman to be accorded the floor in a Republican National Convention and to be elected to committee membership. Beginning with her election to this position in 1924, when she spoke in defense of the Georgia delegation whose seating was being contested, Williams was reelected to the post at the 1928 Republican National Convention. She founded and organized the first and only national political organization among black women in the United States—The National Republican League of Colored Women, which she established in Chicago in 1924.

Williams's election and reelection as a committee member of the national Republican party is best understood in the context of late-nineteenth and early-twentieth century southern politics. Immediately following the Civil War and the death of Abraham Lincoln, the black community channeled its sympathy and sense of indebtedness to the martyred emancipator into support for the Republican party. The party initiated and supported several legislative acts between 1865 and 1879 that directly benefited the welfare of the black population in the United States. The Emancipation Proclamation, the Freedmen's Bureau, the Thirteenth, Fourteenth, and Fifteenth Amendments to the Constitution were the primary measures by which the Republican party secured the allegiance of the black community.

Notwithstanding the party's promotion of these humanitarian policies before 1870, by 1888 the party was divided on state and local levels along racial lines. The term "lily-white" Republicans referred not only to a political faction but also to its set of beliefs. This organization condemned and denounced black Americans in general and their participation in southern politics in particular. Lily-white Republicans upheld the idea of white supremacy and the social system of segregation in the South. The term "black-and-tans" Republicans referred to both the opposing political faction and to its endorsing black suffrage, black participation in politics, and black social equality. Comprised of individuals covering a wide range of skin colors and hues, the black-and-tans protested the disenfranchisement that removed more and more black voters from the Southern political arena.

The black-and-tans and the lily-whites continually fought each other, well into the twentieth century, for recognition by the Republican National Committee as the official party in the various southern states as well as for control over state and local patronage. As a mulatto member of the black-and-tans in Georgia, Williams was deeply embroiled in the effort to discredit the lily-whites. In April 1932 she presided over a meeting called by the black-and-tans and a few of its white supporters in Macon, Georgia, to deplore the "machinations and deceptions of political trickery and demagogy" of the lily-whites who had held a convention in Atlanta the month before to elect delegates to the national convention. The following excerpt from her speech before the group exemplifies the eloquence of Mamie

George Williams and her keen observations of southern racial politics:

> For over half a century the Republican Party had been the Negro's shield and buckler. But lately, in various states of the nation, and now particularly in Georgia, there is prevalent an undercurrent of wicked plotting to establish a regime of lily-white . . . a scheme sought to be inaugurated during the past decade which would drive Negroes from the party councils and take away from them by force and intimidation and by fraud and deception, the official control which they have had for years, and which they have deserved because they represented the Republican majority in such places. . . . The Republican party is being built up and will be built up in the South only by the soundness of American principles and policies. (*The Macon Telegraph*, 28 April 1932).

Unbeknownst to Williams in April 1932 was the fact that in 1928 the Republican president-elect, Herbert Hoover, submitting to the pressures of lily-whiteism, had removed all black Republican officeholders and party officials and placed whites in their place. This act was actually the final blow to what had been a limited participation of the black-and-tans in the party since 1888. The Democratic control of the presidency from 1932 to 1952 and the attraction of the New Deal in Georgia gradually drew blacks into the Democratic fold.

Williams is remembered by those who knew her as a very intelligent and beautiful woman with auburn hair. Pride in her race and especially in the accomplishments and potential of black women accompanied Williams in all of her more than thirty years of work for the black community. She is said to have remarked on many occasions that a black woman "must never live so that she can be humiliated in front of her enemies." To this end she spent the waning years of her life, from the mid- to late 1940s, offering assistance to neglected and homeless black girls residing at the Savannah Federal Women's Home for Girls. She died in Savannah at the Charity Hospital on July 8, 1951.

References

Greene, Gertrude Lovingston. Telephone interview with author, June 1990.

Law, W. W., Archivist, Savannah Branch, Association for the Study of Afro-American Life and History. Telephone interview with author, June 1990.

Macon Telegraph, 28 April 28 1932.

Ravin, Peer Edwin, archivist, Middle Georgia Archives, Macon, Georgia. Interview with author, 28 June 1990.

Savannah City Directory, 1919.

Savannah Tribune, 1932-1951.

Walton, Hanes, Jr. *Black Republicans: The Politics of the Black and Tans*. Metuchen, N.J.: Scarecrow Press, 1975.

Who's Who in Colored America, 2nd ed. New York: Who's Who in Colored America, 1929.

Alice A. Deck

Mary Lou Williams

(1910-1981)

Pianist, composer, arranger, educator

Popularly known as the "First Lady of Jazz," Mary Lou Williams, born Mary Lou Scruggs, was one of the most respected musicians of her time. Pianist, composer, arranger, and teacher, she played a major role in the history of jazz as a contributor to the establishment of the Kansas City-Southwest Territory Big Band jazz style in the 1930s and as a member of the inner circle of musicians that were primarily responsible for the development of the bebop style in the early 1940s.

William's earliest music education came from her mother, a pianist who would sit the infant Mary Lou on her lap and play a repertoire of ragtime and spirituals. It was in this

Mary Lou Williams

position that the two-and-a-half-year-old Mary began to play melodies at the keyboard— an event that both shocked and delighted her mother and began what was to become an extraordinary musical career.

Her mother, who felt her own creativity had been stifled by formal music education, believed strongly that one should learn music first by ear, rather than by learning to read, and that attitude profoundly shaped Mary Lou Williams's ideas about music as a vital art to be deeply felt and intensely experienced in an immediate rather than abstract manner.

At the age of four, Williams, her mother, and sister moved to Pittsburgh, a city in which there was a great variety of music and one that was to present her with many opportunities. By this time, the prodigy with perfect pitch and an uncommon musical memory began to dazzle her immediate family and friends by displays of exceptional musicianship. Her stepfather, Fletcher Burley, purchased a player piano and piano rolls of James P. Johnson and Jelly Roll Morton for her and took her into bars to play ragtime, blues, and boogie woogie for his friends. Her uncle urged her to play Irish tunes, and her grandfather wanted her to play music from the classical European repertoire, and they each paid her for performing. In addition, her mother encouraged her performances and brought professional musicians into her home to play for the gifted child.

In such a musically rich and supportive environment, Williams developed rapidly as a musician. Learning primarily by ear from her mother, the piano rolls, and the musicians who visited her home, she soon developed into an exceptional pianist and earned a reputation as "The Little Piano Girl" before she was ten years old. Among her earliest influences, she cites Atlanta pianist Jack Howard:

> He played stride piano, blues, ragtime—just about everything. He had a tremendous left-hand stretch; played a lot of tenths. With his brute strength he would tear up anybody's piano. Well, I began imitating him (Handy, "Conversations with Mary Lou Williams," 198).

In the early twenties, her brother-in-law, Hugh Floyd, took young Williams into the theaters to see and hear the dynamic popular music of the day that was then dominated by classic blues queens such as Ma Rainey. The pianist-arranger Lovie Austin was among the performers Williams saw during this period, and this multitalented woman made an indelible impression on Williams that both inspired her and shaped her career goals:

> There was this woman, sitting at the piano, with a cigarette in her mouth and her legs crossed, playing with her left hand, writing music for the next act with the other . . . and conducting the band with her head. Although I was just a little baby, I said to myself: "I'm going to do that one day." And I patterned myself on her. On one-nighters with Kirk, if I'd get bored, I'd be writing arrangements for say, Benny Goodman with my right hand and playing [piano] with my left (Britt, 11).

Williams Becomes Professional Performer

Williams's informal childhood performances for family members expanded into performances for neighbors and eventually for the wealthy families of Pittsburgh, including the Mellons, all of whom rewarded her graciously. Her first professional experience with bands came at the age of twelve in 1922 when she substituted for a pianist in the Buzz and Harris Revue, a Theatre Owners Booking Agency (TOBA) show that was visiting Pittsburgh. She was so successful that her parents were persuaded to allow her to perform with the revue on tour for two weeks. Thus, Mary Lou Burley—she had taken her stepfather's name—began her professional career with bands.

For the next few years, while still attending high school, she toured with several shows, the most notable of which was the Seymour and Jeanette Show, one of two black shows that performed on the B.F. Keith circuit (the other was the Bill "Bojangles" Robinson Show). It was during this period that she met and subsequently, in 1926, married John Williams, an alto and baritone saxophone player and the leader of the Seymour and Jeanette show band.

Mary Lou Williams had been exposed to and impressed by the music of Earl Hines, a native of Pittsburgh, who frequently performed with his small group for high school dances in the East Liberty section of Pittsburgh where she lived. During her tours with various circuit shows while still a juvenile, she visited New York, where she met and performed for Jelly Roll Morton, Willie the Lion Smith, Fats Waller, and was even invited to "sit in" with Duke Ellington's Washingtonians at the Lincoln Theater for a week. All these musicians were amazed and impressed by "The Little Piano Girl" who played with the strength of a man. They, in turn, encouraged, influenced, and inspired her. She thus had the opportunity to learn from the major pianists of her time at a formative stage of her career.

In 1927, the Seymour and Jeanette Show settled in Memphis, Tennessee, for an extended period, and Williams made her first recordings as a pianist with the Jeanette James Synco Jazzers on Paramount recordings and the John Williams Synco Jazzers on Paramount, Gennett, and Champion labels. Mary Lou Williams became leader of the Synco Jazzers when John Williams moved to Oklahoma City to join the Terrence Holder Band, a band that soon became the very successful band known as Andy Kirk and the Twelve Clouds of Joy.

In 1929 Williams also joined the Andy Kirk band in Oklahoma. She served the band as an occasional pianist, part-time chauffeur, and most importantly, she began her career as an arranger, learning initially from Andy Kirk and later from Don Redman and Edgar Sampson. The Kirk band moved to Kansas City by November 1929 and became one of the most outstanding bands of the region, due in no small measure to the unique Mary Lou Williams arrangements and outstanding solo piano performances.

By 1930, Mary Lou Williams had become the principal pianist for the band and had established a national reputation as one of the best arrangers in the new style of jazz associated with the hard-driving, blues-based bands of the Southwest region. In addition to being Kirk's principal arranger, she wrote arrangements for Earl Hines, Louis Armstrong, Duke Ellington, Tommie Dorsey, Benny Goodman, Jimmie Lunceford, Cab Calloway, and many others. She remained with the Kansas City-based Andy Kirk band until 1942 and was a significant musical personality in the heyday of Kansas City jazz.

In 1942, she moved to New York and organized a band with trumpeter Harold "Shorty" Baker, her second husband. Subsequently, the couple joined the Duke Ellington Band. Williams toured with the band for six months as staff arranger, creating, among other notable works, the very successful arrangement of "Trumpet No End" (1943) that Ellington recorded in 1946. The marriage to Baker lasted approximately one year and thereafter Williams organized several groups and embarked on an active career as a featured performer in the booming nightclub circuit.

Williams Supports Bebop

During this period in New York she developed very close personal and professional relationships with the young bebop musicians, particularly the pianists Bud Powell, Thelonious Monk, and Tadd Dameron, as well as the principal leaders of the bop movement, Charlie Parker and Dizzy Gillespie. And although she was an established artist in the swing tradition, she rapidly mastered the bop style, became a major exponent of this new music and helped the careers of her younger associates. Her New York apartment became a workshop for the inner circle of creative bebop musicians, and she was a regular performer at bebop jam sessions.

In 1945 she composed the first version of *Zodiac Suite*, a twelve-movement work of musical portraits of various musicians based on astrological themes. She introduced the suite one movement per week on her new radio show, the "Mary Lou Williams Piano Workshop." Later in the year she scored the piece for eighteen instruments for a performance in Town Hall, and in 1946 the three-movement orchestral version of the piece was premiered by the New York Philharmonic Orchestra.

Williams contributed several important compositions to the repertoire of bebop musicians, including the bebop fairy tale "In the Land of Oo-Blah-Dee," written in 1946 with Milton Orent for Dizzy Gillespie, as well as "Tisherome," "Knowledge," "Lonely Moments," and "Waltz Boogie." The latter piece was recorded with one of her Girl Stars all-female groups in 1946 and was one of the earliest blues pieces to be written in a triple meter.

In 1952, Williams moved to Europe, where she had an extended series of appearances in London and Paris. She left Europe in 1954, frustrated with the life of a jazz musician, and returned to the United States, where she began a three-year self-imposed hiatus as a performing musician. During this time, she underwent a period of spiritual and religious awakening and devoted her energies to religious and charitable activities and working with young people in Harlem. In 1956, she converted to Catholicism and afterwards maintained a close association with the Catholic church. She founded the Bel Canto Foundation in 1957, an organization devoted to assisting musicians with medical, drug, and alcohol problems, and was active in many other charitable activities.

Williams resumed her career as a performing artist in 1957, appearing with Dizzy Gillespie at the Newport Jazz Festival and then organizing her trio and establishing her own record company, Mary Records (the first established by a woman). Williams continued an active performance schedule throughout the sixties and the seventies and began to compose extended liturgical works for jazz ensembles, orchestra, and voices. Among these were her cantata *Black Christ of the Andes* (1962) in honor of Saint Martin de Porres, three masses, including her *Mass for the Lenten Season*, premiered in 1968 at St. Thomas the Apostle Church in Harlem, and her *Music for Peace* (1970), commissioned by the Vatican and popularly known as "Mary Lou's Mass." The latter work was adapted for ballet and premiered by the Alvin Ailey American Dance Theater in 1971 at New York's City Center.

Williams began teaching in a Catholic High School in Pittsburgh in the sixties and subsequently was appointed to the faculty of the University of Massachusetts, Amherst (1975-1977) and Duke University from 1977 until her death in 1981. In 1970, she recorded *The History of Jazz* (Folkways, 2860) a solo piano performance-lecture that revealed her extraordinary knowledge and musical mastery of the entire span of jazz history.

Williams's significance to the history of jazz rests on her achievements as both a pianist and an arranger-composer. As a performer, she consolidated the major innovations of the stride pianist with those of the jazz pianists of the twenties and thirties and evolved a style that was eminently personal. While her early technique was based on the dominance of a strong and rhythmically vital left hand, as exemplified by her scintillating performances of stride and boogie woogie, she also developed the rich subtleties of melodic phrasing, pianistic touch, and timbral variety that characterized the performance of pianists of the forties and fifties. Moreover, her sense of harmony was highly imaginative and easily accommodated the complex harmonic innovations associated with both bebop and avant-garde style. Nevertheless, her musical essence remained rooted in her unique interpretation of the spirituality of the blues.

As an arranger, William's sensitivity for dynamic balance, timbral integration and contrast, and control of the subtleties of each section of the band while consistently getting the entire ensemble to swing hard in the foot-patting blues tradition, was what characterized her style and made Andy Kirk's group one of the most important in Kansas City. Her arrangements of "Froggy Bottom" (1936), "Walking and Swinging" (1936), "Little Joe from Chicago" (1936), "Roll Em" (1936), and "Mary's Idea" (1938) are generally considered among the most important of the period.

She was awarded many honors for her accomplishments, including two Guggenheim Fellowships (1972 and 1977) and honorary doctorates from Boston, Fordham, and Loyola (New Orleans) universities and Manhattan, Bates, and Rockhurst colleges, among others. She was also invited to perform at the White House by President Jimmy Carter in 1978 and made frequent appearances as a featured artist at the major international jazz festivals, on television, and on university campuses.

Mary Lou Williams was a major figure in the history of jazz who played an important role in both the establishment of the Kansas City Big Band style and the emergence of bebop, while maintaining a position as one of the premiere creative artists of her time for more than six decades. Duke Ellington expressed, perhaps most cogently, the significance of this black American artist when he said:

> Mary Lou Williams is perpetually contemporary. Her writing and performing are and have always been just a little ahead throughout her career . . . [and] her music retains—and maintains—a standard of quality that is timeless. She is like soul on soul (167).

Selected Discography

Andy Kirk and His Clouds of Joy: Walkin' and Swingin'. Afinity AFS1101, Rec. 1936-1941; *The Asch Recordings, 1944-1947*. (Comp. and ed. Peter O' Brien) Folkways 2966, 1977; *Dizzy Gillespie*. Vintage LRV-530, Recorded July 6, 1949 ("In the Land of Oo-Blah-Dee"); *Embraced: Mary Lou Williams and Cecil Taylor*. (Bob Cranshaw, bass; Mickey Roker, drums) Pablo 2620-108, Recorded April 17, 1977); *Forty Years of Women in Jazz: the Instrumentalists, All Women Groups and Bands* (5 records) Stash STB-001, 1981; *From the Heart*. Chiaroscuro CR 103, Recorded June 9-9, 1971; *The History of Jazz*. (Solo with piano narration) Folkways FJ 2860, recorded late 1970; *Jazz, Vol. 9*. Folkways FJ 2809, recorded May 1945 ("Libra"); *Jazz, Vol. 10*. Folkways FJ 2810, recorded March 1936 ("Froggy Bottom"); *Kansas City Piano (1936-1941)*. (Booker Collins, bass; Ed Thigpen, drums) recorded 1936, 1938;*A Jazz Piano Anthology*. Columbia KG 32355, 1973. Includes "Little Joe from Chicago," recorded live at the Cookery, 1939; *Chiaroscuro*. (Brian Torff, bass) CR 146, recorded October 1975; *Mary Lou Williams: A Keyboard History*. (Wendell Marshall, bass; Ossise Johnson, drums) Jazztone J-1206, recorded early 1955; *My Mama Pinned a Rose on Me*. Pablo 2310-819, recorded December 27, 1977; *Rehersal, Vol.1*. (Frank Newton, trumpet; Edmond Hall, clarinet; Vic Dickenson, trombone; Jack Parker, drums) Folkways FJ 2292, recorded 1944; *Solo Recital: Montreux Jazz Festival 1978*. Pablo 2308 218; *Zodiac Suite*. Folkways 32844, recorded May 1945 (a reissue).

References

Balliett, Whitney. "Out Here." *Such Sweet Thunder*. New York: Bobbs-Merrill, 1966.

——. "Out Here Again." *Improvising: Sixteen Jazz Musicians and Their Art*. New York: Oxford University Press, 1977.

Britt, Stan. "The First Lady of Jazz: Mary Lou Williams." *Jazz Journal* 34 (August 1981): 10-12.

Dahl, Linda. *Stormy Weather: The Music and Lives of a Century of Jazzwomen*. New York: Pantheon, 1984.

Ellington, Duke E. *Music is My Mistress*. New York: Da Capo, 1973.

Feather, Leonard. *Encyclopedia of Jazz in the 60s*. New York: Horizon, 1966.

Gillespie, Dizzy, with A. Fraser. *To Be or Not to Bop*. New York: Da Capo, 1979.

Handy, D. Antoinette. *Black Women in American Bands and Orchestras*. Metuchen, N.J. London: Scarecrow, 1981.

——. "Conversations with Mary Lou Williams: First Lady of the Jazz Keyboard," *Black Perspective in Music* 8 (Fall 1980): 195-214.

Hentoff, Nat and N. Shapiro, eds. *Hear me Talkin' to Ya*. New York: Dover, 1955.

Holmes, Lowell and John Thomas. *Jazz Greats: Getting Better with Age*. New York: 1986.

Lyons, Len. *The Great Jazz Pianists: Speaking of Their Lives and Music*. New York: Quill, 1983.

McCarthy, Albert. *Big Band Jazz*. New York: Purnam, 1974.

McCarthy, Albert, ed. *Jazz on Record*. London: Hanover, 1968.

McManus, Jill. "Women Jazz Composers and Arrangers." In J. L. Zamont, C. Overhauser and J. Gottlieb, comps. *The Musical Woman: an International Perspective 1983*. Westport, Conn: Greenwood, 1984.

McMillan, Lewis. "Grand Lady of Jazz," *Music Journal* 32 (September: 1974): 50-51, 60.

McPartland, Marian. "Mary Lou: Marina McPartland Salutes One Pianist Who Remains Modern and Communicative." *Downbeat* 24 (17 October 1957): 12, 41.

O'Brien, Peter, comp. and ed. Record notes to "The History of Jazz: Mary Lou Williams." Folkways FA 2966 (1977).

——. Record Notes to "Mary Lou Williams, the Asch Recordings, 1944-47." Folkways FA 2966 (1977).

Pease, Sharon. *Boogie-woogie Piano Styles*. Chicago, 1940.

Pierce, N. Record notes to "Kansas City Jazz." Decca 79226.

Placksin, Sally. *American Women in Jazz, 1900 to the Present*. New York: Seaview Books, 1982.

Russell, Ross. *Jazz Style in Kansas City and the Southwest*. Berkeley: University of California Press, 1971.

Shaw, Arnold. *The Street that Never Slept: New York's Fabled 52nd Street*. New York: Coward, McCann and Geoghegan, 1971.

Smith, Arnold. "Mary Lou Williams/Cecil Taylor: Carnegie Hall, New York." *Downbeat* 44 (14 July 1977): 54, 56.

Smith, Charles Edward *The Jazz Record Book*. New York, 1942.

Taylor, Billy. *Jazz Piano: a Jazz History*. Dubuque, Iowa: William C. Brown, 1982.

Thomas, B. and Lowell Holmes. "Jazz Greats: Getting Better with Age." *Jazz Educators Journal* 14 (1981-82): 22, 78-82.

Unterbrink, Mary. *Jazz Women at the Keyboard*. Jefferson, N.C.: McFarland, 1983.

Williams, Mary Lou. "How this Concert Came About." Record Notes to "Mary Lou Williams & Cecil Taylor Embraced." Pablo 2620-108 (1978).

——. "Some Notes on 'The Blues' and 'Jazz'. " Record notes to " 'My Mama Pinned a Rose on Me.''' Pablo 2310 819 (1978).

——. "Mary Lou Williams." In Max Harris *Talking Jazz*. New York: Norton, 1988.

Olly Wilson

Edith Wilson

(1896-1981)

Singer

Despite the versatility that Edith Wilson displayed throughout her long and multifaceted career, she is remembered primarily for her blues singing. She did, after all, begin and end her long run in numerous areas of show business by singing. Her remarkable longevity in this perilous world was due, in fact, to three qualities: versatility, fierce independence (she refused to be "contracted" to anyone, always negotiating her own terms), and talent.

In the often-sleazy world of blues singing, Wilson was controversial because she refused to sing the rough, low-down gutbucket blues of many of her contemporaries, preferring instead to be a sweet singer of less-naughty lyrics that easily crossed over to appeal to white audiences. Her repertoire of show tunes and foreign-language selections further distinguished her from her peers. She and singers like Alberta Hunter were thought to be sophisticated cabaret types.

Edith Wilson's position among the classic blues singers of the 1900s and 1920s is assured, but some are cynical about Wilson's success. Bruce Cook in *Listen to the Blues* opines that many songs sold as blues weren't really blues, and that any song that had blues in its title would sell in great volume to the public. He lumped Wilson into the category of "Harlem honeys who had never been south of Newark (who) suddenly found fame as blues singers when all they knew about it was that they sang the words and notes just as they appeared on the page" (187). Derrick Stewart-Baxter counters: "Amid all the refinement and histrionics there is hidden deep down in the roots of the blues, another Edith Wilson, a jazz singer, who can shout out a song with feeling and conviction."

Edith Goodall Wilson was born well south of Newark to a musically talented family in Louisville, Kentucky. On September 6, 1896, Susan Jones Goodall, a housekeeper, and Hundley Goodall, a teacher, welcomed Edith Goodall to their family as the third of three children. They lived in a quiet, cohesive neighborhood of well-maintained homes and yards. The church was the center of social activity and the first to benefit from Wilson's vocal and performing talents. Louisville produced several entertainers of note during this time, including the tap-dancing comedy team of Buck and Bubbles, jazz musicians Dickie Wells, Jonah Jones, John Wickley, and Elmo Dunn, and blues singers Helen Humes, Edmonia Henderson, and Sara Martin, the latter credited by Wilson as one of her early influences. Show producer Joe Clark put Wilson onstage before her parents even knew about it in "a little show down at White City Park" (Harrison, 173). After her mother learned of her daughter's subterfuge, she accompanied her to the show and discovered her talent—at age thirteen, Wilson was knockin' 'em dead. Her dad and mother immediately hired a music tutor for her and extracted a promise that Wilson would continue her schooling, which she did, for a short while. Thirty-five dollars a week for singing was too much for any of them to resist, and the die was cast: Edith Wilson was destined to be on the stage.

Pianist Danny Wilson took both a professional and personal interest in young Edith Goodall, expanding her song repertoire and booking her into shows in Chicago and Milwaukee. By the end of the Milwaukee show run, she and

Danny Wilson were married. Danny Wilson continued his mentoring and soon had Edith Wilson playing all the clubs in Chicago, on the bill with him and his sister, Lena Wilson. From there they went to Washington, D.C. and Atlantic City, and then New York, where she caught the ear of composer and record executive Perry Bradford. Bradford made a deal with Columbia Records, and Wilson recorded her first single, Bradford's "Nervous Blues," on September 12, 1921. Columbia rejected her first effort but pulled her back into the studio on September 15 and got acceptable takes of "Nervous Blues" and "Vampin' Liza Jane." After a few more unsuccessful tries, her band, Johnny Dunn's Original Jazz Hounds, with Danny Wilson on piano, recorded "Frankie" and "Old Time Blues" on October 6. After these danceable and cheery numbers began to sell, she hit the road with the Theatre Owners Booking Association (TOBA).

At several clubs she drew the line at raunchy performances and song lyrics, though a few songs in her repertoire at the time, such as "He May Be Your Man" and "My Handy Man," were classic double entendre pieces. For her Cotton Club appearances in 1925, Wilson did adult songs and some double entendre comedy skits, but these were within her limits of good taste and propriety. She continued to record for Columbia, which produced thirty-two sides and issued twenty-six. In her vaudeville appearances she did essentially blackface numbers that at the time appealed to some blacks and many whites, who still demanded plantation stereotypes. One of Wilson's first stage triumphs was a revue in the Dixieland Plantation Room of the Winter Garden in New York, where she developed her acting and comedy skills. A revised version of the revue, repackaged into the *Dover Street to Dixie* musical comedy, headlined Florence Mills and featured Wilson in several prominent set-pieces. She and the other black talent were the toast of Europe when the show played there.

On her return to the United States in 1924, Wilson teamed with "Doc" Straine, a highly-regarded comic, and for two years played the Cotton Club and other big venues to excellent reviews. Occasionally she would sing as a single on the vaudeville circuit when the price was right. She and she alone made the deals. This cost her a lot of money in her career with Columbia, as she would agree to fixed and modest prices for each record, some as low as $125. Others who wrangled part of the royalties made much more, but no one owned the woman who was then often billed as the Queen of the Blues.

Entertainer Prominent in Vaudeville and Musical Revues

For much of the next decade Wilson remained prominent both in vaudeville and musical revues. Lew Leslie's *Blackbirds* in 1926 was particularly good for her career. When it closed after a tumultuous tour of Europe, Wilson stayed behind to perform in several cities. Paris was especially taken with her: It "welcomed the 'colored chanteuse' with her naughty lyrics and impertinent humor" (Harrison, 187). She returned to the United States to work as a singer at the Cotton Club and elsewhere and got lots of radio exposure on the CBS network when the Cotton Club's weekly radio shows played. By then Duke Ellington was the leader of the house band. Though her music appealed to many whites, Wilson often did benefits for various Negro charities, where she performed with such luminaries as Ted Lewis, Buck and Bubbles, the Hall Johnson Singers, Fletcher Henderson, Ada Ward, Will Marion Cook, Eddie Cantor, Adam Clayton Powell, Sr., George Gershwin, James Weldon Johnson, J. Rosamond Johnson, and Clifton Webb. (Blacks and whites could perform together for any charity.)

In 1928 while she was abroad with *The Black Revue*, her husband, Danny Wilson, died of complications of his tubercular condition after an all-day work session with composer Andy Razaf. Edith Wilson's career continued after only a brief period of mourning, and soon she was sharing the stage with the likes of Louis Armstrong and Thomas "Fats" Waller, who wrote "(What Did I Do To Be So) Black and Blue" for the Brunswick label and later two versions of "My Handy Man Ain't Handy No More" and "I'll Get Even With You" for the Victor label. These were to be her last recordings until a 1972 album with Eubie Blake, for whom she had appeared in several "Shuffle Along" shows in the 1930s.

Wilson survived the Depression years by singing with big bands and appearing in revues, some of them her own. While other blues singers fell by the wayside, Wilson was able by sheer talent and perseverance to keep going. She was a survivor. Europe was always a place she could be received well, so she did several overseas tours, returning to the Apollo Theatre in Harlem for "trucking and singing." Though whites regained much control of show business and appeared often even at the Apollo, Wilson was singled out by Charlie Barnet and his racially mixed big band. He, along with many others, was convinced of her superstar talent, though she had been upstaged by the many other top-flight singers of the time. At this critical point in her career she had been rediscovered and her visibility was maintained on the East Coast. When she was offered engagements on the West Coast, she went for the first time. Then:

> . . . Los Angeles would see those sparkling eyes and that mischievous smile as she sang one of her favorites, "He May Be Your Man, But He Comes to See Me Sometimes." She worked the Orpheum and Bert Levy circuits while out west, covering Los Angeles, Denver, Seattle, Salt Lake City, and some cities in Canada. The press hailed her as 'a blues singer of international reputation' (Harrison, 192).

And then her career took some amazing turns. She was offered a couple of minor roles in films, the most noteworthy of which was a French-speaking and singing part in the Bacall-Bogart classic *To Have and Have Not*. Though in post-production her scenes were cut, she was most proud of her work in that film. Radio also beckoned, although with stereotypical roles: Kingfish's mother-in-law on "Amos 'n' Andy" and bit parts in "The Great Gildersleeve." From her role as the voice of Aunt Jemima on "The Breakfast Club," the Quaker Oats people signed her to appear as Aunt Jemima and raise funds for charity. Despite objections from civil rights groups, Edith Wilson saw this as just another role and was phenomenally successful, raising close to three million dollars before civil rights groups persuaded Quaker Oats to halt the Aunt Jemima appearances in 1965.

While on the West Coast she'd married Millard Wilson in 1947. In the fifties they moved to Chicago and were active in civic and cultural activities, especially black community organizations. In the sixties and throughout the seventies she was welcomed with great delight at numerous folk festivals as the blues and folk revival boomed.

By the mid-seventies Wilson's heart was failing and she began to confront her mortality. She then had two driving ambitions: to sing as long as her body would let her and to found a home for indigent performers. Though she had been careful with her money over the years, she knew many who hadn't been. But she could still summon up strength when she wanted to:

> Backed by a jazz combo with 'Little Brother' Montgomery at the piano, she romped through some blues and jazz classics on her 1976 album on Delmark Records with an ease that belied her age. The mischievousness was still there in a voice that was mellow and darker. In the late 1970s that elegant older lady, clad in purple chiffon with matching turban, sang blues and ballads in a Chicago Northside lounge as often as they called her, thoroughly enjoying herself, just like the patrons (Harrison, 195-96).

She and Sippie Wallace worked together as artists-in-residence at the University of Maryland in 1978, and it was hard to tell who enjoyed it more: the artists or the students. As late as 1980 Edith Wilson appeared in the musical *Black Broadway* at New York's Town Hall. Staged originally at the Newport Jazz Festival in 1979, it was regarded by the critics as "the most authentic old-time revue" (Shaw, 299). The 1980 Newport Jazz Festival honored her, and she responded with "He May Be Your Man" and brought the house down.

In Chicago on March 30, 1981, Wilson succumbed to a brain tumor. Her dream of a home for indigent performers—she had planned to call it Star Haven—died with her. But she had sung on America's stages during eight decades—ample testament to her versatility, independence, and prodigious talent.

References

Bogle, Donald. *Brown Sugar: Eighty Years of America's Black Female Superstars*. New York: Harmony Books, 1980.

Cook, Bruce. *Listen To The Blues*. New York: Charles Scribner's Sons, 1973.

Dahl, Linda. *Stormy Weather: The Music and Lives of a Century of Jazzwomen*. New York: Pantheon Books, 1984.

Fox, Ted. *Showtime At The Apollo*. New York: Holt, Rinehart and Winston, 1983.

Harris, Sheldon. *Blues Who's Who: A Biographical Dictionary of Blues Singers*. New Rochelle, N.Y.: Arlington House Publishers, 1979.

Harrison, Daphne Duval. *Black Pearls: Blues Queens of the 1920s*. New Brunswick, New Jersey: Rutgers University Press, 1988.

Kinkle, Roger D. *The Complete Encyclopedia of Popular Music and Jazz, 1900-1950*. Vol. 1. *Music Year by Year 1900-1950*. New York: Arlington House, Publisher, 1974.

Oliver, Paul. *The Story of the Blues*. Philadelphia: Chilton Book Company, 1969.

Rust, Brian. *Jazz Records 1987-1942*. 4th Revised and Enlarged Ed. Vol. 2. New Rochelle, N.Y.: Prometheus Books, 1984.

Schiffman, Jack. *Harlem Heyday: A Pictorial History of Modern Black Show Business and the Apollo Theatre*. Buffalo, New York: Prometheus Books, 1984.

Shaw, Arnold. *Black Popular Music in America: From the Spirituals, Minstrels, and Ragtime to Soul, Disco, and Hip-Hop*. New York: Schirmer Books, 1986.

Stewart-Baxter, Derrick. *Ma Rainey and the Classic Blues Singers*. New York: Stein and Day, 1970.

Walton, Ortiz. *Music: Black, White & Blue: A Sociological Survey of the Use and Misuse of Afro-American Music*. New York: Morrow, 1972.

Denis Mercier

Harriet E. Adams Wilson

(1827?-c. 1870)

Writer

Not only has the twenty-year period from 1970 to 1990 produced a proliferation of exceptional fiction written by black American women, it has also been a period of time in which literary historians have rediscovered many of the previously silenced black American female voices of the past. One of the most fascinating works that reemerged during the past two decade is, *Our Nig; or Sketches from the Life of a Free Black, in a Two-Story White House, North. Showing That Slavery's Shadows Fall Even There*, Harriet E. Adams Wilson's fictional autobiography originally published in 1859.

Historian and critic Henry Louis Gates's rediscovery of *Our Nig* in the early 1980s in a Manhattan bookstore, more than one-hundred years after its publication, restructured the black American literary canon. Before Gates's establishment of Wilson's novel as the first black American novel published in the United States, it was commonly asserted that the distinction of being the first black American novelist belonged to William Wells Brown because of his book *Clotel; or, The President's Daughter*, which was published in London in 1853. In 1857 another novel by a black American was published in London. Unlike Wilson's *Our Nig*, the novel *The Garies and Their Friends*, enjoyed wide readership, as did *Clotel* before it. Before Gates's discovery, it was also widely assumed that the first novel published by a black American woman was Francis Ellen Watkins Harper's *Iola LeRoy, Or Shadows Uplifted*, published in 1892.

Although Wilson is described as a black woman in census reports, the plot of her literary landmark revolves around a mulatto protagonist, Alfrado. Abandoned by her mother at an early age, Alfrado is taken in by a white family as a servant. After suffering throughout her childhood at the hands of the cruel mother and sister of this family, Alfrado's personal misfortunes continue into adulthood in the guise of illness and a wandering husband who eventually dies, leaving her destitute and unable to support herself or her sickly child. As Gates has demonstrated, many of the events of Wilson's life overlap with the life of her protagonist, Alfrado. Gates's extensive research has uncovered several primary documents that partially illuminate the 120-year obscurity of the life of the first black American woman novelist. Wilson states in her preface to *Our Nig* that her purpose in writing the novel was to "aid me in maintaining myself and child" (4). Given this raison d'être, it is sadly ironic that the death certificate of this same child should provide the most substantial piece of information about Wilson. From this document, Wilson's birthplace has been tentatively established as Milford, New Hampshire. This document also provided the names of Wilson's son and husband, George M. Wilson and Thomas Wilson, respectively. A census report revealed the approximate date of her birth as 1827 or 1828. Additionally, a marriage record for Thomas and Harriet Wilson was rediscovered giving the date of their marriage as October 6, 1851. Beyond the information revealed in these few pieces of hard documentation uncovered by Gates and his assistants, little else is known about the life story of Wilson.

Novel Spurs Critical Inquiry

Although many of the facts of Wilson's life continue to elude researchers, the single text she left as her legacy, *Our Nig*, is increasingly the subject of critical inquiry. Through her exposition of Alfrado's life experiences, Wilson demonstrates both the fictional and the historical ways in which race, class, and gender interacted to prohibit the development of true autonomy in the nineteenth-century society of which she found herself a member. *Our Nig* is a particularly important text because often so much attention is focused upon slavery in historical texts and in the literature of the period that the northern, free black is frequently neglected. Wilson demonstrates that during her lifetime racism was as virulent in the North as in the South. She reinforces this by noting in her title that *Slavery's Shadows Fall Even There*.

The early to middle 1800s, the period Wilson covers in *Our Nig*, was a particularly difficult one for the free black American woman. Not only was the black woman's situation complicated by lack of economic opportunities, which was a common denominator for most blacks of the time, but additionally, she was subject to the oppressive expectations placed upon her sex. The nineteenth-century's elevation of femininity into a cult created a particularly problematic situation for the black woman. It was the rare black woman of the period who was able to conform to the expectation outlined for women by the larger society. Certainly Wilson's fictional portrayal of Alfrado's life reflects her own frustration at this real-life double-bind situation in which she found herself.

The genre in which *Our Nig* is written, fictionalized autobiography, demonstrates Wilson's awareness of the literary conventions of the day and of the black literary formats that had proven to be most palatable to the white readers who were the major consumers of literary material. Although *Our Nig* bears some resemblance to other black novels of the period, *(Clotel* and *Iola LeRoy)*, particularly in their characterization of a mulatto heroine's struggle in the face of adversity, Wilson's tale has a ring of authenticity (in dialogue and plausibility of storyline), which is not present in any of the aforementioned works.

As such, it is apparent that Wilson appropriated the older traditions of black autobiography and slave narrative in her creation of *Our Nig*. There have been black slave narratives for almost as long as the diaspora itself. Black men as well as women were participants in the creation of this genre. *Our Nig* does indeed bear some similarity to the works of this genre. Wilson episodically details the despicable treatment of Alfrado in much the way the former slaves described the treatment they received at the hands of their respective masters and mistresses. Another common theme is the yearning for freedom expressed by both the slave narrators and Alfrado. In many slave narratives and in *Our Nig*, the acquisition of education is perceived to be the key to escape from bondage; however, *Our Nig* is not a slave narrative. Although Alfrado acquires education and freedom, the dual primary objectives of the slave narrators, she never becomes an autonomous, self-sufficient individual. Furthermore, although *Our Nig* is presumed to be largely autobiographical, it is still a work of fiction.

It is apparent that in writing *Our Nig*, Wilson borrowed not only from the conventions of slave narration but also from those of the sentimental novel. Possibly Wilson chose to wrap her autobiography in the thin veil of sentimental fiction in order to avoid the public castigation that might have occurred had she acknowledged the narrative to be entirely true. In Linda Brent's later narrative, *Incidents in the Life of a Slave Girl*, the attempts to tell her tale and yet remain within the constraints of gender and not offend her "gentle" readers becomes a tension that strains the credibility of the tale. Wilson, by making her tale a fictional one, is able to expose the barbaric treatment she endured while at the same time not impugning her femininity. By incorporating various literary genres into a cohesive body, Wilson created the black woman's novel; a format in which she could delineate the complex and devastating interaction of race, gender, and class in her protagonist's life and, more importantly, in terms of her own bitter reality as an black American woman in the nineteenth century.

References

Bell, Bernard W. "Harriet E. Wilson." *The Afro-American Novel and Its Tradition.* Amherst: University of Massachusetts Press, 1987.

Foster, Frances Smith. "Adding Color and Contour to Early American Self-Portraitures: Autobiographical Writings of Afro-American Women." In *Conjuring: Black Women, Fiction, and Literary Tradition.* Edited by Marjorie Pryse and Hortense J. Spillers. Bloomington: Indiana University Press, 1985.

Gates, Henry Louis. "Harriet E. Adams Wilson." *Dictionary of Literary Biography.* Vol. 50: *Afro-American Writers.* Detroit: Gale Research, 1985.

———. "Introduction." In Harriet E. Wilson, *Our Nig; or, Sketches from the Life of a Free Black, in a Two-Story White House, North. Showing That Slavery's Shadows Fall Even There.* Boston: George C. Rand and Avery, 1859. Reprinted. New York: Vintage Books, 1983.

Gates, Henry Louis and David Ames Curtis. "Establishing the Identity of the Author of *Our Nig.*" In *Wild Women in the Whirlwind: Afra-American Culture and the Contemporary Literary Renaissance.* Edited by Joanne Braxton and Andree Nicola McLaughlin. New Brunswick, N.J.: Rutgers University Press, 1990.

Shockley, Ann Allen. "Harriet E. Adams Wilson." *Afro-American Women Writers, 1746-1933.* Boston: G. K. Hall, 1988.

Wilson, Harriet. *Our Nig; or, Sketches from the Life of a Free Black, in a Two-Story White House, North. Showing That Slavery's Shadows Fall Even There.* Boston: George C. Rand and Avery, 1859. Reprinted. New York: Vintage Books, 1983.

Carmen Renee Gillespie

Margaret Bush Wilson

(1919-)

Lawyer, civil rights leader

Margaret Berenice Bush Wilson, eminent activist lawyer and civil rights leader who served as chairperson of the board of directors of the NAACP for nine years and has used her legal expertise to advance equal rights for blacks throughout her career, was born on January 30, 1919, in Saint Louis to James Thomas Bush, a real estate broker, and Margaret Berenice (Casey) Bush. One of three children in the prominent black middle-class family (which included her sister, Ermine, and brother, James, Jr.), she grew up in Saint Louis ghetto, a black belt that ran through the middle of the city and whose bleak surroundings were a constant reminder of the restrictive social, educational, and employment opportunities encountered by blacks in the 1920s and '30s.

Despite these dismal surroundings, Wilson's childhood home was a gracious and beautiful setting where the foremost stress was on education. Thus she was inspired her to look beyond the barriers of the neighborhood to a bright future as a productive member of society. Wilson attended the local public schools and graduated with honors from Sumner High School in 1935. She then went to Talladega College, Alabama, where in 1940 she earned a B.A. degree cum laude in economics and mathematics. While at Talladega she was awarded a Juliette Derricotte Fellowship for her senior year; a subsequent scholarship offer from Lincoln University School of Law in Jefferson City spurred her to further study. Wilson's formal education culminated in 1943 with the conferral of an LL.B. degree. One year later she and a fellow law student, Robert Edmund Wilson, Jr., were married. Divorced since 1968, they have one son, Robert III, also a lawyer.

When Margaret Wilson succeeded the late Bishop Steven Gill Spottswood as chair of the board of directors of the 450,000-member National Association for the Advancement of Colored People (NAACP) in 1975, it was the "Year of the Woman," and she was the first black woman to assume the position (Mary White Ovington, a white woman who had been one of the organization's founders, served as chair from 1917 to 1932). One board member who had envisioned Wilson's election stated: "I think it's tremendous that the country's oldest civil rights organization, whose history is rooted in fighting race and sex discrimination, would pioneer in choosing a black woman to lead it—particularly now in these days of affirmative action" ("Woman Lawyer is Elected Chairman of NAACP Board," 46). For most who knew her, though, it was clear that this election was in no manner a gesture meant to satisfy concerns about race and sex discrimination. Her fellow board members, commenting that the vote was "practically unanimous" along with her wide circle of professional associates and the press, were of the general sentiment that the organization's selection was the natural outcome of Wilson's professionalism and expertise as a lawyer and social activist. Wilson, preferring to regard her race and gender as "accidents of my birth. I take them for granted" ("Battlefront," 100), simply labeled herself an "aristocrat," one who, by her definition, demonstrates "character, competence, accomplishment" ("Transition," 45). These were indeed the qualities that enabled her to build a very successful legal career and to make invaluable contributions to the black community, most notably through her work with the NAACP.

After finishing law school and being admitted to the Missouri bar association in 1943, Wilson took up the civil rights cause in an assignment that propelled her into the field that became her specialty: real-estate law. Helping her father, who was considered the first successful black real estate broker in Saint Louis, she assisted the black realtors' Real Estate Brokers Association in obtaining a charter and served as counsel for the group, which had been organized by her father. She played a major role in the legal battle initiated by the association which contested the racially restrictive covenants that existed in housing contracts. The struggle concluded in 1948 with the landmark Supreme Court decision, *Shelley v. Kraemer*, whereby such restrictions in housing were deemed unenforceable under the Constitution.

While Wilson has specialized in real-estate law, her brilliant career reflects experience in a wide range of areas of the legal profession and at various levels of local, state, and federal organizations. After finishing law school, she worked for two years (1943-1945) in Saint Louis as an attorney for the Rural Electrification Administration for the United States Department of Agriculture. Wilson then turned to private practice as a partner of Wilson and Wilson, a partnership with which she was involved from 1947 to 1965. That practice was interrupted briefly from 1961 to 1962, when she worked as assistant attorney general for the state of Missouri. A fleeting attraction to political aspirations lured Wilson to run for Congress in 1948 on Henry Wallace's Progressive ticket. The first black woman from Missouri to run for Congress, she was soundly defeated by the Democratic candidate and has since that time been an active Democrat.

Wilson Battles Housing Problems for Blacks

From 1965 to 1967, through her work with the Missouri Office of Urban Affairs, Wilson was once again immersed in the battle to relieve the housing problems of the black poor. Her close ties to the community continued in her next position, from 1967 to 1968, as an administrator for the Missouri Department of Community Affairs, where she was in charge of community services and continuing education programs. First as deputy, then as acting director of the Saint Louis Model City Agency, a corporation she was instrumental in establishing Wilson aided the poor in obtaining better housing by assisting them in securing federal funds. Wilson's concentration on the housing problem continued for the next three years (1969-1972) while she served as director of the Saint Louis Lawyers for Housing. She resumed private practice in 1972 and remains a partner in the firm Wilson and Associates in Saint Louis.

As a result of her fine legal achievements and contributions to the community throughout the years and the respect that she commanded among her colleagues, Wilson has been sought out for service on local, state, and national boards and institutes. In 1972 she was appointed a member of the Council on Criminal Justice and served in that capacity for five years. The next year, 1973, she assumed the post of vice-chair of the Land Reutilization Authority of Saint Louis; that same year Wilson participated in Saint Louis University's Council on Legal Opportunities Institute by joining the law school faculty as an instructor in civil procedure. She was asked in 1975 to serve as chair of the Saint Louis Land Reutilization Authority, a post she occupied for two years. She has been an active participant on the Arts and Education Council of Saint Louis and is a member of Alpha Kappa Alpha sorority.

Wilson has been accepted in a number of bar associations: the American and National bar associations, as well as branches in Illinois, where she worked briefly while her husband completed law school, Missouri, Saint Louis, and Mound City (Missouri). Wilson was on the general advisory committee for the Arms Control and Disarmament Agency from 1978 to 1981 and served on the President's Commission on White House Fellowships. She has been a board director for the Monsanto Corporation, the American Red Cross (1975-1981), United Way (1978-1984), the Mutual Life Insurance Company of New York, and the Intergroup Corporation (1986-1987). In addition, she has served as chair of the board of trustees for Saint Augustine's College (1986-1988) and Talladega College (1988 to the present). She is a member of the board of trustees of Washington University in Saint Louis. These career achievements, however, were all attained in close concert with her steadfast involvement with the work and goals of the NAACP, the nation's largest and oldest civil rights organization.

Wilson's impressive accomplishments as a lawyer and her dedication to the concerns of racial justice both enhanced and were enhanced by her lifelong commitment to the NAACP, which, founded in 1909, aims to "end all barriers to racial justice and guarantee full equality of opportunity and achievement in the United States" (Wynar, 48). Her dedication and commitment to the fundamental principles of the organization developed naturally because, Wilson noted, "In a literal sort of way, I was born and raised in the NAACP, and the issues that it faces have been a part of my life from my very earliest experiences" ("Woman Power at the NAACP," 89). Thus, her involvement grew out of a "family affair": Her father had been a longtime member; her mother served on the executive committee of the Saint Louis branch; in 1924 her sister, Ermine, was voted the NAACP "Baby of the Year"; and her brother, James, Jr., was a faithful and active member of the organization. Feeling as though she had been a member since childhood, Wilson began actively working with the NAACP in 1956, when she played a key role in organizing the Job Opportunities Council in Saint Louis. The group, supporting the increased hiring of blacks in white businesses, targeted specific business owners, whom the group assisted in the hiring of black employees. Wilson not only provided legal advice to the council but also worked side-by-side with members of the community in solving the everyday problems encountered in achieving the goal. In a leaflet campaign mounted against one of the businesses, for instance, she joined the efforts of the Youth Council of the NAACP as she "chauffeured the kids, sat in the car while they paraded, gave them sandwiches and did all the things you do to support a picket line" (Perlez, 81).

Having won the admiration and support of local leaders in the NAACP organization, in 1958 Wilson became the first woman to assume the presidency of the Saint Louis branch. In 1962, she accepted another leadership role in the organization, this time as president of the Missouri conference of the state NAACP branches. Wilson rose higher among the ranks in 1963 when she was elected to the NAACP national board of directors. As an organization leader she joined the March on Washington in 1963 and worked ardently on the task forces organized to monitor the antipoverty program and the Civil Rights Act ratified by President Johnson in 1964. In 1971 Wilson became treasurer of the NAACP National Housing Corporation. In this position, which she held for thirteen years, she was able to help minority groups gain increased involvement in housing construction, and in particular, to obtain contracts for housing projects. The next year, 1972, Wilson turned her attention to another civil rights issue that continues to have far-reaching repercussions: She was asked to participate in the organization's national board hearings that eventually led to complete desegregation of the Atlanta city school system. Criticizing Atlanta's compromise policy, which essentially allowed for a partially segregated system, she asserted "You can't be committed to the principle of integration and equal opportunity and then condone a plan that seems expedient" (*New York Post* cited in *Current Biography*, 445). In 1974 she once again demonstrated her serious resolve to apply long-established legal and judicial principles equally to all when she took command as chair of the NAACP committee that called for the impeachment of former President Nixon.

Permanent Chairmanship of NAACP Convention Held

The year 1973 was the key year for the top leadership role Wilson played as chief policymaker of the organization. She was elected to succeed the late William Robert Ming, Jr., in the highly-coveted and powerful post of permanent chair of the NAACP annual convention. The death of Bishop Steven Gill Spottswood in 1974, who had served as board chair for thirteen years, forced an election in January 1975. Despite rumors, denied by Wilson, of an internal power struggle, she was elected with great approbation from executive director Roy Wilkins, from the press, and from the organization as a whole. She announced that she had no plans to undertake major reforms in the manner in which the NAACP went about pursuing its goals of full equality of opportunity and achievement, that is, by using legal tactics to change outdated legislative and judicial policies. Wilson advocated revitalizing the organization's membership to further enhancing its effectiveness. Approaching the formidable post with vigor and determination, she proposed to update membership operation through automation, to realign and increase the staff responsible for monitoring national developments in housing, employment, and education as they related to the black community, and, above all, to bring new energy to the organization's strength and spirit by attracting more young people. Many of them she felt, were working at cross-purposes rather than progressing because of their involvement in the various militant activist groups such as the Congress on Racial Equality (CORE) and the Student Nonviolent Coordinating Committee (SNCC).

Described as diminutive, soft-spoken, seeming ten years younger than her age, and not particularly aggressive in demeanor, Wilson's initial impression often belied the candid, tough-minded administrator and cagey negotiator. She had come to be known, during her work with the Model Cities Agency, as "Mary Poppins—with a razor blade" (*Current Biography*, 446). She tackled each challenge with an intrepid sense of purpose that proved her quite capable of enduring the "arduous duties of bluffing, lobbying, and other parliamentary in-fighting" and enabled her "usually [to have] her way among the men of that body" ("Woman Power at the NAACP," 89). Despite problems with management within the organization, declining enrollment, and differences with the board's executive director, Benjamin Hooks (1977 successor to the late Roy Wilkins), Wilson's tenure as organization leader set a standard that reached beyond the immediate needs of housing, job opportunities, and education for blacks. For her, ending discrimination by providing more jobs and better housing was not enough; she insisted on the necessity of involving blacks in a broader variety of fields and more prominently in policy-making positions, especially in government. She stated to the *Washington Post*:

> I'm getting a little weary of public officials assuming the only spot we can hold is in civil rights or equal employment. It's cynical and insulting. Blacks should be providing some leadership not only on the problems of blacks, but all problems. We should be respected and heard (Prince, cited in *Current Biography*, 446).

Wilson remained the NAACP national board chair until 1984, when Kelly Alexander was elected.

Wilson has been awarded numerous honors in recognition of the positive and profound impact she has had as a legal adviser and civil rights activist. Among the most prestigious is one conferred upon her in 1963—the Bishop's Award of the Episcopal diocese of Missouri. The American Jewish Congress, a Jewish human rights group, has twice paid tribute to her achievements: in 1975 she was the recipient of the Louise Waterman Wise Laureate Award of the National

Women's Division; in 1978, Wilson received the Democracy in Action Award from the Saint Louis Council of the American Jewish Congress. Along with the academic awards earned in college and law school, several colleges and universities have given her honorary degrees: Alabama State University, Boston University, Kenyon College, Smith College, Saint Paul's College, Talladega College, and Washington University. She has also made appearances on numerous national radio and television shows, including "Meet the Press," "The David Susskind Show," "Today," and "A.M. America" (ABC). Her reflections on her youthful dreams and subsequent success, recorded in an interview in *Essence* in 1982, reveal the principal attributes of integrity, determination, and intelligence that propelled Wilson to the pinnacle and by so doing, opened opportunities for countless others:

> Throughout the years I have advanced professionally but never by design. I just did the job at hand rather than pursue the brass ring. I never sought success but always tried to be successful at what I was doing. There is a difference. . . . I always knew I would be productive in some way. The avenues have changed over the years but the productivity and the need to be a responsible member of society have not (46).

References

"American Jewish Congress Honors Mrs. Wilson." *Crisis* 85 (October 1978): 284.

"Battlefront." *Crisis* 82 (March 1975): 99-101.

Current Biography Yearbook. New York: H. W. Wilson, 1975: 443-46. Photograph, p. 244.

Current, Gloster. ' "Our New Day Begun'—The Transition Convention." *Crisis* 84 (October 1977): 387-89. Photographs, pp. 388-89.

"In the Nation's Press: Margaret Bush Wilson." *Crisis* 82 (March 1975): 83.

"Margaret Wilson." *Essence* 6 (August 1975): 46.

"The NAACP Suspends Hooks." *Newsweek* (30 May 1983): 61.

Perlez, Jane. "Margaret Bush Wilson: NAACP's New Head." *New York Post*, 18 January 1975. Reprinted in *Crisis* 82 (March 1975): 80-82.

"Power Play." *Time* (30 May 1983): 22.

"Transition." *Newsweek* (27 January 1975): 45.

Who's Who Among Black Americans, 1990/91. 6th ed. New York: Gale Research, 1991.

Who's Who in America. 45th ed. Vol 2. Wilmette, Ill.: Marquis, 1989.

"Woman Lawyer is Elected Chairman of NAACP Board." *Washington Post*, 14 January 1975.

"Woman Power at the NAACP." *Ebony* 30 (April 1975): 88-93. Photographs, pp. 88-91.

"Women at the Top." *Ebony* 37 (August 1982): 146.

Wynar, Lubomyr. *Encyclopedic Dictionary of Ethnic Organizations in the United States*. Littleton, Colorado: Libraries Unlimited, 1975.

Carolyn Hodges

Nancy Wilson

(1937-)

Singer, actress

Born the oldest of six children to Olden Wilson and Lillian (Ryan) Wilson on February 20, 1937, singer, actress, and performer Nancy Wilson grew up in Chillicothe, a small city in southern Ohio. She, her brothers Anthony and Michael, and sisters Rita, Brenda, and Karen, spent many of their formative years in the company of their grandmother on "Whiskey Run Road," just outside Columbus. Lillian Wilson worked long hours as a domestic and Olden Wilson worked in an iron foundry.

By the time she was four years old, Nancy Wilson knew that she wanted to become a singer. She sang in the church choir and listened avidly to a litany of musical talent, among them Billy Eckstine, Louis Jordan, Ruth Brown, LaVern Baker, Nat King Cole, and big band vocalists such as Jimmy Rushing and Little Jimmy Scott. Wilson attended Burnside Heights Elementary School and graduated from West High School in Columbus, Ohio. At age fifteen, she began her professional career by performing in local clubs in and around Columbus.

Unsure of her musical career, Wilson decided to play it safe. Entering Central State College, she majored in education, planning to obtain teaching credentials. But in 1956, after a year in college, she decided to pursue her lifelong ambition to become a singer, dropped out of college, and joined the Rusty Bryant Band. During this period Wilson met Julian "Cannonball" Adderly, who became a major influence on her musical career.

After three years of touring with the band throughout the United States and Canada, Wilson decided to move to New York City. She set very specific goals for herself. She wanted to become an independent soloist, she wanted John Levy as her manager, and she wanted to record for Capitol Records. Allotting herself just six months to achieve these goals, she only had to wait for four weeks before her big break came.

She received a telephone call from a New York nightclub asking her to fill in for Irene Reid. Wilson sang so well that she was booked into the club on a permanent basis. Singing four nights a week, she worked as a receptionist during the day to supplement her income. It was not long before John Levy, Cannonball Adderley's manager, came to hear her sing. Impressed, Levy called her the following day and set up a demonstration recording session. She recorded "Guess Who I Saw Today" and "Sometimes I'm Happy." The records were sent to Capitol and within a week she had a positive response. In six weeks Nancy Wilson had accomplished her goals and signed a Capitol contract.

"Guess Who I Saw Today," Wilson's debut single, was a success. Between April 1960 and July 1962 Capitol released five Nancy Wilson albums. Among them is the 1962 historic recording *Nancy Wilson/Cannonball Adderly Quintet*. Her first big hit was released in 1963, "Tell Me The Truth."

Nancy Wilson married drummer Kenny Dennis in 1960. They had one son, Kenneth (Kacy) Dennis, Jr., who was born in Los Angeles on January 24, 1963. Wilson and Dennis divorced and in 1970 Nancy Wilson married Reverend Wiley Burton. They have two daughters, Samantha Burton, born June 4, 1975, and Sheryl Burton, born May 4, 1976.

During the 1970s Wilson seemed to reach her pinnacle. Her shows were booked two years in advance. She worked fifty-two weeks a year performing two shows a night. Wilson recorded on the Capitol label until 1980, when she switched to A. D. I. Records, initiating what became an ongoing relationship with Japanese audiences. She records on Japanese-based labels because of the country's recording techniques. She says, "They've allowed me to sing so that I can sing. I can't sing for a splice in the middle. I say, 'We'll do it from the top until you get what you want.' The day the music died, is the day . . . when they stopped recording live, they started doing things you can't reproduce live" (*Jet*, 28 July 1986).

Wilson is a member of the following organizations: NAACP; SCLS; Operation PUSH, for which she is chairperson; President's Council for Minority Business Enterprises; Committee for the Kennedy Center for Performing Arts; and the United Negro College Fund. She also gives her time and talent to various charities and community projects. Working with the Johnson and Johnson Prenatal Care Promotion, she earned the company's "Red Ruby" Award. She has also worked with the Martin Luther King Center for Social Change, the National Urban Coalition, and the Warwick Foundation, and she and her family have created the Nancy Wilson Foundation to permit inner-city children to see the country and experience alternate lifestyles.

Among her honors, awards, and achievements are an Emmy in 1975 for "The Nancy Wilson Show"; the NAACP Image Award (1986); Grammy Award for "How Glad I Am" (1964); Entertainer of the Year Award presented by *Atlantic City Magazine*; Global Entertainer of the Year Award presented by the World Conference of Mayors (1986); the Paul Robeson Humanitarian Award; first place in the 1983 Japan Song Festival Competition; and an award from the United Negro College Fund (1986).

Wilson Appears in Television Specials

Wilson has appeared extensively on television in addition to her own show in 1967-1968. Her appearances include the "Phil Donahue Show," "The Tonight Show," "The Merv Griffin Show," "The Today Show," "Sunday Morning with Charles Kurault," "Entertainment Tonight," and "Ebony/Jet Showcase." She has made guest appearances on "The Carol Burnett Show," "The Sammy Davis Jr. Show," "The Andy Williams Show," and "The Flip Wilson Show." A television special, "Nancy Wilson in Concert," aired in 1989, and the singer, who gave top comedian and talk show host Arsenio Hall his first break when he opened for her several years back, is a frequent quest on such shows as "The Lou Rawls Parade of Stars" and the "March of Dimes Telethon."

Wilson's acting roles have included both movies and television series. She starred in *The Big Score* with Fred Williamson and Richard Roundtree. She has appeared in "I Spy," "Room 222," "O'Hara: US Treasury," "Police Story," "The FBI," and "Hawaii Five-O."

Producing more than fifty records and forty albums, Wilson confesses that good songs continue to be the key for her. She believes the marketplace has opened up to female stylists and points to Anita Baker, Sade, and Whitney Houston , as examples. At age fifty-three, Wilson says, "There's a whole lot more for me to achieve. I think people are finally beginning to realize that I'm a song stylist; I've been pigeon-holed as a jazz singer, an R & B singer, a pop singer" (Nathan, n.p.), but actually Wilson prefers to be called a "song stylist."

Song stylist is a fitting phrase for it aptly describes what she does with a song. She has won acclaim for her technique, her precise intuition, her faultless intonation, and her sure and deft turning of a phrase. *Time* magazine describes Wilson as "all at once, both cool and sweet, both singer and storyteller" (Nathan, n.p.).

References

DeVeaux, Alexis. "Do be do wows! Jazz's Grand Divas." *Essence* 12 (October 1986): 54.

Hall, Devra. "Sketches from Pros Folios: Nancy Wilson." Factsheet. 1988.

"Nancy Wilson Celebrates Fiftieth Birthday." *Jet* (16 March 1987).

"Nancy Wilson Feted Her Road Manager. *Jet* (11 March 1985).

"Nancy Wilson Tells Why She Records in Japan." *Jet* (28 July 1986).

Nathan, David. "Nancy Wilson." *Music Bio*. Factsheet. John Levy Enterprises, September 1989.

Robinson, Louie, "Home on the Range" *Ebony* 43 (November 1987): 116-118.

Nagueyalti Warren

Oprah Winfrey

(1954-)

Talk show host, actress

Nearly everyone knows Oprah Winfrey from her television program or from her films, but what is less familiar is the story of her rise to stardom, which is the stuff of fiction. Oprah Gail Winfrey was born on January 29, 1954, in Kosciusko, Mississippi, a small town seventy miles north of Jackson, the capital and largest city in the state. Her parents, Vernita Lee and Vernon Winfrey, were never married. Vernon Winfrey was twenty years old and in the service at the time. He was home on furlough from Fort Rucker in Alabama. His leave over, the young father returned to his military duties and had no knowledge of his fatherhood until Vernita Lee mailed a card to him announcing the baby's arrival and scrawled across it a request for clothing for the baby.

The mother had intended to name the baby Orpah after the Biblical woman in the Book of Ruth, but someone, perhaps the midwife who attended the delivery, the clerk at the courthouse, or even Vernita Lee herself, misspelled the name by transposing the "p" and the "r".

There was little work for a young black woman in Kosciusko who had no specific skills and no advanced training in any area of employment. Lee had heard that jobs were more plentiful in Milwaukee and better paid. Shortly after Oprah's birth, Vernita Lee moved to Milwaukee, Wisconsin, leaving the baby in the care of Vernon Winfrey's mother. She hoped to find a job as a domestic worker at wages of $50.00 a week, money that no doubt sounded attractive to a young woman of her background.

Grandmother Winfrey was a woman of strong, disciplined character, closely attached to her church. She lived her life according to a strict interpretation of the Bible and raised her granddaughter to do the same. Much of Oprah Winfrey's early life was spent at church, and the church furnished her with her first opportunities to display and enjoy her talents. It soon became apparent that this child was exceptional. Her ability to read was phenomenal. She had a way with words, whether her own or those of a piece she had memorized. She made her first speaking appearance when she appeared on an Easter program. Later, at Christmas time, she was on the program again. She was three years old.

No doubt the grandmother was pleased at this early evidence of young Winfrey's abilities, and she probably encouraged her to participate in church pageants and other activities that generated many occasions to talk and to read. But outside the church, at home, Oprah Winfrey was made to understand that she was not to be heard so readily. She spent a great deal of time with adults and was to be quiet when in their presence. This kind of restraint was very difficult and discomfiting to a very articulate child who longed for the company and attention of the people around her.

Nevertheless, there was encouragement for this incipient performer, both at home and at church, and the experience of her earliest years was excellent preparation for her later academic, intellectual, and spiritual development. From her first day in kindergarten, she was in her element, even as she objected to the tasks assigned to her and her fellow pupils and sensed that much of her schoolwork did not afford her sufficient mental challenge or pleasure.

When she recalls her childhood, Winfrey indicates that she began to wish that she were white when she was about six years old. She relates that she slept with a clothespin on her nose, and prayed for corkscrew curls. She felt, she says, that being white would have rescued her from all of the physical discipline to which she was subjected in the form of frequent spankings. Though she viewed her life as unsatisfactory, her spirit was not broken. She would not be subdued, and her grandmother would not compromise. Clearly, a change in the arrangements for her care was demanded. The grandmother soon appealed to Vernita Lee for relief. It was decided that Winfrey would go to live with her mother in Milwaukee. She was not to live in Kosciusko again.

If Oprah Winfrey had thought that life in Milwaukee would be more to her liking, she was soon to find that the life there was decidedly different from the semi-rural life she had known in Mississippi. Her mother had only a room in another woman's house and had to work so hard that she had little time or energy to devote to the care of her child. Having been so young and inexperienced when her child was born, Vernita Lee did not have a fully-realized understanding of the parental function and what was required of her as a mother. The combination of welfare money and her wages as a maid was still insufficient to afford them even the minimal comforts of a home. As she became more and more aware of city life, Winfrey became increasingly rebellious and resentful of the lack of material comforts and simple diversions that marked her life with her mother. As she had proven to be too much for her grandmother to control, so too she was more than her mother could handle.

It was Vernon Winfrey's turn now. Perhaps the influence of a father might be brought to bear upon this difficult child with greater success than either grandmother or mother had been able to realize. He had moved to Nashville, Tennessee, upon completing his military commitment. He had married and established a home with his wife, and the two of them welcomed Oprah Winfrey during the summer of 1962, just after she had finished first grade.

The young couple were pleased to have Vernon Winfrey's daughter with them. Oprah Winfrey was soon to find that she would not be able to wear them down as she had done her mother and grandmother. The little girl's stepmother quickly discovered that in spite of her skills in reading, speaking, and writing, Winfrey was lacking the mastery of basic knowledge of arithmetic that should have been hers, so she was firmly set to work at strengthening her performance in computation. The ensuing school year went well.

The church was still a major influence in her life. Vernon Winfrey had not abandoned the religious values that his mother had developed within him. He was active in his church, Progressive Baptist, and brought his daughter with him, not only for Sunday church services, but for youth activities, for holiday programs, and church-sponsored community activities. Oprah Winfrey was a dependable performer in religious pageants, choral presentations, and the activities of the various organizations within the church. Finally it was summer again, and Vernita Lee wanted to see her daughter. The Vernon Winfreys hesitated, but shortly relented because they knew that it was important to support the relationship between the natural mother and her child. Vernon Winfrey's fears of a summertime visit proved to have been well-founded: When summer had ended and he went to retrieve his daughter, he found both her and her mother reluctant to resume the arrangement of the previous year.

Vernita Lee had persuaded Oprah Winfrey that life "at home" could now be much more pleasant than it had been earlier. She was soon to marry a Milwaukee man with whom she had maintained a relationship for several years. The new family would include the man's two children, a son and a daughter. It was for the Winfreys quite a blow, having to return Oprah Winfrey to an environment that they knew did not offer the support and discipline that she needed and deserved, but they felt a certain respect for Lee's wishes, and so the agreement was made. The return to Milwaukee represented a downturn in Oprah Winfrey's fortunes, and the negative aspects of her life became more intolerable to her as she grew older.

Winfrey Suffers in Silence

Again Winfrey developed a painful concern relating to skin color and standards of physical attractiveness. She became convinced that she was neglected in favor of her lighter-skinned stepsister. She felt cast off, and her pain was all the more intense because it seemed to her that her mother was as guilty of her mistreatment as anyone else. Not surprisingly, she more and more often sought refuge in books. Her bookish bent only increased her isolation from the family, who placed little value on superior intelligence and intellectual or scholastic achievement. Having been moved back and forth between her parents according to their preference, she began to fear that neither of them really wanted her as a part of their lives. The seeds of rebellion were soon firmly sowed in her mind, and her conduct began to deteriorate.

It was also during this period, beginning as early as her tenth year, that Winfrey alleges she was made the victim of frequently imposed sexual abuse. She found these outrageous attacks upon her physical and emotional self most confusing and frightening, but she suffered them in silence because she did not know what else to do. In every instance the abusive episodes involved male family members or trusted acquaintances.

In spite of her miserable home life, Winfrey remained a good student. Gene Abrams, one of her teachers at the inner-city Lincoln Middle School, recognized her exceptional abilities and took an active interest in her. He helped her to get a scholarship to a prestigious suburban school in the affluent Fox Point area. Winfrey encountered few scholastic problems there, but her emotional problems were proliferating and her behavior was reflecting the chaos she was experiencing. Out of her fertile mind, Winfrey was hatching and staging one preposterous scheme after another. On several occasions she destroyed family belongings and pretended that their apartment had been burglarized in order to get herself a more fashionable pair of glasses. Twice she ran away from home. Winfrey's mother was constantly bewildered by her increasingly frequent escapades and was brought again to the acknowledgement of her inability to deal with her rebellious daughter. During the summer of 1968 Oprah Winfrey, now fourteen years old, went back to Nashville to live with her father and his wife.

Life Takes a New Course

It was a vastly different Oprah Winfrey who returned to Nashville after the five years spent in Milwaukee. Early adolescence is a period of rapid growth and change for any individual, but the circumstances under which Winfrey had lived had brought great negative influences into her life, which forced her to grow up somewhat more quickly than would have been the case if she had been surrounded by a more congenial environment.

Adjustment between father and daughter was not easy, but Vernon Winfrey was able to prevail. He set high standards of conduct and achievement for his daughter and stuck with her to see that she met them. She enrolled in Nashville's East High School and she was soon involved in numerous school activities, especially those having to do with public speaking and dramatics.

By the time Oprah Winfrey entered her senior year of 1970-1971, she had focused her interests and knew that her future lay in the performing arts. She was chosen to attend the 1970 White House Conference on Youth in Washington. She went to Los Angeles to speak at a church and toured Hollywood while she was there. She won various titles, including "Miss Fire Prevention" and "Miss Black Tennessee."

The local radio station, WVOL, managed and operated by blacks, hired Winfrey to read the news. She was soon ready to enter college and hoped to attend an institution far removed from Nashville, perhaps in New England. But once again, Vernon Winfrey made a decision that countered his daughter's preferences. She would attend Tennessee State University in Nashville. An academic scholarship won in an oratorical contest sponsored by the local Elks lodge helped to finance her college studies, which were to feature a major in the English language arts.

Media Opportunities Open

Winfrey continued her work as a news announcer at WVOL and was soon hired away by WLAC, a major radio station. It was not long before she moved to WLAC-TV (later WTVF) as a reporter-anchor. Although she was earning a five-figure salary while she was in college, her father had not softened his strict requirements of her in terms of conduct or scholarship, and with each succeeding year she was finding his restraints on her social life harder and harder to accept. She began to look beyond Nashville and found a new position at WJZ-TV in Baltimore, Maryland, in 1976. She was only a few months short of her college graduation, but she left Nashville and Tennessee State University without having taken her bachelor's degree.

Winfrey's tenure in Baltimore began less auspiciously than she would have liked. She became the object of an intensive makeover effort on the part of her station. The management sought to develop for her an entirely new persona. The attempt was not completely successful. She had little formal training in journalism or mass communication, and her reporting often failed to achieve the desired degree of objectivity. Indeed, she resisted the necessity to be objective, preferring to approach a story from the inside and react to it in a subjective manner. She had never before accustomed herself to a self-disciplined point of view and seemed unable or unwilling to do so now.

Winfrey Finds Her Niche

Winfrey was well-protected by the contract she had with the station; management was forced to find a better use of her talents. She was assigned to cohost a local morning show called "People Are Talking". Neither she nor her employers recognized the fact right off, but Winfrey had found her niche. Her engaging personality and her amazing ability to communicate with a diverse audience were indisputable assets in her new assignment. Sherry Burns, who was producer of the show, said of her, "Oprah is a wonderful, wonderful person. Who she is on-camera is exactly what she is off-camera. . . . She's a totally approachable, real, warm person." The very traits of emotionalism and subjectivity that had hampered her efforts as a reporter contributed to her ability as an effective and stimulating interviewer.

As the popularity of her show began to grow, as well as her satisfaction and enjoyment with it, Oprah Winfrey began sending tapes of her broadcasts to other markets around the country. She sensed that she was ready for big-time broadcasting. The woman who had been coproducer of "People Are Talking" left Baltimore in 1984 for a new position on "A.M. Chicago," a morning talk show broadcast by the ABC-TV Chicago affiliate, WLS-TV. The station manager had observed Winfrey on some of the tapes his new producer had screened for him and quickly decided to hire her for "A.M. Chicago," which would compete with the "Phil Donahue Show," the well-established favorite in the local and national market. With Winfrey's coming, "A.M. Chicago" took off and quickly outdistanced Donahue in the ratings. In early 1985 Phil Donahue moved his show to New York and left Chicago to Winfrey.

Winfrey Exercises Acting Talent

In high school and college Winfrey had pursued an interest in dramatics and had attracted favorable attention as an actress, so she found the idea of portraying Sofia in the Quincy Jones/Steven Spielberg 1985 film production of Alice Walker's novel *The Color Purple* very appealing. She took leave from her show and went south to create her role. The film opened to mixed reviews and much controversial discussion, but most professional critics praised Winfrey's performance, and it earned her an Academy Award nomination. Close on the heels of *The Color Purple*, she appeared in 1986 in a motion picture based on Richard Wright's novel *Native Son*. Hers was not a major role. The film was neither a critical success not a popular one and was not widely distributed.

Winfrey's "A.M. Chicago" show having become such a sensation, WLS-TV decided to allot it a full hour instead of its former thirty minutes and changed its title to "The Oprah Winfrey Show." By late 1986 the show was in syndication. It was reported that the deal grossed $125,000,000 and that its star would receive more than $30,000,000 in 1987-1988 and become the highest-paid performer in show business. A five-year contract secured her position as a television host through the 1990-1991 season.

Winfrey Forms Own Company

Winfrey had become one of the best-known figures of the 1980s. She could finally devote much of her prodigious energy to the pursuit of the numerous dreams that she had cherished throughout the years of her swift ascent to the pinnacle of her profession. Since the achievement of her full-blown success, Winfrey has formed her own company, Harpo (Oprah spelled backwards) Productions and purchased a gigantic studio to house its operations. Harpo, Inc., has taken over the ownership and production of "The Oprah Winfrey Show," over which she maintains full control and responsibility, thus demonstrating her astuteness as a businesswoman. The company plans to bring to the screen productions that convey important social and spiritual messages that might not be deemed by others to be commercially promising. Already *The Women of Brewster Place*, by Gloria Naylor, has been offered as a television movie, and plans call for presentations of Toni Morrison's Pulitzer Prize-winning novel *Beloved*, Mark Mathabane's autobiographical *Kaffir*

Boy, and Zora Neale Hurston's much-admired novel, *Their Eyes Were Watching God*.

Winfrey speaks to numerous youth groups and urges her audiences on to higher achievement. She presses them to strive for higher standards and to seek to be all that they can be. She seeks to raise the level of confidence and self-esteem of her female listeners of all ages. She speaks of a goal of helping women to win self-empowerment.

In 1988 Winfrey was invited to deliver the main address at commencement exercises at Tennessee State University. At that ceremony the university awarded her a diploma in recognition of her accomplishments, although she had left the institution without having completed degree requirements. For her part, Winfrey established a scholarship fund at her alma mater that will furnish payment of expenses for ten students enrolled in the university each year. Characteristically, she reserves the right to choose the students who receive these annual awards. She maintains a personal relationship with each recipient and requires that each student keep a "B" average. She writes letters to them and reassures them: "I understand that the first year is really difficult, and there are a lot of adjustments to be made. I believe in you. We all made an agreement that it would be a three-point average, not a 2.483, and I know you want to uphold your end of the agreement, because I intend to uphold mine."

She also anticipates establishing a center that would offer counseling and support to women who need assistance. Says Winfrey, "I want to be able to spread the message that you are responsible for your life and to set up a format to teach people how to do that. Right now, I don't know what to call it other than a center for self-improvement."

Oprah Winfrey now lives in a luxury condominium overlooking Chicago's Lake Michigan. Her home reflects a preference for the color white in interior decoration.

"The Oprah Winfrey Show" is viewed by 17,000,000 people each weekday. Winfrey's rise to stardom is an extraordinary story of personal achievement. Her appeal is broad, and her name is among the best-known of any woman now performing on national television.

References

Anderson, Chris."Meet Oprah Winfrey." *Good Housekeeping* (August 1986).

Angelou, Maya. "Oprah Winfrey (Woman of the Year)." *Ms*. 17 (January/February 1989): 88.

Chapelle, Tony. "The Reigning Queen of TV Talk Oprah!! *Black Collegian*, 21 (November-December 1990): 136

Edwards, Audrey. "Stealing the Show," *Essence* (October 1986): 50-52, 123. Photographs, p. 126.

Gillespie, Marcia Ann. "Winfrey Wakes All." *Ms*. 17 (November 1988). 50.

Gross, Linden. "Oprah Winfrey: Wonder Woman." *Ladies Home Journal* 105 (December 1988): 40.

Harrison, Barbara. "The Importance of Being Oprah." *The New York Times Magazine*, 138 (June 11, 1989). 28

King, Norman. *Everybody Loves Oprah!* New York: Morrow, 1987.

Sanders, Charles L. "At Home with Oprah Winfrey." *Ebony* 43 (October 1988).

Lois L. Dunn

Deborah Cannon Partridge Wolfe

(1916-)

Educator, consultant, religious leader

A prominent educator and a tireless advocate of women's equality and civil rights, Deborah Cannon Partridge Wolfe has devoted a lifetime of service to religious, civic, and humanitarian causes and organizations.

Wolfe was born December 22, 1916, in Cranford, New Jersey, one of three children born to David Wadsworth Cannon and Gertrude (Moody) Cannon. Both parents held theological degrees and were active in religious and educational affairs. Her father pastored the First Baptist Church of Cranford, and her mother was a teacher and principal. Their roles as ministers and educators influenced the Wolfe children to pursue careers in education. Her sister, Mary Cannon McLean, was an educational specialist for the mentally retarded, and her brother, David Wadsworth, Jr., was a professor at Virginia State College.

An outstanding student, Wolfe graduated from Cranford High School in 1933, having participated in a variety of activities: the student magazine, the choral group, and sports. Following high school, she attended New Jersey Teachers College in Jersey City, where she majored in education and sociology and minored in social studies and English. She again immersed herself in extracurricular activities. During the summer of 1935 she directed the community center at her father's church, and for the next two summers she directed a community center for migrant workers in Hardlock, Maryland. A year before graduating in 1937, Wolfe taught math and English at a local high school under the Works Progress Administration (WPA) adult education project, of which she later became principal.

While working on the WPA project, Wolfe pursued a master's degree in education and sociology at Teachers College of Columbia University. She received her degree in 1938. Her thesis was entitled "A Background Study and Teacher Training Program for the Education of Migrants."

From 1938 to 1950, she served on the faculty of Tuskegee Institute (now University) in Alabama, teaching education, chairing the department of education, and directing graduate studies. She also worked as principal and teacher-trainer at two of Tuskegee's laboratory schools—Prarie Farms school (1938-1943) and Mitchell's Mill School (1943-1945). In 1940, she married Henry Roy Partridge, a teacher at Tuskegee. One son, Henry Roy Partridge, Jr., was born to the couple before their divorce in 1950. Wolfe married Estemore Avis Wolfe on August 9, 1959.

While Henry Partridge, Sr., was in the service during World War I, Wolfe continued graduate studies at Vassar College and Columbia University, earning an Ed.D. in 1945 from the latter. Her doctoral study was entitled "Redesigning the Curriculum of Rural Schools of Tuskegee Institute."

In 1950 Wolfe and her son returned to Cranford, where she embarked on a long career as a professor of education at Queen's College of the City University of New York. During her summers she taught as a visiting professor at several colleges across the country: New York University, the University of Illinois, Fordam University, the University of Michigan, and Grambling University.

Wolfe's vast experience and expertise in the field of education were increasingly tapped on a national level. In 1955 she was invited by President Dwight D. Eisenhower to take part in the White House Conference on Education and in 1960 was appointed to serve on the Citizens Advisory Committee on Youth Fitness. Her chief appointment, however, came on January 10, 1962, when Representative Adam Clayton Powell, Jr., chair of the House Committee on Education and Labor, named her the committee's chief educational consultant. One of the few women and black Americans to hold a high-ranking staff position on Capitol Hill, she was in charge of research and drafting legislation on education, as well as serving as a liaison between the committee and the Department of Health, Education and Welfare. Despite his often stormy relations with his peers in Congress, Powell's committee produced significant legislation affecting employment practices, public school aid, vocational training, school lunch programs, and federal aid to libraries.

Wolfe left the committee in 1965 to resume teaching at Queen's College and to later direct City University's Center for African and Afro-American Studies (1968-1977). She also continued her consultant work. Among the many organizations and corporations she served were Encyclopedia Britannica, McMillan Publishing Company, and the National Leadership Training Institute, United States Office of Education.

Wolfe's deep roots and active participation in the church led to her ordination in 1970 as an associate minister at First Baptist Church, Cranford. She holds several positions in the Progressive National Baptist Convention and is active in ecumenical activities. She has served as United Nations representative for church women and has chaired its nongovernmental representatives.

Following the tradition of black American educators like Mary McLeod Bethune and Nannie Helen Burroughs, Wolfe has served as vice president of the National Council of Negro Women, member of the board of directors of the American Academy of University Women (1969-1975), grand basileus of Zeta Phi Beta (1954-1965), and member of the New Jersey State Board of Education. Other organizations in which she has been involved include the NAACP, the YWCA, the National Association of Negro Business and Professional Women, and the National Alliance of Black School Educators, of which she was president.

Wolfe had received numerous honors and awards for her many accomplishments. Among them are honorary doctorates from more than eleven colleges, including her alma mater, New Jersey State Teachers College; Distinguished Service Award from Seton Hall University; honorary membership in the Top Ladies of Distinction (1986); Omega Psi Phi Fraternity Sojourner Truth Award; Women of Courage, Radcliffe College; naming of a junior-senior high school in Macon County, Alabama, in her honor (1962); one of New York's Outstanding Ten Women by the *Amsterdam News* (1958); Today's Makers of History Award, the Association for the Study of Negro Life and History (1959); "Woman of the Year," Delta Beta Zeta Chapter of Zeta Phi Beta Sorority (1958); and citation by the National Baptist Convention for outstanding contributions to the religious and civic welfare of America (1952).

Deborah Cannon Partridge Wolfe, who is five feet three inches tall, is a lover of arts and sports. Since her retirement as professor of education at Queens College, Wolfe has remained active in a number of organizations and activities, most notably as an associate minister at her home church. She has pursued postgraduate theological education at Union Theological Seminary and the Jewish Theological Seminary of America in New York, which resulted in her ordination as a Baptist minister.

In addition to her master's and doctoral theses, Wolfe has written numerous articles on education for such publications as the *Journal of Negro Education*, *Understanding the Child*, *School Executive*, and the *Journal of Educational Sociology*. As a member of a team of educators visiting the USSR, her observations appear in "Education in the USSR" (New York State Education, April 1959).

References

Current Biography, 1962. New York: H. W. Wilson, 1962. Photograph, p.470.

Ebony (April 1962): 6.

Who's Who Among Black America, 1990/91. 6th ed. Detroit: Gale Research, 1990.

Who's Who of American Women, 1961-62. Chicago: Marquis, 1962.

Hill, Ruth Edmonds. *Women of Courage*. An Exhibition of Photographs by Judith Sedwick. Based on the Black Women Oral History Project, Cambridge, Mass.: Radcliffe College, 1984.

Collections

The most complete treatment of Wolfe's life, thought, and contributions are contained in a 1979 oral history interview conducted by Marcia McAdoo Greenlee for the Black Women Oral History Project, housed at the Arthur and Elizabeth Schlesinger Library, Radcliffe College.

Raymond R. Sommerville

Geraldine "Jerry" Pittman Woods

(1921-)

Medical consultant, civic leader

The noticeable underrepresentation of blacks in science fields has been a pressing concern of employers, the federal government, and Geraldine Pittman Woods. Her distinguished record as scientist led the federal government in 1969 to appoint her as special consultant to the National Institute of General Medical Sciences, National Institutes of Health (NIH). In that role, Woods helped address the needs of science faculty and potential science students in the black colleges by assisting in the development of two important programs at NIH for minorities—the Minority Biomedical Support Program (MBS) and the Minority Access to Research Careers Program (MARC). Since their initiation in the 1970s, these programs have helped to increase minority participation in the sciences by encouraging students to participate in graduate training in scientific fields. Woods's contributions should be examined by other measures as well, for she has devoted most of her life to improving the quality of life for students, working in education-related activities, and fulfilling important roles in the community that affect a broad spectrum of society.

Born in 1921 in West Palm Beach, Florida, Geraldine Pittman Woods is the daughter of Susie (King) Pittman and Oscar Pittman. Although her parents received only an eighth-grade education, they were determined that their daughter would go as far in school as she wanted. They were established in the restaurant, farming, and lumber businesses, and invested in real estate in West Palm Beach. Apparently their business ventures and investments were wise; after her father died her mother supported Woods throughout her college career without Woods having to work. Woods obtained all of her degrees without interruption in time. She was a student at Talladega College, Talladega, Alabama, from 1938 to 1940. Transferring to Howard University, Washington, D.C., Woods graduated in 1942 with a B.S. degree. Since she had always been attracted to the sciences, one of her Howard professors encouraged her to continue study in his field—embryology. In 1943 she graduated from Radcliffe College with an M.A. degree and in 1945 took her Ph.D. degree from Harvard University. Geraldine Pittman was never the "typical" student that the prestigious institutions expect from black institutions. "I was a good student at Harvard," she said and she became fully involved in her studies:

> I remember walking into a physiology course and seeing all the white students working with various instruments, which I'd never seen before. I said to myself, 'So that's the name of the game,' and I got up early every morning and stayed late every night (Gindick, 12).

She earned has master's and doctorate within three years and was elected to Phi Beta Kappa as well.

She was instructor in biology at Howard University from 1945 to 1946. On January 30, 1945, she married Robert Woods. She soon left the teaching field, and she and her husband moved to California where Woods, a dentist, practiced near Inglewood. In California, where Woods has lived since marriage, she became a homemaker and the mother of two daughters, Jerri and Jan, and a son, Robert, Jr.

Involved at first in raising her family and in community activities, from 1963 to 1967 Geraldine Pittman Woods was on the board of directors, Center for Educational Opportunity, the Claremont Colleges; executive board, YWCA and Family Sevices of Los Angeles; and twice on the Interviewing Panel, Personnel Board, California Department of Employment. In February 1965 Lady Bird Johnson invited her to the White House to launch Project Head Start. In 1968 President Lyndon Johnson appointed her chair of the Defense Advisory Committee on Women in the Services. From 1968 to 1972 she was vice-chairman of the Community Relations Conference of Southern California. In 1969 Woods became special consultant, National Institute of General Medical Sciences, National Institutes of Health—a position that she held until 1987. She was a member of the board of trustees, California Museum Foundation of the California Museum of Science and Industry (1971-79); board of graduate studies advocates, Meharry Medical College, Nashville, Tennessee, 1972-75; member Air Pollution Manpower Development Advisory Committee, Environmental Protection Agency, 1973-75; board of directors, Robert Wood Johnson Health Policy Fellowships, Committee of the Institute of Medicine, National Academy of Sciences, 1973-78; member California Postsecondary Education Commission, 1974-78; board of directors, National Commission for the Certification of Physician's Assistants, 1974; elected to the board of trustees, Atlanta University, 1974; and national board, Girl Scouts, USA, 1975-78. In 1975 Geraldine Pittman Woods was elected chair of the board of trustees of her alma mater, Howard University, and became the first woman to head the board. She held that position until 1988 and now holds chairman emeritus status. She was chair of the Howard University Foundation board of directors from 1984 to 1988. From 1977 to 1976 she was a member of the board of directors of the National Center for Higher Education Management Systems.

Minority Participation in the Sciences Encouraged

Woods has helped to increase minority participation in the sciences through the programs that she innovated at the National Institutes of Health. The Minority Biomedical Support (MBS) and the Minority Access to Research Careers (MARC) help minority schools move into the mainstream of competition for federal research monies and at the same time encourage minority students to seek careers in the sciences. She found that high school counselors discouraged minorities from entering the sciences and mathematics, and that those who do pursue these fields in academia must spend long hours in laboratories while holding jobs to sustain themselves or their families. As a result, the length of time students study was increased. The MBS and MARC problems were designed to help resolve these problems.

There is also a MARC Faculty Fellowship Program that promotes advanced research training for selected faculty at minority institutions and a MARC Visiting Scientist Award that supports outstanding scientists and teachers to serve as visiting scientists in these institutions. The MBS program provides released time from teaching so that a professor may move into research activities and have the equipment and supplies needed. Salaries for undergraduates and graduates to participate in research and training are given. In 1987 NIH produced a documentary, *A Time for Celebration* to demonstrate Woods's work in the initiation and development of MARC and MBRS programs.

Social and civic activities have been equally demanding on Geraldine Pittman Woods. She is a life member of the National Council of Negro Women and served as a member of its national board from 1969 to 1973. She is a life member of the NAACP and has served as president of the auxiliary to the medical, dental, and pharmaceutical association of Southern California. A member of numerous organizations, including the Links and Delta Sigma Theta Sorority, from 1963 to 1967 Woods was national president of Delta Sigma Theta. In that position she furthered the international, mental health, social action, and community service programs, voter registration and education programs, and job-opportunities and career-development programs. She assisted in developing the "Delta Teen-Lift," a program of travel for students fourteen to seventeen years old in various regions of the country to widen their horizons in education, business, and career development. As president of the sorority, she assisted in the passage of civil rights legislation and action.

Geraldine Pittman Woods has received many honors and awards in recognition of her outstanding service to the sciences and to the community. Among these are tributes and plaques for "bold efforts to undergird black colleges in the biomedical sciences" from various chapters of Delta Sigma Theta Sorority, 1977, and the sorority's Mary Church Terrell Award, 1979; "Scroll of Merit," National Medical Association, 1979; a scholarship in her name was given for one of the first chemistry students in a new program at Atlanta University's MBS symposium, 1980; Howard University Achievement Award; and tributes by the Los Angeles City Council, the California Assembly, the California Senate, the Los Angeles County Board of Supervisors, and the Los Angeles mayor, 1980; fellowship in her name established at Howard University by Delta Sigma Theta for students in biology, 1981; selection as one of twenty Famous American Black Scientists, 1981; inclusion in the exhibit "Black Women Achieving Against the Odds," prepared by the Smithsonian Institution, 1983; recognition in *Dollars and Sense* magazine's first annual salute to America's Top 100 Black Business and Professional Women, 1985; founder's award from Delta Headstart, Los Angeles, 1985; recognition by the Undergraduate Student Assembly, Howard University, at the Fifth Annual Salute to Black Women for Service to the Howard University Community, 1985; election as honorary member of Gold Key Society by students at Howard University, 1986; Salute to International Business and Professional Women Award, Nassau, Bahamas, 1987; and Distinguished Leadership Achievement Award, National Association for Equal Opportunity in Higher Education, Washington, D.C., 1987. In addition, she holds honorary degrees from Benedict College, (1977), Talladega College, (1980), and Meharry Medical College, (1988).

The work of Geraldine Pittman Woods to strengthen the presence of minorities in the sciences remains highly visible in the recipient institutions, where the MARC and MBS programs continue to flourish and where students who otherwise may not choose science careers are engaged in study and research. Woods is proud of the number of black students who have reaped the benefit of the programs that she helped to establish.

References

American Men and Women of Science. 16th ed. New York: Bowker, 1983.

Delta Journal (November/December 1974): 7.

Gindick, Tia. "Able Advocate of Higher Education: Dr. Geraldine Woods Works for 'Qualifying' Minorities." *View*, Part V., *Los Angeles Times*, 18 July 1980. 1, 12. Photograph, p. 1.

Who's Who Among Black Americans, 1990/91. Detroit: Gale Research, 1991.

Who's Who of American Women. 10th ed. Chicago: Marquis, 1978.

Collections

Information on Geraldine Pittman Woods can be found in the Biography File, Fisk University Library, Nashville, Tennessee.

Jessie Carney Smith

Elizabeth "Lizzie" Wright

(1872-1906)

School founder, educator

Elizabeth Wright

At a time when the education of black youth in the rural South demanded attention and in an area where white residents opposed the building of a school for that purpose, Elizabeth Evelyn Wright's vision for an educational institution that would project Booker T. Washington's idea of self-help and industrial training would not die. After repeatedly opening schools that were closed because of white opposition, Wright left her last site in Hampton County, moved on to Denmark, South Carolina, and when she was about twenty-five cofounded with Jessie C. Dorsey (later Greene) the Denmark Industrial School in 1897, which later became Voorhees Industrial School and stands today as Voorhees College. It is a monument to the persistence, faith, and love of a young black woman.

Elizabeth "Lizzie" Evelyn (or Evaline) Wright was born on April 3, 1872, on the William Rolfe place located three miles southeast of the courthouse in Talbotton, an out-of-the way town in Georgia (Wright's biographer gives August 18, 1876, as her birthdate.) She was the seventh of a family of twenty-one children, nineteen of whom were Wrights and two, of whom were Fowlkes. Her mother, Virginia "Gini" Rolfe, married Stephen Fowlkes, who died while working in Columbus, Georgia, during the Civil War. She then married John Wesley Wright, a carpenter, and had nineteen additional children. Gini Rolfe was described as "a beautiful Indian woman about five feet tall with long black hair and a light copper complexion." Elizabeth Wright was tall as a girl, with hair and complexion like her mother's. Neither her black slave ancestors nor her Indian ancestors could read or write.

The parents were natives of Talbotton, one of the oldest towns in the state and one known for its long history of cruel treatment of blacks and Indians. A few Cherokees had eluded federal troops when the Cherokee nation was forced from the land, among them the family of Virginia Rolfe, who settled in Talbotton. The town was a stronghold of the crumbling institution of slavery, and for many years after Emancipation it remained a dull and slow farming community, maintaining its original indifference to progress. It was not until 1870 that education for all white children was required. Schools for blacks were even slower to be established, primarily due to the lack of teachers, a school site, and instructional materials.

Life on the Rolfe Place might have been like that on other plantations. According to her biographer, J. F. B. Coleman, until Wright was five, she was often left alone sitting on the cabin floor crying herself to sleep or left under a shade tree or in the sand for the older children to care for. At noon the mothers came from the fields to nurse the babies and fed them no more until night. This was the pattern in the South during Reconstruction. Wright's more recent biographer, J. Kenneth Morris, whose account came from Virginia Rolfe's descendants, said that Gini Rolfe maintained her Indian connections and was absent from the home for weeks at a time. Wesley Wright took a second wife, Mary West, who was black, to care for Virginia's children, but maintained his marriage to Virginia.

At the age of five, Lizzie Wright went to live with her grandmother, Lydia Rolfe, who lived two miles in another direction from Talbotton. The widowed grandmother lived with her son, Jus W. Tolge, who was to become Wright's real guardian. Since she was separated from her brothers and sisters and other children in the nearby community, she was her grandmother's constant companion. The lonely child improvised her playthings and, bright, insightful, and inquisitive, she did not hesitate to seek answers to questions that puzzled her.

In about 1879, at the age of seven or eight, Elizabeth Wright enrolled in a district school, probably conducted in the basement of Saint Philip's Church, and studied the limited curriculum of reading, writing, and arithmetic. The school year was of a short, three-month duration and the cold winter months made attendance difficult for young children. The building was extremely cold during the harsh winter of her first year. She remained there for two years but her education left much to be desired. When Wright was ten the uncle moved her and her grandmother into town, where school facilities were near and better: seats were more comfortable, the school term was longer, and the teacher was better prepared. Wright developed rapidly and performed above average.

The neighborhood children enjoyed playing under a large oak tree with low, thick, wide-spreading branches that stood a little distance from Wright's house. While Wright played there one day, a gentle wind rose and lifted a torn piece of newspaper from the tree. It fell at her feet. Examining the paper, she found that it was an advertisement for Tuskegee Industrial School telling how poor black youth could be educated by working their way through school. The message and accompanying photograph of the early campus buildings appealed to Wright, who showed it to her teacher, a Northern white woman who knew the name of the school but little else about it. After writing for and receiving information on Tuskegee, the teacher counseled Wright and they agreed that she would study there. Only after persistent discussions between the teacher and the grandmother and uncle did the family agree to the idea. Meanwhile, Wright was actively and diligently involved in housework to earn as much as possible toward her Tuskegee studies.

Arriving at Tuskegee in 1888, Elizabeth Wright's savings were insufficient for her to enroll as a day student. Thus, she registered in the night school of the preparatory department and was assigned to kitchen duty. This pattern of work and study became too exacting for the frail Elizabeth Wright but was not to mean failure. Hearing of the matter, Olivia Davidson Washington, Booker T. Washington's second wife, intervened, changed her from the night to the day program, and obtained a scholarship for her, which enabled Wright to remain in school and continue her studies. Her work assignments were also lighter. The experience established a close relationship between Olivia Davidson Washington and Wright, and between Judge George W. Kelley of Massachusetts, her benefactor and Wright. Kelley and Wright maintained a close friendship over the years. Olivia Washington knew Wright's condition well, having suffered from frailties herself. She succumbed to her health problems on May 9, 1989. She had set an example for Wright, who determined to pattern her life after Olivia Washington.

Writing of her early experiences at Tuskegee and of Booker T. Washington's influence on her development, Wright said:

> I was at Tuskegee only a short time before I made up my mind to try to be the same type of woman as Mr. Washington was of a man.
>
> The talks which he gave us on Sunday evenings in the Chapel did more to mold my character than anything else. I made them a part of me while in school and they stick to me now like lead. His talks influenced me to try to help my fellow men to help themselves, and if a way was not opened for me, I must open it (Coleman, 26).

Elizabeth Wright was not to be intimidated by strict rules that prevailed in the college. She and five classmates wrote to college officials on July 26, 1890, acknowledging sorrow for their "brother workman and school-mate" William Connover, who was suspended from school for one month. They called for an alternate penalty for a violation "too large to be passed over in silence," since Connover had no funds for food or housing ("From Six Students to Warren Logan and Washington," *Booker T. Washington Papers*, Vol. 3, 70-71, hereafter *BTW Papers*).

We do not know Elizabeth Wright's whereabouts in the summer of her first year or where she was when the six students wrote to Logan. Because of her financial difficulties, she may have worked in Tuskegee. There is also no evidence that she ever returned to Talbotton. When the fall term opened in 1890, Margaret James Murray had joined the faculty. She also took an interest in Wright, understood her frailties, and knew that she was a protégé of Judge Kelley. Wright continued her studies, registering each year between 1890 and 1892 as "Lizzie" Wright or "Lizzie Eveline," of Talbotton and listing Lydia Rolfe, her grandmother, as her sponsor.

There are conflicting accounts of Elizabeth Wright's life between 1892 and 1895, particularly in two major biographies examined. J. F. B. Coleman's work, *Tuskegee to Voorhees*, is sometimes confusing and presents a difficult chronology. Morris J. Kenneth's *Elizabeth Evelyn Wright* gives a different and clearer chronology. Since the writers used different primary sources, there may be some accuracy on both sides.

Margaret Murray observed Lizzie Wright's weakening condition early in the 1892-93 Tuskegee year and arranged a place for her with Almira S. Steele, a white trustee of Tuskegee, who built a school for "colored" children in McNeill's [sic], South Carolina. Steele financed Wright's travel, which occurred in October 1892, and after a few days of rest Wright was able to assist in the school. Two or three weeks later, she began to teach there. Lulu Davis, another Tuskegee student, accompanied Wright on the trip and also became a teacher. George Kelley visited Steele's school and on January 3, 1893, wrote to the Tuskegee treasurer that he was pleased with the work of Elizabeth Wright and Davis (George W. Kelley to Warren Logan, 3 January 1893, *BTW Papers*, Library of Congress, cited in Morris, 35). In April of that year whites burned the school. It was commonly said in the white community, "negro schools burned because blacks were ignorant, careless, irresponsible" (Morris, 46). Kelley bought the land and a small house from Steele for the purpose of building another schoolhouse. In the meantime, Wright and Davis followed Steele to Chattanooga, Tennessee, where Steele was to open an orphanage for black children. Wright returned to Tuskegee in September 1893 and during the year she had a vision of her goals after graduation: "to build an industrial school [for blacks] patterned after Tuskegee" (Morris, 38).

During Wright's stay at McNeill's, Booker T. Washington and Margaret James Murray had married on October 12, 1892. Still interested in Wright's well-being, Margaret Murray Washington gave her additional responsibilities. Her fondness for Margaret Murray Washington made an equally lasting impact on Wright:

> I always considered myself one of Mrs. Washington's disciples and would sit at her feet as Paul did at Gamaliel. Every Saturday afternoon, she held meetings down town with the country women who came in town to purchase their supplies. It was my duty to go down, ask the women in and serve coffee and bread. Mrs. Washington would then proceed to talk on various subjects which I can never forget. Those meetings trained me to do effectual work among my people. I know if it had not been for Mrs. Washington's training, I could not carry on the work in which I am now engaged (26).

Wright remained reasonably healthy during her senior year, completing her degree in May. Dismayed because she felt her clothing inappropriate for the commencement ceremony, Wright was surprised at the arrival of a beautiful white cotton dress with "a high neck and yoke of tucks and lace meeting in points at the center. The sleeves were full length, puffed at the shoulder. The ankle-length skirt was very full, tucked at the hips and hemmed at the bottom" (Morris, 41). It had been a gift from "a friend up North."

Tuskegee Plan Projected in School's Founding

Elizabeth Wright arrived in McNeill's on June 3, 1893, to prepare to teach at the new school that Judge Kelley promised to build. Local whites were still hostile, while the blacks were fearful. Together with Kelley, however, the new school building was planned. Before construction began, the stacked lumber was burned and the idea of rebuilding in that area was abandoned. Another site under consideration, an old mill located between Early Branch and Cummings, was subsequently burned. They located another site in Hampton County and with Hattie Davidson, a Tuskegee graduate, monies were raised by local blacks to help renovate a log schoolhouse. Local residents volunteered to saw the lumber and renovate the structure. School opened and was scheduled to run from September to November or December. Afterwards night classes were added for men, but Wright still did not have the industrial school that she envisioned. Low attendance during the spring months caused Wright to close the school, first until September, then permanently.

Wright's pattern of opening schools and closing them because of racial incidents was set. She opened another school in the house that she arranged to buy near the Hampton County Courthouse and later moved it to Huspah Baptist Church. With the encouragement of Almira Steele, Jessie C. Dorsey of Coshocton, Ohio, joined Wright as a teacher and replaced Hattie Davidson, who had left when their school closed. Wright spent the summer on a speaking tour among churches, fund-raising to build a school on the site of her home. The women won little approval among local blacks, and whites openly showed their hostility. Wright suffered chronic gastritis, aggravated by the hot summer months, which led to her rest stay at the Battle Creek Sanitarium where Dorsey had worked as a nurse and had met Almira Steele. On January 1, 1897, she returned to Hampton.

Unfair dealing and racial incidents in Hampton caused the women to look elsewhere for a school site. They renovated a one-room log hut in Govan into two apartments—one as a dormitory for the four teachers (Lulu Davis, Anna Marthard, Dorsey, and Wright) and the other as classroom. The site would soon be unsatisfactory, and Wright looked for yet another place. Her visits took her to Denmark, where no black school existed and no plans to rebuild a burned-out school were being made.

They opened in a temporary location on April 14, 1897, and closed permanently at the end of May 1898. In the meantime, Wright, who had solicited funds from sixty-six churches, paid two hundred dollars toward another site in the area, and opened Monday, October 4, 1897. The land was purchased from a South Carolina lawyer and state senator, S. G. Mayfield, and Wright converted an old mansion into the schoolhouse. There was a balance of $1,800. Threats to burn this site were not carried out, perhaps due to the physical support of Mayfield and others. By May 1898 Wright had paid seven hundred dollars on the land and the balance was to be paid without interest.

The school that Elizabeth Wright founded last had the support of her benefactor at Tuskegee, George W. Kelley. She had kept up correspondence with him, informed him about her location, progress, and intention to found an industrial school. According to Coleman, he remained her adviser and provided influence and financial support during her struggles; Morris gives him little place. As soon as the board of trustees was in place, he was elected the first board president. He visited her whenever she was sick, which was not infrequent, and guided and assisted her through the difficult and distressing periods of her illnesses and struggles with the school.

By 1898 there were 4 teachers and 236 pupils. The school had operated for eight months—the longest term for any school in that area at the time—and had operated its own prosperous farm. The closing exercises were successful and a highlight of the area, attracting some five hundred persons. In that same year she was ready to build a three-story structure and wrote to her friend Booker T. Washington for advice. A potential benefactor and supporter of the American Missionary Association advised Wright that he would pay the balance owed to obtain a clear deed on the property if she would sign the property over to the AMA. This was unacceptable to Wright, who said: "I do not believe in denominational schools and feel that I can do more for the uplifting of my race by having it strictly independent under a board of trustees" (Elizabeth Evelyn Wright to Booker T. Washington, 6 June 1898, *BTW Papers,* Vol. 4, 432). Washington was proud of his illustrious graduate, and told the Tuskegee 1990 graduating class:

> I want the girls to go out and do as Miss Lizzie E. Wright is doing. I want you to go into the country districts and build up schools. I would not advise you to be too ambitious. Be willing to begin with a small salary and gradually work your way up ("A Sunday Evening Talk," *Booker T. Washington Papers,* Vol. 5, 503).

At the end of the 1899 school year, mothers' meetings reportedly had been held twice a month—quite similar to those at Tuskegee. Monthly meetings for men were held to persuade them to purchase homes and to plant more food. Wright continued to solicit funds locally and also toured the North to visit prospective donors. The success of the Northern trips is unclear. In response to a request for a note of commendation on behalf of Elizabeth Wright, Booker T. Washington addressed a letter "To Whom It May Concern":

> [She] is doing a very satisfactory and helpful work at Denmark, S.C., for the uplifting of her people. The secretary of our Board of Trustees has visited her and reports that everything is conducted in a splendid manner and that her influence on the people of that section is very marked. I am glad to commend her to such persons as may be interested. (June 2, 1900 (*BTW Papers*, L. C. Morris Collection, quoted in Morris, 119-20).

Jessie C. Dorsey had remained with Wright over the years, aided in the founding of Denmark Industrial School in 1897, and remained at the school as vice-principal after Wright's death. Later the school moved to a site near the outskirts of Denmark and was known as Voorhees Industrial School (1902); the school was renamed in honor of benefactor Ralph Voorhees, and in time was to become known as Voorhees College.

Elizabeth Evelyn Wright, "a tall young woman who was very frail and of sober countenance" (Coleman, 24), married Martin A. Menafee, a Tuskegee graduate, who was either one of her teachers or "stenographer to the Principal" on June 2, 1906, at Voorhees. She continued to use the name Wright. After many years of recurring illness and hospitalization, she died in Battle Creek, Michigan, at age thirty-four on December 14, 1906, of chronic gastric catarrh. Her funeral was held on Tuesday, December 18, in the Voorhees school chapel, and she was buried on the campus. Voorhees College and its students, who have reaped the benefits of her vision, remember her with kind reverence as they view her portrait that hangs on the walls of the administration building.

References

Coleman, J. F. B. *Tuskegee to Voorhees: The Booker T. Washington Idea Projected by Elizabeth Evelyn Wright.* [Columbia, S.C.]: R. L. Bryan, 1922. Portrait on frontispiece. Includes photographs of early school buildings.

Contributions of Black Women to America. Vol. 2. Ed. Marianna W. Davis. Columbia, S.C.: Kenday Press, 1982.

Davis, Marianna W., ed. *South Carolina's Blacks and Native Americans 1776-1976.* Columbia, S.C.: State Human Affairs Commission, 1976. Photograph, p. 291.

Elizabeth Evelyn Wright to Booker T. Washington, 6 June 1898. In Louis R. Harlan, ed. *The Booker T. Washington Papers.* Vol. 4, 1894-98. Urbana: University of Illinois Press, 1975.

"From Six Students to Warren Logan and Washington." In Louis R. Harlan, ed., *The Booker T. Washington Papers.* Vol. 3, 1889-95. Urbana: University of Illinois Press, 1974.

Morris, J. Kenneth. *Elizabeth Evelyn Wright, 1872-1906.* Sewanee, Tenn.: University of the South, 1983. Includes photographs.

[Washington, Booker T]. "A Sunday Evening Talk." In Louis R. Harlan, ed. *The Booker T. Washington Papers.* Vol. 5, 1899-1900. Urbana: University of Illinois Press, 1976.

Collections

Papers of Elizabeth Evelyn Wright are in the archives at Voorhees College, Denmark, South Carolina, and the South Caroliniana Library, Columbia, South Carolina.

Jessie Carney Smith

Jane C. Wright

(1919-)

Physician, researcher, educator

The first of two daughters born to Louis T. Wright and Corinne (Cooke) Wright, Jane Cooke Wright was born in

New York City on November 20, 1919, into a distinguished medical tradition. Her paternal grandfather was one of the first graduates of Meharry Medical College in Nashville, Tennessee, and a step-grandfather, William Penn, was the first black to earn the M.D. degree from Yale Medical School. Penn's son-in-law, Harold D. West, was the first black president of Meharry Medical College. Her father, Louis Tompkins Wright, eminent surgeon and researcher, was one of the first black graduates of Harvard medical school and at his twenty-fifth reunion was voted the man in the class who had contributed the most to medical knowledge. He had been also the first black to become a New York City police surgeon and the first black to be appointed to the staff of a New York City hospital. A pioneer in cancer chemotherapy, he established the Cancer Research Foundation at Harlem Hospital. The second Wright daughter, Barbara, one year younger than Jane, is also a physician.

Jane Wright grew up in New York City in the family residence on 139th Street and was educated in private schools in New York: Ethical Culture, an elementary school, and Fieldston, its affiliated upper school, where she was captain of the swimming team, graduating in 1938. She won a four-year scholarship to Smith College. While there she was an excellent student and varsity swimmer whose records stood for many years.

There had been no pressure on her to go into medicine, and for a while at college she considered becoming a painter. However, her father discouraged this choice because of the uncertainties of a career in art. It was as an upperclassman at Smith that she finally decided on a career in medicine and applied for admission to New York Medical College. She won a four-year scholarship based on her record at Smith, from which she graduated with a B.A. in 1942.

These were the war years, and medical education had been accelerated from the traditional four years to three years of year-round study. In addition to being an exceptionally good student in medical school, she was vice-president of her class, president of the honor society, and literary editor of the yearbook. She received the M.D. degree with honors in June 1945, graduating third in a class of ninety-five. There followed an internship at Bellevue Hospital, 1945-1946, and then an assistant residency in 1946. While interning at Bellevue she was rated by her supervisor as "by all odds the most promising intern I have ever had working with me" (*Crisis*, Vol. 60, 5). A residency in internal medicine at Harlem Hospital, 1947-1948, completed her training.

Meanwhile, on July 27, 1947, she had married David Jones, Jr., a Harvard Law School graduate and son of Bennett College president David D. Jones. They have two daughters, Jane and Alison. Away from the hospital, Jane Cooke Wright is known as Mrs. David Jones or simply Jane Jones.

Her first employment, in 1949, was as a New York City school physician and visiting physician at Harlem Hospital. Later that year she became a clinician at the Cancer Research Foundation at Harlem Hospital, which studied the effects of drugs on tumors and other abnormal growth. When her father died in 1952, she succeeded him as its director. The foundation's work, which contributed to the advancement of cancer chemotherapy, was challenging and exciting, and she seemed to have found her special calling. "There's lots of fun in exploring the unknown. There's no greater thrill than in having an experiment turn out in such a way that you make a positive contribution" (*Current Biography*, 444). In September 1955 Jane Wright joined the faculty of the New York University Medical Center as director of cancer chemotherapy research and instructor of research surgery in the department of surgery. Within five months she was assistant professor, and by 1961, adjunct professor of research surgery. She maintained an affiliation with the two major hospitals in the medical center, Bellevue and University. Her work in analyzing the efficacy of a wide range of drugs in the treatment of cancer produced a greater understanding of the relationship between patient, tissue culture, and animal response, as well as the knowledge that responses to the same drug may differ between research animals and human beings or between extracted malignant tissue and the cancer in the actual patient. Her work was always sustained by the knowledge that with the right drugs, cures are possible.

Administrator Heads Study of Major Diseases

On July 1, 1967, Jane Cooke Wright became associate dean and professor of surgery at her alma mater, New York Medical College, and joined the staff of its affiliated hospitals, Flower-Fifth Avenue, Metropolitan, and Bird S. Coler Memorial. In addition to being able to pursue her own research, her duties included the administration of the medical school and special responsibility for the development of a program to study cancer, heart disease, and stroke. In July 1964 she had been appointed to the President's Commission on Heart Disease, Cancer, and Stroke. The commission's report led to the establishment of a national network of centers for the study and treatment of these diseases—the nation's major killers.

There have been numerous awards and honors. One of the earliest was one of the Merit Awards for 1952 from *Mademoiselle*. *Crisis* gives an account of the award. Presented to young women in their twenties and early thirties "who have already distinguished themselves in their fields and are expected to achieve even greater honors," this award was given to Jane Cooke Wright "for her outstanding contribution to medical science with her evaluations of the efficacy of drugs in cancer treatment—evaluations that are now being translated, abstracted, and quoted all over the world." In accepting, she announced: "My plans for the future are to continue seeking a cure for cancer, to be a good mother to my children, and a good wife to my husband" (*Crisis*, Vol. 60, 5). In recognition of this award, *Crisis* put her on its cover for the January 1953 issue.

In 1965 the Spirit of Achievement Award of the Women's Division of the Albert Einstein College of Medicine was presented to her for her "deep commitment as a scientist and teacher in advancing medical knowledge and research'' (*Crisis*, Vol. 72, 328). Two years later, in 1967, she received, along with Isaac Stern, Senator Ernest Gruening of Alaska, and author Elie Weisel, the Hadassah Myrtle Wreath award for outstanding contribution to her field of endeavor; in 1968, the Smith medal from Smith College; in 1980, she was featured by Ciba Geigy on its Exceptional Black Scientists poster. In observance of International Woman's Year, the December 1975 issue of *Cancer Research* saluted eight senior women scientists, all honored members of the American Association for Cancer Research, whose pictures appeared on its cover. One of the eight was Jane Wright, cited for her contributions to research in clinical cancer chemotherapy.

She has served on the board of trustees of Smith College, of the American Cancer Society (New York City division), and the editorial board of the *Journal of the National Medical Association*. She has served as vice-president of the African Research Foundation and in 1961 went to East Africa to inspect medical conditions. She is a member of numerous professional organizations and has been cited by many civic groups for her outstanding contributions. She is the author of scholarly articles in the field of cancer chemotherapy and is the recipient of honorary degrees from Women's Medical College (now the Medical College of Pennsylvania) in 1965 and from Denison University in 1971. She was elected to Alpha Omega Alpha national honorary medical society in 1966.

In 1983, at the annual convention and scientific assembly of the National Medical Association, she presented the surgical section's distinguished lecture, ''Cancer Chemotherapy: Past, Present, and Future'' (later published in the association's journal), which covered the historical milestones in the development of chemical control of cancer, the present successes with the use of polychemotherapy, and the hopeful trends in research. Beginning in 1984, she published in the *Journal of the National Medical Association* a multipart series of landmark review articles entitled ''Update in Cancer Chemotherapy,'' which included discussions of state-of-the art chemotherapeutic treatment for gastrointestinal, breast, lung, and genito-urinary cancer.

Emeritus professor since 1987, Jane Cooke Wright now has more time to pursue long-postponed interests in watercolor painting, reading mystery stories, and sailing.

References

American Men and Women of Science. 16th ed. Vol. 8. New York: Bowker, 1986.

Crisis 60 (January 1953): 4-5. Photograph, p. 4; Vol. 72 (May 1965): 328. Includes photograph.

Current Biography, 1968. New York: H. W. Wilson, 1969. 443. Includes photograph.

''Homecoming for Jane Wright.'' *Ebony* 23 (May 1968): 72-74, 76-77. Includes photograph.

''Medical Family.'' *Ebony* 6 (January 1951): 71-74.

Who's Who in America. Vol. 2. 45th ed., 1988-1989. Wilmette, Ill.: Marquis, 1989.

Jean Elder Cazort

Y

Josephine Silone Yates

(1859-1912)

Teacher, journalist, clubwoman

Josephine Yates, a woman of formidable energy, took full advantage of the educational opportunities offered her and became a remarkable and well-known educator, as well as a prolific journalist and president of the National Association of Colored Women. Her interests ranged from literature and science to practical concerns of the society in which she lived.

Yates was probably born in 1859 in Mattituck, Suffolk County, on Long Island, the younger daughter of Alexander Silone and Parthenia (Reeve) Silone. The birthdate, 1852, given by Hallie Q. Brown, editor of *Homespun Heroines and Other Women of Distinction*, and others, does not square with the other biographical data. Yates was eleven when she went to Philadelphia to live with her maternal uncle, John Bunyan Reeve, and spend a year at the Institute for Colored Youth. This must have happened in 1870-1871, since the arrangement ended when Reeve resigned his pastorate in September 1871 to accept the invitation to establish a theological department at Howard University.

Yates would have been the fourth generation born near Mattituck, at least in her mother's line. The Silones may have been able to make a similar claim. The family was proud of a pure African ancestry, and there was a family story that they were descended from escapees of a slaveship wrecked off the New England coast, and that they had been free since the middle of the eighteenth century. The family was therefore well-established in their community. Mrs. Silone was a pious woman with a fair education. While the older daughter, Harriett, became a skilled dressmaker, Yates showed great intellectual promise and received strong encouragement in her schooling, during most of which she was the only black American in her class.

Her year at the Institute for Colored Youth when she was eleven, which was directed by Fannie Jackson Coppin, brought her into contact with educated blacks of her own age for the first time, and she made rapid progress in her studies. When the arrangement with her uncle ended, after a two-year interval she went to live with her maternal aunt, Mrs. Girard, in Newport, Rhode Island. Here Yates completed her last year of grade school and entered Rogers High School, where she finished the four-year course in three years. Although she excelled in all of her courses, she took a special interest in chemistry "doing additional laboratory work at odd hours under the guidance of her instructor" (Majors, 46). Yates was the only black in her class, the first to graduate from the school, and valedictorian of the class of 1877. In spite of urging that she attend a university, she decided to take the full teaching course at the Rhode Island State Normal School, from which she graduated with honors, again the only black student in her class of more than twenty. Before she had graduated, she had taken a teachers' examination and received the highest mark recorded in that city up to that date. She thus became the first black American certified to teach in the public schools of Rhode Island.

In the fall of 1879, Yates went to teach chemistry at Lincoln Institute in Jefferson City, Missouri. She eventually became a full professor and head of the department of natural science. When she resigned in 1889 to marry, she was earning a salary of a thousand dollars a year and was possibly the only woman in the country to hold such a position. Although she was already a remarkable teacher, it was her custom to spend her summers in the East, seeking ways to improve her teaching. Her reputation grew to the point that in 1886 Booker T. Washington asked her to become lady principal of Tuskegee; she declined.

Josephine Silone gave up her position in 1889 to marry W. W. Yates, principal of the Wendell Phillips School in Kansas City, Missouri. W. W. Yates was a highly respected person in his own right: the elementary school of which he was principal was renamed in his honor in 1918. The marriage was apparently harmonious. M. A. Majors writes: "She had the full sympathy of her genial husband. He is very proud of his wife's attainments and she feels that his searching criticism aids her not a little in her literary work" (48). The couple had two children, Josephine Silone and William Blyden. Both graduated from the University of Kansas. Josephine Yates became a teacher in the Kansas City schools, continuing her mother's tradition of community work by serving on the first committee of management of the Paseo YWCA. William Yates took his M. D. degree at Northwestern and took up practice in Chicago.

Josephine Silone Yates faced and solved one of the perennial problems of working women. Hallie Q. Brown states: "She never allowed the duties of the home to encroach upon the time set aside for literary work" (180). We know too little of her journalism; she began writing for newspaper publication early and continued. She often used the name R. K. Potter and wrote verse as well as prose. The titles of three poems are known: "The Zephyr," "Royal Today," and "The Isles of Peace" (Majors, 49). She read French and German with ease and wrote a series of articles on German literature. Russian literature also interested her due to the resemblances between the condition of serf and slave. According to Majors, she was wide-ranging, writing on subjects "from the purely literary to the more practical social, economic and scientific questions now confronting us" (49). In addition to writing and lecturing, she also gave private lessons at home and taught intermittently at Lincoln Institute and Lincoln High School in Kansas City.

This work did not absorb all of her formidable energies. Hallie Q. Brown writes: "She had a wonderful capacity for work, and it was no unusual thing for her to write or study all night and teach the following day" (180). She threw herself into the club movement, organizing first in 1893 the Kansas City Women's League, one of the earliest clubs, and soon becoming a state president of the federated clubs. Upon establishment of the National Association of Colored Women (NACW) in 1896, she became an ardent adherent. She served as the second president of the NACW from 1901 to 1906. Her address to the 1904 convention in Saint Louis reveals the spirit in which she and many of her fellows viewed the task before them:

> Careful study . . . forces one to the conclusion that, although the natural outcome of bondage is a cowardly, thieving, brutal, or otherwise totally degraded specimen of humanity, there were even in the darkest hours of the systems, many high born souls, who, at the price of life itself, if necessary, maintained their integrity, rose superior to their surroundings, taught and transmitted to their posterity the same lofty principles that governed their own lives and that formed a goodly heritage for the generations yet unborn.
>
> Also, one is forced to the conclusion that, while emancipation and subsequent enactments brought freedom to the material body of the erstwhile slave, the soul, the higher self, is debased, could not so easily be freed from the evils that slavery had fastened upon it through centuries of soul debasement; and because of this soul debasement, the Negro, on emancipation, not less than the South, hated to be reconstructed. Reconstruction, the irradication of former characteristics, the growth and development of new and more favorable traits and qualities, are still with any race the work of time. . . (Wesley, 61-62).

After her husband's death in November 1910, she taught at Lincoln High School until her sudden death after a two-day illness on September 3, 1912.

References

Brown, Hallie Q., comp. and ed. *Homespun Heroines and Other Women of Distinction*. Xenia, Ohio: Aldine Publishing Co., 1926.

Dannett, Sylvia G. L. *Profiles of Negro Womanhood*. Vol. 1. Yonkers, N. J.: Educational Heritage, 1964.

Major, M. A. *Noted Negro Women*. Chicago: Donohue and Henneberry, 1893.

Simmons, William J. *Men of Mark*. Cleveland, Ohio: George M. Rewell, 1887.

Wesley, Charles Harris. *The History of the National Association of Colored Women's Clubs*. Washington, D.C.: NACW, 1984.

Young, William H. ed. *Your Kansas City and Mine*. Kansas, City, Mo.: The Editors, 1950.

Robert L. Johns

Subject Index

Subject Index

Subject Index